STRE[...]S London

www.philips-maps.co.uk

First published 2000 by

Philip's, a division of
Octopus Publishing Group Ltd
www.octopusbooks.co.uk
2–4 Heron Quays
London E14 4JP
An Hachette Livre UK Company

Third edition 2007
First impression 2007
LONCB

ISBN-10 0-540-09036-0 paperback
ISBN-10 0-540-09035-2 spiral

ISBN-13 978-0-540-09036-5 paperback
ISBN-13 978-0-540-09035-8 spiral

To the best of the Publishers' knowledge, the information in this atlas was correct at the time of going to press. No responsibility can be accepted for any errors or their consequences.

The representation in this atlas of a road, track or path is no evidence of the existence of a right of way.

Ordnance Survey and the OS symbol are registered trademarks of Ordnance Survey, the national mapping agency of Great Britain

This product contains driver restriction information derived from Teleatlas
© TeleatlasDRI

The information for the speed camera locations is used with permission of the London Safety Camera Partnership and is correct at the time of publishing. New sites will be installed by the LSCP, for the latest list visit www.lscp.org.uk

Printed and bound in Spain
by Cayfosa-Quebecor.

Contents

II Our Top 10 tips to avoid parking penalties
V Mobile speed camera sites
VI **Key to map pages**
VIII Administrative and Postcode boundaries
X **Route planning**

XXVIII **Key to map symbols**
1 **Street maps**

228 **Keys to enlarged map pages and symbols**
229 **Enlarged street maps**

271 **Index**
428 **List of numbered locations**

444 Hospitals
445 Places of interest
446 Shopping, theatres, cinemas
448 Central London buses
450 Local rail and London Underground

Digital Data

The exceptionally high-quality mapping found in this atlas is available as digital data in TIFF format, which is easily convertible to other bitmapped (raster) image formats.

The index is also available in digital form as a standard database table. It contains all the details found in the printed index together with the National Grid reference for the map square in which each entry is named.

For further information and to discuss your requirements, please contact
james.mann@philips-maps.co.uk

Our Top 10 Tips to avoid parking penalties

David Willis / Alamy

When it comes to parking, London's streets are mean and its traffic regulators keen. Lucky motorists might find a marked bay, or at night a patch of single line, but that could just be the start of the problem. It's all too easy to pick the wrong space or the wrong time of day.

Getting a ticket for over-staying, or using a suspended bay or a resident's only space, is invariably expensive and sometimes the pain doesn't end there. What's the worst that can happen? Well, the car could be clamped or towed away. But in either case it's excruciatingly costly and time-consuming to retrieve the vehicle, especially after 10pm, when London black cab prices go through the roof.

Why has parking become so hazardous? The whole process used to be much less complex, and far easier to understand. The hours of parking control were fairly standard right across the capital, and enforcement was also uniform, with traffic wardens attached to the police service. Then came the Road Traffic Act 1991, which took responsibility away from the police and into the hands of local authorities.

The post-code lottery

Since 1994 parking in London has been run by the borough councils. Most choose to employ private contractors to operate the parking penalty service. In common with all other companies, these outfits are in pursuit of profit – and they haven't been disappointed. Parking fines are big business in London these days.

Latest figures show that more than five million parking penalties were levied on motorists in 2005/6 (see table). In bald terms, that's nearly one for every person living in Greater London. These penalties produced an income for the boroughs of some £279 million in a year. Once the operators have taken their slice, the money goes into the coffers of London's 33 boroughs as well as Transport for London, which has recently stepped up its enforcement activities, especially on red routes.

There is huge variation among the 32 boroughs, with central London by far the riskiest place to park. Westminster held the 2005 record for issuing the greatest number of fines, even though its total of 715,085 was about 100,000 less than the previous year. The fewest parking fines were given in the City of London.

There is one piece of good news. A third fewer cars were clamped than in 2004/5 – nearly 50,000 fewer. But there was a sharp 18% increase in cars removed to pounds. To acknowledge this grim statistic, Philip's London street atlases are now the first to locate Car Pounds on the maps using this symbol: 🚗

The figures also reveal the trendsetters among the boroughs:

Camden for the most cars clamped.

Parking fines 2005/6

	Borough	fines
1	**Westminster**	715085
2	**Camden**	448085
3	**Kensington and Chelsea**	294932
4	**Lambeth**	255066
5	**Wandsworth**	245475
6	**Ealing**	212656
7	**Islington**	210685
8	**Newham**	188465
9	**Barnet**	168681
10	**Hammersmith and Fulham**	165196
11	**Hackney**	140966
12	**Waltham Forest**	140216
13	**Southwark**	135045
14	**Haringey**	134551
15	**Brent**	133561
16	**Enfield**	100087
17	**Redbridge**	95966
18	**Hounslow**	92764
19	**Croydon**	86534
20	**Harrow**	83303
21	**Tower Hamlets**	72858
22	**Richmond upon Thames**	72526
23	**Bromley**	69538
24	**Bexley**	65739
25	**Kingston upon Thames**	63980
26	**Lewisham**	63250
27	**Hillingdon**	61211
28	**Merton**	56860
29	**Sutton**	48965
30	**Greenwich**	48892
31	**Barking and Dagenham**	42416
32	**Havering**	40141
33	**City of London**	37478
34	**Transport for London**	304305
		5,095,478

Westminster for the most cars removed to pounds.

The boroughs where the number of tickets issued grew the fastest were: Ealing (+55%), Enfield (+47%) and Hackney (+46%)

The boroughs who saw the biggest falls were: Greenwich (-21%), Richmond (-25%) and Islington (-26%)

The sheer number of different authorities shelling out penalties can make the London street parking issue seem baffling. Arrangements in Richmond

Top 10 Tips

1 Check borough boundaries. One common pitfall for London's drivers is to pump cash into a meter belonging to one borough while being parked in another. This is especially problematic around the London museums. Numerous visitors perfectly willing to pay the charge have fed money into a meter belonging to the Royal Borough of Kensington and Chelsea when they have inadvertently parked in a bay operated by Westminster council. The signage, campaigners claim, is inadequate – so beware.

2 Keep plenty of loose change if you intend to use parking meters. If a parking attendant happens along while you have toddled off to find the correct coinage you have no defence against a ticket.

3 If you've been caught fair and square, pay the ticket within 14 days to take advantage of the cash discount scheme. Prompt settlement usually means coughing up just half the full amount.

4 Assume nothing. Just because you are often permitted to park on single yellow lines after 6.30 doesn't mean it is always so. There are an increasing number of parking places reserved for 'residents only' and these are frequently governed by a 10pm rule. Moreover some zones are 24 hour no parking areas. Look for signs to indicate what rules apply to the parking space before moving into it. Don't forget that some parking areas are watched by cameras that can capture your licence plate, so don't imagine you are safe to contravene regulations on the basis that parking attendants will have ended their shift. If you have received a penalty charge notice in an area where the signs outlining the regulations on parking are obscured by trees or even missing then you may have grounds for appeal. Take photographs as evidence before embarking on the appeals process.

5 If you return to your vehicle while a parking attendant is in the process of writing the ticket don't hesitate to drive off if you can do so without endangering anyone. Parking offences are not criminal offences, so you are not leaving the scene of a crime. The relevant legislation makes it clear that the completed ticket must be either given to the driver or attached to the vehicle. If not, the ticket is invalid.

6 There are loopholes in parking regulations to capitalise upon. A ticket is invalid if the parking attendant is not wearing full uniform, including a hat, or if his identification number is not clearly visible. There might be discrepancies in the ticket regarding the timings or your vehicle. Sometimes the markings on the road are awry or the position of the meter is misleading. If the parking attendant is present request that he makes a note of your objections as this may assist in any pending appeals process.

7 Don't be afraid to appeal against a penalty that in your view has been wrongly issued. The number of appeals is surprisingly small (fewer than 1%) and yet more than 60% are successful. It generally costs nothing to appeal so what have you got to lose? At first glance the process is daunting but stick with it if you feel you have been unfairly targeted with a ticket. Whatever you do, don't ignore it! See 'How to appeal' on the following page.

8 When cars are clamped or towed retrieve the vehicle fast – within 24 hours if possible. This is an expensive business because drivers must pay the penalty charge notice as well as a fee to release the vehicle. If it's not recovered promptly expect a daily charge for 'storage' on top. Afterwards, study the timings on the ticket. Most councils permit a 15 or 20 minute grace period after a parking ticket has run out before clamping or towing. Anything less than that is grounds for appeal. Remember, if you return to your vehicle before the clamp is locked or before the wheels are raised from the ground if it is being towed then the penalty charge notice is invalid.

9 Look out for cashless parking zones. Some are already on trial in central London. Drivers can ring a database to establish an arrival time. Then the clock starts running until the driver calls again to signal departure. The amount due is automatically debited from the driver's account. There's no doubt that new technology will play its part on the parking scene in the over-crowded capital. And it's sensible recognition at last that drivers may have many talents but are not as yet blessed with the foresight to know the precise moment that they will return to their vehicles.

10 Don't forget the other offences. London drivers not only have to be careful about parking. There's the congestion charge to consider as well as fines for using bus lanes illegally and other moving traffic fines orchestrated by local authorities. Congestion charge boundaries, bus lanes, red lights and yellow box junctions are generally monitored by enforcement cameras and evidence is extremely difficult to dispute.

At any time
WARNING
Parking
suspension
At any time
WARNING
Parking
suspension
At any time
WARNING

Dominic Burke / Alamy

Parking on a suspended bay will almost certainly result in your car being towed to the borough pound.

may be substantially different to those in Redbridge. Charges and hours of operation for meters and ticket machines vary hugely, sometimes even on opposite sides of the same street. So there's 'stranger danger' not only for those from outside London, or suburbanites driving into central London, but even for Inner Londoners crossing borough borders.

But that isn't what most alarms the average motorist. There's a widely held belief that wardens have quotas to fill, and can get bonuses for over-achieving. Examples of predatory behaviour are

legendary. Favourite times for ticketing are the first and last 10 minutes of the controlled period, when wardens are often seen out in large numbers. There have been reports of tickets being issued to removal vans during house moves, to security company vans when rogue burglar alarms are clanging, and to numerous traders unloading goods for their shops – sometimes in the middle of the night.

In short, it is not only motorists who have broken parking regulations that are being fined, but also the unwary and the downright unlucky - in the right place, at the right time but with a wrong-minded attendant in the vicinity.

Some of the villains have been weeded out. Certain boroughs are ensuring those patrolling the streets have undergone a re-education process that will cast them as a friend to the motorist rather than a foe. It's not in your best interest to assume the whole system is unfair and take out your frustrations upon the parking attendant who just might have ticketed you legitimately.

However, the activities of a few parking regulators deserve close scrutiny. Clampers in particular have earned themselves a cowboy image that is finally arousing the interest of the legislators. A House of Commons Transport Committee Report has urged that operators should 'consider restricting clamping to persistent offenders and unregistered vehicles'. There's even talk in the document that towing a car may be incompatible with our human rights. That's perhaps why the number of cars being clamped in the capital has gone down by some 50,000.

Of course, there are always reasons to justify a harsh parking regime. It keeps London traffic on the move, making journey times more predictable and curtailing traffic mayhem. That's the official line – which never mentions just how valuable the income generated by parking penalties is to the enforcers. Further, authorities don't talk about targets in relation to parking fines, rather 'baseline performance indicators'.

So if you are going to park in London, especially in the centre, beware, be aware – and know your rights. If you do get fined and you think you have a case, be prepared to appeal. Fewer than 1% of motorists did appeal in 2004/5 (do we detect money-raising by inertia?), but over 60% of those appeals were allowed. Remember, if you do not get a response to your appeal within 56 days, your appeal is automatically allowed.

How to appeal

■ Begin with a letter sent by recorded delivery within 14 days. That generally means the clock will stop on the prompt payment discount scheme and it will still be available if the initial appeal is unsuccessful – although some councils claim the reduced amount isn't open to those who embark on this route. Keep copies of the correspondence and any supporting evidence you send with it. Always quote the Penalty Charge Notice number. If you hear nothing for more than 56 days then the council is deemed out of time and the ticket should be cancelled.

■ Do not pay any part of the fine if you are intending to appeal. Once payment is received by the authority the case is closed.

■ If your appeal is turned down don't accept a letter couched in general terms. Write back to ask about the specifics of your case. The council will either stand by the notice and issue a Notice of Rejection or allow the appeal.

■ If the authority endorses the ticket its next step is to issue a Notice to Owner and that should happen within six months. According to the Road Traffic Act of 1991 the owner is liable for violations linked to his vehicle. Disturbingly, it is only at this stage that many motorists discover they are being pursued for a parking offence. If you are the sole driver of a vehicle that hasn't been stolen the ticket has clearly not been either attached to the vehicle or handed to you, the driver, as the law demands. Respond within 28 days filing the relevant information. This is known as Formal Representation. (If you do not answer in the specified time the council may well up the fine and send in the bailiffs to recover the amount.)

■ If this petition is rejected by the local authority then it's time to take the case to the Parking and Traffic Appeals Service. You can select a postal or personal adjudication. Internet advice favours face time with the adjudicator as local councils are known to frequently cave in at the prospect of putting evidence before an official tribunal on the grounds of cost, although there's no guarantee of this happening. The adjudicator's decision is final as there is no recourse to law.

Clamping rates are falling but you are still at risk – especially in Camden and Westminster.

Dominic Burke / Alamy

Helpful information

The Knowledge A telephone advisory service run by off-duty London taxi drivers. They will help with problems including parking and directions. The number is 0906 265 6565 (premium rate) or try *www.theknowledge.com*

Transport for London (TfL) Responsible for 360 miles of roads, 4,600 traffic lights and London's red routes. It is also a fine-issuing authority. Contact Tfl on 0207 2221234 or *www.tfl.gov.uk*.

www.ticketbusters.co.uk is a website devoted to assisting London motorists, offering tailored advice on parking ticket appeals.

www.parkingticket.co.uk also offers support for London drivers.

Mobile speed camera sites

This table lists the sites where the local safety camera partnership may enforce speed limits through the use of mobile cameras or detectors. These are usually set up on the roadside or a bridge spanning the road and operated by a police or civilian enforcement officer.

Barking & Dagenham

A13
Alfreds Way IG11
Alfreds Way IG12
Ripple Rd IG11
Ripple Rd RM9

A406
Barking Relief Rd IG11

A1153
Porters Avenue RM8

B178
Ballards Rd RM10

Barnet

A5
Hendon Broadway NW9

A406
North Circular Rd N3

Unclassified
Oakleigh Rd South N11

Bexley

A20
Sidcup Rd SE9

Unclassified
Abbey Rd DA17
Bellegrove Rd DA16
Erith Rd DA17
Farady Avenue DA14
King Harolds Way DA17
Lower Rd DA17
Penhill Rd DA5
Pickford Lane DA7
Well Hall Rd SE9
Woolwich Rd DA17

Brent

A5
Edgware Rd NW2

A406
North Circular Rd NW2
North Circular Rd NW10

A4006
Kenton Rd HA3

Unclassified
Crest Rd NW2
Fryent Way, Kingsbury NW9
Hillside NW10
Kingsbury Rd NW9
Watford Rd, Wembley HA0
Watford Rd, Sudbury HA0
Woodcock Hill HA3

Bromley

A20
Sidcup By-Pass DA14

A213
Croydon Rd SE20

A222
Bromley Rd BR2
Bromley Rd BR3

Unclassified
Beckenham Rd BR3
Burnt Ash Lane BR1
Crystal Palace Park Rd SE26
Elmers End Rd BR3
Main Rd TN16
Sevenoaks Way BR5
Wickham Way BR3

Camden

A501
Euston Rd NW1

Chadwell

M11
Chadwell IG8

City of Westminster

A40
Westway W2

Unclassified
Great Western Rd W11
Millbank SW1
Vauxhall Bridge Rd SW1

Croydon

A22
Godstone Rd CR8

A215
Beulah Hill SE19

A217
Garratt Lane SW18

Unclassified
Brigstock Rd CR7
Coulsdon Rd, Coulsdon CR5
Long Lane, Addiscombe CR0
Portnalls Rd, Coulsdon CR5
Thornton Rd CR0

Ealing

A40
Perivale UB6
Western Avenue UB5
Western Avenue UB6

Unclassified
Greenford Rd, Greenford UB6
Greenford Rd, Southall UB1
Horn Lane W3
Lady Margaret Rd UB1
Ruislip Rd UB5
Uxbridge Rd UB2

Egham

M25
Egham TW20

Elmbridge

M25
Byfleet KT14

Enfield

A10
Great Cambridge Rd N18

A110
Enfield Rd EN2

Unclassified
Fore Street N9

Forest Hill

Unclassified
Stanstead Rd SE23

Greenwich

A20
Sidcup Rd SE9

Unclassified
Beresford Street SE18
Court Rd SE9
Creek Rd SE10
Glenesk Rd SE9
Rochester Way SE3
Rochester Way SE9
Woolwich Church Street SE18

Hackney

A10
Stamford Hill N16

Unclassified
Clapton Common E5
Seven Sisters Rd N4
Upper Clapton Rd E5

Hammersmith & Fulham

A40
Westway W2
Westway W12

A219
Scrubs Lane W12

Unclassified
Fulham Palace Rd SW6
Uxbridge Rd W12

Haringey

A503
Seven Sisters Rd N15

Unclassified
Belmont Rd N15
Bounds Green Rd N11
Seven Sisters Rd N4
White Hart Lane N22

Harrow

Unclassified
Alexandra Avenue HA2
Harrow View HA3
Honeypot Lane NW9
Porlock Avenue HA2
Uxbridge Rd, Harrow Weald HA3
Watford Rd HA1

Havering

Unclassified
Brentwood Rd, Romford RM1
Chase Cross Rd RM5
Eastern Avenue RM14
Eastern Avenue East RM14
Hall Lane RM14
Ingrebourne Gardens, Upminster RM14
Ockenden Rd RM14
Parkstone Avenue, Hornchurch RM11
Wingletye Lane RM11

Hillingdon

M25
Colnbrook SL3
West Drayton UB7

A40
Western Avenue, Ruislip UB10

A312
Hayes UB3

Unclassified
Church Hill, Harefield UB9
Cowley Rd, Uxbridge UB8
Cowley High Rd UB8
Joel Street, Northwood Hills HA6
Kingshill Avenue, Hayes UB4
Park Rd UB8
Stockley Rd UB7
Uxbridge Rd, Hayes UB4

Hounslow

A4
Great West Rd, Brentford TW8
Great West Rd, Hounslow TW7
Great West Rd, Hounslow W4

A315
High Street TW8

Unclassified
Castle Way, Hanworth TW13
Great West Rd TW5
Harlington Rd West TW14
Hatton Rd, Bedfont TW14

Islington

Unclassified
Holloway Rd N19
Seven Sisters Rd N4
Upper Street N1

Kensington & Chelsea

Unclassified
Barlby Rd W10
Chelsea Embankment SW3
Chesterton Rd W10
Holland Park Avenue W11
Holland Villas Rd W14
Kensington Park Rd W11
Kensington Rd SW7
Ladbroke Grove W11
Latimer Rd W10
Royal Hospital Rd SW3
Sloane Street SW1
St Helens Gardens W10

Kingston upon Thames

A3
Kingston By-Pass SW20

A240
Kingston Rd KT4

Unclassified
Manor Drive North KT3
Richmond Rd KT2

Lambeth

Unclassified
Atkins Rd SW12
Brixton Hill SW2
Brixton Rd SW9
Clapham Rd SW9
Herne Hill Rd SE24
Kennington Park Rd SE11
Kings Avenue SW4
Streatham High Rd SW16

Lewisham

A21
Bromley Rd BR1

Unclassified
Brockley Rd SE4
Brockley Rd SE23
Bromley Rd SE6
Brownhill Rd SE6
Burnt Ash Hill SE12
Lee High Rd SE12
Lewisham Way SE4
Westwood Hill SE26

Merton

A298
Bushey Rd SW20

Unclassified
Central Rd SM4
High Street, Colliers Wood SW19
Hillcross Avenue SM4
London Rd CR4
Martin Way SM4
Martin Way SW20
Ridgway Place SW19
West Barnes Lane SW20

Newham

A13
Alfreds Way IG11

A124
Barking Rd E6

A1020
Royal Albert Dock Way E6
Royal Docks Rd E6

Unclassified
Barking Rd E13
Romford Rd E7

Redbridge

A406
Southend Rd IG8

Unclassified
Manford Way, Hainault IG7
Woodford Avenue IG8
Woodford Rd E18

Richmond upon Thames

A205
Upper Richmond Rd West SW14

Unclassified
Kew Rd TW9
Sixth Cross Rd TW2
Uxbridge Rd TW12

Ruislip

Unclassified
Field End Rd HA4

Runnymeade

M25
Runnymede TW20

Southwark

Unclassified
Albany Rd SE5
Alleyn Park SE21
Brenchley Gardens SE15
Camberwell New Rd SE5
Denmark Hill SE5
Kennington Park Rd SE11
Linden Grove SE15
Old Kent Rd SE1
Old Kent Rd SE14
Old Kent Rd SE17
Peckham Rye SE15
Salter Rd SE16
Southwark Pk Rd SE16
Sunray Avenue SE24

Spelthorne

M25
Staines TW18

Sutton

A232
Cheam Rd SM1

B272
Foresters Drive SM6

B278
Green Lane SM4

B279
Tudor Drive SM4

Unclassified
Malden Rd SM3
Middleton Rd SM5
Beddington Lane CR0
Cheam Common Rd KT4

Tower Hamlets

A102
Homerton High Street E9

Unclassified
Bow Rd E3
Cambridge Heath Rd E2
Manchester Rd E14
Mile End Rd E1
Upper Clapton Rd E5
Westferry Rd E14

Waltham Forest

Unclassified
Chingford Rd E4
Chingford Rd E17
Hoe Street E17
Larkshall Rd E4

Wandsworth

A3
Kingston Rd SW15

A214
Trinity Rd SW18

A3220
Latchmere Rd SW11

Unclassified
Battersea Park Rd SW11
Garratt Lane SW18
Upper Richmond Rd SW15

Windsor & Maidenhead

M25
Wraysbury TW19

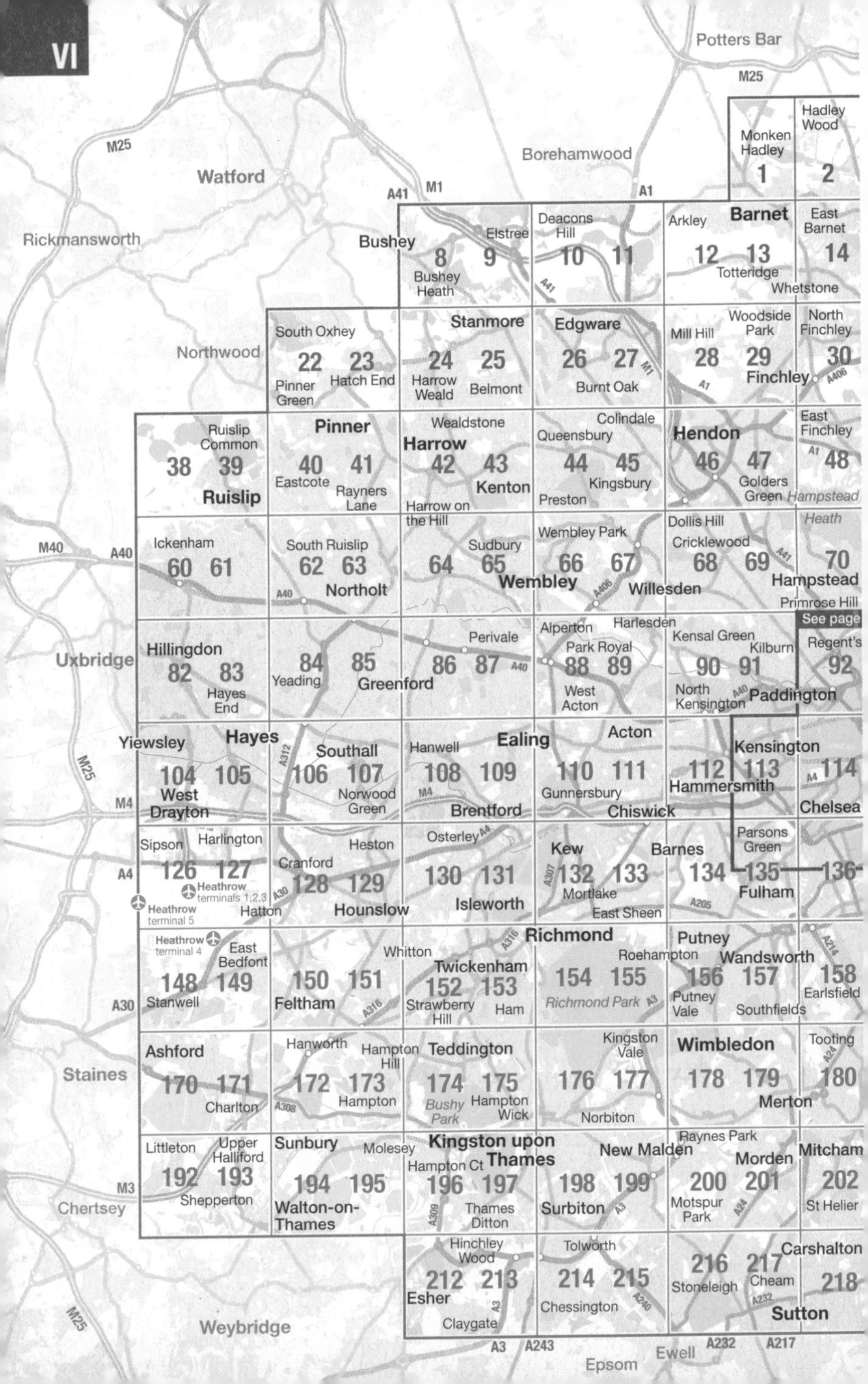

Potters Bar
M25
Hadley Wood
Monken Hadley
1
2
M25
Borehamwood
Watford
A41 M1
A1
Rickmansworth
Bushey
Elstree
8 9
Bushey Heath
Deacons Hill
10 11
A41
Arkley
Barnet
12 13
Totteridge
East Barnet
14
Whetstone
South Oxhey
22 23
Pinner Green
Hatch End
Northwood
Stanmore
24 25
Harrow Weald
Belmont
Edgware
26 27
Burnt Oak
M1
Mill Hill
Woodside Park
28 29
Finchley
A1
North Finchley
30
A406
Ruislip Common
38 39
Ruislip
Pinner
40 41
Eastcote
Rayners Lane
Wealdstone
Harrow
42 43
Kenton
Harrow on the Hill
Colindale
Queensbury
44 45
Kingsbury
Preston
Hendon
46 47
Golders Green
East Finchley
A1
48
Hampstead Heath
M40
A40
Ickenham
60 61
South Ruislip
62 63
Northolt
A40
64
Sudbury
65
Wembley
Wembley Park
66 67
Willesden
A406
Dollis Hill
Cricklewood
68 69
A41
70
Hampstead
Primrose Hill
Uxbridge
Hillingdon
82 83
Hayes End
84 85
Yeading
Greenford
86
Perivale
87
A40
Alperton
Harlesden
Park Royal
88 89
West Acton
Kensal Green
Kilburn
90 91
North Kensington
A40
Paddington
See page
Regent's
92
Yiewsley
Hayes
104 105
West Drayton
M25
M4
A312
Southall
106 107
Norwood Green
Hanwell
108 109
M4
Ealing
Brentford
Acton
110 111
Gunnersbury
Chiswick
112
Hammersmith
Kensington
113
114
A4
Chelsea
Sipson
Harlington
126 127
Heathrow terminals 1,2,3
Heathrow terminal 5
Hatton
A4
Cranford
Heston
128 129
A30
Hounslow
Osterley
A4
130 131
Isleworth
Kew
A307
132 133
Mortlake
East Sheen
Barnes
134
A205
Parsons Green
135
Fulham
136
Heathrow terminal 4
East Bedfont
148 149
Stanwell
A30
150 151
Feltham
Whitton
Twickenham
152 153
Strawberry Hill
Ham
A316
A316
Richmond
154 155
Roehampton
Richmond Park
A3
Putney
Wandsworth
156 157
Putney Vale
Southfields
A214
158
Earlsfield
Ashford
Staines
170 171
Charlton
Hanworth
Hampton Hill
172 173
Hampton
A308
Teddington
174 175
Bushy Park
Hampton Wick
Kingston Vale
176 177
Norbiton
Wimbledon
178 179
Merton
Tooting
A24
180
Littleton
Upper Halliford
192 193
Shepperton
M3
Chertsey
Sunbury
Molesey
194 195
Walton-on-Thames
Kingston upon Thames
Hampton Ct
196 197
Thames Ditton
A309
New Malden
198 199
Surbiton
A3
Raynes Park
200 201
Motspur Park
A24
Morden
Mitcham
202
St Helier
Hinchley Wood
212 213
Esher
A3
Claygate
Tolworth
214 215
Chessington
A240
216 217
Stoneleigh
Cheam
A232
Carshalton
218
Sutton
M25
Weybridge
A3 A243
Epsom
Ewell
A232
A217

Key to map pages

Herne Hill 160 Tulse Hill A23 — Atlas pages at 3½ inches to 1 mile

Central London atlas coverage at 7 inches to 1 mile see page 228

Scale
0 1 2 3 4 5 km
0 1 2 3 miles

M25 A10 Loughton M11 A12 Romford A13 Erith Crayford A2 Swanley A20 M25 A21 A23

3 Cockfosters
4 5 Clay Hill Forty Hill Enfield Town Enfield
6 7 Enfield Wash Enfield Lock Brimsdown A10
15 Osidge Oakwood
16 17 Bush Hill Winchmore Hill Southgate A10
18 19 Ponders End Lower Edmonton
20 21 Epping Forest Chingford Buckhurst Hill
31 Friern Barnet Muswell Hill
32 33 Wood Green Tottenham Edmonton
34 35 A406 Higham Hill
36 37 Chingford Hatch Woodford Woodford Green
49 Highgate
50 51 Hornsey A105 Finsbury Park Stoke Newington
52 53 Walthamstow Upper Clapton
54 55 Snaresbrook Wanstead
56 57 Barkingside A12 Newbury Park
58 59 Little Heath Goodmayes
71 Tufnell Park Camden Town
72 73 Highbury Islington A10
74 75 Lower Clapton Lea Bridge Hackney Hackney Wick
76 77 Leytonstone Leyton Stratford Upton
78 79 A406 Ilford Barking
80 81 Becontree Dagenham
228 for central London
93 Park A501 Marylebone
94 95 Finsbury City of London
96 97 Bethnal Green Bow A12 A11 Stepney Tower Hamlets
98 99 Newham West Ham Canning Town A13
100 101 East Ham A13 Creekmouth Beckton
102 103 Castle Green
115 Mayfair Westminster
116 117 Southwark Walworth Lambeth
118 119 Wapping Canary Wharf Bermondsey
120 121 Blackwall Silvertown Isle of Dogs Greenwich
122 123 London City Woolwich Plumstead
124 125 Thamesmead Abbey Wood Belvedere
137 Battersea Clapham
138 139 A202 Camberwell A3 Brixton
140 141 A2 Deptford New Cross Nunhead
142 143 Charlton Blackheath Lewisham
144 145 Shooters Hill A205 Falconwood Welling
146 147 West Heath Lessness Heath Bexleyheath
159 A205 Balham
160 161 Herne Hill A23 Tulse Hill A205 Dulwich
162 163 Honor Oak Ladywell Forest Hill Catford
164 165 Hither Green Lee Grove Park
166 167 Eltham Avery Hill A20 New Eltham
168 169 A2 Blackfen Old Bexley Sidcup
181 Furzedown Streatham
182 183 Norbury Upper Norwood
184 185 Crystal Palace Penge Beckenham
186 187 Southend Downham Plaistow Bromley
188 189 Elmstead Chislehurst Bickley
190 191 Foots Cray A20 St Paul's Cray
203 Beddington Corner
204 205 Thornton Heath A23 Selhurst
206 207 Elmers End Eden Park Addiscombe
208 209 Shortlands Hayes
210 211 Petts Wood Southborough Broom Hill
219 Wallington Beddington
220 221 Croydon
222 223 Shirley A232 Addington Selsdon
224 225 West Wickham A232 Keston New Addington
226 227 Orpington Farnborough

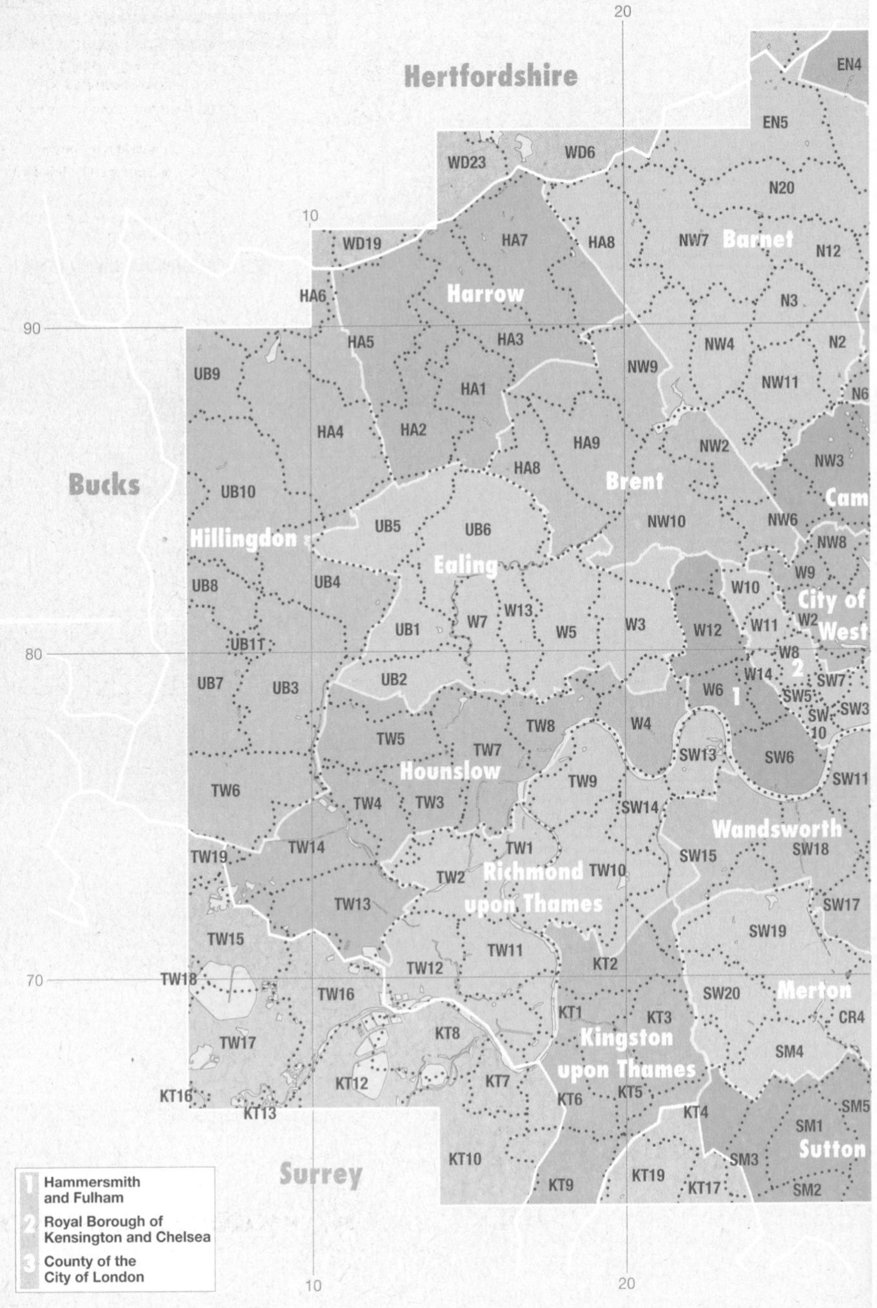
Hertfordshire
Bucks
Surrey
Harrow
Barnet
Brent
Hillingdon
Ealing
Hounslow
Richmond upon Thames
Kingston upon Thames
Wandsworth
Merton
Sutton
City of West
Cam
WD23
WD6
WD19
EN4
EN5
N20
N12
N3
N2
N6
HA7
HA8
HA6
HA5
HA3
HA1
HA2
HA4
HA9
NW7
NW4
NW9
NW11
NW2
NW3
NW6
NW8
NW10
UB9
UB10
UB5
UB6
UB8
UB4
UB1
UB11
UB7
UB3
UB2
W9
W10
W2
W11
W12
W8
W14
W6
W13
W7
W5
W3
W4
SW7
SW5
SW3
SW10
SW13
SW6
SW11
SW14
SW15
SW18
SW17
SW19
SW20
TW5
TW7
TW8
TW9
TW6
TW4
TW3
TW14
TW1
TW19
TW2
TW10
TW13
TW15
TW11
TW12
TW18
TW16
TW17
KT2
KT1
KT3
KT8
KT12
KT7
KT6
KT5
KT4
KT16
KT13
KT10
KT9
KT19
KT17
CR4
SM4
SM5
SM1
SM3
SM2
1
2
10
20
90
80
70
Hammersmith and Fulham
Royal Borough of Kensington and Chelsea
County of the City of London

Major administrative and Postcode boundaries

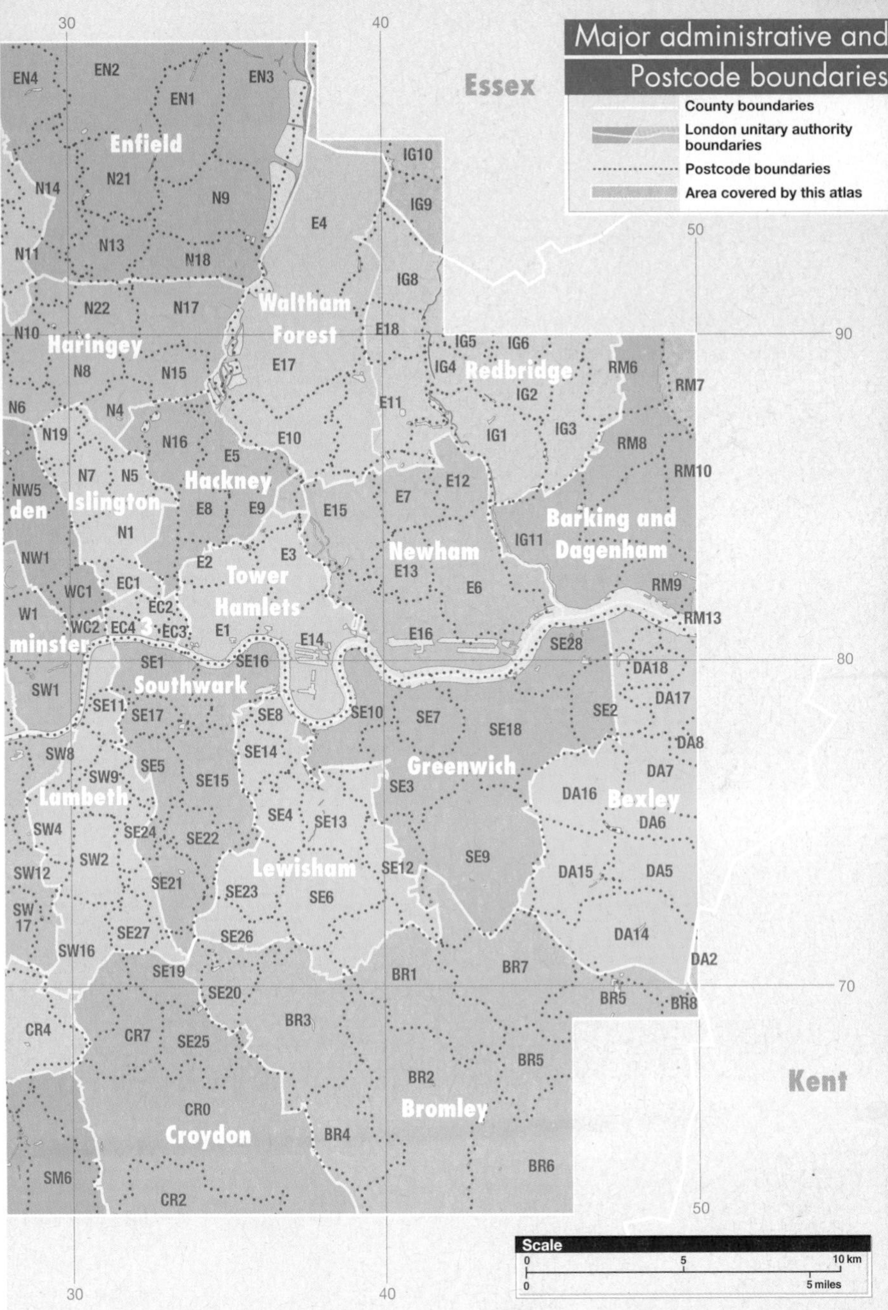

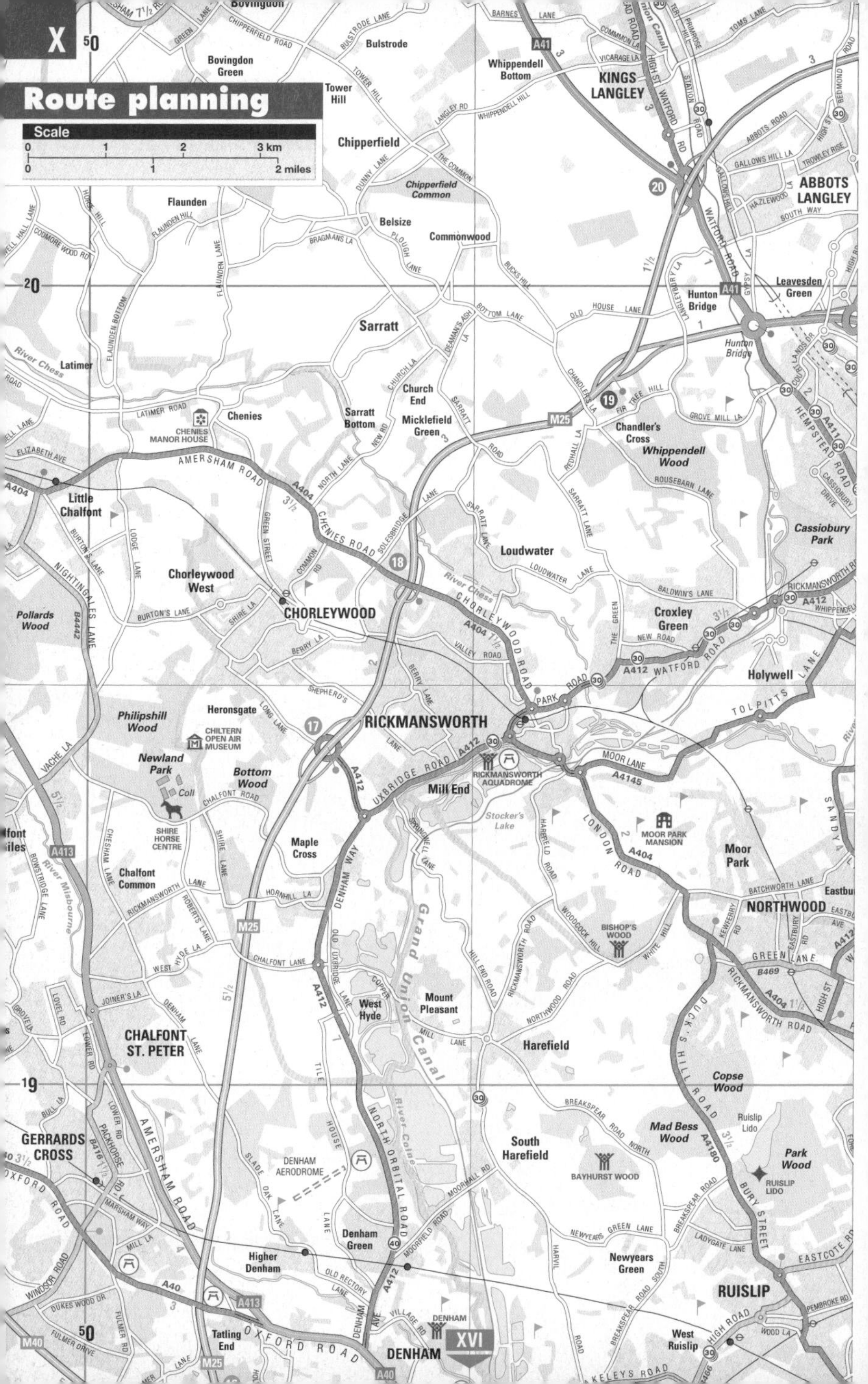

X
Route planning
Scale
0 1 2 3 km
0 1 2 miles
Bovingdon Green
Bulstrode
Tower Hill
Chipperfield
Chipperfield Common
Whippendell Bottom
KINGS LANGLEY
ABBOTS LANGLEY
Flaunden
Belsize
Commonwood
Leavesden Green
Hunton Bridge
Sarratt
Latimer
River Chess
Chenies
CHENIES MANOR HOUSE
Church End
Sarratt Bottom
Micklefield Green
Chandler's Cross
Whippendell Wood
Little Chalfont
Cassiobury Park
Loudwater
Chorleywood West
CHORLEYWOOD
Pollards Wood
Croxley Green
Holywell
Heronsgate
Philipshill Wood
RICKMANSWORTH
CHILTERN OPEN AIR MUSEUM
Newland Park
Bottom Wood
RICKMANSWORTH AQUADROME
Mill End
Stocker's Lake
MOOR PARK MANSION
Moor Park
SHIRE HORSE CENTRE
Maple Cross
Chalfont Common
NORTHWOOD
BISHOP'S WOOD
Grand Union Canal
West Hyde
Mount Pleasant
Harefield
CHALFONT ST. PETER
Copse Wood
Mad Bess Wood
Ruislip Lido
GERRARDS CROSS
DENHAM AERODROME
South Harefield
Park Wood
RUISLIP LIDO
BAYHURST WOOD
Denham Green
Higher Denham
Newyears Green
RUISLIP
Tatling End
DENHAM
West Ruislip
XVI
AMERSHAM ROAD
CHENIES ROAD
CHORLEYWOOD ROAD
UXBRIDGE ROAD
LONDON ROAD
WATFORD ROAD
NORTH ORBITAL ROAD
OXFORD ROAD
DUCK'S HILL ROAD
RICKMANSWORTH ROAD
HEMPSTEAD ROAD
M25
M40
A404
A412
A413
A41
A40
A4145
A4180
B4442
B469
B416

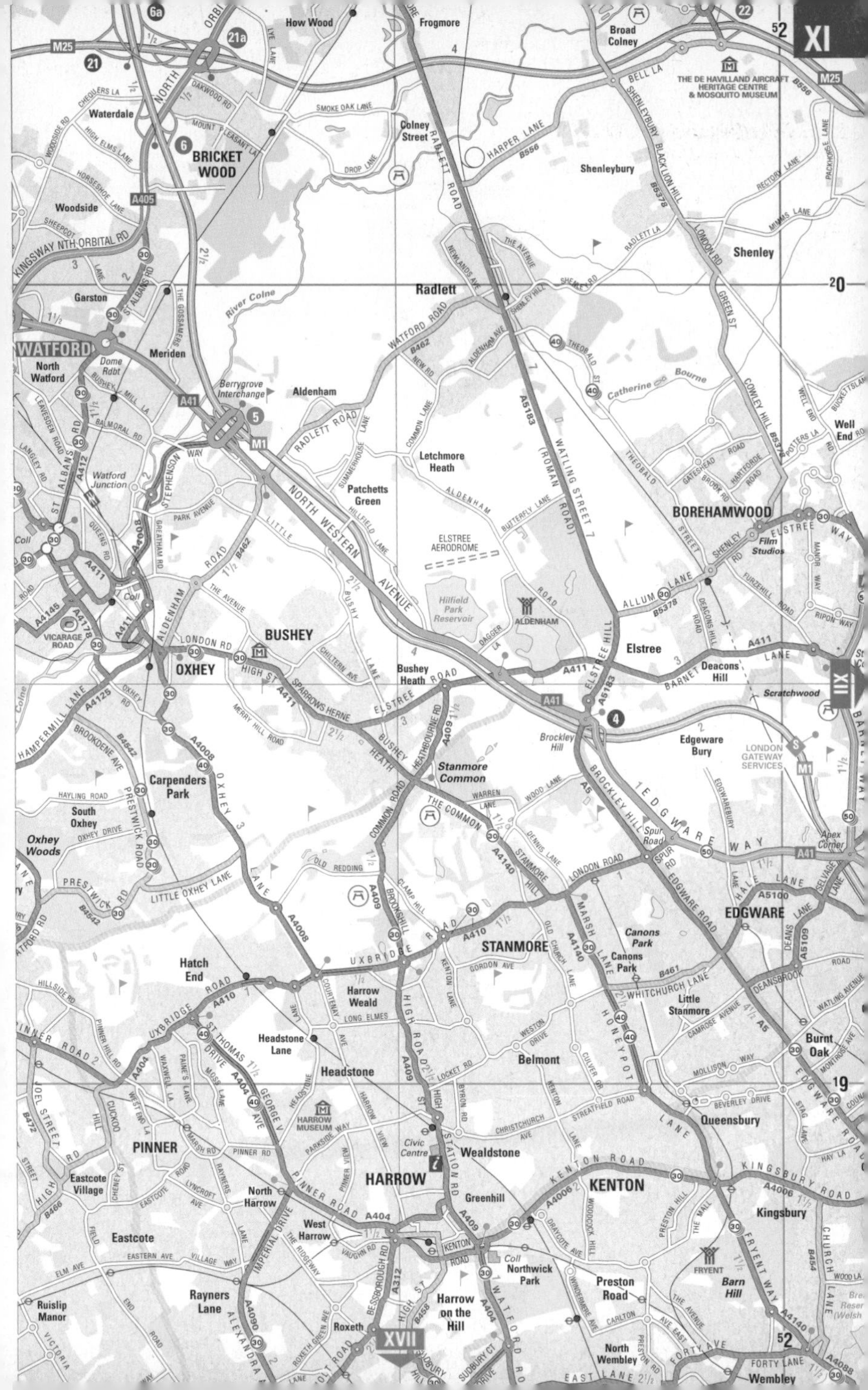

XI
52
How Wood
Frogmore
Broad Colney
M25
21
21a
6a
22
THE DE HAVILLAND AIRCRAFT HERITAGE CENTRE & MOSQUITO MUSEUM
BELL LA
B556
Waterdale
CHEQUERS LA
DAKWOOD RD
MOUNT PLEASANT LA
SMOKE OAK LANE
LYE LANE
Colney Street
NORTH ORBITAL
6
BRICKET WOOD
HIGH ELMS LANE
WOODSIDE RD
HORSESHOE LANE
DROP LANE
RADLETT ROAD
HARPER LANE
Shenleybury
SHENLEYBURY
BLACKLION HILL
B5378
LONDON RD
RECTORY LANE
PACKHORSE LANE
A405
Woodside
SHEEPCOT
KINGSWAY NTH ORBITAL RD
MIMMS LANE
RADLETT LA
Shenley
THE AVENUE
NEWLANDS AVE
Garston
ST ALBANS RD
THE GOSSAMERS
River Colne
Radlett
SHENLEY HILL
20
WATFORD
North Watford
Dome Rdbt
Meriden
WATFORD ROAD
B462
NEW RD
ALDENHAM AVE
THEOBALD ST
GREEN ST
Catherine Bourne
COWLEY HILL
B5378
WELL END
Well End
POTTERS LA
BUCKETTSLAND
BUSHEY MILL LA
LEAVESDEN ROAD
BALMORAL RD
A41
Berrygrove Interchange
5
M1
Aldenham
RADLETT ROAD
SUMMERHOUSE LANE
COMMON LANE
Letchmore Heath
A5183
(ROMAN ROAD)
WATLING STREET
THEOBALD
GATESHEAD ROAD
BROOK RD
HARTFORDE ROAD
LANGLEY RD
ST ALBANS RD
A412
Watford Junction
STEPHENSON WAY
NORTH WESTERN AVENUE
Patchetts Green
ALDENHAM
BUTTERFLY LANE
BOREHAMWOOD
Coll
QUEENS RD
A4008
PARK AVENUE
GREATHAM RD
HILLFIELD LANE
ELSTREE AERODROME
SHENLEY RD
ELSTREE WAY
Film Studios
MANOR WAY
A411
A4145
A4178
VICARAGE ROAD
ALDENHAM ROAD
B462
THE AVENUE
LITTLE BUSHEY LANE
Hilfield Park Reservoir
ALDENHAM
ALLUM LANE
B5378
FURZEHILL ROAD
DEACONS HILL ROAD
RIPON WAY
LONDON RD
OXHEY
BUSHEY
HIGH ST
CHILTERN AVE
DAGGER LA
Elstree
ELSTREE HILL
Bushey Heath
ELSTREE ROAD
BARNET LANE
Deacons Hill
Scratchwood
XII
HAMPERMILL LANE
A4125
OXHEY RD
SPARROWS HERNE
MERRY HILL ROAD
BUSHEY HEATH
HEATHBOURNE RD
A409
4
Brockley Hill
Edgeware Bury
LONDON GATEWAY SERVICES
BROOKDENE AVE
B4542
Carpenders Park
A4008
OXHEY LANE
Stanmore Common
COMMON ROAD
WARREN LANE
WOOD LANE
BROCKLEY HILL
A5
EDGWARE WAY
EDGWAREBURY LANE
HAYLING ROAD
South Oxhey
OXHEY DRIVE
PRESTWICK ROAD
THE COMMON
DENNIS LANE
Spur Road
Apex Corner
Oxhey Woods
OLD REDDING
STANMORE HILL
A4140
LONDON ROAD
SPUR RD
A41
HALE LANE
SELVAGE LA
PRESTWICK RD
LITTLE OXHEY LANE
B4542
CLAMP HILL
BROOKSHILL
A5100
EDGWARE
EDGWARE ROAD
A410
STANMORE
OLD CHURCH LANE
MARSH LANE
Canons Park
DEANS LANE
A5109
Hatch End
UXBRIDGE ROAD
COURTENAY AVE
Harrow Weald
KENTON LANE
GORDON AVE
B461
WHITCHURCH LANE
Little Stanmore
DEANSBROOK ROAD
WATLING AVENUE
HILLSIDE RD
PINNER HILL RD
PINNER ROAD
A404
ST THOMAS DRIVE
LONG ELMES
HEADSTONE LANE
Headstone Lane
HONEYPOT LANE
CAMROSE AVENUE
Burnt Oak
MONTROSE AVE
WAXWELL LA
PAINE'S LANE
MOSS LANE
GEORGE V AVE
Headstone
HIGH ROAD
LOCKET RD
WESTON DRIVE
Belmont
CULVER GR
MOLLISON WAY
19
JOEL STREET
CUCKOO HILL
WEST END LA
MARSH RD
HARROW MUSEUM
PARKSIDE WAY
HARROW VIEW
HIGH ST
BYRON RD
CHRISTCHURCH AVE
STREATFIELD ROAD
BEVERLEY DRIVE
STAG LANE
Queensbury
B472
PINNER
PINNER RD
PINNER VIEW
Civic Centre
STATION RD
Wealdstone
KENTON ROAD
KINGSBURY ROAD
HAY LA
Eastcote Village
CHENEY ST
LYNCROFT AVE
RAYNERS LANE
North Harrow
HARROW
Greenhill
A4006
KENTON
PRESTON HILL
THE MALL
Kingsbury
CHURCH LANE
HIGH RD
B466
EASTCOTE AVE
West Harrow
THE RIDGEWAY
VAUGHAN RD
KENTON ROAD
DRAYCOTT AVE
WOODCOCK HILL
FRYENT WAY
B454
Eastcote
EASTERN AVE
VILLAGE WAY
IMPERIAL DRIVE
Coll
Northwick Park
Preston Road
FRYENT
Barn Hill
WOOD LA
ELM AVE
FIELD END
A312
B458
WATFORD ROAD
A404
WINDERMERE AVE
CARLTON
AVE EAST
THE AVENUE
A4140
Ruislip Manor
Rayners Lane
ALEXANDRA AVE
A4090
ROXETH GREEN AVE
Roxeth
BESSBOROUGH RD
Harrow on the Hill
North Wembley
PRESTON RD
FORTY AVE
FORTY LANE
A4088
52
VICTORIA
XVII
SUDBURY
SUDBURY CT DRIVE
EAST LANE
Wembley

XII
South Mimms
SOUTH MIMMS SERVICES
POTTERS BAR
Shenley
Ridge
Dancers Hill
Bentley Heath
Hadley Wood
Enfield Chase
Well End
ELSTREE
BOREHAMWOOD
Monken Hadley
Monken Hadley Common
Hadley
New Barnet
Cockfosters
Rowley Green
BARNET
Arkley
Underhill
EAST BARNET
Oak Hill Park
Deacons Hill
Barnet Gate
Stirling Corner
Scratchwood
LONDON GATEWAY SERVICES
Totteridge
Whetstone
Osidge
Apex Corner
EDGWARE
Mill Hill
Mill Hill East
Woodside Park
North Finchley
Arnos Grove
FRIERN BARNET
West Finchley
Colney Hatch
Grahame Park
COPTHALL STADIUM
Fiveways Corner
Church End
FINCHLEY
Burnt Oak
RAF MUSEUM
HENDON
CHURCH FARM MUSEUM
Coldfall Wood
Alexandra Palace
Muswell Hill
Queensbury
Henley's Corner
Fortis Green
East Finchley
Colindale
Temple Fortune
Highgate Wood
Queen's Wood
Kingsbury
Crouch End
West Hendon
Brent Cross Shopping Centre
Hampstead Garden Suburb
Golders Green
Brent Cross
Barn Hill
Staples Corner
Brent Reservoir (Welsh Harp)
HAMPSTEAD HEATH
KENWOOD HOUSE
Highgate
Hampstead Heath
Highgate Ponds
Parliament Hill
Golders Hill Park
Child's Hill
Dartmouth Park
Wembley Park
Neasden Circle
Neasden
Dollis Hill
Gladstone Park
Cricklewood
FENTON HOUSE
HAMPSTEAD
KEATS HOUSE
Gospel Oak
Tufnell Park
WEMBLEY ARENA
WEMBLEY STADIUM
GRANGE MUSEUM
WILLESDEN
Belsize Park
XVIII
IX
M25
M1
A1(M)
A1
A41
A406
A5
A1000
A111
A110
A5109
A504
A598

XIII
Bury Green
CHESHUNT
Lee Valley
River Lea
WALTHAM ABBEY
Wood Green
Cattlegate
Waltham Cross
Holdbrook
Crews Hill
Whitewebbs Park
CAPEL MANOR
Freezy Water
M25
Clay Hill
FORTY HALL
Forty Hill
Enfield Wash
Enfield Lock
High Beach
Gordon Hill
Sewardstone
QUEEN ELIZABETH STADIUM
Enfield Highway
Brimsdown
ENFIELD
World's End
Grange Park
Bush Hill Park
Ponders End
King George's Reservoir
Sewardstonebury
Chingford Green
SOUTHGATE
Grovelands Park
Winchmore Hill
William Girling Reservoir
PICKETT'S LOCK
CHINGFORD
Friday Hill
Lower Edmonton
Palmers Green
Great Cambridge Junction
Pymmes Park
Cooks Ferry
Woodford Wells
Broomfield Park
Chingford Hatch
EDMONTON
Angel Edmonton
Hall Lane
Higham's Park
Bowes Park
Clockhouse Junction
NEW RIVER STADIUM
Hale End
Banbury Reservoir
WALTHAMSTOW STADIUM
WOOD GREEN
BRUCE CASTLE MUSEUM
WHITE HART LANE
Crooked Billet
Woodford Green
Higham Hill
Waterworks Corner
Noel Park
TOTTENHAM
Bruce Grove
Reservoirs
West Green
Tottenham Hale
WALTHAMSTOW
Snaresbrook
Seven Sisters
VESTRY HOUSE MUSEUM
HORNSEY
Harringay
South Tottenham
Stroud Green
Finsbury Park
Stamford Hill
Upper Clapton
Green Man Interchange
WANSTEAD
Leytonstone
STOKE NEWINGTON
Clapton
Lea Bridge
R. Lea or Lee
Hackney Marsh
LEYTON
EMIRATES STADIUM
Shacklewell
Highbury
Nags Head
Clapton Park
Lea Interchange
Mkt
Canonbury
Temple Mills
Forest Gate

Claverhambury
Almes Green
Cobbins Brook
EPPING
Coopersale
Coopersale Street
Gaynes Park
Bell Common
Ivy Chimneys
Copthall Green
Upshire
WALTHAM ABBEY
Fiddlers Hamlet
Mount End
Wood Green
Wakearms Rdbt
Theydon Garnon
Hobbs Cross
Theydon Mount
Theydon Bois
Debden Green
High Beach
Epping Forest
STAPLEFORD AERODROME
Abridge
Debden
Sewardstonebury
LOUGHTON
River Roding
Nature Reserve
Lambourne End
CHINGFORD
Friday Hill
Buckhurst Hill
Chigwell Row
HAINAULT FOREST
CHIGWELL
Woodford Wells
Grange Hill
WOODFORD
Hale End
Woodford Bridge
Hainault
Woodford Green
Fairlop
Collier Row
Charlie Browns Rdbt
Clayhall
Fulwell Cross
FAIRLOP WATERS
Marks Gate
Snaresbrook
Barkingside
Little Heath
Redbridge
Gants Hill
Newbury Park
Seven Kings Park
Chadwell Heath
Moby Dick
Redbridge Rdbt
WANSTEAD
Valentines Park
Seven Kings
Green Man Interchange
Wanstead Park
Cranbrook
Goodmayes
Leytonstone
Ilford
REDBRIDGE MUSEUM
Wanstead Flats
M11
M25
XIII
XX

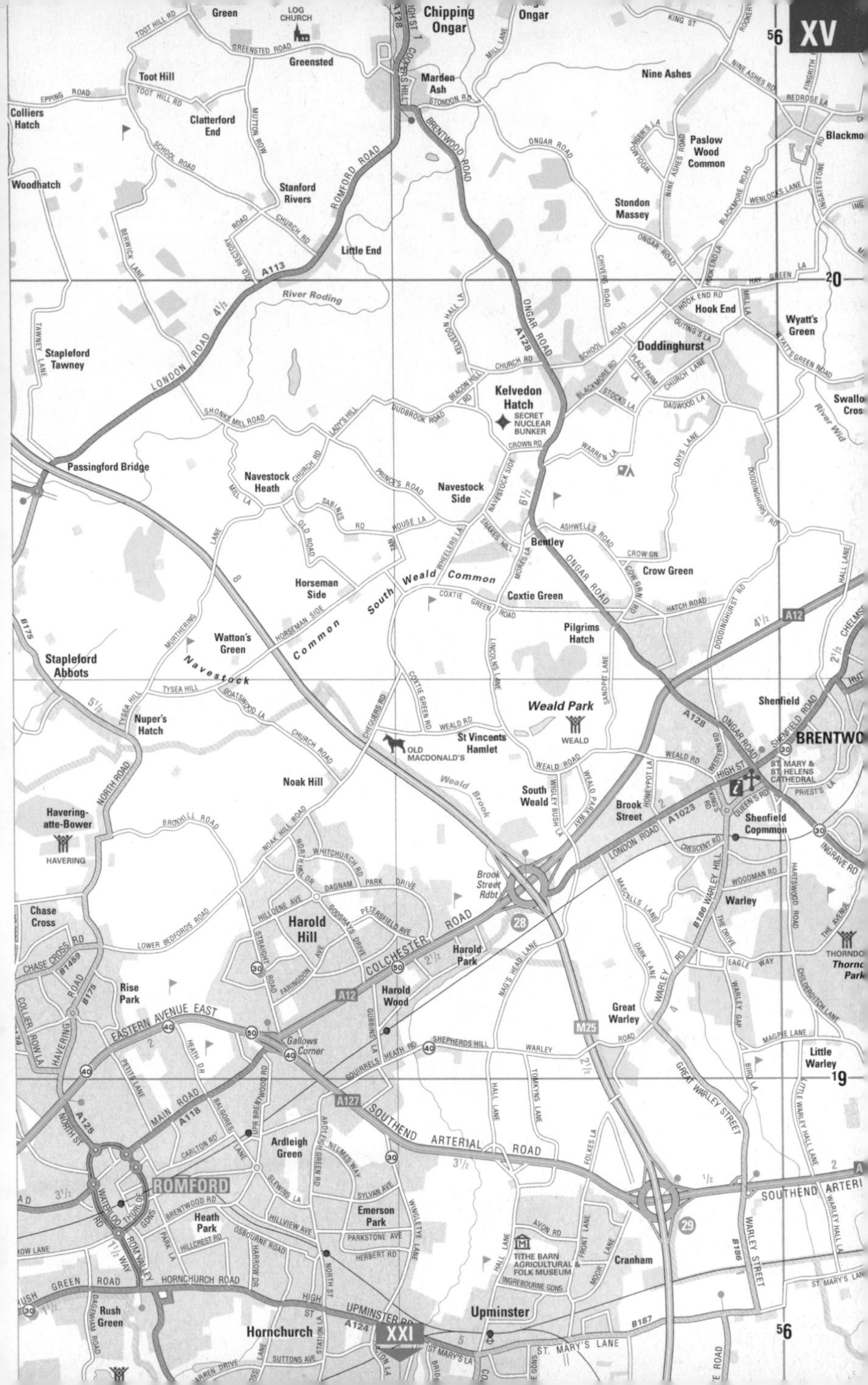
Chipping Ongar
Ongar
Green
LOG CHURCH
Greensted
GREENSTED ROAD
TOOT HILL RD
Toot Hill
Marden Ash
Nine Ashes
NINE ASHES RD
KING ST
FINGRITH
REDROSE LA
Blackmo
Colliers Hatch
EPPING ROAD
TOOT HILL RD
Clatterford End
MUTTON ROW
STONDON RD
BRENTWOOD ROAD
ONGAR ROAD
Paslow Wood Common
NINE ASHES ROAD
BLACKMORE ROAD
WENLOCKS LANE
INGATESTONE RD
Woodhatch
SCHOOL ROAD
ROMFORD ROAD
Stanford Rivers
Stondon Massey
CHURCH RD
OLD RECTORY ROAD
BERWICK LANE
Little End
ONGAR ROAD
HOOK END LA
HAY GREEN LA
A113
River Roding
KELVEDON HALL LA
CHIVERS ROAD
HOOK END RD
Hook End
MILL LA
Wyatt's Green
OUTING'S LA
TAWNEY LANE
LONDON ROAD
Stapleford Tawney
A128
ONGAR ROAD
SCHOOL ROAD
Doddinghurst
WYATT'S GREEN ROAD
CHURCH RD
BEACON HILL RD
Kelvedon Hatch
SECRET NUCLEAR BUNKER
BLACKMORE RD
PLACE FARM LA
CHURCH LANE
STOCKS LA
DAGWOOD LA
Swallo Cros
River Wid
SHONKS MILL ROAD
LADY'S HILL
DUDBROOK ROAD
CROWN RD
WARREN LA
DAYS LANE
Passingford Bridge
Navestock Heath
CHURCH RD
MILL LA
PRINCE'S ROAD
Navestock Side
NAVESTOCK SIDE
DODDINGHURST RD
SABINES RD
HOUSE LA
OLD ROAD
SNAKES HILL
Bentley
ASHWELLS ROAD
CROW GN
Crow Green
COW GRN RD
LANE
8
Horseman Side
South Weald Common
WHEELERS LA
MORES LA
ONGAR ROAD
Coxtie Green
COXTIE GREEN ROAD
HATCH ROAD
DODDINGHURST RD
HALL LANE
A12
B175
MURTHERING LANE
HORSEMAN SIDE
Watton's Green
Navestock Common
Pilgrims Hatch
LINCOLNS LANE
SANDPIT LANE
Stapleford Abbots
TYSEA HILL
GOATSWOOD LA
COXTIE GREEN RD
Weald Park
WEALD
Shenfield
SHENFIELD ROAD
BRENTWO
Nuper's Hatch
CHURCH ROAD
CHEQUERS RD
WEALD RD
St Vincents Hamlet
OLD MACDONALD'S
A128
ONGAR ROAD
WESTERN RD
WEALD RD
HIGH ST
ST MARY & ST HELENS CATHEDRAL
NORTH ROAD
Noak Hill
Weald Brook
WEALD ROAD
South Weald
WIGLEY BUSH LA
WEALD PARK WAY
HONEYPOT LA
Brook Street
KINGS RD
QUEEN'S RD
PRIEST'S LA
Havering-atte-Bower
HAVERING
BROXHILL ROAD
NOAK HILL ROAD
NORTH HILL DR
WHITCHURCH RD
A1023
LONDON ROAD
CRESCENT RD
Shenfield Common
INGRAVE RD
DAGNAM PARK DRIVE
Brook Street Rdbt
MASCALLS LANE
B186 WARLEY HILL
WOODMAN RD
HARTSWOOD ROAD
Warley
THE AVENUE
HILLDENE AVE
GOODSHAYS DRIVE
PETERSFIELD AVE
Harold Hill
ROAD
28
THE DRIVE
THORNDO
Thornd Park
Chase Cross
LOWER BEDFORDS ROAD
STRAIGHT ROAD
FARINGDON AVE
COLCHESTER
Harold Park
NAG'S HEAD LANE
DARK LANE
CHASE CROSS RD
B1459
ROAD
B175
Rise Park
30
50
A12
Harold Wood
WARLEY RD
EAGLE WAY
WARLEY GAP
CHILDERDITCH LANE
COLLIER ROW LA
HAVERING RD
EASTERN AVENUE EAST
40
50
HEATH DR
Gallows Corner
GUBBINS LA
M25
Great Warley
ROAD
MAGPIE LANE
SHEPHERDS HILL
WARLEY
40
40
PETITS LANE
UPR BRENTWOOD RD
SQUIRRELS HEATH RD
HALL LANE
TOMKYNS LANE
GREAT WARLEY STREET
BIRD LA
Little Warley
19
A125
NORTH ST
MAIN ROAD
A118
BALGORES LANE
A127
SOUTHEND ARTERIAL ROAD
LITTLE WARLEY HALL LANE
CARLTON RD
Ardleigh Green
ARDLEIGH GREEN RD
NELMES WAY
30
FOLKES LA
ROMFORD
SLEWINS LA
SYLVAN AVE
WINGLETYE LANE
SOUTHEND ARTERI
WATERLOO RD
THURLOE GDNS
BRENTWOOD RD
Heath Park
Emerson Park
HILLVIEW AVE
PARKSTONE AVE
WARLEY STREET
29
AVON RD
FRONT LANE
MOOR LANE
HALL LANE
PARK LA
HILLCREST RD
OSBOURNE ROAD
HARROW DR
HERBERT RD
NORTH ST
TITHE BARN AGRICULTURAL & FOLK MUSEUM
Cranham
B186
ROM VALLEY WAY
ROW LANE
GREEN ROAD
HORNCHURCH ROAD
INGREBOURNE GDNS
ST. MARY'S LA
Rush Green
DAGENHAM ROAD
HIGH ST
UPMINSTER RD
Upminster
B187
Hornchurch
A124
STATION LA
XXI
ST MARY'S LA
ST. MARY'S LANE
SUTTONS AVE
56
20

X
XXII
Tatling End
DENHAM
West Ruislip
Ickenham
Ruislip Gardens
NORTHOLT AERODROME
Fulmer
Rush Green
Swakeleys Rdbt
Hillingdon Circus
New Denham
North Hillingdon
UXBRIDGE
Civic Centre
Wexham Street
BLACK PARK
Blackpark Lake
Iver Heath
HILLINGDON
Univ
Hayes End
LANGLEY PARK
George Green
Langley Park
Shreding Green
Love Green
IVER
Cowley
Colham Green
SLOUGH
Middle Green
YIEWSLEY
HAYES
Richings Park
Thorney
THORNEY
Langley
WEST DRAYTON
Sutton
HARLINGTON
Harmondsworth
Sipson
Cranford Park
The Queen Mother Reservoir
Colnbrook
Longford
HEATHROW VISITOR CENTRE
Harlington Corner
Heathrow Airport
LONDON HEATHROW
Terminal 1
Terminal 2
Terminal 3
Terminal 4
Terminal 5 u/c
Poyle
Horton
Sunnymeads
Wraysbury Reservoir
Stanwell Moor
Hatton Cross
Wraysbury
STANWELL
West Bedfont
Clockhouse Rdbt
East Bedfont
King George VI Reservoir
Staines Reservoirs
BEDFONT LAKES
The Bull Dog
STAINES
Crooked Billet Roundabout
RUNNYMEDE
Runnymede Park
ASHFORD
Lower Feltham
Ashford Common
EGHAM
Knowle Green
Fordbridge Rdbt
Milton Park
M25
M40
M4
A40
A412
A4020
A4007
A408
A437
A4
A3044
A3113
A30
A308
A320
A328
A315
A244
B470
B376
B378
B3003
B3376
B388
B465
B466
B467
B483
B377
WESTERN AVENUE
OXFORD ROAD
UXBRIDGE ROAD
SLOUGH ROAD
COLNBROOK BY-PASS
GREAT SOUTH-WEST ROAD
LONDON ROAD
STAINES BY-PASS
EGHAM BY-PASS
KINGSTON RD
STAINES RD WEST
River Colne
Colne Brook
Fray's R

XVII
XI
XVIII
XXIII
18
52
Ruislip Manor
Roxeth
Harrow on the Hill
North Wembley
Wembley Park
Wembley Arena
Wembley Stadium
Neasden Circle
South Ruislip
South Harrow
Sudbury
WEMBLEY
Polish War Memorial
NORTHOLT
Target Rdbt
Stonebridge Park
Stonebridge
Alperton
Perivale
White Hart Rdbt
GREENFORD
London Motorcycle Museum
Greenford Rdbt
Hangar Lane
Park Royal
Yeading
EALING
West Acton
Gipsy Corner
Ossie Garvin Rdbt
Hayes Town
Dormer's Wells
Drayton Green
ACTON
SOUTHALL
West Ealing
HANWELL
South Acton
Norwood Green
Northfields
Gunnersbury Park
Chiswick Rdbt
Heston Services
Osterley Park
Osterley Park (N.T.)
BRENTFORD
Griffin Park
Steam Mus.
Music Mus.
Kew Bridge
CHISWICK
HESTON
Gillette Corner
Kew
Public Record Office
North Hyde
Osterley
Syon Park
Syon House
Royal Botanic Gardens (Kew)
Grove Park
Waggoners Rdbt
Cranford
Henlys Rdbt
Civic Centre
North Sheen
Chalkers Corner
Mortlake
Hounslow West
HOUNSLOW
Woodlands
Old Deer Park
Richmond Circus
Manor Circus
ISLEWORTH
East Sheen
RICHMOND
Twickenham Br
Hounslow Heath
Rugby Mus.
Richmond Br
St Margarets
Richmond Hill
Whitton
The Stoop
Marble Hill House
TWICKENHAM
Roads in Richmond Park open in daylight hours only
Richmond Park
FELTHAM
River Thames
Ham House (N.T.)
Petersham
Hanworth Park
Ham
Apex Corner
Robin Hood
Kingston Vale
HANWORTH
TEDDINGTON
KINGSTON UPON THAMES
Grand Union Canal
River Brent
River Crane
A40
A4
M4
A312
A4020
A4127
A406
A3005
A3006
A316
A305
A307
A310
A313
A314
A315
WESTERN AVENUE
GREAT WEST ROAD
UXBRIDGE ROAD
NORTH CIRCULAR ROAD
CHERTSEY ROAD
HANGER LA
GUNNERSBURY AVE

XVIII
XII
XXIV
18
52
Neasden
Gladstone Park
Cricklewood
HAMPSTEAD
KEATS HOUSE
Tufnell Park
GRANGE MUSEUM
WILLESDEN
Belsize Park
Kentish Town
Swiss Cottage
West Hampstead
Stonebridge Park
Brondesbury
Kilburn
Primrose Hill
JEWISH MUSEUM
CAMDEN TOWN
Stonebridge
Harlesden
LONDON ZOO
Regents Park
St Pancras
Kensal Rise
St. John's Wood
Maida Vale
LORDS
Park Royal
Euston
Grand Union Canal
MADAME TUSSAUD'S
Old Oak Common
Marylebone
Wormwood Scrubs Park
LINFORD CHRISTIE STADIUM
Marylebone Flyover
MARYLEBONE
Paddington
West Acton
Gipsy Corner
Westbourne Park
East Acton
MUSEUM OF BRANDS
PADDINGTON
ACTON
Savoy Circus
White City
LOFTUS ROAD
Notting Hill
Bayswater
MARBLE ARCH
Hyde Park
Mayfair
ROYAL ACADEMY
NATIONAL GALLERY
KENSINGTON PALACE
Kensington Gardens
APSLEY HOUSE
Green Park
St James's Palace
Sheperd's Bush
Holland Park
BUCKINGHAM PALACE
St James's Park
South Acton
Bedford Park
Hyde Park Corner
Knightsbridge
ROYAL ALBERT HALL
WESTMINSTER ABBEY
NATURAL HISTORY
Olympia
Victoria
HAMMERSMITH
CHELSEA
Chiswick Rdbt
NATIONAL ARMY MUSEUM
RANELAGH GDNS
Pimlico
Hammersmith Br
Hammersmith Broadway
Earl's Court
Kew Bridge
CHISWICK
Hogarth Rdbt
THE QUEEN'S CLUB
CHISWICK HOUSE
Chelsea Br
Albert Br
Public Record Office
STAMFORD BRIDGE
CHILDREN'S ZOO
Battersea Park
Grove Park
WETLANDS CENTRE
FULHAM
Parsons Green
Battersea Br
River Thames
Barnes Br
CRAVEN COTTAGE
WESTLAND HELIPORT
BATTERSEA
North Sheen
BARNES
Chiswick Br
Putney Br
Hurlingham Park
Clapham Junction
CLAPHAM
Mortlake
Chalkers Corner
Manor Circus
Wandsworth Br
Red Rover
Clapham Common
CHMOND
East Sheen
PUTNEY
Wandsworth Gyratory
WANDSWORTH
Roehampton
Putney Heath
West Hill
Wandsworth Common
Balham
Grange Mills
Roads in Richmond Park open in daylight hours only
Richmond Park
Tibbet's Corner
Southfields
Earlsfield
Tooting Bec Common
Upper Tooting
Robin Hood
Putney Vale
WIMBLEDON L.T.A.
Wimbledon Park
TENNIS MUSEUM
WIMBLEDON STADIUM
Tooting Bec
Kingston Vale
Wimbledon Common
WIMBLEDON
Tooting
Furzedown
Crooked Billet
Collier's Wood
Coombe
NGSTON UPON HAMES
Coombe Lane
Norbiton
NEW MALDEN
Bushey
Morden
MITCHAM
NORTH CIRCULAR ROAD
HARROW ROAD
WESTWAY
UXBRIDGE RD
KENSINGTON ROAD
CROMWELL RD
GREAT WEST ROAD
UPPER RICHMOND ROAD
KINGSTON ROAD
ROBIN HOOD WAY

XIX
XIII
XX
XXV
54
18
17
Shacklewell
Highbury
Canonbury
Highbury Corner
Clapton Park
Temple Mills
STRATFORD
Forest Gate
HACKNEY
Hackney Wick
Dalston
Victoria Park
Upton
West Ham Park
ISLINGTON
SHOREDITCH
Kings Cross
PENTONVILLE
Old Ford
WEST HAM
BETHNAL GREEN
BOW
FINSBURY
Plaistow
Bromley
HOUSE MILL DISTILLERY
GAS MUSEUM
Spitalfields
Holborn
BRITISH MUSEUM
Liverpool St
Stepney
Prince Regent
Law Courts
GUILDHALL
Aldgate
POPLAR
Canning Town
City Thameslink
Blackfriars
Cannon St
Fenchurch St
Blackwall
Blackwall Tunnel
Charing Cross
Waterloo Br
Millennium Br
Southwark Br
London Br
TOWER OF LONDON
Tower Br
HAY'S GALLERIA
Wapping
Rotherhithe Tunnel
Limehouse
EXCEL CENTRE
Royal Victoria
TATE MODERN
GLOBE THEATRE & EXHIBITION
HAYWARD GAL
LONDON EYE
Govt Offices
Westminster
London Bridge
Canary Wharf
West India Docks
MILLENNIUM DOME
North Greenwich
DESIGN MUS
BRUNEL ENGINE HOUSE MUSEUM
Rotherhithe
Waterloo
Houses of Parliament
BERMONDSEY
ISLE OF DOGS
Millwall
Surrey Quays
River Thames
IMPERIAL WAR MUSEUM
Elephant & Castle
Lambeth
LAMBETH
Vauxhall Cross
Walworth
THE NEW DEN
CUTTY SARK
RN Coll
THE OVAL
DEPTFORD
GREENWICH
NATIONAL MARITIME MUSEUM
Greenwich Park
GREENWICH OBSERVATORY
Kennington
LIVESEY MUSEUM
Peckham
New Cross
Camberwell Green
CAMBERWELL
BLACKHEATH
Blackheath Park
BRIXTON
East Dulwich
Nunhead
Brockley
LEWISHAM
Hither Green
Peckham Rye Park
Honor Oak
Ladywell
Brockwell Park
Lee
Dulwich Park
Catford Gyratory
PICTURE GALLERY
HORNIMAN MUSEUM
CATFORD
Tulse Hill
West Dulwich
Forest Hill
STREATHAM
Dulwich
Toll
Bellingham
Bell Green
Downham
CRYSTAL PALACE NATIONAL SPORTS CENTRE
PENGE
Streatham Common
Norwood
Beckenham Place Park
Plaistow
Norbury
Anerley
BECKENHAM
BROMLEY
Elmers End
South Norwood
Eden

XX
XIV
XIX
XXVI
54
ILFORD
Redbridge Museum
Ilford Interchange
Loxford
Little Ilford
Goodmayes
Becontree
Fair Cross
Mayesbrook Park
BARKING
Castle Green
Ripple Road
Heathway
Wanstead Flats
Manor Park
Forest Gate
Plashet
Upton
West Ham Park
Upton Park
WEST HAM
Boleyn Gd (Upton Park)
Barking Flyover
Wallend
EAST HAM
Eastbury Manor House
Movers Lane
Plaistow
Beckton Alps
Beckton
Creekmouth
Barking Creek
River Thames
Crossness Pumping Station
Canning Town
Prince Regent
Custom House
Blackwall
Blackwall Tunnel
Excel Centre
Royal Victoria Dock
Royal Albert Dock
City Airport
King George V Dock
Millennium Dome
18
North Greenwich
Silvertown
Thames Barrier
North Woolwich
Old Station Railway Museum
Woolwich Ferry
Thamesmead
Abbey Wood
Thames Barrier Visitor Centre
WOOLWICH
Plumstead
The Valley
GREENWICH
Charlton
Woolwich Common
East Wickham
Bostall Woods
West Heath
Lessness Heath
Belvedere
Greenwich Park
Shooters Hill
Sun in the Sands Rdbt
Kidbrooke
Eltham Common
Oxleas Wood
Welling
Blackheath
Kidbrooke Intc
Blackheath Park
Falconwood
Bexleyheath
Danson Park
Danson Interchange
The Red House
BEXLEY
Lewisham
Hither Green
Yorkshire Grey
ELTHAM
Avery Hill
Blackfen
Lee
Clifton Rdbt
Eltham Palace
Old Bexley
New Eltham
Mottingham
Longlands
SIDCUP
North Cray
Grove Park
Downham
Elmstead Wood
Elmstead
Plaistow
Sundridge Park
Chislehurst Common
Frognal Corner
Scadbury Park Nature Reserve
Foots Cray
Critnall's Corner
Ruxley
Upper Ruxley
A406
A13
A2
A20
A205
A102
A2213
A112
A206
Sidcup By-Pass
Shooters Hill Road
Rochester Way
Woolwich Road
Ripple Road
Alfred's Way
Newham Way
Eastern Way
Western Way
Sidcup Road
Dover Road
Bellegrove Road

XXI
XV
XXVII
Rush Green
Hornchurch
Upminster
Eastbrookend
Elm Park
Corbets Tey
Hacton
Hornchurch
North Ockendon
Dagenham
South Hornchurch
Rainham
Rainham Hall (N.T.)
Belhus Woods
South Ockendon
Grangewater
Wennington
Belhus Park
Aveley
North Stifford
Thurrock Services
Wennington Marshes
High Speed 1 (Channel Tunnel Rail Link)
Aveley Marshes
Mar Dyke
Lakeside Shopping Centre
Chafford Hundred
Purfleet
West Thurrock
South Stifford
Gray
Erith
North End
Northumberland Heath
Crayford Marshes
Dartford Marshes
Dartford Crossing
Dartford Tunnel
West Thurrock Marshes
Queen Elizabeth II Bridge
River Thames
Barnehurst
Slade Green
River Darent
Swanscombe Marshes
Crayford
Barnes Cray
Temple Hill
Greenhithe
Stone
Stone Lodge Farm Park
Hall Place
Dartford
Swanscombe
Coldblow
Bluewater Shopping Centre
Fleet-Downs
Swanscombe Park
Maypole
Darenth Wood
Bean
Joyden's Wood
Hook Green
Wilmington
Darenth
Lane End
Lords Wood
Beacon Wood
Betsham
Hawley
Southfleet
St John's Jerusalem (N.T.)
Hextable
Clement Street
Green St Green
Sutton-at-
M25
A13
A2
A282
A206
A226
A1306
Thames Gateway
River Ingrebourne
River Beam

XVI
EGHAM
Knowle Green
Milton Park
Callow Hill
Stroude
Longside Lake
Virginia Water
Thorpe
THORPE PARK
River Thames
Marina
Laleham
Littleton
Charlton
Queen Mary Reservoir
Fordbridge Rdbt
KINGSTON RD
STAINES RD WEST
Shepperton Green
Upper Halliford
Shepperton
Lower Halliford
CHERTSEY
CHERTSEY MUSEUM
Chertsey Br
Walton Br
Lyne
Chertsey Common
Addlestonemoor
Woburn Park
Coll
WEYBRIDGE
ELMBRIDGE MUSEUM
Oatlands Park
Broad Water
ADDLESTONE
Ottershaw
Row Town
New Haw
BROOKLANDS MUSEUM
St George's Hill
R Navigation
River Wey
Woodham
FAIROAKS AERODROME
Anningsley Park
Brooklands
Whiteley Village
Dartnell Park
West Byfleet
Byfleet
COBHAM BUS MUSEUM
Silver Mere
Pain's Hill
PAINSHILL PARK
Horsell Common
Sheerwater
Cheapside
Foxwarren Park
Horsell
Pyrford
Wisley
Pyrford Green
Wisley Common
Bolder Mere
Telegraph Hill
Maybury
WOKING
R.H.S. GARDEN WISLEY
Elm Corner
Ripley Green
Hook Heath
Bridge End
Martyr's Green
Ripley
Old Woking
Westfield
Ockham Park
Church End
Ockham
Mayford
Cartbridge
Send
Send Marsh
Hungry Hill
Sutton Green
East Horsley
M25
M3
A3
A308
A320
A317
A318
A319
A245
A247
A3046
A3050
A244
B3376
B388
B377
B376
B375
B3366
B389
B386
B387
B3121
B385
B373
B372
B374
B366
B382
B367
B380
B368
B2215
B2039
B358
RIPLEY BY-PASS
PORTSMOUTH ROAD
OCKHAM ROAD NORTH
GUILDFORD ROAD
CHERTSEY ROAD
CHOBHAM ROAD
WOODHAM LANE
SEND ROAD
BYFLEET ROAD
WEYBRIDGE RD
QUEENS ROAD
SEVEN HILLS ROAD
OATLANDS DRIVE
SHEPPERTON RD
LALEHAM RD
CHRISTCHURCH ROAD
THORPE BY-PASS
STAINES ROAD
CHERTSEY LANE
EGLEY ROAD
OLD WOKING ROAD
50
17
16

XVII
XXIII
XXIV
TEDDINGTON
Hampton
KEMPTON PARK
Sunbury Cross
SUNBURY
Bushy Park
Hampton Wick
Kingston Br
Norbiton
NEW MALDEN
Molesey Reservoirs
Bessborough Res
Knight Res
Hampton Ct Br
HAMPTON COURT PALACE
Hampton Court Park
County Hall
Univ
Hogsmill River
River Thames
East Molesey
SURBITON
Berrylands
Queen Elizabeth II Reservoir
Island Barn Reservoir
Thames Ditton
Coll
Fieldcommon
WALTON-ON-THAMES
River Ember
Rydens
Hinchley Wood
Long Ditton
Tolworth
SANDOWN PARK
Littleworth Common
Govt Offices
Hook Interchange
ESHER
HERSHAM
River Mole
West End Common
CLAREMONT LANDSCAPE GARDEN
CLAYGATE
Arbrook Common
CHESSINGTON
HORTON
West Ewell
CHESSINGTON WORLD OF ADVENTURES
Esher Common
Oxshott Heath
Malden Rushett
Fairmile
Prince's Coverts
Oxshott
Cobham
Stoke Wood
The Forest
Epsom Common
EPSOM
Little Heath
Cobham Park
Stoke D'Abernon
Pachesham Park
Wood Field
Woodcote
Downside
Lower Ashstead
Leatherhead Common
Ashstead
Langley Vale
LEATHERHEAD
Banks Common
Great Bookham Common
Little Bookham Common
Fetcham
Effingham Common
Little Bookham
Tyrell's Wood
Leatherhead Downs
Nower Wood
Givons Grove
BROCKETTS FARM PARK
Great Bookham
Fetcham Downs
Mickleham Downs
Headley
HAMPTON COURT RD
KINGSTON BY-PASS
PORTSMOUTH RD
LEATHERHEAD ROAD
KINGSTON RD
EPSOM RD
DORKING RD
LEATHERHEAD BY-PASS
TOLWORTH RISE
HOOK RISE
HOOK ROAD
A3
A24
A240
A243
A244
A245
A246
A307
A308
A309
A316
A317
A3050
B280
B284
B2122
B2430
M25
9
16
17
52

XVIII
XXIII
NEW MALDEN
Raynes Park
Bushey Mead
MORDEN
Morden Hall Park
MITCHAM
Mitcham Common
Shannon Corner
West Barnes
Morden Park
Berrylands
Motspur Park
Lower Morden
Old Malden
Rosehill
St Helier
Beddington Corner
Hackbridge
Beddington Park
Tolworth
Worcester Park
North Cheam
CARSHALTON
WALLINGTON
Stoneleigh
SUTTON
Nonsuch Park
WHITEHALL
HORTON
West Ewell
Beggars Hill
Organ Crossroads
CHEAM
South Beddington
Ewell
Belmont
Carshalton on the Hill
East Ewell
Little Woodcote
Oaks Park
North Looe
EPSOM
Woodmansterne
Clock House
Nork
BANSTEAD
Coulsdon
Woodcote
Great Burgh
Park Downs
Chipstead
Langley Vale
EPSOM
Burgh Heath
Banstead Wood
Walton Downs
Kingswood
Hooley
Tadworth
Walton on the Hill
Nower Wood
Headley
Banstead Heath
Lower Kingswood
Walton Heath
Merstham
Gatton
Headley Heath
Mogador
Margery
Buckland Hills
A3
A24
A217
A232
A240
A2043
A2022
A23
A237
A239
A297
A298
A236
M25
KINGSTON RD
MALDEN WAY
LONDON ROAD
EPSOM ROAD
REIGATE RD
BRIGHTON ROAD
CARSHALTON ROAD
CHEAM RD
CROYDON LANE
HOLLY LANE
OUTWOOD LANE
WINKWORTH RD
TATTENHAM WAY
REIGATE ROAD
DORKING RD
ASHLEY ROAD
CHESSINGTON RD
16
52

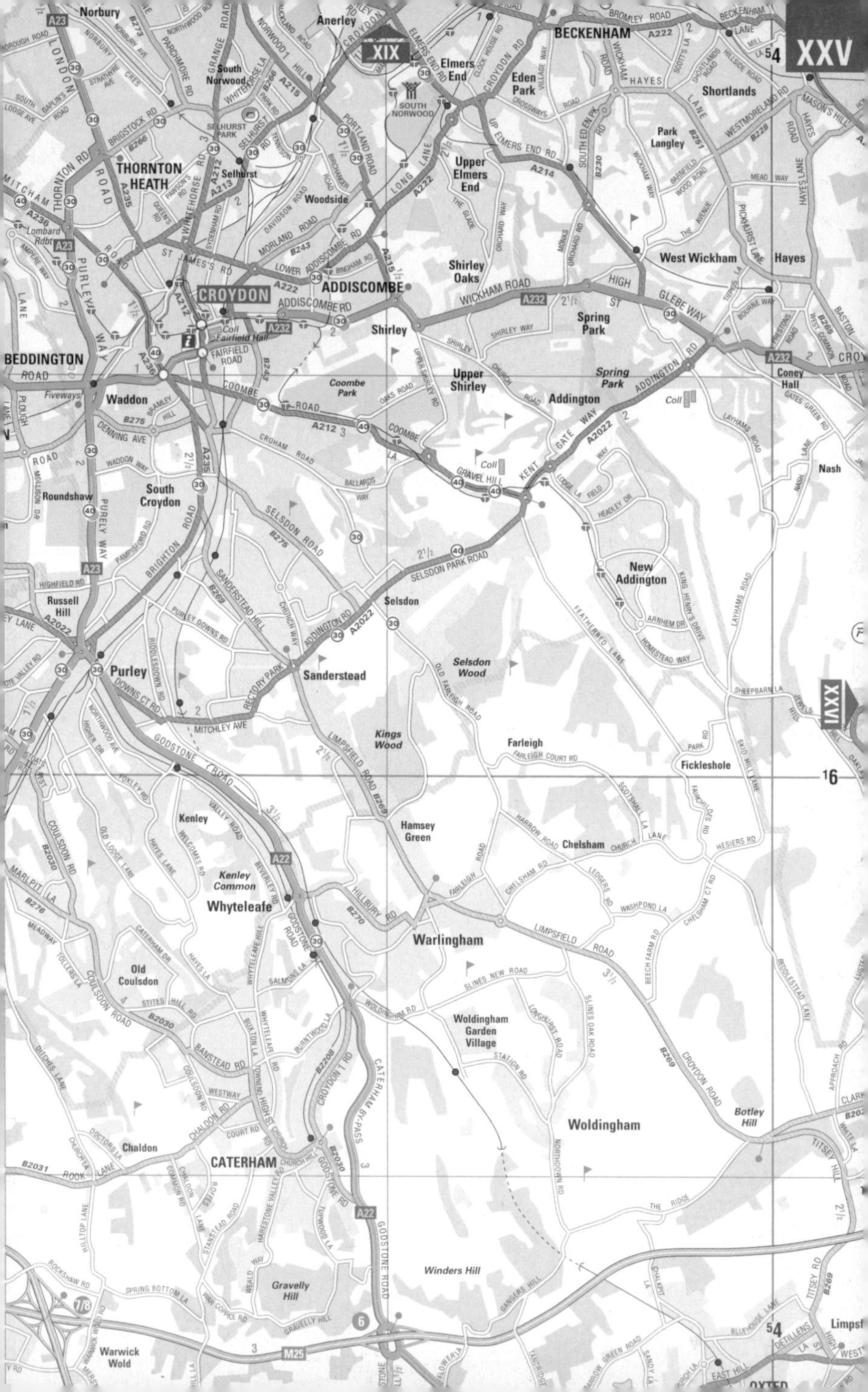
XXV
XIX
XXVI
BECKENHAM
THORNTON HEATH
CROYDON
ADDISCOMBE
BEDDINGTON
CATERHAM
Norbury
Anerley
South Norwood
Elmers End
Eden Park
Shortlands
Park Langley
Upper Elmers End
Selhurst
Woodside
West Wickham
Hayes
Shirley Oaks
Shirley
Spring Park
Upper Shirley
Addington
Coney Hall
Waddon
Nash
South Croydon
Roundshaw
New Addington
Russell Hill
Selsdon
Purley
Sanderstead
Selsdon Wood
Kings Wood
Farleigh
Fickleshole
Kenley
Hamsey Green
Chelsham
Kenley Common
Whyteleafe
Warlingham
Old Coulsdon
Woldingham Garden Village
Woldingham
Botley Hill
Chaldon
Winders Hill
Gravelly Hill
Warwick Wold
Coombe Park
Fairfield Hall
Lombard Rdbt
Fiveways
M25
A22
A23
A232
A2022
A212
A222
16
54

XXVI
XX
XXV
Wood
Coll
Elmstead
Foots Cray
Upper Ruxley
Sundridge Park
Frognal Corner
Scadbury Park Nature Reserve
Critnall's Corner
Ruxley
Chislehurst Common
CHISLEHURST
MAIDSTONE ROAD
CHISLEHURST CAVES
Widmore
Bickley
BROMLEY
St Paul's Cray
Hockenden
Shortlands
Petts Wood
Poverest
JUBILEE
St Mary Cray
Kevingtown
Southborough
Broom Hill
Coll
Bromley Common
Hayes
ORPINGTON
Keston Mark
Crofton
Goddington
Locksbottom
Coney Hall
The Fantail
Keston
Farnborough
Chelsfield
Nash
Maypole
Green Street Green
HIGH ELMS
Pratt's Bottom
Cuckoo Wood
Leaves Green
Downe
DOWN HOUSE (CHARLES DARWIN MUSEUM)
Hazelwood
Halstead
BIGGIN HILL AERODROME
Luxted
Newyears Wood
Fickleshole
Single Street
Cudham
Knockholt Pound
Berry's Green
Knockholt
Letts Green
Biggin Hill
Horns Green
Chevening
South Street
Tatsfield Green
Tatsfield
Botley Hill
Hill Park
Force Green
River Darent
Sundridge
Titsey
QUEBEC HOUSE (N.T.)
Brasted
Farley Common
CLACKET LANE SERVICES
Titsey
A20
A21
A222
A224
A208
A232
A223
A233
A25
B264
B265
B228
B251
B258
B2158
B2024
B2211
M25
CROYDON ROAD
SEVENOAKS ROAD
SEVENOAKS WAY
COURT RD (ORPINGTON BY-PASS)
ORPINGTON BY-PASS
FARNBOROUGH WAY
FARNBOROUGH COMMON
HASTINGS ROAD
WESTERHAM ROAD
WESTERHAM HILL
MAIN ROAD
LEAVES GRN RD
BROMLEY COMMON
CROFTON ROAD
SOUTHBOROUGH LANE
SHIRE LANE
CUDHAM LANE NORTH
CUDHAM LANE SOUTH
JAIL LANE
CLARKS LANE
PILGRIMS LANE
CLACKET LANE
LONDON RD
WESTERHAM RD
BRASTED ROAD
HIGH ST
CHEVENING RD
OVENDEN RD
SUNDRIDGE RD
17
16
54

Hawley
XXI
Hextable
Clement Street
Sutton-at-Hone
St John's Jerusalem (N.T.)
Green St Green
South Darenth
Pinden
Longfield
Swanley Village
Swanley
Farningham Wood
Horton Kirby
Hartley Green
Farningham
Crockenhill
Eynsford Castle
Eynsford
Horton Wood
Fawkham Green
New Ash Green
Bird of Prey Centre
Lullingstone Roman Villa
Lullingstone Castle
Beechen Wood
Maplescombe
Brands Hatch
Ash
Timberden Bottom
River Darent
High Castle Wood
West Kingsdown
Shoreham
Knatts Valley
Romney Street
Magpie Bottom
Woodlands
Twitton
Otford
Kemsing
Crowdleham
Heaverham
Wrotham
Dunton Green
Longford
Greatness
Seal
Styants Bottom
Oldbury
Ightham
Chipstead
Riverhead
Wildernesse
Seal Chart
Godden Green
Stone Street
Ightham Common
Kippington
SEVENOAKS
Knole (N.T.)
Lower Bitchet
Bitchet
Ivy Hatch
Yopps Green
M25
M20
M26
A20
A225
A224
A25
A227
B2173
B258
B260
B2019
17
16

Key to map symbols

Roads

- Motorway with junction number (22a)
- Primary route – single, dual carriageway
- A road – single, dual carriageway
- B road – single, dual carriageway
- Through-route – single, dual carriageway
- Minor road – single, dual carriageway
- Road under construction
- Rural track, private road or narrow road in urban area
- Path, bridleway, byway open to all traffic, road used as public path
- Tunnel, covered road
- Speed camera – single, multiple (30)
- Congestion Charge Zone boundary
  Roads within the zone are outlined in green
- Gate or obstruction, car pound
- Parking, park and ride (P, P&R)
- Road junction name (Crooked Billet)
- Pedestrianised, restricted access area

Public transport

- Railway station, private rail station
- London Underground station, Docklands Light Railway station
- Tramway or miniature railway

- Bus or coach station, tram stop

Scale

3½ inches to 1 mile 1:18103

0 220yds 440yds 660yds ½ mile

0 250m 500m 750m 1km

Emergency services

- Ambulance, police, fire station
- Hospital, accident and emergency entrance (H)

General features

- Market, public amenity site
- Sports stadium
- Information centre, post office (PO)
- Roman, non-Roman antiquity (VILLA, House)
- House number, spot height – metres (100, .304)
- Christian place of worship
- Mosque, synagogue
- Other place of worship
- Houses, important buildings
- Woods, parkland/common
- Adjoining page number (123)

Leisure facilities

- Camp site, caravan site

- Golf course, picnic site, view point

Boundaries

- Postcode boundaries (NW6)
- County and unitary authority boundaries (Westminster)

Water features

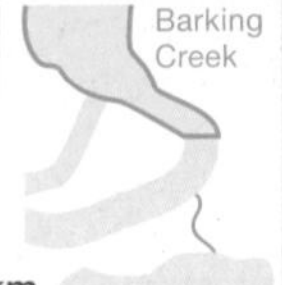

- Water name
- Tidal water
- River or canal – minor, major
- Stream
- Water

Abbreviations

Acad	Academy
Allot Gdns	Allotments
Bndstd	Bandstand
Btcl	Botanical
Bwg Gn	Bowling
Cemy	Cemetery
Ctr	Centre
C Ctr	Civic Centre
CH	Club House
Ctry Pk	Country Park
Coll	College
Ct	Court
Crem	Crematorium
Crkt	Cricket
Ent	Enterprise
Ex H	Exhibition Hall
Fball	Football
Gdns	Gardens
Glf C	Golf Course
Glf Crs	Golf Course
Drv Rng	Golf Driving Range
Gn	Green
Gd	Ground
Hort	Horticultural
Ind Est	Industrial Estate
Inst	Institute
Int	Interchange
Ct	Law Court
L Ctr	Leisure Centre
LC	Level Crossing
Liby	Library
Mkt	Market
Meml	Memorial
Mon	Monument
Mus	Museum
Nat Res	Nature Reserve
Obsy	Observatory
Pav	Pavilion
Pk	Park
Pl Fld	Playing Field
Pal	Royal Palace
PH	Public House
Recn Gd	Recreation Ground
Resr	Reservoir
Ret Pk	Retail Park
Sch	School
Sh Ctr	Shopping Centre
Sp	Sports
Stad	Stadium
Sw Pool	Swimming Pool
Tenn Cts	Tennis
TH	Town Hall
Trad Est	Trading Estate
Univ	University
YH	Youth Hostel

A1000 Potters Bar
Wrotham Park
Home Farm
Lower Kitt's End Farm
Kitt's End
Kitt's End Farm
KITT'S END RD
BARNET RD
A1000
Cockshot Hill
Ganwick Farm
WAGON RD
Bartram's Quash
Hertfordshire Enfield
Pl Fld
Hadley Wood
Great Broad Hill
GREENACRE CL
BEAUMONT PL
Hertfordshire Barnet
EN4
Barnet Enfield
CAMLET WAY
Old Fold Manor
LANGLEY ROW
TAYLOR'S LA
OLD FOLD CL
FOLD LA
HADLEY HIGHSTONE
MILL CNR
Tenn Cts
Monken Hadley CE Prim Sch
St Martha's Senior Sch
HATHERLEIGH CL
PAGITTS GR
BROADGATES AVE
PARKGATE AVE
PARKGATE CRES
EN5
BOUNDARY CL
Hadley Green
Convent
DURY RD
Allot Gdns
Bournwell Hill
Monken Hadley Common
ST ALBANS RD
Monken Hadley
HADLEY GN W
SYDNEY CHAPMAN WAY
HADLEY GREEN RD
HADLEY GN
SUNSET VIEW
Cemy
HADLEY GR
GLADSMUIR RD
HADLEY WOOD RD
Priddeon's Hill
London Loop
BAKERS HILL
THE CRESCENT
THE SPINNEY
HADLEY HTS
The Tudor
Tudor Sp Gd
WROTHAM RD
FALKLAND RD
PULLER RD
CHRIST CHURCH LA
LIVINGSTONE CT
FIRE STATION AL
TA Ctr
A1081
Barnet Mkt
Hadley
King George's Field
LATIMER RD
SHAKESPEARE CT
LOWNDES CT
HADLEYVALE CT
CLIFFORD RD
VINCENT CL
Allot Gdns
TUDOR RD
CH
Tenn Cts
SLADE CT
SEBRIGHT RD
LUCAN RD
ALSTON RD
STRAFFORD RD
CARNARVON RD
Liby
The Spires
High Barnet
HYDE CL
SOUTH CL
HURST RISE
NORFOLK RD
JULIAN CL
SANDFORD CT
RONALD CT
HADLEY RD
ORCHARD CT
Allot Gdns
Cromer Road Sch
PENRAY
WENTWORTH CT
SALISBURY RD
THE DRIVE
THE AVENUE
THORNTON RD
STAPYLTON RD
HART LO
GREAT NORTH RD
MOON LA
MOXON ST
BOSWORTH RD
CATHERINE CT
WOODVILLE RD
DENBY CT
Pl Fld
UNION ST
Sch
GILLINGS CT
Barnet Trad Est
VICTORS WAY
PARK RD
Tenn Cts
MEADWAY CL
BURNSIDE CL
ST MARK'S CL
PEARSON CL
POTTER'S RD
SHERIDAN LO
Pl Flds
WOOD ST
A411
HIGH ST
QUEEN ELIZABETH CT
Queen Elizabeth's Sch
MEADWAY
MARTINS MOUNT
CRABTREE CT
HEXHAM RD
HADRIAN CT
BARNARD LO
SHAFTESBURY AVE
CATTLEY CL
Mus
Barnet Coll
MANOR CL
GORDON WAY
KINGSMEAD
HILLARY RISE
KING EDWARD RD
BARON CT
SHELDON CT
HUGHENDON
BULWER RD
BULWER GDNS
HASTINGS
MASEFIELD CT
SUTHERLAND CL
SCHOLARS CL
Bwg Gns
ORCHARD RD
ELM
VICTORIA LA
High Barnet
A1000
BARNET HILL
LEAF HO
WARWICK RD
VALE CT
LEICESTER RD
MERTON CT
BARNES CT
PLANTAGENET RD
DUNCAN CL
Chipping Barnet
POTTER'S LA
BRACKENWOOD LO
PROSPECT RD
RAVENSCROFT COTTS
ESMOND CT
ABBOTTS RD
WINDERMERE HO
A110
MOWBRAY RD
ASHLEY CT
PINECROFT CR
MANORSIDE
LEECROFT RD
RODINGS ROW
WILLOW DR
MANOR RD
Tenn Cts
FITZJOHN AVE
NEWLYN RD
NORMANDY AVE
BEDFORD AVE
AVENUE MANS
HILLSIDE MANS
WILTON AVE
VALE DR
Sch
TELFORD CT
THE HIGHLANDS
Highlands Gdns
HIGHLANDS RD
HOMESTEAD
HIGHWOOD CT
COLLINGWOOD
STATION RD
SOMERSET RD
NORTH LO
New Barnet
Lyonsdown Sch
RICHMOND
HILLSIDE GDNS
COLGATE CT
THE THOMAS WATSON COTTAGE HOMES
Allot
CEDAR LAWN
ELLESMERE
WOODFALL AVE
ELTON AVE
IMARSTON
13
UNDERHILL CT
POTTERIES
WESTCOMBE DR
BROOK PL
FAIRFIELD
BARNET
A1081 Hatfield (A1(M)), M25
A411 Borehamwood, A1
A B C D

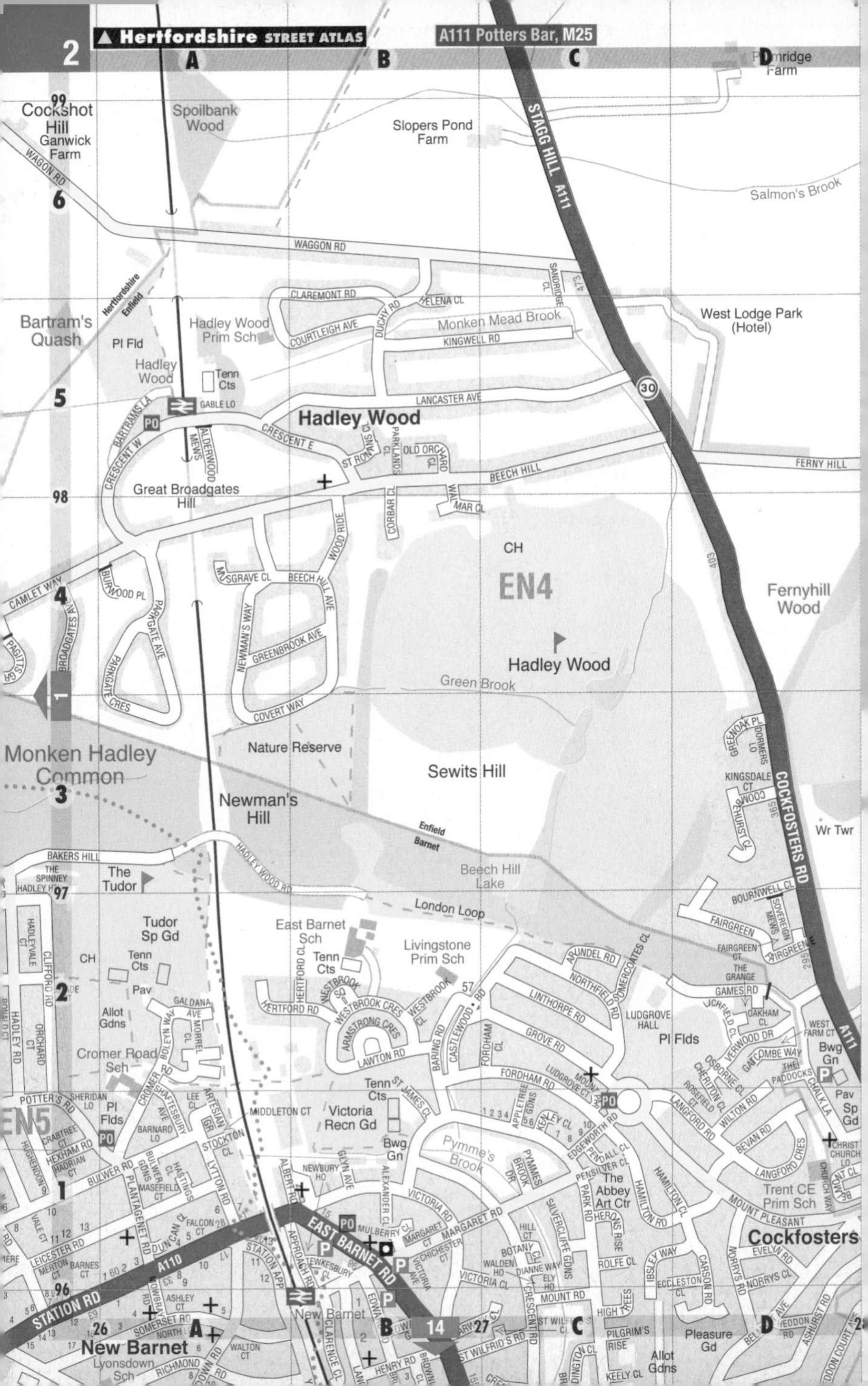

2
Hertfordshire STREET ATLAS
A111 Potters Bar, M25
A
B
C
D
Cockshot Hill
Ganwick Farm
Spoilbank Wood
Slopers Pond Farm
Salmon's Brook
STAGG HILL
A111
WAGGON RD
Hertfordshire
Enfield
Bartram's Quash
Pl Fld
Hadley Wood Prim Sch
Hadley Wood
Tenn Cts
CLAREMONT RD
HELENA CL
COURTLEIGH AVE
DUCHY RD
Monken Mead Brook
KINGWELL RD
SANDRIDGE CL
West Lodge Park (Hotel)
LANCASTER AVE
GABLE LO
Hadley Wood
CRESCENT E
CRESCENT W
BARTRAMS LA
ALDERWOOD MEWS
ST RONANS CL
PARKLANDS
OLD ORCHARD CL
BEECH HILL
FERNY HILL
Great Broadgates Hill
CORBAR CL
MAR CL
CH
EN4
WOOD RIDE
MUSGRAVE CL
BEECH HILL AVE
CAMLET WAY
BURWOOD PL
PARKGATE AVE
NEWMAN'S WAY
GREENBROOK AVE
Fernyhill Wood
Hadley Wood
Green Brook
BROADGATES AV
PARKGATE CRES
COVERT WAY
Monken Hadley Common
Nature Reserve
Sewits Hill
Newman's Hill
GREENOAK PL
DORMERS LO
KINGSDALE CT
COCKFOSTERS RD
Wr Twr
Enfield
Barnet
BAKERS HILL
THE SPINNEY
HADLEY H
The Tudor
HADLEY WOOD RD
Beech Hill Lake
London Loop
BOURNWELL CL
SOVEREIGN MEWS
FAIRGREEN
HADLEYVALE CT
CLIFFORD RD
Tudor Sp Gd
East Barnet Sch
Livingstone Prim Sch
CH
Tenn Cts
Tenn Cts
ARUNDEL RD
SOMERCOATES CL
NORTHFIELD RD
FAIRGREEN CT
THE GRANGE
GAMES RD
Pav
Allot Gdns
GALDANA AVE
MORREL CL
HERTFORD CL
WESTBROOK SQ
HERTFORD RD
WESTBROOK CRES
WESTBROOK CL
ARMSTRONG CRES
LINTHORPE RD
LUDGROVE HALL
Pl Flds
OAKHAM CL
WEST FARM CT
VERWOOD DR
Bwg Gn
ORCHARD CT
HADLEY RD
Cromer Road Sch
LAWTON RD
BARING RD
CASTLEWOOD RD
FORDHAM CL
GROVE RD
GATCOMBE WAY
THE PADDOCKS
CHALK LA
Pav
Sp Gd
POTTER'S RD
SHERIDAN LO
Pl Flds
CROMER RD
SHAFTESBURY AVE
LEE CL
ARTESIAN GR
MIDDLETON CT
ST JAMES CL
Victoria Recn Gd
Tenn Cts
FORDHAM RD
LUDGROVE CT
APPLETREE GDNS
OSBORNE CL
CHERITON CL
ROSEFIELD CL
WILTON RD
LANGFORD RD
EN5
CRABTREE CT
HEXHAM RD
HADRIAN CT
HUGHENDON
BULWER RD
BARNARD LO
BULWER GDNS
MASEFIELD CT
HASTINGS
STOCKTON CL
LYTTON RD
Bwg Gn
Pymme's Brook
PYMMES BROOK DR
EDGEWORTH RD
PENDALL CL
PENSILVER CL
BEVAN RD
LANGFORD CRES
CHRIST CHURCH LO
CHURCH WAY
NEWBURY HO
GLYN AVE
ALEXANDER CL
ALBERT RD
The Abbey Art Ctr
PARK RD
HAMILTON RD
HAMILTON CL
Trent CE Prim Sch
PLANTAGENET RD
DUNCAN CL
FALCON CT
VICTORIA RD
MARGARET RD
MULBERRY CL
MARGARET CT
CHICHESTER CT
SILVERCLIFFE GDNS
HERONS RISE
MOUNT PLEASANT
Cockfosters
LEICESTER RD
MERTON CT
BARNES CT
A110
STATION APP
APPROACH RD
EAST BARNET RD
TEWKESBURY CL
VICTORIA AVE
HILL CT
BOTANY CL
DIANNE WAY
WALDEN HO
ELY HO
VICTORIA CL
ROLFE CL
IBSLEY WAY
CARSON RD
EVELYN RD
NORRYS CL
MORRYS RD
STATION RD
ASHLEY CT
NOWBRAY RD
SOMERSET RD
New Barnet
EDWARD
MOUNT RD
CRESCENT RD
HIGH TREES
ECCLESTON CL
14
ST WILFRID'S RD
PILGRIM'S RISE
Pleasure Gd
ASHURST RD
New Barnet
Lyonsdown Sch
RICHMOND
WALTON CT
CLARENCE CL
HENRY RD
KEELY CL
Allot Gdns

A
B
C
D
Vault Hill Wood
Wood
Botany Bay Farm
Botany Bay
A1005
THE RIDGEWAY
Roundhedge Hill
Salmon's Brook
EN2
Duncan's Wood
Ash Wood
Park Farm
FERNY HILL
Ferny Hill Farm
Obelisk
Moat Wood
Parkside Farm
HADLEY RD
Ride Wood
Leeging Beech
Rough Lot
EN4
Enfield Chase
London Loop
Seedfield Spinney
Icehouse Wood
Williams Wood
Middlesex Univ Trent Park
Trent Country Park
Oak Wood
Shaws Wood
SHAWS WOOD COTTS
ROOKERY COTTS
Pav
Sp Gd
Church Wood
Merryhills Brook
Triangular Wood
South Lodge Farm
Cemy
Cockfosters
SNAKES LA
Trent Park
Trent Park Equestrian Ctr
EASTPOLE COTTS
A110
SOUTH LODGE CRES
LAKESIDE
GREYSTOKE GDNS
LOWTHER
CULGAITH GDNS
NETHERBY GDNS
N14
CH
LONSDALE DR
MERRYHILLS DR
BRAYTON GDNS
CURTHWAITE GDNS
BRANTWOOD GDNS
CLIFTON GDNS
WOODEND GDNS
COCKFOSTERS RD
COCKFOSTERS PAR
GALVA CL
CHADDLEWOOD
MOUNT CL
NORFOLK CL
WEST CL
EAST CL
BRAEMORE CT
HEDDON CT
STATION PAR
GLOUCESTER GDNS
KENT DR
WESTPOLE AVE
BRAMLEY RD
RIDGEVIEW CT
BELGRAVE GDNS
BELGRAVE CL
GROSVENOR GDNS
Oakwood
BETJEMAN CT
TAVERNERS LO
FRESTON GDNS
LEYS GDNS
A111
Southgate Sch
Pl Fld
SUSSEX WAY
MERRYHILLS CT
WOODVILLE CT
STAFFORD CT
HARPER CL
GERRARDS CL
CARLTON AVE
SOUTH LODGE DR
LOWER
BEVERIDGE CT
JENNER CT
ASBURY CT
LONSDALE
99
98
97
96
6
5
4
3
2
1
29
30
15
4
92

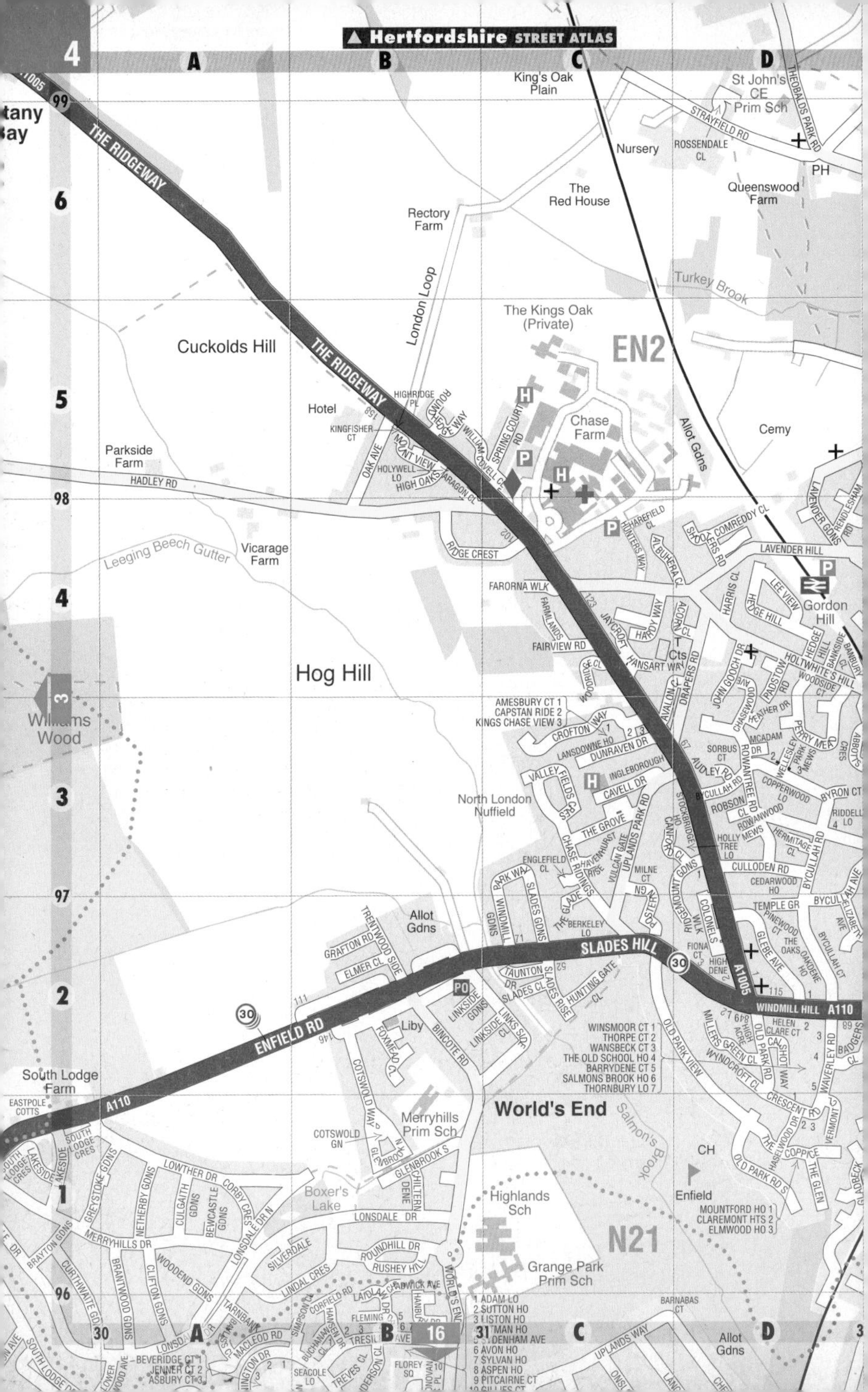
4
Hertfordshire STREET ATLAS
A
B
C
D
King's Oak Plain
St John's CE Prim Sch
THEOBALDS PARK RD
STRAYFIELD RD
ROSSENDALE CL
Nursery
PH
Queenswood Farm
The Red House
Rectory Farm
THE RIDGEWAY
A1005
99
6
Turkey Brook
London Loop
The Kings Oak (Private)
EN2
Cuckolds Hill
5
Hotel
HIGHRIDGE PL
KINGFISHER CT
Chase Farm
Allot Gdns
Cemy
Parkside Farm
HADLEY RD
OAK AVE
HOLYWELL LO
HIGH OAKS
SPRING COURT RD
98
RIDGE CREST
HAREFIELD CL
HUNTERS WAY
ALBUHERA CL
COMREDDY CL
LAVENDER HILL
LAVENDER GDNS
RENDLESHAM RD
Vicarage Farm
Leeging Beech Gutter
FARORNA WLK
HARRIS CL
LEE VIEW
HEDGE HILL
Gordon Hill
4
FARMLANDS
JAYCROFT
HARDY WAY
ACORN CL
FAIRVIEW RD
HANSART WAY
DRAPERS RD
Cts
JOHN GOOCH DR
PADSTOW
HOLTWHITE'S HILL
WOODSIDE CT
BANKSIDE
Hog Hill
3
Williams Wood
AMESBURY CT 1
CAPSTAN RIDE 2
KINGS CHASE VIEW 3
CROFTON WAY
LANSDOWNE HO
DUNRAVEN DR
AVALON CL
CHASEWOOD AVE
HEATHER DR
MCADAM DR
PERRY MEAD
SORBUS CT
AUDLEY RD
ROWANTREE RD
WELLESLEY PARK MEWS
INGLEBOROUGH
VALLEY FIELDS CRES
CAVELL DR
BYCULLAH RD
COPPERWOOD LO
BYRON CT
North London Nuffield
3
THE GROVE
UPLANDS PARK RD
STOCKBRIDGE HO
CANFORD CL
ROBSON CL
ROWANWOOD
RIDDELL LO
HOLLY TREE LO
HERMITAGE CL
ENGLEFIELD CL
PARK WAY
SLADES GDNS
CHASE RIDINGS
HAVENHURST RISE
VULCAN GATE
MILNE CT
CULLODEN RD
CEDARWOOD HO
BYCULLAH AVE
97
WINDMILL GDNS
THE GLADE
BERKELEY LO
POSTERN GN
RIDGEMOUNT GDNS
COLONELS WLK
TEMPLE GR
PINEWOOD CT
THE OAKS
OAKDENE HO
BYCULLAH CT
ELIZABETH AVE
TRENTWOOD SIDE
Allot Gdns
GRAFTON RD
ELMER CL
SLADES HILL
FIONA CT
HIGH DENE
GLEBE AVE
2
TAUNTON DR
SLADES CL
SLADES RISE
HUNTING GATE CL
WINDMILL HILL A110
PO
ENFIELD RD
Liby
FOXMEAD CL
BINCOTE RD
LINKSIDE GDNS
LINKSIDE CL
LINKS SIDE
WINSMOOR CT 1
THORPE CT 2
WANSBECK CT 3
THE OLD SCHOOL HO 4
BARRYDENE CT 5
SALMONS BROOK HO 6
THORNBURY LO 7
OLD PARK VIEW
MILLERS GREEN CL
HIGH ACRE
OLD PARK RD
HELEN CLARE CT
CALSHOT WAY
WYNDCROFT CL
WAVERLEY RD
BADGERS CL
South Lodge Farm
EASTPOLE COTTS
A110
COTSWOLD WAY
Merryhills Prim Sch
World's End
Salmon's Brook
CRESCENT RD
HASEWOOD DR
VERMONT CL
COTSWOLD GN
GLENBROOK N
GLENBROOK S
CH
THE COPPICE
OLD PARK RD S
THE GLEN
SOUTH LODGE CRES
LAKESIDE
GREYSTOKE GDNS
LOWTHER DR
CORBY CRES
CULGAITH GDNS
BEWCASTLE GDNS
CHILTERN DENE
Boxer's Lake
Highlands Sch
Enfield
MOUNTFORD HO 1
CLAREMONT HTS 2
ELMWOOD HO 3
GLADBECK
1
NETHERBY GDNS
LONSDALE DR N
LONSDALE DR
MERRYHILLS DR
BRAYTON GDNS
SILVERDALE
ROUNDHILL DR
RUSHEY HILL
N21
CURTHWAITE GDNS
BRANTWOOD GDNS
CLIFTON GDNS
WOODEND GDNS
LINDAL CRES
WORLD'S END
Grange Park Prim Sch
96
TARNBANK
CORFIELD RD
CHADWICK AVE
1 ADAM LO
2 SUTTON HO
3 LISTON HO
6 AVON HO
7 SYLVAN HO
8 ASPEN HO
9 PITCAIRNE CT
BARNABAS CT
30
31
16
UPLANDS WAY
Allot Gdns
LONSDALE DR
MACLEOD RD
BEVERIDGE CT 1
JENNER CT 2
ASBURY CT 3
SOUTH LODGE DR
TRESILIAN AVE
SEACOLE LO
TREVES CL
FLOREY SQ

Hertfordshire STREET ATLAS
5
A
B
C
D
Whitewebbs Park
Cuffley Brook
Whitewebbs
Brayside Farm
CH
London Loop
PH
Clay Hill
Hilly Fields Park
EN2
Farm
Forty Hall
Allot Gdns
Malden's Bridge
Forty Hill CE Prim Sch
The Clock Ho
Nursery
Worcesters Prim Sch
Old Forge Rd
Cook's Hole Rd
Phipps Hatch La
Clay Hill
Bramley House Ct
St John's Terr
Stratton Ave
Park Nook Gdns
Elm Gdns
Hillside Cres
Gloucester Rd
Cedar Rd
Park Rd
Brodie Rd
Glenville Ave
St Luke's Ave
Morley Hill
Browning Rd
Kilvinton Dr
Woodbine Gr
Myrtle Gr
Violet Ave
Birkbeck Rd
Conway Gdns
Kensington Ct
Henry Cl
Portland Rd
Burnham Cl
Lavender Prim Sch
Enfield Cty Sch
Hawthorn Gr
Rosemary Ave
Primrose Ave
Lavender Rd
Acacia Rd
Ridler Rd
Myddelton Ave
Hallside Rd
Russell Rd
St George's Rd
Goat La
Bridgenhall Rd
Layard Rd
Irkdale Ave
Chimnery Cl
Garnault Rd
Dowland Ho
Holbrook Cl
Mahon Cl
Meyer Gn
98
Lime Tree Wlk
Blossom La
Tudor Cres
Chantry Cl
York Terr
Brigadier Hill
Ripley Rd
Wetherby Rd
Brigadier Ave
Merton Rd
Sterling Rd
Woodlands Rd
Burlington Rd
St Faith's Cl
White House La
Radcliffe Ave
St Michael's CE Prim Sch
PO
Lancaster Rd
Youngmans Cl
Batley Rd
Bank Rd
Lynn St
Walton St
Drake St
Laurel
Lea Rd
Armfield Rd
Philip Ct
Kynaston Rd
York Ho
Weardale Gdns
Lancaster Ho
Radnor Gdns
Kenilworth Cres
Priors Mead
Canonbury Rd
Inverness Ave
Eastbury Ave
Bicknoller Rd
Myddelton Cl
Sinclare Cl
Orchard Cl
Orton Gr
Abercrombie Dr
Linden
Melling Dr
Linwood Cres
Bressey Ave
Gordon Hill
Borrowdale Ct
Whitakers Lo
St Michael's
Gater Dr
John Keats Lo
Shelly Lo
Chase Side Cres
Heene Rd
Farr Rd
The Drive
Baker St
Chace Com Sch
Ivinghoe Cl
Rochester Cl
Forty Hill Cemy
Carisbrook Cl
Tenniswood Rd
Allot Gdns
Sp Gd
Kirkland Dr
Black Fan Cl
Tippetts Cl
Holtwhite Ave
College Gdns
College Rd
Bell Rd
Weston Rd
Gordon Rd
Churchbury Rd
Buckingham Cl
Sandringham Cl
Chailey Ave
Queen Elizabeth Stadium
Sp Ctr
Donkey La
Carterhatch La
Halifax Rd
Manor Rd
Bellamy Rd
St George's RC Prim Sch
Cheviots Hostel
Pilgrims Ct
Bodiam Cl
Cowdrey Cl
Pevensey Ave
Aldersbrook Ave
Willow Rd
Fillebrook Ave
Herongate Cl
Recn Gd
New River
Monks Rd
Trinity St
Chase Side
Nunn's Rd
Cheviot Cl
Cheviot Ct
Graeme Rd
Chase Side Prim Sch
Chase Side Ave
Monastery Gdns
Heath's Cl
Ravens Cl
Connaught Ave
Carnarvon Ave
Lambourne Gdns
3
Cambridge G
Monks Cl
Christchurch Cl
Lambs Wlk
Kings Ct
Conical Cnr
Clere Pl
Riverside Gdns
Parsonage Gdns
Parsonage La
St Andrew's Sch
Churchbury La
Churchbury Cl
Connaught Cl
Newby Cl
Vicar's Cl
Ladysmith Rd
Chase Green Ave
West Bank
Shane Ct
Florence Dr
Chase Side Pl
Horseshoe La
Cricketers Arms Rd
Danby Ct
Enfield Gram Sch
Portcullis Lodge Rd
Riversfield Rd
EN1
97
Pl Fld
Chase Court Gdns
Robinson Cl
Chase Gn
River View
Gentleman's Row
Chapel St
Holly Wlk
Enfield Cty Sch
Offices
C Ctr
Fir Tree Wlk
Orchard Way
Greencroft Gdns
The Vineries
Peartree Rd
Apple Gr
Allot Gdns
2
Cobham Cl
Kingsmead Sch
Chase Hill
Florence Ave
Church La
Silver St
St Andrew's Rd
Fyfield Rd
Calder Cl
Gram Sch
Kimberley Gdns
Craddock Rd
Mafeking Rd
George Spicer Prim Sch
Waverley Gresham Cl
Offices
Shirley Rd
Ct
Little Park Gdns
Burleigh Way
Market Pl
River Front
Skerry Rd
Clydach Rd
Liby
Church St
A110
The Town
Savoy Par
Spicer Ct
Southbury Rd
Enfield Chase
Sarnesfield Rd
Palace Gdns Sh Ctr
Sydney Rd
A105
Genotin Rd
Bovril Ho
Enfield Town Superstore
Eaton Rd
Queen's Rd
Felix Neubergh Ct
Stanley Rd
Fotheringham Rd
Cecil Ave
Bryn-y-Mawr Rd
Jules Thorn Ave
L Ctr
Tempsford
Firbank Way
Tenn Cts
Cecil Rd
Seaford Rd
Halstead Rd
Falmer Rd
Tenn Cts
Old Park Ave
Enfield Town
Bwg Gn
Frobisher Mews
Raleigh Rd
Sydney Rd
London Rd
Rosemary Wlk
Chalkwell Park Ave
Allot Gdns
Beresford Gdns
Lyndhurst Gdns
Camberley Ave
Beverley Cl
Waddington Cl
Burleigh Rd
Cross Rd
Downs Rd
Percival Rd
Bert Way
Bertram Rd
Clive Way
Clive Rd
Southbury Ave
1
Town Park
Essex Rd
Tenn Cts
Old Park Gr
Lincoln Cres
Recn Gd
LC
Salisbury Ct
Park Cres
Walsingham Rd
Pottersfield
Silverthorne Lo
Mornington Lo
Illingworth Way
Kingswood Cl
Lincoln Cres
Lincoln Rd
96
Ridings Ave
Uvedale Rd
Whitethorn Gdns
Ascot Lo
Garfield
33
17
Tenn Cts
Harman Rd
John St
Charles St
James St
Agricola Pl
Hadrian's Ride
Liby
Romany Way
34
Ermine Side
Prim Sch
Princess Ct
Private Rd
Rowley Ct
East Cres
Waterhedge Mews
Karyatis Ct
Main Ave
Bush Hill Park
Tenn

6
A10 Hertford, M25
A1010 Waltham Cross, A10 (A1055)
A
B
C
D
Pav
Myddelton House
Pav
Sp Gd
EN2
99
Malden's Bridge
Bull's Cross
St Ignatius Coll
Forty Hill CE Prim Sch
Forty Hill
The Clock Ho
Nursery
Forty Hill Ho
Worcesters Prim Sch
New River
Severn Dr
Worcesters Ave
Tynemouth Dr
Pentrich Ave
Meyer Gn
Goat La
George's Rd
Garnault Rd
Russell Rd
Dowland Ho
Holbrook Cl
Hoe La
98
Bridgenhall Rd
Layard Rd
Mahon Cl
Magpie Cl
Abercrombie Dr
Linden Ave
Linden Gdns
Orton Gr
Melling Dr
Linwood Cres
Bressey Ave
Baynes Cl
Sinclair
Hill Cemy
Allot Gdns
Carterhatch La
5
Queen Elizabeth Stadium
Sp Ctr
Donkey La
Cambridge Gdns
Great Cambridge Rd
Cambridge Par
Autumn Cl
Carterhatch Jun & Inf Schs
3
97
Pl Fld
2
George Spicer Prim Sch
Kingsmead Sch
Cobham Cl
Skerry Rd
Clydach Rd
Bryn-y-Mawr Rd
Jules Thorn Ave
A110
L Ctr
1
Recn Gd
Percival Rd
Bertram Rd
Bert Way
Clive Way
Clive Rd
Southbury Ave
96
Lincoln Rd
34
Ermine Side
Liby
Prim Sch
Main Ave
Agricola Pl
Roman Way
Karyatis Ct
Hadrian's Ride
A10
Cracknell Cl
Brook Bank
Almshouse La
Brookside Gdns
Hook Gate
Cocker Rd
Dendridge Cl
Auckland Cl
Turkey St
Turkey Street
Teal Cl
Crem
Maltby Dr
Rossington Cl
Maybury Cl
Landridge Dr
Sedley Cl
St Martin's Cl
Boleyn Ave
Northumberland Ave
Sheppard Cl
Stoneleigh Ave
Pembroke Ave
Russet House Sch
Pl Fld
Newland Dr
Monroe Cres
Lakefield Gr
The Approach
Central Ave
Bridge Cl
Oldbury Rd
Gough Rd
Bishops Cl
Ringlewell Cl
Banton Cl
Norton Cl
Wolsey Rd
Barnard Rd
Brick La
Bishop Stopford's Sch
Hammond Rd
Mapleton Rd
Suffolks Prim Sch
EN1
ENFIELD
Broadfield Sq
Tyberry Rd
Wickham Cl
Chalkmill Dr
Crown Rd
Enfield Ret Pk
Superstore
Dearsley Rd
Baird Rd
Colosseum Ret Pk
Works
Northgate Bsns Ctr
Superstore
Southbury Rd
Southbury
Superstores
De Mandeville Gate
Depot
Martinbridge Trad Est
Lincoln Way
Haslemere Bsns Ctr
18
Lockhart Cl
Dove Ct
Kingsway
Emilia Cl
35
Middlesex Univ
Peerglow Est
Cobbett Cl
Lands Sch
Waltham Gdns
Keswick Dr
St George's CE Inf Sch
Meadway
Unity Rd
Gilbert St
A1055
Liby
Joan Player Ho
Putney Rd
Cranborne Ct
Wonnacott Pl
Totteridge Rd
Karens Ct
Raynton Rd
Ordnance Rd
Hartmoor Mews
Kettering Rd
Rotherfield Rd
Fairoaks Gr
Winnington Rd
Goodwood Ave
Ascot Gdns
Elmhurst Rd
Grove Rd W
Lewington Ct
St Stephen's Rd
Hale Ho
Beaconsfield Rd
Bough Beech Ct
Albany Rd
Longfield Ave
Dell Rd
The Loning
Connop Rd
1 Premier Ct
2 Herm Ho
3 Sark Ho
4 Alderney Ho
5 Guernsey Ho
6 Jersey Ho
Enfield Wash
Bouvier Rd
Cherry Rd
Mapleton Cres
Hoecroft Ct
Westcroft Cl
Jasper Cl
Hertford Rd
Phoenix Ct
East Rd
Eastfield Rd
Bell La
Albany Sch
Ingersoll Rd
Templeton Ct
Eastfield Prim Sch
Crest Dr
Riley Rd
Elmore Rd
Lyda Ave
Grove Gdns
Pl Fld
Roedean Ave
Durants Sch
Roedean Cl
Pitfield Way
Midlea Ho
Staintons Rd
Albany Park Ave
EN3
Addis Cl
Nursery Cl
Palmers La
Lytchet Way
Old Rd
Addison Rd
Lombard Ave
Platts Rd
Dison Cl
Shaw Rd
Ian Sq
Nursery Gdns
The Sunny Rd
Moorfield Rd
Lansbury Rd
Oatlands Rd
The Hatch
Logan Cl
Lawson Rd
Carterhatch Rd
Lindhill Cl
Enfield Highway
Hastings Ave
Sherborne Ave
Cedar Ave
Westmoor Gdns
Orchardleigh Ave
Liby
Mildon Ho
Greenmoor Rd
Cres
Frederick Cres
Glenloch Rd
Ashford Cres
Swan Way
Westmoor Rd
Bowood Rd
Prim Sch
Bwg Gn
Sp G
Burywood Ct
Central Par
Shaftesbury Ave
Saville Row
Vista Ave
Mayfield Rd
Enfield Town FC
Yeomans Way
Cuba Dr
Archers Dr
Ashdown Rd
Ashley Rd
Edington Rd
Burncroft Ave
Green St
Cemy
Bwg Gn
Amblesiae Cres
Hunts Mead
Durants Lo
30
Tenn Cts
Enfield Coll
Durants Park
Brimsdown Jun & Inf Sch
Broadlands Ave
Broadlands Cl
Collinwood Ave
Crediton Ho
Exeter Rd
Ashburton Ho
Arbour Rd
Brookfields
Tenby Rd
The Ride
Waverley Sch
Cowland Ave
Moat Side
Durants Park Ave
Bursland Rd
Charcroft Gdns
Alexandra Ct
Anglesey Rd
Aberdare Rd
Brecon Rd
Swansea Rd
Prim Sch
Holmeleigh Ct
Roseacre Lo
Colmore Rd
Holmbridge Gdns
Rossmore Cl
Alexandra Rd
Cardiff Rd
Glyn Rd
Kays Ct
Durants Rd
King Edward's Rd
Hartsway
Superstore
Nags Head Rd
St Mary's RC Prim Sch
Queensway Bsns Ctr
Eagle Cl
Garfield Rd
Walters Rd
Clydesdale
Queensway
Cartons Cl
Swan Ho
Sedcote Rd
Hertford Rd
High St
Tenn Cts
Ponders End
Recn Gd
Allington Ct
Percy Gdns
Keats Cl
Freemantle
Curzon Ave
Derby Rd
College
Stonehorse Rd
Lorraine Cl
Scotland Green Rd
Alma

Enfield Lock
Enfield Island Village
Albany Park
The Arena
EN3
Brimsdown
Sewardstone
Lee Valley Country Pk
King George's Resr
E4
Power Station
Prince of Wales Prim Sch
Chesterfield Sch
Waterways Bsns Ctr
Watermill Bsns Ctr
Innova Bsns Pk
Plaza Bsns Ctr
Sovereign Bsns Ctr
Leaside Bsns Ctr
Delta Pk Ind Est
The Dencora Centre
Mill River Trad Est
Trafalgar Trad Est
Ponders End Ind Est
Luthers Farm
Nurseries
Weirs
The Royal Oak (PH)
The Rifles (PH)
London Loop
MOLLISON AVE
SEWARDSTONE RD
LEA VALLEY RD
A112 Waltham Abbey, M25 (A121)
▲ Essex STREET ATLAS
1 FOGERTY CL
2 McCLINTOCK PL
BENSON CT 1
FULTON CT 2
MAYNARD CT 3
SOPER MEWS 4
RENNIE CT 5
CROMPTON PL 6
LEWISHAM CT 7
WOOLWICH CT 8
HODSON PL 9
River Lea Navigation
Lee Valley Wlk
River Lea or Lee Diversion
Small River Lea or Lee
Turkey Brook
Enterprise Works
ORDNANCE RD
BRANCROFT WAY
LOCKFIELD AVE
MILLMARSH LA
MILL LA
Yardley Hill
Waltham Forest
Essex
Enfield

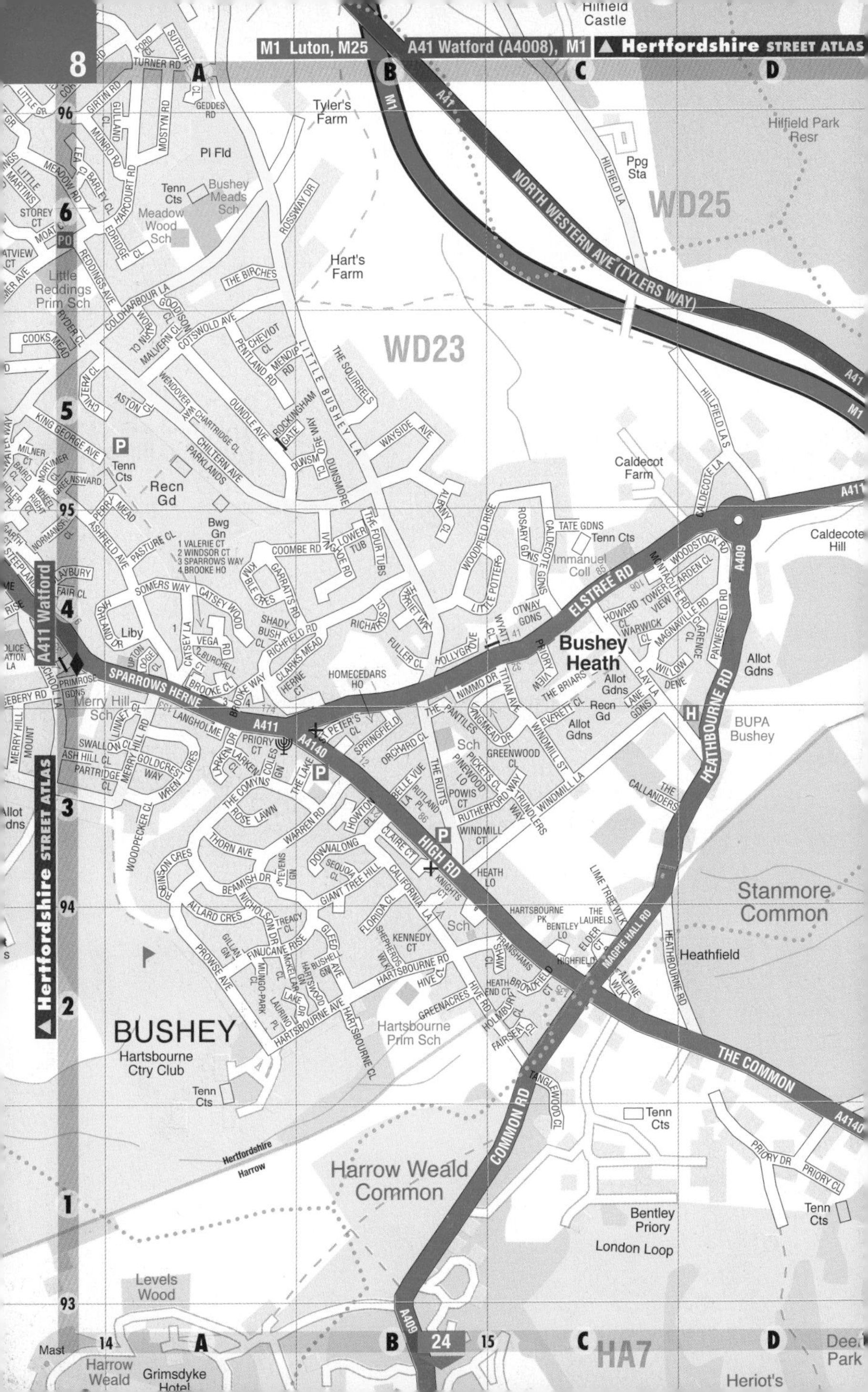
A
B
C
D
Hilfield Castle
Tyler's Farm
Hilfield Park Resr
Ppg Sta
WD25
NORTH WESTERN AVE (TYLERS WAY)
Hart's Farm
WD23
Pl Fld
Bushey Meads Sch
Meadow Wood Sch
Little Reddings Prim Sch
Caldecot Farm
Caldecote Hill
Recn Gd
Bwg Gn
1 VALERIE CT
2 WINDSOR CT
3 SPARROWS WAY
4 BROOKE HO
Immanuel Coll
Bushey Heath
ELSTREE RD
SPARROWS HERNE
HIGH RD
HEATHBOURNE RD
Allot Gdns
BUPA Bushey
Merry Hill Sch
Stanmore Common
Heathfield
BUSHEY
Hartsbourne Ctry Club
Hartsbourne Prim Sch
THE COMMON
COMMON RD
Harrow Weald Common
Bentley Priory
London Loop
Levels Wood
Hertfordshire
Harrow
A411 Watford
Hertfordshire STREET ATLAS
HA7
Harrow Weald
Grimsdyke Hotel
Mast
Heriot's
Deer Park
24
14
15
93
94
95
96

Home Farm
Allot Gdns
Aldenham Ctry Pk
LISTER COTTS
Laboratory
DAGGER LA
ALDENHAM RD
Aldenham Resr
Sailing Club
Pav
Sp Gd
Tenn Cts
WD6
A5183
B5378
ALLUM L
ELSTREE HILL N
ROMELAND CT
THE BARTONS
St Nicholas CE Prim Sch
Elstree
LANDS' END
WATFORD RD
NEW RD
HIGH ST
PO
SCHUBERT RD
A411
PH
ELSTREE RD
Lismirrane Ind Pk
DELIUS CL
WEBBER CL
RODGERS CL
BEETHOVEN RD
SULLIVAN WAY
ELGAR CL
COATES RD
WEST VIEW GDNS
SUMMER GR
VALENTINE CT
MAY GDNS
FORTUNE LA
Tenn Cts
Edgwarebury House Farm
ELSTREE HILL S
NORTH WESTERN AVE (WATFORD BY-PASS)
CENTENNIAL AVE
Centennial Pk
Centennial Ct
WD23
Hertfordshire
Harrow
Brockleyhill Farm
Hertfordshire
Barnet
M1
A5
Sp Gd
Brockley Grange
Tenn Cts
BROCKLEY HILL HO
London Loop
HA8
Annandale
NUTT GR
A41 EDGWARE WAY (WATFORD BY-PASS)
Works
HA7
SIR HENRY FLOYD CT
Royal National Orthopaedic
Grove Farm
Pear Wood Cottages
BROCKLEY HILL
THE LIMES
Limes House
Wood Farm
Pear Wood
WARREN LA
WOOD LA
Crkt Gd
CH
Brockley Hill
Barnet
Harrow
LANCASTER HO
Pav
Tenn Cts
Cloisters Wood
Springbok House
Tenn Cts
SPRINGFIELD CL
PARK LA
HILLTOP WAY
LITTLE COMMON
BROOMFIELD HO 1
FALLOWFIELD CT 2
HILL HO 3
WELLINGTON HO 4
STANMORE HILL
DENNIS LA
Stanmore Hall
FALLOWFIELD
AYLMER CL
AYLWARD RISE
AYLMER DR
A4140
HERIOTS CL
PINE CL
OLD FORGE CL
SPRING LA
HALL FARM
GRANTHAM CL
NEWLANDS CL
HAMLYN CL
PIPERS GREEN LA
JULIUS CAESAR WAY
AUGUSTUS CL
CLAUDIUS CL
FAUNA CL
CHEVALIER CL
BROCKLEY AVE
PARTRIDGE CL
REES DR
BERRY HILL
CLANLEAM RD
REENGLAS
96
6
5
95
4
10
3
94
2
1
93
A
B
C
D

10
Hertfordshire STREET ATLAS
A
B
C
D
Elstree
WOODSIDE
BLATTNER CL
FIR TREE CL
HILL CREST LO
TAUBER CL
KNOWL PK
KNOWL WAY
LODGE AVE
GRANGE RD
BISHOPS AVE
B5378
ALLUM LA
A5183
96
Cemy
6
ELSTREE HILL
London Loop
HARTFIELD AVE
THE RISE
CAVENDISH CRES
LAKESIDE
BERKELEY CL
ASCOT CL
HARTFIELD CL
DEACON'S HILL RD
WENTWORTH AVE
SHIREMEADE
SHERATON CL
LOWTHER CL
NICHOLAS RD
HADLEY CL
ALWYN CL
CLARE CL
BELMOR
SUMMER HILL
AUDEN DR
WORDSWORTH GDNS
BYRON AVE
Furzehill Sch
Allot Gdns
MELROSE AVE
TENNISON AVE
MILTON DR
VALE AVE
MASEFIELD AVE
LULLINGTON GARTH
CARRINGTON AVE
OAKWOOD AVE
ELMWOOD AVE
CEDARS CL
Sch
THE BARTONS
St Nicholas CE Prim Sch
ST NICHOLAS CL
Elstree
NEW RD
OAK TREE CT
GEORGES MEAD
HIGH ST
5
PO
A411
Abbotsbury
BARNET LA
DEACONS HTS
Deacons Hill
WD6
Elstree Tunnel
Woodcock Hill
Tenn Cts
VALENTINE CT
SUMMER GR
FORTUNE LA
MAY GDNS
Tenn Cts
95
Edgwarebury House Farm
The Leys
Penniwells Farm
4
Tenn Cts
Tenn Cts
Edgwarebury Ctry Club
Hertfordshire
Barnet
NW7
9
Hertfordshire
Barnet
M1
3
Edgwarebury Farm
Bury Farm
Edgware Bury
DUNBLANE CL 1
KINROSS CL 2
MOIDART CT 3
MALLAIG CT 4
OBAN CT 5
ARRAN CT 6
TORRIDON CT 7
ROSS CT 8
EDGWAREBURY LA
Clay La
94
A41
EDGWARE WAY (WATFORD BY-PASS)
Cemy
Pl Fld
Pav
MEADFIELD
MEADFIELD GN
BUSHFIELD CL
BUSHFIELD CRES
WARRENS SHAWE LA
BURRELL CL
PENTLAND AVE
HARTLAND CL
Broadfields Prim Sch
HAMONDE CL
CROMARTY RD
MORAY CL
RANNOCH CL
KINGSLEY CT
HARTLAND DR
TAYSIDE DR
ALDRIDGE AVE
2
HA8
GLENDEVON CL
Sch
PO
GLENGALL RD
PARSONS CRES
PARSONS GR
FRANCKLYN GDNS
HARROWES MEADE
BULLESCROFT RD
BROADFIELD CT
BEULAH CL
CRANMER RD
MIDSUMMER CT
ASHFORD CR
MARLBOROUGH AVE
WYRE GR
ROSENS WLK
Edgwarebury Park
Tenn Cts
Pav
WOLMER GDNS
CROSSGATE
PARKSIDE DR
BROADFIELDS AVE
WINDSOR AVE
LYNFORD GDNS
CH
GRANTHAM CL
NEWLANDS CL
HAMLYN CL
PIPERS GREEN LA
CH
Barnet
1
Edgwarebury
JULIUS CAESAR WAY
CLAUDIUS CL
AUGUSTUS CL
BROCKLEY AVE
HA7
PARKLANDS PL 6
COMPASS CL 7
A41
93
FAUNA CL
CHEVALIER CL
A5
PARTRIDGE CL
REES DR
BERRY HILL
A410
SPUR RD
GOLDSMITH CT
COLLINSON CT
SPALDING CT
EATON CT
BLACKWELL GDNS
MOWBRAY RD
WOLMER CL
Sch
BROADHURST AVE
HURSTMEAD CT
GRENVILLE CT
18
A
CANONS CNR
Pl Fld
1 WARE CT
2 WAKEMAN HO
3 ABINGDON CT
4 CHICHELE HO
5 HAVILLAND CT
GARRICK CT
MARTYN CT
RAFFLES
B
26
1950
RANELAGH CL
EDGWARE WAY (WATFORD BY-PASS)
C
D
HAZEL GDNS
WILLOW

BOREHAMWOOD
WD6
EN5
NW7
EDGWARE
Barnet Gate
Arkley
Rowley Bank Nurseries
Memorial Sp Ctr
Scratch Wood
Scratchwood Open Space
Nature Trail
Thistle Wood
Moat Mount Open Space
Barnet Gate Wood
Hyver Hall
Hyver Farm
Mote End Farm
Nut Wood
Mill Hill
Hemmings Wood
Stoney Wood Lake
Mill Hill Cty High Sch
Highwood House
Highwood Hill
London Gateway Service Area
Motel
Fairway Prim Sch
Northway Sch
Stoneyfields Park
Saffron Green Prim Sch
Furze Hill
Stirling Ind Ctr
Stirling Ret Pk
Stirling Cnr
Rowley Lodge
Windmill (dis)
London Loop
Dean's Brook
BARNET LA
BARNET RD
BARNET BY-PASS
BARNET WAY (BARNET BY-PASS)
HIGHWOOD HILL
B552 HIGHWOOD HILL
MARSH LA
EDGWARE WAY (WATFORD BY-PASS)
1 WILLOW GN
2 HUNTER WLK
3 CLYDESDALE PATH
4 DALES PATH
5 SADDLERS PATH
Apex Cnr
St Joseph's Coll
Lawrence Green
12
27

A411 High Barnet
A
B
C
D
96
Arkley
ROWLEY LA
ROWLEY GREEN RD
BARNET RD
A411
CARRINGTON CL
CHARTRIDGE CL
ARKLEY DR
ARKLEY VIEW
HILLCREST
HAZEL MEAD
HEDGEROW LA
SADDLERS CL
RAEBARN GDNS
GARTHLAND DR
ENDERSBY RD
NORTH CL
DENTON CL
ESCOT WAY
AITKEN RD
MALINS CL
QUINTA DR
HILL CL
WEST CL
RYECROFT CRES
ST PETER'S CL
HACKFORTH CL
FARM CL
BRETT RD
1 WEARDALE CT
2 ELVASTON CT
3 DEBENHAM CT
Whitings Hill Prim Sch
VYSE CL
WELLHOUSE LA
WELLSIDE CL
CANTELOWES HO
Cemy
SPRING CL
PEPYS CRES
TRINDER RD
WELL RD
BELLS HILL
DELLORS CL
LINGHOLM WAY
NEWLANDS PL
SUTTON CRES
LEXINGTON WAY
DUNSTER CL
REDWOOD WAY
ST STEPHENS RD
ST ANNA RD
HOWARD WAY
Allot Gdns
CHESTERFIELD FLATS
MATLOCK CL
JUNIPER CL
SELWOOD DR
ELEANOR GDNS
PALMER CL
WHITINGS RD
CHESTERFIELD RD
SAMPSON AVE
DARLANDS DR
JARVIS CL
GOLDA CL
PO
HEALY CT
NITON CL
WILLOWBAY CL
STANHOPE RD
DEXTER RD
DORMER CL
EDWYN CL
MINERVA
NUPTON DR
GREENLAND RD
Allot Gdns
WINDSOR RD
CONNAUGHT RD
SHELFORD RD
BISHOPS CL
SOUTHFIELD
ADRIAN CL
RIDGEVIEW CL
6
Wr Twr
MEADOWBANKS
KATES CL
Arkley
Allot Gdns
Rowley Lodge
LYNFORD CL
EN5
Whitings Hill
WINDMILL LA
A411
GLEBE LA
DINGLE CL
ROCKWAYS
HAWTHORN G
WYLO DR
5
MAYS LA
PARTRIDGE CL
Cottage Farm
Ducks Island
Recn Gd
95
CHANTRY CL
BARNET GATE LA
B552
Sp Gd
Pl Fld
Dollis Brook
London Loop
4
ALTHORP CL
Brent Lodge Farm
N20
11
HENDON WOOD LA
Fairlight Cottage
HORSESHOE LA
Sp Gd
Pav
TOTTERIDGE PK
A5109
3
Abattoir
Tenn Cts
Tenn Cts
38
TOTTERIDGE COMMON
94
Oak Lodge
B552
126
66
Ellern Mead Farm
Totteridge Common
Tenn Cts
Fairlawn
CROWN CL
2
HENDON PK COTTS
A5109
HIGHWOOD HILL
Highwood Hill
B552 HIGHWOOD HILL
Holecombe Dale
•79
NW7
THE LINCOLNS
LAWRENCE GDNS
ABBEY VIEW
1
Allot Gdns
THE REDDINGS
HOLCOMBE HILL
ABBOTSVIEW CT
Belmont Mill Hill Jun Sch
Pl Fld
Folly Farm
Tenn Cts
Tenn Cts
B552
Sp Fld
Pav
93
REDDINGS
Lawrence Green
MILLERS CL
Pav
Sp Gd
22
A
B
28
23
C
D
B1461
Tenn Cts
Pav
Burtonhole
St Joseph's Coll

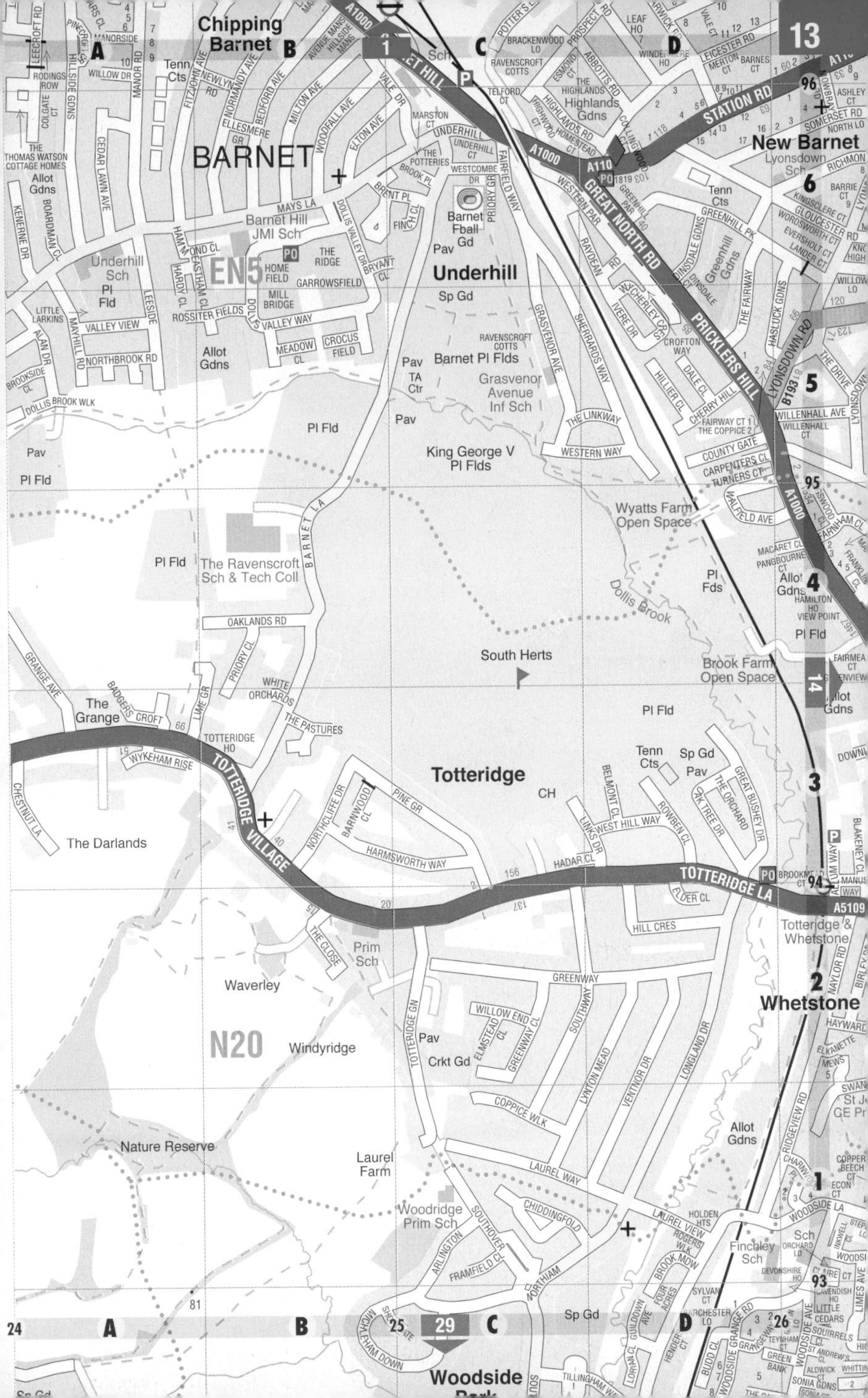

Chipping Barnet
BARNET
New Barnet
Underhill
EN5
Totteridge
Whetstone
N20
Woodside Park
The Ravenscroft Sch & Tech Coll
King George V Pl Flds
Barnet Pl Flds
Grasvenor Avenue Inf Sch
Wyatts Farm Open Space
Brook Farm Open Space
Dollis Brook
South Herts
The Grange
The Darlands
Waverley
Windyridge
Nature Reserve
Laurel Farm
Woodridge Prim Sch
Finchley Sch
Totteridge & Whetstone
Barnet Fball Gd
Underhill Sch
Barnet Hill JMI Sch
Lyonsdown Sch
Highlands Gdns
Greenhill Gdns
TOTTERIDGE LA
TOTTERIDGE VILLAGE
GREAT NORTH RD
PRICKLERS HILL
STATION RD
BARNET LA
A1000
A110
A5109
B193
14
29
24
25
26

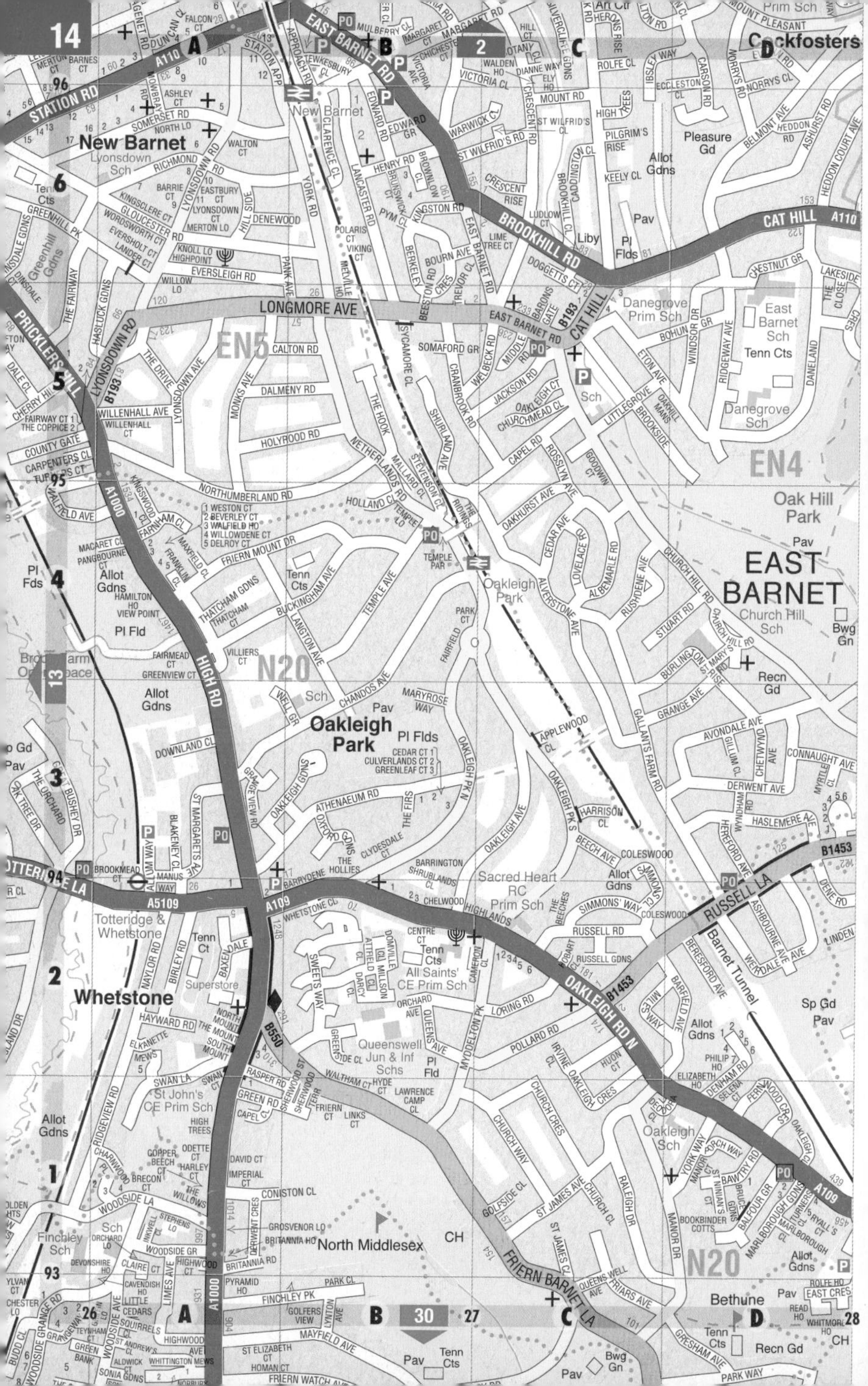
New Barnet
Cockfosters
EN5
EN4
N20
East Barnet
Oakleigh Park
Whetstone
Oak Hill Park
North Middlesex
Station Rd
Longmore Ave
Cat Hill
Brookhill Rd
East Barnet Rd
High Rd
Totteridge La
Oakleigh Rd N
Russell La
Friern Barnet La
Lyonsdown Rd
Northumberland Rd
Church Hill Rd
Gallants Farm Rd
Woodside La
Mayfield Ave
Barnet Tunnel
Danegrove Prim Sch
East Barnet Sch
Church Hill Sch
Sacred Heart RC Prim Sch
All Saints' CE Prim Sch
Queenswell Jun & Inf Schs
St John's CE Prim Sch
Oakleigh Sch
Finchley Sch
Lyonsdown Sch
Totteridge & Whetstone
Pleasure Gd
Recn Gd
Allot Gdns
Bethune
A110
A1000
A109
A5109
B1453
B193
B550
2
13
30

15
N14
A
B
C
D
3
BRAMLEY RD
WESTPOLE AVE
RIDGEVIEW CT
Southgate Sch
Pl Fld
SUSSEX WAY
KENT DR
GLOUCESTER GDNS
FRESTON GDNS
LEYS GDNS
BALMORE CRES
CAT HILL
A110
A111
Middlesex Univ (Cat Hill)
Theatre
De Bohun Prim Sch
Mus
Bramley Sp Gd
Oaktree Sch
MANSFIELD AVE
VERNON CRES
EN4
RUSTON GDNS
Oakhill Coll
CANON MOHAN CL
FARM LA
MONKFRITH AVE
DE BOHUN AVE
TAVISTOCK PL
Monkfrith Prim Sch
CEDAR RISE
MONKFRITH WAY
OAK CL
KNOLL DR
FRIARS WLK
LAWLEY RD
BISHOP RD
EXETER RD
SHAMROCK HO
CHASE SIDE
B1453
OSIDGE LA
ONSLOW PAR
MALLORY GDNS
LANCELOT GDNS
PARKSIDE GDNS
Tenn Cts
EAST RD
WEST RD
EAST WLK
WEST WLK
FERNEY RD
BROOKSIDE S
WOODFIELD DR
Allot Gdns
UPLANDS RD
HAMPDEN SQ
OSIDGE CT
THORNDENE AVE
PREVOST RD
Liby
Brunswick Park Prim Sch
DOWD CL
NURSERYMANS RD
GARDNERS CL
PINE RD
Brunswick Park
BRUNSWICK PARK GDNS
HOWARD CL
GRINDLEFORD AVE
CAMBSTONE CL
BENFLEET WAY
1 COREFIELD CL
2 EXCHANGE CL
CAVERSHAM CT
Brunswick Park
North London Bsns Pk
HAYNES CL
BRUNSWICK CRES
BRUNSWICK AVE
BRUNSWICK GR
BRUNSWICK PARK RD
New Southgate Cemetery & Crematorium
Pymme's Brook
ST MICHAEL'S CT
Recn Gd
Tenn Cts
Pav
DARWIN CL
MARSHALL
PEYTON HO
CHAVILLE CT
NEVILLE HO
ROYSTON HO
OAKLEIGH RD S
FALKLAND AVE
MARNE AVE
FRIERN BARNET
N11
28
29
31
New Southgate
Sports Gd
DALE GREEN RD
RYHOPE RD
A1003
Bwg Gn
MERRYHILLS CT
THE ORCHARD
KENTWINS
SERVITE HO
THE POPLARS
HOMESTEAD PADDOCK
GREEN RD
THE HAVEN
ADDISON AVE
MASEFIELD CRES
THE FAIRWAY
BUSH FAIR CT
COWPER GDNS
HOOD AVE
TRENT GDNS
COVERACK CL
BEARDOW GR
BERKELEY CT
CRICKETERS CL
FRESHFIELD DR
SHERIDAN LO
DORCHESTER CT
ROSEDALE LO
WOODMERE CT
ASHLEIGH CT
LIPTON CT
ORCHID RD
LEWIS CT
NURSERY RD
1 ORCHID LO
2 ORCHID GRANGE
3 HENLEY CT
4 MARLOW CT
5 HEATHDENE
MANOR DR
SHAMROCK WAY
OAKDALE
Osidge Prim Sch
COWPER RD
THE WOODLANDS
CHASE WAY
CECIL RD
ARLINGTON RD
Osidge
Ashmole Sch
Pl Flds
N14
SUMMIT WAY
SUMMIT CL
HAMPDEN WAY
UNDERNE AVE
MANDEVILLE RD
LINCOLN AVE
WHITEHOUSE WAY
MARLBOROUGH
ALLOA CT
ASHFIELD RD
WATERFALL RD
WATERFALL CL
Allot Gdns
ALEXANDRA CT
STAFFORD CL
ASHRIDGE CT
RESERVOIR RD
WOODVILLE CT
MALCOLMS WAY
THE PINES
HARPER CL
THE VINERIES
AVENUE CL
AVENUE RD
LINDEN CL
LOUSADA LO
SPEYSIDE
ORCHARD CT
ORCHARD AVE
GROSVENOR CT
BEVERLEY CT
OLD FARM AVE
FARMLEIGH
ISABELLA CL
GRANT CL
WINDSOR CT
RAMSEY WAY
PINE CL
CHELMSFORD RD
WAGGON MEWS
Oakwood
GERRARDS CL
BELGRAVE CL
BELGRAVE GDNS
GROSVENOR GDNS
CARLTON AVE
SOUTH LODGE DR
PRINCE GEORGE AVE
BRAYTON GDNS
CURTHWAITE GDNS
WOLVERTON WAY
CHESTNUT CL
LAKENHEATH
MERRIVALE
SHERINGHAM AVE
RUSSEL CT
Oakwood
CHASE CT
WAYSIDE CL
ST JOHNS CL
HIGHFIELD CT
SAXON WAY
OAKWOOD CL
CHASE RD
FAIRLAWN CL
CHARTER WAY
IMBER CL
GROVEBURY CT
THE RYE
Chase Side Works
DALRYMPLE CL
Wolfson Hillel Prim Sch
Tenn Cts
Pav
Oakwood Park
OAKWOOD VIEW
OAKWOOD AVE
FOUNTAINS CRES
1 WILLIS YD
2 CHELMSFORD CT
3 NORTHBOURNE HO
4 DENLEIGH CT
5 MANESTY CT
6 DENE HO
West Grove Prim Sch
IVY RD
Allot Gdns
St Andrew's CE Prim Sch
MAYFAIR TERR
REDWOOD CL
HILLSIDE GR
PARK RD
GROVELANDS CT
FERNWOOD CT
COLTSWOOD CT
DEANWOOD CT
PICKARD CL
NICHOL CL
CROWN PAR
BUSH CT
CROWN LA
Southgate
MANOR HO
L Ctr
LANTERN CT
WOOBURN CT
TUDOR WAY
RALEIGH WAY
QUEEN ELIZABETH'S DR
A1004
GRANGE GDNS
JOHN BRADSHAW RD
BURLEIGH GDNS
CHARLES GR
OXFORD AVE
PRINCIPAL CL
BURLEIGH PAR
ASHFIELD PAR
HIGHBURY GR
KINDERTON CL
Liby
Southgate Coll
Southgate Coll
LEIGH HUNT DR
Tenn Cts
BLAGDEN'S LA
BLAGDEN'S CL
BRAMFORD CT
THE CLOSE
HIGH ST
MANOR CT
PRUDEN CL
MAYFIELD AVE
BALAAMS LA
MINCHENDEN CT
1 SHAKESPEARE HO
2 ASHCROFT
3 WHITE HOUSE CT
4 FONTAINE CT
ELLINGTON CT
Crkt Gd
Walker Prim Sch
CHANDOS CT
Pav
Tenn Cts
Cemy
THE GREEN
A1003
HENDEN CRES
MINCHENDEN
CHANDOS AVE
ABBOTSHALL AVE
BRYCEDALE CRES
LANGSIDE CRES
KEITH AVE
FORESTDALE
CORRI AVE
TOWNSEND AVE
MORTON CRES
POWYS LA
93
30
THE BOURNE
BOURNE AVE
PARKWAY
94
95
96
OAKWOOD
ST THOMAS RD
MOUNT PLEASANT COTTS
THE WELLS
16
OVERTON RD
BEVERIDGE CT
JENNER CT
ASBURY CT
LONSDALE
CLIFTON GDNS
BRANTWOOD GDNS
LOWER KENWOOD AVE
KENWOOD AVE
6
5
4
3
2
1
GALVA CL
CHADDLEWOOD
MOUNT CL
BRAEMORE CT
HEDDON CT
HEDDON COURT PAR
BETJEMAN CT
TAVERNERS LO

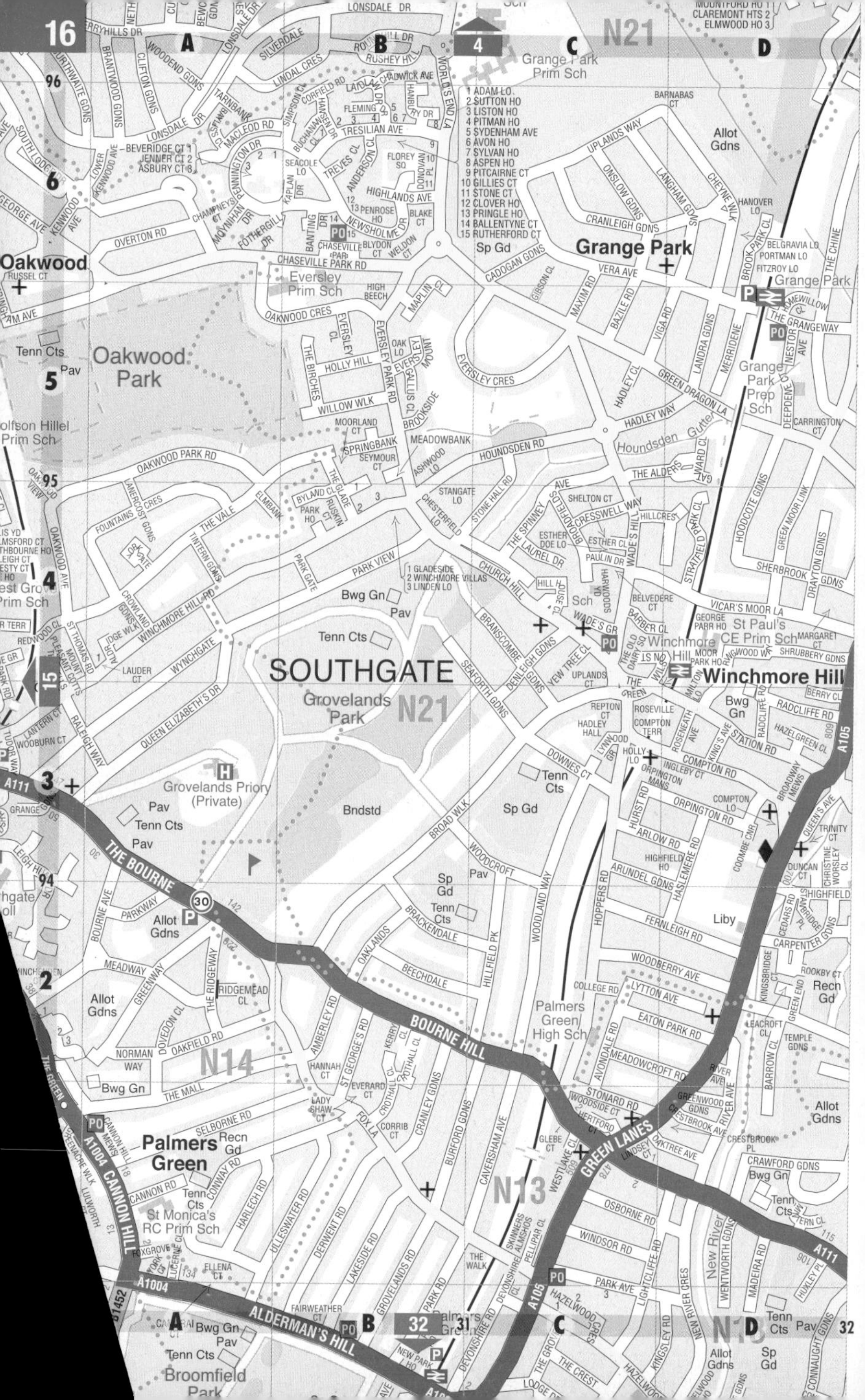
16
A
B
C
D
4
N21
Oakwood
Oakwood Park
Grange Park
Grange Park Prim Sch
SOUTHGATE
Grovelands Park
N21
Grovelands Priory (Private)
Winchmore Hill
St Paul's CE Prim Sch
Palmers Green
Palmers Green High Sch
St Monica's RC Prim Sch
Broomfield Park
N14
N13
Eversley Prim Sch
Grange Park Prep Sch
Houndsden Gutter
1 ADAM LO.
2 SUTTON HO
3 LISTON HO
4 PITMAN HO
5 SYDENHAM AVE
6 AVON HO
7 SYLVAN HO
8 ASPEN HO
9 PITCAIRNE CT
10 GILLIES CT
11 STONE CT
12 CLOVER HO
13 PRINGLE HO
14 BALLENTYNE CT
15 RUTHERFORD CT
1 GLADESIDE
2 WINCHMORE VILLAS
3 LINDEN LO
THE BOURNE
BOURNE HILL
GREEN LANES
ALDERMAN'S HILL
CANNON HILL
A111
A105
A1004
CHASEVILLE PARK RD
OAKWOOD PARK RD
WINCHMORE HILL RD
HOUNDSDEN RD
QUEEN ELIZABETH'S DR
15
32
31

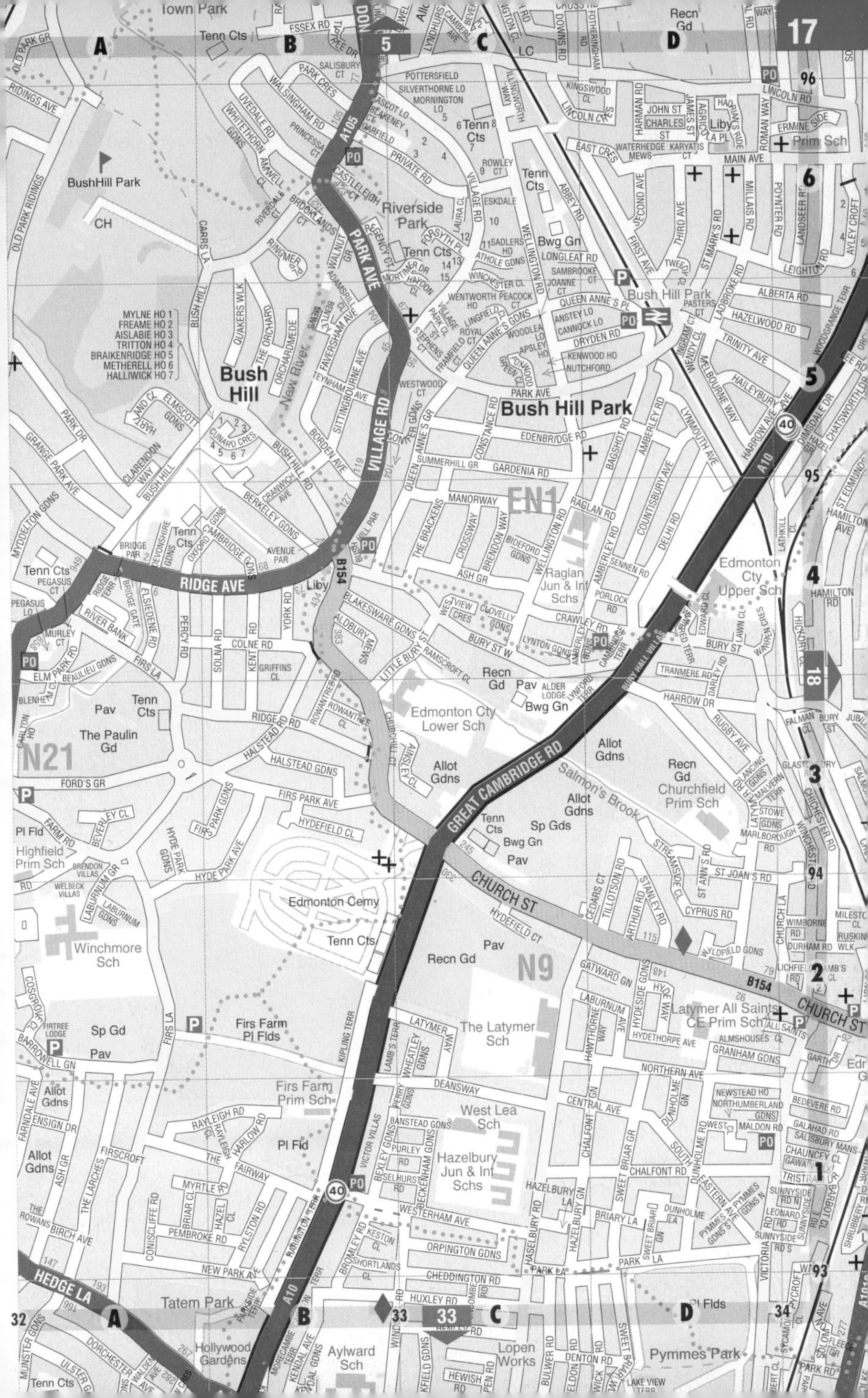

Bush Hill
Bush Hill Park
BushHill Park
Riverside Park
EN1
N21
N9
PARK AVE
VILLAGE RD
RIDGE AVE
GREAT CAMBRIDGE RD
CHURCH ST
HEDGE LA
Edmonton Cemy
Edmonton Cty Lower Sch
Edmonton Cty Upper Sch
The Latymer Sch
West Lea Sch
Hazelbury Jun & Inf Schs
Raglan Jun & Inf Schs
Churchfield Prim Sch
Latymer All Saints CE Prim Sch
Firs Farm Prim Sch
Firs Farm Pl Flds
Winchmore Sch
Highfield Prim Sch
The Paulin Gd
Tatem Park
Hollywood Gardens
Aylward Sch
Lopen Works
Pymmes Park
Salmon's Brook
New River

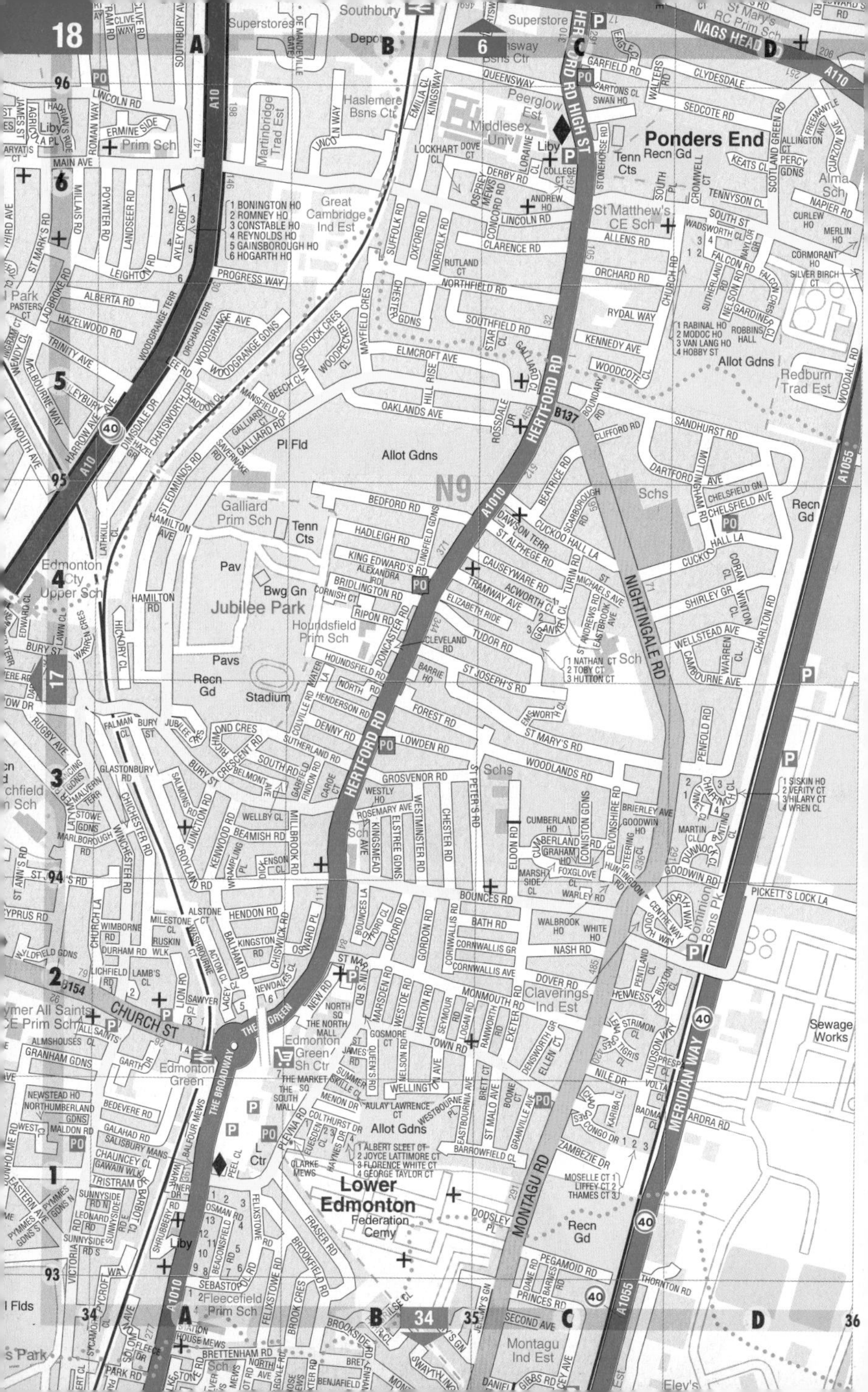
A
B
C
D
6
Southbury
Superstores
Depot
Superstore
Queensway Bsns Ctr
NAGS HEAD
St Mary's RC Prim Sch
A110
Haslemere Bsns Ctr
Martinbridge Trad Est
Peerglow Est
Middlesex Univ
Ponders End
Recn Gd
Tenn Cts
Prim Sch
Great Cambridge Ind Est
1 BONINGTON HO
2 ROMNEY HO
3 CONSTABLE HO
4 REYNOLDS HO
5 GAINSBOROUGH HO
6 HOGARTH HO
St Matthew's CE Sch
Alma Sch
A10
HERTFORD RD
HIGH ST
LINCOLN RD
QUEENSWAY
GARFIELD RD
CLYDESDALE
SEDCOTE RD
KEATS CL
TENNYSON CL
SOUTH ST
NAPIER RD
ALLENS RD
CLARENCE RD
ORCHARD RD
NORTHFIELD RD
SOUTHFIELD RD
RYDAL WAY
KENNEDY AVE
WOODCOTE CL
ELMCROFT AVE
OAKLANDS AVE
PROGRESS WAY
ALBERTA RD
HAZELWOOD RD
TRINITY AVE
WOODGRANGE AVE
WOODGRANGE GDNS
WOODGRANGE TERR
1 RABINAL HO
2 MODOC HO
3 VAN LANG HO
4 HOBBY ST
Allot Gdns
Redburn Trad Est
WOODALL RD
SANDHURST RD
DARTFORD AVE
CHELSFIELD GN
CHELSFIELD AVE
CUCKOO HALL LA
B137
A1010
A1055
N9
Pl Fld
Galliard Prim Sch
Jubilee Park
Pav
Bwg Gn
Pavs
Recn Gd
Stadium
Houndsfield Prim Sch
Edmonton Cty Upper Sch
BEDFORD RD
HADLEIGH RD
KING EDWARD'S RD
BRIDLINGTON RD
RIPON RD
DONCASTER RD
HOUNDSFIELD RD
ST ALPHEGE RD
CAUSEYWARE RD
TRAMWAY AVE
ACWORTH CL
ELIZABETH RIDE
TUDOR RD
ST JOSEPH'S RD
FOREST RD
ST MARY'S RD
WOODLANDS RD
NIGHTINGALE RD
1 NATHAN CT
2 TOBY CT
3 HUTTON CT
SHIRLEY GR
WELLSTEAD AVE
CAMBOURNE AVE
CHARLTON RD
PENFOLD RD
1 SISKIN HO
2 VERITY CT
3 HILARY CT
4 WREN CL
17
HAMILTON AVE
HAMILTON RD
HICKORY CL
BURY ST
LOWDEN RD
GROSVENOR RD
DENNY RD
SOUTH RD
Schs
Sch
CUMBERLAND HO
GRAHAM HO
FOXGLOVE CL
BRIERLEY AVE
GOODWIN HO
HUNTINGDON RD
GOODWIN RD
PICKETT'S LOCK LA
Dominion Bsns Pk
BOUNCES RD
BATH RD
CORNWALLIS RD
CORNWALLIS GR
CORNWALLIS AVE
NASH RD
DOVER RD
MONMOUTH RD
Claverings Ind Est
TOWN RD
Sewage Works
MERIDIAN WAY
HUDSON WAY
NILE DR
ZAMBEZIE DR
CONGO DR
MOSELLE CT
LIFFEY CT
THAMES CT
Recn Gd
MONTAGU RD
PEGAMOID RD
PRINCES RD
SECOND AVE
Montagu Ind Est
THORNTON RD
B154
CHURCH ST
THE GREEN
THE BROADWAY
Edmonton Green
Edmonton Green Sh Ctr
THE NORTH MALL
THE MARKET SQ
THE SOUTH MALL
Latymer All Saints CE Prim Sch
GRANHAM GDNS
BEDEVERE RD
SALISBURY RD
Allot Gdns
1 ALBERT SLEET CT
2 JOYCE LATTIMORE CT
3 FLORENCE WHITE CT
4 GEORGE TAYLOR CT
Lower Edmonton
Federation Cemy
L Ctr
Liby
Fleecefield Prim Sch
FELIXSTOWE RD
BROOKFIELD RD
FRASER RD
BRETTENHAM RD
96
95
94
93
34
35
36
1
2
3
4
5
6

EN3
E4
N9
Ponders End Ind Est
Ponders End
Valleylink Est
Riverside Est
Works
Lee Valley L Ctr
Lee Valley Leisure
Pickett's Lock
William Girling Resr
River Lee Navigation
Lee Valley Wlk
River Lea or Lee Diversion
LEA VALLEY RD
WHARF RD
MORSON RD
LEE PARK WAY
SEWARDSTONE RD
MANSFIELD HILL
OLD CHURCH RD
WALTHAM WAY
KINGS HEAD HILL
THE RIDGEWAY
NEW RD
HALL LA
Yardley Hill
Yardley Prim Sch
Allot Gdns
Chingford Green
Chingford Foundation Sch
Mansfield Pk
Ridgeway Park
Wellington Prim Sch
Larkswood Prim Sch
Cemy
Enterprise
Pl Fld
Liby
Waltham Forest
Enfield

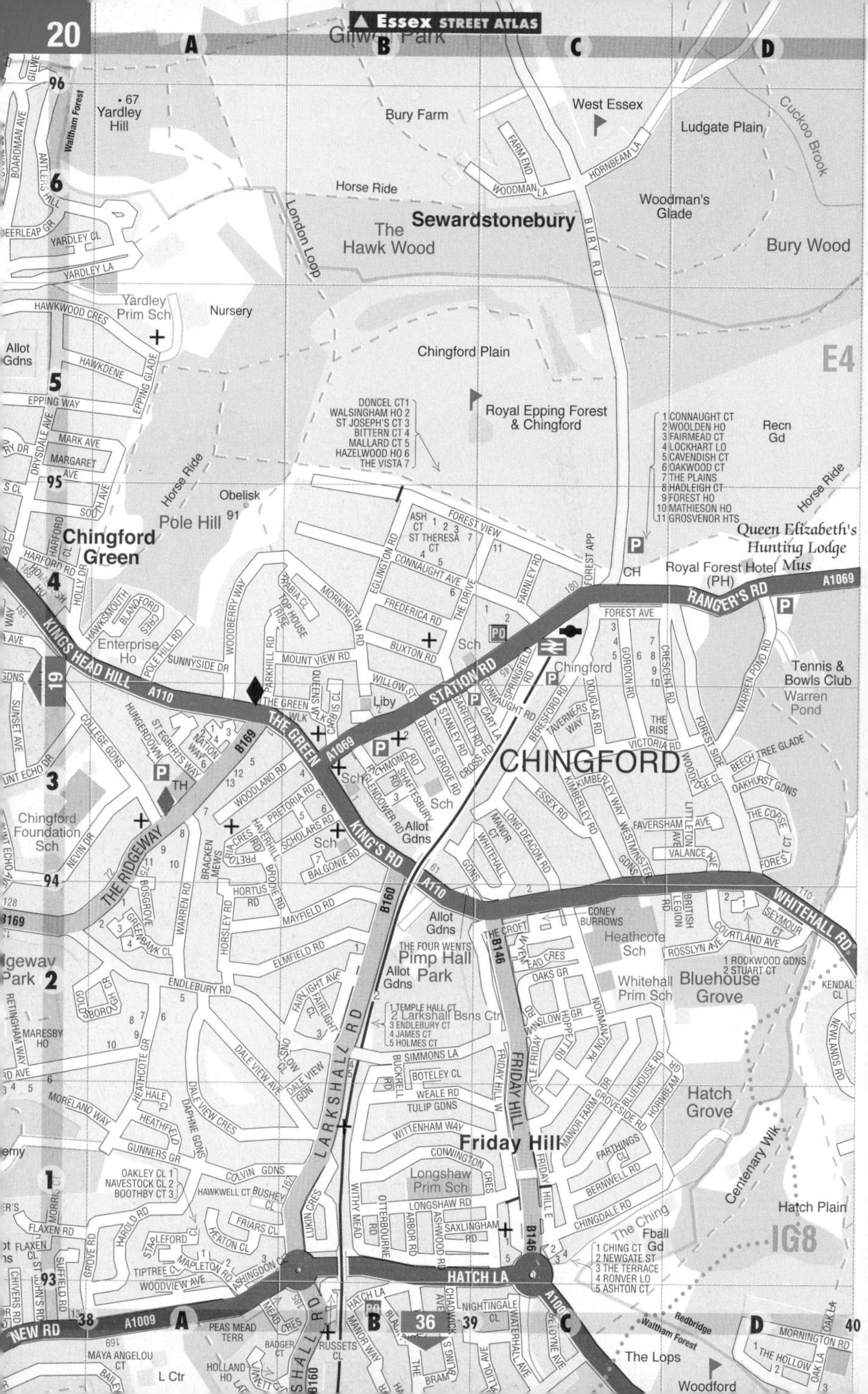
Sewardstonebury
The Hawk Wood
West Essex
Bury Farm
Ludgate Plain
Cuckoo Brook
Woodman's Glade
Bury Wood
Horse Ride
London Loop
Yardley Hill
Yardley Prim Sch
Nursery
Chingford Plain
Royal Epping Forest & Chingford
E4
Recn Gd
Obelisk
Pole Hill
Chingford Green
Queen Elizabeth's Hunting Lodge Mus
Royal Forest Hotel (PH)
RANGER'S RD
A1069
Tennis & Bowls Club
Warren Pond
KINGS HEAD HILL
A110
THE GREEN
STATION RD
CHINGFORD
Chingford
Enterprise Ho
Chingford Foundation Sch
THE RIDGEWAY
B169
KING'S RD
WHITEHALL RD
Heathcote Sch
Whitehall Prim Sch
Bluehouse Grove
Pimp Hall Park
Allot Gdns
LARKSHALL RD
B160
FRIDAY HILL
B146
Friday Hill
Longshaw Prim Sch
Hatch Grove
Centenary Wlk
Hatch Plain
IG8
The Ching
HATCH LA
NEW RD
A1009
The Lops
Woodford
Redbridge
Waltham Forest
36
19

Long Hills
Centenary Wlk
Epping Forest
Palmer's Bridge
Mon
Three Forests
The Warren
Warren Hill
Magpie Hill
Connaught Water
IG10
69 Warren Hill
LOUGHTON
Ranger's Rd
Epping New Rd
High Rd
Manor Rd
Holmehurst
The Warren Wood (PH)
Oak Hall
Powell's Forest
Trinity Terr
The Ching
Waltham Forest
Epping Forest
IG9
St John's CE Prim Sch
Queensbury
Whitehall Plain
The Retreat Cvn Site
Palmerston Rd
Roding La
B170
Buckhurst Hill
The Daiglen Sch
Liby
The Birkbeck
Holly House
Knighton Gn
Reeds Forest
Lord's Bushes
IG8
Knighton Wood
Woodford Wells
Bancrofts Sch
Woodford
Trinity RC High Sch (Upper)
St Antony's Sch
Wells Sch
Roding Valley
Oaklands Sch
Pondfield End
The Stables
Richmond Pk
Allot Gdns
Sp Gd
Buck Cty
A121 Loughton, M11 (A1168)
A110
A104
A121
A1069
Essex
Redbridge
Station Way
1 Station App
2 Station Par
1 Hepworth Ho
2 Whitehall Lo
Tilney Dr 1
Tilney Rd 2
Tilney Ct 3
Hurstcombe 4
The Sidings 1
Lukinstone Cl 2
Seymour Cl 3
A B C D
41 42
37
30
93 94 95 96
1 2 3 4 5 6
▲ Essex STREET ATLAS

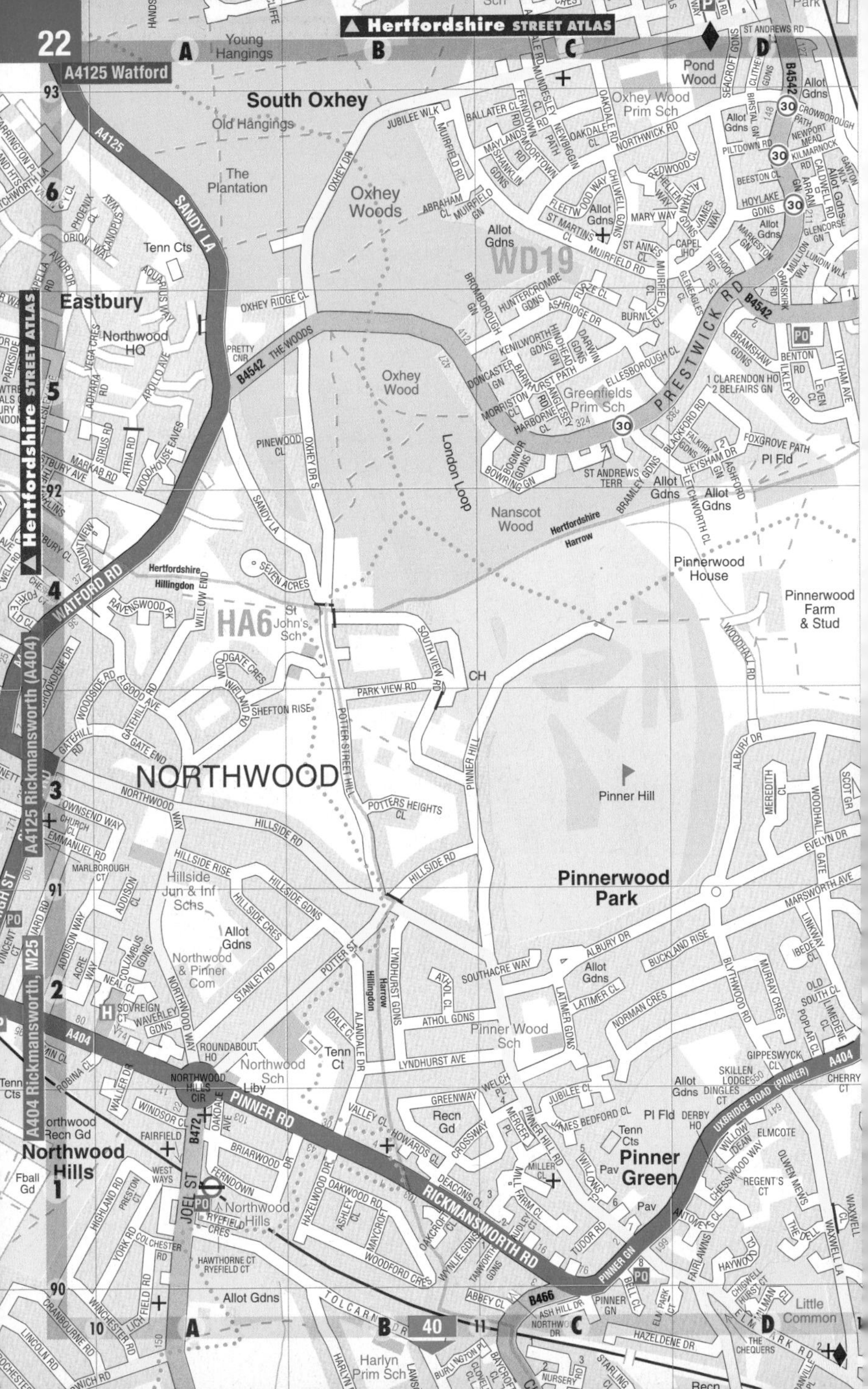
A4125 Watford
Young Hangings
South Oxhey
Old Hangings
The Plantation
Oxhey Woods
Oxhey Wood
Pond Wood
Oxhey Wood Prim Sch
WD19
Eastbury
Northwood HQ
Greenfields Prim Sch
London Loop
Nanscot Wood
Pinnerwood House
Pinnerwood Farm & Stud
HA6
St John's Sch
NORTHWOOD
Pinner Hill
Pinnerwood Park
Hillside Jun & Inf Schs
Northwood & Pinner Com
Pinner Wood Sch
Northwood Sch
Northwood Hills
Pinner Green
Little Common
Harlyn Prim Sch
A404 Rickmansworth, M25
A4125 Rickmansworth (A404)
PINNER RD
RICKMANSWORTH RD
PRESTWICK RD
UXBRIDGE ROAD (PINNER)
WATFORD RD
SANDY LA
40

Mutton Wood
Levels Wood
Carpenders Park Cemy
London Loop
Valley View Farm
Mast
Harrow Weald Common
Grimsdyke Hotel
Weald Wood
Woodhall Prim Sch
LITTLE OXHEY LA
Burnt Oak Farm
CH
Grims Dyke
WD19
HA3
Oxheylane Farm
Stony Wood
CHERRY HILLS
Pl Fld
Sir James Altham Pool
OXHEY LA
ROYSTON PARK RD
Saddlers Mead
Pav
LANGWORTHY
Grimsdyke Fst & Mid Sch
Tenn Cts
Athletics Tk
HA5
Pl Fld
Hatch End
UXBRIDGE ROAD (HATCH END)
Hatch End
Superstore
Pl Flds
Hatch End High Sch
Shaftesbury Sch
St Teresa's Sch
1 DEVONSHIRE CT
2 AVON MEWS
3 BENEDICT CT
4 TRURO HO
Pl Fld
Rugby Gd
Sp Gd
River Pinn
GEORGE V AVE
Headstone Lane
Pinner Park Farm
Model Rly
HA2
Tenn Cts
Bwg Gn
Sp Gd
Allot Gdns
Pl Fld
Pinner Park Schs
Cemy
Nower Hill
Open Air Theatre

A
B
8
C
D
Priory
London Loop
Cts
Levels Wood
93
Mast
Harrow Weald Common
Grimsdyke Hotel
6
Weald Wood
OLD REDDING
A409
The Kiln
HA7
Deer Park
Heriot's Wood
Priory House
Harrow Weald Common
PH
PORTMAN HALL
Tenn Cts
BROOKSHILL DR
Lower Priory Farm
Tenn Cts
HA3
Stony Wood
Copse Farm
5
Hillside
BROOKSHILL AVE
CLAMP HILL
Bentley Wood High Sch
KEMBLE HO
FLECKER CL
BRIDGES RD
AMBERDENE 1
CORONET HO 2
CYGNET HO 3
KIPLING PL 4
SINCLAIR HO 5
FERN HO 6
BROOKSHILL
BROOKSHILL GATE
BINYON CRES
SITWELL GR
MASEFIELD AVE
NEWBOLT RD
WALERAN CL
BROCKHURST CL
92
Allot Gdns
HARROW WEALD PK
Harrow Coll (Harrow Weald Campus)
Tenn Cts
Harrow Weald Cemy
ACACIA CL
A410
30
FORTNUMS ACRE
CAIRN WAY
HOLME WAY
HEATHER WAY
WARBURTON CL
LAKELAND CL
TEMPLARS DR
WEST DR
PO
4
The Bannister Sp Ctr
Athletics Tk
BELLFIELD AVE
PARK DR
Pl Fld
LAVENDER GDNS
ALL SAINTS MEWS
THE COPPINS
CHARLWOOD
GILLIAN HO
WINSTON CL
RICHMOND GDNS
KINGSTON PL
WOODLANDS DR
LAWRIE CT
GORDON AVE
WOODWARD
CASTELLANE
OXHEY LA
23
CARRINGTON SQ
WEST DRIVE GDNS
BIRCH PK
ROSS CL
130
UXBRIDGE RD (HARROW WEALD)
519
416
FONTWELL CL
KELVIN CRES
CHERRY HILL
HILL HO AVE
TREVOR CL
DAVENTER DR
HUTTON WLK
HUTTON GDNS
ARTILLERY PL
MEPHAM GDNS
MEPHAM CRES
WOOD
BOXTREE RD
KYNASTON CL
MONRO GDNS
STAMFORD CL
ELMS RD
WILSMERE DR
WINCHGATE
WHITE GATE GDNS
DROMEY GDNS
KENTON LA
DRUMMOND DR
ALTON AVE
BONIFACE WLK
3
CHICHELEY GDNS
CHICHELEY RD
LANGTON RD
HUTTON LA
BELSIZE RD
SILVER CL
Tenn Cts
PARKVIEW CT
TWICKENHAM GDNS
LORRAINE PK
COLLEGE CL
Weald Fst & Mid Schs
TILLOTSON RD
Kingsley High Sch
Recn Gd
Bwg Gn
Pav
WHITTLESEA CL
STAFFORD RD
BOXTREE LA
COLMER PL
BELMONT LO
BLACKWELL CL
AZURE APPARTMENTS
HIGH VIEW CT
LEONARD CT
TALLACK CL
WHISPERWOOD CL
ROBIN HOOD DR
KINGFISHER CL
WOODPECKER CL
RUSSELL MEAD
THREE MEADOWS MEWS
91
Hatch End High Sch
WHITTLESEA RD
Cedars Fst & Mid Schs
GREER RD
HITHERWELL DR
MARICAS AVE
Harrow Weald
ELM TERR
ALMA ROW
Tenn Cts
BARNVIEW LO
COLLEGE RD
COLLEGE HILL RD
HOLLYBUSH CL
CHESTNUT DR
WEALD RISE
RADNOR WAY
Shaftesbury Sch
St Teresa's Sch
HEADSTONE LA
WHITTLESEA PATH
COURTENAY AVE
ST BARNABAS CT
WEIGHTON RD
HIGH RD
350
PARK CL
PARK CRES
THE AVENUE
JUNIPER CT
WILLOW CT
2
CHANTRY PL
LONG ELMES
MEAD CL
BASLOW CL
ASTALL CL
ORCHID CT
HAREWOOD CT
COLLEGE AVE
COLLEGE HILL RD
BROADWAY
JUXON CL
THEOBALD CRES
BANCROFT GDNS
CARMELITE CL
STOX MEAD
STANHOPE AVE
DERBY AVE
SEFTON AVE
MAISON ALFORT
PARK RISE
THE MEADOW WAY
JOHN LAMB CT
THE BYE WAY
CHURCH LA
ADDERLEY RD
CONNAUGHT RD
Headstone Lane
AUGUSTINE RD
CARMELITE WLK
SECKER CRES
WINDSOR RD
CLEWER CRES
ENDERLEY RD
DURRANT CT
RISINGHOLME CL
NEWTON RD
THE GREEN WAY
DRYDEN RD
BISHOP KEN RD
FERNLEIGH CT
BROADFIELDS
BARMOR CL
BANCROFT RD
HAMPDEN RD
WEALD LA
BARCHESTER RD
FARMSTEAD RD
ENDERLEY CL
QUEENS TERR
207
RISINGHOLME RD
GREEN WAY GDNS
THE CROSS WAY
THE MIDDLE WAY
Allot Gdns
HARKETT CT
FISHER RD
LAURA CL
TEMSFORD CL
PARKFIELD AVE
COURTENAY GDNS
CARMELITE RD
CARMELITE WAY
BRINSLEY RD
BENGARTH DR
NICOLA CL
WHITEFRIARS DR
194
Coll
Sch
SPENCER RD
THE BROADWAY
HARKETT CL
HIBBERT RD
Belmont Fst & Mid Sch
Pav
1
HA2
Sp Gd
FULBECK WAY
PARKFIELD CRES
SARITA CL
CYPRESS RD
TOORACK RD
HARROW
BYRON RD
WARHAM RD
VERWOOD RD
LEIGHTON RD
WICKHAM RD
MARTHORNE CRES
ATHELSTONE RD
WHITEFRIARS AVE
MINSTREL CT
CLAREMONT RD
BRUCE RD
HIGH ST
159
MONTROSE RD
ABERDEEN RD
LORNE RD
ALMOND WAY
WILLOW CT
PINNER PARK AVE
THE CLOSE
HARROW VIEW
PINNER PARK GDNS
TUDOR GDNS
TUDOR RD
LYNN CL
Whitefriars Trad Est
Sch
DAUPHINE CT
LADYSMITH RD
LOCKET RD
TALBOT RD
THE RISE
90
Pinner Park Schs
HOLMWOOD CL
BARRATT WAY
Pl Fld
GRAHAM RD
CARDINAL WAY
STIRLING RD
ARCHERY CL
14
A
Sp Gd
B
42
15
C
D
SHERATON LO
THOMSON WAY
GREENLEAF
GRANT RD
AVONDALE RD
STUART RD
Pav
Bwg Gns
WELLINGTON RD
WOLSELEY RD
HAVELOCK RD
LOMOND CT
CANNING RD
Open Air Theatre
PARKFIELD GDNS
Tenn Cts
Tenn Cts
Headstone
HAILSHAM
CUMBERLAND CT 1
BANNISTER HO 2
CECIL RD
GORDON RD
SUNSET
GEORGE

25
A
B
9
C
D
BROOMFIELD HO 1
ALLOWFIELD CT 2
HILL HO 3
WELLINGTON HO 4
STANMORE HILL
LITTLE COMMON
DENNIS LA
Stanmore Hall
JULIUS CAESAR WAY
CLAUDIUS CL
AUGUSTUS CL
93
A5
FALLOWFIELD
AYLMER CL
AYLWARDS RISE
AYLMER DR
30
A4140
HERIOTS CL
PINE CL
HILL FARM CL
FAUNA CL
CHEVALIER CL
BERRY HILL
BROCKLEYSIDE
REES DR
PARTRIDGE
OLD FORGE CL
SPRING LAKE
DENNIS LA
GLANLEAM RD
REENGLASS RD
56
ADELAIDE CL
St Johns Sch
GREEN LANE COTTS
EATON CL
KNIGHTS RD
KERRY AVE
6
A410
PO
Sch
CULVER LANDS
STANMORE LO
HILL CL
HEWETT CL
Recn Gd
Bwg Gn
LABURNUM CT
OAKMEAD CT
VALENCIA RD
94
LONDON RD
37
SNARESBROOK DR
COURT DR
EMBRY CL
TANGATE GDNS
Pav
WARREN FIELDS
ARRAN DR
RUSPER CL
WHITE HO DR
KERRY CT
Stanmore
MORECAMBE GDNS
TINTAGEL DR
BROCKLEY CL
CAERNAFON HO 1
VARDY HO 2
HODGKINS MEWS 3
DALTON HO 4
SHEPHERDS CL 5
JAVELIN CT 6
MERLIN CT 7
PINEHURST 8
QUEENS LO 9
JUBILEE LO 10
EMBRY WAY
WINSCOMBE WAY
BEN HALE CL
WOODSIDE CL
GREEN LA
HALSBURY CL
THE WOODLANDS
COVERDALE CL
RAINSFORD
Liby
DENNIS GDNS
OAK LODGE CL
16
COPLEY RD
BELMONT
WESTBERE CT
WESTBERE DR
PANGBOURNE DR
DOVERCOURT
HERONSLEA DR
OLDFIELD CL
HOLLAND WALK
HOLLAND CL
T Cts
GREYFELL CL
P
RAY CT
PYNNACLES CL
ALBERT HO
WINDSOR HO
STEWART HO
CHERCHEFELL MEWS
OLD LODGE WAY
BOWLS CL
LINDEN CL
PO
CHURCH RD A410
THE BROADWAY
A4140
DENE GDNS
SANDYMOUNT AVE
CRAIGWEIL DR
MERRION AVE
5
Aylward Schs
DALKEITH GR
DEARNE CT
RIVERINE LO
GLEBE CT
GLEBE RD
CLAIRE GDNS
ALBEMARLE PK
BEAUCHAMP CT
BEECH TREE CL
CHARLBURY AVE
CRAIGWEIL CL
ATKINSON
Tenn Cts
North London Collegiate
THE CHANTRIES
STANMORE
HATHAWAY
BENTLEY WAY
WHITE ORCHARDS
UXBRIDGE RD
GLANVILLE MEWS
RECTORY LA
LADY ALESFORD AVE
WOLSTENHOLME
RECTORY CL
TUDOR WELL CL
MANOR HOUSE EST
ELM PK
HAIG RD
BYWORTH HO
INGRAM CL
PARK CL
MALCOLM CT
MERRYFIELD GDNS
ELIZABETH GDNS
DU CROS DR
92
DOUGLAS CL
WILLIAM DR
GLYN CT
CHAMBERS WALK
CHERRY TREE WAY
LEM
NELSON RD
ORFORD CT
PETERS CL
Tenn Cts
SHERBOURNE PL
ELLIOTT RD
CARR CL
ELLICOE GDNS
CAROLINE CT
EMBRY DR
BOYLE AVE
GOODHALL CL
CHANDOS CT
POND HO
CASTLEREAGH HO
Stanmore Coll
BERNAYS CL
BEATTY RD
TALMAN GR
HA8
QUEENS
WEYMOUTH
SUSSEX
YORK
SURREY
BEDFORD
DOVER
DURHAM
HAMPSHIRE
SUFFOLK
DUDLEY
HEREFORD
RUTLAND
KENT
NORFOLK
GRAHAM
THE CHASE
CONWAY CL
DOWDING PL
ASHDALE GR
ROBB RD
TRENCHARD CL
OAKLAWN CT
SEPTEMBER WAY
NARESBY FOLD
VERSTON WAY
MARSH LA
153
WYCHWOOD AVE
WYCHWOOD CL
CHEYNEYS AVE
Canons Park
4
Allot Gdns
KENNETH GDNS
SALMOND CL
TEMPLE MEAD CL
Temple Pond
WATER GDNS
THE RIDGEWAY
103
LEAVESDEN RD
CAPUCHIN CL
LAURIMEL CL
LINDETH CL
OLD CHURCH LA
BARN CRES
WILDCROFT GDNS
HOWBERRY RD
HOWBERRY CL
GORDON AVE
ROSEDALE CL
SAVERNAKE CT
LANSDOWNE RD
SALISBURY HO
WEYMOUTH WLK
LINKS VIEW CL
SUNNINGDALE CL
WENTWORTH PL
GREENACRES DR
GLENEAGLES
COLMAN CT
KENILWORTH HO
CH
MERTON RD
CLOYSTER WOOD
CORNBURY RD
26
DONNEFIELD AVE
ASH CL
GEORGIAN CL
OLD CHURCH LA
ALGUIN CT
COURTENAY MEWS
CRANMER CL
GREEN VERGES
LONGCROFTE RD
BARTHOLOMEW CT
HA7
THE QUADRANGLE
ABERDEEN COTTS
GOLF CL
TRACY CT
BELMONT LA
ABERCORN RD
Whitchurch Schs
WATERSFIELD WAY
STATION PAR
3
313
Stanmore
Sp Gd
B461
334
THE HIGHWAY
Belmont
105
ACORN CL
OAK TREE CL
Stanburn Schs
AMBER HO
BRAMBLE CL
BRICK LA
PO
Liby
WOODCROFT AVE
HONISTER GDNS
WEMBOROUGH RD
HOMEMEAD
GYLES PK
BROMEFIELD
HONISTER CL
MAYCHURCH CL
Pav
Tenn Cts
91
Allot Gdns
HONISTER PL
VERNON CT
BELLAMY CT
FLORISTON GDNS
FLORISTON CL
BUSH GR
PARR RD
Honeypot Bsns Ctr
GARLAND RD
MOUNTSIDE
VERNON DR
COLEDALE DR
ST ANDREWS DR
Sp Gd
ST EDMUNDS DR
BELLAMY DR
KYNANCE GDNS
BRAITHWAITE GDNS
LYON MEADE
PICKETT CROFT
2
Allot Gdns
HERMITAGE WAY
Allot Gdns
WESTON DR
40
WIGTON GDNS
HA7
BEVERLEY GDNS
FELBRIDGE AVE
PEARESWOOD GDNS
ANNMERSH GR
LADYCROFT WLK
CROWSHOTT AVE
BURNELL GDNS
THISTLECROFT GDNS
LAMORNA GR
Works
DALSTON GDNS
KENTON LA
CURZON AVE
BELMONT CIRC
Belmont
VENTNOR AVE
WETHERAL DR
MOUNTBEL RD
P
STATION PAR
YORK AVE
ST ANDREWS CL
Centenary Park
HONEYPOT LA
BROADCROFT AVE
PO
WARWICK PAR
P
CLIFTON AVE
Sch
DERWENT CRES
Park High Sch
CARISBROOKE CL
PORTLAND CRES
FAIRWAYS
COLLINS AVE
Tenn Cts
GODDARD CT
DOBBIN CL
KENTON LA
GRANGE AVE
UPPINGHAM AVE
1
HA3
GRASMERE GDNS
CROSS RD
ELGIN AVE
KENMORE AVE
KINGSHILL DR
TENBY AVE
ROCKLANDS DR
Sp Gd
CULVER GR
Bwg Gn
Tenn Cts
LANGLAND CRES
ELIZABETH HO
BORROWDALE AVE
RADCLIFFE RD
ASHLEY CT
JERSEY AVE
QUEENS CT
HILIARY GDNS
404
IVANHOE DR
Pl Fld
QUEENS AVE
MORLEY CRES
MORLEY CRES E
CHARMIAN AVE
90
A4140
Priestmead Schs
CLYDESDALE AVE
PORTLAND CRES W
A
B
17
43
C
D
18
PEMBROKE AVE
Recn Gd
PO
FORMBY AVE
STREATFIELD RD
BOOTHMAN HO
QUEENSBURY CIRC PAR
PO
BELMONT RD
IRVINE AVE
HARTFORD AVE
MOORHOUSE RD
Allot
Schs

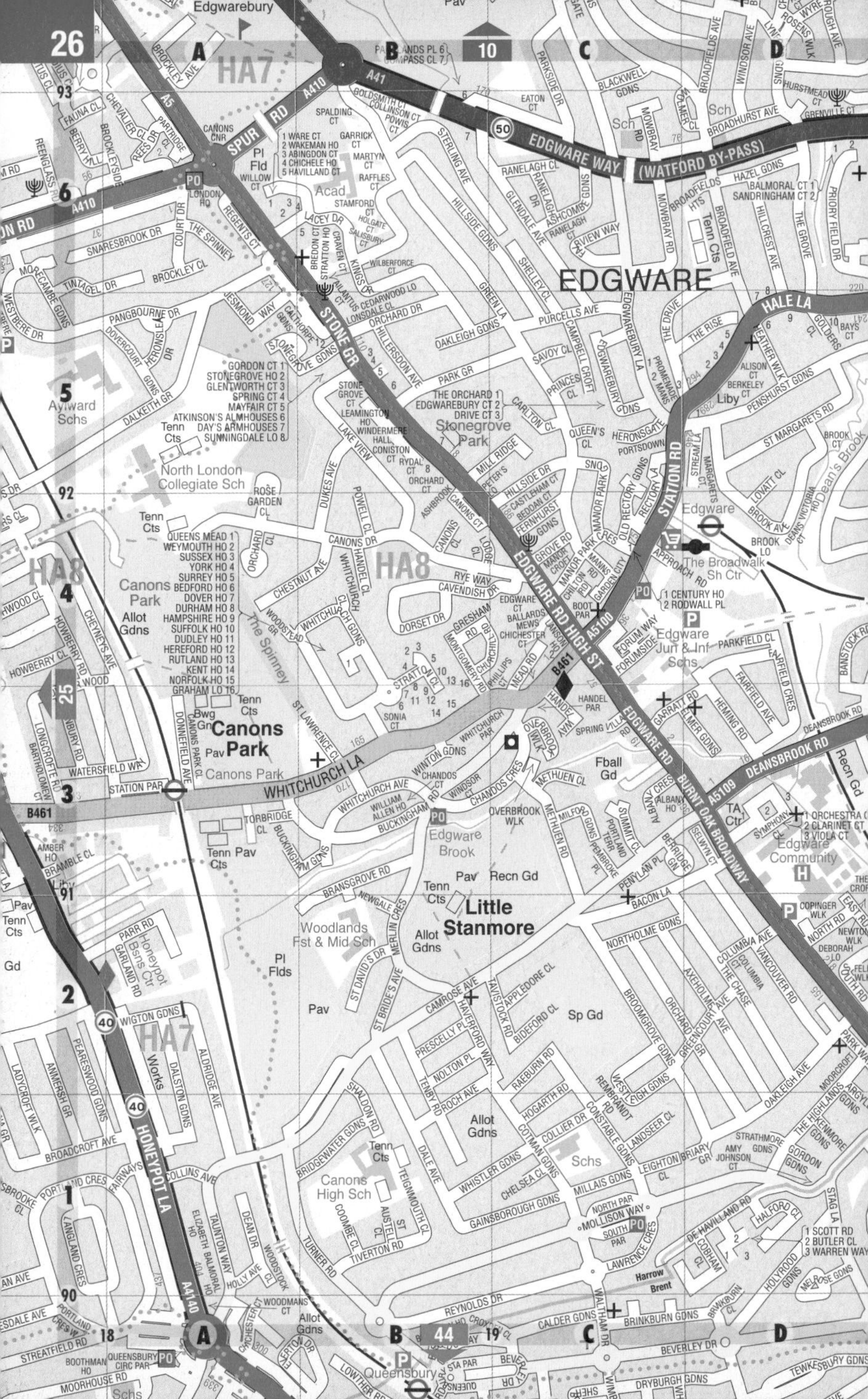
26
10
44
25
EDGWARE
Edgwarebury
Canons Park
Little Stanmore
Stonegrove Park
North London Collegiate Sch
Canons High Sch
Woodlands Fst & Mid Sch
Edgware Jun & Inf Schs
Edgware Community
The Broadwalk Sh Ctr
EDGWARE WAY (WATFORD BY-PASS)
EDGWARE RD HIGH ST
EDGWARE RD BURNT OAK BROADWAY
STONE GR
STATION RD
HALE LA
WHITCHURCH LA
HONEYPOT LA
DEANSBROOK RD
Queensbury

Stoneyfields Park
MARSH LA
WESTFIELD RD
11
Apex Cnr
NORTHWAY CIR
EDGWARE WAY (WATFORD BY-PASS)
A41
A5109
A1
M1
Allot Gdns
THE REDDINGS
REDDINGS CL
Lawrence Green
LAWRENCE ST
LAWRENCE AVE
UPHILL GR
UPHILL RD
TRETAWN PK
TRETAWN GDNS
St Joseph's Coll Mill Hill Missionaries
Tenn Cts
NW7
FOXWOOD CL
ANTHONY CL
DRAPER'S COTTAGE HOMES
SHAKESPEARE RD
TUDOR GABLES
MILTON RD
TAYLORSMEAD
TENNYSON RD
HAMMERS LA
1 LOWLANDS CT
2 FRANCIS CT
3 WILTSHIRE CL
Mill Hill Circus
VICTORIA RD
CONSORT HO
BIRKBECK RD
BYRON RD
B1461
DAWS LA
Liby
HARTLEY AVE
HARTLEY CL
Univ of London Obsy
Pav
Bwg Gn
Tenn Cts
Mill Hill Park
St Martin's Sch
NEWCOMBE PK
GOODWYN AVE
THE BROADWAY
A5100
BROCKENHURST GDNS
MEADOW GATE CL
SYLVAN AVE
WISTERIA CL
OAKLODGE WAY
COURTGATE CL
FLOWER LA
PARK MEAD GDNS
WOODLAND WAY
Mill Hill Broadway
Lyndhurst Park
Granard Bsns Ctr
Mill Hill Ind Est
WATFORD WAY (BARNET BY-PASS)
50
BUNN'S LA
THE RISE
28
HILLSIDE GR
FEATHERSTONE CT
BLOOMSBURY CL
Pentavia Ret Pk
PARKSIDE
HOLMDENE AVE
COPTHALL DR
SUNRISE VIEW
LADYSMITH CL
FARM HOUSE CT
BRANCASTER DR
LONGFIELD AVE
FAKENHAM CL
AYLESHAM CL
BURNHAM CL
TITHE WLK
THE CL
GRAHAME PARK WAY
SELVAGE LA
HALE LA
DEAN'S LA
A5100
SUNBURY AVE
SUNBURY GDNS
MAXWELTON AVE
HIGHWOOD GR
MANOR DR
MANOR CL
BEECHWOOD CL
HALE GROVE GDNS
Sch
ASHBOURNE GR
HOLMWOOD GR
THE HALE DR
DERWENT AVE
DELAMERE GDNS
SEFTON AVE
DOWNHURST AVE
THE CIRCLE
ASHMOOR LO
BEECH WLK
LIMES AVE
SUNNYDALE GDNS
HALE LA
LANGLEY PK
HALE DR
SANDBROOK CL
THE HAWTHORNS
1 TANGLEWOOD LO
2 NIGHTINGALE LO
Nature Reserve
HA8
Allot Gdns
HIGHVIEW AVE
HIGHVIEW GDNS
Dean's Brook
UPCROFT AVE
1 KENDAL HO
2 AMBLESIDE HO
ELMGATE CT
ELMGATE GDNS
BOX ELDER CL
HALE CT
BLUEBERRY CT
2 LAVENDER CT
CLOISTER GDNS
GREENCROFT
ALDERS RD
ORCHARD CRES
GRANGE CL
GRANGE HILL
LANESIDE
DEANS WAY
OAKWOOD DR
STANWAY GDNS
MEADOW GDNS
WEST WAY
CHURCH CL
RUDYARD GR
Schs
DRYFIELD RD
THE MEADS
GOLD HILL
GOLD LA
OLDBERRY RD
BENNINGHOLME RD
BROOK WLK
DEANSBROOK RD
LASHFORD HO
CRISPIN RD
HOMEFIELD RD
GRANGE RD
GOLDBEATERS GR
ELLIS CL
LYNDHURST AVE
WOODCROFT AVE
Woodcroft Park
EVERSFIELD GDNS
SPALDING CL
Sp Gd
BANSTOCK RD
DEANSBROOK RD
EDRICK RD
EDRICK WLK
DEANS CL
LANGHAM RD
HOOK WLK
DEAN WLK
EDWIN RD
ISLIP GDNS
ABBOTS RD
LANGHAM GDNS
CARDINAL CL
RUDDOCK CL
BERNHART CL
BUCKLE CT
Pav
Tenn Ct
Pl Fld
CRESSINGHAM RD
HORSECROFT RD
MILLING RD
WOLSEY GR
ARUNDEL GDNS
GOLDBEATERS GR
STORKSMEAD RD
MAPLE GDNS
RIVINGTON CRES
UNIVERSITY CL
WARDELL CL
FIELD MEAD
DUNN MEAD
LANCASTER CL
WIGGINS MEAD
Burnt Oak
Watling Park
COLCHESTER RD
NORWICH WLK
KIRTON WLK
BRIAR WLK
ORANGE HILL RD
BOSTON RD
LITTLEFIELD RD
PAVILION WAY
BREARLEY CL
GATTING CL
OVAL CT
HEMMINGS CT
GRACE CL
LYNFORD CL
BLESSBURY RD
MOSTYN RD
BLUNDELL RD
Tenn Cts
Sp Gd
FORTESCUE RD
WATLING AVE
Sch
GUNTER GR
HANSHAW DR
THIRLEBY RD
Silk Stream
Liby
GILBERT GR
CRANFIELD DR
BOVINGDON LA
DISHFORTH LA
ACKLINGTON DR
NORTH GN
LINKLEA CL
BIRCH GN
HIGHLEA CL
WILLOW GN
BROOKLEA CL
LARCH GN
PARKLEA CL
SOUTH GN
CLAYTON FIELD
LONG FIELD
GREAT FIELD
SATCHELL MEAD
WITHERS MEAD
CORNER MEAD
LONG MEAD
Barnet Coll (Grahame Pk Ctr)
Grahame Park
Grahame Park
Liby
QUAKERS COURSE
SOUTH MEAD
St James' RC High Sch
EVERGLADE STRAND
NEAR ACRE
BROADHEAD STRAND
Hurricane Trad Ctr
AVION CRES
RAF Mus
NW9
Burnt Oak Fields
COOMS WLK
Burnt Oak
PARK CROFT
SILKSTREAM PARADE
NURSE CL
TREVOR GDNS
TREVOR RD
GLOUCESTER GR
ALBANY CT
PAGEANT AVE
FULBECK DR
HEYWOOD AVE
ELVINGTON LA
TRENCHARD CL
GAYDON LA
HEMSWELL DR
GERVASE RD
Sch
BARNFIELD RD
BACK LA
MARKET LA
SILKSTREAM RD
GASKARTH RD
Barnfield Prim Sch
Silkstream Park
PLAYFIELD RD
MILLFIELD RD
ALPHAGE WLK
MONTROSE AVE
BOOTH RD
ANGUS GDNS
BRAEMAR GDNS
WARMWELL AVE
CONINGSBY AVE
BOSCOMBE CIRCUS
LANACRE AVE
NORTH ACRE
MARTLESHAM WLK
KENLEY AVE
TANGMERE WAY
YELLOWHAMMER CT
KENT CT
JAMES CT
Schs
HAZEL CL
FROBISHER CT
POCKLINGTON CL
KESTREL CL
TURNSTONE CL
WAGTAIL CL
SHELDUCK CL
SWAN DR
FALCON WAY
HARRIER RD
EAGLE DR
MAGPIE CL
KINGFISHER WLK
CHERRY CL
HUNDRED ACRE
LITTLE STRAND
FURTHER ACRE
FIVE ACRE
GREAT STRAND
Pl Fld
LOWER STRAND
BELVEDERE STRAND
Battle of Britain Museum
NW9
Pl Fld
Pav
Allot Gdns
FILTON CL 1
BLACKCAP CT 2
BITTERN CT 3
BUNTING CT 4
LAPWING CT 5
RAVEN CL 6
LISTER CT 7
CURIE GDNS 8
FLEMING WLK 9
AEROVILLE
PRIOR CL
CHANCELLOR PL
Police HQ
HENDON
AERODROME RD
JOHNSON CT 1
WILSHAW CL 2
COLMORE CT 3
Colindale
BURNT OAK BROADWAY
EDGWARE RD THE HYDE
A5
Barnet
Harrow
STABURN CT
OAK GDNS
LIMESDALE GDNS
OAKLEIGH CT
BIRCHWOOD CT
HOLMSTALL PAR
HOLMSTALL AVE
MONTROSE CT
SOUTHBOURNE AVE
SOUTHBOURNE CT
GREENWAY GDNS
PORTMAN GDNS
THE GREENWAY
Tenn Cts
CARLISLE RD
Colindale Bsns Pk
Capitol Ind Pk
Superstore
SHOELANDS CT
SILK HO
Central Public Health Lab
45
COLINDALE AVE
ANNESLEY AVE
British Liby (Newspaper Liby)
Recn Gd
Peel Ctr

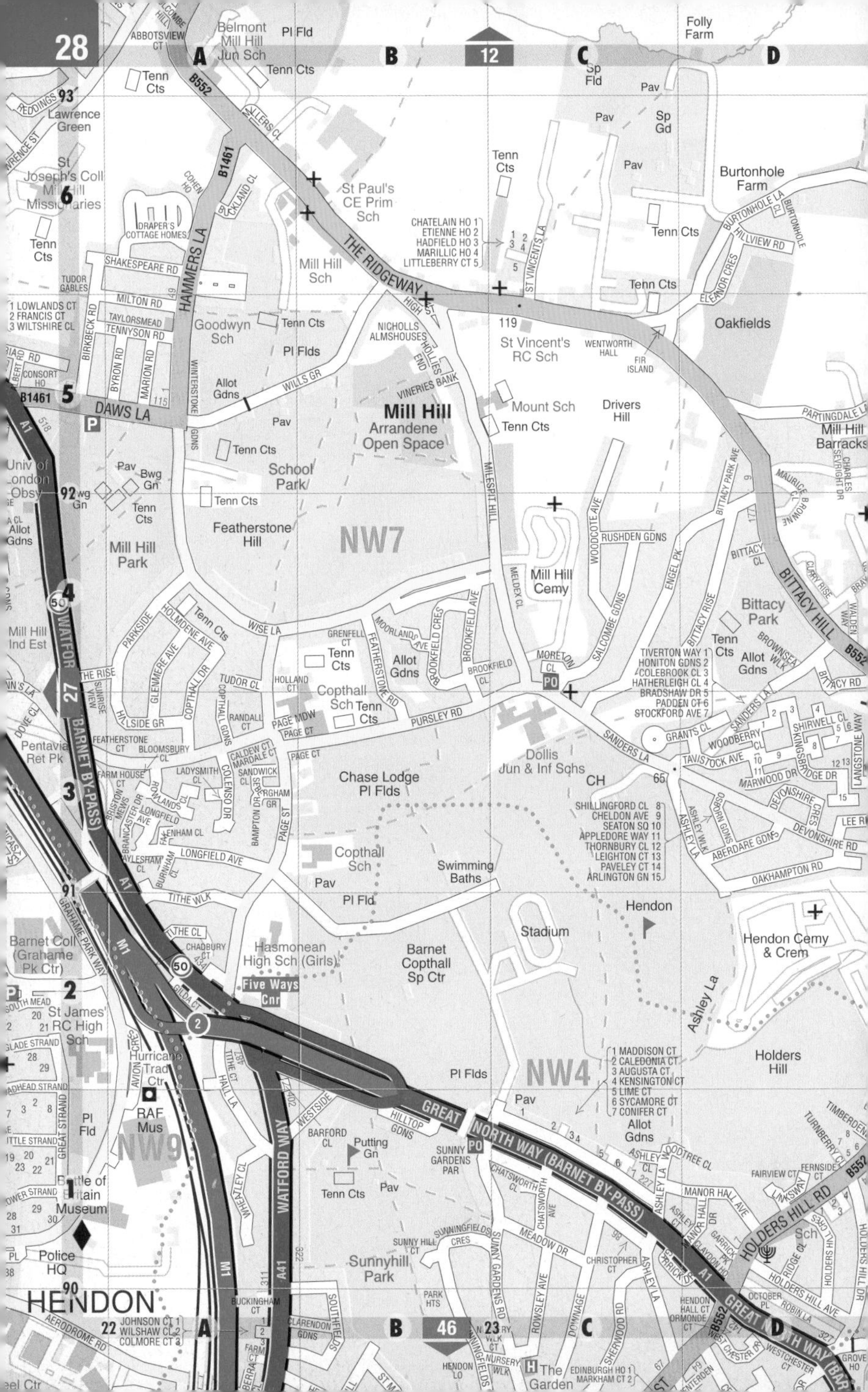
A
B
12
C
D
Belmont Mill Hill Jun Sch
Pl Fld
Folly Farm
Lawrence Green
St Joseph's Coll Mill Hill Missionaries
St Paul's CE Prim Sch
Mill Hill Sch
THE RIDGEWAY
HAMMERS LA
Goodwyn Sch
St Vincent's RC Sch
Burtonhole Farm
Oakfields
Mount Sch
Drivers Hill
Mill Hill
Arrandene Open Space
School Park
Featherstone Hill
Mill Hill Park
NW7
Mill Hill Cemy
Bittacy Park
BITTACY HILL
DAWS LA
WISE LA
Copthall Sch
Dollis Jun & Inf Schs
Chase Lodge Pl Flds
Copthall Sch
Swimming Baths
Hendon Stadium
Barnet Copthall Sp Ctr
Hasmonean High Sch (Girls)
Five Ways Cnr
Hendon Cemy & Crem
Holders Hill
NW4
GREAT NORTH WAY (BARNET BY-PASS)
WATFORD WAY
Sunnyhill Park
Barnet Coll (Grahame Pk Ctr)
St James' RC High Sch
RAF Mus
NW9
Battle of Britain Museum
Police HQ
HENDON
46
Mill Hill Barracks
Mill Hill Ind Est
Pentavia Ret Pk
Univ of London Obsy
CHATELAIN HO 1
ETIENNE HO 2
HADFIELD HO 3
MARILLIC HO 4
LITTLEBERRY CT 5
1 LOWLANDS CT
2 FRANCIS CT
3 WILTSHIRE CL
TIVERTON WAY 1
HONITON GDNS 2
COLEBROOK CL 3
HATHERLEIGH CL 4
BRADSHAW DR 5
PADDEN CT 6
STOCKFORD AVE 7
SHILLINGFORD CL 8
CHELDON AVE 9
SEATON SQ 10
APPLEDORE WAY 11
THORNBURY CL 12
LEIGHTON CT 13
PAVELEY CT 14
ARLINGTON GN 15
1 MADDISON CT
2 CALEDONIA CT
3 AUGUSTA CT
4 KENSINGTON CT
5 LIME CT
6 SYCAMORE CT
7 CONIFER CT
JOHNSON CT 1
WILSHAW CL 2
COLMORE CT 3
EDINBURGH HO 1
MARKHAM CT 2

29
A
B
C
D
13
47
25
26
50
N12
NW7
N3
Woodside Park
FINCHLEY
Church End
Finchley
Woodside Park Sch
West Finchley
Finchley Central
Mill Hill East
Inglis Barracks
Frith Manor Prim Sch
Finchley Sch
Folly Brook
Dollis Brook
Victoria Park
Moss Hall Schs
Middlesex Cty Crkt Sch
St Theresa's RC Prim Sch
Windsor Open Space
Bittacy Bsns Ctr
Superstore
Allot Gdns
Sp Gd
Tenn Cts
Bwg Gn
Pavs
Liby
Sch
Coll
Mus
Pl Fld
CH
Nether Court
Rathgar Schs
Woodridge Prim Sch
Marlex Lo
Manorside Sch
CHIDDINGFOLD
LAUREL VIEW
HOLDEN HTS
ARLINGTON
SOUTHOVER
FRAMFIELD CL
NORTHIAM
SHORTGATE
MICHLEHAM DOWN
BURTONHOLE LA
TILLINGHAM WAY
TWINEHAM GN
RIVERSIDE HO
PYCOMBE CNR
SCAYNES LINK
CHANCTONBURY WAY
CISSBURY RING N
CISSBURY RING S
RODMELL SLOPE
SINGLETON SCARP
LULLINGTON GARTH
OFFHAM SLOPE
WOLSTONBURY
FOLKINGTON CNR
SADDLESCOMBE WAY
POYNINGS WAY
STEYNINGS WAY
WALMINGTON FOLD
LINKSIDE
SUSSEX RING
ARGYLE RD
SPRINGFIELD CL
WESTBURY RD
COURT HOUSE RD
COURT HOUSE GDNS
CHESTERFIELD RD
NETHERCOURT AVE
FURSBY AVE
WEST AVE
BRENT WAY
HAMILTON WAY
FINCHLEY WAY
PENSTEMON CL
THE DRIVE
HOWCROFT CRES
CARLTON CT
CHESTNUT ROW
NETHER CL
SELLERS HALL CL
LANSDOWNE RD
GROSVENOR RD
EVERSLEIGH RD
ELM PARK RD
GORDON RD
OAKDENE PK
ROCKLANDS
HOLDEN RD
HOLDEN AVE
HOPTREE CL
BUDD CL
WOODSIDE GRANGE RD
GRANGEWAY
DORIE MEWS
GUILDOWN AVE
LORIAN CL
FOUR ACRES
BROOK MDW
HENDERSON CT
BARCHESTER LO
SYLVAN CT
WOODSIDE AVE
WOODSIDE PARK RD
LIMES AVE
CLAIRE CT
CAVENDISH HO
LITTLE CEDARS
SQUIRRELS
GREEN BANK
THE OAKS
CLIVEDEN CL
ARDEN GRANGE
AVENUE RD
EMERALD CT
CHOLMELEY CT
DOWNING CT
THE GABLES
FINCHLEY LO
CLARENDON HO
LODGE LA
GAINSBOROUGH RD
GAINSBOROUGH CT
AVONDALE AVE
WORCESTER CT
AVON CT
NETHERFIELD RD
PERCY RD
HUGHES CL
COLERIDGE RD
NETHER ST
VIVIAN CT
QUEENSGATE CT
ALBANY CT
ELLE CT
THE CREST
HILLCOURT AVE
ALEXANDRA GR
MOSSBOROUGH CL
MOSS HALL CT
THYRA GR
GREENLAWNS
MOSS HALL GR
MOSS HALL CRES
HUTTON GR
DALE GR
PUGET CT
BIRKBECK RD
FOLEY CT
BARCLAY CT
KNIGHTSWOOD HO
VINE LO
CHRISTCHURCH
WOODBERRY
GLOWHILL CL
NEWBURN CT
THE LAURELS
WESTLEIGH CT
PAMELA CT
THE LANTERNS
BURNSIDE CL
NORTHUMBERLAND HO
ESSEX PK
HARTLEY HO
FINCHLEY CT
THE FOUNTAINS
WENTWORTH CL
BROWNLOW RD
BALLARDS LA
ROSSANNE HO
SOLAR CT
SEYMOUR RD
NIGEL CT
GRANVILLE RD
ETCHINGHAM CT
HOLLYHURST AVE
HOLDEN
WENTWORTH AVE
WENTWORTH PK
MARWOOD CT
GRUNEISEN RD
CORNWALL AVE
ADAMS CL
GROVE AVE
FALKLAND AVE
THE GROVE
CLAVERLEY VILLAS
CLAVERLEY GR
ST PAUL'S WAY
THE RIDGEWAY
WILLOW WAY
PARKSIDE
MILLERS YD
PRINCES AVE
DORSET MEWS
REDBOURNE AVE
REDBOURNE HO
DUKES AVE
VINES AVE
OAKFIELD CT
OAKFIELD RD
PARK VIEW RD
PARK AVE
PARK CRES
ETCHINGHAM PARK RD
QUEEN'S AVE
WOODLANDS AVE
BARRYMORE
LONG LA
SQUIRES LA
MONTPELIER RD
AVONDALE RD
CROMWELL RD
ABINGDON
NURSERY AVE
DOUGLAS CT
VINEYARD GR
LAKESIDE
BERKELEY CT
CLAIGMAR GDNS
CADOGAN GDNS
STRATHMORE GDNS
HERVEY CL
SHAKESPEARE RD
POPES DR
ALAN RD
ALBERT PL
PREMIER LO
NETHER ST B1462
CRESCENT RD
DOLLIS CT
CRESCENT RISE
DOLLIS PK
DOLLIS MEWS
DOLLIS AVE
DOLLIS RD
LINKS VIEW
LAXMI CT
BRUNSWICK HO
CLIFTON AVE
CHURCH CRES
VICTORIA AVE
PEWTERERS CT
PRIORY CL
RECTORY CL
COLLEGE
REGENCY HO
SPENCER CL
DERBY LO
ELLERTON LO
THE AVENUE
ARCADIA AVE
WOOTTON GR
STATION CL
STATION RD
LICHFIELD GR
GLENHILL CL
SYLVAN AVE
MANOR VIEW
DUDLEY RD
ROSEMARY AVE
BRIARFIELD AVE
PRIMROSE CL
TANGLE TREE CL
MADDISON CL
THE MEAD
MANOR COTTS
RICHMOND RD
BRIAR CL
CRANBOURNE CT
BENEDICT
CECILIA
EAST END RD
SPRING PL
WINDERMERE AVE
PAVILION MEWS
HOLMWOOD GDNS
TEMPLARS CRES
CAVENDISH AVE
EASTGATE CT
STANHOPE CT
COLOSSEUM CT
STANHOPE AVE
MOUNTFIELD RD
LUKES CT
BASING WAY
REMEMBRANCE AVE
THE CRESCENT
AMBERDEN
A504
A598
A5000
A406
B552
B1462
HENDON LA
GRAVEL HILL
REGENTS PARK RD
HENDON AVE
GRENVILLE CL
KINGSWOOD PK
GRASS PK
THE LINTONS
LYNDHURST GDNS
CLAREMONT PK
QUEENSWOOD PK
VILLAGE RD
CYPRUS GDNS
CYPRUS AVE
ST MARY'S AVE
FRESTON PK
SAMUEL LO
BLAKE LO
GOLDA CL
WINDSOR CL
WINDSOR RD
CRANMER CT
PAUL CT
WICKLIFFE AVE
CHARLTON CT
STAFFORDSHIRE HO
ELIZABETHAN HELEN CT
SURREY CL
VOYSEY CL
ARDEN RD
SALISBURY AVE
SALISBURY CT
CROWN LO
ARUNDEL LO
CYPRUS RD
NORTH CRES
TEMPLE CL
ST MICHAEL'S
BIBSWORTH RD
BIBSWORTH LO
EMBASSY LO
FITZALAN RD
WAVERLEY GR
HOLDERS HILL RD
HOLDERS HILL GDNS
HOLDERS HILL PAR
HAWTHORN MEWS
OAKDALE LO
PARAGON CT
FORELAND CT
RYDAL CL
ROCHESTER CT
FREELAND PK
COLERNE CT
CUMBERLAND GDNS
THYME CT
REGEL CT
THORNFIELD PAR
THORNFIELD CT
MILL CT
THORNFIELD AVE
BOSE CL
ABERCORN CL
ABERCORN RD
MALLOW MEAD
FAITH CT
BROOK CL
VINEYARD AVE
DOLLISCROFT
LANGSTONE WAY
NEW RD
BITTACY CT
CRANBOURNE CT
FRITH LA
WESTLINTON CL
WILLIAMSON WAY
WARREN WAY
HOLMES AVE
APPROACH LA
ROSS AVE
HAWTHORNE AVE
READING WAY
HENRY DARLOT DR
ROBERTS RD
LIDBURY RD
KENNY RD
PRICE CL
KELLY RD
DREW AVE
TWINN RD
BARHAM CT
FRITH MANOR COTTS
VICARAGE CT
THE GARTH
BROOKDENE
GARDEN CT
HOLMDENE
HOLDEN RD
SALIX CT
MAPLE CL
CEDAR CT
CHIVINS CT

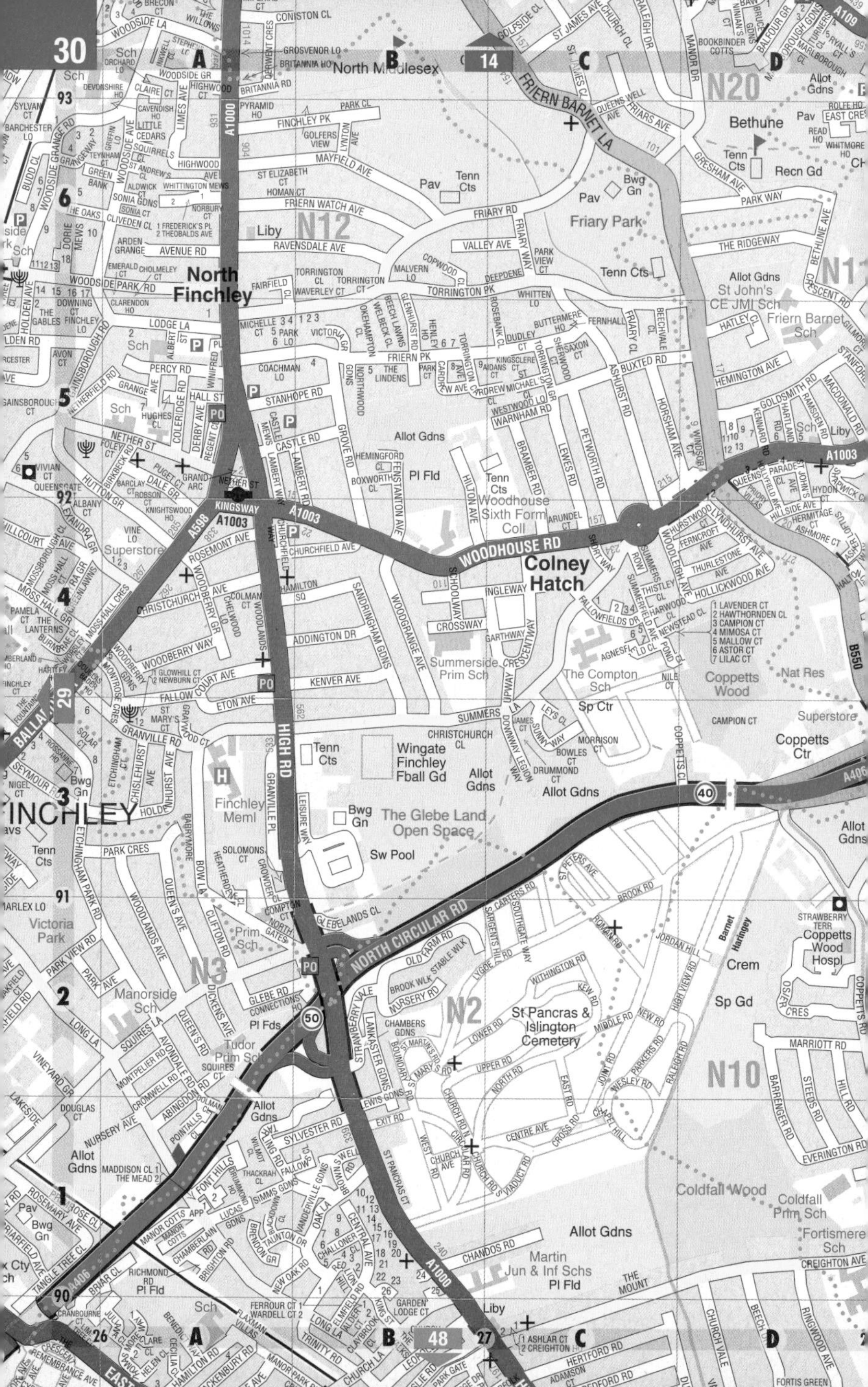

A
B
C
D
14
48
North Middlesex
N20
N12
N3
N2
N10
North Finchley
Colney Hatch
FINCHLEY
Friary Park
Bethune
Recn Gd
Friern Barnet Sch
St John's CE JMI Sch
Woodhouse Sixth Form Coll
Summerside Prim Sch
The Compton Sch
Coppetts Wood
Nat Res
Coppetts Ctr
Superstore
Wingate Finchley Fball Gd
The Glebe Land Open Space
Sw Pool
Finchley Meml
Victoria Park
Manorside Sch
Tudor Prim Sch
St Pancras & Islington Cemetery
Coppetts Wood Hospl
Crem
Sp Gd
Coldfall Wood
Coldfall Prim Sch
Fortismere Sch
Martin Jun & Inf Schs
Allot Gdns
Pl Fld
Tenn Cts
Liby
FRIERN BARNET LA
WOODHOUSE RD
HIGH RD
NORTH CIRCULAR RD
KINGSWAY
A1000
A1003
A598
A406
A109
B550
FRIARY RD
TORRINGTON PK
FRIERN PK
BUXTED RD
PARK WAY
THE RIDGEWAY
SUMMERS LA
ETON AVE
KENVER AVE
ADDINGTON DR
WOODGRANGE AVE
SANDRINGHAM GDNS
CHRISTCHURCH AVE
WOODBERRY WAY
FALLOW COURT AVE
GRANVILLE RD
PARK CRES
WOODLANDS AVE
QUEEN'S AVE
LONG LA
CHURCH LA
CHANDOS RD
CREIGHTON AVE
MARRIOTT RD
EVERINGTON RD
HIGH VIEW RD
RALEIGH RD
BROOK RD
EAST END RD

31
FRIERN BARNET
New Southgate
N11
N14
N13
N22
N10
N8
Arnos Park
Betstyle Circus
BOWES RD
OAKLEIGH RD S
FRIERN BARNET RD
STATION RD
TELFORD RD (NORTH CIRCULAR RD)
PINKHAM WAY NORTH CIRCULAR RD
COLNEY HATCH LA
ALEXANDRA PARK RD
ALBERT RD
DURNSFORD RD
BOUNDS GREEN RD
BROWNLOW RD
WILMER WAY
POWYS LA
MUSWELL HILL RD
Friern Bridge Ret Pk
Bounds Green Ind Est
Superstore
Hollickwood Park
Muswell Hill
Alexandra Park Sch
Rhodes Avenue Prim Sch
Wood Green Tunnel
Alexandra Palace
The Lake
Alexandra Palace Mast
Alexandra Park
Coppetts Wood Prim Sch
Our Lady of Muswell RC Prim Sch
Norfolk House Sch
Fortismere Sch (South Wing)
Colney Hatch
Bounds Green
Arnos Grove
Bowes Prim Sch
Broomfield Sch
St Martin of Porres RC Prim Sch
Hollickwood Prim Sch
15
32
49

32
A
B
C
D
16
50
N13
N22
N8
CANNON HILL
CANNON RD
St Monica's RC Prim Sch
HARLECH RD
ULLESWATER RD
DERWENT RD
LAKESIDE RD
GROVELANDS RD
OLD PARK RD
SKINNERS ALMSHOUSES
PELLIPAR CL
OSBORNE RD
WINDSOR RD
PARK AVE
HAZELWOOD CRES
LIGHTCLIFFE RD
NEW RIVER CRES
New River
WENTWORTH GDNS
MADEIRA RD
HUXLEY PL
A111
FOXGROVE
ELLENA CT
FORESDALE
A1004
B1452
ALDERMAN'S HILL
FAIRWEATHER CL
Palmers Green
DEVONSHIRE RD
A105
CAMBRAI CT
Bwg Gn
Pav
Tenn Cts
Broomfield Park
Sp Gd
Bndstd
CORRI AVE
TOWNSEND AVE
POWYS LA
BROOMFIELD AVE
PILGRIMS CL
THE GROVE
THE CREST
LODGE DR
TRADE CL
St Annes Catholic High Sch for Girls (Upper)
THE RISE
RIVERWAY
HAMILTON CRES
Hazelwood Jun & Inf Schs
HAZELWOOD LA
KINGSLEY RD
Allot Gdns
Sp Gd
DOVERIDGE GDNS
CONNAUGHT GDNS
LYNBRIDGE GDNS
CONNAUGHT GRANGE
LAWRENCE AVE
CALLARD AVE
A406
WILMER WAY
DAWLISH AVE
ASHRIDGE GDNS
SUNNINGDALE
BROOMFIELD LA
ELMWOOD AVE
BELMONT AVE
BRIDGE DR
Liby
SHAPLAND WAY
CYRIL SMITH HO
BOURNE MANS
OAKTHORPE RD
CHIMES AVE
ARNOLD GDNS
CHERRY BLOSSOM CL
Pymme's Brook
HAWTHORN AVE
CRANFORD AVE
1 RIVERSIDE APARTMENTS
2 BOWES HO
3 CLAYBEE CT
4 ANNADALE
5 WENDOVER HO
PALMERSTON CRES
SOUTHCHURCH CT
ECCLESBOURNE GDNS
FELSTEAD CL
NORTH CIRCULAR RD
BIRCHWOOD CT
MELVILLE GDNS
Broomfield Sch
Pl Fld
BROOMFIELD COTTS
BROOMFIELD CT
WESTMINSTER DR
POWYS CT
ELMDALE RD
BROADWAY MEWS
REGENTS AVE
MILLSTREAM CL
HEREWARD GDNS
PANTILES CL
BEALE CL
BOWES RD (NORTH CIRCULAR RD)
LYNTON MEWS
PYMMES
OMFIELD
STANLEY RD
HIGHWORTH RD
WAKEFIELD RD
BOSWORTH RD
UNION RD
NATAL RD
HARDWICKE RD
LIVINGSTONE RD
MOFFAT RD
PYMMES RD
Allot Gdns
1 CLOCKHOUSE PAR
2 CLOCKHOUSE MANS
Clockhouse Junction
SIDNEY AVE
RAVENSWOOD
PARKSIDE CT
PRINCES AVE
FAIRBROOK RD
TOTTENHALL RD
Tottenhall Inf Sch
St Michael-at-Bowes CE Jun Sch
MELBOURNE AVE
GRENOBLE GDNS
ST CUTHBERTS RD
LANCASTER RD
ELVENDON RD
WISHAW WLK
GRANVILLE RD
COLLINGS CL
KELVIN AVE
WILDE PL
SANDCROFT CL
ST PAULS RISE
DEANS DR
COLET CL
MEDESENGE WAY
WILLIAM HO
GODOLPHIN CL
Bowes Park
BEECH RD
WHITTINGTON RD
PALMERSTON RD
BELSIZE AVE
UPSDELL AVE
YORK RD
HAYWOOD CT
Haringey
Enfield
BROWNLOW RD
Tenn Cts
GORING RD
WESTBURY RD
WYNAUD CT
SPENCER AVE
BERKSHIRE GDNS
NORFOLK AVE
ACORN CT
TEWKESBURY CT
PARKDALE
EMBASSY CT
BOUNDS GREEN CT
RIDGEON CT
ELEANOR RD
GRASMERE CT
LASCOTT'S RD
LYNDHURST RD
THETFORD CL
MANOR RD
LAWRENCE HO
MAXWELL HO
LIONEL HO
PALM CT
GARWOOD LO
SPACE APARTMENTS
MARQUIS RD
MARYLAND RD
WOLVES LA
RICHMOND RD
HERBERT RD
IRELAND PL
Bowes Park
NORTHBROOK RD
MARLBOROUGH RD
CHESHIRE RD
PARKHURST RD
ARCADIAN GDNS
CROSS RD
31
A109
B106
QUEEN'S PAR
FLETTON RD
Bounds Green
Schs
BOUNDS GREEN RD
WHITTINGTON RD
MYDDLETON MEWS
MYDDLETON RD
SHROPSHIRE RD
HAMPSHIRE RD
GLENDALE AVE
SYLVAN AVE
New River Sp & Recn Ctr
St Georges Ind Est
THOROLD RD
Allot Gdns
SIDNEY RD
HIGH RD
WOODSIDE RD
Woodside Park
CROFTS LA
MALBURY CT
FERNWOOD
CLARENCE RD
BARNES CT
ORCHARD CT
KINGSLEY CT
REDRUTH CL
FALMOUTH CL
Bwg Gn
St Thomas More Sch
Tenn Cts
White Hart Lane Sec Sch
THE CROSSWAY
PORTERS AND WALTERS ALMSHOUSES
MOHR CT
PORTREE CL
1 ADAMS MEWS
2 ROBIN CT
3 THOMAS HARDY HO
Tenn Cts
Earlham Prim Sch
Pl Fld
WHITE HART LA
CORBETT GR
TRINITY RD
AVONDALE
GRACEDYER HO
TRURO RD
NIGHTINGALE RD
EARLHAM GR
Pl Fld
FIFE RD
LOUISA CT
PARK GR
PALACE RD
EDITH RD
ANEURIN BEVAN CT
BAILEY CL
FIREMAN'S FLATS
IMPERIAL RD
FINSBURY HO
NEWBURY HO
JOHN KEATS HO
COMMERCE RD
JANET CT
NEWNHAM RD
CANNING CRES
1 MAURICE CT
2 NEWNHAM MEWS
3 CHAPMAN GN
PARK VIEW GDNS
STIRLING RD
FORFAR RD
BERWICK RD
PERTH RD
PAISLEY RD
MADDERFIELDS CT
BOLSTER GR
WOODRIDINGS CT
PARTRIDGE WAY
ROSECROFT
JOYCE BUTLER HO
BASIL SPENCE HO
NEVILLE PL
KINGS RD
RIVERSDALE GDNS
DOUGLAS RD
ELIZABETH BLACKWELL HO
ACACIA HO
CEDAR HO
DUNBAR RD
LEITH RD
SOLWAY RD
SAXON RD
EASTERN RD
NORTHCOTT AVE
CORNWALL AVE
BRAEMAR AVE
TRINITY RD
PROGRESS WAY
MOWBRAY CT
COLAB CT
EWART GR
GEORGE LANSBURY HO
WINKFIELD RD
MELROSE AVE
Tenn Ct
Bwg Gn
GRANVILLE RD
PRINCES AVE
WOOD GREEN
Nightingale Gardens
Allot Gdns
Sch
C Ctr
STUART CRES
WILLIAMS GR
PELLATT GR
ALBERT VICTORIA HO
BRACKNELL CL
OLYMPUS GR
CROWN CL
KHALSA CT
ELM RD
PICKERING CT
ELLENBOROUGH RD
LOUISE CT
MERLIN CT
PALACE GATES RD
BUCKINGHAM RD
BRIDGE RD
DORSET RD
TERRICK RD
ST MICHAEL'S TERR
RANELAGH RD
SELBORNE RD
WOODLEIGH CT
GREENWOOD HO
CRANBROOK CT
CAMBRIDGE CL
ST ALBANS CRES
LORDSHIP LA
ANDRULA CT
COLDHAM CT
VERA CT
LYNDUM CT
ALEXANDRA PARK RD
ANDERTON CT
Alexandra Palace
BEDFORD RD
STATION RD
Avenue Gdns
PARK AVE
WOLSELEY RD
WARBERRY RD
RINGSLADE RD
WATSONS RD
SYLVIA LAWLA CT
RIVER PARK RD
HARDY PAS
BERNERS RD
GATHORNE RD
VINCENT SQ
WELLESLEY RD
TEMPLE RD
COOMBE RD
MOSELLE AVE
MORLEY AVE
SALISBURY RD
DARWIN RD
GLADSTONE AVE
Sch
BARRATT AVE
BRADLEY RD
B138
STATION RD
ECLIPSE RD
BRABANT RD
Wood Green
THE BROADWAY
BULLER RD
REDVERS RD
VINCENT RD
FARRANT AVE
Noel Park Prim Sch
LYMINGTON AVE
HEWITT AVE
Wood Green Common
PARKLAND RD
JACK BARNETT WAY
SAXTON RD
GLADSTONE AVE
PELHAM RD
ASHLEY CRES
Rec Gd
Noel Park
SOUTH TERR
Alexandra Prim Sch
TOWER TERR
MAYES RD
Liby
UMOJA HO
Sh City
PARK RD
BARBARA HUCKLESBURY CL
RUSSELL AVE
ALFRED FINDLEY HO
GARDNER CL
WILLINGDON RD
WESTERN RD
CLARENDON RD
JOHN ALDIS HO
CORBURG RD
SILSOE RD
BROOK RD
GLYNNE RD
MEADS RD
A105
WESTBURY AVE
Olympia Ind Est
HORNSEY PARK RD
PARK RIDINGS
PAGE HIGH
BURY RD
WESTBEECH RD
THE SANDLINGS
COBHAM RD
SIRDAR RD
HAWKE PARK RD
1 KOBLENZ HO
2 WAT TYLER HO
3 NEWLAND HO
4 GOODWIN CT
5 GILLETT HO
6 MYDDELTON HO
7 CAMPSFIELD HO
Pl Fld
A1080
COURCY RD
ALEXANDRA PARK
6
5
4
3
2
1
93
92
91
90
30
31

EDMONTON
TOTTENHAM
N17
STERLING WAY (NORTH CIRCULAR RD)
THE ROUNDWAY
LORDSHIP LA
HIGH RD
FORE ST
BRUCE GR
HEDGE LA
DOWNHILLS WAY
Tatem Park
Pymmes Park
Great Cambridge Junction
North Middlesex University
Bruce Castle Park
Lordship Recn Gd
Tower Gardens
Tottenham Hotspur Fball Club
17
51
34
Enfield
Haringey

Lower Edmonton
Federation
18
Recn Gd
EDMONTON
Angel Edmonton
ANGEL ROAD (NORTH CIRCULAR ROAD)
CONDUIT LA
Kenninghall
Cooks Ferry
A406
A1055
A1010
B137
MONTAGU
Montagu Ind Est
Eley's Est
N18
Angel Rd Works
Angel Road
Raynham Prim Sch
Upper Edmonton
Ravenside Ret Pk
Stonehill Bsns Pk
Superstore
GLOVER DR
Lea Valley Trad Est
Kingsway Est
Elm Lea Trad Est
MERIDIAN WAY
Triumph Trad Est
Royal London Est
Hotspur Ind Est
Lake Bsns Ctr
Edmonton Wharf
Canal Bridge
Leeside Works
Mowlem Trad Est
Leeside Trad Est
Nrthmbrlnd Park Ind Est
N17
Northumberland Pk Sp Ctr
Tottenham Hotspur Fball Club
Northumberland Park
Unicorn Works
Allot Gdns
Tottenham Marshes
River Lee Navigation
River Lea or Lee Diversion
Lee Flood Relief Channel
Depot
Coleraine Park Prim Sch
Rosebery Ind Pk
TOTTENHAM
Silver Ind Est
Pymme's Brook
Haringey
Waltham Forest
Lockwood Reservoir
WATERMEAD WAY
BLACKHORSE LA
B179
Uplands Bsns Pk
Lea Valley Technopark
Down Lane Park
Millmead Ind Ctr
Lockwood
Bruce Grove
HIGH RD
A109
A10
33
52
35

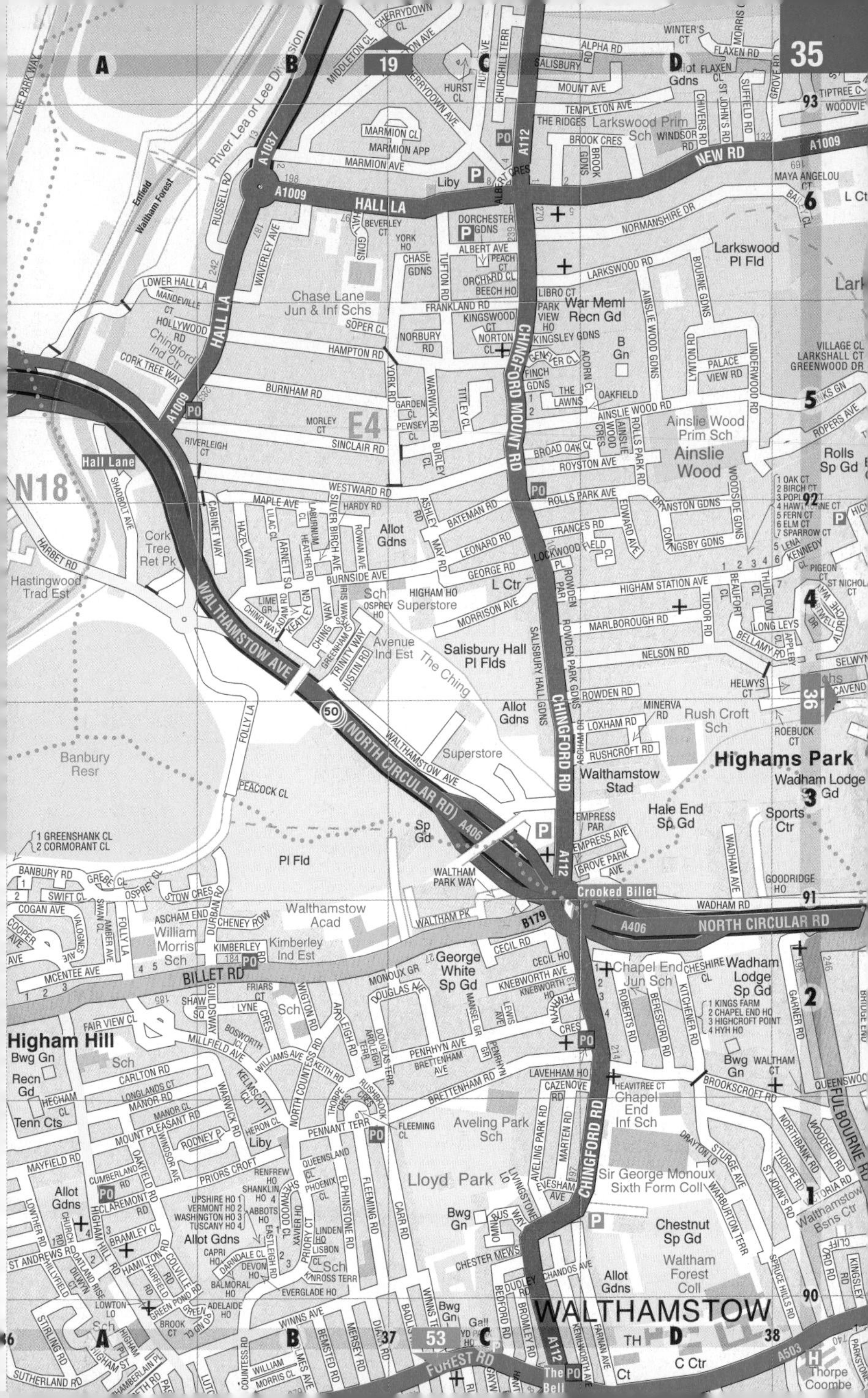
35
A
B
C
D
19
53
36
37
38
93
92
91
90
6
5
4
3
2
1
N18
E4
LEE PARK WAY
River Lea or Lee Diversion
Enfield
Waltham Forest
CHERRYDOWN CL
MIDDLETON CL
CHERRYDOWN AVE
HURST CL
CHURCHILL TERR
SALISBURY RD
ALPHA RD
WINTER'S CT
MORRIS CT
FLAXEN RD
FLAXEN CL
Allot Gdns
MOUNT AVE
ST JOHN'S RD
SUFFIELD RD
GROVE RD
TIPTREE CR
WOODVIEW
TEMPLETON AVE
THE RIDGES
Larkswood Prim Sch
CHIVERS RD
WINDSOR RD
BROOK CRES
BROOK GDNS
NEW RD
A1009
A1037
A112
A406
A503
B179
MARMION CL
MARMION APP
MARMION AVE
RUSSELL RD
HALL LA
Liby
ALBERT CRES
MAYA ANGELOU CT
BAILEY CL
L Ctr
DORCHESTER GDNS
BEVERLEY CT
HALL GDNS
YORK HO
CHASE GDNS
ALBERT AVE
PEACH CT
ORCHARD CL
BEECH HO
NORMANSHIRE DR
Larkswood Pl Fld
LARKSWOOD RD
WAVERLEY AVE
LOWER HALL LA
MANDEVILLE CT
HOLLYWOOD RD
Chingford Ind Ctr
CORK TREE WAY
Chase Lane Jun & Inf Schs
TUFTON RD
LIBRO CT
PARK VIEW HO
War Meml Recn Gd
FRANKLAND RD
KINGSWOOD CT
KINGSLEY GDNS
SOPER CL
NORBURY RD
NORTON CL
HAMPTON RD
YORK RD
WARWICK RD
TITLEY CL
GENEVER CL
FINCH GDNS
THE LAWNS
ACORN CL
OAKFIELD
B Gn
AINSLIE WOOD GDNS
BOURNE GDNS
LINTON RD
UNDERWOOD RD
PALACE VIEW RD
VILLAGE CL
LARKSHALL CT
GREENWOOD DR
JENKINS GN
ROPERS AVE
BURNHAM RD
CHINGFORD MOUNT RD
GARDEN CL
PEWSEY CL
MORLEY CT
SINCLAIR RD
BURLEY CL
RIVERLEIGH CT
AINSLIE WOOD RD
AINSLIE WOOD CRES
ROLLS PARK RD
Ainslie Wood Prim Sch
Ainslie Wood
BROAD OAK CL
ROYSTON AVE
Rolls Sp Gd
Hall Lane
WESTWARD RD
MAPLE AVE
HARDY RD
ROLLS PARK AVE
CRANSTON GDNS
WOODSIDE GDNS
1 OAK CT
2 BIRCH CT
3 POPLAR CT
4 HAWTHORNE CT
5 FERN CT
6 ELM CT
7 SPARROW CT
SHADBOLT AVE
CABINET WAY
HAZEL WAY
LILAC CL
LABURNUM CL
SILVER BIRCH AVE
ROWAN AVE
ASHLEY RD
BATEMAN RD
FRANCES RD
EDWARD AVE
CONINGSBY GDNS
LENA
KENNEDY CL
Cork Tree Ret Pk
HARBET RD
Hastingwood Trad Est
ARNETT SQ
HEATHER RD
Allot Gdns
LEONARD RD
MAY RD
LOCKWOOD PL
FIELD CL
GEORGE RD
BURNSIDE AVE
HIGHAM HO
L Ctr
ROWDEN PARK
HIGHAM STATION AVE
BEAUFORT CL
THURLOW CL
PIGEON CT
ST NICHOLAS
LIME GR
ADAM RD
KEATLEY GN
CHING WAY
Sch
OSPREY HO
Superstore
MORRISON AVE
TUDOR RD
CHATSWORTH DR
WALTHAMSTOW AVE
GREENHAM CL
TRINITY WAY
JUSTIN RD
Avenue Ind Est
The Ching
Salisbury Hall Pl Flds
ROWDEN PARK GDNS
MARLBOROUGH RD
LONG LEYS
BELLAMY RD
APPLEBY CL
NELSON RD
SELWYN
HELWYS CT
CAVENDISH
Allot Gdns
SALISBURY HALL GDNS
CHINGFORD RD
ROWDEN RD
LOXHAM RD
MINERVA RD
Rush Croft Sch
ROEBUCK CT
50
(NORTH CIRCULAR RD)
FOLLY LA
Banbury Resr
WALTHAMSTOW AVE
Superstore
RUSHCROFT RD
Highams Park
Walthamstow Stad
Wadham Lodge Gd
PEACOCK CL
Hale End Sp Gd
Sports Ctr
EMPRESS PAR
EMPRESS AVE
GROVE PARK AVE
1 GREENSHANK CL
2 CORMORANT CL
Sp Gd
Pl Fld
WADHAM AVE
WALTHAM PARK WAY
BANBURY RD
GREBE CL
OSPREY CL
SWIFT CL
STOW CRES
Crooked Billet
GOODRIDGE HO
WADHAM RD
COGAN AVE
VALOGNES AVE
SWAN CL
AMBER AVE
FOLLY LA
COOPER AVE
ASCHAM END
DURBAN RD
CHENEY ROW
Walthamstow Acad
WALTHAM PK
NORTH CIRCULAR RD
William Morris Sch
KIMBERLEY RD
Kimberley Ind Est
CECIL RD
CECIL HO
Chapel End Jun Sch
CHESHIRE CL
Wadham Lodge Sp Gd
BRIDGE END
MCENTEE AVE
BILLET RD
George White Sp Gd
KNEBWORTH AVE
KNEBWORTH HO
ROBERTS RD
BERESFORD RD
KITCHENER RD
GARNER RD
1 KINGS FARM
2 CHAPEL END HO
3 HIGHCROFT POINT
4 HYH HO
SHAW SQ
GUILDSWAY
FRIARS CT
LYNE CRES
Sch
WIGTON RD
ARDLEIGH RD
MONOUX GR
DOUGLAS AVE
DOUGLAS TERR
ARDLEIGH TERR
MANSEL GR
LEWIS AVE
PENRHYN AVE
PENRHYN GR
PENRHYN CRES
FAIR VIEW CL
Higham Hill
Bwg Gn
MILLFIELD AVE
BOSWORTH CL
WILLIAMS AVE
NORTH COUNTESS RD
KEITH RD
BRETTENHAM AVE
BRETTENHAM RD
LAVEHHAM HO
Bwg Gn
WALTHAM CT
Sch
Recn Gd
CARLTON RD
KELMSCOTT CL
RUSHBROOK CRES
THORPE CRES
HEAVITREE CT
BROOKSCROFT RD
QUEENSWOOD
LONGLANDS CT
MANOR RD
HECHAM CL
WARWICK RD
CAZENOVE RD
Chapel End Inf Sch
NORTHBANK RD
WOODEND RD
FULBOURNE RD
Tenn Cts
MANOR CL
MOUNT PLEASANT RD
RODNEY RD
HERON CL
PENNANT TERR
FLEEMING CL
Aveling Park Sch
DRAYTON RD
STURGE AVE
THORPE RD
Liby
WINDSOR RD
MAYFIELD RD
OAKFIELD RD
PRIORS CROFT
QUEENSLAND
AVELING PARK RD
MARTEN RD
CUMBERLAND RD
RENFREW HO
PHOENIX CL
Lloyd Park
LIVINGSTONE
Sir George Monoux Sixth Form Coll
ST JOHN'S RD
VICTORIA RD
Allot Gdns
CLAREMONT RD
UPSHIRE HO 1
VERMONT HO 2
WASHINGTON HO 3
TUSCANY HO 4
SHANKLIN HO
ABBOTS HO
SHERWOOD CL
XAVIER HO
ELPHINSTONE RD
FLEEMING RD
CARR RD
EVESHAM AVE
WARBURTON TERR
Walthamstow Bsns Ctr
LOWTHER RD
CHURCH RD
HIGHAM HILL RD
BRAMLEY CL
Allot Gdns
EASTLEIGH RD
LINDEN HO
PRIORY CT
Bwg Gn
OMNIBUS WAY
Chestnut Sp Gd
ST ANDREWS RD
OATLAND RISE
HAMILTON RD
FAIRFIELD RD
COLVILLE RD
CAPRI HO
DARNDALE CL
DEVON HO
LISBON HO
Sch
CHESTER MEWS
CHANDOS AVE
Waltham Forest Coll
CLIFFORD RD
KINGSLEY RD
HILLYFIELD
DILWYN CT
GREEN POND RD
BALMORAL HO
KINROSS TERR
EVERGLADE HO
DUDLEY RD
BROMLEY RD
Allot Gdns
SPRUCE HILLS RD
LOWTON HO
ADELAIDE HO
BROOK CT
WINNS AVE
WINNS TERR
BADLIS RD
Bwg Gn
Gall
BEDFORD RD
WALTHAMSTOW
STIRLING RD
HIGHAM PL
HIGHAM ST
COUNTESS RD
WILLIAM MORRIS CL
HOLMES AVE
BEMSTED RD
MERSEY RD
DIANA RD
FOREST RD
The Bell
KENILWORTH AVE
FARNAN AVE
TH
Ct
C Ctr
Thorpe Coombe
PARKSTON RD
SUTHERLAND RD
CHAMBERLAIN PL

36
A
B
C
D
20
54
HATCH LA
NEW RD
A1009
LARKSHALL RD
B160
Chingford Hatch
Jubilee Sp Gd
Larks Wood
E4
Larkswood Pl Fld
L Ctr
Allot Gdns
Hatch Plain
IG8
The Lops
Woodford
Redbridge
Waltham Forest
CHINGFORD LA
The Highams Park
Boating Lake
Woodford Cty High Sch
Rugby Fball Gd
Hale End
Higham Park
Highams Park
Wadham Lodge Sp Gd
Sports Ctr
Rolls Sp Gd
Bwg Gns
Wks
Schs
WINCHESTER RD
NORTH CIRCULAR RD
SOUTHEND ROAD
(NORTH CIRCULAR ROAD)
WOODFORD NEW RD
A104
HIGH ROAD WOODFORD GN
St Aubyn's Sch
Hotel
Waterworks Cnr
Thorpe Hall Prim Sch
Whitefield Sch
E17
FOREST RD
A503
FULBOURNE RD
Hyland House Sch
Upper Walthamstow
Gilbert's Slade
Walthamstow Bsns Ctr
Woodside Schs
Thorpe Coombe
BROADWALK

37
A
B
C
D
21
55
41
42
Knighton Wood
Woodford Wells
Woodford
Roding Valley
IG9
IG8
E18
WOODFORD
Woodford Green
South Woodford
Ray Park
River Roding
Redbridge
Essex
Sp Gd
Tennis Ct
Pl Fld & Sp Gd
Fball Gd
Pl Fld
Allot Gdns
Crkt Gd
Trinity RC High Sch (Upper)
Trinity RC High Sch (Lower)
St Antony's RC Sch
Wells Sch
Avon House Sch
Woodford Green Prep Sch
Ray Lodge Prim Sch
Woodbridge High Sch
Churchfields Jun & Inf Schs
Queen Mary & Westfield Coll (Halls of Residence)
Oakdale Jun Sch
Commerce Est
Woodford Trad Est
Charlie Browns Rdbt
Liby
Coll
THE WATERGARDENS
THE SQUARE
HIGH ROAD WOODFORD GN
HIGH RD
BROADMEAD RD
CHIGWELL RD
SOUTHEND RD
SNAKES LA EAST
SNAKES LA WEST
GEORGE LA
THE VIADUCT
A104
A110
A1009
A113
A406
A1400
A1199
B168
M11
M11 Stansted Airport, M25
A113 Chigwell, M11 (A1168)
Essex STREET ATLAS
93
92
91
90
6
5
4
3
2
1

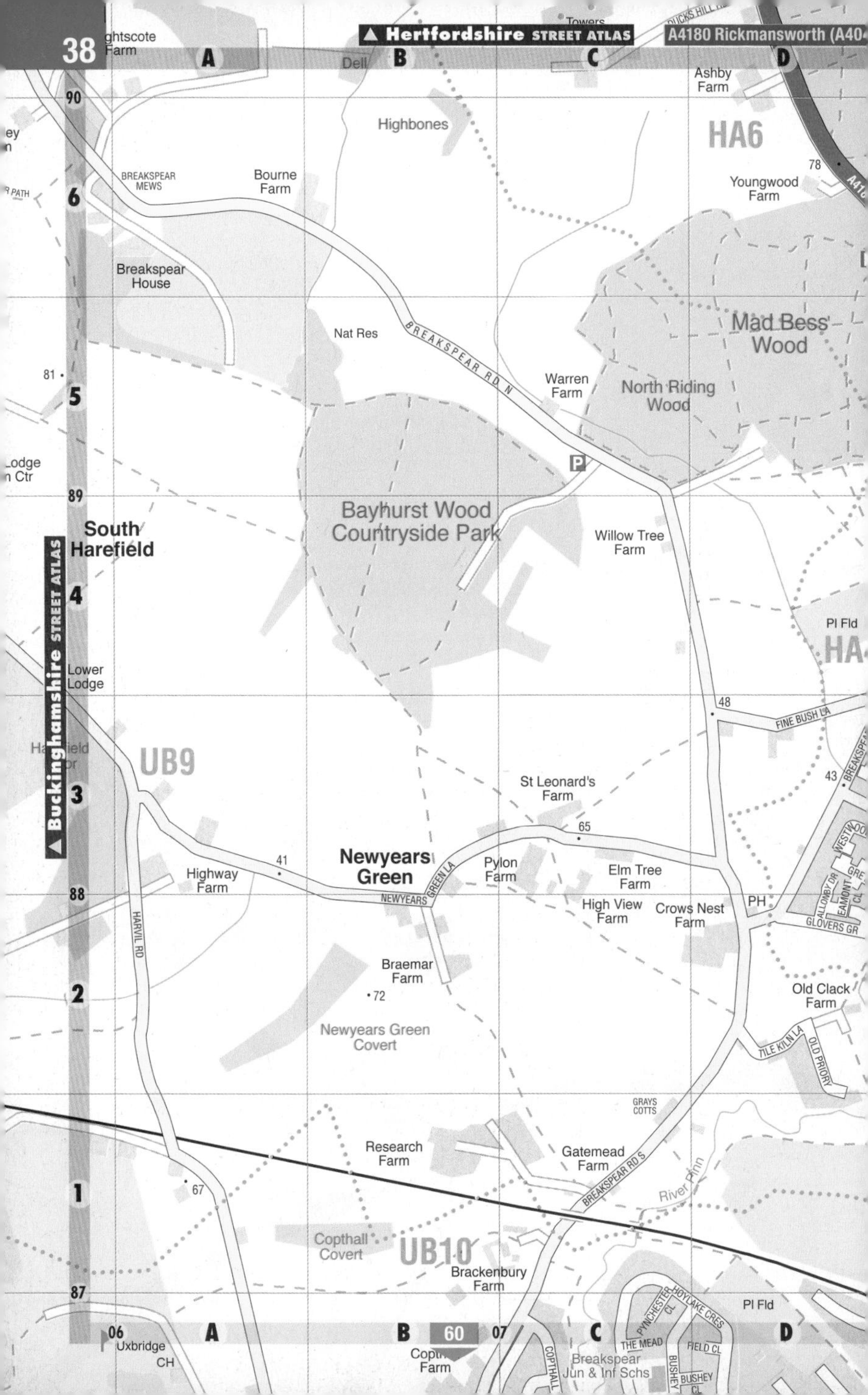
A
B
C
D
ghtscote Farm
Dell
Towers
DUCKS HILL
Ashby Farm
90
Highbones
HA6
78
Youngwood Farm
BREAKSPEAR MEWS
Bourne Farm
6
Breakspear House
Nat Res
BREAKSPEAR RD N
Mad Bess Wood
Warren Farm
North Riding Wood
81
5
Lodge
89
Bayhurst Wood Countryside Park
Willow Tree Farm
South Harefield
4
▲ Buckinghamshire STREET ATLAS
Pl Fld
Lower Lodge
48
FINE BUSH LA
UB9
3
St Leonard's Farm
43
BREAKSPEAR
65
Newyears Green
41
Highway Farm
Pylon Farm
Elm Tree Farm
GREEN LA
NEWYEARS
88
High View Farm
Crows Nest Farm
PH
GLOVERS GR
ALLONBY DR
EAMONT CL
WESTWOOD
HARVIL RD
Braemar Farm
72
2
Old Clack Farm
Newyears Green Covert
TILE KILN LA
OLD PRIORY
GRAYS COTTS
Research Farm
Gatemead Farm
BREAKSPEAR RD S
1
67
River Pinn
Copthall Covert
UB10
Brackenbury Farm
87
Pl Fld
PYNCHESTER CL
HOYLAKE CRES
06
B
60
07
C
D
Uxbridge CH
THE MEAD
FIELD CL
Breakspear Jun & Inf Schs
COPTHALL
BUSHEY
BUSHEY CL

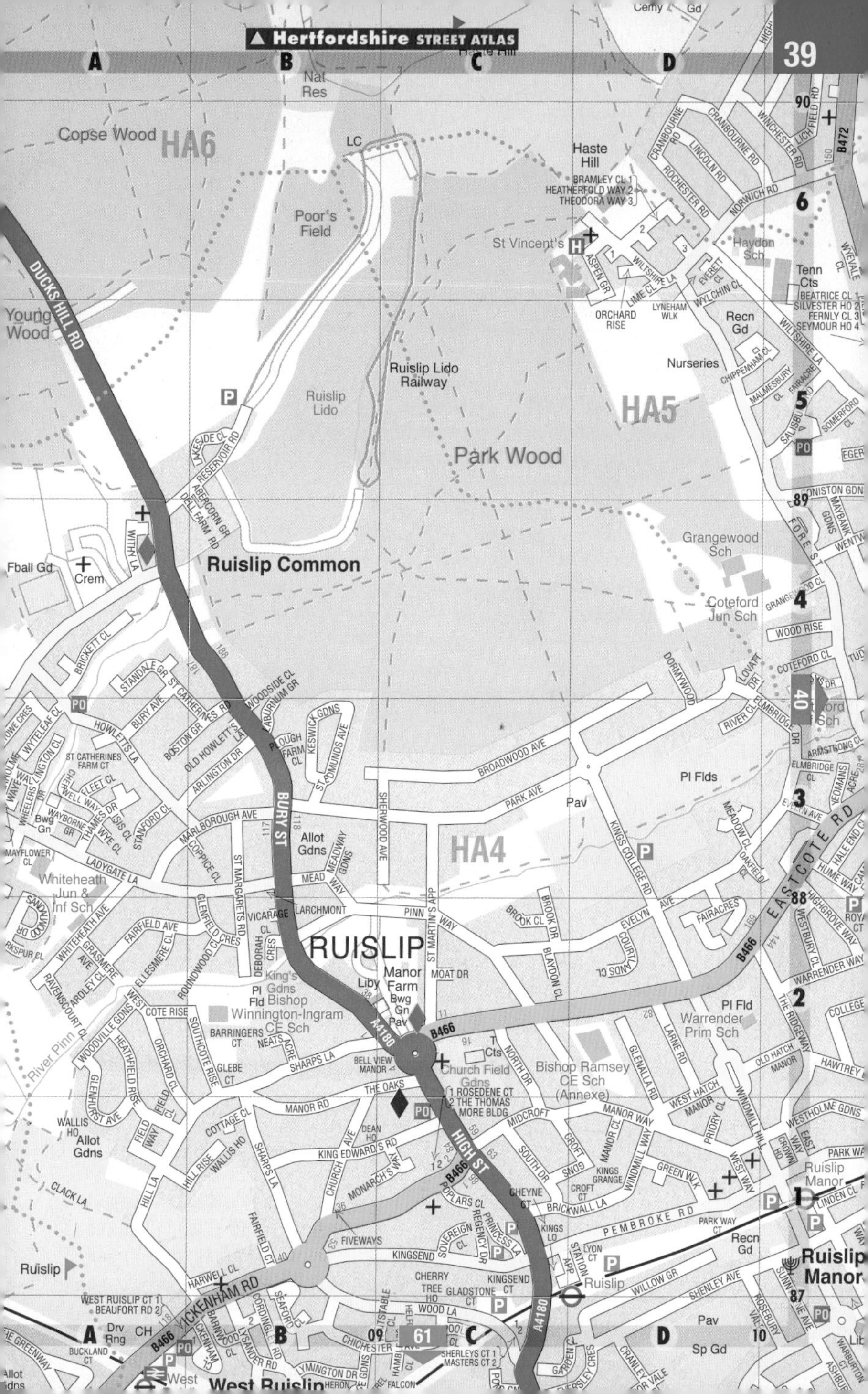
Copse Wood
HA6
Poor's Field
Nat Res
Haste Hill
St Vincent's
Haydon Sch
Young Wood
DUCKS HILL RD
Ruislip Lido
Ruislip Lido Railway
Park Wood
HA5
Nurseries
Recn Gd
Tenn Cts
Ruislip Common
Grangewood Sch
Coteford Jun Sch
Fball Gd
Crem
BROADWOOD AVE
PARK AVE
Pl Flds
Pav
BURY ST
HA4
Allot Gdns
Whiteheath Jun & Inf Sch
RUISLIP
Manor Farm
Liby
King's Gdns
Bishop Winnington-Ingram CE Sch
Church Field Gdns
Bishop Ramsey CE Sch (Annexe)
Warrender Prim Sch
EASTCOTE RD
HIGH ST
Allot Gdns
Ruislip Manor
Ruislip
West Ruislip
Sp Gd

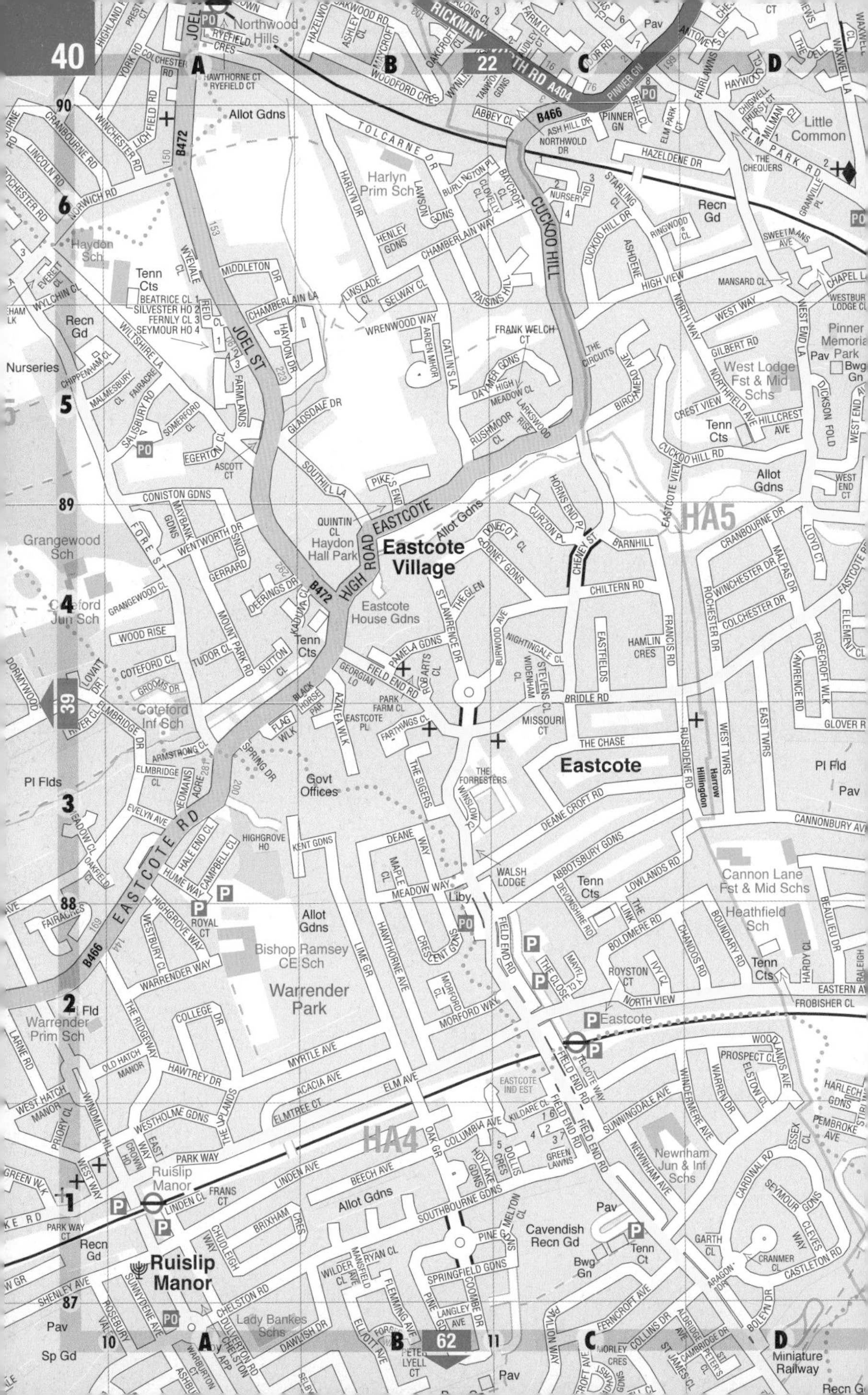

Northwood Hills
Allot Gdns
Harlyn Prim Sch
Haydon Sch
Tenn Cts
Recn Gd
Nurseries
Little Common
Recn Gd
Pinner Memorial Park
West Lodge Fst & Mid Schs
Tenn Cts
Allot Gdns
HA5
Grangewood Sch
Coteford Jun Sch
Quintin CL Haydon Hall Park
Eastcote Village
Eastcote House Gdns
Coteford Inf Sch
Eastcote
Pl Flds
Govt Offices
Cannon Lane Fst & Mid Schs
Heathfield Sch
Allot Gdns
Bishop Ramsey CE Sch
Warrender Park
Warrender Prim Sch
HA4
Ruislip Manor
Newnham Jun & Inf Schs
Cavendish Recn Gd
Lady Bankes Schs
Miniature Railway
JOEL ST
HIGH ROAD EASTCOTE
EASTCOTE RD
CUCKOO HILL
RICKMANSWORTH RD A404
FIELD END RD
B472
B466

22
39
62

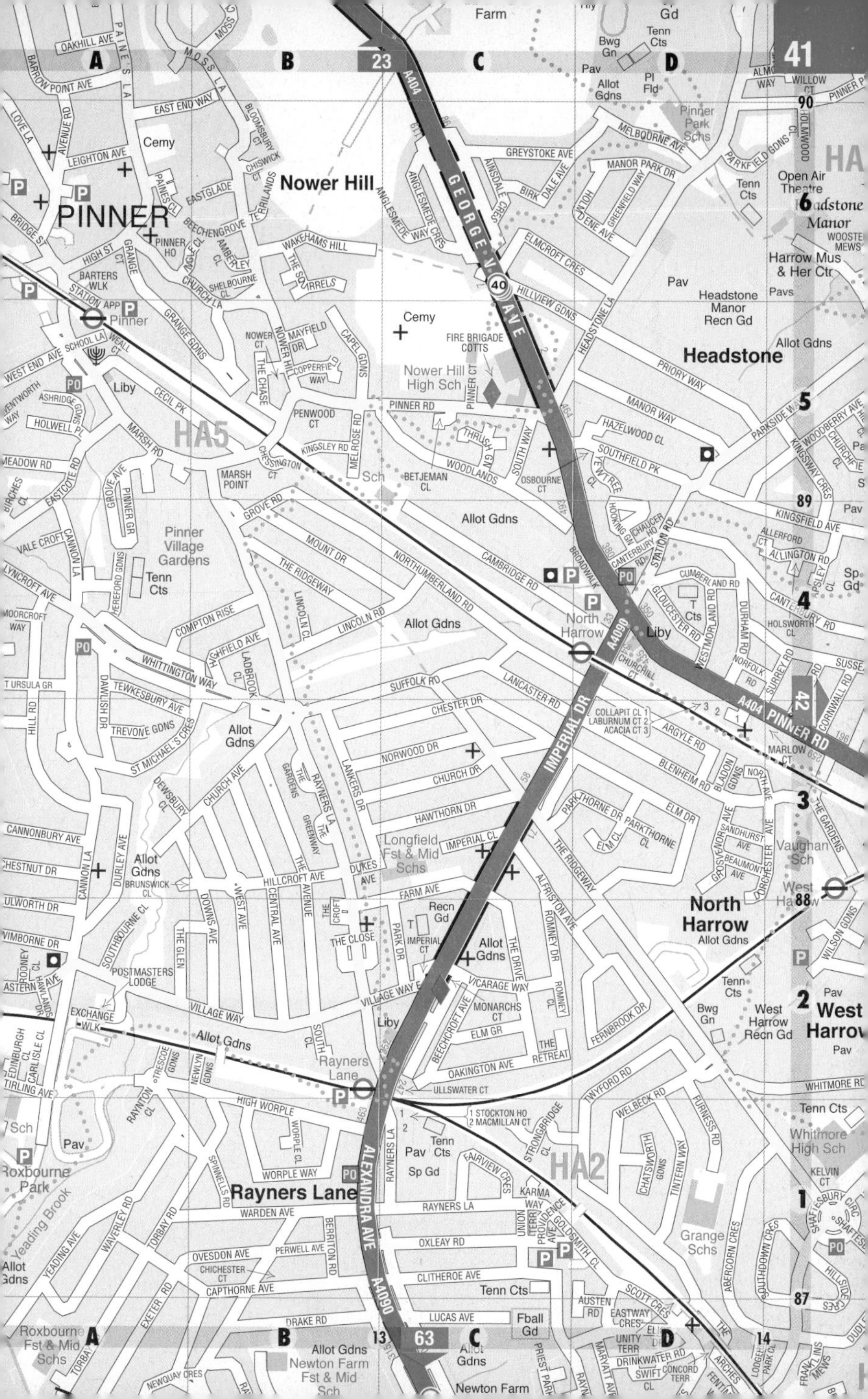
41
A
B
C
D
23
A404
Farm
Gd
Tenn Cts
Bwg Gn
Pav
Allot Gdns
Pl Fld
Pinner Park Schs
ALMOND WAY
WILLOW CT
PINNER PK
90
HOLMWOOD CL
OAKHILL AVE
PAINES LA
MOSS LA
MOSS CL
BARROW POINT AVE
EAST END WAY
LOVE LA
AVENUE RD
BLOOMSBURY CT
CHISWICK CT
Cemy
LEIGHTON AVE
PINNER
PAINES CL
EASTGLADE
TERRILANDS
Nower Hill
BEECHENGROVE
AMBERLEY CL
PINNER HO
BRIDGE ST
HIGH ST
GRANGE CT
INGLE CL
SHELBOURNE CL
CHURCH LA
BARTERS WLK
STATION APP
Pinner
WEALL CT
SCHOOL LA
WEST END AVE
GRANGE GDNS
WAKEHAMS HILL
THE SQUIRRELS
ANGLESMEDE CRES
ANGLESMEDE WAY
GEORGE V AVE
AINSDALE CRES
BIRK DALE AVE
GREYSTOKE AVE
MELBOURNE AVE
MANOR PARK DR
HOLME DENE AVE
GREENFIELD WAY
PARKFIELD GDNS
Tenn Cts
Open Air Theatre
HA
6
Headstone Manor
WOOSTER MEWS
Harrow Mus & Her Ctr
Pavs
ELMCROFT CRES
40
HILLVIEW GDNS
HEADSTONE LA
Pav
Headstone Manor Recn Gd
Allot Gdns
Headstone
Cemy
FIRE BRIDGADE COTTS
Nower Hill High Sch
PINNER CT
NOWER CT
NOWER HILL
MAYFIELD DR
THE CHASE
COPPERFIELD WAY
CAPEL GDNS
PRIORY WAY
MANOR WAY
5
PARKSIDE WAY
WOODBERRY AVE
CHURCHFIELD CL
KINGSWAY CRES
Pa
WENTWORTH WAY
ASHRIDGE GDNS
Liby
CECIL PK
HOLWELL PL
MARSH RD
HA5
PENWOOD CT
KINGSLEY RD
MELROSE RD
PINNER RD
THRUSH GN
SOUTH WAY
HAZELWOOD CL
SOUTHFIELD PK
YEW TREE CL
MEADOW RD
BIRCHES CL
EASTCOTE RD
GROVE AVE
PINNER GR
CHESSINGTON CT
MARSH POINT
Sch
BETJEMAN CL
WOODLANDS
OSBOURNE CT
HOOKING GN
CHAUCER HO
STATION RD
89
Pav
KINGSFIELD AVE
ALLERFORD CT
ALLINGTON RD
APSLEY CL
Sp Gd
VALE CROFT
CANNON LA
Pinner Village Gardens
HEREFORD GDNS
Tenn Cts
GROVE RD
MOUNT DR
THE RIDGEWAY
NORTHUMBERLAND RD
Allot Gdns
CAMBRIDGE RD
BROADWALK
CANTERBURY RD
CUMBERLAND RD
4
CANTERBURY RD
HOLSWORTH CL
LYNCROFT AVE
MOORCROFT WAY
COMPTON RISE
LINCOLN CL
LINCOLN RD
Allot Gdns
North Harrow
A4090
Liby
GLOUCESTER RD
T Cts
WESTMORLAND RD
DURHAM RD
NORFOLK RD
SURREY RD
SUSSEX RD
CORNWALL RD
HIGHFIELD AVE
LADBROOK CL
WHITTINGTON WAY
ST URSULA GR
DAWLISH DR
TEWKESBURY AVE
TREVONE GDNS
ST MICHAEL'S CRES
HILL RD
Allot Gdns
SUFFOLK RD
LANCASTER RD
CHURCHILL CT
CHESTER DR
IMPERIAL DR
COLLAPIT CL 1
LABURNUM CT 2
ACACIA CT 3
ARGYLE RD
A404 PINNER RD
42
MARLOW CT
NORWOOD DR
CHURCH DR
BLENHEIM RD
BLADON GDNS
NORTH AVE
3
THE GARDENS
DEWSBURY CL
CHURCH AVE
THE GARDENS
RAYNERS LA
THE GREENWAY
LANKERS DR
HAWTHORN DR
PARKTHORNE DR
PARKTHORNE CL
ELM CL
ELM DR
GROSVENOR AVE
SANDHURST AVE
BEAUMONT AVE
DORCHESTER AVE
Vaughan Sch
CANNONBURY AVE
CHESTNUT DR
SULWORTH DR
WIMBORNE DR
Allot Gdns
BRUNSWICK CL
DURLEY AVE
Longfield Fst & Mid Schs
IMPERIAL CL
DUKES AVE
HILLCROFT AVE
THE RIDGEWAY
ALFRISTON AVE
West Harrow
88
North Harrow
Allot Gdns
WILSON GDNS
DOWNS AVE
WEST AVE
CENTRAL AVE
THE AVENUE
FARM AVE
THE CROFT
THE CLOSE
PARK DR
Recn Gd
IMPERIAL CT
Allot Gdns
THE DRIVE
ROMNEY DR
ROMNEY CL
SOUTHBOURNE CL
THE GLEN
POSTMASTERS LODGE
RODNEY CL
HAWLANDS DR
EASTERN AVE
VILLAGE WAY
VILLAGE WAY E
VICARAGE WAY
MONARCHS CT
BEECHCROFT AVE
ELM GR
FERNBROOK DR
Tenn Cts
Bwg Gn
2
Pav
West Harrow
West Harrow Recn Gd
Pav
EXCHANGE WLK
Allot Gdns
Liby
THE RETREAT
OAKINGTON AVE
EDINBURGH CL
CARLISLE CL
STIRLING AVE
TRESCOE GDNS
NEWLYN GDNS
SOUTH CL
Rayners Lane
ULLSWATER CT
TWYFORD RD
WELBECK RD
FURNESS RD
WHITMORE RD
Tenn Cts
Whitmore High Sch
Sch
Pav
RAYNTON CL
HIGH WORPLE
WORPLE CL
1 STOCKTON HO
2 MACMILLAN CT
STRONGBRIDGE CL
HA2
CHATSWORTH GDNS
TINTERN WAY
KELVIN CT
Roxbourne Park
Yeading Brook
SPINNELLS RD
WORPLE WAY
ALEXANDRA AVE
RAYNERS LA
Pav
Tenn Cts
Sp Gd
FAIRVIEW CRES
Rayners Lane
KARMA WAY
1
SHAFTESBURY CIRC
WAVERLEY RD
TORBAY RD
WARDEN AVE
BERRITON RD
RAYNERS LA
UNION TERR
PROVIDENCE AVE
GOLDSMITH CL
Grange Schs
ABERCORN CRES
SOUTHDOWN CRES
HILLSIDE CRES
Allot Gdns
YEADING AVE
OVESDON AVE
PERWELL AVE
OXLEAY RD
CHICHESTER CT
CAPTHORNE AVE
CLITHEROE AVE
Tenn Cts
SCOTT CRES
87
EXETER RD
A4090
AUSTEN RD
EASTWAY CRES
Fball Gd
Roxbourne Fst & Mid Schs
TORBAY
DRAKE RD
LUCAS AVE
13
63
Allot Gdns
Newton Farm Fst & Mid Sch
Allot Gdns
Newton Farm
PRIEST PARK
UNITY TERR
DRINKWATER RD
SWIFT CL
CONCORD TERR
MARYATT AVE
ARCHES
14
LODGE PARK CL
FRANKLINS MEWS

A
B
C
D
24
41
64
90
89
88
87
6
5
4
3
2
1
14
15
HA1
HA2
HA3
HARROW
Wealdstone
Headstone
Greenhill
West Harrow
North Harrow
Harrow on the Hill
Headstone Manor
Harrow Mus & Her Ctr
Open Air Theatre
Headstone Manor Recn Gd
Pinner Park Schs
Whitefriars Trad Est
Tudor Ent Pk
Waverley Ind Pk
Phoenix Ind Est
Harrow & Wealdstone
Harrow-on-the-Hill
West Harrow
St Georges Sh & L Ctr
St Ann's Ctr
Quainton Hall Sch
Norbury Sch
Vaughan Sch
Whitmore High Sch
Grange Schs
Harrow Coll
The Grove Open Space
St Anselm's RC Prim Sch
The John Lyon Sch
Harrow Sch
Running Tk
Capital Ring
West Harrow Recn Gd
Palmerston Ctr
PINNER RD
PINNER PARK AVE
PINNER PARK GDNS
PINNER VIEW
HEADSTONE DR
HEADSTONE GDNS
HEADSTONE RD
HARROW VIEW
HIGH ST
GEORGE GANGE WAY
RAILWAY APP
STATION RD
SHEEPCOTE RD
GREENHILL WAY
COLLEGE RD
LOWLANDS RD
KENTON RD
TYBURN LA
PETERBOROUGH RD
BESSBOROUGH RD
LOWER RD
ROXETH HILL
WHITMORE RD
KINGSFIELD AVE
CUNNINGHAM PK
MARLBOROUGH HILL
WALTON RD
NEPTUNE RD
VAUGHAN RD
BUTLER AVE
GROVE HILL
CHURCH HILL
SHAFTESBURY CIRC
SHAFTESBURY AVE
PORLOCK AVE
WEST ST
CROWN ST
MIDDLE RD
1 CROWN CT
2 CHILTERN HO
1 JARDINE HO
2 HILLBOROUGH CT
3 DRUMMOND CT
4 LITTLE CT
5 CHESTNUT CT
WORDSWORTH CT 1
CHARLES CRES 2
KINGSFIELD RD 3
BURRELL CT 4
HANOVER CT 5
KINGSFIELD CT 6
LEYS CL 1
CHILTERN CT 2
MILES LO 3
HOLLY LO 4
CUNNINGHAM CT 5
CUMBERLAND CT 1
BANNISTER HO 2
POPPY CT 3
KARMAN CT 4
AMBASSADOR HO 5
CHURCH PAR 6
CENTURY HO 7
REGENCY LO 8
1 CLARENDON HO
2 BEVERLEY CT

43
25
65
44
A
B
C
D
1
2
3
4
5
6
87
88
89
90
HA7
HA3
HA1
HA0
HA9
KENTON
Kenton
Superstore
North Wembley
Northwick Park
South Kenton
Kenton Lane Farm
Priestmead Schs
Recn Gd
Pl Fld
Byron Recn Gd
Cemy
Tenn Cts
Sp Gd
Bwg Gn
Allot Gdns
Pav
Liby
Ind Est
Elmgrove Fst & Mid Schs
Hawthorn Ctr
St Gregory RC High Sch
Woodcock Park
Uxendon Manor Sch
Mount Stewart Schs
John Billam Pl Flds
Kenmore Park Schs
Glebe Sch
Harrow High Sch & Sports Coll
Univ of Westminster (Harrow Campus)
Northwick Park
Capital Ring
Rugby Fball Gds
Preston Park Sch
Preston Park Recn Gd
Preston Road
Byron Court Sch
KENTON RD
A4006
A409
A404
A4140
WATFORD RD
KENTON LA
KENMORE AVE
SANCROFT RD
RADCLIFFE RD
BORROWDALE AVE
GRASMERE GDNS
BELMONT RD
PEMBROKE AVE
IRVINE AVE
RADSTOCK AVE
BEAUFORT AVE
KINGSHILL DR
HARTFORD AVE
ALVESTON AVE
OAKFIELD AVE
LARKFIELD AVE
IVANHOE DR
ROCKLANDS DR
QUEENS AVE
ENNERDALE AVE
FORMBY AVE
DUDLEY AVE
STREATFIELD RD
HILIARY GDNS
MORLEY CRES E
MORLEY CRES W
CHARMIAN AVE
CLYDESDALE AVE
LANGLAND CRES
MOORHOUSE RD
QUEENSBURY CIRC PAR
ROWLAND AVE
SHOOTERS AVE
BRANCKER RD
HINKLER RD
KENMORE RD
WAGHORN RD
CODY CL
WARNEFORD RD
CHARLTON RD
PAULHAN RD
HUNTERS GR
CHRISTCHURCH AVE
CHRISTCHURCH GDNS
WYKEHAM RD
BOXMOOR RD
BRAMPTON GR
BRADENHAM RD
PRESTWOOD AVE
PRESTWOOD CL
ELMSLEIGH AVE
ALICIA GDNS
ALICIA AVE
KINGSHILL AVE
PENN CL
HUGHENDEN AVE
ADDISCOMBE CL
CULLINGTON CL
DAWTRY CL
MARTOCK CL
COXE PL
BURNHAM CL
THE HOLLIES
KENTON PARK RD
KENTON PARK CL
KENTON PARK AVE
KENTON PARK CRES
KENTON PARK PAR
KENTON PARK MANS
WESTFIELD LA
WESTFIELD DR
WESTFIELD GDNS
D'ARCY DR
D'ARCY GDNS
LODGE AVE
FARRER RD
MORLAND RD
CHELTENHAM
LORETTO
GOOSEACRE LA
LIDDING RD
BROOKSIDE CL
HILLVIEW AVE
BROOKFIELD CRES
CRANLEIGH GDNS
WOODGRANGE AVE
WOODGRANGE MANS
WOODGRANGE CL
PEGASUS CT
WESTGLADE CT
RETREAT CL
KENTON GDNS
ST LEONARDS AVE
ST MARYS VIEW
TOTTERNHOE CL
SEDGECOMBE AVE
BECMEAD AVE
HILLBURY AVE
WILLOWCOURT AVE
MAYFIELD AVE
CARLTON AVE
KENYNGTON PL
BRIAR RD
UPTON GDNS
NORCOMBE GDNS
WINCHFIELD CL
DRAYCOTT CL
DRAYCOTT AVE
NORTHWICK CIRC
DOVEDALE AVE
WELLACRE RD
RADBOURNE CT
MENTMORE CL
GREYSTONE GDNS
LAPSTONE GDNS
ASHRIDGE CL
WOODCOCK HILL
ILMINGTON RD
DONNINGTON RD
EBRINGTON RD
SOUTHWELL RD
SHAFTESBURY AVE
WOODHILL CRES
BOUVERIE GDNS
SHERIDAN GDNS
THE RIDGEWAY
NORTHWICK AVE
ASTON AVE
MOUNT STEWART AVE
CARLISLE GDNS
BULMER GDNS
ABERCORN GDNS
CALVERLEY GDNS
MANNING GDNS
GRENFELL GDNS
TREVELYAN CRES
WOODCOCK DELL AVE
WINDERMERE CT
WINDERMERE AVE
WINDCOTT CT
LULWORTH AVE
KARENZA CT
CONWAY GDNS
DERWENT GDNS
CONISTON GDNS
RYDAL GDNS
AMBLESIDE GDNS
ARNSIDE GDNS
GRASMERE AVE
THIRLMERE GDNS
ENNERDALE GDNS
ALLONBY GDNS
MONTPELIER RISE
COLLEGE RD
SILVERHOLME CL
WOODCOCK CT
VIEWFIELD CL
PRESTON WAY
WOODFORD PL
LONGFIELD AVE
GLENDALE GDNS
CARLTON AVE E
FERNLEIGH CT
LOGAN RD
WALTON GDNS
SECOND AVE
FIRST AVE
WARREN
NORVAL RD
AUDREY GDNS
SPENCER RD
NATHANS RD
ABBOTTS DR
PEBWORTH RD
THE GREEN
STATION CT
THE LINK
ST MARK'S CL
NIGHTINGALE AVE
NORTHWICK CL
FARRANS CT
CHURCHILL AVE
RUSHOUT AVE
HAWTHORNE AVE
ELMWOOD AVE
NASH WAY
NASH CT
DRAYTON WAYE
FRANCIS RD
HILL RD
HILL CRES
RICHARDS CL
ELMGROVE GDNS
ELMGROVE CR
MOELYN MEWS
CROFTS RD
GRANGE RD
BONNERSFIELD LA
BONNERSFIELD CL
CROFT VILLAS
MANOR RD
MANOR ROAD HO
WOODWAY CRES
GERARD RD
FLAMBARD RD
BEAUFORT CT
BLENHEIM CT
ST JAMES'S CT
GAYTON RD
ST GEORGES CT
RUFFORD CL
REMBRANDT CT
BELVOIR CT
FULWOOD CT
MENDIP HO
BOWLES CT
WADDESDON LO
THURLBY CL
KENTON CT
1 PRICE CT
2 HINES CT
3 FENN CT
4 CHALLINER CT
1 SIMPSON HO
2 AYRTON HO
3 WINTOUR HO
4 STEVENSON HO
Harrow
Brent

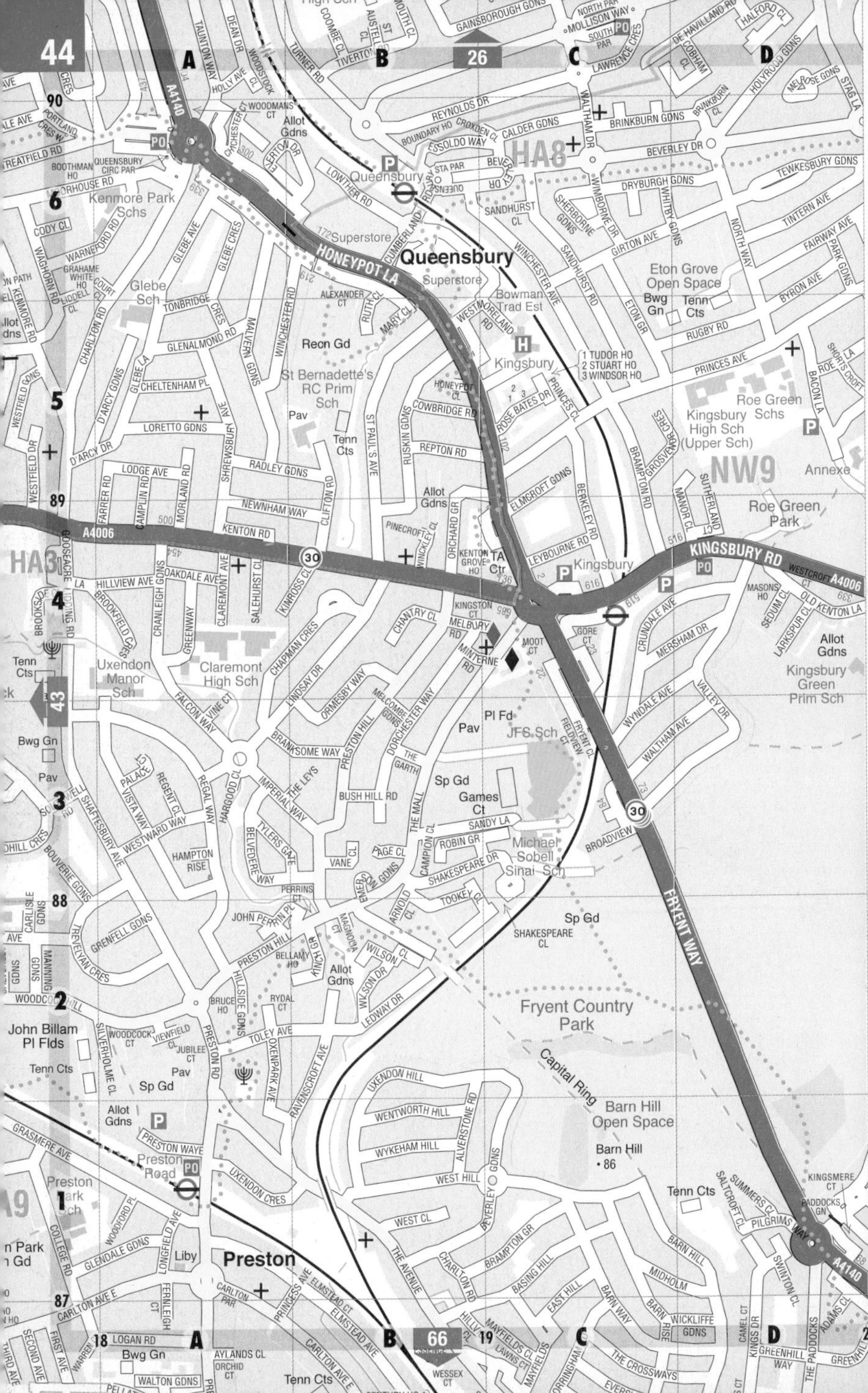
A
B
C
D
26
66
43
1
2
3
4
5
6
87
88
89
90
18
19
HA8
HA3
NW9
Queensbury
Preston
Kingsbury
A4140
A4006
HONEYPOT LA
KINGSBURY RD
FRYENT WAY
Fryent Country Park
Capital Ring
Barn Hill Open Space
Barn Hill
• 86
Kenmore Park Schs
Glebe Sch
Recn Gd
St Bernadette's RC Prim Sch
Superstore
Bowman Trad Est
Eton Grove Open Space
Bwg Gn
Tenn Cts
Kingsbury High Sch (Upper Sch)
Roe Green Schs
Annexe
Roe Green Park
Allot Gdns
Kingsbury Green Prim Sch
Uxendon Manor Sch
Claremont High Sch
JFS Sch
Michael Sobell Sinai Sch
Pl Fd
Pav
Sp Gd
Games Ct
John Billam Pl Flds
Preston Park Sch
Preston Road
Liby
TA Ctr
1 TUDOR HO
2 STUART HO
3 WINDSOR HO
GAINSBOROUGH GDNS
MOLLISON WAY
LAWRENCE CRES
REYNOLDS DR
CALDER GDNS
BRINKBURN GDNS
BEVERLEY DR
TEWKESBURY GDNS
DRYBURGH GDNS
TINTERN AVE
GIRTON AVE
FAIRWAY AVE
BYRON AVE
RUGBY RD
PRINCES AVE
HOLYROOD GDNS
STAG LA
WALTHAM DR
WIMBORNE DR
SANDHURST RD
WINCHESTER AVE
LOWTHER RD
CUMBERLAND RD
WESTMORELAND RD
GLEBE AVE
GLEBE CRES
TONBRIDGE CRES
GLENALMOND RD
MALVERN GDNS
WINCHESTER RD
CHELTENHAM PL
LORETTO GDNS
RADLEY GDNS
LODGE AVE
NEWNHAM WAY
KENTON RD
CLIFTON RD
SHREWSBURY AVE
ST PAUL'S AVE
RUSKIN GDNS
COWBRIDGE RD
REPTON RD
ELMCROFT GDNS
BERKELEY RD
LEYBOURNE RD
BRAMPTON RD
GROSVENOR CRES
SUTHERLAND CT
MANOR CL
CRUNDALE AVE
MERSHAM DR
WYNDALE AVE
VALLEY DR
WALTHAM AVE
BROADVIEW
OLD KENTON LA
LARKSPUR CL
SEDUM CL
HILLVIEW AVE
OAKDALE AVE
CRANLEIGH GDNS
GREENWAY
CLAREMONT AVE
SALEHURST CL
KIMROSS CL
CHAPMAN CRES
LINDSAY DR
ORMESBY WAY
PRESTON HILL
DORCHESTER WAY
BRANKSOME WAY
THE LEYS
IMPERIAL WAY
BUSH HILL RD
THE MALL
SANDY LA
ROBIN GR
SHAKESPEARE DR
TOOKEY CL
FALCON WAY
HARGOOD CL
REGAL WAY
WESTWARD WAY
VISTA WAY
PALACE CT
SHAFTESBURY AVE
BOUVERIE GDNS
TREVELYAN CRES
GRENFELL GDNS
BELVEDERE WAY
TYLERS GATE
HAMPTON RISE
PERRINS CT
JOHN PERRIN PL
PRESTON HILL
HILLSIDE GDNS
TOLEY AVE
OXENPARK AVE
RAVENSCROFT AVE
WILSON DR
LEDWAY DR
PRESTON RD
SILVERHOLME CL
PRESTON WAYE
UXENDON CRES
UXENDON HILL
WENTWORTH HILL
WYKEHAM HILL
WEST HILL
WEST CL
BEVERLEY GDNS
ALVERSTONE RD
THE AVENUE
CHARLTON RD
BRAMPTON GR
BASING HILL
EAST HILL
BARN WAY
BARN RISE
MIDHOLM
BARN HILL
WICKLIFFE GDNS
PILGRIMS WAY
SUMMERS CL
SALTCROFT CL
SWINTON CL
GREENHILL WAY
THE PADDOCKS
GRASMERE AVE
WOODFORD PL
GLENDALE GDNS
LONGFIELD AVE
COLLEGE RD
CARLTON AVE E
FERNLEIGH CT
PRINCESS AVE
ELMSTEAD AVE
LOGAN RD
AYLANDS CL
ORCHID CT
WALTON GDNS
FIRST AVE
SECOND AVE
THE CROSSWAYS
MAYFIELDS
WESSEX CT
Tenn Cts

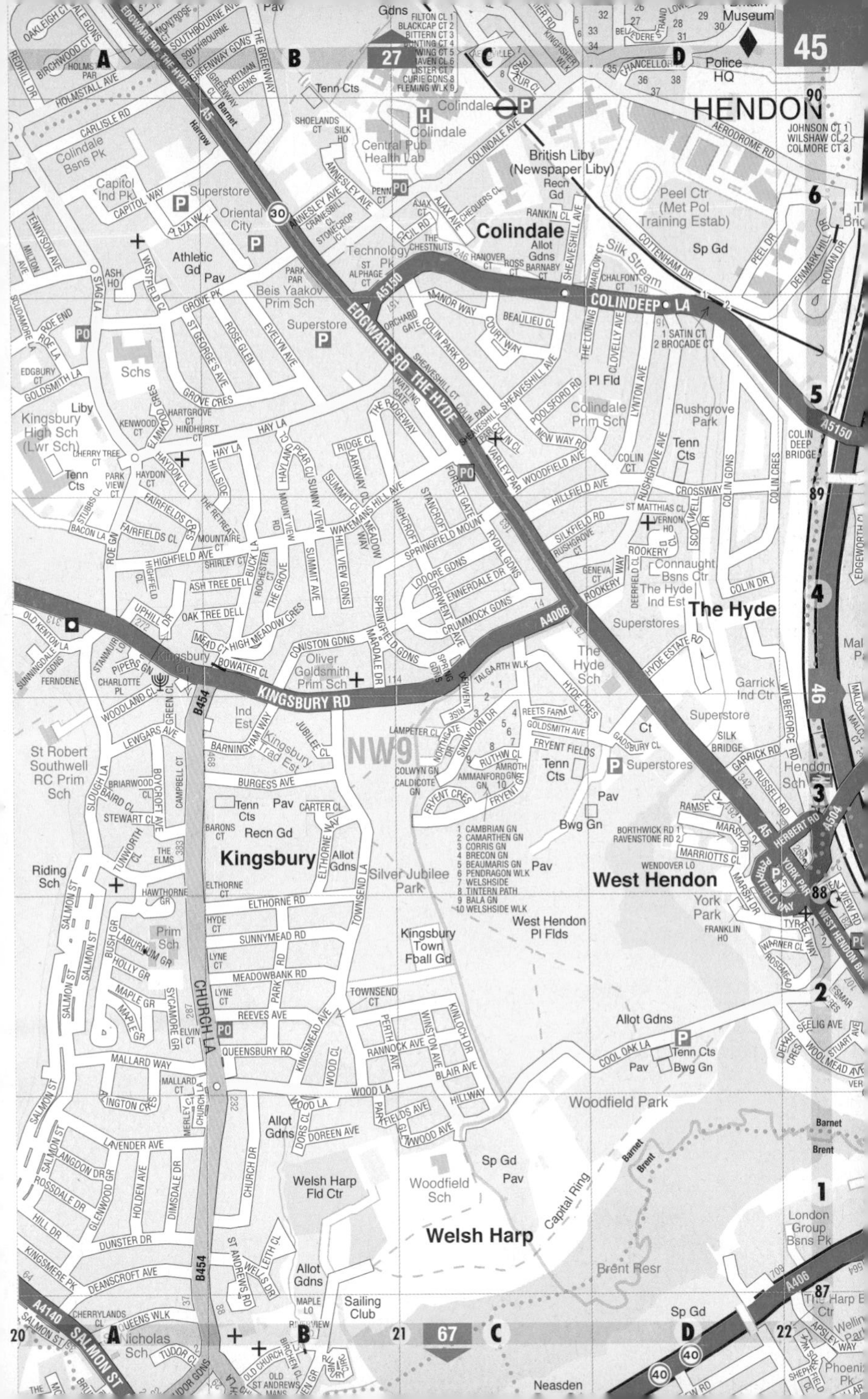

27
67
A
B
C
D
HENDON
Colindale
The Hyde
Kingsbury
West Hendon
Welsh Harp
NW9
EDGWARE RD THE HYDE
KINGSBURY RD
COLINDEEP LA
CHURCH LA
AERODROME RD
A5
A5150
A4006
B454
A4140
A406
A504
Colindale Bsns Pk
Capitol Ind Pk
Superstore
Oriental City
Athletic Gd
Beis Yaakov Prim Sch
Technology Pk
Central Pub Health Lab
British Liby (Newspaper Liby)
Peel Ctr (Met Pol Training Estab)
Police HQ
Museum
Colindale Prim Sch
Rushgrove Park
Kingsbury High Sch (Lwr Sch)
Oliver Goldsmith Prim Sch
Kingsbury Trad Est
Connaught Bsns Ctr
The Hyde Ind Est
Superstores
The Hyde Sch
Garrick Ind Ctr
Hendon Sch
St Robert Southwell RC Prim Sch
Riding Sch
Silver Jubilee Park
Kingsbury Town Fball Gd
West Hendon Pl Flds
York Park
Allot Gdns
Woodfield Park
Woodfield Sch
Welsh Harp Fld Ctr
Sailing Club
Brent Resr
Capital Ring
London Group Bsns Pk
Sp Gd
Silk Stream
Silk Bridge
Colin Deep Bridge
Neasden
Barnet
Brent
1 CAMBRIAN GN
2 CAMARTHEN GN
3 CORRIS GN
4 BRECON GN
5 BEAUMARIS GN
6 PENDRAGON WLK
7 WELSHSIDE
8 TINTERN PATH
9 BALA GN
10 WELSHSIDE WLK
1 SATIN CT
2 BROCADE CT
JOHNSON CT 1
WILSHAW CL 2
COLMORE CT 3
FILTON CL 1
BLACKCAP CT 2
BITTERN CT 3
LISTER CT 7
CURIE GDNS 8
FLEMING WLK 9
BORTHWICK RD 1
RAVENSTONE RD 2

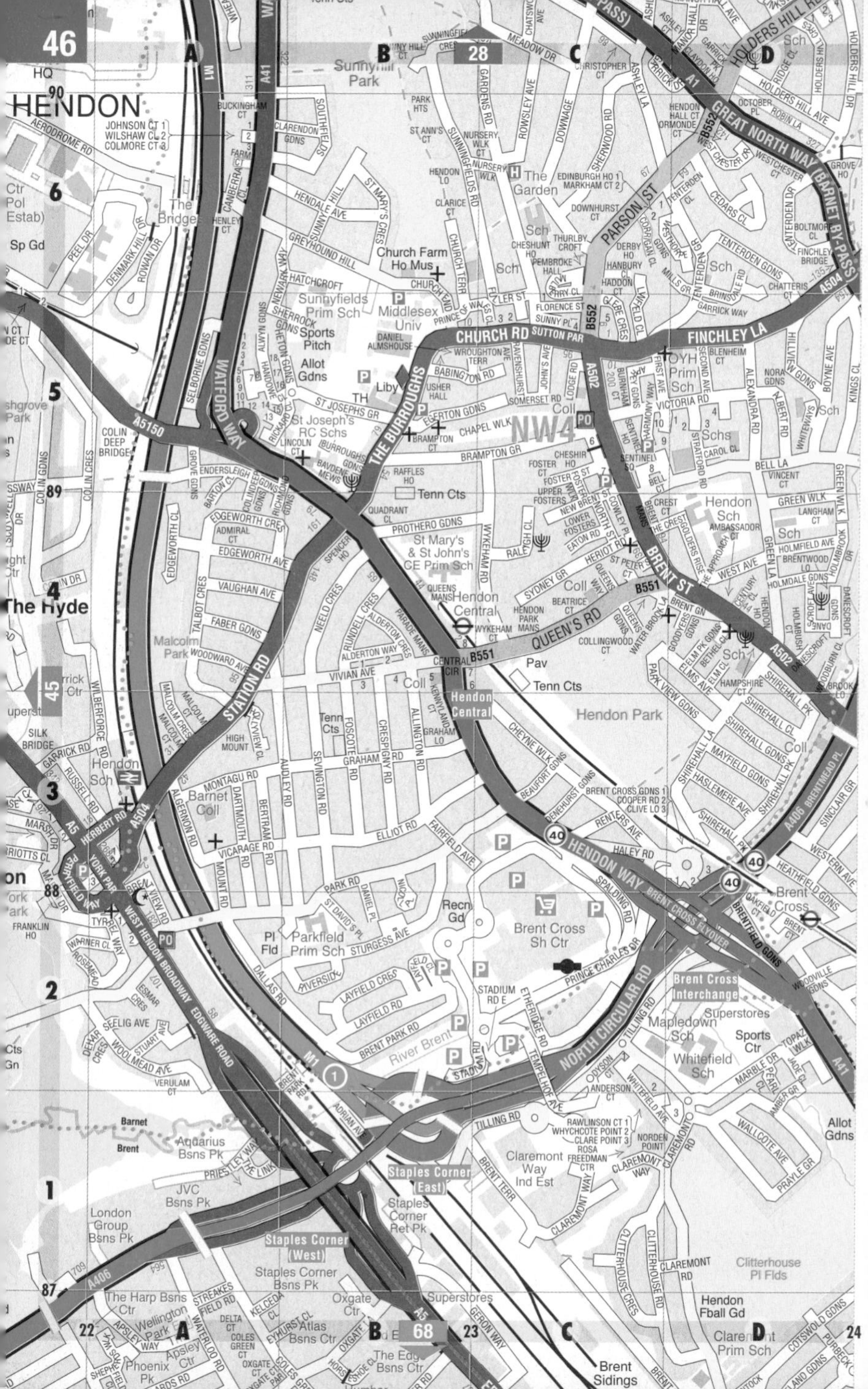
HENDON
NW4
Sunnyhill Park
Church Farm Ho Mus
Sunnyfields Prim Sch
Middlesex Univ
Sports Pitch
Allot Gdns
St Joseph's RC Schs
The Burroughs
Watford Way
Station Rd
Church Rd
Finchley La
Great North Way (Barnet By-Pass)
Parson St
Brent St
Queen's Rd
Hendon Central
Hendon Park
Hendon Sch
Hendon Way
Brent Cross Flyover
Brent Cross Sh Ctr
Brent Cross Interchange
North Circular Rd
Edgware Road
West Hendon Broadway
Colin Deep Bridge
The Hyde
Malcolm Park
Barnet Coll
Parkfield Prim Sch
River Brent
Staples Corner (East)
Staples Corner (West)
Staples Corner Ret Pk
Claremont Way Ind Est
Clitterhouse Pl Flds
Hendon Fball Gd
Mapledown Sch
Whitefield Sch
Aquarius Bsns Pk
JVC Bsns Pk
London Group Bsns Pk
Staples Corner Bsns Pk
The Harp Bsns Ctr
Wellington Park
Atlas Bsns Ctr
The Edge Bsns Ctr
Brent Sidings
Barnet
Brent
A5150
A504
A502
A406
A41
A1
A5
M1
B552
B551
28
45
68
22
23
24

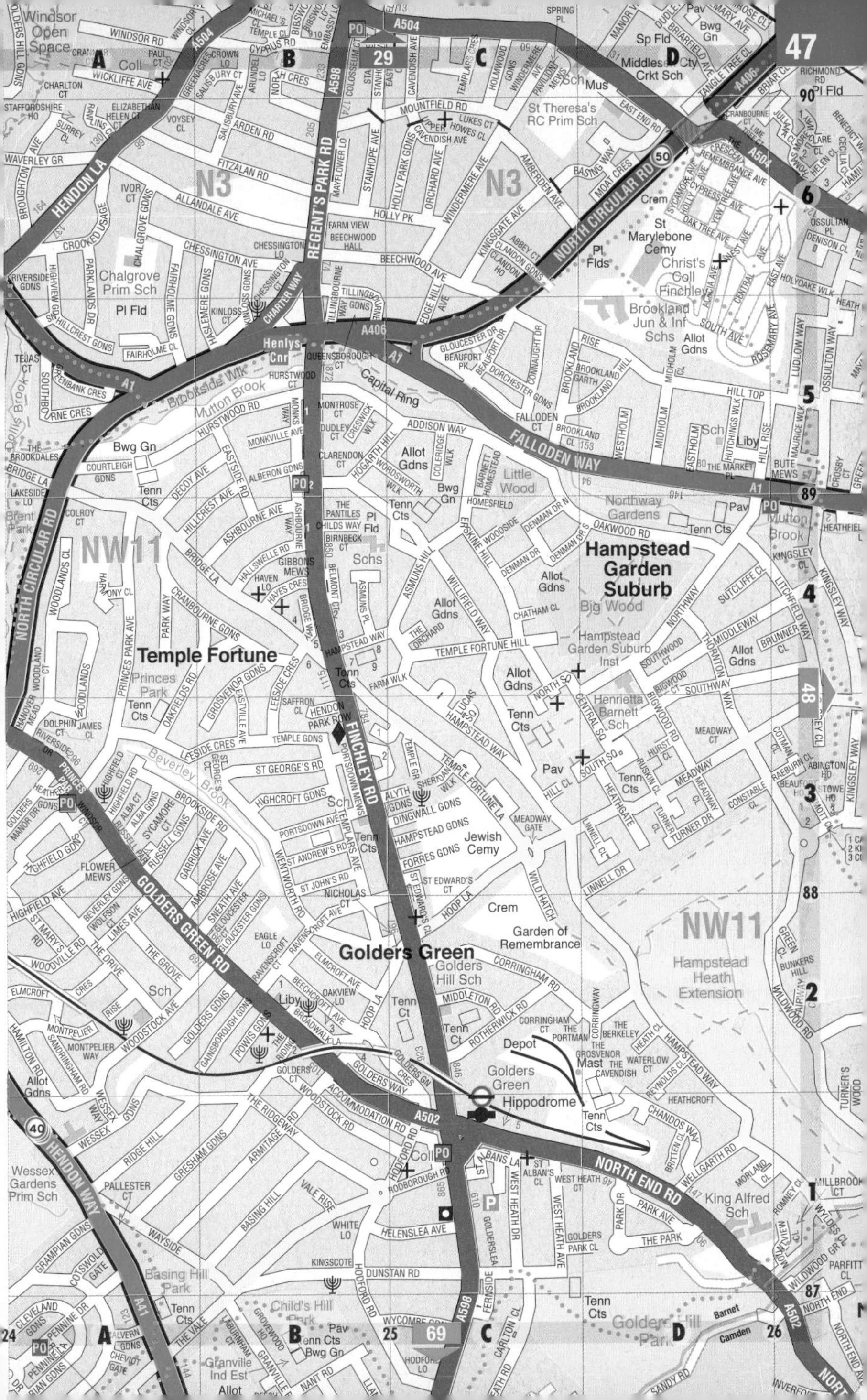

47
29
48
69
A
B
C
D
6
5
4
3
2
1
90
89
88
87
24
25
26
N3
NW11
Hampstead Garden Suburb
Temple Fortune
Golders Green
Hampstead Heath Extension
Windsor Open Space
Chalgrove Prim Sch
St Theresa's RC Prim Sch
St Marylebone Cemy
Christ's Coll Finchley
Brookland Jun & Inf Schs
Middlesex Cty Crkt Sch
Henrietta Barnett Sch
Hampstead Garden Suburb Inst
Big Wood
Little Wood
Northway Gardens
Jewish Cemy
Garden of Remembrance
Golders Hill Sch
Hippodrome
King Alfred Sch
Wessex Gardens Prim Sch
Basing Hill Park
Child's Hill Park
Golders Hill Park
Granville Ind Est
Princes Park
Mutton Brook
Beverley Brook
Capital Ring
Henlys Cnr
NORTH CIRCULAR RD
REGENT'S PARK RD
FINCHLEY RD
HENDON LA
HENDON WAY
FALLODEN WAY
GOLDERS GREEN RD
NORTH END RD
HAMPSTEAD WAY
A1
A41
A406
A502
A504
A598
Barnet
Camden

30
A
B
C
D
Martin Jun & Inf Schs
Allot Gdns
Fortismere Sch
East Finchley
Fortis Green
N2
NW11
N6
East End Rd
High Rd
Great North Rd
Fortis Gn
Lyttelton Rd
Aylmer Rd
Cherry Tree Hill
Hampstead La
Spaniards Rd
Holy Trinity CE Prim Sch
Oak Lodge Sch
Kerem Sch
Annemount Sch
Lyttelton Plg Flds
Cherry Tree Wood
Highgate CH
Highgate Prim Sch
Highgate Private
Highgate Sch
Hampstead
Hampstead Heath Extens
Turner's Wood
Kenwood House
The Spaniards Inn (PH)
Athlone House
Sandy Heath
Ken Wood
Open Air Stage
North End
King Alfred Sch
Hampstead Heath
47
70
A1
A1000
A504
A406
A502
B519
Haringey
Barnet
Camden

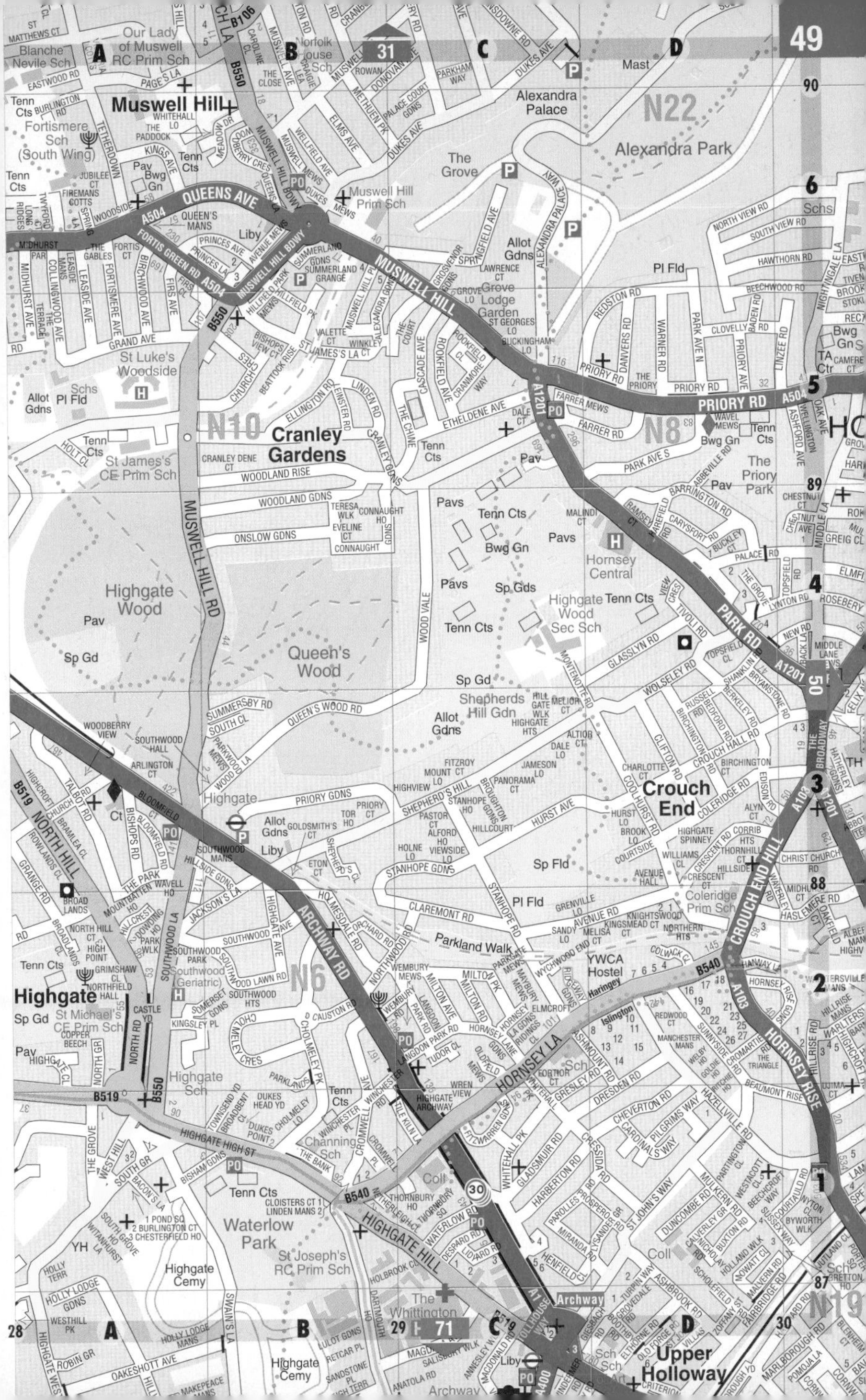
A
B
C
D
31
Muswell Hill
Alexandra Palace
Alexandra Park
N22
Mast
The Grove
Muswell Hill Prim Sch
Our Lady of Muswell RC Prim Sch
Blanche Nevile Sch
Fortismere Sch (South Wing)
QUEENS AVE
A504
MUSWELL HILL
MUSWELL HILL BDWY
FORTIS GREEN RD
PRIORY RD
Grove Lodge Garden
Allot Gdns
St Luke's Woodside
N10
Cranley Gardens
St James's CE Prim Sch
N8
Hornsey Central
The Priory Park
Highgate Wood
Queen's Wood
MUSWELL HILL RD
Highgate Wood Sec Sch
Shepherds Hill Gdn
PARK RD
A1201
Crouch End
Coleridge Prim Sch
Parkland Walk
YWCA Hostel
Haringey
Islington
N6
ARCHWAY RD
Highgate
Southwood (Geriatric)
St Michael's CE Prim Sch
Highgate Sch
Channing Sch
HIGHGATE HIGH ST
HIGHGATE HILL
Waterlow Park
St Joseph's RC Prim Sch
Highgate Cemy
The Whittington
Archway
CROUCH END HILL
HORNSEY RISE
HORNSEY LA
Upper Holloway
N19
71
29
30
A
B
C
D
28

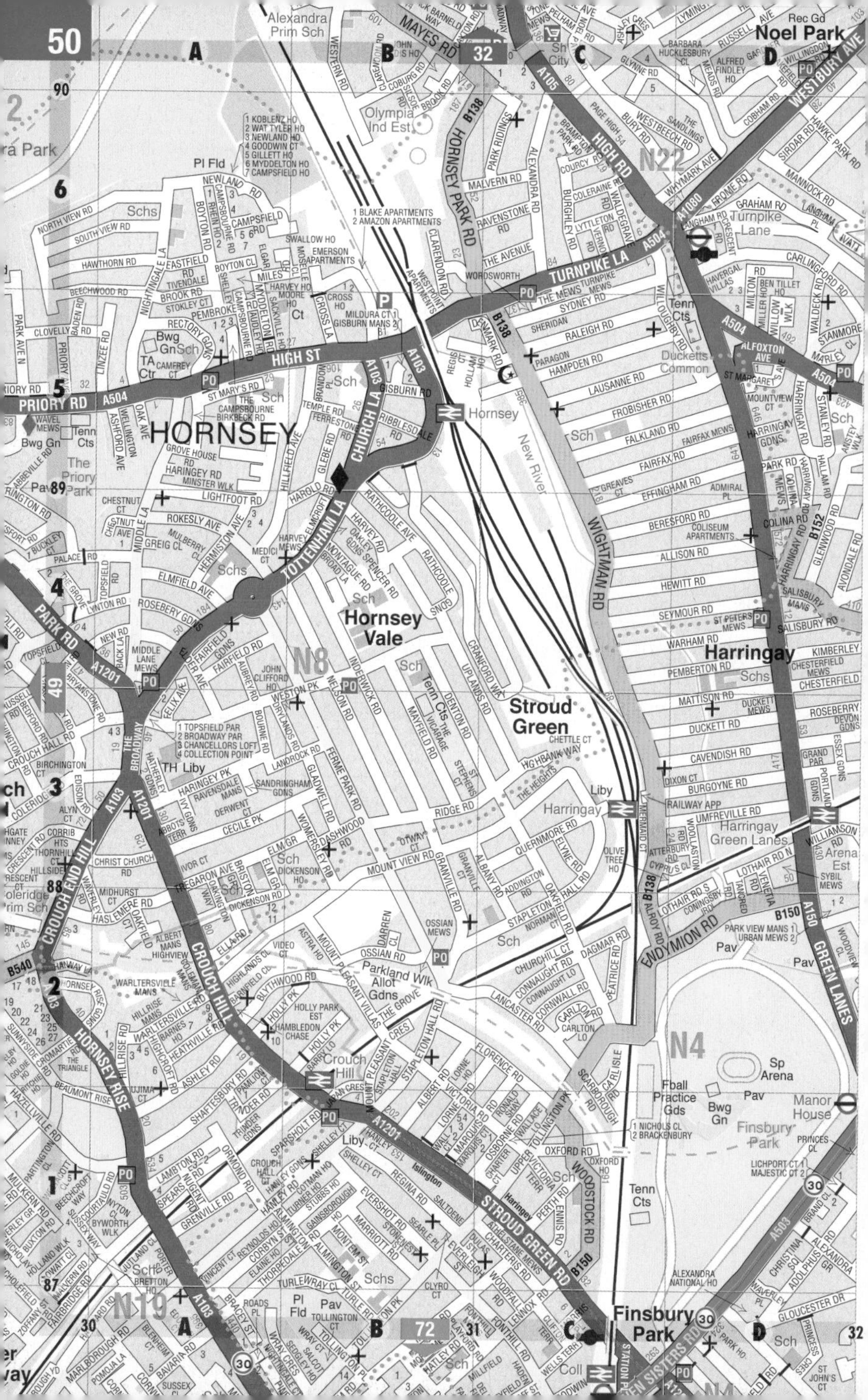

50
A
B
C
D
32
Alexandra Prim Sch
Noel Park
Mayes Rd
Western Rd
Clarendon Rd
Olympia Ind Est
Hornsey Park Rd
B138
High Rd
A105
N22
Westbury Ave
Turnpike Lane
Turnpike La
A504
Westbeech Rd
Whymark Ave
Frome Rd
Graham Rd
Carlingford Rd
Mannock Rd
Sirdar Rd
Hawke Park Rd
Page High
Park Ridings
Malvern Rd
Ravenstone Rd
The Avenue
Alexandra Rd
Wordsworth
Pl Fld
1 Koblenz Ho
2 Wat Tyler Ho
3 Newland Ho
4 Goodwin Ct
5 Gillett Ho
6 Myddelton Ho
7 Campsfield Ho
1 Blake Apartments
2 Amazon Apartments
Newland Rd
Campsfield Rd
North View Rd
South View Rd
Hawthorn Rd
Beechwood Rd
Nightingale La
Eastfield Rd
Tivendale
Brook Rd
Stokley Ct
Pembroke
Rectory Gdns
Boyton Rd
Boyton Cl
Miles
Harvey Ho
Moore Ct
Cross La
Swallow Ho
Emerson Apartments
Mildura Ct
Gisburn Mans
High St
Priory Rd
Clovelly Rd
Park Ave N
Priory Ave
Linzee Rd
Bwg Gn
Sch
TA Ctr
St Mary's Rd
The Campsbourne
Birkbeck Rd
HORNSEY
Wavel Mews
Bwg Gn
Tenn Cts
The Priory Park
Oak Ave
Ashford Ave
Wellington
Grove House Rd
Haringey Rd
Minster Wlk
Lightfoot Rd
Hillfield Ave
Glebe Rd
Brandon
Temple Rd
Ferrestone
Gisburn Rd
Ribblesdale
Church La
A103
Hornsey
New River
Harold Rd
Rathcoole Ave
Chestnut Ct
Rokesly Ave
Greig Cl
Mulberry Ct
Elmfield Ave
Rosebery Gdns
Middle La
Hermiston Ave
Tottenham La
Medici Ct
Harvey Mews
Oakley Gdns
Spencer Rd
Montague Rd
Broad La
Rathcoole Gdns
Hornsey Vale
Palace Rd
The Grove
Lynton Rd
Topsfield Rd
Park Rd
A1201
New Rd
Back La
Middle Lane Mews
Fairfield Gdns
Fairfield Rd
Elder Ave
Felix Ave
John Clifford Ho
Weston Pk
Nelson Rd
Inderwick Rd
Mayfield Rd
Denton Rd
Uplands Rd
Cranford Wk
N8
Tenn Cts
Stroud Green
Chettle Ct
Highbank Way
The Heights
Wightman Rd
Harringay
Sheridan
Raleigh Rd
Hampden Rd
Lausanne Rd
Frobisher Rd
Falkland Rd
Fairfax Mews
Fairfax Rd
Greaves Ct
Effingham Rd
Admiral Pl
Beresford Rd
Coliseum Apartments
Allison Rd
Hewitt Rd
Seymour Rd
St Peters Mews
Warham Rd
Pemberton Rd
Mattison Rd
Duckett Rd
Cavendish Rd
Dixon Ct
Burgoyne Rd
Railway App
Umfreville Rd
Woollaston
Harringay Green Lanes
Duckett Mews
Willoughby Rd
Ducketts Common
St Margaret
Alfoxton Ave
Mountview Ct
Harringay Gdns
Park Rd
Colina Rd
Colina Mews
Harringay Rd
B152
Glenwood Rd
Avondale Rd
Salisbury Mans
Salisbury Rd
Kimberley
Chesterfield Mews
Chesterfield
Rosebery
Devon Gdns
Essex Gdns
Grand Par
Portland Gdns
Williamson Rd
Arena Est
Sybil Mews
Lothair Rd N
Lothair Rd S
Venetia Rd
Tancred Rd
Coningsby Rd
Endymion Rd
B150
A105
Green Lanes
Park View Mans
Urban Mews
Stanley Rd
Hallam Rd
Stanmore
Marley Cl
Waldeck Rd
Milton
Miller Ho
Willow Wlk
Ben Tillet Ho
Havergal Villas
Langham Pl
1 Topsfield Par
2 Broadway Par
3 Chancellors Loft
4 Collection Point
The Broadway
TH Liby
Crouch Hall Rd
Birchington Ct
Hatherley Gdns
Haringey Pk
Ravensdale Mans
Sandringham Gdns
Derwent Ct
Landrock Rd
Gladwell Rd
Ferme Park Rd
Ridge Rd
Cecile Pk
Abbots Terr
Ivy Gdns
Dashwood Rd
Womersley Rd
Elm Gr
Otway Ct
Mount View Rd
Granville Rd
Albany Rd
Addington Rd
Stapleton Hall Rd
Norman Ct
Oakfield Rd
Quernmore Rd
Elyne Rd
Olive Tree Ho
Cyprus Cl
Atterbury Rd
Alroy Rd
Mermaid Ct
Liby
Crouch End Hill
Edison Rd
Alyn Ct
Corrib Hts
Thornhill Ct
Hillside
Coleridge Rd
Christ Church Rd
Ivor Ct
Tregaron Ave
Briston Gr
Dickenson Ho
Dickenson Rd
Midhurst Ct
Haslemere Rd
Waverley
Oakfield Ct
Albert Mans
Highview
Ella Rd
Video Ct
Astra Ho
Mount Pleasant Rd
Ossian Rd
Ossian Mews
Darren Cl
Parkland Wlk
Allot Gdns
The Grove
Churchill Ct
Connaught Rd
Connaught Lo
Cornwall Rd
Lancaster Rd
Carlton Rd
Carlton Lo
Dagmar Rd
Beatrice Rd
N4
Crouch Hill
B540
Hanway La
Hornsey Rise Gdns
Waltersville Mans
Hillrise Mans
Highlands Cl
Blythwood Rd
Holly Pk
Holly Park Est
Hambledon Chase
Hornsey Rise
Hillrise Rd
Highcroft Rd
Ashley Rd
Heathville Rd
Barnes Ho
Sunnyside Rd
Cromartie Rd
The Triangle
Beaumont Rise
Hazellville Rd
Shaftesbury Rd
Trinder Rd
Pamlion Ct
Crouch Hill
Japan Cres
Mount Pleasant Cres
Stapleton Hall
Albert Rd
Lorne Rd
Victoria Rd
Florence Rd
Ronald Shay
Marquis Rd
Osborne Rd
Charter Ct
Upper Tollington Pk
Wallace Rd
Scarborough Rd
Carlisle Rd
Fball Practice Gds
Bwg Gn
Pav
Sp Arena
Finsbury Park
Manor House
1 Nicholls Cl
2 Brackenbury
Oxford Rd
Oxford Ho
Woodstock Rd
Victoria Terr
Perth Rd
Ennis Rd
Tenn Cts
Princes Cl
Lichport Ct
Majestic Ct
30
A503
Christina Sq
Adolphus Rd
Alexandra Gr
Brand Cl
Alexandra National Ho
Waverley Pl
Gloucester Dr
Princess Cres
St John's Ct
Seven Sisters Rd
Park Ho
Station Pl
Finsbury Park
Clifton Terr
Wells Terr
Coll
Fonthill Rd
Lennox Rd
Woodfall Rd
Everleigh St
Dulas St
Charteris Rd
Athelstane Mews
Stroud Green Rd
B150
Islington
Haringey
Hanley Rd
Shelley Ct
Regina Rd
Saltdene
Searle Pl
Evershot Rd
Marriott Rd
Stonenest
Montem St
Almington St
Thorpedale Rd
Corbyn St
Reynolds Ho
Elaine Ho
Gainsborough Ho
Stubbs Ho
Turner Ho
Cotman Ho
Sparsholt Rd
Crouch Hall Ct
Hanley Gdns
Ormond Rd
Lambton Rd
Spears Rd
Nugent Rd
Grenville Rd
Partington Cl
Mulkern Rd
Beechcroft Way
Courtauld Rd
Nyton Cl
Byworth Wlk
Sussex Way
Buxton Rd
Holland Wlk
Wyatt Cl
Malvern Rd
Fairbridge Rd
Zoffany St
Jutland Cl
Porter
Bretton Ho
N19
A103
Turlewray Cl
Turle Rd
Tollington Pk
Tollington Ct
Clyro Ct
Pl Fld
Pav
Roads Pl
Sch
Marlborough Rd
Blenheim Ct
Bavaria Rd
Pomoja La
Sussex Cl
Bracey St
Wray Cres
Sedgley Ho
Salcot
Tollington Pl
Hatley Rd
Millfield
Playford Rd
Haden Ct
Schs
72
31
30
87
88
89
90
1
2
3
4
5
6
49
2

51
A
B
C
D
33
Open Air Theatre
The Moselle
TOTTENHAM
Recn Gd
N17
Bruce Grove
Bruce Grove Prim Sch
HIGHAM RD
HASTINGS RD
WILMOT RD
DOWNHILLS PARK RD
DOWNHILLS AVE
Downhills Park Recn Gd
Tenn Cts
Bwg Gn
Pav
PHILIP LA
WEST GREEN RD
West Green
Sp Ctr
Acad
Sch
Liby
N15
Allot Gdns
Seven Sisters
A503
A504
BROAD LA
HIGH RD
MONUMENT WAY
A1055
B153
B155
BELMONT RD
B152
ST ANN'S RD
St Ann's General
Chestnuts Recn Gd
Arts Ctr
Superstore
South Tottenham
South Tottenham
Arena Bsns Ctr
Crusader Ind Est
N4
N16
Tenn Ct
Stamford Hill
AMHURST PK
A107
SEVEN SISTERS RD
STAMFORD HILL
A10
Haringey
Hackney
East Resr
West Resr
Capital Ring
MANOR RD
Stamford Hill
Abney Park Cemy
STOKE NEWINGTON
Stoke Newington
LORDSHIP PK
B105
A105
CLAPTON COMM
52
73
1
2
3
4
5
6
87
88
89
90
30
40

Tottenham Hale
Upper Clapton
South Tottenham
Lockwood Reservoir
High Maynard Resr
Low Maynard Resr
Resr No 1
Resr No 2
Resr No 3
Resr No 4
Resr No 5
Warwick Resr East
Warwick Resr West
Water Works
Walthamstow Marshes
Leyton Marshes
Springfield Park
Springfield Marina
Lea Valley Walk
Lee Valley Regional Park
River Lea or Lee
River Lee Navigation
Lee Flood Relief Channel
Coppermill Stream
Blackhorse Road
FERRY LA
FOREST RD
BROAD LA
MONUMENT WAY
HALE RD
WATERMEAD WAY
BLACKHORSE LA
CLAPTON COMM
UPPER CLAPTON
N15
N16
N17
E5
E10
E17
34
74
51

53
WALTHAMSTOW
Chestnut Sp Gd
Waltham Forest Coll
Allot Gdns
TH
C Ctr
The Bell
Thorpe Coombe
FOREST RD
CHINGFORD RD
A112
A503
HOE ST
HIGH ST
BLACKHORSE RD
MARKHOUSE RD
LEA BRIDGE RD
CHURCH RD
HIGH ROAD LEYTON
A112 HIGH RD
A104
A1006
B159
B161
LEYTON GREEN RD
E17
E10
Walthamstow Central
Walthamstow Queens Road
St James Street
Queens Road Cemy
South Grove Prim Sch
Kelmscott L Ctr
Kelmscott Sch
St Saviour's CE Prim Sch
Barn Croft Prim Sch
Leyton Link Est
Roxwell Trad Pk
Cromwell Est
Eastgate Bsns Pk
East 10 Ent Pk
Period Wks
Sybourn Inf Sch Annexe
Fairways Bsns Pk
The Lammas Sch
Willow Brook Prim Sch
St Joseph's RC Inf Sch
Lea Park Trad Est
Fball Gd
George Mitchell Sch
Vestry Ho (Mus)
The Holy Family RC Coll
Leyton Midland Road
Dawlish Prim Sch
Orient Ind Pk
Tenn Cts
Sp Gd
Liby
35
54
75
A
B
C
D
1
2
3
4
5
6

54
36
53
76
FOREST RD
Upper Walthamstow
Snaresbrook
E18
E17
E11
E10
Gilbert's Slade
Eagle Pond
Hollow Pond
Centenary Walk
Whipps Cross
WHIPPS CROSS RD
WOODFORD NEW RD
LEA BRIDGE RD
HIGH RD
HIGH ROAD LEYTON
GAINSBOROUGH RD
SNARESBROOK RD
Leyton Midland Road
Leytonstone
Wood Street
Leyton Sixth Form Coll
Wanstead Flats
Norlington Sch for Boys

South Woodford
Woodford Trad Est
E18
IG8
Roding Valley Park
Nightingale Prim Sch
Hatton Sch
Beal High Sch
Roding
Wanstead
Snaresbrook
IG4
Redbridge Prim Sch
Redbridge
Redbridge Rdbt
EASTERN AVE
NORTH CIRCULAR RD
Wanstead High Sch
WANSTEAD
E11
Lincoln Island
River Roding
The Basin
Bush Wood
Wanstead Park
Reservoir Wood
Heronry Pond
Aldersbrook Prim Sch
Boat House
E12
HERMON HILL
WOODFORD RD
CHIGWELL RD
HIGH ST
BLAKE HALL RD
BUSH RD
CAMBRIDGE PK
WOODLANDS AVE
NORTHUMBERLAND AVE
SOUTHEND RD
37
77
56
90
89
88
87
42
41

Essex STREET ATLAS
A
B
C
D
EWELLHURST RD
ST CLAIR CL
COTTESMORE
KIRKLAND AV
PURLEY CL
DUNSPRING LA
BELVEDERE
PEEL PL
CLAYHALL AVE
CORBURG GDNS
WINNINGALES CT
PEEL DR
STRADBROKE GR
MELLOWS RD
DYMCHURCH CL
TIVERTON AVE
SANDPIPER TERR
BEAMINSTER GDNS
WINCANTON
MOSSFORD CT
1 PUFFIN TERR
2 OYSTER CATCHER TERR
TIPTREE CRES
RUSHDEN GDNS
LESSINGHAM AVE
STRADBROKE GR
HATFIELD CL 1
LOOE GDNS 2
CHERRY CT 3
LICHEN CT 4
Cemy
A1400
90
PO
BRINKWORTH RD
MARLBOROUGH DR
MARLANDS RD
GAYFERE RD
CHADACRE AVE
HEATHERLEY DR
CLAYBURY BROADWAY
ANDERSON RD
Hatton Sch
6
Pl Fld
LANSDOWNE CT 1
STONELEIGH CT 2
OLEASTOR CT 3
ASPEN CT 4
HAWTHORN CT 5
STONELEIGH DR
HERENT DR
LORD AVE
Schs
WERNETH HALL RD
ABBOTSWOOD GDNS
MONKSWOOD GDNS
WRAY AVE
EVESHAM WAY
LONGWOOD PAR
OAKLEAFE GDNS
GAYSHAM HALL
MAPLELEAFE GDNS
GREENLEAFE DR
Sp Gd
DELLWOOD GDNS
LONGWOOD GDNS
GLENTHORNE GDNS
WOODVILLE GDNS
ORIEL GDNS
EARLSWOOD GDNS
Beal High Sch
WOODFORD BRIDGE RD
IG5
Clayhall Park
CARSWELL CL
BORROWDALE
LODGE HILL
PARKVIEW GDNS
FORD GDNS
THORPEDALE GDNS
BEATTYVILLE GDNS
ROSEDENE GDNS
QUEENBOROUGH GDNS
GEORGEVILLE GDNS
HAIGVILLE GDNS
EARLSVILLE GDNS
BRANDVILLE
Recn Gd
WIDECOMBE GDNS
CONISTON GDNS
BABBACOMBE GDNS
NORTHWOOD GDNS
SUNNYMEDE DR
5
TORQUAY GDNS
WOODFORD AVE
B Gn
1 REDGELEY
2 QUEENS GATE
HIGHWOOD GDNS
LITTLE GEARIES
SOUTHWOOD GDNS
A123
PO
FALMOUTH GDNS
MERRIVALE AVE
DERWENT GDNS
KESWICK GDNS
BRANTWOOD GDNS
WYCHWOOD GDNS
BEECHWOOD GDNS
COLLINWOOD GDNS
BRONTE CL
BRAINTREE AVE
PEAKETON AVE
89
BERGHOLT AVE
AMBLESIDE GDNS
GRASMERE GDNS
HEDGEWOOD GDNS
GLENWOOD GDNS
KENWOOD GDNS
SWALLOW CT
BUTE RD
LOUDOUN AV
MICHELL AVE
FOWEY AVE
Redbridge Prim Sch
RIDGEWAY GDNS
COLLEGE GDNS
Prep Sch
GOSFORD GDNS
B192
HIGHWOOD GDNS
GANTSHILL CRES
Schs
Sch
BRYFAN CL
GRANGEWAY GDNS
SOMERSBY GDNS
LIMEWOOD CT
SHERE RD
WAREMEAD RD
PERSHORE CL
CHALFORD CT
ICKNIELD DR
4
COBBETTS AVE
VISTA DR
FAIRMEAD GDNS
HIGHCLIFFE GDNS
INGLEHURST GDNS
CROMBIE CL
WYCOMBE RD
ROLL GDNS
SEVEN WAYS PAR
GAYSHAM AVE
GLENHAM DR
MARTLEY DR
FERNHALL DR
EDWINA GDNS
DANEHURST GDNS
RADNOR CRES
SUSSEX CL
AVERY GDNS
WAYSIDE MEWS
HEADLEY APP
PARHAM DR
Liby
ASHURST DR
ROSEMARY DR
MEWS
AVON
55
REDBRIDGE LA E
WINDERMERE GDNS
ELLESMERE GDNS
ETHELBERT GDNS
A1400
Gants Hill
A123
OTLEY DR
MARGARET WAY
EASTERN AVE
40
BEEHIVE LA
333
Redbridge
PO
A12
EVANSTON GDNS
CASTLEVIEW GDNS
BEEHIVE CT
Coll
CLARENCE AVE
PANFIELD MEWS
THE CRESCENT
CRANBROOK RD
FRINTON MEWS
BRAMLEY CRES
LONSDALE CRES
SOUTH VIEW CRES
LYNTON CRES
OTLEY APP
HEADLEY DR
ALBEMARLE
ALBEMARLE APP
3
STUDLEY DR
STUDLEY CT
CASTLE DR
PRESTON GDNS
DEVONPORT GDNS
HILLVIEW CRES
BLENHEIM AVE
Gants Hill
Valentines High Sch (Upper)
Pl Fld
Min Glf Crs
IG2
MIDDLETON GDNS
MIDDLEFIELD GDNS
BLOOMFIELD
CARLISLE HO
STONEHALL AVE
CARLISLE GDNS
Sp Gd
ST HELEN'S RD
ST EDMUND'S RD
1 BRAMLEY HO
2 CHARLOTTE CT
3 VI & JOHN RUBENS HO
4 ABRAHAM COHEN CT
PERTH RD
ROOK LO
88
WAKEFIELD GDNS
WANSTEAD LA
IG1
CRANBROOK RISE
FAIRHOLME RD
MORNINGTON AVE
RIPON GDNS
WORCESTER GDNS
HEREFORD GDNS
ELY GDNS
Sp Gd
A406
NORTH CIRCULAR RD
WELLS GDNS
GLOUCESTER GDNS
Bwg Gn
1 GLOUCESTER CT
2 LINCOLN CT
3 PAVILION RD
ST GEORGE'S RD
MISTLEY THORN
TILLOTSON RD
EMERSON RD
Valentines Park
River Roding
PETERBOROUGH GDNS
LINCOLN GDNS
CANTERBURY AVE
THE DRIVE
ST ANDREW'S RD
WILSON RD
VAUGHAN GDNS
BETHELL AVE
THE SQUARE
2
Allot Gdns
TRURO GDNS
CHELMSFORD GDNS
CHICHESTER GDNS
ROCHESTER GDNS
COWLEY RD
HOLCOMBE RD
Bwg Gn
Pav
QUEBEC
50
WHITFIELD CT
CLARENDON GDNS
Crkt Gd
EXETER GDNS
RANELAGH GDNS
ARLINGTON GDNS
REDCLIFFE GDNS
Cranbrook
HIGHLANDS GDNS
WANSTEAD PARK RD
LENNOX GDNS
STANHOPE GDNS
SACKVILLE GDNS
CAVENDISH GDNS
BEAUFORT GDNS
The Lake
Bwg Gn
1
Highlands Prim Sch
SEYMOUR GDNS
KENSINGTON GDNS
ENDSLEIGH GDNS
VALENTINES RD
INGLEBY RD
MELBOURNE
COVENTRY RD
WARWICK GDNS
CH
PO
GREENWAY CT
BELGRAVE RD
DE VERE GDNS
PARK AVE
Park Sch
AIRLIE GDNS
BATHURST RD
WELLESLEY RD
Allot Gdns
PORTLAND AVE
MAYFAIR AVE
A123
GRANVILLE RD
Coll
MARK WADE CL
WESTMORLAND CL
87
UNDERLAND WAY
42
Redbridge
Newham
A
B
78
43
BELGRAVE
C
D
EMPRESS AVE
MARKET
Coll
MANSFIELD
PO
Sch
MORLAND RD
50
Ilford
WANSTEAD
WESTBURY
ARGYLE
HERON CT
BALFOUR RD
HAINAULT ST

Barkingside
Newbury Park
Aldborough Hatch
Seven Kings
Fairlop Waters Ctry Pk
Fairlop Plain
Sch of Riding
Ilford Jewish Prim Sch
Aldborough Hall Farm
Aldborough House Farm
William Torbitt Prim Sch
Oaks Park High Sch
Seven Kings Park
Farnham Green Prim Sch
Downshall Prim Sch
Westwood Rec Gd
Seven Kings High Sch
St Aidan's RC Sch
Canon Palmer RC Sch
Christchurch Prim Sch
Fullwood Prim Sch
EASTERN AVE
HIGH RD
HIGH ST
IG1
IG2
IG3
IG6

58
79

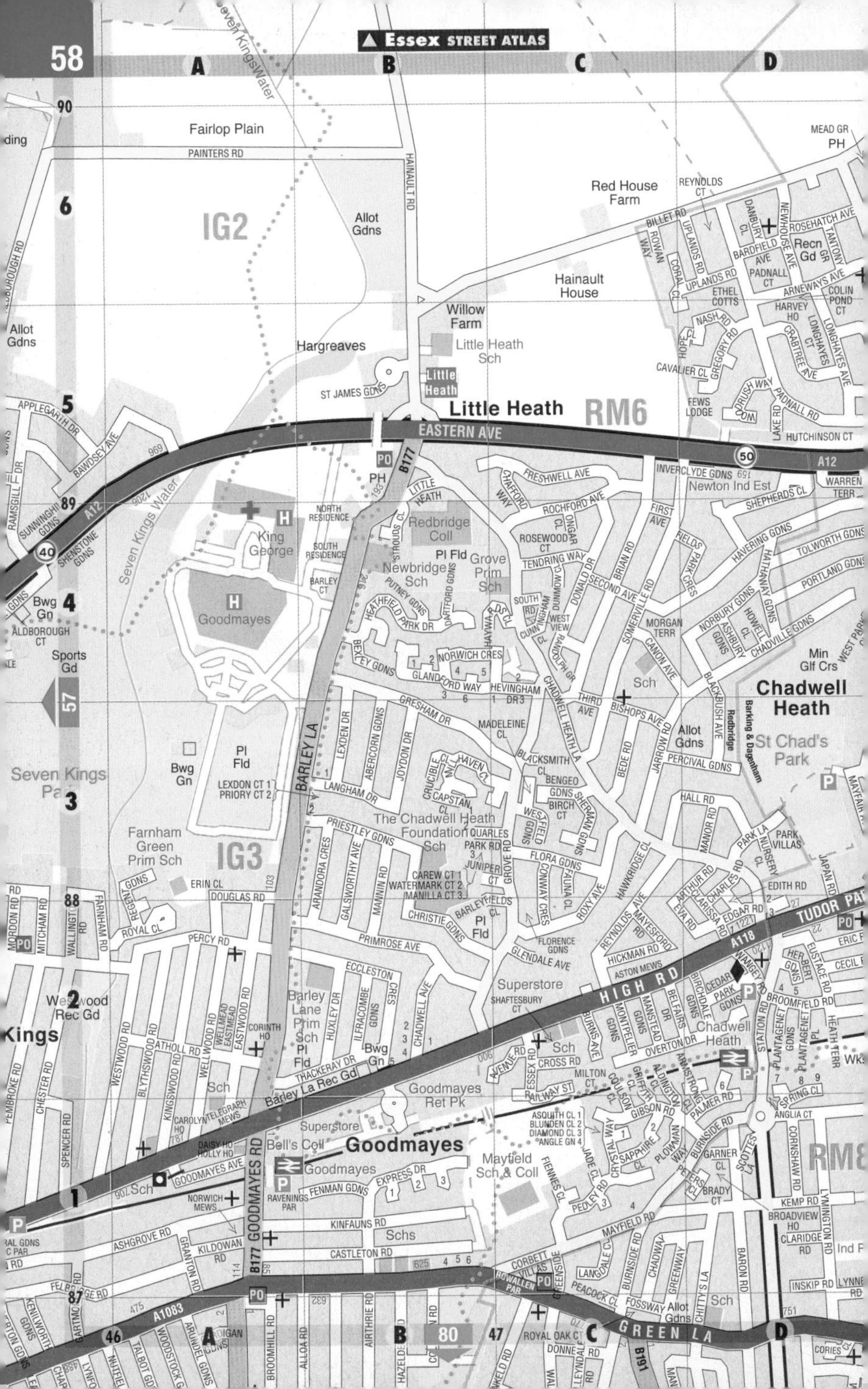
A
B
C
D
Fairlop Plain
PAINTERS RD
IG2
Allot Gdns
Red House Farm
Hainault House
Willow Farm
Little Heath Sch
Hargreaves
Little Heath
RM6
EASTERN AVE
A12
King George
Goodmayes
Seven Kings Water
Redbridge Coll
Newbridge Sch
Grove Prim Sch
Chadwell Heath
St Chad's Park
Seven Kings Park
Farnham Green Prim Sch
IG3
BARLEY LA
The Chadwell Heath Foundation Sch
Westwood Rec Gd
Barley Lane Prim Sch
HIGH RD
TUDOR PAR
Goodmayes Ret Pk
Superstore
Bell's Coll
Goodmayes
Mayfield Sch & Coll
Chadwell Heath
GOODMAYES RD
B177
A1083
GREEN LA
RM8
80
57

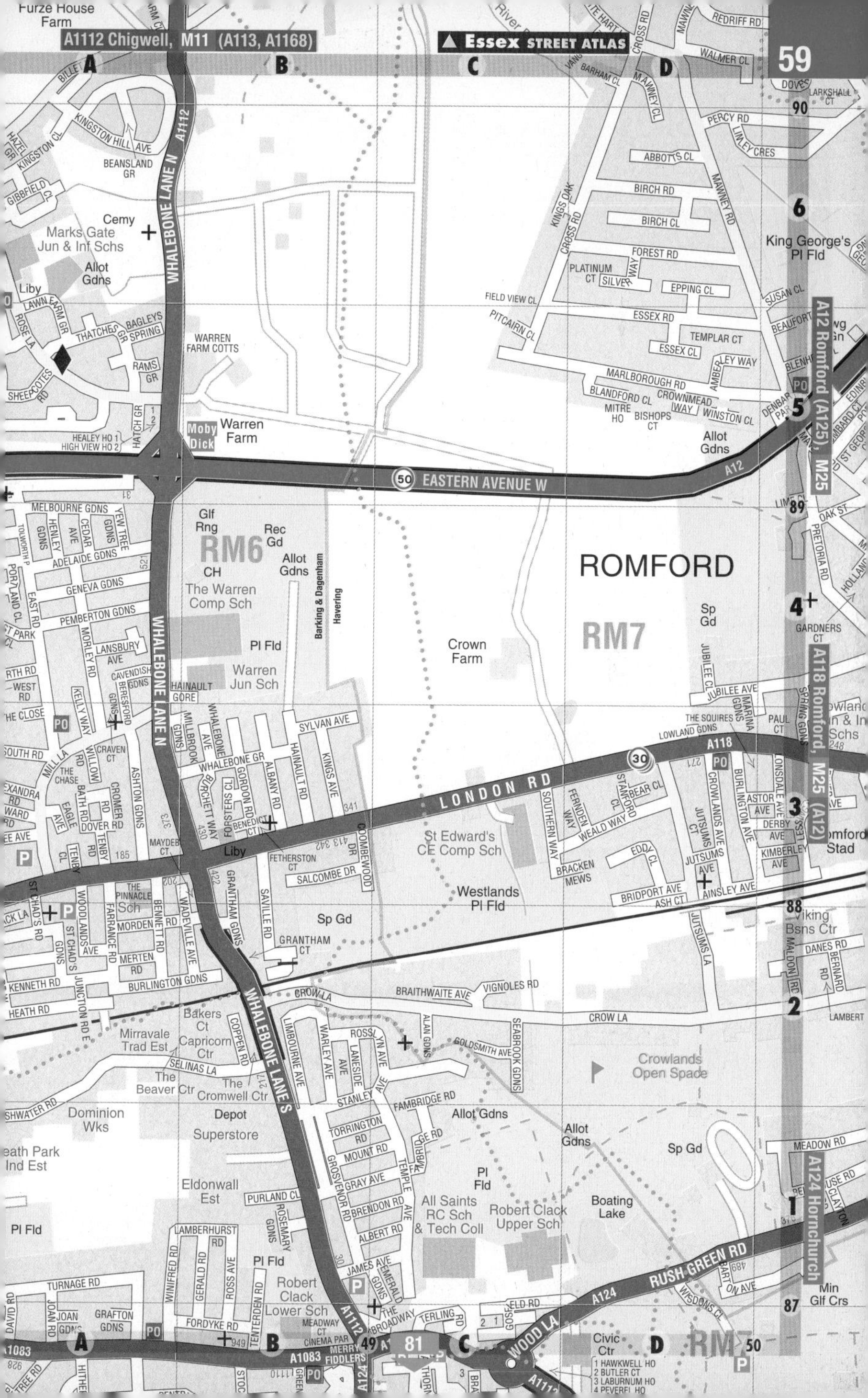
A1112 Chigwell, M11 (A113, A1168)
A
B
C
D
Furze House Farm
Marks Gate Jun & Inf Schs
Cemy
Allot Gdns
Liby
Warren Farm
Moby Dick
WARREN FARM COTTS
WHALEBONE LANE N
EASTERN AVENUE W
ROMFORD
RM6
RM7
Glf Rng
Rec Gd
CH
The Warren Comp Sch
Warren Jun Sch
Pl Fld
Allot Gdns
Barking & Dagenham
Havering
Crown Farm
Sp Gd
LONDON RD
St Edward's CE Comp Sch
Westlands Pl Fld
King George's Pl Fld
A12 Romford (A125), M25
A118 Romford, M25 (A12)
A124 Hornchurch
Romford Stad
Viking Bsns Ctr
CROW LA
WHALEBONE LANE S
Crowlands Open Space
Mirravale Trad Est
Bakers Ct
Capricorn Ctr
The Beaver Ctr
The Cromwell Ctr
Dominion Wks
Depot
Superstore
Heath Park Ind Est
Eldonwall Est
Pl Fld
All Saints RC Sch & Tech Coll
Robert Clack Upper Sch
Robert Clack Lower Sch
Boating Lake
Allot Gdns
Sp Gd
RUSH GREEN RD
WOOD LA
Civic Ctr
Min Glf Crs
1 HAWKWELL HO
2 BUTLER CT
3 LABURNUM HO
4 PEVEREL HO
81
90
89
88
87
6
5
4
3
2
1
50
49

Copthall Covert
UB10
38
Brackenbury Farm
Uxbridge CH
Copthall Farm
Breakspear Jun & Inf Schs
Harvil Farm
THE COTTAGES
Harefield Place
Ickenham
UB10
Swakeleys
The Douay Martyrs RC Sch
The Douay Martyrs RC Sch (Annexe)
Vyners Sch
Tenn Cts
Park Wood
WESTERN AVE
SWAKELEYS RD
Swakeleys Rdbt
A40 Beaconsfield (M40), M25
Buckinghamshire STREET ATLAS
Uxbridge Common
Ski Ctr
Pl Flds
UB8
Uxbridge Coll
Hermitage Prim Sch
Hillingdon Circus
Motel
FREEZELAND WAY
LONG LA
PARK RD
HARVIL RD
UXBRIDGE
Athletic Gd
St Helens Coll
Oak Farm Jun & Inf Schs
Hillingdon Court Park (Recn Gd)
Big Clump
Hillingdon International Sch
82

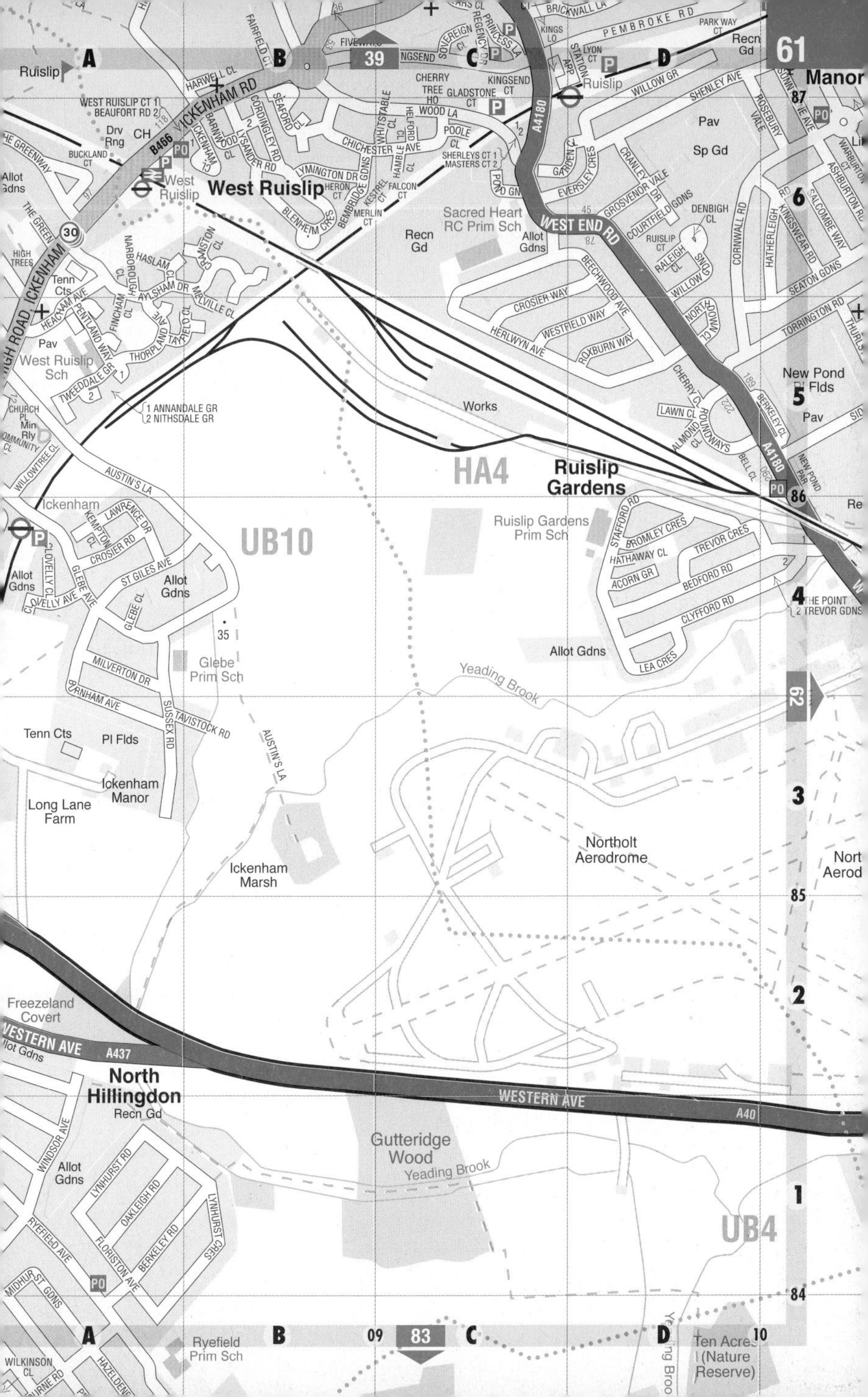

West Ruislip
Ruislip Gardens
Ickenham
North Hillingdon
Northolt Aerodrome
HA4
UB10
UB4
WESTERN AVE
A40
A437
A4180
B466
HIGH ROAD, ICKENHAM
ICKENHAM RD
WEST END RD
Sacred Heart RC Prim Sch
Ruislip Gardens Prim Sch
Glebe Prim Sch
West Ruislip Sch
Ryefield Prim Sch
Works
Ickenham Marsh
Ickenham Manor
Long Lane Farm
Freezeland Covert
Gutteridge Wood
Yeading Brook
Ten Acres (Nature Reserve)
New Pond Pl Flds
Allot Gdns
Recn Gd
39
83
62

62
Ruislip Manor
40
Cavendish Recn Gd
Tenn Ct
Lady Bankes Schs
Liby
Pav
Sp Gd
Bwg Gn
Bessingby Pl Flds
HA4
Miniature Railway
Recn Gd
Allot Gdns
Field End Jun & Inf Schs
New Pond Pl Flds
St Swithun Wells RC Prim Sch
Ruislip Gardens
Braintree Ind Est
Deane Park
Tenn Cts
Deansfield Prim
South Ruislip
Queensmead Sch
Pl Flds
Sp Ctr
Superstore
Odyssey Bsns Pk
Brook Retail Park
Victoria Retail Park
Northolt Aerodrome
Bourne Prim Sch
Priors Farm
Polish War Meml
Glebe Farm
Western Ave
A40
A4180
West End Rd
Yeading Brook
London Ctr
CH
UB4
UB5
Peacock Park
Hillingdon
Ealing
Downe Barns Farm
Ten Acres (Nature Reserve)
84
61
Sharvel La
Whitby Rd
Bessingby Rd
Torrington Rd
Sidmouth Dr
Victoria Rd
Long Dr
Station App
Great Central Ave
1 The Point
2 Trevor Gdns

A
B
C
D
41
85
64
Allot Gdns
Yeading Bro
Yeading Ave
Waverley Rd
Torbay Rd
Warden Ave
Rayners La
Ovesdon Ave
Chichester Ct
Capthorne Ave
Berriton Rd
Oxleay Rd
Clitheroe Ave
Goldsmith Cl
Union Terr
Providence Ave
Grange Schs
Abercorn Cres
Southdown Cres
Hillside Cres
87
A4090
Tenn Cts
Exeter Rd
Drake Rd
Lucas Ave
Fball Gd
Austen Rd
Eastway Cres
Scott Cres
Eliot Dr
Unity Terr
Drinkwater Rd
Swift Cl
Concord Terr
The Arches
Lodgehill Park Cl
Franklins Mews
Roxbourne Fst & Mid Schs
Allot Gdns
Newton Farm Fst & Mid Sch
Newton Park
Allot Gdns
Newton Farm Ecology Pk
Priest Park Ave
Maryatt Ave
Rayners La
Fentiman Way
Torbay Rd
Harrow
Hillingdon
Newquay Cres
Widdicombe Ave
Exeter Rd
Lynton Rd
Lulworth Gdns
Kings Rd
Ravenswood Cres
Tenn Cts
Pav
The Roxbourne
Alexandra Sch
Newton Cl
Learner Dr
Jasmine Gdns
Abbots Dr
Monks Cl
Coles Cres
Thornley Dr
Roxeth Green Ave
Eastcote Ave
Archdale Bsns Ctr
Brember Rd
Stanley Rd
Rosslyn
Sherwood
Greenwood
Eastleigh Ave
Maple Ave
Barnaby Cl
The Viaduct
St Margaret's Ave
Recn Gd
Parkfield Cres
Dunster Way
Clovelly Way
Lulworth Cl
Malvern Ave
Minehead Ct
HA2
Merlins Ave
Minehead Rd
Tithe Farm Cl
Tithe Farm Ave
Sandringham Cres
Cross Rd
Reverend Cl
Cemy
Meadow Gate
Beechwood Circ
Beechwood Ave
Beechwood Gdns
Crane Cl
Whitby Rd
Well Cl
Leamington Cres
Hodson Cl
Hamilton Cres
Jordan Cl
Schs
Rowe Wlk
Eastcote La
Winkley Ct
Alexandra Ave
Alexandra Cl
Grovelands Cl
Findon Cl
Corbin's La
Valentine Rd
Liby
Wargrave Rd
Carsdale Rd
Thistlecroft
Stuart Ave
Veldene Way
Stiven Cres
Bodmin Cl
Kings Road Bglws
1 Cornell Ho
2 Mead Field
3 Stradbrook Cl
Windsor Ave
Windsor Cres
Windsor Cl
Park Mead
Park La
Torrington Ct
Barnetts
Leath
Sale Rd
A312 Northolt Rd
Duncan Rd
Wyvenhoe Rd
86
Pav
Royal Cres
Brookside Cl
Primrose Cl
Mirren Cl
Salter Cl
Rosebery Ave
South Harrow
1 Tregenna Ct
2 Park Gates
3 Arundel Ct
Torrington Dr
Brendon Gdns
Palace Rd
Ind Est
Tregenna Ave
Corfe Ave
Ivy Cl
Alexandra Park
Roxeth Gr
Welldon Park Schs
Jubilee Dr
Princes Way
Brackenhill
Kenilworth Ave
Ludlow Cl
Balmoral Rd
Paddocks Cl
Station Par
Wood End Ave
Westwood Ave
Diamond Rd
The Court
PO
Field End Rd
Earlsmead
Carlyon Ave
Raglan Terr
Stroud Gate
Cadogan Cl
Victoria Rd
Superstores
Warwick Ave
Holyrood Ave
Walton Ave
Earlsmead Fst & Mid Sch
Fball Gd
Arundel Dr
A312
Northolt Park
Haddock Gr
HA4
Hollydale Cl
New Ct
Dorchester Rd
Dorchester Ct
Halsbury Rd W
Tenn Cts
Chancerygate Bsns Ctr
Stonefield Cl
Ind Est
Stonefield Way
Bradfield Rd
Somervell Rd
1 Salisbury Ct
2 Folkestone Ct
3 Pontefract Ct
4 Sedgefield Ct
Station Par
Clauson Ave
Petts Hill
Reading Rd
Floriston Ct
Morton Ct
The Heights
Wincanton Cres
Danemead Gr
Greenacre Gdns
Doncaster Gdns
Martin Dr
Mallet Dr
Allot Gdns
Harrow
Ealing
Gaylor Rd
Dabbs Hill La
Newmarket Ave
Bangor Cl
Sheridan Terr
Mildred Ave
Rabournmead Dr
Graham Ct
Silverdale Cl
Hornbeam Cl
Epsom Cl
Hurst Cl
Perceval Ct 1
Hill Ct 2
Churchill Ct 3
Warwick Ct 4
Lanark Ct 5
Wheatsheaf Cl
Wilsmere Dr
Sandown Way
The Link
Doncaster Dr
Eastcote La
Kempton Ave
Sch
The Mount
Redcar Cl
Wood End La
Grainger Cl
85
Newnham Cl
Hillingdon
Ealing
Newbury Way
Newbury Cl
Cartmel Ct
Pl Fld
Perth Cl
Ascot Cl
Huntingdon Cl
Plumpton Cl
Fontwell Cl
Ripon Cl
Wetherby Cl
Bayshill Rise
Eggardon Ct
Lancaster Rd
Girton Rd
Northolt High Sch
Haydock Ave
Haydock Gn
Southwell Ave
Thirsk Cl
Cheltenham Cl
Holmwood Cl
Anson Terr
Masts
Blenheim Rd
Coneygrove Path 1
Vincents Path 2
Priors Field 3
Ridgeway Wlk 4
Shepherds Path 5
Forlong Path 6
Willow Tree Prim Sch
Pl Fld
Owen Cl
Buttercup Cl
Abbott Cl
Goodwood Dr
Sussex Cres
Lewes Cl
Allot Gdns
UB5
Siverst Cl
Ribblesdale Ave
Briar Cres
Tenby Gdns
Eastcote Lane N
Millway Gdns
Sch
Arnold Rd
New Park Cl
Laymead Cl
Acre Path
Hollowfield Wlk
Field
Stroud
Attwood Rd
Winnings Wlk
Bruffs Mdw
Fortunes Mead
Palmer Cl
Willow Tree Cl
Poppy Cl
Bluebell Cl
Cowings Mead
Eastcote La
The Farmlands
Moat Farm Rd
Wellington Ho
Northolt
Mandeville Rd
Badminton Cl
Conville Cres
Girton Cl
Glamis Way
Castle Rd
Oriel Way
Freeman Cl
Gauntlet Cl
Yeoman Rd
Manor Gate
Lordship Rd
Islip Manor Rd
Islip Manor Park
Belvue Cl
Belvue Rd
Carr Rd
Cherry Gdns
Allot Gdns
1
Petworth Cl
PO
Station Par
Sandringham Rd
Summit Rd
Belvue Bsns Ctr
Northolt Trad Est
Grand Union Canal
Islip Gdns
Dukes Ave
Manor Ave
Dale Ct
Alderney Gdns
Lytton Cl
Kingsmead Dr
Court Farm Rd
Grand Union Canal Wlk
Fairway Dr
John Chilton Sch
West London Acad
Western Ave
Harewood Cl
Harewood Ave
Church Ave
Church Lo
Church Rd
Church Rd
Vicarage Cl
Ealing Rd
NORTHOLT
Fort Rd
84
Target Rdbt
Carisbrooke Ct
Kingston Cl
Belvue Park
Rowdell Rd
Mohammedi Pk Complex
Taunton Rd
Fairway Dr
Aladdin Workspace
West London Acad
A
Dias Ho
Bishops Dr
Moorlands
Godfrey Ave
Garden
Sarah Ct
A312
B
Eskdale Ave
A40
Rectory
Westway Ct
C
D
Golf
Bridport
Derby Rd
The Metropolitan Ctr
Halifax Rd
Long Dr
Stanley Ave
Allot Gdns

Harrow on the Hill
1 CROWN CT
2 CHILTERN HO
Running Tk
Tenn Cts
The John Lyon Sch
42
A312
HIGH ST
B458
SHAFTESBURY AVE
SOUTHDOWN CRES
HILLSIDE CRES
DUDLEY RD
DUDLEY GDNS
JOLLYS LA
MIDDLE RD
RIVERSTONE CL
GRANGE FARM CL
WESLEY CL
FRANKLINS MEWS
OSMOND CL
LODGEHILL PARK CL
ARCHES
HA2
Roxeth
Superstore
Archdale Bsns Ctr
BREMBER RD
STANLEY RD
ROSE CT
SHERWOOD RD
ROXETH GREEN AVE
EASTCOTE AVE
MAPLE AVE
THE VIADUCT
THE GREENWOODS
ST MARGARET'S AVE
BARNABY CL
A4005
ROXETH HILL
ASHBOURNE AVE
BRICKFIELDS
GLASFRYN CT
HAMSON CT
WEST HILL
BYRON HILL RD
CHARTWELL PL
CLONMEL CL
GEORGIAN WAY
ABBOTTS CT
COTTAGE CL
ELMFIELD CL
MOUNT PARK AVE
ATHENA CL 1
BRICKFIELDS 2
WEST HILL HALL 3
THE MOAT LODGE 4
EDWARD CT 5
CHYNGTON CT 6
BLAKE HO 7
KEATS HO 8
LANGTON HO 9
SYCAMORE LODGE 10
COWEN AVE
Allot Gdns
THE MOUNT
St Dominic's Coll(RC)
HARROW PK
KENNETT HO
Bowden House (Private)
THE WOODLANDS
LONDON RD
RAMA CT
JULIAN HILL
HERGA CT
The Clementine Churchill
SUDBURY HILL
CHASEWOOD PK
GRANTCHESTER CL
HERITAGE VIEW
St George's RC Prim Sch
A4127
HIGHLAWN HALL
FIRCROFT GDNS
PENAIR LODGE
ROWSHAM CT
HARROW FIELDS GDNS
LADBANK CL
Capital Ring
Tenn Cts
Sp Gds
LANFRANC CT
ASHTON CT
GRANGE CT
ASSISI CT
ST FRANCIS LODGE
THORNCROFT
BROOKE AVE
ASHNEAL GDNS
PENKETH DR
INGLEBY DR
MOUNT PARK RD
BERMUDA HO
South Harrow
PARKFIELD RD
EASTCOTE RD
WHITBY RD
NARGRAVE RD
SCARSDALE RD
DUNCAN HO
WYVENHOE RD
KINGSLEY RD
A312 NORTHOLT RD
BEECHWOOD CIRC
BEECHWOOD GDNS
CRANE CL
VALENTINE CT
CORBIN'S LA
Liby
TORRINGTON CT
BRENDON GDNS
SACKVILLE CL
ARDEN CL
Orley Farm Sch
HA1
Pl Fld
SOUTH HILL AVE
OAKMEAD
Toll Gates
Bwg Gn
Roxeth Recn Gd
Pav
ORLEY FARM RD
HILL CL
RUNNELFIELD
SOUTH VALE
SOUTH HILL GR
Tenn Ct
Pav
GREVILLE CT
NEW RD
MONTAGUE FELL
SADDLERS MEWS
HUSSAIN CL
KIDMORE
PRIORY CL
Sudbury Hill Pl Flds
THE BOLTONS
A4005
1 HUTTON CL
2 BRASHER CL
3 HEMERY RD
4 TESSA SANDERSON WAY
5 HAMMOND CL
Welldon Park Schs
ROXETH GR
Harrow
Ealing
UB5
WOOD END RD
TYRELL CL
Sudbury Hill Harrow
HARTINGTON CL
CAVENDISH AVE
Sudbury Hill
TOWER BRIDGE MEWS
ROSEBANK AVE
FERNBANK AVE
Allot Gdns
WOOD END AVE
RAGLAN TERR
CADOGAN CL
STROUD GATE
Northolt Park
ACOCK GR
HALSBURY RD E
ROSS CL
CASSANDRA CL
Recn Gd
Tenn Cts
RUSSELL RD
KILLOWEN AVE
CLAUSON AVE
63
BANNISTER CL
Ealing Northern Sp Ctr
THOMAS HEWLETT HO 1
JEM PATERSON CT 2
GREENBANKS 3
LYDIA LODGE 4
WALTON CROFT 5
HORSENDEN AVE
HIGHFIELD AVE
HORSENDEN CRES
RIDDING LA
ALLEN CT
ROSEHILL GDNS
NORTHOLT GDNS
MORDEN GDNS
NORTHWOOD GDNS
GAINSBORO GDNS
UB6
GREENFORD RD
WOOD END GDNS
WOOD END WAY
MARY PETERS DR
BEDSER DR
LILIAN BOARD WAY
DIMMOCK DR
RAMSEY CL
LARWOOD CL
HENDREN CL
MATTHEWS CL
VERNON RISE
Schs
Pl Fld
READING RD
FLORISTON CT
MORTON CT
A4090
SHERIDAN TERR
MILDRED AVE
MERTON AVE
KEBLE CL
PILGRIMS CL
QUANTOCK CT
A4090
Allot Gdns
CAMBRIDGE AVE
MELVILLE AVE
BOURNE VIEW
Liby
WHITTON AVE W
CARLTON CL
NEWNHAM GDNS
NEWNHAM CL
ORCHARD CL
OLDFIELDS CIRC
GRAINGER CL
BAYSHILL RISE
Masts
ANSON TERR
BLENHEIM RD
LANCASTER RD
GIRTON RD
THE FAIRWAY
RAGLAN WAY
GLAMIS WAY
GIRTON CL
WADHAM GDNS
WORCESTER GDNS
CURREY RD
ROTHESAY AVE
HADDEN WAY
CLARE RD
RUGBY AVE
MALDEN AVE
OLDFIELD CL
OLDFIELD LANE N
WILLIAM PERKIN CT
BERKELEY AVE
ENNISMORE AVE
SHERWOOD AVE
BURWELL AVE
HORSENDEN LA N
LINDEN CRES
ELTON AVE
Horsenden Prim Sch
DREW GDNS
HAVERSHAM CT
SHEPPARD'S CT
ROBIN HOOD WAY
Tenn Cts
Bwg Gn
The Ballot Box (PH)
CONVILLE CRES
CASTLE RD
ORIEL WAY
CARR RD
CHERRY GDNS
Pl Fld
Recn Gd
HORSENDEN LANE S
Allot Gdns
Grand Union Canal Paddington Branch
AURIOL DR
Grand Union Canal Walk
Northolt Trad Est
Grand Union Canal Wlk
FAIRWAY DR
STATION APP
ALLINGTON CL
HILL RISE
BELLE VUE
Greenford
OLDFIELD LANE N
ROCKWARE AVE
Rockware Bsns Ctr
GREEN PARK WAY
Sears Ret Pk
TAUNTON RD
FAIRWAY DR
Aladdin Workspace
86
A4127
BIRKBECK AVE
HILLBECK WAY
STATION VIEW
UNEEDA DR
LEXHAM
Allot Gdns
HALIFAX RD
Perivale

North Wembley
Sudbury
WEMBLEY
HA0
HA9
UB6
Horsenden Hill
Vale Farm Sp Ctr
Vale Farm Sp Gd
Sudbury & Harrow Road
Sudbury Town
North Wembley
South Kenton
Wembley Commercial Ctr
East Lane Bsns Pk
Barham Park
Old Court (Mus & Liby)
Maybank Open Space
Grand Union Canal Paddington Branch
Grand Union Canal Walk
Alperton Cemy
Alperton Lower Sch
Alperton
Wembley High Tech Coll
Byron Court Sch
Sudbury Prim Sch
Barham Prim Sch
Horsenden Farm
King Edward VII Park
Preston Park Recn Gd
Rugby Fball Gds
Northwick Park
WATFORD RD
HARROW RD
EAST LA
BRIDGEWATER RD
EALING RD
WHITTON AVE E
SUDBURY COURT DR
A404
A4088
A4005
A4090
A4089
A4127
1 SIMPSON HO
2 AYRTON HO
3 WINTOUR HO
4 STEVENSON HO
BRIDGEWATER CT 1
SUNNYDENE GDNS 2
ATHERTON HTS 3
1 CRESSWELL
2 LOXLEY
3 KIRK H
4 BELL H
43
87
66
A B C D
1 2 3 4 5 6

Preston
44
88
65
WEMBLEY
Wembley Park
Tokyngton
HA9
HA0
Alperton
Forty Ave
Forty La
Bridge Rd
Empire Way
Wembley Park Dr
Park La
High Rd
Harrow Rd
Ealing Rd
South Way
Wembley Hill Rd
Preston Manor High Sch
Wembley Prim Sch
King Edward VII Park
Park Lane Sch
St Christopher's Sch
Wembley Arena
Wembley Stadium
Conference Centre
Exhibition Halls
Palace of Ind
Wembley Stadium Ind Est
Stadium Ret Pk
Olympic Ret Pk
The Junction Wembley Ret Pk
Wembley Park Bsns Ctr
Chalkhill Prim Sch
Wembley Central
Copland Sch
St Joseph's RC Schs
Elsley Prim Sch
Sherrans Farm Open Space
Oakington Manor Sch
Stonebridge Park
Alperton Com Sch
Lyon Park Jun & Inf Schs
Alperton Lower Sch
Northfield Ind Est
Abbey Manufacturing Est
Liberty Ctr
Pop In Bsns Ctr
Adams Bridge Bsns Ctr
Towers Bsns Pk
Cannon Trad Est
The Mirage Ctr
Metro Trad Ctr
A4088
A4089
A479
A404
B4557
A4140
A4005
A406

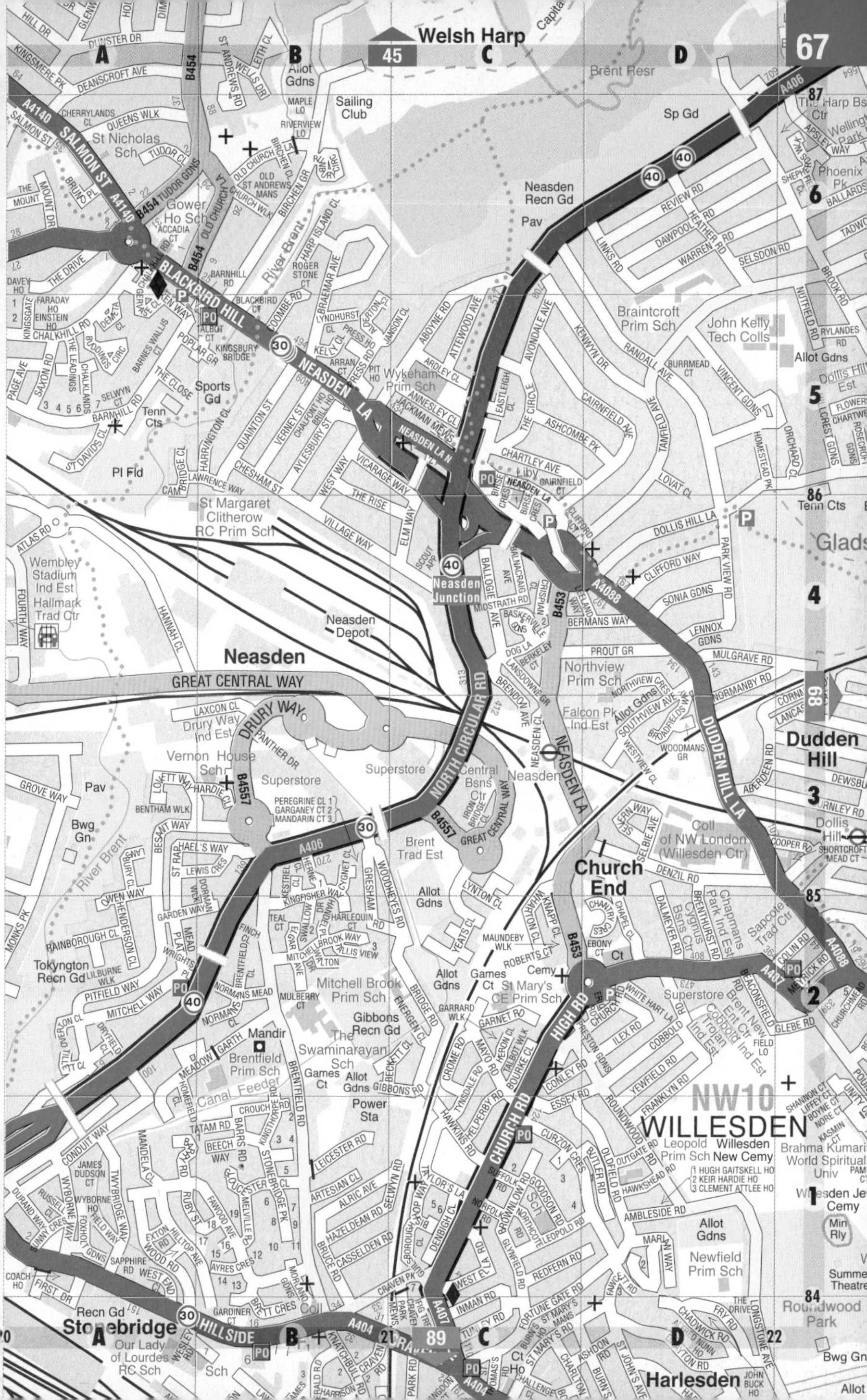
Welsh Harp
45
A
B
C
D
Brent Resr
Sp Gd
Allot Gdns
Sailing Club
St Nicholas Sch
Gower Ho Sch
SALMON ST
A4140
B454
BLACKBIRD HILL
NEASDEN LA
Neasden Recn Gd
Pav
Sports Gd
Tenn Cts
Pl Fld
St Margaret Clitherow RC Prim Sch
Wykeham Prim Sch
Braintcroft Prim Sch
John Kelly Tech Colls
Allot Gdns
Dollis Hill Est
Tenn Cts
Glads
Wembley Stadium Ind Est
Hallmark Trad Ctr
Neasden Depot
Neasden
Neasden Junction
GREAT CENTRAL WAY
DRURY WAY
Drury Way Ind Est
Vernon House Sch
Superstore
Central Bsns Ctr
Northview Prim Sch
Falcon Pk Ind Est
DUDDEN HILL LA
Dudden Hill
NORTH CIRCULAR RD
A406
A4088
B453
B4557
Pav
Bwg Gn
River Brent
Brent Trad Est
Church End
Coll of NW London (Willesden Ctr)
Tokyngton Recn Gd
Mitchell Brook Prim Sch
Gibbons Recn Gd
The Swaminarayan Sch
Mandir
Brentfield Prim Sch
Canal Feeder
Allot Gdns
Games Ct
Power Sta
Cemy
St Mary's CE Prim Sch
Superstore
Brent New Ent Ctr
Cobbold Ind Est
Trojan Ind Est
Chapmans Park Ind Est
Sapcote Trad Ctr
HIGH RD
CHURCH RD
NW10
WILLESDEN
Leopold Prim Sch
Willesden New Cemy
Brahma Kumari World Spiritual Univ
Willesden Jewish Cemy
Allot Gdns
Newfield Prim Sch
Summer Theatre
Roundwood Park
Bwg Gn
Recn Gd
Stonebridge
HILLSIDE
Our Lady of Lourdes RC Sch
Sch
Coll
A404
A407
89
Harlesden
Allot
1 HUGH GAITSKELL HO
2 KEIR HARDIE HO
3 CLEMENT ATTLEE HO
6
5
4
3
2
1
87
86
85
84
21
22
68
40
30

A
B
C
D
46
90
NW2
NW10
Staples Corner (West)
Staples Corner Ret Pk
Staples Corner Bsns Pk
London Group Bsns Pk
The Harp Bsns Ctr
Wellington Park Est
The Apsley Ctr
Phoenix Pk
Atlas Bsns Ctr
Oxgate Ctr
Ind Est
The Edge Bsns Ctr
Humber Trad Est
Millennium Bsns Ctr
Superstores
Brent Sidings
Hendon Fball Gd
Claremont Prim Sch
Clitterhouse Pl Flds
Our Lady of Grace RC Inf Sch
Donoghue Bsns Pk
John Kelly Tech Colls
Allot Gdns
Dollis Hill Est
Tenn Cts
Bwg Gn
Gladstone Park
Dollis Hill
Pl Fld
Games Ct
Mora Prim Sch
Cricklewood
Broadway Ret Pk
Superstore
Liby
Dudden Hill
Gladstone Park Sch
Ind Est
Anson Prim Sch
Coll of N W London (Willesden Ctr)
Sapcote Trad Ctr
Chapmans Park Ind Est
Willesden Green
Schs
Liby & Mus
Coll
Crkt Gd
Pav
WILLESDEN
Willesden New Cemy
Brahma Kumaris World Spiritual Univ
Willesden Jewish Cemy
Min Rly
The Willesden Com
Summer Theatre
Newfield Prim Sch
Roundwood Park
Capital City Acad
Queens Park Com Sch
Malorees Jun & Inf Schs
Brondesbury
Willesden
EDGWARE RD
A5
A406
A407
A4003
A4088
CRICKLEWOOD BROADWAY
CHICHELE RD
WALM LA
WILLESDEN LA
HIGH RD
DUDDEN HILL LA
DOLLIS HILL LA
DOLLIS HILL AVE
GLADSTONE PARK GDNS
OXGATE GDNS
COLES GREEN RD
BROOK RD
CREST RD
TADWORTH RD
BALLARDS RD
SELSDON RD
PADDOCK RD
WATERLOO RD
KENDAL RD
GEARY RD
HELENA RD
FLEETWOOD RD
ELLESMERE RD
DEWSBURY RD
BURNLEY RD
CULLINGWORTH RD
SHERRICK GREEN RD
MELROSE AVE
ANSON RD
OLIVE RD
IVY RD
MORA RD
WALM LA
ST GABRIEL'S RD
TEIGNMOUTH RD
DARTMOUTH RD
CHATSWORTH ROAD
BRONDESBURY PARK
STATION PAR
ST PAUL'S AVENUE
CHAPTER RD
DEACON RD
HARLESDEN RD
DONNINGTON RD
STAVERTON ROAD
SIDMOUTH ROAD
CHAMBERS LANE
MOUNT PLEASANT RD
ALEXANDER AVE
DOBREE AVE
ROWDON AVE
KINGS RD
PARKFIELD RD
PARK AVE N
PARK AVE
CHURCHILL RD
SANDRINGHAM RD
CLAREMONT RD
BRENT TERR
CLITTERHOUSE RD
CLITTERHOUSE CRES
GERON WAY
CONWAY RD
MOUNT RD
ROMAN RD
TEMPLE RD
NEWTON RD
WOTTON RD
CHILTERN GDNS
COTSWOLD GDNS
KEYES RD
HEBER RD
BLACKSTONE RD
DAWSON RD
WREN AVE
SNEYD RD
DICEY AVE
OMAN AVE
JEYMER AVE
GRIFFIN CL
ELVIS RD
LENNON RD
CRANHURST RD
CHANDOS RD
RIFFEL RD
BLENHEIM GDNS
LYDFORD RD
87
86
85
84
22
23
6
5
4
3
2
1
67

A
B
C
D
47
Basing Hill Park
Child's Hill Park
Golders Hill Park
Leg of Mutton Pond
West Heath
Child's Hill
WEST HEATH RD
NW3
NW2
NW6
West Hampstead
Hampstead Cemy
Fortune Green
FINCHLEY RD
HENDON WAY
CRICKLEWOOD LA
FORTUNE GREEN RD
NORTH END WAY
SHOOT-UP HILL
WILLESDEN LA
WEST END LA
IVERSON RD
BELSIZE RD
ABBEY RD
Brondesbury
HAMPSTEAD
South Hampstead
Kilburn
Kilburn Grange Park
West Hampstead Thameslink
Fenton House
King's Coll London
St Margaret's Sch
Beckford Prim Sch
Hampstead Sch
Barnet
Camden
Brent
70
91

48
69
229
92
230

Waterlow Park
St Joseph's RC Prim Sch
Highgate Cemy
The Whittington
Archway
Upper Holloway
N19
Highgate Cemy
Brookfield Prim Sch
HOLLY LODGE GDNS
OAKESHOTT AVE
MAKEPEACE AVE
LANGBOURNE AVE
BROMWICH AVE
HIGHGATE WEST HILL
SWAIN'S LA
MILLFIELD PL
HIGHGATE HILL
DARTMOUTH PARK HILL
JUNCTION RD
HOLLOWAY RD
ST JOHN'S GR
Whittington Park
Yerbury Prim Sch
N6
Dartmouth Park
La Saint Union RC Sec Sch
Tenn Cts
Bwg Gn
William Ellis Sch
Parliament Hill Sch
Athletics Gd
Sw Pool
Gospel Oak
Tufnell Park Hall
Sp Gd
Tufnell Park
TUFNELL PARK RD
ST GEORGE'S AVE
N7
Acland Burghley Sch
DARTMOUTH PARK RD
CHETWYND RD
SPENCER RISE
CHURCHILL RD
HIGHGATE RD
GORDON HOUSE RD
FORTESS RD
BRECKNOCK RD
Tufnell Park Prim Sch
Holloway Sch
CAMDEN RD
HILLDROP RD
NW5
City Farm
Carlton Prim Sch
THE INTERCHANGE
Kentish Town
KENTISH TOWN RD
LEIGHTON RD
TORRIANO AVE
CAMDEN PARK RD
YORK WAY
Kentish Town West
MALDEN RD
PRINCE OF WALES RD
CASTLE RD
HAWLEY RD
CHALK FARM RD
Roundhouse Theatre
Chalk Farm
The Camden Sch for Girls
CAMDEN SQ
AGAR GR
CAMDEN TOWN
NW1
Superstore
ROYAL COLLEGE ST
ST PANCRAS WAY
N1
Britannia Junction
Camden Mkt
Fball Gd
Caledonian Park
49
93
231
72
84
85
86
87
30
A
B
C
D
1
2
3
4
5
6

A
B
C
D
50
STROUD GREEN RD
B150
A503
Finsbury Park
SEVEN SISTERS RD
STATION PL
ROCK ST
A1201
N4
BLACKSTOCK RD
B105
N19
A103
HORNSEY RD
HOLLOWAY RD
A1
TOLLINGTON PK
TOLLINGTON RD
ISLEDON RD
TUFNELL PARK RD
PARKHURST RD
CAMDEN RD
A503
A5203
Nags Head
Gillespie Park
Arsenal
Highbury
Emirates (Arsenal FC)
Drayton Park
QUEENSLAND RD
HIGHBURY PK
HIGHBURY GR
N5
Tenn Cts
Highbury Fields
Highbury Pool
ISLINGTON
Highbury & Islington
Highbury Corner
A1201
A1200
UPPER STREET
CANONBURY RD
ESSEX RD
A104
LIVERPOOL RD
B515
N1
N7
Holloway Road
HM Prison
Lower Holloway
HILLMARTON RD
CALEDONIAN RD
Caledonian Road
Caledonian Park
Hall of Residence
MARKET RD
Fball Gd
YORK WAY
A5200
Barnsbury
Acorn Production Ctr
Caledonian Road & Barnsbury
Copenhagen Junction
Paradise Park
BARNSBURY RD
BARNSBURY PK
Liby
Sch
Univ
Coll
PO
30
71
233
94
234
84
85
86
87
1
2
3
4
5
6

A
B
C
D
51
STOKE NEWINGTON
Abney Park Cemy
MANOR RD
LORDSHIP PK
BROWNSWOOD RD
N4
N16
Clissold Park
Capital Ring
Tenn Cts
Bwg Gn
GREEN LANES
STOKE NEWINGTON CHURCH ST
STOKE NEWINGTON HIGH ST
STOKE NEWINGTON RD
RECTORY RD
Stoke Newington
Rectory Road
Shacklewell
N5
Frogmore Ind Est
Aberdeen Ctr
Canonbury
ST PAUL'S RD
NEWINGTON GREEN RD
ALBION RD
BALLS POND RD
Dalston Kingsland
KINGSLAND HIGH ST
Dalston Jct
Dalston
Kingsland
The Petchey Acad
Ridley
E8
ESSEX RD
SOUTHGATE RD
KINGSLAND RD
QUEENSBRIDGE RD
De Beauvoir Town
N1
Essex Road
Kingsland Basin
235
95
33
34
74
87
86
85
84
6
5
4
3
2
1
A10
A105
A104
A1199
A1200
A1207
B104
B105
B108
B111
B102

74
Upper Clapton
A
B
52
C
D
Lee Valley Riding Ctr
Pl Fld
Leyton Marshes
River Lea or Lee
Capital Ring
Stoke Newington
Keir Hardie Est
Jessam Ave
Moresby Rd
Grosvenor Ho
Wigan Ho
Warwick Gr
Cazenove Rd
Upper Clapton Rd
A107
Dehavilland Studios
Riverside Cl
Lea Valley Ice Ctr
A104
Morley Ho
Fountayne Rd
Muston Rd
Sach Rd
Mount Pleasant Hill
Grosvenor Way
Theydon Rd
Northwold Rd
B111
Southwold Rd
Recn Gd
Lea Bridge Rd
Lea Bridge
Clapton
Gunton Rd
Cleveleys Rd
Casimir Rd
N16
Rectory Rd
Ickburgh Rd
Brooke Rd
Nature Reserve
E5
Lea Valley Wlk
Lea Bridge
Rectory Road
Evering Rd
Kenninghall Rd
Walsingham Rd
Mandeville Prim Sch
Thornby Rd
Fletching Rd
Millfields Rd
Manse Rd
Shacklewell
Downs Rd
Lower Clapton Rd
Cricketfield Rd
Chatsworth Rd
Lockhurst St
Rushmore Rd
Shacklewell Rd
Hackney Downs
Pav
Bwg Gn
Tenn Cts
Clapton Girls Tec Coll
Glenarm Rd
Lower Clapton
Clapton Park
Blurton Rd
Mossbourne Com Acad
Downs Park Rd
The Petchey Acad
Pembury Rd
Clifden Rd
Homerton University
Homerton Gr
Homerton Row
Homerton High St
A106
Dalston La
Amhurst Rd
Sutton House
Urswick Rd
A102
Hackney Downs
Hackney Central
Morning La
Superstore
Wick Rd
Homerton
Graham Rd
A1207
Dalston
Queensbridge Rd
B108
E8
HACKNEY
Mare St
Kenton Rd
B113
Cassland Rd
Homerton
E9
Well Street Common
Mapledene Est
London Fields
Pl Flds
Well St
Victoria Park Rd
96
A
B
C
D
Royal Gate

A
B
C
D
53
E10
Sybourn Inf Sch Annexe
The Lammas Sch
Willow Brook Prim Sch
Fairways Bsns Pk
St Joseph's RC Inf Sch
Leyton Bsns Ctr
Orient Ind Pk
Pl Flds
CHURCH RD
HIGH ROAD LEYTON
Running Track
ORIENT WAY
Waltham Forest
Hackney
Allot Gdns
Leyton Orient Fball Gd
Bndstd
RUCKHOLT RD
MARKET PAVILION
New Spitalfields Market
Hackney Marsh
Recn Gds
Lea Valley Wlk
E5
COW BRIDGE
1 ASHBOURNE CT
2 MELBORNE CT
3 KEDELSTON CT
4 MONSAL CT
1 IRONSIDE HO
2 EDRED HO
3 ETHELBERT HO
4 TEMPLEMEAD HO
5 RUNNYMEDE HO
6 FAIRMEAD HO
7 KINGSMEAD HO
8 EDWY HO
9 ATHELSTAN HO
10 WATERMEAD HO
11 MALMSMEAD HO
12 ASHMEAD HO
13 RIVERMEAD HO
River Lee Navigation Hackney Cut
River Lea or Lee
Kingsmead Prim Sch
HOMERTON RD
EASTWAY
Lee Valley Sp Ctr
Tenn Cts
Temple Mills
76
E9
1 ADELAIDE CT
2 CASTLE CL
3 BRENTON CT
4 TYNTE CT
5 SALISBURY CT
6 HILLYFIELD CL
7 BERESFORD CT
Fball Gds
EAST CROSS ROUTE
1 SOUTHMOOR WAY
2 WINDSOR WHARF
Cycle Circuit
Depot
Hackney Stadium
Gainsborough Prim Sch
Hackney Wick
E15
WICK RD
CHAPMAN RD
East Cross Ctr
Tower Hamlets
Newham
CARPENTER'S RD
WHITE POST LA
Hamlet Ind Est
Carpenters Bsns Pk
Omega Works
Bow Ind Pk
Victoria Park Ind Ctr
Tenn Cts
Bwg Gn
Sp Gd
Victoria Park
Waterworks River
City Mill River
97
Swan Wharf
Crown Wharf
Stratford Marsh
Victoria Fntn
Gunmakers Gate

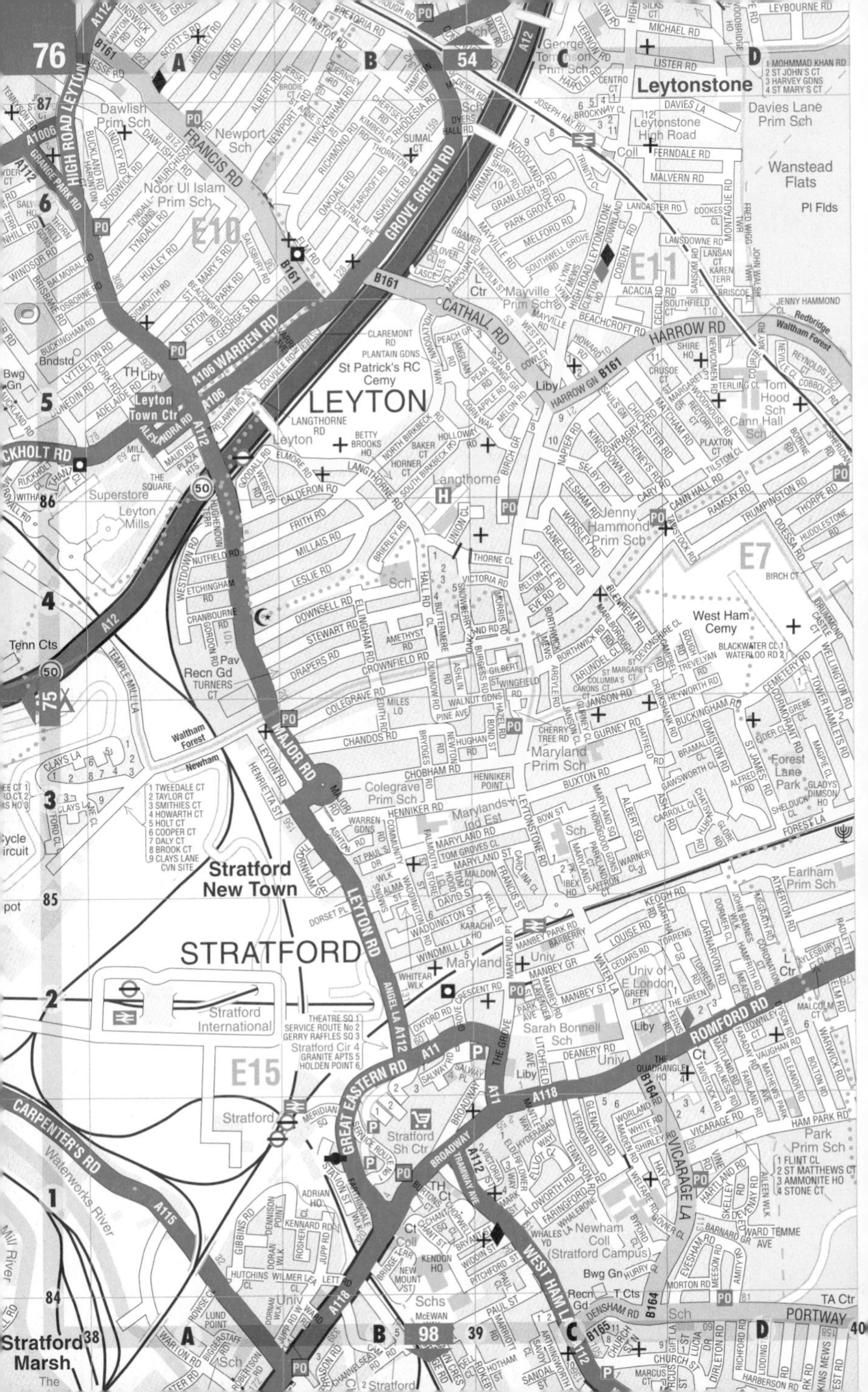

76
54
98
A
B
C
D
Leytonstone
LEYTON
STRATFORD
Stratford New Town
E10
E11
E7
E15
HIGH ROAD LEYTON
GROVE GREEN RD
FRANCIS RD
A106 WARREN RD
CATHALL RD
HARROW RD
HARROW GN B161
CANN HALL RD
LEYTON RD
MAJOR RD
ROMFORD RD
GREAT EASTERN RD
BROADWAY
WEST HAM LA
VICARAGE LA
CARPENTER'S RD
PORTWAY
LEYTONSTONE RD
ANGEL LA A112
THE GROVE
DENSHAM RD
Dawlish Prim Sch
Newport Sch
Noor Ul Islam Prim Sch
Leyton Town Ctr
Superstore
Leyton Mills
St Patrick's RC Cemy
Langthorne
Mayville Prim Sch
Davies Lane Prim Sch
Leytonstone High Road
Wanstead Flats
Pl Flds
George Tomlinson Prim Sch
Tom Hood Sch
Cann Hall Sch
Jenny Hammond Prim Sch
West Ham Cemy
Forest Lane Park
Earlham Prim Sch
Maryland Prim Sch
Marylands Ind Est
Colegrave Prim Sch
Maryland
Univ of E London
Sarah Bonnell Sch
Stratford International
Stratford Sh Ctr
Stratford
Newham Coll (Stratford Campus)
Ham Park Rd
Park Prim Sch
Recn Gd
Tenn Cts
Waltham Forest
Newham
Waterworks River
Stratford Marsh
1 MOHAMMAD KHAN RD
2 ST JOHN'S CT
3 HARVEY GDNS
4 ST MARY'S CT
1 TWEEDALE CT
2 TAYLOR CT
3 SMITHIES CT
4 HOWARTH CT
5 HOLT CT
6 COOPER CT
7 DALY CT
8 BROOK CT
9 CLAYS LANE CVN SITE
THEATRE SQ 1
SERVICE ROUTE No 2
GERRY RAFFLES SQ 3
Stratford Cir 4
GRANITE APTS 5
HOLDEN POINT 6
1 FLINT CL
2 ST MATTHEWS CT
3 AMMONITE HO
4 STONE CT
6
5
4
3
2
1
87
86
85
84
38
39
40

Wood
Boat House
Aldersbrook Prim Sch
55
A
B
C
D
Allot Gdns
87
6
5
4
3
2
1
84
86
85
E12
E7
Aldersbrook
Wanstead Flats
Centenary Walk
Crem
City of
Manor Park
The Manor Park Cemy & Crem
Redbridge Horse Ride
Manor Park
Wanstead Park
Godwin Sch
Woodgrange Sch
Kubrick Bsns Est
Forest Gate
Woodgrange Park
Woodgrange Park Cemy
78
Monega Sch
Plashet
Plashet Jewish Cemy
William Davies Sch
Tenn Cts
Plashet Park
East Ham Meml
Bwg Gn
St Angela's Sch
Stratford Sch
Elmhurst Sch
Upton
West Ham Park
St Bonaventure's Sch
Bndstd
Fball Gd
Azhar Acad
Schs
Liby
Upton Park
99
40
41
42
A114
A116
A117
A118
B161
B165
B167
B109
CENTRE RD
WOODFORD RD
WOODGRANGE RD
ALDERSBROOK RD
FOREST DR
STATION RD
ROMFORD RD
GREEN ST
KATHERINE RD
UPTON LA
PLASHET RD
PLASHET GR
DAMES RD
NORTHUMBERLAND AVE
WOODLANDS AVE
LAKE HOUSE RD
BELGRAVE RD
WINDSOR RD
RICHMOND WAY
BLAKE HALL CRES
PARK RD
INGATESTONE RD
DOVER RD
HERONGATE RD
WANSTEAD PARK AVE
CLAVERING RD
SUNDERLAND WAY
WESTMORLAND CL
CAPEL RD
HAMPTON RD
OSBORNE RD
CLAREMONT RD
WINDSOR RD
BALMORAL RD
RIDLEY RD
TYLNEY RD
LATIMER RD
CRANMER RD
SEBERT RD
DURHAM RD
CLARENCE RD
SALISBURY RD
QUEENSBERRY PL
EARLHAM GR
SPROWSTON MEWS
SPROWSTON RD
VALE RD
GLENPARKE RD
WHYTEVILLE RD
STUDLEY RD
KITCHENER RD
GROSVENOR RD
CHAUCER RD
GOWER RD
DUNBAR RD
SKELTON RD
ST GEORGE'S RD
UPTON PARK RD
BOLEYN RD
NEVILLE RD
HENDERSON RD
SHERRARD RD
HALLEY RD
MONEGA RD
STRONE RD
BRISTOL RD
LINCOLN RD
STAFFORD RD
DERBY RD
RUTLAND RD
CHESTER RD
DORSET RD
CROMWELL RD
WOODSTOCK RD
SHAFTESBURY RD
ELIZABETH RD
GRANGEWOOD ST
MILTON AVE
KNOX RD
MARGERY PARK RD
YORK RD
STORK RD
UPTON AVE
LANCASTER RD
KINGSLEY RD
Upton Park

56
100
A
B
C
D
6
5
4
3
2
1
87
86
85
84
42
43
44
Allot Gdns
Redbridge
Newham
Ilford
City of London Cemy
Crem
Alders Brook
Manor Park
Maytime Sch
Ilford Interchange
ILFORD
IG1
Ilford
The Exchange
Park Sch
Coll
Sch
A123
A118
A406
A116
A117
A124
B165
B109
FOREST DR
STATION RD
ROMFORD RD
NORTH CIRCULAR RD
ILFORD HILL
ILFORD LA
LITTLE ILFORD LA
HIGH ST N
EAST AVE
BROWNING RD
PLASHET GR
ABBEY RD
LONDON RD
HIGHBRIDGE RD
Barking Flyover
E12
E6
IG11
Little Ilford
Little Ilford Park
Wks
Rec Gd
Allot Gdns
Pl Fld
Uphall Prim Sch
Plashet
Plashet Jewish Cemy
Plashet Park
East Ham Meml
Plashet Sch
Tenn Cts
Bwg Gn
Monega Sch
Essex Prim Sch
Kensington Prim Sch
Avenue Prim Sch
Prim Sch
St Mary's Sch
Urdgrange Park Cemy
Sports Gd
Riverside Works
Pacific Wharf
River Roding
Superstore
The Willows
Recn Gd
East Ham
Liby & Mus
The Birches
Barking & Dagenham
Newham

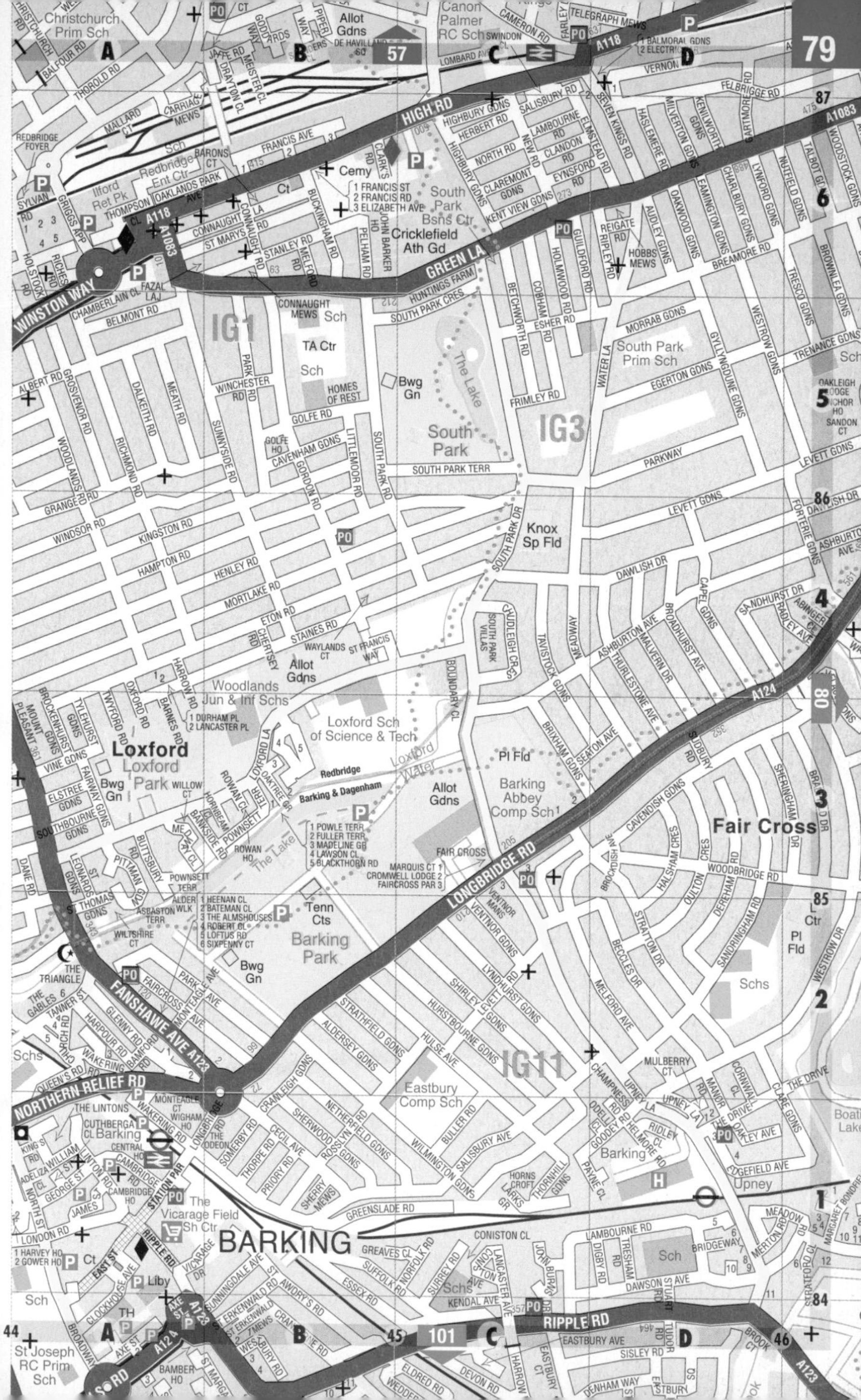
A
B
C
D
57
87
86
85
84
6
5
4
3
2
1
44
45
46
101
80
Christchurch Prim Sch
Canon Palmer RC Sch
Allot Gdns
TELEGRAPH MEWS
CAMERON RD
SWINDON CL
LOMBARD AVE
BALMORAL GDNS
ELECTRIC
VERNON
FELBRIGGE RD
BALFOUR RD
THOROLD RD
JAFFE RD
DRAYTON CL
MEISTER CL
DE HAVILLAND
MALLARD CT
CARRIAGE MEWS
REDBRIDGE FOYER
HIGH RD
HIGHBURY GDNS
SALISBURY RD
SEVEN KINGS RD
HASLEMERE RD
MILVERTON GDNS
KENILWORTH GDNS
GARTMORE RD
A1083
A118
FRANCIS AVE
BARONS CT
Redbridge Ent Ctr
Ilford Ret Pk
OAKLANDS PARK AVE
THOMPSON
SYLVAN
GRIGGS APP
Sch
Cemy
Ct
HERBERT RD
NORTH RD
NEW RD
LAMBOURNE RD
CLANDON RD
EYNSFORD RD
ELMSTEAD RD
CLAREMONT GDNS
KENT VIEW GDNS
South Park Bsns Ctr
1 FRANCIS ST
2 FRANCIS RD
3 ELIZABETH AVE
CONNAUGHT LA
CONNAUGHT RD
ST MARYS RD
STANLEY RD
BUCKINGHAM RD
MELFORD RD
PELHAM RD
JOHN BARKER HO
Cricklefield Ath Gd
GREEN LA
HUNTINGS FARM
SOUTH PARK CRES
REIGATE RD
RIPLEY RD
HOBBS MEWS
AUDLEY GDNS
OAKWOOD GDNS
LEAMINGTON GDNS
CHARLBURY GDNS
LYNFORD GDNS
NUTFIELD GDNS
TALBOT GDNS
WOODSTOCK GDNS
BREAMORE RD
BROWNLEA GDNS
TRESCO GDNS
WESTROW GDNS
HOLMWOOD RD
GUILDFORD RD
BETCHWORTH RD
COBHAM RD
ESHER RD
WINSTON WAY
FAZAL LAJ
CHAMBERLAIN CL
BELMONT RD
HOLSTOCK RD
RICHES RD
CONNAUGHT MEWS
IG1
TA Ctr
HOMES OF REST
Bwg Gn
The Lake
South Park
MORRAB GDNS
South Park Prim Sch
GYLLYNGDUNE GDNS
EGERTON GDNS
TRENANCE GDNS
OAKLEIGH LODGE
SANDON CT
FRIMLEY RD
IG3
WATER LA
PARKWAY
LEVETT GDNS
ALBERT RD
GROSVENOR RD
DALKEITH RD
MEATH RD
WINCHESTER RD
PARK RD
SUNNYSIDE RD
GOLFE RD
GOLFE HO
CAVENHAM GDNS
GORDON RD
LITTLEMOOR RD
SOUTH PARK RD
SOUTH PARK TERR
WOODLANDS RD
RICHMOND RD
GRANGE RD
WINDSOR RD
KINGSTON RD
HAMPTON RD
HENLEY RD
MORTLAKE RD
ETON RD
STAINES RD
CHERTSEY RD
WAYLANDS CT
ST FRANCIS WAY
Knox Sp Fld
SOUTH PARK DR
DAWLISH DR
FORTERIE GDNS
ASHBURTON AVE
SANDHURST DR
ABINGER CL
RADLEY AVE
CAPEL GDNS
BROADHURST AVE
MALVERN DR
THURLESTONE AVE
MEADWAY
TAVISTOCK GDNS
CHUDLEIGH CRES
SOUTH PARK VILLAS
BOUNDARY CL
Allot Gdns
HARROW RD
Woodlands Jun & Inf Schs
BARNES RD
1 DURHAM PL
2 LANCASTER PL
OXFORD RD
TWYFORD RD
TYLEHURST GDNS
BROCKENHURST GDNS
MOUNT PLEASANT
Loxford
Loxford Park
Bwg Gn
VINE GDNS
FAIRWAY GDNS
ELSTREE GDNS
SOUTHBOURNE GDNS
Loxford Sch of Science & Tech
LOXFORD LA
Loxford Water
Redbridge
Barking & Dagenham
ROWAN CL
WILLOW CT
HORNBEAM
BANKSIDE RD
POWNSETT TERR
OAKTREE GR
1 POWLE TERR
2 FULLER TERR
3 MADELINE GR
4 LAWSON CL
5 BLACKTHORN RD
Allot Gdns
FAIR CROSS
MARQUIS CT 1
CROMWELL LODGE 2
FAIRCROSS PAR 3
Pl Fld
Barking Abbey Comp Sch
BRIXHAM GDNS
SEATON AVE
A124
SUDBURY RD
CAVENDISH GDNS
SHERINGHAM DR
Fair Cross
WOODBRIDGE RD
BROCKDISH AVE
HALSHAM CRES
OULTON CRES
DERHAM RD
SANDRINGHAM RD
WESTROW DR
L Ctr
Pl Fld
Schs
LONGBRIDGE RD
VENTNOR MANS
VENTNOR GDNS
STRATTON DR
BECCLES DR
MELFORD AVE
LYNDHURST GDNS
LEVETT RD
SHIRLEY GDNS
HURSTBOURNE GDNS
HULSE AVE
STRATHFIELD GDNS
ALDERSEY GDNS
IG11
Eastbury Comp Sch
MULBERRY CT
CORNWALL CL
CLARE GDNS
THE DRIVE
MANOR RD
UPNEY LA
CHAMPNESS RD
ODELL CL
GOODEY RD
HELMORE RD
RIDLEY CL
Barking
LEY AVE
EDGEFIELD AVE
Upney
Boating Lakes
DANE RD
ST LEONARDS GDNS
PITTMAN GDNS
BUTTSBURY RD
ROWAN HO
The Lake
1 HEENAN CL
2 BATEMAN CL
3 THE ALMSHOUSES
4 ROBERT CL
5 LOFTUS RD
6 SIXPENNY CT
ALDER WLK
ST THOMAS GDNS
ASBASTON TERR
WILTSHIRE CT
Tenn Cts
Barking Park
Bwg Gn
THE TRIANGLE
THE GABLES
TANNER ST
HARPOUR RD
GLENNY RD
FAIRCROSS AVE
PARK AVE
MONTEAGLE AVE
FANSHAWE AVE A123
CHURCH RD
WAKERING RD
BAMFORD RD
QUEEN'S RD
NORTHERN RELIEF RD
LONGBRIDGE
Schs
THE LINTONS
MONTEAGLE CT
WIGHAM HO
CUTHBERGA CL
Barking
CENTRAL HO
CAMBRIDGE RD
KING'S RD
ADELIZA
WILLIAM ST
LINTON RD
GEORGE ST
NORTH ST
ST JAMES
CAMBRIDGE HO
STATION PAR
THE ODEON
SOMERBY RD
THORPE RD
CECIL AVE
PRIORY RD
CRANLEIGH GDNS
SHERWOOD GDNS
ROSSLYN RD
NETHERFIELD GDNS
SHERRY MEWS
WILMINGTON GDNS
BULLER RD
SALISBURY AVE
HORNS CROFT
LARKS GR
THORNHILL GDNS
PAYNE CL
H
The Vicarage Field Sh Ctr
BARKING
GREENSLADE RD
LONDON RD
1 HARVEY HO
2 GOWER HO
Ct
EAST ST
RIPPLE RD
VICARAGE DR
SUNNINGDALE AVE
ST ERKENWALD RD
ST AWDRY'S RD
GREAVES CL
SUFFOLK RD
NORFOLK RD
ESSEX RD
SURREY RD
CONISTON CL
Schs
KENDAL AVE
LANCASTER AVE
JOHN BURNS DR
LAMBOURNE RD
DIGBY RD
TRESHAM RD
Sch
DAWSON AVE
STUART RD
BRIDGEWAY
MERTON RD
MEADOW RD
STRATFORD CL
MARGARET BONDFIELD AVE
Liby
CLOCKHOUSE AVE
Sch
TH
AXE ST
A123
A124
St Joseph RC Prim Sch
BAMBER HO
ST ERKENWALD MEWS
WESTBURY RD
CRANLEY RD
EASTBURY AVE
SISLEY RD
TUDOR RD
EASTBURY CT
HARROW RD
DEVON RD
ELDRED RD
WEDDERBURN RD
DENHAM WAY
EASTBURY
BROOK CT
RIPPLE RD

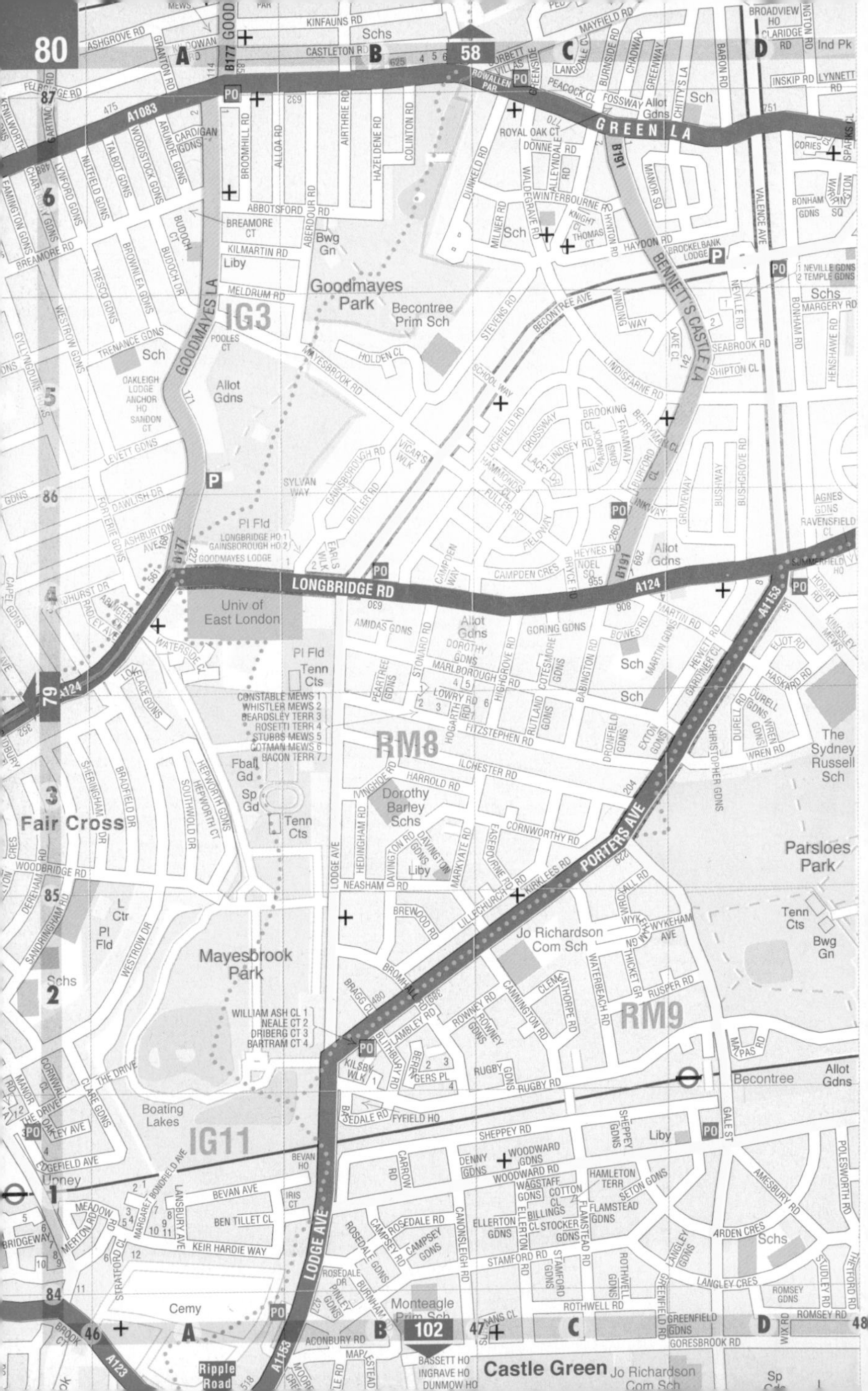

Goodmayes Park
Becontree Prim Sch
IG3
GREEN LA
LONGBRIDGE RD
Univ of East London
RM8
Dorothy Barley Schs
Fair Cross
Mayesbrook Park
Boating Lakes
IG11
RM9
PORTERS AVE
LODGE AVE
Jo Richardson Com Sch
Parsloes Park
The Sydney Russell Sch
Becontree
Monteagle Prim Sch
Castle Green
Ripple Road
58
79
102

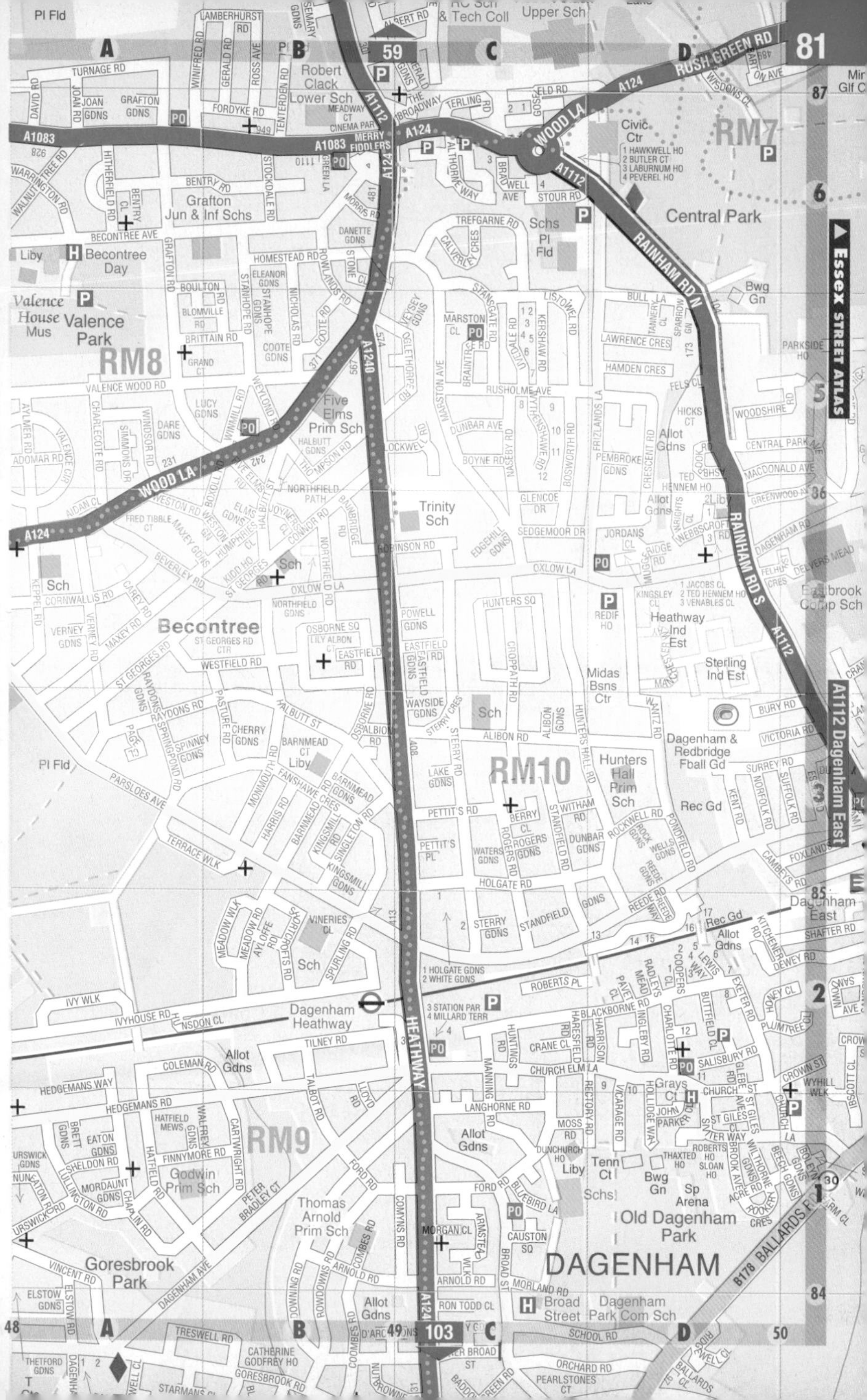

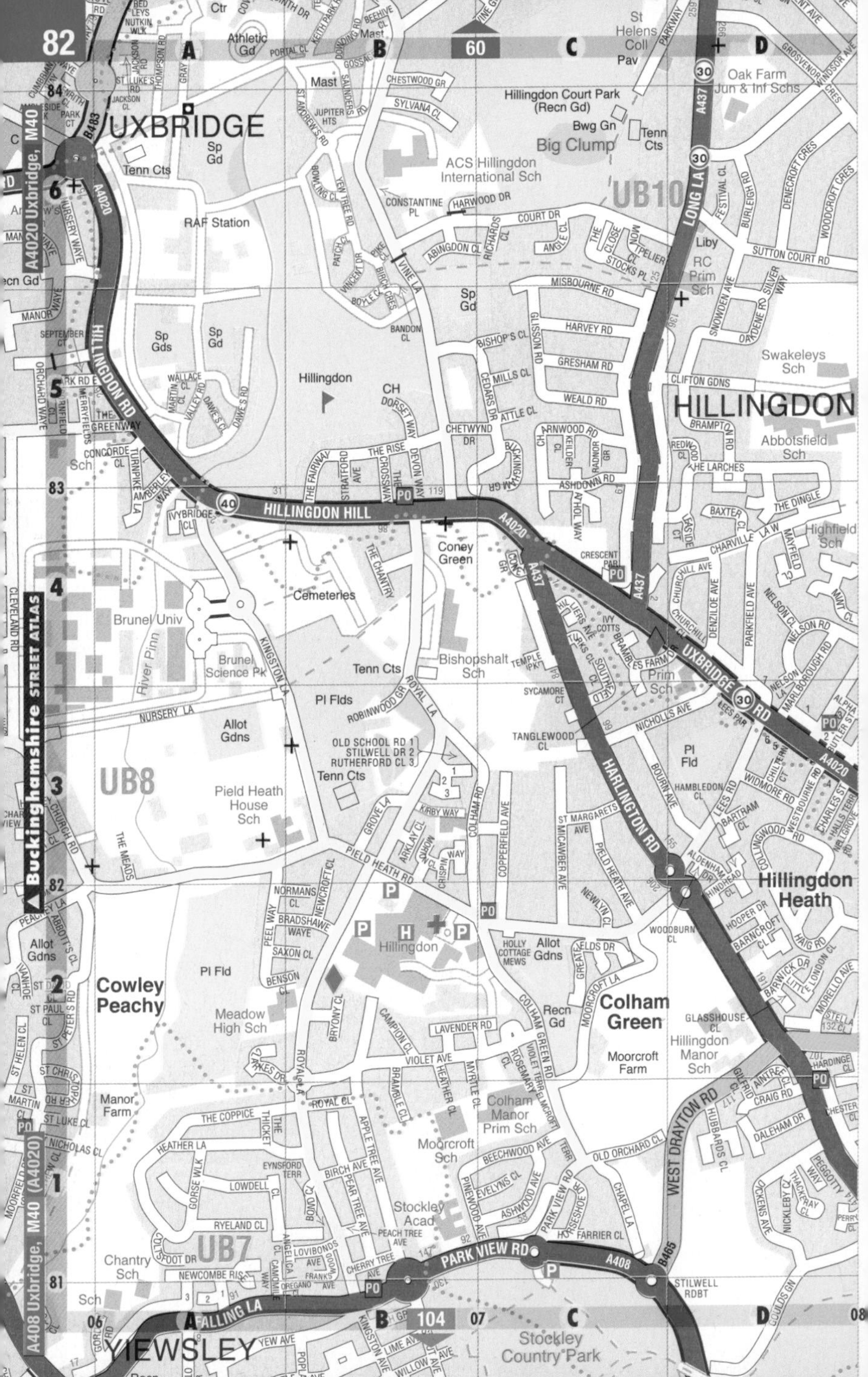
UXBRIDGE
HILLINGDON
Hillingdon Heath
Colham Green
Cowley Peachy
YIEWSLEY
UB10
UB8
UB7
HILLINGDON HILL
HILLINGDON RD
UXBRIDGE RD
HARLINGTON RD
LONG LA
PARK VIEW RD
FALLING LA
WEST DRAYTON RD
Brunel Univ
Brunel Science Pk
Cemeteries
Hillingdon
Stockley Country Park
A4020 Uxbridge, M40
A408 Uxbridge, M40 (A4020)
Buckinghamshire STREET ATLAS

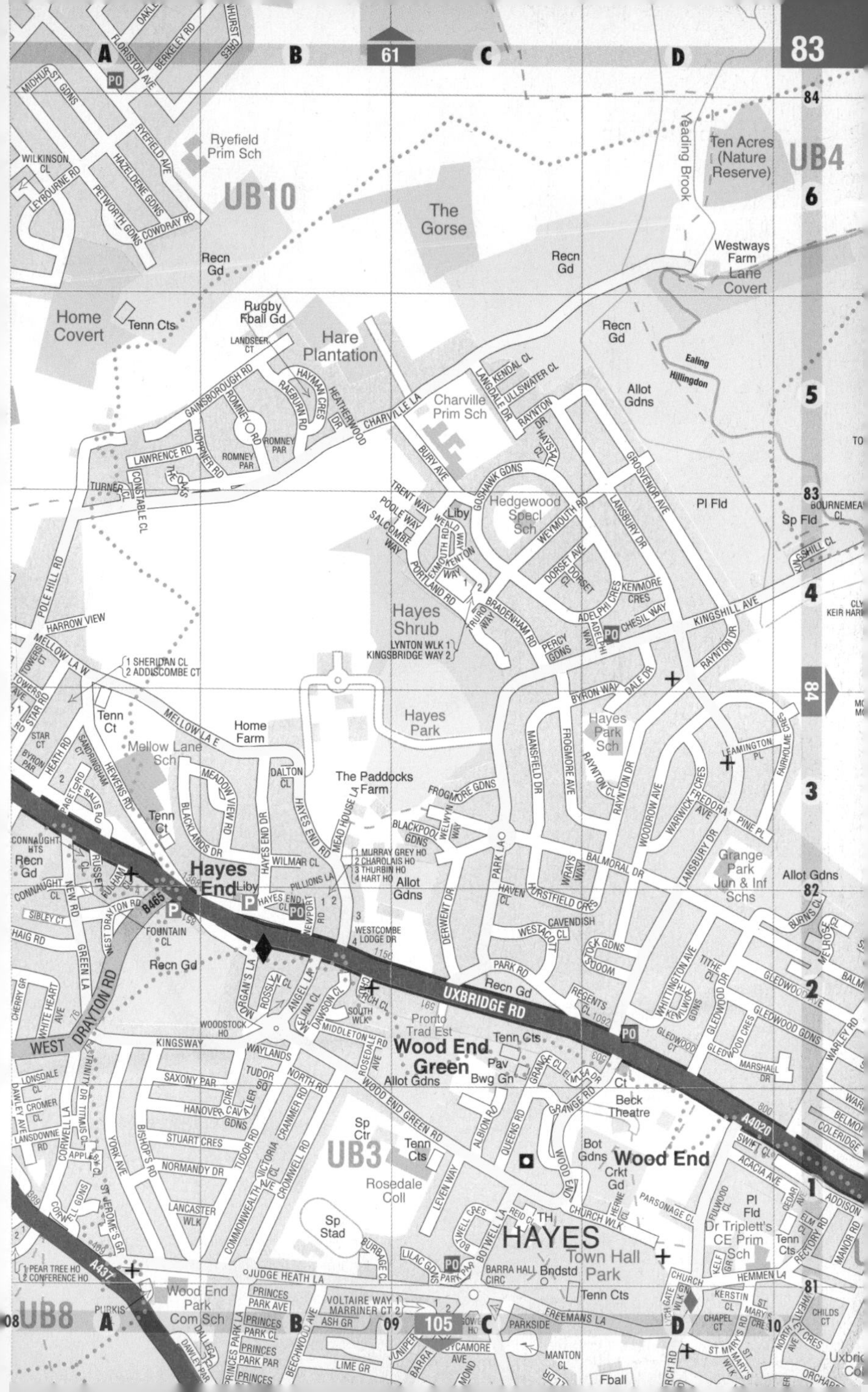
83
A
B
61
C
D
84
UB4
6
5
4
3
2
1
83
82
81
84
105
08
09
10
UB10
UB3
UB8
Ryefield Prim Sch
The Gorse
Ten Acres (Nature Reserve)
Yeading Brook
Westways Farm Lane Covert
Recn Gd
Home Covert
Tenn Cts
Rugby Fball Gd
Hare Plantation
Ealing
Hillingdon
Allot Gdns
Charville Prim Sch
Hedgewood Specl Sch
Liby
Pl Fld
Sp Fld
Hayes Shrub
LYNTON WLK 1
KINGSBRIDGE WAY 2
1 SHERIDAN CL
2 ADDISCOMBE CT
Hayes Park
Hayes Park Sch
Home Farm
Mellow Lane Sch
Tenn Ct
The Paddocks Farm
Grange Park Jun & Inf Schs
Hayes End
1 MURRAY GREY HO
2 CHAROLAIS HO
3 THURBIN HO
4 HART HO
Pronto Trad Est
Wood End Green
Pav
Bwg Gn
Beck Theatre
Sp Ctr
Rosedale Coll
Sp Stad
Bot Gdns
Wood End
Crkt Gd
HAYES
Town Hall Park
Bndstd
Dr Triplett's CE Prim Sch
Tenn Cts
1 PEAR TREE HO
2 CONFERENCE HO
Wood End Park Com Sch
VOLTAIRE WAY 1
MARRINER CT 2
Fball
UXBRIDGE RD
A4020
B465
A437
WEST DRAYTON RD
CHARVILLE LA
KINGSHILL AVE
GROSVENOR AVE
RAYNTON DR
BALMORAL DR
KINGSWAY
WOOD END GREEN RD
JUDGE HEATH LA
FREEMANS LA
CHURCH WLK
COLDHARBOUR LA
POLE HILL RD
MELLOW LA W
MELLOW LA E
HARROW VIEW
HAYES END RD
HAYES END DR
MEAD HOUSE LA
PARK LA
WOODROW AVE
LANSBURY DR
FROGMORE AVE
MANSFIELD DR
DERWENT DR
HEWENS RD
NEW RD
GREEN LA
CONNAUGHT RD
HAIG RD
SIBLEY CT
FOUNTAIN CL
WOODSTOCK HO
NORTH RD
TUDOR RD
CRANMER RD
CROMWELL RD
COMMONWEALTH AVE
VICTORIA CL
YORK AVE
BISHOP'S RD
NORMANDY DR
STUART CRES
SAXONY PAR
HANOVER CIRC
LANCASTER WLK
CORWELL LA
DAWLEY AVE
LANSDOWNE RD
LONSDALE CL
CROMER CL
ST JEROME'S GR
PRINCES PARK LA
LIME GR
ASH GR
BEECHWOOD AVE
SYCAMORE AVE
PARKSIDE
MANTON CL
LEVEN WAY
ALBION RD
QUEENS RD
GRANGE RD
BOTWELL LA
BOTWELL CRES
LILAC GDNS
BURBAGE CL
HEMMEN LA
ST MARY'S RD
CHAPEL CT
KERSTIN CL
CHILDS CT
WHEATLEY CRES
RECTORY RD
MANOR RD
ACACIA AVE
SWIFT CL
PARSONAGE CL
FULWOOD CL
GLEDWOOD DR
GLEDWOOD GDNS
GLEDWOOD CRES
MARSHALL DR
WARLEY RD
WHITTINGTON AVE
KENILWORTH GDNS
TITHE CL
BURNS CL
MELROSE CL
REGENTS CL
PARK RD
WESTACOTT
CAVENDISH
HURSTFIELD CRES
HAVEN CL
BLACKPOOL GDNS
WELWYN WAY
FROGMORE GDNS
WARWICK CRES
FREDORA AVE
PINE PL
LEAMINGTON PL
FAIRHOLME CRES
BYRON WAY
DALE DR
PERCY GDNS
BRADENHAM RD
ADELPHI WAY
ADELPHI CRES
CHESIL WAY
KENMORE CRES
DORSET AVE
DORSET CL
WEYMOUTH RD
LANSBURY DR
GOSHAWK GDNS
BURY AVE
TRENT WAY
POOLE WAY
SALCOMBE WAY
PORTLAND RD
EXMOUTH RD
KENTON WAY
WEALD WAY
TRURO WAY
HAYSTALL CL
RAYNTON DR
LANGDALE DR
KENDAL CL
ULLSWATER CL
HEATHERWOOD DR
HAYMAN CRES
RAEBURN RD
ROMNEY RD
ROMNEY PAR
GAINSBOROUGH RD
HOPPNER RD
LAWRENCE RD
CONSTABLE CL
TURNER CL
THE OAKS
LANDSEER CT
WILKINSON CL
LEYBOURNE RD
PETWORTH GDNS
HAZELDENE GDNS
RYEFIELD AVE
COWDRAY RD
MIDHURST GDNS
FLORISTON AVE
BERKELEY RD
MEADOW VIEW RD
BLACKLANDS DR
DALTON CL
WILMAR CL
PILLIONS LA
NEWPORT RD
WESTCOMBE LODGE DR
MORGAN'S LA
ROSSLYN CL
ANGEL LA
NEELINA CL
DAWSON CL
CHURCH CL
SOUTH WLK
MIDDLETON RD
ROSEDALE AVE
WAYLANDS
TUDOR SQ
CAVALIER GDNS
ST JEROME'S GR
HEATH RD
SANDRINGHAM
STAR RD
TOWERS CT
BYRON PAR
STAR CT
PAGET RD
DE SALIS RD
RUSSET CL
FULHAM CL
CHERRY GR
WHITE HEART AVE
TRINITY DR
TITMUS CL
APPLE CL
MELLOW LA
BARRA HALL CIRC
PRINCES PARK AVE
PRINCES PARK CL
PRINCES PARK PAR
DAWLEY PAR
DALLEGA CL
PURKIS
ORCHARD
NORTH HYDE AVE

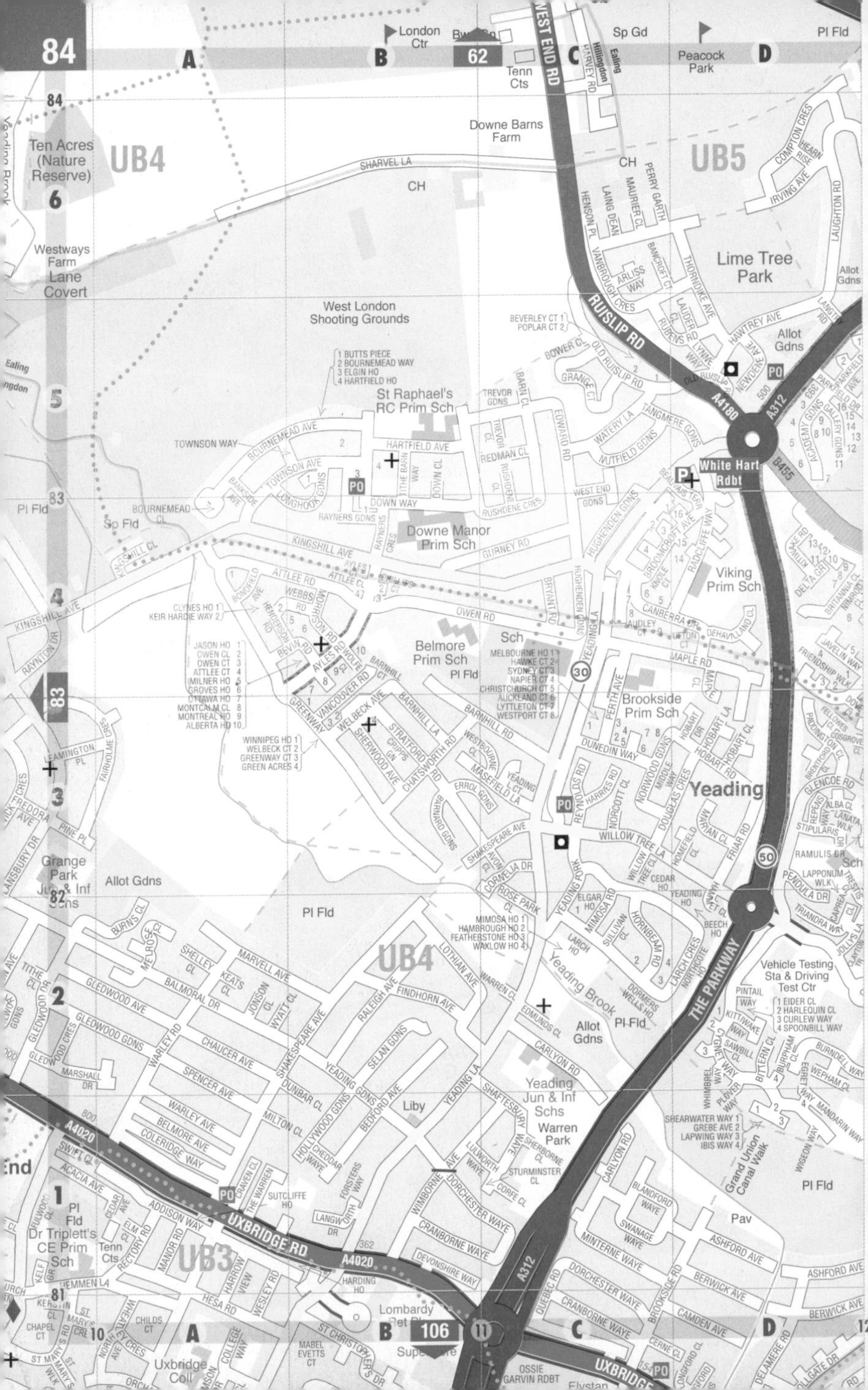
A
B
C
D
London Ctr
62
Tenn Cts
WEST END RD
Hillingdon
Ealing
HARVEY RD
Sp Gd
Peacock Park
Pl Fld
Ten Acres (Nature Reserve)
UB4
Downe Barns Farm
SHARVEL LA
CH
UB5
COMPTON CRES
HEARN RISE
IRVING AVE
LAUGHTON RD
PERRY GARTH
MAURIER CL
LAING DEAN
HENSON PL
VANBROUGH CRES
ARLISS WAY
BANCROFT CT
THORNDIKE AVE
Lime Tree Park
Allot Gdns
Westways Farm Lane Covert
West London Shooting Grounds
RUISLIP RD
LAUDER CL
RUBENS RD
LYNNE WAY
HAWTREY AVE
NEWDENE AVE
BEVERLEY CT 1
POPLAR CT 2
BOWER CL
OLD RUISLIP RD
GRANGE CT
1 BUTTS PIECE
2 BOURNEMEAD WAY
3 ELGIN HO
4 HARTFIELD HO
St Raphael's RC Prim Sch
TREVOR GDNS
BARN CL
EDWARD RD
WATERY LA
TANGMERE GDNS
NUTFIELD GDNS
A4180
A312
PO
White Hart Rdbt
B455
TOWNSON WAY
BOURNEMEAD AVE
HARTFIELD AVE
TOWNSON AVE
LONGHOOK GDNS
TITHE BARN WAY
DOWN CL
REDMAN CL
TREVOR CL
RUSHDENE CL
RUSHDENE CRES
WEST END GDNS
BANKSIDE AVE
BOURNEMEAD CL
DOWN WAY
RAYNERS GDNS
RAYNERS CRES
Downe Manor Prim Sch
GURNEY RD
HUGHENDEN GDNS
BROOMCROFT AVE
RADCLIFFE WAY
Viking Prim Sch
Pl Fld
Sp Fld
KINGSHILL CL
KINGSHILL AVE
AYLES CT
ATTLEE RD
ATTLEE CL
PHILLIPS CT
BONDFIELD AVE
WEBBS RD
MORRISON RD
CLYNES HO 1
KEIR HARDIE WAY 2
HENDERSON RD
OWEN RD
BRYANT RD
KNOLE CL
CANBERRA DR
AUDLEY CT
UPTON CT
DEHAVILLAND CL
JAVELIN WAY
FRIENDSHIP WLK
KINGSHILL AVE
RAYNTON DR
JASON HO 1
OWEN CL 2
OWEN CT 3
ATTLEE CT 4
MILNER HO 5
GROVES HO 6
OTTAWA HO 7
MONTCALM CL 8
MONTREAL HO 9
ALBERTA HO 10
BEVIN RD
AYLES RD
WOLFE CL
BARNHILL CT
Belmore Prim Sch
Sch
MELBOURNE HO 1
HAWKE CT 2
SYDNEY CT 3
NAPIER CT 4
CHRISTCHURCH CT 5
AUCKLAND CT 6
LYTTLETON CT 7
WESTPORT CT 8
YEADING LA
MAPLE RD
MAPLE CL
PERTH AVE
Brookside Prim Sch
HOBART LA
HOBART RD
HOBART CL
83
GREENWAY
VANCOUVER RD
WELBECK AVE
BARNHILL LA
BARNHILL RD
STRATFORD RD
CRIPPS GN
SHERWOOD AVE
CHATSWORTH RD
WESTBOURNE CL
MASEFIELD LA
YEADING CT
DUNEDIN WAY
NORWOOD GDNS
MIDDLE WAY
DOUGLAS CRES
WINNIPEG HO 1
WELBECK CT 2
GREENWAY CT 3
GREEN ACRES 4
LEAMINGTON CRES
FAIRHOLME CRES
LEAMINGTON PL
FREDORA AVE
PINE PL
LANSBURY DR
ERROL GDNS
BARNARD GDNS
REYNOLDS RD
HARRIES RD
NORCOTT CL
Yeading
GLENCOE RD
ALBA CL
LANATA WLK
STIPULARIS DR
RAMULIS DR
SHAKESPEARE AVE
AVON CL
CORNELIA DR
ROSE PARK CL
WILLOW TREE LA
WILLOW TREE CL
CEDAR HO
HOMEFIELD CL
MIRIAN CL
FRIAR RD
YEADING FORK
YEADING HO
HAWTHORN CT CL
BEECH HO
PENDULA DR
TRIANDRA WAY
Grange Park Jun & Inf Schs
Allot Gdns
Pl Fld
MIMOSA HO 1
HAMBROUGH HO 2
FEATHERSTONE HO 3
WAXLOW HO 4
ELGAR HO
MIMOSA RD
SULLIVAN CL
HORNBEAM RD
LARCH HO
LARCH CRES
NORTHCOTE HO
Vehicle Testing Sta & Driving Test Ctr
BURNS CL
MELROSE CL
SHELLEY CL
MARVELL AVE
KEATS CL
JONSON CL
WYATT CL
BALMORAL DR
LOTHIAN AVE
UB4
RALEIGH AVE
FINDHORN AVE
WARREN CL
EDMUNDS CL
Yeading Brook
DORMERS WELLS HO
Pl Fld
Allot Gdns
THE PARKWAY
PINTAIL WAY
KITTIWAKE WAY
1 EIDER CL
2 HARLEQUIN CL
3 CURLEW WAY
4 SPOONBILL WAY
SAWBILL CL
BITTERN CL
BURPHAM CL
EGRET WAY
BURNDELL WAY
WEPHAM CL
MANDARIN WAY
TITHE CL
GLEDWOOD DR
GLEDWOOD AVE
GLEDWOOD CRES
GLEDWOOD GDNS
WARLEY RD
CHAUCER AVE
SPENCER AVE
WARLEY AVE
BELMORE AVE
COLERIDGE WAY
MARSHALL DR
SHAKESPEARE AVE
DUNBAR CL
MILTON CL
YEADING GDNS
SELAN GDNS
BEDFORD AVE
HOLLYWOOD GDNS
CHEDDAR WAYE
Liby
YEADING LA
SHAFTESBURY WAYE
Yeading Jun & Inf Schs
Warren Park
SHERBORNE CL
STURMINSTER CL
CORFE CL
LULWORTH WAYE
CARLYON RD
CYGNET WAY
PLOVER WAY
WHIMBREL WAY
SHEARWATER WAY 1
GREBE AVE 2
LAPWING WAY 3
IBIS WAY 4
WIGEON WAY
Grand Union Canal Walk
Pl Fld
A4020
SWIFT CL
ACACIA AVE
CRAVEN CL
THE WARREN
SUTCLIFFE HO
FORSTERS WAY
LANGWORTH DR
WIMBORNE AVE
DORCHESTER WAYE
CRANBORNE WAYE
DEVONSHIRE WAY
BLANDFORD WAYE
SWANAGE WAYE
MINTERNE WAYE
ASHFORD AVE
Pav
BERWICK AVE
Pl Fld
Dr Triplett's CE Prim Sch
Tenn Cts
ADDISON WAY
CEDAR AVE
ELM CL
RECTORY RD
MANOR RD
UB3
UXBRIDGE RD
HARROW VIEW
WESLEY RD
A4020
HARDING HO
A312
QUEBEC RD
DORCHESTER WAYE
CRANBORNE WAYE
BROOKSIDE RD
CAMDEN AVE
CERNE CL
BERWICK AVE
HEMMEN LA
KERSTIN CL
CHAPEL CT
ST MARY'S CRES
ST MARY'S RD
HESA RD
CHILDS CT
NORTHCOTE AVE
WHEATLEY CRES
COLLEGE WAY
Lombardy Ret Pk
ST CHRISTOPHERS DR
MABEL EVETTS CT
106
Superstore
OSSIE GARVIN RDBT
UXBRIDGE RD
LONGFORD CL
DELAMERE RD
Uxbridge Coll
Elystan

NORTHOLT
Northolt Trad Est
63
A
B
C
D
84
John Chilton Sch
West London Acad
West London Acad
Target Rdbt
A40
A312
CHURCH RD
WESTERN AVE
Belvue Park
Belvue Sch
Golf Range
Mohammedi Pk Complex
The Metropolitan Ctr
Aladdin Workspace
Superstore
Fball Gd
Liby
Pl Fld
Pav
Smith's Farm
Kensington Lodge
CH
Rectory Park
Gifford Prim Sch
UB5
Rectory Park
Crome Ho
1 ARROW SCOUT WLK
2 CHIPMUNK GR
3 CONCORD CL
4 DAKOTA GDNS
5 MONTGOLFIER WLK
6 BEAVER GR
7 FLAMINGO GDNS
8 SEALAND WLK
9 GEMINI GR
10 NEWSTEAD CT
11 PINE CT
12 REDWOOD CT
13 MAYTREE CT
14 HIGHVIEW
15 APPLETREE CT
1 JACQUELINE CL
2 HAWTHORN FARM AVE
3 ASHLEY CT
4 BEECH CT
5 CHICHESTER CT
6 PENTLAND PL
7 BUCKINGHAM CT
8 KENTFORD WAY
9 FOX HO
10 ELY HO
11 CALDER HO
12 HEBBLE HO
13 ORWELL CT
1 LINGFIELD CT
2 HERMES WLK
3 BANBURY WLK
4 MERSEY WLK
5 STAR PATH
6 CONDOR PATH
7 HAMBLE WLK
8 CATHAY WLK
Grand Union Canal Paddington Branch
Grand Union Canal Wk
UB6
Ravenor Prim Sch
RUISLIP RD
B455
Sp Ctr
Greenford High Sch
Pl Fld
Ravenor Park
GREENFORD
London Motorcycle
98
Tenn Cts
Allot Gdns
Pav
Crkt Gd
King George's Field
1 WILSTONE CL
2 DUNSMORE CL
3 NAPTON CL
4 HELMSDALE CL
5 PIKESTONE CL
6 COULTER CL
7 CHIRK CL
8 BLISWORTH CL
9 AVON HO
10 BRIDGEWATER HO
11 CALEDONIAN CT
Higham Mews
Tenn Cts Sp Fld
Hillingdon
Ealing
Recn Gd
Schs
Pl Fld
83
82
Superstore
Lady Margaret Prim Sch
Durdans Park Prim Sch
UB1
Jubilee Park
Liby
Allot Gdns
Cemy
UB4
Marina
Cranleigh Gdns Ind Est
Grand Union Canal Paddington Branch
Tenn Cts
Allot Gdns
Sp Gd
Pav
Mini Glf Crs
Bwg Gn
Ath Gd
Allenby Prim Sch
Dormer's Wells High Sch
Sp Ctr
Mount Pleasant L Gdns
Almshouses
81
A4127
107
Dormer's Wells
Allot Gdns
Dormer's Wells
1 PRESTWICK CT
2 DENHAM CT
3 FULWELL CT
4 BRAMLEY CT
5 SAUNTON CT

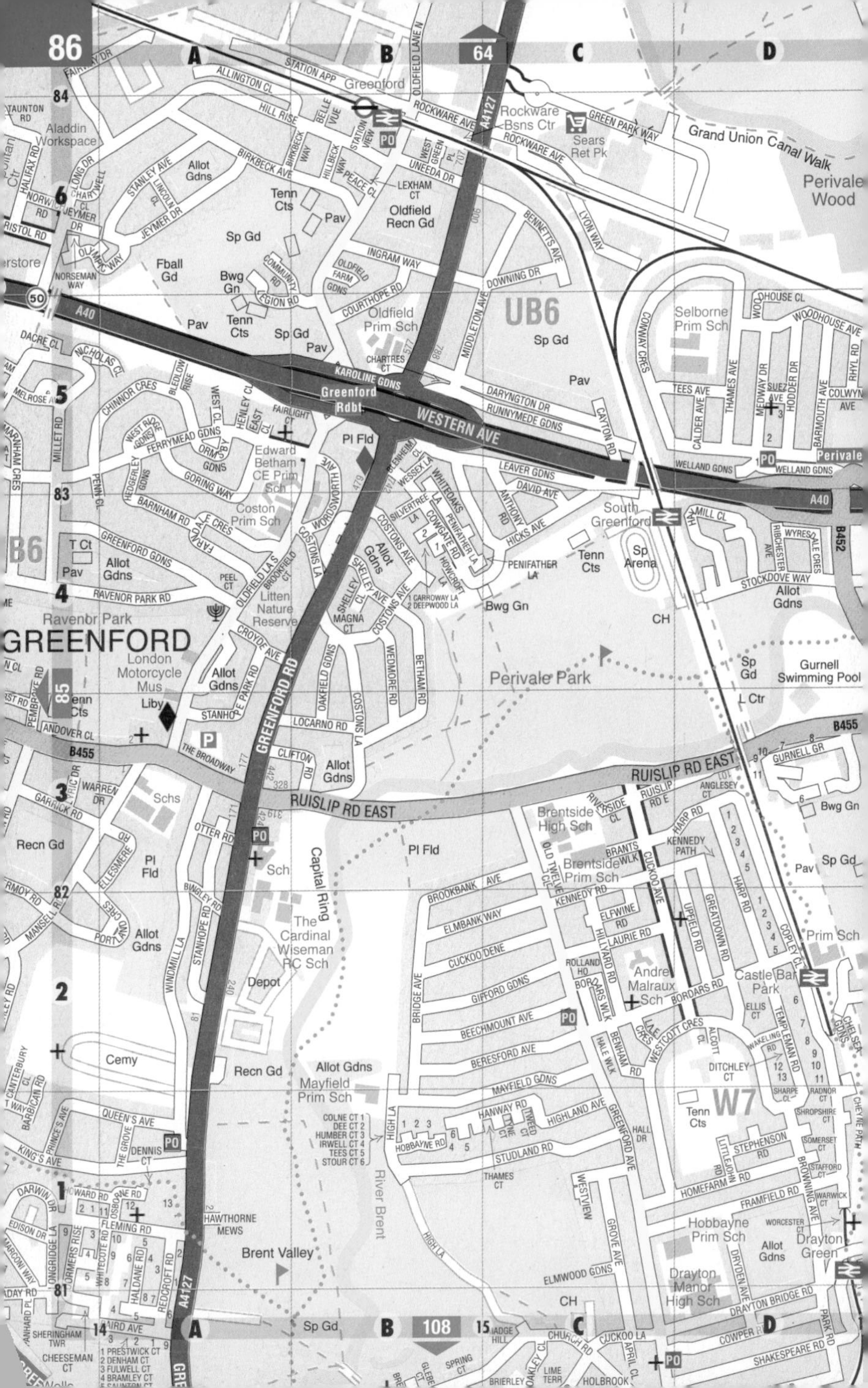

Greenford
Station App
Allington Cl
Hill Rise
Rockware Ave
Rockware Bsns Ctr
Green Park Way
Sears Ret Pk
Grand Union Canal Walk
Perivale Wood
Aladdin Workspace
Birkbeck Ave
Oldfield Recn Gd
Uneeda Dr
Lexham Ct
Ingram Way
Courthope Rd
Oldfield Prim Sch
Downing Dr
Bennetts Ave
Lyon Way
UB6
Selborne Prim Sch
Woodhouse Ave
Conway Cres
Karoline Gdns
Greenford Rdbt
Western Ave
A40
Darvngton Dr
Runnymede Gdns
Cayton Rd
Tees Ave
Calder Ave
Thames Ave
Medway Dr
Hodder Dr
Barmouth Ave
Colwyn Ave
Welland Gdns
Perivale
Edward Betham CE Prim Sch
Coston Prim Sch
Greenford Gdns
Ravenor Park Rd
Ravenor Park
GREENFORD
London Motorcycle Mus
Litten Nature Reserve
Costons Ave
Leaver Gdns
David Ave
Hicks Ave
South Greenford
Sp Arena
Perivale Park
Gurnell Swimming Pool
Greenford Rd
B455
Ruislip Rd East
The Broadway
Gurnell Gr
Brentside High Sch
Brentside Prim Sch
Capital Ring
The Cardinal Wiseman RC Sch
Andre Malraux Sch
Castle Bar Park
Cuckoo Ave
Mayfield Prim Sch
River Brent
Brent Valley
Hobbayne Prim Sch
Drayton Green
Drayton Manor High Sch
W7
Cemy
Queen's Ave
Windmill La
Greenford Ave
Drayton Bridge Rd
Church Rd
Cuckoo La
64
108
85
A
B
C
D

65
Horsenden Farm
Grand Union Canal Paddington Branch
Recn Gd
Liby
UB6
Allot Gdns
Perivale Ind Pk
Perivale
Perivale Prim Sch
Perivale New Bsns Ctr
Wadsworth Bsns Ctr
Fleetway West
Sheraton Bsns Ctr
Vicar's Green Prim Sch
Silicone Bsns Ctr
Alperton Cemy
Alperton Lower Sch
Alperton
Phoenix Trad Est
Abercorn Trad Est
Grand Union Canal Walk
Wharfside
Superstore
HA0
Capital Bsns Ctr
Athlon Ind Est
Met Police Traffic Unit
BRIDGEWATER RD
EALING RD
ALPERTON LA
WESTERN AVE
A40
B456
River Brent
Manhattan Bsns Pk
Ealing
Bwg Gn
Fball Gd
T Cts
Tenn Cts
Allot Gdns
Sp Gd
Pav
Pl Fld
CH
ARGYLE RD
B455
B452
SCOTCH COMM
KENT GDNS
CASTLEBAR HILL
CASTLEBAR RD
Cleveland Park
Castlebar Sch
Hostel
High Sch
St Benedict's Sch
Jun Sch
Prim Sch
Aston House Sch
Schs
Coll
W13
W5
West Ealing
EALING
Ealing Broadway
Christ Church CE Mid Sch
Shop Ctrs
Drayton Green Prim Sch
THE BROADWAY A4020
THE MALL
88
109

A
B
C
D
66
Stonebridge Park
Stonebridge Park
Braemar Ave
Alperton Com Sch
Lyon Park Jun & Inf Schs
Pl Flds
Allot Gdns
84
Alperton Lower Sch
Ealing Rd
A4089
Stanley Ave
Russell Ct
Anne Carver Lo
Lightley Ct
Mount Pleasant
Woodstock Rd
Stanley Park Dr
Belmont Ave
Highcroft Ave
Kenmere Gdns
Laburnham Cl
Heather Park Dr
Blackmore Dr
Beresford Ave
Wycombe Rd
50
A406
Alperton
Woodside Cl
Abbey Manufacturing Est
Liberty Ctr
Liby
Grand Union Canal Wlk
Capitol Ring
Northfields Ind Est
HA0
Alperton
Carlyon Ct
Water Rd
Abbeydale Rd
Park Royal
Abercorn Trad Est
Grand Union Canal Walk
Wharfside
Middlesex Ho
Northwick Rd
Superstore
Glacier Way
Carlyon Rd
Brentvale Ave
Bamford Ave
Norwood Ave
Fulwood Ave
Crabtree Ave
Abbey Ave
Longley Ave
Montague Works
Queensbury Rd
North Circular Rd
Premier Park Rd
Premier Pk
Capital Bsns Ctr
Ealing Rd
Cromwell Rd
Tiverton Rd
Seaton Cl
Vicars Bridge Cl
Elmore Cl
Burns Rd
Elveden Pl
Elveden Rd
Iveagh Ave
Iveagh Cl
Brent
Ealing
Tudor Est
Grand Union Ind Est
Rainsford Ct
Met Police Traffic Unit
5
Tenn Cts
Bwg Gn
Riverside Gdns
B456
Alperton La
1 Norbreck Gdns
Beechwood Gdns
Norbreck Par
Allot Gdns
West Twyford Prim Sch
Twyford Abbey Rd
Abbeyfields Cl
Moyne Pl
Rainsford Rd
NW 10
Abbey Rd
Eldon Way
Genesis Bsns Pk
Commercial Way
Superstore
Hanger La
Quill St
St Augustines Ave
Priory Gdns
Cleveley Cres
Park Ave
Brent Cres
Waverley Gdns
Huxley Gdns
Park Cl
Spencer Cl
Brentmead Gdns
Toucan Cl
Whitby Ave
83
Marsh Rd
River Brent
Manhattan Bsns Pk
West Gate
A4005
A406
St Annes Gdns
Abbey Par
Twyford Abbey Rd
Boonam Way
Recn Gd
Lakeside Dr
Space Bsns Pk
Park Royal
Cumberland Ave
AMC Bsns Ctr
Hanger Lane
Hanger Lane
40
A40
Greystoke Park Terr
Greystoke Park Terr
Fernlea Ho
Rosall Cres
Bispham Rd
1 Ritz Par
2 Churchill Ct
Cumberland Bsns Pk
Vascroft Est
Brunswick Rd
87
Lynwood Rd
Clarendon Rd
Brunswick Gdns
Greystoke Gdns
Sandall Rd
Sandall Cl
Garrick Cl
PO
Connell Cres
Coronation Rd
Hanger Gn
Johnsons Way
Radnor Way
Britannia Way
Park Royal Metro Ctr
Kingfield Rd
Moorfield Rd
Sovereign Pk
Western Ave
628
670
Hill Malcolm Ct
Haymills Ct
Heathcroft
Cresta Ct
Greystoke Gdns
Garth Mews 1
Greystoke Lo 2
Greystoke Ct 3
Hanger Hill Park
Chatsworth Rd
Heathcroft
Ashbourne Rd
Heath Cl
Hanger Ct
East Cl
Park Royal
Park Royal South L Complex
Dukes Rd
Westwood Park Trad Est
Concord Bsns Ctr
Concord Rd
Alliance Rd
Mansfield Rd
Western Avenue Bsns Pk
3
Dale Rd
Birkdale Rd
Mountwood Ho
Daver Ct
82
Cecil Cl
Fox La
Pav
Chatsworth Rise
The Ridings
Rotherwick Hill
Ashbourne Cl
Kendal Ave
Westpoint Trad Est
Heron Trad Est
Alliance Ct
Meadway Ct
Hillcrest Rd
Osborne Ct
Hogarth Cl
The Orchard
Magnolia Pl
Nicholas Gdns
Helena Rd
Prim Sch
1 Marcourt Lawns
2 Chiltern Ho
3 Hillcrest Hts
4 Minster Ct
Dallas Rd
Beaufort Cl
Beaufort Rd
Audley Ct
Corringway
Princes Gdns
T Cts
Bwg Gn
Kenda Ct
Kendal Ave
Northfield Rd
2
Montpelier Rd
St Peter's Way
West Rd
The Croft
Beechcroft Ho
Audley Rd
Cherry Wood Way
W3
Park Hill
Park Hill Ct
Hall Cl
Beaulieu Ct
Thorntree Ct
Hillside Rd
Park View Rd
Wester Gate
Corfton Lo
Red Lo
Hanger Vale La
Vale La
Ayr Ct
T Cts
Grovesides Cl
Walton Way
Saxon Dr
Norman Way
Kings Rd
Regal Cl
Corfton Rd
Queen's Rd
Sp Gd
Westmount Ct
Hanger View Way
Monks Dr
Tudor Gdns
Moat Pl
Howard Cl
Wynton Pl
The Link
Allot Gdns
Westfields Rd
Balmoral Ct
Mount Park Rd
Kings Ave
W5
Roselle Ct
Tree Cl
Marryatt Ct 1
Gilbert Ct 2
Thackery Ct 3
Chatsfield Pl
Tenn Cts
Hanger Vale La
Boileau Rd
Golf Cl
Sp Gd
West Acton
Links Rd
Princes Gdns
West Acton
Allot Gdns
Noel Rd
Alwyn Gdns
Sp Gd
Aston House Sch
1
Woodville Rd
Mountfield Rd
Westbury Rd
Pav
Woodville Gdns
Regency Cl
Boileau Par 4
Balcon Ct 5
Eden Court 6
Hanger Lane (North Circular Road)
North Ealing
Deena Cl
Kent Ct
Pav
Queen's Dr
Garage Rd
Station Par
West Acton Prim Sch
Allot Gdns
Station Rd
Haven La
Denham Lo
Madeley Rd
Madeley Ct
Queens Par
Miranda Ct
Ellen Wilkinson Sch for Girls
Churchill Gdns
Ealing Village
Roberts Ct
Allot Gdns
Haven Gn
PO
81
Ealing Broadway
B455
Waldegrave Rd
Tenn Cts
Lynton Rd
Addison Ct
Oakley Ho
G
18
Haven Pl
A
Parkside
B
110
19
Oakley Ave
C
D
Farnell Pl
The Japanese Sch
Mayfield Rd
Rosemount Lo
Creswick
Twyford Ct
Shop Ctrs
College Ct
Hamilton Rd
The Broadway A4020
The Mall
Mall Ct
Hamilton Ct
Freeland Rd
Western
Bwg Gn
Montague Gdns
A406

Stonebridge
Harlesden
Lower Place
NW10
North Acton
Old Oak Common
W3
W12
Acton Main Line
East Acton
Willesden Junction
Grand Union Canal (Paddington Branch)
Grand Union Canal Wlk
HILLSIDE
CRAVEN PK
CHURCH RD
MANOR PARK RD
CRAVEN PARK RD
HIGH STREET HARLESDEN
STATION RD
OLD OAK LA
VICTORIA RD
ACTON LA
PARK ROYAL RD
WALES FARM RD
HORN LA
WESTERN AVE
WESTWAY
Gipsy Corner
Savoy Circus
Central Middlesex
Hanover West Ind Est
The Royal London Est
Kingham Ind Est
Powergate Bsns Pk
Freightliner Terminal
The New Bsns Ctr
Old Oak Sidings
Gateway Trad Est
Cumberland Pk Ind Est
Apex Ind Est
Old Oak Common Sidings
Chase Road Trad Est
Park Royal Bsns Ctr
North Acton
John Perryn Prim Sch
Old Oak Prim Sch
HM Prison Wormwood Scrubs
Roundwood Park
Harlesden
67
111
90

Harlesden
Willesden Green
Brondesbury Park
Kensal Rise
Kensal Green
College Park
North Kensington
W10
W12
NW6
Roundwood Park
Capital City Acad
Willesden Sp Ctr
Cardinal Hinsley RC High Sch (Boys)
Kensal Green Cemy (All Souls)
Grand Union Canal (Paddington Branch)
Grand Union Canal Wlk
Wormwood Scrubs Park
Little Wormwood Scrubs (Recn Gd)
The Linford Christie Stadium
HM Prison Wormwood Scrubs
Hammersmith
Queen Charlottes & Chelsea
Wood Lane High Sch
Burlington Danes Sch
White City
WESTWAY
WESTWAY (ELEVATED ROAD)
HIGH STREET HARLESDEN
HARROW RD
SCRUBS LA
WOOD LA
ST QUINTIN AVE
LADBROKE GR
KILBURN LA
DU CANE RD
Mitre Bridge Ind Pk
Hythe Road Ind Est
Star Works
Old Oak Sidings
Willesden Junction
Gas Works
Kensington Meml Pk
St Charles'
Canberra Prim Sch
Latimer Road
Rutland Studios
Cumberland Pk Ind Est
Westgate Bsns Ctr
Hogarth Ind Est

68
112

A
B
C
D
69
Willesden La
A4003
A5
Kilburn
NW6
Paddington Cemy
Salusbury Prim Sch
Quadrant Bsns Ctr
Islamia Schs
Brondesbury Park
Queen's Park
Brondesbury Rd
B451
Kilburn High Rd
Kilburn High Road
Belsize Rd
Abbey Rd
B507
B509
B510
Harvist Rd
Premier Corner
Kilburn La
Carlton Vale
Kilburn Park Rd
Maida Vale
NW 8
229
Paddington Recn Gd
West Kilburn
Shirland Rd
B413
B414
Walterton Rd
Harrow Rd
Westbourne Green
W9
92
Kensal Town
Grand Union Canal
Westway (Elevated Rd)
Great Western Rd
Westbourne Park
A404
A40
236
Royal Oak
Porchester Rd
Westbourne Gr
Chepstow Rd
A4207
A4206
Bishop's Bridge Rd
W2
W10
W11
Ladbroke Gr
Ladbroke Grove
Portobello Rd
Kensington Park Rd
Queensway
Bayswater
Warwick Avenue
Little Venice
244
113
245
25
26
1
2
3
4
5
6
81
82
83
84

NW6
NW3
NW8
NW1
W9
W2
South Hampstead
Primrose Hill
Primrose Hill Tunnels
Barrow Hill
St John's Barracks
St John's Wood
The Wellington
St John & Elizabeth
Marlborough Day
Lord's (MCC & Middlesex Cty Crkt Gd)
Crkt Mus
London Central Mosque
Winfield House
Boating Lake
London Business Sch
Maida Vale
Warwick Avenue
Little Venice
Lisson Grove
Marylebone
Baker Street
Edgware Road
Charter Nightingale
Western Eye
Govt Offices
St Mary's Gardens Coll
PADDINGTON
Paddington Basin
Paddington
St Mary's
Marylebone Flyover
Royal Oak
Dominican Republic
Bayswater
Marble Arch
Speakers' Corner
FINCHLEY RD
WELLINGTON RD
AVENUE RD
PRINCE ALBERT RD
PARK RD
MAIDA VALE
ABBEY RD
GROVE END RD
ST JOHN'S WOOD ROAD
LISSON GR
CLIFTON GDNS
WESTWAY (ELEVATED)
HARROW RD (UNDER)
A40 MARYLEBONE FLYOVER
EDGWARE RD
PRAED ST
SUSSEX GDNS
BISHOP'S BRIDGE RD
EASTBOURNE TERR
GLOUCESTER PL
MARYLEBONE RD
PORCHESTER RD
QUEENSWAY
NORTH CARRIAGE DR
Grand Union Canal
Regent's Canal
BELSIZE RD
OUTER CIRCLE
70
230
229
91
236
114
237
A
B
C
D
1
2
3
4
5
6

CAMDEN TOWN
A
B
C
D
71
231
232
84
6
N1
5
4
3
2
1
83
82
81
94
238
115
239
Superstore
Camden Mkt
Camden Town
Britannia Junc
JAMESTOWN RD
GLOUCESTER AVE
GLOUCESTER CRES
OVAL RD
PARKWAY A4201
ARLINGTON RD
DELANCEY ST
CAMDEN HIGH ST
CAMDEN ST
ROYAL COLLEGE ST
ST PANCRAS WAY
Grand Union Canal
St Pancras
Depot
MALDEN LANE BRIDGE
St Pancras Gardens
PANCRAS RD
King's Cross
(Regent's Canal)
CRESCENT
CROWNDALE RD
OAKLEY SQ
Mornington Crescent
MORNINGTON ST
MORNINGTON TERR
PARK VILLAGE E
Regents Park Barracks
NW1
London Zoo
GLOUCESTER GATE BRIDGE
OUTER CIRCLE
BROAD WLK
Refreshment Room
Regent's Park
Cumberland Gate
Regent's Park
ALBANY ST
CHESTER TERR
CHESTER RD
INNER CIRCLE
Open Air Theatre
Queen Mary's Gardens
Refreshment Room
New Lodge
Royal Coll of Physicians
Pav
Tenn Cts
Regent's Coll
YORK BRIDGE
Royal Acad of Music
HAMPSTEAD RD
EVERSHOLT ST
Somers Town
The British Liby
St Pancras International
Euston
Govt Offices
EUSTON ROAD
Euston Underpass
Euston Square
University Coll London
GOWER ST
TOTTENHAM COURT RD
UPPER WOBURN PL
TAVISTOCK SQ
University of London
RUSSELL SQ
Bloomsbury
British Mus
BLOOMSBURY ST
RADA
Great Portland Street
Warren Street
PARK CRES
PORTLAND PL
GREAT PORTLAND ST
Fitzrovia
BT Twr
MORTIMER ST
Goodge Street
NEW OXFORD ST
Tottenham Court Road
St Giles
ST GILES HIGH ST
Soho
Berwick St
CHARING CROSS RD
CAMBRIDGE CIR
SHAFTESBURY AVE
Leicester Square
LONG ACRE
Oxford Circus
OXFORD CIR
OXFORD ST
MARYLEBONE
Bond Street
WIGMORE ST
CAVENDISH SQUARE
MARYLEBONE HIGH ST
BAKER ST
JAMES ST
NEW BOND ST
REGENT ST
CONDUIT ST
Grosvenor Sq Gardens
UPPER BROOK ST
Piccadilly
W1

94
72
233
234
240
116
241
A
B
C
D
1
2
3
4
5
6
N1
WC1
WC2
ISLINGTON
Pentonville
FINSBURY
King's Cross
St Pancras
Somers Town
Bloomsbury
St Giles
Holborn
Gray's Inn
Clerkenwell
Camden Pas
Angel
YORK WAY
CALEDONIAN RD
COPENHAGEN ST
LIVERPOOL RD
UPPER ST
PENTONVILLE RD
KING'S CROSS RD
GRAY'S INN RD
FARRINGDON RD
ROSEBERY AVE
GOSWELL RD
ST JOHN ST
CLERKENWELL RD
THEOBALD'S RD
GUILFORD ST
SOUTHAMPTON ROW
HIGH HOLBORN
HOLBORN
HOLBORN VIADUCT
NEW OXFORD ST
KINGSWAY
CHANCERY LA
ALDWYCH
STRAND
VICTORIA EMBANKMENT
LONG ACRE
CHARING CROSS RD
PANCRAS RD
EUSTON RD
HUNTER ST
JUDD ST
RUSSELL SQ
BLOOMSBURY ST
FLEET ST
FARRINGDON ST
NEW BRIDGE ST
ESSEX RD
Barnard Park
Chapel Mkt
King's Cross (Thameslink)
St Pancras International
The British Liby
Coram's Fields
Eastman Dental
Family Records Ctr
City Univ
Russell Square Garden
British Mus
Lincoln's Inn Fields
Royal Courts of Justice
Smithfield Mkt
Farringdon
Leather Lane
Chancery Lane
Covent Garden
Leicester Square
Somerset House
Temple
Blackfriars
City Thameslink
Chapel
Mkt

A
B
C
D
73
235
Essex Road
SHOREDITCH
Hoxton
Haggerston
Haggerston Park
St Luke's
Barbican
Barbican Arts & Con Ctr
Broadgate
Spitalfields
Old Spitalfields
Whitechapel
Aldgate
Aldgate East
Brick Lane
Columbia Rd
Petticoat Lane
Liverpool Street
Moorgate
Old Street
Shoreditch Park
Kingsland Basin
Grand Union Canal
(Regent's Canal)
City Road Basin
Guildhall
Mansion House
Cannon Street
Fenchurch Street
Tower Hill
Tower Gateway
Monument
Bank
Tower 42
Swiss Re Bldg
Lloyds Bldg
Bunhill Fields Burial Gd
E8
E2
E1
EC2
EC3
EC4
NEW NORTH RD
KINGSLAND RD
SHOREDITCH HIGH ST
CITY RD
EAST RD
OLD ST
PITFIELD ST
HACKNEY RD
GREAT EASTERN ST
COMMERCIAL ST
BISHOPSGATE
BETHNAL GREEN RD
COLUMBIA RD
QUEENSBRIDGE RD
BRICK LA
LONDON WALL
CHISWELL ST
BUNHILL ROW
ALDERSGATE ST
UPPER THAMES ST
MINORIES
WHITECHAPEL HIGH ST
GRACECHURCH ST
EAGLE WHARF RD
SHEPHERDESS WLK
CANAL WLK
CHESHIRE
ALBION DR
84
83
82
81
6
5
4
3
2
1
96
243
242
117
33
34
CITY OF

74
A
B
C
D
HACKNEY
South Hackney
Haggerston
BETHNAL GREEN
STEPNEY
Spitalfields
E8
E9
E2
E1
QUEENSBRIDGE RD
HACKNEY RD
A1208
VICTORIA PARK RD
A106 WELL ST
BISHOP'S WAY
SEWARDSTONE RD
OLD FORD RD
ROMAN RD
OLD BETHNAL GREEN RD
BETHNAL GREEN RD
A1209
GOSSET ST
CAMBRIDGE HEATH RD
WARNER PL
CHESHIRE ST
DUNBRIDGE ST
VALLANCE RD
BRICK LA
WHITECHAPEL RD
MILE END RD
STEPNEY GN
GLOBE RD
NEW RD
COMMERCIAL RD
CANNON STREET RD
CABLE ST
THE HIGHWAY
Regent's Canal
Haggerston Park
Weavers Fields
Royal London
Cambridge Heath
Bethnal Green
Whitechapel
Stepney Green
Shadwell
Globe Town
Meath Gardens
Royal Gate East
Royal Gate West
Gore Gate
Crown Gate West
Morpeth Sec Sch
Anchor Ret Pk
Swanlea Sec Sch
Osmani Sch
Allen Gdns
Art Gall
Columbia Rd
Brick Lane
Aldgate East
Watney
Ratcliff
6
5
4
3
2
1
84
83
82
81
95
243
118
34
35

97
A
B
C
D
75
Bwg Gn
Sp Gd
Victoria Park
Victoria Fntn
Gunmakers Gate
Hertford Union Canal
Swan Wharf
Crown Wharf
Iceland Wharf
Stratford Marsh
The Marshgate Ctr
Pudding Mill Lane
St Clement's Wharf
City Mill River
Vanguard Trad Ctr
Marsh Gate Bsns Ctr
Axis Bsns Ctr
Heron Ind Est
Vulcan Wharf
Bow Back River
River Lea or Lee
Lea Valley Wlk
Old Ford
OLD FORD RD
B118
B119
B142
PARNELL RD
EAST CROSS ROUTE
A12
FAIRFIELD RD
WICK LA
BOW
BOW RD
A11
Bow Road
Bow Church
Bromley
Grove Hall Park
Meeson's Wharf
Tredegar Wharf
Works
GROVE RD
Mile End Park
Mile End
Univ of London
A1205
The Royal London (St Clements)
Tower Hamlets Cemy
Coll (Annexe)
E3
Gas Works
DEVONS RD
Devons Road
Hackney Coll
BLACKWALL TUNNEL NORTHERN APPROACH
98
Allot Gdns
St Andrew's
TOWER HAMLETS
East London Stadium
Mile End Park (South)
Regent's Canal
Shandy Park
Halley Prim Sch
BEN JONSON RD
BURDETT RD
ST PAUL'S WAY
B140
Com Sch
Bow Common
Furze Green
Langdon Park
Locksons Wharf
Bartlett Park
Brickfield Gardens
Quebec & Crown Wharves Cut
Limehouse Cut
POPLAR
EAST INDIA DOCK RD
A13
COMMERCIAL RD
Limehouse
Limehouse Basin
A1261
119
All Saints
A1206 COTTON ST
Westferry
LIMEHOUSE
Recn Gd

98
76
A
B
C
D
Stratford Marsh
Marshgate Ctr
Vanguard Trad Ctr
Marsh Gate Bsns Ctr
Axis Bsns Ctr
Vulcan Wharf
City Mill River
Waterworks River
HIGH ST
A118
A115
A112 WEST HAM LA
Newham Coll (Stratford Campus)
VICARAGE LA
PORTWAY
B165
B164
Channelsea River
Stratford Workshops
Depot
UNION ST
RICK ROBERTS WAY
ABBEY RD
ABBEY LA
NEW PLAISTOW RD
PLAISTOW RD
A1011
Plaistow
CORPORATION ST
Ranelagh Prim Sch
E15
Mill Meads
Allot Gdns
Abbey Creek
Channelsea Bsns Ctr
Prescott Channel
Three Mills Green
Three Mills Wall River
THREE MILLS STUDIOS
Meeson's Wharf
BOW BRIDGE
Works
Tredegar Wharf
Superstore
THREE MILL LA
A11
West Ham
CROWS RD
Memorial Recn Gd
Crem
East London Cemy
NEWHAM
PARK VISTA APARTMENTS
MANOR RD
Gas Works
Bromley-by-Bow
Bow Locks
TWELVETREES CRES
Mus
Twelvetrees Bsns Pk
Depot
E16
Lea Valley Wlk
Barratt Ind Pk
Data Point Bsns Ctr
Gemini Bsns Ctr
Pylon Trad Est
STEPHENSON ST
Eastlea Com Sch
Star Prim Sch
Star Park
Recn Gd
Tenn Cts
BLACKWALL TUNNEL NORTHERN APPROACH
Hackney Coll
St Leonard's Wharf
Islay Wharf
South Bromley
Devon Wharf
River Lea or Lee
Bow Creek
Blackwall Trad Est
Gas Works
ABBOTT RD
B125
EAST INDIA DOCK RD
A13
A12
A124
A1261
A1263
Canning Town
Bow Creek Mills
LOWER LEA CROSSING
A1020
East India Dock Basin
Hercules Wharf
East India
120
Langdon Park
All Saints
Coll
COTTON ST
A1206
VICTORIA DOCK RD
Canning Town
Prim Sch
Liby
Cycleway

Upton
BOLEYN RD
STUKELEY RD
77
NEVILLE RD
PLASHET RD
PLASHET GR
ST STEPHENS RD
WYNDHAM
WORTLEY RD
B109
B165
B167
A114
UPTON CROSS
STOPFORD RD
E15
Tenn Cts
Bndstd
A
B
C
D
Liby
ELIZABETH RD
VICTORIA AVE
GRANGEWOOD ST
EVERSLEIGH RD
LAWRENCE RD
OUTRAM RD
MALVERN RD
STAMFORD RD
OAKFIELD RD
WAKEFIELD ST
84
6
CRESCENT RD
DACRE RD
CLAUDE RD
GWENDOLINE AVE
CHURSTON AVE
LUCAS AVE
THORNGROVE RD
PENGE RD
RAYMOND RD
DONALD RD
Upton Park
Queen's Mkt
KING'S RD
REDCLYFFE RD
WILLIAM MORLEY CL
CEARNS HO
Priory Park
Cleves Prim Sch
HAROLD RD
WEST HAM
TERRACE RD
CARTER RD
QUEENS TERR
ROCHESTER AVE
WAGHORN RD
GREEN ST
TUDOR RD
ARRAGON RD
ABBOTS RD
ST BERNARD'S RD
KATHERINE RD
HARTLEY AVE
AINTREE AVE
PRIORY CT
Boleyn Gd (West Ham Utd FC)
SEYMOUR RD
CLEVES RD
PARR RD
PRIORY RD
STRATFORD RD
PELLY RD
CLEGG ST
HIGH ST
QUEEN'S RD W
MAY WLK
MAY RD
OPUS STUDIOS
Lister Com Sch
NORTHERN RD
Allot Gdns
Plaistow Prim Sch
JUNCTION RD
WESTERN RD
ORWELL RD
KIRTON RD
WALTON RD
FAWN RD
ELGAR CL
BUSHEY RD
CREDON RD
RAVENHILL RD
SELSDON RD
PURAN HO
CASTLE ST
A124
30
KIMBERLEY AVE
MAFEKING AVE
LADYSMITH AVE
GILLETT AVE
MACAULAY RD
THACKERAY RD
DICKENS RD
LOXFORD AVE
COMPTON AVE
CREIGHTON AVE
ST MARTIN'S AVE
5
ST MARY'S RD
SHAFTESBURY POINT
GLASGOW RD
TWEEDMOUTH RD
EDINBURGH RD
STIRLING RD
DUNDEE RD
EASTERN RD
Prim Sch
SOUTHERN RD
T Ct
Plaistow
Pl Fld
EDINBURGH CT
DAVIS ST
SAMSON ST
PARSONS RD
PRAGEL ST
NILE RD
CLAUGHTON RD
CENTRAL PARK RD
CHELTENHAM GDNS
GEOFFREY GDNS
COTSWOLD GDNS
MONTPELIER GDNS
HENNIKER GDNS
HALDANE RD
BURFORD RD
BUXTON RD
83
RICHMOND ST
KENNEDY CL
Curwen Prim Sch
HERBERT ST
STOCK ST
CHESTERTON TERR
CHESTERTON RD
HOWARD'S RD
SECOND AVE
FIRST AVE
SOLENT RISE
SEWELL ST
LACEWING CL
THE BROADWAY
WINKFIELD RD
FENTON'S AVE
ROUTEMASTER CL
DARWIN CT
Recn Gd
Plaistow
BURKE LODGE
B116
BALAAM ST
GREENGATE ST
A112
HOLLYBUSH ST
DRAGONFLY CL
CAVE RD
SPECTACLE WORKS
JEDBURGH RD
HAIG RD W
UPPERTON RD W
JACOBS HO
SUTTON CT RD
KINGSLAND RD
OLIVE RD
PATRICK RD
CORONATION RD
INNISKILLING RD
BOUNDARY RD
BENSON AVE
WILSON RD
GROSVENOR GDNS
BLENHEIM RD
WELBECK RD
HUBERT RD
HATHERLEY GDNS
CLACTON RD
E6
BEVERLEY RD
FRINTON RD
LICHFIELD RD
DENBIGH RD
BRAMPTON RD
Brampton Prim Sch
4
100
E13
DONGOLA RD
KHARTOUM RD
BARKING RD
NICHOLAS CT
BEAUMONT RD
KENT ST
SUSSEX ST
TUNMARSH LA
HUMBERSTONE RD
ANGUS RD
OBAN RD
MORSE CL
CHENAPPA CL
GRANT ST
COLNE ST
GORDON ST
MEREDITH ST
AYRES CL
NEWMAN RD
LIDDON RD
ST ANDREW'S RD
ISOM CL
PRINCE REGENT LA
BELGRAVE RD
WHITWELL RD
FOSTER RD
KELLAND RD
ANNE ST
BOYCE WAY
FALCON ST
St Helen's RC Prim Sch
L Ctr
LAWRENCE HALL
CROFTON RD
WIGSTON RD
WANLIP RD
Newham General
DENBIGH CT
BOUNDARY LA
1 LARCH CL
2 BELGRAVE CT
GLEN RD
WOODSIDE RD
Cumberland Sch
Roman Road Prim Sch
Brampton Manor Sch
Newham Ctr for Mental Health
LONSDALE AVE
STOKES RD
3
AMY WARNE CL
ESK RD
GARDNER RD
CUMBERLAND RD
APPLEWOOD DR
Newham Sixth Form Coll
1 NEWPORT AVE
2 JONES RD
PORT CRES
Sch
ELKINGTON RD
LINCOLN RD
NEW BARN ST
JUTLAND RD
FAIRBAIRN HALL
AVENONS RD
HAYDAY RD
JENKINS RD
PALMER RD
OBAN CL
MAYBURY RD
BENNETT RD
BARCLAY RD
Tollgate Prim Sch
Stadium
A13
50
DAKOTA GDNS
FIREFLY GDNS
VIKING GDNS
82
STUBBS POINT
TINTO RD
CAMBUS RD
LING RD
KILDARE RD
RAVENSCROFT RD
HOLBORN RD
BROCK RD
SELBY RD
CHADWIN RD
CHALK RD
EGHAM RD
BOTHA RD
SHONA HO
Games Ct
L Ctr
East Ham Ind Est
Pav
Horse Ride
RIDGWELL RD
MACGREGOR RD
SULLIVAN AVE
FLEETWOOD CL
GOLDCREST CL
HURST CT
NEWHAM WAY
Prince Regent
2
TOLLGATE RD
PINTAIL CL
KESTREL AVE
WATFORD RD
CHARFORD RD
Prim Sch
Tenn Cts
Canning Town
Rosetta Prim Sch
Recn Gd
Liby
1 PEACOCK WLK
2 RUSTIC WLK
E16
COLMAN RD
CROOMBS RD
ATKINSON RD
GIRALDA CL
HICKMAN CL
FULMER RD
GREENCROFT CL
VANGUARD CL
SOPHIA RD
MILLENNIUM CL
OYSTER CATCHERS CL
MORTLAKE RD
RUSSELL RD
VARLEY RD
HIGH HEADS RD 1
BROADGATE RD 2
Scott Wilkie Prim Sch
King George V Park
Becton District Park
CRAYFORD CL
REMINGTON RD
MAPLECROFT CL
ROOK WLK
DEVONSHIRE RD
LAMBERT RD
HOSKIN'S CL
CHURCHILL RD
ALESTAN BECK RD
STANSFELD RD
RANDOLPH APP
KING GEORGE AVE
CASPIAN WLK
ANDOVER AVE
1
Will Thorne Pav
Hallsville Prim Sch
GOLDWING CL
HOOPER RD
ADAMSON RD
BOREHAM AVE
ELBURY DR
COOLFIN RD
KERRY CL
MANCHESTER CT
GRESHAM RD
SHIPMAN RD
TALLIS CL
LESLIE RD
ETHEL RD
BERWICK RD
CUNDY RD
ANCHOR HO
Recn Gd
ALNWICK RD
PRINCE OF WALES RD
Com Sch
FELSTED RD
ROYAL RD
LEYES RD
Custom House
Allot Gdns
Calverton Prim Sch
RICHARD HOUSE DR
JASPER RD
81
Allot Gdns
VICTORIA DOCK RD
MASON CL
POLLARD CL
Custom House for ExCeL
41
121
CONNAUGHT RD
A112
A1020
42
Prince Regent
SEAGULL LA
Royal Victoria
Hotel
1 WOOD ST
2 BETTS RD
3 CHAUNTLER CL
4 SANDSTONE LA
ROYAL ALBERT WAY
DOCKSIDE RD
FESTOON
Royal Albert

BARKING
79
Vicarage Field Sh Ctr
RIPPLE RD
ST PAULS RD
ALFRED'S WAY (EAST HAM AND BARKING BY-PASS)
A13
A123
A124
IG11
Greatfields Park
Movers Lane (Flyover)
Gascoigne Prim Sch
St Joseph's RC Prim Sch
Abbey Park Ind Est
Cuckold's Haven
New England Est
Barking Creek
Barking & Dagenham
Newham
Kingsbridge Ind Est
Lyon Bsns Pk
Katella Trad Est
Cromwell Trad Ctr
River Road Bsns Pk
Creekmouth Ind Pk
Thames View Jun Sch
Thames View Inf Sch
Barking Ind Pk
Barking Bsns Ctr
Wayside Commercial Est
Alfred's Way Ind Est
Trafalgar Bsns Ctr
Anglian Ind Est
Balmoral Trad Est
Buzzard Creek Ind Est
Sewage Works
Creekmouth
River Roding
Barking Barrier
Horse End
Jetty
Pier
Superstore
Gallions Reach Shp Pk
Depot
E6
ARMADA WAY
JENKINS LA
ERIC CLARKE LA
THAMES RD
RIVER RD
Margaret or Tripcock Ness
Mast
Thamesmead Sh Ctr
102
123
45
46
81
82
83
84

A
B
C
D
80
Castle Green
RM9
Jo Richardson Com Sch
Monteagle Prim Sch
Cemy
Ripple Road
LODGE AVE
A123
A1153
RIPPLE RD
A13 ALFRED'S WAY (EAST HAM AND BARKING BY-PASS)
Barking Ind Pk
Alfred's Way Ind Est
The Invicta Ctr
Wayside Commercial Est
Davenport Ctr
Rippleside Commercial Est
Portland Commercial Est
Maybells Commercial Est
Freightliner Terminal
Thames View Inf Sch
Thames View Jun Sch
Barking Bsns Ctr
Riverside Ind Est
Bankside Pk
City Farm & Eco Pk
IG11
Allot Gdns
RENWICK RD
CHOATS RD
RIVER RD
RM9
Buzzard Creek Ind Est
Balmoral Trad Est
Anglian Ind Est
Pier
Barking or False Point
River Thames
Barking Reach
Cross Ness
Crossway Lake Nature Reserve
Castilion Prim Sch
Green Chain Wlk
Bishop John Robinson Prim Sch
Linton Mead Prim Sch
Thamesmead Sh Ctr
CENTRAL WAY
124
101
1
2
3
4
5
6
81
82
83
84
46
47
5 GREAT FLEETE WAY
6 BREDO HO
7 BELLINGHAM CT
8 ARNCROFT CT
1 HORNBEAM CL
2 VICTORY CT
GILSTEAD HO 1
NAVESTOCK HO 2
STANFORD HO 3
ST AIDANS CT 4
POSEIDON CT 1
NEPTUNE CT 2
SALTERN CT 3
OULTON CL 1
SALHOUSE CL 2

A
B
C
D
81
DAGENHAM
Goresbrook Park
Old Dagenham Park
Thomas Arnold Prim Sch
Allot Gdns
Broad Street
Dagenham Park Com Sch
RM10
RM9
IG11
RIPPLE RD
A1306
A1240
B178
BALLARDS RD
NEW RD
Heathway
Marsh Green Prim Sch
Merrielands Ret Pk
Superstore
Motor Works
Dagenham Dock
LC
Channel Tunnel Rail Link
Dagenham Breach
Thames Gateway Pk
HINDMANS WAY
CHEQUERS LA
KENT AVE
CHOATS MANOR WAY
BREACH LA
Horse Shoe Corner
Power Sta
Ind Est
Motor Works
Works
Jetties
Jetty
River Thames
Beam River
Halfway Reach
THUNDERER RD
Crossness Pumping Station
Drv Rng
SE28
SE2
Riverside
A1306 Rainham
A13 Stanford-le-Hope, M25 Tilbury (A1089)
A13
Essex STREET ATLAS
84
6
5
83
4
3
82
2
1
81
49
50
125

YIEWSLEY
WEST DRAYTON
Harmondsworth
Stockley Country Park
Stockley Park
UB7
UB11
UB3
FALLING LA
PARK VIEW RD
A408
HOLLOWAY LA
A3044
SIPSON RD
STOCKLEY RD
M4
Grand Union Canal
Grand Union Canal Wlk
West Drayton
R A F Station
Heathrow Express Tunnel
Holiday Inn
STILWELL RDBT
82
126
A408 Uxbridge, M40 (A4020)
Buckinghamshire STREET ATLAS
M4 Slough, M25

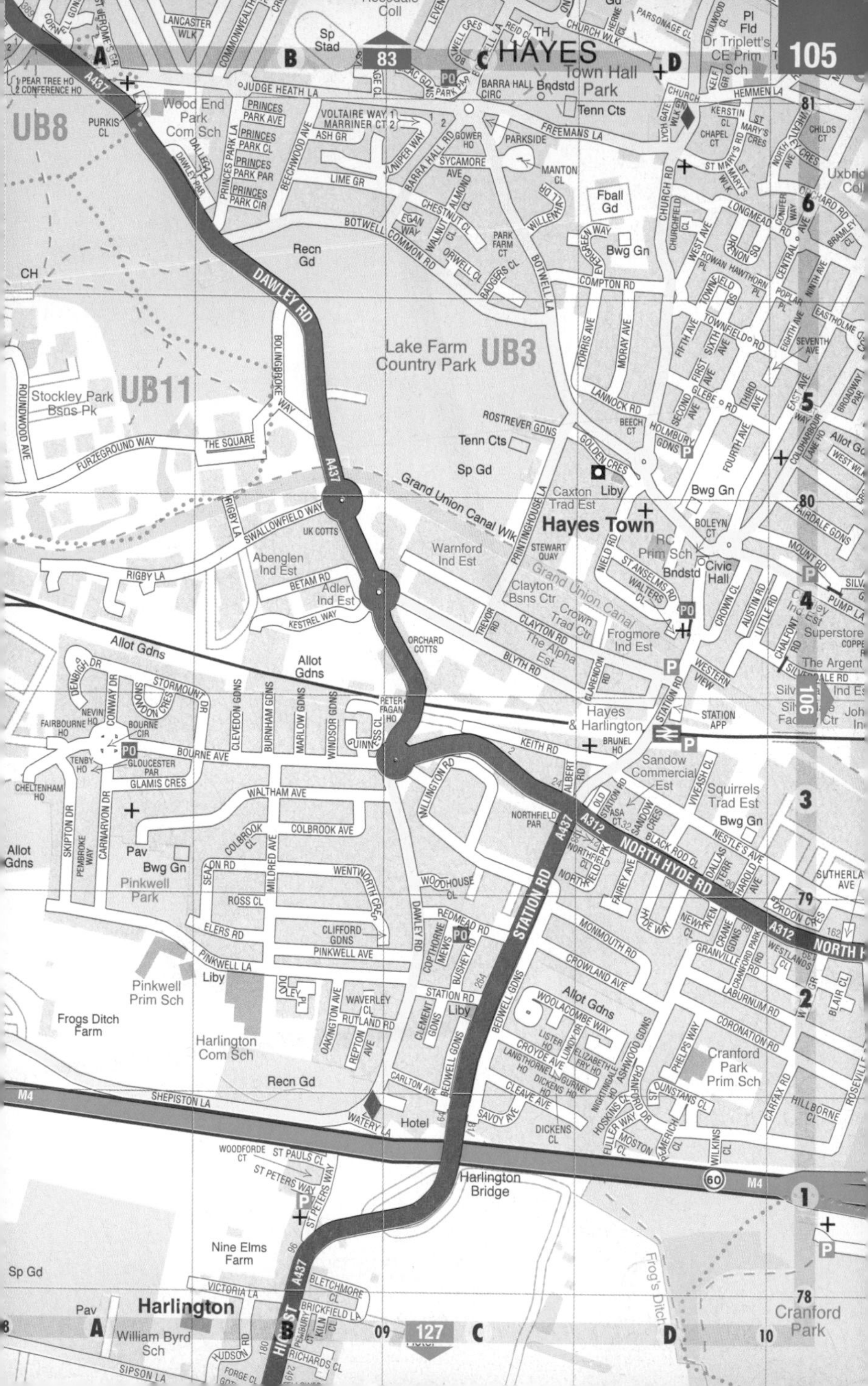
HAYES
Town Hall Park
Hayes Town
Harlington
Hayes & Harlington
UB8
UB3
UB11
Lake Farm Country Park
Stockley Park Bsns Pk
Wood End Park Com Sch
Dr Triplett's CE Prim Sch
Pinkwell Prim Sch
Harlington Com Sch
Cranford Park Prim Sch
Cranford Park
William Byrd Sch
Frogs Ditch Farm
Nine Elms Farm
Harlington Bridge
Grand Union Canal Wlk
Grand Union Canal
Abenglen Ind Est
Adler Ind Est
Warnford Ind Est
Caxton Trad Est
Clayton Bsns Ctr
Crown Trad Ctr
The Alpha Est
Frogmore Ind Est
Sandow Commercial Est
Squirrels Trad Est
Pinkwell Park
Frog's Ditch
DAWLEY RD
STATION RD
NORTH HYDE RD
HIGH ST
A437
A312
M4
BOTWELL LA
BOTWELL COMMON RD
JUDGE HEATH LA
FREEMANS LA
COMPTON RD
FURZEGROUND WAY
THE SQUARE
RIGBY LA
SWALLOWFIELD WAY
BOLINGBROKE WAY
ROUNDWOOD AVE
BOURNE AVE
WALTHAM AVE
COLBROOK AVE
PINKWELL LA
PINKWELL AVE
SHEPISTON LA
WATERY LA
BLYTH RD
CLAYTON RD
KEITH RD
CROWLAND AVE
MONMOUTH RD
CORONATION RD
LABURNUM RD
VICTORIA LA
SIPSON LA
83
127
106
A
B
C
D
1
2
3
4
5
6
78
79
80
81
09
10

UXBRIDGE RD
A4020
84
Lombardy Ret Pk
Superstore
Uxbridge Coll
Hayes Town
Minet Jun & Inf Schs
Minet Country Park
OSSIE GARVIN RDBT
Elystan Bsns Ctr
Hexagon Bsns Ctr
Metro Ctr
Hayes Bridge Ret Pk
Swallowbrook Bsns Ctr
Brook Ind Est
Bsns Pk
Guru Nanak Sikh Prim & Sec Schs
Blair Peach Prim Sch
UB3
UB4
UB1
UB2
TW5
1 GLENISTER HO
2 FITZGERALD HO
3 WELLINGS HO
Yeading Brook
Grand Union Canal Paddington Branch
Grand Union Canal Wlk
Civic Hall
Provident Ind Est
Regent Bsns Ctr
Peter James Bsns Ctr
Halls Bsns Ctr
Silverdale Ind Est
Silverdale Factory Ctr
Johnson's Ind Est
The Argent Ctr
Balfour Bsns Ctr
Brent Park Ind Est
International Trad Est
Featherstone Prim Sch
THE PARKWAY
NORTH HYDE RD
A312
Bulls Bridge Ind Est
Western International Market
THE MARKET CTR
Grand Union Canal
Cranford Park Prim Sch
River Crane
Airlinks
Airlinks Ind Est
The Heston Ctr
The Spitfire Est
Lower Park Farm
Cranford Park
Heston Motorway Service Area
M4
105
128

107
A
B
C
D
85
Allot Gdns
Sp Gd
Mini Glf Crs
Pav
Bwg Gn
Ath Gd
Dormer's Wells High Sch
Sp Ctr
Mount Pleasant L Gdns
TENNYSON RD
CHEPSTOW GDNS
THURSTON RD
BRITTEN DR
PURCELL HO
ELGAR HO
MOUNT AVE
ALMSHOUSES
MOUNT PLEASANT COTTS
GREENFIELDS
NORTH PAR
SHELLEY CRES
TELFORD RD
FARADAY RD
EDISON DR
LONGRIDGE LA
DORMERS RISE
WHITECOTE RD
REDCROFT RD
A4127
ORCHID CL
SPIKES BRIDGE RD
SAHARA CT
MARIGOLD CL
HONEYSUCKLE CL
FOXGLOVE CL
LANCASTER RD
JASMINE CT
VIKING RD
NORMAN AVE
CARLYLE AVE
CARLYLE GDNS
WEST AVE
EAST AVE
LADY MARGARET RD
SOUTHALL CT
FREDERICK HO
NORTH RD
WOODLANDS CT
MASEFIELD AVE
DORMER'S WELLS LA
Dormer's Wells
FARM
BRINDLEY WAY
PANHARD PL
SHERINGHAM TWR
CHEESEMAN CT
BAIRD AVE
1 PRESTWICK CT
2 DENHAM CT
3 FULWELL CT
4 BRAMLEY CT
5 SAUNTON CT
6 ST ANDREW'S TWR
7 ASHRIDGE CT
8 PEEBLES CT
9 TROON CT
GREENFORD RD
LOWDEN RD
ALMA RD
SAXON GDNS
DANE RD
NORTHCOTE AVE
NORTH AVE
UB1
BURNS AVE
WAVERLEY RD
KENTON AVE
Allot Gdns
Dormer's Wells Jun Sch
Tudor Prim Sch
RUSKIN RD
THOMPSON HO
STANLEY RD
HAMBLIN HO
TUDOR RD
SAXON RD
SOUTH AVE
SOUTH AVE GDNS
GREENFORD AVE
SHACKLETON RD
MEADOW RD
PALGRAVE AVE
KINGSLEY AVE
OAKWOOD AVE
MILFORD RD
ADDISON PL
ATHERTON PL
LONGFORD AVE
Dormer's Wells Inf Sch
BELVEDERE CT
CRAVEN CT
West Middlesex
6
THE BROADWAY
ALFRED GDNS
ALEXANDRA AVE
ST GEORGE'S AVE
JOYNER CT
EATON CT
FAIRLAWN GDNS
SCHOOL PAS
GROVE TERR
DOROTHY VILLAS
SHRUBBERY RD
CHARTER CT
PARK VIEW RD
STAMFORD CL
MELROSE DR
MARK CL
1 SEPTEMBER CT
2 UPTON CT
3 BLACKTHORNE CT
4 AMBER CT
5 TIMOR CT
SOUTHALL
A4020
HIGH ST
Coll
Sch
LONGFORD CT 1
MILFORD CT 2
GREEN DR
A4020 UXBRIDGE RD
TRINITY RD
TOWNSEND RD
WEST END RD
HAMBROUGH RD
ABBOTTS RD
OSWALD RD
ORCHARD AVE
BEACHCROFT AVE
HERBERT RD
ANDMARK CT
HAMILTON RD
CAMBRIDGE RD
OXFORD RD
BOYD AVE
Southall Park
ARGYLL AVE
KNOWSLEY AVE
LYNDHURST AVE
MORLAND GDNS
5
WINDMILL PL
Windmill Bsns Ctr
ST JOSEPH'S DR
RAYNOR CL
BEATRICE RD
SOUTH RD
A3005
DENVER RD
WILK RD
AVENUE RD
VILLIERS RD
Villiers High Sch
Tenn Cts
Bwg Gn
Sch
Southall & West London Coll
BEACONSFIELD RD
OAKLEIGH CT
PARK AVE
Barratt Ind Pk
Great Western Ind Pk
80
Great Western Ind Pk
Allot Gdns
GRANGE RD
LEWIS RD
HANSON GDNS
RANDOLPH RD
COPLAND HO
MILAN RD
COLLETT WAY
JACKSON WAY
DEAN WAY
WINDMILL LA
Southall Railway Ctr
Southall
The Arches Bsns Ctr
Middlesex Bsns Ctr
THE CRESCENT
ARMSTRONG WAY
Three Bridges Bsns Ctr
4
THE STRAIGHT
Featherstone Ind Est
MARTIN CT
SOUTHBRIDGE WAY
MAYPOLE CT
HORTUS RD
Grand Union Way
CHARLES HO
Decimal Ctr
The Bridge Bsns Ctr
Glade Lane Canalside Park
QUEEN'S RD
Dominion Ind Est
FEATHERSTONE TERR
DILLOWAY YD
THE GREEN
KINGSTON RD
DRAYSIDE MEWS
Liby
OSTERLEY LODGE
BRIDGE RD
Cemy
Southall Ent Ctr
WHITTLE RD
GLADE LA
POST RD
CAYLEY RD
McNAIR RD
COOKHAM CL
BAXTER CL
108
Dokal Ind Est
SANGAM CL
HARTINGTON RD
GLADSTONE RD
DOMINION RD
OSTERLEY PARK RD
Southall Norwood
JERSEY CT
Dairy Meadow Prim Sch
WATERSIDE RD
QUAKER LA
PENARD RD
FEATHERSTONE RD
ELMFIELD RD
PORTLAND RD
GROSVENOR RD
SWIFT RD
HUNT RD
HILLARY RD
WYLIE RD
TRUBSHAW RD
TYLER RD
POPLAR AVE
Sports Gd
WALTHAM RD
ST JOHN'S RD
CHURCH AVE
Sch
Cemy
MARLOW CT
CHURCH RD
MERRICK RD
WARWICK RD
Havelock Prim Sch
TENSING RD
CLEARMOUNT HO
GREGORY RD
LANGDONS CT
TENTELOW LA
3
WESTERN RD
BELMONT AVE
WESTERN CT
KING ST
HAVELOCK RD
Sybil Elgar Sch
HAVELOCK RD
Grand Union Canal Wlk
Three Bridges Prim Sch
Allot Gdns
DAGMAR RD
DAGMAR MEWS
HAVELOCK CT
HAMMOND RD
MONTAGUE WAYE
VICTORIA RD
RECTORY RD
1 WINDSOR RD
2 CASTLE RD
Allot Gdns
DAMSONWOOD RD
Grand Union Canal
MELBURY AVE
Featherstone High Sch
BEVERLEY RD
NORWOOD RD
SHAFTESBURY AVE
STOUR AVE
MINTERNE AVE
WILLOWBROOK RD
79
Pl Flds
MONTAGUE RD
ADELAIDE RD
CLIFTON RD
ENDSLEIGH RD
Sch
BIDWELL HO
ELLISON GDNS
NORWOOD GDNS
WITLEY GDNS
WREN AVE
BIXLEY CL
BRYANSTON CL
BLANDFORD RD
DORSET AVE
SHERBORNE AVE
UB2
RECREATION RD
GEORGE ST
TALBOT RD
Endsleigh Ind Est
Witley Ind Est
WITLEY CT
HAREWOOD TERR
BRADBURY CL
Playing Field
OLD FARM CT
2
STRATFORD RD
REGINA RD
INVERNESS RD
SALISBURY RD
Wolf Fields Prim Sch
HAREWOOD
WIMBORNE AVE
CRANBORNE AVE
Norwood Green
BISCOE HO
ST MARYS AVE
BRENDON CT
LEA RD
GORDON RD
ROSAMUN
HOLLY LODGE
MANSTON AVE
CAMBRIAN CT
WILLIAMS RD
BURKET CL
BARNES AVE
JESSOP AVE
Allot Gdns
Bwg Gn
Tenn Cts
FROGMORE CT
NORWOOD RD
ELM VIEW CT
Ealing
Hounslow
Allot Gdns
KINGSBRIDGE RD
NORWOOD GREEN RD
Bwg Gn
PENBURY RD
COURT RD
DITTON RD
NORWOOD CL
1 VINE COTTS
2 NORWOOD TERR
3 GREENSLEEVES HO
4 CLEVELAND CT
5 CHEVIOT CT
RALEIGH RD
NEWLANDS CL
Norwood Green Inf Sch
THORNCLIFFE RD
CRANESWATER PK
ALLEYN PK
A4127
THE LAWN
OSTERLEY LA
M4
Norwood Green Jun Sch
NORTH HYDE LA
THE GLEN
GREEN WALK
BOUNDARY CL
1
Osterl
HOLLY FARM RD
PRESTWICK CL
TREVOR GDNS
DADE WAY
HADLEY GDNS
CROSSLANDS AVE
HESTON RD
Recn Gd
KINGS ARBOUR
ROSTREVOR
RINGWAY
CLUNBURY AVE
BRANDON RD
Ealing
Hounslow
FERN LA
OXFORD AVE
TW5
A3005
North Hyde
DURHAM AVE
THE ALDERS
78
GRANGE CL
M4
THE GABLES
2
A
B
13
129
C
D
14
WINCHESTER
FERRARO CL
ETON AVE
1 ASHMORE CT
2 BOSTOCK HO
3 PASSINGHAM HO
4 SPOONER HO
60
HESTON GRANGE
HESTON GRANGE LA
BISCOE CL

86
130
107
Brent Valley
Sp Gd
Churchfields Recn Gd
Bwg Gn
GREENFORD RD
A4127
UXBRIDGE RD
A4020
UB1
UB2
W7
TW7
West Middlesex
Hanwell
Hobbayne Prim Sch
Drayton Manor High Sch
Drayton Green
Triangle Ctr
Windmill Bsns Ctr
Great Western Ind Pk
Three Bridges Bsns Ctr
Glade Lane Canalside Park
Grand Union Canal Wlk
Ealing
Capital Ring
Sports Gd
Sp Ctr
Pl Fld
The Aviary
WINDMILL LA
BOSTON RD
LOWER BOSTON RD
A3002
A4001
Waterside Trad Ctr
Boston Bsns Pk
River Brent Bsns Pk
Elthorne Park
Elthorne Park High Sch
City of Westminster Cemy
River Brent
Grand Union Canal
Osterley Lock
Trumper's Wood
M4
OSTERLEY LA
Osterley Park Farm
Osterley Park
Osterley Park House
Hare & Hounds (PH)
Wyke Green
B454 SYON LA

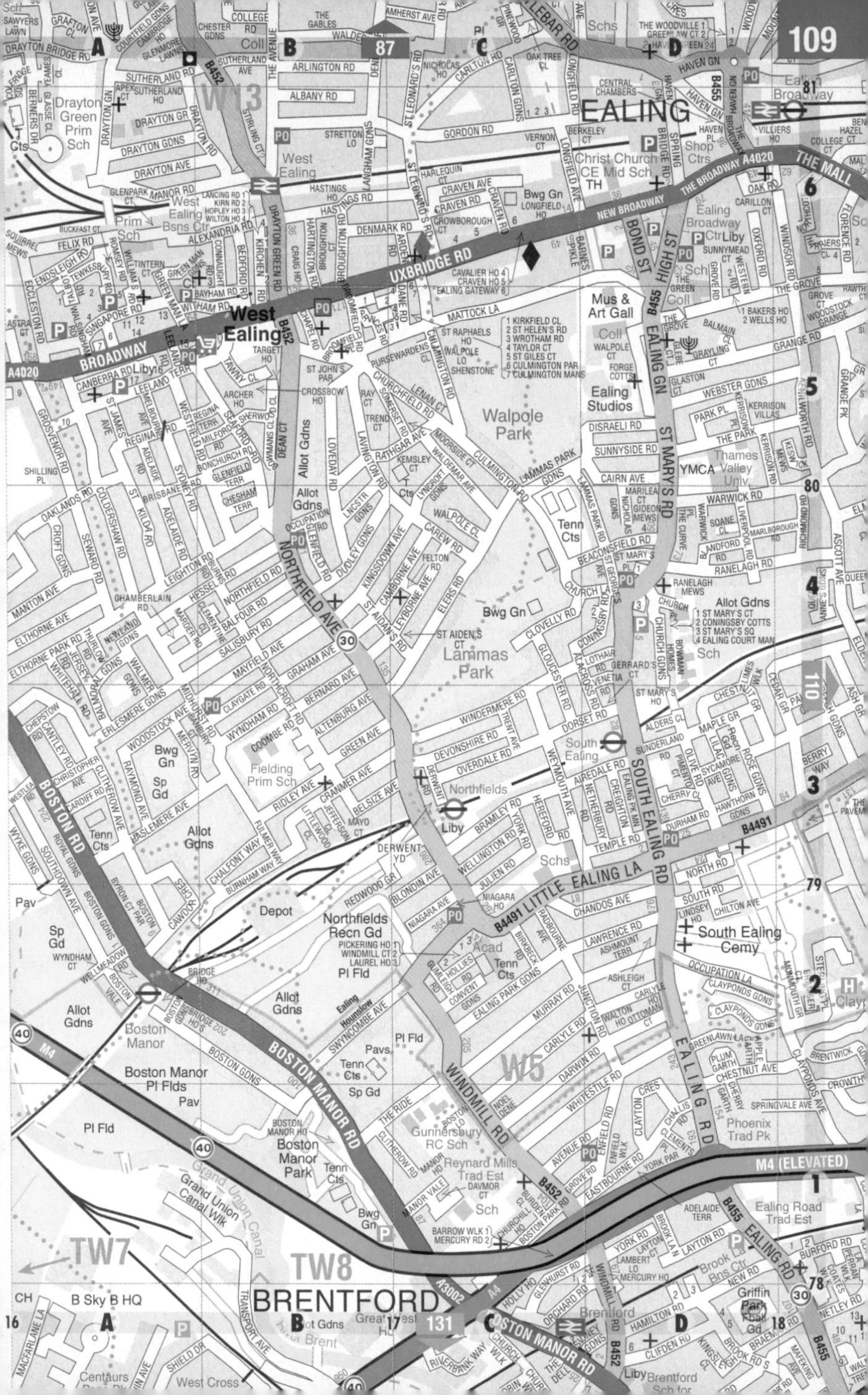

87
A
B
C
D
EALING
W13
W5
TW7
TW8
BRENTFORD
West Ealing
Ealing Broadway
THE MALL
THE BROADWAY
NEW BROADWAY
UXBRIDGE RD
BROADWAY
A4020
B452
B455
B4491
A3002
A4
M4
M4 (ELEVATED)
DRAYTON BRIDGE RD
Drayton Green Prim Sch
DRAYTON GR
DRAYTON GDNS
DRAYTON AVE
DRAYTON GREEN RD
SUTHERLAND RD
COLLEGE RD
THE AVENUE
ARLINGTON RD
ALBANY RD
STRETTON LO
West Ealing
GORDON RD
CARLTON RD
CARLTON GDNS
PINEWOOD
LEBAR RD
LONGFIELD RD
OAK TREE CL
CENTRAL CHAMBERS
HAVEN GN
HAVEN LA
Christ Church CE Mid Sch
CRAVEN AVE
CRAVEN RD
HASTINGS RD
DENMARK RD
ST LEONARD'S RD
LANGHAM GDNS
Bwg Gn
BOND ST
HIGH ST
Mus & Art Gall
Ealing Studios
Walpole Park
MATTOCK LA
CULMINGTON RD
ST MARY'S RD
YMCA
Thames Valley Univ
WARWICK RD
THE PARK
DISRAELI RD
SUNNYSIDE RD
CAIRN AVE
LAMMAS PARK GDNS
Tenn Cts
BEACONSFIELD RD
CHURCH LA
CLOVELLY RD
Lammas Park
Allot Gdns
NORTHFIELD AVE
LOVEDAY RD
LAVINGTON RD
DUDLEY GDNS
KINGSDOWN AVE
CAMBORNE AVE
LEYBORNE AVE
ELERS RD
NORTHFIELD RD
BALFOUR RD
SALISBURY RD
MAYFIELD AVE
GRAHAM AVE
BERNARD AVE
ALTENBURG AVE
GREEN AVE
COOMBE RD
Fielding Prim Sch
RIDLEY AVE
CRANMER AVE
BELSIZE AVE
Northfields
Liby
BRAMLEY RD
YORK RD
HEREFORD RD
WEYMOUTH AVE
South Ealing
SOUTH EALING RD
LITTLE EALING LA
CHANDOS AVE
LAWRENCE RD
South Ealing Cemy
OCCUPATION LA
CLAYPONDS GDNS
EALING RD
Phoenix Trad Pk
Ealing Road Trad Est
WINDMILL RD
Gunnersbury RC Sch
Reynard Mills Trad Est
Northfields Recn Gd
Pl Fld
Depot
BOSTON RD
BOSTON MANOR RD
Boston Manor
Boston Manor Pl Flds
Boston Manor Park
Grand Union Canal Wlk
Grand Union Canal
MANTON AVE
ELTHORNE AVE
ELTHORNE PARK RD
LEIGHTON RD
OAKLANDS RD
SEWARD RD
CROFT GDNS
COLDERSHAW RD
ST KILDA RD
ADELAIDE RD
SYDNEY RD
WOODSTOCK AVE
HASLEMERE AVE
CHALFONT WAY
Sp Gd
Pav
Allot Gdns
Tenn Cts
B Sky B HQ
Brentford
BOSTON MANOR RD
EALING RD
131
110
30
40
1
2
3
4
5
6
79
80
81
78
16
17
18

88
Ellen Wilkinson Sch for Girls
Allot Gdns
Ealing Broadway
Tenn Cts
THE BROADWAY A4020
THE MALL
UXBRIDGE RD
NORTH COMMON RD
Ealing Common
The Japanese Sch
Bwg Gn
Pav
Sp Gd
Coll
RC Prim Sch
Twyford CE High Sch
UXBRIDGE RD
HIGH ST A4020
A4000
W5
Thames Valley
Acton
Acton High Sch
GUNNERSBURY AVENUE (NORTH CIRCULAR ROAD)
GUNNERSBURY LA
North Korea
Pl Fld
Allot Gdns
Acton Town
POPE'S LA
B4491
Gunnersbury Park
Gunnersbury Park Mus
Bwg Gns
W3
South Acton
Rowley Ind Pk
109
South Ealing Cemy
TW8
Lionel Road Prim Sch
International Sch of London
Gunnersbury Cemy
Gunnersbury
W4
Chiswick Pk
Claypands
Potomac
Superstore
Chiswick Rdbt
CHISWICK HIGH RD
A315
GREAT WEST RD (UNDER)
M4 (ELEVATED)
M4
WELLESLEY RD A3000
Phoenix Trad Pk
Brentford Fountain L Ctr
Kew Bridge Dist Ctr
Kew Bridge
Ealing Road Trad Est
EALING RD
B455
Brook La Bns Ctr
Griffin Park Fball Gd
Mus
KEW BRIDGE RD
HIGH ST
132
Kew Pier
Strand on the Green
Brentford Ait
Recn Gd
Allot Gdns
Schs
A
B
C
D
1
2
3
4
5
6

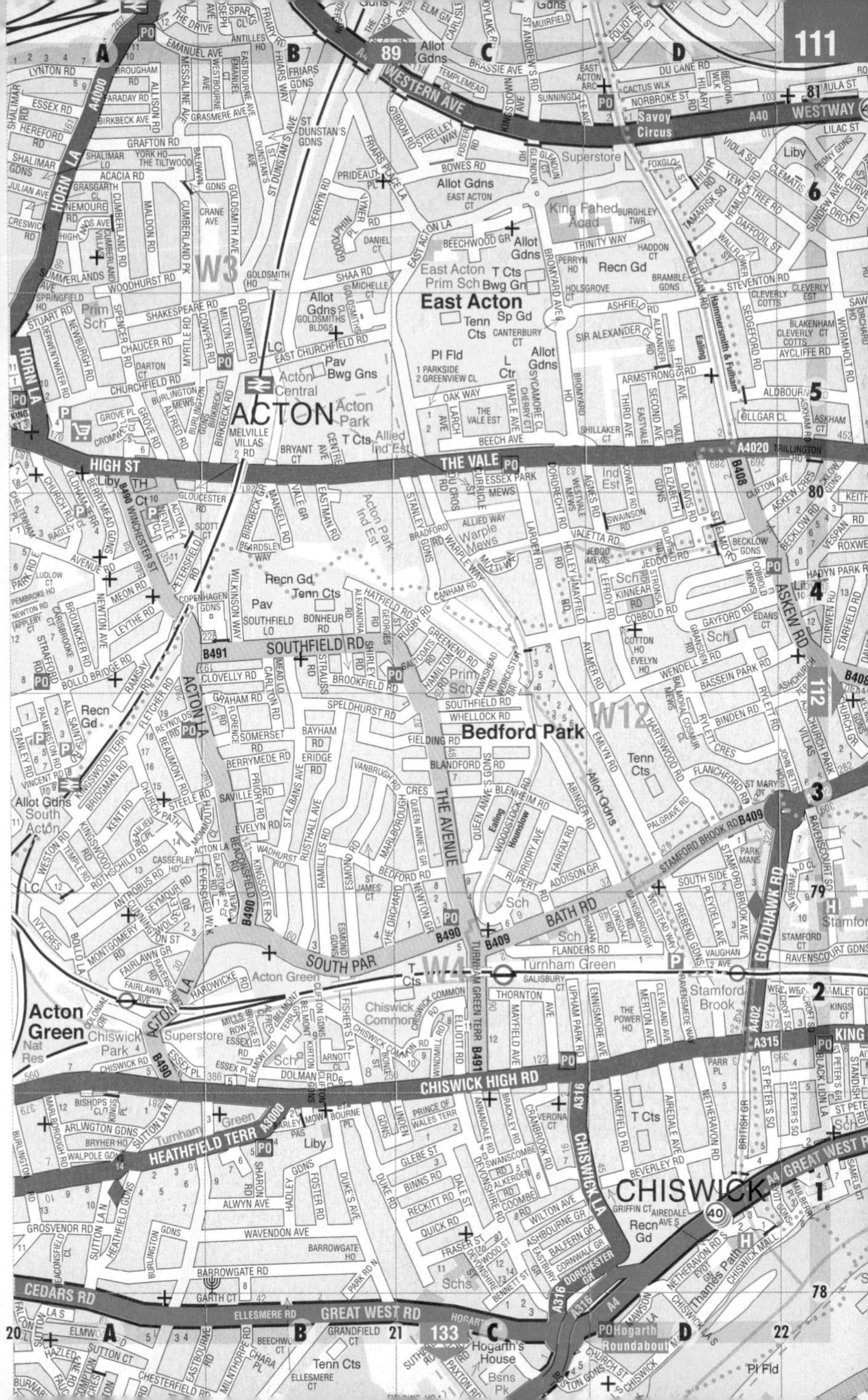

111
A
B
C
D
89
WESTERN AVE
WESTWAY
A40
Savoy Circus
W3
East Acton
ACTON
Acton Central
Acton Park
HIGH ST
THE VALE
A4020
HORN LA
A4000
B408
ASKEW RD
80
4
5
6
81
112
Bedford Park
W12
THE AVENUE
SOUTHFIELD RD
B491
ACTON LA
B490
SOUTH PAR
W4
Turnham Green
Stamford Brook
Acton Green
Chiswick Common
GOLDHAWK RD
A402
A315
KING
CHISWICK HIGH RD
HEATHFIELD TERR
A3000
CHISWICK LA
A316
CHISWICK
GREAT WEST RD
A4
CEDARS RD
Hogarth Roundabout
Hogarth's House
133
20
21
22
78
79
3
2
1

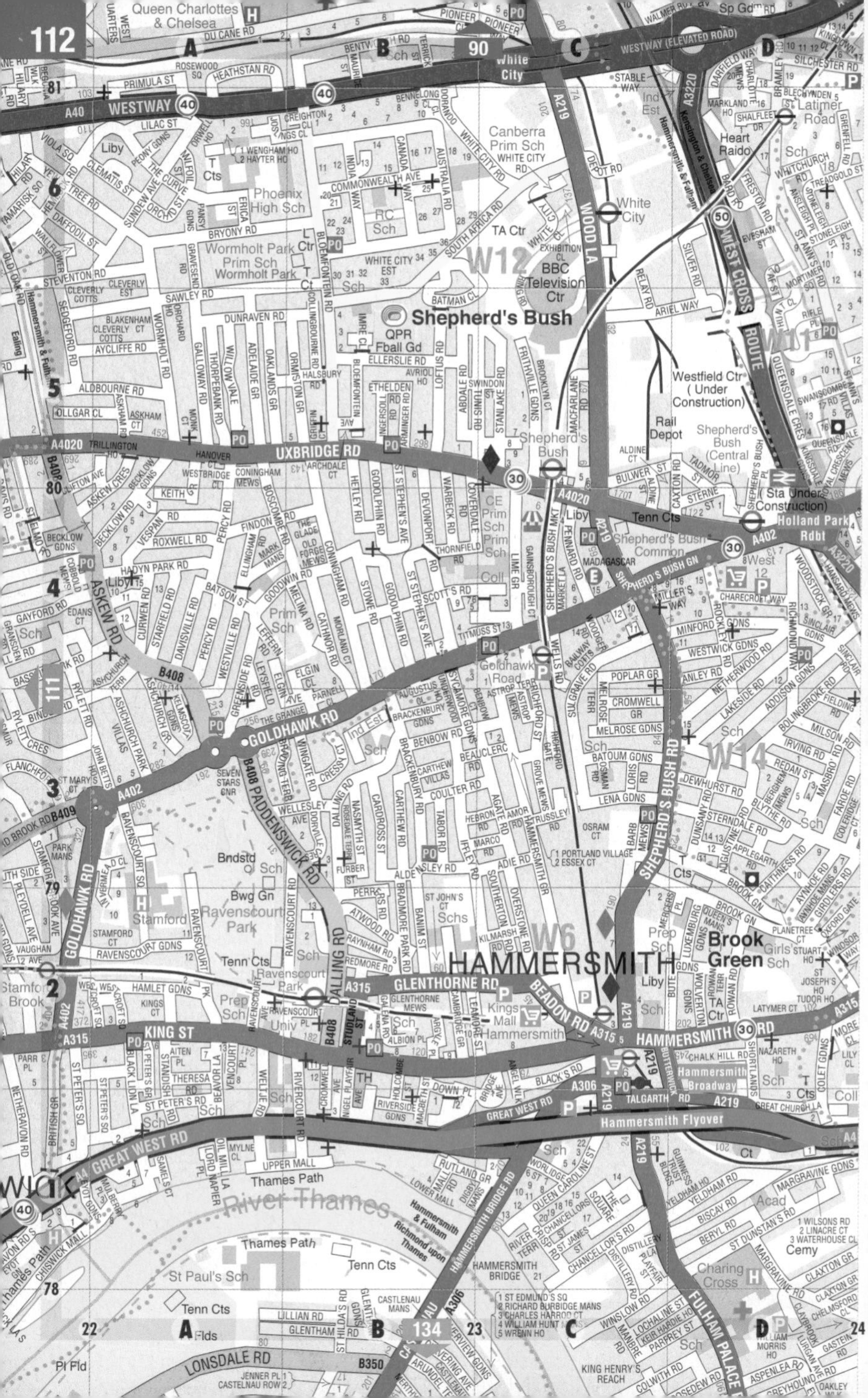

Queen Charlottes & Chelsea
WESTWAY
White City
WESTWAY (ELEVATED ROAD)
Phoenix High Sch
Wormholt Park Prim Sch
Canberra Prim Sch
BBC Television Ctr
Shepherd's Bush
QPR Fball Gd
W12
WOOD LA
WEST CROSS ROUTE
W11
Westfield Ctr (Under Construction)
Rail Depot
Shepherd's Bush (Central Line)
UXBRIDGE RD
Shepherd's Bush Common
SHEPHERD'S BUSH GN
Holland Park Rdbt
GOLDHAWK RD
Goldhawk Road
SHEPHERD'S BUSH RD
W14
ASKEW RD
PADDENSWICK RD
Ravenscourt Park
Stamford Brook
GLENTHORNE RD
HAMMERSMITH
W6
Brook Green
KING ST
Kings Mall
HAMMERSMITH RD
Hammersmith Broadway
Hammersmith Flyover
GREAT WEST RD
River Thames
Thames Path
HAMMERSMITH BRIDGE RD
Charing Cross
FULHAM PALACE RD
St Paul's Sch
LONSDALE RD

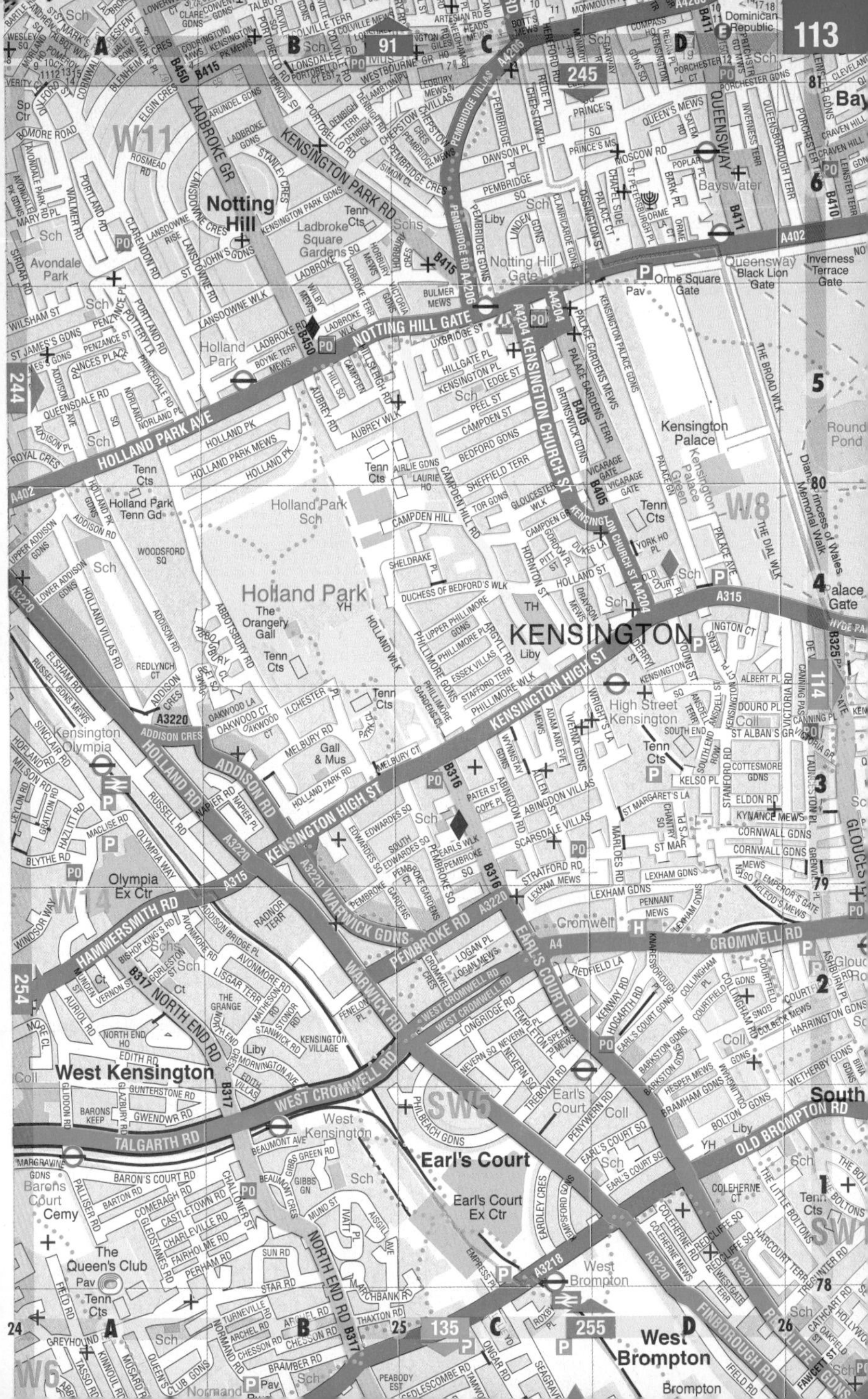

Notting Hill
Kensington
Holland Park
West Kensington
Earl's Court
West Brompton
W11
W8
W14
SW5
Notting Hill Gate
Kensington Palace
High Street Kensington
Kensington Olympia
Olympia Ex Ctr
Earl's Court Ex Ctr
The Queen's Club
Barons Court Cemy
Bayswater
Queensway
Holland Park Ave
Kensington High St
Kensington Church St
Cromwell Rd
Hammersmith Rd
Talgarth Rd
West Cromwell Rd
Old Brompton Rd
North End Rd
Warwick Rd
Earl's Court Rd
Ladbroke Gr
Kensington Park Rd
Pembridge Villas
Holland Rd
Addison Rd
Pembroke Rd
Finborough Rd
Redcliffe Gdns
Ladbroke Square Gardens
Avondale Park
Round Pond
Diana Princess of Wales Memorial Walk
91
245
244
254
114
135
255

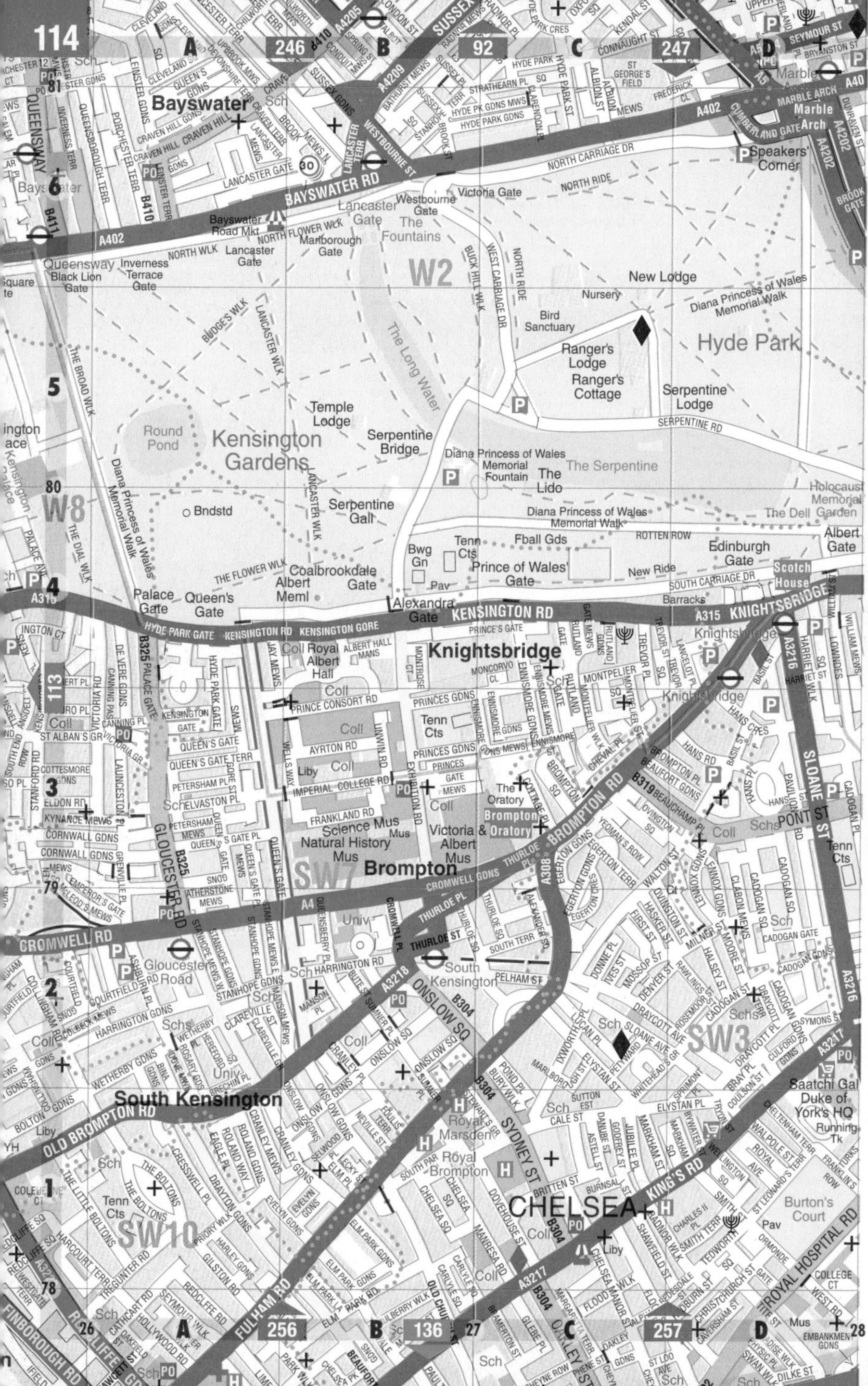

Bayswater
Hyde Park
Kensington Gardens
The Serpentine
The Long Water
Round Pond
Speakers' Corner
Marble Arch
Knightsbridge
Brompton
South Kensington
CHELSEA
Royal Albert Hall
Science Mus
Natural History Mus
Victoria & Albert Mus
Brompton Oratory
Royal Marsden
Royal Brompton
Saatchi Gal
Duke of York's HQ
Burton's Court
Serpentine Gall
Albert Meml
Diana Princess of Wales Memorial Fountain
Diana Princess of Wales Memorial Walk
The Lido
Holocaust Memorial Garden
The Dell
Bird Sanctuary
New Lodge
Ranger's Lodge
Ranger's Cottage
Serpentine Lodge
Temple Lodge
Serpentine Bridge
The Fountains
Victoria Gate
Lancaster Gate
Marlborough Gate
Westbourne Gate
Queensway Black Lion Gate
Inverness Terrace Gate
Palace Gate
Queen's Gate
Alexandra Gate
Prince of Wales' Gate
Edinburgh Gate
Albert Gate
Scotch House
Barracks
Bayswater Road Mkt
Gloucester Road
South Kensington
W2
W8
SW7
SW3
SW10
BAYSWATER RD
KENSINGTON RD
KNIGHTSBRIDGE
BROMPTON RD
CROMWELL RD
OLD BROMPTON RD
FULHAM RD
KING'S RD
SLOANE ST
SYDNEY ST
GLOUCESTER RD
QUEENSWAY
ROYAL HOSPITAL RD
SERPENTINE RD
NORTH CARRIAGE DR
SOUTH CARRIAGE DR
ROTTEN ROW
THE BROAD WLK
246
92
247
256
136
257
113
A
B
C
D
1
2
3
4
5
6

MARYLEBONE
248
93
249
A
B
C
D
Mayfair
Grosvenor Sq Gardens
Royal Academy of Arts
Piccadilly Circus
Eros
National Gallery
Leicester Square
Trafalgar
Nelson's Mon
Charing Cross
St James
Green Park
Diana, Princess of Wales Memorial Walk
Hyde Park Corner
Clarence House
St James's Palace
SW1
Duck Island
St James's Park
St James's Park Lake
Admiralty Arch
Art Galls
Horse Guards Parade
Cabinet War Rooms & Churchill Mus
Queen Victoria Meml
Buckingham Palace Gardens
Buckingham Palace
Queens Gall
The Royal Mews
Wellington Barracks
WESTMINSTER
New Scotland Yard
Westminster Abbey
Constitution Hill
(Closed to traffic on Sundays)
Horse Ride
Victoria
Cath
Belgravia
Victoria Coach
Sloane Square
Pimlico
Chelsea Barracks
Royal Hospital (Army Pensioners)
Ranelagh Gardens (Site of Chelsea Flower Show)
Tate Britain
Vauxhall Bridge
River Thames
Chelsea Bridge
Grosvenor Bridge
Oxford St
Regent St
New Bond St
Conduit St
Piccadilly
Pall Mall
Park Lane
Grosvenor Pl
Victoria St
Buckingham Palace Rd
Vauxhall Bridge Rd
Belgrave Rd
Warwick Way
Pimlico Rd
Chelsea Bridge Rd
Chelsea Embankment
Grosvenor Rd
Whitehall
Horseferry Rd
Marsham St
John Islip St
Eaton Sq
Eccleston St
Shaftesbury Ave
Charing Cross Rd
Haymarket
The Mall
Birdcage Wlk
Great George St
Parliament St
Millbank
258
137
259
116
28
29
30
1
2
3
4
5
6
78
79
80
81

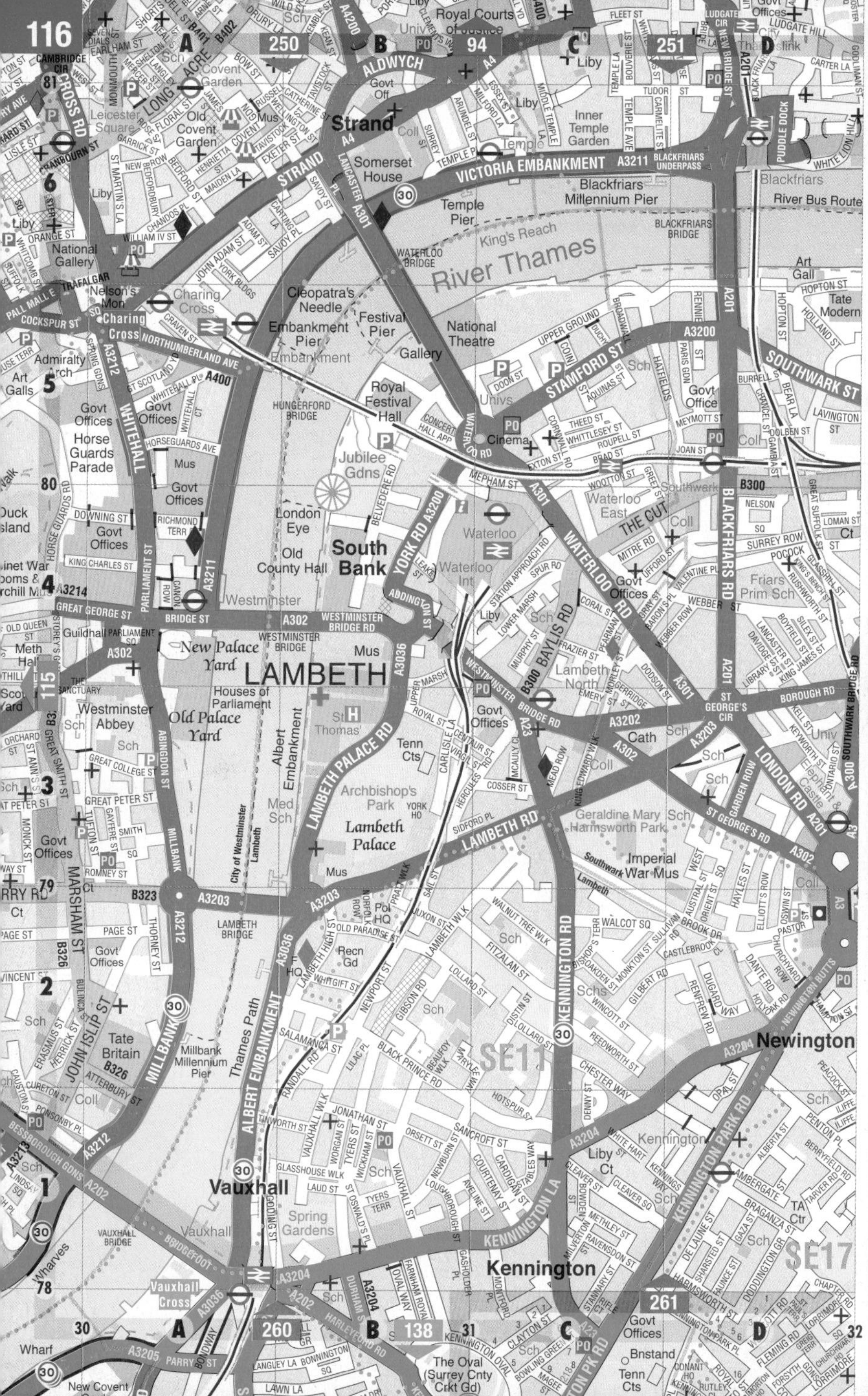
250
94
251
A
B
C
D
Royal Courts of Justice
Covent Garden
LONG ACRE
Leicester Square
Old Covent Garden
ALDWYCH
Strand
STRAND
Somerset House
VICTORIA EMBANKMENT
Temple
Inner Temple Garden
Temple Pier
Blackfriars Millennium Pier
BLACKFRIARS BRIDGE
Blackfriars
River Bus Route
King's Reach
River Thames
WATERLOO BRIDGE
National Gallery
TRAFALGAR SQ
Nelson's Mon
Charing Cross
PALL MALL E
COCKSPUR ST
Cleopatra's Needle
Embankment Pier
Festival Pier
Embankment
National Theatre
Gallery
Art Gall
Tate Modern
SOUTHWARK ST
STAMFORD ST
UPPER GROUND
NORTHUMBERLAND AVE
Admiralty Arch
Art Galls
WHITEHALL
HORSEGUARDS AVE
Horse Guards Parade
Govt Offices
HUNGERFORD BRIDGE
Royal Festival Hall
Jubilee Gdns
London Eye
Old County Hall
South Bank
YORK RD
WATERLOO RD
Cinema
Waterloo
Waterloo Int
Waterloo East
THE CUT
BLACKFRIARS RD
Southwark
Friars Prim Sch
DOWNING ST
KING CHARLES ST
PARLIAMENT ST
GREAT GEORGE ST
BRIDGE ST
Westminster
WESTMINSTER BRIDGE RD
WESTMINSTER BRIDGE
New Palace Yard
LAMBETH
Houses of Parliament
Old Palace Yard
Westminster Abbey
Guildhall
Meth Hall
115
ABINGDON ST
MILLBANK
Albert Embankment
St Thomas'
LAMBETH PALACE RD
Archbishop's Park
Lambeth Palace
BAYLIS RD
Lambeth North
ST GEORGE'S CIR
BOROUGH RD
LONDON RD
Elephant & Castle
LAMBETH RD
Geraldine Mary Harmsworth Park
Imperial War Mus
ST GEORGE'S RD
MARSHAM ST
HORSEFERRY RD
LAMBETH BRIDGE
GREAT PETER ST
JOHN ISLIP ST
Tate Britain
Millbank Millennium Pier
Thames Path
ALBERT EMBANKMENT
KENNINGTON RD
KENNINGTON LA
KENNINGTON PARK RD
SE11
SE17
Newington
NEWINGTON BUTTS
Kennington
Vauxhall
VAUXHALL BRIDGE
Vauxhall Cross
Spring Gardens
BESSBOROUGH GDNS
Wharves
The Oval (Surrey Cnty Crkt Gd)
KENNINGTON OVAL
New Covent Garden
260
138
261
30
31
32
78
79
80
81

A
B
C
D
252
95
EC4
EC3
CITY OF LONDON
St Paul's Cath
Mansion House
Cannon Street
Bank
Aldgate
Whitechapel
Fenchurch Street
Tower Hill
Tower Gateway
Monument
UPPER THAMES ST
LOWER THAMES ST
BYWARD ST
TOWER HILL A3211
ROYAL MINT ST
EAST SMITHFIELD
MILLENNIUM FOOTBRIDGE
Bankside Pier
The Globe Theatre
Swan Lane Pier
City of London
Southwark
SOUTHWARK BRIDGE
LONDON BRIDGE
Custom House
Thames Path
Tower Millennium Pier
The Tower
Traitors Gate
TOWER BRIDGE
E1
St Katharine Docks
East Dock
St Katharine's Pier
Tower Hamlets
Southwark
253
Tower Bridge Wharf
Butler's Wharf Pier
Upper Pool
The London Dungeon Mus
London Bridge City Pier
London Bridge
City Hall
TOOLEY ST
SOUTHWARK BRIDGE RD
SOUTHWARK ST
BOROUGH HIGH ST
UNION ST
Guy's
THOMAS ST
CRUCIFIX LA
BERMONDSEY ST
LONG LA
TOWER BRIDGE RD
BERMONDSEY
DRUID ST
The Borough
Borough
SE1
HARPER RD
GREAT DOVER ST
ABBEY ST
Caledonian Market
GRANGE RD
SE16
118
NEW KENT RD
Bricklayers Arms
Elephant & Castle
WALWORTH RD
OLD KENT RD
Walworth
DUNTON RD
ROLLS RD
263
2
3
4
5
6
1
80
79
78
81
262
139
33
34
Burgess Park
Cobourg Prim Sch
Superstore
TRAFALGAR AV
MANDELA WAY

118
96
253
117
263
140
A
B
C
D
6
5
4
3
2
1
E1
SE16
SE1
Shadwell
Ratcliff
St George in the East
Tobacco Dock Sh Vill
Wapping
BERMONDSEY
Rotherhithe
Canada Water
Surrey Quays Sh Ctr
River Thames
Thames Path
River Bus Route
Upper Pool
Lower Pool
Tower Gateway
St Katharine Docks
St Katharine Pier
Tower Bridge Wharf
Butler's Wharf Pier
Wapping Pier Head
Wapping Old Stairs
Wapping Pier
King Henry's Wharves
Metropolitan Wharf
New Crane Wharf
Shadwell Basin
Shadwell New Basin
London Docks
Shadwell Old Basin
Shadwell Entrance
Free Trade Wharf
Surrey Entrance
Sterling Wharf Stairs
Cherry Garden Pier
King George's Field
Southwark Park
St Joseph's RC Prim Sch
Sports Complex
Tower Bridge Bsns Complex
Tower Bridge Bsns Sq
Admiral Hyson Ind Est
Bermondsey Trad Est
South Bermondsey
The New Den (Millwall FC)
Orion Bsns Ctr
British Wharf Ind Est
Excelsior Ind Est
Elizabeth Ind Est
Mulberry Bsns Ctr
Albion Channel
Paterson Park
Lynton Est
Wevco Wharf
Ruby Triangle
Cantium Ret Pk
Kent Pk Ind Est
Sandgate Trad Est
Canal Bridge
Tower Hamlets
Southwark
Lewisham
THE HIGHWAY
CABLE ST
EAST SMITHFIELD
JAMAICA RD
LOWER RD
SOUTHWARK PARK RD
RAYMOUTH RD
ROTHERHITHE NEW RD
OLD KENT RD
ROLLS RD
CATLIN ST
BUSH RD
ROTHERHITHE TUNNEL
BERMONDSEY WALL E
BERMONDSEY WALL W
WAPPING HIGH ST
WAPPING LA
CANNON STREET RD
LEMAN ST
ROYAL MINT ST
DOCK ST
TRUNDLEYS RD
1 HYNDMAN ST
2 MURDOCK ST
3 SKENFRITH HO

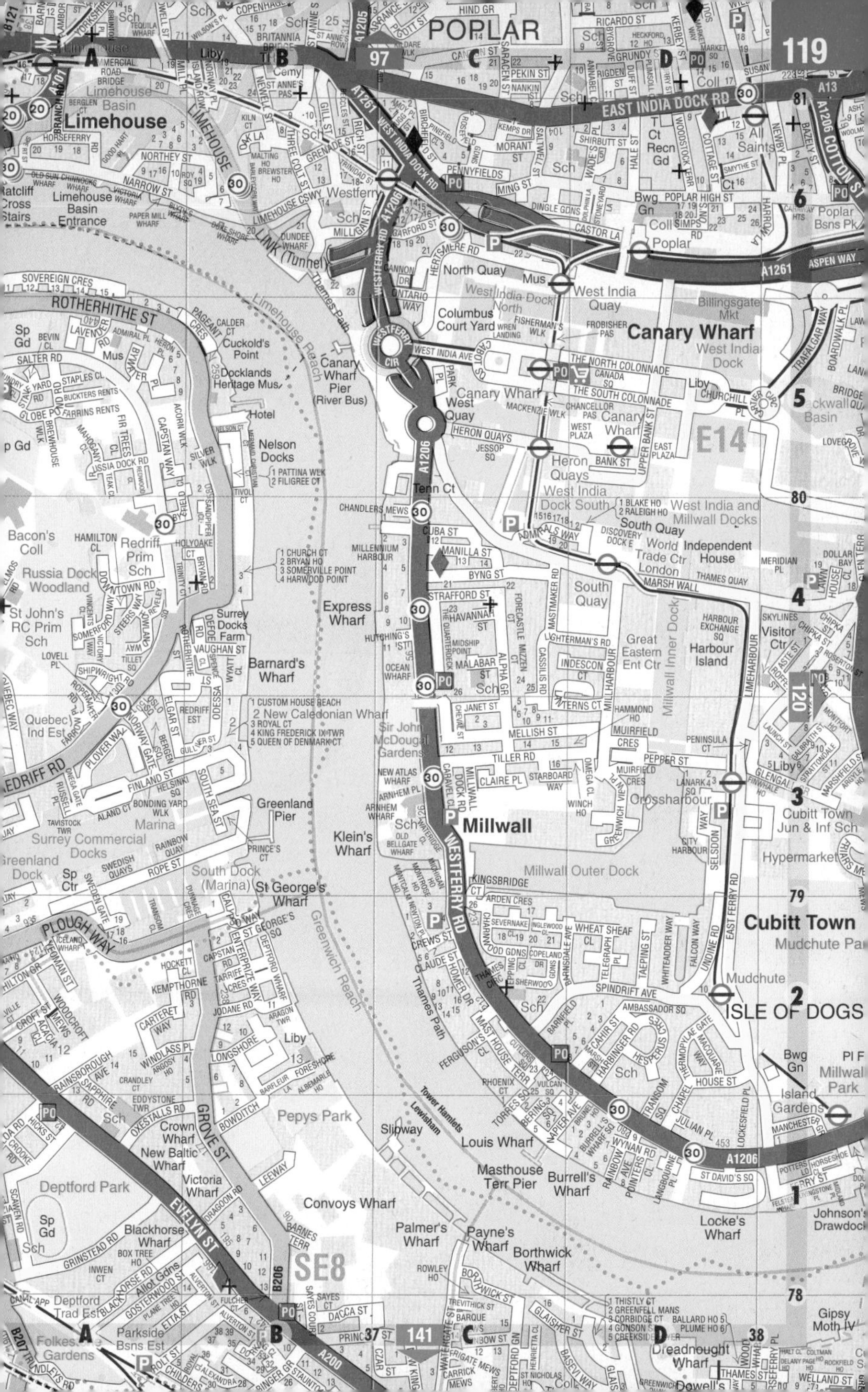

119
POPLAR
Limehouse
Limehouse Basin
LIMEHOUSE LINK (Tunnel)
EAST INDIA DOCK RD
WEST INDIA DOCK RD
POPLAR HIGH ST
Poplar
All Saints
Poplar Bsns Pk
ASPEN WAY
A1261
A1206
A13
COTTON ST
97
Westferry
NARROW ST
Limehouse Basin Entrance
Ratcliff Cross Stairs
ROTHERHITHE ST
Limehouse Reach
Canary Wharf Pier (River Bus)
Docklands Heritage Mus
Cuckold's Point
North Quay
West India Quay
Billingsgate Mkt
Canary Wharf
West India Dock
WEST INDIA AVE
WESTFERRY CIR
THE NORTH COLONNADE
THE SOUTH COLONNADE
Heron Quays
West India Dock South
E14
South Quay
Independent House
West India and Millwall Docks
MARSH WALL
Nelson Docks
Hotel
Russia Dock Woodland
Redriff Prim Sch
Bacon's Coll
St John's RC Prim Sch
Surrey Docks Farm
Express Wharf
Barnard's Wharf
Great Eastern Ent Ctr
Millwall Inner Dock
Harbour Island
Visitor Ctr
120
Quebec Ind Est
REDRIFF RD
Surrey Commercial Docks
Greenland Pier
Sir John McDougal Gardens
Crossharbour
Cubitt Town Jun & Inf Sch
Millwall
Klein's Wharf
Millwall Outer Dock
Hypermarket
South Dock (Marina)
St George's Wharf
Greenland Dock
PLOUGH WAY
Cubitt Town
Mudchute Park
Mudchute
ISLE OF DOGS
Greenwich Reach
WESTFERRY RD
Thames Path
Island Gardens
Millwall Park
Pepys Park
Louis Wharf
Masthouse Terr Pier
Burrell's Wharf
Crown Wharf
New Baltic Wharf
Victoria Wharf
Deptford Park
Convoys Wharf
GROVE ST
EVELYN ST
Blackhorse Wharf
SE8
Palmer's Wharf
Payne's Wharf
Borthwick Wharf
Locke's Wharf
Johnson's Drawdock
Gipsy Moth IV
Deptford Trad Est
Parkside Bsns Est
Folkestone Gardens
141
Dreadnought Wharf
A200
B206
A
B
C
D
1
2
3
4
5
6

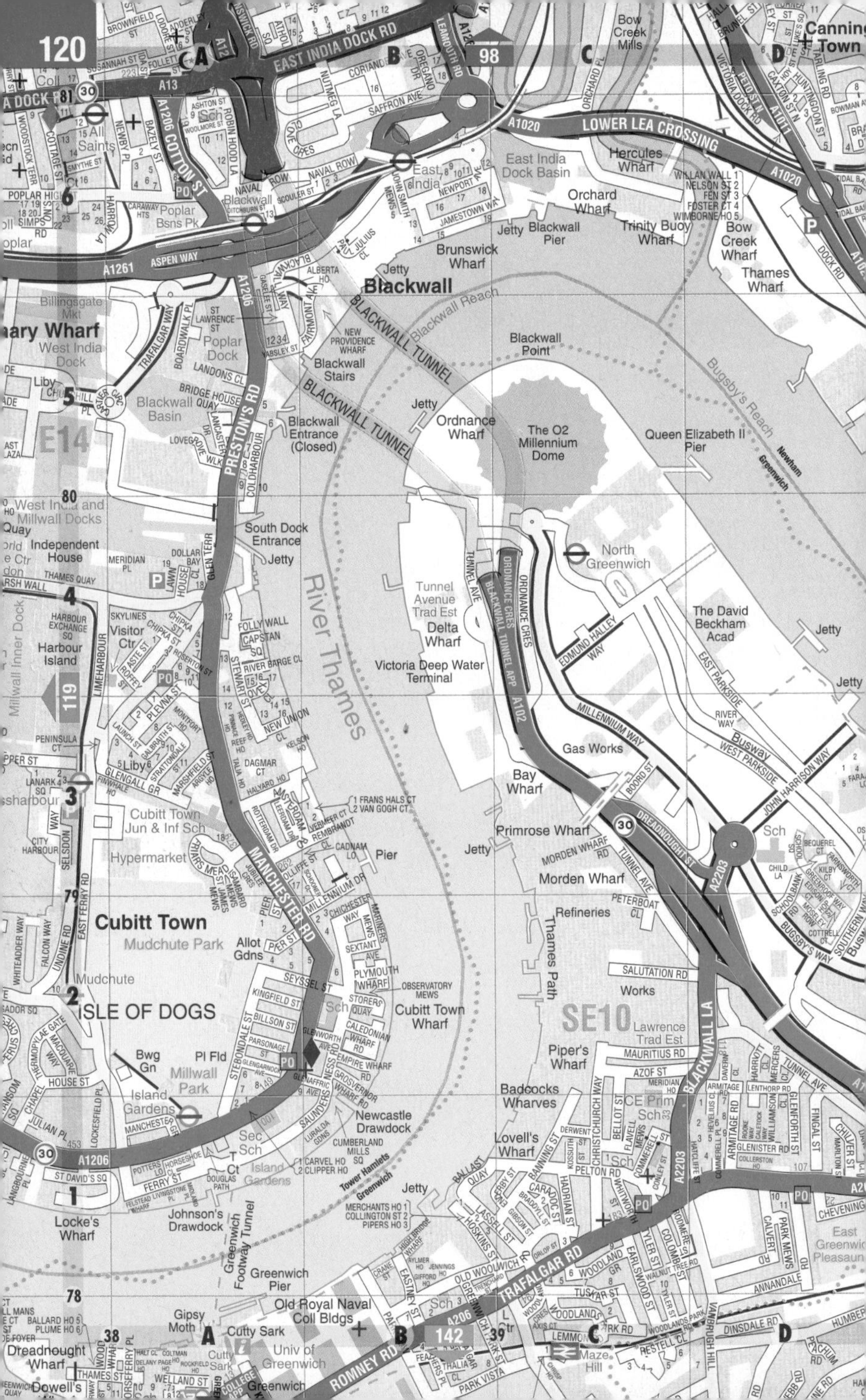
98
A
B
C
D
Canning Town
EAST INDIA DOCK RD
A13
A12
A1206 COTTON ST
ROBIN HOOD LA
BAZELY ST
NEWBY PL
COTTAGE ST
WOODSTOCK TERR
All Saints
Poplar
Poplar Bsns Pk
NUTMEG LA
CORIANDER AVE
OREGANO DR
SAFFRON AVE
LEAMOUTH RD
LOVE CRES
NAVAL ROW
East India
NEWPORT AVE
JAMESTOWN WAY
JOHN SMITH MEWS
Blackwall
ASPEN WAY
A1261
A1020
LOWER LEA CROSSING
Bow Creek Mills
ORCHARD PL
VICTORIA DOCK RD
CAXTON ST N
HUNTINGDON ST
TARLING RD
East India Dock Basin
Hercules Wharf
Orchard Wharf
Trinity Buoy Wharf
Bow Creek Wharf
Thames Wharf
DOCK RD
Jetty
Blackwall Pier
Brunswick Wharf
JULIUS CL
ALBERTA HO
Blackwall
Blackwall Reach
Billingsgate Mkt
Canary Wharf
West India Dock
TRAFALGAR WAY
BOARDWALK PL
ST LAWRENCE ST
Poplar Dock
YABSLEY ST
FAIRMONT AVE
NEW PROVIDENCE WHARF
BLACKWALL TUNNEL
Blackwall Stairs
Blackwall Point
LANDONS CL
BRIDGE HOUSE QUAY
Blackwall Basin
PRESTON'S RD
Blackwall Entrance (Closed)
LOVEGROVE WLK
COLDHARBOUR
Ordnance Wharf
The O2 Millennium Dome
Queen Elizabeth II Pier
Bugsby's Reach
Newham
Greenwich
E14
West India and Millwall Docks
Independent House
South Dock Entrance
MERIDIAN PL
THAMES QUAY
DOLLAR BAY CL
GLEN TERR
River Thames
TUNNEL AVE
ORDNANCE CRES
BLACKWALL TUNNEL APP
North Greenwich
Tunnel Avenue Trad Est
Delta Wharf
Victoria Deep Water Terminal
EDMUND HALLEY WAY
The David Beckham Acad
EAST PARKSIDE
RIVER WAY
WEST PARKSIDE
Busway
MILLENNIUM WAY
JOHN HARRISON WAY
Gas Works
A102
Harbour Island
Visitor Ctr
LIMEHARBOUR
CHIPKA ST
FOLLY WALL
CAPSTAN SQ
RIVER BARGE CL
STEWART ST
NEW UNION CL
PLEVNA ST
Millwall Inner Dock
119
PENINSULA CT
Liby
GLENGALL GR
MARSHFIELD ST
DAGMAR CT
HALYARD HO
Cubitt Town Jun & Inf Sch
Hypermarket
SELSDON WAY
CITY HARBOUR
MANCHESTER RD
ROTTERDAM DR
AMSTERDAM RD
LEERDAM DR
1 FRANS HALS CT
2 VAN GOGH CT
VERMEER CT
REMBRANDT CL
CADNAM LO
Pier
Bay Wharf
BOORD ST
DREADNOUGHT ST
Primrose Wharf
Jetty
MORDEN WHARF RD
TUNNEL AVE
Morden Wharf
PETERBOAT CL
Refineries
Sch
A2203
BUGSBY'S WAY
SOUTHERN WAY
EAST FERRY RD
UNDINE RD
FALCON WAY
WHITEADDER WAY
Cubitt Town
Mudchute Park
Allot Gdns
PIER ST
MILLENNIUM DR
CHICHESTER WAY
MARINERS MEWS
SEXTANT AVE
PLYMOUTH WHARF
OBSERVATORY MEWS
Mudchute
ISLE OF DOGS
SEYSSEL ST
KINGFIELD ST
BILLSON ST
PARSONAGE ST
STEBONDALE ST
STOREYS QUAY
CALEDONIAN WHARF
Cubitt Town Wharf
Thames Path
SALUTATION RD
Works
SE10
Lawrence Trad Est
Piper's Wharf
MAURITIUS RD
AZOF ST
BLACKWALL LA
TUNNEL AVE
Bwg Gn
Pl Fld
Millwall Park
Island Gardens
EMPIRE WHARF RD
GROSVENOR WHARF RD
SAUNDERS NESS RD
Newcastle Drawdock
CUMBERLAND MILLS SQ
Badcocks Wharves
CHRISTCHURCH WAY
CE Prim Sch
LENTHORP RD
ARMITAGE RD
WILLIAMSON CL
GLENFORTH ST
FINGAL ST
CHILVER ST
MANCHESTER GR
HOUSE ST
JULIAN PL
LOCKESFIELD PL
A1206
ST DAVID'S SQ
FERRY ST
Sec Sch
Island Gardens
1 CARVEL HO
2 CLIPPER HO
Tower Hamlets
Greenwich
Lovell's Wharf
PELTON RD
HADRIAN ST
BANNING ST
GLENISTER RD
PARK MEWS
CALVERT RD
CHEVENING RD
Locke's Wharf
Johnson's Drawdock
Greenwich Footway Tunnel
Jetty
MERCHANTS HO 1
COLLINGTON ST 2
PIPERS HO 3
BALLAST QUAY
HOSKINS ST
LASSELL ST
TRAFALGAR RD
WOODLAND GR
EARLSWOOD ST
East Greenwich Pleasaunce
ANNANDALE RD
Greenwich Pier
OLD WOOLWICH RD
HIGHBRIDGE WHARF
EASTNEY ST
CRANE ST
Old Royal Naval Coll Bldgs
Sch
TUSKAR ST
WOODLAND PK RD
VANBRUGH HILL
DINSDALE RD
HUMBER RD
Gipsy Moth
Cutty Sark
Univ of Greenwich
A206
ROMNEY RD
142
39
38
LEMMON RD
RESTELL CL
Maze Hill
PARK VISTA
Dreadnought Wharf
Dowell's
THAMES ST
WELLAND ST
COLLEGE APP
Greenwich
PEACHUM RD
80
79
78
6
5
4
3
2
1

Custom House
Custom House for ExCeL
Prince Regent
Royal Victoria
CONNAUGHT RD
A1020
Royal Albert
ExCel Ex Ctr
Royal Victoria Dock
E16
CONNAUGHT BRIDGE
SILVERTOWN WAY
NORTH WOOLWICH RD
West Silvertown
Pontoon Dock
Silvertown
Thames Barrier Park
London City Airport
Thameside Ind Est
Thames Road Ind Est
Lyle Park
Wharves
Bugsby's Reach
Woolwich Reach
The Thames Barrier
Newham
Greenwich
River Thames
Barrier Gdns Pier
Thames Barrier Visitor Ctr
Thames Path
GREENWICH
SE10
SE7
Anchorage Point Ind Est
VIP Trad Est
Meridian Trad Est
Lombard Trad Est
Stone Lake Ind Pk
Stone Lake Ret Pk
New Charlton
Charlton Gate Bsns Pk
Greenwich Sh Pk
Maritime Ind Est
WOOLWICH RD
A206
Maryon Park
The Valley (Charlton Athletic FC)
Maryon Wilson Park
Charlton
Westcombe Park
SE3
A102
CHARLTON PARK RD
99
122
143

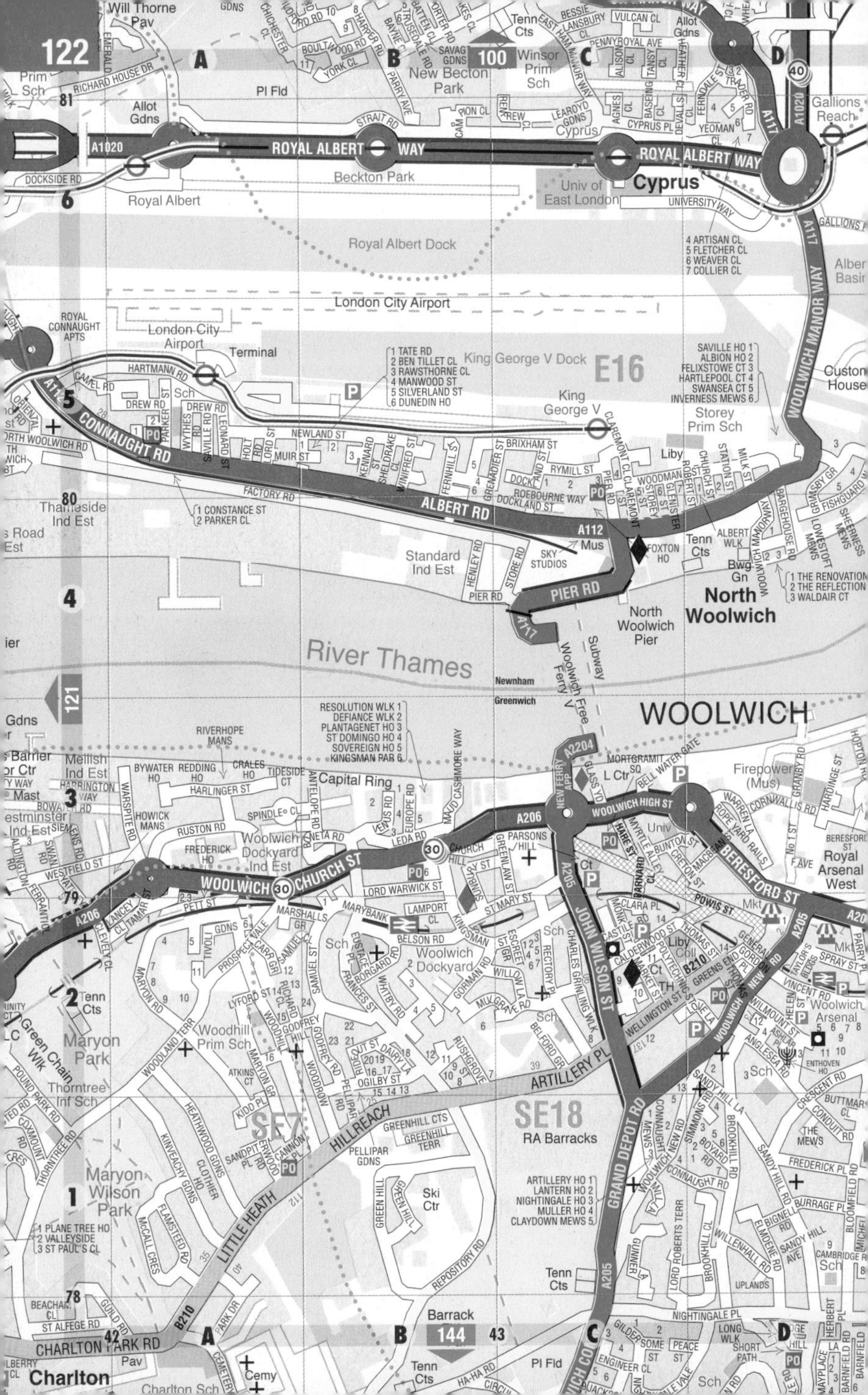

A
B
C
D
100
Will Thorne Pav
New Beckton Park
Winsor Prim Sch
Gallions Reach
ROYAL ALBERT WAY
Beckton Park
Royal Albert
Cyprus
Univ of East London
Royal Albert Dock
London City Airport
King George V Dock
E16
King George V
CONNAUGHT RD
ALBERT RD
PIER RD
North Woolwich Pier
North Woolwich
WOOLWICH MANOR WAY
River Thames
Woolwich Free Ferry
Subway
WOOLWICH
WOOLWICH CHURCH ST
WOOLWICH HIGH ST
BERESFORD ST
JOHN WILSON ST
GRAND DEPOT RD
Woolwich Dockyard
Royal Arsenal West
Woolwich Arsenal
Maryon Park
Maryon Wilson Park
SE7
SE18
RA Barracks
ARTILLERY PL
HILLREACH
LITTLE HEATH
CHARLTON PARK RD
Charlton
121
144
Barrack

A
B
101
C
D
E6
Mast
Newham
Greenwich
Margaret or Tripcock Ness
Thamesmead Sh Ctr
NAVIGATION CT
EBB CT
Gallions Reach
SE28
E16
River Thames
BRIDGE HO
DEFENCE CL
HILL HO
MURRAY CL
WARRIOR CL
TUMP HO
BAILEY CL
TOR GR
1 MARTINS WLK
2 MARTINS PL
3 SHEPHERDS LA
4 CROWFOOT CL
5 LONGMARSH LA
HIGH TOR VIEW
BARNHAM DR
WATERSIDE CL
BARNHAM DR
GRASSHAVEN WAY
NEWMARSH RD
TRICORN HO 1
TIDEHAM HO 2
TRIDENT HO 3
STRAND HO 4
TIDESLEA PATH
MILES CL
MILES DR
MARTIN ST
HILL VIEW DR
TEASEL CRES
FOXGROVE PATH
1 HULL PL
2 SUNDERLAND POINT
3 INVERNESS MEWS
NARROW BOAT CL
MERBURY CL
BLUEBIRD WAY
DELISLE RD
NEW ACRES RD
BATTERY RD
MARATHON WAY
BELLERMINE CL
A2041
A2016
PRINCESS ALICE WAY
WARE POINT DR
RIDGE CL
MERBURY RD
TUGBOAT ST
THAMES REACH
BATTERY RD
KENTLEA RD
ANSON PL
FISHERMANS WLK
WESTERN WAY
Cobalt
HARNESS RD
NATHAN WAY
TIDESLEA TWR 1
SARK TWR 2
GRANARY MANS 3
BENDISH POINT 4
TIDELOCK HO
GALLIONS VIEW RD
CUMBERLAND HO
GADWALL WAY
NUTHATCH GDNS
WREN PATH
Ct
HARRIER MEWS
REDWING PATH
CHARLESMERE GDNS
HM Prison Belmarsh
PURLAND RD
124
MARLBOROUGH RD
EREBUS DR
CAMELOT CL
LIVESEY CL
TEMPLE CL
PIER WAY
TUPPY ST
WHINCHAT RD
WIDGEON PATH
GOLDFINCH RD
MERGANSER GDNS
AVOCET MEWS
GRIFFIN WAY
NATHAN WAY
Mast
ARGYLL RD
HARDINGE CRES
CARRONADE PL
GOOSANDER WAY
KELLNER RD
CADOGAN RD
ARMSTRONG RD
Heronsgate Prim Sch
Royal Arsenal East
BOUGHTON RD
West Thamesmead Bsns Pk
WHITE HART AVE
Sienna
HASTINGS ST
Io Ctr
ALLENBY RD
PETTACRE CL
BROADWATER RD
GARRICK DR
CHAMBERLAIN CL
A2016
GRIFFIN MANOR WAY
St Thomas a Beckett RC Prim Sch
Royal Arsenal West
HADDEN RD
Allot Gdns
DUKE OF WELLINGTON AVE
A206 PETTMAN CRES
Works
GUNNERY TERR
CORNWALLIS RD
SKEFFINGTON ST
SEYMOUR ST
TOM CRIBB RD
GARSIDE CL
Gateway Bsns Ctr
1 PASSFIELD HO
2 LENTON ST
3 FORELAND ST
Sports Gd
Bwg Gn
Tenn Cts
79
PLUMSTEAD RD
NORTH RD
Plumstead
Coll
POLTHORNE GR
DAVE RAMSEY HO
CHURCH MANOR WAY
GILL CT
JESSUP CL
WALKER CL
MAXEY RD
SAMSON HO
VILLAS RD
CLENDON WAY
MARMADON RD
BIRKDALE RD
BURRAGE GR
INVERMORE PL
BARTH MEWS
HEVERHAM RD
WHITE HART RD
SE18
WALMER TERR
REIDHAVEN RD
GUNNING ST
HARTVILLE RD
BALGOWAN ST
HYLTON ST
Plumstead
BROOKDENE RD
ARTHUR GR
RICHMOND PL
OLIVER CT
ROBERT ST
ELMLEY ST
SOUTHPORT RD
MOUNT PLEASANT RD
ABERY ST
GARIBALDI ST
KENTMERE RD
BARTH RD
BANNOCKBURN RD
BENARES RD
MANTON RD
MYRA ST
DAWSON CL
ANN ST
GLYNDON RD
Sch
MINERAL ST
HECTOR ST
BEBBINGTON RD
PO
PLUMSTEAD HIGH ST
Bannockburn Prim Sch
AMAR CT
ABEL HO 1
MAYNARD HO 2
CROWN HO 3
RISE WAY
CONWAY RD
GALLOSSON RD
OLD TRAMYARD
Liby & Mus
RASHGAR RD
CERES RD
ST NICHOLAS RD
CAMROSE ST
SANDBACH PL
PATTISON WLK
SWETENHAM WLK
EARL RISE
SOUTH RISE
GRIFFIN RD
COXWELL RD
INGLEDEW RD
LIFFLER RD
MIRIAM RD
ORISSA RD
WILLOW FIELDS CL
STRANDFIELD CL
STRAND CT
SPERANZA ST
QUILTER ST
AMARDEEP CT
MYRTLEDENE
BURRAGE RD
RAGLAN RD
VICARAGE RD
ROBERT ST
DRAWELL CL
A206
HUDSON PL
DURHAM RISE
WAVERLEY RD
MAENDIE RD
ANCONA RD
BREWERY RD
TEWSON RD
Sports Ctr
RIPPOLSON RD
GRANITE ST
A209
ST JAMES'S CL
CONGLETON GR
COUPLAND PL
VICARAGE PK
MANTHORPE RD
BRAMBLEBURY RD
BURWASH RD
EMMANUEL HO
CONGO RD
LEGHORN RD
LAKEDALE RD
HAWKSMOOR CL
TYNEMOUTH RD
RIVERDALE RD
SAUNDERS RD
PURRETT RD
BARGATE CL
SPINEL CL
FELSPAR CL
GROSMONT RD
ROCKMOUNT RD
GATLING RD
THE DELL
DENEHOLE HO
GLENDOWN RD
BASTION RD
ST MARGARET'S TERR
HEAVITREE CL
WAVERLEY CRES
GOSSAGE RD
TUSCAN RD
PIEDMONT RD
CHESTNUT RISE
PARKDALE RD
ROYDENE RD
SLADEDALE RD
PHILIMORE CL
MARBLE HO 1
CRYSTAL HO 2
BERYL HO 3
GALENA HO 4
LAND RD
VIEW
HEATH VILLAS
Gallions Mount Prim Sch
Allot Gdns
St Margaret's CE Prim Sch
Tenn Cts
HEAVITREE RD
Sch
THE OAKS
ST MARGARET'S GR
TERR
BLENDON
Bwg Gn
ST JOHN'S TERR
Tenn Cts
INVERARY PL
78
GLOBE
PO
WERNBROOK ST
MILL RD
WARWICK TERR
45
145
C
WINN COMMON RD
Plumstead Common
D
46
RUTHERGLEN RD
SANDYCROFT
PLUMSTEAD COMMON RD
Plumstead Manor/Negus Sch
CHURCH HYDE
BLEAK HILL LA
Pav

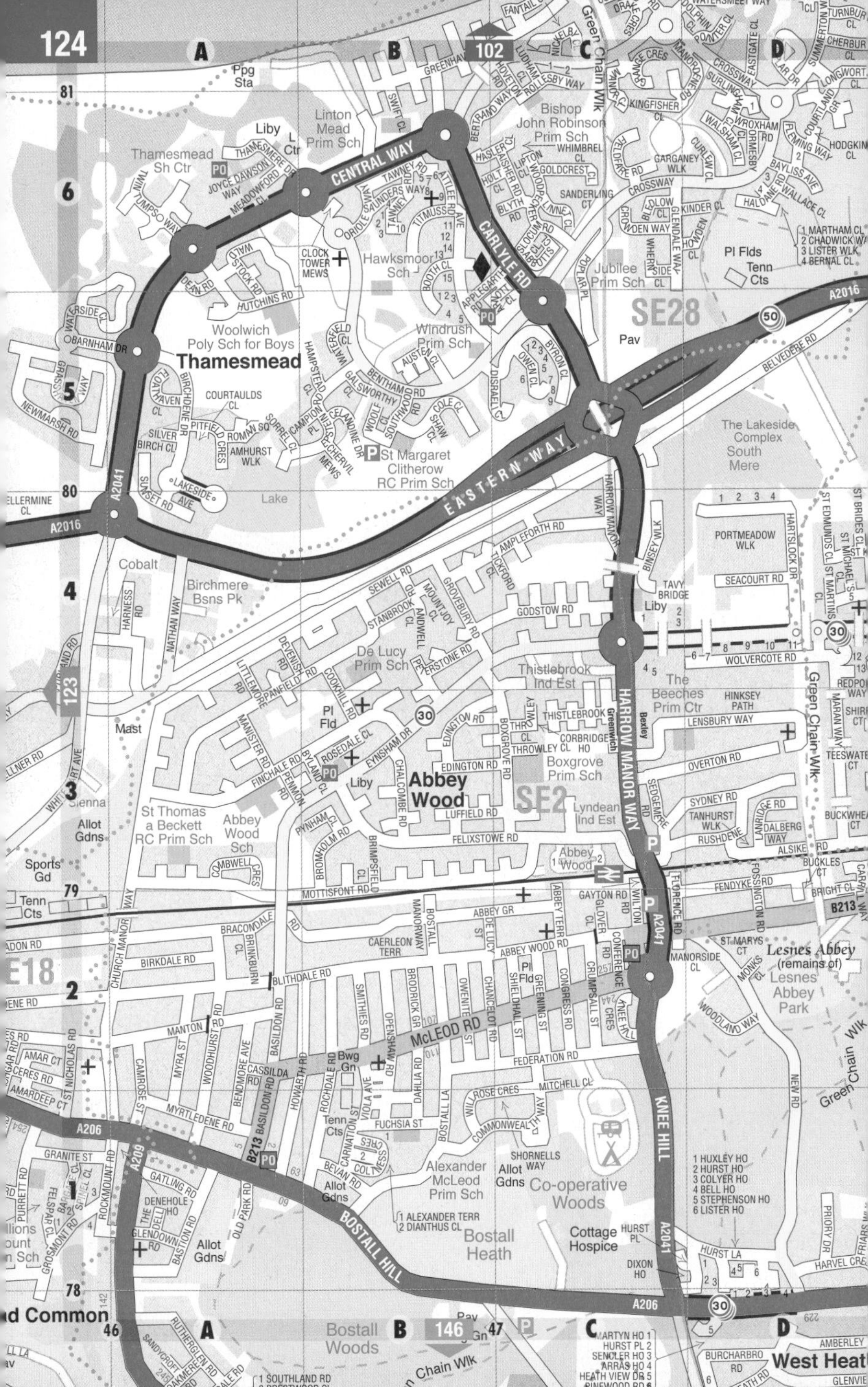
A
B
C
D
102
Ppg Sta
81
Linton Mead Prim Sch
Liby
L Ctr
Thamesmead Sh Ctr
PO
THAMESMERE DR
JOYCE DAWSON WAY
MEADOWFORD CL
NIMUL
TUMPSON WAY
CENTRAL WAY
GREENHAVEN DR
SWIFT CL
FANTAIL CL
LUDHAM CL
HOVETON RD
NICKELBY CL
ROLLESBY WAY
BERTRAND WAY
Bishop John Robinson Prim Sch
WHIMBREL CL
HASLER CL
GOLDCREST CL
SANDERLING CT
Green Chain Wlk
DRAKE CRES
WATERSMEET WAY
DOLPHIN CL
POINTER CL
GRANGE CRES
MANORDENE RD
KINGFISHER CL
CROSSWAY
SURLINGHAM CL
EASTGATE CL
TURNBUR CL
CHERBUR CL
SUMMERTON WAY
LONGWORTH CL
COURTLAND GR
FLEMING WAY
HODGKIN CL
BAYLISS AVE
WALLACE CL
HALDANE RD
WROXHAM RD
ORMESBY CL
WALSHAM CL
CURLEW CL
GARGANEY WLK
FELDFARE RD
BLEDLOW CL
KINDER CL
GLENDALE WAY
HOWDEN CL
CROWDEN WAY
WHERNSIDE CL
1 MARTHAM CL
2 CHADWICK WAY
3 LISTER WLK
4 BERNAL CL
Pl Flds
Tenn Cts
Jubilee Prim Sch
POPLAR PL
SE28
A2016
50
BELVEDERE RD
Pav
6
CLOCK TOWER MEWS
ORIOLE WAY
SAUNDERS WAY
TAWNEY RD
TITMUSS AVE
ATTLEE RD
Hawksmoor Sch
BOOTH CL
APPLEGARTH RD
CARLYLE RD
HOLT CL
BLYTH RD
SLOCUM CL
LINNET CL
WOODPECKER RD
WALDSTOCK RD
DEAN RD
HUTCHINS RD
WATERSIDE CL
BARNHAM DR
Woolwich Poly Sch for Boys
Thamesmead
Windrush Prim Sch
WATERFIELD CL
HAMPSTEAD CL
AUSTEN CL
BENTHAM RD
BYRON CL
OWEN CL
DISRAELI CL
GALSWORTHY CL
SOUTHWOOD RD
COLE CL
SHAW CL
WOOLF CL
5
GRASSWAY
NEWMARSH RD
FLOATHAVEN CL
BIRCHDENE DR
COURTAULDS CL
PITFIELD CRES
ROMAN SQ
SORREL CL
CAMPION PL
CELANDINE DR
CHERVIL MEWS
SILVER BIRCH CL
AMHURST WLK
St Margaret Clitherow RC Prim Sch
EASTERN WAY
The Lakeside Complex
South Mere
LAKESIDE AVE
SUNSET RD
Lake
A2041
80
ELLERMINE CL
HARROW MANOR WAY
AMPLEFORTH RD
TICKFORD CL
BINSEY WLK
PORTMEADOW WLK
HARTSLOCK DR
ST EDMUNDS CL
ST BRIDES CL
ST MICHAELS CL
ST MARTINS CL
SEACOURT RD
Cobalt
Birchmere Bsns Pk
HARNESS RD
NATHAN WAY
4
SEWELL RD
STANBROOK RD
MOUNTJOY CL
GROVEBURY RD
GODSTOW RD
TAVY BRIDGE
Liby
30
WOLVERCOTE RD
123
De Lucy Prim Sch
DEVENISH RD
LITTLEMORE RD
PANFIELD RD
COOKHILL RD
ANDWELL CL
PERSTONE RD
Thistlebrook Ind Est
The Beeches Prim Ctr
HINKSEY PATH
REDPOLL WAY
Mast
Pl Fld
EYNSHAM DR
ROSEDALE CL
EDINGTON RD
BOXGROVE RD
THROWLEY CL
THISTLEBROOK
CORBRIDGE HO
LENSBURY WAY
Green Chain Wlk
MARIAN WAY
TEESWATER CT
MANISTER RD
FINCHALE RD
BYLAND CL
PENMON RD
CHALCOMBE RD
Abbey Wood
EDINGTON RD
Boxgrove Prim Sch
OVERTON RD
SE2
Greenwich
Bexley
WHITEHART AVE
3
Sienna
St Thomas a Beckett RC Prim Sch
Abbey Wood Sch
PYNHAM CL
BROMHOLM RD
BRIMPSFIELD CL
LUFFIELD RD
Lyndean Ind Est
SEDGEMERE RD
SYDNEY RD
TANHURST WLK
LANRIDGE RD
DALBERG WAY
RUSHDENE
BUCKWHEAT CT
ALSIKE RD
Allot Gdns
Sports Gd
COMBWELL CRES
FELIXSTOWE RD
Abbey Wood
BUCKLES CT
79
Tenn Cts
MOTTISFONT RD
GAYTON RD
WILTON RD
FLORENCE RD
FENDYKE RD
FOSSINGTON RD
BRIGHT CL
B213
CHURCH MANOR WAY
BRACONDALE RD
BRINKBURN CL
MANORWAY
BOSTALL
ABBEY GR
DE LUCY ST
ABBEY TERR
GLOVER CL
A2041
CAERLEON TERR
ABBEY WOOD RD
CONFERENCE RD
PO
ST MARYS CT
MANORSIDE CL
MONKS CL
Lesnes Abbey (remains of)
Lesnes Abbey Park
E18
BIRKDALE RD
2
BLITHDALE RD
SMITHIES RD
OPENSHAW RD
BRODRICK GR
OWENITE ST
CHANCELOT RD
SHIELDHALL ST
GREENING ST
CONGRESS RD
CRUMPSALL ST
KNEE HILL CRES
Pl Fld
WOODLAND WAY
MANTON RD
WOODHURST RD
MYRA ST
BENDMORE AVE
BASILDON RD
HOWARTH RD
McLEOD RD
ROCHDALE RD
Bwg Gn
FEDERATION RD
AMAR CT
CERES RD
AMARDEEP CT
ST NICHOLAS RD
CAMROSE ST
CASSILDA RD
MYRTLEDENE RD
VIOLA AVE
DAHLIA RD
BOSTALL LA
WILLROSE CRES
MITCHELL CL
COMMONWEALTH WAY
Tenn Cts
FUCHSIA ST
CARNATION ST
COLTNESS CRES
BEVAN RD
KNEE HILL
NEW RD
Green Chain Wlk
A206
GRANITE ST
A209
B213 BASILDON RD
PO
SHORNELLS WAY
Allot Gdns
Co-operative Woods
1 HUXLEY HO
2 HURST HO
3 COLYER HO
4 BELL HO
5 STEPHENSON HO
6 LISTER HO
1
PURRETT RD
FELSPAR CL
SPINEL CL
GROSMONT RD
ROCKMOUNT RD
GATLING RD
THE DELL
DENEHOLE HO
GLENDOWN RD
BASTION RD
OLD PARK RD
Alexander McLeod Prim Sch
Allot Gdns
1 ALEXANDER TERR
2 DIANTHUS CL
Bostall Heath
Cottage Hospice
HURST PL
DIXON HO
A2041
PRIORY DR
HURST LA
HARVEL CRES
Allot Gdns
BOSTALL HILL
78
A206
30
Common
46
A
Bostall Woods
B
146
47
Pav
Gn
C
D
Chain Wlk
SANDYCROFT
RUTHERGLEN RD
OAKMERE RD
1 SOUTHLAND RD
2 PRESTWOOD CL
MARTYN HO 1
HURST PL 2
SENCLER HO 3
ARRAS HO 4
HEATH VIEW DR 5
PINEWOOD RD 6
BURCHARBRO RD
AMBERLEY
West Heath
GLENVIEW

Barking & Dagenham
Bexley
Halfway Reach
Jetties
103
A
B
C
D
SE28
SE2
Crossness Pumping Station
Riverside
Sewage Works
Jetty
Kent STREET ATLAS
DA17
NORMAN RD
Pl Fld
EASTERN WAY
A2016
PICARDY MANORWAY
BRONZE AGE WAY
DA18
Erith Marshes
East Thamesmead Bsns Pk
Hailey Rd Bsns Pk
The Business Acad
1 CLYDESDALE HO
2 TREFOIL HO
3 TIMOTHY HO
4 MUSCOVY HO
Capital Ind Est
Elbourne Trad Est
A2016 Dartford (A206)
St John Fisher RC Prim Sch
YARNTON WAY
Northwood Prim Sch
Parkway Prim Sch
Belvedere
Allot Gdns
GILBERT RD
PICARDY ST
ABBEY RD
LOWER RD
Belvedere Jun & Inf Sch
Woodside Sch
Tenn Cts
St Augustine CE Prim Sch
Green Chain Wlk
Lesnes Abbey Woods
PICARDY RD
Frank's Park
Trinity Sch
A206 Dartford, M25 (A282)
ERITH RD
A206
WOOLWICH RD
Lessness Heath Prim Sch
Bexley Coll
Lessness Heath
DA8
147
Cemy

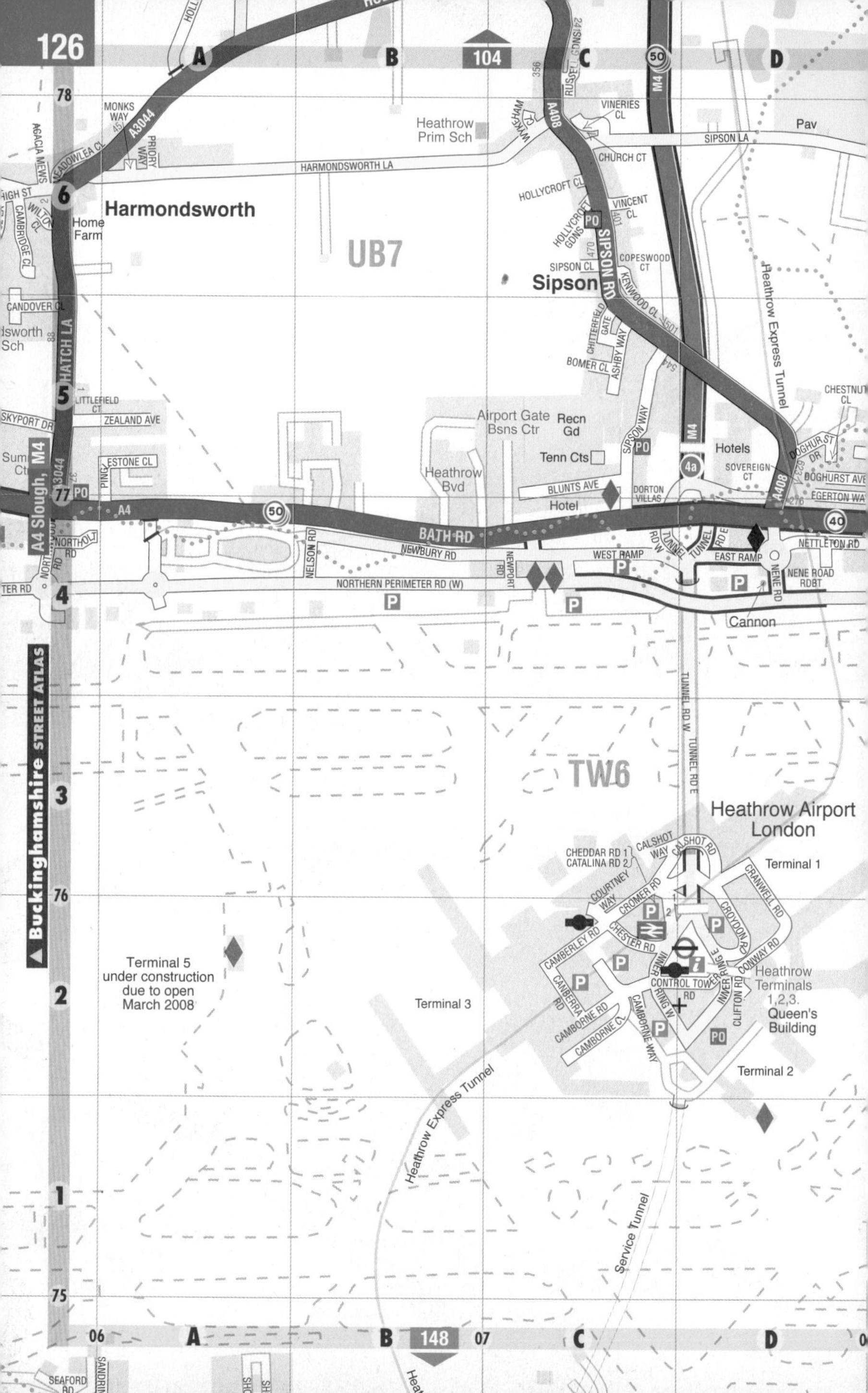
Harmondsworth
UB7
Sipson
TW6
Heathrow Airport London
Terminal 1
Terminal 2
Terminal 3
Terminal 5 under construction due to open March 2008
Heathrow Terminals 1,2,3. Queen's Building
Heathrow Express Tunnel
Service Tunnel
BATH RD
NORTHERN PERIMETER RD (W)
HARMONDSWORTH LA
SIPSON RD
SIPSON LA
HATCH LA
A4 Slough, M4
Buckinghamshire STREET ATLAS

A
B
C
D
105
Nine Elms Farm
Sports Gd
Pav
William Byrd Sch
Harlington
VICTORIA LA
BLETCHMORE CL
BRICKFIELD LA
PEMBURY CT
KILN CL
HUDSON RD
RICHARDS CL
SIPSON LA
FORGE CL
GOTHIC CT
FELLOWES CT
SHORTLANDS
HIGH ST
A437
PO
FELBRIDGE CT
MANOR LA
POND SIDE
MANSE CL
OAKLEY CT
THE CRESCENT
GILPIN WAY
PROVIDENCE CT
PROVIDENCE LA
HIGH STREET HARLINGTON
WEST END LA
FIELD CL
RAYWOOD CL
TASKER CL
CROFT CL
HARLINGTON CL
GRAMPIAN CL
QUANTOCK CL
WARNER CL
Poultry Farm
LITTLE ELMS
Sp Gd
BROWNGRAVES RD
PENNINE WAY
NEW RD
BREWDON CL
CHEVIOT CL
HALL LA
HEATH CL
MENDIP CL
MARLBOROUGH CRES
DAVID CL
CAROLINE PL
NOBEL DR
BULTON'S LA
MONDIAL WAY
Hotel
TRIUMPH CL
Hotels
Harlington Cnr
Hotel
Visitor Ctr
World Bsns Ctr
NEWALL RD
NEPTUNE RD
BATH RD
HATTON RD N
NORTHROP RD
NORTHERN PERIMETER RD
Hotel
Gravel Pits
Frog's Ditch
CRANFORD LA
The White House
ACORN GR
SAUNTON AVE
PENDELL AVE
STRATHEARN AVE
LANGLEY CRES
VANTAGE CT
OXFORD AVE
WINCHESTER RD
ETON RD
WINDSOR PARK RD
MALVERN RD
CRANESWATER
PARK LA
The White Hart (PH)
DUDSET LA
Cranford Park
UB3
6
5
4
3
2
1
78
77
76
75
P
CRANFORD LA
ENFIELD ROAD RDBT
ENFIELD RD
EPSOM SQ
ELY RD
ESHER CRES
ELGIN CRES
EASTERN PERIMETER RD
Eastern Bsns Pk
TW6
128
London Loop
Hillingdon
Hounslow
EASTCHURCH ROAD RDBT
VANGUARD WAY
EXETER WAY
EXETER RD
EASTCHURCH RD
ELECTRA AVE
EAGLE RD
ELMDON RD
CRANFORD LA
Hotel
HATTON CROSS RDBT
VISCOUNT WAY
Hatton Cross
LITHGOW'S RD
A30
GREAT SOUTH-WEST RD
SOUTHERN PERIMETER RD
STEAM FARM LA
DICK TURPIN WAY
Radius Pk
Hatton
HATTON RD
ST THERESA'S RD
ST ANTHONY'S WAY
FAGG'S RD
DOCKWELL CL
GREEN MAN LA
MYRTLE AVE
WELLINGTON RD
Tenn Cts
Fball
Cemy
Playground
09
10
149

A
B
C
D
106
M4
A312
50
78
6
5
4
3
2
1
76
75
77
10
11
127
150
30
40
Lower Park Farm
WATERSPLASH LA
THE HARTLANDS
CHURCH RD
SOUTHALL LA
Bwg Gn
Tenn Cts
The Heston Ctr
INTERNATIONAL AVE
RECTORY WAY
The Spitfire Est
Airlinks
Airlinks Ind Est
Heston Motorway Service Area
Sp Gd
CRANE LODGE RD
Cranford Park
Cranford Com Coll
UB3
REDWOOD EST
Parkway Trad Est
Heston Phoenix Distribution Pk
NORTH RD
SOUTH RD
AERODROME WAY
HARLECH GDNS
PHOENIX WAY
NORTH FIELD RD
FAIRMEAD CL
Berkeley Prim Sch
CRANFORD LA
BRABAZON RD
PEGG RD
QUINTON CL
HIGH ST
The Queen's Head (PH)
Rectory Farm
BLERIOT RD
DE HAVILLAND RD
SOPWITH RD
COBHAM RD
WRIGHT RD
WHITTLE RD
JOHNSON RD
ALCOCK RD
ARMYTAGE RD
NORMAN CRES
SCOTT GDNS
WHITECROFT
The Cedars Prim Sch
Tenn Cts
Avenue Park
Bwg Gn
BRUNEL CL
Allot Gdns
ACORN GR
SAUNTON AVE
PENDELL AVE
STRATHEARN AVE
LANGLEY CRES
KEYSHAM AVE
SHEEPCOTE CL
HAWTHORN CL
AVENUE GDNS
FIRS DR
THE PARKWAY
CRANESWATER
PARK LA
COLE GDNS
SANDRINGHAM GDNS
THE AVENUE
AVENUE CL
PINE TREE CL
ROYSTON CL
MORNINGTON CRES
LYNCHEN CL
The White Hart (PH)
A4
DUDSET LA
WAYE AVE
SANDOWN CL
BLOOMSBURY CT
TREFUSIS CT
COMMUNITY CL
TW5
Cranford
Waggoners Rdbt
ASH GR
LYNMOUTH GDNS
BROWNING WAY
SPRINGWELL RD
CHAILEY CL
MARCHSIDE CL
BROADWELL CT
ALL SAINTS CT
ALMORAH RD
Allot Gdns
BURNS WAY
SHELLEY CRES
PARKLANDS PAR
Henleys Rdbt
Hounslow
Hillingdon
London Loop
MEADOWBANK GDNS
CLEVEDON GDNS
BURNHAM GDNS
Liby
REGENT CL
FIELD CL
BERKELEY AVE
WESTWICK GDNS
BATH RD
RECTORY RD
RECTORY CT
ACTON GN
CEDAR RD
HASLEMERE AVE
TRAVELLERS WAY
HURN CT
PARKLANDS CT
HURN COURT RD
SPRINGWELL CT
A3006
EASTERN PERIMETER RD
BYRON AVE
WOODFIELD RD
STANSFIELD RD
WINDSOR RD
CHAUCER AVE
Allot Gdns
Cranford Jun & Inf Schs
GRANTLEY RD
ST DUNSTAN'S RD
A30
LANCASTER PL
ANN PARKES CT
LEGRACE AVE
LELA AVE
KEVIN CL
FRANCIS RD
The Haslemere & Heathrow Est
SILVER JUBILEE WAY
Cranebank
River Crane
TW6
GREAT SOUTH-WEST RD
MUSQUASH WAY
RACCOON WAY
CHINCHILLA DR
BADGER CL
SABLE CL
OPOSSUM WAY
ERMINE CL
SQUIRREL CL
MINK CT
MARMOT RD
VINCENT RD
WILTON RD
BASILDENE RD
MANOR AVE
ROSEMARY AVE
IVANHOE RD
CLIFFORD RD
Recn Gd
CHESTER RD
ELY RD
WARWICK RD
ARIEL WAY
Heathrow Causeway Est
Heathrow International Trad Est
ARUNDEL RD
BEAVERS LA
Beavers Com Prim Sch
PRINCESS CT
MARNELL WAY
Hounslow West
Barracks
TW4
CRANFORD LA
Hotel
GIRLING WAY
Sun Life Trad Est
Wallbrook Bsns Ctr
LICHFIELD RD
SALISBURY RD
Prologis Pk
CAUSEWAY
Resr
Sp Gd
DICK TURPIN WAY
DOCKWELL CL
TW14
STEYNING WAY
GREEN LA
Beavers Lane Camp
CAVALRY CRES
BEAVERS CRES
HINTON AVE
Radius Pk
FAGG'S RD
THERESA'S RD
ST ANTHONY'S WAY
GREEN MAN LA
HATTON GN
Lawrence Est
LAWRENCE RD
Maple Gr Bsns Ctr
PULBOROUGH WAY
Allot Gdns
CARDINGTON SQ
HERON WAY
North Feltham Trad Est
SPUR RD
River Gdns Bsns Ctr
Tamian Ind Est
TAMIAN WAY
CLEMENTS CT
Central Pk Est
Allot Gdns
Haslemere Ind Est
ARMADALE RD
WAYE AVE
SPACE WAY
PIER RD
DELL RD
Freehold Ind Ctr
AMBERLEY WAY
Fairway Est
FAIRWAY CL
Dockwell's Ind Est
North Feltham
ISLAY GDNS
A315
Garden Ctr

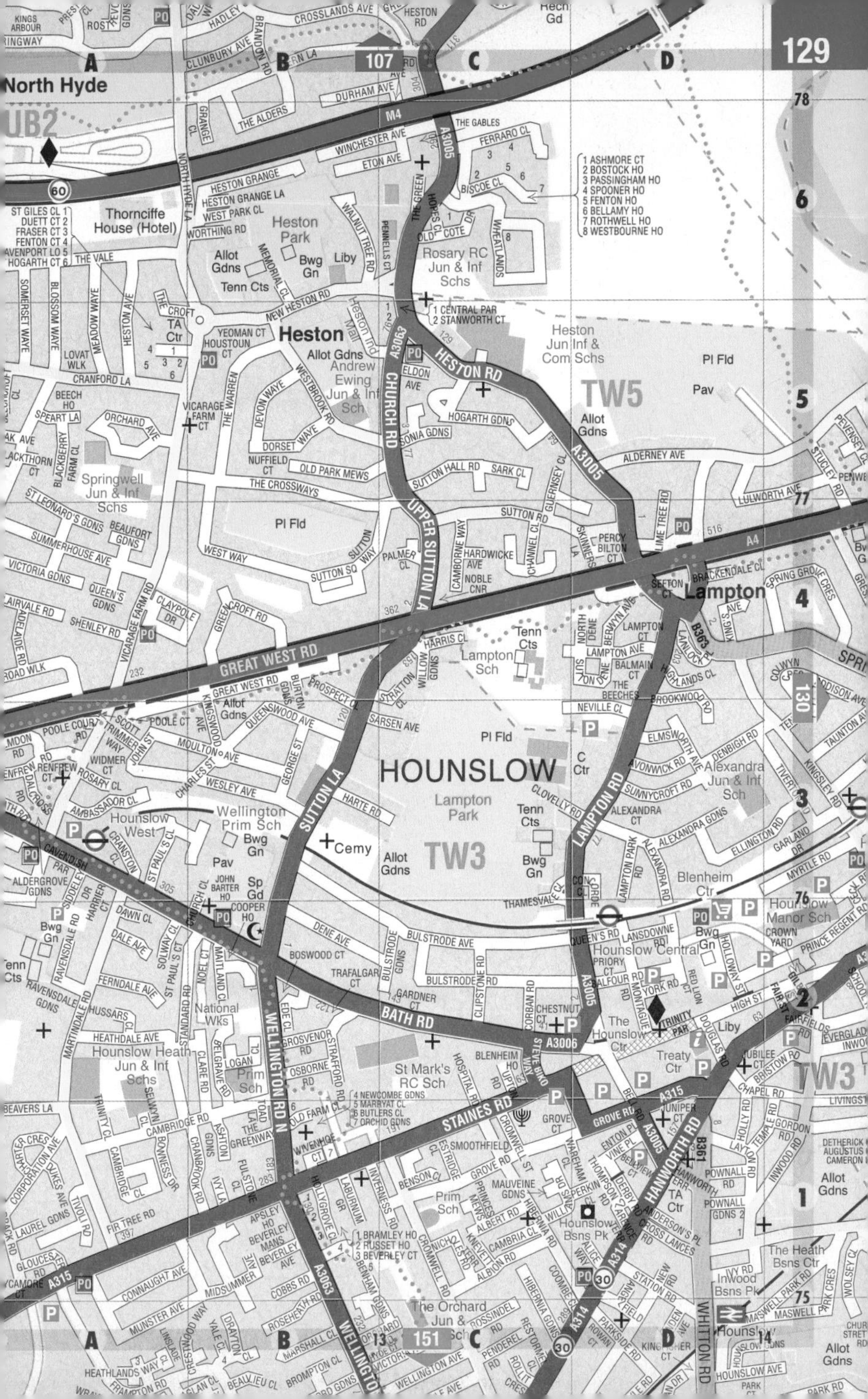
North Hyde
Heston
HOUNSLOW
Lampton
Hounslow West
Hounslow Central
TW5
TW3
UB2
A3005
A3063
A4
A315
A3006
A314
B363
B361
M4
GREAT WEST RD
HESTON RD
CHURCH RD
UPPER SUTTON LA
SUTTON LA
LAMPTON RD
BATH RD
STAINES RD
WELLINGTON RD N
HANWORTH RD
WHITTON RD
NORTH HYDE LA
NEW HESTON RD
CRANFORD LA
THE CROSSWAYS
WEST WAY
SUTTON HALL RD
ALDERNEY AVE
LULWORTH AVE
BULSTRODE AVE
HIGH ST
GROVE RD
1 ASHMORE CT
2 BOSTOCK HO
3 PASSINGHAM HO
4 SPOONER HO
5 FENTON HO
6 BELLAMY HO
7 ROTHWELL HO
8 WESTBOURNE HO
ST GILES CL 1
DUETT CT 2
FRASER CT 3
FENTON CT 4
AVENPORT LO 5
HOGARTH CT 6
1 CENTRAL PAR
2 STANWORTH CT
4 NEWCOMBE GDNS
5 MARRYAT CL
6 BUTLERS CL
7 ORCHID GDNS
1 BRAMLEY HO
2 RUSSET HO
3 BEVERLEY CT
Thorncliffe House (Hotel)
Heston Park
Rosary RC Jun & Inf Schs
Heston Jun Inf & Com Schs
Andrew Ewing Jun & Inf Sch
Springwell Jun & Inf Schs
Lampton Sch
Lampton Park
Alexandra Jun & Inf Sch
Wellington Prim Sch
Hounslow Heath Jun & Inf Schs
St Mark's RC Sch
The Orchard Jun & Inf Sch
Hounslow Manor Sch
Blenheim Ctr
The Hounslow Ctr
Treaty Ctr
Hounslow Bsns Pk
The Heath Bsns Ctr
InWood Bsns Pk
Hounslow
107
151
130
78
77
76
75
A
B
C
D
1
2
3
4
5
6

A
B
C
D
108
152
129
TW7
TW3
Osterley Park
Osterley Park House
Farm
Bwg Gn
Tenn Cts
Sp Gd
CH
Wyke Green
B454
SYON LA
OAKLANDS AVE
GOWER RD
MACFARLANE LA
CROWNTREE CL
STAGS WAY
WYKE CL
Allot Gdns
SYON PARK GDNS
BRAYBOURNE DR
ASHLEY DR
RIDGEWAY RD N
LINGWOOD GDNS
LEIGHAM DR
Pav
Pl Fld
JERSEY RD
HERM CL
BASSETT GDNS
CRANMORE AVE
THISTLEWORTH CL
Osterley
Liby
ST MARY'S CRES
OSTERLEY AVE
GREAT WEST RD
A4
PEVENSEY CL
PENWERRIS AVE
PENWERRIS CT
WEST CT
STUCLEY RD
LULWORTH AVE
THORNBURY AVE
ORCHARD CT
OSTERLEY CT
Campion House (Seminary)
Isleworth & Syon Sch for Boys
CAROLINE CL
CHURCH RD
THORNBURY CT
Running Tk
Brunel Univ Coll Osterley Campus
WOOD LA
ROXBOROUGH AVE
ALBURY AVE
HAREWOOD RD
NORTHUMBERLAND AVE
CAMPION RD
PARKWOOD RD
1 OSTERLEY LO
2 ST ANDREW'S CL
3 PARKFIELD
BOROUGH RD
OSTERLEY CRES
HIGHFIELD RD
MUSGRAVE RD
1 FOXTAIL HO
2 MARYGOLD HO
3 CLOVER HO
4 SORREL HO
5 GRESHAM CT
6 BALDWIN GDNS
7 CHAMBERLAIN GDNS
FAIRACRE
MORETON AVE
DEBORAH CL
APLIN WAY
KILBERRY CL
THORNBURY RD
WYNDHAM LO
OAKLEY CL
THE BROOKLANDS
DAVIES WLK
ST CHRISTOPHER'S CL
THE GROVE
RAVENSWOOD GDNS
COLLEGE RD
Lampton
BRACKENDALE CL
SPRING GROVE CRES
GRESHAM RD
GLADSTONE GDNS
PALMERSTON RD
SPENCER RD
BURLINGTON RD
EVERSLEY CRES
COPPER BEECHES
VINCENT RD
WITHAM RD
WESTON GDNS
West Thames Coll
HARVARD RD
NASEBY CL
GROVE RD
PARKLAND GR
LC
B363
LAYLOCK PL
KINGS AVE
TAYLOR CL
SPRING GROVE RD
COLWYN CRES
ADDISON AVE
TENNYSON RD
TAUNTON AVE
KINGSLEY AVE
THE CLOSE
HERBERT PL
4 FAIRWAYS
5 GRANWOOD CT
6 GROVEWOOD CT
FIRE STATION FLATS
JORDANS CL
WAYSIDE CT
AVENUE RD
HENLEY CL
A315
DENBIGH RD
Alexandra Jun & Inf Sch
TIVERTON RD
KINGSLEY RD
WORTON GDNS
WORTON WAY
BANKS HO
OFFLEY PL
DRAPER CL
STANLEYCROFT CL
VILLIERS RD
CLIFTON RD
PEMBROKE PL
WIGHTON MEWS
Spring Grove
MEON CT
CRAWFORD CL
SIDMOUTH AVE
Metro Ind Ctr
Isleworth
1 OVERTON CL
2 BEECHEN CLIFF WAY
3 THURZA CT
4 PRIMROSE PL
LORING RD
NEWTON RD
CASTLE WAY
LINKFIELD RD
SMALLBERRY AVE
RAYBELL CT
ST JOHN'S RD
ALEXANDRA GDNS
ELLINGTON RD
GARLAND DR
STIRLING GR
Hounslow East
THE ORCHARD
NORTH DR
Sch
KINGFISHER CT 1
GOLDEN CT 2
STAR RD
HONITON GDNS
LONDON RD
Tenn Cts
AYLETT RD
WOODLANDS GR
NOTTINGHAM RD
COPPER MILL DR
GRAINGER RD
Blenheim Ctr
MYRTLE RD
DOMINION CL
RICHENS CL
DERWENT LO
KELVIN CT 1
HAWKFIELD CT 2
COOPERS CT 3
WOODLANDS RD
THE WOODLANDS
Isleworth Bsns Complex
BRADDOCK CL
GREEN HO
Hounslow Manor Sch
CROWN YARD
PRINCE REGENT RD
CECIL RD
ALDERWICK DR
BIRCH CL
STANBOROUGH RD
GREENHAM HO
OCTAVIA RD
FARNELL'S ALMSHOUSES
HOWARD RD
2 3 PANKHURST CL
DRAYMANS WAY
MALTING WAY
CLYDESDALE CL
SHIRE HORSE WAY
Bwg Gn
Central
HOLLOWAY ST
RED LION CT
Hounslow Town Prim Sch
DEPOT RD
WOODLAND GDNS
Woodlands
GREENWOOD RD
MORRIS RD
KENNET RD
CLOCK TOWER RD
HIGH ST
FAIR ST
GILBERT ST
DEVONSHIRE HO
SCHOOL RD
PEARS RD
JAMES ST
GLENWOOD RD
BRIDGE RD
RIVERSIDE WLK
UNWIN RD
WHEATLEY RD
TRINITY PAR
DOUGLAS RD
Liby
FAIRFIELDS RD
EVERGLADES
INWOOD AVE
HYDE HO
Allot Gdns
Oaklands Sch
GIBSON CL
SUSSEX AVE
ABINGER GDNS
ESSEX AVE
CLAYTON RD
BOURNE CL
RUSKIN RD
HIPPISLEY CT
Treaty Ctr
JUBILEE CT
BRISTOW RD
Inwood Park
1 DASHWOOD CT
2 VERNEY HO
3 HANNING LO
4 MACDONALD CT
ELMER GDNS
FARNELL RD
PAGET LA
CHRISTABEL CL
WORTON RD
OAK LA
WEAVERS CL
FLEMING WAY
1 LESTOR CT
2 TRIMMER CT
3 STEINMAN CT
4 WILKINSON HO
5 BOOTHROYD HO
6 RICHARDSON HO
7 ALLCOTT HO
8 ANTHONY CT
9 OLIVER CT
10 WOODALL HO
CHAPEL RD
LIVINGSTONE RD
HOLLY RD
TEMPLE RD
GORDON RD
STANLEY RD
CHATSWORTH CRES
HELDMANN CL
WORTON CT
The Victory Bsns Ctr
MEADOWBROOK CT
Redlees Park
B361
JUNIPER CT
LAYTON RD
INWOOD RD
DETHERICK CT 5
AUGUSTUS CT 6
CAMERON LO 7
Chatsworth Inf Sch
DALMENY CRES
TUDOR RD
Worton Hall Ind Est
Duke of Northumberland's River
POWNALL RD
POWNALL GDNS
HANWORTH TERR
ELLERDINE RD
HEATH RD
ATCHAM RD
Chatsworth Jun Sch
LEIGH RD
CATHERINE GDNS
Sewage Works
LYNTON CL
The Heath Bsns Ctr
IVY RD
Inwood Bsns Pk
MASWELL PARK RD
PARK CRES
WOLSEY CL
LYNCROFT GDNS
CENTRAL AVE
NORBURY AVE
EATON RD
WAINWRIGHT GR
BANKSIDE CL
HILLARY DR
Hounslow
MASWELL PK
CHURCH STREET TN
BRACKEN END
HARVEY DR
WHITTON RD
LINDEN AVE
HOUNSLOW GDNS
HOUNSLOW AVE
PARK CT
PARK RD
PRIORY RD
LEAMINGTON CL
REAPERS WAY
GLEN WLK
TREVOR CL
MANNS CL
BRIAR CL
BEAUMONT PL
MOGDEN LA
Ivybridge
A310
A316

BRENTFORD
Brentford End
ISLEWORTH
RICHMOND
TW8
TW7
TW9
TW1
Syon Park
Syon House & Gdns
River Thames
Old Deer Park
Kew Observatory
Royal Mid-Surrey
Queen Charlotte's Cottage
King's Steps Gate
Isleworth Ait
Richmond Lock
Old Deer Park Recn Gd
London Butterfly House
West Middlesex Univ
Richmond Green
Richmond Circus
GREAT WEST RD
LONDON RD
HIGH ST
BOSTON MANOR RD
M4 (ELEVATED)
TWICKENHAM RD
SOUTH ST
RICHMOND RD
SPUR RD
Grand Union Canal
Thames Path
109
132
153
A
B
C
D
1
2
3
4
5
6

BRENTFORD
Strand on the Green
Kew
Kew Palace
Royal Botanic Gardens
Palm House
Arboretum
Temperate House
Pagoda
Old Deer Park
North Sheen
RICHMOND
TW9
The National Archives
Kew Gardens
Lots Ait
Brentford Ait
Thames Path
KEW RD
MORTLAKE RD
SANDYCOMBE RD
LOWER RICHMOND RD
LOWER MORTLAKE RD
CLIFFORD AVE
MANOR RD
SHEEN RD
HIGH ST
EALING RD
KEW BRIDGE RD
Kew Bridge
Richmond Circus
Manor Circus
Chalkers Cnr
North Sheen Cemy (Fulham)
Sandycombe Ctr
Richmond Athletic Gd
Richmond Healthcare Hamlet
Holy Trinity CE Prim Sch
Marlborough Trad Est
Kew Ret Pk
Herbarium Liby
Kew Green Prep Sch
Marina
1 ARUNDEL HO
2 MARLBOROUGH HO
3 BUCKINGHAM HO
4 OSBOURNE HO
5 YORK HO
6 SANDRINGHAM HO
7 KENT HO
8 NORFOLK HO
1 MORTLAKE TERR
2 SANDSTONE
3 BROADLANDS CT
4 FABYC HO
5 ASPEN HO
6 ASPEN CT
1 WATCOMBE COTTS
2 CAMBRIDGE COTTS
3 WILLOW COTTS
4 THETIS TERR
BLENHEIM CT 1
WOBURN CT 2
FINUCANE CT 3
WINCHESTER CT 4
TRINITY COTTS 5
110
131
154

CHISWICK
GREAT WEST RD
CEDARS RD
Hogarth Roundabout
Hogarth's House
Chiswick House
Chiswick
Grove Park
W4
The Quintin Hogg Meml Gd
GREAT CHERTSEY RD
Riverside Lands School Pl Flds
Duke's Meadows
Civil Service Sp Gd
Riverside Recn Gd
River Thames
Thames Path
Corney Reach
Chiswick Pier
The Harrodian Sch
The Swedish Sch
BARNES
BARNES HIGH ST
STATION RD
THE TERRACE
Barnes Bridge
Mortlake
MORTLAKE HIGH ST
SW13
SW14
East Sheen
UPPER RICHMOND RD
UPPER RICHMOND RD W
Milestone Green
Barnes Common
Red Rover
Rosslyn Park
Roehampton Sports Club
The Priory
SW15
Roehampton
Chiswick Bridge
Barnes Bridge
CLIFFORD AVE
Hounslow
Richmond upon Thames
111
155
134
78
77
76
75
A
B
C
D
1
2
3
4
5
6
21
22

River Thames
Richmond upon Thames
Thames Path
Tenn Cts
St Paul's Sch
112
HAMMERSMITH BRIDGE
A
B
C
D
78
Pl Flds
LONSDALE RD
B350
Pl Fld
The Swedish Sch
6
LILLIAN RD
GLENTHAM RD
ST HILDA'S RD
GLENTHAM GDNS
CASTELNAU MANS
A306
RIVERVIEW GDNS
CLAVERING AVE
ARUNDEL TERR
CASTELNAU GDNS
1 ST EDMUND'S SQ
2 RICHARD BURBIDGE MANS
3 CHARLES HARROD CT
4 WILLIAM HUNT MANS
5 WRENN HO
W6
KING HENRY'S REACH
JENNER PL 1
CASTELNAU ROW 2
NOWELL RD
KILMINGTON RD
ALDERBURY RD
HOWSMAN RD
EVERDON RD
STILLINGFLEET RD
BOILEAU RD
Lowther Prim Sch
THE SPINNEY
FIELDING MEWS
TRINITY CHURCH RD
MERTHYR TERR
SOMERVILLE AVE
BRASENOSE DR
ORIEL DR
ARUNDEL CT 1
ARUNDEL MANS 2
KEBLE PL 3
HARDING HO 4
Hammersmith & Fulham
Richmond upon Thames
Thames Path
THAMES REACH
WINDERMERE CT
B350
1 GRASMERE CT
2 QUEENSMERE CT
BARNES AVE
VERDUN RD
KENTWODE GN
Recn Gd
Tenn Cts
Sp Gd
Allot Gdns
DEVEREUX LA
WYATT DR
BURGES GR
CARTWRIGHT WAY
HOLST MANS
HANDEL MANS
GARRAWAY CT
HEIDEGGER CRES
CASTELNAU
WASHINGTON RD
5
ATHERTON RD
ULLSWATER RD
MADRID RD
Liby
GALATA RD
SUFFOLK RD
CONISTON CL
Recn
77
PARKE RD
BERKELEY RD
WALSINGHAM LODGE
FERRY RD
NEWPORT RD
London Wetland Centre
London Wetland Visitor Ctr
CUMBERLAND RD
BARONSMEAD RD
LOWTHER RD
4
WESTMORELAND RD
ELLERTON RD
BYFELD GDNS
MELVILLE RD
KITSON RD
KING EDWARD MEWS
QUEEN ELIZABETH WLK
BARNES
THE HERMITAGE
CHURCH WLK
CHURCH RD
A3003
PO
133
Bwg Gn
Tenn Cts
Pav
Running Tk
Barn Elms Pl Flds
THE CRESCENT
HILLERSDON AVE
GLEBE RD
BRACKEN GDNS
MEREDYTH RD
CARDIGAN RD
BELLEVUE RD
RECTORY RD
ELM GROVE RD
LAUREL RD
RANELAGH AVE
B349
STATION RD
3
BEVERLEY CL
CEDARS RD
SW13
Beverley Brook
Allot Gdns
Putney Lower Common
Richmond upon Thames
Wandsworth
MILL HILL RD
ROCKS LA
MILL HILL
Barnes Common
30
76
BROOKWOOD AVE
WILLOW AVE
ORCHARD CT
SCARTH RD
STATION RD
COMMON RD
Old Barnes Cemy
Bwg Gn
Pav
Barn Elms Schs Sp Ctr
1 PEARSON HO
2 HUNTINGFORD HO
3 KNOX HO
4 LANCASTER HO
5 HEWETT HO
BONTHRON HO
FORREST HO
FAULKNER HO
HORNE WAY
STOCKHURST CL
JAY HO
WATERS PL
FLOSS ST
COMMONDALE
JERROLD ST
SEFTON ST
PENITLOW ST
DANEMERE ST
ASHLONE RD
FESTING RD
ROTHERWOOD RD
BENDEMEER RD
EMBANKMENT
B349
B306
LOWER RICHMOND RD
Bwg Gn
Pavs
LCs
2
Barnes
Barnes Common
MELINA CT 1
SYCAMORE LO 2
LIME CT 3
WILLOW LO 4
HAWTHORN CT 5
FIR LO 6
MARCH CT 7
ROEHAMPTON CT
QUEEN'S RIDE
CHESTER CL
HALLAM RD
SHERWOOD CL
ST MARY'S GR
CRESSY HO
LOWER COMMON S
EGLISTON MEWS
All Saints CE Prim Sch
PUTNEY COMMON
WILLOW FARM LA
ERPINGHAM RD
Tenn Cts
DRYBURGH MANS
EGLISTON RD
1 LOUISA HO
2 ESME HO
3 SARAH HO
Red Rover
A306
B306
QUEEN'S CT
WARWICK
GIPSY LA
DRYBURGH RD
LANDFORD RD
HOTHAM RD
CLARENDON DR
MAC LAREN MEWS
WELLWOOD CT
HARWOOD CT
RICHMOND RD
A205
Rosslyn Park Pav
Sch
DUNGARVAN AVE
DAYLESFORD AVE
CORNERWAYS
PUTNEY PARK AVE
BALFOUR PL
FAIRDALE GDNS
QUEENSGATE GDNS
SW15
UPPER RICHMOND RD
BELVEDERE CT
ORMONDE CT
LANGSIDE AVE
GLENTHORPE
NEWNES PATH
CHEVAL CT
SEYMOUR
Tenn Cts
1
CH
Roehampton
Roehampton Sports Club
Allot Gdns
Putney Park Sch
WOODBOROUGH RD
SOMERSET LODGE
PEAR TREE CT
MALBROOK RD
PETTIWARD CL
COLINETTE RD
DEALTRY RD
PARKFIELDS
FAIRFAX MEWS
BALMUIR GDNS
BRITTANY HO
CARMALT GDNS
WOODTHORPE RD
HOWARD'S LA
COALECROFT RD
HOLROYD RD
ENMORE RD
TIDESWELL RD
GWENDOLEN AVE
Lion House Sch
NURSERY CL
FAIRACRES
CROMWELL HO
75
SWINBURNE RD
GIBBON WLK
ST MARGARET'S CT
Tenn Cts
HUNTINGFIELD RD
Allot Gdns
PLEASANCE RD
DOVER HOUSE RD
22
Tenn Ct
Roehampton Univ (Southlands Coll)
ELMSHAW RD
HAWKESBURY RD
156
23
HAZLEWELL RD
PUTNEY
GWENDOLEN CL
Schs
Allot
A
B
C
D
Richmond upon Thames
Hammersmith & Fulham
River Thames
Wandsworth
FULHAM
Craven Cottage (Fulham FC)
Eternit Wharf
Stevenage Wharves
Blakes Wharves
CEDAR LO 1
ASH LO 2
ELM LO 3
ALDER LO 4
WILLOW LO 5
CRABTREE HALL 1
ADAM WLK 2
ROSEBANK 3
LYSIA CT 4
WHEATSHEAF LA
HOLYPORT RD
MEADOWBANK
ROWBERRY CL
MILLSHOTT CL
WATERS EDGE
PALEMEAD CL
ETERNIT WLK
STEVENAGE RD
Sch
CRABTREE LA
NITON ST
LYSIA ST
QUEENSMILL RD
LANGTHORNE ST
KENYON ST
INGLETHORPE ST
WOODLAWN RD
HARBORD ST
GRESWELL ST
FINLAY ST
ELLERBY ST
DONERAILE ST
CLONCURRY ST
BISHOP'S MANSIONS
BISHOP'S PARK RD
Bwg Gn
SW6
30
Recn Gd
PURCELL CRES
STRODE RD
Cemy
CLIFFORD HAIGH HO
Liby
KINGWOOD RD
CRAVEN LO
ROBERT OWEN HO
ATALANTA ST
A219
FULHAM PALACE RD
A3218 LILLIE RD
PO
COLWITH RD
ROSEDEW RD
SKELWITH RD
RANNOCH RD
NELLA RD
BOWFELL RD
WINGRAVE RD
LARNACH RD
RAINVILLE RD
PETLEY RD
ELLALINE RD
SILVERTON RD
WINSLOW RD
LOCHALINE ST
KEIR HARDIE HO
PARFREY ST
MANBRE RD
Sch
CHANCELLOR'S RD
DISTILLERY RD
DISTILLERY LA
PLAYFAIR ST
RIVER TERR
CRISP RD
BISCAY RD
BERYL RD
ST DUNSTAN'S RD
Charing Cross
H
Cemy
1 WILSONS RD
2 LINACRE CT
3 WATERHOUSE CL
CLAXTON GR
GRAVINE RD
CLAYBROOK RD
CHELMSFORD CL
WILLIAM MORRIS HO
GASTEIN RD
LURGAN AVE
ASPENLEA RD
GREYHOUND RD
OAKLEY WLK
AVERILL ST
DELORME ST
EVERINGTON ST
ADENEY CL
1 GRIFFIN GATE
2 DARFUR ST
3 JOHN KEALL HO
4 HENRY JACKSON HO
5 FELSHAM HO
6 ARDSHIEL CL
7 RUVIGNY MANS
8 STAR & GARTER MANS
9 UNIVERSITY MANS
10 LOCKYER HO
11 PHELPS HO
12 PRINCETON CT
13 KINGSMERE CL
14 FELSHAM MEWS
GLENDARVON ST
GLADWYN RD
RD
PO
WYMOND ST
STANBRIDGE RD
FARLOW RD
ROSKELL RD
SALVIN RD
HENRY JACKSON RD
BIGG'S ROW
WEISS RD
BEMISH RD
THAMES PL
WATERMAN ST
GAY ST
FELSHAM RD
WESTHORPE RD
ABBOTSTONE RD
BORNEO ST
BANGALORE ST
BLACKETT ST
DRYAD ST
EARLDOM RD
ROSSDALE RD
GAMLEN RD
CHARLWOOD RD
REDGRAVE RD
GWALIOR RD
LACY RD
Hotham Prim Sch
CARLYLE PL
MODDER PL
QUILL LA
CARDINAL PL
LIFFORD ST
STRATFORD GR
Putney Exch
CHELVERTON RD
SPENCER WLK
NORROY RD
JORDAN CT
Lion House
PO
A205
AVENNA RD
ULVA RD
BURSTON RD
ST JOHN'S AV
A219
BURLEIGH PL
ASHDOWN
CAMBALT RD
FAIRLAWNS

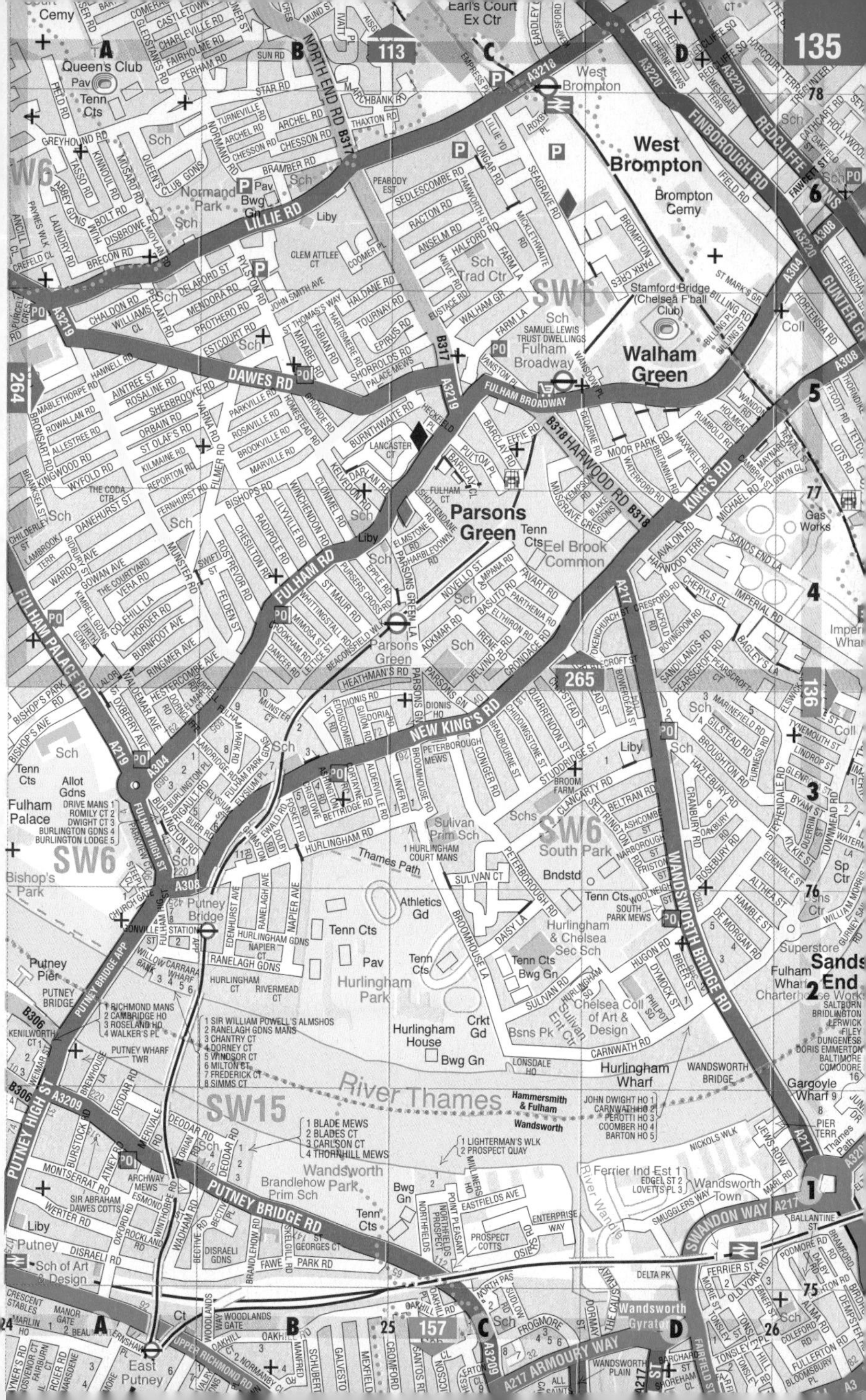
Earl's Court Ex Ctr
113
West Brompton
West Brompton
Brompton Cemy
Queen's Club
W6
Normand Park
LILLIE RD
NORTH END RD
FINBOROUGH RD
REDCLIFFE GDNS
Stamford Bridge (Chelsea F'ball Club)
Walham Green
SW6
Fulham Broadway
FULHAM BROADWAY
DAWES RD
264
FULHAM RD
Parsons Green
Eel Brook Common
KING'S RD
HARWOOD RD
Gas Works
SANDS END LA
IMPERIAL RD
FULHAM PALACE RD
NEW KING'S RD
265
136
Fulham Palace
Bishop's Park
SW6
South Park
Sulivan Prim Sch
HURLINGHAM RD
Thames Path
Athletics Gd
Hurlingham Park
Hurlingham House
Hurlingham & Chelsea Sec Sch
Chelsea Coll of Art & Design
Hurlingham Wharf
WANDSWORTH BRIDGE RD
WANDSWORTH BRIDGE
Fulham Wharf
Sands End
Putney Bridge
Putney Pier
PUTNEY BRIDGE
PUTNEY HIGH ST
River Thames
SW15
Hammersmith & Fulham
Wandsworth
Wandsworth Park
Brandlehow Prim Sch
PUTNEY BRIDGE RD
Ferrier Ind Est
Wandsworth Town
SWANDON WAY
River Wandle
Putney
Sch of Art & Design
UPPER RICHMOND RD
East Putney
157
A217 ARMOURY WAY
Wandsworth Gyratory
A
B
C
D
1
2
3
4
5
6

CHELSEA
SW10
SW11
BATTERSEA
114
266
267
135
158
A
B
C
D
6
5
4
3
2
1
FULHAM RD
KING'S RD
CHEYNE WLK
CHELSEA EMB
OAKLEY ST
BEAUFORT ST
OLD CHURCH ST
REDCLIFFE GDNS
FINBOROUGH RD
EDITH GR
GUNTER GR
CREMORNE RD
LOTS RD
Chelsea & Westminster
Cadogan Pier
Thames Path
Chelsea Reach
ALBERT BRIDGE (SUSPENSION)
Terrace Wlk
THE PARADE
Fountain Lake
CARRIAGE DRIVE N
CENTRAL AVE
Festival Pleasure Gardens
Recn Gd
Pav
Sp Gd
BATTERSEA BRIDGE
Bridge Wharf
Ransome's Dock
Kensington & Chelsea
Wandsworth
Hammersmith & Fulham
Old Ferry Wharf
Chelsea Wharf
Cremorne Wharf
River Thames
Chelsea Creek
Gas Works
Imperial Wharf
Chelsea Harbour Pier
Regent Wharf
BATTERSEA BRIDGE RD
ALBERT BRIDGE RD
WESTBRIDGE RD
SURREY LA
PARKGATE RD
Govt Offices
PRINCE OF WALES DR
BATTERSEA PARK RD
VICARAGE CRES
BATTERSEA HIGH ST
LOMBARD RD
York Road Bsns Ctr
Heliport
The Heliport Est
YORK RD
Battersea Reach
Sands End
Fulham Wharf
Charterhouse Works
Sherwood Wharf
Gargoyle Wharf
WANDSWORTH BRIDGE
WANDSWORTH BRIDGE RD
SWANDON WAY
Wandsworth Town
EAST HILL
NORTH SIDE WANDSWORTH COMMON
ST JOHN'S HILL
Clapham Junction
BATTERSEA RISE
FALCON RD
LATCHMERE RD
Falcon Park
Christ Church CE Prim Sch
ELSPETH RD
LAVENDER HILL
CLAPHAM COMMON
Belleville Prim Sch
1 GREENSWARD HO
2 CHAPLOW CL
3 ARCADIAN HO
4 POTTERS RD
SALTBURN HO 2
BRIDLINGTON HO 3
LERWICK HO 4
FILEY HO 5
DUNGENESS HO 6
DORIS EMMERTON CT 7
BALTIMORE HO 8
COMODORE HO 9
BARNARD MEWS 1
CARRINGTON CT 2
ABYSSINIA CL 3
THE VILLAGE 1
BATTERSEA HTS 2
GILMORE HO 1
GROVE MANS 2
CLAPHAM JUNCTION EST

Royal Hospital (Army Pensioners)
Ranelagh Gardens (Site of Chelsea Flower Show)
Pimlico
Pimlico Sch
115
Grosvenor Road
A3212
Chelsea Bridge
Grosvenor Bridge
River Thames
Thames Path
City of Westminster
Wandsworth
Battersea Wharf
Battersea Power Station (disused)
Nine Elms
Nine Elms La
John Milton Prim Sch
Battersea Dogs Home
SW8
New Covent Garden Flower Mkt
South Bank Bsns Ctr
New Covent Garden Fruit & Vegetable Market
Queenstown Rd
Battersea Park
Boating Lake
Children's Zoo
Queen's Cir
Battersea Park Rd
Queenstown Road
Sir James Barrie Prim Sch
268
269
Wandsworth Road
Wandsworth Rd
Silverthorne Rd
Heathbrook Park
Parkfield Ind Est
Larkhall Park
138
SW4
Lavender Hill
Clapham
Cedars Rd
North St
Old Town
Clapham High St
Clapham High Street
Clapham Park Rd
Clapham Common North Side
Long Rd
Clapham Common
Bedford Rd
1 St Saviours
2 Lyncott Cres
3 Salcombe Gdns
4 Barker Mews
5 Woodlands
6 Okeover Manor
Windmill on the Common (PH)
159
Lambeth Coll
Lambeth Acad
Mount Pond
Ellerslie Ind Est

Vauxhall
Spring Gardens
Kennington
SE17
SE11
Vauxhall Cross
Wharves
Wharf
New Covent Garden Flower Mkt
South Bank Bsns Ctr
Vauxhall Park
The Oval
Kennington Park
Kennington Oval
Govt Offices
KENNINGTON LA
KENNINGTON OVAL
KENNINGTON PK RD
HARLEYFORD RD
CAMBERWELL NEW RD
WANDSWORTH RD
SOUTH LAMBETH RD
CLAPHAM RD
BRIXTON RD
STOCKWELL RD
SW8
SW9
SW4
South Lambeth
Stockwell Park
Stockwell
Larkhall Park
Myatt's Fields Pk
Mostyn Gdns
BRIXTON
Clapham North
Clapham High Street
Lambeth
COLDHARBOUR LA
ACRE LA
ATLANTIC RD
EFFRA RD
BEDFORD RD
MILKWOOD RD
Ellerslie Ind Est
Loughborough Junc
Brixton
116
261
270
137
160
A
B
C
D
1
2
3
4
5
6

262
117
263
140
161
CAMBERWELL
SE15
SE5
Burgess Park
CAMBERWELL RD
CAMBERWELL CHURCH ST
PECKHAM RD
SOUTHAMPTON WAY
ALBANY RD
TRAFALGAR AVE
DENMARK HILL
COLDHARBOUR LA
CHAMPION PK
GROVE LA
DOG KENNEL HILL
GROVE VALE
EAST DULWICH GR
HERNE HILL
Camberwell Green
The Maudsley
King's College
Ruskin Park
East Dulwich
Herne Hill
East D
Peckham Rye

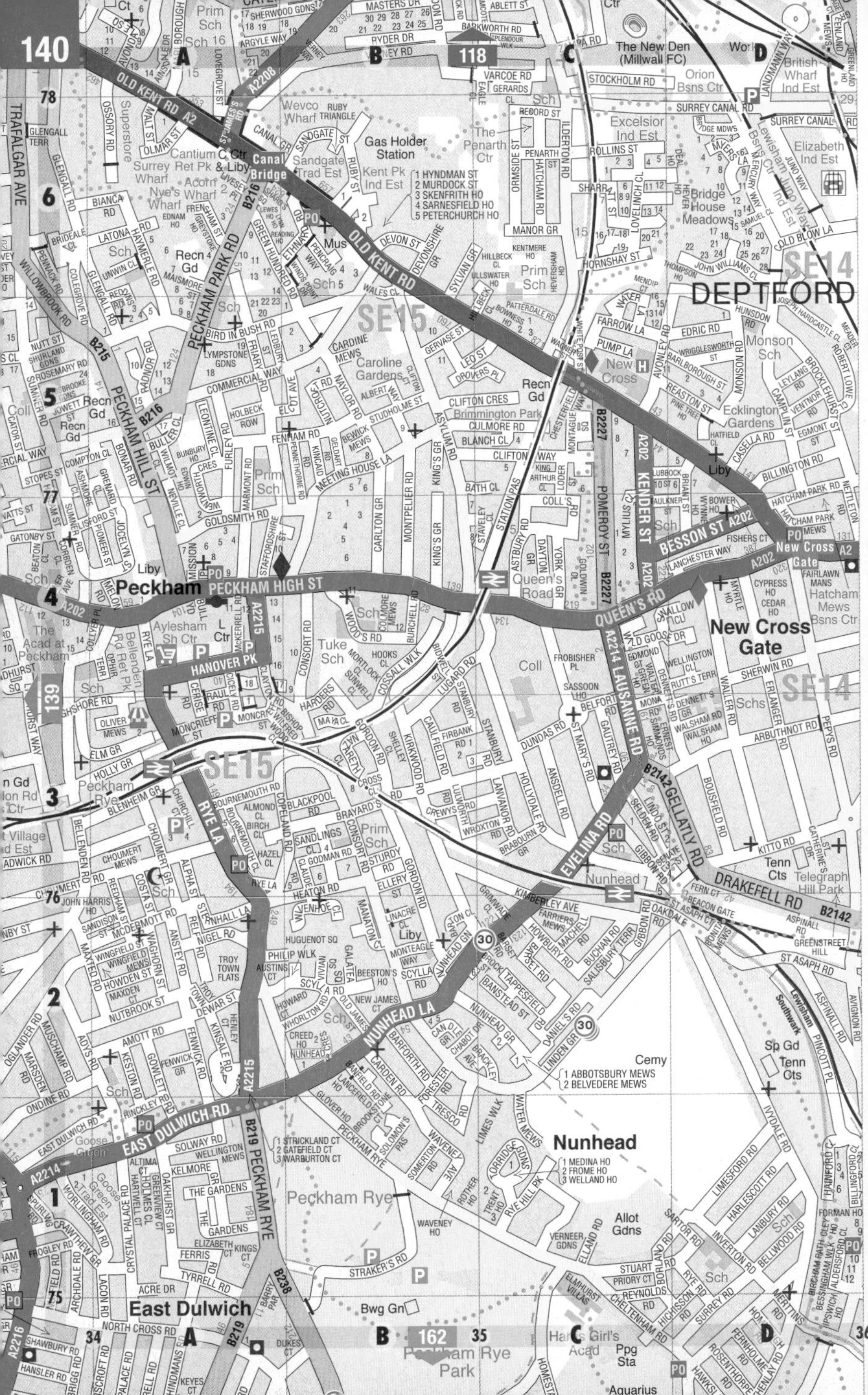

Peckham
DEPTFORD
New Cross Gate
Nunhead
East Dulwich
SE15
SE14
OLD KENT RD
PECKHAM HIGH ST
QUEEN'S RD
RYE LA
PECKHAM RYE
NUNHEAD LA
EAST DULWICH RD
DRAKEFELL RD
KENDER ST
LAUSANNE RD
EVELINA RD
PECKHAM HILL ST
PECKHAM PARK RD
The New Den (Millwall FC)
Peckham Rye
Cemy
Allot Gdns

118
162
139

River Thames
Locke's Wharf
Palmer's Wharf
Payne's Wharf
Borthwick Wharf
Convoys Wharf
Deptford Park
Blackhorse Wharf
119
SE8
EVELYN ST
A200
Trad Est
Folkestone Gardens
Parkside Bsns Est
Dreadnought Wharf
Dowell's Wharf
CREEK RD
Thames Path
Univ Campus
DEPTFORD CHURCH ST
A2209
Deptford Creek
NORMAN RD
SE10
Greenwich Ind Est
GREENWICH HIGH RD
GREENWICH SOUTH ST
A2211
Faircharm Trad Est
Greenwich Bsns Ctr
SANFORD ST
Fordham Park
PAGNELL ST
New Cross Gate
Superstore
NEW CROSS RD
A2
New Cross
DEPTFORD BROADWAY
DEPTFORD BRIDGE
Deptford Bridge
BLACKHEATH RD
A2210
BROOKMILL RD
SE14
Goldsmiths Coll Univ of London
New Cross
LEWISHAM WAY
FLORENCE RD
B218
St Johns
Ravensbourne Park
Ravensbourne River
ELVERSON RD
Elverson Road
142
LEWISHAM RD
LOAMPIT HILL
LOAMPIT VALE
THURSTON RD
Ind Est
MALPAS RD
Brockley Cross Bsns Ctr
Crossways Acad
B2142
ENDWELL RD
Brockley
SE4
Hilly Fields Park
Bwg Gn
Tenn Cts
Prendergast Sch
ADELAIDE AVE
B236
Brockley
Ladywell Cemy
Brockley Cemy
BROCKLEY RD
LADYWELL RD
Ladywell
Leis Ctr
MOLESWORTH ST
A21
LEWISHAM HIGH ST
Depot
Brockley Prim Sch
163
36
37
38
A
B
C
D
1
2
3
4
5
6

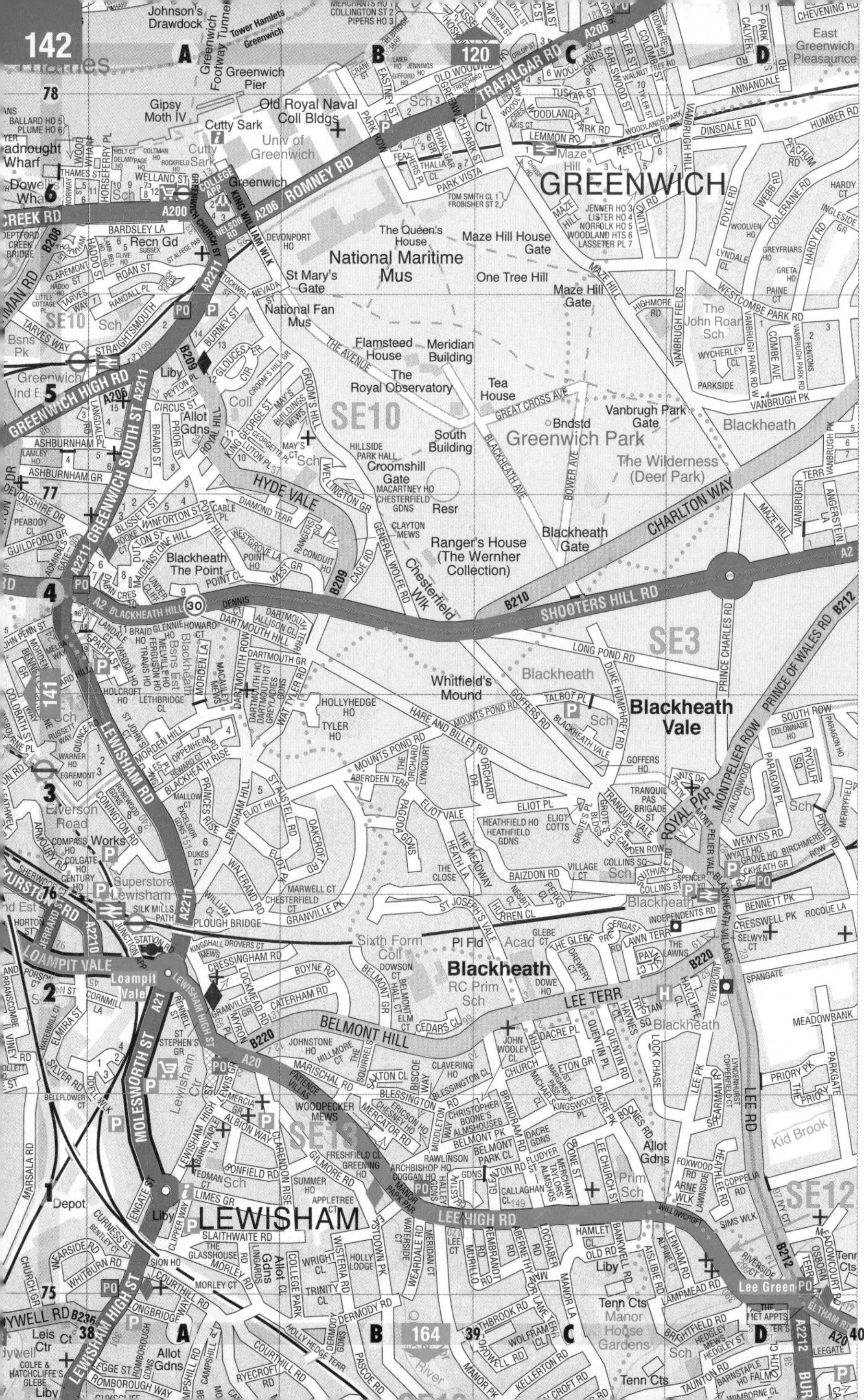

GREENWICH
LEWISHAM
Blackheath
Blackheath Vale
SE10
SE3
SE13
SE12
Greenwich Park
National Maritime Mus
The Royal Observatory
Flamsteed House
Meridian Building
The Queen's House
Old Royal Naval Coll Bldgs
Univ of Greenwich
Cutty Sark
Gipsy Moth IV
Greenwich Pier
Greenwich Footway Tunnel
Ranger's House (The Wernher Collection)
The Wilderness (Deer Park)
One Tree Hill
Maze Hill House Gate
Maze Hill Gate
Blackheath Gate
Vanbrugh Park Gate
St Mary's Gate
Croomshill Gate
National Fan Mus
Whitfield's Mound
TRAFALGAR RD
ROMNEY RD
GREENWICH HIGH RD
GREENWICH SOUTH ST
SHOOTERS HILL RD
CHARLTON WAY
BLACKHEATH HILL
LEWISHAM RD
LEWISHAM HIGH ST
MOLESWORTH ST
LEE HIGH RD
LEE TERR
BELMONT HILL
LEE RD
PRINCE OF WALES RD
HYDE VALE
MAZE HILL
LOAMPIT VALE
CREEK RD
120
141
164
A
B
C
D

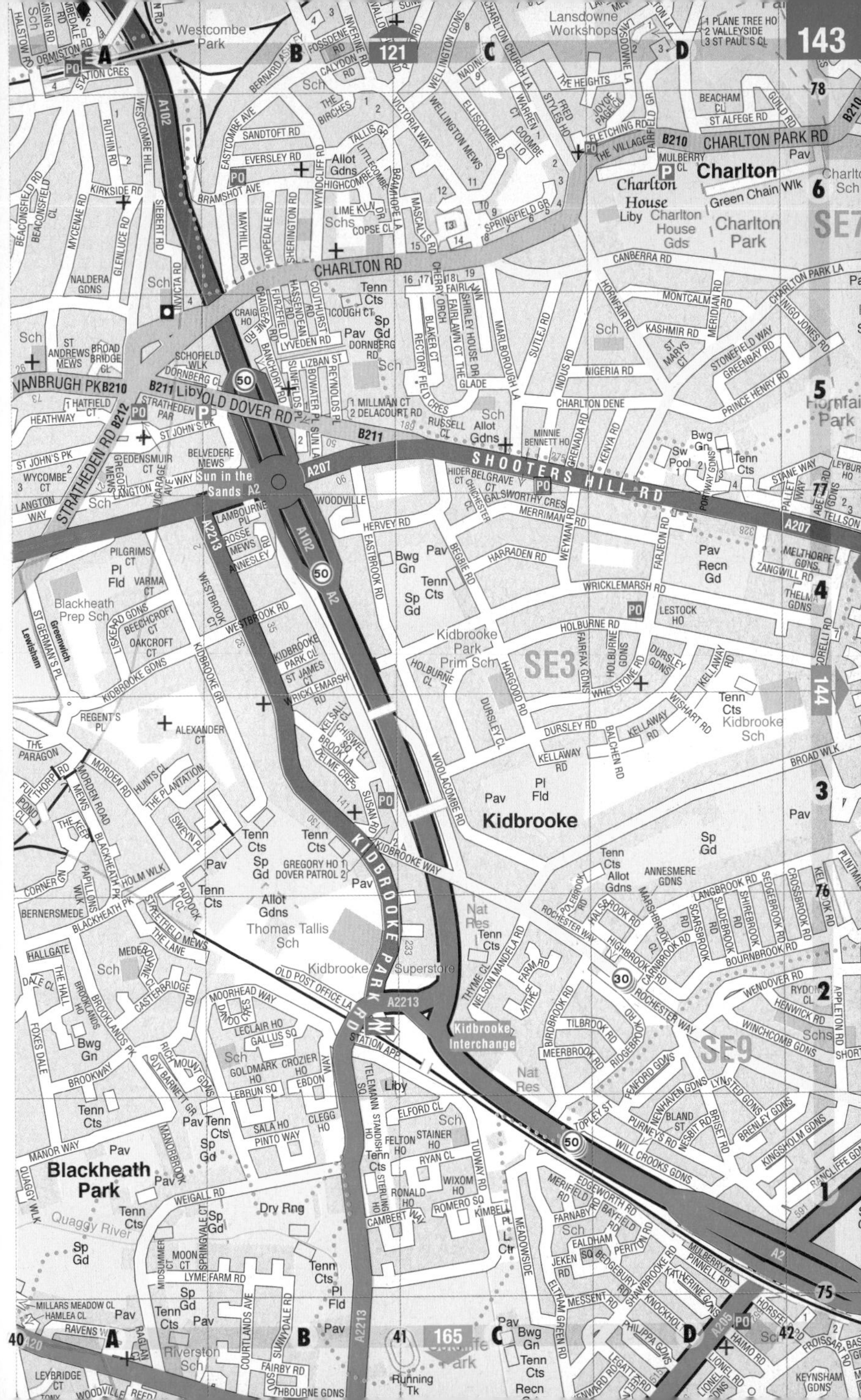
143
A
B
C
D
121
165
Westcombe Park
Lansdowne Workshops
1 PLANE TREE HO
2 VALLEYSIDE
3 ST PAUL'S CL
HALSTOW RD
ORMISTON RD
STATION CRES
FOSSDENE RD
INVERINE RD
CALYDON RD
BERNARD ASHLEY DR
WELLINGTON GDNS
CHARLTON CHURCH LA
LANSDOWNE LA
NADINE ST
THE HEIGHTS
BEACHAM CL
ST ALFEGE RD
GUILD RD
CHARLTON PARK RD
B210
A102
WESTCOMBE HILL
EASTCOMBE AVE
SANDTOFT RD
EVERSLEY RD
THE BIRCHES
VICTORIA WAY
TALLIS GR
WELLINGTON MEWS
ELLISCOMBE RD
WARREN LA
COOMBE LO
FRED STYLES HO
JOYCE PAGE CL
FLETCHING RD
THE VILLAGE
FAIRFIELD GR
MULBERRY CL
Charlton
Charlton House
Liby
Charlton House Gds
Green Chain Wlk
Charlton Park
Charlton Sch
SE7
RUTHIN RD
BEACONSFIELD RD
BEACONSFIELD CL
MYCENAE RD
KIRKSIDE RD
GLENLUCE RD
SIEBERT RD
BRAMSHOT AVE
HIGHCOMBE
LITTLECOMBE
WYNDCLIFF RD
BRAMHOPE LA
MASCALLS RD
LIME KILN DR
COPSE CL
Schs
MAYHILL RD
HOPEDALE RD
SHERINGTON RD
SPRINGFIELD GR
Allot Gdns
CHARLTON RD
CANBERRA RD
CHARLTON PARK LA
NALDERA GDNS
INVICTA RD
Sch
CRAIGHOLM RD
CRAIGERNE RD
FURZEFIELD RD
HASSENDEAN RD
COUTHURST RD
Tenn Cts
ICOUGH CT
CHERRY ORCH
FAIRLAWN
SHIRLEY HOUSE DR
MONTCALM RD
MERIDIAN RD
HORNFAIR RD
INIGO JONES RD
ST ANDREWS MEWS
BROAD BRIDGE CL
SCHOFIELD WLK
DORNBERG CL
LYVEDEN RD
Pav
Sp Gd
DORNBERG RD
BLAKER CT
RECTORY FIELD CRES
FAIRLAWN CT
THE GLADE
MARLBOROUGH LA
SUTLEJ RD
INDUS RD
KASHMIR RD
ST MARYS CT
STONEFIELD WAY
GREENBAY RD
NIGERIA RD
VANBRUGH PK
B210
B211
OLD DOVER RD
HATFIELD CT
HEATHWAY
STRATHEDEN PAR
LIZBAN ST
SUNFIELDS PL
BOWATER PL
REYNOLDS PL
BANCHORY RD
1 MILLMAN CT
2 DELACOURT RD
CHARLTON DENE
PRINCE HENRY RD
Hornfair Park
STRATHEDEN RD
B212
ST JOHN'S PK
GEDENSMUIR CT
BELVEDERE MEWS
SUN LA
RUSSELL CL
MINNIE BENNETT HO
GRENADA RD
KENYA RD
Bwg Gn
Sw Pool
PORTWAY GDNS
WYCOMBE CT
LANGTON WAY
GREGORY MEWS
VICARAGE AVE
Sun in the Sands
A2
A207
B211
SHOOTERS HILL RD
HIDER CT
BELGRAVE CT
CHICHESTER CL
GALSWORTHY CRES
STANE WAY
PALLET WAY
ABERY GDNS
LEYBURN HO
TELLSON AVE
LANGTON WAY
WOODVILLE
MERRIMAN RD
A2213
LAMBOURNE PL
BOSSE MEWS
ANNESLEY RD
HERVEY RD
EASTBROOK RD
BEGBIE RD
HARRADEN RD
WEYMAN RD
FARJEON RD
Recn Gd
MELTHORPE GDNS
ZANGWILL RD
PILGRIMS CT
Pl Fld
VARMA CT
WESTBROOK CT
Blackheath Prep Sch
LISKEARD GDNS
BEECHCROFT CT
OAKCROFT CT
WESTBROOK RD
WRICKLEMARSH RD
LESTOCK HO
THELMA GDNS
ST GERMAN'S PL
Greenwich
Lewisham
KIDBROOKE GDNS
KIDBROOKE GR
KIDBROOKE PARK CL
ST JAMES CT
Kidbrooke Park Prim Sch
HOLBURNE RD
HOLBURNE CL
HARGOOD RD
SE3
FAIRFAX GDNS
HOLBURNE GDNS
DURSLEY GDNS
WHETSTONE RD
KELLAWAY RD
DURSLEY CL
MORELLI RD
144
Kidbrooke Sch
REGENT'S PL
ALEXANDER CT
KELSALL CL
CHISWELL SQ
BROOK LA
DELME CRES
WOOLACOMBE RD
DURSLEY RD
BALCHEN RD
WISHART RD
BROAD WLK
THE PARAGON
MORDEN RD
MORDEN ROAD MEWS
HUNTS CL
THE PLANTATION
SWEYN PL
THORPE RD
POND RD
THE KEEP
BLACKHEATH PK
Kidbrooke
SUSAN RD
KIDBROOKE PARK RD
GREGORY HO
DOVER PATROL
KIDBROOKE WAY
Thomas Tallis Sch
Nat Res
Tenn Cts
Allot Gdns
ANNESMERE GDNS
CORNER GN
PAPILLONS WLK
HOLM WLK
PADDOCK CL
BERNERSMEDE
STREETFIELD MEWS
THE LANE
POLEBROOK RD
HALSBROOK RD
MARSHBROOK CL
LANGBROOK RD
SEDGEBROOK RD
CROSSBROOK RD
SHIREBROOK RD
SLADEBROOK RD
SCARSBROOK RD
ROCHESTER WAY
HIGHBROOK RD
CARNBROOK RD
BOURNBROOK RD
HALLGATE
THE HALL
DALE CL
BROOKLANDS HO
MEDEBOURNE CL
CASTERBRIDGE RD
Kidbrooke Superstore
OLD POST OFFICE LA
A2213
NELSON MANDELA RD
THYME CL
FARM RD
HITHE
WENDOVER RD
RYDON CL
HENWICK RD
APPLETON RD
BROOKLANDS PK
FOXES DALE
Bwg Gn
MOORHEAD WAY
DANDO CRES
LECLAIR HO
GALLUS SQ
Kidbrooke Interchange
STATION APP
BIRDBROOK RD
TILBROOK RD
RIDGEBROOK RD
MEERBROOK RD
WINCHCOMB GDNS
SE9
SHORT
BROOKWAY
RICH
GUY BARNETT GR
MOUNT GDNS
GOLDMARK HO
CROZIER HO
EBDON WAY
LEBRUN SQ
TELEMANN SQ
Liby
PENFORD GDNS
NEWHAVEN GDNS
LYNSTED GDNS
BLAND ST
BRISET RD
NESBIT RD
BRENLEY GDNS
KINGSHOLM GDNS
SALA HO
PINTO WAY
CLEGG HO
ELFORD CL
STANDISH HO
STAINER HO
FELTON HO
TUDWAY RD
TOPLEY ST
PURNEYS RD
WILL CROOKS GDNS
MANOR WAY
Blackheath Park
MANORBROOK
RYAN CL
WIXOM HO
RONALD HO
STERLING HO
ROMERO SQ
CAMBERT WAY
KIMBELL PL
L Ctr
MEADOWSIDE
MERIFIELD RD
EDGEWORTH RD
BAYFIELD RD
FARNABY RD
RANCLIFFE GDNS
QUAGGY WLK
WEIGALL RD
Dry Rng
Quaggy River
SPRINGVALE CT
MIDSUMMER CT
MOON CT
LYME FARM RD
EALDHAM SQ
JEKEN RD
PERITON RD
BEDGEBURY RD
SHAWBROOKE RD
KATHERINE GDNS
MULBERRY PL
PINNELL RD
MILLARS MEADOW CL
HAMLEA CL
RAVENS WAY
COURTLANDS AVE
SUNNYDALE RD
Riverston Sch
FAIRBY RD
SOUTHBOURNE GDNS
41
Running Tk
Sutcliffe Park
Recn Gd
ELTHAM GREEN RD
MESSENT RD
KNOCKHOLT RD
PHILIPPA GDNS
A205
HORSFELD RD
HAIMO RD
FROISSART RD
LIONEL RD
KEYNSHAM GDNS
LEYBRIDGE CT
WOODVILLE
REEDHAM
RAGLAN
40
42
A20
1
2
3
4
5
6
75
76
77
78
Pav
Sp Gd
Pl Fld

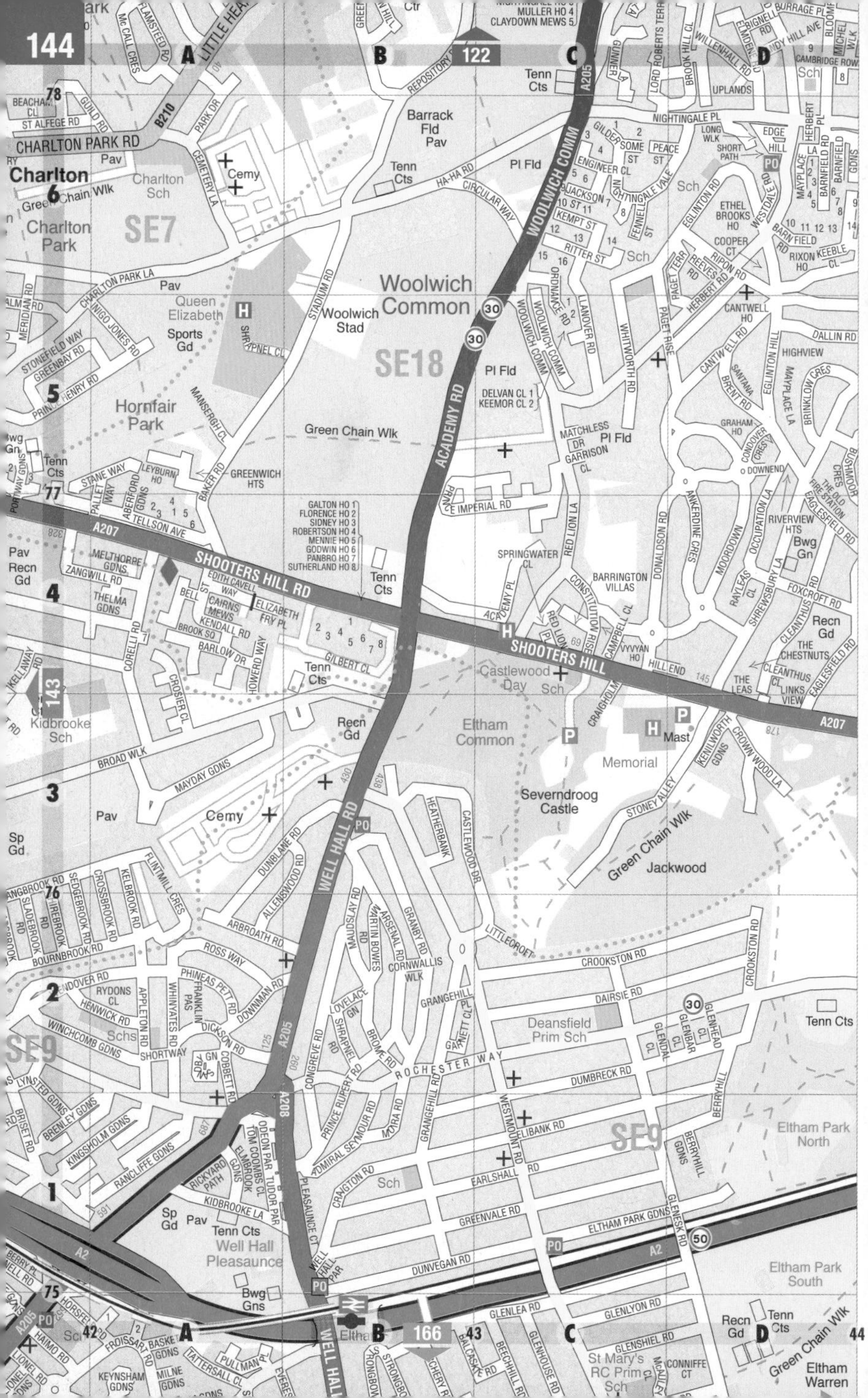
A
B
122
C
D
MULLER HO 4
CLAYDOWN MEWS 5
Tenn Cts
BURRAGE PL
CAMBRIDGE ROW
UPLANDS
Sch
78
BEACHAM CL
GUILD RD
ST ALFEGE RD
CHARLTON PARK RD
B210
LITTLE HEATH
PARK DR
CEMETERY LA
Cemy
Barrack Fld Pav
REPOSITORY RD
Tenn Cts
HA-HA RD
CIRCULAR WAY
Pl Fld
WOOLWICH COMM
A205
NIGHTINGALE PL
GILDERSOME ST
PEACE ST
ENGINEER CL
JACKSON ST
KEMPT ST
RITTER ST
NIGHTINGALE VALE
FENNELL ST
EGLINTON RD
ETHEL BROOKS HO
COOPER CT
WESTDALE RD
EDGE HILL
LONG WLK
SHORT PATH
PO
MAYPLACE LA
BARNFIELD RD
HERBERT PL
BARNFIELD
RIXON HO
KEEBLE CL
Pav
Charlton
6
Green Chain Wlk
Charlton Sch
Charlton Park
SE7
CHARLTON PARK LA
Queen Elizabeth
H
Sports Gd
SHRAPNEL CL
STADIUM RD
Woolwich Stad
Woolwich Common
30
SE18
Pl Fld
ORDNANCE RD
LLANOVER RD
WHITWORTH RD
PAGET RISE
PAGET TERR
REEVES RD
RIPON RD
HERBERT RD
CANTWELL HO
CANTWELL RD
DALLIN RD
HIGHVIEW
EGLINTON HILL
SANTANA
BRENT RD
MAYPLACE LA
BRINKLOW CRES
MERIDIAN RD
INIGO JONES RD
STONEFIELD WAY
GREENBAY RD
PRINCE HENRY RD
5
Hornfair Park
MANSERGH CL
ACADEMY RD
DELVAN CL 1
KEEMOR CL 2
Green Chain Wlk
MATCHLESS DR
GARRISON CL
Pl Fld
GRAHAM HO
CONDOVER CRES
DOWNEND
BUSHMOOR CRES
THE OLD FIRE STATION
EAGLESFIELD RD
Tenn Cts
STANE WAY
LEYBURN HO
BAKER RD
GREENWICH HTS
PALLET WAY
ABERFORD GDNS
TELLSON AVE
77
A207
PRINCE IMPERIAL RD
RED LION LA
DONALDSON RD
ANKERDINE CRES
MOORDOWN
OCCUPATION LA
RIVERVIEW HTS
Bwg Gn
GALTON HO 1
FLORENCE HO 2
SIDNEY HO 3
ROBERTSON HO 4
MENNIE HO 5
GODWIN HO 6
PANBRO HO 7
SUTHERLAND HO 8
Pav
Recn Gd
MELTHORPE GDNS
ZANGWILL RD
THELMA GDNS
4
SHOOTERS HILL RD
EDITH CAVELL WAY
BELL ST
CAIRNS MEWS
ELIZABETH FRY PL
KENDALL RD
BROOK SQ
BARLOW DR
HOWERD WAY
CORELLI RD
GILBERT CL
Tenn Cts
SPRINGWATER CL
ACADEMY PL
BARRINGTON VILLAS
CONSTITUTION RISE
CAMPBELL CL
RED LION PL
VYVYAN HO
SHOOTERS HILL
HILL END
RAYLEAS CL
SHREWSBURY LA
CLEANTHUS RD
FOXCROFT RD
Recn Gd
THE CHESTNUTS
CLEANTHUS CL
LINKS VIEW
THE LEAS
143
Kidbrooke Sch
CROSIER CL
Castlewood Day Sch
Eltham Common
CRAIGHOLM
Mast
Memorial
KENILWORTH GDNS
CROWN WOOD LA
BROAD WLK
MAYDAY GDNS
Recn Gd
3
Pav
Cemy
Sp Gd
WELL HALL RD
PO
HEATHERBANK
CASTLEWOOD DR
Severndroog Castle
STONEY ALLEY
Green Chain Wlk
Jackwood
DUNBLANE RD
ALLENSWOOD RD
76
SEDGEBROOK RD
CROSSBROOK RD
KELBROOK RD
FLINTMILL CRES
SLADEBROOK RD
CIREBROOK RD
BOURNBROOK RD
ARBROATH RD
ROSS WAY
MAUDSLAY RD
MARTIN BOWES RD
ARSENAL RD
GRANBY RD
CORNWALLIS WLK
LITTLECROFT
CROOKSTON RD
CROOKSTON RD
2
ENDOVER RD
RYDONS CL
HENWICK RD
APPLETON RD
WHINYATES RD
FRANKLIN PAS
PHINEAS PETT RD
DOWNMAN RD
DICKSON RD
LOVELACE GN
SHRAPNEL RD
BROME RD
GRANGEHILL PL
GARNETT CL
DAIRSIE RD
Deansfield Prim Sch
GLENBAR CL
GLENDALE CL
GLENHEAD CL
Tenn Cts
SE9
WINCHCOMB GDNS
Schs
SHORTWAY
COBBETT RD
A205
CONGREVE RD
ROCHESTER WAY
DUMBRECK RD
BERRYHILL
LYNSTED GDNS
BRENLEY GDNS
BRISET RD
KINGSHOLM GDNS
RANCLIFFE GDNS
A208
PRINCE RUPERT RD
ADMIRAL SEYMOUR RD
MORA RD
GRANGEHILL RD
WESTMOUNT RD
ELIBANK RD
SE9
BERRYHILL GDNS
Eltham Park North
1
RICKYARD PATH
ELMBROOK GDNS
ODEON PAR
TOM COOMBS CL
TUDOR PAR
KIDBROOKE LA
PLEASAUNCE CT
CRAGTON RD
Sch
EARLSHALL RD
GREENVALE RD
ELTHAM PARK GDNS
GLENESK RD
Sp Gd
Pav
Tenn Cts
Well Hall Pleasaunce
A2
50
WELL HALL PAR
DUNVEGAN RD
A2
Eltham Park South
Bwg Gns
75
HORSFELD
A205
PO
Sch
42
HAIMO RD
FROISSART RD
BASKET GDNS
TATTERSALL CL
PULLMAN PL
KEYNSHAM GDNS
MILNE GDNS
WELL HALL
B
166
43
GLENLEA RD
GLENLYON RD
BALCASKIE RD
BEECHILL RD
GLENHOUSE RD
C
GLENSHIEL RD
St Mary's RC Prim Sch
CONNIFFE CT
Recn Gd
Tenn Cts
D
Green Chain Wlk
Eltham Warren
44

Plumstead Common
SE18
Shrewsbury Park
Green Chain Wlk
Shooters Hill
Shooters Hill
Woodlands Farm
DOVER RD
Oxleas Wood
Nature Reserve
DA16
Falconwood Field
Falconwood
SE9
Falconwood
Bishop Ridley CE Prim Sch
Coll
EAST ROCHESTER WAY
BELLEGROVE RD
A207
Eastcote Prim Sch
Willow Dene Sch
East Wickham Schs
Rockliffe Manor Prim Sch
Plumstead Manor/Negus Sch
St Margaret's CE Prim Sch
Gallions Mount Prim Sch
Crown Woods Sch
DA15
123
146
167
A
B
C
D
1
2
3
4
5
6
44
45
46
75
76
77
78

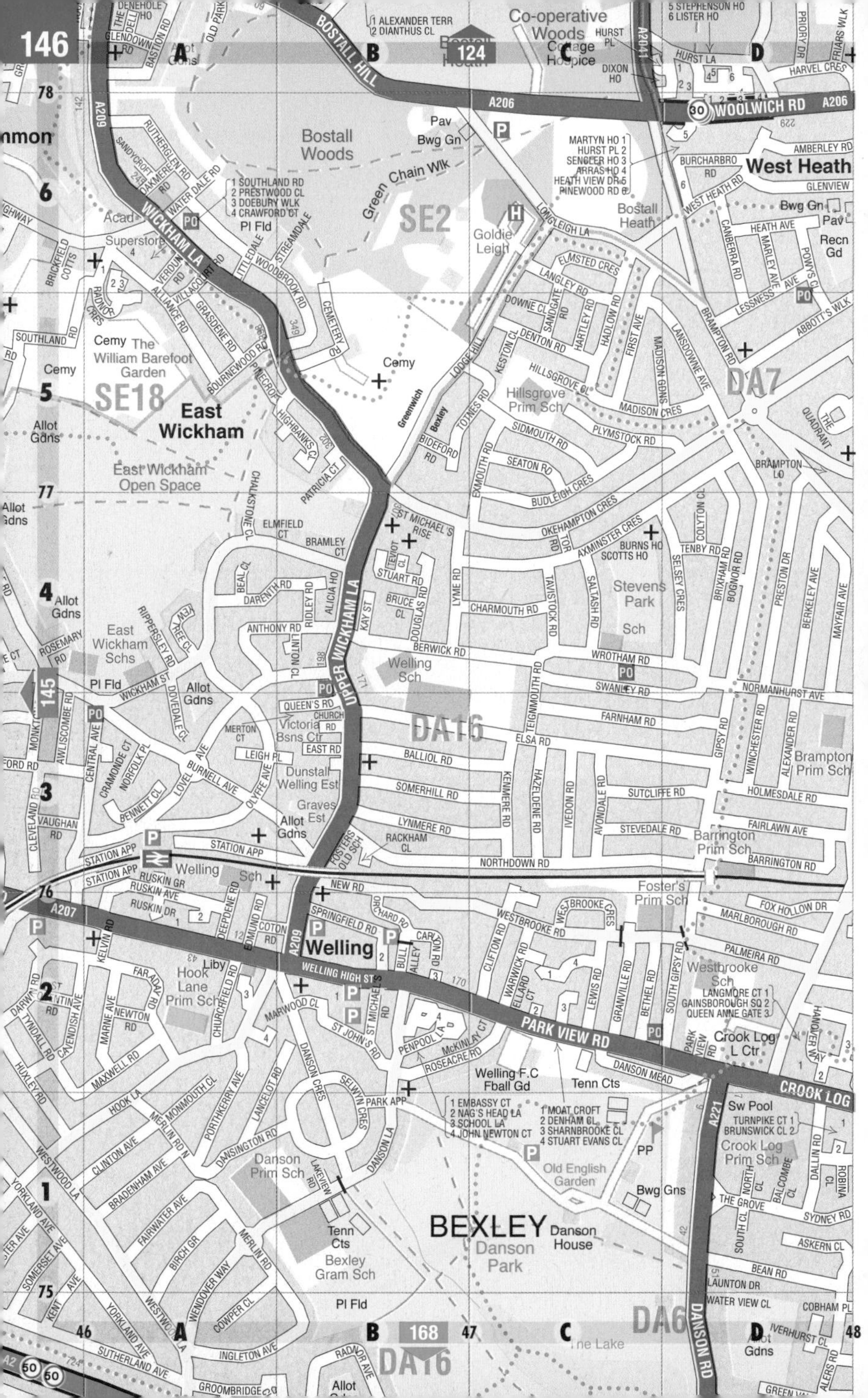
A
B
C
D
124
145
168
78
6
5
77
4
3
76
2
1
75
46
47
48
Bostall Hill
Co-operative Woods
Cottage Hospice
Bostall Heath
A206
Woolwich Rd
1 Alexander Terr
2 Dianthus Cl
5 Stephenson Ho
6 Lister Ho
Hurst PL
Dixon Ho
Hurst La
Harvel Cres
A2041
Bostall Woods
Pav
Bwg Gn
Green Chain Wlk
SE2
Goldie Leigh
Longleigh La
Bostall Heath
Martyn Ho 1
Hurst Pl 2
Sengler Ho 3
Arras Ho 4
Heath View Dr 5
Pinewood Rd 6
West Heath
Amberley Rd
Burcharbro Rd
Glenview
West Heath Rd
Heath Ave
Recn Gd
Canberra Rd
Marley Ave
Powys Cl
Lessness Ave
Abbott's Wlk
A209
Wickham La
Rutherglen Rd
Sandycroft
Oakmere Rd
Water Dale Rd
1 Southland Rd
2 Prestwood Cl
3 Doebury Wlk
4 Crawford Ct
Acad
Superstore
Pl Fld
Littledale
Streamdale
Woodbrook Rd
Villacourt Rd
Verdun Rd
Alliance Rd
Grasdene Rd
Bournewood Rd
Brickfield Cotts
Radnor Cres
Southland Rd
Cemy
The William Barefoot Garden
SE18
East Wickham
Allot Gdns
East Wickham Open Space
Cemetery Rd
Pinecroft
Highbanks Cl
Patricia Ct
Greenwich
Bexley
Lodge Hill
Totnes Rd
Bideford Rd
Elmsted Cres
Langley Rd
Downe Cl
Sandgate Rd
Hartley Rd
Hadlow Rd
First Ave
Denton Rd
Keston Ct
Hillsgrove Cl
Hillsgrove Prim Sch
Madison Gdns
Lansdowne Ave
Brampton Rd
DA7
Madison Cres
Plymstock Rd
Sidmouth Rd
Seaton Rd
Exmouth Rd
Budleigh Cres
Okehampton Cres
The Quadrant
Brampton Lo
Chalkstone Cl
Elmfield Ct
Bramley Ct
St Michael's Rise
Teviot Cl
Stuart Rd
Bruce Cl
Douglas Rd
Kay St
Lyme Rd
Tor Rd
Axminster Cres
Burns Ho
Scotts Ho
Colyton Cl
Tenby Rd
Selsey Cres
Brixham Rd
Bognor Rd
Preston Dr
Berkeley Ave
Mayfair Ave
Beal Cl
Darenth Rd
Ridley Rd
Alicia Ho
Upper Wickham La
Anthony Rd
Linton Cl
Charmouth Rd
Tavistock Rd
Saltash Rd
Stevens Park
Sch
Rippersley Rd
Yew Tree Cl
Berwick Rd
Wrotham Rd
Rosemary Rd
East Wickham Schs
Welling Sch
Teignmouth Rd
Swanley Rd
Normanhurst Ave
Pl Fld
Wickham St
Allot Gdns
Dovedale Cl
Queen's Rd
Church Rd
Victoria Bsns Ctr
Merton Ct
East Rd
Farnham Rd
DA16
Elsa Rd
Gipsy Rd
Winchester Rd
Alexander Rd
Brampton Prim Sch
Awliscombe Rd
Central Ave
Cramonde Ct
Norfolk Pl
Lovel Ave
Burnell Ave
Olyffe Ave
Leigh Pl
Dunstall Welling Est
Balliol Rd
Somerhill Rd
Kenmere Rd
Hazeldene Rd
Ivedon Rd
Avondale Rd
Sutcliffe Rd
Holmesdale Rd
Monkton
Cleveland Rd
Vaughan Rd
Bennett Cl
Graves Est
Allot Gdns
Lynmere Rd
Rackham Cl
Fosters Old Sch
Stevedale Rd
Fairlawn Ave
Barrington Prim Sch
Station App
Welling
Northdown Rd
Barrington Rd
Ruskin Gr
Ruskin Ave
Ruskin Dr
Deepdene Rd
Edmund Rd
Coton Rd
New Rd
Orchard Rd
Springfield Rd
Carlton Rd
Bull Alley
Westbrooke Rd
Westbrooke Cres
Clifton Rd
Foster's Prim Sch
Fox Hollow Dr
Marlborough Rd
Palmeira Rd
A207
Kelvin Rd
Welling
Welling High St
Liby
Hook Lane Prim Sch
Far Aday Rd
Churchfield Rd
Newton Rd
Marine Ave
Maxwell Rd
Cavendish Ave
Tyndall Rd
Darwin Rd
St Constantine Rd
Huxley Rd
Marwood Cl
St Michael's Rd
St John's Rd
Penpool La
McKinlay Ct
Roseacre Rd
Warwick Rd
Ellard Ct
Lewis Rd
Granville Rd
Bethel Rd
South Gipsy Rd
Westbrooke Sch
Langmore Ct 1
Gainsborough Sq 2
Queen Anne Gate 3
Park View Rd
Hanover Way
Crook Log L Ctr
Danson Mead
Welling F.C Fball Gd
Tenn Cts
Crook Log
Hook La
Monmouth Cl
Merlin Rd N
Porthkerry Ave
Lancelot Rd
Danson Cres
Selwyn Cres
Park App
1 Embassy Ct
2 Nag's Head La
3 School La
4 John Newton Ct
1 Moat Croft
2 Denham Cl
3 Sharnbrooke Cl
4 Stuart Evans Cl
Dansington Rd
Danson Prim Sch
Lakeview Rd
Danson La
Old English Garden
PP
Bwg Gns
Sw Pool
Turnpike Ct 1
Brunswick Cl 2
Crook Log Prim Sch
Dallin Rd
Robina Cl
North Cl
Balcombe Cl
The Grove
Sydney Rd
South Cl
Askern Cl
A221
Westwood La
Clinton Ave
Bradenham Ave
Fairwater Ave
Birch Gr
Merlin Rd
Yorkland Ave
Somerset Ave
Kent Ave
Wendover Way
Cowper Cl
Westwood La
BEXLEY
Danson House
Danson Park
Tenn Cts
Bexley Gram Sch
Pl Fld
Bean Rd
Launton Dr
Water View Cl
Cobham Pl
DA6
Danson Rd
The Lake
Allot Gdns
Iverhurst Cl
Ingleton Ave
Sutherland Ave
Groombridge
Radnor Ave
DA16
Green

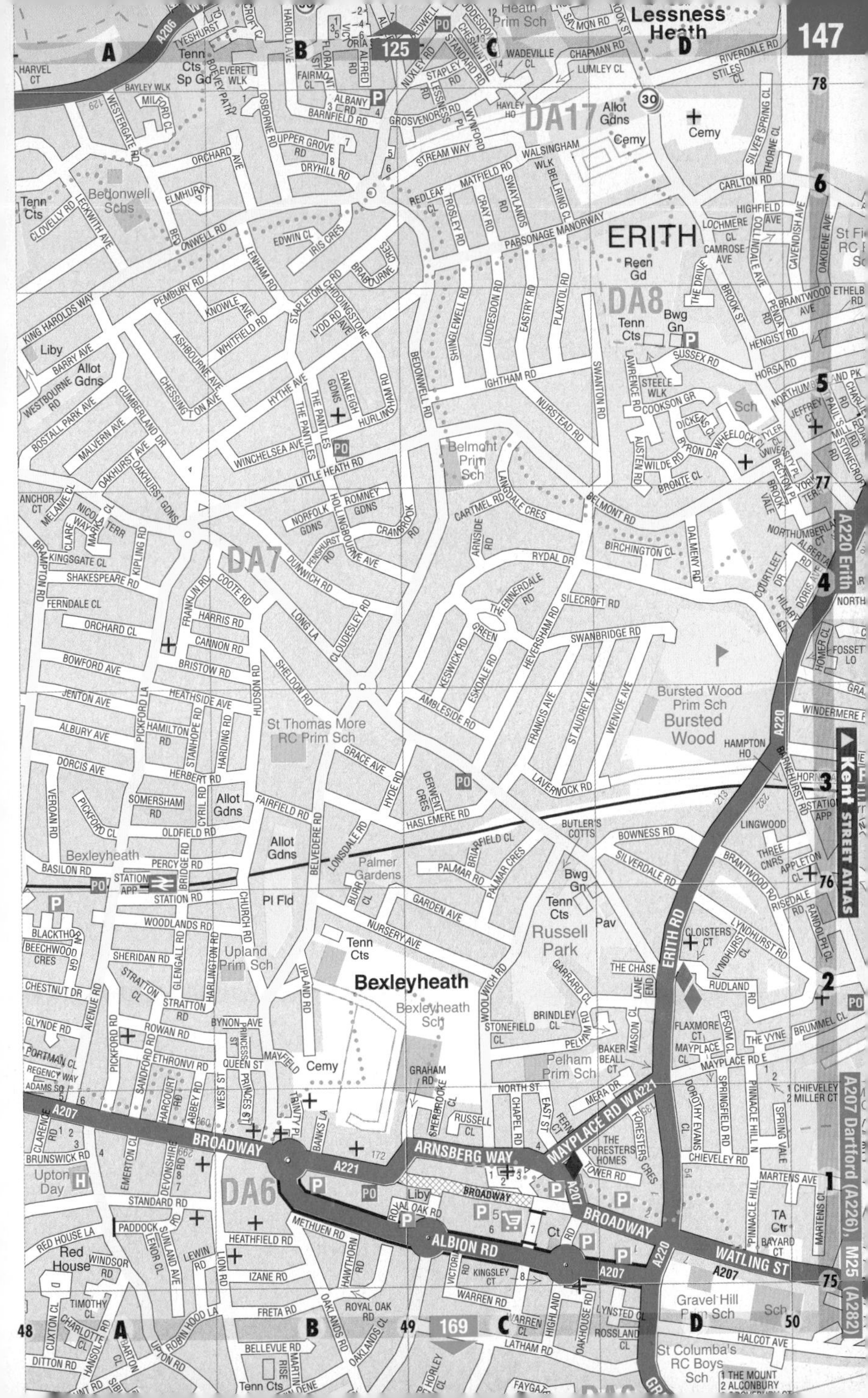

147
125
169
Lessness Heath
ERITH
Bexleyheath
DA17
DA8
DA7
DA6
A
B
C
D
78
77
76
75
48
49
50
6
5
4
3
2
1
A220 Erith
Kent STREET ATLAS
A207 Dartford (A226), M25 (A282)
A206
A207
A220
A221
BROADWAY
ARNSBERG WAY
ALBION RD
WATLING ST
ERITH RD
MAYPLACE RD W
Tenn Cts Sp Gd
Bedonwell Schs
Tenn Cts
Liby
Allot Gdns
Belmont Prim Sch
Recn Gd
Bwg Gn
Sch
St Thomas More RC Prim Sch
Bursted Wood Prim Sch
Bursted Wood
Palmer Gardens
Pl Fld
Upland Prim Sch
Bexleyheath Sch
Russell Park
Pelham Prim Sch
Cemy
Upton Day
Red House
Gravel Hill Prim Sch
St Columba's RC Boys Sch
HAMPTON HO
BUTLER'S COTTS
THE FORESTERS HOMES
LINGWOOD
THREE CNRS
TA Ctr
HAYLEY HO
Heath Prim Sch
Bexleyheath
HARVEL CT
TYESHURST
BAYLEY WLK
EVERETT WLK
BOVEY PATH
MILFORD CL
WESTERGATE RD
OSBORNE RD
HAROLD AVE
FLORA ST
FAIRMONT CL
ALFRED RD
ALBANY RD
BARNFIELD RD
UPPER GROVE RD
DRYHILL RD
NUXLEY RD
STAPLEY RD
LESSNESS RD
STANDARD RD
CHESTNUT RD
GROSVENOR RD
WYNFORD PL
WADEVILLE CL
CHAPMAN RD
LUMLEY CL
RIVERDALE RD
STILES CL
SALMON RD
STREAM WAY
WALSINGHAM WLK
BELLRING CL
SILVER SPRING CL
THORNE CL
CARLTON RD
HIGHFIELD AVE
LOCHMERE CL
CAMROSE AVE
COLLINDALE AVE
CAVENDISH AVE
OAKDENE AVE
THE DRIVE
BROOK ST
PENDA RD
BRANTWOOD AVE
HENGIST RD
HORSA RD
SUSSEX RD
LAWRENCE RD
STEELE WLK
COOKSON GR
DICKENS CL
WHEELOCK CL
BYRON DR
WILDE RD
BRONTE CL
AUSTEN RD
NORTHUMBERLAND PK
JEFFREY CT
PAUL'S RD
MILL RD
STONECROFT
UNIVERSITY PL
BECTON PL
BROOK VALE
TYLER CL
YORK TERR
ORCHARD AVE
ELMHURST
BEDONWELL RD
TENN CTS
CLOVELLY RD
LECKWITH AVE
EDWIN CL
IRIS CRES
LENHAM RD
REDLEAF CL
TROSLEY RD
MATFIELD RD
CRAY RD
SWAYLANDS RD
PARSONAGE MANORWAY
BRADBOURNE CRES
KING HAROLDS WAY
PEMBURY RD
KNOWLE AVE
WHITFIELD RD
ASHBOURNE AVE
STAPLETON RD
CHIDDINGSTONE AVE
LYDD RD
SHINGLEWELL RD
LUDDESDON RD
EASTRY RD
PLAXTOL RD
SWANTON RD
BARRY AVE
WESTBOURNE RD
BOSTALL PARK AVE
CUMBERLAND DR
CHESSINGTON AVE
HYTHE AVE
THE PANTILES
RANLEIGH GDNS
HURLINGHAM RD
BEDONWELL RD
IGHTHAM RD
NURSTEAD RD
MALVERN AVE
OAKHURST AVE
OAKHURST GDNS
WINCHELSEA AVE
LITTLE HEATH RD
ANCHOR CT
MELANIE CL
NICOLA TERR
CLARE WAY
MARK CL
BRAMPTON RD
KINGSGATE CL
KIPLING RD
SHAKESPEARE RD
FERNDALE CL
ORCHARD CL
BOWFORD AVE
JENTON AVE
ALBURY AVE
DORCIS AVE
VEROAN RD
PICKFORD CL
PICKFORD LA
HOLLINGBOURNE AVE
NORFOLK GDNS
ROMNEY GDNS
CRANBROOK RD
PENSHURST RD
DUNWICH RD
COOTE RD
FRANKLIN RD
HARRIS RD
CANNON RD
BRISTOW RD
HEATHSIDE AVE
HAMILTON RD
STANHOPE RD
HARDING RD
HUDSON RD
LONG LA
SHELDON RD
CLOUDESLEY RD
CARTMEL RD
LANGDALE CRES
ARNSIDE RD
BELMONT RD
BIRCHINGTON CL
DALMENY RD
RYDAL DR
THE ENNERDALE RD
GREEN
SILECROFT RD
HEVERSHAM RD
SWANBRIDGE RD
KESWICK RD
ESKDALE RD
AMBLESIDE RD
FRANCIS AVE
ST AUDREY AVE
WENVOE AVE
LAVERNOCK RD
GRACE AVE
HYDE RD
DERWENT CRES
HASLEMERE RD
FAIRFIELD RD
BELVEDERE RD
LONSDALE RD
HERBERT RD
SOMERSHAM RD
CYRIL RD
OLDFIELD RD
BASILON RD
PERCY RD
STATION APP
STATION RD
BRIDGE RD
CHURCH RD
BRIARFIELD CL
PALMAR CRES
PALMAR RD
BURR CL
GARDEN AVE
NURSERY AVE
UPLAND RD
WOOLWICH RD
BOWNESS RD
SILVERDALE RD
BRANTWOOD RD
APPLETON CL
RISEDALE RD
RANDOLPH CL
LYNDHURST RD
CLOISTERS CT
RUDLAND
THE CHASE
LANE END
GARRARD CL
BRINDLEY CL
PELHAM RD
MASON CL
STONEFIELD CL
BAKER BEALL CT
FLAXMORE CT
MAYPLACE CL
MAYPLACE RD E
EPSOM CL
THE VYNE
BRUMMEL CL
CHIEVELEY RD
1 CHIEVELEY
2 MILLER CT
DOROTHY EVANS CL
SPRINGFIELD RD
PINNACLE HILL N
PINNACLE HILL
SPRING VALE
MARTENS AVE
MARTENS CL
BAYARD CT
HORNBEAM
STATION APP
COURTLEET DR
ALBERTA RD
DORIS AVE
HILARY CL
HOMER CL
FOSSETT LO
WINDERMERE RD
NORTHUMBERLAND CT
BLACKTHORN GR
BEECHWOOD CRES
WOODLANDS RD
SHERIDAN RD
GLENGALL RD
HARLINGTON RD
CHESTNUT DR
AVENUE RD
STRATTON CL
STRATTON RD
GLYNDE RD
PICKFORD RD
ROWAN RD
BYNON AVE
PRINCESS ST
PORTMAN CL
REGENCY WAY
ADAMS SQ
SANDFORD RD
ETHRONVI RD
QUEEN ST
MAYFIELD
HARCOURT RD
ABBEY RD
WEST ST
PRINCES ST
TRINITY PL
BANKS LA
GRAHAM RD
SHERBROOKE CL
RUSSELL CL
NORTH ST
CHAPEL RD
EAST ST
FERN CT
MERA DR
FORESTERS CRES
TOWER RD
CLARENCE RD
BRUNSWICK RD
EMERTON CL
DEVONSHIRE RD
STANDARD RD
PADDOCK
LENOR CL
SUNLAND AVE
HEATHFIELD RD
LEWIN RD
LION RD
RED HOUSE LA
WINDSOR RD
METHUEN RD
ROYAL OAK RD
HAWTHORN RD
IZANE RD
FRETA RD
VICTORIA RD
KINGSLEY CT
WARREN RD
WARREN CL
HIGHLAND RD
OAKHOUSE RD
LYNSTED CL
ROSSLAND CL
TIMOTHY CL
CHARLOTTE CL
CUXTON CL
HANSOL RD
BARTON CL
UPTON RD
ROBIN HOOD LA
OAKLANDS RD
OAKLANDS CL
BELLEVUE RD
RISE
MARTIN DENE
HORLEY CL
LATHAM RD
HALCOT AVE
DITTON RD
1 THE MOUNT
2 ALCONBURY
Ct

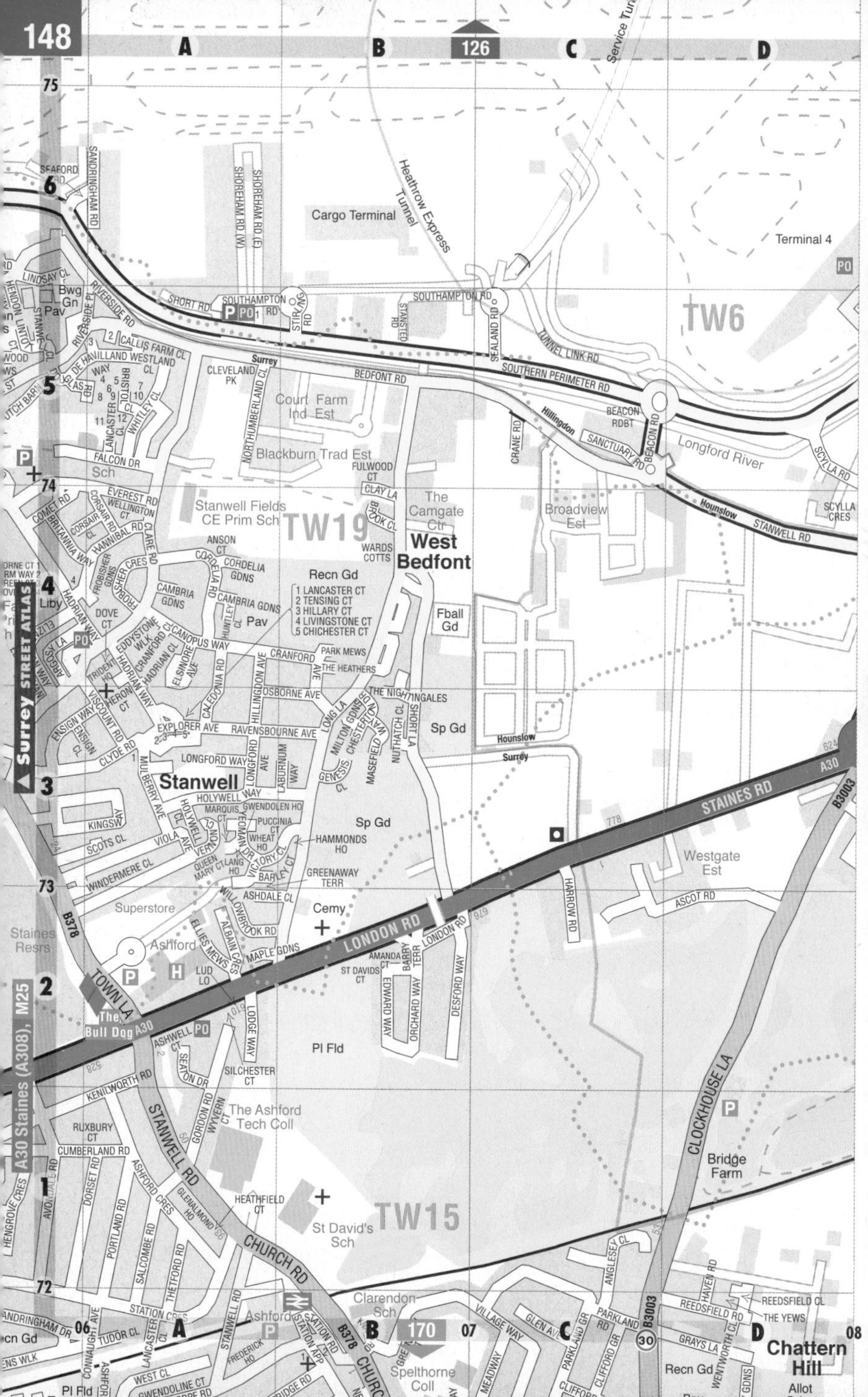
A
B
126
C
D
Cargo Terminal
Heathrow Express Tunnel
Terminal 4
TW6
SOUTHAMPTON RD
SHORT RD
STIRLING RD
STANSTED RD
SEALAND RD
TUNNEL LINK RD
SOUTHERN PERIMETER RD
BEDFONT RD
Court Farm Ind Est
Blackburn Trad Est
BEACON RDBT
SANCTUARY RD
Longford River
SCYLLA RD
SCYLLA CRES
STANWELL RD
Broadview Est
Stanwell Fields CE Prim Sch
TW19
West Bedfont
The Camgate Ctr
Recn Gd
Fball Gd
1 LANCASTER CT
2 TENSING CT
3 HILLARY CT
4 LIVINGSTONE CT
5 CHICHESTER CT
Stanwell
Sp Gd
STAINES RD
A30
B3003
Westgate Est
ASCOT RD
HARROW RD
LONDON RD
Cemy
Superstore
Staines Resrs
Ashford
TOWN LA
The Bull Dog
Pl Fld
The Ashford Tech Coll
St David's Sch
TW15
CLOCKHOUSE LA
Bridge Farm
STANWELL RD
CHURCH RD
Clarendon Sch
Spelthorne Coll
Ashford
170
Chattern Hill
Recn Gd
Allot
Surrey STREET ATLAS
A30 Staines (A308), M25
75
74
73
72
06
07
08

A
B
127
C
D
Hatton
Radius Pk
75
6
5
74
4
150
3
73
2
1
72
TW6
TW14
TW15
TW13
GREAT SOUTH-WEST RD
SOUTHERN PERIMETER RD
A30
Hounslow
Hillingdon
HATTON RD
WELLINGTON RD
MYRTLE AVE
Playground
CAIN'S LA
UNWIN AVE
IVERNA GDNS
EDWARD RD
ORCHARD AVE
Tenn Cts
Fball Gd
Bwg Gn
Pav
Recn Gd
Cemy
Masts
Superstore
DUKES
Marjory Kinnon Sch
Bedfont Jun & Inf Schs
Allot Gdns
Duke of Northumberland's River
Heathrow Terminal 4
Hotel
SWINDON RD
SNOWDON RD
SHEFFIELD RD
SHEFFIELD WAY
SWANSEA RD
SHREWSBURY RD
CARBOROUGH RD
HATFORD RD
1 SHETLAND RD
2 TERMINAL FOUR RDBT
THE GARDENS
HAZELMERE CL
MARRIOTT CL
PENINSULAR CL
NORTHUMBERLAND CRES
TARGET CL
RICHMOND AVE
WELWYN AVE
KINGSTON AVE
LONGFORD AVE
CARLTON HO
WHITE BRIDGE CL
TURPIN RD
ELMCROFT CL
ENGLEHEART DR
PENTELOW GDNS
CLIVE
A315
TENNYSON CL
BURNS
Allot Gdns
RUSKIN AVE
SHAKESPEARE AVE
CASSIOBURY AVE
Pl Fld
LETCHWORTH AVE
Longford Com Sch
TACHBROOK RD
LINK RD
FRUEN RD
EDWARD PAULING HO
BEDFONT LA
B3377
Bwg Gn
T Cts
OWEN HO
GLEBELANDS
SHORE CL
ROWAN HO
THACKERY LO
REGIS CT
BENSINGTON CT
EDITH CT
NORTH CL
NORTH RD
NEW RD
BRAMLEY CT
DORCHESTER DR
BETHANY WAYE
BEDFONT CL
MONTROSE RD
HORSHAM RD
BISHOPS DR
BENEDICT DR
WEST RD
EAST RD
PAGE RD
LEWIN TERR
GOULD RD
WARFIELD RD
COLONIAL RD
IMPERIAL RD
Hillingdon
Hounslow
STANWELL RD
LONGLEAT WAY
PATES MANOR DR
BURLINGTON CL
STAINES RD
Liby
FAIRHOLME
WEST VIEW
SPINNEY DR
VICARAGE CT
ST MARY'S DR
SAFFRON CT
LINDSEY GDNS
NATALIE CL
ELM RD
GROVESTILE WAYE
SHERBORNE RD
BEECH RD
MONARCH CL
SOUTHVILLE RD
WALKER CL
STONE CRES
VEITCH CL
RUSCOMBE WAY
CHANDLERS CL
CHURCHILL CL
BEATTIE CL
PACIFIC CL
WESTMINSTER CL
ASHMEAD RD
PROCTOR CL
DAVID HENRY WARING CT
HATCHETT RD
FAWNS MANOR CL
FAWNS MANOR RD
CEDAR RD
BRIDLEPATH WAY
SOUTHVILLE CL
Clockhouse Rdbt
A315
BEDFONT GREEN CL
DUDLEY RD
PEACOCK AVE
PADBURY CT
KILLROSS RD
CLEEVE CT
BOWDEN CL
ROUTH CT
SLEDMERE CT
LOXWOOD CL
GRAFTON CT
ELDRICK CT
CRAMOND CT
ELSWORTH CL
SOUTHVILLE CRES
SANDY DR
ASH GR
OAK WAY
INVICTA CL
ALLCOT CL
POPE CL
Southville Jun & Inf Schs
ENNERDALE CL
GRASMERE CL
NINE ELMS CL
TREVITHICK CL
BRADLEY CL
ANDOVER CL
JUBILEE WAY
WINDERMERE CL
WESTMACOTT DR
WATERLOO CL
NELSON CL
PADSTOW WALK
Fairholme Prim Sch
East Bedfont
KENDAL CL 1
APPLEBY GDNS 2
DERWENT CL 3
MISSENDEN CL 4
BUTTERMERE CL 5
Cemy
ST CATHERINES CT
IVORY CT
HAMMER AVE
TAYLORS CT
GUILDFORD AVE
Edward Pauling Prim Sch
ROSEMEAD AVE
Pav
T Cts
Grosvenor Park
SOUTHCOTE AVE
GRANVILLE AVE
ROCHESTER AVE
Bedfont Lakes Country Park
Ind Est
BEDFONT RD
Vineyard Nurseries
BEDFORD CL
RALEIGH RD
LANCING RD
VERNON RD
PERCIVAL RD
PRINCES RD
AVENUE RD
WESTBOURNE RD
FRANCIS AVE
AMBER CT 1
RUSSET CT 2
GARNET CT 3
OCHRE CT 1
SIENNA CT 2
VERMILLION CT 3
FUSCIA CT 4
INDIGO CT 5
VIRIDIAN CT 6
TOPAZ CT 7
THE HERMITAGE 8
SPRING CNR 9
QUEENS PARK GDNS 10
PH
NORBURY RD
RUBY CL
ELVEDON RD
AZURE CT
Schs
Recn Gd
ST DUNSTAN'S RD
A244
SPRING RD
HAYLING AVE
CRAIGWELL AVE
HAM CROFT CL
HARVEST RD
PARKFIELD
HM Young Offender Institution & Remand Ctr
Court Two
Court Three
Court One
Bedfont Ind Pk N
Bedfont Ind Pk
CHALLENGE RD
Surrey
Hounslow
ASHFORD RD
B377
LARTHAM CL
BRIARWOOD
PHOENIX CT
WALTON GDNS
SHELSON AVE
Cemy
Lower Feltham
RYLAND CL
SUNBURY CRES
SUNBURY RD
LUDLOW RD
Ashford Ind Est
Mereside Pk
PORTLAND CRES
FIELD VIEW
GATE AVE
THE CLUMPS
Recn Gd
09
171
10
ELLINGTON RD
DENISON
ALLIANCE CT
SHIELD RD

North Feltham
FELTHAM
Lower Feltham
Hanworth
TW14
TW13
Hounslow Heath
Hanworth Park
Hanworth Park House
Feltham Com Sch
Feltham Arena
Sparrow Farm Schs
Victoria Jun Sch
Southville Jun & Inf Schs
Longford Com Sch
Grosvenor Park
STAINES RD
HARLINGTON RD W
HARLINGTON RD E
HOUNSLOW RD
HIGH ST
FAGG'S RD
UXBRIDGE RD
BEDFONT LA
HANWORTH RD
NEW RD
1 FRANK TOWELL CT
2 BRASSEY CL
3 EASTLEIGH WAY
4 ORCHARD RD
5 PEACH RD
6 ALMOND CL
7 HAZEL GR
8 HUNTER HO
9 HAWTHORN RD
10 TILLEY RD
11 PLUM CL
12 ARCHER CT
13 MAGNOLIA CT
14 LEMON GR
15 BELVEDERE HO
16 QUINCE HO
17 CAMELLIA HO
1 BERGENIA HO
2 AZALEA HO
3 HAMLYN HO
1 BROOKLYN CT
2 DEVONSHIRE CT
1 PARKFIELD PAR
2 ROCHESTER PAR
3 THE VINEYARDS
4 CHERVIL CL
1 BLAKEWOOD CL
2 SHAKESPEARE WAY
128
149
172

129
173
152
A
B
C
D
1
2
3
4
5
6
13
14
72
73
74
75
TW4
TW2
TW13
Hounslow Heath Nature Reserve
London Loop
The Heathland Sch
The Orchard Jun & Inf Sch
Hounslow Bsns Pk
Inwood Bsns Pk
Hounslow
Allot Gdns
Recn Gd
Cemy
Millfarm Bsns Pk
Hounslow
Richmond upon Thames
River Crane
Crem
Tenn Cts
Pav
Sp Gd
Heathfield Jun & Inf Schs
Bishop Perrin CE Prim Sch
St Edmund's RC Prim Sch
Nursery
Liby
Whitton Sch
Games Ct
Crane Park
Hospital Bridge Rdbt
Crane Park Prim Sch
Pl Fld
Hampton Farm Ind Est
The Lion Ctr
Hanworth Trad Est
Apex Ret Pk
Links Ind Est
Oriel Prim Sch
Apex Cnr
Sp Ctr
CH Twickenham
Drv Rng
Fulwell Park
Fulwell
HANWORTH RD
WELLINGTON RD S
NELSON RD
HOSPITAL BRIDGE RD
GREAT CHERTSEY RD
STAINES RD
TWICKENHAM RD
HAMPTON RD W
HOUNSLOW RD
WHITTON RD
POWDER MILL LA
A3063
A314
A315
A316
A305
A312
B358
B361
SHERIDAN CT 1
PICKWICK CL 2
HEATHLANDS CT 3
BRAMLEY WAY 4
ALLIANCE CL 5
BODICEA MEWS 1
SHELBURNE DR 2
FOUR SQUARE CT 3
SLADE HO 1
JAMIESON HO 2
ATHERLEY WAY 1
DUNLEARY CL 2
DANIEL CL 3
1 MALLARD CL
2 BRUNEL WLK
3 BRACKEN CL
4 HEATHER WLK
CORFE CL 1
RISBROOKE CL 2
1 TOWFIELD CT
2 NORMAN HO
3 RIVER CRANE WAY
1 WHITELY CT
2 BUTTS COTTS
1 EDWIN STRAY HO
2 CRANE HO
3 GLEBE HO
4 CHERTSEY HO
5 WHITELEYS HO
6 BUTTS HO
7 GLEBE COTTS
COURT CLOSE AVE

130
151
174
A
B
C
D
1
2
3
4
5
6
Chatsworth Jun Sch
The Heath Bsns Ctr
Inwood Bsns Pk
Hounslow
HOUNSLOW GDNS
HOUNSLOW AVE
MASWELL PARK RD
MASWELL PK
WHITTON RD
PARK RD
PARK CT
PARK CRES
WOLSEY CL
LYNCROFT GDNS
CENTRAL AVE
NORBURY AVE
CATHERINE GDNS
EATON RD
WAINWRIGHT GR
BRACKEN END
HARVESTERS CL
HALL RD
CHURCH STRETTON RD
Allot Gdns
LEAMINGTON CL
PRIORY RD
ROSEBERY RD
SOUTHLAND WAY
REAPERS WAY
HEATHER CL
GLEN WLK
PLOUGHMANS END
THATCHERS WAY
CROFTERS CL
GAINSBOROUGH GDNS
CONSTABLE GDNS
MUNNINGS GDNS
ARNOLD CRES
1 YEOMANS MEWS
2 REGENCY MEWS
Sewage Works
Duke of Northumberland's River
BEAUMONT PL
MOGDEN LA
Superstore
EASEDALE HO
Ivybridge Ret Pk
TREVOR CL
HILLARY DR
BRIAR CL
MANNS CL
BANKSIDE CL
LYNTON
MILLWOOD RD
SHIRLEY DR
SHIRLEY CL
PARK CL
DEAN RD
MURRAY AVE
SANDRA CL
Hounslow
Richmond upon Thames
MARZENA CT
COLONIAL AVE
WHITTON MANOR RD
WHITTON DENE
AMBERSIDE CL
KNELLER GDNS
Pav
CONSORT MEWS
QUEENSBRIDGE PK
HARLEQUIN CL
Museum of Rugby
Twickenham Rugby Football Union Ground
RUGBY RD
VARSITY DR
SUMMERWOOD RD
Twickenham Trad Ctr
BUTTERFIELD CL
1 THIRLMERE HO
2 HAWESWATER HO
3 WINDERMERE HO
Ivybridge Prim Sch
CEDAR AVE
OLD MANOR DR
Bnstand
Tenn Cts
Pl Fld
Royal Military Sch of Music (Kneller Hall)
Sp Gd
DUKE OF CAMBRIDGE CL
1 SULLIVAN HO
2 PURCELL HO
3 HANDEL HO
4 ELGAR HO
Chase Bridge Prim Sch
PALMERSTON RD
CHUDLEIGH RD
Whitton Road Rdbt
MARLOW CRES
GLEBE SIDE
ERNCROFT WAY
B361
RYDAL GDNS
RUNNYMEDE RD
DERWENT RD
CONISTON RD
HOUNSLOW RD
KESWICK RD
VICARAGE RD
BRAMLEY CL
PROSPECT CRES
SHIRE MEWS
NELSON RD
SEATON RD
SEATON CL
KNELLER RD
SALLIESFIELD
WHITTON RD
TAYBEN AVE
RUSSELL RD
CHUDLEIGH RD
Sch
ST VINCENT RD
SOUTH LO
WARREN RD
PALGRAVE HO
CRANE WAY
Whitton
HAZEL CL
THE RIDGE
MILNER DR
HALL FARM DR
GODFREY AVE
ALTON GDNS
CHASE GDNS
KENDREY GDNS
TALMA GDNS
EGERTON RD
HEATHFIELD N
HEATHFIELD S
MILTON LO
COURT WAY
Richmond upon Thames Coll
NELSON RD
WILLOWDENE CL
ASHDALE CL
ASHDALE WAY
Liby
HIGH ST
CYPRESS AVE
OAKLANDS AVE
ST EDMUNDS LA
St Edmund's RC Prim Sch
TRANMERE RD
MELROSE AVE
MAYFAIR AVE
OAKLANDS DR
BRITANNIA LA
CONSTANCE RD
REDWAY DR
SHORT WAY
40
ROSEBINE AVE
GLADSTONE AVE
LANGHORN DR
TWICKENHAM
CHALLENGE CT
CRANEFORD WAY
CRANEFORD CL
CRANEMERE CT
CARLING CT 1
WHITEHEAD CT 2
SWANSTON CT 3
Stoop Memorial Gd (Rugby Gd)
River Crane
Pl Fld
HEATHAM PK
MONTROSE AVE
Whitton
BRIDGE WAY
CHERTSEY RD
DENEHURST GDNS
ROSECROFT GDNS
SIMBA CT 1
LANSDOWNE CL 2
STATION RD
ASHLEY DR
JUBILEE AVE
BLANDFORD AVE
FAIRFIELD AVE
RYECROFT AVE
STRATHEARN AVE
PERCY WAY
PAULINE CRES
PARK CRES
POSY LA
Kneller Gardens
Bishop Perrin Prim Sch
COLLEGE CL
DEVON AVE
DORSET WAY
Pav
BARNEBY CL
ROWNTREE RD
MEREWAY RD
GOULD RD
CRANE RD
NORCUTT RD
WARWICK RD
HAMILTON RD
TALBOT RD
MARSH FARM RD
ALBERT RD
STATEN GDNS
FORMAN CT
Coll
TUDOR GDNS
CLIFDEN RD
LION RD
LAUREL AVE
GROVE AVE
STABLE MEWS
LION AVE
EDWIN RD
Cemy
PERCY RD
GLOUCESTER RD
WILTSHIRE GDNS
MELBOURNE CT
MEADWAY
Tenn Cts
ANDOVER RD
GRAVEL RD
MAY RD
KNIGHT'S PL
ALBION RD
KNOWLE RD
HEATH RD
Mereway Ind
COLNE RD
HUNTING GATE MEWS
BRIAR RD
ROSS HO
Whitton Sch
ROSS RD
HEREFORD GDNS
SELKIRK RD
CAMPBELL CL
BRINSWORTH CL
ANDOVER RD
CAMAC RD
THE GREEN
SYCAMORE HO
HEATHLANDS CL
HEATH GDNS
SAVILLE RD
BRADLEY HO
RADNOR RD
TENNYSON AVE
LINCOLN AVE
MORECROFT
CHURCHVIEW RD
WALSINGHAM HO
CAMPBELL RD
ELMSLEIGH HO
WILKINSON HO
CHERRY TREE HO
SECOND CROSS RD
CHESTNUT RD
FIRST CROSS RD
Twickenham Green
POPES CT
TRINITY CT
HOLLIES CL
Allot Gdns
RADNOR GDNS
CROSS DEEP
A316
Liby
CRANEBROOK
BELMONT RD
SELBY CT
ABBEY CT
MELBURY HO
GOTHIC RD
ELMSLEIGH RD
THIRD CROSS RD
LOUISA CT
CHILVERS CL
VICARAGE RD
GRANGE AVE
UPPER GROTTO RD
GROTTO
CEASORS CT
Games Ct
Sp Gd
TW2
MANOR CT
MANOR RD
GREYSTONES
MURRAY CT
MILL RD
RUTLAND RD
WOODBINE CL
FOURTH CROSS RD
TRAFALGAR RD
BOX CNR
Inf & Jun Schs
KENILWORTH CT
A311 THE GREEN
GRACE CT
Sch
CORTAYNE CT
POPE'S AVE
ALEXANDER CL
POPE'S GR
ABBOTSMEDE CL
TW1
HOLMES RD
River Crane
Crane Park
HOSPITAL BRIDGE RD
FULWELL PARK AVE
NAMOEL RD
PORTUGAL GDNS
AUGUSTA RD
LISBON AVE
OSBOURNE HO
NORWOOD CL
APPLEBY CL
FIFTH CROSS RD
HAMPTON RD
WALPOLE CT
WALPOLE RD
CARPENTERS CT
SPENCER RD
MANOR HO
ORFORD GDNS
BONSER RD
RADNOR RD
RIVER VIEW GDNS
WILLOW WAY
RYE WAYS
WARWICK LO
STAINES RD
A305
BEDFORD RD
DENMARK RD
AUDLEY CT
PRESTON CL
WELLESLEY CRES
WALPOLE GDNS
JORDANS MEWS
Strawberry Hill
LC
TOWER RD
WALDEGRAVE GDNS
CHILLINGWORTH GDNS
A30
Waldegrave Sch
Tenn Cts
FORTESCUE AVE
FIELDING AVE
TURNER AVE
TWINING AVE
BRUNSWICK CL
THURNBY CT
WELLESLEY RD
MILTON CT
DOWNSIDE
STRAWBERRY HILL RD
1 STANGATE MANS
COURT CLOSE AVE
30
SHAFTESBURY WAY
Sch
CLARENDON CRES
GOLF SIDE
STANLEY RD
QUEEN ANNES CL
St James's RC Prim Sch
WELLESLEY CT 1
WENTWORTH CT 2
BERKLEY CL 3
ROYMOUNT CT 4
RUTLAND CT 5
CH
Strawberry H
MULBERRY CT
Pl F
Fulwell Park
SIXTH CROSS RD
B358
Allot Gdns
NATALIE MEWS
GROVE RD
SOUTH RD
Strawberry Hill
STRAWBERRY HILL CL
St Mary's Coll
Tenn Cts
72
73
74
75
14
15
Garden Ctr
Superstore
WELLINGTON GDNS
SOUTHFIELD GDNS
WALDEGRAVE RD
STRATHMORE RD
Stanley Inf & Jun Schs
Sch
WALDEGRAVE PK
1 CUSACK CL
2 BRIDGE CL
Fulwell
CH
WILCOX RD
Cemy

RICHMOND
Richmond Lock
Richmond Green
TWICKENHAM BRIDGE
TWICKENHAM RD
THE AVENUE
ST MARGARET'S RD
St Margarets Rdbt
London Road Rdbt
CHERTSEY RD
St Margarets
Twickenham
Moor Mead Gd
River Crane
TW7
TW1
TW10
St Helena Pier
Richmond Landing Stage
RICHMOND BRIDGE
Cambridge Park
Marble Hill Park
Marble Hill House
Thames Path
Ferry P
River Thames
Eel Pie Island
York House
Orleans House Gallery
Orleans Park Sch
St Mary's CE Prim Sch
The German Sch
The Russell Sch
Strathmore Sch
Ham House
Sp Gd
Grey Court Sch
Ham
PETERSHAM RD
Richmond Hill
RICHMOND HILL
Sudbrook P
St Catherine's Sch
St James Ind Sch for Boys
CROSS DEEP
STRAWBERRY VALE
KING ST
YORK ST
RICHMOND RD
HAM COMM
RIVERSIDE
THE EMBANKMENT
1 WINCHESTER HO
2 PARKVIEW CT
3 BIRNHAM HO
1 CAMBRIDGE PARK CT
2 MEADOWSIDE
1 SUTHERLAND HO
2 SCOTT HO
3 WIGGINS LA
ALBANY CT 1
ST RICHARDS CT 2
1 HAWKESLEY CL
2 CLAVERING CL
3 CHATSWORTH PL
4 WOODVILLE CL
5 MARLOW HO
6 FAIRWATER HO
7 REGATTA HO
8 FAIRMILE HO
9 ADMIRAL HO
131
154
175
A
B
C
D
1
2
3
4
5
6

RICHMOND
SHEEN RD
Richmond Hill
Petersham
TW10
Sidmouth Wood
Saw Pit Plantation
East Sheen Common
The Bog
Bog Lodge
Horse Ride
Capital Ring
Sawyer's Hill
Richmond Gate
Star & Garter Home
Richmond Coll
The Vineyard Sch
King's House Sch
Christ's Sch
Pembroke Lodge
Petersham Park
Sudbrook Park
Pond Slade
Hamcross Plantation
Pond Plantation
Pen Ponds
Isabella Plantation
Ham Gate
HAM GATE AVE
PETERSHAM RD
QUEEN'S RD
CHURCH RD
STAR AND GARTER HILL
RICHMOND HILL
FRIARS STILE RD
Richmond Landing Stage
The German Sch
The Russell Sch
1 ARUNDEL HO
2 MARLBOROUGH HO
3 BUCKINGHAM HO
4 OSBOURNE HO
5 YORK HO
6 SANDRINGHAM HO
7 KENT HO
8 NORFOLK HO
9 RUNNYMEDE HO
10 CARISBROOKE HO
11 GLOUCESTER HO
1 CAMBRIDGE PARK CT
2 MEADOWSIDE

132
153
176

A
B
C
D
133
SW15
Roehampton Sports Club
The Priory
Roehampton
Richmond Park
SW14
TW10
Richmond Park
Roehampton
Old House
Polo Field
The Royal Ballet Sch (White Lodge)
Deer Park
Pen Ponds
Spankers Hill Wood
Palewell Common
Palewell Fields
East Sheen Gate
Adam's Pond
Roehampton Gate
Horse Ride
Beverley Brook
Chohole Gate
ROEHAMPTON VALE
KINGSTON VALE
Robin Hood Gate
Kingston Univ Roehampton Vale Campus
Superstore
War Meml
Kingston Vale
ROEHAMPTON LA
SHEEN LA
B351
A306
A3
A308
1 MARTINDALE
2 SPENCER GDNS
ALLENFORD HO 1
SWAYTHLING HO 2
TATCHBURY HO 3
PENWOOD HO 4
BRAMLEY HO 5
SHALDEN HO 6
DUNBRIDGE HO 7
DENMEAD HO 8
CHARCOT HO 9
PORTSWOOD PL 10
BROCKBRIDGE HO 11
HURSTBOURNE HO 12
FINCHDEAN HO 1
HOLMSLEY HO 2
OVERTON HO 3
REDENHAM HO 4
MOUNT ANGELUS RD 5
FLORENCE TERR 1
EBOR COTTS 2
1 SHEENGATE MANS
2 PARKWAY HO
Roehampton Univ (Southlands Coll)
Roehampton Univ (Digby Stuart Coll)
Roehampton Univ (Froebel Coll)
Ibstock Place Sch
South Thames Coll
The Huntercombe Roehampton
156
177
KT2
6
5
4
3
2
1
75
74
73
72
22

Roehampton
Allot Gdns
Putney Park Sch
134
A
B
C
D
PUTNEY
SW15
SW19
Roehampton Univ (Southlands Coll)
Sacred Heart RC Prim Sch
Roehampton Univ (Digby Stuart Coll)
Roehampton Univ (Froebel Coll)
Queen Mary's Univ
Granard Prim Sch
Elliott Sch
Lion House Sch
Putney Heath
Tibbet's Corner
Roehampton CE Prim Sch
The Huntercombe Roehampton
Wildcroft Manor
King's Mere
Jerry's Hill
Roehampton Lane
Choholeh Gate
Crem
Cemy
Superstore
Putney Vale
Queen's Mere
Wimbledon Windmill Mus
The Clockhouse
Hall Sch Wimbledon
London Scottish
War Meml
Parkside (private)
Wimbledon Common
ROEHAMPTON LA
KINGSTON RD
ROEHAMPTON VALE
WIMBLEDON PARK SIDE
PARKSIDE
TIBBET'S RIDE
PUTNEY HILL
WEST HILL
PUTNEY HEATH
PUTNEY PARK LA
HAZLEWELL RD
CHARTFIELD AVE
WESTLEIGH AVE
TELEGRAPH RD
WILDCROFT RD
WINDMILL RD
Horse Ride
A306
A3
A219
Wandsworth
Merton
Richmond upon Thames
155
178
75
6
5
74
4
3
73
2
1
72
22
23

157
A
B
C
D
135
158
179
6
5
4
3
2
1
75
74
73
72
26
25
WANDSWORTH
West Hill
Southfields
SW15
SW18
SW19
East Putney
Putney
Wandsworth Gyratory
WANDSWORTH HIGH ST
WANDSWORTH PLAIN
ARMOURY WAY
UPPER RICHMOND RD
WEST HILL
MERTON RD
BUCKHOLD RD
GARRATT LA
DURNSFORD RD
WIMBLEDON PARK RD
SWANDON WAY
EAST HILL
FAIRFIELD ST
RAM ST
OLD YORK RD
KIMBER RD
REPLINGHAM RD
REVELSTOKE RD
ST JOHN'S DR
HALDANE PL
WANDLE WAY
VANDERBILT RD
KING George's Park
The Sergeant Ind Est
The Kimber Ctr
Merton Road Ind Est
Southfields Com Coll
Sheringdale Prim Sch
Riversdale Prim Sch
St Cecilia's CE Sch
Linden Lodge Sch
Albermarle Prim Sch
Royal Hospl
ADT Coll
Southside Sh Ctr
Visitor Ctr
Earlsfield
Earlsfield Prim Sch
Haslemere Ind Est
Rufus Bsns Ctr
Wimbledon Park Prim Sch
Gresham Way Est
Wimbledon Stadium Bsns Ctr
Garratt Sch
River Wandle
Wimbledon Park
Wimbledon Park Lake
Athletics Gd
The All England Lawn Tennis & Croquet Club
Wimbledon Lawn Tennis Mus
Superstore
Wimbledon
Summ
Wandsworth
Merton
A3
A205
A217
A218
A3209
B229
B234
B235

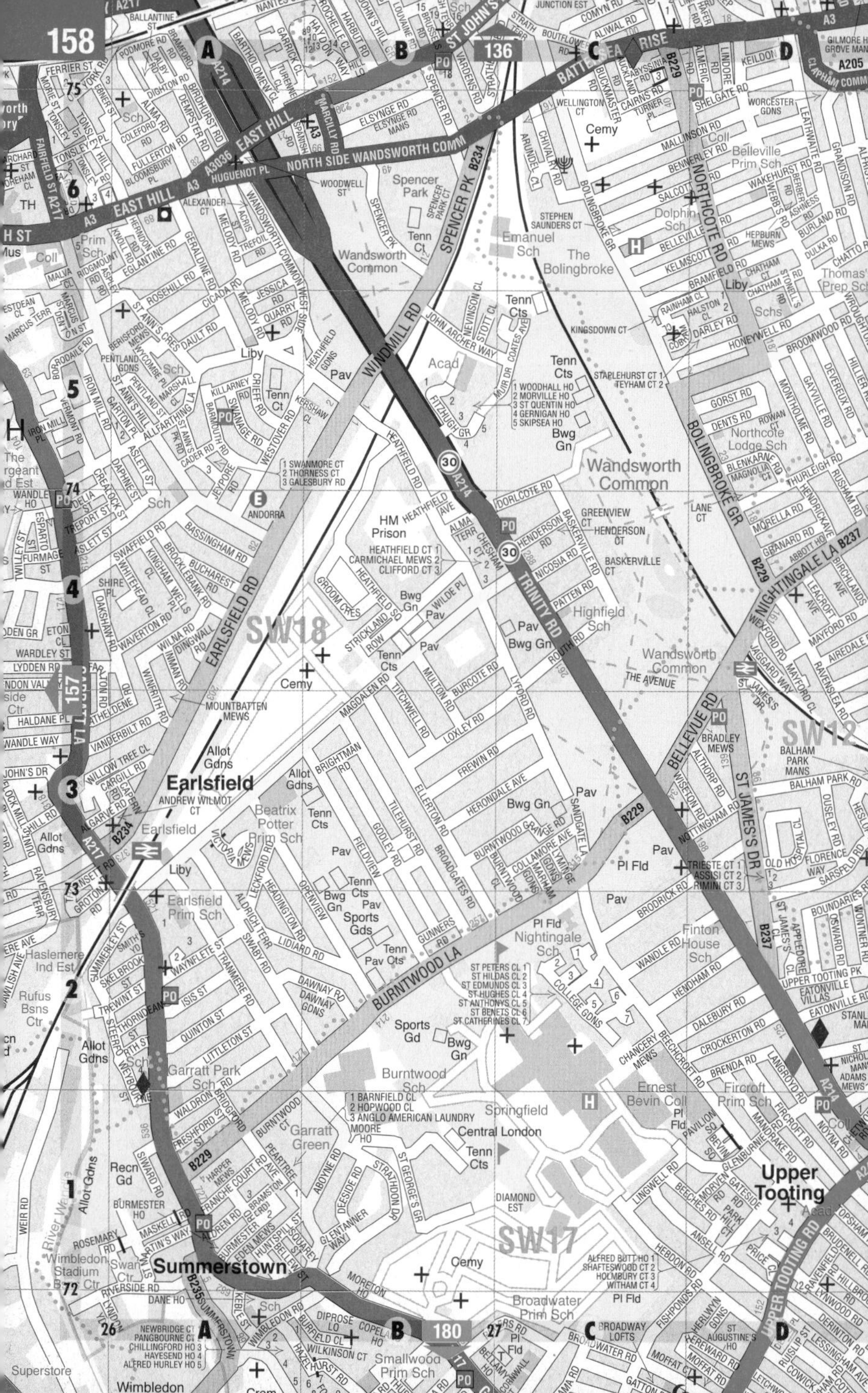

158
A
B
C
D
136
157
180
1
2
3
4
5
6
SW18
SW12
SW17
Earlsfield
Summerstown
Upper Tooting
Wandsworth Common
Spencer Park
The Bolingbroke
HM Prison
Emanuel Sch
Belleville Prim Sch
Dolphin Sch
Northcote Lodge Sch
Highfield Sch
Beatrix Potter Prim Sch
Earlsfield Prim Sch
Garratt Park Sch
Nightingale Sch
Burntwood Sch
Springfield
Central London
Ernest Bevin Coll
Fircroft Prim Sch
Finton House Sch
Broadwater Prim Sch
Smallwood Prim Sch
Haslemere Ind Est
Rufus Bsns Ctr
Wimbledon Stadium Bsns Ctr
Garratt Green
Thomas' Prep Sch
Wimbledon
Superstore
ST JOHN'S
BATTERSEA RISE
EAST HILL
NORTH SIDE WANDSWORTH COMM
SPENCER PK
WINDMILL RD
TRINITY RD
EARLSFIELD RD
BURNTWOOD LA
NIGHTINGALE LA
BELLEVUE RD
NORTHCOTE RD
BOLINGBROKE GR
ST JAMES'S DR
UPPER TOOTING RD
GARRATT LA
MAGDALEN RD
ALLFARTHING LA
HEATHFIELD RD
ST ANN'S HILL
HUGUENOT PL
FAIRFIELD ST
WANDSWORTH COMMON WEST SIDE
MELODY RD
GERALDINE RD
ELSYNGE RD
MARCILLY RD
BROOMWOOD RD
HONEYWELL RD
THURLEIGH RD
HENDERSON RD
BASKERVILLE RD
NICOSIA RD
ROUTH RD
LYFORD RD
BURCOTE RD
FREWIN RD
HERONDALE AVE
ELLERTON RD
BROADGATES RD
TILEHURST RD
GODLEY RD
FIELDVIEW
OPENVIEW
HEADINGTON RD
LIDIARD RD
DAWNAY RD
BURMESTER RD
SUMMERSTOWN
WIMBLEDON RD
BLACKSHAW RD
MORETON RD
BROADWATER RD
FISHPONDS RD
HEBDON RD
LINGWELL RD
BEECHCROFT RD
CHANCERY MEWS
WANDLE RD
HEMDHAM RD
DALEBURY RD
CROCKERTON RD
BRENDA RD
NOTTINGHAM RD
BALHAM PARK RD
WEXFORD RD
MAYFORD RD
RAVENSLEA RD
BRODRICK RD
THE AVENUE
B229
B234
B235
B237
A3
A205
A214
A217
A3036

CLAPHAM COMMON NORTH SIDE
SW4
137
Clapham Common
Windmill on the Common (PH)
Recn Gd
Bndstd
Mount Pond
THE AVENUE
CLAPHAM COMMON SOUTH SIDE
CLAPHAM COMMON WEST SIDE
WINDMILL DR
CAVENDISH RD
Clapham South
Lambeth Coll
Lambeth Acad
Clapham Park
CLAPHAM PARK RD
Ellerslie Ind Est
KINGS AVE
POYNDERS RD
NIGHTINGALE LA
BALHAM HILL
SW12
Balham
Grange Mills
BALHAM HIGH RD
BALHAM STATION RD
BEDFORD HILL
Streatham Hill
THORNTON AVE
STERNHOLD AVE
160
Streatham & Clapham High Sch
Tooting Bec Common
Capital Ring
SW16
SW17
TOOTING BEC RD
181
Streatham Park
Tooting Bec Lido
GARRAD'S RD
STREATHAM HIGH RD

138
182
159
A
B
C
D
A
B
C
D
6
5
4
3
2
1
75
74
73
72
30
31
SW2
SE24
SW16
SE27
ACRE LA
A2217
Works
Ellerslie Ind Est
MAGNOLIA PL
ST PAUL'S CT
WEST RD
BRIARWOOD RD
NORTHBOURNE RD
MAYFIELD CL
SANDHURST CT
GLENELG RD
STRATHLEVEN RD
BRANKSOME RD
KILDORAN RD
MARGATE RD
MAULEVERER RD
MANDRELL RD
TA Ctr
PRAGUE PL
GLANVILLE RD
CRESCENT CT
RODENHURST CT
CLAUDIA JONES WAY
RAMILLES CL
KINGS AVE
KINGS CROFT
ROBIN'S CT
OAKFIELD CT
PETER'S CT
ROSEBERY
THORNBURY RD
THORNCLIFFE RD
PINEWOOD CT
MAPLE CL
MORTEN CL
CLARENCE CRES
HELBY RD
MULLER RD
HEADLAM RD
BOWIE CL
B221
Allot Gdns
JOHN ASHBY CL
LOATS RD
LYHAM RD
Sp Gd
JEBB AVE
THORNCLIFFE CT
HM Prison
LYHAM CL
WINGFORD RD
CHALE RD
DUMBARTON RD
TILSON HO
MORLEY HO
KINGSWOOD RD
DOVERFIELD RD
FELSBERG RD
SAXBY RD
Sch
NEW PARK RD
TILSON GDNS
FORSTER RD
BRIXTON HILL PL
MORRISH RD
RODMILL LA
SULINA RD
A205
STREATHAM PL
LANGHOLM CL
ASPINALL HO
HAYES CT
TENBURY CT
LEYTON GDNS
FORTROSE GDNS
KIRKSTALL GDNS
KIRKSTALL RD
TIERNEY RD
MONTRELL RD
TIERNEY TERR
Streatham Hill
TELFORD AVE
THORNTON AVE
SALFORD RD
CRIFFEL AVE
BELLASIS AVE
GOODMAN CRES
Tenn Cts
ERNHOLD AVE
HANNAY WLK
DORRIEN WLK
DREWSTEAD RD
B221 STERNHOLD AVE
KILLIESER AVE
BARRHILL RD
BLAIRDERRY RD
ARDWELL RD
STREATHAM HILL
A23
WHEATLEY CT
AUGUSTUS RD
COLIN CL
DINGLEY LA
Bwg Gn
BROADLANDS AVE
DE MONTFORT RD
CROMER CT
MOUNT EPHRAIM RD
CHALCOT MEWS
WOODLAND MEWS
STREATHAM CT
ALBANS CL
GARETH CT
WOODFIELD GR
MOORCROFT RD
BLAKEMORE RD
BRANCASTER RD
NORFOLK HOUSE RD
KINGSCOURT RD
WOODBOURNE GDNS
WOODBOURNE AVE
STEEP HILL
ST GILES HO
OCKLEY RD
BECMEAD AVE
NUNEHAM
PRENTIS RD
THE GLEBE
TOOTING BEC GDNS
STREATHAM HIGH RD
ASTORIA PAR
THE HIGH PAR
WOODLEIGH GDNS
LEIGHAM AVE
BUTTERWORTH CT
PENDENNIS RD
Liby
PINFOLD RD
FARM AVE
UJIMA HO
UJIMA CT
SHRUBBERY
NEWCOME GDNS
GRACEFIELD GDNS
ANGLES RD
SUNNYHILL
MANOR CT
CHERRY TREE DR
GARDEN FLATS
The Adare Ctr
STREATHAM CL
ADARE WLK
MOUNTEARL GDNS
BELENOYD CT
LEIGHAM COURT RD
CONIFER GDNS
CULVERHOUSE GDNS
LEIGH ORCHARD CL
IVYDAY GR
LEITHCOTE GDNS
LEITHCOTE PATH
Dunraven Sch
PEREGRINE CT
BARNARD CT
ROSEDENE AVE
ROMEYN RD
MOUNT NOD RD
STOCKFIELD RD
KEYMER RD
HAILSHAM AVE
LYDHURST AVE
HITHERFIELD RD
MILFORD MEWS
CAROLINE CL
CAREW HO
ELLBRIDGE CL
SAMUEL JOHNSON CL
SOUTH OAK RD
CURTIS FIELD RD
Julian's
SCARBOROUGH RD
Streatham Hill
AMESBURY AVE
BARCOMBE AVE
CRICKLADE AVE
DOWNTON AVE
WYATT PARK RD
EMSWORTH ST
FAYGATE RD
TREDWELL CL
1 DESPARD HO
2 PALACE CT
Prim Sch
NORMANHURST RD
NUTHURST AVE
WAVERTREE RD
DAYSBROOK RD
CORNER FIELDE
PULLMAN CT
GARDEN LA
BATY HO
BARSTOW CRES
PRESENTATION MEWS
BUSHELL CL
PONTON HO
PALACE RD
HILLSIDE RD
HILLSIDE GDNS
REDHILL CT
LANERCOST RD
LANERCOST CL
CHALNER HO
KINGSMEAD RD
MAYTREE WLK
NORTHSTEAD RD
KINFAUNS RD
ULVERSTONE RD
ST MARTIN'S CT
LEIGHAM VALE
CAMERON
CANUTE CT
TRAEMORE CT
KNOLLY'S RD
KNOLLY'S CL
TINA CT
PEVENSEY CT
PORTAL CL
ROYAL CIR
CAMBRIAN CL
YORK HILL
THURLOW TOWERS
GLYN CT
BROXHOLM RD
GLENNIE RD
EGREMONT RD
IVYMOUNT RD
ST PETER'S GDNS
CHICHESTER MEWS
CANTERBURY GR
THURLESTONE RD
DODBROOKE RD
SELSDON RD
CHATHAM
PYRMONT GR
FRIAR MEWS
WALDECK GR
VILLAS RD
MOUNT RD
LANSDOWNE HILL
CANTERBURY GR
BLOOM GR
YEOMAN CL
HAINTHORPE RD
PRIORESS RD
FRANKLIN CL
WOLFINGTON RD
SAINTS CL
NETTLEFOLD PL
Pl Fld
COTSWOLD ST
BEADMAN PL
KNIGHT'S HILL SQ
ROCKHAMPTON CL
ROCKHAMPTON RD
UFFINGTON RD
Sp Gd
FARM RD
A215
HARPENDEN RD
PENRITH RD
ULLSWATER RD
SNOWE RD
WAYLETT PL
DALTON ST
HAWKLEY GDNS
ORFORD CT
WILLIAM BROWN CT
LANCASTER AVE
ELMCOURT RD
FAWLEY CT
MALEY AVE
AVENUE PARK RD
Tulse Hill
STATION RISE
PARADE MEWS
PROBYN RD
LUPIN
PERRAN RD
HARDEL RISE
NORWOOD RD
ST FAITH'S RD
Allot Gdns
BERWYN RD
DERONDA RD
DEERBROOK RD
ROMOLA RD
TRUST WLK
ABBESS CL
JARRETT CL
COPPIN HO
SKIFFINGTON CL
SCOLES CRES
1 DUTTON HO
2 CONSTANTINE HO
3 POULLETT HO
4 AXFORD HO
TRINITY RISE
BROCKWELL PARK GDNS
BELLO CL
Liby
T Cts
BODLEY MANOR WAY
HARDEL WLK
HAMBRIDGE WAY
PAPWORTH WAY
CROSBY WLK
Tulse Hill
TULSE HILL
A204
ABBOTS PK
HIGH TREES
MORRISON HO
ROYCROFT CL
MASKALL CL
HART HO
TERRY HO
GAYWOOD CL
RICKARD CL
TA Ctr
HUGGINS PL
MARNFIELD CRES
BANNISTER CL
EWEN CRES
ATWATER CL
HILLWORTH RD
MACKIE RD
ATHLONE RD
CLAVERDALE RD
CRAIGNAIR RD
ELM PK
CRASTER RD
OSTADE RD
WIMBART RD
BRADING RD
Prim Sch
UPPER TULSE HILL
ROMAN RISE
ROMAN FIELD RD
SAXONFIELD CL
CHALLICE WAY
ROUPELL RD
LIMETREE CL
CHRISTCHURCH RD
COBURG CRES
DUCAVEL HO
ARBORFIELD CL
VIBART GDNS
MAPLESTEAD RD
COTHERSTONE RD
HOLMEWOOD RD
HOLMEWOOD GDNS
BROCKHAM DR
FAIRVIEW PL
DEERDENE GDNS
REDLANDS WAY
SOMERS PL
HYPERION HO
TUDOR CL
MERREDENE ST
SOMERS RD
BEWLEY CT
RENTON CL
BRIXTON HILL
ENDYMION RD
CALIDORE CL
BEECHDALE RD
VIRGINIA WLK
FAIRMOUNT RD
RALEIGH GDNS
WATERWORKS RD
CHERRY LAUREL WLK
WINDMILL GDNS
BLENHEIM GDNS
HALLIWELL RD
ST SAVIOUR'S RD
LAMBERT RD
HERMES HO
HELIX GDNS
ARODENE RD
HELIX RD
JOSEPHINE AVE
APPACH RD
LEANDER RD
POVEY HO
BARTELL HO
MEDORA RD
WASHBROOK HO
IRBY HO
HOLT HO
Prim Sch
TENDRING HO
BROCKWELL PARK ROW
Brockwell Park
Brockwell Lido
PARK VIEW HO 1
HERNE HILL HO 2
Pav
Bwg Gn
Tenn Cts
DULWICH RD
A2214
BRIXTON WATER LA
MORVAL RD
TRELAWN RD
BAILEY MEWS
FITCH CT
Bsns Ctr
Ret Pk
EFFRA RD
A204
EFFRA MANS
CROWNSTONE RD
ST MATTHEW'S RD
KETT GDNS
DRAY GDNS
BRIXTON WATER LA
Lambeth Coll
HORSFORD RD
TRENT RD
TORRENS RD
BONHAM RD
HAYCROFT RD
WINTERWELL RD
WINSLADE RD
HAYTER RD
BEVERSTONE RD
Prim Sch
EFFRA CT
SUDBOURNE RD
BAYTREE RD
ARLINGTON LO
RAEBURN ST
PLATO RD
HERRINGTON
SALTOUN RD
KELLETT RD
MERVAN RD
TALMA RD
BANKTON RD
RATTRAY RD
PROBERT RD
JELF RD
CHAPLETON HO
DALBERG RD
BARNWELL RD
EFFRA PAR
CHAUCER RD
SPENSER RD
SHAKESPEARE RD
MILTON RD
MUMFORD RD
REGENT RD
HERNE PL
MEATH HO
HURST ST
RYMER ST
SHARDCROFT AVE
RAILTON RD
MAYALL RD
B223
1 FARMLEIGH HO
2 HOLMBURY HO
WALCOTT CL
DEREK WALCOTT CL
CORRY DR
EATON DR
MILKWOOD RD
GUBYON AVE
Herne Hill
Sch

A
B
C
D
139
183
162
Herne Hill
Dulwich
East Dulwich
North Dulwich
Dulwich Village
Dulwich College
West Dulwich
West Norwood
Knight's Hill
Dulwich & Sydenham
Sydenham Hill
SE22
SE24
SE21
SE27
HERNE HILL
HALF MOON LA
VILLAGE WAY
EAST DULWICH GR
LORDSHIP LA
BARRY RD
DULWICH COMM
CROXTED RD
SOUTH CROXTED RD
COLLEGE RD
DULWICH VILLAGE
GALLERY RD
THURLOW PARK RD
RED POST HILL
BURBAGE RD
TURNEY RD
COURT LA
TOWNLEY RD
CALTON AVE
WOODWARDE RD
GRANGE LA
PARK HALL RD
HUNTS SLIP RD
ALLEYN PK
ALLEYN RD
ROSENDALE RD
GIANT ARCHE RD
FRANK DIXON WAY
HAMBLEDON PL
POND COTTS
Belair Park
Dulwich Park
Dulwich Wood
Herne Hill Stadium
Alleyn's Sch
The Charter Sch
James Allens Pre-Prep Sch
Dulwich Hamlet Jun Sch
Rosendale Prim Sch & Turney Prim Sch
Oakfield Prep Sch
Dulwich Coll
Dulwich Coll Prep Sch
Kingsdale Sec Sch
Art Gall
Cemy
Crem
West Norwood
Low Cross Wood La
Knight's Hill Tunnel
A2214
A2216
A2199
A205
A215
B219

A
B
140
C
D
East Dulwich
Peckham Rye Park
Harris Girl's Acad
Ppg Sta
Aquarius
Honor Oak
Camberwell New Cem
Bwg Gn
Pl Fld
SE22
SE23
SE26
Camberwell Old Cemetery
Cemy
One Tree Hill (Recn Gd)
Allot Gdns
Honor Oak Park
HONOR OAK PK
Brenchley Gardens
FOREST HILL RD
BARRY RD
LORDSHIP LA
A2216
B219
B238
A205
B227
LONDON RD
DARTMOUTH RD
WALDRAM PARK RD
PERRY VALE
The Grove
Horniman Sch
Horniman Mus
Forest Hill
Fairlawn Prim Sch
Nat Res
Malham Road Ind Est
Dulwich Bsns Ctr
Dulwich & Sydenham
Dulwich Wood
Sydenham Hill Wood (Nat Res)
Eliot Bank Prim Sch
Sydenham High Sch
Forest Hill Ind Est
Forest Hill Bsns Ctr
Forest Hill Sec Sch
Willow Bsns Pk
Sydenham Wells Park
Mayow P
RC Prim Sch
Liby
Tenn Cts
Sp Gd
Pav
161
184
NORTH CROSS RD
SHAWBURY RD
WHATELEY RD
SILVESTER RD
PELLATT RD
RODWELL RD
HEBER RD
JENNINGS RD
GOODRICH RD
ETHEROW ST
PLOUGH LA
UPLAND RD
DUNSTAN'S RD
COLYTON RD
DOVEDALE RD
MUNDANIA RD
BRENCHLEY GDNS
NETHERBY RD
SYDENHAM HILL
WELLS PARK RD
WOODSYRE
COUNTISBURY HO
PECKARMANS WOOD
CRESCENT WOOD RD
THORPEWOOD AVE
DACRES RD
DEVONSHIRE RD
WOODLANDS
SOUTHWARK
Lewisham
LANGTON RISE
ROUNDHAY CL
INGLEMERE RD
BISHOPSTHORPE RD
COLLINGTREE RD

163
141
164
185
37
38
A
B
C
D
6
5
4
3
2
1
75
74
73
72
Brockley
Brockley Cemy
Brockley Prim Sch
Ladywell Cemy
Ladywell
Lewisham Park
Lewisham
SE4
SE13
SE23
SE6
SE26
Crofton Park
Crofton L Ctr
Crofton Sch
Ladywell Arena
Ladywell Fields
Greyhound Stadium
Guy's Hospital Athletic Gd
Stillness Jun & Inf Schs
Holbeach Prim Sch
Catford
Catford Gyratory
Catford Bridge Pav
St Dunstan's Coll
Rushey Green Prim Sch
CATFORD
Forest Hill
Rathfern Prim Sch
Kilmorie Prim Sch
Athelney Prim Sch
Bellingham
Bellingham Trad Est
Bromley Road Ret Pk
Bell Green
Superstore
Greenvale Sch
Adamsrill Prim Sch
Elfrida Sch
Holy Cross RC Prim
Ravensbourne River
Pool River
BROCKLEY RD
STONDON PK
BROCKLEY RISE
STANSTEAD RD
CATFORD HILL
PERRY HILL
PERRY RISE
BELL GN
ADELAIDE AVE
LADYWELL RD
LEWISHAM HIGH ST
RUSHEY GN
CATFORD RD
BROMLEY RD
CATFORD BR
PLASSY RD
STANTON WAY
B236
B218
B238
B227
A205
A21
A212
A2218

LEWISHAM
LEE HIGH RD
142
A
B
C
D
Lee Green
SE13
SE12
SE6
BR1
Hither Green
Lee
Ladywell
Lewisham
LEWISHAM HIGH ST
LADYWELL RD
Lewisham Park
Manor Park
Quaggy River
Manor House Gardens
Mountsfield Park
BROWNHILL RD
ST MILDREDS RD
BURNT ASH RD
RUSHEY GN
PLASSY RD
Catford Gyratory
163
Rushey Green Prim Sch
Holy Cross RC Prim Sch
Sandhurst Jun & Inf Schs
Torridon Jun & Inf Schs
Catford High Sch
Forster Park
Forster Park Prim Sch
Chiltonian Ind Est
Brindishe Prim Sch
Cemy
Crem
Downham Ent Ctr
WHITEFOOT LA
Green Chain Wlk
Bonus Pastor RC Sch
New Woodlands Sch
Downderry Prim Sch
St John Baptist CE Prim Sch
Southend
BROMLEY RD
186
38
39
75
6
5
74
4
3
73
2
1
72

Quaggy River
143
Sutcliffe Park
Running Tk
Riverston Sch
ELTHAM RD
A210
A20
A2213
A205
WESTHORNE AVE
Eltham Green
A210 ELTHAM HILL
Yorkshire Grey
Eltham Green Specialist Sports Coll
Eltham Hill Tech Coll for Girls
Moatbridge Sch
Cliftons Roundabout
Colfe's Sch
CROWN CT
ELTHAM PALACE RD
UPWOOD RD
MIDDLE PARK AVE
GREGORY CRES
JOAN CRES
CHURCHBURY RD
CAMPFIELD RD
FERNDOWN RD
A2212
HORN PARK LA
Horn Park
WINN RD
MOTTINGHAM LA
Mottingham Farm
Hadlow Coll
Hadlow Coll Nature Reserve
Eltham Coll Jun Sch
Eltham Coll
SIDCUP RD
166
Greenwich
Bromley
BARING RD
SE12
SE9
Mottingham
Green Chain Wk
GROVE PARK RD
Grove Park
CHINBROOK RD
B226
BR1
Lewisham
Greenwich
Northbrook Park
Haberdashers' Aske's Knights Acad
187
A
B
C
D
1
2
3
4
5
6

ELTHAM
ELTHAM HIGH ST
ELTHAM HILL
Eltham Palace
Royal Blackheath
SE9
COURT RD
SIDCUP RD
FOOTSCRAY RD
MOTTINGHAM RD
GREEN LA
WELL HALL RD
Mottingham
New Eltham
Eltham Warren
Well Hall Pleasaunce
Eltham Park South
Coldharbour Sp Ctr
Fiveways
144
165
188

A
B
C
D
145
189
168
Avery Hill
Avery Hill Park
New Eltham
Longlands
Sidcup
SE9
DA15
BR7
BEXLEY RD
BLACKFEN RD
EAST ROCHESTER WAY
AVERY HILL RD
HALFWAY ST
SIDCUP RD
MAIN RD
SIDCUP BY PASS RD
STATION RD
Univ of Greenwich Avery Hill Campus Mansion Site
Univ of Greenwich Avery Hill Campus Southwood Site
Crown Woods Sch
Our Lady of the Rosary RC Prim Sch
Hollyoak Wood Park
Willersley Park
Burnt Oak Jun Sch
Dulverton Prim Sch
King George's Field
Longlands Prim Sch
West Lodge Sch
Sparrow's Farm L Ctr
Green Chain Wlk
DARLAND HO 1
WOOTTON HO 2
WAYFIELD LINK 3
TEYNHAM HO 4
OSPRINGE CT 5
TRINITY MEWS 6
LONGLANDS CT 1
THE FIRS 2
SANDALWOOD HO 3
BUCKTHORN HO 4
MOAT CT 5

BEXLEY
146
190
167
Blackfen
Sidcup
Foots Cray
DA16
DA6
DA5
DA15
DA14
EAST ROCHESTER WAY
BLACKFEN RD
PENHILL RD
HURST RD
STATION RD
DANSON RD
BLENDON RD
HIGH ST
Danson House
Danson Park
The Lake
Bexley Gram Sch
Blackfen Sch for Girls
Sherwood Park Prim Sch
Penhill Park
Marlborough Park
Willersley Park
Hollyoak Wood Park
River Shuttle
Chatsworth Inf Sch
Rose Bruford Coll
Lamorbey Park
Holy Trinity Lamorbey CE Prim Sch
Chislehurst & Sidcup Gram Sch
Hurstmere Sch for Boys
Burnt Oak Jun Sch
Abbeyhill Park
Albany Park
Birkbeck Prim Sch
Waring Park
West Lodge Sch
Cleeve Park Sch
North Cray Wood
Hurst Prim Sch
Recn Gd
Cemy
Allot Gdns
Pl Fld
Tenn Cts
DANSON UNDERPASS 1
KESTLAKE RD 2
LONGLANDS CT 1
THE FIRS 2
SANDALWOOD HO 3
BUCKTHORN HO 4
MOAT CT 5

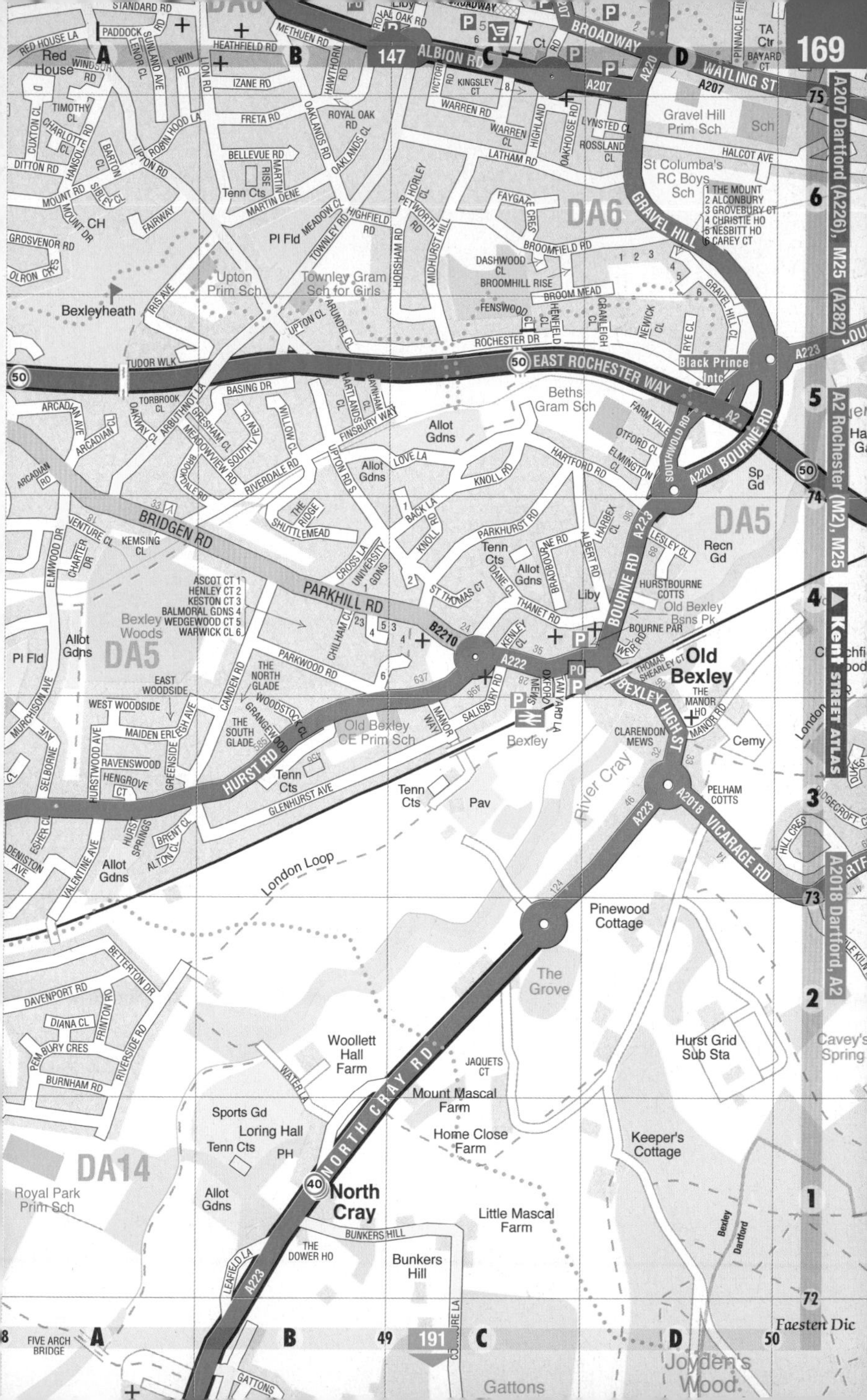
A207 Dartford (A226), M25 (A282)
A2 Rochester (M2), M25
A2018 Dartford, A2
Kent STREET ATLAS
BROADWAY
ALBION RD
WATLING ST
147
DA6
DA5
DA14
GRAVEL HILL
Gravel Hill Prim Sch
St Columba's RC Boys Sch
1 THE MOUNT
2 ALCONBURY
3 GROVEBURY CT
4 CHRISTIE HO
5 NESBITT HO
6 CAREY CT
Red House
Bexleyheath
Upton Prim Sch
Townley Gram Sch for Girls
EAST ROCHESTER WAY
Black Prince Intc
Beths Gram Sch
BOURNE RD
BRIDGEN RD
PARKHILL RD
ASCOT CT 1
HENLEY CT 2
KESTON CT 3
BALMORAL GDNS 4
WEDGEWOOD CT 5
WARWICK CL 6
Bexley Woods
Old Bexley
Old Bexley Bsns Pk
BEXLEY HIGH ST
Bexley
Old Bexley CE Prim Sch
HURST RD
River Cray
VICARAGE RD
London Loop
Pinewood Cottage
The Grove
Hurst Grid Sub Sta
Woollett Hall Farm
Mount Mascal Farm
Home Close Farm
Keeper's Cottage
NORTH CRAY RD
North Cray
Loring Hall
Royal Park Prim Sch
Little Mascal Farm
Bunkers Hill
Cavey's Spring
Joyden's Wood
Gattons
Faesten Dic
FIVE ARCH BRIDGE
191
A B C D
49 50
75 6 5 74 4 3 73 2 1 72

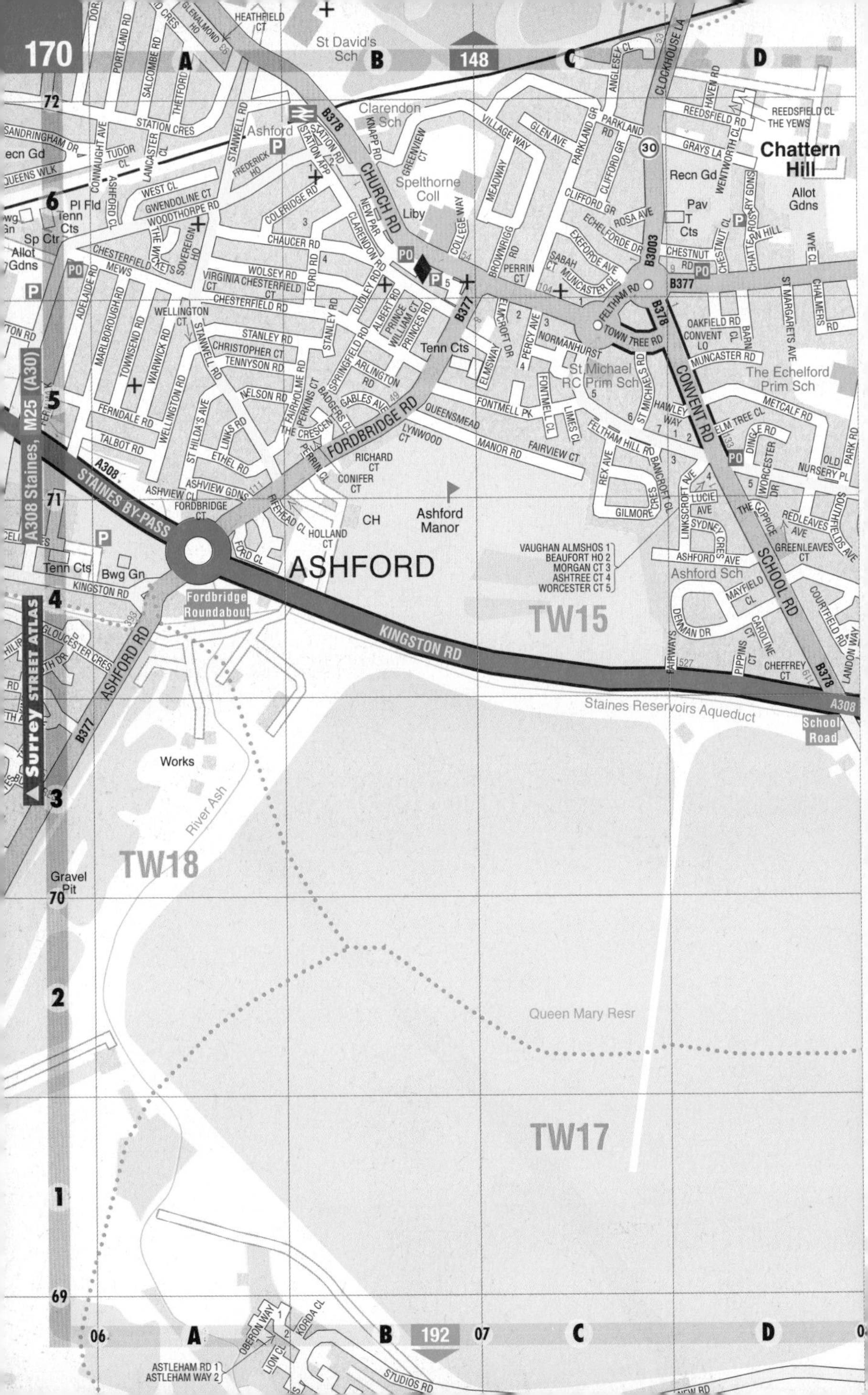
148
A
B
C
D
ASHFORD
Ashford Manor
Chattern Hill
Fordbridge Roundabout
TW15
TW17
TW18
Queen Mary Resr
Staines Reservoirs Aqueduct
STAINES BY-PASS
KINGSTON RD
FORDBRIDGE RD
CHURCH RD
CONVENT RD
SCHOOL RD
ASHFORD RD
CLOCKHOUSE LA
Spelthorne Coll
Clarendon Sch
St David's Sch
St Michael RC Prim Sch
The Echelford Prim Sch
Ashford Sch
School Road
A308 Staines, M25 (A30)
VAUGHAN ALMSHOS 1
BEAUFORT HO 2
MORGAN CT 3
ASHTREE CT 4
WORCESTER CT 5
ASTLEHAM RD 1
ASTLEHAM WAY 2
Works
Gravel Pit
River Ash
192

171
149
193
172
A
B
C
D
A
B
C
D
09
10
6
5
4
3
2
1
72
71
70
69
Surrey
Hounslow
Three Court One
Bedfont Ind Pk N
Bedfont Ind Pk
VIRIDIAN CT 6
TOPAZ CT 7
THE HERMITAGE 8
SPRING CNR 9
QUEENS PARK GDNS 10
PH
HIGH ST
B377
A244
Cemy
HAM CRES
HARVEST
SPRING RD
LUDLOW RD
SUNBURY RD
RYLAND CL
SUNBURY CRES
SHELSON AVE
WALTON GDNS
LARKHAM CL
BRIARWOOD CL
PHOENIX CT
CHALLENGE RD
FIELD VIEW
GATE AVE
SOUTH CRES
Recn Gd
PORTLAND
THE CLUMPS
Ashford Ind Est
Mereside Pk
ASHFORD RD
SHIELD RD
ALLIANCE CT
DUKES CL
ANDERSON DR
JOHNS CL
FERNHURST RD
CHATTERN RD
Allot Gdns
TW13
ELLINGTON RD
Lower Feltham
DENISON RD
CRANLEIGH RD
CHERTSEY RD
HAMILTON RD
HIGHLAND PK
HAMILTON CL
HAMILTON
Works
FELTHAM RD
Ashford Bsns Complex
SANDELLS AVE
WRENS AVE
KINGSWOOD CL
CHALMERS RD E
SUNDOWN RD
LYNEGROVE AVE
TW15
Allot Gdns
Sp Gd
Felthamhill
HALLOWS GR
OAKHALL CT
Bwg Gn
KINROSS DR
KINROSS CL
GROVELEY RD
OAKHALL DR
CUMBERNAULD GDNS
Meadhurst Sports Club
Tenn Cts
THE ROWANS
Kenyngton Manor Prim Sch
COOLGARDIE RD
ST PAUL'S CL
KENNEDY CT
ASPEN GDNS
NEIL CL
BEAUMONT DR
NEWHAVEN CRES
PRIORY GDNS
Hounslow
Surrey
NEW PARK RD
POPLAR RD
OSTLERS DR
BURLEIGH GDNS
ROMNEY CL
MORNINGTON RD
PEARTREE RD
BEECH CL
ASHGROVE RD
CHESTER CL
STAINFORD CL
MEADOW RD
RIPSTON RD
LYNN CL
JUNCTION RD
GOFFS RD
DORIS RD
APPROACH RD
MONTROSE CL
FELTHAM HILL RD
Ashford Common
Spelthorne Inf & Jun Schs
KING GEORGE CL
CAMILLA CL
CHESTNUT CL
BRACKEN CL
KING'S AVE
Felthamhill Brook
CAVENDISH CL
FISK CL
BRYONY WAY
VICARAGE RD
BEECHWOOD
CAVENDISH RD
CAVENDISH CT
MARLIN CL
BROAD OAK
CHESSHOLME RD
GARDEN CL
WOODLANDS PAR
ORCHARD AVE
ORCHARD CL
HOGARTH AVE
DANE RD
Allot Gdns
HENDON TERR
SAXON RD
SAVILLE CRES
CHERTSEY RD
ALEXANDRA CT
HYDE TERR
HYDE CL
CHAPLIN CRES
ROSSLYN CL
BURGOYNE RD
GREEN CT
TW16
HEATHERLANDS
GLENFIELD RD
STROUD WAY
CAREW RD
SELBY RD
CONWAY DR
HUGHES RD
ELGIN AVE
TUDOR RD
ALBANY CT
TEMPLECROFT
STAVELEY RD
BEARD'S RD
CADBURY RD
CLEVES WAY
CATHERINE DR
WYCHWOOD
Recn Gd
NAPIER LO
MEADHURST PK
HOWARD CL
GREEN LEAS
WOLSEY RD
JUNIPER GDNS
CECIL RD
MAXWELL RD
NORMAN RD
MAPLE CT
DENNIS CL
CECIL CL
STAINES RD W
THE DRIVE
CHEYNE RD
NAPIER RD
SQUIRES WLK
NAPIER WLK
ALEXANDRA RD
WARREN RD
CARDINAL'S WLK
SCOTT'S WAY
SCOTT'S AVE
SEYMOUR WAY
ARAGON CL
AVON RD
GREEN LA
CARLTON RD
WOLSEY RD
LEY RD
SADDLEBROOK PK
HELGIFORD GDNS
CADBURY CL
THE WALK
HEATH GR
BRYAN CL
OXFORD CL
BENJAMIN CT
COMPASS CL
HAWTHORN CT
GDNS
BRIDGE
CAMBRIDGE RD
ASHDENE CL
ROWLAND WAY
STAINES RD W
TASMAN CT
CHESSHOLME CT
The Shears
SHEARS CT
PRINCE ALBERT CT
Sunbury Common
DALE RD
HEATHCROFT AVE
THE HAVEN
LITTLETON RD
THORNE CL
Spelthorne Sports Club
Sp Gd
T Cts
1 ALEXANDRA CL
2 REDWOOD MEWS
CEDAR WAY
CASTLE CL
PERCY AVE
BRYANT CT
Liby
THE PARADE
A308
M3
Littleton Common
Wks
WILLOW CT 1
KILLIGREW HO 2
GRANTHAM HO 3
MILL FARM AVE
SHEARS WAY
ESCOT RD
SPELTHORNE GR
SUNNA LO
CEDAR HO
FOREST DR
CROSSWAYS
Sunbury Cross
ASHFORD RD
CORNERSIDE
LITTLETON HO
SPELTHORNE LA
Action Ct
WINDMILL CL
INTERNATIONAL WAY
BROOKLANDS CL
Windmill Bsns Village
BROOKLANDS CL
Superstore
DOWNSIDE
BENWELL CT
BRACKENWOOD
Sunbury
MEADOWS END
West Surrey Est
MERCIA HO
MILLFIELD
LINCOLN WAY
DOLPHIN RD N
CRAYONNE CL
HARRIS WAY
WINDMILL RD
Tenn Cts
L Ctr
Sunbury Int Bsns Ctr
EVELYN CRES
EVELYN WAY
BEVERLEY RD
ALMSHOS
RAVENSCOURT
HOMEWATERS AVE
HERITAGE CL
SPRINGFIELD GR
THE RIDINGS
St Ignat Prim
Water Works
The Dolphin Est
DOLPHIN RD W
DOLPHIN RD
DOLPHIN RD S
Mast
Sch
Springfield Prim Sch
MANOR GDNS
WINDMILL LO
WINDMILL RD W
NURSERY RD
NURSERY GDNS
SUTHERLAND AVE
HEATHL
QUEEN MARY RD
30
CHARLTON HO
CHARLTON RD
HETHERINGTON RD
GENEVA CL
KELLY CL
Upper Halliford
PEREGRINE RD
LAYTON'S LA
RAVENDALE RD
SUTHERLAND GDNS
STRATTON RD
GREEN ST
MANOR DR
GRIFFIN WAY
Cedars Recn Gd
WALNUT TREE RD
HARROW WAY
LODGE WAY
HETHERINGTON RD
Charlton
HASLETT RD
UPPER HALLIFORD RD
FALCON WAY
PEREGRINE RD
T Cts
Pav
ROOKSMEAD RD
ALMOND CL
CROSSWELL CL
BIRCH GR
The Bishop Wand CE Sch
PARKWOOD GR
WALNUT TREE RD
Recn Gd
40
Pl Fld
Hawkedale Inf Sch
AIRLAWNS
CROYSDALE AVE
Sports Gd
ORCHARD DR

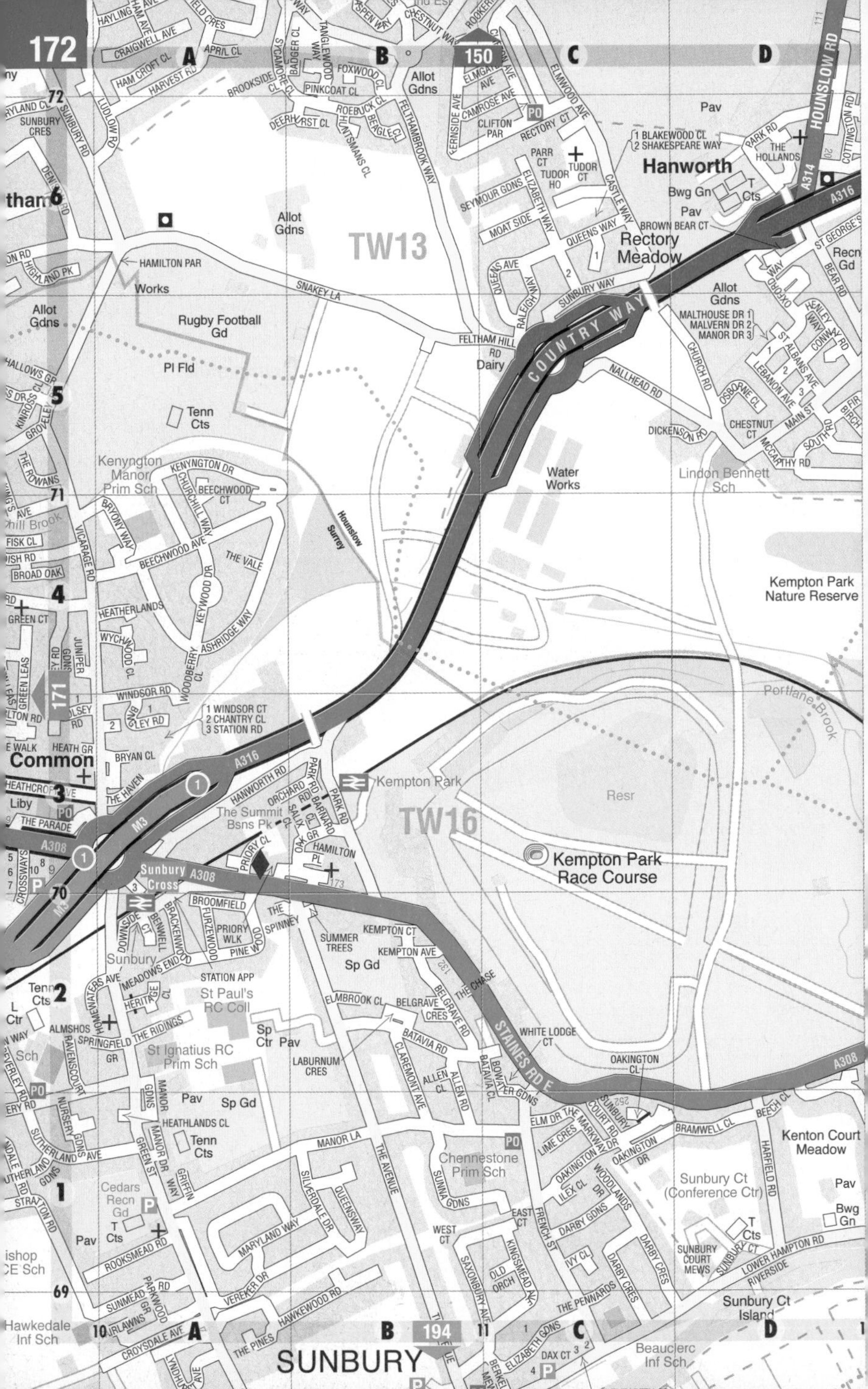
A
B
C
D
150
194
171
Hanworth
TW13
TW16
Rectory Meadow
Kempton Park Nature Reserve
Kempton Park Race Course
Kempton Park
Resr
Portlane Brook
Water Works
Lindon Bennett Sch
Rugby Football Gd
Pl Fld
Tenn Cts
Works
Allot Gdns
Kenyngton Manor Prim Sch
Common
Sunbury Cross
Sunbury
St Paul's RC Coll
St Ignatius RC Prim Sch
Chennestone Prim Sch
Sunbury Ct (Conference Ctr)
Kenton Court Meadow
Sunbury Ct Island
Beauclerc Inf Sch
Hawkedale Inf Sch
Cedars Recn Gd
The Summit Bsns Pk
SUNBURY
COUNTRY WAY
HOUNSLOW RD
STAINES RD E
A316
A308
A314
M3
SNAKEY LA
HAMILTON PAR
FELTHAM HILL RD
Dairy
HANWORTH RD
PARK RD
NALLHEAD RD
CHURCH RD
DICKENSON RD
VICARAGE RD
KENYNGTON DR
BEECHWOOD AVE
THE VALE
KEYWOOD DR
ASHRIDGE WAY
HEATHERLANDS
WYCHWOOD CL
WINDSOR RD
BRYAN CL
THE HAVEN
1 WINDSOR CT
2 CHANTRY CL
3 STATION RD
1 BLAKEWOOD CL
2 SHAKESPEARE WAY
MALTHOUSE DR 1
MALVERN DR 2
MANOR DR 3
BROWN BEAR CT
QUEENS WAY
CASTLE WAY
SUNBURY WAY
SEYMOUR GDNS
MOAT SIDE
ELIZABETH WAY
RALEIGH WAY
QUEENS AVE
ELMWOOD AVE
RECTORY CT
CLIFTON PAR
CAMROSE AVE
ELMGATE AVE
KERNSIDE AVE
FELTHAMBROOK WAY
HUNTSMANS CL
BEAGLE CL
ROEBUCK CL
DEERHURST CL
PINKCOAT CL
FOXWOOD CL
TANGLEWOOD WAY
BADGER CL
SYCAMORE CL
BROOKSIDE
CHESTNUT WAY
HAM CROFT CL
HARVEST RD
CRAIGWELL AVE
APRIL CL
LUDLOW RD
SUNBURY RD
HIGHLAND PK
THE ROWANS
GROVELEY RD
FISK CL
BROAD OAK
GREEN CT
JUNIPER GDNS
HEATH GR
THE PARADE
CROSSWAYS
BROOMFIELD
FURZEWOOD
PRIORY WLK
PINE WOOD
THE SPINNEY
SUMMER TREES
KEMPTON CT
KEMPTON AVE
Sp Gd
THE CHASE
BELGRAVE RD
BELGRAVE CRES
ELMBROOK CL
BATAVIA RD
CLAREMONT AVE
LABURNUM CRES
ALLEN CL
ALLEN RD
BATAVIA CL
WHITE LODGE CT
OAKINGTON CL
OAKINGTON DR
BOWATER GDNS
ELM DR
THE MARKWAY
SUNBURY COURT RD
BRAMWELL CL
BEECH CL
HARFIELD RD
LOWER HAMPTON RD
RIVERSIDE
SUNBURY COURT MEWS
SUNBURY CT
DARBY GDNS
DARBY CRES
WOODLANDS DR
ILEX CL
IVY CL
LIME CRES
FRENCH ST
KINGSMEAD AV
SAXONBURY AVE
OLD ORCH
THE PENNARDS
EAST CT
WEST CT
SUNNA GDNS
THE AVENUE
MANOR LA
SILVERDALE DR
QUEENSWAY
MARYLAND WAY
VEREKER DR
HAWKEWOOD RD
THE PINES
CROYSDALE AVE
SUNMEAD RD
PARKWOOD GR
ROOKSMEAD RD
GRIFFIN WAY
MANOR DR
GREEN ST
MANOR GDNS
HEATHLANDS CL
SUTHERLAND AVE
NURSERY GDNS
RAVENSCOURT
SPRINGFIELD GR
THE RIDINGS
HOMEWATERS AVE
MEADOWS END
STATION APP
HERITAGE CL
DOWNSIDE
BENWELL
BRACKENWOOD
PRIORY CL
HAMILTON PL
OAK GR
SALIX CL
BARNARD CL
ORCHARD RD
PARK RD
STRATTON RD
DAX CT
ELIZABETH GDNS
LYNDHURST AVE
Pav
Bwg Gn
Recn Gd
Sp Ctr
Sch
Liby
OXFORD WAY
HENLEY WAY
CONWAY RD
ST ALBANS AVE
LEBANON AVE
OSBORNE CL
CHESTNUT CT
MAIN ST
SOUTH RD
MCCARTHY RD
BIRCH
ST GEORGE'S
BEAR RD
COTTINGTON RD
PARK RD
THE HOLLANDS
PARR CT
TUDOR HO
TUDOR CT

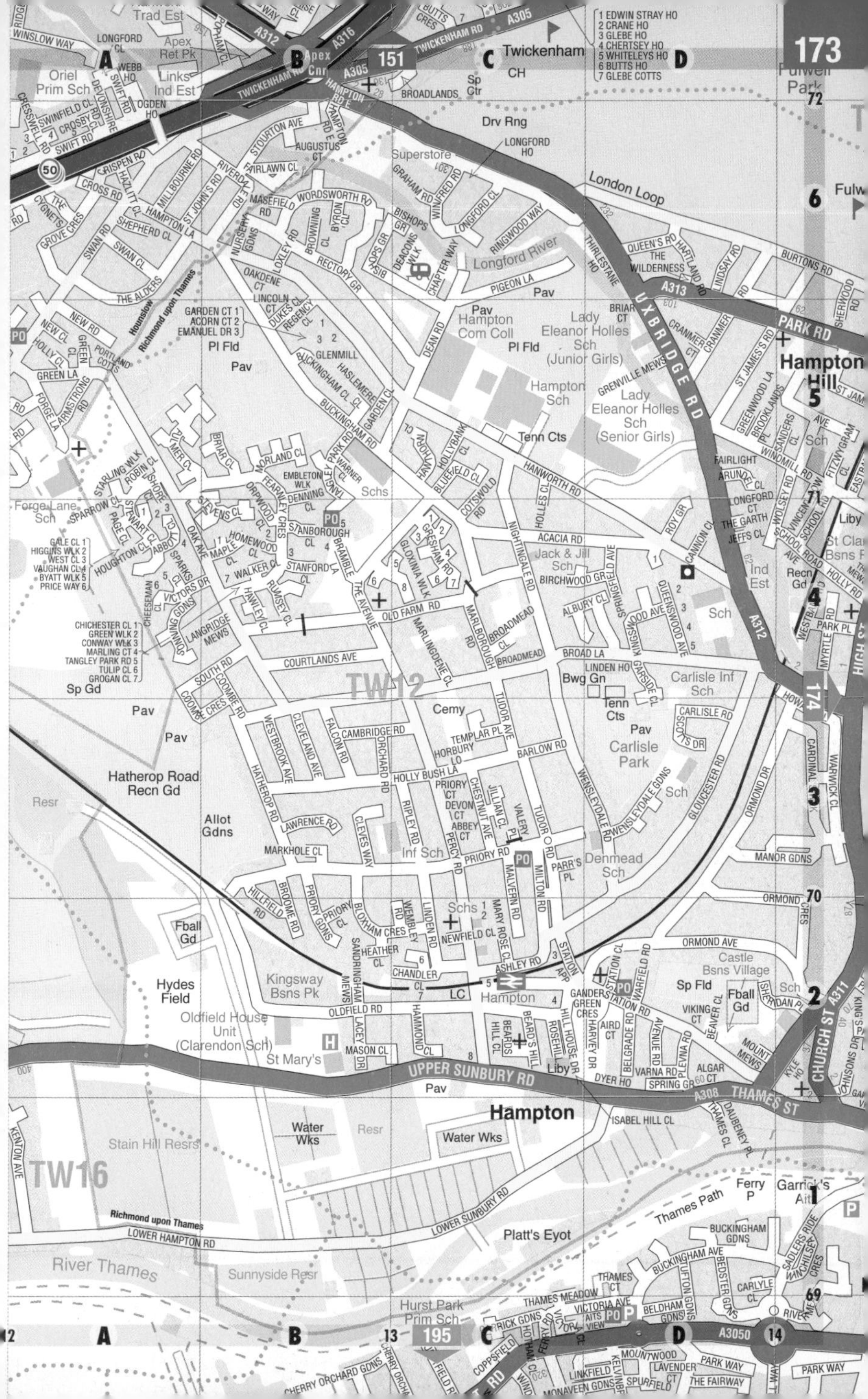
A
B
C
D
151
195
174
Twickenham
Apex Cnr
Apex Ret Pk
Trad Est
Links Ind Est
Oriel Prim Sch
1 EDWIN STRAY HO
2 CRANE HO
3 GLEBE HO
4 CHERTSEY HO
5 WHITELEYS HO
6 BUTTS HO
7 GLEBE COTTS
Fulwell Park
Drv Rng
Superstore
LONGFORD HO
London Loop
Longford River
Hampton Com Coll
Lady Eleanor Holles Sch (Junior Girls)
Hampton Sch
Lady Eleanor Holles Sch (Senior Girls)
Hampton Hill
GARDEN CT 1
ACORN CT 2
EMANUEL DR 3
GALE CL 1
HIGGINS WLK 2
WEST CL 3
VAUGHAN CL 4
BYATT WLK 5
PRICE WAY 6
CHICHESTER CL 1
GREEN WLK 2
CONWAY WLK 3
MARLING CT 4
TANGLEY PARK RD 5
TULIP CL 6
GROGAN CL 7
Forge Lane Sch
Jack & Jill Sch
Ind Est
TW12
Cemy
Carlisle Inf Sch
Carlisle Park
Hatherop Road Recn Gd
Allot Gdns
Inf Sch
Denmead Sch
Kingsway Bsns Pk
Hampton
Oldfield House Unit (Clarendon Sch)
St Mary's
Castle Bsns Village
UPPER SUNBURY RD
THAMES ST
CHURCH ST A311
UXBRIDGE RD
Hydes Field
Water Wks
Stain Hill Resrs
TW16
Richmond upon Thames
LOWER HAMPTON RD
LOWER SUNBURY RD
River Thames
Sunnyside Resr
Platt's Eyot
Thames Path
Garrick's Ait
Hurst Park Prim Sch
A3050
A308
A312
A313
A316
A305

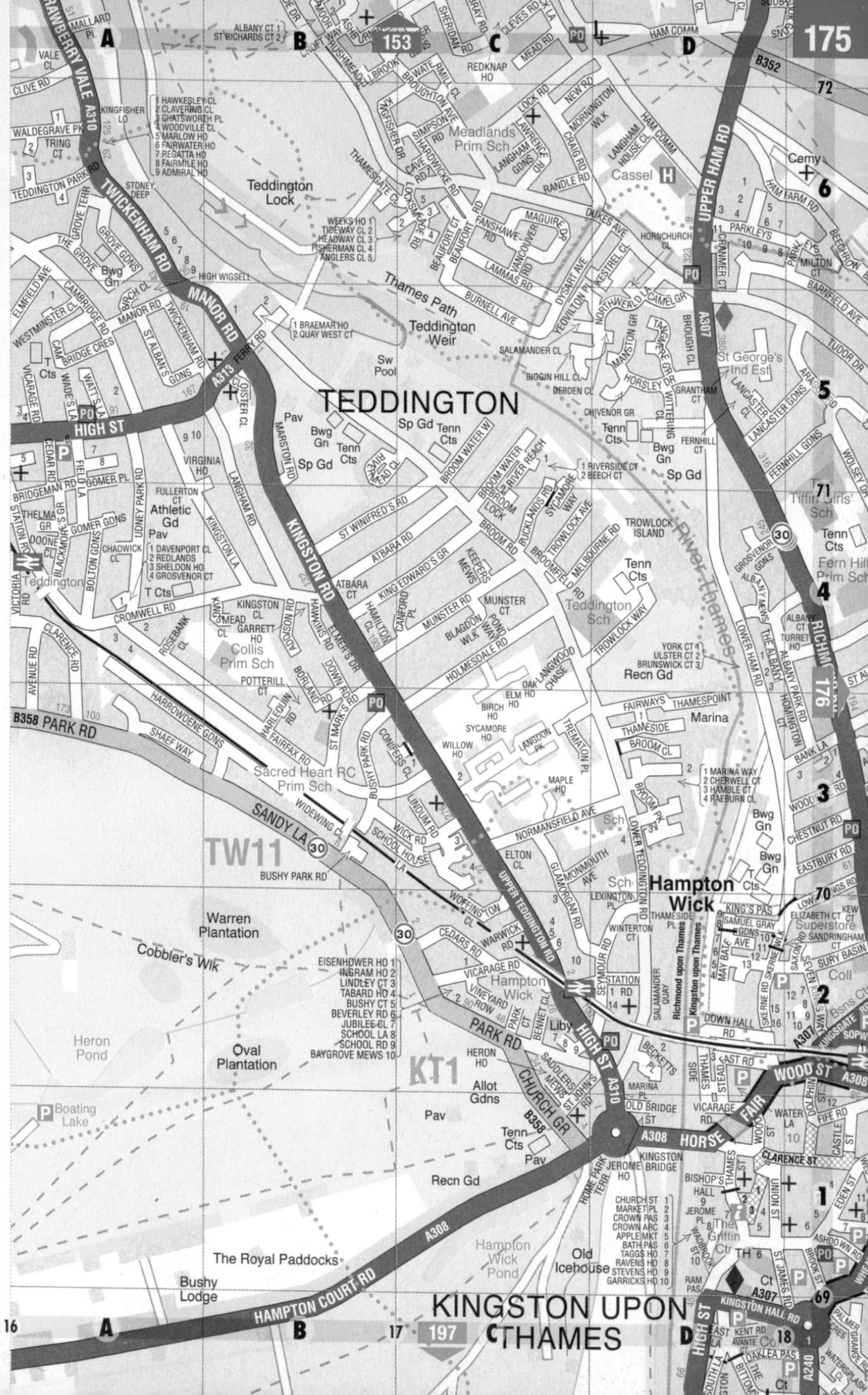

175
153
176
197
A
B
C
D
72
71
70
69
6
5
4
3
2
1
16
17
18
TEDDINGTON
KINGSTON UPON THAMES
Hampton Wick
TW11
KT1
Teddington Lock
Teddington Weir
Thames Path
River Thames
Trowlock Island
Marina
Meadlands Prim Sch
Cassel
Collis Prim Sch
Sacred Heart RC Prim Sch
Teddington Sch
Tiffin Girls' Sch
Fern Hill Prim Sch
St George's Ind Est
Warren Plantation
Oval Plantation
Cobbler's Wlk
Heron Pond
Boating Lake
The Royal Paddocks
Bushy Lodge
Hampton Wick Pond
Old Icehouse
Recn Gd
Allot Gdns
Athletic Gd
Superstore
The Griffin Ctr
Kingston Bridge
Richmond upon Thames
Kingston upon Thames
TWICKENHAM RD
MANOR RD
HIGH ST
KINGSTON RD
UPPER TEDDINGTON RD
UPPER HAM RD
PARK RD
SANDY LA
HAMPTON COURT RD
CHURCH GR
HORSE FAIR
WOOD ST
KINGSTON HALL RD
LOWER HAM RD
LOWER TEDDINGTON RD
STRAWBERRY VALE
HAM COMM
FERRY RD
STATION RD
BROOM RD
ATBARA RD
ST WINIFRED'S RD
MUNSTER RD
HOLMESDALE RD
CROMWELL RD
NORMANSFIELD AVE
VICARAGE RD
DUKES AVE
BURNELL AVE
LAMMAS RD
1 HAWKESLEY CL
2 CLAVERING CL
3 CHATSWORTH PL
4 WOODVILLE CL
5 MARLOW HO
6 FAIRWATER HO
7 REGATTA HO
8 FAIRMILE HO
9 ADMIRAL HO
WEEKS HO 1
TIDEWAY CL 2
HEADWAY CL 3
FISHERMAN CL 4
ANGLERS CL 5
1 BRAEMAR HO
2 QUAY WEST CT
1 DAVENPORT CL
2 REDLANDS
3 SHELDON HO
4 GROSVENOR CT
1 RIVERSIDE CT
2 BEECH CT
YORK CT 1
ULSTER CT 2
BRUNSWICK CT 3
1 MARINA WAY
2 CHERWELL CT
3 HAMBLE CT
4 RAEBURN CL
EISENHOWER HO 1
INGRAM HO 2
LINDLEY CT 3
TABARD HO 4
BUSHY CT 5
BEVERLEY RD 6
JUBILEE CL 7
SCHOOL LA 8
SCHOOL RD 9
BAYGROVE MEWS 10
CHURCH ST 1
MARKET PL 2
CROWN PAS 3
CROWN ARC 4
APPLE MKT 5
BATH PAS 6
TAGGS HO 7
RAVENS HO 8
STEVENS HO 9
GARRICKS HO 10

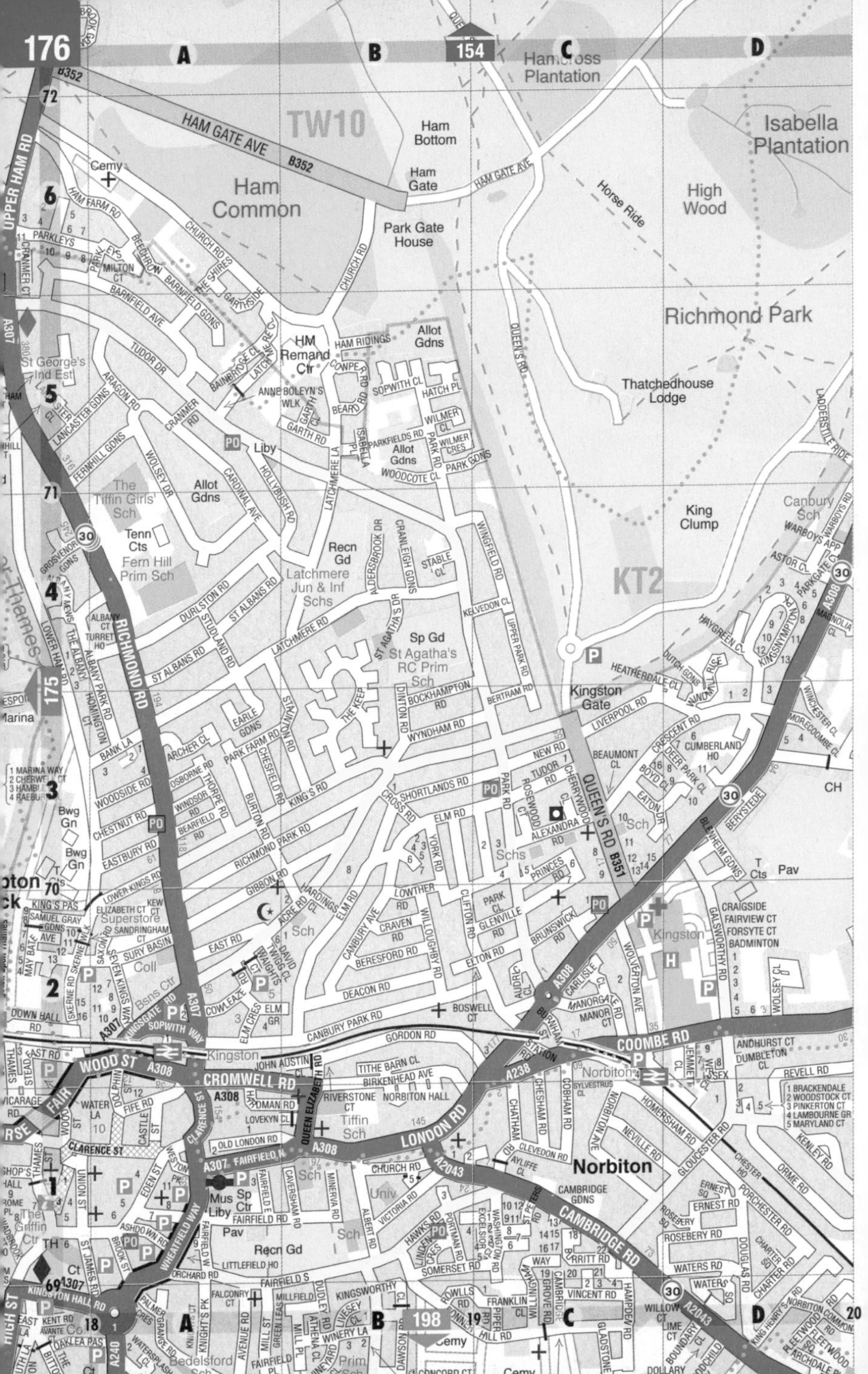

176
A
B
154
C
D
Hamcross Plantation
Isabella Plantation
TW10
HAM GATE AVE
B352
Ham Bottom
Ham Gate
Ham Common
Cemy
Horse Ride
High Wood
Park Gate House
UPPER HAM RD
HAM FARM RD
PARKLEYS
CHURCH RD
THE SHIRES
GARTHSIDE
BEECHROW
BARNFIELD GDNS
BARNFIELD AVE
MILTON CT
CRANMER CT
Richmond Park
QUEEN'S RD
HM Remand Ctr
Allot Gdns
HAM RIDINGS
SOPWITH CL
HATCH PL
TUDOR DR
ARAGON RD
LANCASTER GDNS
St George's Ind Est
ANNE BOLEYN'S WLK
GARTH RD
BEARD RD
WILMER CL
WILMER CRES
PARKFIELDS RD
PARK RD
PARK GDNS
WOODCOTE CL
Thatchedhouse Lodge
LADDERSTILE RIDE
FERNHILL GDNS
WOLSEY DR
CARDINAL AVE
HOLLYBUSH RD
LATCHMERE LA
Liby
The Tiffin Girls' Sch
Tenn Cts
Fern Hill Prim Sch
Recn Gd
Latchmere Jun & Inf Schs
ALDERSBROOK DR
CRANLEIGH GDNS
STABLE CL
WINGFIELD RD
King Clump
Canbury Sch
KT2
GROSVENOR GDNS
RICHMOND RD
DURLSTON RD
STUDLAND RD
ST ALBANS RD
LATCHMERE RD
ST AGATHA'S DR
Sp Gd
St Agatha's RC Prim Sch
KELVEDON CL
UPPER PARK RD
HAYGREEN CL
KINGSNYMPTON PK
MAGNOLIA
175
Marina
THE ALBANY
ALBANY PARK RD
HOMINGTON CT
LOWER HAM RD
Thames
BOCKHAMPTON RD
DINTON RD
WYNDHAM RD
BERTRAM RD
Kingston Gate
LIVERPOOL RD
HEATHERDALE CL
DUTCH GDNS
WINDMILL RISE
WINCHESTER CL
MORECOOMBE CL
EARLE GDNS
PARK FARM RD
CHESFIELD RD
STINTON RD
THE KEEP
ARCHER CL
BANK LA
NEW RD
TUDOR RD
CHERRYWOOD
BEAUMONT CL
CRESCENT RD
DEER PARK CL
BOYD CL
EATON DR
CUMBERLAND HO
BERYSTEDE
CH
1 MARINA WAY
2 CHERWELL CT
3 HAMBLE
4 RAEBURN
WOODSIDE RD
OSBORNE RD
WINDSOR RD
THORPE RD
BURTON RD
KING'S RD
SHORTLANDS RD
CROSS RD
ELM RD
YORK RD
ROSEWOOD CT
ALEXANDRA RD
QUEEN'S RD
B351
BLENHEIM GDNS
Bwg Gn
CHESTNUT RD
BEARFIELD RD
RICHMOND PARK RD
EASTBURY RD
Schs
PRINCES RD
Sch
T Cts
Pav
LOWER KINGS RD
KING'S PAS
ELIZABETH CT
KEW CT
Superstore
SAMUEL GRAY GDNS
SANDRINGHAM CT
GIBBON RD
HARDINGS CL
LOWTHER RD
CRAVEN RD
CANBURY AVE
WILLOUGHBY RD
CLIFTON RD
PARK CL
GLENVILLE RD
BRUNSWICK RD
CRAIGSIDE
FAIRVIEW CT
FORSYTE CT
BADMINTON
Kingston
H
GALSWORTHY RD
WOLSEY CL
MAY BATE AVE
SKERNE RD
SAXON RD
SEVEN KINGS WAY
SURY BASIN
EAST RD
ACRE RD
DAVID TWIGG CL
BERESFORD RD
ELTON RD
AUDRIC CL
A308
CARLISLE CL
WOLVERTON AVE
Coll
Bsns Ctr
COWLEAZE RD
ELM CRES
ELM GR
DEACON RD
CANBURY PARK RD
BOSWELL CT
MANORGATE RD
MANOR CT
DOWN HALL RD
KINGSGATE RD
SOPWITH WAY
A307
GORDON RD
BURNHAM ST
COOMBE RD
ANDHURST CT
DUMBLETON CL
REVELL RD
Kingston
JOHN AUSTIN CL
STATION RD
Norbiton
JEMMETT CL
WESSEX
WOOD ST
THAMES ST
CROMWELL RD
TITHE BARN CL
BIRKENHEAD AVE
NORBITON HALL
A238
SYLVESTRUS CL
1 BRACKENDALE
2 WOODSTOCK CT
3 PINKERTON CT
4 LAMBOURNE GR
5 MARYLAND CT
FAIR
VICARAGE RD
WATER LA
DOLPHIN
FIFE RD
CASTLE ST
HARDMAN RD
RIVERSTONE CT
QUEEN ELIZABETH RD
Tiffin Sch
CHATHAM
CHESHAM RD
COBHAM RD
NORBITON AVE
HOMERSHAM RD
NEVILLE RD
GLOUCESTER RD
KENLEY RD
CLARENCE ST
LOVEKYN CL
OLD LONDON RD
LONDON RD
FAIRFIELD N
A2043
CLEVEDON RD
AYLIFFE CL
Norbiton
CHESTER HO
ORME RD
EDEN ST
CLARENCE ST
Sch
CHURCH RD
VICTORIA RD
CAMBRIDGE GDNS
PORCHESTER RD
UNION ST
Mus
Liby
Sp Ctr
FAIRFIELD E
CAVERSHAM RD
MINERVA RD
Univ
ST PETERS
ERNEST SQ
ERNEST RD
The Griffin Ctr
WHEATFIELD WAY
FAIRFIELD RD
Pav
ALBERT RD
HAWKS RD
LINDEN CRES
PORTMAN RD
EXCELSIOR CL
WASHINGTON RD
CAMBRIDGE RD
ROSEBERY SQ
ROSEBERY RD
CHARTER SQ
TH
ST JAMES RD
BROOK ST
Recn Gd
LITTLEFIELD HO
Sch
SOMERSET RD
WAY
BARRITT RD
WATERS RD
DOUGLAS RD
CHARTER RD
Ct
A307
ORCHARD RD
FAIRFIELD S
ROWLLS RD
FRANKLIN CL
GROVE RD
VINCENT RD
HAMPDEN RD
WATERS SQ
KINGSTON HALL RD
KENT RD
AVANTE CT
OAKLEA PAS
HIGH ST
A240
FALCONRY CT
MILLFIELD
KINGSWORTHY CL
WILLOW CT
LIME CT
A2043
NORBITON COMMON RD
KING HENRY'S RD
FLEETWOOD RD
FLEETWOOD SQ
ARCHDALE PL
20
198
19
PALMER CRES
GRANGE RD
KNIGHT'S PK
AVENUE RD
MILL ST
GREEN LEAS
MILL PL
ATHENA CL
DUDLEY RD
LIVESEY CL
WINERY LA
VINEYARD
DAWSON RD
Cemy
PIPER RD
HILL RD
WILLINGHAM WAY
GLADSTONE
BOUNDARY CL
DOLLARY
CONCORD CT
Bedelsford Sch
Prim Sch
Cemy
WATERSPLASH

177
155
178
199
KT2
SW15
SW19
SW20
KT3
A308 KINGSTON VALE
A3
ROBIN HOOD WAY KINGSTON BY PASS
KINGSTON HILL
COOMBE LA WEST
A238
B283
TRAPS LA
COOMBE RD
Kingston Vale
Robin Hood
Coombe Hill
Coombe Wood
Warren House
Coombe
Mill Corner
Malden
Coombehurst (Kingston University)
Kingston Univ
Holy Cross Prep Sch
Coombe Hill Jun & Inf Schs
Coombe Girls Sch
Corpus Christi RC Prim Sch
New Victoria
Coombe Lane
COOMBE LANE FLYOVER 1
BEVERLEY CT 2
War Meml
Horse Ride
Allot Gdns
Pl Fld
Tenn Cts
Nat Res
Coombe Brook
Richmond upon Thames
Kingston upon Thames
Merton
Wandsworth
WOODVIEW CL
CEDAR CL
KINGSTON HILL PL
ROBINWOOD PL
MARY ADELAIDE CL
DERWENT AVE
ROBIN HOOD LA
VALE CRES
GRASMERE AVE
ULLSWATER CL
ULLSWATER CRES
WINDERMERE RD
ROBIN HOOD LA
BOWNESS CRES
RYDAL GDNS
KESWICK AVE
COOMBE PK
COOMBE RIDINGS
CORSCOMBE CL
PAGET PL
FAIRLAWN CL
COTSWOLD CL
THE WATERGARDENS
WARREN PK
WARREN RD
HIGH COOMBE PL
WARREN CUTTING
RENFREW RD
STOKE RD
GEORGE RD
COOMBE NEVILLE
EDGECOOMBE CL
GOLF CLUB DR
COOMBE END
COOMBE HILL RD
GREENWOOD PK
THE LEIGH
HENLEY DR
BEVERLEY LA
COOMBE HILL GLADE
NOOR PARK GDNS
WARBANK LA
GATEHOUSE CL
THE DRIVE
BALLARD CL
LORD CHANCELLOR WLK
FITZGEORGE AVE
WARREN RISE
COOMBE HOUSE CHASE
NEVILLE AVE
THE FAIRWAY
OAKCOMBE CL
COOMBE BANK
WONFORD CL
THE CHESTERS
THE MOAT
BURGHLEY AVE
CROMFORD WAY
BUXTON DR
SOAMES WLK
BADGERS WLK
BAKEWELL WAY
DARLEY DR
MATLOCK WAY
BRANKSOME WAY
WOODLANDS AVE
CROWN RD
SOUTHWOOD AVE
WEST RD
COOMBE RISE
ORCHARD RISE
BROOK GDNS
ALBION RD
CARDINAL CRES
BEECHCROFT AVE
DICKERAGE RD
ARUNDEL RD
HIGH DR
OVERDALE AVE
OAK RD
LANGLEY GR
CARLTON RD
SELBORNE RD
GOLF SIDE CL
DELL WLK
CLARENCE AVE
OLIVER RD
ASH CL
MYRTLE GR
THE CLOSE
LABURNUM GR
THE CRESCENT
BARTON GN
BURBERRY CL
WOODSIDE RD
POPLAR GDNS
LAWN CL
ROWAN CL
BEACONSFIELD RD
SALISBURY RD
SYCAMORE GR
EDGAR CT
LINKSIDE
FORSYTH CT
HOPPINGWOOD AVE
ORCHARD AVE
ROSEBERY AVE
CAMBRIDGE AVE
ALRIC AVE
THE TRIANGLE
MUYBRIDGE RD
MIDDLETON RD
ASHCOMBE SQ
LONG WLK
DICKERAGE HILL
WARWICK RD
LINCOLN RD
ROSEMONT RD
MOUNT PLEASANT RD
BEECH GR
ELM RD
POPLAR GR
LIME GR
ST MARYS CT
LINCOLN HO
CHESTNUT GR
CHESTNUT GROVE CT
STAFFORD RD
CRAMER CT
PHOENIX HO
VANFAME CT
Beverley
ELLERTON RD
PRESTON RD
HOOD RD
BEVERLEY AVE
HOLLAND AVE
MELVILLE AVE
BURDETT AVE
COTTENHAM PARK RD
WESTCOOMBE AVE
BEVERLEY WAY
ELY CL
ABOYNE DR
1 PERTH CL
2 HUNTLEY WAY
Pl Flds
Sp Gd
Pav
Sch
Schs
CH
PO
Bwg Gn

Wimbledon Common
SW15
SW19
SW20
London Scottish
Gravelly Hill
Wimbledon Common
Caesar's Camp
Royal Wimbledon
Crooked Billet
Cannizaro Park
The Study Prep Sch
King's Coll Sch
Wimbledon Common Prep Sch
Wimbledon Coll
Copse Hill
Cottenham Park
The Norwegian Sch
Ursuline High Sch
Hollymount Sch
St Matthew's CE Prim Sch
The Buddhapadipa Temple
Raynes Park
Rainbow Ind Est
Bushey Mead
PARKSIDE
HIGH ST
CANNIZARO RD
WOODHAYES RD
COTTENHAM PARK RD
COPSE HILL
COOMBE LA
DURHAM RD
WORPLE RD
KINGSTON RD
BUSHEY RD
BEVERLEY WAY KINGSTON BY PASS
ST BARNES LA
THE CAUSEWAY
CAMP RD
SUNSET RD
WEST SIDE COMM
SOUTHSIDE COMM
EDGE HILL
RIDGWAY
CAMBRIDGE RD
DRAX AVE
ELLERTON RD
BARHAM RD
Horse Ride
156
177
200

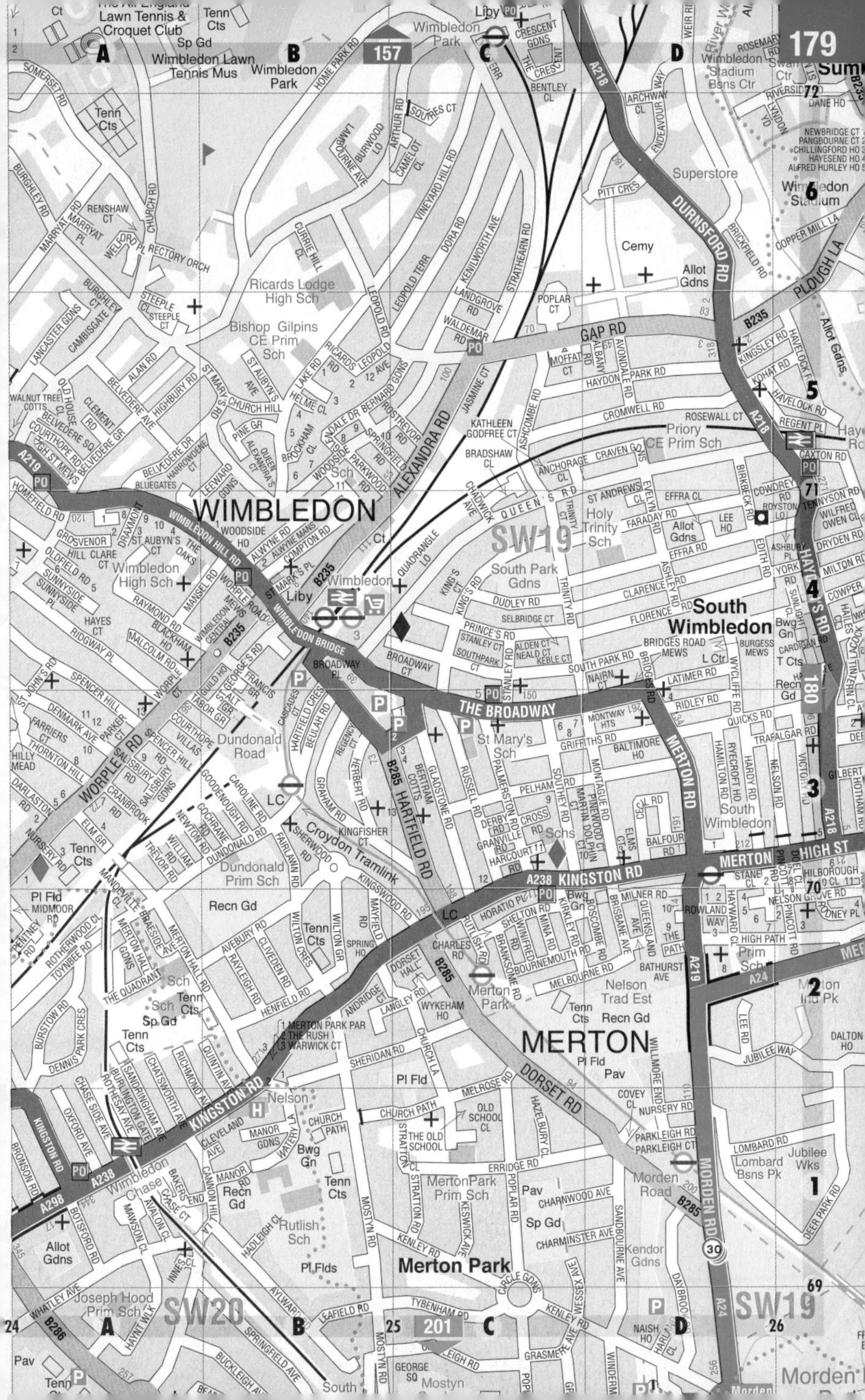
179
157
180
201
A
B
C
D
1
2
3
4
5
6
The All England Lawn Tennis & Croquet Club
Wimbledon Lawn Tennis Mus
Wimbledon Park
WIMBLEDON
SW19
SW20
South Wimbledon
MERTON
Merton Park
Wimbledon Stadium
Wimbledon Stadium Bsns Ctr
Superstore
Cemy
Allot Gdns
Ricards Lodge High Sch
Bishop Gilpins CE Prim Sch
Wimbledon High Sch
Priory CE Prim Sch
Holy Trinity Sch
South Park Gdns
St Mary's Sch
Dundonald Road
Dundonald Prim Sch
Croydon Tramlink
Recn Gd
Merton Park
Nelson Trad Est
Merton Ind Pk
Lombard Bsns Pk
Jubilee Wks
Morden Road
MertonPark Prim Sch
Rutlish Sch
Joseph Hood Prim Sch
Wimbledon Chase
Kendor Gdns
Nelson
Morden
WIMBLEDON HILL RD
WORPLE RD
KINGSTON RD
MERTON RD
MERTON HIGH ST
MORDEN RD
HARTFIELD RD
DORSET RD
THE BROADWAY
ALEXANDRA RD
DURNSFORD RD
HAYDONS RD
GAP RD
PLOUGH LA
QUEENS RD
WIMBLEDON BRIDGE
HOME PARK RD
CHURCH RD
VINEYARD HILL RD
STRATHEARN RD
SOUTH PARK RD
PALMERSTON RD
KINGSWOOD RD
CHURCH LA
CHURCH PATH
ERRIDGE RD
A218
A219
A238
A24
A298
B235
B285
B286

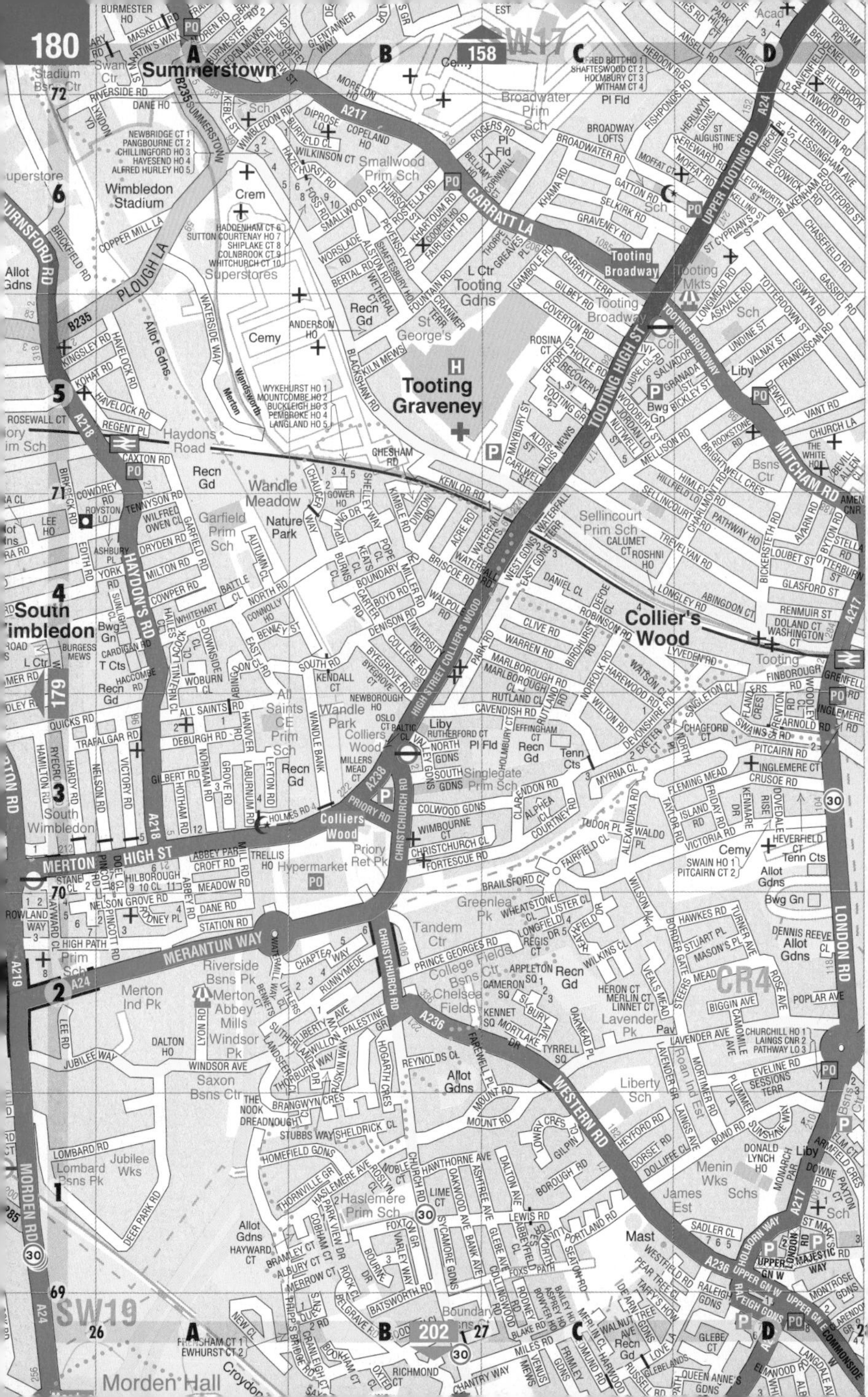

Summerstown
SW17
158
Wimbledon Stadium
Crem
Superstores
Cemy
Tooting Graveney
Tooting Broadway
Tooting Gdns
St George's
L Ctr
Smallwood Prim Sch
Broadwater Prim Sch
Tooting Mkts
Haydons Road
Wandle Meadow Nature Park
Garfield Prim Sch
South Wimbledon
All Saints CE Prim Sch
Wandle Park
Colliers Wood
Collier's Wood
Sellincourt Prim Sch
Singlegate Prim Sch
Tooting
Priory Ret Pk
Hypermarket
Greenlea Pk
Tandem Ctr
College Fields Bsns Ctr
Chelsea Fields
Riverside Bsns Pk
Merton Abbey Mills
Merton Ind Pk
Windsor Pk
Saxon Bsns Ctr
Lavender Pk
Liberty Sch
Menin Wks
James Est
Roan Ind Est
Haslemere Prim Sch
Jubilee Wks
Lombard Bsns Pk
Boundary Bsns Ctr
Morden Hall
SW19
CR4
202
179
PLOUGH LA
GARRATT LA
UPPER TOOTING RD
TOOTING HIGH ST
HIGH STREET COLLIER'S WOOD
MITCHAM RD
HAYDON'S RD
MERTON HIGH ST
MERANTUN WAY
CHRISTCHURCH RD
WESTERN RD
LONDON RD
MORDEN RD
DURNSFORD RD

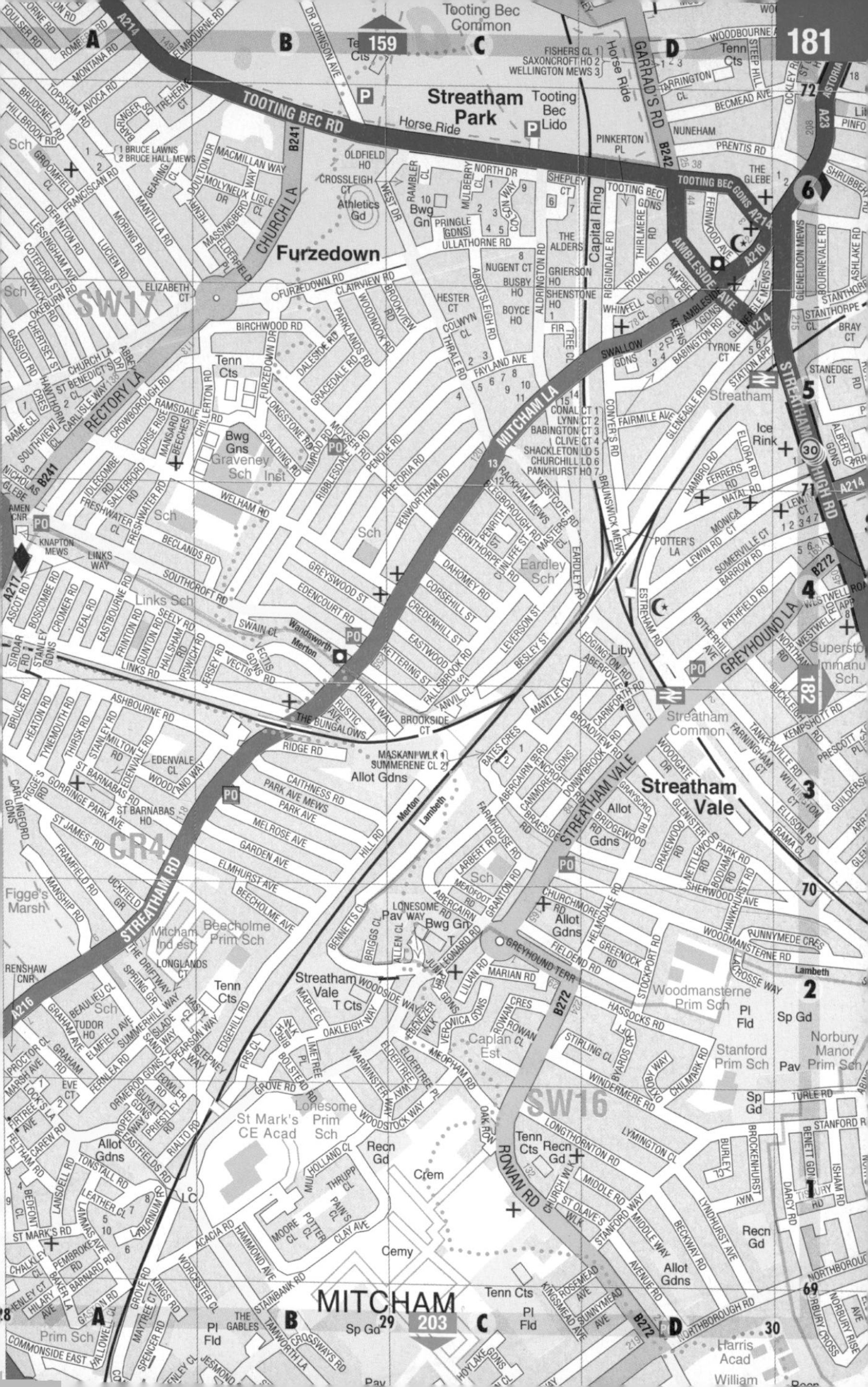
Tooting Bec Common
Streatham Park
Tooting Bec Lido
TOOTING BEC RD
Furzedown
SW17
MITCHAM LA
Streatham
STREATHAM HIGH RD
GREYHOUND LA
Streatham Common
Streatham Vale
STREATHAM VALE
STREATHAM RD
CR4
SW16
Figge's Marsh
MITCHAM
159
182
203

160
A
B
C
D
STREATHAM
Streatham Common
Streatham
Norbury
Norwood Grove
Norbury Park
SW16
SE27
STREATHAM COMMON N
CROWN LA
STREATHAM HIGH RD
LONDON RD
GREEN LA
Capital Ring
Horse Ride
1 ELPHINSTONE CT
2 RIDLEY CT
3 BLADON CT
4 COMMONSIDE CT
5 SANDERS HO
6 BYRON CL
7 HAMBLY MANS
8 ST JOHNS HO
Bishop Thomas Grant RC Sec Sch
Sunnyhill Prim Sch
Julian's Prim Sch
Crown Lane Prim Sch
St Joseph's RC Coll
St Andrews RC Prim Sch
Norbury Manor Bsns & Enterprise Coll for Girls
Kensington Avenue Prim Sch
Norbury Manor Prim Sch
Stanford Prim Sch
St James The Great RC Prim Sch
Norbury Trad Est
181
204
6
5
4
3
2
1
72
71
70
69
30
31

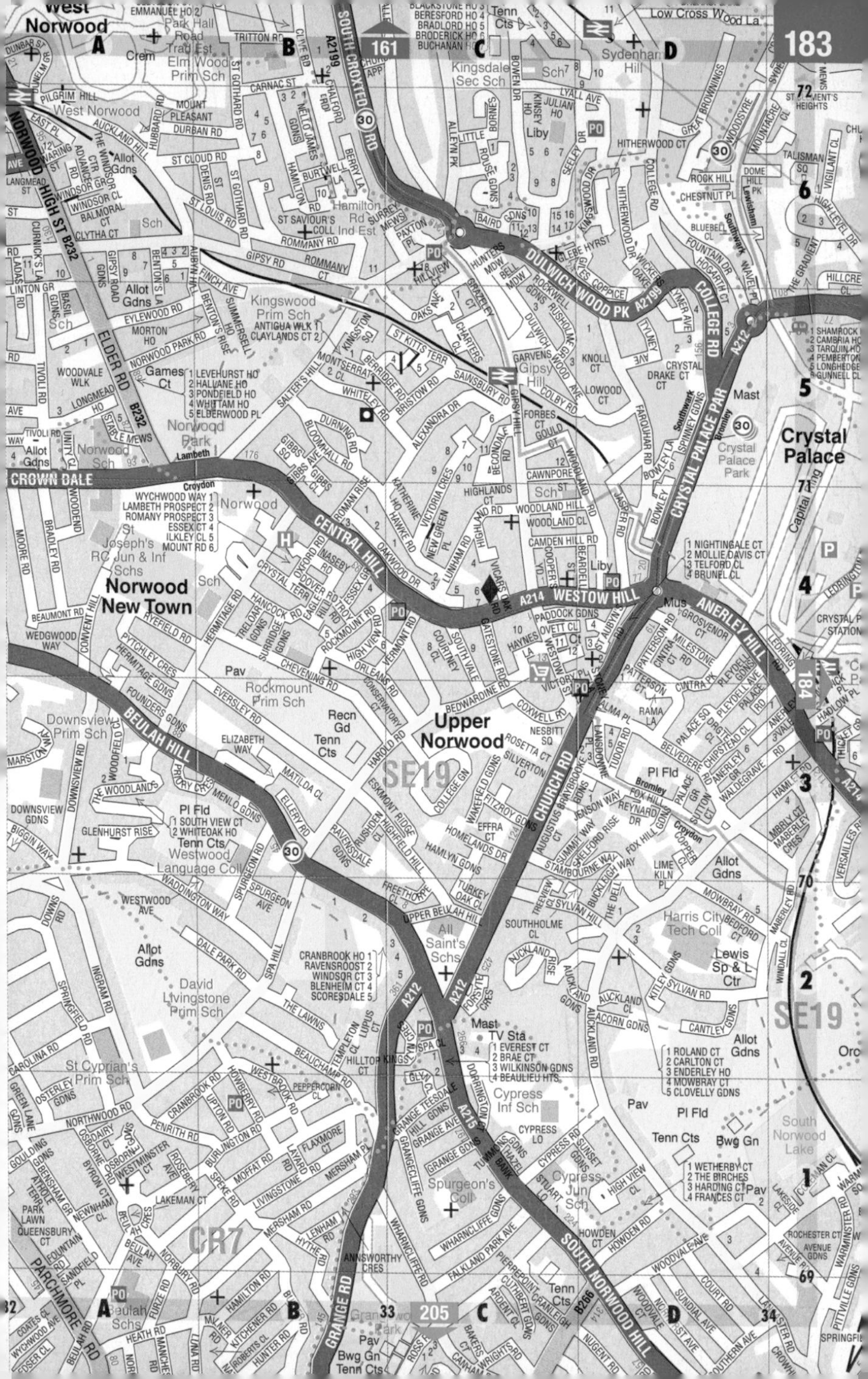
West Norwood
Norwood New Town
Upper Norwood
Crystal Palace
SE19
CR7
161
184
205

162
SE26
Forest Hill Sec Sch
Sydenham Wells Park
Upper Sydenham
WESTWOOD HILL
Sydenham
SYDENHAM RD
KIRKDALE
A2216
A212
A213
A234
A214
Mayow Park
Tenn Cts
Allot Gdns
CRYSTAL PALACE PARK RD
Crystal Palace
Crystal Palace Park
Crystal Palace National Sports Ctr
Capital Ring
CRYSTAL PALACE STATION RD
Crystal Palace
COLLEGE RD
CRYSTAL PALACE PAR
ANERLEY HILL
183
NEWLANDS PK
PENGE
Penge East
Penge West
PARISH LA
HIGH ST
GREEN LA
Alexandra Jun Sch
Green Chain Walk
Recn Gd
Hospice
SE20
Malcolm Prim Sch
Ind Est
Anerley
ANERLEY RD
CROYDON RD
Franklin Ind Est
Royston Prim Sch
SE19
Anerley Prim Sch
Orchard School Sp Ctr
Betts Park
South Norwood Lake
Avenue Road
Croydon Tramlink
Birkbeck
ELMERS END RD
Churchfields Prim Sch
Elmers End
206
A
B
C
D
1
2
3
4
5
6
34
35
69
70
71
72

185
163
186
207
Bell Green
Lower Sydenham
SE26
SE6
Bellingham
New Beckenham
BR3
BECKENHAM
Lower Sydenham Sydenham Ind Est
Broomsleigh Bsns Pk
Kangley Bridge Ctr
Orchard Bsns Ctr
Gardner Ind Est
The Metro Bsns Ctr
Abbey Trad Est
Beckenham Bsns Ctr
Beckenham Junction
Beckenham Hill
Beckenham Place
Beckenham Place Pk
Beckenham Green
Kent House
Clock House
Beckenham Rd
Cator Park Sch
Sedgehill Sch
Elfrida Sch
Kelsey Park
Green Chain Wlk
Pool River
Chaffinch Brook
Lewisham
Bromley
SYDENHAM RD
STANTON WAY
SOUTHEND LA
SOUTHEND RD
BECKENHAM HILL RD
BECKENHAM RD
BELL GN
RECTORY RD
HIGH ST
MANOR RD
BROMLEY RD
WICKHAM RD
KENT HOUSE RD
KENT HOUSE LA
KANGLEY BRIDGE RD
WORSLEY BRIDGE RD
COPERS COPE RD
BRACKLEY RD
PARK RD
CHURCH AVE
CROMWELL RD
CROCKERS COPE
A2218
A212
A2015
A234
A222
B227
B230

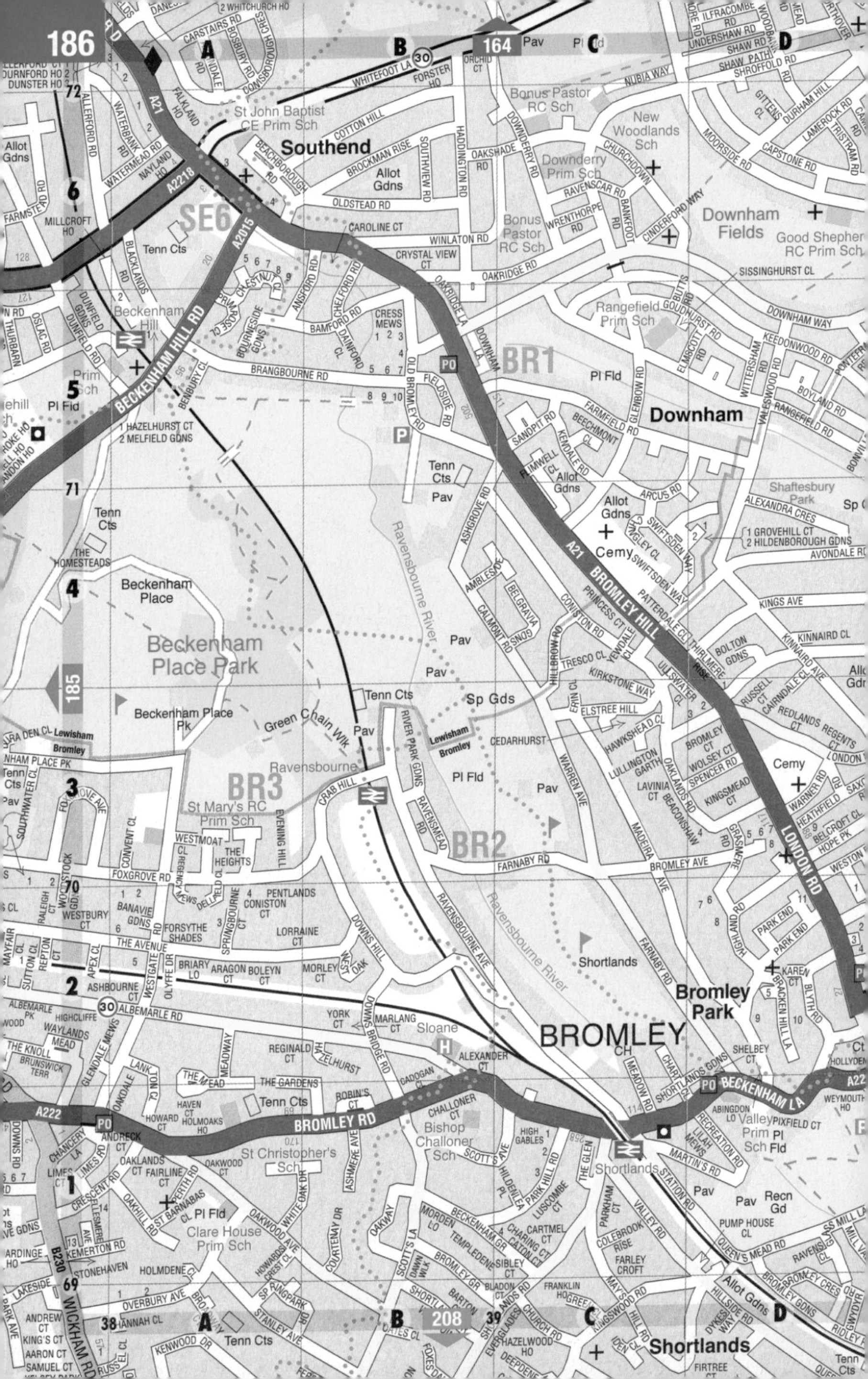

164
185
208
Southend
SE6
BR1
BR2
BR3
Downham
Downham Fields
Beckenham Place Park
Beckenham Place
Beckenham Hill
BROMLEY HILL
BECKENHAM HILL RD
BROMLEY RD
LONDON RD
BECKENHAM LA
Ravensbourne River
Ravensbourne
Green Chain Wlk
Shortlands
Bromley Park
BROMLEY
Sloane
Bishop Challoner Sch
St Christopher's Sch
Clare House Prim Sch
St Mary's RC Prim Sch
Rangefield Prim Sch
Downderry Prim Sch
New Woodlands Sch
Bonus Pastor RC Sch
St John Baptist CE Prim Sch
Good Shepherd RC Prim Sch
Shaftesbury Park
Valley Prim Sch
Lewisham
Bromley

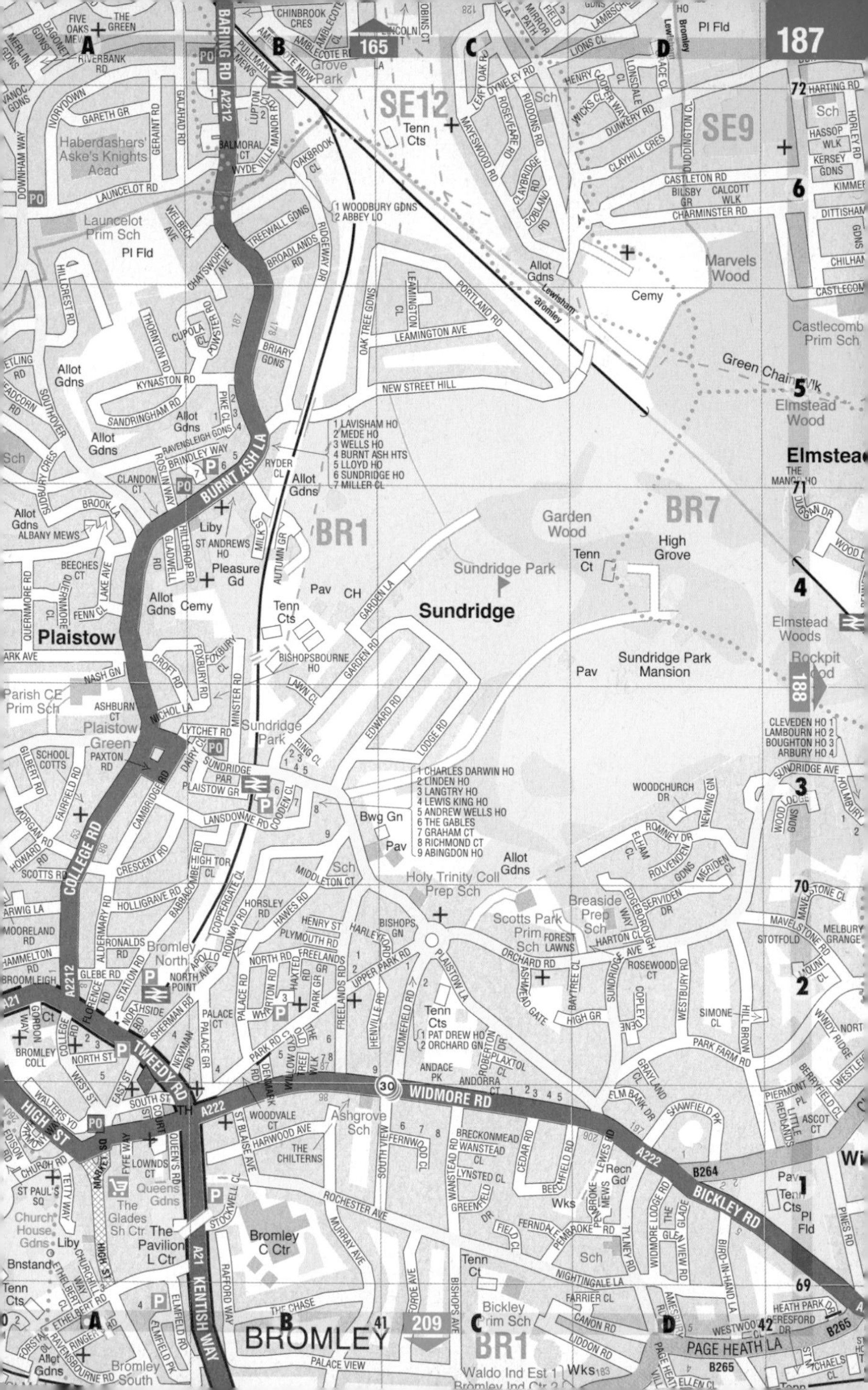
SE12
SE9
BR1
BR7
Sundridge
Plaistow
Elmstead
Sundridge Park
Sundridge Park Mansion
Garden Wood
High Grove
Marvels Wood
Elmstead Wood
Elmstead Woods
Castlecombe Prim Sch
Haberdashers' Aske's Knights Acad
Launcelot Prim Sch
Grove Park
Bromley North
Bromley South
Sundridge Park
Holy Trinity Coll Prep Sch
Scotts Park Prim Sch
Breaside Prep Sch
Ashgrove Sch
Bickley Prim Sch
Parish CE Prim Sch
Plaistow Green
Bromley C Ctr
The Glades Sh Ctr
The Pavilion L Ctr
Queens Gdns
Green Chain Wlk
BARING RD
A2212
BURNT ASH LA
COLLEGE RD
WIDMORE RD
A222
BICKLEY RD
TWEEDY RD
HIGH ST
KENTISH WAY
A21
B264
B265
PAGE HEATH LA
BROMLEY
165
188
209
1 WOODBURY GDNS
2 ABBEY LO
1 LAVISHAM HO
2 MEDE HO
3 WELLS HO
4 BURNT ASH HTS
5 LLOYD HO
6 SUNDRIDGE HO
7 MILLER CL
1 CHARLES DARWIN HO
2 LINDEN HO
3 LANGTRY HO
4 LEWIS KING HO
5 ANDREW WELLS HO
6 THE GABLES
7 GRAHAM CT
8 RICHMOND CT
9 ABINGDON HO
1 PAT DREW HO
2 ORCHARD GN
CLEVEDEN HO 1
LAMBOURN HO 2
BOUGHTON HO 3
ARBURY HO 4
Waldo Ind Est 1
Bromley Ind Ctr 2

SE9
Marvels Wood
Castlecombe Prim Sch
Green Chain Wlk
Elmstead Wood
Elmstead
THE MANOR HO
BR7
Elmstead Woods
Rockpit Wood
Ravensbourne Coll
Babington House Sch
Chislehurst West
Red Hill Prim Sch
Camden Park
Chislehurst
Bullers Wood Sch
Widmore
Bickley
Bickley Park Sch
WHITE HORSE HILL
RED HILL
CHISLEHURST HIGH ST
GREEN LA
OLD HILL
SUMMER HILL
CHISLEHURST RD
BICKLEY RD
BICKLEY PARK RD
BROMLEY RD
PAGE HEATH LA
166
187
210

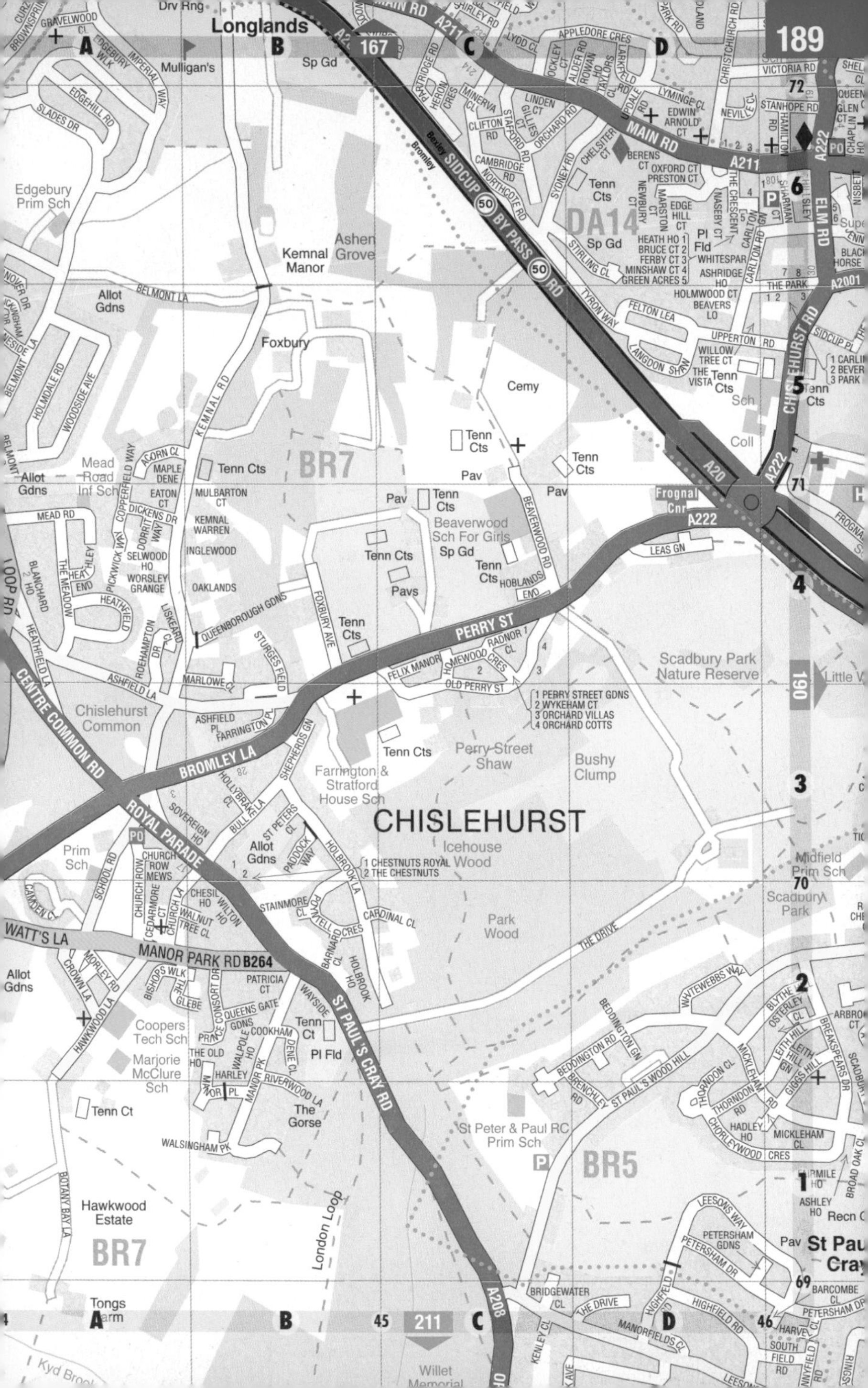
Longlands
Mulligan's
Sp Gd
167
MAIN RD
A211
Edgebury Prim Sch
Kemnal Manor
Ashen Grove
SIDCUP BY PASS RD
DA14
Tenn Cts
Sp Gd
Allot Gdns
Foxbury
KEMNAL RD
Cemy
BR7
Tenn Cts
Mead Road Inf Sch
Beaverwood Sch For Girls
Frognal Cnr
A222
A20
PERRY ST
Scadbury Park Nature Reserve
190
Chislehurst Common
CENTRE COMMON RD
BROMLEY LA
ROYAL PARADE
Farrington & Stratford House Sch
Perry Street Shaw
Bushy Clump
CHISLEHURST
Icehouse Wood
Park Wood
Midfield Prim Sch
Scadbury Park
WATT'S LA
MANOR PARK RD B264
ST PAUL'S CRAY RD
Coopers Tech Sch
Marjorie McClure Sch
The Gorse
St Peter & Paul RC Prim Sch
BR5
Hawkwood Estate
BR7
London Loop
Tongs Farm
211
A208
Willet Memorial

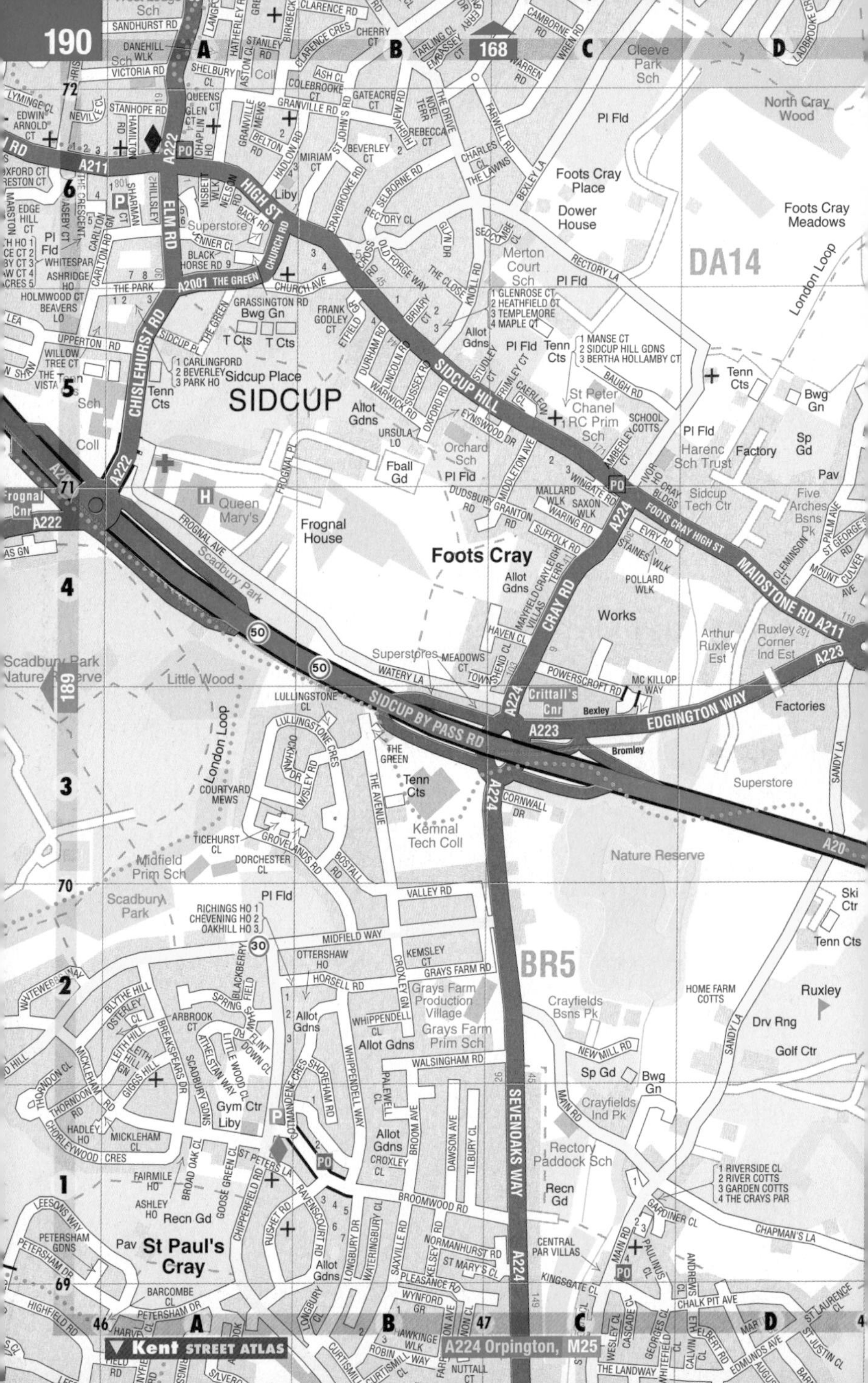
190
A
B
168
C
D
SANDHURST RD
DANEHILL WLK
VICTORIA RD
HATHERLEY RD
STANLEY RD
SHELBURY CL
ASTON CL
BIRKBECK
CLARENCE RD
CLARENCE CRES
CHERRY CT
TARLING CL
EMBASSEY CT
CAMBORNE RD
WREN RD
Cleeve Park Sch
LADBROOKE CR
WARREN RD
ASH CL
COLEBROOKE CT
GRANVILLE RD
GATEACRE CT
ST JOHN'S RD
NOEL TERR
THE DRIVE
FARWELL RD
North Cray Wood
72
LYMINGE CL
EDWIN ARNOLD CT
NEVILLE CL
STANHOPE RD
HAMILTON RD
QUEENS CT
GLEN CT
CHAPLIN HO
GRANVILLE MEWS
BELTON RD
HADLOW RD
MIRIAM CT
REBECCA CT
BEVERLEY CT
CHARLES CL
THE LAWNS
Pl Fld
Foots Cray Place
Dower House
Foots Cray Meadows
A211
A222
PO
OXFORD CT
PRESTON CT
6
THE CRESCENT
SHARMAN CT
HILLSLEY
ELM RD
NISBETT WLK
NELSON RD
HIGH ST
Liby
CRAYBROOKE RD
SELBORNE RD
RECTORY CL
BEXLEY LA
EDGE HILL CT
MARSTON
ASEBY CT
CARLTON RD
Superstore
BACK RD
JENNER CL
BLACK HORSE RD
CHURCH RD
CROSS RD
OLD FORGE WAY
GLYN DR
SECCOMBE CL
Merton Court Sch
RECTORY LA
DA14
London Loop
Pl Fld
WHITESPAR
ASHRIDGE HO
THE PARK
A2001 THE GREEN
CHURCH AVE
THE CLOSE
KNOLL RD
HOLMWOOD CT
BEAVERS LO
GRASSINGTON RD
Bwg Gn
FRANK GODLEY CT
ETFIELD
BRIARY CT
1 GLENROSE CT
2 HEATHFIELD CT
3 TEMPLEMORE
4 MAPLE CT
UPPERTON RD
SIDCUP PL
THE GREEN
T Cts
T Cts
DURHAM RD
LINCOLN RD
SUSSEX RD
SIDCUP HILL
Allot Gdns
Pl Fld
Tenn Cts
1 MANSE CT
2 SIDCUP HILL GDNS
3 BERTHA HOLLAMBY CT
Tenn Cts
Bwg Gn
WILLOW TREE CT
THE VISTA
5
Sch
1 CARLINGFORD
2 BEVERLEY
3 PARK HO
Sidcup Place
SIDCUP
Tenn Cts
CHISLEHURST RD
WARWICK RD
OXFORD RD
STUDLEY CT
FRIMLEY CT
CAERLEON CL
BAUGH RD
St Peter Chanel RC Prim Sch
SCHOOL COTTS
Pl Fld
Sp Gd
Harenc Sch Trust
Factory
Pav
Coll
Allot Gdns
URSULA LO
EYNSWOOD DR
Orchard Sch
Fball Gd
Pl Fld
MIDDLETON AVE
AMBERLEY CT
WINGATE RD
IVOR HO
CRAY BLDGS
Sidcup Tech Ctr
Five Arches Bsns Pk
A20
71
Frognal Cnr
A222
FROGNAL PL
H
Queen Mary's
Frognal House
DUDSBURY RD
GRANTON RD
MALLARD WLK
SAXON WLK
WARING RD
SUFFOLK RD
A224
FOOTS CRAY HIGH ST
EVRY RD
STAINES WLK
PALM AVE
ST GEORGE'S RD
CLEMINSON CT
MOUNT CULVER AVE
FROGNAL AVE
Scadbury Park
Foots Cray
Allot Gdns
MAYFIELD VILLAS
CRAYLEIGH TERR
CRAY RD
POLLARD WLK
Works
MAIDSTONE RD A211
4
50
Scadbury Park Nature Reserve
189
Little Wood
Superstores
MEADOWS CT
HAVEN CL
TOWNSHEND CL
POWERSCROFT RD
Arthur Ruxley Est
Ruxley Corner Ind Est
A223
50
WATERY LA
MC KILLOP WAY
Crittall's Cnr
Bexley
EDGINGTON WAY
Factories
LULLINGSTONE CL
SIDCUP BY PASS RD
A223
LULLINGSTONE CRES
OCKHAM DR
WISLEY RD
THE GREEN
Bromley
London Loop
3
COURTYARD MEWS
THE AVENUE
Tenn Cts
A224
CORNWALL DR
Superstore
SANDY LA
Kemnal Tech Coll
TICEHURST CL
GROVELANDS RD
Nature Reserve
A20
Midfield Prim Sch
DORCHESTER CL
BOSTALL RD
70
Scadbury Park
Pl Fld
VALLEY RD
Ski Ctr
RICHINGS HO 1
CHEVENING HO 2
OAKHILL HO 3
30
MIDFIELD WAY
Tenn Cts
OTTERSHAW HO
KEMSLEY CT
CROXLEY GN
GRAYS FARM RD
BR5
2
WHITEWEBBS WAY
BLYTHE HILL
OSTERLEY CL
BLACKBERRY FIELD
SPRING SHAW RD
HORSELL RD
Grays Farm Production Village
HOME FARM COTTS
Ruxley
ARBROOK CT
FLINT DOWN CL
Allot Gdns
WHIPPENDELL CL
Crayfields Bsns Pk
Drv Rng
LEITH HILL
LEITH HILL GN
BREAKSPEARS DR
ATHELSTAN WAY
LITTLE WOOD CL
Allot Gdns
Grays Farm Prim Sch
NEW MILL RD
SANDY LA
Golf Ctr
MICKLEHAM RD
THORNDON CL
THORNDON RD
GIGGS HILL
SCADBURY GDNS
SHOREHAM RD
WHIPPENDELL WAY
WALSINGHAM RD
Sp Gd
Bwg Gn
Gym Ctr
Liby
COTMANDENE CRES
PALEWELL CL
BROOM AVE
DAWSON AVE
TILBURY CL
SEVENOAKS WAY
MAIN RD
Crayfields Ind Pk
HADLEY HO
MICKLEHAM CL
CHORLEYWOOD CRES
P
Allot Gdns
CROXLEY CL
Rectory Paddock Sch
BROAD OAK CL
GOOSE GREEN CL
CHIPPERFIELD RD
ST PETERS LA
PO
1 RIVERSIDE CL
2 RIVER COTTS
3 GARDEN COTTS
4 THE CRAYS PAR
1
FAIRMILE HO
Recn Gd
ASHLEY HO
Recn Gd
RAVENSCOURT RD
BROOMWOOD RD
GARDINER CL
LEESONS WAY
RUSHET RD
CHAPMAN'S LA
PETERSHAM GDNS
PETERSHAM DR
Pav
St Paul's Cray
Allot Gdns
LONGBURY DR
WATERINGBURY CL
SAXVILLE RD
KELSEY RD
NORMANHURST RD
ST MARY'S CL
CENTRAL PAR VILLAS
A224
PAULINUS CL
MAIN RD
ANDREWS CL
69
BARCOMBE CL
PLEASANCE RD
WYNFORD GR
KINGSGATE CL
CHALK PIT AVE
ST LAURENCE CL
HIGHFIELD RD
PETERSHAM DR
46
A
LONGBURY CL
B
HAWKINGE WLK
47
C
WESLEY CL
CASCADE CL
GEORGES CL
WHITEFIELD CL
CALVIN CL
ELBERT RD
D
EDMUNDS AVE
ST JUSTIN CL
Kent STREET ATLAS
ROBIN CL
CURTISMILL WAY
A224 Orpington, M25
NUTTALL CT
THE LANDWAY

▼ Kent STREET ATLAS

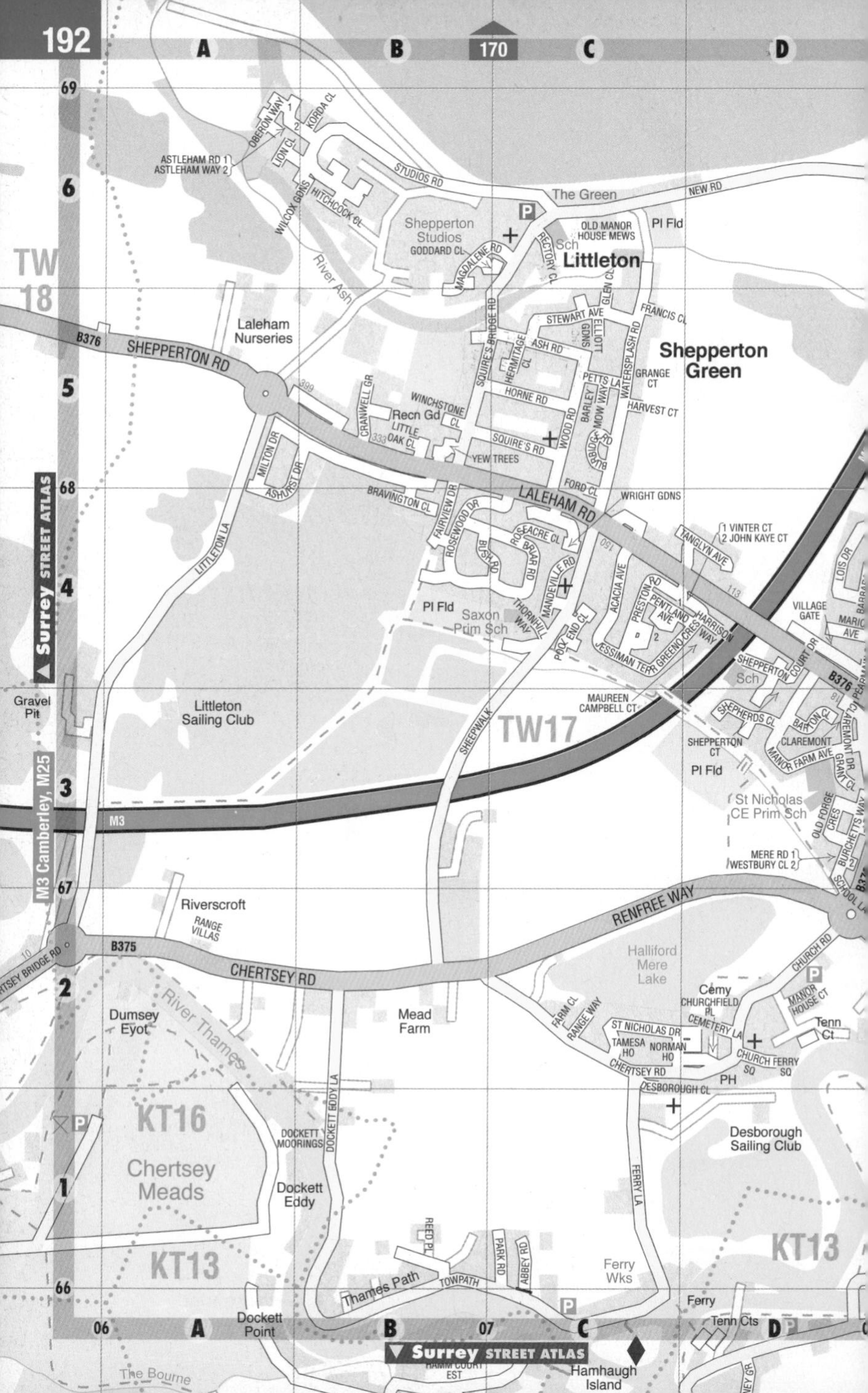
A
B
170
C
D
69
6
5
68
4
3
67
2
1
66
TW
18
OBERON WAY
KORDA CL
ASTLEHAM RD 1
ASTLEHAM WAY 2
LION CL
WILCOX GDNS
HITCHCOCK CL
STUDIOS RD
The Green
NEW RD
P
Shepperton
Studios
GODDARD CL
MAGDALENE RD
RECTORY CL
OLD MANOR
HOUSE MEWS
Pl Fld
Sch
Littleton
River Ash
GLEN CL
STEWART AVE
ELLIOTT GDNS
FRANCIS CL
Laleham
Nurseries
B376
SHEPPERTON RD
SQUIRE'S BRIDGE RD
HERMITAGE CL
ASH RD
WATERSPLASH RD
Shepperton
Green
PETTS LA
GRANGE CT
399
CRANWELL GR
WINCHSTONE CL
Recn Gd
HORNE RD
BARLEY MOW WAY
HARVEST CT
LITTLE OAK CL
333
WOOD RD
SQUIRE'S RD
BURBIDGE RD
YEW TREES
MILTON DR
ASHURST DR
BRAVINGTON CL
FAIRVIEW DR
FORD CL
LALEHAM RD
WRIGHT GDNS
ROSEWOOD DR
ROSEACRE CL
BUSH RD
BALAR RD
MANDEVILLE RD
150
1 VINTER CT
2 JOHN KAYE CT
TANGLYN AVE
LITTLETON LA
ACACIA AVE
PRESTON RD
PENTLAND AVE
HARRISON WAY
113
LOIS DR
VILLAGE GATE
Pl Fld
Saxon
Prim Sch
THORNHILL WAY
POOL END CL
JESSIMAN TERR
GREENO CRES
SHEPPERTON COURT DR
Sch
B376
MAUREEN
CAMPBELL CT
SHEPHERDS CL
BARTON CL
Gravel
Pit
Littleton
Sailing Club
TW17
SHEEPWALK
CLAREMONT
SHEPPERTON CT
MANOR FARM AVE
GRANT CL
Pl Fld
St Nicholas
CE Prim Sch
OLD FORGE CRES
BURCHETTS WAY
M3
MERE RD 1
WESTBURY CL 2
SCHOOL LA
Surrey STREET ATLAS
M3 Camberley, M25
Riverscroft
RANGE VILLAS
RENFREE WAY
B375
CHERTSEY BRIDGE RD
CHERTSEY RD
Halliford
Mere
Lake
CHURCH RD
Dumsey
Eyot
River Thames
Mead
Farm
FARM CL
RANGE WAY
Cemy
CHURCHFIELD PL
CEMETERY LA
MANOR HOUSE CT
Tenn
Ct
ST NICHOLAS DR
TAMESA HO
NORMAN HO
CHERTSEY RD
CHURCH FERRY SQ
CHURCH SQ
PH
DESBOROUGH CL
KT16
DOCKETT MOORINGS
DOCKETT EDDY LA
Desborough
Sailing Club
Chertsey
Meads
Dockett
Eddy
FERRY LA
KT13
REED PL
PARK RD
ABBEY RD
Ferry
Wks
KT13
Thames Path
TOWPATH
Ferry
Dockett
Point
Tenn Cts
06
07
Surrey STREET ATLAS
HAMM COURT EST
Hamhaugh
Island
The Bourne

Charlton
171
The Bishop Wand CE Sch
Recn Gd
Sports Gd
Hawkedale Inf Sch
Grange Farm Est
Hazelwood
Allot Gdns
Sunbury
Recn Gd
CH
Upper Halliford
TW17
TW16
Vicarage Farm
Cemy
River Ash
Rodd Est
Shepperton Bsns Pk
Shepperton
Longwood Bsns Pk
Campasps Bsns Pk
Watersplash Farm
Nursery
Lower Halliford
Shepperton
Thamesmead Sec Sch
Tenn Cts
Recn Gd
Allot Gdns
Halliford Sch
Marina
Gravel Pit
Bishop Duppas Park
Bwg Gn
Las Palmas Est
Desborough Island
Pl Fld
Pav
River Thames
Thames Meadow
Works
Desborough Channel
Engine River
Thames Path
The Heart
KT12
KT13
Ashley Park
194
UPPER HALLIFORD RD
GASTON BRIDGE RD
WALTON BRIDGE RD
GREEN LA
RUSSELL RD
WALTON LA
CHARLTON LA
HALLIFORD RD
FORDBRIDGE RD
NEW ZEALAND AVE
OATLANDS DR
CHURCH ST
HEPWORTH WAY
BRIDGE ST
M3
A
B
C
D
09
10

A
B
C
D
172
SUNBURY
Sunbury Ct Island
Beauclerc Inf Sch
Hawkedale Inf Sch
ROOKSMEAD RD
MARYLAND WAY
VEREKER DR
HAWKEWOOD RD
SUNMEAD RD
PARKWOOD GR
FAIRLAWNS
CROYSDALE AVE
THE PINES
LYNDHURST AVE
THE AVENUE
SAXONBURY AVE
OLD ORCH
KINGSMEAD AV
FRENCH ST
DARBY GDNS
DARBY CRES
THE PENNARDS
ELIZABETH GDNS
DAX CT
BERKELEY MEWS
SUNBURY COURT MEWS
SUNBURY CT
LOWER HAMPTON RD
RIVERSIDE
1 ELIZABETH CT
2 THAMES CNR
3 RIVERMEAD HO
4 CASTLE WLK
AVENUE PAR
The Walled Garden
THAMES ST
Tenn Cts
SCHOOL WLK
Cemy
GREEN ST
Allot Gdns
ANVIL RD
BRIDLE CL
FORGE LA
FORGE MEWS
CHURCH VILLA
CHURCH ST
Sunbury Lock
FARRIER CL
STILE PATH
MARTINGALE CL
GREEN WAY
ST MARY'S CL
MONTFORD RD
CUMBERLAND PL
HALLIFORD RD
TW16
River Thames
Thames Path
LOUDWATER CL
LOUDWATER RD
PARKE RD
FORDBRIDGE RD
WILLOW WAY
TADMOR CL
HURST RD
A3050
Apps Court Farm
Nursery
THE CREEK
Wheatley's Ait
Fball Gd
Leisure Ctr
Riverrnook Farm
SUNNYSIDE
RIVERNOOK CL
Bramble Hill Farm
Knight Resr
B369
WALTON RD
WATERSIDE DR
DUNSMORE RD
FRANKLYN RD
KT12
BEASLEY'S AIT LA
BEASLEY'S AIT
193
ARMSTRONG
THE HALLIARDS
TUMBLING BAY
RIVER WLK
SUNBURY LA
WEIR RD
LITTLE HALLIARDS
FELIX RD
FRANKLIN RD
SUNBURY CL
CAMBRIDGE RD
Thamesfield Farm
Allot Gdns
MONTPELLIER CT
TERRACE RD
Sch
KILSHA RD
SPICER CL
THORNEYCROFT CL
TANNERS CL
TITHE CL
FIRST AVE
SANDY LA
VICARAGE FIELDS
VINERS CL
VANBRUGH DR
1 LUSHINGTON HO
2 LYNDE HO
3 CROXALL HO
4 KIRBY WAY
Queen Elizabeth 2 Storage Resr
Recn Gd
RUSSELL RD
THAMES VIEW HO
THAMES MEAD
GARDEN RD
SECOND AVE
ORCHARD CL
TELFORD DR
EMMELINE CT
VANBRUGH MEWS
DUDLEY RD
ANNETT RD
ENTERPRISE HO
CRANBOURNE CT
LANCASTER CT
THE GROVE
GROVE CRES
CARLTON RD
PANKHURST RD
PAYTON CL
STONEBANKS
MANOR RD
BISHOPS HILL
1 COURTLANDS
2 MANOR PL
KINGSBRIDGE RD
COTTIMORE TERR
KIMBERLEY WLK
NIGHTINGALE RD
FLORENCE CL
FLORENCE RD
FOX GR
CROWN CL
WALTON-ON-THAMES
HARVEY RD
DALE RD
MAYO RD
THAMES ST
ALPINE RD
MONTAGUE CL
WILLOWHAYNE DR
EGMONT RD
COTTIMORE CRES
BRAYCOURT AVE
SHAW DR
BRIDGE ST
WELLINGTON CL
CHURCH ST
Cemy
REGNOLRUF CT
FIR CL
CHURCHFIELD RD
ESHER AVE
ROYSTON CL
SIDNEY RD
COTTIMORE AVE
FAIRFAX CL
COTTIMORE LA
MONKS CRES
CROMWELL CL
HILLARY CRES
REGENCY GDNS
ST CLEMENTS HO
HIGHFIELD RD
NELSON CL
MISTYS FIELD
HIGH ST
The Heart
BRASSEY HO
CHURCH WLK
WINCHESTER RD
OSBORNE RD
Allot Gdns
Recn Gd
KINGS CL
STUART AVE
LANGPORT CT
1 RODNEY CL
2 EDGEHILL CT
3 WORCESTER CT
4 DUNBAR CT
HOLLY AVE
CARDINAL DR
WOLSEY DR
NEW ZEALAND AVE
ASHLEY RD
HIGH ST
COLBY RD
Bwg Gn
1 RYLTON HO
2 BLATCHFORD CT
3 ASHLEY PL
KINGS RD
STRATTON CT
PRESTON CT
NEWARK CT
CHERITON CT
Sch
WINDSOR WLK
TUDOR DR
NORMANHURST RD
RYDENS RD
ASHLEY PARK AVE
ASHLEY PARK CRES
WOODSIDE
Sch
Liby
A244
HERSHAM RD
OAKFIELDS
T Cts
THE CHESTNUTS
CRUTCHFIELD LA
MARSTON CT
CROMWELL RD
LANSDOWNE CT
ST JOHNS DR
INWOOD CT
RODNEY RD
AMBLESIDE AVE
KING GEORGE AVE
WILTON GDNS
BRANKSOME CL
Ashley Park
B365
RED HOUSE LA
GRANGE CT
LINDEN GR
CLEMENTS CT
NOSEBY
THE FURROWS
MEADOWSIDE
RYDENS PK
WALTON PARK
YORK GDNS
A244 Esher
Surrey STREET ATLAS
Walton Comm
10
11
12
69
68
67
66
6
5
4
3
2
1

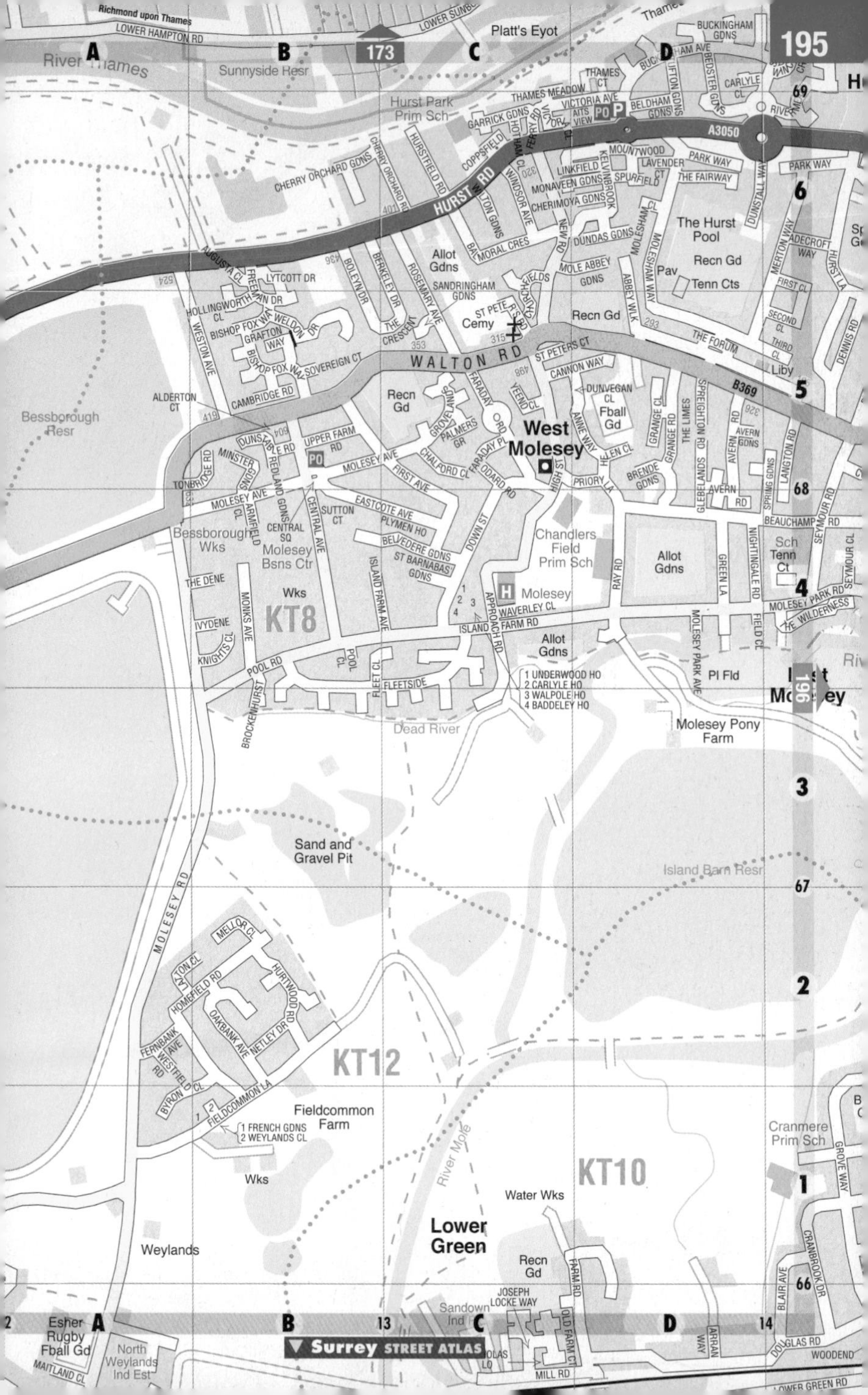
Richmond upon Thames
LOWER HAMPTON RD
173
Platt's Eyot
River Thames
Sunnyside Resr
Hurst Park Prim Sch
A3050
HURST RD
WALTON RD
B369
The Hurst Pool
Recn Gd
Tenn Cts
Allot Gdns
Cemy
West Molesey
Bessborough Resr
Bessborough Wks
Molesey Bsns Ctr
Wks
KT8
Chandlers Field Prim Sch
Molesey
1 UNDERWOOD HO
2 CARLYLE HO
3 WALPOLE HO
4 BADDELEY HO
Dead River
Molesey Pony Farm
Pl Fld
196
Sand and Gravel Pit
Island Barn Resr
KT12
Fieldcommon Farm
1 FRENCH GDNS
2 WEYLANDS CL
Wks
Weylands
River Mole
KT10
Water Wks
Lower Green
Recn Gd
Cranmere Prim Sch
Sandown Ind Est
Esher Rugby Fball Gd
North Weylands Ind Est
Surrey STREET ATLAS
MOLESEY RD
MILL RD
LOWER GREEN RD
A B C D
1 2 3 4 5 6
66 67 68 69
13 14

Hurst Park
Taggs Island
Nursery
174
A
B
C
D
Hampton Court House
Hampton Court Green
Hampton Court
Molesey Lock
Hampton Court Landing Stage
Hampton Court Palace
Maze
Tenn Cts
HAMPTON COURT RD
HURST RD
A3050
A308
A309
Richmond upon Thames
Surrey
The Hurst Pool
Recn Gd
Sp Gd
Pl Fld
Sch
PALACE RD
WOLSEY RD
WESTLANDS CT
WALTON RD
B369
BRIDGE RD
B3379
River Thames
Thames Path
KT8
East Molesey
River Mole
River Ember
Molesey Pony Farm
195
ESHER RD
HAMPTON COURT WAY
Ditton Field
Hampton Court Crossing
KT7
Thames Ditton Fst Sch
Island Barn Resr
Imber Court Trad Est
Met. Police Rugby Fball Gd
B364
EMBERCOURT RD
STATION RD
Thames Ditton
St Paul's RC Prim Sch
Esher Coll
Weston Green
KT10
EMBER LA
Cranmere Prim Sch
Ditton Common
Weston Green
PORTSMOUTH RD
A307
Thames Ditton Jun Sch
212
Esher
Thames Ditton & Esher
6
5
4
3
2
1
68
67
66
14
15

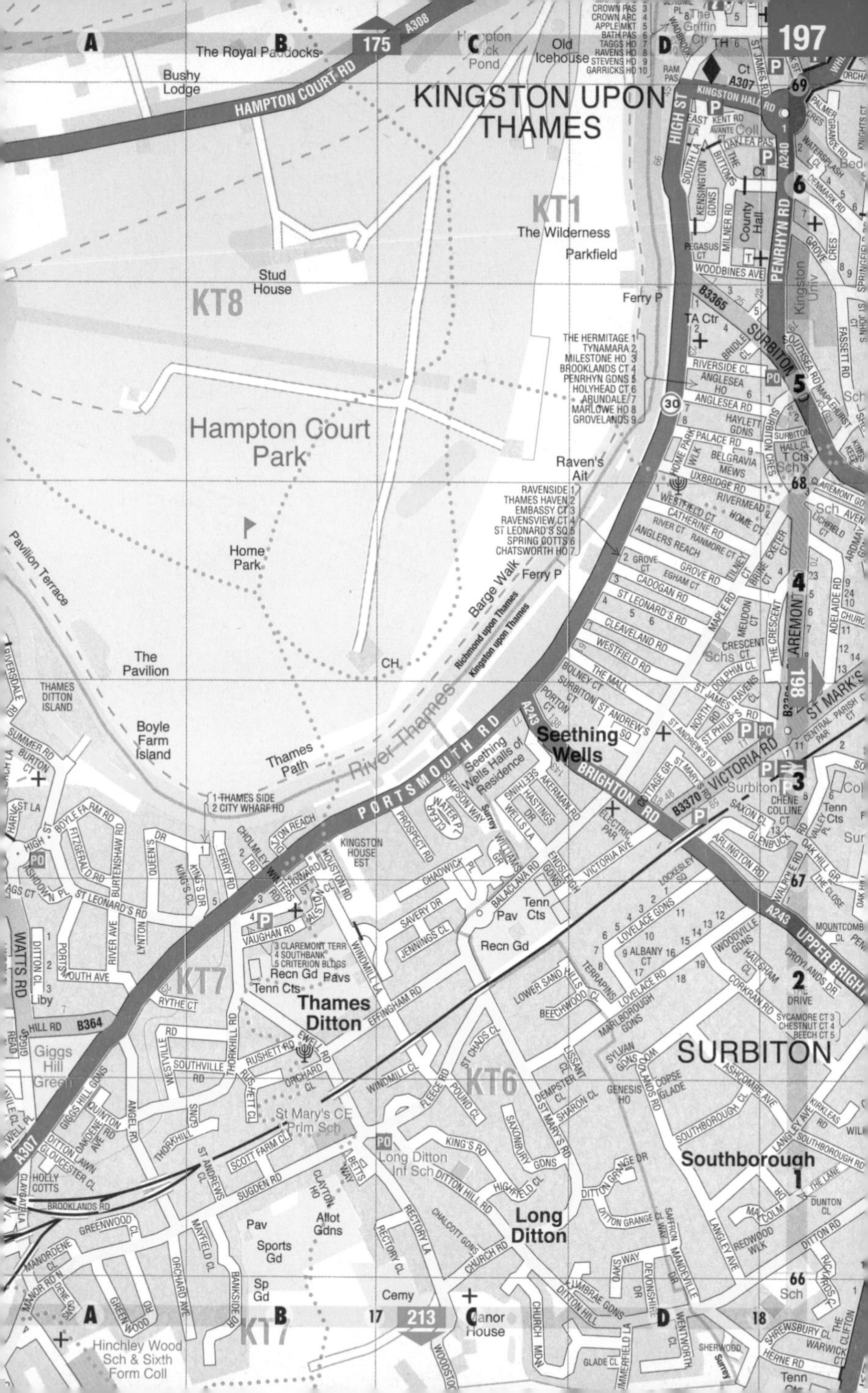
A
B
C
D
175
A308
The Royal Paddocks
Bushy Lodge
HAMPTON COURT RD
Old Icehouse
CROWN PAS 3
CROWN ARC 4
APPLE MKT 5
BATH PAS 6
TAGGS HO 7
RAVENS HO 8
STEVENS HO 9
GARRICKS HO 10
The Griffin Ctr
TH
RAM PAS
ST JAMES RD
KINGSTON UPON THAMES
A307
KINGSTON HALL RD
HIGH ST
EAST LA
KENT RD
AVANTE CT
OAKLEA PAS
SOUTH LA
KENSINGTON GDNS
THE BITTOMS
Coll
Ct
A240
PENRHYN RD
County Hall
MILNER RD
PEGASUS CT
WOODBINES AVE
KT1
The Wilderness
Parkfield
Stud House
KT8
Ferry P
B3365
TA Ctr
SURBITON RD
BRIDLE CL
Kingston Univ
THE HERMITAGE 1
TYNAMARA 2
MILESTONE HO 3
BROOKLANDS CT 4
PENRHYN GDNS 5
HOLYHEAD CT 6
ARUNDALE 7
MARLOWE HO 8
GROVELANDS 9
RIVERSIDE CL
ANGLESEA HO
ANGLESEA RD
SOUTHSEA RD
MAPLEHURST
FASSETT RD
PALMER CRES
GRANGE RD
WATERSPLASH CL
DENMARK RD
GROVE CRES
KNIGHTS CT
ST JOHN'S
30
HAYLETT GDNS
PALACE RD
SURBITON CRES
SURBITON HALL CL
T Cts
Schs
BELGRAVIA MEWS
UXBRIDGE RD
HOME PARK WALK
Hampton Court Park
Raven's Ait
RAVENSIDE 1
THAMES HAVEN 2
EMBASSY CT 3
RAVENSVIEW CT 4
ST LEONARD'S SQ 5
SPRING COTTS 6
CHATSWORTH HO 7
WESTFIELD CT
CATHERINE RD
RIVER CT
RANMORE CT
RIVERMEAD
HOME CT
68
CLAREMONT GDNS
LICHFIELD CT
ARDMAY GDNS
ANGLERS REACH
GROVE CT
GROVE RD
EGHAM CT
TILNEY CT
BRINE CT
EXETER CT
CADOGAN RD
ST LEONARD'S RD
MAPLE RD
MEUDON CT
CLEAVELAND RD
WESTFIELD RD
CRESCENT CT
THE CRESCENT
CLAREMONT
ADELAIDE RD
Home Park
Pavilion Terrace
Barge Walk
Ferry P
Richmond upon Thames
Kingston upon Thames
CH
The Pavilion
THAMES DITTON ISLAND
Boyle Farm Island
River Thames
Thames Path
BOLNEY CT
THE MALL
SURBITON CT
PORTON CT
ST ANDREW'S SQ
DOLPHIN CL
RAVENS CL
ST JAMES' RD
NORTH RD
ST PHILIP'S RD
ST ANDREW'S RD
198
ST MARK'S
CENTRAL PAR
PARISH CT
A243
PORTSMOUTH RD
Seething Wells Halls of Residence
Seething Wells
BRIGHTON RD
SIMPSON WAY
CLEAR WATER PL
SEETHING WELLS LA
HASTINGS DR
AKERMAN RD
COTTAGE GR
ST MARY'S RD
B3370
VICTORIA RD
Surbiton
SAXON CL
CHENE COLLINE CT
GLENBUCK RD
ARLINGTON RD
VALLEY PL
OAK HILL GR
THE CLOSE
Tenn Cts
3
1 THAMES SIDE
2 CITY WHARF HO
RIVERSDALE RD
SUMMER RD
BURTON CT
HARVEST LA
BOYLE FARM RD
FITZGERALD RD
BURTENSHAW RD
QUEEN'S DR
KING'S DR
KING'S CL
FERRY RD
CHOLMLEY RD
LYTON REACH
WINTERS RD
HOWARD ST
HOUSTON RD
ALSTON CL
PROSPECT RD
KINGSTON HOUSE EST
CHADWICK PL
WILLIAMS GR
BALACLAVA RD
ENDSLEIGH GDNS
ELECTRIC PAR
VICTORIA AVE
LOCKESLEY SQ
WALPOLE RD
67
MOUNTCOMBE CL
HIGH ST
ASHDOWN RD
ST LEONARD'S RD
RIVER AVE
LYNTON RD
PORTSMOUTH AVE
DITTON CL
WATTS RD
Liby
VAUGHAN RD
3 CLAREMONT TERR
4 SOUTHBANK
5 CRITERION BLDGS
Recn Gd
Pavs
Tenn Cts
SAVERY DR
JENNINGS CL
WINDMILL LA
Pav
Tenn Cts
Recn Gd
LOVELACE GDNS
ALBANY CT
WOODVILLE GDNS
HAILSHAM CL
UPPER BRIGH
CROYLANDS DR
KT7
RYTHE CT
EFFINGHAM RD
Thames Ditton
LOWER SAND HILLS
TERRAPINS
LOVELACE RD
CORKRAN RD
2
DRIVE
BEECHWOOD CL
MARLBOROUGH GDNS
SYCAMORE CT 3
CHESTNUT CT 4
BEECH CT 5
HILL RD
B364
Giggs Hill Green
WESTVILLE RD
SOUTHVILLE RD
THORKHILL RD
RUSHETT RD
EWELL RD
ORCHARD CL
WINDMILL CL
FLEECE RD
POUND CL
ST CHADS CL
KT6
LISSANT CL
SYLVAN GDNS
COOMBE LANDS RD
COPSE GLADE
SURBITON
DEMPSTER CL
SHARON CL
GENESIS HO
ASHCOMBE AVE
KIRKLEAS RD
SOUTHBOROUGH CL
LANGLEY AVE
SOUTHBOROUGH RD
GIGGS HILL GDNS
QUINTON RD
OAKDENE AVE
ANGEL RD
RUSHETT CL
THORKHILL GDNS
St Mary's CE Prim Sch
SAXONBURY GDNS
ST MARY'S RD
Southborough
1
A307
DITTON LAWN
GLOUCESTER CL
HOLLY COTTS
ST ANDREWS CL
SCOTT FARM CL
SUGDEN RD
CLAYTON HO
BETTS WAY
Long Ditton Inf Sch
KING'S RD
DITTON HILL RD
HIGHFIELD CL
DITTON GRANGE DR
DITTON GRANGE CL
SAFFRON WAY
MANDEVILLE DR
MALCOLM DR
THE LANE
DUNTON CL
REDWOOD WLK
DITTON RD
BROOKLANDS RD
GREENWOOD CL
MANORDENE CL
MANOR RD N
DENE GDNS
MAYFIELD CL
ORCHARD AVE
BANKSIDE DR
Pav
Sports Gd
Allot Gdns
RECTORY CL
RECTORY LA
CHALCOTT GDNS
CHURCH RD
Long Ditton
OAKS WAY
DEVONSHIRE DR
66
Sch
RICKARDS CL
GREENWOOD RD
Sp Gd
Cemy
17
213
Manor House
CHURCH MDW
LIMBRAE GDNS
DITTON HILL
WENTWORTH CL
18
SHREWSBURY CL
WARWICK CL
THE CLIFTON
HERNE RD
Hinchley Wood Sch & Sixth Form Coll
GLADE CL
SHERWOOD
Tenn

198
176
197
214
A
B
C
D
1
2
3
4
5
6
KT1
KT5
KT6
SURBITON
Southborough
Berrylands
Surbiton
Tolworth
CAMBRIDGE RD
A2043
HIGH ST
KINGSTON HALL RD
PENRHYN RD
A240
SURBITON RD
SURBITON HILL RD
B3365
B3370
B3363
ST MARK'S HILL
VICTORIA RD
UPPER BRIGHTON RD
A243
HOOK RD
KINGSDOWNE RD
A3210
EWELL RD
DITTON RD
B3364
TOLWORTH BROADWAY
WARREN DR N
A3
Recn Gd
Cemy
Crem
Kingstonians FC
Sewage Works
Thames Down Link
London Loop
Fairfield Ind Est
Kingsmill Bsns Pk
County Hall
Kingston Univ
Bedelsford Sch
Christ Church CE Prim Sch
Dysart Sch
Tolworth Jun & Inf Schs
Allot Gdns
Nat Res
LOWER MARSH LA
VILLIERS RD
ADDISON GDNS
CRANES PARK AVE
LINGFIELD AVE
SURBITON HILL PK
THE RIDGE
THE CREST
THE ROYSTONS
PEMBROKE AVE
BERRYLANDS RD
MANOR DR
KINGS DR
QUEENS DR
ALEXANDRA DR
COURTLANDS
AVENUE S
CLAREMONT RD
MAPLE RD
ANGLESEA RD
BROWN'S RD
LANGLEY AVE
SOUTHBOROUGH RD
ASHCOMBE AVE
CHAMBERLAIN WAY
ST MATTHEW'S AVE
DOUGLAS RD
RAVENSCAR RD
KINGSMEAD AVE
PRINCES AVE
OAKLEIGH AVE
HAMILTON AVE
TANKERTON RD
GREENFIELD AVE
LYNDHURST AVE
BERESFORD AVE
ELGAR AVE
MORESBY AVE
NORTON AVE

199
177
200
215
A
B
C
D
1
2
3
4
5
6
NEW MALDEN
Old Malden
New Malden
Malden Manor
KT3
KT4
KT5
KINGSTON RD
A2043
HIGH ST
B283
BURLINGTON RD
B282
MALDEN RD
COOMBE RD
MALDEN WAY KINGSTON BY PASS
KINGSTON BY-PASS
A3
Malden
CHURCH RD
B284
Hogsmill River
London Loop & Thames Down Link
Corpus Christi RC Prim Sch
Superstores
Kingspark Bsns Ctr
LC Ind Est
Allot Gdns
Recn Gd
Sp Gd
Pavs
T Cts
Bwg Gn
Liby
Sch
The Study Sch
Richard Challoner Sch
Malden CE Prim Sch
Knollmead Prim Sch
Coombe Boys' Sch
Shannon Cnr Ret Pk
Shannon Commercial Ctr
Beverley Brook
Beverley Pk
Kingston upon Thames
Merton
Manor Pk
Tenn Cts
Pl Fld
Mobile Home
Grand Avenue Prim Sch
MOUNT PLEASANT RD
STAFFORD RD
BEECH GR
ELM RD
MOUNT RD
POPLAR GR
CHESTNUT GR
LIME GR
SYCAMORE GR
BEACONSFIELD RD
SALISBURY RD
DUKES AVE
MALDEN HILL
KINGS AVE
COOMBE GDNS
BLAGDON RD
CAMBRIDGE RD
GROVE
ALRIC AVE
ORCHARD AVE
ROSEBERY AVE
CAMBRIDGE AVE
POTTERS GR
FRANKS AVE
GREEN LA
COTSFORD AVE
WINDSOR AVE
SOUTH LA
NELSON RD
THETFORD RD
LYNTON RD
SELWYN RD
ETON AVE
WESTBURY RD
CAVENDISH RD
CROMWELL AVE
KNIGHTWOOD CRES
BRAMSHAW RISE
AMBERWOOD RISE
MINSTEAD WAY
ALDRIDGE RISE
LYNDHURST DR
PORTLAND AVE
HOLLINGTON CRES
PURBECK AVE
BROADLANDS WAY
SHEEPHOUSE WAY
NEWHOUSE CL
BROCKENHURST AVE
FULLBROOKS AVE
FOREST SIDE
THE MANOR DR
LEYFIELD
HIGHDOWN
MANOR DR N
LAWRENCE AVE
ELMBRIDGE AVE
ELGAR AVE
GRENVILLE CL
RALEIGH DR
WARREN DR S
KNOLLMEAD
ELMDENE
ALPINE AVE
COLLINGWOOD AVE
SOUTHWOOD DR
BURFORD RD
BROADMEAD AVE
MALDEN GREEN AVE
MAYFAIR AVE
DOWNFIELD
THE HOLLANDS
6 TREVELYAN CT
7 MARLFIELD CT
8 RYEHILL CT
9 COLUMBIA CT
NEVADA CL 1
OREGON CL 2
CKWOOD CT 3
WINDRUSH 4

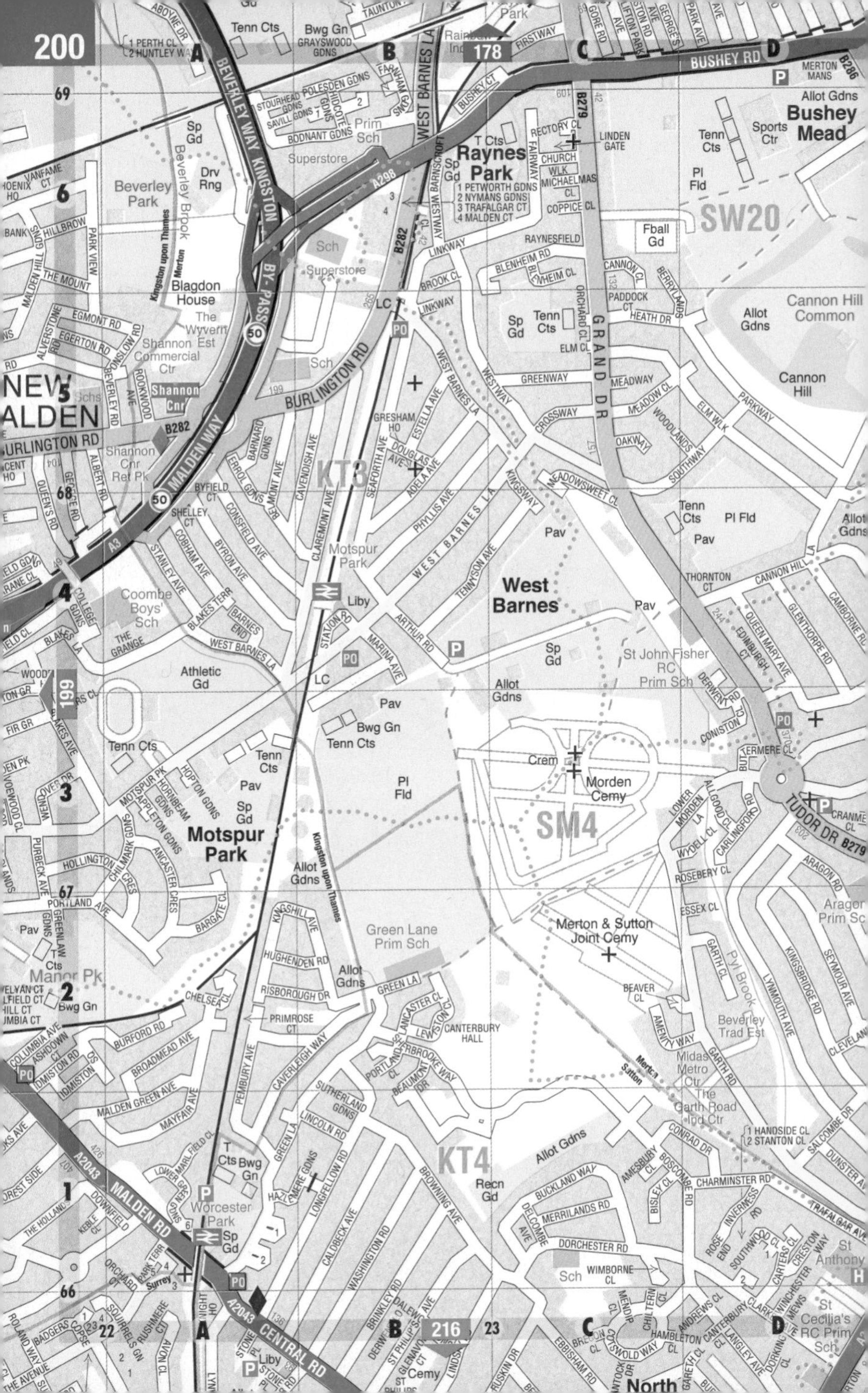
A
B
C
D
178
BUSHEY RD
MERTON MANS
B286
ABOYNE DR
1 PERTH CL
2 HUNTLEY WAY
Tenn Cts
Bwg Gn
GRAYSWOOD GDNS
TAUNTON
FIRSTWAY
Raynes Park
Allot Gdns
Bushey Mead
Sports Ctr
Tenn Cts
Pl Fld
SW20
BEVERLEY WAY KINGSTON BY-PASS
WEST BARNES LA
BUSHEY CT
STOURHEAD GDNS
POLESDEN GDNS
SAVILL GDNS
HIDCOTE GDNS
BODNANT GDNS
FARNHAM GDNS
Prim Sch
Superstore
Sp Gd
Drv Rng
Beverley Park
Beverley Brook
T Cts
Raynes Park
RECTORY CL
LINDEN GATE
CHURCH WLK
MICHAELMAS CL
COPPICE CL
FAIRWAY
WESTWAY
1 PETWORTH GDNS
2 NYMANS GDNS
3 TRAFALGAR CT
4 MALDEN CT
A298
B282
B279
Sch
Superstore
LINKWAY
RAYNESFIELD
BLENHEIM RD
BROOK CL
Fball Gd
CANNON CL
BERRYLANDS
PADDOCK CT
HEATH DR
ORCHARD CL
ELM CL
GRAND DR
Cannon Hill Common
Allot Gdns
Cannon Hill
VANFAME CT
PHOENIX HO
HILLBROW
PARK VIEW
THE MOUNT
MALDEN HILL GDNS
Kingston upon Thames
Merton
Blagdon House
The Wyvern Est
Shannon Commercial Ctr
EGMONT RD
EGERTON RD
ALVERSTONE RD
ONSLOW RD
ROOKWOOD AVE
BEVERLEY RD
NEW MALDEN
Schs
Shannon Cnr
BURLINGTON RD
Sch
LC
PO
Sp Gd
Tenn Cts
GREENWAY
MEADWAY
MEADOW CL
WOODLANDS
ELM WLK
PARKWAY
CROSSWAY
OAKWAY
SOUTHWAY
Shannon Cnr Ret Pk
MALDEN WAY
A3
50
GRESHAM HO
ESTELLA AVE
DOUGLAS AVE
ADELA AVE
SEAFORTH AVE
KT3
BARNARD GDNS
ERROL GDNS
BELMONT AVE
CAVENDISH AVE
CLAREMONT AVE
BYFIELD CT
SHELLEY CT
CONSFIELD AVE
QUEEN'S RD
GEORGE RD
ALBERT RD
68
PHYLLIS AVE
WEST BARNES LA
KINGSWAY
MEADOWSWEET CL
TENNYSON AVE
Pav
Tenn Cts
Pl Fld
Pav
Allot Gdns
THORNTON CT
CANNON HILL LA
GLENTHORPE RD
CAMBORNE RD
QUEEN MARY AVE
EDINBURGH CT
STANLEY AVE
COBHAM AVE
BYRON AVE
Motspur Park
Liby
West Barnes
Pav
4
COLLEGE GDNS
Coombe Boys' Sch
BLAKES TERR
BARNES END
THE GRANGE
WEST BARNES LA
STATION RD
MARINA AVE
ARTHUR RD
P
Sp Gd
St John Fisher RC Prim Sch
DERWENT RD
CONISTON CL
BUTTERMERE CL
Athletic Gd
199
LC
Pav
Bwg Gn
Tenn Cts
Allot Gdns
Crem
Morden Cemy
SM4
TUDOR DR
CRANMER CL
Tenn Cts
Tenn Cts
Pav
Sp Gd
Pl Fld
3
MOTSPUR PK
HORNBEAM GDNS
HOPTON GDNS
APPLETON GDNS
Motspur Park
LOWER MORDEN LA
ALLGOOD CL
CARLINGFORD RD
WYDELL CL
ROSEBERY CL
ARAGON RD
Aragon Prim Sc
HOLLINGTON CRES
CHILMARK GDNS
ANCASTER CRES
BARGATE CL
PURBECK AVE
PORTLAND AVE
67
Kingston upon Thames
Allot Gdns
KINGSHILL AVE
Green Lane Prim Sch
ESSEX CL
GARTH CL
Merton & Sutton Joint Cemy
Pav
T Cts
Manor Pk
GREENLAW GDNS
2
Bwg Gn
HUGHENDEN RD
RISBOROUGH DR
Allot Gdns
GREEN LA
BEAVER CL
Pyl Brook
LYMOUTH AVE
KINGSBRIDGE RD
SEYMOUR AVE
CHELSEA CL
PRIMROSE CT
LANCASTER CL
LEWSTON CL
CANTERBURY HALL
AMENITY WAY
Beverley Trad Est
CLEVELAND
COLUMBIA AVE
ASHDOWN CT
BURFORD RD
BROADMEAD AVE
IDMISTON RD
PO
PEMBURY AVE
CAVERLEIGH WAY
PORTLAND CL
SHERBROOKE WAY
BEAUMONT DR
Midas Metro Ctr
The Garth Road Ind Ctr
GARTH RD
Merton
Sutton
MALDEN GREEN AVE
MAYFAIR AVE
SUTHERLAND GDNS
LINCOLN RD
1 HANDSIDE CL
2 STANTON CL
SALCOMBE DR
CONRAD DR
DUNSTER AVE
A2043
MALDEN RD
MARLFIELD CL
T Cts
Bwg Gn
LOWER GREEN GDNS
HAZLEMERE GDNS
LONGFELLOW RD
KT4
Allot Gdns
BUCKLAND WAY
AMESBURY CL
BOSCOMBE RD
CHARMINSTER RD
TRAFALGAR AVE
1
THE HOLLANDS
KEBLE CL
DOWNFIELD
P
Worcester Park
Sp Gd
CALDBECK AVE
WASHINGTON RD
BROWNING AVE
Recn Gd
MERRILANDS RD
DELCOMBE AVE
BISLEY CL
INVERNESS RD
ROSE END
SOUTHWOOD CL
CARTERS CL
CRESTON WAY
St Anthony
66
ORCHARD CT
PARK TERR
Surrey
PO
DORCHESTER RD
Sch
WIMBORNE CL
MENDIP CL
CHILTERN CL
ANDREWS CL
CANTERBURY CL
CLARKS MEWS
WINCHESTER
St Cecilia's RC Prim Sch
H
A2043 CENTRAL RD
A
B
216
23
C
D
22
ROLAND WAY
BADGERS COPSE
SQUIRRELS GN
RUSHMERE CT
AVON CL
THE AVENUE
NIGHT HO
STONE PL
Liby
P
BRINKLEY RD
DALEWOOD
ST PHILIP'S AVE
GLENAVON CT
Cemy
RUSKIN DR
EBBISHAM RD
BRECON CL
COTSWOLD WAY
HAMBLETON CL
GARETH CL
LANGLEY AVE
DORKING CL
North

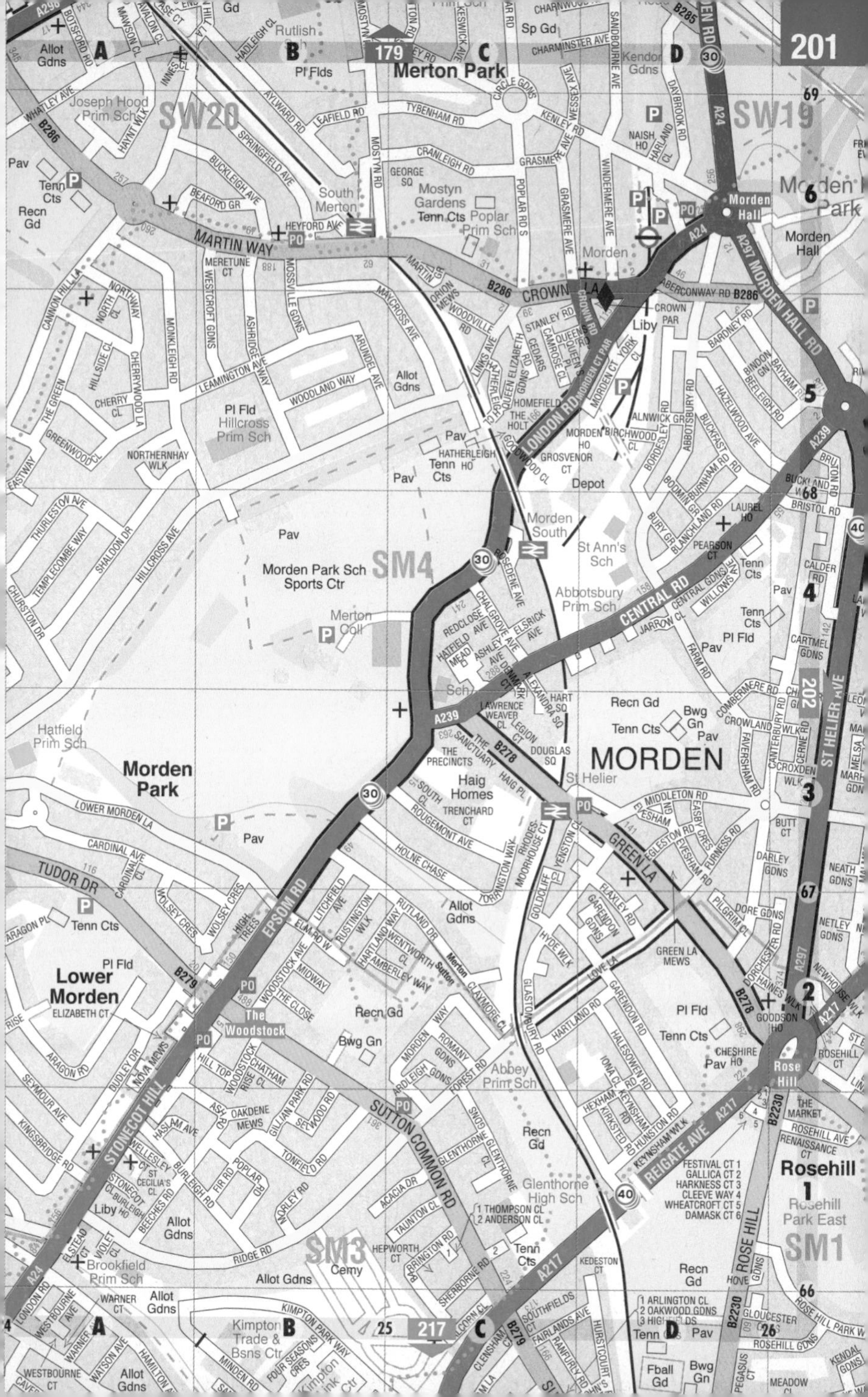

Merton Park
SW20
SW19
SM4
SM3
SM1
MORDEN
Morden Park
Lower Morden
Rosehill
Morden Hall
South Merton
Morden South
St Helier
Rose Hill
MARTIN WAY
CROWN LA
LONDON RD
MORDEN HALL RD
CENTRAL RD
EPSOM RD
STONECOT HILL
SUTTON COMMON RD
REIGATE AVE
ROSE HILL
ST HELIER AVE
GREEN LA
TUDOR DR
Morden Park Sch Sports Ctr
Merton Coll
Hillcross Prim Sch
Joseph Hood Prim Sch
Poplar Prim Sch
Abbotsbury Prim Sch
St Ann's Sch
Abbey Prim Sch
Glenthorne High Sch
Brookfield Prim Sch
Hatfield Prim Sch
Haig Homes
The Woodstock
Kimpton Trade & Bsns Ctr
Rosehill Park East
1 THOMPSON CL
2 ANDERSON CL
FESTIVAL CT 1
GALLICA CT 2
HARKNESS CT 3
CLEEVE WAY 4
WHEATCROFT CT 5
DAMASK CT 6
1 ARLINGTON CL
2 OAKWOOD GDNS
3 HIGHFIELDS
179
202
217

202
A
B
C
D
180
218
SW19
CR4
SM4
SM5
SM1
Morden Hall Park
Morden Hall
Croydon Tramlink
Phipps Bridge
Belgrave Walk
Puma Trade Pk
Denvale Trade Pk
Ravensbury Park
River Wandle
Benedict Prim Sch
Boundary Bsns Ct
Cricket Green Sch
Melrose Sch
MITCHAM
Mitcham
Cranmer Prim Sch
The Canons
Abbey Ind Est
Connaught Bsns Ctr
Chancery Gate Bsns Ctr
Capital Ind Est
Eagle Trad Est
Grace Bsns Ctr
Poulter Park
Wandle Trad Est & Tech Pk
Bishopsford Com Sch
Green Wrythe Prim Sch
St Helier
Sutton Arena
Tweeddale Prim Sch
Wandle Valley Sch
Moreton Gn
Rosehill
Rosehill Park East
Rose Hill
Greenshaw High Sch
Merton
Sutton
MORDEN HALL RD
MORDEN RD
ST HELIER AVE
BISHOPSFORD RD
LONDON RD
CRICKET GN
MADEIRA RD
CRANMER RD
WRYTHE LA
ROSE HILL
MIDDLETON RD
UPPER GN W
A24
A297
A239
A217
A236
B2230
B278
B286

MITCHAM
Mitcham Common
Mitcham Junction
CROYDON RD
WINDMILL RD
CARSHALTON RD
LONDON RD
BEDDINGTON LA
COMMONSIDE EAST
MANOR RD
Croydon Tramlink
Beddington Lane
Beddington Corner
Beddington Sewage Treatment Works
Beddington Farm
Hackbridge
CR4
CR0
SM6
181
204
219
A
B
C
D

A
B
C
D
182
203
220
SW16
CR4
CR7
CR0
Thornton Heath
Broad Green
LONDON RD
A23
A235
A236
MITCHAM RD
B266
BRIGSTOCK RD
THORNTON RD
PURLEY WAY
SUMNER RD
A213
B272
Thornton Heath Pond
Lombard Rdbt
Croydon Tramlink
Therapia Lane
Ampere Way
Waddon Marsh
Harris Acad
William Morris Prim Sch
Recn Gd
Liby
Winterbourne Jun & Inf Schs
Gonville Prim Sch
Crem
Cemy
Allot Gdns
Fball Gd
The Archbishop Lanfranc Sch
Peall Rd Ind Est
Thornton Rd Ind Est
Mayday University
The Tramsheds Ind Est
Valley Point Ind Est
Prologis Pk
Pioneers Ind Pk
Beddington Trad Est
Lombard Bsns Pk
Superstore
Elmwood Schs
St James the Great RC Prim Sch
TA Ctr
The Pilton Est
Peterwood Pk
Ind Est
1 POWELL TERR
2 PERALTE TERR
3 BUCKINGHAM RD
4 BUCKINGHAM CT
5 LINCOLN CT
6 SUSSEX CT
7 LINCOLN RD
WESTFIELD RD 1
LOWER CHURCH ST 2
BOURNE ST 3

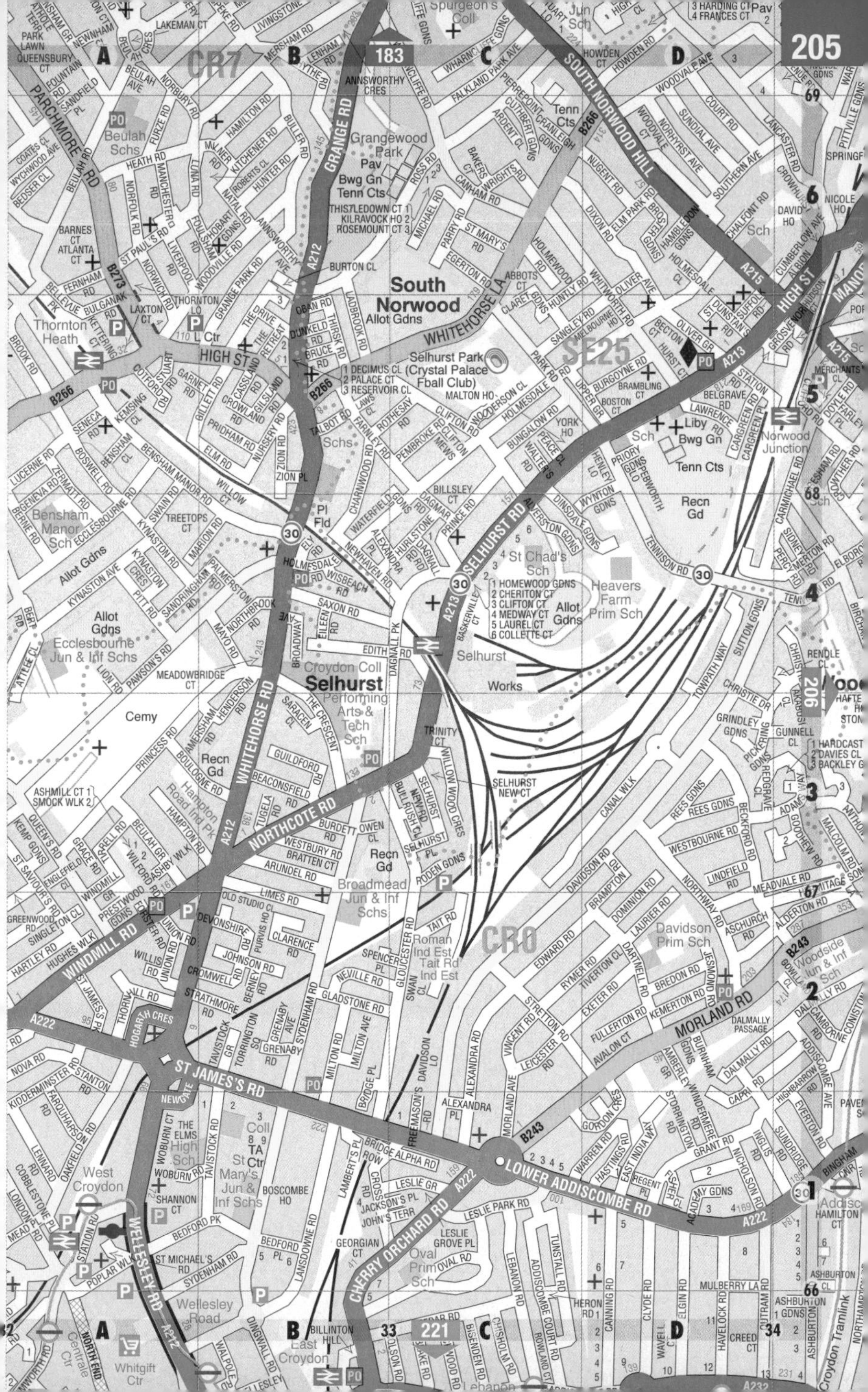

South Norwood
Selhurst
SE25
CR7
CR0
Thornton Heath
West Croydon
East Croydon
Norwood Junction
Selhurst Park (Crystal Palace Fball Club)
Grangewood Park
Croydon Coll
Cemy
Allot Gdns
Recn Gd
Heavers Farm Prim Sch
Davidson Prim Sch
Ecclesbourne Jun & Inf Schs
Bensham Manor Sch
Broadmead Jun & Inf Schs
Selhurst Performing Arts & Tech Sch
Roman Ind Est
Tait Rd Ind Est
Oval Prim Sch
Wellesley Road
Whitgift Ctr
Centrale Ctr
Beulah Schs
St Chad's Sch
Woodside Jun & Inf Sch
WHITEHORSE RD
SELHURST RD
GRANGE RD
SOUTH NORWOOD HILL
HIGH ST
WHITEHORSE LA
NORTHCOTE RD
WINDMILL RD
ST JAMES'S RD
LOWER ADDISCOMBE RD
MORLAND RD
CHERRY ORCHARD RD
WELLESLEY RD
PARCHMORE RD
A212
A213
A215
A222
A232
B266
B273
B243
183
206
221

Woodside
Addiscombe
Shirley
Elmers End
South Norwood Country Park
SE25
BR3
CR0
Norwood Junction
Birkbeck
Harrington Road
Arena
Woodside
Blackhorse Lane
Addiscombe
Ashburton Park
Ashburton Learning Village
Shirley Oaks
Long Lane Wood
Sports Arena
Ryelands Prim Sch
Croydon Road Ind Est
Chaffinch Bsns Pk
Monks Orchard Sch
Churchfields Prim Sch
Superstore
PENGE RD
PORTLAND RD
SPRING LA
LONG LA
LOWER ADDISCOMBE RD
SHIRLEY RD
ELMERS END RD
HIGH ST
MANOR RD
WOODSIDE GN
PRIMROSE LA
184
205
222

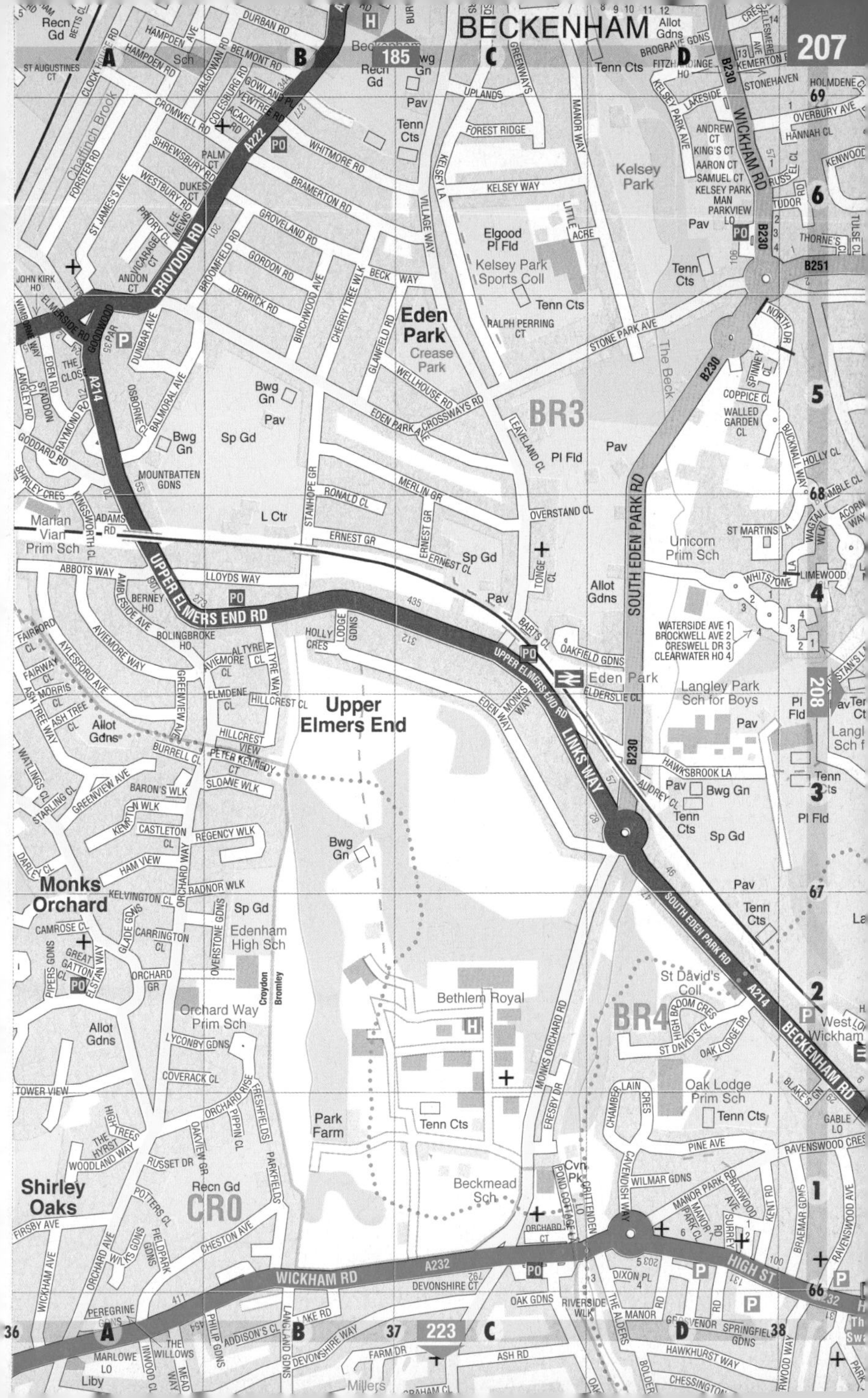
Upper Elmers End
Eden Park
Monks Orchard
Shirley Oaks
Kelsey Park
BR3
BR4
CR0
Crease Park
Bethlem Royal
Edenham High Sch
Orchard Way Prim Sch
Unicorn Prim Sch
Langley Park Sch for Boys
Kelsey Park Sports Coll
St David's Coll
Oak Lodge Prim Sch
Beckmead Sch
Park Farm
Marian Vian Prim Sch
CROYDON RD
UPPER ELMERS END RD
SOUTH EDEN PARK RD
WICKHAM RD
LINKS WAY
BECKENHAM RD
HIGH ST
185
208
223
36
37
38

186
Shortlands
BR2
BR3
Park Langley
BR4
Langley Park
Langley Park Sch for Girls
Highfield Jun & Inf Schs
Cupola Wood
Pickhurst Jun Sch
Pickhurst Inf Sch
Pickhurst Green
Hawes Down Schs
West Wickham
Hayes
Oak Lodge Prim Sch
WICKHAM RD
HAYES LA
WESTMORELAND RD
PICKHURST LA
BECKENHAM RD
STATION RD
HIGH ST
B230
B251
B228
A214
A232
207
224

BROMLEY
BR1
BR2
Bromley South
Masons Hill
Kentish Way
Westmoreland Rd
Hayes Rd
Hayes La
Hayes St
Homesdale Rd
Bromley Common
Page Heath La
Norman Park
Fisher's Wood
Scrogginhill Wood
Brook Wood
Mazzards Wood
Hayes
Hayes Street Farm
Bromley Coll of F & H Ed
Rookery Lake
Oakley House
Ravens Bourne
187
225
210

Bickley
BICKLEY PARK RD
A222
PAGE HEATH LA
Bickley Park Sch
Bickley
BR1
Bromley High Sch
Jubilee Park Country Park
Thornet Wood
BR5
St James RC Prim Sch
Southborough Prim Sch
BR2
Southborough
Bromley Common
Parkfield Recn Gd
Bishop Justus CE Sch
Princes Plain Prim Sch
Prince's Plain
Scrubs Farm
Crofton Heath
Sparrow Wood
London Loop
BROMLEY COMMON
A21
A233
Knowlehill Wood
Knowl Wood
188
209
226

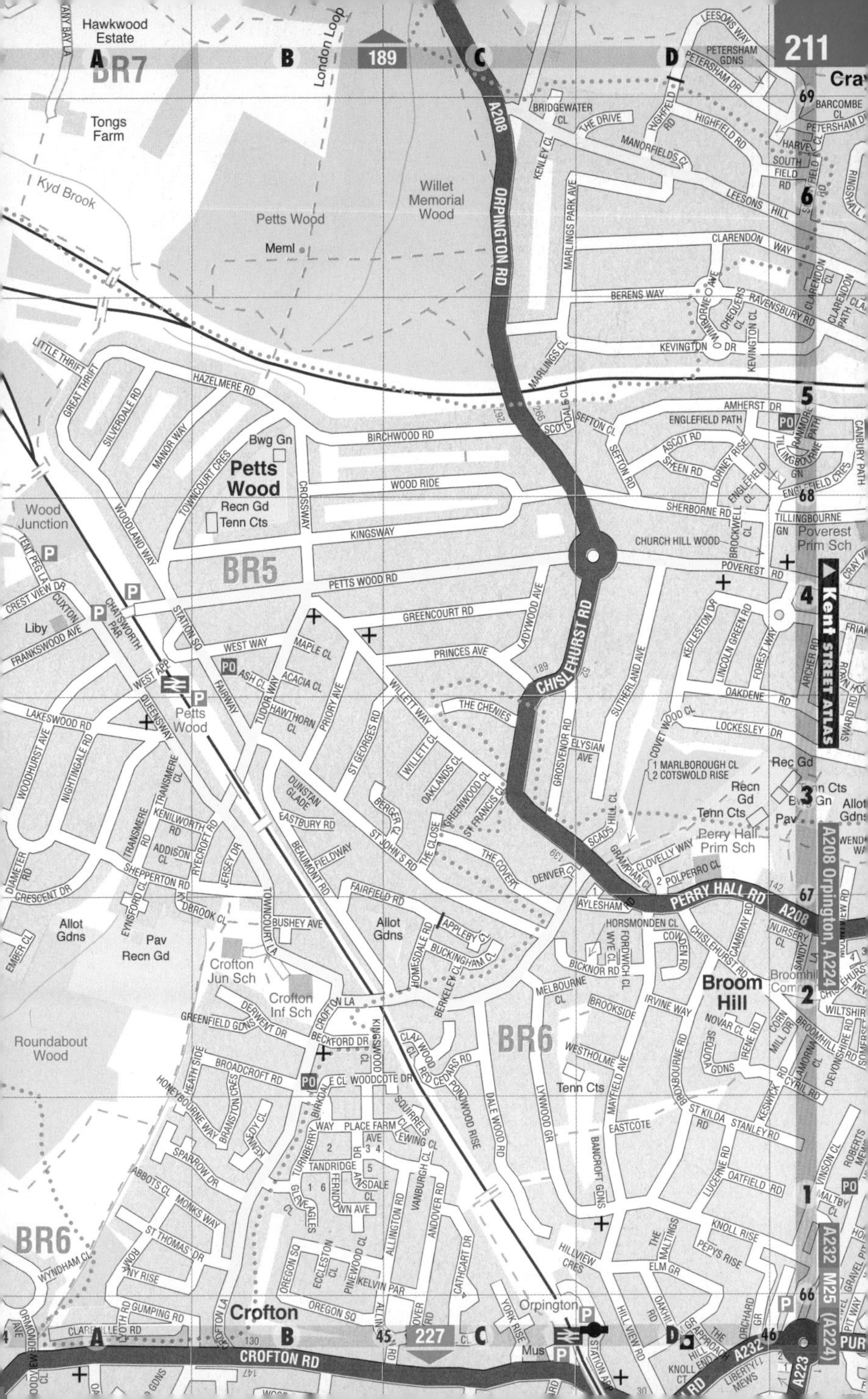

Hawkwood Estate
BR7
Tongs Farm
Kyd Brook
Petts Wood
Meml
Willet Memorial Wood
London Loop
189
A208
ORPINGTON RD
BRIDGEWATER CL
THE DRIVE
KENLEY CL
MARLINGS PARK AVE
HIGHFIELD RD
MANORFIELDS CL
LEESONS WAY
PETERSHAM GDNS
PETERSHAM DR
LEESONS HILL
CLARENDON WAY
BERENS WAY
RAVENSBURY RD
KEVINGTON DR
KEVINGTON CL
CHEQUERS CL
MARLINGS CL
LITTLE THRIFT
GREAT THRIFT
HAZELMERE RD
SILVERDALE RD
MANOR WAY
BIRCHWOOD RD
Bwg Gn
Petts Wood
Recn Gd
Tenn Cts
TOWNCOURT CRES
CROSSWAY
WOOD RIDE
KINGSWAY
BR5
PETTS WOOD RD
WOODLAND WAY
Wood Junction
TENT PEG LA
CREST VIEW DR
CUXTON
Liby
FRANKSWOOD AVE
CHATSWORTH PAR
STATION SQ
GREENCOURT RD
WEST WAY
MAPLE CL
ASH CL
ACACIA CL
PRINCES AVE
LADYWOOD AVE
CHISLEHURST RD
SCOTSDALE CL
SEFTON CL
SEFTON RD
AMHERST DR
ENGLEFIELD PATH
ASCOT RD
SHEEN RD
DORNEY RISE
ENGLEFIELD CL
ENGLEFIELD CRES
TILLINGBOURNE GN
SHERBORNE RD
CHURCH HILL WOOD
BROCKWELL CL
Poverest Prim Sch
POVEREST RD
KEDLESTON DR
LINCOLN GREEN RD
FOREST WAY
OAKDENE RD
LOCKESLEY DR
COVET WOOD CL
SUTHERLAND AVE
ELYSIAN AVE
GROSVENOR RD
1 MARLBOROUGH CL
2 COTSWOLD RISE
Rec Gd
Recn Gd
Tenn Cts
Perry Hall Prim Sch
WEST APP
QUEENSWAY
Petts Wood
LAKESWOOD RD
WOODHURST AVE
NIGHTINGALE RD
TRANSMERE CL
TRANSMERE RD
KENILWORTH RD
ADDISON CL
RYECROFT RD
JERSEY DR
FAIRWAY
TUDOR WAY
HAWTHORN CL
PRIORY AVE
ST GEORGES RD
WILLETT WAY
WILLETT CL
OAKLANDS CL
GREENWOOD CL
ST FRANCIS CL
THE CHENIES
DUNSTAN GLADE
EASTBURY RD
BERGER CL
ST JOHN'S RD
THE CLOSE
THE COVERT
DENVER CL
SCADS HILL CL
GRAMPIAN CL
CLOVELLY WAY
2 POLPERRO CL
PERRY HALL RD
A208
AYLESHAM RD
DIAMETER RD
CRESCENT DR
SHEPPERTON RD
EYNSFORD CL
BEAUMONT RD
FIELDWAY
FAIRFIELD RD
APPLEBY CL
BUSHEY AVE
Allot Gdns
Pav
Recn Gd
EMBER CL
TOWNCOURT LA
HOMESDALE RD
BUCKINGHAM CL
BERKELEY CL
Crofton Jun Sch
Crofton Inf Sch
CROFTON LA
HORSMONDEN CL
WYE CL
FORDWICH CL
COWDEN RD
BICKNOR RD
MELBOURNE CL
CHISLEHURST RD
CAMBRAY RD
Broom Hill
IRVINE WAY
BROOKSIDE
NURSERY CL
SANDY LA
Broomhill Com
NOVAR CL
IRENE RD
SEQUOIA GDNS
CORN MILL DR
BROOMHILL RD
WILTSHIRE RD
DEVONSHIRE RD
CYRIL RD
Roundabout Wood
GREENFIELD GDNS
DERWENT DR
BROADCROFT RD
HEATH SIDE
BECKFORD DR
KINGSWOOD CL
CLAY WOOD CL
RED CEDARS RD
WESTHOLME
MAYFIELD AVE
BROXBOURNE RD
BR6
PO
WOODCOTE DR
HONEYBOURNE WAY
BRANSTON CRES
KENNEDY CL
PONDWOOD RISE
DALE WOOD RD
LYNWOOD GR
Tenn Cts
EASTCOTE
ST KILDA RD
STANLEY RD
BIRKDALE CL
SQUIRRELS CL
PLACE FARM AVE
EWING CL
TURNBERRY WAY
SPARROW DR
TANDRIDGE DR
FERNDOWN AVE
ANSDALE CL
VANBURGH CL
ANDOVER RD
BANCROFT GDNS
LUCERNE RD
OATFIELD RD
VINSON CL
ROBERTS MEWS
MALTBY CL
ABBOTS CL
MONKS WAY
GLENEAGLES CL
ALLINGTON RD
BR6
ST THOMAS' DR
WYNDHAM CL
KNOLL RISE
PEPYS RISE
THE MALTINGS
ELM GR
HILLVIEW CRES
OREGON SQ
ECCLESTON CL
PINEWOOD CL
KELVIN PAR
CATHCART DR
YORK RISE
Orpington
HILL VIEW RD
OAKHILL RD
ORCHARD GR
GUMPING RD
Crofton
CLAREVILLE RD
CROFTON LA
CROFTON RD
227
Mus
STATION APP
KNOLL END CT
GR APPROACH
THE HILL
A232
LIBERTY MEWS
A223
M25 (A224)
A232
A208 Orpington, A224
Kent STREET ATLAS
PUR
Cray
BARCOMBE CL
PETERSHAM DR
HARVEL
SOUTHFIELD RD
RINGSHALL
CLARENDON CL
CLARENDON PATH
CANBURY PATH
RANMORE PATH
Allot Gdns
Bwls Gn
Pav
A
B
C
D
A
B
C
D
69
6
5
68
4
3
67
2
1
66
45
46

A
B
C
D
196
66
6
5
65
4
3
64
2
1
63
14
15
Ditton Common
IMBER CL
CARLETON CL
VILLAS
WESTON PARK CL
WESTON GN
WESTON RD
Sp Gd
Games Ct
Pav
BRUNSWICK CL 2
PORTSMOUTH RD
PAGET PL
WESTON LO
LYNWOOD RD
CRANLEIGH RD
CRANBROOK DR
BLAIR AVE
THE WOODLANDS
WESTON GREEN RD
B3379
A309
HAMPTON COURT WAY
WOODFIELD HO 1
TWICKENHAM PL 2
A307
Allot Gdns
KT7
ARRAN WAY
DOUGLAS RD
WOODEND
LOWER GREEN RD
Esher
Thames Ditton & Esher
ORLEANS CL
STATION RD
CH
HAVEN PL
HAVEN CT
MACAULAY AVE
WOODFIELD RD
BOURNE CL
LYNN
WESSEX CL
Recn Gd
PRIORS WOOD
Scilly Isles
YEW TREE COTTS
COUCHMORE AVE
Race Course
GRANTS COTTS
WESTMONT RD
SOUTHMONT RD
MONTGOMERY AVE
EASTMONT RD
Hinchley Wood
ROYSTON CT
COTSWOLD CL
MANOR RD N
MANOR DR
SANDOWN GATE
HILLMONT RD
GIBSON CT
MEADOW CL
Hinchley Wood
KINGSTON BY-PASS
STATION APP
PO
HINCHLAY MANOR
MANOR DR
Surrey STREET ATLAS
Sandown Park
PORTSMOUTH RD
WEMBLEY CL
LITTLEWORTH COMMON RD
Littleworth Common
LITTLEWORTH RD
HEATHSIDE CL
HEATHSIDE
MEDINA AVE
HAREFIELD
HINCHLEY DR
HILLCREST GDNS
HINCHLEY CL
A244 Walton-on-Thames
PEMBERTON PL
CARRICK GATE
HILLBROW RD
HILLBROW CT
SANDOWN HO
ASHBURNHAM PK
LITTLEWORTH PL
RENATES
GREENWAYS
Telegraph Hill
MANOR RD S
ESHER GN
WARREN
A307
Civic Office
SANDOWN RD
LITTLEWORTH LA
CH
Rugby Gd
Semaphore House
PO
Liby
HIGH ST
OLD CHURCH PATH
Bwg Gn
WILLOWMERE
NEW RD
MARTINEAU CL
LITTLEMEAD
WOOTTON
ESHER
Tenn Cts
Sp Gd
Tenn Cts
VICTORIA PL
A244
CARRINGTON PL
SANDOWN AVE
LITTLEWORTH RD
KT10
TELEGRAPH LA
A307 Cobham, A3 (A245)
CLAREMONT LA
GRANTLEY PL
SIMMONS GATE
CRANFORD RISE
ESHER PARK AVE
ACORNS WAY
BROOMFIELDS
LITTLEWORTH AVE
Bwg Gn
STOCKFIELD RD
CAVENDISH DR
OAKEN LA
BROOM CL
HOMESTEAD GDNS
Allot Gdns
FIR TREE CL
Esher CE Prim Sch
ROSEBRIARS
Tenn Cts
RYTHE RD
Slough Farm
CHARLOTTE CT
LYNNE WLK
HEATHERSET CL
RALEIGH DR
ROSE COTTS
ASTON RD
SIMMIL RD
APPLEGARTH
CLARE HILL
BRACONDALE
MILBOURNE LA
CHADWORTH WAY
LOSEBERRY RD
STATION RD
NORFOLK RD
THE AVENUE
Jun Sch
COMPTON CL
ARBROOK LA
MEADOW RD
WOODBOURNE DR
THE ROUNDWAY
CLAREMONT DR
Pl Fld
ORCHARD WAY
BRENDON CL
The Rythe
JUDGE WLK
Tenn Cts
WESTBURY AVE
HAYMEADS DR
BRENDON DR
STATION WAY
HARE LA
OAKEN DR
BROOKFIELD GDNS
TORRINGTON RD
BROOKFIELD
HOME FARM CL
HIGH GARTH
ARBROOK CHASE
THE PARADE
TORRINGTON CL
CEDAR WLK
WOODWARD CL
DERWENT CL
ELM RD
ST LEONARD'S RD
LAKESIDE DR
Milbourne Lodge Sen Sch
Claygate
THE WILLOWS
SYDNEY TERR 1
SYDNEY COTTS 2
SIM'S COTTS 3
HIGH ST
THE GREEN
PO
COPSEM DR
ALBANY CRES
ATHLONE
FOLEY COTTS
ARBROOK HALL
CLAREMONT
ELM GDNS
HURSTBOURNE
COPSEM WAY
MALBROOK
FIRS CL
FAWCUS CL
THE FIRS
DALMORE AVE
BLAKEDEN DR
CLAREMONT END
FOLEY RD
FOLEY MEWS
CHURCH RD
THE ELMS
Stable Pond
COPSEM LA
Loseberry Farm
KINGS MEAD PK
CORNWALL AVE 1
REDRUTH GDNS 2
THE CAUSEWAY
Claygate Prim Sch
Recn Gd
Claremont Park
GORDON RD
Rowan Prep Sch
Claygate
FEE FARM RD
CLAREMONT RD
FOLEY RD
FITZALAN RD
MEADWAY
CLAYGATE LODGE CL
WOODLANDS CL
Arbrook Common
BEACONSFIELD RD
BEACONSFIELD GDNS
Rowan Prep Sch
COVERTS RD
A244
QUEEN ANNE DR
VALE RD
LANE GDNS
FOXWARREN
VALE CROFT
Allot Gdns
A244 Leatherhead, A3
Homingdon Farm

Long Ditton
197
KT7
KT6
KT10
KT9
Hinchley Wood Sch & Sixth Form Coll
Hinchley Wood Prim Sch
Hill Park Nurseries
Ditton Hill Nurseries
Manor House
Cemy
KINGSTON BY-PASS
A309
A3
A243
HOOK RD
LEATHERHEAD RD
WOODSTOCK LANE S
WOODSTOCK LANE N
The Waffrons
Surbiton
Manor Farm
Elm Farm
Lower Wood
Barwell
Barwell Bsns Pk
Lovelace Prim Sch
St Philip's Sch
Ellingham Prim Sch
Chessington South
Chessington
Claygate Common
214

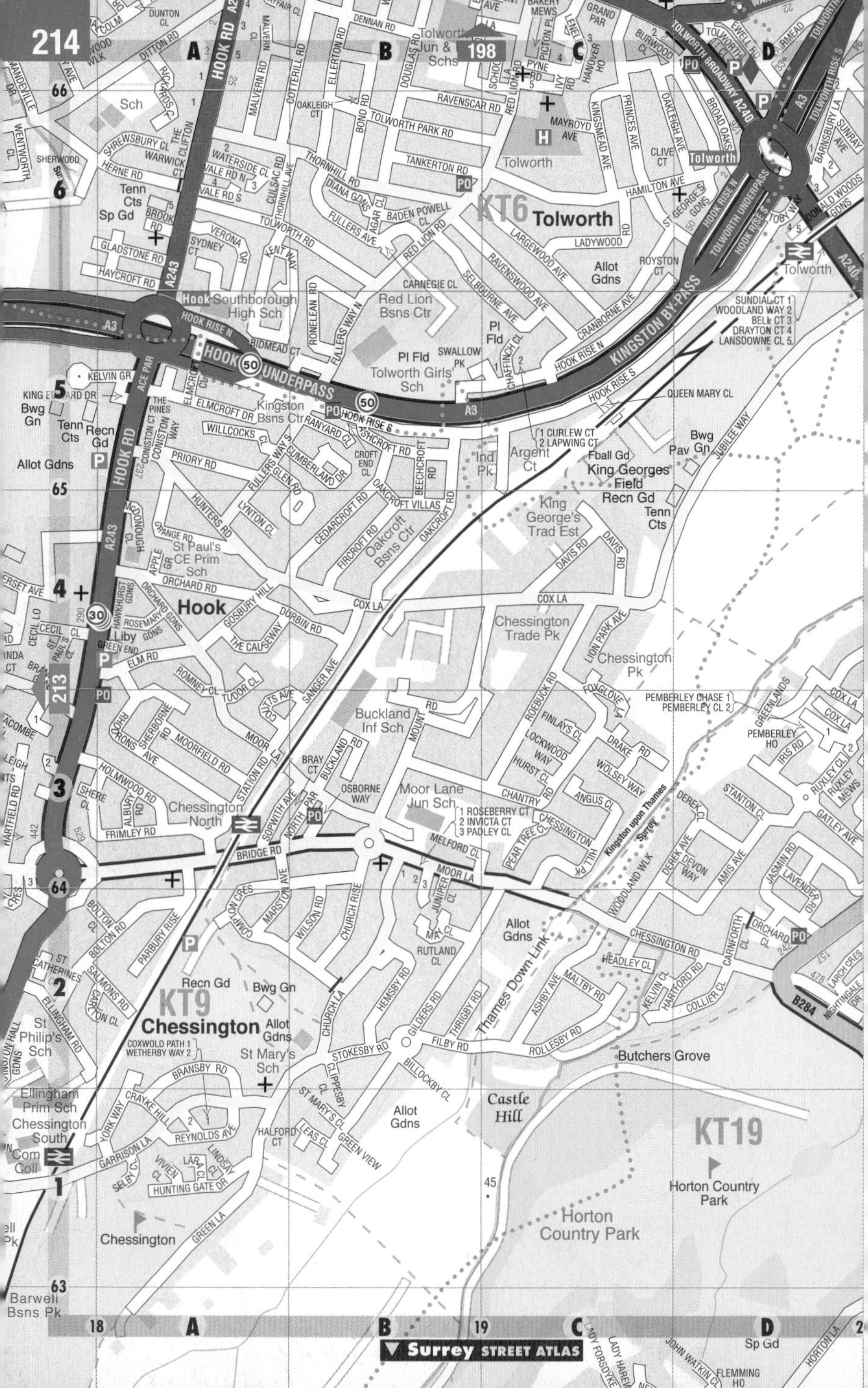
A
B
C
D
198
Tolworth Jun & Inf Schs
HOOK RD
A243
DITTON RD
DUNTON CL
MALVERN RD
COTTERILL RD
ELLERTON RD
DOUGLAS RD
DENNAN RD
BAKERY MEWS
GRAND PAR
PICTON PL
PYNE RD
IVY RD
HANOVER HO
BURWOOD CL
TOLWORTH BROADWAY
A240
EWELL RD
FAIRMEAD
66
Sch
RICHARDS CL
THE CLIFTON
WENTWORTH CL
SHERWOOD
SHREWSBURY CL
WARWICK CL
HERNE RD
WATERSIDE CL
VALE RD N
VALE RD S
CULSAC RD
THORNHILL AVE
OAKLEIGH CT
BOND RD
RAVENSCAR RD
TOLWORTH PARK RD
TANKERTON RD
THORNHILL RD
DIANA GDNS
AGAR CL
BADEN POWELL CL
FULLERS AVE
MAYROYD AVE
KINGSMEAD AVE
PRINCES AVE
OAKLEIGH AVE
BROAD OAKS
CLIVE CT
Tolworth
HAMILTON AVE
ST GEORGE'S GDNS
HOOK RISE N
TOLWORTH UNDERPASS
HOOK RISE S
TOLWORTH RISE S
A3
BARNSBURY LA
SUNRAY AVE
DONALD WOODS GDNS
TOBY WAY
6
Tenn Cts
Sp Gd
BROOK RD
VERONA DR
SYDNEY CT
KENT WAY
TOLWORTH RD
RED LION RD
KT6
Tolworth
LARGEWOOD AVE
LADYWOOD RD
Allot Gdns
ROYSTON CT
GLADSTONE RD
HAYCROFT RD
RAVENSWOOD AVE
SELBOURNE AVE
CARNEGIE CL
Red Lion Bsns Ctr
Hook
Southborough High Sch
RONELEAN RD
FULLERS WAY N
CRANBORNE AVE
KINGSTON BY-PASS
SUNDIAL CT 1
WOODLAND WAY 2
BELL CT 3
DRAYTON CT 4
LANSDOWNE CL 5
HOOK RISE N
BIDMEAD CT
Pl Fld
SWALLOW PK
CHAFFINCH CL
Tolworth Girls' Sch
HOOK UNDERPASS
5
KELVIN GR
KING EDWARD DR
ACE PAR
THE PINES
ELMCROFT CL
ELMCROFT DR
Kingston Bsns Ctr
RANYARD CL
HOOK RISE S
ASHCROFT RD
QUEEN MARY CL
Bwg Gn
Tenn Cts
Recn Gd
WILLCOCKS CL
CONISTON CT
CONISTON WAY
PRIORY RD
FULLERS WAY S
CUMBERLAND DR
CROFT END CL
BEECHCROFT RD
1 CURLEW CT
2 LAPWING CT
Ind Pk
Argent Ct
Fball Gd
King Georges Field
Recn Gd
Pav
Bwg Gn
JUBILEE WAY
Allot Gdns
65
HUNTERS RD
GLEN RD
LYNTON CL
CEDARCROFT RD
OAKCROFT VILLAS
OAKCROFT RD
Tenn Cts
King George's Trad Est
DAVIS RD
McDONOUGH CL
GRANGE RD
St Paul's CE Prim Sch
APPLE GR
FIRCROFT RD
Oakcroft Bsns Ctr
ORCHARD RD
4
SOMERSET AVE
HAWKHURST GDNS
ORCHARD GDNS
GOSBURY HILL
COX LA
Hook
CECIL CL
CECIL LO
ST PAUL'S CL
ROSEMARY GDNS
Liby
DURBIN RD
THE CAUSEWAY
Chessington Trade Pk
LION PARK AVE
Chessington Pk
GREEN END
ELM RD
213
ROMNEY CL
TUDOR CL
COUTTS AVE
SANGER AVE
ROEBUCK RD
FOXGLOVE LA
PEMBERLEY CHASE 1
PEMBERLEY CL 2
GREENLANDS
COX LA
RHODRONS AVE
SHERBORNE RD
MOORFIELD RD
MOOR LA
STATION RD
Buckland Inf Sch
MOUNT RD
FINLAYS CL
LOCKWOOD WAY
DRAKE RD
WOLSEY WAY
PEMBERLEY HO
IRIS RD
RUXLEY CL
RUXLEY MEWS
3
HOLMWOOD RD
SHERE CL
ALBURY RD
FRIMLEY RD
Chessington North
BRAY CT
BUCKLAND RD
OSBORNE WAY
Moor Lane Jun Sch
HURST CL
CHANTRY RD
ANGUS CL
DEREK CL
STANTON CL
GATLEY AVE
SOPWITH AVE
NORTH PAR
1 ROSEBERRY CT
2 INVICTA CT
3 PADLEY CL
PEAR TREE CL
CHESSINGTON HILL PK
Kingston upon Thames
Surrey
DEREK AVE
DEVON WAY
AMIS AVE
JASMIN RD
LAVENDER RD
HARTFIELD RD
BRIDGE RD
MELFORD CL
MOOR LA
64
BOLTON CL
BOLTON RD
PARBURY RISE
COMPTON CRES
MARSTON AVE
WILSON RD
CHURCH RISE
JUNIPER CL
MAY CL
Allot Gdns
WOODLAND WLK
ORCHARD CL
CHESSINGTON RD
CARNFORTH CL
LARCH CRES
ST CATHERINES CT
2
SALMONS RD
CARLTON CL
ELLINGHAM RD
Recn Gd
Bwg Gn
RUTLAND CL
HEMSBY RD
GILDERS RD
THRIGBY RD
Thames Down Link
ASHBY AVE
MALTBY RD
HEADLEY CL
KELVIN CL
HARTFORD RD
COLLIER CL
B284
NIGHTINGALE DR
KT9
Chessington
St Philip's Sch
COXWOLD PATH 1
WETHERBY WAY 2
Allot Gdns
St Mary's Sch
CHURCH LA
STOKESBY RD
FILBY RD
ROLLESBY RD
Butchers Grove
BRANSBY RD
CLIPPESBY CL
BILLOCKBY CL
Ellingham Prim Sch
Chessington South
Com Coll
YORK WAY
CRAYKE HILL
REYNOLDS AVE
HALFORD CT
ST MARY'S CL
LEAS CL
GREEN VIEW
Allot Gdns
Castle Hill
KT19
GARRISON LA
SELBY CL
VIVIEN CL
LARA CL
LINDSAY CL
HUNTING GATE DR
1
45
Horton Country Park
Horton Country Park
Chessington
GREEN LA
63
Barwell Bsns Pk
18
19
LADY FORSDYKE
LADY HAREMYS
JOHN WATKIN CL
FLEMMING HO
Sp Gd
HORTON LA

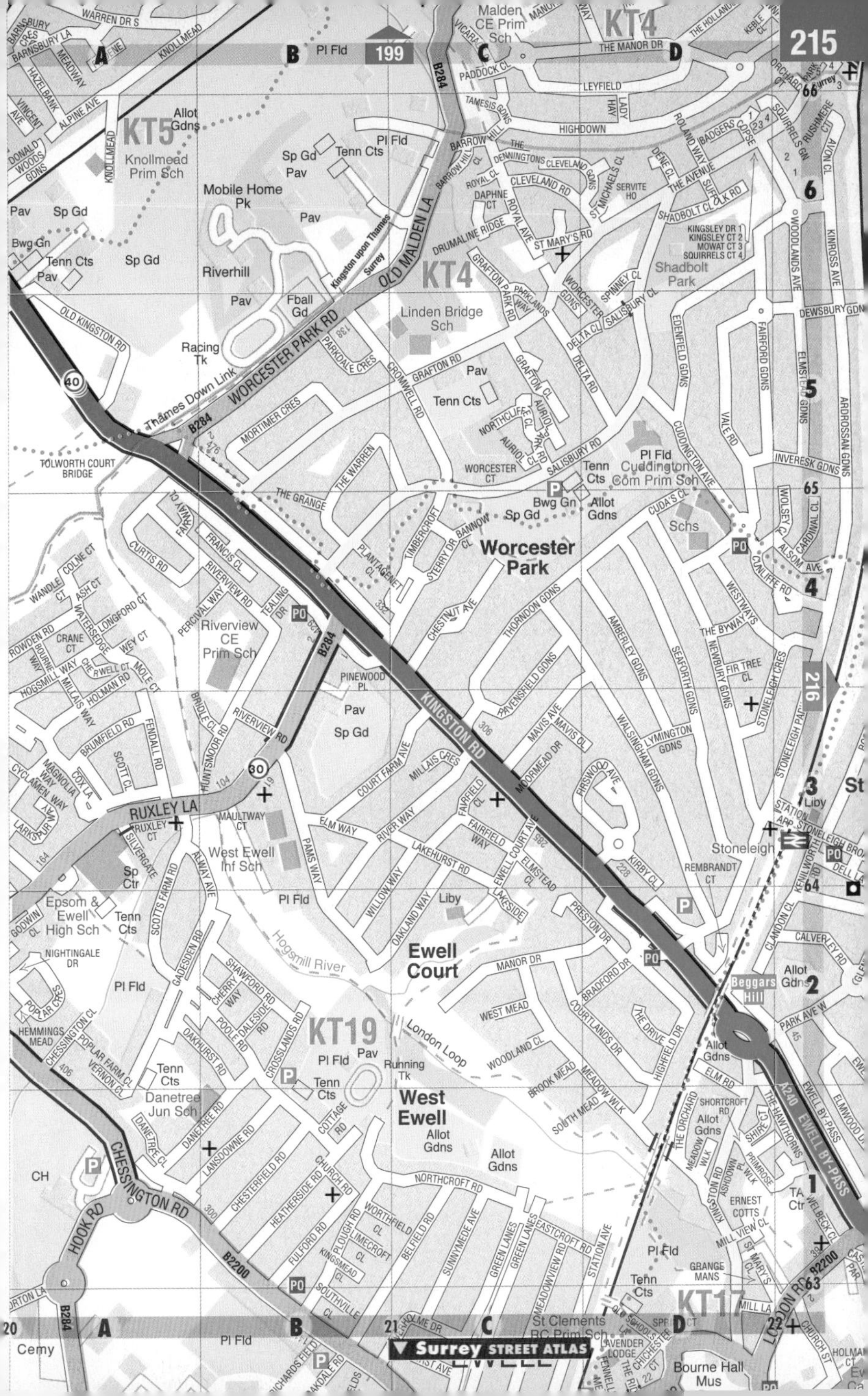

KT4
KT5
KT4
KT19
KT17
199
216
Worcester Park
Ewell Court
West Ewell
Stoneleigh
Knollmead Prim Sch
Mobile Home Pk
Riverhill
Racing Tk
Linden Bridge Sch
Shadbolt Park
Cuddington Com Prim Sch
Riverview CE Prim Sch
West Ewell Inf Sch
Epsom & Ewell High Sch
Danetree Jun Sch
Malden CE Prim Sch
Servite Ho
Hogsmill River
London Loop
Beggars Hill
Bourne Hall Mus
St Clements RC Prim Sch
Lavender Lodge
Tolworth Court Bridge
Thames Down Link
Kingston upon Thames
Surrey
KINGSTON RD
WORCESTER PARK RD
OLD MALDEN LA
RUXLEY LA
CHESSINGTON RD
HOOK RD
EWELL BY-PASS
LONDON RD
A240
B284
B2200
Surrey STREET ATLAS

Worcester Park
Stoneleigh
North Cheam
KT4
KT17
SM3
SM2
Nonsuch Park
Cheam Park
Recn Gd
Nonsuch Prim Sch
Nonsuch High Sch for Girls
Harefield Bridge
Organ Crossroads
CENTRAL RD
CHEAM COMMON RD
LONDON RD
MALDEN RD
EWELL BY-PASS
THE AVENUE
A24 Epsom
A232 Epsom (A24)

A
B
C
D
201
218
SM3
SM1
SM2
A217
A232
A24
A2043
B279
B2230
B283
Liby
Allot Gdns
Brookfield Prim Sch
Cemy
Tenn Cts
Recn Gd
Pav
Fball Gd
Bwg Gn
Kimpton Trade & Bsns Ctr
Kimpton Link Bsns Ctr
Superstore
Cheam Park Farm Inf Sch
Cheam Park Farm Jun Sch
Oldfields Trad Est
Westbourne Prim Sch
Sutton Common
West Sutton
F Ball Gd
Cheam
Cheam High Sch
Cheam Fields Prim Sch
Works
Pl Fld
Homefield Prep Sch
Sch
Games Ct
Coll
C Ctr
Sutton
Manor Park
Schs
Ben
Cheam Village
Glaisdale Sch
Cuddington Croft Prim Sch
Belmont
1 THOMPSON CL
2 ANDERSON CL
WHEATCROFT CT 5
DAMASK CT 6
1 ARLINGTON CL
2 OAKWOOD GDNS
3 HIGHFIELDS
CHAUCER HO 1
MILTON HO 2
ANDREWES HO 1
BALAAM HO 2
DENNIS HO 3
GIBSON HO 4
COLLINGWOOD CT 5
KINGFISHER CT 1
OSPREY CL 2
TEAL PL 3
KITTIWAKE PL 4
1 CARLTON HO
2 WRIGHTON CT
1 STEPHENSON CT
2 FROBISHER CT
3 CARISBROOKE CT
ROSE HILL
ANGEL HILL
SUTTON COMMON RD
OLDFIELDS RD
ST DUNSTAN'S HILL
HIGH ST
ST NICHOLAS WAY
THROWLEY WAY
CHEAM RD
SUTTON PARK RD
BRIGHTON RD
BELMONT RISE
MALDEN RD
THE BROADWAY
STATION WAY
BURDON LA
KIMPTON PARK WAY
GANDER GREEN LA
WINDSOR AVE
SALISBURY AVE
WOODLAND
MULGRAVE RD
LONDON RD
WESTBOURNE AVE
WARNER AVE
WATSON AVE
HAMILTON AVE
MOLESEY DR
HENLEY AVE
BROCKS DR
ST MARGARET'S AVE
KINGSTON AVE
WALTON AVE
WHITTAKER RD
ALCORN CL
CLENSHAM LA
FAIRLANDS AVE
HURSTCOURT RD
RANFURLY RD
CONIFER GDNS
WAVERLEY AVE
HAWTHORNE
ALL SAINTS RD
BENHILL AVE
BENHILL WOOD RD
LODGE RD
GREYHOUND
ELMSLEIGH CT
VICARAGE RD
BUSHEY RD
VALE RD
CROWN RD
OLD MARKET CT
WESTERN RD
GROVE RD
GROVE AVE
CHRISTCHURCH PK
DEVONSHIRE AVE
CAVENDISH
BRENDON HO
ARGYLE HO
SUTTON CT
KEMPSTON HO
TRICKETT HO
FELBRIDGE
EGMONT
PENARTH CT
THE DOWNSWAY
HOLLAND AVE
YORK RD
CORNWALL RD
BERESFORD RD
MANOR RD
HILLSIDE RD
UPPER MULGRAVE RD
GLEBE RD
PEACHES CL
OLD BARN
SANDY LA
WEST DR
THE GLADE
COURTENAY AVE
KINGSWOOD DR
CHIPSTEAD
TOLL BAR CT
SINCLAIR DR
LYNDHURST WAY
EASTLEIGH
VENTNOR RD
A217 Banstead, M25
Surrey STREET ATLAS
25
26
40
63
64
65
66

SM1
A
B
C
D
202
St Helier
Benhilton
Royston Park
The Wrythe
CARSHALTON
SUTTON
SM5
SM2
Carshalton
Carshalton Beeches
Greenshaw High Sch
Muschamp Prim Sch
Carshalton High Sch for Girls
Carshalton Coll
Honeywood Heritage Ctr
Barrow Hedges Prim Sch
Stanley Park Jun & Inf Schs
War Memorial
Superstore
Manor Park
ANGEL HILL
HIGH ST
ST NICHOLAS WAY
THROWLEY WAY
BRIGHTON RD
CARSHALTON RD
WRYTHE LA
PARK HILL
BEECHES AVE
WOODMANSTERNE RD
NORTH ST
WEST ST
POUND ST
NIGHTINGALE RD
BENHILL AVE
BENHILL RD
WESTMEAD RD
ERSKINE RD
GREYHOUND RD
CAVENDISH RD
MULGRAVE RD
DOWNSIDE RD
WAVERLEY WAY
GORDON RD
STANLEY PARK RD
HILLCROOME RD
CHALGROVE RD
THE DOWNSWAY
CROSSWAYS
MUSCHAMP RD
GREEN WRYTHE LA
WRYTHE GREEN RD
ROSE HILL PARK W
WESTMINSTER RD
A232
B2230
B278
B271
B277
217
Surrey STREET ATLAS

Hackbridge
Beddington Park
Bandonhill
SM6
SM5
WALLINGTON
South Beddington
Carshalton on the Hill
Wallington Green
Carshalton Park
Westcroft Sports Ctr
Felnex Trad Est
Soho Mills
River Wandle
A237 Coulsdon, A23

Beddington
Waddon
Roundshaw
Wandle Park
CR0
SM6
CR2
PURLEY WAY
CROYDON RD
DUPPAS HILL RD
STAFFORD RD
DENNING AVE
BEDDINGTON LA
PLOUGH LA
ROMAN WAY
OLD TOWN
Croydon Tramlink
Croydon Airport Ind Est
Roundshaw Park
Haling Manor High Sch
Purley Way Pl Fld
204
219
Surrey STREET ATLAS
A23 Redhill, M23, M25

221
CROYDON
East Croydon
Wellesley Road
Whitgift Ctr
Centrale Ctr
Drummond Ctr
George St
Church Street
Fairfield Halls
Coll
Lebanon Road
Sandilands
Park Hill
Park Hill Inf & Jun Schs
CR0
Lloyd Park
Coombe Park
Vanguard Way
Croydon Tramlink
CE High Sch
Howard Prim Sch
South Croydon
Whitgift Sch
Haling Park
Croham Hurst Sch
Croham Hurst
CR2
Breakneck Hill
South Croydon
Selsdon Road Ind Est
Two Bridges Ind Est
Capital Bsns Ctr
Sanderstead
WELLESLEY RD
ADDISCOMBE RD
FAIRFIELD RD
CHEPSTOW RD
COOMBE RD
PARK LA
PARK HILL RD
SOUTH PARK HILL RD
ST PETER'S RD
SOUTH END
BRIGHTON RD
SELSDON RD
UPPER SELSDON RD
WARHAM RD
LOWER COOMBE ST
BARCLAY RD
THE CROYDON FLYOVER
CROHAM RD
HAREWOOD RD
CROHAM MANOR RD
MANOR WAY
SANDERSTEAD RD
A212
A232
A222
A235
A236
B243
B274
B275
B269
205
222
A235 Purley, A23
Surrey STREET ATLAS

206
A
B
C
D
Shirley
PRIMROSE LA
ADDISCOMBE RD
SHIRLEY RD
WICKHAM RD
A232
Croydon Tramlink
Sandilands
Trinity Sch
Shirley Park
Oaks Farm
Windmill (dis)
Coloma Convent Girls' Sch
Shirley High Sch
Upper Shirley
Coombe Park
Lloyd Park
Coombe Farm
CR0
Addington Hills
Vanguard Way
COOMBE RD
A212
COOMBE LA
Coombe Lane
SUNKEN RD
Royal Russell Sch
Heathfield
Bramley Bank
Nat Res
London Loop
CR2
Croham Hurst
Selsdon High Sch
Littleheath Woods
Selsdon
221
6
5
4
3
2
1
65
64
63
34
35

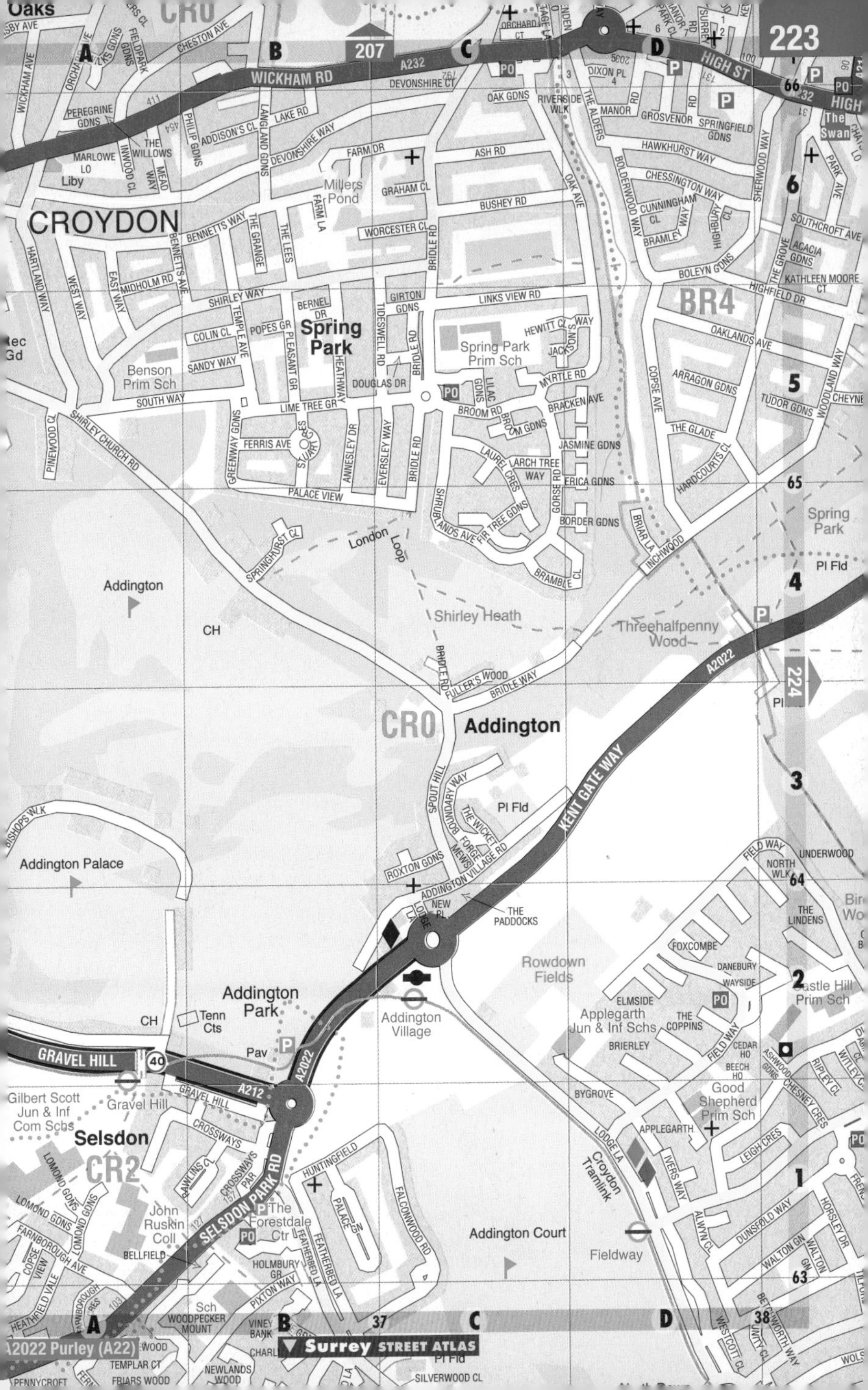
CROYDON
Spring Park
Addington
Shirley Heath
Threehalfpenny Wood
Addington Palace
Addington Park
Addington Village
Rowdown Fields
Selsdon
Addington Court
Fieldway
BR4
CR0
CR2
WICKHAM RD
HIGH ST
KENT GATE WAY
GRAVEL HILL
SELSDON PARK RD
SHIRLEY CHURCH RD
London Loop
Croydon Tramlink
Benson Prim Sch
Spring Park Prim Sch
Applegarth Jun & Inf Schs
Good Shepherd Prim Sch
Castle Hill Prim Sch
Gilbert Scott Jun & Inf Com Schs
John Ruskin Coll
The Forestdale Ctr
207
224
A2022 Purley (A22)
Surrey STREET ATLAS

West Wickham
Coney Hall
New Addington
HIGH ST
GLEBE WAY
CROYDON RD
ADDINGTON RD
LAYHAMS RD
Coney Hall Rdbt
Wickham Court
Sparrows Den Sp Gd
Spring Park
Fox Hill
Wickham Court Farm
Well Wood
Birch Wood
Castlehill Ruffs
Bradmanshill Wood
West Wickham Common
Coney Hall Recn Gd
All Saints RC Sch
Wickham Court Sch
Castle Hill Prim Sch
Good Shepherd Prim Sch
Wolsey Jun & Inf Schs
Hawes Down Schs
Glebe Sch
BR4
BR2
CR0
Bromley
Croydon
KING HENRY'S DR
CASTLE HILL AVE
FIELD WAY
HEADLEY DR
GOLDCREST WAY
MICKLEHAM WAY
QUEENSWAY
KINGSWAY
SYLVAN WAY
CHESTNUT AVE
BIRCH TREE AVE
HAWTHORN DR
CHURCH DR
WOOD LODGE LA
CORKSCREW HILL
STAMBOURNE WAY
COURTFIELD RISE
WOODLAND WAY
OAKLANDS AVE
HIGHFIELD DR
BOLEYN GDNS
SOUTHCROFT AVE
PARK AVE
SHERWOOD WAY
WICKHAM COURT RD
ADDINGTON RD
HAYES HILL
HEPBURN GDNS
LINKS RD
THE MEAD
A232
A2022
A214
208
223
Surrey STREET ATLAS

Keston Mark
Keston
Nash
Hayes Common
Keston Common
BR2
BR4
CROYDON RD
BASTON RD
HEATHFIELD RD
WESTERHAM RD
OAKLEY RD
Hayes Court
Baston Manor
Hast Hill House
Rouse Farm
Barnet Wood
Colyers Wood
Simpson's Cott
Ravens Wood Sch
Ravensbourne Bsns Ctr
Keston CE Prim Sch
Windmill
London Loop
Fuller's Wood
James's Wood
ROMAN MAUSOLEUM
Keston Court
Milchden
Wickham Common Prim Sch
JACKASS LA
CHURCH RD
BLACKNESS LA
ORCHARD PL
DOWNE RD
A233 Biggin Hill

210
A
B
C
D
66
6
5
65
4
3
64
2
1
63
42
43
Keston Mark
BR2
BR6
Locksbottom
OAKLEY RD
HASTINGS RD
FARNBOROUGH COMM.
CROYDON RD
CROFTON RD
FARNBOROUGH COMMON
WESTERHAM RD
SHIRE LA
Knowl Wood
Knowlehill Wood
Hollydale Recn Gd
Princess Royal University
Darrick Wood Sch
Darrick Wood Inf Sch
Darrick Wood Jun Sch
Ravens Wood Sch
The Fantail
Ninhams Wood
Lake Wood
Broom Bank
The Larches
Caesar's Camp
Holwood
Lower Hook Farm
North End Farm
Holwood Farm
Farthing Street
London Loop
DOWNE RD
NEW ROAD HILL
FARTHING ST
BOGEY LA
NORTH END LA
PRUDENCE LA 1
SANDRINGHAM LO 2
BALMORAL LO 3
SUMMERLANDS LO 4
FLEETWOOD CT 5
TUGMUTTON CL 1
HARLANDS GR 2
ELGAL CL 1
LIMES ROW 2

BR6
A
B
C
D
211
Crofton
CROFTON RD
Orpington
Mus
ORPINGTON
STATION RD
A232
A232 M25 (A224)
A223
6
5
4
3
2
1
66
65
64
63
45
46
Kent STREET ATLAS
WYNDHAM CL
ST THOMAS' DR
ECCLESTON CL
PINEWOOD CL
KELVIN PAR
OREGON SQ
ALLINGTON RD
ANDOVER RD
YEOVIL CL
CATHCART DR
GUMPING RD
CLAREVILLE RD
LYOTH RD
CROFTON LA
ORMONDE AVE
HILLVIEW CRES
THE MATTINGS
KNOLL RISE
PEPYS RISE
ELM GR
OAKHILL RD
HILL VIEW RD
YORK RISE
STATION APP
ELM GR
HILL APPROACH
THE
ORCHARD GR
KNOLL END CT
LIBERTY MEWS
THE DRIVE
BADGERS COPSE
THE AVENUE
SYCAMORE LO
TOWER RD
TOWER CL
ST AUBYNS GDNS
ST AUBYNS CL
GODDINGTON LA
CHARTERHOUSE
CRANLEIGH
REPTON RD
CHELTENHAM RD
OAKWOOD GDNS
OAKWOOD RD
OAKLANDS CT
HIGHWOOD DR
HIGHWOOD CL
BLUEBELL CL
WOODVIEW CL
WOOD RD
DARRICK
POUND COURT DR
POUND CL
THE RIDGE
HILLTOP GDNS
TELSCOMBE CL
THORPE CL
SHERLIES AVE
ORCHARD GN
NORTHOLME RISE
LUBBOCK HO
TUBBENDEN CL
WOODHEAD DR
SPENCER CL
RIDGEWAY CRESCENT GDNS
CRESCENT
BECKETTS CL
MAXWELL GDNS
SHELLEY CL
DALTON CL
GRANGE RD
FOXFIELD RD
BROUGHTON RD
TORVER WAY
HAVERTHWAITE RD
RUSLAND AVE
NEWSTEAD AVE
MORRIS CL
BARRY CL
RUSKIN DR
PILKINGTON RD
CROFTON AVE
AVONSTOWE CL
LA TOURNE GDNS
PARTRIDGE DR
MASEFIELD VIEW
STABLES END
NORMAN CL
MOSSLEA RD
DARRICK WOOD HO
SLOANE GDNS 1
LYSANDER WAY 2
Newstead Wood Sch for Girls
AVEBURY RD
WINTERBORNE AVE
TILE FARM RD
WILLERSLEY AVE
REED AVE
SANDY BURY
PO
TUBBENDEN LA
SOUTHCROFT RD
ROSEBERRY GDNS
CROMFORD CL
RIDGEWAY CRES
MARCELLINA WAY
STEPHEN CL
AMBROSE CL
STAPLETON RD
ARNE GR
WAYNE CL
Sch
BISHOP BUTT CL
SHEPHERDS CL
BENEDICT CL
Darrick Wood Sp Ctr
Darrick Wood
Pl Fld
Tubbenden Jun & Inf Schs
SUMMERHILL CL
LEAMINGTON AVE
OTTERDEN CL
SOUTHFLEET RD
ST JOSEPHS CL
MITCHELL RD
BUCKLAND RD
WORTH CL
TUNSTALL CL
Recn Gd
ASHBOURNE RISE
CURZON CL
DEACONS LEAS
STOWTING RD
CHARING CL
KINGS RD
SEVENOAKS RD
HELEGAN CL
TREGONY RD
PADSTOW CL
PORTHALLOW CL
NEWLYN CL
TREGONY RD
1 BRIDLE WAY
2 GREENACRES CL
3 HUNTER'S GR
4 FIELDSIDE CL
5 BRICKFIELD FARM GDNS
6 BEEKEN DENE
7 RIDLEY CT
BROADWATER GDNS
SHURLOCK DR
SUMNER CL
THYER CL
ARTINGTON CL
HALE CL
AVARD GDNS
SHALFORD CL
SABELLA DR
STATE FARM AVE
BEECHCROFT CL 1
TOPCLIFFE DR 2
WALMER CL 3
CHERRYCOT HILL 4
WORLEYS DR
TUBBENDEN DR
BORKWOOD WAY
HARLEY GDNS
DYMCHURCH CL
RYARSH CRES
BORKWOOD PK
NORTHLANDS AVE
CHERRYCOT RISE
BEECHCROFT RD
FAIRVIEW DR
ST LEONARDS RISE
NORTH DR
OAKLEIGH GDNS
Orpington
H
VANCOUVER CL
GLEESON DR
Warren Road Prim Sch
CLOONMORE AVE
CONIFER
FARNBOROUGH WAY
MELROSE CRES
SOUTHLANDS AVE
HAYWOOD RISE
CRESCENT WAY
ASHLEY GDNS
SOUTH DR
COBDEN RD
PITT RD
PALMERSTON RD
TUBBENDEN LA S
PEEL RD
GLADSTONE RD
HARTINGTON CL
LADYCROFT WAY
GREEN GDNS
CHARTWELL DR
DAME CL
DARWIN CL
SAPHORA CL
HILBOROUGH WAY
FERNDALE WAY
OLEANDER CL
DURRANT WAY
WARREN RD
WARREN AVE
OSGOOD AVE
WOLSEY MEWS
WARNFORD RD
WARREN GDNS
MARTINDALE AVE
CHESTNUT CL
FOX CL
EDGEWOOD DR
HIGH ST
FARNBOROUGH HILL
PINEWOOD DR
SHIRE LA
APRIL CL
HOME LEA
BRIARSWOOD WAY
FREESIA CL
GREEN FARM CL
GLENTRAMMON CL
FULLER CL
HIGHFIELD AVE
ATKINSON CL
TYE LA
ST GILES CL
Farnborough
Farnborough Prim Sch
Allot Gdns
1 PLEASANT VIEW PL
2 PLEASANT VIEW
Pl Fld
DOWNSWAY 1
WENTWORTH CL 2
CONTESSA CL 3
AMETHYST CT
RAMUS WOOD AVE
COCKSETT AVE
CLEAVE AVE
BEECHWOOD AVE
KENT CL
B2158
CHURCH RD
BR6
London Loop
BRITTENDEN PAR
GLENTRAMMON GDNS
GLENTRAMMON AVE
GLENTRAMMON RD
STEEP CL
PINCHBECK RD
WARING DR
WARING CL
LAXEY RD
LEZAYRE RD
Green Street Green
Green Street Green Prim Sch
VINE RD
MOAT CT
LINSLADE RD
WOODLANDS RD
WINDSOR
SHIRE LA
OLD HILL
KINGSLEY RD
COAL POST CL
A21
A223
WELLHURST CL
DOWLERVILLE RD
WORLDS END LA
FARRANT CL
Chelsfield Hall Farm
ASH RD
ELM RD
OAK RD
BEECH RD
High Elms Country Park
HIGH ELMS RD
CH
High Elms
High Elms Clockhouse
CUDHAM LA N
SEVENOAKS RD
Rounds Wood
A21 Sevenoaks (A224), M25
Recn Gd

Key to enlarged map pages

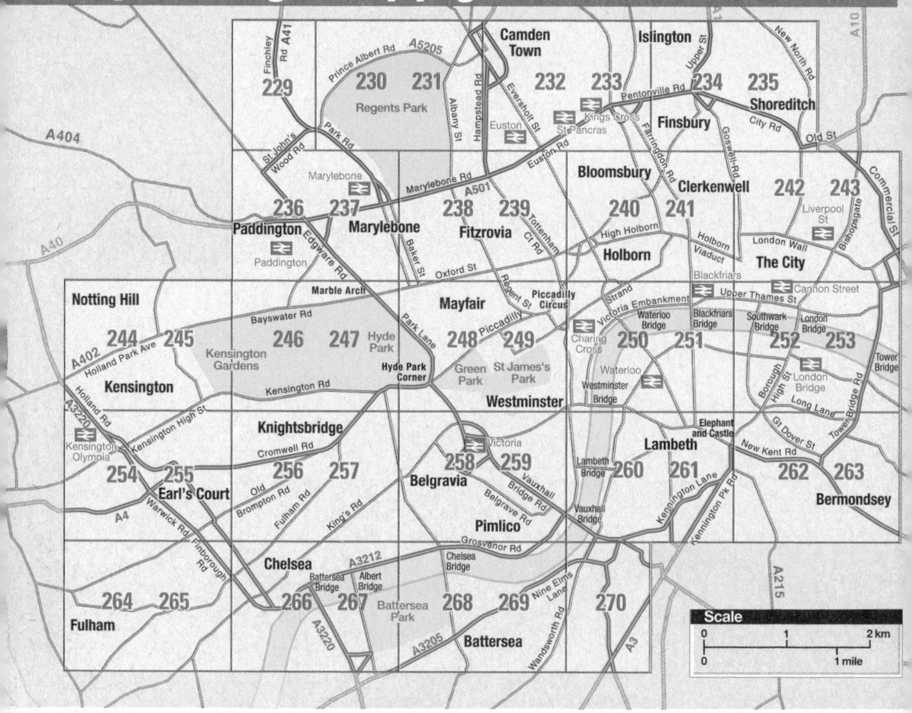

229 Finchley Rd A41
230 231 Regents Park, Prince Albert Rd A5205, Albany St
232 233 Camden Town, Hampstead Rd, Eversholt St, Euston, Kings Cross, St Pancras
234 235 Islington, Upper St, Pentonville Rd, New North Rd, Shoreditch, Finsbury, City Rd, Old St
236 237 Paddington, Marylebone, St John's Wood Rd, Park Rd, Edgware Rd, Marylebone Rd
238 239 Fitzrovia, A501, Euston Rd, Tottenham Ct Rd, Baker St
240 241 Bloomsbury, Holborn, Clerkenwell, High Holborn, Farringdon Rd, Goswell Rd, Holborn Viaduct
242 243 The City, Liverpool St, London Wall, Bishopsgate, Commercial St
244 245 Notting Hill, Kensington, Holland Park Ave, A402, Holland Rd
246 247 Kensington Gardens, Hyde Park, Bayswater Rd, Marble Arch, Kensington Rd, Hyde Park Corner
248 249 Mayfair, Oxford St, Park Lane, Regent St, Piccadilly, Piccadilly Circus, Green Park, St James's Park, Westminster
250 251 Charing Cross, Strand, Victoria Embankment, Waterloo Bridge, Blackfriars Bridge, Waterloo, Westminster Bridge, Blackfriars
252 253 Cannon Street, Upper Thames St, Southwark Bridge, London Bridge, Tower Bridge, Borough High St, Long Lane, Tower Bridge Rd
254 255 Kensington Olympia, Kensington High St, Earl's Court, A3220, A4, Warwick Rd
256 257 Knightsbridge, Cromwell Rd, Old Brompton Rd, Fulham Rd, King's Rd
258 259 Belgravia, Victoria, Vauxhall Bridge Rd, Belgrave Rd, Pimlico
260 261 Lambeth, Lambeth Bridge, Vauxhall Bridge, Elephant and Castle, Kennington Lane, Kennington Pk Rd
262 263 Bermondsey, New Kent Rd, Gt Dover St
264 265 Fulham, Finborough Rd
266 267 Chelsea, A3212, Battersea Bridge, Albert Bridge, Battersea Park, A3220
268 269 Chelsea Bridge, Grosvenor Rd, Nine Elms Lane, Battersea, A3205, Wandsworth Rd
270 A3

A404, A40, A1, A10, A215

Scale: 0 – 1 – 2 km; 0 – 1 mile

Additional symbols on enlarged maps

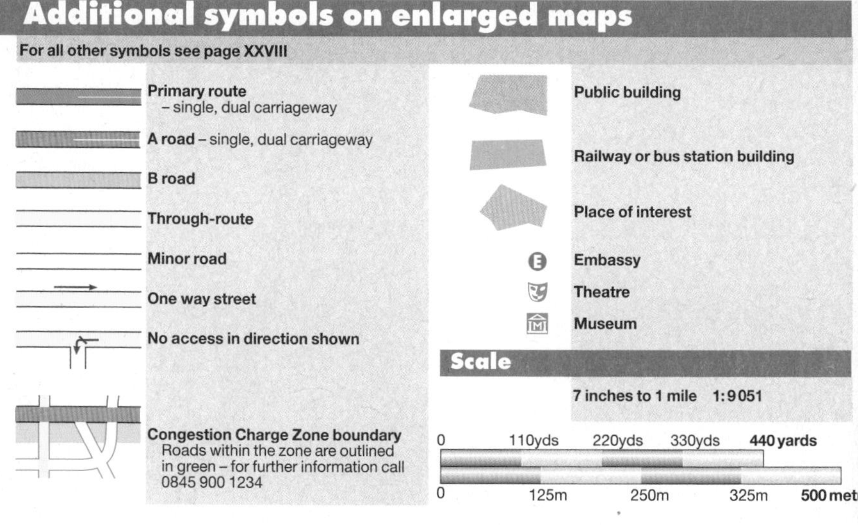

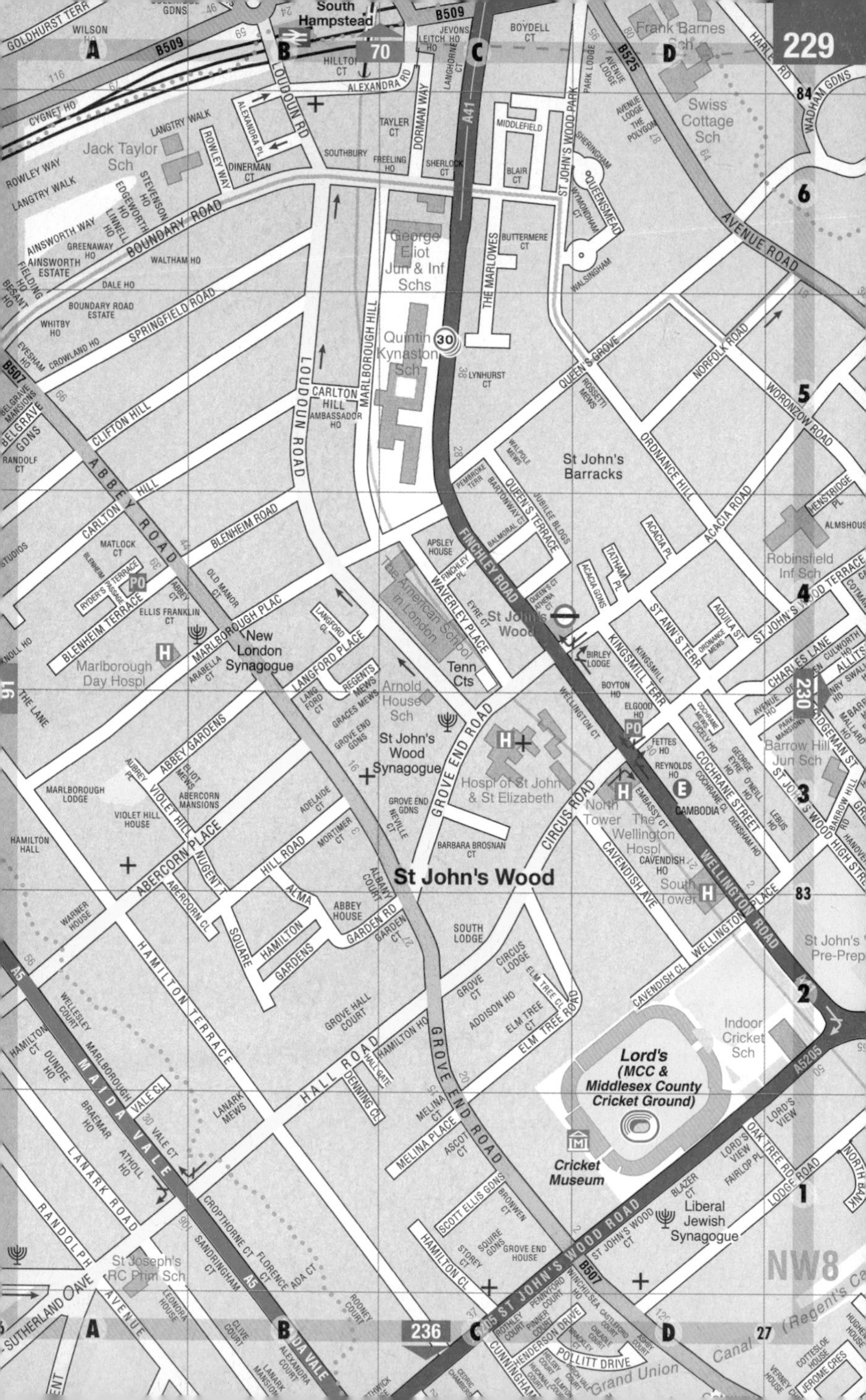
South Hampstead
70
B509
A
B
C
D
Frank Barnes Sch
Swiss Cottage Sch
Jack Taylor Sch
LOUDOUN RD
ALEXANDRA RD
DORMAN WAY
A41
B525
ST JOHN'S WOOD PARK
QUEENSMEAD
BOUNDARY ROAD
ROWLEY WAY
LANGTRY WALK
AINSWORTH WAY
AINSWORTH ESTATE
BOUNDARY ROAD ESTATE
SPRINGFIELD ROAD
George Eliot Jun & Inf Schs
Quintin Kynaston Sch
THE MARLOWES
AVENUE ROAD
6
QUEEN'S GROVE
NORFOLK ROAD
WORONZOW ROAD
5
B507
CLIFTON HILL
CARLTON HILL
LOUDOUN ROAD
MARLBOROUGH HILL
ABBEY ROAD
BLENHEIM ROAD
St John's Barracks
ORDNANCE HILL
ACACIA ROAD
Robinsfield Inf Sch
ST JOHN'S WOOD TERRACE
4
FINCHLEY ROAD
QUEEN'S TERRACE
WAVERLEY PLACE
The American School in London
St John's Wood
New London Synagogue
Marlborough Day Hospl
BLENHEIM TERRACE
MARLBOROUGH PLACE
91
LANGFORD PLACE
Arnold House Sch
Tenn Cts
St John's Wood Synagogue
GROVE END ROAD
Hospl of St John & St Elizabeth
KINGSMILL TERR
CIRCUS ROAD
North Tower
The Wellington Hospl
South Tower
CAMBODIA
COCHRANE STREET
230
Barrow Hill Jun Sch
3
ABBEY GARDENS
ABERCORN PLACE
HILL ROAD
St John's Wood
WELLINGTON ROAD
WELLINGTON PLACE
83
St John's Pre-Prep
CAVENDISH AVE
HAMILTON TERRACE
HAMILTON GARDENS
GARDEN RD
SOUTH LODGE
2
A5
MAIDA VALE
HALL ROAD
ELM TREE ROAD
Indoor Cricket Sch
Lord's (MCC & Middlesex County Cricket Ground)
A5205
Cricket Museum
LANARK ROAD
RANDOLPH AVENUE
MELINA PLACE
ST JOHN'S WOOD ROAD
Liberal Jewish Synagogue
LODGE ROAD
1
NW8
St Joseph's RC Prim Sch
SUTHERLAND AVE
236
27
POLLITT DRIVE
Grand Union Canal (Regent's Canal)

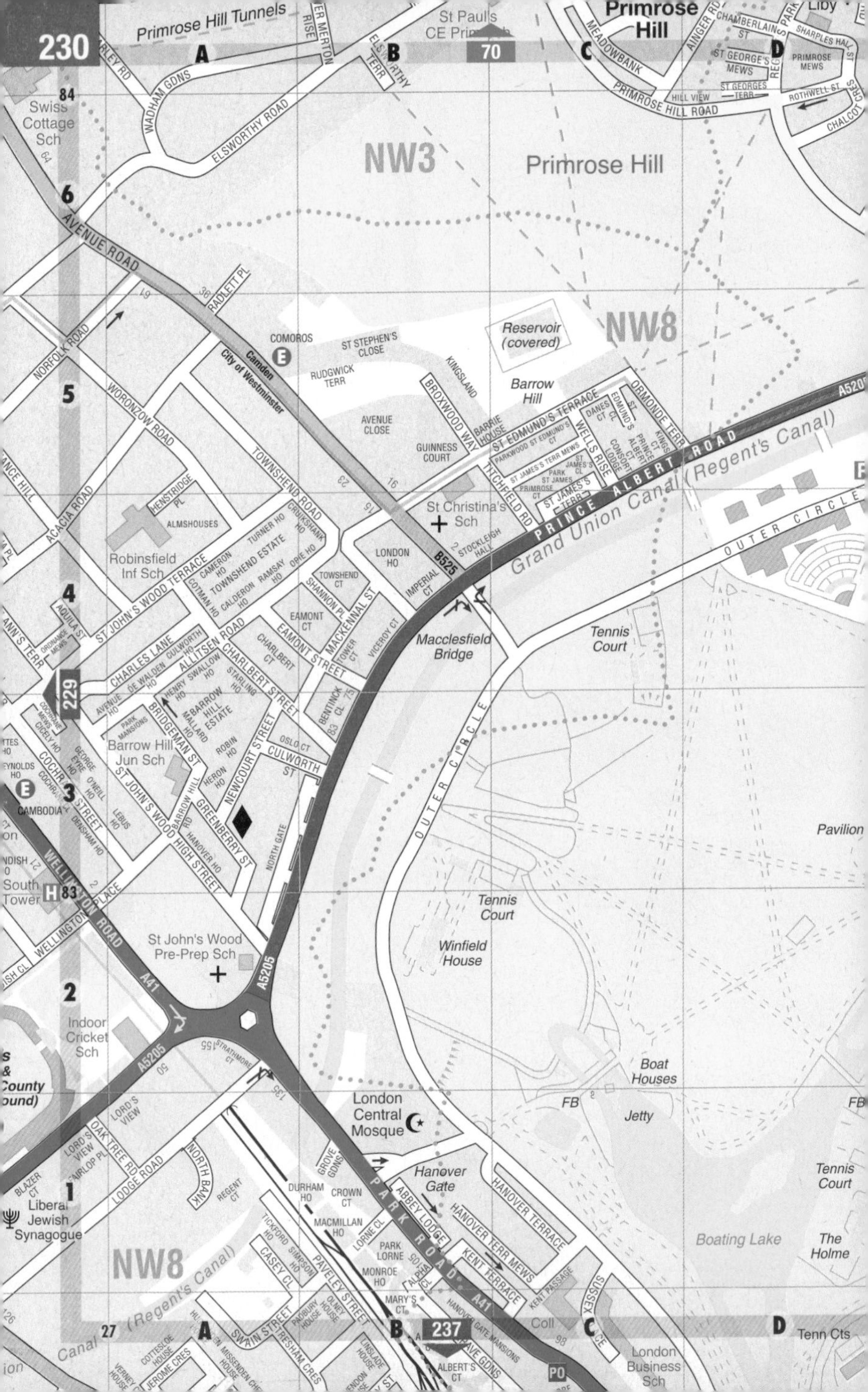
230
Primrose Hill Tunnels
A
B
70
C
D
Primrose Hill
St Pauls CE Prim Sch
Swiss Cottage Sch
Wadham Gdns
Elsworthy Road
Elsworthy Terr
Meadowbank
Chamberlain St
Sharples Hall St
St George's Mews
Primrose Mews
Regents Park Rd
Primrose Hill Road
Hill View
St Georges Terr
Rothwell St
Chalcot Cres
Liby
NW3
Primrose Hill
84
6
Avenue Road
Radlett Pl
Norfolk Road
5
Woronzow Road
Camden
City of Westminster
Comoros
St Stephen's Close
Rudgwick Terr
Kingsland
Broxwood Way
Avenue Close
Guinness Court
Barrie House
Reservoir (covered)
Barrow Hill
NW8
St Edmund's Terrace
Ormonde Terrace
Danes Ct
Edmund's Cl
Wells Rise
Consort Lodge
Prince Albert Ct
Kings Ct
St James's Terr Mews
Primrose Ct
St James's Terr
Titchfield Rd
Townshend Road
Acacia Road
Henstridge Pl
Almshouses
Robinsfield Inf Sch
Townshend Estate
Turner Ho
Cruikshank Ho
Cameron Ho
Cotman Ho
Calderon Ho
Ramsay Ho
Orde Ho
Townshend Ct
Shannon Pl
London Ho
Imperial Ct
B525
St Christina's Sch
Stockleigh Hall
Prince Albert Road
A5205
Grand Union Canal (Regent's Canal)
Outer Circle
4
St John's Wood Terrace
Aquila St
Ordnance Mews
Charles Lane
Allitsen Road
Culworth Ho
De Walden Ho
Avenue Ho
Swallow Ho
Henry Ho
Starling Ho
Charlbert Street
Charlbert Ct
Eamont Ct
Eamont Street
Mackennal St
Tower Ct
Viceroy Ct
Bentinck Cl
Macclesfield Bridge
Tennis Court
229
Barrow Hill Estate
Mallard Ho
Park Mansions
Bridgeman St
Robin Ho
Newcourt Street
Oslo Ct
Culworth St
Barrow Hill Jun Sch
St John's Wood High Street
Barrow Hill Rd
Heron Ho
Greenberry St
Hanover Ho
North Gate
3
Cochrane Mews
Cicely Ho
George Eyre Ho
O'Neill Ho
Cochrane Street
Lebus Ho
Densham Ho
Cambodia
Wellington Road
Wellington Place
83
South Tower
Pavilion
Tennis Court
Winfield House
St John's Wood Pre-Prep Sch
2
A41
Indoor Cricket Sch
A5205
Strathmore Ct
Boat Houses
FB
Jetty
London Central Mosque
Lord's View
Oak Tree Rd
Lodge Road
North Bank
Regent Ct
Grove Gdns
Hanover Gate
Hanover Terrace
1
Blazer Ct
Liberal Jewish Synagogue
Durham Ho
Crown Ct
Macmillan Ho
Park Road
Abbey Lodge
Hanover Terr Mews
Tennis Court
Boating Lake
The Holme
NW8
Tickford Ho
Simpson Ho
Casey Cl
Lorne Cl
Park Lorne
Monroe Ho
Alpha Cl
Kent Terrace
Kent Passage
Paveley Street
Mary's Ct
Hanover Gate Mansions
Sussex Place
Coll
Canal (Regent's Canal)
27
A
Swain Street
Stresham Cres
Padbury House
Olney House
B
237
C
D
Tenn Cts
Cottesloe House
Jerome Cres
Verney House
Missenden House
Linslade House
Albert's Ct
Gave Gdns
PO
London Business Sch

231
A
B
C
D
71
238
1
2
3
4
5
6
Primrose Hill
Primrose Hill Sch
Utopia Village
Chalcot Road
Chalcot Sq
Fitzroy Road
Fitzroy Yd
Egbert St
Manley St
Calvert St
Edis Street
Princess Road
Waterside Pl
Kingstown St
Auden Pl
Hopkinson's Pl
Primrose Hill Studios
Regent's Park Road
Albert Terr
Albert Terr Mews
St Mark's Sq
St Mark's Cres
Gloucester Avenue
Darwin Ct
Regal Lane
Oval Road
Regent's Park Terr
Gloucester Crescent
Jamestown Rd
Inverness Street
Camden Mkt
Early Mews
Camden Town
Camden High St
Kentish Town Rd
Hawley Cres
Hawley Inf Sch
Stucley Pl
Buck St
Camden Rd
Greenland Rd
Britannia Junc
The Cavendish Sch
Parkway
Stanmore Pl
Underhill Pas
Underhill St
Arlington Road
Pleasant Row
Signmakers Yd
Greenland Pl
Greenland St
St Martin's Almshouses
Brehon Ho
Pratt Mews
Latitude Ho
North Bridge House Senior Sch
The Jewish Mus
Delancey Street
Delancey Pas
Mary Terrace
Fairfield
Delancey Studios
Albert Street
Foxfield
Brierfield
Miller St
Carlow St
Cobden House
Beatty St
Mornington Street
Mornington Terrace
Mornington Pl
Mornington Crescent
London Zoo
Gloucester Gate Bridge
Gloucester Gate Mews
Gloucester Gt
Park Village West
Park Village East
St Katharine's Precinct
Silsoe House
Regent's Park Barracks
Richmond House
NW1
Camberley House
Granby Terr
Harrington St
Eskdale
Augustus Ho
Augustus Street
Langdale
Ambleside
Tintern Ho
Kendal
Buttermere
Cumberland Terrace
Cumberland Terrace Mews
Outer Circle
Stones
Broad Walk
Regent's Park
Refreshment Room
Cumberland Gate
Chester Pl
Cmbrlnd Pl
Albany Street
Edward Mews
Christ Church Sch
Redhill St
Little Edward St
Swinley House
Bagshot Ho
Ascot House
Allot Gdns
Datchet Ho
Windsor Ho
St George's Cathedral
Rothay
Cumberland Market
Chester Cl N
Chester Terrace
Chester Ct
Chester Cl S
Chester Gt
Nash Street
Thirlmere
Windermere
Wasdale
Grasmere
Griesdale
Borrowdale
Mosedale
Patterdale
Stanhope Street
Stanhope Par
Mackworth Ho
Mackworth St
Harrington Ho
Kirkstone
Hawkshead
Staveley
Scafell
Derwent
Robert Street
Liby
Compton Cl
Clarence Gardens
Englefield
Troutbeck
Tilehurst
Swallowfield
Marlston
The Combe
Pangbourne
Netley Prim Sch
Everton
Westminster Kingsway Coll
City of Westminster
Camden
Chester Road
Inner Circle
Open Air Theatre
Queen Mary's Gardens
New Lodge
Cambridge Terr
Cambridge Terr Mews
Cambridge Gate
Cambridge Gate Mews
Colosseum Terr
Munster Sq
Little Albany St
Laxton Pl
Albert St
Longford St
Royal College of Physicians
Pav
Tenn Cts
A5205
A4201
A503
A502
A400
Bayham

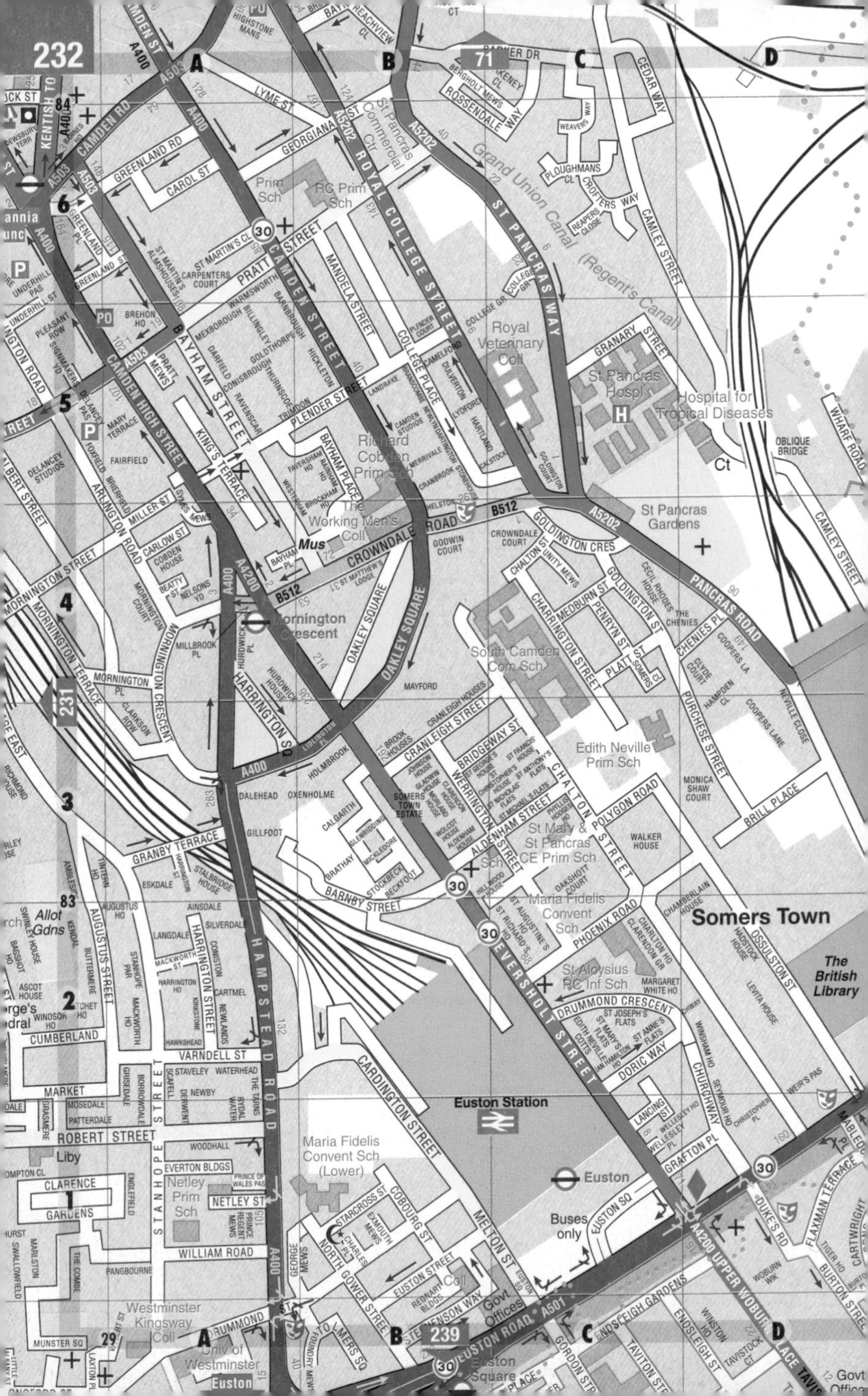

CAMDEN ST
KENTISH TOWN RD
CAMDEN RD
LYME ST
GEORGIANA ST
ROYAL COLLEGE STREET
ST PANCRAS WAY
St Pancras Commercial Ctr
Grand Union Canal (Regent's Canal)
BARKER DR
BERGHOLT MEWS
ROSSENDALE WAY
CEDAR WAY
WEAVERS WAY
PLOUGHMANS CL
CROFTERS WAY
REAPERS CLOSE
CAMLEY STREET
GREENLAND RD
CAROL ST
Prim Sch
RC Prim Sch
PRATT STREET
CAMDEN STREET
MANDELA STREET
ST MARTIN'S CL
ST MARTIN'S ALMSHOUSES
CARPENTERS COURT
UNDERHILL PAS
UNDERHILL ST
PLEASANT ROW
SIGNMAKERS YD
BREHON HO
BAYHAM STREET
PRATT MEWS
CAMDEN HIGH STREET
MEXBOROUGH
WARMSWORTH
BILLINGLEY
BARNBOROUGH
GOLDTHORPE
CONISBOROUGH
DARFIELD
RAVENSCAR
THURNSCOE
TRIMDON
HICKLETON
PLENDER STREET
COLLEGE PLACE
COLLEGE GR
CAMELFORD
DULVERTON
LYDFORD
HARTLAND
CALSTOCK
Royal Veterinary Coll
GRANARY STREET
St Pancras Hospl
Hospital for Tropical Diseases
GOLDINGTON COURT
OBLIQUE BRIDGE
WHARF ROAD
Ct
DELANCEY PAS
MARY TERRACE
FAIRFIELD
DELANCEY STUDIOS
ALBERT STREET
ARLINGTON ROAD
KING'S TERRACE
FAVERSHAM HO
RAINHAM HO
WESTERHAM
BROCKHAM HO
BAYHAM PLACE
Richard Cobden Prim Sch
CAMDEN STUDIOS
MERRIVALE
CRANBROOK
STONEHOUSE
HELSTON
The Working Men's Coll
Mus
MILLER ST
SYMES MEWS
CARLOW ST
COBDEN HOUSE
BEATTY ST
NELSONS YD
BAYHAM PL
CROWNDALE ROAD
B512
GODWIN COURT
CROWNDALE COURT
GOLDINGTON CRES
A5202
St Pancras Gardens
ST MATTHEW'S LODGE
MORNINGTON STREET
MORNINGTON COURT
MORNINGTON TERRACE
MORNINGTON PL
MORNINGTON CRESCENT
Mornington Crescent
MILLBROOK PL
HURDWICK PL
HURDWICK HOUSE
HARRINGTON SQ
OAKLEY SQUARE
CHALTON ST
UNITY MEWS
CHARRINGTON STREET
MEDBURN ST
PENRYN ST
GOLDINGTON ST
CECIL RHODES HOUSE
THE CHENIES
CHENIES PL
PANCRAS ROAD
South Camden Com Sch
PLATT ST
SOMERS CL
CLYDE COURT
COOPERS LA
HAMPDEN CL
COOPERS LANE
NEVILLE CLOSE
PURCHESE STREET
CLARKSON ROW
MAYFORD
CRANLEIGH HOUSES
CRANLEIGH STREET
BRIDGEWAY ST
LIDLINGTON PL
HOLMBROOK
BROOK HOUSES
JOHNSON HOUSE
GLADWIN HOUSE
MORLAND HOUSE
CLARENDON HOUSE
ST GEORGE'S
ST CHRISTOPHER'S HOUSE
ST FRANCIS' HOUSE
ST ANTHONY'S FLATS
ST NICHOLAS' FLATS
ST MICHAEL'S FLATS
WERRINGTON STREET
CHALTON STREET
Edith Neville Prim Sch
POLYGON ROAD
MONICA SHAW COURT
BRILL PLACE
A400
DALEHEAD
OXENHOLME
SOMERS TOWN ESTATE
CALGARTH
GLENRIDDING
MICKLEDORE
WOLCOT HOUSE
ALDENHAM HOUSE
ALDENHAM STREET
PHYLLIS HODGES HO
St Mary & St Pancras CE Prim Sch
WALKER HOUSE
GILLFOOT
BRATHAY
STOCKBECK
BECKFOOT
GRANBY TERRACE
HARRINGTON ST
STALBRIDGE HOUSE
ESKDALE
TINTERN HO
AMBLESIDE
Sch
HILLWOOD HOUSE
OAKSHOTT COURT
Maria Fidelis Convent Sch
BARNBY STREET
AINSDALE
AUGUSTUS HO
AUGUSTUS STREET
Allot Gdns
KENDAL
SWINLEY HOUSE
BASSHOT HO
LANGDALE
SILVERDALE
CONISTON
STANHOPE PAR
MACKWORTH ST
MACKWORTH HO
HARRINGTON HO
KIRKSTONE
CARTMEL
NEWLANDS
HAWKSHEAD
HAMPSTEAD ROAD
ST RICHARD'S HO
ST AUGUSTINE'S HO
PHOENIX ROAD
CHARLTON HO
CLARENDON GR
St Aloysius RC Inf Sch
MARGARET WHITE HO
CHAMBERLAIN HOUSE
Somers Town
HADSTOCK HOUSE
OSSULSTON ST
LEVITA HOUSE
The British Library
EVERSHOLT STREET
DRUMMOND CRESCENT
ST JOSEPH'S FLATS
ST MARY'S FLATS
EDITH NEVILLE COTTS
ST ANNE'S FLATS
DORIC WAY
WINSHAM HO
CHURCHWAY
SEYMOUR HO
CHRISTOPHER PL
WEIR'S PAS
BUTTERMERE
ASCOT HOUSE
WINDSOR HO
CUMBERLAND
MARKET
MOSEDALE
PATTERDALE
GRASMERE
GRISEDALE
BORROWDALE
STANHOPE STREET
SCAFELL
STAVELEY
WATERHEAD
DERWENT
NEWBY
RYDAL WATER
THE TARNS
VARNDELL ST
CARDINGTON STREET
Euston Station
LANCING ST
WELLESLEY HO
WELLESLEY PL
GRAFTON PL
MABLEDON PL
FLAXMAN TERRACE
CARTWRIGHT
ROBERT STREET
Liby
CLARENCE GARDENS
ENGLEFIELD
WOODHALL
EVERTON BLDGS
PRINCE OF WALES PAS
Netley Prim Sch
NETLEY ST
PRINCE REGENT MEWS
Maria Fidelis Convent Sch (Lower)
STARCROSS ST
EXMOUTH MEWS
COBOURG ST
Euston
EUSTON SQ
Buses only
DUKE'S RD
TIGER HO
BURTON STREET
WILLIAM ROAD
PANGBOURNE
THE COMBE
MARLSTON
SWALLOWFIELD
GEORGE MEWS
NORTH GOWER STREET
CHARLES PL
EUSTON STREET
MELTON ST
Coll
REDNAP BLDGS
STEPHENSON WAY
Govt Offices
A501
EUSTON ROAD
ENDSLEIGH GARDENS
ENDSLEIGH ST
WINSTON HO
TAVISTOCK CT
UPPER WOBURN PLACE
A4200
WOBURN WALK
Westminster Kingsway Coll
DRUMMOND ST
MUNSTER SQ
TOLMERS SQ
FOUNDRY MEWS
Univ of Westminster
Euston Square
GORDON ST
TAVITON ST
Govt Offices
A B C D
1 2 3 4 5 6
71
231
239
30

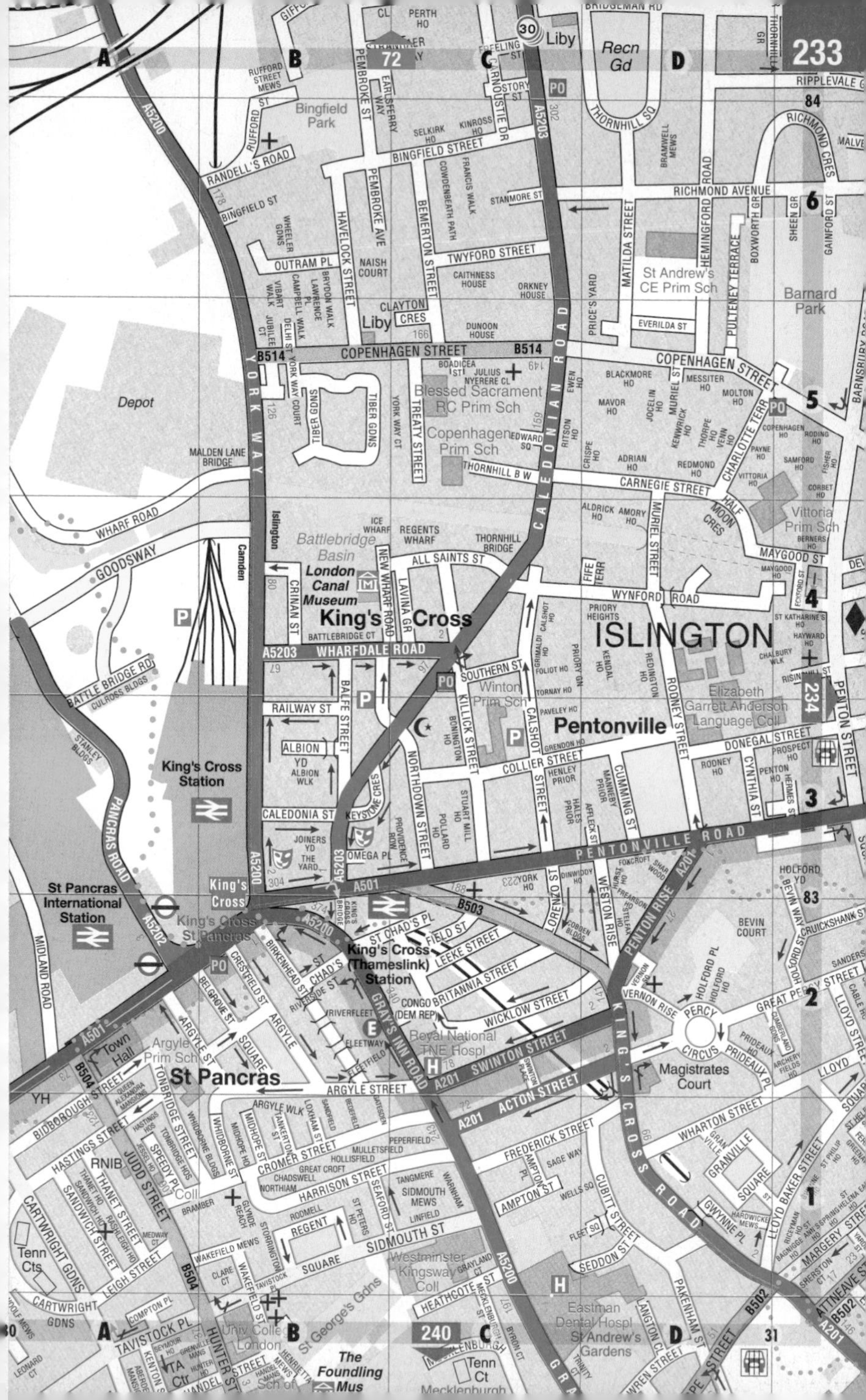
72
York Way
Caledonian Road
Copenhagen Street
Bingfield Park
Bingfield Street
Randell's Road
Outram Pl
Havelock Street
Bemerton Street
Twyford Street
Richmond Avenue
Matilda Street
Hemingford Road
St Andrew's CE Prim Sch
Barnard Park
Thornhill Sq
Recn Gd
Depot
Wharf Road
Goodsway
Blessed Sacrament RC Prim Sch
Copenhagen Prim Sch
Carnegie Street
Vittoria Prim Sch
Battlebridge Basin
London Canal Museum
King's Cross
All Saints St
Wynford Road
ISLINGTON
Wharfdale Road
Islington
Camden
King's Cross Station
Pentonville
Winton Prim Sch
Elizabeth Garrett Anderson Language Coll
Donegal Street
Collier Street
Northdown Street
Caledonia St
Pentonville Road
Penton Street
Pancras Road
St Pancras International Station
King's Cross St Pancras
King's Cross (Thameslink) Station
Gray's Inn Road
Swinton Street
Acton Street
King's Cross Road
Penton Rise
Percy Circus
Magistrates Court
Wharton Street
Granville Square
Lloyd Baker Street
Argyle Street
St Pancras
Argyle Prim Sch
Town Hall
Judd Street
Cromer Street
Harrison Street
Sidmouth St
Regent Square
Westminster Kingsway Coll
Eastman Dental Hospl
St Andrew's Gardens
Royal National TNE Hospl
Midland Road
Cartwright Gdns
Tavistock Pl
Hunter St
Univ Coll London
St George's Gdns
The Foundling Mus
Tenn Cts
240
234
Islington

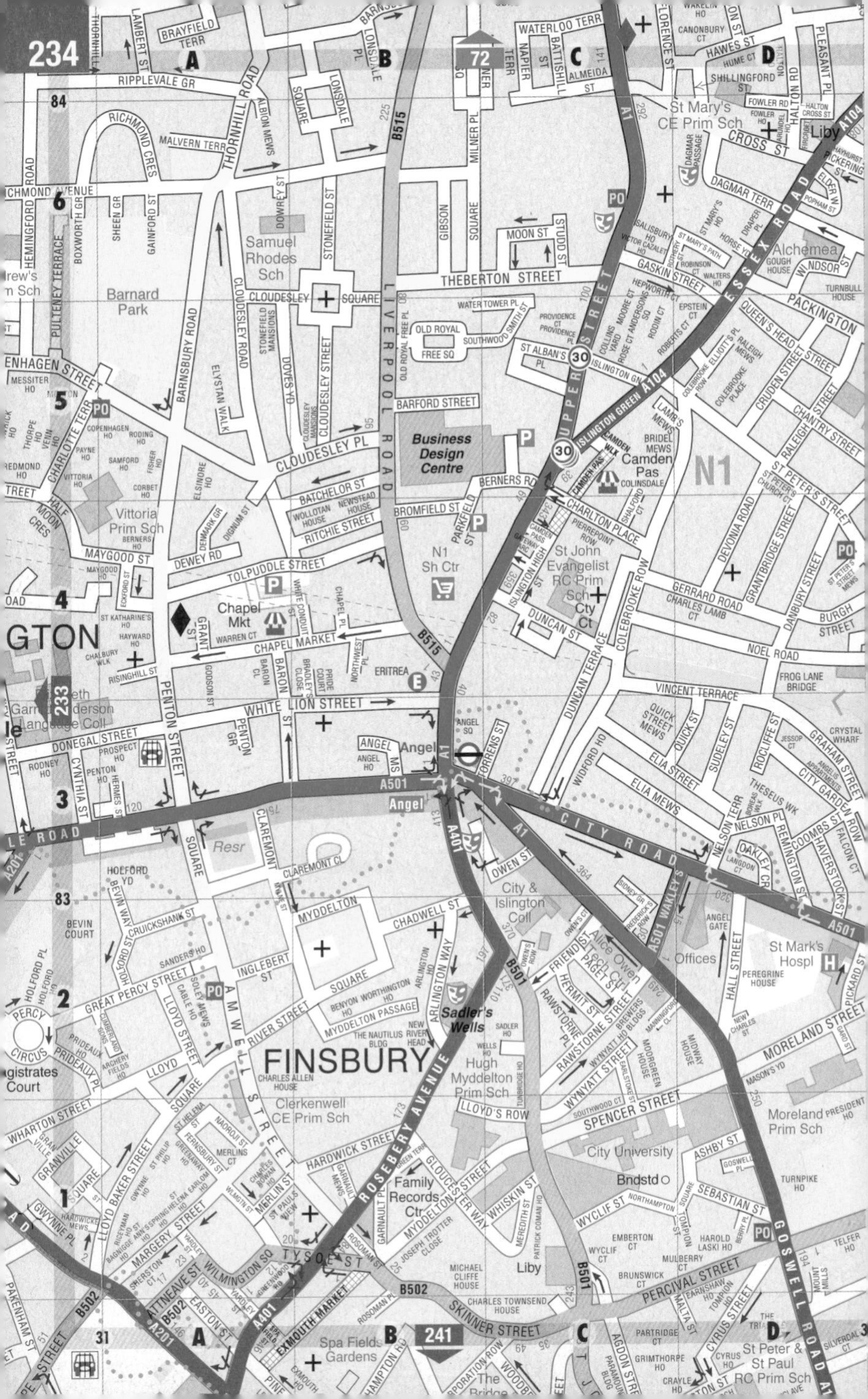

FINSBURY
N1
Angel
Business Design Centre
Sadler's Wells
City University
Chapel Mkt
N1 Sh Ctr
Family Records Ctr
LIVERPOOL ROAD
UPPER STREET
CITY ROAD
ESSEX ROAD
ROSEBERY AVENUE
GOSWELL ROAD
PENTONVILLE ROAD
WHITE LION STREET
CHAPEL MARKET
AMWELL STREET
SKINNER STREET
PERCIVAL STREET
SPENCER STREET
MYDDELTON SQUARE
CLOUDESLEY SQUARE
BARNSBURY ROAD
COLEBROOKE ROW
DUNCAN TERRACE
NOEL ROAD
ST PETER'S STREET
PACKINGTON
CROSS ST
THEBERTON STREET
RICHMOND AVENUE
COPENHAGEN STREET
MAYGOOD ST
TOLPUDDLE STREET
DONEGAL STREET
GREAT PERCY STREET
LLOYD BAKER STREET
EXMOUTH MARKET
Barnard Park
Samuel Rhodes Sch
Vittoria Prim Sch
Hugh Myddelton Prim Sch
Clerkenwell CE Prim Sch
St Mary's CE Prim Sch
Moreland Prim Sch
St Mark's Hospl
City & Islington Coll
Spa Fields Gardens
72
233
241

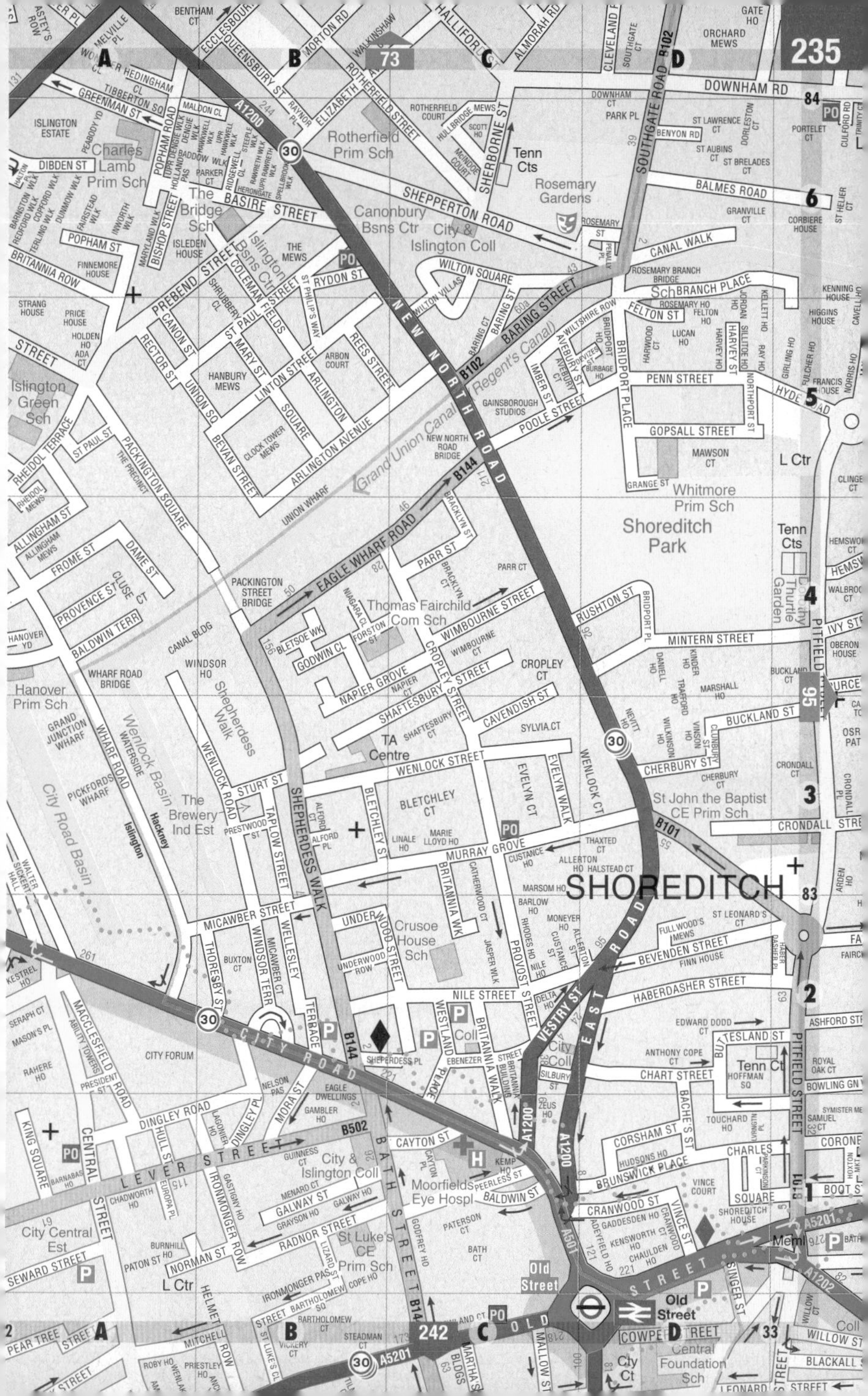
SHOREDITCH
NEW NORTH ROAD
CITY ROAD
EAST ROAD
OLD STREET
LEVER STREET
EAGLE WHARF ROAD
SHEPHERDESS WALK
PITFIELD STREET
SOUTHGATE ROAD
DOWNHAM RD
BASIRE STREET
SHEPPERTON ROAD
WILTON SQUARE
BARING STREET
CANAL WALK
BRANCH PLACE
PENN STREET
GOPSALL STREET
POOLE STREET
ARLINGTON AVENUE
PACKINGTON SQUARE
WIMBOURNE STREET
MINTERN STREET
WENLOCK STREET
MURRAY GROVE
NILE STREET
HABERDASHER STREET
CHART STREET
BEVENDEN STREET
BUCKLAND ST
CHERBURY ST
CRONDALL STREET
Grand Union Canal
Regent's Canal
Shoreditch Park
Whitmore Prim Sch
Rotherfield Prim Sch
Rosemary Gardens
Thomas Fairchild Com Sch
Crusoe House Sch
Moorfields Eye Hospl
City & Islington Coll
St Luke's CE Prim Sch
St John the Baptist CE Prim Sch
Hanover Prim Sch
Charles Lamb Prim Sch
Islington Green Sch
City Road Basin
Wenlock Basin
Shepherdess Walk
The Brewery Ind Est
City Central Est
Central Foundation Sch
Old Street
A1200
B102
B144
B101
B502
A5201
A501
A1202
73
84
95
242
33
A
B
C
D
1
2
3
4
5
6

229
246
91
W9
W2
PADDINGTON
Little Venice
Bayswater
Warwick Avenue
Paddington
Paddington (Hammersmith & City)
Heathrow Express Terminal Paddington Station
Hilton London Paddington Hotel
Alexander Fleming Laboratory Mus
St Mary's Hosp
Medical Sch
Paddington Basin
Paddington Acad
Paddington Green Prim Sch
St Mary's Gardens
City of Westminster Coll
St Joseph's RC Prim Sch
Liberal Jewish Synagogue
Gateway Prim Sch
Hallfield Jun & Inf Schs
Grand Union Canal
Grand Union Canal Wlk
Paddington Branch
HARROW ROAD
WESTWAY (ELEVATED)
HARROW RD (UNDER)
MAIDA VALE
A5205 ST JOHN'S WOOD ROAD
CLIFTON ROAD
CLIFTON GARDENS
WARWICK AVENUE
RANDOLPH AVENUE
WARRINGTON CRESCENT
SUTHERLAND AVE
MAIDA AVENUE
BLOMFIELD ROAD
WARWICK CRESCENT
BISHOP'S BRIDGE ROAD
EASTBOURNE TERRACE
WESTBOURNE TERRACE
GLOUCESTER TERRACE
PRAED STREET
SUSSEX GARDENS
CRAVEN ROAD
NORTH WHARF ROAD
SOUTH WHARF ROAD
EDGWARE ROAD
PORCHESTER TERRACE
CLEVELAND SQUARE
LEINSTER GARDENS
SPRING ST
LONDON ST
CHURCH STREET
PENFOLD STREET
LYONS PLACE
ABERDEEN PLACE
CUNNINGHAM PL
CAPLAND STREET
FISHERTON STREET
HALL PLACE
BOSCOBEL ST
A B C D
1 2 3 4 5 6

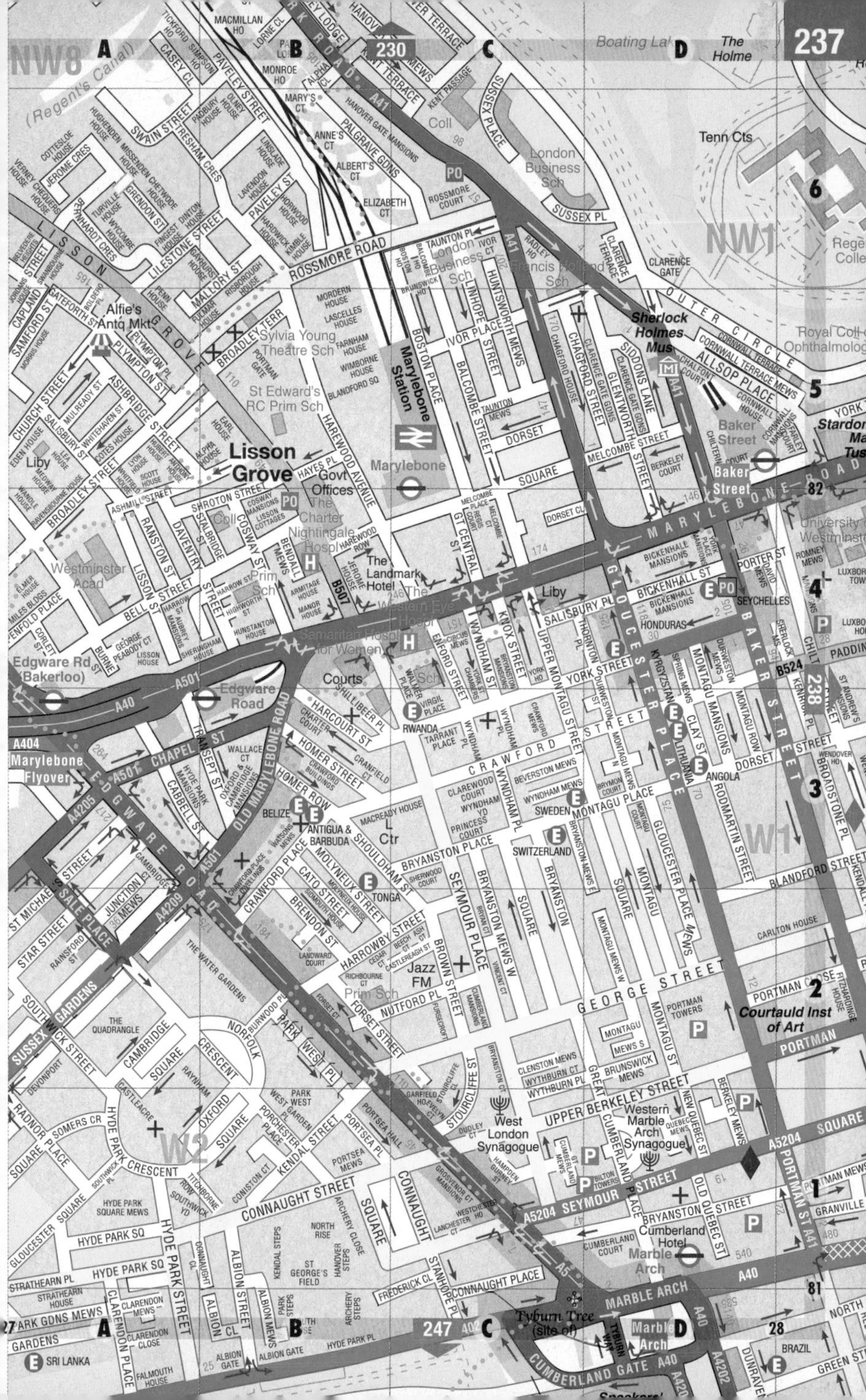

237
NW8
A
B
C
D
230
(Regent's Canal)
Boating Lake
The Holme
Tenn Cts
London Business Sch
Sussex Place
Sussex Pl
Clarence Gate
Outer Circle
NW1
Regent's College
6
Royal Coll of Ophthalmologists
Sherlock Holmes Mus
Allsop Place
Cornwall Terrace
Cornwall Terrace Mews
Chalfont Court
Baker Street
5
York
Stardome
Madame Tussauds
Park Road
Hanover Terrace
Kent Terrace
Kent Passage
Hanover Gate Mansions
Palgrave Gdns
Coll
Rossmore Court
Rossmore Road
Lisson Grove
Alfie's Antq Mkt
Sylvia Young Theatre Sch
St Edward's RC Prim Sch
Marylebone Station
Marylebone
Harewood Avenue
Boston Place
Balcombe Street
Huntsworth Mews
Francis Holland Sch
Chagford Street
Dorset Square
Ivor Place
Taunton Mews
Melcombe Street
Glentworth Street
Siddons Lane
Clarence Gate Gdns
Marylebone Road
Govt Offices
The Charter Nightingale Hospl
The Landmark Hotel
The Western Eye Hospl
Samaritan Hospl for Women
Liby
Church Street
Broadley Street
Broadley Terr
Bell Street
Lisson St
Cosway St
Shroton Street
Ashmill Street
Westminster Acad
Penfold Place
Edgware Rd (Bakerloo)
Edgware Road
A501
A40
A404
Marylebone Flyover
Chapel St
Transept St
Old Marylebone Road
Edgware Road
Courts
Gloucester Place
Baker Street
Bickenhall Mansions
Bickenhall St
Porter St
University of Westminster
4
Salisbury Pl
York Street
Upper Montagu Street
Crawford Street
Wyndham Pl
Montagu Place
Montagu Mansions
Rodmartin Street
Dorset Street
B524
238
Seychelles
Honduras
Kyrgyzstan
Lithuania
Angola
Sweden
Switzerland
Rwanda
Belize
Antigua & Barbuda
Tonga
3
W1
Homer Street
Homer Row
Harcourt St
Shouldham St
Molyneux Street
Bryanston Place
Bryanston Square
Seymour Place
Montagu Square
Blandford Street
Carlton House
George Street
Portman Close
2
Courtauld Inst of Art
Portman Towers
Jazz FM
Brown Street
Nutford Pl
Forset Street
Harrowby Street
Crawford Place
Sale Place
Junction Mews
Star Street
Sussex Gardens
Southwick Street
The Quadrangle
Cambridge Square
Norfolk Crescent
Oxford Square
Hyde Park Crescent
W2
Somers Cr
Radnor Place
Park West Pl
Kendal Street
Portsea Place
Connaught Street
Connaught Square
West London Synagogue
Western Marble Arch Synagogue
Upper Berkeley Street
Great Cumberland Place
Brunswick Mews
New Quebec St
Portman Square
A5204
Seymour Street
Bryanston Street
Cumberland Hotel
Marble Arch
Portman St A41
Granville
1
Hyde Park Square
Hyde Park Sq
Hyde Park Square Mews
Gloucester Square
Strathearn Pl
Hyde Park Street
Albion Street
Connaught Place
Tyburn Tree (site of)
Marble Arch
A40
A5
North Row
Hyde Park Gdns Mews
Gardens
Clarendon Place
Albion Gate
Hyde Park Pl
247
Cumberland Gate
Sri Lanka
Brazil
Green Street
Dunraven

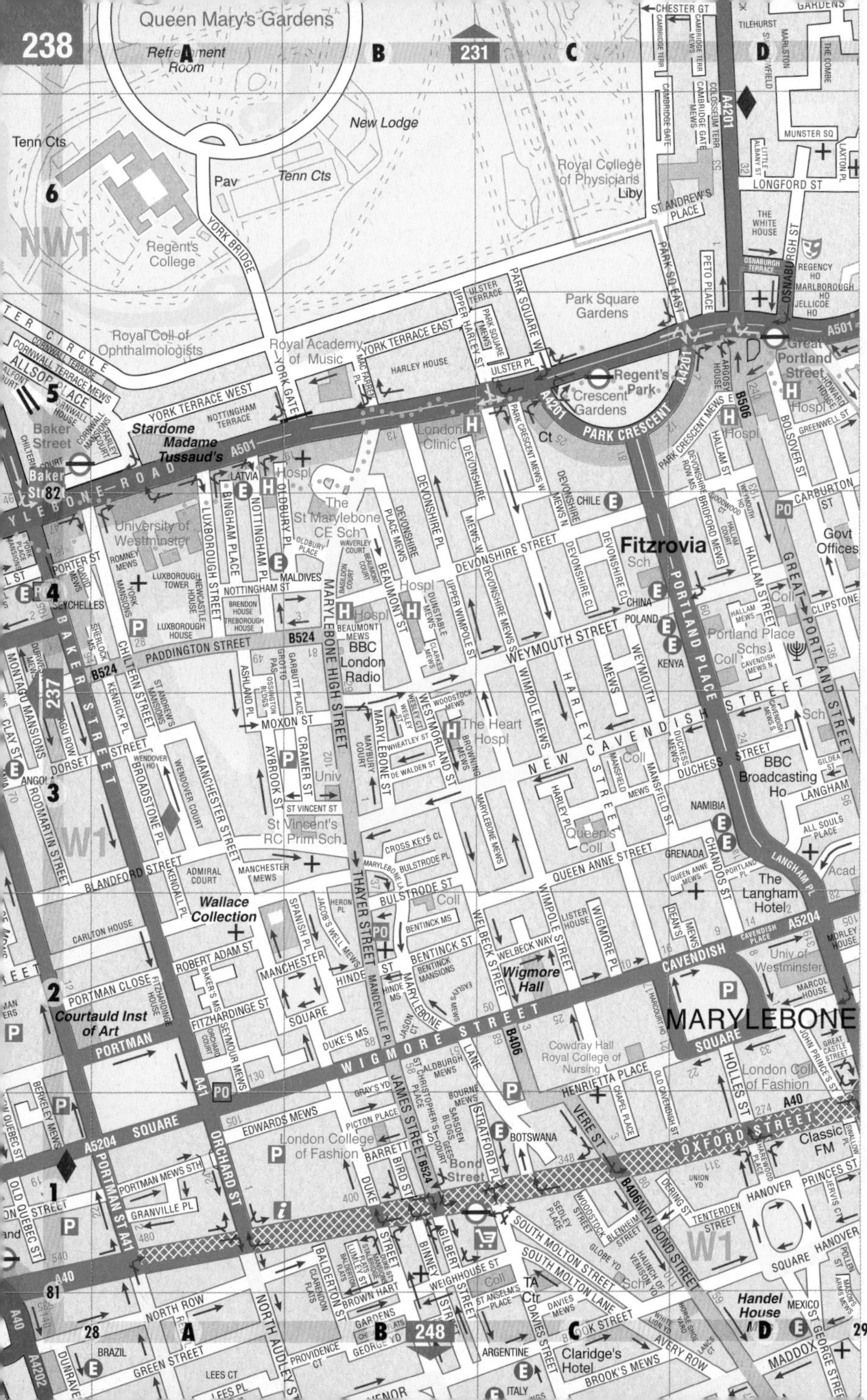
Queen Mary's Gardens
A
B
231
C
D
Refreshment Room
New Lodge
Tenn Cts
Pav
Tenn Cts
Royal College of Physicians
Liby
6
NW1
Regent's College
YORK BRIDGE
CHESTER GT
CAMBRIDGE TERR
CAMBRIDGE TERR MEWS
CAMBRIDGE GATE
CAMBRIDGE GATE MEWS
COLOSSEUM TERR
A4201
TILEHURST
MARLSTON
THE COMBE
MUNSTER SQ
LITTLE ALBANY ST
LAXTON PL
LONGFORD ST
ST ANDREW'S PLACE
THE WHITE HOUSE
OSNABURGH ST
OSNABURGH TERRACE
REGENCY HO
MARLBOROUGH HO
JELLICOE HO
PARK SQ EAST
PETO PLACE
Park Square Gardens
A501
Great Portland Street
ULSTER TERRACE
UPPER HARLEY ST
PARK SQUARE MEWS
PARK SQUARE W
ULSTER PL
Regent's Park
Crescent Gardens
PARK CRESCENT
A4201
ARGOSY HOUSE
B506
Royal Coll of Ophthalmologists
Royal Academy of Music
YORK TERRACE EAST
HARLEY HOUSE
MACFARREN PL
YORK GATE
CORNWALL TERRACE
CORNWALL TERRACE MEWS
ALLSOP PLACE
5
YORK TERRACE WEST
NOTTINGHAM TERRACE
Stardome
Madame Tussaud's
A501
Baker Street
MARYLEBONE ROAD
London Clinic
Hospl
Hospl
LATVIA
The St Marylebone CE Sch
DEVONSHIRE PLACE MEWS
DEVONSHIRE PL
DEVONSHIRE MEWS W
PARK CRESCENT MEWS W
Ct
DEVONSHIRE MEWS N
PARK CRESCENT MEWS E
DEVONSHIRE ROW MS
BRIDFORD MEWS
GOODWOOD CT
HALLAM CT
WEYMOUTH MS
HALLAM ST
BOLSOVER ST
GREENWELL ST
CARBURTON ST
Hospl
PO
CHILE
Fitzrovia
Sch
Govt Offices
University of Westminster
LUXBOROUGH STREET
BINGHAM PLACE
NOTTINGHAM PL
OLDBURY PL
OLDBURY PLACE
WAVERLEY COURT
BEAUMONT COURT
BASILDON COURT
PORTER ST
DAVID MEWS
ROMNEY MEWS
YORK MANSIONS
LUXBOROUGH TOWER
NEWCASTLE HOUSE
NOTTINGHAM ST
MALDIVES
BEAUMONT ST
Hospl
DUNSTABLE MEWS
UPPER WIMPOLE ST
DEVONSHIRE STREET
DEVONSHIRE MEWS S
DEVONSHIRE CL
DEVONSHIRE CL
CHINA
POLAND
KENYA
PORTLAND PLACE
Coll
CLIPSTONE
HALLAM MEWS
Portland Place Schs
CAVENDISH MEWS N
GREAT PORTLAND STREET
4
SEYCHELLES
BRENDON HOUSE
TREBOROUGH HOUSE
LUXBOROUGH HOUSE
SHERLOCK MS
P
Hospl
BEAUMONT MEWS
BBC London Radio
CLARKES MEWS
WEYMOUTH STREET
WIMPOLE MEWS
HARLEY STREET
MEWS
WEYMOUTH
PADDINGTON STREET
B524
MARYLEBONE HIGH STREET
GARBUTT PLACE
GROTTO PAS
OSSINGTON BLDGS
ASHLAND PL
CHILTERN STREET
KENRICK PL
ST ANDREW'S MANSIONS
BAKER STREET
MONTAGU MANSIONS
237
WOODSTOCK MEWS
WESTMORLAND ST
WESLEY ST
WESLEY CT
The Heart Hospl
NEW CAVENDISH STREET
DUCHESS MEWS
CAVENDISH MEWS S
Sch
MOXON ST
AYBROOK ST
CRAMER ST
MARYLEBONE ST
MAYBURY COURT
WHEATLEY ST
DE WALDEN ST
BROWNING MEWS
Univ
Coll
MANSFIELD MEWS
MANSFIELD ST
DUCHESS STREET
BBC Broadcasting Ho
LANGHAM
GILDEA ST
DORSET STREET
WENDOVER HO
BROADSTONE PL
WENDOVER COURT
MANCHESTER STREET
ST VINCENT ST
St Vincent's RC Prim Sch
MARYLEBONE MEWS
HARLEY PL
Queen's Coll
NAMIBIA
ALL SOULS PLACE
CLAY ST
ANGOLA
3
RODMARTIN STREET
W1
CROSS KEYS CL
BULSTRODE PL
MARYLEBONE LA
QUEEN ANNE STREET
GRENADA
QUEEN ANNE MEWS
CHANDOS ST
PORTLAND PL
LANGHAM PL
Acad
The Langham Hotel
BLANDFORD STREET
KENDALL PL
ADMIRAL COURT
MANCHESTER MEWS
THAYER STREET
BULSTRODE ST
Coll
HERON PL
JACOB'S WELL MEWS
Wallace Collection
SPANISH PL
CARLTON HOUSE
ROBERT ADAM ST
BENTINCK MS
BENTINCK ST
BENTINCK MANSIONS
WELBECK STREET
WELBECK WAY
LISTER HOUSE
WIMPOLE STREET
WIGMORE PL
DEAN'S MEWS
CAVENDISH PLACE
A5204
MORLEY HOUSE
Univ of Westminster
CAVENDISH
PO
HINDE ST
MANCHESTER SQUARE
BAKER'S MS
PORTMAN CLOSE
FITZHARDINGE HOUSE
2
Courtauld Inst of Art
FITZHARDINGE ST
ORCHARD COURT
SEYMOUR MEWS
HINDE MS
MANDEVILLE PL
MARYLEBONE LANE
EASLEY'S MEWS
Wigmore Hall
HARCOURT HO
P
MARCOL HOUSE
MARYLEBONE
DUKE'S MS
JASON CT
WIGMORE STREET
B406
Cowdray Hall Royal College of Nursing
SQUARE
HOLLES ST
GREAT CASTLE STREET
JOHN PRINCE'S ST
London Coll of Fashion
PORTMAN
A41
PO
ST CHRISTOPHER'S PLACE
ALDBURGH MEWS
JAMES STREET
HENRIETTA PLACE
CHAPEL PLACE
OLD CAVENDISH ST
GRAY'S YD
BOURNE MEWS
SARSDEN BLDGS
GEES COURT
P
BERKELEY MEWS
EDWARDS MEWS
PICTON PLACE
London College of Fashion
VERE ST
A40
OXFORD STREET
Classic FM
SWALLOW PL
A5204
SQUARE
ORCHARD ST
P
BARRETT ST
STRATFORD PL
BOTSWANA
HAREWOOD PLACE
UNION YD
PORTMAN MEWS STH
DUKE ST
BIRD ST
B524
Bond Street
DERING ST
HANOVER
PRINCES ST
JERVIS CT
1
OLD QUEBEC ST
GRANVILLE PL
PORTMAN ST A41
P
B406 NEW BOND STREET
SEDLEY PLACE
WOODSTOCK STREET
BLENHEIM STREET
TENTERDEN STREET
W1
SOUTH MOLTON STREET
SOUTH MOLTON LANE
GLOBE YD
HAUNCH OF VENISON YD
SQUARE
HANOVER
POLLEN ST
BALDERTON ST
CLARENDON FLATS
BALDERTON FLATS
LUMLEY ST
LUMLEY FLATS
STRATFORD FLATS
DUNCAN FLATS
BINNEY ST
GILBERT ST
WEIGHHOUSE ST
Coll
TA Ctr
Sch
BROWN HART GARDENS
ST ANSELM'S PLACE
DAVIES MEWS
DAVIES ST
A40
81
NORTH ROW
NORTH AUDLEY ST
Handel House
MEXICO
MADDOX ST
MASON'S ARMS MEWS
28
A
B
248
C
D
29
BROOK STREET
WHITE LION YD
HORSE SHOE YARD
LANCS CT
AVERY ROW
A40
A4202
DUNRAVEN
BRAZIL
GREEN STREET
LEES CT
LEES PL
PROVIDENCE CT
GEORGE YD
ARGENTINE
Claridge's Hotel
BROOK'S MEWS
ST GEORGE ST
ITALY

232
249
240
A
B
C
D
1
2
3
4
5
6
Buses only
Euston Road
Euston Square
Euston Underpass
Euston Twr
Regent's Pl
Triton Sq
William Road
Drummond St
Westminster Kingsway Coll
Univ of Westminster
North Gower Street
Euston Street
Stephenson Way
Govt Offices
Gower Place
Gower Ct
Univ Coll Hospl
Beaumont Place
Warren Street
Grafton Way
University College London
Petrie Mus of Egyptian Archaeology
Grant Mus of Zoology
Elizabeth Garrett Anderson Hospl
University St
Huntley Street
Chenies Mews
Gordon Street
Endsleigh Gardens
Endsleigh St
Taviton Street
Gordon Square
Gordon Square Gdn
Tavistock Square
Tavistock Square Gdn
Upper Woburn Place
Woburn Place
Woburn Square
Bedford Way
Torrington Square
University of London
Byng Pl
Malet Pl
Malet Street
Royal Academy of Dramatic Art
Russell Square
Bloomsbury Street
British Museum
Montague Place
Keppel St
Aga Khan Univ
Bedford Square
Bayley St
Morwell Street
Bedford Avenue
Adeline Pl
Time Out Magazine
Gower Street
Gower Mews
Store Street
South Cr
Cavendish Coll
Ridgmount St
Ridgmount Gdns
Chenies Street
North Cres
RADA
Alfred Place
Alfred Ms
Torrington Place
Tottenham Court Road
Goodge Street
Goodge St
Tottenham St
Scala St
Whitfield St
Charlotte St
Charlotte Mews
Chitty St
Howland St
Maple St
Fitzroy Street
Fitzroy Sq
Conway St
Warren St
Cleveland Street
Clipstone Mews
Holcroft Court
BT Tower
Univ of Westminster
Hanson Street
Ogle Street
Great Titchfield St
Gosfield St
Foley Street
Riding House Street
Nassau St
Bolsover St
Mortimer St
Middlesex House
Blake Coll
All Souls Sch
St Luke's Hospl
Bell Language Sch
Croatia
Mozambique
Liberia
Windmill St
Percy Street
Rathbone St
Rathbone Pl
Newman Street
Berners Mews
Berners St
Wells Street
Wells Mews
New Acad Gall
Stephen Ms
Stephen St
Gresse St
Birkbeck Coll
Nickelodeon
Hanway St
Hanway Pl
Tottenham Court Road
St Giles' Circus
Barbados
Bainbridge St
Streatham St
Dyott St
Congress House
Centre Point
St Giles High St
Earnshaw St
Bucknall St
Denmark St
Flitcroft St
Stacey St
New Compton St
Shaftesbury Ave
Monmouth Street
Seven Dials
Tower St
West St
Cambridge Circus
Charing Cross Road
Moor St
Phoenix St
Caxton Wlk
Law Ct
St Andrews Chambers
Little Portland St
Elsalvador
Turkmenistan
Marylebone Passage
Margaret Street
Eastcastle Street
Plaza Sh Ctr
Winsley St
Magic Kiss FM
Oxford Street
Oxford Circus
Regent Street
Argyll St
Great Marlborough Street
Ramillies Place
Radcliffe Coll
The Callan Sch
Noel St
YH
Poland Street
D'Arblay St
Berwick Street
Wardour Street
London Coll of Beauty Therapy
Carnaby Street
Kingly Street
Marshall Street
Broadwick St
Lexington St
Westminster Coll
Soho
Soho Square
Soho St
Carlisle St
Dean Street
Frith St
Greek St
Sutton Row
Manette St
Coll of Art & Design
Bateman St
Old Compton Street
Romilly Street
Meard St
Bourchier St
Shaftesbury Avenue
Soho Parish CE Prim
Berwick Street
Hollen St
Sheraton St
St Anne's Ct
Blooms
Russell Sq Gdn
Govt Offices

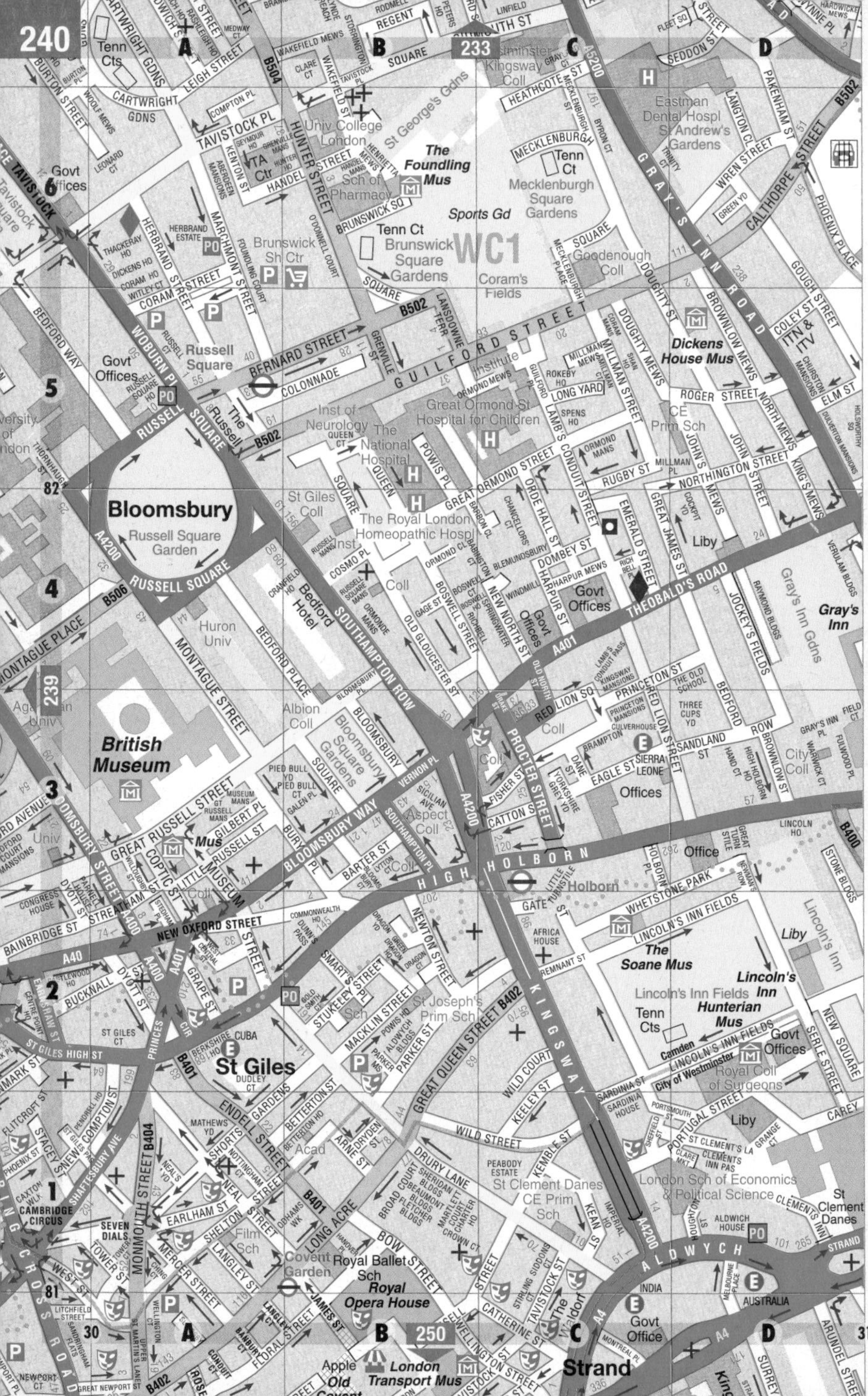
A
B
C
D
233
Tenn Cts
Cartwright Gdns
Leigh Street
Regent Square
Wakefield Mews
Clare Ct
Kingsway Coll
Heathcote St
Mecklenburgh
Seddon St
Eastman Dental Hospl
St Andrew's Gardens
Langton Cl
Pakenham St
Wren Street
Calthorpe Street
Phoenix Place
Burton Street
Burton Pl
Woolf Mews
Compton Pl
Tavistock Pl
Univ College London
St George's Gdns
Hunter Street
B504
Handel Street
Henrietta Mews
The Foundling Mus
Sch of Pharmacy
Brunswick Sq
Tenn Ct
Mecklenburgh Square Gardens
Sports Gd
Gray's Inn Road
Green Yd
Leonard Ct
Govt Offices
6
Tavistock
Thackeray Ho
Dickens Ho
Coram Ho
Witley Ct
Herbrand Street
Herbrand Estate
Marchmont Street
Foundling Court
O'Donnell Court
Brunswick Sh Ctr
Brunswick Square Gardens
WC1
Coram's Fields
Goodenough Coll
Mecklenburgh Place
Doughty St
Brownlow Mews
Gough Street
Coram Street
Bedford Way
Woburn Pl
B502
Lansdowne Terr
Guilford Street
Bernard Street
Russell Square
Colonnade
Grenville St
Dickens House Mus
Coley St
ITN & ITV
5
Govt Offices
Russell Square Ho
The Russell
Ormond Mews
Great Ormond St Hospital for Children
Institute
Millman Mews
Millman Street
Doughty Mews
Rokeby Ho
Long Yard
Roger Street
North Mews
Elm St
Inst of Neurology
Queen Ct
The National Hospital
Powis Pl
Spens Ho
Lamb's Conduit Street
CE Prim Sch
John's Mews
John Street
Kings Mews
Millman Pl
Northington Street
Rugby St
Ormond Mans
Great Ormond Street
82
Thornhaugh St
Bloomsbury
Russell Square Garden
St Giles Coll
Queen Square
The Royal London Homeopathic Hospl
Barbon Cl
Chancellors Ct
Orde Hall St
Emerald Street
Great James St
Cockpit Yd
Liby
A4200
Russell Square
4
B506
Cosmo Pl
Cranfield Ho
Bedford Hotel
Ormond Cl
Blemundsbury
Dombey St
Rich Bell Pl
Theobald's Road
Jockey's Fields
Raymond Bldgs
Gray's Inn Gdns
Gray's Inn
Verulam Bldgs
Montague Place
Huron Univ
Coll
Gage St
Boswell Street
Boswell Ct
Windmill
Harpur Mews
Harpur St
Govt Offices
New North St
Southampton Row
Bedford Place
Montague Street
239
Old Gloucester St
A401
Old North St
Lamb's Conduit Pass
Kingsway Mansions
Princeton St
The Old School
Three Cups Yd
Bedford Row
British Museum
Albion Coll
Bloomsbury Square Gardens
Bloomsbury Pl
Red Lion Sq
Coll
Princeton Mansions
Culverhouse
Red Lion Street
Sandland St
Brownlow Row
Gray's Inn Pl
City Coll
Warwick Ct
Fulwood Pl
Field Ct
3
Great Russell Street
Gt Russell Mans
Museum Mans
Gilbert Pl
Pied Bull Yd
Pied Bull Ct
Galen Pl
Bloomsbury Way
Vernon Pl
Sicilian Ave
Aspect Coll
Fisher St
Procter Street
Brampton
Dane St
Yorkshire Grey Yd
Eagle St
Sierra Leone
Offices
Hand Ct
High Holborn Ho
Catton St
A4200
Bloomsbury Street
Mus
Russell St
Coptic St
Little Russell
Museum
Bury Pl
Barter St
Southampton Pl
Lytton Ct
Coll
High Holborn
Holborn Pl
Office
Great Turnstile
Lincoln Ho
B400
Stone Bldgs
Congress House
Dyott St
Streatham St
New Oxford Street
Commonwealth Ho
Dunn's Pass
Little Turnstile
Holborn
Gate St
Whetstone Park
Newman's Row
Bainbridge St
A40
A400
Dragon Yd
Newton Street
Africa House
Lincoln's Inn Fields
The Soane Mus
Liby
Lincoln's Inn
2
Castlewood Ho
Bucknall
Dyott St
Grape St
Smart's Pl
Stukeley Street
Macklin Street
Powis Ho
St Joseph's Prim Sch
Remnant St
Kingsway
Lincoln's Inn Fields
Tenn Cts
Hunterian Mus
Lincoln's Inn
Centre Point
St Giles Ct
St Giles High St
Princes Cir
Berkshire Ho
Cuba
St Giles
Dudley Ct
Aldwych Bldgs
Parker Ms
Parker St
Great Queen Street
B402
Wild Court
Camden
City of Westminster
Lincoln's Inn Fields
Govt Offices
Royal Coll of Surgeons
Serle Street
New Square
Denmark St
Flitcroft St
Stacey St
New Compton St
Pendrell Ho
St Giles Pas
Shaftesbury Ave
B401
Endell Street
Gardens
Betterton St
Betterton Ho
Mathews Yd
Shorts
Acad
Arne St
Dryden St
Keeley St
Sardinia St
Sardinia House
Portsmouth St
Portugal Street
Carey
Phoenix St
Monmouth Street
B404
Neal's Yd
Nottingham Ct
Wild Street
Kemble St
Peabody Estate
St Clement Danes CE Prim Sch
Sheffield St
Clare Mkt
Clements Inn Pas
St Clement's La
Grange Ct
Liby
London Sch of Economics & Political Science
1
Caxton Wlk
Cambridge Circus
Earlham St
Neal
Shelton
Street
Odhams Wk
Long Acre
Drury Lane
Sheridan Bldgs
Beaumont Bldgs
Fletcher Bldgs
Broad Court
Martlett Court
Charter Ho
Crown Ct
Kean St
Imperial Ho
A4200
Houghton St
Aldwych House
St Clements Inn
St Clement Danes
Seven Dials
Tower St
Mercer Street
Langley St
Film Sch
Covent Garden
Royal Ballet Sch
Bow Street
Hanover Pl
Street
Stirling Siddons Ct
Tavistock St
The Waldorf
Aldwych
India
Melbourne Place
Australia
Strand
Charing Cross Road
West St
81
Litchfield Street
Sandringham Flats
30
St Martin's Lane
Upper St Martin's Lane
Wellington
Banbury Ct
Langley Ct
Floral Street
James St
Royal Opera House
250
Catherine St
Wellington St
Govt Office
Montreal Pl
A4
Strand
Arundel Street
Surrey
King
Newport Ct
Great Newport St
B402
Rose
Conduit Ct
Apple
Old Covent
London Transport Mus
Tavistock St

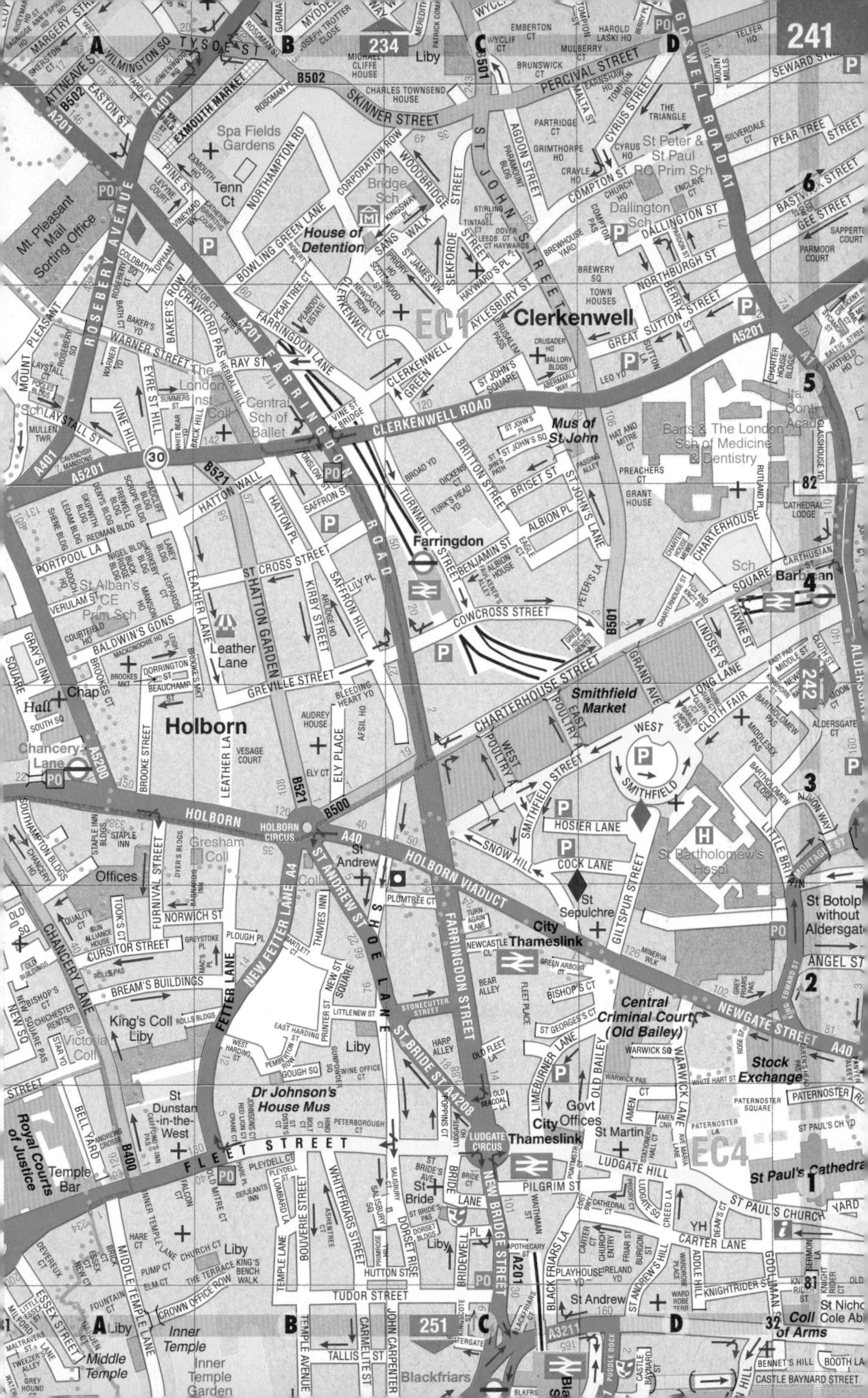
241
234
242
251
A
B
C
D
1
2
3
4
5
6
82
81
Clerkenwell
Holborn
EC1
EC4
Margery Street
Tysoe St
Wilmington Sq
Attneave St
Easton St
Exmouth Market
Rosoman St
Skinner Street
Percival Street
Goswell Road A1
Seward Street
Pear Tree Street
Bastwick Street
Gee Street
Spa Fields Gardens
Northampton Rd
Corporation Row
Woodbridge Street
St John Street
Agdon Street
Cyrus Street
Compton St
Dallington St
Northburgh St
Great Sutton Street
Clerkenwell Road
Rosebery Avenue
Mt. Pleasant Mail Sorting Office
Mount Pleasant
Warner Street
Ray St
Farringdon Road
Farringdon Lane
Bowling Green Lane
House of Detention
The Bridge Sch
Clerkenwell Green
Aylesbury St
Sekforde Street
St James Wk
Britton Street
St John's Square
Mus of St John
St John's Lane
Charterhouse Square
Barts & The London Sch of Medicine & Dentistry
Barbican
Carthusian St
Hatton Wall
Hatton Garden
Leather Lane
Saffron Hill
Kirby Street
Cowcross Street
Turnmill Street
Farringdon
Greville Street
Charterhouse Street
Smithfield Market
Long Lane
Cloth Fair
West Smithfield
Smithfield
Holborn
Holborn Circus
Holborn Viaduct
Snow Hill
Hosier Lane
Cock Lane
Giltspur Street
St Bartholomew's Hospl
Little Britain
Montague St
Aldersgate St
St Botolph without Aldersgate
Angel St
Newgate Street
Chancery Lane
Gray's Inn Square
Brooke Street
Ely Place
Furnival Street
Fetter Lane
New Fetter Lane
St Andrew St
Shoe Lane
Farringdon Street
St Bride St
Old Bailey
Central Criminal Court (Old Bailey)
City Thameslink
Warwick Lane
Stock Exchange
Paternoster Row
St Paul's Cathedral
St Paul's Church Yard
Ludgate Hill
Ludgate Circus
New Bridge Street
Fleet Street
Royal Courts of Justice
Temple Bar
Bell Yard
Middle Temple Lane
Inner Temple
Middle Temple
Essex Street
Whitefriars Street
Bouverie Street
Tudor Street
Carmelite St
John Carpenter
Blackfriars
Black Friars La
Carter Lane
Creed La
Godliman St
Knightrider St
Coll of Arms
Castle Baynard Street
Queen Victoria St
Dr Johnson's House Mus
St Dunstan in-the-West
King's Coll Liby
Victoria Coll
Gresham Coll
St Andrew
St Sepulchre
St Bride
St Martin
Govt Offices
Offices
Liby
Chap
Hall
Cursitor Street
Bream's Buildings
Pilgrim St
Bride Lane
Puddle Dock

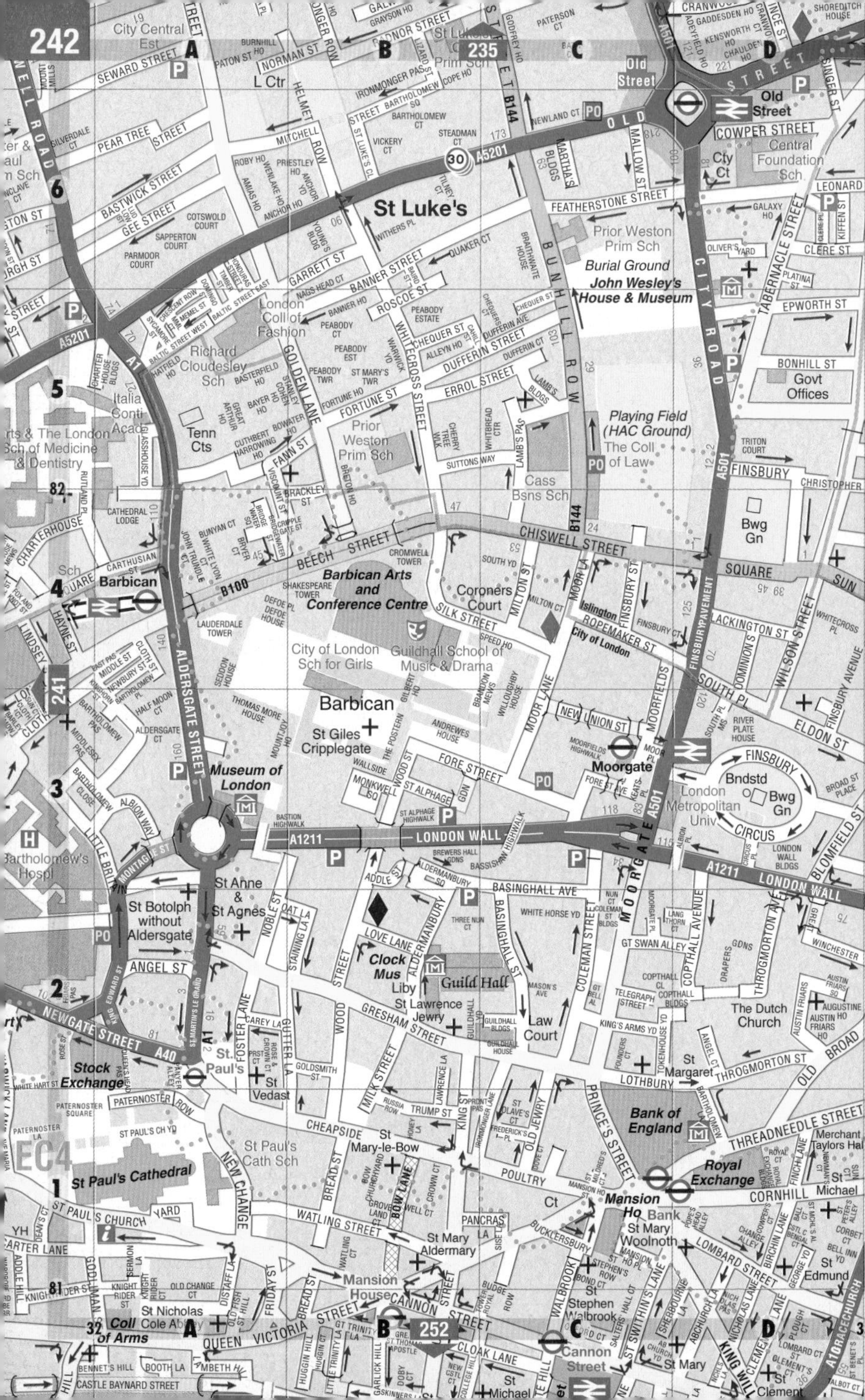
St Luke's
Barbican
Barbican Arts and Conference Centre
City of London Sch for Girls
Guildhall School of Music & Drama
Museum of London
St Giles Cripplegate
Moorgate
Old Street
Burial Ground
John Wesley's House & Museum
Playing Field (HAC Ground)
The Coll of Law
Prior Weston Prim Sch
Richard Cloudesley Sch
London Coll of Fashion
Coroners Court
London Metropolitan Univ
Guild Hall
Clock Mus
Bank of England
Royal Exchange
Mansion Ho
Bank
Stock Exchange
St Paul's Cathedral
St Paul's Cath Sch
Coll of Arms
Mansion House
Cannon Street
The Dutch Church
Govt Offices
Central Foundation Sch
ALDERSGATE STREET
CITY ROAD
OLD STREET
CHISWELL STREET
BEECH STREET
LONDON WALL
MOORGATE
NEWGATE STREET
CHEAPSIDE
QUEEN VICTORIA STREET
CANNON STREET
THREADNEEDLE STREET
CORNHILL
LOMBARD STREET
BUNHILL ROW
WHITECROSS STREET
GOLDEN LANE
FINSBURY PAVEMENT
FINSBURY SQUARE
FINSBURY CIRCUS
235
241
252
EC4

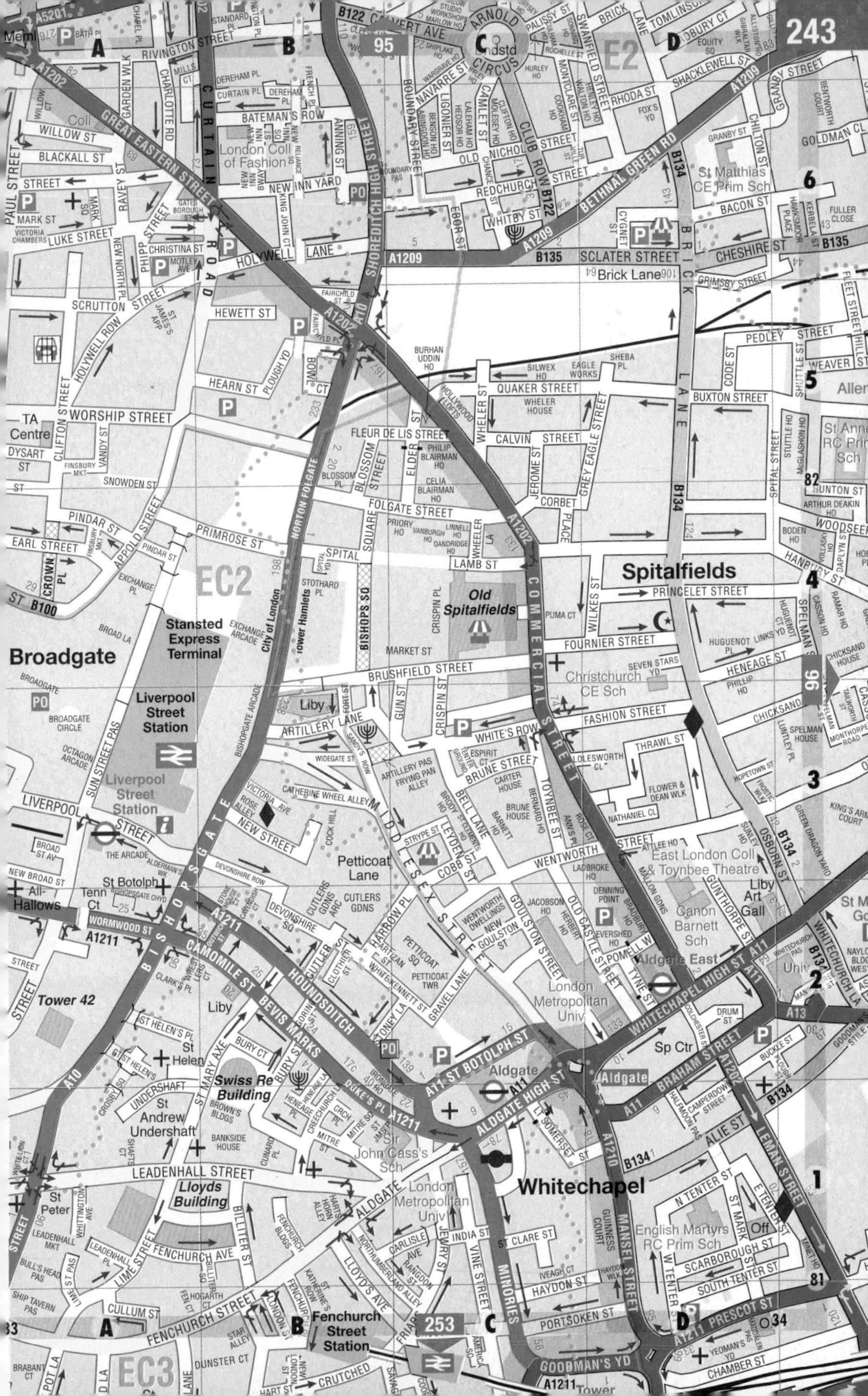
A
B
C
D
E2
95
ARNOLD CIRCUS
CALVERT AVE
RIVINGTON STREET
GREAT EASTERN STREET
CURTAIN ROAD
CHARLOTTE RD
WILLOW ST
BLACKALL ST
PAUL STREET
LUKE STREET
SCRUTTON STREET
HOLYWELL LANE
HOLYWELL ROW
WORSHIP STREET
HEWETT ST
HEARN ST
PLOUGH YD
BATEMAN'S ROW
London Coll of Fashion
NEW INN YARD
SHOREDITCH HIGH STREET
BOUNDARY STREET
LIGONIER ST
CAMLET ST
NICHOL ST
REDCHURCH STREET
CLUB ROW
BETHNAL GREEN RD
SCLATER STREET
CHESHIRE ST
Brick Lane
BRICK LANE
St Matthias CE Prim Sch
BACON ST
GRANBY ST
CHILTON ST
PEDLEY STREET
WEAVER ST
BUXTON STREET
QUAKER STREET
WHEELER ST
CALVIN STREET
GREY EAGLE STREET
FLEUR DE LIS STREET
BLOSSOM STREET
FOLGATE STREET
NORTON FOLGATE
CORBET PLACE
HANBURY ST
Spitalfields
PRINCELET STREET
FOURNIER STREET
LAMB ST
Old Spitalfields
BRUSHFIELD STREET
Christchurch CE Sch
FASHION STREET
THRAWL ST
WENTWORTH STREET
EC2
Stansted Express Terminal
Broadgate
Liverpool Street Station
LIVERPOOL STREET
PRIMROSE ST
APPOLD STREET
EARL STREET
SUN STREET PAS
City of London
Tower Hamlets
BISHOPSGATE
ARTILLERY LANE
MIDDLESEX STREET
Petticoat Lane
COMMERCIAL STREET
TOYNBEE ST
East London Coll & Toynbee Theatre
Canon Barnett Sch
OSBORN ST
Aldgate East
WHITECHAPEL HIGH ST
A11
DEVONSHIRE SQ
HOUNDSDITCH
CAMOMILE ST
BEVIS MARKS
WORMWOOD ST
Tower 42
St Helen
Swiss Re Building
St Andrew Undershaft
ST MARY AXE
DUKE'S PL
Aldgate
ALDGATE HIGH ST
ST BOTOLPH ST
Sir John Cass's Sch
London Metropolitan Univ
LEADENHALL STREET
Lloyds Building
FENCHURCH AVE
BILLITER ST
LIME STREET
FENCHURCH STREET
Fenchurch Street Station
253
MINORIES
Whitechapel
MANSELL STREET
ALIE ST
LEMAN STREET
BRAHAM STREET
English Martyrs RC Prim Sch
PRESCOT ST
PORTSOKEN ST
GOODMAN'S YD
HAYDON ST
CRUTCHED FRIARS
EC3
1
2
3
4
5
6

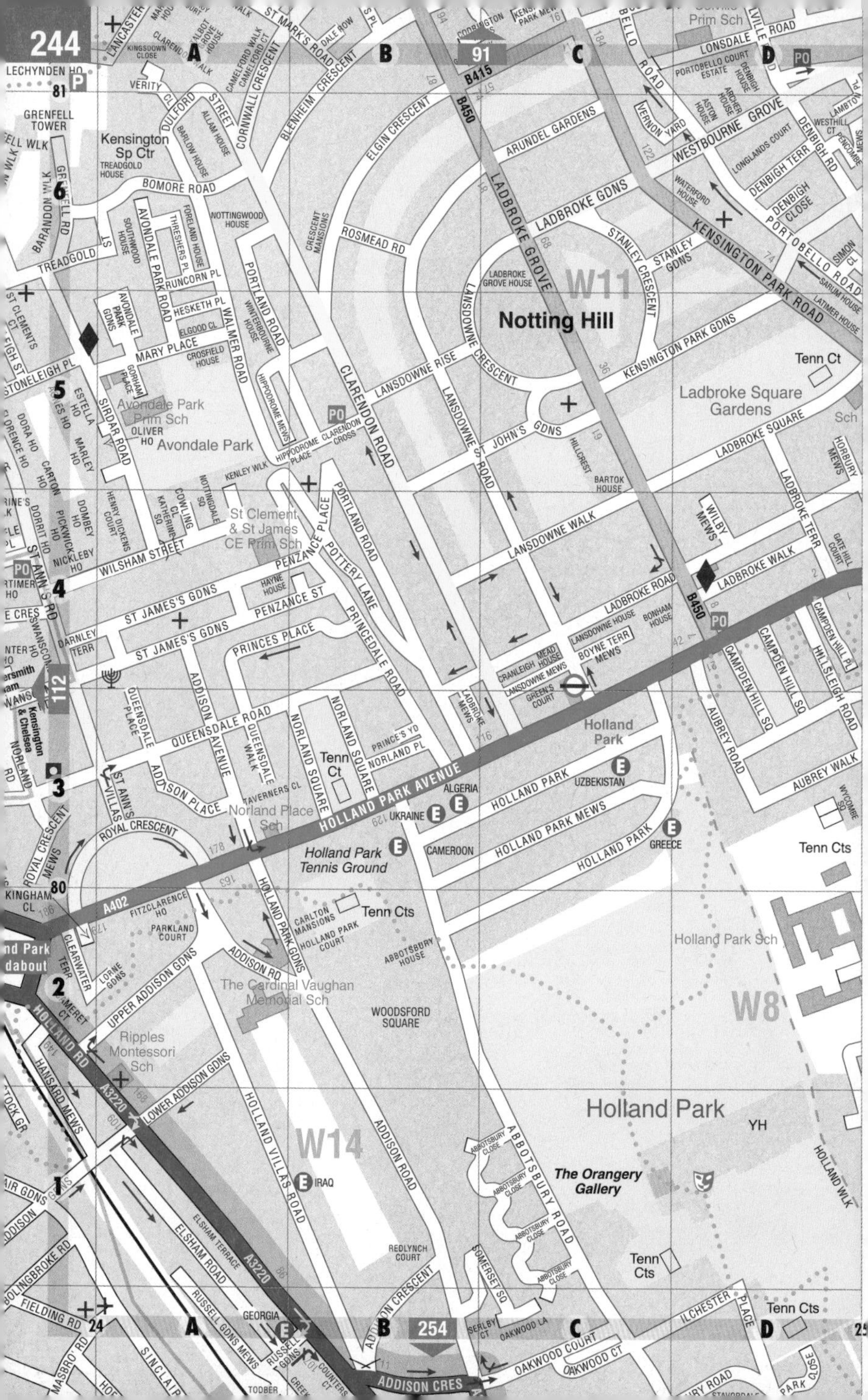
A
B
C
D
91
Notting Hill
W11
Kensington Sp Ctr
Grenfell Tower
Avondale Park
Avondale Park Prim Sch
St Clement & St James CE Prim Sch
Ladbroke Square Gardens
Holland Park Avenue
Holland Park
Holland Park Tennis Ground
The Cardinal Vaughan Memorial Sch
Ripples Montessori Sch
Norland Place Sch
Holland Park Sch
W8
W14
The Orangery Gallery
Ladbroke Grove
Kensington Park Road
Westbourne Grove
Ladbroke Road
Clarendon Road
Portland Road
Addison Road
Abbotsbury Road
Holland Villas Road
Holland Road
Addison Crescent
Royal Crescent
Lansdowne Crescent
Lansdowne Road
Ladbroke Square
Walmer Road
Pottery Lane
Princedale Road
Queensdale Road
St James's Gdns
Woodsford Square
Ilchester Place
Addison Cres
112
254
80
81
24

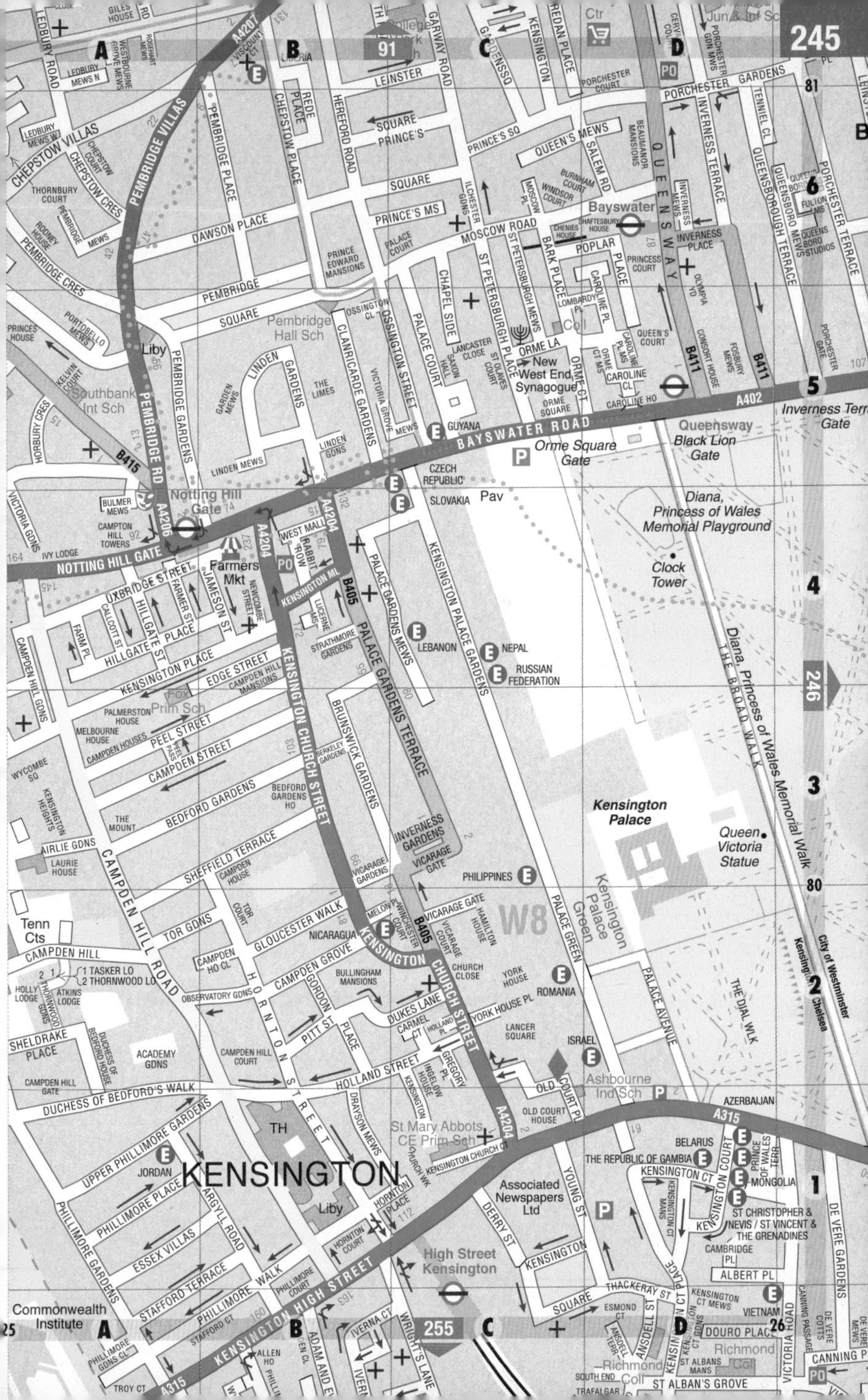

KENSINGTON
Kensington Palace
Kensington Palace Green
W8
BAYSWATER ROAD
NOTTING HILL GATE
KENSINGTON CHURCH STREET
KENSINGTON HIGH STREET
QUEENSWAY
PEMBRIDGE VILLAS
PEMBRIDGE RD
PEMBRIDGE SQUARE
PEMBRIDGE GARDENS
PEMBRIDGE CRES
PEMBRIDGE PLACE
CHEPSTOW VILLAS
CHEPSTOW PLACE
LEDBURY ROAD
DAWSON PLACE
HEREFORD ROAD
PRINCE'S SQUARE
LEINSTER SQUARE
GARWAY ROAD
MOSCOW ROAD
ST PETERSBURGH PLACE
PORCHESTER GARDENS
PORCHESTER TERRACE
INVERNESS TERRACE
QUEENSBOROUGH TERRACE
Bayswater
Notting Hill Gate
High Street Kensington
Inverness Terr Gate
Queensway Black Lion Gate
Orme Square Gate
Diana, Princess of Wales Memorial Playground
Clock Tower
Diana, Princess of Wales Memorial Walk
THE BROAD WALK
Queen Victoria Statue
THE DIAL WLK
New West End Synagogue
Pembridge Hall Sch
Southbank Int Sch
Farmers Mkt
Liby
PALACE GARDENS TERRACE
KENSINGTON PALACE GARDENS
PALACE GREEN
PALACE AVENUE
CAMPDEN HILL ROAD
CAMPDEN HILL
CAMPDEN GROVE
CAMPDEN STREET
PEEL STREET
EDGE STREET
KENSINGTON PLACE
BEDFORD GARDENS
SHEFFIELD TERRACE
HORNTON STREET
HOLLAND STREET
DUKES LANE
GLOUCESTER WALK
VICARAGE GATE
Tenn Cts
ACADEMY GDNS
DUCHESS OF BEDFORD'S WALK
PHILLIMORE GARDENS
UPPER PHILLIMORE GARDENS
PHILLIMORE PLACE
ESSEX VILLAS
STAFFORD TERRACE
ARGYLL ROAD
Commonwealth Institute
St Mary Abbots CE Prim Sch
Associated Newspapers Ltd
KENSINGTON SQUARE
KENSINGTON COURT
YOUNG ST
DERRY ST
THACKERAY ST
DE VERE GARDENS
VICTORIA ROAD
ST ALBAN'S GROVE
Ashbourne Ind Sch
Richmond Coll
City of Westminster
Kensington & Chelsea
CZECH REPUBLIC
SLOVAKIA
LEBANON
NEPAL
RUSSIAN FEDERATION
PHILIPPINES
NICARAGUA
ROMANIA
ISRAEL
JORDAN
AZERBAIJAN
BELARUS
THE REPUBLIC OF GAMBIA
MONGOLIA
ST CHRISTOPHER & NEVIS / ST VINCENT & THE GRENADINES
VIETNAM
GUYANA
A
B
C
D
1
2
3
4
5
6
91
246
255

Bayswater
Kensington Gardens
W2
SW7
Round Pond
The Long Water
Bayswater Road Mkt
Lancaster Gate
Marlborough Gate
Lancaster Gate
Victoria Gate
Westbourne Gate
Inverness Terrace Gate
St Agnes' Well
The Fountains
Bayard's Watering Place (site of)
Speke's Monument
Peter Pan Statue
Diana, Princess of Wales Memorial Walk
Physical Engery Statue
Temple Lodge
Serpentine Bridge
Queen Victoria Statue
Bandstand
Serpentine Gallery
Diana, Princess of Wales Memorial Fountain
Albert Memorial
Coalbrookdale Gate
Alexandra Gate
Queen's Gate
Palace Gate
Royal Coll of Art
Royal Albert Hall
Royal Geographical Society
Polish Inst & Sikorski Museum
Royal Coll of Organists
Royal College of Science
Royal College of Music
Royal Lancaster Hotel
St James's & St Michael's CE Prim Sch
BAYSWATER ROAD
KENSINGTON ROAD
HYDE PARK GATE
KENSINGTON GORE
THE FLOWER WALK
NORTH FLOWER WALK
NORTH WALK
BUDGE'S WALK
LANCASTER WALK
BUCK HILL WALK
City of Westminster
Kensington & Chelsea
236
245
256

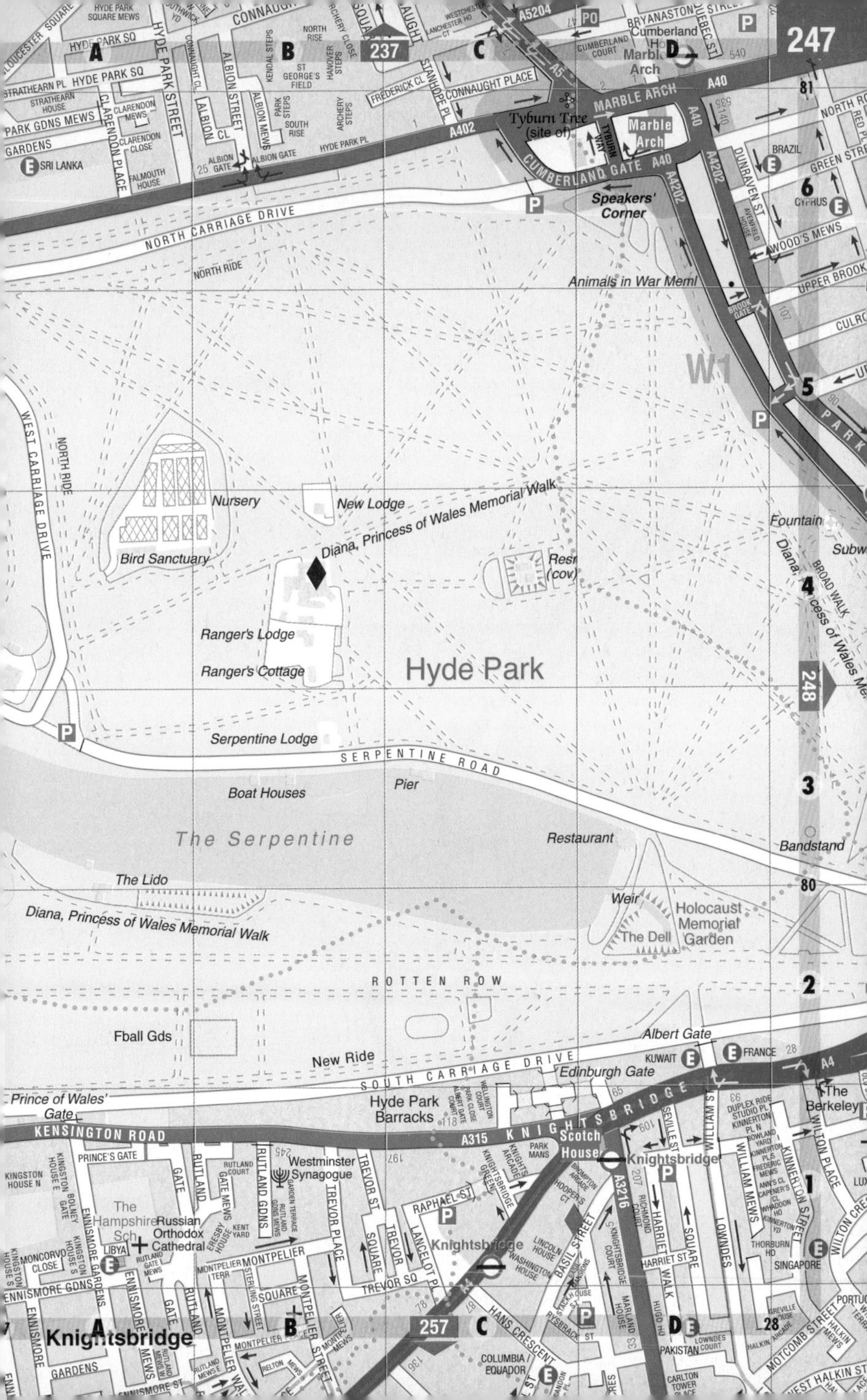

Hyde Park
The Serpentine
Marble Arch
Tyburn Tree (site of)
Speakers' Corner
Animals in War Meml
W1
Nursery
New Lodge
Bird Sanctuary
Diana, Princess of Wales Memorial Walk
Ranger's Lodge
Ranger's Cottage
Resr (cov)
Serpentine Lodge
SERPENTINE ROAD
Boat Houses
Pier
Restaurant
Bandstand
The Lido
Weir
The Dell
Holocaust Memorial Garden
ROTTEN ROW
Fball Gds
New Ride
Albert Gate
SOUTH CARRIAGE DRIVE
Edinburgh Gate
Prince of Wales' Gate
Hyde Park Barracks
KENSINGTON ROAD
KNIGHTSBRIDGE
Scotch House
Knightsbridge
Westminster Synagogue
The Hampshire Sch
Russian Orthodox Cathedral
The Berkeley
NORTH CARRIAGE DRIVE
NORTH RIDE
WEST CARRIAGE DRIVE
BROAD WALK
PARK LANE
CUMBERLAND GATE
HYDE PARK SQ
CONNAUGHT PLACE
HYDE PARK STREET
ALBION STREET
STANHOPE PL
FREDERICK CL
HYDE PARK PL
SRI LANKA
BRAZIL
CYPRUS
KUWAIT
FRANCE
LIBYA
SINGAPORE
PAKISTAN
COLUMBIA / EQUADOR
TREVOR SQ
MONTPELIER SQUARE
HANS CRESCENT
BASIL STREET
SLOANE STREET
ENNISMORE GARDENS
WILTON PLACE
237
248
257
Knightsbridge

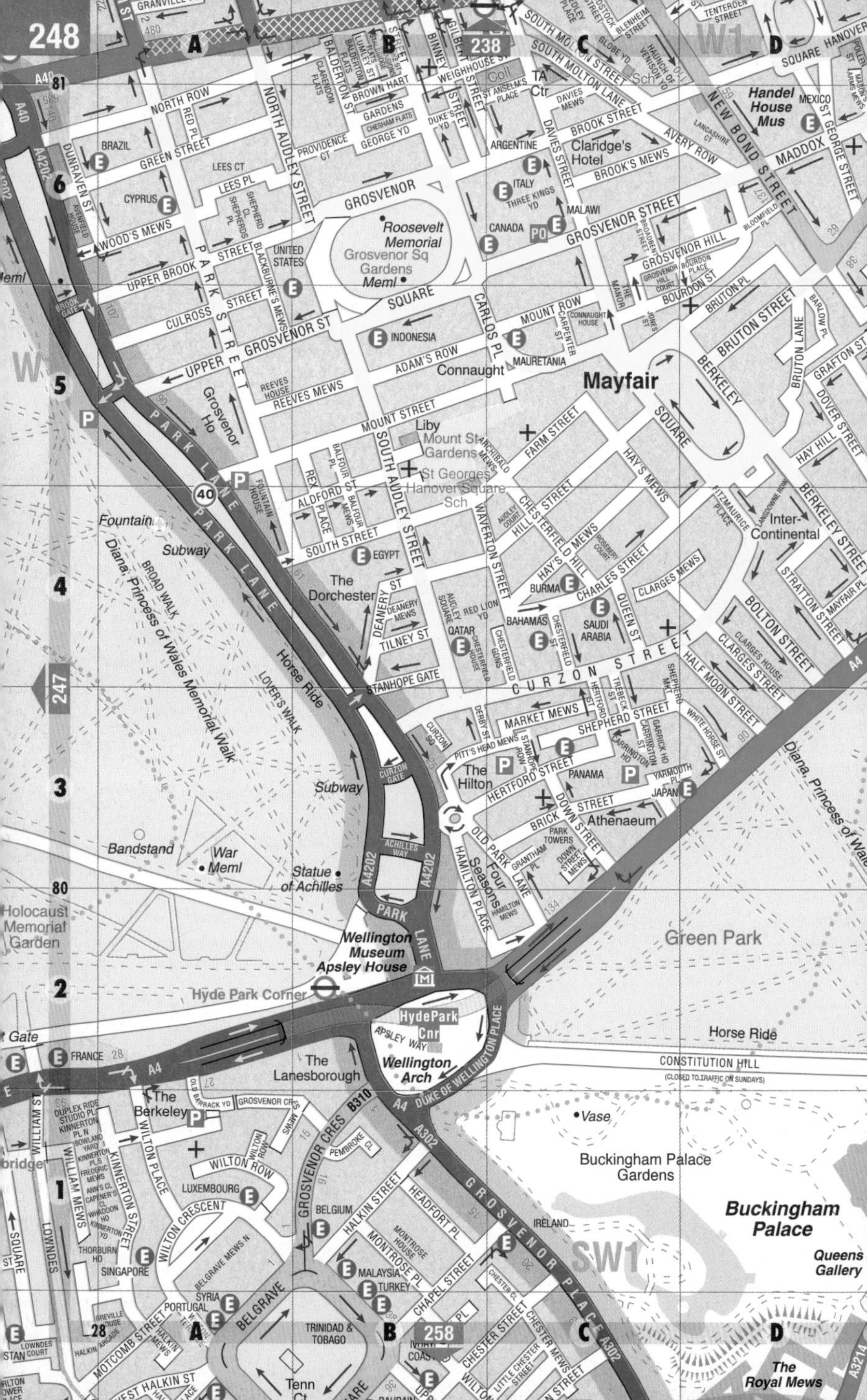
Mayfair
Grosvenor Square
Roosevelt Memorial
Grosvenor Sq Gardens
Claridge's Hotel
Handel House Mus
Connaught
The Dorchester
Grosvenor Ho
Mount St Gardens
St Georges Hanover Square Sch
Inter-Continental
The Hilton
Athenaeum
Four Seasons
Hyde Park Corner
Wellington Museum
Apsley House
Wellington Arch
Statue of Achilles
The Lanesborough
The Berkeley
Green Park
Buckingham Palace Gardens
Buckingham Palace
Queens Gallery
The Royal Mews
Constitution Hill
(CLOSED TO TRAFFIC ON SUNDAYS)
Horse Ride
Diana, Princess of Wales Memorial Walk
Holocaust Memorial Garden
Bandstand
War Meml
Fountain
Subway
Broad Walk
Lover's Walk
Park Lane
Grosvenor Place
Curzon Street
South Audley Street
North Audley Street
Park Street
Brook Street
Grosvenor Street
Berkeley Square
New Bond Street
Piccadilly
Belgrave Square
Wilton Crescent
Vase
W1
SW1
238
247
258

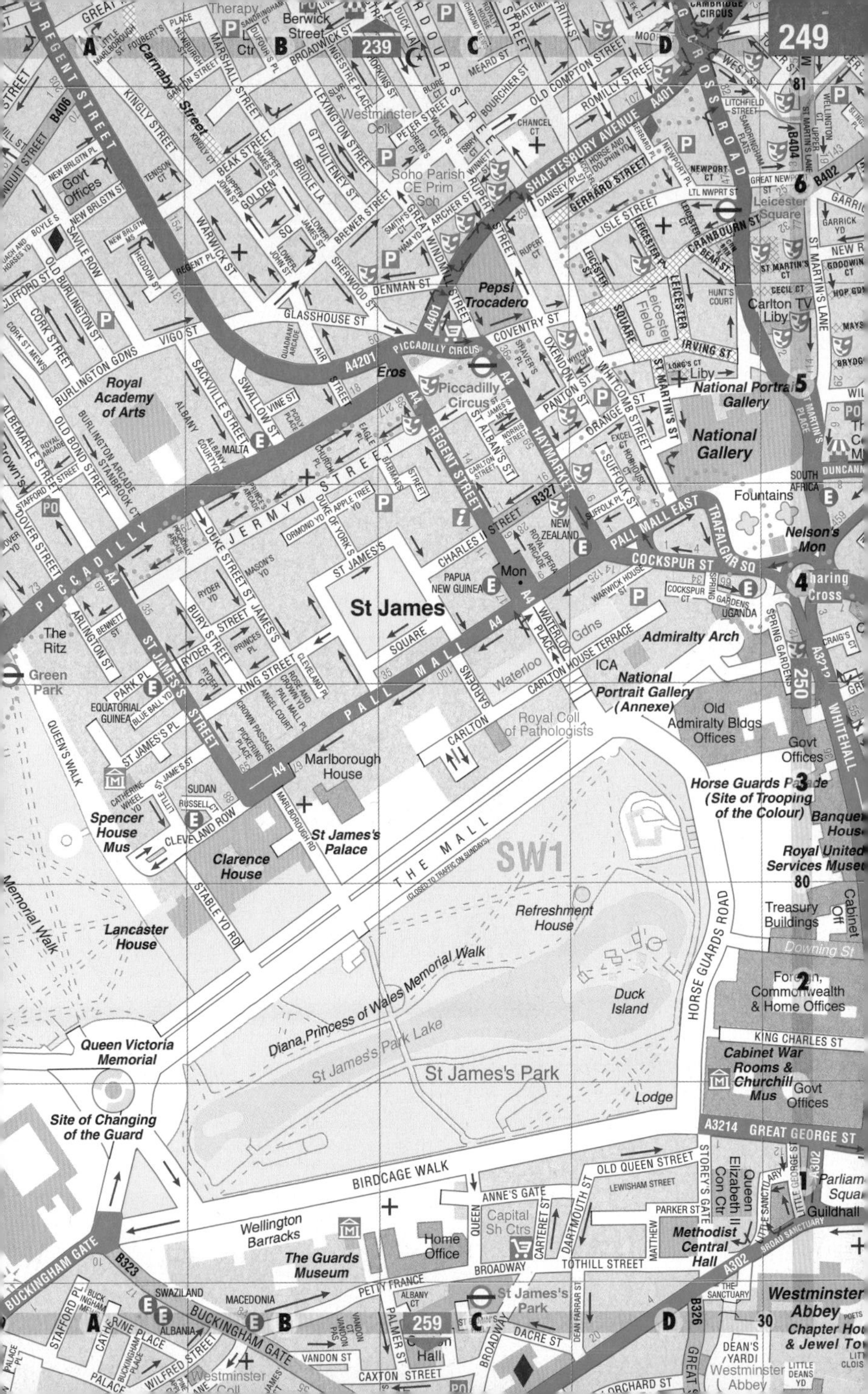

239
Carnaby Street
Regent Street
Berwick Street
Broadwick St
Wardour Street
Old Compton Street
Shaftesbury Avenue
Charing Cross Road
Cambridge Circus
Westminster Coll
Soho Parish CE Prim Sch
Govt Offices
Golden Sq
Beak Street
Brewer Street
Glasshouse St
Vigo St
Leicester Square
Cranbourn St
Gerrard Street
Lisle Street
Leicester Fields
Pepsi Trocadero
Coventry St
Piccadilly Circus
Eros
Royal Academy of Arts
Piccadilly
Jermyn Street
Haymarket
National Portrait Gallery
National Gallery
Carlton TV
Trafalgar Sq
Pall Mall East
Cockspur St
Fountains
Nelson's Mon
Charing Cross
St James
St James's Square
Pall Mall
St James's Street
The Ritz
Green Park
Admiralty Arch
ICA
National Portrait Gallery (Annexe)
Old Admiralty Bldgs Offices
Royal Coll of Pathologists
Marlborough House
St James's Palace
Clarence House
Spencer House Mus
Lancaster House
The Mall
SW1
Horse Guards Parade (Site of Trooping of the Colour)
Banqueting House
Royal United Services Museum
Whitehall
Treasury Buildings
Downing St
Foreign, Commonwealth & Home Offices
King Charles St
Cabinet War Rooms & Churchill Mus
Govt Offices
Horse Guards Road
Refreshment House
Duck Island
Diana, Princess of Wales Memorial Walk
St James's Park Lake
St James's Park
Lodge
Queen Victoria Memorial
Site of Changing of the Guard
Memorial Walk
Queen's Walk
Birdcage Walk
Wellington Barracks
The Guards Museum
Home Office
Capital Sh Ctrs
Old Queen Street
Great George St
Queen Elizabeth II Con Ctr
Methodist Central Hall
Tothill Street
Broadway
Petty France
St James's Park
Buckingham Gate
Westminster Abbey
Chapter House & Jewel Tower
Parliament Square
Guildhall
Caxton Hall
Caxton Street
Victoria Street
259
250

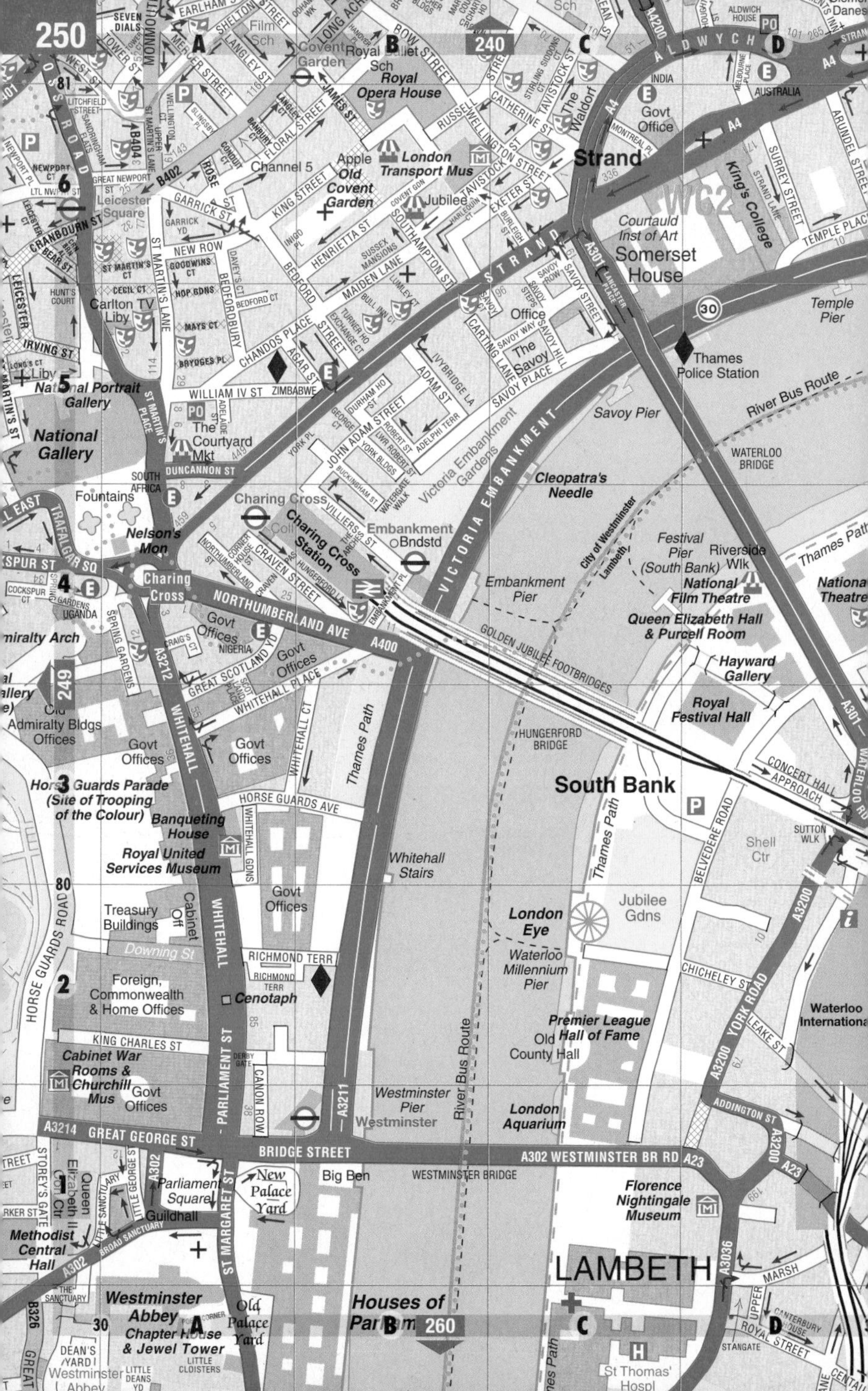
Charing Cross
National Gallery
National Portrait Gallery
Royal Opera House
London Transport Mus
Old Covent Garden
Strand
Somerset House
King's College
Courtauld Inst of Art
Trafalgar Sq
Nelson's Mon
Charing Cross Station
Embankment
Victoria Embankment
Cleopatra's Needle
Golden Jubilee Footbridges
Hungerford Bridge
Waterloo Bridge
South Bank
National Film Theatre
Queen Elizabeth Hall & Purcell Room
Hayward Gallery
Royal Festival Hall
London Eye
Jubilee Gdns
Whitehall
Horse Guards Parade (Site of Trooping of the Colour)
Banqueting House
Royal United Services Museum
Treasury Buildings
Downing St
Foreign, Commonwealth & Home Offices
Cenotaph
Cabinet War Rooms & Churchill Mus
Parliament St
Westminster
Bridge Street
A302 Westminster Br Rd
Westminster Bridge
Big Ben
Houses of Parliament
Westminster Abbey
Chapter House & Jewel Tower
Parliament Square
Methodist Central Hall
Florence Nightingale Museum
London Aquarium
Premier League Hall of Fame
Old County Hall
LAMBETH
St Thomas' Hospl
Waterloo International
Thames Police Station
Temple Pier
Savoy Pier
Embankment Pier
Festival Pier (South Bank)
Waterloo Millennium Pier
Westminster Pier
River Bus Route
Thames Path
Leicester Square
Covent Garden
Aldwych
The Savoy
The Waldorf
240
249
260

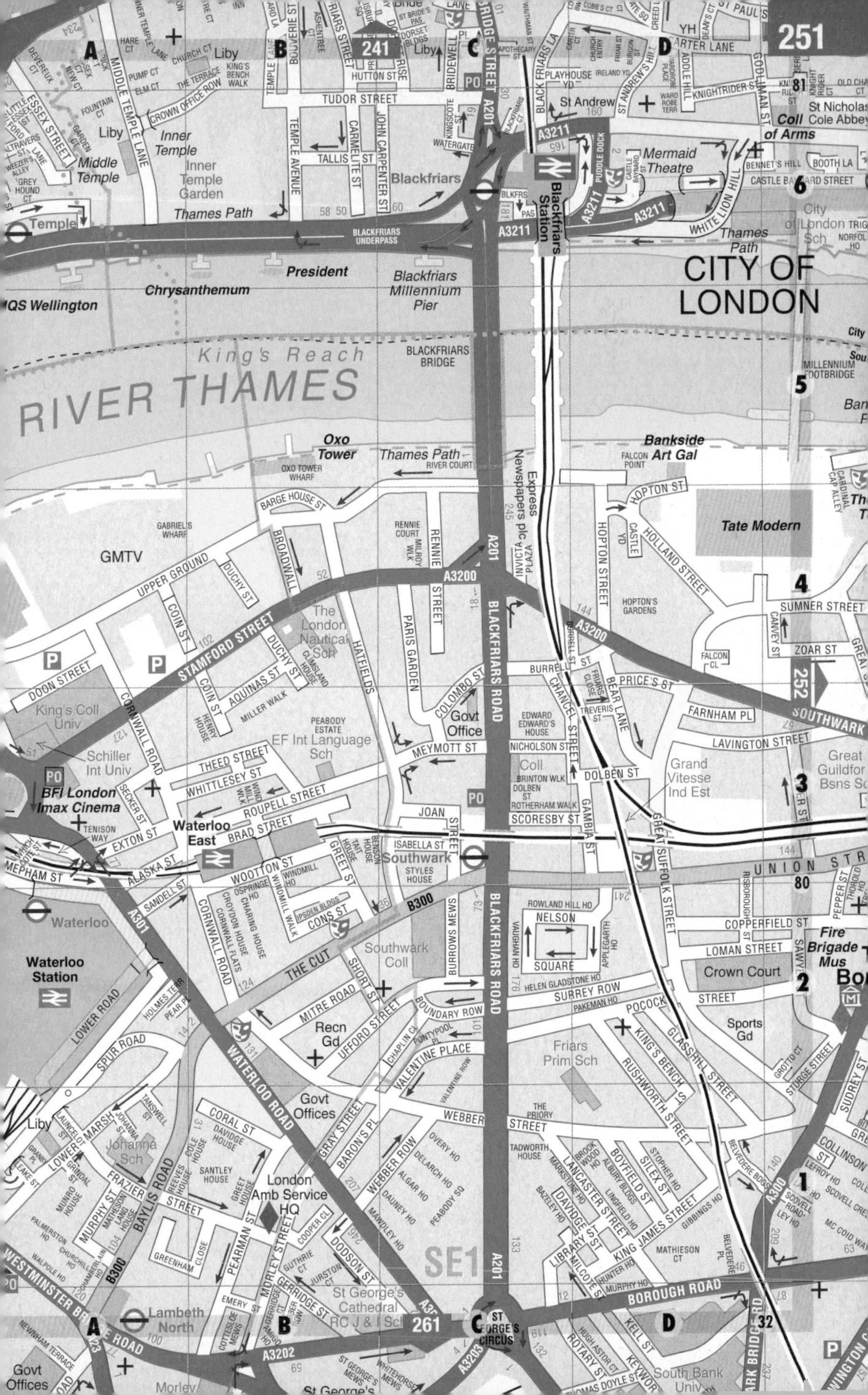
RIVER THAMES
King's Reach
CITY OF LONDON
BLACKFRIARS BRIDGE
BLACKFRIARS ROAD
Blackfriars Station
Blackfriars Millennium Pier
Tate Modern
Bankside Art Gal
Oxo Tower
Thames Path
STAMFORD STREET
UPPER GROUND
Waterloo East
Southwark
Waterloo Station
WATERLOO ROAD
THE CUT
UNION STREET
SOUTHWARK
BOROUGH ROAD
ST GEORGE'S CIRCUS
Lambeth North
St George's Cathedral RC J & I Sch
London Amb Service HQ
Crown Court
Fire Brigade Mus
SE1
Inner Temple
Middle Temple
Temple
Mermaid Theatre
President
Chrysanthemum
HQS Wellington
GMTV
King's Coll Univ
BFI London Imax Cinema
The London Nautical Sch
Southwark Coll
Friars Prim Sch
Grand Vitesse Ind Est
Sports Gd
Recn Gd
Govt Offices
241
261
252

A
B
C
D
242
262
6
5
4
3
2
1
81
80
32
CITY OF LONDON
City of London
Southwark
SE1
The Borough
Watling Street
Pancras
Bank
St Mary Woolnoth
Lombard Street
King William Street
Gracechurch
St Edmund
Mansion House
St Mary Aldermary
Cannon Street
Queen Victoria Street
St Nicholas Cole Abbey
Coll of Arms
Knightrider St
Godliman St
Distaff La
Friday St
Bread St
Old Change Ct
Mermaid Theatre
Bennet's Hill
Booth La
Lambeth Hill
Castle Baynard Street
White Lion Hill
Queen St
Cloak Lane
St Michael
St James
College Street
St Stephen Walbrook
Walbrook
Oxford Ct
Dowgate Hill
Cannon Street Station
St Swithin's Lane
Abchurch La
Nicholas Lane
Clement's Lane
St Clement
St Mary
Monument
The Monument
Fish St Hill
Arthur St
Martin Lane
Laurence Pountney Hill
Bush Lane
Suffolk La
Upper Thames Street
High Timber St
Trig La
Broken Wf
City of London Sch
Norfolk Ho
Gardners La
Globe View
Stew Lane
Queen's Quay
Queenhithe
Kennett Wf La
Vintners Ct
Queen St Pl
Bell Wharf La
Cousin Lane
Allhallows La
Angel Pass
Swan Lane
A300
A3
A3211
A10
A200
A3200
A3201
A3202
A2
A2198
B300
B240
Thames Path
Queenhithe Stairs
Southwark Bridge Stairs
Millennium Footbridge
Bankside Pier
Southwark Bridge
Princess Elizabeth
Swan Lane Pier
River Bus Route
London Bridge
St Magnus the Martyr
Bankside Art Gal
Tate Modern
Bankside
Cardinal Cap Alley
The Globe Theatre
New Globe Wlk
Bear Gdns
Rose Alley
The Financial Times Ltd
Shakespeare's Globe Theatre (site of)
Bank End
Park Street
Winchester Palace
The Golden Hinde
Clink St
Vinopolis
Old London Bridge (site of)
Thames Path
London Bridge
Winchester Sq
Montague Cl
Southwark Cathedral
Tooley St
London Br Wlk
Duke St Hill
The London Dungeon
Bear Gardens Mus
Emerson St
Park
Sumner Street
Canvey St
Zoar St
Great Guildford Street
Sumner Bldgs
Congo (Hon Consul)
Southwark Bridge Road
Anchor Terrace
Old Theatre Ct
Porter St
Perkins Square
Gatehouse Sq
Maiden Lane
Lucy Brown Ho
Riverside Workshops
Stoney Street
Rochester Wk
Winchester Wlk
Cathedral St
Borough
Borough Market
Bedale St
Green Dragon Ct
Railway Approach
London Br St
London Bridge Station
Falcon
251
Farnham Pl
Southwark Street
Peabody Estate
Hotels
Bramah Mus
Thrale St
Redcross Way
Lavington Street
Grand Vitesse Ind Est
Great Guildford Bsns Sq
Ewer St
Keppel Row
Wardens Gr
America St
Crowne Ho
Flatiron Sq
Omeara St
Triangle Ct
Borough High Street
Coll
King's Head Yd
White Hart Yard
George Inn Yd
Talbot Yd
Calvert's Buildings
St Margaret's Court
Maidstone Bldgs
Queen's Head Yd
Kentish Bldgs
Guy's Hospl Sch
St Thomas Street
Joiner St
Stainer St
Guy's Hospl
Great Maze Pond
Union Street
Risborough St
Thorold Ho
Trelawney Ho
Farnham Ho
Tomline Ho
Pepper St
Flatiron Yd
Ayres Street
Cathedral Sch of St Saviour & St Mary Overie Prim Sch
St Joseph's RC Prim Sch
Copperfield St
Doyce St
Fire Brigade Mus
Loman Street
Sawyer St
Crown Court
Quilp St
Glennam St
Pattison Ho
Red Cross Cotts
Marshalsea Road
Little Dorrit Ct
Babington House
Dorrit St
Disney Pl
Disney St
Newcomen Street
Betsham Ho
Mermaid Ct
Chapel Ct
Northfleet Ho
Bowling Green Pl
Snowsfields
City Banking Coll
Sports Gd
Ilfracombe Flats
Mint St
Caleb St
Trundle St
Weller St
Douglas Buildings
Gaitskell Way
Issac Way
Little Dorrit Park
Liby
Chaloner Ct
Kellow Ho
Angel Pl
Govt Offices
Tennis Street
Boughton Ho
Crosby Ct
Baden Pl
Crosby Row
Hamilton Sq
Sarah Swift Ho
Kipling Street
Guy Street
Weston Street
Porlock St
Brenley Ho
Balin Ho
Plantain Pl
Eynsford Ho
Beormund Prim Sch
Hamlet Way
Mulvaney Way
Burwash Ho
Grotto Ct
Sturge Street
Sudrey St
Bittern St
Lant House
Toulmin St
Lant Street
Sanctuary St
Vine Yd
Borough
Glasshill Street
Bittern Ho
Pickwick Street
Charles Dickens Prim Sch
Signal House
Redman House
Silvester St
Nebraska Street
Southall Pl
Halling Ho
Hankey Place
Lockyer St
Lockyer Estate
Long Lane
Great Suffolk Street
Collinson St
Collinson Ho
Lefroy Ho
Lake Ho
Scovell Road
Scovell Cres
Ley Ho
Collinson Walk
Mc Coid Way
Borough Square
Stones End St
Belvedere Bdgs
Gibbings Ho
Belvedere Pl
Hulme Place
Avon Place
Swan Street
Trinity St
Cole Street
Horsemongers Mews
Sterry St
Pilgrimage Street
Abinger Ho
Tabard Gardens
Harbledown Ho
Munro Ho
Aylesford Ho
Medway Ho
Strood Ho
Staple Street
Otford Ho
Rochester Ho
Manciple Street
Crayford Ho
Lenham Ho
Kemsing Ho
Rudyard Ct
Dunsterville Way
Heldar Ct
Borough Road
Trio Place
King's Pl
Cty Ct
Gloucester Ct
Globe St
Selborne Ho
Becket Ho
Shere Ho
Great Dover Street
Becket St
Tabard Street
Fball Gd
Trinity Street
Merrick Square
Brockham St
Newington Causeway
Avonmouth St
Inner London & Southwark Crown Cts
South Bank Univ
Harper Road
Gardner Street
Tabard Ho
Hubert Ho
Eastwell
Weston Street
Elim St
Seal Ho
Godstone Ho
Charlwood Ho

243
A
B
C
D
EC3
Fenchurch Street Station
Tower Gateway
Tower Hill
London Wall
Trinity Sq Gdns
TOWER HILL
BYWARD ST
LOWER THAMES ST
Custom House
All-Hallows
St Peter ad Vincula
Royal Fusiliers Mus
The Royal Armouries
St John's Chapel
The Tower
Tenn Ct
TOWER BR APPROACH
EAST SMITHFIELD
ROYAL MINT ST
E1
West Dock
East Dock
St Katharine Docks
IVORY HOUSE
ST KATHARINE'S WAY
RIVER THAMES
Pontoon
Tower Stairs
Tower Millennium Pier
Traitors Gate
Thames Path
London Bridge City Pier
River Bus Route
HMS Belfast
TOWER BRIDGE
Jetty
St Katharine's Pier
Dock Entrance
Upper Pool
West India Dock Pier 4km
London City Airport 11km
Greenwich Pier 5km
Horselydown Old Stairs
Butler's Wharf Pier
Hay's Galleria
Crown Court
The Scoop
City Hall
London Bridge City Park
Britain at War Experience
TOOLEY STREET
Unicorn
Lambeth Tertiary Coll (Tower Bridge Centre)
TOWER BRIDGE RD
SHAD THAMES
Design Museum
Wharves
St Saviour's Dock
Glass House
Snowsfields Prim Sch
Leathermarket Com Park
Leathermarket Gdns
The Fashion & Design Museum
BERMONDSEY STREET
Tower Bridge Prim Sch
BERMONDSEY
DRUID STREET
JAMAICA ROAD
St Joseph's RC Jun & Inf
Tenn Cts
Caledon Market
ABBEY STREET
263

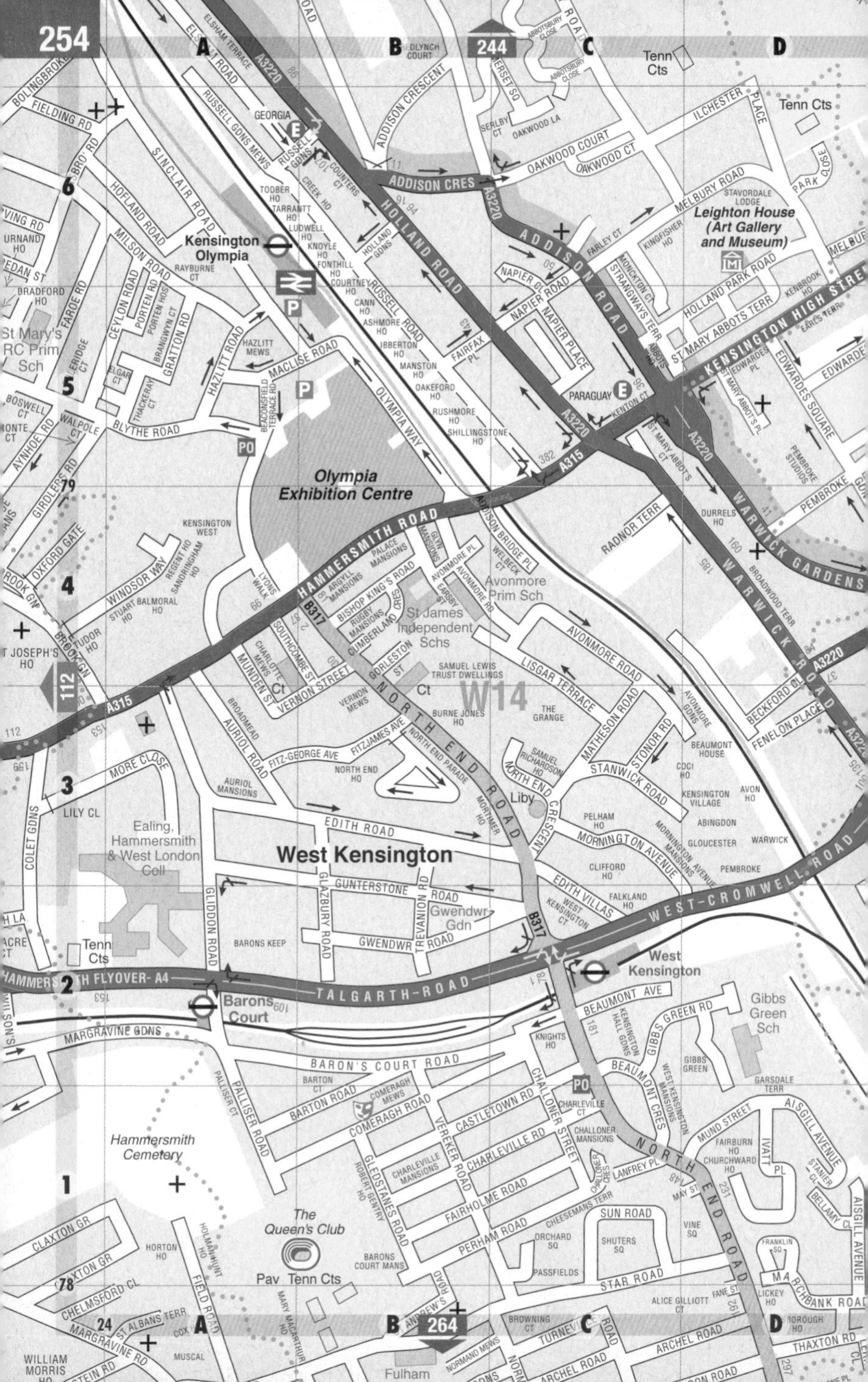
A
B
C
D
244
264
112
6
5
4
3
2
1
A3220
A315
B317
A4
W14
ELSHAM ROAD
RUSSELL GDNS MEWS
GEORGIA
ADDISON CRESCENT
ADDISON CRES
HOLLAND ROAD
OAKWOOD COURT
OAKWOOD CT
OAKWOOD LA
ILCHESTER PLACE
Tenn Cts
MELBURY ROAD
PARK CLOSE
STAVORDALE LODGE
Leighton House (Art Gallery and Museum)
ADDISON ROAD
NAPIER ROAD
NAPIER PLACE
FAIRFAX PL
HOLLAND PARK ROAD
ST MARY ABBOTS TERR
KENSINGTON HIGH STREET
EDWARDES SQUARE
PARAGUAY
KENTON CT
WARWICK GARDENS
WARWICK ROAD
PEMBROKE STUDIOS
DURRELS HO
RADNOR TERR
BROADWOOD TERR
BOLINGBROKE
FIELDING RD
SINCLAIR ROAD
HOFLAND ROAD
MILSON ROAD
Kensington Olympia
RAYBURNE CT
CEYLON ROAD
PORTEN RD
BRANGWYN CT
GRATTON RD
FAROE RD
St Mary's RC Prim Sch
BRADFORD HO
HAZLITT ROAD
HAZLITT MEWS
MACLISE ROAD
OLYMPIA WAY
BEACONSFIELD TERRACE RD
BLYTHE ROAD
WALPOLE CT
THACKERAY CT
GIRDLERS RD
OXFORD GATE
Olympia Exhibition Centre
HAMMERSMITH ROAD
ADDISON BRIDGE PL
KENSINGTON WEST
WINDSOR WAY
LYONS WALK
ARGYLL MANSIONS
PALACE MANSIONS
BISHOP KING'S ROAD
AVONMORE PL
Avonmore Prim Sch
St James Independent Schs
AVONMORE ROAD
LISGAR TERRACE
SAMUEL LEWIS TRUST DWELLINGS
BECKFORD CL
FENELON PLACE
ST JOSEPH'S HO
BROOK GN
BROADMEAD
AURIOL ROAD
MUNDEN ST
VERNON STREET
SOUTHCOMBE ST
GORLESTON ST
NORTH END ROAD
NORTH END PARADE
FITZ-GEORGE AVE
FITZJAMES AVE
BURNE JONES HO
THE GRANGE
MATHESON ROAD
STONOR RD
STANWICK ROAD
NORTH END CRESCENT
Liby
BEAUMONT HOUSE
MORE CLOSE
LILY CL
COLET GDNS
AURIOL MANSIONS
NORTH END HO
Ealing, Hammersmith & West London Coll
EDITH ROAD
West Kensington
MORNINGTON AVENUE
EDITH VILLAS
WEST-CROMWELL ROAD
GUNTERSTONE ROAD
GLAZBURY ROAD
TREVANION RD
Gwendwr Gdn
GWENDWR ROAD
GLIDDON ROAD
BARONS KEEP
HAMMERSMITH FLYOVER- A4
TALGARTH-ROAD
Barons Court
West Kensington
BEAUMONT AVE
GIBBS GREEN RD
Gibbs Green Sch
MARGRAVINE GDNS
BARON'S COURT ROAD
BARTON ROAD
COMERAGH ROAD
PALLISER ROAD
CASTLETOWN RD
CHARLEVILLE RD
CHALLONER STREET
FAIRHOLME ROAD
PERHAM ROAD
GLEDSTANES ROAD
VEREKER ROAD
Hammersmith Cemetery
The Queen's Club
Pav
SUN ROAD
STAR ROAD
MUND STREET
AISGILL AVENUE
IVATT PL
CLAXTON GR
CHELMSFORD CL
MARGRAVINE RD
ST ALBANS TERR
FIELD ROAD
ARCHEL ROAD
TURNEVILLE ROAD
THAXTON RD
MARCHBANK ROAD
Fulham

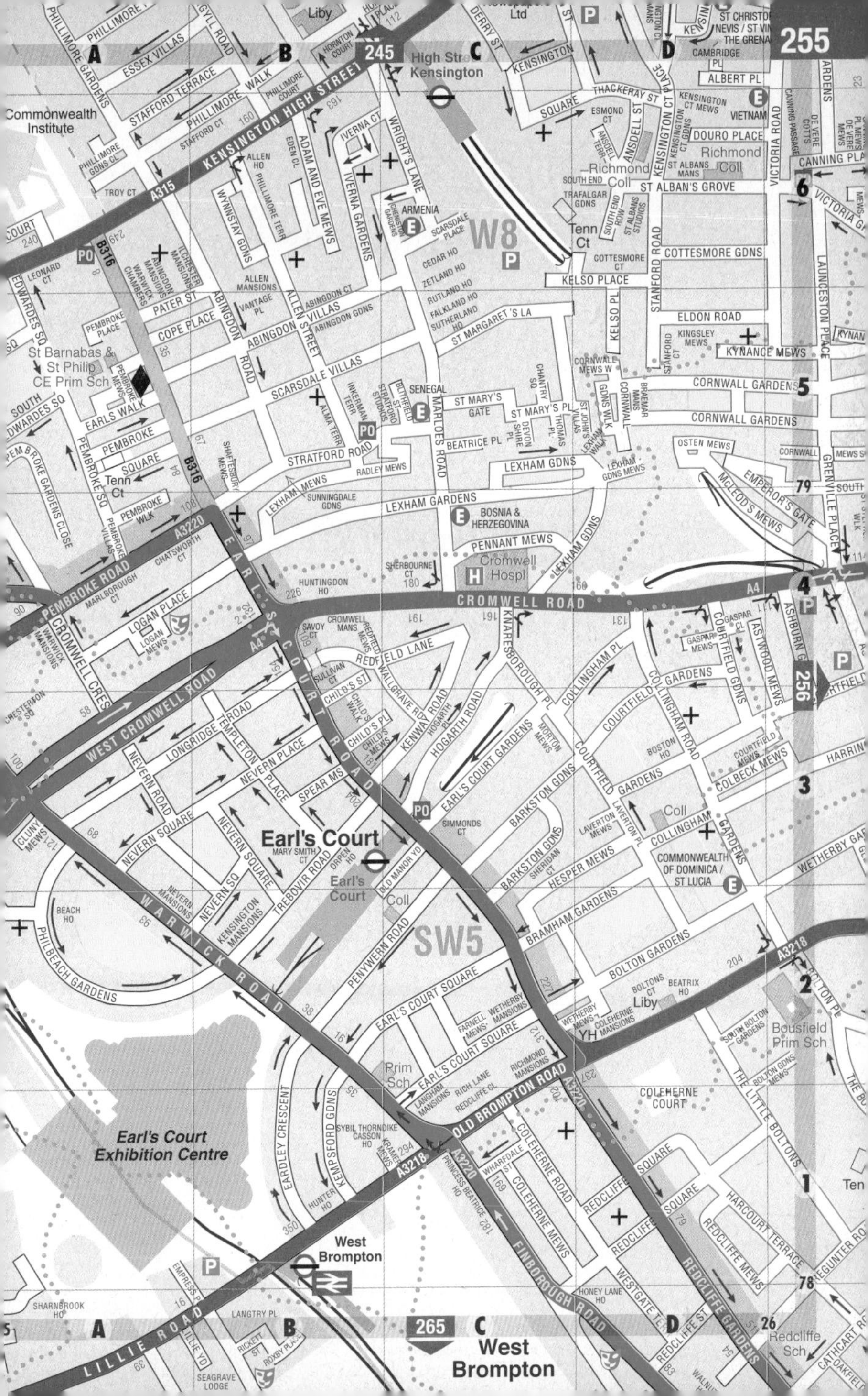
Commonwealth Institute
KENSINGTON HIGH STREET
High Street Kensington
W8
CROMWELL ROAD
WEST CROMWELL ROAD
EARL'S COURT ROAD
Cromwell Hospl
Earl's Court
SW5
WARWICK ROAD
OLD BROMPTON ROAD
Earl's Court Exhibition Centre
West Brompton
LILLIE ROAD
FINBOROUGH ROAD
REDCLIFFE GARDENS
245
256
265

Royal Albert Hall
Royal Geographical Society
Polish Inst & Sikorski Museum
246
Royal College of Organists
Royal College of Science
PRINCE CONSORT ROAD
Royal College of Music
Imperial College London
IMPERIAL COLLEGE ROAD
Science Museum
Earth Galleries
Natural History Museum
Victoria & Albert Museum
Royal College of Art
SW7
PRINCES GARDENS
EXHIBITION ROAD
QUEEN'S GATE
PALACE GATE
KENSINGTON GATE
QUEEN'S GATE TERRACE
PETERSHAM PLACE
ELVASTON PLACE
GLOUCESTER ROAD
CROMWELL ROAD
Gloucester Road
Lycee Francaise Charles de Gaulle (French Univ Coll)
THURLOE PLACE
THURLOE ST
South Kensington
PELHAM STREET
HARRINGTON ROAD
STANHOPE GARDENS
COURTFIELD ROAD
ASHBURN PLACE
HARRINGTON GARDENS
WETHERBY PLACE
OLD BROMPTON ROAD
South Kensington
ONSLOW SQUARE
ONSLOW GARDENS
FULHAM ROAD
Royal Marsden Hospl
Royal Brompton Hospl
THE BOLTONS
DRAYTON GARDENS
CRESSWELL PLACE
TREGUNTER ROAD
REDCLIFFE GARDENS
ELM PARK GARDENS
OLD CHURCH STREET
CHELSEA SQUARE
Cameron House Sch
Redcliffe Sch
266
255
A
B
C
D
1
2
3
4
5
6

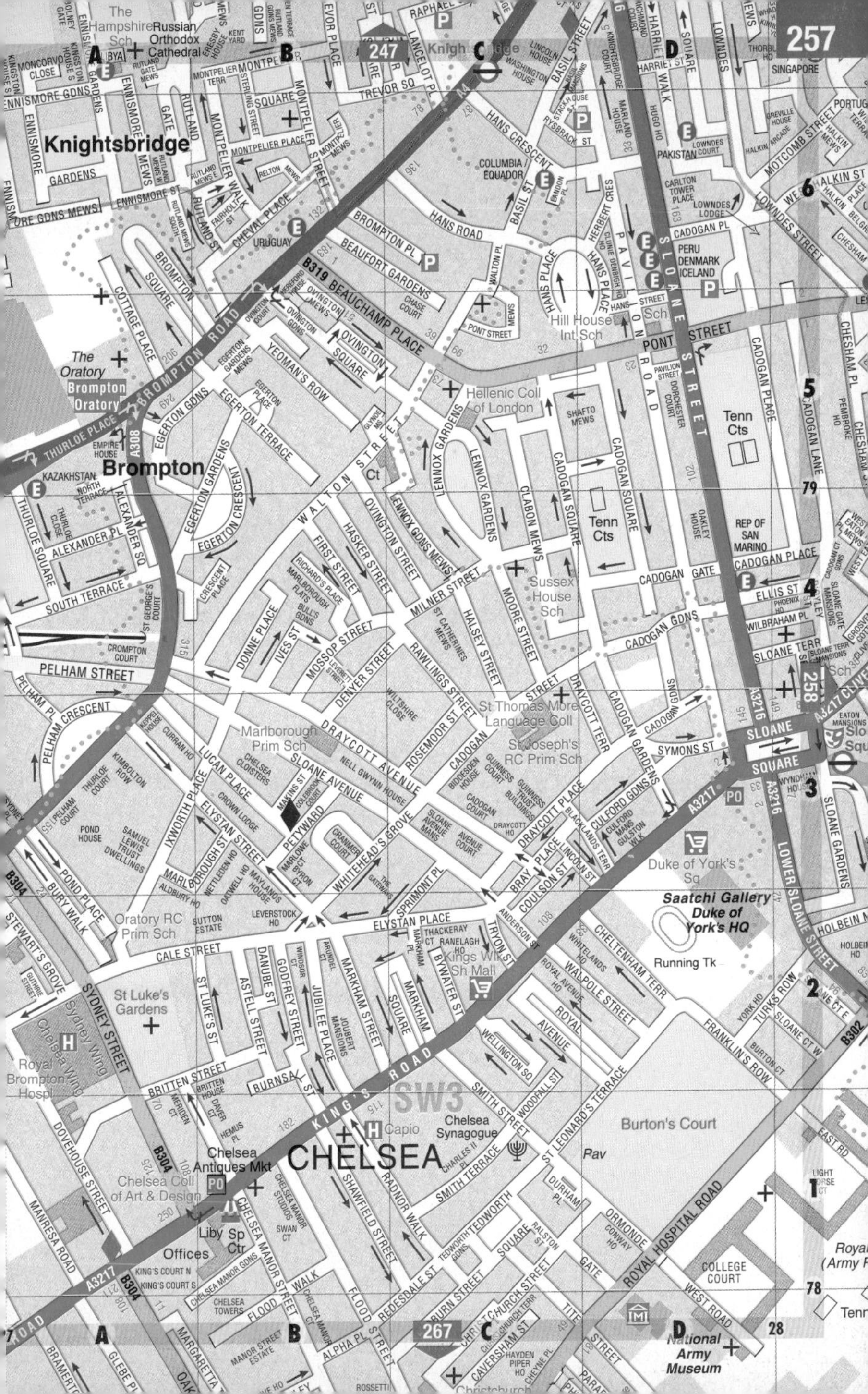

Knightsbridge
Brompton
CHELSEA
SW3
The Hampshire Sch
Russian Orthodox Cathedral
The Oratory
Brompton Oratory
Hellenic Coll of London
Hill House Int Sch
Sussex House Sch
St Thomas More Language Coll
St Joseph's RC Prim Sch
Marlborough Prim Sch
Oratory RC Prim Sch
St Luke's Gardens
Royal Brompton Hospl
Sydney Wing
Chelsea Wing
Chelsea Antiques Mkt
Chelsea Coll of Art & Design
Liby
Sp Ctr
Offices
Capio
Chelsea Synagogue
Kings Wk Sh Mall
Duke of York's Sq
Saatchi Gallery
Duke of York's HQ
Running Tk
Burton's Court
Pav
College Court
National Army Museum
Royal Army
Tenn Cts
Ct
PO
KAZAKHSTAN
URUGUAY
COLUMBIA / EQUADOR
PAKISTAN
PERU
DENMARK
ICELAND
REP OF SAN MARINO
SINGAPORE
LIBYA
A4
A308
A3217
A3216
B319
B304
B302
247
258
267
BROMPTON ROAD
KING'S ROAD
SLOANE STREET
SLOANE SQUARE
LOWER SLOANE STREET
BEAUCHAMP PLACE
PONT STREET
WALTON STREET
DRAYCOTT AVENUE
SLOANE AVENUE
FULHAM ROAD
PELHAM STREET
SYDNEY STREET
CADOGAN SQUARE
CADOGAN GARDENS
CADOGAN PLACE
CADOGAN GATE
CADOGAN LANE
HANS CRESCENT
HANS ROAD
HANS PLACE
BASIL STREET
ROYAL HOSPITAL ROAD
ROYAL AVENUE
SMITH STREET
FLOOD STREET
OAKLEY STREET
CHELTENHAM TERR
FRANKLIN'S ROW
WALPOLE STREET
ST LEONARD'S TERRACE
MARKHAM STREET
ELYSTAN PLACE
CALE STREET
LUCAN PLACE
IXWORTH PLACE
ELYSTAN STREET
PETYWARD
WHITEHEAD'S GROVE
MILNER STREET
LENNOX GARDENS
CLABON MEWS
MOORE STREET
HALSEY STREET
RAWLINGS STREET
OVINGTON SQUARE
YEOMAN'S ROW
EGERTON GARDENS
EGERTON CRESCENT
EGERTON TERRACE
ENNISMORE GARDENS
MONTPELIER SQUARE
MONTPELIER STREET
RUTLAND GATE
LOWNDES SQUARE
MOTCOMB STREET
CHESHAM PLACE
HOLBEIN MEWS
TURKS ROW
WEST ROAD
TITE STREET
TEDWORTH SQUARE
RADNOR WALK
SHAWFIELD STREET
CHELSEA MANOR STREET
MANRESA ROAD
DOVEHOUSE STREET
A B C D
1 2 3 4 5 6

258
248
257
268
A
B
C
D
SW1
1
2
3
4
5
6
Buckingham Palace
Queens Gallery
The Royal Mews
BELGRAVE SQUARE
TRINIDAD & TOBAGO
Tenn Ct
BELGIUM
HALKIN ST
MONTROSE HOUSE
MONTROSE PL
MALAYSIA
TURKEY
CHAPEL STREET
GROOM PL
IVORY COAST
CHESTER STREET
CHESTER MEWS
LITTLE CHESTER STREET
WILTON MEWS
WILTON STREET
WILTON CRESCENT
SINGAPORE
SYRIA
PORTUGAL
WILTON TERRACE
GREVILLE HOUSE
HALKIN ARCADE
LOWNDES COURT
MOTCOMB STREET
HALKIN MEWS
WEST HALKIN ST
HALKIN PLACE
BELGRAVE MEWS N
BELGRAVE MEWS WEST
CHESHAM MEWS
GHANA
AUSTRIA
GERMANY
NORWAY
BAHRAIN
SERBIA/ MONTENEGRO
BRUNEI
UPPER BELGRAVE STREET
DORSET MEWS
GROSVENOR PLACE A302
IRELAND
LR GROSVENOR PL
HOBART PLACE
GROSVENOR GARDENS
B312
BEESTON PL
VICTORIA SQUARE
EATON LANE
LAKE VIEW CT
ALLINGTON
VICTORIA ARCADE
A3217
A3214
Victoria
TERMINUS PL
A302
Gatwick Express Terminal
Victoria Station
Victoria Place Sh Ctr
ECCLESTON BRIDGE
Passport Office
LESOTHO
SPAIN
FINLAND
BOLIVIA
HUNGARY
B319
B310
LOWNDES STREET
LOWNDES PLACE
LOWNDES SQUARE
CADOGAN PL
PERU
DENMARK
ICELAND
STREET
SLOANE STREET
CHESHAM PLACE
CHESHAM PL
CHESHAM ST
LYALL MEWS
LYALL MEWS WEST
LYALL STREET
ROBERTS MEWS
EATON PLACE
BELGRAVE PLACE
BELGRAVE MEWS S
ECCLESTON MEWS
EATON MEWS NORTH
EATON SQUARE
Eaton Square Gardens
EATON MEWS N
EATON ROW
LOWER BELGRAVE ST
GROSVENOR GDNS MEWS NORTH
BELGRAVE YD
LYGON PLACE
CHESTER SQ MEWS
EATON MEWS SOUTH
CHESTER SQUARE
EBURY MEWS EAST
BELGRAVIA COURT
ECCLESTON PLACE
Eaton Square Sch
ECCLESTON STREET
A3213
BUCKINGHAM PALACE ROAD
A3215
PO
Sch
CADOGAN PLACE
CADOGAN LANE
PEMBROKE HO
Tenn Cts
REP OF SAN MARINO
OAKLEY HOUSE
ELLIS ST
WILBRAHAM PL
SLOANE TERR
D'OYLEY ST
SLOANE GATE MANSIONS
WEST EATON PL MEWS
WEST EATON PL
EATON PL
EATON TERRACE MEWS
EATON SQ
BOSCOBEL PL
ELIZABETH STREET
EATON MEWS WEST
EBURY MEWS
HILDRED HOUSE
EBURY STREET
Belgravia
ECCLESTON PLACE
Liby
CHESTER ROW
MINERA MEWS
GERALD RD
GERALD MEWS
BURTON MEWS
EATON TERRACE
CLIVEDEN PLACE
A3217
GROSVENOR COTTAGES
SEDDING ST
SLOANE TERR MANSIONS
Sch
EATON CLOSE
CAROLINE TERR
EATON MANSIONS
Sloane Square
SLOANE SQUARE
A3216
WYNDHAM HOUSE
SKINNER PL
TARNBROOK COURT
WHITTAKER ST
BOURNE STREET
GRAHAM TERRACE
KILMUIR HOUSE
PALACE MEWS
Francis Holland Sch
JOHNSON HOUSE
SEMLEY HOUSE
SEMLEY PLACE
Victoria Coach Station
CUNDY ST
LOCHMORE HO
EBURY SQUARE
KYLESTROME HO
COLESHILL FLATS
LOXFORD HO
WALDEN HO
STACK HO
AVERY FARM ROW
FOUNTAIN COURT
National Audit Offices
ELIZABETH BRIDGE
BULLEID WAY
ROYAL BELGRAVE HO
HUGH STREET
HUGH MEWS
ECCLESTON SQUARE
ST GEORGE'S DRIVE
LOWER SLOANE STREET
SLOANE GARDENS
HOLBEIN PLACE
ST MICHAEL'S MEWS
REMBRANT CL
LUMLEY FLATS
PASSMORE ST
ORMONDE PL
BUNHOUSE PL
PIMLICO ROAD
St Barnabas CE Prim Sch
HOLBEIN MS
HOLBEIN HO
DOVE WLK
BLOOMFIELD TERR
RANELAGH GR
ST BARNABAS ST
B313
B324
BRIDGE HO
PIMLICO HO
RYE HO
WESTBOURNE HO
MERCER HO
BUCKNILL HO
VICTORIA HO
DALTON HO
WAINWRIGHT HO
EDISON HO
HILLERSDON HO
TINTERN HOUSE
GLASTONBURY HO
DRYBURGH HO
EBURY BRIDGE
WARWICK WAY
FURNESS HO
KIRKSTALL HO
MELROSE HO
FONTHILL HO
EVESHAM HO
SHERBORNE HO
SUTHERLAND ROW
ALDERNEY STREET
CLARENDON STREET
WINCHESTER STREET
CUMBERLAND STREET
SUSSEX STREET
SUTHERLAND STREET
WESTMORELAND TERR
WESTMORELAND PL
TURPENTINE LANE
PEABODY AVENUE
SUSSEX ST
LUPUS STREET
NASH HO
GILBERT HO
CHIPPENDALE HO
ELGAR HO
SULLIVAN HO
SHERATON HO
PAXTON TERR
PEABODY CL
Churchill Gdns
GROSVENOR RD
A3212
Dock
Saatchi Gallery
Duke of York's HQ
Duke of York's Sq
York's Sq
YORK HO
TURKS ROW
SLOANE CT E
SLOANE CT W
FRANKLIN'S ROW
BURTON CT
B302
Chelsea Barracks
City of Westminster
Kensington & Chelsea
CHELSEA BRIDGE ROAD
EBURY BRIDGE ROAD
CHEYLESMORE HO
DONERAILE HO
GATLIFF ROAD
GATCLIFF CL
CHELSEA GATE
WELLINGTON BLDGS
CHELSEA GDNS
HEPWORTH CT
Lister Hospl
HIRST CT
CUBITT BLDG
PAVILLION CT
EAST RD
LIGHT HORSE CT
Court
Royal Hospital (Army Pensioners)
Ranelagh Gardens (Site of Chelsea Flower Show)
COLLEGE COURT
WEST ROAD
National Army Museum
Tenn Cts
Thames Path

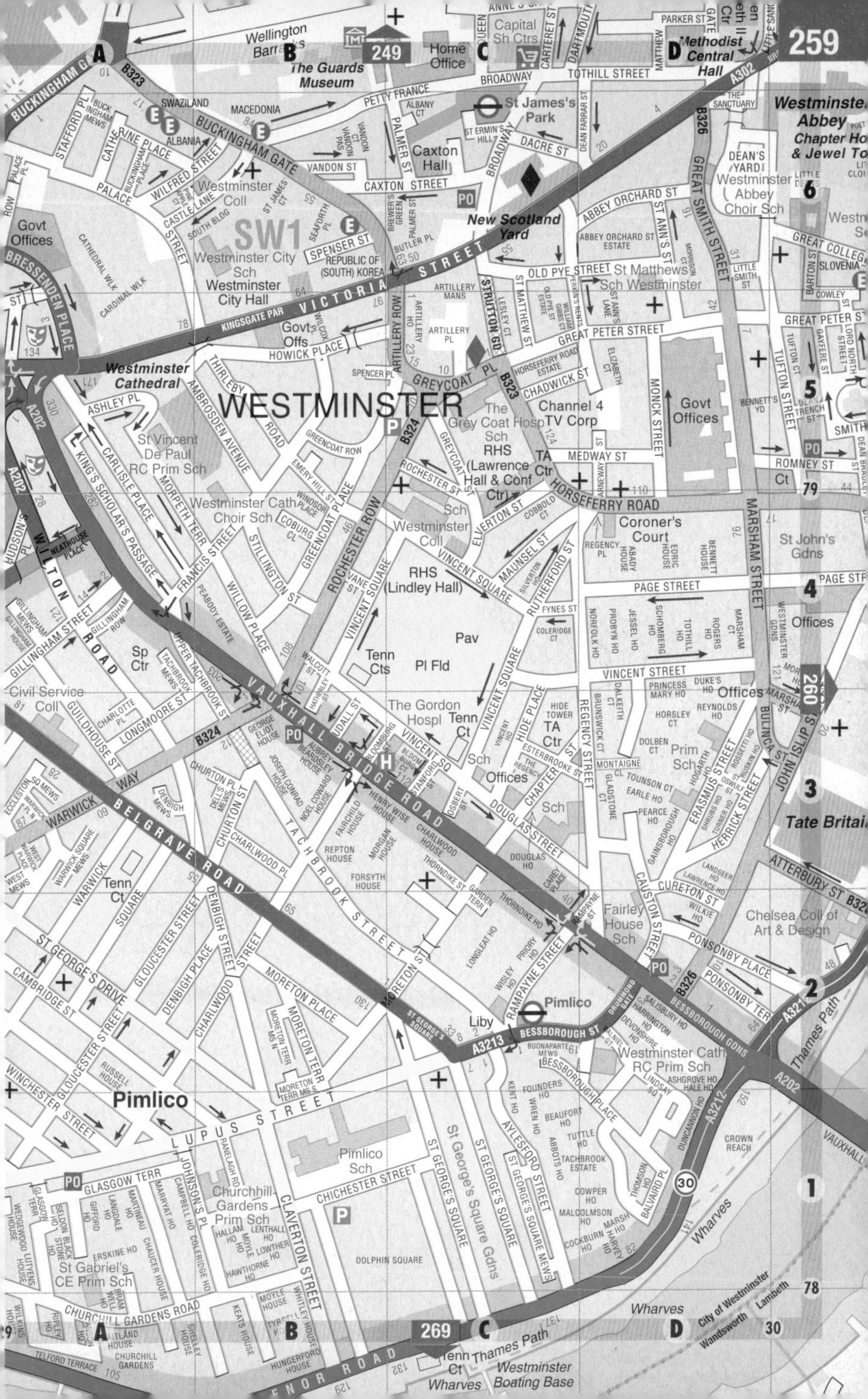
259
249
260
269
A
B
C
D
1
2
3
4
5
6
WESTMINSTER
SW1
Pimlico
Wellington Barracks
The Guards Museum
Home Office
Capital Sh Ctrs
Methodist Central Hall
Westminster Abbey
Chapter House & Jewel Tower
Dean's Yard
Westminster Abbey Choir Sch
St James's Park
Caxton Hall
New Scotland Yard
Westminster Coll
Westminster City Sch
Westminster City Hall
Republic of (South) Korea
Govt Offices
Govt Offs
Westminster Cathedral
St Vincent De Paul RC Prim Sch
Westminster Cath Choir Sch
The Grey Coat Hosp Sch
RHS (Lawrence Hall & Conf Ctr)
Channel 4 TV Corp
TA Ctr
Westminster Coll
RHS (Lindley Hall)
Coroner's Court
St John's Gdns
Offices
Tenn Cts
Pl Fld
Pav
The Gordon Hospl
Tenn Ct
Sp Ctr
Civil Service Coll
Prim Sch
Sch
Tate Britain
Chelsea Coll of Art & Design
Fairley House Sch
Pimlico
Liby
Westminster Cath RC Prim Sch
Pimlico Sch
Churchhill Gardens Prim Sch
St Gabriel's CE Prim Sch
St George's Square Gdns
Dolphin Square
Crown Reach
Thames Path
Wharves
Westminster Boating Base
City of Westminster
Wandsworth
Lambeth
Buckingham Gate
Petty France
Broadway
Tothill Street
Victoria Street
Kingsgate Par
Caxton Street
Old Pye Street
Great Peter Street
Great Smith Street
Abbey Orchard St
Horseferry Road
Marsham Street
Page Street
Vincent Street
Vincent Square
Rochester Row
Greycoat Place
Greycoat Pl
Howick Place
Artillery Row
Strutton Gd
Monck Street
Regency Street
Medway St
Romney St
Chadwick St
Thirleby Road
Ambrosden Avenue
Morpeth Terr
Francis Street
Carlisle Place
Ashley Pl
Bressenden Place
Wilton Road
Vauxhall Bridge Road
Belgrave Road
Warwick Way
Tachbrook Street
Upper Tachbrook St
Willow Place
Stillington St
Douglas Street
Causton Street
Ponsonby Place
Ponsonby Ter
John Islip St
Bulinca St
Herrick Street
Erasmus Street
Atterbury St
Cureton St
Bessborough St
Bessborough Gdns
Bessborough Place
Rampayne Street
Moreton St
Moreton Place
Moreton Terr
Lupus Street
Claverton Street
Chichester Street
St George's Square
Aylesford Street
St George's Drive
Gloucester Street
Denbigh Street
Denbigh Place
Charlwood Street
Churton St
Cambridge St
Winchester Street
Glasgow Terr
Johnson's Pl
Churchill Gardens Road
Grosvenor Road
Telford Terrace
Guildhouse St
Longmoore St
Gillingham Street
Hudson's Pl
Warwick Square
Palace Street
Stafford Pl
Catherine Place
Wilfred Street
Castle Lane
Palmer St
Vandon St
Dacre St
Tufton St
Great College St
Barton St
Cowley St
Lord North St
Smith Sq
B323
B324
B326
A202
A302
A3212
A3213
A321
B322
PO
P
H

LAMBETH
Westminster Abbey
Chapter House & Jewel Tower
Houses of Parliament
Old Palace Yard
Victoria Tower
The Victoria Tower Gardens
Westminster Sch
Westminster Abbey Choir Sch
St Johns Concert Hall
Smith Sq
St John's Gdns
Govt Offices
Offices
Tate Britain
Millbank Tower
Millbank Millennium Pier
Chelsea Coll of Art & Design
RIVER THAMES
Lambeth Bridge
Lambeth Pier
Fire Brigade Pier
Fire Brigade HQ
Albert Embankment
Thames Path
St Thomas's Hospital Medical School
St Thomas' Hospl
Lambeth Palace
Archbishop's Park
Mus of Garden History
Nightingale Museum
Lambeth Palace Road
Police HQ
Recn Gd
Pedlers Park
Tenn Cts
Gunhouse Stairs (site of)
Vauxhall
Vauxhall Cross
Vauxhall Bridge
Vauxhall City Farm
Spring Gardens
Vauxhall Prim Sch
Lilian Baylis Tech Sch
St Anne's RC Prim Sch
Westminster Bsns Sq
St Mark's CE Prim Sch
Millbank
Abingdon Street
Great Smith Street
Marsham Street
Horseferry Road
Page Street
Thorney Street
Great Peter Street
Great College Street
Tufton Street
Romney St
Atterbury St
John Islip Street
Ponsonby Place
Bessborough Gdns
Kennington Lane
Black Prince Road
Old Paradise Street
Lambeth High Street
Lambeth Walk
Salamanca Street
Randall Road
Tinworth St
Glasshouse Walk
Vauxhall Walk
Jonathan Street
Goding Street
Durham St
Harleyford Road
Wharves
A B C D
250 259 270
1 2 3 4 5 6

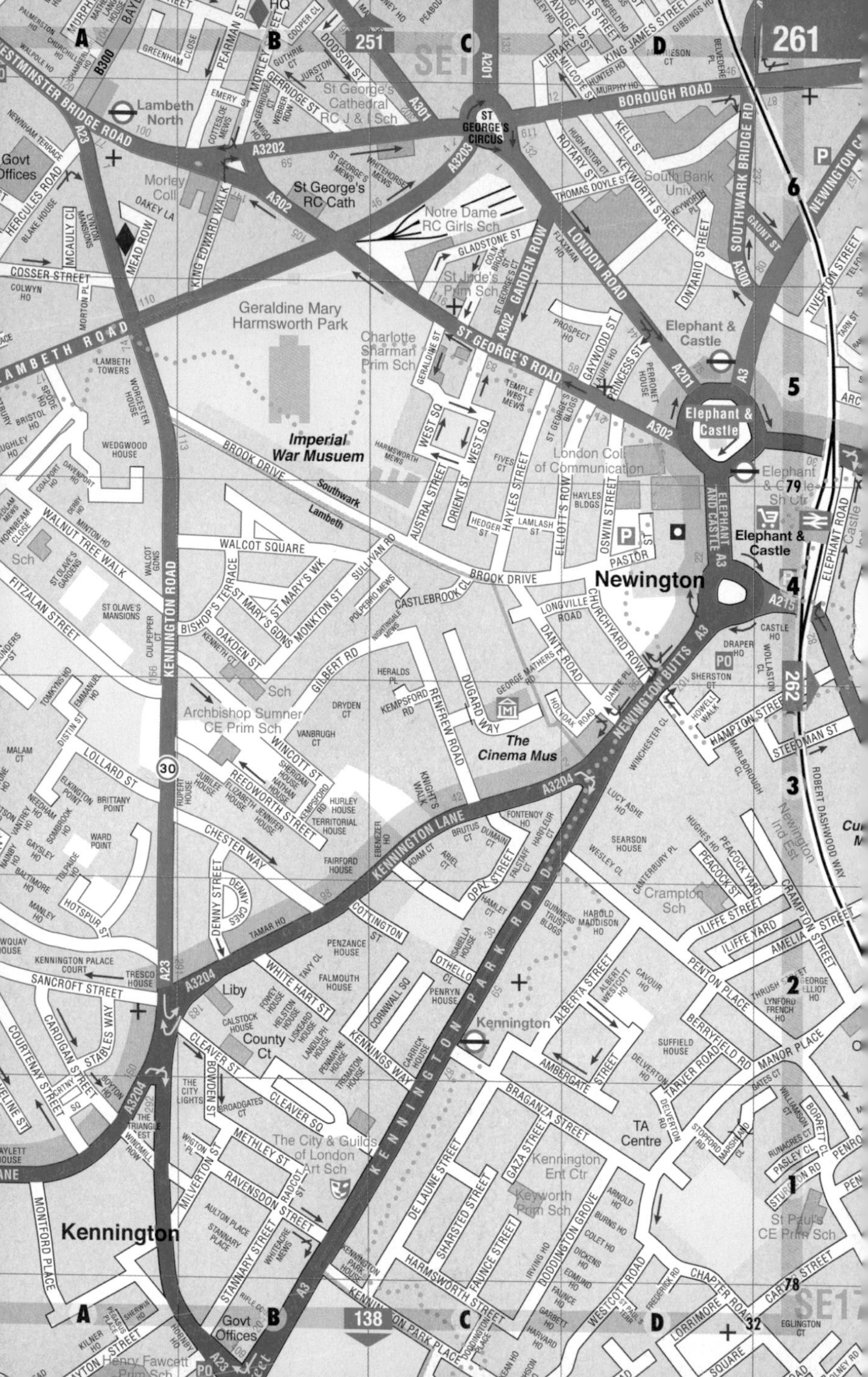

A
B
C
D
251
261
SE1
HQ
Lambeth North
WESTMINSTER BRIDGE ROAD
B300
A23
Govt Offices
HERCULES ROAD
Morley Coll
OAKEY LA
MEAD ROW
KING EDWARD WALK
A3202
A302
St George's RC Cath
ST GEORGE'S CIRCUS
A201
A3203
A301
St George's Cathedral RC J & I Sch
BOROUGH ROAD
SOUTHWARK BRIDGE RD
KING JAMES STREET
LIBRARY ST
ROTARY ST
THOMAS DOYLE ST
KEYWORTH STREET
South Bank Univ
LONDON ROAD
Notre Dame RC Girls Sch
GLADSTONE ST
St Jude's Prim Sch
GARDEN ROW
ONTARIO STREET
GAUNT ST
A300
NEWINGTON CAUSEWAY
COSSER STREET
LAMBETH ROAD
Geraldine Mary Harmsworth Park
Charlotte Sharman Prim Sch
ST GEORGE'S ROAD
Elephant & Castle
A3
Imperial War Musuem
BROOK DRIVE
Southwark
Lambeth
WEST SQ
AUSTRAL STREET
ORIENT ST
HAYLES STREET
ELLIOTT'S ROW
OSWIN STREET
London Coll of Communication
Elephant & Castle Sh Ctr
ELEPHANT AND CASTLE
ELEPHANT ROAD
A215
Newington
WALCOT SQUARE
ST MARY'S GDNS
MONKTON ST
OAKDEN ST
BISHOP'S TERRACE
KENNINGTON ROAD
WALNUT TREE WALK
FITZALAN STREET
LOLLARD ST
Archbishop Sumner CE Prim Sch
GILBERT RD
RENFREW ROAD
DUGARD WAY
The Cinema Mus
DANTE ROAD
CHURCHYARD ROW
NEWINGTON BUTTS
HAMPTON STREET
STEEDMAN ST
ROBERT DASHWOOD WAY
262
Newington Ind Est
REEDWORTH STREET
CHESTER WAY
KENNINGTON LANE
A3204
KENNINGTON PARK ROAD
HOTSPUR ST
DENNY STREET
COTTINGTON ST
WHITE HART ST
SANCROFT STREET
Liby
County Ct
CLEAVER ST
CLEAVER SQ
The City & Guilds of London Art Sch
KENNINGS WAY
Kennington
ALBERTA STREET
AMBERGATE STREET
BRAGANZA STREET
Crampton Sch
ILIFFE STREET
PENTON PLACE
BERRYFIELD RD
MANOR PLACE
TA Centre
Kennington Ent Ctr
Keyworth Prim Sch
DE LAUNE STREET
SHARSTED STREET
FAUNCE STREET
HARMSWORTH STREET
DODDINGTON GROVE
WESTCOTT ROAD
CHAPTER ROAD
St Paul's CE Prim Sch
CARTER STREET
SE17
METHLEY ST
RAVENSDON STREET
MILVERTON ST
STANNARY STREET
MONTFORD PLACE
COURTENAY STREET
CARDIGAN STREET
Kennington
Govt Offices
138
Henry Fawcett Prim Sch
KENNINGTON PARK PLACE
30
1
2
3
4
5
6

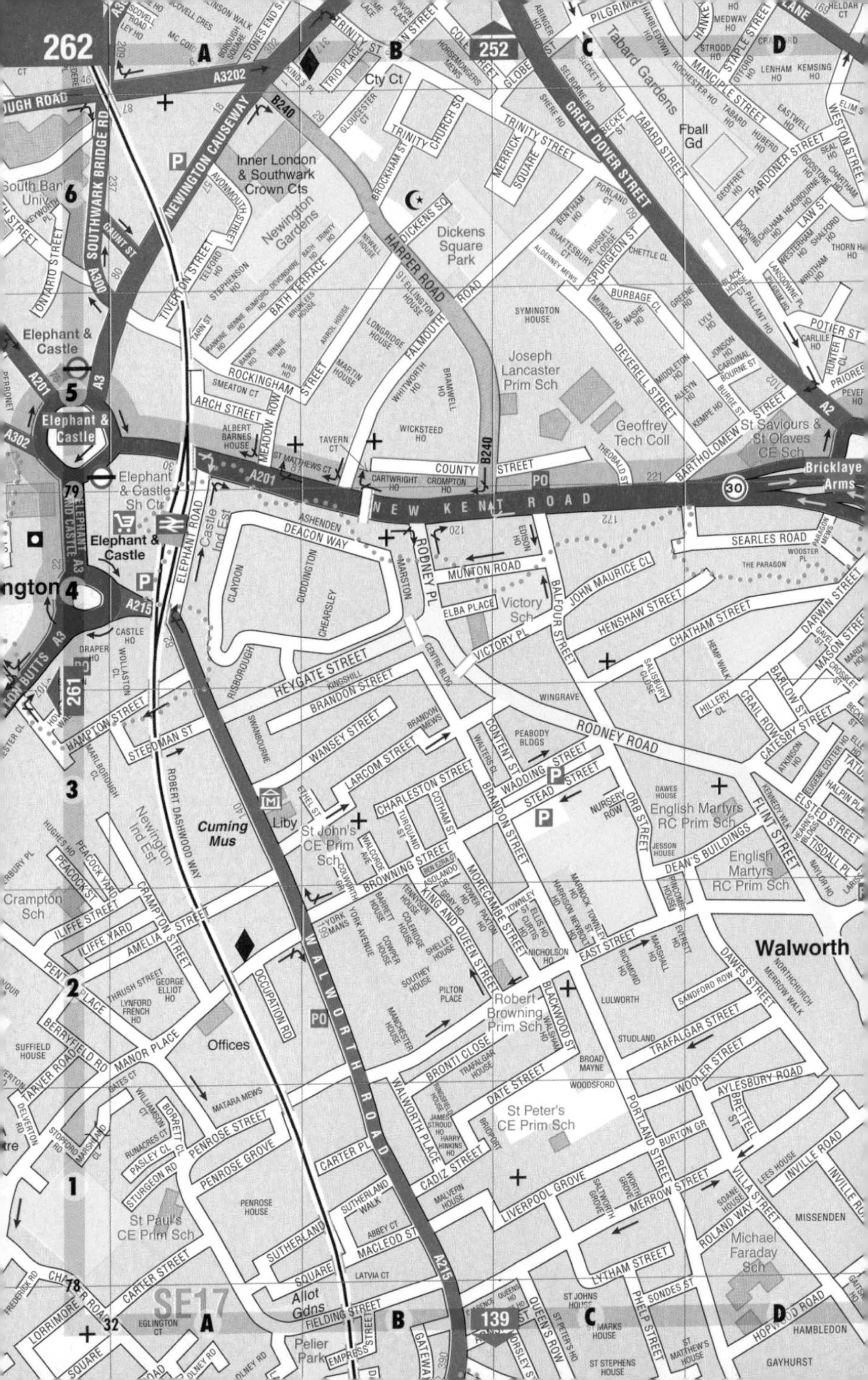

262
A
B
C
D
252
261
139
A3202
A3
A201
A302
A215
A300
A2
B240
NEWINGTON CAUSEWAY
SOUTHWARK BRIDGE RD
BOROUGH ROAD
TRINITY ST
TRIO PLACE
KINGS PL
Cty Ct
GLOUCESTER CT
TRINITY CHURCH SQ
HORSEMONGERS MEWS
GLOBE ST
PILGRIMAGE ST
Tabard Gardens
TABARD STREET
GREAT DOVER STREET
MANCIPLE STREET
STAPLE STREET
Fball Gd
PARDONER STREET
WESTON STREET
LAW ST
TRINITY STREET
MERRICK SQUARE
Inner London & Southwark Crown Cts
Newington Gardens
AVONMOUTH STREET
TIVERTON STREET
BATH TERRACE
HARPER ROAD
DICKENS SQ
Dickens Square Park
BROCKHAM ST
South Bank Univ
ONTARIO STREET
GAUNT ST
Elephant & Castle
ROCKINGHAM STREET
SMEATON CT
ARCH STREET
MEADOW ROW
FALMOUTH ROAD
SPURGEON ST
BURBAGE CL
DEVERELL STREET
SYMINGTON HOUSE
Joseph Lancaster Prim Sch
Geoffrey Tech Coll
BARTHOLOMEW STREET
St Saviours & St Olaves CE Sch
POTIER ST
COUNTY STREET
ST MATTHEWS CT
TAVERN CT
CARTWRIGHT HO
CROMPTON HO
WICKSTEED HO
NEW KENT ROAD
Bricklayers Arms
30
PO
Elephant & Castle Sh Ctr
ELEPHANT AND CASTLE
ELEPHANT ROAD
Castle Ind Est
DEACON WAY
ASHENDEN
CLAYDON
CHEARSLEY
RODNEY PL
MUNTON ROAD
ELBA PLACE
Victory Sch
VICTORY PL
BALFOUR STREET
JOHN MAURICE CL
HENSHAW STREET
CHATHAM STREET
SEARLES ROAD
THE PARAGON
DARWIN STREET
MASON STREET
HEYGATE STREET
BRANDON STREET
HAMPTON STREET
STEEDMAN ST
WANSEY STREET
LARCOM STREET
CHARLESTON STREET
CONTENT ST
WADDING STREET
STEAD STREET
RODNEY ROAD
PEABODY BLDGS
WINGRAVE
ORB STREET
FLINT STREET
DEAN'S BUILDINGS
English Martyrs RC Prim Sch
CATESBY STREET
ELSTED STREET
TISDALL PL
Walworth
ROBERT DASHWOOD WAY
Cuming Mus
Liby
St John's CE Prim Sch
BROWNING STREET
KING AND QUEEN STREET
MORECAMBE STREET
YORK AVENUE
EAST STREET
Newington Ind Est
Crampton Sch
ILIFFE STREET
ILIFFE YARD
AMELIA STREET
CRAMPTON STREET
PENTON PLACE
MANOR PLACE
OCCUPATION RD
WALWORTH ROAD
Offices
Robert Browning Prim Sch
BLACKWOOD ST
DAWES STREET
SANDFORD ROW
TRAFALGAR STREET
WOOLER STREET
AYLESBURY ROAD
BRETTELL ST
BRONTI CLOSE
DATE STREET
WALWORTH PLACE
St Peter's CE Prim Sch
PORTLAND STREET
BURTON GR
BERRYFIELD RD
TARVER ROAD
MATARA MEWS
PENROSE STREET
PENROSE GROVE
PASLEY CL
STURGEON RD
St Paul's CE Prim Sch
CARTER PL
CADIZ STREET
SUTHERLAND WALK
SUTHERLAND SQUARE
LIVERPOOL GROVE
MERROW STREET
VILLA STREET
ROLAND WAY
INVILLE ROAD
MISSENDEN
Michael Faraday Sch
MACLEOD ST
LATVIA CT
LYTHAM STREET
SONDES ST
PHELP STREET
QUEEN'S ROW
HOPWOOD ROAD
HAMBLEDON
GAYHURST
Allot Gdns
FIELDING STREET
Pelier Park
EMPRESS ST
CARTER STREET
LORRIMORE ROAD
CHAPTER ROAD
SE17
1
2
3
4
5
6

263
253
139
118
A
B
C
D
1
2
3
4
5
6
Caledonian Market
BERMONDSEY SQ
TOWER BRIDGE ROAD
ABBEY STREET
B202
A2198
A2205
A2206
A100
A2
B203
B204
B214
B215
GRANGE ROAD
GRANGE WALK
GRANGE YARD
SPA ROAD
NECKINGER
NECKINGER ESTATE
ENID STREET
MILLSTREAM RD
MALTBY STREET
RILEY ROAD
PURBROOK ST
STEVENS ST
FENDALL ST
THE GRANGE
PAGE'S WALK
CRIMSCOTT STREET
DECIMA STREET
ROTHSAY STREET
ALICE ST
WILD'S RENTS
WEBB STREET
SWAN MEAD
LEROY STREET
CLUNY PLACE
MEAKIN ESTATE
ROYAL OAK YD
NEWHAM'S ROW
Southwark Coll (Grange Centre)
Grange Prim Sch
Bermondsey Spa Gdns
Liby
ALSCOT ROAD
ALSCOT WAY
Alscot Rd Ind Est
HENLEY DRIVE
Aylwin Girls Sch
Boutcher CE Prim Sch
CURTIS STREET
CURTIS WAY
SETCHELL WAY
SETCHELL RD
WILLOW WALK
MANDELA WAY
HAZEL WAY
BACON GROVE
DUNTON ROAD
LYNTON ROAD
FORT ROAD
BALACLAVA ROAD
VAUBAN ST
DUNLOP PLACE
ROUEL ROAD
WOOLSTAPLERS WAY
VALDING ROAD
REVERDY RD
JAMAICA RD
LUCEY
TA Ctr
Dockley Ind
SOUTH
MILTON CL
CHAUCER DRIVE
LONGFELLOW WAY
BUSHWOOD DR
OXLEY CLOSE
ROLLS ROAD
CADET DR
LYNTON ESTATE
Tenn Cts
Superstore
OLD KENT ROAD
HUMPHREY ST
ROWCROSS STREET
COOPER'S ROAD
MAWBEY PLACE
HARMAN CLOSE
AVONDALE SQ
TRAFALGAR AVENUE
GLENGALL ROAD
GLENGALL TERR
NILE TERRACE
OAKLEY PLACE
COBOURG ROAD
Cobourg Jun & Inf Sch
PEPLER MEWS
Burgess Park
SE5
SE15
SE17
Surrey Square Park
Surrey Square Jun & Inf Schs
SURREY SQUARE
MADRON STREET
MARCIA ROAD
HENDRE RD
KINGLAKE STREET
SMYRK'S ROAD
MINA ROAD
UPNOR WAY
BAGSHOT STREET
RAVENSTONE
THURLOW STREET
WENDOVER
ALSACE RD
ALVEY STREET
CONGREVE STREET
EAST STREET
EXON ST
FREMANTLE ST
SEDAN WAY
ALBANY ROAD
CALMINGTON ROAD
LONCROFT ROAD
WAITE STREET
Walworth Sch
SHORNCLIFFE RD
Amazonas
Pl Fld
BEACONSFIELD ROAD
LATIMER
CALVERTON
WOLVERTON
Liby
PO

The Queen's Club
254
134
135
W6
SW6
FULHAM
Fulham Prep Sch
Normand Park
Normand Croft Com Sch
St Augustine's RC Prim Sch
St John Lillie Prim Sch
St Thomas of Canterbury RC Prim Sch
Fulham Cross Sec Sch
Henry Compton Sec Sch
St John's CE Prim Sch
Kensington Prep Sch
Al-Muntada Islamic Sch
Recn Ground
Cemetery
LILLIE ROAD
DAWES ROAD
FULHAM PALACE RD
FULHAM RD
MUNSTER ROAD
GREYHOUND ROAD
MARGRAVINE RD
NORMAND ROAD
HOMESTEAD ROAD
FILMER ROAD
A3218
A3219
A219
A304
B317

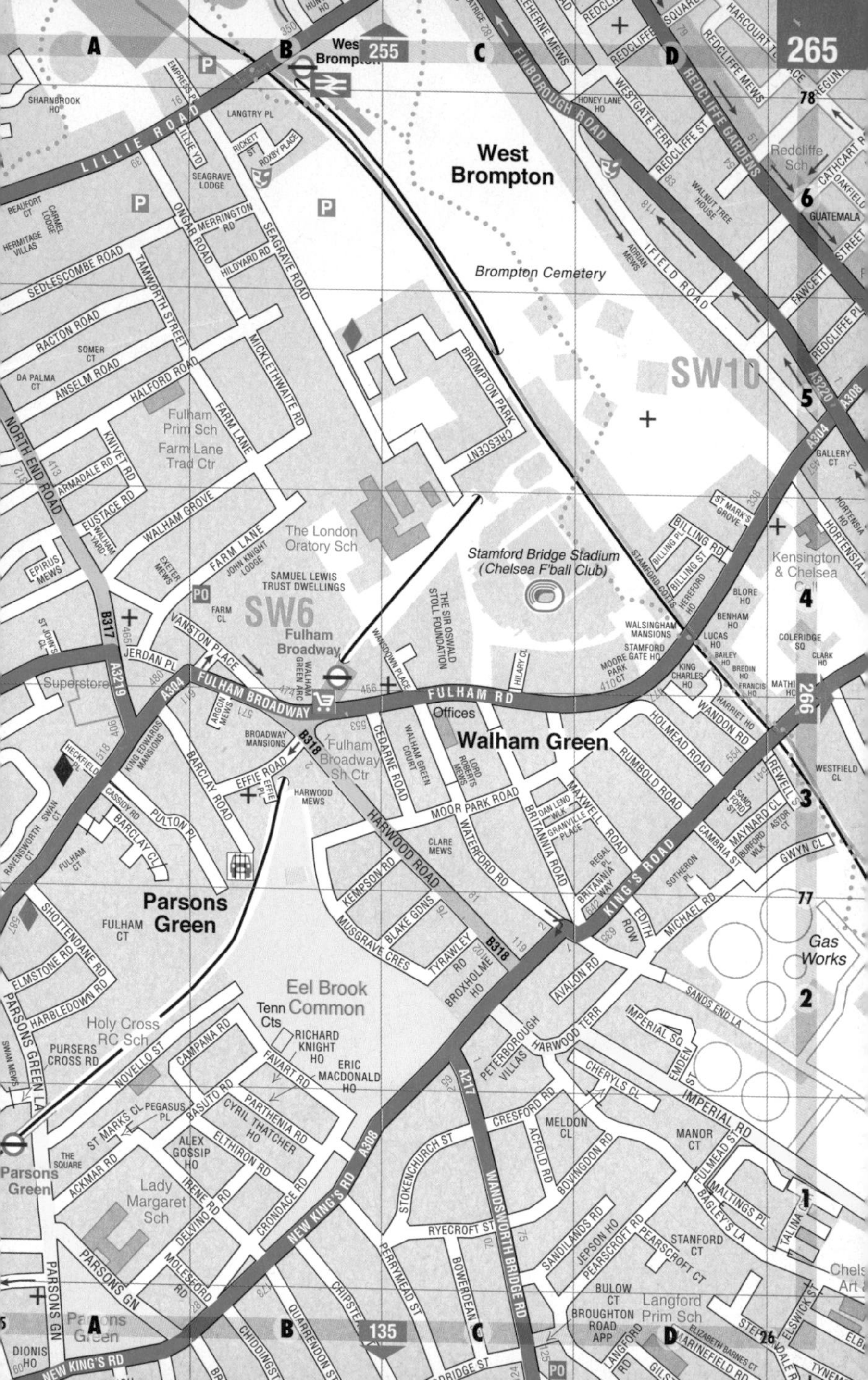

255
West Brompton
West Brompton
Brompton Cemetery
SW10
SW6
Stamford Bridge Stadium (Chelsea F'ball Club)
The London Oratory Sch
SAMUEL LEWIS TRUST DWELLINGS
THE SIR OSWALD STOLL FOUNDATION
Fulham Broadway
Fulham Broadway Sh Ctr
Walham Green
Offices
Parsons Green
Eel Brook Common
Tenn Cts
Holy Cross RC Sch
Lady Margaret Sch
Fulham Prim Sch
Farm Lane Trad Ctr
Superstore
Redcliffe Sch
Kensington & Chelsea Coll
Gas Works
Langford Prim Sch
LILLIE ROAD
FINBOROUGH ROAD
REDCLIFFE GARDENS
REDCLIFFE SQUARE
REDCLIFFE MEWS
IFIELD ROAD
SEAGRAVE ROAD
ONGAR ROAD
SEDLESCOMBE ROAD
TAMWORTH STREET
RACTON ROAD
ANSELM ROAD
HALFORD ROAD
MICKLETHWAITE RD
FARM LANE
NORTH END ROAD
WALHAM GROVE
BROMPTON PARK CRESCENT
FULHAM BROADWAY
FULHAM RD
KING'S ROAD
HARWOOD ROAD
MOOR PARK ROAD
WATERFORD RD
BRITANNIA ROAD
MAXWELL ROAD
HOLMEAD ROAD
RUMBOLD ROAD
WANDON RD
CEDARNE ROAD
KEMPSON RD
MUSGRAVE CRES
BLAKE GDNS
TYRAWLEY RD
BROXHOLME HO
NEW KING'S RD
WANDSWORTH BRIDGE RD
IMPERIAL RD
SANDS END LA
STOKENCHURCH ST
RYECROFT ST
PERRYMEAD ST
BOWERDEAN ST
PARSONS GREEN LA
PARSONS GN
SHOTTENDANE RD
ELMSTONE RD
HARBLEDOWN RD
NOVELLO ST
CAMPANA RD
FAVART RD
PARTHENIA RD
CRONDACE RD
ELTHIRON RD
IRENE RD
DELVINO RD
MOLESFORD RD
CYRIL THATCHER HO
ALEX GOSSIP HO
RICHARD KNIGHT HO
ERIC MACDONALD HO
PEARSCROFT RD
SANDILANDS RD
BOVINGDON RD
ACFOLD RD
CRESFORD RD
MELDON CL
MANOR CT
STANFORD CT
135
266
B317
B318
A304
A308
A217
A219
A3220
SW10

A
B
C
D
256
SW10
REDCLIFFE GARDENS
TREGUNTER ROAD
GILSTON ROAD
REDCLIFFE ROAD
SEYMOUR WALK
CATHCART ROAD
HOLLYWOOD ROAD
Redcliffe Sch
GUATEMALA STREET
Servite RC Prim Sch
FULHAM ROAD
Chelsea & Westminster Hospl
ELM PARK GARDENS
ELM PARK LANE
ELM PARK ROAD
CALLOW STREET
PARK WALK
BEAUFORT STREET
Cameron House Sch
MULBERRY WALK
MALLORD STREET
THE VALE
CARLYLE SQ
KING'S ROAD
PAULTONS SQUARE
DANVERS STREET
THE PORTICOS
Park Walk Prim Sch
LIMERSTON STREET
NETHERTON GROVE
GERTRUDE STREET
HOBURY ST
LAMONT ROAD
LANGTON STREET
SLAIDBURN STREET
EDITH GROVE
FERNSHAW ROAD
GUNTER GROVE
EDITH TERRACE
MILMAN'S STREET
Lindsey House
CHEYNE WALK
WORLD'S END PL
Ashburnham Com Sch
BLANTYRE STREET
DARTREY WALK
CREMORNE ROAD
ASHBURNHAM ROAD
Kensington & Chelsea Coll
HORTENSIA ROAD
Westfield Park
LOTS ROAD
TETCOTT ROAD
UVERDALE ROAD
UPCERNE ROAD
BURNABY STREET
TADEMA ROAD
STADIUM STREET
Thames Path
Cremorne Gdns
Old Ferry Wharf
Chelsea Wharf
Cremorne Wharf
RIVER THAMES
Heatherley Sch of Fine Art
Kensington & Chelsea
Hammersmith & Fulham
Wandsworth
Gas Works
SANDS END LA
IMPERIAL RD
CHELSEA HARBOUR DR
THE QUADRANGLE
KING'S QUAY
THAMES QUAY
Chelsea Harbour Design Ctr
HARBOUR AVE
Imperial Wharf
THE BOULEVARD
THE BELVEDERE
CHELSEA CRES
Chelsea Harbour Pier
Fulham Bsns Exchange
Chelsea Coll of Art & Design
TOWNMEAD RD
VICARAGE CRES
THE RIVERAINS
OLD SWAN WHARF
VICARAGE WLK
BATTERSEA CHURCH RD
WHISTLERS AVENUE
THORNEY CRES
SUNBURY LA
Royal Academy of Dance
Thomas's London Day Schs
BATTERSEA HIGH ST
GRANFIELD ST
VICARAGE CT
Tenn Cts
Fred Wells
ORVILLE RD
136
265
77
78
1
2
3
4
5
6

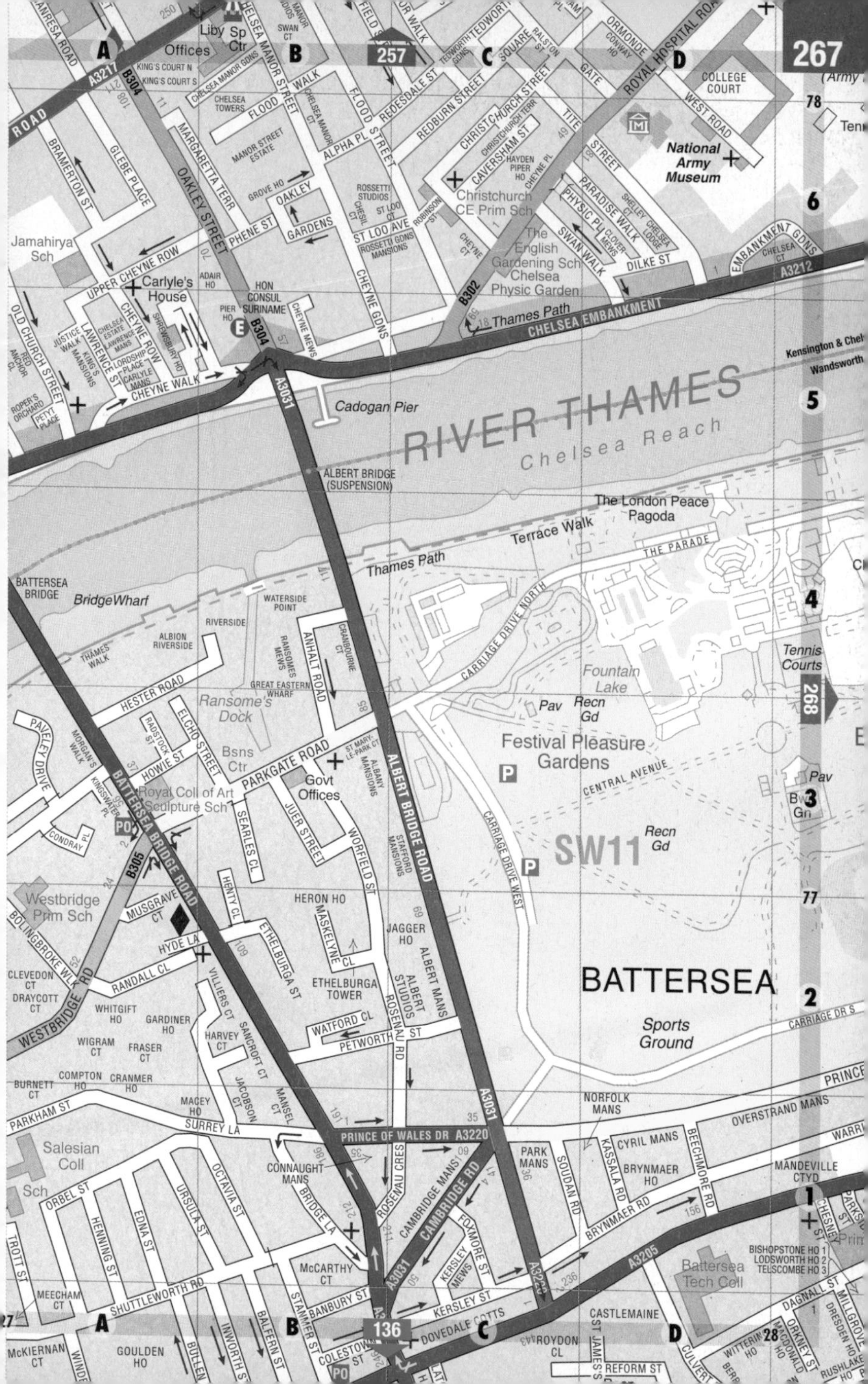
257
A
B
C
D
Liby
Sp Ctr
Offices
KING'S COURT N
KING'S COURT S
A3217
B304
ROAD
SWAN CT
ROYAL HOSPITAL ROAD
ORMONDE GATE
CONWAY HO
TEDWORTH SQUARE
TEDWORTH GDNS
RALSTON ST
COLLEGE COURT
WEST ROAD
National Army Museum
TITE STREET
CHELSEA MANOR STREET
CHELSEA MANOR GDNS
CHELSEA TOWERS
FLOOD WALK
FLOOD STREET
CHELSEA MANOR CT
REDESDALE ST
REDBURN STREET
CHRISTCHURCH STREET
CHRISTCHURCH TERR
CAVERSHAM ST
HAYDEN PIPER HO
CHEYNE PL
ALPHA PL
MANOR STREET ESTATE
GROVE HO
OAKLEY GARDENS
MARGARETTA TERR
OAKLEY STREET
PHENE ST
BRAMERTON ST
GLEBE PLACE
ROSSETTI STUDIOS
CHESIL CT
ST LOO CT
ST LOO AVE
ROBINSON ST
ROSSETTI GDNS MANSIONS
Christchurch CE Prim Sch
The English Gardening Sch
Chelsea Physic Garden
PARADISE WALK
PHYSIC PL
SWAN WALK
CLOVER MEWS
SHELLEY CT
CHELSEA LODGE
DILKE ST
EMBANKMENT GDNS
CHELSEA CT
A3212
Jamahirya Sch
UPPER CHEYNE ROW
Carlyle's House
ADAIR HO
HON CONSUL SURINAME
PIER HO
CHEYNE GDNS
CHEYNE MEWS
CHEYNE CT
B302
Thames Path
CHELSEA EMBANKMENT
OLD CHURCH STREET
JUSTICE WALK
LAWRENCE ST
KING'S MANSIONS
CHELSEA ESTATE
LAWRENCE MANS
LORDSHIP PLACE
CARLYLE MANS
CHEYNE ROW
SHREWSBURY HO
CHEYNE WALK
ROPER'S ORCHARD
PETYT PLACE
RED ANCHOR CL
E
A3031
Cadogan Pier
Kensington & Chelsea
Wandsworth
RIVER THAMES
Chelsea Reach
ALBERT BRIDGE (SUSPENSION)
The London Peace Pagoda
Terrace Walk
THE PARADE
Thames Path
BATTERSEA BRIDGE
BridgeWharf
WATERSIDE POINT
RIVERSIDE
ALBION RIVERSIDE
THAMES WALK
RANSOMES MEWS
ANHALT ROAD
CRANBOURNE CT
GREAT EASTERN WHARF
HESTER ROAD
Ransome's Dock
CARRIAGE DRIVE NORTH
Fountain Lake
Tennis Courts
Pav
Recn Gd
Festival Pleasure Gardens
CENTRAL AVENUE
Pav
Bwls Gn
268
PAVELEY DRIVE
MORGAN'S WALK
RADSTOCK ST
ELCHO STREET
HOWIE ST
Bsns Ctr
PARKGATE ROAD
ST MARY-LE-PARK CT
ALBANY MANSIONS
Govt Offices
ALBERT BRIDGE ROAD
KINGSWATER PL
BATTERSEA BRIDGE ROAD
Royal Coll of Art Sculpture Sch
SEARLES CL
JUER STREET
WORFIELD ST
STAFFORD MANSIONS
CARRIAGE DRIVE WEST
Recn Gd
SW11
CONDRAY PL
PO
B305
Westbridge Prim Sch
MUSGRAVE CT
HENTY CL
HERON HO
MASKELYNE CL
JAGGER HO
BOLINGBROKE WLK
HYDE LA
ETHELBURGA ST
ALBERT STUDIOS
ALBERT MANS
RANDALL CL
ETHELBURGA TOWER
CLEVEDON CT
DRAYCOTT CT
VILLIERS CT
BATTERSEA
WESTBRIDGE RD
WHITGIFT HO
GARDINER HO
HARVEY CT
SANCROFT CT
WATFORD CL
ROSENAU RD
PETWORTH ST
Sports Ground
CARRIAGE DR S
WIGRAM CT
FRASER CT
COMPTON HO
CRANMER HO
BURNETT CT
JACOBSON CT
MACEY HO
MANSEL CT
PRINCE
PARKHAM ST
SURREY LA
PRINCE OF WALES DR A3220
NORFOLK MANS
OVERSTRAND MANS
Salesian Coll
Sch
CONNAUGHT MANS
ROSENAU CRES
CAMBRIDGE MANS
CAMBRIDGE RD
PARK MANS
SOUDAN RD
KASSALA RD
CYRIL MANS
BRYNMAER HO
BEECHMORE RD
MANDEVILLE CTYD
ORBEL ST
OCTAVIA ST
URSULA ST
HENNING ST
EDNA ST
BRIDGE LA
FOXMORE ST
KERSLEY MEWS
BRYNMAER RD
A3205
CHESNEY ST
BISHOPSTONE HO
LODSWORTH HO
TELSCOMBE HO
Battersea Tech Coll
TROTT ST
McCARTHY CT
A3220
MEECHAM CT
SHUTTLEWORTH RD
BANBURY ST
KERSLEY ST
DAGNALL ST
MILLGROVE
DRESDEN HO
ORKNEY ST
STAMMER ST
CASTLEMAINE
136
DOVEDALE COTTS
ROYDON CL
JAMES'S
MACDONALD HO
McKIERNAN CT
GOULDEN HO
BULLEN
INWORTH ST
BALFERN ST
COLESTOWN ST
REFORM ST
CULVERT
WITTERING HO
RUSHLAKE HO
A
B
C
D
1
2
3
4
5
6
77
78
28
27

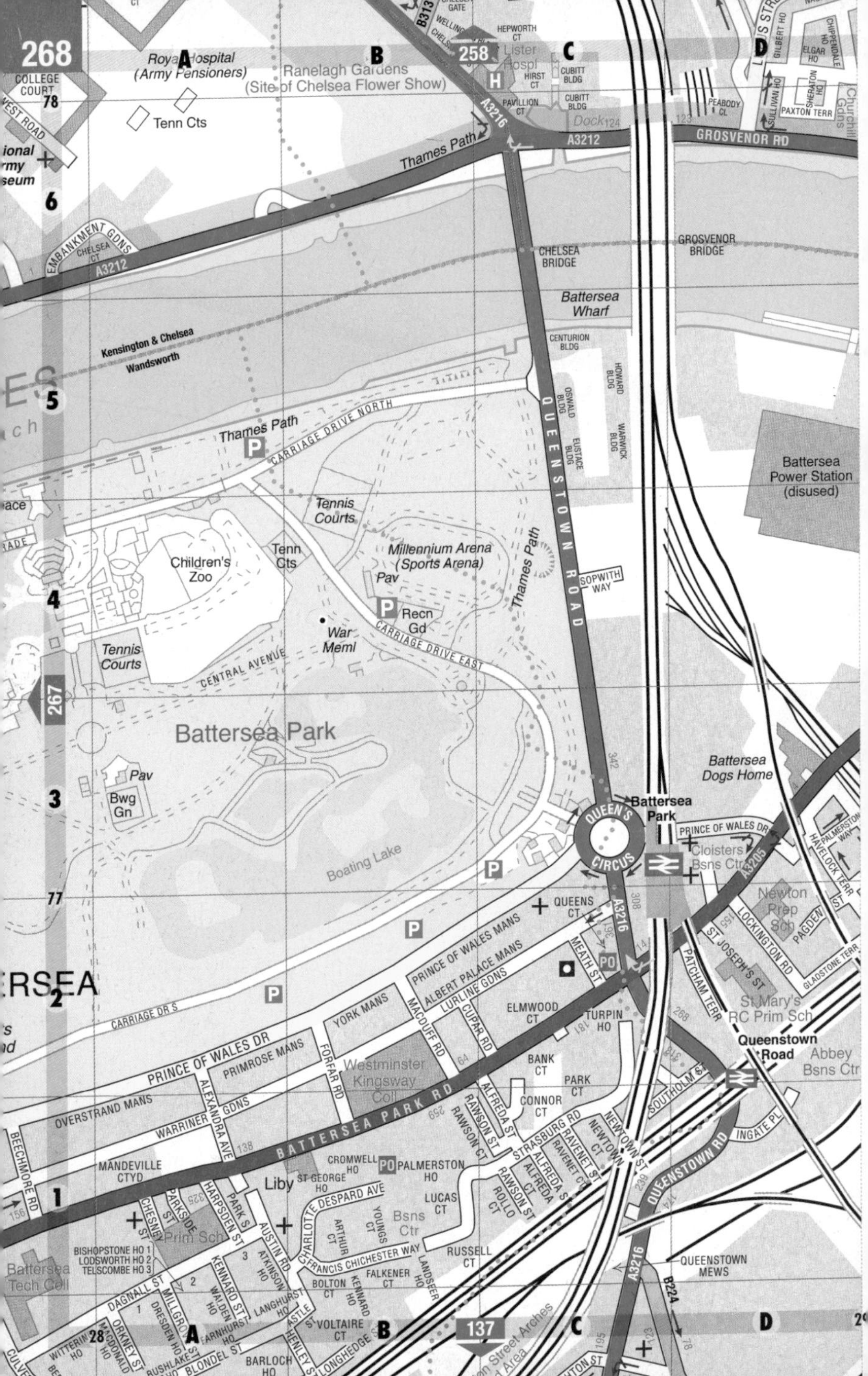

268
A
B
C
D
Royal Hospital (Army Pensioners)
Ranelagh Gardens (Site of Chelsea Flower Show)
258
Lister Hospl
HEPWORTH CT
HIRST CT
CUBITT BLDG
PAVILLION CT
COLLEGE COURT
78
Tenn Cts
Thames Path
A3216
A3212
Dock
GROSVENOR RD
PEABODY CL
PAXTON TERR
GILBERT HO
ELGAR HO
CHIPPENDALE HO
SULLIVAN HO
SHERATON HO
Churchill Gdns
6
EMBANKMENT GDNS
CHELSEA CT
CHELSEA BRIDGE
GROSVENOR BRIDGE
Battersea Wharf
Kensington & Chelsea
Wandsworth
5
CENTURION BLDG
HOWARD BLDG
OSWALD BLDG
EUSTACE BLDG
WARWICK BLDG
QUEENSTOWN ROAD
CARRIAGE DRIVE NORTH
Battersea Power Station (disused)
Tennis Courts
Children's Zoo
Tenn Cts
Millennium Arena (Sports Arena)
Pav
SOPWITH WAY
4
Recn Gd
War Meml
CARRIAGE DRIVE EAST
CENTRAL AVENUE
Tennis Courts
267
Battersea Park
Pav
Bwg Gn
3
Battersea Dogs Home
Battersea Park
QUEEN'S CIRCUS
PRINCE OF WALES DR
Cloisters Bsns Ctr
A3205
HAVELOCK TERR
PALMERSTON WAY
Boating Lake
77
QUEENS CT
Newton Prep Sch
LOCKINGTON RD
PAGDEN ST
ST JOSEPH'S ST
GLADSTONE TERR
PRINCE OF WALES MANS
ALBERT PALACE MANS
LURLINE GDNS
MEATH ST
PO
2
CARRIAGE DR S
YORK MANS
MACDUFF RD
CUPAR RD
ELMWOOD CT
TURPIN HO
PATCHAM TERR
St Mary's RC Prim Sch
Queenstown Road
Abbey Bsns Ctr
PRINCE OF WALES DR
PRIMROSE MANS
FORFAR RD
Westminster Kingsway Coll
BANK CT
PARK CT
SOUTHOLM ST
OVERSTRAND MANS
ALEXANDRA AVE
WARRINER GDNS
BATTERSEA PARK RD
ALFREDA ST
RAWSON ST
CONNOR CT
STRASBURG RD
NEWTOWN ST
RAVENET ST
INGATE PL
QUEENSTOWN RD
BEECHMORE RD
MANDEVILLE CTYD
CROMWELL HO
PALMERSTON HO
ST GEORGE HO
Liby
CHARLOTTE DESPARD AVE
1
CHESNEY ST
PARKSIDE ST
HARPSDEN ST
PARK S
AUSTIN RD
LUCAS CT
ROLLO CT
Prim Sch
ARTHUR CT
YOUNGS CT
Bsns Ctr
BISHOPSTONE HO 1
LODSWORTH HO 2
TELSCOMBE HO 3
FRANCIS CHICHESTER WAY
RUSSELL CT
QUEENSTOWN MEWS
Battersea Tech Coll
KENNARD ST
WALDEN HO
ATKINSON HO
BOLTON CT
FALKENER CT
KENNARD HO
LANDSEER HO
B224
DAGNALL ST
MILLGROVE ST
DRESDEN HO
LANGHURST HO
ASTLE ST
VOLTAIRE CT
28
ORKNEY ST
MACDONALD HO
WITTERING HO
FARNHURST HO
RUSHLAKE HO
BLONDEL ST
BARLOCH HO
HENLEY ST
LONGHEDGE ST
137
Arches

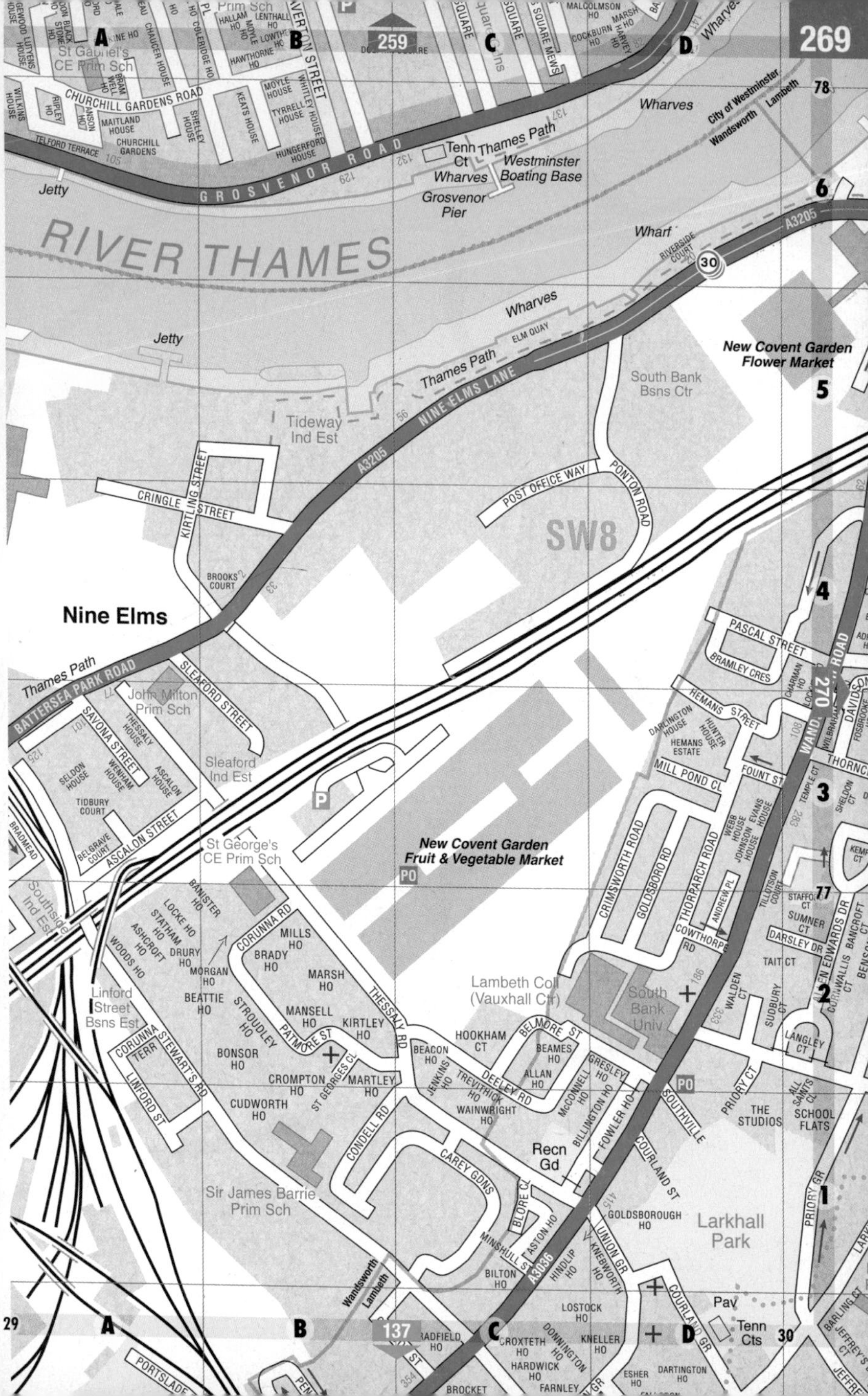

259
River Thames
Grosvenor Road
Churchill Gardens Road
St Gabriel's CE Prim Sch
Jetty
Wharves
Thames Path
Westminster Boating Base
Grosvenor Pier
Tenn Ct
City of Westminster
Lambeth
Wandsworth
Wharf
Riverside Court
A3205
Nine Elms Lane
Elm Quay
New Covent Garden Flower Market
South Bank Bsns Ctr
Tideway Ind Est
Post Office Way
Ponton Road
SW8
Cringle Street
Kirtling Street
Brooks Court
Nine Elms
Battersea Park Road
John Milton Prim Sch
Sleaford Street
Savona Street
Sleaford Ind Est
Ascalon Street
St George's CE Prim Sch
New Covent Garden Fruit & Vegetable Market
Southside Ind Est
Linford Street Bsns Est
Corunna Rd
Thessaly Rd
Patmore St
Stewart's Rd
Linford St
Lambeth Coll (Vauxhall Ctr)
South Bank Univ
Pascal Street
Bramley Cres
Hemans Street
Hemans Estate
Mill Pond Cl
Fount St
Crimsworth Road
Goldsboro Rd
Thorparch Road
Cowthorpe Rd
Wandsworth Road
270
Belmore St
Deeley Rd
Condell Rd
Carey Gdns
Blore Cl
Minshull St
Sir James Barrie Prim Sch
Recn Gd
A3036
Southville
Courland St
Priory Ct
The Studios
School Flats
Larkhall Park
Priory Gr
Union Gr
Courland Gr
Pav
Tenn Cts
137
Portslade
29
30
77
78

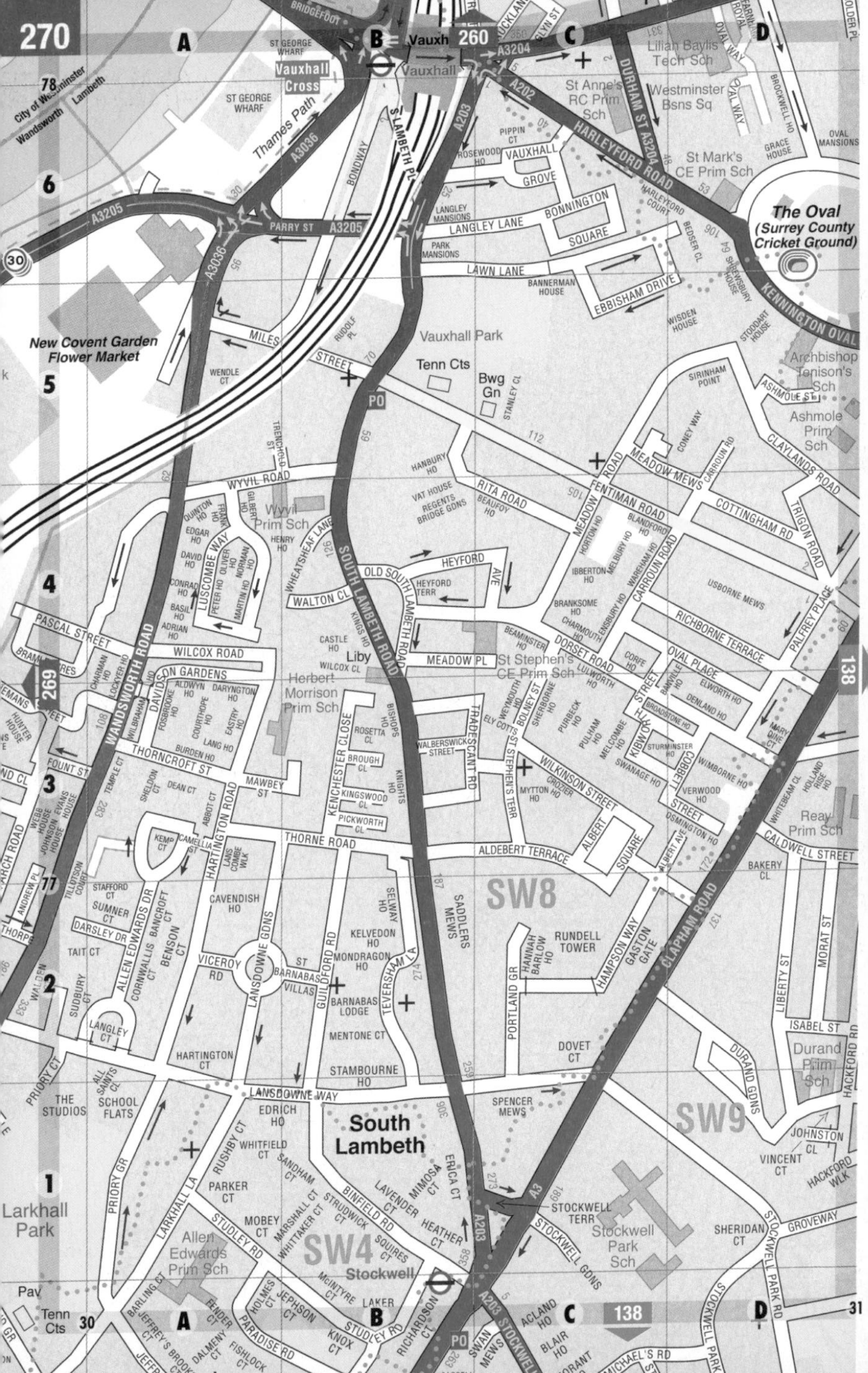

270
A
B
C
D
260
Vauxhall
Vauxhall Cross
BRIDGEFOOT
ST GEORGE WHARF
City of Westminster
Lambeth
Wandsworth
Thames Path
A3036
A3205
A3204
A202
A203
PARRY ST
BONDWAY
S LAMBETH PL
MILES STREET
RUDOLF PL
New Covent Garden Flower Market
WENDLE CT
Lillian Baylis Tech Sch
St Anne's RC Prim Sch
Westminster Bsns Sq
DURHAM ST
HARLEYFORD ROAD
OVAL WAY
BROCKWELL HO
OVAL MANSIONS
GRACE HOUSE
St Mark's CE Prim Sch
The Oval (Surrey County Cricket Ground)
KENNINGTON OVAL
PIPPIN CT
ROSEWOOD HO
VAUXHALL GROVE
BONNINGTON SQUARE
LANGLEY MANSIONS
LANGLEY LANE
PARK MANSIONS
LAWN LANE
BANNERMAN HOUSE
EBBISHAM DRIVE
HARLEYFORD COURT
BEDSER CL
SHREWSBURY HOUSE
WISDEN HOUSE
STODDART HOUSE
Vauxhall Park
Tenn Cts
Bwg Gn
STANLEY CL
PO
Archbishop Tenison's Sch
ASHMOLE ST
Ashmole Prim Sch
SIRINHAM POINT
CONEY WAY
CARROUN RD
CLAYLANDS ROAD
MEADOW MEWS
MEADOW ROAD
FENTIMAN ROAD
COTTINGHAM RD
TRIGON ROAD
TRENCHOLD ST
WYVIL ROAD
Wyvil Prim Sch
HANBURY HO
VAT HOUSE
REGENTS BRIDGE GDNS
RITA ROAD
BEAUFOY HO
QUINTON HO
FRANK HO
GILBERT HO
EDGAR HO
DAVID HO
CONRAD HO
BASIL HO
ADRIAN HO
LUSCOMBE WAY
PETER HO
OLIVER HO
MARTIN HO
MORMAN HO
HENRY HO
WHEATSHEAF LANE
SOUTH LAMBETH ROAD
OLD SOUTH LAMBETH ROAD
HEYFORD AVE
HEYFORD TERR
WALTON CL
HORTON HO
MELBURY HO
BLANDFORD HO
WAREHAM HO
IBBERTON HO
BRANKSOME HO
CHARMOUTH HO
TENSBURY HO
USBORNE MEWS
RICHBORNE TERRACE
PALFREY PLACE
PASCAL STREET
WANDSWORTH ROAD
WILCOX ROAD
269
DAVIDSON GARDENS
CHARMAN HO
LOCKYER HO
WILBRAHAM HO
ALDWYN HO
DARYNGTON HO
FOSBROOKE HO
COURTHOPE HO
EASTRY HO
LANG HO
BURDEN HO
THORNCROFT ST
FOUNT ST
TEMPLE CT
SHELDON CT
DEAN CT
ABBOT CT
MAWBEY ST
HARTINGTON ROAD
CASTLE HO
WILCOX CL
KINGS HO
Liby
Herbert Morrison Prim Sch
MEADOW PL
St Stephen's CE Prim Sch
BEAMINSTER HO
DORSET ROAD
LULWORTH HO
CORFE HO
OVAL PLACE
ELWORTH HO
DENLAND HO
BISHOPS HO
ROSETTA CL
BROUGH CL
KINGSWOOD CL
PICKWORTH CL
KENCHESTER CLOSE
KNIGHTS HO
TRADESCANT RD
WALBERSWICK STREET
ELY COTTS
WEYMOUTH HO
BOLNEY ST
ST STEPHEN'S TERR
SHERBORNE HO
PURBECK HO
PULHAM HO
MELCOMBE HO
SWANAGE HO
KIBWORTH STREET
BROADSTONE HO
STURMINSTER HO
COBBETT STREET
WIMBORNE HO
VERWOOD HO
MARY DINE CT
WILKINSON STREET
MYTTON HO
CROZIER HO
OSMINGTON HO
ALBERT SQUARE
ALBERT AVE
138
WHITEBEAM CL
HOLLAND RISE HO
Reay Prim Sch
CALDWELL STREET
BAKERY CL
KEMP CT
CAMELLIA ST
THORNE ROAD
ALDEBERT TERRACE
SW8
LAMS COMBE WLK
CAVENDISH HO
SELWAY HO
SADDLERS MEWS
STAFFORD CT
SUMNER CT
DARSLEY DR
TAIT CT
TILLOTSON COURT
ALLEN EDWARDS DR
BANCROFT CT
CORNWALLIS CT
BENSON CT
VICEROY RD
LANSDOWNE GDNS
ST BARNABAS VILLAS
GUILDFORD RD
KELVEDON HO
MONDRAGON HO
TEVERSHAM LA
HANNAH BARLOW HO
RUNDELL TOWER
HAMPSON WAY
GASTON GATE
PORTLAND GR
CLAPHAM ROAD
LIBERTY ST
MORAT ST
ISABEL ST
HACKFORD RD
WEBB HOUSE
JOHNSON HOUSE
EVANS HOUSE
ANDREW PL
THORPE
WALDEN
SUDBURY CT
LANGLEY CT
BARNABAS LODGE
MENTONE CT
HARTINGTON CT
DOVET CT
DURAND GDNS
Durand Prim Sch
PRIORY CT
ALL SAINTS CL
THE STUDIOS
SCHOOL FLATS
STAMBOURNE HO
LANSDOWNE WAY
EDRICH HO
SPENCER MEWS
South Lambeth
SW9
JOHNSTON CL
VINCENT CT
HACKFORD WLK
Larkhall Park
PRIORY GR
LARKHALL LA
RUSHBY CT
WHITFIELD CT
SANDHAM CT
PARKER CT
MOBEY CT
MARSHALL CT
WHITTAKER CT
STRUDWICK CT
BINFIELD RD
LAVENDER CT
MIMOSA CT
ERICA CT
HEATHER CT
SQUIRES CT
A3
STOCKWELL TERR
Stockwell Park Sch
SHERIDAN CT
STOCKWELL PARK RD
GROVEWAY
STOCKWELL GDNS
SW4
Allen Edwards Prim Sch
STUDLEY RD
Stockwell
Pav
Tenn Cts
BARLING CT
FENDER CT
JEFFREY'S BROOKS CT
DALMENY CT
FISHLOCK CT
HOLMES CT
JEPHSON CT
PARADISE RD
MCINTYRE CT
LAKER CT
KNOX CT
STUDLEY RD
RICHARDSON CT
SWAN MEWS
STOCKWELL
ACLAND HO
BLAIR HO
MORANT
MICHAEL'S RD
STOCKWELL PARK
CASSELL
1
2
3
4
5
6
30
31
77
78

Place name May be abbreviated on the map

Location number Present when a number indicates the place's position in a crowded area of mapping

Locality, town or village Shown when more than one place has the same name

Postcode district District for the indexed place

Standard-scale reference Page number and grid reference for the standard-scale mapping on pages 1–227

Large-scale reference Page number and grid reference for the large-scale central London mapping on pages 229–270, underlined in red

Church Rd 6 Beckenham BR2......53 C6 228 C6

Cities, towns and villages are listed in **CAPITAL LETTERS** **Public and commercial buildings** are highlighted in magenta
Places of interest are highlighted in blue with a star★

Abbreviations used in the index

Acad	**Academy**	Comm	**Common**	Gd	**Ground**	L	**Leisure**	Prom	**Promenade**
App	**Approach**	Cott	**Cottage**	Gdn	**Garden**	La	**Lane**	Rd	**Road**
Arc	**Arcade**	Cres	**Crescent**	Gn	**Green**	Liby	**Library**	Recn	**Recreation**
Ave	**Avenue**	Cswy	**Causeway**	Gr	**Grove**	Mdw	**Meadow**	Ret	**Retail**
Bglw	**Bungalow**	Ct	**Court**	H	**Hall**	Meml	**Memorial**	Sh	**Shopping**
Bldg	**Building**	Ctr	**Centre**	Ho	**House**	Mkt	**Market**	Sq	**Square**
Bsns, Bus	**Business**	Ctry	**Country**	Hospl	**Hospital**	Mus	**Museum**	St	**Street**
Bvd	**Boulevard**	Cty	**County**	HQ	**Headquarters**	Orch	**Orchard**	Sta	**Station**
Cath	**Cathedral**	Dr	**Drive**	Hts	**Heights**	Pal	**Palace**	Terr	**Terrace**
Cir	**Circus**	Dro	**Drove**	Ind	**Industrial**	Par	**Parade**	TH	**Town Hall**
Cl	**Close**	Ed	**Education**	Inst	**Institute**	Pas	**Passage**	Univ	**University**
Cnr	**Corner**	Emb	**Embankment**	Int	**International**	Pk	**Park**	Wk, Wlk	**Walk**
Coll	**College**	Est	**Estate**	Intc	**Interchange**	Pl	**Place**	Wr	**Water**
Com	**Community**	Ex	**Exhibition**	Junc	**Junction**	Prec	**Precinct**	Yd	**Yard**

Index of towns, villages, streets, hospitals, industrial estates, railway stations, schools, shopping centres, universities and places of interest

A

Aaron Ct BR3 ....207 D6
Aaron Hill Rd E6.....100 C2
Abady Ho SW1...... 259 D4
Abberley Mews 9 SW8.................137 B2
Abberton IG8.........37 C5
Abbess Cl
11 Newham E6 ..... 100 A2
Streatham SW2..... 160 D3
Abbeville Mews 3 SW4...............137 D1
Abbeville Rd
Clapham Pk SW4.... 159 C6
Hornsey N8 ....49 D5
Abbey Ave HA0 ....88 A5
Abbey Bsns Ctr SW8........ 137 B4 268 D2
Abbey Cl Hayes UB3 ..106 B5
Northolt UB5 ....85 B4
Pinner HA5 ....40 C6
Abbey Cres DA17 ....125 C2
Abbey Ct
6 Bedford Pk W12 .... 111 C3
Camberwell SE17 ... 262 B1
Church End N3.........47 C6
5 Edgware HA8.......26 D5
Hampton TW12 ..... 173 C3
St John's Wood NW8 229 A4
Twickenham TW2......152 B2
Abbeydale Rd HA0 ....88 C6
Abbey Dr SW17 ....181 A5
Abbeyfield Cl CR4....180 C1
Abbeyfield Rd SE16 ..118 C2
Abbeyfields Cl NW10..88 C5
Abbey Gdns
10 Bermondsey SE16............ 118 A2
Chislehurst BR7..... 188 C2
St John's Wood NW8.......92 A5 229 B3
West Kensington W6...... 135 A6 264 A5
Abbey Gr SE2..........124 B2
Abbeyhill Rd DA15 ...168 C2
Abbey Ho
Newham E15..........98 C5
St John's Wood NW8. 229 B2
Abbey Ind Est CR4.. 202 D4
Abbey La
Beckenham BR3 .... 185 C3
Mill Meads E15 ....98 B5
Abbey Lane Commercial Est 1 E15 ....98 C5
Abbey Lo
Bromley SE12 ....187 B6
1 Ealing W5....... 109 C6
Lisson Gr NW8 ..... 230 B1
Abbey Manufacturing Est HA0..............88 B6
Abbey Mews
Brentford TW7........131 B4
Walthamstow E17......53 C4
Abbey Mount DA17...125 B1
Abbey Orchard Street Est SW1 .... 259 D6
Abbey Orchard St SW1....... 115 D3 259 D6
Abbey Par NW10.......88 B4
Abbey Park Ind Est IG11............... 101 A6
Abbey Par SW19 ......180 A3
Abbey Pk BR3 ....185 C3
Abbey Prim Sch SM4............... 201 C2
Abbey Rd
Barking IG11....... 100 D6
Bexley DA7 .... 147 A1
Croydon CR0 .... 220 D5
Enfield EN1 ....17 C6
Erith DA17......... 125 A3
Ilford IG2 ....57 B4
Lower Halliford TW17 .... 192 C1
Merton SW19 ...... 180 A2
Abbey Rd Motorist Ctr 4 NW6..............91 D6
Abbey Rd
Newham E15..........98 C5
St John's Wood NW8...... 92 A5 229 A4
Wembley NW10.......88 D5
Abbey St
Bermondsey SE1...... 117 D3 263 C6
Newham E13..........99 A3
Abbey Terr SE2 ....124 C2
Abbey Trad Est SE26................185 B5
Abbey View NW7......11 D1
Abbey Wlk KT8 ....195 D5
ABBEY WOOD 124 B3
Abbey Wood Rd SE2.................124 C2
Abbey Wood Sch SE2............... 124 A3
Abbey Wood Sta SE2............... 124 C3
Abbot Cl HA4.........62 D5
Abbot Ct SW8 ...... 270 A3
Abbot Ho 14 E14.....119 D6
Abbotsbury Cl
Kensington W14..... 113 B4 244 C1
Mill Meads E15 ....98 A5
Abbotsbury Gdns HA5 ....40 C3
Abbotsbury Ho W14. 244 B2
Abbotsbury Mews SE15................140 C2
Abbotsbury Prim Sch SM4............... 201 D4
Abbotsbury Rd
Coney Hall BR2, BR4............. 224 D6
Kensington W14..... 113 B4 244 C1
Morden SM4 .... 201 D5
Abbots Cl BR5 ....211 A1
Abbots Ct SE25 ......205 C6
Abbots Dr HA2........63 C6
Abbotsfield Sch UB10 ....82 D5
Abbotsford Ave N15...51 A5
Abbotsford Gdns IG8..................37 A3
Abbotsford Rd IG3....80 B6
Abbots Gdns N2 ......48 B5
Abbots Gn CR0, CR2 ..222 D2
Abbots Green CR2 ...222 D2
Abbotshade Rd 15 SE16................118 D5
Abbotshall Ave N14...15 C1
Abbotshall Rd SE6 ...164 B2
Abbots Ho
Kensington W14 .... 254 C5
Pimlico SW1 .... 259 C1
Walthamstow E17.....35 B1
Abbots La SE1.........117 C5 253 B3
Abbotsleigh Cl SM2..217 D1
Abbotsleigh Rd SW16...............181 C5
Abbotsmede Cl TW1................152 D2
Abbots Pk SW2 ......160 C3
Abbot's Pl NW6.......91 D6
Abbots Rd
Burnt Oak HA8 ....27 B3
Cheam SM3........ 217 A4
Newham E6..........99 D6
Abbots Terr N8 ....50 A3
Abbot St E8 ....73 D2
Abbotstone Ho 4 E5..74 A6
Abbotstone Rd SW15...............134 C2
Abbotsview Ct NW7...12 A1
Abbots Way BR3 .....207 A4
Abbotswell Rd SE4...163 B6
Abbotswood Cl 7 DA17 ....125 A3
Abbotswood Gdns IG5..................56 B6
Abbotswood Rd
London SE22 .... 139 C1
Streatham SW16.... 159 D1
Abbotswood Way UB3 ....106 B5
Abbott Ave SW20 ....178 D2
Abbott Cl
Hampton TW12 ..... 173 A4
Northolt UB5 ....63 B2
Abbott Ho SW12 .....158 D4
Abbott Rd E14.........98 B1
Abbotts Cl
Canonbury N1 ....73 A2
Romford RM7 ....59 D6
Woolwich SE28 ..... 124 C6
Abbotts Cres
Chingford E4 ....36 B6
Enfield EN2 ....4 D3
Abbotts Ct HA2 ....64 B6
Abbotts Dr HA0.......65 B6
Abbotts Park Rd E10..54 A2
Abbotts Rd Barnet EN5..1 D1
Mitcham CR4....... 203 C5
Southall UB1 .... 107 A5
Abbotts Wharf 4 E14.................97 C1
Abbott's Wlk DA7....146 D5
Abchurch La EC2, EC4 ....117 B6 252 D6
Abchurch Yd EC4 ... 252 C6
Abdale Rd W12 ......112 B5
Abel Ho
7 Kennington SE11............ 138 C6
Woolwich SE18 ..... 123 A2
Abenglen Ind Est UB3 ....105 B4
Aberavon Rd E3 ......97 A4
Abercairn Rd SW16 ..181 C3
Aberconway Rd SM4................201 D5
Abercorn Cl
Finchley NW7 ....29 A3
St John's Wood NW8...... 92 A4 229 A2
Abercorn Cres HA2 ...41 D1
Abercorn Gdns
Harrow HA3 ....43 D2
Ilford RM6...........58 B3
Abercorn Gr HA4 .....39 B5

Abercorn Mans NW8 229 B3
Abercorn Mews 10 TW10 132 B1
Abercorn Pl NW8 92 A5 229 A3
Abercorn Rd
Finchley NW7 29 A3
Stanmore HA7 25 C3
Abercorn Trad Est HA0 87 D6
Abercorn Way SE1 118 A1
Abercrombie Dr EN1 6 A4
Abercrombie Ho 1 W12 112 B6
Abercrombie St SW11 136 C3
Aberdale Ct 22 SE16 118 D4
Aberdare Cl BR4 224 A6
Aberdare Gdns
Finchley NW7 28 D3
South Hampstead NW6 69 D1
Aberdare Rd EN3 6 C1
Aberdeen Cotts HA7 25 C3
Aberdeen Ct
Canonbury N5 73 A3
Paddington W2 236 C5
Aberdeen Ctr N5 73 A3
Aberdeen La N5 73 A3
Aberdeen Mans WC1 240 A6
Aberdeen Par N18 34 B5
Aberdeen Pk N5 73 A3
Aberdeen Pl NW8 92 B3 236 C6
Aberdeen Rd
Canonbury N5 73 A4
Croydon CR0 221 B4
Dudden Hill NW10 67 D3
Edmonton N18 34 B5
Harrow HA3 24 D1
Aberdeen Terr SE3 142 B3
Aberdour Rd IG3 80 B6
Aberdour St SE1 117 C2 263 A4
Aberfeldy Ho SE5 138 D5
Aberfeldy St E14 98 A1
Aberford Gdns SE18 144 A4
Aberfoyle Rd SW16 181 D4
Abergeldie Rd SE12 165 B5
Abernethy Rd SE13 142 C1
Abersham Rd E8 73 D3
Abery St SE18 123 C2
Ability Plaza 8 E8 73 D1
Ability Twrs EC1 235 A2
Abingdon Cl
Fulham SE1 263 D2
Hillingdon UB10 82 B6
Kentish Town NW1 71 D2
Wimbledon SW19 180 A4
Abingdon Ct
Earl's Ct W8 255 B5
Edgware HA8 26 A6
Upper Tooting SW17 180 D4
Abingdon Gdns W8 255 B5
Abingdon Ho
Bromley BR1 187 B3
Spitalfields E2 243 C6
Abingdon Lo
2 Barnet EN5 1 A1
Bromley BR2 186 D1
Abingdon Mans W8 255 A6
Abingdon Rd
Finchley N3 30 A1
Kensington W8 113 C3 255 B5
Thornton Heath SW16 182 A2
Abingdon St SW1 116 A3 260 A6
Abingdon Villas W8 113 C3 255 B5
Abingdon W14 254 D3
Abinger Cl
Barking IG11 80 A4
Bickley BR1 210 A6
New Addington CR0 224 A2
Wallington SM6 220 A3
Abinger Ct
3 Ealing W5 109 C6
Thornton Heath CR0 204 D2
Wallington SM6 220 A3
Abinger Gdns TW7 130 C2
Abinger Gr SE8 141 B6
Abinger Ho
Borough The SE1 252 C1
2 Kingston u T KT2 176 D3
Abinger Mews W9 91 C3
Abinger Rd W4 111 C3
Abington Ho NW11 48 A3
Ablett St SE16 118 C1
Abney Gdns 5 N16 73 D6
Abney Park Cemetery* N16 73 C6
Abney Park Ct N16 73 D6
Aborfield 6 NW5 71 C3
Aboyne Dr SW20 178 A1
Aboyne Rd
Neasden NW10 67 C5
Wandsworth SW17 158 B1
Abraham Cl WD19 22 B6
Abraham Cohen Ct IG1 56 C3
Abraham Fisher Ho 2 E12 78 C3
Abridge Way IG11 102 B5
Abyssinia Cl SW11 136 C1
Abyssinia Rd SW11 136 C1
Acacia Ave
Brentford TW8 131 B5
East Finchley N2 47 D6
Hayes UB3 83 D1
Littleton TW17 192 C4
Ruislip HA4 40 B2
Tottenham N17 33 B3
Wembley HA9 66 A3
Yiewsley UB7 104 B6
Acacia Bsns Ctr 1 E11 76 C5
Acacia Cl
Penge SE20 184 A1
Petts Wood BR5 211 B4
Rotherhithe SE8 119 A2
Stanmore HA7 24 C4
Acacia Ct Harrow HA1 41 D3
5 West Norwood SW16 182 C5
Acacia Dr SM3 201 C1
Acacia Gdns
St John's Wood NW8 229 D4
West Wickham BR4 224 A6
Acacia Gr
Dulwich SE21 161 B2
Kingston u T KT3 199 C6
Acacia Ho
Brockley SE4 141 B1
1 New Malden KT3 199 C5
Stoke Newington N16 73 B6
Wood Green N22 32 C2
Acacia Lo 6 N3 29 B1
Acacia Pl NW8 92 B5 229 D4
Acacia Rd Acton W3 111 A6
Beckenham BR3 207 B6
Enfield EN2 5 B4
Hampton TW12 173 C4
Leyton E11 76 C6
Mitcham CR4 181 B1
St John's Wood NW8 92 B5 229 D4
Thornton Heath SW16 182 A2
Walthamstow E17 53 A3
Wood Green N22 32 C2
Acacias Lo EN4 14 B6
Acacias The EN4 14 B6
Acacia Way DA15 167 D3
Acacia Wlk SW10 266 B3
Acad at Peckham The SE15 139 D4
Academy Ct 13 E2 96 C4
Academy Gdns
Croydon CR0 205 D1
Kensington W8 245 A2
Northolt UB5 84 D5
Academy Pl SE18 144 C4
Academy Rd SE18 144 B5
Academy Sch The NW3 70 B4
Academy The 2 N19 49 C1
Acad of Live & Recorded Arts The SW18 158 B5
Acanthus Dr SE1 118 A1
Acanthus Rd SW11 137 A2
Accadia Ct NW9 67 A6
Accommodation Rd NW11 47 B1
Ace Par KT9 214 A5
Acer Ave UB4 85 A2
Acer Ct
2 Cricklewood NW2 68 D4
3 Enfield EN3 7 A2
Acers BR7 188 A3
Acfold Rd SW6 265 C1
Achilles Cl SE1 118 A1
Achilles Ho 16 E2 96 B5
Achilles Rd NW6 69 C3
Achilles St SE14 141 A5
Achilles Way W1 248 B3
Acklam Rd W10 91 B2
Acklington Dr NW9 27 C2
Ackmar Rd SW6 135 C4 265 A1
Ackroyd Dr E3 97 C2
Ackroyd Rd SE23 163 A4
Acland Burghley Sch NW5 71 B4
Acland Cl SE18 145 B5
Acland Cres SE5 139 B2
Acland Ho SW9 138 B3
Acland Rd NW2 68 B2
Acock Gr UB5 64 A4
Acol Cres HA4 62 B3
Acol Ct 3 NW6 69 C1
Acol Rd NW6 69 D1
Aconbury Rd RM9 102 B6
Acorn Cl Chingford E4 35 D5
Chislehurst BR7 189 A5
Enfield EN2 4 D4
1 Hampton TW12 173 D4
Stanmore HA7 25 B3
Acorn Ct 5 Bow E3 97 C5
Hampton TW12 173 B5
Ilford IG2 57 C4
Upton Pk E6 78 A1
Wood Green N11 31 D4
Acorn Gdns
North Acton W3 89 B2
South Norwood SE19 183 D2
Acorn Gr
Harlington UB3 127 D5
Ruislip HA4 61 D4
Acorn Par 7 SE15 140 B5
Acorn Production Ctr N7 72 A1
Acorns The 21 SW19 156 D3
Acorns Way KT10 212 A3
Acorn Way
Beckenham BR3 208 A4
Forest Hill SE23 162 D1
Orpington BR6 226 D4
Acorn Wharf SE15 140 A6
Acorn Wlk SE16 119 A5
Acqua Ho TW9 132 D5
Acre Dr SE22 140 A1
Acrefield Ho 4 NW4 46 D5
Acre La Brixton SW2 138 B1
Wallington SM5 219 A4
Acre Path UB5 63 A2
Acre Rd
Dagenham RM10 81 D1
Kingston u T KT2 176 B2
Mitcham SW19 180 B4
Acre Way HA6 22 A2
Acris St SW18 158 A6
ACS Hillingdon International Sch UB10 82 B6
Action Ct TW15 171 A2
ACTON 111 B5
Acton Bsns Ctr NW10 89 B3
Acton Central Ind Est 4 W3 110 D5
Acton Central Sta W3 111 B5
Acton Cl N9 18 A2
ACTON GREEN 111 A2
Acton High Sch W3 110 C4
Acton Hill Mews W3 110 D5
Acton Ho
5 Acton W3 89 A1
16 Haggerston E8 95 D6
Acton Hospl W3 110 C4
Acton La
Acton Green W4 111 A2
Acton W3 111 A4
Harlesden NW10 89 B5
Acton Main Line Sta W3 89 A1
Acton Mews E8 95 D6
Acton Park Ind Est W3 111 B4
Acton St WC1 94 B4 233 C1
Acton Town Sta W3 110 C4
Acton Vale Ind Pk W3 111 D5
Acuba Ho SW18 157 D3
Acuba Rd SW18 157 D2
Acworth Cl N9 18 C4
Acworth Ho 1 SE18 144 D6
Ada Ct Islington N1 235 A5
St John's Wood W9 92 A4 229 B1
Ada Gdns
Plaistow E15 98 D6
South Bromley E14 98 B1
Ada Ho 23 E2 96 A6
Adair Cl SE25 206 B6
Adair Ho SW3 267 B6
Adair Rd W10 91 A3
Adair Twr 7 W10 91 A3
Ada Kennedy Ct 6 SE10 142 A5
Ada Lewis Ho HA9 66 B4
Adam Cl SE6 185 C6
Adam Ct
Newington SE11 261 C3
15 Sutton SM1 218 A4
Adam & Eve Ct W1 239 B2
Adam & Eve Mews W8 113 C3 255 B6
Adamfields NW3 70 B1
Adam Lo N21 16 B6
Adam Rd E4 35 B4
Adams Bridge Bsns Ctr HA9 66 D3
Adams Cl Finchley N3 29 C3
Surbiton KT5 198 B3
Wembley Pk NW9 66 D6
Adams Ct E17 53 A3
Adams Gardens Est 5 SE16 118 C4
Adams Ho
3 South Bromley E14 98 B1
3 Streatham SW16 181 C5
Adams Mews
Upper Tooting SW17 158 D2
Wood Green N22 32 B3
Adamson Ct N2 48 C6
Adamson Rd
Hampstead NW3 70 B1
Newham E16 99 A1
Adamson Way BR3 208 A4
Adams Pl N7 72 B3
Adams Qtr TW8 131 C6
Adams Rd
Beckenham BR3 207 A4
Tottenham N17 33 B1
Adamsrill Cl EN1 17 B5
Adamsrill Prim Sch SE26 163 A1
Adamsrill Rd SE26 185 A6
Adam's Row W1 115 A6 248 B5
Adams Sq DA6 147 A2
Adam St WC2 116 A6 250 B5
Adams Way CR0 206 A3
Adams Wlk 11 KT1 176 A1
Adam Wlk SW6 134 C5
Ada Pl E2 96 A6
Ada Rd
Camberwell SE5 139 C5
Wembley HA0, HA9 65 D5
Adare Ctr The SW16 160 A1
Adare Wlk SW16, SW2 160 B2
Ada St E8 96 B6
Adcot Wlk 6 BR6 227 D4
Adderley Gdns SE9 188 C6
Adderley Gr SW11 159 A6
Adderley Rd HA3 24 D2
Adderley St E14 98 A1
Addey Ho SE8 141 B5
Addey & Stanhope Sch SE14 141 C4
ADDINGTON 223 C3
Addington Ct 7 SW14 133 B2
Addington Dr N12 30 B4
Addington Gr SE26 185 A6
Addington Ho 13 SW9 138 B3
Addington Rd Bow E3 97 C4
Newham E16 98 C3
Stroud Green N4 50 C3
Thornton Heath CR0 204 C1
West Wickham BR4 224 C6
West Wickham BR4, CR0 224 B4
Addington Sq SE5 139 B5
Addington St SE1 116 B4 250 D1
Addington Village Rd CR0 223 C3
Addington Village Sta CR0 223 C2
Addis Cl EN3 6 D4
ADDISCOMBE 206 A1
Addiscombe Ave CR0 206 A2
Addiscombe Cl HA3 43 C4
Addiscombe Court Rd CR0 221 C6
Addiscombe Ct UB10 83 A3
Addiscombe Rd CR0 222 B6
Addiscombe Sta CR0 206 A1
Addis Ho 18 E1 96 C2
Addison Ave
Hounslow TW3 130 A4
Notting Hill W11 113 A5 244 A3
Southgate N14 15 C5
Addison Bridge Pl W14 113 B2 254 C4
Addison Cl
Northwood HA6 22 A2
Addison Cl *continued*
Orpington BR5 211 A3
Addison Cres W14 113 A3 254 B6
Addison Ct
3 Belmont SM2 217 D1
Ealing W5 110 C6
Twickenham TW1 153 A3
Addison Dr SE12 165 B6
Addison Gdns
Hammersmith W14 112 D3
Kingston u T KT5 198 B5
Addison Gr W4 111 C3
Addison Ho NW8 92 B4 229 C2
Addison Park Mans 12 W14 112 D4
Addison Pl
Notting Hill W11 113 A5 244 A3
Southall UB1 107 C6
Addison Prim Sch W14 112 D3
Addison Rd
Bromley BR2 209 D4
Croydon SE25 206 A5
Enfield EN3 6 D4
Kensington W14 113 B3 254 C6
Teddington TW11 175 B4
Walthamstow E17 54 A4
Wanstead E11 55 A3
Addison's Cl CR0 223 B6
Addison Way
Hampstead Garden Suburb NW11 47 C5
Hayes UB3 84 A1
Northwood HA6 22 A2
Addle Hill EC4 241 D1
Addle St EC2 242 B3
Addlestone Ho 4 W10 90 C2
Addy Ho SE16 118 C2
Adecroft Way KT8 196 A6
Adela Ave KT3 200 B5
Adela Ho 9 W6 112 C1
Adelaide Ave SE4 141 C1
Adelaide Cl
Brixton SW9 138 C1
Enfield EN1 5 C5
Stanmore HA7 25 A6
Adelaide Ct
15 Beckenham BR3 185 C3
Hackney E5 75 A3
Hanwell W7 108 D4
St John's Wood NW8 229 B3
Adelaide Gdns RM6 59 A4
Adelaide Gr W12 112 A5
Adelaide Ho E17 53 B6
Adelaide Rd
Ashford TW15 170 A6
Chislehurst BR7 188 D5
Ealing W13 109 A4
Heston TW5 129 A4
Ilford IG1 78 D6
Kingston u T KT6 198 A4
Leyton E10 76 A5
Primrose Hill NW3 70 C1
Richmond TW9 132 B1
Southall UB2 107 A2
Teddington TW11 174 D4
2 Wandsworth SW18 157 C6
Adelaide St WC2 250 A5
Adelaide Terr TW8 109 D1
Adela St W10 91 A3
Adelina Gr E1 96 C2
Adelina Mews SW12 159 D3
Adeline Pl WC1 93 D2 239 D3
Adelphi Cres UB4 83 D4
Adelphi Ct
19 Finchley N2 30 B1
20 Rotherhithe SE16 118 D4
Adelphi Terr WC2 250 B5
Adelphi Way UB4 83 D4
Adeney Cl W6 134 D6
Aden Gr N16 73 B4
Aden Ho 18 E1 96 D2
Aden Lo N16 73 B4
Adenmore Rd SE6 163 C4
Aden Rd Enfield EN3 7 A1
Ilford IG1 57 A2
Adeyfield Ho EC1 235 D1
Adhara Rd HA6 22 A5
Adie Rd W6 112 C3
Adine Rd E13 99 B3
Adisham Ho 4 E5 74 B3
Adler Ind Est UB3 105 B4
Adler St E1 96 A1
Adley St E5 75 A3
Adlington Cl N18 33 C5
Admaston Rd SE18 145 A6
Admiral Ct
Barking IG11 102 C5
Carshalton SM5 202 C1
Chelsea SW10 136 A4 266 B2
Hendon NW4 46 A4
Marylebone W1 238 A3
Admiral Ho TW11 175 A6
Admiral Hyson Ind Est SE16 118 B1
Admiral Mews W10 90 D3
Admiral Pl
Harringay N8 50 D5
Rotherhithe SE16 119 A5
Admirals Cl E18 55 B5
Admirals Ct
Bermondsey SE1 253 C3
3 Newham E6 100 D1
32 Putney SW19 156 D3
Admiral Seymour Rd SE9 144 B1
Admirals Gate SE10 141 D4
Admiral Sq SW10 136 A4 266 B2
Admiral St SE8 141 C4
Admirals Way E14 119 C4
Admiral's Wlk NW3 70 A5
Admiralty Arch* SW1 249 D4
Admiralty Cl 1 SE8 141 C4
Admiralty Rd TW11 174 D4
Admiralty Way TW11 174 D4
Admiral Wlk W9 91 C2
Adolf St SE6 185 D6
Adolphus Rd N4 50 D1
Adolphus St SE8 141 B5
Adomar Rd RM8 81 A5
Adpar St W2 92 B2 236 C4
Adrian Ave NW2 46 B1
Adrian Bolt Ho 2 E2 96 B4
Adrian Cl EN5 12 D5
Adrian Ho
Islington N1 233 D5
South Lambeth SW8 270 A4
Stratford E15 76 B1
Adrian Mews SW10 265 D6
Adriatic Bldg 18 E14 119 A6
Adriatic Ho 18 E1 96 D3
Adrienne Ave UB1 85 B4
Adron Ho 13 SE16 118 C2
Adstock Ho 5 N1 72 D1
ADT Coll SW15 157 B6
Advance Rd SE27 183 A6
Advent Ct IG8 36 D5
Adventurers Ct 17 E14 120 B6
Advent Way N18 34 D5
Adyar Ct 7 SW19 179 A3
Adys Lawn NW2 68 B2
Adys Rd SE15 139 D2
Aegean Apts 7 E16 121 A6
Aegon Ho 3 E14 119 D3
Aerodrome Rd NW4, NW9 45 D6
Aerodrome Way TW5 128 C6
Aeroville NW9 27 C1
Affleck St N1 233 D3
Afghan Rd SW11 136 C3
Africa Ho WC2 240 C2
Afsil Ho EC1 241 B3
Aga Khan Univ WC1 239 D3
Agamemnon Rd NW6 69 B3
Agar Cl KT6 214 B6
Agar Gr NW1 71 D1
Agar Ho 6 KT1 198 A6
Agar Pl NW1 71 C1
Agar St WC2 250 B5
Agate Cl E16 99 D1
Agate Ho
New Malden KT4 199 C1
12 Penge SE26 184 B5
Agate Rd W6 112 C3
Agatha Cl E1 118 C5
Agaton Rd SE9 167 A2
Agave Rd NW2 68 C4
Agdon St EC1 94 D3 241 C6
Agincourt E11 54 D3
Agincourt Rd NW3 70 D4
Agnes Ave IG1 78 D4
Agnes Cl E6 122 C6
Agnes Ct 11 SW18 136 B1
Agnesfield Cl N12 30 C4
Agnes Gdns RM8 80 D4
Agnes Ho 13 W11 112 D6
Agnes Rd W3 111 D4
Agnes St E14 97 B1
Agnew Rd SE23 162 D4
Agricola Pl EN1 17 D6
Aidan Cl RM8 81 A4
Aidans Ct N12 30 C5
Aigburth Mans 5 SW9 138 C5
Ailantus Ct HA8 26 B5

Aileen Wlk E15 . . . . .76 D1
Ailsa Ave TW1 . . . . . . .153 B6
Ailsa Rd TW1 . . . . .153 B6
Ailsa St E14 . . . . .98 A2
Ainger Rd NW3 . . . . .70 D1
Ainsdale Cl BR6. . . . . .211 B1
Ainsdale Cres HA5 . . . .41 C6
Ainsdale Dr SE1 . . . . .118 A1
Ainsdale NW1 . . . . . . 232 A2
Ainsdale Rd W5 . . . . . . .87 D3
Ainsley Ave RM7 . . . . . .59 D3
Ainsley Cl N9 . . . . .17 C3
Ainsley St E2 . . . . .96 B4
Ainslie Ct 2 HA0 . . . . .88 A5
Ainslie Ho 1 E4 . . . . . .35 C5
Ainslie Wlk 8
SW12. . . . . .159 B4
Ainslie Wood Cres
E4. . . . . .35 D5
Ainslie Wood Gdns
E4. . . . . .35 D5
Ainslie Wood Prim Sch
E4. . . . . .35 D5
Ainslie Wood Rd E4. . . .35 D5
Ainsty St 20 SE16 . . . . .118 C4
Ainsworth Cl
Camberwell SE5 . . . . 139 C3
Dollis Hill NW2 . . . . . . .68 A5
Ainsworth Est
NW8. . . . . . . .92 A6 229 A6
Ainsworth Ho NW8. . . .91 D6
Ainsworth Rd
Croydon CR0 . . . . 220 D6
Hackney E9 . . . . .74 C1
Ainsworth Way
NW8. . . . . . . .92 A6 229 A6
Aintree Ave E6. . . . . . .100 A6
Aintree Cl UB8. . . . . . . .82 D2
Aintree Ho SE26 . . . . .184 B4
Aintree Rd UB6 . . . . . . .87 B5
Aintree St
SW6. . . . . . . .135 A5 264 B4
Airborne Ho 10
SM6. . . . . .219 B4
Aird Ct TW12 . . . . .173 D2
Aird Ho SE1 . . . . 262 A5
Airdrie Cl
Barnsbury N1 . . . . .72 B1
Hayes UB4. . . . . .85 A2
Airedale Ave W4. . . . . .111 D1
Airedale Ave S W4 . . . .111 D1
Airedale Rd
Balham SW12 . . . . . . 158 D4
Ealing W5 . . . . 109 D3
Airlie Gdns Ilford IG1. . .56 D1
Kensington
W8 . . . . . . 113 C5 245 A3
Airlinks Ind Est
TW5. . . . . 106 C1
Air Park Way TW13. . .150 B2
Airport Gate Bsns Ctr
UB7 . . . . 126 C5
Airport Ho CR0 . . . . . .220 C2
Airport Rdbt E16. . . . .121 D5
Air St W1 . . . . 249 B5
Airthrie Rd IG3 . . . . . . .80 B6
Aisgill Ave
SW5. . . . . . . .113 B1 254 D1
Aisher Rd SE28 . . . . . .124 C6
Aislabie Ho N21 . . . . . . .17 B5
Aislibie Rd SE12 . . . . .142 C1
Aiten Pl W6 . . . . .112 A2
Aithan Ho 15 E14 . . . . .97 B1
Aitken Cl
Carshalton CR4 . . . . . 202 D2
Hackney E8 . . . . .96 A6
Aitken Rd Barnet EN5 . .12 C6
Catford SE6. . . . . 163 D2
Aits View KT8 . . . . . . .195 D6
Ajax Ave NW9. . . . . .45 C6
Ajax Ct NW9. . . . . .45 C6
Ajax Ho 15 E2. . . . . .96 B5
Ajax Rd NW6 . . . . .69 C3
Akabusi Cl SE25 . . . . .206 A3
Akbar Ho 7 E14 . . . . .119 D2
Akehurst St SW15. . . .156 A4
Akenside Ct 3 NW3. . . .70 B3
Akenside Rd NW3. . . . . .70 B3
Akerman Rd
Brixton SW9 . . . . 138 D4
Kingston u T KT6. . . . . 197 C3
Akintaro Ho 7 SE8 . .141 B6
Akiva Sch N3. . . . . .29 D1
Alabama St SE18. . . . .145 C5
Alacross Rd W5. . . . . .109 D4
Aladdin Workspace
UB6 . . . . .85 D6
Alamaro Lo 5 SE10 . .120 D3
Alandale Dr HA5 . . . . . .22 B2
Aland Ct SE16 . . . . . . .119 A3
Alander Mews E17 . . . .54 A5
Alan Dr EN5 . . . . .13 A5
Alan Gdns RM7 . . . . . . .59 C2
Alan Hocken Way
E15. . . . . .98 C5
Alan Lo N3 . . . . .29 C2
Alan Preece Ct NW6 . .68 D1
Alan Rd SW19 . . . . . . .179 A5
Alanthus Cl SE12. . . . .165 A5
Alaska Bldg 12
SE13. . . . . .141 D4
Alaska St SE1. . . . . . . 251 A3
Alastor Ho 10 E14. . . .120 A3
Alba Cl UB4 . . . . .84 D3
Albacore Cres SE13 . .163 D5
Alba Gdns NW11 . . . . . .47 A3
Albain Cres TW15. . . .148 A2
Alba Mews SW18,
SW19. . . . . .157 C2
Alban Ho
Hampstead NW3 . . . . . .70 A2
New Cross SE14 . . . . .141 B4
Albans Cl SW16. . . . . .160 A1
Albany Cl Bushey WD23. . 8 B5
Ickenham UB10. . . . . . . .60 C3
Mortlake SW14 . . . . . 132 D1
Sidcup DA5 . . . . 168 D4
West Green N15 . . . . . . .51 A5
Albany Coll Hendry Ho
NW4. . . . . .46 B4
Albany Coll NW4 . . . . .46 C4
Albany Cres
Claygate KT10. . . . . . . 212 C2
Edgware HA8. . . . . .26 C3
Albany Ct
Ashford TW15 . . . . . . .171 B4
Cheam SM1. . . . . .217 B4
Chingford E4 . . . . .19 D5
College Pk NW10 . . . . .90 B4
Finchley N12 . . . . .29 D4
Grahame Pk HA8. . . . . . .27 B2
Kingston u T KT2. . . . . 176 A4
NW8 . . . . 229 C3
Richmond TW10. . . . . .153 B1
Surbiton KT6 . . . . 197 D2
Walthamstow E10 . . . . .53 C2
Westminster SW1. . . . 259 C6
8 Whitechapel E1 . . . . .96 A1
Albany Ctyd W1 . . . . 249 B5
Albany Ho
6 Brentford
TW8 . . . . 132 A6
Edgware HA8. . . . . .26 C3
Upper Clapton E5 . . . . .74 C6
Albany Mans SW11. . 267 B3
Albany Mews
Camberwell SE5 . . . . 139 A6
Islington N1 . . . . .72 C1
Kingston u T KT2. . . . . 175 D4
Plaistow BR1. . . . . 187 A4
Sutton SM1 . . . . 217 D3
Albany Par 4 TW8. . . .132 A6
Albany Park Ave EN3. . . 6 D4
Albany Park Rd KT2. . .176 A4
Albany Park Sta
DA14 . . . . 168 D2
Albany Pas 12
TW10. . . . . .154 A6
Albany Pl TW8. . . . . . .131 D6
Albany Rd
Brentford TW8. . . . . . 131 D6
Camberwell SE5 . . . . 139 C6
Chislehurst BR7. . . . . . 188 D5
Dagenham RM6. . . . . . .59 B3
Ealing W13 . . . . .109 B6
Enfield EN3 . . . . .6 D5
Erith DA17. . . . . .147 B6
Leyton E10. . . . . .53 C2
Manor Pk E12 . . . . .77 D4
New Malden KT3. . . . .199 B5
Richmond TW10. . . . . . 154 A6
Sidcup DA5 . . . . 168 C4
Stroud Green N4. . . . . . .50 C3
Upper Edmonton N18 . . .34 C5
Walthamstow E17 . . . . . .53 A3
Wimbledon SW19 . . . . 179 D5
Albany Reach KT7 . . . .196 D4
Albany Sch EN3 . . . . .6 D5
Albany St
NW1. . . . . . . .93 B4 231 D2
Albany Terr 6
TW10. . . . . .154 B6
Albany The
Kingston u T KT2. . . . . 175 D4
Woodford IG8 . . . . .36 D6
Albany View IG9 . . . . . .21 A3
Albany W1 . . . . 249 A5
Albany Wlk N15. . . . . . . .50 D5
Alba Pl W11 . . . . .91 B1
Albatross Cl E6 . . . . . . .100 B3
Albatross 31 NW9 . . . . .27 D1
Albatross St SE18 . . . . .145 C5
Albemarle App IG2 . . . .56 D3
Albemarle Ave TW2. . .151 B3
Albemarle Gdns
Ilford IG2 . . . . .56 D3
New Malden KT3. . . . .199 B5
Albemarle Ho
2 Brixton SW9. . . . . 138 C2
Rotherhithe SE8 . . . . .119 B2
Albemarle Lo SE26. . .185 A5
Albemarle Mans
NW3. . . . . .69 D4
Albemarle Pk
Beckenham BR3 . . . . 185 D2
Stanmore HA7. . . . . .25 C5
Albemarle Prim Sch
SW19. . . . . 157 A2
Albemarle SW19 . . . . .156 D2
Albemarle Rd
Beckenham BR2,
BR3. . . . . 186 A2
East Barnet EN4 . . . . . .14 C4
Albemarle St
W1. . . . . .115 C6 249 A5
Albemarle Way EC1. . 241 C5
Alberon Gdns NW11. . . .47 B5
Alberta Ave SM1 . . . . .217 B3
Alberta Ct 1 TW10. . . .154 B6
Alberta Ho
Blackwall E14 . . . . . . 120 A5
Hayes UB4. . . . . .84 B4
Alberta Rd EN1 . . . . .18 A5
Alberta St
SE17. . . . . . . 116 D1 261 D2
Albert Ave
Chingford E4 . . . . .35 C6
South Lambeth SW8 . . 270 C3
Albert Barnes Ho
SE1. . . . . 262 A5
Albert Bigg Point
E15. . . . . .98 A6
Albert Bridge Rd
SW11. . . . . . . .136 D5 267 C3
Albert Carr Gdns
SW16. . . . . .182 A5
Albert Cl
11 Hackney E9 . . . . . . 96 B6
Wood Green N22. . . . . . .31 D2
Albert Cotts 2 E1 . . . . .96 A2
Albert Cres E4. . . . . .35 C6
Albert Ct
Knightsbridge
SW7 . . . . 246 C1
9 Putney SW19. . . . . . 157 A3
Albert Dr SW19 . . . . . .157 A3
Albert Emb
SE1. . . . . .116 A2 260 B3
Albert Gate Ct SW1 . . 247 C1
Albert Gdns E1 . . . . . . .96 D1
Albert Gray Ho
SW10. . . . . 266 C4
Albert Gr SW20 . . . . . .178 D2
Albert Hall Mans
SW7. . . . . . . .114 B4 246 C1
Albert Ho
Stanmore HA7. . . . . .25 B5
5 Wanstead E18 . . . . . .55 B6
2 Woolwich SE28 . . . 123 A3
Albert Mans
Battersea SW11 . . . . 267 C2
Hornsey N8 . . . . .50 A2
Albert Meml*
SW7. . . . . . . 114 B4 246 C1
Albert Mews W8. . . . . 256 A6
Albert Palace Mans
SW11. . . . . 268 B2
Albert Pl Finchley N3 . . .29 C2
Kensington
W8 . . . . . . 113 D4 245 D1
Albert Rd
Ashford TW15 . . . . . . .170 B5
Bromley Comm BR2. . 209 D4
Buckhurst Hill IG9. . . . . .21 D2
Chislehurst SE9. . . . . . 166 A1
Croydon SE25 . . . . . . .206 B5
Dagenham RM8. . . . . . . .59 C1
Ealing W5 . . . . .87 B3
East Barnet EN4 . . . . .2 A1
Erith DA17. . . . . .125 B1
Finsbury Pk N4 . . . . .50 B2
Hampton TW12 . . . . . . 174 A5
Harrow HA2 . . . . .42 A6
Hayes UB3. . . . . 105 C3
Hendon NW4. . . . . .46 D5
Hounslow TW3 . . . . . . 129 C1
Ilford IG1 . . . . .79 A5
Kilburn NW6 . . . . .91 B5
Kingston u T KT1. . . . . .176 B1
Leyton E10. . . . . .54 A1
Mill Hill NW7. . . . . .27 D5
Mitcham CR4. . . . . 202 D6
Newham E16 . . . . .122 B4
New Malden KT3. . . . . 199 D5
Penge SE20. . . . . 184 D4
Richmond TW10. . . . . . .154 B6
Sidcup DA5 . . . . 169 D4
Southall UB2 . . . . 106 D3
South Tottenham N15 . . .51 C3
Sutton SM1 . . . . .218 B3
Teddington TW11. . . . . 174 D4
Twickenham TW1. . . . . 152 D3
Walthamstow E17 . . . . . .53 C4
4 Wanstead E18 . . . . . . .55 B6
Wood Green N22. . . . . . .31 C2
Yiewsley UB7. . . . . 104 A5
Albert's Ct NW1 . . . . . 237 B6
Albert Sleet Ct N9 . . . . .18 B1
Albert Sq Leyton E15. . . .76 C3
Albert Sq *continued*
South Lambeth
SW8 . . . . . 138 B5 270 C3
Albert Starr Ho 7
SE8. . . . . .118 D2
Albert St
Camden Town
NW1. . . . . . . 93 B6 231 D5
North Finchley N12 . . . .30 A5
Albert Studios SW11 267 C2
Albert Terr
Buckhurst Hill IG9. . . . .21 D2
Camden Town
NW1. . . . . . . 93 A6 231 A5
Albert Terr Mews
NW1. . . . . 231 A5
Albert Terr NW10 . . . . . .89 A6
Albert Victoria Ho
N22 . . . . .32 C2
Albert Way SE15 . . . . .140 B5
Albert Westcott Ho
SE17. . . . . 261 D2
Albert Whicher Ho 3
E17. . . . . .54 A5
Albert Wlk E16 . . . . . . .122 D4
Albion Ave
Clapham SW8 . . . . . . 137 D3
Muswell Hill N10. . . . . . .31 A2
Albion Cl W2 . . . . 247 B6
Albion Coll
WC1. . . . . .94 A2 240 B3
Albion Ct
7 Hammersmith
W6 . . . . .112 B2
Sutton SM2 . . . . .218 B1
2 Woolwich SE7 . . . . 122 A2
Albion Dr E8 . . . . .74 A1
Albion Est SE16. . . . . . .118 C4
Albion Gate W2. . . . . . 247 B6
Albion Gdns 1 W6. . . .112 B2
Albion Gr N16 . . . . .73 C4
Albion Hill IG10 . . . . . . .21 D6
Albion Ho
17 Deptford SE8 . . . . 141 C5
EC1 . . . . 241 C4
Newham E16 . . . . 122 D5
Albion Mews
Bayswater
W2 . . . . . . 114 C6 247 B6
6 Hammersmith
W6 . . . . .112 B2
Islington N1 . . . . 234 A6
Albion Pk IG10 . . . . .21 D6
Albion Pl
Broadgate EC2 . . . . . 242 D3
Clerkenwell EC1 . . . . 241 C4
Hammersmith W6 . . . .112 B2
South Norwood
SE25. . . . . 206 A6
Albion Prim Sch
SE16. . . . . 118 C4
Albion Rd
Bexley DA6 . . . . 147 C1
Dagenham RM10. . . . . . .81 B3
Hayes UB3. . . . . .83 C1
Hounslow TW3 . . . . . 129 C1
Kingston u T KT2. . . . . 177 A2
Stoke Newington N16 . .73 B4
Sutton SM2 . . . . .218 B1
Tottenham N17 . . . . .34 A1
Twickenham TW2. . . . . 152 C3
Walthamstow E17 . . . . .54 A6
Albion Riverside
SW11. . . . . 267 A4
Albion Sq E8 . . . . .73 D1
Albion St
Bayswater
W2 . . . . . . 114 C6 247 B6
Rotherhithe SE16 . . . . 118 C4
Thornton Heath CR0 . . 204 D1
Albion Terr
Hackney E8 . . . . .73 D1
Sewardstone E4 . . . . .7 D1
Albion Villas Rd SE23,
SE26. . . . . .162 C1
Albion Way
Barbican EC1. . . . . . . 242 A3
Lewisham SE13. . . . . . 142 A1
Wembley HA9 . . . . .66 C5
Albion Wlk N1. . . . . . . 233 B3
Albion Works Studios
14 E8. . . . . .74 A3
Albion Yd N1 . . . . 233 B3
Albon Ho SW18 . . . . . .157 D5
Albrighton Rd SE5,
SE22. . . . . .139 C2
Albuhera Cl EN2 . . . . . . .4 C4
Albury Ave
Bexleyheath DA7. . . . . 147 A3
Hounslow TW7 . . . . . . 130 D5
Albury Bldgs SE1 . . . . 251 D1
Albury Cl TW12 . . . . . .173 D4
Albury Ct
4 Croydon CR0 . . . . . 221 A4
Deptford SE8. . . . . 141 C6
Mitcham CR4. . . . . .180 B1
6 Northolt UB5 . . . . . .84 C4
Albury Ct *continued*
Ruislip HA4 . . . . .62 C3
Sutton SM1 . . . . 218 A4
Albury Dr HA5 . . . . .22 D3
Albury Lo 7 SW2. . . . . .160 B4
Albury Mews E12 . . . . . .77 C6
Albury Rd KT9 . . . . . . .214 A3
Albury St SE8. . . . . . . .141 C6
Albyfield BR1. . . . . . . .210 B6
Albyn Rd SE8 . . . . .141 C4
Alcester Cres E5. . . . . . .74 B6
Alcester Ct 4 SM6. . . .219 B4
Alcester Rd SM6 . . . . .219 B4
Alchemea Coll of Audio
Engineering
N1 . . . . 94 D6 234 D6
Alcock Cl SM6 . . . . . . .219 D1
Alcock Rd TW5 . . . . . .128 D5
Alconbury DA6 . . . . . . .169 D6
Alconbury Rd E5. . . . . . .74 A6
Alcorn Cl SM3. . . . . . . .217 C6
Alcott Cl W7. . . . . .86 D2
Aldborough Ct
Chingford E4 . . . . .19 D1
Ilford IG2 . . . . .57 D4
ALDBOROUGH HATCH
. . . . .57 C5
Aldborough Rd IG2 . . . .57 D6
Aldborough Rd N
IG2. . . . . .57 D4
Aldborough Rd S
IG3. . . . . .57 C2
Aldbourne Rd W12. . . .112 A5
Aldbridge St
SE17. . . . . . . .117 C1 263 B2
Aldburgh Mews W1. . . 238 B2
Aldbury Ave HA9. . . . . . .66 D1
Aldbury Ho SW3 . . . . . 257 A3
Aldbury Mews N9. . . . . .17 B4
Aldebert Terr
SW8. . . . . . . .138 B5 270 C3
Aldeburgh Cl 16 E5 . . . .74 B6
Aldeburgh Pl
Greenwich SE10 . . . . . 121 A2
Woodford IG8 . . . . .37 A6
Aldeburgh St SE10 . . . .121 A1
Alden Ave E15 . . . . .98 D4
Alden Ct
South Croydon
CR0. . . . . 221 C5
Wimbledon SW19 . . . . 179 C4
Aldenham Ctry Pk
WD6. . . . . .9 B6
Aldenham Dr UB8. . . . . .82 D3
Aldenham Ho NW1. . . . 232 B3
Aldenham Rd WD6. . . . . .9 C6
Aldenham St
NW1. . . . . .93 D5 232 C3
Alden Ho E8. . . . . .96 B6
Aldensley Rd W6 . . . . .112 B3
Alderbrook Prim Sch
SW12. . . . . .159 B4
Alderbrook Rd
SW12. . . . . .159 B5
Alderbury Rd SW13 . . .134 A6
Alder Ct
East Finchley N2 . . . . . .48 B6
3 West Norwood
SW16 . . . . 182 C5
Alder Gr NW2. . . . . .68 B6
Aldergrove Gdns
TW4. . . . . .129 A3
Aldergrove Ho 3 E5 . . .74 A6
Alder Ho
Camberwell SE15 . . . 139 D6
1 Maitland Pk NW3. . . .70 D2
St Johns SE4 . . . . 141 C2
Alderley Ho 36 SW8 . .137 D3
Alder Lodge N9. . . . . . . .17 C3
Alder Lo SW6. . . . . .134 D4
Alderman Ave IG11 . . . .102 A4
Aldermanbury
EC2 . . . . .95 A1 242 B2
Aldermanbury Sq
EC2 . . . . 242 B3
Alderman Ct 13 N11. . . .30 D5
Alderman Judge Mall
6 KT1. . . . . .176 A1
Alderman's Hill N13 . . .32 B6
Alderman's Wlk EC2 243 A3
Aldermary Rd BR1 . . . .187 A2
Aldermead 2 TW3. . . .129 D1
Alder Mews 12 N19 . . . .71 C6
Aldermoor Rd SE6 . . . .163 B1
Alderney Ave TW5 . . . .129 D5
Alderney Gdns UB5 . . . 63 B1
Alderney Ho
20 Canonbury N1 . . . . .73 A2
Enfield EN3 . . . . .6 D5
Alderney Mews SE1. . 262 C6
Alderney Rd E1 . . . . .96 D3
Alderney St
SW1. . . . . . . .115 B1 258 D2
Alder Rd
Mortlake SW14 . . . . . . .133 B2
Sidcup DA14 . . . . 167 D1
Alders Ave IG8 . . . . .36 C4
ALDERSBROOK 77 C6
Aldersbrook Ave EN1. . . .5 C3
Aldersbrook Dr KT2. . .176 B4
Aldersbrook La E12 . . . .78 B5
Aldersbrook Prim Sch
E12. . . . . .77 C6
Aldersbrook Rd E11,
E12. . . . . .77 C6
Alders Cl Ealing W5 . . .109 D3
Edgware HA8. . . . . .27 A5
Wanstead E11. . . . . .77 B6
Alders Ct N17 . . . . .52 B5
Aldersey Gdns IG11 . . .79 B2
Aldersford Cl SE4 . . . .140 D1
Aldersgate Ct EC1 . . 242 A3
Aldersgate St
EC1 . . . . 95 A2 242 A3
Aldersgrove Ave SE9,
SE12. . . . . .165 D1
Aldersgrove KT8. . . . . .196 B4
Aldershot Rd NW6 . . . . .91 B6
Aldersmead Ave
CR0 . . . . .206 D3
Aldersmead Rd BR3. . .185 A3
Alderson Pl UB2 . . . . .108 A5
Alderson St W10. . . . . . .91 A3
Alders Rd HA8 . . . . .27 A5
Alders The
Feltham TW13 . . . . . . 173 A6
Heston TW5. . . . . .129 B6
Southgate N21. . . . . . . .16 C5
Streatham SW16. . . . . 181 C6
West Wickham BR4 . . 223 D6
Alderton Cl NW10. . . . . .67 B5
Alderton Cres NW4 . . . .46 B4
Alderton Ct KT8 . . . . . .195 B5
Alderton 9 KT2 . . . . . .176 D2
Alderton Rd
Croydon CR0 . . . . 206 A2
Herne Hill SE24. . . . . . 139 A2
Alderton Way NW4. . . . .46 B4
Alderville Rd SW6 . . . .135 B3
Alderwick Ct N7 . . . . . . .72 B2
Alderwick Dr TW3 . . . .130 B2
Alder Wlk IG11 . . . . .79 A2
Alderwood Mews EN4. . 2 A5
Alderwood Prim Sch
SE9. . . . . 167 C5
Alderwood Rd SE9 . . . .167 B5
Aldford St
W1. . . . . .115 A5 248 B4
Aldgate East Sta
E1. . . . . 95 D1 243 D2
Aldgate EC3 . . . 95 C1 243 B1
Aldgate High St
EC3 . . . . .95 D1 243 C1
Aldgate Sta
EC3 . . . . 95 D1 243 C1
Aldham Hall 1 E11 . . . .55 A3
Aldham Ho SE4 . . . . . .141 B4
Aldine Ct W12 . . . . . . .112 C5
Aldine St W12 . . . . . . .112 C4
Aldington Cl RM8 . . . . .58 C1
Aldington Ct 1 E8. . . . .74 A1
Aldington Rd SE18 . . .121 D3
Aldis Mews
3 Holdbrook EN3. . . . . .7 C6
Upper Tooting
SW17 . . . . 180 C5
Aldis St SW17. . . . . . . .180 C5
Aldred Rd NW6 . . . . .69 C3
Aldren Rd SW17 . . . . . .158 A1
Aldriche Way E4. . . . . . .36 A4
Aldrich Gdns SM3. . . . .217 B5
Aldrich Terr SW18. . . . .158 A2
Aldrick Ho N1 . . . . . . 233 D4
Aldridge Ave
Edgware HA8. . . . . .10 D1
Holdbrook EN3 . . . . .7 C5
Ruislip HA4 . . . . .62 D6
Stanmore HA7. . . . . .26 A2
Aldridge Ct W11 . . . . . . .91 B2
Aldridge Rd Villas
W11. . . . . .91 B2
Aldridge Rise KT3. . . . .199 C3
Aldridge Wlk N14. . . . . .16 A4
Aldrington Rd
SW16. . . . . .181 C6
Aldsworth Cl W9. . . . . . .91 D3
Aldwich Ho WC2. . . . . 240 D1
Aldwick Cl SE9 . . . . . . .167 B1
Aldwick Ct N12 . . . . .30 A6
Aldwick Rd CR0. . . . . . .220 B4
Aldworth Gr SE13 . . . .164 A5
Aldworth Rd E15. . . . . . .76 C1
Aldwych Ave IG6 . . . . . .57 A5
Aldwych Bldgs WC2. . 240 B2
Aldwych WC2. . . 94 B1 240 D1
Aldwyn Ho SW8. . . . . . 270 A3
Alers Rd DA6 . . . . .168 D6
Alesia Cl N22. . . . . .32 A3
Alestan Beck Rd E16 . . .99 D1
Alexa Ct 4 SM2. . . . . . .217 C2
Alexander Ave NW10 . . 68 B1

Alexander Cl
Barnet EN4 2 B1
Hayes BR2 209 A1
Sidcup DA15 167 C5
Southall UB2 108 A5
Twickenham TW2 152 D2
Alexander Ct
Beckenham BR3 186 B2
Greenwich SE3 143 B3
Stanmore HA7 44 B6
14 Surbiton KT6 197 D2
Wandsworth SW18 158 A6
Alexander Evans Mews SE23 162 D2
Alexander Fleming Laboratory Mus* W2 236 D2
Alexander Ho
8 Kingston u T KT2 176 A2
15 Millwall E14 119 C3
16 Sutton SM2 218 A2
Alexander Lo SM1 217 B3
Alexander McLeod Prim Sch SE2 124 B1
Alexander Mews 2 W2 91 D1
Alexander Pl SW7 257 A4
Alexander Rd
Bexley DA7 146 D3
Chislehurst BR7 188 D5
Upper Holloway N19 72 A6
Alexander Sq SW3 114 C2 257 A4
Alexander St W2 91 C1
Alexander Terr SE2 124 B1
Alexandra Ave
Battersea SW11 268 A1
Harrow HA2 63 C5
Southall UB1 107 B6
Sutton SM1 217 C5
Wood Green N22 31 D2
Alexandra Bsns Ctr EN3 6 D1
Alexandra Cl
Ashford TW15 171 B3
Deptford SE8 141 B6
Harrow HA2 63 D5
Alexandra Cotts
New Cross SE14 141 B4
Penge SE20 184 D4
Alexandra Cres BR1 186 D4
Alexandra Ct
Ashford TW15 171 B4
Ealing W5 87 C2
Greenford UB6 85 D5
Hounslow TW3 129 D3
Paddington W9 236 B6
4 Shacklewell N16 73 D4
5 Shepherd's Bush W12 112 A4
Southgate N14 15 C6
Wembley HA9 66 B4
Alexandra Dr
Surbiton KT5 198 C2
West Norwood SE19 183 C5
Alexandra Gdns
Chiswick W4 133 C5
Cranley Gdns N10 49 B5
Hounslow TW3 129 D3
Wallington SM5 219 A1
Alexandra Gr
Finchley N12 29 D4
Finsbury Pk N4 50 D1
Alexandra Ho 13 W6 112 C1
Alexandra Inf Sch
Kingston u T KT2 176 C3
Penge BR3 184 D3
Alexandra Jun & Inf Sch TW3 129 D3
Alexandra Jun Sch SE26 184 D4
Alexandra Mans
Chelsea SW3 266 C5
Cricklewood NW2 68 D3
6 Hampstead NW6 69 C3
9 Shepherd's Bush W12 112 C5
Alexandra Mews N2 48 D6
Alexandra National Ho N4 72 D6
Alexandra Palace Sta N22 32 A1
Alexandra Palace Way N10 49 C6
Alexandra Pal* N22 31 D1
Alexandra Park Rd N10, N22 31 D2
Alexandra Park Sch N11 31 C2
Alexandra Pl
Croydon CR0 205 C1
Alexandra Pl *continued*
South Norwood SE25 205 B4
St John's Wood NW8 92 A6 229 B6
Alexandra Prim Sch N22 32 B1
Alexandra Rd
Acton W4 111 B4
Ashford TW15 171 C4
10 Brentford TW8 131 D6
Croydon CR0 205 C2
Dagenham RM6 59 A3
Edmonton N9 18 B4
Enfield EN3 6 D1
Hampstead NW8 70 B1
Hendon NW4 46 D5
Hornsey N8, N22 50 C6
Hounslow TW3 129 D3
Kingston u T KT2 176 C3
Leyton E10 76 A5
Mitcham SW19 180 C3
Mortlake SW14 133 B2
Muswell Hill N10 31 B3
Penge SE26 184 D4
Richmond TW9 132 B3
Thames Ditton KT7 196 D4
Tottenham N15 51 B4
Twickenham TW1 153 C5
Wallend E6 100 C4
Walthamstow E17 53 B2
Wanstead E18 55 B6
Wimbledon SW19 179 C5
Alexandra Sch HA2 63 C6
Alexandra Sq SM4 201 C4
Alexandra St
5 Deptford SE14 141 A5
Newham E16 99 A2
Alexandra Wlk 8 SE19 183 C5
Alexandria Rd W13 109 B6
Alex Gossip Ho SW6 265 A1
Alexis St SE16 118 A2
Alfearn Rd E5 74 C4
Alford Ct
18 Belmont SM2 217 D1
Shoreditch N1 235 B3
Alford Gn CR0 224 B2
Alford Ho
Crouch End N6 49 C3
6 Woolwich SE18 144 D6
Alford Pl N1 235 B3
Alfoxton Ave N8, N15 50 D5
Alfreda Ct SW11 268 C1
Alfreda St SW11 137 B4 268 C1
Alfred Butt Ho SW17 158 D1
Alfred Cl W4 111 B2
Alfred Findley Ho N22 32 D1
Alfred Gdns UB1 107 A6
Alfred Ho E9 75 A3
Alfred Hurley Ho SW17 180 A6
Alfred Mews W1, WC1 239 C4
Alfred Nunn Ho NW10 89 D6
Alfred Pl WC1 93 D2 239 C4
Alfred Prior Ho 7 E12 78 C4
Alfred Rd Acton W3 111 A5
Buckhurst Hill IG9 21 D2
Croydon SE25 206 A4
Erith DA17 125 B1
Feltham TW13 150 C2
Kingston u T KT1 198 B6
Leyton E15 76 D3
Paddington W2 91 C2
Sutton SM1 218 A3
Alfred Salter Ho SE1 263 D3
Alfred Salter Prim Sch SE16 118 D4
Alfred's Gdns IG11 101 C5
Alfred St E3 97 B4
Alfred's Way (East Ham & Barking By-Pass) IG11 101 B5
Alfred's Way Ind Est IG11 102 A6
Alfred Villas 9 E17 54 A5
Alfreton Cl SW19 156 D1
Alfriston Ave
Harrow HA2 41 C2
Thornton Heath CR0 204 A2
Alfriston Cl KT5 198 B3
Alfriston Rd SW11 158 D6
Alfriston KT5 198 B3
Algar Cl
Isleworth TW7 131 A2
Stanmore HA7 24 D5
Algar Ct TW12 173 D2
Algar Ho SE1 251 C1
Algar Rd TW7 131 A2
Algarve Rd SW18 157 D3
Algernon Rd
Hendon NW4 46 A3
Kilburn NW6 91 C6
Lewisham SE13 141 D1
Algers Cl IG10 21 D6
Algers Rd IG10 21 D6
Alghers Mead IG10 21 D6
Algiers Rd SE13 141 C1
Alguin Ct HA7 25 C3
Alibon Gdns RM10 81 C3
Alibon Rd RM10 81 C3
Alice Cl 13 EN5 2 A1
Alice Ct 10 N3 29 C2
Alice Gilliott Ct W14 264 D6
Alice La E3 97 B6
Alice Mews 3 TW11 174 D5
Alice Owen Tech Ctr EC1 234 C2
Alice Shepherd Ho 12 E14 120 A4
Alice St SE1 117 C3 263 A5
Alice Thompson Cl SE12 165 C2
Alice Walker Cl 8 SE24 138 D1
Alice Way TW3 129 D1
Alicia Ave HA3 43 C5
Alicia Cl HA3 43 C5
Alicia Gdns HA3 43 C5
Alicia Ho DA16 146 B4
Alie St E1 95 D1 243 D1
Alington Cres NW9 45 A1
Alison Cl
Croydon CR0 206 D1
Newham E6 100 C1
Alison Ct HA8 26 D5
Aliwal Rd SW11 136 C1
Alkerden Rd W4 111 C1
Alkham Rd N16 73 D6
Allam Ho W11 244 A6
Allan Barclay Cl N15 51 D3
Allanbridge N16 51 C2
Allan Cl KT3 199 B4
Allandale Ave N3 47 B6
Allan Ho SW8 269 C2
Allanson Ct E10 75 C6
Allan Way W3 89 A2
Allard Cres WD23 8 A2
Allard Gdns SW4 159 D6
Allardyce St SW4, SW9 138 B1
Allbrook Cl TW11 174 C5
Allbrook Ho 4 SW15 156 A4
Allcot Cl TW14 149 D3
Allcott Ho TW7 130 D2
Allcroft Rd NW5 71 A2
Allder Way CR2 220 D1
Allenby Cl UB6 85 C4
Allenby Prim Sch UB1 85 C1
Allenby Rd
Forest Hill SE23 163 A1
Southall UB1 85 C3
Woolwich SE28 123 A3
Allen Cl
Streatham CR4 181 C2
Sunbury TW16 172 B2
Allen Ct
Greenford UB6 64 D3
Walthamstow E17 53 C3
Allendale Ave UB1 85 C1
Allendale Cl
Camberwell SE5 139 B4
Forest Hill SE26 184 D5
Allendale Rd UB6 65 B2
Allen Edwards Dr SW8 138 A4 270 A2
Allen Edwards Prim Sch SW4 138 A4 270 A1
Allenford Ho SW15 155 D5
All England Lawn Tennis & Croquet Club The SW19 157 A1
Allen Ho W8 255 B6
Allen Mans W8 255 B6
Allen Rd Old Ford E3 97 B5
Penge BR3 184 D1
Stoke Newington N16 73 C4
Sunbury TW16 172 B1
Thornton Heath CR0 204 C1
Allensbury Pl
7 Camden Town NW1 71 D1
Camden Town NW1 72 A1
Allens Rd EN3 18 C6
Allen St W8 113 C3 255 B5
Allenswood 12 SW19 157 A3
Allenswood Rd SE9 144 B3
Allerdale Ho 7 N4 51 B2
Allerford Ct
Catford SE6 163 D1
Harrow HA2 42 A4
Allerford Rd SE6 185 D6
Allerton Ct
5 Hendon NW4 28 D1
North Cheam SM3 216 D6
Allerton Ho
4 Merton SW19 180 A3
Shoreditch N1 235 D3
Allerton Rd N16 73 A6
Allerton St N1 235 D2
Allerton Wlk 11 N7 72 B6
Allestree Rd SW6 135 A5 264 A3
Alleyn Cres SE21 161 B2
Alleyndale Rd RM8 80 C6
Alleyn Ho
Bermondsey SE1 262 C5
St Luke's EC1 242 B5
Alleyn Pk
Dulwich SE21 161 C1
Southall UB2 107 C1
Alleyn Rd SE21 161 C1
Alleyn's Sch SE22 161 C6
Allfarthing La SW18 158 A5
Allfarthing Prim Sch SW18 158 A5
Allgood Cl SM4 200 D3
Allgood St 10 E2 95 D5
Allhallows La EC4 252 C5
Allhallows Rd E6 100 A1
All Hallows Rd N17 33 C2
Alliance Cl
Twickenham TW4 151 B6
Wembley HA0 65 D4
Alliance Ct Acton W3 88 D2
Ashford TW15 171 A6
Alliance Rd Acton W3 88 D3
East Wickham SE18 146 A5
1 Newham E16 99 C2
Allied Ind Est W3 111 C5
Allied Way W3 111 C4
Allingham Cl W7 108 D6
Allingham Ct NW3 70 C3
Allingham Mews N1 235 A4
Allingham St N1 95 A5 235 A4
Allington Ave
Tottenham N17 33 C4
Upper Halliford TW17 193 C6
Allington Cl
Greenford UB6 64 A1
3 Wimbledon SW19 178 D5
Allington Ct
6 Clapham SW8 137 C3
Croydon CR0 206 C3
Enfield EN3 18 D6
Allington Rd
Harrow HA2 42 A4
Hendon NW4 46 B3
Kensal Rise W10 91 A5
Orpington BR6 211 C1
Allington St SW1 258 D5
Allison Cl SE10 142 A4
Allison Gr SE21 161 C3
Allison Rd Acton W3 111 A6
Harringay N8 50 D4
Alliston Ho 27 E2 95 D4
Allitsen Rd NW8 92 C5 230 A4
All Nations Ho 10 E8 74 B1
Allnutt Way SW4 159 D6
Alloa Ct N14 15 C2
Alloa Rd IG3 80 A6
Allom Ct 11 SW4 138 A3
Allonby Dr HA4 38 D2
Allonby Gdns HA9 43 C1
Allonby Ho E14 97 A2
Alloway Rd E3 97 A4
Allport Ho SE5 139 B2
Allport Mews 44 E1 96 C3
All Saints' Benhilton CE Prim Sch SM1 217 D5
All Saint's CE Jun Sch SE19 183 C2
All Saints' CE Prim Sch
Blackheath Vale SE3 142 C3
Child's Hill NW2 69 B5
East Barnet N20 14 B2
All Saints CE Prim Sch
Merton SW19 180 A3
Putney SW15 134 C2
All Saints' CE Prim Sch SM5 219 A3
All Saints Church 9 N19 71 D5
All Saints' Cl N9 18 A2
All Saints Ct
Heston TW5 128 D4
Lower Clapton E5 74 C4
10 Shadwell E1 118 C6
All Saints Dr SE3 142 D3
All Saints Ho 2 W11 91 B2
All Saint's Inf Sch SE19 183 C2
All Saints Mews HA3 24 C4
All Saints Pas SW18 157 C6
All Saints RC Sch BR4 224 B4
All Saints RC Sch & Tech Coll RM8 59 C1
All Saints' Rd W3 111 A3
All Saints Rd
Merton SW19 180 A3
Notting Hill W11 91 B1
Sutton SM1 218 A5
All Saints Sta E14 119 D6
All Saints St N1 94 B5 233 C4
All Saints Twr 19 E10 53 D2
Allsop Pl NW1 92 D3 237 D5
All Souls' Ave NW10 90 B6
All Souls CE Prim Sch W1 93 C2 239 A4
All Souls Pl W1 238 D3
Allum La WD6 10 A6
Allum Way N20 14 A3
Allwood Cl SE26 184 D6
Alma Ave E4 36 A3
Alma Birk Ho 1 NW6 69 B1
Almack Rd E5 74 C4
Alma Cl N10 31 B2
Alma Cres SM1 217 A3
Alma Gr SE1 117 D2 263 D3
Alma Ho
7 Brentford TW8 132 A6
2 Edmonton N9 34 A6
Alma Pl
College Pk NW10 90 B4
Penge SE19 183 D3
Thornton Heath CR7 204 C4
Alma Prim Sch
Bermondsey SE16 118 A2
Enfield EN3 18 D6
Alma Rd
Carshalton SM5 218 C3
Enfield EN3 7 A1
Muswell Hill N10 31 B3
Sidcup DA14 168 A1
Southall UB1 107 A6
Thames Ditton KT10, KT7 196 C1
Wandsworth SW18 158 A6
Alma Row HA3 24 B2
Alma Sq NW8 92 A4 229 B2
Alma St
Camden Town NW5 71 B2
Stratford New Town E15 76 B2
Alma Terr
Earl's Ct W8 255 B5
Wandsworth SW18 158 B4
Almeida St 10 N1 72 D1
Almeric Rd SW11 136 D1
Almer Rd SW20 178 A3
Almington St N4 50 B1
Almond Ave
Carshalton SM5 218 D6
Ealing W5 110 A3
Uxbridge UB10 60 D5
West Drayton UB7 104 C3
Almond Cl
Bromley BR2 210 C2
Charlton TW17 171 A1
Feltham TW14 150 A3
Hayes UB3 105 C6
Peckham SE15 140 A3
Ruislip HA4 61 D5
Almond Gr TW8 131 B5
Almond Ho SE4 141 B3
Almond Rd
Bermondsey SE16 118 B2
Tottenham N17 34 A3
Almonds Ave IG9 21 A2
Almond Way
Bromley BR2 210 C2
Harrow HA2 24 A1
Mitcham CR4 203 D5
Almorah Rd
De Beauvoir Town N1 73 B1
Heston TW5 128 D4
Almshouse La EN1 6 B6
Almshouses
Edmonton N9 17 D2
Leyton E10 75 D6
Southall UB1 85 C1
Sunbury TW16 171 D2
Almshouses The IG11 79 A2
Al-Muntada Islamic Sch SW6 135 B4 264 D2
Alnmouth Ct 10 UB1 86 A1
Al-Noor Muslim Prim Sch IG3 58 B1
Alnwick Gr SM4 201 D5
Alnwick Rd
Eltham SE12 165 B4
Newham E16 99 C1
Alnwick 8 N17 34 B3
Alonso Ho 4 DA17 125 C1
ALPERTON 88 A6
Alperton Com Sch HA0 66 B1
Alperton La UB6 87 D5
Alperton Lower Sch HA0 87 D6
Alperton Sta HA0 88 A6
Alperton St W10 91 B3
Alphabet Gdns SM5 202 B3
Alphabet Sq E3 97 C2
Alpha Bsns Ctr E17 53 B4
Alpha Cl NW8 92 C4 230 B1
Alpha Ct 6 NW5 71 B2
Alpha Est The UB3 105 C4
Alpha Gr E14 119 C4
Alpha Ho
10 Brixton SW4 138 B1
Kilburn NW6 91 C5
Lisson Gr NW8 237 B5
Alpha Pl
Chelsea SW3 136 C6 267 B6
Kilburn NW6 91 C5
Alpha Rd Chingford E4 19 D1
Croydon CR0 205 C1
Edmonton N18 34 A4
Enfield EN3 7 A1
Hillingdon UB10 82 D3
New Cross SE14 141 B4
Surbiton KT5 198 B3
Teddington TW12 174 B5
Alpha St SE15 140 A3
Alphea Cl SW19 180 C3
Alpine Ave KT5 215 A6
Alpine Bsns Ctr E6 100 C2
Alpine Cl CR0 221 C5
Alpine Copse BR1 188 C1
Alpine Ct SE12 142 D1
Alpine Gr 37 E9 74 C1
Alpine Rd
Deptford SE16 118 D1
Leyton E10 75 D6
Walton-on-T KT12 194 A2
Alpine View SM5 218 C3
Alpine Way E6 100 C2
Alpine Wlk HA7 8 C2
Alric Ave
Kingston u T KT3 199 D6
Willesden NW10 67 B1
Alroy Rd N4 50 C2
Alsace Rd SE17 117 C1 263 A2
Al Sadiq & Al Zahra Schs NW6 91 A6
Alscot Rd SE1 117 D3 263 D5
Alscot Road Ind Est SE1 263 D5
Alscot Way SE1 263 C4
Alsike Rd DA18 125 A3
Alsom Ave KT19, KT4 216 A4
Alston Cl KT7 197 B2
Alston Ct 2 EN5 1 A2
Alstone Ct N9 18 A2
Alston Rd
Edmonton N18 34 B5
High Barnet EN5 1 A2
Upper Tooting SW17 180 B6
Altair Cl N17 33 D4
Altair Ct N1 73 B2
Altash Way SE9 166 C2
Altenburg Ave W13 109 B3
Altenburg Gdns SW11 136 D1
Alt Gr SW19 179 B3
Altham Gdns WD19 22 D6
Altham Rd HA5 23 A3
Althea St SW6 135 D2
Althorne Gdns E18 54 D5
Althorne Way RM10 81 C6
Althorp Cl EN5 12 A4
Althorpe Mews SW11 266 D1
Althorpe Rd HA1 42 A4
Althorp Rd SW17 158 D3
Altima Ct SE22 140 A1
Altior Ct N6 49 C3
Altmore Ave E6 100 B6
Altmore Inf Sch E6 100 B6
Alton Ave HA7 24 D3
Alton Cl
Isleworth TW7 130 D3
Sidcup DA5 169 A3
Alton Ct 18 BR3 185 C3
Alton Gdns
Beckenham BR3 185 C3
Twickenham TW2 152 B4
Alton Ho 3 E3 97 D4
Alton Rd
Croydon CR0 220 C5

lton Rd *continued*
Richmond TW10,
TW9 ... 132 A1
Roehampton SW15 .. 156 A3
Tottenham N17 ... 51 B6
lton St E14 ... 97 D2
tyre Cl BR3 ... 207 B4
tyre Rd CR0 ... 221 B6
tyre Way BR3 ... 207 B4
lum Ct KT5 ... 198 B3
lumni Ct SE1 ... 253 D2
lvanley Ct NW3 ... 69 D3
lvanley Gdns NW6 ... 69 D3
lvanley Ho 14 SW9 .. 138 C4
lvernia Lo SM1 ... 217 D5
lverstone Ave
East Barnet EN4 ... 14 C4
Wimbledon SW18,
SW19 ... 157 C2
lverstone Gdns
SE9 ... 167 A3
lverstone Ho 11
SE11 ... 138 C6
lverstone Rd
Little Ilford E12 ... 78 C4
New Malden KT3 ... 199 D5
Wembley HA9 ... 44 B1
Willesden NW2 ... 68 C1
lverston Gdns
SE25 ... 205 C4
lverton St SE8 ... 141 B6
lveston Ave HA3 ... 43 B6
lveston Sq 5 E18 ... 37 A1
lvey St SE17 ... 263 A2
lvia Gdns SM1 ... 218 A4
lvington Cres E8 ... 73 D3
lway Ave KT19 ... 215 B3
lwen Cotts CR0 ... 222 D4
lwold Cres SE12 ... 165 C5
lwyn Ave W4 ... 111 B1
lwyn Cl
Borehamwood
WD6 ... 10 B5
New Addington CR0 .. 223 D1
lwyne La N1 ... 72 D1
lwyne Mans SW19 .. 179 B4
lwyne Pl N1 ... 73 A1
lwyne Rd
Canonbury N1 ... 73 A1
Ealing W7 ... 108 C6
Wimbledon SW19 ... 179 B4
lwyne Sq N1 ... 73 A2
lwyne Villas N1 ... 72 D1
lwyn Gdns Acton W3 .. 88 D1
Hendon NW9 ... 46 A5
lyn Ct N8 ... 49 D3
lyth Gdns NW11 ... 47 C3
lzette Ho 11 E2 ... 96 D5
Amalgamated Dr
TW8 ... 131 B6
Amanda Ct
Ashford TW15 ... 148 B2
Chingford E4 ... 36 C4
Aman Dalvi Ho
SW18 ... 157 A4
Amar Ct SE18 ... 123 D2
Amardeep Ct SE18 ... 123 D1
Amazon Apartments
N8 ... 50 B6
Amazonas
SE1 ... 117 C2 263 B3
Amazon St E1 ... 96 B1
Ambassador Cl
TW3 ... 129 A3
Ambassador Ct
9 Hampstead
NW6 ... 69 C3
Hendon NW4 ... 46 D4
Ambassador Gdns
E6 ... 100 B2
Ambassador Ho
Harrow HA3 ... 42 C6
St John's Wood NW8. 229 B5
Ambassador Sq
E14 ... 119 D2
Amber Ave E17 ... 35 A2
Amber Ct
Feltham TW13 ... 149 C1
Islington N7 ... 72 C2
Mitcham CR4 ... 202 C5
Southall UB1 ... 107 D5
Amberden Ave N3 ... 47 C6
Amberdene HA7 ... 24 D4
Ambergate St
SE17 ... 116 D1 261 D2
Amber Gr NW2 ... 46 D1
Amber Ho HA7 ... 25 D3
Amberley Cl
2 Orpington
BR6 ... 227 D3
Pinner HA5 ... 41 B6
Amberley Ct
2 Brixton SW9 ... 138 D2
Sidcup DA14 ... 190 C5
Sutton SM2 ... 218 A1
Amberley Gdns
Enfield EN1 ... 17 C4
Amberley Gdns *continued*
Worcester Pk KT19 .. 215 D4
Amberley Gr
Croydon CR0 ... 205 D2
Penge SE26 ... 184 B5
Amberley Ho
8 Barnet EN5 ... 1 D1
7 Ealing W7 ... 108 C5
Amberley Rd
Buckhurst Hill IG9 ... 21 C3
Enfield EN1 ... 17 D5
Palmers Green N13 ... 16 B2
Walthamstow E10 ... 53 D2
Westbourne Green
W9 ... 91 C2
West Heath SE2 ... 146 D6
Amberley Way
Heston TW4 ... 150 C6
Morden SM4 ... 201 B2
Romford RM7 ... 59 D5
Uxbridge UB10 ... 82 A5
Amberside Cl TW2 ... 152 B5
Amber Wharf 29 E2 ... 95 D6
Amberwood Cl SM6 .. 220 A3
Amberwood Rise
KT3 ... 199 C3
Amblecote Cl SE12 ... 165 B1
Amblecote Mdws
SE12 ... 165 B1
Amblecote Rd SE12 .. 165 B1
Ambler Prim Sch N4 .. 72 D6
Ambler Rd N4 ... 72 D5
Ambleside Ave
Beckenham BR3 ... 207 A4
Streatham SW16 ... 181 D6
Walton-on-T KT12 ... 194 C1
Ambleside BR1 ... 186 B4
Ambleside Cl
Lower Clapton E9 ... 74 C3
5 Tottenham N17 ... 51 D6
Walthamstow E10 ... 53 D2
Ambleside Cres EN3 ... 6 D2
Ambleside Dr TW14 .. 149 D3
Ambleside Gdns
Redbridge IG4 ... 56 A4
Streatham SW16 ... 181 D5
Sutton SM2 ... 218 A2
Wembley HA9 ... 43 D1
Ambleside Ho HA8 ... 27 A5
Ambleside Point 1
SE15 ... 140 C5
Ambleside 13 SW19 .. 157 A3
Ambleside Rd
Bexleyheath DA7 ... 147 C3
Willesden NW10 ... 67 D1
Ambleside NW1 ... 231 D3
Ambrook Ct SM1 ... 218 B3
Ambrook Rd DA17 ... 125 C3
Ambrosden Ave
SW1 ... 115 C3 259 B5
Ambrose Ave NW11 ... 47 B3
Ambrose Cl
6 Newham E6 ... 100 B2
Orpington BR6 ... 227 D5
Ambrose Ho 9 E14 ... 97 C2
Ambrose Mews 2
SW11 ... 136 D3
Ambrose St SE16 ... 118 B2
Ambrose Wlk E3 ... 97 C5
AMC Bsns Ctr NW10 .. 88 D4
Amelia Cl W3 ... 110 D4
Amelia Ho 5 W6 ... 112 C1
Amelia St
SE17 ... 117 A1 262 A2
Amen Cnr
Holborn EC4 ... 241 D1
Streatham SW17 ... 181 A4
Amen Ct EC4 .. 94 D1 241 D1
Amenity Way SM4 ... 200 C2
American
Intercontinental Univ
W1 ... 93 A2 238 B3
American Sch in
London The
NW8 ... 92 B5 229 C4
American Univ in
London The N7 ... 72 B5
America Sq EC3 ... 253 C6
America St SE1 ... 252 A3
Amerland Rd SW18 .. 157 B5
Amersham Ave N18 ... 33 B4
Amersham Gr SE14 .. 141 B5
Amersham Rd
New Cross SE14 ... 141 B4
Thornton Heath CR0 .. 205 B3
Amersham Vale SE14,
SE8 ... 141 B5
Amery Gdns NW10 ... 90 B6
Amery Ho SE17 ... 263 B2
Amery Rd HA1 ... 65 A6
Amesbury Ave SW2 .. 160 B2
Amesbury Cl KT4 ... 200 C1
Amesbury Ct EN2 ... 4 C3
Amesbury Dr E4 ... 19 D5
Amesbury Rd
Bromley BR1 ... 209 D6
Dagenham RM9 ... 80 D1
Amesbury Rd *continued*
Feltham TW13 ... 150 D2
Amesbury Twr 4
SW8 ... 137 C3
Ames Cotts 12 E3 ... 97 A2
Ames Ho 10 E2 ... 96 D5
Amethyst Ct 1 EN3 ... 7 A2
Amethyst Cl N11 ... 31 D3
Amethyst Ct BR6 ... 227 C3
Amethyst Rd E15 ... 76 B4
Amherst Ave W13 ... 87 C1
Amherst Dr BR5 ... 211 D5
Amherst Gdns 2
W13 ... 87 C1
Amherst Rd W13 ... 87 C1
Amhurst Ct N4 ... 51 B2
Amhurst Gdns TW7 .. 131 A3
Amhurst Par N16 ... 51 D2
Amhurst Pk N4, N16 ... 51 C2
Amhurst Rd E8, N16 ... 74 A4
Amhurst Terr E8 ... 74 A4
Amhurst Wlk SE28 ... 124 A5
Amias Ho EC1 ... 242 A6
Amidas Gdns RM8 ... 80 B4
Amiel St 15 E1 ... 96 C3
Amies St SW11 ... 136 D2
Amigo Ho SE1 ... 261 B6
Amina Way SE16 ... 118 A3
Amis Ave KT19 ... 214 D3
Amity Gr SW20 ... 178 C2
Amity Rd E15 ... 76 D1
Ammanford Gn NW9 .. 45 C3
Ammonite Ho 3 E15 .. 76 D1
Amner Rd SW11 ... 159 A5
Amora 8 HA7 ... 25 C6
Amor Rd W6 ... 112 C3
Amory Ho N1 ... 233 D4
Amott Rd SE15 ... 140 A2
Amoy Pl E14 ... 119 C6
Ampere Way CR0 ... 204 B1
Ampleforth Rd SE2 .. 124 C4
Ampton Pl WC1 ... 233 C1
Ampton St
WC1 ... 94 B4 233 C1
Amroth Cl SE23 ... 162 B3
Amroth Gn NW9 ... 45 C3
Amstel Ct 12 SE15 ... 139 D5
Amsterdam Rd E14 .. 120 A3
Amundsen Ct 7
E14 ... 119 C1
Amundsen Ho 6
NW10 ... 67 B1
Amwell Cl EN2 ... 17 B6
Amwell St
EC1 ... 94 C4 234 A2
Amyand Cotts 12
TW1 ... 153 B5
Amyand Park Gdns 2
TW1 ... 153 B4
Amyand Park Rd
TW1 ... 153 B4
Amy Cl SM6 ... 220 A1
Amy Johnson Ct HA8 .. 26 D1
Amy Johnson Prim Sch
SM6 ... 220 A1
Amyruth Rd SE4 ... 163 C6
Amy Warne Cl E6 ... 100 A3
Anarth Ct KT13 ... 193 C1
Anatola Rd N19 ... 71 C6
Ancaster Cres KT3 ... 200 A3
Ancaster Mews
CR0 ... 206 D6
Ancaster Rd BR3 ... 206 D6
Ancaster St SE18 ... 145 C5
Anchorage Cl SW19 .. 179 C5
Anchorage Point 1
E14 ... 119 C4
Anchorage Point Ind Est
SE7 ... 121 C3
Anchor Bsns Pk CR0,
SM6 ... 220 A5
Anchor Cl IG11 ... 102 B4
Anchor Ct
Bexley DA7 ... 147 A4
5 Enfield EN1 ... 17 C6
Anchor Ho Ilford IG3 .. 80 A5
Newham E16 ... 99 C1
Anchor & Hope La
SE7 ... 121 C2
Anchor Ho EC1 ... 242 A6
Anchor Mews SW12 .. 159 B5
Anchor Ret Pk E1 ... 96 C3
Anchor St SE16 ... 118 B2
Anchor Terr SE1 ... 252 B4
Anchor Yd EC1 ... 242 B6
Ancill Cl W6 .. 135 A6 264 A5
Ancona Rd
Plumstead SE18 ... 123 B1
Willesden Green
NW10 ... 90 A5
Andace Pk BR1 ... 187 C2
Andalus Rd SW9 ... 138 A2
Andaman Ho 3 E1 ... 97 A2
Ander Cl HA0 ... 65 D4
Andersens Wharf 9
E14 ... 97 B1
Anderson Cl
Morden SM3 ... 201 C1
North Acton W3 ... 89 B1
Southgate N21 ... 16 B6
Anderson Ct NW2 ... 46 C2
Anderson Dr TW15 .. 171 A6
Anderson Ho
1 Barking IG11 ... 101 B5
10 Blackwall E14 ... 120 A6
Upper Tooting SW17 .. 180 B5
Anderson Rd
Homerton E9 ... 74 D2
Redbridge IG8 ... 55 D6
Anderson's Pl TW3 .. 129 D1
Andersons Sq N1 ... 234 C5
Anderson St SW3 ... 257 C2
Anderson Way
Erith DA17 ... 125 D4
Erith DA17 ... 125 D4
Anderton Cl SE5 ... 139 B2
Anderton Ct N22 ... 31 D1
Andhurst Ct KT2 ... 176 D2
Andmark Ct UB1 ... 107 B5
Andon Ct BR3 ... 207 A6
Andorra Ct BR1 ... 187 C2
Andover Ave E16 ... 99 D1
Andover Cl
East Bedfont
TW14 ... 149 D3
Greenford UB6 ... 85 D3
Andover Ho 5 N7 ... 72 B6
Andover Pl NW6 ... 91 D5
Andover Rd
Finsbury Pk N7 ... 72 B6
Orpington BR6 ... 211 C1
Twickenham TW2 ... 152 B3
Andoversford Ct 2
SE15 ... 139 C6
Andrecht Terr CR4 .. 203 D5
Andreck Ct BR3 ... 186 A1
Andre Malraux Sch
W7 ... 86 C2
Andre St E8 ... 74 A3
Andrew Borde St
WC2 ... 239 D2
Andrew Ct
Beckenham BR3 ... 207 D6
2 Forest Hill SE23 .. 162 D2
Andrewes Ct 2 W7 .. 108 C5
Andrewes Gdns E6 .. 100 A1
Andrewes Ho
Barbican EC2 ... 242 B3
Sutton SM1 ... 217 C4
Andrew Ewing Jun & Inf
Sch TW5 ... 129 B5
Andrew Ho
Enfield EN3 ... 18 C6
New Cross SE4 ... 141 B3
Putney SW15 ... 156 A6
Andrew Logan's Glass
Ho* SE1 ... 253 A2
Andrew Marvell Ho 12
N16 ... 73 C4
Andrew Pl SW8 ... 269 D2
Andrew Reed Ho
SW18 ... 157 A4
Andrews Cl
Buckhurst Hill IG9 ... 21 C2
Harrow HA1 ... 42 B2
North Cheam KT4 ... 216 D6
Sidcup BR5 ... 190 D1
Andrews Crosse
WC2 ... 241 A1
Andrew's Rd E8 ... 96 B6
Andrew St E14 ... 98 A1
Andrews Wharf 14
E8 ... 96 B6
Andrews Wlk SE17 .. 138 D6
Andrew Wells Ho
BR1 ... 187 B3
Andrew Wilmot Ct
SW18 ... 158 A3
Andridge Ct SW19 .. 179 B2
Andringham Lo 4
BR1 ... 187 B2
Andrula Ct N22 ... 32 D2
Andwell Cl SE2 ... 124 B4
ANERLEY ... 184 B2
Anerley Ct SE20 ... 184 B3
Anerley Gr SE19 ... 183 D3
Anerley Hill SE19 ... 183 D4
Anerley Park Rd
SE20 ... 184 B3
Anerley Pk SE20 ... 184 B3
Anerley Rd SE20 ... 184 B2
Anerley Sta SE20 ... 184 B2
Anerley Station Rd
SE20 ... 184 B2
Anerley Vale SE19 .. 184 A3
Aneurin Bevan Ct
NW2 ... 68 B6
Aneurin Bevan Ho
N11 ... 31 D3
Anfield Cl SW12 ... 159 C4
Angela Ct 2 SE23 ... 162 C3
Angela Davis Ind Est 20
SW9 ... 138 D1
Angel Cl N18 ... 34 A6
Angel Corner Par 6
N18 ... 34 A6
Angel Ct
Broadgate EC2 ... 242 D2
St James SW1 ... 249 B3
5 Willesden NW2 ... 68 A2
Angel EC1 ... 94 D5 234 D3
Angel Edmonton
N18 ... 34 A5
Angelfield TW3 ... 151 D6
Angel Gate EC1 ... 234 D2
Angel Hill Dr SM1 ... 217 D5
Angel Hill SM1 ... 217 D5
Angel Ho N1 ... 234 B3
Angelica Cl UB7 ... 82 B1
Angelica Dr E6 ... 100 C2
Angelica Gdns CR0 .. 206 D1
Angelina Ho 2
SE15 ... 140 A4
Angelis Apartments
N1 ... 234 D3
Angel La Hayes UB3 ... 83 B2
Stratford E15 ... 76 B2
Angell Park Gdns 4
SW9 ... 138 C2
Angell Rd SW9 ... 138 D2
Angel Mews
Finsbury N1 ... 234 B3
Putney SW15 ... 156 A4
Stepney E1 ... 118 B6
Angel Pas
EC4 ... 117 B6 252 C5
Angel Pl
Borough The SE1 ... 252 C2
1 Edmonton N18 ... 34 A5
Angel Rd HA1 ... 42 C3
Angel Rd (North
Circular Rd) N18 ... 34 B5
Angel Rd KT7 ... 197 A1
Angel Rd Works N18 .. 34 C5
Angel Road Sta N18 .. 34 C5
Angel Sq N1 ... 234 B3
Angel Sta EC1 94 C5 234 B3
Angel St EC1 .. 95 A1 242 A2
Angel Wlk W6 ... 112 C2
Angerstein Bsns Pk
SE10 ... 121 A2
Angerstein La SE3 ... 142 D4
Anglebury 5 W2 ... 91 C1
Angle Cl UB10 ... 82 C6
Angle Gn RM8 ... 58 C1
Anglers Cl TW10 ... 175 C6
Anglers La NW5 ... 71 B2
Anglers Reach KT6 .. 197 D4
Anglesea Ave 4
SE18 ... 122 D2
Anglesea Ho KT1 ... 197 D5
Anglesea Mews 12
SE18 ... 122 D2
Anglesea Rd
Kingston u T KT1 ... 197 D5
Woolwich SE18 ... 122 D2
Anglesey Cl TW15 ... 148 C1
Anglesey Court Rd
SM5 ... 219 A2
Anglesey Ct W7 ... 86 D3
Anglesey Gdns SM5 .. 219 A2
Anglesey Ho 13 E14 ... 97 C1
Anglesey Rd
Enfield EN3 ... 6 B1
South Oxhey WD19 ... 22 C5
Anglesmede Cres
HA5 ... 41 C6
Anglesmede Way
HA5 ... 41 C6
Angles Rd SW16 ... 182 A6
Anglia Cl N17 ... 34 B3
Anglia Ct RM8 ... 58 D1
Anglia Ho 13 E14 ... 97 A1
Anglian Ind Est
IG11 ... 101 D2
Anglian Rd E11 ... 76 B5
Anglia Wlk E6 ... 100 C6
Anglo American
Laundry SW17 ... 158 A1
Anglo Rd 16 E3 ... 97 B5
Angrave Ct 4 E8 ... 95 D6
Angrave Pas 5 E8 ... 95 D6
Angus Cl KT9 ... 214 C3
Angus Dr HA4 ... 62 C4
Angus Gdns NW9 ... 27 B2
Angus Ho 12 SW12 .. 159 D4
Angus Rd E13 ... 99 C4
Angus St SE14 ... 141 A5
Anhalt Rd
SW11 ... 136 C5 267 B4
Animals in War Meml*
W1 ... 247 D6
Ankerdine Cres
SE18 ... 144 D4
Anlaby Rd TW11 ... 174 C5
Anley Rd W14 ... 112 D4
Anmersh Gr HA7 ... 25 D2
Annabel Cl E14 ... 97 D1
Anna Cl E8 ... 95 D6
Annadale N22 ... 32 B5
Annandale Gr UB10 ... 61 A5
Annandale Rd
Chiswick W4 ... 111 C1
Croydon CR0 ... 222 A6
Greenwich SE10 ... 120 D1
Sidcup DA15 ... 167 D4
Anna Neagle Cl 2
E7 ... 77 A4
Anne Boleyn's Wlk
Belmont SM3 ... 217 A1
Kingston u T KT2 ... 176 A5
Anne Compton Mews
SE12 ... 164 D4
Anne Goodman Ho 3
E1 ... 96 C1
Anne Kerr Ct 18
SW15 ... 156 D5
Annemount Sch N2 ... 48 B3
Anne's Ct NW8 ... 237 B6
Annesley Ave NW9 ... 45 B6
Annesley Cl NW10 ... 67 C5
Annesley Dr CR0 ... 223 B5
Annesley Ho
31 Brixton SW9 ... 138 C4
15 Kennington SW9 .. 138 C5
Annesley Rd SE3 ... 143 B4
Annesley Wlk N19 ... 71 C6
Annesmere Gdns
SE3 ... 143 D2
Anne St E13 ... 99 A3
Annett Cl TW17 ... 193 C5
Annette Cl HA3 ... 24 C1
Annette Cres 16 N1 ... 73 A1
Annette Ct N7 ... 72 B5
Annette Rd N7 ... 72 B4
Annette White Lo 20
N2 ... 30 B1
Annett Rd KT12 ... 194 A2
Anne Way KT8 ... 195 D5
Annie Besant Cl E3 ... 97 B6
Annie Taylor Ho 2
E12 ... 78 C4
Anning St E2 ... 243 B6
Annington Rd N2 ... 48 D6
Annis Rd E9 ... 75 A2
Ann La
SW10 ... 136 B6 266 C5
Ann Moss Way
SE16 ... 118 C3
Ann Parkes Ct TW5 .. 128 D3
Ann's Cl SW1 ... 248 A1
Ann's Pl E1 ... 243 C3
Ann Stroud Ct SE12 .. 165 A6
Ann St SE18 ... 123 B2
Annsworthy Ave
CR7 ... 205 B6
Annsworthy Cres
CR7 ... 183 B1
Annunciation RC Inf
Sch The HA8 ... 27 B2
Annunciation RC Jun
Sch The HA8 ... 27 B4
Ansar Gdns E17 ... 53 B4
Ansdell Rd SE15 ... 140 C3
Ansdell St
W8 ... 113 D3 255 D6
Ansdell Terr
W8 ... 113 D3 255 D6
Ansell Gr SM5 ... 203 A1
Ansell Ho E1 ... 96 C2
Ansell Rd SW17 ... 158 D1
Anselm Cl CR0 ... 221 D5
Anselm Rd
Hatch End HA5 ... 23 B3
West Brompton
SW6 ... 135 C6 265 A5
Ansford Rd BR1, SE6 .. 186 B6
Ansleigh Pl W11 ... 112 D6
Anson Ct TW19 ... 148 A4
Anson Ho
Pimlico SW1 ... 269 A6
6 Tower Hamlets E1 .. 97 A3
Anson 30 NW9 ... 27 D1
Anson Pl SE28 ... 123 B4
Anson Prim Sch
NW2 ... 68 D3
Anson Rd
Cricklewood NW2 ... 68 C3
Tufnell Pk N7 ... 71 D4
Anson Terr UB5 ... 63 D2
Anstey Ct 6 W3 ... 110 D4
Anstey Ho 7 E9 ... 96 C6
Anstey Lo EN1 ... 17 C5
Anstey Rd SE15 ... 140 A2
Anstey Wlk N15 ... 51 A5
Anstice Cl W4 ... 133 C5
Anstridge Rd SE9 ... 167 B5
Antelope Rd SE18 ... 122 B3
Antenor Ho 11 E2 ... 96 B5
Anthony Cl NW7 ... 27 C6
Anthony Cope Ct
N1 ... 235 D2
Anthony Ct
Harrow HA1 ... 42 B2

Anthony Ct *continued*
Isleworth TW7...130 D2
Anthony Ho NW8...237 A5
Anthony Kendal Ho 4
E5...74 B5
Anthony Rd
Croydon SE25...206 A3
East Wickham DA16...146 A4
Greenford UB6...86 C4
Anthony St E1...96 B1
Antigua Wlk SE19...183 B5
Antilles Bay 19 E14...120 A4
Antilles Ho W3...89 B1
Antill Rd Mile End E3...97 A4
Tottenham Hale N15...52 A5
Antill Terr 5 E1...96 D1
Antlers Hill E4...19 D6
Anton Cres SM1...217 C5
Antoneys Cl HA5...22 D1
Antonine Hts SE1...253 A1
Anton Pl HA9...66 D5
Anton St E8...74 A3
Antony Ho
4 Deptford SE14...140 D5
2 Rotherhithe SE16...118 C2
Antrim Gr NW3...70 D2
Antrim Ho SW11...137 A2
Antrim Mans NW3...70 D2
Antrim Rd NW3...70 D2
Antrobus Cl SM1...217 B3
Antrobus Rd W4...111 A3
Anvil Cl SW16...181 C3
Anvil Ho 10 N9...18 A1
Anvil Rd TW16...194 A6
Anworth Cl IG8...37 B4
Apex Cl BR3...185 D2
Apex Cnr
Edgware NW7...27 B6
Twickenham TW13...151 B1
Apex Ct W13...87 A1
Apex Ind Est NW10...89 D3
Apex Lo 10 EN5...14 A6
Apex Ret Pk TW13...151 B1
Aphrodite Ct 11
E14...119 C2
Aplin Ct 4 SM1...217 D2
Aplin Way TW7...130 C4
Apollo Ave
Bromley BR1...187 B2
Loughton HA6...22 A5
Apollo Bldg 2 E14...119 C2
Apollo Ho
Chelsea SW10...266 C5
32 Hackney E2...96 B5
Highgate N6...48 D2
Apollo Ind Bsns Ctr 29
SE8...140 D6
Apollo Pl
Chelsea SW10...266 C4
6 Leyton E11...76 C5
Apollo Studios 18
NW5...71 D3
Apollo Way 1 SE18...123 B3
Apostle Way CR7...182 D1
Apothecary St EC4...241 C1
Appach Rd SW2...160 C5
Appin Ct HA1...42 C2
Appleby Cl
Chingford E4...36 A4
Hayes UB3, UB8...83 A1
Orpington BR5...211 C2
Twickenham TW2...152 B2
West Green N15...51 B4
Appleby Ct W3...111 A4
Appleby Gdns
TW14...149 D3
Appleby Rd
Hackney E8...74 A1
Newham E16...99 A1
Appleby St E2...95 D5
Appledore Ave HA4...62 C5
Appledore Cl
Bromley BR2...209 A4
Edgware HA8...26 C2
Upper Tooting SW12, SW17...158 D2
Appledore Cres
DA14...167 D1
Appledore Way NW7...28 D3
Appleford Ho 6
W10...91 A3
Appleford 8 NW5...71 C3
Appleford Rd W10...91 A3
Apple Garth TW8...109 D2
Applegarth KT10...212 D3
Applegarth Dr IG2...57 D5
Applegarth Ho
Borough The SE1...251 D2
9 Camberwell SE15...140 A5
Applegarth Inf Sch
CR0...223 D2
Applegarth Jun Sch
CR0...223 D2
Applegarth CR0...223 D1
Applegarth Rd
Hammersmith W14...112 D3
Woolwich SE28...124 C6
Apple Gr
Chessington KT9...214 A4
Enfield EN1...5 C2
Apple Lo HA0...65 C5
Apple Mkt KT1...175 D1
Apple Mkt WC2...250 B6
Apple Rd E11...76 C5
Appleshaw Ho 4
SE5...139 C2
Appleton Ct 30 E8...74 B3
Appleton Gdns KT3...200 A3
Appleton Rd SE9...144 A2
Appleton Sq CR4...180 C2
Apple Tree Ave UB7...82 B1
Appletree Cl 5
SE20...184 B2
Appletree Ct
Lewisham SE13...142 B1
Northolt UB5...85 A4
Appletree Gdns EN4...2 C1
Apple Tree Yd SW1...249 B4
Applewood Cl
Dollis Hill NW2...68 B5
Ickenham UB10...60 A4
Oakleigh Pk N20...14 C3
Applewood Dr E13...99 B3
Appold St
EC2...95 C2 243 A4
Apollo Ct 7 SW9...138 C4
Apprentice Gdns
UB5...85 B4
Apprentice Way 5
E5...74 B4
Approach Cl N16...73 C4
Approach La NW7...29 A5
Approach Rd
Ashford TW15...171 A4
Bethnal Green E2...96 C5
East Molesey KT8...195 C4
Edgware HA8...26 C4
Merton SW20...178 C1
New Barnet EN4, EN5...2 B1
Approach The
Acton W3...89 B1
Enfield EN1...6 B3
Hendon NW4...46 D4
Orpington BR6...227 D6
Aprey Gdns NW4...46 C5
April Cl Ealing W7...108 C6
Feltham TW13...150 A1
Orpington BR6...227 D3
April Ct 20 E2...96 A5
April Glen SE23...162 D1
April St E8...73 D4
Apsley Cl HA2...42 A4
Apsley Ctr The NW2...68 A6
Apsley Ct SM2...218 A2
Apsley Ho Enfield EN1...17 C5
Hounslow TW4...129 B1
Stepney E1...96 C2
St John's Wood NW8...229 C4
Apsley Rd
Croydon SE25...206 B5
Kingston u T KT3...199 A6
Apsley Way
Dollis Hill NW2...68 A6
Mayfair W1...248 B2
Aquarius Bsns Pk
NW2...46 A1
Aquarius TW1...153 B3
Aquarius Way HA6...22 A6
Aquila St
NW8...92 B5 229 D4
Aquinas St
SE1...116 C5 251 B3
Arabella Ct NW8...229 B4
Arabella Dr SW15...133 C1
Arabia Cl E4...20 B4
Arabian Ho 3 E1...97 A3
Arabin Rd SE4...141 B1
Aragon Ave KT7...196 D4
Aragon Cl
Ashford TW16...171 D3
Bromley BR2...210 B1
Enfield EN2...4 B5
Aragon Ct
Beckenham BR3...186 A2
East Molesey KT8...196 A5
Aragon Dr HA4...40 D1
Aragon Pl SM4...201 A2
Aragon Prim Sch
SM4...200 D2
Aragon Rd
Kingston u T KT2...176 A5
West Barnes SM4...201 A2
Aragon Twr SE8...119 B2
Arakan Ho 4 N16...73 B4
Aral Ho 14 E1...96 D3
Arandora Cres RM6...58 B2
Aranya Ct 3 E17...35 A1
Arapiles Ho 6 E14...98 B1
Arbery Rd E3...97 A5
Arbon Ct N1...235 B5
Arbor Cl BR3...185 D1
Arbor Ct N16...73 B6
Arborfield Cl SW2...160 B3
Arborfield Ho 7
E14...119 C6
Arbor Rd E4...20 B1
Arbour Ho 3 E1...96 D1
Arbour Rd EN3...6 D2
Arbour Sq E1...96 D1
Arbroath Rd SE9...144 A2
Arbrook Chase
KT10...212 A2
Arbrook Ct
Chessington KT9...213 D3
St Paul's Cray BR5...190 A2
Arbrook Hall KT10...212 D2
Arbrook La KT10...212 B2
Arbury Ho BR1...188 A3
Arbury Terr 3 SE26...162 B1
Arbuthnot La DA5...169 A5
Arbuthnot Rd SE14...140 D3
Arbutus St E8...95 D6
Arcade Ho 7 NW11...47 B4
Arcade The
Broadgate EC2...243 A3
2 Eltham SE9...166 C5
1 Tufnell Pk N7...72 A4
Walthamstow E17...53 C5
Arcadia Ave N3...29 C2
Arcadia Centre The
W5...109 D6
Arcadia Cl SM5...219 A4
Arcadian Ave DA5...169 A5
Arcadian Cl DA5...169 A5
Arcadian Gdns N22...32 C3
Arcadian Ho SW6...136 A3
Arcadian Pl SW18...157 B4
Arcadian Rd DA5...169 A5
Arcadia St E14...97 C1
Archangel St SE16...118 D4
Archbishop Coggan Ho
SE13...142 B1
Archbishop Lanfranc Sch The CR0...204 A3
Archbishop Michael Ramsey Tech Coll
SE5...138 D5
Archbishop's Pl 1
SW2...160 B4
Archbishop Sumner CE Prim Sch
SE11...116 C2 261 B3
Archbishop Tenison's CE High Sch CR0...221 D5
Archbishop Tenison's Sch SE11...138 B6 270 D5
Archdale Bsns Ctr
HA2...64 A6
Archdale Ct W12...112 B5
Archdale Ho SE1...263 A6
Archdale Pl KT3...198 D6
Archdale Rd SE22...139 D1
Archdeacon Cambridge's CE Prim Sch TW2...152 C2
Archel Rd
W14...135 B6 264 C6
Archer Cl KT2...176 A3
Archer Ct TW13...150 A3
Archer Ho
1 Battersea SW11...136 B3
Ealing W13...109 B5
24 Hoxton N1...95 C6
1 New Cross SE14...141 A4
Notting Hill W11...244 D6
Archer Mews TW12...174 A4
Archer Rd SE25...206 B5
Archers Ct 3 CR2...221 A3
Archers Dr EN3...6 C3
Archers Lo 22 SE16...118 A1
Archer Sq SE14...141 A6
Archer St W1...249 C6
Archer Terr UB7...104 A6
Archery Cl
Harrow HA3...42 D6
Paddington W2...237 B1
Archery Fields Ho
WC1...234 A2
Archery Rd SE9...166 B6
Archery Stps W2...247 B6
Arches Bsns Ctr The
UB2...107 B4
Arches The
Harrow HA2...63 D6
Strand WC2...250 B4
Archgate Bsns Ctr 1
N12...30 A5
Archibald Mews W1...248 C5
Archibald Rd N7...71 D4
Archibald St E3...97 C4
Archie Cl UB7...104 C4
Archie St SE1...253 B1
Arch St SE1...117 A3 262 A5
Archway Bsns Ctr 5
N19...71 D5
Archway Cl
North Kensington W10...90 D2
2 Upper Holloway N19...71 C6
Wallington SM6...220 A5
Wimbledon SW19...179 D6
Archway Hts 5 N19...49 C1
Archway N19...71 C6
Archway Mews
SW15...135 A1
Archway Rd N6...49 B2
Archway Sta N19...71 C6
Archway St SW13, SW14...133 C2
Arcola St E8...73 D3
Arcon Dr UB5...85 A3
Arctic St NW5...71 B3
Arcus Rd BR1...186 C4
Ardbeg Rd SE24...161 B6
Arden Cl
Bushey Heath WD23...8 D4
Erith SE28...102 D1
Harrow HA1...64 B5
Arden Court Gdns
N2...48 B3
Arden Cres
Dagenham RM9...80 D1
Millwall E14...119 C2
Arden Grange N12...30 A6
Arden Gr BR6...226 D4
Arden Ho
21 Hoxton N1...95 C5
29 Stockwell SW9...138 A3
Vauxhall SE11...260 C3
Arden Mews E17...53 D4
Arden Mhor HA5...40 B5
Arden 17 SW19...156 D3
Arden Rd
Ealing W13...109 C6
Finchley N3...47 B6
Ardent Cl SE25...205 C6
Ardent Ho 30 E3...97 A5
Ardfern Ave SW16...204 C6
Ardfillan Rd SE6...164 B2
Ardgowan Rd SE6...164 C3
Ardilaun Rd N5...73 A4
Ardingly Cl CR0...222 D5
Ardleigh Gdns SM3...201 C2
Ardleigh Ho 5
IG11...101 A6
Ardleigh Rd
Kingsland N1...73 C2
Walthamstow E17...35 B2
Ardleigh Terr E17...35 B2
Ardley Cl
Forest Hill SE6...163 A1
Neasden NW10...67 C5
Ruislip HA4...39 A2
Ardlui Rd SE27...161 A2
Ardmay Gdns KT6...198 A4
Ardmere Rd SE13...164 B5
Ardmore La IG9...21 B4
Ardmore Pl IG9...21 B4
Ardoch Rd SE6...164 B2
Ardra Rd N9...18 D1
Ardrossan Gdns
KT4...216 A5
Ardshiel Cl SW15...134 D2
Ardwell Ave IG6...57 A4
Ardwell Rd SW2...160 A2
Ardwick Rd NW2...69 C4
Arena Bsns Ctr N4...51 A3
Arena Est N4...50 D3
Arena Sta SE25...206 C4
Arena The EN3...7 B5
Ares Ct 16 E14...119 C2
Arethusa Ho 8 E14...119 D2
Argali Ho 3 DA18...125 A3
Argall Ave E10...52 D1
Argall Way E10...53 A1
Argenta Way NW10...66 D1
Argent Ctr The UB3...106 A4
Argent Ct KT6...214 C5
Argent Ho HA5...23 B4
Argo Bsns Ctr 7
NW6...91 C4
Argon Mews SW6...265 B3
Argon Rd N18...34 D5
Argos Ct 5 SW9...138 C4
Argos Ho 8 E2...96 B5
Argosy Ho
Fitzrovia W1...238 D5
Rotherhithe SE8...119 A2
Argus Way UB5...85 A4
Argyle Cl W13...87 A3
Argyle Ho
Cubitt Town E14...120 A3
Richmond TW10...153 C2
Sutton SM2...218 A2
Teddington TW11...174 C5
Argyle Mans 4 NW2...68 D4
Argyle Pl W6...112 B2
Argyle Prim Sch
WC1...94 A4 233 A2
Argyle Rd Ealing W13...87 A2
Edmonton N18...34 A6
Harrow HA2...41 D3
Hounslow TW3...151 D6
Ilford IG1...78 C6
Leyton E15...76 C4
Newham E16...99 B1
Stepney E1...96 D3
Tottenham N17...34 A2
Woodside Pk N12...29 C5
Argyle Sq
WC1...94 A4 233 B2
Argyle St
WC1...94 A4 233 B2
Argyle Way SE16...118 A1
Argyle Wlk WC1...233 B1
Argyll Ave UB1...107 D5
Argyll Cl SW9...138 B2
Argyll Ct 15 SW2...160 A4
Argyll Gdns HA8...26 D2
Argyll Mans
Chelsea SW3...266 D6
West Kensington W14...254 B4
Argyll Rd
Kensington W8...113 C4 245 B1
Woolwich SE18...123 A3
Argyll St W1...93 C1 239 A1
Aria Ct IG2...57 A3
Arica Ho SE16...118 B3
Arica Rd SE4...141 A2
Ariel Ct
5 Belvedere DA17...125 C1
5 Hammersmith W12...112 A3
Newington SE11...261 C3
Ariel Rd NW6...69 C2
Ariel Way
Hounslow TW4...128 B2
Shepherd's Bush W12...112 C5
Aristotle Rd SW4...137 D2
Arizona Bldg 10
SE13...141 D4
Arkansas Ho 21 N19...49 D2
Ark Ct N16...73 D6
Arkell Gr SW16...182 D3
Arkindale Rd SE6...164 A1
Arklay Cl UB8...82 B3
ARKLEY...12 A6
Arkley Cres E17...53 B4
Arkley Dr EN5...12 B6
Arkley Pk EN5...11 B5
Arkley Rd E17...53 B4
Arklow Ho SE17...139 B6
Arklow Mews 4
KT6...214 A6
Arklow Rd SE14...141 B6
Arklow Road Trad Est
SE14...141 B6
Arkwright Ho 23
SW2...160 A4
Arkwright Mans
NW3...70 A3
Arkwright Rd NW3...70 A3
Arlesey Cl SW15...157 A6
Arlesford Rd SW9...138 A2
Arless Ho 8 HA1...42 D4
Arlidge Ho EC1...241 B4
Arlingford Rd SW2...160 C5
Arlington Ave
N1...95 A6 235 B5
Arlington Cl
Lewisham SE13...164 B6
Sidcup DA15...167 C4
Sutton SM1...217 C6
Twickenham TW1...153 C5
Arlington Ct
13 Acton W3...110 D5
Highgate N6...49 A3
4 Twickenham TW1...153 C5
Arlington Dr
Carshalton SM5...218 D6
Ruislip HA4...39 B3
Arlington Gdns
Acton Green W4...111 A1
Ilford IG1...56 C1
Arlington Gn NW7...28 D3
Arlington Ho
3 Deptford SE8...141 B6
Finsbury EC1...234 B2
1 Shepherd's Bush W12...112 B5
Arlington Lo SW2...138 B1
Arlington N12...13 C1
Arlington Park Mans 1
W4...111 A1
Arlington Pl 7
SE10...142 A5
Arlington Rd
Ashford TW15...170 B5
Camden Town NW1...93 B6 231 D5
Ealing W13...87 B1
Arlington Rd *continued*
Osidge N14...15 C
Richmond TW10...153 D
Surbiton KT6...197 D
Teddington TW11...174 D
Twickenham TW1...153 C
Woodford IG8...37 B
Arlington Sq
N1...95 A6 235 B
Arlington St
SW1...115 C5 249 A
Arlington Way
EC1...94 C4 234 B
Arliss Way UB5...84 C
Arlow Rd N21...16 C
Armada Ct 11 SE8...141 C
Armadale Cl N17...52 B
Armadale Rd
Feltham TW14...150 A
West Brompton SW6...265 A
Armada St 10 SE8...141 C
Armada Way E6...101 B
Armagh Rd E3...97 B
Armeston KT3...199 B
Armfield Cl KT8...195 B
Armfield Cotts 3
SW19...180 D
Armfield Cres CR4...180 D
Armfield Rd EN2...5 B
Arminger Rd W12...112 B
Armistice Gdns
SE25...206 A
Armitage Ho
NW1...92 C2 237 B
Armitage Rd
Golders Green NW11...47 B
Greenwich SE10...120 D
Armour Cl N7...72 B
Armoury Ho E3...97 A
Armoury Rd SE8...141 D
Armoury Way SW18...157 C
Armsby Ho 17 E1...96 C
Armstead Wlk RM10...81 C
Armstrong Ave IG8...36 C
Armstrong Cl
Bickley BR1...210 A
Dagenham RM8...58 D
Newham E6...100 B
Pinner HA5...40 A
Walton-on-T KT12...194 A
Armstrong Cres EN4...2 B
Armstrong Ho 8
SW15...156 D
Armstrong Rd
East Acton W3...111 D
Feltham TW13...173 A
Knightsbridge SW7...256 C
Woolwich SE18...123 A
Armstrong Way
UB2...107 D
Armytage Rd TW5...128 D
Arnal Cres SW18...157 A
Arncliffe Cl N11...31 A
Arncliffe NW6...91 D
Arncroft Ct IG11...102 B
Arndale Wlk 6
SW18...157 D
Arndell Ho 16 SM1...218 A
Arne Gr BR6...227 D
Arne Ho SE11...260 C
Arne St WC2...94 A1 240 B
Arnett Sq E4...35 B
Arneways Ave RM6...58 D
Arneway St SW1...259 D
Arne Wlk SE3...142 D
Arnewood Cl SW15...156 A
Arney's La CR4...203 A
Arngask Rd SE6...164 B
Arnhem Pl E14...119 C
Arnhem Way 3
SE22...161 C
Arnhem Wharf E14...119 C
Arnhem Wharf Prim Sch E14...119 C
Arnison Rd KT8...196 B
Arnold Ave E EN3...7 C
Arnold Ave W EN3...7 B
Arnold Cir E2...95 D
Arnold Cl HA3...44 B
Arnold Cres TW7...152 B
Arnold Ct E18...36 D
Arnold Dr KT9...213 D
Arnold Est SE1...253 D
Arnold Gdns N13...32 D
Arnold Ho
Croydon CR0...220 D
Newington SE17...261 D
9 Stoke Newington N16...73 C
Arnold House Sch
NW8...92 B5 229 C
Arnold Rd Bow E3...97 C
Dagenham RM10...81 C
Mitcham SW17...180 D
Northolt UB5...63 A
Tottenham N15...51 D

Arnos Gr N14 15 D1
Arnos Grove Ct 4 N11 31 C5
Arnos Grove Sta N11 31 C6
Arnos Rd N11 31 C6
Arnot Ho 27 SE5 139 A5
Arnott Cl
Acton Green W4 111 B2
Thamesmead SE28 124 C5
Arnould Ave SE5 139 B1
Arnsberg Way DA6, DA7 147 C1
Arnside Gdns HA9 43 D1
Arnside Ho 2 SE17 139 B6
Arnside Rd DA7 147 C4
Arnside St SE17 139 A6
Arnulf St SE6 185 D6
Arnull's Rd SW16 182 D4
Arodene Rd SW2 160 B5
Arosa Rd 8 TW1 153 D5
Arragon Gdns
Streatham SW16 182 A3
West Wickham BR4 223 D5
Arragon Rd
Newham E6 99 D6
4 Twickenham TW1 153 A3
Wandsworth SW18 157 C3
Arran Cl SM6 219 C4
Arran Ct Edgware HA8 10 D2
32 Hendon NW9 27 D1
Neasden NW10 67 B5
Arrandene Ho 3 BR5 190 B1
Arran Dr
Stanmore HA7 25 C6
Wanstead E12 77 D6
Arran Ho
5 Canary Wharf E14 120 A5
Stoke Newington N16 51 D1
Arran Mews W5 110 B5
Arran Rd SE6 164 A2
Arran Wlk N1 73 A1
Arras Ave SM4 202 A4
Arras Ho SE2 146 D6
Arrol Ho SE1 262 B5
Arrol Rd BR3 206 D6
Arrowe Ct 6 E5 74 B4
Arrow Ho 23 N1 95 C6
Arrow Rd E3 97 D4
Arrow Scout Wlk UB5 85 A4
Arrowsmith Ho SE11 260 C2
Arsenal Rd SE9 144 B2
Arsenal Sta N5 72 C5
Arsenal Way SE18 123 A3
Arta Ho 26 E1 96 C1
Artemis Ct 14 E14 119 C2
Artemis Pl SW18 157 B4
Arterberry Rd SW20, SW19 178 D2
Artesian Cl NW10 67 B1
Artesian Gr EN5 2 A1
Artesian Rd W2 91 C1
Artesian Wlk 4 E11 76 C5
Arthingworth St E15 98 C6
Arthur Ct
Battersea SW11 268 B1
10 North Kensington W10 90 D1
Paddington W2 91 D1
South Croydon CR0 221 B5
Arthur Deakin Ho 1 E1 96 A2
Arthurdon Rd SE4 163 C6
Arthur Gr SE18 123 A2
Arthur Henderson Ho
9 Crouch End N19 49 D2
9 Fulham SW6 135 B3
Arthur Newton Ho 20 SW11 136 B2
Arthur Rd
Dagenham RM6 58 D3
Edmonton N9 17 D2
6 Kingston u T KT2 176 C3
Lower Holloway N7 72 B4
Newham E6 100 B5
West Barnes KT3 200 B4
Wimbledon SW19 179 C6
Arthur Ruxley Est DA14 190 D4
Arthur St EC4 117 B6 252 D6
Arthur Wade Ho 7 E2 95 D4
Arthur Walls Ho 3 E12 78 C5
Artichoke Hill 8 E1 118 B6
Artichoke Mews 5 SE5 139 B4
Artichoke Pl SE5 139 B4
Artillery Cl IG2 57 A3
Artillery Ho Bow E3 97 A6
Westminster SW1 259 C5
Woolwich SE18 122 C1
Artillery La
Broadgate E1 95 C2 243 B3
North Kensington W12 90 A1
Artillery Pas E1 243 B3
Artillery Pl
Harrow Weald HA3 24 A3
Westminster SW1 259 C5
Woolwich SE18 122 C2
Artillery Row SW1 259 C5
Artington Cl BR6 227 A4
Artisan Cl E16 122 D6
Artisan Ct E8 74 A2
Artisan Mews 9 NW10 90 D4
Artisan Quarter 10 NW10 90 D4
Artizan St E1 243 B2
Arton Wilson Ho 12 SW15 156 A6
Arts Educational Sch The W4 111 C2
Arundale KT1 197 D5
Arundel Ave SM4 201 B5
Arundel Bldgs SE1 263 B5
Arundel Cl
Croydon CR0 220 D5
Hampton TW12 173 D5
Leyton E15 76 C4
Sidcup DA5 169 B5
Wandsworth SW11 158 C6
Arundel Ct
Barnes SW13 134 B6
4 Beckenham BR2 186 C1
2 Bexley DA6 147 A1
Chelsea SW3 257 B2
Colney Hatch N12 30 C4
3 Croydon CR0 220 D5
Harrow HA2 63 C4
Putney SW15 156 D6
Tottenham N17 34 A2
Arundel Dr
Borehamwood WD6 11 A6
Harrow HA2 63 C4
Woodford IG8 37 A3
Arundel Gdns
Burnt Oak HA8 27 B3
Ilford IG3 80 A6
Notting Hill W11 113 B6 244 C6
Southgate N21 16 C3
Arundel Gr N16 73 C3
Arundel Ho
Croydon CR0 221 B3
Islington N1 94 D6 234 D6
Richmond TW10 154 C6
3 South Acton W3 110 D4
Arundel Lo
Church End N3 29 B1
9 Upper Holloway N19 72 A6
Arundel Mans
Barnes SW13 134 B6
Fulham SW6 264 D2
Arundel Pl N1, N7 72 C2
Arundel Rd
Belmont SM2 217 B1
Cockfosters EN4 2 C2
Hounslow TW4 128 C2
Kingston u T KT1 177 A1
Thornton Heath CR0 205 B3
Arundel Sq N7 72 C2
Arundel St WC2 116 B6 250 D6
Arundel Terr SW13 134 B6
Arun Ho 5 KT2 175 D2
Arvon Rd N5 72 C3
Asa Ct UB3 105 D3
Asaph Ho SE14 141 B4
Asbaston Terr IG11 79 A2
Asbury Ct N21 16 A6
Ascalon Ct 16 SW2 160 B4
Ascalon Ho SW8 269 A3
Ascalon St SW8 137 C5 269 A3
Ascham Dr E4 35 C3
Ascham End E17 35 A2
Ascham St NW5 71 C3
Aschurch Rd CR0 205 D2
Ascot Cl
Borehamwood WD6 10 C6
Northolt UB5 63 C3
Ascot Ct
8 Brixton SW4 138 A1
Bromley BR1 188 A1
Old Bexley DA5 169 B4
St John's Wood NW8 229 C1
Ascot Gdns Enfield EN3 6 C6
Southall UB1 85 C2
Ascot Ho
6 Acton Green W4 111 A1
1 Paddington W9 91 C2
Penge SE26 184 B4
Ascot Ho *continued*
Regent's Pk NW1 231 D2
Paddington NW6 91 D5
Ascot Lo Enfield EN1 17 B6
Ascot Par 9 SW4 138 A1
Ascot Pl 12 HA7 25 C5
Ascot Rd
East Bedfont TW14 148 D2
Edmonton N18 34 A6
Newham E6 100 B4
Orpington BR5 211 D5
Streatham SW17 181 A4
Tottenham N15 51 B4
Ascott Ave W5 110 A4
Ascott Ct HA5 40 A5
Ashbourne Ave
East Barnet N20 14 D2
Erith DA7 147 A5
Harrow HA2 64 B6
Temple Fortune NW11 47 B4
Wanstead E18 55 B5
Ashbourne Cl
Ealing W5 88 C2
18 Woodside Pk N12 29 D6
Ashbourne Ct
Beckenham BR3 186 A2
Clapton Pk E5 75 A4
13 Woodside Pk N12 29 D6
Ashbourne Gr
Chiswick W4 111 C1
East Dulwich SE22 139 D1
Edgware NW7 27 B5
Ashbourne Ind Sch W8 113 D4 245 C1
Ashbourne Lo 2 N13 32 C6
Ashbourne Par 2 NW11 47 B5
Ashbourne Rd
Ealing W5 88 B3
Mitcham CR4 181 A3
Ashbourne Rise BR6 227 C4
Ashbourne Terr 1 SW19 179 C3
Ashbourne Way NW11 47 B4
Ashbridge Ct 3 W6 112 B3
Ashbridge Rd E11 54 D2
Ashbridge St NW8 92 C3 237 A5
Ashbrook HA8 26 B4
Ashbrook Rd
Dagenham RM10 81 D5
Upper Holloway N19 71 D6
Ashburn Ct BR1 187 A3
Ashburn Gdns SW7 256 A4
Ashburnham Ave HA1 42 D3
Ashburnham Cl N2 48 B5
Ashburnham Com Sch SW10 266 C4
Ashburnham Gdns HA1 42 D3
Ashburnham Gr SE10 141 D5
Ashburnham Pk KT10 212 A4
Ashburnham Pl SE10 141 D5
Ashburnham Rd
Chelsea SW10 136 A5 266 B3
Kensal Rise NW10 90 C5
Richmond TW10 153 B1
Ashburnham Retreat 4 SE10 141 D5
Ashburnham Twr SW10 266 C4
Ashburn Pl SW7 114 A2 256 A3
Ashburton Ave
Croydon CR0 206 B1
Ilford IG3 79 D4
Ashburton Cl CR0 206 A1
Ashburton Ct 1 HA5 40 D6
Ashburton Gdns CR0 222 A6
Ashburton Ho
Enfield EN3 6 D2
2 Wallington SM6 219 D3
Ashburton Jun & Inf Sch CR0 206 B3
Ashburton Learning Village CR9 206 B2
Ashburton Mans SW10 266 B4
Ashburton Rd
Croydon CR0 222 A6
Newham E16 99 A1
Ruislip HA4 62 A6
Ashburton Terr 2 E13 99 A5
Ashbury Dr UB10 60 D5
Ashbury Gdns RM6 58 D4
Ashbury Pl SW19 180 A4
Ashbury Rd SW11 137 A2
Ashby Ave KT19, KT9 214 C2
Ashby Ct NW8 236 D6
Ashby Grange 7 SM6 219 C2
Ashby Gr N1 73 A1
Ashby Ho
6 Brixton SW9 138 D3
17 Islington N1 73 A1
3 Northolt UB5 85 B3
14 Surbiton KT6 198 A3
Ashby Mews
10 Clapham Pk SW2 160 A6
New Cross SE4 141 B3
Ashby Rd
New Cross SE4 141 B3
South Tottenham N15 52 A4
Ashby St EC1 94 D4 234 D1
Ashby Way UB7 126 C5
Ashby Wlk CR0 205 A3
Ashchurch Ct 2 W12 112 A3
Ashchurch Gr W12 112 A3
Ashchurch Park Villas W12 112 A3
Ashchurch Terr W12 112 A3
Ash Cl
Carshalton SM5 218 D6
Edgware HA8 27 A6
Kingston u T KT3 177 B1
Penge SE20 184 C1
Petts Wood BR5 211 B4
Sidcup DA14 168 B1
Stanmore HA7 25 A4
Ashcombe Ave KT6 197 D2
Ashcombe Ct 4 SW15 157 A6
Ashcombe Gdns HA8 26 C6
Ashcombe Ho 39 E3 97 D4
Ashcombe Pk NW2 67 C5
Ashcombe Rd
Wallington SM5 219 A2
Wimbledon SW19 179 C5
Ashcombe Sq KT3 199 A6
Ashcombe St SW6 135 D3
Ashcroft Ave DA15 168 A5
Ashcroft Cres DA15 168 A5
Ashcroft Ct
5 Eltham SE9 166 C5
Wembley HA0 65 A4
3 Whetstone N20 14 B2
Ashcroft HA5 23 C4
Ashcroft Ho SW8 269 A2
Ashcroft N14 15 D2
Ashcroft Rd Bow E3 97 A4
Chessington KT9 214 B5
Ashcroft Sq 8 W6 112 C2
Ash Ct Chingford E4 20 B4
Clapham SW11 159 A6
Lee SE12 165 A4
Marylebone W1 237 C2
Romford RM7 59 D3
6 Rotherhithe SE16 119 A5
Upper Holloway N19 71 C6
West Ewell KT19 215 A4
2 West Norwood SW16 182 C5
9 Wimbledon SW19 179 A3
Woodford E18 37 C2
Ashdale Cl
Stanwell TW19 148 A2
Twickenham TW2 152 A4
Ashdale Gr HA7 24 D4
Ashdale Ho N4 51 B2
Ashdale Rd SE12 165 B3
Ashdale Way TW2 151 D4
Ashdene Cl TW15 171 A3
Ashdene
6 Deptford SE15 140 B5
Pinner HA5 40 C6
Ashdon Cl IG8 37 B4
Ashdon Rd NW10 89 D6
Ashdown Cl 13 BR3 185 D1
Ashdown Cres NW5 71 A3
Ashdown Ct
Dulwich SE22 162 A3
Ilford IG1 78 D2
New Malden KT4 199 D2
Sutton SM2 218 A2
Ashdown W13 87 B2
Ashdowne Ct N17 34 A2
Ashdown Ho 7 E5 74 A6
Ashdown Pl
Ewell KT17 215 D1
Thames Ditton KT7 197 A2
Ashdown SW15 156 D6
Ashdown Rd
Enfield EN3 6 C3
Hillingdon UB10 82 C5
Kingston u T KT1 176 A1
Ashdown Way SW17 159 A2
Ashdown Wlk 20 E14 119 C2
Ashe Ho 9 TW1 153 D5
Ashenden Rd E5 75 A3
Ashenden SE17 262 B4
Ashen Gr SW19 157 C2
Ashen E6 100 C1
Ashentree Ct EC4 241 B1
Asher Loftus Way N11 30 D4
Asher Way E1 118 A6
Ashfield Ave
Bushey WD23 8 A4
Feltham TW13 150 B3
Ashfield Cl
Beckenham BR3 185 C3
Richmond TW10 154 A3
Ashfield Ct SW9 138 A3
Ashfield Ho 5 N5 73 A3
Ashfield La BR7 189 A3
Ashfield Par N14 15 D3
Ashfield Pl BR7 189 B3
Ashfield Rd
East Acton W3 111 D5
New Southgate N14 15 C1
Tottenham N4 51 A3
Ashfield St E1 96 C2
Ashfield Yd 21 E1 96 C2
ASHFORD 170 B4
Ashford Ave
Ashford TW15 170 D4
Hayes UB4 84 D1
Hornsey N8 50 A5
Ashford Bsns Complex TW15 171 A6
Ashford CE Prim Sch TW15 170 D4
Ashford Cl
Ashford TW15 170 A6
Walthamstow E17 53 B3
ASHFORD COMMON 171 B4
Ashford Cres EN3 6 C3
Ashford Ct
Cricklewood NW2 68 D4
Edgware HA8 10 D1
Ashford Gn WD19 22 D5
Ashford Ho
14 Brixton SW9 138 D1
11 Deptford SE8 141 B6
Ashford Hospl TW15 148 A2
Ashford Ind Est TW15 171 A6
Ashford Mews N17 34 A2
Ashford Rd
Cricklewood NW2 68 D4
Feltham TW13, TW15 171 B6
Littleton TW15, TW17 171 A3
Staines TW18 170 A4
Wallend E6 78 C1
Woodford E18 37 B1
Ashford St N1 95 C4
Ash Gr
Cricklewood NW2 69 A4
Ealing W5 110 A3
East Bedfont TW14 149 C3
Edmonton N13 17 A1
Enfield EN1 17 C4
Hackney E8 96 B6
Hayes UB3 105 B6
Heston TW5 128 D5
Ashgrove Ct 2 W9 91 C2
Ashgrove Ho SW1 259 D2
Ashgrove SE12 165 A3
Ashgrove Rd
Ashford TW15 171 B5
Catford BR1 186 B4
Ashgrove Sch BR1 187 B1
Ash Gr Penge SE20 184 C1
Southall UB1 85 C2
Wembley HA0 65 A4
West Wickham BR4 208 A1
Yiewsley UB7 104 B6
Ash Hill Dr HA5 40 C6
Ash Ho
3 Canary Wharf E14 120 A4
Fulham SE1 263 D3
Kenton NW9 45 A6
Lewisham SE12 165 A3
2 Teddington TW11 175 C3
Ashingdon Cl E4 20 A1
Ashington Ho 16 E1 96 B3
Ashington 1 NW5 71 B2
Ashington Rd SW6 135 B3
Ashlake Rd SW16 182 A6
Ashland Pl W1 238 A4
Ashlar Ct N2 48 C6
Ashlar Pl SE18 122 D2
Ashleigh Commercial Est SE7 121 D3
Ashleigh Ct
Ealing W5 109 D2
Osidge N14 15 C4
Penge SE26 184 B4
Ashleigh Gdns SM1 217 D6
Ashleigh Ho
Mortlake SW14 133 C2
1 Streatham SW16 182 B6
Ashleigh Point 8 SE26 162 D1
Ashleigh Rd
Mortlake SW14 133 C2
Penge SE20 206 B6
Ashley Ave SM4 201 C4
Ashley CE Prim Sch KT12 194 A1
Ashley Cl
Hendon NW4 28 C1
Oatlands Pk KT12, KT13 193 D1
Pinner Green HA5 22 B1
Ashley Cres
Clapham SW11 137 A2
Wood Green N22 32 C1
Ashley Ct
Hampstead NW3 69 D3
Hendon NW4 28 C1
19 Kingsland N16 73 C3
New Barnet EN5 14 A6
Northolt UB5 85 A6
Stanmore HA7 25 B1
Yiewsley UB7 104 A5
Ashley Dr
Borehamwood WD6 11 B6
Hounslow TW7 130 C6
Twickenham TW2 151 D3
Ashley Gdns
Edmonton N13 33 A6
Orpington BR6 227 C3
Richmond TW10 153 D2
Wembley HA9 66 A6
Ashley Ho BR5 190 A1
Ashley La
Croydon CR0 220 D4
Edgware NW7 28 D3
Hendon NW4 28 C1
Ashley Park Ave KT12 193 D1
Ashley Park Cres KT12 194 A1
Ashley Pl
Walton-on-T KT12 194 A1
Westminster SW1 115 C3 259 A5
Ashley Rd
Chingford E4 35 C4
Enfield EN3 6 C3
Hampton TW12 173 C2
Hornsey N19 50 A2
Richmond TW9 132 A2
Thames Ditton KT7 196 D3
Thornton Heath CR7 204 B5
Tottenham Hale N17 52 A6
Upton E7 77 C1
Walton-on-T KT12 194 A1
Wimbledon SW19 179 D4
Ashleys Alley N15 51 A5
Ashley Wlk NW7 28 D3
Ashling Ho 2 N17 33 D1
Ashling Rd CR0 206 A1
Ashlin Rd E15 76 B4
Ash Lo
2 Ashford TW16 171 D3
Fulham SW6 134 D4
Ashlone Rd SW15 134 D2
Ashlyns Way KT9 213 D2
Ashmead Bsns Ctr 2 E16 98 B3
Ashmead Gate BR1 187 C2
Ashmead Ho E9 75 A3
Ashmead Prim Sch SE8 141 C3
Ashmead Rd
East Bedfont TW14 150 A3
St Johns SE8 141 C3
Ashmead 4 N14 15 C6
Ashmere Ave BR3 186 B1
Ashmere Cl SM3 216 D3
Ashmere Gr 11 SW2, SW4 138 A1
Ashmere Ho 10 SW2 138 A1
Ashmill Ct CR0 205 A3
Ashmill St NW8 92 C2 237 A4
Ashmole Prim Sch SW8 138 B6 270 D5
Ashmole Sch N14 15 C3
Ashmole St SW8 138 B6 270 D5
Ashmoor Lo NW7 27 B4

Ashmore Cl SE15 ....139 D5
Ashmore Ct
Catford SE6 ....164 C3
Colney Hatch N11 ....30 D4
Heston TW5 ....129 C6
Ashmore Gr DA16 ....145 C2
Ashmore Ho 4 W14 ....254 B5
Ashmore NW1 ....71 D1
Ashmore Rd W9 ....91 B4
Ashmount Prim Sch N19 ....49 C2
Ashmount Rd
Crouch End N19 ....49 D2
South Tottenham N15 ..51 D4
Ashmount Terr W5 ....109 D2
Ashneal Gdns HA1 ....64 B5
Ashness Gdns UB6 ....65 B2
Ashness Rd SW11 ....158 D6
Ashpark Ho 4 E14 ....97 B1
Ash Rd Cheam SM3 ....201 B1
Croydon CR0 ....223 C6
Littleton TW17 ....192 C5
Orpington BR6 ....227 D1
Plashet E15 ....76 D3
Ashridge Cl HA3 ....43 C3
Ashridge Cres SE18 ..145 A5
Ashridge Ct
Southall UB1 ....108 A6
Southgate N14 ....15 C6
Ashridge Dr WD19 ....22 C5
Ashridge Gdns
Bowes Pk N13 ....32 A5
Pinner HA5 ....41 A5
Ashridge Ho DA14 ....189 D6
Ashridge Way
Ashford TW16 ....172 A4
Merton SM4 ....201 B5
Ash Row BR2 ....210 C3
Ashtead Ct 15 SW19 ....156 D3
Ashtead Rd E5 ....52 A2
Ash Tech Coll The TW15 ....148 A1
Ashton Cl SM1 ....217 C4
Ashton Ct
1 Beckenham BR3 ....185 B2
Chingford E4 ....20 C1
Harrow HA1 ....64 D5
Ashton Gdns
Dagenham RM6 ....59 A3
Hounslow TW4 ....129 B1
Ashton Ho
13 Kennington SW9 ....138 C5
Roehampton SW15 ....156 B4
Ashton Rd E15 ....76 B3
Ashton St E14 ....120 A6
Ashtree Ave CR4 ....180 B1
Ash Tree Cl CR0 ....207 A3
Ashtree Cl BR6 ....226 D4
Ash Tree Cl 1 KT6 ....198 A1
Ashtree Ct TW15 ....170 D5
Ash Tree Dell NW9 ....45 B4
Ash Tree Villas CR0 ....204 B3
Ash Tree Way CR0 ....207 A3
Ashurst Cl SE20 ....184 B2
Ashurst Dr
Ilford IG2, IG6 ....57 A4
Littleton TW17 ....192 A4
Ashurst Lo 4 N5 ....72 D3
Ashurst Rd
Cockfosters EN4 ....14 D6
Colney Hatch N12 ....30 C5
Ashurst Wlk CR0 ....222 B6
Ashvale Rd SW17 ....180 D5
Ashview Cl TW15 ....170 A5
Ashview Gdns TW15 ....170 A5
Ashville Rd E11 ....76 B6
Ashwater Rd SE12 ....165 A3
Ashway Ctr 5 KT2 ....176 A2
Ashwell Cl 8 E6 ....100 A1
Ashwell Ct TW15 ....148 A2
Ashwin St E8 ....73 D2
Ash Wlk HA0 ....65 C4
Ashwood Ave UB8 ....82 C1
Ashwood Ct HA9 ....66 B4
Ashwood Gdns
Hayes UB3 ....105 D2
New Addington CR0 ....224 A2
Ashwood Ho 10 NW4 ..46 C5
Ashwood Lo
9 New Barnet EN5 ....13 D6
Southgate N21 ....16 B5
Ashwood Pk 6 SM2 ....217 C1
Ashwood Rd E4 ....20 B1
Ashworth Cl SE5 ....139 B3
Ashworth Mans W9 ....91 D4
Ashworth Rd W9 ....91 D4
Aske Ho 2 N1 ....95 C4
Asker Ho N7 ....72 A4
Askern Cl DA6 ....146 D1
Aske St N1 ....95 C4
Askew Cres W12 ....112 A4
Askew Mans 14 W12 ....112 A4
Askew Rd W12 ....112 A4
Askham Ct W12 ....112 A5
Askham Lo 5 SE12 ....165 A4
Askham Rd W12 ....112 A5
Askill Dr SW15 ....157 A6
Asland Rd E15 ....98 B6
Aslett St SW18 ....158 A4
Asmara Rd NW2 ....69 A3
Asmuns Hill NW11 ....47 C4
Asmuns Pl NW11 ....47 B4
Asolando Dr SE17 ....262 B3
Aspect Coll WC1 ....94 A2 240 B3
Aspect Ho 7 E14 ....120 A4
Aspects SM1 ....217 D3
Aspen Cl Ealing W5 ....110 B4
13 Upper Holloway N19 ....71 C6
Yiewsley UB7 ....104 B5
Aspen Copse BR1 ....188 B1
Aspen Ct 10 Acton W3 ..89 A1
12 Hackney E8 ....74 A3
Redbridge IG5 ....56 A6
Richmond TW9 ....132 C5
Aspen Dr HA0 ....65 A5
Aspen Gdns
Ashford TW15 ....171 A5
2 Hammersmith W6 ....112 B1
Mitcham CR4 ....203 A4
Aspen Gn DA18 ....125 B3
Aspen Gr HA5 ....39 D6
Aspen Ho
8 Deptford SE15 ....140 C6
4 Maitland Pk NW3 ....70 D2
Richmond TW9 ....132 C5
2 Sidcup DA15 ....168 A1
Southgate N21 ....16 B6
Aspen La UB5 ....85 A4
Aspenlea Rd W6 ....134 D6
Aspen Lo 1 SW19 ....179 B4
Aspen Way
Canary Wharf E14 ....120 A6
Feltham TW13 ....150 B1
Aspern Gr NW3 ....70 C3
Aspinall Ho SW12 ....160 A3
Aspinall Rd SE4 ....140 D2
Aspinden Rd SE16 ....118 B2
Aspire Bld 10 SW15 ....157 B6
Aspley Rd SW18 ....157 D6
Asplins Rd N17 ....34 B2
Asprey Ho CR4 ....202 C6
Asquith Cl RM8 ....58 C1
Assam SE1 ....253 D3
Assam St E1 ....96 A1
Assata Mews N1 ....72 D2
Assembly Pas E1 ....96 C2
Assembly Wlk SM5 ....202 C2
Assheton-Bennett Ho 15 KT6 ....198 A4
Ass House La HA3 ....23 D6
Assisi Ct
Upper Tooting SW12 ....158 D3
Wembley HA0 ....64 D5
Astall Cl HA3 ....24 C2
Astbury Bsns Pk 5 SE15 ....140 C4
Astbury Ho SE11 ....261 A5
Astbury Rd SE15 ....140 C4
Astell St SW3 ....114 C1 257 B2
Aster Ct 3 HA8 ....27 A6
Aster Ho 3 SE13 ....142 A3
Aste St E14 ....120 A4
Astey's Row 1 N1 ....73 A1
Asthall Gdns IG6 ....57 A5
Astins Ho 4 E17 ....53 D5
Astleham Rd TW17 ....192 A6
Astleham Way TW17 ....192 A6
Astle St SW11 ....137 A3
Astley Ave NW2 ....68 C3
Astley Ho Fulham SE1 263 D2
39 Paddington W2 ....91 C2
8 West Norwood SE27 ....183 A6
Aston Ave HA3 ....43 C2
Aston Cl Bushey WD23 ....8 A5
Sidcup DA14 ....168 A1
Aston Ct
Stoke Newington N4 ....73 A6
3 Wimbledon SW19 ....178 C3
10 Woodford IG8 ....37 A4
Aston Gn TW5 ....128 C3
Aston Ho
Notting Hill W11 ....244 D6
South Lambeth SW8 ....269 C1
Aston House Sch W5 ....87 D1
Aston Mews RM6 ....58 C2
Aston Pl SW16 ....182 D4
Aston Rd
Claygate KT10 ....212 C3
Ealing W5 ....87 D1
Merton SW20 ....178 C1
Aston St E14 ....97 A2
Astonville St SW18 ....157 C3
Astor Ave RM7 ....59 D3
Astor Cl KT2 ....176 D4
Astor Ct
Colney Hatch N12 ....30 C4
Newham E16 ....99 C1
Walham Green SW6 ....266 A3
Astoria Mans 18 SW16 ....160 A1
Astoria Par SW16 ....160 A1
Astoria Wlk SW9 ....138 C2
Astra Ct W13 ....109 A5
Astra Ho 4 Bow E3 ....97 B4
Hornsey N4 ....50 B2
Astrid Ho TW13 ....150 C2
Astrop Mews W6 ....112 C3
Astrop Terr W6 ....112 C4
Astwood Mews SW7 ....256 A4
Asylum Rd SE15 ....140 B5
Atalanta St SW6 ....134 D5 264 A3
Atbara Ct TW11 ....175 B4
Atbara Rd TW11 ....175 B4
Atcham Rd TW3 ....130 A1
Atcost Rd IG11 ....102 A2
Atheldene Rd SW18 ....158 A3
Athelney Prim Sch SE6 ....163 C1
Athelney St SE6 ....163 C1
Athelstan Ct E6 ....100 C5
Athelstane Gr E3 ....97 B5
Athelstane Mews N4 ....50 C1
Athelstan Gdns 8 NW6 ....69 A1
Athelstan Ho
Hackney Wick E9 ....75 B3
Kingston u T KT1 ....198 B5
Stoke Newington N16 ....73 C4
Athelstan House Sch TW12 ....173 C2
Athelstan Rd KT1 ....198 B5
Athelstan Way BR5 ....190 A2
Athelstone Rd HA3 ....24 B1
Athena Cl
Harrow HA2 ....64 C6
Kingston u T KT1 ....198 B6
Athena Ct
Bermondsey SE1 ....253 A1
St John's Wood NW8 ....229 C4
Athenaeum Pl 3 N10 ....49 B6
Athenaeum Rd N20 ....14 B3
Athenia Ho 7 E14 ....98 B1
Athenlay Rd SE15 ....162 D6
Athenoeum Ct N5 ....73 A4
Athens Gdns W9 ....91 C3
Atherden Rd E5 ....74 C4
Atherfield Ct SW18 ....157 D5
Atherfold Rd SW9 ....138 A2
Atherley Way TW4 ....151 B4
Atherstone Ct W2 ....91 D2
Atherstone Mews SW7 ....114 A2 256 B4
Atherton Dr SW19 ....178 D6
Atherton Ho CR2 ....221 C2
Atherton Hts HA0 ....65 C2
Atherton Mews E7 ....77 A2
Atherton Pl
Harrow HA2 ....42 B6
Southall UB1 ....107 C6
Atherton Rd
Barnes SW13 ....134 A5
Stratford E7 ....76 D2
Atherton St SW11 ....136 C3
Athlone KT10 ....212 C2
Athlone Cl 24 E5 ....74 B3
Athlone Ct
Lewisham SE6 ....164 B4
Upper Walthamstow E17 ....54 B6
Athlone Ho
16 Camden Town NW5 ....71 A2
9 Stepney E1 ....96 C1
Athlone House N6 ....48 D1
Athlone Rd SW2 ....160 C4
Athlone St NW5 ....71 A2
Athlon Ind Est HA0 ....87 D5
Athlon Rd HA0 ....87 D5
Athol Cl HA5 ....22 B2
Athol Ct 15 N4 ....72 B6
Athole Gdns EN1 ....17 C6
Athole Terr CR7 ....183 A1
Athol Gdns HA5 ....22 B2
Atholl Ho W9 ....229 A1
Atholl Rd IG3 ....58 A2
Athol Sq E14 ....98 A1
Athol Way UB10 ....82 C4
Atkins Ct
13 Old Ford E3 ....97 B6
Atkins Ct *continued*
Woolwich SE7 ....122 A2
Atkins Dr BR4 ....224 B6
Atkins Lo W8 ....245 A2
Atkinson Ct 3 E10 ....53 D2
Atkinson Ho
11 Battersea SW11 ....137 A3
Battersea SW11 ....268 A1
15 Hackney E2 ....96 A5
Newham E13 ....98 D3
Walworth SE17 ....262 D3
Atkinson Rd E16 ....99 C2
Atkinson's Almhouses HA8 ....26 B5
Atkins Rd
Streatham SW4, SW12 ....159 D4
Walthamstow E10 ....53 D3
Atlanta Bldg 8 SE13 ....141 D4
Atlanta Ct CR7 ....205 A6
Atlantic Ct 19 E14 ....120 B6
Atlantic Ho
5 Putney SW15 ....157 B6
4 Tower Hamlets E1 ....97 A2
Atlantic Rd SW2, SW9, SE24 ....138 C1
Atlas Cl IG11 ....102 B4
Atlas Bsns Ctr NW2 ....68 B6
Atlas Gdns SE7 ....121 C2
Atlas Mews
Dalston E8 ....73 D2
Islington N7 ....72 B2
Atlas Rd
Friern Barnet N11 ....31 A4
Newham E13 ....99 A5
North Acton NW10 ....89 C4
Wembley HA9 ....67 A4
Atley Rd E3 ....97 C6
Atlip Rd HA0 ....88 A6
Atney Rd SW15 ....135 A1
Atria Rd HA6 ....22 A5
Atrium 9 IG9 ....21 D2
Atterbury Rd N4 ....50 D3
Atterbury St SW1 ....116 A2 260 A3
Attewood Ave NW10 ....67 C5
Attewood Rd UB5 ....63 A2
Attfield Cl N20 ....14 B2
Attilburgh Ho SE1 ....263 C6
Attleborough Ct 4 SE21 ....162 B2
Attle Cl UB10 ....82 C5
Attlee Cl Hayes UB4 ....84 B4
Thornton Heath CR7 ....205 A4
Attlee Ct UB4 ....84 B4
Attlee Ho E1 ....243 D3
Attlee Rd Hayes UB4 ....84 B4
Thamesmead SE28 ....124 B6
Attlee Terr 3 E17 ....53 D5
Attneave St WC1 ....234 A1
Atwater Cl SW2 ....160 C3
Atwell Cl E10 ....53 D3
Atwell Pl KT7 ....197 A1
Atwell Rd 6 SE15 ....140 A3
Atwood Ave TW9 ....132 C3
Atwood Ho SE21 ....161 C1
Atwood Rd W6 ....112 B2
Aubert Ct N5 ....72 D4
Aubert Pk N5 ....72 D4
Aubert Rd N5 ....72 D4
Aubrey Beardsley Ho SW1 ....259 B3
Aubrey Mans NW1 ....237 A4
Aubrey Moore Point E15 ....98 A5
Aubrey Pl NW8 ....229 A3
Aubrey Rd
Hornsey N8 ....50 A4
Kensington W14 ....113 B5 244 D3
Walthamstow E17 ....53 D6
Aubrey Wlk W14 ....113 B5 244 D3
Auburn Cl SE14 ....141 A5
Aubyn Hill SE27 ....183 B6
Aubyn Sq SW15 ....156 A6
Auckland Cl
Enfield EN1 ....6 B6
South Norwood SE19 ....183 D2
Auckland Ct UB4 ....84 C3
Auckland Gdns SE19 ....183 D2
Auckland Hill SE27 ....183 A6
Auckland Ho 11 W12 ....112 B6
Auckland Rd
Clapham SW11 ....136 C1
Ilford IG1 ....57 A2
Kingston u T KT1 ....198 B5
Leyton E10 ....75 D5
South Norwood SE19 ....183 D2
Auckland Rise SE19 ....183 C2
Auckland St SE11 ....260 C1
Audax 29 NW9 ....27 D1
Auden Dr WD6 ....10 C6
Auden Pl NW1 ....231 A6
Audley Cl
8 Clapham SW11 ....137 A2
Muswell Hill N10 ....31 B3
Audley Ct Ealing W5 ....88 C2
Mayfair W1 ....248 C4
Northolt UB5 ....84 C4
Pinner Green HA5 ....22 C1
Snaresbrook E11, E18 ....54 D5
Surbiton KT5 ....198 B3
Twickenham TW2 ....152 B1
Audley Dr 3 E16 ....121 B5
Audley Gdns IG3 ....79 D6
Audley Ho N8 ....50 A5
Audley Pl SM2 ....217 D1
Audley Rd Ealing W5 ....88 B2
Enfield EN2 ....4 D3
Hendon NW4 ....46 B3
Richmond TW10 ....154 B6
Audley Sq W1 ....248 B4
Audrey Cl BR3 ....207 D3
Audrey Gdns HA0 ....65 B6
Audrey Ho EC1 ....241 B3
Audrey Rd IG1 ....78 D5
Audrey St E2 ....96 A5
Audric Cl KT2 ....176 C2
Augurs La 3 E13 ....99 B4
Augusta Cl KT8 ....195 B6
Augusta Ct NW4 ....28 C1
Augusta Rd TW2 ....152 A2
Augusta St E14 ....97 D1
Augustine Ho
Broadgate EC2 ....242 D2
New Cross SE4 ....141 B4
Augustine Rd
Hammersmith W14 ....112 D3
Harrow Weald HA3 ....24 A2
Augustines Ct E9 ....74 C3
Augustus Cl
Brentford TW8 ....131 D5
Hammersmith W12 ....112 B3
Stanmore HA7 ....9 D1
Augustus Ct
Feltham TW13 ....173 B6
Isleworth TW3 ....130 A1
8 Putney SW19 ....157 A3
South Norwood SE19 ....183 C3
Streatham SW16 ....159 D2
Augustus Ho NW1 ....232 A2
Augustus Rd SW19 ....157 A3
Augustus St NW1 ....93 B4 231 D2
Aulay Lawrence Ct N9 ....18 B1
Aultone Way
Carshalton SM5 ....218 D5
Sutton SM1 ....218 A6
Aultone Yd Ind Est SM5 ....218 D5
Aulton Pl SE11 ....261 B1
Aura Ho 3 TW9 ....132 D4
Aurelia Gdns CR0 ....204 B3
Aurelia Rd CR0 ....204 B3
Auriga Mews N1 ....73 B3
Auriol Cl KT4 ....215 C5
Auriol Dr
Greenford UB6 ....64 B1
Hillingdon UB10 ....60 D2
Auriol Jun Sch KT19 ....215 D4
Auriol Mans W14 ....254 A3
Auriol Park Rd KT4 ....215 C5
Auriol Rd W14 ....113 A2 254 A3
Aurora Bldg 4 E14 ....120 A5
Aurora Ct IG8 ....36 D6
Aurora Ho E14 ....97 D1
Austell Gdns NW7 ....11 C1
Austell Hts NW7 ....11 C1
Austen Cl SE28 ....124 B5
Austen Ho 5 NW6 ....91 C4
Austen Rd Erith DA8 ....147 D5
Harrow HA2 ....63 D6
Austin Ave BR1, BR2 ....210 A4
Austin Cl
Forest Hill SE23 ....163 B4
Twickenham TW1 ....153 C6
Austin Ct
9 Enfield EN1 ....17 C6
9 Newham E6 ....99 C6
Austin Friars EC2 ....242 D2
Austin Friars Ho EC2 ....242 D2
Austin Friars Sq EC2 ....242 D2
Austin Ho
6 Brixton SW2 ....160 B6
19 Kingston u T KT6 ....198 A4
1 New Cross SE14 ....141 B5
Austin Rd
Battersea SW11 ....137 A4 268 A1
Austin Rd *continued*
Hayes UB3 ....105 D4
Austins Ct SE15 ....140 A2
Austin's La UB10 ....61 A5
Austin St E2 ....95 D4
Austral Cl DA15 ....167 D1
Australia Rd W12 ....112 B6
Austral St SE11 ....116 D2 261 C4
Austyn Gdns KT5 ....198 D1
Autumn Cl Enfield EN1 ....6 A4
Wimbledon SW19 ....180 A4
Autumn Gr BR1 ....187 B4
Autumn Lo CR2 ....221 C4
Autumn Rise 9 W4 ....111 B1
Autumn St E3 ....97 C6
Avalon BR7 ....188 C1
Avalon Cl Ealing W13 ....87 A2
Enfield EN2 ....4 C3
Merton SW20 ....179 A1
Avalon Ct CR0 ....205 D2
Avalon Rd Ealing W13 ....87 A3
Parsons Green SW6 ....135 D4 265 C2
Avante Ct KT1 ....197 D6
Avard Gdns BR6 ....227 A4
Avarn Rd SW17 ....180 D4
Avebury Ct N1 ....235 C5
Avebury Rd
Leytonstone E11 ....54 B1
Merton SW19 ....179 B2
Orpington BR6 ....227 B5
Avebury St N1 ....235 C5
Aveley Ct 15 E5 ....74 B6
Aveley Mans 1 IG11 ....78 D1
Aveline St SE11 ....116 C1 261 A1
Aveling Ho 12 N19 ....71 C5
Aveling Park Rd E17 ....35 C1
Aveling Park Sch E17 ....35 C1
Ave Maria La EC4 ....241 D1
Avenell Mans N5 ....72 D4
Avenell Rd N5 ....72 D5
Avenfield Ho W1 ....247 D6
Avening Rd SW18 ....157 C4
Avening Terr SW18 ....157 C4
Avenons Rd E13 ....99 A3
Avenue Cl
Cranford TW5 ....128 B4
Primrose Hill NW8 ....92 C6 230 B5
Southgate N14 ....15 C5
Avenue Cres
Cranford TW5 ....128 B5
South Acton W3 ....110 D4
Avenue Ct
Chelsea SW3 ....257 C3
Cricklewood NW2 ....69 A5
Ealing W5 ....87 D2
Penge SE20 ....184 C2
Redbridge IG5 ....56 A6
Southgate N14 ....15 C5
Avenue Elmers KT6 ....198 A4
Avenue Gate IG10 ....21 C5
Avenue Gdns
Cranford TW5 ....128 B5
Mortlake SW14 ....133 C2
South Acton W3 ....110 D4
South Norwood SE25 ....184 A1
Teddington TW11 ....174 D4
Avenue Hall N6 ....49 D3
Avenue Ho
St John's Wood NW8 ....230 A3
Upper Clapton N16 ....74 A6
Willesden Green NW10 ....90 B5
Avenue Ind Est E4 ....35 B4
Avenue Lo 12 NW8 ....70 B1
Avenue Mans
Barnet EN5 ....1 B1
Clapham SW11 ....137 A1
Hampstead NW3 ....69 D3
Muswell Hill N10 ....31 C1
Willesden NW2 ....68 B2
Avenue Mews N10 ....49 B6
Avenue Park Rd SE21, SE27 ....160 D2
Avenue Par
Southgate N21 ....17 B4
Sunbury TW16 ....194 B6
Avenue Prim Sch E12 ....78 A3
Avenue Rd
Bexley DA6, DA7 ....147 A2
Brentford TW8 ....109 C1
Crouch End N6 ....49 D2
Feltham TW13 ....149 D1
Forest Gate E7 ....77 B4
Hampton TW12 ....173 D2
Harlesden NW10 ....89 D5
Hounslow TW7 ....130 D4
Ilford RM6 ....58 C2
Kingston u T KT1 ....198 A6
Mitcham SW16 ....181 D1

Avenue Rd *continued*
New Malden KT3 .... 199 C5
North Finchley N12 .... 30 A6
Penge BR3, SE20 .... 184 D2
Pinner HA5 .... 41 A6
Primrose Hill
NW8 .... 92 C6 230 A6
South Acton W3 .... 110 D4
Southall UB1 .... 107 B5
Southgate N14 .... 15 C5
South Norwood
SE25 .... 184 A1
Teddington TW11 .... 175 A4
Tottenham N15 .... 51 B4
Wallington SM6 .... 219 C1
Wimbledon SW20 .... 178 B1
Woodford IG8 .... 37 C4
Avenue Road Sta
BR3 .... 184 D1
Avenue Sch The
NW6 .... 69 A1
Avenue S KT5 .... 198 C2
Avenue Terr
Ilford IG2 .... 57 C3
Kingston u T KT3 .... 199 A6
Avenue The
Barnet EN5 .... 1 A2
Beckenham BR3 .... 186 A2
Bedford Pk W4 .... 111 C3
Bromley BR1 .... 209 D6
Brondesbury Pk NW6 .... 91 A6
8 Buckhurst Hill IG9 .... 21 C2
Chingford E4 .... 36 B5
Clapham SW4 .... 159 A6
Claygate KT10 .... 212 C3
Cranford TW5 .... 128 A4
Ealing W13 .... 87 B1
Finchley N3 .... 29 C1
Friern Barnet N11 .... 31 B5
Greenwich SE10 .... 142 B5
Hampton TW12 .... 173 B4
Harrow HA3 .... 24 D2
Hatch End HA5 .... 23 B4
Hornsey N8 .... 50 C6
Hounslow TW3 .... 151 D6
Isleworth TW1 .... 153 B6
Keston Mark BR2 .... 225 D5
Loughton IG10 .... 21 D5
Muswell Hill N10 .... 31 C1
4 New Malden KT4 .... 200 A1
Orpington BR6 .... 227 D6
Pinner HA5 .... 41 B3
Richmond TW9 .... 132 B3
Sidcup DA5 .... 168 D4
South Croydon CR0 .... 221 C5
Stoneleigh KT17,
SM3 .... 216 C1
St Paul's Cray BR5 .... 190 B3
Sunbury TW16 .... 172 B1
Surbiton KT5 .... 198 B3
Tottenham N17 .... 33 C1
Uxbridge UB10 .... 60 D5
Wallington SM5 .... 219 A1
Wandsworth SW18,
SW12 .... 158 C4
Wanstead E11 .... 55 B4
Wembley HA9 .... 44 B1
West Wickham BR4 .... 208 C2
Worcester Pk KT4 .... 215 D6
Averil Gr SW16 .... 182 D4
Averill St W6 .... 134 D6
Avern Gdns KT8 .... 195 D5
Avern Rd KT8 .... 195 D5
Avery Ct 1 SE20 .... 184 B3
Avery Farm Row
SW1 .... 258 C3
Avery Gdns IG2 .... 56 B4
AVERY HILL 167 B5
Avery Hill Coll (Mile
End Annexe) E3 .... 97 B3
Avery Hill Rd SE9 .... 167 B3
Avery Row
W1 .... 115 B6 248 D6
Aviary Cl E16 .... 98 D2
Aviemore Cl BR3 .... 207 B4
Aviemore Way BR3 .... 207 A4
Avignon Rd SE4 .... 140 D2
Avingdor Ct 10 W3 .... 111 A5
Avington Ct SE1 .... 263 B3
Avington Gr SE20 .... 184 C3
Avion Cres NW7,
NW9 .... 28 A2
Avis Sq E1 .... 96 D1
Avoca Rd SW17 .... 181 A6
Avocet Cl SE1 .... 118 A1
Avocet Mews SE28 .... 123 B3
Avon Cl Hayes UB4 .... 84 C3
Sutton SM1 .... 218 A4
Worcester Pk KT4 .... 216 A6
Avon Ct 1 Acton W3 .... 89 A1
13 Chingford E4 .... 20 A3
Greenford UB6 .... 85 D3
North Finchley N12 .... 29 D5
11 Putney SW15 .... 157 A6
Wembley HA0 .... 65 A4
Avondale Ave
Barnet EN4 .... 14 D3

Avondale Ave *continued*
Finchley N12 .... 29 D5
Hinchley Wood KT10 .... 213 A5
Neasden NW2 .... 67 C5
New Malden KT4 .... 199 D1
Avondale Cres
Enfield EN3 .... 7 A2
Redbridge IG4 .... 55 D4
Avondale Ct
Canning Town E16 .... 98 C2
Leytonstone E11 .... 54 C1
9 Sutton SM2 .... 218 A1
Woodford E18 .... 37 B2
Avondale Dr UB3 .... 106 B5
Avondale Gdns
TW4 .... 151 B6
Avondale Ho
11 Bermondsey
SE1 .... 118 A1
6 Mortlake SW14 .... 133 B2
Avondale Mans SW6 264 C2
Avondale Park Gdns
W11 .... 113 A6 244 A5
Avondale Park Prim Sch
W11 .... 113 A6 244 A5
Avondale Park Rd
W11 .... 113 A6 244 A6
Avondale Pavement 7
SE1 .... 118 A1
Avondale Rd
Bexley DA16 .... 146 C3
Bromley BR1 .... 186 D4
Chislehurst SE9 .... 166 A2
Finchley N3 .... 30 A2
Harringay N15 .... 50 D4
Harrow HA3 .... 42 D6
Mortlake SW14 .... 133 B2
Newham E16 .... 98 C2
South Croydon CR2 .... 221 A2
Southgate N13 .... 16 C2
Walthamstow E17 .... 53 C2
Wimbledon SW19 .... 179 D5
Avondale Rise SE15 .... 139 D2
Avondale Sq SE1 .... 118 A1
Avondale N22 .... 32 A3
Avonfield Ct E17 .... 54 B6
Avon Ho
2 Islington N1 .... 72 C1
7 Kingston u T KT2 .... 175 D2
Northolt UB5 .... 85 A3
Southgate N21 .... 16 B6
14 Stoke Newington
N16 .... 73 B4
Avon House Sch IG8 .... 37 A6
Avon Ho W14 .... 254 D3
Avonhurst Ho NW6 .... 69 A1
Avonley Rd SE14 .... 140 C5
Avon Mews HA5 .... 23 B2
Avonmore Gdns
W14 .... 254 D3
Avonmore Pl W14 .... 254 B4
Avonmore Prim Sch
W14 .... 113 A2 254 B4
Avonmore Rd
W14 .... 113 B2 254 C4
Avonmouth St SE1 .... 262 A6
Avon Path CR0 .... 221 A1
Avon Pl SE1 .... 252 B1
Avon Rd
Ashford TW16 .... 171 D3
Greenford UB6 .... 85 D3
St Johns SE4 .... 141 C2
Upper Walthamstow
E17 .... 54 B6
Avonstowe Cl BR6 .... 227 A5
Avon Way E18 .... 55 A6
Avonwick Rd TW3 .... 129 D3
Avril Way E4 .... 36 A5
Avriol Ho W12 .... 112 B5
Avro Ct E9 .... 75 A3
Avro Way SM6 .... 220 A1
Awlfield Ave N17 .... 33 B2
Awliscombe Rd
DA16 .... 145 D3
Axeholm Ave HA8 .... 26 D2
Axe St IG11 .... 101 A6
Axford Ho SW2 .... 160 D3
Axiom Apartments 5
BR2 .... 209 B5
Axis Bsns Ctr E15 .... 97 D6
Axis Ct
7 Bermondsey
SE16 .... 118 A4
Greenwich SE10 .... 142 C6
Axminster Cres
DA16 .... 146 C4
Axminster Rd N7 .... 72 B5
Axon Pl 5 IG1 .... 79 A6
Aybrook St
W1 .... 93 A2 238 A3
Aycliffe Cl BR1 .... 210 B5
Aycliffe Rd W12 .... 112 A5
Ayerst Ct 1 E10 .... 54 A2
Aylands Cl HA9 .... 66 A6
Aylesbury Cl E7 .... 76 D2
Aylesbury Ct SM1 .... 218 A5

Aylesbury Ho 13
SE15 .... 140 A6
Aylesbury Rd
Bromley BR2 .... 209 A6
Walworth
SE17 .... 117 B1 262 D1
Aylesbury St
Clerkenwell
EC1 .... 94 D3 241 C5
Neasden NW10 .... 67 B5
Ayles Ct UB4 .... 84 B4
Aylesford Ave BR3 .... 207 A4
Aylesford Ho SE1 .... 252 D1
Aylesford St
SW1 .... 115 D1 259 C1
Aylesham Cl NW7 .... 28 A3
Aylesham Rd BR6 .... 211 D2
Aylesham Sh Ctr
SE15 .... 140 A4
Ayles Rd UB4 .... 84 B4
Aylestone Ave NW6 .... 90 D6
Aylestone Ct 10 HA0 .... 66 A2
Aylett Rd
Croydon SE25 .... 206 B5
Isleworth TW7 .... 130 C3
Ayley Croft EN1 .... 18 A6
Ayliffe Cl KT1 .... 176 C1
Aylmer Cl HA7 .... 25 A6
Aylmer Ct N2 .... 48 D4
Aylmer Dr HA7 .... 25 A6
Aylmer Ho SE10 .... 120 B1
Aylmer Par N2 .... 48 D4
Aylmer Rd
Acton W12 .... 111 D4
Dagenham RM8 .... 81 A5
East Finchley N2 .... 48 C4
Leytonstone E11 .... 54 D1
Ayloffe Rd RM9 .... 81 B2
Aylsham Dr UB10 .... 61 A6
Aylton Est 28 SE16 .... 118 C4
Aylward Fst & Mid Schs
HA7 .... 25 D5
Aylward Rd
Forest Hill SE23 .... 162 D2
Merton SW20 .... 201 B6
Aylward Sch N18 .... 33 B6
Aylwards Rise HA7 .... 25 A6
Aylward St E1 .... 96 D1
Aylwin Est SE1 .... 263 B6
Aylwin Girls Sch
SE1 .... 117 D2 263 D4
Aynhoe Mans W14 .... 112 D2
Aynhoe Rd W14 .... 112 D3
Ayr Ct W3 .... 88 C2
Ayres Cl E13 .... 99 A4
Ayres Cres NW10 .... 67 B1
Ayres St SE1 .... 117 A4 252 B2
Ayrsome Rd N16 .... 73 C5
Ayrton Gould Ho 9
E2 .... 96 D4
Ayrton Ho HA9 .... 65 D6
Ayrton Rd
SW7 .... 114 B3 256 C6
Aysgarth Ct SM1 .... 217 D5
Aysgarth Rd SE21 .... 161 C4
Ayshford Ho E1 .... 96 B4
Ayston Ho 19 SE8 .... 118 D2
Aytoun Ct 17 SW9 .... 138 B3
Aytoun Pl SW9 .... 138 B3
Aytoun Rd SW9 .... 138 B3
Azalea Cl Ealing W7 .... 108 D5
Ilford IG1 .... 78 D3
Azalea Ct
Chingford IG8 .... 36 C3
Ealing W7 .... 108 D5
Azalea Ho
Feltham TW13 .... 150 B3
New Cross SE14 .... 141 B5
Azalea Wlk HA5 .... 40 B3
Azania Mews NW5 .... 71 B2
Azenby Rd SE15 .... 139 D3
Azhar Acad E7 .... 77 A2
Azof St SE10 .... 120 C2
Azov Ho 10 E1 .... 97 A3
Aztec Ct 8 N16 .... 73 C2
Azure Appartments
HA3 .... 24 B3
Azure Ct TW13 .... 149 D1
Azure Ho 28 E2 .... 96 A4

B

Baalbec Rd N5 .... 72 D3
Babbacombe Cl
KT9 .... 213 D3
Babbacombe Gdns
IG4 .... 56 A5
Babbacombe Rd
BR1 .... 187 A2
Baber Bridge Par
TW14 .... 150 C5
Baber Dr TW14 .... 150 C5
Babington Ct
Bloomsbury WC1 .... 240 B4
Streatham SW16 .... 181 D5
Babington Ho SE1 .... 252 B2

Babington House Sch
BR7 .... 188 B4
Babington Rd
Dagenham RM8 .... 80 C4
Hendon NW4 .... 46 B5
Streatham SW16 .... 181 D5
Babington Rise HA9 .... 66 C2
Babmaes St SW1 .... 249 C5
Bacchus Wlk 12 N1 .... 95 C5
Bache's St N1 .... 95 B4 235 D1
Back Church La E1 .... 96 A1
Back Hill EC1 .... 241 B5
Backhouse Pl SE1 .... 263 B3
Back La
Brentford TW8 .... 131 D6
Buckhurst Hill IG9 .... 21 D2
Burnt Oak HA8 .... 27 A2
Dagenham RM6 .... 59 A2
Hampstead NW3 .... 70 A4
Hornsey N8 .... 50 A4
Richmond TW10 .... 153 C2
Sidcup DA5 .... 169 C4
Backley Gdns SE25 .... 206 A3
Back Rd Sidcup DA14 .... 190 A6
Teddington TW11 .... 174 C3
Bacon Gr
SE1 .... 117 D3 263 C5
Bacon La
Edgware HA8 .... 26 C2
Queensbury NW9 .... 44 D5
Bacon's Coll SE16 .... 119 A4
Bacon's La N6 .... 49 A1
Bacon St E2 .... 95 D3 243 D6
Bacon Terr RM8 .... 80 B3
Bacton NW5 .... 71 A3
Bacton St E2 .... 96 C4
Baddeley Cl 11 EN3 .... 7 C6
Baddeley Ho
East Molesey KT8 .... 195 C4
Vauxhall SE11 .... 260 D2
Baddow Cl
Dagenham RM10 .... 103 C6
Woodford IG8 .... 37 D4
Baddow Wlk N1 .... 235 A6
Baden Ct N11 .... 31 D3
Baden Pl SE1 .... 252 C2
Baden Powell Cl
Dagenham RM9 .... 103 A6
Surbiton KT6 .... 214 B6
Baden Powell Ho 11
DA17 .... 125 C3
Baden Powell Sch
E5 .... 74 B5
Baden Rd Hornsey N8 .... 49 D5
Ilford IG1 .... 78 D3
Badger Cl
Feltham TW13 .... 150 B1
Hounslow TW4 .... 128 C2
Ilford IG2 .... 57 A2
Badger Ct
Chingford E4 .... 36 B6
Dollis Hill NW2 .... 68 C5
Badgers Cl
Ashford TW15 .... 170 B5
Enfield EN2 .... 4 D2
Harrow HA1 .... 42 B3
Hayes UB3 .... 105 C6
Badgers Copse
Orpington BR6 .... 227 D6
Worcester Pk KT4 .... 215 D6
Badgers Croft
Barnet N20 .... 13 A3
Chislehurst SE9 .... 166 C1
Badgers Hole CR0 .... 222 D4
Badgers Wlk KT3 .... 177 C1
Badlis Rd E17 .... 53 C6
Badma Cl N9 .... 18 C1
Badminton Cl
Harrow HA1 .... 42 C5
Northolt UB5 .... 63 C2
Badminton Ct 9 N4 .... 51 A2
Badminton Ho SE22 .... 139 C1
Badminton KT2 .... 176 D2
Badminton Mews 9
E16 .... 121 A5
Badminton Rd
SW12 .... 159 A5
Badric Ct SW11 .... 136 B3
Badsworth Rd 3
SE5 .... 139 A4
Bagley Cl UB7 .... 104 A4
Bagley's La
SW6 .... 135 D4 265 D1
Bagleys Spring RM6 .... 59 A5
Bagnigge Ho WC1 .... 234 A1
Bagshot Ho NW1 .... 231 D2
Bagshot Rd EN1 .... 17 D5
Bagshot St
SE17 .... 117 C1 263 B1
Baildon 27 E2 .... 96 C5
Baildon St SE8 .... 141 B5
Bailey Cl Chingford E4 .... 36 A6
Wood Green N11 .... 31 D3
Woolwich SE28 .... 123 C5
Bailey Cres KT9 .... 213 D1
Bailey Ct
4 Chingford E4 .... 36 B5

Bailey Ct *continued*
9 Shepherd's Bush
W12 .... 112 A4
Bailey Ho
Mitcham CR4 .... 202 C6
11 Penge SE26 .... 184 B5
Walham Green
SW10 .... 265 D4
Bailey Mews
Brixton SW2 .... 160 C6
Chiswick W4 .... 132 D6
Bailey Pl SE26 .... 184 D4
Bainbridge cl KT2 .... 176 A5
Bainbridge Rd RM9 .... 81 B4
Bainbridge St WC1 .... 239 D2
Baines Cl CR2 .... 221 B3
Bain Ho 23 SW9 .... 138 A3
Baird Ave UB1 .... 108 A6
Baird Cl
Kingsbury NW9 .... 45 A3
Walthamstow E10 .... 53 C1
Baird Gdns SE19 .... 183 C6
Baird Ho
12 Belvedere
DA17 .... 125 C3
29 Shepherd's Bush
W12 .... 112 B6
Baird Rd EN1 .... 6 B1
Baird St EC1 .... 242 B6
Bairny Wood App
IG8 .... 37 B4
Baizdon Rd SE3 .... 142 C3
Baker Beall Ct DA7 .... 147 D2
Baker Ct E11 .... 76 B5
Baker Ho
12 Bromley E3 .... 97 D4
Ealing W7 .... 108 D5
Baker La CR4 .... 203 A6
Baker Rd
Harlesden NW10 .... 89 C6
Kidbrooke SE18 .... 144 A4
Bakers' Almshouses
E10 .... 53 D3
Bakers Ave E17 .... 53 D3
Bakers Ct RM8 .... 59 B2
Bakers Ct SE25 .... 205 C6
Bakers End SW20 .... 179 A1
Bakers Field N7 .... 72 A4
Bakers Gdns SM5 .... 218 C6
Bakers Hall Ct EC3 .... 253 B5
Bakers Hill Barnet EN5 .... 1 D3
Upper Clapton E5 .... 52 C1
Bakers Ho W5 .... 109 D5
Baker's La N6 .... 48 D3
Bakers Mews 9
BR6 .... 227 D2
Baker's Mews W1 .... 238 A2
Bakers Pas 22 NW3 .... 70 A4
Bakers Rents 18 E2 .... 95 D4
Bakers Row E15 .... 98 C5
Baker's Row
EC1 .... 94 C3 241 A5
Baker St Enfield EN1 .... 5 B4
Marylebone
W1 .... 92 D2 237 D4
Baker Street Sta
NW1 .... 92 D3 237 D5
Baker Street
W1 .... 92 D2 237 D4
Baker's Yd EC1 .... 241 A5
Bakery Cl SW9 .... 270 D3
Bakery Mews KT6 .... 198 C1
Bakewell Way KT3 .... 177 C1
Balaam Ho SM1 .... 217 C4
Balaams La N14 .... 15 D2
Balaam St E13 .... 99 B4
Balaclava Rd
Bermondsey
SE1 .... 117 D2 263 D3
Kingston u T KT6 .... 197 C2
Bala Gn NW9 .... 45 C3
Balcaskie Rd SE9 .... 166 B6
Balchen Rd SE3 .... 143 D3
Balchier Rd SE22 .... 162 B5
Balcombe Cl DA6 .... 146 D1
Balcombe Ho
Lisson Gr NW1 .... 237 C6
3 Streatham SW2 .... 160 B3
Balcombe St
NW1 .... 92 D3 237 C5
Balcon Ct W5 .... 88 B1
Balcorne St E9 .... 74 C1
Balder Rise SE12 .... 165 B2
Balderton Flats W1 .... 238 B1
Balderton St
W1 .... 93 A1 238 B1
Baldewyne Ct N17 .... 34 A2
Baldock Ho 31 SE5 .... 139 A3
Baldock St E3 .... 97 D5
Baldrey Ho 1 SE10 .... 120 D1
Baldry Gdns SW16 .... 182 B4
Baldwin Cres SE5 .... 139 A4
Baldwin Gdns TW3 .... 130 A4
Baldwin Ho
15 Streatham
SW2 .... 160 C3
Wallend E12 .... 78 C1

Baldwin's Gdns
EC1 .... 94 C2 241 A4
Baldwin St EC1 .... 235 C1
Baldwin Terr
N1 .... 95 A5 235 A4
Baldwyn Gdns W3 .... 111 B6
Balearic Apts 3
E16 .... 121 A6
Bale Rd E1 .... 97 A2
Bales Coll W10 .... 90 D4
Balfern Gr W4 .... 111 C1
Balfern St SW11 .... 136 C3
Balfe St N1 .... 94 A5 233 B3
Balfour Ave W7 .... 108 D5
Balfour Bsns Ctr
UB2 .... 106 D3
Balfour Gr N20 .... 14 D1
Balfour Ho W10 .... 90 D2
Balfour Mews
Edmonton N9 .... 18 A1
Mayfair W1 .... 248 B4
Balfour Pl
Mayfair W1 .... 248 B5
Putney SW15 .... 134 B1
Balfour Rd
Bromley Comm
BR2 .... 209 D4
Croydon SE25 .... 206 A5
Ealing W13 .... 109 B4
Harrow HA1 .... 42 B4
Highbury N5 .... 73 A4
Hounslow TW3 .... 129 D2
Ilford IG1 .... 57 A1
Merton SW19 .... 179 D3
North Acton W3 .... 89 A2
Southall UB2 .... 106 D3
Wallington SM5 .... 218 D1
Balfour St
SE17 .... 117 B2 262 C4
Balfron Twr 4 E14 .... 98 A1
Balgonie Rd E4 .... 20 B3
Balgowan Cl KT3 .... 199 C5
Balgowan Prim Sch
BR3 .... 185 A1
Balgowan Rd BR3 .... 185 B1
Balgowan St SE18 .... 123 D2
BALHAM 159 A3
Balham Gr SW12 .... 159 A4
Balham High Rd SW12,
SW17 .... 159 A3
Balham Hill SW12 .... 159 B5
Balham New Rd
SW12 .... 159 B4
Balham Park Mans
SW12 .... 158 D3
Balham Park Rd SW12,
SW17 .... 159 A3
Balham Rd N9 .... 18 A2
Balham Sta SW12 .... 159 B3
Balham Station Rd
SW12 .... 159 B3
Balin Ho SE1 .... 252 C2
Balkan Wlk E1 .... 118 B6
Balladier Wlk E14 .... 97 D2
Ballamore Rd BR1 .... 165 A1
Ballance Rd E9 .... 75 A2
Ballantine St SW18 .... 136 A1
Ballantrae Ho NW2 .... 69 B4
Ballard Cl KT2 .... 177 B3
Ballard Ho SE10 .... 141 D6
Ballards Cl RM10 .... 103 D6
Ballards Farm Rd CR0,
CR2 .... 222 A2
Ballards La N3 .... 29 D3
Ballards Mews HA8 .... 26 C4
Ballards Rd
Dagenham RM10 .... 103 D6
Dollis Hill NW2 .... 68 A6
Ballards Rise CR2 .... 222 A2
Ballards Way CR0,
CR2 .... 222 B2
Ballast Quay SE10 .... 120 B1
Ballater Cl WD19 .... 22 C6
Ballater Rd
Brixton SW2,
SW4 .... 138 A1
South Croydon CR2 .... 221 D3
Ball Ct EC3 .... 242 D1
Ballentyne Ct N21 .... 16 B6
Ballina St SE23 .... 162 D4
Ballin Ct 14 E14 .... 120 A4
Ballingdon Rd
SW11 .... 159 A5
Ballinger Point 18
E3 .... 97 D4
Ballinger Way UB5 .... 85 A3
Balliol Ave E4 .... 36 C6
Balliol Ho 11 SW15 .... 156 D5
Balliol Rd
Bexley DA16 .... 146 B3
North Kensington
W10 .... 90 D1
Tottenham N17 .... 33 C2
Balloch Rd SE6 .... 164 B2

Ballogie Ave NW10 ....67 C4
Ballow Cl 15 SE5 ....139 C5
Ball's Pond Pl 3 N1 ....73 B2
Ball's Pond Rd N1 ....73 B2
Balmain Cl W5 ....109 D5
Balmain Ct TW3 ....129 D4
Balman Ho 3 SE16 ....118 D2
Balmer Rd E3 ....97 B5
Balmes Rd N1 ....95 B6 235 D6
Balmoral Ave
Beckenham BR3 ....207 A5
Friern Barnet N11 ....31 B5
Balmoral Cl 1 SW15 ....156 D5
Balmoral Cres KT8 ....195 C6
Balmoral Ct
18 Belmont SM2 ....217 C1
Ealing W5 ....87 D1
Edgware HA8 ....26 D6
Grove Pk SE12 ....187 B6
North Cheam KT4 ....216 B6
21 Rotherhithe SE16 ....118 D5
St John's Wood NW8 229 C4
Wembley HA9 ....66 B5
West Norwood SE27 . 183 A6
Balmoral Dr
Borehamwood WD6 ....11 B6
Hayes UB4 ....83 D3
Southall UB1 ....85 B3
Balmoral Gdns
Ealing W13 ....109 A3
Ilford IG3 ....57 D1
Old Bexley DA5 ....169 B4
Balmoral Gr N7 ....72 B2
Balmoral Ho
2 Isle Of Dogs E14 ....119 D3
Stanmore HA7 ....26 A1
Stoke Newington N4 ....51 A1
Walthamstow E17 ....35 B1
West Kensington W14 ....254 A4
Balmoral Lo BR6 ....226 C4
Balmoral Mews W12 ....111 D3
Balmoral Rd
Forest Gate E7 ....77 C3
Harrow HA2 ....63 C4
Kingston u T KT1 ....198 B5
Leyton E10 ....75 D6
North Cheam KT4 ....216 B6
Willesden NW2 ....68 B2
Balmoral Trad Est IG11 ....101 D2
Balmore Cl E14 ....98 A1
Balmore Cres EN4 ....15 A6
Balmore St N19 ....71 B6
Balmuir Gdns SW15 ....134 C1
Balnacraig Ave NW10 ....67 C4
Balniel Gate SW1 ....259 D2
Balsam Ho 9 E14 ....119 D6
Baltic Apts 5 E16 ....121 A6
Baltic Cl SW19 ....180 B3
Baltic Ho 7 SE5 ....139 A3
Baltic St E EC1 ....95 A3 242 A5
Baltic St W EC1 ....95 A3 242 A5
Baltimore Ho
Clapham SW18 ....136 A1
Kennington SE11 ....261 A2
Merton SW19 ....179 D3
Baltimore Pl DA16 ....145 D3
Balvaird Pl SW1 ....259 D1
Balvernie Gr SW18 ....157 C4
Bamber Ho IG11 ....101 A6
Bamber Rd 5 SE15 ....139 D4
Bamborough Gdns 12 W12 ....112 C4
Bamburgh 9 N17 ....34 B3
Bamford Ave HA0 ....88 B5
Bamford Ct E15 ....75 D3
Bamford Rd
Barking IG11 ....79 A2
Catford BR1 ....186 B5
Bampfylde Cl SM6 ....219 C5
Bampton Ct W5 ....87 D1
Bampton Dr NW7 ....28 A3
Bampton Rd SE23 ....162 D1
Banavie Gdns BR3 ....186 A2
Banbury Cl EN2 ....4 D4
Banbury Ct
11 Belmont SM2 ....217 C1
Ealing W13 ....109 A3
Strand WC2 ....250 A6
Banbury Ho 5 E9 ....74 D1
Banbury Rd
Higham Hill E17 ....35 A3
Homerton E9 ....74 D1
Banbury St 3 SW11 ....136 C3
Banbury Wlk UB5 ....85 C5
Banchory Rd SE3 ....143 B5
Bancroft Ave
East Finchley N2 ....48 C4
Woodford IG9 ....21 A2
Bancroft Cl TW15 ....170 C5
Bancroft Ct
Northolt UB5 ....84 C6
South Lambeth SW8 . 270 A2
Bancroft Gdns
Harrow Weald HA3 ....24 A2
Orpington BR6 ....211 D1
Bancroft Ho 11 E1 ....96 C3
Bancroft Rd
Bethnal Green E1 ....96 D3
Harrow Weald HA3 ....24 A1
Bancrofts Sch IG8 ....21 A1
Bandon Cl UB10 ....82 B5
BANDONHILL 219 D3
Bandon Hill Prim Sch SM6 ....219 D2
Bandon Rise SM6 ....219 D3
Banff Ho 1 NW3 ....70 C2
Banfield Rd SE15 ....140 B2
Banfor Ct SM6 ....219 C3
Bangabandhu Prim Sch E2 ....96 C4
Bangalore St SW15 ....134 D2
Bangor Cl UB5 ....63 D3
Banim St W6 ....112 B2
Banister Ho
Hackney E9 ....74 D3
Nine Elms SW8 ....269 B2
9 West Kilburn W10 ....91 A4
Banister Rd W10 ....90 D4
Bank Ave CR4 ....180 B1
Bank Bldgs 13 SW16 ....181 C5
Bank Ct SW11 ....268 C2
Bank End SE1 ....252 B4
Bankfoot Rd BR1 ....186 C6
Bankhurst Rd SE6 ....163 B4
Bank La
Kingston u T KT2 ....176 A3
Roehampton SW15 ....155 C6
Bank Mews SM1 ....218 A2
Bank of England* EC2 ....95 B1 242 C1
Bank of England Mus* EC2 ....95 B1 242 C1
Bank Par N11 ....31 B5
Banks Ho
Isleworth TW7 ....130 C3
Newington SE1 ....262 A5
Banksia Rd N18 ....34 D5
Bankside Art Gal* SE1 ....116 D6 251 D5
Bankside Ave
1 Lewisham SE13 ....142 A2
Northolt UB5 ....84 A5
Bankside
Borough The SE1 ....117 A6 252 A5
Borough The SE1 ....252 B4
Bankside Cl
Carshalton SM5 ....218 C2
Isleworth TW7 ....130 D1
Bankside Dr KT7 ....213 B6
Bankside EN2 ....4 D4
Bankside Ho EC3 ....243 B1
Bankside Pier SE1 ....117 A6 252 A5
Bankside Pk IG11 ....102 A4
Bankside Rd IG1 ....79 B3
Bankside
Southall UB1 ....106 D5
South Croydon CR2 ....221 D2
Bankside Way 6 SE19 ....183 C4
Banks La DA6 ....147 B1
Bank Sta EC3. 95 B1 242 D1
Bank St E14 ....119 D5
Banks Way E12 ....78 C4
Bank The N6 ....49 B1
Bankton Rd SW2 ....138 C1
Bankwell Rd SE13 ....142 C1
Banner Ct 5 SE16 ....118 C2
Banner Ho EC1 ....242 B5
Bannerman Ho SW8 270 C5
Banner St EC1 ....95 A3 242 B6
Banning Ho 4 SW19 ....156 D3
Banning St SE10 ....120 C1
Bannister Cl
Greenford UB6 ....64 B3
Streatham SW2 ....160 C3
Bannister Ho
28 Deptford SE14 ....140 D6
Harrow HA3 ....42 C6
Bannister Sports Ctr The HA3 ....24 A4
Bannockburn Prim Sch SE18 ....123 D2
Bannockburn Rd SE18 ....123 D2
Bannow Cl KT19 ....215 C4
Banqueting Ho* SW1 ....250 A3
Banstead Ct
Stoke Newington N4 ....51 A1
Walthamstow E10 ....53 D1
Banstead Gdns N9 ....17 C1
Banstead Rd SM5 ....218 C1
Banstead St SE15 ....140 C2
Banstead Way SM6 ....220 A3
Banstock Rd HA8 ....26 D4
Banting Dr N21 ....16 B6
Banting Ho 6 NW2 ....68 A5
Bantock Ct 1 N20 ....14 D2
Bantock Ho 8 W10 ....91 A4
Banton Cl EN1 ....6 B3
Bantry Ho 13 E1 ....96 D3
Bantry St SE5 ....139 B5
Banville Ho SW8 ....270 D3
Banwell Rd DA5 ....168 D5
Banyan Ho 8 NW3 ....69 D2
Banyard Rd SE16 ....118 B3
Baptist Gdns NW5 ....71 A2
Barandon Wlk 6 W11 ....112 D6
Barbanel Ho 26 E1 ....96 C3
Barbara Brosnan Ct NW8 ....229 C3
Barbara Castle Cl SW6 ....264 D5
Barbara Cl TW17 ....192 D4
Barbara Hucklesbury Cl N22 ....32 D1
Barbara Martin Ho 1 N11 ....31 C5
Barbara Rudolph Ct 5 N19 ....50 A2
Barbara Ward Ct 3 E11 ....76 C6
Barbauld Rd N16 ....73 C5
Barber Beaumont Ho 21 E1 ....96 D4
Barber Cl N21 ....16 C4
Barberry Ct E15 ....76 C2
Barbers Alley 1 E13 ....99 B4
Barbers Rd E15 ....97 D5
BARBICAN 95 A2
Barbican Arts & Con Ctr* EC2 ....95 A2 242 B4
Barbican* EC2 ....95 A2 242 B3
Barbican Rd UB1 ....85 D1
Barbican Sta EC1 ....95 A2 242 A4
Barb Mews W6 ....112 C3
Barbon Cl WC1 ....240 C4
Barbot Cl N9 ....18 A1
Barbrook Ho E9 ....74 C2
Barchard St SW18 ....157 D6
Barchester Cl W7 ....108 D5
Barchester Lo N12 ....29 D6
Barchester Rd HA3 ....24 B1
Barchester St E14 ....97 D2
Barclay Cl SW6 ....135 C5 265 A3
Barclay Ct N12 ....30 A5
Barclay Ho 21 E9 ....74 C1
Barclay Oval IG8 ....37 A6
Barclay Prim Sch E10 ....54 B3
Barclay Rd
Edmonton N18 ....33 B4
Leyton E11 ....54 D1
Newham E13 ....99 C3
Parsons Green SW6 ....135 C5 265 B3
South Croydon CR0 ....221 B5
Walthamstow E17 ....54 A4
Barcombe Ave SW2 ....160 B2
Barcom Trad Est 1 CR0 ....204 A2
Bardell Ho 17 SE1 ....118 A4
Barden St SE18 ....145 C5
Bardfield Ave RM6 ....58 D6
Bardney Rd SM4 ....201 D5
Bardolph Rd
Richmond TW9 ....132 B2
Tufnell Pk N7 ....72 A4
Bard Rd W10 ....112 D6
Bardsey Pl 41 E1 ....96 C3
Bardsey Wlk 5 N1 ....73 A2
Bardsley Cl CR0 ....221 D5
Bardsley Ho 6 SE10 ....142 A6
Bardsley La SE10 ....142 A6
Barents Ho 10 E1 ....96 D3
Barfett St W10 ....91 B3
Barfield Ave N20 ....14 D2
Barfield Rd
Bromley BR1, BR7 ....210 C6
Leytonstone E11 ....54 D1
Barfleur La SE8 ....119 B2
Barford Cl NW4 ....28 A2
Barford Ho 23 E3 ....97 B5
Barford St N1 . 94 C6 234 B5
Barforth Rd SE15 ....140 B2
Barfreston Way SE20 ....184 B2
Bargate Cl
New Malden KT3 ....200 A2
Plumstead Comm SE18 ....123 D1
Bargehouse Rd E16 ....122 D4
Barge House St SE1 . 251 B4
Barge La 10 E3 ....97 B6
Bargery Rd SE6 ....163 D3
Bargrove Cl 8 SE20 ....184 A3
Bargrove Cres SE6 ....163 B2
Barham Cl
Chislehurst BR7 ....188 D5
Keston Mark BR2 ....210 A1
Wembley HA0 ....65 C2
Barham Ct
8 Croydon CR2 ....221 A4
Keston Mark BR2 ....210 A1
Wembley HA0 ....65 C2
Woodside Pk N12 ....29 B5
Barham Ho SE17 ....263 B2
Barham Prim Sch HA0 ....65 C2
Barham Rd
Chislehurst BR7 ....188 D5
Croydon CR2 ....221 A3
Wimbledon SW20 ....178 A3
Baring Cl SE12 ....165 A2
Baring Ct N1 ....235 C5
Baring Ho 15 E14 ....97 C1
Baring Prim Sch SE12 ....165 A4
Baring Rd Barnet EN4 ....2 B2
Croydon CR0 ....206 A1
Grove Pk SE12 ....165 A2
Baring St N1 ....95 B6 235 C5
Barker Cl
Kingston u T KT3 ....198 D5
Richmond TW9 ....132 D3
Barker Dr NW1 ....71 D1
Barker Ho
Dulwich SE21 ....161 C1
3 Harringay N15 ....50 D5
Walthamstow E17 ....53 B2
Walworth SE17 ....263 A3
Barker Mews SW4 ....137 B1
Barker St SW10 ....266 A6
Barker Wlk SW16 ....159 D1
Barkham Rd N17 ....33 C3
BARKING 79 B1
Barking Abbey Comp Sch (Sports & Humanities Coll)) IG11 ....79 C3
Barking Abbey Sch (Sports & Humanities Coll) IG11 ....79 D2
Barking Bsns Ctr IG11 ....102 A4
Barking Flyover IG11 ....78 D1
Barking Hospl IG11 ....79 D1
Barking Ind Pk IG11 ....102 A6
Barking Rd
East Ham E6 ....100 B6
Plaistow E13 ....99 B4
BARKINGSIDE 57 A6
Barkingside Sta IG6 ....57 B6
Barking Sta IG11 ....79 A1
Bark Pl W2 ....113 D6 245 C6
Barkston Gdns SW5 ....113 D2 255 C3
Barkway Cl BR6 ....226 C4
Barkway Ct N4 ....73 A6
Barkwith Ho 27 SE14 ....140 D6
Barkworth Rd SE16 ....118 C1
Barlborough St SE14 ....140 D5
Barlby Gdns W10 ....90 D3
Barlby Prim Sch W10 ....90 D3
Barlby Rd W10 ....90 D2
Barley Cl WD23 ....8 A6
Barleycorn Way E14 ....119 B6
Barley Ct Ilford IG3 ....58 B4
Stanwell TW19 ....148 A3
Barleyfields Cl RM6 ....58 C2
Barley La IG3 ....58 B3
Barley Lane Prim Sch RM6 ....58 B2
Barley Mow Pas
Chiswick W4 ....111 B1
Clerkenwell EC1 ....241 D3
Barley Mow Way TW17 ....192 C5
Barley Shotts Bsns Pk W10 ....91 B2
Barling Ct 1 SW4 ....138 A3
Barling 6 NW1 ....71 B1
Barlings Ho 2 SE4 ....140 D1
Barloch Ho 14 SW11 ....137 A3
Barlow Cl SM6 ....220 A1
Barlow Dr SE18 ....144 A4
Barlow Ho
14 Bermondsey SE16 ....118 B2
Notting Hill W11 ....244 A6
Shoreditch N1 ....235 C2
Barlow Pl W1 ....248 D5
Barlow Rd Acton W3 ....110 D5
Brondesbury NW6 ....69 B2
Hampton TW12 ....173 C3
Barlow St SE17 ....117 B2 262 D3
Barmeston Rd SE6 ....163 D2
Barmor Cl HA2 ....23 D1
Barmouth Ave UB6 ....86 D5
Barmouth Ho 6 N7 ....72 B6
Barmouth Rd
Croydon CR0 ....222 D6
Wandsworth SW18 ....158 A5
Barnabas Ct N21 ....16 D6
Barnabas Ho EC1 ....235 A1
Barnabas Lo SW8 ....270 B2
Barnabas Rd E9 ....74 D3
Barnaby Cl HA2 ....64 A6
Barnaby Ct NW9 ....45 C6
Barnaby Pl SW7 ....256 C3
Barnard Cl
Chislehurst BR7 ....189 B2
Sunbury TW16 ....172 B3
Wallington SM6 ....219 D1
Woolwich SE18 ....122 C3
Barnard Ct SW16 ....160 B1
Barnard Gdns
Hayes UB4 ....84 B3
West Barnes KT3 ....200 A5
Barnard Gr E15 ....76 D1
Barnard Hill N10 ....31 B2
Barnard Ho 17 E2 ....96 B4
Barnard Lo
New Barnet EN5 ....2 A1
10 Paddington W9 ....91 C2
Barnard Mews SW11 ....136 C1
Barnardo Dr IG6 ....57 A5
Barnardo Gdns 1 E1 ....118 D6
Barnardo St E1 ....96 D1
Barnard Rd
Clapham SW11 ....136 C1
Enfield EN1 ....6 B3
Mitcham CR4 ....181 A1
Barnard's Inn EC4 ....241 B2
Barnbrough NW1 ....232 A5
Barnby Sq 1 E15 ....98 C6
Barnby St
Somers Town NW1 ....93 C4 232 B2
2 West Ham E15 ....98 C6
Barn Cl
Ashford TW15 ....170 D5
19 Kentish Town NW5 ....71 D3
Northolt UB5 ....84 C5
Barn Cres HA7 ....25 C4
Barncroft Cl UB8 ....82 D2
Barn Croft Prim Sch E17 ....53 A3
Barneby Cl TW2 ....152 C3
Barnehurst Rd DA7 ....147 D3
Barnersbury Ho N7 ....72 A4
BARNES 133 D4
Barnes Ave
Barnes SW13 ....134 A5
Southall UB2 ....107 B2
Barnes Bridge Sta SW13 ....133 C3
Barnes Cl E12 ....77 D4
Barnes Common* SW13 ....134 A2
Barnes Ct Barnet EN5 ....1 D1
Islington N1 ....72 C1
3 Newham E16 ....99 C2
South Norwood CR7 . 205 A6
Woodford IG8 ....37 D5
Wood Green N22 ....32 A3
Barnes End KT3 ....200 A4
Barnes High St SW13 ....133 D3
Barnes Ho
8 Barking IG11 ....101 B6
14 Bethnal Green E2 ....96 C5
Camden Town NW1 ....231 D6
26 Deptford SE14 ....140 D6
Hornsey N19 ....50 A2
Barnes Hospl SW14. 133 C2
Barnes Prim Sch SW13 ....133 D2
Barnes Qtr 6 TW8 ....131 C5
Barnes Rd
Edmonton N18 ....34 C6
Ilford IG1 ....79 A3
Barnes Sta SW13 ....134 A2
Barnes St E14 ....97 A1
Barnes Terr SE8 ....119 B
Barnes Wallis Ct HA9 ....67 A
BARNET ....13 B
Barnet By-Pass WD6 ....11 C
Barnet Coll EN5 ....1 B
Barnet Coll (Grahame Park Ctr) NW9 ....27 D
Barnet Coll (Montagu Rd) NW4 ....46 A
Barnet Dr BR2 ....226 A
BARNET GATE ....11 C
Barnet Gate La EN5 ....11 D
Barnet Gr E2 ....96 A
Barnet Hill EN5 ....1 C
Barnet Hill JMI Sch EN5 ....13 B
Barnet Ho 35 SE5 ....139 A
Barnet La
Barnet EN5, N20 ....13 B
Borehamwood WD6 ....10 B
Barnet Mus* EN5 ....1 A
Barnet Rd Barnet EN5 ....1 B
Edgware EN5 ....11 C
Barnett Ho E1 ....243 C
Barnett Homestead NW11 ....47 C
Barnet Trad Est EN5 ....1 B
Barnetts Ct HA2 ....63 D
Barnett St 18 E1 ....96 B
Barnet Way (Barnet By-Pass) EN5, NW7, WD6 ....11 B
Barnet Wood Rd BR2 ....225 C
Barney Cl SE7 ....121 C
Barnfield Ave
Croydon CR0 ....222 C
Kingston u T KT2 ....176 A
Mitcham CR4 ....203 B
Barnfield Cl
London N4 ....50 A
Wandsworth SW17 ....158 A
Barnfield Gdns
Kingston u T KT2 ....176 A
Shooters Hill SE18 ....144 D
Barn Field NW3 ....70 D
Barnfield KT3 ....199 C
Barnfield Pl E14 ....119 C
Barnfield Prim Sch HA8 ....27 A
Barnfield Rd
Burnt Oak HA8 ....27 A
Ealing W5 ....87 C
Erith DA17 ....147 B
Shooters Hill SE18 ....144 D
Barnfield Wood Cl BR3 ....208 B
Barnfield Wood Rd BR3 ....208 B
Barnham Dr SE28 ....123 D
Barnham Rd UB6 ....86 A
Barnham St SE1 ....253 B
Barnhill Ave BR2 ....208 D
Barnhill Com High Sch UB4 ....84 C
Barnhill Ct UB4 ....84 B
Barnhill La UB4 ....84 B
Barnhill HA5 ....40 C
Barnhill Rd
Hayes UB4 ....84 C
Wembley HA9 ....67 A
Barn Hill HA9 ....44 D
Barnhurst Path WD19 ....22 C
Barningham Way NW9 ....45 B
Barnlea Cl TW13 ....151 A
Barnmead Ct RM9 ....81 B
Barnmead Gdns RM9 ....81 B
Barnmead Rd
Dagenham RM9 ....81 B
Penge BR3 ....185 A
Barn Rise HA9 ....66 C
BARNSBURY ....72 A
Barnsbury Cl KT3 ....199 A
Barnsbury Cres KT5 ....199 A
Barnsbury Gr N7 ....72 B
Barnsbury Ho 12 SW4 ....159 D
Barnsbury La KT5 ....199 A
Barnsbury Pk N1 ....72 C
Barnsbury Rd N1 ....94 C6 234 A
Barnsbury Sq N1 ....72 C
Barnsbury St N1 ....72 C
Barnsbury Terr N1 ....72 B
Barnscroft SW20 ....200 B
Barnsdale Ave E14 ....119 C
Barnsdale Rd W9 ....91 B
Barnsley St E1 ....96 B
Barnstaple Ho SE12 ....164 D
Barnstaple La SE13 ....142 A
Barnstaple Rd HA4 ....62 C
Barn St N16 ....73 C
Barnston Wlk N1 ....235 A
Barnview Lo HA3 ....24 C

Barn Way HA9 66 C6
Barnwell Ho 1 SE5 139 C4
Barnwell Rd SW2 160 C6
Barnwood Cl
Barnet N20 13 B3
Ruislip HA4 61 B6
Westbourne Green W9 91 D3
Baron Cl
Friern Barnet N11 31 B5
Islington N1 234 A4
Baron Ct Barnet EN5 1 D1
Mitcham CR4 202 C5
Baroness Rd 5 E2 95 D4
Baronet Gr N17 34 A2
Baronet Rd N17 34 A2
Baron Gdns IG6 57 A6
Baron Gr CR4 202 C5
Baron Ho 6 SW19 180 B2
Baron Rd RM8 58 D1
Barons 14 BR3 185 D1
Barons Court Mans W14 254 B1
Baron's Court Rd W14 113 A1 254 B2
Barons Court Sta W14 113 A1 254 A2
Barons Ct Ilford IG1 79 B6
Kingsbury NW9 45 B3
Wallington SM6 219 D5
Baronsfield Rd TW1 153 B5
Barons Gate
East Barnet EN4 14 C5
13 South Acton W4 111 A3
Barons Keep W14 113 A1 254 A2
Barons Lo 9 E14 120 A2
Barons Mead HA1 42 C5
Baronsmead Rd SW13 134 A4
Baronsmede W5 110 B4
Baronsmere Ct 9 EN5 1 A1
Baronsmere Rd N2 48 C5
Baron's Pl SE1 116 C4 251 B1
Barons The TW1 153 B5
Baron St N1 94 C5 234 A4
Baron's Wlk CR0 207 A3
Baron Wlk E16 98 D2
Barque Mews SE8 141 C6
Barrack Rd TW4 129 A1
Barradell Ho 13 W14 112 D3
Barra Hall Cir UB3 83 C1
Barra Hall Rd UB3 105 C6
Barrass Cl 7 EN3 7 C6
Barratt Ave N22 32 B1
Barratt Ho 15 N1 72 D1
Barratt Ind Pk
Poplar E3 98 A3
Southall UB1 107 C5
Barratt Way HA3 42 B6
Barr Beacon SE23 162 C4
Barrenger Rd N10 30 D1
Barret Ho NW6 91 C6
Barrett Ct 2 NW10 89 C5
Barrett Rd E17 54 A5
Barrett's Green Rd NW10 89 B5
Barrett's Gr N16 73 C3
Barrett St W1 93 A1 238 B1
Barrhill Rd SW2 160 A2
Barrie Ct EN5 14 A6
Barriedale SE14 141 A3
Barrie Ho Acton W3 111 A4
Bayswater W2 246 B5
Edmonton N9 18 B4
Primrose Hill NW8 230 B5
8 Stoke Newington N16 73 C5
Barrier Gdns Pier SE18 121 D3
Barrier Point Rd E16 121 C4
Barringers Ct HA4 39 B2
Barringer Sq SW17 181 A6
Barrington Cl NW5 71 A3
Barrington Ct
9 Acton W3 110 D4
Kentish Town NW5 71 A3
4 Muswell Hill N10 31 B1
31 South Lambeth SW9 138 A3
Barrington N20 14 B3
Barrington Prim Sch DA7 146 D3
Barrington Rd
Bexley DA7 146 D3
Brixton SW9 138 D2
Cheam SM3 201 C1
Hornsey N8 49 D4
Little Ilford E12 78 C2
Barrington Villas SE18 144 C4
Barrington Wlk 9 SE19 183 C4
Barrow Ave SM5 218 D1
Barrow Cl N21 16 D2
Barrow Ct 6 SE6 164 D3
Barrowdene Cl HA5 23 A1
Barrowell Gn N21 17 A2
Barrowfield Cl N9 18 C1
Barrowgate Ho W4 111 B1
Barrowgate Rd W4 111 B1
Barrow Hedges Cl SM5 218 C1
Barrow Hedges Prim Sch SM5 218 C1
Barrow Hedges Way SM5 218 C1
Barrow Hill Cl KT4 215 C6
Barrow Hill Est NW8 92 C5 230 A3
Barrow Hill Jun Sch NW8 92 C5 230 A3
Barrow Hill Rd NW8 230 A3
Barrow Hill KT4 215 C6
Barrow Point Ave HA5 23 A1
Barrow Point La HA5 23 A1
Barrow Rd
Croydon CR0 220 C3
Streatham SW16 181 D4
Barrow Wlk TW8 109 C1
Barrs Rd NW10 67 B1
Barry Ave Erith DA7 147 A5
South Tottenham N15 51 D3
Barry Cl BR6 227 C5
Barry Ct SW4 159 C5
Barrydene Ct EN2 4 D2
Barrydene N20 14 B2
Barry Ho 4 SE16 118 B1
Barry Lo N4 50 B2
Barrymore N12 30 A3
Barry Par SE22 140 A1
Barry Rd
London SE22 162 A6
Newham E6 100 A1
Willesden NW10 67 A1
Barry Terr TW15 148 B2
Barset Rd SE15 140 C2
Barsons Cl SE20 184 C3
Barston Rd SE27 161 A1
Barstow Cres SW2 160 B3
Bartell Ho SW2 160 C5
Barter St WC1 94 A2 240 B3
Barters Wlk HA5 41 A6
Barth Mews SE18 123 C2
Bartholomew Cl
Barbican EC1 242 A3
Wandsworth SW18 136 A1
Bartholomew Ct
16 Blackwall E14 120 B6
Edgware HA8 25 D3
St Luke's EC1 242 B6
Bartholomew Ho
22 Camberwell SE5 139 A3
Enfield EN3 7 A6
Bartholomew La EC2 242 D1
Bartholomew Pas EC1 241 D3
Bartholomew Pl EC1 242 A3
Bartholomew Rd NW5 71 C2
Bartholomew Sq
18 Bethnal Green E1 96 B3
St Luke's EC1 242 B6
Bartholomew St SE1 117 B3 262 D5
Bartholomew Villas NW5 71 C2
Barth Rd SE18 123 C2
Bartle Ave E6 100 A5
Bartle Rd W11 91 A1
Bartlett Cl E14 97 C1
Bartlett Ct EC4 241 B2
Bartletts Cotts 4 EN5 1 A2
Bartletts Ho 10 RM10 81 D2
Bartlett St CR2 221 B3
Bartok Ho W11 244 C5
Barton Ave RM7 59 D1
Barton Cl
Bexley DA6 169 A6
Hackney E9 74 C3
Hendon NW4 46 A5
2 Newham E6 100 B1
Peckham SE15 140 B2
Shepperton TW17 192 D3
Barton Ct
Beckenham BR2 208 B6
10 South Lambeth SW4 138 A3
3 Sutton SM1 217 D2
West Kensington W14 254 B2
Barton Gn KT3 177 B1
Barton Ho
8 Bromley E3 97 D4
Islington N1 72 D1
Barton Ho *continued*
Sands End SW6 135 D2
Barton Mdws IG6 57 A5
Barton Rd
Sidcup DA14 191 A4
West Kensington W14 113 A1 254 B1
Bartons The WD6 9 D5
Barton St SW1 260 A6
Bartonway NW8 229 C4
Bartram Cl UB8 82 D3
Bartram Ct RM9 80 B2
Bartram Rd SE4 163 A5
Bartrams La EN4 2 A5
Bartrip St E9 75 B2
Barts Cl BR3 207 C4
Barts & The London Sch of Medicine & Dentistry EC1 94 D3 241 D5
Barville Cl SE4 141 A1
Barwell Bsns Pk KT9 213 D1
Barwell Ho 7 E2 96 A3
Barwell La KT9 213 C1
Barwick Dr UB8 82 D2
Barwick Ho 7 W3 111 A4
Barwick Rd E7 77 B4
Barwood Ave BR4 207 D1
Bascome St 13 SW2 160 C5
Basden Gr TW13 151 C2
Base Apartments 8 N1 73 A1
Basedale Rd RM9 80 B1
Baseing Cl E6 122 C6
Baseline Business Studios 18 W11 112 D6
Basevi Way SE8 141 D6
Bashley Rd NW10 89 B3
Basil Ave E6 100 A4
Basil Ct 11 EN5 2 A1
Basildene Rd TW4, TW5 128 D2
Basildon Ct W1 238 B4
Basildon Rd SE2 124 A1
Basil Gdns
Croydon CR0 206 D1
West Norwood SE27 183 A5
Basil Ho
South Lambeth SW8 270 A4
22 Whitechapel E1 96 A1
Basil Mans SW1 247 C1
Basilon Rd DA7 147 A3
Basil Spence Ho N22 32 B2
Basil St
Knightsbridge SW1 114 D4 247 C1
Knightsbridge SW1, SW3 114 D3 257 C6
Basin App 20 E14 97 A1
Basing Cl KT7 196 D2
Basing Ct 13 SE15 139 D4
Basingdon Way SE5 139 B1
Basing Dr DA5 169 B5
Basingfield Rd KT7 196 D2
Basinghall Ave EC2 95 B1 242 C2
Basinghall St EC2 95 B1 242 C2
Basing Hill
London NW11 47 B1
Wembley HA9 44 C1
Basing Ho
7 Barking IG11 101 B6
Catford SE6 185 C6
Basing House Yd 22 E2 95 C4
Basing Pl E2 95 C4
Basing St W11 91 B1
Basing Way
London N3 47 D6
Thames Ditton KT7 196 D2
Basire St N1 95 A6 235 B6
Baskerville Ct
South Norwood SE25 205 C4
Wandsworth SW18 158 C4
Baskerville Gdns NW10 67 C4
Baskerville Rd SW18 158 C4
Basket Gdns SE9 166 A6
Basle Ho 3 E15 76 C3
Baslow Cl HA3 24 B2
Baslow Wlk E5 74 D4
Basnett Rd 9 SW11 137 A2
Basque Ct 21 SE16 118 D4
Bassano St SE22 161 D6
Bassant Rd SE18 145 D6
Bassein Park Rd W12 111 D4
Bassett Gdns TW7 130 A5
Bassett Ho RM9 102 B6
Bassett Rd W10 90 D1
Bassetts Cl BR6 226 D4
Bassett St NW5 71 A2
Bassetts Way BR6 226 D4
Bassett Way UB1 85 D1
Bassingbourn Ho 3 N1 72 D1
Bassingham Rd
Wandsworth SW18 158 A4
Wembley HA0 65 D2
Bassishaw Highwalk EC2 242 C3
Basswood Cl 5 SE15 140 B2
Bastable Ave IG11 102 A5
Basterfield Ho EC1 242 A5
Bastion Highwalk EC2 242 A3
Bastion Rd SE18, SE2 124 A1
Baston Manor Rd BR2, BR4 225 B4
Baston Rd BR2 225 B5
Baston Sch BR2 225 B6
Bastwick St EC1 95 A3 242 A6
Basuto Rd SW6 135 C4 265 B1
Batavia Cl TW16 172 C2
Batavia Ho 1 SE14 141 A5
Batavia Mews 3 SE14 141 A5
Batavia Rd
Deptford SE14 141 A5
Sunbury TW16 172 B2
Batchelor St N1 94 C6 234 B5
Bateman Cl IG11 79 A2
Bateman Ho 8 SE17 138 D6
Bateman Rd E4 35 C4
Bateman's Bldgs W1 239 C1
Bateman's Row EC2 95 C3 243 B6
Bateman St W1 93 D1 239 C1
Bates Cres
Croydon CR0 220 C3
Streatham SW16 181 C3
Bateson St 3 SE18 123 C2
Bate St 10 E14 119 B6
Bath Cl SE15 140 B5
Bath Ct Finsbury EC1 235 C1
3 Forest Hill SE26 162 A1
Holborn EC1 241 A5
Bathgate Ho 8 SW9 138 D4
Bathgate Rd SW19 156 D1
Bath Gr E2 96 A5
Bath Ho
Bethnal Green E2 96 A3
Borough The SE1 262 B6
Bath House Rd CR0 204 A1
Bath Pas KT1 175 D1
Bath Pl Barnet EN5 1 B2
14 Hammersmith W6 112 C1
11 Shoreditch EC2 95 C4
Bath Rd Acton W4 111 C2
Cranford TW3, TW4, TW5 128 C4
Dagenham RM6 59 A3
Harlington TW6, UB7, TW5 127 B4
Harmondsworth TW6, UB7 126 B4
Lower Edmonton N9 18 C2
Upton E7 77 D2
Baths Rd BR1, BR2 209 D5
Bath St EC1 95 B4 235 C1
Bath Terr SE1 117 A3 262 A6
Bathurst Ave SW19 179 D2
Bathurst Gdns NW10 90 B5
Bathurst Ho 2 W12 112 B6
Bathurst Mews W2 114 B6 246 D6
Bathurst Rd IG1 56 D1
Bathurst St W2 246 D6
Bathway 11 SE18 122 C2
Batley Cl CR4 202 D2
Batley Pl 3 N16 73 D5
Batley Rd Enfield EN2 5 B4
Shacklewell N16 73 D5
Batman Cl W12 112 B5
Batoum Gdns W6 112 C3
Batson Ho 29 E1 96 A1
Batson St W12 112 A4
Batsworth Rd CR4 202 B6
Battenburg Wlk 10 SE19 183 C5
Batten Cl E6 100 B1
Batten Ho
7 London SW4 159 C6
8 Walthamstow E17 53 D6
10 West Kilburn W10 91 A4
Batten St SW11 136 C2
Battersby Rd SE6 164 B1
BATTERSEA 136 D4
Battersea Bridge Rd SW11 136 C5 267 A3
Battersea Bsns Ctr SW11 137 A2
Battersea Church Rd SW11 136 B4 266 D2
Battersea Dogs Home SW8 137 B5 268 D3
Battersea High St SW11 136 B3
Battersea Hts SW11 136 D2
Battersea Park* SW11 137 A5 268 A3
Battersea Park Rd SW11, SW8 267 D1
Battersea Park Sta SW8 137 B5 268 C3
Battersea Power Station(dis) SW8 137 B6 268 D6
Battersea Rise SW11 136 C1
Battersea Sq SW11 266 D1
Battery Rd SE28 123 C4
Battishill St 9 N1 72 D1
Battlebridge Ct NW1 233 B4
Battle Bridge La SE1 117 C5 253 A3
Battle Bridge Rd NW1 94 A5 233 A4
Battle Cl SW19 180 A4
Battledean Rd N5 72 D3
Battle Ho 8 SE15 140 A6
Battle House Mews 7 EN5 2 A1
Battle of Britain Mus* NW9 27 D1
Batty St E1 96 A1
Baty Ho SW2 160 B3
Baudwin Rd SE6 164 C2
Baugh Rd DA14 190 C5
Baulk The SW18 157 C4
Bavant Rd SW16 182 B1
Bavaria Rd N19 72 A6
Bavdene Mews NW4 46 B5
Bavent Rd SE5 139 A3
Bawdale Rd SE22 161 D6
Bawdsey Ave IG2 57 D5
Bawtree Rd SE14 141 A5
Bawtry Rd N20 14 D1
Baxendale N20 14 A2
Baxendale St E2 96 A4
Baxter Cl
Bromley BR1 210 D6
Hillingdon UB10 82 D4
Southall UB2 107 D3
Baxter Ho 11 E3 97 D4
Baxter Rd
Edmonton N18 34 B6
Ilford IG1 78 D3
Islington N1 73 B2
Newham E16 99 C1
Bayard Ct DA7 147 D1
Baycliffe Ho 8 E9 74 D2
Baycroft Cl HA5 40 C6
Bay Ct Ealing W5 110 A3
7 Stepney E1 96 D3
Baydon Ct BR2 208 D6
Bayer Ho EC1 242 A5
Bayes Ct NW3 70 D1
Bayeux Ho 10 SE7 143 C6
Bayfield Ho 3 SE4 140 D1
Bayfield Rd SE9 143 D1
Bayford Lodge HA5 23 B2
Bayford Rd NW10 90 D4
Bayford St Ind Ctr 4 E8 74 B1
Bayford St 5 E8 74 B1
Baygrove Mews KT1 175 C2
Bayham Pl NW1 93 C6 232 B5
Bayham Rd
Acton W4 111 B3
Ealing W13 109 B5
Morden SM4 202 A5
Bayham St NW1 93 C6 232 A5
Bay Ho UB10 60 C4
Bayhurst Ho N4 51 A2
Bayhurst Wood Countryside Park UB9 38 B4
Bayleaf Cl TW12 174 B5
Bayley St WC1 239 C3
Bayley Wlk SE2 125 A1
Baylis Mews TW1 153 A4
Baylis Rd SE1 116 C4 251 A1
Bayliss Ave SE28 124 D6
Bayliss Cl
4 Southall UB1 85 D1
Southgate N21 16 A6
Bayne Cl E6 100 B1
Baynes Cl EN1 6 A4
Baynes Mews 2 NW3 70 B2
Baynes St NW1 71 C1
Baynham Cl DA5 169 B5
Bayon Ho 27 N19 49 D2
Bayonne Rd W6 264 A5
Bays Cl SE26 184 C5
Bays Ct HA8 26 D5
Bayshill Rise UB5 63 D2
Bayston Rd N16 73 D5
BAYSWATER 114 A6
Bayswater Rd W2 114 B6 246 C5
Bayswater Sta W2 113 D6 245 D6
Bayton Ct 2 E8 74 A1
Baytree Cl
Bromley BR1 187 D2
Sidcup DA15 167 D3
Baytree Ho E4 19 D4
Baytree Rd SW2 138 B1
Bazalgette Cl KT3 199 B4
Bazalgette Gdns KT3 199 B4
Bazalgette Ho NW8 236 D6
Bazeley Ho SE1 251 C1
Bazely St E14 120 A6
Bazile Rd N21 16 C5
BBC Television Ctr W12 112 C5
Beacham Cl SE7 143 D6
Beachborough Rd BR1 186 A6
Beachcroft Ave UB1 107 B5
Beachcroft Rd E11 76 C5
Beach Ct SE9 166 A5
Beach Gr TW13 151 C2
Beach Ho SW5 255 A2
Beachy Rd E3 75 C1
Beaconfield Terrace Rd W14 254 A5
Beacon Gate SE14 140 D2
Beacon Gr SM5 219 A4
Beacon Hill N7 72 A3
Beacon Ho
11 Camberwell SE5 139 C5
7 Isle Of Dogs E14 119 D1
10 Penge SE26 184 B5
South Lambeth SW8 269 C2
Beacon House Sch W5 110 B5
Beacon Pl CR0 220 A5
Beacon Rdbt TW6 148 C5
Beacon Rd
Harlington TW19, TW6 148 C5
Hither Green SE13 164 B5
Beacons Cl 10 E6 100 A2
Beaconsfield Cl
Acton Green W4 111 A1
Friern Barnet N11 31 A5
Greenwich SE3 143 A6
Beaconsfield Ct N11 31 A5
Beaconsfield Gdns KT10 212 C1
Beaconsfield Par 1 SE9 188 A6
Beaconsfield Prim Sch UB2 107 A5
Beaconsfield Rd
Acton W4 111 B3
Bromley BR1 209 D6
Claygate KT10 212 C1
Ealing W5 109 D4
Edmonton N9 18 A1
Elmstead SE9 188 A6
Enfield EN3 6 D6
Friern Barnet N11 31 A6
Greenwich SE3 143 A5
Hayes UB4 106 C5
Kingston u T KT3 177 B1
Leyton E10 76 A5
Newham E16 98 D3
Southall UB1 107 A5
South Tottenham N15 51 C5
Surbiton KT5 198 B2
Thornton Heath CR0 205 B3
Twickenham TW1 153 B5
Walthamstow E17 53 B3
Walworth SE17 117 C1 263 A1
Willesden NW10 67 D2
Beaconsfield Wlk SW6 135 B4 264 D1
Beaconshaw BR1 186 C3
Beacontree Ave E17 36 B1
Beacontree Rd E11 54 D2
Beadle Ct CR4 202 C6
Beadlow Cl SM4 202 B3
Beadman Pl SE27 182 D6
Beadman St SE27 182 D6
Beadnell Rd SE23 162 D3

Beadon Rd
Bromley BR2 209 A4
Hammersmith W6 112 C2
Beaford Gr SW20 201 B6
Beagle Cl TW13 172 B6
Beak St W1 115 C6 249 B6
Beal Cl DA16 146 A4
Beale Cl N13 32 D5
Beale Ho 7 SW9 138 B3
Beale Pl E3 97 B5
Beale Rd E3 97 B6
Beal High Sch IG5 56 A5
Beal Rd IG1 78 C6
Beam Ave RM10 103 D6
Beames Ho SW8 269 C2
Beames Rd NW10 89 B6
Beaminster Ct N15 51 B4
Beaminster Gdns IG6 56 D6
Beaminster Ho SW8 270 C4
Beamish Dr WD23 8 A3
Beamish Ho 7 SE16 118 C2
Beamish Rd N9 18 A3
Beanacre Cl E9 75 B2
Bean Rd DA6 146 D1
Beanshaw SE9 188 C6
Beansland Gr RM6 59 A6
Bear Alley EC4 241 C2
Bear Cl RM7 59 D3
Bear Croft Ho 6 SW6 135 B3
Beardell St SE19 183 D4
Beardow Gr N14 15 C5
Beard Rd KT2 176 B5
Beardsfield E13 99 A5
Beards Hill Cl TW12 173 C2
Beard's Hill TW12 173 C2
Beardsley Terr RM8 80 B3
Beardsley Way W3 111 B4
Beard's Rd TW15, TW16 171 C4
Bearfield Rd KT2 176 A3
Bear Gardens Mus* SE1 117 A5 252 A4
Bear Gdns SE1 117 A5 252 A4
Bear La SE1 116 D5 251 D3
Bear Rd TW13 172 D6
Bearstead Rise SE4 163 B6
Bearsted Terr 7 BR3 185 C2
Bear St WC2 249 D6
Beasley's Ait La TW16, TW17 193 D3
Beasley's Ait TW17 193 D3
Beaton Cl SE15 139 D4
Beatrice Ave
Thornton Heath SW16 182 B1
Wembley HA9 66 A3
Beatrice Cl
Newham E13 99 A3
Pinner HA5 40 A5
Beatrice Ct
Buckhurst Hill IG9 21 D2
Hendon NW4 46 C4
Beatrice Ho
1 Brixton SW2 160 B6
Forest Hill SE6 163 C2
4 Hammersmith W6 112 C1
2 Stepney E1 96 D2
Beatrice Lo 3 N12 30 A4
Beatrice Pl W8 255 C5
Beatrice Rd
Bermondsey SE1 118 A2
Edmonton N9 18 C4
Finsbury Pk N4 50 C2
2 Richmond TW10 154 B6
Southall UB1 107 B5
Walthamstow E17 53 C4
Beatrice Tate Sch E2 96 B4
Beatrice Webb Ho 4 E3 97 A5
Beatrix Ho SW5 255 D2
Beatrix Potter Prim Sch SW18 158 A3
Beatson Wlk 23 SE16 118 D5
Beattie Cl TW14 149 D3
Beattie Ho SW8 269 B2
Beattock Rise N10 49 B5
Beatty Ho 16 E14 119 C4
Beatty Rd
Stanmore HA7 25 C4
Stoke Newington N16 73 C4
Beatty St NW1 232 A4
Beattyville Gdns IG6 56 D5
Beauchamp Cl 17 W4 111 A3
Beauchamp Ct HA7 25 C5
Beauchamp Pl SW3 114 C3 257 B5
Beauchamp Rd
Clapham SW11 136 D1
East Molesey KT8 196 A4
South Norwood SE19 183 B2
Sutton SM1 217 C4
Twickenham TW1 153 A4
Upton E7 77 B1
Beauchamp St EC1 241 A3
Beauchamp Terr SW15 134 B2
Beauclerc Inf Sch TW16 194 C6
Beauclerc Rd W6 112 B3
Beauclere Ho 1 SM2 218 A1
Beauclerk Cl TW13 150 B3
Beauclerk Ho 10 SW16 160 A1
Beaudesert Mews UB7 104 A4
Beaufort Ave HA3 43 B6
Beaufort Cl
Chingford E4 35 D4
Ealing W5 88 B2
Putney SW19 156 B4
Beaufort Ct
Friern Barnet N11 31 B5
Harrow HA3 43 A3
3 New Barnet EN5 14 A6
Richmond TW10 175 C6
West Brompton SW6 265 A6
Beaufort Dr NW11 47 C5
Beaufort Gdns
Hendon NW4 46 C3
Heston TW5 129 A4
Ilford IG1 56 C1
Knightsbridge SW3 114 C3 257 B6
South Norwood SW16 182 B3
Beaufort Ho
Ashford TW15 170 D5
Battersea SW11 136 C3
Chelsea SW3 266 D5
Hampstead Garden Suburb NW11 48 A3
20 Millwall E14 119 C4
Pimlico SW1 259 C1
8 South Tottenham N15 51 D5
1 Wimbledon SW20 178 D2
Beaufort Mans SW3 266 D5
Beaufort Mews SW6 264 D6
Beaufort E6 100 C2
Beaufort Pk NW11 47 C5
Beaufort Rd
Ealing W5 88 B2
Kingston u T KT1, KT5, KT6 198 A5
Richmond TW10 175 C6
Ruislip HA4 61 B6
Twickenham TW1 153 C4
Beaufort St SW3 136 B6 266 C6
Beaufort Way KT17 216 A1
Beaufoy Ho
South Lambeth SW8 270 C4
3 West Norwood SE27 160 D1
Beaufoy Rd
11 London SW8 137 B2
Tottenham N17 33 C3
Beaufoy Wlk SE11 116 B2 260 D3
Beaulieu Ave
Forest Hill SE26 184 B6
1 Newham E16 121 B5
Beaulieu Cl
Camberwell SE5 139 B2
Colindale NW9 45 C5
Hounslow TW4 151 B6
Mitcham CR4 181 A2
14 Twickenham TW1 153 D5
Beaulieu Ct W5 88 A2
Beaulieu Dr HA5 40 D2
Beaulieu Gdns N21 17 A4
Beaulieu Ho 6 NW4 28 D1
Beaulieu Hts CR7 183 C2
Beaulieu Pl W4 111 A3
Beaumanor Gdns SE9 188 C6
Beaumanor Mans W2 245 D6
Beaumaris 5 N11 32 A4
Beaumaris Dr IG8 37 D3
Beaumaris Gn NW9 45 C3
Beaumaris Twr 2 W3 110 D4
Beaumont Ave
Harrow HA2 41 D3
Richmond TW9 132 B2
Wembley HA0 65 C4
Beaumont Ave *continued*
West Kensington W14 113 B1 254 C2
Beaumont Bldgs WC2 240 B1
Beaumont Cl KT2 176 C3
Beaumont Cres W14 113 B1 254 C1
Beaumont Ct
10 Acton Green W4 111 A1
16 Hendon NW9 27 D1
Lower Clapton E5 74 B5
Marylebone W1 238 B4
7 Mile End E1 97 A4
6 Mitcham CR4 181 A1
Wembley HA0 65 C3
17 Wimbledon SW19 178 D3
Beaumont Dr
Ashford TW15 171 B5
New Malden KT4 200 B2
Beaumont Gdns NW3 69 C5
Beaumont Gr E1 96 D3
Beaumont Ho
12 Leyton E10 53 D2
1 Streatham SW2 160 A3
West Kensington W14 254 D3
Wimbledon SW19 157 C1
Beaumont Lo E8 74 A2
Beaumont Pl
Barnet EN5 1 B4
Fitzrovia NW1, WC1, W1 93 C3 239 B6
Isleworth TW7 152 D6
Beaumont SW15 157 A6
Beaumont Rd
Leyton E10 53 D2
Newham E13 99 B4
Orpington BR5 211 B3
Putney SW15, SW19 157 A4
South Acton W4 111 A3
South Norwood SE19 183 A4
Beaumont Rise N19 49 D1
Beaumont Sch The E10 53 D1
Beaumont Sq E1 96 D2
Beaumont St W1 238 B4
Beaumont Terr 1 SE13 164 C4
Beaumont Wlk NW3 70 D1
Beauvais Terr UB5 84 D4
Beauvale 6 NW1 71 A1
Beauval Rd SE22 161 D5
Beaverbank Rd SE9 167 B3
Beaver Cl
Hampton TW12 173 D2
9 Penge SE20 184 A3
West Barnes SM4 200 C2
Beaver Ctr The RM8 59 A2
Beaver Gr UB5 85 A4
Beavers Com Prim Sch TW4 128 C2
Beavers Cres TW4 128 D1
Beavers La TW4 128 C2
Beavers Lo DA14 189 D5
Beaverwood Rd BR7 189 C4
Beaverwood Sch for Girls BR7 189 C4
Beavis Ho N16 73 C5
Beavor La W6 112 A1
Bebbington Rd SE18 123 C2
Beblets Cl 4 BR6 227 D3
Beccles Dr IG11 79 D2
Beccles St E14 119 B6
Bec Cl HA4 62 D5
Bechervaise Ct 2 E10 53 D1
Beck Cl SE13 141 D4
Beck Ct BR3 206 D6
BECKENHAM 185 C1
Beckenham Bsns Ctr BR3 185 A4
Beckenham Ct BR3 185 C2
Beckenham Gdns N9 17 C1
Beckenham Gr BR2 186 B1
Beckenham Hill Rd BR3, SE6 186 A5
Beckenham Hill Sta SE6 186 A5
Beckenham Hospl BR3 185 B1
Beckenham Junction Sta BR3 185 C2
Beckenham La BR1, BR2 186 D1
Beckenham Place Pk BR3 185 D3
Beckenham Rd BR3 185 A2
Beckenham Rd Sta BR3 185 A2
Beckenham Rd BR3, BR4 208 A2
Beckers The N16 74 A4
Becket Ave E6 100 C4
Becket Cl
Croydon SE25 206 A3
2 Merton SW19 179 D2
Becket Fold 10 HA1 42 D4
Becket Ho SE1 252 C1
Becket Rd N18 34 C6
Becket St SE1 262 C6
Beckett Cl
Abbey Wood DA17 125 B3
Streatham SW16 159 D2
Willesden NW10 67 C2
Beckett Ho
28 London SW9 138 A3
15 Stepney E1 96 C2
Becketts Cl
Feltham TW14 150 B5
Orpington BR6 227 D5
Becketts Pl KT1 175 D2
Beckett Wlk BR3 185 A4
Beckfoot NW1 232 B3
Beckford Cl W14 254 D3
Beckford Dr BR5 211 B2
Beckford Ho 18 N16 73 C3
Beckford Prim Sch NW6 69 B3
Beckford Rd CR0 205 D3
Beckham Ho SE11 260 D3
Beck Ho
4 Edmonton N18 34 A5
Stoke Newington N16 73 C5
Beckington 18 NW5 71 A2
Beck La BR3 206 D6
Beckley Ho E3 97 B3
Becklow Gdns
Chiswick W4 111 D4
1 Shepherd's Bush W12 112 A4
Becklow Mews 7 W12 112 A4
Becklow Rd W12 112 A4
Beckmead Sch BR3 207 C1
Beck Rd E8 96 B6
Beck River Pk 10 BR3 185 C2
Becks Rd DA14 168 A1
BECKTON 100 D2
Beckton Alps E6 100 C3
Beckton Alps Ski Ctr E6 100 C3
Beckton Park Sta E6 122 B6
Beckton Rd E16 98 D2
Beckton Ret Pk E6 100 C2
Beckton Sta E6 100 C2
Beckton Triangle Ret Pk E6 100 D3
Beck Way BR3 207 B6
Beckway Rd SW16 181 D1
Beckway St SE17 117 C2 263 A3
Beckwith Ho 22 E2 96 B5
Beckwith Rd SE24 161 B6
Beclands Rd SW17 181 A4
Becmead Ave
Harrow HA3 43 B4
Streatham SW16 181 D6
Becondale Rd SE19 183 C5
BECONTREE 81 A4
Becontree Ave RM8 80 C5
Becontree Day Hospl RM8 81 A6
Becontree Prim Sch RM8 80 B5
Becontree Sta RM9 80 D2
Bective Pl SW15 135 B1
Bective Rd
Forest Gate E7 77 A4
Putney SW15 135 B1
Becton Pl DA8 147 D5
Bedale Rd EN2 5 A5
Bedale St SE1 252 C3
Beddan Ct HA8 26 C4
BEDDINGTON 220 A6
BEDDINGTON CORNER 203 A2
Beddington Cross CR0 204 A2
Beddington Farm Rd CR0 204 A1
Beddington Gdns SM5, SM6 219 A2
Beddington Gn BR5 189 D2
Beddington Gr SM6 219 D3
Beddington Inf Sch SM6 219 C4
Beddington Lane Sta CR0 203 C3
Beddington La
Wallington CR0 203 D2
Wallington CR0 220 A6
Beddington Manor SM2 218 B2
Beddington Park Cotts SM6 219 D5
Beddington Park Prim Sch CR0 219 D5
Beddington Rd
Ilford IG3 57 D2
St Paul's Cray BR5 189 D2
Beddington Terr CR0 204 B2
Beddington Trad Est CR0 204 A1
Bede Cl HA5 22 D2
Bedefield WC1 233 B1
Bede Ho
London SE14 141 B4
5 Putney SW15 156 D5
Bedelsford Sch KT1 198 A6
Bedens Rd DA14 191 A5
Bede Rd RM6 58 C3
Bedevere Rd N9 18 A1
Bedfont Cl
East Bedfont TW14 149 A5
Mitcham CR4 181 A1
Bedfont Green Cl TW14 149 A3
Bedfont Ind Pk TW15 149 B1
Bedfont Ind Pk N TW15 149 A1
Bedfont Jun & Inf Schs TW14 149 C5
Bedfont La TW14, TW13 149 D4
Bedfont Lakes Ctry Pk TW14 149 A2
Bedfont Rd
East Bedfont TW13, TW14 149 B2
Stanwell TW19 148 B5
Bedford Ave
Barnet EN5 13 B6
Bloomsbury WC1 93 D2 239 D3
Hayes UB4 84 B1
Bedfordbury WC2 116 A6 250 A5
Bedford Cl
Chiswick W4 133 D6
Muswell Hill N10 31 A3
Bedford Cnr 3 W4 111 C2
Bedford Court Mans WC1 239 D3
Bedford Ct
6 Richmond TW9 132 B1
South Norwood SE19 183 D2
St James WC2 250 A5
Wembley HA0 65 D4
Bedford Gardens Ho W8 245 B3
Bedford Gdns W8 113 C5 245 B3
Bedford Hill SW12 159 B2
Bedford Ho
2 Acton W4 111 C2
Edgware HA8 26 B3
7 Stockwell SW4 138 A1
Bedford Mews SE6 163 D2
BEDFORD PARK 111 C3
Bedford Park Cnr 5 W4 111 C2
Bedford Park Mans 4 W4 111 B2
Bedford Pas SW6 264 B4
Bedford Pk CR0 205 A1
Bedford Pl
Bloomsbury WC1 94 A2 240 A4
Croydon CR0 205 B1
Bedford Rd
Acton W4 111 C3
Barking E6 100 C6
Crouch End N8 49 D3
Ealing W13 109 B6
East Finchley N2 48 C6
Edgware NW7 11 C1
Edmonton N9 18 B4
Harrow HA1 42 A3
Ilford IG1 78 D5
North Cheam KT4 216 C6
Ruislip HA4 61 D4
Sidcup DA15 167 C1
South Tottenham N15 51 C5
Stockwell SW2, SW4 138 A1
Twickenham TW2 152 B1
Walthamstow E17 53 C6
Woodford E18 37 A1
Wood Green N22 32 A1
Bedford Row WC1 94 B2 240 D3
Bedford Sq WC1 93 D2 239 D3
Bedford St WC2 116 A6 250 B5
Bedford Terr SM2 218 A
Bedford Villas 3 SM5 218 D
Bedford Way WC1 93 D3 239 D
Bedgebury Gdns SW19 157 A
Bedgebury Rd SE9 143 D
Bedivere Rd BR1 165 A
Bedlam Mews SE11 261 A
Bedlow Cl NW8 236 D
Bedlow Way CR0 220 B
Bedonwell Inf Sch DA17 147 A
Bedonwell Jun Sch DA17 147 A
Bedonwell Rd
Bexley DA17 147 A
Erith DA7 147 C
Bedser Cl
Kennington SE11 270 D
South Norwood CR7 205 A
Bedser Ct 7 SW4 138 A
Bedser Dr UB6 64 B
Bedster Gdns KT8 195 D
Bedwardine Rd SE19 183 C
Bedwell Ct 4 RM6 58 D
Bedwell Gdns UB3 105 C
Bedwell Ho 18 SW9 138 C
Bedwell Rd
Belvedere DA17 125 C
Tottenham N17 33 C
Beeby Rd E16 99 B
Beech Ave Acton W3 111 C
Brentford TW8 131 B
4 Chigwell IG9 21 B
East Barnet N20 14 C
Ruislip HA4 40 B
Sidcup DA15 168 A
Beech Cl
Ashford TW15 171 B
Carshalton SM5 218 D
Deptford SE8 141 B
Enfield N9 18 B
Putney SW15 156 A
Sunbury TW16 172 D
West Drayton UB7 104 C
Wimbledon SW19 178 C
Beech Copse
Bickley BR1 188 B
South Croydon CR2 221 C
Beechcroft Ave
Golders Green NW11 47 B
Harrow HA2 41 C
Kingston u T KT1, KT3 177 A
Beechcroft BR7 188 C
Beechcroft Cl
Heston TW5 129 A
Orpington BR6 227 B
Streatham SW16 182 B
Beechcroft Ct
3 Golders Green NW11 47 B
Greenwich SE3 143 A
Beech Croft Ct N5 72 D
Beechcroft Ct 8 N12 29 D
Beechcroft Gdns HA9 66 B
Beechcroft Ho W5 88 A
Beechcroft 3 KT2 176 D
Beechcroft Lo 6 SM2 218 A1
Beechcroft Mans SW16 182 B
Beechcroft Rd
Chessington KT9 214 B
Mortlake SW14 133 A2
Orpington BR6 227 B4
Upper Tooting SW17 158 C2
Woodford E18 37 B1
Beechcroft Way N19 49 D1
Beech Ct
Beckenham BR3 185 B3
3 Buckhurst Hill IG9 21 D2
Child's Hill NW2 69 B6
Hayes UB3 105 D5
6 Ilford E12 78 C5
Marylebone W1 237 C2
Northolt UB5 85 A6
43 Notting Hill W2 91 C2
7 Rotherhithe SE16 119 A5
Surbiton KT6 198 A2
Teddington TW11 175 C4
Walthamstow E17 54 B6
4 West Norwood SW16 182 C5
Beechdale Rd SW2 160 B5
Beechdale N21 16 B2
Beech Dell BR2, BR6 226 B4
Beechdene 4 SE15 140 B4
Beech Dr N2 48 D6

echen Cliff Way
W7 ... 130 D3
echengrove HA5 ... 41 B6
echen Pl SE23 ... 162 C2
eches Ave SM5 ... 218 C1
eches Cl SE20 ... 184 C2
eches Ct BR1 ... 187 A4
eches Prim Ctr The
E2 ... 124 C3
eches Rd
heam SM3 ... 201 A1
pper Tooting
SW17 ... 158 D1
eches The
aling W7 ... 108 D4
ast Barnet N20 ... 14 C2
ast Ham E12 ... 78 B1
lounslow TW3 ... 129 D4
Aitcham CR4 ... 202 C4
1 Upper Holloway
N19 ... 50 A1
echey Ho 30 E1 ... 118 B5
ech Farm Cotts
G8 ... 36 B3
echfield Cotts 5
R1 ... 187 C1
echfield Ct 7
R2 ... 221 A4
echfield Rd
Bromley BR1 ... 187 C1
orest Hill SE6 ... 163 B3
Harringay N4 ... 51 A3
ech Gdns
Dagenham RM10 ... 81 D1
Ealing W5 ... 110 A3
ech Gr
Kingston u T KT3 ... 199 B6
Mitcham CR4 ... 203 D5
ech Hall Cres E4 ... 36 B3
ech Hall Rd E4 ... 36 B3
ech Hill Ave EN4 ... 2 B4
ech Hill EN4 ... 2 C5
echhill Rd SE9 ... 166 C6
ech Ho
Chingford E4 ... 35 C6
Hayes UB4 ... 84 D2
Heston TW5 ... 129 A5
6 Maitland Pk NW3 ... 70 D2
New Addington CR0 . 223 D2
2 Rotherhithe
SE16 ... 118 C4
7 Sidcup DA15 ... 168 A1
5 Stoke Newington
N16 ... 73 B6
ech House Rd
CR0 ... 221 B5
ech Ho 12 SM6 ... 219 C2
ech La IG9 ... 21 B2
ech Lawns N12 ... 30 B5
echmont Cl BR1 ... 186 C5
echmore Gdns
SM3 ... 216 D6
echmore Rd
SW11 ... 136 D4 267 D1
echmount Ave W7 ... 86 C2
echolme Ave
CR4 ... 181 B2
echolme Est E5 ... 74 B5
echolme 15 N12 ... 29 D6
echolme Prim Sch
CR4 ... 181 B2
ech Rd
Bowes Pk N11 ... 32 A4
East Bedfont TW14 ... 149 C4
Thornton Heath
SW16 ... 204 B6
echrow KT2 ... 176 A6
ech St EC2 ... 95 A2 242 B4
ech Tree Cl
Islington N1 ... 72 C1
Stanmore HA7 ... 25 C5
ech Tree Glade
E4 ... 20 D3
ech Tree Pl SM1 ... 217 D3
echvale Cl N12 ... 30 C5
echway DA5 ... 168 D5
ech Way
Twickenham TW2 ... 151 C1
Willesden NW10 ... 67 B1
ech Wlk NW7 ... 27 C4
echwood Ave
Ashford TW16 ... 172 A4
East Finchley N3 ... 47 C6
Greenford UB6 ... 85 D4
Harrow HA2 ... 63 D5
Hayes UB3 ... 105 B6
Hillingdon UB8 ... 82 C1
Orpington BR6 ... 227 C2
Richmond TW9 ... 132 C4
Ruislip HA4 ... 61 D6
Thornton Heath CR7 ... 204 D5
echwood Circ
HA2 ... 63 D5
echwood Cl
Edgware NW7 ... 27 C5
Fortis Green N2 ... 48 D5
Surbiton KT6 ... 197 D2

Beechwood Cres
DA7 ... 147 A2
Beechwood Ct
Ashford TW16 ... 172 A5
Carshalton SM5 ... 218 D4
Cheam SM1 ... 217 C3
Chiswick W4 ... 133 B6
Stamford Hill N16 ... 51 C2
Sutton SM2 ... 218 B2
Beechwood Dr
Keston BR2 ... 225 D4
Woodford IG8 ... 36 D5
Beechwood Gdns
Ealing NW10 ... 88 B4
Harrow HA2 ... 63 D5
Ilford IG5 ... 56 C5
Beechwood Gr W3 ... 111 C6
Beechwood Hall N3 ... 47 B6
Beechwood Ho 23
E2 ... 96 A5
Beechwood Mews 2
N9 ... 18 A2
Beechwood Pk E18 ... 55 A6
Beechwood Rd
Dalston E8 ... 73 D2
London N8 ... 50 A5
South Croydon CR2 ... 221 C1
Beechwood Rise
BR7 ... 188 D6
Beechwoods Ct 5
SE19 ... 183 D5
Beechworth Cl NW3 ... 69 C6
Beecroft La SE4 ... 163 A6
Beecroft Mews SE4 ... 163 A6
Beecroft Rd SE4 ... 163 A6
Beehive Cl Dalston E8 ... 73 D1
Elstree WD6 ... 9 D5
Hillingdon UB10 ... 60 B1
Beehive Ct IG1 ... 56 B3
Beehive La IG1 ... 56 B3
Beehive Pl SW9 ... 138 C2
Beehive Prep Sch
IG4 ... 56 B4
Beeken Dene BR6 ... 227 A4
Beeleigh Rd SM4 ... 201 D5
Beemans Row 1
SW18 ... 158 A2
Beeston Cl
5 Dalston E8 ... 74 A3
South Oxhey WD19 ... 22 D6
Beeston Pl SW1 ... 258 D6
Beeston Rd EN4 ... 14 B5
Beeston's Ho SE15 ... 140 B2
Beeston Way TW14 ... 150 C5
Beethoven Rd WD6 ... 9 D5
Beethoven St W10 ... 91 A4
Beeton Cl HA5 ... 23 C3
Begbie Ho SW9 ... 138 B3
Begbie Rd SE3 ... 143 C4
Beggars Hill KT17 ... 215 D2
Beggar's Roost La
SM1 ... 217 C2
Begonia Cl E6 ... 100 B3
Begonia Pl 1 TW12 ... 173 C4
Begonia Wlk W12 ... 89 D1
Beira St SW12 ... 159 B4
Beis Chinuch Lebonos
Girls Sch N4 ... 51 A2
Beis Rochel d'Satmar
Girls Sch N16 ... 51 C2
Beis Soroh Schneirer
(Sch) NW4 ... 46 A3
Beis Yaakov Prim Sch
NW9 ... 45 B6
Bekesbourne St 17
E14 ... 97 A1
Belcroft Cl BR1 ... 186 D3
Beldanes Lo NW10 ... 68 A1
Beldham Gdns KT8 ... 195 D6
Belenoyd Ct SW16 ... 160 B1
Belfairs Dr RM6 ... 58 C2
Belfairs Gn WD19 ... 22 D5
Belfast Rd
Croydon SE25 ... 206 B5
Stoke Newington N16 ... 73 D6
Belfield Rd KT19 ... 215 C1
Belfont Wlk N7 ... 72 A4
Belford Gr SE18 ... 122 C2
Belford Ho 7 E8 ... 95 D6
Belfort Rd SE15 ... 140 C3
Belfry Cl 33 SE16 ... 118 B1
Belgrade Ho N16 ... 73 C4
Belgrade Rd
Hampton TW12 ... 173 D2
Stoke Newington N16 ... 73 C4
Belgrave Cl
1 Acton W3 ... 111 A4
Burnt Oak NW7 ... 27 B5
Southgate N14 ... 15 C6
Belgrave Cres
TW16 ... 172 B2
Belgrave Ct
8 Acton Green
W4 ... 111 A1
Charlton SE3 ... 143 C5
22 Limehouse E14 ... 119 B6
Newham E13 ... 99 C3

Belgrave Ct *continued*
Nine Elms SW8 ... 269 A3
Belgrave Gdns
Kilburn NW8 ... 91 D6
Southgate N14 ... 3 D1
1 Stanmore HA7 ... 25 C5
St John's Wood NW8 229 A5
Belgrave Ho SW9 ... 138 C5
Belgrave Hts E11 ... 55 A1
Belgrave Mans NW8 229 A5
Belgrave Market IG1 ... 78 C6
Belgrave Mews N
SW1 ... 248 A1
Belgrave Mews S
SW1 ... 115 A3 258 B6
Belgrave Mews W
SW1 ... 258 A6
Belgrave Pl
SW1 ... 115 A3 258 B5
Belgrave Rd
Barnes SW13 ... 133 D5
Hounslow TW4 ... 129 B2
Leyton E10 ... 54 A1
Mitcham CR4 ... 202 B6
Newham E13 ... 99 C3
Redbridge IG1 ... 56 B1
South Norwood
SE25 ... 205 D5
Sunbury TW16 ... 172 B2
Walthamstow E17 ... 53 C3
Wanstead E11 ... 55 A1
Westminster
SW1 ... 115 C2 259 A3
Belgrave Sq
SW1 ... 115 A3 258 A6
Belgrave St E1 ... 96 D1
Belgrave Terr IG8 ... 21 A1
Belgrave Wlk CR4 ... 202 B6
Belgrave Wlk Sta
CR4 ... 202 B5
Belgrave Yd SW1 ... 258 C5
BELGRAVIA ... 115 B2
Belgravia Cl EN5 ... 1 B2
Belgravia Ct SW1 ... 258 C5
Belgravia Gdns BR1 ... 186 C4
Belgravia Ho
11 London SW4 ... 159 D5
1 Teddington
TW11 ... 175 C3
Belgravia Lo N21 ... 16 D6
Belgravia Mews
KT1 ... 197 D5
Belgrove St WC1 ... 233 B2
Belham Wlk 13 SE5 ... 139 B4
Belinda Rd 8 SW9 ... 138 D2
Belitha Villas N1 ... 72 C1
Bel La TW13 ... 151 B1
Bellamy Cl
Edgware HA8 ... 11 A1
13 Millwall E14 ... 119 C4
Uxbridge UB10 ... 60 C5
West Kensington
SW5 ... 254 D1
Bellamy Ct HA7 ... 25 B2
Bellamy Dr HA7 ... 25 B2
Bellamy Ho
Harrow HA3 ... 44 A2
Heston TW5 ... 129 C6
Upper Tooting SW17 ... 180 B6
Bellamy Rd
Chingford E4 ... 35 D4
Enfield EN2 ... 5 B3
Bellamy's Ct 16
SE16 ... 118 D5
Bellamy St SW12 ... 159 B4
Bellasis Ave SW2 ... 160 A2
Bell Ave UB7 ... 104 B3
Bellclose Rd UB7 ... 104 A4
Bell Cl Pinner HA5 ... 40 C6
Ruislip HA4 ... 61 D5
Bell Ct Hendon NW4 ... 46 C5
Ladywell SE13 ... 163 C6
Tolworth KT5 ... 214 D6
Bell Dr SW18 ... 157 A4
Bellefields Rd SW9 ... 138 B2
Bellegrove Cl DA16 ... 145 D3
Bellegrove Par
DA16 ... 145 D2
Bellegrove Rd DA16 ... 145 D3
Bellenden Prim Sch
SE15 ... 140 A3
Bellenden Rd SE15 ... 139 D3
Bellenden Rd Ret Pk
SE15 ... 140 A4
Bellendon Road Bsns
Ctr SE15 ... 139 D3
Bellerbys Coll SE8 ... 141 C6
Bellermine Cl SE28 ... 123 D4
Belle Staines
Pleasaunce E4 ... 19 C2
Belleville Prim Sch
SW11 ... 158 D6
Belleville Rd SW11 ... 158 D6
Belle Vue Gdns
SW9 ... 138 A3
Belle Vue UB6 ... 86 B6
Belle Vue La WD23 ... 8 B3

Bellevue Mews N11 ... 31 A5
Bellevue Pk CR7 ... 205 A5
Bellevue Pl E1 ... 96 C3
Bellevue Rd
Barnes SW13 ... 134 A3
Bexley DA6 ... 169 B6
Belle Vue Rd E17 ... 36 B1
Bellevue Rd
Ealing W13 ... 87 B3
Friern Barnet N11 ... 31 A5
Belle Vue Rd 8 NW4 ... 46 C5
Bellevue Rd
Kingston u T KT1 ... 198 A6
Upper Tooting
SW17 ... 158 D3
Bellew St SW17 ... 158 A1
Bellfield Ave HA3 ... 24 B4
Bellfield CR0 ... 223 B1
Bell Flats 4 NW2 ... 68 A2
Bellflower Cl 2 E6 ... 100 A2
Bellflower Ct SE13 ... 141 D1
Bellgate Mews NW5 ... 71 B5
Bell Gn SE26 ... 185 B6
Bellgrave Lo 9 W4 ... 110 D1
BELL GREEN ... 163 B1
Bell Green La SE26 ... 185 B6
Bell Ho
6 Dagenham
RM10 ... 81 D2
Greenwich SE10 ... 142 A6
15 Streatham SW2 ... 160 C4
Wembley HA9 ... 66 A5
West Heath SE2 ... 124 D1
Bellina Mews NW5 ... 71 C4
Bell Ind Est 2 W4 ... 111 A2
BELLINGHAM ... 185 C5
Bellingham Ct IG11 ... 102 B4
Bellingham Gn SE6 ... 163 C1
Bellingham Rd SE6 ... 164 A1
Bellingham Sta SE6 ... 163 D1
Bellingham 10 N17 ... 34 B3
Bellingham Trad Est
SE6 ... 163 D2
Bell Inn Yd EC3 ... 242 D1
Bell La Enfield EN3 ... 6 D5
Hendon NW4 ... 46 D5
Bell Lane Prim Sch
NW4 ... 46 D5
Bell La E16 ... 121 A5
Bell Language Sch
W1 ... 93 C3 239 A5
Bell La
Spitalfields
E1 ... 95 D2 243 C3
Twickenham TW1 ... 153 A3
Wembley HA9 ... 65 D6
Bellmaker Ct 18 E3 ... 97 C2
Bell Mdw SE19 ... 183 C6
Bell Moor NW3 ... 70 A5
Bellmore Ct 5 CR0 ... 205 D1
Bello Cl SE24, SW2 ... 160 D3
Bellot Gdns 1 SE10 ... 120 C1
Bellot St SE10 ... 120 C1
Bell Rd
East Molesey KT8 ... 196 B4
Enfield EN1 ... 5 B4
Hounslow TW3 ... 129 D1
Bellring Cl DA17 ... 147 C6
Bell's Coll IG3 ... 58 A1
Bells Hill EN5 ... 12 D6
Bell St
Kidbrooke SE18 ... 144 A4
Paddington
NW1 ... 92 C2 237 A4
Bell The E17 ... 53 C6
Bell View BR3 ... 185 B3
Bellview Ct TW3 ... 129 D1
Bell View Manor
HA4 ... 39 C2
Bell Water Gate
SE18 ... 122 C3
Bell Wharf La EC4 ... 252 B6
Bellwood Rd SE15 ... 140 D1
Bell Yard Mews SE1 ... 253 B1
Bell Yd WC2 ... 94 C1 241 A1
BELMONT ... 25 B2
Belmont Ave
Bowes Pk N13 ... 32 B5
Cockfosters EN4 ... 14 D6
Edmonton N9 ... 18 A3
Falconwood DA16 ... 145 C2
Southall UB2 ... 107 A3
Tottenham N17 ... 51 A6
Wembley HA0 ... 88 B6
West Barnes KT3 ... 200 A5
Belmont Circ HA3 ... 25 B2
Belmont Cl
Chingford E4 ... 36 B5
Clapham SW4 ... 137 C2
Cockfosters EN4 ... 2 D1
Totteridge N20 ... 13 D3
Uxbridge UB8 ... 60 A2
Woodford IG8 ... 37 B6
Belmont Ct
Highbury N5 ... 73 A4
6 Stamford Hill N16 ... 51 C1

Belmont Ct *continued*
Temple Fortune
NW11 ... 47 B4
1 Whetstone N20 ... 14 A1
Wood Green N11 ... 31 D3
Belmont Fst & Mid Schs
HA3 ... 24 D1
Belmont Gr
Chiswick W4 ... 111 B2
Lewisham SE13 ... 142 B2
Belmont Hall Ct
SE13 ... 142 B2
Belmont Hill SE13 ... 142 B2
Belmont Jun & Inf Schs
N22 ... 51 A6
Belmont La
Chislehurst BR7 ... 189 A5
Stanmore HA7 ... 25 C3
Belmont Lo
Harrow HA3 ... 24 B3
Stanmore HA7 ... 25 C6
Belmont Mews
SW19 ... 156 D2
Belmont Mill Hill Jun
Sch NW7 ... 12 A1
Belmont Par BR7 ... 189 A5
Belmont Park Cl
SE13 ... 142 C1
Belmont Park Rd
E10 ... 53 D3
Belmont Par 2
NW11 ... 47 B4
Belmont Pk SE13 ... 142 C1
Belmont Pk Sch E10 ... 54 A3
Belmont Prim Sch
Chiswick W4 ... 111 B2
Erith DA8 ... 147 C5
Belmont Rd
Beckenham BR3 ... 185 B1
Chislehurst BR7 ... 188 D5
Clapham SW4 ... 137 C2
Croydon SE25 ... 206 B4
Erith DA8 ... 147 D4
Harrow HA3 ... 43 A6
Ilford IG1 ... 79 A5
London W4 ... 111 B2
Twickenham TW2 ... 152 B2
Uxbridge UB8 ... 60 A2
Wallington SM6 ... 219 C3
West Green N15, N17 ... 51 A5
Belmont Rise SM1,
SM2 ... 217 B1
Belmont St NW1 ... 71 A1
Belmont Terr W4 ... 111 B2
Belmor WD6 ... 10 C5
Belmore Ave UB4 ... 84 A1
Belmore Ho N7 ... 71 D3
Belmore La N7 ... 71 D3
Belmore Prim Sch
UB4 ... 84 B4
Belmore St
SW8 ... 137 D4 269 C2
Beloe Cl SW15 ... 134 A1
Belper Ct 11 E5 ... 74 D4
Belsham St E9 ... 74 C2
Belsize Ave
Bowes Pk N13 ... 32 B4
Ealing W13 ... 109 B3
Maitland Pk NW3 ... 70 C3
Belsize Court Garages
1 NW3 ... 70 B3
Belsize Cres NW3 ... 70 B2
Belsize Ct NW3 ... 70 B3
Belsize Gdns SM1 ... 217 D4
Belsize Gr NW3 ... 70 C2
Belsize La NW3 ... 70 B3
Belsize Mews NW3 ... 70 B2
Belsize Park Gdns
NW3 ... 70 C2
Belsize Park Mews 1
NW3 ... 70 B2
Belsize Park Sta
NW3 ... 70 C3
Belsize Pk NW3 ... 70 B2
Belsize Pl NW3 ... 70 B3
Belsize Rd
Harrow HA3 ... 24 B3
Kilburn NW6 ... 91 D6
Belsize Sq NW3 ... 70 B2
Belsize Terr NW3 ... 70 B2
Belson Rd SE18 ... 122 B2
Beltane Dr SW19 ... 156 D1
Belthorn Cres
SW12 ... 159 C4
Belton Rd Leyton E11 ... 76 C4
Sidcup DA14 ... 190 A6
Tottenham N17 ... 51 C6
Upton E7 ... 77 B1
Willesden NW2 ... 68 A2
Belton Way E3 ... 97 C2
Beltran Rd SW6 ... 135 D3
BELVEDERE ... 125 D2
Belvedere Ave
SW19 ... 179 A5
Belvedere Bldgs
SE1 ... 251 D1
Belvedere Cl TW11 ... 174 C5

Belvedere Ct
Abbey Wood
DA17 ... 125 B3
Brondesbury NW2 ... 68 D2
7 Clapham Pk SW4 ... 159 D5
East Finchley N2 ... 48 B4
8 Kingston u T KT2 ... 176 C3
Putney SW15 ... 134 C1
33 Shoreditch N1 ... 95 C6
Southall UB1 ... 107 D6
Southgate N21 ... 16 C4
Belvedere Dr SW19 ... 179 A5
Belvedere Gdns
KT8 ... 195 C4
Belvedere Gr SW19 ... 179 A5
Belvedere Ho TW14 ... 150 A3
Belvedere Htss NW8 ... 237 A6
Belvedere Jun & Inf Sch
DA17 ... 125 D3
Belvedere Mews
Greenwich SE3 ... 143 B5
Nunhead SE15 ... 140 C2
Belvedere Pl
Brixton SW2 ... 138 B1
Lambeth SE1 ... 251 D1
Belvedere Rd
Bexleyheath DA7 ... 147 B3
Erith SE2, SE28 ... 124 D5
Hanwell W7 ... 108 D3
Lambeth
SE1 ... 116 B5 250 D3
Penge SE19 ... 183 D3
Walthamstow E10 ... 53 A1
Belvedere Sq SW19 ... 179 A5
Belvedere Sta DA17 ... 125 D3
Belvedere Strand
NW9 ... 27 D1
Belvedere The
SW10 ... 266 B1
Belvedere Way HA3 ... 44 A3
Belvoir Cl SE9 ... 166 A1
Belvoir Ct HA3 ... 43 A3
Belvoir Lo SE22 ... 162 A4
Belvoir Rd SE22 ... 162 A4
Belvue Bsns Ctr UB5 ... 63 D1
Belvue Cl UB5 ... 63 C1
Belvue Rd UB5 ... 63 C1
Belvue Sch UB5 ... 85 C6
Bembridge Cl NW6 ... 69 A1
Bembridge Gdns
HA4 ... 61 B6
Bembridge Ho
9 Deptford SE8 ... 119 B2
Wandsworth SW18 ... 157 D5
Bemersyde Point 6
E13 ... 99 B4
Bemerton St
N1 ... 94 B6 233 C6
Bemish Rd SW15 ... 134 D2
Bempton Dr HA4 ... 62 B5
Bemsted Rd E17 ... 53 B6
Benabo Ct 6 E8 ... 74 A3
Benares Rd SE18,
SE2 ... 123 D2
Benbow Ct W6 ... 112 B3
Benbow Ho 12 SE8 ... 141 C6
Benbow Rd W6 ... 112 B3
Benbow St SE8 ... 141 C6
Benbury Cl BR1 ... 186 A5
Bence Ho 18 SE8 ... 119 A2
Bench Field CR2 ... 221 D3
Bencroft Rd SW16 ... 181 C3
Bencurtis Pk BR4 ... 224 B6
Bendall Mews NW1 ... 237 B4
Bendemeer Rd
SW15 ... 134 D2
Benden Ho SE13 ... 164 A6
Bendish Point SE28 ... 123 A4
Bendish Rd E6 ... 78 A1
Bendmore Ave SE2 ... 124 A2
Bendon Valley
SW18 ... 157 D4
Benedict Cl
2 Erith DA17 ... 125 A3
Orpington BR6 ... 227 C5
Benedict Ct
Dagenham RM9 ... 59 B3
Pinner HA5 ... 23 B2
Benedict Dr TW14 ... 149 B4
Benedict House Prep
Sch DA15 ... 168 A1
Benedict Prim Sch
CR4 ... 202 B6
Benedict Rd
London SW9 ... 138 B2
Mitcham CR4 ... 202 B6
Benedict Way N2 ... 48 A6
Benedict Wharf
CR4 ... 202 C6
Benenden Gn BR2 ... 209 A4
Benenden Ho SE17 ... 263 B2
Benett Gdns SW16 ... 182 A1
Beney Ct BR3 ... 185 C1
Ben Ezra Ct SE17 ... 262 B3

Benfleet Cl SM1 218 A5
Benfleet Ct 6 E8 95 D6
Benfleet Way N11 15 A2
Bengal Ct EC3 242 D1
Bengal Ho E1 96 D2
Bengal Rd IG1 78 D5
Bengarth Dr HA3 24 B1
Bengarth Rd UB5 85 A6
Bengeo Gdns RM6 58 C3
Bengeworth Rd
Camberwell SE5 139 A2
Harrow HA1 65 A5
Ben Hale Cl HA7 25 B5
Benham Cl
1 Battersea SW11 136 B2
Chessington KT9 213 C2
Benham Gdns TW3, TW4 151 B6
Benham Ho SW10 265 D4
Benham Rd W7 86 C2
Benham's Pl 11 NW3 70 A4
Benhill Ave SM1 218 A4
Benhill Rd
London SE5 139 B4
Sutton SM1 218 B4
Benhill Wood Rd SM1 218 A4
BENHILTON 218 A5
Benhilton Ct SM1 218 A5
Benhilton Gdns SM1 217 D5
Benhurst Ct
Ealing W5 110 A6
12 Penge SE20 184 B2
West Norwood SW16 182 C5
Benhurst La SW16 182 C5
Benington Ct N4 73 A6
Benin St SE13 164 B4
Benjafield Cl N18 34 B6
Benjamin Cl E8 96 A6
Benjamin Ct
4 Ealing W7 108 C5
4 Erith DA17 147 B6
Littleton TW15 171 A3
Benjamin Ho 12 W3 110 D5
Benjamin Mews SW12 159 C4
Benjamin St EC1 241 C4
Ben Jonson Ct 30 N1 95 C5
Ben Jonson Prim Sch E1 97 A3
Ben Jonson Rd E1 97 A2
Benledi Rd E14 98 B1
Bennelong Cl W12 90 B1
Bennerley Rd SW11 158 D6
Bennet Cl KT1 175 C2
Bennets Ct SW19 180 A2
Bennetsfield Rd UB11 104 D5
Bennet's Hill EC4 251 D6
Bennets Lo EN2 5 A2
Bennett Cl
Twickenham TW4 151 A6
Welling DA16 146 A3
Bennett Ct
Hampstead NW6 69 D2
Lower Holloway N7 72 B5
7 South Acton W3 110 D4
Bennett Gr SE13 141 D4
Bennett Ho
2 Streatham SW4 159 D4
Westminster SW1 259 D4
Bennett Pk SE3 142 D2
Bennett Rd
Brixton SW9 138 C3
Dagenham RM6 59 A2
Newham E13 99 C3
Bennetts Ave
Croydon CR0 223 A6
Greenford UB6 86 C6
Bennett's Castle La RM8 80 D5
Bennetts Cl
Mitcham CR4, SW16 181 B2
Tottenham N17 33 D4
Bennetts Copse BR7 188 A4
Bennett St
Chiswick W4 111 C1
St James SW1 249 A4
Bennetts Way CR0 223 B6
Bennett's Yd SW1 259 D5
Benn Ho
Bethnal Green E2 96 A4
7 Greenwich SE7 121 C1
Benningholme Rd HA8 27 C4
Bennington Rd
Chingford IG8 36 C3
Bennington Rd *continued*
Tottenham N17 33 C2
Benn St E9 75 A2
Benns Wlk 8 TW9 132 A1
Bensbury Cl SW15 156 C4
Bensham Cl CR7 205 A5
Bensham Gr CR7 183 A1
Bensham La CR0, CR7 204 D3
Bensham Manor Rd CR7 205 A5
Bensham Manor Sch CR7 205 A4
Bensington Ct TW14 149 B5
Bensley Cl 7 N11 30 D5
Ben Smith Way 21 SE16 118 A3
Benson Ave E13, E6 99 D5
Benson Cl
Hillingdon UB8 82 A2
Hounslow TW3 129 C1
Benson Ct
Holdbrook EN3 7 C5
South Lambeth SW8 270 A2
1 Tufnell Pk N19 71 C4
Benson Ho
Lambeth SE1 251 B3
1 Richmond TW10 153 C1
Shoreditch E2 243 C6
Benson Prim sch CR0 223 A5
Benson Quay E1 118 C6
Benson Rd
Croydon CR0 220 C5
Forest Hill SE23 162 C3
Bentall Sh Ctr The 10 KT1 176 A1
Bentfield Gdns SE9 165 D1
Benthal Ct N16 74 A5
Benthal Prim Sch N16 74 A5
Benthal Rd N16 74 A5
Bentham Ct 11 N1 73 A1
Bentham Ho SE1 262 C6
Bentham Rd
Homerton E9 74 D2
Woolwich SE28 124 B5
Bentham Wlk NW10 67 A3
Ben Tillet Cl E16 122 B5
Ben Tillet Ho N15 50 D6
Bentinck Cl NW8 230 B3
Bentinck Ho
4 Richmond TW10 153 C1
4 Shepherd's Bush W12 112 B6
Bentinck Mans W1 238 B2
Bentinck Mews W1 238 B2
Bentinck Rd UB7 104 A5
Bentinck St W1 93 A1 238 B2
Bentley Cl SW19 157 C1
Bentley Ct SE13 142 A1
Bentley Dr IG2 57 A3
Bentley Ho
6 Bow E3 97 C3
4 Camberwell SE5 139 C4
Bentley Lo WD23 8 C2
Bentley Mews EN1 17 B5
Bentley Rd N1 73 C2
Bentley Way
Stanmore HA7 25 A5
Woodford IG8 21 A1
Bentley Wood High Sch HA7 24 D5
Benton Rd
Ilford IG1, IG2 57 B1
South Oxhey WD19 22 D5
Benton's La SE27 183 A6
Benton's Rise SE27 183 B5
Bentry Cl RM8 81 A6
Bentry Rd RM8 81 B6
Bentworth Ct 1 E2 96 A3
Bentworth Prim Sch W12 90 B1
Bentworth Rd W12 90 B1
Benwell Ct TW16 172 A2
Benwell Rd N7 72 C3
Benwick Cl SE16 118 B2
Benwick Ct SE20 184 C2
Benwood Ct SM1 218 A5
Benworth St E3 97 B4
Benyon Ho EC1 234 B2
Benyon Rd N1 95 B6 235 D6
Benyon Wharf 31 E8 95 C6
Beormund Prim Sch SE1 117 B4 252 D1
Bequerel Ct SE10 120 D3
Berberis Ct IG1 78 D2
Berberis Ho 17 E3 97 C2
Berberis Wlk UB7 104 A2
Berber Pl 2 E14 119 C6
Berber Rd SW11 158 D6
Berberry Cl 5 HA8 27 A6
Bercta Rd SE9 167 A2
Berebinder Ho 21 E3 97 B5
Berengers Pl RM9 80 B2
Berenger Twr SW10 266 C4
Berenger Wlk SW10 266 C4
Berens Ct DA14 189 D6
Berens Rd NW10 90 D4
Berens Way BR5, BR7 211 D6
Beresford Ave
Ealing W7 86 C2
Friern Barnet N20 14 D2
Tolworth KT5 199 A2
Twickenham TW1 153 C5
Wembley HA0 88 C6
Beresford Ct
Homerton E9 75 A3
11 Twickenham TW1 153 C5
Beresford Dr
Bickley BR1 210 A6
Woodford IG8 37 C6
Beresford Gdns
Dagenham RM6 59 A4
Enfield EN1 5 C1
Hounslow TW4 151 B6
Beresford Ho
Dulwich SE21 161 C1
15 Stockwell SW4 138 A1
Beresford Lo N4 73 B3
Beresford Rd
Belmont SM2 217 B1
Canonbury N5 73 B3
Chingford E4 20 C3
East Finchley N2 48 C6
Harringay N8 50 D4
Harrow HA1 42 B4
Kingston u T KT2 176 B2
New Malden KT3 199 A5
Southall UB1 106 D5
Walthamstow E17 35 D2
Beresford Square Mkt SE18 122 D2
Beresford Sq 1 SE18 122 D2
Beresford St SE18 122 D3
Beresford Terr 3 N5 73 A3
Bere St E1 118 D6
Berestede Rd 4 W6 111 D1
Bergen Ho 1 SE5 139 A3
Bergenia Ho TW13 150 B3
Bergen Sq SE16 119 A3
Berger Cl BR5 211 C3
Berger Prim Sch E9 74 D2
Berger Rd E9 74 D2
Berghem Mews W14 112 D3
Bergholt Ave IG4 56 A4
Bergholt Cres N16 51 C2
Bergholt Mews 4 NW1 71 D1
Berglen Ct E14 119 A6
Berica Ct IG6 57 A6
Bering Sq E14 119 C1
Bering Wlk E16 99 D1
Berisford Mews SW18 158 A5
Berkeley Ave
Cranford TW4 128 A3
Erith DA16 146 D4
Northolt UB6 64 C2
Berkeley Cl
Borehamwood WD6 10 C6
Broom Hill BR5 211 C2
2 Kingston u T KT2 176 A3
Ruislip HA4 62 A5
Berkeley Cres EN4 14 B6
Berkeley Ct
Ealing W5 109 C6
Edgware HA8 26 D5
Finchley N3 29 D2
1 Golders Green NW11 47 B2
Marylebone NW1 237 D5
Southgate N14 15 C5
Wallington SM6 219 C4
Willesden NW10 67 C4
Berkeley Dr KT8 195 C6
Berkeley Gdns
Claygate KT10 213 A2
Kensington W8 245 B3
Southgate N21 17 B4
Walton-on-T KT12 193 D2
Berkeley Ho
17 Bow E3 97 C4
11 Brentford TW8 131 D6
8 Deptford SE8 119 B1
Berkeley Lo
Enfield EN2 4 C2
New Malden KT3 199 C5
Berkeley Mews
Marylebone W1 237 D1
Sunbury TW16 194 C6
Berkeley Pl SW19 178 D4
Berkeley Prim Sch TW5 128 D5
Berkeley Rd
Barnes SW13 134 A4
Crouch End N8 49 D3
Hillingdon UB10 61 A1
Manor Pk E12 78 A3
Queensbury NW9 44 C4
Stamford Hill N15 51 B3
Berkeley Sq W1 115 B6 248 D5
Berkeleys The SE25 206 A5
Berkeley St W1 115 B5 248 D4
Berkeley The NW11 47 D2
Berkeley Waye TW5 128 D5
Berkeley Wlk 1 N7 72 B6
Berkhampstead Rd DA17 125 C1
Berkhamsted Ave HA9 66 C2
Berkley Cl TW2 152 C1
Berkley Ct 8 TW1 153 A4
Berkley Gr NW1 71 A1
Berkley Rd NW1 70 D1
Berkshire Ct 1 W7 86 D3
Berkshire Gdns
Bowes Pk N13 32 C4
Upper Edmonton N18 34 B5
Berkshire Ho
Catford SE6 185 C6
St Giles WC2 240 A2
Berkshire Rd E9 75 B2
Berkshire Way CR4 204 A5
Bermans Way NW10 67 D4
BERMONDSEY 118 A4
Bermondsey Leather Mkt SE1 253 A1
Bermondsey Mkt* SE1 117 C3 263 B6
Bermondsey Sq SE1 263 B6
Bermondsey St SE1 117 C4 253 A1
Bermondsey Trad Est SE16 118 C1
Bermondsey Wall E SE16 118 B4
Bermondsey Wall W SE1, SE16 118 A4
Bermuda Ho HA1 64 B5
Bernal Cl SE28 124 D6
Bernard Angell Ho 4 SE10 142 B6
Bernard Ashley Dr SE7 121 B1
Bernard Ave W13 109 B3
Bernard Cassidy St 2 E16 98 D2
Bernard Gdns SW19 179 B5
Bernard Ho E1 243 C3
Bernard Rd
South Tottenham N15 51 D4
Wallington SM5, SM6 219 B4
Bernard Shaw Ct 5 NW1 71 C1
Bernard Shaw Ho 2 NW10 89 B6
Bernard St WC1 94 A3 240 B5
Bernays Cl HA7 25 C4
Bernay's Gr SW9 138 B1
Bernel Dr CR0 223 B5
Berne Rd CR7 205 A4
Berners Dr W13 109 A6
Berners Ho N1 234 A4
Bernersmede SE3 143 A2
Berners Mews W1 93 C2 239 B3
Berners Pl W1 239 B2
Berners Rd
Islington N1 234 C5
Wood Green N22 32 C1
Berners St W1 93 C1 239 B2
Berner Terr 27 E1 96 A1
Berney Ho BR3 207 A4
Berney Rd CR0 205 B2
Bernhard Baron Ho 23 E1 96 A1
Bernhardt Cres NW8 237 A6
Bernhart Cl HA8 27 A3
Bernie Grant Ho 40 E9 74 C1
Bernwell Rd E4 20 C1
Bernwood Ho 6 N4 51 B2
Berridge Gn HA8 26 C3
Berridge Mews NW6 69 C3
Berridge Rd SE19 183 C5
Berriman Rd N7 72 B5
Berrite Works UB7 104 C4
Berriton Rd HA2 41 B1
Berrybank Cl 4 E4 20 A2
Berry Cl
Dagenham RM10 81 C3
Southgate N21 16 D3
Berry Cotts 2 E14 97 A1
Berry Ct TW4 151 B6
Berrydale Rd UB4 85 A3
Berryfield Cl BR1 188 A1
Berry Field Cl 8 E17 53 D5
Berryfield Rd SE17 116 D1 261 D2
Berryhill Gdns SE9 144 D1
Berryhill SE9 144 D1
Berry Hill HA7 25 D6
Berry Ho
10 Battersea SW11 136 D3
25 Bethnal Green E1 96 B3
BERRYLANDS 198 C3
Berrylands Ct 16 SM2 217 D1
Berrylands Rd KT5 198 B3
Berrylands Sta KT5 198 D5
Berrylands
Surbiton KT5 198 C3
West Barnes SW20 200 C5
Berry La SE21 183 B6
Berryman Cl RM8 80 C5
Berryman's La SE26 184 D6
Berrymead Gdns W3 111 A4
Berrymede Inf Sch W3 110 D4
Berrymede Jun Sch W3 110 D4
Berrymede Rd W4 111 B3
Berry Pl EC1 234 D1
Berry St EC1 241 D5
Berry Way W5 110 A3
Bertal Rd SW17 180 B6
Bertha Hollamby Ct DA14 190 C5
Bertha James Ct BR2 209 B5
Bertha Neubergh Ho 1 SE5 139 A4
Berthan Gdns E17 54 B4
Berthon St SE8 141 C6
Bertie Rd
Penge SE26 184 D4
Willesden NW10 68 A2
Bertram Cotts SW19 179 C3
Bertram Rd Enfield EN1 6 A1
Hendon NW4 46 A3
Kingston u T KT2 176 C3
Bertram St N19 71 B6
Bertrand Ho 11 SW16 160 A1
Bertrand St SE13 141 D2
Bertrand Way SE28 124 C6
Bert Rd CR7 205 A4
Bert Reilly Ho 1 SE18 123 B1
Bertrum House Sch SW17 159 A2
Bert Way EN1 5 D1
Berwick Ave UB4 106 D6
Berwick Cl
Harrow HA7 24 D4
Twickenham TW2 151 C3
Berwick Cres DA15 167 C5
Berwick Ct 8 BR3 185 C2
Berwick Gdns SM1 218 A5
Berwick Ho 10 N2 30 B1
Berwick Rd
Newham E16 99 C1
Tottenham N22 32 D2
Welling DA16 146 B4
Berwick St W1 93 C1 239 B1
Berwyn Ave TW3 129 D4
Berwyn Ho 3 N16 51 D1
Berwyn Rd
Mortlake SW14, TW10 132 D1
Streatham SE24 160 D3
Beryl Ave E6 100 A2
Beryl Harding Ho 3 SW19 178 D3
Beryl Ho SE18 123 D1
Beryl Rd W6 112 D1
Berystede KT2 176 D3
Besant Cl NW2 69 A5
Besant Ct
Canonbury N1 73 B3
15 Thamesmead SE28 124 B6
Besant Ho NW8 229 A5
Besant Pl SE22 139 D1
Besant Rd NW2 69 A4
Besant Way NW10 67 A3
Besant Wlk N7 72 B6
Besford Ho 26 E2 96 A5
Besley St SW16 181 C4
Bessant Dr TW9 132 D4
Bessborough Gdns SW1 115 D1 259 D2
Bessborough Pl SW1 115 D1 259
Bessborough Rd
Harrow HA1 42
Roehampton SW15 156
Bessborough St SW1 115 D1 259
Bessborough Wks KT8 195
Bessemer Ct 7 NW1 71
Bessemer Grange Prim Sch SE5 139
Bessemer Park Ind Est 3 SE24 138
Bessemer Rd SE5 139
Bessie Lansbury Cl E6 100
Bessingby Rd HA4 62
Bessingham Wlk SE4 162
Besson St SE14 140
Bessy St E2 96
Bestwood St SE8 118
Beswick Mews 1 NW6 69
Betam Rd UB3 105
Beta Pl 20 SW4 138
Betchworth Cl SM1 218
Betchworth Ho 8 N7 71
Betchworth Rd IG3 79
Betham Rd UB6 86
Bethany Ct 8 DA6 147
Bethany Waye TW14 149
Bethecar Rd HA1 42
Bethel Cl NW4 46
Bethell Ave Ilford IG1 56
Newham E13, E16 98
Bethel Lo N11 31
Bethel Rd DA16 146
Bethersden Cl BR3 185
Bethersden Ho SE17 263
Bethesda Ct 5 SE20 184
Beth Jacob Gram Sch NW4 46
Bethlehem Ho 13 E14 119
Bethlem Royal Hospl BR3 207
BETHNAL GREEN 96
Bethnal Green Rd
Bethnal Green E2 96
Shoreditch E1, E2 95 D3 243
Bethnal Green Sta
Bethnal Green E1 96
Bethnal Green E2 96
Bethnal Green Tech Coll E2 95
Beths Gram Sch DA5 169
Bethune Ave N11 30
Bethune Rd
North Acton NW10 89
Stamford Hill N16 51
Bethwin Rd SE5 139
Betjeman Cl HA5 41
Betjeman Ct EN4 15
Betony Cl CR0 206
Betoyne Ave E4 36
Betsham Ho SE1 252
Betspath Ho 6 N11 31
Betstyle Circus N11 31
Betstyle Ho 2 N10 31
Betstyle Rd N11 31
Betterton Dr DA14 169
Betterton Ho WC2 240
Betterton St WC2 94 A1 240
Bettons Pk E15 98
Bettridge Rd SW6 135
Betts Cl BR3 185
Betts Ho E1 118
Betts Mews E17 53
Betts Rd E16 121
Betts St E1 118
Betts Way
Long Ditton KT6 197
Penge SE20 184
Bettswood Ct 15 SE20 184
Betty Brooks Ho E11 76
Betty Layward Prim Sch N16 73
Betty May Gray Ho 2 E14 120
Beulah Ave CR7 183
Beulah Cl HA8 10
Beulah Cres CR7 183
Beulah Gr CR0 205
Beulah Hill SE19 183
Beulah Inf Sch CR7 205
Beulah Jun Sch CR7 205

ulah Rd
erton SW19 179 B3
outh Norwood CR7 205 A6
utton SM1 217 C4
/althamstow E17 53 D4
uleigh Ct E17 54 B4
van Ave IG11 80 A1
van Ct
roydon CR0 220 C3
Twickenham
TW1 153 D5
van Ho IG11 80 B1
van Rd
ockfosters EN4 2 D1
lumstead Comm
SE2 124 B1
van St N1 95 A6 235 B5
v Callender Cl 4
W8 137 B2
venden St
1 95 B4 235 D2
vercote Wlk 1
A17 147 B6
veridge Ct
outhgate N21 16 A6
1 Thamesmead
SE28 124 B6
everidge Rd 1
W10 67 C1
everley Ave
ounslow TW4 129 B1
idcup DA15 167 D4
Vimbledon SW20 177 D2
everley Cl
Barnes SW13 134 A3
Chessington KT9 213 C4
Edmonton N21 17 A3
Enfield EN1 5 C1
6 Wandsworth
SW11 136 B1
everley Cotts
SW15 155 C1
everley Cres IG8 37 B2
everley Ct
9 Acton Green
W4 111 A1
5 Acton W12 111 C4
Brockley SE4 141 B2
6 Cheam SM2 217 C2
Chingford Hatch E4 35 B6
Fortis Green N2 48 D5
Harrow HA2 42 B6
Hounslow TW4 129 B1
Islington N5 72 D2
Northolt UB5 84 C5
Oakleigh Pk N20 14 A4
Oakwood N14 15 C4
Sidcup DA14 190 B6
Wimbledon SW20 177 D2
everley Dr HA8 44 C6
everley Gdns
Barnes SW13 133 D2
Hendon NW11 47 A2
2 New Malden KT4 200 A1
Stanmore HA7 25 A2
Wembley HA9 44 C1
everley Ho 5 BR1 186 B5
everley Hyrst 10
CR0 221 D6
everley La KT2 177 C3
everley Lo 6
TW10 154 A6
everley Mans TW4 129 B1
everley Path 9
SW13 133 D3
everley Rd
Barnes SW13 133 D2
Chingford E4 36 B4
Chiswick W4 111 D1
Dagenham RM9 81 A4
Keston Mark BR2 226 A6
Mitcham CR4 203 D5
Newham E6 99 D4
North Cheam KT4 216 C6
Penge SE20 184 B1
Ruislip HA4 62 B6
Southall UB2 107 A3
Sunbury TW16 171 D2
Teddington KT1 175 C2
West Barnes KT3 200 A5
everley DA14 190 A5
everley Trad Est
SM4 200 D2
everley Way (Kingston
By Pass) KT3,
SW20 200 A6
Beverley Way KT3, SW20,
KT2 177 D2
everly Ct HA3 43 C5
eversbrook Rd N19 71 D5
Beverstone Rd
London SW2 160 B6
Thornton Heath CR7 204 D5
Beverston Mews
NW1 237 C3
Bevill Allen Cl
SW17 180 D5
Bevill Cl SE25 206 A6
Bevin Cl SE16 119 A5
Bevin Ct WC1 233 D2
Bevington Prim Sch
W10 91 A2
Bevington Rd
Beckenham BR3 185 D1
Kensal Town W10 91 A2
Bevington St SE16 118 A4
Bevin Ho
35 Bethnal Green
E2 96 C4
8 Bow E3 97 C4
Bevin Rd UB4 84 B4
Bevin Sq SW17 158 D1
Bevin Way WC1 234 A2
Bevis Marks
EC3 95 C1 243 B2
Bewcastle Gdns EN2 4 A1
Bew Ct SE21 162 A4
Bewdley Ho N4 51 A2
Bewdley St N1 72 C1
Bewick Mews SE15 140 B5
Bewick St SW8 137 B3
Bewley Ct SW2 160 B5
Bewley Ho 7 E1 118 B6
Bewley St
Stepney E1 118 B6
Wimbledon SW19 180 A4
Bewlys Rd SE27 182 D5
Bexhill Cl TW13 151 A2
Bexhill Rd
Catford SE4 163 B5
Mortlake SW14 133 A2
Wood Green N11 31 D5
Bexhill Wlk 6 E15 98 C6
BEXLEY 146 B1
Bexley Coll (Erith Rd
Campus) DA17 125 D1
Bexley Gdns
Edmonton N9 17 B1
Ilford RM6 58 B4
Bexley Gram Sch
DA16 146 B1
BEXLEYHEATH 147 B2
Bexleyheath Sch
DA8 147 C2
Bexleyheath Sta
DA7 147 A3
Bexley High St DA5 169 D3
Bexley Ho SE4 141 A1
Bexley La DA14 168 C1
Bexley Rd SE9 167 A6
Bexley Sta DA5 169 C3
Beynon Rd SM5 218 D3
BFI London Imax
Cinema
SE1 116 C5 251 A3
Bglws The SM6 219 B3
Bianca Rd SE1, SE15 140 A6
Bibsworth Lo N3 29 B1
Bibsworth Rd N3 29 B1
Bicester Rd TW9 132 D2
Bickenhall Mans
W1 237 D4
Bickenhall St
W1 92 D2 237 D4
Bickersteth Rd
SW17 180 D4
Bickerton Rd N19 71 C6
BICKLEY 188 B1
Bickley Cres BR1 210 A5
Bickley Ct
10 Merton SW19 179 C3
1 Stanmore HA7 25 C6
Bickley Park Rd BR1,
BR7 210 B6
Bickley Park Sch
BR1 210 A6
Bickley Prim Sch
BR1 209 C6
Bickley Rd
Bromley BR1 187 D1
Leyton E10 53 D2
Bickley Sta BR1 210 A6
Bickley St SW17 180 D5
Bicknell Ho 34 E1 96 A1
Bicknell Rd SE5 139 A2
Bicknoller Rd EN1 5 D4
Bicknor Ho 2 E5 74 B3
Bicknor Rd BR6 211 D2
Bidborough Cl 3
BR2 208 D4
Bidborough St N1,
WC1 94 A4 233 A1
Biddenden Way
SE9 188 C6
Biddenham Ho 18
SE16 118 D2
Bidder St E16 98 C2
Biddesden Ho SW3 257 C3
Biddestone Rd N7 72 B4
Biddulph Ho 22
SE18 122 B2
Biddulph Mans W9 91 D4
Biddulph Rd W9 91 D4
Bideford Ave UB6 87 B5
Bideford Cl
Edgware HA8 26 C2
Twickenham TW13 151 B1
Bideford Gdns EN1 17 C4
Bideford Rd
Catford BR1 164 D1
East Wickham DA16 146 B5
Enfield EN3 7 B5
Ruislip HA4 62 B5
Bidmead Ct KT6 214 A5
Bidwell Gdns N11 31 C3
Bidwell Ho
Southall UB2 107 A2
3 Willesden NW2 68 A5
Bidwell St SE15 140 B4
Big Ben* SW1 250 B1
Bigbury Cl N17 33 C3
Biggerstaff Rd E15 98 A6
Biggerstaff St N4 72 C6
Biggin Ave CR4 180 D2
Biggin Hill Cl KT2 175 C5
Biggin Hill SE19 182 D3
Biggin Way SE19 183 A3
Bigginwood Rd
SW16 182 D2
Bigg's Row SW15 134 D2
Big Hill E5 52 B1
Bigland Green Prim Sch
E1 96 B1
Bigland St E1 96 B1
Bignell Rd SE18 122 D1
Bignold Rd E7 77 A4
Bigwood Ct NW11 47 D4
Bigwood Rd NW11 47 D3
Biko Ho 1 NW10 67 B1
Bilberry Ho 18 E3 97 C2
Bilberry Manor
SM2 218 A1
Billet Rd Ilford RM6 58 C6
Walthamstow E17 35 B2
Billetts Hart Cl W7 108 C4
Bill Hamling Cl SE9 166 B2
Billie Holiday Ct
NW10 89 B5
Billingford Cl SE4 140 D1
Billing Ho 7 E1 96 D1
Billingley NW1 232 A5
Billing Pl
SW10 135 D5 265 D4
Billing Rd
SW10 135 D5 265 D4
Billings Cl RM9 80 C1
Billingsgate Mkt
E14 119 D5
Billing St
SW10 135 D5 265 D4
Billington Ho SW8 269 D1
Billington Rd SE14 140 D5
Billinton Hill CR0 221 B6
Billiter Sq EC3 243 B1
Billiter St EC3 95 C1 243 B1
Bill Nicholson Way
N17 33 D3
Billockby Cl KT9 214 B2
Billsley Ct SE25 205 C5
Billson St E14 120 A2
Bilsby Gr SE9 187 D6
Bilton Ho SW8 269 C1
Bilton Rd UB6 87 B6
Bilton Twrs W1 237 D1
Bilton Way Enfield EN3 7 B5
Hayes UB3 106 B4
Bina Gdns
SW5 114 A2 256 A3
Binbrook Ho 13 W10 90 C2
Bincote Rd EN2 4 B2
Binden Rd W12 111 D3
Bindon Gn SM4 201 D5
Binfield Ct SE5 139 A3
Binfield Rd
London
SW4 138 A4 270 B1
South Croydon CR2 221 D3
Bingfield St
N1 94 B6 233 C6
Bingham Cnr CR0 206 A1
Bingham Pl
W1 93 A2 238 A4
Bingham Point 11
SE18 122 D2
Bingham Rd CR0 206 B1
Bingham St N1 73 B2
Bingley Rd
Ashford TW16 172 A3
Newham E16 99 C1
Southall UB6 86 A2
Binley Ho SW15 155 D5
Binney St W1 93 A1 238 B1
Binnie Ct SE10 141 D5
Binnie Ho SE1 262 A5
Binns Rd W4 111 C1
Binns Terr 3 W4 111 C1
Binsey Wlk 1 SE2 124 C4
Binstead Cl UB4 85 A2
Binstead Ho SW18 157 D5
Binyon Cres HA7 24 D5
Binyon Ho 8 N16 73 C4
Birbeck Ho 4 N19 49 D1
Birbetts Rd SE9 166 B2
Bircham Path SE4 140 D1
Birchanger Rd SE25 206 A4
Birch Ave
Edmonton N13 17 A1
Hillingdon UB7 82 B1
Birch Cl
Brentford TW8 131 B5
Buckhurst Hill IG9 21 D1
Hounslow TW3 130 B3
Newham E16 98 C2
Peckham SE15 140 A3
Romford RM7 59 D6
Teddington TW11 175 A5
Upper Holloway N19 71 C6
Birch Cres UB10 82 B6
Birch Ct Chingford E4 35 D4
Forest Gate E7 76 D4
Ilford RM6 58 C3
Sutton SM1 218 A4
9 Wallington SM6 219 B4
7 Woodside Pk N12 29 D6
Birchdale Gdns RM6 58 D2
Birchdale Rd E7 77 C3
Birchdene Dr SE28 124 A5
Birchdown Ho 32 E3 97 D4
Birchen Cl NW9 67 B6
Birchend Cl CR2 221 B2
Birchen Gr NW9 67 B6
Birches Cl
Mitcham CR4 202 D6
Pinner HA5 41 A4
Birches The
2 Beckenham
BR2 208 D5
Bushey WD23 8 A6
Camberwell SE5 139 C3
Greenwich SE7 143 B6
Manor Pk E12 78 A4
Orpington BR6 226 C4
Southgate N21 16 B5
South Norwood
SE25 183 D1
Twickenham TW4 151 B4
Birchfield Ho 3
E14 119 C6
Birchfield St E14 119 C6
Birch Gn NW9 27 C3
Birch Gr Acton W3 110 C6
Bexley DA16 146 A1
Lewisham SE12 164 D4
Leyton E11 76 C5
Birchgrove Ho TW9 132 D5
Birch Gr TW17 171 C1
Birch Hill CR0 222 D3
Birch Ho
New Cross Gate
SE14 141 B4
Teddington TW11 175 C3
8 Tulse Hill SW2 160 C5
Birchington Cl DA7 147 D4
Birchington Ct
Crouch End N8 49 D3
2 Kilburn NW6 91 D6
Birchington Ho 1
E5 74 B3
Birchington Rd
Crouch End N8 49 D3
Kilburn NW6 91 C6
Surbiton KT5 198 B2
Birchin La EC3 242 D1
Birchlands Ave
SW12 158 D4
Birchmead Ave HA5 40 C5
Birch Mead BR2,
BR6 226 C6
Birchmere Bsns Pk
SE2 124 A4
Birchmere Lo 18
SE16 118 B1
Birchmere Row
SE3 142 D3
Birchmore Wlk N5 73 A5
Birch Pk HA3 24 A3
Birch Rd
Feltham TW13 172 D5
Romford RM7 59 D6
Birch Row BR2 210 C3
Birch Tree Ave BR4 224 D4
Birch Tree Ho 16
SE7 143 C6
Birch Tree Way CR0 222 B6
Birch Vale Ct NW8 236 D6
Birchway UB3 106 A5
Birch Wlk CR4 181 B2
Birchwood Ave
Beckenham BR3 207 B5
Hackbridge SM5,
SM6 219 B5
Muswell Hill N10 49 A6
Sidcup DA14 168 C1
Birchwood Cl SM4 201 D5
Birchwood Ct
Burnt Oak HA8 27 A1
Edmonton N13 32 D5
Birchwood Dr NW3 69 D5
Birchwood Gr
TW12 173 C4
Birchwood Rd
Orpington BR5 211 C5
Streatham SW17 181 B5
Birdbrook Rd SE3 143 C2
Birdcage Wlk
SW1 115 D4 249 C1
Bird Coll DA14 168 A1
Birdham Cl BR1 210 A4
Birdhurst Ave CR2 221 B4
Birdhurst Ct SM6 219 C1
Birdhurst Gdns CR2 221 B4
Birdhurst Rd
London SW18 158 A6
Mitcham SW19 180 C4
South Croydon CR2 221 C3
Birdhurst Rise CR2 221 C3
Bird In Bush Rd
SE15 140 A5
Bird-in-Hand La
BR1 187 D1
Bird-In-Hand Pas
SE23 162 C2
Bird In Hand Yd 24
NW3 70 A4
Birdsall Ho 5 SE5 139 C2
Birdsfield La 12 E3 97 B6
Bird St W1 238 B1
Bird Wlk TW2 151 B3
Birdwood Cl TW11 174 C6
Birkbeck Ave
Acton W3 111 A6
Greenford UB6 86 A6
Birkbeck Coll
W1 93 D1 239 C2
Birkbeck Ct W3 111 B5
Birkbeck Gdns IG8 21 A2
Birkbeck Gr W3 111 B4
Birkbeck Hill SE21 160 D3
Birkbeck Mews 5
E8 73 D3
Birkbeck Pl SE21 161 A2
Birkbeck Prim Sch
DA14 168 B1
Birkbeck Rd
Acton W3 111 B5
Dalston E8 73 D3
Ealing W5 109 C2
Edgware NW7 27 D5
Enfield EN2 5 B5
Hornsey N8 50 A5
Ilford IG2 57 B4
North Finchley N12 30 A5
Penge BR3 184 D1
Sidcup DA14 168 A1
Tottenham N17 33 D2
Wimbledon SW19 179 D4
Birkbeck Sta SE20 206 C6
Birkbeck St E2 96 B4
Birkbeck Way UB6 86 B6
Birkdale Ave HA5 41 C6
Birkdale Cl
30 Bermondsey
SE16 118 B1
Crofton BR6 211 B2
Erith SE28 102 D1
Birkdale Ct 3 UB1 86 A1
Birkdale Gdns CR0 222 D4
Birkdale Rd
Abbey Wood SE2 124 A2
Ealing W5 88 A3
Birkenhead Ave
KT2 176 B2
Birkenhead Ho 11
N7 72 C3
Birkenhead St
WC1 94 A4 233 B2
Birkhall Rd SE6 164 B2
Birkwood Cl SW12 159 D4
Birley Lo NW8 229 D4
Birley Rd N20 14 A2
Birley St SW11 137 A3
Birnam Rd N4 72 B6
Birnbeck Ct NW11 47 B4
Birnham Ho TW1 153 C4
Birrell Ho 9 SW9 138 B3
Birse Cres NW10 67 C4
Birstal Gn WD19 22 D6
Birstall Rd N15 51 C4
Birtwhistle Ho 5 E3 97 B6
Biscay Ho 11 E1 96 D3
Biscay Rd W6 112 D1
Biscoe Cl TW5 129 C6
Biscoe Ho UB2 107 D2
Biscoe Way SE13 142 B2
Biscott Ho 8 E3 97 D3
Bisenden Rd CR0 221 C6
Bisham Cl CR4 202 D1
Bisham Gdns N6 49 A1
Bishop Butt Cl BR6 227 D5
Bishop Challoner
Collegiate Sch E1 96 C1
Bishop Challoner Sch
BR2 186 B1
Bishop Ct 20 SW2 160 C5
Bishop Douglass RC
High Sch N2 48 A6
Bishop Duppa's
Almshouses 7
TW10 154 A6
Bishop Duppas Pk
TW17 193 C2
Bishop Fox Way
KT8 195 B5
Bishop Gilpins CE Prim
Sch SW19 179 B5
Bishop John Robinson
CE Prim Sch
SE28 124 C6
Bishop Justus CE Sch
BR2 210 A2
Bishop Ken Rd HA3 24 D2
Bishop King's Rd
W14 113 A2 254 B4
Bishop Perrin CE Prim
Sch TW2 151 D3
Bishop Ramsey CE Sch
(Annexe) HA4 39 D2
Bishop Ramsey CE Sch
HA4 40 A2
Bishop Rd N14 15 B4
Bishop Ridley CE Prim
Sch DA16 145 C1
Bishops Ave
Borehamwood
WD6 10 B6
Bromley BR1 209 C6
Bishop's Ave SW6 135 A3
Bishops Ave
Ilford RM6 58 C3
Newham E13 99 B6
Bishops Ave The N2 48 B3
Bishopsbourne Ho
BR1 187 B3
Bishop's Bridge Rd
W2 92 A1 236 A2
Bishops Cl
Acton Green W4 111 A1
Barnet EN5 12 D5
Bishop's Cl N19 71 C5
Bishops Cl EN1 6 B3
Bishop's Cl UB10 82 C5
Bishops Cl
New Eltham SE9 167 A2
Richmond TW10 153 D1
Sutton SM1 217 C5
Bishop's Cl E17 53 D5
Bishopscourt 8
CR0 221 D6
Bishops Ct
1 Ashford TW16 171 D3
13 Bayswater W2 91 D1
East Finchley N2 48 C5
Bishop's Ct
Holborn EC4 241 C2
Holborn WC2 241 A2
Bishops Ct
Richmond TW9 132 A2
Romford RM7 59 D5
Wembley HA0 65 B4
Bishopsdale Ho 8
NW6 91 C6
Bishops Dr
East Bedfont
TW14 149 B5
Northolt UB5 85 A6
Bishopsford Com Sch
SM4 202 B3
Bishopsford Ho
SM4 202 C3
Bishopsford Rd
SM4 202 B3
Bishopsgate Arc E1 243 B3
Bishopsgate
Churchyard EC2 243 A2
Bishopsgate
EC2 95 C1 243 A2
Bishops Gn BR1 187 C2
Bishops Gr
East Finchley N2 48 C3
Feltham TW12 173 B6
Bishop's Hall KT1 175 D1
Bishopshalt Sch UB8 82 B4
Bishops Hill KT12 194 A2
Bishops Ho SW8 270 B3
Bishop's Mans SW6 134 D3
Bishops Mead SE5 139 A5
Bishop's Park Rd
SW6 134 D3
Bishops Park Rd
SW16 182 A2
Bishop's Pl SM1 218 A3
Bishops Rd
SW6 135 B4 264 C2
Bishop's Rd
Hanwell W7 108 C4
Hayes UB3 83 A1
Bishops Rd N6 49 A3
Bishop's Rd CR0 204 D2

Bishops Sq E1 243 B4
Bishop's Terr SE11 116 C2 261 B4
Bishopsthorpe Rd SE26 184 D6
Bishop St N1 95 A6 235 A6
Bishopstone Ho 4 SW11 137 A3
Bishop Stopford's Sch EN1 6 B3
Bishops View Ct N10 49 B5
Bishop's Way E2 96 C5
Bishops Wlk
Chislehurst BR7 189 A2
South Croydon CR0, CR9 223 A3
Bishopswood Rd N6 48 D2
Bishop Thomas Grant RC Sec Sch SW16 182 B5
Bishop Wand CE Sch The TW16 171 D1
Bishop Way NW10 67 C1
Bishop Wilfred Wood Cl SE15 140 A3
Bishop Wilfred Wood Ct 3 E13 99 C5
Bishop Winnington-Ingram CE Prim Sch HA4 39 B2
Bisley Cl KT4 200 C1
Bisley Ho SW19 156 D2
Bispham Rd NW10 88 B4
Bissextile Ho SE13 141 D3
Bisson Rd E15 98 A5
Bisterne Ave E17 54 B6
Bittacy Bsns Ctr NW7 29 A3
Bittacy Cl NW7 28 D4
Bittacy Ct NW7 29 A3
Bittacy Hill NW7 28 D4
Bittacy Park Ave NW7 28 D5
Bittacy Rd NW7 28 D4
Bittacy Rise NW7 28 D4
Bittern Cl UB4 84 D2
Bittern Ct
Chingford E4 20 B4
7 Deptford SE8 141 C6
Hendon NW9 27 C1
Bittern Ho SE1 252 A1
Bittern St SE1 252 A1
Bittoms The KT1 197 D6
Bixley Cl UB2 107 B2
Blackall St EC2 243 A6
Blackberry Cl TW17 193 C5
Blackberry Farm Cl TW5 129 A5
Blackberry Field BR5 190 A2
Blackbird Ct NW9 67 B5
Blackbird Hill NW9 67 B5
Blackborne Rd RM10 81 D2
Black Boy La N15 51 A4
Blackbrook La BR1, BR2 210 C5
Blackburn Ct 21 SW2 160 C5
Blackburne's Mews W1 248 A5
Blackburn 28 NW9 27 D1
Blackburn Rd NW6 69 D2
Blackburn Trad Est TW19 148 B5
Blackburn Way TW4 151 A6
Blackbush Ave RM6 58 D4
Blackbush Cl SM2 217 D1
Blackcap Ct NW9 27 C1
Blackdown Cl N2 30 A1
Blackdown Ho E8 74 A4
Blackett St SW15 134 D2
Black Fan Cl EN2 5 A4
BLACKFEN 168 A5
Blackfen Par DA15 168 A5
Blackfen Rd DA15 168 B5
Blackfen Sch for Girls DA15 168 B5
Blackford Rd WD19 22 D5
Blackfriars Bridge EC4 251 C5
Blackfriars Ct EC4 251 C6
Black Friars La EC4 94 D1 241 C1
Blackfriars Pas EC4 251 C6
Blackfriars Pier EC4 251 C6
Blackfriars Rd SE1 116 D5 251 C3
Blackfriars Sta EC4 116 D6 251 C6
Blackfriars Underpass EC4 116 C6 251 B6
Blackham Ho SW19 179 A4
BLACKHEATH 142 C2
Blackheath Ave SE3 142 C5
Blackheath Bluecoat CE Sec Sch SE3 143 B5
Blackheath Bsns Est SE10 142 A4
Blackheath Gr SE3 142 D3
Blackheath High Sch
Blackheath SE3 142 D3
Greenwich SE3 143 A5
Blackheath Hill SE10 142 A4
Blackheath Hospl SE3 142 C2
Blackheath* SE3 142 C4
BLACKHEATH PARK 143 A1
Blackheath Pk SE3 143 A2
Blackheath Prep Sch SE3 143 A4
Blackheath Rd SE10 141 D4
Blackheath Rise SE13 142 A3
Blackheath Sta SE3 142 D2
BLACKHEATH VALE 142 D3
Blackheath Vale SE3 142 C3
Blackheath Village SE3 142 D3
Black Horse Ct SE1 262 D6
Blackhorse La
Croydon CR0 206 A2
Higham Hill E17 34 D1
Blackhorse La Sta CR0 206 A2
Blackhorse Mews E17 52 D6
Black Horse Par HA5 40 B4
Blackhorse Rd SE8 141 A6
Black Horse Rd DA14 190 A6
Blackhorse Rd E17 53 A5
Blackhorse Road Sta E17 52 D5
Blackhorse Road E17 52 D5
Blacklands Dr UB4 83 A3
Blacklands Rd SE6 186 A6
Blacklands Terr SW3 257 D3
Black Lion La W6 112 A2
Black Lion Mews 4 W6 112 A2
Blackmore Ave UB1 108 B5
Blackmore Dr NW10 66 D1
Blackmore Ho
Forest Hill SE23 163 B3
Islington N1 233 D5
2 Wandsworth SW18 157 D6
Blackmore's Gr TW11 175 A4
Blackmore Twr 1 W3 111 A3
Blackness La BR2 225 D1
Blackpool Gdns UB4 83 C3
Blackpool Rd SE15 140 B3
Black Prince Intc DA6 169 D5
Black Prince Rd SE1, SE11 116 B2 260 D3
Black Rod Cl UB3 105 D3
Black Roof Ho 9 SE5 138 D4
Blackshaw Rd SW17 180 B5
Blacksmith Cl RM6 58 C3
Blacksmiths Ho 7 E17 53 C5
Black's Rd W6 112 C2
Blackstock Ho 2 N5 72 D5
Blackstock Mews N4 72 D5
Blackstock Rd N4, N5 72 D6
Blackstone Ho
Dulwich SE21 161 C1
Pimlico SW1 259 A1
Blackstone Rd NW2 68 C4
Black Swan Yd SE1 253 A2
Blackthorn Ave UB7 104 C3
Blackthorn Ct
20 Camberwell SE15 139 D5
Heston TW5 129 A5
4 Leyton E15 76 B4
6 West Norwood SW16 182 C5
Blackthorne Ave CR0 206 C1
Blackthorne Ct
2 Littleton TW15 171 A3
Southall UB1 107 D5
Blackthorne Dr E4 36 B6
Blackthorn Gr DA7 147 A2
Blackthorn Rd IG1 79 B3
Blackthorn St E3 97 C3
Blacktree Mews 11 SW9 138 C2
BLACKWALL 120 B6
Blackwall Sta E14 120 A6
Blackwall Trad Est E14 98 B2
Blackwall Tunnel App SE10 120 C4
Blackwall Tunnel E14, SE10 120 B5
Blackwall Tunnel Northern Approach E14, E3 98 A3
Blackwall Way E14 120 A6
Blackwater Cl E7 76 D4
Blackwater Ho NW8 236 D4
Blackwater St SE22 161 D6
Blackwell Cl
10 Clapton Pk E5 74 D4
Harrow HA3 24 B3
Blackwell Gdns HA8 10 C1
Blackwell Ho 3 SW4 159 D5
Blackwood Ho 11 E1 96 B3
Blackwood St SE17 117 B1 262 C2
Blade Ho TW1 153 D5
Blade Mews SW15 135 B1
Bladen Ho 4 E1 96 D1
Blades Ct
4 Hammersmith W6 112 B1
Putney SW15 135 B1
Blades Ho 12 SE11 138 C6
Blades Lo 16 SW2 160 C5
Bladindon Dr DA5 168 D4
Bladon Ct
Beckenham BR2 208 C6
Streatham SW16 182 A4
Bladon Gdns HA2 41 D3
Blagden's Cl N14 15 D2
Blagden's La N14 15 D2
Blagdon Ct W7 108 C6
Blagdon Rd
London SE13 163 D5
New Malden KT3 199 D5
Blagdon Wlk TW11 175 C4
Blagrove Rd 1 W10 91 B2
Blair Ave London NW9 45 C2
Thames Ditton KT10 212 A6
Blair Cl
Avery Hill DA15 167 C6
Canonbury N1 73 A2
Hayes UB3 106 A2
Blair Ct
Beckenham BR3 185 D2
8 Carshalton SM5 218 D5
7 Catford SE6 164 D3
St John's Wood NW8 229 C6
Blairderry Rd SW2 160 A2
Blairgowrie Ct 13 E14 98 B1
Blair Ho SW9 138 B3
Blair Peach Prim Sch UB1 106 D5
Blair St E14 98 B1
Blake Apartments N8 50 B6
Blake Ave IG11 101 D6
Blake Cl
Bexley DA16 145 C4
Carshalton SM5 202 C1
Blake Coll W1 93 C2 239 A4
Blake Ct
8 Bermondsey SE16 118 B1
9 Clapham SW8 137 C3
Croydon CR2 220 D3
Kilburn NW6 91 C4
Southgate N21 16 B6
Blakeden Dr KT10 212 D2
Blake Gdns SW6 135 D4 265 C2
Blake Hall Cres E11 55 A1
Blakehall Rd SM5 218 D2
Blake Hall Rd E11 55 A2
Blake Ho
6 Beckenham BR3 185 D4
2 Deptford SE8 141 C6
Harrow HA1 64 C6
Isle Of Dogs E14 119 D4
1 Kentish Town N19 71 D3
Lambeth SE1 261 A6
14 Stoke Newington N16 73 C4
Blake Lo N3 29 B1
Blake Mews 15 TW9 132 C4
Blakemore Rd
Streatham SW16 160 A1
Thornton Heath CR7 204 B4
Blakemore Way DA17 125 A3
Blakeney Ave BR3 185 B2
Blakeney Cl
5 Camden Town NW1 71 D1
4 Dalston E8 74 A3
Whetstone N20 14 A3
Blakeney Ct EN2 17 B6
Blakeney Rd BR3 185 B2
Blakenham Ct W12 112 A5
Blakenham Rd SW17 180 D6
Blaker Ct SE7 143 C5
Blake Rd
Croydon CR0 221 C6
Mitcham CR4 202 C6
Newham E16 98 D3
Wood Green N11 31 C3
Blaker Rd E15 98 A6
Blakes Ave KT3 199 D3
Blakes Cl W10 90 C2
Blake's Gn BR4 208 A1
Blakes La KT3 199 D4
Blakesley Ave W5 87 C1
Blakesley Ct W5 87 C1
Blakesley Ho 4 E12 78 C5
Blake's Rd SE15 139 C5
Blakes Terr KT3 200 A4
Blakesware Gdns N9 17 B4
Blakewood Cl TW13 172 C6
Blakewood Ct 5 SE20 184 B3
Blanca Ho 16 N1 95 C5
Blanchard Cl SE9 166 A1
Blanchard Gr EN3 7 D5
Blanchard Ho
Chislehurst BR7 189 A4
7 Twickenham TW1 153 D5
Blanchard Way E8 74 A2
Blanch Cl SE15 140 C5
Blanchedowne SE5 139 B1
Blanche Nevile Sch N10 31 A1
Blanche St E16 98 D3
Blanchland Rd SM4 201 D4
Blandfield Rd SW12 159 A4
Blandford Ave
2 Beckenham BR3 185 A1
Twickenham TW2 151 D3
Blandford Cl
London N2 48 A5
Romford RM7 59 D5
Wallington CR0 220 A5
Blandford Cres E4 20 A4
Blandford Ct
Brondesbury Pk NW6 69 A1
6 De Beauvoir Town N1 73 C1
Blandford Ho SW8 270 C4
Blandford Rd
Acton W4 111 C3
Ealing W5 109 D4
Penge BR3 184 D1
Southall UB2 107 C2
Teddington TW11 174 C5
Blandford Sq NW1 237 B5
Blandford St W1 93 A2 238 A3
Blandford Waye UB4 84 C1
Bland Ho SE11 260 D2
Bland St SE9 143 D1
Blaney Cres E6 100 D4
Blanmerle Rd SE9 166 D3
Blann Cl SE9 165 D5
Blantyre St SW10 136 B5 266 C4
Blantyre Twr SW10 266 C4
Blantyre Wlk SW10 136 B5 266 C4
Blashford NW3 70 D1
Blashford St SE13 164 B4
Blasker Wlk 8 E14 119 D1
Blatchford Ct KT12 194 A1
Blatchford Ho 8 RM10 81 C5
Blawith Rd HA1 42 D5
Blaxland Ho 12 W12 112 B6
Blaydon Cl HA4 39 C2
Blaydon Ct 4 UB5 63 C2
Blaydon Wlk N17 34 B3
Blazer Ct NW8 229 D1
Bleak Hill La SE18 145 D6
Blean Gr SE20 184 C3
Bleasdale Ave UB6 87 A5
Blechynden Ho 17 W10 90 D1
Blechynden St W10 112 D6
Bledlow Cl SE28 124 C6
Bledlow Rise UB6 86 A5
Bleeding Heart Yd EC1 241 B3
Blegborough Rd SW16 181 C4
Blemundsbury WC1 240 C4
Blendon Dr DA5 168 D5
Blendon Path 9 BR1 186 D3
Blendon Rd DA5 168 D5
Blendon Terr SE18 145 A6
Blendworth Point 4 SW15 156 B3
Blenheim Ave IG2 56 C3
Blenheim Bsns Ctr CR4 180 D1
Blenheim Centre 7 SE20 184 D3
Blenheim Cl
Edmonton N21 17 A3
Eltham SE12 165 B3
Greenford UB6 86 B5
Wallington SM6 219 C1
West Barnes SW20 200 C6
Blenheim Cres
Notting Hill W11 91 A1
Notting Hill W11 244 B6
Ruislip HA4 61 B6
South Croydon CR2 221 A1
Blenheim Ct
Barnsbury N7 72 A2
Beckenham BR2 208 D5
5 Hampton TW12 173 C2
Harrow HA3 43 A3
Hendon NW4 46 D5
Longlands DA14 167 B1
Blenheim Ctr TW3 129 D2
Blenheim Ct
Richmond TW9 132 B2
17 Rotherhithe SE16 118 D5
South Norwood SE19 183 C2
Sutton SM2 218 A2
Upper Holloway N19 72 A6
Woodford IG8 37 B3
Blenheim Dr DA16 145 D4
Blenheim Gdns
Clapham Pk SW2 160 B5
Dollis Hill NW2 68 C3
Kingston u T KT2 176 D3
Wallington SM6 219 C1
Wembley HA9 66 A5
Blenheim Gr SE15 140 A3
Blenheim Ho
6 Edmonton N9 18 A1
Hounslow TW3 129 C2
8 Woolwich SE18 123 A3
Blenheim Par 2 UB10 82 D3
Blenheim Park Rd CR2 221 A1
Blenheim Pas NW8 229 A4
Blenheim Pl TW11 174 D5
Blenheim 26 SW19 156 D3
Blenheim Rd
Acton W4 111 C3
Bromley BR1, BR2 210 A5
Harrow HA2 41 D3
Leyton E15 76 C4
Newham E6 99 D4
Northolt UB5 63 D2
Penge SE20 184 C3
Sidcup DA15 168 C3
St John's Wood NW8 92 A5 229 B4
Sutton SM1 217 D5
Walthamstow E17 53 A6
West Barnes SW20 200 C6
Blenheim Rise N15 51 D5
Blenheim St W1 238 C1
Blenheim Terr NW8 92 A5 229 A4
Blenheim Way TW7 131 A4
Blenkarne Rd SW11 158 D5
Bleriot 27 NW9 27 D1
Bleriot Rd TW5 128 C5
Blessbury Rd HA8 27 A2
Blessed Dominic RC Sch NW9 27 D1
Blessed Sacrament RC Prim Sch N1 94 B6 233 C5
Blessington Cl SE13 142 B2
Blessington Rd SE13 142 B1
Blessing Way IG11 102 C5
Bletchingley Cl CR7 204 D5
Bletchington Ct 2 DA17 125 C2
Bletchley Ct N1 235 C3
Bletchley St N1 95 A5 235 B3
Bletchmore Cl UB3 105 B1
Bletsoe Wlk N1 235 B4
Blewbury Ho 3 SE2 124 C4
Blick Ho 1 SE16 118 C3
Bligh Ho 4 SE27 183 A6
Blincoe Cl SW19 156 D2
Blissett St SE10 142 A4
Blissland Ct 5 N12 30 A4
Bliss Mews 14 W10 91 A4
Blisworth Cl UB4 85 A3
Blisworth Ho 12 E2 96
Blithbury Rd RM9 80
Blithdale Rd SE2 124
Blithfield St W8 255
Blockley Rd HA0 65
Bloemfontein Ave W12 112
Bloemfontein Rd W12 112
Blomfield Ct
Battersea SW11 266
Paddington W9 236
Blomfield Ho 4 E14 119
Blomfield Mans 3 W12 112
Blomfield Rd W9 92 A2 236
Blomfield St EC2 95 B2 242
Blomfield Villas W9 236
Blomville Rd RM8 81
Blondel St SW11 137
Blondin Ave W5 109
Blondin St E3 97
Bloomburg St SW1 259
Bloomfield Cres IG2 56
Bloomfield Ct N6 49
Bloomfield Ho 19 E1 96
Bloomfield Pl W1 248
Bloomfield Rd
Bromley Comm BR2 209
Highgate N6 49
Kingston u T KT1 198 A
Woolwich SE18 122
Bloomfield Terr SW1 115 A1 258
Bloom Gr SE27 160
Bloomhall Rd SE19 183
Bloom Park Rd SW6 264 C
BLOOMSBURY 93
Bloomsbury Cl
Ealing W5 110
Edgware NW7 28 A
Bloomsbury Ct
Cranford TW5 128
Leytonstone E11 54
Pinner HA5 41
St Giles WC1 240
Bloomsbury Ho 10 SW4 159 D
Bloomsbury Pl
London SW18 158 A
St Giles WC1 240
Bloomsbury Sq WC1 94 A2 240
Bloomsbury St WC1 93 D2 239 D
Bloomsbury Way WC1 94 A2 240
Blore Cl SW8 269 C
Blore Ct W1 249 C
Blore Ho SW10 265 D
Blossom Cl
Dagenham RM9 103 B
Ealing W5 110 A
South Croydon CR2 221 D
Blossom La EN2 5 A
Blossom Pl E1 243 B
Blossom St E1 95 C3 243 B
Blossom Waye TW5 129 A
Blossom Way
Hillingdon UB10 60 B
West Drayton UB7 104 C
Blount St E14 97 A
Bloxam Gdns SE9 166 A
Bloxhall Rd E10 53 B
Bloxham Cres TW12 173 B
Bloxworth Cl SM6 219 C
Blucher Rd SE5 139 A
Blue Anchor Alley 4 TW9 132 A
Blue Anchor La SE16 118 B
Blue Anchor Yd E1 118 A
Blue Ball Yd SW1 249 A
Bluebell Ave E12 78 A
Bluebell Cl
Forest Hill SE26 183 D
Hackbridge SM6 203 B
10 Hackney E9 96 C
Northolt UB5 63 B
Orpington BR6 227 A
Bluebell Ct 4 N12 14 A
Bluebell Way IG1 78 D
Blueberry Cl IG8 37 A
Blueberry Ct
Edgware HA8 27 A
3 Enfield EN2 4 D
Bluebird La RM10 81 C
Bluebird Way SE28 123 B
Bluefield Cl TW12 173 C
Blue Gate Fields Jun & Inf Schs E1 118 C
Bluegate Mews E1 118 B

uegates
Stoneleigh KT17 216 A1
Wimbledon SW19 179 A5
luehouse Rd E4 20 C1
lue Lion Pl SE1 263 A6
lue Point Ct 2 HA1 42 D4
lueprint Apartments 15 SW12 159 B4
lue Sch The TW7 131 A2
lundell Cl E8 74 A4
lundell Rd HA8 27 C3
lundell St N7 72 A2
lunden Cl RM8 58 C1
lunt Rd CR0 221 B3
lunts Ave UB7 126 C5
lunts Rd SE9 166 C6
lurton Rd E5 74 D4
lydon Ct N21 16 B6
lyth Cl
4 Cubitt Town E14 120 B2
Twickenham TW1 152 D5
lythe Cl SE23 163 B4
lythe Hill SE6 163 B4
lythe Hill La SE6 163 B3
lythe Hill BR5 190 A2
lythe Ho 8 SE11 138 C6
lythe Mews 2 W14 112 D3
lythendale Ho 34 E2 96 A5
lythe Rd W14 113 A3 254 A5
lythe St E2 96 B4
lytheswood Pl 4 SW16 182 B6
lythe Vale SE6 163 B3
lythewood 5 SM1 218 B3
lyth Rd
Bromley BR1 186 D2
Hayes UB3 105 C4
Walthamstow E17 53 B2
Woolwich SE28 124 C6
lyth's Wharf E14 119 A6
lythswood Rd IG3 58 A2
lythwood Pk 10 BR1 186 D2
lythwood Rd
London N4 50 A2
Pinner HA5 22 D2
nois Jerusalem Sch N16 51 B2
oades Mews 3 NW3 70 B4
oadicea St N1 233 C5
oardman Ave E4 19 D6
oardman Cl EN5 13 A6
oardwalk Pl E14 120 A5
oarhound 25 NW9 27 D1
oarley Ho SE17 263 A3
oatemah Wlk 21 SW9 138 C3
oathouse Ctr The W10 90 D3
oathouse Wlk 24 SE15 139 D5
oat Lifter Way 19 SE16 119 A2
ob Anker Cl 1 E13 99 A4
obbin Cl SW4 137 C2
obby Moore Bridge The HA9 66 C5
ob Marley Way 11 SE24 138 C1
ob Thompson Ct HA9 66 D5
ockhampton Rd KT2 176 B3
ocking St E8 96 B6
oddicott Cl SW19 157 A2
oddington Gdns W3 110 C4
oddington Ho 2 SE14 140 C4
odeney Ho 10 SE5 139 C4
oden Ho 4 E1 96 A2
odiam Cl EN1 5 C3
odiam Ct
Beckenham BR2 208 D5
Sutton SM1 218 B4
odiam Rd SW16 181 D3
odiam Way NW10 88 B4
Bodicea Mews TW4 151 C5
Bodington Ct 2 W12 112 D4
Bodley Cl KT3 199 C4
Bodley Manor Way SE24 160 C4
Bodley Rd KT3 199 C4
Bodmin Cl HA2 63 B5
Bodmin Gr SM4 201 D4
Bodmin 26 NW9 27 D1
Bodmin St SW18 157 C3
Bodnant Gdns SW20 200 B6
Bodney Rd E5, E8 74 B3
Boeing Way UB2 106 B3
Boevey Path DA17 125 B1
Bogart Ct 13 E14 119 C6
Bognor Gdns WD19 22 C5
Bognor Rd DA16 146 D4
Bohemia Pl 1 E8 74 B2
Bohn Rd E1 97 A2
Bohun Gr EN4 14 D5
Boileau Par W5 88 B1
Boileau Rd
Barnes SW13 134 B6
Ealing W5 88 B1
Boilerhouse SE1 253 C3
Boisseau Ho 31 E1 96 C2
Bolden St SE8 141 D3
Boldero Pl NW8 237 A5
Bolderwood Way BR4 223 D6
Boldmere Rd HA5 40 C2
Boleyn Ave EN1 6 B4
Boleyn Ct
Beckenham BR3 186 A2
Buckhurst Hill IG9 21 B3
East Molesey KT8 196 B5
Hayes UB3 105 D4
Walthamstow E17 53 C5
Boleyn Dr
East Molesey KT8 195 B6
Ruislip HA4 62 D6
Boleyn Gdns BR4 223 D6
Boleyn Ground(Upton Park) (West Ham Utd FC) E13, E6 99 D5
Boleyn Rd
Newham E6 99 D5
Stoke Newington N16 73 C3
Upton E7 77 B1
Boleyn Way EN5 2 A2
Bolina Rd SE16 118 C1
Bolingbroke Gr SW11 158 D5
Bolingbroke Ho
Beckenham BR3 207 A4
Catford BR3 185 D5
Bolingbroke Hospl The SW11 158 C6
Bolingbroke Rd W14 112 D3
Bolingbroke Way UB3, UB11 105 B5
Bolingbroke Wlk SW11 136 C4 267 A2
Bollo Bridge Rd W3 111 A4
Bollo Ct 2 W3 111 A3
Bollo La W3 110 D3
Bolney Ct KT6 197 D4
Bolney Gate SW7 247 A1
Bolney St SW8 138 B5 270 C3
Bolsover St W1 93 B3 238 D5
Bolstead Rd CR4 181 B2
Bolster Gr N22 31 D2
Bolt Ct EC4 241 B1
Boltmore Cl NW4 46 D6
Bolton Cl
Chessington KT9 214 A2
Penge SE20 184 A1
Bolton Cres SE5 138 D5
Bolton Ct SW11 268 B1
Bolton Dr SM4 202 B2
Bolton Gdns
Bromley BR1 186 D4
Kensal Rise NW10 90 D5
Bolton Gdns Mews SW10 256 A2
Bolton Gdns
South Kensington SW5 113 D1 255 D2
Teddington TW11 175 A4
Bolton Ho 4 SE10 120 C1
Bolton Pl SW5 256 A2
Bolton Rd
Chessington KT9 214 A2
Chiswick W4 133 A5
Edmonton N18 33 D5
Harlesden NW10 89 C6
Harrow HA1 42 B5
Kilburn NW8 91 D6
Stratford E15 76 D2
Boltons Ct SW5 255 D2
Bolton's La TW6, UB7 127 A5
Boltons The
Harrow HA1 42 A5
South Kensington SW10 114 A1 256 A2
6 Stratford E15 76 D2
Wembley HA0 64 D4
Woodford IG8 37 A6
Bolton Studios SW10 256 B1
Bolton St W1 115 B5 248 D4
Bolton Wlk N7 72 B6
Bombay Ct 8 SE16 118 C4
Bombay St SE16 118 B2
Bomer Cl UB7 126 C5
Bomore Rd W11 113 A6 244 A6
Bonar Pl BR7 188 A3
Bonar Rd SE15 140 A5
Bonchester Cl BR7 188 C3
Bonchurch Cl SM2 217 D1
Bonchurch Rd
Ealing W13 109 B5
Kensal Town W10 91 A2
Bond Cl UB7 82 B1
Bond Ct EC4 242 C1
Bondfield Ave UB4 84 A4
Bondfield Rd 4 E6 100 B2
Bond Gdns SM6 219 C4
Bond Ho 4 NW6 91 B5
Bonding Yard Wlk SE16 119 A3
Bond Prim Sch CR4 180 D1
Bond Rd
Mitcham CR4 180 D1
Surbiton KT6 214 B6
Bond St Chiswick W4 111 B2
Ealing W5 109 D6
Bond Street Sta W1 93 A1 238 B1
Bond St E15 76 C3
Bondway SW8 138 A6 270 B6
Boneta Rd SE18 122 B3
Bonfield Rd SE13 142 A1
Bonham Gdns RM8 80 D6
Bonham Ho W11 244 C4
Bonham Rd
Brixton SW2 160 B6
Dagenham RM8 80 D5
Bonheur Rd W4 111 B4
Bonhill St EC2 95 B3 242 D5
Boniface Gdns HA3 23 D3
Boniface Rd UB10 60 D5
Boniface Wlk HA3 23 D3
Bonington Ho
Enfield EN1 18 A6
Pentonville N1 233 C3
Bonita Mews SE15 140 D2
Bonne Marche Terr Mews 18 SE27 183 C6
Bonner Hill Rd KT1 198 C6
Bonner Ho 3 SW15 156 A6
Bonner Prim Sch E2 96 C4
Bonner Rd E2 96 C5
Bonnersfield Cl HA1 43 A3
Bonnersfield La
Greenhill HA1 42 D3
Kenton HA1, HA3 43 A3
Bonner St E2 96 C5
Bonneville Gdns SW4 159 C5
Bonneville Prim Sch SW4 159 C5
Bonnington Ct 14 UB5 84 D5
Bonnington Ho 9 SM2 217 D2
Bonnington Sq SW8 138 B6 270 C6
Bonnington Twr BR2 210 A3
Bonny St NW1 71 C1
Bonser Rd TW1 152 D2
Bonsor Ho SW8 269 B2
Bonsor St SE5 139 C5
Bonthron Ho SW15 134 C3
Bonus Pastor RC Sch BR1 186 C6
Bonville Gdns 17 NW4 46 A5
Bonville Rd BR1 186 D5
Bookbinder Cotts N20 14 D1
Booker Cl 11 E3 97 B2
Booker Rd 5 N18 34 A5
Bookham Ct CR4 202 B6
Boone Ct N9 18 C1
Boones Rd SE13 142 C1
Boone St SE13 142 C1
Boord St SE10 120 C3
Boothby Ct E4 20 A1
Boothby Ho 2 SW16 181 C5
Boothby Rd N19 71 D6
Booth Cl
10 Hackney E9 96 B6
Thamesmead SE28 124 B6
Booth Ho
9 Brentford TW8 131 C5
2 Streatham SW2 160 C4
Booth La EC4 252 A6
Boothman Ho HA3 43 D6
Booth Rd
Croydon CR0 220 D6
Hendon NW9 27 C1
Boothroyd Ho TW7 130 D2
Booth's Pl W1 239 B3
Boot Par HA8 26 C4
Boot St N1 95 C4
Bordars Rd W7 86 D2
Bordars Wlk W7 86 C2
Bordeaux Ho 1 E15 76 C3
Borden Ave EN1 17 B5
Border Cres SE26 184 B5
Border Gate CR4 180 D2
Border Gdns CR0 223 D4
Border Rd SE26 184 B5
Bordesley Rd SM4 201 D5
Bordeston Ct 11 TW8 131 C5
Bordley Ct 4 N20 14 D2
Bordon Wlk 5 SW15 156 A4
Boreas Wlk N1 234 D3
Boreham Ave E16 99 A1
Boreham Cl E11 54 A1
Boreham Rd N22 33 A1
BOREHAMWOOD 11 A5
Boreman Ho 11 SE10 142 A6
Borgard Rd SE18 122 B2
Borkwood Pk BR6 227 D4
Borkwood Way BR6 227 C4
Borland Rd
London SE15 140 C1
Teddington TW11 175 B3
Borneo St SW15 134 C2
Borough High St SE1 117 B5 252 C4
Borough Hill CR0 220 D5
Borough Mkt* SE1 252 C3
Borough Rd
Hounslow TW7 130 D4
7 Kingston u T KT2 176 C3
Lambeth SE1 116 D3 261 D6
Mitcham CR4 180 C1
Borough Sq SE1 252 A1
Borough Sta SE1 117 A4 252 B1
BOROUGH THE 117 A4
Borrett Cl SE17 117 A1 262 A1
Borrodaile Rd SW18 157 D5
Borrowdale Ave HA3 25 A1
Borrowdale Cl IG4 56 A5
Borrowdale Ct EN2 5 A4
Borrowdale NW1 232 A1
Borthwick Mews E15 76 C4
Borthwick Rd
Leyton E15 76 C4
London NW9 45 D3
Borthwick St SE8 119 C1
Borwick Ave E17 53 B6
Bosbury Rd SE6 164 A1
Boscastle Rd NW5 71 B5
Boscobel Cl BR1 188 B1
Boscobel Ho 4 E8 74 B2
Boscobel Pl SW1 258 B4
Boscobel St NW8 92 B3 236 D5
Boscombe Ave E10 54 B2
Boscombe Circus NW9 27 B1
Boscombe Cl E5 75 A3
Boscombe Gdns SW16 182 A4
Boscombe Ho CR0 205 B1
Boscombe Rd
Merton SW19 179 D2
North Cheam KT4 200 D1
Shepherd's Bush W12 112 A4
Streatham SW17 181 A4
Bose Cl N3 29 A2
Bosgrove E4 20 A2
Boss Ho SE1 253 C2
Boss St SE1 253 C2
Bostall Hill SE2 124 B1
Bostall La SE2 124 B1
Bostall Manorway SE2 124 B2
Bostall Park Ave DA7 147 A5
Bostall Rd BR5 190 B3
Bostock Ho TW5 129 C6
Boston Bsns Pk W7 108 C3
Boston Ct
South Norwood SE25 205 D5
Sutton SM2 218 A1
Boston Gdns
Brentford TW8 109 B2
Chiswick W4 133 C6
Boston Gr HA4 39 A3
Boston Ho
24 Camberwell SE5 139 A3
Earl's Ct SW5 255 D3
Lisson Gr NW1 237 C6
Boston Lo W13 109 C1
Boston Manor Ho TW8 109 B1
Boston Manor Rd TW8 109 B1
Boston Manor Sta TW8 109 A2
Boston Park Rd TW8 109 C1
Boston Par W7 109 A2
Boston Pl NW1 92 D3 237 C5
Boston Rd
Burnt Oak HA8 27 A3
Ealing W7 109 A3
Newham E6 100 A4
Thornton Heath CR0 204 C3
Bostonthorpe Rd W7 108 C4
Boston Vale W7 109 A2
Bosun Cl 22 E14 119 C4
Boswell Ct
Bloomsbury WC1 240 B4
9 Hammersmith W14 112 D3
Kingston u T KT2 176 C2
Boswell Ho
Bloomsbury WC1 240 B4
Bromley Comm BR2 209 D4
5 Streatham SW16 181 C5
Boswell Rd CR7 205 A5
Boswell St WC1 94 A2 240 B4
Boswood Ct TW4 129 B2
Bosworth Cl E17 35 B2
Bosworth Ho 4 W10 91 A3
Bosworth Rd
Barnet EN5 1 C2
Dagenham RM10 81 C5
Kensal Town W10 91 A3
Wood Green N11 31 D4
Botany Bay La BR7 189 A1
Botany Cl EN4 2 C1
Boteley Cl E4 20 B2
Botham Cl 6 HA8 27 A3
Botha Rd E13 99 C2
Bothwell Cl E16 98 D2
Bothwell St 4 W6 134 D6
Botolph Alley EC3 253 A6
Botolph La EC3 253 A6
Botsford Rd SW20 179 A1
Bott's Mews W2 91 C1
Botwell Common Rd UB3 105 C6
Botwell Cres UB3 83 C1
Botwell House RC Prim Sch UB3 105 D4
Botwell La UB3 105 C6
Boucher Cl TW11 174 D5
Bouchier Ho 6 N2 30 B1
Bough Beech Ct EN3 6 D6
Boughton Ave BR2 208 D2
Boughton Ho
Borough The SE1 252 C2
Bromley BR1 188 A3
Boughton Rd SE28 123 C3
Boulcott St E1 96 D1
Boulevard The
Chelsea SW6 266 B1
4 Upper Tooting SW17 159 A2
Boullen Ct SM1 218 A4
Boulogne Ho SE1 263 C6
Boulogne Rd CR0 205 A3
Boulter Ho 4 SE14 140 C4
Boulters Ct HA0 65 A4
Boulton Ho TW8 110 A1
Boulton Rd RM8 81 B6
Boultwood Rd E6 100 B1
Bounces La N9 18 B2
Bounces Rd N9 18 C2
Boundaries Mans 3 SW12 159 A3
Boundaries Rd
Feltham TW13 150 C3
Upper Tooting SW12 159 A3
Boundary Ave E17 53 B2
Boundary Bsns Ct CR4 202 B6
Boundary Cl
Barnet EN5 1 B4
Ilford IG3 79 C4
Kingston u T KT1 198 D6
Penge SE20 184 A1
Southall UB2 107 C1
Boundary Ct
3 Edmonton N18 33 D4
9 New Southgate N11 31 B6
Boundary Ho
Balham SW12 159 B3
1 Camberwell SE5 139 A5
Edgware HA8 44 B6
Isleworth TW1 153 B6
15 Notting Hill W11 112 D5
Boundary La
Camberwell SE17 139 A6
Newham E13, E6 99 D3
Boundary Pas E2 243 C6
Boundary Rd
Avery Hill DA15 167 C6
Barking IG11 101 A5
London N2 30 B2
Mitcham SW19 180 B4
Newham E13 99 D4
Pinner HA5 40 D2
Ponders End N9 18 C5
St John's Wood NW8 92 A6 229 B6
Tottenham N22 33 A1
Wallington SM5, SM6 219 A1
Walthamstow E17 53 C3
Boundary Road Est NW8 92 A6 229 A5
Boundary Row SE1 251 C2
Boundary St E2 95 D3 243 C6
Boundary Way CR0 223 C3
Boundfield Rd SE6 164 C2
Bounds Green Ct N11 31 D4
Bounds Green Ind Est N11 31 C4
Bounds Green Jun & Inf Schs N11 32 A3
Bounds Green Rd
London N11 31 D4
Wood Green N22 32 A3
Bounds Green Sta N11 31 D3
Bourbon Ho 9 SE6 186 A6
Bourchier St W1 249 C6
Bourdillon Ct 2 SE9 166 A2
Bourdon Pl W1 248 D6
Bourdon Rd SE20 184 C1
Bourdon St W1 115 B6 248 D5
Bourke Cl
London SW4 160 A5
Willesden NW10 67 C2
Bourlet Cl W1 239 A3
Bourn Ave
Hillingdon UB8 82 C3
New Barnet EN4 14 B6
West Green N15 51 B5
Bournbrook Rd SE3, SE9 143 D2
Bourne Ave
Hayes UB3 105 B3
Palmers Green N14 16 A2
Ruislip HA4 62 C3
Bourne Cir UB3 105 A3
Bourne Cl
Hinchley Wood KT7 212 D6
Isleworth TW7 130 C2
Bourne Ct
Chiswick W4 133 A6
Ruislip HA4 62 B3
Wanstead E11 55 A4
Woodford IG8 37 D1
Bourne Dr CR4 180 B1
Bourne Gdns E4 35 D6
Bourne Hill N13 16 B2
Bourne Ho
4 Ashford TW15 170 C5
3 Buckhurst Hill IG9 21 D1
5 Clapham SW4 137 C1
1 Dollis Hill NW2 68 A5
Bourne Mans N13 32 C5
Bournemead Ave UB5 84 A5
Bournemead Cl UB5 84 A4
Bournemead Way UB5 84 B5
Bourne Mews W1 238 B1
Bournemouth Cl SE15 140 A3
Bournemouth Ct 6 SM1 218 A3
Bournemouth Rd
London SE15 140 A3
Merton SW19 179 C2
Bourne Par DA5 169 D4
Bourne Pl W4 111 B1
Bourne Prim Sch HA4 62 C2
Bourne Rd
Bexley DA5 169 D5
Bromley BR2 209 D5
Hornsey N8 50 A3
Leyton E7, E11 76 D5
Bournes Ho 4 N15 51 C3
Bourneside Cres 6 N14 15 D3
Bourneside Gdns SE6 186 A5
Bourneside 5 N14 15 D3
Bourne St
Belgravia SW1 115 A2 258 A3

Bourne St *continued*
Croydon CR0 ... 220 D6
Bourne Terr W2 ... 91 D2
Bourne The N14 ... 16 A3
Bourne Vale BR2 ... 209 A2
Bournevale Rd SW16 ... 182 A6
Bourne View UB6 ... 64 D3
Bourne Way
Cheam SM1 ... 217 B3
Coney Hall BR2, BR4 ... 224 D6
West Ewell KT19 ... 215 A4
Bournewood Rd SE18 ... 146 A5
Bournville Rd SE6 ... 163 C4
Bournwell Cl EN4 ... 2 D3
Bourton Cl UB3 ... 106 A5
Bousfield Prim Sch SW10 ... 114 A1 256 A2
Bousfield Rd SE14 ... 140 D3
Boutcher CE Prim Sch SE1 ... 117 D2 263 C4
Boutflower Rd SW11 ... 136 C1
Bouverie Ct 4 SW16 ... 182 A5
Bouverie Gdns HA3 ... 43 D3
Bouverie Mews N16 ... 73 C6
Bouverie Pl W2 ... 236 D2
Bouverie Rd
Harrow HA1 ... 42 A3
Stoke Newington N16 ... 73 C6
Bouverie St EC4 ... 94 C1 241 B1
Bouvier Rd EN3 ... 6 C5
Boveney Rd SE23 ... 162 D4
Bovill Rd SE23 ... 162 D4
Bovingdon Ave HA9 ... 66 C2
Bovingdon Cl 4 N19 ... 71 C6
Bovingdon La NW9 ... 27 C2
Bovingdon Rd SW6 ... 135 D4 265 D1
Bovril Ho EN1 ... 5 C2
BOW ... 97 B5
Bowater Cl
Clapham Pk SW2 ... 160 A5
Kingsbury NW9 ... 45 B4
Bowater Gdns TW16 ... 172 C2
Bowater Ho EC1 ... 242 B5
Bowater Pl SE3 ... 143 B5
Bowater Rd
Greenwich SE18 ... 121 D3
Wembley HA9 ... 66 D5
Bow Brook The 20 E2 ... 96 D5
Bow Church Sta E3 ... 97 C4
BOW COMMON ... 97 D2
Bow Common La E3 ... 97 B3
Bowden Cl TW14 ... 149 C3
Bowden Ct HA4 ... 62 C3
Bowden Ho 29 E3 ... 97 D4
Bowden House Hospl (Private) HA1 ... 64 C6
Bowden St SE11 ... 116 C1 261 B1
Bowditch SE8 ... 119 B1
Bowdon Rd E17 ... 53 C2
Bowen Ct 2 N5 ... 72 D4
Bowen Dr SE21 ... 161 C1
Bowen Rd HA1 ... 42 A2
Bowen St E14 ... 97 D1
Bower Ave SE3 ... 142 C5
Bower Cl UB5 ... 84 C5
Bowerdean St SW6 ... 135 D3
Bower Ho SE14 ... 140 D4
Bowerman Ave SE14 ... 141 A6
Bowerman Ct 1 N19 ... 71 D6
Bowers Ho 5 IG11 ... 78 D1
Bower St E1 ... 96 D1
Bowers Wlk 1 E6 ... 100 B1
Bowery Ct 10 RM10 ... 81 D2
Bowes Cl DA15 ... 168 B5
Bowes Ho N13 ... 32 B5
Bowes-Lyon Hall 13 E16 ... 121 A5
Bowes Lyon Ho 2 TW10 ... 153 C1
BOWES PARK ... 32 A4
Bowes Park Sta N22 ... 32 A3
Bowes Prim Sch N11 ... 31 D5
Bowes Rd Acton W3 ... 111 C6
Dagenham RM8 ... 80 C4
New Southgate N11 ... 31 C5
Bowes Rd (North Circular Rd) N13 ... 32 A5
Bowes Rd KT12 ... 194 B1
Bowfell Rd W6 ... 134 C6
Bowford Ave DA7 ... 147 A4
Bowhill Cl SW9 ... 138 C5
Bow Ho 1 E3 ... 97 C4
Bowie Cl SW4 ... 159 D4
Bow Ind Pk E15 ... 75 C1
Bow La
Barbican EC2, EC4 ... 95 A1 242 B1
Finchley N12 ... 30 A3
Bowland Ho N4 ... 51 A2
Bowland Rd
London SW4 ... 137 D1
Woodford IG8 ... 37 C4
Bowland Yd SW1 ... 247 D1
Bowl Ct EC2 ... 243 B5
Bowles Ct
Finchley N12 ... 30 C3
Harrow HA3 ... 43 A3
Bowles Rd 1 SE1 ... 140 A6
Bowley Cl SE19 ... 183 D4
Bowley Ho 6 SE16 ... 118 A3
Bowley La SE19 ... 183 D5
Bowling Cl UB10 ... 82 B6
Bowling Green Cl SW19 ... 156 B4
Bowling Green Ct HA9 ... 66 B6
Bowling Green Ho SW10 ... 266 C4
Bowling Green La EC1 ... 94 C3 241 B6
Bowling Green Pl SE1 ... 252 C2
Bowling Green Row 1 SE18 ... 122 B2
Bowling Green St SE11 ... 138 C6
Bowling Green Wlk N1 ... 95 C4
Bowls Cl HA7 ... 25 B5
Bowman Ave E16 ... 120 D6
Bowman Homes W5 ... 109 D4
Bowman Mews
St George in t East E1 ... 118 A6
Wandsworth SW18 ... 157 B3
Bowmans Cl W13 ... 109 B5
Bowmans Lea SE23 ... 162 C4
Bowman's Meadow SM6 ... 219 B5
Bowman's Mews N7 ... 72 A5
Bowman's Pl N7 ... 72 A5
Bowman Trad Est NW9 ... 44 C5
Bowmar Lo 13 EN5 ... 1 D1
Bowmead SE9 ... 166 B2
Bowmore Wlk NW1 ... 71 D1
Bowness Cl 5 E8 ... 73 D2
Bowness Cres KT2, SW15 ... 177 C5
Bowness Dr TW4 ... 129 A1
Bowness Ho SE15 ... 140 C5
Bowness Rd
Catford SE6 ... 163 D4
Erith DA7 ... 147 D3
Bowood Rd
Clapham SW11 ... 159 A6
Enfield EN3 ... 6 D3
Bow Rd E3 ... 97 C4
Bowring Gn WD19 ... 22 C5
Bow Road Sta E3 ... 97 C4
Bowrons Ave HA0 ... 65 D1
Bowry Ho 14 E14 ... 97 B2
Bow Sch E3 ... 97 C4
Bowsley Ct TW13 ... 150 A2
Bowsprit Point 1 E14 ... 119 C3
Bowstead Ct SW11 ... 266 D1
Bow St
St Giles WC2 ... 94 A1 240 B1
Stratford E15 ... 76 C3
Bow Triangle Bsns Ctr 17 E3 ... 97 C3
Bowyer Cl E6 ... 100 B2
Bowyer Ct 4 E4 ... 20 A3
Bowyer Ho
Mitcham CR4 ... 202 C6
27 Shoreditch N1 ... 95 C6
Wandsworth SW18 ... 157 D5
Bowyer Pl SE5 ... 139 A5
Bowyer St 15 SE5 ... 139 A5
Boxall Rd SE21 ... 161 C5
Box Cnr TW2 ... 152 C2
Box Elder Cl HA8 ... 27 A5
Boxgrove Prim Sch SE2 ... 124 C3
Boxgrove Rd SE2 ... 124 C3
Box La IG11 ... 102 C5
Boxley Ho 3 E5 ... 74 B3
Boxley Rd SM4 ... 202 A5
Boxley St E16 ... 121 B5
Boxmoor Ho
18 Hackney E2 ... 96 A6
9 Shepherd's Bush W11 ... 112 D5
Boxmoor Rd HA3 ... 43 B5
Boxoll Rd RM9 ... 81 B5
Boxshall Ho 7 SE18 ... 144 D6
Box Tree Ho SE8 ... 119 A1
Boxtree La HA3 ... 24 B3
Boxtree Rd HA3 ... 24 B3
Boxwood Cl UB7 ... 104 B4
Boxworth Cl N12 ... 30 B5
Boxworth Gr N1 ... 94 B6 233 D6
Boyard Rd SE18 ... 122 D1
Boyce Ho
Streatham SW16 ... 181 C5
1 West Kilburn W10 ... 91 B4
Boyce Way E13 ... 99 A3
Boycroft Ave NW9 ... 45 A3
Boyd Ave UB1 ... 107 B5
Boyd Cl KT2 ... 176 C3
Boyd Ct SW15 ... 156 C5
Boydell Ct NW8 ... 70 B1
Boyden Ho 8 E17 ... 54 A6
Boyd Rd SW19 ... 180 B4
Boyd St E1 ... 96 A1
Boyfield St SE1 ... 116 D4 251 D1
Boyland Rd BR1 ... 186 D5
Boyle Ave HA7 ... 25 A4
Boyle Cl UB10 ... 82 B5
Boyle Farm Rd KT7 ... 197 A3
Boyle Ho
13 Belvedere DA17 ... 125 C3
Wembley HA9 ... 66 D5
Boyle St W1 ... 249 A6
Boyne Ave NW4 ... 46 D5
Boyne Ct NW10 ... 68 A1
Boyne Ho 10 E5 ... 74 B6
Boyne Rd
Dagenham RM10 ... 81 C5
Lewisham SE13 ... 142 B2
Boyne Terr Mews W11 ... 113 B5 244 C4
Boyson Rd 10 SE17 ... 139 B6
Boyton Cl London N8 ... 50 A6
Stepney E1 ... 96 D3
Boyton Ho
Kennington SE11 ... 261 A1
St John's Wood NW8 ... 229 D4
Boyton Rd N8 ... 50 A6
Brabant Ct EC3 ... 253 A6
Brabant Rd N22 ... 32 B1
Brabazon Ave SM6 ... 220 A1
Brabazon Rd
Heston TW5 ... 128 D5
Northolt UB5 ... 85 C5
Brabazon St E14 ... 97 D2
Brabner Ho 8 E2 ... 96 A4
Brabourne Cl 7 SE19 ... 183 C5
Brabourne Cres DA7 ... 147 B6
Brabourne Hts NW7 ... 11 C1
Brabourne Rise BR3 ... 208 B4
Brabourn Gr SE15 ... 140 C3
Brabrook Ct SM6 ... 219 B3
Brabstone Ho 2 UB6 ... 86 D5
Bracer Ho 1 N1 ... 95 C5
Bracewell Ave UB6 ... 65 A2
Bracewell Rd W10 ... 90 C2
Bracewood Gdns CR0 ... 221 D5
Bracey Mews 1 N4 ... 72 A6
Bracey St N4 ... 72 A6
Bracken Ave
Balham SW12 ... 159 A4
Croydon CR0 ... 223 C5
Brackenbridge Dr HA4 ... 62 D5
Brackenbury Gdns W6 ... 112 B3
Brackenbury N4 ... 50 B1
Brackenbury Prim Sch W6 ... 112 B3
Brackenbury Rd
East Finchley N2 ... 48 A6
Hammersmith W6 ... 112 B3
Bracken Cl
Ashford TW16 ... 171 D4
Newham E6 ... 100 B2
Twickenham TW4 ... 151 C4
Brackendale Cl TW5 ... 129 D4
Brackendale Ct 2 BR3 ... 185 C3
Brackendale
Kingston u T KT1 ... 176 D1
Southgate N21 ... 16 B2
Bracken End TW7 ... 152 B6
Brackenfield Cl E5 ... 74 B5
Bracken Gdns SW13 ... 134 A3
Bracken Hill Cl 5 BR1 ... 186 D2
Bracken Hill La BR1 ... 186 D2
Brackenhill HA4 ... 63 A4
Bracken Ho 15 E3 ... 97 C2
Bracken Mews
Chingford E4 ... 20 A3
Bracken Mews *continued*
Romford RM7 ... 59 D3
Brackens BR3 ... 185 C3
Brackens The EN1 ... 17 C4
Bracken The E4 ... 20 A2
Brackenwood Lo EN5 ... 1 C1
Brackenwood TW16 ... 172 A2
Brackley Ave SE15 ... 140 C2
Brackley Cl SM6 ... 220 A1
Brackley Ct NW8 ... 236 D6
Brackley Rd
Beckenham BR3 ... 185 C3
Chiswick W4 ... 111 C1
Brackley Sq IG8 ... 37 D3
Brackley St EC1 ... 242 B4
Brackley Terr 6 W4 ... 111 C1
Bracklyn Ct N1 ... 235 C4
Bracklyn St N1 ... 235 C4
Bracknell Cl N22 ... 32 C2
Bracknell Gate NW3 ... 69 D3
Bracknell Gdns NW3 ... 69 D4
Bracknell Way NW3 ... 69 D4
Bracondale KT10 ... 212 A3
Bracondale Rd SE2 ... 124 A2
Braconhyrst HA1 ... 42 C2
Bradbeer Ho 24 E2 ... 96 C4
Bradbourne Ct 11 SM2 ... 217 D2
Bradbourne Rd DA5 ... 169 C4
Bradbourne St SW6 ... 135 C3
Bradbury Cl UB2 ... 107 B2
Bradbury Ct
4 Barnet EN5 ... 1 D1
2 Greenwich SE3 ... 143 A5
Merton SW20 ... 178 C1
Bradbury Ho E1 ... 243 D2
Bradbury St 28 N16 ... 73 C3
Bradby Ho NW8 ... 91 D5
Braddock Cl TW7 ... 130 D3
Braddon Rd TW9 ... 132 B2
Braddyll St SE10 ... 120 C1
Bradenham Ave DA16 ... 146 A1
Bradenham Cl SE17 ... 139 B6
Bradenham Rd
Harrow HA3 ... 43 B5
Hayes UB4 ... 83 C4
Bradenham 11 SE17 ... 139 B6
Braden St W9 ... 91 D3
Bradfield Ct 14 NW1 ... 71 B1
Bradfield Dr IG11 ... 80 A3
Bradfield Ho 15 SW8 ... 137 D3
Bradfield Rd
Newham E16 ... 121 B4
Ruislip HA4 ... 63 A3
Bradford Cl
Bromley BR2 ... 210 B1
Forest Hill SE26 ... 184 B6
Tottenham N17 ... 33 D4
Bradford Dr KT19 ... 215 D2
Bradford Ho 4 W14 ... 112 D3
Bradford Rd
Acton W3 ... 111 C4
Ilford IG1 ... 57 C1
Bradgate Rd SE6 ... 163 D5
Brading Cres E11 ... 77 B6
Brading Rd
Streatham SW2 ... 160 B4
Thornton Heath CR0 ... 204 B3
Brading Terr W12 ... 112 A3
Bradiston Rd W9 ... 91 B4
Bradley Cl N7 ... 72 B2
Bradley Ct CR0 ... 220 C4
Bradley Gdns W13 ... 87 B1
Bradley Ho
Bermondsey SE16 ... 118 B2
1 Bromley E3 ... 97 D4
Twickenham TW1 ... 152 D3
Woodford IG8 ... 37 A3
Bradley Mews SW12 ... 158 D3
Bradley Rd Enfield EN3 ... 7 A6
South Norwood SE19 ... 183 A4
Wood Green N22 ... 32 B1
Bradley's Cl N1 ... 234 B4
Bradley Stone Rd E6 ... 100 B2
Bradlord Ho SE21 ... 161 C1
Bradman Row 7 HA8 ... 27 A3
Bradmead SW8 ... 137 C5 269 A3
Bradmore Ct 2 EN3 ... 7 A2
Bradmore Park Rd W6 ... 112 B2
Bradon 24 NW9 ... 27 D1
Bradshaw Cl SW19 ... 179 C4
Bradshaw Dr NW7 ... 28 D3
Bradshawe Waye UB8 ... 82 B2
Bradshaws Cl SE25 ... 206 A6
Bradsole Ho 10 BR3 ... 185 C3
Bradstock Ho E9 ... 75 A1
Bradstock Rd
Homerton E9 ... 74 D2
Stoneleigh KT17 ... 216 B3
Brad St SE1 ... 116 C5 251 B3
Bradwell Ave RM10 ... 81 C6
Bradwell Cl E18 ... 54 D5
Bradwell Ho
8 Kilburn NW6 ... 91 D6
9 Walthamstow E17 ... 53 D6
Bradwell Mews 5 N18 ... 34 A6
Brady Ct RM8 ... 58 D1
Brady Dr BR1 ... 210 C6
Brady Ho
London SW4 ... 159 D6
South Lambeth SW8 ... 269 B2
Bradymead E6 ... 100 D1
Brady St E1 ... 96 B3
Braeburn Ct 1 EN4 ... 2 C1
Brae Ct
2 Kingston u T KT2 ... 176 C2
South Norwood SE25 ... 183 C2
Braefoot Ct SW15 ... 156 D6
Braemar Ave
Thornton Heath CR7 ... 204 D6
Welsh Harp NW10 ... 67 B6
Wembley HA0 ... 66 A1
Wimbledon SW18, SW19 ... 157 C2
Wood Green N22 ... 32 A2
Braemar Ct
4 Brentford TW8 ... 131 D6
5 Catford SE6 ... 164 D3
Braemar Gdns
Hendon NW9 ... 27 B2
Longlands DA15 ... 167 B1
West Wickham BR4 ... 208 A1
Braemar Ho
Richmond TW11 ... 175 B5
St John's Wood W9 ... 229 A1
Braemar Mans W8 ... 255 D5
Braemar SW15 ... 156 D5
Braemar Rd
Brentford TW8 ... 131 D6
Newham E13 ... 98 D3
North Cheam KT4 ... 216 B5
South Tottenham N15 ... 51 C4
Braemore Ct EN4 ... 3 A1
Braeside Ave SW19 ... 179 A2
Braeside BR3 ... 185 D5
Braeside Cl HA5 ... 23 C3
Braeside Rd SW16 ... 181 C3
Braeside Sch
Buckhurst Hill IG9 ... 21 B3
Buckhurst Hill IG9 ... 21 C2
Braes St N1 ... 72 D1
Braesyde Cl DA17 ... 125 B2
Brafferton Rd CR0 ... 221 A4
Braganza St SE17 ... 116 D1 261 C1
Bragg Cl RM8 ... 80 B2
Bragg Rd TW11 ... 174 D4
Braham Ho SE11 ... 260 D1
Braham St E1 ... 243 D2
Brahma Kumaris World Spiritual Univ NW10 ... 68 A1
Braid Ave W3 ... 89 C1
Braid Cl TW13 ... 151 B2
Braid Ho SE10 ... 142 A4
Braidwood Ho 2 CR7 ... 204 D5
Braidwood Rd SE6 ... 164 B3
Braidwood St SE1 ... 117 C5 253 A3
Braikenridge Ho N21 ... 17 B5
Brailsford Cl SW19 ... 180 C3
Brailsford Rd SW2 ... 160 C5
Braintcroft Prim Sch NW2 ... 67 D5
Brainton Ave TW14 ... 150 C4
Braintree Ave IG4 ... 56 A5
Braintree Ho 6 E1 ... 96 C3
Braintree Ind Est HA4 ... 62 B4
Braintree Rd
Dagenham RM10 ... 81 C5
Ruislip HA4 ... 62 B4
Braintree St E2 ... 96 C4
Braithwaite Ave RM7 ... 59 C2
Braithwaite Gdns HA7 ... 25 C2
Braithwaite Ho EC1 ... 242 C6
Braithwaite Rd EN3 ... 7 B2
Braithwaite Twr W2 ... 236 C4
Brake Shear Ho 1 EN5 ... 1 B2
Bramah Gn SW9 ... 138 C4
Bramah Mus of Tea & Coffee* SE1 ... 252 B3
Bramalea Cl N6 ... 49 A3
Bramall Cl E15 ... 76 D3
Bramall Ct N7 ... 72 B
Bramber Ct TW8 ... 110 A
Bramber Ho 9 KT2 ... 176 A
Bramber Rd
Colney Hatch N12 ... 30 C
Fulham W14 ... 135 B6 264 C
Bramber WC1 ... 233 A
Bramble Acres Cl SM2 ... 217 C
Bramblebury Rd SE18 ... 123 A
Bramble Cl
Beckenham BR3 ... 208 A
Croydon CR0 ... 223 D
Hillingdon UB8 ... 82 B
South Tottenham N15 ... 52 A
Stanmore HA7 ... 25 D
Upper Halliford TW17 ... 193 B
Brambledown Cl BR2, BR4 ... 208 C
Brambledown 8 N4 ... 50 A
Brambledown Rd
South Croydon CR2 ... 221 C
Wallington SM5, SM6 ... 219 B
Bramble Gdns W12 ... 111 D
Bramble Ho 16 E3 ... 97 C
Bramble La TW12 ... 173 B
Brambles Cl TW7, TW8 ... 131 B
Brambles Farm Dr UB10 ... 82 C
Brambles The
West Drayton UB7 ... 104 A
8 Wimbledon SW19 ... 179 B
Bramblewood Cl SM5 ... 202 C
Brambling Ct
25 Deptford SE8 ... 141 B
South Norwood SE25 ... 205 D
Bramblings The E4 ... 36 B
Bramcote Ave CR4 ... 202 D
Bramcote Ct CR4 ... 202 D
Bramcote Gr SE16 ... 118 C
Bramcote Rd SW15 ... 134 B
Bramdean Cres SE12 ... 165 A
Bramdean Gdns SE12 ... 165 A
Bramerton NW6 ... 68 D
Bramerton Rd BR3 ... 207 B
Bramerton St SW3 ... 136 C6 267 A
Bramfield Ct N4 ... 73 A
Bramfield Rd SW11 ... 158 D
Bramford Ct N14 ... 15 D
Bramford Rd SW18 ... 136 A
Bramham Gdns
Chessington KT9 ... 213 D
South Kensington SW5 ... 113 D1 255 D
Bramham Ho SE22 ... 139 C
Bramhope La SE7 ... 143 B
Bramlands Cl SW11 ... 136 C
Bramley Ave TW17 ... 193 C
Bramley Cl
Croydon CR2 ... 221 A
East Barnet N14 ... 15 B
Hayes UB3 ... 106 A
Higham Hill E17 ... 35 A
Orpington BR6 ... 210 D
Pinner HA5 ... 39 D
Twickenham TW2 ... 152 A
Woodford IG8 ... 37 C
Bramley Cres
Ilford IG2 ... 56 C
Nine Elms SW8 ... 137 D5 269 D
Bramley Ct
2 Barnet EN4 ... 2 C
9 Chingford E4 ... 20 A
Dollis Hill NW2 ... 68 B
Feltham TW14 ... 149 C
Hither Green SE13 ... 164 B
Mitcham CR4 ... 180 B
Southall UB1 ... 108 A
Wallington SM6 ... 219 C
Welling DA16 ... 146 B
Bramley Gdns WD19 ... 22 C
Bramley Hill CR2 ... 221 A
Bramley Ho
Hounslow TW3 ... 129 B
Ilford IG2 ... 56 C
1 Kingston u T KT2 ... 176 D
19 North Kensington W10 ... 90 D
Roehampton SW15 ... 155 D
Bramley House Ct EN2 ... 5 B
Bramleyhyrst CR2 ... 221 A
Bramley Lo HA0 ... 65 D

ramley Rd
Ealing W5 ... 109 C3
North Kensington
W10 ... 90 D1
Southgate N14 ... 15 C6
Sutton SM1 ... 218 B3
ramley Way
Hounslow TW4 ... 151 B6
West Wickham BR4 ... 223 D6
rampton Cl 14 E5 ... 74 B6
rampton Coll NW4 ... 46 C5
rampton Ct NW4 ... 46 B5
rampton Gr
Harrow HA3 ... 43 B5
Hendon NW4 ... 46 C5
Wembley HA9 ... 44 C1
rampton La 6 NW4 ... 46 C5
rampton Lo DA7 ... 146 D5
rampton Manor Sch
E6 ... 99 D3
rampton Park Rd
N22 ... 50 C6
rampton Prim Sch
Bexley DA7 ... 146 D3
Newham E6 ... 100 A4
rampton Rd
Bexleyheath DA7 ... 147 A4
Croydon CR0 ... 205 D3
Harringay N15 ... 51 A4
Hillingdon UB10 ... 82 D5
Newham E6 ... 99 D4
Queensbury NW9 ... 44 C5
rampton WC1 ... 240 C3
ramshaw Gdns
WD19 ... 22 D5
ramshaw Rd E9 ... 74 D2
ramshaw Rise KT3 ... 199 C3
ramshill Gdns NW5 ... 71 B5
ramshill Rd NW10 ... 89 D5
ramshot Ave SE7 ... 143 B6
ramshott Ct 3
KT6 ... 198 A3
ramshurst NW8 ... 91 D6
ramston Rd
Harlesden NW10 ... 90 A5
Wandsworth SW17 ... 158 A1
ramwell Cl TW16 ... 172 D1
ramwell Ho
Borough The SE1 ... 262 B5
Chelsea SW1 ... 269 A6
Bramwell Mews N1 ... 233 D6
Brancaster Dr NW7 ... 28 A3
Brancaster Ho
22 Globe Town E1 ... 96 D4
Islington N5 ... 72 D3
Brancaster Rd
Ilford E12 ... 78 B4
Newbury Pk IG2 ... 57 C3
Streatham SW16 ... 160 A1
Brancepeth Gdns
IG9 ... 21 A2
Branch Hill NW3 ... 70 A5
Branch Ho 18 SM1 ... 218 A4
Branch Pl N1 .. 95 B6 235 D6
Branch Rd E14 ... 119 A6
Branch St SE15 ... 139 C5
Brancker Rd HA3 ... 43 D6
Brancroft Way EN3 ... 7 B4
Brandan Ho 11 HA1 ... 42 D4
Brand Cl N4 ... 50 D1
Branden Lo 18 W4 ... 111 A1
Brandlehow Rd
SW15 ... 135 B1
Brandon Ho BR3 ... 185 D5
Brandon Mews
Barbican EC2 ... 242 C4
Walworth SE17 ... 262 B3
Brandon Pl N8 ... 50 B5
Brandon Rd
Barnsbury N7 ... 72 A1
Southall UB2 ... 107 B1
Sutton SM1 ... 217 D4
Walthamstow E17 ... 54 A6
Brandon St
SE17 ... 117 A2 262 B3
Brandram Rd SE13 ... 142 C1
Brandrams Wharf
SE16 ... 118 C4
Brandreth Ct HA1 ... 42 D3
Brandreth Rd
Newham E6 ... 100 B1
Upper Tooting SW17 ... 159 B2
Brandries The SM6 ... 219 D5
Brand St SE10 ... 142 A5
Brandville Gdns IG6 ... 56 D5
Brandville Rd UB7 ... 104 A4
Brandy Way SM2 ... 217 C1
Brangbourne Rd
BR1 ... 186 A5
Brangton Rd SE11 ... 260 D1
Brangwyn Cres
SW19 ... 180 B1
Brangwyn Ct W14 ... 254 A5
Branham Ho 1
SE18 ... 122 D1
Branksea St
SW6 ... 135 A5 264 A3
Branksome Ave N18 ... 33 D5
Branksome Cl
Teddington TW11 ... 174 B6
Walton-on-T KT12 ... 194 D1
Branksome Ct 6 N2 ... 48 A6
Branksome Ho SW8 ... 270 C4
Branksome Rd
London SW2 ... 160 A6
Merton SW19 ... 179 C2
Branksome Way
Harrow HA3 ... 44 B3
Kingston u T KT3 ... 177 B2
Bransby Ct 4 N16 ... 73 C4
Bransby Rd KT9 ... 214 A2
Branscombe Ct
BR2 ... 208 C4
Branscombe Gdns
N21 ... 16 C4
Branscombe NW1 ... 232 B5
Branscombe St
SE13 ... 141 D2
Bransdale Cl NW6 ... 91 C6
Bransgrove Rd HA8 ... 26 B3
Branston Cres BR5 ... 211 B1
Branstone Ct 9
TW9 ... 132 B4
Branstone Rd TW9 ... 132 B4
Branston Ho N7 ... 72 C3
Brants Wlk W7 ... 86 C3
Brantwood Ave
Erith DA8 ... 147 D5
Isleworth TW7 ... 131 A1
Brantwood Cl E17 ... 53 D6
Brantwood Gdns
Enfield EN2 ... 16 A6
Redbridge IG4 ... 56 A5
Brantwood Ho 9
SE5 ... 139 A5
Brantwood Rd
Erith DA7 ... 147 D3
Herne Hill SE24 ... 161 A6
Tottenham N17 ... 34 A4
Brasenose Dr SW13 ... 134 C6
Brasher Cl UB6 ... 64 B3
Brashley Road Cvn Site
NW10 ... 89 C4
Brassett Point 3
E15 ... 98 C6
Brassey Cl TW14 ... 150 A3
Brassey Ho
1 Millwall E14 ... 119 D2
Walton-on-T KT12 ... 194 A1
Brassey Rd NW6 ... 69 B2
Brassey Sq SW11 ... 137 A2
Brassie Ave W3 ... 89 C1
Brass Talley Alley 31
SE16 ... 118 D4
Brasted Cl
Bexley DA6 ... 168 D6
Forest Hill SE26 ... 184 C6
Brasted Lo 11 BR3 ... 185 C3
Brathay NW1 ... 232 B3
Brathway Rd SW18 ... 157 C4
Bratley St 11 E1 ... 96 A3
Bratten Ct CR0 ... 205 B3
Braund Ave UB6 ... 85 D3
Braundton Ave
DA15 ... 167 D3
Braunston Dr UB4 ... 85 A3
Braunston Ho TW8 ... 131 C6
Bravington Cl TW17 ... 192 B4
Bravington Pl W9 ... 91 B3
Bravington Rd W9 ... 91 B4
Brawne Ho 12 SE17 ... 138 D6
Braxfield Rd SE4 ... 141 B1
Braxted Pk SW16 ... 182 B4
Brayard's Rd SE15 ... 140 B3
Braybourne Dr
TW7 ... 130 D5
Braybrooke Gdns
SE19 ... 183 C3
Braybrook St W12 ... 89 D1
Brayburne Ave SW4 ... 137 C3
Braycourt Ave KT12 ... 194 C2
Bray Cres SE16 ... 118 D4
Bray Ct
Chessington KT9 ... 214 B3
Streatham SW16 ... 182 A5
Braydon Rd N16 ... 52 A1
Bray Dr E16 ... 120 D6
Brayfield Terr N1 ... 72 C1
Brayford Sq 12 E1 ... 96 C1
Bray NW3 ... 70 C1
Bray Pl SW3 .. 114 D2 257 C3
Bray Rd NW7 ... 28 D4
Brayton Gdns EN2 ... 3 D1
Braywick Ct 9 KT2 ... 176 C3
Braywood Rd SE9 ... 145 B1
Brazier Cres UB5 ... 85 B3
Brazil Cl CR0 ... 204 A2
Breach La RM9 ... 103 C4
Bread St EC2, EC4 ... 242 B1
Breakspeare SE21 ... 161 D1
Breakspear Jun & Inf
Schs UB10 ... 60 C6
Breakspear Rd N
UB9 ... 38 B5
Breakspear Rd HA4,
UB9 ... 38 D3
Breakspear Rd S UB9,
UB10 ... 38 C1
Breakspears Dr
BR5 ... 190 A2
Breakspears Mews
SE4 ... 141 C3
Breakspears Rd
SE4 ... 141 C2
Breakwell Ct 10 W10 ... 91 A3
Bream Cl N17 ... 52 B5
Bream Gdns E6 ... 100 C4
Breamore Cl SW15 ... 156 A3
Breamore Ct IG3 ... 80 A6
Breamore Ho 21
SE15 ... 140 A5
Breamore Rd IG3 ... 79 D6
Bream's Bldgs
EC4 ... 94 C1 241 A2
Bream St E3 ... 75 C1
Breamwater Gdns
TW10 ... 153 B1
Brearley Cl
Burnt Oak HA8 ... 27 A3
Uxbridge UB8 ... 60 A2
Breaside Prep Sch
BR1 ... 187 D2
Breasley Cl SW15 ... 134 B1
Brechin Pl
SW7 ... 114 A2 256 B3
Brecknock Prim Sch
N7 ... 71 D2
Brecknock Rd N19 ... 71 D3
Breckonmead BR1 ... 187 C1
Brecon Cl
Mitcham CR4 ... 204 A6
North Cheam KT4 ... 216 C6
Brecon Ct
7 Eltham SE9 ... 166 C5
Whetstone N12 ... 14 A1
Brecon Gn NW9 ... 45 C3
Brecon Ho
Stamford Hill N16 ... 51 D1
Wandsworth SW18 ... 157 C4
Brecon Rd Enfield EN3 .. 6 C1
Fulham W6 . 135 A6 264 B5
Brede Cl E6 ... 100 C4
Bredel Ho 1 E14 ... 97 C2
Bredgar SE13 ... 163 D6
Bredgar Rd N19 ... 71 C6
Bredhurst Cl SE20 ... 184 C4
Bredinghurst SE22 ... 162 A4
Bredinghurst Sch
SE15 ... 140 D1
Bredin Ho SW10 ... 265 D4
Bredo Ho IG11 ... 102 B4
Bredon Ct HA8 ... 26 B6
Bredon Rd CR0 ... 205 D2
Breer St SW6 ... 135 D2
Breezer's Ct 22 E1 ... 118 A6
Breezer's Hill E1 ... 118 A6
Brehon Ho NW1 ... 232 A5
Brember Rd HA2 ... 64 A6
Bremer Mews E17 ... 53 D5
Bremner Rd SW7 ... 256 B6
Brenchley Cl
Chislehurst BR7 ... 188 C2
Hayes BR2 ... 208 D3
Brenchley Gdns SE15,
SE22, SE23 ... 162 D5
Brenchley Rd BR5 ... 189 D1
Bren Ct 27 EN3 ... 7 C6
Brenda Rd SW17 ... 158 D2
Brende Gdns KT8 ... 195 D5
Brendon Ave NW10 ... 67 C4
Brendon Cl
Esher KT10 ... 212 A2
Harlington UB7 ... 127 A5
Brendon Ct
3 London N20 ... 14 C2
Southall UB2 ... 107 D2
Brendon Dr KT10 ... 212 A2
Brendon Gdns
Harrow HA2 ... 63 D4
Ilford IG2 ... 57 C4
Brendon Gr N2 ... 30 A1
Brendon Ho
Marylebone W1 ... 238 A4
Sutton SM2 ... 218 A2
Brendon Rd
Dagenham RM8 ... 59 C1
New Eltham SE9 ... 167 B2
Brendon St
W1 ... 92 C1 237 B2
Brendon Villas N21 ... 17 A3
Brendon Way EN1 ... 17 C4
Brenley Cl CR4 ... 203 A6
Brenley Gdns SE9 ... 143 D1
Brenley Ho SE1 ... 252 C2
Brennands Ct 14 N19 ... 71 C5
Brent Adult Comm
Education Service
Coll NW10 ... 89 B6
Brent Cl DA5 ... 169 A3
Brentcot Cl W13 ... 87 B3
Brent Cres NW10 ... 88 B5
Brent Cross Flyover NW2,
NW4 ... 46 D2
Brent Cross Gdns
NW4 ... 46 D3
Brent Cross
Interchange NW2,
NW4 ... 46 D2
Brent Cross Sh Ctr
NW4 ... 46 C2
Brent Cross Sta
NW11 ... 46 D2
Brent Ct
3 Acton W12 ... 111 C3
Ealing W7 ... 108 B6
Hendon NW11 ... 46 D2
Brentfield Cl NW10 ... 67 B2
Brentfield Gdns
NW2 ... 46 D2
Brentfield Ho 7
NW10 ... 67 B1
Brentfield Prim Sch
NW10 ... 67 B2
Brentfield Rd NW10 ... 67 B2
Brentfield NW10 ... 66 D1
BRENTFORD ... 131 B6
Brentford Bsns Ctr
TW8 ... 131 C5
Brentford Cl UB4 ... 84 D3
BRENTFORD END ... 131 C4
Brentford Fountain L
Ctr W4 ... 110 C1
Brentford Ho 6
TW1 ... 153 B4
Brentford Sch for Girls
TW8 ... 131 D6
Brentford Sta TW8 ... 131 C6
Brent Gn NW4 ... 46 D4
Brentham Way W5 ... 87 D3
Brent Ho
3 Catford BR1 ... 186 B5
16 Hackney E9 ... 74 C2
Brenthouse Rd E9 ... 74 C1
Brent Ho HA9 ... 66 B3
Brenthurst Rd NW10 ... 67 D2
Brent Knoll Sch
SE26 ... 162 D1
Brent Lea TW8 ... 131 C5
Brent Mans NW4 ... 46 C4
Brentmead Cl W7 ... 108 C6
Brentmead Gdns
NW10 ... 88 B5
Brentmead Pl NW11 ... 46 D3
Brent Mus* NW10 ... 68 B2
Brent New Ent Ctr
NW10 ... 67 D2
Brenton Ct E9 ... 75 A3
Brenton St E14 ... 97 A1
Brent Park Ind Est
UB2 ... 106 C3
Brent Park Rd NW4 ... 46 B2
Brent Pl EN5 ... 13 B6
Brent Rd
Brentford TW8 ... 131 C6
Newham E16 ... 99 A2
Southall UB2 ... 106 C3
Woolwich SE18 ... 144 D5
Brentside TW8 ... 131 C6
Brentside Cl W13 ... 87 A3
Brentside Executive Ctr
TW8 ... 131 B6
Brentside High Sch
W7 ... 86 C3
Brentside Prim Sch
W7 ... 86 C3
Brent St NW4 ... 46 C4
Brent Trad Est NW10 ... 67 C3
Brentvale Ave
Southall UB1 ... 108 B5
Wembley HA0 ... 88 B6
Brent View Rd NW9 ... 46 A2
Brentwaters Bsns Pk
TW8 ... 131 C5
Brent Way
Brentford TW8 ... 131 D5
Finchley N3 ... 29 C4
Wembley HA9 ... 66 D2
Brentwick Gdns
TW8 ... 110 A2
Brentwood Cl SE9 ... 167 A3
Brentwood Ho 2
SE18 ... 143 D5
Brentwood Lo NW4 ... 46 D4
Brereton Ho 4
SW2 ... 160 C4
Brereton Rd N17 ... 33 D3
Bressenden Pl
SW1 ... 115 C3 259 A6
Bressey Ave EN1 ... 6 A4
Bressey Gr E18 ... 36 D1
Bretherton Ct CR2 ... 221 C2
Breton Ho
Bermondsey SE1 ... 263 C6
St Luke's EC2 ... 242 B5
Brett Cl
15 Northolt UB5 ... 84 D4
Stoke Newington N16 ... 73 C6
Brett Cres NW10 ... 89 B6
Brett Ct N9 ... 18 C2
Brettell St SE17 ... 262 D1
Brettenham Ave E17 ... 35 C2
Brettenham Prim Sch
N18 ... 34 A6
Brettenham Rd
Edmonton N18 ... 34 A6
Walthamstow E17 ... 35 C2
Brett Ho 1 SW15 ... 156 D4
Brett House Cl 2
SW15 ... 156 D4
Brettinghurst 8
SE1 ... 118 A1
Bretton Ho N19 ... 50 A1
Brett Pas 28 E8 ... 74 B3
Brett Rd Barnet EN5 ... 12 C6
Hackney E8 ... 74 B3
Brewers Bldgs EC1 ... 234 C2
Brewers Ct W2 ... 236 A2
Brewer's Gn SW1 ... 259 C6
Brewers Hall Gdns
EC2 ... 242 B3
Brewers La 11 TW9 ... 153 D6
Brewer St
W1 ... 115 C6 249 B6
Brewery Cl HA0 ... 65 A4
Brewery Ind Est The
N1 ... 235 B3
Brewery Mews Bsns Ctr
1 TW7 ... 131 A2
Brewery Rd
Islington N7 ... 72 A2
Keston Mark BR2 ... 210 A1
Plumstead SE18 ... 123 B1
Brewery Sq
Bermondsey SE1 ... 253 C3
Clerkenwell EC1 ... 241 D6
Brewhouse La
Putney SW15 ... 135 A2
Wapping E1 ... 118 B5
Brewhouse Rd 3
SE18 ... 122 B2
Brewhouse Wlk
SE16 ... 119 A5
Brewhouse Yd EC1 ... 241 C6
Brewood Rd RM8 ... 80 B2
Brewster Gdns W10 ... 90 C2
Brewster Ho
Bermondsey SE1 ... 263 D4
Poplar E14 ... 119 B6
Brewster Rd E10 ... 53 D1
Brian Ct N10 ... 31 B2
Brian Rd RM6 ... 58 C4
Briant Ho SE1 ... 260 D5
Briants Cl HA5 ... 23 B1
Briant St SE14 ... 140 D5
Briar Ave SW16 ... 182 B3
Briarbank Rd W13 ... 87 A1
Briar Cl
Buckhurst Hill IG9 ... 21 D2
Edmonton N13 ... 17 A1
Finchley N2 ... 30 A1
Hampton TW12 ... 173 B5
Isleworth TW7 ... 152 D6
Briar Cres UB5 ... 63 D2
Briar Ct 3 Bow E3 ... 97 C5
Cheam SM3 ... 216 C4
Dalston E8 ... 73 D1
Hampton TW12 ... 173 D5
Leytonstone E11 ... 54 B2
Briardale HA8 ... 27 B6
Briardale Gdns NW3 ... 69 C5
Briardale Ho 12 N16 ... 51 C1
Briardale SW19 ... 157 B3
Briarfield Ave N3 ... 29 D1
Briarfield Cl DA7 ... 147 C3
Briar Gdns BR2 ... 208 D1
Briaris Cl 11 N17 ... 34 B3
Briar La CR0 ... 223 D4
Briar Lo E18 ... 37 C2
Briar Rd
Cricklewood NW2 ... 68 C4
Harrow HA3 ... 43 C4
Littleton TW17 ... 192 C4
Thornton Heath
SW16 ... 204 B6
Twickenham TW2 ... 152 C3
Briars The WD23 ... 8 C4
Briarswood Way
BR6 ... 227 D3
Briar The 11 SM1 ... 218 A4
Briarview Ct E4 ... 36 B4
Briar Way UB7 ... 104 C4
Briar Wlk
Burnt Oak HA8 ... 27 A3
Putney SW15 ... 134 B1
West Kilburn W10 ... 91 A3
Briarwood Cl
Feltham TW13 ... 149 C1
Kingsbury NW9 ... 45 A3
Briarwood Ct 5
KT4 ... 200 A1
Briarwood Dr HA6 ... 22 A1
Briarwood Rd
London SW4 ... 159 D6
Stoneleigh KT17 ... 216 A2
Briary Cl NW3 ... 70 C1
Briary Ct
10 Canning Town
E16 ... 98 D1
Sidcup DA14 ... 190 B5
Briary Gdns BR1 ... 187 B5
Briary Gr HA8 ... 26 D1
Briary La N9 ... 17 D1
Briary Lo BR3 ... 186 A2
Brickbarn Cl SW10 ... 266 B4
Brick Ct EC4 ... 241 A1
Brickett Cl HA4 ... 39 A4
Brick Farm Cl TW9 ... 132 D4
Brickfield Cl TW8 ... 131 C5
Brickfield Cotts
SE18 ... 145 D6
Brickfield Farm Gdns
BR6 ... 227 A4
Brickfield La
Edgware EN5 ... 11 D5
Harlington UB3 ... 127 B6
Brickfield Rd
South Norwood CR7,
SW16 ... 182 D2
Wimbledon SW19 ... 179 D6
Brickfields HA2 ... 64 B6
Brickfields Way
UB7 ... 104 B3
Brick La Enfield EN1 ... 6 B3
Northolt UB5 ... 85 B4
Shoreditch E2 ... 95 D4
Spitalfields
E1 ... 95 D3 243 D5
Stanmore HA7 ... 25 D3
Bricklayers Arms
SE1 ... 262 D5
Brick St W1 .. 115 B5 248 C3
Brickwall La HA4 ... 39 D1
Brickwood Cl SE26 ... 162 B1
Brickwood Rd CR0 ... 221 C6
Brickworth Ho 26
SW9 ... 138 C4
Brideale Cl SE15 ... 139 D6
Bride Ct EC4 ... 241 C1
Bride La EC4 .. 94 D1 241 C1
Bridel Mews N1 ... 234 C5
Bride St N7 ... 72 B2
Bridewain St SE1 ... 263 C6
Bridewell Pl
Holborn EC4 ... 241 C1
20 Wapping E1 ... 118 B5
Bridford Mews W1 ... 238 D4
Bridge App NW3 ... 71 A1
Bridge Ave Ealing W7 .. 86 B2
Hammersmith W6 ... 112 C1
Bridge Avenue Mans 1
W6 ... 112 C1
Bridge Bsns Ctr The
UB2 ... 107 C4
Bridge Cl Enfield EN1 ... 6 B3
13 North Kensington
W10 ... 90 D1
Teddington TW11 ... 174 D6
Walton-on-T KT12 ... 193 D1
Bridge Ct
9 Blackwall E14 ... 120 B6
Leyton E10 ... 53 B2
2 Walton-on-T
KT12 ... 193 D1
7 Willesden NW10 ... 67 C1
Bridge Dr N13 ... 32 B6
Bridge End E17 ... 36 A2
Bridge Field Ho 7
W2 ... 91 D1
Bridgefield Rd SM1 ... 217 C2
Bridgefoot
SE1 ... 116 A1 260 B1
Bridge Gate N21 ... 17 A4
Bridge Gdns
Canonbury N16 ... 73 B4
East Molesey KT8 ... 196 B5
Littleton TW15 ... 171 A3
Bridge Ho
Brockley SE4 ... 141 B1
1 Camden Town
NW1 ... 71 A1
Ealing TW8 ... 109 A2
Homerton E9 ... 74 D3
Bridge Ho S TW8 ... 109 A2
Bridge House Quay
E14 ... 120 A5
Bridge Ho SE28 ... 123 C5
Bridge La
SW11 ... 136 C4 267 B1
Bridgeland Rd E16 ... 121 A6
Bridgelands Cl BR3 ... 185 B3
Bridge La NW11 ... 47 B4
Bridgeman Ho 19 E9 ... 74 C1
Bridgeman Rd
Islington N1 ... 72 B1
Teddington TW11 ... 175 A4
Bridgeman St
NW8 ... 92 C5 230 A3

Bridge Meadows SE14 ... 140 D6
Bridgend Rd SW18 ... 136 A1
Bridgenhall Rd EN1 ... 5 D4
Bridgen Ho 9 E1 ... 96 B1
Bridgen Rd DA5 ... 169 A4
Bridge Par
7 Croydon CR0 ... 220 D5
Edmonton N21 ... 17 A4
Bridge Pk
7 London SW18 ... 157 C6
Wembley NW10 ... 66 D1
Bridge Pl
Belgravia SW1 ... 115 B2 258 D4
Croydon CR0 ... 205 B1
Bridgepoint Lofts 2 E7 ... 77 C1
Bridgeport Pl 4 E1 ... 118 A5
Bridge Rd
Beckenham BR3 ... 185 B3
Bexleyheath DA7 ... 147 A3
Chessington KT9 ... 214 A3
East Ham E6 ... 78 B1
East Molesey KT8 ... 196 C5
Isleworth TW3, TW7 ... 130 B2
Southall UB2 ... 107 C4
Stratford Marsh E15 ... 98 B6
Sutton SM2 ... 217 D2
Twickenham TW1 ... 153 B5
Wallington SM6 ... 219 C3
Walthamstow E17 ... 53 B2
Wembley HA9 ... 66 C5
Willesden NW10 ... 67 C2
Wood Green N22 ... 32 A2
Bridge Row CR0 ... 205 B1
Bridge Sch The
Clerkenwell EC1 ... 94 D3 241 C6
Shoreditch N1 ... 95 A6 235 B6
Bridges Ct SW11 ... 136 B3
Bridges Ho 15 SE5 ... 139 B5
Bridges La CR0 ... 220 A4
Bridges Rd
Stanmore HA7 ... 24 D5
Wimbledon SW19 ... 179 D4
Bridges Road Mews SW19 ... 179 D4
Bridge St W4 ... 111 B2
Bridges The NW4 ... 46 A6
Bridge St Pinner HA5 ... 41 A6
Richmond TW10 ... 153 D6
Walton-on-T KT12 ... 193 D2
Westminster SW1 ... 116 A4 250 B1
Bridge Terr E15 ... 76 B1
Bridge The HA3 ... 42 D5
Bridgetown Cl 5 SE19 ... 183 C5
Bridgeview 2 W6 ... 112 C1
Bridgewater Cl BR7 ... 211 C6
Bridgewater Ct HA0 ... 65 C2
Bridgewater Gdns HA8 ... 26 B1
Bridgewater Ho UB5 ... 85 A3
Bridgewater Rd
Ruislip HA4 ... 62 B4
Stratford Marsh E15 ... 98 A6
Wembley HA0 ... 65 C1
Bridgewater Sq EC2 ... 242 A4
Bridgewater St EC2 ... 242 A4
Bridgeway IG11 ... 79 D1
Bridge Way NW11 ... 47 B4
Bridgeway St NW1 ... 93 C5 232 B3
Bridge Way
Twickenham TW2 ... 152 A4
Uxbridge UB10 ... 60 D3
Bridgeway HA0 ... 66 B1
Bridge Wharf 18 E2 ... 96 D5
Bridge Wharf Rd TW7 ... 131 B2
Bridgewood Cl SE20 ... 184 B3
Bridgewood Rd
North Cheam KT17, KT4 ... 216 A4
Streatham SW16 ... 181 D3
Bridge Yd SE1 ... 252 D4
Bridgford St SW17, SW18 ... 158 A1
Bridgman Rd W4 ... 111 A3
Bridgnorth Ho 10 SE15 ... 140 A6
Bridgwater Ho W2 ... 236 A2
Bridle Cl Enfield EN3 ... 7 B6
Kingston u T KT1 ... 197 D5
Sunbury TW16 ... 194 A6
West Ewell KT19 ... 215 B3
Bridle La
Marylebone W1 ... 115 C6 249 B6
Bridle La *continued*
Twickenham TW1 ... 153 B5
Bridle Path The IG8 ... 36 C3
Bridle Path CR0 ... 220 A5
Bridlepath Way TW14 ... 149 C3
Bridle Rd
Addington CR0 ... 223 C4
Claygate KT10 ... 213 B2
Croydon CR0 ... 223 C6
Pinner HA5 ... 40 C4
Bridle Way
Addington CR0 ... 223 C3
Orpington BR6 ... 227 A4
Bridle Way The SM6 ... 219 C3
Bridlington Ho SW18 ... 136 A1
Bridlington Rd N9 ... 18 B4
Bridport Ave RM7 ... 59 D3
Bridport Ho
6 Edmonton N18 ... 34 A5
Shoreditch N1 ... 235 D5
Bridport Pl N1 ... 95 B6 235 D5
Bridport Rd
Edmonton N18 ... 33 D5
Greenford UB6 ... 85 D6
Thornton Heath CR7 ... 204 D6
Bridport SE17 ... 262 B1
Bridstow Pl W2 ... 91 C1
Brief St SE5 ... 138 D4
Brierfield NW1 ... 232 A5
Brierley Ave N9 ... 18 C3
Brierley Cl SE25 ... 206 A5
Brierley Ct W7 ... 108 C6
Brierley CR0 ... 223 D2
Brierley Rd
Leyton E11 ... 76 B4
Upper Tooting SW12 ... 159 C2
Brierly Gdns E2 ... 96 C5
Brigade Cl HA2 ... 64 B6
Brigade St SE3 ... 142 D3
Brigadier Ave EN2 ... 5 A4
Brigadier Hill EN2 ... 5 A5
Briggeford Cl 5 E5 ... 74 A6
Briggs Cl CR4 ... 181 B2
Briggs Ho 20 E2 ... 95 D4
Bright Cl DA17 ... 124 D2
Bright Ct 8 SE28 ... 124 C5
Brightfield Rd SE12 ... 164 D6
Brightling Rd SE4 ... 163 B5
Brightlingsea Pl 5 E14 ... 119 B6
Brightman Rd SW18 ... 158 B3
Brighton Ave E17 ... 53 B4
Brighton Bldgs SE1 ... 263 A5
Brighton Cl UB10 ... 60 D1
Brighton Ct SW15 ... 157 B5
Brighton Dr 3 UB5 ... 63 C2
Brighton Gr SE14 ... 141 A4
Brighton Ho 7 SE5 ... 139 B4
Brighton Rd
Belmont SM2 ... 217 D1
Finchley N2 ... 30 A1
South Croydon CR2 ... 221 B2
Stoke Newington N16 ... 73 C4
Surbiton KT6 ... 197 D3
Sutton SM2 ... 218 A1
Wallend E6 ... 100 C4
Brighton Terr SW9 ... 138 B1
Brightside Rd SE13 ... 164 B5
Brightside The EN3 ... 7 A4
Bright St E14 ... 97 D2
Brightwell Cl CR0 ... 204 C1
Brightwell Cres SW17 ... 180 D5
Brightwell Ct N7 ... 72 B3
Brightwells 1 SW6 ... 135 D3
Brig Mews SE8 ... 141 C6
Brigstock Ho SE5 ... 139 A3
Brigstock Par 1 CR7 ... 204 C4
Brigstock Rd
Belvedere DA17 ... 125 D2
Thornton Heath CR7 ... 204 D4
Brill Ho NW10 ... 67 B5
Brill Pl NW1 ... 93 D5 232 D3
Brim Hill N2 ... 48 B5
Brimpsfield Cl SE2 ... 124 B3
BRIMSDOWN ... 7 B3
Brimsdown Ave EN3 ... 7 A4
Brimsdown Ho E3 ... 98 A3
Brimsdown Jun & Inf Sch EN3 ... 6 D2
Brimsdown Sta EN3 ... 7 A3
Brimstone Ho 4 E15 ... 76 C1
Brindishe Prim Sch SE12 ... 164 D6
Brindle Gate DA15 ... 167 C3
Brindley Cl
Bexleyheath DA7 ... 147 D2
Wembley HA0 ... 87 D6
Brindley Ho
Carshalton SM1 ... 218 C3
37 Notting Hill W2 ... 91 C2
Brindley Ho *continued*
22 Streatham SW12 ... 160 A4
Brindley St SE14 ... 141 B4
Brindley Way
Bromley BR1 ... 187 B5
Southall UB1 ... 107 D6
Brindwood Rd E4 ... 19 C1
Brine Ct KT6 ... 197 D4
Brine Ho 11 E3 ... 97 A5
Brinkburn Cl
Abbey Wood SE2 ... 124 A2
Edgware HA8 ... 44 D6
Brinkburn Gdns HA8 ... 44 C6
Brinkley 18 KT1 ... 176 C1
Brinkley Rd KT4 ... 216 B6
Brinklow Cres SE18 ... 144 D5
Brinklow Ho W2 ... 91 D2
Brinkworth Rd IG5 ... 56 A6
Brinkworth Way E9 ... 75 B2
Brinsdale Rd NW4 ... 46 D6
Brinsley Ho 17 E1 ... 96 C1
Brinsley Rd HA3 ... 24 B1
Brinsley St 35 E1 ... 96 B1
Brinsworth Cl TW2 ... 152 B2
Brinton Wlk SE1 ... 251 C3
Brion Pl E14 ... 98 A2
Brisbane Ave SW19 ... 179 D2
Brisbane Ct N10 ... 31 B3
Brisbane Ho 3 W12 ... 112 B6
Brisbane Rd
Ealing W13 ... 109 A4
Ilford IG1 ... 57 A1
Leyton E10 ... 75 D6
Brisbane St SE5 ... 139 B5
Briscoe Cl E11 ... 76 D6
Briscoe Rd SW19 ... 180 B4
Briset Rd SE9 ... 143 D1
Briset St EC1 ... 94 D3 241 C5
Briset Way N7 ... 72 B6
Bristol Cl
Stanwell TW19 ... 148 A5
Wallington SM6 ... 220 A1
Bristol Ct 11 TW19 ... 148 A5
Bristol Gdns
Putney SW15 ... 156 C4
Westbourne Green W9 ... 91 D3
Bristol Ho
1 Barking IG11 ... 80 A1
SE11 ... 261 A5
Bristol Mews W9 ... 91 D3
Bristol Park Rd 1 E17 ... 53 A5
Bristol Rd
Greenford UB6 ... 85 D6
Morden SM4 ... 202 A4
Upton E7 ... 77 D2
Briston Gr N8 ... 50 A3
Briston Mews NW7 ... 28 A3
Bristowe Cl 24 SW2 ... 160 C5
Bristow Rd
Bexleyheath DA7 ... 147 A4
Hounslow TW3 ... 130 A2
Wallington CR0 ... 220 A4
West Norwood SE19 ... 183 C5
Britain at War Experience* SE1 ... 253 A3
Britannia Building N1 ... 235 C2
Britannia Cl
London SW4 ... 137 D1
Northolt UB5 ... 84 D4
Britannia Gate 11 E16 ... 121 A5
Britannia Ho N20 ... 14 A1
Britannia Junc NW1 ... 231 D6
Britannia La TW2 ... 152 A4
Britannia Rd
Ilford IG1 ... 78 D5
23 Millwall E14 ... 119 C2
Surbiton KT5 ... 198 B2
Walham Green SW6 ... 135 D5 265 C3
Whetstone N12 ... 14 A1
Britannia Row N1 ... 95 A6 235 A6
Britannia St WC1 ... 94 B4 233 C2
Britannia Village Prim Sch E16 ... 121 B5
Britannia Way NW10 ... 88 D3
Britannia Wlk N1 ... 235 C2
British Coll of Osteopathic Medicine NW3 ... 70 A2
British Gr W4 ... 111 D1
British Grove Pas 2 W4 ... 111 D1
British Grove S 3 W4 ... 111 D1
British Home & Hospl for Incurables SE27 ... 182 D5
British Legion Rd E4 ... 20 D2
British Library (Newspaper Library) NW9 ... 45 C6
British Library The* WC1 ... 93 D4 232 D2
British Mus* WC1 ... 94 A2 240 A3
British St E3 ... 97 B4
British Wharf Ind Est SE14 ... 140 D6
Britley Ho 16 E14 ... 97 B1
Brittain Ct SE9 ... 166 A3
Brittain Rd RM8 ... 81 B5
Brittany Ho SW15 ... 134 C1
Brittany Point SE11 ... 261 A3
Britten Cl Elstree WD6 ... 9 D5
Golders Green NW11 ... 47 D1
Brittenden Cl 1 BR6 ... 227 D2
Brittenden Par BR6 ... 227 D2
Britten Dr UB1 ... 85 C1
Britten Ho SW3 ... 257 B2
Britten St SW3 ... 114 C1 257 A2
Britton Cl SE6 ... 164 B4
Britton St EC1 ... 94 D3 241 C5
Brixham Cres HA4 ... 40 A1
Brixham Gdns IG3 ... 79 C3
Brixham Rd DA16 ... 146 D4
Brixham St E16 ... 122 C5
BRIXTON ... 138 C2
Brixton Day Coll SW9 ... 138 A2
Brixton Hill Ct 5 SW2 ... 160 B6
Brixton Hill SW2 ... 160 B5
Brixton Hill Pl SW2 ... 160 A4
Brixton Mkt SW9 ... 138 C1
Brixton Oval 7 SW2 ... 138 C1
Brixton Rd SW9 ... 138 C4
Brixton Sta SW9 ... 138 C1
Brixton Station Rd SW9 ... 138 C2
Brixton Water La SW2 ... 160 B6
Broadacre Cl UB10 ... 60 D5
Broadbent Cl N6 ... 49 B1
Broadbent St W1 ... 248 C6
Broadberry Ct N18 ... 34 B5
Broadbridge Cl SE3 ... 143 A5
Broad Common Est N16 ... 52 A1
Broadcoombe CR2 ... 222 D1
Broadcroft Ave HA7 ... 25 D1
Broadcroft Rd BR5 ... 211 B2
Broad Ct WC2 ... 240 B1
Broadeaves Cl CR2 ... 221 C3
Broadfield Cl
Croydon CR0 ... 220 B6
Dollis Hill NW2 ... 68 C5
Broadfield Ct
Bushey WD23 ... 8 C2
Edgware HA8 ... 10 D1
Broadfield La NW1 ... 72 A1
Broadfield NW6 ... 69 D2
Broadfield Rd SE6 ... 164 C3
Broadfields Ave
Edgware HA8 ... 10 D1
Southgate N21 ... 16 C4
Broadfields HA2 ... 23 D1
Broadfields Hts HA8 ... 26 D6
Broadfields Prim Sch HA8 ... 10 C2
Broadfield Sq EN1 ... 6 B3
Broadfields KT8 ... 196 C3
Broadfields Way NW10 ... 67 D3
Broadfield Way IG9 ... 21 C1
Broadford Ho 12 E1 ... 97 A3
BROADGATE ... 95 C2
Broadgate Circ EC2 ... 95 C2 243 A3
Broadgate EC2 ... 95 C2 243 A4
Broadgate Rd E16 ... 99 D1
Broadgates Ave EN4 ... 1 D4
Broadgates Ct SE11 ... 261 B1
Broadgates Rd SW18 ... 158 B3
BROAD GREEN ... 204 D3
Broad Green Ave CR0 ... 204 D2
Broadhead Strand NW9 ... 27 D2
Broadheath Dr BR7 ... 188 B5
Broadhinton Rd SW4 ... 137 C2
Broadhurst Ave
Edgware HA8 ... 26 D6
Ilford IG3 ... 79 D4
Broadhurst Cl
Hampstead NW6 ... 70 A2
9 Richmond TW10 ... 154 B6
Broadhurst Gdns
Hampstead NW6 ... 69 D2
Broadhurst Gdns *continued*
Ruislip HA4 ... 62 C6
Broadhurst Mans NW6 ... 69 D2
Broad La
Broadgate EC2 ... 243 A4
Hampton TW12 ... 173 C4
Hornsey Vale N8 ... 50 B4
Broadlands Ave
Enfield EN3 ... 6 B2
Shepperton TW17 ... 193 A3
Streatham SW16 ... 160 A2
Broadlands Cl
Enfield EN3 ... 6 C2
Highgate N6 ... 49 A2
Streatham SW16 ... 160 A2
Broadlands Ct TW9 ... 132 C5
Broadlands
Feltham TW13 ... 151 C1
Highgate N6 ... 49 A2
Broadlands Lo N6 ... 48 D2
Broadlands Mans 2 SW16 ... 160 A2
Broadlands Rd
Grove Pk BR1 ... 187 B6
Highgate N6 ... 48 D2
Broadlands Way KT3 ... 199 D3
Broad La
South Tottenham N15 ... 51 D5
South Tottenham N15 ... 52 A5
Broadlawns Ct HA3 ... 24 D2
Broad Lawn SE9 ... 166 C3
Broadley St NW8 ... 92 C2 237 A4
Broadley Terr NW1 ... 92 C3 237 B5
Broadmayne SE17 ... 262 C2
Broadmead Ave KT4 ... 200 A2
Broadmead SE6 ... 163 C1
Broadmead Cl
Hampton TW12 ... 173 C4
Pinner HA5 ... 23 A3
Broadmead Ct 6 IG8 ... 37 A4
Broadmead TW12 ... 173 C4
Broadmead Inf Sch CR0 ... 205 B2
Broadmead Jun Sch CR0 ... 205 B3
Broadmead Rd
Northolt UB5 ... 85 A3
Woodford IG8 ... 37 B3
Broadmead W14 ... 254 A3
Broad Oak TW16 ... 171 D4
Broad Oak Cl
Chingford E4 ... 35 C5
St Paul's Cray BR5 ... 190 A1
Broadoak Ct 8 SW9 ... 138 C2
Broadoak Ho 11 NW6 ... 91 D6
Broadoaks BR7 ... 188 D4
Broad Oaks KT6 ... 214 D6
Broadoaks Way BR2 ... 208 D4
Broad Oak IG8 ... 37 B5
Broad St Ave EC2 ... 243 A3
Broad Sanctuary SW1 ... 250 A1
Broad St RM10 ... 81 C1
Broadstone Ho SW8 ... 270 C3
Broadstone Pl W1 ... 238 A3
Broad Street Health Ctr RM10 ... 103 C6
Broad Street Pl EC2 ... 242 D3
Broad St TW11 ... 174 D4
Broadview Est TW19 ... 148 C4
Broadview Ho RM8 ... 58 D1
Broadview NW9 ... 44 C3
Broadview Rd SW16 ... 181 D3
Broadwalk HA2 ... 41 D4
Broadwalk Ho SW7 ... 246 A1
Broadwalk La NW11 ... 47 B2
Broadwalk Sh Ctr The HA8 ... 26 D4
Broadwalk E18 ... 54 D6
Broadwall SE1 ... 116 C5 251 B4
Broadwater Farm Prim Sch N17 ... 33 B1
Broadwater Gdns BR6 ... 227 A4
Broadwater Prim Sch SW17 ... 180 C6
Broadwater Rd
Plumstead SE18 ... 123 B3
Tottenham N17 ... 33 C1
Upper Tooting SW17 ... 180 C6
Broadway Arc 3 W6 ... 112 C2
Broadway Ave
Thornton Heath CR0 ... 205 B
Twickenham TW1 ... 153 B
Broadway
Barking IG11 ... 101 A
Bexley DA6 ... 147 C
Bexleyheath DA6 ... 147 B
Broadway Bldgs 5 W7 ... 108 C
Broadway Cl IG8 ... 37 B
Broadway Ct BR3 ... 208 A
Broadway Ctr The 6 W6 ... 112 C
Broadway Ct SW19 ... 179 C
Broadway Gdns
Mitcham CR4 ... 202 C
Woodford IG8 ... 37 B
Broadway W7 ... 108 C
Broadway Ho 2 E8 ... 96 B
Broadway Ho 5 SW19 ... 179 C
Broadway Lofts SW17 ... 180 C
Broadway Mans SW6 ... 265 B
Broadway Market E8 ... 96 B
Broadway Market Mews 21 E8 ... 96 A
Broadway Mews
Bowes Pk N13 ... 32 B
Southgate N21 ... 16 D
Stamford Hill E5 ... 51 D
Broadway Par
Chingford E4 ... 36 A
Hayes UB3 ... 106 A
Hornsey N8 ... 50 A
West Drayton UB7 ... 104 A
Broadway Pl SW19 ... 179 B
Broadway Ret Pk NW2 ... 68 D
Broadway Sh Ctr 5 DA6 ... 147 C
Broadway E15 ... 76 B
Broadway The
Barnes SW13 ... 133 C
Cheam SM3 ... 217 A
Chingford E4 ... 36 B
Dagenham RM8 ... 81 C
Ealing W5 ... 109 D
Edgware NW7 ... 27 D
Edmonton N9 ... 18 A
Friern Barnet N11 ... 31 A
Greenford UB6 ... 86 A
Harrow HA3 ... 24 D
Hornsey N8 ... 50 A
Merton SW19 ... 179 C
Newham E13 ... 99 B
Pinner HA5 ... 23 B
South Acton W3 ... 110 C
Southall UB1 ... 107 A
2 Southgate N14 ... 15 D
Stanmore HA7 ... 25 C
Sutton SM1 ... 218 A
Thames Ditton KT10 ... 196 C
Tolworth KT6 ... 198 C
Wallington SM6 ... 220 A
Wembley HA9 ... 66 A
Woodford IG8 ... 37 B
Wood Green N22 ... 32 C
Broadway
West Ealing W13 ... 109 A5
Westminster SW1 ... 115 D3 259 C6
Broadway Wlk 4 E14 ... 119 C3
Broadwell Ct TW5 ... 128 D4
Broadwick St W1 ... 93 C1 239 B1
Broad Wlk
Eltham SE3, SE18 ... 144 A3
Heston TW5 ... 129 A4
Mayfair W1 ... 115 A5 248 A4
Regent's Pk NW1 ... 93 A5 231 B3
Richmond TW9 ... 132 B5
Southgate N21 ... 16 B3
Broad Wlk The W8 ... 113 D5 245 D3
Broadwood Ave HA4 ... 39 C3
Broadwood Terr W14 ... 254 D4
Broad Yd EC1 ... 241 C5
Brocade Ct NW9 ... 45 D5
Brocas Cl NW3 ... 70 C1
Brockbridge Ho SW15 ... 155 D5
Brockdene Dr BR2 ... 225 D4
Brockdish Ave IG11 ... 79 D3
Brockelbank Lo RM8 ... 80 D6
Brockenhurst Ave KT4 ... 199 C1
Brockenhurst KT8 ... 195 B3
Brockenhurst Gdns
Edgware NW7 ... 27 C5
Ilford IG1 ... 79 A3

Brockenhurst Mews 9 N18 34 A6
Brockenhurst Rd CR0 206 B2
Brockenhurst Way SW16 181 D1
Brocket Ho 16 SW8 137 D3
Brockham Cl SW19 179 B5
Brockham Cres CR0 224 B1
Brockham Ct
17 Belmont SM2 217 D1
8 South Croydon CR2 221 A3
Brockham Dr
Ilford IG2 57 A4
Streatham SW2 160 B4
Brockham Ho
Camden Town NW1 232 B5
11 Streatham SW2 160 B4
Brockham St SE1 262 B6
Brockhurst Cl HA7 24 D4
Brockhurst Ho N4 51 B2
Brockill Cres SE4 141 A1
Brocklebank Ho 7 E16 122 C5
Brocklebank Rd
Greenwich SE7 121 B2
Wandsworth SW18 158 A4
Brocklebank Road Ind Est SE7 121 A2
Brocklehurst St SE14 140 D5
Brocklesby Rd SE25 206 B5
BROCKLEY 141 B1
Brockley Ave HA7 10 A1
Brockley Cl HA7 26 A6
Brockley Cross Bsns Ctr SE4 141 A2
Brockley Cross SE4 141 B2
Brockley Gdns SE4 141 B3
Brockley Gr SE4 163 B6
Brockley Hall Rd SE4 163 A6
Brockley Hill Ho HA7 9 C3
Brockley Hill HA7, HA8 9 D2
Brockley Ho SE17 263 A2
Brockley Mews SE4 163 A6
Brockley Pk SE23 163 A4
Brockley Prim Sch SE4 163 B6
Brockley Rd SE4 163 B6
Brockley Rise SE23 163 A4
Brockleyside HA7 26 A6
Brockley Sta SE4 141 A2
Brockley View SE23 163 A4
Brockley Way SE4 163 A6
Brockman Rise BR1 186 B6
Brockmer Ho 5 E1 118 B6
Brock Pl E3 97 D3
Brock Rd E13 99 B2
Brocks Dr SM3 217 A5
Brockshot Cl 1 TW8 131 D6
Brock St SE15 140 C2
Brockway Cl E11 76 C6
Brockweir 28 E2 96 C5
Brockwell Ave BR3 207 D4
Brockwell Cl BR5 211 D4
Brockwell Ct
2 London SW2 160 C6
Thornton Heath CR0 204 D2
Brockwell Ho SE11 270 D6
Brockwell Park Gdns SE24 160 D4
Brockwell Park Row SW2 160 C5
Brockwell Park* SE24 160 D5
Brockworth 8 KT2 176 D2
Broderick Ho SE21 161 C1
Brodia Rd N16 73 C5
Brodick Ho 12 E3 97 B5
Brodie Ct E10 54 B1
Brodie Ho
Bermondsey SE1 263 D2
7 Wallington SM6 219 B4
Brodie Rd
Chingford E4 20 A2
Enfield EN2 5 A5
Brodie St SE1 117 D1 263 D2
Brodlove La E1 118 D6
Brodrick Gr SE2 124 B2
Brodrick Rd SW17 158 C2
Brody Ho E1 243 C3
Brograve Gdns BR3 185 D1
Broken Wharf EC4 252 A6
Brokesley St E3 97 B4
Broke Wlk
Hackney E8 95 D6
1 Hackney E8 96 A6
Bromar Rd SE5 139 C2
Bromborough Gn WD19 22 C5
Bromefield HA7 25 C2
Bromehead St 8 E1 96 C1
Bromell's Rd SW4 137 C1
Brome Rd SE9 144 B2
Bromfelde Rd SW4 137 D3
Bromfield Ct 20 SE16 118 A3
Bromfield St N1 234 B4
Bromhall Rd RM8 80 B2
Bromhedge SE9 166 B1
Bromholm Rd SE2 124 B3
Bromleigh Ct 1 SE21, SE22 162 B2
Bromleigh Ho SE1 263 C6
BROMLEY E3 97 D4
BR1 186 C2
Bromley Ave BR1 186 C3
Bromley-by-Bow Sta E3 98 A4
Bromley Coll BR1 187 A2
Bromley Coll of F & H Ed BR2 209 D3
Bromley Comm BR2 209 D4
BROMLEY COMMON 210 A3
Bromley Cres
Beckenham BR2 208 D6
Ruislip HA4 61 D4
Bromley Ct BR1 186 D3
Bromley Gdns BR2 208 D6
Bromley Gr BR2 186 B1
Bromley Hall Rd E14 98 A2
Bromley High Sch BR1 210 C5
Bromley High St E3 97 D4
Bromley Hill BR1 186 C4
Bromley Ho 5 BR1 187 A2
Bromley Ind Ctr BR1 209 D6
Bromley La BR7 189 B3
Bromley Lo 2 W3 89 A1
Bromley Manor Mans 3 BR1 209 A6
Bromley North Sta BR1 187 A2
BROMLEY PARK 186 D2
Bromley Pk 11 BR1 186 D2
Bromley Pl W1 239 A4
Bromley Rd
Beckenham BR3 185 D2
Bromley BR2, BR3 186 B1
Catford SE6 163 D1
Chislehurst BR7 188 D2
Edmonton N18 17 B1
Leyton E10 53 D3
Tottenham N17 34 A2
Walthamstow E17 53 C6
Bromley Road Inf Sch BR3 185 D2
Bromley Road Ret Pk SE6 163 D2
Bromley South Sta BR2 209 A6
Bromley St E1 96 D1
BROMPTON 114 B3
Brompton Arc SW1 247 D1
Brompton Cl
Hounslow TW4 151 B6
Penge SE20 184 A1
Brompton Ct 4 HA7 25 C6
Brompton Gr N2 48 C5
Brompton Ho 3 N9 34 A6
Brompton Oratory SW3 114 C3 257 A5
Brompton Park Cres SW6 135 D6 265 C5
Brompton Pl SW3 114 C3 257 B6
Brompton Rd SW3 114 C3 257 A5
Brompton Sq SW3 114 C3 257 A6
Bromstone Ho 19 SW9 138 C4
Bromwich Ave N6 71 A6
Bromwich Ho 3 TW10 154 A5
Bromyard Ave W3 111 C6
Bromyard Ho
Acton W3 111 C5
3 Peckham SE15 140 B5
Bron Ct NW6 91 C6
BRONDESBURY 69 A2
Brondesbury Coll for Boys NW6 69 A1
Brondesbury Ct NW2 68 D2
Brondesbury Mews 11 NW6 69 C1
BRONDESBURY PARK 90 D6
Brondesbury Park Sta NW6 91 A6
Brondesbury Pk NW2 68 D1
Brondesbury Rd NW6 91 C5
Brondesbury Sta NW6 69 B1
Brondesbury Villas NW6 91 C5
Bronhill Terr N17 34 A2
Bronsart Rd SW6 135 A5 264 A3
Bronson Rd SW20 179 A1
Bronte Cl Erith DA8 147 D5
1 Forest Gate E7 77 A4
Ilford IG2 56 C5
Bronte Ct 8 W14 112 D3
Bronte Ho
Kilburn NW6 91 C4
6 Stoke Newington N16 73 C3
Bronti Cl SE17 117 A1 262 B2
Bronwen Ct NW8 229 C1
Bronze Age Way DA17 125 D4
Bronze St SE8 141 C5
Brook Ave
Dagenham RM10 81 D1
Edgware HA8 26 D4
Wembley HA9 66 C5
Brookbank Ave W7 86 B2
Brook Bank EN1 6 B6
Brookbank Rd SE13 141 D2
Brook Cl Acton W3 110 C5
Finchley N12 29 A3
Ruislip HA4 39 C2
Stanwell TW19 148 B4
Upper Tooting SW17 159 A2
West Barnes SW20 200 B6
Brook Com Prim Sch E8 74 A3
Brook Cres
Chingford E4 35 D6
Edmonton N9 34 B6
Brook Ct
Barking IG11 101 D6
Beckenham BR3 185 B2
5 Brentford TW8 131 D6
Cheam SM3 216 C4
Edgware HA8 26 D5
2 Leyton E11 76 C5
Mortlake SW14 133 C2
Stratford New Town E15 76 A3
Walthamstow E17 53 A6
Brookdale N11 31 C6
Brookdale Rd
Catford SE6 163 D4
Lewisham SE6 163 D5
Sidcup DA5 169 A5
Walthamstow E17 53 C6
Brookdales The NW4 47 A5
Brookdene N12 29 D6
Brookdene Rd SE18, SE2 123 D2
Brook Dr Harrow HA1 42 A5
Newington SE11 116 D2 261 C4
Ruislip HA4 39 C2
Brooke Ave HA2 64 A5
Brooke Cl WD23 8 A4
Brooke Ct
Kilburn W10 91 A5
7 Kingston u T KT2 175 D6
Brooke Ho
Bushey WD23 8 A4
4 New Cross Gate SE14 141 A4
Brookehowse Rd SE6 163 D1
Brookend Rd DA15 167 C3
Brooke Rd
Shacklewell E5, N16 74 A5
Walthamstow E17 54 A5
Brookes Ct EC1 241 A4
Brooke's Mkt EC1 241 B4
Brooke St EC1 94 C2 241 A3
Brooke Way WD23 8 A4
Brookfield Ave
Carshalton SM1, SM5 218 C5
Ealing W5 87 D3
Mill Hill NW7 28 B4
Walthamstow E17 54 A5
Brookfield Cl NW7 28 B4
Brookfield Cres
Harrow HA3 44 A4
Mill Hill NW7 28 B4
Brookfield Ct
Greenford UB6 86 A4
1 London N12 29 D6
Brookfield
Dartmouth Pk N6 71 A5
1 Finsbury Pk N4 72 C6
Brookfield Gdns KT10 212 D2
Brookfield Ho 23 E2 96 B5
Brookfield House Sch IG8 36 C4
Brookfield Path IG8 36 C4
Brookfield Pk NW5 71 B5
Brookfield Prim Sch
Cheam SM3 201 A1
Dartmouth Pk N19 71 B6
Brookfield Rd
Acton W4 111 B4
Edmonton N9 18 B1
Homerton E9 75 A2
Brookfields Ave CR4 202 C4
Brookfields EN3 6 D1
Brookgate N16 73 B6
Brook Gate W1 114 D6 247 D5
Brook Gdns
Barnes SW13 133 D2
Chingford E4 35 D6
Kingston u T KT2 177 A2
Brook Gn W6 112 D2
BROOK GREEN 112 D2
Brook Green Flats 11 W14 112 D3
Brookhill Cl
East Barnet EN4 14 C6
Woolwich SE18 122 D1
Brookhill Ct 2 EN4 14 C5
Brookhill Rd
East Barnet EN4 14 C6
Woolwich SE18 122 D1
Brook Ho
3 Clapham Pk SW4 159 C6
Ealing W3 110 C4
3 Edmonton N9 18 A1
4 Hammersmith W6 112 C2
Marylebone WC1 239 C4
Brook Hos NW1 232 B3
Brook Ho 4 TW1 153 A4
Brookhouse Gdns E4 36 C6
Brook House Sixth Form Coll E5 74 B5
Brook Ind Est UB4 106 C5
Brooking Cl RM8 80 C5
Brooking Rd E7 77 A3
Brook La Bexley DA5 168 D5
Greenwich SE3 143 B3
Brook La N 3 TW8 131 D6
Brookland Cl NW11 47 C5
Brookland Garth NW11 47 D5
Brookland Hill NW11 47 D5
Brookland Jun & Inf Schs NW11 47 D5
Brookland Rise NW11 47 C5
Brooklands Ave
New Eltham DA15 167 B2
Wandsworth SW18 157 D2
Brooklands Cl TW16 171 C2
Brooklands Court Apartments 3 NW6 69 B1
Brooklands Ct
10 Clapham SW8 137 C3
Enfield N21 17 B6
Kingston u T KT1 197 D5
2 London NW6 69 B1
2 Mitcham CR4 180 B1
Brooklands Dr UB6 87 D6
Brooklands Ho SE3 143 A2
Brooklands Pk SE3 143 A2
Brooklands Pl TW12 173 D5
Brooklands Prim Sch SE3 143 A2
Brooklands Rd KT7 197 A1
Brooklands The TW7 130 B4
Brook Lane Bns Ctr TW8 109 D1
Brook La BR1 187 A4
Brooklea Cl NW9 27 C2
Brook Lo
Crouch End N8 49 D3
Edgware HA8 26 D4
Hendon NW4 46 D4
Brooklyn Ave SE25 206 B5
Brooklyn Cl SM5 218 C6
Brooklyn Ct
Feltham TW13 150 B2
Shepherd's Bush W12 112 C5
Brooklyn Gr SE25 206 B5
Brooklyn SE20 184 A3
Brooklyn Rd
Bromley BR2 210 A4
Croydon SE25 206 B5
Brookmarsh Ind Est SE10 141 D5
Brook Mdw N12 13 D1
Brookmead Ave BR1, BR2 210 B4
Brookmead Ct N20 14 A2
Brookmead Ind Est CR4 203 C3
Brook Meadow Cl IG8 36 C4
Brookmead Rd CR0 203 C3
Brook Mead KT19 215 C2
Brook Mews N W2 114 A6 246 B6
Brookmill Rd SE8 141 C4
Brook Park Cl N21 16 D6
Brook Pl EN5 13 C6
Brook Rd
Buckhurst Hill IG9 21 A3
Dollis Hill NW2 68 A6
Finchley N12 30 C3
Hornsey N8 50 A5
Ilford IG2 57 C3
Brook Rd S TW8 131 D6
Brook Rd
South Norwood CR7 205 A5
Surbiton KT6 214 A6
Twickenham TW1 153 A5
Wood Green N22 50 B6
Brook Ret Pk HA4 62 D3
Brooks Ave E6 100 B3
Brooksbank Ho 7 E9 74 C2
Brooksbank St 9 E9 74 C2
Brooksby Ho 9 N1 72 C1
Brooksby Mews N1 72 C1
Brooksby St N1 72 C1
Brooksby's Wlk E9 74 D3
Brooks Cl SE9 166 C2
Brookscroft Rd E17 35 D2
Brookscroft E17 53 D6
Brooks Ct
3 London SW4 138 A3
Nine Elms SW8 269 B4
Brookshill Ave HA3 24 C5
Brookshill Dr HA3 24 B5
Brookshill Gate HA3 24 B5
Brookshill HA3 24 B5
Brooks Ho 6 SW2 160 C3
Brookside BR6 211 D2
Brookside Cl
Barnet EN5 13 A5
Feltham TW13 150 A1
Harrow HA3 43 D4
South Harrow HA2, HA4 63 A4
Brookside Cres 1 KT4 200 A1
Brookside Ct SW16 181 C3
Brookside EN4 14 C5
Brookside Gdns EN1 6 C6
Brookside UB10 60 B1
Brookside Ho N17 33 C1
Brookside Prim Sch UB4 84 C4
Brookside Rd
Edmonton N9 34 B6
Hayes UB4 106 C6
Temple Fortune NW11 47 B3
Upper Holloway N19 71 C6
Brookside S EN4 15 A4
Brookside
Southgate N21 16 B5
Wallington SM5 219 A3
Brookside Way CR0 206 D3
Brooks La W4 132 C6
Brook's Mans 5 IG3 58 B1
Brook's Mews W1 115 B6 248 C6
Brook's Par 6 IG3 58 B1
Brook Sq SE18 144 A4
Brooks Rd W4 110 C1
Brook's Rd E13 99 A6
Brook St
Bayswater W2 114 B6 246 D6
Erith DA8 147 D5
Kingston u T KT1 176 A1
Mayfair W1 115 B6 248 C6
Brookstone Ct SE15 140 B1
Brook St 7 N17 33 D1
Brooksville Ave NW6 91 A6
Brook Vale DA8 147 D4
Brookview Ct 11 EN1 17 C6
Brookview Rd SW16 181 C5
Brookville Rd SW6 135 B5 264 C3
Brookway SE3 143 A2
Brook Wlk
Burnt Oak HA8 27 B4
Finchley N2 30 B2
Brookwood Ave SW13 133 D3
Brookwood Cl BR2 208 D5
Brookwood Ho SE1 251 D1
Brookwood Rd
Hounslow TW3 129 D4
Wandsworth SW18 157 C3
Broom Ave BR5 190 B1
Broom Cl
Bromley Comm BR2 210 A3
Broom Cl *continued*
Teddington KT1, TW11 175 D3
Broomcroft Ave UB5 84 C4
Broome Ct 3 TW9 132 C4
Broome Ho 7 E5 74 B3
Broome Rd TW12 173 B2
Broome Way SE5 139 B5
Broom Farm SW6 135 C3
Broomfield Ave N13 32 B5
Broomfield 7 NW1 71 A1
Broomfield Cotts N13 32 A5
Broomfield Ct N13 32 A5
Broomfield Ho
Stanmore HA7 9 A1
4 St Paul's Cray BR5 190 B1
Broomfield House Sch TW9 132 B4
Broomfield Ho SE17 263 A3
Broomfield La N13 32 B6
Broomfield Pl W13 109 B5
Broomfield Rd
Beckenham BR3 207 B6
Bexley DA6 169 C6
Bowes Pk N13 32 A5
Dagenham RM6 58 D2
Ealing W13 109 B5
Richmond TW9 132 B4
Surbiton KT5 198 B1
Teddington TW11 175 C4
Broomfield Sch N14 31 D5
Broomfields KT10 212 A3
Broomfield St E14 97 D2
Broomfield
Sunbury TW16 172 A2
Walthamstow E17 53 B2
Broom Gdns CR0 223 C5
Broomgrove Gdns HA8 26 C2
Broomgrove Rd SW9 138 B3
BROOM HILL 211 D2
Broomhill Ct 2 IG8 37 A4
Broomhill Rd
Broom Hill BR6 211 D2
Ilford IG3 80 A6
Wandsworth SW18 157 C6
Woodford IG8 37 A4
Broomhill Rise DA6 169 C6
Broomhill Wlk IG8 36 D3
Broomhouse La SW6 135 C2
Broomhouse Rd SW6 135 C3
Broomleigh BR1 187 A2
Broomloan La SM1 217 C6
Broom Lock TW11 175 C4
Broom Mead DA6 169 C6
Broom Pk KT1 175 D3
Broom Rd
Croydon CR0 223 C5
Teddington TW11 175 C4
Broomsleigh Bsns Pk SE26 185 B5
Broomsleigh St NW6 69 B3
Broom Water TW11 175 C5
Broom Water W TW11 175 C5
Broomwood Cl CR0 206 D4
Broomwood Hall Sch SW12 159 A4
Broomwood Rd
London SW11 159 A6
St Paul's Cray BR5 190 B1
Broseley Gr SE26 185 A5
Broster Gdns SE25 205 D6
Brougham Rd
Acton W3 89 A1
Hackney E8 96 A6
Brougham St SW11 136 D3
Brough Cl
Kingston u T KT2 175 D5
South Lambeth SW8 270 B3
Broughton Ave
London N3 47 A6
Richmond TW10 175 C6
Broughton Ct W13 109 B6
Broughton Dr 19 SW9 138 D1
Broughton Gdns N6 49 C3
Broughton Ho 10 SW19 179 A3
Broughton Rd
Ealing W13 109 B6
Orpington BR6 227 B6
Sands End SW6 135 D3
Thornton Heath CR7 204 C3
Broughton Road App 2 SW6 135 D3
Broughton St SW8 137 B3
Brouncker Rd W3 111 A4
Browells La TW13 150 B2

Brown Bear Ct TW13 172 D6
Brown Cl SM6 220 A1
Browne Ho
  13 Deptford SE8 141 C5
  9 Penge SE26 184 B5
Brownfield St E14 98 A1
Brownflete Ho SE4 141 A1
Browngraves Rd UB7 127 A5
Brown Hart Gdns W1 248 B6
Brownhill Rd SE6 164 A4
Browning Ave
  Carshalton SM1 218 C4
  Ealing W7 86 D1
  North Cheam KT4 200 B1
Browning Cl
  Bexley DA16 145 C4
  Feltham TW12 173 B6
  Paddington W9 236 B5
  Walthamstow E17 54 A5
Browning Ct W14 264 C6
Browning Ho
  2 London SE14 141 A4
  7 Shepherd's Bush W12 90 C1
  10 Stoke Newington N16 73 C4
Browning Mews W1 238 B3
Browning Rd
  Enfield EN2 5 B5
  Leytonstone E11 54 D2
  Plashet E12 78 B2
Browning St SE17 117 A2 262 B3
Browning Way TW5 128 D4
Brownlea Gdns IG3 80 A6
Brownlow Cl EN4 14 B6
Brownlow Ct
  2 Bowes Pk N11 32 A4
  Hampstead Garden Suburb N2 48 A4
Brownlow Ho 10 SE16 118 A4
Brownlow Lo 1 N11 32 A4
Brownlow Mews WC1 94 B3 240 D5
Brownlow Rd
  Bowes Pk N11 32 A4
  6 Ealing W13 109 A5
  Finchley N3 29 D3
  3 Forest Gate E7 77 A4
  Hackney E8 96 A6
  South Croydon CR0 221 D4
  Willesden NW10 67 C1
Brownlow St WC1 94 B2 240 D3
Brownrigg Rd TW15 170 C6
Brown's Bldgs EC3 243 B1
Brownsea Wlk NW7 28 D4
Brownspring Dr SE9 166 D1
Brown's Rd
  Surbiton KT5, KT6 198 B2
  Walthamstow E17 53 C6
Brown St W1 92 D1 237 C2
Brownswell Rd N2 30 B1
Brownswood Rd N4 73 A6
Broxash Rd SW11 159 A5
Broxbourne Ave E18 55 B5
Broxbourne Ho 1 E3 97 D3
Broxbourne Rd
  Broom Hill BR6 211 D2
  Wanstead E7 77 A5
Broxholme Ho SW6 265 C2
Broxholm Rd SE27, SW16 160 C1
Broxted Rd SE6 163 B2
Broxwood Way NW8 92 C6 230 B5
Bruce Ave TW17 193 A3
Bruce Castle Ct N17 33 C2
Bruce Castle Mus* N17 33 C2
Bruce Castle Rd N17 33 D2
Bruce Cl
  North Kensington W10 90 D2
  Welling DA16 146 B4
Bruce Ct DA15 189 D6
Bruce Gdns N20 14 D1
Bruce Glasier Ho 13 N19 49 D2
Bruce Grove Prim Sch N17 33 D1
Bruce Grove Sta N17 33 D1
Bruce Grove N17 33 D1
Bruce Gr N17 33 D1
Bruce Hall Mews SW17 181 A6
Bruce Ho
  4 Clapham Pk SW4 159 D5
  5 Greenhill HA1 42 D4
  North Kensington W10 90 D2
  Preston HA3 44 A2
  Putney SW15 156 B6
Bruce Lawns SW17 181 A6
Bruce Rd Barnet EN5 1 A2
  Bromley E3 97 D4
  Harrow HA3 24 C1
  Mitcham CR4 181 A3
  South Norwood SE25 205 B5
  Willesden NW10 67 B1
Bruckner St W10 91 B4
Brudenell Rd SW17 181 A6
Bruffs Meadow UB5 63 A2
Bruges Pl 16 NW1 71 C1
Brumfield Rd KT19 215 A3
Brune Ho E1 243 C3
Brunel Cl
  Cranford TW5 128 B5
  Northolt UB5 85 B4
  Penge SE19 183 D4
Brunel Ct 8 SW13 133 D3
Brunel Engine House Rotherhithe* SE16 118 C4
Brunel Est W2 91 C2
Brunel Ho
  Chelsea SW10 266 D4
  4 Gospel Oak NW5 71 B4
  Hayes UB3 105 D3
  Millwall E14 119 D1
  New Cross SE8 141 B5
  25 Streatham SW2 160 A4
Brunel Mews NW10 90 D4
Brunel Pl 7 UB1 85 D1
Brunel Rd Acton W3 89 C2
  Walthamstow E17 53 A3
  Wapping SE16 118 C5
Brunel Science Pk UB8 82 A4
Brunel St E16 98 D1
Brunel Univ Coll Gate Osterley Campus TW7 130 D5
Brunel Univ UB8 82 A4
Brunel Wlk
  South Tottenham N15 51 C5
  Twickenham TW4 151 C4
Brune St E1 95 D2 243 C3
Brunlees Ho SE1 262 B5
Brunner Cl NW11 48 A4
Brunner Ho 6 SE6 186 A6
Brunner Rd
  Ealing W5 87 D3
  Walthamstow E17 53 B4
Bruno Ct 5 E8 74 A2
Bruno Pl NW9 67 A6
Brunswick Ave N11 15 A1
Brunswick Cl
  Bexley DA6 146 D1
  Pinner HA5 41 A3
  Thames Ditton KT7 196 D1
  Twickenham TW2 152 B1
Brunswick Cres N11 15 A1
Brunswick Ct
  Bermondsey SE1 117 C4 253 B2
  Finsbury EC1 234 C1
  Kingston u T KT2 175 D4
  New Barnet EN4 14 B6
  2 Penge SE19 184 A3
  Westminster SW1 259 D3
  2 Wimbledon SW19 179 A3
Brunswick Gdns
  Ealing W5 88 A3
  Kensington W8 113 C5 245 B3
Brunswick Gr N11 15 A1
Brunswick Ho
  Church End N3 29 B2
  4 Haggerston E2 95 D5
  Lisson Gr NW1 237 C6
Brunswick Lo 6 E4 20 A2
Brunswick Manor SM1 218 A4
Brunswick Mews
  Marylebone W1 237 D2
  Streatham SW16 181 D4
BRUNSWICK PARK 15 A1
Brunswick Park Gdns N11 15 A2
Brunswick Park Prim Sch
  Brunswick Pk N14 15 A2
  Camberwell SE5 139 B5
Brunswick Park Rd N11 15 A1
Brunswick Pk SE5 139 C4
Brunswick Pl
  Penge SE19 184 A3
  Shoreditch N1 95 B4 235 D1
Brunswick Quay SE16 118 D3
Brunswick Rd
  Bexley DA6 147 A1
  Ealing W5 88 A4
  Holdbrook EN3 7 C5
  Kingston u T KT2 176 C2
  Leyton E10 54 A1
  Poplar E14 98 A1
  South Tottenham N15 51 C4
  South Tottenham N15 51 C5
  Sutton SM1 217 D4
Brunswick Sh Ctr WC1 94 A3 240 B6
Brunswick Sq
  St Pancras WC1 94 A3 240 B6
  Tottenham N17 33 D4
Brunswick St E17 54 A4
Brunswick Terr BR3 185 D2
Brunswick Villas 2 SE5 139 C4
Brunswick Way N11 31 B6
Brunton Pl E14 97 A1
Brushfield St E1 95 D2 243 C4
Brushwood Lo 1 DA17 125 C2
Brussels Ct N18 33 C5
Brussels Rd SW11 136 B1
Bruton Cl BR7 188 B3
Bruton La W1 115 B6 248 D5
Bruton Pl W1 115 B6 248 D5
Bruton Rd SM4 202 A5
Bruton St W1 115 B6 248 D5
Bruton Way W13 87 A2
Brutus Ct SE11 261 C3
Bryan Ave NW10 68 B1
Bryan Cl TW16 172 A3
Bryan Ct W1 237 C2
Bryan Ho SE16 119 B4
Bryan Rd SE16 119 B4
Bryanston Ave TW2 151 D3
Bryanston Cl UB2 107 B2
Bryanston Ct W1 237 C2
Bryanstone Ct SM1 218 A5
Bryanstone Rd N8 49 D4
Bryanston Ho 12 SE15 139 D4
Bryanston Mans W1 237 C4
Bryanston Mews E W1 237 C3
Bryanston Mews W W1 92 D1 237 C2
Bryanston Pl W1 92 D2 237 C3
Bryanston Sq W1 92 D1 237 C2
Bryanston St W1 92 D1 237 D1
Bryant Cl EN5 13 B6
Bryant Ct Acton W3 111 B5
  Haggerston E2 95 D5
Bryant Rd UB5 84 C4
Bryant St E15 76 C1
Bryantwood Rd N5, N7 72 C3
Brycedale Cres N14 15 D1
Bryce Ho 25 SE14 140 D6
Bryce Rd RM8 80 C4
Brydale Ho 2 SE16 118 D2
Bryden Cl SE26 185 A5
Brydges Pl WC2 250 A5
Brydges Rd E15 76 B3
Brydon Wlk N1 233 B6
Bryer Ct EC2 242 A4
Bryett Rd N7 72 A5
Bryher Ho W4 111 A1
Brymay Cl E3 97 C5
Brymon Ct W1 237 D3
Brynmaer Ho SW11 267 D1
Brynmaer Rd SW11 136 D4 267 D1
Bryn-y-Mawr Rd EN1 5 D1
Bryony Cl UB8 82 B2
Bryony Rd W12 112 A6
Bryony Way TW16 172 A4
B Sky B Hq TW7 131 A6
BT Telecom Twr* W1 93 C2 239 A4
Buccleuch Ho E5 52 A2
Buchanan Cl N21 16 B6
Buchanan Ct 18 SE16 118 D2
Buchanan Gdns NW10 90 B5
Buchanan Ho
  Dulwich SE21 161 C1
  Wandsworth SW18 157 C4
Buchan Ho W3 110 D4
Buchan Rd SE15 140 C2
Bucharest Rd SW18 158 A4
Buckden Cl
  Fortis Green N2 48 D5
  Lee SE12 165 A5
Buckfast Ct W13 109 A6
Buckfast Ho N14 15 C6
Buckfast Rd SM4 201 D5
Buckfast St E2 96 A4
Buck Hill Wlk W2 114 B6 246 D5
Buckhold Rd SW18 157 C5
Buckhurst Ave CR4, SM5 202 D1
Buckhurst Ct 7 IG9 21 D2
BUCKHURST HILL 21 C2
Buckhurst Hill Ho 3 IG9 21 B2
Buckhurst Hill Sta IG9 21 D2
Buckhurst Ho 15 N7 71 D3
Buckhurst St E1 96 B3
Buckhurst Way IG9 21 D1
Buckingham Ave
  East Molesey KT8 173 D1
  Falconwood DA16 145 C1
  Feltham TW14 150 B5
  Oakleigh Pk N20 14 B4
  South Norwood CR7 182 C2
  Wembley UB6 87 A6
Buckingham Cl
  Broom Hill BR5 211 C2
  Ealing W5 87 C2
  Enfield EN1 5 C3
  Hampton TW12 173 B5
Buckingham College Sch HA1 42 C4
Buckingham Ct
  2 Ealing W7 86 D3
  Hendon NW4 46 A6
  Mitcham CR4 204 A4
  Northolt UB5 85 A6
  Wembley HA0 65 C2
Buckingham Dr BR7 189 A5
Buckingham Gate SW1 115 C3 259 B6
Buckingham Gdns
  East Molesey KT8 173 D1
  Edgware HA8 26 B3
  South Norwood CR7 182 C1
Buckingham Gr UB10 82 C5
Buckingham Ho
  1 Acton W3 88 C1
  Finsbury Pk N4 51 A1
  Richmond TW10 154 C6
Buckingham La SE23 163 A4
Buckingham Lo N10 49 C5
Buckingham Mans NW6 69 D3
Buckingham Mews
  Harlesden NW10 89 D5
  7 Kingsland N1 73 C2
  Westminster SW1 259 A6
Buckingham Palace Rd SW1 115 B2 258 D4
Buckingham Pal* SW1 115 C4 249 A1
Buckingham Par 19 HA7 25 C5
Buckingham Pl SW1 259 A6
Buckingham Prim Sch TW12 173 B5
Buckingham Rd
  Edgware HA8 26 B3
  Hampton TW12, TW13 173 B5
  Harlesden NW10 89 D5
  Harrow HA1 42 B4
  Ilford IG1 79 B6
  Kingsland N1 73 C2
  Kingston u T KT1 198 B5
  Leyton E10 75 D5
  Mitcham CR4 204 A4
  Richmond TW10 153 D2
  Stratford E15 76 D3
  Wanstead E11 55 C4
  Woodford E18 36 D2
  Wood Green N22 32 A2
Buckingham St WC2 250 B5
Buckingham Way SM6 219 C1
Buckingham Yd NW10 89 D5
Buck La NW9 45 B4
Buckland Cl NW7 28 A6
Buckland Cres NW3 70 B2
Buckland Ct
  6 Shoreditch N1 95 C5
  Uxbridge UB10 61 A6
Buckland Ho 3 N1 72 C1
Buckland Inf Sch KT9 214 B3
Buckland Rd
  Chessington KT9 214 B3
  Leyton E10 76 A6
  Orpington BR6 227 C4
Buckland Rise HA5 22 D2
Bucklands Rd TW11 175 C4
Buckland St N1 95 B5 235 D3
Buckland Way KT4 200 C1
Buckland Wlk
  2 Acton W3 111 A4
  Morden SM4 202 A5
Buckle Ct HA8 27 A3
Buckleigh Ave SW20 201 B6
Buckleigh Ho SW17 180 B5
Buckleigh Rd SW16 182 A3
Buckleigh Way SE19 183 D3
Buckler Gdns SE9 166 B1
Buckler's Alley SW6 264 D4
Bucklersbury EC2, EC4 242 C1
Bucklers' Way SM5 218 D5
Buckles Ct DA17 124 D2
Buckle St
  15 Whitechapel E1 96 A1
  Whitechapel E1 243 D2
Buckley Cl SE23 162 B4
Buckley Ct
  5 Brondesbury NW6 69 B1
  London N8 49 D4
Buckley Ho W3 110 C5
Buckley Rd NW6 69 B1
Buckmaster Cl 1 SW9 138 C2
Buckmaster Ho 1 N7 72 B4
Buckmaster Rd SW11 136 C1
Bucknall St WC1 240 A2
Bucknall Way BR3 208 A5
Bucknell Cl SW2 138 B1
Buckner Rd SW2 138 B1
Buckrell Rd E4 20 B2
Buckridge Bldg EC1 241 A4
Buckshead Ho 19 W2 91 C2
Buck St NW1 71 B1
Buckstone Cl SE23 162 C5
Buckstone Rd N18 34 A5
Buckters Rents SE16 119 A5
Buckthorne Rd SE4 163 A6
Buckthorn Ho DA15 167 D1
Buckwheat Ct DA18 124 D3
Budd Cl N12 29 D6
Buddings Circ HA9 67 A5
Bude Cl E17 53 B4
Budge La CR4 202 D2
Budge Row EC4 242 C1
Budge's Wlk W2 114 A5 246 B4
Budleigh Cres DA16 146 C4
Budleigh Ho 19 SE15 140 A5
Budoch Ct IG3 80 A6
Budoch Dr IG3 80 A6
Buer Rd SW6 135 A3
Bugsby's Way SE10 120 D2
Buick Ho 4 E3 97 C3
Building 36 7 SE18 123 A3
Building 47 6 SE18 123 A3
Building 48 5 SE18 123 A3
Building 49 4 SE18 123 A3
Building 50 3 SE18 123 A3
Bulbarrow NW8 91 D6
Bulganak Rd CR7 205 A5
Bulinca St SW1 115 D2 259 D3
Bullace Row SE5 139 B4
Bull Alley DA16 146 B2
Bullard Rd TW11 174 D4
Bullards Pl 13 E2 96 D4
Bull Dog The (Juct) TW15 148 A2
Bulleid Way SW1 115 B2 258 D3
Bullen Ho 13 E1 96 B3
Bullen St SW11 136 C3
Buller Cl SE15 140 A5
Buller Rd
  Barking IG11 79 C1
  Kensal Green NW10 90 D4
  South Norwood CR7 205 B6
  Tottenham N17 34 A1
  Wood Green N22 32 C1
Bullers Cl DA14 191 A5
Bullers Wood Dr BR7 188 B3
Bullers Wood Sch BR7 188 A2
Bullescroft Rd HA8 10 D1
Bullfinch Ct 4 SE21 161 B2
Bullingham Mans W8 245 B2
Bull Inn Ct WC2 250 B5
Bullivant St 9 E14 120 A6
Bull La
  Chislehurst BR7 189 B3
  Dagenham RM10 81 D5
  Edmonton N18 33 C5
Bull Rd E15 98 D5
Bullrush Cl
  Carshalton SM5 218 C6
  Thornton Heath CR0 205 C3
Bulls Alley SW14 133 B3
Bulls Bridge Ind Est UB2 106 B2
Bulls Bridge Rd UB2 106 B2
Bullsbrook Rd UB4 106 C5
Bull's Cross EN1, EN2 6 A6
Bull's Gdns SW3 257 B4
Bulls Head Pas EC3 243 A1
Bull Yd SE15 140 A4
Bulmer Gdns HA3 43 D2
Bulmer Mews W11 113 C5 245 A4
Bulow Ct 3 SW6 135 D3
Bulstrode Ave TW3 129 C2
Bulstrode Gdns TW3 129 C2
Bulstrode Pl W1 238 B3
Bulstrode Rd TW3 129 C2
Bulstrode St W1 93 A1 238 B2
Bulwer Court Rd E11 54 B1
Bulwer Ct E11 54 B1
Bulwer Gdns EN5 2 A1
Bulwer Rd
  Edmonton N18 33 C6
  Leytonstone E11 54 B1
  New Barnet EN5 2 A1
Bulwer St W12 112 C5
Bunbury Ho SE15 140 A5
Bunces La IG8 36 D3
Bungalow Rd SE25 205 C5
Bungalows The
  Leyton E10 54 A3
  Mitcham SW16 181 B3
Bunhill Row EC1 95 B3 242 C5
Bunhouse Pl SW1 258 B2
Bunker's Hill DA17 125 C2
Bunkers Hill
  London NW11 48 A2
  North Cray DA14 169 B1
Bunning Ho N7 72 A4
Bunning Way N7 72 B1
Bunn's La NW7 27 D4
Bunsen Ho 2 E3 97 A5
Bunsen St 3 E3 97 A5
Buntingbridge Rd IG2 57 B4
Bunting Cl London N9 18 D3
  Mitcham CR4 202 D4
Bunting Ct NW9 27 C1
Bunton St SE18 122 C3
Bunyan Ct EC2 242 A4
Bunyan Rd E17 53 A6
Buonaparte Mews SW1 259 C2
BUPA Bushey Hospl WD23 8 D3
Burbage Cl
  Bermondsey SE1 117 B3 262 C5
  Hayes UB3 83 B1
Burbage Ho
  16 Deptford SE14 140 D6
  Shoreditch N1 235 D5
Burbage Rd SE21, SE24 161 B4
Burbage Sch N1 95 C5
Burbank KT3 199 D6
Burberry Cl KT3 177 C1
Burberry Ct 8 N3 29 D3
Burbidge Rd TW17 192 C5
Burbridge Way N17 34 A1
Burcham St E14 98 A1
Burcharbro Rd SE2 146 D6
Burchell Ct WD23 8 A4
Burchell Ho SE11 260 D2
Burchell Rd
  Leyton E10 53 D1
  London SE15 140 B4
Burcher Gale Gr 5 SE15 139 D5
Burchetts Way TW17 192 D3
Burchett Way RM6 59 B3
Burcote Rd SW18 158 B4
Burden Cl TW8 109 C1
Burden Ho SW8 270 A3
Burdenshott Ave TW10 132 D1
Burden Way E11 77 B6
Burder Cl N1 73 C2
Burder Rd N1 73 C2
Burdett Ave SW20 178 A2

urdett Cl
2 Ealing W7 ... 108 D5
Sidcup DA14 ... 191 A5
urdett Coutts & Townshend CE Prim Sch SW1 ... 115 D2 259 D3
urdett Mews 4 W2 ... 91 D1
urdett Rd
Richmond TW9 ... 132 B2
Thornton Heath CR0 ... 205 B3
Tower Hamlets E3 ... 97 B2
urdetts Rd RM9 ... 103 B6
urdock Cl CR0 ... 206 D1
urdock Rd N17 ... 52 A6
urdon Ct 3 E8 ... 74 A2
urdon La SM2 ... 217 A1
ure Ct 17 EN5 ... 13 D6
urfield Cl SW17 ... 180 B6
urford Cl
Dagenham RM8 ... 80 C5
Ickenham UB10 ... 60 A4
Ilford IG6 ... 57 A5
urford Ct SE8 ... 141 C6
urford Gdns N13 ... 16 B1
urford Ho
1 Brentford TW8 ... 110 A1
11 South Lambeth SW9 ... 138 B3
urford Rd
Brentford TW8 ... 110 A1
Bromley BR1 ... 210 A5
Forest Hill SE6 ... 163 B2
Newham E6 ... 100 A4
New Malden KT4 ... 200 A2
5 Stratford Marsh E15 ... 98 B6
Sutton SM1 ... 217 C6
urford Way CR0 ... 224 A2
urford Wlk SW6 ... 265 D3
urgate Ct 9 SW9 ... 138 C2
urges Gr SW13 ... 134 B5
urges Rd E6 ... 78 B1
urgess Ave NW9 ... 45 B3
urgess Cl 4 TW13 ... 173 A6
urgess Ct
2 London N20 ... 14 D2
3 Southall UB1 ... 85 D1
Wallend E12 ... 78 C1
urgess Hill NW2 ... 69 C4
urgess Ho 3 SE5 ... 139 A5
urgess Ind Pk SE5 ... 139 B5
urgess Mews SW19 ... 179 D4
urgess Park Mans NW6 ... 69 C4
urgess Rd
Leyton E15 ... 76 C4
Sutton SM1 ... 217 D4
urgess St E14 ... 97 C2
urge St SE1 ... 262 D5
urghill Rd SE26 ... 185 A6
urghley Ave
Borehamwood WD6 ... 11 A6
Kingston u T KT3 ... 177 B2
urghley Ct SW19 ... 179 A5
urghley Hall Cl SW19 ... 157 A3
urghley Ho SW19 ... 157 A1
urghley Pl CR4 ... 202 D5
urghley Rd
Camden Town NW5 ... 71 B4
Leytonstone E11 ... 54 C1
London N8 ... 50 C6
Wimbledon SW19 ... 179 A6
urghley Twr W3 ... 111 D6
urgh St N1 ... 94 D5 234 D4
urgon St EC4 ... 241 D1
urgos Cl CR0 ... 220 C2
urgos Gr SE10 ... 141 D4
urgoyne Rd
Ashford TW16 ... 171 D4
Brixton SW9 ... 138 B2
Harringay N4 ... 50 D3
South Norwood SE25 ... 205 D5
urham Cl SE20 ... 184 C3
urhan Uddin Ho E1 ... 243 C5
urhill Gr HA5 ... 23 A1
uriton Ho 9 SW15 ... 156 B3
urke Cl SW15 ... 133 C1
urke Ho 1 SW11 ... 136 B1
urke Lodge E13 ... 99 B4
urke St E16 ... 98 D2
urket Cl UB2 ... 107 B2
urland Rd SW11 ... 158 D6
urleigh Ave
Bexley DA15 ... 167 D6
Hackbridge SM6 ... 219 B5
urleigh Ct N17 ... 34 A4
urleigh Gdns
Ashford TW15 ... 171 A5
Osidge N14 ... 15 C3
urleigh Ho
Cheam SM3 ... 201 A1
Burleigh Ho *continued*
Chelsea SW3 ... 266 D5
North Kensington W10 ... 90 D2
Burleigh Lo 3 SW19 ... 179 D3
Burleigh Par N14 ... 15 D3
Burleigh Pl SW15 ... 156 D6
Burleigh Rd
Cheam SM3 ... 201 A1
Enfield EN1 ... 5 C1
Hillingdon UB10 ... 82 D6
Burleigh St WC2 ... 250 C6
Burleigh Way EN2 ... 5 B2
Burleigh Wlk SE6 ... 164 A3
Burley Cl Chingford E4 ... 35 C5
Mitcham SW16 ... 181 D1
Burley Ho E1 ... 96 D1
Burley Rd E16 ... 99 C2
Burlington Apartments SE20 ... 184 B3
Burlington Arc W1 ... 249 A5
Burlington Ave
Richmond TW9 ... 132 C4
Romford RM7 ... 59 D3
Burlington Cl
East Bedfont TW14 ... 149 B4
5 Newham E6 ... 100 A1
Orpington BR6 ... 226 D6
Paddington W9 ... 91 C3
Pinner HA5 ... 40 B6
Burlington Ct
Chiswick W4 ... 133 A5
Highgate N6 ... 49 A1
Burlington Danes Sch W12 ... 90 B1
Burlington Gate SW20 ... 179 A1
Burlington Gdns
Acton Green W4 ... 111 A1
Acton W3 ... 111 A5
Dagenham RM6 ... 59 A2
Fulham SW6 ... 135 A3
Marylebone W1 ... 115 C6 249 A5
Burlington Ho NW3 ... 70 B3
Burlington Inf Sch KT3 ... 199 D5
Burlington Jun Sch KT3 ... 199 D5
Burlington La W4 ... 133 B5
Burlington Lo BR7 ... 188 B3
Burlington Mews
Acton W3 ... 111 A5
2 Putney SW15 ... 157 B6
Burlington Park Ho 6 HA7 ... 25 C6
Burlington Pl
Fulham SW6 ... 135 A3
Woodford IG8 ... 21 A1
Burlington Rd
Acton Green W4 ... 111 A1
Enfield EN2 ... 5 B4
Fulham SW6 ... 135 A3
Hounslow TW7 ... 130 B4
Muswell Hill N10 ... 49 A6
New Malden KT3 ... 199 D5
South Norwood CR7 ... 183 B1
Tottenham N17 ... 34 A2
Burlington Rise EN4 ... 14 D4
Burma Rd N16 ... 73 B4
Burmarsh Ct SE20 ... 184 C2
Burmarsh 6 NW5 ... 71 A2
Burma Terr 11 SE19 ... 183 C5
Burmester Ho SW17 ... 158 A1
Burmester Rd SW17 ... 158 A1
Burnaby Cres W4 ... 133 A6
Burnaby Ct 31 SE16 ... 118 A4
Burnaby Gdns W4 ... 132 D6
Burnaby St SW10 ... 136 A5 266 B3
Burnand Ho 3 W14 ... 112 D3
Burnbrae Cl N12 ... 29 D4
Burnbury Rd SW12 ... 159 C3
Burncroft Ave EN3 ... 6 C3
Burndell Way UB4 ... 84 D2
Burne Jones Ho W14 ... 254 B3
Burnell Ave
Richmond TW10 ... 175 C5
Welling DA16 ... 146 A3
Burnell Gdns HA7 ... 25 D1
Burnell Ho 18 SW2 ... 160 C3
Burnell Rd SM1 ... 217 D4
Burnell Wlk SE1 ... 263 D2
Burnels Ave E6 ... 100 C4
Burness Cl N7 ... 72 B2
Burne St NW1 ... 237 A4
Burnett Cl E9 ... 74 C3
Burnett Ct SW11 ... 267 A1
Burnett Ho 6 SE13 ... 142 A3
Burney Ave KT5 ... 198 B4
Burney Ho 4 SW16 ... 181 C5
Burney St SE10 ... 142 A5
Burnfoot Ave SW6 ... 135 A4 264 B1
Burnham Ave UB10 ... 61 A4
Burnham Cl
Bermondsey SE1 ... 263 D3
Enfield EN1 ... 5 C5
Harrow HA3 ... 43 A5
Hendon NW7 ... 28 A3
Burnham Cres E11 ... 55 C5
Burnham Ct
Bayswater W2 ... 245 D6
Hendon NW4 ... 46 C5
15 Stanmore HA7 ... 25 C5
Burnham Dr KT4 ... 216 D6
Burnham Est 8 E2 ... 96 C4
Burnham Gdns
Cranford TW4 ... 128 B4
Croydon CR0 ... 205 D2
Hayes UB3 ... 105 B3
Burnham NW3 ... 70 C1
Burnham Rd
Chingford Hatch E4 ... 35 B5
Dagenham RM9 ... 102 B6
Morden SM4 ... 201 D5
Sidcup DA14 ... 169 A2
Burnham St
Bethnal Green E2 ... 96 C4
Kingston u T KT2 ... 176 C2
Burnham Way
Ealing W13 ... 109 B3
Penge SE26 ... 185 B5
Burnhill Ho EC1 ... 235 A1
Burnhill Rd BR3 ... 185 C1
Burnley Cl WD19 ... 22 C5
Burnley Rd
London SW9 ... 138 B3
Willesden NW10 ... 68 A3
Burnsall St SW3 ... 114 C1 257 B2
Burns Ave
Blackfen DA15 ... 168 B5
Feltham TW14 ... 150 A5
Ilford RM6 ... 58 C2
Southall UB1 ... 107 C6
Burns Cl
Bexley DA16 ... 145 D4
Hayes UB4 ... 84 A2
Mitcham SW17 ... 180 B4
Walthamstow E17 ... 54 A5
Burns Ct
Tottenham N17 ... 34 B3
Wallington SM6 ... 219 B1
Burns Ho
18 Bethnal Green E2 ... 96 C4
Bexley DA16 ... 146 C4
1 Islington N7 ... 72 B2
Kennington SE17 ... 261 D1
Burn's Ho NW10 ... 89 C6
Burns Ho 11 N16 ... 73 C4
Burnside Ave E4 ... 35 B4
Burnside Cl Barnet EN5 ... 1 C2
Rotherhithe SE16 ... 118 D5
Twickenham TW1 ... 153 A5
Burnside Cres HA0 ... 87 D6
Burnside Ct 1 SM6 ... 219 A5
Burnside Rd RM8 ... 58 D1
Burns Rd
Battersea SW11 ... 136 D3
Ealing W13 ... 109 B4
Burn's Rd NW10 ... 89 D6
Burns Rd HA0 ... 88 A5
Burns Way TW5 ... 128 D4
Burnt Ash Hill
Lee SE12 ... 164 D5
Lewisham SE12 ... 165 A3
Burnt Ash Hts BR1 ... 187 B5
Burnt Ash La BR1, SE12 ... 187 B5
Burnt Ash Prim Sch BR1 ... 187 A5
Burnt Ash Rd SE12 ... 164 D6
Burnthwaite Rd SW6 ... 135 B5 264 D3
BURNT OAK ... 27 B3
Burnt Oak Broadway HA8 ... 26 D2
Burnt Oak Fields HA8 ... 27 A2
Burnt Oak Jun Sch DA15 ... 168 A3
Burnt Oak La DA15 ... 168 B3
Burnt Oak Sta HA8 ... 27 A2
Burntwood Cl SW18 ... 158 C3
Burntwood Ct SW17 ... 158 A1
Burntwood Grange Rd SW18 ... 158 C3
Burntwood La SW17 ... 158 B2
Burntwood Sch SW17 ... 158 B2
Burntwood View 6 SE19 ... 183 D5
Buross St E1 ... 96 B1
Burpham Cl UB4 ... 84 D2
Burrage Ct 17 SE16 ... 118 D2
Burrage Gr SE18 ... 123 A2
Burrage Pl SE18 ... 122 D1
Burrage Rd SE18 ... 123 A1
Burrard Ho 11 E2 ... 96 C5
Burrard Rd
Newham E16 ... 99 B1
West Hampstead NW6 ... 69 C4
Burr Cl
Bexleyheath DA7 ... 147 B2
St George in t East E1 ... 118 A5
Burrell Cl
Croydon CR0 ... 207 A3
Edgware HA8 ... 10 D2
Burrell Ct HA1 ... 42 B2
Burrell Ho 4 TW1 ... 153 B4
Burrell Row BR3 ... 185 C1
Burrells 9 BR3 ... 185 D1
Burrell St SE1 ... 116 D5 251 C4
Burrell's Wharf Sq E14 ... 119 D1
Burrell Twrs E10 ... 53 C2
Burrhill Ct SE16 ... 118 D3
Burritt Rd KT1 ... 176 C1
Burrmead Ct NW2 ... 67 D5
Burroughs Gdns NW4 ... 46 B5
Burroughs The NW4 ... 46 B5
Burrow Ho 19 SW9 ... 138 B3
Burrow Rd SE22 ... 139 C1
Burrows Mews SE1 ... 251 C2
Burrows Rd NW10 ... 90 C4
Burrow Wlk SE21 ... 161 A4
Burr Rd SW18 ... 157 C4
Bursar St SE1 ... 253 A3
Bursdon Cl DA15 ... 167 D2
Bursland Rd EN3 ... 6 D1
Burslem St E1 ... 96 A1
Bursted Wood Prim Sch DA7 ... 147 D3
Burstock Rd SW15 ... 135 A1
Burston Rd SW15 ... 156 D6
Burstow Rd SW20 ... 179 A2
Burtenshaw Rd KT7 ... 197 A3
Burtley Cl N4 ... 51 A1
Burton Bank N1 ... 73 B1
Burton Cl
Chessington KT9 ... 213 D1
South Norwood CR7 ... 205 B6
Burton Ct
Chelsea SW3 ... 257 D2
10 Friern Barnet N11 ... 30 D5
Thames Ditton KT7 ... 197 A3
Burton Dr EN3 ... 7 C6
Burton Gdns TW5 ... 129 B4
Burton Gr SE17 ... 262 C1
Burton Ho
8 Bermondsey SE16 ... 118 B4
Brixton SE5 ... 138 D4
Burtonhole Cl NW7 ... 28 D6
Burtonhole La
Finchley NW7 ... 29 A6
Mill Hill NW7 ... 28 D6
Burton Ho SE26 ... 184 B5
Burton La 3 SW9 ... 138 C3
Burton Lo 6 SW15 ... 157 B6
Burton Mews SW1 ... 258 B3
Burton Pl WC1 ... 232 D1
Burton Rd
7 Brixton SW9 ... 138 C3
Brixton SW9 ... 138 D3
Brondesbury NW6 ... 69 B1
Kingston u T KT2 ... 176 A3
Wanstead E18 ... 55 B6
Burtons Ct E15 ... 76 B1
Burtons Rd TW12 ... 174 A6
Burton St WC1 ... 93 D3 239 D6
Burtonwood Ho N4 ... 51 B2
Burt Rd E16 ... 121 C5
Burtt Ho 6 N1 ... 95 C4
Burtwell La SE21, SE27 ... 183 B6
Burvill Ct SW20 ... 178 C2
Burwash Ho SE1 ... 252 D1
Burwash Rd SE18 ... 123 B1
Burwell Ave UB6 ... 64 C2
Burwell Cl 27 E1 ... 96 B1
Burwell 2 KT1 ... 176 C1
Burwell Rd E10 ... 53 A1
Burwell Wlk 14 E3 ... 97 C3
Burwood Ave
Hayes BR2 ... 225 B6
Pinner HA5 ... 40 C4
Burwood Cl KT6 ... 198 C1
Burwood Ct SE23 ... 162 C4
Burwood Ho 11 SW9 ... 138 D1
Burwood Lo SW19 ... 179 B6
Burwood Pl Barnet EN4 ... 2 A4
Paddington W2 ... 237 B2
Bury Ave Hayes UB4 ... 83 C5
Ruislip HA4 ... 39 A3
Bury Cl SE16 ... 118 D5
Bury Ct EC3 ... 243 B2
Buryfield Ct 23 SE8 ... 118 D2
Bury Gr SM4 ... 201 D4
Bury Hall Villas N9 ... 17 D4
Bury Pl WC1 ... 94 A2 240 B3
Bury Rd Chingford E4 ... 20 C6
Dagenham RM10 ... 81 D3
Hornsey N22 ... 50 C6
Bury St W N9 ... 17 C4
Buryside Cl IG2 ... 57 D5
Bury St Edmonton N9 ... 18 A3
Ruislip HA4 ... 39 B3
St James SW1 ... 115 C5 249 B4
Whitechapel EC3 ... 95 C1 243 B2
Bury Wlk SW3 ... 114 C1 257 A2
Burywood Ct EN3 ... 6 C3
Busbridge Ho 24 E14 ... 97 C2
Busby Ho SW16 ... 181 C6
Busby Mews 5 NW1 ... 71 D2
Busby Pl NW5 ... 71 D2
Busch Cl TW7 ... 131 B4
Busch Cnr TW7 ... 131 B4
Bushbaby Cl SE1 ... 263 A5
Bushberry Rd E9 ... 75 A2
Bush Cl IG2 ... 57 B4
Bush Cotts 12 SW18 ... 157 C6
Bush Ct London N14 ... 15 C3
7 Shepherd's Bush W12 ... 112 D4
Bushell Cl SW2 ... 160 B2
Bushell Gn WD23 ... 8 B2
Bushell Ho 3 SE27 ... 183 A6
Bushell Way BR7 ... 188 C5
BUSHEY ... 8 A2
Bushey Ave
Crofton BR5 ... 211 B2
Snaresbrook E18 ... 54 D6
Bushey Cl
Chingford E4 ... 20 A1
Ickenham UB10 ... 60 C6
Bushey Ct SW20 ... 178 B1
Bushey Down SW12 ... 159 B2
Bushey Hall SE5 ... 139 D4
BUSHEY HEATH ... 8 C4
Bushey Heath Prim Sch WD23 ... 8 B3
Bushey Hill Rd SE5 ... 139 D4
Bushey Ho SE12 ... 165 C1
Bushey La SM1 ... 217 C4
Bushey Lees DA15 ... 167 D5
BUSHEY MEAD ... 200 D6
Bushey Meads Sch WD23 ... 8 A6
Bushey Rd
Croydon CR0 ... 223 C6
Hayes UB3 ... 105 C2
Ickenham UB10 ... 60 C6
Newham E13 ... 99 C5
South Tottenham N15 ... 51 C3
Sutton SM1 ... 217 C4
West Barnes SW20 ... 178 D1
Bushey Way BR3 ... 208 B4
Bush Fair Ct N14 ... 15 B5
Bushfield Cl HA8 ... 10 D2
Bushfield Cres HA8 ... 10 D2
Bushfield Ho N5 ... 73 A3
Bush Gr NW9 ... 45 A2
Bushgrove Rd RM8 ... 80 D5
Bush Gr HA7 ... 25 D2
BUSH HILL ... 17 B5
Bush Hill N21 ... 17 A5
Bush Hill Par EN1 ... 17 B4
BUSH HILL PARK ... 17 C5
Bush Hill Park Prim Sch EN1 ... 18 A6
Bush Hill Park Sta EN1 ... 17 D5
Bush Hill Rd
Enfield N21 ... 17 B5
Harrow HA3 ... 44 B3
Bush Ind Est NW10 ... 89 B3
Bush La EC4 ... 117 B6 252 C6
Bushmead Ci 7 N15 ... 51 D5
Bushmoor Cres SE18 ... 144 D5
Bushnell Rd SW17 ... 159 B1
Bush Rd
Bermondsey SE8 ... 118 D2
Hackney E8 ... 96 B6
Littleton TW17 ... 192 B4
Richmond TW9 ... 132 B6
Wanstead E11 ... 55 A2
Woodford IG9 ... 37 D6
Bushway RM8 ... 80 D5
Bushwood Dr SE1 ... 117 D2 263 D3
Bushwood Rd TW9 ... 132 C6
Bushwood E11 ... 55 A1
Bushy Ct KT1 ... 175 C2
Bushy Park Gdns TW12 ... 174 B5
Bushy Park Rd TW11 ... 175 B3
Bushy Rd TW11 ... 174 D3
Business Acad Bexley The DA18 ... 125 A4
Business Design Ctr* N1 ... 94 C6 234 B5
Buspace Studios 3 W10 ... 91 A3
Butcher Row E1 ... 96 D1
Butchers Rd E16 ... 99 A1
Bute Ave TW10 ... 154 A2
Bute Ct SM6 ... 219 C3
Bute Gardens W SM6 ... 219 C3
Bute Gdns
Hammersmith W6 ... 112 D2
Wallington SM6 ... 219 C3
Bute House Prep Sch W6 ... 112 D2
Bute Mews NW11 ... 48 A4
Bute Rd Ilford IG6 ... 56 D4
Thornton Heath CR0 ... 204 C1
Wallington SM6 ... 219 C4
Bute St SW7 ... 114 B2 256 C4
Bute Wlk 18 N1 ... 73 B2
Butfield Ho 6 E9 ... 74 C2
Butler Ave HA1 ... 42 B2
Butler Cl HA8 ... 26 D1
Butler Ct
Dagenham RM8 ... 81 C6
Wembley HA0 ... 65 A4
Butler Ho
32 Bethnal Green E2 ... 96 C4
5 Brixton SW9 ... 138 D4
11 Poplar E14 ... 97 B1
Butler Pl SW1 ... 259 C6
Butler Rd
Dagenham RM8 ... 80 B4
Harrow HA1 ... 42 A2
Willesden NW10 ... 67 D1
Butlers Cl TW3 ... 129 B1
Butlers & Colonial Wharf SE1 ... 253 D2
Butler's Cotts DA7 ... 147 C3
Butler St
33 Bethnal Green E2 ... 96 C4
Hillingdon UB10 ... 82 D3
Butler's Wharf W SE1 ... 253 C3
Butley Ct 8 E3 ... 97 A5
Butt Ct SM4 ... 202 A3
Buttercup Cl UB5 ... 63 B2
Butterfield Cl
1 Bermondsey SE16 ... 118 B4
Tottenham N17 ... 33 A4
Twickenham TW1 ... 152 D5
Butterfield Ho 4 EN2 ... 4 D3
Butterfields E17 ... 54 A4
Butterfield Sq 10 E6 ... 100 B1
Butterfly Ct E6 ... 100 B4
Butterfly La SE9 ... 166 D5
Butterfly Wlk 2 SE5 ... 139 B4
Butter Hill SM5, SM6 ... 219 A4
Butteridges Cl RM9 ... 103 B6
Buttermere Cl
Bermondsey SE1 ... 263 C3
East Bedfont TW14 ... 149 D3
Leyton E11 ... 76 B4
West Barnes SM4 ... 200 D3
Buttermere Ct NW8 ... 229 C6
Buttermere Dr SW15 ... 157 A6
Buttermere Ho
London N12 ... 30 C5
13 Tower Hamlets E3 ... 97 B4
Buttermere NW1 ... 231 D2
Buttermere Wlk 9 E8 ... 73 D2
Butterwick W6 ... 112 C2
Butterworth Ct SW16 ... 160 A1
Butterworth Gdns IG8 ... 37 A5
Buttesland St N1 ... 95 B4 235 D2
Buttfield Cl RM10 ... 81 D2
Buttmarsh Cl SE18 ... 122 D1
Buttsbury Rd IG1 ... 79 A3
Butts Cotts TW13 ... 151 B1
Butts Cres TW13 ... 151 C1
Butts Ho TW13 ... 151 C1
Butts Piece UB5 ... 84 B5
Butts Rd BR1 ... 186 C5
Butts The TW8 ... 131 D6
Buxhall Cres E9 ... 75 B2
Buxlow Prep Sch HA9 ... 66 A5

Buxted Rd
Camberwell SE22 ... 139 C1
Colney Hatch N12 ... 30 C5
Dalston E8 ... 73 D1
Buxton Cl London N9 ... 18 C2
Woodford IG8 ... 37 D4
Buxton Cres SM3 ... 217 A4
Buxton Ct
1 Leyton E11 ... 54 D2
Shoreditch N1 ... 235 B2
Buxton Dr
Kingston u T KT3 ... 177 B1
Leytonstone E11 ... 54 C5
Buxton Gdns W3 ... 110 D6
Buxton Ho
Leytonstone E11 ... 54 C5
3 London SW11 ... 136 B1
Buxton Lo E11 ... 77 B6
Buxton Mews SW4 ... 137 D3
Buxton Rd
Chingford E4 ... 20 B4
Ilford IG2 ... 57 C3
Mortlake SW14 ... 133 C2
Newham E6 ... 100 A4
Stratford E15 ... 76 C3
Thornton Heath CR7 ... 204 D4
Upper Holloway N19 ... 49 D1
Walthamstow E17 ... 53 A5
Willesden NW2 ... 68 B2
Buxton St E1 ... 95 D3 243 D5
Buzzard Creek Ind Est IG11 ... 102 A2
Byam Shaw Sch of Art N19 ... 71 D6
Byam St SW6 ... 136 A3
Byards Croft SW16 ... 181 D2
Byards Ct SE16 ... 118 D3
Byas Ho 6 E3 ... 97 B4
Byatt Wlk TW12 ... 173 A4
Bychurch End 11 TW11 ... 174 D5
Bycroft Rd UB1 ... 85 C3
Bycroft St SE20 ... 184 D3
Bycullah Ave EN2 ... 4 D3
Bycullah Ct EN2 ... 4 D2
Bycullah Rd EN2 ... 4 D3
Byefield Cl SE16 ... 119 A4
Byegrove Ct SW19 ... 180 B4
Byegrove Rd SW19 ... 180 B4
Byelands Cl 12 SE16 ... 118 D5
Bye The W3 ... 89 C1
Byeways The KT5 ... 198 D4
Bye Ways TW2 ... 151 D1
Bye Way The HA3 ... 24 D2
Byeway The SW14 ... 133 A2
Byfeld Gdns SW13 ... 134 A4
Byfield Ct KT3 ... 200 A5
Byfield Rd TW7 ... 131 A2
Byford Cl E15 ... 76 C1
Bygrove CR0 ... 223 D1
Bygrove Prim Sch E14 ... 97 D1
Bygrove St E14 ... 97 D1
Byland Cl
Abbey Wood SE2 ... 124 B3
Carshalton SM4 ... 202 B2
Southgate N21 ... 16 B4
Byne Rd
Carshalton SM5 ... 218 C6
Forest Hill SE26 ... 184 C5
Bynes Rd CR2 ... 221 B1
Byng Pl WC1 ... 93 D3 239 C5
Byng St E14 ... 119 C4
Bynon Ave DA7 ... 147 B2
Byre Rd N14 ... 15 B5
Byrne Ho 11 SW2 ... 160 B6
Byrne Rd SW12 ... 159 B2
Byron Ave
Borehamwood WD6 ... 10 C6
Cranford TW4 ... 128 B3
Byron Ave E SM1 ... 218 B4
Byron Ave
Plashet E12 ... 78 A2
Queensbury NW9 ... 44 D6
Sutton SM1 ... 218 B4
West Barnes KT3 ... 200 A4
Woodford E18 ... 36 D1
Byron Cl
Feltham TW12 ... 173 B6
Forest Hill SE26 ... 185 A6
Hackney E8 ... 96 A6
Streatham SW16 ... 182 A4
Thamesmead SE28 ... 124 C5
Walton-on-T KT12 ... 195 A1
Byron Court Prim Sch HA0 ... 65 C6
Byron Ct
Chelsea SW3 ... 257 B3
Dulwich SE21 ... 162 A3
Ealing W7 ... 109 A2
Enfield EN2 ... 4 D3
3 Hampstead NW6 ... 70 A1
Byron Ct *continued*
Harrow HA1 ... 42 C3
4 New Barnet EN5 ... 2 A1
Paddington W9 ... 91 C3
1 Richmond TW10 ... 175 D6
South Norwood CR7 ... 183 A1
St Pancras WC1 ... 240 C6
11 Wanstead E11 ... 55 A5
Woodford E18 ... 37 B2
Byron Dr
East Finchley N2 ... 48 B3
Erith DA8 ... 147 D5
Byron Gdns SM1 ... 218 B4
Byron Hill Rd HA1, HA2 ... 64 C6
Byron Ho 5 BR3 ... 185 D4
Byron Mews
Hampstead NW3 ... 70 C4
2 Maida Vale W9 ... 91 C3
Byron Par UB10 ... 83 A3
Byron Rd
Dollis Hill NW2 ... 68 B6
Ealing W5 ... 110 B5
Edgware NW7 ... 28 A5
Harrow HA1 ... 42 C3
Leyton E10 ... 53 D1
Walthamstow E17 ... 53 C6
Wealdstone HA3 ... 24 D1
Wembley HA0 ... 65 C5
Byron St E14 ... 98 A1
Byron Way
Hayes UB4 ... 83 D3
Northolt UB5 ... 85 A4
West Drayton UB7 ... 104 B2
Bysouth Cl N15 ... 51 B5
Bythorn St SW9 ... 138 B1
Byton Rd SW17 ... 180 D4
Byward Ave TW14 ... 150 C5
Byward St EC3 ... 117 C6 253 B5
Bywater Ho SE18 ... 122 A3
Bywater Pl SE16 ... 119 A5
Bywater St SW3 ... 114 D1 257 C2
Byway The KT19 ... 215 D4
Bywell Pl W1 ... 239 A3
Bywood Ave CR0 ... 206 D3
Bywood Terr CR0 ... 206 C3
Byworth Ho HA7 ... 25 C4
Byworth Wlk N19 ... 50 A1

C

Cabbell St NW1 ... 92 C2 237 A3
Cabinet Off SW1 ... 250 A2
Cabinet War Rooms & Churchill Mus* SW1 ... 115 D4 249 D2
Cabinet Way E4 ... 35 B4
Cable Ho WC1 ... 234 A2
Cable Pl SE10 ... 142 A4
Cable St E1 ... 118 B6
Cabot Ct SE16 ... 118 D3
Cabot Sq E14 ... 119 C5
Cabot Way 3 E6 ... 99 D6
Cabul Rd SW11 ... 136 C3
Cactus Cl SE5 ... 139 C3
Cactus Wlk W12 ... 89 D1
Cadbury Cl
Ashford TW16 ... 171 C3
Isleworth TW7 ... 131 A4
Cadbury Rd TW16 ... 171 C4
Cadbury Way 1 SE16 ... 118 A2
Caddington Cl EN4 ... 14 C6
Caddington Rd NW2 ... 69 A5
Caddis Cl HA7 ... 24 D3
Cadell Cl E2 ... 95 D5
Cadell Ho 12 E2 ... 95 D5
Cade Rd SE10 ... 142 B4
Cader Rd SW18 ... 158 A5
Cadet Dr SE1 ... 117 D1 263 D2
Cade Tyler Ho 10 SE10 ... 142 A4
Cadiz St SE17 ... 117 A1 262 B1
Cadley Terr SE23 ... 162 C2
Cadman Cl SW9 ... 138 D5
Cadmer Cl KT3 ... 199 C5
Cadmore Ho 4 N1 ... 72 D1
Cadmus Cl 9 SW4 ... 137 D2
Cadmus Ct 6 SW9 ... 138 C4
Cadnam Lo E14 ... 120 B3
Cadnam Point 15 SW15 ... 156 B3
Cadogan Cl
Beckenham BR3 ... 186 B1
Hackney Wick E9 ... 75 B1
Harrow HA2 ... 63 D4
Teddington TW11 ... 174 C5
Cadogan Ct SW3 ... 257 C3
Cadogan Ct Gdns SW1 ... 258 A4
Cadogan Ct
New Malden KT3 ... 199 C5
Sutton SM2 ... 217 D2
Cadogan Gate SW1 ... 114 D2 257 D4
Cadogan Gdns
Chelsea SW3 ... 114 D2 257 D3
Finchley N3 ... 29 D2
Southgate N21 ... 16 C6
Wanstead E18 ... 55 B6
Cadogan Ho SW3 ... 266 D5
Cadogan La SW1 ... 115 A3 258 A5
Cadogan Pl SW1 ... 114 D3 257 D5
Cadogan Rd
Kingston u T KT6 ... 197 D4
Woolwich SE18 ... 123 A3
Cadogan Sq SW1 ... 114 D3 257 D5
Cadogan St SW3 ... 114 D2 257 C3
Cadogan Terr E9 ... 75 B1
Cadoxton Ave 3 N15 ... 51 D3
Cadwallon Rd SE9 ... 167 A2
Caedmon Rd N7 ... 72 B4
Caerleon Cl
Claygate KT10 ... 213 B1
Sidcup DA14 ... 190 C5
Caerleon Terr SE2 ... 124 B2
Caernafon Ho HA7 ... 25 A5
Caernarvon Cl CR4 ... 204 A6
Caernarvon Ct 3 KT5 ... 198 B4
Caernarvon Ho W2 ... 236 A2
Caesar Ct 25 E2 ... 96 D5
Caesar's Way TW17 ... 193 B3
Caesars Wlk CR4 ... 202 D4
Cahill St EC1 ... 242 B5
Cahir St E14 ... 119 D2
Cain Ct 2 W5 ... 87 C2
Caine Ho W3 ... 110 D4
Cain's La TW14 ... 149 C6
Caird St W10 ... 91 B4
Cairn Ave W5 ... 109 D5
Cairndale Cl BR1 ... 186 D3
Cairnfield Ave NW2 ... 67 D5
Cairnfield Ct NW2 ... 67 C5
Cairngorm Cl 3 TW11 ... 175 A5
Cairn Ho 3 SW19 ... 180 C3
Cairns Ho 3 N7 ... 72 B4
Cairns Mews SE18 ... 144 A4
Cairns Rd SW11 ... 158 C6
Cairn Way HA7 ... 24 D4
Cairo New Rd CR0 ... 220 D6
Cairo Rd E17 ... 53 C5
Caister Ho N7 ... 72 B2
Caistor Ho
10 Balham SW12 ... 159 B4
5 West Ham E15 ... 98 D6
Caistor Mews SW12 ... 159 B4
Caistor Park Rd E15 ... 98 D6
Caistor Rd SW12 ... 159 B4
Caithness Gdns DA15 ... 167 D5
Caithness Ho N1 ... 233 C6
Caithness Rd
Hammersmith W14 ... 112 D3
Mitcham CR4 ... 181 B3
Calabria Rd N5 ... 72 D3
Calais Gate SE5 ... 138 D4
Calais St SE5 ... 138 D4
Calbourne Rd SW12 ... 159 A4
Calcott Wlk SE9 ... 187 D6
Calcraft Ho 10 E2 ... 96 C5
Caldbeck Ave KT4 ... 200 B1
Caldecot Ct SE5 ... 139 A3
Caldecote Gdns WD23 ... 8 C4
Caldecote 3 KT1 ... 176 C1
Caldecote La WD23 ... 8 D5
Caldecot Rd SE5 ... 139 A3
Caldecott Way E5 ... 74 D5
Calder Ave UB6 ... 86 D5
Calder Cl EN1 ... 5 C2
Calder Ct SE16 ... 119 B5
Calder Gdns HA8 ... 44 C6
Calder Ho UB5 ... 85 A6
Calderon Ho NW8 ... 230 A4
Calderon Pl 20 W10 ... 90 C2
Calderon Rd E11 ... 76 B5
Calder Rd SM4 ... 202 A4
Caldervale Rd SW4 ... 159 D6
Calderwood St SE18 ... 122 C2
Caldew Ct NW7 ... 28 A3
Caldew St SE5 ... 139 B5
Caldicote Gn NW9 ... 45 C3
Caldon Ho 2 UB5 ... 85 B3
Caldwell Rd WD19 ... 22 D6
Caldwell St SW9 ... 138 B5 270 D3
Caldy Rd DA17 ... 125 D3
Caldy Wlk 10 N1 ... 73 A2
Caleb St SE1 ... 252 B2
Caledonia Ct
Barking IG11 ... 102 C5
Hendon NW4 ... 28 C1
Caledonia Ho 15 E14 ... 97 A1
Caledonian Cl 1 IG3 ... 58 B1
Caledonian Ct UB5 ... 85 A3
Caledonian Market SE1 ... 117 C3 263 B6
Caledonian Rd
Islington N1 ... 94 B6 233 C5
Lower Holloway N7 ... 72 B2
Caledonian Road & Barnsbury Sta N7 ... 72 B1
Caledonian Road Sta N7 ... 72 B2
Caledonian Sq 6 NW1 ... 71 D2
Caledonian Wharf Rd E14 ... 120 B2
Caledonia Rd TW19 ... 148 A3
Caledonia St N1 ... 233 B3
Caledon Rd
East Ham E6 ... 78 B1
Hackbridge SM5, SM6 ... 219 A4
Cale St SW3 ... 114 C1 257 A2
Caletock Way SE10 ... 120 D1
Calgarth NW1 ... 232 B3
Calgary Ct 30 SE16 ... 118 C4
Caliban Twr 9 N1 ... 95 C5
Calico Ho 4 SW11 ... 136 A2
Calico Row 5 SW11 ... 136 A2
Calidore Cl SW2 ... 160 B5
California Bldg 2 SE13 ... 141 D4
California La WD23 ... 8 B3
California Rd KT3 ... 199 A6
Callaby Terr 11 N1 ... 73 B2
Callaghan Cl SE13 ... 142 C1
Callahan Cotts 8 E1 ... 96 C2
Callander Rd SE6 ... 164 A2
Callanders The WD23 ... 8 C3
Callan Sch The W1 ... 93 C1 239 B2
Callard Ave N13 ... 32 D6
Callcott Ct NW6 ... 69 B1
Callcott Rd NW6 ... 69 B1
Callcott St W8 ... 245 A4
Callendar Rd SW7 ... 256 C6
Callingham Cl 13 E14 ... 97 B2
Callingham Ho 1 SW4 ... 138 A2
Callis Farm Cl TW19 ... 148 A5
Callis Rd E17 ... 53 B3
Callonfield 3 E17 ... 53 A5
Callow St SW3 ... 136 B6 266 C6
Calmington Rd SE5 ... 139 C6
Calmont Rd BR1 ... 186 C4
Calonne Rd SW19 ... 178 D6
Calshot Ho N1 ... 233 C4
Calshot Rd TW6 ... 126 D3
Calshot St N1 ... 94 B5 233 C3
Calshot Way
Enfield EN2 ... 4 D2
Harlington TW6 ... 126 C3
Calstock Ho SE11 ... 261 B2
Calstock NW1 ... 232 C5
Calthorpe Gdns
Edgware HA8 ... 26 B5
Sutton SM1 ... 218 A5
Calthorpe St WC1 ... 94 B3 240 D6
Calton Ave SE21 ... 161 C5
Calton Rd EN5 ... 14 B5
Calumet Ct SW17 ... 180 C4
Calver Ct E17 ... 54 B6
Calverley Cl BR3 ... 185 D4
Calverley Cres RM10 ... 81 C6
Calverley Gdns HA3 ... 43 D2
Calverley Gr N19 ... 49 D1
Calverley Rd KT17 ... 216 A2
Calver 13 NW5 ... 71 B4
Calvert Ave E2 ... 95 D4
Calvert Cl
Belvedere DA17 ... 125 D2
Sidcup DA14 ... 191 A4
Calvert Ct
1 London N19 ... 49 C1
5 Richmond TW9 ... 132 B1
Calvert Ho 9 W12 ... 112 B6
Calverton Prim Sch E16 ... 99 D1
Calverton Rd E6 ... 100 C6
Calverton SE5 ... 139 C6
Calvert Rd SE10 ... 120 D1
Calvert's Bldgs SE1 ... 252 C3
Calvert St NW1 ... 93 A6 231 A6
Calvin St E1 ... 95 D3 243 C5
Calydon Rd SE7 ... 121 B1
Calypso Cres 6 SE15 ... 139 D5
Calypso Way SE8, SE16 ... 119 B2
Camac Rd TW2 ... 152 B3
Camarthen Gn NW9 ... 45 C3
Cambalt Ho 3 SW15 ... 156 D6
Cambalt Rd SW15 ... 156 D6
Cambay Ho 7 E1 ... 97 A3
Cambell Jun & Inf Schs RM9 ... 80 D1
Camber Ho 4 SE15 ... 140 C6
Camberley Ave
Enfield EN1 ... 5 C1
Wimbledon SW20 ... 178 B1
Camberley Cl SM3 ... 216 D5
Camberley Ct 15 SM2 ... 217 D1
Camberley Ho NW1 ... 231 D3
Camberley Rd TW6 ... 126 C2
Cambert Way SE9 ... 143 B1
CAMBERWELL ... 139 A4
Camberwell Bsns Ctr SE5 ... 139 B5
Camberwell Church St SE5 ... 139 B4
Camberwell Coll of Arts
Camberwell SE5 ... 139 C4
Camberwell SE15 ... 139 D5
Camberwell Glebe SE5 ... 139 C4
Camberwell Gn SE5 ... 139 B4
Camberwell Green SE5 ... 139 A4
Camberwell Gr SE5 ... 139 C3
Camberwell New Rd SW9 ... 138 D5
Camberwell Rd SE5 ... 139 A5
Camberwell Station Rd SE5 ... 139 A4
Camberwell Trad Est SE5 ... 139 A4
Cambeys Rd RM10 ... 81 D3
Cambisgate SW19 ... 179 A5
Camborne Ave W13 ... 109 C4
Camborne Cl TW6 ... 126 C2
Camborne Rd
Belmont SM2 ... 217 D1
Bexley DA16 ... 145 D3
Croydon CR0 ... 206 A2
Harmondsworth TW6 ... 126 C2
Sidcup DA14 ... 168 C1
Wandsworth SW18 ... 157 C4
West Barnes SM4 ... 200 D4
Camborne Way
Harlington TW6 ... 126 C2
Heston TW5 ... 129 C4
Cambourne Ave N9 ... 18 D4
Cambourne Mews 6 W11 ... 91 A1
Cambrai Ct N13 ... 32 A6
Cambray Rd
Broom Hill BR6 ... 211 D2
Streatham SW12 ... 159 C3
Cambria 6 BR3 ... 185 D1
Cambria Cl
Hounslow TW3 ... 129 C1
Sidcup DA15 ... 167 C3
Cambria Ct TW14 ... 150 B4
Cambria Gdns TW19 ... 148 A4
Cambria Ho
Forest Hill SE26 ... 184 A6
10 Limehouse E14 ... 97 A1
Cambria Lo 3 SW15 ... 157 B6
Cambrian Ave IG2 ... 57 C4
Cambrian Cl SE27 ... 160 D1
Cambrian Ct UB2 ... 107 D2
Cambrian Gn NW9 ... 45 C4
Cambrian Rd
Leyton E10 ... 53 C1
Richmond TW10 ... 154 B5
Cambria Rd SE5 ... 139 A2
Cambria St SW6 ... 135 D5 265 D3
Cambridge Ave
Falconwood DA16 ... 145 D1
Greenford UB6 ... 64 D3
Kilburn NW6 ... 91 C5
Kingston u T KT3, SW20 ... 177 D1
Cambridge Barracks Rd 11 SE18 ... 122 B2
Cambridge Cir WC2 ... 93 D1 239 D1
Cambridge Cl
Hounslow TW4 ... 129 A1
Walthamstow E17 ... 53 B3
Willesden NW10 ... 67 A5
Wimbledon SW20 ... 178 B2
Wood Green N22 ... 32 C2
Cambridge Cotts TW9 ... 132 C6
Cambridge Cres
20 Bethnal Green E2 ... 96 B
Teddington TW11 ... 175 A
Cambridge Ct
4 Barnet EN5 ... 1 B
26 Bethnal Green E2 ... 96 B
7 Hammersmith W6 ... 112 C
2 Kilburn NW6 ... 91 C
Marylebone W2 ... 237 A
Stamford Hill N16 ... 51 C
Wembley HA0 ... 65 D
Wimbledon SW20 ... 178 B
Cambridge Dr
Lee SE12 ... 165 A
Ruislip HA4 ... 62 D
Cambridge Gate Mews NW1 ... 238 D
Cambridge Gate NW1 ... 238 C
Cambridge Gdns
Enfield EN1 ... 6 A
Kilburn NW6 ... 91 C
Kingston u T KT1 ... 176 C
Muswell Hill N10 ... 31 B
North Kensington W10 ... 91 A
Southgate N21 ... 17 B
Tottenham N17 ... 33 B
Cambridge Gn SE9 ... 166 D
Cambridge Gr W6 ... 112 B
Cambridge Grove Rd
13 Kingston u T KT1 ... 176 C
Kingston u T KT1 ... 198
Cambridge Gr SE20 ... 184
Cambridge Heath Rd E1, E2 ... 96
Cambridge Heath Sta E2 ... 96
Cambridge Ho
Barking IG11 ... 79
Ealing W13 ... 87
Fulham SW6 ... 135
2 Teddington TW11 ... 175
8 Woolwich SE18 ... 122
Cambridge Mans SW11 ... 267
Cambridge Par EN1 ... 6
CAMBRIDGE PARK ... 153
Cambridge Park Ct TW1 ... 153
Cambridge Park Rd E11 ... 55
Cambridge Pas 9 E9 ... 74
Cambridge Pk
Twickenham TW1 ... 153
Wanstead E11 ... 55
Cambridge Pl W8 ... 245
Cambridge Rd
Barking IG11 ... 79
Barnes SW13 ... 133
Battersea SW11 ... 136 D4 267
Carshalton SM5 ... 218
3 Chingford E4 ... 20
East Molesey KT8 ... 195
Hampton TW12 ... 173
Hanwell W7 ... 108
Harrow HA2 ... 41
Hounslow TW4 ... 129
Ilford IG3 ... 57
Kilburn NW6 ... 91
Kilburn NW6 ... 91
Kingston u T KT1 ... 176
Leytonstone E11 ... 54
Littleton TW15 ... 171
Mitcham CR4 ... 203
New Malden KT3 ... 199
Cambridge Rd N W4 ... 110
Cambridge Rd
Penge SE20 ... 206
Plaistow BR1 ... 187
Richmond TW9 ... 132
Sidcup DA14 ... 189
Cambridge Rd S 3 W4 ... 110
Cambridge Rd
Southall UB1 ... 107
Teddington TW11 ... 175
Twickenham TW1 ... 153
Walton-on-T KT12 ... 194
Wimbledon SW20 ... 178
Cambridge Row SE18 ... 122
Cambridge Sch W6 ... 112
Cambridge Sq W2 ... 92 C1 237
Cambridge St SW1 ... 115 C1 259
Cambridge Terr N9 ... 17

Cambridge Terr Mews NW1 .... 231 D1
Cambridge Terr NW1 .... 231 C1
Cambstone Cl N11 .... 15 A2
Cambus Cl UB4 .... 85 A2
Cambus Rd E16 .... 99 A2
Cam Ct 2 SE15 .... 139 D6
Camdale Rd SE18 .... 145 D5
Camden Ave
Feltham TW13 ...... 150 C3
Hayes UB4 .... 106 D6
Camden Cl BR7 .... 189 A2
Camden Coll of English NW1 .... 71 A1
Camden Ct 9 DA17 .. 125 C1
Camden Gdns
Camden Town NW1 .... 71 B1
Sutton SM1 .... 217 D3
Thornton Heath CR7 . 204 D6
Camden Gr BR7 .... 188 D4
Camden High St NW1 .... 93 C6 232 A5
Camden Hill Rd SE19 .... 183 C4
Camden Ho
6 Deptford SE8 ...... 119 B1
Wallington CR6 ...... 220 A5
Camdenhurst St E14 .. 97 A1
Camden Jun Sch SM5 .... 218 D4
Camden Lock Pl NW1 .... 71 B1
Camden Mews NW1 .... 71 D2
Camden Mkt* NW1 .... 93 B6 231 D6
Camden Park Rd
Camden Town NW1 .... 71 D2
Chislehurst West BR7 .... 188 C3
Camden Pas N1 .... 94 D6 234 C5
Camden Rd
Camden Town NW1 ...... 93 B6 231 D6
Carshalton SM5 ...... 218 D4
Old Bexley DA5 ...... 169 B4
Sutton SM1 .... 217 D3
Walthamstow E17 ...... 53 B3
Wanstead E11 .... 55 B3
Camden Road Sta NW1 .... 71 C1
Camden Row SE3 .... 142 C3
Camden Sch for Girls The NW5 .... 71 C2
Camden Sq NW1 .... 71 D2
Camden St NW1 .... 93 C6 232 B5
Camden Studios NW1 .... 232 B5
Camden Terr 17 NW1 .... 71 D2
CAMDEN TOWN 71 B1
Camden Town Sta NW1 .... 93 B6 231 D6
Camden Way
Chislehurst West BR7 .... 188 C3
Thornton Heath CR7 . 204 D6
Camden Wlk N1 .... 234 C5
Cameford Ct 20 SW12 .... 160 A4
Camelford Ct 15 W11 .... 91 A1
Camelford Ho SE1 .. 260 B1
Camelford NW1 ...... 232 B5
Camelford Wlk 13 W11 .... 91 A1
Camel Gr KT2 .... 175 D5
Camelia Ct IG8 .... 36 C4
Camellia Ct 20 BR3 .. 185 C3
Camellia Ho
Feltham TW13 ...... 150 A3
New Cross SE8 ...... 141 B5
Camellia Pl TW2 ...... 151 D4
Camellia St SW8 .... 270 A3
Camelot Cl
Plumstead SE18 ...... 123 B4
Wimbledon SW19 ... 179 C6
Camelot Ho 15 NW1 ... 71 D2
Camelot Prim Sch SE15 .... 140 B6
Camel Rd E16 .... 121 D5
Camera Pl SW10 .... 266 C6
Cameret Ct 6 W11 .. 112 D4
Cameron Cl
East Barnet N20 ...... 14 C2
Edmonton N18 .... 34 B5
Cameron Ct 3 SW19 .... 157 A3
Cameron Ho
8 Bromley BR1 .... 186 D2
Camberwell SE5 .... 139 A5
St John's Wood NW8 230 A4
Cameron House Sch SW10 .... 266 D6
Cameron Lo TW3 .... 130 A1
Cameron Pl SW16 .... 160 C2
Cameron Rd
Bromley BR2 .... 209 A4
Forest Hill SE6 .... 163 B2
Ilford IG3 .... 57 C1
Thornton Heath CR0 . 204 D3
Cameron Sq CR4 ...... 180 C2
Camerton Cl 8 E8 .... 73 D2
Camfrey Ct N8 .... 50 A5
Camgate Ctr The TW19 .... 148 B4
Camilla Cl TW16 ...... 171 D4
Camilla Ct 12 SM2 .. 217 C1
Camilla Rd SE16 ...... 118 B2
Camille Cl SE25 ...... 206 A6
Camlan Rd BR1 ...... 186 D6
Camlet St E2 .... 243 C6
Camlet Way EN4 .... 1 D4
Camley St NW1 .... 93 D5 232 D4
Camm Gdns
5 Kingston u T KT1 .... 176 B1
Thames Ditton KT7 .. 196 D2
Camm 23 NW9 .... 27 D1
Camomile Ave CR4 ... 180 D2
Camomile St EC3 .... 95 C1 243 B2
Camomile Way UB7 ... 82 A1
Campaign Ct W9 ...... 91 B3
Campana Rd SW6 .... 135 C4 265 B2
Campasps Bsns Pk TW16 .... 193 D4
Campbell Ave IG6 .... 57 A5
Campbell Cl
Ruislip HA4 .... 40 A3
Shooters Hill SE18 ... 144 C4
Streatham SW16 .... 181 D6
Twickenham TW2 ...... 152 B3
Campbell Croft HA8 ... 26 C5
Campbell Ct
Dulwich SE21 .... 162 A3
Ealing W7 .... 108 C6
Kingsbury NW9 .... 45 A3
South Kensington SW7 .... 256 A5
Tottenham N17 .... 33 D2
Campbell Gordon Way NW2 .... 68 B4
Campbell Ho
Paddington W2 ...... 236 C5
Pimlico SW1 .... 259 A1
30 Shepherd's Bush W12 .... 112 B6
6 Wallington SM6 ... 219 B4
Campbell Rd Bow E3 .. 97 C4
Ealing W7 .... 108 C6
Newham E6 .... 100 A6
Stratford E15 .... 76 D4
Thornton Heath CR0 . 204 D3
Tottenham N17 .... 34 A2
Twickenham TW2 ...... 152 B2
Walthamstow E17 ...... 53 B5
Campbell Wlk N1 ... 233 B6
Campdale Rd N7 ...... 71 D5
Campden Cres
Dagenham RM8 .... 80 C4
Wembley HA0 .... 65 B5
Campden Gr W8 .... 113 C4 245 B2
Campden Hill Ct W8 245 B2
Campden Hill Gate W8 .... 245 A2
Campden Hill Gdns W8 .... 245 A4
Campden Hill Mans W8 .... 245 B4
Campden Hill Pl W14 .... 244 D4
Campden Hill Rd W8 .... 113 C4 245 A2
Campden Hill Sq W14 .... 113 B5 244 D4
Campden Hill W8 .... 113 C4 245 A2
Campden Ho 4 NW6 .. 70 B1
Campden Hos W8 .. 245 A3
Campden House Cl W8 .... 245 B2
Campden Rd
Ickenham UB10 .... 60 B4
South Croydon CR2 .. 221 C3
Campden St W8 .... 113 C5 245 A3
Campden Way RM8 ... 80 B4
Campe Ho 1 N10 .... 31 A3
Campen Cl SW19 .... 157 A2
Camperdown St E1 . 243 D1
Campfield Rd SE9 .... 165 D4
Campion Cl
Harrow HA3 .... 44 B3
Hillingdon UB8 .... 82 B2
Newham E6 .... 122 B6
South Croydon CR2 .. 221 C4
Campion Ct
London N12 .... 30 C4
10 Wembley HA0 ...... 88 A5
Campion Gdns IG8 .... 37 A5
Campion Ho 15 N16 ... 73 C3
Campion House (Seminary) TW7 ... 130 B4
Campion Pl SE28 .... 124 B5
Campion Rd
Hounslow TW7 ...... 130 D4
Putney SW15 .... 156 C6
Campion Terr NW2 .... 68 D5
Campion Way HA8 .... 27 A6
Camplin Rd HA3 ...... 44 A4
Camplin St SE14 ...... 140 D5
Camp Rd SW19 ...... 178 C5
Campsbourne Ho 3 N8 .... 50 A5
Campsbourne Jun & Inf Schs N8 .... 50 A6
Campsbourne Rd
Hornsey N8 .... 50 A5
Hornsey N8 .... 50 A6
Campsbourne The N8 .... 50 A5
Campsey Gdns RM9 ... 80 B1
Campsey Rd RM9 .... 80 B1
Campsfield Ho N8 .... 50 A6
Campsfield Rd N8 .... 50 A6
Campshill Pl SE13 .... 164 A6
Campshill Rd SE13 ... 164 A6
Camp Site The BR8 ... 191 C3
Campton Hill Twrs W8 .... 245 A4
Campus Rd E17 .... 53 B3
Camp View SW19 .... 178 B5
Cam Rd E15 .... 98 B6
Camrose Ave
Edgware HA8 .... 26 B2
Erith DA8 .... 147 D6
Feltham TW13 ...... 172 C6
Camrose Cl
Croydon CR0 .... 207 A2
Morden SM4 .... 201 C5
Camrose St SE2 ...... 124 A2
Camsey Ho 8 SW2 ... 160 B6
Canada Ave N18 .... 33 A4
Canada Cres W3 ...... 89 A3
Canada Gdns SE13 ... 164 A6
Canada Rd W3 .... 89 A2
Canada Sq E14 ...... 119 D5
Canada St SE16 ...... 118 D4
Canada Water Sta SE16 .... 118 D3
Canada Way W12 .... 112 B6
Canadian Ave SE6 .... 163 D3
Canal App SE8 .... 141 A6
Canal Bldg N1 ...... 235 A4
Canal Bridge SE15 ... 140 A6
Canal Bvd 7 NW1 .... 71 D2
Canal Cl Mile End E1 ... 97 A3
North Kensington W10 .... 90 D3
Canal Gr SE15 .... 140 B6
Canal Head Public Sq 1 SE15 .... 140 A4
Canal Path 22 E2 ...... 95 D6
Canalside Studios 29 N1 .... 95 C6
Canal St SE5 .... 139 B6
Canal Way W10 .... 90 D3
Canal Wlk
Croydon CR0 .... 205 D3
Forest Hill SE26 ...... 184 C5
Shoreditch N1 .... 95 B6 235 D6
CANARY WHARF 119 D5
Canary Wharf* E14 .... 119 D5
Canary Wharf Pier (River Bus) E14 .... 119 B5
Canary Wharf Sta E14 .... 119 D5
Canary Wharf Sta (DLR) E14 .... 119 C5
Canberra Cl NW4 .... 46 A6
Canberra Dr UB4 ...... 84 C4
Canberra Ho 7 HA4 .. 40 C1
Canberra Prim Sch W12 .... 112 B6
Canberra Rd
Charlton SE7 .... 143 D6
Ealing W13 .... 109 A5
Erith DA7 .... 146 D6
Harlington TW6 ...... 126 C2
Newham E6 .... 100 B6
Canbury Ave KT2 .... 176 B2
Canbury Bsns Pk 3 KT2 .... 176 A2
Canbury Ct 3 KT2 ... 176 A3
Canbury Mews SE26 .... 162 A1
Canbury Park Rd KT2 .... 176 B2
Canbury Sch KT2 .... 176 D4
Cancell Rd SW9 ...... 138 C4
Candahar Rd SW11 .. 136 C3
Candida Ct 9 NW1 ... 71 B1
Candishe Ho SE1 .... 253 C2
Candle Gr SE15 ...... 140 B2
Candlelight Ct 5 E15 .... 76 D2
Candlemakers 25 SW11 .... 136 B2
Candler Mews TW1 .. 153 A4
Candler St N15 .... 51 B3
Candover St W1 .... 239 A3
Candy St E3 .... 97 B6
Caney Mews NW2 ...... 68 D6
Canfield Dr HA4 ...... 62 B3
Canfield Gdns NW6 ... 69 D1
Canfield Ho N15 ...... 51 C3
Canfield Pl NW6 ...... 70 A2
Canford Ave UB5 ...... 85 A6
Canford Cl EN2 .... 4 C3
Canford Gdns KT3 .. 199 C3
Canford Pl TW11 .... 175 C4
Canford Rd SW11 .... 159 A6
Canham Rd
Acton W3 .... 111 C4
South Norwood SE25 .... 205 C6
Canmore Gdns SW16 .... 181 C3
Cann Hall Prim Sch E11 .... 76 D5
Cann Hall Rd E11 ...... 76 D4
Cann Ho W14 .... 254 B5
Canning Cres N22 .... 32 B2
Canning Cross SE5 ... 139 C3
Canning Ct N22 .... 32 B2
Canning Ho 23 W12 .. 112 B6
Canning Pas W8 .... 114 A3 256 A6
Canning Pl Mews W8 .... 256 A6
Canning Pl W8 .... 114 A3 256 A6
Canning Rd
Croydon CR0 .... 221 D6
Harrow HA3 .... 42 D6
Highbury N5 .... 72 D5
Walthamstow E17 ...... 53 A6
West Ham E15 .... 98 C5
Cannington 14 NW5 ... 71 A2
Cannington Rd RM9 ... 80 C2
CANNING TOWN 99 B2
Canning Town E16 ...... 98 C1
Canning Town Sta E16 .... 98 C1
Cannizaro Rd SW19 .. 178 D5
Cannock Ho N4 .... 51 B2
Cannock Lo EN1 ...... 17 C5
Cannonbury Ave HA5 .... 40 D3
Cannon Cl
Hampton TW12 ...... 173 D4
West Barnes SW20 .. 200 C6
Cannon Dr 21 E14 .... 119 C6
Cannon Hill La SM4, SW20 .... 201 A5
Cannon Hill Mews N14 .... 16 A1
Cannon Hill
Palmers Green N14 .... 16 A1
West Hampstead NW6 .... 69 C3
Cannon Ho
Lambeth SE11 ...... 260 D3
Penge SE26 .... 184 B4
Cannon La NW3 ...... 70 B5
Cannon Lane Fst & Mid Schs HA5 .... 40 D3
Cannon La HA5 .... 41 A3
Cannon Pl
Hampstead NW3 ...... 70 B5
Woolwich SE7 ...... 122 A1
Cannon Rd
Erith DA7 .... 147 B4
Palmers Green N14 .... 16 A1
Cannon St EC4 .... 117 A6 252 B6
Cannon Street Rd E1 .. 96 B1
Cannon Street Sta EC4 .... 117 B6 252 C6
Cannon Trad Est HA9 .... 66 D4
Cannon Way KT8 .... 195 D5
Cannon (W End of General Roy's Base Line)* TW6 ...... 126 D4
Cannon Wharf Bsns Ctr 12 SE8 .... 119 A2
Canon Ave RM6 ...... 58 C4
Canon Barnett Prim Sch E1 .... 95 D1 243 D2
Canon Beck Rd SE16 .... 118 C4
Canonbie Rd SE23 ... 162 C4
CANONBURY 73 A2
Canonbury Bsns Ctr N1 .... 235 B6
Canonbury Cres N1 ... 73 A1
Canonbury Ct 21 N1 ... 72 D1
Canonbury Gr N1 ...... 73 A1
Canonbury Hts 6 N1 .. 73 B2
Canonbury La N1 ...... 72 D1
Canonbury Pk N N1 .... 73 A2
Canonbury Pk S N1 ... 73 A2
Canonbury Pl N1 ...... 72 D2
Canonbury Prim Sch N1 .... 72 D2
Canonbury Rd
Enfield EN1 .... 5 C4
Islington N1 .... 72 D1
Canonbury Sq N1 ...... 72 D1
Canonbury Sta N1, N5 .... 73 A3
Canonbury St N1 ...... 73 A1
Canonbury Villas N1 .. 72 D1
Canon Mohan Cl N14 .. 15 B5
Canon Murnane Rd SE1 .... 263 C5
Canon Palmer RC Sch IG3 .... 57 C1
Canon Rd BR1 .... 209 D6
Canon Row SW1 .... 116 A4 250 A1
Canons Cl
East Finchley N2 ...... 48 B2
Edgware HA8 .... 26 B4
Canons Cnr HA8 ...... 26 A6
Canons Ct
Edgware HA8 .... 26 B4
Leyton E15 .... 76 C4
Canons Dr HA8 .... 26 B4
Canons High Sch HA8 .... 26 B1
Canons L Ctr The CR4 .... 202 D5
Canonsleigh Rd RM9 .. 80 B1
CANONS PARK 26 A3
Canons Park Cl HA8 .. 26 A3
Canons Park Sta HA8 .... 26 A3
Canon St N1 .... 95 A6 235 A5
Canon's Wlk CR0 .... 222 D5
Canopus Way
Northwood HA6 .... 22 A6
Stanwell TW19 ...... 148 A4
Canrobert St E2 ...... 96 B4
Cantelowes Ho EN5 ... 12 D6
Cantelowes Rd NW1 .. 71 D2
Canterbury Ave
Redbridge IG1 .... 56 A2
Sidcup DA15 .... 168 C2
Canterbury Cl
Beckenham BR3 .... 185 D2
16 Camberwell SE5 .. 139 A3
7 Newham E6 ...... 100 B1
North Cheam KT4 ... 216 D6
Southall UB6 .... 85 D2
Canterbury Cres SW9 .... 138 C2
Canterbury Ct
Acton W3 .... 111 C5
4 Ashford TW15 .... 170 B6
Eltham SE12 .... 165 B1
15 Hendon NW9 ...... 27 D1
Kilburn NW6 .... 91 C5
South Croydon CR2 .. 221 A1
Thornton Heath CR0 . 204 C2
Canterbury Gr SE27, SW16 .... 160 C1
Canterbury Hall KT4 .... 200 B2
Canterbury Ho
2 Barking IG11 ...... 80 A1
6 Bromley E3 .... 97 D4
Lambeth SE1 .... 260 D6
Canterbury Ind Pk 15 SE15 .... 140 C6
Canterbury SE13 ...... 164 A6
Canterbury Mans NW6 .... 69 D2
Canterbury Pl SE17 . 261 D3
Canterbury Rd
Feltham TW13 ...... 151 A2
Harrow HA1, HA2 ...... 42 A4
Kilburn NW6 .... 91 C5
Leyton E10 .... 54 A3
Morden SM4 .... 202 A3
Thornton Heath CR0 . 204 C2
Canterbury Terr NW6 .... 91 C5
Cantium Ret Pk SE1 .... 140 A6
Cantley Gdns
Ilford IG2 .... 57 A3
South Norwood SE19 .... 183 D2
Cantley Rd W7 .... 109 A3
Canton St E14 .... 97 C1
Cantrell Rd E3 .... 97 C3
Cantwell Ho SE18 .... 144 D5
Cantwell Rd SE18 .... 144 D5
Canute Ct SW16 ...... 160 C1
Canute Gdns SE16 ... 118 D2
Canute Ho 1 TW8 ... 131 C5
Canvey St SE1 ...... 252 A4
Cape Cl IG11 .... 78 D1
Cape Henry Ct 15 E14 .... 120 B6
Capel Ave SM6 .... 220 B3
Capel Cl
Keston Mark BR2 ... 210 A1
Whetstone N20 .... 14 A1
Capel Ct SE20 .... 184 C2
Capel Gdns Ilford IG3 .. 79 D4
Pinner HA5 .... 41 B5
Capel Ho
17 Hackney E9 .... 74 C1
South Oxhey WD19 .... 22 D6
Capella Ho 1 SE7 ... 143 B6
Capel Lo
5 Richmond TW9 .... 132 B4
12 Streatham SW2 ... 160 B4
Capel Point E7 .... 77 B4
Capel Rd
East Barnet EN4 ...... 14 C5
Forest Gate E7, E12 ... 77 C4
Capel KT5 .... 198 B2
Capener's Cl SW1 ... 248 A1
Cape Rd N17 .... 52 A6
Capern Rd SW18 ..... 158 A3
Cape Yd 6 E1 .... 118 A5
Capio Nightingale Hospl SW3 .... 257 B1
Capital Bsns Ctr
South Croydon CR0 .... 221 B1
Wembley HA0 .... 87 D5
Capital City Acad NW10 .... 90 B6
Capital East Apts 8 E16 .... 121 A6
Capital Ind Est
Belvedere DA17 .... 125 D3
Mitcham CR4 .... 202 D4
Capital Interchange Way TW8 .... 110 C1
Capital Sh Ctrs SW1 249 C1
Capital Wharf 15 E1 .... 118 A5
Capitol Ind Pk NW9 ... 45 A6
Capitol Way NW9 ...... 45 A6
Capland Ho NW8 ... 236 D6
Capland St NW8 .... 92 B3 236 D6
Caplan Est CR4 ...... 181 C2
Caple Ho SW10 ...... 266 B4
Caple Rd NW10 .... 89 D5
Capper St WC1 .... 93 C3 239 B5
Caprea Cl UB4 .... 84 D2
Capricorn Ctr RM8 .... 59 B2
Capri Ho E17 .... 35 B1
Capri Rd CR0 .... 205 D2
Capstan Cl RM6 ...... 58 B3
Capstan Ho 6 E14 .. 120 A2
Capstan Rd SE8 ...... 119 B2
Capstan Ride EN2 ...... 4 C3
Capstan Sq E14 ...... 120 A4
Capstan Way SE16 ... 119 A5
Capstone Rd BR1 ... 186 D6
Capthorne Ave HA2 ... 41 B1
Capuchin Cl HA7 ...... 25 B4
Capulet Mews 1 E16 .... 121 A5
Capworth St E10 ...... 53 D2
Caradoc Cl W2 .... 91 C1
Caradoc Evans Cl N11 .... 31 B5
Caradoc St SE10 .... 120 C1
Caradon Cl 4 E11 .... 76 C6
Caradon Ct 7 TW1 .. 153 C5
Caradon Way N15 ..... 51 B5
Cara Ho 10 N1 .... 72 C1
Caranday Villas 5 W11 .... 112 D5
Caravel Cl E14 ...... 119 C3
Caravelle Gdns 1 UB5 .... 84 D4
Caravel Mews 14 SE8 .... 141 C6
Caraway Cl E13 ...... 99 B2
Caraway Hts E14 .... 120 A6
Caraway Pl SM6 ...... 219 B5
Carberry Rd 12 SE19 .... 183 C4
Carbery Ave W3 ...... 110 B4
Carbis Cl E4 .... 20 B3
Carbis Rd E14 .... 97 B1
Carbroke Ho 9 E9 .... 96 C6
Carburton St W1 .... 93 B3 238 D5
Cardale St 1 E14 .... 120 A3
Cardamom Ct 1 E12 .. 78 C4
Carden Rd SE15 ...... 140 B2
Cardiff Ho 9 SE15 ... 140 A6
Cardiff Rd Ealing W7 .. 109 A3
Enfield EN3 .... 6 B1
Cardiff St SE18 ...... 145 C5

Cardigan Ct 3 W7....86 D3
Cardigan Gdns IG3...80 A6
Cardigan Rd
Barnes SW13......134 A3
Bow E3............97 B5
Richmond TW10.....154 A5
Wimbledon SW19...180 A4
Cardigan St
SE11........116 C1 261 A2
Cardigan Wlk 19 N1...73 A1
Cardinal Ave
Kingston u T KT2....176 A4
West Barnes SM4....201 A3
Cardinal Bourne St
SE1...............262 D5
Cardinal Cap Alley
SE1...............252 A5
Cardinal Cl
Burnt Oak HA8.......27 B3
Chislehurst BR7......189 B2
West Barnes SM4....201 A3
Worcester Pk KT19,
KT4............216 A4
Cardinal Cres KT3....177 A1
Cardinal Ct KT8......196 B5
Cardinal Dr KT12.....194 D1
Cardinal Hinsey Cl
NW10..............90 A5
Cardinal Hinsley RC
High Sch (Boys)
NW10..............90 A6
Cardinal Pl SW15....134 D1
Cardinal Pole RC Sch
London E9..........74 D1
London E9..........75 A3
Cardinal Rd
Feltham TW13.......150 B3
Ruislip HA4.........40 D1
Cardinal Road Inf Sch
TW13..............150 B3
Cardinals Way N19....49 D1
Cardinal's Wlk
Ashford TW16......171 C4
Hampton TW12.....174 A3
Cardinal Vaughan Meml
Sch The W14......244 A2
Cardinal Way HA3.....42 C6
Cardinal Wiseman RC
Sch The UB6........86 A2
Cardinal Wlk SW1..259 A5
Cardine Mews SE15..140 B5
Cardington Sq TW4..128 D1
Cardington St
NW1........93 C4 232 B1
Cardozo Rd N7.......72 A3
Cardrew Ave N12.....30 B5
Cardrew Cl N12.......30 B5
Cardrew Ct 8 N12....30 B5
Cardross St W6......112 B3
Cardwell Prim Sch
SE18..............122 B2
Cardwell Rd 3 N7....72 A4
Career Ct 11 SE16....118 D4
Carew Cl N7..........72 B6
Carew Ct
15 Deptford SE14...140 D6
Ilford RM6...........58 B3
Carew Ho
West Norwood
SW16...........160 C1
23 Woolwich SE18...122 B2
Carew Manor Sch
SM6..............219 D5
Carew Rd
Ashford TW15......171 A4
Ealing W13........109 C4
Mitcham CR4.......181 A1
Thornton Heath CR7.204 D5
Tottenham N17.......34 A1
Wallington SM6.....219 C2
Carew St SE5........139 A3
Carey Ct Bexley DA6...169 D6
20 Camberwell SE5..139 A5
Carey Gdns
SW8........137 D4 269 C1
Carey Ho E5..........74 B5
Carey La EC2........242 A2
Carey Pl SW1........259 C3
Carey Rd RM9........81 A4
Carey St WC2..94 B1 240 D1
Carey Way HA9.......66 D4
Carfax Pl SW4.......137 D1
Carfax Rd UB3.......106 A2
Carfree Cl 5 N1......72 C1
Cargill Rd SW18.....158 A3
Cargreen Pl SE25....205 D5
Cargreen Rd SE25....205 D5
Cargrey Ho 9 HA7....25 C5
Carholme Rd SE23...163 B3
Carillon Ct W5.......109 D6
Carinthia Ct 5 SE8...119 A2
Carisbrook Cl EN1.....5 D4
Carisbrooke Ave
DA5..............168 D3
Carisbrooke Cl
Stanmore HA7........25 D1
Twickenham TW4....151 A4
Carisbrooke Ct
Acton W3..........111 A4
Belmont SM2........217 B1
Northolt UB5........85 B6
1 Streatham SW16..160 B1
Carisbrooke Gdns
SE15..............139 D5
Carisbrooke Ho
10 Kingston u T
KT2............176 A2
Richmond TW10.....154 C6
Carisbrooke Rd
Bromley BR2.......209 C5
Mitcham CR4.......204 A5
Walthamstow E17.....53 A4
Carisbrook 2 N10....31 B1
Carleton Ave SM6....219 D1
Carleton Cl KT10.....196 B1
Carleton Gdns N19....71 C3
Carleton Ho 4 N8.....50 A4
Carleton Rd N7.......71 D4
Carley Ct 6 N12......30 B5
Carlile Cl E3..........97 B5
Carlile Ho SE1......262 D5
Carlina Gdns IG8.....37 B5
Carling Ct TW1......152 D4
Carlingford Gdns
CR4...............181 A3
Carlingford Rd
Hampstead NW3......70 B4
London N15..........50 D6
West Barnes SM4....200 D3
Carlingford DA14....190 A5
Carlisle Ave
Acton W3............89 C1
Whitechapel EC3....243 C1
Carlisle Cl
Kingston u T KT2....176 C2
Pinner HA5..........41 A2
Carlisle Gdns
Harrow HA3..........43 D2
Redbridge IG1........56 A3
Carlisle Ho
6 Dartmouth Pk
NW5..............71 C5
Redbridge IG1........56 A3
Carlisle Inf Sch
TW12..............173 D4
Carlisle La
SE1........116 B3 260 D6
Carlisle Lo 1 N3......29 B1
Carlisle Pl
London N11..........31 B6
Westminster
SW1.....115 C3 259 A5
Carlisle Rd
Cheam SM1.........217 B2
Finsbury Pk N4.......50 C2
Hampton TW12......173 D3
Hendon NW9.........45 A6
Kilburn NW6.........91 A6
Leyton E10...........53 C1
Carlisle St
W1..........93 D1 239 C1
Carlisle Way SW17...181 A5
Carlisle Wlk 6 E8....73 D2
Carlos Pl
W1.........115 B6 248 C5
Carlow St NW1......232 A4
Carlson Ct SW15.....135 B1
Carlton Ave E HA9....65 D6
Carlton Ave
Feltham TW14.......150 C5
Harrow HA3..........43 B4
Hayes UB3..........105 C2
South Croydon CR2..221 C1
Southgate N14........15 D6
Carlton Ave W HA0....65 B6
Carlton Cl
Chessington KT9.....213 D2
Child's Hill NW3......69 C6
Edgware HA8.........26 C5
Northolt UB5.........64 A3
Carlton Cres SM3....217 A4
Carlton Ct
Brixton SW9........138 D4
Ealing W7..........108 D4
Finchley N3..........29 C3
Ilford IG6............57 B6
Kilburn NW6.........91 D5
11 Penge SE20......184 B2
South Norwood
SE19............183 D2
8 Willesden NW2....68 C2
Carlton Dr Ilford IG6...57 B6
Putney SW15........157 A6
Carlton Gdns
Ealing W5..........109 C6
St James
SW1......115 D5 249 C3
Carlton Gn DA14.....189 D6
Carlton Gr SE15......140 B4
Carlton Hill
NW8.........92 A5 229 A4
Carlton Ho
Cheam SM1.........217 B2
Edmonton N21........17 A3
Feltham TW14.......149 D5
Hounslow TW4......151 C5
8 Kilburn NW6.......91 B5
Kilburn NW6.........91 C5
Marylebone W1.....237 D2
Carlton House Terr
SW1......115 D5 249 D4
Carlton Lo N4........50 C2
Carlton Mans
Brixton SW9........138 C1
Cricklewood NW2.....68 D3
Kensington W14.....244 B2
Maida Vale W9.......91 D4
7 South Hampstead
NW6..............69 C1
Stamford Hill N16.....51 D1
Carlton Park Ave
SW20..............178 D1
Carlton Par HA9......44 A1
Carlton Prim Sch
NW5...............71 A3
Carlton Rd Acton W4..111 B4
Ashford TW16......171 D3
Ealing W5...........87 C1
Erith DA8..........147 D6
Finsbury Pk N4.......50 C2
Friern Barnet N11.....31 A5
Higham Hill E17......35 A2
Kingston u T KT3....177 C1
Leytonstone E11......54 D1
Manor Pk E12........77 D4
Mortlake SW14......133 A1
Sidcup DA14........189 D6
South Croydon CR2...221 B1
Walton-on-T KT12....194 B2
Welling DA16........146 B2
Carlton Sq E1........96 D3
Carltons The 5
SW15..............157 A6
Carlton St SW1.....249 C5
Carlton Terr
Edmonton N18........33 B6
Forest Hill SE26.....162 C1
Upton E7.............77 C1
Wanstead E11........55 B4
Carlton Tower Pl
SW1...............257 D6
Carlton Twrs SM5....218 D5
Carlton Vale Inf Sch
NW6...............91 B4
Carlton Vale NW6.....91 C5
Carlwell St SW17....180 C5
Carlyle Ave
Bromley BR1.......209 D6
Southall UB1.......107 B6
Carlyle Cl
East Molesey KT8...173 D1
Hampstead Garden
Suburb N2.........48 A3
Carlyle Gdns UB1....107 B6
Carlyle Ho
4 Camberwell
SE5............139 A5
Chelsea SW3.......266 D6
Ealing W5..........109 D2
East Molesey KT8...195 C4
12 Stoke Newington
N16...............73 C5
Carlyle Lo 6 EN5.....14 A6
Carlyle Mans SW3...267 A5
Carlyle Mews 24 E1...96 D3
Carlyle Pl SW15.....134 D1
Carlyle Rd
Croydon CR0.......222 A6
Ealing W5..........109 C2
Manor Pk E12........78 A4
1 Stonebridge
NW10.............89 B6
Woolwich SE28......124 C6
Carlyle's Ho* SW3...267 A5
Carlyle Sq
SW3........114 B1 256 D1
Carlyon Ave HA2......63 C4
Carlyon Cl HA0.......88 A6
Carlyon Ct HA0.......88 B6
Carlyon Mans 1
HA0................88 A5
Carlyon Rd
Hayes UB4...........84 C2
Wembley HA0........88 A6
Carlys Cl BR3.......184 D1
Carmalt Gdns SW15..134 C1
Carmarthen Ct 4
W7.................86 D3
Carmarthen Ho 8
SW15..............156 C4
Carmarthen Pl SE1...253 A2
Carmel Ct
Kensington W8......245 C2
Wembley Pk HA9......66 D6
Carmelite Cl HA3......24 A2
Carmelite Rd HA3......24 A1
Carmelite St
EC4........116 C6 251 B6
Carmelite Way HA3...24 A1
Carmelite Wlk HA3....24 A2
Carmel Lo SW6.......265 A6
Carmen St E14.......97 D1
Carmichael Cl
9 London SW11.....136 B2
Ruislip HA4..........62 A4
Carmichael Ct 5
SW13..............133 D3
Carmichael Ho
17 Dulwich SE21.....183 C6
6 Poplar E14.......120 A6
Carmichael Mews
SW18..............158 B4
Carmichael Rd
SE25..............206 A5
Carminia Rd SW17...159 B2
Carnaby St*
W1.........93 C1 239 A1
Carnac St SE21,
SE27..............161 B1
Carna Ct TW9........132 A2
Carnanton Rd E17....36 B2
Carnarvon Ave EN1....5 D3
Carnarvon Dr UB3...105 A3
Carnarvon Rd
Barnet EN5...........1 A2
Leyton E10...........54 A4
Stratford E15.........76 D2
Woodford E18.........36 D2
Carnation St SE2.....124 B1
Carnbrook Rd SE3...143 D2
Carnecke Gdns SE9..166 A6
Carnegie Cl
Holdbrook EN3........7 D5
Surbiton KT6........214 B6
Carnegie Ho NW3.....70 B5
Carnegie Pl SW19....156 D1
Carnegie St
N1.........94 B6 233 D5
Carnforth Cl KT19....214 D2
Carnforth Rd SW16..181 D3
Carnicot Ho 9
SE15..............140 B4
Carnoustie Cl SE28..102 D1
Carnoustie Dr N1.....72 B1
Carnwath Ho SW6....135 D2
Carnwath Rd SW6....135 D2
Caroe Ct N9..........18 B3
Carol Cl NW4.........46 D5
Carole Ho 15 SE20....184 B2
Carolina Cl E15.......76 C3
Carolina Rd CR7.....183 A2
Caroline Cl
Bayswater W2......245 D5
Hounslow TW7......130 C5
Muswell Hill N10.....31 B1
South Croydon CR0..221 C4
Streatham SW16.....160 B1
Caroline Ct
Ashford TW15......170 D4
Catford SE6........186 B6
Stanmore HA7........25 A4
17 Surbiton KT6.....197 D2
23 Woodside Pk N12...29 D6
Caroline Gdns E2.....95 C4
Caroline Ho
Bayswater W2......245 D5
20 Hammersmith
W6..............112 C1
Caroline Martyn Ho 8
N19...............49 D2
Caroline Pl
Bayswater W2......245 D5
Clapham SW11......137 A3
Harlington UB3......127 C5
Caroline Pl Mews
W2................245 D5
Caroline Rd SW19....179 B3
Caroline St E1........96 D1
Caroline Terr
SW1.......115 A2 258 A3
Caroline Wlk W6....264 A5
Carol St NW1..93 C6 232 A6
Carolyn Ho IG3.......58 A1
Caronia Ct 4 SE16....119 A2
Carpenter Gdns N21..16 D2
Carpenter Ho
London NW11........48 A3
11 Tower Hamlets
E14...............97 C2
5 Tufnell Pk N19.....71 D4
Carpenters Bsns Pk
E15................75 D1
Carpenters Cl EN5....13 D5
Carpenters Ct
Camden Town
NW1..............232 A6
5 Dagenham RM10....81 D2
Twickenham TW2....152 C2
Carpenter's Pl SW4..137 D1
Carpenters Prim Sch
E15................98 A6
Carpenter's Rd E15...75 D1
Carpenter St W1.....248 C5
Carradale Ho 2 E14...98 A1
Carrara Cl 18 SW9...138 D1
Carrara Wharf SW6..135 A2
Carr Cl HA7...........25 A4
Carr Gr SE18.........122 A2
Carriage Dr E
SW11.......137 A5 268 B4
Carriage Drive E
SW11.......137 A5 268 B4
Carriage Drive N SW11,
SW8........137 A6 268 B5
Carriage Dr N
Battersea SW8,
SW11....136 D5 267 C4
Battersea SW8,
SW11....137 A6 268 B5
Carriage Dr S
SW11.......137 A4 268 A2
Carriage Dr W
SW11.......136 D5 267 C3
Carriage Mews IG1...79 A6
Carriage Pl 14
SW16..............181 C5
Carrick Cl TW7......131 A2
Carrick Gate KT10...212 A5
Carrick Gdns N17.....33 C3
Carrick Ho
Islington N7.........72 B2
Kennington SE11....261 C2
Carrick Mews SE8...141 C6
Carrill Way DA17....124 D3
Carrington Ave
Borehamwood
WD6..............10 D6
Hounslow TW3......151 D6
Carrington Cl
Barnet EN5..........12 A6
Borehamwood WD6....11 A6
Croydon CR0.......207 A2
Carrington Ct
London SW11......136 C1
3 New Malden KT3.199 C5
Southgate N21........16 D5
Carrington Gdns 4
E7.................77 A4
Carrington Ho
Mayfair W1........248 C3
7 Merton SW19....179 C3
Carrington Lo
3 Richmond
TW10...........154 A6
Wembley HA9........66 B5
Carrington Pl KT10...212 A4
Carrington Rd
TW10..............132 C1
Carrington Sq HA3....24 A3
Carrington St W1....248 C3
Carrol Cl NW5........71 B4
Carroll Cl E15........76 D3
Carroll Ct Acton W3...110 D3
4 Shacklewell E5.....74 A5
Carroll Ho W2.......246 C6
Carronade Pl SE18...123 B3
Carron Cl E14........97 D1
Carroun Rd
SW8........138 B5 270 C4
Carroway La UB6.....86 B4
Carrow Rd RM9.......80 B1
Carr Rd Northolt UB5...64 A1
Walthamstow E17.....35 C1
Carrs La N21.........17 B6
Carr St 5 E14........97 A1
CARSHALTON.......218 C4
Carshalton, Beddington
& Wallington War
Meml Hospl SM5..218 D2
Carshalton Beeches Sta
SM5..............218 D2
Carshalton Boys Sports
Coll SM5.........218 C6
Carshalton Coll
SM5..............218 D5
Carshalton Gr SM1...218 B3
Carshalton High Sch for
Girls SM5.........218 C5
CARSHALTON ON THE
HILL..............219 B1
Carshalton Park Rd
SM5..............218 D3
Carshalton Pl SM5...219 A3
Carshalton Rd
Mitcham CR4.......203 A4
Sutton SM1, SM5....218 B3
Carshalton Sta SM5..218 D4
Carslake Rd SW15...156 C5
Carson Rd
Cockfosters EN4.......2 D1
Dulwich SE21.......161 B2
Newham E16..........99 A2
Carstairs Rd SE6....164 A1
Carston Cl SE12.....164 D6
Carswell Cl IG4.......55 D5
Carswell Rd SE6.....164 A4
Carter Cl Kenton NW9..45 B3
Wallington SM6.....219 D1
Carter Ct EC4.......241 D1
Carteret Ho 8 W12...112 B6
Carteret St SW1.....249 C1
Carteret Way SE8....119 A2
Carterhatch Jun & Inf
Schs EN1.............6 B4
Carterhatch La EN1....6 A4
Carterhatch Rd EN3....6 D4
Carter Ho
11 London SW2.....160 C6
Spitalfields E1......243 C3
Carter La EC4..94 D1 241 D1
Carter Pl
SE17.......117 A1 262 B1
Carter Rd
Mitcham SW19......180 B4
Newham E13..........99 B6
Carters Cl
10 Kentish Town
NW5..............71 D2
North Cheam KT4...200 D1
Carters Hill Cl SE9...165 C3
Carters La SE23......163 B1
Carters Rd N2.........30 C3
Carter St
SE17.......117 A1 262 A1
Carter's Yd SW18....157 C6
Carthew Rd W6......112 B3
Carthew Villas W6...112 B3
Carthusian St EC1...242 A4
Cartier Circ E14.....120 A5
Carting La
WC2........116 A6 250 B5
Cart La E4...........20 C3
Cartmel Cl N17.......34 B3
Cartmel Ct
Beckenham BR2.....186 C1
Northolt UB5.........63 A2
Cartmel Gdns SM4...202 A4
Cartmel NW1........232 A2
Cartmel Rd DA7.....147 C4
Carton Ho
4 Bermondsey
SE16.............118 A3
2 Dollis Hill NW2.....68 A5
12 Shepherd's Bush
W11.............112 D6
Cartoon Mus The*
WC1........94 A2 240 A3
Cartwright Gdns
WC1........94 A4 233 A1
Cartwright Ho SE1...262 B5
Cartwright Rd RM9...81 B1
Cartwright St
E1.........117 D6 253 D
Cartwright Way
SW13..............134 B5
Carvel Ho E14.......120 A1
Carver Cl 15 W4.....111 A
Carver Rd SE24......161 A5
Carville Cres TW8....110 A
Caryl Ho 6 SW19....156 D
Cary Rd E11..........76 C
Carysfort Rd
Canonbury N16.......73 B
London N8...........49 D
Casby Ho 7 SE16....118 A
Cascade Ave N10.....49 C
Cascade Cl IG9.......21 D
Cascade Rd IG9.......21 D
Cascadia Ho 22 KT1..176 C
Casella Rd SE14.....140 D
Casewick Rd SE27....182 D
Casey Cl NW8..92 C4 230 B
Casimir Rd E5........74 C
Casino Ave SE24.....161 B
Caspian Ho 10 E1.....96 D
Caspian St SE5......139 B
Caspian Wlk E16......99 D
Cassandra Cl UB5.....64 B
Cassandra Ct 7
NW2................68 C
Cass Bsns Sch
EC1........95 B3 242 C
Casselden Rd NW10...67 B
Cassel Hospl TW10..175 D
Cassell Ho 21 SW9...138 A
Casserley Ho W4.....111 B
Cass Ho 23 E9........74 D
Cassidy Rd SW6.....265 A
Cassilda Rd SE2.....124 A
Cassilis Rd
Millwall E14........119 C
Twickenham TW1.....153 B
Cassinghurst SE24...161 B
Cassiobury Ave
TW14..............149 D
Cassiobury Rd E17....53 A
Cassland Rd
Homerton E9.........74 D
South Norwood CR7..205 B
Casslee Rd SE6......163 B
Cassocks Sq TW17....193 B
Casson Ho 11 E1......96 A
Casson St E1..........96 A
Castalia Sq 6 E14....120 A
Castellain Mans W9...91 D
Castellain Rd W9.....91 D
Castellane Cl HA7....24 D
Castell Ho 11 SE8....141 C
Castello Ave SW15...156 C

Castelnau SW13 134 B5
Castelnau Gdns
SW13 134 B6
Castelnau Mans
SW13 134 B6
Castelnau Row
SW13 134 B6
Casterbridge
Kilburn NW6 91 D6
3 Notting Hill W11 91 C1
Casterbridge Rd
SE3 143 A2
Casterton St E8 74 B2
Castile Rd SE18 122 C2
Castilion Prim Sch
SE28 102 C1
Castillon Rd SE6 164 C2
Castlands Rd SE6 163 B2
Castleacre W2 237 A1
Castle Ave
Chingford E4 36 B5
Yiewsley UB7 104 B6
Castlebar Ct 5 W5 87 C2
Castlebar Hill W5 87 C2
Castlebar Mews W5 87 C2
Castle Bar Park Sta
W7 86 D2
Castlebar Pk W5 87 B2
Castlebar Rd W5 87 C1
Castlebar Sch W13 87 A2
Castle Baynard St
EC4 117 A6 252 A6
Castlebrook Cl
SE11 116 D2 261 C4
Castle Bsns Village
TW12 173 D2
Castle Cl
12 Acton W3 111 A4
Ashford TW16 171 C3
Beckenham BR2 208 C6
Homerton E9 75 A3
South Acton W3 110 D4
Wimbledon SW19 156 D1
Castlecombe Dr
SW19 156 D4
Castlecombe Prim Sch
SE9 188 A5
Castlecombe Rd
SE9 188 A6
Castle Ct
Belmont SM2 217 C2
City of London EC3 242 D1
Dagenham RM9 103 A6
Forest Hill SE26 185 A6
Morden SM4 202 B4
Castleden Ho NW6 70 B1
Castledine Rd SE20 184 B3
Castle Dr IG4 56 A3
Castleford Ave SE9 166 D3
Castleford Cl N17 33 D4
Castleford Ct NW8 236 D6
Castlefrank Ho 20
N1 95 C4
Castlegate TW9 132 B2
CASTLE GREEN 102 C6
Castleham Ct HA8 26 C4
Castlehaven Rd NW1 71 B1
Castle Hill Ave CR0 224 A1
Castle Hill Prim Sch
CR0 224 A2
Castle Ho
17 Belmont SM2 217 C1
3 Chingford E4 36 B5
Newington SE1 262 A4
South Lambeth SW8 270 B4
Castle Hts RM9 102 B6
Castle Ind Est SE17 262 A4
Castle La
SW1 115 C3 259 A6
Castleleigh Ct EN2 17 B6
Castlemaine Ave
CR2 221 D3
Castlemaine 8
SW11 136 D3
Castlemaine St 2 E1 96 B2
Castle Mead SE5 139 A5
Castle Mews
Camden Town NW1 71 B2
North Finchley N12 30 A5
Castle Par KT17 216 A1
Castle Pl
6 Acton W4 111 C2
Camden Town NW1 71 B2
Castle Point 4 E13 99 C5
Castle Rd
Camden Town NW1 71 B2
Dagenham RM9 102 B6
Enfield EN3 7 A5
Isleworth TW7 130 D3
North Finchley N12 30 B5
Northolt UB5 63 D1
Southall UB2 107 B3
Castlereagh Ho HA7 25 B4
Castlereagh St W1 237 C2
Castle St
Kingston u T KT2 176 A1
Newham E6 99 C5
Castleton Ave HA9 66 A4
Castleton Cl CR0 207 A3
Castleton Ct KT5 198 B4
Castleton Gdns HA9 66 A5
Castleton Ho 3
E14 120 A2
Castleton Rd
Chingford E17 36 B1
Ilford IG3 58 B1
Mitcham CR4 203 D5
Mottingham SE12,
SE9 187 D6
Ruislip HA4 40 D1
Castletown Rd
W14 113 A1 254 B1
Castleview Cl N4 73 A6
Castleview Gdns IG1 56 B3
Castle Way
Feltham TW13 172 C6
Wimbledon SW19 156 D1
Castle Wlk TW16 194 C6
Castlewood Day Hospl
SE18 144 C4
Castlewood Dr SE9 144 B3
Castlewood Ho WC1 239 D2
Castlewood Rd
Barnet EN4 2 B2
Stamford Hill N16 52 A3
Castle Yd Highgate N6 49 A2
Lambeth SE1 251 D4
18 Richmond TW10 153 D6
Castor La E14 119 D6
Catalina Rd TW6 126 C2
Catalpa Ct SE13 164 B5
Caterham Rd SE13 142 B2
Catesby Ho 25 E9 74 C1
Catesby St
SE17 117 B2 262 D3
CATFORD 163 C3
Catford Br SE6 163 C4
Catford Bridge Sta
SE6 163 C4
Catford Broadway
SE6 163 D4
Catford Gyratory
SE6 163 D4
Catford High Sch
SE6 164 A1
Catford Hill SE6 163 C3
Catford Rd SE6 163 C4
Catford Sh Ctr SE6 163 D4
Catford Sta SE6 163 C4
Cathall Rd E11 76 B5
Cathay Ho SE16 118 B4
Cathay St 12 SE16 118 B4
Cathay Wlk UB5 85 C5
Cathcart Dr BR6 211 C1
Cathcart Hill N19 71 C5
Cathcart Rd
SW10 136 A6 266 A6
Cathcart St NW5 71 B2
Cathedral Ct EC4 241 D1
Cathedral Lo EC1 242 A4
Cathedral Sch of St
Saviour & St Mary
Overie Prim Sch
SE1 117 A4 252 B2
Cathedral St
SE1 117 B5 252 C4
Cathedral Wlk SW1 259 A6
Catherall Rd N5, N16 73 A5
Catherine Baird Ct 12
SW12 159 B4
Catherine Ct
Barnet EN5 1 D2
1 Ilford IG2 57 A3
2 Southgate N14 15 C6
3 Wimbledon
SW19 179 B5
Catherine Dr
Ashford TW16 171 D4
Richmond TW9 132 A1
Catherine Gdns
TW3 130 B1
Catherine Godfrey Ho
RM9 103 B6
Catherine Griffiths Ct
EC1 241 B6
Catherine Gr SE10 141 D4
Catherine Ho
Isleworth TW7 131 B4
16 Shoreditch N1 95 C6
Catherine Lo E18 37 C2
Catherine Pl
Harrow HA1 42 D4
Westminster
SW1 115 C3 259 A6
Catherine Rd
Enfield EN3 7 A6
Kingston u T KT6 197 D4
Catherine St
WC2 116 B6 250 C6
Catherine Wheel Alley
E1 243 B3
Catherine Wheel Rd
TW8 131 D5
Catherine Wheel Yd
SW1 249 A3
Catherwood Ct N1 235 C3
Cat Hill EN4 14 D6
Cathles Rd SW12 159 B5
Cathnor Rd W12 112 B4
Catisfield Rd EN3 7 A6
Catlin Cres TW17 193 B4
Catling Cl SE23 162 D1
Catlin's La HA5 40 B5
Catlin St SE16 118 B1
Catman Ho N4 50 B1
Caton Ct BR2 186 C1
Cato Rd SW4 137 D1
Cator La BR3 185 B2
Cator Park Sch BR3 185 A3
Cator Rd
Penge SE20,
SE26 184 D5
Wallington SM5 218 D3
Cator St
Camberwell SE15 139 D5
Camberwell SE15 139 D6
Cato St W1 92 C1 237 B2
Catsey La WD23 8 A4
Catsey Wood WD23 8 A4
Catterick Cl N11 31 A4
Cattistock Rd SE9 188 B5
Cattley Cl EN5 1 A1
Catton St WC1 240 C3
Caughley Ho SE11 261 A5
Caulfield Ct 15 NW1 71 C1
Caulfield Rd
East Ham E6 78 B1
London SE15 140 B3
Causeway TW14,
TW4 128 B1
Causeway The
Carshalton SM5 219 A6
Chessington KT9 214 A4
Claygate KT10 212 D1
East Finchley N2 48 C5
Teddington TW11 174 D4
Wandsworth SW18 157 D6
Wimbledon SW19 178 C5
Causeyware Rd N9 18 C4
Causton Cotts 3
E14 97 A1
Causton Ho SE5 139 A5
Causton Rd N6 49 B2
Causton Sq RM10 81 C1
Causton St
SW1 115 D1 259 D2
Cautley Ave SW4 159 C6
Cavalier Cl RM6 58 D5
Cavalier Gdns UB3 83 B1
Cavalier Ho W5 109 C6
Cavalry Cres TW4 128 D1
Cavalry Gdns SW15 157 B6
Cavan Pl HA5 23 B2
Cavaye Ho SW10 266 B6
Cavaye Pl SW10 256 B1
Cavell Ct 5 N19 71 C6
Cavell Dr EN2 4 C3
Cavell Ho 8 N1 95 C6
Cavell Rd N17 33 B3
Cavell St E1 96 B2
Cavendish Ave
Ealing W13 87 A1
Falconwood DA16 145 D2
Finchley N3 29 C1
Harrow HA1 64 C4
Ruislip HA4 62 B3
Sidcup DA15 168 A4
St John's Wood
NW8 92 B5 229 D3
West Barnes KT3 200 B5
Woodford IG8 37 B3
Cavendish Cl
Ashford TW16 171 D4
Brondesbury NW6 69 B2
Edmonton N18 34 B5
Hayes UB4 83 C2
3 Putney SW15 157 A6
St John's Wood
NW8 92 B4 229 D2
Cavendish Coll
WC1 93 D2 239 C4
Cavendish Cres WD6 10 C6
Cavendish Ct
Ashford TW16 171 D4
Catford SE6 163 D3
5 Chingford E4 20 C4
Wallington SM6 219 B2
Wembley HA0 65 D3
Whitechapel EC2 243 B2
Cavendish Dr
Claygate KT10 212 C3
Edgware HA8 26 B4
Leytonstone E11 54 B1
Cavendish Gdns
Barking IG11 79 D3
Clapham Pk SW4 159 C5
Dagenham RM6 59 A4
Ilford IG1 56 C1
Cavendish Ho
London N12 30 A6
Cavendish Ho *continued*
5 Muswell Hill N10 31 A3
3 Richmond TW10 153 C1
South Lambeth SW8 270 A2
St John's Wood NW8 229 D3
Twickenham TW1 153 A5
Cavendish Mans
2 Clapham Pk
SW12 159 C5
Hackney E5 74 C3
Holborn EC1 241 A5
8 West Hampstead
NW6 69 C3
Cavendish Mews N
W1 238 D4
Cavendish Mews S
W1 238 D3
Cavendish Par
Balham SW12 159 B5
Hounslow TW4 129 A3
Cavendish Pl
Balham SW4 159 B5
Bromley BR1 210 B6
Brondesbury NW2 68 D2
Marylebone W1 238 D2
Cavendish Prim Sch
W4 133 C5
Cavendish Rd
Ashford TW16 171 D4
Brondesbury NW6 69 B1
Chingford E4 36 A4
Chiswick W4 133 A4
Clapham Pk SW12 159 C5
Edmonton N18 34 B5
Harringay N4 50 D3
Mitcham SW19 180 C3
New Malden KT3 199 D5
Sutton SM2 218 A1
Thornton Heath CR0 204 D1
Cavendish Sch The
NW1 93 B6 231 D6
Cavendish Sq
W1 93 B1 238 D2
Cavendish St
N1 95 B5 235 C3
Cavendish Terr
Feltham TW13 150 A2
11 Tower Hamlets E3 97 B4
Cavendish The NW11 47 D2
Cavendish Way BR4 207 D1
Cavenham Gdns IG1 79 B5
Cave Rd Newham E13 99 B4
Richmond TW10 175 C6
Caverleigh Way
KT4 200 B2
Caversham Ave
Cheam SM3 217 A6
Palmers Green N13 16 C1
Caversham Ct N11 15 A1
Caversham Ho
8 Kingston u T
KT1 176 A1
7 Peckham SE15 140 A6
Wallington CR0 220 A5
West Green N15 51 A5
Caversham Lo N10 31 C1
Caversham Rd
Kentish Town NW5 71 C2
Kingston u T KT1 176 B1
West Green N15 51 A5
Caversham St
SW3 136 D6 267 C6
Caverswall St W12 90 C1
Caveside Cl BR7 188 C2
Cavour Ho SE17 261 D2
Cawdor Cres W7 109 A2
Cawnpore St SE19 183 C5
Cawston Ct 8 BR1 186 D3
Caxton Gr E3 97 C4
Caxton Hall* SW1 259 C6
Caxton Rd
Shepherd's Bush
W12 112 D4
Southall UB2 106 D3
Wimbledon SW19 180 A5
Wood Green N22 32 B1
Caxton St N E16 98 D1
Caxton St
SW1 115 D3 259 C6
Caxton Trad Est
UB3 105 C5
Caxton Wlk WC2 239 D1
Cayford Ho 1 NW3 70 D3
Caygill Cl BR2 208 D5
Cayley Cl SM6 220 A1
Cayley Prim Sch E14 97 A1
Cayley Rd UB2 107 D3
Cayton Pl EC1 235 C1
Cayton Rd UB6 86 C5
Cayton St EC1 235 C1
Cazenove Mans 1
N16 74 A6
Cazenove Rd
Stoke Newington
N16 74 A6
Walthamstow E17 35 C2
Cearns Ho E6 99 D6
Ceasors Ct TW1 152 D2
Cecil Ave
Barking IG11 79 B1
Enfield EN1 5 D1
Wembley HA9 66 B3
Cecil Cl
Chessington KT9 213 D4
Ealing W5 87 D2
Littleton TW15 171 A3
Cecil Ct
Chelsea SW10 266 A6
12 Croydon CR0 221 D6
Ealing W5 87 D2
South Hampstead
NW6 69 D1
St James WC2 250 A5
Cecile Pk N8 50 A3
Cecil Ho E17 35 C2
Cecilia Cl N2 48 A6
Cecilia Rd E8 74 A3
Cecil Lo KT9 213 D4
Cecil Mans 2
SW17 159 A2
Cecil Pk HA5 41 A5
Cecil Pl CR4 202 D4
Cecil Rd Acton W3 89 A2
Ashford TW15 171 A4
Cheam SM1, SM2 217 B2
Colindale NW9 45 C6
Dagenham RM6 58 D2
Enfield EN2 5 B1
Harlesden NW10 89 C6
Harrow HA3 42 C6
Hounslow TW3 130 A3
Ilford IG1 78 D4
Leyton E11 76 C5
Merton SW19 179 D3
Muswell Hill N10 31 B1
Newham E13 99 A6
Osidge N14 15 C3
Thornton Heath CR0 204 B3
Walthamstow E17 35 C2
Cecil Rhodes Ho
NW1 232 C4
Cecil Rosen Ct HA0 65 B5
Cecil Way BR2 209 A1
Cedar Ave
Dagenham RM6 59 A4
East Barnet EN4 14 C4
Enfield EN3 6 C3
Hayes UB3 84 A1
Ruislip HA4 62 C3
Sidcup DA15 168 A4
Twickenham TW2 152 A5
Yiewsley UB7 104 B6
Cedar Cl
Buckhurst Hill IG9 21 D2
East Molesey KT8 196 C5
Keston Mark BR2 226 A5
Kingston u T KT2 177 B6
Old Ford E3 97 B6
Wallington SM5 218 D2
West Norwood SE21 161 A2
Cedar Copse BR1 188 B1
Cedar Cres BR2 226 A5
Cedarcroft Rd KT9 214 B4
Cedar Ct
7 Brentford
TW8 131 D6
19 Charlton SE7 143 C6
Edgware HA8 11 A1
Eltham SE9 166 A5
Finchley N3 29 C3
Islington N1 73 A1
Marylebone W1 237 B2
Mortlake SW14 133 A1
1 Muswell Hill N10 31 B1
5 New Southgate
N11 31 C5
Oakleigh Pk N20 14 B3
Stoneleigh KT17 216 A1
3 Sutton SM2 218 A2
6 Wanstead E11 55 B4
Wembley HA0 65 B4
Wimbledon SW19 156 D1
5 Woodford E18 37 A2
Cedar Dr London N2 48 C5
Pinner HA5 23 C4
Cedar Gdns SM2 218 A2
Cedar Grange 10
EN1 17 C6
Cedar Gr Ealing W5 110 A3
Sidcup DA5 168 D5
Southall UB1 85 C2
Cedar Ho
Ashford TW16 171 D3
5 Cubitt Town E14 120 A4
Hayes UB4 84 C3
Kensington W8 255 C6
New Addington CR0 223 D2
New Cross Gate
SE14 140 D4
5 Richmond TW9 132 D4
16 Rotherhithe
SE16 118 D4
Wood Green N22 32 C2
Cedar Hts TW10 154 A3
Cedarhurst BR1 186 C3
Cedarhurst Dr SE9 165 C6
Cedar Lawn Ave EN5 13 A6
Cedar Lo
Brondesbury NW2 69 B2
Fulham SW6 134 D4
Cedarmore Ct BR7 189 A2
Cedar Mount SE9 165 D3
Cedarne Rd
SW6 135 D5 265 C3
Cedar Park Gdns
RM6 58 D2
Cedar Park Rd EN2 5 A5
Cedar Pl 3 SE7 121 C1
Cedar Rd
Bromley BR1 187 C1
Cranford TW5 128 C3
Cricklewood NW2 68 C4
Croydon CR0 221 C6
East Bedfont TW14 149 B3
East Molesey KT8 196 C5
Enfield EN2 5 A5
Sutton SM2 218 A2
Teddington TW11 175 A5
Tottenham N17 33 D2
Cedar Rise N14 15 A4
Cedars Ave
Mitcham CR4 203 A6
Walthamstow E17 53 C4
Cedars Cl
Hendon NW4 46 D6
Lewisham SE13 142 B2
Cedars Ct
Edmonton N9 17 D2
Putney SW15 156 A5
Cedars Dr UB10 82 C5
Cedars Fst & Mid Schs
HA3 24 A2
Cedars Ho
21 London SW2 138 B1
15 Walthamstow E17 53 D6
5 West Norwood
SW27 182 D5
Cedars Mews SW4 137 B1
Cedars Prim Sch The
TW5 128 A5
Cedars Rd
Barnes SW13 134 A3
Beckenham BR3 185 B1
Clapham SW4 137 B1
4 Lower Edmonton
N9 18 A2
Morden SM4 201 C5
Stratford E15 76 C2
Teddington KT8 175 C2
Wallington CR0 220 A4
Winchmore Hill N21 16 D2
Cedars The
Buckhurst Hill IG9 21 A3
Ealing W13 87 C1
Hackney E9 74 D1
4 Kingston u T KT2 176 D2
Teddington TW11 174 D4
Wallington SM6 219 C4
Cedar Terr
9 Dagenham RM8 58 D2
Richmond TW9 132 A1
Cedar Tree Gr SE27 182 D5
Cedarville Gdns
SW16 182 B4
Cedar Way
Ashford TW16 171 C3
Camden Town
NW1 93 D6 232 C6
Cedar Wlk KT10 212 D2
Cedarwood BR3 185 B3
Cedarwood Ho EN2 4 D3
Cedarwood Lo HA8 26 B5
Cedra Ct N16 52 A1
Cedric Chambers
NW8 236 C6
Cedric Rd SE9 167 A1
Celadon Cl EN3 7 A2
Celandine Cl E3, E14 97 C2
Celandine Ct E4 19 D1
Celandine Dr
Dalston E8 73 D1
Woolwich SE28 124 B5
Celandine Gr N14 15 C6
Celandine Way E15 98 C4
Celbridge Mews W2 91 D1
Celestial Gdns SE13 142 B1
Celia Blairman Ho
E1 243 C4
Celia Ct 7 TW9 132 B4
Celia Ho 10 N1 95 C5
Celia Rd N19 71 C4
Celtic Ave BR2 208 C6
Celtic St E14 97 D2
Cemetery La
Lower Halliford
TW17 192 D2
Woolwich SE7 144 A6

Cemetery Rd
East Wickham SE2 146 B5
Forest Gate E7 76 D4
Tottenham N17 33 C3
Cenacle Cl NW3 69 C5
Cenotaph* SW1 250 A2
Centaur Ct 3 TW8 110 A1
Centaurs Bsns Pk TW7 131 A6
Centaur St SE1 116 B3 260 D6
Centenary Rd EN3 7 B1
Centennial Ave WD6 9 C4
Centennial Ct WD6 9 C4
Centennial Pk HA7, WD6 9 C4
Central Ave
Battersea SW11 136 D5 267 D3
East Finchley N2 47 D6
East Molesey KT8 195 B4
Edmonton N9 17 D1
Enfield EN1 6 B3
Finchley N2 30 B1
Hayes UB3 106 A6
Isleworth TW3, TW7 130 A1
Leyton E11 76 B6
Pinner HA5 41 B2
Wallington SM6 220 A3
Welling DA16 146 A3
Central Bsns Ctr NW10 67 C3
Central Chambers W5 109 D6
Central Cir NW4 46 B4
Central Criminal Court (Old Bailey)* EC4 94 D1 241 D2
Central Ct 2 SE18 122 D2
Centrale Ctr CR0 221 A6
Central Foundation Boys' Sch EC2 95 B3 242 D6
Central Foundation Lower Girls Sch The E3 97 A4
Central Foundation Upper Girls Sch The E3 97 B4
Central Gdns SM4 201 D4
Central Hill SE19 183 B4
Central Ho
Barking IG11 79 A1
Mill Meads E15 98 A5
Central Mans
8 London NW4 46 B4
1 Streatham SW16 182 A6
Central Middlesex Hospl NW10 89 A4
Central Par
Croydon CR0 220 C4
Ealing UB6 87 A4
Enfield EN3 6 C3
Feltham TW14 150 C4
Harrow HA1 42 D4
Heston TW5 129 C5
Ilford IG2 57 B3
Central Park Ave RM10 81 D5
Central Park Prim Sch E6 99 D5
Central Park Rd E6 99 D5
Central Par
Penge SE20 184 D3
South Acton W3 110 D4
2 Streatham SW16 182 A6
Surbiton KT6 198 A3
Central Par Villas BR5 190 C1
Central Par 8 E17 53 C5
Central Pk Est TW4 128 D1
Central Public Health Laboratories NW9 45 C6
Central Rd
Morden SM4 201 D4
Wembley HA0 65 B3
Worcester Pk KT4 216 A6
Central St Martins Coll EC1 94 C3 241 B5
Central St Martins Coll of Art & Design (The London Inst) WC1 94 B2 240 C3
Central St Martin's Coll of Art & Design W1 93 D1 239 D1
Central Sch of Ballet EC1 94 C3 241 B5
Central Sch of Speech & Drama The NW3 70 B1
Central Sq
East Molesey KT8 195 B5
Central Sq *continued*
Hampstead Garden Suburb NW11 47 D3
4 Wembley HA9 66 A3
Central St EC1 95 A4 235 A1
Central Terr BR3 206 D6
Central Way
Feltham TW14 150 B6
Lower Place NW10 89 A4
Sutton SM5 218 C1
Thamesmead SE28 124 B6
Centre Ave
Acton W3 111 B5
Finchley N2 30 C1
Centre Bldg SE17 262 B4
Centre Common Rd BR7 189 A3
Centre Court Sh Ctr 3 SW19 179 B4
Centre Ct N20 14 B2
Centre Dr E7 77 C4
Centre Hts 5 NW3 70 B1
Centre Point Ho WC2 239 D2
Centre Point 3 SE1 118 A1
Centre Rd
Dagenham RM10 103 D5
Wanstead E7, E11 77 A6
Centre St E2 96 B5
Centre The TW13 150 B3
Centreway 4 IG1 79 A6
Centre Way N9 18 D2
Centro Ct E11 54 C1
Centurian Way DA18 125 C3
Centurion Bldg SW8 268 C5
Centurion Cl N7 72 B1
Centurion Ct
Hackbridge SM6 219 B6
7 Woolwich SE18 122 B2
Centurion La E3 97 B5
Centurion Lodge 2 RM10 81 D2
Century Cl NW4 46 D4
Century Ho
Edgware HA8 26 C3
Harrow HA3 42 C6
Lewisham SE13 141 D3
Wembley HA9 66 B6
Century Rd E17 53 A6
Century Yd SE23 162 C2
Cephas Ave E1 96 C3
Cephas Ho 9 E1 96 C3
Cephas St E1 96 C3
Ceres Ct 12 KT1 176 A1
Ceres Rd SE18 123 D2
Cerise Rd SE15 140 A4
Cerne Cl UB4 106 C6
Cerne Rd SM4 202 A3
Cerney Mews W2 246 C6
Cervantes Ct 12 W2 91 D1
Cester St E2 96 A6
Ceylon Rd
6 Hammersmith W14 112 D3
Kensington W14 254 A5
Chabot Dr SE15 140 B2
Chace Com Sch EN1 5 C4
Chadacre Ave IG5 56 B6
Chadacre Ct E15 99 A6
Chadacre Ho 10 SW9 138 D1
Chadacre Rd KT17 216 B3
Chadbourn St E14 97 D2
Chadbury Ct NW7 28 A2
Chad Cres N9 18 C1
Chadd Dr BR1 210 A6
Chadd Gn E13 99 A6
Chaddlewood EN4 3 A1
Chadston Ho 17 N1 72 D1
Chadswell WC1 233 B1
Chadview Ct 2 RM6 58 D2
Chadville Gdns RM6 58 D4
Chadway RM8 58 C1
Chadwell Ave RM6 58 B2
CHADWELL HEATH 58 D4
Chadwell Heath Foundation Sch The RM6 58 B3
Chadwell Heath Hospl RM6 58 B4
Chadwell Heath Ind Pk RM8 58 D1
Chadwell Heath La RM6 58 C3
Chadwell Heath Sta RM6 58 D2
Chadwell Prim Sch RM6 58 C2
Chadwell St EC1 94 C4 234 B2
Chadwick Ave
Chingford E4 36 B6
Enfield N21 4 B1
Wimbledon SW19 179 C4
Chadwick Cl
12 Ealing W7 86 D2
Roehampton SW15 155 D4
Teddington TW11 175 A4
Chadwick Ct 4 SE28 124 B5
Chadwick Pl KT6 197 C3
Chadwick Rd
Harlesden NW10 89 D6
Ilford IG1 78 D5
Leytonstone E11 54 D3
Peckham SE15 139 D3
Chadwick St SW1 115 D3 259 C5
Chadwick Way SE28 124 D6
Chadwin Rd E13 99 B2
Chadworth Ho
Finsbury EC1 235 A1
Finsbury Pk N4 51 A1
Chadworth Way KT10 212 B3
Chaffey Ho 6 SE7 121 C1
Chaffinch Ave CR0 206 D3
Chaffinch Bsns Pk CR0 206 D5
Chaffinch Cl
Croydon CR0 206 D3
Edmonton N9 18 D3
Tolworth KT6 214 C5
Chaffinch Rd BR3 185 A2
Chafford Way RM6 58 C5
Chagford Ct SW19 180 C3
Chagford Ho
38 Bromley E3 97 D4
Marylebone NW1 237 C5
Chagford St NW1 92 D3 237 D5
Chailey Ave EN1 5 D3
Chailey Cl TW5 128 D4
Chailey Ind Est UB3 106 A4
Chailey St E5 74 C5
Chalbury Ho 8 SW9 138 B1
Chalbury Wlk N1 234 A4
Chalcombe Rd SE2 124 B3
Chalcot Cl SM2 217 C1
Chalcot Cres NW1 92 D6 230 D6
Chalcot Gdns NW3 70 D2
Chalcot Mews SW16 160 A1
Chalcot Rd NW1 93 A6 231 A6
Chalcot Sch NW1 71 B1
Chalcot Sq NW1 71 A1
Chalcott Gdns KT6 197 C1
Chalcroft Rd SE13 164 C6
Chaldon Rd SW6 135 A5 264 B4
Chale Rd SW2 160 A5
Chalfont Ave HA9 66 D2
Chalfont Ct
3 Belvedere DA17 125 C1
12 Harrow HA1 42 D3
Hendon NW9 45 D6
Marylebone NW1 237 D5
Chalfont Gn N9 17 C1
Chalfont Ho
2 Bermondsey SE16 118 B3
Willesden NW10 67 B5
Chalfont Rd
Edmonton N9 17 D1
Hayes UB3 106 A4
South Norwood SE25 205 D6
Chalfont Way W13 109 B3
Chalfont Wlk 5 HA5 22 C1
Chalford Cl KT8 195 C5
Chalford Ct Ilford IG2 56 D4
15 Putney SW15 156 D5
Surbiton KT6 198 B2
Chalford 7 NW3 70 A2
Chalford Rd SE21 183 B6
Chalford Wlk IG8 37 D3
Chalgrove Ave SM4 201 C4
Chalgrove Gdns N3 47 A6
Chalgrove Prim Sch N3 47 A6
Chalgrove Rd
Sutton SM2 218 B1
Tottenham N17 34 B2
Chalice Cl SM6 219 D2
Chalice Ct N2 48 C5
Chalkenden Cl SE20 184 B3
Chalkers Cnr TW9 132 D2
Chalk Farm Rd NW1 71 A1
Chalk Farm Sta NW3 71 A1
Chalkhill Prim Sch HA9 66 D5
Chalk Hill Rd W6 112 D2
Chalkhill Rd HA9 67 A5
Chalk La EN4 2 D1
Chalklands HA9 67 A5
Chalkley Cl CR4 181 A1
Chalkmill Dr EN1 6 B2
Chalk Pit Ave BR5 190 C1
Chalk Pit Way SM1 218 A3
Chalk Rd E13 99 C2
Chalkstone Cl DA16 146 A4
Chalkwell Ho 10 E1 96 D1
Chalkwell Park Ave EN1 5 C1
Challenge Cl NW10 89 C6
Challenge Ct TW2 152 C4
Challenge Rd TW15 149 B1
Challenger Ho 7 E14 119 A6
Challice Way SW2 160 B3
Challiner Ct HA1 43 A4
Challin St 1 SE20 184 C2
Challis Rd TW8 109 D1
Challoner Cl N2 30 B1
Challoner Cres W14 254 C1
Challoner Ct BR2 186 B1
Challoner Mans W14 254 C1
Challoners Cl KT8 196 B5
Challoner St W14 113 B1 254 C1
Chalmers Ho
13 London SW11 136 A2
Walthamstow E17 53 D4
Chalmers Rd TW15 170 D5
Chalmers Rd E TW15 171 A5
Chalmers Way TW14 150 B6
Chalmer's Wlk 14 SE17 138 D6
Chalner Ho SW2 160 C3
Chaloner Ct SE1 252 C2
Chalsey Lodge SE4 141 B1
Chalsey Rd SE4 141 B1
Chalton Dr N2 48 B3
Chalton St NW1 93 D5 232 C3
Chamberlain Cl
Ilford IG1 79 A5
Plumstead SE18 123 B3
Chamberlain Cotts SE5 139 B4
Chamberlain Cres BR4 207 D1
Chamberlain Gdns TW3 130 A4
Chamberlain Ho 6 E1 118 C6
Chamberlain La HA5 40 A5
Chamberlain Pl E17 53 A6
Chamberlain Rd
Ealing W13 109 A4
Finchley N2 30 A1
Chamberlain St 7 NW1 70 D1
Chamberlain Way
Pinner HA5 40 B6
Surbiton KT6 198 A2
Chamberlain Wlk 5 TW13 173 A6
Chamberlayne Ave HA9 66 A6
Chamberlayne Mans 3 NW10 90 D4
Chamberlayne Rd NW10 90 C6
Chambers Gdns N2 30 B2
Chambers Ho 2 SW16 181 C6
Chambers La NW10 68 C1
Chambers Pl CR2 221 B1
Chambers Rd N7 72 A4
Chambers St SE16 118 A4
Chamber St E1 117 D6 253 D6
Chambers Walk HA7 25 B5
Chambon Pl 7 W6 112 A2
Chambord Ho 24 E2 95 D4
Chambord St E2 95 D4
Chamomile Ct E17 53 C3
Champa Cl N17 33 D1
Champion Cres SE26 185 A6
Champion Gr SE5 139 B2
Champion Hill SE5 139 B2
Champion Pk SE5 139 B3
Champion Rd SE26 185 A6
Champlain Ho 28 W12 112 B6
Champness Cl 9 SE27 183 B6
Champness Rd IG11 79 D1
Champneys Cl SM2 217 B1
Champneys Ct N21 16 A6
Chancel Ct W1 249 C6
Chancellor Gr SE21 161 A1
Chancellor Ho
South Kensington SW7 256 B6
29 Wapping E1 118 B5
Chancellor Pas E14 119 C5
Chancellor Pl NW9 27 D1
Chancellors' Ct WC1 240 C4
Chancellors Loft N8 50 A3
Chancellor's Rd W6 112 C1
Chancellors St W6 112 C1
Chancellors Wharf 21 W6 112 C1
Chancelot Rd SE2 124 B2
Chancel St SE1 116 D5 251 C3
Chancery Bldgs 14 E1 118 C6
Chancery Gate Bsns Ctr CR4 202 D4
Chancerygate Bsns Ctr HA4 63 A3
Chancery Ho WC2 241 A3
Chancery La
Beckenham BR3 185 D1
Holborn EC4 94 C1 241 A2
Chancery Lane Sta WC1 94 C2 241 A3
Chancery Mews SW17 158 C2
Chance St E2 243 C6
Chanctonbury Cl SE9 166 D1
Chanctonbury Gdns SM2 217 D1
Chanctonbury Way N12 29 C6
Chanderia Ct 5 CR0 221 A5
Chand Ho 7 N12 30 A5
Chandler Ave E16 99 A2
Chandler Cl TW12 173 C2
Chandler Ct
Feltham TW14 150 A5
Thornton Heath CR7 204 D4
2 Tolworth KT5 198 D1
8 Wallington SM6 219 B2
Chandlers Cl TW14 149 D4
Chandlers Field Prim Sch KT8 195 C4
Chandlers Mews E14 119 C4
Chandler St E1 118 B5
Chandlers Way 11 SE24 160 C4
Chandler Way SE15 139 D5
Chandlery Ho 26 E1 96 A1
Chandos Lo SM2 218 A1
Chandos Ave
Ealing W5 109 D2
New Southgate N14 15 C1
Oakleigh Pk N20 14 B3
Walthamstow E17 35 C1
Chandos Bsns Ctr 11 SM6 219 C2
Chandos Cl IG9 21 B2
Chandos Cres HA8 26 C3
Chandos Ct
Edgware HA8 26 B3
Palmers Green N14 15 D2
Stanmore HA7 25 B4
Chandos Pl WC2 116 A6 250 A5
Chandos Rd
Cricklewood NW2 68 C3
Finchley N2 30 C1
Harrow HA1 42 A4
Old Oak Common NW10 89 C3
Pinner HA5 40 D2
Stratford New Town E15 76 B3
Tottenham N17 33 C1
Chandos St W1 93 B2 238 D3
Chandos Way NW11 47 D1
Change Alley EC3 242 D1
Channel Cl TW5 129 C4
Channel Gate Rd NW10 89 C4
Channel Ho E14 97 A2
Channelsea Bsns Ctr E15 98 B5
Channelsea Rd E15 98 B6
Channing Sch N6 49 B1
Channon Ct 3 KT6 198 A4
Chantrey Rd SW9 138 B2
Chantries The HA7 25 A5
Chantry Cl
2 Abbey Wood SE2 124 C3
Edgware NW7 11 D4
Enfield EN2 5 A5
Harrow HA3 44 B4
Sidcup DA14 191 A5
Sunbury TW16 172 A3
West Kilburn W9 91 B3
Chantry Cres NW10 67 D2
Chantry Ct SM5 218 C5
Chantry Ct SW6 135 A2
Chantry La BR2 209 D4
Chantry Pl HA3 23 D2
Chantry Rd
Chessington KT9 214 C3
Harrow HA3 23 D2
Chantry Sch UB7 104 A6
Chantry Sq W8 113 D3 255 C5
Chantry St N1 94 D6 234 D5
Chantry The
3 Chingford E4 20 A3
Hillingdon UB8 82 B4
Chantry Way CR4 202 B6
Chant Sq E15 76 B1
Chant St E15 76 B1
Chapel Cl NW10 67 D2
Chapel Ct
Borough The SE1 252 C2
East Finchley N2 48 C6
Hayes UB3 105 D6
Chapel End Ho E17 35 D2
Chapel End Inf Sch E17 35 D2
Chapel End Jun Sch E17 35 D2
Chapel Farm Rd SE9 166 B2
Chapel Hill N2 30 C1
Chapel House St E14 119 D2
Chapel La
5 Dagenham RM6 58 D2
Hillingdon UB8 82 C1
Pinner HA5 40 D6
Chapel Market N1 94 C5 234 A4
Chapel Mill Rd KT1 198 B6
Chapel Pl
Islington N1 234 B4
Marylebone W1 238 C1
12 Shoreditch EC2 95 C4
Tottenham N17 33 D3
Chapel Rd
Bexleyheath DA7 147 C1
Ealing W13 109 B5
Hounslow TW3 129 D2
Ilford IG1 78 D5
Twickenham TW1 153 B4
West Norwood SE27 182 D6
Chapel Side W2 113 D6 245 C5
Chapel St Enfield EN2 5 B2
Paddington NW1 92 C2 237 A3
Westminster SW1 115 A4 248 B1
Chapel View CR2 222 C1
Chapel Wlk NW4 46 C5
Chapleton Ho SW2 160 C6
Chaplin Cl
Lambeth SE1 251 C2
Wembley HA0 65 D2
Chaplin Cres TW16 171 C4
Chaplin Ho
6 London SW9 138 C1
Sidcup DA14 190 A6
Chaplin Rd
Dagenham RM9 81 A1
3 Tottenham N17 51 D6
Wembley HA0 65 D2
West Ham E15 98 D6
Willesden NW2 68 A2
Chaplow Cl SW6 136 A3
Chapman Cl UB7 104 B3
Chapman Cres HA3 44 B4
Chapman Gn N22 32 C2
Chapman Ho
26 Stepney E1 96 B1
2 West Norwood SE27 160 D1
Chapman Rd
Belvedere DA17 125 D1
Hackney Wick E9 75 B2
Thornton Heath CR0 204 C1
Chapmans End BR5 191 A1
Chapman's La BR5 190 D1
Chapmans Park Ind Est NW10 67 D2
Chapman Sq SW19 156 D2
Chapman St E1 118 B6
Chapone Pl W1 239 C1
Chapter Cl
Hillingdon UB10 60 B1
16 South Acton W4 111 A3
Chapter House & Jewel Twr* SW1 260 A6
Chapter Rd
Kennington SE17 116 D1 261 D1
Willesden NW2 68 A3
Chapter St SW1 259 C3
Chapter Way
Hampton TW12 173 C6
Mitcham SW19 180 B2
Chara Pl W4 133 B6
Charcot Ho SW15 155 D5
Charcroft Ct 11 W14 112 D4
Charcroft Gdns EN3 6 D1
Chard Ho 7 N7 72 B6
Chardin Ho 30 SW9 138 C4

Chardin Rd 11 W4 ....111 C2
Chardmore Rd N16 ....52 A1
Chardwell Cl E6 .....100 B1
Charecroft Way
W12 ....112 D4
Charfield Ct W9 .....91 D3
Charford Rd E16 ......99 A2
Chargeable La E13 ....99 A3
Chargeable St E16 ....98 D3
Chargrove Cl 24
SE16 ....118 D4
Charing Cl BR6 ......227 D4
Charing Cross Hospl
W6 ....112 D1
Charing Cross Rd
WC2 ......93 D1 239 D1
Charing Cross Sta
WC2 ......116 A5 250 B4
Charing Cross
SW1 ......116 A5 250 A4
Charing Ct BR2 ......186 C1
Charing Ho SE1 ......251 B2
Chariot Cl 3 E3 ......97 C6
Charlbert Ct NW8 ...230 A4
Charlbert St
NW8 ......92 C5 230 A4
Charlbury Ave HA7 ....25 D5
Charlbury Gdns IG3 ...79 D6
Charlbury Gr W5 .....87 C1
Charlbury Ho 1 E12 ..78 C5
Charlbury Rd UB10 ....60 B5
Charldane Rd SE9 ....166 D1
Charlecote Gr SE26 ..162 B1
Charlecote Rd RM8 ...81 A5
Charlemont Rd E6 ...100 C4
Charles Allen Ho
EC1 ....234 A2
Charles Auffray Ho 30
E1 ....96 C2
Charles Babbage Cl
KT9 ....213 C1
Charles Barry Cl
SW4 ....137 C2
Charles Bradlaugh Ho
2 N17 ....34 B3
Charles Burton Ct
E5 ....75 A4
Charles Cl DA14 .....190 B6
Charles Cobb Gdns
CR0 ....220 C3
Charles Coveney Rd 4
SE15 ....139 D4
Charles Cres HA1 .....42 B2
Charles Ct 5 TW11 ..174 C5
Charles Darwin Ho
8 Bethnal Green
E2 ....96 B4
Bromley BR1 ....187 B3
Charles Dickens Ct
SE25 ....206 A5
Charles Dickens Ho 1
E2 ....96 B4
Charles Dickens Prim
Sch SE1 ...117 A4 252 A1
Charles Edward Brooke
Sch (Dennen Site)
SE5 ....138 D4
Charles Edward Brooke
Sch SW9 ....138 D4
Charlesfield SE12 ....165 C1
Charles Flemwell Mews
7 E16 ....121 A5
Charles Goddard Ho 3
HA0 ....65 D3
Charles Grinling Wlk
SE18 ....122 C2
Charles Gr N14 ....15 C3
Charles Haller St 25
SW2 ....160 C4
Charles Harrod Ct
SW13 ....134 C6
Charles Hobson Ho 4
NW10 ....67 C1
Charles Hocking Ho 8
W3 ....111 A4
Charles Ho
Southall UB2 ....107 C4
1 Tottenham N17 ....33 D3
Charles II Pl
SW3 ......114 D1 257 C1
Charles II St
SW1 ......115 D5 249 C4
Charles Lamb Ct N1 .234 D4
Charles Lamb Prim Sch
N1 ......95 A6 235 A6
Charles La
NW8 ......92 C5 230 A4
Charles Lesser KT9 ..213 D3
Charles Mackenzie Ho
7 SE16 ....118 A2
Charlesmere Gdns
SE28 ....123 C4
Charles Mills Ct
SW16 ....182 A4
Charles Pl NW1 .....232 B1
Charles Rd
Dagenham RM6 ....58 D3
Charles Rd *continued*
Ealing W13 ....87 A1
Merton SW19 ....179 C2
Upton E7 ....77 C1
Charles Rowan Ho
WC1 ....234 A1
Charles Sevright Dr
NW7 ....28 D5
Charles Sq
N1 ......95 B4 235 D1
Charles Staunton Ho 3
SE27 ....183 B6
Charles St
Barnes SW13 ....133 C3
Croydon CR0 ....221 A5
Enfield EN1 ....17 D6
Hillingdon UB10 ......82 D3
Hounslow TW3 ....129 B3
Mayfair W1 ..115 B5 248 C4
Newham E16 ....121 C5
Charleston Cl TW13 ..150 A1
Charleston St SE17 ..262 B3
Charles Townsend Ho
EC1 ....241 C6
Charles Utton Ct E8 ...74 A4
Charles Whincup Rd 2
E16 ....121 B5
Charlesworth Ho 6
E14 ....97 C1
Charleville Cir SE26 .184 A5
Charleville Ct SW5 ..254 C1
Charleville Mans
W14 ....254 B1
Charleville Mews
TW7 ....131 B1
Charleville Rd
W14 ......113 B1 254 C1
Charlie Browns Rdbt
E18 ....37 C1
Charlmont Rd
SW17 ....180 D4
Charlotte Cl DA6 .....169 A6
Charlotte Ct
Crouch End N8 ....49 D3
Esher KT10 ....212 A3
10 Hammersmith
W6 ....112 A2
Ilford IG2 ....56 C3
11 Wembley HA0 .....66 A2
Charlotte Despard Ave
SW11 ......137 A4 268 B1
Charlotte Ho 12 W6 ..112 C1
Charlotte Mews
Marylebone W1 .....239 B4
North Kensington
W10 ....90 D1
West Kensington
W14 ....254 A4
Charlotte Par SE23 ..163 A2
Charlotte Park Ave
BR1 ....210 A6
Charlotte Pl
Kenton NW9 ....45 A4
Marylebone W1 .....239 B3
Westminster SW1 ...259 A3
Charlotte Rd
Barnes SW13 ....133 D4
Dagenham RM10 ......81 D2
Shoreditch
EC2 ......95 C3 243 A6
Wallington SM6 .....219 C2
Charlotte Row SW4 ..137 C2
Charlotte Sharman Prim
Sch SE11 ..116 D3 261 C5
Charlotte Sq 5
TW10 ....154 B5
Charlotte St
W1 ......93 C2 239 B4
Charlotte Terr
N1 ......94 B6 233 D5
CHARLTON 143 D6
171 B1
Charlton Church La
SE7 ....121 C1
Charlton Cl UB10 .....60 D6
Charlton Cres IG11 ..101 D5
Charlton Ct
Finchley N3 ....29 A1
25 Hackney E2 ....95 D6
17 Kentish Town N7 ...71 D3
Newham E6 ....100 B4
Charlton Dene SE7 ...143 D5
Charlton Gate Bsns Pk
SE7 ....121 C2
Charlton Ho
5 Brentford
TW8 ....132 A6
Charlton TW17 ......171 A1
Somers Town NW1 ..232 C2
Charlton King's Rd
NW5 ....71 D3
Charlton La
Greenwich SE7 .....121 D1
Upper Halliford
TW17 ....193 B5
Upper Halliford
TW17 ....193 C5
Charlton Lo 1 NW11 ..47 B3
Charlton Manor Prim
Sch SE7 ....143 D5
Charlton Park La
SE7 ....144 A6
Charlton Park Rd
SE7 ....143 D6
Charlton Pl
N1 ......94 D5 234 C4
Charlton Rd
Charlton TW17 ......171 A1
Edmonton N9 ....18 D4
Greenwich SE3, SE7 ..143 B6
Harlesden NW10 ......89 C6
Harrow HA3 ....43 D5
Wembley HA9 ....44 B1
Charlton Sch SE7 ...144 A6
Charlton Way SE10,
SE3 ....142 C4
Charlwood Cl HA3 ....24 C4
Charlwood Ho
Richmond TW9 ......132 D5
1 Streatham SW2 ...160 B3
Westminster SW1 ...259 C3
Charlwood Pl
SW1 ......115 C2 259 B3
Charlwood Rd
SW15 ....134 D1
Charlwood St
SW1 ......115 C1 259 B2
Charlwood Terr 5
SW15 ....134 D1
Charman Ho
18 London SW2 ......160 C5
South Lambeth SW8 .270 A4
Charmian Ave HA7 ....25 D1
Charmian Ho 19 N1 ...95 C5
Charminster Ave
SW19 ....179 D1
Charminster Ct 3
KT6 ....197 D2
Charminster Rd
Mottingham SE12,
SE9 ....187 D6
North Cheam KT4 ...200 D1
Charmouth Ct
TW10 ....154 B6
Charmouth Ho SW8 .270 C4
Charmouth Rd
DA16 ....146 C4
Charnock Ho 22
W12 ....112 B6
Charnock Rd E5 ......74 B5
Charnwood Ave
SW19 ....179 D1
Charnwood Cl KT3 ...199 C5
Charnwood Dr E18 ....55 B5
Charnwood Gdns
E14 ....119 C2
Charnwood Ho 9 E5 ..74 B6
Charnwood Pl N20 ....14 A1
Charnwood Rd
Hillingdon UB10 ......82 C5
South Norwood
SE25 ....205 B5
Charnwood St E5 .....74 B6
Charolais Ho UB4 .....83 B2
Charrington Ho 42
E1 ....96 C3
Charrington Rd 2
CR0 ....221 A6
Charrington St
NW1 ......93 D5 232 C4
Charsley Rd SE6 .....163 D2
Chart Cl
Bromley BR2 ....186 C2
Croydon CR0 ....206 C3
Mitcham CR4 ....202 D5
Charter Ave IG2 ......57 B2
Charter Bldgs 14
SE10 ....141 D4
Charter Cres TW4 ....129 A1
Charter Ct
Finsbury Pk N4 ....50 C1
Kingston u T KT3 ....199 C6
Marylebone W1 .....237 B3
Southall UB1 ....107 C5
Wood Green N22 ......31 D2
Charter Dr DA5 ......169 A4
Charterhouse Ave
HA0 ....65 C3
Charterhouse Bldgs
EC1 ....242 A5
Charterhouse Mews
EC1 ....241 D4
Charterhouse Rd E8 ...74 A3
Charterhouse Sq
EC1 ......94 D2 241 D4
Charterhouse Square
Sch EC1 ....94 D2 241 D4
Charterhouse St
EC1 ....241 C3
Charterhouse Works
SW18 ....136 A1
Charter Ho WC2 .....240 B1
Charteris Rd
Finsbury Pk N4 ....50 C1
Kilburn NW6 ....91 B6
Woodford IG8 ....37 B4
Charter Nightingale
Hospl The
NW1 ......92 C2 237 B4
Charter Rd KT1 ......198 D6
Charter Rd The IG8 ...36 D4
Charter Sch The
SE24 ....161 B6
Charters Cl SE19 ....183 C5
Charter Sq KT1 ......176 D1
Charter Way
London NW3 ....47 B5
Southgate N14 ....15 D5
Chartes Ho SE1 .....263 B6
Chartfield Ave
SW15 ....156 C6
Chartfield Sch
SW15 ....156 B6
Chartfield Sq SW15 ..156 D6
Chartham Ct 12
SW9 ....138 C2
Chartham Gr SE27 ...160 D1
Chartham Ho SE1 ...262 D6
Chartham Rd SE25 ...206 B6
Chart Hills Cl SE28 ..103 A1
Chart Ho 7 SW19 ....180 D1
Chart House The 5
E14 ....119 D1
Chartley Ave
Harrow HA7 ....24 D4
Neasden NW2 ....67 C5
Charton Cl 5 DA17 ..147 B6
Chartres Ct UB6 ......86 B5
Chartridge Cl
Barnet EN5 ....12 A6
Bushey WD23 ....8 A5
Chartridge Ct 6 HA7 ..25 C5
Chartridge SE17 .....139 B6
Chart St N1 ...95 B4 235 D2
Chartwell Bsns Ctr
BR1 ....209 D6
Chartwell Cl
2 Croydon CR0 .....205 B1
Greenford UB6 ....85 D6
Sidcup SE9 ....167 B2
Chartwell Ct
10 Barnet EN5 ....1 A1
Dollis Hill NW2 ......68 A5
2 Woodford IG8 .....37 A3
Chartwell Dr BR6 ....227 B3
Chartwell Gdns
SM3 ....217 A4
Chartwell Lo 5
BR3 ....185 C3
Chartwell Pl
Cheam SM3 ....217 B4
Harrow HA2 ....64 B6
Chartwell 25 SW19 ...156 D3
Chartwell Way 3
SE20 ....184 B2
Charville Ct 8 HA1 ...42 D3
Charville La UB4 .....83 C5
Charville La W UB10 ..82 D4
Charville Prim Sch
UB4 ....83 C5
Charwood SW16 .....182 C6
Chase Bridge Prim Sch
TW2 ....152 C5
Chase Court Gdns
EN2 ....5 A2
Chase Ct
Chelsea SW3 ....257 C5
Isleworth TW7 ......131 A3
Merton SW20 ....179 A1
Chase Ctr The NW10 ..89 B4
Chase Ct
Southgate N14 ....15 C5
Wembley HA0 ....65 D2
Chase Farm Hospl
EN2 ....4 C5
Chasefield Rd
SW17 ....180 D6
Chase Gdns
Chingford E4 ....35 C6
Twickenham TW2 ....152 B4
Chase Gn EN2 ....5 A2
Chase Green Ave EN2 ..5 A3
Chase Hill EN2 ....5 A2
Chase La IG6 ....57 B4
Chase Lane Inf Sch
E4 ....35 B6
Chase Lane Jun Sch
E4 ....35 B6
Chaseley Ct
Gunnersbury W4 ....110 D1
Oatlands Pk KT13 ...193 C1
Chaseley St E14 ......97 A1
Chasemore Cl CR4 ..202 D2
Chasemore Gdns
CR0 ....220 C3
Chasemore Ho SW6 .264 B4
Chase Rd
North Acton NW10 ....89 B3
Southgate N14 ....15 D5
Chase Ridings EN2 .....4 C3
Chase Road Trad Est
NW10 ....89 B3
Chase Side Ave
Enfield EN2 ....5 A3
Merton SW20 ....179 A1
Chase Side Cres EN2 ...5 A4
Chase Side
East Barnet N14 ......15 B4
Enfield EN2 ....5 A3
Chase Side Pl EN2 .....5 A3
Chase Side Prim Sch
EN2 ....5 A3
Chase Side Works
N14 ....15 D4
Chase The
Bromley BR1 ....209 B6
Clapham SW4 ....137 B2
Dagenham RM6 ....59 A3
Eastcote HA5 ....40 C3
Edgware HA8 ....26 D2
Erith DA7 ....147 D2
Ickenham UB10 ....60 C3
Loughton IG10 ....21 D4
Manor Pk E12 ....77 D4
Pinner HA5 ....41 B5
South Norwood
SW16 ....182 C3
Stanmore HA7 ....25 A4
Sunbury TW16 ......172 B2
Wallington CR0,
SM6 ....220 B3
Chaseville Park Rd
N21 ....16 B6
Chaseville Par N21 ....16 B6
Chase Way N14 ....15 C3
Chasewood Ave EN2 ...4 D3
Chasewood Ct 4
NW7 ....27 B5
Chasewood Pk HA1 ...64 C5
Chateau The 4
SM5 ....218 D5
Chatelain Ho NW7 ....28 C6
Chater Ho 6 E2 ......96 D4
Chatfield Rd
London SW11 ....136 A2
Thornton Heath CR0 .204 D1
Chatham Ave BR2 ....209 A2
Chatham Cl
Cheam SM3 ....201 B2
Hampstead Garden
Suburb NW11 ....47 C4
Chatham Ct SW11 ....158 D6
Chatham Ho
7 London SE5 ......139 C3
6 Wallington SM6 ...219 B3
21 Woolwich SE18 ...122 B2
Chatham Pl E9 ....74 C2
Chatham Rd
Clapham SW11 .....158 D6
Kingston u T KT1,
KT2 ....176 C1
Walthamstow E17 .....53 A6
1 Woodford E18 .....36 D1
Chatham St
SE17 ......117 B2 262 D4
Chatsfield Pl W5 ......88 A1
Chatsworth Ave
Grove Pk BR1 ....187 B6
Hendon NW4 ....28 C1
Merton SW20 ....179 A1
Sidcup DA15 ....168 A3
Wembley HA9 ....66 B3
Chatsworth Cl
Coney Hall BR2,
BR4 ....224 D6
Hendon NW4 ....28 C1
Chatsworth Cres TW3,
TW7 ....130 B2
Chatsworth Ct
Brondesbury NW2 ....68 D2
Clapton Pk E5 ....74 D4
Earl's Ct W8 ....255 A4
5 Stanmore HA7 .....25 C5
Thornton Heath
SW16 ....204 B6
Chatsworth Dr EN1 ...18 A5
Chatsworth Est E5 ....74 D4
Chatsworth Gdns
Acton W3 ....110 D5
Harrow HA2 ....41 D1
New Malden KT3 ....199 D4
Chatsworth Ho
2 Bromley BR2 .....209 A5
Kingston u T KT6 ....197 D4
Chatsworth Inf Sch
Isleworth TW3 ......130 A1
Sidcup DA15 ....168 A3
Chatsworth Jun Sch
TW3 ....130 A1
Chatsworth Lo
1 Chiswick W4 ......111 B1
West Wickham BR4 ..224 A6
Chatsworth Par
BR5 ....211 A4
Chatsworth Pl
Mitcham CR4 ....202 D6
Chatsworth Pl *continued*
Teddington TW11 ....175 A6
Chatsworth Rd
Brondesbury NW2 ....68 D2
Cheam SM3 ....217 A4
Chiswick W4 ....133 A6
Clapton Pk E5 ....74 D4
Ealing W5 ....88 B3
Hayes UB4 ....84 B3
South Croydon CR0 ..221 B5
Stratford E15 ....76 D3
Chatsworth Rise W5 ..88 B3
Chatsworth Way
SE27 ....161 A1
Chattenden Ho 8
N4 ....51 B2
Chatteris Ct NW4 .....46 D6
CHATTERN HILL 170 D6
Chattern Hill TW15 ..170 D6
Chattern Rd TW15 ...171 A6
Chatterton Ct TW9 ...132 B3
Chatterton Rd
Bromley Comm
BR2 ....209 D4
Highbury N4 ....72 D5
Chatton Ct 5 NW9 ....46 A5
Chatto Rd SW11 .....158 D6
Chaucer Ave
Cranford TW4 ....128 B3
Hayes UB4 ....84 A2
Richmond TW9 ......132 C3
Chaucer Cl N11 ....31 D5
Chaucer Ct
14 New Barnet
EN5 ....13 D6
17 Stoke Newington
N16 ....73 C4
Chaucer Dr
SE1 ......117 D2 263 D3
Chaucer Gdns SM1 ..217 C5
Chaucer Gn CR0 .....206 C2
Chaucer Ho
Harrow HA2 ....41 D4
Pimlico SW1 ....259 A1
Sutton SM1 ....217 C5
2 West Norwood
SE27 ....183 A6
Chaucer Rd
Acton W3 ....111 A5
Ashford TW15 ......170 B6
Bexley DA16 ....145 D4
Chingford E17 ....36 A1
Herne Hill SE24 .....160 D6
Sidcup DA15 ....168 C3
Sutton SM1 ....217 C4
Upton E7 ....77 A2
Wanstead E11 ....55 A3
Chaucer Way SW17 ..180 B5
Chaulden Ho EC1 ...235 D1
Chauncey Cl N9 ....18 A1
Chaundrye Cl SE9 ...166 B5
Chauntler Cl E16 .....121 B6
Chaville Ct N11 ....31 A6
Cheadle Ct NW8 .....236 D6
Cheadle Ho 17 E14 ....97 B1
CHEAM 217 B3
Cheam Common Inf Sch
KT4 ....216 B6
Cheam Common Jun
Sch KT4 ....216 B6
Cheam Common Rd
KT4 ....216 C5
Cheam Court Flats 1
SM3 ....217 A2
Cheam Fields Prim Sch
SM3 ....217 A3
Cheam High Sch
SM3 ....217 A4
Cheam Mans SM3 ....217 A1
Cheam Park Farm Inf
Sch SM3 ....217 A5
Cheam Park Farm Jun
Sch SM3 ....217 A5
Cheam Park Way
SM3 ....217 A2
Cheam Rd
Belmont SM2,
SM3 ....216 D1
Cheam SM1 ....217 C2
Cheam Sta SM2 .....217 A1
Cheam St 6 SE15 ....140 B2
Cheam Village SM3 ..217 A2
Cheapside
Barbican
EC2 ......95 A1 242 B1
Edmonton N13 ....33 A6
Chearsley SE17 .....262 B4
Cheddar Cl 1 N11 ....31 A4
Cheddar Rd TW6 .....126 C3
Cheddar Waye UB4 ...84 B1
Cheddington Ho 9
E2 ....96 A6
Cheddington Rd N18 ..33 C6
Chedworth Cl E16 ....98 D1

Chedworth Ho
London N15 ... 51 B5
2 Stoke Newington E5 ... 74 A6
Cheeseman Cl TW12 ... 173 A4
Cheeseman Ct UB1 ... 107 D6
Cheesemans Terr W14 ... 254 C1
Cheffrey Ct TW15 ... 170 D4
Cheldon Ave NW7 ... 28 D3
Chelford Rd BR1 ... 186 B5
Chelmer Cres IG11 ... 102 B5
Chelmer Ct E18 ... 37 B2
Chelmer Rd E9 ... 74 D3
Chelmsford Cl
Fulham W6 ... 134 D6
Newham E6 ... 100 B1
Chelmsford Ct N14 ... 15 D4
Chelmsford Gdns IG1 ... 56 B2
Chelmsford Ho 5 N7 ... 72 B4
Chelmsford Rd
Leytonstone E11 ... 54 B1
London N14 ... 15 C4
Walthamstow E17 ... 53 C3
Woodford E18 ... 36 D2
Chelmsford Sq NW10 ... 90 C6
CHELSEA ... 114 C1
Chelsea Barracks* SW1 ... 115 A1 258 B1
Chelsea Bridge Rd SW1 ... 115 A1 258 B1
Chelsea Bridge SW1 ... 137 B6 268 C6
Chelsea Cl
Edgware HA8 ... 26 C1
Hampton TW12 ... 174 A5
New Malden KT4 ... 200 A2
Chelsea Cloisters SW3 ... 257 B3
Chelsea Cl NW10 ... 89 B6
Chelsea Coll of Art & Design
Chelsea SW3 ... 114 C1 257 A1
Pimlico SW1 ... 116 A1 260 A2
Chelsea Cres
Brondesbury NW2 ... 69 B2
Chelsea SW10 ... 266 B1
Chelsea Ct
Chelsea SW3 ... 268 A6
8 Chingford E4 ... 20 A3
Sutton SM2 ... 217 D2
Chelsea Emb SW3 ... 136 D6 267 C5
Chelsea Est SW3 ... 267 A5
Chelsea Farm Ho SW10 ... 266 D5
Chelsea Fields SW19 ... 180 B2
Chelsea Gate SW1 ... 258 B1
Chelsea Gdns
Cheam SM3 ... 217 A4
Chelsea SW1 ... 258 B1
Ealing W13 ... 86 D2
Chelsea Harbour Design Ctr SW10 ... 266 B2
Chelsea Harbour Dr SW10 ... 136 A4 266 B2
Chelsea Harbour Pier SW10 ... 266 C1
Chelsea Lo SW3 ... 267 D6
Chelsea Manor Ct SW3 ... 267 B6
Chelsea Manor Gdns SW3 ... 257 B1
Chelsea Manor St SW3 ... 114 C1 257 B1
Chelsea Manor Studios SW3 ... 257 B1
Chelsea Park Gdns SW3 ... 136 B6 266 C6
Chelsea Physic Gdn* SW1 ... 267 C6
Chelsea Reach Twr SW10 ... 266 C4
Chelsea Sq SW3 ... 114 B1 256 D1
Chelsea Twrs SW3 ... 267 B6
Chelsea & Westminster Hospl SW10 ... 136 A6 266 B5
Chelsfield Ave N9 ... 18 D4
Chelsfield Gdns SE26 ... 162 C1
Chelsfield Gn N9 ... 18 D4
Chelsfield Ho SE17 ... 263 A3
Chelsfield Point 3 E9 ... 74 D1
Chelsham Ho 1 SW4 ... 137 D2
Chelsham Rd
London SW4 ... 137 D2
South Croydon CR2 ... 221 B2
Chelsiter Ct DA14 ... 189 D6
Chelston App HA4 ... 62 A6
Chelston Ct 2 E11 ... 55 B4
Chelston Rd HA4 ... 40 A1
Chelsworth Dr SE18 ... 145 B6
Cheltenham Ave 10 TW1 ... 153 A4
Cheltenham Cl
Kingston u T KT3 ... 199 A6
Northolt UB5 ... 63 D2
Cheltenham Ct 8 HA7 ... 25 C5
Cheltenham Gdns E6 ... 100 A5
Cheltenham Ho UB3 ... 105 A3
Cheltenham Pl
10 Acton W3 ... 110 D5
Acton W3 ... 111 A4
Harrow HA3 ... 44 A5
1 South Acton W3 ... 110 D4
Cheltenham Rd
Leyton E10 ... 54 A3
London SE15 ... 162 C6
Cheltenham Terr SW3 ... 114 D1 257 D2
Cheltenham Villas CR7 ... 204 C3
Chelverton Ct SW15 ... 134 D1
Chelverton Rd SW15 ... 134 D1
Chelwood Cl E4 ... 19 D5
Chelwood Ct
Battersea SW11 ... 266 D2
9 South Croydon CR2 ... 221 A3
Chelwood Gdns TW9 ... 132 C3
Chelwood NW5 ... 71 A3
Chelwood Ho W2 ... 236 D1
Chelwood Lo N12 ... 30 A4
Chelwood N20 ... 14 B2
Chenappa Cl E13 ... 99 A4
Chenduit Way HA7 ... 24 D5
Chene Colline Ct KT6 ... 198 A3
Cheney Ct SE23 ... 162 D3
Cheney Row E17 ... 35 B2
Cheneys Rd E11 ... 76 C5
Cheney St HA5 ... 40 C4
Chenies Ho W2 ... 245 C6
Chenies Mews WC1 ... 239 C5
Chenies Pl NW1 ... 232 D4
Chenies St WC1 ... 93 D2 239 C4
Chenies The
Orpington BR6 ... 211 C3
Somers Town NW1 ... 232 D4
Cheniston Gdns W8 ... 255 C6
Chennestone Prim Sch TW16 ... 172 B1
Chepstow Cl SW15 ... 157 A6
Chepstow Cres
Ilford IG3 ... 57 C3
Notting Hill W11 ... 113 C6 245 A6
Chepstow Ct W11 ... 245 A6
Chepstow Gdns UB1 ... 85 B1
Chepstow Pl W2 ... 113 C6 245 B6
Chepstow Rd
Croydon CR0 ... 221 D6
Ealing W7 ... 109 A3
Paddington W2 ... 91 C1
Chepstow Rise CR0 ... 221 C5
Chepstow Villas W11 ... 113 C6 245 A6
Chequers IG9 ... 21 B3
Chequers Cl
London NW9 ... 45 C6
Orpington BR5 ... 211 D5
Chequers Ct
7 Croydon CR0 ... 205 D1
St Luke's EC1 ... 242 C5
Chequers Ho NW8 ... 237 A6
Chequers La RM9 ... 103 C5
Chequers Par
Dagenham RM9 ... 103 C6
Edmonton N13 ... 33 A5
Chequer St EC1 ... 95 A3 242 B5
Chequers The HA5 ... 40 D6
Chequers Way N13 ... 32 D5
Cherbury Cl SE28 ... 102 D1
Cherbury Ct N1 ... 235 D3
Cherbury St N1 ... 95 B5 235 D3
Cherchefells Mews HA7 ... 25 B5
Cherimoya Gdns KT8 ... 195 D6
Cherington Rd W7 ... 108 D5
Cheriton Ave BR2 ... 209 A4
Cheriton Cl
Cockfosters EN4 ... 2 D1
10 Ealing W5 ... 87 C2
Cheriton Ct
4 Lee SE12 ... 165 A4
South Norwood SE25 ... 205 C4
Walton-on-T KT12 ... 194 C1
Cheriton Dr SE18 ... 145 B6
Cheriton Ho 9 E5 ... 74 B3
Cheriton Sq SW17 ... 159 A2
Cherry Ave UB1 ... 106 D5
Cherry Blossom Cl N13 ... 32 D5
Cherry Cl
Carshalton SM5 ... 218 D6
Ealing W5 ... 109 D3
Merton SM4 ... 201 A5
Ruislip HA4 ... 61 D5
7 Streatham SW2 ... 160 C4
Walthamstow E17 ... 53 D4
Cherrycot Hill BR6 ... 227 B4
Cherrycot Rise BR6 ... 227 A4
Cherry Cres TW8 ... 131 B5
Cherry Croft Gdns 3 HA5 ... 23 B3
Cherry Ct Acton W3 ... 111 C5
Hackbridge CR4 ... 203 A1
Ilford IG6 ... 56 D6
Pinner HA5 ... 22 D2
5 Rotherhithe SE16 ... 119 A5
Sidcup DA14 ... 168 B1
Cherrydeal Ct E11 ... 54 B2
Cherrydown Ave E4 ... 19 C1
Cherrydown Cl E4 ... 19 C1
Cherrydown Rd DA14 ... 168 D2
Cherry Garden Ho 7 SE16 ... 118 B4
Cherry Garden Sch SE16 ... 118 A2
Cherry Garden St SE16 ... 118 B4
Cherry Garth TW8 ... 109 D1
Cherry Gdns
Dagenham RM9 ... 81 B3
Northolt UB5 ... 63 D1
Cherry Gr
Hayes UB3 ... 106 B5
Hillingdon UB8 ... 83 A2
Cherry Hill Gdns CR0 ... 220 B4
Cherry Hill EN5 ... 13 D5
Cherry Hills WD19 ... 23 A5
Cherry Hill HA3 ... 24 C4
Cherrylands Cl NW9 ... 67 A6
Cherry Lane Prim Sch UB7 ... 104 B2
Cherry Laurel Wlk SW2 ... 160 B5
Cherry La UB7 ... 104 C2
Cherry Orchard Gdns
7 Croydon CR0 ... 205 B1
East Molesey KT8 ... 195 B6
5 South Croydon CR0 ... 221 B6
Cherry Orchard Prim Sch SE7 ... 143 C5
Cherry Orchard Rd
Croydon CR0 ... 205 C1
East Molesey KT8 ... 195 C6
Keston Mark BR2 ... 226 A6
Cherry Orch
Charlton SE7 ... 143 C6
West Drayton UB7 ... 104 A4
Cherry Rd EN3 ... 6 C5
Cherry Tree Ave UB7 ... 82 B1
Cherry Tree Cl
11 Hackney E9 ... 96 C6
Wembley HA0 ... 65 A4
Cherry Tree Ct
1 Camden Town NW1 ... 71 C1
17 Charlton SE7 ... 143 C6
Kingsbury NW9 ... 45 A5
11 Peckham SE15 ... 140 B4
3 Woodford E18 ... 36 D1
Cherry Tree Dr SW16 ... 160 A1
Cherry Tree Hill N6 ... 48 D4
Cherry Tree Ho SE14 ... 141 B3
Cherrytree Ho 8 W10 ... 90 D4
Cherry Tree Ho
Ruislip HA4 ... 39 C1
Twickenham TW2 ... 152 B2
Wood Green N22 ... 32 A3
Cherry Tree Rd
London N2 ... 48 D5
Stratford E15 ... 76 C3
Cherry Tree Rise IG9 ... 37 D6
Cherry Trees Sch The E3 ... 97 C4
Cherry Tree Terr SE1 ... 253 B2
Cherry Tree Way HA7 ... 25 B4
Cherry Tree Wlk
Beckenham BR3 ... 207 B5
Coney Hall BR4 ... 224 D4
St Luke's EC1 ... 242 B5
Cherry Way
Upper Halliford TW17 ... 193 C5
West Ewell KT19 ... 215 B2
Cherry Wlk BR2 ... 209 A1
Cherrywood Cl
Bow E3 ... 97 A4
Kingston u T KT2 ... 176 C3
Cherrywood Ct 1 TW11 ... 175 A5
Cherrywood Dr SW15 ... 156 D6
Cherrywood La SM4, SW20 ... 201 A5
Cherry Wood Way W5 ... 88 C2
Chertsey Ct SW14 ... 132 D2
Chertsey Dr SM3 ... 217 A6
Chertsey Ho
Feltham TW13 ... 151 C1
37 Shoreditch E2 ... 95 D4
Chertsey Rd
Ashford TW15, TW16 ... 171 B4
Feltham TW13, TW16 ... 171 C6
Ilford IG1 ... 79 B4
Leyton E11 ... 76 B6
Lower Halliford TW17 ... 192 C2
Shepperton TW17 ... 192 A2
Twickenham TW2 ... 152 B4
Chertsey St SW17 ... 181 A5
Chervil Cl TW13 ... 150 A1
Chervil Mews SE28 ... 124 B5
Cherwell Ct
Teddington KT1 ... 175 D3
West Ewell KT19 ... 215 A4
Cherwell Ho NW8 ... 236 D5
Cherwell Way HA4 ... 39 A3
Cheryls Cl SW6 ... 135 D4 265 D2
Cheseman St SE26 ... 162 B1
Chesfield Rd KT2 ... 176 A3
Chesham Ave BR2, BR5 ... 210 D3
Chesham Cl SW1 ... 258 A5
Chesham Cres SE20 ... 184 C2
Chesham Ct SW18 ... 158 B4
Chesham Flats W1 ... 248 B6
Chesham Ho SW1 ... 258 A5
Chesham Mews SW1 ... 258 A6
Chesham Pl SW1 ... 115 A3 258 A5
Chesham Rd
Kingston u T KT1, KT2 ... 176 C1
Mitcham SW19 ... 180 B4
Penge SE20 ... 184 C2
Chesham St
Westminster SW1 ... 115 A3 258 A5
Willesden NW10 ... 67 B5
Chesham Terr W13 ... 109 B4
Cheshire Cl
Chingford E17 ... 35 D2
Mitcham CR4, SW16 ... 204 A6
Cheshire Gdns KT9 ... 213 D2
Cheshire Ho SM4 ... 201 D2
Cheshire Rd N22 ... 32 B4
Cheshire St E2 ... 95 D3 243 D6
Cheshir Ho NW4 ... 46 C5
Chesholm Rd N16 ... 73 C5
Cheshunt Ho
Hendon NW4 ... 46 C6
9 Kilburn NW6 ... 91 D6
Cheshunt Rd
Belvedere DA17 ... 125 C1
Upton E7 ... 77 B2
Chesil Ct
17 Bethnal Green E2 ... 96 C5
Chelsea SW3 ... 267 B6
Chesil Ho BR7 ... 189 B2
Chesilton Rd SW6 ... 135 B4 264 C2
Chesil Way UB4 ... 83 D4
Chesley Gdns E6 ... 100 A4
Chesney Cres CR0 ... 224 A1
Chesney Ct W9 ... 91 C3
Chesney Ho SE13 ... 142 B1
Chesney St SW11 ... 268 A1
Chesnut Gr N17 ... 51 D6
Chesnut Rd N17 ... 51 D6
Chessell Cl CR7 ... 204 D5
Chessholme Ct TW16 ... 171 C3
Chessholme Rd TW15 ... 171 A4
Chessing Ct N2 ... 48 D6
CHESSINGTON ... 214 A2
Chessington Ave
Church End N3 ... 47 B6
Erith DA7 ... 147 A5
Chessington Cl KT19 ... 215 A2
Chessington Com Coll KT9 ... 213 D1
Chessington Ct
London N3 ... 47 B6
Pinner HA5 ... 41 B5
Chessington Hall Gdns KT9 ... 213 D1
Chessington Hill Pk KT9 ... 214 C3
Chessington Ho 19 SW8 ... 137 D3
Chessington Lo N3 ... 47 B6
Chessington Mans
Leyton E10 ... 53 C2
Leytonstone E11 ... 54 C2
Chessington North Sta KT9 ... 214 A3
Chessington Par KT9 ... 213 D3
Chessington Pk KT9 ... 214 C4
Chessington Rd KT19 ... 215 B1
Chessington South Sta KT9 ... 213 D1
Chessington Trade Pk KT9 ... 214 C4
Chessington Way BR4 ... 223 D6
Chesson Rd W14 ... 135 B6 264 D6
Chessum Ho E8 ... 74 A2
Chesswood Way HA5 ... 22 D1
Chestbrook Ct 12 EN1 ... 17 C6
Chester Ave
Richmond TW10 ... 154 B5
Twickenham TW2 ... 151 B3
Chester Cl
Ashford TW15 ... 171 B5
Barnes SW13 ... 134 B2
Hayes UB8 ... 82 D1
Knightsbridge SW1 ... 248 C1
Chester Close N NW1 ... 231 D2
Chester Close S NW1 ... 231 D1
Chester Cl
1 Richmond TW10 ... 154 B5
Sutton SM1 ... 217 C6
Chester Cres E8 ... 73 D3
Chester Ct
2 Acton W3 ... 88 C1
Bermondsey SE8 ... 118 D1
4 Camberwell SE5 ... 139 B5
Gospel Oak NW5 ... 71 A4
Harrow HA1 ... 42 D3
Regent's Pk NW1 ... 231 D1
Chester Dr HA2 ... 41 C3
Chesterfield Ct
Ashford TW15 ... 170 A6
Kingston u T KT6 ... 198 A4
Lewisham SE13 ... 142 A2
Chesterfield Dr KT10 ... 213 A6
Chesterfield Flats EN5 ... 12 D6
Chesterfield Gdns
Greenwich SE10 ... 142 B5
Harringay N4 ... 50 D4
Mayfair W1 ... 248 C4
Chesterfield Gr SE22 ... 161 D6
Chesterfield Hill W1 ... 115 B5 248 C4
Chesterfield Ho
Highgate N6 ... 49 A1
Mayfair W1 ... 248 B4
6 Streatham SW16 ... 181 C5
Chesterfield Lo N21 ... 16 B4
Chesterfield Mews
Ashford TW15 ... 170 A6
Harringay N4 ... 50 D4
Chesterfield Rd
Ashford TW15 ... 170 A5
Barnet EN5 ... 12 D6
Chiswick W4 ... 133 A6
Enfield EN3 ... 7 A6
Finchley N3 ... 29 C4
Leyton E10 ... 54 A3
West Ewell KT19 ... 215 B1
Chesterfield Sch EN3 ... 7 A6
Chesterfield St W1 ... 248 C4
Chesterfield Way
Hayes UB3 ... 106 A4
Chesterfield Way continued
Peckham SE15 ... 140 C5
Chesterford Gdns NW3 ... 69 D4
Chesterford Ho 4 SE18 ... 143 D5
Chesterford Rd E12 ... 78 B3
Chester Gate NW1 ... 231 D1
Chester Gdns
Ealing W13 ... 87 B1
Enfield EN3 ... 18 B5
Morden SM4 ... 202 A3
Chester Ho
5 Barnet EN5 ... 1 D1
Dartmouth Pk N19 ... 71 B6
1 Deptford SE8 ... 141 B6
Kingston u T KT1 ... 176 D1
Chesterman Ct W4 ... 133 C5
Chester Mews
Belgravia SW1 ... 258 C6
Walthamstow E17 ... 35 C1
Chester Pl NW1 ... 231 C2
Chester Rd
Avery Hill DA15 ... 167 C6
Dartmouth Pk N19 ... 71 B6
Edmonton N9 ... 18 B3
Harlington TW6 ... 126 C2
Hounslow TW4 ... 128 B2
Ilford IG3 ... 57 D2
Newham E16 ... 98 C3
Regent's Pk NW1 ... 93 B4 231 C2
Tottenham N17 ... 51 C6
Upton E7 ... 77 D1
Walthamstow E17 ... 52 D4
Wanstead E11 ... 55 B3
Wimbledon SW19, SW20 ... 178 C4
Chester Row SW1 ... 115 A2 258 B4
Chester Sq Mews SW1 ... 258 C5
Chester Sq SW1 ... 115 B2 258 C4
Chester St E2 ... 96 A3
Chesters The KT3 ... 177 C2
Chester St SW1 ... 115 A3 258 B6
Chester Terr NW1 ... 93 B4 231 C2
Chesterton Cl
Greenford UB6 ... 85 D5
Wandsworth SW18 ... 157 C6
Chesterton Ct W3 ... 110 D3
Chesterton Dr TW19 ... 148 B3
Chesterton Ho
21 Battersea SW11 ... 136 B2
3 Kensal Town W10 ... 91 A2
3 Sutton SM1 ... 218 A4
Chesterton Prim Sch SW11 ... 137 A4 268 A1
Chesterton Rd
Kensal Town W10 ... 91 A2
Newham E13 ... 99 A4
Chesterton Sq W8 ... 255 A3
Chesterton Terr
6 Kingston u T KT1 ... 176 C1
Newham E13 ... 99 A4
Chester Way SE11 ... 116 C2 261 B3
Chesthunte Rd N17 ... 33 A2
Chestnut Alley SW6 ... 264 D5
Chestnut Ave
Brentford TW8 ... 109 D2
Buckhurst Hill IG9 ... 21 D1
Coney Hall BR4 ... 224 C4
Edgware HA8 ... 26 B4
Forest Gate E7 ... 77 B4
Hampton TW12 ... 173 C3
Hornsey N8 ... 50 A4
Kingston u T KT8, KT11 ... 174 D2
11 Mortlake SW14 ... 133 B2
Chestnut Ave N E17 ... 54 B5
Chestnut Ave S E17 ... 54 B4
Chestnut Ave
Thames Ditton KT10 ... 196 B1
Wembley HA0 ... 65 B3
Worcester Pk KT19 ... 215 C4
Yiewsley UB7 ... 104 B6
Chestnut Cl
Buckhurst Hill IG9 ... 21 D2
Carshalton SM5 ... 202 D1
Catford SE6 ... 186 A6
Chattern Hill TW15 ... 170 D6
Harlington UB7 ... 126 D5
Hayes UB3 ... 105 C6
New Cross Gate SE14 ... 141 B4
Sidcup DA15 ... 168 A2
Southgate N14 ... 15 D6

Chestnut Cl *continued*
1 Stoke Newington N16 73 B6
Sunbury Comm TW16 171 D4
West Norwood SW16 182 C6
Chestnut Ct
Beckenham BR3 185 C3
7 Cheam SM2 217 C2
5 Croydon CR0 221 A4
Feltham TW13 172 D5
Harrow HA1 42 C2
Hornsey N8 50 A4
Hounslow TW3 129 C2
Kingston u T KT3 199 C6
Surbiton KT6 198 A2
Wembley HA0 65 B3
West Brompton SW6 264 D6
Chestnut Dr
Bexley DA7 147 A2
Harrow HA3 24 D2
Pinner HA5 41 A3
Wanstead E11 55 A3
Chestnut Gr
Cockfosters EN4 14 D6
Ealing W5 109 D3
Isleworth TW7 131 A1
Kingston u T KT3 199 B6
Mitcham CR4 203 D5
Chestnut Grove Sch SW12 159 A3
Chestnut Gr
Penge SE20 184 C3
South Croydon CR2 222 B1
Upper Tooting SW12 159 A3
Wembley HA0 65 B3
Chestnut Ho
1 Acton W4 111 C2
Brockley SE4 141 B2
7 Maitland Pk NW3 70 D2
West Norwood SE27 161 A1
Chestnut La N20 13 A3
Chestnut Pl SE19 183 D6
Chestnut Rd
Ashford TW15 170 D6
Kingston u T KT2 176 A3
Twickenham TW2 152 C2
West Barnes SW20 178 D1
West Norwood SE21, SE27 161 A1
Chestnut Rise SE18 123 C1
Chestnut Row N3 29 C3
Chestnuts Ct 3 E17 54 A6
Chestnuts Prim Sch N15 51 A4
Chestnuts Royal BR7 189 B3
Chestnuts The
Chislehurst BR7 189 B3
Colindale NW9 45 C6
East Finchley N2 48 D4
7 Erith DA17 125 B1
1 Highbury N5 72 D4
Penge BR3 206 D6
8 Pinner HA5 23 B3
Shooters Hill SE18 144 D4
Uxbridge UB10 60 A1
Walton-on-T KT12 194 B1
Chestnut Way TW13 150 B1
Chestnut Wlk
Upper Halliford TW17 193 C5
Woodford IG8 37 A5
Cheston Ave CR0 207 B1
Chestwood Gr UB10 60 B1
Chettle Cl SE1 262 C6
Chettle Ct N8 50 C3
Chetwode Ho NW8 237 A6
Chetwode Rd SW17 158 D1
Chetwood Wlk 13 E6 100 A2
Chetwynd Ave EN4 14 D3
Chetwynd Dr UB10 82 B5
Chetwynd Rd NW5 71 B5
Cheval Ct SW15 134 B1
Chevalier Cl HA7 26 A6
Cheval Pl SW7 114 C3 257 B6
Cheval St E14 119 C3
Chevender BR7 188 D3
Cheveney Wlk 2 BR2 209 A6
Chevening Ho BR5 190 A2
Chevening Rd
Cubitt Town SE10 120 D1
Kilburn NW6 91 A6
South Norwood SE19 183 B4
Chevenings The DA14 168 C1
Cheverell Ho 25 E2 96 A5
Cheverton Rd N19 49 D1
Chevet St E9 75 A3
Chevington NW2 69 B2
Cheviot Cl
Bushey WD23 8 A5
Enfield EN1 5 B3
Harlington UB3 127 B5
Cheviot Ct
16 Deptford SE14 140 C5
Enfield EN2 5 B3
Southall UB2 107 D2
Cheviot Gate NW2 69 A6
Cheviot Gdns
Cricklewood NW2 69 A6
West Norwood SE27 182 D6
Cheviot Ho N16 51 D1
Cheviot Rd SE27 182 D5
Cheviots Hostel EN1 5 B3
Cheviot 4 N17 34 B3
Cheviot Way IG2 57 C5
Chevron Cl E16 99 A1
Chevy Rd UB2 108 A4
Chewton Rd E17 53 A5
Cheylesmore Ho SW1 258 C2
Cheyne Ave
Snaresbrook E18 54 D6
Twickenham TW2 151 B3
Cheyne Cl
6 Hendon NW4 46 B4
Keston Mark BR2 226 A5
Cheyne Ct
Chelsea SW3 267 C6
1 Croydon CR0 221 D6
Ruislip HA4 39 C1
4 Wallington SM6 219 B2
Cheyne Gdns SW3 136 C6 267 B5
Cheyne Hill KT5 198 B5
Cheyne Mews SW3 136 C6 267 B5
Cheyne Park Dr BR4 224 A5
Cheyne Path W7 86 D1
Cheyne Pl SW3 267 C6
Cheyne Rd TW15 171 B4
Cheyne Row SW3 136 C6 267 A5
Cheyne Wlk
Chelsea SW10 136 B5 266 C4
Croydon CR0 222 A6
Hendon NW4 46 C3
Southgate N21 16 D6
Cheyney Ho 2 E9 74 D2
Cheyneys Ave HA8 25 D4
Chichele Gdns CR0 221 C4
Chichele Ho HA8 26 B6
Chichele Mans NW2 68 D3
Chichele Rd NW2 68 D3
Chicheley Gdns HA3 24 A3
Chicheley Rd HA3 24 A3
Chicheley St SE1 250 D2
Chichester Ave HA4 61 B6
Chichester Cl
Hampton TW12 173 B4
Kidbrooke SE3 143 C4
Newham E6 100 A1
Chichester Ct
Barnet EN4 2 B1
2 Camden Town NW1 71 C1
Edgware HA8 26 C4
Harrow HA2 41 B1
Northolt UB5 85 A6
3 Sidcup DA5 169 C4
Stanmore HA7 44 A6
Stanwell TW19 148 A3
Chichester Gdns IG1 56 B2
Chichester Ho
Kilburn NW6 91 C5
2 Kingston u T KT2 176 D2
Chichester Mews SE27 182 C6
Chichester Rd
Bayswater W2 91 D2
Edmonton N9 18 A3
Kilburn NW6 91 C5
Leyton E11 76 C5
South Croydon CR0 221 C5
Chichester Rents WC2 241 A2
Chichester St SW1 115 C1 259 B1
Chichester Way
Cubitt Town E14 120 B2
Feltham TW14 150 C4
Chicksand Ho 14 E1 96 A2
Chicksand St E1 95 D2 243 D3
Chicksand Street E1 96 A2
Chiddingfold N12 13 C1
Chiddingstone Ave DA7 147 B5
Chiddingstone SE13 164 A6
Chiddingstone St SW6 135 C3
Chieveley Par DA7 147 D2
Chieveley Rd DA7 147 D1
Chignell Pl 7 W13 109 A5
Chigwell Ct 1 E9 75 A2
Chigwell Hill E1 118 B6
Chigwell Hurst Ct HA5 40 D6
Chigwell Rd
Wanstead E18 55 B6
Woodford IG8 37 D3
Chiham Ho 5 SE15 140 C6
Chilchester Ct 3 BR3 207 D6
Chilcombe Ho 6 SW15 156 A4
Chilcot Cl 13 E14 97 D1
Chilcott Cl HA0 65 C4
Child Ct E11 54 B2
Childebert Rd SW17 159 B2
Childeric Prim Sch SE14 141 A5
Childeric Rd SE14 141 A5
Childerley St SW6 135 A4 264 A2
Childerly KT1 198 C6
Childers St SE8 141 B6
Child La SE10 120 D3
Childs Ct UB3 106 A6
CHILD'S HILL 69 C6
Child's Hill Prim Sch NW2 69 A5
Childs La 11 SE19 183 C4
Child's Mews SW5 255 B3
Child's Pl SW5 255 B3
Child's St SW5 255 B3
Childs Way NW11 47 B4
Child's Wlk SW5 255 B3
Chilham Cl
Old Bexley DA5 169 B4
Wembley UB6 87 A5
Chilham Ct 15 SW9 138 C2
Chilham Ho SE1 262 D6
Chilham Rd SE9 188 A6
Chilham Way BR2 209 A2
Chillerton Rd SW17 181 B5
Chillingford Ho SW17 180 A6
Chillington Dr SW11 136 B1
Chillingworth Gdns TW1 152 D1
Chillingworth Rd N7 72 C3
Chilmark Gdns KT3 200 A3
Chilmark Rd SW16 181 D2
Chiltern Ave
Bushey WD23 8 A5
Twickenham TW2 151 C3
Chiltern Cl Bus WD23 8 A5
Ickenham UB10 60 C6
North Cheam KT4 216 C6
South Croydon CR0 221 C5
Chiltern Ct
15 Deptford SE14 140 C5
6 East Barnet N20 14 C2
11 Eltham SE9 166 C5
Harrow HA1 42 B4
Hillingdon UB8 82 D3
Marylebone NW1 237 D5
Muswell Hill N10 31 A1
1 New Barnet EN5 14 A6
Chiltern Dene EN2 4 B1
Chiltern Dr KT5 198 D4
Chiltern Gdns
Beckenham BR2 208 D5
Cricklewood NW2 68 D5
Chiltern Ho
Camberwell SE17 139 B6
Ealing W5 88 A2
5 Edmonton N9 18 A1
Harrow HA1 42 C1
4 Kensal Town W10 91 A2
5 Stamford Hill N16 51 D1
Chiltern Rd Bow E3 97 C3
Ilford IG2 57 C4
Pinner HA5 40 C4
Chilterns The BR1 187 B1
Chiltern St W1 93 A2 238 A4
Chiltern Way IG8 21 A1
Chilthorne Cl SE6 163 B4
Chilton Ave W5 109 D2
Chilton Gr SE8 119 A2
Chiltonian Ind Est SE12 164 D5
Chilton Rd
Edgware HA8 26 C4
Richmond TW9 132 C2
Chilton St E2 95 D3 243 D6
Chiltons The 1 E18 37 A1
Chilvers Cl TW2 152 C2
Chilver St SE10 120 D1
Chilwell Gdns WD19 22 C6
Chilworth Ct 8 SW19 156 D3
Chilworth Gdns SM1 218 A5
Chilworth Mews W2 92 B1 236 C1
Chilworth St W2 92 A1 236 B1
Chimes Ave N13 32 D6
Chimney Ct 23 E1 118 B5
Chimneys Ct 2 SW19 178 C3
China Ct 1 E1 118 B5
China Hall Mews 16 SE16 118 C3
China Mews 17 SW2 160 B4
Chinbrook Cres SE12 165 B1
Chinbrook Rd SE12 165 B1
Chinchilla Dr TW4 128 C3
Chindit Ho 11 N16 73 B4
Chine The
London N10 49 C5
Southgate N21 16 D6
Wembley HA0 65 B3
Ching Ct Chingford E4 20 C1
St Giles WC2 240 A1
Chingdale Rd E4 20 C1
CHINGFORD 20 C3
Chingford Ave E4 19 D2
Chingford CE Inf Sch E4 20 B3
Chingford CE Jun Sch E4 20 B3
Chingford Foundation Sch E4 19 D3
CHINGFORD GREEN 20 A4
Chingford Hall Com Prim Sch E4 35 B4
CHINGFORD HATCH 36 B6
Chingford Hospl E4 20 A1
Chingford Ind Ctr E4 35 A5
Chingford La IG8 36 D5
Chingford Mount Rd E4 35 C5
Chingford Rd
Highams Pk E4 35 C3
Walthamstow E17 35 D1
Chingford Sta E4 20 C4
Chingley Cl BR1 186 C4
Ching Way E4 35 B4
Chinnery Cl EN1 5 D4
Chinnocks Wharf E14 119 A6
Chinnor Cres UB6 86 A5
Chipka St E14 120 A4
Chipley St SE14 141 A6
Chipmunk Gr UB5 85 A4
Chippendale Ho SW1 258 D1
Chippendale St E5 74 D5
Chippenham Ave HA9 66 D3
Chippenham Cl HA5 39 D5
Chippenham Gdns NW6 91 C4
Chippenham 4 KT1 176 B1
Chippenham Mews W9 91 C3
Chippenham Rd W9 91 C3
Chipperfield Rd BR5 190 A1
CHIPPING BARNET 1 B1
Chipping Cl EN5 1 A2
Chipstead Ave CR7 204 D5
Chipstead Cl SE19 183 D3
Chipstead Gdns NW2 68 B6
Chipstead Ho 4 SW2 160 A3
Chipstead St SW6 135 C3
Chip St SW4 137 D1
Chirk Cl UB4 85 A3
Chirk Ct SE4 141 B3
Chisenhale Prim Sch E3 97 A5
Chisenhale Rd E3 97 A5
Chisholm Ct 1 W6 112 A1
Chisholm Rd
Croydon CR0 221 C6
13 Richmond TW10 154 B5
Chisledon Wlk E9 75 B2
CHISLEHURST 189 C3
Chislehurst Ave N12 30 A3
Chislehurst High St BR7 188 D4
Chislehurst Rd
Bromley BR1, BR7 188 A2
Broom Hill BR6 211 D2
Orpington BR5, BR6, BR7 211 C4
Richmond TW10 154 A6
Sidcup DA14 190 A5
Chislehurst St Nicholas CE Prim Sch BR7 189 A3
Chislehurst & Sidcup Gram Sch DA15 168 B2
Chislehurst Sta BR7 188 C1
CHISLEHURST WEST 188 C4
Chislet Cl BR3 185 C3
Chislet 5 NW5 71 A2
Chisley Rd 5 N15 51 C3
Chiswell Sq SE3 143 B3
Chiswell St
Barbican EC1 95 B2 242 C4
Camberwell SE5 139 B5
CHISWICK 111 D1
Chiswick & Bedford Park Prep Sch W4 111 C2
Chiswick Cl CR0 220 B5
Chiswick Common Rd W4 111 B2
Chiswick Com Sch W4 133 B5
Chiswick Ct HA5 41 B6
Chiswick Green Studios 1 W4 111 A2
Chiswick High Rd W4 111 C2
Chiswick High Road (North Circular Rd) W4 110 C1
Chiswick Ho* W4 133 B6
Chiswick La W4 111 C1
Chiswick La S W4 133 D6
Chiswick Mall W4 111 D1
Chiswick Maternity Hospl W4 111 D1
Chiswick Park Sta W4 111 A2
Chiswick Pier W4 133 D5
Chiswick Pk W4 110 D2
Chiswick Plaza W4 133 A6
Chiswick Quay W4 133 A4
Chiswick Rd W4 111 A2
Chiswick Rdbt W4 110 C1
Chiswick Rd N9 18 A2
Chiswick Sq W4 133 C6
Chiswick Sta W4 133 A5
Chiswick Staithe W4 133 A4
Chiswick Terr 6 W4 111 A2
Chiswick Village W4 132 D6
Chiswick Wharf W4 133 D6
Chitterfield Gate UB7 126 C5
Chitty's La RM8 80 D6
Chitty St W1 93 C2 239 B4
Chivalry Rd SW11 158 C6
Chivelston 27 SW19 156 D3
Chivenor Gr KT2 175 D5
Chivers Rd E4 35 D6
Chivins Ct N3 29 C3
Choats Manor Way RM9 103 B4
Choats Rd IG11 102 D4
Chobham Gdns SW19 156 D2
Chobham Rd E15 76 B3
Cholmeley Cres N6 49 B2
Cholmeley Ct N12 30 A6
Cholmeley Lo N6 49 B1
Cholmeley Pk N6 49 B2
Cholmley Gdns NW6 69 C3
Cholmley Rd KT7 197 B3
Cholmondeley Ave NW10 90 A5
Cholmondeley Wlk TW9 153 C6
Chopin's Ct 13 E1 118 B5
Chopwell Cl E15 76 B1
Chorleywood Cres BR5 190 A1
Choumert Gr SE15 140 A3
Choumert Mews SE15 140 A3
Choumert Rd SE15 139 D3
Choumert Sq 4 SE15 140 A3
Chow Sq 2 E8 73 D3
Chrisp Ho SE10 142 C6
Chrisp St E14 97 D1
Christabel Cl TW7 130 C2
Christchurch Ave
Brondesbury Pk NW6 69 A1
Finchley N12 30 A4
Harrow HA3 42 D5
Harrow HA3 43 A5
5 Teddington TW11 175 A5
Wembley HA0 66 A2
Christ Church Bentinck CE Prim Sch NW1 92 C2 237 B4
Christ Church CE Mid Sch W5 109 D6
Christ Church CE Prim Sch
Battersea SW11 136 C2
Brondesbury NW6 69 B1
Camberwell SW9 138 C4
Cubitt Town SE10 120 C1
Christ Church CE Prim Sch *continued*
Forest Hill SE23 162 D2
Shooters Hill SE18 144 C4
Surbiton KT5 198 C3
Christchurch CE Prim Sch SW3 136 D6 267 C6
Christchurch CE Sch E1 95 D2 243 D3
Christchurch Cl
Enfield EN2 5 A3
Finchley N12 30 B3
Mitcham SW19 180 B3
Christ Church Ct
1 Brondesbury Pk NW6 69 A1
Harlesden NW10 89 C6
Christchurch Ct UB4 84 C3
Christchurch Gdns HA3 43 A5
Christchurch Gn HA0 66 A2
Christchurch Hill NW3 70 B4
Christchurch Ho 2 SW2 160 A3
Christ Church La EN5 1 A3
Christchurch Lo EN4 2 D1
Christ Church New Malden CE Prim Sch KT3 199 C6
Christchurch Pas NW3 70 A5
Christchurch Pk SM2 218 A1
Christ Church Prim Sch, Hampstead NW3 70 B5
Christchurch Prim Sch IG1 57 A1
Christ Church Rd
1 Beckenham BR3 185 C1
Hornsey N8 50 A3
Christchurch Rd
Ilford IG1 57 A1
Mitcham SW19 180 B3
Mortlake SW14 155 A6
Sidcup DA15 167 D1
Streatham SW2 160 C3
Christ Church Rd KT5 198 B3
Christ Church TW9 132 A2
Christ Church Sch NW1 93 B4 231 D2
Christchurch Sq 2 E9 96 C6
Christ Church Streatham CE Prim Sch SW2 160 B3
Christchurch St SW3 136 D6 267 C6
Christchurch Terr SW3 267 C6
Christchurch Way SE10 120 C1
Christian Ct SE16 119 B5
Christian Fields SW16 182 C3
Christian St E1 96 A1
Christie Ct
Maitland Pk NW3 70 C3
2 Upper Holloway N19 72 A6
Christie Dr SE25 206 A4
Christie Gdns RM6 58 B2
Christie Ho
Bexley DA6 169 D6
2 Cubitt Town SE10 120 D1
Harrow HA3 42 D6
4 West Wickham BR4 207 D1
Christie Rd E9 75 A2
Christina Sq N4 50 D1
Christina St EC2 243 A6
Christine Worsley Cl N21 16 D3
Christopher Ave W7 109 A3
Christopher Boone's Almshouses SE13 142 B1
Christopher Cl
Bexley DA15 167 D6
Rotherhithe SE16 118 D4
Christopher Ct
Ashford TW15 170 A5
12 Barnet EN5 1 D1
6 Croydon CR0 206 A1
Hendon NW4 28 C1
23 Surbiton KT6 198 A4
Sutton SM1 217 C3
Christopher France Ho 6 E1 97 A4
Christopher Gdns RM9 80 D3

Christopher Hatton Prim Sch EC1 94 C3 241 A5
Christopher Lo 2 N6 49 D2
Christopher Pl NW1 232 D1
Christopher Rd UB2 106 B2
Christopher St EC2 95 B3 242 D5
Christ's Coll Finchley NW11 47 D6
Christ's Coll Upper Sch N3 29 B1
Christ's Sch TW10 154 C6
Christ the King RC Fst Sch TW19 148 A5
Christ the King RC Prim Sch N4 72 B6
Christ the King Sixth Form Coll SE13 142 B2
Chryssell Rd SW9 138 C5
Chubworthy St 5 SE14 141 A6
Chudleigh Cres IG3 79 C4
Chudleigh Gdns SM1 218 A5
Chudleigh Rd
Hampstead NW6 68 D1
London SE4 163 C6
Twickenham TW1, TW2 152 D4
Chudleigh 1 DA14 190 B6
Chudleigh St E1 96 D1
Chudleigh Way HA4 40 A1
Chulsa Rd SE26 184 B5
Chumleigh Gdns SE5 139 C6
Chumleigh St SE5 139 C6
Chumleigh Wlk KT5 198 B5
Church App SE21 161 B1
Church Ave
Beckenham BR3 185 C2
Camden Town NW1 71 B2
Chingford E4 36 B4
Finchley N2 30 B2
Mortlake SW14 133 B2
Northolt UB5 63 B1
Pinner HA5 41 B3
Ruislip HA4 39 B1
Sidcup DA14 190 B5
Southall UB2 107 A3
Churchbank E17 53 C5
Churchbury Cl EN1 5 C3
Churchbury La EN1 5 C3
Churchbury Rd
Eltham SE9 165 D4
Enfield EN1 5 C3
Church Cl
Edgware HA8 27 A5
Friern Barnet N20 14 C1
Hayes UB4 83 B2
Hounslow TW4 129 B3
Kensington W8 245 C2
West Drayton UB7 104 A3
Church Cres
Church End N3 29 B2
Cranley Gdns N10 49 B5
Friern Barnet N20 14 C1
Hackney E9 74 D1
Churchcroft Cl SW12 159 A4
Church Ct
East Finchley N2 48 B6
Forest Hill SE26 185 A5
Harmondsworth UB7 126 C6
Holborn EC4 241 B1
16 Richmond TW10 153 D6
Rotherhithe SE16 119 B4
Ruislip HA4 62 D5
5 West Norwood SE27 182 D6
Churchdale Ct 1 W4 110 D1
Churchdown BR1 186 C6
Church Dr
Coney Hall BR4 224 C5
Harrow HA2 41 C3
Welsh Harp NW9 45 B1
Church Elm La RM10 81 C2
CHURCH END N3 29 C1
NW10 67 D3
Church End
Hendon NW4 46 B6
Walthamstow E17 53 D5
Church Entry EC4 241 D1
Church Estate Almshouses 8 TW9 132 B1
Church Farm House Mus* NW4 46 B6
Church Farm La SM3 217 A2
Churchfield Ave N12 30 B4
Churchfield Cl
Harrow HA2 42 A5
Hayes UB3 105 D6
Churchfield Ho W2 236 C5
Churchfield Mans 5 SW6 135 B3
Churchfield Pl TW17 192 D2
Churchfield Prim Sch N9 17 D3
Churchfield Rd
Acton W3 111 A5
Ealing W13 109 C5
Hanwell W7 108 C4
Walton-on-T KT12 194 A1
Welling DA16 146 A2
Churchfields Ave TW13 151 C1
Churchfields
East Molesey KT8 195 C6
Greenwich SE10 142 A6
Churchfields Jun & Inf Sch E18 37 A2
Churchfields Prim Sch BR3 206 D6
Churchfields Rd BR3 185 A1
Churchfields E18 37 A2
Churchfield Way N12 30 A4
Church Garth 4 N19 71 D6
Church Gate SW6 135 A2
Church Gdns
Ealing W5 109 D4
Wembley HA0 65 A4
Church Gn
4 Brixton SW9 138 C3
Hayes UB3 83 D1
Church Gr
London SE13 163 D6
Teddington KT1 175 C1
Churchhill Gardens Prim Sch SW1 115 C1 259 B1
Church Hill HA1 42 C1
Church Hill Rd
Cheam SM1, SM3 217 A4
East Barnet EN4 14 D4
Kingston u T KT6 198 A4
Walthamstow E17 53 D5
Church Hill Sch EN4 14 D4
Church Hill
Southgate N21 16 C4
Wallington SM5 218 D3
Walthamstow E17 53 D5
Wimbledon SW19 179 B5
Church Hill Wood BR5 211 D4
Church Hill SE18 122 B3
Church Ho EC1 241 D6
Church Hyde SE18 145 C6
Churchill Ave
Harrow HA3 43 B3
Hillingdon UB10 82 D4
Churchill Cl
East Bedfont TW14 149 D3
Hillingdon UB10 82 D4
Churchill Ct
Ealing W5 88 B3
Edmonton N9 17 B3
4 Farnborough BR6 227 A3
Finsbury Pk N4 50 C2
Harrow HA2 41 D4
7 Ilford IG1 78 D5
Northolt UB5 63 C3
Peckham SE15 140 A3
Willesden NW2 68 B3
9 Woolwich SE18 122 B2
Churchill Gdns
Acton W3 88 C1
Pimlico SW1 137 C6 269 A6
Churchill Gdns Rd SW1 137 C6 269 A6
Churchill Ho
Brentford TW8 109 C1
Mitcham CR4 180 D2
Churchill Lodge IG6 57 A5
Churchill Lo
Streatham SW16 181 D5
Woodford IG8 36 D4
Churchill Mews IG8 36 D4
Churchill Pl
Canary Wharf E14 119 D5
Harrow HA1 42 C5
Churchill Rd
Edgware HA8 26 C4
Gospel Oak NW5 71 B4
Newham E16 99 C1
South Croydon CR2 221 A1
Willesden NW2 68 B2
Churchill Terr E4 19 C1
Churchill Way
Ashford TW16 172 A4
Churchill Way *continued*
Bromley BR1 187 A1
Churchill Wlk E9 74 C3
Church La
Chessington KT9 214 B2
Chislehurst BR7 189 A2
Dagenham RM10 81 D1
Ealing W5 109 D4
East Finchley N2 48 B6
Edmonton N9 18 A2
Enfield EN1 5 B2
Harrow HA3 24 D2
Hornsey N8 50 B5
Keston Mark BR2 210 A1
Kingsbury NW9 45 B2
Leytonstone E11 54 C1
Merton SW19 179 C2
Pinner HA5 41 B6
Teddington TW11 174 D5
Thames Ditton KT7 197 A3
Tottenham N17 33 C2
Twickenham TW1 153 A3
Upper Tooting SW17 181 A5
Wallington SM6 219 D5
Walthamstow E17 53 D5
Churchley Rd SE26 184 B6
Churchley Villas SE26 184 B6
Church Lo UB5 63 B1
Church Manor Way SE18, SE2 124 A2
Church Mdw KT6 213 C6
Churchmead Cl EN4 14 C5
Church Mead Inf Sch E10 53 C1
Churchmead Rd NW10 68 A2
Church Mead SE5 139 A5
Churchmore Rd SW16 181 D2
Church Mount N2 48 B4
Church Paddock Ct SM6 219 D5
Church Par
5 Ashford TW15 170 B6
Harrow HA3 42 C6
Church Path
Merton SW19 179 C1
Mitcham CR4 202 C6
South Acton W4 111 A3
Walthamstow E17 53 D5
Wanstead E11 55 A4
Church Pl Ealing W5 109 D4
Mitcham CR4 202 C6
St James SW1 249 B5
Uxbridge UB10 61 A5
Church Rd Acton W3 111 A4
Ashford TW15 170 B6
Barking IG11 79 A2
Barnes SW13 134 A4
Beckenham BR2 208 C6
Bexleyheath DA7 147 B2
Bromley BR1, BR2 187 A1
Buckhurst Hill IG9 21 B3
24 Canonbury N1 73 A2
Cheam SM3 217 A2
Claygate KT10 212 D1
Cranford TW5 128 B6
Croydon CR0 221 A5
Ealing W7 108 C6
East Molesey KT8 196 B6
Enfield EN3 18 C6
Farnborough BR6 227 B3
Feltham TW13 172 D5
Hayes UB3 105 D6
Hendon NW4 46 C5
Heston TW5 129 C5
Higham Hill E17 35 A1
Highgate N6 49 A3
Hillingdon UB8 82 A3
Hounslow TW7 130 C5
Ilford IG2 57 C3
Keston BR2 225 D1
Kingston u T KT1 176 B1
Leyton E10 75 C6
Long Ditton KT6 197 C1
Lower Halliford TW17 192 D2
Manor Pk E12 78 A3
Mitcham CR4 202 C6
Mitcham CR4, SW19 180 B1
New Malden KT4 199 C1
Church Rd N N2 30 B2
Church Rd
Northolt UB5 85 A6
Richmond TW10 176 A6
Richmond TW10, TW9 154 A6
Sidcup DA14 190 A6
Church Rd S N2 30 B2
Church Rd
Southall UB2 107 B3
South Norwood SE19 183 C3
Stanmore HA7 25 B5
Teddington TW11 174 D5
Church Rd *continued*
Tottenham N17 33 D3
Wallington SM6 219 D5
Welling DA16 146 B3
West Drayton UB7 104 A3
West Ewell KT19 215 B1
Willesden NW10 67 C1
Wimbledon SW19 179 A6
Church Rise
Chessington KT9 214 B2
Forest Hill SE23 162 D2
Church Row
Chislehurst BR7 189 A2
Hampstead NW3 70 A4
Church Row Mews BR7 189 A3
Church St N E15 98 C6
Church St Sta CR0 221 A6
Church Sq TW17 192 D2
Church St
Chiswick W4 133 D6
Croydon CR0 220 D6
Croydon CR0 221 A6
Dagenham RM10 81 D2
Edmonton N9 17 C2
Enfield EN2 5 B2
Hampton TW12 174 A2
Isleworth TW7 131 B3
Kingston u T KT1 175 D1
Lisson Gr NW8 92 C3 237 A5
Newham E16 122 D5
Church Street Est NW8 236 D5
Church Stretton Rd TW3 152 A6
Church St
Sunbury TW16 194 B6
Twickenham TW1 153 A3
Church Studios 16 NW1 71 D2
Church St
Walton-on-T KT12 194 A2
West Ham E15 98 D6
Church Terr
Hendon NW4 46 B6
Lewisham SE13 142 C2
21 Richmond TW10 153 D6
Church Vale
Forest Hill SE23 162 D2
Muswell Hill N2 48 D6
Churchview Rd TW2 152 B2
Church Villa TW16 194 B6
Churchward Ho
Camberwell SE17 138 D6
West Kensington SW5 254 D1
Church Way
Cockfosters EN4 2 D1
Friern Barnet N20 14 C1
Churchway NW1 232 D2
Church Wlk
Barnes SW13 134 A4
Brentford TW8 131 C6
Canonbury N16 73 B4
Child's Hill NW2 69 B5
Dartmouth Pk N6 71 A5
Hayes UB3 83 D1
Mitcham SW16 181 C1
15 Richmond TW10 153 D6
Thames Ditton KT7 196 D3
Walton-on-T KT12 194 A1
Welsh Harp NW9 67 B6
West Barnes SW20 200 C6
Churchwood Gdns IG8 37 A6
Churchyard Row SE11 116 D2 261 D4
Churnfield 2 N4 72 C6
Churston Ave E13 99 B6
Churston Cl 16 SW2 160 C3
Churston Dr SM4 201 A4
Churston Gdns N11 31 C4
Churston Mans WC1 240 D5
Churton Pl
Brentford W4 132 D6
Pimlico SW1 259 B3
Churton St SW1 115 C2 259 B3
Chute Ho 17 SW9 138 C3
Chuter Ede Ho SW6 264 D5
Chyngton Cl DA15 167 D1
Chyngton Ct HA1 64 C6
Cibber Rd SE23 162 D2
Cicada Rd SW18 158 A6
Cicely Ho NW8 229 D3
Cicely Rd SE15 140 A4
Cinderford Way BR1 186 C6
Cinema Mus The* SE11 261 C3
Cinema Par RM8 81 B6
Cinnabar Wharf Central 17 E1 118 A5
Cinnabar Wharf East 16 E1 118 A5
Cinnabar Wharf West 18 E1 118 A5
Cinnamon Cl
8 Camberwell SE15 139 D5
Thornton Heath CR0 204 A2
Cinnamon Row 3 SW11 136 A2
Cinnamon St E1 118 B5
Cinnamon Wharf SE1 253 D2
Cinque Cotts SW19 178 C4
Cintra Ct SE19 183 D4
Cintra Pk SE19 183 D3
Circle Ct HA0 65 D4
Circle Gdns SW19 179 C1
Circle Ho 14 E14 98 B1
Circle The
Bermondsey SE1 253 D2
Burnt Oak NW7 27 B4
Neasden NW2 67 C5
Circuits The HA5 40 C5
Circular Rd
London N2 30 B2
Tottenham N17 51 D6
Circular Way SE18 144 C6
Circus Lo NW8 229 C2
Circus Mews W1 237 C4
Circus Pl EC2 242 D3
Circus Rd NW8 92 B5 229 C3
Circus St SE10 142 A5
Cirencester St W2 91 D2
Cirrus Cl 4 SM6 220 A1
Cirrus 17 NW9 27 D1
Cissbury Ho 6 SE26 162 A1
Cissbury Rd N15 51 B4
Cissbury Ring N N12 29 C5
Cissbury Ring S N12 29 B5
Citadel Pl SE11 260 C2
Citizen Ho N7 72 C4
Citizen Rd N7 72 C4
Citron Terr 4 SE15 140 B2
Citrus Ho 14 SE8 119 B1
City Banking Coll SE1 117 B4 252 D2
City Bsns Ctr 33 SE16 118 C4
City Central Est EC1 235 A1
City Coll N1 235 C2
City Coll of London The WC1 240 D3
City Forum EC1 95 A4 235 A2
City Garden Row N1 94 D5 234 D3
City Gate E1 96 C3
City & Guilds of London Art Sch The SE11 116 C1 261 B1
City Harbour E14 119 D3
City & Islington 6th Form Coll EC1 94 D4 234 C2
City & Islington Coll
Finsbury Pk N4 72 D6
Lower Holloway N7 72 A4
Lower Holloway N7 72 B4
Shoreditch EC1 95 A4 235 B1
Shoreditch N1 95 B6 235 C6
City Lights The SE11 261 B1
CITY OF LONDON 117 A6
City of London Sch EC4 117 A6 252 A6
City of London Sch for Girls EC2 95 A2 242 B4
City of Westminster Coll, Maida Vale Ctr W9 91 D4
City of Westminster Coll
Paddington NW1 92 C2 237 B4
Paddington W2 92 B2 236 C4
City of Westminster Coll, Queens Park Ctr W9 91 C4
City Prospect 5 SE19 183 C4
City Rd EC1 95 A4 235 B2
City Thameslink Sta EC4 94 D1 241 C1
City University EC1 94 D4 234 C1
City View 3 IG1 79 A6
City Wharf Ho KT7 197 B3
City Wlk SE1 253 A1
Civic Way Ilford IG6 57 A5
Ruislip HA4 62 D3
Civil Service Coll SW1 115 C2 259 A3
Clabon Mews SW1 114 D2 257 C4
Clack St SE16 118 C4
Clacton Rd
Newham E6 99 D4
Tottenham N17 33 D1
Walthamstow E17 53 A3
Claigmar Gdns N3 29 D2
Claire Ct
Brondesbury NW2 69 A2
Bushey WD23 8 B3
4 Pinner HA5 23 B3
Whetstone N12 14 A1
Claire Gdns HA7 25 C5
Claire Pl E14 119 C3
Clairvale Rd TW5 129 A4
Clairview Rd SW16 181 B5
Clairville Gdns W7 108 C5
Clairville Point 12 SE23 162 D1
Clamp Hill HA7 24 C5
Clancarty Rd SW6 135 C3
Clandon Cl
South Acton W3 110 D4
Stoneleigh KT17 216 A2
Clandon Ct
Plaistow BR1 187 A4
Sutton SM2 218 B2
Clandon Gdns N3 47 C6
Clandon Ho
East Finchley N3 47 C6
12 Kingston u T KT2 176 D4
Clandon Rd IG3 79 C6
Clandon St SE8 141 C3
Clanfield Ho 12 SW15 156 A3
Clanricarde Gdns W2 113 C6 245 B5
CLAPHAM 137 B2
Clapham Common* SW4 137 B1
Clapham Common North Side SW4 137 A1
Clapham Common South Side SW4 159 C6
Clapham Common Sta SW4 137 C1
Clapham Common West Side
Clapham SW4, SW11 136 D1
Clapham SW11 159 A6
Clapham Computer & Secretarial Coll SW11 158 D6
Clapham Court Terr 2 SW4 160 A6
Clapham Cres SW4 137 D1
Clapham Ct 3 SW4 160 A6
Clapham High St SW4 137 D1
Clapham High Street Sta SW4 137 D2
Clapham Junction Est SW11 136 C1
Clapham Junction Sta SW11 136 C1
Clapham Manor Ct 1 SW4 137 C2
Clapham Manor Prim Sch SW4 137 C2
Clapham Manor St SW4 137 D2
Clapham Mans SW4 159 B5
Clapham North Bsns Ctr 10 SW4 137 D2
Clapham North Sta SW4 138 A2
CLAPHAM PARK 159 D6
Clapham Park Rd SW4 137 D1
Clapham Park Terr 4 SW2 160 A6
Clapham Rd SW9 138 B5 270 D4
Clapham South Sta SW4 159 B5
Claps Gate La E6 100 D3
Clapton Comm E5 52 A2
Clapton Girls Tec Coll E5 74 C4
CLAPTON PARK 74 D4
Clapton Pas E5 74 C3
Clapton Sq E5 74 C3
Clapton Sta E5 74 B6
Clapton Terr E5 52 A1
Clapton Way E5 74 A4
Clara Grant Ho 10 E14 119 C3
Clara Grant Prim Sch The E3 97 C3
Clara Pl SE18 122 C2

Clare Cl
Borehamwood
WD6 10 B5
East Finchley N2 48 A6
Clare Cnr SE9 166 D4
Clare Ct
Chislehurst BR7 188 B2
St Pancras WC1 233 B1
Wimbledon SW19 179 A4
Claredale Ct SM2 218 A1
Claredale Ho 3 E2 96 B5
Claredale St E2 96 A5
Clare Gdns
Barking IG11 80 A1
Forest Gate E7 77 A4
Notting Hill W11 91 A1
Clare Ho
Bermondsey SE1 263 D2
4 Burnt Oak HA8 27 A1
5 Ealing W7 108 D5
6 Old Ford E3 97 B6
Clare House Prim Sch
BR3 186 A1
Clare La N1 73 A1
Clare Lawn Ave
SW14 155 B6
Clare Mews SW6 265 C3
Clare Mkt WC2 240 D1
Claremont Ave
Harrow HA3 44 A4
Sunbury TW16 172 B2
West Barnes KT3 200 B4
Claremont Cl
Finsbury
N1 94 C5 234 B3
Newham E16 122 C5
Orpington BR6 226 C4
4 Streatham SW2 160 B3
Claremont Ct 1 W9 91 B5
Claremont Dr TW17 192 D3
Claremont Gdns
Ilford IG3 79 C6
Kingston u T KT6 198 A4
Claremont Gr
Chiswick W4 133 C5
Woodford IG8 37 C4
Claremont High Sch
HA3 44 A4
Claremont Ho 15
SM2 217 C1
Claremont Hts EN2 4 D1
Claremont La KT10 212 A3
Claremont Lo 12
SW19 178 D3
Claremont Pk N3 29 A2
Claremont Pl KT10 212 D2
Claremont Prim Sch
NW2 68 D6
Claremont 1 SW15 157 A6
Claremont Rd
Bromley BR1 210 B5
Claygate KT10 212 C1
Croydon CR0 206 A1
Ealing W13 87 A2
Forest Gate E7 77 C3
Hadley Wood EN4 2 B6
Harrow HA3 24 C1
Hendon NW2 68 D6
Higham Hill E17 35 A1
Highgate N6 49 C2
Kingston u T KT6 198 A4
Leyton E7 76 B5
Teddington TW11 174 D6
Twickenham TW1 153 C5
West Kilburn W9 91 B5
Claremont TW17 192 D3
Claremont Sq
N1 94 C5 234 A3
Claremont St
Edmonton N18 34 A4
Greenwich SE10 141 D6
Newham E16 122 C4
Claremont Terr KT7 197 B2
Claremont Way NW2 46 C1
Claremont Way Ind Est
NW2 46 C1
Clarence Ave
Bromley BR1,
BR2 210 A5
Clapham Pk SW4 159 D5
Ilford IG2 56 C3
Kingston u T KT3 177 B1
Clarence Cl
Bushey WD23 8 D4
New Barnet EN4 14 B6
Clarence Cres
Clapham Pk SW4 159 D5
Sidcup DA14 168 B1
Clarence Ct
Edgware NW7 27 D5
10 Hammersmith
W6 112 B2
5 North Finchley
N12 30 B5
Clarence Gate Gdns
NW1 237 D5
Clarence Gate NW1 237 D6
Clarence Gdns
NW1 93 B4 231 D1
Clarence Ho SE17 139 A6
Clarence Ho*
SW1 115 C5 249 B3
Clarence La SW15 155 D5
Clarence Mews
Balham SW12 159 B4
Hackney E5 74 B3
1 Rotherhithe
SE16 118 D5
Clarence Pl 25 E5 74 B3
Clarence Rd
Bexley DA6 147 A1
Brentford W4 110 C1
Bromley BR1, BR2 210 A6
Brondesbury NW6 69 B1
Chislehurst SE9 166 A2
Enfield EN3 18 C6
Harringay N15 51 A4
Higham Hill E17 34 D1
Lower Clapton E5 74 B4
Manor Pk E12 77 D3
Newham E16 98 C3
Richmond TW9 132 C4
Sidcup DA14 168 B1
Sutton SM1 217 D3
Teddington TW11 175 A4
Thornton Heath CR0 205 B2
Wallington SM6 219 B3
Wimbledon SW19 179 D4
Wood Green N22 32 A3
Clarence St
Kingston u T KT1,
KT2 176 A1
5 Richmond TW9 132 A1
Southall UB2 106 D3
Clarence Terr
Hounslow TW3 129 D1
Lisson Gr NW1 237 D6
Clarence Way NW1 71 B1
Clarence Wlk 9
SW4 138 A3
Clarendon Cl
Bayswater W2 247 A6
38 Hackney E9 74 C1
Clarendon Cres
TW2 152 B1
Clarendon Cross
W11 244 B5
Clarendon Ct
London NW11 47 B5
Mitcham SM4 202 C4
Paddington W9 236 B6
1 Richmond TW9 132 C4
Willesden NW2 68 C1
Clarendon Dr SW15 134 C1
Clarendon Flats W1 238 B1
Clarendon Gdns
Hendon NW4 46 B6
Paddington
W9 92 A3 236 B5
Redbridge IG1 56 B2
Wembley HA9 66 A4
Clarendon Gr
Mitcham CR4 202 D6
Somers Town NW1 232 C2
Clarendon Ho
Harrow HA2 42 B6
North Finchley N12 30 A5
Somers Town NW1 232 B3
South Oxhey WD19 22 D5
Clarendon Mews
Bayswater W2 247 A6
Old Bexley DA5 169 D3
Clarendon Pl
W2 114 C6 247 A6
Clarendon Prim Sch
TW15 170 B6
Clarendon Rd
Ashford TW15 170 B6
Croydon CR0 220 D6
Ealing W5 88 A3
Edmonton N18 34 A5
Harrow HA1 42 C3
Hayes UB3 105 D4
Hornsey N8 50 B6
Leytonstone E11 54 B1
Mitcham SW19 180 C3
Notting Hill
W11 113 A6 244 B5
Wallington SM6 219 C2
Walthamstow E17 53 D3
Wanstead E18 55 A6
West Green N15 51 A5
Wood Green N22 32 B1
Clarendon Rise
SE13 142 A1
Clarendon Sch
TW12 173 D4
Clarendon St
SW1 115 B1 258 D2
Clarendon Terr W9 236 B6
Clarendon Way
Enfield N21 17 A5
Orpington BR5, BR7 211 D6
Clarendon Wlk 11
W11 91 A1
Clarens St SE6 163 B2
Clare Pl SW15 155 D4
Clare Point NW2 46 D1
Clare Rd
Hounslow TW4 129 B2
Leytonstone E11 54 B3
New Cross Gate
SE14 141 B4
Northolt UB6 64 B2
Stanwell TW19 148 A4
Willesden NW10 68 A1
Clare St E2 96 B5
Claret Gdns SE25 205 C5
Clareville Ct SW7 256 B3
Clareville Grove Mews
SW7 256 B3
Clareville Gr
SW7 114 A2 256 B3
Clareville Rd BR5 227 A6
Clareville St
SW7 114 A2 256 B3
Clare Way DA7 147 A4
Clarewood Ct W1 237 C3
Clarewood Wlk
SW9 138 C1
Clarges Ho W1 248 D4
Clarges Mews
W1 115 B5 248 C4
Clarges St
W1 115 B5 248 D4
Clariat Ct W3 110 C4
Claribel Rd SW9 138 D3
Clarice Ct NW4 46 B6
Claridge Ct SW6 264 C1
Claridge Rd RM8 58 D1
Clarinet Ct HA8 26 D3
Clarissa Ho 7 E14 97 D1
Clarissa Rd RM6 58 D2
Clarissa St E8 95 D6
Clark Ct 17 NW10 67 B1
Clarke Ho
2 London SW4 137 C2
5 Richmond TW10 153 C1
Clarke Mans 9 IG11 79 D1
Clarke Mews N9 18 B1
Clarke Path N16 52 A1
Clarke's Ave KT4,
SM3 216 D6
Clarkes Dr UB8 82 A2
Clarkes Mews W1 238 B4
Clark Ho SW10 266 A4
Clark Lawrence Ct 11
SW11 136 B2
Clarks Mead WD23 8 B4
Clarkson Rd E16 98 D1
Clarkson Row NW1 232 A3
Clarkson St E2 96 B4
Clarksons The IG11 101 A5
Clark's Pl EC2 243 A2
Clark's Rd IG1 79 B6
Clark St E1 96 C2
Clark Way TW5 128 D5
Classic Mans 33 E9 74 C1
Classinghall Ho 14
SW15 156 D5
Classon Cl UB7 104 A4
Claude Rd Leyton E10 54 A1
London SE15 140 B3
Newham E13 99 B6
Claude St E14 119 C2
Claudia Jones Way
SW2 160 A5
Claudia Pl SW19 157 A3
Claudius Cl HA7 9 D1
Claughton Rd E13 99 C5
Clauson Ave UB5 64 A3
Clavell St 8 SE10 142 A6
Claverdale Rd SW2 160 C4
Clavering Ave SW13 134 B6
Clavering Cl TW1 175 A6
Clavering Ho SE13 142 B1
Clavering Rd E12 77 D6
Claverings Ind Est
N9 18 C2
Claverley Gr N3 29 D2
Claverley Villas N3 29 D3
Claverton St
SW1 115 C1 259 B1
Clave St E1 118 C5
Claxton Gr
W6 112 D1 254 A1
Clay Ave CR4 181 B1
Claybank Gr SE13 141 D2
Claybee Ct N22 32 B5
Claybourne Mews 2
SE19 183 D3
Claybridge Rd SE12 187 C6
Claybrook Cl N2 48 B6
Claybrook Rd W6 134 D6
Claybury Broadway
IG5 56 A6
Clay Ct E17 54 B6
Claydon Dr CR0 220 A4
Claydon Ho NW4 28 D1
Claydon SE17 262 A4
Claydown Mews
SE18 122 C1
Clayfarm Rd SE9 167 A2
CLAYGATE 212 D1
Claygate Cres CR0 224 B2
Claygate Ct SM1 218 A5
Claygate La
Hinchley Wood
KT10 213 A6
Thames Ditton KT7 197 A1
Claygate Lodge Cl
KT10 212 C1
Claygate Prim Sch
KT10 212 C1
Claygate Rd W13 109 B3
Claygate Sta KT10 212 C2
CLAYHALL 56 B6
Clayhall Ct 20 E3 97 B5
CLAY HILL 5 A6
Clayhill Cres SE12,
SE9 187 D6
Clay Hill EN2 5 B6
Clay La WD23 8 C4
Claylands Ct SE19 183 B5
Claylands Pl SW8 138 C5
Claylands Rd
SW8 138 B6 270 D5
Clay La TW19 148 B4
Claymill Ho 2 SE18 123 A1
Claymore Cl SM3,
SM4 201 C2
Claymore Ct 4 E17 35 A2
Claypole Ct E17 53 C4
Claypole Dr TW5 129 A4
Claypole Rd E15 98 A5
Clayponds Ave TW8 110 A2
Clayponds Gdns
W5 109 D2
Clayponds Hospl & Day
Treatment Ctr
TW8 110 A2
Clayponds La TW8 110 A1
Clays Ct N16 51 D1
Clays La E15 75 D3
Clays Lane Cl E15 75 D3
Clays Lane Cvn Site
E15 76 A3
Clay St W1 92 D2 237 D3
Clayton Ave HA0 66 A1
Clayton Bsns Ctr
UB3 105 C4
Clayton Cl 3 E6 100 B1
Clayton Cres
Brentford TW8 109 D1
Islington N1 233 C5
Clayton Ct
1 Higham Hill E17 35 A1
Stamford Hill N16 52 A2
Clayton Field NW9 27 C2
Clayton Ho
22 Hackney E9 74 C1
Long Ditton KT7 197 B1
Clayton Mews SE10 142 B4
Clayton 22 NW9 27 D1
Clayton Rd
Chessington KT10,
KT9 213 D4
Hayes UB3 105 C4
Isleworth TW7 130 C2
Peckham SE15 140 A4
Clayton St SE11 138 C6
Clayton Terr UB4 84 D2
Claytonville Terr
DA17 125 D4
Clay Wood Cl BR6 211 C2
Clayworth Cl DA15 168 B5
Cleanthus Cl SE18 144 D4
Cleanthus Rd SE18 144 D4
Clearbrook Way 13
E1 96 C1
Clearmont Ho UB2 107 C3
Clear Water Ho 9
TW10 154 A6
Clearwater Ho BR3 207 D4
Clearwater Pl KT6 197 C3
Clearwater Terr 4
W11 112 D4
Clearwell Dr W9 91 D3
Cleave Ave
Hayes UB3 105 C2
Orpington BR6 227 C2
Cleaveland Rd KT6 197 D4
Cleaverholme Cl
SE25 206 B3
Cleaver Ho 6 NW3 70 D1
Cleaver Sq
SE11 116 C1 261 B1
Cleaver St
SE11 116 C1 261 B2
Cleave's Almshos 1
KT2 176 A1
Cleeve Ct
East Bedfont
TW14 149 C3
Muswell Hill N10 31 B3
Cleeve Hill SE23 162 B3
Cleeve Ho 15 E2 95 C4
Cleeve Park Gdns
DA14 168 B2
Cleeve Park Sch
DA14 168 C1
Cleeve Way
Cheam SM1 201 D1
Roehampton SW15 155 D4
Cleeve Workshops 14
E2 95 C4
Clegg Ho SE3 143 B1
Clegg St Newham E13 99 A5
16 Wapping E1 118 B5
Cleland Ho 19 E2 96 C5
Clematis Gdns IG8 37 A5
Clematis St W12 112 A6
Clem Atlee Par SW6 264 D5
Clem Attlee Ct
SW6 135 B6 264 D5
Clemence St E14 97 B2
Clement Attlee Ho
NW10 67 D1
Clement Ave SW4 137 D1
Clement Cl
Acton W4 111 B2
Hampstead NW6 68 C1
Clement Danes Ho 2
W12 90 B1
Clement Gdns UB3 105 C2
Clement Ho
14 Deptford SE8 119 A2
17 North Kensington
W10 90 C2
Clementhorpe Rd
RM9 80 C2
Clementina Rd E10 53 B1
Clementine Churchill
Hospl The HA1 64 D5
Clementine Cl W13 109 B4
Clementine Wlk 4
IG8 37 A3
Clement Rd
Penge BR3 184 D1
Wimbledon SW19 179 A5
Clements Ave 1
E16 121 A6
Clements Cl 19 N12 29 D6
Clements Ct
Hounslow TW4 128 D1
5 Ilford IG1 78 D5
Clements Ho N17 34 A2
Clements Inn Pas
WC2 240 D1
Clements Inn
WC2 94 B1 240 D1
Clement's La EC2,
EC4 117 B6 252 D6
Clements La IG1 78 D5
Clements Pl TW8 109 D1
Clements Rd
East Ham E6 78 B1
Ilford IG1 78 D5
Clement's Rd SE16 118 B3
Cleminson Ct DA14 190 D4
Clemson Ho 9 E8 95 D6
Clendon Way SE18 123 B2
Clennam St SE1 252 B2
Clensham Ct SM3 217 C6
Clensham La SM1 217 C6
Clenston Mews W1 237 C2
Clent Ho 4 N16 51 D1
Cleopatra's Needle*
WC2 116 B6 250 C5
Clephane Rd 13 N1 73 A2
Clephane Rd N N1 73 A2
Clephane Rd S N1 73 B2
Clere Pl EC2 242 D6
Clere St EC2 95 B3 242 D6
Clerics Wlk TW17 193 B3
CLERKENWELL 94 D3
Clerkenwell Cl
EC1 94 C3 241 B5
Clerkenwell Gn
EC1 94 D3 241 C5
Clerkenwell Parochial
CE Prim Sch
EC1 94 C4 234 A1
Clerkenwell Rd
EC1 94 D3 241 C5
Clermont Rd E9 96 C6
Cleveden Ct CR2 221 C3
Cleveden Ho BR1 188 A3
Clevedon Ct
Battersea SW11 267 A2
Dulwich SE21 161 B1
Clevedon Gdns
Cranford TW5 128 B4
Hayes UB3 105 B3
Clevedon Ho 4
SM1 218 A4
Clevedon Mans NW5 71 A4
Clevedon Rd
Kingston u T KT1 176 C1
Penge SE20 184 D2
Twickenham TW1 153 D5
Cleve Ho NW6 69 D1
Cleveland Ave
Chiswick W4 111 D2
Cleveland Ave *continued*
Hampton TW12 173 B3
Merton SW20 179 B1
Cleveland Cres WD6 11 A6
Cleveland Ct
Ealing W13 87 B2
Marylebone W1 239 B5
Southall UB2 107 D2
Cleveland Gdns
Barnes SW13 133 D3
Harringay N4, N15 51 A4
Hendon NW2 68 D6
Paddington
W2 92 A1 236 A1
Worcester Pk KT4 215 D6
Cleveland Gr 39 E1 96 C3
Cleveland Ho 7 N2 30 B1
Cleveland Inf Sch
IG1 78 D5
Cleveland Jun Sch
IG1 78 D5
Cleveland Mans
8 Brixton SW9 138 C5
4 Brondesbury NW6 69 B1
Paddington W9 91 C3
Cleveland Mews W1 239 A4
Cleveland Park Ave
E17 53 C5
Cleveland Park Cres
E17 53 C5
Cleveland Pk TW19 148 A5
Cleveland Pl SW1 249 B4
Cleveland Rd
Barnes SW13 133 D3
Bexley DA16 145 D3
Ealing W13 87 B2
Edmonton N9 18 B4
Ilford IG1 78 D5
Isleworth TW7 131 A1
Islington N1 73 B1
New Malden KT3 199 C5
14 South Acton W4 111 A3
Wanstead E18 55 A6
Worcester Pk KT4 215 C6
Cleveland Rise SM4 200 D2
Cleveland Row
SW1 115 C5 249 B3
Cleveland Sq
W2 92 A1 236 A1
Cleveland St
W1 93 C3 239 A5
Cleveland Terr
W2 92 A1 236 B2
Cleveland Way E1 96 C3
Cleveley Cres W5 88 B5
Cleveleys Rd E5 74 B5
Clevely Cl SE7 121 D2
Clevendon Cl N16 73 D5
Cleve Rd
Sidcup DA14 168 D1
South Hampstead
NW6 69 D1
Cleverly Cotts W12 111 D5
Cleverly Est W12 112 A6
Cleves Ct KT6 198 A3
Cleves Prim Sch E6 99 D6
Cleves Rd Newham E6 99 D5
Richmond TW10 153 C1
Cleves Way
Ashford TW16 171 D4
Hampton TW12 173 B3
Ruislip HA4 40 D1
Clewer Cres HA3 24 B2
Clewer Ct 2 E10 53 C1
Clewer Ho 1 SE2 124 D4
Cley Ho SE4 140 D1
Clichy Ho 32 E1 96 C2
Clifden Centre
(Richmond Adult &
Com Coll) TW1 152 D3
Clifden Ho 6 TW8 131 D6
Clifden Mews E5 74 D3
Clifden Rd
Brentford TW8 131 D6
Homerton E5 74 D3
Twickenham TW1 152 D3
Cliff Ct 14 NW1 71 D2
Cliffe Ho 4 SE10 120 D1
Cliffe Rd CR2 221 B3
Cliffe Wlk 2 SM1 218 A3
Clifford Ave
Elmstead BR7 188 B4
Mortlake SW14 133 A3
Mortlake SW14,
TW9 132 D2
Wallington SM6 219 C4
Clifford Cl UB5 85 A6
Clifford Ct
Bayswater W2 91 D2
Wandsworth SW18 158 B4
Willesden NW10 67 C4
Clifford Dr SW9 138 D1
Clifford Gdns
Hayes UB3 105 B2

Clifford Gdns *continued*
Kensal Green NW10 ... 90 C5
Clifford Gr TW15 ... 170 C6
Clifford Haigh Ho SW6 ... 134 D5
Clifford Ho
2 Beckenham BR3 ... 185 D4
West Kensington W14 ... 254 C3
Clifford Lo 5 N3 ... 29 B1
Clifford Rd Barnet EN5 .. 1 D2
Chingford E17 ... 36 A1
Croydon SE25 ... 206 A5
Hounslow TW4 ... 128 D2
Newham E16 ... 98 D3
Ponders End N9 ... 18 C5
Richmond TW10 ... 153 D2
Wembley HA0 ... 87 D6
Clifford's Inn Pas EC4 ... 241 A1
Clifford St W1 ... 115 C6 249 A5
Clifford Way NW10 ... 67 D4
Cliff Rd NW1 ... 71 D2
Cliff Road Studios 13 NW1 ... 71 D2
Cliffsend Ho 23 SW9 ... 138 C4
Cliff Terr SE8 ... 141 C3
Cliffview Rd SE13 ... 141 C2
Cliff Villas NW1 ... 71 D2
Cliff Wlk E16 ... 98 D2
Clifton Ave
Church End N3 ... 29 B2
Feltham TW13 ... 150 C1
Shepherd's Bush W12 ... 111 D5
Stanmore HA7 ... 25 B1
Walthamstow E17 ... 52 D6
Wembley HA9 ... 66 B2
Clifton Cl 8 BR6 ... 227 A3
Clifton Cres SE15 ... 140 B5
Clifton Ct
1 Beckenham BR3 ... 185 D2
Finsbury Pk N4 ... 72 C6
Paddington NW8 ... 236 C6
Peckham SE15 ... 140 B5
Putney SW15 ... 156 D6
South Norwood SE25 ... 205 C4
9 Stanwell TW19 ... 148 A5
Surbiton KT5 ... 198 B2
3 Woodford IG8 ... 37 A4
Clifton Gate SW10 ... 266 A6
Clifton Gdns
Chiswick W4 ... 111 B2
Enfield EN2 ... 16 A6
Hillingdon UB10 ... 82 D5
Paddington W9 ... 92 A3 236 A5
South Tottenham N15 .. 51 D3
2 Temple Fortune NW11 ... 47 B3
Clifton Gr E8 ... 74 A2
Clifton Hill NW8 ... 92 A6 229 A5
Clifton Ho Leyton E11 .. 76 C6
Shoreditch E2 ... 243 C6
Clifton Mans 4 SW9 ... 138 C1
Clifton Mews SE25 ... 205 C5
Clifton Par TW13 ... 172 C6
Clifton Park Ave SW20 ... 178 C1
Clifton Pl
Paddington W2 ... 236 D1
Rotherhithe SE16 ... 118 C4
Clifton Prim Sch UB2 ... 107 A2
Clifton Rd
Bexley DA16 ... 146 C2
Crouch End N8 ... 49 D3
Finchley N3 ... 30 A2
Greenford UB6 ... 86 B3
Harlesden NW10 ... 90 A5
Harlington TW6 ... 126 D2
Harrow HA3 ... 44 B4
Ilford IG2 ... 57 B3
Isleworth TW7 ... 130 C3
Kingston u T KT2 ... 176 B2
Newham E16 ... 98 C2
Paddington W9 ... 92 A3 236 B6
Sidcup DA14 ... 189 C6
Southall UB2 ... 107 A2
South Norwood SE25 ... 205 C5
Teddington TW11 ... 174 C6
Upton E7 ... 77 D2
Wallington SM6 ... 219 B3
Wimbledon SW19 ... 178 D4
Wood Green N22 ... 31 C2
Clifton Rise SE14 ... 141 A5
Cliftons Roundabout SE9, SE12 ... 165 C5
Clifton St EC2 . 95 C3 243 A5
Clifton Terr N4 ... 72 C6
Clifton The KT6 ... 214 A6
Clifton Villas W9 ... 92 A2 236 A4
Cliftonville Ct SE12 .. 165 A3
Clifton Way
Peckham SE15 ... 140 C5
Wembley HA0 ... 88 A6
Climsland Ho SE1 ... 251 B4
Clinch Ct 11 E16 ... 99 A2
Cline Ho SW15 ... 156 A6
Cline Rd N11 ... 31 C4
Clinger Ct N1 ... 95 C6
Clink St SE1 .. 117 B5 252 C4
Clinton Ave
Bexley DA16 ... 146 A1
East Molesey KT8 ... 196 A5
Clinton Ho
New Malden KT3 ... 199 B1
6 Surbiton KT6 ... 197 D2
Clinton Rd Bow E3 ... 97 A4
Forest Gate E7 ... 77 A4
West Green N15 ... 51 B5
Clipper Appts 12 SE10 ... 142 A6
Clipper Cl 3 SE16 ... 118 D4
Clipper Ho E14 ... 120 A1
Clipper Way SE13 ... 142 A1
Clippesby Cl KT9 ... 214 B2
Clipstone Ho 10 SW15 ... 156 A6
Clipstone Mews W1 . 239 A4
Clipstone Rd TW3 ... 129 C2
Clipstone St W1 ... 93 C2 239 A4
Clissold Cl N2 ... 48 D6
Clissold Cres N16 ... 73 B4
Clissold Ct N4 ... 73 A6
Clissold Ho 4 N16 ... 73 B6
Clissold Rd N16 ... 73 B5
Clitheroe Ave HA2 ... 41 C1
Clitheroe Rd SW9 ... 138 A3
Clitherow Ave W7 ... 109 A3
Clitherow Rd TW8 ... 109 C1
Clitterhouse Cres NW2 ... 46 C1
Clitterhouse Rd NW2 .. 46 C1
Clive Ave N18 ... 34 A4
Clive Ct
Paddington W9 ... 236 B6
Streatham SW16 ... 181 D5
Tolworth KT6 ... 214 C6
Cliveden Cl N12 ... 30 A6
Cliveden Ho SW1 ... 258 A4
Cliveden Pl
Belgravia SW1 ... 115 A2 258 A4
Shepperton TW17 ... 193 A3
Cliveden Rd SW19 ... 179 B2
Clivedon Ct
Ealing W13 ... 87 B2
6 New Barnet EN5 ... 2 A1
Clivedon Rd E4 ... 36 C5
Clive Ho
18 Clapham SW8 ... 137 D3
3 Croydon CR0 ... 205 D1
Greenwich SE10 ... 142 A6
Clive Lloyd Ho N15 ... 51 A4
Clive Lo NW4 ... 46 D3
Clive Rd
Belvedere DA17 ... 125 C2
Enfield EN1 ... 6 A1
Feltham TW14 ... 150 A5
Mitcham SW19 ... 180 C4
Teddington TW1 ... 175 A6
West Norwood SE21, SE27 ... 161 B1
Clivesdale Dr UB3 ... 106 B5
Clive Way EN1 ... 6 A1
Cloak La EC4 ... 117 B6 252 C6
Clochar Ct NW10 ... 89 D6
Clock Ct 2 E11 ... 55 B5
Clock Ho N16 ... 51 D2
Clock Ho The EN2 ... 5 D6
Clockhouse Ave IG11 ... 101 A6
Clockhouse Cl SW19 ... 156 C2
Clock House Ct 1 BR3 ... 185 A1
Clockhouse Junc N13 ... 32 C5
Clockhouse La TW14, TW15 ... 148 D2
Clockhouse Mans N13 ... 32 C5
Clockhouse Par N13 .. 32 C5
Clock House Par E11 .. 55 B3
Clockhouse Pl SW15 ... 157 A5
Clock House Rd BR3 ... 185 A1
Clockhouse Rdbt TW14 ... 149 A3
Clock House Sta BR3 ... 185 A2
Clockhouse The SW19 ... 156 C1
Clock Ho E17 ... 54 B5
Clock Mus* EC2 ... 95 A1 242 B2
Clock Tower Mews N1 ... 235 B5
Clocktower Mews 6 W7 ... 108 C5
Clock Tower Mews SE28 ... 124 B6
Clock Tower Pl N7 ... 72 A2
Clock Tower Rd TW7 ... 130 D2
Cloister Cl TW11 ... 175 B5
Cloister Gdns
Croydon SE25 ... 206 B3
Edgware HA8 ... 27 A5
Cloister Rd Acton W3 .. 89 A2
Child's Hill NW2 ... 69 B6
Cloisters Ave BR1, BR2 ... 210 B4
Cloisters Ct
Erith DA7 ... 147 D2
Highgate N6 ... 49 B1
Cloisters Ho 8 SW19 ... 179 C3
Cloisters The 22 SW9 ... 138 C4
Clonard Way HA5 ... 23 C4
Clonbrock Rd N16 ... 73 C4
Cloncurry St SW6 ... 134 D3
Clone Ct 4 W12 ... 111 C3
Clone The 5 KT2 ... 176 D3
Clonmel Cl HA2 ... 42 B1
Clonmell Rd N17 ... 51 B6
Clonmel Rd
Fulham SW6 ... 135 B4 264 D2
Teddington TW11 ... 174 B6
Clonmore St SW18 ... 157 B3
Cloonmore Ave BR6 ... 227 D4
Clorane Gdns NW3 ... 69 C5
Close The
Beckenham BR3 ... 207 A5
Cheam SM3 ... 201 B2
Chingford E4 ... 36 A3
Cockfosters EN4 ... 14 D6
Croydon SE25 ... 206 A3
Dagenham RM6 ... 59 A3
Eastcote HA5 ... 40 C2
Harrow HA2 ... 24 A1
Hillingdon UB10 ... 82 C6
Hounslow TW7 ... 130 B3
Ilford IG2 ... 57 C3
Kingston u T KT3 ... 177 A1
Lewisham SE3 ... 142 B3
Mitcham CR4 ... 202 D5
Mortlake TW9 ... 132 D2
Muswell Hill N10 ... 31 B1
1 Old Bexley DA5 .. 169 C4
Palmers Green N14 ... 15 D2
Petts Wood BR5 ... 211 C3
Rayners La HA5 ... 41 B2
Sidcup DA14 ... 190 B5
Surbiton KT6 ... 198 A3
Totteridge N20 ... 13 B2
Wembley HA0 ... 66 A2
Wembley Pk HA9 ... 67 A5
Cloth Ct EC1 ... 241 D3
Cloth Fair EC1 ... 94 D2 241 D3
Clothier Ho SE7 ... 122 A1
Clothier St EC3 ... 243 B2
Cloth St EC1 ... 95 A2 242 A4
Clothworkers Rd SE18 ... 145 B5
Cloudesdale Rd SW17 ... 159 B2
Cloudesley Mans N1 ... 234 B5
Cloudesley Pl N1 ... 94 C6 234 B5
Cloudesley Rd
Erith DA7 ... 147 B4
Islington N1 . 94 C6 234 A5
Cloudesley Sq N1 ... 94 C6 234 B6
Cloudesley St N1 ... 94 C6 234 B5
Clouston Cl SM6 ... 220 A3
Clova Rd E7 ... 77 A3
Clove Cres E14 ... 120 B6
Clovelly Ave
London NW9 ... 45 D5
Uxbridge UB10 ... 61 A4
Clovelly Cl
Pinner HA5 ... 40 C6
Uxbridge UB10 ... 61 A4
Clovelly Ct NW2 ... 68 C3
Clovelly Gdns
Enfield EN1 ... 17 C4
Clovelly Gdns *continued*
South Norwood SE19 ... 183 D2
Clovelly Ho W2 ... 236 A2
Clovelly Rd
Acton W4 ... 111 B4
Ealing W5 ... 109 C4
Erith DA7 ... 147 A6
Hornsey N8 ... 49 D5
Hounslow TW3 ... 129 C3
Clovelly Way
Harrow HA2 ... 63 B6
Orpington BR6 ... 211 D3
Stepney E1 ... 96 C1
Clover Cl E11 ... 76 B6
Clover Ct Enfield EN3 ... 7 A1
Sutton SM2 ... 217 D2
Cloverdale Gdns DA15 ... 167 D5
Clover Ho
Hounslow TW3 ... 130 A4
Southgate N21 ... 16 B6
Cloverleys IG10 ... 21 D6
Clover Mews SW3 ... 267 D6
Clover Way SM6 ... 203 A1
Clove St 9 E13 ... 99 A3
Clowders Rd SE6 ... 163 B1
Clowes Ho 3 SW4 ... 138 A1
Clowser Cl 4 SM1 ... 218 A3
Cloysters Gn E1 ... 118 A5
Cloyster Wood HA8 ... 25 D4
Club Gardens Rd BR2 ... 209 A2
Club Row E2 .. 95 D3 243 C6
Clumps The TW15 ... 171 B6
Clunbury Ave UB2 ... 107 B1
Clunbury St N1 ... 235 D3
Clunie Ho SW1 ... 257 D6
Cluny Mews SW5 ... 255 A3
Cluny Pl SE1 .. 117 C3 263 A6
Cluse Ct N1 ... 235 A4
Clutton St E14 ... 97 D2
Clydach Rd EN1 ... 5 D1
Clyde Cir N15 ... 51 C5
Clyde Ct NW1 ... 232 D4
Clyde Flats SW6 ... 264 C4
Clyde Ho 9 KT2 ... 175 D2
Clyde Pl E10 ... 53 D2
Clyde Rd
Croydon CR0 ... 221 D6
South Tottenham N15 .. 51 C5
Stanwell TW19 ... 148 A3
Sutton SM1 ... 217 C3
Wallington SM6 ... 219 C2
Wood Green N22 ... 31 D2
Clydesdale Ave HA7 ... 43 D6
Clydesdale Cl
Borehamwood WD6 ... 11 B6
Isleworth TW7 ... 130 D2
Clydesdale Ct N20 ... 14 B3
Clydesdale EN3 ... 6 D1
Clydesdale Gdns TW10 ... 132 D1
Clydesdale Ho
Abbey Wood DA18 ... 125 A4
4 Notting Hill W11 ... 91 B1
Clydesdale Path WD6 ... 11 B6
Clydesdale Rd W11 ... 91 B1
Clyde St SE8 ... 141 B6
Clyde Terr SE23 ... 162 C2
Clyde Vale SE23 ... 162 C2
Clyde Works 10 SM6 ... 219 C2
Clyfford Rd HA4 ... 61 D4
Clymping Dene TW14 ... 150 B4
Clynes Ho
6 Dagenham RM10 ... 81 C5
3 Globe Town E2 ... 96 D4
Hayes UB4 ... 84 A4
Clyro Ct N4 ... 50 B1
Clyston St SW8 ... 137 C3
Clytha Ct SE27 ... 183 A6
Coach & Horses Yd W1 ... 249 A6
Coach House La
Highbury N5 ... 72 D4
Wimbledon SW19 ... 156 D1
Coach House Mews SE23 ... 162 D5
Coach House Yd 5 NW3 ... 70 B4
Coach Ho NW10 ... 67 A1
Coachmaker Mews 5 SW9 ... 138 A2
Coachman Lo N12 ... 30 A5
Coalbrook Mans 3 SW12 ... 159 B3
Coaldale Wlk SE21 ... 161 A4
Coalecroft Rd SW15 ... 156 C6
Coalport Ho SE11 ... 261 A4
Coal Post Cl BR6 ... 227 D2
Coatbridge Ho 8 N1 .. 72 B1
Coates Ave SW18 ... 158 C5
Coates Cl CR7 ... 205 A6
Coates Ct NW3 ... 70 C3
Coates Hill Rd BR1 ... 188 C1
Coates Rd WD6 ... 9 D4
Coate St E2 ... 96 A5
Coates Wlk TW8 ... 110 A1
Cobalt SE2 ... 124 A4
Cobalt Cl CR0 ... 206 D5
Cobb Cl WD6 ... 11 A6
Cobbett Rd
Kidbrooke SE9 ... 144 A2
Twickenham TW2 ... 151 C3
Cobbetts Ave IG4 ... 55 D4
Cobbett St SW8 ... 138 B5 270 D3
Cobble La N1 ... 72 D1
Cobble Mews N4, N5 .. 73 A5
Cobbler's Wlk TW11 ... 174 D3
Cobblestone Pl CR0 .. 205 A1
Cobbold Ct SW1 ... 259 C4
Cobbold Ind Est NW10 ... 67 D2
Cobbold Mews W12 ... 111 D4
Cobbold Rd
Bedford Pk W12 ... 111 D4
Leyton E11 ... 76 D5
Willesden NW10 ... 67 D2
Cobb's Hall 1 SW6 .. 134 D6
Cobbs Rd TW4 ... 129 B1
Cobb St E1 ... 243 C3
Cobden Bldgs WC1 . 233 C2
Cobden Ct
Bromley BR2 ... 209 C5
9 Thamesmead SE28 ... 124 C5
Cobden Ho
11 Bethnal Green E2 ... 96 A4
Regent's Pk NW1 ... 232 A4
Cobden Mews SE26 .. 184 B5
Cobden Rd
Croydon SE25 ... 206 A4
Leyton E11 ... 76 C6
Orpington BR6 ... 227 B4
Cobham Ave KT3 ... 200 A4
Cobham Cl
2 Blackfen DA15 ... 168 B5
Bromley BR2 ... 210 A2
Clapham SW11 ... 158 C5
Edgware HA8 ... 26 D1
Enfield EN1 ... 6 A2
Wallington SM6 ... 220 A2
Cobham Ct CR4 ... 180 B1
Cobham Ho IG11 ... 101 A6
Cobham Mews 3 NW1 ... 71 D1
Cobham 21 NW9 ... 27 D1
Cobham Pl DA6 ... 168 D6
Cobham Rd
Chingford E17 ... 36 A2
Harringay N22 ... 50 D6
Heston TW5 ... 128 C5
Ilford IG3 ... 79 C5
Kingston u T KT1, KT2 ... 176 C1
Cobland Rd SE12 ... 187 C6
Coborn Mews 9 E3 ... 97 B4
Coborn Rd E3 ... 97 B4
Coborn St E3 ... 97 B4
Cobourg Prim Sch SE5 ... 139 D6
Cobourg Rd SE5 ... 139 D6
Cobourg St NW1 ... 93 C4 232 B1
Coburg Cl SW1 ... 259 B4
Coburg Cres SW2 ... 160 C3
Coburg Dwellings 11 E1 ... 118 C6
Coburg Gdns IG5 ... 37 D1
Coburg Rd N22 ... 32 B1
Cochrane Cl NW8 ... 229 D3
Cochrane Ct 3 E10 ... 53 C1
Cochrane Ho 15 E14 ... 119 C4
Cochrane Mews NW8 ... 92 B5 229 D3
Cochrane Rd SW19 .. 179 B3
Cochrane St NW8 ... 92 B5 229 D3
Coci Ho W14 ... 254 D3
Cockburn Ho SW1 ... 259 D1
Cockerell Rd E17 ... 53 A3
COCKFOSTERS ... 2 D1
Cockfosters Par EN4 ... 3 A1
Cockfosters Rd EN4 ... 2 D3
Cockfosters Sta EN4 ... 3 A1
Cock Hill E1 ... 243 B3
Cock La EC1 ... 94 D2 241 D3
Cockpit Yd WC1 ... 240 D4
Cocks Cres KT3 ... 199 D5
Cocksett Ave BR6 ... 227 C2
Cockspur Ct SW1 ... 249 D4
Cockspur St SW1 ... 115 D5 249 D4
Cocksure La DA14 ... 191 C6
Coda Ctr The SW6 ... 135 A4 264 B2
Code St E1 ... 95 D3 243 D5
Codicote Ho 22 SE8 .. 118 D2
Codicote Terr N4 ... 73 A6
Codling Cl 18 E1 ... 118 A5
Codling Way HA0 ... 65 D4
Codrington Ct 3 SE16 ... 119 A5
Codrington Hill SE23 ... 163 A4
Codrington Ho 7 E1 .. 96 B3
Codrington Mews W11 ... 91 A1
Cody Cl Harrow HA3 ... 43 D6
Wallington SM6 ... 219 D1
Cody Rd E16 ... 98 B3
Coe Ave SE25 ... 206 A3
Coe's Alley EN5 ... 1 A1
Coffey St SE8 ... 141 C5
Cogan Ave E17 ... 35 A2
Cohen Ho NW7 ... 28 A6
Cohen Lo E5 ... 75 A3
Coin St SE1 .. 116 C5 251 A4
Coity Rd NW5 ... 71 A2
Cokers La SE21 ... 161 B3
Coke St E1 ... 96 A1
Colab Ct N22 ... 32 C2
Colas Mews 7 NW6 .. 91 C6
Colbeck Mews SW5 ... 113 D2 255 D3
Colbeck Rd HA1 ... 42 A2
Colberg Pl N16 ... 51 D2
Colbert 1 SE5 ... 139 D4
Colborne Ct 8 SW19 ... 179 D2
Colborne Ho 8 E14 .. 119 C6
Colborne Way KT4 .. 216 C6
Colbrook Ave UB3 ... 105 B3
Colbrook Cl UB3 ... 105 B3
Colburn Ave HA5 ... 23 A4
Colburn Way SM1 ... 218 B5
Colby Rd
Walton-on-T KT12 ... 194 A1
West Norwood SE19 . 183 C5
Colchester Ave E12 ... 78 B5
Colchester Dr HA5 ... 40 D4
Colchester Ho 17 SW8 ... 137 D3
Colchester Rd
Burnt Oak HA8 ... 27 A3
Leyton E10 ... 54 A2
Pinner HA6 ... 22 A1
Walthamstow E17 ... 53 C3
Colchester St E1 ... 243 D2
Colchester Villas CR7 ... 204 C3
Coldbath Sq EC1 ... 241 A6
Coldbath St SE13 ... 141 D3
Cold Blow La SE14 ... 140 D6
Coldershaw Rd W13 ... 109 A4
Coldfall Ave N10 ... 31 A1
Coldfall Prim Sch N10 ... 30 D1
Coldham Ct N22 ... 32 D2
Coldham Gr EN3 ... 7 A6
Coldharbour Crest SE9 ... 166 C1
Coldharbour E14 ... 120 A5
Coldharbour Ind Est SE5 ... 139 A3
Coldharbour La
Brixton SW9 ... 138 D2
Bushey WD23 ... 8 A6
Hayes UB3 ... 106 A5
Coldharbour Lane Ho UB3 ... 106 A5
Coldharbour Pl SE5 .. 139 B3
Coldharbour Rd CR0 ... 220 C3
Coldharbour Sports Ctr SE9 ... 166 C2
Coldharbour Way CR0 ... 220 C3
Coldstream Gdns SW18 ... 157 B5
Colebeck Mews N1 ... 72 D2
Colebert Ave E1 ... 96 C3
Colebert Ho 21 E1 ... 96 C3
Colebrook Cl
Edgware NW7 ... 28 D3
Putney SW19 ... 156 D4
Colebrook Ct SW3 ... 257 B3
Colebrooke Ave W13 .. 87 B1
Colebrooke Ct DA14 ... 190 B6
Colebrooke Dr E11 ... 55 C2
Colebrooke Pl N1 ... 234 D5
Colebrooke Row
Islington N1 ... 94 D5 234 C4
Islington N1 ... 234 D5

Colebrook Ho 1 E14...97 D1
Colebrook Rd SW16...182 A2
Colebrook Rise BR2...186 C1
Colebrook Way N11...31 B5
Coleby Path 21 SE5...139 B5
Colechurch Ho 9 SE1...118 A1
Cole Cl SE28...124 B5
Cole Court Lo 9 TW1...153 A4
Coledale Dr HA7...25 C2
Colefax Bldg 12 E1...96 A1
Coleford Rd SW18...158 A6
Cole Gdns TW5...128 A5
Colegrave Prim Sch E15...76 B3
Colegrave Rd E15...76 B3
Colegrove Rd SE15...139 D6
Coleherne Ct SW10...113 D1 255 D1
Coleherne Mans SW5...255 D2
Coleherne Mews SW10...113 D1 255 C1
Coleherne Rd SW10...113 D1 255 C1
Colehill Gdns SW6...264 A1
Colehill La SW6...135 A4 264 B1
Cole Ho SE1...251 B1
Coleman Cl SE25...184 A1
Coleman Ct SW18...157 C4
Coleman Fields N1...95 A6 235 B6
Coleman Mans N19...50 A2
Coleman Rd
Belvedere DA17...125 C2
Camberwell SE5...139 C5
Dagenham RM9...81 A2
Colemans Heath SE9...166 D1
Coleman St EC2...95 B1 242 C2
Coleman Street Bldgs EC2...242 C2
Colenso Dr NW7...28 A3
Colenso Rd Ilford IG2...57 C2
Lower Clapton E5...74 C4
Cole Park Gdns TW1...153 A5
Cole Park Rd TW1...153 A5
Cole Park View 2 TW1...153 A5
Colepits Wood Rd SE9...167 B6
Coleraine Park Prim Sch N17...34 B2
Coleraine Rd
Greenwich SE3...142 D6
Hornsey N8, N22...50 C6
Cole Rd TW1...153 A5
Coleridge Ave
Carshalton SM1...218 C4
Plashet E12...78 A2
Coleridge Cl SW8...137 B3
Coleridge Ct
Hammersmith W14...112 D3
15 New Barnet EN5...13 D6
2 Richmond TW10...175 D6
Coleridge Gdns NW6...70 A1
Coleridge Ho
Pimlico SW1...259 B1
Walworth SE17...262 B2
Wembley HA9...65 D6
Coleridge Prim Sch N8...49 D2
Coleridge Rd
Ashford TW15...170 B6
Crouch End N8...49 D3
Croydon CR0...206 C2
Finsbury Pk N4, N7...72 C6
North Finchley N12...30 A5
Walthamstow E17...53 B5
Coleridge Sq
Chelsea SW10...266 A4
Ealing W13...87 A1
Coleridge Way
Borehamwood WD6...10 C6
Hayes UB4...84 A1
West Drayton UB7...104 B2
Coleridge Wlk NW11...47 C5
Colerne Ct NW4...29 A1
Colesburg Rd BR3...185 B1
Coles Cres HA2...63 D6
Coles Ct SW11...266 D1
Coles Gn WD23...8 A3
Coles Green Ct NW2...68 A6
Coles Green Rd NW2...68 B6
Coleshill Flats SW1...258 B3
Coleshill Rd TW11...174 C4
Colestown St 4 SW11...136 C3
Cole St SE1...117 A4 252 B1
Coleswood N20...14 C3
Colesworth Ho 1 HA8...27 A1
Colet Cl N13...32 D4
Colet Gdns W14...112 D2
Colet Ho SE17...261 D1
Colette Ct 5 SE16...118 D4
Coley St WC1...94 B3 240 D5
Colfe & Hatchcliffe's Glebe SE13...163 D6
Colfe Rd SE23...163 A3
Colfe's Sch SE12...165 A5
Colgate Ct EN5...13 A6
Colgate Ho SE13...141 D3
Colgate Pl 10 EN3...7 C6
Colham Ave UB7...104 A5
COLHAM GREEN...82 C2
Colham Green Rd UB8...82 C2
Colham Manor Prim Sch UB8...82 C1
Colham Rd UB8...82 B3
Colina Mews N8, N15...50 D5
Colina Rd N8, N15...50 D4
Colin Blanchard Ho SE4...141 C3
Colin Cl
Colindale NW9...45 C5
Coney Hall BR4...224 D5
Croydon CR0...223 B5
Colin Cres NW9...45 D5
Colin Ct
Forest Hill SE6...163 B4
Hendon NW9...45 D5
Streatham SW16...159 D2
COLINDALE...45 C6
Colindale Ave NW9...45 C6
Colindale Bsns Pk NW9...45 A6
Colindale Hospl NW9...45 C6
Colindale Prim Sch NW9...45 D5
Colindale Sta NW9...45 C6
Colindeep Gdns NW4...46 A5
Colindeep La NW9, NW4...45 D5
Colin Dr NW9...45 D4
Colinette Rd SW15...134 C1
Colin Gdns NW9...45 D5
Colin Park Rd NW9...45 C5
Colin Par NW9...45 C5
Colin Pond Ct RM6...58 D6
Colin Rd NW10...68 A2
Colinsdale N1...234 C5
Colinton Rd IG3...80 B6
Colin Winter Ho 45 E1...96 C3
Coliseum Apartments N8...50 D4
Coliston Pas SW18...157 C4
Coliston Rd SW18...157 C4
Collamore Ave SW18...158 C3
Collapit Cl HA1...41 D3
Collard Pl NW1...71 B1
Collard's Almshouses 1 E17...54 A4
Collcutt Lo SW4...138 A1
Collection Point N8...50 A3
College App SE10...142 A6
College Ave HA3...24 C2
College Cl
Edmonton N18...33 D5
Hackney E5...74 C3
Harrow HA3...24 C3
Twickenham TW2...152 B3
College Cres NW3...70 B2
College Cross N1...72 C1
College Ct
Chelsea SW3...114 D1 257 D1
Croydon CR0...222 A6
Ealing W5...110 A6
Enfield EN3...18 C6
3 Hammersmith W6...112 C1
Hampstead NW3...70 B2
College Dr
Ruislip HA4...40 A2
Thames Ditton KT7...196 C2
College Fields Bsns Ctr SW19...180 B2
College Gdns
Chingford E4...20 A3
Dulwich SE21...161 C3
Edmonton N18...34 A5
Enfield EN2...5 B4
New Malden KT3...199 D4
Redbridge IG4...56 A4
Upper Tooting SW17...158 C2
College Gn SE19...183 C3
College Green Ct SW9...138 D2
College Gr NW1...232 C6
College Hill EC4...252 B6
College Hill Rd HA3...24 C3
College La NW5...71 B4
College Mews 5 SW18...157 D6
COLLEGE PARK...90 B4
College Park Cl SE13...142 B1
College Park Rd N17...33 D4
College Park Sch W2...91 D1
College Pl
Camden Town NW1...93 C6 232 B5
Chelsea SW10...266 A4
Walthamstow E17...54 C5
College Pt 3 E15...76 D2
College Rdbt 1 KT1...198 A6
College Rd
Dulwich SE19, SE21...161 C2
Ealing W13...87 B1
Enfield EN2...5 B3
Harrow HA1...42 C3
Harrow Weald HA3...24 C2
Hounslow TW7...130 D4
Kensal Green NW10...90 C5
Mitcham SW19...180 B4
Plaistow BR1...187 A3
South Croydon CR0...221 B6
Southgate N21...16 C2
Tottenham N17...33 D4
Walthamstow E17...54 A4
Wembley HA9...43 D1
College St EC4...117 A6 252 B6
College Terr Bow E3...97 B4
Church End N3...29 B1
College View SE9...165 D3
College Way
Ashford TW15...170 B6
Hayes UB3...106 A6
College Wlk 10 KT1...198 A6
Collent Ho 12 E9...74 C2
Collent St E9...74 C2
Collerston Ho SE10...120 D1
Colless Rd N15...51 D4
Collette Ct SE25...205 C4
Collette Ho N16...51 D1
Collett Ho SE13...141 D2
Collett Rd SE16...118 A3
Collett Way UB2...107 D4
Colley Ho 12 N7...71 D3
Collier Cl
Newham E16...122 D6
West Ewell KT19...214 D2
Collier Dr HA8...26 C1
Colliers Shaw BR2...225 D3
Collier St N1...94 B5 233 C3
Colliers Water La CR7...204 C4
COLLIER'S WOOD...180 C4
Colliers Wood SW19...180 B3
Collier's Wood Sta SW19...180 B3
Collindale Ave
Erith DA8...147 D6
Sidcup DA15...168 A3
Collingbourne Rd W12...112 B5
Collingham Gdns SW5...113 D2 255 D3
Collingham Pl SW5...113 D2 255 D4
Collingham Rd SW5...113 D2 255 D3
Collingham Sixth Form Coll SW5...113 D2 255 D3
Collings Cl N22...32 B4
Collington Ho 2 SE7...143 B6
Collington St SE10...120 B1
Collingtree Rd SE26...184 C6
Collingwood Ave
London N10...49 A5
Tolworth KT5...199 A1
Collingwood Cl
2 Penge SE20...184 B2
Twickenham TW2, TW4...151 C4
Collingwood Ct
London NW4...46 C4
New Barnet EN5...13 D6
Sutton SM1...217 C4
Collingwood Ho
27 Bethnal Green E1...96 B3
Marylebone W1...239 A4
Collingwood Rd
Hillingdon UB8...82 D3
Mitcham CR4...202 C6
South Tottenham N15...51 C5
Sutton SM1...217 C4
Collingwood Sch SM6...219 B3
Collingwood St E1...96 B3
Collins Ave HA7...26 A1
Collins Ct Dalston E8...74 A2
3 Loughton IG10...21 D6
Collins Dr HA4...62 C6
Collins Ho
8 Barking IG11...78 D1
6 Cubitt Town SE10...120 D1
4 Poplar E14...120 A6
Collinson Ct
Borough The SE1...252 A1
Edgware HA8...26 B6
Collinson Ho 14 SE15...140 A5
Collinson St SE1...252 A1
Collinson Wlk SE1...252 A1
Collins Rd N5, N16...73 A4
Collins Sq SE3...142 D3
Collins St SE3...142 C3
Collins Yd N1...234 C5
Collinwood Ave EN3...6 C2
Collinwood Gdns IG5...56 C5
Collison Pl N16...51 C1
Collis Prim Sch TW11...175 B4
Coll of Arms* EC4...117 A6 252 A6
Coll of Central London The EC2...243 A6
Coll of Law The EC1...95 B3 242 C5
Coll of North East London The N15...51 D5
Coll of NW London NW6...91 C6
Coll of NW London (Willesden Centre) NW10...67 D3
Coll of Optometrists The SW1...250 A4
Coll Sharp Ct 42 E2...95 D4
Coll's Rd SE15...140 C4
Collyer Ave CR0...220 A4
Collyer Pl SE15...140 A4
Collyer Rd CR0...220 A4
Colman Ct
London N12...30 A4
Stanmore HA7...25 B4
Colman Rd E16...99 C2
Colmans Wharf 5 E14...97 D2
Colmar Cl 3 E1...96 D3
Colmer Pl HA3...24 B3
Colmer Rd SW16...182 A3
Colmore Ct NW4...46 A6
Colmore Mews SE15...140 B4
Colmore Rd EN3...6 C1
Colnbrook Ct SW17...180 B6
Colnbrook St SE1...261 C6
Colne Ct Ealing W7...86 B1
West Ewell KT19...215 A4
Colne Ho
Barking IG11...78 D2
Paddington NW8...236 D5
Colne Rd
Clapton Pk E5...75 A4
Southgate N21...17 B4
Twickenham TW1, TW2...152 C3
Colne St E13...99 A4
COLNEY HATCH...30 C4
Colney Hatch La N10...31 A3
Colney Hatch N10...31 A3
Cologne Rd SW11...136 B1
Coloma Convent Girls Sch CR0...222 D5
Colombo Rd IG1...57 A2
Colombo St SE1...251 C3
Colomb St SE10...120 C1
Colonades The 4 SE5...139 B4
Colonels Wlk EN2...4 D2
Colonial Ave TW2...152 A5
Colonial Dr W4...111 A2
Colonial Rd TW14...149 C4
Colonnade Ho SE3...142 D3
Colonnades The
Croydon CR0...220 C2
6 Hackney E8...74 B2
Colonnade The 12 SE8...119 B2
Colonnade WC1...240 B5
Colorado Bldg 9 SE13...141 D4
Colosseum Ct N3...29 B1
Colosseum Ret Pk EN1...6 A1
Colosseum Terr NW1...238 D6
Colour Ho SE1...253 B1
Colroy Ct NW4...47 A4
Colson Rd CR0...221 C6
Colson Way SW16...181 C6
Colstead Ho 22 E1...96 B1
Colsterworth Rd N15...51 D5
Colston Ave SM1, SM5...218 C4
Colston Ct SM5...218 D4
Colston Rd
Mortlake SW14...133 A1
Upton E7...77 D2
Colthurst Cres N4...73 A6
Colthurst Dr N9...18 B1
Coltman Ho SE10...142 A6
Coltman St E14...97 A2
Colt Mews 5 EN3...7 C6
Coltness Cres SE2...124 B1
Colton Gdns N17...51 A6
Colton Rd HA1...42 C4
Coltsfoot Dr UB7...82 A1
Coltswood Ct N14...15 D3
Colts Yd E11...54 D2
Columba Ho SE14...141 B4
Columbas Dr NW3...48 B1
Columbia Ave
Edgware HA8...26 D2
New Malden KT4...199 D2
Ruislip HA4...40 B1
Columbia Ct
Edgware HA8...26 D2
New Malden KT3...199 D2
Columbia Ho 18 E3...97 C4
Columbia Point 7 SE16...118 C3
Columbia Prim Sch E2...95 D4
Columbia Rd
9 Hackney E2...96 A5
Newham E13...98 D3
Shoreditch E2...95 D4
Columbia Road Mkt E2...95 D4
Columbine Ave
Croydon CR2...220 D1
Newham E6...100 A2
Columbus Gdns HA6...22 A2
Colveiw Ct SE9...165 D3
Colverson Ho 14 E1...96 C2
Colvestone Cres E8...73 D3
Colvestone Prim Sch E8...73 D3
Colville Gdns W11...91 B1
Colville Ho
32 Bethnal Green E2...96 C5
Notting Hill W11...91 B1
Colville Mews W11...91 B1
Colville Pl W1...239 B3
Colville Prim Sch W11...91 B1
Colville Rd
Edmonton N9...18 B3
Higham Hill E17...35 A1
Leyton E11...76 A5
Notting Hill W11...91 B1
South Acton W3...110 D3
Colville Sq W11...91 B1
Colville Terr W11...91 B1
Colvin Cl SE26...184 C5
Colvin Gdns
Chingford E4...20 A1
Wanstead E11...55 B5
Colvin Rd
Thornton Heath CR7...204 C4
Upton Pk E6...78 A1
Colwall Gdns IG8...37 A5
Colwall Ho 18 SW9...138 B3
Colwell Rd SE22...161 D6
Colwick Cl N6...49 D2
Colwith Rd W6...134 C6
Colwood Gdns SW19...180 B3
Colworth Gr SE17...262 B3
Colworth Rd
Croydon CR0...206 A1
Leytonstone E11...54 C2
Colwyn Ave UB6...86 D5
Colwyn Cl SW16...181 C5
Colwyn Cres TW3...130 A4
Colwyn Gn NW9...45 C3
Colwyn Ho SE1...261 A5
Colwyn Rd NW2...68 B5
Colyer Cl SE9...166 D2
Colyer Ho SE2...124 D1
Colyton Cl
Erith DA16...146 D4
Wembley HA0...65 C2
Colyton La 14 SW16...182 C5
Colyton Rd SE22...162 B6
Colyton Way N18...34 A5
Combe Ave SE3...142 D5
Combedale Rd SE10...121 A1
Combe Ho
Mortlake SW14...133 A3
20 Paddington W2...91 C2
Combe Lane Sta CR0...222 C3
Combemartin Rd SW18...157 A3
Combe Mews 4 SE3...142 D5
Comber Cl NW2...68 B6
Comber Grove Prim Sch SE5...139 A5
Comber Gr SE5...139 A5
Comber Ho SE5...139 A5
Combermere Rd
London SW9...138 B2
Morden SM4...201 D4
Comberton 10 KT1...176 C1
Comberton Rd E5...74 B6
Combeside SE18...145 D5
Combes Rd RM9...81 B1
Combe The NW1...231 D1
Combwell Cres SE2...124 A3
Com Coll Hackney The E8...96 B6
Comely Bank Rd E17...54 A4
Comeragh Mews W14...254 B1
Comeragh Rd W14...113 A1 254 B1
Comer Cres UB2...108 A4
Comerford Rd SE4...141 B1
Comer Ho 10 EN5...2 A1
Comet Cl E12...77 D4
Comet Pl SE8...141 C5
Comet St SE8...141 C5
Comins Ho SW4...159 C6
Commerce Est E18...37 C1
Commerce Pk CR0...220 B6
Commerce Rd
Brentford TW8...131 C5
Wood Green N22...32 B2
Commerce Way CR0...220 B6
Commercial Rd
Edmonton N18...33 C4
Stepney E1...96 C1
Whitechapel E1...96 A1
Commercial St E1...95 D2 243 C4
Commercial Way
Peckham SE15...140 A5
Wembley NW10...88 D5
Commerell Pl SE10...120 D1
Commerell St SE10...120 C1
Commodity Quay E1...253 D5
Commodore Ct SE8...141 C4
Commodore Ho 7 E14...120 A6
Commodore St E1...97 A3
Commondale SW15...134 C2
Common La KT10...213 A1
Common Rd
Barnes SW13...134 A2
Claygate KT10...213 A1
Stanmore HA7...8 C1
Commonside BR2...225 C4
Commonside Ct SW16...182 A4
Commonside E CR4...203 B6
Commonside W CR4...203 A6
Common The
Ealing W5...110 A5
Southall UB2...106 D2
Stanmore HA7...8 D2
1 Stratford E15...76 D2
Common View SW15...134 C2
Commonwealth Ave
Hayes UB3...83 B1
21 Shepherd's Bush W12...112 B6
25 Shepherd's Bush W12...112 B6
Commonwealth Ho WC1...240 B2
Commonwealth Rd N17...34 A3
Commonwealth Way SE2...124 C1
Community Cl
Cranford TW5...128 B4
Uxbridge UB10...61 A5
Community Rd
Greenford UB6...86 A6
Stratford New Town E15...76 B3
Comodore Ho SW18...136 A1
Como Rd SE23...163 A2
Compania Bldg 12 E1...118 D6
Compass Cl
Edgware HA8...26 B6
Littleton TW15...171 A3
Compass Ct SE1...253 C3
Compass Hill TW10...153 D5
Compass Ho
Bayswater W2...91 D1
London SE8...141 D3

Compass Point 10 E14 119 C6
Compayne Gdns NW6 69 D1
Compton Ave
Islington N1 72 D2
London N6 48 C2
Newham E6 99 D5
Wembley HA0 65 C4
Compton Cl
5 Burnt Oak HA8 27 A3
Camberwell SE15 139 D5
Cricklewood NW11 68 D5
Ealing W13 87 A1
Esher KT10 212 B3
Regent's Pk NW1 231 D1
Compton Cres
Chessington KT9 214 A2
Chiswick W4 133 A6
Northolt UB5 84 D6
Tottenham N17 33 A3
Compton Ct
London N12 30 A2
Sutton SM1 218 A4
9 West Norwood SE19 183 C5
Compton Ho SW11 267 A2
Compton Lo N21 16 D3
Compton Pas EC1 241 D6
Compton Pl
Bloomsbury WC1 240 A6
South Oxhey WD19 23 A6
Compton Rd
Croydon CR0 206 B1
Hayes UB3 105 D6
Islington N1 72 D2
Kensal Green NW10 90 D4
Southgate N21 16 D3
Wimbledon SW19 179 B4
Compton Rise HA5 41 B4
Compton Sch The N12 30 C4
Compton St EC1 94 D3 241 D6
Compton Terr
Islington N1 72 D2
Southgate N21 16 C3
Comreddy Cl EN2 4 D4
Comus Ho SE17 263 A3
Comus Pl SE17 117 C2 263 A3
Comyn Rd SW11 136 C1
Comyns Cl E16 98 D2
Comyns Rd RM9 81 C1
Comyns The WD23 8 A3
Conal Ct SW16 181 D5
Conant Ho SE11 138 D6
Conant Mews 1 E1 118 A6
Concanon Rd SW2, SW4 138 B1
Concert Hall App SE1 116 B5 250 D3
Concord Bsns Ctr W3 88 D2
Concord Cl UB5 85 A4
Concord Ct KT1 198 B6
Concorde Cl
Hounslow TW3 129 D3
Uxbridge UB10 82 A5
Concorde Dr E6 100 B2
Concorde Way SE16 118 D2
Concord Ho
Kingston u T KT3 199 C6
5 Tottenham N17 33 D3
Concordia Wharf 10 E14 120 A5
Concord Rd
Acton W3 88 D3
Enfield EN3 18 C6
Concord Terr HA2 63 D6
Concourse The
32 Edgware NW9 27 D2
7 Edmonton N9 18 A2
Condell Rd SW8 137 C4 269 B1
Conder St E14 97 A1
Condor Path UB5 85 C5
Condover Cres SE18 144 D5
Condray Pl SW11 267 A3
Conduit Ct WC2 250 A6
Conduit Ho SE10 142 B4
Conduit La
London N18 34 C5
South Croydon CR0 222 A3
Conduit Mews W2 92 B1 236 C1
Conduit Pas W2 236 C1
Conduit Pl W2 236 C1
Conduit Rd SE18 122 D1
Conduit St W1 115 C6 249 A6
Conduit Way NW10 67 A1
Conewood St N5 72 D5
Coney Acre SE21 161 A3
Coney Burrows E4 20 C2
Coney Gr UB8 82 C4
Coneygrove Path UB5 63 A2
CONEY HALL 224 D5
Coney Hall Par BR4 224 C5
Coney Hall Rdbt BR4 224 C5
Coney Hill Rd BR4 224 D6
Coney Way SW8 270 D5
Conference Cl 3 E4 20 A2
Conference Ho UB8 83 A1
Conference Rd SE2 124 C2
Congers Ho SE8 141 C5
Congleton Gr SE18 123 A1
Congo Dr N9 18 C1
Congo Rd SE18 123 B1
Congress Ho WC1 239 D2
Congress Rd SE2 124 C2
Congreve Ho 10 N16 73 C3
Congreve Rd SE9 144 B2
Congreve St SE17 117 C2 263 A3
Congreve Wlk 6 E16 99 D2
Conical Cnr EN2 5 A3
Conifer Cl BR6 227 B4
Conifer Ct
Ashford TW15 170 B5
Hendon NW4 28 C1
Ilford IG1 78 D2
23 Putney SW19 156 D3
Sutton SM2 218 B2
Conifer Gdns
Enfield EN1 17 C5
Streatham SW16 160 B1
Sutton SM1 217 D6
Conifer Ho SE4 141 B1
Conifers Cl TW11 175 C3
Conifer Way
Hayes UB3 106 A6
Wembley HA0 65 C5
Coniger Rd SW6 135 C3
Coningham Ct SW10 266 B4
Coningham Mews W12 112 A5
Coningham Rd W12 112 B4
Coningsby Ave NW9 27 C1
Coningsby Cotts W5 109 D4
Coningsby Ct 4 CR4 181 A1
Coningsby Gdns E4 35 D4
Coningsby Rd
Ealing W5 109 D4
Harringay N4 50 D2
Conington Rd SE13 142 A3
Conisbee Ct 3 N14 15 C6
Conisborough Cres SE6 164 A1
Conisbrough NW1 232 A5
Coniscliffe Cl BR7 188 C2
Coniscliffe Rd N13 17 A1
Coniston Ave
Barking IG11 79 C1
Ealing UB6 87 B4
Falconwood DA16 145 C2
Coniston Cl
Barking IG11 79 C1
Barnes SW13 133 D5
Chiswick W4 133 A5
West Barnes SM4 200 D3
Whetstone N20 14 A1
Coniston Ct
Beckenham BR3 186 A2
Chessington KT9 214 A5
Edgware HA8 26 B5
4 Finchley NW7 29 A3
Marylebone W2 237 B1
Penge SE26 184 B4
6 Rotherhithe SE16 118 D4
3 Wallington SM6 219 B4
Conistone Way N7 72 A1
Coniston Gdns
Edmonton N9 18 C3
Kingsbury NW9 45 B4
Pinner HA5 40 A5
Redbridge IG4 56 A5
Sutton SM2 218 B2
Wembley HA9 43 C1
Coniston Ho
14 Bow E3 97 B4
18 Camberwell SE5 139 A5
Coniston NW1 232 A2
Coniston Rd
Catford BR1 186 C4
Croydon CR0 206 A2
Muswell Hill N10 31 B1
Tottenham N17 34 A4
Twickenham TW2 151 D5
Coniston Way KT9 214 A5
Coniston Wlk E9 74 C3
Conlan St W10 91 A3
Conley Rd NW10 67 C2
Conley St SE10 120 C1
Connaught Ave
Ashford TW15 170 A6
Barnet EN4 14 D3
Chingford E4 20 B4
Enfield EN1 5 C3
Hounslow TW4 129 A1
Mortlake SW14 133 A1
Connaught Bridge E16 121 D6
Connaught Bsns Ctr
London NW9 45 D4
Mitcham CR4 202 D4
Wallington CR0 220 B2
Connaught Cl
Carshalton SM1 218 B6
Enfield EN1 5 C3
Hillingdon UB8 83 A3
Lea Bridge E10 75 A6
Marylebone W2 237 B1
Connaught Ct
1 Chingford E4 20 C4
9 Walthamstow E17 53 D5
Connaught Day Hospl E11 54 C3
Connaught Dr NW11 47 C5
Connaught Gdns
Cranley Gdns N10 49 B4
Edmonton N13 32 D6
Morden SM4 202 A5
Connaught Grange N13 32 D6
Connaught Ho
College Pk NW10 90 B4
London N10 49 B4
Mayfair W1 248 C5
Connaught Hts UB10 83 A3
Connaught La IG1 79 B6
Connaught Lo N4 50 C2
Connaught Mans
Battersea SW11 267 B1
3 Brixton SW9 138 C1
15 Canonbury N16 73 B4
Fulham SW6 264 A2
Connaught Mews
Ilford IG1 79 B6
Woolwich SE18 122 C1
Connaught Pl W2 237 C1
Connaught Rd
Barnet EN5 12 D5
Carshalton SM1 218 B6
Chingford E4 20 C3
Ealing W13 109 B6
Finsbury Pk N4 50 C2
Harlesden NW10 89 C5
Harrow HA3 24 D2
Ilford IG1 79 B6
Leytonstone E11 54 B1
Newham E16 121 D5
New Malden KT3 199 C5
5 Richmond TW10 154 B6
Teddington TW11, TW12 174 B5
Walthamstow E17 53 C4
Woolwich SE18 122 D1
Connaught Sch for Girls (Annexe) E11 76 C6
Connaught Sch for Girls E11 54 C1
Connaught Sq W2 92 D1 237 C1
Connaught St W2 92 C1 237 B1
Connaught Way N13 32 D6
Connaught Works E3 97 A6
Connections Ho N2 30 B2
Connell Cres W5 88 B3
Connell Ct 6 SE14 140 D6
Connell Ho 6 SM6 219 C2
Connemara Cl WD6 11 B5
Conniffe Ct SE9 166 D6
Connington Cres E4 20 B1
Connington 5 KT1 176 C1
Connolly Ho SW19 180 A4
Connoly Ct NW2 68 B5
Connop Rd EN3 6 D5
Connor Cl E11 54 C2
Connor Ct SW11 268 C1
Connor Rd RM9 81 B4
Connor St E9 96 D6
Conolly Rd W7 108 C5
Conrad Dr KT4 200 D1
Conrad Ho
8 Limehouse SE16 119 A6
South Lambeth SW8 270 A4
12 Stoke Newington N16 73 C3
Conrad Twr W3 110 D3
Conroy Ct 6 DA14 190 A6
Conservatory Ct SE19 183 C3
Consfield Ave KT3 200 A4
Consort Ho
Bayswater W2 245 D5
Edgware NW7 27 D5
Consort Lo NW8 230 C5
Consort Mews TW7 152 B6
Consort Rd SE15 140 B3
Cons St SE1 251 B2
Constable Ave E16 121 B5
Constable Cl
12 Friern Barnet N11 30 D5
Hampstead Garden Suburb NW11 47 D3
Hayes UB4 83 A5
Constable Cres N15 52 A4
Constable Ct 11 SE16 118 B1
Constable Gdns
Edgware HA8 26 C1
Isleworth TW7 152 B6
Constable Ho
Enfield EN1 18 A6
25 Millwall E14 119 C4
13 Northolt UB5 84 D5
Primrose Hill NW3 70 D1
Constable Mews RM8 80 B4
Constable Wlk SE21 161 C1
Constance Cres BR2 208 D1
Constance Ct N10 31 B3
Constance Rd
Enfield EN1 17 C5
Sutton SM1 218 A4
Thornton Heath CR0 204 D2
Twickenham TW2 151 D4
Constance St E16 122 A5
Constant Ho 26 E14 119 D6
Constantine Ho SW2 160 D3
Constantine Pl UB10 82 B6
Constantine Rd NW3 70 C4
Constitution Hill SW1, W1 115 B4 248 D2
Constitution Rise SE18 144 C4
Consul Ho 5 E3 97 C3
Content St SE17 117 B2 262 C3
Contessa Cl BR6 227 C3
Control Tower Rd TW6 126 D2
Convair Wlk 11 UB5 84 D4
Convent Cl BR3 186 A3
Convent Gdns
Ealing W5 109 C2
Notting Hill W11 91 B1
Convent Hill SE19 183 A4
Convent Lo TW15 170 D5
Convent of Jesus & Mary Language Coll NW10 89 D6
Convent of Jesus & Mary RC Inf Sch NW2 68 C2
Convent Rd TW15 170 D5
Convent Way UB2 106 D2
Conway Cl HA7 25 A4
Conway Cres
Dagenham RM6 58 C3
Greenford UB6 86 C5
Conway Dr
Ashford TW15 171 A4
Hayes UB3 105 A3
Sutton SM2 217 D2
Conway Gdns
Enfield EN2 5 C5
Mitcham CR4 204 A5
Wembley HA9 43 C2
Conway Gr W3 89 B2
Conway Ho
Chelsea SW3 257 D1
5 Millwall E14 119 D2
6 Streatham SW2 160 A3
Conway Mews W1 239 A5
Conway Prim Sch SE18 123 C2
Conway Rd
Dollis Hill NW2 68 C6
Feltham TW13 172 D5
Harlington TW6 126 D2
Harringay N15 51 A4
Palmers Green N14 16 A1
Plumstead SE18 123 C2
Twickenham TW4 151 C4
Wimbledon SW20 178 C2
Conway St W1 93 C3 239 A5
Conway Wlk TW12 173 B4
Conybeare NW3 70 C1
Conyers Cl IG8 36 C4
Conyer's Rd SW16 181 D5
Conyer St 21 E3 97 A5
Cooden Cl BR1 187 B3
Cookes Cl E11 76 D6
Cookes La SM3 217 A2
Cooke St 3 IG11 101 A6
Cookham Cl UB2 107 D4
Cookham Cres SE16 118 D4
Cookham Dene Cl BR7 189 B2
Cookham Ho E2 243 C6
Cookham Rd BR8, DA14 191 C2
Cookhill Rd SE2 124 B3
Cooks Ferry N18 34 D5
Cook's Hole Rd EN2 5 A5
Cookson Gr DA8 147 D5
Cook's Rd
Camberwell SE17 138 D6
Stratford Marsh E15 97 D5
Coolfin Rd E16 99 B1
Coolgardie Ave E4 36 B5
Coolgardie Rd TW15 171 A5
Coolhurst Rd N8 49 D3
Cool Oak La NW9 45 D2
Coomassie Rd W9 91 B3
COOMBE 177 B3
Coombe Ave CR0 221 C4
Coombe Bank KT2, KT3 177 C2
Coombe Boys' Sch KT3 200 A4
Coombe Cl
Edgware HA8 26 B1
Hounslow TW3 129 C1
Coombe Cnr N21 16 D3
Coombe Cres TW12 173 A3
Coombe Ct 2 BR3 185 B2
Coombe Dr HA4 40 B1
Coombe End KT2 177 B3
Coombefield Cl KT3 199 C4
Coombe Gdns
New Malden KT3 199 D5
Wimbledon SW20 178 A2
Coombe Girls Sch KT3 177 B1
Coombe Hill Glade KT2 177 C3
Coombe Hill Inf Sch KT2 177 B2
Coombe Hill Jun Sch KT2 177 B2
Coombe Hill Rd KT2 177 C3
Coombe Ho 13 N7 71 D3
Coombe House Chase KT3 177 B2
Coombehurst Cl EN4 2 D3
Coombehurst (Kingston University) KT2 177 A5
Coombe Lane Flyover SW20 177 D2
Coombe La CR0 222 B3
Coombe La W KT2 177 B2
Coombe Lea BR1 210 A6
Coombe Lo SE7 143 C6
Coombe Neville KT2 177 B3
Coombe Pk KT2 177 B5
Coombe Pl KT2 177 A5
Coombe Rd
Bushey WD23 8 B4
Chiswick W4 111 C1
Ealing W13 109 B3
Forest Hill SE26 184 B6
Hampton TW12 173 B4
New Malden KT3 199 C6
Norbiton KT2 176 C2
South Croydon CR0, CR2 221 C4
Willesden NW10 67 B5
Wood Green N22 32 C2
Coomber Ho SW6 135 D2
Coombe Ridings KT2 177 A5
Coombe Rise KT2 177 A2
Coomber Way CR0 203 D3
Coombes Rd RM9 103 B6
Coombe Wlk SM1 217 D5
Coombewood Dr RM6 59 B3
Coombe Wood Rd KT2 177 A5
Coombs St N1 234 D3
Coomer Mews SW6 264 D5
Coomer Pl SW6 135 B6 264 D5
Cooms Wlk HA8 27 A2
Cooperage Cl 5 N17 33 D4
Cooperage The SE1 253 C3
Cooper Ave E17 35 A2
Cooper Cl SE1 251 B1
Cooper Cres SM5 218 D5
Cooper Ct
Shooters Hill SE18 144 D6
Stratford New Town E15 76 A3
Cooper Ho
Hounslow TW4 129 B2
Paddington NW8 236 C5
Upper Tooting SW17 180 B6
Cooper Ho *continued*
7 West Norwood SW27 182 D5
Cooper Rd
Croydon CR0, CR9 220 D4
Hendon NW4 46 D3
Willesden NW10 68 A3
Coopersale Cl 3 IG8 37 C3
Coopersale Rd E9 74 D3
Coopers Cl
Bethnal Green E1 96 C3
Dagenham RM10 81 D2
Coopers Ct
9 Acton W3 111 A5
4 Friern Barnet N20 14 D1
Isleworth TW7 130 D3
Tower Hamlets E3 97 B3
Coopers La SE12 165 B2
Cooper's La E10 54 A1
Cooper's Lane Prim Sch SE12 165 B2
Coopers La NW1 232 D3
Coopers Lo SE1 253 C2
Coopers Mews BR3 185 C1
Cooper's Rd SE1 117 D1 263 D2
Cooper's Row EC3 117 D6 253 C6
Cooper St 10 E16 98 D2
Coopers Tech Sch BR7 189 A2
Coopers Yd N1 72 D1
Cooper's Yd SE19 183 C4
Coote Gdns RM8 81 B5
Coote Rd
Dagenham RM8 81 B5
Erith DA7 147 B4
Cope Ho EC1 235 B1
Copeland Dr E14 119 C2
Copeland Ho
Lambeth SE11 260 D5
Upper Tooting SW17 180 B6
Copeland Rd
London SE15 140 B3
Walthamstow E17 53 D3
Copelands BR3 185 B3
Copeman Cl SE26 184 C5
Copenhagen Gdns W4 111 B4
Copenhagen Ho N1 234 A5
Copenhagen Pl E14 97 B1
Copenhagen Prim Sch N1 94 B6 233 C5
Copenhagen St N1 94 B6 233 C5
Cope Pl W8 113 C3 255 A5
Copers Cope Rd BR3 185 B3
Cope St SE16 118 D2
Copeswood Ct UB7 126 C5
Copford Wlk N1 235 A6
Copgate Path SW16 182 C4
Copinger Wlk HA8 26 D2
Copland Ave HA0 65 D3
Copland Cl HA0 65 C3
Copland Com Sch & Tech Ctr HA9 66 B3
Copland Ho UB1 107 B4
Copland Mews 8 HA0 66 A2
Copland Rd HA0 66 A2
Copleston Rd SE15 139 D2
Copley Cl
15 Camberwell SE17 138 D6
Ealing W7 86 D2
Copley Dene BR1 187 D2
Copley Pk SW16 182 B4
Copley Rd HA7 25 C5
Coppard Gdns KT9 213 C2
Coppedhall 2 SE21 161 B2
Coppelia Rd SE3 142 D1
Coppen Rd RM8 59 B2
Copperas St SE8 141 D6
Copperbeech Cl NW3 70 B3
Copper Beech Ct N20 14 A1
Copper Beeches TW7 130 B4
Copper Beech N6 49 A2
Copper Cl
Penge SE19 183 D3
Tottenham N17 34 B3
Copperdale Rd UB3 106 A4
Copperfield Ave UB8 82 C3
Copperfield Ct
Blackheath SE3 142 D2
Ilford IG6 57 A6
Copperfield Dr N15 51 D5
Copperfield Ho 12 SE1 118 A4
Copperfield Mews N18 33 C5

Copperfield Rd
Stepney E3 97 A2
Thamesmead SE28 102 C1
Copperfields 5 BR3 186 A2
Copperfields Ct W3 110 C4
Copperfields HA1 42 C2
Copperfield St SE1 117 A4 252 A2
Copperfield Way
Chislehurst BR7 189 A4
Pinner HA5 41 B5
Coppergate Cl BR1 187 B2
Coppermead Cl NW2 68 C5
Copper Mews 19 W4 111 A3
Copper Mill Dr TW7 130 D3
Coppermill La E17 52 D4
Copper Mill La SW17 180 A6
Coppermill Prim Sch E17 52 D4
Copper Row SE1 253 C3
Copperwood Lo EN2 4 D3
Coppetts Cl N12 30 D3
Coppetts Ctr N12 30 D3
Coppetts Rd N10 30 D2
Coppetts Wood Hospl N10 30 D2
Coppetts Wood Prim Sch N10 31 A2
Coppice Cl
Beckenham BR3 207 D5
Harrow HA7 24 D4
Ruislip HA4 39 B3
West Barnes SW20 200 C6
Coppice Dr SW15 156 B5
Coppice The
Ashford TW15 170 D4
Enfield EN2 4 D1
Hillingdon UB7 82 A1
New Barnet EN5 13 D5
Coppice Way E18 54 D6
Coppice Wlk N20 13 C1
Coppies Gr N11 31 B6
Copping Cl CR0 221 C4
Coppin Ho SW2 160 D3
Coppins The
2 Ilford RM6 58 B2
New Addington CR0 223 D2
Stanmore HA3 24 C4
Coppock Cl SW11 136 C3
Coppsfield KT8 195 C6
Copse Ave BR4 223 D5
Copse Cl SE7 143 B6
Copse Ct SW15 157 A6
Copse Glade KT6 197 D1
COPSE HILL 178 B3
Copse Hill
Belmont SM2 217 D1
Wimbledon SW20 178 B3
Copsem Dr KT10 212 A2
Copsem La KT10 212 A1
Copsem Way KT10 212 A2
Copse The
Chingford E4 20 D3
Muswell Hill N2 48 D6
Copse View CR2 223 A1
Copsewood Cl DA15 167 C5
Coptefield Dr DA17 125 A3
Copthall Ave EC2 95 B1 242 D2
Copthall Bldgs EC2 242 D2
Copthall Cl EC2 242 C2
Copthall Dr NW7 28 A4
Copthall Gdns
Hendon NW7 28 A3
Twickenham TW1 152 D3
Copthall Rd E UB10 60 C5
Copthall Rd W UB10 60 C6
Copthall Sch NW7 28 B3
Copthall Sports Ctr NW4 28 B2
Copthorne Ave
Bromley BR2 226 B6
Streatham SW12 159 D4
Copthorne Chase 3 TW15 170 B6
Copthorne Cl TW17 193 A3
Copthorne Ct SM1 218 A5
Copthorne Mews UB3 105 C2
Coptic St WC1 94 A2 240 A3
Copton Cl E3 97 C2
Copwood Cl N12 30 B6
Coral Apts 6 E16 121 A6
Coral Cl RM6 58 C6
Coral Ho 5 E1 97 A3
Coraline Cl UB1 85 B4
Coralline Wlk 4 SE2 124 C4
Coral Row 14 SW11 136 A2
Coral St SE1 116 C4 251 B1
Coram Ho
Bloomsbury WC1 240 A6
9 Chiswick W4 111 C1
Coram Mans WC1 240 C5
Coram St WC1 94 A3 240 A5
Coran Cl N9 18 D4
Corban Rd TW3 129 C2
Corbar Cl EN4 2 B4
Corbden Cl SE15 139 D4
Corbet Cl CR4, SM6 219 A6
Corbet Ct EC3 242 D1
Corbet Ho N1 234 A5
Corbet Pl E1 95 D2 243 C4
Corbett Ct SE26 185 B6
Corbett Gr N22 32 A3
Corbett Ho SW10 266 A6
Corbett Rd
Walthamstow E17 54 A6
Wanstead E11 55 C3
Corbett's La SE16 118 C2
Corbetts Pas 8 SE16 118 C2
Corbett Villas RM8 58 C1
Corbicum E11 54 C2
Corbidge Ct SE8 141 D6
Corbiere Ct SW19 178 D4
Corbiere Ho 5 N1 95 C6
Corbin Ho 7 E3 97 D4
Corbin's La HA2 63 D5
Corbridge Cres E2 96 B5
Corbridge Ho SE2 124 C3
Corbridge 5 N17 34 B3
Corby Cres EN2 4 A1
Corbylands Rd DA15 167 C3
Corbyn St N4, N19 50 A1
Corby Rd NW10 89 B5
Corby Way E3 97 C3
Cordelia Cl SE24 138 D1
Cordelia Gdns TW19 148 A4
Cordelia Ho 26 N1 95 C5
Cordelia Rd TW19 148 A4
Cordelia St E14 97 D1
Cordell Ho N15 51 D4
Cordingley Rd HA4 61 B6
Cording St E14 97 D2
Cordwainers Ct 18 E9 74 C1
Cordwainers Wlk 9 E13 99 A5
Cordwain Ho 7 N18 34 A5
Cordwell Rd SE13 164 C6
Corefield Cl N11 15 A2
Corelli Rd SE3 144 A4
Corfe Ave HA2 63 C4
Corfe Cl Hayes UB4 84 C1
Twickenham TW4 151 A3
Corfe Ho SW8 270 C4
Corfe Lodge 15 SE21 161 B2
Corfe Twr 6 W3 111 A4
Corfield Rd N21 16 B6
Corfield St E2 96 B4
Corfton Lo W5 88 A2
Corfton Rd W5 88 A2
Coriander Ave E14 98 B1
Coriander Ct SE1 253 D2
Cories Cl RM8 80 D6
Corigan Ct 6 E11 76 C6
Corinium Cl HA9 66 B4
Corinne Rd N19 71 C4
Corinth Rd IG3 58 A2
Cork St Mews W1 249 A5
Corkscrew Hill BR4 224 B5
Cork Sq E1 118 B5
Cork St W1 115 C6 249 A5
Cork Tree Ho 3 SW27 182 D5
Cork Tree Ret Pk N18 35 A4
Cork Tree Way E4 35 A5
Corlett St NW1 237 A4
Cormont Rd SE5 138 D4
Cormorant Cl E17 35 A3
Cormorant Ct
36 Deptford SE8 141 B6
13 Dulwich SE21 161 B2
Cormorant Ho EN3 18 D6
Cormorant Pl SM1 217 B3
Cormorant Rd E7 76 D3
Cornbury Ho 5 SE8 141 B6
Cornbury Rd HA8 25 D3
Cornel Ho 4 DA15 168 A1
Cornelia Dr UB4 84 C3
Cornelia St N7 72 B2
Cornelion Cotts 1 SM6 219 B3
Cornelius Ct 4 N12 30 A5
Cornell Bldg 9 E1 96 A1
Cornell Cl DA14 191 A4
Cornell Ct 4 EN3 7 A2
Cornell Ho HA2 63 B5
Corner Fielde SW2 160 B3
Corner Gn SE3 143 B3
Corner House St WC2 250 A4
Corner Mead NW9 27 D2
Cornerside TW15 171 A3
Cornerstone Ct 13 E1 96 A3
Cornerways
Harrow HA1 65 A5
Putney SW15 134 A1
Corney Rd W4 133 C6
Corney Reach Way W4 133 C5
Cornflower La CR0 206 D1
Cornflower Terr SE22 162 B5
Cornford Cl BR2 209 A4
Cornford Gr SW12 159 B2
Cornhill Dr EN3 7 A6
Cornhill EC3 95 B1 242 D1
Cornick Ho 7 SE16 118 B3
Cornish Ct N9 18 B4
Cornish Gr SE20 184 B2
Cornish Ho
Brentford TW8 110 B1
7 Camberwell SE17 138 D6
Cornmill La SE13 142 A2
Cornmow Dr NW10 68 A3
Cornshaw Rd RM8 58 D1
Cornthwaite Rd E5 74 C5
Cornwall Ave
Bethnal Green E2 96 C4
Claygate KT10 212 D1
Falconwood DA16 145 D2
Finchley N3 29 C3
Southall UB1 85 C2
Wood Green N22 32 A2
Cornwall Cl IG11 79 D2
Cornwall Cres W11 91 A1
Cornwall Ct
5 Ealing W7 86 D3
5 Pinner HA5 23 B3
Upper Tooting SW17 180 C6
Cornwall Dr BR5 190 C3
Cornwall Flats SE1 251 B2
Cornwall Gdns
Kensington SW7 113 D3 255 D5
Willesden NW10 68 B2
Cornwall Gdns Wlk SW7 255 D5
Cornwall Gr W4 111 C1
Cornwall Ho
Marylebone NW1 237 D5
3 Putney SW15 156 C4
Cornwallis Ave
London N9 18 C2
New Eltham SE9 167 B2
Cornwallis Ct SW8 270 A2
Cornwallis Gr N9 18 C2
Cornwallis Ho 24 W12 112 B6
Cornwallis Rd
Dagenham RM9 81 A4
Edmonton N9 18 B2
Upper Holloway N19 72 A6
Walthamstow E17 52 D5
Woolwich SE18 122 D3
Woolwich SE18 123 A3
Cornwallis Sq N19 72 A6
Cornwallis Wlk SE9 144 B2
Cornwall Mans
Chelsea SW10 266 B4
Marylebone NW1 237 D5
Cornwall Mews S SW7 256 A5
Cornwall Mews W SW7 255 D5
Cornwall Rd
Belmont SM2 217 B1
Croydon CR0 220 D6
Edmonton N18 34 A5
Finsbury Pk N4 50 C2
Harrow HA1 42 A3
Lambeth SE1 116 C4 251 B2
Pinner HA5 23 B3
Ruislip HA4 61 D6
Twickenham TW1 153 A3
West Green N15 51 B4
Cornwall Sq SE11 261 C2
Cornwall St 4 E1 118 B6
Cornwall Terrace Mews NW1 237 D5
Cornwall Terr NW1 237 D5
Corn Way E11 76 C5
Cornwood Cl N2 48 B5
Cornwood Dr E1 96 C1
Cornworthy Rd RM8 80 C3
Corona Rd SE12 165 A4
Coronation Ave 1 N16 73 D4
Coronation Cl
Bexley DA5 168 D5
Ilford IG6 57 A5
Coronation Ct
19 North Kensington W10 90 C2
Stratford E15 76 D2
Coronation Rd
Acton NW10 88 C3
Hayes UB3 105 D2
Newham E13 99 C4
Coronet Ho HA7 24 D4
Coronet Par 9 HA0 66 A2
Coronet St N1 95 C4
Corporation Ave TW4 129 A1
Corporation Row EC1 241 B6
Corporation St
Lower Holloway N7 72 A3
West Ham E15 98 D5
Corpus Christi RC Prim Sch
Brixton SW2 160 B6
Kingston u T KT3 199 A6
Corrance Rd SW2, SW4 138 A1
Corri Ave N14 31 D6
Corrib Ct N13 16 B1
Corrib Dr SM1 218 C3
Corrib Hts N8 49 D3
Corrigan Cl NW4 46 C6
Corringham Ct NW11 47 C2
Corringham Ho 11 E1 96 D1
Corringham Rd
London NW11 47 C2
Wembley HA9 66 C6
Corringway Ealing W5 88 C2
Golders Green NW11 47 D2
Corris Gn NW9 45 C3
Corry Dr SW9 138 D1
Corry Ho 2 E14 119 D6
Corsair Cl TW19 148 A4
Corsair Rd TW19 148 A4
Corscombe Cl KT2 177 A5
Corsehill St SW16 181 C4
Corsell Ho 5 TW8 131 C5
Corsham Ho HA9 66 C2
Corsham St N1 95 B4 235 D1
Corsica St N5 72 D2
Corsley Way E9 75 B2
Cortayne Ct TW2 152 C2
Cortayne Rd SW6 135 B3
Cortis Rd SW15 156 B5
Cortis Terr SW15 156 B5
Corunna Rd SW8 137 C4 269 B2
Corunna Terr SW8 269 A2
Corvette Sq 5 SE10 142 B6
Corwell Gdns UB8 83 A1
Corwell La UB8 83 A1
Coryton Path W9 91 B3
Cosbycote Ave SE24 161 A6
Cosdach Ave SM6 219 D1
Cosedge Cres CR0, CR9 220 D3
Cosgrove Cl
Edmonton N21 17 A2
Hayes UB4 84 D3
Cosgrove Ho 11 E2 96 A6
Cosmo Pl WC1 240 B4
Cosmur Cl W12 111 D3
Cossall Wlk SE15 140 B4
Cossar Mews 10 SW2 160 C6
Cosser St SE1 116 C3 261 A6
Costa St SE15 140 A3
Coston Prim Sch UB6 86 A4
Costons Ave UB6 86 B4
Costons La UB6 86 B4
Coston Wlk 4 SE4 140 D1
Cosway Ho NW11 48 A3
Cosway Mans NW1 237 B4
Cosway St NW1 92 C2 237 B4
Cotall St E14 97 C2
Coteford Cl HA5 40 A4
Coteford Inf Sch HA5 40 A3
Coteford Jun Sch HA5 39 D4
Coteford St SW17 181 A6
Cotelands CR0 221 C5
Cotesbach Rd E5 74 C5
Cotes Ho NW8 237 A5
Cotesmore Gdns RM8 80 C4
Cotford Rd CR7 205 A5
Cotham St SE17 262 B3
Cotherstone Rd SW2 160 B3
Cotleigh Ave DA5 168 D2
Cotleigh Rd NW6 69 C1
Cotman Cl
London NW11 48 A3
Cotman Cl *continued*
Putney SW15 156 D6
Cotman Ct BR3 185 B2
Cotmandene Cres BR5 190 A1
Cotman Gdns HA8 26 C1
Cotman Ho
5 Northolt UB5 84 D5
St John's Wood NW8 230 A4
Cotman Mews RM8 80 C3
Cotmans Cl UB3 106 A5
Coton Rd DA16 146 A2
Cotrill Gdns E8 74 B2
Cotsford Ave KT3 199 B4
Cotswold Ave WD23 8 A5
Cotswold Cl
Hinchley Wood KT10 212 D6
Kingston u T KT2 177 A4
Cotswold Ct
London N11 31 A6
St Luke's EC1 242 A6
3 Wembley UB6 86 D5
Cotswold Gate NW2 47 A1
Cotswold Gdns
Hendon NW2 68 D6
Ilford IG2 57 B2
Newham E6 99 D5
Cotswold Gn EN2 4 B1
Cotswold Ho N16 51 D1
Cotswold Mews SW11 266 D1
Cotswold Rd TW12 173 C4
Cotswold Rise BR6 211 D3
Cotswold St SE27 182 D6
Cotswold Way
Enfield EN2 4 B2
North Cheam KT4 216 C6
Cottage Ave BR2 210 A1
Cottage Cl
Harrow HA2 64 C6
Ruislip HA4 39 B1
Cottage Field Cl DA14 168 C3
Cottage Gn SE5 139 B5
Cottage Gr
London SW9 138 A2
Surbiton KT6 197 D3
Cottage Pl SW3 114 C3 257 A5
Cottage Rd KT19 215 B1
Cottage St E14 119 D6
Cottages The
Ickenham UB10 60 A6
Lambeth SE1 260 C5
Uxbridge UB10 60 D5
Cottage Wlk 2 N16 73 D5
Cottenham Dr
London NW9 45 D6
Wimbledon SW20 178 B3
Cottenham Ho 5 N19 72 A6
COTTENHAM PARK 178 B2
Cottenham Park Rd SW20 178 C3
Cottenham Par SW20 178 B1
Cottenham Pl SW20 178 B3
Cottenham Rd E17 53 B5
Cotterill Rd KT6 198 B1
Cottesbrook St 9 SE14 141 A5
Cottesloe Ho NW8 237 A6
Cottesloe Mews SE1 261 B6
Cottesmore Ct W8 255 D6
Cottesmore Gdns W8 113 D3 255 D6
Cottimore Ave KT12 194 B1
Cottimore Cres KT12 194 B2
Cottimore La KT12 194 B2
Cottimore Terr KT12 194 B2
Cottingham Chase HA4 62 A5
Cottingham Rd
Penge SE20 184 D3
South Lambeth SW8 138 B5 270 D4
Cottington Rd TW13 172 D6
Cottington St SE11 261 C2
Cotton Ave W3 89 B1
Cotton Cl
Dagenham RM9 80 C1
12 Leyton E11 76 C6
Cottongrass Cl 1 CR0 206 D1
Cotton Hill BR1 186 B6
Cotton Ho
Bedford Pk W12 111 D4
18 Streatham SW12 160 A4
Cotton Row SW11 136 B2
Cotton's Gdns E2 95 C4
Cottons La SE1 252 D4
Cotton St E14 120 A6
Cottrell Ct SE10 120 D2
Cotts Cl 13 W7 86 D2
Couchman Ho 8 SW4 159 C5
Couchmore Ave KT10 212 C6
Coulgate St SE4 141 A2
Coulsdon Ct 4 N8 49 D4
Coulsdon Ho 5 SW2 160 A3
Coulson Cl RM8 58 C1
Coulson St SW3 114 D1 257 C2
Coulter Cl UB4 85 A3
Coulter Rd W6 112 B3
Coulthurst Ct SW16 182 A3
Coults Cres NW5 71 A5
Councillor St SE5 139 A5
Counters Ct W14 254 B6
Counter St SE1 253 A3
Countess Rd NW5 71 C3
Countisbury Ave EN1 17 D4
Countisbury Ho SE26 162 A1
Country Way TW13, TW16 172 C5
County Gate
Longlands SE9 167 A1
New Barnet EN5 13 D5
County Gr SE5 139 A4
County Ho
22 Herne Hill SE24 138 D1
9 South Lambeth SW9 138 C4
County Par TW8 131 D5
County Rd
Newham E6 100 D2
South Norwood CR7 182 D1
County St SE1 117 A3 262 B5
Coupland Pl SE18 123 A1
Courcy Rd N8, N22 50 C6
Courier Ho 17 SW2 160 C4
Courland Gr SW8 137 D3
Courland St SW8 137 D4 269 D1
Course The SE9 166 C1
Courtauld Ho 12 E2 96 A5
Courtauld Inst of Art*
Marylebone W1 237 D2
Strand WC2 250 C6
Courtauld Rd N19 50 A1
Courtaulds Cl SE28 124 A5
Court Ave DA17 125 B1
Court Cl HA3 44 A6
Court Close Ave TW13, TW2 151 D1
Court Cl
Twickenham TW13, TW2 151 D1
Wallington SM6 219 D1
Court Cres KT9 213 D2
Court Downs Rd BR3 185 D1
Court Dr
Carshalton SM1 218 C4
Edgware HA7 26 A6
Hillingdon UB10 82 C6
Wallington CR0 220 B4
Courtenay Ave
Harrow HA3 24 A2
Highgate N6 48 C2
Courtenay Dr BR3 186 B1
Courtenay Gdns HA3 24 A1
Courtenay Mews E17 53 A4
Courtenay Pl E17 53 A4
Courtenay Rd
Leyton E11 76 D5
North Cheam KT4, SM3 216 C5
Penge BR3, SE20 184 D4
Walthamstow E17 52 D5
Courtenay Rd HA9 65 D5
Courtenay Sq SE11 261 A1
Courtenay St SE11 116 C1 261 A2
Courtens Mews HA7 25 C3
Court Farm Ave KT19 215 B3
Court Farm Ind Est TW19 148 B5
Court Farm Rd
Chislehurst SE9 166 A1
Northolt UB5 63 C1
Courtfield Ave HA1 42 D4
Courtfield Cres HA1 42 D4
Courtfield W13 87 C2
Courtfield Gdns
Ealing W13 87 A1
Ruislip HA4 61 D6
South Kensington SW5 113 D2 255 D3

Courtfield Ho EC1 241 A4
Courtfield Mews
SW7 255 D3
Courtfield Rd
Ashford TW15 170 D4
South Kensington
SW7 114 A2 256 A3
Courtfield Rise BR4 224 B5
Courtgate Cl NW7 27 D4
Court Gdns N7 72 C2
Courthill Rd SE13 142 A1
Courthope Ho
14 Rotherhithe
SE16 118 C3
South Lambeth SW8 270 A3
Courthope Rd
Gospel Oak NW3 70 D4
Greenford UB6 86 B5
Wimbledon SW19 179 A5
Courthope Villas
SW19 179 A3
Court House Gdns
N3 29 C4
Court House Rd N12 29 D4
Court La SE21 161 D4
Courtland Ave
Chingford E4 20 D2
Edgware NW7 11 C1
Redbridge IG1 78 B6
South Norwood
SW16 182 B3
Courtland Gr SE28 124 D6
Courtland Rd E6 100 A6
Courtlands Ave
Hampton TW12 173 B4
Hayes BR2 208 D1
Lee SE12 165 B6
Richmond TW9 132 D3
Courtlands
11 Beckenham
BR3 185 D1
8 Belmont SM2 217 D1
Courtland Sch NW7 11 C2
Courtlands Cl HA4 39 D2
Courtlands Dr KT19 215 D2
Courtlands W5 87 C2
Courtlands Rd KT5 198 C2
Courtlands
Richmond TW10 154 C6
5 Upper Clapton E5 52 B1
Walton-on-T KT12 194 A2
Court Lane Gdns
SE21 161 C4
Courtleet Dr DA8 147 D4
Courtleigh Ave EN4 2 B5
Courtleigh Gdns
NW11 47 A5
Courtleigh 6 NW11 47 B4
Court Lo 11 DA17 125 C1
Courtman Rd N17 33 A3
Court Mans 8 W6 112 A2
Courtmead Cl SE24 161 A5
Court Mead UB5 85 B4
Courtnell St W2 91 C1
Courtney Cl SE19 183 C4
Courtney Cres SM5 218 D1
Courtney Ct N7 72 C3
Courtney Ho
1 Hendon NW4 46 C5
Kensington W14 254 B6
Courtney Pl CR0 220 C5
Courtney Rd
Croydon CR0 220 C5
Islington N7 72 C3
Mitcham SW19 180 C3
Courtney Twrs IG2 57 B3
Courtney Way TW6 126 C2
Court One TW15 149 A1
Court Par HA0 65 B5
Courtrai Rd SE23 163 A5
Court Rd Eltham SE9 166 B4
Southall UB2 107 B1
South Norwood
SE25 205 D6
Uxbridge UB10 60 D4
Court Royal SW15 157 A6
Courtside
Crouch End N8 49 D3
Forest Hill SE23 162 C1
Court St
Bromley BR1 187 A1
3 Stepney E1 96 B2
Court The London N10 49 C5
Ruislip HA4 63 A4
Court Three TW15 149 A1
Court Two TW15 149 A1
Courtville Ho 12 W10 91 A4
Court Way Acton W3 89 A2
Colindale NW9 45 C5
Ilford IG6 57 A6
Twickenham TW1,
TW2 152 D4
Courtway IG8 37 C5
Courtyard Apartments
TW11 174 B5
Courtyard Mews
BR5 190 A3
Courtyard The
Fulham
SW6 135 A4 264 A1
Islington N1 72 B1
Keston BR2 226 A2
Thornton Heath CR0 204 B3
13 Wandsworth
SW18 136 B1
Court Yd SE9 166 B5
Cousin La
EC4 117 B6 252 C5
Cousins Cl 2 UB7 104 A6
Cousins Ct 2 NW9 46 A5
Couthurst Rd SE3 143 B5
Coutts Ave KT9 214 A3
Couzens Ho 8 E3 97 B2
Coval Gdns SW14 132 D1
Coval La SW14 132 D1
Coval Pas SW14 133 A1
Coval Rd SW14 133 A1
Covardale Ct EN3 7 A6
Covelees Wall E6 100 C1
Covell Ct 16 SE8 141 C5
Covent Garden Sta
WC2 94 A1 240 B1
Covent Gdn*
WC2 116 A6 250 B6
Coventry Cl
Kilburn NW6 91 C6
9 Newham E6 100 B1
Coventry Rd
Bethnal Green E1 96 B3
Croydon SE25 206 A5
Ilford IG1 56 D1
Coventry St W1 249 C5
Coverack Cl
Croydon CR0 207 A2
Southgate N14 15 C5
Coverdale Cl HA7 25 B5
Coverdale Gdns
CR0 221 D5
Coverdale Rd
Brondesbury NW2 69 A2
Friern Barnet N11 31 A4
Hammersmith W12 112 B4
Hampstead NW6 68 D1
Coverdales The
IG11 101 B5
Coverham Ho 5
SE4 140 D1
Coverley Cl E1 96 A2
Coverley Point SE11 260 C3
Coverton Rd SW17 180 C5
Coverts Rd KT10 212 D1
Covert The BR6 211 C3
Covert Way EN4 2 A3
Covet Wood Cl BR5 211 D3
Covey Cl SW19 179 D1
Covington Gdns
SW16 182 D3
Covington Way
South Norwood
SW16 182 C3
South Norwood
SW16 182 D3
Cowan Cl E6 100 A2
Cowan Ct 14 NW10 67 B1
Cowan Lo 6 IG8 37 C4
Cowbridge La IG11 78 D1
Cowbridge Rd HA3 44 B5
Cowcross St
EC1 94 D2 241 C4
Cowdenbeath Path
N1 233 C6
Cowden Rd BR6 211 D2
Cowden St SE6 185 C6
Cowdray Hall Royal Coll
of Nursing
W1 93 B1 238 C2
Cowdray Ho 22
SE22 139 C2
Cowdray Rd UB10 83 A6
Cowdrey Cl EN1 5 C3
Cowdrey Rd SW19 180 A5
Cowdry Rd E9 75 B2
Cowell Lo E4 36 D5
Cowen Ave HA2 64 B6
Cowen Ho 4 SE18 144 D6
Cowgate Rd UB6 86 B4
Cowick Rd SW17 180 D6
Cowings Mead UB5 63 A2
Cowland Ave EN3 6 C1
Cow Leaze E6 100 C1
Cowleaze Rd KT2 176 A2
Cowley Ct 8 E18 37 A1
Cowley La E11 76 C5
COWLEY PEACHY 82 A2
Cowley Pl NW4 46 C4
Cowley Rd
Brixton SW9 138 C4
East Acton W3 111 D5
18 Kennington SW9 138 C5
Mortlake SW14 133 C2
Cowley Rd *continued*
Redbridge IG1 56 B2
Wanstead E11 55 B4
Cowley St SW1 260 A5
Cowling Cl W11 244 A4
Cowper Ave
Sutton SM1 218 B4
Upton Pk E6 78 A1
Cowper Cl
Bexley DA16 168 A6
Bromley BR2 209 D5
Cowper Gdns
Southgate N14 15 C5
Wallington SM6 219 C2
Cowper Ho
Pimlico SW1 259 D1
Walworth SE17 262 B2
Cowper Rd
Acton W3 111 B5
6 Belvedere DA17 125 C2
Bromley BR2 209 D5
Ealing W7 108 D6
East Barnet N14 15 B3
Edmonton N18 34 A5
Kingston u T KT2 176 B5
Stoke Newington N16 73 C4
Wimbledon SW19 180 A4
Cowper's Ct EC3 242 D1
Cowper St EC1,
EC2 95 B3 242 D6
Cowper Terr W10 90 D2
Cowslip Cl UB10 60 A1
Cowslip Rd E18 37 B1
Cowthorpe Rd SW8 269 D2
Cox Ct 3 EN4 2 C1
Coxe Pl HA3 43 A5
Cox Ho W6 264 A6
Cox La
Chessington KT9 214 B4
West Ewell KT19 215 A3
Coxmount Rd SE7 121 D1
Coxs Ave TW17 193 C6
Coxson Way SE1 253 C1
Coxwell Rd
Plumstead SE18 123 B1
South Norwood
SE19 183 C3
Coxwold Path KT9 214 A1
Coysh Ct 8 SW15 157 A6
Crabbs Croft Cl 7
BR6 227 A3
Crab Hill BR3 186 B3
Crabtree Ave
Dagenham RM6 58 D5
Wembley HA0 88 B5
Crabtree Cl E2 95 D5
Crabtree Ct Barnet EN5 1 D1
Temple Mills E15 75 D3
Crabtree Hall SW6 134 C5
Crabtree La SW6 134 D5
Cracknell Cl EN1 6 B6
Craddock Rd EN1 5 D2
Craddock St NW5 71 A2
Cradley Rd SE9 167 B3
Cragie Ho SE1 263 D3
Craig Dr UB8 82 D1
Craigen Ave CR0 206 B1
Craigerne Rd SE3 143 B5
Craig Gdns E18 36 D1
Craig Ho Ealing W13 109 B6
Greenwich SE3 143 B5
Craigholm SE18 144 C4
Craigie Lea N10 31 B1
Craigleith SW15 156 D5
Craigmuir Pk HA0 88 B6
Craignair Rd SW2 160 C4
Craignish Ave SW16 182 B1
Craig Park Rd N18 34 B6
Craig Rd TW10 175 C6
Craig's Ct SW1 250 A4
Craigside KT2 176 D2
Craigton Rd SE9 144 B1
Craigweil Cl HA7 25 D5
Craigweil Dr HA7 25 D5
Craigwell Ave
TW13 150 A1
Craik Ct NW6 91 B5
Crail Row
SE17 117 B2 262 D3
Crales Ho SE18 122 A3
Cramer Ct KT3 199 A6
Cramer St W1 93 A2 238 B3
Cramhurst Ho 3
SM1 218 B3
Crammond Cl W6 264 A5
Cramond Ct TW14 149 C3
Cramonde Ct DA16 146 A3
Crampton Rd SE20 184 C4
Crampton Sch
SE17 116 D1 261 D2
Crampton St
SE17 117 A1 262 A2
Cranberry Cl 2 UB5 84 D5
Cranberry La E16 98 C3
Cranborne Ave
Southall UB2 107 C2
Tolworth KT6, KT9 214 C5
Cranborne Rd IG11 101 B6
Cranborne Waye
Hayes UB4 84 B1
Hayes UB4 106 C6
Cranbourn Alley
WC2 249 D6
Cranbourne Cl
SW16 204 A6
Cranbourne Ct
East Finchley N2 47 D6
2 Edgware HA8 26 D5
Finchley NW7 29 A3
SW11 267 B4
Walton-on-T KT12 194 B2
Wanstead E18 55 B5
Cranbourne Dr HA5 40 D4
Cranbourne Gdns
Ilford IG6 57 A6
Temple Fortune
NW11 47 B4
Cranbourne Rd
Leyton E15 76 A4
London N10 31 B1
Manor Pk E12 78 A3
Northwood HA6 39 D6
Cranbourn Ho 6
SE16 118 B4
Cranbourn Pas 5
SE16 118 B4
Cranbourn St
WC2 115 D6 249 D6
CRANBROOK 56 C1
Cranbrook Cl BR2 209 A3
Cranbrook Coll (Boys)
IG1 78 C6
Cranbrook Ct
8 Brentford
TW8 131 D6
South Croydon CR2 221 C3
Cranbrook Dr
Thames Ditton
KT10 196 A1
Twickenham TW2 151 D3
Cranbrook Ho
5 Hackney E5 74 B3
South Norwood
SE19 183 B2
Cranbrook La N11 31 B6
Cranbrook Mews
E17 53 B4
Cranbrook NW1 232 B5
Cranbrook Pk N22 32 C2
Cranbrook Rd
Chiswick W4 111 C1
Erith DA7 147 B4
Hounslow TW4 129 B1
Ilford IG1, IG2 56 C3
New Barnet EN4 14 B5
South Norwood CR7 183 A1
St Johns SE8 141 C4
Wimbledon SW19 179 A3
Cranbrook Rise IG1 56 B2
Cranbrook St E2 96 D5
Cranbury Rd SW6 135 D3
Crandale Ho 8 E5 74 B3
Crandley Ct SE8 119 A2
Crane Ave Acton W3 111 A6
Isleworth TW7 153 A6
Cranebank TW4 128 B2
Cranebank Mews
TW1 131 A1
Cranebrook TW2 152 A2
Crane Cl
Dagenham RM10 81 C2
Harrow HA2 64 A5
Crane Ct
7 Acton W12 111 C4
Holborn EC4 241 B1
West Ewell KT19 215 A4
Craneford Cl TW2 152 D4
Craneford Way
TW2 152 D4
Crane Gdns UB3 105 D2
Crane Gr N7 72 C2
Crane Ho 24 Bow E3 97 A5
9 Catford BR1 186 B5
Feltham TW13 151 C1
10 Peckham SE15 139 D4
Crane Lodge Rd
TW5 128 B6
Crane Mead Ct
TW1 152 D4
Crane Mead SE16 118 D2
Crane Park Prim Sch
TW13 151 B2
Crane Park Rd TW2 151 D2
Crane Rd
Stanwell TW19 148 C5
Twickenham TW2 152 C3
Cranesbill Cl NW9 45 B6
Cranes Dr KT5 198 B5
Cranes Park Ave KT5,
KT6 198 B5
Cranes Park Cres
KT5 198 B5
Cranes Pk KT5, KT6 198 A4
Crane St
Greenwich SE10 120 B1
6 Peckham SE15 139 D4
Craneswater TW6 127 D5
Craneswater Pk
UB2 107 B1
Cranes Way WD6 11 A6
Crane Way TW2 152 A4
Cranfield Ct
Marylebone NW1 237 B3
2 Woodford IG8 37 A6
Cranfield Dr NW9 27 C3
Cranfield Ho WC1 240 B4
Cranfield Rd SE4 141 B2
CRANFORD 128 C4
Cranford Ave
Bowes Pk N13 32 A5
Stanwell TW19 148 B4
Cranford Cl
Stanwell TW19 148 A4
Wimbledon SW20 178 B3
Cranford Com Coll
TW5 128 B6
Cranford Cotts 8
E1 118 D6
Cranford Ct SM1 218 A4
Cranford Dr UB3 105 D2
Cranford Jun & Inf Schs
TW4 128 B3
Cranford La
Harlington TW6 127 D4
Harlington UB3 127 C5
Hatton TW6 127 D2
Heston TW5 128 C5
Cranford Lo SW19 156 D2
Cranford Park Prim Sch
UB3 105 D2
Cranford Park Rd
UB3 105 D2
Cranford Rise KT10 212 A3
Cranford St E1 118 D6
Cranford Way N8 50 C4
Cranhurst Rd NW2 68 C3
Cranleigh Cl
Bexley DA5 169 D5
Penge SE20 184 B1
Cranleigh Ct
1 Barnet EN5 1 D1
Mitcham CR4 202 B6
Richmond TW9 132 C2
Southall UB1 85 B1
4 Stamford Hill N16 51 C1
Cranleigh Gardens Ind
Est UB1 85 B2
Cranleigh Gdns
Barking IG11 79 B2
Harrow HA3 44 A4
Kingston u T KT2 176 B4
Southall UB1 85 B1
Southgate N21 16 C6
South Norwood
SE25 205 C6
Sutton SM1 217 D6
Cranleigh Hos NW1 232 B3
Cranleigh Ho SW20 178 B1
Cranleigh Mews
SW11 136 D3
Cranleigh Rd
Feltham TW13 171 D6
Harringay N15 51 A4
Merton SW19 201 C6
Thames Ditton KT10 196 A1
Cranleigh St
NW1 93 C5 232 B3
Cranleigh W11 244 C4
Cranley Dene Ct N10 49 B5
Cranley Dr Ilford IG2 57 A2
Ruislip HA4 61 D6
CRANLEY GARDENS
49 B5
Cranley Gdns
London N10 49 B5
Palmers Green N13 16 B1
South Kensington
SW7 114 B1 256 C2
Wallington SM6 219 C1
Cranley Mews
SW7 114 A1 256 B2
Cranley Par 2 SE9 188 A6
Cranley Pl
SW7 114 B2 256 C3
Cranley Rd Ilford IG2 57 A2
Newham E13 99 B2
Cranmer Ave W13 109 B3
Cranmer Cl
Ruislip HA4 40 D1
Stanmore HA7 25 C3
West Barnes SM4 200 D3
Cranmer Ct
Chelsea SW3 257 B3
Church End N3 29 A1
Hampton TW12 173 D5
Kingston u T KT2 175 D6
Cranmere Prim Sch
KT10 196 A1
Cranmer Farm Cl
CR4 202 D5
Cranmer Ho SW11 267 A2
Cranmer Prim Sch
CR4 202 D5
Cranmer Rd
Brixton SW9 138 C5
Croydon CR0 221 A5
Edgware HA8 10 D1
Forest Gate E7 77 B4
Hampton TW12 173 D5
Hayes UB3 83 B1
Kingston u T KT2 176 A5
Mitcham CR4 202 D5
Cranmer Terr SW17 180 B5
Cranmore Ave TW7 130 A5
Cranmore Rd
Catford BR1 164 D1
Elmstead BR7 188 B5
Cranmore Way N10 49 C5
Cranston Cl
Hounslow TW3,
TW4 129 A3
Uxbridge UB10 61 B6
Cranston Ct 6 N20 14 D2
Cranston Gdns E4 35 D4
Cranston Rd SE23 163 A2
Cranswick Rd SE16 118 B1
Crantock Rd SE6 164 A2
Cranwell Cl E3 97 D3
Cranwell Ct
Croydon CR0 222 D6
6 Hendon NW9 27 D3
Cranwell Gr TW17 192 B5
Cranwell Rd TW6 126 D3
Cranwich Ave N21 17 B4
Cranwich Rd N16 51 C2
Cranwood Ct EC1 235 D1
Cranwood St
EC1 95 B4 235 D1
Cranworth Cres 7
E4 20 B3
Cranworth Gdns
SW9 138 C4
Cranworth Ho 6 N7 72 B4
Craster Rd SW2 160 B4
Craston Ho 2 SE5 139 C3
Crathie Rd SE12 165 B5
Crathorne Ho N2 30 B1
Cravan Ave TW13 150 A2
Craven Ave
Ealing W5 109 C6
Southall UB1 85 B2
Craven Cl Hayes UB4 84 A1
Stamford Hill N16 52 A2
Craven Cottage (Fulham
FC) SW6 134 D4
Craven Ct
Dagenham RM6 59 A3
Edgware HA8 26 B6
Harlesden NW10 89 C6
Southall UB1 107 D5
Craven Gdns
Barking IG11 101 C5
Ilford IG6 57 B6
Wimbledon SW19 179 D5
Craven Hill Gdns
W2 114 A6 246 A6
Craven Hill Mews
W2 246 B6
Craven Hill
W2 114 A6 246 B6
Craven Ho
Ealing W5 109 C6
16 Finchley N2 30 B1
2 Mortlake SW14 133 B2
Craven Lo
Bayswater W2 246 B6
Fulham SW6 134 D4
Craven Mews 6
SW11 137 A2
Craven Park Mews
NW10 89 C6
Craven Park Rd
Harlesden NW10 89 C6
South Tottenham N15 52 A3
Craven Pas WC2 250 A4
Craven Pk NW10 89 C6
Craven Rd
Croydon CR0 206 B1
Ealing W5 109 C6
Kingston u T KT2 176 B2
Paddington
W2 92 A1 236 B1
Stonebridge NW10 89 B6
Craven St
WC2 116 A5 250 A4
Craven Terr
W2 114 A6 246 B6
Craven Wlk E5, N16 52 A2
Crawford Ave HA0 65 D3
Crawford Bldgs
NW1 237 B3
Crawford Cl TW7 130 C3
Crawford Ct SE18 146 A6
Crawford Gdns
Edmonton N13 16 D1
Northolt UB5 85 B4
Crawford Mews W1 237 C3

Crawford Pas EC1 ... 241 B5
Crawford Place Dwellings NW1 ... 237 B3
Crawford Pl W1 ... 92 C2 237 B3
Crawford Point 4 E16 ... 98 D1
Crawford Prim Sch SE5 ... 139 A4
Crawford Rd SE5 ... 139 A3
Crawford St
Marylebone W1 ... 92 D2 237 C3
16 Willesden NW10 ... 67 B1
Crawley Rd
Enfield EN1 ... 17 D4
Leyton E10 ... 53 D1
Tottenham N22 ... 33 A1
Crawshay Ct SW9 ... 138 C4
Crawshay Ho 13 N16 ... 73 B4
Crawthew Gr SE22 ... 139 D1
Cray Bldgs DA14 ... 190 C4
Craybrooke Rd DA14 ... 190 B6
Craybury End SE9 ... 167 A2
Crayfields Bsns Pk BR5 ... 190 C2
Crayfields Ind Pk BR5 ... 190 C1
Crayford Cl E6 ... 100 A1
Crayford Ho
Bermondsey SE1 ... 252 D1
5 Lower Holloway N7 ... 72 A4
Crayford Rd N7 ... 72 A4
Crayke Hill KT9 ... 214 A1
Crayle Ho EC1 ... 241 D6
Crayleigh Terr DA14 ... 190 C4
Crayonne Cl TW16 ... 171 C2
Cray Rd Erith DA17 ... 147 C6
Sidcup DA14 ... 190 C4
Crays Par The BR5 ... 190 C1
Crealock Gr IG8 ... 36 D5
Crealock St SW18 ... 157 D5
Creasy Est SE1 ... 263 A5
Crebor St SE22 ... 162 A5
Credenhall Dr BR2 ... 210 B1
Credenhill Ho 2 SE15 ... 140 B5
Credenhill St SW16 ... 181 C4
Crediton Hill NW6 ... 69 D3
Crediton Ho EN3 ... 6 D2
Crediton Rd
Brondesbury Pk NW10 ... 90 D6
Newham E16 ... 99 A1
Crediton Way KT10 ... 213 A3
Credon Rd
Bermondsey SE16 ... 118 B1
Newham E13 ... 99 C5
Creechurch La EC3 ... 243 B1
Creechurch Pl EC3 ... 243 B1
Creed Ct 5 E1 ... 97 A4
Creed Ho SE15 ... 140 B2
Creed La EC4 ... 241 D1
Creek Ho W14 ... 254 B6
CREEKMOUTH ... 101 D2
Creekmouth Ind Pk IG11 ... 101 D3
Creek Rd
Barking IG11 ... 101 D4
East Molesey KT8 ... 196 C5
Greenwich SE10, SE8 ... 141 D6
Creek Road Ind Est SE8 ... 141 D6
Creekside Foyer SE8 ... 141 D6
Creekside SE8 ... 141 D5
Creek The TW16 ... 194 A4
Creeland Gr SE6 ... 163 B3
Crefeld Cl W6 ... 135 A6 264 A5
Creffield Rd W3, W5 ... 110 C6
Creighton Ave
London N2, N10 ... 30 D1
Newham E6 ... 99 D5
Creighton Cl W12 ... 112 B6
Creighton Ho N2 ... 48 C6
Creighton Rd
Ealing W5 ... 109 D3
Kensal Rise NW6 ... 90 D5
Tottenham N17 ... 33 C3
Cremer Bsns Ctr 8 E2 ... 95 D5
Cremer Ho 9 SE8 ... 141 C5
Cremer St E2 ... 95 D5
Cremorne Rd SW10 ... 136 B5 266 C4
Creon Ct 3 SW9 ... 138 C4
Crescent Arc 1 SE10 ... 142 A6
Crescent Court Bsns Ctr 1 E16 ... 98 B3
Crescent Ct
Clapham Pk SW4 ... 159 D6
Crouch End N8 ... 49 D3
Kingston u T KT6 ... 197 D4
14 Sidcup DA15 ... 168 A1
Crescent Dr BR5 ... 211 A3
Crescent EC3 ... 253 C6
Crescent E EN4 ... 2 A5
Crescent Gdns
Ruislip HA4 ... 40 B2
Wimbledon SW19 ... 157 C1
Crescent Gr
London SW4 ... 137 C1
Mitcham CR4 ... 202 C5
Crescent Ho
London SE13 ... 141 D3
5 Wimbledon SW20 ... 178 D2
Crescent La SW4 ... 159 D6
Crescent Mans
Islington N5 ... 72 D3
Notting Hill W11 ... 244 B6
Crescent Par UB10 ... 82 C4
Crescent Pl SW3 ... 257 B4
Crescent Rd
Beckenham BR3 ... 185 D1
Chingford E4 ... 20 C4
Church End N3 ... 29 B2
Crouch End N8 ... 49 D3
Dagenham RM10 ... 81 D5
East Barnet EN4 ... 14 C6
Edmonton N9 ... 18 A3
Enfield EN2 ... 4 D1
Friern Barnet N11 ... 30 D6
Harringay N15 ... 50 D6
Kingston u T KT2 ... 176 D3
Leyton E10 ... 75 D6
Plaistow BR1 ... 187 A3
Shepperton TW17 ... 193 A4
Sidcup DA15 ... 167 D1
Upton Pk E6 ... 99 C6
West Ham E13 ... 99 A6
Wimbledon SW20 ... 178 D2
Woodford E18 ... 37 C2
Wood Green N22 ... 31 D2
Woolwich SE18 ... 122 D2
Crescent Rise
East Barnet EN4 ... 14 C6
3 Finchley N3 ... 29 C2
Wood Green N22 ... 31 D2
Crescent Row EC1 ... 242 A5
Crescent Stables SW15 ... 157 A6
Crescent St N1 ... 72 B1
Crescent The
Acton W3 ... 89 C1
Ashford TW15 ... 170 B5
Barnes SW13 ... 134 A3
Barnet EN5 ... 1 D3
Beckenham BR3 ... 185 C2
Bexley DA5 ... 168 C4
Coombe KT3 ... 177 A1
Dollis Hill NW2 ... 68 B5
East Finchley N2 ... 47 D6
East Molesey KT8 ... 195 C5
Friern Barnet N11 ... 31 A6
Harlington UB7 ... 127 B5
Harrow HA2 ... 42 A1
Ilford IG2 ... 56 C3
Loughton IG10 ... 21 D5
Lower Halliford TW17 ... 193 D2
Sidcup DA14 ... 189 D6
Southall UB1 ... 107 A4
Surbiton KT6 ... 198 A4
Sutton SM1 ... 218 B3
Thornton Heath CR0 ... 205 B3
Walthamstow E17 ... 53 A4
Wembley HA0 ... 65 B6
West Wickham BR4 ... 208 C3
Wimbledon SW19 ... 157 C1
Crescent View IG10 ... 21 D6
Crescentway N12 ... 30 C4
Crescent Way
London SE4 ... 141 C2
Orpington BR6 ... 227 C3
South Norwood SW16 ... 182 C3
Crescent W EN4 ... 2 A5
Crescent Wood Rd SE21, SE26 ... 162 A1
Cresford Rd SW6 ... 135 D4 265 C1
Crespigny Rd NW4 ... 46 B3
Cressage Cl UB1 ... 85 C3
Cressage Ho 9 TW8 ... 132 A6
Cressall Ho 14 E14 ... 119 C3
Cresset Ho 8 E9 ... 74 C2
Cresset Rd E9 ... 74 C2
Cresset St SW4 ... 137 D2
Cressfield Cl NW5 ... 71 A3
Cressida Rd N19 ... 49 D1
Cressingham Ct 1 DA17 ... 125 C3
Cressingham Gr SM1 ... 218 A4
Cressingham Rd
Burnt Oak HA8 ... 27 B3
Lewisham SE13 ... 142 A2
Cressington Cl 4 N16 ... 73 C3
Cress Mews BR1 ... 186 B5
Cresswell Gdns SW5 ... 256 A2
Cresswell Ho HA9 ... 66 A5
Cresswell Pk SE3 ... 142 D2
Cresswell Pl SW10 ... 114 A1 256 B2
Cresswell Rd
Croydon SE25 ... 206 A5
Feltham TW13 ... 173 A6
Twickenham TW1 ... 153 D5
Cresswell Way N21 ... 16 C4
Cressy Ct
Hammersmith W6 ... 112 B3
6 Stepney E1 ... 96 C2
Cressy Ho SW13 ... 134 B2
Cressy Hos 7 E1 ... 96 C2
Cressy Pl E1 ... 96 C2
Cressy Rd NW3 ... 70 D4
Cresta Ct W5 ... 88 B3
Cresta Ho 7 Bow E3 ... 97 C3
Hampstead NW6 ... 70 B1
Crestbrook Ave N13 ... 16 D1
Crestbrook Pl N13 ... 16 D1
Crest Ct NW4 ... 46 C4
Crest Dr EN3 ... 6 C5
Crestfield St N1, WC1 ... 233 B2
Crest Gdns HA4 ... 62 C5
Crest Ho 3 TW15 ... 170 C5
Creston Way KT4 ... 200 D1
Crest Rd
Dollis Hill NW2 ... 68 A6
Hayes BR2 ... 208 D2
South Croydon CR2 ... 222 B1
Crest The
Edmonton N13 ... 32 C6
Finchley N12 ... 29 D4
Hendon NW4 ... 46 C4
Surbiton KT5 ... 198 C4
10 West Norwood SW27 ... 182 D5
Crest View Dr BR5 ... 211 A4
Crestview NW5 ... 71 B5
Crest View HA5 ... 40 D5
Crestway SW15 ... 156 B5
Crestwood Way TW4 ... 151 A6
Creswell Dr BR3 ... 207 D4
Creswick Ct W3 ... 110 D6
Creswick Rd W3 ... 110 D6
Creswick Wlk
7 Bow E3 ... 97 C4
Temple Fortune NW11 ... 47 B5
Creton St SE18 ... 122 C3
Crewdson Rd SW9 ... 138 C5
Crewe Pl NW10 ... 89 D4
Crewkerne Ct SW11 ... 266 D2
Crews St E14 ... 119 C2
Crewys Rd
Child's Hill NW2 ... 69 B6
London SE15 ... 140 B3
Crichton Ave SM6 ... 219 D4
Crichton Rd SM5 ... 218 D1
Crichton St SW8 ... 137 C3
Cricket Ct E6 ... 100 B4
Cricketers Arms Rd EN2 ... 5 A3
Cricketers Cl
Chessington KT9 ... 213 D4
Oakwood N14 ... 15 C4
Cricketers Mews 4 SW18 ... 157 D6
Cricketers Terr SM5 ... 218 C5
Cricketers Wlk SE26 ... 184 C5
Cricketfield Rd E5 ... 74 B4
Cricket Gn CR4 ... 202 D5
Cricket Green Sch CR4 ... 202 C6
Cricket Ground Rd BR7 ... 188 D2
Cricket La BR3 ... 185 A4
Cricket Row N2 ... 48 B6
Cricklade Ave SW2 ... 160 B2
CRICKLEWOOD ... 68 D4
Cricklewood Broadway NW2 ... 68 D4
Cricklewood La NW2 ... 69 B5
Cricklewood Sta NW2 ... 68 D4
Cridland St E15 ... 98 D6
Crieff Ct 3 TW11 ... 175 C3
Crieff Rd SW18 ... 158 A5
Criffel Ave SW2 ... 159 D3
Crimscott St SE1 ... 117 C3 263 B5
Crimsworth Rd SW8 ... 137 D5 269 D3
Crinan St N1 ... 94 A5 233 B4
Cringle St SW8 ... 137 C5 269 A4
Cripplegate St EC1 ... 242 B4
Cripps Gn UB4 ... 84 B3
Crispe Ho
4 Barking IG11 ... 101 B5
Islington N1 ... 233 D5
Crispen Rd TW13 ... 173 A6
Crispian Cl NW10 ... 67 C4
Crispin Cl SM6 ... 220 A6
Crispin Cres SM6 ... 219 D6
Crispin Ct SE17 ... 263 A3
Crispin Pl E1 ... 243 C4
Crispin Rd HA8 ... 27 A4
Crispin St E1 ... 95 D2 243 C3
Crispin Way UB8 ... 82 B3
Crisp Rd W6 ... 112 C1
Cristowe Rd SW6 ... 135 B3
Criterion Bldgs KT7 ... 197 B2
Criterion Mews N19 ... 71 D6
Crittall's Cnr DA14 ... 190 C3
Crittenden Lo BR4 ... 207 C1
Crockerton Rd SW17 ... 158 D2
Crockham Way SE9 ... 188 C6
Crocus Cl CR0 ... 206 D1
Crocus Field EN5 ... 13 B5
Croft Ave BR4 ... 208 A1
Croft Cl Edgware NW7 ... 11 C1
Elmstead BR7 ... 188 B5
Erith DA17 ... 125 B1
Harlington UB7 ... 127 A5
Hillingdon UB10 ... 60 C1
Croft Ct London SE13 ... 164 A5
Ruislip HA4 ... 39 D1
Croftdown Rd NW5 ... 71 B5
Croft End Cl KT9 ... 214 B5
Crofters Cl TW7 ... 152 B6
Crofters Ct 9 SE8 ... 119 A2
Crofters Way NW1 ... 93 D6 232 C6
Croft Gdns
Ealing W7 ... 109 A4
Ruislip HA4 ... 39 D1
Croft Ho
Putney SW15 ... 157 A5
11 West Kilburn W10 ... 91 A4
Croft Lodge Cl IG8 ... 37 B4
Croft Mews 3 N12 ... 14 A1
CROFTON ... 227 B6
Crofton Ave
Chiswick W4 ... 133 B5
Orpington BR6 ... 227 A6
Sidcup DA5 ... 168 D4
Crofton Gate Way SE4 ... 163 A6
Crofton Gr E4 ... 36 B6
Crofton Inf Sch BR5 ... 211 B2
Crofton Jun Sch BR5 ... 211 B2
Crofton La BR5, BR6 ... 211 B2
Crofton L Ctr SE4 ... 163 C5
Crofton Park Rd SE4 ... 163 B5
Crofton Park Sta SE4 ... 163 A6
Crofton Rd
Camberwell SE5 ... 139 C3
Locksbottom BR6 ... 226 C5
Newham E13 ... 99 B3
Crofton Roman Villa* BR6 ... 227 C6
Crofton Sch SE4 ... 163 C5
Crofton Terr
Homerton E5 ... 75 A3
Richmond TW9 ... 132 B1
Crofton Way
Enfield EN2 ... 4 C3
New Barnet EN5 ... 13 D5
Croft Rd
Carshalton SM1 ... 218 C3
Enfield EN3 ... 7 A4
Merton SW19 ... 180 A3
Plaistow BR1 ... 187 A4
South Norwood SW16 ... 182 C3
Crofts Ho 21 E2 ... 96 A5
Croftside The 3 SE25 ... 206 A6
Crofts La N22 ... 32 C3
Crofts Rd HA1 ... 43 A4
Crofts St E1 ... 118 A6
Crofts The TW17 ... 193 C5
Croft St SE8 ... 119 A2
Croft The Barnet EN5 ... 1 A1
Chingford E4 ... 20 C2
Ealing W5 ... 88 A2
Edgware HA8 ... 26 D3
Harlesden NW10 ... 89 D5
Heston TW5 ... 129 A5
New Malden KT3 ... 199 C4
Pinner HA5 ... 41 B2
Ruislip HA4 ... 62 C4
Wembley HA0 ... 65 C3
Croft Villas HA1 ... 43 A3
Croft Way
Richmond TW10 ... 153 B1
Croft Way *continued*
Sidcup DA15 ... 167 C1
Crogsland Rd NW1 ... 71 A1
Croham Cl CR2 ... 221 C1
Croham Hurst Sch CR2 ... 221 D3
Croham Manor Rd CR2 ... 221 C2
Croham Mount CR2 ... 221 C1
Croham Park Ave CR2 ... 221 D3
Croham Rd CR2 ... 221 C3
Croham Valley Rd CR2 ... 222 B1
Croindene Rd SW16 ... 182 A2
Crokesley Ho 2 HA8 ... 27 A1
Cromartie Rd N19 ... 49 D2
Cromarty Ct 7 BR1 ... 187 C1
Cromarty Ho 8 E1 ... 97 A2
Cromarty Rd HA8 ... 10 D2
Cromberdale Ct N17 ... 34 A2
Crombie Cl IG4 ... 56 B4
Crombie Mews 5 SW11 ... 136 C3
Crombie Rd DA15 ... 167 B3
Cromdale Ct N16 ... 51 D2
Crome Ho UB5 ... 85 A5
Cromer Cl UB8 ... 83 A1
Cromer Ct
Streatham SW16 ... 160 A1
Wandsworth SW18 ... 157 B5
Crome Rd NW10 ... 67 C2
Cromer Mans 6 SM1 ... 217 D3
Cromer Pl 5 BR6 ... 211 B1
Cromer Rd Barnet EN5 ... 2 A2
Croydon SE25 ... 206 B6
Dagenham RM6 ... 59 A3
Harlington TW6 ... 126 C3
Leyton E10 ... 54 B2
Streatham SW17 ... 181 A4
Tottenham N17 ... 34 A1
Woodford IG8 ... 37 A6
Cromer Road Prim Sch EN5 ... 2 A2
Cromer St WC1 ... 94 A4 233 B1
Cromer Terr
Dalston E8 ... 74 A3
3 Ilford RM6 ... 58 B4
Cromer Villas Rd SW18 ... 157 B5
Cromford Cl BR6 ... 227 C5
Cromford Path 1 E5 ... 74 D4
Cromford Rd SW18 ... 157 C6
Cromford Way KT3 ... 177 B2
Cromlix Cl BR7 ... 188 D1
Crompton Ct SW3 ... 257 A4
Crompton Ho
Borough The SE1 ... 262 B5
Paddington W2 ... 236 C5
South Lambeth SW8 ... 269 B1
Crompton Pl EN3 ... 7 C5
Crompton St W2 ... 92 B3 236 C5
Cromwell Ave
Bromley BR2 ... 209 B5
Hammersmith W6 ... 112 B2
Highgate N6 ... 49 B1
New Malden KT3 ... 199 D4
Cromwell Cl
Acton W3 ... 111 A5
Bromley BR2 ... 209 B5
East Finchley N2 ... 48 B5
2 Gunnersbury W4 ... 110 D1
Walton-on-T KT12 ... 194 B1
Cromwell Cres SW5 ... 113 C2 255 A4
Cromwell Ct
Enfield EN3 ... 18 D6
15 Kingston u T KT2 ... 176 C3
Cromwell Ctr
Barking IG11 ... 102 A4
North Acton NW10 ... 89 B4
Cromwell Ctr The RM8 ... 59 B2
Cromwell Ct HA0 ... 88 A5
Cromwell Est E10 ... 53 A1
Cromwell Gdns SW7 ... 114 B3 256 D5
Cromwell Gr W6 ... 112 C3
Cromwell Ho
Battersea SW11 ... 268 B1
2 Croydon CR0 ... 220 D5
Muswell Hill N10 ... 31 B3
Putney SW15 ... 134 A1
Cromwell Hospl SW5 ... 113 D2 255 C4
Cromwell Lo
Barking IG11 ... 79 C3
40 Bethnal Green E1 ... 96 C3
Cromwell Mans SW5 ... 255 B4
Cromwell Mews SW7 ... 256 D4
Cromwell Pl
5 Acton W3 ... 111 A5
Cromwell Pl *continued*
Highgate N6 ... 49 B1
Mortlake SW14 ... 133 A2
South Kensington SW7 ... 114 B2 256 D4
Cromwell Rd
Beckenham BR3 ... 207 A6
Brixton SW9 ... 138 D4
Feltham TW13 ... 150 B3
Finchley N3 ... 30 A2
Hayes UB3 ... 83 B1
Hounslow TW3 ... 129 C1
Kingston u T KT2 ... 176 A2
Muswell Hill N10 ... 31 A3
South Kensington SW7 ... 256 B4
Teddington TW11 ... 175 A4
Thornton Heath CR0 ... 205 B2
Upton E7 ... 77 C1
Walthamstow E17 ... 54 A4
Walton-on-T KT12 ... 194 B1
Wembley HA0 ... 88 A5
Wimbledon SW19 ... 179 D5
Worcester Pk KT4 ... 215 C5
Cromwell St TW3 ... 129 C1
Cromwell Trad Ctr IG11 ... 101 C4
Cromwell Twr EC2 ... 242 B4
Crondace Rd SW6 ... 135 C4 265 B1
Crondall Ct 7 N1 ... 95 C5
Crondall Ho SW15 ... 156 A3
Crondall Pl 15 N1 ... 95 C5
Crondall St N1 ... 95 C5
Crone Ct 5 NW6 ... 91 B5
Cronin St SE15 ... 139 D5
CROOKED BILLET ... 178 C4
Crooked Billet
Chingford E4 ... 35 C3
Wimbledon SW19 ... 178 C4
Crooked Billet Yd 18 E2 ... 95 C4
Crooked Usage N3 ... 47 A6
Crooke Rd SE8 ... 119 A1
Crookham Rd SW6 ... 135 B4 264 C1
Crook Log DA6 ... 146 D1
Crook Log L Ctr DA7 ... 146 D2
Crook Log Prim Sch DA6 ... 146 D1
Crookston Rd SE9 ... 144 C2
Croombs Rd E16 ... 99 C2
Croom's Hill Gr SE10 ... 142 A5
Croom's Hill SE10 ... 142 B5
Cropley Ct N1 ... 235 C4
Cropley St N1 ... 95 B5 235 C4
Croppath Rd RM10 ... 81 C4
Cropthorne Ct W9 ... 229 B1
Crosbie Ho 20 E17 ... 53 D6
Crosbie 10 NW9 ... 27 D1
Crosby Cl TW13 ... 173 A6
Crosby Ct
Borough The SE1 ... 252 C2
East Finchley N2 ... 48 A5
7 New Southgate N11 ... 31 B6
Crosby Ho
18 Cubitt Town E14 ... 120 A3
Forest Gate E7 ... 77 A2
Crosby Rd
Dagenham RM10 ... 103 D6
Upton E7 ... 77 A2
Crosby Row SE1 ... 117 B4 252 C2
Crosby Sq EC3 ... 243 A2
Crosby Wlk
3 Dalston E8 ... 73 D2
Streatham SE24 ... 160 C4
Crosfield Ct 3 W10 ... 90 D1
Crosfield Ho W11 ... 244 A5
Crosier Cl SE3 ... 144 A3
Crosier Rd UB10 ... 61 A4
Crosier Way HA4 ... 61 C5
Crosland Pl 5 SW11 ... 137 A2
Crossbow Ho
Ealing W13 ... 109 B5
15 Shoreditch N1 ... 95 C6
Crossbrook Rd SE3 ... 144 A2
Cross Cl SE15 ... 140 B3
Cross Ct London SE5 ... 139 B2
11 Thamesmead SE28 ... 124 B6
Cross Deep Gdns TW1 ... 152 D2
Cross Deep TW1 ... 153 A2
Crossfield Rd
Hampstead NW3 ... 70 B2
London N17 ... 51 A6
Crossfield St SE8 ... 141 C5
Crossford St SW9 ... 138 B3

Crossgate
Edgware HA8 10 C1
Wembley UB6 65 B2
Crossharbour Sta E14 119 D3
Cross Ho N8 50 B5
Cross Keys Cl
5 Edmonton N9 18 A2
Marylebone W1 238 B3
Cross La
City of London EC3 253 A5
Hornsey N8 50 B5
Cross Lances Rd TW3 129 D1
Crossland Rd CR7 204 D3
Crosslands Ave
Ealing W5 110 B5
Southall UB2 107 B1
Crosslands Rd KT19 215 B2
Cross La DA5 169 B4
Crossleigh Ct
3 New Cross SE14 141 B5
Streatham SW16 181 B6
Crosslet St SE17 262 D4
Crosslet Vale SE10 141 D4
Crossley St N7 72 C2
Crossman Hos 19 SW12 160 A4
Crossmead Ave UB6 85 C4
Crossmead SE9 166 B3
Crossmount Ho 13 SE5 139 A5
Crossness Rd IG11 101 D4
Cross Rd Belmont HA3 25 A1
Camberwell SE5 139 C3
Chingford E4 20 C3
Croydon CR0 205 B1
Enfield EN1 5 C1
Feltham TW13 173 A6
Finchley N2 30 C1
Friern Barnet N11 31 B5
Harrow HA1 42 B4
Ilford RM6 58 C2
Keston Mark BR2 226 A6
Kingston u T KT2 176 B3
Merton SW19 179 C3
Romford RM7 59 C6
Sidcup DA14 190 B6
South Harrow HA2 63 D5
Sutton SM1 218 B3
Wood Green N22 32 C3
Cross St
2 Edmonton N18 34 A5
Hampton TW12 174 A5
Islington N1 94 D6 234 D6
Mortlake SW13 133 C2
Crossthwaite Ave SE5, SE24 139 B1
Crosstrees Ho 7 E14 119 C3
Crosswall EC3 117 D6 253 C6
Crossway Ct SE4 141 A3
Crossway
Dagenham RM8 80 C5
Ealing W13 87 A3
Enfield EN1 17 C4
Finchley N12 30 B4
Hayes UB3 106 A5
Hendon NW9 45 D5
Kingsland E8, N16 73 C3
Crossway Par N22 32 D3
Crossway
Petts Wood BR5 211 B4
Pinner HA5 22 B1
Ruislip HA4 62 C4
Crossways Acad SE4 141 A3
Crossways TW16 171 D3
Crossways Par CR2 223 B1
Crossways Rd
Beckenham BR3 207 C5
Mitcham CR4 203 B6
Crossways
South Croydon CR2 223 B1
Sutton SM2 218 B1
Crossways The
Heston TW5 129 B5
Wembley HA9 66 C6
Crossway SE28 102 D1
Crossway The SE9 165 D2
Cross Way The HA3 24 C1
Crossway The
Hillingdon UB10 82 B5
Tottenham N22 32 D3
Crossway
West Barnes KT3, SW20 200 C5
Woodford IG8 37 C6
Crosswell Cl TW17 171 A1
Croston St E8 96 A6
Crothall Cl N13 16 B1
Crouch Ave IG11 102 B5
Crouch Cl BR3 185 C4
Crouch Croft SE9 166 C1
CROUCH END 49 D3
Crouch End Hill N8 49 D2
Crouch Hall Ct N19 50 A1
Crouch Hall Rd N8 49 D3
Crouch Hill N4, N8, N19 50 A2
Crouch Hill Sta N4 50 B2
Crouchmans Cl SE21, SE26 162 A1
Crouch Rd NW10 67 B1
Crowborough Ct W13 109 C6
Crowborough Path WD19 22 D6
Crowborough Rd SW17 181 A5
Crowden Way SE28 124 C6
Crowder Cl N12 30 A3
Crowder St E1 118 B6
Crowfield Ho N5 73 A4
Crowfoot Cl
Hackney Wick E9 75 B3
Woolwich SE28 123 C5
Crowhurst Cl SW9 138 C3
Crowhurst Ct N17 34 B2
Crowhurst Ho 21 SW9 138 B3
Crowhurst SE25 206 A6
Crowland Ave UB3 105 D2
Crowland Gdns N14 16 A4
Crowland Ho NW8 229 A5
Crowland Prim Sch N15 52 A4
Crowland Rd
South Norwood CR7 205 B5
South Tottenham N15 51 D4
Crowlands Ave RM7 59 D3
Crowland Terr N1 73 B1
Crowland Wlk SM4 202 A3
Crow La RM7, RM8 59 D2
Crowley Cres CR0 220 C3
Crowline Wlk 1 N1 73 A2
Crowmarsh Gdns SE23 162 C4
Crown Arc KT1 175 D1
Crown Bldgs 4 E4 20 B3
Crownbourne Ct SM1 217 D4
Crown Cl Bow E3 97 C6
Edgware NW7 11 D2
Hampstead NW6 69 D2
Hayes UB3 105 D4
Crown Close Bsns Ctr 12 E3 97 C6
Crown Cl
Walton-on-T KT12 194 C2
Wood Green N22 32 C2
Crown Ct
Bromley BR1 209 D4
City of London EC4 242 B1
Harrow HA2 42 C1
Lee SE12 165 B5
11 Muswell Hill N10 31 A3
4 Putney SW15 134 D1
St Giles WC2 240 B1
St John's Wood NW8 230 B1
3 Twickenham TW1 153 B4
Crowndale Ct NW1 232 C4
Crowndale Rd NW1 93 C5 232 B4
Crown Dale SE19 183 A5
Crowne Ho SE1 252 B3
Crownfield Ave IG2 57 C4
Crownfield Rd E15 76 B4
Crowngate Ho 33 E3 97 B5
Crown Hill CR0 221 A5
Crownhill Rd NW10 89 D6
Crown Ho Ruislip HA4 40 A1
Wembley HA9 66 B3
Woolwich SE18 123 A2
Crown La
Bromley Comm BR2 209 D4
Chislehurst BR7 189 A2
Merton SM4 201 C6
Crown Lane Gdns SE27 182 C5
Crown Lane Prim Sch SE27 182 D5
Crown Lane Spur BR2 209 D3
Crown La Osidge N14 15 C3
South Norwood SE19, SW16 182 C5
Crownleigh Ct SW2 160 C6
Crown Lo
Chelsea SW3 257 B3
Finchley N3 29 B1
Crownmead Way RM7 59 D5
Crown Mews
2 Newham E13 99 C6
9 Stepney E1 96 D2
Crown Mill CR4 202 C4
Crown Office Row EC4 251 A6
Crown Par
London N14 15 C3
Morden SM4 201 D5
Crown Pas
Kingston u T KT1 175 D1
St James SW1 249 B3
Crown Pl
Broadgate EC2 243 A4
Kentish Town NW5 71 B2
Crown Point Par SE19 182 D4
Crown Rd Enfield EN1 6 B2
Ilford IG6 57 B5
Kingston u T KT3 177 A2
Morden SM4 201 D5
Muswell Hill N10 31 A3
Ruislip HA4 62 D3
Sutton SM1 217 D4
Twickenham TW1 153 B5
Crown Reach SW1 259 D1
Crown St Acton W3 110 D5
Camberwell SE5 139 A5
Dagenham RM10 81 D2
Harrow HA2 42 C1
Crownstone Ct 1 SW2 160 C6
Crownstone Rd SW2 160 C6
Crown Terr TW9 132 B1
Crown Trad Ctr UB3 105 C4
Crowntree Cl TW7 130 D6
Crown Way UB7 104 B5
Crown Wlk HA9 66 B5
Crown Wood La SE18 144 D3
Crown Woods Sch SE9 167 A6
Crown Woods Way SE9 167 B6
Crown Yard TW3 130 A2
Crowshott Ave HA7 25 D2
Crows Rd
Barking IG11 78 D2
Mill Meads E15 98 B4
Crowther Ave TW8 110 A2
Crowther Cl SW6 135 B6 264 D5
Crowther Rd SE25 206 A5
Crowthorne Cl SW18 157 B3
Crowthorne Rd W10 90 D1
Croxall Ho KT12 194 C3
Croxden Cl HA8 44 C6
Croxden Wlk SM4 202 A3
Croxford Gdns N22 32 D3
Croxley Cl BR5 190 B1
Croxley Gn BR5 190 B2
Croxley Rd W9 91 B4
Croxted Cl SE21 161 A4
Croxted Rd SE21, SE24 161 B3
Croxteth Ho 11 SW8 137 D3
Croxton 17 KT1 176 C1
Croyde Ave
Greenford UB6 86 A4
Hayes UB3 105 C2
Croyde Cl DA15 167 B4
Croyden Ct HA0 65 D2
CROYDON 221 B5
Croydon Airport Ind Est CR0 220 B2
Croydon Coll Annexe CR0 205 B1
Croydon Coll (Selhurst Tertiary Ctr) SE25 205 B4
Croydon Coll CR0 221 B6
Croydon Flyover The CR0 221 A5
Croydon Gr CR0 204 D1
Croydon Ho
Lambeth SE1 251 B2
Thornton Heath CR0 204 B3
Croydon Rd
Bandonhill CR0, SM5, SM6 219 C5
Beckenham BR3 207 A6
Coney Hall BR2, BR4 224 D5
Harlington TW6 126 D2
Croydon Rd Ind Est BR3 206 D5
Croydon Rd
Keston Mark BR2, BR4, BR6 225 C5
Mitcham CR0, CR4 203 C4
Newham E13 98 D3
Penge SE20 184 C2
Waddon CR0 220 B4
Croydon N17 33 B1
Croydon Valley Trade Pk 2 CR0 204 A2
Croyland Rd N9 18 A3
Croylands Dr KT6 198 A2
Croysdale Ave TW16 194 A6
Crozier Ho
Blackheath Pk SE3 143 B2
South Lambeth SW8 270 C3
Crozier Terr E9 74 D3
Crucible Cl RM6 58 B3
Crucifix La SE1 117 C4 253 A2
Cruden Ho 15 Bow E3 97 B5
11 Camberwell SE17 138 D6
Cruden St N1 94 D6 234 D5
Cruickshank St WC1 234 A2
Cruikshank Ho NW8 230 B4
Cruikshank Rd E15 76 C3
Crummock Gdns NW9 45 C4
Crumpsall St SE2 124 C2
Crundale Ave NW9 44 C4
Crunden Rd CR2 221 B1
Crusader Gdns CR0 221 C5
Crusader Ho EC1 241 C5
Crusader Ind Est N4 51 A3
Crusoe Ct E11 76 D5
Crusoe House Sch N1 95 B4 235 C2
Crusoe Mews N16 73 B6
Crusoe Rd CR4 180 D3
Crutched Friars EC3 117 C6 253 B6
Crutchfield La KT12 194 B1
Crutchley Rd SE6 164 C2
Crystal Ct SE19 183 D5
Crystal Ctr The 1 HA1 42 D4
Crystal Ho SE18 123 D1
CRYSTAL PALACE 184 A5
Crystal Palace Mus* SE19 183 D4
Crystal Palace National Sports Ctr SE20 184 A4
Crystal Palace Par SE19 183 D5
Crystal Palace Park Rd SE26 184 B5
Crystal Palace Rd SE22 162 A6
Crystal Palace Sta SE19 184 A4
Crystal Palace Station Rd SE19 184 A4
Crystal Terr SE19 183 B4
Crystal View Ct BR1 186 B6
Crystal Way
Dagenham RM8 58 C1
Harrow HA1 42 D4
Crystal Wharf N1 234 D3
Cuba Dr EN3 6 C3
Cuba St E14 119 C4
Cubitt Bldg SW1 258 C1
Cubitt Ho 4 SW4 159 C5
Cubitt Sq UB2 108 A5
Cubitt St WC1 94 B4 233 D1
Cubitt Terr SW4 137 C2
CUBITT TOWN 120 A2
Cubitt Town Jun & Inf Sch E14 120 A3
Cuckoo Ave W7 86 C3
Cuckoo Dene W7 86 B2
Cuckoo Hall La N9 18 D4
Cuckoo Hall Prim Sch N9 18 C4
Cuckoo Hill Dr HA5 40 C6
Cuckoo Hill HA5 40 C6
Cuckoo Hill Rd HA5 40 D5
Cuckoo La W7 108 C6
Cuda's Cl KT19 215 D4
Cuddington Ave KT19, KT4 215 D5
Cuddington Com Prim Sch KT4 215 D5
Cuddington SE17 262 B4
Cudham La N BR6 227 C1
Cudham St SE6 164 A4
Cudworth Ho SW8 269 B1
Cudworth St E1 96 B3
Cuff Cres SE9 165 D5
Cuffley Ho 3 W10 90 C2
Cuff Point 12 E2 95 D4
Culand Ho SE17 263 A3
Culford Gdns SW3 114 D2 257 D3
Culford Gr N1 73 C2
Culford Mans SW3 257 D3
Culford Mews N1 73 C2
Culford Rd
Kingsland N1 73 C2
Shoreditch N1 95 C6
Culgaith Gdns EN2 4 A1
Culham Ho
21 Paddington W2 91 C2
Culham Ho *continued*
33 Shoreditch E2 95 D4
Cullen Ho W9 91 B5
Cullen Way NW10 89 A3
Culling Rd SE16 118 C3
Cullington Cl HA3 43 A5
Cullingworth Rd NW10 68 B3
Culloden Cl 21 SE16 118 A1
Culloden Prim Sch E14 98 A1
Culloden Rd EN2 4 D3
Cullum St EC3 253 A6
Culmington Mans W13 109 C6
Culmington Par W13 109 C6
Culmington Rd
Ealing W13, W5 109 C5
South Croydon CR2 221 A1
Culmore Rd SE15 140 C5
Culmstock Rd SW11 159 A6
Culpepper Cl N18 34 B5
Culpepper Ct SE11 261 A4
Culross Bldgs NW1 233 A4
Culross Cl N15 51 A5
Culross St W1 115 A6 248 A5
Culsac Rd KT6 214 A6
Culver Ct SW18 157 D5
Culverden Rd SW12 159 C2
Culver Gr HA7 25 C1
Culverhouse Gdns SW16 160 B1
Culverhouse WC1 240 C3
Culverin Ct 1 N7 72 B3
Culverlands Cl HA7 25 B6
Culverlands Ct N20 14 B3
Culverley Rd SE6 164 A3
Culvers Ave SM5 218 D6
Culvers House Prim Sch CR4 203 A1
Culvers Retreat SM5 218 D6
Culverstone Cl BR2 208 D4
Culvers Way SM5 218 D6
Culvert Ct SW11 137 A3
Culverton Ct 8 DA14 190 A6
Culvert Pl SW11 137 A3
Culvert Rd
London SW11 136 D3
South Tottenham N15 51 C4
Culworth Ho NW8 230 A4
Culworth St NW8 230 A3
Cumber Ho SW18 157 C3
Cumberland Ave
Falconwood DA16 145 D1
Wembley NW10 88 D4
Cumberland Bsns Pk NW10 88 D4
Cumberland Cl
Dalston E8 73 D2
2 Twickenham TW1 153 B5
8 Wimbledon SW20 178 D3
Cumberland Cres W14 254 B4
Cumberland Ct
4 Croydon CR0 205 B1
7 Finchley N3 29 B1
Harrow HA1 42 C6
Marylebone W1 237 D1
Woodford IG8 37 B3
Cumberland Dr
Chessington KT9 214 B5
Erith DA7 147 A5
Hinchley Wood KT10 213 A6
Cumberland Gate W1 114 D6 247 D6
Cumberland Gdns
Church End NW4 29 A1
Finsbury WC1 234 A2
Cumberland Ho
Edmonton N9 18 C3
Kingston u T KT2 176 D3
Paddington W9 236 A5
1 Putney SW15 156 C4
Woolwich SE28 123 B4
Cumberland Mans
Marylebone W1 237 C2
7 West Hampstead NW6 69 C3
Cumberland Market NW1 93 B4 231 D2
Cumberland Mills Sq E14 120 B1
Cumberland Park Ind Est NW10 90 A4
Cumberland Pk W3 111 A6
Cumberland Pl
Catford SE6 164 D3
Regent's Pk NW1 231 C2
Sunbury TW16 194 A5
Cumberland Rd
Acton W3 111 A6
Ashford TW15 148 A1
Barnes SW13 134 A4
Beckenham BR2 208 D6
Croydon SE25 206 B3
Edmonton N9 18 C3
Hanwell W7 108 D4
Harrow HA1 41 D4
Higham Hill E17 35 A1
Manor Pk E12 77 D4
Newham E13 99 B3
Richmond TW9 132 C5
Stanmore HA7, HA8 44 B6
Wood Green N22 32 B1
Cumberland Sch E13 99 C3
Cumberland St SW1 115 B1 258 D2
Cumberland Terrace Mews NW1 231 C3
Cumberland Terr NW1 231 C3
Cumberland Villas W3 111 A6
Cumberland Wharf 12 SE16 118 C4
Cumberlow Ave SE25 206 A6
Cumbernauld Gdns TW16 171 D5
Cumberton Rd N17 33 B2
Cumbrae Gdns KT6 213 D6
Cumbrian Gdns NW2 69 A6
Cuming Mus* SE17 262 A3
Cumming St N1 233 D3
Cumnor Cl 23 SW9 138 B3
Cumnor Gdns KT17 216 A2
Cumnor Rd SM2 218 A2
Cunard Cres N21 17 B5
Cunard Pl EC3 243 B1
Cunard Rd NW10 89 B4
Cunard Wlk 3 SE16 119 A2
Cundy Rd E16 99 C1
Cundy St SW1 115 A2 258 B3
Cunliffe Rd KT19 215 D4
Cunliffe St SW16 181 C4
Cunningham Cl
Dagenham RM6 58 C4
West Wickham BR4 223 D6
Cunningham Ct
Harrow HA1 42 B4
Paddington W2 236 C5
Cunningham Ho 16 SE5 139 B5
Cunningham Pk HA1 42 B4
Cunningham Pl NW8 92 B3 236 C6
Cunningham Rd N15 52 A5
Cunnington St W4 111 A2
Cupar Rd SW11 268 B2
Cupola Cl BR1 187 B5
Cureton St SW1 115 D2 259 D3
Curie Gdns NW9 27 C1
Curie Ho 1 HA9 67 A5
Curlew Cl SE28 124 D6
Curlew Ct KT6 214 C5
Curlew Ho
Brockley SE4 141 A1
Enfield EN3 18 D6
2 Peckham SE15 139 D4
Curlew St SE1 117 D4 253 D2
Curlew Way UB4 84 D2
Curness St SE13 142 A1
Curnick's La SE27 183 A6
Curran Ave
Bexley DA15 167 D6
Hackbridge SM6 219 A5
Curran Ho SW3 257 A3
Currey Rd UB6 64 B2
Curricle St W3 111 C5
Currie Hill Cl SW19 179 B6
Currie Ho 13 SW12 159 D4
Curry Rise NW7 28 D4
Cursitor St EC4 94 C1 241 A2
Curtain Pl EC2 243 B6
Curtain Rd EC2 95 C3 243 B6
Curthwaite Gdns EN2 15 D6
Curtis Dr W3 89 B1
Curtis Field Rd SW16 182 C6
Curtis Ho
7 London N11 31 C5
Walworth SE17 262 C2
Curtis La HA0 66 A3
Curtis Rd
Twickenham TW4 151 B4
West Ewell KT19 215 A4
Curtis St SE1 117 D2 263 C4

urtis Way
Bermondsey SE1 263 C4
7 Thamesmead SE28 124 B6
urtlington Ho 8 HA8 27 A1
urve Bldg The SE4 163 B6
urve The
Ealing W5 109 D4
Shepherd's Bush W12 112 A6
urwen Ave E7 77 B4
urwen & New Acad Gall* W1 239 C3
urwen Prim Sch E13 99 A5
urwen Rd W12 112 A4
urzon Ave
Enfield EN3 18 D6
Stanmore HA7 25 A2
urzon Cl BR6 227 B4
urzon Cres
Barking IG11 101 D4
Willesden NW10 67 C1
urzon Ct SE9 167 A1
urzon Gate W1 248 B3
urzon Ho W5 87 B3
urzon Pl HA5 40 C4
urzon Rd Ealing W5 87 B3
Muswell Hill N10 31 B1
Thornton Heath CR7 204 C3
urzon Sq W1 248 B3
urzon St
W1 115 B5 248 C4
usack Cl TW1 174 D6
ustance Ho N1 235 C3
ustance St N1 235 C2
USTOM HOUSE 121 C6
ustom House EC3 117 C6 253 A5
ustom House for ExCeL Sta E16 121 B6
ustom House Reach SE16 119 B3
utbush Ho N7 71 D3
utcombe Rd SE5 139 A3
uthberga Cl IG11 79 A1
uthbert Gdns SE25 205 C6
uthbert Harrowing Ho EC1 242 A5
uthbert Ho W2 236 C4
uthbert Rd
Croydon CR0 220 D6
8 Edmonton N18 34 A6
Walthamstow E17 54 A6
uthbert St W2 236 C5
uthill Wlk 3 SE5 139 B4
utlers Gdns Arc EC2 243 B2
utlers Gdns EC2 243 B2
utlers Sq E14 119 C2
utler St EC2 243 B2
ut The SE1 116 C4 251 B2
utty Sark Ho 10 E14 119 D2
utty Sark Ret Development SE10 142 A6
utty Sark* SE10 142 A6
utty Sark Sta SE10 142 A6
uxton BR5 211 A4
uxton Cl DA6 169 A6
uxton Ho SE17 263 B2
yclamen Cl 4 TW12 173 C4
yclamen Way KT19 215 A3
yclops Mews 12 E14 119 C2
ygnet Ave TW14 150 D4
ygnet Cl NW10 67 B3
ygnet Ct EN3 7 A4
ygnet Ho
Harrow HA7 24 D4
St John's Wood NW8 229 A6
ygnet House N 18 E14 97 D1
ygnet House S 19 E14 97 D1
ygnet St E1 243 D6
ygnets The TW13 173 A6
ygnet Way UB4 84 D2
ygnus Bsns Ctr NW10 67 D2
ymbeline Ct 6 HA1 42 D3
yna Ct 5 E11 55 A3
ynthia St N1 233 D3
yntra Pl 8 E8 74 B1
ypress Ave
London N2 47 D6
Twickenham TW2 152 A4
ypress Cl 9 E5 74 A6
ypress Ct
Cheam SM1 217 C2
5 Leyton E11 76 B4

Cypress Ct *continued*
7 West Norwood SW16 182 C5
Cypress Gdns SE4 163 A6
Cypress Ho SE14 140 D4
Cypress Inf Sch SE25 183 C1
Cypress Jun Sch SE25 183 C1
Cypress Lo SE25 183 C1
Cypress Pl W1 239 B5
Cypress Rd
Harrow HA3 24 B1
South Norwood SE25 183 C1
Cypress Tree Cl DA15 167 D3
CYPRUS 122 C6
Cyprus Ave N3 29 A1
Cyprus Cl N4 50 C3
Cyprus Ct 9 N3 29 B1
Cyprus Gdns N3 29 A1
Cyprus Ho 10 N3 29 B1
Cyprus Pl
23 Bethnal Green E2 96 C5
Newham E6 122 C6
Cyprus Rd
Church End N3 29 B1
Edmonton N9 17 D2
Cyprus Sta E6 122 C6
Cyprus St E2 96 C5
Cyrena Rd SE22 161 D6
Cyril Jackson Prim Sch (North Bldg) E14 119 B6
Cyril Jackson Prim Sch (South Bldg) E14 119 B6
Cyril Lo 2 DA14 190 A6
Cyril Mans SW11 267 D1
Cyril Rd DA7 147 A3
Cyril Smith Ho N13 32 B5
Cyril Thatcher Ho SW6 265 B1
Cyrus Ho EC1 241 D6
Cyrus St EC1 94 D3 241 D6
Czar St SE8 141 C6

D

Dabbs Hill La UB5 63 C3
Dabb's La EC1 241 B5
Dabin Cres SE10 142 A4
Dacca St SE8 141 B6
Dace Rd E3 97 C6
Dacre Cl UB6 85 D5
Dacre Gdns
Borehamwood WD6 11 B6
Lewisham SE13 142 C1
Dacre Ho SW3 266 D5
Dacre Pk SE13 142 C1
Dacre Pl SE13 142 C2
Dacre Rd
Leytonstone E11 54 D1
Newham E13 99 B6
Thornton Heath CR0 204 A2
Dacres Rd SE23 162 D1
Dacre St SW1 115 D3 259 C6
Dade Way UB2 107 B1
Daerwood Cl BR2 210 B1
Daffodil Cl CR0 206 D1
Daffodil Gdns IG1 78 D3
Daffodil Pl 7 TW12 173 C4
Daffodil St W12 111 D6
Dafforne Rd SW17 159 A1
DAGENHAM 81 D1
Dagenham Ave
Dagenham RM9 81 B1
Dagenham RM9 103 A6
Dagenham Dock Sta RM9 103 B5
Dagenham East Sta RM10 81 D3
Dagenham Heathway Sta RM9 81 B2
Dagenham Park Com Sch RM10 103 D6
Dagenham Rd
Dagenham RM10 81 D4
London E10 53 B1
Dagger La WD23 9 A6
Dagmar Ave HA9 66 B4
Dagmar Ct
Cubitt Town E14 120 A3
South Tottenham N15 51 B5
Dagmar Gdns NW10 90 D5
Dagmar Mews UB2 107 A3
Dagmar Pas N1 234 D6
Dagmar Rd
Camberwell SE5 139 C4
Finsbury Pk N4 50 C2
4 Kingston u T KT2 176 C3
Southall UB2 107 A3
South Norwood SE25 205 C4

Dagmar Rd *continued*
West Green N15 51 B5
Wood Green N22 31 D2
Dagmar Terr N1 94 D6 234 D6
Dagnall Pk SE25 205 C4
Dagnall Rd SE25 205 C4
Dagnall St SW11 137 A4 268 A1
Dagnan Rd SW12 159 C4
Dagobert Ho 27 E1 96 C2
Dagonet Gdns BR1 165 A1
Dagonet Rd BR1 165 A1
Dahlia Gdns
Ilford IG1 78 D2
Mitcham CR4 203 D5
Dahlia Rd SE2 124 B2
Dahomey Rd SW16 181 C4
Daiglen Sch The IG9 21 C2
Daimler Ho 8 E3 97 C3
Daimler Way SM6 220 A1
Daines Cl E12 78 B5
Dainford Cl BR1 186 B5
Dainton Cl 1 BR1 187 B2
Dainton Ho 22 W2 91 C2
Daintry Cl HA3 43 A5
Daintry Way E9 75 B2
Dairsie Ct 3 BR1 187 C1
Dairsie Rd SE9 144 C2
Dairy Cl Bromley BR1 187 B3
South Norwood CR7 183 A1
Willesden NW10 90 A6
Dairy La SE18 122 B2
Dairyman Cl NW2 69 A5
Dairy Meadow Prim Sch UB2 107 B3
Daisy Cl CR0 206 D1
Daisy Dormer Ct 11 SW9 138 B1
Daisy Ho IG3 58 A1
Daisy La SW6 135 C2
Daisy Rd Newham E16 98 C3
Woodford E18 37 B1
Dakin Pl 9 E1 97 A2
Dakota bldg 6 SE13 141 D4
Dakota Cl SM6 220 B1
Dakota Gdns
Newham E6 100 A3
Northolt UB5 85 A4
Dalberg Rd SW2 160 C6
Dalberg Way SE2 124 D3
Dalbury Ho 6 SW9 138 B1
Dalby Rd SW18 136 A1
Dalbys Cres N17 33 C4
Dalby St NW5 71 B2
Dalcross Rd TW4, TW5 129 A3
Dale Ave
Edgware HA8 26 B1
Hounslow TW4 129 A2
Dalebury Rd SW17 158 D2
Dale Cl
Blackheath Pk SE3 143 A2
New Barnet EN5 13 D5
Pinner HA5 22 B2
Dale Croft N4 73 A5
Dale Ct
Cranley Gdns N8 49 C5
3 Kingston u T KT2 176 B3
Northolt UB5 63 B1
Wembley HA0 65 D4
Woodford E18 37 A1
Dale Dr UB4 83 D4
Dalefield IG9 21 D3
Dale Gdns IG8 37 B6
Dale Green Rd N11 15 B1
Dale Gr N12 30 A5
Dalehead NW1 232 A3
Daleham Dr UB8 82 D1
Daleham Gdns NW3 70 B2
Daleham Mews NW3 70 B2
Dale Ho London SE4 141 A1
St John's Wood NW8 229 A6
Dale Lo N6 49 C3
Dalemain Ho 5 SW8 137 D3
Dalemain Mews 12 E16 121 A5
Dale Park Ave SM5 218 D6
Dale Park Rd SE19 183 B2
Dale Rd
Ashford TW16 171 D3
Camberwell SE17 138 D6
Cheam SM1 217 B4
Gospel Oak NW5 71 A3
Southall UB6 85 D2
Walton-on-T KT12 193 D2
Dale Row W11 91 A1
Daleside Rd
Streatham SW17 181 B5
West Ewell KT19 215 B2
Dales Path WD6 11 B6
Dales Rd WD6 11 B6
Dale St W4 111 C1
Dale The BR2 225 D4

Dale View Ave E4 20 A2
Dale View Cres E4 20 A1
Dale View Gdns E4 20 B1
Daleview Rd N15 51 C3
Dalewood Gdns KT4 216 B6
Dale Wood Rd BR6 211 C1
Daley Ho 6 W12 90 B1
Daley St E9 74 D2
Daley Thompson Way 7 SW8 137 B2
Dalgarno Gdns W10 90 C2
Dalgarno Way W10 90 C3
Daling Way E3 97 A5
Dalkeith Ct SW1 259 D3
Dalkeith Gr HA7 26 A5
Dalkeith Ho 6 SW9 138 D4
Dalkeith Rd
Ilford IG1 79 A5
West Norwood SE21 161 A4
Dallas Ct SM3 217 A2
Dallas Rd
Cheam SM3 217 A2
Ealing W5 88 B2
Forest Hill SE26 162 B1
Hendon NW4 46 A2
Dallas Terr UB3 105 D3
Dallega Cl UB3 105 B6
Dallinger Rd SE12 164 D5
Dalling Rd W6 112 B2
Dallington Sch EC1 94 D3 241 D6
Dallington St EC1 94 D3 241 D6
Dallin Rd
Bexley DA6 146 D1
Woolwich SE18 144 D5
Dalmain Prim Sch SE23 163 A3
Dalmain Rd SE23 162 D3
Dalmally Pas CR0 205 D2
Dalmally Passage CR0 205 D3
Dalmally Rd CR0 206 A2
Dalmeny Avenue Est 3 N7 71 D4
Dalmeny Ave
Thornton Heath SW16 182 C1
Tufnell Pk N7 71 D4
Dalmeny Cl HA0 65 C2
Dalmeny Cres TW3 130 B1
Dalmeny Ct 4 SW4 138 A3
Dalmeny Rd
Erith DA8 147 D4
New Barnet EN5 14 A5
North Cheam KT4 216 B5
Tufnell Pk N7 71 D4
Wallington SM5 219 A1
Dalmeyer Rd NW10 67 D2
Dalmore Ave KT10 212 D2
Dalmore Rd SE21 161 A2
Dalrymple Cl N14 15 D4
Dalrymple Rd SE4 141 A1
DALSTON 74 A2
Dalston Gdns HA7 26 A1
Dalston Jct E8 73 D2
Dalston Kingsland Sta E8 73 D3
Dalston La E8 74 A3
Dalton Ave CR4 180 C1
Dalton Cl Hayes UB4 83 B3
Orpington BR6 227 C5
Dalton Ho
7 Balham SW12 159 B4
10 Bow E3 97 A5
19 Deptford SE14 140 D6
Merton SW19 180 A2
Stanmore HA7 25 B5
Dalton St SE27 160 D1
Daltry Ho HA1 42 D5
Dalwood St SE5 139 C4
Daly Ct E15 76 A3
Daly Dr BR1 210 C6
Dalyell Rd SW9 138 B2
Damascene Wlk SE21 161 A3
Damask Cres E16 98 C3
Damask Ct SM1 201 D1
Damer Ho 9 TW10 154 B5
Damer Terr SW10 266 B3
Dames Rd E7 77 A5
Dame St N1 95 A5 235 A4
Damien Ct 12 E1 96 B1
Damien St E1 96 B1
Damon Cl DA14 168 B1
Damon Ct DA14 168 B1
Damon Ho 2 N12 30 B5
Damory Ho 1 SE16 118 C2
Damson Dr UB3 106 A6
Damsonwood Rd UB2 107 C3
Danbrook Rd SW16 182 A3
Dan Bryant Ho 5 SW12 159 C4
Danbury Cl RM6 58 D6

Danbury Mans 3 IG11 78 D1
Danbury Mews SM5, SM6 219 B4
Danbury St N1 94 D5 234 D4
Danbury Way IG8 37 C4
Danby Ct EN2 5 A2
Danby Ho
23 Hackney E9 74 C1
3 West Kilburn W10 91 B4
Danby St SE15 139 D2
Dancastle Ct 7 N3 29 C2
Dancer Rd
Fulham SW6 135 B4 264 C1
Richmond TW9 132 C2
Dando Cres SE3 143 B2
Dandridge Cl SE10 120 D1
Dandridge Ho E1 243 C4
Danebury Ave SW15 155 D5
Danebury
New Addington CR0 223 D2
18 North Kensington W10 90 C2
Daneby Rd SE6 164 A2
Dane Cl
Farnborough BR6 227 B3
Sidcup DA5 169 C4
Danecourt Gdns CR0 221 D5
Danecroft Rd SE24 161 B6
Daneglen Ct 18 HA7 25 C5
Danegrove Prim Sch EN4 14 C5
Danegrove Sch EN4 14 D5
Danehill Wlk DA14 168 A1
Dane Ho
15 London SE5 139 A3
Upper Tooting SW17 180 A6
Danehurst TW8 131 C5
Danehurst Gdns IG4 56 B4
Danehurst St SW6 135 A4 264 A2
Daneland EN4 14 D5
Danemead Gr UB5 63 D3
Danemere St SW15 134 C2
Dane Pl E3 97 B5
Dane Rd
Ashford TW15 171 B4
Ealing W13 109 C5
Ilford IG1 79 A3
Lower Edmonton N18 18 C1
Merton SW19 180 A2
Southall UB1 107 A6
Danesbury Rd TW13 150 B3
Danescombe SE12 165 A3
Danescourt Cres SM1 218 A6
Danescroft Ave NW4 46 D4
Danescroft Gdns NW4 46 D4
Danescroft
Hendon NW4 46 D4
3 North Finchley N12 30 A5
Danes Ct
Primrose Hill NW8 230 C5
Wembley HA9 66 D5
Danesdale Rd E9 75 A2
Danesfield SE5 139 C6
Danes Gate HA1 42 C6
Danes Ho 10 W10 90 C2
Dane St WC1 240 C3
Daneswood Ave SE6 164 A1
Danethorpe Rd HA0 65 D2
Danetree Cl KT19 215 A1
Danetree Jun Sch KT19 215 A1
Danetree Rd KT19 215 A1
Danette Gdns RM8 81 B6
Daneville Rd SE5 139 B4
Danford Ho 9 N11 31 C5
Dangan Rd E11 55 A3
Daniel Almshouse NW4 46 B5
Daniel Bolt Cl E14 97 D2
Daniel Cl London N18 34 C6
Twickenham TW4 151 B4
Upper Tooting SW17 180 C4
Daniel Ct Acton W3 111 C6
3 Beckenham BR3 185 C3
7 Edgware HA8 26 D5
10 Hendon NW9 27 C2
Daniel Gdns SE15 139 D5
Daniel Ho 1 HA5 22 C1
Daniell Ho N1 235 D4
Daniell Way CR0 204 B1
Daniel Pl NW4 46 B2
Daniel Rd W5 110 B6
Daniel's Rd SE15 140 C2

Dan Leno Wlk SW6 265 C3
Dansey Pl W1 249 C6
Dansington Rd DA16 146 A1
Danson Cres DA16 146 B2
Danson House* DA6 146 C1
Danson Intc DA5 168 C5
Danson La DA16 146 B1
Danson Mead DA16 146 C2
Danson Prim Sch DA16 146 A1
Danson Rd DA5 168 D6
Danson Underpass DA5 168 C5
Dante Pl SE11 261 D3
Dante Rd SE11 116 D2 261 C4
Danube Ct 13 SE15 139 D5
Danube St SW3 114 C1 257 B2
Danvers Ho 35 E1 96 A1
Danvers Rd N8 49 D5
Danvers St SW3 136 B6 266 D5
Da Palma Ct SW6 265 A5
Daphne Ct Ealing W5 87 C1
Wembley HA0 65 D3
Worcester Pk KT4 215 C6
Daphne Gdns E4 20 A1
Daphne Ho N22 32 C2
Daphne St SW18 158 A5
Daplyn St 6 E1 96 A2
D'arblay St W1 93 C1 239 B1
Darby Cres TW16 172 C1
Darby Gdns TW16 172 C1
Darcy Ave SM6 219 C4
Darcy Cl N20 14 B2
D'arcy Dr HA3 43 D5
D'arcy Gdns
Dagenham RM9 103 B6
Harrow HA3 44 A5
Darcy Ho E8 96 B6
D'arcy Pl BR2 209 A5
D'arcy Rd SM3 216 D4
Darcy Rd
Isleworth TW7 131 A4
Thornton Heath SW16 182 A1
Dare Ct 2 E10 54 A2
Dare Gdns RM8 81 A5
Darell Prim Sch TW9 132 C2
Darell Rd TW9 132 C2
Daren Ct N7 72 A4
Darent Ho
4 Catford BR1 186 B5
Lisson Gr NW8 236 D4
Darenth Rd
Stamford Hill N16 51 D1
Welling DA16 146 A4
Darfield NW1 232 A5
Darfield Rd SE4 163 B6
Darfield Way W10 90 D1
Darfur St SW15 134 D2
Dargate Cl SE19 183 D3
Darien Ho
17 London SW11 136 B2
11 Stepney E1 96 D2
Darien Rd SW11 136 B2
Daring Ho 23 E3 97 A5
Darland Ho SE9 167 B5
Darlands Dr EN5 12 D6
Darlan Rd SW6 135 B5 264 D3
Darlaston Rd SW19 179 A3
Darley Cl CR0 207 A3
Darley Dr KT3 177 B1
Darley Gdns SM4 201 D3
Darley Ho SE11 260 C1
Darley Rd
Clapham SW11 158 D5
Edmonton N9 17 D3
Darling Ho 12 TW1 153 D5
Darling Rd SE4 141 C2
Darling Row E1 96 B3
Darlington Ct 8 SE6 164 D3
Darlington Ho
South Lambeth SW8 269 D3
2 Surbiton KT6 197 D2
Darlington Rd SE27 182 D5
Darmaine Cl CR2 221 A1
Darnall Ho 4 SE10 142 A4
Darnay Ho 3 SE16 118 A3
Darndale Cl E17 35 B1
Darnell Ho 9 SE10 142 A5
Darnley Ho 7 E14 97 A1
Darnley Rd
Hackney E9 74 C2
Woodford IG8 37 B2

Darnley Terr 12 W11 112 D5
Darrell Ct BR2 208 C6
Darrell Rd SE22 162 A6
Darren Cl N4 50 B2
Darrick Wood Ho BR6 227 A5
Darrick Wood Inf Sch BR6 226 D5
Darrick Wood Jun Sch BR6 226 D4
Darrick Wood Rd BR6 227 B6
Darrick Wood Sch BR6 226 D5
Darrick Wood Sports Ctr BR6 227 A5
Darris Cl UB4 85 A3
Darsley Dr SW8 138 A4 270 A2
Dartford Ave N9 18 D5
Dartford Gdns RM6 58 B4
Dartford Ho SE1 263 D4
Dartford St SE17 139 A6
Dartington Ho
Bayswater W2 91 D2
7 London SW8 137 D3
Dartington NW1 232 B5
Dartle Ct 23 SE16 118 A4
Dartmoor Wlk 18 E14 119 C2
Dartmouth Cl W11 91 C1
Dartmouth Ct SE10 142 A4
Dartmouth Gr SE10 142 A4
Dartmouth Hill SE10 142 A4
Dartmouth Ho
Dartmouth Pk N19 71 B6
11 Kingston u T KT2 176 A2
Lewisham SE10 142 A3
Thornton Heath CR0 204 D2
DARTMOUTH PARK 71 B5
Dartmouth Park Ave NW5 71 B5
Dartmouth Park Hill N19 71 B6
Dartmouth Park Rd NW5 71 B5
Dartmouth Pl
Chiswick W4 133 C6
Forest Hill SE23 162 C2
Dartmouth Rd
Brondesbury NW2 68 D2
Forest Hill SE23, SE26 162 C1
Hayes BR2 209 A2
Hendon NW4 46 A3
Ruislip HA4 62 A5
Dartmouth Row SE10 142 A4
Dartmouth St SW1 115 D4 249 D1
Dartmouth Terr SE10 142 B4
Dartnell Rd CR0 205 D2
Darton Ct W3 111 A5
Dartrey Twr SW10 266 C4
Dartrey Wlk SW10 136 A5 266 B4
Dart St W10 91 B4
Darville Rd N16 73 D5
Darwell Cl E6 100 C5
Darwen Pl E2 96 B6
Darwin Cl
Farnborough BR6 227 B3
New Southgate N11 15 B1
Darwin Ct
Eltham SE9 166 C5
Newham E13 99 B4
Primrose Hill NW1 231 B6
Darwin Dr UB1 85 D1
Darwin Gdns WD19 22 C5
Darwin Ho
8 London SE13 142 A3
2 Wembley HA9 67 A5
Darwin Rd
Ealing W5 109 C2
Falconwood DA16 145 D2
Tottenham N22 32 D1
Darwin St SE17 117 B2 262 D4
Daryngton Dr UB6 86 C5
Daryngton Ho SW8 270 A3
Dashwood Cl DA6 169 C6
Dashwood Ct TW3 130 A1
Dashwood Ho SE21 161 D1
Dashwood Rd N8 50 B3
Dassett Rd SE27 182 D5
Data Point Bsns Ctr E16 98 B3
Datchelor Pl 14 SE5 139 B4
Datchet Ho NW1 231 D2
Datchet Rd SE6 163 B2
Datchett Ho 40 E2 95 D4
Datchwood Ct N4 73 A5
Datchworth Ct 7 EN1 17 C6
Datchworth Ho 8 N1 72 D1
Date St SE17 117 B1 262 C1
Daubeney Gdns N17 33 A3
Daubeney Pl TW12 173 D1
Daubeney Prim Sch E5 75 A4
Daubeney Rd
Clapton Pk E5 75 A4
Tottenham N17 33 A3
Daubeney Twr 2 SE8 119 B1
Dault Rd SW18 158 A5
Dauney Ho SE1 251 C1
Dauphine Ct HA3 24 C1
Dave Adams Ho 8 E3 97 B5
Davenant Ho 20 E1 96 A2
Davenant Rd
Croydon CR0, CR9 220 D4
Upper Holloway N19 71 D6
Davenant St E1 96 A2
Davenport Cl TW11 175 A4
Davenport Ctr IG11 102 B5
Davenport Ho SE11 261 A5
Davenport Lo TW3 129 A5
Davenport Mews 6 W12 112 B5
Davenport Rd
London SE6 164 A5
Sidcup DA14 169 A2
Daventer Dr HA7 24 D3
Daventry Ave E17 53 C3
Daventry St NW1 92 C2 237 A4
Dave Porter Hts SW19 157 A4
Dave Ramsey Ho SE18 123 B2
Daver Ct
Chelsea SW3 257 B1
Ealing W5 87 D3
Davern Cl SE10 120 D2
Davey Cl
Bowes Pk N13 32 B5
Islington N7 72 B2
Davey Ho HA9 67 A6
Davey Rd E9 75 C1
Davey's Ct WC2 250 A6
Davey St SE15 139 D6
David Ave UB6 86 C5
David Beckham Acad The SE10 120 D4
David Cl UB3 127 C5
David Coffer Ct DA17 125 D2
David Ct N20 14 A1
David Devine Ho 7 E8 74 A3
David Game Coll SW7 256 C3
Davidge Ho SE1 251 B1
Davidge St SE1 116 D4 251 D1
David Henry Waring Ct TW14 149 A3
David Hewitt Ho 2 E3 97 D2
David Ho
8 Putney SW15 156 A6
South Lambeth SW8 270 A4
South Norwood SE25 206 A6
David Lee Point 4 E15 98 C6
David Livingstone Prim Sch CR7 183 A2
David Mews W1 237 D4
David Rd RM8 81 A6
Davidson Gdns SW8 138 A5 270 A4
Davidson Ho 7 N19 71 C4
Davidson Lo CR0 205 C2
Davidson Prim Sch CR0 205 D2
Davidson Rd CR0 205 D3
Davidson Terrs E7 77 B3
David's Rd SE23 162 C3
David St E15 76 B3
David Twigg Cl KT2 176 A2
Davies Cl CR0 206 A3
Davies Laing & Dick Coll W1 93 A1 238 B2
Davies La E11 76 D6
Davies Lane Prim Sch E11 76 D6
Davies Mews W1 248 C6
Davies St W1 115 B6 248 C6
Davies Walk TW7 130 B4
Davina Ho
Brondesbury NW2 69 B2
14 Hackney E5 74 B3
Da Vinci Ct 12 SE16 118 B1
Davington Ct 19 SM2 217 C1
Davington Gdns RM8 80 B3
Davington Rd RM8 80 B3
Davis Ct 1 N20 14 B2
Davis Ho 35 W12 112 B6
Davis Rd
Bedford Pk W3 111 D4
Chessington KT9 214 C4
Davis Sch The E10 53 D1
Davis St E13 99 B5
Davisville Rd W12 112 A4
Davmor Ct TW8 109 C1
Dawes Ave TW7 131 A1
Dawe's Cl UB10 82 A5
Dawes Ho SE17 262 C3
Dawes Rd SW6 135 B5 264 C4
Dawe's Rd UB10 82 A5
Dawes St SE17 117 B1 262 D2
Dawley Ave UB8 83 A1
Dawley Par UB3 105 A6
Dawley Rd
Harlington UB3 105 C2
Hayes UB3 105 B6
Dawlish Ave
Bowes Pk N13 32 A5
Wandsworth SW18 157 D2
Wembley UB6 87 A5
Dawlish Dr Ilford IG3 79 D4
Pinner HA5 41 A3
Ruislip HA4 62 B6
Dawlish Prim Sch E10 54 A1
Dawlish Rd
Brondesbury NW2 68 D2
Leyton E10 76 A6
Tottenham Hale N17 52 A6
Dawnay Gdns SW18 158 B2
Dawnay Rd SW17, SW18 158 B2
Dawn Cl TW4 129 A2
Dawn Cres E15 98 B6
Dawn Wlk BR2 186 B1
Dawpool Rd NW2 67 D6
Daws La NW7 28 A5
Dawson Ave
Barking IG11 79 D1
St Paul's Cray BR5 190 B1
Dawson Cl Hayes UB3 83 B2
Woolwich SE18 123 A2
Dawson Gdns 10 IG11 79 D1
Dawson Ho
23 Bethnal Green E2 96 C4
5 Camberwell SE5 139 C4
Dawson Pl W2 113 C6 245 B6
Dawson Rd
Cricklewood NW2 68 C4
Kingston u T KT1 198 B6
Dawson St E2 95 D5
Dawson Terr N9 18 C4
Dax Ct TW16 194 C6
Daybrook Rd SW19 201 D6
Day Ho 2 SE5 139 A5
Daylesford Ave SW15 134 A1
Daymer Gdns HA5 40 C5
Daynor Ho 4 NW6 91 C6
Day's Armhouses HA8 26 B5
Daysbrook Rd SW2 160 B3
Days La DA15 167 C4
Days Lane Prim Sch DA15 167 D5
Daytone Ho SW20 178 D2
Dayton Gr SE15 140 C4
Deaconess Ct 5 N15 51 D5
Deacon Ho SE11 260 D3
Deacon Mews N1 73 B1
Deacon Rd
Kingston u T KT2 176 B2
Willesden NW2 68 A2
Deacons Cl HA5 22 B1
DEACONS HILL 10 C5
Deacon's Hill Rd WD6 10 C6
Deacons Hts WD6 10 C5
Deacons Leas BR6 227 B4
Deacons Rise N2 48 B4
Deacons Wlk TW12 173 C6
Deacon Way SE17 117 A2 262 B4
Deal Ct
13 Hendon NW9 27 D1
7 Southall UB1 86 A1
Deal Ho
Deptford SE15 140 D6
Walworth SE17 263 B2
Deal Porters Way SE16 118 D3
Deal Rd SW17 181 A4
Deal St E1 96 A2
Dealtry Rd SW15 134 C1
Deal Wlk 3 SW9 138 C5
Dean Bradley St SW1 260 A5
Dean Cl Hackney E9 74 C3
Hillingdon UB10 60 B1
Rotherhithe SE16 118 D5
Dean Coll of London N7 72 B5
Deancross St E1 96 C1
Dean Ct Acton W3 89 B1
Ealing W13 109 B5
10 Kingston u T KT2 176 C3
South Lambeth SW8 270 A3
Wembley HA0 65 B5
Dean Dr HA7 26 A1
Deane Ave HA4 62 C3
Deane Croft Rd HA5 40 C3
Deanery Cl N2 48 C5
Deanery Mews W1 248 B4
Deanery Rd E15 76 C2
Deanery St W1 115 A5 248 B4
Deanesfield Prim HA4 62 D4
Deane Way HA4 40 B3
Dean Farrar St SW1 259 D6
Deanfield Gdns CR0 221 B4
Dean Gdns E17 54 B5
Deanhill Ct 2 SW14 132 D1
Deanhill Rd SW14 132 D1
Dean Ho London N4 51 A2
New Cross SE14 141 B5
Ruislip HA4 39 B1
Stamford Hill N16 51 D1
18 Stepney E1 96 C1
Dean Rd
Croydon CR0 221 B4
Hampton TW12 173 C5
Hounslow TW3 151 D6
Thamesmead SE28 124 A6
Willesden NW2 68 C2
Dean Ryle St SW1 260 A4
Dean's Bldgs SE17 117 B2 262 D3
Deansbrook Cl HA8 27 A3
Deansbrook Jun & Inf Schs NW7 27 A4
Deansbrook Rd
Burnt Oak HA8 27 B4
Edgware HA8 26 D3
Deans Cl
Burnt Oak HA8 27 A4
Chiswick W4 132 D6
South Croydon CR0 221 D5
Deanscroft Ave NW9 45 A1
Dean's Ct EC4 241 D1
Deans Ct HA8 26 D4
Deans Dr N13 32 D4
Dean's Dr HA8 27 B5
Deansfield Prim Sch
Eltham SE9 144 C2
Ruislip HA4 62 D4
Deans Gate Cl SE23 162 D1
Deanshanger Ho 21 SE8 118 D2
Dean's La HA8 27 A4
Dean's Mews W1 238 D2
Dean's Rd W7 108 D4
Deans Rd SM1 217 D5
Dean Stanley St SW1 260 A5
Dean St
Forest Gate E7 77 A3
Soho W1 93 D1 239 C1
Deansway
East Finchley N2 48 B5
Edmonton N9 17 C1
Deans Way HA8 27 A5
Deanswood N11 31 D4
Dean's Yd SW1 259 D6
Dean Trench St SW1 260 A5
Dean Way UB2 107 D4
Dean Wlk HA8 27 B3
Deanwood Ct N14 15 C3
Dearmer Ho 6 SW2 160 C4
Dearne Cl HA7 25 A5
De'arn Gdns CR4 202 C6
Dearsley Rd EN1 6 A2
Deason St E15 98 A6
Deauville Ct
14 London SW4 159 C5
4 Rotherhithe SE16 118 D4
Deauville Mans 13 SW4 159 C5
De Barowe Mews 1 N5 72 D3
Debdale Ho 20 E2 96 A6
Debden Cl
7 Edgware NW9 27 C2
Kingston u T KT2 175 D5
Woodford IG8 37 D3
Debden N17 33 B1
De Beauvoir Cres N1 95 C6
De Beauvoir Ct N1 73 B1
De Beauvoir Pl 5 N1 73 C2
De Beauvoir Prim Sch N1 73 C2
De Beauvoir Rd N1 73 C1
De Beauvoir Sq N1 73 C1
DE BEAUVOIR TOWN 73 C1
Debenham Ct
Barnet EN5 12 C6
Hackney E8 96 A6
Debham Ct NW2 68 C5
Debnams Rd SE16 118 C2
De Bohun Ave N14 15 B5
De Bohun Prim Sch N14 15 B6
Deborah Cl TW7 130 C4
Deborah Cres HA4 39 B2
Deborah Ct 7 E18 55 B6
Deborah Lo HA8 26 D2
De Broome Rd TW13 150 C3
De Burgh Ho 10 SW19 180 A3
Deburgh Rd SW19 180 A3
Debussy 9 NW9 27 D1
Decimal Ctr UB2 107 C4
Decima St SE1 117 C3 263 A6
Decimus Cl CR7 205 B5
Deck Cl SE16 118 D5
Decoy Ave NW11 47 A5
De Crespigny Pk SE5 139 B3
Dedham Ho 1 SE6 186 A6
Dee Ct W7 86 B1
Deeley Rd SW8 137 D4 269 C2
Deena Cl W3 88 B1
Deepdale Ave BR2 208 D5
Deepdale Cl N11 31 A4
Deepdale Highbury N4 72 D5
Wimbledon SW19 178 D6
Deepdene Ave CR0 221 D5
Deepdene Cl E11 55 A5
Deepdene Ct
Beckenham BR2 208 C6
Southgate N21 16 D5
Deepdene Gdns SW2 160 B4
Deepdene Ho N16 51 B1
Deepdene N12 30 C6
Deepdene Lo 5 SW2 160 B4
Deepdene Mans SW6 264 C2
Deepdene Point 9 SE26 162 D1
Deepdene Rd
London SE5, SE24 139 B1
Welling DA16 146 A2
Deepwell Cl TW7 131 A4
Deepwood La UB6 86 B4
Deerbrook Rd SE24, SW2 160 D3
Deerdale Rd SE24 139 A1
Dee Rd TW9 132 B1
Deerfield Cl NW9 45 D4
Deerhurst Cl TW13 172 B6
Deerhurst Cres TW12 174 A5
Deerhurst Ct CR0 204 D1
Deerhurst Ho 6 SE15 140 A6
Deerhurst 7 KT2 176 D2
Deerhurst Rd
Brondesbury NW2 68 D2
Streatham SW16 182 B5
Deerhurst 5 SW16 182 A5
Deerings Ct 2 N20 14 B2
Deerings Dr HA5 40 A4
Deerleap Gr E4 19 D6
Deer Lo SW6 135 A2
Deer Park Cl KT2 176 D3
Deer Park Gdns CR4 202 B5
Deer Park Rd SW19 180 A1
Deer Park Way BR4 224 D6
Deesdale Ct CR2 221 B4
Deeside Rd SW17 158 B1
Dee St E14 98 A1
Defence Cl SE28 123 C5
Defiance Wlk SE18 122 B3
Defiant 18 NW9 27 D1
Defiant Way SM6 220 A1
Defoe Ave TW9 132 C5
Defoe Cl SW17 180 C4
Defoe Ho
Barbican EC2 242 A4
5 Stoke Newington N16 73 C5
Defoe Pl
Barbican EC2 242 A4
Upper Tooting SW17 180 D6
Defoe Rd
Rotherhithe SE16 119
Stoke Newington N16 73
De Frene Rd SE26 163
De Gama Pl 8 E14 119
Degema Rd BR7 188
Dehar Cres NW9 46
De Haviland Dr 8 SE18 122
Dehavilland Cl UB5 84
De Havilland Rd
Edgware HA8 26
Heston TW5 128
De Havilland Sq IG1 57
Dehavilland Studios E5 74
De Havilland Way TW19 148
Dekker Ho 19 SE5 139
Dekker Rd SE21 161
Delacourt Rd SE3 143
Delafield Ho 28 E1 96
Delafield Rd SE7 121
Delaford Rd SE16 118
Delaford St SW6 135 A6 264
Delamare Cres CR0 206
Delamere Gdns NW7 27
Delamere Ho 4 N4 51
Delamere Rd
Ealing W5 110
Hayes UB4 106
Wimbledon SW20 178
Delamere St W2 236
Delamere Terr W2 91
Delancey Pas NW1 231
Delancey St NW1 93 B6 231
Delancey Studios NW1 231
Delany Ho SE10 142
Delarch Ho SE1 251
De Laune St SE17 116 D1 261
Delaware Rd W9 91
Delawyk Cres SE24 161
Delcombe Ave KT4 200
Delft Ho 8 KT2 176
Delft Way 2 SE22 161
Delhi Rd EN1 17
Delhi St N1 94 A6 233
Delia St SW18 157
Delisle Rd SE28 123
Delius Cl WD6 9
Delius Gr E15 98
Dellafield N4 72
Della Path E5 74
Dellbow Rd TW14 150
Dell Cl
Stratford Marsh E15 98
Wallington SM6 219
Woodford IG8 21
Dellfield Cl BR3 186
Dell La KT17 216
Dellors Cl EN5 12
Dellow Cl IG2 57
Dellow Ho 6 E1 118
Dellow St E1 118
Dell Rd Enfield EN3 6
Stoneleigh KT17 216
West Drayton UB7 104
Dells Cl Chingford E4 19
Teddington TW11 174
Dell's Mews SW1 259
Dell The
Brentford TW8 131
Feltham TW14 150
Pinner HA5 22
Plumstead Comm SE2 124
South Norwood SE19 183
Wembley HA0 65
Woodford IG8 21
Dell Way W13 87
Dell Wlk KT3 177
Dellwood Gdns IG5 56
Delme Cres SE3 143
Delmey Cl CR0 221
Deloraine Ho SE8 141
Deloraine St SE8 141
Delorme St W6 134
Delphian Ct 5 SW16 182
Delroy Ct N20 14
Delta Bldg 7 E14 98
Delta Cl KT4 215
Delta Ct NW2 68
Delta Gr UB5 84
Delta Ho N1 235
Delta Pk Ind Est EN3 7
Delta Pk SW18 135
Delta Point 5 E2 96
Delta Rd KT4 215
Delta St 4 E2 96

e Lucy Prim Sch
SE2 124 B4
e Lucy St SE2 124 B2
elvan Cl SE18 144 C5
elverton Ho SE17 261 D2
elverton Rd SE17 261 D1
elvino Rd
SW6 135 C4 265 B1
e Mandeville Gate
EN1 6 B1
emesne Rd SM6 219 D4
emeta Cl HA9 67 A5
e Montfort Ct 1
SW16 160 A1
e Montfort Rd
SW16 160 A2
e Morgan Rd SW6 135 D2
empster Cl KT6 197 C1
empster Rd SW18 158 A6
enberry Dr DA14 168 B1
enbigh Cl
Cheam SM1 217 B3
Elmstead BR7 188 B4
Notting Hill
W11 113 B6 244 D6
Ruislip HA4 61 D6
Southall UB1 85 B1
Willesden NW10 67 C1
enbigh Ct
1 Ealing W7 86 D2
Newham E6 99 D4
enbigh Dr UB3 105 A4
enbigh Gdns
TW10 154 B6
enbigh Ho
Knightsbridge
SW1 257 D6
7 Notting Hill W11 91 B1
Notting Hill W11 244 D6
enbigh Mews SW1 259 A3
enbigh Pl
SW1 115 C1 259 A2
enbigh Rd
Ealing W13 87 B1
Hounslow TW3 129 D3
Newham E6 99 D4
Notting Hill
W11 113 B6 244 D6
Southall UB1 85 B1
enbigh St
SW1 115 C1 259 B2
enbigh Terr
W11 113 B6 244 D6
enbridge Rd BR1,
BR7 188 B1
enbury Ho 48 E3 97 D4
enby Ct Barnet EN5 1 D2
Lambeth SE11 260 D4
ence Ho 15 E2 96 A4
enchworth Ho 14
SW9 138 C3
en Cl BR2, BR3 208 B6
encliffe 2 TW15 170 C5
encora Centre The
EN3 7 A2
endridge Cl EN1 6 B6
ene Ave
Blackfen DA15 168 B4
Hounslow TW3 129 B2
ene Cl Brockley SE4 141 A1
Hayes BR2 208 D1
Worcester Pk KT4 215 D6
enecroft Cres UB10 82 D6
ene Ct Ealing W5 87 C2
Hanwell W7 108 D4
ene Gdns
Hinchley Wood
KT7 213 A6
Stanmore HA7 25 C5
enehole Ho SE18 124 A1
ene Ho N14 15 D4
enehurst Gdns
Acton W3 110 D5
Hendon NW4 46 C3
Richmond TW10 132 C1
Twickenham TW2 152 B4
Woodford IG8 37 B6
ene Mans 1 NW6 69 C2
ene Rd
Buckhurst Hill IG9 21 D3
Friern Barnet N11 14 D2
enesmead SE24 161 A6
ene The Ealing W13 87 B2
East Molesey KT12,
KT8 195 B4
South Croydon CR0 222 D4
Wembley HA9 66 A4
enewood Ho 6
SM1 218 A4
enewood EN5 14 A6
enewood Rd N6 48 D2
engie Wlk N1 235 A6
enham Cl DA16 146 C2
enham Cres CR4 202 D5
enham Ct
Forest Hill SE26 162 B1
Southall UB1 108 A6

Denham Dr IG2 57 A3
Denham Ho 32 W12 112 B6
Denham Lo W5 88 A1
Denham Rd
Feltham TW14 150 C4
Friern Barnet N20 14 D1
Denham St SE10 121 A1
Denham Way IG11 101 D6
Denholme Rd W9 91 B4
Deniel Lo TW9 153 C6
Denise Ct HA0 65 C4
Denison Cl N2 48 A6
Denison Rd Ealing W5 87 C3
Feltham TW13 171 D6
Mitcham SW19 180 B4
Deniston Ave DA5 169 A3
Denland Ho SW8 270 D3
Denleigh Ct N14 15 D4
Denleigh Gdns
Southgate N21 16 C4
Thames Ditton KT7 196 C3
Denman Dr
Ashford TW15 170 D4
Claygate KT10 213 A3
Hampstead Garden
Suburb NW11 47 C4
Denman Dr N NW11 47 C4
Denman Dr S NW11 47 C4
Denman Ho N16 73 C6
Denman Rd SE15 139 D3
Denman St W1 249 C5
Denmark Ave SW19 179 A3
Denmark Ct SM4 201 C4
Denmark Gdns SM5 218 D5
Denmark Gr N1 234 A4
Denmark Hill Dr
NW9 46 A6
Denmark Hill SE5 139 B3
Denmark Hill Sta
SE5 139 B3
Denmark Ho 9 SE7 122 A2
Denmark Mans 14
SE5 139 A3
Denmark Pl
2 Bromley E3 97 C4
Soho WC2 239 D2
Denmark Rd
Bromley BR1 187 B2
Camberwell SE5 139 A3
Carshalton SM5 218 D5
Croydon SE25 206 B4
Ealing W13 109 B6
Hornsey N8 50 C5
Kilburn NW6 91 B5
Kingston u T KT1 198 A6
Twickenham TW2 152 B1
Wimbledon SW19 178 D4
Denmark St
8 Leyton E11 76 C5
Newham E13 99 B2
Soho WC2 239 D2
Tottenham N17 34 B3
Denmark Terr NW2 48 D6
Denmead Ho SW15 155 D5
Denmead Rd CR0 204 D1
Denmead Sch
TW12 173 D3
Denmead Upper Sch
TW12 173 D3
Denmore Ct SM6 219 B3
Dennan Rd KT6 198 B1
Dennard Way BR6 226 C4
Denner Rd E4 19 C2
Denne Terr E8 95 D6
Dennett Rd CR0 204 C2
Dennett's Gr SE14 140 D3
Dennett's Rd SE14 140 C4
Denning Ave CR0 220 C3
Denning Cl
Hampton TW12 173 B5
St John's Wood
NW8 92 A4 229 B1
Denning Point E1 243 D2
Denning Rd NW3 70 B4
Dennington Cl 17 E5 74 B6
Dennington Park
Mansions 12 NW6 69 C3
Dennington Park Rd
NW6 69 C2
Denningtons The
KT4 215 C6
Dennis Ave HA9 66 B3
Dennis Cl TW15 171 B3
Dennis Ct
Chingford E17 36 B1
Greenford UB6 86 A1
Lewisham SE10 142 A4
Dennis Gdns HA7 25 C5
Dennis Ho 4 Bow E3 97 B5
Sutton SM1 217 C4
Dennis La HA7 25 B6
Dennison Point E15 76 A1
Dennis Park Cres
SW20 179 A2
Dennis Par 1 N14 15 D3
Dennis Rd KT8 196 A5

Dennis Reeve Cl
CR4 180 D2
Dennis Way SW4 137 D2
Denny Cl 15 E6 100 A2
Denny Cres SE11 261 B2
Denny Gdns RM9 80 B1
Denny Rd N9 18 B3
Denny St
SE11 116 C1 261 B2
Den Rd BR2 208 B6
Densham Ho NW8 229 D3
Densham Rd E15 98 C6
Densole Cl BR3 185 A2
Denstone Ho 5
SE15 140 A6
Densworth Gr N9 18 C2
Dent Ho SE17 263 A3
Denton Cl EN5 12 C6
Denton Ct BR2 210 C2
Denton Ho N1 72 D1
Denton NW1 71 A2
Denton Rd
Bexley DA16 146 C5
Edmonton N18 33 C6
Hornsey N8 50 B3
Twickenham TW1 153 D5
Denton St SW18 157 D5
Denton Way E5 74 D5
Dents Rd SW11 158 D5
Denvale Trade Pk
CR4 202 B5
Denver Cl BR6 211 C3
Denver Ct UB1 107 B5
Denver Rd N16 51 C2
Denwood SE23 162 D1
Denyer Ho 1 NW5 71 B4
Denyer St
SW3 114 C2 257 B4
Denys Bldg EC1 241 A4
Denziloe Ave UB10 82 D4
Denzil Rd NW10 67 D3
Deodar Rd SW15 135 A1
Deodora Cl N20 14 D1
Depot App NW2 68 D4
Depot Rd
Isleworth TW3,
TW7 130 B2
Shepherd's Bush
W12 112 C6
Depot St SE5 139 B6
DEPTFORD 140 D6
Deptford Bridge
SE8 141 C4
Deptford Bridge Sta
SE8 141 C4
Deptford Broadway SE8,
SE14 141 C4
Deptford Church St
SE8 141 C5
Deptford Ferry Rd 24
E14 119 C2
Deptford Gn SE8 141 C6
Deptford Green Sch
(Annex) SE14 141 A5
Deptford Green Sch
SE14 141 B5
Deptford High St
SE8 141 C5
Deptford Park Prim Sch
SE8 119 A1
Deptford Sta SE8 141 C5
Deptford Trad Est
SE8 141 A6
Deptford Wharf
SE8 119 B2
Dept of Transport &
Environment SW1 259 D5
De Quincey Mews 3
E16 121 A5
De Quincey Rd N17 33 B2
Derby Ave
Harrow HA3 24 B2
North Finchley N12 30 A5
Romford RM7 59 D3
Derby Ct
8 Clapton Pk E5 74 D4
Woodford E18 36 D2
Derby Gate SW1 250 A2
Derby Hill Cres
SE23 162 C2
Derby Hill SE23 162 C2
Derby Ho
Hendon NW4 46 C6
Lambeth SE11 261 A4
Pinner HA5 22 D1
4 Wallington SM6 219 B3
Derby Lo N3 29 B1
Derby Rd
Cheam SM1, SM2 217 B2
Edmonton N18 34 C5
Enfield EN3 18 C6
Greenford UB6 85 D6
Hounslow TW3 129 D1
Merton SW19 179 C3
Mortlake SW14 132 D1
South Hackney E9 96 D6
Surbiton KT5, KT6 198 C1

Derby Rd *continued*
Thornton Heath CR0 204 D1
Upton E7 77 D1
Woodford E18 36 D2
Derbyshire St E2 96 A4
Derby St W1 248 B3
Dereham Ho 7
SE4 140 D1
Dereham Pl EC2 243 B6
Dereham Rd IG11 79 D3
Derek Ave
Chessington
KT19 214 D3
Wallington SM6 219 B4
Wembley HA9 66 D1
Derek Cl KT19 214 D3
Derek Walcott Cl
SE24 160 D6
Dericote St E8 96 B6
Deri Dene Cl 2
TW19 148 A5
Derifall Cl E6 100 B2
Dering Pl CR0 221 A4
Dering Rd CR0 221 A4
Dering St W1 238 D1
Derinton Rd SW17 181 A6
Derley Rd UB2 106 D3
Dermody Gdns
SE13 164 B6
Dermody Rd SE13 164 B6
Deronda Rd SE24,
SW2 160 D3
Deroy Cl SM5 218 D2
Derrick Gdns SE7 121 C2
Derrick Ho 13 SW2 160 C3
Derrick Rd BR3 207 B5
Derrycombe Ho 18
W2 91 C2
Derry Rd CR0, SM6 220 A5
Derry St W8 113 D4 245 C1
Dersingham Ave E12 78 C4
Dersingham Inf Sch
E12 78 C3
Dersingham Rd NW2 69 A5
Derwent Ave
Barnet EN4 14 D3
Burnt Oak NW7 27 B4
Edmonton N18 33 B5
Hyde The NW9 45 C4
Kingston u T SW15 177 C6
Pinner HA5 23 A4
Uxbridge UB10 60 C5
Derwent Cl
Claygate KT10 212 D2
East Bedfont TW14 149 D3
Derwent Cres
Bexleyheath DA7 147 C3
Stanmore HA7 25 C1
Whetstone N20 14 A1
Derwent Ct
2 Hammersmith
W6 112 A2
Hornsey N8 50 A3
8 Rotherhithe
SE16 118 D4
Derwent Dr
Crofton BR5 211 B2
Hayes UB4 83 C2
Derwent Gdns
Redbridge IG4 56 A5
Wembley HA9 43 C2
Derwent Gr SE22 139 D1
Derwent Ho
Penge SE20 184 B1
South Kensington
SW7 256 B4
Tower Hamlets E3 97 B3
Derwent Lo
Hounslow TW7 130 B3
North Cheam KT4 216 B6
Derwent NW1 232 A1
Derwent Rd
Ealing W5 109 C3
Palmers Green N13 16 B1
Penge SE20 184 B1
Southall UB1 85 B1
Twickenham TW2 151 D5
West Barnes SM4 200 D3
Derwent Rise NW9 45 C3
Derwent St SE10 120 C1
Derwentwater Mans 2
W3 111 A5
Derwentwater Prim Sch
W3 111 A5
Derwentwater Rd
W3 111 A5
Derwent Wlk SM6 219 B1
Derwent Yd W5 109 C3
De Salis Rd UB10 83 A3
Desborough Cl
Bayswater W2 91 D2
Lower Halliford
TW17 192 C2
Desborough Ct
SE25 206 B5
Desborough Ho
W14 264 D6

Desenfans Rd SE21 161 C5
Deseret Ho 6 CR4 202 D6
Desford Rd E16 98 C3
Desford Way TW15 148 B2
Desmond Ho 4 EN4 14 C5
Desmond St SE14 141 A6
Desmond Tutu Dr
SE23 163 A3
Despard Ho SW2 160 C2
Despard Rd N19 49 C1
Dessouter 19 NW9 27 D1
Desvignes Dr SE13 164 B5
Detherick Ct TW3 130 A1
Dethick Ct E3 97 A6
Detling Ho SE17 263 A3
Detling Rd BR1 187 A5
Detmold Rd E5 74 C6
Devalls Cl E6 122 C6
Devana End SM5 218 D5
Devas Rd SW20 178 C2
Devas St E3 97 D3
Devema Cl BR7 188 C2
Devenay Rd E15 76 D1
Devenish Rd SE2 124 A4
Deventer Cres 8
SE22 161 C6
Deveraux Cl BR3 208 A4
De Vere Cotts W8 256 A6
De Vere Ct 1 E5 74 B5
De Vere Gdns
Kensington
W8 114 A4 246 A1
Redbridge IG1 56 B1
Deverell St
SE1 117 B3 262 C5
De Vere Mews W8 256 A6
Devereux Ct WC2 241 A1
Devereux Ho 7
SW15 156 A6
Devereux La SW13 134 B5
Devereux Rd SW11 158 D5
Deverill Ct SE20 184 C2
Devey Cl KT2 177 B5
Devitt Ho 5 E14 119 D6
Devizes St N1 235 D5
Devon Ave TW2 152 A3
Devon Cl Chigwell IG9 21 B2
Tottenham N17 51 D6
Wembley UB6 87 C6
Devoncroft Gdns
TW1 153 A4
Devon Ct
3 Acton W3 88 C1
2 Ealing W7 86 D2
Hampton TW12 173 C3
Devon Gdns N4 50 D3
Devon Ho
9 Penge SE20 184 B3
Walthamstow E17 35 B1
6 Wanstead E11 55 A4
Devonhurst Pl 4
W4 111 B1
Devonia Gdns N18 33 A4
Devonia Rd
N1 94 D5 234 D4
Devon Mans SE1 253 B2
Devon Par HA3 43 C4
Devonport Gdns IG1 56 B3
Devonport Ho
Greenwich SE10 142 A6
23 Paddington W2 91 C2
Devonport Rd W12 112 B4
Devonport St E1 96 D1
Devonport W2 237 A2
Devon Rd IG11 101 C6
Devon Rise N2 48 B5
Devonshire Ave
SM2 218 A1
Devonshire Cl
Edmonton N13 32 C6
Leyton E15 76 C4
Marylebone W1 238 C4
Devonshire Cres
NW7 28 D3
Devonshire Ct
14 Balham SW12 159 B4
Croydon CR0 207 C1
Feltham TW13 150 B2
Pinner HA5 23 B2
6 Richmond TW9 132 B4
Tottenham N17 33 A4
Devonshire Dr
London SE10 141 D4
Long Ditton KT6 213 D6
Devonshire Gdns
Chiswick W4 133 A5
Edmonton N21 17 A4
Tottenham N17 33 A4
Devonshire Gr SE15 140 B6
Devonshire Hall 15
E9 74 C2
Devonshire Hill La
N17 33 A4
Devonshire Hill Prim
Sch N17 33 B4
Devonshire Ho
Brondesbury NW6 69 B2

Devonshire Ho *continued*
Hounslow TW3 130 A2
Newington SE1 262 A6
Paddington W2 236 D4
2 Putney SW15 156 C4
Devonshire Hospl
W1 93 A2 238 B4
Devonshire Ho 10
SM2 218 A1
Devonshire House Prep
Sch NW3 70 B3
Devonshire House Sch
NW3 70 A3
Devonshire Ho
Westminster SW1 259 D2
Whetstone N12 14 A1
Devonshire Mews 2
W4 111 C1
Devonshire Mews N
W1 238 C4
Devonshire Mews S
W1 238 C4
Devonshire Mews W
W1 238 B4
Devonshire Place Mews
W1 238 B4
Devonshire Pl
Child's Hill NW2 69 C5
Kensington W8 255 C5
Marylebone
W1 93 A2 238 B4
Devonshire Prim Sch
SM2 218 A1
Devonshire Rd
Bexley DA6 147 A1
Chislehurst SE9 166 A2
Chiswick W4 111 C1
Ealing W5 109 C3
Eastcote HA5 40 C2
Edmonton N9 18 C3
Feltham TW13 173 A6
Forest Hill SE23 162 C4
Hackbridge SM5,
SM6 219 A4
Harrow HA1 42 B3
Hatch End HA5 23 B2
Ilford IG2 57 C2
Mill Hill NW7 28 D3
Mitcham SW19 180 C3
Newham E16 99 B1
Palmers Green N13 32 C6
Southall UB1 85 C2
Sutton SM2 218 A1
Thornton Heath CR0 205 B2
Tottenham N17 33 A4
Walthamstow E17 53 C3
Devonshire Row
EC2 243 B3
Devonshire Row Mews
W1 238 D5
Devonshire Sq
Bromley BR2 209 B5
Whitechapel
EC2 95 C1 243 B2
Devonshire St
Chiswick W4 111 C1
Marylebone
W1 93 B2 238 C4
Devonshire Terr
W2 92 A1 236 B1
Devonshire Way
Croydon CR0, CR9 223 B6
Hayes UB4 84 B1
Devons Rd E3 97 D3
Devons Road Sta E3 97 D3
Devon St SE15 140 B6
Devon Way KT9 213 C3
Devon Way TW5 129 B5
Devon Way
Ewell KT19 214 D3
Hillingdon UB10 82 B5
De Walden Ho NW8 230 A4
De Walden St W1 238 B3
Dewar Ho 2 SW17 180 C5
Dewar St SE15 140 A2
Dewberry Gdns E6 100 A2
Dewberry St E14 98 A2
Dewey Rd
Dagenham RM10 81 D2
Islington N1 94 C5 234 A4
Dewey St SW17 180 D5
Dewhurst Rd W14 112 D3
Dewlands Ct 7 NW4 28 D1
Dewsbury Cl HA5 41 A3
Dewsbury Ct 5 W4 111 A2
Dewsbury Gdns
KT4 216 A5
Dewsbury Rd NW10 68 A3
Dewsbury Terr NW1 231 D6
Dexter Ho 2 DA18 125 A3
Dexter Rd EN5 12 D5
Deyncourt Rd N17 33 A2
Deyncourt Gdns
E11 55 C5

D'eynsford Rd SE5 139 B4
Dhonau Ho SE16 263 D4
Diadem Ct W1 239 C2
Dial Wlk The
W8 113 D4 245 D2
Diameter Rd BR5 211 A3
Diamond Cl RM8 58 C1
Diamond Ct 8 W7 108 C5
Diamond Est SW17 158 C1
Diamond Ho 22 E3 97 A5
Diamond Rd HA4 63 A4
Diamond St
18 London NW10 67 B1
SE15 139 C5
Diamond Terr SE10 142 A4
Diana Cl
27 Deptford SE8 141 B6
Sidcup DA14 169 A2
Woodford E18 37 B2
Diana Ct SM5 219 A1
Diana Gdns KT6 214 B6
Diana Ho
Barnes SW13 133 D4
4 Brixton SW2 160 B6
Diana, Princess of Wales Mml Wlk
W2 114 A5 246 A3
Diana Rd E17 53 B6
Dianne Ct SE12 165 A3
Dianne Way EN4 2 C1
Dianthus Cl SE2 124 B1
Dias Ho UB5 85 A6
Dibden Ho 8 SE5 139 C5
Dibden St N1 95 A6 235 A6
Dibdin Cl SM1 217 C5
Dibdin Ho W9 91 D5
Dibdin Rd SM1 217 C6
Dicey Ave NW2 68 C4
Dickens Ave
Finchley N3 30 A2
Hayes UB8 82 D1
Dickens Cl Erith DA8 147 D5
Hayes UB3 105 C2
Richmond TW10 154 A2
Dickens Ct
Clerkenwell EC1 241 C5
10 Wanstead E11 55 A5
Wembley HA0 65 C5
Dickens Dr BR7 189 A4
Dickens Ho
Bloomsbury WC1 240 A6
3 Erith DA17 125 B1
Hayes UB3 105 C2
Kennington SE17 261 D1
Kilburn NW6 91 C4
Paddington NW8 236 D6
Dickens House Mus*
WC1 94 B3 240 D5
Dickens La N18 33 C5
Dickenson Cl N9 18 A3
Dickenson Ho N8 50 B3
Dickenson Rd
Feltham TW13 172 D5
Hornsey N8 50 A2
Dickenson's La
SE25 206 A3
Dickenson's Pl
SE25 206 A3
Dickens Rd E6 99 D5
Dickens Sq
SE1 117 A3 262 B6
Dickens St SW8 137 B3
Dickenswood Cl
SE19 182 D3
Dickerage Hill
Kingston u T KT3 177 A1
Kingston u T KT3 199 A6
Dickerage La KT3 199 A6
Dickerage Rd KT1, KT2,
KT3 177 A1
Dickinson Ho 18 E2 96 A4
Dicksee Ho NW8 236 C5
Dick Shepherd Ct 17
SW2 160 C5
Dickson Fold HA5 40 D5
Dickson Ho
3 Charlton SE18 144 A4
4 Stepney E1 96 B1
Dickson Rd SE9 144 A2
Dick Turpin Way
TW14 127 D1
Didbin Ho N7 72 B6
Didsbury Cl E6 100 B6
Digby Bsns Ctr E9 74 D2
Digby Cres N4 73 A6
Digby Gdns RM10 103 C6
Digby Mans W6 112 C1
Digby Pl CR0 221 D5
Digby Rd
Barking IG11 79 D1
Homerton E9 74 D2
Digby St E2 96 C4
Diggon St E1 96 D2
Dighton Ct SE17 139 A6
Dighton Rd SW18 136 A1
Dignum St N1 234 A4
Digswell St N7 72 C2
Dilhorne Cl SE12 165 B1
Dilke St
SW3 136 D6 267 D6
Dilloway Yd UB2 107 A4
Dillwyn Cl SE26 185 A6
Dilston Cl 1 UB5 84 C4
Dilston Gr SE16 118 C2
Dilton Gdns SW15 156 B3
Dilwyn Ct E17 35 A1
Dimes Pl 9 W6 112 B2
Dimmock Dr UB6 64 B3
Dimond Cl E7 77 A4
Dimsdale Dr
Enfield EN1 18 A5
Welsh Harp NW9 45 A1
Dimsdale Wlk 4 E13 99 A5
Dimson Cres E3 97 C4
Dinerman Ct NW8 229 B6
Dingle Cl EN5 11 D5
Dingle Ct 10 HA7 25 C5
Dingle Gdns E14 119 C6
Dingle Rd TW15 170 D5
Dingles Ct HA5 22 D1
Dingle The UB10 82 D4
Dingley La SW16 159 D2
Dingley Pl
EC1 95 A4 235 B1
Dingley Rd
EC1 95 A4 235 A1
Dingwall Ave CR0 221 A6
Dingwall Gdns NW11 47 C3
Dingwall Rd
South Croydon
CR0 221 B6
Wandsworth SW18 158 A4
Dinmont Ho 27 E2 96 A5
Dinmont St 1 E2 96 B5
Dinmore Ho 6 E9 96 C6
Dinnington Ho 17 E1 96 B3
Dinorben SM6 219 C1
Dinsdale Ct EN5 13 D6
Dinsdale Gdns
New Barnet EN5 13 D6
South Norwood
SE25 205 C4
Dinsdale Rd SE3 142 D6
Dinsmore Rd SW12 159 B4
Dinton Ho NW8 237 A6
Dinton Rd
Kingston u T KT2 176 B3
Mitcham SW19 180 B4
Dinwiddy Ho N1 233 C3
Dionis Ho SW6 135 C3
Diploma Ave N2 48 C5
Diploma Ct N2 48 C5
Diprose Lo SW17 180 B6
Dirleton Rd E15 98 D6
Disbrowe Rd
W6 135 A6 264 B5
Discovery Bsns Pk 13
SE16 118 A3
Discovery Dock E
E14 119 D4
Discovery Ho 1
E14 120 A6
Dishforth La NW9 27 C2
Disley Ct 2 UB1 85 D1
Disney Pl SE1 252 B2
Disney St SE1 252 B2
Dison Cl EN3 6 D4
Disraeli Cl
1 Acton W4 111 B2
Thamesmead SE28 124 C5
Disraeli Gdns SW15 135 B1
Disraeli Rd
Acton NW10 89 B5
Ealing W5 109 D5
Putney SW15 135 A1
Upton E7 77 A2
Diss St E2 95 D4
Distaff La EC4 252 A6
Distillery La W6 112 C1
Distillery Rd W6 112 C1
Distillery Wlk 14
TW8 132 A6
Distin Ct 3 SM1 217 D3
Distin St
SE11 116 C2 261 A3
District Rd HA0 65 B3
Ditchburn St E14 120 A6
Ditchfield Rd UB4 85 A3
Ditchley Ct W7 86 D2
Dittisham Rd SE9 188 A6
Ditton Cl KT7 197 A2
Dittoncroft Cl CR0 221 C4
Ditton Grange Cl
KT6 197 D1
Ditton Grange Dr
KT6 197 D1
Ditton Hill KT6 213 D6
Ditton Hill Rd KT6 197 C1
Ditton Ho 10 E5 74 B3
Ditton Lawn KT7 197 A1
Ditton Pl 6 SE20 184 B2
Ditton Rd
Bexley DA6 169 A6
Southall UB2 107 B1
Surbiton KT6 198 B1
Ditton Reach KT7 197 B3
Divis Way SW15 156 B5
Dixon Clark Ct N1 72 D2
Dixon Cl 4 E6 100 B1
Dixon Ct N4 50 C3
Dixon Ho
20 North Kensington
NW10 90 D1
West Heath SE2 124 C1
Dixon Pl BR4 207 D1
Dixon Rd
London SE14 141 A4
South Norwood
SE25 205 D6
Dixon's Alley 10
SE16 118 B4
Dobbin Cl HA3 25 A1
Dobell Rd SE9 166 B6
Dobree Ave NW10 68 B1
Dobson Cl NW6 70 B1
Dobson Ho 18 SE14 140 D6
Doby Ct EC4 252 B6
Dockers Tanner Rd 26
E14 119 C2
Dockett Eddy La KT16,
TW17 192 B1
Dockett Moorings
KT16 192 B1
Dockhead
SE1 117 D4 253 D1
Dockhead Wharf
SE1 253 D2
Dock Hill Ave SE16 118 D4
Docklands Ct 20 E14 97 B1
Docklands Heritage
Mus* SE16 119 B5
Dockland St E16 122 C5
Dockley Rd SE16 118 A3
Dockley Road Ind Est 11
SE16 118 A3
Dock Offices 12
SE16 118 C3
Dock Rd
Brentford TW8 131 D5
Canning Town E16 120 D6
Dockside Rd E16 121 D6
Dock St E1 118 A6
Dockwell Cl TW14 128 A1
Dockwell's Ind Est
TW14 150 B6
Doctor Johnson Ho 2
SW16 181 D6
Doctors Cl SE26 184 C5
Doctor Spurstowe
Almshouses 9 E8 74 B2
Docura Ho N7 72 B6
Docwras Bldgs N1 73 C2
Dodbrooke Rd
SE27 160 D1
Dodd Ho 18 SE16 118 B2
Doddington Gr
SE17 116 D1 261 D1
Doddington Pl 4
SE17 138 D6
Dodsley Pl N9 18 C1
Dodson St
SE1 116 C4 251 B1
Dod St E14 97 C1
Doebury Wlk SE18 146 A6
Doel Cl SW19 180 A3
Doggett Rd SE6 163 C4
Doggetts Ct EN4 14 C6
Doghurst Ave UB3 126 D5
Doghurst Dr UB7 126 D5
Dog Kennel Hill
SE22 139 C2
Dog Kennel Hill Sch
SE22 139 C2
Dog La NW10 67 C4
Dogrose Ct 14 NW9 46 A5
Doherty Rd E13 99 A3
Dokal Ind Est UB2 107 A4
Doland Ct SW17 180 D4
Dolben Ct SW1 259 D3
Dolben St
SE1 116 D5 251 D3
Dolby Rd SW6 135 B3
Doleman Ho 19
SE10 141 D4
Dolland Ho SE11 260 D1
Dolland St SE11 260 D1
Dollar Bay E14 120 A4
Dollary Ct KT3 198 D6
Dolliffe Cl CR4 180 D1
Dollis Ave N3 29 B2
Dollis Brook Wlk
EN5 13 A5
Dollis Cres HA4 40 C1
Dolliscroft NW7 29 A3
Dollis Ct N3 29 B2
DOLLIS HILL 68 B5
Dollis Hill Ave NW2 68 B5
Dollis Hill Est NW2 68 A5
Dollis Hill La NW2 68 A5
Dollis Hill Sta NW2 68 A3
Dollis Hts NW2 68 B5
Dollis Jun & Inf Schs
NW7 28 C3
Dollis Mews N3 29 C2
Dollis Pk N3 29 B2
Dollis Rd N3, NW7 29 B3
Dollis Valley Dr EN5 13 B6
Dollis Valley Way
EN5 13 B5
Dolman Cl N3 30 A1
Dolman Rd W4 111 B2
Dolman St SW4 138 B1
Dolphin Cl
Kingston u T KT6 197 D4
2 Rotherhithe
SE16 118 D4
Thamesmead SE28 102 D1
Dolphin Ct
London NW11 47 A3
Merton SW19 179 C3
Tufnell Pk N7 71 D4
2 Wallington SM6 219 B2
Dolphin Est The
TW16 171 B2
Dolphin La E14 119 D6
Dolphin Rd TW16 171 C2
Dolphin Rd N TW16 171 C2
Dolphin Rd UB5 85 B5
Dolphin Rd S TW16 171 C2
Dolphin Rd W
TW16 171 C2
Dolphin Sch SW11 158 D6
Dolphin Sq
SW1 115 C1 259 B1
Dolphin St KT2 176 A2
Dolphin Twr 21 SE8 141 B6
Dombey Ho
13 Bermondsey
SE1 118 A4
4 Shepherd's Bush
W11 112 D5
Dombey St WC1 240 C4
Dome Hill Pk SE26 183 D6
Domelton Ho SW18 157 D5
Domett Cl SE5 139 B1
Domfe Pl E5 74 C4
Domingo St EC1 242 A5
Dominica Cl 6 E6 99 D5
Dominion Bsns Pk
N9 18 D2
Dominion Cl TW3 130 B3
Dominion Ind Est
UB2 107 A4
Dominion Par HA1 42 D4
Dominion Rd
Croydon CR0 205 D2
Southall UB2 107 A3
Dominion St
EC2 95 B2 242 D4
Dominion Wks RM8 59 A1
Domonic Dr SE9 166 D1
Domville Cl N20 14 B2
Donaghue Cotts 11
E14 97 A2
Donald Dr RM6 58 C4
Donald Lynch Ho
CR4 180 D1
Donald Rd
Newham E13 99 B6
Thornton Heath CR0 204 B2
Donaldson Rd
Kilburn NW6 91 B6
Shooters Hill SE18 144 C4
Donald Woods Gdns
KT5 215 A6
Doncaster Dr UB5 63 B3
Doncaster Gdns
London N4 51 A3
Northolt UB5 63 B3
Doncaster Gn WD19 22 C5
Doncaster Rd N9 18 B4
Doncel Ct E4 20 B4
Donegal Ho 2 E1 96 C3
Donegal St
N1 94 B5 233 D3
Doneraile Ho SW1 258 C1
Doneraile St SW6 134 D4
Dongola Rd
Newham E13 99 B4
Tottenham N17 51 C6
Tower Hamlets E1 97 A2
Dongola Rd W 5
E13 99 B4
Don Gratton Ho 23
E1 96 A2
Donington Ave IG6 57 A4
Donkey Alley SE22 162 A5
Donkey La EN1 6 A3
Donkin Ho 15 SE16 118 B2
Donne Ct SE24 161 A5
Donnefield Ave HA8 26 A3
Donne Ho
18 Canonbury N16 73 B4
14 Deptford SE14 140 D6
11 Poplar E14 97 C1
Donnelly Ct SW6 264 B4
Donne Pl
Chelsea
SW3 114 C2 257 B4
Mitcham CR4 203 B5
Donne Rd RM8 80 C6
Donnington Ct
11 Camden Town
NW1 71 B1
Willesden NW10 68 B1
Donnington Ho 12
SW8 137 D3
Donnington Prim Sch
NW10 90 B6
Donnington Rd
Harrow HA3 43 D3
Willesden Green
NW10 90 B6
Worcester Pk KT4 216 A6
Donnybrook Rd
SW16 181 D3
Donoghue Bsns Pk
NW2 68 D5
Donovan Ave N10 31 C1
Donovan Ct SW7 256 C1
Donovan Ho 4 E1 118 C6
Donovan Pl N21 16 B6
Don Phelan Cl SE5 139 B4
Doone Cl TW11 175 A4
Doon St SE1 116 C5 251 A4
Doradus Ct 20
SW19 156 D3
Dora Ho
11 Shepherd's Bush
W11 112 D6
1 Tower Hamlets
E14 97 B1
Doral Way SM5 218 D3
Doran Ct E6 100 B5
Dorando Cl W12 112 B6
Doran Gr SE18 145 C5
Doran Manor N2 48 D4
Doran Wlk
Stratford E15 76 A1
Stratford Marsh E15 98 A6
Dora Rd SW19 179 C6
Dora St E14 97 B1
Dora Way SW9 138 C3
Dorcas Ct 9 SW18 136 B1
Dorchester Ave
Edmonton N13 33 A6
Harrow HA2 42 A3
Sidcup DA5 168 D4
Dorchester Cl
Northolt UB5 63 D3
St Paul's Cray BR5 190 B3
Dorchester Ct
Cricklewood NW2 68 D5
1 De Beauvoir Town
N1 73 C1
East Barnet N14 15 B4
Herne Hill SE24 161 A6
Knightsbridge SW1 257 D5
1 Muswell Hill N10 49 B6
5 Streatham SW16 160 A2
2 Woodford E18 36 D2
Dorchester Dr
Feltham TW14 149 C5
Herne Hill SE24 161 A6
Dorchester Gdns
Chingford E4 35 C6
East Finchley NW11 47 C5
Dorchester Gr W4 111 D1
Dorchester Ho
Richmond TW9 132 D5
Wallington SM5 218 D3
Dorchester Mews
New Malden KT3 199 B5
Twickenham TW1 153 C5
Dorchester Prim Sch
KT4 200 C1
Dorchester Rd
Cheam SM4 202 A2
North Cheam KT4 200 C1
Northolt UB5 63 D3
Dorchester Waye
Hayes UB4 84 B1
Hayes UB4 84 C1
Dorchester Way HA3 44 B3
Dorcis Ave DA7 147 A3
Dordrecht Rd W3 111 C5
Dore Ave E12 78 C3
Doreen Ave NW9 45 B1
Doreen Capstan Ho 5
E11 76 C5
Dore Gdns SM4 201 D2
Dorell Cl UB1 85 B2
Dorey Ho 7 TW8 131 C5
Doria Rd SW6 135 B3
Doric Ho 7 E2 96 D5
Doric Way
NW1 93 D4 232 C2
Dorie Mews N12 29 D6
Dorien Rd SW20 178 D1
Doris Emmerton Ct
SW18 136 A1
Doris Rd
Ashford TW15 171
Upton E7 77
Dorking Cl
Deptford SE8 141
North Cheam KT4 216
Dorking Ct N17 34
Dorking Ho SE1 262
Dorland Ct SW15 157
Dorlcote Rd SW18 158
Dorleston Ct N1 235
Dorly Cl TW17 193
Dorman Pl 6 N9 18
Dorman Way
NW8 92 B6 229
Dorman Wlk NW10 67
Dorma Trad Pk E10 52
Dormay St SW18 157
Dormer Cl Barnet EN5 12
Stratford E15 76
Dormer's Ave UB1 85
Dormers Lo EN4 2
Dormers Rise UB1 85
DORMER'S WELLS 107
Dormer's Wells High
Sch UB1 85
Dormers Wells Ho
UB4 84
Dormer's Wells Inf Sch
UB1 107
Dormer's Wells Jun Sch
UB1 107
Dormer's Wells La
UB1 107
Dormstone Ho SE17 263
Dormywood HA4 39
Dornberg Cl SE3 143
Dornberg Rd SE3 143
Dorncliffe Rd SW6 135
Dorney Ct SW6 135
Dorney NW3 70
Dorney Rise BR5 211
Dorney Way TW4 151
Dornfell St NW6 69
Dornoch Ho 26 E3 97
Dornton Rd
South Croydon
CR2 221
Upper Tooting SW12,
SW17 159
Dorothy Ave HA0 66
Dorothy Barley Schs
RM8 80
Dorothy Charrington Ho
1 SE22 162
Dorothy Evans Cl
DA7 147
Dorothy Gdns RM8 80
Dorothy Pettingel Ho 1
SM1 217
Dorothy Rd SW11 136
Dorothy Villas UB1 107
Dorrien Wlk SW16 159
Dorrington Ct SE25 183
Dorrington Point 20
E3 97
Dorrington St EC1 241
Dorrington Way
BR3 208
Dorrit Ho 2 W11 112
Dorrit Mews N18 33
Dorrit St SE1 252
Dorrit Way BR7 189
Dorryn Ct SE26 184
Dors Cl NW9 45
Dorset Ave
Falconwood DA16 145
Hayes UB4 83
Southall UB2 107
Dorset Bldgs EC4 241
Dorset Cl Hayes UB4 83
Marylebone NW1 237
Dorset Ct
3 Ealing W7 86
3 London N1 73
4 Northolt UB5 85
Dorset Dr HA8 26
Dorset Gdns SW16 204
Dorset Hall SW19 179
Dorset Ho 1 SE20 184
Dorset Mans 2 W6 134
Dorset Mews
Belgravia SW1 258
Finchley N3 29
Dorset Pl E15 76
Dorset Rd
Ashford TW15 148
Chislehurst SE9 166
Ealing W5 109
Harrow HA1 42
Merton SW19 179
Mitcham CR4 180
Penge BR3 206
South Lambeth
SW8 138 B5 270
Upton E7 77
West Green N15 51

rset Rd continued
Vood Green N22 32 A2
rset Rise
C4 94 D1 241 C1
rset Road Inf Sch
E9 166 A2
rset Sq
W1 92 D3 237 C5
rset St W1 92 D2 237 D3
rset Waye TW5 129 B5
rset Way
illingdon UB10 82 B5
wickenham TW2 152 B3
rton Cl 6 SE15 139 C5
rton Villas UB7 126 C4
rville Cres W6 112 B3
rville Rd SE12 165 A6
thill Rd SE18 145 A5
uai Gr TW12 174 A2
uay Martyrs RC Sch
Annexe) The
B10 60 D3
uay Martyrs RC Sch
he UB10 60 D4
ughty Ct 11 E1 118 B5
ughty Mews
Cl 94 B3 240 C5
ughty St
Cl 94 B3 240 C5
uglas Ave
althamstow E17 35 C2
embley HA0 66 A1
est Barnes KT3 200 B5
uglas Bader Ho
3 29 D4
uglas Bldgs SE1 252 B2
uglas Cl
tanmore HA7 25 A5
allington SM6 220 A2
uglas Cres UB4 84 D3
uglas Ct London N3 29 D1
South Hampstead
NW6 69 C1
Upper Tooting
SW17 180 C4
uglas Dr CR0 223 C5
uglas Gracey Ho
W18 157 A4
uglas Ho
sleworth TW1 153 B6
utney SW15 156 A5
estminster SW1 259 C3
uglas Johnstone Ho
W6 264 C5
uglas Mews NW2 69 A5
uglas 20 NW9 27 D1
uglas Path E14 120 A1
uglas Rd
hingford E4 20 C3
ounslow TW3 129 D2
ford IG3 58 A3
slington N1 73 A1
ilburn NW6 91 B6
ingston u T KT1 176 D1
Newham E16 99 A2
uglas Rd N N1 73 A2
uglas Rd S N1 73 A2
uglas Rd
tanwell TW19 148 A5
urbiton KT6 198 B1
hames Ditton KT10 212 A6
elling DA16 146 B4
Vood Green N22 32 C2
uglas Robinson Ct
W16 182 A3
uglas Sq SM4 201 C3
uglas St
W1 115 D2 259 C3
uglas Terr E17 35 B2
uglas Waite Ho
W6 69 D1
uglas Way SE8 141 B5
ulton Ho SE11 260 D4
ulton Mews 4
W6 69 D2
unesforth Gdns
W18 157 D3
uro Pl
8 113 D3 255 D6
uro St E3 97 C5
uthwaite Sq 12
1 118 A5
ve App E6 100 A2
ve Cl Hendon NW7 27 D3
ortholt UB5 84 D3
Vallington SM6 220 B1
vecot Cl HA5 40 C4
vecote Gdns 8
W14 133 B2
ve Ct
ity of London EC2 242 C1
nfield EN3 18 B6
tanwell TW19 148 A4
vedale Ave HA3 43 C3
vedale Cl DA16 146 A3
vedale Cotts 6
W11 136 D3

Dovedale Ho N16 51 B2
Dovedale Rd SE22 162 B5
Dovedale Rise CR4 180 D3
Dovedon Cl N14 16 A2
Dove House Gdns E4 19 C2
Dovehouse Mead
IG11 101 B5
Dovehouse St
SW3 114 C1 257 A1
Dove Mews
SW7 114 A1 256 B2
Dove Pk HA5 23 C3
Dover Cl NW2 68 D6
Dovercourt Ave
CR7 204 C5
Dovercourt Gdns
HA7 26 A5
Dovercourt La SM1 218 A5
Dovercourt Rd
SE22 161 D5
Dover Ct
Clerkenwell EC1 241 C6
17 Greenwich SE10 141 D4
Sutton SM1 218 B4
Dove Rd N1 73 B2
Doverfield Rd SW2 160 A4
Dover Flats SE1 263 B3
Dover Gdns SM5 218 D5
Dover Ho
7 Beckenham
BR3 185 C3
Brixton SE5 138 D4
11 Deptford SE15 140 C6
Edgware HA8 26 B3
14 Penge SE20 184 B2
Dover House Rd
SW15 156 B6
Doveridge Gdns N13 32 D6
Dover Mans 16
SW9 138 C2
Dove Row E2 96 A6
Dover Park Dr
SW15 156 B5
Dover Patrol SE3 143 C3
Dover Rd
Dagenham RM6 59 A3
Lower Edmonton N9 18 C2
South Norwood
SE19 183 B4
Wanstead E12 77 C6
Woolwich SE18 145 A3
Dover St W1 115 C5 249 A4
Dover Terr TW9 132 C3
Dover Yd W1 249 A4
Doves Cl BR2 226 A6
Doves Yd N1 94 C6 234 A5
Dovet Ct SW8 270 C2
Doveton Ho 7 E1 96 C3
Doveton Rd CR2 221 B3
Doveton St 8 E1 96 C3
Dove Wlk SW1 258 A2
Dovey Lo 4 N1 72 C1
Dowanhill Rd SE6 164 B3
Dowd Cl N11 15 A2
Dowdeny Cl 12 NW5 71 C3
Dowdeswell Cl
SW15 133 C1
Dowding Ho N6 49 A2
Dowding Pl HA7 25 A4
Dowding Rd UB10 60 B1
Dowe Ho SE3 142 C2
Dowell Ho SE21 161 D1
Dower Ho The
DA14 169 B1
Dowes Ho 13 SW16 160 A1
Dowgate Hill EC4 252 C6
Dowland Ho EN1 5 D5
Dowland St W10 91 A4
Dowlas St SE5 139 C5
Dowlen Ct 14 E14 119 C4
Dowler Ct 2 KT2 176 B2
Dowler Ho 32 E1 96 A1
Dowlerville Rd BR6 227 D2
Dowling Ho DA17 125 B3
Dowman Cl 2
SW19 179 D3
Downage NW4 46 C6
Downalong WD23 8 B3
Down Barns Rd HA4 62 D5
Downbarton Ho 11
SW9 138 C4
Downbury Mews 13
SW18 157 C6
Down Cl UB5 84 B5
Downderry Prim Sch
BR1 186 C6
Downderry Rd BR1 186 C6
Downe Cl DA16 146 C5
Downe Ho 9 SE7 143 C6
Downe Manor Prim Sch
UB5 84 B4
Downend Ct 1
SE15 139 C6
Downend SE18 144 D5
Downe Rd CR4 180 D1
Downer's Cotts
SW4 137 C1

Downes Cl TW1 153 B5
Downes Ct N21 16 C3
Downes Ho CR0 220 D4
Downey Ho 6 E1 96 D3
Downfield Cl W9 91 D3
Downfield Ho KT3 199 B1
Downfield KT4 200 A1
Down Hall Rd KT2 175 D2
DOWNHAM 186 C5
Downham Ct 1 N1 73 B1
Downham Ent Ctr
SE6 164 D2
Downham La BR1 186 B5
Downham Rd N1 73 B1
Downham Way BR1 186 C6
Downhills Ave N17 51 B6
Downhills Park Rd
N17 51 A6
Downhills Prim Sch
N15 51 B5
Downhills Way N17 33 A1
Downhurst Ave NW7 27 B5
Downhurst Ct NW4 46 C6
Downing Cl HA2 42 A6
Downing Ct N12 29 D5
Downing Dr UB6 86 C6
Downing Ho
9 Merton SW19 179 C3
2 North Kensington
W10 90 D1
4 Putney SW15 156 A6
Downing Rd RM9 81 B1
Downings E6 100 C1
Downing St*
SW1 116 A4 250 A2
Downland Cl N20 14 A3
Downland Ct E11 76 C6
Downleys Cl SE9 166 B2
Downman Rd SE9 144 A2
Down Pl W6 112 B1
Down Rd TW11 175 B4
Down St Mews W1 248 C3
Downs Ave
Elmstead BR7 188 B5
Pinner HA5 41 B2
Downs Bridge Rd
BR3 186 B2
Downs Ct
16 Hackney E8 74 B3
13 Wimbledon
SW19 178 D3
Downsell Prim Sch
E15 76 B4
Downsell Rd E15 76 B4
Downsfield Rd E17 53 A3
Downshall Ave IG3 57 C3
Downshall Ct IG3 57 C3
Downshall Prim Sch
IG3 57 C2
Downs Hill BR2, BR3 186 B2
Downshire Hill NW3 70 B4
Downside Cl SW19 180 A4
Downside Cres
Ealing W13 87 A3
Maitland Pk NW3 70 C3
Downside 2 SW15 157 A6
Downside Rd SM2 218 C2
Downside
Sunbury TW16 172 A2
Twickenham TW1 152 D1
Downside Wlk UB5 85 B4
Downs La 2 E5 74 B4
Downs Park Rd E5,
E8 74 A3
Downs Rd
Beckenham BR3 185 D1
Enfield EN1 5 C1
Shacklewell E5, N16 74 A4
South Norwood CR7 183 A2
Down St KT8 195 C4
Downs The SW19,
SW20 178 D3
Down St W1 115 B5 248 C3
Downsview Gdns
SE19 183 A3
Downs View TW7 131 A4
Downs View Lo 9
KT6 198 A3
Downsview Prim Sch
SE19 183 A3
Downsview Rd
SE19 183 A3
Downsview Sch E5 74 B4
Downsway BR6 227 C3
Downton Ave SW2 160 B2
Downtown Rd SE16 119 A4
Downway N12 30 C3
Down Way UB5 84 B4
Dowrey St N1 234 A6
Dowsett Rd N17 34 A1
Dowson Cl SE5 139 B1
Dowson Ct SE13 142 B2
Dowson Ho 8 E1 96 D1
Doyce St SE1 252 A2
Doyle Gdns NW10 90 B6
Doyle Ho W3 110 D4
Doyle Rd SE25 206 A5

D'Oyley St SW1 258 A4
Doynton St N19 71 B6
Draco St SE17 139 A6
Dragon Ct WC2 240 B2
Dragonfly Cl E13 99 B4
Dragon Rd SE15 139 C6
Dragon Yd WC1 240 B2
Dragoon Rd SE8 119 B1
Dragor Rd NW10 89 A3
Drake Cl 30 SE16 118 D4
Drake Cres SE28 102 C1
Drake Croft N16 73 B6
Drake Ct
Dulwich SE19 183 D5
5 Hammersmith
W12 112 B4
Kingston u T KT5 198 B5
Drakefell Rd SE4,
SE14 140 D2
Drakefield Rd
SW17 159 A1
Drake Hall 18 E16 121 B5
Drake Ho
2 Limehouse
E14 119 A6
20 Stepney E1 96 C2
Drakeley Ct N5 72 D4
Drake Mews BR2 209 C5
Drake Rd
Brockley SE4 141 C2
Chessington KT9 214 C3
Harrow HA2 63 B6
Mitcham CR4 203 A3
Thornton Heath CR0 204 B2
Drakes Ct SE23 162 C3
Drakes Ctyd NW6 69 B1
Drake St Enfield EN2 5 B4
Holborn WC1 240 C3
Drakes Wlk E6 100 B6
Drakewood Rd
SW16 181 D3
Draper Cl
Belvedere DA17 125 B2
Hounslow TW7 130 B3
Draper Ct BR1 210 A5
Draper Ho SE1 261 D4
Draper Pl N1 234 D6
Drapers Almhouses 5
E3 97 C4
Draper's Cottage Homes
NW7 28 A6
Drapers Gdns EC2 242 D2
Drapers Rd Enfield EN2 4 D4
Leyton E15 76 B4
Tottenham N17 51 D6
Drappers Way 8
SE16 118 A2
Draven Cl BR2 208 D2
Drawell Cl SE18 123 C1
Drax Ave SW20 178 A3
Draxmont SW19 179 A4
Draycot Rd
Tolworth KT6 198 C1
Wanstead E11 55 B2
Draycott Ave
Chelsea
SW3 114 C2 257 B3
Harrow HA3 43 C3
Draycott Cl
Camberwell SE5 139 B5
Cricklewood NW2 68 D5
Harrow HA3 43 B3
Draycott Ct SW11 267 A2
Draycott Ho SW3 257 C3
Draycott Pl
SW3 114 D2 257 C3
Draycott Terr
SW3 114 D2 257 D3
Drayford Cl W9 91 B3
Dray Gdns SW2 160 B6
Draymans Ct 4
SW9 138 B2
Draymans Way
TW7 130 D2
Drayside Mews UB2 107 B4
Drayson Mews
W8 113 C4 245 B1
Drayton Ave
Ealing W13 109 A6
Orpington BR6 210 D1
Drayton Bridge Rd
Ealing W7, W13 108 D6
Ealing W13 87 A1
Drayton Cl
Hounslow TW4 151 B6
Ilford IG1 57 B1
Drayton Ct
South Kensington
SW10 256 B1
Tolworth KT5 214 D6
West Drayton UB7 104 B2
Drayton Gdns
Ealing W13 109 A6
Southgate N21 16 D4
South Kensington
SW10 114 A1 256 B1
West Drayton UB7 104 A4

Drayton Gn W13 109 A6
Drayton Gr W13 109 A6
Drayton Green Prim Sch
W13 109 A6
Drayton Green Rd
W13 109 B6
Drayton Green Sta
W7 86 D1
Drayton Ho
14 Camberwell
SE5 139 B5
Leytonstone E11 54 B1
Drayton Lo E17 35 D1
Drayton Manor High
Sch W7 86 D1
Drayton Park Mews 12
N5 72 C3
Drayton Park Prim Sch
N5 72 C3
Drayton Park Sta N5 72 C3
Drayton Pk N5, N7 72 C4
Drayton Rd
Croydon CR0 220 D6
Ealing W13 109 B6
Harlesden NW10 89 D6
Leytonstone E11 54 B1
Tottenham N17 33 C1
Drayton Waye HA3 43 B3
Dreadnought Cl
SW19 180 B1
Dreadnought St
SE10 120 C3
Drenon Sq UB3 105 D6
Dresden Cl NW6 69 D2
Dresden Ho
5 Clapham
SW11 137 A3
Lambeth SE11 260 D4
Dresden Rd N19 49 D1
Dressington Ave
SE4 163 C5
Drew Ave NW7 29 A4
Drewery Ct SE3 142 C2
Drewett Ho 31 E1 96 A1
Drew Gdns UB6 64 D2
Drew Ho 12 SW16 160 A1
Drew Prim Sch E16 122 A5
Drew Rd E16 122 A5
Drewstead La
SW16 159 D2
Drewstead Rd
SW16 159 D2
Driberg Ct RM9 80 B2
Driffield Ct 4 NW9 27 C2
Driffield Rd E3 97 A5
Drift The BR2 225 D5
Driftway Ho 19 E3 97 B5
Driftway The CR4 181 A2
Drinkwater Ho 11
SE5 139 B5
Drinkwater Rd HA2 63 D6
Drive Ct HA8 26 C5
Drive Ho CR4 202 C5
Drive Mans SW6 135 A3
Drive The Acton W3 89 A1
Ashford TW15 171 B3
Barking IG11 79 D1
Barking IG11 80 A2
Barnet EN5 1 A2
Beckenham BR3 185 C2
Bexley DA5 168 D4
Buckhurst Hill IG9 21 C4
Chingford E4 20 B4
Chislehurst BR7 189 D2
Edgware HA8 26 C5
Enfield EN2 5 B4
Erith DA8 147 D6
Feltham TW14 150 C4
Finchley N3 29 C3
Fortis Green N6 48 D4
Harlesden NW10 89 D6
Harrow HA2 41 C2
Hendon NW11 47 A2
Hounslow TW3,
TW7 130 B3
Ickenham UB10 60 A5
Islington N7 72 B2
Kingston u T KT2 177 A3
Morden SM4 202 B4
New Barnet EN5 14 A5
Orpington BR6 227 D6
Redbridge IG1 56 B2
Sidcup DA14 190 B6
South Norwood CR7 205 B5
St Paul's Cray BR7 211 D6
Surbiton KT6 198 A2
Thames Ditton KT10 196 A1
Walthamstow E17 53 D6
Wanstead E18 55 A6
Wembley Pk HA9 67 A6
West Ewell KT19 215 D2
West Wickham BR4 208 B2
Wimbledon SW19,
SW20 178 C3
Wood Green N11 31 D4
Dr Johnson Ave
SW17 159 B1

Dr Johnson's House
Mus* EC4 241 B1
Droitwich Cl SE26 162 A1
Dromey Gdns HA3 24 D3
Dromore Rd SW15 157 A5
Dronfield Gdns RM8 80 C3
Dron Ho E1 96 C2
Droop St W10 91 A3
Drovers Ct
3 Kingston u T
KT1 176 A1
Lewisham SE13 142 A2
Drovers Pl SE15 140 B5
Drovers Rd CR2 221 B3
Dr Triplett's CE Prim
Sch UB3 83 D1
Druce Rd SE21 161 C5
Druid St SE1 117 D4 253 C1
Druids Way BR2 208 B5
Drumaline Ridge
KT4 215 C6
Drummer Lo N7 72 B5
Drummond Castle Ct
E7 76 D4
Drummond Cres
NW1 93 D4 232 C2
Drummond Ct
Finchley N12 30 C3
Harrow HA1 42 C2
Drummond Ctr CR0 221 A6
Drummond Dr HA7 24 D3
Drummond Gate
SW1 259 D2
Drummond Ho
13 Bethnal Green
E2 96 A5
Finchley N2 30 A1
Drummond Rd
Bermondsey SE16 118 B3
Croydon CR0 221 A6
Wanstead E11 55 C3
Drummonds Pl
TW9 132 A1
Drummonds The IG9 21 B2
Drummond St
NW1 93 C3 239 A6
Drum St E1 243 D2
Drury Cres CR0 220 C6
Drury Ho SW8 269 A2
Drury La WC2 94 A1 240 B1
Drury Rd HA1 42 A2
Drury Way Ind Est
NW10 67 B3
Drury Way NW10 67 B3
Dryad St SW15 134 D2
Dryburgh Gdns NW9 44 C6
Dryburgh Ho SW1 258 D2
Dryburgh Mans
SW15 134 C2
Dryburgh Rd SW15 134 C2
Dryden Ave W7 86 D1
Dryden Bldg 10 E1 96 A1
Dryden Ct
Lambeth SE11 261 B3
11 Richmond TW10 175 D6
Dryden Ho
Bromley Comm
BR2 209 D4
6 Camberwell SE5 139 C4
16 Stoke Newington
N16 73 C5
Dryden Rd
Bexley DA16 145 D4
Enfield EN1 17 D5
Harrow HA3 24 D2
Wimbledon SW19 180 A4
Dryden St WC2 240 B1
Dryer Ct 21 EN3 7 C6
Dryfield Cl NW10 67 A2
Dryfield Rd HA8 27 A4
Dryfield Wlk 1 SE8 141 C6
Dryhill Rd DA17 147 B6
Dryland Ave 5 BR6 227 D4
Drylands Rd N8 50 A3
Drysdale Ave E4 19 D5
Drysdale Flats 3 E8 73 D3
Drysdale Ho 19 E2 95 C4
Drysdale Pl N1 95 C4
Drysdale St N1 95 C4
Dublin Ave E8 96 A6
Du Burstow Terr
W7 108 C4
Ducal St 25 E2 95 D4
Ducane Cl 6 W12 90 C1
Du Cane Ct SW12 159 A3
Du Cane Rd W12 90 A1
Ducavel Ho SW2 160 B3
Duchess Cl
London N11 31 B5
Sutton SM1 218 A4
Duchess Gr IG9 21 B2
Duchess Mews W1 238 D3
Duchess of Bedford Ho
W8 245 A2

Duchess of Bedford's Wlk W8 113 C4 245 A1
Duchess St W1 93 B2 238 D3
Duchy Rd EN4 2 B5
Duchy St SE1 116 C5 251 B4
Ducie Ho
8 Charlton SE7 143 C6
2 Putney SW15 156 C6
Ducie St SW4 138 B1
Duckett Mews N4 50 D3
Duckett Rd N4 50 D3
Duckett St E1 97 A2
Duck La W1 239 C1
Duck Lees La EN3 7 A1
Ducks Hill Rd HA4, HA6 39 A5
DUCKS ISLAND 12 D5
Duck's Wlk TW1 153 C6
Du Cros Dr HA7 25 D4
Du Cros Rd W3 111 C5
DUDDEN HILL 68 A3
Dudden Hill La NW10 67 D3
Duddington Cl SE9 187 D6
Dudley Ave HA3 43 C6
Dudley Ct
Colney Hatch N12 30 C5
Marylebone W1 237 C1
St Giles WC2 240 A2
Temple Fortune NW11 47 B5
14 Wanstead E11 55 A4
Wembley HA0 65 D3
Dudley Dr Ruislip HA4 62 B3
West Barnes SM4 201 A2
Dudley Gdns
Ealing W13 109 B4
Harrow HA2 42 B1
Dudley Ho
18 Brixton SW9 138 C3
Edgware HA8 26 B3
Paddington W2 236 C3
Dudley Mews 14 SW2 160 C5
Dudley Pl UB3 105 B2
Dudley Rd
Ashford TW15 170 B6
East Bedfont TW14 149 B3
Finchley N3 29 D1
Harrow HA2 64 A6
Ilford IG1 78 D4
Kilburn NW6 91 B5
Kingston u T KT1 198 B6
Richmond TW9 132 B3
Southall UB2 106 D3
Walthamstow E17 35 C1
Walton-on-T KT12 194 A2
Wimbledon SW19 179 C4
Dudley St W2 236 C3
Dudlington Rd E5 74 C6
Dudmaston Mews SW3 256 D2
Dudsbury Rd DA14 190 B4
Dudset La TW5 128 A4
Duett Ct TW3 129 A5
Duffell Ho SE11 260 D1
Dufferin Ave EC1 242 C5
Dufferin Ct EC1 242 C5
Dufferin St EC1 95 A3 242 B5
Duffield Cl HA1 42 D4
Duffield Dr N15 51 D5
Duffield Ho N4 51 A2
Duff St E14 97 D1
Dufour's Pl W1 239 B1
Dugard Way SE11 116 D2 261 C3
Dugdale Ho 10 N7 71 D3
Duggan Dr BR7 188 A4
Dugolly Ave HA9 66 D5
Duke Gdns IG6 57 B5
Duke Humphrey Rd SE3 142 C3
Duke Of Cambridge Cl TW2 152 B5
Duke Of Edinburgh Rd SM1 218 B6
Duke Of Wellington Ave SE18 123 A3
Duke of Wellington Pl SW1, W1 248 B2
Duke of York's Sq SW3 114 D2 257 D3
Duke of York St SW1 249 B4
Duke Rd
Chiswick W4 111 B1
Ilford IG6 57 B5
Duke St Hill SE1 252 D4
Duke St St James's SW1 115 C5 249 B4

Dukes Ave
Edgware HA8 26 B5
Finchley N3 29 D2
Hornsey N10 49 C6
Hounslow TW4 129 A1
Kingston u T KT3 199 D6
Duke's Ave W4 111 B1
Dukes Ave
Northolt UB5 63 A1
Rayners La HA2, HA5 41 B3
Richmond KT2, TW10 175 D6
Wealdstone HA1 42 C5
Dukes Cl
Ashford TW15 171 A6
Hampton TW12 173 B5
Dukes Ct Barking E6 100 C6
Beckenham BR3 207 A6
Dulwich SE22 162 A3
Ealing W13 87 B2
East Dulwich SE22 162 B6
Lewisham SE13 142 A3
Mortlake SW14 133 B3
Dukes Gate 4 W4 111 A2
Dukes Green Ave TW14 150 A6
Dukes Head Yd N6 49 B1
Duke Shore Wharf E14 119 B6
Duke's Ho SW1 259 D4
Dukes La W8 113 D4 245 C2
Dukes Mews N10 49 B6
Duke's Mews W1 238 B2
Duke's Pl EC3 95 C1 243 B1
Dukes Point N6 49 B1
Dukes Rd Acton W3 88 C3
Barking E6 100 C6
Duke's Rd WC1 93 D4 232 D1
Dukes Ride UB10 60 A4
Dukesthorpe Rd SE26 184 D6
Duke St W1 93 A1 238 B1
Duke Street Mans W1 238 B1
Duke St
Richmond TW10, TW9 153 D6
Sutton SM1 218 B4
Dukes Way BR4 224 C5
Duke's Yd W1 248 B6
Dulas St N4 50 B1
Dulford St W11 113 A6 244 A6
Dulka Rd SW11 158 D6
Dulverton Ct 12 KT6 198 A4
Dulverton Mans WC1 240 D5
Dulverton NW1 232 B5
Dulverton Prim Sch SE9 167 B2
Dulverton Rd
New Eltham SE9 167 B2
Ruislip HA4 62 A6
DULWICH 161 C1
Dulwich Bsns Ctr SE23 162 D3
Dulwich Coll SE21 161 C2
Dulwich Coll Picture Gall* SE21 161 C4
Dulwich Coll Prep Sch SE21 161 C1
Dulwich Comm SE21 161 C3
Dulwich Ct SE22 162 B3
Dulwich Hamlet Jun Sch SE21 161 B5
Dulwich Hospl SE22 139 C1
Dulwich Lawn Cl SE22 161 D6
Dulwich Mead SE24 161 A5
Dulwich Mews
1 East Dulwich SE22 139 D1
East Dulwich SE22 161 D6
Dulwich Oaks The SE21 161 D1
Dulwich Rd SE24 160 D5
DULWICH VILLAGE 161 C4
Dulwich Village CE Inf Sch SE21 161 C5
Dulwich Village SE21 161 C5
Dulwich Wood Ave SE19 183 C5
Dulwich Wood Pk SE19 183 C6
Dumain Ct SE11 261 C3
Du Maurier Ho 2 NW3 70 D3
Dumbarton Ct 16 SW2 160 A4
Dumbarton Rd SW2 160 A5

Dumbleton Cl KT2 176 D2
Dumbreck Rd SE9 144 C2
Dumont Rd N16 73 C5
Dumphreys Ho 5 SW4 159 D4
Dumpton Pl NW1 71 A1
Dunally Pk TW17 193 B2
Dunbar Ave
Beckenham BR3 207 A5
Dagenham RM10 81 C5
Thornton Heath SW16 182 C1
Dunbar Cl UB4 84 A2
Dunbar Ct
3 London N12 29 D6
Sutton SM1 218 B3
Walton-on-T KT12 194 C1
Dunbar Gdns RM10 81 D3
Dunbar Rd
New Malden KT3 199 A5
Tottenham N22 32 D2
Upton E7 77 A2
Dunbar St SE27 161 A1
Dunbar Wharf 20 E14 119 B6
Dunblane Cl HA8 10 D2
Dunblane Rd SE9 144 A3
Dunboe Pl TW17 193 A2
Dunboyne Rd NW3 70 D3
Dunbridge Ho SW15 155 D5
Dunbridge St
Bethnal Green E2
Bethnal Green E2 96 B3
Duncan Cl EN5 2 A1
Duncan Ct
5 London N12 29 D5
3 Poplar E14 98 A2
Southgate N21 16 D3
Duncan Gr W3 89 C1
Duncan Ho
Harrow HA2 64 A5
3 Primrose Hill NW3 70 D1
Duncannon Ho SW1 259 D1
Duncannon St WC2 250 A5
Duncan Rd
Hackney E8 96 B6
Richmond TW9 132 A1
Duncan St N1 94 D5 234 C4
Duncan Terr N1 94 D5 234 C4
Dunch St 33 E1 96 B1
Dunchurch Ho RM10 81 C1
Duncombe Hill SE23 163 A4
Duncombe Ho 7 SW19 156 D3
Duncombe Prim Sch N19 50 A1
Duncombe Rd N19 49 D1
Duncrievie Rd SE13 164 B5
Duncroft SE18 145 C5
Dundalk Ho 2 E1 96 C1
Dundalk Rd SE4 141 A2
Dundas Gdns KT8 195 D6
Dundas Ho 12 E2 96 C5
Dundas Mews 4 EN3 7 C6
Dundas Rd SE15 140 C3
Dundee Ct 36 E1 118 B5
Dundee Ho W9 229 A2
Dundee Rd
Croydon SE25 206 B4
Newham E13 99 B5
Dundee St E1 118 B5
Dundee Way EN3 7 A2
Dundee Wharf E14 119 B6
Dundela Gdns KT17, KT4 216 B4
Dundonald Cl 6 E6 100 A1
Dundonald Prim Sch SW19 179 B3
Dundonald Rd
Brondesbury Pk NW10 90 D6
Merton SW19 179 B3
Dundonald Road Sta SW19 179 B3
Dundry Ho 8 SE26 162 A1
Duneaves HA1 64 C5
Dunedin Ho E16 122 B5
Dunedin Rd
Ilford IG1 57 A1
Leyton E10 75 D5
Dunedin Way UB4 84 C3
Dunelm Gr SE27 161 A1
Dunelm St E1 96 D1
Dunfield Gdns SE6 185 D5
Dunfield Rd SE6 185 D5
Dunford Ct 9 HA5 23 B3
Dunford Rd N7 72 B4
Dungarvan Ave SW15 134 A1
Dungeness Ho SW18 136 A1
Dunheved Cl CR7 204 C3

Dunheved Ct 2 CR7 204 C3
Dunheved Rd N CR7 204 C3
Dunheved Rd S CR7 204 C3
Dunheved Rd W CR7 204 C3
Dunhill Point 12 SW15 156 B3
Dunholme Gn N9 17 D1
Dunholme La N9 17 D1
Dunholme Rd N9 17 D1
Dunkeld Ho 15 E14 98 B1
Dunkeld Rd
Dagenham RM8 80 C6
South Norwood SE25 205 B5
Dunkery Rd SE9 166 A1
Dunkirk St 12 SE27 183 A6
Dunlace Rd E5 74 D4
Dunleary Cl TW4 151 B4
Dunley Dr CR0 224 A2
Dunlin Ct 12 SE21 161 B2
Dunlin Ho 18 SE16 118 D2
Dunloe Ave N17 51 B6
Dunloe Ct 7 E2 95 D5
Dunloe St E2 95 D5
Dunlop Pl SE16 117 D3 263 D5
Dunmore Point 15 E2 95 D4
Dunmore Rd
Kilburn NW6 91 A6
Wimbledon SW20 178 D2
Dunmow Cl
Dagenham RM6 58 C4
3 Feltham TW13 173 A6
Dunmow Ho
Dagenham RM9 102 B6
Vauxhall SE11 260 D2
Dunmow Rd E15 76 B4
Dunmow Wlk N1 235 A6
Dunnage Cres SE16 119 A2
Dunne Mews 11 NW5 71 C3
Dunnet Ho 27 E3 97 B5
Dunnico Ho SE17 263 A2
Dunn Mead NW9 27 D3
Dunnock Cl N9 18 D3
Dunnock Ct 11 SE21 161 B2
Dunnock Rd E6 100 A1
Dunn's Pas WC1 240 B2
Dunn St E8 73 D3
Dunollie Pl NW5 71 C3
Dunollie Rd NW5 71 C3
Dunoon Gdns SE23 162 D4
Dunoon Ho N1 233 C5
Dunoon Rd SE23 162 C4
Dunraven Dr EN2 4 C3
Dunraven Ho 12 TW9 132 B4
Dunraven Rd W12 112 A5
Dunraven Sch SW16 160 B1
Dunraven St W1 114 D6 247 D6
Dunrobin Ct NW3 69 D3
Dunsany Rd W14 112 D3
Dunsfold Ct 14 SM2 217 D1
Dunsfold Ho
10 Kingston u T KT2 176 D4
4 Streatham SW2 160 B4
Dunsfold Way CR0 223 D1
Dunsford Way SW15 156 B5
Dunsmore Cl
Bushey WD23 8 B5
Hayes UB4 85 A3
Dunsmore Rd KT12 194 B3
Dunsmore Way WD23 8 B5
Dunsmure Rd N16 51 C1
Dunstable Ct 3 SE3 143 A5
Dunstable Mews W1 238 B4
Dunstable Rd
East Molesey KT8 195 B5
Richmond TW10, TW9 132 A1
Dunstall Ho 9 SE15 140 A4
Dunstall Rd SW19, SW20 178 C4
Dunstall Way KT8 195 D6
Dunstall Welling Est DA16 146 B3
Dunstan Cl 2 N2 48 A6
Dunstan Glade BR5 211 B3
Dunstan Ho SE4 141 B3
Dunstan Hos 5 E1 96 C2
Dunstan Rd NW11 47 C1
Dunstan's Gr SE22 162 B5
Dunstan's Rd SE22 162 A5
Dunster Ave SM4 200 D1
Dunster Ct EC3 253 B6
Dunster Dr NW9 45 A1

Dunster Gdns NW6 69 B1
Dunster Ho SE6 163 D1
Dunsterville Way SE1 252 D1
Dunster Way
Carshalton CR4 203 A1
Harrow HA2 63 A5
Dunston Rd
Clapham SW11 137 A3
Hackney E8 95 D6
Dunston St E8 95 D6
Dunton Cl KT6 198 A1
Dunton Ct 5 SE26 162 B2
Dunton Ho 14 SW16 160 A1
Dunton Rd
Bermondsey SE1 117 D2 263 C3
Leyton E10 53 D2
Duntshill Rd SW18 157 D3
Dunvegan Cl KT8 195 D5
Dunvegan Rd SE9 144 B1
Dunwich Ct 2 RM6 58 B4
Dunwich Rd DA7 147 B4
Dunworth Mews W11 91 B1
Duplex Ride SW1 247 D1
Dupont Rd SW20 178 D1
Duppas Ave CR0 220 D4
Duppas Cl TW17 193 B4
Duppas Ct CR0 220 D5
Duppas Hill La CR0 220 D4
Duppas Hill Rd CR0 220 D4
Duppas Hill Terr CR0 220 D5
Duppas Jun Sch CR0 220 D3
Duppas Rd CR0 220 D5
Dupree Rd SE7 121 B1
Dura Den Cl BR3 185 D3
Durand Cl SM5 202 D1
Durand Gdns SW9 138 B4 270 D1
Durand Prim Sch SW9 138 B4 270 D2
Durand Way NW10 67 A1
Durants Lo EN3 6 D2
Durants Park Ave EN3 6 D1
Durants Rd EN3 6 D1
Durants Sch EN3 6 C4
Durant St E2 96 A4
Durban Ct E7 77 D1
Durban Ho 28 W12 112 B6
Durban Rd
Beckenham BR3 185 B1
Ilford IG2 57 C1
Newham E15 98 C4
Tottenham N17 33 D4
Walthamstow E17 35 B2
West Norwood SE27 183 B6
Durbin Ho 13 N9 18 A1
Durbin Rd KT9 214 B4
Durdan Cotts UB5 85 B1
Durdans Ho 3 NW1 71 C1
Durdans Park Prim Sch UB1 85 B2
Durdans Rd UB1 85 B1
Durell Gdns RM9 80 D3
Durell Rd RM9 80 D3
Durfey Pl SE5 139 B5
Durford Cres SW15 156 B3
Durham Ave
Beckenham BR2 208 D5
Hounslow TW5 107 B1
Woodford IG8 37 D5
Durham Cl SW20 178 B1
Durham Ct
2 Barnet EN5 1 B2
Brockley SE4 141 C2
4 Kilburn NW6 91 C5
Teddington TW11 174 C6
Durham Hill BR1 186 D6
Durham Ho
3 Barking IG11 80 A1
7 Dartmouth Pk NW5 71 C5
Edgware HA8 26 B3
Lisson Gr NW8 230 B1
Durham House St WC2 250 B5
Durham Pl
Chelsea SW3 257 C1
Ilford IG1 79 A4
Durham Rd
Beckenham BR2 208 D6
Ealing W5 109 D3
Edmonton N9 18 A2
Feltham TW14 150 C4
Harrow HA1 41 D4
Lower Holloway N4, N7 72 B6
Manor Pk E12 77 D4
Muswell Hill N2 48 D6
Newham E16 98 C3
Sidcup DA14 190 B5
Wimbledon SW20 178 B2
Durham Rise SE18 123 B1
Durham Row E1 97 A2

Durham St SE11 138 B6 270
Durham Terr W2 91
Durham Wharf Dr TW8 131
Durley Ave HA5 41
Durley Rd N16 51
Durlock Ho 16 SW9 138
Durlston Rd
Kingston u T KT2 176
Stoke Newington E5 74
Durnford Ho SE6 163
Durnford St
4 Greenwich SE10 142
South Tottenham N15 51
Durning Rd SE19 183
Durnsford Ave SW18, SW19 157
Durnsford Ct 5 EN3 7
Durnsford Rd
London N11 31
Wimbledon SW18, SW19 157
Durnston Ct 2 SM1 217
Durrant Ct HA3 24
Durrant Way BR6 227
Durrell Rd SW6 264
Durrell Way TW17 193
Durrels Ho W14 254
Durrington Ave SW20 178
Durrington Park Rd SW20 178
Durrington Rd E5 75
Durrington Twr 3 SW8 137
Durrisdeer Ho NW2 69
Dursley Cl SE3 143
Dursley Gdns SE3 143
Dursley Rd SE3 143
Durston House Middleton's Sch W5 87
Durston House Prep Sch W5 87
Durston NW5 71
Durward St E1 96
Durweston Mews W1 237
Durweston St W1 237
Dury Rd EN5 1
Dutch Gdns KT2 176
Dutch Yd SW18 157
Dutton Ho SW2 160
Dutton St SE10 142
Duxberry Cl BR2 210
Duxford Ho 10 SE2 124
Duxford 21 KT1 176
Dwight Ct SW6 135
Dycer Ho 19 E9 74
Dye House La E3 97
Dyer Ho
Hampton TW12 173
New Cross SE14 141
Dyer's Bldgs EC1 241
Dyers Hall Rd
Leyton E11 76
Leytonstone E11 54
Dyer's La SW15 134
Dykes Ct 11 SW2 160
Dykes Way BR2 208
Dylan Cl WD6 9
Dylan Rd
Belvedere DA17 125
2 Brixton SE24 138
Dylways SE5 139
Dymchurch Cl
Ilford IG5 56
Orpington BR6 227
Dymchurch Ho 12 E5 74
Dymes Path SW19 156
Dymock St SW6 135
Dyneley Rd SE12 165
Dyne Rd NW6 69
Dynevor Rd
Richmond TW10 154
Shacklewell N16 73
Dynham Rd NW6 69
Dyott St Soho WC1 239
St Giles WC1, WC2 94 A1 240
Dysart Ave KT2, TW10 175
Dysart Sch KT6 198
Dysart St EC2 95 C3 243
Dyson Ct London NW2 46
Wembley HA0 65
Dyson Ho 3 SE10 120
Dyson Rd
Leytonstone E11 54
Stratford E15 76
Dyson's Rd N18 34

de Rd N4 ....51 A2
gans Cl N2 ....48 B6
gle Ave RM6 ....59 A3
gle Cl
ermondsey
SE16 ....118 C1
nfield EN3 ....6 C1
Vallington SM6 ....220 A2
gle Ct
Dulwich SE21 ....161 B2
dmonton N18 ....33 D4
Holborn EC1 ....241 C4
[3] Wanstead E11 ....55 A5
gle Dr NW9 ....27 C1
gle Dwellings EC1 235 B2
gle Hill SE19 ....183 B4
gle Ho
[2] Bethnal Green
E1 ....96 B3
insbury Pk N7 ....72 B5
gle House Sch
R4 ....180 D1
gle Hts [10] SW11 ...136 C2
gle La E11 ....55 A5
gle Lo
eytonstone E11 ....54 D5
ondon NW11 ....47 B2
gle Mans N16 ....73 D3
gle Mews N1 ....73 C2
gle Pl
South Kensington
SW7 ....114 A1 256 B2
St James SW1 ....249 B5
gle Rd
Hatton TW6 ....127 D2
Wembley HA0 ....65 D1
glesfield Rd SE18 ..144 D4
gle Star Ho SM1 ...217 D4
gle St WC1 ..94 B2 240 C3
gle Terr IG8 ....37 B3
gle Trad Est CR4 .. 202 D3
gle Wharf Rd
N1 ....95 A5 235 B4
gle Wharf SE1 ....253 C3
gle Works E1 ....243 D5
gling Cl E3 ....97 C4
lcom Ct W5 ....110 B5
ldham Prim Sch
SE9 ....143 C1
ldham Sq SE9 ....143 C1
LING 109 D6
aling Broadway Ctr
W5 ....109 D6
aling Broadway Sta
W5 ....109 D6
aling Coll W13 ....87 B1
aling Coll of Higher Ed
W5 ....109 D5
aling Common W5 ..110 B6
aling Common Sta
W5 ....110 B5
aling Court Man
W5 ....109 D4
aling Gateway W5 ..109 C6
aling Gn W5 ....109 D5
aling, Hammersmith &
West London Coll
W14 ....113 A1 254 A2
aling Hospl UB1,
UB2 ....108 B4
aling Park Gdns
W5 ....109 C2
aling Park Lo UB6 ..87 A5
aling Park Mans
W5 ....109 D3
aling Rd
Brentford TW8 ....109 D2
Northolt UB5 ....63 C1
Wembley HA0 ....66 A1
aling Road Trad Est
TW8 ....109 D1
aling Tertiary Coll
W3 ....110 D5
aling Village W5 ....88 A1
aling & West London
Coll W5 ....109 D5
amann Casey Ho [34]
SW9 ....138 C4
amont Cl HA4 ....38 D2
amont Ct NW8 ....230 B4
amont St
NW8 ....92 C5 230 B4
ardley Cres
SW5 ....113 C1 255 B1
ardley Point [9]
SE18 ....122 D2
ardley Rd
Belvedere DA17 ....125 C1
Streatham SW16 ....181 C4
ardley Sch SW16 ..181 C4
arl Cl N11 ....31 B5
arldom Rd SW15 ....134 C1
arle Gdns KT2 ....176 A3
arle Ho SW1 ....259 D3

Earlham Gr
Forest Gate E7 ....77 A3
Wood Green N22 ....32 B3
Earlham Prim Sch
Stratford E7 ....76 D3
Wood Green N22 ....32 C3
Earlham St
WC2 ....94 A1 240 A1
Earl Ho NW1 ....237 B5
Earlom Ho WC1 ....234 A1
Earl Rd SW14 ....133 A1
Earl Rise SE18 ....123 B2
EARL'S COURT 113 C1
Earl's Court Ex Ctr*
SW5 ....113 C1 255 A1
Earl's Court Gdns
SW5 ....113 D2 255 C3
Earl's Court Rd SW5,
W8 ....113 C2 255 B4
Earl's Court Sq
SW5 ....113 D1 255 C2
Earl's Court Sta
SW5 ....113 C2 255 B3
Earls Cres HA1 ....42 C5
Earlsdown Ho [6]
IG11 ....101 B5
Earlsferry Way N1 ....72 A1
EARLSFIELD 158 A3
Earlsfield Ho [16]
KT2 ....175 D2
Earlsfield Prim Sch
SW18 ....158 A2
Earlsfield Rd SW18 ..158 A4
Earlsfield Sta SW18. 158 A3
Earlshall Rd SE9 ....144 C1
Earlsmead Fst & Mid
Sch HA2 ....63 B4
Earlsmead HA2 ....63 B4
Earlsmead Prim Sch
N15 ....51 D5
Earlsmead Rd
Kensal Green
NW10 ....90 C4
South Tottenham N15 ..51 D4
Earl St EC2 ....95 C2 243 A4
Earls Terr W8 ....254 D5
Earlsthorpe Mews [3]
SW12 ....159 A5
Earlsthorpe Rd
SE26 ....184 D6
Earlstoke St EC1 ....234 C2
Earlston Gr E9 ....96 B6
Earls Wlk
Dagenham RM8 ....80 B4
Kensington
W8 ....113 C3 255 A5
Earlswood Ave CR7 ..204 C4
Earlswood Cl [10]
SE10 ....120 C1
Earlswood Gdns IG5 ..56 C6
Earlswood Ho [2]
SW2 ....160 B3
Earlswood St SE10 ...120 C1
Early Mews NW1 ....231 D6
Earnshaw Ho EC1 ....234 D1
Earnshaw St WC1,
WC2 ....239 D2
Earsby St W14 ....254 B4
Earth Galleries*
SW7 ....114 B3 256 D5
Easby Cres SM4 ....201 D3
Easebourne Rd RM8 ..80 C3
Easedale Ho TW7 ....152 D6
Eashing Point [5]
SW15 ....156 B3
Easleys Mews W1 ....238 B2
East 10 Ent Pk E10 ...53 A1
EAST ACTON 111 C5
East Acton Arc W3 ....89 D1
East Acton Ct W3 ....111 C6
East Acton La W3 ....111 C6
East Acton Prim Sch
W3 ....111 C6
East Acton Sta W12 ..89 D1
East Arbour St E1 ....96 D1
East Ave
Croydon CR0 ....220 B3
East Finchley NW2 ....48 A6
Hayes UB3 ....106 A5
Plashet E12 ....78 A1
Southall UB1 ....107 B6
Walthamstow E17 ....53 D5
East Bank N16 ....51 C2
Eastbank Rd TW12 ...174 A5
EAST BARNET 14 D4
East Barnet Rd EN4 ....2 B1
East Barnet Sch
Barnet EN4 ....2 B2
East Barnet EN4 ....14 D5
East Beckton District
Ctr E6 ....100 B2
EAST BEDFONT 149 C3
East Block [5] E1 ....118 D6
Eastbourne Ave W3 ...89 B1
Eastbourne Gdns
SW14 ....133 A2

Eastbourne Mews
W2 ....92 A1 236 B2
Eastbourne Rd
Brentford TW8 ....109 D1
Chiswick W4 ....133 A6
Feltham TW13 ....150 D2
South Tottenham N15 ..51 C3
Streatham SW17 ....181 A4
Wallend E6 ....100 C4
West Ham E15 ....98 C6
Eastbourne Terr
W2 ....92 A1 236 B2
Eastbournia Ave N9 ...18 B1
Eastbrook Ave N9 ....18 C4
Eastbrook Rd SE3 ....143 B4
EASTBURY 22 A5
Eastbury Ave
Barking IG11 ....101 C6
Enfield EN1 ....5 D4
Mo Pk HA6 ....22 A5
Eastbury Comp Sch
IG11 ....79 C2
Eastbury Ct
Barking IG11 ....101 C6
New Barnet EN5 ....14 A6
Eastbury Gr W4 ....111 C1
Eastbury Inf Sch
IG11 ....79 D1
Eastbury Rd
Kingston u T KT2 ....176 A3
Newham E6 ....100 C3
Orpington BR5 ....211 B3
Eastbury Sq IG11 ....101 D6
Eastbury Terr E1 ....96 D3
Eastcastle St
W1 ....93 C1 239 B2
Eastcheap
EC3 ....117 C6 253 A6
East Churchfield Rd
W3 ....111 B5
Eastchurch Rd TW6 ..127 C2
Eastchurch Road Rdbt
TW6 ....127 C3
East Cl Cockfosters EN4 ..3 A1
Ealing W5 ....88 C3
Greenford UB6 ....86 A5
Eastcombe Ave SE7 ..143 B6
EASTCOTE 40 C3
Eastcote Ave
East Molesey KT8 ....195 C4
Harrow HA2 ....64 A6
Wembley UB6 ....65 A3
Eastcote BR6 ....211 D1
Eastcote Ind Est HA4 ..40 C2
Eastcote La HA2 ....63 C5
Eastcote La N UB5 ....63 C2
Eastcote La UB5 ....63 B2
Eastcote Pl HA5 ....40 B3
Eastcote Prim Sch
DA16 ....145 B2
Eastcote Rd
Bexley DA16 ....145 B3
Harrow HA2 ....64 A5
Pinner HA5 ....40 D4
Ruislip HA4 ....40 A3
Eastcote Sta HA5 ....40 C2
Eastcote St SW9 ....138 B3
Eastcote View HA5 ....40 C5
EASTCOTE VILLAGE ..40 B4
Eastcourt Ind Sch
IG3 ....58 A1
East Cres Enfield EN1 ..17 D6
Friern Barnet N11 ....30 D6
Eastcroft Rd KT19 ....215 C1
East Cross Ctr E15 ....75 C2
East Cross Route
Bow E3 ....97 C6
Hackney Wick E9 ....75 B3
East Croydon Sta
CR0 ....221 B6
East Ct
Sunbury TW16 ....172 C1
Wembley HA0 ....65 C6
Eastdown Ho E8 ....74 A4
Eastdown Pk SE13 ....142 B1
East Duck Lees La
EN3 ....7 B1
EAST DULWICH 162 A6
East Dulwich Gr
SE22 ....161 C6
East Dulwich Rd SE15,
SE22 ....140 A1
East Dulwich Sta
SE22 ....139 C1
East End Rd
East Finchley N2,
N3 ....48 A6
Finchley N3 ....29 C1
East End Way HA5 ....41 A6
East Entrance
RM10 ....103 D5
Eastern Ave
Gants Hill IG1, IG2,
IG4 ....56 C3
Newbury Pk IG2 ....57 B3
Eastern Avenue W
RM7 ....59 C5

Eastern Ave
Pinner HA5 ....40 D2
Wanstead E11 ....55 C3
Eastern Bsns Pk
TW16 ....127 D3
Eastern Perimeter Rd
TW14 ....127 D3
Eastern Quay [15]
E16 ....121 B5
Eastern Rd
Brockley SE4 ....141 C1
Fortis Green N2 ....48 D5
Newham E13 ....99 B5
Walthamstow E17 ....54 A4
Wood Green N22 ....32 A2
Easternville Gdns
IG2 ....57 A3
Eastern Way SE28 ....124 B4
East Ferry Rd E14 ....119 D2
Eastfield Gdns RM10 ..81 C4
Eastfield Prim Sch
EN3 ....6 D5
Eastfield Rd
Dagenham RM9 ....81 B4
Dagenham RM10 ....81 C4
Enfield EN3 ....6 D5
Hornsey N8 ....50 A6
Walthamstow E17 ....53 C5
Eastfields Ave
SW18 ....135 C1
Eastfields HA5 ....40 C4
Eastfields Rd
Acton W3 ....89 A2
Mitcham CR4 ....181 A1
Eastfield St E14 ....97 A2
EAST FINCHLEY 48 B5
East Finchley Sta N2 ..48 C5
Eastgate Bsns Pk
E10 ....53 A1
Eastgate Cl SE28 ....102 D1
Eastgate Ct N3 ....29 C1
East Gdns SW17 ....180 C4
Eastglade HA5 ....41 B6
EAST HAM 100 A5
Eastham Cl EN5 ....13 B6
East Ham Ind Est
E6 ....100 A2
East Ham Manor Way
E6 ....100 C1
East Ham Meml Hospl
E7 ....77 D1
East Ham Sta E6 ....78 A1
East Harding St EC4. 241 B2
East Heath Rd NW3 ...70 B5
East Hill
London SW18 ....158 A6
Wembley HA9 ....44 C1
Eastholme UB3 ....106 A5
Eastholm NW11 ....47 D5
East India Bldgs [9]
E14 ....119 C6
East India Ct [7]
SE16 ....118 C4
East India Dock Basin*
E14 ....120 C6
East India Dock Rd
E14 ....119 D6
East India Dock Road
Tunnel [18] E14 ....98 B1
East India Sta E14 ...120 B6
East India Way CR0 ..205 D1
East La
[5] Bermondsey
SE16 ....118 A4
Bermondsey SE16 ....118 A4
Eastlake Ho NW8 ....236 D5
Eastlake Rd SE5 ....139 A3
East La KT1 ....197 D6
Eastland Ct [2] BR1 ...187 C1
Eastlands Cres
SE21 ....161 D5
East Lane Bsns Pk
HA9 ....65 D5
East La HA0, HA9 ....65 D5
Eastlea Com Sch E16 .98 C3
Eastlea Mews E16 ....98 C3
Eastleigh Ave HA2 ....63 D6
Eastleigh Cl
Belmont SM2 ....217 D1
Neasden NW2 ....67 C5
Eastleigh Rd E17 ....35 B1
Eastleigh Way
TW14 ....150 A3
Eastleigh Wlk [9]
SW15 ....156 A4
East London Coll
E11 ....76 C6
East London Coll &
Toynbee Theatre
E1 ....95 D2 243 D3
East London Stad E3 .97 B2
Eastman Dental Hospl
WC1 ....94 B3 240 C6
Eastman Ho [7]
SW4 ....159 C5
Eastman Rd W3 ....111 B4

East Mascalls [15]
SE7 ....143 C6
Eastmead Ave UB6 ....85 D4
Eastmead Cl BR1 ....188 A1
Eastmead IG3 ....58 A2
East Mead HA4 ....62 D5
Eastmearn Rd SE21,
SE27 ....161 A2
EAST MOLESEY 196 A4
Eastmont Rd KT10 ....212 D6
Eastmoor Pl SE7 ....121 D3
Eastmoor St SE7 ....121 D3
East Mount St E1 ....96 B2
Eastney Rd CR0 ....204 D1
Eastney St SE10 ....120 B1
Eastnor Rd SE9 ....167 A3
Easton Ho [4] SE27 ....160 D1
Easton St WC1 ....241 A6
East Park Cl RM6 ....59 A4
East Parkside SE10 ..120 D4
East Pas EC1 ....242 A4
East Plaza E14 ....119 D5
East Pl SE27 ....183 A6
East Point [4] SE1 ....118 A1
Eastpole Cotts N14 ....3 D1
East Poultry Ave
EC1 ....241 C3
East Putney Sta
SW15 ....157 A6
East Ramp TW6 ....126 D4
East Rd Burnt Oak HA8 ..27 A2
Chelsea
SW1 ....115 A1 258 A1
Dagenham RM6 ....59 A4
East Barnet EN4 ....15 A3
East Bedfont TW14 ....149 B4
Enfield EN3 ....6 C5
Finchley N2 ....30 C2
Kingston u T KT2 ....176 A2
Newham E15 ....99 A6
Shoreditch
N1 ....95 B4 235 D2
Welling DA16 ....146 B3
West Drayton UB7 ....104 C2
Wimbledon SW19 ....180 A4
East Rochester Way DA5,
DA15, SE9 ....168 C5
East Row
Kensal Town W10 ....91 A3
Wanstead E11 ....55 A3
Eastry Ave BR2 ....208 D3
Eastry Ho SW8 ....270 A3
Eastry Rd DA8 ....147 C5
EAST SHEEN 133 B1
East Sheen Ave
SW14 ....133 B1
East Sheen Prim Sch
SW14 ....133 C1
Eastside Rd NW11 ....47 B5
East Smithfield
E1 ....117 D6 253 D5
East St Barking IG11 ....79 A1
Bexleyheath DA7 ....147 C1
Brentford TW8 ....131 C5
Bromley BR1 ....187 A1
Walworth
SE17 ....117 B1 262 C2
East Surrey Gr
SE15 ....139 D5
East Tenter St
E1 ....95 D1 243 D1
East Terr DA15 ....167 C3
East Thamesmead Bsns
Pk DA18 ....125 B4
East Towers HA5 ....40 D3
Eastvale W3 ....111 D5
Eastview Ave SE18 ...145 C5
East View Barnet EN5 ....1 B2
Chingford E4 ....36 A5
Hampstead NW3 ....70 B6
East View Ho [13] N2 ...30 B1
Eastville Ave NW11 ....47 B3
Eastway Cres HA2 ....63 D6
East Way CR0 ....223 A5
Eastway BR2 ....209 A2
East Way UB3 ....106 A5
Eastway SM4, SW20 ..201 A5
East Way HA4 ....40 A1
Eastway
South Hackney E3,
E9 ....97 A6
Temple Mills E9, E10 ...75 C4
Wallington SM6 ....219 C4
Wanstead E11 ....55 B4
Eastwell Cl BR3 ....185 A2
Eastwell Ho SE1 ....262 D6
Eastwick Ct [2]
SW19 ....156 D3
EAST WICKHAM 146 A5
East Wickham Inf Sch
DA16 ....145 D4
East Wickham Jun Sch
DA16 ....146 A4
East Wlk
East Barnet EN4 ....15 A3
Hayes UB3 ....106 A5

Eastwood Cl
[2] Islington N7 ....72 C3
[7] Tottenham N17 ....34 B3
Woodford E18 ....37 A1
Eastwood Rd
Ilford IG3 ....58 A2
Muswell Hill N10 ....31 A1
West Drayton UB7 ....104 C4
Woodford E18 ....37 A1
East Woodside DA5 ..169 A3
Eastwood St SW16 ...181 C4
Eatington Rd E10 ....54 B4
Eaton Cl
Belgravia SW1 ....258 A3
Stanmore HA7 ....25 B6
Eaton Ct
Chislehurst BR7 ....189 A4
Ealing W5 ....87 D1
Edgware HA8 ....26 C6
Southall UB1 ....107 B6
Sutton SM2 ....218 B2
[6] Woodford E18 ....37 A1
Eaton Dr
Brixton SW9 ....138 D1
Kingston u T KT2 ....176 C3
Eaton Gate
SW1 ....115 A2 258 A4
Eaton Gdns RM9 ....81 A1
Eaton Ho
Battersea SW11 ....266 D1
Ealing W5 ....87 D1
[23] Limehouse E14 ....119 B6
Eaton House Sch
SW1 ....115 A2 258 A4
Eaton House The Manor
Sch SW4 ....137 B1
Eaton La
SW1 ....115 B3 258 D5
Eaton Lo SM2 ....218 B2
Eaton Mans SW1 ....258 A3
Eaton Mews N
SW1 ....115 A3 258 B5
Eaton Mews S
SW1 ....115 B3 258 C5
Eaton Mews W SW1. 258 B4
Eaton Park Rd N13 ....16 D2
Eaton Pl
SW1 ....115 A3 258 B5
Eaton Rd Enfield EN1 ....5 C1
Hendon NW4 ....46 C4
Isleworth TW3, TW7 ..130 B1
Sidcup DA14 ....168 D2
Sutton SM2 ....218 B2
Eaton Rise Ealing W5 ..87 D1
Wanstead E11 ....55 C4
Eaton Row
SW1 ....115 B3 258 C5
Eatons Mead E4 ....19 C2
Eaton Sq
SW1 ....115 A3 258 B5
Eaton Square Sch
SW1 ....115 B2 258 C4
Eaton Terr
Belgravia
SW1 ....115 A2 258 B4
Bow E3 ....97 A4
Eaton Terr Mews
SW1 ....258 A4
Eatonville Rd SW17 ..158 D2
Eatonville Villas
SW17 ....158 D2
Ebb Ct E16 ....123 A6
Ebbisham Dr
SW8 ....138 B6 270 C5
Ebbisham Rd KT4 ....216 C6
Ebbsfleet Rd NW2 ....69 A4
Ebdon Way SE3 ....143 B2
Ebenezer Ho SE11 ....261 C3
Ebenezer Mussel Ho [5]
E2 ....96 C5
Ebenezer St N1 ....235 C2
Ebenezer Wlk CR4 ....181 C2
Ebley Cl SE15 ....139 D6
Ebner St SW18 ....157 D6
Ebony Ct NW10 ....67 D2
Ebony Ho
[27] Bethnal Green
E2 ....96 A4
[10] West Hampstead
NW3 ....69 D2
Ebor Cotts SW15 ....155 C1
Ebor St E1, E2 ....243 C6
Ebrington Rd HA3 ....43 D3
Ebsworth St SE23 ....162 D4
Eburne Rd N7 ....72 A5
Ebury Bridge Rd
SW1 ....115 A1 258 B1
Ebury Cl BR2 ....226 A5
Ebury Mews
SW1 ....115 B2 258 C4
Ebury Mews E SW1 . 258 C5
Ebury Mews SE27 ....160 D1
Ebury Sq SW1 ....258 B3

Ebury St SW1 115 B2 258 C4
Ecclesbourne Cl N13 32 C5
Ecclesbourne Gdns N13 32 C5
Ecclesbourne Inf Sch CR7 205 A4
Ecclesbourne Jun Sch CR7 205 A4
Ecclesbourne Rd
Islington N1 73 A1
Thornton Heath CR7 205 A4
Eccles Ct SE11 260 D1
Eccleshill 3 BR2 208 D5
Eccles Rd SW11 136 D1
Eccleston Cl
Cockfosters EN4 2 D1
Crofton BR6 211 B1
Eccleston Cres RM6 58 B2
Ecclestone Ct HA9 66 A3
Ecclestone Mews HA9 66 A3
Ecclestone Pl HA9 66 B3
Eccleston Ho 1 SW2 160 C5
Eccleston Mews SW1 115 A3 258 B5
Eccleston Pl SW1 115 B2 258 C4
Eccleston Rd W13 109 A5
Eccleston Sq Mews SW1 259 A3
Eccleston Sq SW1 115 B2 258 D3
Eccleston St SW1 115 B2 258 C4
Echelforde Dr TW15 170 C6
Echelford Prim Sch The TW15 170 D5
Echo Hts E4 19 D3
Eckford St N1 234 A4
Eckington Ho N15 51 B3
Eckstein Rd SW11 136 C1
Eclipse Ho N22 32 B1
Eclipse Rd E13 99 B2
Ector Rd SE6 164 C2
Edam Ct 11 DA14 168 A1
Edans Ct W12 111 D4
Edbrooke Rd W9 91 C3
Eddisbury Ho 7 SE26 162 A1
Eddiscombe Rd SW6 135 B3
Eddison Ct N19 72 A6
Eddy Cl RM7 59 D3
Eddystone Rd SE4 163 A6
Eddystone Twr SE8 119 A1
Eddystone Wlk TW19 148 A4
Ede Cl TW4 129 B2
Edenbridge Cl 29 SE16 118 B1
Edenbridge Rd
Enfield EN1 17 C5
Hackney E9 74 D1
Eden Cl
Child's Hill NW3 69 C6
Enfield EN3 7 C5
Kensington W8 255 B6
Wembley HA0 87 D6
Edencourt W5 88 B1
Edencourt Rd SW16 181 B4
Eden Ct 3 N3 29 B1
Edendale W3 110 D6
Edenfield Gdns KT4 215 D5
Eden Gr Islington N7 72 B3
Walthamstow E17 53 D4
Edenham High Sch CR0 207 B2
Edenham Way W10 91 B2
Eden Ho
15 Battersea SW11 136 C2
Lisson Gr NW8 237 A5
Edenhurst Ave SW6 135 B2
Eden Lodge NW6 68 D1
Eden Mews SW17 158 A1
EDEN PARK 207 C5
Eden Park Ave BR3 207 C4
Eden Park Sta BR3 207 C4
Eden Rd
Croydon CR0 221 B4
Penge BR3 185 A2
Walthamstow E17 53 D4
West Norwood SE27 182 D5
Edensmuir Ct SE3 143 A5
Edensor Gdns W4 133 C5
Edensor Rd W4 133 C5
Eden St KT1, KT2 176 A1
Edenvale Cl CR4 181 A3
Edenvale Rd CR4 181 A3
Edenvale St SW6 136 A3
Eden Way
Beckenham BR3 207 C3
Bow E3 97 B6
Eden Wlk 5 KT1 176 A1
Ederline Ave SW16 182 C1
Edgar Ct KT3 199 C6
Edgar Ho
Homerton E9 75 A3
South Lambeth SW8 270 A4
Wanstead E11 55 A2
Edgar Kail Way SE22 139 C1
Edgarley Terr SW6 264 A1
Edgar Rd Bromley E3 97 D4
Dagenham RM6 58 D2
Twickenham TW4 151 B4
Yiewsley UB7 104 A5
Edgar Wallace Cl 4 SE15 139 C5
Edgbury Ct NW9 45 A5
Edgcott Ho 2 W10 90 C2
Edgeborough Way BR1 187 D2
Edge Bsns Ctr The NW2 68 B6
Edgebury BR7, SE9 188 D6
Edgebury Prim Sch BR7 189 A6
Edgebury Wlk BR7 167 A1
Edgecombe Ho
4 London SE5 139 C3
Putney SW19 157 A4
Edgecoombe Cl KT2 177 B3
Edgecoombe CR2 222 C1
Edgecote Cl 7 W3 111 A5
Edgecot Gr N15 51 C4
Edgecumbe Ct 2 CR0 206 A1
Edgefield Ave IG11 79 D1
Edgefield Ct 3 IG11 79 D1
Edge Hill Ave N3 47 C5
Edge Hill Ct DA14 189 D6
Edgehill Ct KT12 194 C1
Edge Hill Ct SW19 178 D3
Edgehill Gdns RM10 81 C4
Edgehill Ho 4 SW9 138 D3
Edgehill Rd
Ealing W13 87 C2
Longlands BR7 189 A6
Mitcham CR4 181 B2
Edge Hill
Shooters Hill SE18 144 D6
Wimbledon SW19 178 D3
Edgeley La SW4 137 D2
Edgeley Rd SW4 137 D2
Edgel St SW18 135 D1
Edge Point Cl SE27 182 D5
Edge St W8 113 C5 245 B4
Edgewood Dr BR6 227 D3
Edgewood Gn CR0 206 D1
Edgeworth Ave NW4 46 A4
Edgeworth Cl NW4 46 A4
Edgeworth Cres NW4 46 A4
Edgeworth Ct 10 EN4 2 C1
Edgeworth Ho NW8 229 A6
Edgeworth Rd
Barnet EN4 2 C1
Eltham SE9 143 D1
Edgington Rd SW16 181 D4
Edgington Way DA14 190 D3
Edgson Ho SW1 258 C2
EDGWARE 26 C6
Edgware Acad WC2 240 B1
EDGWARE BURY 10 B3
Edgwarebury Ct HA8 26 C5
Edgwarebury Gdns HA8 26 C5
Edgwarebury La
Edgware Bury HA8 10 C2
Edgware HA8 26 C5
Edgware Community Hospl HA8 26 D3
Edgware Ct HA8 26 C4
Edgware Jun & Inf Schs HA8 26 C4
Edgware Rd Burnt Oak Broadway HA8 26 D3
Edgware Rd NW2 68 C6
Edgware Rd High St HA8 26 C4
Edgware Rd W1, W2, NW1, NW8 92 C2 237 A3
Edgware Road Sta (Bakerloo) NW1 92 C2 237 A3
Edgware Road Sta (Met, Distr, Circle) NW1 237 B3
Edgware Road The Hyde NW9 45 C5
Edgware Road West Hendon Broadway NW9 46 A2
Edgware Sta HA8 26 D4
Edgware Way (Watford By-Pass) HA8 27 A6
Edinburgh Cl
7 Bethnal Green E2 96 C5
Pinner HA5 41 A2
Uxbridge UB10 60 D4
Edinburgh Ct
1 Catford SE6 164 D3
2 Kingston u T KT1 198 A6
Newham E13 99 B5
10 Rotherhithe SE16 118 D5
West Barnes SM4 200 D4
Edinburgh Dr UB10 60 D4
Edinburgh Ho
3 Acton W3 89 B1
Carshalton SM1 218 B6
Hendon NW4 46 C6
Maida Vale W9 91 D4
Edinburgh Prim Sch E17 53 B4
Edinburgh Rd
Carshalton SM1 218 B6
Edmonton N18 34 A5
Hanwell W7 108 D4
Newham E13 99 B5
Walthamstow E17 53 C4
Edington 20 NW5 71 A2
Edington Rd
Abbey Wood SE2 124 B3
Enfield EN3 6 C3
Edison Bldg 7 E14 119 C4
Edison Cl
Walthamstow E17 53 C4
West Drayton UB7 104 B4
Edison Ct SE10 120 D3
Edison Dr
Southall UB1 85 D1
Wembley HA9 66 A6
Edison Gr SE18 145 D5
Edison Ho
Walworth SE1 262 C4
7 Wembley HA9 67 A5
Edison Rd
Bexley DA16 145 D4
Brimsdown EN3 7 B3
Bromley BR2 187 A1
Crouch End N8 49 D3
Edis St NW1 93 A6 231 B6
Editha Mans SW10 266 A5
Edith Cavell Cl 2 N19 50 A2
Edith Cavell Way SE18 144 A4
Edith Ct TW14 149 B5
Edith Gdns KT5 198 D2
Edith Gr SW10 136 A5 266 B4
Edith Ho 6 W6 112 C1
Edithna St SW9 138 A2
Edith Neville Cotts NW1 232 C2
Edith Neville Prim Sch NW1 93 D5 232 C3
Edith Pond Ct SE9 166 D2
Edith Ramsay Ho 2 E1 97 A2
Edith Rd
Dagenham RM6 58 D2
South Norwood SE25 205 B4
Stratford New Town E15 76 B3
Upton Pk E6 77 D1
West Kensington W14 113 A2 254 B3
Wimbledon SW19 179 D4
Wood Green N11 31 D3
Edith Row SW6 265 D2
Edith St E2 96 A5
Edith Summerskill Ho SW6 264 C4
Edith Terr SW10 136 A5 266 A4
Edith Villas W14 113 B1 254 C2
Edith Yd SW10 266 B4
Edmansons' Cl N17 33 D2
Edmeston Cl E9 75 A2
Edmond Ct SE14 140 C4
Edmonscote W13 87 A2
EDMONTON 33 D6
Edmonton Ct 5 SE16 118 C3
Edmonton Cty Lower Sch N9 17 C3
Edmonton Cty Upper Sch EN1 17 D4
Edmonton Green Sh Ctr N9 18 B2
Edmonton Green Sta N9 18 A2
Edmonton Wharf N18 34 D4
Edmund Gr TW13 151 B2
Edmund Halley Way SE10 120 C4
Edmund Ho
Kennington SE17 261 D1
New Cross Gate SE14 141 B4
Edmund Hurst Dr E6 100 D2
Edmund Rd
Mitcham CR4 202 C6
Welling DA16 146 A2
Edmundsbury Ct Est 16 SW9 138 B1
Edmunds Cl UB4 84 C2
Edmund St SE5 139 B5
Edmunds Wlk N2 48 C5
Edmund Waller Prim Sch SE14 140 D3
Ednam Ho SE15 140 A6
Edna Rd SW20 178 D1
Edna St SW11 136 C4 267 A1
Edred Ho E9 75 A4
Edrich Ho SW4 270 A1
Edric Ho SW1 259 D4
Edrick Rd HA8 27 A4
Edrick Wlk HA8 27 A4
Edric Rd SE14 140 D5
Edridge Cl WD23 8 A6
Edridge Ho 9 SE27 160 D1
Edridge Rd CR0 221 B5
Edward Alleyn Ho SE21 161 C4
Edward Ave
Chingford E4 35 D4
Morden SM4 202 B4
Edward Betham CE Prim Sch UB6 86 A5
Edward Cl
Edmonton N9 17 D4
Hampton TW12 174 A5
Edward Ct
2 Ealing W5 87 B3
Harrow HA1 64 C6
2 Newham E16 99 A2
Edward Dodd Ct N1 235 D2
Edward Edward's Ho SE1 251 C3
Edwardes Pl W8 254 D5
Edwardes Sq W8 113 B3 254 D5
Edward Friend Ho 6 N16 73 C5
Edward Gr EN4 14 B6
Edward Harvey Ct DA17 125 B1
Edward Ho
Paddington W2 236 C5
Vauxhall SE11 260 D2
Edward Kennedy Ho 18 W10 91 A3
Edward Mann Cl 13 E1 96 D1
Edward Mans 8 IG11 79 D1
Edward Mews NW1 231 D3
Edward Pauling Ho TW14 149 D4
Edward Pauling Prim Sch TW13 149 C2
Edward Pinner Ct 5 KT6 214 A6
Edward Pl SE8 141 B6
Edward Rd
Bromley BR1 187 C3
Chislehurst BR7 188 D5
Croydon CR0 205 C2
Dagenham RM6 59 A3
Hampton TW12 174 A5
Harrow HA2 42 A6
Hatton TW14 149 C6
New Barnet EN4 14 B6
Northolt UB5 84 C5
Penge SE20 184 D4
Walthamstow E17 52 D4
Edward Robinson Ho 3 SE14 140 D5
Edward's Ave HA4 62 C2
Edwards Cl KT4 216 D6
Edward's Cotts 11 N1 72 D1
Edwards Dr N11 31 D3
Edwards Ho 7 TW10 153 C1
Edward's La N16 73 C6
Edwards Language Sch W5 110 A6
Edwards Mews
Islington N1 72 C1
Marylebone W1 93 A1 238 A1
Edward Sq
Islington N1 233 C5
1 Rotherhithe SE16 119 A5
Edwards Rd DA17 125 C2
Edward St
New Cross SE14 141 B5
10 Newham E16 99 A3
Edward Temme Ave E15 76 D1
Edward Tyler Rd SE12 165 C2
Edward VII Mans NW10 90 D4
Edward Way TW15 148 B2
Edward Wilson Prim Sch W2 91 D2
Edwina Ct SM1 217 D4
Edwina Gdns IG4 56 A4
Edwin Arnold Ct DA15 189 D6
Edwin Ave E6 100 C5
Edwin Cl DA7 147 B6
Edwin Ho SE15 140 A5
Edwin Rd
Burnt Oak HA8 27 B4
Twickenham TW1, TW2 152 C3
Edwin's Mead E9 75 A4
Edwin St
Bethnal Green E1 96 C3
Newham E16 99 A2
Edwin Stray Ho TW13 151 C1
Edwin Ware Ct 4 HA5 22 C1
Edwy Ho E9 75 B4
Edwyn Cl EN5 12 D5
Edwyn Ho SW18 157 D5
Eel Pie Island* TW1 153 A3
Effie Pl SW6 265 B3
Effie Rd SW6 135 C5 265 B3
Effingham Cl SM2 217 D1
Effingham Ct SW19 180 C3
Effingham Ho
37 Clapham SW8 137 D3
9 Kingston u T KT2 176 D4
Effingham Lo 1 KT6 198 A4
Effingham Rd
Hornsey N8 50 C5
Lewisham SE12 164 D6
Thames Ditton KT6, KT7 197 C2
Thornton Heath CR0 204 B2
Effort St SW17 180 C5
Effra Cl SW19 179 D4
Effra Ct London SW2 160 B6
South Norwood SE19 183 C3
Effra Mans SW2 160 C6
Effra Par SW2 160 C6
Effra Rd London SW2 160 C6
Wimbledon SW19 179 D4
Effra Road Ret Pk SW2 160 C6
EF International Language Sch SE1 251 B3
Egan Way UB3 105 C6
Egbert Ho E9 75 A3
Egbert St NW1 93 A6 231 A6
Egbury Ho SW15 155 D5
Egerton Cl HA5 40 A5
Egerton Cres SW3 114 C2 257 B4
Egerton Ct
Leytonstone E11 54 B2
5 Richmond TW10 154 A6
Egerton Dr SE10 141 D4
Egerton Gdns
Ealing W13 87 B1
Hendon NW4 46 B5
Ilford IG3 79 D5
Knightsbridge SW3 114 C3 257 A5
Egerton Gdns Mews SW3 257 B5
Egerton Gdns NW10 90 C6
Egerton Ho W4 133 A6
Egerton Pl SW3 257 B5
Egerton Rd
New Malden KT3 199 D5
South Norwood SE25 205 C6
Stamford Hill N16 51 D2
Twickenham TW2 152 C4
Wembley HA0 66 B1
Egerton Terr SW3 114 C3 257 B5
Egerton Way UB3 126 D5
Eggardon Ct UB5 64 A2
Egham Cl
Cheam SM3 217 A6
Putney SW19 157 A2
Egham Cres SM3 217 A6
Egham Ct KT6 197 D4
Egham Rd E13 99 B2
Eglantine Rd SW18 158 A6
Egleston Rd SM4 201
Eglington Ct SE17 139
Eglington Rd E4 20
Eglinton Hill SE18 144
Eglinton Prim Sch SE18 144
Eglinton Rd SE18 144
Egliston Mews SW15 134
Egliston Rd SW15 134
Egmont Ave KT6 198
Egmont Rd
New Malden KT3 199
Sutton SM2 218
Tolworth KT6 198
Walton-on-T KT12 194
Egmont St SE14 140
Egremont Ho SE13 141
Egremont Rd SE27 160
Egret Ho 11 SE16 118
Egret Way UB4 84
Eider Cl Hayes UB4 84
Stratford E7 76
Eider Ct 33 SE8 141
Eighteenth Rd CR4 204
Eighth Ave
Hayes UB3 106
Ilford E12 78
Eileen Ct BR7 188
Eileen Rd SE25 205
Eindhoven Cl SM5 203
Einstein Ho HA9 67
Eisenhower Dr E6 100
Eisenhower Ho KT8 175
Elaine Ct 13 NW3 70
Elaine Gr NW5 71
Elaine Ho N4 50
Elam Cl SE5 138
Elam St SE5 138
Elan Ct E1 96
Eland Pl CR0 220
Eland Rd
Clapham SW11 136
Croydon CR0 220
Elba Pl SE17 117 A2 262
Elberon Ave CR0 203
Elbe St SW6 136
Elborough Rd SE25 206
Elborough St SW18 157
Elbourne Trad Est DA17 125
Elbury Dr E16 99
Elcho St SW11 136 C5 267
Elcot Ave SE15 140
Elder Ave N8 50
Elderberry Ct 2 EN2 4
Elderberry Gr 10 SE27 183
Elderberry Rd W5 110
Elderberry Way E6 100
Elder Cl Barnet N20 13
Sidcup DA15 167
Yiewsley UB7 104
Elder Ct WD23 8
Elderfield Ho 4 E14 119
Elderfield Pl SW17 181
Elderfield Rd E5 74
Elderfield Wlk E11 55
Elderflower Way E15 76
Elder Gdns 9 SE27 183
Elder Oak Cl SE20 184
Elder Rd SE27 183
Elderslie Cl BR3 207
Elderslie Rd SE9 166
Elder St E1 95 D3 243
Elderton Rd SE26 185
Eldertree Pl CR4 181
Eldertree Way CR4 181
Elder Wlk
Islington N1 234
2 Lewisham SE13 142
Elderwood Pl SE27 183
Eldon Ave
Croydon CR0 222
Heston TW5 129
Eldon Ct NW6 91
Eldon Gr NW3 70
Eldon Ho SW9 138
Eldon Jun & Inf Schs N9 18
Eldon Pk SE25 206
Eldon Rd
Edmonton N9 18
Kensington W8 113 D3 255
Tottenham N22 32
Walthamstow E17 53
Eldon St EC2 95 B2 242
Eldonwall Est RM8 59
Eldon Way NW10 88
Eldred Rd IG11 101
Eldrick Ct TW14 149
Eldridge Cl TW14 150

dridge Ct
Bermondsey SE16 118 A3
14 Dagenham RM10 81 D2
eanor Cl
Rotherhithe SE16 118 D4
South Tottenham N15 51 D6
eanor Cres NW7 28 D6
eanor Ct 13 E2 96 A6
eanor Gdns
Barnet EN5 12 D6
Dagenham RM8 81 B6
eanor Gr
Mortlake SW13 133 C2
Uxbridge UB10 60 D5
eanor Ho
18 Hammersmith W6 112 C1
1 Kentish Town NW5 71 C3
6 Merton SW19 179 D2
eanor Palmer Prim Sch NW5 71 C4
eanor Rathbone Ho 1 N6 49 D2
eanor Rd
Bowes Pk N11 32 A4
Hackney E8 74 B1
Stratford E15 76 D2
eanor Smith Sch E13 99 B5
eanor Smith Sch (West Beckton Site) E16 99 C2
eanor St E3 97 C4
eanor Wlk 24 SE18 122 B2
ectra Ave TW6 127 D2
ectra Ct 6 NW2 68 C2
ectric Ave SW9 138 C1
ectric Ho
13 Bow E3 97 C4
Walthamstow E17 53 C5
ectric La 2 SW9 138 C1
ectric Mans 1 SW9 138 C1
ectric Par
Ilford IG3 57 D1
Surbiton KT6 197 D3
Woodford E18 37 A1
enmore Ct BR1 210 A5
ephant & Castle
Newington SE1 116 D3 261 D5
Newington SE1 261 D4
ephant & Castle Sh Ctr SE1 117 A2 262 A4
ephant & Castle Sta
Lambeth SE1 116 D3 261 D5
Newington SE17 117 A2 262 A4
ephant La SE16 118 C4
ephant Rd SE17 117 A2 262 A4
ers Rd Ealing W13 109 C4
Hayes UB3 105 B2
ey Rd N18 34 D5
ey's Est N18 34 D6
lfindale Rd SE24 161 A6
lfin Gr TW11 174 D5
lford Cl SE9 143 C1
lfort Rd N5 72 C4
lfrida Cres SE6 185 C6
lfrida Prim Sch SE6 185 C6
lf Row E1 118 C6
lfwine Rd W7 86 C2
lgal Cl BR6 226 D3
lgar Ave Ealing W5 110 A4
Thornton Heath SW16 204 A6
Tolworth KT5, KT6 198 D2
Willesden NW10 67 B2
lgar Cl
Buckhurst Hill IG9 21 D2
Deptford SE8 141 C5
Elstree WD6 9 D4
Ickenham UB10 60 C6
Newham E13 99 C5
lgar Ct W14 254 A5
lgar Ho Hayes UB4 84 C2
Isleworth TW2 152 B5
Pimlico SW1 258 D1
Southall UB1 85 C1
South Hampstead NW6 70 A1
lgar N8 50 A6
lgar St SE16 119 A3
lgin Ave
Ashford TW15 171 A4
Hammersmith W12 112 B3
Harrow HA3 25 B1

Elgin Ave *continued*
Westbourne Green W9 91 D3
Elgin Cl W12 112 B4
Elgin Cres
Hatton TW6 127 C3
Notting Hill W11 113 A6 244 B6
Elgin Ct
6 Croydon CR0 221 A4
Westbourne Green W9 91 D3
Elgin Ho Northolt UB5 84 B5
8 Poplar E14 97 D1
Elgin Mans W9 91 D4
Elgin Mews N W9 91 D4
Elgin Mews S W9 91 D4
Elgin Mews W11 91 A1
Elgin Rd
Croydon CR0 221 D6
Ilford IG3 57 C2
Sutton SM1 218 A5
Wallington SM6 219 C2
Wood Green N22 31 C1
Elgood Ave HA6 22 A3
Elgood Cl W11 244 A3
Elgood Ho NW8 229 D3
Elham Cl BR1 187 D3
Elham Ho 13 E5 74 B3
Elia Mews N1 94 D5 234 C3
Elias Pl SW8 138 C6
Elia St N1 94 D5 234 C3
Elibank Rd SE9 144 C1
Elim Est SE1 263 A6
Elim St SE1 263 A6
Elim Way E13 98 D4
Eliot Bank SE23, SE26 162 B2
Eliot Bank Prim Sch SE26 162 B2
Eliot Cotts SE3 142 C3
Eliot Ct SW18 157 D5
Eliot Dr HA2 63 D6
Eliot Gdns SW15 134 A1
Eliot Hill SE13 142 A3
Eliot Ho 10 TW10 154 B5
Eliot Mews NW8 229 A3
Eliot Pk SE13 142 A3
Eliot Pl SE3 142 C3
Eliot Rd RM9 80 D4
Eliot Vale SE3 142 B3
Elis David Almshouses CR0 220 D4
Elizabethan Ct N3 47 A6
Elizabeth Ave
Enfield EN2 4 D2
Ilford IG1 79 B6
Islington N1 73 B1
Shoreditch N1 95 A6 235 B6
Elizabeth Barnes Ct 5 SW6 135 D3
Elizabeth Blackwell Ho N22 32 C2
Elizabeth Blount Ct 4 E14 97 A1
Elizabeth Cl
Cheam SM1 217 B4
Paddington W9 236 B5
12 Poplar E14 97 D1
Elizabeth Clyde Cl N15 51 C5
Elizabeth Cooper Lo SW12 159 A5
Elizabeth Cotts 5 TW9 132 C4
Elizabeth Ct
Buckhurst Hill IG9 21 B3
Chelsea SW10 266 D5
East Dulwich SE22 140 A1
Kingston u T KT2 176 A2
Marylebone NW8 237 B6
South Croydon CR0 221 C5
Sunbury TW16 194 C6
3 Teddington TW11 174 C5
Upper Tooting SW17 181 A5
West Barnes SM4 201 A2
Westminster SW1 259 D5
6 Woodford Green E18 37 A2
2 Woodford Green IG8 37 C3
10 Woolwich SE18 122 B2
Elizabeth Finn Ho 1 W12 112 A3
Elizabeth Fry Ho UB3 105 D2
Elizabeth Fry Pl SE18 144 A4
Elizabeth Garrett Anderson Ho 9 DA17 125 C3
Elizabeth Garrett Anderson Hospl NW1 93 C3 239 B5

Elizabeth Garrett Anderson Language Coll N1 94 B5 233 D3
Elizabeth Gdns
East Acton W3 111 D5
Isleworth TW7 131 A1
Stanmore HA7 25 C5
Sunbury TW16 194 C6
Elizabeth Ho
Cheam SM3 217 A2
Friern Barnet N20 14 D1
15 Hammersmith W6 112 C1
Lambeth SE11 261 B3
Stanmore HA7 26 A1
Wembley HA9 66 B3
Elizabeth Ind Est SE14 140 D6
Elizabeth Kenny Ho N1 73 A2
Elizabeth Mews
28 Hackney E2 96 A5
Maitland Pk NW3 70 D2
Elizabeth Pl N15 51 B5
Elizabeth Rd
Newham E6 99 D6
South Tottenham N15 51 C4
Elizabeth Ride N9 18 B4
Elizabeth Selby Inf Sch E2 96 A4
Elizabeth Sq 13 SE16 119 A6
Elizabeth St SW1 115 A2 258 B4
Elizabeth Terr SE9 166 B5
Elizabeth Way
Feltham TW13 172 C6
South Norwood SE19 183 B3
Elkanette Mews N20 14 A2
Elkington Point SE11 261 A3
Elkington Rd E13 99 B3
Elkstone Rd W10 91 B2
Ella Cl BR3 185 C1
Ellacombe Ho 1 SW2 160 C4
Ellaline Rd W6 134 D6
Ella Mews NW3 70 D4
Ellanby Cres N18 34 B5
Elland Ho 18 E14 97 B1
Elland Rd SE15 140 C1
Ellard Ct DA16 146 C2
Ella Rd N4, N8 50 A2
Elle Ct N12 29 D5
Ellement Cl HA5 40 D4
Ellena Ct N14 16 A1
Ellenborough Ct N22 32 D2
Ellenborough Ho 5 W12 112 B6
Ellenborough Pl SW15 134 A1
Ellenborough Rd
Sidcup DA14 191 A5
Tottenham N22 33 A2
Ellen Cl BR1 209 D6
Ellen Ct
6 Chingford E4 20 A3
Lower Edmonton N9 18 C2
Ellen Miller Ho 2 E17 54 A4
Ellen St E1 96 A1
Ellen Webb Dr HA3 42 C6
Ellen Wilkinson Ho
12 Dagenham RM10 81 C5
7 Globe Town E2 96 D4
West Brompton SW6 264 D5
Ellen Wilkinson Prim Sch E6 100 A2
Ellen Wilkinson Sch for Girls W3 88 B1
Elleray Rd TW11 174 D4
Ellerby St SW6 134 D4
Ellerdale Cl 15 NW3 70 A4
Ellerdale Rd NW3 70 A3
Ellerdale St SE13 141 D2
Ellerdine Rd TW3 130 B1
Ellerker Gdns TW10 154 A5
Ellerman Ave TW2, TW4 151 B3
Ellerslie Ct 6 SM6 219 B2
Ellerslie Gdns NW10 90 A6
Ellerslie Ind Est SW2 160 A6
Ellerslie Rd W12 112 B5
Ellerton Ct W3 110 D4
Ellerton Gdns RM9 80 C1
Ellerton Lo N3 29 C1
Ellerton Rd
Barnes SW13 134 A4
Dagenham RM9 80 C1
Surbiton KT6 198 B1
Wandsworth SW17, SW18 158 B3
Wimbledon SW20 178 A3
Ellery Cl 5 NW10 89 D5

Ellery Ho SE17 262 D3
Ellery Rd SE19 183 B3
Ellery St SE15 140 B3
Ellesborough Cl WD19 22 C5
Ellesmere Ave
Beckenham BR3 185 D1
Edgware NW7 11 B1
Ellesmere Cl
Leytonstone E11 54 D4
Ruislip HA4 39 A2
Ellesmere Ct
Chiswick W4 133 B6
Lewisham SE12 165 A3
Penge SE20 184 B1
Ellesmere Gdns IG4 56 A3
Ellesmere Gr EN5 13 B6
Ellesmere Rd Bow E3 97 A5
Chiswick W4 133 B6
Greenford UB6 86 A3
Twickenham TW1 153 C5
Willesden NW10 68 A3
Ellesmere St E14 97 D1
Ellies Mews TW15 148 A2
Ellingfort Rd E8 74 B1
Ellingham Prim Sch KT9 213 D1
Ellingham Rd
Chessington KT9 213 D2
Leyton E15 76 B4
Shepherd's Bush W12 112 A4
Ellington Ct N14 15 D2
Ellington Ho SE1 262 B5
Ellington Rd
Cranley Gdns N10 49 B5
Feltham TW13 171 D6
Hounslow TW3 129 D3
Ellington St N7 72 C2
Elliot Cl Stratford E15 76 C1
Wembley HA9 66 C5
Woodford IG8 37 D4
Elliot Ct 6 N15 51 D5
Elliot Rd NW4 46 B3
Elliott Ave HA4 62 B6
Elliott Gdns TW17 192 C5
Elliott Ho 8 CR7 204 D5
Elliott Rd Acton W4 111 C2
Brixton SW9 138 D4
Bromley BR2 209 D5
Camberwell SW9 138 D4
Stanmore HA7 25 A4
Thornton Heath CR7 204 D5
Elliott Sch SW15 156 C5
Elliott's Pl N1 234 D5
Elliott Sq NW3 70 C1
Elliott's Row SE11 116 D2 261 D4
Ellis Cl Burnt Oak HA8 27 C4
New Eltham SE9 167 A2
Willesden NW10 68 C2
Elliscombe Mount 11 SE7 143 C6
Elliscombe Rd SE7 143 C6
Ellis Ct W7 86 D2
Ellisfield Dr SW15 156 A4
Ellis Franklin Ct NW8 229 A4
Ellis Ho
Walthamstow E17 54 A4
Walworth SE17 262 C2
Ellison Gdns UB2 107 B2
Ellison Ho 1 SE13 142 A3
Ellison Rd
Barnes SW13 133 D3
New Eltham DA15 167 B3
Streatham SW16 182 A3
Ellis Rd Mitcham CR4 202 D3
Southall UB2 108 A5
Ellis St SW1 115 A2 258 A4
Elliston Ho 8 SE18 122 C2
Ellora Rd SW16 181 D5
Ellswood Ct 18 KT6 197 D2
Ellsworth St E2 96 B4
Ellwood Ct 1 W9 91 D3
Elmar Ct SW6 135 A3
Elmar Rd N15 51 B5
Elm Ave Ealing W5 110 B5
Ruislip HA4 40 B2
Elm Bank Dr BR1 187 D1
Elm Bank Gdns SW13 133 C3
Elm Bank Mans SW13 133 C3
Elmbank N14 16 A4
Elmbank Way W7 86 B2
Elmbourne Dr DA17 125 D2
Elmbourne Rd SW17 159 B1
Elmbridge Ave KT5 199 A3
Elmbridge Cl HA4 40 A3
Elmbridge Dr HA4 40 A3
Elmbridge Wlk E8 74 A1
Elmbrook Cl TW16 172 B2
Elmbrook Gdns SE9 144 A1
Elmbrook Rd SM1 217 B4
Elmbrook 3 E18 55 A6

Elm Cl
Buckhurst Hill IG9 21 D2
Carshalton SM5 202 D1
Harrow HA2 41 D3
Hayes UB3 84 A1
Hendon NW4 46 D4
South Croydon CR2 221 C2
Tolworth KT5 199 A2
Twickenham TW13, TW2 151 D2
Upper Holloway N19 71 C6
Wanstead E11 55 B3
West Barnes SW20 200 C5
Elmcote HA5 22 D1
Elmcourt Rd SE21, SE27 160 D2
Elm Court Sch SE27 161 A2
Elm Cres Ealing W5 110 A4
Kingston u T KT2 176 A2
Elmcroft Ave
Blackfen DA15 168 A5
Enfield N9 18 B5
Golders Green NW11 47 B2
Wanstead E11 55 B5
Elmcroft Cl
Chessington KT9 214 A5
Ealing W5 87 D1
Feltham TW14 149 D5
Wanstead E11 55 B5
Elmcroft Cres
Harrow HA2 41 C6
Hendon NW11 47 A2
Elmcroft Dr
Ashford TW15 170 C5
Chessington KT9 214 A5
Elmcroft Gdns NW9 44 C4
Elmcroft Highgate N6 49 C2
Hornsey Vale N8 50 B4
Elmcroft St E5 74 C4
Elmcroft Terr UB8 82 C1
Elm Ct
5 Ashford TW16 171 D3
Brixton SW9 138 C4
Catford SE6 163 D3
Chingford E4 36 A4
4 Finchley N3 29 C2
Lewisham SE13 142 B2
Mitcham CR4 180 D1
42 Notting Hill W2 91 C2
Strand EC4 251 A6
Elmdale Rd N13 32 B5
Elmdene Cl BR3 207 B4
Elmdene Rd SE18 122 D1
Elmdene KT5 199 A1
Elmdon Rd
Hatton TW6 127 D2
Hounslow TW5 129 A3
Elm Dr Harrow HA2 41 D3
Sunbury TW16 172 C1
Elmer Cl EN2 4 B2
Elmer Ct HA1 42 D3
Elmer Gdns
Edgware HA8 26 D3
Isleworth TW7 130 B2
Elmer Ho NW1 237 A4
Elmer Rd SE6 164 A4
Elmer's Dr TW11 175 B4
ELMERS END 206 D6
Elmers End Rd BR3, SE20 206 C6
Elmers End Sta BR3 206 D5
Elmerside Rd BR3 207 A5
Elmers Rd SE25 206 A2
Elmfield Ave
London N8 50 A4
Mitcham CR4 181 A2
Teddington TW11 174 D5
Elmfield Cl HA1 64 C6
Elmfield Ct DA16 146 B4
Elmfield Ho
6 Canonbury N5 73 A3
22 London N2 30 B1
Paddington W9 91 C3
Elmfield Mans 5 SW17 159 A2
Elmfield Pk BR1 209 A6
Elmfield Rd
Bromley BR1 209 A6
Chingford E4 20 B2
East Finchley N2 48 B6
Southall UB2 107 A3
Upper Tooting SW17 159 B2
Walthamstow E17 52 D3
Elmfield Way
Paddington W9 91 C2
South Croydon CR2 221 D1
Elm Friars Wlk NW1 71 D1
Elmgate Ave TW13 150 C1
Elmgate Ct HA8 27 A5
Elmgate Gdns HA8 27 B6
Elm Gdns
Claygate KT10 212 D2
East Finchley N2 48 A6
Enfield EN2 5 B5
Mitcham CR4 203 D5
Elm Gn W3 89 C1

Elm Gr NW2 68 D4
Elmgreen Cl 8 E15 98 C6
Elm Gr Harrow HA2 41 C2
Hornsey N8 50 A3
Kingston u T KT2 176 A2
Orpington BR6 211 D1
Elmgrove Cres HA1 43 A4
Elmgrove Fst & Mid Schs HA3 43 A5
Elmgrove Gdns HA1 43 A4
Elm Grove Par SM6 219 A5
Elm Grove Rd SW13 134 A3
Elmgrove Rd CR0 206 B2
Elm Grove Rd W5 110 A4
Elmgrove Rd HA1 42 D4
Elm Gr
Peckham SE15 140 A3
Sutton SM1 217 D4
Wimbledon SW19 179 A3
Woodford IG8 36 D5
Yiewsley UB7 104 B6
Elm Hall Gdns E11 55 B3
Elm Hatch HA5 23 B3
Elm Ho
4 Cubitt Town E14 120 A4
2 Kingston u T KT2 176 B3
Teddington TW11 175 C3
Elmhurst Ave
London N2 48 B6
Mitcham CR4 181 B3
Elmhurst Cres N2 48 B5
Elmhurst Ct
Carshalton SM5 218 B6
Croydon CR0 221 B3
Elmhurst DA17 147 A6
Elmhurst Dr E18 37 A1
Elmhurst Lo 3 SM2 218 A1
Elmhurst Mans SW4 137 D2
Elmhurst Prim Sch E7 77 B1
Elmhurst Rd
Chislehurst SE9 166 A1
Enfield EN3 6 C6
Tottenham N17 33 D1
Upton E7 77 B1
Elmhurst Sch CR2 221 B3
Elmhurst St SW4 137 D2
Elmhurst Villas SE15 140 C1
Elmington Cl DA5 169 D5
Elmington Rd SE5 139 B5
Elmira St SE13 141 D2
Elm La SE6 163 B2
Elm Lawn Cl UB8 60 A1
Elmlea Dr UB3 83 D2
Elm Lea Trad Est N17 34 B4
Elmlee Cl BR7 188 B4
Elmley Cl 12 E6 100 A2
Elmley St SE18 123 B2
Elm Lo SW6 134 D4
Elmore Cl HA0 88 A5
Elmore Ho SW9 138 D3
Elmore Rd Enfield EN3 6 D5
Leyton E11 76 B5
Elmore St N1 73 B1
Elm Park Ave N15 52 A3
Elm Park Ct HA5 40 C6
Elm Park Gdns
Chelsea SW10 114 B1 256 C1
Hendon NW4 46 D4
Elm Park Ho SW10 256 C1
Elm Park La SW3 114 B1 256 C1
Elm Park Mans SW10 266 B6
Elm Park Rd
Chelsea SW3 136 B6 266 C6
Edmonton N21 17 A4
Finchley N3 29 B3
Pinner HA5 40 D6
South Norwood SE25 205 D6
Walthamstow E10 53 A1
Elm Pk Stanmore HA7 25 C5
Streatham SW2 160 B4
Elm Pl SW7 114 B1 256 C2
Elm Quay SW8 269 C5
Elm Rd Barnet EN5 1 B1
Beckenham BR3 185 B1
Chessington KT9 214 A4
Claygate KT10 212 D2
East Bedfont TW14 149 B4
Hackbridge SM6 203 A1
Kingston u T KT2 176 B2
Leyton E11 76 B6
Mortlake SW14 133 A1
New Malden KT3 199 B6
Sidcup DA14 190 A6
South Norwood CR7 205 B5

Elm Rd *continued*
Stoneleigh KT17 ... 215 D2
Stratford E7 ... 76 D2
Tottenham N22 ... 32 D2
Walthamstow E17 ... 54 A4
Wembley HA9 ... 66 A3
Elm Rd W SM4 ... 201 B2
Elm Row NW3 ... 70 A5
Elms Ave
Hendon NW4 ... 46 D4
Muswell Hill N10 ... 49 B6
Elmscott Gdns N21 ... 17 A5
Elmscott Rd BR1 ... 186 D5
Elms Cotts 1 CR4 ... 180 D1
Elms Cres SW4 ... 159 D5
Elms Ct
Merton SW19 ... 179 D3
Wembley HA0 ... 65 A4
Elmsdale Rd E17 ... 53 B5
Elms Gdns
Dagenham RM9 ... 81 B4
Wembley HA0 ... 65 A4
Elmshaw Rd SW15 ... 156 A6
Elmside CR0 ... 223 D2
Elmside Rd HA9 ... 66 C5
Elms La HA0 ... 65 A5
Elmsleigh Ave HA3 ... 43 C5
Elmsleigh Ct SM1 ... 217 D5
Elmsleigh Ho TW2 ... 152 B2
Elmsleigh Rd TW2 ... 152 B2
Elmslie Ct SE9 ... 166 C5
Elmslie Point 2 E3 ... 97 B2
Elms Mews W2 ... 246 C6
Elms Park Ave HA0 ... 65 A4
Elms Rd
Clapham Pk SW4 ... 159 C6
Harrow HA3 ... 24 C3
ELMSTEAD ... 188 A5
Elmstead Ave
Elmstead BR7 ... 188 B5
Wembley HA9 ... 66 B6
Elmstead Cl
Totteridge N20 ... 13 C2
West Ewell KT19 ... 215 C3
Elmstead Ct HA9 ... 44 B1
Elmstead Gdns KT4 ... 216 A5
Elmstead Glade
BR7 ... 188 B4
Elmstead La BR7 ... 188 B5
Elmstead Rd IG3 ... 79 D6
Elmstead Woods Sta
BR7 ... 188 A4
Elmsted Cres DA16 ... 146 C6
Elms The
5 Ashford TW15 ... 170 C5
Barnes SW13 ... 133 D2
Claygate KT10 ... 212 D1
Croydon CR0 ... 205 A1
3 Harlesden NW10 ... 89 C5
Kingsbury NW9 ... 45 A3
Plashet E12 ... 78 A2
Wallington SM6 ... 219 C4
Elmstone Rd SW6 ... 265 A2
Elm St WC1 ... 94 B3 240 D5
Elmsway TW15 ... 170 C5
Elmsworth Ave
TW3 ... 129 D3
Elm Terr
Child's Hill NW2 ... 69 C5
3 Eltham SE9 ... 166 C5
Harrow HA3 ... 24 B2
Elmton Ct NW8 ... 236 C6
Elm Tree Ave KT10 ... 196 C2
Elm Tree Cl
Ashford TW15 ... 170 D5
Northolt UB5 ... 85 B5
St John's Wood
NW8 ... 92 B4 229 C2
Elm Tree Ct
5 Camberwell
SE5 ... 139 A4
18 Charlton SE7 ... 143 C6
Elmtree Ct HA4 ... 40 A1
Elm Tree Ct NW8 ... 229 C2
Elm Tree Rd
NW8 ... 92 B4 229 C2
Elmtree Rd TW11 ... 174 C5
Elm View Ct UB2 ... 107 C2
Elm Way London N11 ... 31 A4
North Cheam KT4 ... 216 C5
West Ewell KT19 ... 215 B3
Willesden NW10 ... 67 C4
Elm Wlk
Child's Hill NW3 ... 69 C6
Orpington BR6 ... 226 B5
West Barnes SW20 ... 200 D5
Elmwood Ave
Bowes Pk N13 ... 32 A5
Feltham TW13 ... 150 B1
Harrow HA3 ... 43 B3
Elmwood Cl
Hackbridge SM6 ... 219 B6
Stoneleigh KT17 ... 216 A1
Elmwood Cres NW9 ... 45 A5
Elmwood Ct
Battersea SW11 ... 268 C2
Walthamstow E10 ... 53 C1
Wembley HA0 ... 65 A5
Elmwood Dr
Sidcup DA5 ... 169 A4
Stoneleigh KT17 ... 216 A1
Elmwood Gdns W7 ... 86 C1
Elmwood Ho
Enfield EN2 ... 4 D1
Feltham TW13 ... 150 B1
Elmwood Inf Sch
CR0 ... 204 D3
Elmwood Jun Sch
CR0 ... 204 D2
Elm Wood Prim Sch
SE27 ... 161 B1
Elmwood Rd
Chiswick W4 ... 133 A6
Herne Hill SE24 ... 161 B6
Mitcham CR4 ... 202 D6
Thornton Heath CR0 ... 204 D2
Elmworth Gr SE21 ... 161 B2
Elnathan Mews W9 ... 91 D3
Elphinstone Ct
SW16 ... 182 A4
Elphinstone Rd E17 ... 35 B1
Elphinstone St N5 ... 72 D4
Elrington Rd
Dalston E8 ... 74 A2
Woodford IG8 ... 37 A5
Elsa Ct BR3 ... 185 B2
Elsa Rd DA16 ... 146 C3
Elsa St E1 ... 97 A2
Elsdale Ho 14 E9 ... 74 C2
Elsdale St E9 ... 74 C1
Elsden Mews E2 ... 96 C5
Elsden Rd N17 ... 33 D2
Elsenham Rd E12 ... 78 C3
Elsenham St SW18,
SW19 ... 157 B2
Elsfield NW5 ... 71 B3
Elsham Rd
Kensington
W14 ... 113 A4 244 A1
Leyton E11 ... 76 C4
Elsham Terr W14 ... 244 A1
Elsiedene Rd N21 ... 17 A4
Elsie Lane Ct W2 ... 91 D2
Elsiemaud Rd SE4 ... 163 B6
Elsie Rd SE22 ... 139 D1
Elsinge Rd EN1 ... 6 B6
Elsinore Ave TW19 ... 148 A4
Elsinore Gdns NW2 ... 69 A5
Elsinore Ho
12 Camberwell
SE5 ... 139 A3
Islington N1 ... 234 A5
7 Woolwich SE7 ... 122 A2
Elsinore Rd SE23 ... 163 A3
Elsinore Way TW9 ... 132 D2
Elsley Ct HA9 ... 66 D2
Elsley Prim Sch HA9 ... 66 B2
Elsley Rd SW11 ... 137 A2
Elsley Sch SW11 ... 137 A2
Elspeth Rd
London SW11 ... 136 D1
Wembley HA0 ... 66 A3
Elsrick Ave SM4 ... 201 C4
Elstan Way CR0 ... 207 A2
Elstead Ct SM3 ... 201 A1
Elstead Ho 9 SW2 ... 160 B4
Elsted St
SE17 ... 117 B2 262 D3
Elstow Cl Eltham SE9 ... 166 B6
Ruislip HA4 ... 40 D2
Elstow Gdns RM9 ... 103 A6
Elstow Grange NW6 ... 68 D1
Elstow Rd RM9 ... 103 A6
ELSTREE ... 10 A5
Elstree Gdns
Abbey Wood
DA17 ... 125 A2
Edmonton N9 ... 18 B3
Ilford IG1 ... 79 A3
Elstree Hill BR1 ... 186 C3
Elstree Hill N WD6 ... 9 D6
Elstree Hill S WD6 ... 9 D4
Elstree Ho 3 HA7 ... 25 C6
Elstree Pk WD6 ... 11 B5
Elstree Rd
Bushey WD23 ... 8 C4
Elstree WD6 ... 9 A5
Elswick Rd SE13 ... 141 D3
Elswick St SW6 ... 136 A3
Elsworth Cl TW14 ... 149 C3
Elsworthy Rd
NW3 ... 92 C6 230 A6
Elsworthy Rise NW3 ... 70 C1
Elsworthy Terr NW3 ... 70 C1
Elsworthy KT7 ... 196 C3
Elsynge Rd SW18 ... 158 B6
Elsynge Road Mans
SW18 ... 158 B6
ELTHAM ... 166 B6
Eltham CE Prim Sch
SE9 ... 166 B6
Eltham Coll Jun Sch
SE9 ... 165 D3
Eltham Coll SE9 ... 165 D2
Eltham Green Rd
SE9 ... 165 C6
Eltham Green Specialist
Sports Coll SE9 ... 165 D5
Eltham High St SE9 ... 166 B5
Eltham Hill SE9 ... 166 A6
Eltham Hill Tech Coll
for Girls SE9 ... 166 A5
Eltham Palace Rd
SE9 ... 165 D5
Eltham Pal* SE9 ... 166 A4
Eltham Park Gdns
SE9 ... 144 C1
Eltham Rd SE9, SE12 ... 165 B6
Eltham Sta SE9 ... 166 B6
Elthiron Rd
SW6 ... 135 C4 265 B1
Elthorne Ave W7 ... 109 A4
Elthorne Ct
Feltham TW13 ... 150 C3
Kingsbury NW9 ... 45 B3
Elthorne Park High Sch
W7 ... 108 D3
Elthorne Park Rd
W7 ... 109 A4
Elthorne Rd
London NW9 ... 45 B2
Upper Holloway N19 ... 71 D6
Elthorne Way NW9 ... 45 B3
Elthruda Rd SE13 ... 164 B5
Eltisley Rd IG1 ... 78 D4
Elton Ave Barnet EN5 ... 13 B6
Wembley HA0 ... 65 B3
Wembley UB6 ... 64 D2
Elton Cl KT1 ... 175 C3
Elton Ho 3 E3 ... 97 B6
Elton Lo 4 W5 ... 110 A6
Elton Pl N16 ... 73 C3
Elton Rd KT2 ... 176 C2
Elton St 11 N16 ... 73 C3
Eltringham St
SW18 ... 136 A1
Elvaston Ct EN5 ... 12 C6
Elvaston Mews SW7 ... 256 B6
Elvaston Pl
SW7 ... 114 A3 256 B5
Elveden Ho 17 SW9 ... 138 D1
Elveden Pl NW10 ... 88 C5
Elveden Rd NW10 ... 88 C5
Elvedon Rd TW13 ... 149 D1
Elvendon Rd N13 ... 32 A4
Elver Gdns 10 E2 ... 96 A4
Elverson Rd SE8 ... 141 D3
Elverson Rd Sta
SE8 ... 141 D3
Elverton St
SW1 ... 115 D2 259 C4
Elvin Ct NW9 ... 45 A2
Elvington Gn BR2 ... 208 D4
Elvington La NW9 ... 27 C2
Elvin Ho 2 E9 ... 74 C2
Elvino Rd SE26 ... 185 A5
Elvis Rd NW2 ... 68 C2
Elwill Way BR3 ... 208 B5
Elwin St E2 ... 96 A4
Elwood Ho N5 ... 72 D5
Elwood St N4, N5 ... 72 D5
Elworth Ho SW8 ... 270 D3
Elwyn Gdns SE12 ... 165 A4
Ely Cl SW20 ... 177 D1
Ely Cotts SW8 ... 270 C3
Ely Court Flats SW6 ... 264 A1
Ely Ct Holborn EC1 ... 241 B3
3 Maida Vale NW6 ... 91 C5
Ely Gdns
Borehamwood
WD6 ... 11 B6
Redbridge IG1 ... 56 A2
Ely Ho Barnet EN4 ... 2 C1
Northolt UB5 ... 85 A6
22 Peckham SE15 ... 140 A5
Elyne Rd N4 ... 50 C3
Ely Pl EC1 ... 94 C2 241 B3
Ely Rd Hatton TW6 ... 127 D3
Hounslow TW4 ... 128 C2
Leyton E10 ... 54 A2
Thornton Heath CR0 ... 205 B4
Elysian Ave BR5 ... 211 D3
Elysium Gate 7
SW6 ... 135 B3
Elysium Pl SW6 ... 135 B3
Elysium St SW6 ... 135 B3
Elystan Bsns Ctr
UB4 ... 106 C6
Elystan Ct SW15 ... 156 B6
Elystan Pl
SW3 ... 114 D1 257 C2
Elystan St
SW3 ... 114 C2 257 B3
Elystan Wlk N1 ... 234 A5
Emanuel Ave W3 ... 89 A1
Emanuel Ct Acton W3 ... 89 B1
10 Leyton E10 ... 53 D2
Emanuel Dr TW12 ... 173 B5
Emanuel Sch SW11 ... 158 C6
Embankment Gdns
SW3 ... 136 D6 267 D6
Embankment Pier
WC2 ... 116 A5 250 B4
Embankment Pl
WC2 ... 250 B4
Embankment SW15 ... 134 D3
Embankment Sta
WC2 ... 116 A5 250 B4
Embankment The
TW1 ... 153 A3
Embassy Ct
Ealing W5 ... 110 B6
Kingston u T KT6 ... 197 D4
Sidcup DA14 ... 168 B1
St John's Wood NW8 ... 229 D3
7 Wallington SM6 ... 219 B2
8 Wanstead E18 ... 55 A6
Welling DA16 ... 146 B2
Wood Green N11 ... 31 D4
Embassy Gdns BR3 ... 185 B2
Embassy Ho 2 NW6 ... 69 C1
Embassy Lo N3 ... 29 B1
Emba St SE16 ... 118 A4
Ember Cl BR5 ... 211 A2
Embercourt Rd KT10, KT7,
KT8 ... 196 C3
Ember Ct
2 Acton W12 ... 111 C3
14 Hendon NW9 ... 27 D1
Ember Farm Ave
KT8 ... 196 B3
Ember Farm Way
KT8 ... 196 B4
Ember Gdns KT10,
KT8 ... 196 C2
Ember Ho 8 BR1 ... 186 B5
Ember La KT10, KT8 ... 196 B2
Emberson Ho 7 E17 ... 54 A5
Emberton Ct EC1 ... 234 C1
Emberton SE5 ... 139 C6
Embleton Rd SE13 ... 141 D1
Embleton Wlk
TW12 ... 173 B5
Embry Cl HA7 ... 25 A6
Embry Dr HA7 ... 25 A4
Embry Way HA7 ... 25 A6
Emden Cl UB7 ... 104 C4
Emden St SW6 ... 265 D2
Emerald Cl E16 ... 100 A1
Emerald Ct N12 ... 30 A6
Emerald Gdns RM8 ... 59 C1
Emerald Rd NW10 ... 89 B6
Emerald Sq UB2 ... 106 D3
Emerald St
WC1 ... 94 B2 240 C4
Emerson Apartments
N8 ... 50 B6
Emerson Ct 8
SW19 ... 179 A4
Emerson Gdns HA3 ... 44 B3
Emerson Ho N16 ... 73 C3
Emerson Rd IG1 ... 56 C2
Emerson St
SE1 ... 117 A5 252 A4
Emerton Cl DA6 ... 147 A1
Emery Hill St SW1 ... 259 B5
Emery St
SE1 ... 116 C3 261 B6
Emilia Cl EN3 ... 18 B6
Emily St 7 E16 ... 98 D1
Emirates Stad (Arsenal
FC) N7 ... 72 C4
Emlyn Gdns 3 W12 ... 111 C3
Emlyn Rd W12 ... 111 D3
Emmanual Ho SE18 ... 123 B1
Emmanuel CE Prim Sch
NW6 ... 69 C3
Emmanuel Ct 3 EN4 ... 14 D3
Emmanuel Ho
Dulwich SE21 ... 161 B1
Lambeth SE11 ... 261 A3
Emmanuel Rd
Northwood HA6 ... 22 A3
Streatham SW12 ... 159 D3
Emma Rd E13 ... 98 D5
Emma St E2 ... 96 B5
Emmeline Ct KT12 ... 194 C2
Emminster NW6 ... 91 D6
Emmott Ave IG6 ... 57 A4
Emmott Cl
London NW11 ... 48 A3
Mile End E1 ... 97 A3
Emperor's Gate
SW7 ... 114 A2 256 A4
Empingham Ho 20
SE8 ... 118 D2
Empire Ave N18 ... 33 A4
Empire Ct HA9 ... 66 D5
Empire Ho
Brompton SW3 ... 257 A5
Edmonton N18 ... 33 B4
Empire Par
Edmonton N18 ... 33 B4
Wembley HA9 ... 66 C5
Empire Rd UB6 ... 65 C1
Empire Sq N19 ... 72 A5
Empire Way HA9 ... 66 C4
Empire Wharf E3 ... 97 A6
Empire Wharf Rd
E14 ... 120 B2
Empress Ave
Chingford E4 ... 35 D3
Ilford IG1 ... 78 C6
Wanstead E12 ... 77 D6
Woodford IG8 ... 36 D3
Empress Dr BR7 ... 188 D4
Empress Mews 36
SE5 ... 139 A3
Empress Par E4 ... 35 C3
Empress Pl
SW5 ... 113 C1 255 A1
Empress St SE17 ... 139 A6
Empson St E3 ... 97 D3
Emsworth Cl N9 ... 18 C3
Emsworth St SW2 ... 160 B2
Emu Rd SW8 ... 137 B3
Enard Ho 28 E3 ... 97 B5
Ena Rd SW16 ... 204 A6
Enbrook St W10 ... 91 A4
Enclave Ct EC1 ... 241 D6
Endale Cl SM5 ... 218 D6
Endeavour Way
Barking IG11 ... 102 A5
Thornton Heath CR0 ... 204 A2
Wimbledon SW19 ... 179 D6
Endell St
WC2 ... 94 A1 240 A1
Enderby St SE10 ... 120 C1
Enderfield Ct BR7 ... 188 C2
Enderley Cl HA3 ... 24 C2
Enderley Ho SE19 ... 183 D2
Enderley Rd HA3 ... 24 C2
Endersby Rd EN5 ... 12 C6
Endersleigh Gdns
NW4 ... 46 A5
Endlebury Ct E4 ... 20 B2
Endlebury Rd E4 ... 20 A2
Endlesham Ct 2
SW12 ... 159 A4
Endlesham Rd
SW12 ... 159 A4
Endsleigh Gdns
Bloomsbury
WC1 ... 93 D3 239 C6
Ilford IG1 ... 56 D1
Kingston u T KT6 ... 197 C3
Endsleigh Ind Est
UB2 ... 107 B2
Endsleigh Mans 4
SW16 ... 160 A1
Endsleigh Pl WC1 ... 239 D6
Endsleigh Rd
Ealing W13 ... 109 A6
Southall UB2 ... 107 A2
Endsleigh St
WC1 ... 93 D3 239 D6
Endway KT5 ... 198 D2
Endwell Rd SE4 ... 141 A3
Endymion Rd
Harringay N4 ... 50 D2
Tulse Hill SW2 ... 160 B5
Energen Cl NW10 ... 67 C2
ENFIELD ... 6 B2
Enfield Chase Sta EN2 ... 5 A2
Enfield Cloisters 7
N1 ... 95 C4
Enfield Coll EN3 ... 6 C2
Enfield Gram Sch EN2 ... 5 B2
Enfield Gram Sch Lower
EN1 ... 5 B3
ENFIELD HIGHWAY ... 6 C3
Enfield Ho 24 SW9 ... 138 A3
ENFIELD LOCK ... 7 B6
Enfield Lock Sta EN3 ... 7 A6
Enfield Rd
Brentford TW8 ... 109 D1
De Beauvoir Town E8,
N1 ... 73 C1
Enfield EN2 ... 4 A2
Hatton TW6 ... 127 C3
South Acton W3 ... 110 D4
Enfield Ret Pk EN1 ... 6 A2
Enfield Road Rdbt
TW6 ... 127 C3
Enfield Sec Tuition Ctr
PRU N9 ... 18 C3
ENFIELD TOWN ... 5 B1
Enfield Town Sta EN1 ... 5 B2
ENFIELD WASH ... 6 D5
Enfield Wlk TW8 ... 109 D1
Enford St W1 ... 92 D2 237 C4
Engadine Cl CR0 ... 221 D5
Engadine St SW18 ... 157 C3
Engate St SE13 ... 142 A1
Engel Pk NW7 ... 28 C4
Engineer Cl SE18 ... 144 C6
Engineers Way HA9 ... 66 C4
England's La NW3 ... 70 D2
England Way KT3 ... 199 A5
Englefield BR1 ... 188 A1
Englefield Cl
Enfield EN2 ... 4
Orpington BR5 ... 211
Thornton Heath CR0 ... 205
Englefield Path
BR5 ... 211
Englefield Rd N1 ... 73
Englefield NW1 ... 232
Engleheart Dr
TW14 ... 149
Engleheart Rd SE6 ... 164
Englewood Rd
SW12 ... 159
English Gardening Sch
The SW3 ... 136 D6 267
English Grounds
SE1 ... 253
English Martyrs RC
Prim Sch
E1 ... 95 D1 243
English St E3 ... 97
Enid Stacy Ho 11
N19 ... 49
Enid St SE16 ... 117 D3 263
Enmore Ave SE25 ... 206
Enmore Ct SW14 ... 155
Enmore Gdns SW14 ... 155
Enmore Rd
Croydon SE25 ... 206
Putney SW15 ... 156
Southall UB1 ... 85
Ennerdale Ave HA3,
HA7 ... 43
Ennerdale Cl
Cheam SM1 ... 217
East Bedfont TW14 ... 149
Ennerdale Ct E11 ... 55
Ennerdale Dr NW9 ... 45
Ennerdale Gdns HA9 ... 43
Ennerdale Ho 3 N4 ... 51
Ennerdale Rd
Erith DA7 ... 147
Richmond TW9 ... 132
Ennersdale Rd SE13 ... 164
Ennis Ho 16 E14 ... 97
Ennismore Ave
Chiswick W4 ... 111
Greenford UB6 ... 64
Ennismore Gdns
SW7 ... 114 C3 257
Ennismore Gdns Mews
SW7 ... 114 C3 257
Ennismore Gdns
KT7 ... 196
Ennismore Mews
SW7 ... 114 C3 257
Ennismore St
SW7 ... 114 C3 257
Ennis Rd London N4 ... 50
Shooters Hill SE18 ... 145
Ennor Ct KT4 ... 216
Ensbury Ho SW8 ... 270
Ensign Cl TW19 ... 148
Ensign Ct 12 E1 ... 118
Ensign Dr N13 ... 17
Ensign Ho 19 E14 ... 119
Ensign St E1 ... 118
Ensign Way
Stanwell TW19 ... 148
2 Wallington SM6 ... 220
Enslin Rd SE9 ... 166
Ensor Mews SW7 ... 256
Enstone Rd Enfield EN3 ... 7
Ickenham UB10 ... 60
Enterprise Cl CR0 ... 204
Enterprise Ho IG11 ... 101
Enterprise Ho E4 ... 20
Enterprise Ho
36 Hackney E9 ... 74
Walton-on-T KT12 ... 194
Enterprise Row N15 ... 51
Enterprise Way
College Pk NW10 ... 90
Teddington TW11 ... 174
Wandsworth SW18 ... 135
Enterprise Works EN3 ... 7
Enterprize Way SE8 ... 119
Enthoven Ho SE18 ... 122
Enton Pl TW3 ... 129
Enversham Ct SE23 ... 163
Epirus Mews SW6 ... 265
Epirus Rd
SW6 ... 135 B5 264
Epping Cl
Millwall E14 ... 119
Romford RM7 ... 59
Epping Forest* IG10 ... 21
Epping Glade E4 ... 20
Epping Ho 8 E5 ... 74
Epping New Rd IG9 ... 21
Epping Pl N1 ... 72
Epping Way E4 ... 19
Epple Rd
SW6 ... 135 B4 264
Epsom Cl Erith DA7 ... 147
Northolt UB5 ... 63

som & Ewell High
ch KT19 215 A3
som Ho SM1 217 D4
som Rd
roydon CR0 220 C4
lford IG3 57 D3
eyton E10 54 A3
Morden SM3, SM4 201 B2
som Sq TW6 127 D3
stein Ct N1 234 D5
stein Rd SE28 124 B5
worth Rd TW7,
W8 131 B5
worth St
C2 95 B3 242 D5
uity Sq 28 E2 95 D4
asmus St
W1 115 D2 259 D3
conwald St W12 89 D1
ebus Dr SE28 123 B4
esby Dr BR3 207 C1
esby Ho SW7 247 B1
esby Pl NW6 69 C1
ica Ct SW4 270 B1
ica Gdns CR0 223 D5
ica Ho London SE4 141 B2
6 Wimbledon
SW19 179 A3
Wood Green N22 32 C2
ica St W12 112 A6
ic Clarke La IG11 101 A4
ic Cl E7 77 A4
iccson Cl SW18 157 C6
ic Fletcher Ct 15
N1 73 A1
ic Macdonald Ho
SW6 265 B1
ic Rd
Dagenham RM6 58 D2
Forest Gate E7 77 A4
Willesden NW10 67 D2
ic Shipman Terr 2
E13 99 A3
icson Ho
London SE13 142 B1
Stamford Hill N16 51 D1
ic St E3 97 B3
ic Wilkins Ho 14
SE1 118 A1
idge Ho SE22 139 D2
idge Rd W4 111 B3
in Cl Bromley BR1 186 C3
Ilford IG3 58 A3
in Ct NW2 68 C2
indale Ct 1 BR3 185 C2
indale SE18 145 B6
indale Terr SE18 145 B6
RITH 147 D6
ith Rd
Belvedere DA17 125 D1
Erith DA7 147 D2
langer Rd SE14 140 D3
lesmere Gdns
W13 109 A3
mine Cl TW4 128 C3
mine Ho 3 N17 33 D3
mine Rd
London SE13 141 D1
South Tottenham N15 51 D3
mine Side EN1 18 A6
mington Rd SE9 167 A2
nald Ave E6 100 A5
ncroft Way TW1 152 D5
nest Ave SE27 182 D6
nest Bevin Coll
SW17 158 C2
nest Cl BR3 207 C4
nest Cotts KT17 215 D1
nest Gdns W4 132 D6
nest Gr BR3 207 B4
nest Rd KT1 176 D1
nest Richards Twr
E17 53 B3
nest Simmonds Ho
SE14 140 C3
nest Sq KT1 176 D1
nest St E1 96 D3
nle Rd SW20 178 C3
nshaw Pl SW15 157 A6
os Ho SE6 163 D4
os (Shaftesbury
Meml)*
W1 115 D6 249 C5
rpingham Rd
SW15 134 C2
rridge Rd SW19 179 C1
rrington Manor 6
SM5 218 D5
rrington Rd W9 91 B3
rrol Gdns Hayes UB4 84 B3
West Barnes KT3 200 A5
rrol St EC1 95 A3 242 B5
rskine Cl SM1 218 C5
rskine Cres N17 52 B5
rskine Hill NW11 47 C4
rskine Ho
7 Charlton SE7 143 C6

Erskine Ho *continued*
Pimlico SW1 259 A1
Erskine Rd
Carshalton SM1 218 B5
Primrose Hill NW3 70 D1
Walthamstow E17 53 B5
Erwood Rd SE7 122 A1
Esam Way SW16 182 C5
Escot Rd TW16 171 C3
Escott Gdns SE9 188 A6
Escot Way EN5 12 C6
Escreet Gr SE18 122 C2
Escuan Lo N5 73 A3
ESHER 212 A4
Esher Ave
Cheam SM3 216 D5
Walton-on-T KT12 194 A1
Esher CE Prim Sch
KT10 212 A3
Esher Cl DA5 169 A3
Esher Coll KT7 196 C2
Esher Cres TW6 127 D3
Esher Gdns SW19 156 D2
Esher Ho 8 SW8 137 D3
Esher Mews 4 CR4 202 D6
Esher Park Ave
KT10 212 A3
Esher Rd
East Molesey KT8 196 B4
Ilford IG3 79 C5
Esher Sta KT10 212 B6
Eskdale Ave UB5 85 B6
Eskdale Cl HA9 65 D6
Eskdale EN1 17 C6
Eskdale Rd DA7 147 C4
Eskdale NW1 232 A3
Esk Ho E3 97 B3
Eskmont Ridge
SE19 183 C3
Esk Rd E13 99 B3
Esmar Cres NW9 46 A2
Esme Ho SW15 133 D1
Esmeralda Rd SE1 118 A2
Esmond Ct Barnet EN5 1 C1
Kensington W8 255 D6
Esmond Gdns W4 111 B2
Esmond Rd
Acton W4 111 B3
Kilburn NW6 91 B6
Esmond St SW15 135 A1
Esparto St SW18 157 D4
Espirit Ct E1 243 C3
Espirit Ho 6 SW15 157 A6
Essan Ho W13 87 B2
Essence Ct HA9 66 B6
Essenden Rd
Belvedere DA17 125 C1
South Croydon CR2 221 C1
Essendine Mans W9 91 C4
Essendine Prim Sch
W9 91 C4
Essendine Rd W9 91 C4
Essex Ave TW7 130 C2
Essex Cl Romford RM7 59 D5
Ruislip HA4 40 D1
Walthamstow E17 53 A5
West Barnes SM4 200 D2
Essex Ct
Barnes SW13 133 D3
Hammersmith W6 112 C3
Holborn EC4 241 A1
South Norwood
SE19 183 B4
Essex Gdns N4 50 D3
Essex Gr SE19 183 B4
Essex Ho 4 Acton W3 88 C1
2 Poplar E14 97 D1
Essex Lo 5 N10 31 B1
Essex Mans E11 54 B2
Essex Park Mews
W3 111 C5
Essex Pk N3 29 D4
Essex Place Sq 5
W4 111 B2
Essex Pl W4 111 A2
Essex Prim Sch E12 78 A3
Essex Rd Acton W3 111 A6
Barking IG11 79 B1
Chingford E4 20 C3
Chiswick W4 111 B2
Enfield EN2 5 B1
Ilford RM6 58 C2
Islington N1 94 D6 234 D6
Leyton E10 54 A3
Plashet E12 78 A2
Romford RM7 59 D5
Essex Rd S E11 54 B2
Essex Rd
Walthamstow E17 53 A3
Willesden NW10 67 C1
Woodford E18 37 B1
Essex Road Sta N1 73 A1
Essex St
Forest Gate E7 77 A3
Strand WC2 116 C6 251 A6
Essex Twr 4 SE20 184 B2

Essex Villas
W8 113 C4 245 A1
Essian St E1 97 A2
Essington SW15 157 A5
Essoldo Way HA8 44 B6
Estate Way E10 53 B1
Estcourt Rd
Croydon SE25 206 B3
Fulham
SW6 135 B5 264 C4
Estella Ave KT3 200 B5
Estella Ho 15 W11 112 D6
Estelle Rd NW3 70 D4
Esterbrooke St SW1 259 C3
Este Rd SW11 136 C2
Esther Cl N21 16 C4
Esther Doe Lo N21 16 C4
Esther Rd E11 54 C2
Estoria Cl 22 SW2 160 C4
Estreham Rd SW16 181 D4
Estridge Cl TW3 129 C1
Estuary Cl IG11 102 B4
Eswyn Rd SW17 180 D5
Etal Ho N1 72 D1
Etchingham Ct N12 30 A3
Etchingham Park Rd
N3 29 D3
Etchingham Rd E15 76 A4
Eternit Wlk SW6 134 D4
Etfield Gr DA14 190 B5
Ethelbert Cl BR1 209 A6
Ethelbert Gdns IG2 56 C4
Ethelbert Ho E9 75 A4
Ethelbert Rd
Bromley BR1,
BR2 209 A6
Wimbledon SW20 178 D2
Ethelbert St SW12 159 B3
Ethel Brooks Ho
SE18 144 D6
Ethelburga St
SW11 136 C4 267 B2
Ethelburga Twr
SW11 267 B2
Ethel Cotts RM6 58 D6
Etheldene Ave N10 49 C5
Ethelden Rd W12 112 B5
Ethel Rankin Ct 8
SW6 135 B3
Ethel Rd
Ashford TW15 170 A5
Newham E16 99 B1
Ethel St SE17 262 B3
Ethelworth Ct 4
SW2 160 C3
Etheridge Rd NW2 46 C2
Etherley Rd N15 51 A4
Etherow St SE22 162 A4
Etherstone Gn
SW16 182 C6
Etherstone Rd
SW16 182 C6
Ethnard Rd SE15 140 B6
Ethronvi Rd DA7 147 A2
Etienne Ho NW7 28 C6
Etloe Ho E10 53 C1
Etloe Rd E10 75 C6
Eton Ave
East Barnet EN4 14 C5
Finchley N12 30 A3
Heston TW5 129 C6
New Malden KT3 199 B5
Primrose Hill NW3 70 C1
Wembley HA0 65 C4
Eton Cl SW18 157 D4
Eton College Rd
NW3 70 D2
Eton Ct
Hampstead NW3 70 B1
Highgate N6 49 B3
Wembley HA0 65 C4
Eton Garages 11
NW3 70 C2
Eton Gr
Lewisham SE13 142 C2
Queensbury NW9 44 C5
Eton Hall NW3 70 D2
Eton Ho Hackney E9 75 B2
Highbury N5 72 D4
Eton Manor Ct E10 75 C6
Eton Pl NW1 71 A1
Eton Rd
Harlington UB3 127 D5
Ilford IG1 79 B4
Maitland Pk NW3 70 D2
Eton Rise NW3 70 D2
Eton St TW10 154 A6
Eton Villas NW3 70 D2
Etta St SE8 141 A6
Ettrick Ho 8 E5 74 B6
Ettrick St E14 98 A1
Etwell Pl KT5 198 B3
Euesden Cl N9 18 B1
Eugene Cotter Ho
SE17 262 D3
Eugenia Rd SE16 118 C2
Eugenie Mews BR7 188 D2

Eureka Rd 8 KT1 176 C1
Euro Bsns Ctr 3 E15 98 D6
Euro Cl NW10 68 A2
Eurolink Bsns Ctr
SW2 160 C6
Europa Pl EC1 235 A1
Europe Rd SE18 122 B3
Eustace Bldg SW8 268 C5
Eustace Ho SE11 260 C4
Eustace Pl SE18 122 B2
Eustace Rd
Dagenham RM6 58 D2
Newham E6 100 A4
Walham Green
SW6 135 C5 265 A4
Euston Ct 5 HA0 66 A2
Euston Rd
Fitzrovia
NW1 93 C3 239 B6
Thornton Heath CR0 204 C1
Euston Sq NW1 232 C1
Euston Square Sta
WC1 93 C3 239 B6
Euston Sta
NW1 93 D4 232 C1
Euston St
NW1 93 C4 232 B1
Euston Underpass
NW1 239 A6
Evandale Rd SW9 138 C3
Evangelist Rd NW5 71 B4
Evans Cl E8 73 D2
Evans Gr TW13 151 C2
Evans Ho
34 Shepherd's Bush
W12 112 B6
South Lambeth SW8 269 D3
Evans Rd SE6 164 C2
Evanston Ave E4 36 A3
Evanston Gdns IG4 56 A3
Eva Rd RM6 58 D2
Eve Ct CR4 181 A1
Evelina Mans 9
SE5 139 B5
Evelina Rd
London SE15 140 C3
Penge SE20 184 D3
Eveline Ct N10 49 B4
Eveline Lowe Prim Sch
SE1 118 A1
Eveline Rd CR4 180 D2
Evelyn Ave
London NW9 45 B5
Ruislip HA4 39 D2
Evelyn Cl TW2 151 D4
Evelyn Cres TW16 171 D2
Evelyn Ct
Chislehurst SE9 166 A2
Marylebone W1 237 C1
Shacklewell E8 74 A4
Shoreditch N1 235 C3
Evelyn Denington Ct 2
N1 72 D1
Evelyn Denington Rd
E6 100 A3
Evelyn Dr HA5 22 D3
Evelyn Fox Ct W10 90 C2
Evelyn Gdns
Richmond TW9 132 A1
South Kensington
SW7 114 B1 256 C1
Evelyn Gr Ealing W5 110 B5
Southall UB1 85 B1
Evelyn Ho
Bedford Pk W12 111 D4
3 Brixton SW2 160 B6
Harrow HA1 42 B4
18 Spitalfields E1 96 A2
Evelyn Rd Acton W4 111 B3
Cockfosters EN4 2 D1
Ham TW10 153 C1
Newham E16 121 B5
Richmond TW9 132 A2
Walthamstow E17 54 A5
Wimbledon SW19 179 D4
Evelyns Cl UB8 82 C1
Evelyn St SE8 119 A1
Evelyn Terr TW9 132 A2
Evelyn Way
Sunbury TW16 171 D2
Wallington SM6 219 D4
Evelyn Wlk
N1 95 B5 235 C3
Evelyn Yd W1 239 C2
Evening Hill BR3 186 A3
Evenlode Ho 5 SE2 124 C4
Evenwood Cl SW15 157 A6
Everard Ave BR2 209 A1
Everard Ct N13 16 B1
Everard Ho 38 E1 96 A1
Everard Way HA9 66 A5
Everatt Cl SW18 157 B6
Everdale Ct N2 48 C5
Eve Rd
Isleworth TW7 131 A1
Leyton E11 76 C4
Everdon Rd SW13 134 A6

Eve Rd Tottenham N17 51 C6
West Ham E15 98 C5
Everest Ct
6 Chislehurst
SE9 166 A2
South Norwood
SE19 183 C2
Everest Pl E14 98 A2
Everest Rd
Eltham SE9 166 B6
Stanwell TW19 148 A4
Everett Cl
Bushey WD23 8 C3
Pinner HA5 39 D6
Everett Ho
Islington N7 72 C4
Walworth SE17 262 C2
Everett Wlk DA17 125 B1
Everglade Ho E17 35 B1
Everglades
Beckenham BR2 208 C6
Hounslow TW3 130 A2
Everglade Strand
NW9 27 D2
Evergreen Cl SE20 184 C3
Evergreen Ct 6
SM2 218 A2
Evergreen Sq 3 E8 73 D1
Evergreen Way
UB3 105 D6
Everilda St N1 233 D5
Evering Rd E5, N16 74 A5
Everington Rd N10 30 D1
Everington St W6 134 D6
Everitt Rd NW10 89 B4
Everleigh St N4 50 B1
Eversfield Ct SE12 165 B2
Eversfield Gdns HA8,
NW7 27 C3
Eversfield Rd TW9 132 B3
Evershed Ho E1 243 D2
Evershed Wlk W4 111 B2
Eversholt Ct EN5 14 A6
Eversholt St
NW1 93 D4 232 C2
Evershot Rd N4 50 B1
Eversleigh Ct N3 29 C3
Eversleigh Rd
Clapham SW11 137 A3
Finchley N3 29 B3
New Barnet EN5 14 A6
Newham E6 99 D6
Eversley Ave HA9 66 C6
Eversley Cl N21 16 B5
Eversley Cres
Hounslow TW7 130 B4
Ruislip HA4 61 D6
Southgate N21 16 C5
Eversley Ho 12 E2 96 A4
Eversley Mount N21 16 B5
Eversley Park Rd
N21 16 B5
Eversley Pk SW19 178 B5
Eversley Prim Sch
N21 16 B5
Eversley Rd
Greenwich SE7 143 B6
Kingston u T KT5 198 B4
South Norwood
SE19 183 B3
Eversley Way CR0 223 C5
Everthorpe Rd SE15 139 D2
Everton Bldgs NW1 232 A1
Everton Ct HA0 65 D4
Everton Dr HA7 44 A6
Everton Rd CR0 206 A1
Evesham Ave E17 35 C1
Evesham Cl
Belmont SM2 217 C1
Greenford UB6 85 D5
Evesham Ct
2 Ealing W13 109 A5
2 Richmond TW10 154 B5
Evesham Gn SM4 201 D3
Evesham Ho
1 Bethnal Green
E2 96 C5
Pimlico SW1 258 D2
St John's Wood NW8 229 A5
Evesham Rd
London N11 31 D5
Morden SM4 201 D3
Stratford E15 76 D1
Evesham St W11 112 D6
Evesham Way
Clapham SW11 137 A2
Ilford IG5 56 C6
Evesham Wlk
Brixton SW9 138 C3
Camberwell SE5 139 B3
Evry Rd DA14 190 C4
Ewald Rd SW6 135 B3
Ewanrigg Terr IG8 37 C5
Ewart Gr N22 32 C2
Ewart Pl 13 E3 97 B5
Ewart Rd SE23 162 D4
Ewe Cl N7 72 A2

EWELL 215 C1
Ewell By-Pass KT17 216 A1
EWELL COURT 215 C2
Ewell Court Ave
KT19 215 C3
Ewell Park Gdns
KT17 216 A1
Ewell Park Way
KT17 216 A1
Ewell Rd
Cheam SM2, SM3 216 D2
Surbiton KT6 198 B2
Thames Ditton KT6,
KT7 197 B2
Tolworth KT6 198 D1
Ewelme Rd SE23 162 C3
Ewen Cres SW2 160 C4
Ewen Henderson Ct 10
SE14 141 A5
Ewen Ho N1 233 C5
Ewer St SE1 117 A5 252 A3
Ewhurst Cl E1 96 C2
Ewhurst Ct CR4 202 B6
Ewhurst 19 SW15 156 D5
Ewhurst Rd SE4 163 B5
Exbury Ho Hackney E9 74 C2
4 London SW9 138 B1
Exbury Rd SE6 163 C2
Excel Ct WC2 249 D5
Excel Ex Ctr E16 121 B6
Excelsior Cl KT1 176 C1
Excelsior Gdns
SE13 142 A3
Excelsior Ind Est
SE16 140 C6
Exchange Apartments
4 BR2 209 B5
Exchange Arc EC2 243 B4
Exchange Cl N11 15 A2
Exchange Ct WC2 250 B5
Exchange Mans 2
NW11 47 B2
Exchange Pl EC2 243 A4
Exchange The IG1 78 D6
Exchange Wlk HA5 41 A2
Exeforde Ave TW15 170 C6
Exeter Cl E6 100 B1
Exeter Ct Kilburn NW6 91 C5
Kingston u T KT6 198 A4
Mitcham SW19 180 C3
Exeter Gdns IG1 56 B1
Exeter Ho
7 Barking IG11 80 A1
Feltham TW13 151 C2
Paddington W2 236 A2
11 Peckham SE15 140 A6
Putney SW15 156 C5
Exeter Mans NW2 69 A2
Exeter Mews
Fulham SW6 265 A4
12 Hampstead NW6 69 D2
Exeter Rd
Bexley DA16 145 D3
Brondesbury NW2 69 A2
Croydon CR0 205 D2
Dagenham RM10 81 D2
East Barnet N14 15 B4
Enfield EN3 6 D2
Harrow HA2 63 A6
Hatton TW6 127 C2
Lower Edmonton N9 18 C2
Newham E16 99 A2
Twickenham TW13 151 B1
Walthamstow E17 53 C4
Exeter St
WC2 116 B6 250 C6
Exeter Way
Hatton TW6 127 C3
2 New Cross SE14 141 B5
Exford Ct SW11 266 D2
Exford Gdns SE12 165 B3
Exford Rd SE12 165 B3
Exhibition Cl W12 112 C6
Exhibition Rd
SW7 114 B3 256 D6
Exit Rd N2 30 B1
Exmoor Ho 25 E3 97 A5
Exmoor St W10 90 D2
Exmouth Ho
Clerkenwell EC1 241 B6
6 Millwall E14 119 D2
Exmouth Market
EC1 94 C3 241 B6
Exmouth Mews
NW1 232 B1
Exmouth Pl E8 74 B1
Exmouth Rd
Bexley DA16 146 C5
Hayes UB4 83 C4
Ruislip HA4 62 C5
Walthamstow E17 53 B4
Exmouth St E1 96 C1
Exning Rd E16 98 D3
Exonbury NW8 91 D6

Exon St
SE17 117 C2 263 A3
Explorer Ave TW19 148 A3
Explorers Ct 6 E14 120 B6
Express Dr IG3 58 B1
Express Wharf 10
E14 119 C4
Exton Cres NW10 67 A1
Exton Gdns RM8 80 C3
Exton Rd NW10 67 A1
Exton St SE1 116 C5 251 A3
Eyebright Cl 3 CR0 206 D1
Eyhurst Cl NW2 68 A6
Eylewood Rd SE27 183 A5
Eynella Rd SE21 161 D4
Eynham Rd W12 90 C1
Eynsford Cl BR5 211 A3
Eynsford Cres DA5 168 D3
Eynsford Ho
Borough The SE1 252 C2
12 Deptford SE15 140 C6
Walworth SE17 263 A3
Eynsford Rd IG3 79 C6
Eynsford Terr UB7 82 B1
Eynsham Dr SE2 124 B3
Eynswood Dr DA14 190 C5
Eyot Gdns W6 111 D1
Eyot Gn W4 111 D1
Eyre Ct NW8 229 C4
Eyre St Hill
EC1 94 C3 241 A5
Eysham Ct 12 EN5 13 D6
Eythorne Rd SW9 138 C4
Ezra St E2 95 D4

F

Faber Gdns NW4 46 A4
Fabian Rd
SW6 135 B5 264 D4
Fabian St E6 100 B3
Fabyc Ho TW9 132 C5
Factory La
Croydon CR0 220 D6
Tottenham N17 33 D1
Factory Rd E16 122 A5
Factory Yd W7 108 C5
Fagg's Rd TW14 150 A6
Fairacre
Hounslow TW7 130 B4
Kingston u T KT3 199 C6
Pinner HA5 40 A5
Fair Acres BR2 209 A4
Fairacres
Putney SW15 134 A1
Ruislip HA4 39 D2
Fairbairn Gn 1
SW9 138 D4
Fairbairn Hall E13 99 A3
Fairbank Ave BR6 226 D6
Fairbanks Rd N17 52 A6
Fairbourne Ho UB3 105 A3
Fairbourne Rd N17 51 C6
Fairbriar Residence
SW7 256 B4
Fairbridge Rd N19 71 D6
Fairbrook Cl N13 32 C5
Fairbrook Rd N13 32 C4
Fairburn Ct SW15 157 A6
Fairburn Ho
9 Stamford Hill
N16 51 C1
West Kensington
SW5 254 D1
Fairby Ho SE1 263 D4
Fairby Rd SE12 165 B6
Faircharm Trad Est
SE8 141 D5
Fairchild Cl 6
SW11 136 B3
Fairchild Ho
13 Hackney E9 74 C1
Pimlico SW1 259 B3
5 Shoreditch N1 95 C4
Fairchild Pl EC2 243 B5
Fairchild St EC2 243 B5
Fairclough Cl UB5 85 B3
Fairclough St E1 96 A1
Faircourt 14 NW3 70 D2
Faircroft
6 Forest Hill
SE26 184 C6
Stoke Newington N16 51 B1
FAIR CROSS 79 D3
Faircross Ave IG11 79 A2
Fair Cross IG11 79 C3
Faircross Par IG11 79 C3
Fairdale Gdns
Hayes UB3 106 A4
Putney SW15 134 B1
Fairdene Ct N7 72 A3
Fairey Ave UB3 105 D3
Fairfax Cl KT12 194 B1
Fairfax Gdns SE3 143 C4
Fairfax Ho
11 Brixton SW9 138 C3
5 Ealing W5 88 A4
6 Putney SW15 156 A6
Fairfax Mews
London N8 50 D5
Newham E16 121 B5
Putney SW15 134 C1
Fairfax Pl
Kensington W14 254 B5
South Hampstead
NW6 70 A1
Fairfax Rd Acton W4 111 C3
Hornsey N8 50 C5
South Hampstead
NW6 70 A1
Teddington TW11 175 B3
Fairfax Way N10 31 A3
Fairfield Ave
Edgware HA8 26 D3
Hendon NW4 46 B3
Ruislip HA4 39 A2
Twickenham TW2 151 D3
Fairfield NW1 232 A5
Fairfield Cl
Blackfen DA15 167 D5
Enfield EN3 7 A1
Mitcham SW19 180 C3
North Finchley N12 30 A6
West Ewell KT19 215 C3
Fairfield Cres HA8 26 D4
Fairfield Ct
Harlesden NW10 90 A6
1 London SW18 157 D6
Ruislip HA4 39 B1
8 Woodford IG8 37 A4
Fairfield Dr
Harrow HA2 42 A6
Wandsworth SW18 157 D6
Wembley UB6 87 C6
Fairfield E KT1 176 A1
Fairfield Gdns N8 50 A4
Fairfield Gr SE7 143 D6
Fairfield Ind Est
KT1 198 B6
Fairfield N KT1, KT2 176 A1
Fairfield N20 14 B4
Fairfield Path CR0 221 B5
Fairfield HA6 22 A1
Fairfield Pl KT1 198 A6
Fairfield Rd
Beckenham BR3 185 C1
Bexleyheath DA7 147 B3
Bow E3 97 C5
Edmonton N18 34 A6
Higham Hill E17 35 A1
Hornsey N8 50 A4
Ilford IG1 78 D2
Kingston u T KT1 176 A1
Petts Wood BR5 211 B3
Plaistow BR1 187 A3
Southall UB1 85 B1
South Croydon CR0 221 C5
Woodford IG8 37 A4
Yiewsley UB7 104 A6
Fairfields SE6 163 D4
Fairfields Cl NW9 45 A4
Fairfields Cres NW9 45 A4
Fairfield S KT1 176 B1
Fairfields Rd TW3 130 A2
Fairfield 4 E1 96 C2
Fairfield St SW18 157 D6
Fairfield Way
Barnet EN5 13 C6
West Ewell KT19 215 C3
Fairfield W KT1 176 A1
Fairfoot Rd E3 97 C3
Fairford Ave CR0 206 D4
Fairford Cl CR0 207 A4
Fairford Ct SM2 217 D1
Fairford SE6 163 C3
Fairford Gdns KT4 215 D5
Fairford Ho SE11 261 B3
Fairgreen EN4 2 D2
Fairgreen Ct EN4 2 D2
Fair Green Ct 1
CR4 202 D6
Fairgreen E EN4 2 D2
Fairgreen Rd CR7 204 D4
Fairhall Ct KT6 198 B2
Fairhaven Ave CR0 206 D3
Fairhaven Ct 7
CR2 221 A3
Fairhazel Gdns NW6 70 A1
Fairheathe SW15 156 D5
Fairholme Cl N3 47 A5
Fairholme Cres UB4 84 A3
Fairholme TW14 149 C4
Fairholme Gdns N3 47 A5
Fairholme Ho 4
KT3 199 C5
Fairholme Prim Sch
TW14 149 B3
Fairholme Rd
Ashford TW15 170 B5
Cheam SM1 217 B2
Fairholme Rd *continued*
Harrow HA1 42 D4
Ilford IG1 56 C2
Thornton Heath CR0 204 C2
West Kensington
W14 113 A1 254 B1
Fairholt Cl N16 51 C1
Fairholt Rd N16 51 B1
Fairholt St SW7 257 B6
Fairhurst 4 NW6 70 A2
Fairland Ho BR2 209 B5
Fairland Rd E15 76 D1
Fairlands Ave
Sutton SM1 217 C6
Thornton Heath CR7 204 C4
Woodford IG9 21 A2
Fairlands Ct 6 SE9 166 C5
Fairlawn Ave
Acton W4 111 A2
Bexley DA7 146 D3
East Finchley N2 48 C5
Fairlawn Cl
Claygate KT10 212 D2
Feltham TW13 173 B6
Kingston u T KT2 177 A4
Southgate N14 15 D5
Fairlawn Ct
3 Acton W4 111 A2
Charlton SE7 143 C5
Fairlawn Dr IG8 37 A3
Fairlawnes SM6 219 B3
Fairlawn Gdns UB1 107 B6
Fairlawn Gr W4 111 A2
Fairlawn Mans
SE14 140 D4
Fairlawn Pk SE26 185 A5
Fairlawn Prim Sch
(Annexe) SE23 162 C3
Fairlawn Prim Sch
SE23 162 C4
Fairlawn Rd SW19 179 B3
Fairlawns
4 Bowes Pk N11 32 A4
10 Chingford E4 20 A2
Fairlawn SE7 143 C6
Fairlawns Pinner HA5 22 D1
Putney SW15 156 D6
Sunbury TW16 194 A6
Twickenham TW1 153 C5
Fairlead Ho 6 E14 119 C3
Fair Lea Pl W5 87 C2
Fairlea Pl W5 87 D3
Fairleas 12 BR3 185 D1
Fairley Ct HA0 65 D3
Fairley House Sch
SW1 259 D2
Fairlie Ct
22 Bromley E3 97 D4
1 Tufnell Pk N7 71 D4
Fairlie Gdns SE23 162 C4
Fairlight Ave
Chingford E4 20 B2
Harlesden NW10 89 C5
Woodford IG8 37 A4
Fairlight Cl
Cheam KT4 216 C4
Chingford E4 20 B2
Fairlight Ct
Greenford UB6 86 B5
4 Harlesden NW10 89 C5
Fairlight TW12 173 D5
Fairlight Rd SW17 180 B6
Fairline Ct BR3 186 A1
Fairlop Ct E11 54 C1
Fairlop Pl NW8 229 D1
Fairlop Rd E11 54 B2
Fairmark Cl UB10 60 C2
Fairmead BR1 210 B5
Fairmead Cl
Bromley BR1 210 B5
Heston TW5 128 D5
Kingston u T KT3 199 B6
Fairmead Cres HA8 11 A1
Fairmead Ct
3 Chingford E4 20 C4
Oakleigh Pk N20 14 A4
Fairmead Gdns IG4 56 A4
Fairmead Ho E9 75 A4
Fairmead Rd
Lower Holloway N7,
N19 72 A5
Thornton Heath CR0 204 C2
Fairmeadside IG10 21 C6
Fairmead KT5, KT6 198 D1
Fairmile Ave SW16 181 D5
Fairmile Ho
St Paul's Cray
BR5 190 A1
Teddington TW11 175 A6
Fairmont Ave E14 120 B5
Fairmont Cl DA17 125 B1
Fairmont Ho 1 E3 97 C3
Fairmount Rd SW2 160 B5
Fairoak Cl BR5 210 D2
Fairoak Dr SE9 167 B6
Fairoaks Gr EN3 6 D6
Fairseat Cl WD23 8 C2
Fair St SE1 117 D4 253 C2
Fairstead Lo 4 IG8 37 A4
Fairstead Wlk N1 235 A6
Fair St TW3 130 A2
Fairthorn Rd SE7,
SE10 121 A1
Fairview Ave HA0 65 D2
Fairview Cl SE26 185 A5
Fair View Cl E17 35 A2
Fairview Cres HA2 41 C1
Fairview Ct
Ashford TW15 170 C5
Hendon NW4 28 D1
Kingston u T KT2 176 D2
Fairview Dr
Littleton TW17 192 B4
Orpington BR6 227 B4
Fairview Gdns IG8 37 B2
Fairview Ho 14 SW2 160 B4
Fairview Pl SW2 160 B4
Fairview Rd
Carshalton SM1,
SM5 218 C3
Enfield EN2 4 C4
South Tottenham N15 51 D3
Thornton Heath
SW16 182 B2
Fairview Way HA8 26 C6
Fairwall Ho 9 SE5 139 C4
Fairwater Ave DA16 146 A1
Fairwater Ho TW11 175 A6
Fairway Ave NW9 44 D6
Fairway DA6 169 A6
Fairway Cl
Croydon CR0 207 A4
Heston TW4 150 C6
Hounslow TW4 150 D6
North End NW11 48 A2
West Ewell KT19 215 A4
Fairway Ct
Edgware NW7 11 B1
12 Eltham SE9 166 C5
New Barnet EN5 13 D5
13 Rotherhithe
SE16 118 D4
Fairway Dr
Erith SE28 103 A1
Greenford UB6 63 D1
Fairway Est TW4 150 C6
Fairway Gdns
Ilford IG1 79 A3
West Wickham BR3 208 B3
Fairway BR5 211 B4
Fairway Prim Sch
NW7 11 B2
Fairways TW15 170 D4
Fairways Bsns Pk
E10 75 A6
Fairways
12 Chingford E4 20 A3
4 Hounslow TW7 130 C4
Stanmore HA7 26 A1
Teddington TW11 175 D3
Walthamstow E17 54 A5
Fairway The
Acton W3 89 C1
Bromley BR1, BR2 210 B4
East Molesey KT8 195 D6
Edgware NW7 11 B1
Edmonton N13 17 B1
Hillingdon UB10 82 B5
Kingston u T KT3 177 B2
New Barnet EN5 13 D5
Northolt UB5 64 A2
Ruislip HA4 62 D5
Southgate N14 15 C5
Wembley HA0 65 B6
Fairway
West Barnes
SW20 200 C6
Woodford IG8 37 C5
Fairweather Cl N15 51 C5
Fairweather Ct N13 32 B6
Fairweather Ho N7 72 A4
Fairweather Rd N16 52 A3
Fairwood Ct E11 54 B2
Fairwyn Rd SE26 185 A6
Faith Ct NW2 68 B2
Faithfull Ho N5 73 A3
Fakenham Cl
Hendon NW7 28 A3
6 Northolt UB5 63 C2
Fakruddin St E1 96 A3
Falcon Ave BR1 210 A5
Falconberg Ct W1 239 D2
Falconberg Mews
W1 239 D2
Falconbrook Prim Sch
SW11 136 B2
Falcon Cl
Chiswick W4 133 A6
Lambeth SE1 251 D4
Falcon Cres EN3 18 D6
Falcon Ct
9 Dulwich SE21 161 B2
Holborn EC4 241 A1
Islington N1 234 D3
Falcon Ct *continued*
New Barnet EN5 2 A1
Ruislip HA4 61 C6
6 Wanstead E18 55 B6
Falcon Dr TW19 148 A5
Falconer Ct N17 33 A3
Falconer Wlk 12 N7 72 B6
Falcon Gr SW11 136 C2
Falcon Ho
11 London SE15 139 D4
9 Merton SW19 179 D2
Falconhurst 4 KT6 198 A4
Falcon La SW11 136 C2
Falcon Lo
11 Paddington W9 91 C2
West Hampstead
NW3 69 D4
Falcon Pk Ind Est
NW10 67 C3
Falcon Point SE1 251 D5
Falcon Rd
Battersea SW11 136 C2
Enfield EN3 18 D6
Hampton TW12 173 B3
Falconry Ct KT1 198 A6
Falcon St E13 99 A3
Falcon Terr SW11 136 C2
Falcon Way
Feltham TW14 150 B6
Harrow HA3 44 A3
Hendon NW9 27 C1
Millwall E14 119 D2
Sunbury TW16 171 C1
Wanstead E11 55 A5
FALCONWOOD 145 C1
Falconwood Ave
DA16 145 C3
Falconwood Ct SE3 142 D3
Falconwood Par
DA16 145 D1
Falconwood Rd
CR0 223 C1
Falconwood Sta
SE9 145 B1
Falcourt Cl SM1 217 D3
Falkener Ct SW11 268 B1
Falkirk Ct 11 SE16 118 D5
Falkirk Gdns WD19 22 D5
Falkirk Ho W9 91 D4
Falkirk St N1 95 C5
Falkland Ave
Finchley N3 29 C3
Friern Barnet N11 31 B6
Falkland Ho
Catford SE6 186 A6
Kensington W8 255 C5
West Kensington
W14 254 C2
Falkland Park Ave
SE25 183 C1
Falkland Pl 2 NW5 71 C3
Falkland Rd
Barnet EN5 1 A3
Hornsey N8 50 C5
Kentish Town NW5 71 C3
Falkner House Sch
SW7 256 B2
Fallaize Ave IG1 78 D4
Falling La UB7 104 A6
Falloden Ct NW11 47 C5
Falloden Way NW11 47 C5
Fallodon Ho
6 London SW8 137 D3
Paddington W11 91 B2
Fallow Court Ave
N12 30 A4
Fallow Ct 20 SE16 118 A1
Fallowfield Ct HA7 9 A1
Fallowfield N4 72 B6
Fallowfields Dr N12 30 C4
Fallow Fields IG10 21 C4
Fallowfield HA7 9 A1
Fallows Cl N2 30 B1
Fallsbrook Rd
SW16 181 C4
Falman Cl N9 18 A3
Falmer Rd Enfield EN1 5 C1
Walthamstow E17 53 D6
West Green N15 51 B4
Falmouth Ave E4 36 C5
Falmouth Cl
London SE12 164 D6
Wood Green N22 32 B3
Falmouth Gdns IG4 55 D5
Falmouth Ho
Bayswater W2 247 A6
Kennington SE11 261 B2
15 Kingston u T KT2 175 D2
6 Pinner HA5 23 B3
Falmouth Rd
SE1 117 A3 262 B5
Falmouth St E15 76 B3
Falmouth Way E17 53 B4
Falstaff Ct SE11 261 C3
Falstaff Ho 18 N1 95 C5
Fambridge Cl SE26 185 B6
Fambridge Rd RM8 59 C1
Fane St W14 264
Fann St EC1 95 A3 242
Fanshawe Ave IG11 79
Fanshawe Cres RM9 81
Fanshawe Rd TW10 175
Fanshaw Ho 6 E17 53
Fanshaw St N1 95
Fantail Cl SE28 102
Fantail The BR6 226
Fanthorpe St SW15 134
Faraday Ave DA14 168
Faraday Cl N7 72
Faraday Ho
2 Balham SW12 159
4 Belvedere DA17 125
6 Gospel Oak NW5 71
5 Hampton TW12 173
Kensal Town W10 91
6 Poplar E14 119
Wembley HA9 67
Faraday Lo SE10 120
Faraday Pl KT8 195
Faraday Rd
Acton W3 111
East Molesey KT8 195
Kensal Town W10 91
Southall UB1 107
Stratford E15 76
Welling DA16 146
Wimbledon SW19 179
Faraday Way
Greenwich SE18 121
Thornton Heath CR0 204
Fareham Ho 13
SW15 156
Fareham Rd TW14 150
Fareham St W1 239
Farendon Ho 15
SM2 218
Farewell Pl CR4 180
Faringdon Ave BR2 210
Faringford Rd E15 76
Farjeon Ho NW6 70
Farjeon Rd SE3 143
Farleigh Ave BR2 209
Farleigh Ct CR2 221
Farleigh Ho 7 KT2 176
Farleigh Pl N16 73
Farleigh Rd N16 73
Farley Croft BR2 186
Farleycroft 1 CR0 206
Farley Ct
Kensington W14 254
Marylebone NW1 238
Farley Dr IG3 57
Farley Ho SE26 162
Farley Mews SE6 164
Farley Pl SE25 206
Farley Rd
Catford SE6 164
South Croydon CR2 222
Farlington Pl SW15 156
Farlow Rd SW15 134
Farlton Rd SW18 157
Farman Gr 2 UB5 84
Farman Terr HA3 43
Farm Ave
Child's Hill NW2 69
Harrow HA2, HA5 41
Streatham SW16 182
Wembley HA0 65
Farmborough Cl HA1 42
Farm Cl Barnet EN5 12
Buckhurst Hill IG9 21
Coney Hall BR4 224
Lower Halliford
TW17 192
Southall UB1 107
Sutton SM2 218
Uxbridge UB10 60
Walham Green SW6 265
Farmcote Rd SE12 165
Farm Cotts E17 53
Farm Ct NW4 46
Farmdale Rd
Greenwich SE10 121
Sutton SM5 218
Farm Dr CR0 223
Farm End E4 20
Farmer Ho 4 SE16 118
Farmer Rd E10 53
Farmers Rd SE5 138
Farmer St W8 245
Farmfield Rd BR1 186
Farm House Ct NW7 28
Farmhouse Rd
SW16 181
Farmilo Rd E17 53
Farmington Ave
SM1 218
Farm La
Croydon CR0 223
East Barnet N14 15
Farmlands Enfield EN2 4
Pinner HA5 40
Farmlands The UB5 63
Farmland Wlk BR7 188

Farm Lane Trad Ctr SW6 135 C6 265 B5
Farm La SW6 135 C5 265 B4
Farmleigh Ho SW9 160 D6
Farmleigh N14 15 C4
Farm Pl W8 245 A4
Farm Rd Edgware HA8 27 A5
Edmonton N21 17 A3
Morden SM4 201 D4
Stonebridge NW10 89 B6
Sutton SM2 218 B1
Thames Ditton KT10 195 C1
Twickenham TW4 151 A3
Farmstead Ct 3 SM6 219 B3
Farmstead Rd
Catford SE6 185 D6
Harrow HA3 24 B1
Farm St W1 115 B6 248 C5
Farm Vale DA5 169 D5
Farm View N3 47 B6
Farm Way IG9 37 C6
Farmway RM8 80 C5
Farm Way KT4 216 C5
Farm Wlk NW11 47 C4
Farnaby Ho 2 W10 91 B4
Farnaby Rd
Bromley BR1, BR2 186 C2
Kidbrooke SE9 143 C1
Farnan Ave E17 53 D6
Farnan Hall 6 SW16 182 A5
Farnan Rd SW16 182 A5
FARNBOROUGH 227 B3
Farnborough Ave
South Croydon CR2 223 A1
Walthamstow E17 53 A6
Farnborough Cl HA9 66 D6
Farnborough Comm
Keston Mark BR2, BR6 226 B5
Orpington BR6 226 C4
Farnborough Cres
3 Hayes BR2 208 D1
South Croydon CR2 223 A1
Farnborough Ct 2 BR6 227 A3
Farnborough Hill BR6 227 C3
Farnborough Ho 1 SW15 156 A3
Farnborough Prim Sch BR6 227 A3
Farnborough Way BR6 227 B3
Farncombe St SE16 118 A4
Farndale Ave N13 17 A1
Farndale Cres UB6 86 A4
Farndale Ho 3 NW6 91 D6
Farnell Mews SW5 255 C2
Farnell Pl W3 110 D6
Farnell Rd TW7 130 B2
Farnell's Almshouses TW7 130 D3
Farnfield Ho 12 SW2 160 B6
Farnham Cl N20 14 A4
Farnham Ct
2 Cheam SM3 217 A2
1 Southall UB1 86 A1
2 Stamford Hill N16 51 C1
Farnham Gdns SW20 178 B1
Farnham Green Prim Sch IG3 58 A3
Farnham Ho
Borough The SE1 252 A3
Marylebone NW1 237 B5
Farnham Pl SE1 251 D3
Farnham Rd
Bexley DA16 146 C3
Ilford IG3 57 D2
Farnham Royal SE11 116 B1 260 D1
Farnhurst Ho 7 SW11 137 A3
Farningham Ct SW16 181 D3
Farningham Ho 9 N4 51 B2
Farningham Rd N17 34 A3
Farnley Ho 15 SW8 137 D3
Farnley Rd
Chingford E4 20 C4
South Norwood SE25 205 B5
Farnsworth Ct SE10 120 D3
Farnsworth Ho 8 SW27 182 D5
Farnworth Ho 5 E14 120 B2
Faro Cl BR1 188 C1
Faroe Rd W14 112 D3
Farorna Wlk EN2 4 C4
Farquhar Rd
Dulwich SE19 183 D5
Wimbledon SW19 157 C1
Farquharson Rd CR0 205 A1
Farrance Rd RM6 59 A2
Farrance St E14 97 C1
Farrans Ct HA3 43 B2
Farrant Ave N22 32 D1
Farrant Cl BR6 227 D1
Farrant Ho 15 SW11 136 B2
Farrants Ct BR1 188 B1
Farr Ave IG11 102 A5
Farrell Ho E1 96 C1
Farren Rd SE23 163 A2
Farrer Ho SE8 141 C5
Farrer Mews N8 49 C5
Farrer Rd Harrow HA3 44 A5
Hornsey N8 49 D5
Farrer's Pl CR0 222 D4
Farrier Cl
Bromley BR1 209 D6
Hillingdon UB8 82 C1
Sunbury TW16 194 A5
Farrier Pl SM1 217 D6
Farrier Rd UB5 85 C5
Farriers Ct
Belmont SM2 217 A1
Wimbledon SW19 179 A3
Farriers Mews SE15 140 C2
Farrier St NW1 71 C1
Farriers Way WD6 11 B6
Farrier Wlk SW10 136 A6 266 A6
Farringdon La EC1 94 C3 241 B5
Farringdon Rd EC1 94 C3 241 B5
Farringdon Sta EC1 94 D2 241 C4
Farringdon St EC4 94 D1 241 C2
Farrington Pl BR7 189 B3
Farrington & Stratford House Sch BR7 189 B3
Farrins Rents SE16 119 A5
Farrow La SE14 140 C5
Farrow Pl SE16 119 A3
Farr Rd EN2 5 B4
Farthingale Wlk E15 76 B1
Farthing Alley 8 SE1 118 A4
Farthing Ct 3 NW7 29 A3
Farthing Fields 8 E1 118 B5
Farthings Cl
Chingford E4 20 C1
Pinner HA5 40 B3
Farthing St BR6 226 B1
Farthings The 1 KT2 176 C2
FARTHING STREET 226 B1
Farwell Rd DA14 190 C6
Farwig La BR1 187 A2
Fashion & Design Mus The* SE1 253 A2
Fashion Retail Acad The W1 239 C2
Fashion St E1 95 D2 243 D3
Fashoda Rd BR2 209 D5
Fassett Rd Dalston E8 74 A2
Kingston u T KT1 198 A5
Fassett Sq E8 74 A2
Fauconberg Ct W4 133 A6
Fauconberg Rd W4 133 A6
Faulkner Cl 6 RM8 58 D2
Faulkner Ho SW15 134 C3
Faulkner's Alley EC1 241 C4
Faulkner St SE14 140 C4
Fauna Cl
Dagenham RM6 58 C3
Stanmore HA7 25 D6
Faunce Ho 1 SE17 138 D6
Faunce St SE17 116 D1 261 C1
Favart Rd SW6 135 C4 265 B2
Faversham Ave
Chingford E4 20 D3
Enfield EN1 17 B5
Faversham Ct SE6 163 B3
Faversham Ho
Camden Town NW1 232 B5
Walworth SE17 263 A1
Faversham Rd
Beckenham BR3 185 B1
Forest Hill SE6 163 B3
Morden SM4 201 D3
F Ave SE18 122 D3
Fawcett Cl
London SW11 136 B3
West Norwood SW16 182 C6
Fawcett Est E5 52 A1
Fawcett Ho 25 SW9 138 A3
Fawcett Rd
Croydon CR0 221 A5
Willesden NW10 67 D1
Fawcett St SW10 136 A6 266 A6
Fawcus Cl KT10 212 C2
Fawe Park Rd SW15 135 B1
Fawe St E14 97 D2
Fawkham Ho SE1 263 D3
Fawley Ct SE27 160 D2
Fawley Lo 2 E14 120 B2
Fawley Rd NW6 69 D3
Fawnbrake Ave SE24 161 A6
Fawn Rd E13 99 C5
Fawns Manor Cl TW14 149 A3
Fawns Manor Rd TW14 149 B3
Fawood Ave NW10 67 B1
Fayetville Ho 26 N19 49 D2
Faygate Cres DA6 169 C6
Faygate Ct CR2 220 D1
Faygate Rd SW2 160 B2
Fayland Ave SW16 181 C5
Fazal Laj IG1 79 A6
Fazerley Ct 49 W2 91 C2
Fearnley Cres TW12 173 B4
Fearnley Ho SE5 139 C3
Fearon St SE10 121 A1
Featherbed La CR0 223 B1
Feathers Pl SE10 142 B6
Featherstone Ave 4 SE23 162 C2
Featherstone Ct NW7 28 A3
Featherstone High Sch UB2 107 A3
Featherstone Ho UB4 84 C2
Featherstone Ind Est UB2 107 A3
Featherstone Prim Sch UB2 106 C2
Featherstone Rd
Mill Hill NW7 28 B4
Southall UB2 107 A3
Featherstone St EC1 95 B3 242 C6
Featherstone Terr UB2 107 A3
Featley Rd SW9 138 D2
Federal Rd UB6 87 C5
Federation Rd SE2 124 C2
Fee Farm Rd KT10 212 D1
Felbridge Ave HA7 25 B2
Felbridge Cl SW16 182 C6
Felbridge Ct
Croydon CR2 221 A1
Feltham TW13 150 B3
Harlington UB3 127 B6
Felbridge Ho 21 SE22 139 C2
Felbrigge Rd IG3 57 D1
Felday Rd SE13 163 D5
Felden Cl HA5 23 A3
Felden St SW6 135 B4 264 C1
Feldman Cl N16 52 A1
Feldspar Ct 6 EN3 7 A2
Felgate Mews 4 W6 112 B2
Felhampton Rd SE9 166 D1
Felhurst Cres RM10 81 D4
Feline Ct 1 EN4 14 C5
Felix Ave N8 50 A3
Felix Ct E17 53 D4
Felix La TW17 193 D3
Felix Manor BR7 189 C4
Felix Neubergh Ct EN1 5 C1
Felix Rd Ealing W13 109 A6
Walton-on-T KT12 194 A3
Felix St 19 E2 96 B5
Felixstowe Ct E16 122 D5
Felixstowe Rd
Abbey Wood SE2 124 B3
College Pk NW10 90 B4
Edmonton N9 34 A6
Tottenham N17 51 D6
Fellbrigg Rd SE22 161 D6
Fellbrigg St 21 E1 96 B3
Fellbrook TW10 153 B1
Fell Ho 11 N19 71 C5
Fellmongers Yd 1 CR0 221 A5
Fellowes Cl UB4 84 D3
Fellowes Ct UB3 127 B6
Fellowes Rd SM5 218 C6
Fellows Ct E2 95 D5
Fellows Rd NW3 70 C1
Fell Rd CR0 221 A5
Fells Haugh 6 W3 89 A1
Felltram Way SE7 121 A1
Fell Wlk HA8 26 D2
Felmersham Cl 2 SW4 137 D1
Felmingham Rd SE20 184 C1
Felnex Trad Est SM6 219 A6
Felpham Ct HA9 65 D4
Felsberg Rd SW2 160 A4
Fels Cl RM10 81 D5
Felsham Ho SW15 134 D2
Felsham Mews SW15 134 D2
Felsham Rd SW15 134 D2
Felspar Cl SE18 123 D1
Felstead Cl N13 32 C5
Felstead Rd E11 55 A2
Felstead St E9 75 B2
Felstead Wharf E14 120 A1
Felsted Rd E16 99 D1
FELTHAM 150 B2
Feltham Ave KT8 196 C5
Felthambrook Ind Est TW13 150 B1
Felthambrook Way TW13 172 B6
Feltham Bsns Complex TW13 150 B2
Feltham Com Sch TW13 150 C2
Feltham Corporate Ctr TW13 150 B1
FELTHAMHILL 171 D5
Feltham Hill Jun & Inf Schs TW13 149 D1
Feltham Hill Rd
Ashford TW15 171 A4
Feltham TW13 172 C5
Feltham Rd
Ashford TW15 171 A6
Mitcham CR4 181 A1
Feltham Sta TW13 150 B3
Felton Cl BR5 210 D3
Felton Gdns IG11 101 C5
Felton Ho
Kidbrooke SE9 143 C1
Shoreditch N1 235 D5
Felton Lea DA14 189 D5
Felton Rd
Barking IG11 101 C5
Ealing W13 109 C4
Felton St N1 95 B6 235 D5
Fenchurch Ave EC3 95 C1 243 A1
Fenchurch Bldgs EC3 243 B1
Fenchurch Pl EC3 253 B6
Fenchurch St EC3 117 C6 253 B6
Fenchurch Street Sta EC3 117 C6 253 B6
Fen Ct EC3 253 A6
Fendall Rd KT19 215 A3
Fendall St SE1 117 C3 263 B5
Fender Ct 5 SW4 138 A3
Fendt Cl 8 E16 98 D1
Fendyke Rd SE2, DA17 124 D3
Fenelon Pl W14 113 B2 254 D3
Fen Gr DA15 167 D5
Fenham Rd SE15 140 B5
Fenman Ct N17 34 B2
Fenman Gdns IG3 58 B1
Fenn Cl BR1 187 A4
Fenn Ct HA1 43 A4
Fennel Cl
Croydon CR0 206 D1
Newham E16 98 C3
Fennell St SE18 144 C6
Fenner Cl SE16 118 B2
Fenner Ho 25 E1 118 B5
Fenner Sq 10 SW11 136 B2
Fenn Ho TW7 131 B4
Fenning Ct CR4 202 C5
Fenning St SE1 253 A2
Fenn St E9 74 C3
Fenstanton Ave N12 30 B5
Fenstanton 3 N4 50 B1
Fenstanton Prim Sch SW2 160 C3
Fen St E16 120 D6
Fenswood Cl DA5 169 C5
Fentiman Rd SW8 138 B5 270 C4
Fentiman Way HA2 63 D6
Fenton Cl Dalston E8 73 D2
Elmstead BR7 188 B5
South Lambeth SW9 138 B3
Fenton Ct TW3 129 A5
Fenton Ho
Deptford SE14 141 A5
Heston TW5 129 C6
Fenton House* NW3 70 A5
Fenton Rd N17 33 A3
Fenton's Ave E13 99 B5
Fentons SE3 142 D5
Fenton St E1 96 B1
Fenwick Cl 16 SE18 144 C6
Fenwick Gr SE15 140 A2
Fenwick Pl
Croydon CR2 220 D1
Stockwell SW9 138 A2
Fenwick Rd SE15 140 A2
Ferby Ct DA15 189 D6
Ferdinand Ho 1 NW1 71 B1
Ferdinand Pl NW1 71 A1
Ferdinand St NW1 71 A1
Ferguson Ave KT5 198 B4
Ferguson Cl BR2, BR3 208 B6
Ferguson Dr W3 89 B1
Ferguson Ho SE10 142 A4
Ferguson's Cl E14 119 C2
Fergus Rd N5 72 D3
Fermain Ct E N1 95 C6
Fermain Ct N N1 95 C6
Fermain Ct W N1 95 C6
Ferme Park Rd N4, N8 50 B3
Fermor Rd SE23 163 A3
Fermoy Rd
Greenford UB6 85 D3
West Kilburn W9 91 B3
Fern Ave CR4 203 D5
Fernbank Ave
Walton-on-T KT12 195 A2
Wembley HA0 64 D3
Fernbank IG9 21 B3
Fernbank Mews SW12 159 C5
Fernbrook Cres SE13 164 C5
Fernbrook Dr HA2 41 D2
Fernbrook Rd SE13 164 C5
Ferncliff Rd E8 74 A3
Fern Cl 3 N1 95 C5
Ferncroft Ave
London N12 30 D4
Ruislip HA4 62 C6
West Hampstead NW3 69 C4
Fern Ct
Bexleyheath DA7 147 C1
Chingford E4 36 A4
New Cross Gate SE14 140 D3
Ferndale Ave
Hounslow TW4 129 A2
Walthamstow E17 54 B4
Ferndale BR1 187 C1
Ferndale Cl DA7 147 A4
Ferndale Ct 3 SE3 142 D5
Ferndale Ho N16 51 B1
Ferndale Rd
Ashford TW15 170 A5
Brixton SW4, SW9 138 B1
Croydon SE25 206 B4
Enfield EN3 7 A6
Leyton E11 76 D6
South Tottenham N15 51 D4
Upton E7 77 B1
Ferndale St E6 100 D1
Ferndale Way BR6 227 B3
Fern Dene W13 87 B2
Ferndene NW9 45 A4
Ferndene Rd SE24 139 A1
Fernden Way RM7 59 D3
Ferndown Ave BR6 211 B1
Ferndown Cl
Pinner HA5 23 A3
Sutton SM2 218 B2
Ferndown Ct 6 UB1 86 A1
Ferndown 5 KT6 198 A4
Ferndown Lo 17 E14 120 A3
Ferndown HA6 22 A1
Ferndown Rd
Eltham SE9 165 D4
South Oxhey WD19 22 C6
Ferndown 7 E18 55 A6
Ferney Meade Way TW7 131 A3
Ferney Rd EN4 15 A3
Fern Gr TW14 150 B4
Fernhall Dr IG4 55 D3
Fernhall N12 30 C5
Fernham Rd CR7 205 A6
Fernhead Rd W9 91 B4
Fernhead 12 SM1 218 A4
Fernhill Ct
Chingford E17 36 B1
Kingston u T KT2 175 D5
Fernhill Gdns KT2 176 A5
Fernhill Ho E5 74 A6
Fern Hill Pl 3 BR6 227 A3
Fern Hill Prim Sch KT2 176 A4
Fernhill St E16 122 B5
Fern Ho HA7 24 D4
Fernholme Rd SE15 162 D6
Fernhurst Gdns HA8 26 C4
Fernhurst Rd
Ashford TW15 171 A6
Croydon CR0 206 B1
Fulham SW6 135 A4 264 B2
Fernie Ho SE22 139 D2
Fern La TW5 107 B1
Fernlea Ho NW10 88 B4
Fernlea Rd
Balham SW12 159 B3
Mitcham CR4 181 A2
Fernleigh Cl
Croydon CR0 220 C4
West Kilburn W9 91 B4
Fernleigh Ct
Harrow HA2 23 D1
Wembley HA9 44 A1
Fernleigh Rd N21 16 D2
Fern Lo 13 SW16 182 C5
Fernly Cl HA5 40 A5
Fernsbury St WC1 234 A1
Fernshaw Mans SW10 266 A5
Fernshaw Rd SW10 136 A6 266 A5
Fernside Ave
Edgware NW7 11 B1
Feltham TW13 172 B6
Fernside IG9 21 B3
Fernside Ct NW4 28 D1
Fernside NW11 47 C1
Fernside Rd SW12 159 A4
Ferns Rd E15 76 D2
Fern St E3 97 C3
Fernthorpe Rd SW16 181 C4
Ferntower Rd N5 73 B3
Fernways IG1 78 D4
Fern Wlk 18 SE16 118 A1
Fernwood Ave
Streatham SW16 181 D6
Wembley HA0 65 C2
Fernwood Cl BR1 187 C1
Fernwood Cres N20 14 D1
Fernwood Ct N14 15 D3
Fernwood
Wandsworth SW19 157 B3
Wood Green N22 32 A3
Ferny Hill EN4 3 A5
Ferranti Cl SE18 121 D3
Ferraro Cl TW5 129 C6
Ferrers Ave
Wallington SM6 219 D4
West Drayton UB7 104 A4
Ferrers Rd SW16 181 D5
Ferrestone Rd N8 50 B5
Ferrey Mews 19 SW9 138 C3
Ferriby Cl N1 72 C1
Ferrier Ind Est SW18 135 D1
Ferrier Point 6 E16 99 A2
Ferrier St SW18 135 D1
Ferring Cl HA2 42 A1
Ferrings SE21 161 C1
Ferris Ave CR0 223 B5
Ferris Rd SE22 140 A1
Ferron Rd E5 74 B5
Ferrour Ct N2 48 B6
Ferrybridge Ho SE11 260 D5
Ferrydale Lo 4 NW4 46 C5
Ferry Ho E5 52 B1
Ferry Island Ret Pk N17 52 A6
Ferry La
Barnes SW13 133 D6
Brentford TW8 132 A6
Lower Halliford TW17 192 C1
Ferry Lane Ind Est E17 52 D5
Ferry Lane Prim Sch N17 52 B5
Ferry La
Richmond TW9 132 B6
Tottenham Hale N17 52 B5
Ferrymead Ave UB6 85 C5
Ferrymead Dr UB6 85 C5
Ferrymead Gdns UB6 86 A5
Ferrymoor TW10 153 B1
Ferry Quays Ctyd 13 TW8 131 D6
Ferry Rd
Barnes SW13 134 A4
East Molesey KT8 195 C6
Richmond TW11 175 B5
Thames Ditton KT7 197 B3
Twickenham TW1 153 B3
Ferry Sq
1 Brentford TW8 132 A6

Ferry Sq *continued*
Lower Halliford TW17 192 D2
Ferry St E14 120 A1
Ferry Wks TW17 192 C1
Festing Rd SW15 134 D2
Festival Cl
Hillingdon UB10 82 D6
Sidcup DA5 168 D3
Festival Ct
Cheam SM1 201 D1
5 Dalston E8 73 D1
Festival Pier
SE1 116 B5 250 C4
Festival Pleasure Gdns
SW11 136 D5 267 C3
Festoon Way E16 121 D6
Fetherston Ct RM6 59 B3
Fetter La EC4 94 C1 241 B2
Fettes Ho NW8 229 D3
Fews Lodge RM6 58 D5
Ffinch St SE8 141 C5
Fidgeon Cl BR1 210 C6
Field Cl Bromley BR1 187 C1
Buckhurst Hill IG9 21 C1
Chessington KT9 213 C3
Chingford E4 35 D4
Cranford TW4 128 B4
East Molesey KT8 195 D4
Harlington UB7 127 A5
Ruislip HA4 39 A1
Uxbridge UB10 60 D6
Willesden NW2 68 A6
Fieldcommon La
KT12 195 B1
Field Ct
Hampstead NW3 70 A3
Holborn WC1 240 D3
Lower Holloway N7 72 A3
Wimbledon SW19 157 C1
Field End Jun & Inf
Schs HA4 62 D6
Field End Rd HA5,
HA4 40 C1
Fieldend Rd SW16 181 C2
Field End HA4 62 C2
Fieldend TW11 174 D6
Fielders Cl
2 Enfield EN1 5 C1
Harrow HA2 42 A1
Fieldfare Rd SE28 124 C6
Fieldgate Mans 25
E1 96 A2
Fieldgate St E1 96 A2
Field Ho
4 Edmonton N9 34 A6
Kensal Green NW10 90 D4
8 Richmond TW10 153 C1
Fieldhouse Cl E18 37 B2
Fieldhouse Rd
SW12 159 C3
Fielding Ave TW2 152 A1
Fielding Ho
Chiswick W4 133 C6
6 Kilburn NW6 91 C4
St John's Wood NW8 229 A6
Fielding Mews
SW13 134 B6
Fielding Prim Sch
W13 109 B3
Fielding Rd
Acton W4 111 C3
Hammersmith W14 112 D3
Fieldings The SE23 162 C3
Fielding St SE17 139 A6
Fielding Terr W5 110 B6
Field La
Brentford TW8 131 C5
Teddington TW11 175 A5
Field Lo NW10 67 D2
Field Mead NW9,
NW7 27 D3
Fieldpark Gdns CR0 207 A1
Field Pl KT3 199 D3
Field Point E7 77 A4
Field Rd
Feltham TW14 150 B5
Forest Gate E7 77 A4
Fulham W6 135 A6 264 A6
Tottenham N17 51 C6
Fieldsend Rd SM3 217 A3
Fields Est E8 74 A1
Fieldside Cl BR6 227 A4
Fieldside Rd BR1 186 B5
Fields Park Cres
RM6 58 D4
Field St WC1 233 C2
Fieldsway Ho N5 72 C3
Field View Cl RM7 59 C6
Fieldview Ct
2 Islington N5 72 D3
London NW9 44 C3
Field View TW13 171 B6
Fieldview SW17,
SW18 158 B3
Fieldway Cres N5, N7 72 C3
Fieldway RM8 80 C4
Field Way
Greenford UB6 85 D6
New Addington CR0 223 D2
Fieldway BR5 211 B3
Field Way HA4 39 A1
Fieldway Sta CR0 223 D1
Field Way NW10 67 A1
Fieldwick Ho 14 E9 74 D2
Fiennes Cl RM8 58 C1
Fife Ct 5 W3 88 C1
Fifehead Cl TW15 170 A4
Fife Rd
Kingston u T KT2 176 A1
Mortlake SW14 155 A6
Newham E16 99 A2
Tottenham N22 32 D3
Fife Terr N1 233 D4
Fifield Path SE23 162 D1
Fifteenpenny Fields
SE9 166 C6
Fifth Ave Hayes UB3 105 D5
Ilford E12 78 B4
West Kilburn W10 91 A4
Fifth Cross Rd TW2 152 B2
Fifth Way HA9 66 D4
Figge's Rd CR4 181 A3
Fig Tree Cl NW10 89 C6
Filanco Ct W7 108 D5
Filby Rd KT9 214 B2
Filey Ave N16 52 A1
Filey Cl SM2 218 A1
Filey Ho SW18 136 A1
Filey Waye HA4 62 B6
Filigree Ct SE16 119 B5
Fillebrook Ave EN1 5 D3
Fillebrook Rd E11 54 C1
Filmer Ho SW6 264 B2
Filmer Mews SW6 264 B2
Filmer Rd
SW6 135 B5 264 C3
Filston Rd DA8 125 D1
Filton Cl NW9 27 C1
Filton Ct 14 SE14 140 C5
Finborough Rd
Upper Tooting
SW17 180 D4
West Brompton
SW10 135 D6 265 D6
Finchale Rd SE2 124 A3
Fincham Cl UB10 61 A5
Finch Ave SE27 183 B6
Finch Cl Barnet EN5 13 C6
Willesden NW10 67 B2
Finch Ct DA14 168 B1
Finchdean Ho
SW15 155 D4
Finch Dr TW14 150 D4
Finch Gdns E4 35 C5
Finch Ho 1 SE8 141 D5
Finchingfield Ave
IG8 37 C3
Finch La EC2, EC3 242 D1
FINCHLEY 29 D3
Finchley Cath High Sch
N12 13 D1
Finchley Central Sta
N3 29 C2
Finchley Ct N3 29 D4
Finchley La NW4 46 D5
Finchley Lo N12 29 D5
Finchley Meml Hospl
N12 30 A3
Finchley Pk N12 30 B6
Finchley Pl NW8 229 C4
Finchley Rd
Hampstead NW3 70 A2
London NW11 47 B3
St John's Wood NW8 229 C4
Finchley Road &
Frognal Sta NW3 70 A3
Finchley Road Sta
NW3 70 A2
Finchley Way N3 29 C3
Finch Lo 15 W9 91 C2
Finch Mews 8
SE15 139 D4
Finch's Ct 10 E14 119 D6
Finden Rd E7 77 C3
Findhorn Ave UB4 84 B2
Findhorn St 8 E14 98 A1
Findon Cl
Harrow HA2 63 D5
Wandsworth SW18 157 C5
Findon Rd
Edmonton N9 18 B3
Shepherd's Bush
W12 112 A4
Fine Bush La HA4 38 D3
Fineran Ct 6 SW11 136 B1
Fingal St SE10 120 D1
Fingest Ho NW8 237 A6
Finians Cl UB10 60 B1
Finland Rd SE4 141 A2
Finland St SE16 119 A3
Finlays Cl KT9 214 C3
Finlay St SW6 134 D4
Finley Ct 21 SE5 139 A5
Finmere Ho 1 N4 51 A2
Finnemore Ho N1 235 A6
Finney La TW7 131 A4
Finn Ho N1 235 D2
Finnis St E2 96 B3
Finnymore Rd RM9 81 A1
FINSBURY 94 C4
Finsbury Ave EC2 242 D3
Finsbury Cir
EC2 95 B2 242 D3
Finsbury Coll N4 72 C6
Finsbury Cotts N22 32 A3
Finsbury Ct EC2 242 C4
Finsbury Ho N22 32 A2
Finsbury Market
EC2 243 A4
Finsbury Mkt EC2 243 A5
FINSBURY PARK 72 C6
Finsbury Park Ave
N4 51 A3
Finsbury Park Rd N4,
N5 72 D6
Finsbury Park Sta
N4 72 C6
Finsbury Pavement
EC2 95 B2 242 D4
Finsbury Rd N22 32 B2
Finsbury Sq
EC2 95 B2 242 D4
Finsbury St EC2 242 C4
Finsbury Way DA5 169 B5
Finsen Rd SE5 139 A2
Finstock Rd W10 90 D1
Finton House Sch
SW17 158 D2
Finucane Ct TW9 132 B2
Finucane Rise WD23 8 A2
Finwhale Ho E14 119 D3
Fiona Ct Enfield EN2 4 D2
9 Kilburn NW6 91 B5
Firbank Cl Enfield EN2 5 A1
Newham E16 99 D2
Firbank Rd SE15 140 B3
Fir Cl KT12 194 A2
Fircroft Gdns HA1 64 C5
Fircroft N1 94 D6 234 D6
Fircroft Prim Sch
SW17 158 D1
Fircroft Rd
Chessington KT9 214 B4
Upper Tooting
SW17 158 D1
Fir Dene BR6 226 C5
Firdene KT5 199 A1
Fire Bell Alley KT6 198 A3
Firebell Mews KT6 198 A3
Fire Brigade Cotts
HA5 41 C5
Fire Brigade Pier
SE1 260 B4
Firecrest Dr NW3 69 D5
Firefly Gdns E6 100 A3
Firefly 7 NW9 27 D1
Firemans Cotts N10 49 A6
Fireman's Flats N22 32 A2
Firepower (The Royal
Artillery Mus)*
SE18 122 D3
Fire Station Alley EN5 1 A3
Fire Station Flats
TW7 130 C3
Fire Station Mews 4
BR3 185 D2
Firethorn Cl 4 HA8 27 A6
Fir Gr KT3 199 D3
Fir Grove Rd 25
SW9 138 C3
Firhill Rd SE6 163 C1
Fir Island NW7 28 C5
Firle Ho 7 W10 90 C2
Fir Lo SW15 134 B1
Firmans Ct E17 54 B5
Firmston Ho 9
SW14 133 B2
Fir Rd Cheam SM3 201 B1
Feltham TW13 172 D5
Firs Ave
Fortis Green N10 49 A5
Friern Barnet N11 31 A4
Mortlake SW14 133 A1
Firsby Ave CR0 207 A1
Firsby Rd N16 52 A1
Firs Cl Claygate KT10 212 C2
Forest Hill SE23 163 A4
Mitcham CR4 181 B2
Muswell Hill N10 49 A6
Firscroft N13 17 A1
Firs Dr TW5 128 B5
Firs Farm Prim Sch
N13 17 B1
Firs Ho N22 32 C2
Firside Gr DA15 167 D3
Firs La N21, N13 17 A2
Firs Park Ave N21 17 B3
Firs Park Gdns N21 17 B3
First Ave Bexley DA7 146 C5
Chadwell Heath RM6 58 C4
Dagenham RM10 103 D5
East Acton W3 111 D5
East Molesey KT8 195 C5
Edmonton N18 34 C6
Enfield EN1 17 D6
Hayes UB3 105 D5
Hendon NW4 46 C5
Manor Pk E12 78 A3
Mortlake SW14 133 C2
Newham E13 99 A4
Walthamstow E17 53 D4
Walton-on-T KT12 194 B3
Wembley HA9 65 D6
West Kilburn W10 91 B3
First Cl KT8 196 A6
First Cross Rd TW2 152 C2
First Dr NW10 67 A1
Firs The
Belmont SM2 217 D1
Claygate KT10 212 C2
Ealing W5 87 D2
Forest Hill SE26 184 C5
Oakleigh Pk N20 14 B3
2 Penge SE26 184 B5
Sidcup DA15 167 D1
Upton Pk E6 78 A1
Wimbledon SW20 178 A3
Woodford IG8 37 C3
First St SW3 114 C2 257 B4
Firstway SW20 178 C1
First Way HA9 66 D4
Firs Wlk IG8 37 A5
Firswood Ave KT19 215 D3
Firth Gdns
SW6 135 A4 264 A1
Firtree Ave CR4 181 A1
Fir Tree Ave UB7 104 C3
Fir Tree Cl Ealing W5 88 A1
Esher KT10 212 A3
5 Orpington BR6 227 D3
Streatham SW16 181 C5
Worcester Pk KT19 215 D4
Firtree Ct BR2 208 D6
Fir Tree Gdns CR0 223 C4
Fir Tree Gr SM5 218 D1
Firtree Ho SE13 164 B4
Fir Tree Ho 11 SE14 140 C5
Firtree Lodge N21 17 A2
Fir Tree Rd TW4 129 A1
Fir Trees Cl SE16 119 A5
Fir Tree Wlk EN1 5 B2
Fir Wlk KT17, SM3 216 D2
Fisher Cl
Croydon CR0 205 D1
Holdbrook EN3 7 C6
Southall UB6 85 C4
Fisherdene KT10 213 A1
Fisher Ho
Islington N1 234 A5
9 Shadwell E1 118 C6
2 Tufnell Pk N19 71 C5
Fisherman Cl TW10 175 C6
Fishermans Dr
SE16 118 D4
Fisherman's Wlk
E14 119 C5
Fishermans Wlk
SE28 123 C4
Fisher Rd HA3 24 D1
Fishers Cl SW16 159 D1
Fishers Ct
London SE14 140 D4
6 Teddington
TW11 174 D5
Fisher's La W4 111 B2
Fisher St
Holborn WC1 240 C3
Newham E16 99 A2
Fisherton St
NW8 92 B3 236 D6
Fisherton Street Est
NW8 92 B3 236 D5
Fishguard Way E16 122 D5
Fishlock Ct 6 SW4 138 A3
Fishponds Rd
Keston BR2 225 D3
Upper Tooting
SW17 180 C6
Fish St Hill EC3 252 D5
Fisk Cl TW16 171 D4
Fiske Ct
Barking IG11 101 B5
1 Merton SW19 180 A3
Sutton SM2 218 A1
Tottenham N17 34 A2
Fitch Ct London SW2 160 C6
8 Mitcham CR4 181 A1
Fitzalan Rd
Church End N3 47 B6
Claygate KT10 212 C1
Fitzalan St
SE11 116 C2 261 A4
Fitzclarence Ho
W11 244 A2
Fitzgeorge Ave KT2,
KT3 177 B2
Fitz-George Ave
W14 254 A3
Fitzgerald Ave
SW14 133 C2
Fitzgerald Ct 1 E10 53 D1
Fitzgerald Ho
15 Brixton SW9 138 C3
Hayes UB3 106 B5
14 Poplar E14 97 D1
Fitzgerald Rd
Mortlake SW14 133 B2
Thames Ditton KT7 197 A3
Wanstead E11 55 A4
Fitzhardinge Ho
Beckenham BR3 185 D1
Marylebone W1 238 A2
Fitzhardinge St W1 238 A2
Fitzherbert Ho 11
TW10 154 B5
Fitzhugh Gr SW18 158 B5
Fitzjames Ave
Croydon CR0 222 A6
West Kensington
W14 254 B3
Fitzjohn Ave EN5 1 B1
Fitzjohn's Ave NW3 70 B3
Fitzjohns Mans NW3 70 A2
Fitzjohns Prim Sch
NW3 70 B3
Fitzmaurice Ho 17
SE16 118 B2
Fitzmaurice Pl W1 248 D4
Fitzneal St W12 89 D1
FITZROVIA 93 C2
Fitzroy Cl N6 48 D1
Fitzroy Cres W4 133 B5
Fitzroy Ct London N6 49 C3
Marylebone W1 239 B5
Fitzroy Gdns SE19 183 C3
Fitzroy Ho
Bermondsey SE1 263 D2
12 Tower Hamlets
E14 97 B1
Fitzroy Lo N21 16 D6
Fitzroy Mews W1 239 A5
Fitzroy Pk N6 48 D1
Fitzroy Rd
NW1 93 A6 231 A6
Fitzroy Sq W1 239 A5
Fitzroy St W1 93 C3 239 A5
Fitzroy Yd NW1 231 A6
Fitzstephen Rd RM8 80 C3
Fitzwarren Gdns N19 49 C1
Fitzwilliam Ave
TW9 132 B3
Fitzwilliam Ho
4 Higham Hill E17 35 A1
Richmond TW9 131 D1
Fitzwilliam Hts 1
SE23 162 C2
Fitzwilliam Mews
E16 121 A5
Fitzwilliam Rd SW4 137 C2
Fitzwygram Cl
TW12 174 A5
Fiveacre Cl CR7 204 C3
Five Acre NW9 27 D1
Five Arch Bridge
DA14 191 A6
Five Arches Bsns Pk
DA14 190 D4
Five Elms Prim Sch
RM8 81 B5
Five Elms Rd
Dagenham RM9 81 B5
Keston Mark BR2 225 C5
Five Oaks Mews
BR1 165 A1
Fives Ct SE11 261 C5
Fiveways SE9 166 D2
Five Ways Cnr NW4 28 A2
Fiveways CR0 220 C4
Fiveways Rd SW9 138 C3
Fiveways HA4 39 B1
Flack Ct 15 E10 53 D2
Fladbury Rd N15 51 B3
Fladgate Rd E11 54 C3
Flag Cl CR0 206 D1
Flag Wlk HA5 40 A3
Flambard Rd HA1,
HA3 43 A3
Flamborough Ho 12
SE15 140 A4
Flamborough Rd
HA4 62 A5
Flamborough St E14 97 A1
Flamingo Ct 2 SE8 141 C5
Flamingo Gdns UB5 85 A4
Flamstead Gdns RM9 80 C1
Flamstead Rd RM9 80 C1
Flamsted Ave HA9 66 C2
Flamsteed Ct 15
SE13 141 D4
Flamsteed Ho*
SE10 142 B
Flamsteed Rd SE7 122 A
Flanchford Rd W12 111 D
Flanders Cres
SW17 180 D
Flanders Ct E17 53 A
Flanders Ho N16 73 C
Flanders Mans 1
W4 111 D
Flanders Rd
Acton W4 111 C
Wallend E6 100 C
Flanders Way E9 74 D
Flandrian Cl EN3 7 D
Flank St 9 E1 118 A
Flansham Ho 2 E14 97 B
Flash La EN2 5 A
Flask Cotts 4 NW3 70 B
Flask Wlk NW3 70 B
Flatford Ho 2 SE6 186 A
Flather Cl 12 SW16 181 C
Flatiron Sq SE1 252 B
Flatiron Yd SE1 252 B
Flavell Mews SE10 120 C
Flaxen Cl E4 19 D
Flaxen Rd E4 19 D
Flaxley Rd SM4 201 D
Flaxman Ct
12 Belvedere
DA17 125 C
Soho W1 239 C
Flaxman Ho
10 Chiswick W4 111 C
Newington SE1 261 D
Flaxman Rd SE5 138 D
Flaxman Terr
WC1 93 D4 232 D
Flaxman Villas N2 48 A
Flaxmore Ct
Erith DA7 147 D
South Norwood CR7 183 B
Flaxton Rd SE18 145 C
Flecker Cl HA7 24 D
Flecker Ho 6 SE5 139 B
Fleece Dr N9 34 A
Fleecefield Prim Sch
N18 34 A
Fleece Rd KT6 197 C
Fleece Wlk N7 72 A
Fleeming Cl E17 35 B
Fleeming Rd E17 35 B
Fleet Cl
East Molesey KT8 195 B
Ruislip HA4 39 A
Fleet Ct 1 W12 111 C
Fleetfield WC1 233 B
Fleet Ho
6 Brixton SW2 160 C
4 Limehouse E14 119 A
Fleet Pl EC4 241 C
Fleet Prim Sch NW3 70 D
Fleet Rd NW3 70 D
Fleetside KT8 195 C
Fleet Sq WC1 233 D
Fleet St EC4 94 C1 241 B
Fleet Street Hill 10
E1 96 A3
Fleet Terr SE6 164 A
Fleetway WC1 233 B2
Fleetway West Bsns Pk
UB6 87 B5
Fleetwood Cl
Chessington KT9 213 D
Newham E16 99 D2
South Croydon CR0 221 D5
Fleetwood Ct
1 Newham E6 100 B2
Orpington BR6 226 C4
8 Stanwell TW19 148 A5
Fleet Wood 6 N16 73 D6
Fleetwood Rd
Kingston u T KT3 198 D6
Willesden NW10 68 A3
Fleetwood Sq KT3 198 D6
Fleetwood St N16 73 C6
Fleetwood Way
WD19 22 C6
Fleming Cl 4 W9 91 C3
Fleming Ct
Croydon CR0 220 C3
Paddington W2 236 C4
Fleming Dr N21 16 B6
Fleming Ho
14 Bermondsey
SE16 118 A4
Finsbury Pk N4 51 A1
5 Wembley HA9 67 A5
Fleming Mead CR4 180 D3
Fleming Rd
Camberwell SE17 138 D6
Southall UB1 86 A1
Fleming Way
Isleworth TW7 130 D1
Thamesmead SE28 124 D6
Fleming Wlk NW9 27 C1
Flemming Ave HA4 62 B6

Flempton Rd E10 53 A1
Fletcher Bldgs WC2 240 B1
Fletcher Cl E16 122 D6
Fletcher Ct 9 NW5 71 B4
Fletcher Ho 16 N16 73 C4
Fletcher La E10 54 A2
Fletcher Path 7 SE8 141 C5
Fletcher Rd W4 111 A3
Fletchers Cl BR2 209 B5
Fletcher St 16 E1 118 A6
Fletching Rd
Charlton SE7 143 D6
Lower Clapton E5 74 C5
Fletton Rd N11 32 A3
Fleur De Lis St E1 243 C5
Fleur Gates 7 SW19 156 D4
Flexmere Rd N17 33 C2
Flimwell Cl BR1 186 C5
Flinders Ho 28 E1 118 B5
Flint Cl
8 Green Street Green BR6 227 D2
1 Stratford E15 76 D1
Flint Ct CR0 204 B3
Flint Down Cl BR5 190 A2
Flintmill Cres SE3, SE9 144 A3
Flinton St SE17 117 C1 263 B2
Flint St SE17 117 B2 262 D3
Flitcroft St WC2 239 D1
Flitton Ho 7 N1 72 D1
Floathaven Cl SE28 124 A5
Flock Mill Pl SW18 157 D3
Flockton St
20 Bermondsey SE16 118 A4
3 Bermondsey SE16 118 A4
Flodden Rd SE5 139 A4
Flood La 5 TW1 153 A3
Flood St SW3 136 C6 267 B6
Flood Wlk SW3 136 C6 267 B6
Flora Cl E14 97 D1
Flora Gardens Prim Sch W6 112 B2
Flora Gdns
Dagenham RM6 58 C3
2 Hammersmith W6 112 B2
Floral St WC2 116 A6 250 A6
Flora St DA17 125 B1
Florence Ave
Enfield EN2 5 A2
Morden SM4 202 A4
Florence Cl KT12 194 B2
Florence Ct
18 New Barnet EN5 13 D6
St John's Wood W9 229 B1
Wanstead E11 55 C5
5 Wimbledon SW19 179 A4
Florence Dr EN2 5 A2
Florence Elson Cl E12 78 C4
Florence Gdns
Chiswick W4 133 A6
Ilford RM6 58 C2
Florence Ho
20 Bermondsey SE16 118 B1
2 Brixton SW2 160 B6
Kidbrooke SE18 144 B4
5 Kingston u T KT2 176 B3
10 Shepherd's Bush W11 112 D6
7 Wandsworth SW18 136 B1
Florence Mans
Fulham SW6 264 C2
4 Hendon NW4 46 B4
Florence Nightingale Ho 14 N1 73 A2
Florence Nightingale Mus* SE1 250 D1
Florence Rd
Abbey Wood SE2 124 C2
Acton W4 111 B3
5 Beckenham BR3 185 A1
Bromley BR1 187 A2
Ealing W5 110 A6
Feltham TW13 150 B3
Finsbury Pk N4 50 C2
6 Kingston u T KT2 176 B3
New Cross Gate SE14 141 B4
Southall UB2 106 D3
7 Upton Pk E6 99 C6
Walton-on-T KT12 194 B2
West Ham E13 99 A5
Wimbledon SW19 179 D4
Florence Root Ho 3 IG4 56 B4
Florence St
Islington N1 72 D1
London NW4 46 C5
Newham E16 98 D3
Florence Terr
Kingston u T SW15 155 C1
New Cross Gate SE14 141 B4
Florence Way SW12 158 D3
Florence White Ct N9 18 B1
Florentine Ho 3 IG1 78 D6
Flores Ho 13 E1 96 D2
Florey Sq N21 16 B6
Florfield Rd E8 74 B2
Florian Ave SM1 218 B4
Florian SE5 139 C4
Florian Rd SW15 135 A1
Florida Cl WD23 8 B2
Florida Ct BR2 208 D5
Florida Rd CR7 182 D2
Florida State Univ WC1 93 D2 239 D3
Florida St E2 96 A4
Florin Ct
Bermondsey SE1 253 C1
Edmonton N18 33 C6
8 St George in t East SE1 118 A6
Floris Pl 7 SW4 137 C2
Floriston Ave UB10 61 A1
Floriston Cl HA7 25 B2
Floriston Ct UB5 63 D3
Floriston Gdns HA7 25 B2
Florys Ct 7 SW19 157 A3
Floss St SW15 134 C3
Flower & Dean Wlk E1 243 D3
Flower La NW7 27 D4
Flower Mews NW11 47 A3
Flower Pot Cl N15 51 D3
Flowers Cl NW2 68 A5
Flowersmead SW17 159 A2
Flowers Mews 1 N19 71 C6
Flower Wlk The SW7 114 A4 246 B2
Floyd Rd SE7 121 C1
Floyer Cl TW10 154 B6
Fludyer St SE13 142 C1
Flynn Ct 19 E14 119 C6
Fogerty Cl EN3 7 D6
Foley Cotts KT10 212 D2
Foley Ct N12 30 A5
Foley Ho 19 E1 96 C1
Foley Mews KT10 212 C2
Foley Rd KT10 212 C1
Foley St W1 93 C2 239 A3
Folgate St E1 95 D2 243 C4
Foliot Ho N1 233 C4
Foliot St W12 89 D1
Folkestone Ct UB5 63 D3
Folkestone Rd
Edmonton N18 34 A6
Wallend E6 100 C4
Walthamstow E17 53 D5
Folkingham La 6 NW9 27 C2
Folkington Cnr N12 29 B5
Folland 6 NW9 27 D1
Follett Ho SW10 266 C4
Follett St E14 98 A1
Folly La
Higham Hill E17 35 A2
Walthamstow E4 35 B3
Folly Wall E14 120 A4
Fonda Ct 14 E14 119 C6
Fontaine Ct
3 Beckenham BR3 185 B2
Southgate N14 15 D2
Fontaine Rd SW16 182 B3
Fontarabia Rd SW11 137 A1
Fontenelle SE5 139 C4
Fontenoy Ho SE11 261 C3
Fontenoy Rd SW12, SW17 159 C2
Fonteyne Gdns IG8 37 D1
Fonthill Cl SE20 184 A1
Fonthill Ct SE23 162 C4
Fonthill Ho
Kensington W14 254 B6
Pimlico SW1 258 D2
Fonthill Mews N4 72 B6
Fonthill Rd N4 72 C6
Font Hills N2 30 A1
Fontley Way SW15 156 A4
Fontmell Cl TW15 170 C5
Fontmell Pk TW15 170 C5
Fontwell Cl
Harrow HA3 24 C3
Northolt UB5 63 C2
Fontwell Dr BR2 210 C4
Football La HA1 42 C1
Footpath The SW15 156 A6
FOOTS CRAY 190 B4
Foots Cray High St DA14 190 D4
Foots Cray La DA14 168 C3
Footscray Rd SE9 166 D3
Forber Ho 25 E2 96 C4
Forbes Cl NW2 68 A5
Forbes Ct SE19 183 C5
Forbes Ho 2 W4 110 C1
Forbes St E1 96 A1
Forbes Way HA4 62 B6
Forburg Rd N16 52 A1
Fordbridge Ct TW15 170 A4
Fordbridge Rd TW15 170 B5
Fordbridge Rdbt TW15 170 A4
Fordbridge Rd
Lower Halliford TW16, TW17 193 D3
Sunbury TW16 194 A5
Ford Cl
Ashford TW15 170 A4
12 Bow E3 97 A5
Harrow HA1 42 B2
Littleton TW17 192 C4
Thornton Heath CR7 204 D4
Fordcombe 13 NW5 71 A2
Forde Ave BR1 209 C6
Fordel Rd SE6 164 B3
Ford End IG8 37 B4
Fordham Cl EN4 2 C2
Fordham Ho 11 SE14 141 A5
Fordham 4 KT1 176 C1
Fordham Rd EN4 2 C2
Fordham St 13 E1 96 A1
Ford Ho 2 EN5 13 D6
Fordhook Ave W5 110 C6
Ford Ho 2 SE18 122 D1
Fordingley Rd W9 91 B4
Fordington Ho 2 SE26 162 B1
Fordington Rd N6 48 D5
Fordmill Rd SE6 163 C2
Ford Rd
Ashford TW15 170 B6
Bow E3 97 B5
Dagenham RM10 81 C1
Ford's Gr N21 17 A3
Fords Park Rd E16 99 A1
Ford Sq E1 96 B2
Ford St Bow E3 97 A5
Canning Town E16 98 D1
Fordwich Cl BR6 211 D2
Fordwych Ct NW2 69 A2
Fordwych Rd NW2 69 A3
Fordyce Ho 3 SW16 181 C6
Fordyce Rd SE13 164 A6
Fordyke Rd RM8 81 B6
Forecastle Ct E14 119 C4
Foreign, Commonwealth & Home Offices SW1 250 A2
Foreland Ct NW4 29 A2
Foreland Ho W11 244 A6
Foreland St SE18 123 B2
Foreshore SE8 119 B2
Forest App
Chingford E4 20 C4
Woodford IG8 37 A3
Forest Ave E4 20 C4
Fore St EC2 95 A2 242 B3
Forest Bsns Pk E17 52 D2
Forest Cl
Brondesbury NW6 69 A1
Chislehurst BR7 188 C2
Wanstead E11 55 A4
Woodford IG8 37 B6
Forest Croft SE23 162 B2
Forest Ct Chingford E4 20 D3
Leytonstone E11 54 C5
14 Woodside Pk N12 29 D6
Forestdale Ctr The CR0 223 B1
Forestdale N14 31 D6
Forest Dene Ct 2 SM2 218 A2
Forest Dr
Ashford TW16 171 D3
Chingford IG8 36 C3
Forest Dr E E11 54 B3
Forest Dr
Keston Mark BR2 226 A4
Wanstead E12 77 D5
Forest Dr W E11 54 B2
Forest Edge IG9 21 D1
Fore St N18 34 A6
Forester Rd SE15 140 B2
Foresters Cl SM6 219 D1
Foresters Cres DA7 147 D1
Foresters Dr
Wallington SM6 219 D1
Walthamstow E17 54 B5
Foresters Homes The DA7 147 D1
Foresters Prim Sch SM6 219 D1
FOREST GATE 77 A3
Forest Gate Com Sch E7 77 A3
Forest Gate NW9 45 C4
Forest Gate Sta E7 77 A3
Forest Gdns N17 33 D1
Forest Glade
Chingford E4 36 C5
Leytonstone E11 54 C3
Forest Gr E8 73 D2
FOREST HILL 163 A3
Forest Hill Bsns Ctr SE23 162 C2
Forest Hill Ct 6 SE26 162 B1
Forest Hill SE23 162 C3
Forest Hill Ind Est SE23 162 C2
Forest Hill Rd SE22 162 B5
Forest Hill Sec Sch SE23 162 D1
Forest Hill Sta SE23 162 C2
Forest Ho 9 E4 20 C4
Forestholme Cl SE23 162 C2
Forest Ho The SE23 163 A3
Forest Hts IG9 21 A2
Forest La E7, E15 76 D3
Forest Lawns BR1 187 C2
Forest Lea 3 E11 54 D2
Forest Lo 1 SE23 162 C1
Forest Mount Rd IG8 36 B3
Fore St HA5 40 A4
Forest Point E7 77 B3
Forest Rd Dalston E8 73 D2
Edmonton N9 18 B3
Feltham TW13 150 C1
Forest Gate E7 77 A4
Leytonstone E11 54 B2
Morden SM3, SM4 201 C2
Richmond TW9 132 C5
Romford RM7 59 D6
Walthamstow E17 53 C6
Woodford IG8 21 A1
Fore Street Ave EC2 242 C3
Forest Ridge
Beckenham BR3 207 C6
Bromley BR2 226 B4
Forest Rise E17 54 B5
Forest Sch E17 54 C5
Forest Side
Buckhurst Hill IG9 21 C3
Chingford E4 20 D3
Forest Gate E7 77 B4
New Malden KT4 199 D1
Forest St E7 77 A3
Forest The E11 54 C5
Forest Trad Est E17 52 D6
Forest View Ave E10 54 B4
Forest View
Chingford E4 20 B4
Leytonstone E11 54 D2
Forest View Rd
Chingford E17 36 A2
Manor Pk E12 78 A4
Forest Way
Orpington BR5 211 D4
Sidcup DA15 167 B4
9 Upper Holloway N19 71 C6
Woodford IG8 37 B6
Forest Wlk N10 31 B2
Forfar Rd
London SW11 137 A4 268 B2
Tottenham N22 32 D2
Forge Cl
Harlington UB3 127 B6
Hayes BR2 209 A1
Forge Cotts W5 109 D5
Forge Dr KT10 213 A1
Forge La
Belmont SM3 217 A1
Feltham TW13 173 A5
Forge Lane Prim Sch TW13 173 A5
Forge La
Richmond TW10 154 A3
Sunbury TW16 194 A6
Forge Lo 2 TW7 131 A2
Forge Mews
Addington CR0 223 C3
Sunbury TW16 194 A6
Forge Pl NW1 71 A2
Forlong Path UB5 63 A2
Forman Ct TW1 152 D3
Forman Ho SE4 140 D1
Forman Pl N16 73 D4
Formby Ave HA3, HA7 43 C6
Formby Ct 9 N7 72 C3
Formosa Ho 1 E1 97 A3
Formosa St W9 91 D3
Formunt Cl E16 98 D2
Forres Gdns NW11 47 C3
Forrest Ct N7 72 C2
Forrester Path SE26 184 C6
Forresters The HA5 40 B3
Forrest Gdns SW16 204 B6
Forrest Ho SW15 134 C3
Forris Ave UB3 105 D5
Forset Ct W1 237 B2
Forset St W1 92 C1 237 B2
Forstal Cl BR2 209 A6
Forster Cl IG8 36 B3
Forster Ho SE6 164 B1
Forster Park Prim Sch SE6 164 C1
Forster Rd
Beckenham BR3 207 A6
Streatham SW2 160 A4
Thornton Heath CR0 205 A2
Tottenham N17 51 D6
Walthamstow E17 53 A3
Forsters Cl RM6 59 B3
Forsters Way UB4 84 B1
Forston St N1 95 A5 235 B4
Forsyte Cres SE19 183 C2
Forsyte Ct KT2 176 D2
Forsyth Ct
13 Dagenham RM10 81 D2
Harrow HA1 42 B3
Kingston u T KT3 177 C1
Forsythe Shades BR3 186 A2
Forsyth Gdns SE17 138 D6
Forsyth Ho
14 Hackney E9 74 C1
Pimlico SW1 259 B3
Forsythia Cl IG1 78 D3
Forsythia Ho SE4 141 A2
Forsyth Pl EN1 17 C6
Forterie Gdns IG3 80 A4
Fortescue Ave
1 Hackney E8 74 B1
Twickenham TW2 152 A1
Fortescue Rd
Burnt Oak HA8 27 B3
Mitcham SW19 180 B3
Fortess Gr NW5 71 C3
Fortess Rd NW5 71 C4
Fortess Wlk NW5 71 B3
Forthbridge Rd SW11 137 A1
Forth Ho 30 E3 97 B5
Forties The 9 NW5 71 C3
Fortior Ct N6 49 C2
Fortis Cl E16 99 C1
Fortis Ct N10 49 A6
Fortis Gn N2, N10 48 D6
FORTIS GREEN 48 D5
Fortis Green Ave N2 48 D5
Fortis Green Cotts N2 48 D6
Fortismere Ave N10 49 A6
Fortismere Sch N10 30 D1
Fortismere Sch (South Wing) N10 49 A6
Fortnam Rd N19 71 D6
Fortnums Acre HA7 24 D4
Fort Rd
Bermondsey SE1 117 D2 263 D3
Northolt UB5 63 C1
Fortrose Cl E14 98 B1
Fortrose Gdns SW12, SW2 160 A3
Fort St Broadgate E1 243 B3
Newham E16 121 B5
Fortuna Cl N7 72 B2
Fortune Ct
Barking IG11 102 B5
6 Dalston E8 73 D1
Fortune Gate Rd NW10 89 C6
Fortune Green Rd NW6 69 C4
Fortune Ho
Lambeth SE11 261 A3
St Luke's EC1 242 B5
Fortune La WD6 9 D5
Fortunes Mead UB5 63 A2
Fortune St EC1 95 A3 242 B5
Fortune Way NW10 90 A4
Fortune Wlk 4 SE28 123 B3
Forty Acre La E16 99 A2
Forty Ave HA9 66 B6
Forty Cl HA9 66 B5
Forty Hall* EN2 5 D6
FORTY HILL 5 D4
Forty Hill CE Prim Sch EN2 6 A6
Forty Hill EN2 5 D5
Forty Hill Ho EN1 5 D5
Forty La HA9 66 D6
Forum Cl 7 E3 97 C6
Forumside HA8 26 C4
Forum The KT8 195 D5
Forum Way HA8 26 C4
Forval Cl CR4 202 D4
Forward Bsns Ctr The 3 E16 98 B3
Forward Dr HA3 42 D5
Fosbrooke Ho SW8 270 A3
Fosbury Ho 7 SW9 138 B1
Fosbury Mews W2 245 D5
Foscote Mews W9 91 C2
Foscote Rd NW4 46 B3
Foskett Ho 21 N2 30 B1
Foskett Rd SW6 135 B3
Foss Ave CR0, CR9 220 C3
Fossdene Prim Sch SE7 121 B1
Fossdene Rd SE7 121 B1
Fossdyke Cl UB4 85 A2
Fosse Way W13 87 A2
Fossil Rd SE13 141 C2
Fossington Rd DA17 124 D2
Foss Rd SW17 180 B6
Fossway RM8 80 C6
Foster Ct
6 Camden Town NW1 71 C1
Canning Town E16 120 D6
Hendon NW4 46 C5
Foster Ho SE14 141 B4
Foster La EC2 95 A1 242 A2
Foster Rd Acton W3 111 C6
Chiswick W4 111 B1
Newham E13 99 A3
Fosters Cl
Elmstead BR7 188 B5
Woodford E18 37 B2
Fosters Old Sch DA16 146 B3
Foster's Prim Sch DA16 146 C2
Foster St NW4 46 C5
Foster Wlk NW4 46 C5
Fothergill Cl E13 99 A5
Fothergill Dr N21 16 A6
Fotheringham Ct EN1 5 D1
Fotheringham Rd EN1 5 D1
Foubert's Pl W1 239 A1
Foulden Rd N16 73 D4
Foulden Terr N16 73 D4
Foulis Terr SW7 114 B1 256 D2
Foulser Rd SW17 159 A1
Foulsham Rd CR7 205 B6
Foundary Ho 6 E14 97 D2
Founder Cl 8 E6 100 D1
Founders Cl UB5 85 B4
Founders Ct EC2 242 C2
Founders Gdns SE19 183 A3
Founders Ho SW1 259 C2
Foundling Ct WC1 240 A6
Foundling Mus The* WC1 94 A3 240 B6
Foundry Cl SE16 119 A5
Foundry Mews NW1 239 B6
Foundry Pl
Stepney E1 96 C2
Wandsworth SW18 157 D4
Fountain Cl UB8 83 A2
Fountain Ct
Belgravia SW1 258 C3
Blackfen DA15 168 B5
New Malden KT3 199 A5
5 Penge SE26 184 C4
14 Shepherd's Bush W11 112 D4
Strand EC4 251 A6
Fountain Dr
Dulwich SE19 183 D6
Wallington SM5 218 D1
Fountain Green Sq 34 SE16 118 A4
Fountain Ho
33 Bermondsey SE16 118 A4
3 Brondesbury Pk NW6 69 A1
Mayfair W1 248 A4
5 Mitcham SW19 180 D1
Fountain Mews
1 Highbury N5 73 A4
Maitland Pk NW3 70 D2
Fountain Pl SW9 138 C4
Fountain Rd
South Norwood CR7 183 A1
Upper Tooting SW17 180 B6
Fountains Ave TW13 151 B1

Fountains Cl TW13 ... 151 B1
Fountains Cres N14 ... 16 A4
Fountains The
London N3 ... 29 D3
Loughton IG10 ... 21 D4
Fountayne Bsns Ctr N15 ... 52 A5
Fountayne Rd
South Tottenham N15 ... 52 A5
Stoke Newington N16 ... 74 A6
Fount St SW8 ... 137 D5 269 D3
Fouracres EN3 ... 7 A4
Four Acres N12 ... 29 D6
Fourland Wlk HA8 ... 27 A4
Fournier St E1 ... 95 D2 243 D4
Fourscore Mans E8 ... 74 A1
Four Seasons Cl E3 ... 97 C5
Four Seasons Cres SM3 ... 217 B6
Four Square Ct TW4 ... 151 C5
Fourth Ave
Hayes UB3 ... 105 D5
Ilford E12 ... 78 B4
West Kilburn W10 ... 91 A4
Fourth Cross Rd TW2 ... 152 B2
Fourth Way
Wembley HA9 ... 66 D4
Wembley HA9 ... 67 A4
Four Tubs The WD23 ... 8 B4
Fourways 2 CR0 ... 221 D6
Four Wents The E4 ... 20 B2
Fovant Ct 5 SW8 ... 137 C3
Fowey Ave IG4 ... 55 D4
Fowey Cl E1 ... 118 B5
Fowey Ho SE11 ... 261 B2
Fowler Cl
London SW11 ... 136 B2
Sidcup DA14 ... 191 A5
Fowler Ho
5 Camberwell SE5 ... 139 C3
Islington N1 . 94 D6 234 D6
South Lambeth SW8 . 269 D1
West Green N15 ... 51 B4
Fowler Rd
Forest Gate E7 ... 77 A4
Islington N1 . 94 D6 234 D6
Mitcham CR4 ... 181 A1
Fowler's Wlk W5 ... 87 D3
Fownes St SW11 ... 136 C2
Fox and Knot St EC1 241 D4
Foxberry Ct SE4 ... 141 B1
Foxberry Rd SE4 ... 141 A2
Foxborough Gdns SE4 ... 163 C6
Foxbourne Rd SW17 ... 159 A2
Foxbury Ave BR7 ... 189 B4
Foxbury Cl BR1 ... 187 B4
Foxbury Rd BR1 ... 187 B4
Fox Cl
Bethnal Green E1 ... 96 C3
Elstree WD6 ... 9 D5
Newham E16 ... 99 A2
Foxcombe Cl 1 E6 ... 99 D5
Foxcombe CR0 ... 223 D2
Foxcombe Rd 6 SW15 ... 156 A3
Foxcote SE5 ... 263 B1
Foxcroft N1 ... 233 D3
Foxcroft Rd SE18 ... 144 D4
Foxes Dale
Beckenham BR2 ... 208 B6
Blackheath Pk SE3 .. 143 A2
Foxfield NW1 ... 231 D5
Foxfield Prim Sch SE18 ... 123 A1
Foxfield Rd BR6 ... 227 B6
Foxglove Cl
Bexley DA15 ... 168 A5
Edmonton N9 ... 18 C3
Southall UB1 ... 107 A6
Foxglove Ct 11 HA0 ... 88 A5
Foxglove Gdns E11 ... 55 C5
Foxglove La KT9 ... 214 C4
Foxglove Path SE28 .. 123 C5
Foxglove St W12 ... 111 D6
Foxglove Way SM6 ... 203 B1
Foxgrove Ave BR3 ... 185 D3
Foxgrove N14 ... 16 A1
Foxgrove Path WD19 .. 22 D5
Foxgrove Rd BR3 ... 186 A3
Fox Gr KT12 ... 194 B2
Foxham Rd N19 ... 71 D5
Fox Hill Gdns SE19 ... 183 D3
Fox Hill SE19 ... 183 D3
Foxhole Rd 2 SE9 ... 166 A6
Fox Hollow Cl 1 SE18 ... 123 C1
Fox Hollow Dr DA7 ... 146 D2
Fox Ho 2 SW11 ... 136 B1
Foxholt Gdns NW10 ... 67 A1
Foxhome Cl BR7 ... 188 C4
Fox Ho UB5 ... 85 A6
Fox House Rd DA17 .. 125 D1
Fox La Ealing W5 ... 88 A3
Keston BR2 ... 225 C3
Palmers Green N13 ... 16 B1
Foxlees HA0 ... 65 A4
Foxley Cl E8 ... 74 A3
Foxley Ct SM2 ... 218 A1
Foxley Ho 4 E3 ... 97 D4
Foxley Rd
Camberwell SW9 ... 138 D5
Thornton Heath CR7 . 204 D5
Foxley Sq 3 SW9 ... 138 D4
Foxmead Cl EN2 ... 4 B2
Foxmore St SW11 ... 267 C1
Fox Prim Sch W8 ... 113 C5 245 A3
Fox Rd E16 ... 98 D2
Foxs Path CR4 ... 180 C1
Fox's Yd E2 ... 243 D6
Foxtail Ho TW3 ... 130 A4
Foxton Gr CR4 ... 180 B1
Foxton Ho E16 ... 122 C4
Foxton KT1 ... 198 C6
Foxwarren KT10 ... 212 D1
Foxwell Mews SE4 ... 141 A2
Foxwell St SE4 ... 141 A2
Foxwood Cl
Edgware NW7 ... 27 C6
Feltham TW13 ... 150 B1
Foxwood Green Cl EN1 ... 17 C5
Foxwood Rd SE3 ... 142 D1
Foyle Rd
Greenwich SE3 ... 142 D6
Tottenham N17 ... 34 A2
Fradel Lo N16 ... 51 B1
Framfield Cl N12 ... 13 C1
Framfield Ct EN1 ... 17 C5
Framfield Rd
Ealing W7 ... 86 D1
Islington N5 ... 72 D3
Mitcham CR4 ... 181 A3
Framlingham Cl 2 E5 ... 74 C6
Framlingham Cres SE9 ... 188 B6
Framlingham Ct 5 RM6 ... 58 B4
Frampton Cl SM2 ... 217 C1
Frampton Ct 3 W3 .. 111 A4
Frampton Ho NW8 .. 236 D5
Frampton NW1 ... 71 D1
Frampton Park Rd E9 ... 74 C1
Frampton Rd TW4 ... 151 A6
Frampton St NW8 ... 92 B3 236 D5
Francemary Rd SE4 .. 163 C6
Frances Ct
South Norwood SE25 ... 183 D1
Walthamstow E17 ... 53 C3
Frances & Dick James Ct 2 NW7 ... 29 A3
Frances Rd E4 ... 35 C4
Frances St SE18 ... 122 B2
Franche Court Rd SW17 ... 158 A1
Francis Ave
Bexleyheath DA7 ... 147 C3
Feltham TW13 ... 150 A1
Ilford IG1 ... 79 B6
Francis Barber Cl SW16 ... 182 B6
Franciscan Prim Sch SW17 ... 181 A5
Franciscan Rd SW17 ... 181 A6
Francis Chichester Way SW11 ... 137 A4 268 B1
Francis Cl
6 Cubitt Town E14 ... 120 B2
Littleton TW17 ... 192 C5
West Ewell KT19 ... 215 B4
Francis Ct
12 Deptford SE14 ... 140 D6
Ealing W5 ... 110 B6
Edgware NW7 ... 27 D5
Kingston u T KT5 ... 198 A5
Francis Gr SW19 ... 179 B4
Francis Ho NW10 ... 89 D6
Francis Holland Sch
Belgravia SW1 ... 115 A2 258 B3
Marylebone NW1 ... 92 D3 237 C6
Francis Ho
11 Shoreditch N1 ... 95 C6
Walham Green SW10 ... 265 D4
Francis Rd
Fortis Green N2 ... 48 D5
Harrow HA1 ... 43 A4
Hounslow TW4 ... 128 D3
Ilford IG1 ... 79 B6
Leyton E10 ... 76 A6
Pinner HA5 ... 40 C4
Thornton Heath CR0 . 204 D2
Wallington SM6 ... 219 C2
Wembley UB6 ... 87 C6
Francis Snary Lo 11 SW18 ... 157 C6
Francis St Ilford IG1 ... 79 B6
Stratford E15 ... 76 C3
Westminster SW1 ... 115 C2 259 B4
Francis Terrace Mews 16 N19 ... 71 C5
Francis Terr N19 ... 71 C5
Francis Wlk N1 ... 233 C6
Francklyn Gdns HA8 .. 10 C1
Franconia Rd SW4 ... 159 D6
Frank Bailey Wlk E12 ... 78 C2
Frank Barnes Sch NW3 ... 70 B1
Frank Beswick Ho SW6 ... 264 D5
Frank Burton Cl 4 SE7 ... 121 B1
Frank Dixon Cl SE21 ... 161 C3
Frank Dixon Way SE21 ... 161 C3
Frankfurt Rd SE24 ... 161 A6
Frank Godley Ct DA14 ... 190 B5
Frankham Ho 8 SE8 ... 141 C5
Frankham St SE8 ... 141 C5
Frank Ho SW8 ... 270 A4
Frankland Cl
Bermondsey SE16 ... 118 B2
Woodford IG8 ... 37 C5
Frankland Ho 4 SW12 ... 159 B4
Frankland Rd
Brompton SW7 ... 114 B3 256 C5
Chingford E4 ... 35 C5
Franklin Bldg 5 E14 ... 119 C4
Franklin Cl
Greenwich SE13 ... 141 D4
Kingston u T KT1 ... 198 C6
Oakleigh Pk N20 ... 14 A4
West Norwood SE27 ... 160 D1
Franklin Cres CR4 ... 203 C5
Franklin Ho
Beckenham BR2 ... 208 C6
New Cross SE4 ... 141 A3
26 Wapping E1 ... 118 B5
West Hendon NW9 ... 45 D2
Franklin Ind Est SE20 ... 184 C2
Franklin Pas SE9 ... 144 A2
Franklin Pl SE13 ... 141 D4
Franklin Rd
Bexleyheath DA7 ... 147 A4
Penge SE20 ... 184 C3
Walton-on-T KT12 ... 194 A3
Franklins Mews HA2 .. 64 A6
Franklin Sq SW5 ... 254 D1
Franklin's Row SW3 ... 114 D1 257 D2
Franklin St
43 Bromley E3 ... 97 D4
South Tottenham N15 .. 51 C3
Franklin Way CR0 ... 204 A2
Franklyn Rd
Walton-on-T KT12 ... 194 B3
Willesden NW10 ... 67 D2
Franks Ave KT3 ... 199 A5
Franks Ho TW7 ... 131 B1
Frank Slater Ho 4 IG3 ... 58 B1
Frank Soskice Ho SW6 ... 264 D5
Frank St 5 E13 ... 99 A3
Frankswood Ave
Hillingdon UB7 ... 82 B1
Petts Wood BR2, BR5 ... 211 A4
Frank Towell Ct TW14 ... 150 A3
Frank Welch Ct HA5 ... 40 C5
Frank Whymark Ho 4 SE16 ... 118 C4
Franlaw Cres N13 ... 33 A6
Frans Ct HA4 ... 40 A1
Fransfield Gr SE26 ... 162 B1
Frans Hals Ct E14 ... 120 B3
Franshams WD23 ... 8 C2
Frant Cl SE20 ... 184 C3
Franthorne Way SE6 ... 163 D1
Frant Rd CR7 ... 204 D4
Fraserburgh Ho 29 E3 ... 97 B5
Fraser Cl 3 E6 ... 100 A1
Fraser Ct
Battersea SW11 ... 267 A2
Heston TW3 ... 129 A5
Fraser Ho
Brentford TW8 ... 110 B1
40 Clapham SW8 ... 137 D3
3 Woolwich SE18 ... 122 C2
Fraser Rd
Edmonton N9 ... 18 B1
Walthamstow E17 ... 53 D3
Wembley UB6 ... 87 C6
Fraser Regnart Ct 12 NW5 ... 70 D3
Fraser St W4 ... 111 C1
Frating Cres IG8 ... 37 B4
Frazer Ave HA4 ... 62 C3
Frazier St SE1 ... 116 C4 251 A1
Freame Ho N21 ... 17 B5
Frean St SE16 ... 118 A3
Frearson Ho WC1 ... 233 D2
Freda Corbett Cl 10 SE15 ... 140 A5
Frederica Rd E4 ... 20 B4
Frederica St 4 N7 ... 72 B1
Frederick Blg N1 ... 73 C2
Frederick Charrington Ho 4 E1 ... 96 C3
Frederick Cl
Cheam SM1 ... 217 B3
Marylebone W2 ... 114 D6 247 C6
Frederick Cres
Camberwell SW9 ... 138 D5
Enfield EN3 ... 6 C3
Frederick Ct SW6 ... 135 A2
Frederick Gdns
Cheam SM1 ... 217 B3
Thornton Heath CR0 . 204 D3
Frederick Ho
Ashford TW15 ... 170 A6
Southall UB1 ... 107 B6
Woolwich SE7 ... 122 A3
Frederick Pl SE18 ... 122 D1
Frederick Rd SM1 ... 217 B3
Frederick's Pl
City of London EC2 .. 242 C1
North Finchley N12 ... 30 A6
Frederick Sq 11 SE16 ... 119 A6
Frederick's Row EC1 234 C2
Frederick St WC1 ... 94 B4 233 C1
Frederick Terr E8 ... 73 D1
Frederic Mews SW1 . 248 A1
Frederic St E17 ... 53 A4
Fredora Ave UB4 ... 83 D3
Fred Styles Ho SE7 ... 143 C6
Fred Tibble Ct RM9 ... 81 A4
Fred Wigg Twr E11 ... 76 D6
Freedom Cl E17 ... 53 A5
Freedom St SW11 ... 136 D3
Freegrove Rd N7 ... 72 A3
Freehold Ind Ctr TW4 ... 150 C6
Freeland Ct
Ealing W5 ... 110 B6
15 Sidcup DA14 ... 168 A1
Freeland Pk N3 ... 29 A1
Freeland Rd W5 ... 110 B6
Freelands Ave CR2 ... 222 D1
Freelands Gr BR1 ... 187 B2
Freelands Rd BR1 ... 187 B2
Freeling Ho NW8 ... 229 C6
Freeling St 7 N1 ... 72 B1
Freeman Cl
Northolt UB5 ... 63 A1
Upper Halliford TW17 ... 193 C5
Freeman Ct SW16 ... 182 A1
Freeman Dr KT8 ... 195 B5
Freeman Ho 13 SW2 ... 160 A4
Freeman Rd SM4 ... 202 B4
Freemans La UB3 ... 105 C6
Freemantle Ave EN3 ... 18 D6
Freemantle St SE17 ... 117 C1 263 A2
Freemason's Rd CR0 ... 205 C1
Freemasons Rd E16 ... 99 B1
Freemens Hos 1 SW9 ... 138 B1
Freesia Cl BR6 ... 227 D3
Freethorpe Cl SE19 .. 183 C2
Freezeland Way UB10 ... 60 D2
Freke Rd SW11 ... 137 A2
Fremantle Ho 14 E1 ... 96 B3
Fremantle Rd
Belvedere DA17 ... 125 C2
Ilford IG6 ... 57 A6
Fremont St E9 ... 96 C6
French Gdns KT12 ... 195 B1
French Pl E1 ... 243 B6
French St TW16 ... 172 C1
Frendsbury Rd SE4 ... 141 A1
Frensham Cl UB1 ... 85 B4
Frensham Ct
Canonbury N5 ... 73 A3
4 London NW9 ... 46 A5
Mitcham CR4 ... 202 B6
Frensham Dr
New Addington CR0 ... 224 A1
Roehampton SW15 ... 156 A2
Frensham Ho 7 KT6 ... 198 A4
Frensham Rd SE9 ... 167 B2
Frensham St SE15 ... 140 A6
Frere St 6 SW11 ... 136 C3
Fresham Ho BR2 ... 208 D6
Freshfield Ave E8 ... 73 D1
Freshfield Cl SE13 ... 142 B1
Freshfield Dr N14 ... 15 B4
Freshfields CR0 ... 207 B1
Freshford St SW17, SW18 ... 158 A1
Freshwater Cl SW17 ... 181 A4
Freshwater Ct UB1 ... 85 C4
Freshwater Rd
Dagenham RM8 ... 59 A1
Streatham SW17 ... 181 A4
Freshwell Ave RM6 ... 58 C5
Fresh Wharf Est IG11 ... 100 D6
Fresh Wharf Rd IG11 ... 100 D5
Freshwood Cl BR3 ... 185 D2
Freston Gdns EN4 ... 15 A6
Freston Pk N3 ... 29 B1
Freston Rd W10, W11 ... 112 D6
Freswick Ho 6 SE8 .. 119 A2
Freta Rd DA6 ... 169 B6
Freud Mus The* NW3 ... 70 A2
Frewell Bldg EC1 ... 241 A4
Frewing Cl BR7 ... 188 C5
Frewin Rd SW18 ... 158 B3
Friar Mews SE27 ... 160 D1
Friar Rd UB4 ... 84 D3
Friars Ave
London N20 ... 30 C6
Roehampton SW15 .. 155 D1
Friars Cl Chingford E4 .. 20 A1
Ilford IG1 ... 57 B1
Lambeth SE1 ... 251 D3
16 Northolt UB5 ... 84 D4
Friars Ct
5 Wallington SM6 ... 219 B4
Walthamstow E17 ... 35 B2
Friars Gate Cl IG8 ... 37 A6
Friars Gdns W3 ... 89 B1
Friars La TW9 ... 153 D6
Friars Mead E14 ... 120 A3
Friars Mews SE9 ... 166 C6
Friars Place La W3 ... 111 B6
Friars Prim Sch SE1 ... 116 D4 251 D1
Friar's Rd E6 ... 99 D6
Friars Stile Pl 9 TW10 ... 154 A5
Friars Stile Rd TW10 ... 154 A5
Friar St EC4 ... 241 D1
Friars Way W3 ... 89 B1
Friars Wlk
London N14 ... 15 B4
West Heath SE2 ... 124 D1
Friary Cl N12 ... 30 C5
Friary La IG8 ... 37 A6
Friary Park Ct 12 W3 .. 89 A1
Friary Rd Acton W3 ... 89 B1
London N12 ... 30 C6
Peckham SE15 ... 140 A5
Friary Way N12 ... 30 C6
Friday Grove Mews 11 SW12 ... 159 C4
FRIDAY HILL ... 20 C1
Friday Hill E4 ... 20 C1
Friday Hill E E4 ... 20 C1
Friday Hill W E4 ... 20 C2
Friday Rd CR4 ... 180 D3
Friday St EC4 ... 117 A6 252 A6
Frideswide Pl NW5 ... 71 C3
Friendly Pl 16 SE13 ... 141 D4
Friendly St SE8 ... 141 C4
Friendly Street Mews SE8 ... 141 C3
Friendship Way E15 ... 98 A6
Friendship Wlk UB5 ... 84 D4
Friends' Rd CR0 ... 221 B5
Friend St EC1 .. 94 D4 234 C2
FRIERN BARNET ... 31 A6
Friern Barnet La N20 .. 30 C6
Friern Barnet Rd N11 ... 31 A5
Friern Barnet Sch N11 ... 30 D5
Friern Bridge Ret Pk N11 ... 31 B4
Friern Ct N20 ... 14 B1
Friern Mount Dr N20 .. 14 A4
Friern Pk N12 ... 30 B5
Friern Rd SE22 ... 162 A5
Friern Watch Ave N12 ... 30 B6
Frigate Ho 7 E14 ... 120 A2
Frigate Mews SE8 ... 141 C6
Frimley Ave SM6 ... 220 B3
Frimley Cl
New Addington CR0 ... 224 A1
Putney SW19 ... 157 A2
Frimley Cres CR0 ... 224 A1
Frimley Ct DA14 ... 190 C5
Frimley Gdns CR4 ... 202 C6
Frimley Ho CR4 ... 202 C6
Frimley Rd
Chessington KT9 ... 214 A3
Ilford IG3 ... 79 C5
Frimley Way E1 ... 96 D3
Frinstead Ho 1 W10 ... 112 D6
Frinton Ct W13 ... 87 B2
Frinton Dr IG8 ... 36 B3
Frinton Mews IG2 ... 56 C3
Frinton Rd
Newham E6 ... 99 D4
Sidcup DA14 ... 169 A2
South Tottenham N15 .. 51 C3
Streatham SW17 ... 181 A4
Friston St SW6 ... 135 D3
Friswell Pl 1 DA6 ... 147 C1
Fritham Cl KT3 ... 199 C3
Frith Ct NW7 ... 29 A3
Frith Ho
Bethnal Green E2 ... 96 A4
Paddington NW8 ... 236 D5
Frith La NW7 ... 29 A4
Frith Manor Cotts N12 ... 29 B5
Frith Manor Prim Sch N12 ... 29 B5
Frith Rd
Croydon CR0 ... 221 A6
Leyton E11 ... 76 B4
Frith St W1 ... 93 D1 239 C1
Frithville Ct 2 W12 .. 112 C5
Frithville Gdns W12 .. 112 C5
Frizlands La RM10 ... 81 D5
Frobisher Cl HA5 ... 40 D2
Frobisher Cres TW19 ... 148 A4
Frobisher Ct
Belmont SM2 ... 217 B1
6 Forest Hill SE23 ... 162 B2
1 Greenwich SE10 ... 142 B6
Hendon NW9 ... 27 C1
3 Shepherd's Bush W12 ... 112 C4
Frobisher Gdns TW19 ... 148 A4
Frobisher Ho
3 Ealing W5 ... 88 A4
27 Wapping E1 ... 118 B5
Frobisher Mews EN2 ... 5 B1
Frobisher Pas E14 ... 119 C5
Frobisher Pl SE14 ... 140 C4
Frobisher Rd
London N8 ... 50 C5
Newham E6 ... 100 B1
Frobisher St SE10 ... 142 C6
Froghall Cotts EN5 ... 11 B5
Frogley Rd SE22 ... 139 D1
Frogmore Ave UB4 ... 83 C3
Frogmore Cl SM3 ... 217 A5
Frogmore Ct UB2 ... 107 B2
Frogmore Est NW10 .. 89 A4
Frogmore Gdns
Cheam SM3 ... 217 A4
Hayes UB4 ... 83 C3
Frogmore Ind Est
Hayes UB3 ... 105 D4
Highbury N5 ... 73 A4
Frogmore SW18 ... 157 C6
Frognal Ave
Harrow HA1 ... 42 D5
Sidcup DA14 ... 190 A4
Frognal Cl NW3 ... 70 A3
Frognal Cnr BR7 ... 189 D4
Frognal Ct NW3 ... 70 A2
Frognal Gdns NW3 ... 70 A4
Frognal La NW3 ... 69 D3
Frognal NW3 ... 70 A3
Frognal Par NW3 ... 70 A2
Frognal Pl DA14 ... 190 A5
Frognal Rise NW3 ... 70 A4
Frognal Way NW3 ... 70 A4
Froissart Rd SE9 ... 166 A6
Frome Ho SE15 ... 140 C3
Frome Rd N22 ... 50 D6

Frome St N1 ... 95 A5 235 A4
Fromondes Rd SM3 ... 217 A3
Fromow's Cnr 14 W4 ... 111 A1
Frontenac NW10 ... 68 B1
Frontier Works N17 ... 33 C4
Frosbery Ct 23 EN3 ... 7 C6
Frostic Wlk E1 ... 243 D3
Froude St SW8 ... 137 B3
Fruen Rd TW14 ... 149 D4
Fryatt Rd N17 ... 33 B3
Frye Ct 5 E3 ... 97 B4
Fryent Cl NW9 ... 44 C3
Fryent Cres NW9 ... 45 C3
Fryent Ctry Park HA3, HA9, NW9 ... 44 C2
Fryent Fields NW9 ... 45 C3
Fryent Gr NW9 ... 45 C3
Fryent Prim Sch NW9 ... 45 A2
Fryent Way HA9, NW9 ... 44 D2
Fry Ho E6 ... 77 C1
Frying Pan Alley E1 ... 243 C3
Fry Rd
Harlesden NW10 ... 89 D6
Upton Pk E6 ... 77 D1
Fryston Ave CR0 ... 222 A6
Fuchsia St SE2 ... 124 B1
Fulbeck Dr NW9 ... 27 C2
Fulbeck Ho N7 ... 72 B2
Fulbeck Way HA2 ... 24 A1
Fulbourne Rd E17 ... 36 A1
Fulbourne St E1 ... 96 B2
Fulbourn 9 KT1 ... 176 C1
Fulbrook Rd N19 ... 71 C4
Fulcher Ct SE8 ... 141 B6
Fulcher Ho
13 Deptford SE8 ... 119 B1
10 Shoreditch N1 ... 95 C6
Fulford Mans 3 N19 ... 72 A5
Fulford Rd KT19 ... 215 B1
Fulford St SE16 ... 118 B4
FULHAM ... 134 D3
Fulham Broadway Sh Ctr SW6 ... 265 B3
Fulham Broadway Sta SW6 ... 135 C5 265 B4
Fulham Broadway SW6 ... 135 C5 265 B3
Fulham Bsns Exchange SW6 ... 266 B1
Fulham Cl UB10 ... 83 A3
Fulham Cross Sec Sch SW6 ... 135 A5 264 A3
Fulham Ct SW6 ... 135 C4 265 A2
Fulham High St SW6 ... 135 A3
Fulham Palace Rd SW6, W6 ... 134 D6
Fulham Pal* SW6 ... 135 A3
Fulham Park Gdns SW6 ... 135 B3
Fulham Park Rd SW6 ... 135 B3
Fulham Prep Sch
Fulham SW6 ... 135 A3
Fulham W14 ... 135 A6 264 B6
Fulham Prim Sch SW6 ... 135 C6 265 A5
Fulham Rd
Chelsea SW10 ... 136 A6 266 B6
Fulham SW6 ... 135 B4 264 D2
Fulke Ho E5 ... 74 B5
Fullbrooks Ave KT4 ... 199 D1
Fuller Cl
4 Bethnal Green E2 ... 96 A3
Bushey WD23 ... 8 B4
Orpington BR6 ... 227 D3
Fuller Rd RM8 ... 80 C4
Fullers Ave KT6 ... 214 B6
Fuller's Ave IG8 ... 36 D3
Fullers Ho 6 SW18 ... 157 C6
Fuller's Rd E18 ... 36 D3
Fuller St NW4 ... 46 C5
Fullers Way N KT6 ... 214 B5
Fullers Way S KT9 ... 214 A5
Fuller's Wood CR0 ... 223 C3
Fuller Terr IG1 ... 79 B3
Fullerton Ct TW11 ... 175 A4
Fullerton Rd
Croydon CR0 ... 205 D2
Wandsworth SW18 ... 158 A6
Fuller Way UB3 ... 105 D1
Fullwood Prim Sch IG6 ... 57 A5
Fullwood's Mews N1 ... 235 D2
Fulmar Ct
6 Dulwich SE21 ... 161 B2
10 Ealing W13 ... 86 D3
Surbiton KT5 ... 198 B3
Fulmar Ho
12 Bermondsey SE16 ... 118 D2
Marylebone NW8 ... 237 B5
Fulmead St SW6 ... 265 D1
Fulmer Cl TW12 ... 173 A5
Fulmer Rd E16 ... 99 D2
Fulmer Way W13 ... 109 B3
Fulneck 1 E1 ... 96 C2
Fulready Rd E10 ... 54 B4
Fulstone Cl TW4 ... 129 B1
Fulthorp Rd SE3 ... 143 A3
Fulton Ct EN3 ... 7 C5
Fulton Mews W2 ... 246 A6
Fulton Rd HA9 ... 66 C5
Fulwell Ct
Southall UB1 ... 108 A6
Teddington TW11 ... 174 C6
Fulwell Park Ave TW2 ... 152 A2
Fulwell Rd TW11, TW12 ... 174 B6
Fulwell Sta TW11 ... 174 B6
Fulwood Ave HA0 ... 88 B5
Fulwood Cl UB3 ... 83 D1
Fulwood Ct
Harrow HA3 ... 43 A3
Stanwell TW19 ... 148 B5
Fulwood Gdns TW1 ... 153 A5
Fulwood Pl WC1 ... 240 D3
Fulwood Wlk SW19 ... 157 A3
Furber St W6 ... 112 B3
Furham Field HA5 ... 23 C3
Furley Ho 7 SE15 ... 140 A5
Furley Rd SE15 ... 140 A5
Furlong Cl SM6 ... 203 B1
Furlong Rd N7 ... 72 C2
Furmage St SW18 ... 157 D4
Furneaux Ave SE27 ... 182 D5
Furness Ho SW1 ... 258 C2
Furness Lo 4 SW14 ... 132 D1
Furness Prim Sch The NW10 ... 90 A5
Furness Rd
Harlesden NW10 ... 90 A5
Harrow HA2 ... 41 D1
Morden SM4 ... 201 D3
Sands End SW6 ... 135 D3
Furnival St EC4 ... 94 C1 241 A2
Furrow La E9 ... 74 C3
Furrows The KT12 ... 194 C1
Fursby Ave N3 ... 29 C4
Fursecroft W1 ... 237 C2
Further Acre NW9 ... 27 D1
Furtherfield Cl CR0 ... 204 C3
Further Green Rd SE6 ... 164 C3
Furze Cl WD19 ... 22 C5
Furze Ct CR0 ... 222 A6
FURZEDOWN ... 181 B6
Furzedown Dr SW17 ... 181 B5
Furzedown Prim Sch SW17 ... 181 A4
Furzedown Rd SW17 ... 181 B5
Furzefield Cl BR7 ... 188 D4
Furzefield Rd SE3 ... 143 B5
Furzeground Way UB11 ... 105 A5
Furzeham Rd UB7 ... 104 A4
Furzehill Rd WD6 ... 11 A6
Furze Inf Sch RM6 ... 59 A3
Furzeland Ho 2 KT3 ... 199 C2
Furze Rd CR7 ... 205 A6
Furze St E3 ... 97 C2
Furzewood TW16 ... 172 A2
Fuschia Ct IG8 ... 36 C4
Fuscia Ct TW13 ... 149 D1
Fusion Ct SW15 ... 155 C1
Futters Ct 1 NW10 ... 89 C5
Fyfe Way BR1 ... 187 A1
Fyfield Cl BR2, BR3 ... 208 B5
Fyfield Ct E7 ... 77 A2
Fyfield Ho RM9 ... 80 B1
Fyfield N4 ... 72 C6
Fyfield Rd
5 Brixton SW9 ... 138 C2
Enfield EN1 ... 5 C2
Walthamstow E17 ... 54 B6
Woodford IG8 ... 37 C3
Fynes St SW1 ... 259 C4

G

Gable Cl HA5 ... 23 C3
Gable Ct SE26 ... 184 B6
Gable Ho 12 W4 ... 111 C2
Gable Lo
Hadley Wood EN4 ... 2 A5
5 North Finchley N12 ... 30 A5
West Wickham BR4 ... 208 A1
Gables Ave TW15 ... 170 B5
Gables Cl
Camberwell SE5 ... 139 C4
Lewisham SE12 ... 165 A3
Gables The
Barking IG11 ... 79 A2
Bromley BR1 ... 187 B3
3 Clapham SW4 ... 137 C2
Ealing W13 ... 87 B1
Hampstead NW3 ... 70 B6
Heston TW5 ... 129 C6
Mitcham CR4 ... 203 B6
Muswell Hill N10 ... 49 A6
North Finchley N12 ... 29 D5
Wembley HA9 ... 66 B5
Gabriel Cl 1 TW13 ... 173 A6
Gabriel Ho SE11 ... 260 C4
Gabrielle Cl HA9 ... 66 B5
Gabrielle Ct NW3 ... 70 B2
Gabriel Mews NW2 ... 69 B6
Gabriel St SE23 ... 163 A4
Gabriel's Wharf SE1 ... 251 A4
Gad Cl E13 ... 99 B4
Gaddesden Ave HA9 ... 66 B2
Gaddesden Ho EC1 ... 235 D1
Gade Cl UB3 ... 106 B5
Gadesden Rd KT19 ... 215 A2
Gadsbury Cl NW9 ... 45 D3
Gadsden Ho
6 Homerton E9 ... 74 D2
8 Kensal Town W10 ... 91 A3
Gadwall Cl E16 ... 99 B1
Gadwall Way SE28 ... 123 B4
Gagarin Ho SW11 ... 136 B2
Gage Rd E16 ... 98 C2
Gage St WC1 ... 240 B4
Gainford Ho 18 E2 ... 96 B4
Gainford St N1 ... 94 C6 234 A6
Gainsboro Gdns UB6 ... 64 C3
Gainsborough Ave E12 ... 78 C3
Gainsborough Cl
Beckenham BR3 ... 185 C3
Thames Ditton KT10 ... 196 C1
Gainsborough Ct
11 Barnet EN5 ... 1 D1
6 Bermondsey SE16 ... 118 B1
Bromley BR2 ... 209 C5
Dulwich SE21 ... 161 C2
North Finchley N12 ... 29 D5
Shepherd's Bush W12 ... 112 C4
Gainsborough Gdns
Edgware HA8 ... 26 C1
Golders Green NW11 ... 47 B2
Hampstead NW3 ... 70 B5
Isleworth TW7 ... 152 B6
Gainsborough Ho
Dagenham RM8 ... 80 B4
Enfield EN1 ... 18 A6
Finsbury Pk N4 ... 50 B1
3 Hampstead NW3 ... 70 A4
5 Limehouse E14 ... 119 A6
Westminster SW1 ... 259 D3
Gainsborough Lodge HA1 ... 42 C4
Gainsborough Mews 5 SE26 ... 162 B1
Gainsborough Prim Sch
Hackney Wick E9 ... 75 C2
Newham E15 ... 98 C4
Gainsborough Rd
Bedford Pk W4 ... 111 D2
Dagenham RM8 ... 80 B5
Hayes UB4 ... 83 B5
Leytonstone E11 ... 54 C2
Newham E15 ... 98 C4
New Malden KT3 ... 199 B2
North Finchley N12 ... 29 D5
Richmond TW9 ... 132 B2
Gainsborough Sq DA6 ... 146 D2
Gainsborough St 3 E9 ... 75 B2
Gainsborough Studios N1 ... 235 C5
Gainsborough Twr 7 UB5 ... 84 D5
Gainsfield Ct 3 E11 ... 76 C5
Gainsford Rd E17 ... 53 B5
Gainsford St SE1 ... 117 D4 253 D2
Gairloch Ho 2 NW1 ... 71 D1
Gairloch Rd SE5 ... 139 C3
Gaisford St NW5 ... 71 C2
Gaitskell Ct SW11 ... 136 C3
Gaitskell Ho
Camberwell SE17 ... 139 B6
2 Newham E6 ... 99 D6
3 Walthamstow E17 ... 53 D6
Gaitskell Rd SE9 ... 167 A3
Gaitskell Way SE1 ... 252 A2
Galahad Rd
Edmonton N9 ... 18 A1
Galahad Rd *continued*
Grove Pk BR1 ... 187 A6
Galata Rd SW13 ... 134 A5
Galatea Sq SE15 ... 140 B2
Galaxy Bldg 6 E14 ... 119 C2
Galaxy Ho EC2 ... 242 D6
Galba Ct 1 TW8 ... 131 D5
Galbraith St E14 ... 120 A3
Galdana Ave EN5 ... 2 A2
Galeborough Ave IG8 ... 36 B3
Gale Cl
Hampton TW12 ... 173 A4
Mitcham CR4 ... 202 B6
Gale Ho
10 Brixton SW2 ... 160 B6
Carshalton SM5 ... 218 C3
Galena Ho
5 Hammersmith W6 ... 112 B2
Plumstead Comm SE18 ... 123 D1
Galena Rd W6 ... 112 B2
Galen Pl WC1 ... 240 B3
Galesbury Rd SW18 ... 158 A5
Gales Gdns E2 ... 96 B4
Gale St
Dagenham RM9 ... 80 D1
Tower Hamlets E3 ... 97 C2
Galgate Cl 4 SW19 ... 157 A3
Gallants Farm Rd EN4 ... 14 C3
Galleon Cl SE16 ... 118 D4
Galleon Ho 8 E14 ... 120 A2
Galleons Dr IG11 ... 102 A4
Gallery Ct SW10 ... 266 A5
Gallery Gdns UB5 ... 84 D5
Gallery Rd SE21 ... 161 B3
Galleywall Rd SE16 ... 118 B2
Galleywall Road Trad Est 12 SE16 ... 118 B2
Galleywood Ho 1 W10 ... 90 C2
Galliard Cl N9 ... 18 C5
Galliard Ct N9 ... 18 A5
Gallia Rd N5 ... 72 D3
Galliard Prim Sch N9 ... 18 A4
Galliard Rd N9 ... 18 A5
Gallica Ct SM1 ... 201 D1
Gallions Cl IG11 ... 102 A4
Gallions Mount Prim Sch SE18 ... 123 D1
Gallions Prim Sch E6 ... 100 D1
Gallions Rd E16 ... 122 D6
Gallions Reach Shp Pk IG11 ... 101 A2
Gallions Reach Sta E16 ... 122 D6
Gallions View Rd SE28 ... 123 C4
Gallon Cl SE7 ... 121 C2
Gallop The
South Croydon CR2 ... 222 B1
Sutton SM2 ... 218 A1
Gallosson Rd SE18 ... 123 C2
Galloway Rd W12 ... 112 A5
Gallus Cl N21 ... 16 B5
Gallus Sq SE3 ... 143 B2
Galpin's Rd CR4, CR7 ... 204 B5
Galsworthy Ave
Ilford RM6 ... 58 B2
Tower Hamlets E14 ... 97 A2
Galsworthy Cl SE28 ... 124 B5
Galsworthy Cres SE3 ... 143 C4
Galsworthy Ct W3 ... 110 D3
Galsworthy Ho 4 W11 ... 91 A1
Galsworthy Rd
Cricklewood NW2 ... 69 A4
Kingston u T KT2 ... 176 D2
Galton Ho SE18 ... 144 B4
Galton St W10 ... 91 A4
Galva Cl EN4 ... 3 A1
Galvani Way CR0 ... 204 B1
Galveston Ho 2 E1 ... 97 A3
Galveston Rd SW15 ... 157 B6
Galway Cl 28 SE16 ... 118 B1
Galway Ho
Finsbury EC1 ... 235 B1
7 Stepney E1 ... 96 D2
Galway St EC1 ... 95 A4 235 B1
Galy 5 NW9 ... 27 D1
Gambetta St 3 SW8 ... 137 B3
Gambia St SE1 ... 116 D5 251 D3
Gambler Ho EC1 ... 235 B1
Gambole Rd SW17 ... 180 C6
Games Ho 6 SE7 ... 143 C6
Games Rd EN4 ... 2 D2
Gamlen Rd SW15 ... 134 D1
Gamma Ct 9 CR0 ... 205 B1
Gamuel Cl E17 ... 53 C3
Gander Green Cres TW12 ... 173 C2
Gander Green La KT4, SM1, SM3 ... 217 B5
Gandhi Cl E17 ... 53 C3
Gandolfi St 5 SE15 ... 139 C6
Ganley Ct 19 SW11 ... 136 B2
Gannet Ct 5 SE21 ... 161 B2
Gannet Ho SE15 ... 139 D4
Ganton St W1 ... 239 B1
Ganton Wlk WD19 ... 22 D6
GANTS HILL ... 56 C3
Gantshill Cres IG2 ... 56 C4
Gants Hill IG2 ... 56 C3
Gants Hill Sta IG2 ... 56 C3
Gap Rd SW19 ... 179 D5
Garage Rd W3 ... 88 C1
Garand Ct 2 N7 ... 72 B3
Garbett Ho 2 SE17 ... 138 D6
Garbutt Pl W1 ... 238 B3
Garden Ave
Bexleyheath DA7 ... 147 C2
Mitcham CR4 ... 181 B3
Garden City HA8 ... 26 C4
Garden Cl
Ashford TW15 ... 171 A4
Chingford E4 ... 35 C5
Grove Pk SE12 ... 165 B1
Hampton TW12 ... 173 B5
Northolt UB5 ... 85 A6
Roehampton SW15 ... 156 B4
Ruislip HA4 ... 61 D6
Wallington SM6 ... 220 A3
Garden Cotts BR5 ... 190 C1
Garden Ct
5 Belmont SM2 ... 217 C1
10 Eltham SE9 ... 166 C5
Hampton TW12 ... 173 B5
North Finchley N12 ... 29 D5
4 Richmond TW9 ... 132 B4
12 South Acton W4 ... 111 A3
South Croydon CR0 ... 221 D5
4 Stanmore HA7 ... 25 C5
St John's Wood NW8 ... 229 C2
Strand EC4 ... 251 A6
Wembley HA0 ... 65 C5
Wimbledon SW20 ... 178 D2
Gardeners Cl SE9 ... 166 A1
Gardeners Rd CR0 ... 204 D1
Garden Flats SW16 ... 160 A1
Garden Ho
2 Finchley N2 ... 30 B1
12 South Lambeth SW9 ... 138 A3
Garden Hospl The NW4 ... 46 C6
Gardenia Ct 1 BR3 ... 185 C3
Gardenia Rd
Bromley BR1 ... 210 C6
Enfield EN1 ... 17 C5
Gardenia Way IG8 ... 37 A5
Garden La
Bromley BR1 ... 187 B4
Streatham SW2 ... 160 B3
Garden Lodge Ct N2 ... 48 B6
Garden Mews W2 ... 245 B5
Garden Pl 28 E2 ... 95 D6
Garden Prim Sch CR4 ... 203 D6
Garden Rd
Bromley BR1 ... 187 B4
Penge SE20 ... 184 C2
Richmond TW9 ... 132 C2
St John's Wood NW8 ... 92 A4 229 B2
Walton-on-T KT12 ... 194 B2
Garden Row SE1 ... 116 D3 261 C6
Garden Royal 10 SW15 ... 156 D5
Garden St E1 ... 96 D2
Gardens The
Beckenham BR3 ... 186 A2
East Bedfont TW14 ... 149 B5
East Dulwich SE22 ... 140 A1
Harrow HA1, HA2 ... 42 A3
Pinner HA5 ... 41 B3
Stamford Hill N16 ... 51 D2
Garden Suburb Jun & Inf Schs NW11 ... 47 B4
Garden Terr
Knightsbridge SW7 ... 247 B1
Pimlico SW1 ... 259 C2
Garden Way NW10 ... 67 A2
Garden Wlk
Beckenham BR3 ... 185 B2
Shoreditch EC2 ... 95 C3 243 A6
Gardiner Ave NW2 ... 68 C3
Gardiner Cl
Chislehurst BR5 ... 190 C1
Dagenham RM8 ... 80 D4
Enfield EN3 ... 18 D5
Gardiner Ct NW10 ... 89 B6
Gardiner Ho SW11 ... 267 A2
Gardner Cl E11 ... 55 B3
Gardner Ct
Highbury N5 ... 73 A4
Hounslow TW3 ... 129 C2
Tottenham N22 ... 32 D1
Gardner Ho
Feltham TW13 ... 151 B2
Southall UB1 ... 106 D6
Gardner Ind Est SE26 ... 185 B5
Gardner Pl TW14 ... 150 B5
Gardner Rd E13 ... 99 B3
Gardners Cl N11 ... 15 A2
Gardners La EC4 ... 252 A6
Gardnor Mans 14 NW3 ... 70 A4
Gardnor Rd NW3 ... 70 B4
Gard St EC1 ... 234 D2
Garendon Gdns SM4 ... 201 D2
Garendon Rd SM4 ... 201 D2
Garenne Ct 10 E4 ... 20 A3
Gareth Cl KT4 ... 216 D6
Gareth Ct SW16 ... 159 D1
Gareth Gr BR1 ... 187 A6
Garfield Edmonton N9 ... 18 B3
Enfield EN2 ... 17 B6
Garfield Ho W2 ... 237 C1
Garfield Mews 7 SW11 ... 137 A2
Garfield Prim Sch
London N11 ... 31 C5
Wimbledon SW19 ... 180 A4
Garfield Rd
Chingford E4 ... 20 B3
Clapham SW11 ... 137 A2
Enfield EN3 ... 6 C1
Newham E13 ... 98 D3
3 Twickenham TW1 ... 153 A3
Wimbledon SW19 ... 180 A4
Garford St E14 ... 119 C6
Garganey Ct NW10 ... 67 B2
Garganey Wlk SE28 ... 124 C6
Garibaldi St SE18 ... 123 C2
Garland Ct 12 E14 ... 119 C6
Garland Dr TW3 ... 130 A3
Garland Ho
12 Kingston u T KT2 ... 176 A2
Stoke Newington N16 ... 73 B5
Garland Rd
Plumstead Comm SE18 ... 145 B5
Stanmore HA7 ... 26 A2
Garlands Ct CR0 ... 221 B4
Garlands Ho NW8 ... 91 D5
Garlands La HA1 ... 42 D1
Garlands The HA1 ... 42 D2
Garlick Hill EC4 ... 117 A6 252 B6
Garlies Rd SE23 ... 163 A1
Garlinge Ho 12 SW9 ... 138 C4
Garlinge Rd NW2 ... 69 B2
Garman Cl N18 ... 33 B5
Garman Rd N17 ... 34 C3
Garnault Mews EC1 ... 234 B1
Garnault Pl EC1 ... 234 B1
Garnault Rd EN1 ... 5 D5
Garner Cl RM8 ... 58 D1
Garner Rd E17 ... 36 A2
Garner St E2 ... 96 A5
Garnet Ct TW13 ... 149 C1
Garnet Ho KT4 ... 199 B1
Garnet Rd
South Norwood CR7 ... 205 B5
Willesden NW10 ... 67 C2
Garnet St E1 ... 118 C6
Garnett Cl SE9 ... 144 B2
Garnett Ho 5 NW3 ... 70 D3
Garnett Rd NW3 ... 70 D3
Garnett Way 3 E17 ... 35 A2
Garnet Wlk 8 E6 ... 100 A2
Garnham Cl 2 N16 ... 73 D6
Garnham St 1 N16 ... 73 D6
Garnies Cl SE15 ... 139 D5
Garrad's Rd SW16 ... 159 D1
Garrard Cl
Bexleyheath DA7 ... 147 C2
Chislehurst BR7 ... 188 D5
Garrard Ho BR2 ... 209 C5
Garrard Wlk NW10 ... 67 C2
Garratt Cl CR0 ... 220 A4
Garratt Ho 8 N16 ... 51 C1
Garratt La
Upper Tooting SW17, SW18 ... 180 C6
Wandsworth SW18 ... 157 D3
Garratt Park Sch SW18 ... 158 A1
Garratt Rd HA8 ... 26 C3

Garratts Rd WD23 8 A4
Garratt Terr SW17 180 C6
Garraway Ct SW13 134 C5
Garraway Ho SE21 161 D1
Garrett Cl W3 89 B2
Garrett Ho
8 Shepherd's Bush W12 90 B1
Teddington TW11 175 B4
Garrett St
EC1 95 A3 242 B6
Garrick Ave NW11 47 A3
Garrick Cl Ealing W5 88 A3
1 Richmond TW9 153 D6
Wandsworth SW18 136 A1
Garrick Cres CR0 221 C6
Garrick Ct HA8 26 B6
Garrick Dr
Hendon NW4 28 C1
Plumstead SE18 123 B3
Garrick Gdns KT8 195 C6
Garrick Ho
Chiswick W4 133 C6
2 Kingston u T KT1 198 A5
Mayfair W1 248 C3
7 Streatham SW16 181 C5
Garrick Ind Ctr NW9 45 D4
Garrick Pk NW4 28 D1
Garrick Rd
Greenford UB6 85 D3
Richmond TW9 132 C3
West Hendon NW9 45 D3
Garrick's Ait KT8 174 A1
Garricks Ho KT1 175 D1
Garrick St
WC2 116 A6 250 A6
Garrick's Villa
TW12 174 A1
Garrick Way NW4 46 D5
Garrick Yd WC2 250 A6
Garrison Cl
Hounslow TW4 151 B6
Shooters Hill SE18 144 C5
Garrison La KT9 214 A1
Garrowsfield EN5 13 B6
Garsdale Cl N11 31 A4
Garsdale Terr SW5 254 D2
Garside Cl
Hampton TW12 173 D4
Plumstead SE28 123 B3
Garside Ct 5 N20 14 D2
Garsington Mews
SE4 141 B2
Garson Ho W2 246 C6
Garston Ho 6 N1 72 D1
Garter Way SE16 118 D4
Garth Cl
Kingston u T KT2 176 B5
Ruislip HA4 40 D1
West Barnes SM4 200 D2
Garth Ct
Chiswick W4 133 B6
11 Harrow HA1 42 D3
Garth Dr N9 18 A2
Garth Ho NW2 69 B6
Garthland Dr EN5 12 C6
Garth Mews W5 88 A3
Garthorne Rd SE23 162 D4
Garth Rd
Child's Hill NW2 69 B6
8 Chiswick W4 111 B1
Kingston u T KT2 176 B5
West Barnes SM4 200 D2
Garth Road Ind Ctr The
SM4 200 D1
Garthside TW10 176 A5
Garth The
Hampton TW12 173 D4
Harrow HA3 44 B3
North Finchley N12 29 D5
Garthway N12 30 C4
Gartmoor Gdns
SW19 157 B3
Gartmore Rd IG3 79 D6
Garton Ho 6 N6 49 D2
Garton Pl SW18 158 A5
Gartons Cl EN3 6 C1
Gartons Way SW11 136 A2
Garvary Rd E16 99 B1
Garvens SE19 183 C5
Garway Rd W2 91 D1
Garwood Cl N17 34 B2
Garwood Lo N22 32 B3
Gascoigne Gdns IG8 36 C3
Gascoigne Pl 17 E2 95 D4
Gascoigne Prim Sch
IG11 101 A6
Gascoigne Rd IG11 101 A5
Gascony Ave NW6 69 C1
Gascoyne Ho 2 E9 74 D1
Gascoyne Rd E9 74 D1
Gaselee St E14 120 A6
Gasholder Pl
SE11 116 B1 260 D1
Gaskarth Rd
Balham SW12 159 B5
Burnt Oak HA8 27 A1
Gaskell Rd N6 48 D3
Gaskell St SW4 138 A3
Gaskin Ho N16 73 B5
Gaskin St N1 94 D6 234 C6
Gaspar Cl SW7 255 D4
Gaspar Mews SW5 255 D4
Gassiot Rd SW17 180 D6
Gassiot Way SM1 218 B5
Gasson Ho 24 SE14 140 D6
Gastein Rd W6 134 D6
Gastigny Ho EC1 235 B1
Gaston Bell Cl TW9 132 B2
Gaston Bridge Rd
TW17 193 B3
Gaston Gate SW8 270 C2
Gaston Rd CR4 203 A6
Gaston Way TW17 193 B4
Gataker Ho 5 SE16 118 B3
Gataker St 6 SE16 118 B3
Gatcliff Cl SW1 258 B1
Gatcombe Ct BR3 185 C3
Gatcombe Ho 20
SE22 139 C2
Gatcombe Mews
W5 110 B6
Gatcombe Rd
8 Newham E16 121 A5
Tufnell Pk N19 71 D5
Gatcombe Way EN4 2 D2
Gateacre Ct DA14 190 B6
Gate End HA6 22 A3
Gatefield Ct SE15 140 A2
Gateforth St NW8 237 A5
Gate Hill Ct W11 244 D4
Gatehill Rd HA6 22 A3
Gate Ho 4 KT6 198 A1
Gatehouse Cl KT2 177 A3
Gatehouse Sch E2 96 D5
Gatehouse Sq SE1 252 B4
Gateley Ho 6 SE4 140 D1
Gateley Rd SW9 138 B2
Gate Mews
SW7 114 C4 247 B1
Gater Dr EN2 5 B4
Gatesborough St
EC2 243 A6
Gates Ct SE17 262 A2
Gatesden WC1 233 B1
Gates Green Rd BR2,
BR4 225 A4
Gateside Rd SW17 158 D1
Gates 4 NW9 27 D1
Gatestone Ct 10
SE19 183 C4
Gatestone Rd SE19 183 C4
Gate St WC2 94 B1 240 C2
Gateway Arc N1 234 C4
Gateway Bsns Ctr
SE28 123 B3
Gateway Ho
Balham SW12 159 B5
4 Barking IG11 101 A6
3 Upper Tooting
SW17 180 C4
Gateway Mews 4
E8 73 D3
Gateway Prim Sch
NW8 92 B3 236 D6
Gateway Ret Pk E6 100 D3
Gateways Ct SM6 219 B3
Gateway SE17 139 A6
Gateways KT6 198 A4
Gateways The
Chelsea SW3 257 B3
Richmond TW9 131 D1
Gateway Trad Est
NW10 89 D4
Gatfield Gr TW13 151 C2
Gatfield Ho TW13 151 C2
Gathorne Rd N22 32 C2
Gathorne St 19 E2 96 D5
Gatley Ave KT19 214 D3
Gatliff Rd
SW1 115 B1 258 C1
Gatling Rd SE18,
SE2 124 A1
Gatonby St SE15 139 D4
Gatting Cl HA8 27 A3
Gatting Way UB8 60 A2
Gatton Prim Sch
SW17 180 C6
Gatton Rd SW17 180 C6
Gattons Way DA14 191 B6
Gatward Cl N21 16 D5
Gatward Gn N9 17 D2
Gatwick Ho 3 E14 97 B1
Gatwick Rd SW18 157 B4
Gauden Cl SW4 137 D2
Gauden Rd SW4 137 D2
Gaugin Ct 18 SE16 118 B1
Gauntlet Cl UB5 63 A1
Gauntlet 1 NW9 27 D1
Gauntlett Ct HA0 65 B3
Gauntlett Rd SM1 218 B3
Gaunt St SE1 262 A6
Gautrey Rd SE15 140 C3
Gautrey Sq 5 E6 100 B1
Gavel St SE17 262 D4
Gaven Ho N17 33 C1
Gaverick Mews 3
E14 119 C2
Gavestone Cres
SE12 165 B4
Gavestone Rd SE12 165 B4
Gavestone Terr
SE12 165 B4
Gaviller Pl 3 E5 74 B4
Gavina Cl SM4 202 C4
Gavin Ho 1 SE18 123 C2
Gawain Wlk N9 18 A1
Gawber St E2 96 C4
Gawsworth Cl E15 76 D3
Gawthorne Ave NW7 29 A5
Gawthorne Ct E3 97 C5
Gay Cl NW2 68 B3
Gaydon Ho W2 91 D2
Gaydon La NW9 27 C2
Gayfere Rd
Redbridge IG5 56 B6
Stoneleigh KT17 216 A3
Gayfere St
SW1 116 A3 260 A5
Gayford Rd W12 111 D4
Gay Ho N16 73 C3
Gayhurst Ct 9 UB5 84 C4
Gayhurst Ho NW8 237 B6
Gayhurst Prim Sch
E8 74 A1
Gayhurst Rd E8 74 A1
Gayhurst SE17 139 B6
Gaylor Rd UB5 63 B3
Gaymead NW8 91 D6
Gaynesford Rd
Forest Hill SE23 162 D2
Wallington SM5 218 D1
Gay Rd E15 98 B5
Gaysham Ave IG2 56 D4
Gaysham Hall IG5 56 D6
Gaysley Ho SE11 261 A3
Gay St SW15 134 D2
Gayton Cres NW3 70 B4
Gayton Ct
3 Harrow HA1 42 D3
New Malden KT3 199 D4
Gayton Ho E3 97 C3
Gayton Rd
Abbey Wood SE2 124 C3
Hampstead NW3 70 B4
Harrow HA1 43 A3
Gayville Rd SW11 158 D5
Gaywood Cl SW2 160 C3
Gaywood Rd E17 53 C6
Gaywood St SE1 261 D5
Gaza St
SE17 116 D1 261 C1
Gaze Ho 11 E14 98 B1
Gean Ct 3 E11 76 B4
Gearies Inf Sch IG2 56 D4
Gearies Jun Sch IG2 56 D4
Geariesville Gdns
IG6 56 D5
Gearing Cl SW17 181 A6
Geary Ho N7 72 B3
Geary Rd NW10 68 A3
Geary St N7 72 B3
GEC Est HA9 65 D6
Geddes Pl 3 DA6 147 C1
Gedeney Rd N17 33 A2
Gedge Ct CR4 202 C5
Gedling Ho SE22 139 D2
Gedling Pl SE1 263 D6
Geere Rd E15 98 D6
Gees Ct W1 238 B1
Gee St EC1 95 A3 242 A6
Geffrey's Ct SE9 166 A1
Geffrye Ct N1 95 C5
Geffrye Mus* E2 95 D5
Geffrye St E2 95 D5
Geldart Rd SE15 140 B5
Geldeston Rd E5 74 A6
Gellatly Rd SE14 140 D3
Gell Cl UB10 60 B5
Gemima Ct SM1 217 C3
Gemini Bsns Ctr E16 98 B3
Gemini Gr UB5 85 A4
Gemini Ho 11 E3 97 C6
Gemma Ct BR3 185 B1
General Gordon Pl
SE18 122 D2
Generals Wlk The EN3 7 A6
General Wolfe Rd
SE10 142 B4
Genesis Bsns Pk
NW10 88 D5
Genesis Cl TW19 148 B3
Genesis Ho KT6 197 D1
Genesta Rd SE18 145 A6
Geneva Cl TW17 171 C1
Geneva Ct
Hendon NW9 45 D4
1 Putney SW15 156 D6
Geneva Ct continued
Stoke Newington N16 51 B1
Geneva Dr SW9 138 C1
Geneva Gdns RM6 59 A4
Geneva Rd
Kingston u T KT1 198 A5
Thornton Heath CR7 205 A4
Genever Cl E4 35 C5
Genista Rd N18 34 B5
Genoa Ave SW15 156 C6
Genoa Ho 19 E1 96 D3
Genoa Rd SE20 184 C2
Genotin Rd EN1 5 B2
Genotin Terr EN1 5 B2
Gentleman's Row EN2 5 A2
Gentry Gdns E13 99 A4
Geoffrey Chaucer Tech
Coll SE1 117 B3 262 D5
Geoffrey Cl SE5 139 A3
Geoffrey Ct SE4 141 B2
Geoffrey Gdns E6 100 A5
Geoffrey Ho SE1 262 D6
Geoffrey Jones Ct
NW10 90 A6
Geoffrey Rd SE4 141 B2
George Akass Ho 5
SE18 123 A1
George Beard Rd 11
SE8 119 B2
George Beare Lo 9
SW4 159 C6
George Belt Ho 8
E2 96 D4
George Carver Ho
E7 77 A3
George Comberton Wlk
4 E12 78 C3
George Cres N10 31 A3
George Ct
Buckhurst Hill IG9 21 D2
St James WC2 250 B5
George Davies Lodge
IG6 57 A4
George Downing Est
N16 73 D6
George Eliot Ho
SW1 259 B3
George Eliot Jun & Inf
Schs NW8 92 B6 229 C6
George Elliot Ho
SE17 262 A2
George Elliston Ho 13
SE1 118 A1
George Eyre Ho
NW8 229 D3
George Gange Way
HA3 42 D6
George Green's Sec Sch
E14 120 A1
George Groves Rd
SE20 184 A2
George Ho 8 SE26 184 B5
George Inn Yd SE1 252 C3
George La
Hayes BR2 209 B1
Lewisham SE13 164 A5
George Lansbury Ho
7 Bow E3 97 B4
8 Willesden NW10 67 C1
Wood Green N22 32 C2
George Lashwood Ct 12
SW9 138 B1
George La
Wanstead E18 55 B6
Woodford E18 37 A1
George Leybourne Ho
15 E1 118 A6
George Lindgren Ho
SW6 264 D4
George Loveless Ho 4
E2 95 D4
George Lovell Dr EN3 7 C6
George Mathers Rd
SE11 261 C4
George Mews NW1 232 A1
George Mitchell Sch
E10 53 D1
George Parr Ho N21 16 D4
George Peabody Ct
NW1 237 A4
George Rd
Chingford E4 35 C4
Kingston u T KT2 177 A3
New Malden KT3 199 D4
George Row SE16 118 A4
Georges Mead WD6 10 A5
George Spicer Prim Sch
EN1 5 D2
George Sq SW19 201 C6
George's Rd N7 72 B3
George's Sq SW6 264 D6
George St
Barking IG11 79 A1
6 Canning Town E16 98 D1
Ealing W7 108 C5
Hounslow TW3,
TW5 129 B3
George St continued
Marylebone
W1 92 D1 237 D2
George Street Sta
CR0 221 A6
George St
Richmond TW10 153 D6
Southall UB2 107 A2
South Croydon CR0 221 B6
George Taylor CT N9 18 B1
George Tingle Ho
SE1 263 D6
George Tomlinson Prim
Sch E11 54 C1
Georgetown Cl 4
SE19 183 C5
Georgette Pl SE10 142 A5
George Vale Ho 35
E2 96 A5
George V Ave HA2,
HA5 41 C6
Georgeville Gdns
IG6 56 D5
George V Way UB6 87 B6
George Walter Ho 11
SE16 118 C2
George Wyver Cl
SW18 157 A4
George Yd
City of London EC3 242 D1
Mayfair W1 115 A6 248 B6
Georgiana St
NW1 93 C6 232 B6
Georgian Cl
Hayes BR2 209 B1
Ickenham UB10 60 A4
Stanmore HA7 25 A3
Georgian Ct
Croydon CR0 205 B1
12 Hackney E9 96 C6
3 Hendon NW4 46 B4
Wembley HA9 66 D2
Georgian Ho HA0 65 A5
Georgian Lo HA5 40 B4
Georgian Village The
E17 54 A6
Georgian Way HA1 64 B6
Georgia Rd
New Malden KT3 199 A5
South Norwood CR7 182 D2
Georgina Ct 5
TW1 153 C5
Georgina Gdns 10
E2 95 D4
Geraint Rd BR1 187 A6
Geraldine Ct 6 NW9 46 A5
Geraldine Rd
Brentford W4 132 C6
Wandsworth SW18 158 A6
Geraldine St SE11 261 C5
Gerald Mews SW1 258 B4
Gerald Rd
Belgravia
SW1 115 A2 258 B4
Dagenham RM8 59 B1
Newham E16 98 D3
Gerard Ave TW4 151 C4
Gerard Ct NW2 68 D3
Gerard Rd
Barnes SW13 133 D4
Harrow HA1 43 A3
Gerards Cl SE16 118 C1
Gerboa Ct 6 E4 36 B5
Gerda Rd SE9 167 A2
Germander Way E15 98 C4
German Sch The
TW10 153 D3
Gernigan Ho SW18 158 B5
Gernon Rd E3 97 A5
Geron Way NW2 68 C6
Gerrard Gdns HA5 40 A4
Gerrard Ho 5 SE14 140 D5
Gerrard Pl W1 249 D6
Gerrard Rd
N1 94 D5 234 D4
Gerrards Cl N14 15 C6
Gerrard's Ct W5 109 D3
Gerrard St
W1 115 D6 249 D6
Gerridge Ct SE1 261 B6
Gerridge St
SE1 116 C3 261 B6
Gerry Raffles Sq E15 76 B2
Gertrude Rd DA17 125 C2
Gertrude St
SW10 136 A6 266 B5
Gervase Cl HA9 67 A5
Gervase Rd HA8 27 B2
Gervase St SE15 140 B5
Getters Talmud Torah
N16 51 B2
Ghent St SE6 163 C2
Ghent Way E8 73 D2
Giant Arches Rd
SE24 161 A5
Giant Tree Hill WD23 8 B3
Gibbards Cott 1
IG11 79 D1
Gibbfield Cl RM6 59 A6
Gibbings Ho SE1 251 D1
Gibbins Rd E15 76 A1
Gibbon Ho NW8 236 D5
Gibbon Rd Acton W3 111 C6
Kingston u T KT2 176 A3
Nunhead SE15 140 C3
Gibbons Mews NW11 47 B4
Gibbons Rd NW10 67 C2
Gibbon's Rents SE1 253 A3
Gibbon Wlk SW15 134 A1
Gibbs Ave SE19 183 B5
Gibbs Cl SE19 183 B5
Gibbs Gn
Edgware HA8 27 A6
West Kensington
W14 113 B1 254 D2
Gibbs Green Rd
W14 113 B1 254 C2
Gibbs Green Sch
W14 113 B1 254 D2
Gibbs Ho
6 Balham SW12 159 B4
2 Bromley BR1 186 D2
Gibbs Rd N18 34 C6
Gibbs Sq SE19 183 B5
Gibraltar Ho NW10 89 C5
Gibraltar Wlk 28 E2 95 D4
Gibson Bsns Ctr 10
N17 33 D3
Gibson Cl
Bethnal Green E1 96 C3
Chessington KT9 213 C3
Isleworth TW7 130 B2
Southgate N21 16 C5
Gibson Ct
9 Friern Barnet
N11 30 D5
Hinchley Wood
KT10 212 D5
Gibson Gdns N16 73 D6
Gibson Ho
South Croydon
CR2 221 A2
Sutton SM1 217 C4
Gibson Rd
Dagenham RM8 58 C1
Ickenham UB10 60 B4
Lambeth SE11 260 D3
Sutton SM1 217 D3
Gibson's Hill SW16 182 C3
Gibson Sq N1 94 C6 234 B6
Gibson St SE10 120 C1
Gideon Cl DA17 125 D2
Gideon Mews W5 109 D4
Gideon Rd SW11 137 A2
Giesbach Rd N19 71 D6
Giffard Rd N18 33 C4
Giffen Square Mkt
SE8 141 C5
Giffin St SE8 141 C5
Gifford Gdns W7 86 C2
Gifford Ho
5 Clapham SW4 137 D1
Greenwich SE10 120 B1
Pimlico SW1 259 A1
Gifford Prim Sch
UB5 85 B5
Gifford St N1 72 A1
Gift La E15 98 D6
Giggs Hill BR5 190 A2
Giggs Hill Gdns KT7 197 A1
Giggs Hill Rd KT7 197 A2
Gilbert Cl
Kidbrooke SE18 144 B4
1 Merton SW19 179 D2
Gilbert Ct W5 88 B1
Gilbert Gr HA8 27 B2
Gilbert Ho
Barbican EC2 242 B3
Deptford SE8 141 C6
5 Globe Town E2 96 D4
Pimlico SW1 258 D1
South Lambeth SW8 270 A4
5 Walthamstow E17 54 A6
Gilbert Pl
WC1 94 A2 240 A3
Gilbert Rd
Belvedere DA17 125 C3
Lambeth
SE11 116 C2 261 B4
Merton SW19 180 A3
Pinner HA5 40 D5
Plaistow BR1 187 A3
Gilbert Scott Inf Com
Sch CR2 223 A1
Gilbert Scott Jun Com
Sch CR2 223 A1
Gilbert Sheldon Ho
W2 236 D4
Gilbertson Ho 11
E14 119 C3
Gilbert St Enfield EN3 6 C6
Hounslow TW3 130 A2
Leyton E15 76 C4

Gilbert St *continued*
Marylebone W1 93 A1 238 B1
Gilbey Cl UB10 60 D4
Gilbey Rd SW17 180 C5
Gilbeys Yd NW1 71 A1
Gilbourne Rd SE18 145 D6
Gilby Ho 5 E9 74 D2
Gilda Ave EN3 19 A6
Gilda Cres N16 52 A1
Gilda Ct NW7 28 A2
Gildea Cl HA5 23 C3
Gildea St W1 238 D3
Gilden Cres NW5 71 A3
Gildersome St SE18 144 C6
Gilders Rd KT9 214 B2
Giles Coppice SE19 183 D6
Giles Ho
5 Bermondsey SE16 118 A3
Notting Hill W11 91 C1
Gilesmead SE5 139 B4
Gilfrid Cl UB8 82 D1
Gilkes Cres SE21 161 C5
Gilkes Pl SE21 161 C5
Gillam Ho 9 SE16 118 C2
Gillan Ct SE12 165 B1
Gillan Gn WD23 8 A2
Gillards Mews 6 E17 53 C5
Gillards Way E17 53 C5
Gill Ave E16 99 A1
Gill Ct SE18 123 A2
Gillender St E3 98 A3
Gillespie Prim Sch N5 72 D5
Gillespie Rd N4, N5 72 D5
Gillett Ave E6 100 A5
Gillette Cnr TW7 131 A5
Gillett Ho N8 50 A6
Gillett Pl 27 E8 73 C3
Gillett Rd CR7 205 B5
Gillett St E8, N16 73 C3
Gillfoot NW1 232 A3
Gillham Terr N17 34 A3
Gillian Ho HA3 24 C4
Gillian Park Rd SM3 201 B1
Gillian St SE13 163 D6
Gillies Ct
Sidcup DA14 189 C6
Southgate N21 16 B6
Gillies St NW5 71 A3
Gilling Ct 5 NW3 70 C2
Gillingham Ho SW1 259 A4
Gillingham Mews SW1 259 A4
Gillingham Rd NW2 69 A5
Gillingham Row SW1 259 A4
Gillingham St SW1 115 C2 259 A4
Gillings Ct EN5 1 A1
Gillison Wlk 19 SE16 118 A3
Gillman Dr E15 98 D6
Gillman Ho 24 E2 96 A5
Gillray Ho
Chelsea SW10 266 C5
2 Sutton SM1 218 B3
Gills Ct 2 EN5 14 A6
Gill St E14 119 B6
Gillum Cl EN4 14 D3
Gilmore Cl UB10 60 C5
Gilmore Cres TW15 170 C4
Gilmore Ct N11 30 D5
Gilmore Ho SW4 136 D1
Gilmore Rd SE13 142 B1
Gilpin Ave SW14 133 B1
Gilpin Cl
Mitcham CR4 180 C1
Paddington W2 236 B4
Gilpin Cres
Edmonton N18 33 D5
Twickenham TW2 151 D4
Gilpin Ho
9 Edmonton N9 18 A1
New Malden KT3 199 C4
Gilpin Rd E5 75 A4
Gilpin Way UB3 127 B5
Gilray Ho W2 246 C6
Gilsland Rd CR7 205 B5
Gilstead Ho IG11 102 B5
Gilstead Rd SW6 135 D3
Gilston Rd SW10 114 A1 256 B1
Gilton Rd SE6 164 C1
Giltspur St EC1 94 D1 241 D2
Gilwell Cl E4 7 D1
Gilwell Ct 7 E5 74 B4
Gippeswyck Cl HA5 22 D2
Gipsy Cnr W3 89 B2
Gipsy Hill Sta SE19 183 C5
Gipsy Hill SE19 183 C5
Gipsy La SW15 134 B2
Gipsy Moth IV* SE10 142 A6
Gipsy Rd
Bexley DA16 146 D3
West Norwood SE27 183 B6
Gipsy Road Gdns SE27 183 A6
Giralda Cl E16 99 D2
Giraud St E14 97 D1
Girdlers Rd W14 112 D2
Girdlestone Wlk N19 71 C6
Girdwood Rd SW18, SW19 157 A4
Girling Ho 9 N1 95 C6
Girling Way TW14 128 A2
Gironde Rd SW6 135 B5 264 D3
Girtin Ho
6 Belmont SM2 217 D1
4 Northolt UB5 84 D5
Girton Ave NW9 44 C6
Girton Cl UB5 64 A2
Girton Gdns CR0 223 C5
Girton Ho SW15 156 D5
Girton Rd
Forest Hill SE26 184 D5
Northolt UB5 64 A2
Girton Villas 6 W10 90 D1
Gisbourne Cl SM6 219 D5
Gisburn Ho 23 SE15 140 A5
Gisburn Mans N8 50 B5
Gisburn Rd N8 50 B5
Gissing Wlk N1 72 C1
Gittens Cl BR1 186 D6
Given-Wilson Wlk E13 98 D5
Glacier Way HA0 87 D5
Gladbeck Way EN2 4 D1
Gladding Rd E12 77 D4
Gladebury Ct 2 SW19 179 B4
Glade Cl KT6 213 D6
Glade Gdns CR0 207 A2
Glade La UB2 107 D4
Gladeside Cl KT9 213 D1
Gladeside
Croydon CR0 206 D3
Southgate N21 16 B4
Gladesmore Com Sch N15 52 A4
Gladesmore Rd N15 51 D3
Glades Sh Ctr The BR1 187 A1
Gladeswood Rd DA17 125 D2
Glade The
Bromley BR1 187 D1
Charlton SE7 143 C5
Croydon CR0 206 D3
Enfield EN2 4 C3
Hammersmith W12 112 B4
Southgate N21 16 B4
Stoneleigh KT17 216 A2
West Wickham BR4 223 D5
Woodford IG8 21 B1
Gladiator St SE23 163 A4
Glading Terr N16 73 D5
Gladioli Cl 6 TW12 173 C4
Gladsdale Dr HA5 40 B5
Gladsmuir Rd
Barnet EN5 1 A3
Upper Holloway N19 49 C1
Gladstone Ave
Feltham TW14 150 B5
Plashet E12 78 A1
Tottenham N22 32 D1
Twickenham TW2 152 B4
Gladstone Ct
12 Merton SW19 179 C3
Ruislip HA4 61 C6
Westminster SW1 259 D3
Willesden NW2 68 B3
Gladstone Gdns TW3 130 A4
Gladstone Ho
6 Mitcham SW19 180 D1
16 Poplar E14 97 C1
Gladstone Mews
3 Penge SE20 184 C3
Wood Green N22 32 C1
Gladstone Park Gdns NW2 68 B5
Gladstone Park Sch NW10 68 B3
Gladstone Par NW2 68 C5
Gladstone Pl KT8 196 C4
Gladstone Rd
Acton W4 111 B3
Buckhurst Hill IG9 21 C3
Farnborough BR6 227 A3
Kingston u T KT1 198 C6
Merton SW19 179 C3
Southall UB2 107 A4
Surbiton KT6 214 A6
Thornton Heath CR0 205 B2
Gladstone St SE1 261 C6
Gladstone Terr SW8 137 B4 268 D2
Gladstone Way HA3 42 C6
Gladwell Rd
London N8 50 B3
Plaistow BR1 187 A4
Gladwin Ho NW1 232 B3
Gladwyn Rd SW15 134 D2
Gladys Dimson Ho E7 76 D3
Gladys Rd NW6 69 C1
Glaisdale Sch SM2 217 B1
Glaisher St SE8 141 D6
Glamis Cres UB3 105 A3
Glamis Ct W3 110 D4
Glamis Est 3 E1 118 D6
Glamis Pl E1 118 C6
Glamis Rd E1 118 C6
Glamis Way UB5 64 A2
Glamorgan Cl CR4, SW16 204 A6
Glamorgan Ct 4 W7 86 D2
Glamorgan Rd KT1 175 C3
Glandford Way RM6 58 B4
Glanfield Rd BR3 207 B5
Glanleam Rd HA7 25 D6
Glanville Ho 4 SW12 159 C4
Glanville Mews HA7 25 A5
Glanville Rd
Bromley BR2 209 B6
Clapham Pk SW2 160 A6
Glasbrook Ave TW2 151 B3
Glasbrook Rd SE9 165 D4
Glasbury Ho 5 SW9 138 B1
Glaserton Rd N16 51 C2
Glasford St SW17 180 D4
Glasfryn Ct HA2 64 B6
Glasgow Ho W9 91 D5
Glasgow Rd
Edmonton N18 34 B5
Newham E13 99 B5
Glasgow Terr SW1 115 C1 259 A1
Glasier Ct 6 E15 76 C1
Glasse Cl W13 109 A6
Glasshill St SE1 116 D4 251 D2
Glasshouse Cl UB8 82 D2
Glasshouse Fields E1 118 D6
Glasshouse St W1 115 C6 249 B5
Glasshouse The SE13 142 A1
Glasshouse Wlk SE11 116 B1 260 C2
Glasshouse Yd EC1 242 A5
Glasslyn Rd N8 49 D4
Glassmill La BR2 186 D1
Glass St 4 E2 96 B3
Glass Yd SE18 122 C3
Glastonbury Ave IG8 37 D4
Glastonbury Ct
12 Deptford SE14 140 C5
1 Ealing W13 109 A5
Glastonbury Ho
London SE12 164 D6
Pimlico SW1 258 C2
Glastonbury Pl 22 E1 96 C1
Glastonbury Rd
Edmonton N9 18 A3
Morden SM4 201 C2
Glastonbury St NW6 69 B3
Glaston Ct W5 109 D5
Glaucus St E3 97 D2
Glazbury Rd W14 113 A1 254 B2
Glazebrook Cl SE21 161 B2
Glazebrook Rd TW11 174 D3
Gleave Ct 7 N20 14 D2
Glebe Ave Enfield EN2 4 D2
Harrow HA3 44 A6
Mitcham CR4 180 C1
Ruislip HA4 62 B2
Uxbridge UB10 61 A4
Woodford IG8 37 A4
Glebe Cl
1 Chiswick W4 111 C1
Uxbridge UB10 61 A4
Glebe Cotts
Feltham TW13 151 C1
Sutton SM1 217 D4
Glebe Cres
Harrow HA3 44 A6
Hendon NW4 46 C5
Glebe Ct
15 Bromley E3 97 D4
Ealing W5 109 D5
Hanwell W7 108 B6
Lewisham SE3 142 C2
Mitcham CR4 202 D6
Palmers Green N13 16 C1
Ruislip HA4 39 B2
Stanmore HA7 25 C5
Glebe Fst & Mid Sch HA3 44 A5
Glebe Gdns KT3 199 C2
Glebe Ho
8 Bermondsey SE16 118 B3
Feltham TW13 151 C1
Glebe House Dr BR2 209 B1
Glebe Ho 7 SE18 122 C2
Glebehyrst SE19 183 C6
Glebe La Barnet EN5 12 A5
Harrow HA3 44 A5
Glebeland Gdns TW17 193 A3
Glebelands Ave
Ilford IG2 57 B2
Woodford E18 37 A1
Glebelands Cl
Camberwell SE5 139 C2
Finchley N2 30 B2
Glebelands
East Molesey KT8 195 D5
Leyton E10 75 D6
Mitcham CR4 202 C6
Glebelands Rd TW14 150 A4
Glebe Path CR4 202 D6
Glebe Pl SW3 136 C6 267 A6
Glebe Prim Sch UB10 61 B4
Glebe Rd
Barnes SW13 134 A3
Belmont SM2 217 A1
Bromley BR1 187 A2
Dagenham RM10 81 D2
Dalston E8 73 D1
Finchley N3 30 A2
Hayes UB3 105 D5
Hornsey N8 50 B5
Stanmore HA7 25 C5
Wallington SM5 218 D2
Willesden NW10 68 A2
Glebe Sch BR4 224 B6
Glebe Side TW1 152 D5
Glebe Sq CR4 202 D6
Glebe St W4 111 C1
Glebe The
Chislehurst BR7 189 A2
Lewisham SE3 142 C2
New Malden KT4 199 D1
Streatham SW16 181 D6
West Drayton UB7 104 B2
Glebe Way
Feltham TW13 151 C1
West Wickham BR4 224 A6
Glebeway IG8 37 C5
Gledhow Gdns SW5 256 A3
Gledstanes Rd W14 113 A1 254 B1
Gledwood Ave UB4 84 A2
Gledwood Cres UB4 83 D2
Gledwood Ct UB4 83 D2
Gledwood Dr UB4 83 D2
Gledwood Gdns UB4 84 A2
Gleed Ave WD23 8 B2
Gleeson Dr BR6 227 D4
Glegg Pl 3 SW15 134 D1
Glenaffric Ave E14 120 B2
Glen Albyn Rd SW19 156 D2
Glenalla Rd HA4 39 D2
Glenalmond Ho
Ashford TW15 148 A1
2 Putney SW15 156 D5
Glenalmond Rd HA3 44 A5
Glenalvon Way 5 SE7 122 A2
Glena Mount SM1 218 A4
Glenarm Coll IG1 78 D6
Glenarm Rd E5 74 C4
Glen Ave TW15 170 C6
Glenavon Cl KT10 213 A1
Glenavon Ct KT4 216 B6
Glenavon Lo 5 E18 55 A6
Glenavon Rd E15 76 C1
Glenbarr Cl SE9 144 D2
Glenbow Rd BR1 186 C5
Glenbrook N EN2 4 B1
Glenbrook Prim Sch SW4 159 D5
Glenbrook Rd NW6 69 C3
Glenbrook S EN2 4 B1
Glenbuck Ct 6 KT6 198 A3
Glenbuck Rd KT6 198 A3
Glenburnie Rd SW17 158 D1
Glencairn Dr W5 87 C3
Glencairne Cl E16 99 D2
Glencairn Rd SW16 182 A3
Glen Cl TW17 192 C5
Glencoe Ave IG2 57 C2
Glencoe Dr RM10 81 C4
Glencoe Mans 6 SW9 138 C5
Glencoe Rd UB4 84 D3
Glencorse Gn WD19 22 D6
Glen Cres IG8 37 B4
Glencroft Ct SM1 217 C3
Glen Ct
6 Bromley BR1 186 D3
9 Penge SE20 184 B2
Sidcup DA14 190 A6
Glendale Ave
Edgware HA8 26 C6
Ilford RM6 58 C2
Wood Green N22 32 C3
Glendale Cl SE9 144 C2
Glendale Dr SW19 179 B5
Glendale Gdns HA9 44 A1
Glendale Mews BR3 185 D2
Glendale Way SE28 124 C6
Glendall St SW9 138 B1
Glendarvon St SW15 134 D2
Glendevon Cl HA8 10 D1
Glendish Rd N17 34 B2
Glendor Gdns NW7 27 B6
Glendower Gdns 10 SW14 133 B2
Glendower Pl SW7 256 C4
Glendower Prep Sch SW7 114 B2 256 C4
Glendower Rd
Chingford E4 20 B3
Mortlake SW14 133 B2
Glendown Ho 2 E8 74 A3
Glendown Rd SE2 124 A1
Glendun Ct W3 111 C6
Glendun Rd W3 111 C6
Gleneagle Lo BR3 185 C2
Gleneagle Mews SW16 181 D5
Gleneagle Rd SW16 181 D5
Gleneagles Cl
21 Bermondsey SE16 118 B1
Crofton BR6 211 B1
South Oxhey WD19 22 D6
Gleneagles Ct 4 TW11 175 A5
Gleneagles W13 87 B2
Gleneagles Gn 1 BR6 211 B1
Gleneagles HA7 25 B4
Gleneagles Twr 2 UB1 86 A1
Gleneldon Mews SW16 182 A6
Gleneldon Rd SW16 182 A6
Glenelg Rd SW2 160 A6
Glenesk Rd SE9 144 D1
Glenfarg Rd SE6 164 B3
Glenfield Cres HA4 39 B2
Glenfield Rd
Ashford TW15 171 A4
Ealing W13 109 B4
Streatham SW12 159 C3
Glenfield Terr W13 109 B5
Glenfinlas Way SE5 138 D5
Glenforth St SE10 120 D1
Glengall Ct SE23 163 A4
Glengall Gr E14 120 A3
Glengall Pass 2 NW6 91 C6
Glengall Rd
Bexley DA7 147 A2
Camberwell SE15 139 D6
Edgware HA8 10 D1
Kilburn NW6 91 B6
Woodford IG8 37 B4
Glengall Terr SE15 139 D6
Glengarnock Ave E14 120 A2
Glengarry Rd SE22 161 D6
Glen Gdns CR0 220 C4
Glenham Dr IG2 56 D4
Glenhead Cl SE9 144 D2
Glenhill Cl N3 29 C1
Glen Ho 6 E16 122 C5
Glenhouse Rd SE9 166 C6
Glen Ho SM6 219 C4
Glenhurst Ave
Gospel Oak NW5 71 A4
Ruislip HA4 39 A1
Sidcup DA5 169 B3
Glenhurst 4 BR3 186 A2
Glenhurst Ct 1 SE19 183 D5
Glenhurst Rd
Brentford TW8 109 C1
North Finchley N12 30 B5
Glenhurst Rise SE19 183 A3
Glenilla Rd NW3 70 C2
Glenister Ho UB3 106 B5
Glenister Park Rd SW16 181 D3
Glenister Rd SE10 120 D1
Glenister St E16 122 C5
Glenkerry Ho 1 E14 98 A1
Glenlea Rd SE9 166 C6
Glenloch Ct 2 NW3 70 C2
Glenloch Rd
Enfield EN3 6 C3
Maitland Pk NW3 70 C3
Glenluce Rd SE3 143 A6
Glenlyon Rd SE9 166 C6
Glenmead IG9 21 C3
Glenmere Ave NW7 28 A4
Glen Mews E17 53 B4
Glenmill TW12 173 B5
Glenmore Ho 6 TW10 154 A5
Glenmore Lawns W13 87 A1
Glenmore SW15 156 D5
Glenmore Rd
Bexley DA16 145 D4
Maitland Pk NW3 70 C2
Glenmore Way IG11 102 A5
Glenmount Path 1 SE18 123 A1
Glennie Ct SE21 162 A3
Glennie Ho SE10 142 A4
Glennie Rd SE27, SW16 160 C1
Glenny Rd IG11 79 A2
Glenorchy Cl UB4 85 A2
Glenpark Ct W13 109 A6
Glenparke Rd E7 77 B2
Glen Rd
Chessington KT9 214 A5
Newham E13 99 C3
Walthamstow E17 53 B4
Glenridding NW1 232 B3
Glen Rise IG8 37 B4
Glenrosa St SW6 136 A3
Glenrose Ct DA14 190 B5
Glenrose Ho 9 SM1 218 A4
Glenroy St W12 90 C1
Glensdale Rd SE4 141 B2
Glenshaw Mans 7 SW9 138 C5
Glenshiel Rd SE9 166 C6
Glentanner Way SW17 158 B1
Glen Terr E14 120 A4
Glentham Gdns SW13 134 B6
Glentham Rd SW13 134 B6
Glen The
Beckenham BR2 186 C1
Eastcote Village HA5 40 B4
Enfield EN2 4 D1
Locksbottom BR6 226 C5
Rayners La HA5 41 A2
Southall UB2 107 B1
South Croydon CR0 222 D5
Wembley HA9 65 D4
Glenthorne Ave CR0 206 C1
Glenthorne Cl SM3 201 C1
Glenthorne Gdns
Cheam SM3 201 C1
Ilford IG6 56 D5
Glenthorne High Sch SM3 201 C1
Glenthorne Mews W6 112 B2
Glenthorne Rd
Friern Barnet N11 31 A5
Hammersmith W6 112 B2
Kingston u T KT1 198 B5
Walthamstow E17 53 A4
Glenthorpe SW15 134 A1
Glenthorpe Rd SM4 200 D4
Glenton Rd SE13 142 C1
Glentrammon Ave BR6 227 D2
Glentrammon Cl BR6 227 D3
Glentrammon Gdns BR6 227 D2
Glentrammon Rd BR6 227 D2
Glentworth Ct HA8 26 B5
Glentworth St NW1 92 D3 237 D5
Glenure Rd SE9 166 C6
Glen View Rd BR1 187 D1
Glenview SE2 146 D6
Glenville Ave EN2 5 A5
Glenville Gr SE8 141 B5
Glenville Mews SW18 157 C4
Glenville Rd KT2 176 C2
Glen Wlk TW7 152 B6
Glenwood Ave NW9 45 C1
Glenwood Cl HA1 42 D4
Glenwood Ct
7 Sidcup DA14 190 A6
6 Wanstead E18 55 A6
Glenwood Gdns IG2 56 C4
Glenwood Gr NW9 45 A1

Glenwood Ho 3 EN5 . . 13 D6
Glenwood Rd
Edgware NW7 . . . 11 C1
Forest Hill SE6 . . . 163 C3
Harringay N15 . . . 50 D4
Hounslow TW3 . . . 130 B2
Stoneleigh KT17 . . . 216 A2
Glenwood Way CR0 . . 206 D3
Glenworth Ave E14 . . 120 B2
Gliddon Dr E5 . . . 74 B4
Gliddon Rd
W14 . . . 113 A1 254 A2
Glimpsing Gn DA18 . . 125 A3
Glisson Rd UB10 . . . 82 C5
Globe Ct SE18 . . . 145 A6
Globe Pond Rd
SE16 . . . 119 A5
Globe Prim Sch E2 . . . 96 C4
Globe Rd
Bethnal Green E1,
E2 . . . 96 C3
Stratford E15 . . . 76 D3
Woodford IG8 . . . 37 C4
Globe St SE1 . 117 B4 252 C1
Globe Terr 9 E2 . . . 96 C4
Globe Theatre The*
SE1 . . . 252 A5
GLOBE TOWN . . . 96 D4
Globe View EC4 . . . 252 A6
Globe Yd W1 . . . 238 C1
Glossop Ho TW7 . . . 131 A1
Gloster Rd KT3 . . . 199 C5
Gloucester Ave
Camden Town
NW1 . . . 93 A6 231 B6
Falconwood DA16 . . . 145 D1
Sidcup DA15 . . . 167 C2
Gloucester Cir SE10 . . 142 A5
Gloucester Cl
Thames Ditton
KT7 . . . 197 A1
Willesden NW10 . . . 67 B1
Gloucester Cres
Camden Town
NW1 . . . 93 B6 231 C6
Staines TW18 . . . 170 A4
Gloucester Ct
6 Acton W3 . . . 88 C1
10 Belmont SM2 . . . 217 C1
Borough The SE1 . . . 262 B6
City of London EC3 . . 253 B5
Dulwich SE22 . . . 162 A3
5 Ealing W7 . . . 86 D2
Golders Green NW11 . . 47 B2
Harrow HA1 . . . 42 C6
Redbridge IG1 . . . 56 B2
Richmond TW9 . . . 132 C5
8 Surbiton KT6 . . . 197 D2
Gloucester Dr
Finsbury Pk N4 . . . 72 D6
London NW11 . . . 47 C5
Gloucester Gate Mews
NW1 . . . 231 C4
Gloucester Gate
NW1 . . . 231 C4
Gloucester Gdns
Cockfosters EN4 . . . 15 A6
Golders Green NW11 . . 47 B2
Paddington W2 . . . 236 A2
Redbridge IG1 . . . 56 A2
Sutton SM1 . . . 217 D6
Gloucester Gr HA8 . . . 27 B2
Gloucester Ho
Kilburn NW6 . . . 91 C5
Richmond TW10 . . . 154 C6
Gloucester Lo 9
CR0 . . . 221 D6
Gloucester Mews
Paddington W2 . . . 236 B1
Walthamstow E17 . . . 53 C2
Gloucester Mews W
W2 . . . 236 B1
Gloucester Par
Bexley DA15 . . . 168 A6
Hayes UB3 . . . 105 A3
Gloucester Pk SW7 . 256 A4
Gloucester Pl Mews
W1 . . . 92 D2 237 D3
Gloucester Pl
W1 . . . 92 D2 237 D4
Gloucester Prim Sch
SE15 . . . 139 C5
Gloucester Rd
Acton W3 . . . 111 A4
Croydon CR0 . . . 205 C2
Ealing W5 . . . 109 C4
Edmonton N18 . . . 33 D5
Enfield EN2 . . . 5 A5
Erith DA17 . . . 125 B1
Feltham TW13 . . . 150 C3
Hampton TW12 . . . 173 D3
Harrow HA1 . . . 41 D4
Higham Hill E17 . . . 34 D1
Hounslow TW4 . . . 129 A1

Gloucester Rd *continued*
Ilford E12 . . . 78 B4
Kingston u T KT1,
KT2 . . . 176 D1
Leyton E10 . . . 53 C2
New Barnet EN5 . . . 14 A6
Richmond TW9 . . . 132 C5
South Kensington
SW7 . . . 114 A2 256 A4
Teddington TW11 . . . 174 C5
Tottenham N17 . . . 51 B6
Twickenham TW2 . . . 152 A3
Wanstead E11 . . . 55 C4
Gloucester Road Sta
SW7 . . . 114 A2 256 A4
Gloucester Sq
6 Hackney E2 . . . 96 A6
Paddington
W2 . . . 92 C1 237 A1
Gloucester St
SW1 . . . 115 C1 259 A2
Gloucester Terr
W2 . . . 92 A1 236 B1
Gloucester W14 . . . 254 D3
Gloucester Way EC1 . 234 B1
Gloucester Wlk
W8 . . . 113 C4 245 B2
Glover Cl SE2 . . . 124 C2
Glover Dr N18 . . . 34 C4
Glover Ho
London SE15 . . . 140 B1
2 South Hampstead
NW6 . . . 70 A1
Glover Rd HA5 . . . 40 D3
Glovers Gr HA4 . . . 38 D2
Glovers Lo 24 TW10 . . 153 D6
Glowhill Ct N12 . . . 30 A3
Gloxinia Wlk TW12 . . . 173 C4
Glycena Rd SW11 . . . 136 D2
Glyn Ave EN4 . . . 2 B1
Glyn Cl SE25 . . . 183 C2
Glyn Ct Stanmore HA7 . . 25 B4
West Norwood SE27 . 160 C1
Glyndale Grange
SM2 . . . 217 D2
Glyndebourne Ct 5
UB5 . . . 84 C4
Glyndebourne Pk
BR6 . . . 226 D6
Glynde Mews SW3 . . 257 B5
Glynde Rd DA7 . . . 147 A2
Glynde Reach WC1 . . 233 B1
Glynde St SE4 . . . 163 B5
Glyndon Rd SE18 . . . 123 B2
Glyn Dr DA14 . . . 190 B6
Glynfield Rd NW10 . . . 67 C1
Glyn Mans W14 . . . 254 B4
Glynne Rd N22 . . . 32 C1
Glyn Rd Clapton Pk E5 . . 74 D4
Enfield EN3 . . . 6 C1
North Cheam KT4,
SM3 . . . 216 D6
Glyn St SE11 . . . 260 C1
Glynwood Ct 7
SE23 . . . 162 C2
Goater's Alley SW6 . 264 D3
Goat La EN1 . . . 5 D5
Goat Rd CR4 . . . 202 D2
Goat Wharf TW8 . . . 132 A6
Godalming Ave
SM6 . . . 220 B3
Godalming Rd E14 . . . 97 D2
Godbold Rd E15 . . . 98 C4
Goddard Cl TW17 . . . 192 B6
Goddard Ct HA3 . . . 25 A1
Goddard Ho SW19 . . . 156 D2
Goddard Pl N19 . . . 71 C5
Goddard Rd BR3 . . . 207 A5
Goddards Way IG1 . . . 57 B1
Goddarts Ho E17 . . . 53 C6
Godfrey Ave
Northolt UB5 . . . 85 A6
Twickenham TW2 . . . 152 B4
Godfrey Hill SE18 . . . 122 A2
Godfrey Ho EC1 . . . 235 C1
Godfrey Rd SE18 . . . 122 B2
Godfrey St
Chelsea
SW3 . . . 114 C1 257 B2
Mill Meads E15 . . . 98 A5
Godfrey Way TW4 . . . 151 B4
Goding St
SE11 . . . 116 A1 260 B1
Godley Rd SW18 . . . 158 B3
Godliman St EC4 . . . 252 A6
Godman Rd SE15 . . . 140 B3
Godolphin Cl N13 . . . 32 D4
Godolphin Ho
Primrose Hill NW3 . . . 70 C1
7 Streatham SW2 . . 160 C3
Godolphin & Latymer
Sch W6 . . . 112 B2
Godolphin Pl W3 . . . 111 B6
Godolphin Rd W12 . . . 112 B4
Godson Rd CR0 . . . 220 C5
Godson St N1 . . . 234 A4
Godstone Ct 1 N16 . . . 51 C1

Godstone Ho
Borough The SE1 . . . 262 D6
1 Kingston u T KT2 . 176 D4
Godstone Rd
Sutton SM1 . . . 218 A4
Twickenham TW1 . . . 153 B5
Godstow Rd SE2 . . . 124 C4
Godwin Cl
Shoreditch N1 . . . 235 B4
West Ewell KT19 . . . 215 A2
Godwin Ct NW1 . . . 232 B4
Godwin Ho
2 Haggerston E2 . . . 95 D5
Kidbrooke SE18 . . . 144 B4
Kilburn NW6 . . . 91 D5
Godwin Jun Sch E7 . . . 77 B4
Godwin Prim Sch
RM9 . . . 81 A1
Godwin Rd
Bromley BR1,
BR2 . . . 209 C6
Forest Gate E7 . . . 77 B4
Godwyn Ho 13 KT6 . . . 198 A3
Goffers Ho SE3 . . . 142 C3
Goffers Rd SE3,
SE13 . . . 142 C3
Goffs Rd TW15 . . . 171 B4
Goffton Ho 14 SW9 . . . 138 B3
Goidel Cl SM6 . . . 219 D4
Golborne Gdns
5 Kensal Town
W10 . . . 91 A3
West Kilburn W10 . . . 91 B3
Golborne Mews 9
W10 . . . 91 A2
Golborne Rd W10 . . . 91 A2
Golda Cl EN5 . . . 12 D5
Golda Ct N3 . . . 29 B1
Goldbeaters Gr HA8 . . . 27 C3
Goldbeaters Prim Sch
HA8 . . . 27 B2
Goldcliff Cl SM4 . . . 201 C2
Goldcrest Cl
Newham E16 . . . 99 D2
Woolwich SE28 . . . 124 C6
Goldcrest Mews W5 . . 87 D2
Goldcrest Way
Bushey WD23 . . . 8 A3
New Addington CR0 . . 224 B1
Golden Cres UB3 . . . 105 D5
Golden Cross Mews 2
W11 . . . 91 B1
Golden Ct
4 Barnet EN4 . . . 2 C1
Ealing W7 . . . 108 C6
Hounslow TW3 . . . 130 B3
10 Richmond TW9 . . . 153 D6
Golden Hinde The*
SE1 . . . 252 C4
Golden Hind Pl 5
SE8 . . . 119 B2
Golden La
EC1 . . . 95 A3 242 B5
Golden Manor W7 . . . 108 C6
Golden Mews SE20 . . . 184 C2
Golden Par 2 E17 . . . 54 A6
Golden Plover Cl
E16 . . . 99 A1
Golden Sq
W1 . . . 115 C6 249 B6
Golders Cl HA8 . . . 26 D5
Golders Ct NW11 . . . 47 B2
Golders Gdns NW11 . . . 47 B2
GOLDERS GREEN . . . 47 B2
Golders Green Coll
NW11 . . . 47 C1
Golders Green Cres
NW11 . . . 47 C2
Golders Green Rd
NW11 . . . 47 A2
Golders Green Sta
NW11 . . . 47 C1
Golders Hill Sch
NW11 . . . 47 C2
Golderslea NW11 . . . 47 C1
Golders Manor Dr
NW11 . . . 47 A3
Golders Park Cl
NW11 . . . 47 C1
Golders Rise NW4 . . . 46 D4
Golders Way NW11 . . . 47 B2
Golderton 2 NW4 . . . 46 C5
Goldfinch Rd SE28 . . . 123 B3
Goldhawk Ind Est The
W6 . . . 112 B3
Goldhawk Mews 2
W12 . . . 112 B4
Goldhawk Rd W12 . . . 112 A3
Goldhawk Road Sta
W12 . . . 112 C4
Goldhaze Cl IG8 . . . 37 D3
Gold Hill HA8 . . . 27 B4
Goldhurst Terr NW6 . . . 70 A1
Goldie Ho N19 . . . 49 D2
Goldie Leigh Hospl
SE2 . . . 146 C6
Golding Cl KT9 . . . 213 C2

Golding Ct 7 IG1 . . . 78 C5
Golding St E1 . . . 96 A1
Goldington Cres
NW1 . . . 232 C4
Goldington Ct NW1 . 232 C5
Goldington St
NW1 . . . 93 D5 232 C4
Gold La HA8 . . . 27 B4
Goldman Cl E2 . . . 96 A3
Goldmark Ho SE3 . . . 143 B2
Goldney Rd W9 . . . 91 C3
Goldrill Dr N11 . . . 15 A2
Goldsboro Rd
SW8 . . . 137 D5 269 D3
Goldsborough Cres
E4 . . . 20 A2
Goldsborough Ho
SW8 . . . 269 D1
Goldsdown Cl EN3 . . . 7 A3
Goldsdown Rd EN3 . . . 7 A3
Goldsmid St 2
SE18 . . . 123 C1
Goldsmith Ave
Acton W3 . . . 111 B6
Dagenham RM7 . . . 59 C2
Hyde The NW9 . . . 45 C3
Plashet E12 . . . 78 A2
Goldsmith Cl HA2 . . . 41 D1
Goldsmith Ct
Edgware HA8 . . . 26 B6
St Giles WC1 . . . 240 B2
Goldsmith Ho W3 . . . 111 B6
Goldsmith La NW9 . . . 45 A5
Goldsmith Rd
Acton W3 . . . 111 B5
Friern Barnet N11 . . . 30 D5
Higham Hill E17 . . . 34 D1
Leyton E10 . . . 53 D1
Peckham SE15 . . . 140 A4
Goldsmiths Bldgs
W3 . . . 111 B5
Goldsmiths Cl W3 . . . 111 B5
Goldsmiths Coll, Univ of
London SE14 . . . 141 A4
Goldsmith's Ct N6 . . . 49 B3
Goldsmith's Pl 6
NW6 . . . 91 D6
Goldsmith's Row E2 . . 96 A5
Goldsmith's Sq 17 E2 . 96 A5
Goldsmith St EC2 . . . 242 B2
Goldthorpe NW1 . . . 232 A5
Goldwell Ho SE22 . . . 139 C1
Goldwell Rd CR7 . . . 204 B5
Goldwin Cl SE14 . . . 140 C4
Goldwing Cl E16 . . . 99 A1
Golf Cl
South Norwood
SW16 . . . 182 C2
Stanmore HA7 . . . 25 C3
Golf Club Dr KT2 . . . 177 B3
Golfe Ho IG1 . . . 79 B5
Golfe Rd IG1 . . . 79 B5
Golfers View N12 . . . 30 B6
Golf Rd Bromley BR1 . . 210 C6
Ealing W5 . . . 88 B1
Golf Side Cl KT3 . . . 177 C1
Golfside Cl N20 . . . 14 C1
Golf Side TW2 . . . 152 B1
Gollogly Terr 9
SE7 . . . 121 C1
Gomer Gdns TW11 . . . 175 A4
Gomer Pl TW11 . . . 175 A4
Gomm Rd SE16 . . . 118 C3
Gomshall Ave SM6 . . . 220 A3
Gondar Gdns NW6 . . . 69 B3
Gondar Mans NW6 . . . 69 B3
Gonson St SE8 . . . 141 D6
Gonston Cl SW19 . . . 157 A2
Gonville Cres UB5 . . . 63 D2
Gonville Ct 6 EN4 . . . 14 D3
Gonville Ho 6
SW15 . . . 156 D5
Gonville Prim Sch
CR7 . . . 204 B4
Gonville Rd CR7 . . . 204 B4
Gonville St SW6 . . . 135 A2
Gooch Ho
Holborn EC1 . . . 241 A4
Lower Clapton E5 . . . 74 B5
Goodall Ho 10 SE4 . . . 140 D1
Goodall Rd E11 . . . 76 A5
Goodbehere Ho 7
SE27 . . . 183 A6
Gooden Ct HA1 . . . 64 C5
Goodenough Coll
WC1 . . . 94 B3 240 C6
Goodenough Rd
SW19 . . . 179 B3
Goodey Rd IG11 . . . 79 D1
Goodfaith Ho 18
E14 . . . 119 D6
Goodge Pl W1 . . . 239 B3
Goodge Street Sta
W1 . . . 93 D2 239 C4
Goodge St
W1 . . . 93 C2 239 B3
Goodhall Cl HA7 . . . 25 B4

Goodhall St NW10 . . . 89 D4
Good Hart Pl E14 . . . 119 A6
Goodhart Way BR4 . . . 208 C3
Goodhew Rd CR0 . . . 206 A3
Goodhope Ho 17
E14 . . . 119 D6
Gooding Cl KT3 . . . 199 A4
Goodinge Cl N7 . . . 72 A2
Goodinge Rd N7 . . . 72 A2
Gooding Ho 4 SE7 . . . 121 C1
Goodison Cl WD23 . . . 8 A6
Goodland Ho 1
KT3 . . . 199 C2
Goodman Cres
SW2 . . . 159 D2
Goodman Rd E10 . . . 54 A2
Goodmans Ct HA0 . . . 65 D4
Goodman's Stile 17
E1 . . . 96 A1
Goodman's Yd E1,
EC3 . . . 117 D6 253 C6
GOODMAYES . . . 58 B1
Goodmayes Ave IG3 . . 58 A1
Goodmayes Hospl
IG3 . . . 58 A4
Goodmayes La IG3 . . . 80 A5
Goodmayes Lodge
RM8 . . . 80 A4
Goodmayes Prim Sch
IG3 . . . 58 B1
Goodmayes Rd IG3 . . 58 A1
Goodmayes Ret Pk
RM6 . . . 58 B2
Goodmayes Sta IG3 . . 58 A1
Goodrich Com Sch
SE22 . . . 162 A5
Goodrich Ct 9 W10 . . . 90 D1
Goodrich Ho
20 Bethnal Green
E2 . . . 96 C5
Stamford Hill N16 . . . 51 C2
Goodrich Rd SE22 . . . 162 A5
Goodridge Ho E17 . . . 36 A3
Good Shepherd RC
Prim Sch
Catford BR1 . . . 186 D6
New Addington CR0 . 223 D1
Good Shepherd RC
Prim Sch The
W12 . . . 111 D4
Goodson Ho SM4 . . . 202 A2
Goodson Rd NW10 . . . 67 C1
Goodspeed Ho 20
E14 . . . 119 D6
Goodsway
NW1 . . . 94 A5 233 A4
Goodway Gdns E14 . . . 98 B1
Goodwill Ho 22 E14 . . 119 D6
Goodwin Cl
Bermondsey
SE16 . . . 117 D3 263 D5
Mitcham CR4 . . . 202 B6
Goodwin Ct
East Barnet EN4 . . . 14 C5
Hornsey N8 . . . 50 A6
2 Mitcham SW19 . . . 180 C3
Goodwin Dr DA14 . . . 168 D2
Goodwin Gdns CR0,
CR2 . . . 220 D2
Goodwin Ho
Edmonton N9 . . . 18 C3
2 Peckham SE15 . . . 140 B2
Goodwin Rd
Croydon CR0 . . . 220 D3
Edmonton N9 . . . 18 D3
Shepherd's Bush
W12 . . . 112 A4
Goodwins Ct WC2 . . . 250 A6
Goodwin St N4 . . . 72 C6
Goodwood Ave EN3 . . . 6 C6
Goodwood Cl
Morden SM4 . . . 201 C5
11 Stanmore HA7 . . . 25 C5
Goodwood Ct W1 . . . 238 D4
Goodwood Dr UB5 . . . 63 C2
Goodwood Ho
3 Acton Green
W4 . . . 111 A1
Penge SE26 . . . 184 B4
Goodwood Lo 1
SM6 . . . 219 D5
Goodwood Mans 3
SW9 . . . 138 C2
Goodwood Par BR3 . . 207 A5
Goodwood Rd SE14 . . 141 A5
Goodwyn Ave NW7 . . . 27 C5
Goodwyn Sch NW7 . . . 28 A5
Goodwyn's Vale N10 . . . 31 B2
Goodyear Ho 8 N2 . . . 30 B1
Goodyers Gdns NW4 . . 46 D4
Goosander Ct 34
NW9 . . . 27 D1
Goosander Way SE18,
SE28 . . . 123 B3
Gooseacre La HA3 . . . 43 D4

Goose Green Cl
BR5 . . . 190 A1
Goose Green Prim Sch
SE22 . . . 139 D1
Goose Green Trad Est
SE22 . . . 140 A1
Gooseley La E6 . . . 100 C4
Goose Sq 8 E6 . . . 100 B1
Goossens Cl 1
SM1 . . . 218 A3
Gophir La EC4 . . . 252 C6
Gopsall St N1 . . 95 B6 235 D5
Gordon Ave
Chingford E4 . . . 36 C4
Isleworth TW1 . . . 153 B6
Mortlake SW14 . . . 133 C1
Stanmore HA7 . . . 25 A4
Gordonbrock Prim Sch
SE4 . . . 163 C6
Gordonbrock Rd
SE4 . . . 163 C6
Gordon Cl E17 . . . 53 C3
Gordon Cres
Croydon CR0 . . . 205 D1
Hayes UB3 . . . 106 A2
Gordon Ct
Edgware HA8 . . . 26 B5
Hampton TW12 . . . 174 A5
5 Shepherd's Bush
W12 . . . 90 C1
18 Wimbledon
SW20 . . . 178 D3
Gordondale Rd SW18,
SW19 . . . 157 C2
Gordon Dr TW17 . . . 193 B2
Gordon Gdns HA8 . . . 26 D1
Gordon Gr SE5 . . . 138 D3
Gordon Hill EN2 . . . 5 A4
Gordon Hill Sta EN2 . . . 4 D4
Gordon Ho
2 Ealing W5 . . . 88 A4
Lee SE12 . . . 165 A4
17 Shadwell E1 . . . 118 C6
Gordon Hospl The
SW1 . . . 115 D2 259 C3
Gordon House Rd
NW5 . . . 71 A4
Gordon Inf Sch IG1 . . . 79 B5
Gordon Lo N16 . . . 51 B1
Gordon Mans
3 Barnet EN5 . . . 1 B1
Marylebone WC1 . . . 239 C5
Gordon Pl
W8 . . . 113 C4 245 B2
Gordon Prim Sch
SE9 . . . 144 B1
Gordon Rd
Ashford TW15 . . . 148 A1
Avery Hill DA15 . . . 167 C6
Barking IG11 . . . 101 C6
Beckenham BR3 . . . 207 B6
Chingford E4 . . . 20 C4
Chiswick W4 . . . 132 D6
Claygate KT10 . . . 212 C1
Dagenham RM6 . . . 59 B3
Ealing W13 . . . 109 C6
Edmonton N9 . . . 18 B2
Enfield EN2 . . . 5 B3
Finchley N3 . . . 29 B3
Harrow HA3 . . . 42 C6
Ilford IG1 . . . 79 B5
Isleworth TW3 . . . 130 A1
Kingston u T KT2 . . . 176 B2
Leyton E15 . . . 76 A4
Peckham SE15 . . . 140 B3
Richmond TW9 . . . 132 B3
Shepperton TW17 . . . 193 B3
Southall UB2 . . . 107 A2
Surbiton KT5 . . . 198 B2
Wallington SM5 . . . 218 D2
Wanstead E11 . . . 55 A3
Woodford E18 . . . 37 B2
Wood Green N11 . . . 31 D3
Yiewsley UB7 . . . 104 A6
Gordon Sq
WC1 . . . 93 D3 239 D6
Gordon St
Bloomsbury
WC1 . . . 93 D3 239 C6
Newham E13 . . . 99 A4
Gordon Way
Barnet EN5 . . . 1 B1
Bromley BR1 . . . 187 A2
Gore Ct NW9 . . . 44 C4
Gorefield Ho NW6 . . . 91 C5
Gorefield Pl NW6 . . . 91 C5
Gore Rd Hackney E9 . . . 96 C6
Merton SW20 . . . 178 C1
Goresbrook Rd
RM9 . . . 102 D6
Gore St SW7 . . 114 A3 256 B6
Gorham Ho 12 SW4 . . 159 C5
Gorham Pl W11 . . . 244 A5
Goring Gdns RM8 . . . 80 C4
Goring Rd N11 . . . 32 A4
Goring St EC3 . . . 243 B2
Goring Way UB6 . . . 86 A5

Gorleston Rd N15 51 B4
Gorleston St
W14 113 A2 254 B4
Gorman Rd SE18 122 B2
Gorringe Park Ave
CR4 181 A3
Gorringe Park Prim Sch
CR4 181 A2
Gorse Cl E16 99 A1
Gorsefield Ho 6
E14 119 C6
Gorse Rd CR0 223 C5
Gorse Rise SW17 181 A5
Gorse Wlk UB7 82 A1
Gorst Rd
London SW11 158 D5
North Acton NW10 89 B3
Gorsuch Pl 1 E2 95 D4
Gorsuch St E2 95 D4
Gosberton Rd SW12 159 A3
Gosbury Hill KT9 214 A4
Gosfield Rd RM8 59 C1
Gosfield St
W1 93 C2 239 A3
Gosford Gdns IG4 56 B4
Gosford Ho 25 E3 97 B5
Goshawk Gdns UB4 83 C5
Goslett Yd WC2 239 D2
Gosling Cl UB6 85 C4
Gosling Ho 2 E1 118 C6
Gosling Way SW9 138 C4
Gosmore Ct N9 18 B2
Gospatric Home Ho
SW14 133 C2
Gospatrick Rd N17 33 A2
GOSPEL OAK 71 A4
Gospel Oak Prim Sch
NW5 71 A4
Gospel Oak Sta NW5 71 A4
Gosport Ho 9
SW15 156 A3
Gosport Rd E17 53 B4
Gosport Wlk N17 52 B5
Gossage Rd
Hillingdon UB10 60 B1
Plumstead SE18 123 B1
Gosset St E2 96 A4
Gosshill Rd BR7 188 C1
Gossington Cl BR7 188 D6
Gosterwood St SE8 141 A6
Gostling Rd TW2 151 C3
Goston Gdns CR7 204 C6
Goswell Pl EC1 234 D1
Goswell Rd
EC1 94 D4 234 D2
Gothic Ct
17 Camberwell
SE5 139 A5
Harlington UB3 127 B6
Gothic Rd TW2 152 B2
Gottfried Mews NW5 71 C4
Goudhurst Ho 7
SE20 184 C3
Goudhurst Rd BR1 186 D5
Gough Ho
Islington N1 234 D6
4 Kingston u T KT1 176 A1
Gough Rd Enfield EN1 6 B3
Stratford E15 76 D4
Gough Sq EC4 94 C1 241 B2
Gough St
WC1 94 B3 240 D5
Gough Wlk 14 E14 97 C1
Gould Ct SE19 183 C5
Goulden Ho SW11 136 C3
Goulding Gdns CR7 183 A1
Gouldman Ho 33 E1 96 C3
Gould Rd
East Bedfont
TW14 149 C4
Twickenham TW2 152 C3
Gould's Gn UB8 104 D6
Gould Terr 26 E8 74 B3
Goulston St
E1 95 D1 243 C2
Goulton Rd E5 74 B4
Gourley Pl N15 51 C4
Gourley St N15 51 C4
Gourock Rd SE9 166 C6
Govan St E2 96 A6
Gover Ct 8 SW4 138 A3
Government Row EN3 7 C6
Govett Ave TW17 193 A4
Govier Cl E15 76 C1
Gowan Ave
SW6 135 A4 264 A2
Gowan Ho 22 E2 95 D4
Gowan Lea 4 E18 55 A5
Gowan Rd NW10 68 B2
Gower Cl SW4 159 C5
Gower Ct WC1 239 C6
Gower Ho
Barking IG11 79 A1
Hayes UB3 105 C6
Upper Tooting SW17 180 B4
Gower House Sch
NW9 67 A6

Gower Ho
12 Walthamstow
E17 53 D6
Walworth SE17 262 B2
Gower Mews WC1 239 D4
Gower Pl NW1,
WC1 93 D3 239 C6
Gower Rd
Hounslow TW7 130 D6
Upton E7 77 A2
Gower Sch The N7 72 A2
Gower St
WC1 93 D3 239 C5
Gower's Wlk E1 96 A1
Gowland Pl BR3 185 B1
Gowlett Rd SE15 140 A2
Gowlland Cl CR0 206 A2
Gowrie Rd SW11 137 A2
Graburn Way KT8 196 B6
Grace Ave DA7 147 B3
Grace Bsns Ctr CR4 202 D3
Gracechurch St EC2,
EC4 252 D6
Grace Cl
Burnt Oak HA8 27 A3
Mottingham SE9 165 D1
Grace Ct
5 Croydon CR0 220 D5
Twickenham TW2 152 C2
Gracedale Rd SW16 181 B5
Gracedyer Ho N22 32 A3
Gracefield Gdns
SW16 160 A1
Gracehill 2 E1 96 C2
Grace Ho
Kennington SE11 270 D6
Penge SE26 184 B5
Grace Jones Cl E8 74 A2
Grace Path 2 SE26 184 C6
Grace Pl E3 97 D4
Grace Rd CR0 205 A3
Graces Alley 14 SE1 118 A6
Grace's Mews SE5 139 C3
Graces Mews NW8 229 B3
Grace's Rd SE5 139 C3
Grace St E3 97 D4
Gradient The SE26 184 A6
Graeme Ct UB6 85 D4
Graeme Rd EN1 5 C3
Graemesdyke Ave
SW14 132 D1
Grafton Cl Ealing W13 87 A1
Twickenham TW4 151 B3
Worcester Pk KT4 215 C5
Grafton Cres NW1 71 B2
Grafton Ct
10 Dalston E8 74 A3
East Bedfont TW14 149 B3
Grafton Gdns
Dagenham RM8 81 A6
Harringay N4 51 A3
Grafton Ho
16 Bow E3 97 C4
12 Deptford SE8 119 B1
Grafton Jun & Inf Schs
RM8 81 B6
Grafton Mans SW4 137 C1
Grafton Mews W1 239 A5
Grafton Park Rd
KT4 215 C6
Grafton Pl
NW1 93 D4 232 D1
Grafton Prim Sch N7 72 A5
Grafton Rd
Acton W3 111 A6
Dagenham RM8 81 A6
Enfield EN2 4 B2
Gospel Oak NW5 71 A3
Harrow HA1 42 A4
Kingston u T KT3 199 C6
Thornton Heath CR0 204 C1
Worcester Pk KT4 215 C5
Grafton Sq SW4 137 C2
Grafton St
W1 115 B6 248 D5
Grafton Terr NW5 71 A3
Grafton Way
East Molesey KT8 195 B5
Marylebone W1 239 B5
Grafton Yd NW5 71 B2
Graham Ave
Ealing W13 109 B4
Mitcham CR4 181 A2
Graham Cl CR0 223 C6
Graham Ct
Bromley BR1 187 B3
5 Deptford SE14 140 D6
Northolt UB5 63 B3
GRAHAME PARK 27 C2
Grahame Park Way NW7,
NW9 27 D2
Grahame White Ho
HA3 43 D6
Graham Gdns KT6 198 A1
Graham Ho
5 Balham SW12 159 B4
6 Barnet EN5 1 D1

Graham Ho *continued*
Edmonton N9 18 C3
6 Tufnell Pk N19 71 D4
Woolwich SE18 144 D5
Graham Lo
Edgware HA8 26 B4
Hendon NW4 46 B3
Graham Mans
11 Barking IG11 80 A1
2 Hackney E8 74 B2
Graham Rd
Acton W4 111 B3
Bexleyheath DA6 147 C1
Dalston E8 74 A2
Hampton TW12 173 C6
Harringay N15 50 D6
Harrow HA3 42 C6
Hendon NW4 46 B3
Merton SW19 179 B3
Mitcham CR4 181 A2
Newham E13 99 A3
Graham St
N1 94 D5 234 D3
Graham Terr
SW1 115 A2 258 B3
Graham Twr W3 110 D3
Grainger Cl UB5 64 A3
Grainger Ct 22 SE5 139 A5
Grainger Rd
Isleworth TW7 130 D3
Tottenham N22 33 A2
Gramer Cl E11 76 B6
Grampian Cl
Harlington UB3 127 B5
Orpington BR6 211 D3
15 Sutton SM2 218 A1
Grampian Gdns NW2 47 A1
Grampians The 10
W14 112 D4
Gramsci Way SE6 163 D1
Granada St SW17 180 D5
Granard Ave SW15 156 B6
Granard Bsns Ctr
NW7 27 C4
Granard Ho 20 E9 74 D2
Granard Prim Sch
SW15 156 B5
Granard Rd SW11,
SW12 158 D4
Granary Cl N9 18 C4
Granary Ct 3 RM6 58 D2
Granary Mans SE28 123 A4
Granary Rd E1 96 B3
Granary Sq N1 72 C2
Granary St
NW1 93 D6 232 C5
Granary The SE8 141 C5
Granby Ho 13 SE18 122 B2
Granby Pl SE1 251 A1
Granby Rd
Eltham SE9 144 B2
Woolwich SE18 122 D3
Granby St
Bethnal Green E2 96 A3
Shoreditch E2 243 D6
Granby Terr
NW1 93 C5 232 A3
Grand Arc N12 30 A5
Grand Ave EC1 241 D4
Grand Ave E HA9 66 D3
Grand Ave N10 49 A5
Grand Avenue Prim Sch
KT5 199 A3
Grand Ave
Tolworth KT5 198 D3
Wembley HA9 66 C3
Grand Ct RM8 81 A5
Grand Depot Rd
SE18 122 C1
Grand Dr
Southall UB2 108 A4
West Barnes SM4,
SW20 200 C5
Granden Rd SW16 182 A1
Grandfield Ct W4 133 B6
Grandison Rd
London SW11 158 D6
North Cheam KT4 216 C5
Grand Junction Wharf
N1 235 A3
Grand Par London N4 50 D3
Mortlake SW14 133 A1
Tolworth KT6 198 C1
Wembley HA9 66 C6
Grand Union Cl W9 91 B2
Grand Union Cres E8 96 A6
Grand Union Ind Est
NW10 88 D5
Grand Union Way
UB2 107 C4
Grand Vitesse Ind Est
SE1 251 D3
Granfield St SW11 266 D1
Grange Ave
East Barnet EN4 14 D3
North Finchley N12 30 A5

Grange Ave *continued*
South Norwood
SE25 183 C1
Stanmore HA7 25 C1
Totteridge N20 13 A4
Twickenham TW2 152 C2
Woodford IG8 37 A3
Grange Cl
East Molesey KT8 195 D5
Edgware HA8 27 A5
Hayes UB3 83 C2
Heston TW5 129 B6
Grangecliffe Gdns
SE25 183 C1
Grange Cl
Sidcup DA15 168 A1
Woodford IG8 37 A3
Grangecourt Rd N16 51 C1
Grange Cres SE28 102 C1
Grange Ct
Belmont SM2 217 D1
4 Finchley N12 30 A4
Hackbridge SM6 219 B5
Harrow HA1 64 D5
Ilford IG6 57 A6
Littleton TW17 192 C5
Loughton IG10 21 D6
Northolt UB5 84 C5
Peckham SE15 139 D3
Pinner HA5 41 A6
Strand WC2 240 D1
Wembley HA0 65 C3
1 Willesden NW10 67 C4
Grange Dr BR7 188 B4
Grange Farm Cl HA2 64 A6
Grange Farm Est
TW17 193 C6
Grangefield NW1 72 A1
Grange Fst & Mid Schs
HA2 41 D1
Grange Gdns
London N14 15 D3
Pinner HA5 41 A5
South Norwood
SE25 183 C1
West Hampstead
NW3 69 D5
Grange Gr N1 73 A2
Grange Hill HA8 27 A5
Grangehill Pl SE9 144 B2
Grangehill Rd SE9 144 B1
Grange Hill SE25 183 C1
Grange Ho
6 Barking IG11 101 B6
Bermondsey SE1 263 C5
Willesden NW10 68 B1
Grange La SE21 161 D2
Grange Lo SW19 178 D4
Grange Mans KT17 215 D1
Grangemill 11 NW5 71 B4
Grangemill Rd SE6 163 C2
GRANGE MILLS 113 C3
Grange Mills SW12 159 C3
Grangemill Way
SE6 163 C2
GRANGE PARK 16 C6
Grange Park Ave
N21 17 A5
Grange Park Jun & Inf
Schs UB4 83 D3
Grange Park Pl
SW20 178 B3
Grange Park Prep Sch
N21 16 D5
Grange Park Prim Sch
N21 4 C1
Grange Park Rd
Leyton E10 53 D1
South Norwood CR7 205 B6
Grange Park Sta N21 16 D5
Grange Pk W5 110 A5
Grange Pl NW6 69 C1
Grange Prim Sch
Bermondsey
SE1 117 C3 263 A5
Ealing W5 109 D4
Newham E13 98 D4
Grange Rd
Barnes SW13 134 A4
Belmont SM2 217 C1
Bermondsey
SE1 117 D3 263 C5
Borehamwood WD6 10 B6
Burnt Oak HA8 27 B4
Chessington KT9 214 A4
Ealing W5 110 A5
East Molesey KT8 195 D5
Greenhill HA1 43 A4
Gunnersbury W4 110 D1
Hayes UB3 83 C1
Highgate N6 49 A3
Ilford IG1 79 A4
Kingston u T KT1 198 A6
Leyton E10 53 C1
Newham E13 98 D4
Orpington BR6 227 A6

Grange Rd *continued*
Roxeth HA2 64 B6
Southall UB1 107 A4
South Norwood SE19,
SE25 183 B1
Tottenham N17 34 A4
Walthamstow E17 53 A4
Willesden NW10 68 B2
Grange St N1 235 D5
Grange The
Bermondsey
SE1 117 D3 263 C5
Cockfosters EN4 2 D2
Croydon CR0 223 B6
Ealing W13 87 C2
7 Gunnersbury W4 110 D1
Hammersmith W12 112 B3
19 Maitland Pk NW3 70 D2
South Acton W3 110 D4
3 Walthamstow E17 53 A4
4 Wanstead E18 55 A6
Wembley HA0 66 C1
West Barnes KT3 200 A4
West Ewell KT19 215 B4
West Kensington
W14 113 B2 254 C3
Wimbledon SW19 178 D4
Grange Vale SM2 217 D1
Grange View Rd N20 14 A3
Grangeway Gdns
IG4 56 A4
Grangeway
London N12 29 D6
South Hampstead
NW6 69 C1
Grangeway The N21 16 D5
Grangeway IG8 37 C6
Grange Wlk
SE1 117 D3 263 C5
Grangewood Cl HA5 40 A4
Grangewood DA5 169 B3
Grangewood Ind Sch
E7 77 D1
Grangewood La
BR3 185 B4
Grangewood Sch
HA5 39 D4
Grangewood St E6 99 D6
Grange Yd
SE1 117 D3 263 C5
Granham Gdns N9 17 D2
Granite Apts E15 76 B2
Granite St SE18 123 D1
Granleigh Rd E11 76 C6
Grannary The 10
SE16 118 C4
Gransden Ave E8 74 B1
Gransden Ho 1
SE8 119 B1
Gransden Rd W12 111 D4
Grantbridge St
N1 94 D5 234 D4
Grantchester Cl HA1 64 D5
Grantchester 12
KT1 176 C1
Grant Cl London N14 15 C4
Shepperton TW17 192 D3
Tottenham N17 33 C1
Grant Ct
2 Chingford E4 20 A3
11 Hendon NW9 27 D1
Grantham Cl HA8 10 A1
Grantham Ct
Dagenham RM6 59 B2
Kingston u T KT2 175 D5
9 Rotherhithe
SE16 118 D4
Grantham Gdns RM6 59 B2
Grantham Gn WD6 11 A6
Grantham Ho
Ashford TW16 171 C3
12 Peckham SE15 140 A6
Grantham Pl W1 248 C3
Grantham Rd
Chiswick W4 133 C5
Little Ilford E12 78 C4
South Lambeth SW9 138 A3
Grant Ho
38 Clapham SW8 137 D3
Clerkenwell EC1 241 D4
Grantley Ho
2 Deptford SE14 140 D6
5 Putney SW19 156 D3
Grantley Pl KT10 212 A3
Grantley Rd TW4,
TW5 128 C3
Grantley St E1 96 D3
Grant Mus of Zoology &
Comparative
Anatomy*
WC1 93 D3 239 C5
Grantock Rd E17 36 B2
Granton Prim Sch
SW16 181 C3
Granton Rd Ilford IG3 58 A1
Sidcup DA14 190 C4
Streatham SW16 181 C2

Grant Pl 2 CR0 205 D1
Grant Rd
Battersea SW11 136 C2
Croydon CR0 205 D1
Harrow HA3 42 D6
Grants Cl NW7 28 D3
Grants Cotts KT10 212 B6
Grant St Islington N1 234 A4
Newham E13 99 A4
Grantully Rd W9 91 D4
Grant Way TW7 131 A6
Granville Ave
Feltham TW13 150 A2
Hounslow TW3,
TW4 151 C6
Lower Edmonton N9 18 C1
Granville Cl CR0 221 C6
Granville Ct
8 Deptford SE14 141 A5
Hornsey N4 50 B3
Shoreditch N1 235 D6
Granville Gdns
Ealing W5 110 B5
South Norwood
SW16 182 B3
Granville Gr SE13 142 A2
Granville Ho 18 E14 97 C1
Granville Ind Est
NW2 69 B6
Granville Mans 8
W12 112 C4
Granville Mews
DA14 190 A6
Granville Pk SE13 142 B2
Granville Pl
London N12 30 A3
Marylebone
W1 93 A1 238 A1
Pinner HA5 40 D6
Walham Green SW6 265 C3
Granville Point NW2 69 B6
Granville Rd
Bexley DA16 146 C2
Bowes Pk N13 32 B4
Child's Hill NW2 69 B6
Finchley N12 30 A3
Hayes UB3 105 D2
Hillingdon UB10 60 D2
Hornsey N4, N8 50 B3
Ilford IG1 78 D6
Kilburn NW6 91 C5
Merton SW19 179 C3
Sidcup DA14 190 B6
Tottenham N22 32 D2
Walthamstow E17 53 D3
Wandsworth SW18 157 B4
Woodford E18 37 B1
Granville Sq
3 Camberwell
SE15 139 C5
Finsbury
WC1 94 B4 233 D1
Granville St WC1 233 D1
Granwood Ct 5
TW7 130 C4
Grape St WC2 240 A2
Grapsome Cl KT9 213 C1
Grasdene Rd SE18 146 A5
Grasgarth Cl W3 111 A6
Grasmere Ave
Acton W3 111 B6
Kingston u T SW15 177 C6
Locksbottom BR6 226 D5
Merton SW19 201 C6
Ruislip HA4 39 A2
Twickenham TW3 151 D5
Wembley HA9 43 D1
Grasmere Cl TW14 149 D3
Grasmere Ct
Barnes SW13 134 A6
Bowes Pk N22 32 B4
Forest Hill SE26 184 A5
7 Sutton SM2 218 A2
Grasmere Gdns
Harrow HA3 25 A1
Locksbottom BR6 226 D5
Redbridge IG4 56 B4
Grasmere Ho 20 N16 73 B4
Grasmere NW1 231 D1
Grasmere Point 2
SE15 140 C5
Grasmere Prim Sch
N16 73 B4
Grasmere Rd
Bromley BR1 186 D3
Croydon SE25 206 B4
Locksbottom BR6 226 D5
Muswell Hill N10 31 B2
3 Newham E13 99 A5
Streatham SW16 182 B5
Tottenham N17 34 A4
Grasshaven Way
SE28 123 D5
Grassington Cl N11 31 A4

Grassington Rd DA14 . . . 190 A6
Grassmere Ct 6 EN1 . . 17 C6
Grassmount SE23 . . . 162 B2
Grass Pk N3 . . . 29 B2
Grassway SM6 . . . 219 C4
Grasvenor Ave EN5 . . . 13 C5
Grasvenor Avenue Inf Sch EN5 . . . 13 C5
Grateley Ho 10 SW15 . . . 156 B3
Gratton Rd W14 . . . 113 A3 254 A5
Gratton Terr NW2 . . . 68 D5
Graveley Ave WD6 . . . 11 A6
Graveley Ho 7 SE8 . . . 119 A2
Graveley 16 KT1 . . . 176 C1
Gravel Hill
Bexley DA6 . . . 169 D6
Church End N3 . . . 29 B1
Gravel Hill Cl DA6 . . . 169 D5
Gravel Hill Prim Sch DA6 . . . 169 D6
Gravel Hill CR0, CR2 . . 223 B1
Gravel Hill Sta CR0 . 223 A2
Gravel La E1 . . . 95 D1 243 C2
Gravel Rd
Keston Mark BR2 . . . 226 A6
Twickenham TW2 . . . 152 C3
Gravelwood Cl BR7 . . 167 A1
Gravenel Gdns 5 SW17 . . . 180 C5
Graveney Gr SE20 . . . 184 C3
Graveney Rd SW17 . . . 180 C6
Graveney Sch SW17 . 181 B5
Gravesend Rd W12 . . . 112 A6
Graves Est DA16 . . . 146 B3
Gray Ave RM8 . . . 59 B1
Gray Ct 8 KT2 . . . 175 D6
Grayfriars Pas EC1 . . 241 D2
Grayham Cres KT3 . . . 199 B5
Grayham Rd KT3 . . . 199 B5
Gray Ho SE17 . . . 262 B2
Grayland Cl BR1 . . . 187 D2
Grayland Ct WC1 . . . 233 C1
Grayling Cl E16 . . . 98 C3
Grayling Ct
Ealing W5 . . . 109 D5
Tottenham Hale N17 . . . 52 B5
Grayling Rd N16 . . . 73 B6
Grayling Sq E2 . . . 96 A4
Grays Cotts UB9 . . . 38 C1
Grays Court Hospl RM10 . . . 81 D1
Grayscroft Rd SW16 . . . 181 D3
Grays Farm Prim Sch BR5 . . . 190 B2
Grays Farm Production Village BR5 . . . 190 B2
Grays Farm Rd BR5 . . 190 B2
Grayshott Ct 10 SM2 . . . 217 D1
Grayshott Rd SW11 . . 137 A2
Gray's Inn Pl WC1 . . . 240 D3
Gray's Inn Rd WC1 . . . 94 B3 240 D6
Gray's Inn Sq WC1 . . . 94 C2 241 A4
Gray's Inn* WC1 . . . 94 B2 240 D4
Grays La TW15 . . . 170 D6
Grayson Ho EC1 . . . 235 B1
Gray's Rd UB10 . . . 60 A1
Gray St SE1 . . . 116 C4 251 B1
Grayswood Gdns SW20 . . . 178 B1
Grayswood Point 14 SW15 . . . 156 A3
Gray's Yd W1 . . . 238 B2
Graywood Ct N12 . . . 30 A3
Grazebrook Prim Sch N16 . . . 73 C6
Grazebrook Rd N16 . . . 73 B6
Grazeley Ct SE19 . . . 183 C5
Great Arthur Ho EC1 242 A5
Great Bell Alley EC2. 242 C2
Great Benty UB7 . . . 104 A2
Great Brownings SE21 . . . 183 D6
Great Bushey Dr N20 . . 13 D3
Great Cambridge Ind Est EN1 . . . 18 B6
Great Cambridge Junction N13, N18 . . . 33 B6
Great Cambridge Rd
Edmonton N9, N18 . . . 17 C3
Enfield EN1 . . . 6 A3
Great Castle St W1 . . 239 A2
Great Central Ave HA4 . . . 62 C3
Great Central St NW1 . . . 92 D2 237 C4
Great Central Way NW10 . . . 67 B4
Great Chapel St W1 . . . 93 D1 239 C2
Great Chart St SW11 . . . 136 A1
Great Chertsey Rd
Chiswick SW14, W4 . . . 133 B4
Feltham TW13, TW2 . 151 C1
Great Church La W6 . . . 112 D1
Great College St SW1 . . . 116 A3 260 A6
Great Croft WC1 . . . 233 B1
Great Cross Ave SE3 . . . 142 C5
Great Cumberland Mews W1 . . . 237 C1
Great Cumberland Pl W1 . . . 92 D1 237 D1
Great Dover St SE1 . . . 117 B3 262 C6
Greatdown Rd W7 . . . 86 D2
Great Eastern Bldgs 10 E8 . . . 74 B2
Great Eastern Ent Ctr E14 . . . 119 D4
Great Eastern Pier E14 . . . 119 C1
Great Eastern Rd E15 . . . 76 B2
Great Eastern St EC2 . . . 95 C3 243 A6
Great Eastern Wharf SW11 . . . 267 B3
Great Elms Rd BR2 . . . 209 C5
Greatfield Ave E6 . . . 100 B3
Greatfield Cl
London SE4 . . . 141 C1
4 Tufnell Pk N19 . . . 71 C4
Great Field
Hendon NW9 . . . 27 D2
7 Kentish Town NW5 . . . 71 C3
Greatfields Dr UB8 . . . 82 C2
Greatfields Rd IG11 . . . 101 B5
Great Fleete Way IG11 . . . 102 C5
Great Galley Cl IG11 . . . 102 C4
Great Gatton Cl CR0 . . . 207 A2
Great George St SW1 . . . 116 A4 250 A1
Great Guildford Bsns Sq SE1 . . . 252 A3
Great Guildford St SE1 . . . 117 A5 252 A3
Great Hall The 1 E11 . . . 55 B5
Greatham Wlk 8 SW15 . . . 156 A3
Great Harry Dr SE9 . . . 166 C1
Great James St WC1 240 C4
Great Marlborough St W1 . . . 93 C1 239 A1
Great Maze Pond SE1 . . . 117 B4 252 D2
Great Newport St WC2 . . . 250 A6
Great North Rd
Barnet EN5 . . . 1 A2
East Finchley N2 . . . 48 C5
New Barnet EN5 . . . 13 D6
Great North Way (Barnet By-Pass) NW4 . . . 46 D6
Greatorex Ho 13 E1 . . . 96 A2
Greatorex St E1 . . . 96 A2
Great Ormond St Hospl for Children WC1 . . . 94 B3 240 C5
Great Ormond St WC1 . . . 94 B3 240 C5
Great Percy St WC1 . . . 94 C4 234 A2
Great Peter St SW1 . . . 115 D3 259 D5
Great Portland Street Sta W1 . . . 93 B3 238 D5
Great Portland St W1 . . . 93 B2 238 D4
Great Pulteney St W1 . . . 249 B6
Great Queen St WC2 . . . 94 A1 240 B2
Great Russell Mans WC1 . . . 240 A3
Great Russell St WC1 . . . 94 A2 240 A3
Great St Helen's EC3 . . . 243 A2
Great St Thomas Apostle EC4 . . . 252 B6
Great Scotland Yd SW1, WC2 . . . 116 A5 250 A4
Great Smith St SW1 . . . 115 D3 259 D6
Great South West Rd TW6, TW14, TW4 . . . 148 B6
Great South-West Rd TW5 . . . 128 B2
Great Spilmans SE22 . . . 161 C6
Greatstone Ho 10 SE20 . . . 184 C3
Great Strand NW9 . . . 27 D1
Great Suffolk St SE1 . . . 116 D5 251 D3
Great Sutton St EC1 . . . 94 D3 241 D5
Great Swan Alley EC2 . . . 242 C2
Great Thrift BR5 . . . 211 A5
Great Titchfield St W1 . . . 93 C2 239 A3
Great Tower St EC3 . . . 117 C6 253 A6
Great Trinity La EC4 . 252 B6
Great Turnstile WC2. 240 D3
Great Western Ind Pk UB2 . . . 108 A4
Great Western Rd W2, W9 . . . 91 B2
Great West Ho TW8. 131 C6
Great West Rd
Brentford TW7, TW8 . . . 131 B6
Chiswick W4, W6 . . . 133 B6
Heston TW5, TW7 . . . 129 B4
Hounslow TW5, TW7 . . . 130 B5
Great West Road Cedars Rd W4 . . . 133 A6
Great West Road Hogarth La W4 . . . 133 C6
Great West Trad Est TW8 . . . 131 B6
Great Winchester St EC2 . . . 95 B1 242 D2
Great Windmill St W1 . . . 115 D6 249 C6
Greatwood BR7 . . . 188 C3
Great Yd SE1 . . . 253 B2
Greaves Cl IG11 . . . 79 C1
Greaves Cotts 10 E14 . . . 97 A2
Greaves Ct N8 . . . 50 C5
Greaves Pl SW17 . . . 180 C6
Greaves Twr SW10 . . 266 B4
Grebe Ave UB4 . . . 84 D1
Grebe Cl
Barking IG11 . . . 102 A3
Higham Hill E17 . . . 35 A3
Stratford E7 . . . 76 D3
Grebe Ct Cheam SM1 . . 217 B3
16 Cubitt Town E14 . . 120 A4
Grebe 3 NW9 . . . 27 D1
Grebe Terr 4 KT1 . . . 198 A6
Grecian Cres SE19 . . 182 D4
Greek Ct W1 . . . 239 D1
Greek St W1 . . . 93 D1 239 D1
Greenacre Cl
Barnet EN5 . . . 1 B5
Northolt UB5 . . . 63 B3
Greenacre Ct E8 . . . 74 A3
Greenacre Gdns E17 . . 54 A5
Greenacre Pl SM6 . . . 219 B6
Greenacres Ave UB10 . . . 60 C5
Greenacres
Bushey WD23 . . . 8 B2
Church End N3 . . . 29 A1
Greenacres Cl BR6 . . . 227 A4
Greenacres Dr HA7 . . . 25 B3
Greenacres SE9 . . . 166 C5
Green Acres UB4 . . . 84 B3
Greenacres Prim Sch SE9 . . . 166 C2
Greenacre Sq 26 SE16 . . . 118 D4
Green Acres
Sidcup DA14 . . . 189 D6
South Croydon CR0 . . 221 D5
Greenacre Wlk N14 . . . 15 D1
Green Arbour Ct EC1 . . . 241 C2
Green Ave
Ealing W13 . . . 109 B3
Edgware NW7 . . . 27 C6
Greenaway Gdns NW3 . . . 69 D4
Greenaway Ho
Finsbury WC1 . . . 234 A1
St John's Wood NW8 229 A6
Greenaway Terr TW19 . . . 148 A3
Greenbank Ave HA0 . . . 65 A3
Greenbank Cl E4 . . . 20 A2
Greenbank Cres NW4 . . . 47 A5
Greenbank Lo 2 BR7 . . . 188 C2
Green Bank N12 . . . 29 D6
Greenbanks HA1 . . . 64 C4
Green Bank E1 . . . 118 B5
Greenbay Rd SE7 . . . 143 D5
Greenberry St NW8 . 230 A3
Greenbrook Ave EN4 . . . 2 A4
Green CE Prim Sch The N17 . . . 51 D6
Green CE Sch Holy Trinity (Inf Annexe) The N15 . . . 51 D5
Green Cl
Beckenham BR2 . . . 208 C6
Carshalton SM5 . . . 218 D6
Feltham TW13 . . . 173 A5
Kingsbury NW9 . . . 45 A3
North End NW11 . . . 48 A2
Greencoat Pl SW1 . . . 115 C2 259 B4
Greencoat Row SW1 . . . 259 B5
Green Court Ave CR0 . . . 222 B6
Greencourt Ave HA8 . . 26 D2
Green Court Gdns CR0 . . . 222 B6
Greencourt Ho 25 E1 . . . 96 D3
Greencourt Rd BR5 . . 211 C4
Greencroft Ave HA4 . . . 62 C6
Greencroft Cl E16 . . . 99 D2
Greencroft Gdns
Enfield EN1 . . . 5 C2
South Hampstead NW6 . . . 70 A1
Greencroft HA8 . . . 27 A5
Greencroft Rd TW5 . . 129 B4
Green Ct
Ashford TW16 . . . 171 D4
2 Willesden NW10 . . . 67 C4
Greendale Cl SE22 . . . 161 C6
Greendale Ct CR2 . . . 221 A2
Green Dale SE22 . . . 161 C6
Greendale NW7 . . . 27 C6
Green Dragon Ct SE1 . . . 252 C3
Green Dragon Ho WC1 . . . 240 B2
Green Dragon La
Brentford TW8 . . . 110 B1
Southgate N21 . . . 16 D5
Green Dragon Prim Sch TW8 . . . 132 A6
Green Dragon Yd 24 E1 . . . 96 A2
Green Dr UB1 . . . 107 C5
Greene Ct 20 SE14 . . . 140 D6
Greene Ho SE1 . . . 262 C5
Green Elms IG6 . . . 57 A6
Green End
Chessington KT9 . . . 214 A4
Edmonton N21 . . . 16 D2
Greenend Rd W4 . . . 111 C4
Greener Ct 26 EN3 . . . 7 C6
Greener Ho 3 SW4 . . 137 D2
Green Farm Cl BR6 . . 227 D3
Greenfell Mans SE8 . . 141 D6
Greenfield Ave KT5 . . 198 D3
Greenfield Ct SE9 . . . 166 A1
Greenfield Dr
Bromley BR1 . . . 187 C1
Fortis Green N2 . . . 48 D5
Greenfield Gdns
Cricklewood NW2 . . . 69 A5
Crofton BR5 . . . 211 B2
Dagenham RM9 . . . 102 D6
Greenfield Ho 28 SW19 . . . 156 D3
Greenfield Rd
Dagenham RM9 . . . 102 C6
South Tottenham N15 . . 51 C4
Whitechapel E1 . . . 96 A1
Greenfields Prim Sch WD19 . . . 22 C5
Greenfields UB1 . . . 85 C1
Greenfield Way HA2 . . . 41 D6
GREENFORD . . . 86 A4
Greenford Ave
Ealing W7 . . . 86 C1
Southall UB1 . . . 107 B6
Greenford Gdns UB6 . . 86 A4
Greenford High Sch UB6 . . . 85 C4
Greenford Rdbt UB6 . . 86 B5
Greenford Rd
Greenford UB6 . . . 86 A3
Sudbury HA1, UB6 . . . 64 C3
Sutton SM1 . . . 217 D4
Greenford Sta UB6 . . . 86 B6
Greengate St E13 . . . 99 B4
Greengate UB6 . . . 65 B2
Green Gdns BR6 . . . 227 A3
Greenhalgh Wlk N2 . . . 48 A5
Greenham Cl SE1 . . . 251 A1
Greenham Cres E4 . . . 35 B4
Greenham Ho
5 Hackney E9 . . . 96 C6
Isleworth TW7 . . . 130 B2
Greenham Rd N10 . . . 31 A1
Greenhaven Dr SE28 . . . 102 B1
Greenheath Bsns Ctr 3 E2 . . . 96 B3
Green Hedges 8 TW1 . . . 153 C5
Greenheys Dr E18 . . . 54 D6
GREENHILL . . . 42 D4
Greenhill IG9 . . . 21 C3
Greenhill Cts SE7 . . . 122 B1
Greenhill Gdns UB5 . . . 85 B5
Greenhill Gr E12 . . . 78 A4
Greenhill NW3 . . . 70 B4
Greenhill Par EN5 . . . 13 D6
Greenhill Pk
Harlesden NW10 . . . 89 C6
New Barnet EN5 . . . 13 D6
Greenhill Rd
Harlesden NW10 . . . 89 C6
Harrow HA1 . . . 42 C3
Greenhill's Rents EC1 . . . 241 C4
Greenhills Terr 16 N1 . . . 73 B2
Greenhill SM1 . . . 218 A6
Greenhill Terr
Northolt UB5 . . . 85 B5
Woolwich SE18 . . . 122 B1
Greenhill Way
Harrow HA1 . . . 42 C3
Wembley Pk HA9 . . . 66 D6
Greenhill HA9 . . . 66 D6
Green Hill SE18 . . . 122 B1
Greenhithe Cl DA15 . . 167 C4
Green Ho TW7 . . . 130 D3
Greenholm Rd SE9 . . . 166 D6
Green Ho The 5 SW19 . . . 157 A3
Green Hundred Rd SE15 . . . 140 A6
Greenhurst Rd SE27 . . . 182 C5
Greening Ho SE13 . . . 142 B1
Greening St SE2 . . . 124 C2
Green La
Ashford TW16 . . . 171 D4
Chessington KT9 . . . 214 A1
Chislehurst SE9 . . . 166 D1
Dagenham RM8 . . . 81 B6
East Molesey KT8 . . . 195 D4
Edgware HA8 . . . 26 C5
Feltham TW13 . . . 173 A5
Hanwell W7 . . . 108 C4
Hendon NW4 . . . 46 D4
Hillingdon UB8 . . . 83 A2
Hounslow TW4 . . . 128 C1
Ilford IG1, IG3 . . . 79 C6
Morden SM4 . . . 201 D3
Greenland Cres UB2 . . . 106 D3
Greenland Ho
Bermondsey SE8 . . . 118 D1
4 Mile End E1 . . . 97 A3
Greenland Mews SE8 . . . 118 D1
Greenland Pl NW1 . . 231 D6
Greenland Quay SE16 . . . 118 D2
Greenland Rd
Barnet EN5 . . . 12 C5
Camden Town NW1 . . . 93 C6 232 A6
Greenlands
Borehamwood WD6 . . . 11 B5
Chessington KT19 . . . 214 D3
Greenland St NW1 . . 231 D6
Greenland Way CR0 . . . 203 D2
Green Lane Bsns Pk SE9 . . . 166 C2
Green Lane Cotts HA7 . . . 25 B6
Green Lane Gdns CR7 . . . 183 A1
Green Lane Mews SM4 . . . 201 D3
Green Lane Prim Sch KT4 . . . 200 B2
Green Lanes
London N4, N8, N15 . . . 50 D2
Palmers Green N13 . . . 16 C1
West Ewell KT19 . . . 215 C1
Green La
New Malden KT3 . . . 199 A4
New Malden KT4 . . . 200 A1
Penge SE20 . . . 184 D3
Shepperton TW17 . . . 193 A4
South Norwood CR7, SW16 . . . 182 C2
Stanmore HA7 . . . 25 B5
Greenlaw Ct W5 . . . 87 D1
Greenlaw Gdns KT3 . . 199 D2
Greenlawn La TW8 . . . 109 D2
Greenlawns N12 . . . 29 D4
Green Lawns
Ruislip HA4 . . . 40 C1
8 Woolwich SE18 . . 122 D2
Greenlaw St SE18 . . . 122 C3
Green Leaf Ave SM6 . . . 219 D4
Greenleaf Cl 8 SW2 . . . 160 C4
Greenleaf Ct N20 . . . 14 B3
Greenleafe Dr IG6 . . . 56 D6
Greenleaf Prim Sch E17 . . . 53 B6
Greenleaf Rd
5 Newham E6 . . . 99 C6
Walthamstow E17 . . . 53 B6
Greenleaf Way HA3 . . . 42 D6
Greenlea Pk SW19 . . 180 C2
Green Leas TW16 . . . 171 D4
Green Leas Cl TW16 . . . 171 D4
Green Leas KT1 . . . 198 A6
Greenleaves Ct TW15 . . . 170 D4
Green Link Wlk TW9 . . . 132 D4
Green Man Gdns W13 . . . 109 A6
Green Man Intc E11 . . . 54 D2
Green Man La
Ealing W13 . . . 109 A5
Hatton TW14 . . . 128 A1
Greenman St N1 . . . 95 A6 235 A6
Greenmead Cl SE25 . . 206 A4
Greenmead Sch SW15 . . . 156 B6
Green Moor Link N21 . . . 16 D4
Greenmoor Rd EN3 . . . 6 C1
Greenoak Pl EN4 . . . 2 D1
Green Oaks UB2 . . . 106 D2
Greenoak Way SW19 . . . 178 D6
Greenock Rd
Mitcham SW16 . . . 181 D2
11 South Acton W3 . . 111 A3
Greeno Cres TW17 . . . 192 C4
Greenpark Ct HA0 . . . 65 C1
Green Park Sta W1 . . . 115 C5 249 A4
Green Park* SW1, W1 . . . 115 B4 248 D2
Green Park Way UB6 . . 86 C
Green Pond Cl E17 . . . 53 B
Green Pond Rd E17 . . . 53 A
Green Pt E15 . . . 76 C2
Green Rd
East Barnet N14 . . . 15 B
Whetstone N20 . . . 14 A1
Green Ride IG10, E4 . . . 21 A
Greenroof Way SE10 . . . 120 D
Green Sch (Girls) The TW7 . . . 131 A
Greens Ct W1 . . . 249 C
Green's Ct W11 . . . 244 C
Greens Ct HA9 . . . 65 D
Greens End SE18 . . . 122 D
Greenshank Cl E17 . . . 35 A
Greenshaw High Sch SM1 . . . 218 A
Greenshields Ind Est E16 . . . 121 B
Greenside Cl
Catford SE6 . . . 164 B
Whetstone N20 . . . 14 B
Greenside RM8 . . . 58 C
Greenside Prim Sch W12 . . . 112 A
Greenside Rd
Shepherd's Bush W12 . . . 112 A
Thornton Heath CR0 . 204 C
Greenside DA5 . . . 169 A
Greenslade Prim Sch SE18 . . . 145 B
Greenslade Rd IG11 . . . 79 B
Greensleeves Ho UB2 . . . 107 D
Greensleeves Manor SM2 . . . 217 D
Greenstead Ave IG8 . . . 37 C
Greenstead Cl IG8 . . . 37 C
Greenstead Gdns
Putney SW15 . . . 156 B
Woodford IG8 . . . 37 C
Green St Enfield EN3 . . . 6 D
Mayfair W1 . 115 A6 248 A
Newham E13 . . . 99 C
Greenstone Mews E11 . . . 55 A
GREEN STREET GREEN . . . 227 C
Green Street Green Prim Sch BR6 . . . 227 D
Greenstreet Hill SE4 . . . 140 D

Green St
Sunbury TW16 172 A1
Upton E7 77 C1
Greensward Ho
SW6 136 A3
Green Terr EC1 234 B1
Green The Acton W3 89 C1
Buckhurst Hill IG9 21 B3
Chingford E4 20 B3
Claygate KT10 212 D2
Ealing W5 109 D6
Edmonton N9 18 A2
Erith DA7 147 C4
Falconwood DA16 145 C1
Feltham TW13 150 B2
Grove Pk BR1 165 A1
Hackbridge SM6 219 A6
Hayes BR2 209 A2
Heston TW5 129 C6
Kingston u T KT3 177 A1
Merton SM4 201 A5
Palmers Green N14 15 D1
Richmond TW9 131 D1
[7] Richmond TW9 153 D6
Sidcup DA14 190 A5
Southall UB2 107 B4
Southgate N21 16 C4
St Paul's Cray BR5 190 B3
Stratford E15 76 D2
Sutton SM1 217 D5
Tottenham N17 33 A4
Twickenham TW2 152 C2
Upper Halliford
TW17 193 C5
Uxbridge UB10 61 A6
Wallington SM5 219 A4
Wanstead E11 55 B3
Wembley HA0 65 A6
Wimbledon SW19 178 D5
Woodford IG8 37 A5
Green Vale
Bexley DA6 168 D6
Ealing W5 88 B1
Greenvale Rd SE9 144 C1
Greenvale Sch SE23 163 A1
Green Verges HA7 25 D3
Greenview Ave CR0 207 A3
Green View KT9 214 B1
Greenview Cl W3 111 C5
Greenview Ct
Ashford TW15 170 B6
East Dulwich SE22 140 A1
Oakleigh Pk N20 14 A4
Wandsworth SW18 158 C4
Greenway Ave E17 54 B5
Green Way BR2 210 A3
Greenway BR7 188 D5
Greenway Cl
Finsbury Pk N4 73 A6
Friern Barnet N11 31 A4
Hendon NW9 27 B1
[2] South Tottenham
N15 51 D5
Totteridge N20 13 C2
Greenway Ct
Hayes UB4 84 B3
Ilford IG1 56 D1
[2] Newham E15 98 C5
Greenway RM8 58 C1
Green Way SE9 165 D6
Greenway Gdns
Croydon CR0 223 B5
Greenford UB6 85 D4
Green Way Gdns
HA3 24 C1
Greenway Gdns NW9 27 B1
Greenway
Harrow HA3 44 A4
Hayes UB4 84 B3
Palmers Green N14 16 A2
Pinner HA5 22 B1
Greenways
Beckenham BR3 185 C1
[5] Forest Hill SE26 184 C6
Hinchley Wood KT10 212 C4
Greenways The [1]
TW1 153 A5
Green Way TW16 194 A5
Greenway The
Harrow HA3 24 C2
Hendon NW9 27 B1
Hounslow TW4 129 B1
Pinner HA5 41 B3
Uxbridge UB8 82 A5
West Ruislip UB10 61 A6
Greenway
Totteridge N20 13 C2
Wallington SM6 219 C4
West Barnes SW20 200 C5
Woodford IG8 37 C5
Greenwell St W1 238 D5
GREENWICH 142 C6
Greenwich Acad
SE10 141 D4
Greenwich Borough
Mus* SE18 123 D1
Greenwich Bsns Ctr
SE10 141 D5
Greenwich Bsns Pk
SE10 141 D5
Greenwich Church St
SE10 142 A6
Greenwich Coll
SE10 142 A5
Greenwich Com Coll
Plumstead Ctr
SE18 123 A2
Greenwich Cres E6 100 A2
Greenwich Ct [11] E1 96 B1
Greenwich High Rd
SE10 141 D5
Greenwich Ho SE13 164 B5
Greenwich Hts
SE18 144 A5
Greenwich Ind Est
SE10 141 D5
Greenwich London Coll
SE18 122 D2
Greenwich Mkt [2]
SE10 142 A6
Greenwich Mkt
SE10 142 A6
Greenwich Park*
SE10 142 C5
Greenwich Park St
SE10 142 B6
Greenwich Quay
SE8 141 D6
Greenwich Sh Pk
SE7 121 B2
Greenwich South St
SE10 142 A4
Greenwich Sta
SE10 141 D5
Greenwich View Pl
E14 119 D3
Green Wlk
Bermondsey SE1 263 A5
Hampton TW12 173 B4
Hendon NW4 46 D4
Ruislip HA4 39 D1
Southall UB2 107 C1
Green Wlk The E4 20 B3
Greenwood Ave
Dagenham RM10 81 D4
Enfield EN3 7 A4
Greenwood Cl
Bushey WD23 8 C3
Merton SM4 201 A5
Orpington BR5 211 C3
Sidcup DA15 168 A2
Thames Ditton KT7 197 A1
Greenwood Dr E4 36 B5
Greenwood Gdns
N13 16 D1
Greenwood Ho
Finsbury WC1 234 A1
[8] Nunhead SE4 140 D1
Wood Green N22 32 C2
Greenwood La
TW12 173 D5
Green Wood NW5 71 C3
Greenwood Mans [9]
IG11 80 A1
Greenwood Pk KT2 177 C3
Greenwood Pl NW5 71 B3
Greenwood Prim Sch
UB5 64 A3
Greenwood [8]
SW19 156 D4
Greenwood Rd
Dalston E8 74 A2
Hinchley Wood KT7 213 A6
Isleworth TW7 130 D2
Mitcham CR4 203 D6
Thornton Heath CR0 205 A2
West Ham E13 98 D5
Greenwoods The
HA2 64 A5
Greenwood Terr
NW10 89 B5
Greenwood [3] IG8 37 A3
Green Wrythe Cres
SM5 202 C1
Green Wrythe La
SM5 202 C2
Green Wrythe Prim Sch
SM5 202 B3
Green Yd WC1 240 D6
Greer Rd HA3 24 A2
Greet Ho SE1 251 B1
Greet St SE1 116 C5 251 B3
Greg Cl E10 54 A3
Gregor Mews SE3 143 A5
Gregory Cres SE9 165 D4
Gregory Ho SE3 143 B3
Gregory Pl W8 245 C2
Gregory Rd
Dagenham RM6 58 D5
Southall UB2 107 C3
Greig City Acad N8 50 A5
Greig Cl N8 50 A4
Greig Ho [9] TW10 153 C1
Greig Terr SE17 138 D6
Grenaby Ave CR0 205 B2
Grenaby Rd CR0 205 B2
Grenada Ho [18] E14 119 B6
Grenada Rd SE7 143 C5
Grenade St E14 119 B6
Grenadier St E16 122 C5
Grena Gdns TW9 132 B1
Grenard Cl SE15 140 A5
Grena Rd TW10,
TW9 132 B1
Grendon Gdns HA9 66 C6
Grendon Ho
[29] Hackney E9 74 C1
Pentonville N1 233 C3
Grendon St
NW8 92 C3 237 A6
Grenfell Ct NW7 28 B4
Grenfell Gdns
Harrow HA3 44 A2
Ilford IG2 57 D4
Grenfell Ho SE5 139 A5
Grenfell Rd
Mitcham CR4,
SW17 180 D4
Shepherd's Bush
W11 112 D6
Grenfell Twr [5]
W11 112 D6
Grenfell Wlk [4]
W11 112 D6
Grengate Lodge [2]
E13 99 B4
Grenier Apartments [11]
SE15 140 B5
Grennell Cl SM1 218 B6
Grennell Rd SM1 218 A6
Grenoble Gdns N13 32 C4
Grenville Cl
Church End N3 29 B2
Tolworth KT5 199 A1
Grenville Ct
[3] Dulwich SE19 183 D5
Ealing W13 87 B2
Edgware HA8 26 D6
Grenville Gdns IG8 37 C3
Grenville Ho
[26] Bow E3 97 A5
[4] Deptford SE8 141 C6
Grenville Lo N6 49 C2
Grenville Mans WC1 240 A6
Grenville Mews
Hampton TW12 173 D5
South Kensington
SW7 256 A3
Grenville Pl
Burnt Oak NW7 27 B5
South Kensington
SW7 114 A2 256 A4
Grenville Rd N19 50 A1
Grenville St WC1 240 B5
Gresham Almshouses
[3] SW9 138 B1
Gresham Ave N20 30 D6
Gresham Cl Enfield EN2 5 A2
Sidcup DA5 169 B5
Gresham Coll
EC1 94 C2 241 B3
Gresham Ct TW3 130 A4
Gresham Dr RM6 58 B3
Gresham Gdns NW11 47 A1
Gresham Ho
[4] Teddington
TW11 174 D5
[3] Thames Ditton
KT7 197 A2
West Barnes KT3 200 B5
Gresham Lo E17 53 D4
Gresham Pl [2] N19 71 D6
Gresham Rd
Beckenham BR3 185 A1
Brixton SW9 138 C2
Canning Town E16 99 B1
Croydon SE25 206 A5
East Ham E6 100 B5
Edgware HA8 26 B4
Hampton TW12 173 C4
Hillingdon UB10 82 C5
Hounslow TW3,
TW5 130 A4
Willesden NW10 67 B3
Gresham St
EC2 95 A1 242 B2
Gresham Way Est
SW19 157 D1
Gresham Way
SW19 157 C1
Gresley Cl London N15 51 B5
Walthamstow E17 53 A3
Gresley Ho SW8 269 D2
Gresley Rd N19 49 C2
Gressenhall Rd
SW18 157 B4
Gressenham Ct [7]
HA7 25 C6
Gresse St W1 93 D1 239 C2
Gresswell Cl DA14 168 A1
Greswell St SW6 134 D4
Greta Ho SE3 142 D6
Gretton Ho [2] E2 96 C4
Gretton Rd N17 33 D3
Greville Cl TW1 153 B4
Greville Ct
Harrow HA1 64 C4
[3] Lower Clapton E5 74 B5
Greville Hall NW6 91 D5
Greville Ho
Harrow HA2 42 B1
Knightsbridge SW1 258 A6
Putney SW15 134 D2
Greville Lo
[5] Bayswater W2 91 D1
[16] London N12 29 D6
Greville Mews [5]
NW6 91 D6
Greville Pl W9 91 D5
Greville Rd
Kilburn NW6 91 D5
Richmond TW10 154 B5
Walthamstow E17 54 A5
Greville St
EC1 94 C2 241 B4
Grey Cl NW11 48 A3
Grey Coat Hospital Sch
(St Michaels) The
SW1 115 D2 259 C3
Grey Coat Hospital Sch
The SW1 115 D3 259 C5
Greycoat Pl
SW1 115 D3 259 C5
Greycoat St
SW1 115 D3 259 C5
Greycot Rd BR3 185 C5
Grey Court Sch
TW10 153 C1
Grey Eagle St
E1 95 D3 243 D5
Greyfell Cl HA7 25 B5
Greyfriars [18] SE26 162 A1
Greyfriars Ho SE3 142 D6
Grey Ho [27] W12 112 B6
Greyhound Ct WC2 251 A6
Greyhound Hill NW4 46 B6
Greyhound La
SW16 181 D4
Greyhound Rd
College Pk NW10 90 B4
Fulham W6 135 A6 264 A6
Sutton SM1 218 A3
Tottenham N17 51 C6
Greyhound Terr
SW16 181 C2
Greyladies Gdns
SE10 142 A3
Greys Park Cl BR2 225 D3
Greystead Rd SE23 162 C4
Greystoke Ave HA5 41 C6
Greystoke Ct W5 88 B3
Greystoke Dr HA4 38 D3
Greystoke Gdns
Ealing W5 88 B3
Enfield EN2 3 D1
Greystoke Ho
Ealing W5 88 A3
Peckham SE15 140 A6
Greystoke Lo W5 88 B3
Greystoke Park Terr
W5 88 A4
Greystoke Pl EC4 241 B2
Greystone Gdns HA3 43 C3
Greystones TW2 152 A2
Greyswood St SW16 181 B4
Greytiles TW11 174 D4
Grey Turner Ho W12 90 A1
Grice Ct N1 73 A2
Grierson Ho SW16 181 C6
Grierson Rd
Forest Hill SE23 162 D4
Forest Hill SE23 163 A5
Griffin Cl NW10 68 B3
Griffin Ct
[8] Brentford
TW8 132 A6
Chiswick W4 111 D1
Griffin Ctr TW14 150 B5
Griffin Ctr The KT1 175 D1
Griffin Ct W12 112 B5
Griffin Gate SW15 134 D2
Griffin Lo N12 30 A6
Griffin Manor Way
SE28 123 B3
Griffin Park (Brentford
FC) TW8 131 D6
Griffin Rd
Plumstead SE18 123 B1
Tottenham N17 33 C1
Griffins Cl N21 17 B4
Griffin Way
Sunbury TW16 172 A1
Woolwich SE28 123 C3
Griffith Cl RM8 58 C1
Griffiths Cl KT4 216 B6
Griffiths Ho [2]
SE18 144 D6
Griffiths Rd SW19 179 D3
Griffon Ho [3] SW11 136 C2
Griggs App IG1 79 A6
Grigg's Pl SE1 263 B5
Griggs Rd E10 54 A3
Grilse Cl N9 34 B6
Grimaldi Ho N1 233 C4
Grimsby Gr E16 122 D5
Grimsby St
[8] Bethnal Green
E2 96 A3
Shoreditch E2 243 D6
Grimsdyke Fst & Mid
Sch HA5 23 B4
Grimsdyke Rd HA5 23 A3
Grimsel Path SE5 138 D5
Grimshaw Cl N6 49 A2
Grimston Rd SW6 135 B3
Grimthorpe Ho EC1 241 C6
Grimwade Ave CR0 222 A5
Grimwade Cl SE15 140 C2
Grimwood Rd TW1 152 D4
Grindall Cl CR0 220 D4
Grindall Ho [26] E1 96 B3
Grindal St SE1 251 A1
Grindleford Ave N11 15 A2
Grindley Gdns CR0 205 D3
Grindley Ho [3] E3 97 B2
Grinling Gibbons Prim
Sch SE8 141 B6
Grinling Ho [6] SE18 122 C2
Grinling Pl SE8 141 C6
Grinstead Rd SE8 119 A1
Grisedale NW1 232 A2
Grittleton Ave HA9 66 D2
Grittleton Rd W9 91 C3
Grizedale Terr [8]
SE23 162 B2
Grogan Cl TW12 173 B4
Groombridge Cl
DA16 168 A6
Groombridge Ho [1]
SE20 184 D3
Groombridge Rd E9 74 D1
Groom Cl BR2 209 B5
Groom Cres SW18 158 B4
Groome Ho SE11 260 D3
Groomfield Cl
SW17 181 A6
Groom Pl
SW1 115 A3 258 B6
Grooms Dr HA5 40 A4
Grosmont Rd SE18 123 D1
Grosse Way SW15 156 B5
Grosslea SM4 202 B4
Grosvenor Ave
Canonbury N5 73 A3
Harrow HA2 41 D3
Hayes UB4 83 D5
Mortlake SW14 133 C2
Richmond TW10 154 A6
Wallington SM5,
SM6 219 A2
Grosvenor Bridge
SW1 137 B6 268 D6
Grosvenor Cotts
SW1 258 A4
Grosvenor Court Mans
W2 237 C1
Grosvenor Cres
UB10 82 D6
Grosvenor Cres Mews
SW1 248 A1
Grosvenor Cres
Queensbury NW9 44 C5
Westminster
SW1 115 A4 248 B1
Grosvenor Ct
[4] Acton W3 110 C5
Brondesbury Pk NW6 90 D6
[3] Ealing W5 110 A6
[3] Edgware NW7 27 B5
Gunnersbury W4 110 D1
Leyton E10 53 D1
Morden SM4 201 C5
Oakwood N14 15 C4
Penge SE19 183 D4
[22] Poplar E14 97 B1
Putney SW15 157 A6
[1] Sutton SM2 218 A2
Teddington TW11 175 A4
[3] Wanstead E11 55 B4
[2] Wimbledon
SW19 179 A4
Grosvenor Gdns
Cricklewood NW2 68 C3
Hornsey N10 49 C6
Kingston u T KT2 175 D4
Grosvenor Gdns Mews E
SW1 258 D6
Grosvenor Gdns Mews
N SW1 258 C5
Grosvenor Gdns Mews S
SW1 258 D5
Grosvenor Gdns
Mortlake SW14 133 C2
Newham E6 99 D4
Grosvenor Gdns
continued
Southgate N14 15 D6
Temple Fortune
NW11 47 B4
Wallington SM6 219 C1
Westminster
SW1 115 B3 258 D5
Woodford IG8 37 B4
Grosvenor Hill Ct
W1 248 C6
Grosvenor Hill
Mayfair
W1 115 B6 248 C6
Wimbledon SW19 179 A4
Grosvenor Ho
[5] Sutton SM1 217 D3
Upper Clapton E5 52 A1
Grosvenor Hts E4 20 C4
Grosvenor Lo
London N20 14 A1
[4] Woodford E18 36 D1
Grosvenor Par [1]
W5 110 C5
Grosvenor Park Rd
E17 53 D4
Grosvenor Park
SE5 139 A5
Grosvenor Pier SW1 269 C6
Grosvenor Pk SE5 139 A6
Grosvenor Pl
SW1 115 B4 248 C1
Grosvenor Rd
Acton Green W4 111 A1
Bexley DA6 169 A6
Brentford TW8 131 D6
Croydon SE25 206 A5
Dagenham RM8 59 B1
Ealing W7 109 A5
Edmonton N9 18 B3
Erith DA17 147 C6
Finchley N3 29 C3
Hounslow TW3,
TW4 129 B2
Ilford IG1 79 A5
Leyton E10 54 A1
Muswell Hill N10 31 B2
Newham E6 99 D6
Orpington BR6 211 C3
Pimlico
SW1 137 C6 269 B6
Richmond TW10 154 A6
Southall UB2 107 B3
Twickenham TW1 153 A3
Upton E7 77 B2
Wallington SM6 219 B3
Wanstead E11 55 B4
West Wickham BR4 223 D6
Grosvenor Residences
[1] W14 112 D3
Grosvenor Rise E
E17 53 D4
Grosvenor Sq
W1 115 A6 248 B6
Grosvenor St
W1 115 B6 248 C6
Grosvenor Terr SE5 139 A6
Grosvenor The
NW11 47 D2
Grosvenor Vale HA4 61 D6
Grosvenor Way E5 74 C6
Grosvernor Wharf Rd
E14 120 B2
Grote's Bldgs SE3 142 C3
Grote's Pl SE3 142 C3
Groton Rd SW18 157 D2
Grotto Ct SE1 252 A2
Grotto Pas W1 238 A4
Grotto Rd TW1 152 D2
Grove Ave
Cheam SM1 217 C2
Ealing W7 86 C1
Finchley N3 29 C3
Pinner HA5 41 A5
Twickenham TW1 152 D3
Wood Green N10 31 C1
Grovebury Ct
Bexley DA6 169 D6
Southgate N14 15 D4
Grovebury Rd SE2 124 B4
Grove Cl
East Barnet N14 15 B4
Forest Hill SE23 163 A3
Hayes BR2 225 A6
Ickenham UB10 60 C3
Kingston u T KT1 198 B5
Grove Crescent Rd
E15 76 B2
Grove Cres
Feltham TW13 173 A6
Kingsbury NW9 45 B5
Kingston u T KT1 198 A6
Walton-on-T KT12 194 B2
Woodford E18 36 D1

Grove Ct Barnet EN5 1 B2
Camberwell SE5 139 C3
Clapham SW4 137 C2
Ealing W5 110 A5
East Molesey KT8 196 B4
3 Forest Hill SE26 185 A6
Hounslow TW3 129 C1
8 Kingston u T KT1 198 A6
New Malden KT3 199 C6
Penge SE20 184 B3
Seething Wells KT6 197 D4
South Kensington SW10 256 B1
St John's Wood NW8 229 C2
Grovedale Rd N19 71 D6
Grove Dwellings E1 96 C2
Grove End Gdns NW8 229 B3
Grove End NW5 71 B4
Grove End Ho NW8 229 C1
Grove End La KT10 196 B1
Grove End Rd NW8 92 B4 229 C1
Grove End E18 36 D1
Grove Farm Ct CR4 202 D4
Grovefield 1 N11 31 B6
Grove Footpath KT5 198 A5
Grove Gdns Enfield EN3 6 D5
Hendon NW4 46 A5
Lisson Gr NW8 92 C4 230 B1
Teddington TW11 175 A6
Grove Glade Shop Hall W13 109 A5
Grove Green Rd E11 76 B6
Grove Hall Ct Bow E3 97 C5
St John's Wood NW8 92 A4 229 B2
Grovehill Ct BR1 186 D4
Grove Hill HA1 42 C2
Grove Hill Rd
Camberwell SE5 139 C2
Harrow HA1 42 D2
Grove Hill E18 36 D1
Grove Ho
Blackheath SE3 142 D3
Chelsea SW3 267 B6
Hendon N3 46 D6
Grove House Rd N8 50 A5
Grove La
Camberwell SE5 139 C2
Hillingdon UB8 82 B3
Kingston u T KT1 198 A5
Groveland Ave SW16 182 B3
Groveland Ct EC4 242 B1
Groveland Rd BR3 207 B6
Grovelands Cl
Camberwell SE5 139 C3
Harrow HA2 63 D5
Grovelands Ct N14 15 D4
Grovelands KT8 195 C5
Grovelands Inf Sch KT12 194 B3
Grovelands KT1 197 D5
Grovelands Priory (Private Hospl) N14 16 A3
Grovelands Rd
Palmers Green N13 16 B1
South Tottenham N15 52 A3
St Paul's Cray BR5 190 A3
Groveland Way KT3 199 B4
Grove Lane Terr SE5 139 B3
Groveley Ho 7 N4 51 A2
Groveley Rd TW13, TW16 171 D5
Grove Lo
Clapham SW4 137 C1
Cranley Gdns N10 49 C5
Grove Mans
London SW4 136 D1
2 Shepherd's Bush W6 112 C4
3 Stamford Hill N16 52 A1
Grove Market Pl SE9 166 B5
Grove Mews W6 112 C3
Grove Mill CR4 202 C4
Grove Mill Pl SM5 219 A5
GROVE PARK W4 133 A4
SE9 165 B1
Grove Park Ave E4 35 D3
Grove Park Bridge W4 133 A5
Grove Park Gdns W4 133 A5
Grove Park Mews W4 133 A5
Grove Park Prim Sch W4 133 A6
Grove Park Rd
Chiswick W4 132 D5
Mottingham SE9, SE12 165 D2
South Tottenham N15 51 C5
Grove Park Sch NW9 45 A5
Grove Park Sta SE12 165 B1
Grove Park Terr W4 132 D6
Grove Pk
Camberwell SE5 139 C3
Kingsbury NW9 45 B5
Wanstead E11 55 B4
Grove Pl Acton W3 111 A5
Balham SW12 159 B5
Hampstead NW3 70 B5
Grove Prim Sch RM6 58 C4
Grover Ct SE13 141 D3
Grove Rd Acton W3 111 A5
Barnes SW13 133 D3
Belmont SM2 217 C2
Bow E3 97 A5
Brentford TW8 109 C1
Chingford E4 20 A1
Cockfosters EN4 2 C2
Dagenham RM6 58 C3
Ealing W5 109 D6
East Molesey KT8 196 B5
Edgware HA8 26 C4
8 Erith DA17 147 B6
Friern Barnet N11 31 B5
Hounslow TW3 129 C1
Kingston u T KT6 197 D4
Leytonstone E11 54 D2
Merton SW19 180 A3
Mitcham CR4 181 B1
North Finchley N12 30 B5
Pinner HA5 41 B4
Grove Rd Prim Sch TW3 129 C1
Grove Rd
Richmond TW10 154 B5
Shepperton TW17 193 A3
South Tottenham N15 51 C4
Spring Gr TW7 130 C4
Thornton Heath CR7 204 C5
Twickenham TW2 152 B1
Uxbridge UB8 60 A1
Walthamstow E17 53 D4
Grove Rd W EN3 6 C6
Grove Rd
Willesden NW2 68 C2
Woodford E18 36 D1
Grover Ho
4 London SW4 159 C6
Vauxhall SE11 260 D1
Groves Ho UB4 84 B4
Groveside Cl
Acton W3 88 C1
Carshalton SM5 218 C6
Groveside Ct SW11 136 B3
Groveside Rd E4 20 C1
Grove St
Deptford SE8 119 B1
Edmonton N18 33 D4
Grovestile Waye TW14 149 B4
Grove Terrace Mews NW5 71 B5
Grove Terr
Gospel Oak NW5 71 B4
Southall UB1 107 C6
Teddington TW11 175 A6
Grove The
Bexley DA6 146 D1
Dulwich SE21 162 A3
Ealing W5 110 A5
Edgware HA8 26 D6
Edmonton N13 32 C6
Enfield EN2 4 C3
Finchley N3 29 C3
Hendon NW11 47 A2
Highgate N6 49 A1
Hornsey N8 49 D4
Hounslow TW7 130 C4
Ickenham UB10 60 C3
Kingsbury NW9 45 B4
Sidcup DA14 191 A6
Southall UB6 86 A1
Stratford E15 76 C2
Stroud Green N4 50 B2
Teddington TW11 175 A6
1 Twickenham TW1 153 B5
Walton-on-T KT12 194 B2
West Wickham BR4 224 A6
Grove Vale
Chislehurst West BR7 188 C4
East Dulwich SE22 139 D1
Groveway
Dagenham RM8 80 D4
South Lambeth SW9 138 B4 270 D1
Grove Way
Thames Ditton KT10 196 A1
Wembley HA9 67 A3
Grovewood Ct 6 TW7 130 C4
Grovewood Ho NW2 69 B6
Grovewood 9 TW9 132 C4
Grummant Rd SE15 139 D4
Grundy St E14 97 D1
Gruneisen Rd N3 29 D3
Guardian Angels RC Prim Sch E3 97 A4
Guardian Ct SE12 164 C6
Guards Mus The* SW1 115 C4 249 B1
Gubyon Ave SE24 160 D6
Guerin Sq E3 97 B4
Guernsey Cl TW5 129 C5
Guernsey Gr SE24 161 A4
Guernsey Ho
10 Canonbury N1 73 A2
Enfield EN3 6 D5
Guernsey Rd
11 Canonbury N1 73 A2
Leytonstone E11 54 B1
Guibal Rd SE12 165 B3
Guildersfield Rd SW16 182 A3
Guildford Ave TW13 150 A2
Guildford Gr SE10 141 D4
Guildford Ho 23 SE5 139 A3
Guildford Rd
Chingford E17 36 A2
Ilford IG3 79 C6
Newham E6 100 B1
South Lambeth SW8 138 A4 270 B2
Thornton Heath CR0 205 B3
Guildford Way SM6 220 A3
Guildhall Bldgs EC2 242 C2
Guild Hall* EC2 95 A1 242 B2
Guildhall Ho EC2 242 C2
Guildhall Sch Music & Drama EC2 95 A2 242 B4
Guildhall Yd EC2 242 B2
Guildhouse St SW1 115 C2 259 A3
Guild Ho SW19 179 B4
Guildown Ave N12 29 D6
Guild Rd SE7 143 D6
Guildsway E17 35 B2
Guilford Ave KT5 198 B4
Guilford Pl WC1 240 C5
Guilford St WC1 94 A3 240 B5
Guilfoyle 2 NW9 27 D1
Guillemot Ct 28 SE8 141 B6
Guilsborough Cl NW10 67 C1
Guinness Cl
Hayes UB3 105 B3
Homerton E9 75 A1
Guinness Ct
Chelsea SW3 257 C3
6 Croydon CR0 221 D6
Finsbury EC1 235 B1
Primrose Hill NW8 230 B5
Whitechapel E1 243 D1
Guinness Sq SE1 263 A4
Guinness Trust Bldgs
Bermondsey SE1 253 A2
7 Bethnal Green E2 96 A5
Chelsea SW3 257 C3
Hammersmith W6 112 C1
Kennington SE11 261 C2
Guion Rd SW6 135 B3
Gujarat Ho 1 N16 73 C5
Gulland Cl WD23 8 A6
Gulland Wlk 21 N1 73 A2
Gullane Ho 24 E3 97 B5
Gull Cl SM6 220 A1
Gulliver Cl UB5 85 B6
Gulliver Ct CR2 220 D1
Gulliver Rd DA15 167 C2
Gulliver St SE16 119 B3
Gulston Wlk SW3 257 D3
Gumleigh Rd W5 109 C2
Gumley Gdns TW7 131 A2
Gumley House RC Convent Sch (Girls) TW7 131 A2
Gumping Rd BR5 227 A6
Gundulph Rd BR2 209 C6
Gunmakers La E3 97 A6
Gunnel Cl SE20 184 A6
Gunnell Cl SE25 206 A3
Gunnell Ct 3 CR4 180 C2
Gunnels Ct & Hastingwood Ct 6 IG9 21 C2
Gunner Dr 9 EN3 7 C6
Gunner La SE18 122 C1
GUNNERSBURY 110 D2
Gunnersbury Avenue (North Circular Rd) W3 110 C3
Gunnersbury Cl 8 W4 110 D1
Gunnersbury Cres W3 110 C4
Gunnersbury Ct 8 W3 110 D4
Gunnersbury Dr W5 110 B4
Gunnersbury Gdns W3 110 C4
Gunnersbury La W3 110 C4
Gunnersbury Manor W5 110 B5
Gunnersbury Mews 6 W4 110 D1
Gunnersbury Park W3 110 C3
Gunnersbury Park Mus* W3 110 C3
Gunnersbury RC Sch TW8 109 C1
Gunnersbury Sta W4 110 D1
Gunners Gr E4 20 A1
Gunners Rd SW18 158 B2
Gunnery Terr SE18 123 A3
Gunning St SE18 123 C2
Gunpowder Sq EC4 241 B2
Gun St E1 243 C3
Gunstor Rd N16 73 C4
Gunter Gr
Chelsea SW6 136 A5 266 A4
Hendon HA8 27 B2
Gunterstone Rd W14 113 A1 254 B2
Gunthorpe St E1 95 D1 243 D2
Gunton Rd
Streatham SW17 181 A4
Upper Clapton E5 74 B6
Gunwhale Cl SE16 118 D5
Gun Wharf
Old Ford E3 97 A6
Wapping E1 118 C5
Gurdon Ho 7 E14 97 C1
Gurdon Rd SE7 121 A1
Gurnell Gr W13 86 D3
Gurney Cl
Barking IG11 78 D2
Higham Hill E17 34 D2
Stratford E15 76 C3
Gurney Cres CR0 204 B1
Gurney Dr N2 48 A5
Gurney Ho
3 Bayswater W2 91 D1
14 Bethnal Green E2 96 A5
Hayes UB3 105 C2
Gurney Rd
London SW6 136 A2
Northolt UB5 84 C4
Stratford E15 76 C3
Wallington SM5 219 A4
Guru Nanak Sikh Prim & Sec Schs UB4 106 C5
Guthrie Ct SE1 251 B1
Guthrie St SW3 257 A2
Gutter La EC2 95 A1 242 A2
Guyatt Gdns CR4 181 A1
Guy Barnett Gr SE3 143 A2
Guy Rd SM6 219 D5
Guyscliff Rd SE13 164 A6
Guy's Hospl Sch SE1 117 B5 252 D3
Guy's Hospl SE1 117 B4 252 D2
Guy's Retreat IG9 21 C4
Guy St SE1 117 B4 252 D2
Gwalior Ho N14 15 C5
Gwalior Rd SW15 134 D2
Gwendolen Ave SW15 156 D6
Gwendolen Cl SW15 156 D6
Gwendolen Ho TW19 148 A3
Gwendoline Ave E13 99 B6
Gwendoline Ct TW15 170 A6
Gwendwr Rd W14 113 A1 254 B2
Gwent Ct 13 SE16 118 D5
Gwillim Cl DA15 168 A6
Gwilym Maries Ho 11 E2 96 B4
Gwydor Rd BR3 206 D6
Gwydyr Rd BR2 208 D6
Gwyn Cl SW6 136 A5 266 A3
Gwyn Jones Prim Sch E11 54 B2
Gwynne Ave CR0 206 D2
Gwynne Cl W4 133 D6
Gwynne Ho
Finsbury WC1 234 A1
6 Streatham SW2 160 B3
3 Wanstead E11 55 A4
Whitechapel E1 96 B2
Gwynne Pl WC1 233 D1
Gwynne Rd SW11 136 B3
Gye Ho 2 SW4 138 A1
Gylcote Cl SE5 139 B1
Gyles Pk HA7 25 C2
Gyllyngdune Gdns IG3 79 D5

H

Haarlem Rd 12 W14 112 D3
Haberdasher Pl 4 N1 95 C4
Haberdashers' Aske's Hatcham Coll SE4 141 A3
Haberdashers' Aske's Knights Acad BR1 187 A6
Haberdasher St N1 95 B4 235 D2
Haccombe Rd SW19 180 A4
HACKBRIDGE 219 B6
Hackbridge Park Gdns SM5 218 D6
Hackbridge Prim Sch SM5 203 A1
Hackbridge Rd SM5, SM6 219 A6
Hackbridge Sta SM6 219 B6
Hackford Rd SW9 138 B4 270 D2
Hackford Wlk SW9 138 C4
Hackforth Cl EN5 12 B6
Hackington Cres BR3 185 C4
HACKNEY 74 B2
Hackney Central Sta E8 74 B2
Hackney Cl WD6 11 B6
Hackney Coll (Poplar Ctr) E3 97 D3
Hackney Com Coll N1 95 C4
Hackney Downs Sta E8 74 B3
Hackney Free & Parochial CE Sec Sch E9 74 C2
Hackney Gr E8 74 B2
Hackney Hospl E9 75 A3
Hackney Rd E2 96 A5
Hackney Stadium Mkt* E15 75 C2
HACKNEY WICK 75 C2
Hackney Wick E9 75 B2
Hackney Wick Sta E9 75 C2
Hackworth Point 24 E3 97 D4
Hacon Sq 12 E8 74 B1
Hadar Cl N20 13 D3
Haddenham Ct SW17 180 B6
Hadden Rd SE28 123 C3
Hadden Way UB6 64 B2
Haddington Rd BR1 186 B6
Haddo Ho
Gospel Oak NW5 71 B4
Greenwich SE10 141 D6
Haddon Cl
Enfield EN1 18 A5
New Malden KT3 199 D4
Haddon Ct
East Acton W3 111 D6
Hendon NW4 46 C6
Haddon Gr DA15 168 A4
Haddon Rd SM1 217 D4
Haddo St SE10 142 A6
Haden Ct N4 72 C6
Hadfield Cl UB1 85 B4
Hadfield Ho
Edgware NW7 28 C6
37 Whitechapel E1 96 A1
Hadleigh Cl
17 Bethnal Green E1 96 C3
Merton SW20 179 B1
Hadleigh Ct 8 E4 20 C4
Hadleigh Ho 16 E1 96 C3
Hadleigh Lo 5 IG8 37 A4
Hadleigh Rd N9 18 B4
Hadleigh St E2 96 C4
Hadleigh Wlk 1 E6 100 A1
HADLEY 1 B2
Hadley Cl
Borehamwood WD6 10 B5
Southgate N21 16 C5
Hadley Ct
1 London N3 29 D3
Stamford Hill N16 52 A1
Hadley Gdns
Chiswick W4 111 B1
Southall UB2 107 B1
Hadley Gn EN5 1 B3
Hadley Gn W EN5 1 B3
Hadley Gr EN5 1 A3
Hadley Green Rd EN5 1 B3
Hadley Hall N21 16 C3
Hadley Highstone EN5 1 B4
Hadley Ho BR5 189 D1
Hadley Hts EN5 1 D3
Hadley Rd Barnet EN5 1 D2
Belvedere DA17 125 B2
Enfield EN2 4 A5
Mitcham CR4 203 D5
Hadley Ridge EN5 1 B2
Hadley St NW1 71 B2
Hadleyvale Ct EN5 1 D2
Hadley View 9 EN5 1 D1
Hadley Way N21 16 C5
HADLEY WOOD 2 B5
Hadley Wood Prim Sch EN4 2 A5
Hadley Wood Rd
Barnet EN4 2 A3
Barnet EN5 1 C3
Hadley Wood Sta EN4 2 A5
Hadlow Coll (Mottingham Ctr) SE12 165 C3
Hadlow Coll Nature Reserve* SE12 165 C3
Hadlow Ho SE17 263 B2
Hadlow Pl SE19 184 A3
Hadlow Rd
Bexley DA16 146 C5
Sidcup DA14 190 A6
Hadrian Cl
5 Old Ford E3 97 C6
Stanwell TW19 148 A4
Hadrian Ct Barnet EN5 1 D1
11 Belmont SM2 217 D1
Brockley SE4 141 C2
Hadrian Est 33 E2 96 A5
Hadrian's Ride EN1 17 D6
Hadrian St SE10 120 C1
Hadrian Way TW19 148 A4
Hadstock Ho NW1 232 D2
Hadyn Park Ct 13 W12 112 A4
Hadyn Park Rd W12 112 A4
Hafer Rd SW11 136 D1
Hafton Rd SE6 164 C2
Haggard Rd TW1 153 B4
Hagger Ct E17 54 B6
HAGGERSTON 95 D5
Haggerston Rd E8 95 D6
Haggerston Sch E2 95 D5
Haggerston Studios 30 E8 95 D6
Hague Prim Sch E2 96 B3
Hague St 30 E2 96 A4
Ha-Ha Rd SE7, SE18 144 B6
Haig Ct BR7 188 D5
Haig Ho 4 E2 96 A5
Haig Pl SM4 201 C3
Haig Rd E E13 99 C5
Haig Rd
Hillingdon UB8 83 A2
Stanmore HA7 25 C5
Haig Rd W E13 99 C4
Haigville Gdns IG6 56 D5
Hailes Cl SW19 180 A4
Haileybury Ave EN1 17 D5
Hailey Rd DA18 125 C4
Hailey Rd Bsns Pk DA18 125 C4
Hailing Mews BR2 209 B6
Hailsham Ave SW2 160 B2
Hailsham Cl KT6 197 D2
Hailsham Dr HA1 42 B6
Hailsham Rd SW17 181 A4
Hailsham Terr N18 33 B5
Haimo Prim Sch SE9 165 D6
Haimo Rd SE9 165 D6
Hainault Bldgs E10 54 A1
Hainault Bridge Par 5 IG1 78 D6
Hainault Ct E17 54 B5
Hainault Gore RM6 59 A4
Hainault Rd
Dagenham RM6 59 B3
Ilford RM6 58 B6
Leytonstone E11 54 B2
Hainault St Ilford IG1 78 D6
New Eltham SE9 166 D3
Haines Wlk SM4 201 D2
Hainford Cl SE4 140 D1
Haining Cl 3 W4 110 C1
Hainthorpe Rd SE27 182 D6
Hainton Cl E1 96 B1

Halberd Mews E5 74 B6
Halbutt Gdns RM9 81 B5
Halbutt St RM9 81 B4
Halcomb St N1 95 C6
Halcot Ave DA6 169 D6
Halcroft Ct SM1 218 B4
Halcrow St E1 96 B2
Halcyon Ho 3 EN1 17 C6
Halcyon Wharf 19 E1 118 A5
Haldane Cl
Holdbrook EN3 7 D5
Muswell Hill N10 31 B3
Haldane Pl SW18 157 D3
Haldane Rd
Fulham SW6 135 B6 264 D5
Newham E6 100 A4
Southall UB1 86 A1
Thamesmead SE28 124 D6
Haldan Rd E4 36 A4
Haldon Rd SW18 157 B5
Hale Cl Chingford E4 20 A1
Edgware HA8 27 A5
Orpington BR6 227 A4
Hale Ct HA8 27 A5
Hale Dr NW7 27 B4
HALE END 36 C4
Hale End Cl HA4 40 A3
Hale End Rd E17 36 B2
Halefield Rd N17 34 B2
Hale Gdns Acton W3 110 C5
Tottenham Hale N17 52 A6
Hale Grove Gdns NW7 27 C5
Hale Ho Enfield EN3 6 D6
Westminster SW1 259 D2
Hale La NW7, HA8 27 B5
Hale Lo HA1 42 C2
Hale Rd Newham E6 100 A3
Tottenham Hale N17 52 A6
Hales Ct 6 TW11 175 A5
Hales Ho 3 SW12 159 B4
Halesowen Rd SM4 201 D2
Hales Prior N1 233 C3
Hales St SE8 141 C5
Hale St E14 119 D6
Halesworth Cl 3 E5 74 C6
Halesworth Rd SE13 141 D2
Hale The Chingford E4 36 B3
Tottenham Hale N17 52 A6
Hale Wlk W7 86 C2
Haley Rd NW4 46 C3
Half Acre TW8 131 D6
Half Acre Mews TW8 131 D6
Half Acre Rd W7 108 C5
Halfacre 14 HA7 25 C5
Half Acre 2 E18 55 A6
Half Moon Cres N1 233 D4
Half Moon Ct EC1 242 A3
Half Moon La SE24 161 A5
Halfmoon Pas E1 243 D1
Half Moon St W1 115 B5 248 D3
Halford Cl HA8 26 D1
Halford Ct KT9 214 A1
Halford Ho 9 SW15 156 D6
Halford Rd
Ickenham UB10 60 C3
Leyton E10 54 B4
Richmond TW10 154 A6
West Brompton SW6 135 C6 265 A5
Halfway St DA15 167 C3
Haliburton Rd TW1, TW7 131 A1
Haliday Ho N1 73 B2
Haliday Wlk 4 N1 73 B2
Halidon Cl E9 74 C3
Halifax Cl TW11 174 C4
Halifax 8 NW9 27 D1
Halifax Rd Enfield EN2 5 B3
Greenford UB6 85 D6
Halifax St SE26 162 B1
Halifield Dr DA17 125 A3
Haling Gr CR2 221 A1
Haling Manor High Sch CR2 220 D1
Haling Park Gdns CR2 220 D2
Haling Park Rd
Croydon CR2 220 D3
South Croydon CR2 221 A2
Haling Rd CR2 221 B2
Haliwell Ho 10 NW6 91 D6
Halkett Ho 1 E2 96 C6
Halkin Arc SW1 114 D3 257 D6
Halkin Mews SW1 258 A6
Halkin Pl SW1 258 A6
Halkin St SW1 115 A4 248 B1
Hallam Cl BR7 188 B5
Hallam Ct W1 238 D4
Hallam Gdns HA5 23 A3
Hallam Ho
17 London SW9 138 C4
Pimlico SW1 259 B1
Hallam Mews W1 238 D4
Hallam Rd
Barnes SW13 134 B2
Harringay N15 50 D5
Hallam St W1 93 B2 238 D4
Hallane Ho SE27 183 A5
Hall Cl W5 88 A2
Hall Ct TW11 174 D5
Hall Dr Ealing W7 86 C1
Forest Hill SE26 184 C5
Halley Gdns SE13 142 B1
Halley Ho
16 Bethnal Green E2 96 A5
8 Cubitt Town SE10 120 D1
Halley Prim Sch E14 97 A2
Halley Rd E7, E12 77 D2
Halley St E14 97 A2
Hall Farm Cl HA7 25 B6
Hall Farm Dr TW2 152 B4
Hallfield Jun & Inf Schs W2 91 D1
Hall Gate NW8 92 A4 229 B2
Hallgate SE3 143 A2
Hall Gdns E4 35 B6
Halliards The KT12 194 A3
Halliday Ho 40 E1 96 A1
Halliday Sq UB2 108 B5
Halliford Cl TW17 193 C6
Halliford Rd
Sunbury TW16 194 A5
Upper Halliford TW16, TW17 193 D5
Halliford Sch TW17 193 A2
Halliford St N1 73 B1
Hallingbury Ct 1 E17 53 D6
Halling Ho SE1 252 D1
Hallings Wharf Studios 2 E15 98 B6
Halliwell Ct 4 SE22 162 A6
Halliwell Rd SW2 160 B5
Halliwick Court Par 2 N12 30 D5
Halliwick Ct 1 N12 30 D5
Halliwick Ho N21 17 B5
Halliwick Rd N10 31 A2
Hall La
Chingford Hatch E4 35 B5
Harlington UB3 127 B5
Hendon NW4 28 A1
Hall Lane E4 35 A5
Hallmark Trad Ctr HA9 67 A4
Hallmead Rd SM1 217 D5
Hall Oak Wlk NW6 69 B2
Hallowell Ave CR0 220 A4
Hallowell Cl CR4 203 A6
Hallowfield Way CR4 202 C6
Hallows Gr TW16 171 D5
Hall Pl W2 92 B3 236 C5
Hall Rd
Dagenham RM6 58 D3
Isleworth TW7 152 B6
Leyton E15 76 B4
Newham E6 100 B6
St John's Wood NW8 92 A4 229 B2
Halls Bsns Ctr UB3 106 A3
Hall Sch The NW3 70 B2
Hall Sch Wimbledon SW15 156 A1
Hall Sch SW20 178 D2
Hallside Rd EN1 5 D5
Halls Terr UB10 82 D3
Hall St
Finsbury EC1 94 D4 234 D2
North Finchley N12 30 A5
Hallsville Prim Sch E16 99 A1
Hallsville Rd E16 98 D1
Hallswelle Par 1 NW11 47 B4
Hallswelle Rd NW11 47 B4
Hall The SE3 143 A2
Hall Twr W2 236 D4
Hall View SE9 165 D2
Hallywell Cres E6 100 B2
Halons Rd SE9 166 C4
Halpin Pl SE17 117 B2 262 D3
Halsbrook Rd SE3 143 D2
Halsbury Cl HA7 25 B6
Halsbury Ct HA7 25 B6
Halsbury Ho 4 N7 72 B4
Halsbury Rd E UB5 64 A4
Halsbury Rd W12 112 B5
Halsbury Rd W UB5 63 D3
Halsend UB3 106 B5
Halsey St SW3 114 D2 257 C4
Halsham Cres IG11 79 D3
Halsmere Rd SE5 138 D4
Halstead Cl 2 CR0 221 A5
Halstead Ct
Shoreditch N1 235 D3
Walthamstow E17 53 B2
Halstead Gdns N21 17 B3
Halstead Rd
Edmonton N21 17 B3
Enfield EN1 5 C1
Wanstead E11 55 B4
Halston Cl SW11 158 D5
Halstow 12 NW5 71 A2
Halstow Prim Sch SE10 121 A1
Halstow Rd
Greenwich SE3, SE10 121 A1
Kensal Green NW10 90 D4
Halsway UB3 106 A5
Halter Cl WD6 11 B6
Halton Cl N11 30 D4
Halton Cross St N1 94 D6 234 D6
Haltone Ho 1 SW4 137 D3
Halton Ho 22 N1 72 D1
Halton Mans N1 72 D1
Halton Pl N1 235 A6
Halton Rd N1 94 D6 234 D6
Halt Robin La DA17 125 D2
Halt Robin Rd DA17 125 D2
Halyard Ho E14 120 A3
HAM 153 C1
Hamara Ghar 4 E13 99 C6
Hambalt Rd SW4 159 C6
Hamble Cl HA4 61 C6
Hamble Ct KT1 175 D3
Hambledon Chase N4 50 A2
Hambledon Cl UB8 82 D3
Hambledon Ct
5 Ealing W5 110 A6
9 Wallington SM6 219 B2
Hambledon Gdns SE25 205 D6
Hambledon Ho
2 Kingston u T KT2 176 D4
Lower Clapton E5 74 B4
Hambledon Pl SE21 161 D3
Hambledon Rd SW18 157 B4
Hambledon SE17 139 B6
Hambledown Rd DA15 167 C4
Hamble St SW6 135 D2
Hambleton Cl KT4 216 C6
Hamble Wlk UB5 85 C5
Hambley Ho 5 SE16 118 B2
Hamblin Ho UB1 107 A6
Hambly Mans SW16 182 A4
Hamblyn Ct N16 51 D2
Hambridge Way SW2 160 C4
Hambro Ave BR2 209 A1
Hambrook Ct 12 NW5 71 B4
Hambrook Rd SE25 206 B6
Hambro Rd SW16 181 D5
Hambrough Ho UB4 84 C2
Hambrough Prim Sch UB1 107 B5
Hambrough Rd UB1 107 A5
Ham Cl TW10 153 C1
Ham Comm TW10 153 D1
Ham Croft Cl TW13 150 A1
Ham Ct 12 NW9 27 D1
Hamden Cres RM10 81 D5
Hamel Cl HA3 43 D5
Hamers Ho 19 SW2 160 C4
Hameway E6 100 C3
Ham Farm Rd KT2, TW10 176 A6
Hamfrith Rd E15 76 D2
Ham Gate Ave TW10 176 A6
Ham Ho* TW10 153 C2
Hamilton Ave
Cheam SM3 217 A6
Edmonton N9 18 A4
Ilford IG6 57 A4
Tolworth KT6, SM3 214 C6
Hamilton Cl
Ashford TW13 171 D5
Cockfosters EN4 2 D1
Rotherhithe SE16 119 A4
St John's Wood NW8 92 B4 229 C1
Teddington TW11 175 B4
Tottenham N17 51 D6
Hamilton Cres
Edmonton N13 32 C6
Harrow HA2 63 B5
Hounslow TW3 151 D6
Hamilton Ct
9 Catford SE6 164 D3
Croydon CR0 206 A1
Ealing W5 110 B6
St John's Wood W9 229 A2
Hamilton Gdns NW8 92 A4 229 B2
Hamilton Hall NW8 92 A5 229 A3
Hamilton Ho
23 Bow E3 97 B4
Chiswick W4 133 C6
Kensington W8 245 C2
Oakleigh Pk N20 14 A4
1 Poplar E14 119 B6
Putney SW15 156 A6
10 Richmond TW9 132 C4
St John's Wood NW8 229 C2
Hamilton La N5 72 D4
Hamilton Lo 37 E1 96 C3
Hamilton Mews W1 248 C2
Hamilton Par TW13 172 A6
Hamilton Pk N5 72 D4
Hamilton Pk W N5 72 D4
Hamilton Pl
Mayfair W1 115 A5 248 B3
Sunbury TW16 172 B3
Tottenham N17 33 D1
Hamilton Rd
Acton W4 111 C4
Barnet EN4 2 C1
Bexleyheath DA7 147 A3
Brentford TW8 131 D6
Ealing W5 110 A6
East Finchley N2 48 A6
Edmonton N9 18 A4
Feltham TW13 171 D6
Harrow HA1 42 C4
Hayes UB3 106 B6
Hendon NW11 47 A2
Higham Hill E17 35 A1
Ilford IG1 78 D4
Merton SW19 179 D3
Newham E15 98 C4
Sidcup DA15 190 A6
Southall UB1 107 B5
South Norwood CR7 205 B6
Twickenham TW2 152 C3
West Norwood SE27 183 B6
Willesden NW10 68 A3
Hamilton Road Ind Est SE27 183 B6
Hamilton Road Mews 1 SW19 179 D3
Hamilton Sq
Bermondsey SE1 252 D2
Finchley N12 30 A4
Hamilton St SE8 141 C6
Hamilton Terr NW8 92 A4 229 B2
Hamilton Way
Edmonton N13 32 D6
Finchley N3 29 C4
Hamlea Cl SE12 165 A6
Hamlet Cl SE13 142 C1
Hamlet Ct
14 Enfield EN1 17 C6
1 Hammersmith W6 112 A2
Kennington SE11 261 C2
Hamlet Gdns W6 112 A2
Hamlet Ho SE9 166 C6
Hamlet Ind Est E9 75 C1
Hamleton Terr RM9 80 C1
Hamlet Rd SE19 184 A3
Hamlet Sq NW2 69 A5
Hamlets Way E3 97 B3
Hamlet The SE5 139 B2
Hamlet Way SE1 252 D2
Hamlin Cres HA5 40 C4
Hamlyn Cl HA8 10 A1
Hamlyn Gdns SE19 183 C3
Hamlyn Ho TW13 150 B3
Hammelton Ct 4 BR1 186 D2
Hammelton Gn 2 SW9 138 D4
Hammelton Rd BR1 187 A2
Hammers La NW7 28 A6
Hammersley Ho 8 SE14 140 C5
HAMMERSMITH 112 C2
Hammersmith Bridge Rd W6, SW13 112 C1
Hammersmith Broadway
Hammersmith W6 112 C1
5 Hammersmith W6 112 C2
Hammersmith Flyover W6 112 C1
Hammersmith Gr W6 112 C3
Hammersmith Hospl W12 90 B1
Hammersmith Rd
Hammersmith W6 112 D2
Kensington W14 254 B4
Hammersmith Sta W6 112 C2
Hammersmith Terr 6 W6 112 A1
Hammet Cl UB4 84 D2
Hammett St EC3 253 C6
Hammond Ave CR4 181 B1
Hammond Cl
Barnet EN5 13 B6
Greenford UB6 64 B3
Hampton TW12 173 C2
Hammond Ct
1 Leyton E10 75 D6
1 Walthamstow E17 53 A4
Hammond Ho
10 Deptford SE14 140 C5
Millwall E14 119 D3
Hammond Lo 6 W9 91 C2
Hammond Rd
Enfield EN1 6 B3
Southall UB2 107 A3
Hammonds Cl RM8 80 C5
Hammonds Ho TW19 148 B3
Hammond St NW5 71 C2
Hammond Way 2 SE28 124 B6
Hamonde Cl HA8 10 D2
Hamond Sq N1 95 C5
Ham Park Rd E15 76 D1
Hampden Ave BR3 185 A1
Hampden Cl NW1 232 D4
Hampden Ct
Harrow HA1 42 A5
10 Muswell Hill N10 31 A3
Hampden Gurney CE Prim Sch W1 92 C1 237 B2
Hampden Gurney St W1 237 C1
Hampden La N17 34 A2
Hampden Rd
Beckenham BR3 185 A1
Harrow HA3 24 A1
Hornsey N8 50 C5
Kingston u T KT1 198 C6
Muswell Hill N10 31 A3
Tottenham N17 34 A2
Upper Holloway N19 71 D6
Hampden Sq N14 15 B3
Hampden Way N14 15 B2
Hampshire Cl N18 34 B5
Hampshire Ct
6 Barnes SW13 133 D3
Hendon NW4 46 D4
Hampshire Ho HA8 26 B3
Hampshire Hog La
3 Hammersmith W6 112 B1
11 Hammersmith W6 112 B2
Hampshire Rd N22 32 B3
Hampshire Sch The SW7 114 C4 247 A1
Hampshire St NW5 71 D2
Hampson Way SW8 138 B4 270 C2
HAMPSTEAD 70 A3
Hampstead Cl SE28 124 B5
Hampstead Coll of Fine Arts & Humanities NW3 70 C2
HAMPSTEAD GARDEN SUBURB 47 D4
Hampstead Garden Suburb Inst NW11 47 D4
Hampstead Gate NW3 70 A3
Hampstead Gdns NW11 47 C3
Hampstead Gn NW3 70 C3
Hampstead Gr NW3 70 A5
Hampstead Heath* NW3 70 B6
Hampstead Heath Sta NW3 70 C4
Hampstead High St NW3 70 B4
Hampstead Hill Gdns NW3 70 C4
Hampstead Hill Sch NW3 70 C3
Hampstead Hts N2 48 A6
Hampstead La N6 48 C2
Hampstead Parochial CE Prim Sch NW3 70 A4
Hampstead Rd NW1 93 C4 232 A2
Hampstead Sch NW2 69 A4
Hampstead Sq 1 NW3 70 A5
Hampstead Sta NW3 70 A4
Hampstead Way NW11 47 A3
Hampstead West 4 NW6 69 C2
Hampstead Wlk 1 E3 97 B6
HAMPTON 173 C1
Hampton Cl
Borehamwood WD6 11 A6
Friern Barnet N11 31 B5
Kilburn NW6 91 C4
Wimbledon SW20 178 C3
Hampton Com Coll TW12 173 C5
Hampton Court Ave KT8 196 C3
Hampton Court Cres KT8 196 B6
Hampton Court Landing Stage KT8 196 C6
Hampton Court Pal* KT8 196 D6
Hampton Court Par KT8 196 C5
Hampton Court Rd KT1, KT8 197 B6
Hampton Court Sta KT8 196 C5
Hampton Court Way KT10, KT7, KT8 196 C3
Hampton Ct
Hampton KT8 196 C6
1 Islington N1 72 D2
19 Rotherhithe SE16 118 D5
Wood Green N22 31 C2
Hampton Farm Ind Est TW13 151 A1
HAMPTON HILL 174 A5
Hampton Hill Bsns Pk TW12 174 A5
Hampton Hill Jun Sch TW12 174 A5
Hampton Ho DA7 147 D3
Hampton Inf Sch TW12 173 C3
Hampton Jun Sch TW12 173 C2
Hampton La TW13 173 A6
Hampton Rd E4 35 B5
Hampton Rd E TW13 151 B1
Hampton Rd
Forest Gate E7 77 C3
Ilford IG1 79 A4
Leytonstone E11 54 B1
North Cheam KT4 216 B6
Teddington TW11, TW12 174 C5
Thornton Heath CR0 205 A3
Twickenham TW2 152 B1
Hampton Rd W TW13 151 A1
Hampton Rise HA3 44 A3
Hampton Road Ind Pk CR0 205 A3
Hampton Sch TW12 173 C5
Hampton Sta TW12 173 C2
Hampton St SE1 116 D2 261 D3
HAMPTON WICK 175 D3
Hampton Wick Inf Sch TW11 175 D3
Hampton Wick Sta KT1 175 C2
Ham Ridings TW10 176 B5
Ham Shades Cl 1 DA15 168 A1
Hamson Ct HA2 64 B6
Hamstead Gates 11 NW5 71 B2
Ham St TW10 153 C1
Ham The TW8 131 C5
Ham View CR0 207 A3
Ham Yd W1 249 C6
Hanameel St E16 121 B5
Hana Mews E5 74 B4
Hanbury Cl NW4 46 C6
Hanbury Ct HA1 42 D3
Hanbury Dr
2 Leyton E11 54 D2
Southgate N21 16 B6
Hanbury Ho
8 Bethnal Green E1 96 A2
South Lambeth SW8 270 B5
Hanbury Mews N1 235 B5
Hanbury Rd
South Acton W3 110 D4
Tottenham N17 34 B1
Hanbury St E1 95 D2 243 D4

Hancocke Ho 4 E17 53 D6
Hancock Nunn Ho 1 NW3 70 D1
Hancock Rd
Bromley E3 98 A4
South Norwood SE19 183 B4
Handa Wlk 3 N1 73 A2
Handcroft Rd CR0 204 D1
Hand Ct WC1 240 D3
Handel Cl HA8 26 B4
Handel Ho TW2 152 B5
Handel Mans
Barnes SW13 134 C5
Bloomsbury WC1 240 B6
Handel Par HA8 26 C3
Handel Pl NW10 67 B2
Handel St WC1 94 A3 240 B6
Handel Way HA8 26 C3
Handen Rd SE12 164 D6
Handforth Rd
Brixton SW9 138 C5
6 Ilford IG1 78 D5
Handley Gr NW2 68 D5
Handley Page Rd SM6 220 B1
Handley Rd E9 96 C6
Handowe Cl NW4 46 A5
Handside Cl KT4 200 D1
Hands Wlk E16 99 A1
Handsworth Ave E4 36 B4
Handsworth Prim Sch E4 36 B4
Handsworth Rd N17 51 B6
Handtrough Way IG11 100 D5
Hanford Cl SW18 157 C3
Hanford Row SW19 178 C4
Hanger Ct W5 88 C3
Hanger Gn W5 88 C3
Hanger Lane Sta W5 88 A4
Hanger La (North Circular Rd) W5 88 B2
Hanger Vale La W5 88 B1
Hanger View Way W3 88 C2
Hangmans Cnr BR7 188 D2
Hankey Pl SE1 117 B4 252 D1
Hankins La NW7 11 C1
Hanley Ct N4 50 B1
Hanley Gdns N4 50 B1
Hanley Pl BR3 185 C3
Hanley Rd N4, N19 50 A1
Hanmer Wlk N7 72 B6
Hannah Cl
Beckenham BR3 208 A6
Wembley NW10 67 A4
Hannah Ct
Palmers Green N13 16 B2
5 Sutton SM1 217 D2
Wimbledon SW19 178 D3
Hannah Mary Way 17 SE1 118 A2
Hannah Mews SM6 219 C1
Hannay La N8 49 D2
Hannay Wlk SW16 159 D2
Hannell Rd SW6 135 A5 264 B4
Hannen Ho SE5 139 B2
Hannen Rd SE27 160 D1
Hannibal Rd
Stanwell TW19 148 A4
Stepney E1 96 C2
Hannibal Way CR0 220 B2
Hanning Lo TW3 130 A1
Hannington Rd SW4 137 B2
Hanover Ave
Feltham TW13 150 A2
Newham E16 121 A5
Hanover Circ UB3 83 B1
Hanover Cl
Cheam SM3 217 B4
Richmond TW9 132 C5
Hanover Ct
Colindale NW9 45 C6
Harrow HA1 42 B2
1 Penge SE19 184 A3
11 Pinner HA5 23 B3
Shepherd's Bush W12 112 A5
Stamford Hill N16 51 D2
Hanover Dr BR7 189 A6
Hanover Gate Mans NW1 237 B6
Hanover Gdns SE11 138 C6
Hanover Ho
1 New Barnet EN5 2 A1
St John's Wood NW8 230 A3
Tolworth KT6 198 C1
Hanover Lo N21 16 D6
Hanover Mans 5 SW2 160 C6
Hanover Mead NW11 47 A3
Hanover Pk SE15 140 A4
Hanover Pl
16 Bow E3 97 B4
St Giles WC2 240 B1
Hanover Prim Sch N1 95 A5 235 A4
Hanover Rd
Merton SW19 180 A3
South Tottenham N15 51 D5
Willesden NW10 90 C6
Hanover Sq W1 93 B1 238 D1
Hanover St
Croydon CR0 220 D5
Marylebone W1 93 B1 238 D1
Hanover Stps W2 237 B1
Hanover Terrace Mews NW1 92 C4 230 B1
Hanover Terr
Isleworth TW7 131 A4
Lisson Gr NW1 92 D4 230 C1
Hanover Way DA6 146 D2
Hanover West Ind Est NW10 89 B4
Hanover Yd N1 235 A4
Hansard Mews W14 112 D4
Hansart Way EN2 4 C4
Hanscomb Mews SW4 137 C1
Hans Cres SW1 114 D3 257 C6
Hanselin Cl HA7 24 D5
Hansen Dr N21 16 B6
Hanshaw Dr HA8 27 B2
Hansler Ct 11 SW19 157 A3
Hansler Gr KT8 196 B5
Hansler Rd SE22 161 D6
Hansol Rd DA6 169 A6
Hanson Cl
Balham SW12 159 B4
Beckenham BR3 185 D4
Mortlake SW14 133 A2
West Drayton UB7 104 B3
Hanson Ct E17 53 D3
Hanson Gdns UB1 107 A4
Hanson Ho 2 E1 118 A6
Hanson St W1 93 C2 239 A4
Hans Pl SW1 114 D3 257 C6
Hans Rd SW3 114 D3 257 C6
Hans St SW1 114 D3 257 D5
Hanway Ho 25 SW9 138 C4
Hanway Pl W1 239 C2
Hanway Rd W7 86 C1
Hanway St W1 239 C2
HANWELL 108 D5
Hanwell Sta W7 108 C6
HANWORTH 172 D6
Hanworth Ho SE5 138 D5
Hanworth Rd
Ashford TW16 172 A3
Feltham TW13 150 B3
Hampton TW12 173 C5
Hounslow TW3, TW4 129 D1
Twickenham TW4 151 B4
Hanworth Terr TW3 129 D1
Hanworth Trad Est TW13 151 A1
Hapgood Cl UB6 64 B3
Harben Rd NW6 70 A1
Harberson Rd
Balham SW12 159 B3
West Ham E15 98 D6
Harberton Rd N19 49 C1
Harbet Rd
Highams Pk N18 35 A4
Paddington W2 92 B2 236 D3
Harbex Cl DA5 169 D4
Harbinger Prim Sch E14 119 D2
Harbinger Rd E14 119 D2
Harbin Ho 5 SW2 160 C3
Harbledown Ho SE1 252 C1
Harbledown Rd SW6 265 A2
Harbord Cl SE5 139 B3
Harbord Ho 5 SE16 118 D2
Harbord St SW6 134 D4
Harborne Cl WD19 22 C5
Harborough Ave DA15 167 D4
Harborough Rd SW16 182 B6
Harborough Sch N19 71 D6
Harbour Ave SW10 136 A4 266 B1
Harbour Exchange Sq E14 119 D4
Harbour Rd SE5 139 A2
Harbridge Ave SW15 156 A4
Harbury Rd SM5 218 C1
Harbut Rd SW11 136 B1
Harcombe Rd N16 73 C5
Harcourt Ave
Edgware HA8 11 A1
Little Ilford E12 78 B3
Sidcup DA15 168 C4
Wallington SM6 219 B4
Harcourt Cl TW7 131 A2
Harcourt Field SM6 219 B4
Harcourt Ho
5 Chingford E4 36 B5
27 Clapham SW8 137 D3
Marylebone W1 238 C2
4 Willesden NW10 68 C2
Harcourt Lo 2 SM6 219 B4
Harcourt Rd
Bexley DA6 147 A1
Brockley SE4 141 B2
Bushey WD23 8 A6
Merton SW19 179 C3
Thornton Heath CR7 204 C3
Wallington SM6 219 B4
West Ham E15 98 D5
Wood Green N22 31 D2
Harcourt St W1 92 C2 237 B3
Harcourt Terr SW10 113 D1 255 D1
Hardcastle Cl SE25 206 A3
Hardcastle Ho
3 New Cross Gate SE14 141 A4
8 Peckham SE15 140 A4
Hardcourts Cl BR4 223 D5
Hard Ct IG8 37 C4
Hardel Rise SW2 160 D3
Hardel Wlk SE24, SW2 160 C4
Harden Ct 1 SE7 122 A2
Harden Ho SE5 139 C3
Harders Rd SE15 140 B3
Hardess St SE24 139 A2
Hardham Ho 5 SW2 160 C5
Hardie Cl NW10 67 B3
Harding Cl
Camberwell SE17 139 A6
South Croydon CR0 221 D5
Harding Ct SE25 183 D1
Hardinge Cl UB8 82 D1
Hardinge Cres SE18 123 A3
Hardinge Rd
Edmonton N18 33 C4
Willesden NW10 90 C6
Hardinge St
Stepney E1 96 C1
Woolwich SE18 122 D3
Harding Ho
Barnes SW13 134 B6
Hayes UB3 84 B1
14 Woolwich SE18 122 B2
Harding Pl SE23 163 A4
Harding Rd DA7 147 B3
Hardings Cl KT2 176 B2
Hardings La SE20 184 D4
Hardington 2 NW1 71 A1
Hardman Rd
Greenwich SE7 121 B1
Kingston u T KT2 176 A1
Hardwick Cl 7 HA7 25 C5
Hardwick Ct 8 E11 55 A3
Hardwicke Ave TW5 129 C4
Hardwicke Ho 14 E3 97 D4
Hardwicke Mews WC1 233 D1
Hardwicke Rd
Acton W4 111 B2
Bowes Pk N13 32 A4
Richmond TW10 175 C6
Hardwicke St IG11 101 A6
Hardwick Gn W13 87 B2
Hardwick Ho
14 London SW8 137 D3
Marylebone NW8 237 B6
Hardwick St EC1 94 C4 234 B1
Hardwick's Way SW18 157 C6
Hardwidge St SE1 253 A2
Hardy Ave
4 Newham E16 121 A5
Ruislip HA4 62 B3
Hardy Cl Barnet EN5 13 A6
Pinner HA5 40 D2
Rotherhithe SE16 118 D4
Hardy Cotts 2 SE10 142 B6
Hardy Ct
Greenwich SE3 142 D6
Hardy Ct *continued*
9 Wanstead E11 55 A5
Hardyng Ho 4 E17 53 A5
Hardy Pas N22 32 C1
Hardy Rd
Greenwich SE3 142 D6
Merton SW19 179 D3
Walthamstow E4 35 B4
Hardys Mews KT8 196 C5
Hardy Way EN2 4 C4
Hare and Billet Rd SE3 142 B3
Harebell Dr E6 100 C2
Harecastle Cl UB4 85 A3
Harecourt Rd N1 73 A2
Hare Ct EC4 241 A1
Haredale Ho 24 SE16 118 A4
Haredale Rd SE24 139 A1
Haredon Cl SE23 162 D4
Harefield Cl EN2 4 C4
Harefield Ct 4 SW19 179 C3
Harefield KT10 212 C5
Harefield Mews SE4 141 B2
Harefield Rd
Brockley SE4 141 B2
Hornsey N8 49 D4
Sidcup DA14 168 D1
South Norwood SW16 182 B3
Uxbridge UB8 60 A3
Hare La KT10 212 C2
Hare Marsh E2 96 A3
Harenc Sch Trust DA14 190 C5
Hare Pl EC4 241 B1
Hare Row E2 96 B5
Haresfield Rd RM10 81 C2
Harestone Ct CR2 221 C2
Hare St SE18 122 C3
Hare Wlk N1 95 C5
Harewood Ave
Lisson Gr NW1 92 C3 237 B5
Northolt UB5 63 B1
Harewood Cl UB5 63 B1
Harewood Ct HA3 24 C2
Harewood Pl W1 238 D1
Harewood Rd
Hounslow TW7 130 D4
Mitcham SW19 180 C4
South Croydon CR2 221 C2
Harewood Row NW1 237 B4
Harewood Terr UB2 107 B2
Harfield Gdns 1 SE5 139 C2
Harfield Rd TW16 172 D1
Harfleur Ct SE11 261 C3
Harford Cl E4 19 D4
Harford Ho
Camberwell SE5 139 A6
Notting Hill W11 91 B2
Harford Mews 6 N19 71 D5
Harford Rd E4 19 D4
Harford St E1 97 A3
Harford Wlk N2 48 B5
Hargood Cl HA3 44 A3
Hargood Rd SE3 143 C4
Hargrave Mans 3 N19 71 D6
Hargrave Park Prim Sch N19 71 C6
Hargrave Pk N19 71 C6
Hargrave Pl N7 71 D3
Hargrave Rd N19 71 C6
Hargraves Ho 14 W12 112 B6
Hargwyne St SW9 138 B2
Haringey Pk N8 50 A3
Haringey Rd N8 50 A5
Harington Terr N18 17 B1
Harkett Cl HA3 24 D1
Harkett Ct HA3 24 D1
Harkness Ct SM1 201 D1
Harkness Ho 30 E1 96 A1
Harland Ave
Sidcup DA15 167 C2
South Croydon CR0 222 A5
Harland Cl SW19 201 D6
Harland Rd SE12 165 A3
Harlands Gr BR6 226 D4
Harlech Ct 1 SE23 162 C3
Harlech Gdns TW5 128 C5
Harlech Rd N14 16 A1
Harlech Twr 5 W3 111 A4
Harlequin Ave TW8 131 A6
Harlequin Cl
Hayes UB4 84 D2
Isleworth TW7 152 C6
Harlequin Ct
Croydon CR2 221 A1
Ealing W5 109 C6
Willesden NW10 67 B2
Harlequin Ho 1 DA18 125 A3
Harlequin Rd TW11 175 B3
Harlescott Rd SE15 140 D1
HARLESDEN 89 D6
Harlesden Gdns NW10 89 D6
Harlesden Plaza 2 NW10 89 D5
Harlesden Prim Sch NW10 89 C5
Harlesden Rd NW10 90 A6
Harlesden Sta NW10 89 B5
Harleston Cl 4 E5 74 C6
Harley BR7 189 B2
Harley Cl HA0 65 D2
Harley Cres HA1 42 B5
Harley Ct Harrow HA1 42 B5
Wanstead E11 55 A2
Whetstone N20 14 A1
Harleyford BR1 187 C2
Harleyford Ct
Kennington SW8 270 C6
Wembley HA0 65 A4
Harleyford Manor 8 W3 111 A5
Harleyford Rd SE11 138 B6 270 C6
Harleyford St SE11 138 C6
Harley Gdns
Orpington BR6 227 C4
South Kensington SW10 114 A1 256 B1
Harley Gr E3 97 B4
Harley Ho
Leytonstone E11 54 B2
Marylebone NW1 238 B5
Harley Pl W1 93 B2 238 C3
Harley Rd
Hampstead NW3 70 B1
Harlesden NW10 89 C5
Harrow HA1 42 B5
Harley St W1 93 B2 238 C3
Harley Villas NW10 89 C5
Harling Ct 3 SW11 136 D3
Harlinger St SE18 122 A3
HARLINGTON 127 A6
Harlington Cl UB7 127 A5
Harlington Cnr UB3 127 B4
Harlington Com Sch UB3 105 B2
Harlington Rd DA7 147 A2
Harlington Rd E TW13, TW14 150 C3
Harlington Rd UB8 82 C3
Harlington Rd W TW14 150 B5
Harlowe Ho 13 E8 95 D6
Harlow Mans 2 IG11 78 D1
Harlow Rd N13 17 B1
Harlyn Dr HA5 40 B6
Harlyn Prim Sch HA5 40 B6
Harlynwood 19 SE5 139 A5
Harman Ave IG8 36 D4
Harman Cl
10 Bermondsey SE1 118 A1
Chingford E4 36 B6
Cricklewood NW2 69 A5
Harman Dr
Blackfen DA15 167 D5
Cricklewood NW2 69 A4
Harman Rd EN1 17 D6
HARMONDSWORTH 126 A6
Harmondsworth La UB7 126 B6
Harmondsworth Rd UB7 104 A2
Harmon Ho 7 SE8 119 B2
Harmony Cl NW11 47 A4
Harmony Way
Bromley BR1 187 A1
Hendon NW4 46 C5
Harmood Gr NW1 71 B1
Harmood Ho 2 NW1 71 B1
Harmood St NW1 71 B1
Harmsworth St SE17 116 D1 261 C1
Harmsworth Way N20 13 C3
Harnage Ho TW8 110 A1
Harness Rd SE28 124 A4
Harney Ct SE14 141 A4
Harold Ave
Erith DA17 125 B1
Hayes UB3 105 D3
Harold Ct
14 Rotherhithe SE16 118 D4
6 Teddington TW11 174 C5
Harold Est SE1 263 B5
Harold Gibbons Ct 12 SE7 143 C6
Harold Ho 16 E2 96 D5
Harold Laski Ho EC1 234 D1
Harold Maddison Ho SE17 261 D2
Harold Rd
Chingford E4 20 A1
Hornsey N8 50 B5
Leytonstone E11 54 C1
Newham E13 99 B6
North Acton NW10 89 B4
South Norwood SE19 183 B3
South Tottenham N15 51 D4
Sutton SM1 218 B4
Woodford IG8 37 A2
Haroldstone Rd E17 53 A4
Harold Wilson Ho SW6 264 D5
Haronton Ct E10 76 A6
Harp Alley EC4 241 C2
Harp Bsns Ctr The NW2 68 A6
Harpenden Rd
Wanstead E12 77 C6
West Norwood SE27, SW16 160 D2
Harpenmead Point NW2 69 B6
Harper Cl N14 15 C6
Harper Ho 3 SW9 138 D2
Harper Mews SW17 158 A1
Harper Rd
Bermondsey SE1 117 A3 262 B6
Newham E6 100 B1
Harper's Yd N17 33 D2
Harp Island Cl NW10 67 B6
Harp La EC3 253 A5
Harpley Sq E1 96 D3
Harpour Rd IG11 79 A2
Harp Rd W7 86 D3
Harpsden St SW11 268 A1
Harpur Mews WC1 240 C4
Harpur St WC1 94 B2 240 C4
Harraden Rd SE3 143 C4
Harrier Ave E11 55 B3
Harrier Ct TW4 129 A3
Harrier Ho 9 SW11 136 C2
Harrier Mews SE28 123 B4
Harrier Rd NW9 27 C1
Harriers Cl W5 110 A6
Harrier Way E6 100 B2
Harries Rd UB4 84 C3
Harriet Cl E8 96 A6
Harriet Gdns CR0 222 A6
Harriet Ho
Walham Green SW6 265 D3
Walthamstow E17 53 D4
Harriet St SW1 114 D4 247 D1
Harriet Tubman Cl 21 SW2 160 C4
Harriet Way WD23 8 B4
Harriet Wlk SW1 114 D4 247 D1
HARRINGAY 50 D4
Harringay Gdns N8 50 D5
Harringay Green Lanes Sta N4 50 D3
Harringay Rd N15 50 D5
Harringay Sta N4 50 C3
Harrington Cl
Wallington CR0 220 A6
Willesden NW10 67 B5
Harrington Ct
6 South Croydon CR0 221 B6
South Kensington SW7 256 D4
9 West Kilburn W9 91 B4
Harrington Gdns SW7 114 A2 256 A3
Harrington Hill E5 52 B1
Harrington Hill Prim Sch E5 52 B1
Harrington Ho
2 Bromley BR1 187 A2
Regent's Pk NW1 232 A2
Upper Clapton E5 52 C1
Westminster SW1 259 D2
Harrington Rd
Croydon SE25 206 B5
Leytonstone E11 54 C1
South Kensington SW7 114 B2 256 C4
Harrington Road Sta SE25 206 C6
Harrington Sq NW1 93 C5 232 A3
Harrington St NW1 93 C4 232 A2
Harrington Way SE18 121 D3
Harriott Cl SE10 120 D2
Harriott Ho 11 E1 96 C1
Harris Acad CR4 203 D6

Harris City Tech Coll
SE19 183 D2
Harris Cl Enfield EN2 4 D4
Heston TW5 129 C4
Harris Cotts 1 E15 98 D6
Harris Ct HA9 66 B5
Harris Girl's Acad
SE15 162 C6
Harris Ho 11 Bow E3 97 C4
7 Brixton SW9 138 C2
Harris Lo SE6 164 A3
Harrison Cl N20 14 C3
Harrison Ho SE17 262 C2
Harrison Rd
Dagenham RM10 81 D2
Stonebridge NW10 89 B6
Harrisons Ct 1
SE14 140 D6
Harrison's Rise CR0 220 D5
Harrison St
WC1 94 A4 233 B1
Harrison Way TW17 192 D4
Harris Rd
Dagenham RM9 81 B3
Erith DA7 147 B4
Harris St
Camberwell SE5 139 B5
Walthamstow E17 53 B2
Harris Way TW16 171 C2
Harrodian Sch The
SW13 133 D5
Harrogate Ct
2 Forest Hill
SE26 162 A1
9 New Southgate
N11 31 A4
Harrold Ho 1 NW3 70 A1
Harrold Rd RM8 80 B3
HARROW 42 B3
Harrow Ave EN1 17 D5
Harroway Rd SW11 136 B3
Harrowby St
W1 92 C1 237 B2
Harrow Cl KT9 213 D1
Harrow Coll HA1 42 C2
Harrow Coll (Harrow
Weald Campus)
HA3 24 C4
Harrowdene Cl HA0 65 D4
Harrowdene Ct
SW19 179 A5
Harrowdene Gdns
TW11 175 A3
Harrowdene Rd HA0 65 D4
Harrow Dr N9 17 D3
Harrowes Meade
HA8 10 C1
Harrow Fields Gdns
HA1 64 C5
Harrowgate Ho 22
E9 74 D2
Harrowgate Rd E9 75 A1
Harrow Gn E11 76 C5
Harrow High Sch &
Sports Coll HA1 43 A3
Harrow La E14 120 A6
Harrow Lo SM2 218 B2
Harrow Manor Way
SE2 124 C3
Harrow Mus & Her Ctr*
HA2 42 A6
HARROW ON THE HILL
42 C1
Harrow-on-the-Hill Sta
HA1 42 C3
Harrow Pk HA1 64 C6
Harrow Pl E1 95 C1 243 B2
Harrow Rd
Ashford TW15 148 C2
Barking IG11 101 C6
Carshalton SM5 218 C2
Ilford IG1 79 A4
Leyton E11 76 D5
Little Venice
W2 92 A2 236 B3
2 Newham E6 100 A6
Sudbury HA0 65 A4
Tokyngton HA9 66 C2
Wembley HA0 65 D3
Westbourne Green W2,
W9 91 C3
Harrow Sch HA1 42 C1
Harrow St NW1 237 A4
Harrow View
Harrow HA1, HA2 42 B5
Hayes UB3 84 A1
Hillingdon UB10 83 A4
Harrow View Rd W5 87 B3
Harrow Way
Charlton TW17 171 A1
South Oxhey WD19 23 A6
HARROW WEALD 24 B2
Harrow Weald Pk
HA3 24 B4
Harrow & Wealdstone
Sta HA1 42 C5
Harry Ct 15 NW9 46 A5
Harry Gosling Prim Sch
E1 96 A1
Harry Hinkins Ho
SE17 262 B1
Harry Lambourn Ho 10
SE15 140 B5
Harston Dr EN3 7 C5
Harston 15 KT1 176 C1
Hart Ct E12 78 C1
Harte Rd TW3 129 B3
Hartfield Ave
Borehamwood
WD6 10 C6
Northolt UB5 84 B5
Hartfield Cl WD6 10 C6
Hartfield Cres
Coney Hall BR4 225 A5
Merton SW19 179 B3
Hartfield Ct CR2 220 D1
Hartfield Gr SE20 184 C2
Hartfield Ho UB5 84 B5
Hartfield Rd
Chessington KT9 213 D3
Hayes BR4 225 A4
Merton SW19 179 C3
Hartfield Terr E3 97 C5
Hartford Ave HA3 43 B6
Hartford Rd
Old Bexley DA5 169 C5
West Ewell KT19 214 D2
Hart Gr W5 110 C5
Hart Grove Ct 3
W5 110 C5
Hartgrove Ct NW9 45 A5
Hart Gr UB1 85 C2
Hartham Cl
Isleworth TW7 131 A4
Lower Holloway N7 72 A3
Hartham Rd
Isleworth TW7 131 A4
Lower Holloway N7 72 A3
Tottenham N17 33 D1
Hart Ho Hayes UB4 83 B2
Streatham SW2 160 C3
Harting Rd SE9 166 A1
Hartington Cl
Farnborough BR6 227 A3
Harrow HA1 64 C4
Hartington Ct
Chiswick W4 132 D5
South Lambeth SW8 270 A2
Hartington Rd
Chiswick W4 133 A4
Ealing W13 109 B6
Newham E16 99 B1
Southall UB2 107 A3
South Lambeth
SW8 138 A5 270 A3
Twickenham TW1 153 B5
Walthamstow E17 53 A3
Hartismere Rd
SW6 135 B5 264 D4
Hartlake Rd E9 75 A2
Hartland Cl
Edgware HA8 10 C2
Enfield N21 17 A5
Hartland Ct 5 N11 30 D5
Hartland Dr
Edgware HA8 10 C2
Ruislip HA4 62 B4
Hartland NW1 232 B5
Hartland Rd
Camden Town NW1 71 B1
Cheam SM4 201 D2
Friern Barnet N11 30 D5
Hampton TW12 173 D6
Isleworth TW7 131 A2
Kilburn NW6 91 B6
Stratford E15 76 D1
Hartlands Cl DA5 169 B5
Hartlands The TW5 128 B6
Hartland Way
Croydon CR0 223 A6
Morden SM4 201 B2
Hartlepool Ct E16 122 D5
Hartley Ave
Edgware NW7 27 D5
Newham E6 100 A6
Hartley Cl
Bickley BR1 188 B1
Edgware NW7 27 D5
Hartley Ct Ealing W5 110 C5
5 Mitcham CR4 180 C2
Hartley Ho
Bermondsey SE1 263 D4
Finchley N3 29 D4
Putney SW15 156 A6
Hartley Prim Sch
E6 100 A6
Hartley Rd
Bexley DA16 146 C5
Leytonstone E11 54 D1
Thornton Heath CR0 205 A2
Hartley St E2 96 C4
Hart Lo EN5 1 A2
Hartmann Rd E16 122 A5
Hartmoor Mews EN3 6 D6
Hartnoll Ho 4 N7 72 C3
Hartnoll St N7 72 B3
Harton Cl BR1 187 D2
Harton Lodge 2
SE8 141 C4
Harton Rd N9 18 B2
Harton St SE8 141 C4
Hartopp Ct 20 N16 73 C5
Hartopp Point SW6 264 B4
Hartsbourne Ave
WD23 8 B2
Hartsbourne Cl WD23 8 B2
Hartsbourne Ct 5
UB1 86 A1
Hartsbourne Pk WD23 8 C2
Hartsbourne Prim Sch
WD23 8 B2
Hartsbourne Rd WD23 8 B2
Harts Gr IG8 37 A5
Hartshill Cl UB10 60 D2
Hartshorn Alley EC3 243 B1
Hartshorn Gdns E6 100 C3
Harts La IG11 78 D2
Hart's La SE14 141 A4
Hartslock Dr SE2 124 D4
Hartsmead Rd SE9 166 B2
Hart Sq SM4 201 C3
Hart St EC3 253 B6
Hartsway EN3 6 C1
Hartswood Gn WD23 8 B2
Hartswood Ho 10
SW2 160 A3
Hartswood Rd W12 111 D3
Hartsworth Cl E13 98 D5
Hartville Rd SE18 123 C2
Hartwell Ct SE22 140 A1
Hartwell Dr E4 36 A4
Hartwell Ho 2 SE7 121 B1
Hartwell St E8 73 D2
Harvard Ct
9 Eltham SE9 166 C5
West Hampstead
NW6 69 D3
Harvard Hill W4 132 D6
Harvard Ho
3 Camberwell
SE17 138 D6
Putney SW15 156 D5
Harvard Mans 18
SW11 136 B1
Harvard Rd
11 Acton Green
W4 111 A1
Gunnersbury W4 110 D1
Hounslow TW7 130 C4
Lewisham SE13 164 A6
Harvel Cres SE2 124 D1
Harvel Ct SE2 125 A1
Harvest Bank Rd
BR4 225 A5
Harvest Ct
Beckenham BR3 185 C3
Littleton TW17 192 C5
Harvesters Cl TW7 152 B6
Harvest La
Loughton IG10 21 D4
Thames Ditton KT7 197 A3
Harvest Rd TW13 150 A1
Harvey Ct
Battersea SW11 267 B2
Walthamstow E17 53 C4
Harvey Dr TW12 173 C2
Harvey Gdns
Greenwich SE7 121 C1
Leytonstone E11 54 D1
Harvey Ho
Barking IG11 79 A1
10 Bethnal Green E1 96 B3
Brentford TW8 110 A1
Dagenham RM6 58 D5
Hornsey N8 50 A6
Pimlico SW1 259 D1
Shoreditch N1 235 D5
Wembley Pk HA9 66 D6
Harvey Lo 8 W9 91 C2
Harvey Mews N8 50 B4
Harvey Point 7 E16 99 A2
Harvey Rd
15 Camberwell
SE5 139 B4
Hillingdon UB10 82 C5
Hornsey Vale N8 50 B4
Ilford IG1 78 D3
Leytonstone E11 54 D1
Ruislip UB5 62 C1
Twickenham TW4 151 B4
Walton-on-T KT12 194 A2
Harvey St N1 235 D5
Harvill Rd
Newyears Green
UB9 38 A2
Sidcup DA14 191 A5
Harvil Rd UB9, UB10 38 A2
Harvington Sch W5 87 D1
Harvington Wlk E8 74 A1
Harvist Rd NW6 91 A5
Harwell Cl HA4 39 B1
Harwood Ave
Bromley BR1 187 B1
Mitcham CR4 202 C6
Harwood Cl
London N12 30 C4
Wembley HA0 65 D4
Harwood Ct
Putney SW15 134 C1
Shoreditch N1 235 D5
Harwood Dr UB10 82 B6
Harwood Point
SE16 119 B4
Harwood Rd
SW6 135 D5 265 C3
Harwoods Yd N21 16 C4
Harwood Terr
SW6 135 D4 265 C2
Hascombe Ho 11
SW15 156 B3
Hascombe Terr 2
SE5 139 B3
Haselbury Rd N9 17 C1
Haseley End SE23 162 C4
Haselrigge Rd SW4 137 D1
Haseltine Prim Sch
SE26 185 B6
Haseltine Rd SE26 185 B6
Haselwood Dr EN2 4 D1
Haskard Rd RM9 80 D4
Hasker St
SW3 114 C2 257 B4
Haslam Ave SM3 201 A1
Haslam Cl
Islington N1 72 C1
Uxbridge UB10 61 A6
Haslam Ct N11 31 B6
Haslam Ho 12 N1 73 A1
Haslam St SE15 139 D4
Haslemere Ave
Barnet EN4 14 D3
Cranford TW5 128 C3
Ealing W13 109 A3
Hendon NW4 46 D3
Mitcham CR4, SW19 180 B1
Wandsworth SW18 157 D2
Haslemere Bsns Ctr
EN1 18 B6
Haslemere Cl
Hampton TW12 173 B5
Wallington SM6 220 A3
Haslemere Ct 5 N16 51 C1
Haslemere Gdns N3 47 B5
Haslemere & Heathrow
Est The TW4 128 B3
Haslemere Ind Est
Feltham TW14 150 A6
Wandsworth SW18 157 D2
Haslemere Prim Sch
CR4 180 B1
Haslemere Rd
Bexleyheath DA7 147 C3
Hornsey N8 50 A2
Ilford IG3 79 D6
Southgate N21 16 D3
Thornton Heath CR7 204 D4
Hasler Cl SE28 124 C6
Hasler Ct E12 78 A4
Haslett Rd TW17 171 C1
Hasluck Gdns EN5 14 A5
Hasmonean High Sch
(Boys) NW4 28 D1
Hasmonean High Sch
(Girls) NW7 28 A2
Hasmonean Prim Sch
NW4 46 D4
Hassard St E2 95 D5
Hassendean Rd SE3 143 B5
Hassett Rd E9 75 A2
Hassocks Cl SE23,
SE26 162 B1
Hassocks Rd SW16 181 D2
Hassock Wood BR2 225 D4
Hassop Rd NW2 68 D4
Hassop Wlk SE9 188 A6
Hasted Rd SE7 121 D1
Hasting Ct TW11 174 B5
Hastings Ave IG6 57 A5
Hastings Cl
New Barnet EN5 2 A1
17 Peckham SE15 140 A5
Wembley HA0 65 C4
Hastings Dr KT6 197 C3
Hastings Ho
Ealing W13 109 B6
Enfield EN3 6 C3
18 Shepherd's Bush
W12 112 B6
Hastings Hos WC1 233 A1
Hastings Ho
Tottenham N17 34 A2
6 Woolwich SE18 122 B2
Hastings Pl 1 CR0 205 D1
Hastings Rd
Croydon CR0 205 D1
Ealing W13 109 B6
Keston Mark BR2 226 A6
Tottenham N17 51 B6
Hastings Rd *continued*
Wood Green N11 31 D5
Hastings St
St Pancras
WC1 94 A4 233 A1
Woolwich SE18 123 A3
Hastingwood Ct
Newham E6 100 B5
Walthamstow E17 53 D4
Hastingwood Trad Est
N18 35 A4
Hastoe Cl UB4 85 A3
Hasty Cl CR4 181 A2
Hatcham Mews Bsns Ctr
SE14 140 D4
Hatcham Park Mews
SE14 140 D4
Hatcham Park Rd
SE14 140 D4
Hatcham Rd SE15 140 C6
Hatchard Rd N19 72 A6
Hatchcroft NW4 46 B6
HATCH END 23 A3
Hatch End High Sch
HA3 23 D2
Hatch End Sta HA5 23 C3
Hatchers Mews SE1 253 B1
Hatchett Rd TW14 149 A3
Hatchfield Ho 8
N15 51 C3
Hatch Gr RM6 59 A5
Hatch Ho
9 Muswell Hill
N10 31 A3
14 Richmond TW10 153 C1
Hatch La E4 20 C1
Hatch Pl KT2 176 B5
Hatch Rd SW16 182 A1
Hatch The EN3 6 D4
Hatchwoods IG8 36 D6
Hatcliffe Almshouses 8
SE10 120 C1
Hatcliffe Cl SE3 142 D2
Hatcliffe St SE10 120 D1
Hatfield Cl
Deptford SE14 140 D5
Ilford IG6 56 D6
Mitcham CR4 202 B5
Hatfield Ct
Greenwich SE3 143 A5
8 Northolt UB5 84 C4
Hatfield Ho
16 Kingston u T
KT6 198 A4
Leytonstone E11 54 D2
St Luke's EC1 242 A5
Hatfield Mead SM4 201 C4
Hatfield Mews RM9 81 A1
Hatfield Prim Sch
SM4 201 A3
Hatfield Rd
Acton W4 111 B4
Dagenham RM9 81 A1
10 Ealing W13, W7 109 A5
Stratford E15 76 C3
Hatfields
SE1 116 C5 251 B4
Hathaway Cl
Bromley BR2 210 B1
Ruislip HA4 61 D4
Stanmore HA7 25 A5
Hathaway Cres E12 78 C2
Hathaway Gdns
Ealing W13 87 A2
Ilford RM6 58 D4
Hathaway Ho 3 N1 95 C4
Hathaway Prim Sch
W13 86 D2
Hathaway Rd CR0 204 D2
Hatherleigh Cl
Barnet EN4 1 D4
Chessington KT9 213 D3
Edgware NW7 28 D3
Morden SM4 201 C5
Hatherleigh Ho
SM4 201 C5
Hatherleigh Rd HA4 62 A6
Hatherley Cres
DA14 168 A2
Hatherley Ct 6 W2 91 D1
Hatherley Gdns
London N8 50 A3
Newham E6 99 D4
Hatherley Gr W2 91 D1
Hatherley Ho 2 E17 53 C5
Hatherley Mews E17 53 C5
Hatherley Rd
Richmond TW9 132 B4
Sidcup DA14 168 A1
Walthamstow E17 53 C5
Hatherley St SW1 259 B3
Hathern Gdns SE9 188 C6
Hatherop Rd TW12 173 B3
Hathersage Ct N1 73 B3
Hathersley Ho 3
SW2 160 C4
Hathorne Cl 3
SE15 140 B3
Hathway Ho 3
SE15 140 C3
Hathway St 4 SE15 140 C3
Hatley Ave IG6 57 A5
Hatley Cl N11 30 D5
Hatley Rd N4, N7 72 B6
Hat & Mitre Ct EC1 241 D5
Hatstone Ct NW3 70 A3
Hatteraick St 6
SE16 118 C4
Hattersfield Cl
DA17 125 B2
HATTON 127 D1
Hatton Cl SE18 145 B5
Hatton Cross Rdbt
TW6 127 D2
Hatton Cross Sta
TW6 127 D1
Hatton Ct BR7 188 B3
Hatton Gdn
EC1 94 C2 241 B4
Hatton Gdns CR4 202 D4
Hatton Gn TW14 128 A1
Hatton Ho 17 E1 118 A6
Hatton Pl EC1 241 B4
Hatton Rd TW14,
TW6 149 C6
Hatton Rd N TW6 127 B4
Hatton Rd CR0 204 C1
Hatton Row NW8 236 D5
Hatton Sch IG8 55 D6
Hatton St NW8 236 D5
Hatton Wall
EC1 94 C2 241 B4
Haughmond 4 N12 29 D6
Haunch of Venison Yd
W1 238 C1
Hauteville Court Gdns
2 W6 111 D3
Havana Rd SW18,
SW19 157 C2
Havannah St E14 119 C4
Havant Rd E17 54 A6
Havelock Cl 13 W12 112 B6
Havelock Ct
8 Peckham SE15 140 B5
Southall UB2 107 B3
Havelock Hall 8
CR0 205 D1
Havelock Ho
4 Croydon CR0 205 D1
Forest Hill SE23 162 C3
Havelock Pl HA1 42 C3
Havelock Prim Sch
UB2 107 B3
Havelock Rd
Belvedere DA17 125 B2
Bromley BR2 209 C5
Croydon CR0 221 D6
Harrow HA3 42 C6
Southall UB2 107 C3
Tottenham N17 34 A1
Wimbledon SW19 180 A5
Havelock St
Ilford IG1 78 D6
Islington N1 94 A6 233 B6
Havelock Terr
SW8 137 B5 268 D3
Havelock Wlk SE23 162 C2
Haven Cl
Chislehurst SE9 166 B1
Hayes UB4 83 C3
Hinchley Wood KT10 212 C6
Sidcup DA14 190 C4
Wimbledon SW19 156 D1
Haven Ct
Beckenham BR3 186 A1
Hinchley Wood KT10 212 C6
Thornton Heath CR7 204 C6
Haven Gn W5 87 D1
Haven Green Ct W5 87 D1
Havenhurst Rise EN2 4 C3
Haven La W5 88 A1
Haven Lo
15 Enfield EN1 17 C6
Temple Fortune
NW11 47 B4
7 Woolwich SE18 122 D2
Haven Pl Ealing W5 109 D6
Hinchley Wood KT10 212 C6
Havenpool NW8 91 D6
Haven Rd TW15 148 D1
Haven St 18 NW1 71 B1
Haven The
Ashford TW16 172 A3
East Barnet N14 15 B5
Richmond TW9 132 C2
Havenwood HA9 66 D5
Havercourt 3 NW3 70 C2
Haverfield Gdns
TW9 132 C5
Haverfield Rd E3 97 A4

Haverford Way HA8 ... 26 B2
Havergal Villas N15 ... 50 D6
Haverhill Rd
Chingford E4 ... 20 A3
Streatham SW12 ... 159 C3
Havering Gdns RM6 ... 58 D4
Havering Ho N4 ... 51 A2
Havering 8 NW1 ... 71 B1
Havering St E1 ... 96 D1
Havering Way IG11 ... 102 B4
Haverley 15 SW20 ... 178 D3
Haversham Cl TW1 ... 153 D5
Haversham Ct UB6 ... 64 D2
Haversham Lo NW2 ... 68 D3
Haversham Pl N6 ... 70 D6
Haverstock Ct 2 BR5 ... 190 B1
Haverstock Hill NW3 ... 70 D2
Haverstock Rd NW5 ... 71 A3
Haverstock Sch NW1 ... 71 A2
Haverstock St N1 ... 94 D5 234 D3
Haverthwaite Rd BR6 ... 227 B5
Havilland Ct HA8 ... 26 B6
Havil St SE5 ... 139 C4
Havisham Ho 25 SE16 ... 118 A4
Havisham Pl SW16 ... 182 D3
Hawarden Gr SE24 ... 161 A4
Hawarden Hill NW2 ... 68 A5
Hawarden Rd E17 ... 52 D5
Hawberry Lo N7 ... 72 A2
Hawbridge Rd E11 ... 54 B1
Hawes Down Inf Sch BR4 ... 208 B1
Hawes Down Jun Sch BR4 ... 208 B1
Hawes La BR4 ... 224 C6
Hawes Rd
Bromley BR1 ... 187 B2
Edmonton N18 ... 34 B4
Hawes St N1 ... 72 D1
Haweswater Ho TW1 ... 152 D6
Hawfinch 28 NW9 ... 27 D2
Hawgood St E3 ... 97 C2
Hawkdene E4 ... 20 A5
Hawke Ct UB4 ... 84 C3
Hawkedale Inf Sch TW16 ... 193 D6
Hawke Ho 20 E1 ... 96 D3
Hawke Park Rd N22 ... 50 D6
Hawke Pl 29 SE16 ... 118 D4
Hawker Ct 14 KT2 ... 176 C3
Hawke Rd SE19 ... 183 C4
Hawker 28 NW9 ... 27 D2
Hawkesbury Rd SW15 ... 156 B6
Hawkesfield Rd SE23 ... 163 B2
Hawkesley Cl TW1 ... 175 A6
Hawkes Rd
Feltham TW14 ... 150 A4
Mitcham CR4 ... 180 D2
Hawkesworth Ho 5 SW4 ... 159 C5
Hawke Twr 4 SE14 ... 141 A6
Hawkewood Rd TW16 ... 194 A6
Hawkfield Ct TW7 ... 130 C3
Hawk Ho 7 SW11 ... 136 C2
Hawkhurst Gdns KT9 ... 214 A4
Hawkhurst Rd SW16 ... 181 D2
Hawkhurst Way
New Malden KT3 ... 199 B4
West Wickham BR4 ... 223 D6
Hawkinge N17 ... 33 B1
Hawkins Cl
Burnt Oak NW7 ... 27 B5
Harrow HA1 ... 42 B2
Hawkins Ho
3 Deptford SE8 ... 141 C6
10 Richmond TW10 ... 153 C1
Hawkins Rd
Teddington TW11 ... 175 B4
Willesden NW10 ... 67 C1
Hawkins Way SE6 ... 185 C5
Hawkley Gdns SE27 ... 160 D2
Hawkridge Cl RM6 ... 58 C3
Hawkridge 19 NW5 ... 71 A2
Hawksbrook La BR3 ... 208 A3
Hawkshaw Cl 28 SW2 ... 160 A4
Hawkshead Cl BR1 ... 186 C3
Hawkshead NW1 ... 232 A2
Hawkshead Rd
Acton W4 ... 111 C4
Willesden NW10 ... 67 D1
Hawkslade Rd SE15 ... 162 D6
Hawksley Rd N16 ... 73 C5
Hawks Mews 10 SE10 ... 142 A5
Hawksmoor Cl
2 Newham E6 ... 100 A1
Plumstead Comm SE18 ... 123 C1
Hawksmoor Mews E1 ... 118 B6
Hawksmoor Pl 2 E2 ... 96 A3
Hawksmoor Sch SE28 ... 124 B6
Hawksmoor St 5 W6 ... 134 D6
Hawksmouth E4 ... 20 A4
Hawks Rd KT1 ... 176 B1
Hawkstone Rd SE16 ... 118 C2
Hawkwell Ct E4 ... 20 A1
Hawkwell Ho RM8 ... 81 C6
Hawkwell Wlk N1 ... 235 B6
Hawkwood Cres E4 ... 19 D5
Hawkwood La BR7 ... 189 A2
Hawkwood Mount 1 E5 ... 52 B1
Hawlands Dr HA5 ... 41 A2
Hawley Cl TW12 ... 173 B4
Hawley Cres NW1 ... 71 B1
Hawley Inf Sch NW1 ... 71 B1
Hawley Mews 4 NW1 ... 71 B1
Hawley Rd
3 Camden Town NW1 ... 71 B1
London N18 ... 34 D5
Hawley St NW1 ... 71 B1
Hawley Way TW15 ... 170 D5
Haworth Ho 7 SW2 ... 160 C5
Hawstead Rd SE6 ... 163 D5
Hawsted IG9 ... 21 B4
Hawthorn Ave
Bowes Pk N13 ... 32 A5
Old Ford E3 ... 97 B6
South Norwood CR7 ... 182 D2
Hawthorn Cl
Cranford TW5 ... 128 B5
Hampton TW12 ... 173 C5
Petts Wood BR5 ... 211 B3
Hawthorn Cres SW17 ... 181 A5
Hawthorn Ct
Littleton TW15 ... 171 A3
2 Pinner HA5 ... 22 C1
Putney SW15 ... 134 B2
Redbridge IG5 ... 56 B6
Hawthorn Ctr HA1 ... 43 A4
Hawthorn Ct
Richmond TW9 ... 132 D4
Sutton SM1 ... 217 C4
8 West Norwood SW16 ... 182 C5
Hawthornden Cl N12 ... 30 C4
Hawthorndene Cl BR2 ... 225 A6
Hawthorndene Rd BR2 ... 225 A6
Hawthorn Dr
Coney Hall BR4 ... 224 C4
Harrow HA2 ... 41 C3
Hawthorne Ave
Harrow HA3 ... 43 A3
Mitcham CR4 ... 180 B1
Ruislip HA4 ... 40 B2
Wallington SM5 ... 219 A1
Hawthorne Cl
Bickley BR1 ... 210 B6
Kingsland N1 ... 73 C2
Sutton SM1 ... 218 A6
Hawthorne Cres UB7 ... 104 B4
Hawthorne Ct
Chingford E4 ... 35 D4
Ealing W5 ... 110 A5
Pinner HA6 ... 22 A1
Hawthorne Gr NW9 ... 45 A2
Hawthorne Ho SW1 ... 259 B1
Hawthorne Mews UB6 ... 86 A1
Hawthorne Rd
Bickley BR1 ... 210 B6
Edmonton N18 ... 33 D5
Walthamstow E17 ... 53 C6
Hawthorne Way N9 ... 17 D2
Hawthorn Farm Ave UB5 ... 85 A6
Hawthorn Gdns W5 ... 109 D3
Hawthorn Gr
Edgware EN5 ... 11 D5
Enfield EN2 ... 5 B5
Penge SE20 ... 184 B2
Hawthorn Hatch TW8 ... 131 B5
Hawthorn Ho SE14 ... 141 B4
Hawthorn Mews NW7 ... 29 A2
Hawthorn Pl UB3 ... 105 D6
Hawthorn Rd
Bexleyheath DA6 ... 147 B1
Hawthorn Rd *continued*
Brentford TW8 ... 131 B5
Carshalton SM1 ... 218 C2
Feltham TW14 ... 150 A3
Hornsey N8 ... 50 A6
Wallington SM5, SM6 ... 219 B1
Willesden NW10 ... 68 A1
Woodford IG9 ... 37 D6
Hawthorns The
2 Cheam SM2 ... 217 C2
Edgware NW7 ... 27 B4
Stoneleigh KT17 ... 216 A1
Hawthorns IG8 ... 21 A1
Hawthorn Terr DA15 ... 167 D6
Hawthorn Way TW17 ... 193 B5
Hawthorn Wlk W10 ... 91 A3
Hawtrey Ave UB5 ... 84 D5
Hawtrey Dr HA4 ... 40 A2
Hawtrey Rd NW3 ... 70 C1
Haxted Rd BR1 ... 187 B2
Haybridge Ho 1 E5 ... 74 C6
Hay Cl E15 ... 76 D1
Haycroft Gdns NW10 ... 90 B6
Haycroft Mans NW10 ... 90 A6
Haycroft Rd
London SW2 ... 160 A6
Surbiton KT6 ... 214 A6
Hay Currie St E14 ... 97 D1
Hayday Rd E16 ... 99 A2
Hayden Piper Ho SW3 ... 267 C6
Hayden's Pl W11 ... 91 B1
Haydock Ave UB5 ... 63 C2
Haydock Gn UB5 ... 63 C2
Haydock Green Flats 2 UB5 ... 63 C2
Haydock Lo 2 SM6 ... 219 D5
Haydon Cl Enfield EN1 ... 17 C6
Kingsbury NW9 ... 45 A5
Haydon Ct NW9 ... 45 A5
Haydon Dr HA5 ... 40 A5
Haydon Ho W7 ... 108 D5
Haydon Park Rd SW19 ... 179 D5
Haydon Rd RM8 ... 80 C6
Haydon Sch HA5 ... 39 D6
Haydon's Rd SW19 ... 180 A4
Haydons Road Sta SW19 ... 180 A5
Haydon St E1, EC3 ... 117 D6 253 C6
Haydon Way SW11 ... 136 B1
Haydon Wlk E1 ... 243 D1
HAYES UB3 ... 83 C1
BR2 ... 209 A2
Hayes Bridge Ret Pk UB4 ... 106 D6
Hayes Chase BR4 ... 208 C3
Hayes Cl BR2 ... 225 A6
Hayes Cres
Cheam SM3 ... 216 D4
Temple Fortune NW11 ... 47 B4
Hayes Ct
23 Camberwell SE5 ... 139 A5
Streatham SW12 ... 160 A3
Wimbledon SW19 ... 179 A4
HAYES END ... 83 B3
Hayes End Cl UB4 ... 83 B2
Hayes End Dr UB4 ... 83 B3
Hayesend Ho SW17 ... 180 A6
Hayes End Rd UB4 ... 83 B3
Hayesford Park Dr BR2 ... 208 D4
Hayes Gdn BR2 ... 209 A1
Hayes Gr SE15, SE22 ... 139 D1
Hayes & Harlington Sta UB3 ... 105 D3
Hayes Hill Rd BR2 ... 208 D1
Hayes Hill BR2 ... 208 C1
Hayes La
Beckenham BR2, BR3 ... 208 B5
Hayes BR2 ... 209 A4
Hayes Mead Rd BR2 ... 208 C1
Hayes Park Sch UB4 ... 83 D3
Hayes Pl NW1 ... 237 B5
Hayes Prim Sch BR2 ... 209 B1
Hayes Rd
Bromley BR2 ... 209 A5
Southall UB2 ... 106 B2
Hayes Sch BR2 ... 225 B6
Hayes Sta BR2 ... 208 D1
Hayes St BR2 ... 209 B1
HAYES TOWN ... 106 B5
Hayes Way BR3 ... 208 B5
Hayes Wood Ave BR2 ... 209 B1
Hayfield Pas E1 ... 96 C3
Hayfield Yd 13 E1 ... 96 C3
Hayford Ct NW2 ... 68 D5
Haygarth Pl 2 SW19 ... 178 D5
Haygreen Cl KT2 ... 176 D4
Hay Hill W1 ... 115 B6 248 D5
Hayhurst N1 ... 234 D6
Hay La NW9 ... 45 B5
Hayland Cl NW9 ... 45 B5
Hay Lane Sch NW9 ... 45 A5
Hayles Bldgs SE11 ... 261 D4
Hayles St SE11 ... 116 D2 261 C4
Haylett Gdns KT1 ... 197 D5
Hayley Ho DA17 ... 147 C6
Hayling Ave TW13 ... 150 A1
Hayling Cl 20 N16 ... 73 C3
Hayling Ct SM3 ... 216 C4
Haymaker Cl UB10 ... 60 B1
Hayman Cres UB4 ... 83 B5
Haymans Point SE11 ... 260 C2
Haymarket SW1 ... 115 D6 249 C5
Haymeads Dr KT10 ... 212 A2
Haymer Gdns KT4 ... 216 A5
Haymerle Ho 6 SE15 ... 140 A5
Haymerle Rd SE15 ... 140 A6
Haymerle Sch SE15 ... 140 A6
Haymill Cl UB6 ... 86 D4
Haymills Ct W5 ... 88 B3
Hayne Ho W11 ... 244 A4
Hayne Rd BR3 ... 185 B2
Haynes Cl
Friern Barnet N11 ... 15 A1
Lewisham SE3 ... 142 C2
Tottenham N17 ... 34 B3
Haynes Dr N9 ... 18 B1
Haynes Ho 3 E9 ... 74 D2
Haynes La SE19 ... 183 C4
Haynes Rd HA0 ... 66 A1
Hayne St EC1 ... 94 D2 241 D4
Haynt Wlk SW20 ... 201 A6
Hay's Galleria* SE1 ... 253 A4
Hay's La SE1 ... 253 A4
Haysleigh Gdns SE20 ... 184 A1
Haysleigh Ho SE20 ... 184 B1
Hay's Mews W1 ... 115 B5 248 C4
Haystall Cl UB4 ... 83 C5
Hay St E2 ... 96 A6
Hayter Ct E11 ... 77 B6
Hayter Ho W12 ... 112 A6
Hayter Rd SW2 ... 160 B6
Haythorn Ho SW11 ... 136 B4 266 D1
Hayton Cl 11 E8 ... 73 D2
Hayward Cl SW19 ... 179 D2
Hayward Ct
14 London SW4 ... 138 A3
Mitcham CR4 ... 180 B1
Hayward Gallery* SE1 ... 116 B5 250 D4
Hayward Gdns SW15 ... 156 C5
Hayward Ho
Islington N1 ... 234 A4
Lower Clapton E5 ... 74 B5
Hayward Rd
London N20 ... 14 A2
Thames Ditton KT7 ... 196 D1
Haywards Cl RM6 ... 58 C4
Haywards Pl EC1 ... 241 C6
Hayward's Pl EC1 ... 241 C6
Haywood Cl HA5 ... 22 D1
Haywood Ct N11 ... 31 D4
Haywood Lo 23 N7 ... 71 D3
Haywood Rd BR2 ... 209 D5
Haywood Rise BR6 ... 227 C3
Hazel Ave UB7 ... 104 C3
Hazelbank Rd SE6 ... 164 C2
Hazel Bank SE25 ... 183 C1
Hazelbank KT5 ... 199 A1
Hazelbourne Rd SW12 ... 159 B5
Hazelbury Cl SW19 ... 179 C1
Hazelbury Gn N9 ... 17 C1
Hazelbury Inf Sch N9 ... 17 C1
Hazelbury Jun Sch N9 ... 17 C1
Hazelbury La N9 ... 17 C1
Hazel Cl
Brentford TW8 ... 131 B5
Croydon CR0 ... 206 D1
Edmonton N13 ... 17 B1
Hendon NW9 ... 27 D1
Mitcham CR4 ... 203 D5
Peckham SE15 ... 140 A3
Twickenham TW2 ... 152 A4
Upper Holloway N19 ... 71 C6
Hazelcroft Cl UB10 ... 60 B1
Hazelcroft HA5 ... 23 D4
Hazel Ct Ealing W5 ... 110 A6
8 Rotherhithe SE16 ... 119 A5
9 West Norwood SW16 ... 182 C5
Hazeldean Rd NW10 ... 67 B1
Hazeldene Dr HA5 ... 40 C6
Hazeldene Gdns UB10 ... 83 A6
Hazeldene Rd
Bexley DA16 ... 146 C3
Ilford IG3 ... 80 B6
Hazeldon Rd SE4 ... 163 A6
Hazel Gdns HA8 ... 26 D6
Hazel Gr RM6 ... 59 A6
Hazelgreen Cl N21 ... 16 D3
Hazel Gr Enfield EN1 ... 18 A5
Feltham TW14 ... 150 A3
Forest Hill SE26 ... 184 D6
Orpington BR6 ... 226 D6
Wembley HA0 ... 88 A6
Hazel Ho London SE4 ... 141 B2
12 Maitland Pk NW3 ... 70 D2
Hazelhurst BR3 ... 186 B2
Hazelhurst Ct SE6 ... 186 A5
Hazelhurst Rd SW17 ... 180 B6
Hazellville Rd N19 ... 49 D1
Hazel Mead EN5 ... 12 B6
Hazelmere Cl
Feltham TW14 ... 149 C5
Northolt UB5 ... 85 B5
Hazelmere Ct 10 SW2 ... 160 B3
Hazelmere Dr UB5 ... 85 B5
Hazelmere Rd
Kilburn NW6 ... 91 B6
Northolt UB5 ... 85 B5
Petts Wood BR5 ... 211 B5
Hazelmere Way BR2 ... 209 A3
Hazelmere Wlk UB5 ... 85 B5
Hazel Rd
Kensal Green NW10 ... 90 C4
Stratford E15 ... 76 C3
Hazeltree La UB5 ... 85 A4
Hazel Way
Bermondsey SE1 ... 263 C4
Walthamstow E4 ... 35 B4
Hazel Wlk BR2 ... 210 C3
Hazelwood Ave SM4 ... 201 D5
Hazelwood Cl
Clapton Pk E5 ... 75 A5
Ealing W5 ... 110 A4
Harrow HA2 ... 41 D5
Hazelwood Cres N13 ... 32 C6
Hazelwood Ct
1 Edmonton N13 ... 32 C6
Surbiton KT6 ... 198 A3
1 Willesden NW10 ... 67 C5
Hazelwood Dr HA5 ... 22 B1
Hazelwood Ho
Beckenham BR2 ... 208 C6
Chingford E4 ... 20 B4
11 Deptford SE8 ... 119 A2
Edmonton N13 ... 32 D6
2 Sutton SM1 ... 218 A4
Hazelwood Jun & Inf Schs N13 ... 32 C6
Hazelwood La N13 ... 32 C6
Hazelwood IG10 ... 21 D6
Hazelwood Lo BR4 ... 208 A2
Hazelwood Mans SW6 ... 264 C2
Hazelwood Rd
Enfield EN1 ... 17 D5
Walthamstow E17 ... 53 A4
Hazlebury Rd SW6 ... 135 D3
Hazledean Rd CR0 ... 221 B6
Hazledene Rd W4 ... 133 A6
Hazlemere Gdns KT4 ... 200 A1
Hazlemere 3 DA14 ... 190 A6
Hazlewell Rd SW15 ... 156 C6
Hazlewood Cres W10 ... 91 A3
Hazlewood Twr W10 ... 91 B3
Hazlitt Cl TW13 ... 173 A6
Hazlitt Ct 4 SE28 ... 124 C5
Hazlitt Mews W14 ... 254 A5
Hazlitt Rd W14 ... 113 A3 254 A5
Heacham Ave UB10 ... 61 A5
Headbourne Ho SE1 ... 262 D6
Headcorn 10 NW5 ... 71 A2
Headcorn Pl CR7 ... 204 B5
Headcorn Rd
Plaistow BR1 ... 187 A5
Thornton Heath CR7 ... 204 B5
Tottenham N17 ... 33 D3
Headfort Pl SW1 ... 115 A4 248 B1
Headington Rd SW18 ... 158 A2
Headlam Rd SW4 ... 159 D4
Headlam St E1 ... 96 B3
Headley App IG2 ... 56 D4
Headley Ave CR0, SM6 ... 220 B3
Headley Cl KT19 ... 214 C2
Headley Ct SE26 ... 184 C5
Headley Dr Ilford IG2 ... 56 D3
New Addington CR0 ... 224 A1
Headley Ho 5 BR5 ... 190 B1
Heads Mews W11 ... 91 C1
Headstart Montessori Sch SW17 ... 180 A6
Head St E1 ... 96 D1
HEADSTONE ... 41 D5
Headstone Dr HA1, HA3 ... 42 C6
Headstone Gdns HA2 ... 42 A5
Headstone La
Harrow HA2, HA3 ... 23 D2
Headstone HA2 ... 41 D5
Headstone Lane Sta HA3 ... 23 D2
Headstone Rd HA1 ... 42 C3
Headway Cl TW10 ... 175 C6
Heald St SE8, SE14 ... 141 C4
Healey Ho RM6 ... 59 A5
Healey St NW1 ... 71 B2
Healy Ct EN5 ... 12 D5
Healy Dr 1 BR6 ... 227 D4
Healy Ho
12 Kennington SW9 ... 138 C5
2 Tower Hamlets E3 ... 97 C3
Heanor Ct 4 E5 ... 74 D4
Hearne Rd W4 ... 132 C6
Hearn Rise UB5 ... 84 D6
Hearn's Bldgs SE17 ... 262 D3
Hearnshaw St 1 E14 ... 97 A1
Hearn St EC2 ... 95 C3 243 B5
Hearnville Rd SW12 ... 159 A3
Heart Hospl The W1 ... 93 A2 238 B3
Heart Raido W11 ... 112 D6
Heart The KT12 ... 193 D1
Heatham Pk TW2 ... 152 D4
Heath Ave DA7 ... 146 D6
Heathbourne Rd WD23 ... 8 D3
Heathbrook Prim Sch SW4 ... 137 C3
Heath Brow NW3 ... 70 A5
Heath Bsns Ctr The TW3 ... 130 A1
Heath Cl
Croydon CR2 ... 220 D2
Ealing W5 ... 88 B3
Golders Green NW11 ... 47 D2
Harlington UB3 ... 127 B5
Heathcote Gr E4 ... 20 A2
Heathcote Point 25 E9 ... 74 D2
Heathcote Rd TW1 ... 153 B6
Heathcote Sch E4 ... 20 C2
Heathcote St WC1 ... 94 B4 233 C1
Heathcroft Ave TW16 ... 171 D3
Heathcroft W5 ... 88 B3
Heathcroft Gdns E4 ... 36 B2
Heathcroft NW11 ... 47 D1
Heath Ct
Carshalton SM5 ... 218 B6
Eltham SE9 ... 167 A3
2 Hampstead NW3 ... 70 A2
Leytonstone E11 ... 54 D3
Stoke Newington N16 ... 51 B1
Uxbridge UB8 ... 60 A1
Heathdale Ave TW4 ... 129 A2
Heathdene Dr DA17 ... 125 D2
Heathdene N14 ... 15 C4
Heathdene Rd
South Norwood SW16 ... 182 B3
Wallington SM5, SM6 ... 219 B1
Heath Dr SW20 ... 200 C5
Heathedge SE23, SE26 ... 162 B2
Heath End Ct WD23 ... 8 C2
Heatherbank
Chislehurst BR7 ... 188 C1
Eltham SE9 ... 144 B3
Heather Cl
Clapham SW8 ... 137 B2
Hampton TW12 ... 173 B2
Hillingdon UB8 ... 82 B2
Hither Green SE13 ... 164 B4
Isleworth TW7 ... 152 B6
Newham E6 ... 100 C1
Heather Ct
South Lambeth SW4 ... 270 B1
6 West Norwood SW16 ... 182 C6
Heatherdale Cl KT2 ... 176 D3
Heatherdene Cl
London N12 ... 30 A2
Mitcham CR4 ... 202 C5
Heatherdene Ct CR4 ... 202 B5
Heatherdene Mans 2 TW1 ... 153 D5

Heather Dr EN2 4 D3
Heatherfold Way HA5, HA6 39 D6
Heather Gdns
Belmont SM2 217 C2
Hendon NW11 47 A3
Heather Ho 11 E14 98 A1
Heather La UB7 82 A1
Heatherlands TW16 172 A4
Heatherley Ct N16 74 A5
Heatherley Dr IG5 56 B6
Heatherley Sch of Fine Art SW10 266 B3
Heather Lo N16 51 C1
Heather Park Dr HA0 66 C1
Heather Park Par HA0 66 B1
Heather Rd
Dollis Hill NW2 67 D6
Lewisham SE12 165 A3
Walthamstow E4 35 B4
Heatherset Cl KT10 212 A3
Heatherset Gdns SW16 182 B3
Heatherside Rd
Sidcup DA14 168 C1
West Ewell KT19 215 B1
Heathers The TW19 148 B4
Heather Way HA7 24 D4
Heather Wlk
Edgware HA8 26 D5
Twickenham TW4 151 C4
West Kilburn W10 91 A3
Heatherwood Cl E12 77 C6
Heatherwood Dr UB4 83 B5
Heathfield Ave SW18 158 B4
Heathfield
Chingford E4 20 A1
Chislehurst BR7 189 A4
Heathfield Cl
Keston BR2 225 C3
Newham E16 99 D2
Heathfield Ct
Ashford TW15 148 A1
3 Bow E3 97 C5
5 Chiswick W4 111 B1
Penge SE20 184 C3
Sidcup DA14 190 B5
8 Sutton SM2 218 A2
Wandsworth SW18 158 B4
Heathfield Dr CR4 180 C2
Heathfielde N2 48 A4
Heathfield Gdns
Acton Green W4 111 A1
Blackheath SE3 142 C3
Croydon CR0 221 B4
Hendon NW11 46 D3
Wandsworth SW18 158 B5
Heathfield Ho SE3 142 C3
Heathfield Inf Sch TW2 151 C3
Heathfield Jun Sch TW2 151 C3
Heathfield La BR7 189 A4
Heathfield N TW1, TW2 152 D4
Heathfield Park Dr RM6 58 B4
Heathfield Pk NW2 68 C2
Heathfield Rd
Bexleyheath DA6 147 B1
Bromley BR1 186 D3
Croydon CR0 221 B4
Keston BR2 225 D3
South Acton W3 110 D4
Wandsworth SW18 158 B5
Heathfield Rise HA4 39 A2
Heathfield Sch HA5 40 D2
Heathfield Sq SW18 158 B4
Heathfield S TW1, TW2 152 D4
Heathfield Terr
Chiswick W4 111 B1
Plumstead Comm SE18 145 D6
Heathfield Vale CR2 223 A1
Heathgate NW11 47 D3
Heathgate Pl NW3 70 D4
Heath Gdns TW1 152 D2
Heath Gr
Ashford TW16 171 D3
Penge SE20 184 C3
Heath Ho
Sidcup DA15 189 D6
Thornton Heath CR7 204 C4
Uxbridge UB10 60 D4
Heath Hurst Rd NW3 70 C4
Heath La SE3 142 B3
Heathland Rd N16 51 C1
Heathland Sch The TW4 151 B5
Heathlands Cl
Sunbury TW16 172 A1
Twickenham TW1 152 D3
Heathlands Ct
Hounslow TW4 151 A6
Mitcham CR4 203 A6
Heathlands Way TW4 151 A6
Heathlee Rd SE3 142 D1
Heathley End BR7 189 A4
Heath Lo WD23 8 B3
Heath Mans
5 Hampstead NW3 70 A4
Putney SW15 156 D5
Heathman's Rd SW6 135 B4 264 D1
Heath Mead SW19 156 D1
Heathmere Prim Sch SW15 156 A3
Heath Park Dr BR1 210 A6
Heath Park Gdns NW3 69 D5
Heath Park Ind Est RM8 59 A1
Heathpool Ct 8 E1 96 B3
Heath Rd
Clapham SW8 137 B3
Dagenham RM6 59 A2
Harrow HA1 42 A2
Hillingdon UB10 83 A3
Isleworth TW3, TW7 130 A1
South Norwood CR7 205 A6
Twickenham TW1 152 D3
Heath Rise
Hayes BR2 209 A3
Putney SW15 156 D5
Heathrow Airport London TW6 126 D3
Heathrow Bvd UB7 126 B5
Heathrow Causeway Est TW4 128 B2
Heathrow International Trad Est TW4 128 B2
Heathrow Prim Sch UB7 126 B6
Heathrow Terminal 4 Sta TW6 149 A5
Heathrow Terminals 1, 2, 3 TW6 126 D2
Heath Royal SW15 156 D5
Heath's Cl EN1 5 C3
Heathshott 8 TW10 154 A5
Heathside Ave DA7 147 A3
Heath Side BR5 211 A2
Heathside Cl
Hinchley Wood KT10 212 C5
Ilford IG2 57 B4
Heathside
Hampstead NW3 70 B4
Hinchley Wood KT10 212 C5
Heathside Prep Sch NW3 70 A4
Heathside TW4 151 B4
Heathstan Rd W12 90 A1
Heath St NW3 70 A5
Heath Terr RM6 58 D2
Heath The W7 108 C5
Heath View Cl N2 48 A5
Heathview Ct SW19 156 D2
Heath View Dr SE2 146 D6
Heathview Gdns SW15 156 C4
Heath View
Gospel Oak NW5 71 A4
London N2 48 A5
Heathview Rd CR7 204 C5
Heath Villas
Hampstead NW3 70 B5
Plumstead Comm SE18 123 D1
Heathville Rd N4, N19 50 A2
Heathwall St SW11 136 D2
Heathway CR0 223 B5
Heathway Ct NW3 69 C6
Heathway
Dagenham RM10 81 C2
Dagenham RM10 103 C6
Greenwich SE3 143 A5
Heathway Ind Est RM10 81 D4
Heathway IG8 37 C5
Heathwood Ct
1 Hounslow TW3 129 D1
Streatham SW12 159 C3
Heathwood Gdns SE7 122 A1
Heathwood Point 7 SE26 162 D1
Heaton Cl E4 20 A1
Heaton Ct 3 N20 14 D2
Heaton Ho
Chelsea SW10 266 B6
6 Peckham SE15 140 B3
Heaton Rd
London SE15 140 B3
Mitcham CR4 181 A3
Heaven Tree Cl N1 73 A3
Heaver Rd 24 SW11 136 B2
Heavers Farm Prim Sch SE25 205 D4
Heavitree Cl SE18 123 B1
Heavitree Ct E17 35 D2
Heavitree Rd SE18 123 B1
Hebble Ho UB5 85 A6
Hebden Ct 24 E2 95 D6
Hebden Terr N17 33 C4
Hebdon Rd SW17 158 C1
Hebe Ct SM1 218 A4
Heber Prim Sch SE22 161 D5
Heber Rd
Cricklewood NW2 68 D4
East Dulwich SE22 161 D5
Hebron Rd W6 112 B3
Hecham Cl E17 35 A2
Heckfield Pl SW6 135 C5 265 A3
Heckford Ho E14 97 D1
Heckford St E1 118 D6
Hector Ct
1 London SW9 138 C4
Putney SW15 156 D6
Hector Ho 14 E2 96 B5
Hector 31 NW9 27 D2
Hector St SE18 123 C2
Heddington Gr N7 72 B3
Heddon Cl TW7 131 A1
Heddon Court Ave EN4 14 D6
Heddon Court Par EN4 15 A6
Heddon Ct EN4 15 A6
Heddon Rd EN4 14 D6
Heddon St W1 249 A6
Hedge Hill EN2 4 D4
Hedge La N13 17 A1
Hedgeley IG4 56 B5
Hedgemans Rd RM9 81 A1
Hedgemans Way RM9 81 A2
Hedgemoor Ct 1 E4 36 B5
Hedgerley Gdns UB6 86 A5
Hedgerow La EN5 12 B6
Hedger's Gr E9 75 A2
Hedger St SE11 261 C4
Hedge Wlk SE6 185 D6
Hedgewood Gdns IG5 56 C4
Hedgewood Specl Sch UB4 83 C4
Hedgley Mews SE12 164 D6
Hedgley St SE12 164 D6
Hedingham Cl 6 N1 73 A1
Hedingham Ho 7 KT2 176 A2
Hedingham Rd RM8 80 B3
Hedley Ct SW15 156 D5
Hedley Ho E14 120 A3
Hedley Rd TW4 151 C4
Hedley Row N5, N16 73 B3
Hedsor Ho E2 243 C6
Heenan Cl IG11 79 A2
Heene Rd EN2 5 B4
Heidegger Cres SW13 134 B5
Heigham Rd E6 78 A1
Heighton Gdns CR0 220 D3
Heights Cl SW20 178 B3
Heights The
Beckenham BR3 186 A3
Greenwich SE7 121 C1
Hampstead NW3 70 A4
Northolt UB5 63 C3
Stroud Green N4 50 C3
Heiron St SE17 138 D6
Helby Rd SW4 159 D5
Heldar Ct SE1 252 D1
Helder Gr SE12 164 D4
Helder St CR2 221 B2
Heldmann Cl TW7 130 B1
Helegan Cl BR6 227 D4
Helena Cl EN4 2 B5
Helena Ct W5 87 D2
Helena Pl 3 E9 96 C6
Helena Rd Ealing W5 87 D2
Newham E13 99 A5
Walthamstow E17 53 C4
Willesden NW10 68 B3
Helena Sq 12 SE16 119 A6
Helen Ave TW14 150 B4
Helen Clare Ct EN2 4 D2
Helen Cl
East Finchley N2 48 A6
East Molesey KT8 195 D5
Helen Ct N3 47 A6
Helen Gladstone Ho SE1 251 C2
Helen Ho 9 E2 96 B5
Helen Mackay Ho 10 E14 98 B1
Helen Peele Cotts 10 SE16 118 C3
Helenslea Ave NW11 47 C1
Helen's Pl E2 96 C4
Helen St SE18 122 D2
Helen Taylor Ho 5 SE16 118 A2
Helford Cl HA4 61 C6
Helgiford Gdns TW16 171 C3
Helios Rd CR4 203 A1
Heliport Est The SW11 136 B3
Helix Ct 17 W11 112 D5
Helix Gdns SW2 160 B5
Helix Ho TW7 131 B3
Helix Rd SW2 160 B5
Helix The SW19 156 D2
Hellenic Coll of London SW1 114 D3 257 C5
Hellen Way WD19 22 D6
Hellings St E1 118 A5
Helme Cl SW19 179 B5
Helmet Row EC1 242 B6
Helmore Rd IG11 79 D1
Helmsdale Cl UB4 85 A3
Helmsdale Ho NW6 91 D5
Helmsdale Rd SW16 181 D2
Helmsley Pl E8 74 B1
Helmsley St 7 E8 74 B1
Helmsley 11 E18 55 A6
Helperby Rd NW10 67 C1
Helsby Ct NW8 236 C6
Helsinki Sq SE16 119 A3
Helston Cl HA5 23 B3
Helston Ct N15 51 C4
Helston Ho SE11 261 B2
Helston NW1 232 B4
Helvetia St SE6 163 B2
Helwys Ct E4 36 A4
Hemans Est SW8 137 D5 269 D3
Hemans St SW8 137 D5 269 D3
Hemberton Rd SW9 138 A2
Hemery Rd UB6 64 B3
Hemingford Cl N12 30 B5
Hemingford Rd
Cheam SM3 216 C4
Islington N1 94 B6 233 D6
Heming Rd HA8 26 D3
Hemington Ave N11 30 D5
Hemlock Rd W12 111 D6
Hemmen La UB3 83 D1
Hemming Cl 6 TW12 173 C2
Hemmings Cl DA14 168 B2
Hemmings Ct HA8 27 A3
Hemmings Mead KT19 215 A2
Hemming St E1 96 A3
Hemmingway Cl NW5 71 A4
Hempstead Cl IG9 21 A2
Hempstead Rd E17 36 B1
Hemp Wlk SE17 262 D4
Hemsby Rd KT9 214 B2
Hemstal Rd NW6 69 C1
Hemswell Dr NW9 27 C2
Hemsworth Ct N1 95 C5
Hemsworth St N1 95 C5
Hemus Pl SW3 257 B1
Henchman St W12 89 D1
Hendale Ave NW4 46 B6
Hendale Ho 13 E5 74 B6
Henderson Cl NW10 67 A2
Henderson Ct
8 Deptford SE14 140 D6
Hampstead NW3 70 B3
Wandsworth SW18 158 C4
Woodside Pk N12 29 D6
Henderson Dr NW8 92 B3 236 C6
Henderson Ho 7 RM10 81 C5
Henderson Rd
Edmonton N9 18 B3
Forest Gate E7 77 C2
Hayes UB4 84 A4
Thornton Heath CR0 205 B3
Wandsworth SW18 158 C4
Hendfield Ct 5 SM6 219 B2
Hendham Rd SW17 158 D2
HENDON 46 C3
Hendon Ave N3 29 A2
Hendon Central NW4 46 B4
Hendon Central Sta NW4 46 B4
Hendon Hall Ct NW4 46 D6
Hendon Ho NW4 46 D4
Hendon La N3 29 B1
Hendon Lo NW4 46 B6
Hendon Park Mans NW4 46 C4
Hendon Park Row NW11 47 B3
Hendon Pk Cotts NW7 11 D2
Hendon Prep Sch NW4 46 D6
Hendon Rd N9 18 A2
Hendon Sch NW4 46 D4
Hendon Sta NW4 46 A3
Hendon Terr TW15 171 B4
Hendon Way NW2, NW4 46 C3
Hendon Wood La NW7 12 A3
Hendre Ho SE1 263 B3
Hendren Cl UB6 64 B3
Hendre Rd SE1 117 C2 263 B3
Hendrick Ave SW12 158 D4
Heneage La EC3 243 B1
Heneage Pl EC3 243 B1
Heneage St E1 95 D2 243 D4
Henfield Cl
London N19 49 C1
Old Bexley DA5 169 C5
Henfield Rd SW19 179 B2
Hengelo Gdns CR4 202 B5
Hengist Rd
Eltham SE12 165 B4
Erith DA8 147 D5
Hengist Way BR2, BR3 208 C5
Hengrave Rd SE23 162 D4
Hengrove Ct DA5 169 A3
Henley Ave SM3 217 A5
Henley Cl
Greenford UB6 86 A5
Hounslow TW7 130 D4
Rotherhithe SE16 118 C4
Henley Ct
Brondesbury NW2 68 D2
Hendon NW4 46 A6
Ilford IG1 78 D4
Mitcham CR4 203 A6
Oakwood N14 15 C4
Peckham SE15 140 A2
Sidcup DA5 169 B4
Henley Dr
Bermondsey SE1 117 D2 263 D4
Kingston u T KT2 177 D3
Henley Gdns
Dagenham RM6 59 A4
Pinner HA5 40 B6
Henley Ho
London N12 30 B5
Shoreditch E2 243 D6
Henley Lo
South Norwood SE25 205 D5
Walthamstow E17 53 B4
Henley Prior N1 233 C3
Henley Rd
Edmonton N18 33 C6
Ilford IG1 79 B4
Newham E16 122 B4
Willesden NW10 90 C6
Henleys Cnr NW11 47 B5
Henleys Rdbt TW5 128 C3
Henley St SW11 137 A3
Henley Way TW13 172 D5
Henlow Pl TW10 153 D2
Hennel Cl SE23 162 C1
Hennessy Rd N9 18 C2
Henniker Gdns E6 100 A4
Henniker Mews SW3 266 C6
Henniker Point E15 76 C3
Henniker Rd E15 76 B3
Henningham Rd N17 33 B2
Henning St SW11 136 C4 267 A1
Henrietta Barnett Sch NW11 47 D3
Henrietta Cl SE8 141 C6
Henrietta Ho
11 Hammersmith W6 112 C1
3 New Barnet EN5 2 A1
3 South Tottenham N15 51 C3
Henrietta Mews WC1 240 B6
Henrietta Pl W1 93 B1 238 C2
Henrietta St
Strand WC2 116 A6 250 B6
Stratford New Town E15 76 A3
Henriques St E1 96 A1
Henry Addlington Cl E6 100 D2
Henry Cavendish Prim Sch SW12 159 C3
Henry Cl EN2 5 C5
Henry Compton Sec Sch SW6 135 A4 264 A2
Henry Cooper Way SE12 187 D6
Henry Darlot Dr NW7 29 A5
Henry Dent Cl SE5 139 B2
Henry Dickens Ct W11 244 A4
Henry Doulton Dr SW17 181 B6
Henry Fawcett Prim Sch SE11 138 C6
Henry Green Prim Sch RM8 80 D6
Henry Hatch Ct SM2 218 A1
Henry Ho
Lambeth SE1 251 B3
South Lambeth SW8 270 A4
St John's Wood NW8 230 A4
Henry Jackson Ho SW15 134 D2
Henry Jackson Rd SW15 134 D2
Henry Macaulay Ave 13 KT2 175 D2
Henry Maynard Inf Sch E17 54 A4
Henry Maynard Jun Sch E17 54 A4
Henry Peters Dr TW11 174 C5
Henry Rd London N4 51 A1
New Barnet EN4 14 B6
Newham E6 100 A5
Henry's Ave IG8 36 D5
Henryson Rd SE4 163 C6
Henry St BR1 187 B2
Henry Tate Mews SW16 182 C5
Henry Wise Ho SW1 259 B3
Hensford Gdns SE26 184 B6
Henshall Point 19 E3 97 D4
Henshall St N1 73 B2
Henshawe Rd RM8 80 D5
Henshaw St SE17 117 B2 262 C4
Hensley Point 28 E9 74 D2
Henslowe Rd SE22 162 A6
Henslow Ho 12 SE15 140 A5
Henson Ave NW2 68 C3
Henson Cl BR6 226 D6
Henson Ct 3 N5 73 A4
Henson Path HA3 43 D6
Henson Pl UB5 84 C6
Henstridge Pl NW8 230 A5
Henty Cl SW11 136 C4 267 B2
Henty Wlk SW15 156 B6
Henville Rd BR1 187 B2
Henwick Prim Sch SE9 144 A2
Henwick Rd SE9 144 A2
Hepburn Gdns BR2 208 D1
Hepburn Mews SW11 158 D6
Hepple Cl TW7 131 B3
Hepplestone Cl SW15 156 B5
Hepscott Rd E9 75 C1
Hepworth Ct
Barking IG11 80 A3
Cheam SM3 201 C1
Chelsea SW1 258 C1
Islington N1 234 C6
Hepworth Gdns IG11 80 A3
Hepworth Ho IG8 21 A1
Hepworth Rd SW16 182 A3
Hepworth Way KT12 193 D1
Heracles Cl SM6 220 A1
Heracles 30 NW9 27 D2
Hera Ct 15 E14 119 C2
Herald Gdns SM6 219 B5
Heralds Pl SE11 261 C4
Herald St 5 E2 96 B3
Herbal Hill EC1 241 B5
Herbert Chapman Ct N5 72 D4
Herbert Cres SW1 257 D6
Herbert Ct 4 KT5 198 B3
Herbert Gdns
Chiswick W4 132 D6
Dagenham RM6 58 D2
Willesden Green NW10 90 B5
Herbert Ho E1 243 C2

Herbert Mews 15 SW2 .... 160 C5
Herbert Morrison Ho SW6 .... 264 C5
Herbert Morrison Prim Sch SW8 ... 138 A5 270 A3
Herbert Pl
Hounslow TW3 .... 130 B3
Shooters Hill SE18 ... 144 D6
Herbert Rd
Bexleyheath DA7 .... 147 A3
Bromley BR2 .... 210 A4
Hendon NW9 .... 46 A3
Ilford IG3 .... 79 C6
Kingston u T KT1 .... 198 B6
Manor Pk E12 .... 78 A4
Merton SW19 .... 179 B3
Shooters Hill SE18 ... 144 D6
Southall UB1 .... 107 B5
South Tottenham N15 .. 51 D4
Walthamstow E17 .... 53 B2
Wood Green N11 .... 32 A3
Herbert St
Camden Town NW5 .... 71 A2
Newham E13 .... 99 A5
Herbrand Est WC1 .... 94 A3 240 A6
Herbrand St WC1 .... 94 A3 240 A6
Hercies Rd UB10 .... 60 C2
Hercules Ct 7 SE14 .... 141 A6
Hercules Pl N7 .... 72 A5
Hercules Rd SE1 .... 116 B3 260 D5
Hercules St N7 .... 72 A5
Hereford Ave EN4 .... 14 D3
Hereford Bldgs SW3 266 D6
Hereford Ct
20 Belmont SM2 .... 217 C1
6 Croydon CR0 .... 205 D1
6 Ealing W7 .... 86 D2
Harrow HA1 .... 42 C6
Hereford Gdns
London SE13 .... 164 C6
Pinner HA5 .... 41 A4
Redbridge IG1 .... 56 A2
Twickenham TW2 .... 152 A3
Hereford Ho
7 Acton W3 .... 88 C1
5 Brixton SW2 .... 138 C1
25 Camberwell SE5 .. 139 A3
Edgware HA8 .... 26 B3
Knightsbridge SW3 .. 257 B6
Walham Green SW10 .... 265 D4
Hereford Mans 10 W2 .... 91 C1
Hereford Mews 11 W2 .... 91 C1
Hereford Pl SE14 .... 141 B5
Hereford Rd
Acton W3 .... 111 A6
Bayswater W2 .... 113 C6 245 B6
Ealing W5 .... 109 C3
Feltham TW13 .... 150 C3
Wanstead E11 .... 55 B4
Hereford Retreat 5 SE15 .... 140 A5
Hereford Sq SW7 .... 114 A2 256 B3
Hereford St E2 .... 96 A3
Hereford Way KT9 .... 213 D3
Herent Dr IG5 .... 56 B6
Hereward Gdns N13 .. 32 C5
Hereward House Sch NW3 .... 70 B2
Hereward Rd SW17 .. 180 D6
Herga Ct HA1 .... 64 C6
Herga Rd HA3 .... 42 D5
Heriot Ave E4 .... 19 C2
Heriot Rd NW4 .... 46 C4
Heriots Cl HA7 .... 25 A6
Heritage Cl
London SW9 .... 138 D2
Sunbury TW16 .... 172 A2
Heritage Ct SE8 .... 118 D1
Heritage Hill BR2 .... 225 C3
Heritage Ho
22 Putney SW19 .... 156 D3
3 Twickenham TW1 .... 153 A4
Heritage View HA1 .... 64 D5
Herlwyn Ave HA4 .... 61 C5
Herlwyn Gdns SW17 .... 180 D6
Herm Cl TW7 .... 130 A5
Hermes Cl 5 W9 .... 91 C3
Hermes Ct 4 SW9 .... 138 C4
Hermes Ho BR3 .... 185 A2
Hermes St N1 .... 234 A3
Hermes Way SM6 .... 219 D1
Hermes Wlk UB5 .... 85 C5
Herm Ho EN3 .... 6 D5
Hermiston Ave N8 .... 50 A4
Hermiston Ct
3 Hornsey N8 .... 50 A4
7 North Finchley N12 .... 30 B5
Hermitage Cl
1 Abbey Wood SE2 .... 124 C3
Claygate KT10 .... 213 A2
Enfield EN2 .... 4 D3
Littleton TW17 .... 192 C5
Snaresbrook E18 .... 54 D5
Hermitage Ct
2 Child's Hill NW2 .... 69 C5
Colney Hatch N11 .... 30 D4
3 Wanstead E18 .... 55 A5
14 Wapping E1 .... 118 A5
Hermitage Gdns
Child's Hill NW2 .... 69 C5
South Norwood SE19 .... 183 A3
Hermitage La
Child's Hill NW2 .... 69 C5
Croydon CR0 .... 206 A3
South Norwood SW16 .... 182 B3
Hermitage Prim Sch E1 .... 118 A5
Hermitage Rd
London N4, N15 .... 51 A3
South Norwood SE19 .... 183 B4
Hermitage Row 9 E8 .... 74 A3
Hermitage St W2 ... 236 C3
Hermitage The
Barnes SW13 .... 133 D4
Feltham TW13 .... 149 D1
Forest Hill SE23 .... 162 C3
Kingston u T KT1 .... 197 D5
Richmond TW10 .... 154 A6
Uxbridge UB8 .... 60 A2
Hermitage Villas SW6 .... 265 A6
Hermitage Wall E1 .. 118 A5
Hermitage Way HA7 .. 25 A2
Hermitage Wlk E18 .. 54 D5
Hermit Pl NW6 .... 91 D6
Hermit Rd E16 .... 98 D3
Hermit St EC1 .... 234 C2
Hermon Gr UB3 .... 106 A5
Hermon Hill E11 .... 55 A5
Herndon Rd SW18 ... 158 A6
Herne Cl Hayes UB3 .... 83 D1
Willesden NW10 .... 67 B3
Herne Ct WD23 .... 8 A4
HERNE HILL 161 A6
Herne Hill SE24 .... 139 A1
Herne Hill Ho SE24 .. 160 D5
Herne Hill Mans SE24 .... 161 A5
Herne Hill Rd SE24 .. 139 A1
Herne Hill Sch SE24 .... 161 A6
Herne Hill Stad SE24 .... 161 B5
Herne Hill Sta SE24. 160 D5
Herne Mews N18 .... 34 A6
Herne Pl SE24 .... 160 D6
Herne Rd KT6 .... 214 A6
Heron Cl
Buckhurst Hill IG9 .... 21 A3
Cheam SM1 .... 217 B3
Walthamstow E17 .... 35 B1
Willesden NW10 .... 67 C2
Heron Cres DA14 .... 189 C6
Heron Ct
Bromley BR2 .... 209 C5
18 Cubitt Town E14 .. 120 A3
7 Dulwich SE21 .... 161 B2
9 Forest Hill SE23 .. 162 C3
Ilford IG1 .... 78 D6
5 Kingston u T KT1 . 198 A6
Merton SW20 .... 178 C1
Mitcham CR4 .... 180 C2
Ruislip HA4 .... 61 B6
Stanwell TW19 .... 148 A3
Herondale Ave SW18 .... 158 C3
Heron Dr N4 .... 73 A6
Herongate N1 .... 235 B6
Herongate Rd E12 .... 77 C6
Heron Hill DA17 .... 125 B2
Heron Ho
Battersea SW11 .... 267 B2
Ealing W13 .... 87 A3
Peckham SE15 .... 139 D4
Sidcup DA14 .... 168 B1
St John's Wood NW8 230 A3
Teddington KT1 .... 175 C2
Heron Ind Est E15 .... 97 D5
Heron Mead EN3 .... 7 C5
Heron Mews IG1 .... 78 D6
Heron Pl
Marylebone W1 .... 238 B2
Heron Pl *continued*
Rotherhithe SE16 .... 119 A5
Heron Quays E14 .... 119 C5
Heron Quays Sta E14 .... 119 C5
Heron Rd
Croydon CR0 .... 221 C6
Herne Hill SE24 .... 139 A1
Isleworth TW1 .... 131 B1
Heronsforde W13 .... 87 C1
Heronsgate HA8 .... 26 C5
Heronsgate Prim Sch SE28 .... 123 B3
Heronslea Dr HA7 .... 26 A5
Heron's Lea N6 .... 48 D3
Herons Pl TW7 .... 131 B2
Heron Sq 27 TW10 ... 153 D6
Herons Rise EN4 .... 2 C1
Herons The E11 .... 54 D3
Heron Trad Est W3 .. 88 D2
Heron Way TW14 .... 128 A1
Heronway IG8 .... 37 C6
Herrick Ct 4 TW10 .. 175 D6
Herrick Ho
18 Camberwell SE5 .... 139 B5
17 Canonbury N16 .... 73 B4
Herrick Rd N5 .... 73 A5
Herrick St SW1 .... 115 D2 259 D3
Herries St W10 .... 91 A5
Herringham Rd SE7 .. 121 C3
Herrongate Cl EN1 .... 5 D3
Hersant Cl NW10 .... 90 A6
Herschell Rd SE23 .. 163 A4
Herschell's Mews SE5 .... 139 A2
Hersham Cl SW15 .... 156 A4
Hersham Rd KT12 .... 194 A1
Hershell Ct 1 SW14 .... 132 D1
Hertford Ave SW14 .. 133 C1
Hertford Cl EN4 .... 2 B2
Hertford Ct
16 London SW11 .... 136 C2
Newham E6 .... 100 B4
Palmers Green N13 .... 16 C1
Hertford Ho 5 UB5 ... 85 B3
Hertford Lo 10 SW19 .... 157 A3
Hertford Pl W1 .... 239 B5
Hertford Rd
Barking IG11 .... 78 D1
Barnet EN4 .... 2 A2
East Finchley N2 .... 48 C6
Edmonton N9 .... 18 B3
Enfield EN3 .... 6 C5
Hertford Rd High St EN3 .... 18 C6
Hertford Rd
Ilford IG2 .... 57 C3
Shoreditch N1 .... 95 C6
Hertford St W1 .... 115 B5 248 C3
Hertford Way CR4 .... 204 A5
Hertford Wlk 13 DA17 .... 125 C1
Hertmitage The 5 SE13 .... 142 A3
Hertslet Rd N7 .... 72 B5
Hertsmere Rd E14 .... 119 C6
Hertswood Ct 1 EN5 ... 1 A1
Hervey Cl N3 .... 29 C2
Hervey Park Rd E17 ... 53 A5
Hervey Rd SE3 .... 143 B4
Hesa Rd UB3 .... 106 A6
Hesewall Cl SW4 .... 137 C3
Hesketh Pl W11 .... 244 A5
Hesketh Rd E7 .... 77 A5
Heslop Ct 1 SW12 .... 159 A3
Heslop Rd SW12 .... 158 D3
Hesper Mews SW5 .... 113 D2 255 C3
Hesperus Cres E14 ... 119 D2
Hessel Rd W13 .... 109 B4
Hessel St E1 .... 96 B1
Hestercombe Ave SW6 .... 135 A4 264 B1
Hester Ct SW16 .... 181 C5
Hesterman Way CR0 .... 204 B1
Hester Rd
Battersea SW11 .... 136 C5 267 A3
Edmonton N18 .... 34 A5
Hester Terr TW9 .... 132 C2
Hestia Ho SE1 .... 253 A1
HESTON 129 B5
Heston Ave TW5 .... 129 A5
Heston Com Sch TW5 .... 129 C5
Heston Ctr The TW5 .... 106 C1
Heston Grange TW5 .... 129 B6
Heston Grange La TW5 .... 129 B6
Heston Ho
Gunnersbury W4 .... 110 D1
5 St Johns SE8 .... 141 C4
Heston Ind Mall TW5 .... 129 B5
Heston Inf Sch TW5 129 C5
Heston Jun Sch TW5 .... 129 C5
Heston Phoenix Distribution Pk TW5 .... 128 C6
Heston Rd TW5 .... 129 C5
Heston St SE14 .... 141 C4
Hetherington Rd
Charlton TW17 .... 171 A1
Stockwell SW2, SW4 .... 138 A1
Hetherington Way UB10 .... 60 A4
Hethpool Ho W2 .... 236 C5
Hetley Gdns 1 SE19 .... 183 D3
Hetley Rd W12 .... 112 B4
Heton Gdns NW4 .... 46 A5
Hetty Rees Ct 6 N19 .. 50 A2
Hevelius Cl SE10 .... 120 D1
Hever Croft SE9 .... 188 C6
Heverfield Ct CR4 .... 180 D3
Hever Gdns BR1 .... 188 C1
Heverham Rd SE18 ... 123 C2
Hever Ho SE15 .... 140 D6
Heversham Ho SE15 .... 140 C6
Heversham Rd DA7 .. 147 C4
Hevingham Dr RM6 .... 58 C4
Heward Ct SE13 .... 142 A3
Hewens Rd UB4 .... 83 A3
Hewer Ho 6 SW4 .... 159 C6
Hewer St W10 .... 90 D2
Hewes Ho E17 .... 52 D5
Hewett Cl HA7 .... 25 B6
Hewett Ho
Putney SW15 .... 134 C3
7 Woolwich SE18 .. 122 D1
Hewett Rd RM8 .... 80 D4
Hewetts Quay 7 IG11 .... 101 A6
Hewett St EC2 . 95 C3 243 B5
Hewish Rd N18 .... 33 C6
Hewison St E3 .... 97 B5
Hewitt Ave N22 .... 32 D1
Hewitt Cl CR0 .... 223 C5
Hewitt Ho 2 E4 .... 36 B5
Hewitt Rd N8 .... 50 D4
Hewlett Rd E3 .... 97 A5
Hewling Ho 1 N16 .... 73 C3
Hexagon Bsns Ctr UB4 .... 106 C6
Hexagon The N6 .... 48 D1
Hexal Rd SE6 .... 164 C1
Hexham Gdns TW7 .... 131 A5
Hexham Rd Barnet EN5 .. 1 D1
Cheam SM4 .... 201 D1
West Norwood SE27 . 161 A2
Hexton Ct N4 .... 73 A6
Heybourne Rd N17 .... 34 B3
Heybridge Ave SW16 .... 182 B4
Heybridge Dr IG6 .... 57 B6
Heybridge 9 NW1 .... 71 B2
Heybridge Way E10 ... 53 B1
Heydon Ct BR4 .... 224 C6
Heydon Ho 3 SE14 .. 140 C4
Heyford Ave
Merton SW20 .... 201 B6
South Lambeth SW8 .... 138 A5 270 B4
Heyford Rd CR4 .... 180 C1
Heyford Terr SW8 ... 270 B4
Heygate St SE17 .... 117 A2 262 B4
Heylyn Sq E3 .... 97 B4
Heynes Rd RM8 .... 80 C4
Heysham Dr WD19 .... 22 D5
Heysham La NW3 .... 69 D5
Heysham Rd N15 .... 51 B3
Heythorp St SW18 ... 157 B2
Heythrop Dr UB10 .... 60 B4
Heyward Ct SM2 .... 217 C2
Heywood Ave NW9 .... 27 C2
Heywood Ct 2 HA7 .... 25 C5
Heywood Ho
11 Deptford SE14 .... 140 D6
6 Tulse Hill SW2 ... 160 C5
Heyworth Rd
Lower Clapton E5 .... 74 B4
Stratford E15 .... 76 D4
Hibbert Ho 18 E14 ... 119 C3
Hibbert Rd
Harrow HA3 .... 24 D1
Walthamstow E17 .... 53 B2
Hibbert St SW11 .... 136 B2
Hibernia Gdns TW3 .. 151 C6
Hibernia Point 9 SE2 .... 124 D4
Hibernia Rd TW3 .... 129 C1
Hibiscus Cl 6 HA8 .... 27 A6
Hibiscus Lo 5 E15 .... 76 C1
Hichisson Rd SE15 ... 162 C6
Hickes Ho 6 NW6 .... 70 B1
Hickey's Almshouses 7 TW9 .... 132 B1
Hickin Cl SE7 .... 121 D2
Hickin St 2 E14 .... 120 A3
Hickleton NW1 .... 232 B5
Hickling Ho 10 SE16 .. 118 B3
Hickling Rd IG1 .... 78 D3
Hickman Ave E4 .... 36 A4
Hickman Cl E16 .... 99 D2
Hickman Rd RM6 .... 58 C2
Hickmore Wlk SW4 .. 137 C2
Hickory Cl N9 .... 18 A4
Hicks Ave UB6 .... 86 C4
Hicks Cl SW11 .... 136 C2
Hicks Ct RM10 .... 81 D5
Hicks St SE8 .... 119 A1
Hidaburn Ct 7 SW16 .... 181 C6
Hidcote Gdns SW20 .. 200 B6
Hidcote Ho 11 SM2 .. 218 A1
Hide E6 .... 100 C1
Hide Pl SW1 .. 115 D2 259 C3
Hider Ct SE3 .... 143 C5
Hide Rd HA1 .... 42 B5
Hide Twr SW1 .... 259 C3
Hieover SE21 .... 161 A2
Higgins Ho 7 N1 .... 95 C6
Higginson Ho 2 NW3 .... 70 D1
Higgins Wlk TW12 ... 173 A4
Higgs Ind Est 9 SE24 .... 138 D2
High Acre EN2 .... 4 D2
Higham Ct 9 IG8 .... 37 A4
HIGHAM HILL 35 A2
Higham Hill Ho E17 ... 34 D2
Higham Hill Rd E17 ... 35 A1
Higham Ho E4 .... 35 C4
Higham Mews UB5 .... 85 B3
Higham Pl E17 .... 53 A6
Higham Rd
Tottenham N17 .... 51 B6
Woodford IG8 .... 37 A4
Highams Lodge Bsns Ctr E17 .... 52 D6
HIGHAMS PARK 36 A3
Highams Park Sch E4 .... 36 B4
Highams Park Sta E4 36 B4
Higham Station Ave E4 .... 35 D4
Highams The E17 .... 36 A2
Higham St E17 .... 53 A6
High Ashton 11 KT2 .. 176 D3
Highbanks Cl DA16 ... 146 B5
Highbanks Rd HA5 .... 23 D4
Highbank Way N8 .... 50 C3
HIGH BARNET 1 B2
High Barnet Sta EN5 ... 1 C1
Highbarrow Rd CR0 .. 206 A1
High Beeches DA14 .. 191 A5
High Beech
South Croydon CR2 .... 221 C1
Southgate N21 .... 16 B5
High Birch Ct 7 EN4 ... 2 C1
Highbridge Ct 13 SE14 .... 140 C5
Highbridge Rd IG11 .... 100 D6
High Bridge Wharf SE10 .... 120 B1
Highbrook Rd SE3 ... 143 D2
High Broom Cres BR4 .... 207 D2
Highburty Mans 24 N1 .... 72 D1
HIGHBURY 72 D4
Highbury Ave CR7 .... 182 D1
Highbury Cl
New Malden KT3 .... 199 A4
West Wickham BR4 .. 223 D6
Highbury Cnr N5 .... 72 D2
Highbury Corner N5 .. 72 D2
Highbury Cres N5 .... 72 C3
Highbury Fields Sch N5 .... 72 D3
Highbury Gdns IG3 ... 79 C6
Highbury Grange N5 .. 73 A4
Highbury Gr N5 .... 72 D3
Highbury Grove Ct N5 .... 72 D2
Highbury Grove Sch N5 .... 73 A3
Highbury Hill N5 .... 72 D4
Highbury & Islington Sta N1 .... 72 D2
Highbury New Pk N5 .. 73 A4
Highbury Pk N5 .... 72 D4
Highbury Pl N5 .... 72 D3
Highbury Quadrant N5 .... 73 A5
Highbury Quadrant Prim Sch N5 .... 73 A4
Highbury Rd SW19 ... 179 A5
Highbury Sq N14 .... 15 C3
Highbury Station Rd N1 .... 72 C2
Highbury Terrace Mews N5 .... 72 D3
Highbury Terr N5 .... 72 D3
High Cedar Dr SW20 .... 178 B3
Highclears 6 IG9 .... 21 B2
Highclere Rd KT3 .... 199 B6
Highclere St SE26 .... 185 A6
Highcliffe BR3 .... 185 D2
Highcliffe Dr SW15 .. 155 D5
Highcliffe W13 .... 87 B2
Highcliffe Gdns IG4 ... 56 A4
Highcombe Cl SE9 .... 166 A3
Highcombe SE7 .... 143 B6
High Coombe Pl KT2 .... 177 B3
Highcroft Ave HA0 .... 88 C6
Highcroft Gdns NW11 .... 47 B3
Highcroft Highgate N6 .. 49 A3
Hyde The NW9 .... 45 C4
2 Kingston u T KT5 .. 198 B4
Highcroft Point E17 ... 35 D2
Highcroft Rd N19 .... 50 A2
High Cross Ctr The N15 .... 52 A5
High Cross Rd N17 .... 52 A6
Highcross Way 4 SW15 .... 156 A3
Highdaun Dr SW16 ... 204 B5
High Dene EN2 .... 4 D2
Highdown Rd SW15 .. 156 B5
Highdown KT4 .... 215 D6
High Dr KT2, KT3 .... 177 A1
High Elms Ctry Pk* BR6 .... 227 A1
High Elms Rd BR6 .... 227 A1
High Elms IG8 .... 37 A5
Highfield Ave
Erith DA8 .... 147 D6
Greenford UB6 .... 64 D3
Hendon NW11 .... 47 A2
Kingsbury NW9 .... 45 A4
Orpington BR6 .... 227 D3
Pinner HA5 .... 41 B4
Wembley HA9 .... 66 B5
Highfield WD23 .... 8 C2
Highfield Cl
Hither Green SE13 .... 164 B5
Kingsbury NW9 .... 45 A4
Long Ditton KT6 .... 197 C1
Wood Green N22 .... 32 C2
Highfield Ct
7 Barnet EN5 .... 1 D1
Hendon NW11 .... 47 A3
Mitcham CR4 .... 202 C5
Southgate N14 .... 15 C5
Wanstead E12 .... 77 C6
Highfield Dr
Beckenham BR2 .... 208 D5
Ickenham UB10 .... 60 A5
West Ewell KT19 .... 215 D2
West Wickham BR4 .. 224 A5
Highfield Gdns NW11 .... 47 A3
Highfield Hill SE19 ... 183 C3
Highfield Ho N21 .... 16 D3
Highfield Inf Sch BR2 .... 208 C5
Highfield Jun Sch BR2 .... 208 C5
Highfield Mews NW6 .. 69 D1
Highfield Prim Sch
Edmonton N21 .... 17 A3
Hillingdon UB10 .... 82 D4
Highfield Rd
Acton W3 .... 89 A2
Bexley DA6 .... 169 B6
Bromley BR1 .... 210 B5
Carshalton SM1 .... 218 C3
Edmonton N21 .... 16 D2
Feltham TW13 .... 150 A2
Hendon NW11 .... 47 A3
Hounslow TW7 .... 130 D4
Orpington BR5, BR7 . 211 D6
St Paul's Cray BR5, BR7 .... 211 D6
Tolworth KT5 .... 199 A2
Upper Halliford TW16 .... 193 D4
Walton-on-T KT12 ... 194 A1
Highfield Sch SW18. 158 C4
Highfields Gr N6 .... 48 D1
Highfields SM1 .... 217 C6
High Foleys KT10 .... 213 B1
High Gables
Beckenham BR2 .... 186 C1
Loughton IG10 .... 21 D6
High Garth KT10 .... 212 A2
HIGHGATE 49 A2
Highgate Archway N6 .... 49 C1

Highgate Ave N6......49 B2
Highgate Ballet Sch NW11......47 D5
Highgate Cemetery* N19......71 B6
Highgate Cl N6......49 A2
High Gate Edge N2......48 C4
Highgate High St N6......49 B1
Highgate Hill N19......49 C1
Highgate Ho 11 SE26......162 A1
Highgate Hts N6......49 C3
Highgate Prim Sch N6......48 D3
Highgate Private Hospl N6......48 D3
Highgate Rd NW5......71 B4
Highgate Sch
  Highgate N6......48 D2
  Highgate N6......49 A2
Highgate Spinney N8......49 D3
Highgate Sta N6......49 B3
Highgate West Hill N6......71 A6
Highgate Wlk SE23......162 C2
Highgate Wood Sec Sch N8......49 C4
High Gr BR1......187 D2
Highgrove Cl
  London N11......31 A5
  Widmore BR7......188 A2
Highgrove Ct BR3......185 C3
Highgrove Ho HA4......40 A3
Highgrove Mews SM5......218 D5
Highgrove Point 2 NW3......70 A4
Highgrove Rd RM8......80 C4
Highgrove Way HA4......40 A2
High Gr SE18......145 B4
High Hill Ferry 3 E5......52 B1
High Holborn Ho WC1......240 D3
High Holborn WC1......94 B2 240 C3
High La W7......86 B1
Highland Ave W7......86 C1
Highland Cotts SM6......219 C4
Highland Croft BR3......185 D4
Highland Ct E18......37 B2
Highland Dr WD23......8 A4
Highland Lo 3 SE19......183 D3
Highland Pk TW13......171 D6
Highland Rd
  Bexley DA6......147 C1
  Bromley BR1......186 D2
  Pinner HA6......22 A1
  West Norwood SE19......183 C4
Highlands Ave
  Acton W3......111 A6
  Southgate N21......16 B6
Highlands Cl
  Hornsey N4......50 A2
  Hounslow TW3......129 D4
Highlands Ct SE19......183 C4
Highlands Gdns IG1......56 B1
Highlands Heath SW15......156 C4
Highlands N20......14 B2
Highlands Prim Sch IG1......56 B1
Highlands Rd EN5......13 C6
Highlands Sch N21......4 C1
Highlands The
  Barnet EN5......1 D1
  Edgware HA8......26 D1
Highlawn Hall HA1......64 C5
Highlea Cl NW9......27 C2
High Level Dr SE26......184 A6
Highlever Rd W10......90 C2
High Limes 2 SE19......183 C4
High London 5 N6......49 D2
Highmead Cres HA0......66 B1
Highmead 9 N18......34 A5
High Mead HA1......42 D4
High Meadow Cl HA5......40 C5
High Meadow Cres NW9......45 B4
Highmead SE18......145 D5
High Meads Rd E16......99 D1
High Mead BR4......224 C6
Highmore Rd SE3......142 C5
High Mount
  Hendon NW4......46 A3
  11 Hornsey N4......50 A2
High Oaks EN2......4 B5
High Oaks Lo 9 E18......37 A1
High Park Ave TW9......132 C4
High Park Rd TW9......132 C4
High Par The SW16......160 A1
High Path SW19......180 A2
High Point
  Chislehurst SE9......166 D1
  Highgate N6......49 A2
Highpoint EN5......14 A6
High Range SW20......178 C3
High Rd
  Buckhurst Hill IG9, IG10......21 C5
  Bushey WD23......8 B3
  Chadwell Heath RM6......58 C2
  East Finchley N2......48 C6
  Finchley N2, N12......30 A3
  Friern Barnet N11......31 B5
  Harrow HA3......24 C3
  Ilford IG1......78 D6
  Leyton E10......53 D3
  Oakleigh Pk N20......14 A4
  Seven Kings IG1, IG3......79 C6
  South Tottenham N15, N17......51 D5
  Tottenham N17......33 D2
  Wembley HA0, HA9......66 A3
  Willesden NW10......68 A2
  Woodford E18......37 A2
  Wood Green N22......32 B3
High Ridge N10......31 B2
Highridge Pl EN2......4 B5
High Road Buckhurst Hill 5 IG9......21 B2
High Road Eastcote HA5......40 B4
High Road, Ickenham UB10......61 A6
High Road Leyton E10......75 D6
High Road Leytonstone E11......76 C6
High Road Woodford Gn IG8......37 A6
High St Mews SW19......179 A5
High St N
  Newham E6......100 A6
  Plashet E12......78 A2
High St S E6......100 B4
High Sheldon N6......48 D3
Highshore Rd SE15......139 D3
Highshore Sch SE15......139 D4
High Silver IG10......21 D6
High St Acton W3......110 D5
  Barnet EN5......1 B1
  Beckenham BR3......185 C1
  Brentford TW8......132 A6
  Bromley BR1......187 A1
  Cheam SM1, KT17......217 A2
  Claygate KT10......212 D2
  Cranford TW5......128 B5
  Croydon CR0......221 A5
  Ealing W5......109 D6
  East Molesey KT8......195 C5
  Elstree WD6......9 D5
  Farnborough BR6......227 A3
  Feltham TW13......150 A2
  Green Street Green BR6......227 D2
  Hampton TW12......174 A4
  Harlington UB3......127 B6
  Harrow on t H HA1......42 C1
  Hornsey N8......50 B5
  Hounslow TW3......129 D2
  Ilford IG6......57 A6
  Kingston u T KT1......175 D2
  Kingston u T KT1......197 D6
  Mill Hill NW7......28 B5
  Newham E13......99 A5
  New Malden KT3......199 C5
Highstone Ave E11......55 A3
Highstone Ct E11......54 D3
High St
  Palmers Green N14......15 D2
  Penge SE20......184 D3
  Pinner HA5......41 A6
High Street Collier's Wood SW17, SW19......180 B4
High Street Harlesden NW10......89 D5
High Street Harlington TW6......127 B5
High Street Kensington Sta W8......113 D4 245 C1
High St Ruislip HA4......39 C1
  Shepperton TW17......193 A3
  Sidcup DA14......190 A6
  Southall UB1......107 B5
  South Norwood CR7......205 B5
  South Norwood SE25......206 A5
  Stratford Marsh E15......98 A6
  Sutton SM1......217 D4
  Sutton SM1, SM2......217 D3
  Teddington TW11......175 A5
  Thames Ditton KT7......197 A3
  Twickenham TW2......152 A4
  Wallington SM5......219 A4
  Walthamstow E17......53 B5
  Walton-on-T KT12......194 A1
  Wanstead E11......55 A4
  Wealdstone HA3......24 C1
High St *continued*
  Wealdstone HA3......42 C6
  Wembley HA9......66 B4
  West Wickham BR4......207 D1
  Wimbledon SW19......178 D5
  Yiewsley UB7......104 A6
High The SW16......160 A1
High Timber St EC4......252 A6
High Tor Cl BR1......187 B3
High Tor View SE28......123 C5
High Trees
  Cheam SM3......201 B2
  Croydon CR0......207 A1
Hightrees Ct W7......108 C6
High Trees EN4......14 C6
Hightrees Ho SW12......159 A5
High Trees
  Streatham SW2......160 C3
  Uxbridge UB10......61 A6
  Whetstone N20......14 A1
Highview Ave HA8......27 A6
High View Ave CR0, SM6......220 B3
High View Cl
  Loughton IG10......21 C6
  South Norwood SE19......183 D1
Highview N6......49 C3
High View Ct HA3......24 C3
Highview Ct
  2 Loughton IG10......21 D6
  2 Putney SW19......157 A3
Highview Gdns
  Edgware HA8......27 A6
  Hendon N3......47 A6
  New Southgate N11......31 C5
Highview Ho
  2 Buckhurst Hill IG9......21 D1
  1 Buckhurst Hill IG9......21 D1
High View Ho RM6......59 A5
Highview Hornsey N8......50 A2
  Northolt UB5......85 A4
High View Par 1 IG4......56 B4
High View
  6 Penge SE19......183 D3
  Pinner HA5......40 C6
High View Prim Sch
  London SW11......136 B1
  Wallington SM6......220 A3
Highview Rd W13......87 A1
High View Rd N10......30 D2
Highview Rd DA14......190 B6
High View Rd
  Snaresbrook E18......54 D6
  South Norwood SE19......183 B4
Highview SE18......144 D5
Highway Bsns Pk The 7 E1......118 D6
Highway The
  Shadwell E1......118 C6
  Stanmore HA7......25 A3
Highway Trad Ctr The 6 E1......118 D6
High Wigsell TW11......175 A5
Highwood Ave N12......30 A6
Highwood Cl
  Dulwich SE22......162 A3
  Orpington BR6......227 A6
Highwood Ct
  Barnet EN5......13 C6
  Whetstone N12......14 A1
Highwood Dr BR6......227 A6
Highwood Gdns IG5......56 B5
Highwood Gr NW7......27 B5
Highwood Hill NW7......11 D2
Highwood Rd N19......72 A5
Highwood IG8......36 D6
High Worple HA2......41 B1
Highworth Rd N11......31 D5
Highworth St NW1......237 B4
Hilary Ave CR4......203 A6
Hilary Cl Bexley DA8......147 D4
  Walham Green SW6......265 C4
Hilary Ct N9......18 D3
Hilary Rd W12......111 D6
Hilbert Rd SM3......216 D5
Hilborough Cl SW19......180 A3
Hilborough Ct 1 E8......95 D6
Hilborough Rd 1 E8......73 D1
Hilborough Way BR6......227 B3
Hilda Lockert Wlk SW9......138 D3
Hilda Rd Newham E16......98 C3
  Upton Pk E6......77 D1
Hilda Terr 2 SW9......138 C3
Hilda Vale Cl BR6......226 D4
Hilda Vale Rd BR6......226 D4
Hildenborough Gdns BR1......186 D4
Hildenbrough Ho BR3......185 B3
Hildenlea Pl BR2......186 C1
Hilditch Ho 7 TW10......154 B5
Hildred Ho SW1......258 C4
Hildreth St SW12......159 B3
Hildreth Street Mews 2 SW12......159 B3
Hildyard Rd SW6......265 B6
Hiley Rd NW10......90 C4
Hilfield La WD23......8 C6
Hilgrove Rd NW6......70 A1
Hiliary Gdns HA7......25 C1
Hillary Cres KT12......194 C1
Hillary Ct
  3 Chislehurst SE9......166 A2
  13 Shepherd's Bush W12......112 C4
  Stanwell TW19......148 A3
Hillary Dr TW7......152 D6
Hillary Rd UB2......107 C3
Hillary Rise EN5......1 C1
Hillbeck Cl
  Deptford SE15......140 C5
  Deptford SE15......140 C6
Hillbeck Way UB6......86 B6
Hillborne Cl UB3......106 A1
Hillboro Ct
  Leytonstone E11......54 B2
  1 Woodford E18......36 D2
Hillborough Ct HA1......42 C2
Hillbrook Rd SW17......181 A6
Hillbrook Sch SW17......181 A6
Hill Brow BR1......187 D2
Hillbrow Ct KT10......212 A4
Hillbrow KT3......199 D6
Hillbrow Rd
  Catford BR1......186 C4
  Esher KT10......212 A4
Hillbrow 7 TW10......154 A5
Hill Bunker's DA17......125 C2
Hillbury Ave HA3......43 B4
Hillbury Rd SW17......159 B1
Hill Cl Barnet EN5......12 C6
  Chislehurst BR7......188 D5
  Dollis Hill NW2......68 B5
  Hampstead Garden Suburb NW11......47 C3
  Harrow HA1......64 C5
  Stanmore HA7......25 B6
Hillcote Ave SW16......182 C3
Hillcourt Ave N12......29 D4
Hillcourt N6......49 C3
Hillcourt Rd SE22......162 B5
Hill Cres Harrow HA1......43 A4
  Kingston u T KT5......198 B4
  North Cheam KT4......216 C6
Hillcrest Ave
  Edgware HA8......26 D6
  Pinner HA5......40 D5
  Temple Fortune NW11......47 B4
Hillcrest SE24......139 B1
Hillcrest Cl
  Beckenham BR3......207 B3
  Forest Hill SE26......184 A6
Hillcrest Ct
  Brondesbury NW2......69 A3
  8 Edgware HA8......26 D5
  Lewisham SE6......164 B4
  Sutton SM2......218 B2
Hill Crest DA15......168 B4
Hillcrest Gdns
  Dollis Hill NW2......68 A5
  Hendon N3......47 A5
  Hinchley Wood KT10......212 D5
Hillcrest N6......49 A2
Hillcrest Hts W5......88 A3
Hillcrest W11......244 C5
Hill Cres N20......13 D2
Hillcrest Rd
  Acton W3......110 D5
  Chingford E17......36 B1
  Ealing W5......88 A2
  Grove Pk BR1......187 A6
  Loughton IG10......21 D5
  Woodford E18......37 A1
Hillcrest N21......16 C4
Hillcrest View BR3......207 B3
Hillcroft Ave HA5......41 B3
Hillcroft Coll KT6......198 A3
Hillcroft Cres
  Ealing W5......87 D1
  Ruislip HA4......62 D5
  Wembley HA9......66 B4
Hillcroft Rd E6......100 D2
Hillcroome Rd SM2......218 B2
Hillcross Ave SM4......201 A4
Hillcross Prim Sch SM4......201 B5
Hill Ct Barnet EN4......2 C1
  Ealing W5......88 B3
  Hampstead NW3......70 C4
  8 Norbiton KT2......176 D3
  Northolt UB5......63 C3
  Putney SW15......156 D6
  14 Surbiton KT6......198 A4
Hill Ct *continued*
  Wembley HA0......65 A4
  9 Wimbledon SW19......179 A4
Hilldale Rd SM1......217 B4
Hilldown Ct SW16......182 A3
Hilldown Rd
  Hayes BR2......208 D1
  South Norwood SW16......182 B3
Hill Dr NW9......45 A1
Hilldrop Cres N7......71 D3
Hilldrop La N7......71 D3
Hilldrop Rd
  Bromley BR1......187 B4
  Kentish Town N7......71 D3
Hill Dr SW16......204 B6
Hill End
  Orpington BR6......227 D6
  Shooters Hill SE18......144 C4
Hillersdon Ave
  Barnes SW13......134 A3
  Edgware HA8......26 B5
Hillersdon Ho SW1......258 C2
Hillery Cl SE17......262 D3
Hill Farm Rd W10......90 D2
Hillfield Ave
  Colindale NW9......45 C5
  Hornsey N8......50 A5
  Mitcham SM4......202 C4
  Wembley HA0......66 B1
Hillfield Cl HA2......42 A5
Hillfield Ct NW3......70 C3
Hillfield Ho N5......73 A3
Hillfield La S WD23......8 D5
Hillfield Lo SW17......180 D5
Hillfield Mans NW3......70 C3
Hillfield Par SM4......202 B3
Hillfield Park Mews N10......49 B5
Hillfield Pk
  London N10......49 B5
  Southgate N21......16 C2
Hillfield Rd
  Hampton TW12......173 B2
  West Hampstead NW6......69 C3
Hillgate Pl
  Balham SW12......159 B4
  Kensington W8......113 C5 245 A4
Hillgate St W8......245 A4
Hill Gate Wlk N6......49 C3
Hill Gr TW13......151 B2
Hill Ho Southall UB1......85 C1
  Stanmore HA7......9 A1
  Upper Clapton E5......52 B1
Hill House Ave HA7......24 D3
Hill House Cl N21......16 C4
Hill House Dr TW12......173 C2
Hill House Rd SW16......182 B5
Hill House Sch SW1......114 D3 257 D5
Hill Ho SE28......123 C5
Hilliard Ct SM6......219 D2
Hilliard Ho 15 E1......118 B5
Hilliard's Ct E1......118 C5
Hillier Cl EN5......13 D5
Hillier Gdns CR0......220 C3
Hillier Ho 1 NW1......71 D1
Hillier Lo TW12......174 B5
Hillier Pl KT9......213 D2
Hillier Rd SW11......158 D5
Hilliers Ave UB8......82 C4
Hillier's La CR0, SM6......220 A5
HILLINGDON......82 D5
Hillingdon Ave TW19......148 A3
Hillingdon Circus UB10......60 D2
HILLINGDON HEATH......82 D2
Hillingdon Hill UB10......82 B4
Hillingdon Hospl UB8......82 B2
Hillingdon Manor Sch UB8......82 D2
Hillingdon Par 6 UB10......82 D3
Hillingdon Prim Sch UB10......82 D4
Hillingdon Rd UB10......82 A5
Hillingdon Sta UB10......60 D3
Hillingdon St SE17......138 D6
Hillington Gdns IG8......37 D1
Hill La HA4......39 A1
Hill Lo SW11......136 B1
Hillman Cl UB8......60 A3
Hillman Dr 12 NW10......90 C3
Hillman St E8......74 B2
Hillmarton Rd N7......72 A3
Hillmead Dr SW9......138 D1
Hill Mead Prim Sch SW9......138 D1
Hillmont Rd KT10......212 C5
Hillmore Ct SE13......142 B2
Hillmore Gr SE26......185 A5
Hill Rd
  Carshalton SM5......218 C2
  Finchley N10......30 D2
  Harrow HA1......43 A4
  Mitcham CR4......181 B3
  Pinner HA5......41 A3
  St John's Wood NW8......92 A5 229 B3
  Sutton SM1......217 D3
  Wembley HA0......65 B5
Hillreach SE7, SE18......122 B1
Hill Rise
  East Finchley NW11......47 D5
  Enfield N9......18 B5
  Forest Hill SE23......162 B3
  Greenford UB6......86 A6
  Hinchley Wood KT10......213 B6
Hillrise Mans N19......50 A2
Hillrise Rd N19......50 A2
Hill Rise
  Richmond TW10......153 D6
  Ruislip HA4......39 B1
Hillrise KT12......193 D2
Hillsboro Rd SE22......161 C6
Hillsborough Ct 13 NW6......91 D6
Hillside 6 SM1......218 B3
Hillsgrove Cl DA16......146 C5
Hillsgrove Prim Sch DA16......146 C5
Hillside Ave
  London N11......30 D4
  Wembley HA9......66 B4
  Woodford IG8......37 C5
Hillside EN5......14 A6
Hillside Cl
  Merton SM4......201 A5
  St John's Wood NW8......91 D5
  Woodford IG8......37 C5
Hillside Cres
  Enfield EN2......5 B5
  Harrow HA2......42 A1
  Northwood HA6......22 A2
Hillside N8......49 D3
Hillside Ct
  Hampstead NW3......69 D3
  7 Kingston u T KT2......176 D3
Hillside Dr HA8......26 C5
Hillside Gdns
  Chipping Barnet EN5......1 A1
  Edgware HA8......26 B6
  Friern Barnet N11......31 C4
  Harrow HA3......44 A2
  Highgate N6......49 B3
  Northwood HA6......22 B2
  Streatham SW2......160 C2
  Wallington SM6......219 C1
  Walthamstow E17......54 B6
Hillside Glen CR0......220 D4
Hillside SE10......142 B5
Hillside Gr
  Hendon NW7......28 A3
  Southgate N14......15 D4
Hillside Ho CR0......220 D4
Hillside Jun & Inf Schs HA6......22 A3
Hillside NW9......45 B5
Hillside La BR2......224 D6
Hillside Mans EN5......1 B1
Hill Side EN5......14 A6
Hillside Rd
  Beckenham BR2......208 D6
  Belmont SM2......217 B1
  Croydon CR0......220 D4
  Ealing W5......88 A2
  Northwood HA6, HA5......22 B3
  Southall UB1......85 C3
  South Tottenham N15......51 C3
  Streatham SW2......160 C2
  Surbiton KT5......198 C4
Hillside Rise HA6......22 A3
Hillside
  Stonebridge NW10......89 B6
  Wimbledon SW19......178 D4
Hillsleigh Rd W14......113 B5 244 D4
Hillsley DA14......190 A6
Hills Mews 2 W5......110 A6
Hills Pl W1......239 A1
Hill's Rd IG9......21 B3
Hill St W1......115 B5 248 C4
Hillstone Ct 5 E3......97 D3
Hillstowe St E5......74 C5
Hill St TW10......153 D6
Hilltop Ave NW10......67 A1
Hill Top SM3......201 B2
Hilltop Ct
  12 London SW18......136 B1
  South Hampstead NW8......70 A1
  South Norwood SE19......183 B2
Hill Top NW11......47 D5

Hilltop Gdns
Hendon NW4 .... 28 B1
Orpington BR6 .... 227 C6
Hilltop Ho 7 N6 .... 49 D2
Hilltop 7 E17 .... 53 D6
Hilltop Rd NW6 .... 69 C1
Hilltop Way HA7 .... 9 A1
Hillview Ave HA3 .... 44 A4
Hillview Cl
Pinner HA5 .... 23 B4
Wembley HA9 .... 66 B6
Hillview Cres
Orpington BR6 .... 211 D1
Redbridge IG1 .... 56 B3
Hillview Ct SE19 .... 183 C6
Hill View Dr
Bexley DA16 .... 145 C3
Woolwich SE28 .... 123 C5
Hillview Gdns
Harrow HA2 .... 41 C5
Hendon NW4 .... 46 D5
Hill View Gdns NW9 .... 45 B4
Hill View
Mitcham CR4 .... 204 A5
Primrose Hill NW1 .... 230 D6
Hillview Rd
Carshalton SM1 .... 218 B5
Chislehurst BR7 .... 188 D6
Hill View Rd KT10 .... 213 A1
Hillview Rd NW7 .... 28 D6
Hill View Rd BR6 .... 227 D6
Hillview Rd HA5 .... 23 B4
Hill View Rd TW1 .... 153 A5
Hillview SW20 .... 178 B3
Hillway Highgate N6 .... 71 A6
London NW9 .... 45 C1
Hill Wood Ho NW1 .... 232 C3
Hillworth 7 BR3 .... 185 D1
Hillworth Rd SW2 .... 160 C4
Hillyard Rd W7 .... 86 C2
Hillyard St SW9 .... 138 C4
Hillyfield Cl E9 .... 75 A3
Hillyfield E17 .... 35 A1
Hillyfield Prim Sch
E17 .... 53 A6
Hilly Fields Cres
SE4 .... 141 C2
Hilly Mead SW19 .... 179 A3
Hilsea Point 7
SW15 .... 156 B3
Hilsea St E5 .... 74 C4
Hilton Ave N12 .... 30 B5
Hilton Ho
4 Ealing W13 .... 87 C1
12 Finchley N2 .... 30 B1
Lower Holloway N7 .... 72 A4
9 Nunhead SE4 .... 140 D1
Hilversum Cres 10
SE22 .... 161 C6
Himley Rd SW17 .... 180 D4
Hinchlay Manor
KT10 .... 212 D5
Hinchley Cl KT10 .... 212 D5
Hinchley Dr KT10 .... 212 D5
Hinchley Way KT10 .... 213 A5
HINCHLEY WOOD 212 D6
Hinchley Wood Prim
Sch KT10 .... 213 A6
Hinchley Wood Sch &
Sixth Form Ctr
KT10 .... 213 A6
Hinchley Wood Sta
KT10 .... 212 D5
Hinckley Rd SE15 .... 140 A1
Hind Ct EC4 .... 241 B1
Hinde Mews W1 .... 238 B2
Hindes Rd HA1 .... 42 C4
Hinde St W1 .... 93 A1 238 B2
Hind Gr E14 .... 97 C1
Hindhead Cl UB8 .... 82 D2
Hindhead Gdns UB5 .... 85 A6
Hindhead Gn WD19 .... 22 C5
Hindhead Point 6
SW15 .... 156 B3
Hindhead Way SM6 .... 220 A3
Hind Ho
13 Deptford SE14 .... 140 D6
Islington N7 .... 72 C4
Hindhurst Ct NW9 .... 45 A5
Hindle Ho E8 .... 73 D3
Hindley Ho N7 .... 72 B5
Hindlip Ho SW8 .... 269 C1
Hindmans Rd SE22 .... 162 A6
Hindmans Way RM9 .... 103 B3
Hindmarsh Cl E1 .... 118 A6
Hindrey Rd E5 .... 74 B3
Hindsley's Pl SE23 .... 162 C2
Hines Ct HA1 .... 43 A4
Hinkler Rd HA3 .... 43 D6
Hinksey Path SE2 .... 124 D3
Hinstock NW6 .... 91 D6
Hinstock Rd SE18 .... 145 A5
Hinton Ave TW4 .... 128 D1
Hinton Cl SE9 .... 166 A3
Hinton Ct 8 E10 .... 75 D6
Hinton Rd
Brixton SE24 .... 138 D2
Edmonton N18 .... 33 C6
Wallington SM6 .... 219 C2
Hippisley Ct TW7 .... 130 D2
Hippodrome Mews
W11 .... 244 A5
Hippodrome Pl W11 .... 244 B5
Hirst Cres HA9 .... 66 A5
Hirst Ct SW1 .... 258 C1
Hispano Mews 17 EN3 .... 7 C6
Hitcham Rd E17 .... 53 B2
Hitchcock Cl TW17 .... 192 B6
Hitchin Sq E3 .... 97 A5
Hithe Gr 15 SE16 .... 118 C3
Hitherbroom Rd
UB3 .... 106 A6
Hither Farm Rd SE3 .... 143 C2
Hitherfield Prim Sch
SW16 .... 160 C2
Hitherfield Rd
Dagenham RM8 .... 81 A6
Streatham SW16,
SW27 .... 160 C1
HITHER GREEN 164 C5
Hither Green La
SE13 .... 164 B5
Hither Green Prim Sch
SE13 .... 164 B5
Hither Green Sta
SE13 .... 164 C5
Hitherlands SW12 .... 159 B2
Hitherwell Dr HA3 .... 24 B2
Hitherwood Ct
SE21 .... 183 D6
Hitherwood Dr
SE19 .... 183 D6
Hive Cl WD23 .... 8 B2
Hive Rd WD23 .... 8 C2
Hive Wood Ho E7 .... 77 A2
HM Prison Wormwood
Scrubs W12 .... 90 A1
HMS Belfast* SE1 .... 253 B4
Hoadly Rd SW16 .... 159 D2
Hobart Cl
East Barnet N20 .... 14 C2
Hayes UB4 .... 84 D3
Hobart Ct
Harrow HA1 .... 42 C2
Woodford IG8 .... 36 D6
Hobart Dr UB4 .... 84 D3
Hobart Gdns CR7 .... 205 B6
Hobart Ho 24 KT6 .... 198 A4
Hobart La UB4 .... 84 D3
Hobart Pl
Richmond TW10 .... 154 B4
Westminster
SW1 .... 115 B3 258 C6
Hobart Rd
Dagenham RM9 .... 80 D4
Hayes UB4 .... 84 D3
North Cheam KT4 .... 216 B5
Hobbayne Prim Sch
W7 .... 86 D1
Hobbayne Rd W7 .... 86 B1
Hobbes Wlk SW15 .... 156 B6
Hobb's Ct SE1 .... 253 D2
Hobbs Gn N2 .... 48 A6
Hobbs Mews IG3 .... 79 D6
Hobbs' Pl N1 .... 95 C6
Hobbs Rd 5 SE27 .... 183 A6
Hobby St EN3 .... 18 D6
Hobday St E14 .... 97 D1
Hobhouse Ct SW1 .... 249 D5
Hobill Wlk KT5 .... 198 B3
Hoblands End BR7 .... 189 C4
Hobsons Pl 7 E1 .... 96 A2
Hobury St
SW10 .... 136 B6 266 C5
Hockenden La BR5,
BR8 .... 191 D1
Hocker St 41 E2 .... 95 D4
Hockett Cl SE8 .... 119 B2
Hockington Ct 7
EN5 .... 13 D6
Hockley Ave E6 .... 100 A5
Hockley Ct 2 E18 .... 37 A2
Hockley Ho 4 E9 .... 74 C2
Hockley Mews IG11 .... 101 C5
Hockliffe Ho 5 W10 .... 90 C2
Hockney Ct 1 SE16 .... 118 B1
Hockworth Ho 7
N16 .... 51 C1
Hocroft Ave NW2 .... 69 B5
Hocroft Ct NW2 .... 69 B5
Hocroft Rd NW2 .... 69 B5
Hocroft Wlk NW2 .... 69 B5
Hodder Dr UB6 .... 86 D5
Hoddesdon Rd
DA17 .... 125 C1
Hodford Lo NW11 .... 69 C6
Hodford Rd NW11 .... 47 B1
Hodgkins Cl SE28 .... 124 D6
Hodgkins Mews HA7 .... 25 B5
Hodister Cl 26 SE5 .... 139 A5
Hodson Cl HA2 .... 63 B5
Hodson Pl EN3 .... 7 C5
Hoecroft Ct EN3 .... 6 C5
Hoe La EN1 .... 6 B5
Hoe St E17 .... 53 C4
Hoffman Gdns CR2 .... 222 B1
Hoffman Sq N1 .... 235 D2
Hofland Rd
W14 .... 113 A3 254 A6
Hogan Mews W2 .... 236 C4
Hogan Way E5 .... 74 A6
Hogarth Ave TW15 .... 171 A4
Hogarth Bsns Pk
W4 .... 133 C6
Hogarth Cl Ealing W5 .... 88 A2
Newham E16 .... 99 D2
Hogarth Cres
Mitcham SW19 .... 180 B2
Thornton Heath CR0 .... 205 A2
Hogarth Ct
8 Camden Town
NW1 .... 71 C1
City of London EC3 .... 253 B6
Dulwich SE19 .... 183 D6
Heston TW5 .... 129 A5
24 Whitechapel E1 .... 96 A1
Hogarth Gdns TW5 .... 129 C5
Hogarth Hill NW11 .... 47 B5
Hogarth Ho
Enfield EN1 .... 18 A6
12 Northolt UB5 .... 84 D5
1 Sutton SM1 .... 218 B3
Westminster SW1 .... 259 D3
6 West Norwood
SE27 .... 183 A6
Hogarth Ind Est
NW10 .... 90 A3
Hogarth La W4 .... 133 C6
Hogarth Pl SW5 .... 255 C3
Hogarth Rd
Barking RM8 .... 80 B3
Earl's Ct
SW5 .... 113 D2 255 C3
Edgware HA8 .... 26 C1
Hogarth Roundabout
W4 .... 133 C6
Hogarth's House*
W4 .... 133 C6
Hogarth Way TW12 .... 174 A2
Hogsmill Way KT19 .... 215 A4
Holbeach Cl 8 NW9 .... 27 C2
Holbeach Gdns
DA15 .... 167 D5
Holbeach Mews 1
SW12 .... 159 B3
Holbeach Prim Sch
SE6 .... 163 C4
Holbeach Rd SE6 .... 163 D4
Holbeck Row SE15 .... 140 A5
Holbein Ho
Chelsea SW1 .... 258 A2
10 Stanmore HA7 .... 25 C5
Holbein Mews
SW1 .... 115 A1 258 A2
Holbein Pl
SW1 .... 115 A2 258 A3
Holberry Ho 5
SE21 .... 183 C6
Holberton Gdns
NW10 .... 90 B4
HOLBORN 94 C2
Holborn Cir
EC1 .... 94 C2 241 B3
Holborn EC1 .... 94 C2 241 B3
Holborn Ho 1 W12 .... 90 B1
Holborn Pl WC1 .... 240 C3
Holborn Rd E13 .... 99 B3
Holborn Sta
WC1 .... 94 B2 240 C3
Holborn Viaduct
EC1 .... 94 D2 241 C3
Holborn Way CR4 .... 180 D1
Holbrook Cl
Enfield EN1 .... 6 A5
Highgate N19 .... 49 B1
Holbrook Ct W7 .... 108 C6
Holbrooke Ct N7 .... 72 A4
Holbrooke Pl 25
TW10 .... 153 D6
Holbrook Ho
Acton W3 .... 89 B2
Chislehurst BR7 .... 189 B2
5 Streatham SW2 .... 160 B3
Holbrook La BR7 .... 189 B3
Holbrook Rd E15 .... 98 D5
Holbrook Way BR2 .... 210 B4
Holburne Cl SE3 .... 143 C4
Holburne Gdns SE3 .... 143 D4
Holburne Rd SE3 .... 143 D4
Holcombe Hill NW7 .... 12 A1
Holcombe Ho SW9 .... 138 A2
Holcombe Pl SE4 .... 141 A2
Holcombe Rd
Ilford IG1 .... 56 C2
Tottenham Hale N17 .... 52 A6
1 Tottenham N17 .... 51 D6
Holcombe St W6 .... 112 B2
Holcote Cl DA17 .... 125 A3
Holcroft Ct W1 .... 239 A4
Holcroft Ho
Battersea SW11 .... 136 B2
Lewisham SE10 .... 142 A4
Holcroft Rd E9 .... 74 C1
Holden Ave
North Finchley N12 .... 29 D5
Welsh Harp NW9 .... 45 A1
Holdenby Rd SE4 .... 163 A6
Holden Cl RM8 .... 80 B5
Holden Ho
12 Deptford SE8 .... 141 C5
Islington N1 .... 235 A5
Holden Hts N12 .... 13 D1
Holdenhurst Ave
N12 .... 30 A3
Holden Lo N11 .... 31 C5
Holden Point E15 .... 76 B2
Holden Rd N12 .... 29 D6
Holden St SW11 .... 137 A3
Holdernesse Rd
Isleworth TW7 .... 131 A4
6 Upper Tooting
SW17 .... 159 A2
Holderness Ho SE5 .... 139 C2
Holderness Way
SE27 .... 182 D5
Holders Hill Ave
NW4 .... 46 D6
Holders Hill Cres
NW4 .... 28 D1
Holders Hill Dr NW4 .... 28 D1
Holders Hill Gdns
NW4 .... 29 A1
Holders Hill Par
NW7 .... 29 A2
Holders Hill Rd
Church End NW4,
NW7 .... 29 A2
Hendon NW4 .... 28 D1
Holdsworth Ho 5
SW2 .... 160 C4
Holford Ho
6 Bermondsey
SE16 .... 118 B2
Finsbury WC1 .... 233 D2
Holford Pl WC1 .... 233 D2
Holford Rd NW3 .... 70 A5
Holford St WC1 .... 234 A2
Holford Yd WC1 .... 234 A3
Holgate Ave SW11 .... 136 B2
Holgate Ct HA8 .... 26 B6
Holgate Gdns RM10 .... 81 C2
Holgate Rd RM10 .... 81 C3
Holgate St SE7 .... 121 D3
Holkham Ho 6 EN5 .... 1 A2
Hollam Ho N8 .... 50 B5
Holland Ave
Belmont SM2 .... 217 C1
Wimbledon SW20 .... 177 D2
Holland Cl
Coney Hall BR2 .... 224 D6
New Barnet EN5 .... 14 B4
Stanmore HA7 .... 25 B5
Holland Ct
Ashford TW15 .... 170 B4
Hendon NW7 .... 28 A4
6 Walthamstow E17 .... 54 A5
Holland Dr SE23 .... 163 A1
Holland Gdns
Brentford TW8 .... 132 A6
Kensington W14 .... 254 B6
Holland Gr SW9 .... 138 C5
Holland Ho E4 .... 36 A6
Holland House Sch
HA8 .... 26 D6
Holland Park Ave
Ilford IG3 .... 57 D4
Notting Hill
W11 .... 113 A5 244 B3
Holland Park Ct
W14 .... 244 B2
Holland Park Gdns
W14 .... 113 A4 244 A2
Holland Park Mews
W11 .... 113 B5 244 C3
Holland Park Rdbt
W12 .... 112 D4
Holland Park Rd
W14 .... 113 B3 254 D5
Holland Park Sch
W8 .... 113 B4 244 D2
Holland Park Sta
W11 .... 113 B5 244 C3
Holland Park
W11 .... 113 B5 244 C3
Holland Pas N1 .... 235 A6
Holland Pl W8 .... 245 C2
Holland Rd
Croydon SE25 .... 206 A4
Newham E15 .... 98 C4
Wallend E6 .... 78 C1
Wembley HA0 .... 65 D2
West Kensington
W14 .... 113 A3 254 B6
Willesden Green
NW10 .... 90 B5
Holland Rise Ho
SW9 .... 270 D3
Hollands The
Feltham TW13 .... 172 D6
New Malden KT4 .... 199 D1
Holland St
Kensington
W8 .... 113 C4 245 B2
Lambeth
SE1 .... 116 D5 251 D4
Holland Villas Rd
W14 .... 113 A4 244 A1
Holland Way BR2 .... 224 D6
Holland Wlk
Kensington
W14 .... 113 B4 244 D1
Stanmore HA7 .... 25 A5
Upper Holloway N19 .... 49 D1
Hollar Rd N16 .... 73 D5
Hollen St W1 .... 239 C2
Holles Cl TW12 .... 173 C5
Holles Ho 8 SW9 .... 138 C3
Holles St W1 .... 93 B1 238 D2
Holley Rd W3 .... 111 C4
Hollickwood Ave
N12 .... 30 D4
Hollickwood Prim Sch
N10 .... 31 B3
Holliday Sq 7
SW11 .... 136 B2
Hollidge Way RM10 .... 81 D1
Hollies Ave DA15 .... 167 D3
Hollies Cl
South Norwood
SW16 .... 182 C4
Twickenham TW1 .... 152 D2
Hollies End NW7 .... 28 B5
Hollies Rd W5 .... 109 C2
Hollies The
Harrow HA3 .... 43 A5
Oakleigh Pk N20 .... 14 B3
Upper Tooting
SW12 .... 159 C2
9 Wanstead E11 .... 55 A4
Wood Green N11 .... 31 D4
Hollies Way 1
SW12 .... 159 A4
Holligrave Rd BR1 .... 187 A2
Hollingbourne Ave
DA7 .... 147 B4
Hollingbourne Gdns
W13 .... 87 B2
Hollingbourne Rd
SE24 .... 161 A6
Hollingsworth Ct 7
KT6 .... 197 D2
Hollingsworth Rd
CR0 .... 222 B2
Hollington Cres
KT3 .... 199 D3
Hollington Ct BR7 .... 188 D4
Hollington Rd
Newham E6 .... 100 B4
Tottenham N17 .... 34 A1
Hollingworth Cl
KT8 .... 195 B5
Hollingworth Rd BR2,
BR5 .... 210 D2
Hollins Ho N7 .... 72 A4
Hollisfield WC1 .... 233 B1
Hollman Gdns
SW16 .... 182 D4
Holloway Cl UB7 .... 104 A1
Holloway La UB7 .... 104 B1
Holloway Rd
Leyton E11 .... 76 B5
Lower Holloway N7 .... 72 B4
Newham E6 .... 100 B4
Upper Holloway N19 .... 71 D6
Holloway Road Sta
N7 .... 72 B3
Holloway Sch N7 .... 71 D3
Holloway St TW3 .... 129 D2
Hollow Combe
SE20 .... 184 B6
Hollowfield Wlk UB5 .... 63 A2
Hollow The IG8 .... 36 D6
Holly Ave London N2 .... 47 D6
Stanmore HA7 .... 26 A1
Walton-on-T KT12 .... 194 D1
Hollybank Cl TW12 .... 173 C5
Holly Berry La 8
NW3 .... 70 A4
Hollybrake Cl BR7 .... 189 B3
Hollybush Cl
Harrow HA3 .... 24 C2
Wanstead E11 .... 55 A4
Hollybush Gdns E2 .... 96 B4
Hollybush Hill E11 .... 54 D3
Holly Bush Hill 4
NW3 .... 70 A4
Hollybush Ho 23 E2 .... 96 B4
Holly Bush La TW12 .... 173 C3
Hollybush Pl E2 .... 96 B4
Hollybush Rd KT2 .... 176 A4
Holly Bush Steps 6
NW3 .... 70 A4
Hollybush St E13 .... 99 B
Holly Bush Vale 10
NW3 .... 70 A
Holly Cl
Beckenham BR3 .... 208 A
Buckhurst Hill IG9 .... 21 D
Feltham TW13 .... 173 A
Wallington SM6 .... 219 B
Holly Cottage Mews
UB8 .... 82 C
Holly Cotts KT7 .... 197 A
Holly Cres
Beckenham BR3 .... 207 B
Chingford IG8 .... 36 B
Hollycroft Ave
Child's Hill NW3 .... 69 C
Wembley HA9 .... 66 B
Hollycroft Cl
Harmondsworth
UB7 .... 126 C
South Croydon CR2 .... 221 C
Hollycroft Gdns
UB7 .... 126 C
Holly Ct
16 Belmont SM2 .... 217 C
Catford SE6 .... 164 A
4 Sidcup DA14 .... 190 B
South Tottenham N15 .... 51 C
Hollydale Cl UB5 .... 63 D
Hollydale Dr BR2 .... 226 B
Hollydale Prim Sch
SE15 .... 140 C
Hollydale Rd SE15 .... 140 C
Hollydene
Bromley BR1 .... 186 D
Hither Green SE13 .... 164 B
5 Peckham SE15 .... 140 B
Hollydown Way E11 .... 76 B
Holly Dr E4 .... 19 D
Holly Farm Rd UB2 .... 107 A
Hollyfield Ave N11 .... 30 D
Hollyfield Rd KT5 .... 198 B
Hollyfield Sch & Sixth
Form Ctr The
KT6 .... 198 A
Holly Gdns UB7 .... 104 B
Holly Gr NW9 .... 45 A
Hollygrove WD23 .... 8 B
Hollygrove Cl TW3 .... 129 B
Holly Gr
Peckham SE15 .... 140 A
Pinner HA5 .... 23 A
Hollyhedge Ho SE3 .... 142 B
Holly Hedge Terr
SE13 .... 164 B
Holly Hill NW3 .... 70 A
Holly Hill Rd DA8,
DA17 .... 125 D
Holly Hill N21 .... 16 B
Holly Ho
Brentford TW8 .... 131 C
Ilford IG3 .... 58 A
Holly House Hospl
IG9 .... 21 B
Holly Lo SW20 .... 178 B
Holly Lodge Gdns
N6 .... 49 A
Holly Lodge SE13 .... 142 B
Holly Lodge Mans
N6 .... 71 A
Holly Lodge UB2 .... 107 B
Holly Lo Harrow HA1 .... 42 B
Kensington W8 .... 245 A
Southgate N21 .... 16 C
4 Wimbledon
SW19 .... 179 A
Hollymead SM5 .... 218 D
Holly Mews SW10 .... 256 B
Hollymount Cl 9
SE10 .... 142 A
Holly Mount NW3 .... 70 A
Hollymount Sch
SW20 .... 178 C
Holly Park Est N4 .... 50 B
Holly Park Gdns N3 .... 47 C
Holly Park Prim Sch
N11 .... 31 A
Holly Park Rd
Ealing W7 .... 108 D
Friern Barnet N11 .... 31 A
Holly Pk
East Finchley N3 .... 47 C
Hornsey N4 .... 50 B
Holly Pl NW3 .... 70 A
Holly Rd
6 Chiswick W4 .... 111 B
Hampton TW12 .... 174 A
Hounslow TW3 .... 129 D
Leytonstone E11 .... 54 D
Twickenham TW1 .... 153 A
Holly St E8 .... 73 D
Holly Terr N6 .... 49 A
Hollytree Cl SW19 .... 156 D
Holly Tree Ho SE4 .... 141 B
Holly Tree Lo EN2 .... 4 D
Hollyview Cl NW4 .... 46 A

Holly Village N6 71 B6
Holly Way CR4 203 D6
Holly Wlk Enfield EN2 5 B2
Hampstead NW3 70 A4
Hollywood Ct W5 110 B6
Hollywood Gdns UB4 84 B1
Hollywood Lofts E1 243 C5
Hollywood Mews SW10 266 A6
Hollywood Rd
Chelsea SW10 136 A6 266 A6
Highams Pk E4 35 A5
Hollywood Way IG8 36 B4
Holman Ho 2 E2 96 D4
Holman Hunt Ho W14 254 A1
Holman Rd
London SW11 136 B3
West Ewell KT19 215 A3
Holmbank Dr TW17 193 C5
Holmbridge Gdns EN3 6 D1
Holmbrook Dr NW4 46 D4
Holmbrook NW1 232 B3
Holmbury Cl WD23 8 C2
Holmbury Ct
Mitcham SW19 180 C3
Upper Tooting SW17 158 D1
Holmbury Gdns UB3 105 D5
Holmbury Gr CR0 223 B1
Holmbury Ho SW9 160 D6
Holmbury Manor 9 DA14 190 A6
Holmbury Pk BR7 188 A3
Holmbury View 2 E5 52 B1
Holmbush Ct NW4 46 D4
Holmbush Rd SW15 157 A5
Holmcote Gdns N5 73 A3
Holmcroft Ho 10 E17 53 D5
Holmcroft Way BR2 210 B4
Holm Ct SE12 165 B1
Holmdale Gdns NW4 46 D4
Holmdale Rd
Chislehurst BR7 189 A5
South Hampstead NW6 69 C3
Holmdale Terr N15 51 C3
Holmdene Ave
Harrow HA2 41 D6
Hendon NW7 28 A4
Herne Hill SE24 161 A6
Holmdene Cl BR3 186 A1
Holmdene Ct BR1 210 A6
Holmdene N12 29 D5
Holmead Rd SW6 135 D5 265 D3
Holme Ct 12 TW7 131 A2
Holmefield Ct 4 NW3 70 C2
Holmefield Ho W10 91 A3
Holme Lacey Rd SE12 164 D5
Holmeleigh Ct EN3 6 C1
Holme Rd E6 100 A6
Holmes Ave
Mill Hill NW7 29 A5
Walthamstow E17 53 B6
Holmes Cl SE22 140 A1
Holmes Ct
Chingford E4 20 B2
18 South Acton W4 111 A3
18 South Lambeth SW4 138 A3
Holmesdale Ave SW14 132 D1
Holmesdale Cl SE25 205 D6
Holmesdale Ho 12 NW6 91 C6
Holmesdale Rd
Bexley DA7 146 D3
Highgate N6 49 B2
Richmond TW9 132 B4
South Norwood SE25 205 C5
Teddington TW11 175 C4
Thornton Heath CR0 205 B4
Holmesley Rd SE23 163 A5
Holmes Pl SW10 266 B6
Holmes Rd
Kentish Town NW5 71 B3
Merton SW19 180 A3
Twickenham TW1 152 D2
Holmes Terr SE1 251 A2
Holmeswood 1 SM2 217 D1
Holmeswood Ct 3 N22 32 C1
Holme Way HA7 24 D4
Holmewood Gdns SW2 160 B4
Holmewood Rd
South Norwood SE25 205 C6

Holmewood Rd *continued*
Streatham SW2 160 B4
Holmfield Ave NW4 46 D4
Holmfield Ho E17 54 B5
Holm Gr UB10 60 C1
Holmhurst SE13 164 B5
Holmhurst Rd DA17 125 D1
Holmhurst SW19 178 C3
Holmlea Ct CR0 221 B4
Holmleigh Prim Sch N16 51 C1
Holmleigh Rd N16 51 C1
Holm Oak Cl SW15 157 B5
Holmoaks Ho BR3 186 A1
Holmsbury Ho 6 N7 71 D3
Holmsdale Ho
6 London N11 31 B6
24 Poplar E14 119 D6
Holmshaw Cl SE26 185 A6
Holmside Ct SW12 159 A5
Holmside Rd SW12 159 A5
Holmsley Cl KT3 199 D2
Holmsley Ho SW15 155 D4
Holmstall Ave HA8 27 A1
Holmstall Par HA8 27 A1
Holm Wlk SE3 143 A3
Holmwood Cl
Cheam SM2 216 D1
Harrow HA2 42 A6
Northolt UB5 63 D2
Holmwood Ct
Kingston u T KT3 199 B6
Sidcup DA14 189 D5
3 Stamford Hill N16 51 D2
Holmwood Gdns
London N3 29 C1
Wallington SM6 219 B2
Holmwood Gr NW7 27 B5
Holmwood Mans W3 110 C5
Holmwood Rd
Chessington KT9 214 A3
Ilford IG3 79 C6
Holmwood 2 KT5 198 B3
Holne Chase
London N2 48 A3
Morden SM4 201 C3
Holne Lo N6 49 C3
Holness Rd E15 76 D2
Holocaust Meml Gdn* W2 114 D4 247 D2
Holroyd Rd SW15 156 C6
Holsgrove Ct W3 111 C5
Holstein Way 6 DA18 125 A3
Holst Mans SW13 134 C5
Holstock Rd IG1 79 A6
Holsworth Cl HA2 42 A4
Holsworthy Ho 49 E3 97 D4
Holsworthy Sq WC1 240 D5
Holsworthy Way KT9 213 C3
Holt Cl London N10 49 A5
Woolwich SE28 124 C6
Holt Ct
Greenwich SE10 142 A6
Stratford New Town E15 76 A3
Holt Ho SW2 160 C5
Holtoake Ct 1 W5 87 C3
Holtoake Ho 8 W5 87 C3
Holton St E1 96 D3
Holt Rd Newham E16 122 A5
Wembley HA0 65 C5
Holt The
Morden SM4 201 C5
Wallington SM6 219 C4
Holtwhite Ave EN2 5 A3
Holtwhite's Hill EN2 4 D4
Holwell Pl HA5 41 A5
Holwood Park Ave BR2, BR6 226 B4
Holwood Pl 7 SW4 137 D1
Holybourne Ave SW15 156 A4
Holy Cross Prep Sch KT2 177 A3
Holy Cross RC Prim Sch SE6 164 A3
Holy Cross RC Sch SW6 135 C4 265 A2
Holy Cross Sch The KT3 199 C4
Holy Family RC Coll The
Walthamstow E17 54 A5
Walthamstow E17 54 A6
Holy Family RC Prim Sch
Kidbrooke SE9 143 C1
Poplar E14 119 C6
Holy Ghost RC Prim Sch SW12 159 A4
Holyhead Cl Bow E3 97 C4
3 Newham E6 100 B2
Holyhead Ct KT1 197 D5

Holy Innocents RC Prim Sch BR6 227 D5
Holyoake Ct SE16 119 B4
Holyoake Wlk
Ealing W5 87 C3
East Finchley N2 48 A6
Holyoak Rd SE11 116 D2 261 D3
Holyport Rd SW6 134 D5
Holyrood Ave HA2 63 B4
Holyrood Gdns HA8 26 D1
Holyrood Ho N4 51 A1
Holyrood Mews 10 E16 121 A5
Holyrood Rd EN5 14 B5
Holyrood St SE1 117 C5 253 A3
Holy Trinity CE Jun Sch SM6 219 C4
Holy Trinity CE Prim Sch
Belgravia SW1 115 A2 258 A4
Dalston E8 73 D2
East Finchley N2 48 B6
Forest Hill SE26 162 C2
Hampstead NW3 70 A2
Richmond TW10 132 C1
Streatham SW2 160 B4
Wimbledon SW19 179 D4
Holy Trinity Coll Prep Sch BR1 187 C2
Holy Trinity Lamorbey CE Prim Sch DA15 168 A3
Holy Trinity & Saint Silas CE Prim Sch NW1 71 B1
Holywell Cl
35 Bermondsey SE16 118 B1
2 Greenwich SE3 143 A6
Stanwell TW19 148 A3
Holywell La EC2 243 B6
Holywell Lo EN2 4 B5
Holywell Row EC2 95 C3 243 A5
Holywell Way TW19 148 A3
Homan Ct N12 30 A6
Homan Ho 6 SW4 159 D4
Homebush Ho E4 19 D4
Homecedars Ho WD23 8 B3
Homecherry Ho 5 IG10 21 D6
Home Cl
Carshalton SM5 218 D6
Northolt UB5 85 B4
Homecoppice Ho 1 BR1 186 D3
Homecroft Rd
Forest Hill SE26 184 C5
Tottenham N22 33 A2
Homecross Ho 7 W4 111 B2
Home Ct KT6 197 D4
Homedale Ho SM1 217 D4
Home Farm Cl
Thames Ditton KT7 196 D2
Upper Halliford TW17 193 C5
Home Farm Cotts BR5 190 D2
Homefarm Rd W7 86 D1
Homefield Ave IG2 57 C4
Home Field EN5 13 B6
Homefield Cl
Hayes UB4 84 D3
Willesden NW10 67 A2
Homefield Ct NW4 46 C5
Homefield Gdns
London N2 48 B6
Mitcham CR4, SW19 180 B1
Homefield Ho SE23 162 D1
Homefield SM4 201 C5
Homefield Pk SM1, SM2 217 D2
Homefield Pl 4 SW19 178 D5
Homefield Prep Sch SM1 217 C3
Homefield Rd
Bromley BR1 187 C2
Burnt Oak HA8 27 B4
Chiswick W4 111 D1
Walton-on-T KT12 195 A2
Wembley HA0 65 B4
Wimbledon SW19 179 A4
Homefield St 14 N1 95 C5
Homefirs Ho HA9 66 B5
Homeheather Ho 5 IG4 56 B4
Homelands Dr SE19 183 C3
Home Lea BR6 227 D3
Homeleigh Ct 8 SW16 160 A1

Homeleigh Rd SE15 162 D6
Homemead SW12 159 B2
Homemead Rd
Bromley BR2 210 B4
Wallington CR0 203 C3
Home Mead HA7 25 C2
Home Office SW1 249 C1
Home Park Rd SW19 157 B1
Home Park Terr KT1 175 D1
Home Park Wlk KT1 197 D5
Home Rd SW11 136 C3
Homer Dr E14 119 C2
Homer Rd
Croydon CR0 206 D3
Homerton E9 75 A2
Homer Row W1 237 B3
Homersham Rd KT1 176 D1
Homer St W1 92 C2 237 B3
HOMERTON 74 D1
Homerton Coll of Technology E9 74 C3
Homerton Ct 2 EN4 14 D3
Homerton Gr E9 74 D3
Homerton High St E9 74 D3
Homerton Rd E9 75 B3
Homerton Row E9 74 C3
Homerton Sta E9 74 D2
Homerton Terr E9 74 C2
Homerton University Hospl E9 74 D3
Homesdale Cl E11 55 A4
Homesdale Rd
Bromley BR1, BR2 209 C6
Orpington BR5 211 C2
Homesfield NW11 47 C4
Homes Of Rest (CE Temperance Society) IG1 79 B5
Homestall Rd SE22 162 C6
Homestead Ct EN5 13 C6
Homestead Gdns KT10 212 C3
Homestead Paddock N14 15 B6
Homestead Pk NW2 67 D5
Homestead Rd
Dagenham RM8 81 B6
Fulham SW6 135 B5 264 D3
Homesteads The BR3 185 D4
Homestead The N11 31 B6
Homewalk Ho 1 SE26 184 C6
Homewaters Ave TW16 171 D2
Homewillow Cl N21 16 D5
Homewood Cl TW12 173 B4
Homewood Cres BR7 189 C4
Homewood Gdns SE25 205 C4
Homewoods 2 SW12 159 C4
Homildon Ho 10 SE26 162 A1
Homington Ct KT2 176 A3
Honduras St EC1 242 A6
Honeybourne Rd NW6 69 D3
Honeybourne Way BR5 211 B1
Honeybrook Rd SW12, SW4 159 C4
Honey Cl RM10 81 D2
Honeycroft Hill UB10 60 A1
Honeyden Rd DA14 191 A4
Honeyfield N4 72 C6
Honey Hill UB10 60 B1
Honey La EC2 242 B1
Honey Lane Ho SW10 265 D6
Honeyman Cl NW6 68 D1
Honeypot Bsns Ctr HA7 26 A2
Honeypot Cl NW9 44 B5
Honeypot La HA3, HA7, NW9 44 B6
Honeysett Rd 3 N17 33 D1
Honeysuckle Cl UB1 107 A6
Honeysuckle Ct
Ilford IG1 78 D2
2 Lee SE12 165 A4
6 Sutton SM2 217 D2
Honeysuckle Gdns CR0 206 D1
Honeywell Jun & Inf Schs SW11 158 D5

Honeywell Rd SW11 158 D5
Honeywood Heritage Ctr* SM5 218 D4
Honeywood Ho 5 SE15 140 A4
Honeywood Rd
Harlesden NW10 89 D5
Isleworth TW7 131 A1
Honeywood Wlk SM5 218 D4
Honister Cl HA7 25 B2
Honister Gdns HA7 25 B2
Honister Pl HA7 25 B2
Honiton Gdns
Edgware NW7 28 D3
1 Nunhead SE15 140 C3
Honiton Ho 23 SE5 139 A3
Honiton Rd
Bexley DA16 145 D3
Kilburn NW6 91 B5
Honley Rd SE6 163 D4
Honnor Gdns TW7 130 B3
HONOR OAK 162 C6
Honor Oak Park Sta SE23 162 D5
Honor Oak Pk SE23 162 D5
Honor Oak Rd SE23 162 C4
Honor Oak Rise SE23 162 C5
Honwell Ho 24 W2 91 C2
Hood Ave
East Barnet N14 15 B5
Mortlake SW14 155 A6
Hood Cl CR0 204 D1
Hoodcote Gdns N21 16 D4
Hood Ct N7 72 B5
Hood Ho 17 SE5 139 B5
Hood Lo E11 77 B6
Hood Rd SW20 177 D3
HOOK 214 A4
Hooke Ct SE10 142 A4
Hooke Ho 32 E3 97 A5
Hooker's Rd E17 52 D6
Hook Farm Rd BR2 209 D4
Hookham Ct SW8 269 C2
Hook Ho 9 SW27 182 D5
Hooking Gn HA2 41 D4
Hook La DA16 146 A1
Hook Lane Prim Sch DA16 146 A2
Hook Rd KT19, KT17 215 A1
Hook Rise N
Surbiton KT6 214 A5
Tolworth KT6 214 D6
Hook Rise South Ind Pk KT6 214 C5
Hook Rise South KT6 214 A5
Hook Rise S KT6, KT9 214 D6
Hooks Cl SE15 140 B4
Hookstone Way IG8 37 D3
Hook KT6 214 A5
Hook The EN5 14 B5
Hook Underpass KT6 214 A5
Hook Wlk HA8 27 A4
Hooper Dr UB8 82 D2
Hooper Ho 9 SW18 157 B6
Hooper Rd E16 99 A1
Hooper's Ct SW1 247 C1
Hooper's Mews 4 W3 111 A5
Hooper St E1 96 A1
Hoop La NW11 47 C2
Hoover Ho 5 SE6 186 A6
Hope Cl
2 Brentford TW8 110 A1
Canonbury N1 73 A2
Dagenham RM6 58 D5
Grove Pk SE12 165 B1
Sutton SM1 218 A3
1 Woodford IG8 37 C4
Hope Ct 1 SE1 118 A1
Hopedale Rd SE7 143 B6
Hopefield Ave NW6 91 A5
Hopefield 3 W7 108 D5
Hope Gdns 10 W3 110 D4
Hope Pk BR1 186 D3
Hopes Cl TW5 129 C6
Hope St SW11 136 B2
Hopetown St E1 243 D3
Hopewell St SE5 139 B5
Hop Gdns WC2 250 A5
Hopgood St 5 W12 112 C5
Hopkins Cl N10 31 A3
Hopkins Ho 17 E14 97 C1
Hopkins Mews E15 98 D6
Hopkinson Ho 1 SW11 137 A3
Hopkinson's Pl NW1 231 A6
Hopkins St W1 93 D1 239 C1
Hopley Ho W13 109 B6
Hoppers Rd N21 16 C2

Hoppett Rd E4 20 C2
Hopping La N1 72 D2
Hoppingwood Ave KT3 199 C6
Hoppner Rd UB4 83 B5
Hop St SE10 120 D2
Hopton Ct BR2 209 A1
Hopton Gdns KT3 200 A3
Hopton Ho 5 SW9 138 D3
Hopton Par 2 SW16 182 A5
Hopton Rd
Streatham SW16 182 A5
Woolwich SE18 122 D3
Hopton's Gdns SE1 251 D4
Hopton St SE1 116 D5 251 D4
Hoptree Cl N12 29 D6
Hopwood Cl SW17 158 A1
Hopwood Rd SE17 139 B6
Hopwood Wlk E8 74 A1
Horace Rd
Forest Gate E7 77 B4
Ilford IG6 57 A6
Kingston u T KT1 198 B6
Horatio Ho
13 Haggerston E2 95 D5
4 Merton SW19 179 D3
Horatio Pl
9 Canary Wharf E14 120 A5
Merton SW19 179 C2
Horatio St 11 E2 95 D5
Horatius Way CR0 220 B2
Horbury Cres W11 113 C6 245 A5
Horbury Lo TW12 173 C3
Horbury Mews W11 113 B6 244 D5
Horder Rd SW6 135 A4 264 B1
Hordle Prom E 15 SE15 139 D5
Hordle Prom N 4 SE15 139 D5
Hordle Prom S 7 SE15 139 D5
Horizon Bldg 22 E14 119 C6
Horizon Sch N16 73 C4
Horle Wlk SE5 138 D3
Horley Cl DA6 169 C6
Horley Rd SE9 188 A6
Hormead Rd W9 91 B3
Hornbeam Cl
Barking IG11 102 B3
Buckhurst Hill IG9 21 D1
Edgware NW7 11 D1
Ilford IG1 79 B3
Lambeth SE11 261 A4
Northolt UB5 63 B3
Hornbeam Cres TW8 131 B5
Hornbeam Gdns KT3 200 A3
Hornbeam Gr E4 20 D1
Hornbeam Ho
1 Buckhurst Hill IG9 21 D1
2 Maitland Pk NW3 70 D2
6 Penge SE20 184 D3
6 Sidcup DA15 168 A1
Hornbeam La E4 20 C6
Hornbeam Rd
Buckhurst Hill IG9 21 D1
Hayes UB4 84 C2
Hornbeam Sq 8 E3 97 B6
Hornbeams Rise N11 31 A4
Hornbeam Terr SM5 202 C1
Hornbeam Way BR2 210 C3
Hornblower Cl 2 SE16 119 A2
Hornbuckle Cl HA2 64 B6
Hornby Cl NW3 70 B1
Hornby Ho
6 Kennington SE11 138 C6
13 Richmond TW10 153 C1
Horncastle Cl SE12 165 A4
Horncastle Rd SE12 165 A4
Hornchurch Cl KT2 175 D6
Hornchurch N17 33 B1
Horndean Cl 3 SW15 156 A3
Horne Ho 4 SE18 144 A4
Horner Ct E11 76 B5
Horne Rd TW17 192 C5
Horner Hos 18 N1 95 C6
Horner La 3 CR4 180 B1
Horne Way SW15 134 C3
Hornfair Rd SE7 143 D5
Horniman Dr SE23 162 C4

Horniman Grange 7 SE23 ... 162 C3
Horniman Mus & Gdns* SE23 ... 162 B3
Horniman Sch SE23 .. 162 B3
Horning Cl SE9 ... 188 A6
Horn La Acton W3 ... 89 A1
Greenwich SE10 ... 121 A2
Woodford IG8 ... 37 A3
Horn Link Way SE10 ... 121 A2
Horn Park Cl SE12 ... 165 B6
Horn Park La SE12 ... 165 B5
Horn Park Prim Sch SE12 ... 165 B4
Hornsby House Sch SW12 ... 159 A3
Horns Croft IG11 ... 79 C1
Horns End Pl HA5 ... 40 C4
HORNSEY ... 50 A5
Hornsey Central Hospl N8 ... 49 D4
Hornsey La N6 ... 49 C2
Hornsey Lane Gdns N6 ... 49 C2
Hornsey Park Rd N8 .. 50 B6
Hornsey Rd N7, N19 ... 72 B6
Hornsey Rise Gdns N19 ... 50 A2
Hornsey Sch for Girls N8 ... 50 B4
Hornsey Sta N8 ... 50 B5
Hornsey St N7 ... 72 B3
HORNSEY VALE ... 50 B4
Hornshay St SE15 ... 140 C6
Horns Rd IG2, IG6 ... 57 A4
Hornton Ct W8 ... 245 B1
Hornton Pl W8 ... 245 B1
Hornton St W8 ... 113 C4 245 B2
Horrocks Ho SW15 ... 156 B6
Horsa Rd
Eltham SE12 ... 165 C4
Erith DA8 ... 147 D5
Horsebridge Cl RM9 ... 103 A6
Horsecroft Rd HA8 ... 27 B3
Horse & Dolphin Yd W1 ... 249 D6
Horse Fair KT1 ... 175 D1
Horseferry Pl SE10 ... 142 A6
Horseferry Rd Est SW1 ... 259 C5
Horseferry Rd
Limehouse E14 ... 119 A6
Westminster SW1 ... 115 D2 259 D4
Horse Guards Ave SW1 ... 116 A5 250 A3
Horse Guards Par* SW1 ... 115 D5 249 D3
Horse Guards Rd SW1 ... 115 D4 249 D2
Horse Leaze E6 ... 100 C1
Horsell Rd
Islington N5 ... 72 C3
St Paul's Cray BR5 ... 190 B2
Horselydown La SE1 ... 117 D5 253 C3
Horselydown Mans SE1 ... 253 C2
Horsemongers Mews SE1 ... 252 B1
Horsenden Ave UB6 ... 64 D3
Horsenden Cres UB6 ... 64 D3
Horsenden La N UB6 ... 64 D1
Horsenden La S UB6 ... 87 A6
Horsenden Prim Sch UB6 ... 64 C2
Horsendon Ho 11 N7 ... 71 D3
Horseshoe Cl
Cubitt Town E14 ... 120 A1
Dollis Hill NW2 ... 68 B6
Horse Shoe Cres UB5 ... 85 C5
Horseshoe Dr UB8 ... 82 C1
Horse Shoe Gn SM1 ... 217 D6
Horseshoe La
Barnet N20 ... 12 D3
Enfield EN2 ... 5 A2
Horse Yd N1 ... 234 D6
Horsfeld Gdns 1 SE9 ... 166 A6
Horsfeld Rd SE9 ... 165 D6
Horsfield Ho 18 N1 ... 73 A1
Horsford Rd SW2 ... 160 B6
Horsham Ave N12 ... 30 C5
Horsham Ct N17 ... 34 A2
Horsham Rd
Bexley DA6 ... 169 C6
East Bedfont TW14 ... 149 A5
Horsley Ct SW1 ... 259 D3
Horsley Dr
Kingston u T KT2 ... 175 D5
New Addington CR0 ... 224 A1
Horsley Ho 11 SE4 ... 140 D1
Horsley Rd
Bromley BR1 ... 187 B2
Chingford E4 ... 20 A2
Horsley St 3 SE17 ... 139 B6
Horsman Ho SE5 ... 139 A6
Horsman St SE5 ... 139 A6
Horsmonden Cl BR6 ... 211 D2
Horsmonden Rd SE4 ... 163 B5
Horston Ho N4 ... 51 A2
Hortensia Ho SW10 ... 266 A4
Hortensia Rd SW10 ... 136 A5 266 A4
Horticultural Pl 6 W4 ... 111 B1
Horton Ave NW2 ... 69 A4
Horton Bridge Rd UB7 ... 104 B5
Horton Cl UB7 ... 104 B5
Horton Ctry Pk KT19 ... 214 C1
Horton Ho
13 Deptford SE15 ... 140 C6
South Lambeth SW8 ... 270 C4
West Kensington W14 ... 254 A1
Horton Ind Pk UB7 ... 104 B5
Horton La KT19 ... 215 A1
Horton Par UB7 ... 104 A5
Horton Rd Hackney E8 ... 74 B2
Yiewsley UB7 ... 104 B5
Horton Road Ind Est UB7 ... 104 B5
Horton St SE13 ... 141 D2
Horton Way CR0 ... 206 D4
Hortus Rd
Chingford E4 ... 20 A2
Southall UB2 ... 107 B4
Horwood Ho
24 Bethnal Green E2 ... 96 B4
Marylebone NW8 ... 237 B6
Hosack Rd SW12, SW17 ... 159 A2
Hoser Ave SE12 ... 165 A2
Hosier La EC1 . 94 D2 241 D3
Hoskins Cl UB3 ... 105 D1
Hoskin's Cl E16 ... 99 C1
Hoskins St SE10 ... 120 B1
Hospital Bridge Rdbt TW2 ... 151 D2
Hospital Bridge Rd TW2 ... 151 D3
Hospital of the Holy Trinity (Almshouses) 5 CR0 ... 221 A6
Hospital Rd TW3 ... 129 C2
Hospital Way SE13 ... 164 B4
Hospl for Tropical Diseases
Fitzrovia WC1 ... 93 C3 239 B5
Somers Town NW1 ... 232 D5
Hospl of St John & St Elizabeth NW8 ... 92 B5 229 C3
Hotham Cl KT8 ... 195 C6
Hotham Prim Sch SW15 ... 134 D1
Hotham Rd
Merton SW19 ... 180 A3
Putney SW15 ... 134 C2
Hotham Road Mews 12 SW19 ... 180 A3
Hotham St E15 ... 98 C6
Hothfield Pl SE16 ... 118 C3
Hotspur Ind Est N17 ... 34 B4
Hotspur Rd UB5 ... 85 C5
Hotspur St SE11 ... 116 C1 261 A2
Houblon Rd TW10 ... 154 A6
Houghton Cl
10 Dalston E8 ... 73 D2
Hampton TW12 ... 173 A4
Houghton Rd N15 ... 51 D5
Houghton Sq SW9 ... 138 A2
Houghton St WC2 ... 240 D1
Houlder Cres CR0 ... 220 D2
Houndsden Rd N21 ... 16 C5
Houndsditch EC3 ... 95 C1 243 B2
Houndsfield Prim Sch N9 ... 18 B4
Houndsfield Rd N9 ... 18 B4
HOUNSLOW ... 129 C3
Hounslow Ave TW3 ... 151 D6
Hounslow Bsns Pk TW3 ... 129 D1
Hounslow Central Sta TW3 ... 129 D2
Hounslow Ctr The TW3 ... 129 D2
Hounslow East Sta TW3 ... 130 A3
Hounslow Gdns TW3 ... 151 D6
Hounslow Heath Jun & Inf Schs TW4 ... 129 A2
Hounslow Heath Nature Reserve TW4 ... 151 A5
Hounslow Manor Sch TW3 ... 130 A2
Hounslow Rd
Feltham TW14 ... 150 B4
Hanworth TW13 ... 151 A2
Twickenham TW2, TW3 ... 152 A5
Hounslow Sta TW3 . 151 D6
Hounslow Town Prim Sch TW3 ... 130 B2
HOUNSLOW WEST ... 128 D2
Hounslow West Sta TW3 ... 129 A3
Houseman Way 20 SE5 ... 139 B5
House of Detention* EC1 ... 94 C3 241 B6
Houses of Parliament* SW1 ... 116 A3 260 B6
Houston Ct 3 CR0 ... 205 C1
Houston Pl KT10 ... 196 C1
Houston Rd
Forest Hill SE23 ... 163 A1
Thames Ditton KT6 ... 197 B3
Houstoun Ct TW5 ... 129 B5
Hove Ave E17 ... 53 B4
Hoveden Rd NW2 ... 69 A3
Hove Gdns SM1 ... 201 D1
Hovenden Ho 6 SE21 ... 183 C6
Hoveton Rd SE28 ... 102 C1
Howard Ave DA5 ... 168 C4
Howard Bldg SW8 ... 268 C5
Howard Cl Acton W3 ... 88 D1
Ashford TW16 ... 171 D4
Brunswick Pk N11 ... 15 A2
Bushey WD23 ... 8 C4
Cricklewood NW2 ... 69 A4
Hampton TW12 ... 174 A4
Howard Ct
12 Barking IG11 ... 101 B6
Beckenham BR3 ... 186 A1
Lewisham SE10 ... 142 A4
Peckham SE15 ... 140 A2
Howard Ho
6 Brixton SW9 ... 138 C2
14 Deptford SE8 ... 141 B6
Fitzrovia W1 ... 238 D5
Penge SE20 ... 184 C2
6 Upper Clapton E5 ... 74 C6
Howard Mans E17 ... 53 D6
Howard Mews N5 ... 72 D4
Howard Prim Sch CR0 ... 221 A4
Howard Rd
Barking IG11 ... 101 B6
Canonbury N16 ... 73 B4
Cricklewood NW2 ... 68 D4
Croydon SE25 ... 206 A3
Ilford IG1 ... 78 D4
Isleworth TW7 ... 130 D2
Leyton E11 ... 76 C5
Newham E6 ... 100 B5
New Malden KT3 ... 199 D5
Penge SE20 ... 184 C2
Plaistow BR1 ... 187 A3
Southall UB1 ... 85 D1
South Tottenham N15 ... 51 C3
Surbiton KT5 ... 198 B3
Walthamstow E17 ... 53 D6
Howards Cl HA5 ... 22 B1
Howards Crest Cl BR3 ... 186 A1
Howard's La SW15 ... 134 C1
Howard's Rd E13 ... 99 A4
Howard St KT7 ... 197 B3
Howard Way EN5 ... 12 D6
Howard Wlk N2 ... 48 B5
Howarth Ct E15 ... 76 A3
Howarth Rd SE2 ... 124 A2
Howberry Cl HA8 ... 25 D4
Howberry Rd
South Norwood CR7 ... 183 B1
Stanmore HA7, H8 ... 25 D4
Howbury Rd SE15 ... 140 C2
Howcroft Cres N3 ... 29 C3
Howcroft Ho 3 E3 ... 97 B4
Howcroft La UB6 ... 86 B4
Howden Cl SE28 ... 124 D6
Howden Ct SE25 ... 183 D1
Howden Rd SE25 ... 183 D1
Howden St SE15 ... 140 A2
Howell Cl RM6 ... 58 D4
Howell Ct 2 E10 ... 53 D2
Howell Ho 5 N7 ... 71 D3
Howell Wlk SE1 ... 261 D3
Howe Lo TW1 ... 153 A4
Howerd Way SE18 ... 144 A4
Howes Cl N3 ... 47 C6
Howeth Ct 7 N11 ... 31 A4
Howfield Pl N17 ... 51 D6
Howgate Rd SW14 ... 133 B2
Howick Mans SE18 ... 122 A3
Howick Pl SW1 ... 115 C3 259 B5
Howie St SW11 ... 136 C5 267 A3
Howitt Cl
6 Maitland Pk NW3 ... 70 C2
Stoke Newington N16 ... 73 C4
Howitt Rd NW3 ... 70 C2
Howland Ho 9 SW16 ... 160 A1
Howland Mews E W1 ... 239 B4
Howland St W1 ... 93 C2 239 B4
Howland Way SE16 ... 119 A4
Howletts La HA4 ... 39 A3
Howletts Rd SE24 ... 161 A5
Howley Pl W2 . 92 A2 236 B4
Howley Rd CR0 ... 221 A5
Howmic Ct 1 TW1 ... 153 C5
Howsman Rd SW13 ... 134 A6
Howson Rd SE4 ... 141 A1
Howson Terr TW10 ... 154 A5
How's St E2 ... 95 D5
Howton Pl WD23 ... 8 B3
HOXTON ... 95 C5
Hoxton Mkt 10 N1 ... 95 C4
Hoxton Point EC1 ... 95 C4
Hoxton Sq N1 ... 95 C4
Hoxton St N1 ... 95 C5
Hoylake Cres UB10 ... 60 D6
Hoylake Gdns
Mitcham CR4 ... 203 C6
Ruislip HA4 ... 40 B1
South Oxhey WD19 ... 22 D6
Hoylake Rd W3 ... 89 C1
Hoyland Cl 4 SE15 ... 140 B5
Hoyle Rd SW17 ... 180 C5
Hoy St E16 ... 98 D1
Hubbard Dr KT9 ... 213 D2
Hubbard Rd SE27 ... 183 A6
Hubbards Cl UB8 ... 82 D1
Hubbard St E15 ... 98 C6
Hub Buildings The 4 SW12 ... 159 B3
Huberd Ho SE1 ... 262 D6
Hubert Gr SW9 ... 138 A2
Hubert Ho NW8 ... 237 A5
Hubert Rd E6 ... 99 D4
Hucknall Ct NW8 ... 236 C6
Huddart St 6 E3 ... 97 B2
Huddleston Cl E2 ... 96 C5
Huddlestone Rd
Forest Gate E7 ... 76 D4
Willesden NW2 ... 68 B2
Huddleston Rd N7 ... 71 C4
Hudson Cl
Newham E15 ... 99 A6
15 Shepherd's Bush W12 ... 112 B6
Hudson Ct
Croydon SE25 ... 206 A5
1 Isle Of Dogs E14 ... 119 C1
4 Merton SW19 ... 179 D2
Hudson Ho
Chelsea SW10 ... 266 A4
5 Notting Hill W11 ... 91 A1
Hudson 27 NW9 ... 27 D2
Hudson Pl SE18 ... 123 A1
Hudson Rd
Erith DA7 ... 147 B4
Harlington UB7 ... 127 B6
Hudsons Ho N1 ... 235 D1
Hudson's Pl SW1 ... 115 C2 259 A4
Hudson Way N9 ... 18 C2
Huggin Ct EC4 ... 252 B6
Huggin Hill EC4 ... 252 B6
Huggins Ho 9 E3 ... 97 C4
Huggins Pl SW2 ... 160 B3
Hughan Rd E15 ... 76 B3
Hugh Astor Ct SE1 ... 261 D6
Hugh Clark Ho 13 W13 ... 109 A5
Hugh Dalton Ave SW6 ... 264 C5
Hughenden Ave HA3 .. 43 B4
Hughenden Gdns UB5 ... 84 C4
Hughenden Ho NW8 ... 237 A6
Hughenden Rd KT4 ... 200 A2
Hughendon EN5 ... 1 D1
Hughendon Terr E15 .. 76 A4
Hughes Cl N12 ... 30 A5
Hughes Ho
26 Bethnal Green E2 ... 96 C4
Camberwell SE5 ... 139 A4
Hughes Ho *continued*
15 Deptford SE8 ... 141 C6
Newington SE17 ... 261 D3
Hughes Mans E1 ... 96 A3
Hughes Rd
Ashford TW15 ... 171 A4
Hayes UB3 ... 106 B6
Hughes Terr 6 E16 ... 98 D2
Hughes Wlk CR0 ... 205 A2
Hugh Gaitskell Cl SW6 ... 264 C5
Hugh Gaitskell Ho
Stoke Newington N16 ... 73 D6
Willesden NW10 ... 67 D1
Hugh Herland KT1 ... 198 A6
Hugh Mews SW1 ... 258 D3
Hugh Morgan Ho 5 SW4 ... 137 D2
Hugh Myddelton Prim Sch EC1 ... 94 C4 234 B1
Hugh Platt Ho 29 E2 ... 96 B5
Hugh St SW1 ... 115 B2 258 D3
Hugo Ho SW1 ... 257 D6
Hugon Rd SW6 ... 135 D2
Hugo Rd N19 ... 71 C4
Huguenot Ct 9 E1 ... 96 A2
Huguenot Pl
London SW18 ... 158 A6
Spitalfields E1 ... 243 D4
Huguenot Sq SE15 ... 140 B2
Hullbridge Mews N1 ... 235 C6
Hull Cl SE16 ... 118 D5
Hull Ct SE5 ... 139 B3
Hull Pl E16 ... 123 A5
Hull St EC1 ... 235 A1
Hulme Pl SE1 ... 252 B1
Hulse Ave IG11 ... 79 C2
Humber Ct W7 ... 86 B1
Humber Dr W10 ... 90 D3
Humber Rd
Dollis Hill NW2 ... 68 B6
Greenwich SE3 ... 142 D6
Humberstone Rd E13 ... 99 C4
Humberton Cl E9 ... 75 A3
Humber Trad Est NW2 ... 68 B6
Humbolt Rd W6 ... 135 A6 264 A5
Hume Ct N1 ... 72 D1
Hume Ho 14 W11 ... 112 D5
Humes Ave W7 ... 108 D4
Hume Terr E16 ... 99 B1
Hume Way HA4 ... 40 A3
Humphrey Ct SW11 . 266 D1
Humphrey St SE1 ... 117 D1 263 C2
Humphries Cl RM9 ... 81 B4
Humphry Ho 10 SW15 ... 156 D6
Hundred Acre NW9 ... 27 D1
Hungerdown E4 ... 20 A3
Hungerford Bridge WC2 ... 250 C4
Hungerford Ho SW1 ... 269 B6
Hungerford La WC2 ... 250 B4
Hungerford Prim Sch N7 ... 71 D2
Hungerford Rd
12 Camden Town N7 ... 71 D2
Lower Holloway N7 ... 72 A3
Hungerford St 21 E1 ... 96 B1
Hunsdon Cl RM9 ... 81 A2
Hunsdon Ho E5 ... 74 B5
Hunsdon Rd SE14 ... 140 D5
Hunslett St 28 E2 ... 96 C5
Hunstanton Ho NW1 ... 237 B4
Hunston Rd SM4 ... 201 D1
Hunt Cl W11 ... 112 D5
Hunt Ct London N14 ... 15 B4
10 Northolt UB5 ... 84 D5
Hunter Cl
Borehamwood WD6 ... 11 A6
Borough The SE1 ... 262 D5
Upper Tooting SW12 ... 159 A3
3 Wallington SM6 ... 220 A1
Huntercombe Roehampton Hospl The SW15 ... 156 A4
Huntercrombe Gdns WD19 ... 22 C5
Hunter Ct
8 London SE5 ... 139 B1
27 Streatham SW2 ... 160 C4
11 Wanstead E11 ... 55 A4
Hunter Ho
Bloomsbury WC1 ... 240 B6
Feltham TW14 ... 150 A3
Lambeth SE1 ... 251 D1
South Lambeth SW8 ... 269 D3
1 Tufnell Pk N19 ... 71 C5
Hunter Ho *continued*
West Brompton SW5. 255
Hunterian Mus* WC2 ... 94 B1 240
Hunter Lo 9 W9 ... 91
Hunter Rd
South Norwood CR7 ... 205
Wimbledon SW20 ... 178
Hunters Ct 5 TW9 ... 153
Hunter's Gr BR6 ... 227
Hunters Gr
Harrow HA3 ... 43
Hayes UB3 ... 106
Hunters Hall Prim Sch RM10 ... 81
Hunters Hall Rd RM10 ... 81
Hunters Hill HA4 ... 62
Hunters Lo
9 Edgware HA8 ... 26
10 Sidcup DA15 ... 168
Hunters Mdw SE19 ... 183
Hunters Rd
Chessington KT9 ... 214
Ilford IG1 ... 78
Hunters Sq RM10 ... 81
Hunters The 2 BR3 .. 186
Hunter St WC1 ... 94 A3 240
Hunters Way
Enfield EN2 ... 4
South Croydon CR0 .. 221
Hunter Wlk
Borehamwood WD6 ... 11
Newham E13 ... 99
Huntingdon Cl
Mitcham CR4, SW16 ... 204
Northolt UB5 ... 63
Huntingdon Ct
3 Barnet EN5 ... 1
Mortlake SW14 ... 133
Huntingdon Gdns
Chiswick W4 ... 133
North Cheam KT4 ... 216
Huntingdon Ho SW5 255
Huntingdon Rd
East Finchley N2 ... 48
Edmonton N9 ... 18
Huntingdon St
Canning Town E16 ... 98
Islington N1 ... 72
Huntingfield CR0 ... 223
Huntingfield Rd SW15 ... 156
Huntingford Ho SW15 ... 134
Hunting Gate Cl EN2 ... 4
Hunting Gate Dr KT9 ... 214
Hunting Gate Mews
Sutton SM1 ... 217
Twickenham TW2 ... 152
Huntings Farm IG1 ... 79
Huntings Rd RM10 ... 81
Huntington Ho NW2 .. 68
Huntley Cl TW19 ... 148
Huntley Ho 7 SE21 .. 183
Huntley St WC1 ... 93 D3 239
Huntley Way SW20 ... 178
Huntly Dr N3 ... 29
Huntly Rd SE25 ... 205
Hunton St E1 ... 96
Hunt Rd UB2 ... 107
Hunts Cl SE3 ... 143
Hunt's Ct WC2 ... 249
Huntshaw Ho 37 E3 ... 97
Hunt's La E15 ... 98
Huntsmans Cl TW13 .. 172
Huntsman St SE17 .. 263
Hunts Mead Cl BR7 .. 188
Hunts Mead EN3 ... 6
Huntsmoor Rd KT19 .. 215
Huntspill St SW17 ... 158
Hunts Slip Rd SE21 ... 161
Huntsworth Ct SE6 ... 163
Huntsworth Mews NW1 ... 92 D3 237
Huon Ct N20 ... 14
Hurdwick Ho NW1 .. 232
Hurdwick Pl NW1 ... 232
Hurleston Ho 11 SE8 ... 119
Hurley Cres SE16 ... 118
Hurley Ct 1 W5 ... 87
Hurley Ho
Lambeth SE11 ... 261
34 Shoreditch E2 ... 95
Hurley Lo SE22 ... 162
Hurley Rd UB6 ... 85
Hurlingham Bsns Pk SW6 ... 135
Hurlingham & Chelsea Sec Sch SW6 ... 135

urlingham Court Mans
SW6 135 C3
'urlingham Ct SW6 135 B2
urlingham Gdns
SW6 135 B2
urlingham Rd
Erith DA7 147 B5
Fulham SW6 135 B3
urlingham Sch
SW15 135 B1
urlingham Sq
SW6 135 D2
urlock Ho 1 N5 72 D5
urlock St N5 72 D5
urlstone Rd SE25 205 C4
urn Court Rd TW5 128 D3
urn Ct TW5 128 D3
uron Cl 5 BR6 227 D2
uron Rd SW17 159 A1
uron Univ
WC1 94 A2 240 A4
urren Cl SE3 142 C2
urricane Rd SM6 220 B1
urricane Trad Ctr
NW9 28 A2
urry Cl E15 76 C1
ursley Ct 11 KT6 197 D2
urst Ave
Chingford E4 19 C1
Highgate N6 49 C3
urstbourne KT10 212 D2
urstbourne Cotts
DA5 169 D4
urstbourne Gdns
IG11 79 C2
urstbourne Ho
SW15 155 D5
urstbourne Priors
CR2 221 C2
urstbourne Rd
SE23 163 A3
urst Cl
Chessington KT9 214 C3
Chingford E4 19 C1
Hampstead Garden
Suburb NW11 47 D3
Hayes BR2 208 D1
Northolt UB5 63 B3
urstcombe IG9 21 A2
urstcourt Rd SM1 217 D6
urst Ct
Beckenham BR3 185 C3
Newham E6 99 D2
South Norwood
SE25 205 D5
Woodford IG8 37 B4
urstdene Ave BR2 208 D1
urstdene Gdns N15 51 C2
urstfield BR2 209 A4
urstfield Cres UB4 83 C2
urstfield Rd KT8 195 C6
urst Gr KT12 193 D1
urst Ho
7 Penge SE26 184 B5
Pentonville N1 233 D3
West Heath SE2 124 D1
urst La
East Molesey KT8 196 A6
West Heath SE2 124 D1
urst Lo London N8 49 D3
Wembley HA0 66 B1
urstmead Ct HA8 26 D6
urstmere Foundation
Sch for Boys
DA15 168 C3
URST PARK 174 A1
urst Park Prim Sch
KT8 195 C6
urst Pl Erith SE2 146 D6
Woolwich SE2 124 C1
urst Prim Sch
DA5 168 D3
urst Rd
Buckhurst Hill IG9 21 D3
Croydon CR0 221 B3
East Molesey KT8,
KT12 195 C6
Sidcup DA5, DA15 168 C3
Southgate N21 16 C3
Walthamstow E17 53 D6
Walton-on-T
KT8&KT12 194 D5
urst Rise EN5 1 C2
urst Springs DA5 169 A3
urst St SE24 160 D5
urst View Grange
CR2 220 D1
urst View Rd CR2 221 C1
urst Way CR2 221 C2
urstway Wlk 2
W11 112 D6
urstwood Ave
Sidcup DA5 169 A3
Wanstead E18 55 B5
urstwood Ct
Colney Hatch N12 30 C4
Hurstwood Ct *continued*
Temple Fortune
NW11 47 B5
Hurstwood Dr BR1 210 B6
Hurstwood Rd NW11 47 B5
Hurtwood Rd KT12 195 B2
Husbourne Ho 8
SE8 119 A2
Huson Cl NW3 70 C1
Hussain Cl HA1 64 D4
Hussars Cl TW4 129 A2
Husseywell Cres
BR2 209 A1
Hutching's St E14 119 C4
Hutching's Wharf 11
E14 119 C4
Hutchings Wlk NW11 47 D5
Hutchins Cl E15 76 A1
Hutchins Ho 8
SW4 159 D4
Hutchinson Ct RM6 58 D5
Hutchinson Ho 9
SE14 140 C5
Hutchinson Terr HA9 65 D5
Hutchins Rd SE28 124 A5
Hutton Cl
Greenford UB6 64 B3
Woodford IG8 37 B4
Hutton Ct
1 Ealing W5 87 C2
Edmonton N9 18 C4
4 Finsbury Pk N4 50 B1
Hutton Gdns HA3 24 A3
Hutton Gr N12 29 D5
Hutton Ho 19 E2 96 A4
Hutton La HA3 24 A3
Hutton Row 4 HA8 27 A3
Hutton St EC4 241 B1
Hutton Wlk HA3 24 A3
Huxbear St SE4 163 B6
Huxley Cl UB5 85 A6
Huxley Dr RM6 58 B2
Huxley Gdns NW10 88 B5
Huxley Ho
4 London SW9 138 B3
Paddington NW8 236 D5
West Heath SE2 124 D1
Huxley Par N18 33 B5
Huxley Pl N13 16 D1
Huxley Rd
Edmonton N18 33 C6
Falconwood DA16 145 D2
Leyton E10 76 A6
Huxley Sayze N18 33 B5
Huxley South N18 33 B5
Huxley St W10 91 A4
Hyacinth Cl
3 Hampton
TW12 173 C4
Ilford IG1 78 D2
Hyacinth Ct 2 HA5 40 C6
Hyacinth Dr UB10 60 A1
Hyacinth Rd SW15 156 A3
Hyde Cl
Ashford TW16 171 C4
Barnet EN5 1 B2
Newham E13 99 A5
Hyde Cres NW9 45 C4
Hyde Ct
Forest Hill SE23 163 A2
Hounslow TW4 151 B6
Kingsbury NW9 45 B2
Whetstone N20 14 B1
Hyde Estate Rd NW9 45 D4
Hyde Farm Mews
SW12 159 D3
Hydefield Cl N21 17 B3
Hydefield Ct N9 17 C2
Hyde Ho
12 Ealing W13 109 A5
Hounslow TW3 130 A2
Hyde Ind Est The
NW9 45 D4
Hyde La
SW11 136 C4 267 A2
Hyde Park Ave N21 17 B3
Hyde Park Cnr SW1 248 B2
Hyde Park Corner Sta
SW1 115 A4 248 B2
Hyde Park Cres
W2 92 C1 237 A1
Hyde Park Gate Mews
SW7 246 B1
Hyde Park Gdns
Bayswater
W2 114 B6 246 D6
Edmonton N21 17 A3
Hyde Park Gdns Mews
W2 114 C6 247 A6
Hyde Park Mans
NW1 237 A3
Hyde Park Pl W2 247 B6
Hyde Park Square
Mews W2 237 A1
Hyde Park Sq
W2 92 C1 237 A1
Hyde Park St
W2 92 C1 237 A1
Hyde Park Twrs W2 246 A5
Hyde Park*
W2 114 D5 247 C3
Hyderabad Way E15 76 C1
Hyde Rd
Bexleyheath DA7 147 B3
Richmond TW10 154 B6
Shoreditch N1 95 C6
Hyde Sch The NW9 45 D4
Hydeside Gdns N9 17 D2
Hyde's Pl 12 N1 72 D1
Hyde St SE8 141 C6
Hyde Terr TW15,
TW16 171 C4
HYDE THE 45 D4
Hydethorpe Ave N9 17 D2
Hydethorpe Rd
SW12 159 C3
Hyde Vale SE10 142 A5
Hyde Way
Edmonton N9 17 D2
Hayes UB3 105 D2
Hyde Wlk SM4 201 C2
Hydon Ct N11 30 D5
Hyh Ho E17 35 D2
Hyland House Sch
E17 36 B1
Hylands Rd E17 36 B1
Hylda Ct NW5 71 A5
Hylton St SE18 123 D2
Hyndewood 14
SE23 162 D1
Hyndman Ho
5 Dagenham
RM10 81 C5
4 Tufnell Pk N19 71 D4
Hyndman St SE15 140 B6
Hynton Rd RM8 80 C6
Hyperion Ho
27 Bow E3 97 A5
Streatham SW2 160 B4
Hyrstdene CR0 220 D4
Hyrst The CR0 207 A1
Hyson Rd SE16 118 B1
Hythe Ave DA7 147 B5
Hythe Cl N18 34 A6
Hythe Ho 14 SE16 118 C4
Hythe Rd
College Pk NW10 90 A3
South Norwood CR7 183 B1
Hythe Road Ind Est
NW10 90 A3
Hyver Hill NW7 11 B4

I

Ian Ct SE23 162 C2
Ian Hamilton Ho
NW1 232 C2
Ian Mikardo Sch E3 97 D4
Ian Sq EN3 6 D4
Ibberton Ho
Kensington W14 254 B5
South Lambeth SW8 270 C4
Ibbotson Ave E16 98 D1
Ibbott St 22 E1 96 C3
Iberia Ho 17 N19 49 D2
Iberian Ave CR0,
SM6 220 A4
Ibex Ho E15 76 C3
Ibis Ct 16 SE8 141 B6
Ibis Ho E12 78 B4
Ibis La W4 133 A4
Ibis Way UB4 84 D1
Ibrox Ct 3 IG9 21 C2
Ibsley Gdns SW15 156 A3
Ibsley Way EN4 2 C1
Ibstock Place Sch
SW15 155 C5
Icarus Ho 21 E3 97 B4
Iceland Rd E3 97 C6
Iceland Wharf SE16 119 A2
Iceni Ct 28 Bow E3 97 B6
Buckhurst Hill IG9 21 B3
Ice Wharf NW1 233 B4
Ickburgh Est E5 74 B6
Ickburgh Rd E5 74 B5
Ickburgh Sch E5 74 B5
ICKENHAM 60 C4
Ickenham Cl HA4 61 B6
Ickenham Rd HA4 39 B1
Ickenham Sta UB10 61 A4
Ickleton Rd SE9 188 A6
Icknield Dr IG2 56 D4
Ickworth Park Rd
E17 53 A5
Icough Ct SE3 143 B5
Idaho Bldg 7 SE13 141 D4
Ida Rd N15 51 B5
Ida St E14 98 A1
Iden Cl BR2 208 C6
Idlecombe Rd
SW17 181 A4
Idmiston Rd
New Malden KT4 199 D2
Stratford E15 76 D3
West Norwood SE21,
SE27 161 A2
Idmiston Sq KT4 199 D2
Idol La EC3 117 C6 253 A5
Idonia St SE8 141 C5
Iffley Ho 47 E2 95 D4
Iffley Rd W6 112 B3
Ifield Ho SE17 263 B2
Ifield Rd
SW10 135 D6 265 D6
Ifor Evans Pl E1 96 D3
Ightham Ho
Beckenham BR3 185 B3
Walworth SE17 263 A3
Ightham Rd DA8 147 C5
Ikon Ho 21 E1 118 C6
Ikra Prim Sch N16 73 D4
Ilbert St W10 91 A4
Ilchester Gdns W2 245 C6
Ilchester Mans W8 255 A6
Ilchester Pl
W14 113 B3 254 D6
Ilchester Rd RM8 80 C3
Ildersly Gr SE21 161 B2
Ilderton Prim Sch
SE16 118 C1
Ilderton Rd SE15,
SE16 140 C6
Ilex Cl TW16 172 C1
Ilex Rd NW10 67 D2
Ilex Way SW16 182 C5
ILFORD 78 D6
Ilford Chambers 10
IG1 78 D5
Ilford Hill IG1 78 C5
Ilford Ho 14 N1 73 B2
Ilford Interchange
IG1 78 C5
Ilford Jewish Prim Sch
IG6 57 B6
Ilford La IG1 78 D4
Ilford Prep Sch IG3 58 A1
Ilford Ret Pk IG1 79 A6
Ilford Sta IG1 78 D6
Ilford Ursuline High Sch
IG1 78 D6
Ilfracombe Flats
SE1 252 B2
Ilfracombe Gdns
RM6 58 B2
Ilfracombe Rd BR1 164 D1
Iliffe St
SE17 116 D1 261 D2
Iliffe Yd
SE17 116 D1 261 D2
Ilkeston Ct 7 E5 74 D4
Ilkley Cl SE19 183 B4
Ilkley Ct N11 31 A4
Ilkley Rd
Newham E16 99 C2
South Oxhey WD19 22 D5
Illingworth Cl CR4 202 B6
Illingworth Way EN1 17 C6
Ilmington Rd HA3 43 D3
Ilminster Gdns
SW11 136 C1
Ilsley Ct 8 SW8 137 C3
Imber Cl
London N14 15 C4
Thames Ditton KT7 196 B1
Imber Court Trad Est
KT8 196 B3
Imber Cross KT7 196 D3
Imber Ct 4 SE9 166 C5
Imber Gr KT10 196 B2
Imber Park Rd KT10 196 B1
Imber St N1 235 C5
Immanuel Coll WD23 8 C4
Immanuel & St Andrew
CE Prim Sch
SW16 182 A4
Impact Ct SE20 184 B1
Imperial Ave 5 N16 73 C4
Imperial Cl HA2 41 C3
Imperial College Rd
SW7 114 B3 256 C6
Imperial College London
SW7 114 B3 256 C6
Imperial Cres SW6 136 A3
Imperial Ct
Chislehurst BR7 188 D4
Harrow HA2 41 C2
St John's Wood NW8 230 B4
Wembley HA9 66 C5
Whetstone N20 14 A1
Imperial Dr HA2 41 C3
Imperial Gdns CR4 203 B6
Imperial Ho
1 Bow E3 97 A4
2 Poplar E14 119 B6
Strand WC2 240 C1
Imperial Mews 5 E6 99 D5
Imperial Pl BR7 188 C2
Imperial Rd
East Bedfont
TW14 149 C4
Walham Green SW6 265 D1
Wood Green N22 32 A2
Imperial Sq SW6 265 D2
Imperial St E3 98 A4
Imperial Twrs 3
NW3 70 A2
Imperial War Mus* SE1,
SE11 116 C3 261 B5
Imperial Way
Croydon CR0, CR9 220 C2
Harrow HA3 44 A3
Longlands BR7 167 A1
Imperial Wharf Sta
SW10 136 A4 266 B1
Impington 19 KT1 176 C1
Imre Cl W12 112 B5
Inca Dr SE9 166 D4
Ince Terr 3 N15 50 D6
Inchmery Rd SE6 164 A3
Inchwood BR4, CR0 223 D4
Independant Jewish
Day Sch NW4 46 D4
Independence Ho 4
SW19 180 B2
Independent Ind Est
UB7 104 C5
Independent Pl E8 73 D3
Independents Rd
SE3 142 D2
Inderwick Rd N8 50 B4
Indescon Ct E14 119 D4
Indiana Bldg 7 SE8 141 C4
India St EC3 243 C1
India Way W12 112 B6
Indigo Ct TW13 149 D1
Indigo Mews N16 73 B5
Indus Ct 16 SE15 139 D5
Indus Rd SE7 143 C5
Ingal Rd E13 99 A3
Ingate Pl
SW8 137 B4 268 D1
Ingatestone Rd
Croydon SE25 206 B5
Wanstead E12 55 C1
Woodford IG8 37 B3
Ingelow Ho W8 245 C2
Ingelow Rd SW8 137 B3
Ingersoll Rd
Enfield EN3 6 C5
Shepherd's Bush
W12 112 B5
Ingestre Pl W1 239 B1
Ingestre Rd
Forest Gate E7 77 A4
Gospel Oak NW5 71 B4
Ingham Rd NW6 69 C4
Inglebert St
EC1 94 C4 234 A2
Ingleborough EN2 4 C3
Ingleborough St
SW9 138 C3
Ingleby Ct N21 16 D3
Ingleby Dr HA1 64 B5
Ingleby Rd
Dagenham RM10 81 D2
Ilford IG1 56 D1
Lower Holloway N7 72 A5
Ingleby Way
Chislehurst West
BR7 188 C5
Wallington SM6 219 D1
Ingle Cl HA5 41 B6
Ingledew Rd SE18 123 B1
Inglefield Sq 12 E1 118 B5
Ingle Ho 3 SW12 159 D3
Inglehurst Gdns IG4 56 B4
Inglemere Ct CR4,
SW17 180 D3
Inglemere Rd
Forest Hill SE23 162 D1
Mitcham CR4, SW17 180 D3
Inglesham Wlk E9 75 B2
Ingleside Cl BR3 185 C3
Ingleside Gr SE3 142 D6
Inglethorpe Ho 6
E5 74 A6
Inglethorpe St SW6 134 D4
Ingleton Ave DA16 168 A6
Ingleton Rd N18 34 A4
Ingleton St SW9 138 C3
Ingleway N12 30 C4
Inglewood BR7 189 B4
Inglewood Cl E14 119 C2
Inglewood Copse
BR1 188 B1
Inglewood Ct 4
BR1 186 D3
Inglewood Mans 11
NW6 69 C3
Inglewood Rd NW6 69 C3
Inglis Ct W5 110 B6
Inglis Ho 1 SW15 156 C6
Inglis Rd
Croydon CR0 205 D1
Inglis Rd *continued*
Ealing W5 110 B6
Inglis St SE5 138 D4
Ingram Ave NW11 48 A2
Ingram Cl
Lambeth SE11 260 D4
Stanmore HA7 25 C5
Ingram Ct EN1 17 D5
Ingram Ho
7 Harrow HA1 42 D4
Old Ford E3 97 A6
Teddington KT8 175 C2
Ingram Lo 8 SW4 159 D5
Ingram Rd London N2 48 C5
South Norwood CR7 183 A2
Ingram Way UB6 86 B6
Ingrave Ho RM9 102 B6
Ingrave St SW11 136 C2
Ingrebourne Ct E4 19 D2
Ingrebourne Ho
2 Catford BR1 186 B5
Lisson Gr NW8 236 D4
Ingress St 4 W4 111 C1
Inigo Jones Rd SE7 144 A5
Inigo Pl WC2 250 A6
Inkerman Rd NW5 71 B2
Inkerman Terr W8 255 B5
Inks Gn E4 36 A5
Inkster Ho 8 SW11 136 C2
Inkwell Cl N12 14 A1
Inman Rd
Harlesden NW10 89 C6
Wandsworth SW18 158 A4
Inmans Row IG8 37 A6
Inner Circ
NW1 93 A4 231 A2
Inner Park Rd
SW19 156 D2
Inner Ring E TW6 126 D2
Inner Ring W TW6 126 C2
Inner Temple* EC4 251 A6
Inner Temple La
EC4 241 A1
Innes Cl SW20 179 A1
Innes Gdns SW15 156 B5
Innes Lo SE23 162 D1
Innes Yd CR0 221 A5
Innisfree Ho NW2 68 D2
Innis Ho SE17 263 A2
Inniskilling Rd E13 99 C5
Innova Bsns Pk EN3 7 B3
Innovation Cl HA0 88 A6
Inskip Cl E10 75 D6
Inskip Rd RM8 58 D1
Insley Ho 13 E3 97 D4
Inst for Child Health
WC1 94 B3 240 C5
Institute Pl E8 74 B3
Instituto Espanol
Vicente Canada
Blanch W10 91 A2
Inst of Neurology
Bloomsbury
WC1 94 A2 240 B4
St Pancras
WC1 94 A3 240 B5
Int Coll of Accountancy
The SW17 158 D1
Integer Gdns E11 54 B2
Interchange The
Kentish Town NW5 71 B3
Thornton Heath CR0 204 D2
International Ave
TW5 106 C1
International House
Language Sch
WC2 94 A1 240 B2
International Sch of
London W3 110 C2
International Trad Est
UB2 106 B3
International Way
TW16 171 C2
Inverary Pl SE18 145 B6
Inver Cl E5 74 C6
Inverclyde Gdns RM6 58 D5
Inver Ct
11 Bayswater W2 91 D1
4 Hammersmith
W6 112 A3
Inveresk Gdns KT4 216 A5
Inverey Ho 2 N12 29 D5
Inverforth Cl NW3 70 A6
Inverforth Ho NW3 70 A6
Inverforth Rd N11 31 B5
Invergarry Ct 11 EN5 13 D6
Invergarry Ho NW6 91 D5
Inverine Rd SE7 121 B1
Invermead Cl W6 112 A2
Invermore Pl SE18 123 A2
Inverness Ave EN1 5 C4
Inverness Ct
8 Acton W3 88 C1

Inverness Ct continued
10 Catford SE6 ... 164 D3
Inverness Gdns W8 . 245 C3
Inverness Mews
Bayswater W2 ... 245 D6
Newham E16 ... 122 D5
North Woolwich E16 . 123 A5
Inverness Pl W2 ... 245 D6
Inverness Rd
Edmonton N18 ... 34 B5
Hounslow TW3 ... 129 C1
North Cheam KT4 ... 200 D1
Southall UB2 ... 107 A2
Inverness St NW1 ... 231 D6
Inverness Terr
W2 ... 113 D6 245 D6
Inverton Rd SE15 ... 140 D1
Invicta Cl
Chislehurst West
BR7 ... 188 C5
East Bedfont TW14 .. 149 D3
21 Tower Hamlets E3 .. 97 C2
Invicta Ct KT9 ... 214 B3
Invicta Ctr The
IG11 ... 102 A6
Invicta Gr UB5 ... 85 B4
Invicta Plaza SE1 ... 251 C4
Invicta Prim Sch
SE3 ... 143 A5
Invicta Rd SE3, SE7 ... 143 A6
Inville Rd
SE17 ... 117 B1 262 D1
Inwen Ct SE8 ... 119 A1
Inwood Ave TW3 ... 130 A2
Inwood Bsns Pk
TW3 ... 129 D1
Inwood Cl CR0 ... 223 A6
Inwood Ct 12 NW1 ... 71 C1
Inwood Ho 19 SE22 ... 139 C2
Inwood Rd TW3 ... 130 A1
Inworth St SW11 ... 136 C3
Inworth Wlk N1 ... 235 A6
Io Ctr Barking IG11 .. 101 D3
Woolwich SE18 ... 123 A3
Iona Cl Catford SE6 ... 163 C4
Morden SM4 ... 201 D2
Ion Ct 8 E2 ... 96 A5
Ionian Bldg 19 E14 ... 119 A6
Ionian Ho 22 E1 ... 96 D3
Ipsden Bldgs SE1 ... 251 B2
Ipswich Ho SE4 ... 162 D6
Ipswich Rd SW17 ... 181 A4
Irby Ho SW2 ... 160 C5
Ireland Cl E6 ... 100 B2
Ireland Pl N22 ... 32 A3
Ireland Yd EC4 ... 241 D1
Irene Rd
Broom Hill BR6 ... 211 D2
Parsons Green
SW6 ... 135 C4 265 B1
Ireton Cl N10 ... 31 A3
Ireton Ho 22 SW9 ... 138 C3
Ireton St 12 E3 ... 97 C3
Iris Ave DA5 ... 169 A5
Iris Cl Croydon CR0 ... 206 D1
Newham E6 ... 100 A3
Surbiton KT6 ... 198 B2
Iris Cres DA7 ... 147 B6
Iris Ct Dagenham IG11 .. 80 B1
8 Peckham SE15 ... 140 B3
4 Pinner HA5 ... 40 C6
Iris Rd KT19 ... 214 D3
Iris Way E4 ... 35 B4
Iris Wlk 1 HA8 ... 27 A6
Irkdale Ave EN1 ... 5 D4
Iroko Ho 7 NW3 ... 69 D2
Iron Bridge Cl
Southall UB2 ... 108 A5
Willesden NW10 ... 67 C3
Iron Bridge Ho NW3 ... 70 D1
Iron Bridge Rd N
UB11 ... 104 C5
Iron Bridge Rd S
UB7 ... 104 C4
Irongate Ho EC3 ... 243 B2
Iron Mill Pl SW18 ... 157 D5
Iron Mill Rd SW18 ... 157 D5
Ironmonger La
EC2 ... 95 B1 242 C1
Ironmonger Pas
EC1 ... 235 B1
Ironmonger Row
EC1 ... 95 A4 235 B1
Ironmonger's Pl 22
E14 ... 119 C2
Ironside Cl SE16 ... 118 D4
Ironside Ho E9 ... 75 A4
Ironworks 1 E3 ... 97 C6
Irvine Ave HA3 ... 43 B6
Irvine Cl N20 ... 14 C2
Irvine Ct
Marylebone W1 ... 239 B5
Thornton Heath CR7 . 204 C3
Irvine Ho N7 ... 72 B2
Irvine Way BR6 ... 211 D2
Irving Ave UB5 ... 84 D6
Irving Ct N22 ... 32 D2
Irving Gr SW9 ... 138 B3
Irving Ho SE17 ... 261 C1
Irving Mews N1 ... 73 A2
Irving Rd W14 ... 112 D3
Irving St WC2 ... 249 D5
Irwell Ct W7 ... 86 B1
Irwell Est 31 SE16 ... 118 C4
Irwin Ave SE18 ... 145 C5
Irwin Cl UB10 ... 60 C5
Irwin Gdns NW10 ... 90 B6
Isabel Hill Cl TW12 ... 173 C2
Isabella Cl N14 ... 15 C4
Isabella Ct 8 TW10 ... 154 B5
Isabella Dr BR6 ... 227 A4
Isabella Ho
18 Hammersmith
W6 ... 112 C1
Kennington SE11 ... 261 C2
Isabella Pl KT2 ... 176 B5
Isabella Rd E9 ... 74 C3
Isabella St SE1 ... 251 C3
Isabel St SW9 ... 270 D2
Isambard Mews
E14 ... 120 A3
Isambard Pl SE16 ... 118 C5
Iseldon Ct N7 ... 72 A4
Isel Way 4 SE22 ... 161 C6
Isham Rd SW16 ... 182 A1
Isis Cl Putney SW15 ... 134 C1
Ruislip HA4 ... 39 A3
Isis Ct W4 ... 132 D5
Isis Ho
2 Edmonton N18 ... 33 D4
Paddington NW8 ... 236 D5
Isis St SW18 ... 158 A2
Islamia Girls' High Sch
NW6 ... 91 A6
Islamia Prim Sch
NW6 ... 91 A6
Islamic Coll for
Advanced Studies
NW10 ... 68 B2
Island Centre Way 16
EN3 ... 7 C6
Island Farm Ave
KT8 ... 195 B4
Island Farm Rd KT8 .. 195 C4
Island Gardens Sta
E14 ... 120 A1
Island Ho Bromley E14 .. 98 A4
Morden SW19 ... 202 A5
Island Rd
Deptford SE16 ... 118 D2
Mitcham CR4 ... 180 D3
Island Row E14 ... 97 B1
Isla Rd SE18 ... 145 A6
Islay Gdns TW4 ... 150 D6
Islay Wlk 17 N1 ... 73 A2
Isleden Ho N1 ... 235 A6
Isledon Rd N4, N7 ... 72 C5
Islehurst Cl BR7 ... 188 C2
ISLE OF DOGS ... 120 A2
ISLEWORTH ... 131 B2
Isleworth Bsns Complex
TW7 ... 130 D3
Isleworth Sta TW7 .. 130 D3
Isleworth & Syon Sch
for Boys TW7 ... 130 C5
Isleworth Town Prim
Sch TW7 ... 131 A3
ISLINGTON ... 72 D2
Islington Arts & Media
Sch N4 ... 50 B1
Islington Bsns Ctr
N1 ... 235 B6
Islington Est
N1 ... 95 A6 235 A6
Islington Gn
N1 ... 94 D6 234 C5
Islington Green Sch
N1 ... 95 A6 235 A5
Islington High St
N1 ... 94 D5 234 C4
Islington Park Mews 1
N1 ... 72 D1
Islington Park St N1 .. 72 D1
Islington Sixth Form Ctr
N7 ... 72 C4
Islip Gdns
Burnt Oak HA8 ... 27 B3
Northolt UB5 ... 63 A1
Islip Manor Rd UB5 ... 63 A1
Islip St NW5 ... 71 C3
Ismailia Rd E7 ... 77 B1
Isobel Ho
10 Ashford TW16 ... 171 D3
Harrow HA1 ... 42 D4
Isokon Flats 3 NW3 .. 70 D3
Isom Cl E13 ... 99 B4
Issac Way SE1 ... 252 B2
Italia Conti Acad of
Theatre Arts EC1 .. 242 A5
Ithell Ct HA0 ... 65 D3
Ivanhoe Dr HA3 ... 25 B1
Ivanhoe Ho
11 Balham SW12 ... 159 B4
31 Bow E3 ... 97 A5
Ivanhoe Rd
Hounslow TW4 ... 128 D2
Peckham SE5 ... 139 D2
Ivatt Pl W14 .. 113 B1 254 D1
Ivatt Way N17 ... 50 D6
Iveagh Ave NW10 ... 88 C5
Iveagh Cl
Ealing NW10 ... 88 C5
South Hackney E9 ... 96 D6
Iveagh Ct
4 Beckenham
BR3 ... 207 D6
Whitechapel EC3 ... 243 C1
Iveagh Ho
2 Brixton SW9 ... 138 D3
Chelsea SW10 ... 266 B4
Ivebury Ct 9 W10 ... 90 C1
Ivedon Rd DA16 ... 146 C3
Ive Farm Cl E10 ... 75 C6
Ive Farm La E10 ... 75 C6
Iveley Rd SW4 ... 137 C3
Iver Ct N1 ... 73 A2
Ivere Dr EN5 ... 13 D5
Iverhurst Cl DA6 ... 168 D6
Iverna Ct W8 ... 255 B6
Iverna Gdns
Hatton TW14 ... 149 B6
Kensington
W8 ... 113 C3 255 B6
Iverson Rd NW6 ... 69 C2
Ivers Way CR0 ... 223 D1
Ives Rd E16 ... 98 C2
Ives St SW3 .. 114 C2 257 B4
Ivestor Terr SE23 ... 162 C4
Ivimey St E2 ... 96 A4
Ivinghoe Cl EN1 ... 5 C4
Ivinghoe Ho 14 N7 ... 71 D3
Ivinghoe Rd
Barking RM8 ... 80 B3
Bushey WD23 ... 8 B4
Ivor Ct Hendon N3 ... 47 A6
Hornsey N8 ... 50 A3
Lisson Gr NW1 ... 237 C6
Ivor Gr SE9 ... 166 D3
Ivor Ho DA14 ... 190 C5
Ivories The N1 ... 73 A1
Ivor Mayor Lo
SW12 ... 159 A5
Ivor Pl NW1 ... 92 D3 237 C5
Ivor St NW1 ... 71 C1
Ivory Ct TW13 ... 150 A3
Ivorydown BR1 ... 187 A6
Ivory Ho
9 London SW11 ... 136 A2
St George in t East
E1 ... 253 D4
Ivory Sq 15 SW18 ... 136 A2
Ivybridge Cl
2 Twickenham
TW1 ... 153 A4
Uxbridge UB8 ... 82 A4
Ivybridge Ct 1 BR7 .. 188 C2
Ivybridge Ho 18
SE22 ... 139 C2
Ivybridge La WC2 ... 250 B5
Ivybridge Prim Sch
TW1 ... 152 D5
Ivybridge Ret Pk
TW7 ... 152 D6
Ivychurch Cl SE20 ... 184 C3
Ivy Church La SE1,
SE17 ... 263 C2
Ivy Cl Harrow HA2 ... 63 B4
Pinner HA5 ... 40 C2
Sunbury TW16 ... 172 C1
Ivy Cotts UB10 ... 82 C4
Ivy Cres W4 ... 111 A2
Ivy Ct
19 Bermondsey
SE16 ... 118 A1
Lewisham SE3 ... 142 D1
Ivydale Prim Sch
SE15 ... 140 D1
Ivydale Rd
Carshalton SM5 ... 218 D6
Nunhead SE15 ... 140 D1
Ivyday Gr SW16 ... 160 B1
Ivydene Cl SM1 ... 218 A4
Ivydene KT12, KT8 ... 195 B4
Ivy Gdns London N8 ... 50 A3
Mitcham CR4 ... 203 D6
Ivy Ho Croydon CR0 ... 206 D1
6 Upper Clapton E5 ... 52 B1
Ivyhouse Rd RM9 ... 81 A2
Ivy House Rd UB10 ... 60 D5
Ivy La TW4 ... 129 B1
Ivy Lo W8 ... 245 A4
Ivymount Rd SE27 ... 160 C1
Ivy Rd Brockley SE4 ... 141 C1
Cricklewood NW2 ... 68 C4
Hounslow TW3 ... 129 D1
Newham E16 ... 99 A1
Southgate N14 ... 15 D4
Tolworth KT6 ... 198 C1
Ivy Rd continued
Upper Tooting
SW17 ... 180 C5
Walthamstow E17 ... 53 C3
Ivy St N1 ... 95 C5
Ivy Terr 3 IG2 ... 57 A3
Ivy Wlk RM9 ... 81 A2
Ixworth Pl
SW3 ... 114 C2 257 A3
Izane Rd DA6 ... 147 B1

J

Jacaranda Cl KT3 ... 199 C6
Jacaranda Gr E8 ... 73 D1
Jack Ashley Ct 5
NW9 ... 27 C2
Jackass La BR2 ... 225 C2
Jack Barnett Way
N22 ... 32 B1
Jack Clow Rd E15 ... 98 C5
Jack Cook Ho 9
IG11 ... 78 D1
Jack Cornwell St
E12 ... 78 C4
Jack Goodchild Way
KT3 ... 198 D6
Jack & Jill Sch
TW12 ... 173 C4
Jacklin Gn IG8 ... 37 A6
Jackman Ho 24 E1 ... 118 B5
Jackman Mews NW2 .. 67 C5
Jackman St E8 ... 96 B6
Jackson Cl
Hackney E9 ... 74 D1
Uxbridge UB10 ... 60 A1
Jackson Ct
Forest Gate E7 ... 77 B2
Wanstead E11 ... 55 B1
Jackson Ho
16 London SW11 ... 136 B2
13 New Southgate
N11 ... 31 C5
Jackson Rd
Barking IG11 ... 101 B6
Bromley BR2 ... 226 B6
East Barnet EN4 ... 14 C5
Lower Holloway N7 ... 72 B4
Uxbridge UB10 ... 60 A1
Jackson's La N6 ... 49 B2
Jackson's Pl CR0 ... 205 C1
Jackson St SE18 ... 144 C6
Jackson's Way CR0 .. 223 C5
Jackson Way UB2 ... 107 D4
Jack Taylor Sch
NW8 ... 92 A6 229 A6
Jack Tizard Sch
W12 ... 112 B5
Jack Walker Ct N5 ... 72 D4
Jacob Ct 24 EN3 ... 7 C6
Jacob Ho 10 DA18 ... 124 D4
Jacobin Lo N7 ... 72 A3
Jacob Mans 15 E1 ... 96 B1
Jacobs Cl RM10 ... 81 D4
Jacobs Ho E13 ... 99 C4
Jacobson Ct SW11 ... 267 B1
Jacobson Ho E1 ... 243 C2
Jacob St SE1 ... 118 A4
Jacob's Well Mews
W1 ... 238 B2
Jacotts Ho W10 ... 90 C3
Jacqueline Cl UB5 ... 85 A6
Jacqueline Ho 8 E1 .. 96 D2
Jade Cl
Dagenham RM8 ... 58 C1
Hendon NW2 ... 46 D2
Newham E16 ... 99 D1
Jaffe Rd IG1 ... 57 B1
Jaffray Rd BR2 ... 209 D5
Jaggard Way SW12 .. 158 D4
Jagger Ho SW11 ... 267 C2
Jago Cl SE18 ... 145 A6
Jago Wlk SE5 ... 139 B5
Jamahirya Sch
SW3 ... 136 C6 267 A6
Jamaica Rd
Bermondsey SE1 ... 253 D1
Bermondsey SE16 ... 118 B3
Thornton Heath CR7 . 204 C3
Jamaica St E1 ... 96 C2
James Allen's Girls' Sch
SE22 ... 161 C6
James Allens Pre-Prep
Sch SE21 ... 161 B5
James Anderson Ct 29
E2 ... 95 C5
James Ave
Cricklewood NW2 ... 68 C3
Dagenham RM8 ... 59 B1
James Bedford Cl
HA5 ... 22 C1
James Boswell Cl 1
SW16 ... 182 C6
James Brine Ho 6
E2 ... 95 D4
James Campbell Ho 2
E2 ... 96 C5
James Cl
London NW11 ... 47 A3
8 Newham E13 ... 99 A5
James Collins Cl W9 .. 91 B3
James Ct Chingford E4 . 20 B2
Finchley N12 ... 30 C3
Hendon NW9 ... 27 C1
Northolt UB5 ... 85 A5
3 Woodford E18 ... 37 B1
James Dixon Prim Sch
SE20 ... 184 B3
James Docherty Ho 4
E2 ... 96 C5
James Dudson Ct
NW10 ... 67 A1
James Est CR4 ... 180 D1
James Gdns N22 ... 32 D3
James Hammett Ho 9
E2 ... 95 D5
James Ho Mile End E1 .. 97 A3
33 Rotherhithe
SE16 ... 118 D4
James Joyce Wlk 7
SE24 ... 138 D1
James La E10, E11 ... 54 B3
James Lee Sq EN3 ... 7 C5
James Leicester Hall of
Residence N7 ... 72 A2
James Lind Ho 6
SE8 ... 119 B2
James Middleton Ho 20
E2 ... 96 B4
James Newman Ct
SE9 ... 166 C1
Jameson Ct 6 E2 ... 96 C5
Jameson Ho SE11 ... 260 C2
Jameson Lo N6 ... 49 C3
Jameson Pl 11 W3 ... 111 A4
Jameson St W8 ... 245 B4
James Pl N17 ... 33 D2
James's Cotts TW9 .. 132 C5
James St
Barking IG11 ... 79 A1
Enfield EN1 ... 17 D6
James Stewart Ho
NW6 ... 69 B1
James St
Hounslow TW3 ... 130 B2
Marylebone
W1 ... 93 A1 238 B1
James Stroud Ho
SE17 ... 262 B1
James St
WC2 ... 116 A6 250 B6
Jamestown Rd
NW1 ... 93 B6 231 C6
Jamestown Way
E14 ... 120 B6
James Way WD19 ... 22 D6
James Wolfe Prim Sch
SE10 ... 142 A5
Jamieson Ho TW4 ... 151 B5
Jamuna Cl E14 ... 97 A2
Jane Austen Hall 14
E16 ... 121 B5
Jane St E1 ... 96 B1
Janet Ct
4 Bexleyheath
DA7 ... 147 C1
Wood Green N22 ... 32 B2
Janet St E14 ... 119 C3
Janeway Pl 2 SE16 .. 118 B4
Janeway St SE16 ... 118 A4
Janice Mews 3 IG1 .. 78 D5
Jansen Ho 5 SW15 .. 156 A6
Jansen Wlk SW11 ... 136 B1
Janson Cl
Stratford E15 ... 76 C3
Willesden NW10 ... 67 C5
Janson Rd E15 ... 76 C3
Jansons Rd N15 ... 51 C6
Japan Cres N4 ... 50 B1
Japanese Sch The
W3 ... 110 C6
Japan Rd RM6 ... 58 D3
Jaquets Ct DA5 ... 169 C2
Jardine Ho HA1 ... 42 C2
Jardine Rd E1 ... 118 D6
Jarman Ho
Bermondsey
SE16 ... 118 D2
16 Stepney E1 ... 96 C2
Jarrett Cl SW2 ... 160 D3
Jarrow Cl SM4 ... 201 D4
Jarrow Rd
Bermondsey
SE16 ... 118 C1
Dagenham RM6 ... 58 C3
Tottenham Hale N17 ... 52 B5
Jarrow Way E9 ... 75 A4
Jarvis Cl
1 Barking IG11 ... 101 B6
Barnet EN5 ... 12 D6
Jarvis Ho 3 SE15 ... 140 A4
Jarvis Rd
London SE22 ... 139
South Croydon CR2 ... 221
Jasmine Cl Ilford IG1 .. 78
Orpington BR6 ... 226
Southall UB1 ... 107
Jasmine Ct
Lee SE12 ... 165
11 Wallington SM6 ... 219
Wimbledon SW19 ... 179
Jasmine Gdns
Harrow HA2 ... 63
West Wickham CR0 .. 223
Jasmine Gr SE20 ... 184
Jasmine Sq 15 E3 ... 97
Jasmine Terr UB7 ... 104
Jasmine Way KT7 ... 196
Jasmin Ho SE4 ... 141
Jasmin Lo 17 SE16 ... 118
Jasmin Rd KT19 ... 214
Jasmin SE1 ... 253
Jason Ct
2 London SW9 ... 138
Marylebone W1 ... 238
Jason Ho UB5 ... 84
Jason Wlk SE9 ... 188
Jasper Cl EN3 ... 6
Jasper Ho KT4 ... 199
Jasper Rd
Newham E16 ... 99
Penge SE19 ... 183
Jasper Wlk N1 ... 235
Java Wharf SE1 ... 253
Javelin Ct HA7 ... 25
Javelin Way UB5 ... 84
Jawahar Bagh
SW16 ... 182
Jaycroft EN2 ... 4
Jay Gdns BR7 ... 188
Jay Ho SW15 ... 134
Jay Mews
SW7 ... 114 A4 246
Jayson Ct 7 CR0 ... 206
Jazzfern Terr HA0 ... 65
Jean Batten Cl SM6 .. 220
Jean Darling Ho
SW10 ... 266
Jean Ho 3 SW17 ... 180
Jean Humbert Ho 2
SE27 ... 183
Jean Pardies Ho 23
E1 ... 96
Jebb Ave SW2 ... 160
Jebb St E3 ... 97
Jedburgh Rd E13 ... 99
Jedburgh St SW11 ... 137
Jeddo Mews W12 ... 111
Jeddo Rd W12 ... 111
Jefferies Ho 13
NW10 ... 67
Jefferson Bldg 3
E14 ... 119
Jefferson Cl
Ealing W13 ... 109
Ilford IG2 ... 56
Jefferson Wlk 13
SE18 ... 144
Jeffrey Row SE12 ... 165
Jeffrey's Ct 2 SW4 .. 138
Jeffrey's Pl NW1 ... 71
Jeffreys Rd EN3 ... 7
Jeffrey's Rd SW4 ... 138
Jeffrey's St NW1 ... 71
Jeffs Cl TW12 ... 173
Jeffs Rd SM1 ... 217
Jeff Wooller Coll
WC1 ... 94 A2 240
Jefton Ct SM6 ... 219
Jeger Ave E2 ... 95
Jeken Rd SE9 ... 143
Jelf Rd SW2 ... 160
Jellicoe Ct E4 ... 36
Jellicoe Gdns HA7 ... 25
Jellicoe Ho
5 Bethnal Green
E2 ... 96
Fitzrovia NW1 ... 238
11 Putney SW15 ... 156
Jellicoe Rd
4 Newham E13 ... 99
Tottenham N17 ... 33
Jemmett Cl KT2 ... 176
Jemotts Ct 9 SE14 ... 140
Jem Paterson Ct
HA1 ... 64
Jengar Cl SM1 ... 217
Jenkins Ho SW8 ... 269
Jenkins La IG11 ... 101
Jenkinson Ho 12 E2 ... 96
Jenkins Rd E13 ... 99
Jenner Ave W3 ... 89
Jenner Cl DA14 ... 190
Jenner Ct N21 ... 16
Jenner Ho
5 Belvedere
DA17 ... 125
Greenwich SE3 ... 142

Jenner Pl SW13 ... 134 B6
Jenner Rd N16 ... 73 D5
Jennett Rd CR0 ... 220 C5
Jennifer Ho SE11 ... 261 B3
Jennifer Rd BR1 ... 164 D1
Jennings Cl KT6 ... 197 C2
Jennings Ho SE10 ... 120 B1
Jennings Rd SE22 ... 161 D5
Jenny Hammond Cl E11 ... 76 D5
Jenny Hammond Prim Sch E11 ... 76 C4
Jensen Ho 10 E3 ... 97 C3
Jenson Way SE19 ... 183 D3
Jenton Ave DA7 ... 147 A3
Jephson Ct 17 SW4 ... 138 A3
Jephson Ho 6 SE17 ... 138 D6
Jephson Rd E7 ... 77 C1
Jephson St SE5 ... 139 B4
Jephtha Rd SW18 ... 157 C5
Jeppo's La CR4 ... 202 D5
Jerdan Pl SW6 ... 265 A4
Jeremiah St 11 E14 ... 97 D1
Jeremy Bentham Ho 24 E2 ... 96 A4
Jeremy's Gn N18 ... 34 C6
Jermyn St SW1 ... 115 C5 249 B4
Jerningham Ct SE14 ... 141 A4
Jerningham Rd SE14 ... 141 A4
Jerome Cres NW8 ... 92 C3 237 A6
Jerome Ct 2 N11 ... 31 C5
Jerome Ho
Kingston u T KT1 ... 175 D1
Lisson Gr NW1 ... 237 B4
Jerome Pl KT1 ... 175 D1
Jerome St E1 ... 95 D3 243 C5
Jerome Twr 5 W3 ... 110 D4
Jerrard St SE13 ... 141 D2
Jerrold Lo SW15 ... 134 C2
Jerrold St 24 N1 ... 95 C5
Jersey Ave HA7 ... 25 C1
Jersey Ct UB2 ... 107 B3
Jersey Dr BR5 ... 211 B3
Jersey Ho
15 Canonbury N1 ... 73 A2
Enfield EN3 ... 6 D5
Jersey Rd
Canonbury N1 ... 73 A2
Ealing W7 ... 109 A4
Hounslow TW5, TW7 ... 130 B5
Ilford IG1 ... 78 D4
Leytonstone E11 ... 54 B1
Mitcham SW17 ... 181 B4
Newham E16 ... 99 C1
Jersey St E2 ... 96 B4
Jerusalem Pas EC1 ... 241 C5
Jervis Bay Ho 9 E14 ... 98 B1
Jervis Ct
9 Dagenham RM10 ... 81 D2
2 Greenwich SE10 ... 142 A4
Marylebone W1 ... 238 D1
Jerviston Gdns SW16 ... 182 C4
Jesmond Ave HA9 ... 66 B2
Jesmond Cl CR4 ... 203 B6
Jesmond Ct HA9 ... 66 C2
Jesmond Rd CR0 ... 205 D2
Jesmond Way HA7 ... 26 A5
Jessam Ave E5 ... 52 B1
Jessamine Rd W7 ... 108 D5
Jessel Ho
St Pancras WC1 ... 233 A1
Westminster SW1 ... 259 D4
Jesse Rd E10 ... 54 A1
Jessica Rd SW18 ... 158 A6
Jessie Blythe La 4 N19 ... 50 A2
Jessie Duffett Ho 11 SE5 ... 139 A5
Jessie's Cotts E17 ... 53 A3
Jessiman Terr TW17 ... 192 C4
Jesson Ho SE17 ... 262 C3
Jessop Ave UB2 ... 107 B2
Jessop Ct N1 ... 234 D3
Jessop Ho 9 W4 ... 111 B2
Jessop Pl CR4 ... 202 C5
Jessop Prim Sch SE24 ... 139 A1
Jessop Sq E14 ... 119 C5
Jessops Way CR0 ... 203 C3
Jessops Wharf 4 TW8 ... 131 C5
Jessup Cl SE18 ... 123 A2
Jeston Ho 10 SE27 ... 160 D1
Jethou Ho 16 N1 ... 73 A2
Jetstar Way UB5 ... 85 A4
Jevington Way SE12 ... 165 B3
Jevons Ho 9 NW8 ... 70 B1
Jewell Ho 3 SW12 ... 159 C4
Jewel Rd E17 ... 53 C6
Jewish Mus The*
Camden Town NW1 ... 93 B6 231 D5
Finchley N3 ... 29 D1
Jewry St EC3 ... 95 D1 243 C1
Jews Row SW18 ... 136 A1
Jews Wlk SE26 ... 184 B6
Jeymer Ave NW2 ... 68 C3
Jeymer Dr UB6 ... 86 A6
Jeypore Rd SW18 ... 158 A5
JFS Sch HA3 ... 44 C3
Jillian Cl TW12 ... 173 C3
Jim Bradley Cl 10 SE18 ... 122 C2
Jim Griffiths Ho SW6 ... 264 D5
Joan Cres SE9 ... 165 D4
Joan Gdns RM8 ... 81 A6
Joanna Ho 7 W6 ... 112 C1
Joanne Ct EN1 ... 17 C5
Joan Player Ho EN3 ... 6 D6
Joan Rd RM8 ... 81 A6
Joan St SE1 ... 116 D5 251 C3
Joan Villas IG2 ... 57 A2
Jocelin Ho N1 ... 233 D5
Jocelyn Rd TW9 ... 132 A2
Jocelyn St SE15 ... 140 A4
Jockey's Fields WC1 ... 94 B2 240 D4
Jodane Rd SE8 ... 119 B2
Jodrell Cl TW7 ... 131 A4
Jodrell Rd E3 ... 75 B1
Joe Hunte Ct 2 SW27 ... 182 D5
Joel St HA5, HA6 ... 40 A5
Johanna Prim Sch SE1 ... 116 C4 251 A1
Johanna St SE1 ... 251 A1
John Adam St WC2 ... 116 A6 250 B5
John Aird Ct W2 ... 92 A2 236 B4
John Aldis Ho N22 ... 32 B1
John Archer Way SW18 ... 158 B5
John Ashby Cl SW2 ... 160 A5
John Austin Cl KT2 ... 176 B2
John Baird Ct SE26 ... 184 D6
John Baird Ho 11 SE20 ... 184 C3
John Ball Prim Sch SE3 ... 142 C3
John Barker Ct NW6 ... 69 A1
John Barker Ho IG1 ... 79 B6
John Barnes Wlk E15 ... 76 D2
John Barter Ho TW3 ... 129 B3
John Betts' Ho W12 ... 112 A3
John Betts Prim Sch W6 ... 112 B3
John Bond Ho 2 E3 ... 97 B5
John Bradshaw Rd N14 ... 15 D3
John Brent Ho 8 SE8 ... 118 D2
John Buck Ho NW10 ... 89 D6
John Burns Dr IG11 ... 79 C1
John Burns Prim Sch SW11 ... 137 A3
Johnby Cl EN3 ... 7 A6
John Campbell Rd 26 N16 ... 73 C3
John Carpenter St EC4 ... 251 C6
John Cartwright Ho 7 E2 ... 96 B4
John Chilton Sch UB5 ... 63 A1
John Clifford Ho N8 ... 50 A3
John Clynes Ct SW15 ... 134 B1
John Conway Ho 23 SW2 ... 160 C5
John Cornwell VC Ho 6 E12 ... 78 C4
John Day Ho TW7 ... 131 B2
John Dee Ho 3 SW14 ... 133 B2
John Donne Prim Sch SE15 ... 140 B4
John Drinkwater Cl E11 ... 54 D2
John Dwight Ho SW6 ... 135 D2
John Fearon Wlk 5 W10 ... 91 A4
John Felton Rd 19 SE16 ... 118 A4
John Fielden Ho 10 E2 ... 96 B4
John Fisher St E1 ... 118 A6
John F. Kennedy Specl Sch E15 ... 98 B6
John Gooch Dr EN2 ... 4 D4
John Harris Ho SE15 ... 140 A2
John Harrison Way SE10 ... 120 D3
John Hunt Ct 5 SE9 ... 166 A2
John Islip St SW1 ... 116 A2 260 A3
John Kaye Ct TW17 ... 192 C4
John Keall Ho SW15 ... 134 D2
John Keats Ho N22 ... 32 B2
John Keats Lo EN2 ... 5 B4
John Keble CE Prim Sch NW10 ... 89 D6
John Kelly Tech Colls NW2 ... 67 D5
John Kennedy Ct 1 N1 ... 73 B2
John Kennedy Ho 1 SE16 ... 118 D2
John Kennedy Lo 2 N1 ... 73 B2
John King Ct 5 N19 ... 71 D6
John Kirk Ho
22 Battersea SW11 ... 136 B2
Beckenham BR3 ... 207 A5
5 Streatham SW16 ... 160 A1
John Knight Lo SW6 ... 265 B4
John Lamb Ct HA3 ... 24 C2
John Loughborough Sch N17 ... 33 D1
John Lyon Sch The HA2 ... 42 B1
John McDonald Ho 3 E14 ... 120 A3
John McKenna Wlk 17 SE16 ... 118 A3
John & Mary Sch NW5 ... 71 D3
John Masefield Ho N15 ... 51 B3
John Maurice Cl SE17 ... 117 B2 262 C4
John Milton Prim Sch SW8 ... 137 C5 269 A3
John Nettleford Ho 14 E2 ... 96 B4
John Newton Ct DA16 ... 146 B2
John Orwell Sports Ctr E1 ... 118 B5
John Parker Cl RM10 ... 81 D1
John Parker Sq 8 SW11 ... 136 B2
John Parry Ct 28 N1 ... 95 C5
John Paul II Sch SW19 ... 156 D4
John Penn Ho SE8 ... 141 B5
John Penn St SE13 ... 141 D4
John Perrin Pl HA3 ... 44 A2
John Perryn Prim Sch W3 ... 89 C1
John Prince's St W1 ... 238 D2
John Pritchard Ho 16 E1 ... 96 A3
John Ratcliffe Ho 8 NW6 ... 91 C4
John Rennie Wlk 1 E1 ... 118 C5
John Roan Sch The SE3 ... 142 C5
John Roll Way SE16 ... 118 A3
John Ruskin Coll CR2 ... 223 A1
John Ruskin Prim Sch SE5 ... 139 A6
John Ruskin St SE5 ... 139 A6
John's Ave NW4 ... 46 C5
Johns Ct TW15 ... 171 A6
John Scurr Ho 18 E14 ... 97 A1
John Scurr Prim Sch E1 ... 96 C3
John Silkin La SE8 ... 118 D1
Johns La SM4 ... 202 A4
John's Mews WC1 ... 94 B3 240 D5
John Smith Ave SW6 ... 135 B5 264 C4
John Smith Mews E14 ... 120 B6
Johnson Cl E8 ... 96 A6
Johnson Ct
Hendon NW4 ... 46 A6
10 Wandsworth SW18 ... 136 B1
Johnson Ho
Belgravia SW1 ... 258 B3
23 Bethnal Green E2 ... 96 A4
Somers Town NW1 ... 232 B3
South Lambeth SW8 ... 269 D3
Johnson Lo 12 W9 ... 91 C2
Johnson Rd
Bromley Comm BR2 ... 209 D4
Heston TW5 ... 128 C5
Stonebridge NW10 ... 89 B6
Thornton Heath CR0 ... 205 B2
Johnson's Cl SM5 ... 218 D5
Johnsons Ct EC4 ... 241 B1
Johnsons Dr TW12 ... 174 A2
Johnson's Ind Est UB3 ... 106 A3
Johnson's Pl SW1 ... 115 C1 259 A1
Johnson St
Southall UB2 ... 106 D3
Stepney E1 ... 96 C1
Johnsons Way NW10 ... 88 D3
John Spencer Sq N1 ... 72 D2
John's Pl E1 ... 96 B1
John Stainer Com Prim Sch SE4 ... 141 A2
John St
Croydon SE25 ... 206 A5
Enfield EN1 ... 17 D6
John's Terr CR0 ... 205 C1
John St
Finsbury WC1 ... 94 B3 240 D5
Hounslow TW3, TW5 ... 129 A3
Johnston Cl SW9 ... 270 D1
Johnstone Ho SE13 ... 142 B2
Johnstone Rd E6 ... 100 B4
Johnston Rd IG8 ... 37 A5
Johnston Terr NW2 ... 68 D5
John Strachey Ho SW6 ... 264 D5
John Strype Ct E10 ... 53 D1
John St E15 ... 98 D6
John Trundle Ct EC2 ... 242 A4
John Tucker Ho 3 E14 ... 119 C3
John Walsh Twr E11 ... 76 D6
John Wesley Ct 6 TW1 ... 153 A3
John Wesley's House & Mus* EC1 ... 242 D6
John Wheatley Ho
14 London N19 ... 49 D2
West Brompton SW6 ... 264 D5
John William Cl 12 KT2 ... 175 D2
John Williams Cl SE14 ... 140 D6
John Wilson St SE18 ... 122 C2
John Wooley Cl SE13 ... 142 C1
Joiners Arms Yd 1 SE5 ... 139 B4
Joiners Ct 5 N20 ... 14 D1
Joiner St SE1 ... 252 D3
Joiners Yd N1 ... 233 B3
Joint Rd N10 ... 30 C2
Jolles Ho 9 E3 ... 97 D4
Jollys La Harrow HA2 ... 42 B1
Hayes UB4 ... 84 D2
Jonathan Ct 9 W4 ... 111 C2
Jonathan St SE11 ... 116 B1 260 C2
Jones Ho
4 South Bromley E14 ... 98 B1
Stamford Hill N16 ... 51 C1
Jones Rd E13 ... 99 B3
Jones St W1 ... 248 C5
Jones Wlk 6 TW10 ... 154 B5
Jonquil Gdns 5 TW12 ... 173 C4
Jonson Cl Hayes UB4 ... 84 A2
Mitcham CR4 ... 203 B6
Jonson Ho
Borough The SE1 ... 262 D5
16 Canonbury N16 ... 73 B4
Jordan Cl HA2 ... 63 B5
Jordan Ct SW15 ... 134 D1
Jordan Hill N10 ... 30 C2
Jordan Ho
12 London SE4 ... 140 D1
Shoreditch N1 ... 235 D5
Jordan Lo SW17 ... 180 C5
Jordan Rd UB6 ... 87 C6
Jordans Cl
Dagenham RM10 ... 81 D4
Hounslow TW7 ... 130 C4
Jordans Ho NW8 ... 237 A5
Jordans Mews TW11 ... 152 C2
Jo Richardson Comm Sch RM9 ... 102 D6
Jo Richardson Com Sch RM9 ... 80 C2
Joscoyne Ho 5 E1 ... 96 B1
Josef Perrin Ho 1 SE27 ... 183 B6
Joseph Ave W3 ... 89 B1
Joseph Clarke Sch E4 ... 36 B4
Joseph Conrad Ho SW1 ... 259 B3
Joseph Ct N16 ... 51 C2
Joseph Hardcastle Cl SE14 ... 140 D5
Joseph Hood Prim Sch SW20 ... 201 A6
Josephine Ave SW2 ... 160 B6
Joseph Irwin Ho 11 E14 ... 119 B6
Joseph Lancaster Prim Sch SE1 ... 117 B3 262 C5
Joseph Lister Ct E7 ... 77 A1
Joseph Lister Lo E11 ... 55 B1
Joseph Powell Cl 1 SW12 ... 159 C5
Joseph Priestley Ho 12 E2 ... 96 B4
Joseph Ray Rd E11 ... 76 C6
Joseph St E3 ... 97 B3
Joseph Trotter Cl EC1 ... 234 B1
Joshua Cl
Croydon CR2 ... 220 D1
Muswell Hill N10 ... 31 B3
Joshua St E14 ... 98 A1
Joslings Cl W12 ... 112 A6
Joslyn Cl EN3 ... 7 C5
Josseline Ct 9 E3 ... 97 A5
Joubert Mans SW3 ... 257 B2
Joubert St SW11 ... 136 D3
Jowett Ho 27 SW9 ... 138 A3
Jowett St SE15 ... 139 D5
Joyce Ave N18 ... 33 D5
Joyce Butler Ho N22 ... 32 B2
Joyce Dawson Way SE28 ... 124 A6
Joyce Lattimore Ct N9 ... 18 B1
Joyce Page Cl SE7 ... 143 D6
Joy Ct NW2 ... 68 D5
Joydon Dr RM6 ... 58 B3
Joyner Ct UB1 ... 107 B6
Joyners Cl RM9 ... 81 B4
Joystone Ct 8 EN4 ... 2 C1
Jubb Powell Ho N15 ... 51 C3
Jubet Ho 9 N16 ... 73 B4
Jubilee Ave
Chingford E4 ... 36 A4
Romford RM7 ... 59 D4
Twickenham TW2 ... 152 A3
Jubilee Bldgs NW8 ... 229 C4
Jubilee Cl
4 Harlesden NW10 ... 89 D5
Kingsbury NW9 ... 45 B3
Pinner HA5 ... 22 C1
Romford RM7 ... 59 D4
Teddington KT1 ... 175 C2
Jubilee Cres
Cubitt Town E14 ... 120 A3
Edmonton N9 ... 18 A3
Jubilee Ct
Harrow HA3 ... 44 A2
Hounslow TW3 ... 129 D2
Islington N1 ... 233 B6
Muswell Hill N10 ... 49 A6
12 Sutton SM2 ... 218 A2
Thornton Heath CR7 ... 204 C5
Jubilee Dr HA4 ... 63 A4
Jubilee Gdns UB1 ... 85 C1
Jubilee Ho
3 Hampton TW12 ... 173 C2
Lambeth SE11 ... 261 B3
Jubilee Hts NW2 ... 69 B2
Jubilee Lo HA7 ... 25 A5
Jubilee Mans 10 E1 ... 96 C1
Jubilee Mkt WC2 ... 250 B6
Jubilee Park Ctry Pk BR2 ... 210 C4
Jubilee Par IG8 ... 37 C4
Jubilee Pl SW3 ... 114 C1 257 B2
Jubilee Prim Sch
London SW2 ... 160 C5
Stamford Hill N16 ... 52 A1
Woolwich SE28 ... 124 C6
Jubilee Rd
Cheam SM3 ... 216 D1
Wembley UB6 ... 87 B6
Jubilee St E1 ... 96 C2
Jubilee The 2 SE10 ... 141 D5
Jubilee Villas KT10 ... 196 C1
Jubilee Way
East Bedfont TW14 ... 150 A3
Merton SW19 ... 179 D2
Sidcup DA14 ... 168 A2
Tolworth KT4, KT9 ... 214 D5
Jubilee Wks SW19 ... 180 A1
Jubilee Wlk WD19 ... 22 B6
Jubilee Yd SE1 ... 253 C2
Judd St WC1 ... 94 A4 233 A1
Jude St E16 ... 98 D1
Judge Heath La UB3 ... 83 B1
Judges' Wlk NW3 ... 70 A5
Judge Wlk KT10 ... 212 C2
Juer St SW11 ... 136 C5 267 B3
Jules Thorn Ave EN1 ... 6 A1
Julia Ct E17 ... 53 D4
Julia Garfield Mews 4 E16 ... 121 B5
Julia Gdns IG11 ... 102 D5
Juliana Cl N2 ... 48 A6
Julian Ave W3 ... 110 D6
Julian Cl EN5 ... 1 D2
Julian Ct SW13 ... 133 D4
Julian Hill HA1 ... 64 C6
Julian Ho SE21 ... 183 C6
Julian Pl E14 ... 119 D1
Julian's Prim Sch SW16 ... 182 C6
Julian Taylor Path 7 SE23 ... 162 B2
Julia St NW5 ... 71 A3
Julien Rd W5 ... 109 C3
Juliet Ho 11 N1 ... 95 C5
Juliette Rd E13 ... 99 A5
Julius Caesar Way HA7 ... 9 D1
Julius Ct TW8 ... 132 A5
Julius Ho 8 E14 ... 98 B1
Julius Nyerere Cl N1 ... 233 C5
Junction App
Battersea SW11 ... 136 C2
Lewisham SE13 ... 142 A2
Junction Mews W2 ... 237 A2
Junction Pl W2 ... 236 D2
Junction Rd
Ashford TW15 ... 171 B5
Brentford TW8 ... 109 D2
Croydon CR2 ... 221 B3
Dartmouth Pk N19 ... 71 C5
Junction Rd E RM6 ... 59 A2
Junction Rd
Edmonton N9 ... 18 A3
Harrow HA1 ... 42 C3
Newham E13 ... 99 B5
Tottenham Hale N17 ... 52 A6
Junction Rd W RM6 ... 59 A2
Junction Wembley Ret Pk The HA9 ... 66 D4
Juniper Cl
Barnet EN5 ... 12 D6
Chessington KT9 ... 214 B3
Wembley HA9 ... 66 C3
Juniper Cres NW1 ... 71 A1
Juniper Ct
Dagenham RM6 ... 58 C3
Harrow HA3 ... 24 D2
Hounslow TW3 ... 129 D1
Stoke Newington N16 ... 73 B6
Thornton Heath CR0 ... 204 C3
Juniper Dr SW18 ... 136 A1
Juniper Gdns
Ashford TW16 ... 171 D4
Streatham CR4 ... 181 C2
Juniper Ho
12 Ealing W5 ... 87 C2
6 Peckham SE14, SE15 ... 140 C5
9 Richmond TW9 ... 132 D4
Juniper La E6 ... 100 A2
Juniper Rd IG1 ... 78 D4
Juniper St 16 E1 ... 118 C6
Juniper Way UB3 ... 105 C6
Juno Ct 11 SW9 ... 138 C5
Juno Ho 2 E3 ... 97 C6
Juno Way Ind Est SE14 ... 140 D6
Juno Way SE14 ... 140 D6
Jupiter Ct
10 Brixton SW9 ... 138 C5
8 Northolt UB5 ... 84 D4
Jupiter Hts UB10 ... 82 B6
Jupiter Way N7 ... 72 B2
Jupp Rd E15 ... 76 B1
Jupp Rd W E15 ... 98 B6
Jura Ho SE16 ... 119 A2
Jurston Ct SE1 ... 251 B1
Justice Wlk SW3 ... 267 A5
Justin Cl TW8 ... 131 D5
Justin Ct 3 CR7 ... 204 C4
Justines Pl E2 ... 96 D4
Justin Plaza CR4 ... 202 C5
Justin Rd E4 ... 35 B4
Jute La EN3 ... 7 A2
Jutland Cl N19 ... 50 A1
Jutland Ho
4 London SE5 ... 139 A3
10 Woolwich SE7 ... 122 A2
Jutland Rd
Catford SE6 ... 164 A4
Newham E13 ... 99 A3
Jutsums Ave RM7 ... 59 D3

Jutsums Ct RM7 59 D3
Jutsums La RM7 59 D2
Juxon Cl HA3 23 D2
Juxon St SE11 116 B2 260 D4
JVC Bsns Pk NW2 46 A1

K

Kaduna Cl HA5 40 B4
Kaizen Prim Sch E13 99 B3
Kale Rd DA18 125 A4
Kambala Rd SW11 136 B2
Kangley Bridge Ctr SE26 185 B5
Kangley Bridge Rd SE26 185 B5
Kaplan Dr N21 16 B6
Karachi Ho E15 76 C2
Kara Way NW2 68 D4
Karen Ct
Bromley BR1 186 D2
2 Camberwell SE5 139 C2
Forest Hill SE23 163 A5
Karen Ho 7 N16 73 B4
Karens Ct EN3 6 D6
Karen Terr Ilford IG2 57 B4
Leyton E11 76 D6
Karenza Ct HA9 43 C2
Kariba Cl N9 18 C1
Karman Ct HA3 42 C6
Karma Way HA2 41 C1
Karoline Gdns UB6 86 B5
Karyatis Ct EN1 17 D6
Kashgar Rd SE18 123 D2
Kashmir Rd SE7 143 D5
Kasmin Ct NW10 68 A1
Kassala Rd SW11 136 D4 267 D1
Katella Trad Est IG11 101 C4
Kates Cl EN5 12 A6
Katharine Rd 1 TW1 153 A3
Katharine St CR0 221 A5
Katherine Cl 3 SE16 118 D5
Katherine Ct
10 Forest Hill SE23 162 C3
Penge SE20 184 C2
Katherine Gdns SE9 143 D1
Katherine Ho
15 Kensal Town W10 91 A3
6 South Croydon CR0 221 A5
South Norwood SE19 183 C4
Katherine Rd E6, E7 77 C1
Katherine Sq W11 244 A4
Kathleen Ave
Acton W3 89 A2
Wembley HA0 66 A1
Kathleen Ferrier Ct 4 N17 33 D3
Kathleen Godfree Ct SW19 179 C5
Kathleen Moore Ct BR4 224 A6
Kathleen Rd SW11 136 D2
Katrine Ct NW2 68 C5
Kayemoor Rd SM2 218 C2
Kay Rd SW9 138 B3
Kays Ct EN3 6 D1
Kay St
Bethnal Green E2 96 A5
Welling DA16 146 B4
Keadby Ho 2 UB5 85 B4
Kean Ho 5 SE17 138 D6
Kean St WC2 94 B1 240 C1
Keates Est N16 73 D6
Keatley Gn E4 35 B4
Keats Ave E16 121 B5
Keats Cl
Bermondsey SE1 263 C3
Enfield EN3 18 D6
Hampstead NW3 70 C4
Hayes UB4 84 A2
Mitcham SW19 180 B4
Wanstead E11 55 B4
Keats Ct HA0 65 C5
Keats Gr NW3 70 C4
Keats Ho
7 Beckenham BR3 185 D4
22 Bethnal Green E2 96 C4
30 Camberwell SE5 139 A5
Chelsea SW1 269 B6
Harrow HA2 64 C6
Keats House Mus* NW3 70 C4
Keats Par 3 N9 18 A2
Keats Pl EC2 242 C3
Keats Rd DA16 145 D4
Keats Way
Croydon CR0 206 C3
Southall UB6 85 D2
West Drayton UB7 104 B2
Kebbell Terr E7 77 B3
Keble Cl
New Malden KT4 199 D1
Northolt UB5 64 A3
Keble Ct SW19 179 C4
Keble Ho 4 SW15 156 D5
Keble Pl SW13 134 B6
Keble Prep Sch N21 16 C4
Keble St SW17 180 A6
Kechill Gdns BR2 209 A2
Kedelston Ct E5 75 A4
Kedeston Ct SM1 201 D1
Kedge Ho 16 E14 119 C3
Kedleston Dr BR5 211 D4
Kedleston Wlk 21 E2 96 B4
Kedyngton Ho 5 HA8 27 A1
Keeble Cl SE18 144 D6
Keedonwood Rd BR1 186 D5
Keel Cl Barking IG11 102 C5
Rotherhithe SE16 118 D5
Keel Ct 8 E14 120 B6
Keeley Rd CR0 221 A6
Keeley St WC2 94 B1 240 C1
Keeling Ct CR0 220 D4
Keeling Ho 4 E2 96 B5
Keeling Rd SE9 165 D6
Keeling 2 TW11 174 C5
Keelson Ho 9 E14 119 C3
Keely Cl EN4 14 C6
Keemor Cl SE18 144 C5
Keens Cl SW16 181 D5
Keen's Rd CR0 221 A4
Keen's Yd N1 72 D2
Keepers Ct 4 CR2 221 A3
Keepers Mews TW11 175 C4
Keeper Wharf E1 118 D6
Keepier Wharf 15 E1 118 D6
Keep The
Forest Hill SE6 163 C3
Kidbrooke SE3 143 A3
Kingston u T KT2 176 B3
Keeton's Rd SE16 118 B3
Keevil Dr SW19 157 A4
Keighley Cl N7 72 A4
Keightley Dr SE9 167 A3
Keilder Cl UB10 82 C5
Keildon Rd SW11 136 D1
Keir Hardie Est E5 52 B1
Keir Hardie Ho
6 Belvedere DA17 125 C3
Fulham W6 134 D6
15 Upper Holloway N19 49 D2
Willesden NW10 67 D1
Keir Hardie Way
Barking IG11 80 A1
Hayes UB4 84 A4
Keir Hardy Prim Sch E16 99 A2
Keir The SW19 178 C5
Keith Connor Cl 5 SW8 137 B2
Keith Gr W12 112 A5
Keith Ho NW6 91 D5
Keith Park Rd UB10 60 B1
Keith Rd
Barking IG11 101 B5
Hayes UB3 105 C3
Walthamstow E17 35 B2
Keith Sutton Ho 3 SE9 167 A2
Kelbrook Rd SE3 144 A2
Kelby Ho N7 72 B2
Kelceda Cl NW2 68 A6
Kelf Gr UB3 83 D1
Kelfield Ct 1 W10 90 D1
Kelfield Gdns W10 90 D1
Kelfield Mews W10 90 D1
Kelham Ho 10 SE18 144 D6
Kelland Cl 1 N8 49 D4
Kelland Rd E13 99 A3
Kellaway Rd SE3 143 D3
Keller Cres E12 77 D4
Kellerton Rd SE13 164 C6
Kellett Ho N1 235 D5
Kellett Rd SW2 138 C1
Kelling Gdns CR0 204 D2
Kellino St SW17 180 D6
Kellner Rd SE28 123 D3
Kellow Ho SE1 252 C2
Kell St SE1 116 D3 261 D6
Kelly Ave SE15 139 D4
Kelly Cl
Upper Halliford TW17 171 C1
Willesden NW10 67 B5
Kelly Ct 18 E14 119 C6
Kelly Mews 4 W9 91 B3
Kelly Rd NW7 29 A4
Kelly St NW1 71 B2
Kelly Way RM6 59 A3
Kelman Cl SW4 137 D3
Kelmore Gr SE22 140 A1
Kelmscott Cl E17 35 B2
Kelmscott Ct 2 HA7 25 C6
Kelmscott 5 SE23 162 D1
Kelmscott Gdns W12 112 A3
Kelmscott L Ctr E17 53 B3
Kelmscott Rd SW11 158 D6
Kelmscott Sch E17 53 B3
Kelross Rd N5 73 A4
Kelsall Cl SE3 143 B3
Kelsall Mews TW9 132 D4
Kelsey Gate 8 BR3 185 D1
Kelsey La BR3 207 C6
Kelsey Park Ave BR3 185 D1
Kelsey Park Man BR3 207 D6
Kelsey Park Rd BR3 185 C1
Kelsey Park Sp Coll BR3 207 C6
Kelsey Rd BR5 190 B1
Kelsey Sq BR3 185 C1
Kelsey St E2 96 A3
Kelsey Way BR3 207 C6
Kelshall Ct N4 73 A6
Kelso Ct SE20 184 B3
Kelso Lo E18 37 B1
Kelson Ho E14 120 A3
Kelso Pl W8 113 D3 255 D6
Kelso Rd SM5 202 A2
Kelvedon Cl KT2 176 C4
Kelvedon Ct HA4 62 C4
Kelvedon Ho SW8 270 B2
Kelvedon Rd SW6 135 B5 264 D3
Kelvin Ave N13 32 B4
Kelvinbrook KT8 195 D6
Kelvin Cl KT19 214 C2
Kelvin Cres HA3 24 C3
Kelvin Ct
Chiswick W4 133 A5
Harrow HA2 42 A1
Isleworth TW7 130 C3
Notting Hill W11 245 A5
7 Penge SE20 184 B2
8 Twickenham TW1 153 B5
Kelvin Dr TW1 153 B5
Kelvin Gdns
Southall UB1 85 C1
Thornton Heath CR0 204 A2
Kelvin Gr SE26 162 B1
Kelvin Grove Prim Sch SE26 162 B1
Kelvin Gr KT6 214 A5
Kelvington Cl CR0 207 A2
Kelvington Rd SE15 162 D6
Kelvin Ho 3 DA17 125 C3
Kelvin Par BR6 211 C1
Kelvin Rd Highbury N5 73 A4
Welling DA16 146 A2
Kelyway Ho 20 SW2 160 C4
Kember St N1 72 B1
Kemble Dr BR2 226 A5
Kemble Ho
London SW9 138 D2
Stanmore HA7 24 D5
Kemble Rd
Croydon CR0 220 D5
Forest Hill SE23 162 D3
Tottenham N17 34 A2
Kemble St WC2 94 B1 240 C1
Kemerton Rd
Beckenham BR3 185 D1
Camberwell SE5 139 A2
Croydon CR0 205 D2
Kemey's St E9 75 A3
Kemnal Rd BR7 189 B5
Kemnal Tech Coll DA14 190 B3
Kemnal Warren BR7 189 B4
Kemp Ct SW8 270 A3
Kempe Ho SE1 262 D5
Kempe Rd NW6 90 D5
Kemp Gdns CR0 205 A3
Kemp Ho
Finsbury EC1 235 C1
1 Globe Town E2 96 D5
Wallend E6 78 C2
Kempis Way 5 SE22 161 C6
Kemplay Rd NW3 70 B4
Kemp 24 NW9 27 D2
Kemp Rd RM8 58 D1
Kemps Ct NW2 68 D5
Kemp's Ct W1 239 C1
Kemps Dr E14 119 C6
Kempsford Gdns SW5 113 C1 255 B1
Kempsford Rd
Lambeth SE11 261 B3
Newington SE11 261 C3
Kemps Gdns SE13 164 A6
Kempshott Rd SW16 182 A3
Kempson Rd SW6 135 C5 265 B3
Kempthorne Rd SE8 119 B2
Kempton Ave
Northolt UB5 63 C3
Sunbury TW16 172 B2
Kempton Cl UB10 61 A4
Kempton Ct
Stepney E1 96 B2
Sunbury TW16 172 B2
Kempton Ho 13 N1 95 C6
Kempton Lo 3 SM6 219 D5
Kempton Park Race Course TW16 172 C3
Kempton Park Sta TW16 172 B3
Kempton Rd E6 100 B6
Kempton Wlk CR0 207 A3
Kempt St SE18 144 C6
Kemsing Cl
Coney Hall BR2 224 D6
Sidcup DA5 169 A4
South Norwood CR7 205 A5
Kemsing Ho SE1 252 D1
Kemsing Rd SE10 121 A1
Kemsley Ct
Ealing W13 109 C5
St Paul's Cray BR5 190 B2
Kemsley SE13 163 D6
Kenbrook Ho
Kensington W14 254 D5
5 Kentish Town NW5 71 C3
Kenbury Cl UB10 60 C5
Kenbury Gdns 10 SE5 139 A3
Kenbury Mans 18 SE5 139 A3
Kenbury St SE5 139 A3
Kenchester Cl SW8 138 A5 270 B3
Kencot Cl DA18 125 B4
Kendal Ave Acton W3 88 D2
Barking IG11 101 C6
Edmonton N18 33 B6
Kendal Cl
Camberwell SE5 138 D5
East Bedfont TW14 149 D3
Hayes UB4 83 C5
Woodford IG8 20 D2
Kendal Ct Acton W3 88 C2
Brondesbury NW2 69 A3
11 Chingford E4 20 A3
Kendale Rd BR1 186 C5
Kendal Gdns
Edmonton N18 33 B6
Sutton SM1 218 A6
Kendal Ho
Edgware HA8 27 A6
Forest Hill SE23 163 B3
32 Hackney E9 74 C1
Islington N1 233 D4
Penge SE20 184 B1
Kendall Ave BR3 185 A1
Kendall Ct
3 London SE22 162 A6
Mitcham SW19 180 B4
5 Penge SE19 183 D3
Sidcup DA15 168 A1
Kendall Ho SE12 164 D4
Kendall Lo 5 BR1 187 B2
Kendall Pl W1 238 A3
Kendall Rd
Beckenham BR3 185 A1
Isleworth TW7 131 A3
Kidbrooke SE18 144 A4
Kendalmere Cl N10 31 B2
Kendal NW1 231 D2
Kendal Par N18 33 B6
Kendal Pl SW15 157 B6
Kendal Rd NW10 68 A4
Kendal Stps W2 237 B1
Kendal St W2 92 C1 237 B1
Kender Prim Sch SE14 140 C4
Kender St SE14 140 C4
Kendoa Rd 1 SW4 137 D1
Kendon Cl E11 55 B4
Kendon Ho E15 76 B1
Kendra Ct CR2 220 D1
Kendra Hall Rd CR2 220 D1
Kendrey Gdns TW2 152 C4
Kendrick Ct 12 SE15 140 B4
Kendrick Mews SW7 256 C3
Kendrick Pl SW7 256 C3
Kenelm Cl HA1 65 A5
Kenerne Dr EN5 13 A6
Kenilford Rd SW12 159 B4
Kenilworth Ave
Harrow HA2 63 B4
Walthamstow E17 53 C6
Wimbledon SW19 179 C6
Kenilworth Cres EN1 5 C4
Kenilworth Ct
7 Chingford E4 20 A2
Fulham SW6 135 A2
Twickenham TW2 152 C2
Kenilworth Gdns
Hayes UB4 83 D2
Ilford IG3 79 D6
Southall UB1 85 B4
South Oxhey WD19 22 C5
Woolwich SE18 144 D3
Kenilworth Ho HA7 25 B3
Kenilworth Rd
Ashford TW15, TW19 148 A1
Bow E3 97 A5
Ealing W5 110 A5
Edgware HA8 11 A1
Kilburn NW6 91 B6
Orpington BR5 211 A3
Penge SE20 184 D2
Stoneleigh KT17 216 A3
Kenilworth Terr 3 SM2 217 C1
Kenley Ave NW9 27 C2
Kenley Cl Barnet EN4 2 C1
Sidcup DA5 169 C4
St Paul's Cray BR7 211 C6
Kenley Gdns CR7 204 D5
Kenley Ho
5 Croydon CR0 206 A1
6 St Paul's Cray BR5 190 B1
Kenley Rd
Kingston u T KT1, KT3 176 D1
Merton SW19 201 C6
Twickenham TW1 153 B5
Kenley N17 33 B1
Kenley Wlk
Cheam SM3 216 D4
Notting Hill W11 244 A5
Kenlor Ct 6 HA8 26 D5
Kenlor Rd SW17 180 B5
Kenmare Ct 5 HA7 25 C6
Kenmare Dr
Mitcham CR4 180 D3
1 Tottenham N17 33 D1
Kenmare Gdns N13 33 A6
Kenmare Rd CR7 204 C3
Kenmere Gdns HA0 88 C6
Kenmere Rd DA16 146 C3
Kenmont Gdns NW10 90 B4
Kenmont Prim Sch NW10 90 B4
Kenmore Ave HA3 43 A6
Kenmore Cl TW9 132 C5
Kenmore Cres UB4 83 D4
Kenmore Ct NW6 69 C1
Kenmore Gdns HA8 26 D1
Kenmore Park Fst & Mid Schs HA3 44 A6
Kenmore Rd HA3 43 D5
Kenmure Mans W5 87 C3
Kenmure Rd E8 74 B3
Kenmure Yd E8 74 B3
Kennacraig Cl 6 E16 121 A5
Kennard Ho 12 SW11 137 A3
Kennard Mans 6 N11 30 D5
Kennard Rd
London N11 30 D5
Stratford E15 76 B1
Kennard St
9 London SW11 137 A3
Newham E16 122 B5
Kennedy Ave EN3 18 C5
Kennedy Cl
Crofton BR5 211 B1
1 Mitcham CR4 181 A1
Newham E13 99 A5
Pinner HA5 23 B4
Kennedy Cox Ho 9 E16 98 D2
Kennedy Ct
Ashford TW15 171 A5
Bushey WD23 8 B2
Kennedy Ho SE11 260 C2
Kennedy Path W7 86 D3
Kennedy Rd
Barking IG11 101 C6
Ealing W7 86 C2
Kennedy Wlk SE17 262 D3
Kennet Cl SW11 136 B1
Kennet Ct 47 W2 91 C2
Kennet Dr UB4 85 A2
Kenneth Ave IG1 78 D
Kenneth Campbell Ho NW8 236 D
Kenneth Cres NW2 68 B
Kenneth Ct SE11 261 B
Kenneth Gdns HA7 25 A
Kenneth More Rd 4 IG1 78 D
Kennet Ho NW8 236 D
Kenneth Rd RM6 59 A
Kenneth Robbins Ho 1 N17 34 B
Kenneth Younger Ho SW6 264 D
Kennet Rd
Isleworth TW7 130 D
West Kilburn W9 91 B
Kennet Sq CR4 180 C
Kennet St E1 118 A
Kennett Ho HA1 64 D
Kennett Wharf La EC4 252 B
Kenninghall N18 34 C
Kenninghall Rd
London N18 34 C
Lower Clapton E5 74 B
Kenning Ho 6 N1 95 C
Kenning St 18 SE16 118 C
Kennings Way SE11 116 C1 261 B
KENNINGTON 116 C
Kennington Ent Ctr SE17 261 C
Kennington La SE11 116 B1 260 D
Kennington Oval SE11 138 B6 270 D
Kennington Palace Ct SE11 261 A
Kennington Park Gdns SE17 138 D
Kennington Park Ho SE11 261 B
Kennington Park Pl SE11 138 D
Kennington Park Rd SE11 116 D1 261 C
Kennington Rd SE11 116 C2 261 A
Kennington Sta SE17 116 D1 261 C
Kennoldes SE21 161 B
Kennyland Ct NW4 46 B
Kenny Rd NW7 29 A
Kenrick Pl W1 238 A
KENSAL GREEN 90 C
Kensal Green Cemy (All Souls)* NW10 90 C
Kensal Green Sta NW10 90 C
Kensal Ho W10 90 D
Kensal Rd W10 91 A
KENSAL RISE 90 D
Kensal Rise Prim Sch NW6 90 D
Kensal Rise Sta NW10 90 D
KENSAL TOWN 91 A
KENSINGTON 113 C
Kensington Avenue Prim Sch CR7 182 C
Kensington Ave
Plashet E12 78 B
South Norwood CR7 182 C
Kensington & Chelsea Coll
Chelsea SW10 136 A5 266 A
Kensal Town W10 91 A
Kensington Church Ct W8 245 C
Kensington Church St W8 113 C5 245 B
Kensington Church Wlk W8 245 C
Kensington Cl N11 31 A
Kensington Court Mans W8 245 D
Kensington Court Mews W8 255 D
Kensington Court Pl W8 113 D3 255 D
Kensington Ct
2 Burnt Oak NW7 27 B
Enfield EN2 5 C
Kensington Ct Gdns W8 255 D
Kensington Ct
Hendon NW4 28 C
Kensington W8 113 D4 245 D
Kensington Dr IG8 37 D
Kensington Gardens* W2 114 A5 246 B
Kensington Gate W8 114 A3 256 A

Kensington Gdns
 Kingston u T KT1 197 D6
 Redbridge IG1 56 B1
Kensington Gdns Sq W2 91 D1
Kensington Gore SW7 114 B4 246 C1
Kensington Hall Gdns W14 254 C2
Kensington High St W8 113 C3 255 B6
Kensington Ho [3] NW5 71 C3
Kensington Hts
 Harrow HA1 42 D3
 Kensington W8 245 A3
Kensington Lodge UB5 85 C5
Kensington Mall W8 245 B4
Kensington Mans SW5 255 B2
Kensington Olympia Sta W14 113 A3 254 A6
Kensington Palace Gdns W8 113 D5 245 C4
Kensington Pal* W8 113 D5 245 D3
Kensington Park Gdns W11 113 B6 244 D5
Kensington Park Mews W11 91 B1
Kensington Park Rd W11 113 B6 244 D6
Kensington Pl W8 113 C5 245 A4
Kensington Prep Sch SW6 135 B4 264 D2
Kensington Prim Sch E12 78 B2
Kensington Rd
 Kensington SW7 114 A4 246 B1
 Northolt UB5 85 C5
Kensington Sports Ctr W11 244 A6
Kensington Sq W8 113 D4 245 C1
Kensington Terr CR2 221 B1
Kensington Village W14 113 B2 254 D3
Kensington W W14 254 A4
Kensit Meml Coll N3 29 A1
Kensworth Ho EC1 235 D1
Kent Ave
 Bexley DA16 167 D6
 Dagenham RM9 103 C3
 Ealing W13 87 B2
Kent Cl
 Mitcham CR4, SW16 204 A5
 Orpington BR6 227 C2
Kent Ct Acton W3 88 B1
 [3] Haggerston E2 95 D5
 Hendon NW9 27 C1
Kent Dr
 Cockfosters EN4 15 A6
 Teddington TW11 174 C5
Kentford Way UB5 85 A6
Kent Gate Way CR0 223 D3
Kent Gdns Ealing W13 87 B2
 Ruislip HA4 40 B3
Kent Ho
 Camberwell SE1 263 D1
 [13] Chiswick W4 111 C1
 Edgware HA8 26 B3
 Marylebone W1 239 A2
 Pimlico SW1 259 C1
 Richmond TW10 154 C6
Kent House La BR3 185 A5
Kent House Rd BR3 185 A4
Kent House Sta BR3 185 A2
Kent House Station App BR3 184 D2
Kentish Bldgs SE1 252 C3
Kentish Rd DA17 125 C2
KENTISH TOWN 71 C3
Kentish Town CE Prim Sch NW5 71 C3
Kentish Town Rd NW1 71 B2
Kentish Town Sta NW5 71 C3
Kentish Town West Sta NW5 71 B2
Kentish Way BR1, BR2 209 B6
Kentlea Rd SE28 123 C4
Kent Lo [9] SW19 156 D3
Kentmere Ho SE15 140 C6
Kentmere Rd SE18 123 C2
KENTON 43 C3
Kenton Ave
 Harrow HA1 42 D2
 Southall UB1 107 C6
Kenton Ave *continued*
 Sunbury TW16 173 A1
Kenton Ct
 [2] Forest Hill SE26 185 A6
 Harrow HA3 43 B3
 [3] Richmond TW10 153 D5
 West Kensington W14 254 C5
Kenton Gdns HA3 43 C4
Kenton Grove Ho HA3 44 B4
Kenton Ho
 [20] Globe Town E1 96 C3
 Highbury N5 72 C5
Kenton La
 Harrow HA3 24 D3
 Kenton HA3 43 C6
Kenton Park Ave HA3 43 D5
Kenton Park Cl HA3 43 C4
Kenton Park Cres HA3 43 D5
Kenton Park Mans HA3 43 C4
Kenton Park Par HA3 43 D4
Kenton Park Rd HA3 43 C5
Kenton Rd
 Harrow HA3 43 C4
 Homerton E9 74 D2
Kenton Sta HA3 43 B3
Kenton St WC1 240 A6
Kenton Way UB4 83 C4
Kent Pas NW1 237 C6
Kent Pk Ind Est SE15 140 B6
Kent Rd
 Dagenham RM10 81 D3
 East Molesey KT8 196 A5
 Kingston u T KT1 197 D6
 Richmond TW9 132 C5
 South Acton W4 111 A3
 Southgate N21 17 B4
 West Wickham BR4 207 D1
Kent St Haggerston E2 95 D5
 Newham E13 99 B4
Kent Terr NW1 92 C4 230 B1
Kent Twr SE20 184 B3
Kent View Gdns IG3 79 C6
Kent Way KT6 214 B6
Kentwell Cl SE4 141 A1
Kentwins N14 15 B6
Kentwode Gn SW13 134 A5
Kent Yard SW7 247 B1
Kenver Ave N12 30 B4
Kenward Rd SE9 165 D6
Kenway Rd SW5 113 D2 255 C3
Ken Way HA9 67 A5
Ken Wilson Ho [19] E2 96 A5
Kenwood Ave N14 15 D6
Kenwood Cl
 North End NW3 48 B1
 Sipson UB7 126 C6
Kenwood Ct NW9 45 A5
Kenwood Dr BR3 208 A6
Kenwood Gdns
 Ilford IG2 56 C4
 [2] Wanstead E18 55 B6
Kenwood Ho
 [15] Brixton SW9 138 D1
 Enfield EN1 17 C5
Kenwood Ho* NW3 48 C1
Kenwood Rd
 Edmonton N9 18 A3
 Highgate N6 48 D3
Kenworthy Rd E9 75 A2
Kenwrick Ho N1 233 D5
Kenwyn Dr NW2 67 D5
Kenwyn Rd
 Clapham SW4 137 D1
 Wimbledon SW20 178 C2
Kenya Rd SE7 143 D5
Kenyngton Dr TW16 172 A5
Kenyngton Manor Prim Sch TW16 172 A4
Kenyngton Pl HA3 43 C4
Kenyon Ho [31] SE5 139 A5
Kenyon St SW6 134 D4
Keogh Rd E15 76 D2
Kepler Ho [9] SE10 120 D1
Kepler Rd SW2, SW4 138 A1
Keppel Ho
 Brompton SW3 257 A3
 [5] Deptford SE8 119 B1
Keppel Rd
 Dagenham RM9 81 A4
 Newham E6 100 B6
Keppel Row SE1 252 A3
Keppel St WC1 239 D4
Kerala Ct N17 33 D2
Kerbela St [3] E2 96 A3
Kerbey St E14 97 D1
Kerem Sch N2 48 B4
Kerfield Cres SE5 139 B4
Kerfield Pl SE5 139 B4
Kerridge Ct N1 73 C2
Kerrier Ho SW10 266 B3
Kerrington Ct [7] W12 112 C4
Kerrison Pl W5 109 D5
Kerrison Rd
 Battersea SW11 136 C2
 Ealing W5 109 D5
 Mill Meads E15 98 B6
Kerrison Villas W5 109 D5
Kerry Ave HA7 25 D6
Kerry Cl Newham E16 99 B1
 Palmers Green N13 16 B2
Kerry Ct HA7 25 D6
Kerry Ho [5] E1 96 C1
Kerry N7 72 A2
Kerry Path SE8 141 B6
Kerry Rd SE8 141 B6
Kerscott Ho [30] E3 97 D4
Kersey Gdns SE9 188 A6
Kersfield Ho SW15 156 D5
Kersfield Rd SW15 156 D5
Kershaw Cl SW18 158 B5
Kershaw Ho [7] SE27 160 D1
Kershaw Rd RM10 81 C5
Kersley Mews SW11 267 C1
Kersley Rd N16 73 C5
Kersley St SW11 136 D3
Kerstin Cl UB3 105 D6
Kerswell Cl N15 51 C4
Kerwick Cl [1] N7 72 B1
Keslake Mans NW10 90 D5
Keslake Rd NW6 90 D5
Kessock Cl N17 52 B4
Kestlake Rd DA5 168 C5
KESTON 225 D4
Keston Ave BR2 225 C3
Keston CE Prim Sch BR2 225 D3
Keston Cl
 Bexley DA16 146 C5
 Edmonton N18 17 B1
Keston Ct DA5 169 B4
Keston Gdns BR2 225 C4
Keston Ho SE17 263 B2
KESTON MARK 225 D6
Keston Mark BR2 226 A5
Keston Park Cl BR2 226 B5
Keston Rd
 East Dulwich SE15 140 A2
 Thornton Heath CR7 204 C3
 West Green N17 51 B5
Kestrel Ave
 East Ham E6 100 A2
 Herne Hill SE24 161 A6
Kestrel Cl
 Grahame Pk NW9 27 C1
 Kingston u T KT2 175 D6
 Neasden NW10 67 B3
Kestrel Ct
 Higham Hill E17 34 D1
 Ruislip HA4 61 B6
 South Croydon CR2 221 A2
 Wallington SM6 219 C3
Kestrel Ho
 [4] Battersea SW11 136 C2
 Enfield EN3 19 A6
 Finsbury EC1 235 A2
Kestrel Pl SE14 141 A6
Kestrel Way UB3 105 B4
Keswick Apartments [4] N17 51 D6
Keswick Ave
 Kingston u T KT2, SW15 177 C5
 Merton SW19 179 C1
 Upper Halliford TW17 193 C6
Keswick Broadway [1] SW15 157 B6
Keswick Cl SM1 218 A4
Keswick Ct
 [13] Catford SE6 164 D3
 [2] East Dulwich SE22 162 A6
Keswick Dr EN3 6 C6
Keswick Gdns
 Redbridge IG4 56 A5
 Ruislip HA4 39 B3
 Wembley HA9 66 A4
Keswick Ho [8] SE5 139 A4
Keswick Hts [9] SW15 157 A6
Keswick Lo E8 73 D2
Keswick Mews W5 110 A5
Keswick Rd
 Bexleyheath DA7 147 C4
 Broom Hill BR6 211 D1
 Putney SW15 157 A6
 Twickenham TW2 152 A5
 West Wickham BR4 224 C6
Kettering Ct CR7 205 A5
Kettering Rd EN3 6 D6
Kettering St SW16 181 C4
Kett Gdns SW2 160 B6
Kettlebaston Rd E10 53 B1
Kettleby Ho SW9 138 D2
Kettlewell Cl N11 31 A4
Ketton Ho [11] W10 90 C3
Kevan Ct [6] E17 53 D5
Kevan Ho SE5 139 A5
Kevelioc Rd N17 33 A2
Kevin Cl TW4 128 D3
Kevington Cl BR5 211 D5
Kevington Dr BR5, BR7 211 D5
KEW 132 C6
Kew Bridge TW8 110 B1
Kew Bridge Ct [8] W4 110 C1
Kew Bridge Distribution Ctr TW8 110 B1
Kew Bridge Rd TW8 110 B1
Kew Bridge Sta TW8 110 B1
Kew Bridge Steam Mus* TW8 110 B1
Kew Coll TW9 132 C5
Kew Cres SM3 217 B5
Kew Ct KT2 176 A2
Kew Foot Rd TW9 132 A2
Kew Gardens Rd TW9 132 C4
Kew Gardens (Royal Botanic)* TW9 132 A4
Kew Gardens Sta TW9 132 C4
Kew Gn TW9 132 B6
Kew Green Prep Sch TW9 132 B6
Kew Green TW9 132 C6
Kew Lo [11] TW9 132 B4
Kew Montessori Sch TW9 132 C4
Kew Obsy* TW9 131 C2
Kew Pal* TW9 132 A5
Kew Pier TW9 132 C6
Kew Rd Finchley N2 30 C2
 Richmond TW9, W4 132 B4
Kew Ret Pk TW9 132 D4
Kew Riverside Prim Sch TW9 132 D3
Key Cl E1 96 B3
Keyes Ct SE22 162 A6
Keyes Rd NW2 68 D3
Keyham Ho [31] W2 91 C2
Key Ho [9] SE11 138 C6
Keymer Rd SW2 160 B2
Keynes Cl N2 48 D6
Keynes Ct [9] SE28 124 B6
Keynsham Ave IG8 36 C6
Keynsham Gdns SE9 166 A6
Keynsham Ho [2] N4 51 A2
Keynsham Rd
 Cheam SM4 201 D1
 Eltham SE9 166 A6
Keynsham Wlk SM4 201 D1
Keyse Rd SE1 117 D3 263 C5
Keysham Ave TW5 128 A4
Keysham Ct HA9 66 A6
Keystone Cres N1 233 B3
Keywood Dr TW16 172 A4
Keyworth Cl E5 75 A4
Keyworth Pl SE1 261 D6
Keyworth Prim Sch SE17 116 D1 261 C2
Keyworth St SE1 116 D3 261 D6
Kezia St SE8 119 A1
Khalsa Ct N22 32 D2
Khama Rd SW17 180 C6
Khartoum Rd
 Ilford IG1 78 D3
 Newham E13 99 B4
 Upper Tooting SW17 180 B6
Khyber Rd SW11 136 C3
Kibworth St SW8 138 B5 270 C3
KIDBROOKE 143 C3
Kidbrooke Gdns SE3 143 A4
Kidbrooke Gr SE3 143 B4
Kidbrooke Interchange SE3 143 C2
Kidbrooke La SE9 144 A1
Kidbrooke Park Cl SE3 143 B4
Kidbrooke Park Prim Sch SE3 143 C4
Kidbrooke Park Rd SE12, SE3 143 B2
Kidbrooke Sch SE3 143 D3
Kidbrooke Sta SE3 143 B2
Kidbrooke Way SE3 143 B3
Kiddens BR8 191 D1
Kidderminster Pl CR0 204 D1
Kidderminster Rd CR0 205 A2
Kidderpore Ave NW3 69 C4
Kidderpore Gdns NW3 69 C4
Kidd Ho RM9 81 B4
Kidd Pl SE7 122 A1
Kidlington Way NW9 27 C2
Kierbeck Bsns Complex E16 121 B4
Kiffen St EC2 242 D6
Kilberry Cl TW7 130 B4
Kilbrennan Ho [9] E14 98 A1
KILBURN 91 C6
Kilburn Bridge [14] NW6 91 C6
Kilburn Gate NW6 91 D5
Kilburn High Rd NW6 91 C6
Kilburn High Road Sta NW6 91 D6
Kilburn Ho [11] W9 91 B4
Kilburn La W10 91 A5
Kilburn Park Foundation Sch The NW6 91 B5
Kilburn Park Rd NW6 91 C4
Kilburn Park Sta NW6 91 C5
Kilburn Pl NW6 91 C6
Kilburn Priory NW6 91 D6
Kilburn Sq NW6 91 C6
Kilburn Sta NW2 69 B2
Kilburn Vale Est [13] NW6 91 C6
Kilburn Vale NW6 91 D6
Kilby Ct SE10 120 D3
Kildare Cl HA4 40 C1
Kildare Ct W2 91 C1
Kildare Gdns W2 91 C1
Kildare Rd E16 99 A2
Kildare Terr W2 91 C1
Kildare Wlk E14 97 C1
Kildoran Rd SW2 160 A6
Kildowan Rd IG3 58 A1
Kilgour Rd SE23 163 A5
Kilkie St SW6 136 A3
Killarney Rd SW18 158 A5
Killburns Mill Cl SM6 219 B6
Killearn Rd SE6 164 B3
Killester Gdns KT17, KT4 216 B4
Killick Ho SM1 217 D4
Killick St N1 94 B5 233 C3
Killieser Ave SW2 160 A2
Killigrew Ho TW16 171 C3
Killip Cl E16 98 D1
Killoran Ho [9] E14 120 A3
Killowen Ave UB5 64 A3
Killowen Rd E9 74 D2
Killyon Rd SW8 137 C3
Kilmaine Rd SW6 135 A5 264 B3
Kilmarnock Gdns RM8 80 C5
Kilmarnock Rd WD19 22 D6
Kilmarsh Rd W6 112 C2
Kilmartin Ave SW16 204 C6
Kilmartin Rd IG3 80 A6
Kilmington Rd SW13 134 A6
Kilmiston Ave TW17 193 A3
Kilmiston Ho TW17 193 A3
Kilmore Ho [17] E14 97 D1
Kilmorey Gdns TW1 131 B1
Kilmorey Rd TW1 131 B1
Kilmorie Prim Sch SE23 163 A2
Kilmorie Rd SE23 163 A2
Kilmuir Ho SW1 258 B3
Kiln Cl UB3 127 B6
Kiln Ct E14 119 B6
Kilner Ho [3] SE11 138 C6
Kilner St E14 97 C2
Kiln Mews SW17 180 B5
Kiln Pl NW5 71 A3
Kilnsey Ct [8] N11 31 A4
Kilnside KT10 213 A1
Kiloh Ct [1] SW11 136 C2
Kilpatrick Ct N16 51 D1
Kilpatrick Way UB4 85 A2
Kilpeck Ho [3] N4 51 A2
Kilravock Ho SE25 205 C6
Kilravock St W10 91 A4
Kilronan [5] W3 89 B1
Kilross Rd TW14 149 C3
Kilsby Wlk RM9 80 B2
Kilsha Rd KT12 194 C3
Kilvinton Dr EN2 5 B5
Kimbell Gdns SW6 135 A4 264 A1
Kimbell Pl SE9 143 C1
Kimber Ctr The SW18 157 C4
Kimber Ho [11] SE18 144 D6
Kimberley Ave
 Ilford IG2 57 C2
 Newham E6 100 A5
 Nunhead SE15 140 C2
Kimberley Ct
 Belvedere DA17 125 B2
 Kilburn NW6 91 A6
Kimberley Dr DA14 168 D2
Kimberley Gate [3] BR1 186 D3
Kimberley Gdns
 Enfield EN1 5 D2
 Harringay N4 50 D4
Kimberley Ho [7] E14 120 A3
Kimberley Ind Est E17 35 B2
Kimberley Rd
 Chingford E4 20 C3
 Edmonton N18 34 B4
 Kilburn NW6 91 A6
 Leyton E11 76 B6
 Newham E16 98 D3
 Penge BR3 184 D1
 Stockwell SW9 138 A2
 Thornton Heath CR0 204 D3
 Tottenham N17 34 A1
 Walthamstow E17 35 B2
Kimberley Way E4 20 C3
Kimberley Wlk KT12 194 B2
Kimber Rd SW18 157 D4
Kimble Cres WD23 8 A4
Kimble Ho
 Lisson Gr NW8 237 B6
 [1] Lower Holloway N7 72 A3
Kimble Rd SW17 180 B4
Kimbolton Cl SE12 164 D5
Kimbolton Row SW3 257 A3
Kimmeridge Gdns [3] SE9 188 A6
Kimmeridge Rd SE9 188 A6
Kimm Ho [16] E17 53 D6
Kimpton Ct [12] SE5 139 B4
Kimpton Ho SW15 156 A4
Kimpton Link Bsns Ctr SM3 217 B6
Kimpton Park Way SM3 217 B6
Kimpton Rd
 Camberwell SE5 139 B4
 Cheam SM3 217 B6
Kimpton Trade & Bsns Ctr SM3 217 B6
Kinburn St SE16 118 D4
Kincaid Rd SE15 140 B5
Kincardine Gdns W9 91 C3
Kinch Gr HA3, HA9 44 B2
Kincraig BR7 188 C2
Kindell Ho [4] SW14 133 B2
Kinder Cl SE28 124 D6
Kinder Ho N1 235 D4
Kindersley Ho [38] E1 96 A1
Kinder St [19] E1 96 B1
Kinderton Cl N14 15 C3
Kinefold Ho N7 72 A2
Kinfauns Rd
 Ilford IG3 58 B1
 Streatham SW2 160 C2
King Alfred Ave
 Catford SE6 163 C1
 Catford SE6 185 C6
King Alfred Sch NW11 47 D1
King Arthur Cl SE15 140 C5
King Athelstan Prim Sch KT1 198 B6
King Charles Cres KT5 198 B2
King Charles Ct [16] SE17 138 D6
King Charles Ho SW6 265 D4
King Charles' Rd KT5, KT6 198 B3
King Charles St SW1 116 A4 250 A2
King Charles Terr [11] E1 118 B6
King Charles Wlk [6] SW19 157 A3
King Ct [16] E10 53 D2
Kingcup Cl CR0 206 D1
King David La E1 118 C6
Kingdon Ho [8] E14 120 A3

Kingdon Rd NW6 ... 69 C2
Kingdown Cl W10 ... 90 D1
King Edward Dr KT6 ... 214 A5
King Edward Mans 12 E8 ... 96 B6
King Edward Mews SW13 ... 134 A4
King Edward Rd
Barnet EN5 ... 1 D1
Leytonstone E10 ... 54 A1
Walthamstow E17 ... 53 A6
King Edward's Gdns W3 ... 110 C5
King Edward's Gr TW11 ... 175 C4
King Edwards Mans SW6 ... 265 A3
King Edward's Rd
Barking IG11 ... 101 B5
Edmonton N9 ... 18 B4
Enfield EN3 ... 6 D1
Ruislip HA4 ... 39 B1
South Hackney E9 ... 96 C6
King Edward St EC1 ... 242 A2
King Edward The Third Mews 11 SE16 ... 118 B4
King Edward VII Hospl-Sister Agnes W1 ... 93 A2 238 B4
King Edward Wlk SE1 ... 116 C3 261 B6
King Fahad Acad The W5 ... 109 C2
King Fahed Acad W3 ... 111 D6
Kingfield Rd W5 ... 87 D3
Kingfield St E14 ... 120 A2
Kingfisher Ave E11 ... 55 B3
Kingfisher Cl
Harrow HA3 ... 24 D3
Woolwich SE28 ... 124 C6
Kingfisher Ct
11 Battersea SW11 ... 136 C2
Cheam SM1 ... 217 B3
17 Cubitt Town E14 ... 120 A4
East Molesey KT8 ... 196 C5
Enfield EN2 ... 4 B5
Hounslow TW3 ... 151 D6
Merton SW19 ... 179 B3
Putney SW19 ... 157 A2
Spring Gr TW3 ... 130 B3
Kingfisher Dr TW10 ... 175 B6
Kingfisher Ho
16 Battersea SW18 ... 136 A2
Peckham SE15 ... 139 D4
West Kensington W14 ... 254 C6
Kingfisher Lo TW11 ... 175 A6
Kingfisher Mews SE13 ... 163 D6
Kingfisher Sq 19 SE8 ... 141 B6
Kingfisher St E6 ... 100 A2
Kingfisher Way
Croydon CR0 ... 206 D4
Neasden NW10 ... 67 B3
Kingfisher Wlk NW9 ... 27 C1
King Frederick IX Twr SE16 ... 119 B3
King Garth Mews SE23 ... 162 C2
King Gdns CR0 ... 220 D3
King George Ave
Ilford IG2 ... 57 B3
Newham E16 ... 99 D1
Walton-on-T KT12 ... 194 D1
King George Cl TW16 ... 171 C5
King George Hospl IG3 ... 58 A4
King George Sq TW10 ... 154 B5
King George's Trad Est KT9 ... 214 C4
King George St SE10 ... 142 A5
King George VI Ave CR4 ... 202 D5
King George V Sta E16 ... 122 C5
Kingham Cl
3 Shepherd's Bush W11 ... 112 D4
Wandsworth SW18 ... 158 A4
Kingham Ind Est NW10 ... 89 B4
King Harolds Way DA7 ... 147 A5
King Henry Mews
Harrow HA2 ... 42 C1
7 Orpington BR6 ... 227 D3
King Henry's Mews EN3 ... 7 C6
King Henry's Rd
Kingston u T KT1, KT3 ... 198 D6
Primrose Hill NW3 ... 70 C1
King Henry's Reach W6 ... 134 C6
King Henry St N16 ... 73 C3
King Henry's Wlk N1 ... 73 C2
King Henry's Yd 5 N16 ... 73 C3
King Henry Terr 10 E1 ... 118 B6
King Ho 5 W12 ... 90 B1
Kinghorn St EC1 ... 242 A3
King James St SE1 ... 116 D4 251 D1
King John Ct EC2 ... 243 B6
King John St E1 ... 96 D2
King John's Wlk SE9 ... 166 A5
Kinglake St SE17 ... 117 C1 263 B2
Kinglet Cl E7 ... 77 A2
Kingly Ct W1 ... 249 B6
Kingly St W1 ... 115 C6 249 A6
King & Queen Cl 4 SE9 ... 188 A6
King & Queen St SE17 ... 117 A1 262 B2
Kingsand Rd SE12 ... 165 A2
Kings Arbour UB2 ... 107 A1
King's Arms Ct E1 ... 96 A2
King's Arms Yd EC2 ... 242 C2
Kingsash Dr UB4 ... 85 A3
King's Ave TW16 ... 171 D4
Kings Ave BR1 ... 186 D4
King's Ave IG9 ... 21 D2
Kings Ave
Clapham Pk SW4 ... 160 A5
Dagenham RM6 ... 59 B3
Ealing W5 ... 87 D1
King's Ave TW3, TW5 ... 129 D4
Kings Ave
Muswell Hill N10 ... 49 A6
New Malden KT3 ... 199 D5
Kings Avenue Sch SW4 ... 160 A6
King's Ave
Southall UB1 ... 85 D1
Southgate N21 ... 16 D3
Kings Ave SM5 ... 218 D1
King's Ave IG8 ... 37 C5
King's Bench St SE1 ... 116 D4 251 D2
King's Bench Wlk EC4 ... 241 B1
Kingsbridge Ave W3 ... 110 B4
Kingsbridge Cres UB1 ... 85 B2
Kingsbridge Ct
Edmonton N21 ... 16 D2
Millwall E14 ... 119 C2
Kingsbridge Dr NW7 ... 28 D3
Kingsbridge Ho 10 SE20 ... 184 B2
Kingsbridge Ind Est IG11 ... 101 C4
Kingsbridge N16 ... 51 B1
Kingsbridge Rd
Barking IG11 ... 101 B5
North Kensington W10 ... 90 C1
Southall UB2 ... 107 B2
Walton-on-T KT12 ... 194 B2
West Barnes SM4 ... 200 D2
Kingsbridge Way UB4 ... 83 C4
KINGSBURY ... 45 B3
Kingsbury Green Prim Sch NW9 ... 44 D4
Kingsbury High Sch (Lower Sch) NW9 ... 45 A5
Kingsbury High Sch (Upper Sch) NW9 ... 44 D5
Kingsbury Hospl NW9 ... 44 C5
Kingsbury Rd
Kingsbury NW9 ... 44 D4
Kingsland N1 ... 73 C2
Kingsbury Sta NW9 ... 44 C4
Kingsbury Terr N1 ... 73 C2
Kingsbury Trad Est NW9 ... 45 B3
Kings Chase KT8 ... 196 A6
Kings Chase View EN2 ... 4 C3
Kingsclere Cl SW15 ... 156 A4
Kingsclere Ct
Colney Hatch N12 ... 30 C5
New Barnet EN5 ... 14 A6
Kingsclere Pl EN2 ... 5 A3
Kings Cl NW4 ... 46 D5
Kingscliffe Gdns SW19 ... 157 B3
King's Cl
Thames Ditton KT7 ... 197 A2
Walthamstow E10 ... 53 D2
Kings Cl KT12 ... 194 B1
King's Coll SE24 ... 161 B5
Kings College Ct NW3 ... 70 C1
King's College Hospl SE5 ... 139 B3
Kings College Rd
Primrose Hill NW3 ... 70 B1
Ruislip HA4 ... 39 D3
King's Coll London (Hampstead) NW3 ... 69 C4
King's Coll Sch SW19 ... 178 D4
King's Coll WC2 ... 116 B6 250 D6
King's Coll Univ SE1 ... 116 C5 251 A3
Kingscote NW11 ... 47 B1
Kingscote Rd
Bedford Pk W4 ... 111 B3
Croydon CR0 ... 206 B2
Kingston u T KT3 ... 199 B6
Kingscote St EC4 ... 251 C6
Kings Court Mews KT8 ... 196 B4
King's Court N SW3 ... 257 A1
Kingscourt Rd SW16 ... 160 A1
King's Court S SW3 ... 257 A1
King's Cres N4, N5 ... 73 A5
Kingscroft SW4 ... 160 A5
Kingscroft Rd NW2 ... 69 B2
KING'S CROSS ... 94 A5
King's Cross Bridge WC1 ... 233 B2
King's Cross Rd WC1 ... 94 B4 233 D1
King's Cross, St Pancras N1 ... 94 A4 233 A2
King's Cross Sta N1 ... 94 A5 233 B3
King's Cross (Thames Link) Sta WC1 ... 94 A4 233 B2
King's Cross WC1 ... 94 A4 233 B2
Kings Ct 6 N7 ... 72 B1
King's Ct BR3 ... 207 D6
Kings Ct
2 Buckhurst Hill IG9 ... 21 D2
Chiswick W6 ... 112 A2
King's Ct 9 W5 ... 87 C2
Kings Ct
East Dulwich SE22 ... 140 A1
18 Kingston u T KT2 ... 176 C3
Newham E13 ... 99 B6
Primrose Hill NW8 ... 230 C5
10 Putney SW15 ... 156 A4
3 Wallington SM6 ... 219 B2
Wembley Pk HA9 ... 66 D6
King's Ct SW19 ... 179 C4
Kingsdale Ct EN4 ... 2 D3
Kingsdale Gdns W11 ... 112 D5
Kingsdale Rd
Penge SE20 ... 184 D3
Plumstead Comm SE18 ... 145 D6
Kingsdale Sec Sch SE21 ... 161 C1
Kingsdown Ave
East Acton W3 ... 111 C6
West Ealing W13 ... 109 B4
Kingsdown Cl
26 Deptford SE16 ... 118 B1
8 Notting Hill W11 ... 91 A1
Kingsdown Ct SW11 ... 158 C5
Kingsdowne Rd KT6 ... 198 B2
Kingsdown Ho 1 E8 ... 74 A3
Kingsdown Rd
Cheam SM3 ... 217 A3
Leyton E11 ... 76 C5
4 Upper Holloway N19 ... 72 A6
Kingsdown Way BR2 ... 209 A3
Kingsdown SW19 ... 178 D3
Kings Dr Edgware HA8 ... 26 B6
Surbiton KT5 ... 198 C3
King's Dr KT7 ... 197 B2
Kings Dr HA9 ... 66 D6
Kingsend Ct HA4 ... 39 C1
Kingsend HA4 ... 39 C1
Kings Farm Ave TW10 ... 132 C1
Kings Farm E17 ... 35 D2
Kingsfield Ave HA1, HA2 ... 42 A4
Kingsfield Ct HA1 ... 42 B2
Kingsfield Ho
Mottingham SE9 ... 165 D1
7 Muswell Hill N10 ... 31 A3
18 Stoke Newington N16 ... 73 C5
Kingsfield Rd HA1 ... 42 B2
Kingsford Com Sch E6 ... 100 B1
Kingsford St NW5 ... 70 D3
Kingsford Way E6 ... 100 B2
Kingsgate Ave N3 ... 47 C6
Kingsgate Bsns Ctr KT2 ... 176 A2
Kingsgate Cl
Erith DA7 ... 147 A4
Sidcup BR5 ... 190 C1
Kingsgate Est N1 ... 73 C2
Kingsgate Ho 29 SW9 ... 138 C4
Kingsgate Par SW1 ... 259 B5
Kingsgate Pl NW6 ... 69 C1
Kingsgate Prim Sch NW6 ... 69 C1
Kingsgate Rd
Hampstead NW6 ... 69 C1
Kingston u T KT2 ... 176 A2
Kingsgate HA9 ... 67 A5
Kings Gdns IG1 ... 57 B1
King's Gdns 6 NW6 ... 69 C1
Kings Grange HA4 ... 39 D1
Kingsground SE9 ... 166 A5
King's Gr
Peckham SE15 ... 140 B4
Peckham SE15 ... 140 B5
Kingshall Mews SE13 ... 142 A2
Kings Hall Rd BR3 ... 185 A2
Kings Head Hill E4 ... 19 D4
King's Head Yd SE1 ... 252 C3
King's Highway SE18 ... 145 D6
Kingshill Ave
Harrow HA3 ... 43 B5
Hayes UB4 ... 83 D4
New Malden KT4 ... 200 B2
Northolt UB5 ... 84 B4
Kingshill Cl UB4, UB5 ... 84 A4
Kingshill Ct 8 EN5 ... 1 A1
Kingshill Dr HA3 ... 43 B6
Kingshill SE17 ... 262 B4
Kingshold Rd E9 ... 74 C1
Kings Ho 19 E14 ... 119 B6
Kingsholm Gdns SE9 ... 144 A1
Kings Ho SW8 ... 270 B4
King's House Sch (Jun) TW10 ... 154 B6
King's House Sch TW10 ... 154 B6
Kingshurst Rd SE12 ... 165 A4
Kings Keep KT6 ... 198 A5
King's Keep 6 SW15 ... 156 D6
KINGSLAND ... 73 C2
Kingsland Gn 1 E8, N1 ... 73 C2
Kingsland High St E8 ... 73 D3
Kingsland NW8 ... 92 C6 230 B5
Kingsland Pas 2 E8 ... 73 C2
Kingsland Rd
Hoxton E2 ... 95 C5
Newham E13 ... 99 C4
Kingsland Sh Ctr 12 E8 ... 73 D2
King's La SM1 ... 218 B3
Kingslawn Cl SW15 ... 156 B6
Kingslee Ct 4 SM2 ... 217 D1
Kingsleigh Cl TW8 ... 131 D6
Kingsleigh Pl CR4 ... 202 D6
Kingsleigh Wlk BR2 ... 208 D5
Kingsley Ave
Ealing W13 ... 87 A1
Hounslow TW3 ... 130 A3
Southall UB1 ... 107 C6
Sutton SM1 ... 218 B4
Kingsley Cl
Dagenham RM10 ... 81 D4
East Finchley N2 ... 48 A4
Kingsley Ct
Bexley DA6 ... 147 C1
Edgware HA8 ... 10 D2
Snaresbrook E11 ... 54 D3
1 Thamesmead SE28 ... 124 C5
Willesden NW2 ... 68 B2
Wood Green N22 ... 32 B3
Worcester Pk KT4 ... 215 D6
Kingsley Dr KT4 ... 215 D6
Kingsley Flats SE1 ... 263 B3
Kingsley Gdns E4 ... 35 C5
Kingsley Grange 1 E11 ... 55 A4
Kingsley High Sch HA3 ... 24 A3
Kingsley Ho
Chelsea SW3 ... 266 D5
3 Clapham SW4 ... 137 D3
East Finchley NW11 ... 48 A3
8 Kingston u T KT6 ... 198 A4
Kingsley Mews
Chislehurst West BR7 ... 188 D4
Dagenham RM9 ... 80 D4
4 Ilford IG1 ... 78 D6
Kensington W8 ... 255 D5
15 St George in t East E1 ... 118 B6
Kingsley Pl N6 ... 49 A2
Kingsley Prim Sch CR9 ... 204 C1
Kingsley Rd
Chingford E17 ... 36 A1
Edmonton N13 ... 32 D6
Harrow HA2 ... 64 A5
Hounslow TW3 ... 130 A3
Kilburn NW6 ... 91 B6
Orpington BR6 ... 227 D1
Pinner HA5 ... 41 B5
Thornton Heath CR0 ... 204 C1
Upton E7 ... 77 A1
Wimbledon SW19 ... 179 D5
Kingsley St SW11 ... 136 D2
Kingsley Way N2 ... 48 A4
Kingsley Wood Dr SE9 ... 166 B1
Kings Lo HA4 ... 39 C1
Kingslyn Cres SE19 ... 183 C2
Kings Mall Sh Ctr W6 ... 112 C2
Kingsman Par SE18 ... 122 B3
King's Mans SW3 ... 267 A5
Kingsman St SE18 ... 122 B2
Kingsmead Ave
Edmonton N9 ... 18 B3
Kingsbury NW9 ... 45 B2
Mitcham CR4 ... 203 C6
North Cheam KT4 ... 216 B5
Sunbury TW16 ... 172 C1
Tolworth KT6 ... 214 C6
Kingsmead EN5 ... 1 C1
Kingsmead Cl
Sidcup DA15 ... 168 A2
Teddington TW11 ... 175 B4
West Ewell KT19 ... 215 B1
Kingsmead Cotts BR2 ... 210 A1
Kingsmead Ct
Bromley BR1 ... 186 D3
Crouch End N6 ... 49 D2
Kingsmead Dr UB5 ... 63 B1
Kingsmead Ho E9 ... 75 A4
Kingsmead Lo
9 Chingford E4 ... 20 A2
Sutton SM2 ... 218 B2
Kings Mead Pk KT10 ... 212 C1
Kingsmead Prim Sch E9 ... 75 A4
Kingsmead Rd SW2 ... 160 C2
Kingsmead TW10 ... 154 B5
Kingsmead Sch EN1 ... 6 A2
King's Mead Way E5, E9 ... 75 A4
Kingsmere SE6 ... 163 D3
Kingsmere Cl SW15 ... 134 D2
Kingsmere Ct NW9 ... 44 D1
Kingsmere Pk NW9 ... 45 A1
Kingsmere Pl N16 ... 51 B1
Kingsmere Rd SW19 ... 156 D2
Kingsmere BR7 ... 188 A2
King's Mews
1 Clapham Pk SW4 ... 160 A6
Gray's Inn WC1 ... 94 B3 240 D5
Kingsmill Bsns Pk KT1 ... 198 B6
Kingsmill Gdns RM9 ... 81 B3
Kingsmill NW8 ... 92 B5 229 D4
Kingsmill Rd RM9 ... 81 B3
Kingsmill Terr NW8 ... 92 B5 229 D4
Kingsmount Ct SM1 ... 217 D4
Kingsnorth Ho 12 W10 ... 90 D1
Kingsnympton Pk KT2 ... 176 D4
Kings Oak Hospl (Private) The EN2 ... 4 C5
Kings Oak RM7 ... 59 C6
King's Orch SE9 ... 166 A5
King's Paddock TW12 ... 174 A2
King's Par 3 W12 ... 112 A3
Kingspark Bsns Ctr KT3 ... 199 A6
Kingspark Ct E18 ... 55 A6
King's Par NW10 ... 90 C6
King's Pas KT2 ... 175 D2
King's Penny Ho 4 KT2 ... 176 A3
Kings Pl
Acton Green W4 ... 111 A2
Buckhurst Hill IG9 ... 21 D2
Loughton IG10 ... 21 D4
King's Pl SE1 ... 252 A1
King Sq EC1 ... 95 A4 235 A1
King's Quay SW10 ... 266 B2
King's Rd
Barking IG11 ... 79 A1
Chelsea SW3 ... 257 B1
Chelsea SW10 ... 136 B6 266 C5
Chingford E4 ... 20 B3
Kings Rd W5 ... 87 D2
King's Rd N18 ... 34 A6
Kings Rd
Feltham TW13 ... 150 C3
Harrow HA2 ... 63 B6
King's Rd
Kingston u T KT2 ... 176 B3
Leytonstone E11 ... 54 C2
Long Ditton KT6 ... 197 C1
Kings Rd CR4 ... 203 A6
King's Rd
Mortlake SW14 ... 133 B2
Newham E6 ... 99 C6
Kings Rd
Orpington BR6 ... 227 D4
Richmond TW10, TW9 ... 154 B6
King's Rd
South Norwood SE25 ... 206 A6
Teddington TW11, TW12 ... 174 B5
Tottenham N17 ... 33 D2
Twickenham TW1 ... 153 B5
Kings Rd
Walton-on-T KT12 ... 194 B1
West Drayton UB7 ... 104 B4
Willesden NW10 ... 68 B1
King's Rd SW19 ... 179 C4
Kings Rd N22 ... 32 B2
Kings Ride Gate TW10 ... 132 C1
Kingsridge SW19 ... 157 A2
Kings Road Bglws HA2 ... 63 B5
King's Scholars' Pas SW1 ... 259 A4
King St W3 ... 111 A5
King Stairs Cl SE16 ... 118 B4
King St N2 ... 48 B6
King's Terr
Camden Town NW1 ... 93 C6 232 A5
10 Isleworth TW7 ... 131 A2
King St W6 ... 112 A2
Kingsthorpe Rd SE26 ... 184 D6
King St Newham E13 ... 98 D3
Newham E13 ... 99 A3
Kingston Ave
Cheam SM3 ... 217 A5
Feltham TW14 ... 149 D5
Yiewsley UB7 ... 104 B6
Kingston Bsns Ctr KT9 ... 214 B5
Kingston By-Pass KT6, KT7, KT9 ... 213 C5
Kingston By - Pass KT6 ... 214 C5
Kingston Cl
Dagenham RM6 ... 59 A6
Northolt UB5 ... 85 B6
Teddington TW11 ... 175 B4
Kingston Coll of F Ed KT1 ... 197 D6
Kingston Coll of F Ed (M V Annex) KT2 ... 176 A2
Kingston Cres BR3 ... 185 B2
Kingston Ct HA3 ... 44 B4
Kingston Gdns CR0 ... 220 A5
Kingston Gram Sch KT2 ... 176 B1
Kingston Hall Rd KT1 ... 197 D6
Kingston Hill Ave RM6 ... 59 A6
Kingston Hill KT2 ... 177 A5
Kingston Hill Pl KT2, TW10 ... 177 A6
Kingston Ho E SW7 ... 247 A1
Kingston Ho 4 NW6 ... 69 A1
Kingston Ho N SW7 ... 247 A1
Kingston Hospl KT2 ... 176 D2
Kingston Ho S SW7 ... 247 A1
Kingston House Est KT6 ... 197 B3
Kingston La
Teddington TW11 ... 175 B4
Uxbridge UB8 ... 82 A4
West Drayton UB7 ... 104 B4
Kingston Lo 2 KT3 ... 199 C5

ngston Mus*
KT1 176 A1
ngston Pl HA3 24 D3
ngston Rd
Ashford TW15 170 A4
Ashford TW15 170 B4
Edmonton N9 18 A2
Ewell KT17 215 D1
Ilford IG1 79 A4
Kingston u T KT1, KT3 199 A5
Merton SW19, SW20 179 B1
New Barnet EN4 14 B6
Roehampton SW15, SW19 156 B3
Southall UB2 107 B4
Teddington TW11 175 B4
ingston Sq SE19 183 B5
ingston Sta KT2 176 A2
ingston Univ Annex KT1 176 B1
ingston Univ
Kingston u T KT1 198 A6
Kingston Vale KT2 177 B5
ingston Univ Roehampton Vale Campus SW15 155 D1
INGSTON UPON THAMES 197 C6
INGSTON VALE 177 B6
ingston Vale SW15 155 C1
ingstown St NW1 93 A6 231 A6
ing Street Cloisters 8 W6 112 B2
ing Street Coll W12 112 C4
ing Street Par 7 TW1 153 A3
ing St
Richmond TW9 153 D6
Southall UB2 107 A3
St James SW1 115 C5 249 B4
Strand WC2 250 A6
Tottenham N17 33 D2
Twickenham TW1 153 A3
Whitechapel EC2 95 A1 242 B1
ings View Ct 1 SW20 178 D3
ingswater Pl SW11 267 A3
ingsway Bsns Pk TW12 173 B2
ingsway Coll NW5 71 B2
ingsway BR4 224 D5
ingsway Cres HA2 42 A5
ings Way CR0 220 B3
ingsway EN3 18 B6
ingsway Est N18 34 D4
ings Way HA1 42 C5
ingsway UB3 83 A2
ingsway Mans WC1 240 C4
ingsway
Mortlake SW14, TW9 132 D2
North Finchley N12 30 A4
Petts Wood BR5 211 B4
ingsway Pl EC1 241 C6
ingsway Rd SM3 217 A1
ingsway
Stanwell TW19 148 A3
St Giles WC2 94 B1 240 C2
Wembley HA9 66 A4
West Barnes KT3 200 C4
Woodford IG8 37 C5
ingswear Ho 5 SE23 162 C2
ingswear Rd
Dartmouth Pk NW5 71 B5
Ruislip HA4 62 A6
ings Well 25 NW3 70 A4
ings Wlk Sh Mall SW3 114 D1 257 C2
ingswood Ave
Beckenham BR2, BR3 208 C5
Belvedere DA17 125 B2
Hampton TW12 173 D4
Hounslow TW3, TW5 129 B3
Kensal Rise NW6 91 A5
Thornton Heath CR7 204 C4
ingswood Cl
Ashford TW15 171 B5
Crofton BR6 211 B2
East Barnet N20 14 A4
Enfield EN1 17 D6
New Malden KT3 199 D3
South Lambeth SW8 270 B3
Surbiton KT6 198 A2
ingswood Ct
Chingford E4 35 C5

Kingswood Ct *continued*
Hither Green SE13 164 B5
Kings Wood Ct 4 NW6 69 C1
Kingswood Ct 7 TW10 154 B6
Kingswood Dr
Carshalton SM5 202 D1
Dulwich SE19, SE21 183 D6
Kingswood 31 E2 96 C5
Kingswood Ho 3 KT2 176 D4
Kingswood Mans 14 SM2 217 C1
Kingswood Pk N3 29 B1
Kingswood Pl SE13 142 C1
Kingswood Prim Sch SE27 183 B5
Kingswood Rd
Beckenham BR2 208 C6
Ilford IG3 58 A2
Leytonstone E11 54 C2
Merton SW19 179 B2
Penge SE20 184 C4
South Acton W4 111 A3
Streatham SW2 160 A4
Wembley HA9 66 C5
Kingswood Terr W4 111 A3
Kingswood Way SM6 220 A3
Kingsworth Cl BR3 207 A4
Kingsworthy Cl KT1 198 B6
Kings Yd E15 75 C2
Kingthorpe Rd NW10 67 B1
Kingthorpe Terr 2 NW10 67 B1
Kington Ho 18 NW6 91 D6
Kingward Ho E1 96 A2
Kingwell Rd EN4 2 B5
Kingweston Cl NW2 69 A5
King William IV Gdns SE20 184 C4
King William La 3 SE10 120 C1
King William St EC4 117 B6 252 D6
King William Wlk SE10 142 A6
Kingwood Rd SW6 135 A5 264 A3
Kinlet Rd SE18 145 A4
Kinloch Dr NW9 45 C2
Kinloch St N7 72 B5
Kinloss Ct NW3 47 B5
Kinloss Gdns NW3 47 B5
Kinloss Rd SM5 202 A2
Kinnaird Ave
Bromley BR1 186 D4
Chiswick W4 133 A5
Kinnaird Cl BR1 186 D4
Kinnear Ct 2 SW20 178 D2
Kinnear Rd W12 111 D4
Kinnerton Pl N SW1 247 D1
Kinnerton Pl S SW1 247 D1
Kinnerton St SW1 115 A4 248 A1
Kinnerton Yd SW1 248 A1
Kinnoull Mans 10 E5 74 B4
Kinnoul Rd W6 135 A6 264 A6
Kinross Ave KT4 216 A6
Kinross Cl
Ashford TW16 171 D5
Edgware HA8 10 D2
Harrow HA3 44 B4
Kinross Ct 1 SE6 164 D2
Kinross Dr TW16 171 D5
Kinross Ho N1 233 C6
Kinross Terr E17 35 B1
Kinsale Grange 10 SM2 218 A2
Kinsale Rd SE15 140 A2
Kinsella Gdns SW19 178 B5
Kinsey Ho SE21 183 C6
Kinsham Ho 5 E2 96 A3
Kintore Way SE1 263 C4
Kintyre Cl SW16 204 B6
Kintyre Ct 17 SW2 160 A4
Kintyre Ho 6 E14 120 A5
Kinveachy Gdns SE7 122 A1
Kinver Ho N4 51 B2
Kinver Rd SE26 184 C6
Kipling Ct W7 108 D6
Kipling Dr SW17 180 B4
Kipling Ho 29 SE5 139 A5
Kipling Pl HA7 24 D4
Kipling Rd DA7 147 A4
Kipling St SE1 117 B4 252 D2
Kipling Terr N9 17 B2
Kipling Twr 3 W3 111 A3
Kippington Dr SE9 165 D3
Kirby Cl KT19 215 D3
Kirby Est SE16 118 B3
Kirby Gr SE1 117 C4 253 A2

Kirby St EC1 94 C2 241 B4
Kirby Way
Hillingdon UB8 82 B3
Walton-on-T KT12 194 C3
Kirchen Rd W13 109 B6
Kirkby Cl N11 31 A4
Kirkdale SE26 162 B1
Kirkdale Rd E11 54 C2
Kirkeby Bldg EC1 241 A4
Kirkfield Cl W13 109 B5
Kirkham Rd E6 100 A1
Kirkham St SE18 145 C6
Kirk Ho HA9 66 A5
Kirkland Cl DA15 167 C5
Kirkland Dr EN2 5 A4
Kirkland Terr BR3 185 C4
Kirkland Wlk 4 E8 73 D2
Kirk La SE18 145 A6
Kirkleas Rd KT6 198 A1
Kirklees Rd
Dagenham RM8 80 C3
Thornton Heath CR7 204 C4
Kirkley Ho N16 51 C1
Kirkley Rd SW19 179 C2
Kirkman Ho W1 239 C3
Kirkman Pl W1 239 C3
Kirkmichael Rd E14 98 A1
Kirk Rd E17 53 B3
Kirk Rise SM1 217 D5
Kirkside Rd SE3 143 A6
Kirkstall Ave N17 51 B5
Kirkstall Gdns SW2 160 A3
Kirkstall Ho SW1 258 C2
Kirkstall Rd SW2 160 A3
Kirkstead Ct E5 75 A4
Kirksted Rd SM4 201 D1
Kirkstone NW1 232 A2
Kirkstone Way BR1 186 C3
Kirkton Rd N15 51 C5
Kirkwall Pl E2 96 C4
Kirkwood Rd SE15 140 B3
Kirn Rd W13 109 B6
Kirrane Cl KT3 199 D4
Kirtley Ho SW8 269 B2
Kirtley Rd SE26 185 A6
Kirtling St SW8 137 C5 269 A4
Kirton Cl W4 111 B2
Kirton Gdns 23 E2 95 D4
Kirton Rd E13 99 C5
Kirton Wlk HA8 27 A3
Kirwin Way SE5 138 D5
Kisharon Day Sch NW11 47 B3
Kitcat Terr E3 97 C4
Kitchener Rd
Dagenham RM10 81 D2
East Finchley N2 48 C6
South Norwood CR7 205 B6
Tottenham N17 51 C6
Upton E7 77 B2
Walthamstow E17 35 D2
Kite Ho 5 SW11 136 C2
Kite Pl 9 E2 96 A4
Kitley Gdns SE19 183 D2
Kitson Rd
Barnes SW13 134 A4
Camberwell SE5 139 A5
Kittiwake Ct 26 SE8 141 B6
Kittiwake Pl SM1 217 B3
Kittiwake Rd UB5 84 D4
Kittiwake Way UB4 84 D2
Kitto Rd SE14 140 D3
KITTS END 1 A5
Kitt's End Rd EN5 1 A6
Kiver Rd N19 72 A6
Klea Ave SW4 159 C5
Kleffens Ct 2 SE3 142 D5
Kleine Wharf 30 N1 95 C6
Knaggs Ho 1 TW11 174 C5
Knapdale Cl SE23 162 B2
Knapmill Rd SE6 163 D2
Knapmill Way SE6 163 D2
Knapp Cl NW10 67 C2
Knapp Rd
Ashford TW15 170 B6
Bow E3 97 C3
Knapton Mews SW17 181 A4
Knaresborough Dr SW18 157 D3
Knaresborough Ho 4 N4 51 A2
Knaresborough Pl SW5 113 D2 255 C4
Knatchbull Rd
Brixton SE5 138 D4
Stonebridge NW10 89 B6
Knebworth Ave E17 35 C2
Knebworth Ho
South Lambeth SW8 269 D1
2 Stoke Newington N16 73 C4
Walthamstow E17 35 C2
Knebworth Rd 3 N16 73 C4

Knee Hill Cres SE2 124 C2
Knee Hill SE2 124 C1
Kneller Gdns TW7 152 B5
Kneller Ho 9 SW8 137 D3
Kneller Rd
Brockley SE4 141 A1
Isleworth TW2 152 B5
New Malden KT3 199 C2
Knevett Terr TW3 129 C1
Knight Cl RM8 80 C6
Knight Ct
1 Chingford E4 20 A3
Stamford Hill N15 51 C4
Knighten St E1 118 B5
Knighthead Point 26 E14 119 C4
Knight Ho
Walworth SE17 263 A3
Worcester Pk KT4 216 A6
Knightland Ho E5 74 B6
Knightland Rd E5 74 B6
Knightleas Ct NW2 68 C2
Knightleys Ct E10 53 A1
Knighton Cl
Croydon CR2 220 D1
Woodford IG8 37 B6
Knighton Dr IG8 37 B6
Knighton Gn IG9 21 B2
Knighton La IG9 21 B2
Knighton Park Rd SE26 184 D5
Knighton Rd E7 77 A4
Knightrider Ct EC4 252 A6
Knightrider St EC4 251 D6
Knights Arc SW1 247 C1
Knight's Ave W5 110 A4
KNIGHTSBRIDGE 114 C4
Knightsbridge Ct SW1 247 D1
Knightsbridge Gn SW1 247 C1
Knightsbridge Mews BR7 188 B3
Knightsbridge SW1, SW7 114 D4 247 C1
Knightsbridge Under Sch SW7 256 B3
Knights Cl
East Molesey KT8 195 B4
Lower Clapton E9 74 C3
Knights Ct WD23 8 B3
Knight's Ct BR1 164 D1
Knights Ct
11 Friern Barnet N11 30 D5
Kingston u T KT1 198 A6
Penge BR3 185 A2
Knightshayes Ho 8 NW4 28 D1
Knight's Hill Sq SE27 182 D6
Knight's Hill SE19, SE27 182 D6
Knights Ho
Bermondsey SE1 253 C2
South Lambeth SW8 270 B3
Knight's Ho SW10 266 A4
Knights Ho SW5 254 C2
Knight's Pk KT1 198 A6
Knight's Pl TW2 152 C3
Knights Rd
Newham E16 121 A4
Stanmore HA7 25 C6
Knight's Wlk SE11 261 C3
Knightswood Cl HA8 11 A2
Knightswood Ct N6 49 D2
Knightswood Ho N12 30 A4
Knightwood Cres KT3 199 C3
Knivet Rd SW6 135 C6 265 A5
Knobs Hill Rd E15 97 D6
Knockholt Rd SE9 165 D6
Knole Cl CR0 206 C3
Knole Ct UB5 84 C4
Knole Gate DA15 167 C1
Knole The SE9 188 C6
Knoll Ct
Dulwich SE19 183 D5
Orpington BR6 227 D6
Knoll Dr N14 15 A4
Knoll Ho NW8 229 A4
Knoll Lo EN5 14 A6
Knollmead Prim Sch KT5 215 A6
Knollmead KT4, KT5 199 A1
Knoll Rd Bexley DA5 169 C5
Sidcup DA14 190 B6
Wandsworth SW18 158 A6
Knoll Rise BR6 211 D1
Knolls Cl KT4 216 B5
Knoll The
Beckenham BR3 185 D2
Ealing W13 87 C2
Hayes BR2 209 A1
Knolly's Cl SE27, SW16 160 C1

Knolly's Rd SE27, SW16 160 C1
Knot Ho SE1 253 C3
Knottisford St E2 96 C4
Knotts Green Mews E10 54 A3
Knotts Green Rd E10 54 A3
Knowlden Ho 5 E1 118 C6
Knowle Ave DA7 147 B5
Knowle Cl SW9 138 C2
Knowledge Point Sch N7 72 B2
Knowle Lo BR7 188 B4
Knowle Rd
Bromley BR2 226 A6
Twickenham TW2 152 C3
Knowles Cl UB7 104 A5
Knowles Ct 7 HA1 42 D3
Knowles Hill Cres SE13 164 B6
Knowles Ho
Wandsworth SW18 157 D5
Willesden Green NW10 90 A6
Knowles Wlk SW4 137 C2
Knowl Pk WD6 10 A6
Knowlton Gn 1 BR2 208 D4
Knowlton Ho 32 SW9 138 C4
Knowl Way WD6 10 B6
Knowsley Ave UB1 107 D5
Knowsley Rd SW11 136 D3
Knox Ct 16 SW4 138 A3
Knox Ho SW15 134 C3
Knox Rd E7 77 A2
Knox St W1 92 D2 237 C4
Knoyle Ho W14 254 B6
Knoyle St SE14 141 A6
Kobi Nazrul Prim Sch E1 96 A1
Koblenz Ho N8 50 A6
Kohat Rd SW19 179 D5
Korda Cl TW17 192 B6
Kossuth St SE10 120 C1
Kotree Way 16 SE1 118 A2
Kramer Mews SW5 255 C1
Kreedman Wlk 8 E8 74 A3
Kreisel Wlk TW9 132 B6
Kristina Ct 5 SM2 217 C2
Kuala Gdns SW16 182 B2
Kubrick Bsns Est E7 77 B4
Kuhn Way E7 77 A3
Kwesi Johnson Ct 4 N22 32 C1
Kydbrook Cl BR5 211 A2
Kyle Ho TW12 174 A2
Kylemore Cl 3 E6 99 D5
Kylemore Ct 4 W12 112 A4
Kylemore Rd NW6 69 C1
Kylestrome Ho SW1 258 B3
Kymberley Rd HA1 42 C3
Kynance Gdns HA7 25 C2
Kynance Mews SW7 113 D3 255 D5
Kynance Pl SW7 256 A5
Kynaston Ave CR7 205 A4
Kynaston Cl HA3 24 B3
Kynaston Cres CR7 205 A4
Kynaston Ho 7 SW2 160 B3
Kynaston Rd
Enfield EN2 5 B4
Plaistow BR1 187 A5
Stoke Newington N16 73 C5
Thornton Heath CR7 205 A4
Kynaston Wood HA3 24 B3
Kynersley Cl 1 SM5 218 D5
Kynoch Rd N18 34 D6
Kyrle Rd SW11 159 A5
Kyverdale Rd N16 51 D1

L

Laburnam Ct 12 SW16 182 C5
Laburnham Cl HA0 88 C6
Laburnham Ct
Child's Hill NW2 69 B6
Sutton SM1 217 C3
Laburnham Pl SE9 166 C6
Laburnum Ave
Carshalton SM1 218 C5
Edmonton N9 17 D2
Tottenham N17 33 B3
Yiewsley UB7 104 B6
Laburnum Cl
Friern Barnet N11 31 A4
5 Nunhead SE15 140 C5
Walthamstow E4 35 B4
Laburnum Cres TW16 172 B2

Laburnum Ct
26 Haggerston E2 95 D6
Harrow HA1 41 D3
5 Mitcham CR4 181 A1
Stanmore HA7 25 C6
Laburnum Gdns
Croydon CR0 206 D1
Edmonton N21 17 A2
Laburnum Gr
Edmonton N21 17 A2
Hounslow TW3 129 B1
Kingsbury NW9 45 A2
Kingston u T KT3 177 B1
Ruislip HA4 39 B3
Southall UB1 85 B3
Laburnum Ho
Dagenham RM10 81 C6
New Cross SE4 141 B3
6 Stoke Newington N16 73 B6
Laburnum JMI Sch E2 95 D6
Laburnum Lo 2 N3 29 B1
Laburnum Rd
Hayes UB3 105 D2
Merton SW19 180 A3
Mitcham CR4 181 A1
Laburnum St E2 95 D6
Laburnums The E6 100 A3
Laburnum Way
Southborough BR2 210 D2
Stanwell TW19 148 B3
Lacebark Cl DA15 167 D4
Lacewing Cl E13 99 A4
Lacey Cl N9 18 A2
Lacey Dr
Dagenham RM8 80 C5
Edgware HA8 26 B6
Hampton TW12 173 B2
Lacey Ho 7 SE13 142 A3
Lacine Ct 12 SE16 118 D4
Lackington St EC2 242 D4
Lackland Ho SE1 263 D2
Lacland Ho SW10 266 C4
Lacock Cl SW19 180 A4
Lacock Ct 3 W13 109 A5
Lacon Rd SE22 140 A1
Lacrosse Way SW16 181 D2
Lacy Rd SW15 134 D1
Ladas Rd SE27 183 A5
Ladbroke Cres W11 91 A1
Ladbroke Gdns W11 113 B6 244 C6
Ladbroke Gr
Kensal Town W10 91 A2
Notting Hill W11 113 B6 244 C6
Ladbroke Grove Ho W11 244 C6
Ladbroke Grove Sta W10 91 A1
Ladbroke Ho E1 243 D3
Ladbroke Mews W11 244 B3
Ladbroke Rd
Enfield EN1 17 D5
Notting Hill W11 113 B5 244 C4
Ladbroke Sq W11 113 B6 244 D5
Ladbroke Terr W11 113 B5 244 D4
Ladbroke Wlk W11 113 B5 244 D4
Ladbrook Cl HA5 41 B4
Ladbrooke Cres DA14 168 D1
Ladbrook Rd SE25 205 B5
Ladderstile Ride KT2, TW10 176 D5
Ladderswood Way N11 31 C5
Ladlands SE22 162 A4
Lady Alesford Ave HA7 25 B5
Lady Bankes Jun & Inf Schs HA4 62 A6
Lady Booth Rd 7 KT1 176 A1
Ladybower Ct 6 E5 74 D4
Ladycroft Gdns 6 BR6 227 A3
Ladycroft Rd SE13 141 D2
Ladycroft Way BR6 227 A3
Ladycroft Wlk HA7 25 D1
Lady Eleanor Holles Sch The (Jun Girls) TW12 173 D5
Lady Eleanor Holles Sch The (Senior Girls) TW12 173 D5

Lady Elizabeth Ho SW14 133 A2
Ladyfern Ho [10] E3 97 C2
Lady Florence Ctyd [13] SE8 141 C5
Ladygate La HA4 39 A3
Lady Hay KT4 215 D6
Lady Helen Seymour Ho [14] E13 99 A5
Lady Margaret Prim Sch UB1 85 B2
Lady Margaret Rd
Kentish Town NW5 71 C3
Southall UB1 85 B2
Lady Margaret Sch SW6 135 C4 265 A1
Lady Shaw Ct N13 16 B1
Ladysmith Ave
Ilford IG2 57 C2
Newham E6 100 A5
Ladysmith Cl NW7 28 A3
Ladysmith Rd
Edmonton N18 34 B5
Eltham SE9 166 C5
Enfield EN1 5 D3
Harrow HA3 24 C1
Newham E16 98 D4
Tottenham N17 34 A1
Lady Somerset Rd NW5 71 B4
LADYWELL 163 C6
Ladywell Cl SE4 141 C1
Ladywell Ho [7] BR5 190 B1
Ladywell Hts SE4 163 B5
Ladywell Rd SE13 163 D6
Ladywell Sta SE13 163 D6
Ladywell St [4] E15 98 D6
Ladywell Water Twr SE4 163 C6
Ladywood Ave BR5 211 C4
Ladywood Rd KT6 214 C6
Lafitte Ho [22] N19 49 D2
Lafone Ave TW13 150 C2
Lafone Ho [11] SW2 160 A4
Lafone St SE1 117 D4 253 C2
Lagado Mews SE16 118 D5
Lagonda Ho [11] E3 97 C3
Lagonier Ho EC1 235 B1
Laidlaw Dr N21 16 B6
Laindon Ho [6] N16 51 D1
Laing Dean UB5 84 C6
Laing Ho SE5 139 A5
Laings Ave CR4 180 D1
Laings Cnr CR4 180 D2
Lainlock Pl TW3 129 D4
Lainson St SW18 157 C4
Lairdale Cl SE21 161 A4
Laird Ho SE5 139 A5
Lairs Cl N7 72 A2
Lait Ho [3] BR3 185 D2
Laitwood Rd SW12 159 B3
Lakanal [11] SE5 139 C4
Lake Ave BR1 187 A4
Lake Bsns Ctr N17 34 A3
Lake Cl
Dagenham RM8 80 D5
[6] Wimbledon SW19 179 B5
Lakedale Ct IG11 102 A3
Lakedale Rd SE18 123 C1
Lake Dr WD23 8 B2
Lake Farm Ctry Pk UB3 105 C5
Lakefield Cl SE20 184 B3
Lakefield Rd N22 32 D1
Lake Gdns
Dagenham RM10 81 C3
Hackbridge SM6 219 B5
Richmond TW10 153 B2
Lakehall Gdns CR7 204 D4
Lakehall Rd CR7 204 D4
Lake Ho SE1 252 A1
Lake House Rd E11 77 A6
Lake Ho [4] SW27 182 D5
Lakehurst Rd KT19 215 C3
Lakeland Cl HA3 24 B4
Lakeman Ct CR7 183 A1
Lakenheath N14 15 D6
Laker Ct SW4 138 A3
Lake Rd Croydon CR0 223 B6
Dagenham RM6 58 D5
Wimbledon SW19 179 B5
Laker Pl SW15 157 A5
Lakeside Ave
Redbridge IG4 55 D5
Thamesmead SE28 124 A5
Lakeside BR3 207 D6
Lakeside Cl
Ruislip HA4 39 B5
Sidcup DA15 168 C6
South Norwood SE25 184 A1
Lakeside Complex The SE2 124 D5
Lakeside Cres EN4 14 D6
Lakeside Ct N4 51 A1
Lakeside WD6 10 C6
Lakeside Dr
Acton NW10 88 B4
Esher KT10 212 A2
Keston Mark BR2 226 A5
Lakeside Ealing W13 87 C1
Enfield EN2 3 D1
Finchley N3 29 D1
[10] Kingston u T KT2 176 D3
Lakeside Lo NW4 47 A5
Lakeside Rd
Brook Green W14 112 D3
Palmers Green N13 16 B1
Lakeside SM6 219 B4
Lakeside Way HA9 66 C4
Lakeside KT19 215 C2
Lakes Rd BR2 225 C3
Lakeswood Rd BR5 211 A3
Lake The WD23 8 B3
Lakeview Ct E4 36 B4
Lake View Ct SW1 258 D6
Lakeview [23] E3 96 D5
Lake View HA8 26 B5
Lakeview Rd
Bexley DA16 146 B1
West Norwood SE27 182 D5
Lake View Terr N18 33 D6
Lakis Cl NW3 70 A4
Laleham Ave NW7 11 B1
Laleham Ho E2 243 C6
Laleham Rd
Catford SE6 164 A4
Littleton TW17 192 C4
Lalor St SW6 135 A3
Lambarde Ave SE9 188 C6
Lambard Ho [4] SE10 142 A5
Lamb Cl UB5 85 A4
Lamb Ct [16] E14 119 A6
Lamberhurst Ho [14] SE15 140 C6
Lamberhurst Rd
Dagenham RM8 59 B1
West Norwood SE27 182 C5
Lambert Ave TW9 132 D2
Lambert Ho
[16] Brixton SW9 138 C3
[19] Crouch End N19 49 D2
Lambert Lo TW8 109 D1
Lambert Rd
Clapham Pk SW2 160 B6
Newham E16 99 B1
North Finchley N12 30 B5
Lambert's Pl CR0 205 B1
Lambert's Rd KT6 198 B4
Lambert St N1 72 C1
Lambert Way N12 30 A5
Lambert Wlk HA9 65 D5
LAMBETH 116 B4
Lambeth Acad SW4 159 C6
Lambeth Coll (Brixton Ctr) SW2 160 B6
Lambeth Coll (Clapham Ctr) SW4 159 C6
Lambeth Coll (Tower Bridge Ctr) SE1 117 C5 253 B3
Lambeth Coll (Vauxhall Ctr) SW8 137 D4 269 C2
Lambeth Ct [8] SW18 157 C6
Lambeth High St SE1 116 B2 260 C4
Lambeth Hill EC4 252 A6
Lambeth Hospl SW9 138 B2
Lambeth North Sta SE1 116 C3 261 A6
Lambeth Palace Rd SE1 116 B3 260 C6
Lambeth Pal* SE1 116 B3 260 C5
Lambeth Pier SE1 260 B5
Lambeth Prospect SE19 183 B4
Lambeth Rd
Lambeth SE1 116 C3 261 B5
Thornton Heath CR0 204 D1
Lambeth Twrs SE11 261 A5
Lambeth Wlk SE11 116 B2 260 D4
Lambfold Ho N7 72 A2
Lamb Ho
[28] Camberwell SE5 139 A5
[11] Camberwell SE5 139 B4
Greenwich SE10 142 A6
Lamb La E8 74 B1
Lamble St NW5 71 A4
Lambley Rd RM9 80 B2
Lambolle Pl NW3 70 C2
Lambolle Rd NW3 70 C2
Lambourn Cl
Hanwell W7 108 D4
[9] Kentish Town NW5 71 C4
Lambourne Ave SW19 179 B6
Lambourne Ct [5] IG8 37 C3
Lambourne Gdns
[5] Barking IG11 79 D1
Chingford E4 19 C2
Enfield EN1 5 D3
Lambourne Gr
Deptford SE16 118 D1
Kingston u T KT1 176 D1
Lambourne Ho NW8 236 D4
Lambourne Pl SE3 143 B4
Lambourne Rd
Barking IG11 79 D1
Ilford IG3 79 C6
Leytonstone E11 54 A2
Lambourn Ho BR1 188 A3
Lambourn Rd SW4 137 B2
Lambrook Ho [13] SE15 140 A4
Lambrook Terr SW6 135 A4 264 A2
Lamb's Bldgs EC1 242 C5
Lamb's Cl N9 18 A2
Lamb's Conduit Pas WC1 240 C4
Lamb's Conduit St WC1 94 B3 240 C5
Lambscroft Ave SE9, SE12 165 D1
Lambs Mdw IG8 37 D1
Lamb's Mews N1 234 C5
Lamb's Pas EC1 95 B3 242 C5
Lamb St E1 95 D2 243 C4
Lamb's Terr N9 17 B2
Lambs Wlk EN2 5 A3
Lambton Ct [2] N19 50 A1
Lambton Mews [4] N19 50 A1
Lambton Pl W11 244 D6
Lambton Rd
Finsbury Pk N19 50 A1
Wimbledon SW20 178 C2
Lamb Wlk SE1 253 A1
Lamerock Rd BR1 186 D6
Lamerton Lo [10] TW9 132 B4
Lamerton St [8] SE8 141 C6
Lamford Cl N17 33 B3
Lamington St [3] W6 112 B2
Lamlash St SE11 261 C4
Lamley Ho SE10 141 D5
Lammas Ave CR4 181 A1
Lammas Gn SE26 162 B1
Lammas Park Gdns W5 109 C5
Lammas Park Rd W5 109 D4
Lammas Rd
Homerton E9 74 D1
Richmond TW10 175 C6
Walthamstow E10 53 A1
Lammas Sch The E10 53 B1
Lammermoor Rd SW12 159 B4
Lamont Rd Pas SW10 266 C5
Lamont Rd SW10 136 B6 266 C5
Lamorbey Cl DA15 167 D2
Lamorna Cl E17 36 A2
Lamorna Gr HA7 25 D1
Lampard Gr N16 51 D1
Lampern Sq [8] E2 96 A4
Lampeter Cl NW9 45 C3
Lampeter Sq W6 264 A5
Lamplighter Cl [34] E1 96 C3
Lampmead Rd SE12 142 D1
Lamport Cl SE18 122 B2
Lampson Ho [6] N19 71 C4
LAMPTON 129 D4
Lampton Ave TW5 129 D4
Lampton Ct TW5 129 D4
Lampton House Cl SW19 178 D6
Lampton Park Rd TW3 129 D3
Lampton Rd TW3, TW5 129 D3
Lampton Sch TW5 129 C4
Lanacre Ave NW9 27 C2
Lanain Ct SE12 164 D4
Lanark Cl W5 87 C2
Lanark Ct UB5 63 C3
Lanark Ho [12] SE1 118 A1
Lanark Mans
Paddington W9 236 B6
Lanark Mans *continued*
[15] Shepherd's Bush W12 112 C4
Lanark Mews NW8 229 B1
Lanark Pl W9 92 A3 236 B6
Lanark Rd W9 92 A4 229 A1
Lanark Sq E14 119 D3
Lanata Wlk UB4 84 D3
Lanbury Rd SE15 140 D1
Lancashire Ct W1 248 D6
Lancaster Ave
Barking IG11 101 C6
Croydon CR4 204 A5
Hadley Wood EN4 2 B5
Wanstead E18 55 B5
West Norwood SE21, SE27 161 A2
Wimbledon SW19 178 D5
Lancaster Cl
Ashford TW15 170 A6
Beckenham BR2 208 D5
[10] De Beauvoir Town N1 73 C1
Grahame Pk NW9 27 D3
Kensington W2 245 C5
Kingston u T KT2 175 D5
New Malden KT4 200 B2
Stanwell TW19 148 A5
Tottenham N17 34 A3
Lancaster Cotts [1] TW10 154 A5
Lancaster Ct
Bayswater W2 246 B6
[1] Belmont SM2 217 C1
Parsons Green SW6 264 D3
Stanwell TW19 148 A3
Walton-on-T KT12 194 B2
West Norwood SE27 160 D2
Lancaster Dr
Canary Wharf E14 120 A5
Maitland Pk NW3 70 C2
Lancaster Gate Sta W2 114 B6 246 C6
Lancaster Gate W2 114 A6 246 B6
Lancaster Gdns
Bromley BR1 210 A4
Kingston u T KT2 175 D5
West Ealing W13 109 B4
Wimbledon SW19 179 A5
Lancaster Gr NW3 70 C2
Lancaster hall [14] E16 121 A5
Lancaster Ho
Enfield EN2 5 B4
Putney SW15 134 C3
Stanmore HA7 9 A1
Lancaster Ho SW1 249 A2
Lancaster Ho SW18 157 D4
Lancasterian Prim Sch N17 33 D2
Lancaster Lo [2] W11 91 A1
Lancaster Mews
Bayswater W2 114 A6 246 B6
[2] Richmond TW10 154 A5
[3] Wandsworth SW18 157 D6
Lancaster Pk TW10 154 A6
Lancaster Pl
Hounslow TW5 128 D3
Ilford IG1 79 A4
Strand WC2 116 B6 250 C5
Twickenham TW1 153 A4
[1] Wimbledon SW19 178 D5
Lancaster Rd
Bowes Pk N11 31 D4
Dudden Hill NW10 68 A3
Edmonton N18 33 D5
Enfield EN2 5 B4
Finsbury Pk N4 50 C2
Harrow HA2 41 C4
Higham Hill E17 34 D1
Leytonstone E11 76 C6
New Barnet EN4 14 B6
Northolt UB5 64 A2
Notting Hill W11 91 A1
Southall UB1 107 A6
South Norwood SE25 206 A6
Upton E7 77 A1
Wimbledon SW19 178 D5
Lancaster Road Ind Est [2] EN4 14 B6
Lancaster Stables [10] NW3 70 C2
Lancaster St SE1 116 D4 251 D1
Lancaster Terr W2 114 B6 246 C6
Lancaster Wlk
Hayes UB3 83 A1
Lancaster Wlk *continued*
Knightsbridge W2 114 A5 246 B4
Lancastrian Rd SM6 220 B1
Lancefield Ho SE15 140 B2
Lancefield St W10 91 B4
Lancell St N16 73 C6
Lancelot Ave HA0 65 D4
Lancelot Cres HA0 65 D4
Lancelot Gdns EN4 15 A4
Lancelot Ho SM5 202 C1
Lancelot Pl SW7 114 D4 247 C1
Lancelot Rd
Welling DA16 146 A2
Wembley HA0 65 D3
Lance Rd HA1 42 A2
Lancer Sq W8 245 C2
Lancey Cl SE7 122 A2
Lanchester Ct W2 237 C1
Lanchester Rd N6 48 D4
Lanchester Way SE14 140 D4
Lancing Gdns N9 17 D3
Lancing Rd
Ealing W13 109 B6
Feltham TW13 149 D2
Ilford IG2 57 B2
Thornton Heath CR0 204 B2
Lancing St NW1 232 C1
Lancresse Ct N1 95 C6
Landale Ct SE10 142 A4
Landale Ho [13] SE16 118 C3
Landau Ct [11] CR2 221 A3
Landcroft Rd SE22 161 D5
Landells Rd SE22 162 A5
Lander Ct EN5 14 A6
Landford Rd SW15 134 C2
Landgrove Rd SW19 179 C5
Landin Ho [1] E14 97 C1
Landleys Field [21] N7 71 D3
Landmann Ho [16] SE16 118 B2
Landmann Way SE14 118 D1
Landmark Commercial Ctr N18 33 C4
Landmark Hts E5 75 A4
Landon Pl SW1 257 C6
Landons Cl E14 120 A5
Landon Way TW15 170 D4
Landon Wlk [16] E14 119 D6
Landor Ct N16 73 C3
Landor Ho [7] SE5 139 B5
Landor Rd SW9 138 A2
Landor Wlk [11] W12 112 A4
Landra Gdns N21 16 D5
Landrake NW1 232 B5
Landridge Dr EN1 6 B5
Landridge Rd SW6 135 B3
Landrock Rd N8 50 B3
Landscape Rd IG8 37 B3
Landsdown Cl [9] EN5 2 A1
Landseer Ave E12 78 C3
Landseer Cl
Edgware HA8 26 C1
Mitcham SW19 180 B2
Landseer Ct
Hayes UB4 83 B5
[10] Upper Holloway N19 72 A6
Landseer Ho
Battersea SW11 268 B1
[16] Northolt UB5 84 D5
Paddington NW8 236 D6
Westminster SW1 259 D3
Landseer Rd
Cheam SM1 217 C2
Enfield EN1 18 A6
New Malden KT3 199 B2
Upper Holloway N19 72 A6
Lands' End WD6 9 D5
Landstead Rd SE18 145 B5
Landulph Ho SE11 261 B2
Landward Ct W1 237 B2
Lane Cl NW2 68 B5
Lane Ct SW11 158 D4
Lane End DA7 147 D2
Lane Gdns
Bushey Heath WD23 8 C4
Claygate KT10 212 D1
Lane Mews E12 78 B5
Lanercost Cl SW2 160 C2
Lanercost Gdns N14 16 A4
Lanercost Rd SW2 160 C2
Laneside Ave RM8 59 B2
Laneside
Chislehurst BR7 189 A5
Edgware HA8 27 A5
Lane The
Blackheath Pk SE3 143 A2
St John's Wood NW8 92 A5 229 A3
Laneway SW15 156 B6
Laney Bldg EC1 241 A4
Lanfranc Ct HA1 64
Lanfranc Rd E3 97
Lanfrey Pl W14 254 C
Langbourn Ct E17 53
Langbourne Ave N6 71
Langbourne Ho [7] SW2 160 C
Langbourne Mans N6 71
Langbourne Pl E14 119 D
Langbourne Prim Sch SE21 161 C
Langbourne Way KT10 213
Langbrook Rd SE3 143
Langcroft Cl SM5 218
Langdale Ave CR4 202 D
Langdale Cl
Camberwell SE17 139
Dagenham RM8 58 C
Locksbottom BR6 226 D
Mortlake SW14 132 D
Langdale Cres DA7 147 C
Langdale Ct
[3] Ealing W5 87 C
[9] Ilford IG1 78 D
Ruislip HA4 62
Langdale Dr UB4 83 C
Langdale Gdns UB6 87
Langdale Ho SW1 259
Langdale NW1 232
Langdale Par [8] CR4 202 D
Langdale Rd
Greenwich SE10 142
Thornton Heath CR7 204 C
Langdale St [25] E1 96
Langdon Cres E6 100 C
Langdon Ct
Finsbury EC1 234 D
Harlesden NW10 89 C
Langdon Dr NW9 45
Langdon Ho [3] E14 98
Langdon Park Rd N6 49 C
Langdon Park Sec Sch E14 98
Langdon Pk TW11 175 C
Langdon Pl SW14 133
Langdon Rd
Barking E6 100 C
Bromley BR2 209 B
Morden SM4 202 A
Langdon Sch E6 100 D
Langdons Ct UB2 107 C
Langdon Shaw DA14 189 D
Langdon Way [18] SE1 118
Langdon Wlk SM4 202
Langford Cl
Shacklewell E8 74
[7] South Tottenham N15 51 C
St John's Wood NW8 229 B
Langford Cres EN4 2 D
Langford Ct NW8 229 B
Langford Gn SE5 139 C
Langford Ho [5] SE8 141 C
Langford Pl
Sidcup DA14 168
St John's Wood NW8 92 A5 229 B
Langford Prim Sch SW6 135 D
Langford Rd
Cockfosters EN4 2 D
[4] Sands End SW6 135 D
Woodford IG8 37 C
Langfords IG9 21 D
Langham Cl [1] N15 50 D
Langham Ct
Hendon NW4 46 D
Merton SW20 178 C
[4] Putney SW15 156 D
Ruislip HA4 62 B
[12] Twickenham TW1 153 C
Langham Dr RM6 58 B
Langham Gdns
Burnt Oak HA8 27 A
Ealing W13 109 B
Richmond TW10 175 C
Southgate N21 16 D
Wembley HA0 65 C
Langham Ho SW4 159 C
Langham House Cl TW10 175 D
Langham Ho [3] E11 55 B
Langham Mans SW5 255 C
Langham Park Pl BR2 208 D
Langham Pl
Chiswick W4 133 C
Fitzrovia W1 93 B2 238 D
Noel Pk N15 50 D
Langham Rd
Burnt Oak HA8 27 A

ngham Rd *continued*
Teddington TW11 175 B4
West Green N15 51 A6
Wimbledon SW20 178 C2
angham St
W1 93 B2 238 D3
anghedge Cl N18 33 D4
anghedge La N18 33 D4
anghedge Lane Ind Est
N18 33 D4
angholm Cl SW12 159 D4
angholme WD23 8 A3
anghorn Dr TW2 152 C4
anghorne Ct 10
NW8 70 B1
anghorne Ho 5
SE7 143 C6
anghorne Rd RM10 81 C1
ang Ho
South Lambeth
SW8 270 A3
Stanwell TW19 148 A3
3 Tufnell Pk N19 71 C5
anghurst Ho 10
SW11 137 A3
angland Cres HA7 25 D1
angland Dr HA5 23 A3
angland Gdns
Croydon CR0 223 B6
West Hampstead
NW3 69 D3
angland Ho 10 SE5 139 B5
Upper Tooting SW17 180 B5
angland Mans NW3 69 D3
angler Rd NW10 90 C5
angley Ave
North Cheam KT4,
SM3 216 D6
Ruislip HA4 62 B6
Surbiton KT6 198 A1
angley Cres
Dagenham RM9 80 D1
Edgware HA8 11 A1
Harlington UB3 127 D5
Wanstead E11 55 C2
angley Ct
South Lambeth
SW8 270 A2
Strand WC2 250 A6
13 Sutton SM2 218 A2
angley Dr
South Acton W3 110 D4
Wanstead E11 55 B2
angley Gdns
Bromley BR2 209 C5
Dagenham RM9 80 D1
Southborough BR5 210 D3
angley Gr KT3 177 C1
angley Ho
11 Lower Clapton
E5 74 B3
36 Paddington W2 91 C2
angley La
SW8 138 A6 270 B6
angley Lawns SM2 218 B1
angley Manor BR3 208 A4
angley Mans SW8 270 B6
angley Park Rd SM1,
SM2 218 A1
angley Park Sch for
Boys BR3 207 D3
angley Park Sch for
Girls BR3 208 A3
angley Pk NW7 27 C4
angley Rd
Beckenham BR3 207 A5
Isleworth TW7 130 D3
Merton SW19 179 C2
Surbiton KT6 198 A2
West Heath DA16 146 C6
angley Row EN5 1 B4
angley St
WC2 94 A1 240 A1
angley Way BR4 208 C2
angmead Dr WD23 8 B3
angmead Ho 34 E3 97 D4
angmead St SE27 183 A6
angmore Ct DA6 146 D2
angmore Ho 39 E1 96 A1
angport Ct KT12 194 C1
angport Ho 1
SW9 138 D3
angridge Mews
TW12 173 B4
angridge 15 NW5 71 A2
angroyd Rd SW17 158 D2
angside Ave SW15 134 A1
angside Cres N14 15 D1
ang St E1 96 C3
angstone Way NW7 28 D3
angston Hughes Cl 5
SE24 138 D1
angthorn Ct EC2 242 D2
angthorne Ct 3
SE6 186 A6
angthorne Ho UB3 105 C2
Langthorne Hospl
E11 76 B5
Langthorne Lo 30
SW2 160 C4
Langthorne Rd E11 76 B5
Langthorne St SW6 134 D5
Langton Ave
Oakleigh Pk N20 14 B4
Wallend E6 100 C4
Langton Cl
WC1 94 B3 240 D6
Langton Ct SW15 157 B5
Langton Ho
Harrow HA2 64 C6
Lambeth SE11 260 D4
5 Streatham SW16 181 C6
Langton Pl SW18 157 C3
Langton Rd
Camberwell SW9 138 D5
Cricklewood NW2 68 C5
East Molesey KT8 196 A5
Harrow Weald HA3 24 A3
Langton Rise SE22,
SE23 162 B4
Langton St
SW10 136 A6 266 B5
Langton Way
Greenwich SE3 143 A5
South Croydon CR0 221 C4
Langtry Ho BR1 187 B3
Langtry Pl SW6 265 B6
Langtry Rd
Northolt UB5 84 D5
Paddington NW8 91 D6
Langtry Wlk
NW8 92 A6 229 A6
Langwood Chase
TW11 175 C4
Langworth Dr UB4 84 B1
Langworthy HA5 23 C4
Lanherne Ho 7
SW19 178 D3
Lanhill Rd W9 91 C3
Lanier Rd SE13 164 B5
Lanigan Dr TW3 151 D6
Lankaster Gdns N2 30 B2
Lankers Dr HA2 41 B3
Lankton Cl BR3 186 A2
Lanner Ho 2 SW11 136 C2
Lannock Ct 2
SW17 180 C4
Lannock Rd UB3 105 D5
Lannoy Point SW6 264 B4
Lannoy Rd SE9 167 A3
Lanrick Rd E14 98 C1
Lanridge Rd SE2 124 D3
Lansan Ct E11 76 D6
Lansbury Ave
Barking IG11 80 A1
Dagenham RM6 59 A4
Edmonton N18 33 C5
Feltham TW14 150 B5
Lansbury Cl NW10 67 A3
Lansbury Ct 4
SE28 124 B6
Lansbury Dr UB4 83 D3
Lansbury Gdns 1
E14 98 B1
Lansbury Ho 5
DA17 125 B1
Lansbury Lawrence
Prim Sch E14 97 D1
Lansbury Rd EN3 6 D4
Lansbury Way N18 33 C5
Lanscombe Wlk
SW8 270 A3
Lansdell Ho 9 SW2 160 C5
Lansdell Rd CR4 181 A1
Lansdown Cl KT12 194 C1
Lansdowne Ave
Orpington BR6 210 D1
West Heath DA7 146 D5
Lansdowne Cl
Tolworth KT5 214 D6
Twickenham TW1 152 D3
Wimbledon SW20 178 D3
Lansdowne Coll W2 245 C5
Lansdowne Copse 1
KT4 216 A6
Lansdowne Cres
W11 113 A6 244 B5
Lansdowne Ct
Redbridge IG5 56 A6
2 Worcester Pk
KT4 216 A6
Lansdowne Dr E8 74 A1
Lansdowne Gdns
SW8 138 A4 270 A2
Lansdowne Gr NW10 67 C4
Lansdowne Hill
SE27 160 D1
Lansdowne Ho
19 Belmont SM2 217 D1
Enfield EN2 4 C3
Notting Hill W11 244 C4
Lansdowne Int Coll Ltd
SW7 256 B5
Lansdowne La SE7 121 D1
Lansdowne Mews
Greenwich SE7 121 D1
Notting Hill W11 244 C4
Lansdowne Pl
Borough The SE1 262 D6
Penge SE19 183 D3
Lansdowne Rd
Chingford E4 19 C2
Croydon CR0 205 B1
Finchley N3 29 C3
Harrow HA1 42 C2
Hayes UB8 83 A1
Hounslow TW3 129 D2
Ilford IG3 57 D2
Leytonstone E11 76 D6
Muswell Hill N10 31 C1
Notting Hill
W11 113 A6 244 B5
Stanmore HA7 25 C4
Sundridge BR1 187 B3
Tottenham N17 34 A2
Walthamstow E17 53 C3
Wanstead E18 55 A6
West Ewell KT19 215 B1
Wimbledon SW19,
SW20 178 C3
Lansdowne Rise
W11 113 A6 244 B5
Lansdowne Row W1 248 D4
Lansdowne Sch
SW9 138 B2
Lansdowne Terr
WC1 240 B5
Lansdowne Way SW4,
SW8 138 A4 270 B1
Lansdowne Wlk
W11 113 B5 244 C4
Lansdowne Wood Cl 11
SE27 160 D1
Lansdowne Workshops
SE7 121 D1
Lansdown Ho 28
SE5 139 A3
Lansdown Rd
Sidcup DA14 168 B1
Upton E7 77 C1
Lansfield Ave N18 34 A6
Lanson Ho HA8 26 C4
Lantern Cl
Orpington BR6 226 D4
Putney SW15 134 A1
Wembley HA0 65 D3
Lantern Ct
Southgate N14 15 D3
4 Wimbledon
SW20 178 D2
Lantern Ho
Millwall E14 119 C4
Woolwich SE18 122 C1
Lanterns Ct E14 119 C3
Lanterns The N12 29 D4
Lantern Way UB7 104 B4
Lant Ho SE1 252 A1
Lantry Ct 1 W3 110 D5
Lant St SE1 117 A4 252 B1
Lanvanor Rd SE15 140 C3
Lanyard Ho 4 SE8 119 B2
Lapford Cl W9 91 B3
Lapponum Wlk UB4 84 D2
Lapsang SE1 253 D3
Lapse Wood Wlk
SE22 162 B3
Lapstone Gdns HA3 43 C3
Lapwing Ct
Grahame Pk NW9 27 C1
Tolworth KT6 214 C5
Lapwing Terr E7 77 D3
Lapwing Twr 31
SE8 141 B6
Lapwing Way UB4 84 D1
Lapworth Ct W2 91 D2
Lapworth 2 N11 31 B6
Lara Cl
Chessington KT9 214 A1
Lewisham SE13 164 A5
Lara Lo SM1 217 C3
Larbert Rd SW16 181 C3
Larch Ave W3 111 C5
Larch Cl
Balham SW12 159 B2
Colney Hatch N11 31 A3
15 Deptford SE8 141 B6
Newham E13 99 C3
10 Upper Holloway
N19 71 C6
Larch Cres
Hayes UB4 84 D2
West Ewell KT19 214 D2
Larch Ct 41 W2 91 C2
Larch Dene BR6 226 C6
Larches Ave SW14 133 B1
Larches The
Edmonton N13 17 A1
Hillingdon UB10 82 D5
Larchfield Ho 2 N5 73 A3
Larch Gn NW9 27 C2
Larch Gr DA15 167 D3
Larch Ho Hayes UB4 84 C2
23 Rotherhithe
SE16 118 C4
Larchmont HA4 39 B2
Larchmore Ct N19 72 A6
Larch Rd
Cricklewood NW2 68 C4
Leyton E10 75 C6
Larch Tree Way
CR0 223 C5
Larchvale Ct 20
SM2 217 D1
Larch Way BR2 210 C2
Larchwood Rd SE9 166 D2
Larcombe Cl CR0 221 D4
Larcom St
SE17 117 A2 262 B3
Larden Rd W3 111 C4
La Retraite RC Girls Sch
SW12 159 C4
Largewood Ave KT6 214 C6
Larissa St SE17 262 D3
Larix Ct NW10 90 A6
Larkbere Rd SE26 185 A6
Larken Cl WD23 8 A3
Larken Dr WD23 8 A3
Larkfield Ave HA3 43 B6
Larkfield Cl BR2 225 A6
Larkfield Rd
Longlands DA14 167 D1
Richmond TW9 132 A1
Larkhall La
SW4 138 A4 270 A1
Lark Hall Prim Sch
SW4 137 D3
Larkhall Rise SW4 137 D3
Larkham Cl TW13 149 C1
Lark Row E2 96 C6
Larksfield Gr EN1 6 B4
Larks Gr IG11 79 C1
Larkshall Bsns Ctr
E4 20 B2
Larkshall Cres E4 36 A6
Larkshall Ct E4 36 A5
Larkshall Rd E4 36 B6
Larkspur Cl
Kingsbury NW9 44 D4
4 Newham E6 100 A2
Ruislip HA4 39 A2
Tottenham N17 33 B3
Larkspur Ct SM6 219 B1
Larkspur Gr HA8 27 A6
Larkspur Way KT19 215 A3
Larkswood Ct E4 36 B5
Larkswood Prim Sch
E4 35 D6
Larkswood Rd E4 35 D6
Larkswood Rise HA5 40 C5
Lark Way SM5 202 C2
Larkway Cl NW9 45 B5
Larmenier & Sacred
Heart RC Prim Sch
W6 112 D2
Larnaca Ho SE1 263 C6
Larnach Rd W6 134 D6
Larne Rd HA4 39 D2
Larpent Ave SW15 156 C6
Larwood Cl UB6 64 B3
La Saint Union RC Sec
Sch NW5 71 A5
Lascelles Ave HA1 42 B2
Lascelles Cl E11 76 B6
Lascelles Ho NW1 237 B5
Lascott's Rd N22 32 B4
Laseron Ho 1 N15 51 D5
Lashford Ho HA8 27 A4
Lassa Rd SE9 166 B6
Lassell St SE10 120 B1
Lasseter Pl SE3 142 D6
Latchett Rd E18 37 B2
Latchingdon Ct E17 52 D5
Latchmere Cl KT2,
TW10 176 A5
Latchmere Jun & Inf
Schs KT2 176 B4
Latchmere La KT2,
TW10 176 B5
Latchmere Rd
Battersea SW11 136 D3
Kingston u T KT2 176 B4
Latchmere St 5
SW11 136 D3
Lateward Rd TW8 131 D6
Latham Cl
Newham E6 100 A1
6 Twickenham
TW1 153 A4
Latham Ct
3 Bowes Pk N11 32 A4
7 Northolt UB5 84 D4
Latham Ho
Stepney E1 96 D1
18 Walthamstow E17 53 D6
Latham Rd
Bexleyheath DA6 169 C6
Twickenham TW1 152 D4
Latham's Way CR0 220 B6
Lathkill Cl EN1 18 A4
Lathkill Ct BR3 185 B2
Lathom Jun Sch E6 78 A1
Lathom Rd E6 78 B1
Lathwood Ho 6
SE26 184 B5
Latimer Ave E6 100 B6
Latimer Cl
North Cheam KT4 216 B4
Pinner Green HA5 22 C2
Latimer Gdns HA5 22 C2
Latimer Ho
11 Homerton E9 74 D2
Notting Hill W11 244 D5
Latimer Ind Est 1
NW10 90 C1
Latimer Pl W10 90 C1
Latimer Rd Barnet EN5 1 D2
1 Croydon CR0 220 D5
Forest Gate E7 77 B4
North Kensington
W10 90 C1
South Tottenham N15 51 C3
Teddington TW11 174 D5
Wimbledon SW19 179 D4
Latimer Road Sta
W10 112 D6
Latimer SE17 263 A1
Latitude Ho NW1 231 C5
Latona Rd SE15 140 A6
La Tourne Gdns
BR6 227 A5
Lattimer Pl W4 133 C6
Latton Cl KT12 195 A2
Latvia Ct SE17 262 B1
Latymer All Saints CE
Prim Sch N9 17 D2
Latymer Ct W6 112 D2
Latymer Rd N9 17 D3
Latymer Sch The N9 17 C2
Latymer Upper Sch
W6 112 A1
Latymer Way N9 17 C2
Laubin Cl TW1 131 B1
Lauder Cl UB5 84 D5
Lauder Ct N14 16 A4
Lauderdale Dr
TW10 153 D1
Lauderdale Mans
W9 91 D4
Lauderdale Rd W9 91 D4
Lauderdale Twr EC2 242 A4
Laud St Croydon CR0 221 A5
Vauxhall
SE11 116 B1 260 C2
Laughton Ho 11
SW2 160 C5
Laughton Rd UB5 84 D6
Launcelot Prim Sch
BR1 187 A6
Launcelot Rd BR1,
SE12 187 A6
Launcelot St SE1 251 A1
Launceston Ct CR7 204 C3
Launceston Gdns
UB6 65 C1
Launceston Pl
W8 114 A3 256 A5
Launceston Rd UB6 87 C6
Launch St E14 120 A3
Laundress La N16 74 A5
Laundry La 7 N1 73 A1
Laundry Mews
SE23 162 D4
Laundry Rd
W6 135 A6 264 A5
Launton Dr DA6 146 D1
Laura Cl Enfield EN1 17 C6
Wanstead E11 55 C4
Laura Ct HA2 24 A1
Lauradale Rd N2 48 D5
Laura Pl E5 74 C4
Laurel Ave TW1 152 D3
Laurel Bank Gdns 3
SW6 135 B3
Laurel Bank Rd EN2 5 B4
Laurel Cl
Sidcup DA14 168 A1
8 Upper Holloway
N19 71 C6
Upper Tooting
SW17 180 C5
Laurel Cres CR0 223 C5
Laurel Ct Dalston E8 73 D1
2 Putney SW15 156 D6
9 Rotherhithe
SE16 119 A5
South Norwood
SE25 205 C4
8 Wembley HA0 88 A5
Laurel Dr N21 16 C4
Laurel Gdns
Bromley BR1 210 A5
Chingford E4 19 D4
Ealing W7 108 C5
Edgware NW7 11 B1
Laurel Gdns *continued*
Hounslow TW4 129 A1
Laurel Gr
Forest Hill SE26 185 A6
Penge SE20 184 C3
Laurel Ho
Brentford W5 109 C2
9 Deptford SE8 141 B6
5 Hamstead NW3 69 D2
Morden SM4 201 D4
Laurel La UB7 104 A2
Laurel Manor SM2 218 A1
Laurel Mead Ct 8
E18 37 A2
Laurel Pk HA3 24 D3
Laurel Rd
Barnes SW13 134 A3
Teddington TW12 174 B5
Wimbledon SW20 178 B2
Laurels The
8 Belvedere
DA17 125 C1
2 Buckhurst Hill IG9 21 C3
Bushey WD23 8 C2
Finchley N3 29 D4
Shortlands BR2 209 A5
9 Sundridge BR1 187 B2
Laurel St E8 73 D2
Laurel View N12 13 D1
Laurel Way
Snaresbrook E18 54 D5
Woodside Pk N20 13 C1
Laurence Ct E10 53 D2
Laurence Mews 12
W12 112 A4
Laurence Pountney Hill
EC4 252 C6
Laurence Pountney La
EC4 252 D6
Laurie Gr SE14 141 A4
Laurie Ho
Newington SE1 261 D5
Notting Hill
W8 113 C5 245 A3
Laurie Rd W7 86 C2
Laurier Rd
Croydon CR0 205 D2
Dartmouth Pk NW5 71 B5
Laurimel Cl HA7 25 B4
Laurino Pl WD23 8 A2
Lauriston Apartments
6 N17 51 D6
Lauriston Ho 6 E9 74 D1
Lauriston Lo NW6 69 B2
Lauriston Rd
Homerton E9 74 D1
Wimbledon SW19 178 D4
Lauriston Sch E9 96 D6
Lausanne Rd
Hornsey N8 50 C5
St Johns SE15 140 C4
Lavehham Ho E17 35 D2
Lavell St N16 73 B4
Lavender Ave
Mitcham CR4 180 D2
North Cheam KT4,
SM3 216 C5
Welsh Harp NW9 45 A1
Lavender Cl
Bromley Comm
BR2 210 A3
South Kensington
SW3 266 D5
Wallington SM5 219 B4
Lavender Ct
Colney Hatch N12 30 C4
East Molesey KT8 195 D6
Edgware HA8 27 A5
Feltham TW14 150 B5
South Lambeth SW4 270 B1
Sutton SM2 218 A1
Lavender Gdns
Clapham SW11 136 D1
Enfield EN2 4 D4
Stanmore HA3 24 C4
Lavender Gr
Dalston E8 74 A1
Mitcham CR4 180 C2
Lavender Hill
Clapham SW11 137 A2
Enfield EN2 4 D4
Lavender Ho
8 Richmond
TW9 132 D4
14 Rotherhithe
SE16 118 D5
Lavender Pl IG1 78 D3
Lavender Prim Sch
EN2 5 C5
Lavender Rd
Battersea SW11 136 B2
Enfield EN2 5 B4
Hillingdon UB8 82 B2
Rotherhithe SE16 119 A5

Lavender Rd *continued*
Sutton SM1 ... 218 B4
Thornton Heath CR0 .. 204 B3
Wallington SM5 ... 219 A4
West Ewell KT19 ... 214 D2
Lavender Rise UB7 ... 104 C4
Lavender St E15 ... 76 C2
Lavender Sweep SW11 ... 136 D1
Lavender Terr 12 SW11 ... 136 C2
Lavender Vale SM6 ... 219 D2
Lavender Way CR0 ... 206 D3
Lavender Wlk SW11 ... 136 D1
Lavendon Ho NW8 .. 237 B6
Lavengro Rd SE27 ... 161 A2
Lavenham Rd SW18 .. 157 C3
Lavernock Rd DA7 ... 147 C3
Lavers Rd N16 ... 73 C5
Laverstoke Gdns SW15 ... 156 A4
Laverton Mews SW5 255 D3
Laverton Pl SW5 ... 255 D3
Lavidge Rd SE9 ... 166 B2
Lavina Gr N1 ... 233 C4
Lavington Cl E9 ... 75 B2
Lavington Rd
Ealing W13 ... 109 B5
Wallington CR0 ... 220 B4
Lavington St SE1 ... 116 D5 251 D3
Lavinia Ct BR1 ... 186 C3
Lavisham Ho BR1 ... 187 B5
Lawdale Jun Sch E2 .. 96 A4
Lawdon Gdns CR0 ... 220 D4
Lawford Rd
Chiswick W4 ... 133 A5
De Beauvoir Town N1 .. 73 C1
Kentish Town NW5 ... 71 C2
Lawfords Wharf 18 NW1 ... 71 C1
Law Ho IG11 ... 102 A5
Lawless Ho 5 E14 ... 120 A6
Lawless St 12 E14 ... 119 D6
Lawley Ho 11 TW1 ... 153 D5
Lawley Rd N14 ... 15 B4
Lawley St E5 ... 74 C4
Lawman Ct 2 TW9 ... 132 B4
Lawn Cl Edmonton N9 .. 17 D4
Kingston u T KT3 ... 177 C1
Ruislip HA4 ... 61 D5
Sundridge BR1 ... 187 B3
Lawn Cres TW9 ... 132 C3
Lawn Farm Gr RM6 ... 59 A5
Lawnfield Ct NW6 ... 68 D1
Lawn Gdns W7 ... 108 C5
Lawn House Cl E14 .. 120 A4
Lawn La SW8 ... 138 B6 270 C6
Lawn Mans EN5 ... 1 B1
Lawn Rd
Beckenham BR3 ... 185 B3
Maitland Pk NW3 ... 70 D3
Lawns Ct HA9 ... 66 C6
Lawnside SE3 ... 142 D1
Lawns The
Belmont SM2 ... 217 A1
Blackheath SE3 ... 142 D2
Chingford E4 ... 35 C5
Harrow HA5 ... 23 D3
Sidcup DA14 ... 190 B6
South Norwood SE19 ... 183 B2
Stoke Newington N16 .. 73 C3
1 Wimbledon SW19 ... 179 B5
Lawn Terr SE3 ... 142 C2
Lawn The UB2 ... 107 C1
Lawn Vale HA5 ... 23 A1
Lawrence Ave
Edmonton N13 ... 32 D6
Higham Hill E17 ... 34 D2
Little Ilford E12 ... 78 C4
Mill Hill NW7 ... 27 D6
New Malden KT3 ... 199 C2
Stonebridge NW10 ... 89 B6
Lawrence Bldgs 1 N16 ... 73 D5
Lawrence Camp Cl N20 ... 14 B1
Lawrence Cl Bow E3 ... 97 C5
6 Shepherd's Bush W12 ... 112 B6
West Green N15 ... 51 C5
Lawrence Cres
Dagenham RM10 ... 81 D5
Edgware HA8 ... 26 C1
Lawrence Ct
Hornsey N10 ... 49 C6
Mill Hill NW7 ... 27 C5
4 South Acton W3 .. 111 A3
Stoke Newington N16 .. 73 D5
5 Woodford IG8 ... 37 C4
Lawrence Dr UB10 ... 61 A4
Lawrence Est TW4 .. 128 C1
Lawrence Gdns NW7 .. 11 D1
Lawrence Hall E13 ... 99 B3
Lawrence Hill E4 ... 19 C2
Lawrence Ho
Bowes Pk N22 ... 32 B4
20 Camden Town NW1 ... 71 B1
Westminster SW1 ... 259 D3
Lawrence La EC2 ... 242 B2
Lawrence Mans SW3 ... 267 A5
Lawrence Pl N1 ... 233 B6
Lawrence Rd
Coney Hall BR4 ... 225 A4
Ealing W5 ... 109 D2
Edmonton N18 ... 34 B6
Erith DA8 ... 147 D5
Hampton TW12 ... 173 B3
Hillingdon UB4 ... 83 A5
Hounslow TW4 ... 128 C1
Pinner HA5 ... 40 D4
Richmond TW10 ... 175 C6
South Norwood SE25 ... 205 D5
Tottenham N15 ... 51 C5
Upton Pk E6 ... 100 A6
West Ham E13 ... 99 B6
Lawrence St
Canning Town E16 ... 98 D2
Chelsea SW3 ... 136 C6 267 A5
Mill Hill NW7 ... 27 D6
Lawrence Trad Est SE10 ... 120 C2
Lawrence Univ SW7 256 B3
Lawrence Way NW10 .. 67 B5
Lawrence Weaver Cl SM4 ... 201 C3
Lawrence Yd N15 ... 51 C5
Lawrie Ct HA3 ... 24 D3
Lawrie Park Ave SE26 ... 184 B5
Lawrie Park Cres SE26 ... 184 B5
Lawrie Park Gdns SE26 ... 184 B5
Lawrie Park Rd SE26 ... 184 C5
Laws Cl SE25 ... 205 B5
Lawson Cl Ilford IG1 ... 79 B3
Newham E16 ... 99 C2
Wimbledon SW19 ... 156 D1
Lawson Ct
1 Finsbury Pk N4 ... 50 B1
13 Surbiton KT6 ... 197 D2
Lawson Gdns HA5 ... 40 B6
Lawson Ho
17 Shepherd's Bush W12 ... 112 B6
1 Woolwich SE18 .. 144 C6
Lawson Rd Enfield EN3 .. 6 C4
Southall UB1 ... 85 C3
Law St SE1 ... 117 B3 262 D6
Lawton Rd Barnet EN4 .. 2 B2
Bow E3 ... 97 A4
Leytonstone E10 ... 54 A1
Laxcon Cl NW10 ... 67 B3
Laxey Rd BR6 ... 227 D2
Laxfield Ct E8 ... 96 A6
Laxley Cl SE5 ... 138 D5
Laxmi Ct N3 ... 29 B2
Laxton Ct CR7 ... 205 A5
Laxton Path 1 SE4 .. 140 D1
Laxton Pl NW1 ... 238 D6
Layard Rd Enfield EN1 ... 5 D4
Rotherhithe SE16 ... 118 B2
South Norwood CR7 .. 183 B1
Layard Sq SE16 ... 118 B2
Laybourne Ho 18 E14 ... 119 C4
Laycock Prim Sch N1 ... 72 D2
Laycock St N1 ... 72 C2
Layer Gdns W3 ... 110 C6
Layfield Cl NW4 ... 46 B2
Layfield Cres NW4 ... 46 B2
Layfield Ho 1 SE10 .. 121 A1
Layfield Rd NW4 ... 46 B2
Laymarsh Cl DA17 ... 125 B3
Laymead Cl UB5 ... 63 A2
Laystall Ct EC1 ... 241 A5
Laystall St EC1 ... 241 A5
Layton Cres CR0 ... 220 D3
Layton Ct TW8 ... 109 D1
Layton Pl TW9 ... 132 C4
Layton Rd
Brentford TW8 ... 109 D1
Hounslow TW3 ... 129 D1
Layton's La TW16 ... 171 D1
Layzell Wlk SE9 ... 165 D3
Lazar Wlk 2 N7 ... 72 B6
Leabank Cl HA1 ... 64 C5
Leabank Sq E9 ... 75 C2
Leabank View N15 ... 52 A3
Leabourne Rd N16 ... 52 A2
LEA BRIDGE ... 74 D5
Lea Bridge Rd E10 ... 53 C2
Lea Cl TW2 ... 151 B4
Lea Cotts 10 CR4 ... 181 A1
Lea Cres HA4 ... 61 D4
Leacroft Ave SW12 ... 158 D4
Leacroft Cl
Southgate N21 ... 16 D2
8 Yiewsley UB7 ... 104 A6
Lea Ct
3 Bedford Pk W12 ... 111 C4
1 Chingford E4 ... 20 A2
3 Hillingdon UB10 ... 82 D3
2 Newham E13 ... 99 A4
Leadale Ave E4 ... 19 C2
Leadale Rd N16 ... 52 A3
Leadbeaters Cl 8 N11 ... 30 D5
Leadbetter Ct 12 NW10 ... 67 B1
Leadenhall Mkt EC3 . 243 A1
Leadenhall Pl EC3 .. 243 A1
Leadenhall St EC3 ... 95 C1 243 A1
Leadenham Ct 15 E3 .. 97 C3
Leader Ave E12 ... 78 C3
Leadings The HA9 ... 67 A5
Leaf Cl KT7, KT8 ... 196 C4
Leaf Gr SE27 ... 182 C5
Leaf Ho Barnet EN5 ... 1 D1
9 Harrow HA1 ... 42 D4
Leafield Cl SW16 ... 182 D4
Leafield La DA14 ... 169 B1
Leafield Rd
Merton SW19, SW20 ... 201 B6
Sutton SM1 ... 217 C6
Leafy Gr BR2 ... 225 C3
Leafy Oak Rd SE12 ... 165 C1
Leafy Way CR0 ... 221 D6
Lea Gdns HA9 ... 66 B4
Leagrave St E5 ... 74 C5
Lea Hall Gdns E10 ... 53 C1
Lea Hall Rd E10 ... 53 C1
Lea Ho
2 Edmonton N9 ... 18 A1
Lisson Gr NW8 ... 237 A5
Leaholme Waye HA4 .. 39 A3
Lea Ho E5 ... 52 C1
Leahurst Rd SE13 ... 164 B6
Lea Int E9 ... 75 C3
Leake St
Lambeth SE1 ... 251 A1
South Bank SE1 ... 116 B4 250 D2
Lealand Rd N15 ... 51 D3
Leamington Ave
Bromley BR1 ... 187 C5
Farnborough BR6 ... 227 C4
Merton SM4 ... 201 B5
Walthamstow E17 ... 53 C4
Leamington Cl
Bromley BR1 ... 187 C5
Hounslow TW3 ... 152 A6
Plashet E12 ... 78 A3
Leamington Cres HA2 ... 63 B5
Leamington Ct
4 Forest Hill SE26 ... 162 A1
North Acton W3 ... 89 B2
Leamington Gdns IG3 ... 79 D6
Leamington Ho
Edgware HA8 ... 26 B5
4 Kensal Town W11 ... 91 B2
Leamington Pk W3 ... 89 B2
Leamington Pl UB4 ... 83 D3
Leamington Rd UB2 ... 106 D2
Leamington Rd Villas W11 ... 91 B2
Leamington Villas SE13 ... 164 C6
Leamore St W6 ... 112 C2
Leamouth Rd
Newham E6 ... 100 A2
South Bromley E14 ... 98 B1
Leander Ct
11 Edgware NW9 ... 27 C2
27 Hackney E9 ... 74 C1
St Johns SE8 ... 141 C4
5 Surbiton KT6 ... 197 D2
Leander Rd
Northolt UB5 ... 85 C5
Thornton Heath CR7 .. 204 B5
Tulse Hill SW2 ... 160 C5
Lea Park Trad Est E10 ... 53 B1
Lea Rd
2 Beckenham BR3 ... 185 C1
Enfield EN2 ... 5 B4
Southall UB2 ... 107 A2
Learner Dr HA2 ... 63 C6
Learoyd Gdns E6 ... 122 C6
Leary Ho SE11 ... 260 D1
Leas Cl KT9 ... 214 B1
Leas Dale SE9 ... 166 C1
Leas Gn BR7 ... 189 D4
Leaside Ave N10 ... 49 A5
Leaside Bsns Ctr EN3 .. 7 B3
Leaside Ct UB10 ... 82 D4
Leaside Ho 4 E5 ... 52 B1
Leaside Mans N10 ... 49 A6
Leaside Rd E5 ... 52 C1
Leasowes Rd E10 ... 53 C1
Lea Sq 22 E3 ... 97 B6
Leas The SE18 ... 144 D4
Leatherbottle Gn DA18 ... 125 B3
Leather Cl CR4 ... 181 A1
Leatherdale St
32 Bethnal Green E1 ... 96 C3
19 Globe Town E1 ... 96 D4
Leather Gdns E15 ... 98 C6
Leatherhead Cl N16 ... 51 D1
Leatherhead Rd KT9 ... 213 D1
Leather La EC1 ... 94 C2 241 B4
Leathermarket Ct SE1 ... 253 A1
Leathermarket St SE1 ... 117 C4 253 A1
Leather Rd SE16 ... 118 D2
Leathersellers Cl 5 EN5 ... 1 A2
Leathsale Rd HA2 ... 63 D5
Leathwaite Rd SW11 ... 158 D6
Leathwell Rd SE8 ... 141 D3
Lea Valley Prim Sch N17 ... 34 A3
Lea Valley Rd EN3 ... 19 B5
Lea Valley Technopark N17 ... 52 A6
Lea Valley Trad Est N18 ... 34 D5
Leaveland Cl BR3 ... 207 C5
Leaver Gdns UB6 ... 86 C5
Leavesden Rd HA7 ... 25 A4
Lea View Ho E5 ... 52 B1
Lebanon Ave TW13 ... 172 D5
Lebanon Ct 10 TW1 .. 153 B4
Lebanon Gdns SW18 ... 157 C5
Lebanon Park Mans TW1 ... 153 B4
Lebanon Pk TW1 ... 153 B4
Lebanon Rd
Croydon CR0 ... 205 C1
Wandsworth SW18 .. 157 C6
Lebanon Road Sta CR0 ... 221 C6
Lebrun Sq SE3 ... 143 B2
Lebus Ho NW8 ... 230 A3
Le Chateau CR0 ... 221 B5
Lechmere App IG8 ... 37 D1
Lechmere Ave IG8 ... 37 D1
Lechmere Rd NW2 ... 68 B2
Leckford Rd SW18 ... 158 A3
Leckhampton Pl 23 SW2 ... 160 C4
Leckwith Ave DA7 ... 147 A6
Lecky Ho NW2 ... 68 B4
Lecky St SW7 ... 114 B1 256 C2
Leclair Ho SE3 ... 143 B2
L'Ecole des Petits Sch SW6 ... 135 D3
Leconfield Ave SW13, SW15 ... 133 D2
Leconfield Ho SE5 ... 139 C2
Leconfield Rd N5 ... 73 B4
Lector Ct EC1 ... 241 B5
Leda Ave EN3 ... 6 D5
Leda Ct 9 SW9 ... 138 C5
Ledalle Ho NW2 ... 68 B5
Ledam Bldg EC1 ... 241 A4
Leda Rd SE18 ... 122 B3
Ledbury Ho 12 SE22 .. 139 C2
Ledbury Mews N W11 ... 91 C1
Ledbury Mews W W11 ... 245 A6
Ledbury Pl 10 CR0 ... 221 A4
Ledbury Rd
Croydon CR0 ... 221 B4
Kensington W11 ... 91 C1
Ledbury St SE15 ... 140 A5
Ledo Ho 1 N16 ... 73 B4
Ledrington Rd SE19 .. 184 A4
Ledway Dr HA9 ... 44 B2
LEE ... 164 D5
Lee Ave RM6 ... 59 A3
Leechcroft Ave DA15 ... 167 D6
Leechcroft Rd SM6 ... 219 A5
Lee Church St SE13 .. 142 C1
Lee Cl Higham Hill E17 ... 34 D2
New Barnet EN5 ... 2 A1
Lee Conservancy Rd E9 ... 75 B3
Leecroft Rd EN5 ... 1 A1
Lee Ct SE13 ... 142 B1
Leeds Ct
7 Carshalton SM5 ... 218 D5
Catford SE6 ... 163 D1
Clerkenwell EC1 ... 241 C6
Leeds Rd IG1 ... 57 B1
Leeds St N18 ... 34 A5
Leegate SE12 ... 164 D6
Lee Green SE12 ... 142 D1
Lee High Rd SE12, SE13 ... 142 C1
Lee Ho
3 Kentish Town N19 ... 71 D3
Wimbledon SW19 ... 179 D4
Leeke St WC1 .. 94 B4 233 C2
Leeland Mans 15 W13 ... 109 A5
Leeland Rd W13 ... 109 A5
Leeland Terr W13 ... 109 A5
Leeland Way NW10 ... 67 D4
Lee Manor Sch SE13 ... 164 C5
Lee Mews BR3 ... 207 A6
Lee Park Way N9, N18 ... 19 A1
Lee Pk SE3 ... 142 D2
Leerdam Dr E14 ... 120 A3
Lee Rd Enfield EN1 ... 18 A5
Lewisham SE3 ... 142 D1
Merton SW19 ... 179 D2
Mill Hill NW7 ... 28 D3
Wembley UB6 ... 87 C6
Lees Ct W1 ... 248 A6
Lees Ho SE17 ... 262 D1
Leeside EN5 ... 13 A5
Leeside Cres NW11 .. 47 C3
Leeside Ind Est N17 .. 34 B3
Leeside Rd N17 ... 34 B4
Leeside Trad Est N17 ... 34 C3
Leeside Works N17 ... 34 C3
Leeson Ho 7 TW1 ... 153 B4
Leeson Rd 12 SE24 ... 138 C1
Leesons Hill BR5, BR7 ... 211 D6
Leesons Way BR5 ... 189 D1
Lees Par UB10 ... 82 D3
Lees Pl W1 ... 115 A6 248 A6
Lees Rd UB8 ... 82 D3
Lee Sta SE12 ... 165 A5
Lee St E8 ... 95 D6
Lees The CR0 ... 223 B6
Leet Ct N16 ... 73 B4
Lee Terr SE3 ... 142 C2
Lee Valley Country Pk EN3 ... 7 C4
Lee Valley L Ctr N9 .. 19 A3
Lee Valley Riding Ctr E10 ... 52 D1
Lee Valley Sp Ctr E10 ... 75 D4
Leeve Ho 7 W9 ... 91 B4
Leeview Ct 7 E4 ... 20 A3
Lee View EN2 ... 4 D4
Leeward Ct 3 E1 ... 118 A5
Leeward Gdns SW19 ... 179 B5
Leeway Cl HA5 ... 23 B3
Leeway SE8 ... 119 B1
Leewood Cl SE12 ... 165 A5
Lefevre Wlk E3 ... 97 C6
Leffern Rd W12 ... 112 A4
Leff Ho 9 NW6 ... 69 A1
Lefroy Ho SE1 ... 252 A1
Lefroy Rd W12 ... 111 D4
Legard Rd N5 ... 72 D5
Legat Ct N4 ... 51 A4
Legatt Rd SE9 ... 165 D6
Leggatt Rd E15 ... 98 A5
Legge St SE13 ... 164 A6
Leghorn Rd
Plumstead SE18 ... 123 B1
Willesden Green NW10 ... 90 A5
Legion Cl N1 ... 72 C1
Legion Ct SM4 ... 201 C3
Legion Rd UB6 ... 86 A5
Legion Terr E3 ... 97 C6
Legion Way N12 ... 30 C3
Legrace Ave TW4, TW5 ... 128 D3
Leicester Ave CR4 ... 204 A5
Leicester Cl KT4 ... 216 C4
Leicester Ct
46 Paddington W2 ... 91 C2
St James WC2 ... 249 D6
5 Twickenham TW1 ... 153 D5
Leicester Gdns IG3 ... 57 C2
Leicester Ho
4 Brixton SW9 ... 138 D2
Carshalton SM5 ... 218 C5
Leicester Ho *continued*
5 Putney SW15 ... 156 C
2 Thames Ditton KT7 ... 197 A
Leicester Mews N2 ... 48 C
Leicester Pl WC2 ... 249 D
Leicester Rd
Barnet EN5 ... 1 D
Croydon CR0 ... 205 C
East Finchley N2 ... 48 C
Stonebridge NW10 ... 67 B
Wanstead E11 ... 55 B
Leicester Square Sta WC2 ... 115 D6 249 D
Leicester Sq* WC2 ... 115 D6 249 D
Leicester St WC2 ... 249 D
Leigham Ave SW16 ... 160 A
Leigham Cl
Streatham SW16 ... 182 B
9 Wallington SM6 .. 219 C
Leigham Court Rd SW16 ... 182 C
Leigham Dr TW7 ... 130 C
Leigham Hall Par 2 SW16 ... 160 A
Leigham Hall 3 SW16 ... 160 A
Leigham Vale SE27, SW16, SW2 ... 160 C
Leigh Ave IG4 ... 55 D
Leigh Cl KT3 ... 199 B
Leigh Close Ind Est KT3 ... 199 B
Leigh Cres CR0 ... 223 D
Leigh Ct Harrow HA2 ... 42 C
22 Tulse Hill SW2 ... 160 C
3 Woodford E18 ... 37 A
Leighfield Ho 5 N4 ... 51 A
Leigh Gdns NW10 ... 90 C
Leigh Ho
4 Kingston u T KT2 ... 176 D
9 Putney SW15 ... 156 A
Leigh Hunt Dr N14 ... 15 D
Leigh Orchard Cl SW16 ... 160 B
Leigh Pl
Feltham TW13 ... 150 C
Holborn EC1 ... 241 A
Welling DA16 ... 146 A
Leigh Rd Highbury N5 .. 72 D
Isleworth TW3 ... 130 B
Leytonstone E10 ... 54 A
Wallend E6 ... 78 C
Leigh St WC1 .. 94 A4 233 A
Leigh The KT2 ... 177 C
Leighton Ave
Little Ilford E12 ... 78 C
Pinner HA5 ... 41 A
Leighton Cl HA8 ... 26 C
Leighton Cres NW5 ... 71 C
Leighton Ct NW7 ... 28 D
Leighton Gdns
Thornton Heath CR0 ... 204 D
Willesden Green NW10 ... 90 C
Leighton Gr NW5 ... 71 C
Leighton Ho 7 KT6 .. 198 A
Leighton House (Art Gall & Mus)* W14 ... 254 D
Leighton Pl NW5 ... 71 C
Leighton Rd
Ealing W13 ... 109 A
Enfield EN1 ... 18 A
Harrow HA3 ... 24 B
Kentish Town NW5 ... 71 C
Leighton St CR0 ... 204 D
Leila Parnell Pl 14 SE7 ... 143 C
Leinster Ave SW14 ... 133 A
Leinster Gdns W2 ... 114 A6 246 A
Leinster Mews
7 Barnet EN5 ... 1 A
Bayswater W2 ... 246 A
Leinster Pl W2 ... 236 A
Leinster Rd N10 ... 49 B
Leinster Sq W2 ... 91 D
Leinster Terr W2 ... 246 A
Leisure Way N12 ... 30 B
Leitch Ho 8 NW8 ... 70 B
Leith Cl NW9 ... 45 B
Leithcote Gdns SW16 ... 182 B
Leithcote Path SW16 ... 160 B
Leith Hill BR5 ... 190 A
Leith Hill Gn BR5 ... 190 A
Leith Ho
7 Kentish Town N7 ... 71 D
13 Streatham SW2 ... 160 B
Leith Mans W9 ... 91 D
Leith Rd N22 ... 32 D

ith Towers 7
M2 217 D1
ith Yd 3 NW6 91 C6
la Ave TW4, TW5 128 C3
litia Cl E8 96 A6
ly Ho 3 UB5 84 D5
man St E1 96 A1
mark Cl HA7 25 C4
May Ave SE12 165 B1
mmon Rd SE10 142 C6
mna Ct E11 54 C2
mna Rd E11 54 C2
Moal Ho 28 E1 96 C2
mon Gr TW14 150 A3
monwell Ct SE9 167 A6
monwell Dr SE9 167 A6
msford Cl N15 52 A4
msford Ct N4 73 A6
na Cres N9 18 C2
na Gardens Prim Sch
W6 112 C3
na Gdns W6 112 C3
na Kennedy Cl E4 36 A4
nan Ct W13 109 C5
n Clifton Ho 12
SE18 122 B2
ndal Terr 7 SW4 137 D2
nelby Rd KT6 198 C1
n Freeman Pl
SW6 264 C5
nham Ho SE1 252 D1
nham 11 NW5 71 A2
nham Rd
Erith DA7 147 B6
Lewisham SE12 142 D1
South Norwood CR7 183 B1
Sutton SM1 218 A3
nnard Ave BR4 224 C6
nnard Cl BR4 224 C6
nnard Rd
Bromley BR2 210 B1
Croydon CR0 205 A1
Penge BR3 185 A4
nnon Rd NW2 68 C2
nnox Gdns
Croydon CR0 220 D4
Knightsbridge
SW1 114 D3 257 C5
nnox Gdns Mews
SW1 257 C4
nnox Gdns
Redbridge IG1 56 B1
Willesden NW10 67 D4
nnox Ho
7 Belvedere
DA17 125 C3
10 Hackney E9 74 C2
4 Twickenham
TW1 153 D5
nnox Rd
Finsbury Pk N4, N7 72 C6
Walthamstow E17 53 C3
nor Cl DA6 147 A1
nsbury Way SE2 124 D3
ns Rd E7 77 C1
nthall Ho SW1 259 B1
nthall Rd E8 74 A1
nthorp Rd SE10 120 D2
ntmead Rd BR1 164 D1
nton Rise TW9 132 A2
nton St SE18 123 B2
n Williams Ct NW6 91 C5
o Ct 4 TW8 131 D5
of Cres SE6 185 D5
ominster Rd SM4 202 A3
ominster Wlk
SM4 202 A3
onard Ave SM4 202 A4
onard Ct
Bloomsbury WC1 240 A6
Harrow HA3 24 C3
Kensington W8 255 A6
onard Day Ho 3
NW5 71 B2
onard Ho 10 E17 54 A5
onard Pl 6 N16 73 C4
onard Rd
Chingford E4 35 C4
Edmonton N9 18 A1
Forest Gate E7 77 A4
Mitcham CR4, SW16 181 C2
Southall UB2 106 D2
onard Robbins Path
3 SE28 124 B6
onard St
Broadgate
EC2 95 B3 242 D6
Newham E16 122 A5
onora Ho W9 236 A6
ontine Cl SE15 140 A5
opards Ct EC1 241 A4
opold Ave SW19 179 B5
opold Bldgs 14 E2 95 D4
opold Ct 12 SW19 179 B5
opold Mews E9 96 C6
eopold Prim Sch
NW10 67 D1

Leopold Rd
Ealing W5 110 B5
East Finchley N2 48 B6
Edmonton N18 34 B5
Walthamstow E17 53 C4
Willesden NW10 67 C1
Wimbledon SW19 179 B5
Leopold St E3 97 B2
Leopold Terr SW19 179 C5
Leopold Wlk SE11 260 C1
Leo St SE15 140 B5
Leo Yd EC1 241 D5
Leppoc Rd SW4 159 D6
Leroy St SE1 117 C2 263 A4
Lerry Cl W14 264 D6
Lerwick Ct 4 EN1 17 C6
Lerwick Ho SW18 136 A1
Lescombe Cl SE23 163 A1
Lescombe Rd SE23,
SE6 163 A1
Lesley Cl DA5 169 D4
Lesley Ct
8 Wallington
SM6 219 B4
Westminster SW1 259 C5
Leslie Gdns SM2 217 C1
Leslie Gr CR0 205 C1
Leslie Grove Pl CR0 205 C1
Leslie Park Rd CR0 205 C1
Leslie Prince Ct 8
SE5 139 B5
Leslie Rd
East Finchley N2 48 B6
Leyton E11 76 B4
Newham E16 99 B1
Leslie Smith Sq 7
SE18 144 C6
Lessar Ave SW4 159 C5
Lessar Ct SW4 159 C5
Lessingham Ave
Ilford IG5 56 D6
Upper Tooting
SW17 181 A6
Lessing St SE23 163 A4
Lessness Ave DA7 146 D5
LESSNESS HEATH 125 D1
Lessness Heath Prim
Sch DA17 125 C1
Lessness Pk DA17 125 C1
Lessness Rd
Belvedere DA17 125 C1
Morden SM4 202 A4
Lester Ave E16 98 C3
Lester Ct 42 E3 97 D4
Lester Ho IG8 36 B3
Lestock Cl 2 SE25 206 A6
Lestock Ho SE3 143 D4
Lestor Ct TW7 130 D2
Leswin Pl N16 73 D5
Leswin Rd N16 73 D5
Letchford Gdns
NW10 90 A4
Letchford Mews
NW10 90 A4
Letchmore Ho 7
W10 90 C3
Letchworth Ave
TW14 149 D4
Letchworth Cl
Bromley BR2 209 A4
South Oxhey WD19 22 D5
Letchworth Dr BR2 209 A4
Letchworth St
SW17 180 D6
Lethaby Ho 15 SW4 138 B1
Lethbridge Cl SE13 142 A3
Letterstone Rd SW6 264 C3
Lettice St
SW6 135 B4 264 D1
Lett Rd E15 76 B1
Lettsom St SE5 139 C3
Lettsom Wlk 1 E13 99 A5
Leucha Rd E17 53 A4
Levana Cl SW19 157 A3
Levant Ho 17 E1 96 D3
Levehurst Ho SE27 183 A5
Levehurst Way SW4,
SW9 138 A3
Leven Cl WD19 22 D5
Levendale Rd SE23 163 B2
Leven Rd E14 98 B1
Leven Way UB3 83 C1
Lever Ct 15 E9 74 D2
Leverett St SW3 257 B4
Leverholme Gdns
SE9 188 C6
Leverington Pl N1 235 D1
Leverson St SW16 181 C4
Lever St EC1 95 A4 235 A1
Leverstock Ho SW3 257 B2
Leverton Pl NW5 71 C3
Leverton St NW5 71 C3
Levett Gdns IG3 80 A5
Levett Ho 8 SW16 181 C5
Levett Rd IG11 79 C2
Levine Gdns IG11 102 D5
Levison Way 2 N19 49 D1

Levita Ho NW1 232 D2
Levyne Ct EC1 241 A6
Lewes Cl UB5 63 C2
Lewes Ct 3 CR4 202 D6
Lewesdon Cl 13
SW19 156 D3
Lewes Ho
Bermondsey SE1 253 B2
Peckham SE15 140 A6
Lewes Rd
Bromley BR1 187 D1
Colney Hatch N12 30 C5
Leweston Pl N16 51 D2
Lewey Ho E3 97 B3
Lewgars Ave NW9 45 A3
Lewin Ct
4 Plumstead
SE18 123 C2
Streatham SW16 182 A4
Lewing Cl BR6 211 C1
Lewington Ct EN3 6 D6
Lewin Rd Bexley DA6 147 A1
Mortlake SW14 133 B2
Streatham SW16 181 D4
Lewin Terr TW14 149 B4
Lewis Ave E17 35 C2
Lewis Cl N14 15 C4
Lewis Cres NW10 67 B3
Lewis Ct 5 SE16 118 B1
Lewis Gdns N2 30 B1
Lewis Gr SE13 142 A2
LEWISHAM 142 A1
Lewisham Bridge Prim
Sch SE13 141 D2
Lewisham Bsns Ctr
SE14 140 D6
Lewisham Coll SE4 141 C3
Lewisham Ct EN3 7 C5
Lewisham Ctr SE13 142 A2
Lewisham High St
SE13 163 D6
Lewisham Hill SE13 142 A3
Lewisham Hospl
SE13 163 D6
Lewisham Pk SE13 164 A5
Lewisham Rd SE13 142 A3
Lewisham Sta SE13 142 A2
Lewisham St SW1 249 D1
Lewisham Way SE4,
SE14 141 B4
Lewis Ho 2 E4 35 C5
Lewis King Ho BR1 187 B3
Lewis Pl E8 74 A3
Lewis Rd
Bexley DA16 146 C2
Mitcham CR4 180 C1
19 Richmond TW10 153 D6
Sidcup DA14 168 C1
Southall UB1 107 A4
Sutton SM1 217 D4
Lewis Silkin Ho 9
SE15 140 C6
Lewis Sports & L Ctr
SE19 183 D2
Lewis St NW1 71 B2
Lewiston Cl KT4 200 B2
Lewis Way RM10 81 D2
Lexden Dr RM6 58 B3
Lexden Rd Acton W3 110 D5
Mitcham CR4 203 D5
Lexdon Ct RM6 58 B3
Lexfield Ho N5 73 A4
Lexham Ct UB6 86 B6
Lexham Gardens Mews
W8 255 D5
Lexham Gdns
W8 113 D2 255 C4
Lexham Ho 8 IG11 101 B6
Lexham Mews
W8 113 C2 255 B4
Lexham Wlk W8 255 D5
Lexington Pl KT1 175 D2
Lexington St
W1 115 C6 249 B6
Lexton Gdns SW12 159 D3
Leyborne Ave W13 109 C4
Leyborne Pk TW9 132 C4
Leybourne Cl BR2 209 A3
Leybourne Ct 1
SE25 206 A6
Leybourne Ho 20
SE15 140 C6
Leybourne Rd
17 Camden Town
NW1 71 B1
Hillingdon UB10 83 A6
Leytonstone E11 54 D1
Queensbury NW9 44 C4
Leybourne St 5
NW1 71 B1
Leybridge Ct SE12 165 A6
Leyburn Cl E17 53 D5
Leyburn Gdns CR0 221 C6
Leyburn Gr N18 34 A4
Leyburn Ho SE18 144 A5
Leyburn Rd N18 34 B4
Leyden Mans 7 N19 50 A2

Leyden St E1 95 D2 243 C3
Leydon Cl SE16 118 D5
Leyes Rd E16 99 D1
Leyfield KT4 199 D1
Ley Ho SE1 252 A1
Leyland Ave EN3 7 A3
Leyland Ct 8 N11 31 B6
Leyland Gdns IG8 37 C5
Leyland Ho
6 Canary Wharf
E14 119 D6
12 Richmond TW10 153 C1
Leyland Rd SE12 165 A6
Leylands SW18 157 B5
Leylang Rd SE14 140 D5
Leys Cl Finchley N12 30 C3
Harrow HA1 42 B4
Leys Ct 9 SW9 138 C3
Leysdown Ho SE17 263 B2
Leysdown 9 NW5 71 A2
Leysdown Rd SE9 166 B2
Leysfield Rd W12 112 A4
Leys Gdns EN4 15 A6
Leyspring Rd E11 54 D1
Leys Rd E EN3 7 A4
Leys Rd W EN3 7 A4
Leys The
East Finchley N2 48 A5
Harrow HA3 44 B3
Ley St Ilford IG1 78 D6
Newbury Pk IG1, IG2 57 B1
Leyswood Dr IG2 57 C4
Leythe Rd W3 111 A4
LEYTON 76 B5
Leyton Bsns Ctr E10 75 C6
Leyton Ct SE23 162 C3
Leyton Grange E10 53 C1
Leyton Green Rd E10 54 A3
Leyton Green Twrs
E10 54 A3
Leyton Ind Village
E10 52 D2
Leyton Link Est E10 53 A2
Leyton Midland Road
Sta E10 54 A1
Leyton Mills E10 76 A4
Leyton Park Rd E10 76 A5
Leyton Rd
Merton SW19 180 A3
Stratford E15 76 B2
Leyton Sixth Form Coll
E10 54 B3
Leyton Stadium (Leyton
Orient FC) E10 75 D5
Leyton Sta E11 76 A5
LEYTONSTONE 54 D1
Leytonstone Bsns &
Spec Sch E11 54 C3
Leytonstone High Road
Sta E11 76 C6
Leytonstone Rd E15 76 C3
Leytonstone Sta E11 54 C1
Leyton Town Ctr E10 76 A5
Leywick St E15 98 C5
Lezayre Rd BR6 227 D2
Liardet St SE14 141 A6
Liberia Rd N5 72 D2
Libert Cl N18 33 D6
Liberty Ave SW19 180 B2
Liberty Ct IG11 102 C5
Liberty Ctr HA0 88 B6
Liberty Ho 11 E1 118 A6
Liberty Mews
Balham SW12 159 B5
Orpington BR6 227 D6
Liberty Sch CR4 180 C1
Liberty St
SW9 138 B4 270 D2
Libra Rd 7 Bow E3 97 B5
Newham E13 99 A5
Library Ct N17 51 D6
Library Mans 4
W12 112 C4
Library Par NW10 89 C6
Library Pl E1 118 B6
Library St
SE1 116 D4 251 D1
Libro Ct E4 35 C6
Lichen Ct IG6 56 D6
Lichfield Cl EN4 2 D2
Lichfield Ct
Kingston u T KT6 198 A4
Richmond TW9 132 A1
Lichfield Gdns TW10,
TW9 154 A6
Lichfield Gr N3 29 C1
Lichfield Ho 27 SE5 139 A3
Lichfield Rd
Dagenham RM8 80 C5
Edmonton N9 18 A2
Hounslow TW4 128 C2
Mile End E3 97 A4
Newham E6 99 D4
Northwood HA6 40 A6
Richmond TW9 132 B4
West Hampstead
NW2 69 A4

Lichfield Rd *continued*
Woodford IG8 36 C6
Lichfield Terr 1
TW9 154 A6
Lichlade Cl 7 BR6 227 D4
Lichport Ct N4 50 D1
Lickey Ho W14 264 D6
Lidbury Rd NW7 29 A4
Lidcote Gdns 22
SW9 138 B3
Liddall Way UB7 104 B5
Liddell Cl HA3 43 D6
Liddell Gdns NW10 90 C5
Liddell Rd NW6 69 C2
Lidding Rd HA3 43 D4
Liddington Rd E15 98 D6
Liddlesdale Ho E 6
KT2 176 D2
Liddlesdale Ho W 5
KT2 176 D2
Liddon Rd
Bromley BR1 209 D6
Newham E13 99 B4
Liden Cl E10, E17 53 B1
Lidfield Rd N16 73 B4
Lidgate Rd 22 SE15 139 D5
Lidiard Rd SW18 158 A2
Lidlington Pl NW1 232 B3
Lido Sq N17 33 B1
Lidyard Rd N19 49 C1
Liffey Ct Edmonton N9 18 C1
Willesden NW10 68 A1
Liffler Rd SE18 123 C1
Liffords Pl SW13 133 D3
Lifford St SW15 134 D1
Lightcliffe Rd N13 16 C1
Lighter Cl 16 SE16 119 A2
Lighterman Mews 15
E1 96 D1
Lighterman's Rd
E14 119 D4
Lighterman's Wlk
SW18 135 C1
Lightfoot Rd N8 50 A4
Light Horse Ct SW1 258 A1
Lightley Cl HA0 88 B6
Ligonier St E2 243 C6
Lilac Cl E4 35 B4
Lilac Ct
Colney Hatch N12 30 C4
3 Newham E13 99 C6
Teddington TW11 174 D6
Lilac Gdns
Croydon CR0 223 C5
Ealing W5 109 D3
Hayes UB3 83 C1
Lilac Ho SE4 141 B2
Lilac Pl
Vauxhall
SE11 116 B2 260 C3
Yiewsley UB7 104 B6
Lilac St W12 112 A6
Lilah Mews BR2 186 D1
Lilburne Gdns SE9 166 A6
Lilburne Rd SE9 166 A6
Lilburne Wlk NW10 67 A2
Lile Cres W7 86 C2
Lilestone Est NW8 236 D5
Lilestone Ho NW8 236 D6
Lilestone St
NW8 92 C3 237 A6
Lilford Ho 21 SE5 139 A3
Lilford Rd SE5 138 D3
Lilian Barker Cl
SE12 165 A6
Lilian Baylis Ho N1 73 A2
Lilian Baylis Tech Sch
SE11 116 B1 260 D1
Lilian Board Way
UB6 64 B3
Lilian Gdns IG8 37 B2
Lilian Rd SW16 181 C2
Lilian Rolfe Ho 5
SE27 183 B6
Lillechurch Rd RM8 80 C2
Lilleshall Rd SM4 202 B3
Lilley Cl E1 118 A5
Lillian Ave W3 110 C4
Lillian Cl 14 N16 73 C5
Lillian Rd SW13 134 B6
Lillie Ho N5 72 C3
Lillie Rd
SW6 135 B6 264 C5
Lillie Road Mans
SW6 264 B5
Lillieshall Rd SW4 137 C2
Lillie Yd
SW6 135 C6 265 A6
Lillingston Ho N7 72 C4
Lilliput Ave UB5 85 B6
Lillywhite 21 NW9 27 D2
Lily Albon Ct RM9 81 B4
Lily Cl W14 112 D2
Lily Gdns HA0 87 C5
Lily Ho 7 HA9 66 A3
Lily Pl EC1 241 B4
Lily Rd E17 53 C3

Lilyville Rd
SW6 135 B4 264 C2
Limavady Ho 12
SE18 122 C2
Limborough Ho 5
E14 97 C2
Limbourne Ave RM8 59 B2
Limburg Rd SW11 136 C1
Lime Ave UB7 104 B6
Limeburner La
EC4 94 D1 241 C2
Lime Cl Bromley BR1 210 A5
Buckhurst Hill IG9 21 D2
Carshalton SM5 218 D6
Harrow HA3 25 A1
Pinner HA5 39 D6
Wapping E1 118 A5
Lime Cres TW16 172 C1
Limecroft Cl KT19 215 B1
Lime Ct
9 Harrow HA1 42 D3
Hendon NW4 28 C1
Kingston u T KT3 198 D6
9 Leyton E11 76 C6
Mitcham CR4 180 B1
Putney SW15 134 B2
Limedene Cl HA5 22 D2
Lime Gr Barnet N20 13 B3
Blackfen DA15 167 D5
Hayes UB3 105 B6
Kingston u T KT3 199 C6
Orpington BR6 226 D6
Ruislip HA4 40 B2
Shepherd's Bush
W12 112 C4
Twickenham TW1 153 A5
Walthamstow E4 35 B4
Limeharbour E14 119 D4
Lime Ho 7 TW9 132 D4
LIMEHOUSE 119 A6
Limehouse Cswy
E14 119 B6
Lime House Ct 23
E14 97 B1
Limehouse Ct 5 E14 97 C1
Limehouse Cut 4
E14 97 D2
Limehouse Fields Est 14
E14 97 A2
Limehouse Link
(Tunnel) E14 119 B6
Limehouse Sta E14 97 A1
Lime Kiln Dr SE7 143 B6
Limekiln Pl SE19 183 D3
Limekiln Wharf 21
E14 119 B6
Limeleaf Ct HA8 27 A6
Lime Lo 3 TW16 171 D3
Limerick Cl SW12 159 C4
Limerick Ct 1
SW12 159 C4
Lime Row DA18 125 B3
Limerston St
SW10 136 A6 266 B5
Lime St Pas EC3 253 A6
Limes Ave
Barnes SW13 133 D3
Carshalton SM5 202 D1
Croydon CR0 220 C5
Edgware NW7 27 C4
Golders Green NW11 47 A2
North Finchley N12 30 A6
Penge SE20 184 B3
Limes Ave The N11 31 C5
Limes Ave E11 55 B5
Limes Cl
Ashford TW15 170 C5
3 Friern Barnet N11 31 C5
Limes Ct
Beckenham BR3 185 D1
Willesden NW6 68 D1
Limesdale Gdns HA8 27 A1
Limes Field Rd
SW14 133 C2
Limesford Rd SE15 140 D1
Limes Gdns SW18 157 C5
Limes Gr SE13 142 A1
Limes Rd
Beckenham BR3 185 D1
Thornton Heath CR0 205 B2
Limes Row BR6 226 D3
Limes The
Camberwell SE5 139 C2
3 Cheam SM2 217 C2
East Molesey KT8 195 D5
Kensington W2 245 B5
Keston Mark BR2 226 A6
Stanmore HA7 9 B2
Limestone Wlk 12
DA18 124 D4
Lime St
Walthamstow E17 53 A5
Whitechapel
EC3 95 C1 243 A1

Limes Wlk
Ealing W5 109 D4
Nunhead SE15 140 C1
Lime Terr W7 108 C6
Lime Tree Ave KT10, KT7 196 C1
Limetree Cl SW2 160 B3
Lime Tree Cl E11 55 C5
Lime Tree Ct
East Barnet EN4 14 C6
East Finchley N2 47 D6
Limetree Ct HA5 23 C3
Lime Tree Ct
14 Poplar E3 97 C2
South Croydon CR2 221 A2
Lime Tree Gr CR0 223 B5
Limetree Pl CR4 181 B2
Lime Tree Rd TW5 129 D4
Lime Tree Wlk
Bushey WD23 8 C2
Coney Hall BR4 224 D4
Enfield EN2 5 A5
Limetree Wlk 2 SW17 181 A5
Lime Wlk 11 E15 98 C6
Limewood Cl
Beckenham BR3 208 A4
Ealing W13 87 B1
Walthamstow E17 53 B5
Limewood Ct IG4 56 B4
Limpsfield Ave
Putney SW19 156 D2
Thornton Heath CR7 204 B4
Limscott Ho 35 E3 97 D4
Linacre Cl SE15 140 B2
Linacre Ct W6 112 D1
Linacre Rd NW2 68 B2
Linale Ho N1 235 C3
Linberry Wlk 3 SE8 119 B2
Linchmere Rd SE12 164 D4
Lincoln Ave
Osidge N14 15 C2
Twickenham TW2 152 A2
Wimbledon SW19 156 D1
Lincoln Cl
Croydon SE25 206 B3
Greenford UB6 86 A6
Harrow HA2 41 B4
Lincoln Cres EN1 17 D6
Lincoln Ct
Borehamwood WD6 11 B6
Enfield EN2 5 B1
Grove Pk SE12 165 C1
Hampton TW12 173 B5
Hendon NW4 46 B5
2 Ilford IG2 57 A3
Mitcham CR4 204 A4
Redbridge IG1 56 B2
5 South Croydon CR2 221 A3
Stoke Newington N16 51 B2
Lincoln Gdns IG1 56 A2
Lincoln Green Rd BR5 211 D4
Lincoln Ho
Bloomsbury WC1 240 D3
9 Dartmouth Pk NW5 71 C5
2 Islington N1 73 A1
Knightsbridge SW1 247 C1
10 Putney SW15 157 A6
Lincoln Lo 10 BR3 185 D1
Lincoln Mews NW6 91 B6
Lincoln Rd
Croydon SE25 206 B6
East Finchley N2 48 C6
Enfield EN1, EN3 18 B6
Harrow HA2, HA5 41 B4
Kingston u T KT3 199 A6
Mitcham CR4 204 A4
Newham E13 99 B3
North Cheam KT4 200 B1
Northwood HA6 39 D6
Plashet E7 77 D2
Sidcup DA14 190 B5
Twickenham TW13 151 B1
Wembley HA0 65 D2
Woodford E18 37 A2
Lincoln's Inn Fields WC2 94 B1 240 D2
Lincoln's Inn* WC2 94 B1 240 D2
Lincoln St SW3 257 C3
Lincolns The NW7 11 D1
Lincoln St E11 76 C6
Lincoln Terr 4 SM2 217 C1
Lincoln Way
Charlton TW16 171 C2
Enfield EN1 18 B6
Lincombe Rd BR1 164 D1
Linda Ct KT9 213 D4

Lindal Cres EN2 4 B1
Lindal Ct 1 E18 37 A2
Lindale SW19 157 A2
Lindales The N17 33 D4
Lindal Rd SE4 163 B6
Lindbergh Rd SM6 220 A1
Linden Ave Enfield EN1 6 A4
Hounslow TW3 151 D6
Kensal Rise NW10 90 D5
Ruislip HA4 40 A1
Thornton Heath CR7 204 D5
Wembley HA9 66 B3
Linden Bridge Sch KT4 215 C5
Linden Cl Ruislip HA4 40 A1
Southgate N14 15 C5
Stanmore HA7 25 B5
Thames Ditton KT7 197 A2
Linden Cotts 6 SW19 179 A4
Linden Cres
Kingston u T KT1 176 B1
Wembley UB6 64 D2
Woodford IG8 37 B4
Linden Ct
8 Battersea SW18 136 B1
1 Beckenham BR3 207 D6
2 Bromley BR1 186 D3
Edgware NW7 27 B5
Penge SE20 184 B3
1 Shepherd's Bush W12 112 C5
Sidcup DA14 189 C6
11 Sutton SM2 218 A2
Lindenfield BR7 188 D1
Linden Gate SW20 200 C6
Linden Gdns
Chiswick W4 111 B1
Enfield EN1 6 A4
Notting Hill W2 113 C6 245 B5
Linden Gr
Kingston u T KT3 199 C6
Nunhead SE15 140 C2
Penge SE20 184 C4
Teddington TW11 174 D5
Linden Ho
Bromley BR1 187 B3
10 Deptford SE8 141 B6
Hampton TW12 173 D4
Walthamstow E17 35 B1
Linden Lawns HA9 66 B4
Lindenlea Ct E17 53 B5
Linden Lea N2 48 A4
Linden Leas BR4 224 B6
Linden Lodge Sch SW19 157 A3
Linden Lo N21 16 B4
Linden Mans N6 49 B1
Linden Mews
Kensington W2 245 B5
Stoke Newington N1 73 B3
Linden Pl CR4 202 C5
Linden Rd
Brunswick Pk N11 15 A2
Cranley Gdns N10 49 B5
Hampton TW12 173 C2
Tottenham N15 51 A5
Lindens The
Chiswick W4 133 A4
New Addington CR0 224 A2
North Finchley N12 30 B5
5 Walthamstow E17 53 D5
Linden Way
Shepperton TW17 193 A4
Southgate N14 15 C5
Lindeth Cl HA7 25 B4
Lindfield Gdns NW3 70 A3
Lindfield Hts NW3 70 A3
Lindfield Rd
Croydon CR0 205 D3
Ealing W5 87 C3
Lindfield St E14 97 C1
Lindford Christie Stadium The W12 90 B2
Lindhill Cl EN3 6 D3
Lindholme Ct 3 NW9 27 C2
Lindisfarne Rd
Dagenham RM8 80 C5
Wimbledon SW20 178 A3
Lindisfarne Way E9 75 A4
Lindley Ct KT1 175 C2
Lindley Ho
13 Peckham SE15 140 A5
9 Stepney E1 96 C2
Lindley Pl TW9 132 C4
Lindley Rd E10 76 A6
Lindley St E1 96 C2
Lindon Bennett Sch TW13 172 D5
Lindop Ho 8 E1 97 A3
Lindore Rd SW11 136 D1
Lindores Rd SM5 202 A1
Lindo St SE15 140 C3

Lind Rd SM1 218 A3
Lindrop St SW6 136 A3
Lindsay Cl KT9 214 A1
Lindsay Ct
Battersea SW11 266 D1
Sutton SM1 217 C3
Lindsay Dr
Harrow HA3 44 B4
Shepperton TW17 193 B3
Lindsay Ho 2 SE18 122 C2
Lindsay Rd
Hampton TW12 173 D6
North Cheam KT4 216 B6
Lindsay Sq SW1 115 D1 259 D2
Lindsell St 6 SE10 142 A4
Lindsey Cl
Bickley BR1 210 A6
Mitcham CR4, SW16 204 A5
Lindsey Ct N13 16 C1
Lindsey Gdns TW14 149 B4
Lindsey Ho W5 109 D2
Lindsey Ho* SW10 266 D4
Lindsey Mews 18 N1 73 A1
Lindsey Rd RM8 80 C5
Lindsey St EC1 94 D2 241 D4
Lind St SE8 141 D3
Lindum Rd TW11 175 C3
Lindums The BR3 185 B4
Lindway SE27 182 D5
Lindwood Cl 8 E6 100 B2
Linear View HA9 66 D6
Linfield Cl NW4 46 C5
Linfield WC1 233 C1
Linford Ct 1 CR4 180 C2
Linford Ho 17 E2 96 A6
Linford Rd E17 54 A6
Linford St SW8 137 C4 269 A1
Linford Street Bsns Est SW8 269 A2
Lingard Ho 11 E14 120 A3
Lingards Rd SE13 142 A1
Lingey Cl DA15 167 D2
Lingfield Ave KT1, KT5 198 B5
Lingfield Cl EN1 17 C5
Lingfield Cres SE9 145 B1
Lingfield Ct
Northolt UB5 85 C5
Wimbledon SW19 178 D4
Lingfield Gdns N9 18 B4
Lingfield Ho
5 Acton Green W4 111 A1
Lambeth SE1 251 D1
Penge SE26 184 B4
Lingfield Rd
North Cheam KT4 216 C5
Wimbledon SW19 178 D4
Lingham St SW9 138 B3
Lingholm Way EN5 12 D6
Ling Rd E16 99 A2
Lingrove Gdns IG9 21 B2
Ling's Coppice SE21 161 B2
Lingwell Rd SW17 158 C1
Lingwood DA7 147 D3
Lingwood Gdns TW7 130 C5
Lingwood Rd E5 52 A2
Linhope St NW1 92 D3 237 C5
Linkenholt Mans 3 W6 111 D2
Linkfield KT8 195 D6
Link Field BR2 209 A3
Linkfield Rd TW7 130 D3
Link La SM6 220 A2
Linklea Cl NW9 27 C3
Link Prim Sch CR0 220 A4
Link Rd
Dagenham RM9 103 D5
East Bedfont TW14 149 D4
Friern Barnet N11 31 A6
Hackbridge SM6 203 A1
Links Ave SM4 201 C5
Linkscroft Ave TW15 170 D4
Links Ct N20 14 B1
Links Dr N20 13 D3
Link Sec Sch CR0 220 B4
Links Gdns SW16 182 C3
Linkside Cl EN2 4 C2
Linkside N12 29 C4
Linkside Gdns EN2 4 B2
Linkside KT3 177 C1
Links Ind Est TW13 151 A1
Links Prim Sch SW17 181 A4
Links Rd Acton W3 88 C1
Ashford TW15 170 A5
Mitcham SW16, SW17 181 A4
West Wickham BR4 208 A1
Willesden NW2 67 D6
Woodford IG8 37 A5

Links Side EN2 4 C2
Links The E17 53 A5
Link St E9 74 C3
Links View Cl HA7 25 A4
Links View N3 29 B3
Linksview N2 48 D4
Links View Rd
Croydon CR0 223 C5
Hampton TW12 174 A6
Links View SE18 144 D4
Links Way BR3 207 C3
Linksway NW4 28 D1
Links Way SW17 181 A4
Links Yd
10 Spitalfields E1 96 A2
Spitalfields E1 243 D4
Link The Acton W3 88 D1
Chislehurst SE9 166 C1
Enfield EN3 7 A4
Hendon NW2 46 A1
Northolt UB5 63 B3
Pinner HA5 40 C2
Teddington TW11 174 D4
Wembley HA0 43 C1
Link Way BR2 210 A2
Linkway
Dagenham RM8 80 C4
Pinner HA5 22 D2
Link Way TW10 153 B2
Linkway N4 51 A2
Linkway The EN5 13 D5
Linkway SW20 200 B5
Linkwood Wlk NW1 71 D1
Linley Cres RM7 59 D6
Linley Ct
1 Dulwich SE21 183 C6
Sutton SM1 218 A4
Linley Rd N17 33 C1
Linnell Cl NW11 47 D3
Linnell Dr NW11 47 D3
Linnell Ho
Spitalfields E1 243 C4
St John's Wood NW8 229 A6
Linnell Rd
Camberwell SE5 139 C3
Edmonton N18 34 A5
Linnet Cl Bushey WD23 8 A3
Lower Edmonton N9 18 D3
Woolwich SE28 124 C6
Linnet Ct CR4 180 C2
Linnet Mews SW12 159 A4
Linnett Cl E4 36 A6
Linom Rd SW4 138 A1
Linscott Rd E5 74 C4
Linsdell Rd IG11 101 A6
Linsey St
Bermondsey SE16 118 A2
Bermondsey SE16 118 A3
Linslade Cl
Hounslow TW4 151 A6
Pinner HA5 40 B6
Linslade Ho
10 Hackney E2 96 A6
Marylebone NW8 237 B6
Linstead St 1 NW6 69 C1
Linstead Way SW18, SW19 157 A4
Linsted Ct SE9 167 C5
Linster Gr WD6 11 A6
Lintaine Cl W6 264 B5
Linthorpe Ave HA0 65 C2
Linthorpe Rd
Cockfosters EN4 2 C2
Stamford Hill N16 51 C2
Linton Cl
Carshalton CR4 202 D2
2 Greenwich SE7 121 C1
Welling DA16 146 B4
Linton Gdns E6 100 A1
Linton Gr SE27 183 A5
Linton Ho
Lower Holloway N7 72 B4
2 Tower Hamlets E3 97 C2
Linton Mead Prim Sch SE28 124 B6
Linton Rd IG11 79 A1
Lintons The
Barking IG11 79 A1
Finchley N3 29 B2
Linton St N1 95 A6 235 B5
Linver Rd SW6 135 C3
Linwood Cl SE5 139 D3
Linwood Cres EN1 6 A4
Linzee Rd N8 50 A5
Lion Ave TW1 152 D3
Lion Cl Ladywell SE4 163 C5
Littleton TW17 192 A6
Lion Ct 12 NW9 46 A5
Lion Ctr The TW13 151 A1
Lionel Gdns SE9 165 D6
Lionel Ho
Bowes Pk N22 32 B4
5 Kensal Town W10 91 A2
Lionel Mans 14 W14 112 D3
Lionel Mews 13 W10 91 A2

Lionel Rd SE9 165 D6
Lionel Road N TW8 110 A2
Lionel Road Prim Sch TW8 110 A2
Lionel Road S TW8 110 B1
Lion Gate Gdns TW9 132 B2
Lion Gate Mews SW18 157 C4
Lion House Sch SW15 134 D1
Lion Mills 35 E2 96 A5
Lion Park Ave KT9 214 C4
Lion Rd
Bexleyheath DA6 147 B1
Edmonton N9 18 A2
Newham E6 100 B2
Thornton Heath CR0 205 A4
Twickenham TW1, TW2 152 D3
Lions Cl SE12 165 D1
Lion Way TW8 131 D5
Lion Wharf Rd TW7 131 B2
Lion Yd SW4 137 D1
Liphook Cres SE23 162 C4
Liphook Rd WD19 22 D6
Lipton Cl SE28 124 C6
Lipton Ct N14 15 C4
Lipton Rd 9 E1 96 D1
Lisa Lo 5 EN5 13 D6
Lisbon Ave TW2 152 A2
Lisbon Cl E17 35 B1
Lisburne Rd NW3 70 D4
Lisford St SE15 139 D4
Lisgar Terr W14 113 B2 254 C4
Liskeard Cl BR7 189 A4
Liskeard Gdns SE3 143 A4
Liskeard Ho SE11 261 B2
Lisle Cl SW17 181 B6
Lisle Ct NW2 69 A5
Lisle St WC2 115 D6 249 D6
Lismirrane Ind Pk WD6 9 B5
Lismore Cir NW5 71 A3
Lismore Cl TW7 131 A3
Lismore Rd
South Croydon CR2 221 C2
Tottenham N17 51 B6
Lismore 9 SW19 179 B5
Lismore Wlk 4 N1 73 A2
Lissant Cl KT6 197 D2
Lisselton Ho 3 NW4 46 D5
Lissenden Gdns NW5 71 A4
Lissenden Mans NW5 71 A4
Lisson Cotts NW1 237 B4
Lisson Gr NW1, NW8 92 C3 237 A6
LISSON GROVE 92 B3
Lisson Ho NW1 237 A4
Lisson St NW1 92 C2 237 A4
Lister Cl
Dagenham W3 89 B2
Mitcham SW19 180 C2
Lister Com Sch E13 99 B5
Lister Cotts WD6 9 A6
Lister Ct Hendon NW9 27 C1
Stoke Newington N16 73 C6
Lister Gdns N18 33 A5
Lister Ho
Greenwich SE3 142 C6
Hayes UB3 105 C2
Marylebone W1 238 C2
Spitalfields E1 96 A2
Lister Hospl SW1 115 B1 258 C1
Lister Ho
6 Wembley HA9 67 A5
West Heath SE2 124 D1
Lister Mews N7 72 B4
Lister Rd E11 54 D1
Lister Wlk SE28 124 D6
Liston Ho N21 16 B6
Liston Rd
Clapham SW4 137 C2
Tottenham N17 34 A2
Liston Way 1 IG8 37 C3
Listowel Cl 2 SW9 138 C5
Listowel Rd RM10 81 C5
Listria Lo N16 73 D6
Listria Pk N16 73 D6
Litcham Ho 23 E1 96 D4
Litchfield Ave
Morden SM4 201 B2
Stratford E15 76 C2
Litchfield Ct E17 53 C3
Litchfield Gdns NW10 68 A2
Litchfield Rd SM1 218 A4
Litchfield St WC2 249 D6
Litchfield Way NW11 48 A4
Lithgow's Rd TW14, TW6 127 D1
Lithos Rd NW3 70 A2

Little Acre BR3 207 C
Little Albany St NW1 238
Little Argyll St W1 239 A
Littleberry Ct NW7 28 C
Little Birches DA15 167 C
Little Boltons The SW10 255 D
Little Bornes SE21 183
Littlebourne 2 SE13 164 C
Little Britain EC1 242 A
Littlebrook Cl CR0 206 D
Little Brownings SE23 162 B
Littlebury Rd SW4 137 D
Little Bury St N9 17 C
Little Bushey La WD23 8 B
Little Cedars N12 30 A
Little Chelsea Ho SW10 266 B
Little Chester St SW1 258 C
Little Cloisters SW1 260 A
Little College St SW1 260 A
Little Combe Cl 13 SW15 156 D
Littlecombe SE7 143 B
Little Common HA7 9 A
Littlecote Cl SW19 157 A
Littlecote Pl HA5 23 B
Little Cottage Pl SE10 141 D
Littlecroft SE9 144 C
Little Ct Harrow HA1 42 C
West Wickham BR4 224 C
Littledale SE2 146 A
Little Deans Yd SW1 260 A
Little Dell Lo 8 N3 29 B
Little Dimocks SW12 159 B
Little Dorrit Ct SE1 252 B
Little Ealing La W5 109 C
Little Ealing Prim Sch W5 109 C
Little Edward St NW1 231 D
Little Elms UB3 127 B
Little Essex St WC2 251 A
Little Ferry Rd TW1 153 B
Littlefield Cl
9 Kingston u T KT1 176 A
Tufnell Pk N19 71 C
Littlefield Ct UB7 126 A
Littlefield Ho KT1 176 A
Littlefield Rd HA8 27 A
Little Friday Rd E4 20 C
Little Gearies IG6 56 D
Little George St SW1 250 A
Little Gn TW9 131 D
Little Grange UB6 87 A
Little Green St NW5 71 B
Littlegrove Ct 3 EN4 14 C
Littlegrove EN4 14 C
Little Halliards KT12 194 A
LITTLE HEATH 58 B
Little Heath RM6 58 B
Little Heath Rd DA7 147 B
Littleheath Rd CR2 222 B
Little Heath Sch RM6 58 B
Little Heath SE7 122 A
Little Holt 10 E11 55 A
LITTLE ILFORD 78 C
Little Ilford La E12 78 B
Little Ilford Sch E12 78 B
Littlejohn Rd W7 86 D
Little Larkins EN5 13 A
Little London Cl UB8 82 D
Little Marlborough St W1 239 A
Littlemead KT10 212 B
Littlemede SE9 166 B
Littlemoor Rd IG1 79 B
Littlemore Rd SE2 124 A
Little Moss La HA5 23 A
Little Newport St WC2 249 D
Little New St EC4 241 B
Little Oak Cl TW17 192 B
Little Orchard Cl HA5 23 A
Little Oxhey La WD19 23 A
Little Park Dr TW13 151 A
Little Park Gdns EN2 5 B
Little Pluckett's Way IG9 21 D
Little Portland St W1 239 A
Little Potters WD23 8 C
Little Queens Rd TW11 174 D
Little Rd UB3 105 D

Little Redlands BR1 188 A1
Littlers Cl SW19 180 B2
Little Russell St WC1 240 A3
Little St James's St SW1 249 A3
Little St Leonards SW14 133 A2
Little Sanctuary SW1 250 A1
Little Smith St SW1 259 D6
Little Somerset St E1 243 C1
LITTLE STANMORE 26 B2
Littlestone Cl BR3 185 C4
Little Strand NW9 27 D1
Little Thrift BR5 211 A5
Little Titchfield St W1 239 A3
LITTLETON 192 C6
Littleton Ave E4 20 D3
Littleton CE Inf Sch TW17 192 C6
LITTLETON COMMON 171 B3
Littleton Cres HA1 64 D6
Littleton Ho TW15 171 A3
Littleton La TW17, TW18 192 A4
Littleton Rd
  Harrow HA1 64 D6
  Littleton TW15, TW17 171 A3
Littleton St SW18 158 A2
Little Trinity La EC4 252 B6
Little Turnstile WC1 240 C3
LITTLE VENICE 92 A2
Little Venice* W9 92 A2 236 A4
Little Wood Cl BR5 190 A2
Littlewood Cl W13 109 B3
Littlewood SE13 164 A5
Littleworth Ave KT10 212 B3
Littleworth Common Rd KT10 212 B5
Littleworth La KT10 212 B4
Littleworth Pl KT10 212 B4
Littleworth Rd KT10 212 C5
Livermere Ct 3 E8 95 D6
Livermere Rd E8 95 D6
Liverpool Gr SE17 117 B1 262 C1
Liverpool Ho N7 72 C2
Liverpool Rd
  Ealing W5 109 D4
  Islington N1 234 B5
  Islington N1, N7 72 C1
  Kingston u T KT2 176 C3
  Leytonstone E10 54 A3
  Newham E16 98 C2
  South Norwood CR7 205 A6
Liverpool St EC2 95 C2 243 A3
Liverpool Street Sta EC2 95 C2 243 A3
Livesey Cl
  Kingston u T KT1 198 B6
  Woolwich SE28 123 A3
Livesey Mus* SE15 140 B6
Livesey Pl SE15 140 A6
Livingstone Ct
  Barnet EN5 1 A3
  Leytonstone E10 54 A3
  Stanwell TW19 148 A3
Livingstone Ho 16 SE5 139 A5
Livingstone Lo
  13 Paddington W9 91 C2
  Walthamstow E17 35 C1
Livingstone Pl E14 120 A1
Livingstone Prim Sch EN4 2 B2
Livingstone Rd
  14 Battersea SW11 136 B2
  Bowes Pk N13 32 A5
  Isleworth TW3 130 A1
  Mill Meads E15 98 A6
  Southall UB1 106 D6
  South Norwood CR7 183 B1
  Walthamstow E17 53 D3
Livity Sch The SW2 160 A6
Livonia St W1 239 B1
Lizard St EC1 95 A4 235 B1
Lizban St SE3 143 B5
Llandovery Ho 1 E14 120 A4
Llanelly Rd NW2 69 B6
Llanover Rd
  Shooters Hill SE18 144 C5
  Wembley HA9 65 D4
Llanthony Rd SM4 202 B4
Llanvanor Rd NW2 69 B6
Llewellyn Ct SE20 184 C2
Llewellyn Ho 10 N19 71 C5
Llewellyn St SE16 118 A4
Lloyd Ave SW16 182 A2
Lloyd Baker St WC1 94 C4 234 A1
Lloyd Ct
  Ladywell SE13 163 D6
  Pinner HA5 40 D4
  6 West Norwood SE27 160 D1
Lloyd Ho
  3 Beckenham BR3 185 D4
  Bromley BR1 187 B5
  Stoke Newington N16 73 B5
Lloyd Mews EN3 7 C5
Lloyd Park Ave CR0 221 D4
Lloyd Park Ho E17 53 C6
Lloyd Park Sta CR0 221 D4
Lloyd Rd
  Dagenham RM9 81 B1
  Newham E6 100 B6
  North Cheam KT4, SM3 216 D5
  Walthamstow E17 52 D5
Lloyd's Ave EC3 243 B1
Lloyd's Bldg* EC3 95 C1 243 A1
Lloyd's Pl SE3 142 C3
Lloyd Sq WC1 94 C4 234 A2
Lloyd's Row EC1 94 D4 234 C1
Lloyd St WC1 94 C4 234 A2
Lloyds Way BR3 207 B4
Lloyd Villas SE4 141 C3
Loampit Hill SE13 141 D3
Loampit Vale SE13 142 A2
Loanda Cl 17 E8 95 D6
Loats Rd SW2 160 A5
Lobelia Cl 5 E6 100 A2
Locarno Cl 15 SW16 181 C5
Locarno Rd
  6 Acton W3 111 A5
  Greenford UB6 86 B3
Lochaber Rd SE13 142 C1
Lochaline St W6 134 C6
Lochan Cl UB4 85 A3
Lochbie 9 N4 50 A2
Lochinvar St SW12 159 B4
Lochleven Ho 9 N2 30 B1
Lochmere Cl DA8 147 D6
Lochmore Ho SW1 258 B3
Lochnagar St E14 98 A2
Lockbridge Ct 3 W9 91 C2
Lock Chase SE3 142 C2
Lock Cl UB2 108 A4
Locke Ho
  Nine Elms SW8 269 A2
  Stamford Hill N16 51 D1
Lockesfield Pl E14 119 D1
Lockesley Dr BR5 211 D3
Lockesley Sq KT6 197 D3
Locket Rd HA3 24 D1
Lockfield Ave EN3 7 B4
Lockgate Cl E9 75 B3
Lockhart Cl
  Barnsbury N7 72 B2
  Enfield EN3 18 B6
Lockhart Lo 4 E4 20 C4
Lockhart St E3 97 B3
Lockhurst St E5 74 D4
Lockier Wlk HA9 65 D5
Lockington Rd SW8 137 B4 268 D2
Lockmead Rd
  Lewisham SE13 142 A2
  South Tottenham N15 52 A3
Lock Mews 9 NW1 71 D2
Lock Rd TW10 175 C6
LOCKSBOTTOM 226 D5
Lockside 17 E14 119 A6
Lock's La CR4 181 A1
Locksley St E14 97 B2
Locksmeade Rd TW10 175 C6
Lock View Ct 9 E14 119 A6
Lockwell Rd RM10 81 C5
Lockwood Cl SE26 184 D6
Lockwood Ct KT3 199 A5
Lockwood Ho 10 SE11 138 C6
Lockwood Ind Pk N17 52 B6
Lockwood Pl E4 35 C4
Lockwood Sq SE16 118 B3
Lockwood Way
  Chessington KT9 214 C3
  Higham Hill E17 34 D1
Lockyer Cl EN3 7 D5
Lockyer Est SE1 252 D1
Lockyer Ho
  7 Greenwich SE10 120 D1
  Putney SW15 134 D2
  South Lambeth SW8 270 A4
Lockyer St SE1 252 D1
Locomotive Dr TW14 150 A3
Locton Gn 4 E3 97 B6
Lodden Lo 13 SM2 218 A1
Loddiges Ho 5 E9 74 C1
Loddiges Rd E9 74 C1
Loddon Ho NW8 236 D5
Loder St SE15 140 C5
Lodge Ave
  Borehamwood WD6 10 B6
  Croydon CR0 220 C5
  Dagenham RM8, RM9, IG11 80 B3
  Harrow HA3 44 A5
  Mortlake SW14 133 C2
Lodge Cl
  Edgware HA8 26 C4
  Edmonton N18 33 A5
  Hackbridge SM6 203 A1
  Isleworth TW7 131 B4
Lodge Ct 3 HA0 66 A3
Lodge Dr N13 32 C6
Lodge Gdns BR3 207 B4
Lodge Hill DA16 146 B5
Lodgehill Park Cl HA2 63 D6
Lodge Hill IG4 56 A5
Lodge La Bexley DA5 168 D5
  New Addington CR0 223 D1
  North Finchley N12 30 A5
Lodge Mead Ct 5 N3 29 D3
Lodge Pl SM1 217 D3
Lodge Rd
  Bromley BR1 187 C3
  Hendon NW4 46 C5
  Lisson Gr NW8 92 C4 230 A1
  Sutton SM1 217 D3
  Thornton Heath CR0 204 D2
  Wallington SM6 219 B3
Lodge The
  9 Chiswick W4 111 C3
  1 Sutton SM1 218 A4
Lodge Villas IG8 36 D4
Lodge Way
  Charlton TW17 171 A1
  Stanwell TW15 148 A2
Lodore Gdns NW9 45 C4
Lodore Gn UB10 60 A5
Lodore St E14 98 A1
Lodsworth Ho SW11 268 A1
Lofthouse Pl KT9 213 C2
Loftie St SE16 118 A4
Lofting Ho 8 N1 72 C1
Lofting Rd N1 72 C1
Lofts on the Park 24 E9 74 D2
Loftus Rd IG11 79 A2
Loftus Rd (Queens Park Rangers FC) W12 112 B5
Loftus Rd W12 112 B5
Logan Cl Enfield EN3 6 D4
  Hounslow TW4 129 B2
Logan Mews W8 255 A4
Logan Pl W8 113 C2 255 A4
Logan Rd
  Edmonton N9 18 B2
  Wembley HA9 66 A6
Loggetts SE21 161 C2
Logs Hill BR1, BR7 188 A2
Logs Hill Cl BR7 188 A2
Lohmann Ho 5 SE11 138 C6
Lois Dr TW17 192 D4
Lolesworth Cl E1 243 D3
Lolland Ho 8 SE7 122 A2
Lollard St SE11 116 C2 261 A3
Lollards Twr SE1 260 C5
Loman St SE1 116 D4 251 D2
Lomas Cl CR0 224 A1
Lomas St E1 96 A2
Lombard Ave
  Enfield EN3 6 C4
  Ilford IG3 57 C1
Lombard Bsns Pk
  Merton SW19 179 D1
  Thornton Heath CR0 204 B2
Lombard Ct
  14 Acton W3 110 D5
  City of London EC3 252 D6
Lombard La EC4 241 B1
Lombard Rd SW11 136 B3
Lombard Rdbt CR0 204 B2
Lombard Rd
  Friern Barnet N11 31 B5
  Merton SW19 179 D1
Lombard St EC3 95 B1 242 D1
Lombard Trad Est SE7 121 B2
Lombard Wall SE7 121 B2
Lombardy Pl W2 245 D5
Lombardy Ret Pk UB3 106 B6
Lomley Ho 10 SW2 160 C5
Lomond Cl
  Tottenham N15 51 C4
  Wembley HA0 66 B1
Lomond Ct HA3 42 D6
Lomond Gdns CR2 223 A1
Lomond Gr SE5 139 B5
Lomond Ho 10 SE5 139 B4
Loncroft Rd SE5 139 C6
Londesborough Ho 1 N16 73 C4
Londesborough Rd N16 73 C4
London Acadamy HA8 26 B6
London Acad of Computing & Electronics SW17 158 D1
London Aquarium* SE1 250 C1
London Bridge City Pier SE1 117 C5 253 A4
London Bridge EC4, SE1 117 B6 252 D5
London Bridge Hospl SE1 117 B5 252 D4
London Bridge Sta SE1 117 B5 252 D3
London Bridge St SE1 117 B5 252 D3
London Bridge Wlk SE1 252 D4
London Britannia Coll N1 95 B4 235 C2
London Business Sch NW1 92 D3 237 C6
London Butterfly Ho* TW8 131 B4
London Canal Mus* N1 94 A5 233 B4
London Central Mosque* NW8 92 C4 230 B1
London Chest Hospl E2 96 C5
London City Airport E16 122 B5
London City Airport Sta E16 122 A5
London Clinic NW1 93 A3 238 B5
London Coll of Advanced Studies SE1 252 C3
London Coll of Beauty Therapy W1 93 C1 239 B1
London Coll of Bsns & Computer Studies SW4 137 D1
London Coll of Communication (Sch of Printing & Publishing) SE11 116 D3 261 D5
London Coll of Economics & Science NW10 89 A3
London Coll of Fashion EC2 95 C3 243 B6
London Coll of Fashion (Mare St) E8 74 B1
London Coll of Fashion
  Marylebone W1 238 D2
  Marylebone W1 238 B1
  Marylebone W1 238 C1
  St Luke's EC1 95 A3 242 A5
London Coll of International Business Studies WC1 240 B3
London Ct 3 SW18 157 C6
London Docklands Visitor Ctr* E14 120 A4
London Dungeon The* SE1 117 B5 252 D4
London Electronics Coll SW5 113 D1 255 C2
London Eye (Millennium Wheel)* SE1 116 B4 250 C2
London Fields East Side E8 74 B1
London Fields Prim Sch E8 96 B6
London Fields Sta E8 74 B1
London Fields West Side E8 74 A1
London Fire Brigade Mus* SE1 252 A2
London Gas Mus The* E3, E16 98 B3
London Group Bsns Pk NW2 46 A1
London Ho
  Edgware HA8 26 A6
  13 Hammersmith W6 112 A2
London Ho TW9 132 B2
London Hospital Dental Inst E1 96 B2
London Ho NW8 230 B4
London Independent Hospl The E1 96 D2
London Inst The SW17 181 B5
London Int Coll N7 72 B5
London International Film Sch WC2 94 A1 240 A1
London IT Coll IG2 56 C3
London La
  Bromley BR1 186 D3
  Hackney E8 74 B1
London Metropolitan Univ (Central Ho) E1 96 A1
London Metropolitan Univ (Commercial Rd) E1 96 A1
London Metropolitan Univ N7 72 C3
London Metropolitan Univ (Ladbrook Ho) N5 72 D3
London Metropolitan Univ (Moorgate) EC2 95 B2 242 D3
London Metropolitan Univ
  Whitechapel E1 95 D1 243 C1
  Whitechapel E1 95 D1 243 C2
  Whitechapel EC3 117 D6 253 C6
London Metropolitan Univ (Spring Ho) N7 72 C2
London Mews W2 236 D2
London Motorcycle Mus* UB6 86 A4
London Nautical Sch The SE1 116 C5 251 B4
London Oratory Sch The SW6 135 C5 265 B4
London Pavilion SW1 249 C5
London Peace Pagoda* SW3 267 D4
London Rd
  Ashford TW15, TW18, TW19, TW14 148 B2
  Brentford TW7, TW8 131 B4
  Bromley BR1 186 D3
  Carshalton CR4 203 A2
  Enfield EN2 5 B1
  Forest Hill SE22, SE23 162 C3
  Hackbridge SM6, CR4 219 B6
  Harrow HA1 64 C6
  Hounslow TW3, TW7, TW1, TW8 130 B3
  Kingston u T KT1, KT2 176 B1
  Lambeth SE1 116 D3 261 D6
  Mitcham CR4 180 D2
  Morden SM4 201 C5
  Newham E13 99 A5
  Romford RM7, RM8 59 C5
  Stanmore HA7 25 D6
  Stoneleigh KT17, KT4, SM3 216 B3
  Thornton Heath CR0, CR7, SW16 204 C3
  Twickenham TW1 153 A4
  Wembley HA9 66 A2
London Road Rdbt TW1 153 A5
London Sch of Economics & Political Science WC2 94 B1 240 D1
London Sch of Jewish Studies NW4 46 D5
London St EC3 253 B6
London Stile 5 W4 110 C1
London Stock Exchange* EC2 242 A2
London Stone Bsns Est 15 SW11 137 A3
London St W2 92 B1 236 C1
London Terr 1 E2 96 A5
London Tottenham Coll N17 33 D3
London Transport Mus* WC2 250 B6
London Wall Bldgs EC2 242 D3
London Wall EC2 95 B2 242 D3
London Wetland Ctr* SW13 134 B5
London Wetland Visitor Ctr* SW13 134 B4
London Wharf 4 E2 96 B6
London Xtra Tuition Coll N4 72 D6
London Zoo* NW1 93 A5 231 A4
Lonesome Prim Sch CR4 181 B1
Lonesome Way CR4 181 C2
Long Acre Ct W13 87 A2
Longacre Pl SM5 219 A2
Longacre Rd E17 36 B2
Long Acre WC2 94 A1 240 B1
Longbeach Rd SW11 136 D2
Longberrys NW2 69 B5
Longboat Row UB1 85 B1
Longbridge Ho RM8 80 B4
Longbridge Rd
  Barking IG11 79 C3
  Dagenham RM8 80 B4
Longbridge Way SE13 164 A6
Longbury Dr BR5 190 B1
Longchamp Ct 13 HA7 25 C5
Longcliffe Ho SW18 157 D6
Longcrofte Rd HA8 25 D3
Longcroft SE9 166 C1
Long Deacon Rd E4 20 C3
LONG DITTON 197 C1
Long Ditton Inf Sch KT6 197 C1
Longdon Wood BR2 226 A4
Longdown Rd SE6 185 C6
Long Dr
  Dagenham W3 89 C1
  Greenford UB6 85 D6
  Ruislip HA4 62 D4
Long Elmes HA3 24 A2
Longfellow Rd
  North Cheam KT4 200 B1
  Walthamstow E17 53 B3
Longfellow Way SE1 263 D3
Longfield Ave
  Ealing W5 109 C6
  Enfield EN3 6 C5
  Hackbridge SM6 203 A1
  Hendon NW7 28 A3
  Walthamstow E17 53 A5
  Wembley HA9 44 A1
Longfield 3 BR1 186 D2
Longfield Cres SE23, SE26 162 C1
Longfield Ct 4 N2 48 A6
Longfield Dr
  Mitcham SW19 180 C2
  Mortlake SW14 154 D6
Longfield Est SE1 263 D3
Longfield Fst & Mid Schs HA2 41 C3
Longfield Ho
  Ealing W5 109 C6
  Walthamstow E17 53 B4
Longfield IG10 21 C6
Long Field NW9 27 D3
Longfield Rd W5 87 C1
Longfield St SW18 157 C4
Longford Ave
  Feltham TW14 149 D5
  Southall UB1 107 D6
  Stanwell TW19 148 A3
Longford Cl
  Feltham TW13 151 A1
  Hampton TW12 173 C6
  Hayes UB4 106 D6
Longford Com Sch TW14 149 D4
Longford Ct
  1 Bedford Pk W12 111 C4
  2 Clapton Pk E5 74 D4
  Hampton TW12 173 D4
  9 Hendon NW4 46 C5
  Southall UB1 107 C5
  West Ewell KT19 215 A4
Longford Gdns
  Hayes UB4 106 D6
  Sutton SM1 218 A6
Longford Ho
  1 Catford BR1 186 B5
  Hampton TW12 173 C6
  7 Stepney E1 96 C1

Longford Ind Est TW12 173 D4
Longford Rd TW2 151 D3
Longford St NW1 93 B3 238 D6
Longford Way TW19 148 A3
Longford Wlk 9 SW2 160 C4
Longhayes Ave RM6 58 D5
Longhayes Ct RM6 58 D5
Longheath Gdns CR0 206 C4
Longhedge Ho SE26 184 A6
Longhedge St SW11 137 A3
Longhill Rd SE6 164 B1
Long Ho SM5 218 C6
Longhook Gdns UB5 84 B4
Longhope Cl SE15 139 D6
Longhurst Ho 8 W9 91 B4
Longhurst Rd
Croydon CR0 206 B3
Lewisham SE13 164 C6
Long La
Bermondsey SE1 117 B4 252 D1
Croydon CR0 206 C3
East Finchley N2 48 B6
Erith DA7 147 B4
Finchley N3 29 D2
Hillingdon UB10 82 D6
Holborn EC1 94 D2 241 D4
Longland Ct
Bermondsey SE1 118 A1
Hackney E9 75 A3
Longland Dr N20 13 D2
LONGLANDS 167 B1
Longlands Ct
Higham Hill E17 35 A2
Mitcham CR4 181 A2
Notting Hill W11 244 D6
Sidcup DA15 167 D1
Longlands Park Cres DA15 167 C2
Longlands Prim Sch DA15 167 C1
Longlands Rd DA15 167 D1
Long La TW15, TW19 148 B3
Longleat Ct 3 DA6 147 A1
Longleat Ho SW1 259 C2
Longleat Rd EN1 17 C6
Longleat Way TW14 149 B4
Longleigh Ho 8 SE5 139 C4
Longleigh La SE2, DA7 146 C6
Longlents Ho 3 NW10 89 B6
Longley Ave HA0 88 B6
Longley Ho 5 N19 71 C4
Longley Rd
Harrow HA1 42 B5
Thornton Heath CR0 204 D2
Upper Tooting SW17 180 D4
Long Leys E4 36 A4
Longley St SE1 118 A2
Longley Way NW2 68 C5
Longman Ho
9 Globe Town E2 96 D5
10 Shoreditch E8 95 D6
Long Mark Rd 5 E16 99 D2
Longmarsh La SE28 123 C5
Longmead BR7 188 C1
Longmead Dr DA14 168 D2
Longmead Ho SE27 183 A5
Long Mead NW9 27 D2
Long Meadow Cl BR3, BR4 208 A2
Long Meadow 20 N7 71 D3
Longmeadow Rd DA15 167 C3
Longmead Prim Sch UB7 104 A2
Longmead Rd
Hayes UB3 105 D6
Thames Ditton KT7 196 D2
Upper Tooting SW17 180 D5
Longmoor Point 14 SW15 156 B3
Longmore Ave EN4, EN5 14 B5
Longmore St SW1 115 C2 259 A3
Longnor Rd E1 96 D4
Long Pond Rd SE3 142 C4
Long Rd SW4 137 C1
Longreach Ct IG11 101 B5
Long Reach Rd IG11 101 D3
Longridge Ho SE1 262 B5
Longridge La UB1 85 D1
Longridge Rd SW5 113 C2 255 B3
Long Ridges N2 49 A6
Longs Ct 2 TW9 132 B1
Long's Ct W1 249 D5
Longshaw Prim Sch E4 20 B1
Longshaw Rd E4 20 B1
Longshore SE8 119 B2
Longstaff Cres SW18 157 C4
Longstaff Rd SW18 157 C5
Long St E2 95 D4
Longstone Ave NW10 89 D6
Longstone Rd SW17 181 B5
Longthorne Ho 18 E3 97 B4
Longthornton Rd SW16 181 D1
Longthorpe Ct 9 W6 112 A2
Longton Ave SE26 184 A6
Longton Gr SE26 184 B6
Longville Rd SE11 261 D4
Longwalk Rd UB11 104 D5
Long Wlk
Bermondsey SE1 263 B6
Kingston u T KT3 199 A6
Shooters Hill SE18 144 D6
Longwood Bsns Pk TW16 193 D4
Longwood Dr SW15 156 A5
Longwood Gdns IG2, IG6, IG5 56 C6
Longwood Par IG6 56 D6
Longworth Cl SE28 102 D1
Long Yd WC1 94 B3 240 C5
Loning The Enfield EN3 6 C5
Hyde The NW9 45 D5
Lonsdale Ave
Newham E6 100 A3
Wembley HA9 66 A3
Lonsdale Cl
Edgware HA8 26 B5
Hillingdon UB8 83 A2
Mottingham SE12 165 D1
Newham E6 100 A3
Pinner HA5 23 A2
Lonsdale Cres IG2 56 D3
Lonsdale Dr EN2 16 A6
Lonsdale Dr N EN2 4 A1
Lonsdale Gdns CR7, SW16 204 B5
Lonsdale Ho
Fulham SW6 135 C2
6 Stoke Newington N4 51 A2
Lonsdale Mews
Notting Hill W11 91 B1
4 Richmond TW9 132 C4
Lonsdale Pl N1 72 C1
Lonsdale Rd
Barnes SW13 133 D5
Bexley DA7 147 B3
Chiswick W4 111 D2
Croydon SE25 206 B5
Kilburn NW6 91 B6
Leytonstone E11 54 D2
Notting Hill W11 91 B1
Southall UB2 106 D3
Lonsdale Sq
Islington N1 72 C1
Islington N1 234 B6
Loobert Rd N15 51 C6
Looe Gdns IG6 56 D6
Loop Rd BR7 189 A4
Lopen Rd N18 33 C6
Lopen Works N18 33 C6
Lopez Ho 4 SW9 138 A2
Lorac Ct 13 SM2 217 C1
Loraine Cl EN3 18 C6
Loraine Ct BR7 188 D5
Loraine Ho 1 SM5 219 B4
Loraine Rd
Chiswick W4 132 D6
Islington N7 72 B4
Lord Ave IG5 56 B6
Lord Chancellor Wlk KT2 177 A2
Lord David Pitt Ho 8 SE24 138 C1
Lordell Pl SW19 178 C4
Lorden Wlk 13 E2 96 A4
Lord Gdns IG5 56 B5
Lord Hills Rd W2 91 D2
Lord Holland La 5 SW9 138 C3
Lord Knyvetts Ct 3 TW19 148 A5
Lord Napier Pl W6 112 A1
Lord North St SW1 260 A5
Lord Roberts Mews SW6 265 C3
Lord Roberts Terr SE18 122 C1
Lords Cl
Feltham TW13 151 A2
West Norwood SE21 161 A2
Lord's Cricket Mus* NW8 92 B4 229 D1
Lords Ct 3 HA8 27 A3
Lordship Gr N16 73 B6
Lordship Ho 3 N16 73 B6
Lordship La SE22 161 D5
Lordship Lane Prim Sch N22 33 A2
Lordship La N22 33 B2
Lordship Park Mews N16 73 A6
Lordship Pk N16 73 B6
Lordship Pl SW3 267 A5
Lordship Rd
Northolt UB5 63 A1
Stoke Newington N16 73 B6
Lordship Terr N16 73 B6
Lord's Indoor Cricket Sch NW8 230 A2
Lord's (MCC & Middlesex Cty Cricket Ground)* NW8 92 B4 229 D2
Lordsmead Rd N17 33 C1
Lord St E16 122 A5
Lord's View NW8 229 D1
Lord Warwick St SE18 122 B3
Loreburn Ho 2 N7 72 B4
Lorenzo St N1, WC1 233 C2
Loretto Gdns HA3 44 A5
Lorian Cl N12 29 D6
Loring Rd
East Barnet N20 14 C2
Isleworth TW7 130 D3
Loris Rd W6 112 C3
Lorn Ct SW9 138 C3
Lorne Ave CR0 206 D2
Lorne Cl NW8 92 C4 230 B1
Lorne Ct Harrow HA1 42 C2
Putney SW15 156 D5
Lorne Gdns
Croydon CR0 206 D2
5 Hammersmith W11 112 D4
Wanstead E11 55 C5
Lorne Ho
Friern Barnet N11 31 B5
Hornsey N4 50 B2
7 Tower Hamlets E1 97 A2
Lorne Rd
Finsbury Pk N4 50 B1
Forest Gate E7 77 C4
Harrow HA3 24 D1
3 Richmond TW10 154 B6
Walthamstow E17 53 C4
Lorn Rd SW9 138 C3
Lorraine Ct
Beckenham BR3 186 A2
9 Belmont SM2 217 C1
10 Camden Town NW1 71 B1
Lorraine Pk HA3 24 C3
Lorrimore Rd SE17 138 D6
Lorrimore Sq SE17 138 D6
Lorton Ho 9 NW6 91 C6
Loseberry Rd KT10 212 B3
Lostock Ho 10 SW8 137 D3
Lothair Rd W5 109 D4
Lothair Rd N N4 50 D3
Lothair Rd S N4 50 D2
Lothbury EC2 95 B1 242 C2
Lothian Ave UB4 84 B2
Lothian Cl HA0 65 A5
Lothian Rd SW9 138 D4
Lothrop St W10 91 A4
Lots Rd SW10 136 A5 266 B3
Loubet St SW17 180 D4
Loudoun Ave IG6 56 D4
Loudoun Rd NW8 92 A6 229 B5
Loudwater Cl TW16 194 A5
Loudwater Rd TW16 194 A5
Loughborough Ct 7 SW9 138 D2
Loughborough Junction Sta SW9 138 D2
Loughborough Pk SW9 138 D1
Loughborough Prim Sch SW9 138 D3
Loughborough Rd SE5, SW9 138 D3
Loughborough St SE11 116 B1 260 D1
Lough Rd N7 72 B2
LOUGHTON 21 D5
Loughton Way IG9 21 D3
Louie Black Ho 4 SW19 179 A3
Louisa Cl E9 96 D6
Louisa Ct
Twickenham TW2 152 C2
Wood Green N11 31 D3
Louisa Gdns E1 96 D3
Louisa Ho SW15 133 D1
Louisa St E1 96 D3
Louis Ct 3 RM10 81 D2
Louise Bennett Cl 9 SE24 138 D1
Louise Ct
7 Bexley DA6 147 A1
4 Wanstead E11 55 B4
Wood Green N22 32 C2
Louise De Marillac Ho 26 E1 96 C2
Louise Graham Ho 5 IG11 101 B6
Louise Rd E15 76 C2
Louise White Ho 1 N19 49 D1
Louis Gdns BR7 188 B6
Louis Mews N10 31 B2
Louisville Rd SW17 159 A1
Lousada Lo N14 15 C5
Louvaine Rd SW11 136 B1
Lovage App E6 100 A2
Lovat Cl NW2 67 D5
Lovat La EC3 253 A5
Lovatt Cl HA8 26 D4
Lovatt Ct SW12 159 B3
Lovatt Dr HA4 39 D4
Lovat Wlk TW5 129 A5
Loveday Ho 2 SW2 160 C3
Loveday Rd W13 109 B5
Lovegrove St SE1 140 A6
Lovegrove Wlk E14 120 A5
Lovekyn Cl KT2 176 B1
Lovelace Ave BR2 210 C3
Lovelace Gdns
Barking IG11 80 A4
Surbiton KT6 197 D2
Lovelace Gn SE9 144 B2
Lovelace Ho 12 E8 95 D6
Lovelace Prim Sch KT9 213 C3
Lovelace Rd
East Barnet EN4 14 C4
Surbiton KT6 197 D2
West Norwood SE21 161 A3
Love La Cheam SM3 217 A2
City of London EC2 95 A1 242 B2
Croydon SE25 206 B6
Long Ditton KT6 213 D6
Mitcham CR4 202 C6
Morden SM4 201 D2
Loveland Mans 7 IG11 79 D1
Love La
Old Bexley DA5 169 C5
Pinner HA5 41 A6
Tottenham N17 33 D3
Lovel Ave DA16 146 A3
Love La SE18 122 D2
Lovelinch Cl SE15 140 C6
Lovell Ho Hackney E8 96 A6
4 Merton SW19 180 A2
Lovell Pl SE16 119 A3
Lovell Rd
Richmond TW10 153 C1
Southall UB1 85 D1
Loveridge Mews NW6 69 B2
Loveridge Rd NW6 69 B2
Lover's Wlk W1 115 A5 248 A3
Lovett Dr SM5 202 B2
Lovette Ho 4 E3 97 C4
Lovetts Pl SW18 135 D1
Lovett Way NW10 67 A3
Love Wlk SE5 139 B3
Lovibonds Ave
Hillingdon UB7 82 B1
Locksbottom BR6 226 D5
Lowbrook Rd IG1 78 D4
Lowdell Cl UB7 82 A1
Lowden Rd
Edmonton N9 18 B3
Herne Hill SE24 139 A1
Southall UB1 107 A6
Lowder Ho 6 E1 118 B5
Lowe Ave E16 99 A2
Lowell Ho 10 SE5 139 A5
Lowell St E14 97 A1
Lower Addiscombe Rd CR0 205 C1
Lower Addison Gdns W14 113 A4 244 A1
Lower Belgrave St SW1 115 B3 258 C5
Lower Boston Rd W7 108 C4
Lower Broad St RM10 103 C6
Lower Camden BR7 188 B2
Lower Church St CR0 220 D6
LOWER CLAPTON 74 C4
Lower Clapton Rd E5 74 C4
Lower Clarendon Wlk 9 W11 91 A1
Lower Comm S SW15 134 B2
Lower Coombe St CR0 221 A4
Lower Downs Rd SW20 178 D2
LOWER EDMONTON 18 B1
LOWER FELTHAM 149 D1
Lower Fosters NW4 46 C4
Lower George St 13 TW10 153 D6
Lower Gn W CR4 202 C6
Lower Gravel Rd BR2 210 B1
LOWER GREEN 195 C1
Lower Green Gdns KT4 200 A1
Lower Green Rd KT10 212 A6
Lower Grosvenor Pl SW1 115 B3 258 D6
Lower Grove Rd TW10 154 B6
LOWER HALLIFORD 193 C3
Lower Hall La E4 35 A6
Lower Hampton Rd TW12, TW16 172 D1
Lower Ham Rd KT2 175 D4
LOWER HOLLOWAY 72 A3
Lower James St W1 249 B6
Lower John St W1 249 B6
Lower Kenwood Ave EN2 16 A6
Lower Kings Rd KT2 176 A3
Lower Lea Crossing E14, E16 120 C6
Lower Maidstone Rd N11 31 C4
Lower Mall W6 112 B1
Lower Marsh La KT1, KT5 198 C5
Lower Marsh SE1 116 C4 251 A1
Lower Merton Rise NW3 70 C1
LOWER MORDEN 201 A2
Lower Morden La SM4 201 A3
Lower Mortlake Rd TW9 132 B2
Lower Park Rd
Belvedere DA17 125 C2
Friern Barnet N11 31 C5
4 Loughton IG10 21 D6
Lower Pk Acton W3 89 A3
5 Putney SW15 156 D6
LOWER PLACE 89 A5
Lower Place Bsns Ctr NW10 89 A5
Lower Queen's Rd IG9 21 D2
Lower Rd
Belvedere DA17 125 D3
Finchley N2 30 B2
Harrow HA2 42 B1
Rotherhithe SE16 118 C4
Sutton SM1 218 A4
Lower Richmond Rd
Mortlake SW14, TW9 132 D2
Putney SW15 134 C2
Lower Robert St WC2 250 B5
Lower Sand Hills KT6 197 C2
Lower Sloane St SW1 115 A1 258 A2
Lower Sq TW7 131 B2
Lower Strand NW9 27 D1
Lower Sunbury Rd TW12 173 C1
LOWER SYDENHAM 185 A6
Lower Sydenham Sta SE26 185 B5
Lower Teddington Rd KT1 175 D2
Lower Terr NW3 70 A5
Lower Thames St EC3 117 C6 253 A5
Lower Tub WD23 8 B4
Lowerwood Ct W11 91 A1
Lower Wood Rd KT10 213 B2
Lowestoft Cl 5 E5 74 C6
Lowestoft Mews E16 122 D4
Loweswater Cl HA9 65 D6
Loweswater Ho E3 97 B
Lowfield Rd
Dagenham W3 89 A
Hampstead NW6 69 C
Low Hall Cl E4 19 D
Low Hall La E17 53 A
Lowick Rd HA1 42 C
Lowland Gdns RM7 59 D
Lowlands Ct NW7 27 D
Lowlands NW3 70 C
Lowlands Rd
Harrow HA1 42 C
Pinner HA5 40 C
Lowman Rd N7 72 B
Lowndes Cl SW1 258 B
Lowndes Ct
Knightsbridge SW1 257 D
Marylebone W1 239 A
Lowndes Lo
Barnet EN5 1 D
SW1 257 D
Lowndes Pl SW1 115 A3 258 A
Lowndes Sq SW1 114 D4 247 D
Lowndes St SW1 115 A3 258 A
Lownds Ct BR1 187 A
Lowood Ct SE19 183 D
Lowood Ho 12 E1 118 C
Lowood St E1 118 B
Lowry Cres CR4 180 C
Lowry Ct 3 SE16 118 B
Lowry Ho N17 33 D
Lowry Lo 1 HA0 65 D
Lowry Rd RM8 80 B
Lowther Cl WD6 10 B
Lowther Dr EN2 4 A
Lowther Hill SE23 163 A
Lowther Ho
Pimlico SW1 259 B
11 Shoreditch E8 95 D
Lowther Prim Sch SW13 134 A
Lowther Rd
Barnes SW13 133 D
Higham Hill E17 35 A
Islington N7 72 C
Kingston u T KT2 176 B
Stanmore HA7 44 B
Lowth Rd SE5 139 A
Lowton Lo E17 53 A
LOXFORD 79 A
Loxford Ave E6 99 D
Loxford Ho SW1 258 B
Loxford La IG1 79 B
Loxford Rd IG11 78 D
Loxford Sch of Science & Tech IG1 79 B
Loxham Rd E4 35 D
Loxham St WC1 233 B
Loxley Cl SE26 184 D
Loxley Hall E11 54 C
Loxley Ho HA9 66 A
Loxley Rd
Feltham TW12 173 B6
Wandsworth SW18 158 B3
Loxton Rd SE23 163 A3
Loxwood Cl TW14 149 B3
Loxwood Rd N17 51 C6
Loyola Prep Sch IG9 21 C3
LTC Coll London W1 239 A2
Lubavitch House Sch (Jun Boys) E5 51 D2
Lubbock Ct BR7 188 B3
Lubbock Ho
21 Canary Wharf E14 119 D6
Orpington BR6 227 C6
Lubbock Rd BR7 188 B3
Lubbock St SE14 140 C5
Lucan Ho N1 235 D5
Lucan Pl SW3 114 C2 257 B3
Lucan Rd EN5 1 A2
Lucas Ave
Harrow HA2 63 C6
Newham E13 99 B6
Lucas Ct
Battersea SW11 268 B1
Forest Hill SE26 185 A5
Lucas Gdns N2 30 A1
Lucas Ho
2 Clapham SW8 137 C3
Walham Green SW10 265 D4
Lucas Rd SE20 184 C4
Lucas Sq NW11 47 C3
Lucas St SE4, SE8 141 C4
Lucas Vale Prim Sch SE8 141 C4
Lucerne Cl N14 16 A1
Lucerne Ct
5 Abbey Wood DA18 125 A3

Lucerne Ct *continued*
8 Beckenham BR3 185 C3
Lucerne Gr E17 54 B5
Lucerne Mews W8 245 B4
Lucerne Rd
Highbury N5 72 D4
Orpington BR6 211 D1
South Norwood CR7 205 A5
Lucey Rd SE16 118 A3
Lucey Way SE16 118 A2
Lucie Ave TW15 170 D4
Lucien Rd
Upper Tooting SW17 181 A6
Wandsworth SW18 157 D2
Lucille Ho SE26 184 B4
Lucknow St SE18 145 C5
Lucorn Cl SE12 164 D5
Lucraft Ho 12 SW2 160 A4
Luctons Ave IG9 21 C3
Lucy Ashe Ho SE17 261 D3
Lucy Brown Ho SE1 252 B3
Lucy Cres W3 89 A3
Lucy Gdns RM8 81 A5
Luddesdon Rd DA8 147 C5
Ludford Cl
Croydon CR0 220 D4
Edgware NW9 27 C1
Ludgate Broadway EC4 241 D1
Ludgate Cir EC4 94 D1 241 C1
Ludgate Hill EC4 94 D1 241 D1
Ludgate Ho EC4 241 C1
Ludgate Sq EC4 241 D1
Ludgrove Ct EN4 2 C1
Ludgrove Hall EN4 2 C2
Ludham Cl SE28 102 C1
Ludham NW5 70 D3
Lud Lo TW15 148 A2
Ludlow Cl
Bromley BR2 209 A6
Harrow HA2 63 B4
Ludlow Ct Acton W3 111 A4
East Barnet EN4 14 C6
Ludlow Rd Ealing W5 87 C3
Feltham TW13 172 A6
Ludlow St EC1 242 A6
Ludlow Way N2 48 A5
Ludovick Wlk SW15 133 C1
Ludwell Ho W14 254 B6
Ludwick Mews SE14 141 A5
Luffield Rd SE2 124 B3
Luffman Rd SE12 165 B1
Lugard Ho 2 W12 112 B5
Lugard Rd SE15 140 B4
Lugg App E12 78 C5
Luke Ho 32 E1 96 B1
Lukes Ct N3 47 C6
Luke St EC2 95 C3 243 A6
Lukin Cres E4 20 B1
Lukin St E1 96 C1
Lullingstone Cl BR5 190 B3
Lullingstone Cres BR5 190 B3
Lullingstone Ho 21 SE15 140 C6
Lullingstone La SE13 164 B5
Lullingstone Rd 3 DA17 147 B6
Lullington Garth
Borehamwood WD6 10 D6
Bromley BR1 186 C3
Finchley N12 29 B5
Lullington Rd
Dagenham RM9 81 A1
Penge SE20 184 A3
Lulot Gdns N19 71 B6
Lulworth Ave
Hounslow TW5, TW7 130 A5
Wembley HA9 43 C2
Lulworth NW1 71 D1
Lulworth Cl HA2 63 B5
Lulworth Cres CR4 180 C1
Lulworth Ct N14 16 A1
Lulworth Dr HA5 41 A2
Lulworth Gdns HA2 63 B6
Lulworth Ho SW8 270 C3
Lulworth Rd
Bexley DA16 145 D3
Chislehurst SE9 166 A2
Peckham SE15 140 B3
Lulworth SE17 262 C2
Lulworth Waye UB4 84 B1
Lumen Rd HA9 65 D6
Lumiere Bldg The E7 77 D3
Lumiere Ct 7 SW17 159 A2
Lumina Bldg 1 E14 120 A5
Lumley Cl DA17 125 C1
Lumley Ct WC2 250 B5
Lumley Flats SW1 258 A2
Lumley Gdns SM3 217 A3
Lumley Ho KT3 199 B1
Lumley Rd SM1, SM3 217 A3
Lumley St W1 238 B1
Lumsdon NW8 91 D6
Luna Ho 6 SE16 118 A4
Lunan Ho 14 E3 97 B5
Luna Rd CR7 205 A6
Lundin Wlk WD19 22 D6
Lund Point E15 98 A6
Lundy Dr UB3 105 C2
Lunham Rd SE19 183 C4
Luntley Pl E1 96 A2
Lupin Cl
Croydon CR0 206 D1
Streatham SW2 160 D2
Lupin Cres IG11 78 D2
Lupino Ct SE11 260 D4
Lupin Point SE1 253 D1
Lupton Cl SE12 187 B6
Lupton St NW5 71 C4
Lupus Ct SE19 183 B2
Lupus St SW1 115 C1 259 B1
Luralda Gdns E14 120 B1
Lurgan Ave W6 134 D6
Lurline Gdns SW11 137 A4 268 B2
Luscombe Ct BR2 186 C1
Luscombe Ho SW18 157 B6
Luscombe Way SW8 138 A5 270 A4
Lusher Ho SW15 156 D5
Lushington Ho KT12 194 C3
Lushington Rd
Catford SE6 185 D5
Willesden Green NW10 90 B5
Lushington Terr 11 E8 74 A3
Lutea Ho SM2 218 A1
Luther Cl HA8 11 A2
Luther King Cl E17 53 A3
Luther Mews 2 TW11 174 D5
Luther Rd TW11 174 D5
Luton Pl SE10 142 A5
Luton Rd Newham E13 99 A3
Sidcup DA14 168 C1
Walthamstow E17 53 B6
Luton St NW8 92 B3 236 D5
Luttrell Ave SW15 156 B6
Lutwyche Rd SE6 163 B2
Lutyens Ho SW1 259 A1
Luxborough Ho W1 238 A4
Luxborough St W1 93 A2 238 A4
Luxborough Twr W1 238 A4
Luxembourg Mews 2 E15 76 C3
Luxemburg Gdns W6 112 D2
Luxfield Rd SE9 166 A3
Luxford St SE16 118 D2
Luxmore St SE4 141 B4
Luxor St SE5 139 A2
Lyall Ave SE21 183 D6
Lyall Mews SW1 115 A3 258 A5
Lyall Mews W SW1 258 A5
Lyall St SW1 115 A3 258 A5
Lyal Rd E3 97 A5
Lyce e Francais Charles de Gaulle (French Univ Coll) SW7 114 B2 256 C4
Lycee The SE11 116 C1 261 B1
Lycett Ho 10 SW2 160 A4
Lycett Pl 3 W12 112 A4
Lychgate Ct 4 N12 30 B5
Lychgate Manor HA1 42 C2
Lych Gate Wlk UB3 105 D6
Lyconby Gdns CR0 207 A2
Lydd Cl DA14 167 C1
Lydden Ct SE9 167 C5
Lydden Gr SW18 157 D4
Lydden Rd SW18 157 D4
Lydd Rd DA7 147 B5
Lydeard Rd E6 78 B1
Lydford Cl 22 N16 73 C3
Lydford NW1 232 B5
Lydford Rd
Brondesbury NW2 68 D2
Paddington W9 91 B3
Tottenham N15 51 B4
Lydgate Ho 8 N16 73 C3
Lydhurst Ave SW2 160 B2
Lydia Ct 2 N12 30 A4
Lydia Lodge HA1 64 C4
Lydney Cl
Camberwell SE15 139 C5
Putney SW19 157 A2
Lydon Rd SW4 137 C2
Lydstep Rd BR7 188 C6
Lydwell Ho 29 SW8 137 D3
Lyford Rd SW18 158 C3
Lyford St SE7 122 A2
Lygoe Ho 18 N6 49 D2
Lygoe Rd N2 30 B2
Lygon Ho 2 E2 96 A4
Lygon Pl SW1 258 C5
Lyham Cl SW2 160 A5
Lyham Rd SW2 160 A5
Lyle Cl CR4 203 A2
Lyle Ct SM4 202 B3
Lyle Pk SW15 156 D5
Lyly Ho SE1 262 D5
Lyme Farm Rd SE12 143 B1
Lyme Gr E9 74 C1
Lyme Grove Ho 2 E9 74 C1
Lymer Ave SE19 183 D5
Lyme Rd DA16 146 B4
Lymescote Gdns SM1 217 C6
Lyme St NW1 93 C6 232 A6
Lyminge Cl DA14 189 D6
Lyminge Gdns SW17, SW18 158 C3
Lymington Ave N22 32 D1
Lymington Cl
Mitcham SW16 181 D1
2 Newham E6 100 B2
Lymington Ct SM1 218 A5
Lymington Dr HA4 61 B6
Lymington Gdns KT19 215 D3
Lymington Mans NW6 69 D2
Lymington Rd
Dagenham RM8 58 D1
Hampstead NW6 69 D2
Lyminster Cl UB4 85 A2
Lympne N17 33 B1
Lympstone Gdns SE15 140 A5
Lynbridge Gdns N13 32 D6
Lynbrook Gr SE15 139 C5
Lynchen Cl TW5 128 B4
Lynch Wlk 2 SE8 141 B6
Lyncott Cres SW4 137 B1
Lyncourt SE3 142 B3
Lyncroft Ave HA5 41 A4
Lyncroft Gdns
Ealing W13 109 C5
Hampstead NW6 69 C3
Hounslow TW3 152 A6
Lyncroft Mans 4 NW6 69 C3
Lyndale Ave NW2 69 B5
Lyndale Cl SE3 142 D6
Lyndale NW2 69 B5
Lyndean Ind Est SE2 124 C3
Lynde Ho
2 Clapham SW4 137 D2
Walton-on-T KT12 194 C3
Lynden Gate SW15 156 B4
Lyndenhurst SE3 142 D2
Lynden Hyrst CR0 221 D6
Lyndhurst Ave
Colney Hatch N12 30 D4
Edgware NW7 27 C4
Mitcham SW16 181 D1
Pinner HA5 22 B2
Southall UB1 107 D5
Sunbury TW16 194 A6
Tolworth KT5 198 D1
Twickenham TW2, TW4 151 C3
Lyndhurst BR7 188 D4
Lyndhurst Cl
Bexleyheath DA7 147 D2
Neasden NW10 67 B5
Orpington BR6 226 D4
South Croydon CR0 221 D5
Lyndhurst Ct
8 Belmont SM2 217 C1
11 Woodford E18 37 A2
Lyndhurst Dr
Leytonstone E10 54 A2
New Malden KT3 199 D2
Lyndhurst Gdns
Barking IG11 79 C2
Enfield EN1 5 C1
Hampstead NW3 70 B3
Hendon N3 29 A2
Ilford IG2 57 B3
Pinner HA5 22 B2
Lyndhurst Gr SE5, SE15 139 D3
Lyndhurst Ho 2 SW15 156 A4
Lyndhurst House Prep Sch NW3 70 B3
Lyndhurst Lo 3 E14 120 B2
Lyndhurst Rd
Bexleyheath DA7 147 D2
Lyndhurst Rd *continued*
Chingford E4 36 A3
Edmonton N18 34 A6
Greenford UB6 85 D3
Hampstead NW3 70 B3
Thornton Heath CR7 204 C5
Tottenham N22 32 C4
Lyndhurst Sch SE5 139 B3
Lyndhurst Sq SE15 139 D4
Lyndhurst Terr NW3 70 B3
Lyndhurst Way
Belmont SM2 217 C1
Camberwell SE15 139 D3
Lyndon Ave
Bexley DA15 167 D6
Hackbridge SM6 219 A5
Pinner HA5 23 A4
Lyndon Rd DA17 125 C2
Lyndon Yd SW17 179 D6
Lyndum Ct N22 32 C2
Lyne Cres E17 35 B2
Lyne Ct NW9 45 B2
Lynegrove Ave TW15 171 A5
Lyneham Wlk
Hackney E5 75 A3
Pinner HA5 39 D6
Lynette Ave SW4 159 C5
Lynfield Ct SE23 162 D4
Lynford Cl
Barnet Gate EN5 11 D6
Burnt Oak HA8 27 A2
Lynford French Ho SE17 262 A2
Lynford Gdns
Edgware HA8 10 D1
Ilford IG3 79 D6
Lynford Terr N9 17 D3
Lyngham Ct 10 N4 50 A2
Lynhurst Cres UB10 61 B1
Lynhurst Ct NW8 229 C5
Lynhurst Rd UB10 61 A1
Lynmere Rd DA16 146 B3
Lyn Mews 12 E3 97 B4
Lynmouth Ave
Enfield EN1 17 D5
West Barnes SM4 200 D2
Lynmouth Dr HA4 62 B5
Lynmouth Gdns
Heston TW5 128 D4
Wembley UB6 65 B1
Lynmouth Rd
Fortis Green N2 48 D5
Stamford Hill N16 51 D1
Walthamstow E17 53 A4
Wembley UB6 87 B6
Lynn Cl
Ashford TW15 171 B5
Harrow HA3 24 B1
Lynn Ct SW16 181 D5
Lynne Cl 7 BR6 227 D2
Lynne Ct
Forest Hill SE23 163 B4
Hampstead NW6 69 D1
South Croydon CR2 221 C4
Wimbledon SW20 178 B2
Lynnett Ct E9 75 A2
Lynnett Rd RM8 58 D1
Lynne Way UB5 84 D5
Lynne Wlk KT10 212 A3
Lynn Ho SE15 140 A6
Lynn Mews E11 76 C6
Lynn Rd
Balham SW12 159 B4
Ilford IG2 57 B2
Leyton E11 76 C5
Lynn St EN2 5 B4
Lynsted Cl
Bexley DA6 169 D6
Bromley BR1 187 C1
Lynsted Ct 4 BR3 185 A1
Lynsted Gdns SE9 143 D2
Lynton Ave
Ealing W13 87 A1
Hyde The NW9 45 D5
North Finchley N12 30 B6
Lynton Cl
Chessington KT9 214 A4
Isleworth TW7 130 D1
Willesden NW10 67 D3
Lynton Cres IG2 56 D3
Lynton Ct
Bowes Pk N13 32 A5
9 Dagenham W3 89 A1
Penge SE20 184 B2
Sutton SM2 218 A2
Lynton Est SE1 118 A2
Lynton Gdns
Enfield EN1 17 C4
Friern Barnet N11 31 D4
Lynton Grange N2 48 D6
Lynton Ho 16 W2 91 D1
Lynton Lo N5 72 D3
Lynton Mans SE1 261 A6
Lynton Mead N20 13 D2
Lynton Rd Acton W3 110 D6
Bermondsey SE1 117 D2
Lynton Rd *continued*
Chingford E4 35 D5
Harrow HA2 63 A6
Hornsey N8 50 A4
New Malden KT3 199 B4
Paddington NW6 91 B5
Thornton Heath CR0 204 C3
Lynton Terr 4 W3 89 A1
Lynton KT7 197 A2
Lynton Wlk UB4 83 C4
Lynwood Cl
Harrow HA2 63 A5
Woodford E18 37 C2
Lynwood Ct TW15 170 B5
Lynwood Dr KT4 216 A6
Lynwood Gdns
Southall UB1 85 B1
Wallington CR0 220 B4
Lynwood Gr
Orpington BR6 211 C1
Southgate N21 16 C3
Lynwood Rd
Ealing W5 88 A3
Thames Ditton KT7 196 D1
Upper Tooting SW17 180 D6
Lynx Terr SW19 157 C1
Lynx Way E16 121 D6
Lyon Bsns Pk IG11 101 C5
Lyon Ct HA4 39 D1
Lyon Ho NW8 237 A5
Lyon Meade HA7 25 C2
Lyon Park Ave HA0 66 B2
Lyon Park Jun & Inf Schs HA0 66 B1
Lyon Rd Harrow HA1 42 D3
Merton SW19 180 A2
Lyonsdown Ave EN5 14 A5
Lyonsdown Ct EN5 14 A6
Lyonsdown Rd EN5 14 A6
Lyonsdown Sch EN5 14 A6
Lyons Pl NW8 92 B3 236 C5
Lyon St N1 72 B1
Lyons Wlk W14 254 A4
Lyon Way UB6 86 C6
Lyoth Rd BR5 227 A6
Lyric Dr UB6 85 D3
Lyric Mews SE26 184 C6
Lyric Rd SW13 133 D4
Lysander Ct 8 EN5 13 D6
Lysander Gdns KT5 198 B3
Lysander Gr N19 49 D1
Lysander Ho 10 E2 96 B5
Lysander 20 NW9 27 D2
Lysander Rd
Ruislip HA4 61 B6
Wallington CR0 220 B2
Lysander Way BR6 227 A5
Lysia Ct SW6 134 D5
Lysias Rd SW12 159 B5
Lysia St SW6 134 D5
Lysons Wlk SW15 156 A6
Lytchet Rd BR1 187 B3
Lytchet Way EN3 6 C4
Lytchgate Cl CR2 221 C1
Lytcott Dr KT8 195 B6
Lytcott Gr SE22 161 D6
Lytham Ave WD19 22 D5
Lytham Cl SE28 103 A1
Lytham Ct 5 UB1 85 D1
Lytham Gr W5 88 B4
Lytham St SE17 117 B1 262 C1
Lyttelton Cl NW3 70 C1
Lyttelton Ct N2 48 A4
Lyttelton Rd
Hampstead Garden Suburb N2 48 A4
Leyton E10 76 A5
Lytten Ct 6 W12 112 A4
Lyttleton Ct UB4 84 C3
Lyttleton Ho 10 E9 74 C1
Lyttleton Rd N8 50 C6
Lytton Ave Enfield EN3 7 A5
Southgate N13 16 C2
Lytton Cl
Hampstead Garden Suburb N2 48 B4
Northolt UB5 63 B1
Lytton Ct WC1 240 B3
Lytton Gdns SM6 219 D4
Lytton Gr SW15 157 A5
Lytton Ho 3 TW12 173 D4
Lytton Rd
Leytonstone E11 54 C2
New Barnet EN5 2 A1
Pinner HA5 23 A3
Lytton Strachey Path 8 SE28 124 B6
Lyveden Rd
Greenwich SE3 143 B5
Mitcham SW17, SW19 180 D4

M

Mabbett Ho 2 SE18 144 C6
Mabel Crout Ct SE9 145 B1
Mabel Evetts Ct UB3 106 B6
Mabel Thornton Ho 12 N16 73 B4
Maberley Cres SE19 184 A3
Maberley Ct SE19 184 A3
Maberley Rd SE19 182 C2
Mabledon Pl NW1, WC1 232 D1
Mablethorpe Rd SW6 264 A3
Mabley St E9 75 A3
Mablin Lo 3 IG9 21 C3
McAdam Dr EN2 4 D3
MacAllister Ho 8 SE18 144 D6
Macaret Cl N20 14 A4
MacArthur Cl E7 77 A2
MacArthur Ho 4 SW2 160 A4
Macartney Ho SE10 142 B5
MacAulay Ave KT10 212 C6
Macaulay CE Prim Sch SW4 137 B1
MacAulay Ct SW4 137 B2
MacAulay Ho
2 Kensal Town W10 91 A2
10 Stoke Newington N16 73 C5
MacAulay Rd
Clapham SW4 137 B2
Newham E6 99 D5
MacAulay Sq SW4 137 B1
MacAulay Way 2 SE28 124 B5
McAuley Cl
Eltham SE9 166 C6
Lambeth SE1 116 C3 261 A6
MacAuley Mews SE13 142 A3
McAusland Ho 5 E3 97 B5
Macbean St SE18 122 D3
Macbeth Ho 4 N1 95 C5
Macbeth St W6 112 B1
McBride Ho 6 E3 97 B5
McCall Cl SW4 138 A3
McCall Cres SE7 122 A1
McCall Ho N7 72 A4
Mccarthy Ct SW11 267 B1
McCarthy Rd TW13 172 D5
Macclesfield Rd
Croydon SE25 206 C4
Shoreditch EC1 95 A4 235 A2
Macclesfield St W1 249 D6
McClintock Pl EN3 7 D6
McCoid Way SE1 252 A1
McConnell Ho SW8 269 C1
McCormick Ho 9 SW2 160 C3
McCrone Mews 3 NW3 70 B2
McCullum Rd E3 97 B6
McDermott Cl SW11 136 C2
McDermott Rd SE15 140 A2
MacDonald Ave RM10 81 D5
MacDonald Ct TW3 130 A1
McDonald Ho 1 KT2 176 B3
MacDonald Ho 2 SW11 137 A3
MacDonald Rd
Chingford E17 36 A1
Dartmouth Pk N19 71 C6
Forest Gate E7 77 A4
Friern Barnet N11 30 D5
McDonough Cl KT9 214 A4
McDougall Ct TW9 132 C3
Mcdougall Ho E2 96 A4
McDowall Cl E16 98 D2
McDowall Rd SE5 139 A4
Macduff Rd SW11 137 A4 268 B2
Mace Cl E1 118 B5
Mace Ho 2 E17 53 D6
McEntee Ave E17 35 A2
Mace St E2 96 D5
McEwan Way E15 98 B6
Macey Ho
Battersea SW11 267 A1
10 Greenwich SE10 142 A6
Macfarlane La TW7 131 A6

Macfarlane Rd W12 112 C5
Macfarren Ho 7 W10 91 A4
MacFarren Pl NW1 238 B5
McGlashon Ho 15 E1 96 A3
McGrath Rd E15 76 D2
McGregor Ct 8 N1 95 C4
MacGregor Ho 2 SW12 159 D3
MacGregor Rd E16 99 C2
McGregor Rd W11 91 B2
Mcguffie Ct E17 53 B6
Machell Rd SE15 140 C2
McIndoe Ct N1 235 C6
McIntosh Cl SM6 220 A1
McIntosh Ho 14 SE16 118 C2
McIntyre Ct 19 SW4 138 A3
Mackay Ho 33 W12 112 B6
Mackay Rd SW4 137 B2
McKay Rd SW20 178 C4
McKellar Cl WD23 8 A2
McKenna Ho 3 E3 97 B5
Mackennal St NW8 92 C5 230 B4
Mackenzie Cl 7 W12 112 B6
Mackenzie Ho
5 Dollis Hill NW2 68 A5
1 Hornsey N8 50 A5
Mackenzie Rd
Barnsbury N7 72 B2
Penge BR3 184 D1
Mackenzie Wlk E14 119 C5
McKerrell Rd SE15 140 A4
Mackeson Rd NW3 70 D4
Mackie Ho 18 SW2 160 C4
Mackie Rd SW2 160 C4
McKiernan Ct 2 SW11 136 C3
Mc Killop Way DA14 190 C3
McKinlay Ct
Beckenham BR3 185 B1
Bexley DA16 146 C2
McKinnon Wood Ho 16 E2 96 A4
Mackintosh La E9 74 D3
Macklin Ho SE23 162 B2
Macklin St WC2 94 A1 240 B2
Mackonochie Ho EC1 241 A4
Mackrow Wlk 11 E14 120 A6
Macks Rd SE16 118 A2
Mackworth Ho NW1 232 A2
Mackworth St NW1 232 A2
Mac Laren Mews SW15 134 C1
Maclean Rd SE23 163 A5
McLeod Ct SE21 162 A3
McLeod Ho 3 SE23 162 C2
McLeod Rd SE2 124 B2
MacLeod Rd N21 16 A6
McLeod's Mews SW7 113 D2 255 D4
MacLeod St SE17 117 A1 262 B1
Maclise Rd W14 113 A3 254 A5
McManus Ho 3 SW11 136 B2
McMillan Ct 2 SE6 164 D3
Macmillan Ct HA2 41 C1
Macmillan Ho
Cricklewood NW4 68 B4
Lisson Gr NW8 230 B1
McMillan Ho SE4 141 A2
McMillan St SE8 141 C6
Macmillan Way SW17 181 B6
Mcmorran Ho 4 N7 72 A4
McNair Rd UB2 107 D3
Macnamara Ho SW10 266 C4
McNeil Rd SE5 139 C3
McNicol Dr NW10 89 A5
Macoma Rd SE18 145 B6
Macoma Terr SE18 145 B6
Maconochies Rd 9 E14 119 D1
Macquarie Way E14 119 D2
McRae La CR4 202 D2
Macready Ho W1 237 B3
Macready Pl 2 N7 72 A4
Macroom Ho W9 91 B4
Macroom Rd W9 91 B4
Mac's Pl EC4 241 B2
Madame Tussaud's* NW1 93 A3 238 A5
Mada Rd BR6 226 D5
Maddams St E3 97 D3
Madderfields Ct N11 31 D2
Maddison Cl
Finchley N2 30 A1
Teddington TW11 174 D4
Maddison Ct NW4 28 C1
Maddocks Cl DA14 191 A5
Maddocks Ho 3 E1 118 B6
Maddock Way SE17 138 D6
Maddox Ct 1 E4 20 B3
Maddox St W1 248 D6
Madeira Ave BR1 186 C3
Madeira Gr IG8 37 C4
Madeira Rd
Edmonton N13 16 D1
Leytonstone E11 54 C1
Mitcham CR4 202 D5
Streatham SW16 182 A5
Madeleine Cl RM6 58 C3
Madeley Ct W5 88 A1
Madeley Rd W5 88 A1
Madeline Gr IG1 79 B3
Madeline Rd SE20 184 A3
Madge Gill Way 4 E6 100 A6
Madge Hill W7 108 C6
Madinah Rd E8 74 A3
Madingley Ct TW1 153 C6
Madingley 11 KT1 176 C1
Madison Apartments N11 31 D3
Madison Cres DA7 146 C5
Madison Ct 15 RM10 81 D2
Madison Gdns
Beckenham BR2 208 D6
Bexley DA7 146 C5
Madison Ho E3 98 A4
Madras Ho IG1 78 D4
Madras Pl N7 72 C2
Madras Rd IG1 78 D4
Madrid Rd SW13 134 A5
Madron St SE17 117 C1 263 B2
Mafeking Ave
Brentford TW8 132 A6
Ilford IG2 57 B2
Newham E6 100 A5
Mafeking Rd
Enfield EN1 5 D2
Newham E16 98 D3
Tottenham N17 34 A1
Magdala Ave N19 71 C6
Magdala Rd
Isleworth TW7 131 A2
South Croydon CR2 221 B1
Magdalen Ct SE25 206 A4
Magdalene Cl 7 SE15 140 B3
Magdalene Gdns E6 100 C3
Magdalene Ho 7 SW15 156 D5
Magdalene Rd TW17 192 B6
Magdalen Pas E1 253 D6
Magdalen Rd SW18 158 B3
Magdalen St SE1 253 A3
Magee St SE11 138 C6
Magellan Ct 11 NW10 67 B1
Magellan Ho 16 E1 96 D3
Magellan Pl 28 E14 119 C2
Magna Ct UB6 86 B4
Magnaville Rd WD23 8 D4
Magnet Rd HA9 65 D6
Magnin Cl 5 E8 96 A6
Magnolia Cl
Kingston u T KT2 176 D4
Leyton E10 75 C6
Magnolia Ct
13 Belmont SM2 217 D1
Feltham TW14 150 A3
2 Finchley N12 29 D6
Forest Hill SE26 184 C5
Harrow HA3 44 B2
Hillingdon UB10 60 D2
Northolt UB5 85 A3
Richmond TW9 132 D4
Wallington SM6 219 B3
Wandsworth SW11 158 D5
Magnolia Gdns HA8 27 A6
Magnolia Ho 13 SE8 141 B6
Magnolia Lo E4 19 D1
Magnolia Pl
Clapham Pk SW4 160 A6
Ealing W5 87 D2
Magnolia Rd W4 132 D6
Magnolia Way KT19 215 A3
Magnolia Wharf W4 132 D6
Magpie Cl
Edgware NW9 27 C1
Enfield EN1 6 A4
Forest Gate E7 76 D3
Magpie Hall Cl BR2 210 A3
Magpie Hall La BR2 210 B3
Magpie Hall Rd WD23 8 C2
Magpie Ho 7 E3 97 B6
Magpie Pl SE14 141 A6
Magri Wlk 22 E1 96 C2
Maguire Dr TW10 175 C6
Maguire St SE1 117 D4 253 D2
Mahatma Gandhi Ind Est 1 SE24 138 D1
Mahlon Ave HA4 62 B2
Mahogany Cl SE16 119 A5
Mahon Cl EN1 5 D4
Mahoney Ho SE14 141 B4
Maida Ave
Chingford E4 19 D4
Little Venice W2 92 A3 236 B5
Maida Rd DA17 125 C3
MAIDA VALE 91 D4
Maida Vale Sta W9 91 D4
Maida Vale W9 92 A4 229 A1
Maida Way E4 19 D4
Maiden Erlegh Ave DA5 169 A3
Maiden La
Borough The SE1 117 A5 252 B4
Camden Town NW1 71 D1
Strand WC2 116 A6 250 B6
Maiden Rd E15 76 C1
Maidenstone Hill SE10 142 A4
Maids of Honour Row 4 TW9 153 D6
Maidstone Bldgs SE1 252 C3
Maidstone Ct N11 31 D4
Maidstone Ho 4 E14 97 D1
Maidstone Rd
Friern Barnet N11 31 D4
Ruxley DA14 191 C3
Mail Coach Yd 23 E2 95 C4
Main Ave EN1 17 D6
Main Dr HA9 65 D5
Main Rd
Chislehurst BR5 190 C1
Sidcup DA14 167 C1
Mainridge Rd BR7, SE9 188 C6
Main St TW13 172 D5
Mainwaring Ct 3 CR4 181 A1
Main Yd E9 75 C2
Mais Ho SE26 162 B2
Maismore St SE15 140 A6
Maison Alfort HA3 24 C2
Maisonettes The SM1 217 B3
Maitland Cl
3 Greenwich SE10 141 D5
Hounslow TW4 129 B2
Maitland Ct W2 246 C6
Maitland Ho
Chelsea SW1 269 A6
16 South Hackney E2 96 C5
MAITLAND PARK 70 D2
Maitland Park Rd NW3 70 D2
Maitland Park Villas NW3 70 D2
Maitland Pl E5 74 C4
Maitland Rd
Penge SE26 184 D4
Stratford E15 76 D2
Majendie Rd SE18 123 B1
Majestic Ct N4 50 D1
Majestic Way CR4 180 D1
Major Cl SW9 138 D2
Majorie Mews 6 E1 96 D1
Major Rd
22 Bermondsey SE16 118 A3
Stratford New Town E15 76 B3
Makepeace Ave N6 71 A6
Makepeace Mans N6 71 A6
Makepeace Rd
Northolt UB5 85 A6
Wanstead E11 55 A5
Makinen Ho 5 IG9 21 C3
Makins St SW3 257 B3
Malabar Ct 20 W12 112 B6
Malabar St E14 119 C4
Malam Ct SE11 261 A3
Malam Gdns 3 E14 119 D6
Malatia CR2 221 A2
Malay Ho 2 E1 118 C5
Malborough Ho 3 N20 14 D1
Malbrook Rd SW15 134 B1
Malbury Ct N22 32 A3
Malcolm Cl SE20 184 C3
Malcolm Cres NW4 46 A3
Malcolm Ct Ealing W5 88 B3
Hendon NW4 46 A3
Stanmore HA7 25 C5
Malcolm Ct *continued*
Stratford E7 76 D2
Malcolm Dr KT6 198 A1
Malcolm Ho 13 N1 95 C5
Malcolm Pl E2 96 C3
Malcolm Prim Sch SE20 184 C3
Malcolm Rd
Bethnal Green E1 96 C3
Croydon SE25 206 A3
Ickenham UB10 60 B4
Penge SE20 184 C3
Wimbledon SW19 179 A4
Malcolmson Ho SW1 259 D1
Malcolms Way N14 15 C6
Malcolm Way E11 55 A5
Malden Ave
Croydon SE25 206 B6
Northolt UB6 64 C2
Malden CE Prim Sch KT4 199 C1
Malden Cres NW1 71 A2
Malden Ct
Stoke Newington N4 51 A3
West Barnes KT3 200 B6
Malden Green Ave KT4 200 A1
Malden Hill Gdns KT3 199 D6
Malden Hill KT3 199 D6
Malden Junc KT3 199 D4
Malden Manor Prim Sch KT3 199 C2
Malden Manor Sta KT3 199 C2
Malden Pk KT3 199 D3
Malden Pl NW5 71 A3
Malden Rd
Camden Town NW5 71 A2
Cheam KT4, SM3 216 D4
New Malden KT3, KT4 199 D2
Malden Way (Kingston By Pass) KT3, KT5 199 C4
Malden Way KT3 200 A5
Maldon Cl
Camberwell SE5 139 C2
Shoreditch N1 235 B6
Stratford New Town E15 76 B3
Maldon Ct
Barking E6 100 C6
Wallington SM6 219 C3
Maldon Rd
Acton W3 111 A6
Edmonton N9 17 D1
Wallington SM6 219 B3
Maldon Wlk IG8 37 C4
Malet Pl WC1 239 C5
Malet St WC1 93 D2 239 D4
Maley Ave SE27 160 D2
Malford Ct E18 37 A1
Malford Gr E18 54 D6
Malfort Rd SE5 139 C2
Malham Cl N11 31 A4
Malham Rd SE23 162 D3
Malham Road Ind Est SE23 162 D3
Malindi Ct N8 49 D4
Malins Cl EN5 12 C6
Malins Ct SW12 159 A5
Mallaig Ct HA8 10 D2
Mallams Mews 1 SW9 138 D2
Mallard Cl
1 Hackney E9 75 B2
Hanwell W7 108 C4
Kilburn NW6 91 C6
New Barnet EN5 14 B5
Twickenham TW4 151 C4
Mallard Ct
Chingford E4 20 B4
Ilford IG1 79 A6
Kingsbury NW9 45 A2
Little Ilford E12 78 B3
14 Richmond TW10 153 D5
Walthamstow E17 54 B6
Mallard Ho
8 Camberwell SE15 139 D4
St John's Wood NW8 230 A3
Mallard Path 3 SE28 123 B3
Mallard Pl TW1 153 A1
Mallard Point 6 E3 97 C4
Mallards Rd
Barking IG11 102 A3
Woodford IG8 37 B3
Mallards E11 55 A2
Mallard Way NW9 45 A2
Mallard Wlk
Beckenham BR3 206 D4
Sidcup DA14 190 C4
Mall Ct W5 110 A6
Mallet Dr UB5 63 B3
Mallet Ho 11 SW15 156 A6
Mallet Rd SE13 164 B5
Malling Cl CR0 206 C3
Malling Gdns SM4 202 A3
Malling Ho 9 BR3 185 C3
Malling SE13 163 D6
Malling Way BR2 208 D2
Mallinson Ct 2 E11 76 C6
Mallinson Rd
Wallington SM6 219 D5
Wandsworth SW11 158 D6
Mallon Gdns E1 243 D3
Mallord St SW3 136 B6 266 D6
Mallory Bldgs EC1 241 C5
Mallory Cl SE4 141 A1
Mallory Gdns EN4 15 A4
Mallory St NW8 92 C3 237 B6
Mallow Cl CR0 206 D1
Mallow Ct
Colney Hatch N12 30 C4
Lewisham SE13 142 A3
Mallow Mead NW7 29 A3
Mallow St EC1 242 C6
Mallows The UB10 60 D5
Mall Rd W6 112 B1
Mall Studios 9 NW3 70 D3
Mall The
6 Bexley DA6 147 C1
Brentford TW8 131 D6
4 Bromley BR1 209 A6
Ealing W5 110 A6
Harrow HA3 44 B3
Kingston u T KT6 197 D4
Mortlake SW14 155 A6
Palmers Green N14 16 A1
Mall The (Prep Sch) TW2 152 B1
Mall The SW1 115 D5 249 C3
Malmains Cl BR3 208 B5
Malmains Way BR3 208 B5
Malmesbury Cl HA5 40 A5
Malmesbury 30 E2 96 C5
Malmesbury Prim Sch
Morden SM4 202 A3
Tower Hamlets E3 97 B4
Malmesbury Rd
Bow E3 97 B5
Morden SM4 202 A3
Newham E16 98 C2
Woodford E18 36 D2
Malmesbury Terr E16 98 D2
Malmsey Ho SE11 260 D2
Malmsmead Ho E9 75 A3
Malorees Jun & Inf Schs NW6 68 D1
Malory Cl BR3 185 A1
Malpas Dr HA5 40 D4
Malpas Rd
Dagenham RM9 80 D2
Hackney E8 74 B2
New Cross SE4 141 B3
Malta Rd E10 53 C2
Malta St EC1 241 D6
Maltby Dr EN1 6 B5
Maltby Rd KT9 214 C2
Maltby St SE1 117 D3 263 C6
Maltham Terr N18 34 B4
Malthouse Dr
Chiswick W4 133 D6
Feltham TW13 172 D5
Malthouse Pas SW13 133 C3
Malthus Path 7 SE28 124 C5
Malting Ho E14 119 B6
Maltings Cl SW13 133 C3
Maltings Lo W4 133 C5
Maltings W4 110 C1
Maltings Pl
Bermondsey SE1 253 B2
Parsons Green SW6 265 D1
Maltings The BR6 211 D1
Malting Way TW7 130 D2
Malt Mill SE1 253 C3
Malton Ho SE25 205 C5
Malton Mews
1 Notting Hill W10 91 A1
Plumstead Comm SE18 145 C6
Malton Rd W10 91 A1
Malton St SE18 145 C6
Maltravers St WC2 251 A6
Malt St SE1 140 A6
Malva Cl SW18 157 D6
Malvern Ave
Chingford E4 36 B3
Erith DA7 147 A5
Harrow HA2 63 B5
Malvern Cl
Bushey WD23 8 A
Ickenham UB10 60 C
Mitcham CR4 203 C
Notting Hill W10 91 B
Penge SE20 184 A
Surbiton KT6 198 A
Malvern Ct
Belmont SM2 217 C
5 East Barnet N20 14 C
15 Shepherd's Bush W12 112 A
South Kensington SW7 256 D
3 Surbiton KT6 198 A
Malvern Dr
Feltham TW13 172 D
Ilford IG3 79 D
Woodford IG8 37 C
Malvern Gdns
Cricklewood NW2 69 A
Harrow HA3 44 A
Malvern Ho
London N16 51 D
SE17 262 B
Malvern Lo N12 30 B
Malvern Mews NW6 91 C
Malvern Pl NW6 91 B
Malvern Rd
Dalston E8 74 A
Enfield EN3 7 A
Hampton TW12 173 C
Harlington UB3 127 C
Hornsey N8 50 C
Leytonstone E11 76 D
Maida Vale NW6 91 C
Newham E6 100 A
Surbiton KT6 198 A
Thornton Heath CR7 204 C
Tottenham Hale N17 52 A
Upper Holloway N19 49 D
Malvern Terr
Edmonton N9 17 D
Islington N1 234 A
Malvern Way W13 87 B
Malwood Rd SW12 159 B
Malyons Rd SE13 163 D
Malyons Terr SE13 163 D
Malyons The TW17 193 B
Managers St 8 E14 120 A
Manatee Pl SM6 219 D
Manaton Cl SE15 140 B
Manaton Cres UB1 85 C
Manbey Gr E15 76 C
Manbey Park Rd E15 76 C
Manbey Rd E15 76 C
Manbey St E15 76 C
Manbre Rd W6 134 C
Manbrough Ave E6 100 C
Manchester Ct E16 99 B1
Manchester Dr W10 91 A3
Manchester Gr E14 120 A1
Manchester Ho SE17 262 B2
Manchester Mans N19 49 D2
Manchester Mews W1 238 A3
Manchester Rd
Cubitt Town E14 120 A3
South Norwood CR7 205 A6
Tottenham N15 51 B3
Manchester Sq W1 93 A1 238 B2
Manchester St W1 93 A2 238 A3
Manchester Way RM10 81 D4
Manchuria Rd SW11 159 A5
Manciple St SE1 117 B3 262 D6
Mandalay Ho 6 N16 73 B4
Mandalay Rd SW4 159 C6
Mandarin Ct
6 Deptford SE8 141 C6
Willesden NW10 67 B2
Mandarin Way UB4 84 D1
Mandela Cl
36 Shepherd's Bush W12 112 B6
Stonebridge NW10 67 A1
Mandela Ho
Plumstead Comm SE18 145 B6
18 Spitalfields E2 95 D4
Mandela Rd E16 99 A1
Mandela St
Camden Town NW1 93 C6 232 B6
Kennington SW9 138 C5
Mandela Way SE1 117 C2 263 B4
Manderville Ho SE1 263 D2
Mandeville Cl
5 Greenwich SE3 142 D5

Mandeville Cl continued
Merton SW19 ... 179 A2
Mandeville Ct
Hampstead NW3 ... 69 D3
Highams Pk E4 ... 35 A6
Mandeville Ctyd
SW11 ... 268 A1
Mandeville Dr KT6 ... 197 D1
Mandeville Ho 8
SW4 ... 159 C6
Mandeville Pl W1 ... 238 B2
Mandeville Prim Sch
E5 ... 74 D5
Mandeville Rd
Enfield EN3 ... 7 A6
Isleworth TW7 ... 131 A3
Littleton TW17 ... 192 C4
Northolt UB5 ... 63 C1
Osidge N14 ... 15 C2
Mandeville Sch UB5 ... 63 B2
Mandeville St E5 ... 75 A5
Mandrake Rd SW17 ... 158 D1
Mandrake Way 3
E15 ... 76 C1
Mandrell Rd SW2 ... 160 A6
Manesty Ct N14 ... 15 D4
Manette St W1 ... 239 D1
Manfred Ct 7
SW15 ... 157 B6
Manfred Rd SW15 ... 157 B6
Manger Rd N7 ... 72 A2
Mangold Way 4
DA18 ... 125 A3
Manilla Ct RM6 ... 58 B3
Manilla St E14 ... 119 C4
Manister Rd SE2 ... 124 A3
Manitoba Ct 29
SE16 ... 118 C4
Manitoba Gdns 6
BR6 ... 227 D2
Manley Ct N16 ... 73 D5
Manley Ho SE11 ... 261 A2
Manley St NW1 ... 231 A6
Manly Dixon Dr EN3 ... 7 A6
Mann Cl 3 CR0 ... 221 A5
Manneby Prior N1 ... 233 D3
Mannering Ho 16
SW2 ... 160 B6
Manning Ct 3 SE28 ... 124 B5
Manningford Cl EC1 ... 234 C2
Manning Gdns HA3 ... 43 D2
Manning Ho
3 Notting Hill
W11 ... 91 A1
6 Walthamstow E17 ... 54 A6
Manning Pl TW10 ... 154 B5
Manning Rd
Dagenham RM10 ... 81 C1
Walthamstow E17 ... 53 A4
Manningtree Cl
SW19 ... 157 A3
Manningtree Rd HA4 ... 62 B4
Manningtree St 2
E1 ... 96 A1
Mannin Rd RM6 ... 58 B2
Mannock Mews IG8 ... 37 B2
Mannock Rd N22 ... 50 D6
Mann's Cl TW7 ... 152 D6
Manns Rd HA8 ... 26 C4
Manny Shinwell Ho
SW6 ... 264 D5
Manoel Rd TW2 ... 152 A2
Manor Ave
Hounslow TW4 ... 128 D3
New Cross SE4 ... 141 B3
Northolt UB5 ... 63 B1
Manorbrook SE12,
SE3 ... 143 A1
Manor Circus TW9 ... 132 C2
Manor Cl Barnet EN5 ... 1 A1
Edgware NW7 ... 27 B5
Higham Hill E17 ... 35 A1
Kingsbury NW9 ... 44 D4
New Malden KT4 ... 199 C1
Ruislip HA4 ... 39 D1
Thamesmead SE28 ... 102 C1
Manor Cottages App
N2 ... 30 A1
Manor Cotts N2 ... 30 A1
Manor Court Lo 12
E18 ... 37 A2
Manor Court Rd
W7 ... 108 C6
Manor Cres KT5 ... 198 C3
Manor Croft HA8 ... 26 C4
Manor Ct
4 Barking IG11 ... 79 D1
7 Brixton SW2 ... 160 B6
Camberwell SE15 ... 139 D4
Chingford E4 ... 20 C3
Fortis Green N2 ... 48 D4
Friern Barnet N20 ... 14 D1
Gunnersbury W3 ... 110 C2
5 Hackbridge SM6 ... 219 A5
Harrow HA1 ... 42 D3
Kingston u T KT2 ... 176 C2
Osidge N14 ... 15 D2
Manor Ct continued
Parsons Green SW6 ... 265 D1
Streatham SW16 ... 160 A1
Surbiton KT5 ... 198 C3
8 Sutton SM1 ... 218 A4
Twickenham TW2 ... 152 A2
Walthamstow E10 ... 53 D1
5 Wembley HA9 ... 66 A3
Manordene Cl KT7 ... 197 A1
Manordene Rd
SE28 ... 102 D1
Manor Dr
East Barnet N14 ... 15 B3
Edgware NW7 ... 27 B5
Feltham TW13 ... 172 D5
Friern Barnet N20 ... 14 D1
Hinchley Wood KT10 ... 213 A5
Manor Dr N KT3,
KT4 ... 199 B2
Manor Dr
Sunbury TW16 ... 172 A1
Surbiton KT5 ... 198 C3
Manor Dr The KT4 ... 199 D1
Manor Dr
Wembley HA9 ... 66 B4
West Ewell KT19 ... 215 C2
Manor Farm Ave
TW17 ... 192 D3
Manor Farm Cl KT4 ... 199 C1
Manor Farm Ct E6 ... 100 B4
Manor Farm Dr E4 ... 20 C1
Manor Farm Rd
Thornton Heath CR7,
SW16 ... 182 C1
Wembley HA0 ... 87 D5
Manorfield Cl 3 N19 ... 71 C4
Manorfield Prim Sch
E14 ... 97 D2
Manorfields Cl BR7 ... 211 D6
Manor Gate UB5 ... 63 A1
Manorgate Rd KT2 ... 176 C2
Manor Gdns
8 Chiswick W4 ... 111 C1
Clapham SW4 ... 137 C3
Gunnersbury W3 ... 110 C2
Hampton TW12 ... 174 A3
Merton SW20 ... 179 B1
Richmond TW10,
TW9 ... 132 B1
Ruislip HA4 ... 62 C3
South Croydon CR2 ... 221 D2
Sunbury TW16 ... 172 A1
Upper Holloway N7 ... 72 A5
Manor Gr
Beckenham BR3 ... 185 D1
Deptford SE15 ... 140 C6
Richmond TW9 ... 132 C2
Manor Gt SW15 ... 157 A6
Manor Hall Ave NW4 ... 28 D1
Manor Hall Dr NW4 ... 28 D1
Manor Hall Gdns E10 ... 53 C1
Manor Ho
Brentford TW8 ... 109 C1
Manor Pk E12 ... 77 D4
Osidge N14 ... 15 D3
Paddington NW1 ... 237 B4
Manor Ho The
Bexley DA5 ... 169 D3
Chislehurst SE9 ... 188 A5
Manor Ho TW2 ... 152 C2
Manor House Ct
Lower Halliford
TW17 ... 192 D2
Paddington W9 ... 236 A5
Manor House Dr
NW6 ... 68 D1
Manor House Est
HA7 ... 25 B5
Manor House Gdns
E11 ... 55 B3
Manor House Sta N4 ... 50 D1
Manor House Way
TW7 ... 131 B2
Manor Ho SM6 ... 219 B3
Manor Jun & Inf Schs
IG11 ... 79 D2
Manor La
Feltham TW13 ... 150 A2
Harlington UB3 ... 127 B6
Hither Green SE12 ... 164 C5
Manor Lane Terr
SE13 ... 164 C6
Manor La
Sunbury TW16 ... 172 B1
Sutton SM1 ... 218 A3
Manor Lo NW2 ... 68 D2
Manor Mans
7 Hampstead
NW3 ... 70 C2
Tufnell Pk N7 ... 72 A5
Manor Mead Sch
TW17 ... 192 D4
Manor Mews
New Cross SE4 ... 141 B3
Paddington NW6 ... 91 C5
Manor Mount SE23 ... 162 C3
Manor Oak Mans
SE22 ... 162 B5
Manor Par HA1 ... 42 D3
MANOR PARK ... 78 A4
Manor Park Cl BR4 ... 207 D1
Manor Park Cres
HA8 ... 26 C4
Manor Park Dr HA2 ... 41 D6
Manor Park Gdns
HA8 ... 26 C4
Manor Park Par
SE13 ... 142 B1
Manor Park Prim Sch
SM1 ... 218 A3
Manor Park Rd
Chislehurst BR7 ... 189 B2
Dagenham NW10 ... 89 D6
East Finchley N2 ... 48 B6
Manor Pk E12 ... 77 D4
Sutton SM1 ... 218 A3
West Wickham BR4 ... 207 D1
Manor Park Sta E12 ... 77 D4
Manor Par N16 ... 73 D6
Manor Pk
Chislehurst BR7 ... 189 B2
Lewisham SE13 ... 164 C6
Richmond TW9 ... 132 B1
Manor Pl
Chislehurst BR7 ... 189 B1
East Bedfont TW14 ... 150 A3
Mitcham CR4 ... 203 C6
Newington
SE17 ... 117 A1 262 A2
Sutton SM1 ... 217 D4
Walton-on-T KT12 ... 194 A2
Manor Prim Sch E15 ... 98 C5
Manor Rd
Ashford TW15 ... 170 C5
Barking IG11 ... 79 D2
Barnet EN5 ... 1 A1
Beckenham BR3 ... 185 D1
Belmont SM2 ... 217 B1
Bowes Pk N22 ... 32 A4
Dagenham RM6 ... 58 D3
Ealing W13 ... 109 A6
East Molesey KT8 ... 196 B5
Enfield EN2 ... 5 B3
Harrow HA1 ... 43 A3
Hayes UB3 ... 84 A1
Higham Hill E17 ... 35 A1
Loughton IG10 ... 21 B5
Merton SW20 ... 179 B1
Mitcham CR4 ... 203 C6
Newham E15, E16 ... 98 C4
Manor Rd N
Hinchley Wood
KT7 ... 213 A6
Wallington SM5,
SM6 ... 219 B4
Manor Rd
Old Bexley DA5 ... 169 D3
Richmond TW10,
TW9 ... 132 B1
Ruislip HA4 ... 39 B1
Manor Rd S KT10 ... 212 C4
Manor Rd
Sidcup DA15 ... 168 A1
South Norwood
SE25 ... 206 A6
Stamford Hill N16 ... 51 C1
Teddington TW11 ... 175 B5
Tottenham N17 ... 34 B2
Twickenham TW2 ... 152 B2
Wallington SM5,
SM6 ... 219 B3
Walthamstow E10 ... 53 C2
Walton-on-T KT12 ... 193 D2
West Wickham BR4 ... 223 D6
Manor Road Ho HA1 ... 43 A3
Manor Sch NW10 ... 90 C6
Manorside EN5 ... 1 A1
Manorside Cl SE2 ... 124 D2
Manorside Prim Sch
N3 ... 30 A2
Manor Sq RM8 ... 80 C6
Manor Street Est
SW3 ... 267 B6
Manor The
Dulwich SE23 ... 162 C4
Mayfair W1 ... 248 C5
Manor Vale TW8 ... 109 C1
Manor View N3 ... 29 D1
Manor Way
Beckenham BR3 ... 207 C6
Bromley BR2 ... 210 A3
Chingford E4 ... 36 B6
Colindale NW9 ... 45 C5
Manorway EN1 ... 17 C4
Manor Waye UB8 ... 82 A6
Manor Way
Greenwich SE3 ... 143 A1
Gunnersbury W3 ... 110 C2
Harrow HA2 ... 41 D5
Mitcham CR4 ... 203 C6
New Malden KT4 ... 199 D1
Orpington BR5 ... 211 A5
Ruislip HA4 ... 39 D1
Manor Way continued
Sidcup DA5 ... 169 C3
Southall UB2 ... 106 D2
South Croydon CR2 ... 221 D2
Manor Way The
SM6 ... 219 B4
Manorway IG8 ... 37 C5
Manpreet Ct E12 ... 78 B3
Manray Ct 2 N8 ... 50 A4
Manresa Rd
SW3 ... 114 C1 257 A1
Mansard Beeches
SW17 ... 181 A5
Mansard Cl HA5 ... 40 D6
Mansard Manor 4
SM2 ... 218 A1
Manse Cl UB3 ... 127 B6
Manse Ct DA14 ... 190 C5
Mansel Ct SW11 ... 267 B1
Mansel Gr E17 ... 35 C2
Mansell Ho SW8 ... 269 B2
Mansell Rd
Acton W3 ... 111 B4
Southall UB6 ... 85 D2
Mansell St E1 ... 95 D1 243 D1
Mansel Rd SW19 ... 179 B4
Manse Rd N16 ... 73 D5
Mansergh Cl SE18 ... 144 A5
Mansfield Ave
East Barnet EN4 ... 15 A5
Ruislip HA4 ... 40 B1
Tottenham N15 ... 51 B5
Mansfield Cl N9 ... 18 A5
Mansfield Ct 27 E2 ... 95 D6
Mansfield Dr UB4 ... 83 C3
Mansfield Hill E4 ... 19 D3
Mansfield Ho SW15 ... 156 D5
Mansfield Hts N2 ... 48 D4
Mansfield Mews W1 ... 238 C3
Mansfield Pl 28 NW3 ... 70 A4
Mansfield Rd
Acton W3 ... 88 D3
Chessington KT9 ... 213 D3
Ilford IG1 ... 78 C6
Maitland Pk NW3 ... 70 D4
South Croydon CR2 ... 221 B2
Walthamstow E17 ... 53 B5
Wanstead E11 ... 55 B3
Mansfield St
W1 ... 93 B2 238 C3
Mansford St E2 ... 96 A5
Manship Rd CR4 ... 181 A2
Mansion Cl SW9 ... 138 C4
Mansion Gdns NW3 ... 69 D5
Mansion Ho* EC4 ... 242 C1
Mansion House Pl EC3,
EC4 ... 242 C1
Mansion House Sta
EC4 ... 117 A6 252 B6
Mansion House St
EC2 ... 242 C1
Mansions The NW6 ... 69 B3
Manson Mews
SW7 ... 114 B2 256 C3
Manson Pl
SW7 ... 114 B2 256 C3
Manstead Gdns RM6 ... 58 C2
Manston Ave UB2 ... 107 C2
Manston NW1 ... 71 C1
Manston Cl SE20 ... 184 C2
Manstone Rd NW2 ... 69 A3
Manston Gr KT2 ... 175 D5
Manston Ho W14 ... 254 B5
Manston N17 ... 33 B1
Mantell Ho SW4 ... 159 C6
Manthorpe Rd SE18 ... 123 A1
Mantilla Rd SW17 ... 181 A6
Mantle Rd SE4 ... 141 A2
Mantlet Cl SW16 ... 181 C3
Mantle Way E15 ... 76 C1
Manton Ave W7 ... 109 A4
Manton Cl UB3 ... 105 C6
Manton Ho N16 ... 73 B5
Manton Rd
Holdbrook EN3 ... 7 C5
Plumstead SE2 ... 124 A2
Mantua St 23 SW11 ... 136 B2
Mantus Cl
Bethnal Green E1 ... 96 C3
19 Stepney E1 ... 96 C3
Mantus Rd E1 ... 96 C3
Manus Way N20 ... 14 A3
Manville Gdns
SW17 ... 159 B1
Manville Rd SW17 ... 159 B1
Manwood Rd SE4 ... 163 B5
Manwood St E16 ... 122 B5
Manygate La TW17 ... 193 A3
Many Gates SW12 ... 159 B2
Mapesbury Ct NW2 ... 69 A3
Mapesbury Mews 1
NW9 ... 46 A3
Mapesbury Rd NW2 ... 69 A2
Mapeshill Pl NW2 ... 68 C2
Mapes Ho 7 NW6 ... 69 A1
Mape St E2 ... 96 B3
Maple Ave
East Acton W3 ... 111 C5
Harrow HA2 ... 63 D6
Walthamstow E4 ... 35 B4
Yiewsley UB7 ... 104 B6
Maple Cl
Buckhurst Hill IG9 ... 21 D1
Clapham Pk SW4 ... 159 D5
Finchley N3 ... 29 C4
Hampton TW12 ... 173 B4
Hayes UB4 ... 84 D4
Mitcham CR4 ... 181 B2
Petts Wood BR5 ... 211 B4
Ruislip HA4 ... 40 B3
South Tottenham N16 ... 52 A3
Maple Cres DA15 ... 168 A5
Maplecroft Cl E6 ... 100 A1
Maple Ct
Ashford TW15 ... 171 B3
Catford SE6 ... 163 D3
2 Croydon CR0 ... 221 A4
7 Dagenham RM8 ... 58 D2
Kingston u T KT3 ... 199 B6
Newham E6 ... 100 C2
6 Pinner HA5 ... 22 C1
Sidcup DA14 ... 190 B5
11 West Norwood
SW16 ... 182 C5
3 Willesden NW2 ... 68 D4
Mapledale Ave CR0 ... 222 A5
Mapledene BR7 ... 189 A5
Mapledene Est E8 ... 74 A1
Mapledene Rd E8 ... 74 A1
Mapledown Sch
NW2 ... 46 C2
Mapledurham Ct 3
N13 ... 32 C6
Maple Gdns
Grahame Pk HA8 ... 27 C3
Stanwell TW19 ... 148 A2
Maple Gr TW8 ... 131 B5
Maple Gr Bsns Ctr
TW4 ... 128 C1
Maple Gr Ealing W5 ... 109 D3
Kingsbury NW9 ... 45 A2
Southall UB1 ... 85 B2
Maple Ho
2 Kingston u T
KT6 ... 198 A4
11 Maitland Pk NW3 ... 70 D2
5 New Cross SE8 ... 141 B5
4 Richmond TW9 ... 132 D4
Teddington KT1 ... 175 C3
13 Walthamstow E17 ... 53 D6
Maplehurst 2 BR2 ... 186 C1
Maplehurst Cl KT1 ... 198 A5
Maple Ind Est TW13 ... 150 A1
Maple Inf Sch KT6 ... 197 D4
Maple Leaf Dr
DA15 ... 167 D3
Mapleleafe Gdns
IG6 ... 56 D6
Maple Leaf Sq 27
SE16 ... 118 D4
Maple Lo
Buckhurst Hill IG9 ... 21 D3
Putney SW15 ... 157 A5
Welsh Harp NW9 ... 67 B6
Maple Mews
Paddington NW6 ... 91 D5
Streatham SW16 ... 182 B5
Maple Pl
Marylebone W1 ... 239 B5
Tottenham N17 ... 34 A3
Yiewsley UB7 ... 104 B6
Maple Rd Hayes UB4 ... 84 D4
Kingston u T KT6 ... 197 D4
Leytonstone E11 ... 54 C3
Penge SE20 ... 184 C2
Maples Pl E1 ... 96 B2
Maple St 5 E2 ... 96 B5
Maplestead Rd
Dagenham RM9 ... 102 B6
Streatham SW2 ... 160 B4
Maple St W1 ... 93 C3 239 B5
Maples The 4 KT1 ... 175 C3
Maplethorpe Rd
CR7 ... 204 D5
Mapleton Cl BR2 ... 209 A3
Mapleton Cres
Enfield EN3 ... 6 C5
Wandsworth SW18 ... 157 D5
Mapleton Rd
Chingford E4 ... 20 A1
Enfield EN1 ... 6 B3
Wandsworth SW18 ... 157 D5
Maple Tree Pl 7
SE3 ... 144 A4
Maple Way TW13 ... 150 B1
Maple Wlk W10 ... 90 D3
Maplin Cl N21 ... 16 B5
Maplin Ho 7 SE2 ... 124 D4
Maplin Rd E16 ... 99 B1
Maplin St E3 ... 97 B4
Mapperley Cl 3 E11 ... 55 A3
Mapperley Dr IG8 ... 36 C3
Marabou Cl E12 ... 78 A3
Marada Ho NW6 ... 69 A1
Marais W4 ... 133 A5
Maran Way DA18 ... 124 D3
Marathon Way
SE28 ... 123 D4
Marban Rd W9 ... 91 B4
Marble Arch Sta
W1 ... 92 D1 237 D1
Marble Arch*
W1 ... 114 D6 247 D6
Marble Cl W3 ... 110 D5
Marble Dr NW2 ... 46 D2
Marbleford Ct 4 N6 ... 49 D2
Marble Hill Cl TW1 ... 153 B4
Marble Hill Gdns
TW1 ... 153 B4
Marble Hill* TW1 ... 153 C4
Marble Ho
Paddington W9 ... 91 B3
Plumstead Comm
SE18 ... 123 D1
Marble Quay SE1 ... 118 A5
Marbrook Ct SE12 ... 165 C1
Marcella Rd SW9 ... 138 C3
Marcellina Way
BR6 ... 227 D5
Marchant Ho 13
SW2 ... 160 B6
Marchant Rd E11 ... 76 B6
Marchant St SE14 ... 141 A6
Marchbank Rd
W14 ... 135 B6 264 D6
March Ct SW15 ... 134 B1
Marchmont Ho 10
SW16 ... 181 C5
Marchmont Rd
Richmond TW10 ... 154 B6
Wallington SM6 ... 219 C1
Marchmont St
WC1 ... 94 A3 240 A6
March 23 NW9 ... 27 D2
March Rd 7 TW1 ... 153 A4
Marchside Cl TW5 ... 128 D4
Marchwood Cl 9
SE5 ... 139 C5
Marchwood Cres
W5 ... 87 D1
Marcia Rd
SE1 ... 117 C2 263 B3
Marcilly Rd SW18 ... 158 B6
Marcol Ho W1 ... 238 D2
Marcon Ct 29 E8 ... 74 B3
Marconi Pl N11 ... 31 B6
Marconi Rd E10 ... 53 C1
Marconi Way UB1 ... 85 D1
Marcon Pl E8 ... 74 B3
Marco Rd W6 ... 112 C3
Marcourt Lawns W5 ... 88 A3
Marcus Ct
Brentford TW8 ... 132 A5
Newham E15 ... 98 C6
Marcus Garvey Mews
SE22 ... 162 B6
Marcus Garvey Way 9
SE24 ... 138 C1
Marcus Ho 14 SE15 ... 139 D4
Marcus St
Wandsworth
SW18 ... 157 D5
West Ham E15 ... 98 D6
Marcus Terr SW18 ... 157 D5
Mardale Ct NW7 ... 28 A3
Mardale Dr NW9 ... 45 B4
Mardell Rd CR0 ... 206 D4
Marden Ave BR2 ... 209 A3
Marden Cres CR0 ... 204 B3
Marden Ho 6 E8 ... 74 B3
Marden Rd
Thornton Heath
CR0 ... 204 B3
Tottenham N17 ... 33 C1
Marden Sq SE16 ... 118 B3
Marder Rd W13 ... 109 A4
Mardon HA5 ... 23 B3
Mardyke Ho SE17 ... 262 D4
Marechal Niel Ave
DA15 ... 167 B1
Marechal Niel Par
DA15 ... 167 B1
Maresby Ho E4 ... 19 D2
Maresfield Gdns
NW3 ... 70 A2
Maresfield CR0 ... 221 C5
Mare St E8 ... 74 B1
Marey Ct 10 CR2 ... 221 A3
Marfleet Cl SM5 ... 218 C6
Margaret Ave E4 ... 19 D5
Margaret Bondfield Ave
IG11 ... 80 A1
Margaret Bondfield
Ho
5 Bow E3 ... 97 A5
22 Kentish Town N7 ... 71 D3

Margaret Ct
Barnet EN4 . . . 2 B1
Marylebone W1 . . . 239 A2
Margaret Gardner Dr SE9 . . . 166 B2
Margaret Herbison Ho SW6 . . . 264 D5
Margaret Hill Ho 1 N8 . . . 50 A4
Margaret Ho
16 Hammersmith W6 . . . 112 C1
2 Sutton SM1 . . . 217 D5
Margaret Ingram Cl SW6 . . . 264 C5
Margaret Lockwood Cl KT5 . . . 198 B5
Margaret Mcmillan Ho 10 N19 . . . 49 D2
Margaret Rd
Barnet EN4 . . . 2 B1
Bexley DA5 . . . 168 D5
Stamford Hill N16 . . . 51 D1
Margarets Ct HA8 . . . 26 D5
Margaret's Ct E11 . . . 54 B2
Margaret St W1 . . . 93 C1 239 A2
Margaretta Terr SW3 . . . 136 C6 267 B6
Margaretting Rd E12 . . 55 C1
Margaret Way IG4 . . . 56 A3
Margaret White Ho NW1 . . . 232 C2
Margate Rd SW2 . . . 160 A6
Margery Fry Ct N7 . . . 72 A5
Margery Park Rd E7 . . 77 A2
Margery Rd RM8 . . . 80 D5
Margery St WC1 . . . 94 C4 234 A1
Margin Dr SW19 . . . 178 D6
Margravine Gdns
Hammersmith W6 . . . 112 D1
West Kensington W14 . . . 254 A2
Margravine Rd W6 . . . 135 A6 264 A6
Marham Gdns
Morden SM4 . . . 202 A3
Wandsworth SW17, SW18 . . . 158 C3
Mar Ho 4 SE7 . . . 143 C6
Maria Cl 13 SE1 . . . 118 A2
Maria Fidelis Convent Sch (Lower) NW1 . . . 93 C4 232 B1
Maria Fidelis Convent Sch (Upper) NW1 . . . 93 D4 232 C2
Marian Cl UB4 . . . 84 D3
Marian Ct Hackney E9 . . 74 C3
1 Sutton SM1 . . . 217 D3
Marian Lo 5 SW20 . . . 178 D3
Marian Pl E2 . . . 96 B5
Marian Rd SW16 . . . 181 C2
Marian Sq E2 . . . 96 B5
Marian St 2 E2 . . . 96 B5
Marian Vian Prim Sch BR3 . . . 207 A4
Marian Way NW10 . . . 67 D1
Maria Terr E1 . . . 96 D3
Maria Theresa Cl KT3 . . . 199 B4
Maribor 13 SE10 . . . 142 A5
Maricas Ave HA3 . . . 24 B2
Marie Curie SE5 . . . 139 C4
Marie Lloyd Ct 13 SW9 . . . 138 B1
Marie Lloyd Gdns 1 N19 . . . 50 A2
Marie Lloyd Ho N1 . . 235 C3
Marien Ct E4 . . . 36 B5
Marie Stopes Ct 3 N19 . . . 50 A2
Marigold Cl UB1 . . . 107 A6
Marigold Rd N17 . . . 34 C3
Marigold St SE16 . . . 118 B4
Marigold Way CR0 . . . 206 D1
Marilea Ct W5 . . . 109 D4
Marillic Ho NW7 . . . 28 C6
Marina App UB4 . . . 85 A2
Marina Ave KT3 . . . 200 B4
Marina Cl 1 BR2 . . . 209 A6
Marina Ct 12 Bow E3 . . . 97 C4
Greenford UB6 . . . 85 D5
Marina Dr DA16 . . . 145 C3
Marina Gdns RM7 . . . 59 D4
Marina Pl KT1 . . . 175 D2
Marina Point 4 E14 . . . 119 D3
Marina Way TW11 . . . 175 D3
Marine Dr
Barking IG11 . . . 102 B4
5 Woolwich SE18 . . . 122 B2
Marinefield Rd SW6 . . . 135 D3
Marinel Ho 25 SE5 . . . 139 A5
Mariner Gdns TW10 . . 153 C1
Mariner Rd E12 . . . 78 C4
Mariners Mews E14 . . 120 B2
Marine St SE16 . . . 118 A3
Marine Twr 20 SE8 . . . 141 B6
Marion Ave TW17 . . . 192 D4
Marion Ct 4 SW17 . . . 180 C5
Marion Gr IG8 . . . 36 C6
Marion Rd
Mill Hill NW7 . . . 28 A5
Thornton Heath CR0 . . 205 B4
Marion Richardson Prim Sch E1 . . . 96 D1
Marischal Rd SE13 . . . 142 B2
Maritime Ho
5 Clapham SW4 . . . 137 C2
14 Woolwich SE18 . . 122 D2
Maritime Ind Est SE7 . . . 121 B2
Maritime Quay 5 E14 . . . 119 C1
Maritime St E3 . . . 97 B3
Marius Mans 3 SW17 . . . 159 A2
Marius Rd SW17 . . . 159 A2
Marjorie Gr SW11 . . . 136 D1
Marjorie McClure Sch BR7 . . . 189 A2
Marjory Kinnon Sch TW14 . . . 149 C6
Markab Rd HA6 . . . 22 A5
Mark Ave E4 . . . 19 D5
Mark Cl
Bexleyheath DA7 . . . 147 A4
Keston Mark BR2 . . . 226 A4
Southall UB1 . . . 107 D5
Markeston Gn WD19 . . 22 D6
Market Ctr The UB2 . . 106 B2
Market Ct W1 . . . 239 A2
Market La
Burnt Oak HA8 . . . 27 A2
Shepherd's Bush W12 . . . 112 C4
Market Mews W1 . . . 115 B5 248 C3
Market Par
Croydon SE25 . . . 206 A5
1 Edmonton N9 . . . 18 A2
Feltham TW13 . . . 151 A2
Leyton E10 . . . 53 D3
Walthamstow E17 . . . 53 B6
Market Pavilion E10 . . 75 C5
Market Pl
3 Acton W3 . . . 111 A5
1 Bermondsey SE16 . . . 118 B2
2 Bexleyheath DA6 . 147 C1
Brentford TW8 . . . 131 C5
East Finchley N2 . . . 48 C6
Enfield EN2 . . . 5 B2
Kingston u T KT1 . . . 175 D1
Marylebone W1 . . . 239 A2
Market Pl The NW11 . . 47 D5
Market Rd
Barnsbury N7 . . . 72 A2
Richmond TW9 . . . 132 C2
Market Sq
Bromley BR1 . . . 187 A1
Poplar E14 . . . 97 D1
Market Sq The N9 . . . 18 B2
Market St E1 . . . 243 C4
Market Studios 14 W12 . . . 112 C4
Market St
Wallend E6 . . . 100 C5
Woolwich SE18 . . . 122 C2
Market The SM1, SM5 . . . 202 A1
Market Way
Poplar E14 . . . 97 D1
2 Wembley HA0 . . . 66 A3
Market Yd Mews SE1 . . . 263 A6
Markfield Beam Engine & Mus* N15 . . . 52 A4
Markfield Gdns E4 . . . 19 D4
Markfield Ho N15 . . . 52 A4
Markfield Rd N15 . . . 52 A4
Markham Ct NW4 . . . 46 C6
Markham Ho
1 Dagenham RM10 . . . 81 C5
9 Dulwich SE21 . . . 183 C6
Markham Pl SW3 . . . 257 C2
Markham Sq SW3 . . . 114 D1 257 C2
Markham St SW3 . . . 114 C1 257 B2
Mark Ho 3 E2 . . . 96 D5
Markhole Cl TW12 . . . 173 B3
Markhouse Ave E17 . . . 53 A3
Markhouse Pas E17 . . . 53 B3
Markhouse Rd E17 . . . 53 B3
Mark La EC3 . . 117 C6 253 B6
Markland Ho W10 . . . 112 D6
Mark Lo 9 EN4 . . . 2 C1
Markmanor Ave E17 . . 53 B2
Mark Mans W12 . . . 112 A4
Mark Rd N22 . . . 32 D1
Marksbury Ave TW9 . . . 132 C2
Marks Gate Jun & Inf Schs RM6 . . . 59 A6
Mark Sq EC2 . . . 243 A6
Mark St EC2 . . . 243 A6
Markstone Ho SE1 . . 251 C1
Mark St E15 . . . 76 C1
Mark Wade Cl E12 . . . 55 D1
Markway The TW16 . . 172 C1
Markwell Cl SE26 . . . 184 B6
Markyate Ho 6 W10 . . 90 C3
Markyate Rd RM8 . . . 80 B3
Marland Ho SW1 . . . 257 D6
Marlands Rd IG5 . . . 56 B6
Marlang Ct BR3 . . . 186 B2
Marlborough Ave
Edgware HA8 . . . 10 D1
3 Hackney E8 . . . 96 A6
New Southgate N14 . . . 15 C1
Ruislip HA4 . . . 39 B3
Marlborough Cl
Broom Hill BR6 . . . 211 D3
Friern Barnet N20 . . . 14 D1
Mitcham SW19 . . . 180 C4
Newington SE17 . . . 261 D3
Marlborough Cres
Bedford Pk W4 . . . 111 C3
Harlington UB3 . . . 127 B5
Marlborough Ct
6 Beckenham BR3 . . . 185 C2
7 Bromley BR1 . . . 186 D3
7 Buckhurst Hill IG9 . . 21 C2
Harrow HA1 . . . 42 B5
Kensington W8 . . . 255 A4
Marylebone W1 . . . 239 A1
Wallington SM6 . . . 219 C1
Marlborough Day Hospl NW8 . . . 92 A5 229 A4
Marlborough Dr IG5 . . 56 A6
Marlborough Flats SW3 . . . 257 B4
Marlborough Fst & Mid Sch HA1 . . . 42 C5
Marlborough Gdns
Friern Barnet N20 . . . 14 D1
Surbiton KT6 . . . 197 D2
Marlborough Gr SE1 . . . 118 A1
Marlborough Hill
Harrow HA1 . . . 42 C5
St John's Wood NW8 . . . 92 A6 229 B5
Marlborough Ho
Marylebone NW1 . . . 238 D6
Richmond TW10 . . . 154 C6
Stoke Newington N4 . . . 51 A1
Marlborough Ho SW1 . . . 249 B3
Marlborough Ho SW19 . . . 156 D1
Marlborough La SE7 . . . 143 C5
Marlborough Lo
36 Stepney E1 . . . 96 C3
St John's Wood NW8 . 229 A3
Marlborough Mans 5 NW6 . . . 69 C3
Marlborough Mews 18 SW2 . . . 138 B1
Marlborough Par 1 UB10 . . . 82 D3
Marlborough Park Ave DA15 . . . 168 A3
Marlborough Pl NW8 . . . 92 A5 229 B4
Marlborough Prim Sch
Chelsea SW3 . . . 114 C2 257 B3
Isleworth TW7 . . . 131 A4
Marlborough 11 SW19 . . . 156 D3
Marlborough Rd
Acton Green W4 . . . 111 A1
Ashford TW15 . . . 170 A5
Bexley DA7 . . . 146 D2
Bowes Pk N22 . . . 32 B4
Brentford TW7 . . . 131 B5
Bromley BR2 . . . 209 C5
Chingford E4 . . . 35 D4
Dagenham RM8 . . . 80 C4
Ealing W5 . . . 109 D4
Edmonton N9 . . . 18 A3
Feltham TW13 . . . 150 D2
Hampton TW12 . . . 173 C4
Hillingdon UB10 . . . 82 D4
Leyton E15 . . . 76 C4
Mitcham SW19 . . . 180 C4
Richmond TW10 . . . 154 B5
Marlborough Rd *continued*
Romford RM7 . . . 59 D5
Southall UB2 . . . 106 C3
South Croydon CR2 . . 221 A1
St James SW1 . . . 115 C5 249 B3
Sutton SM1 . . . 217 C6
Upper Holloway N19 . . . 72 A6
Upton E7 . . . 77 C1
Wanstead E18 . . . 55 A6
Woolwich SE18 . . . 123 A3
Marlborough Sch DA15 . . . 168 A4
Marlborough W9 . . . 229 A2
Marlborough St SW3 . . . 114 C2 257 B3
Marlborough Trad Est TW9 . . . 132 D4
Marlborough Yd N19 . . 71 D6
Marlbury NW8 . . . 91 D6
Marler Rd SE23 . . . 163 B3
Marlesford Ct SM6 . . . 219 C4
Marlex Lo N3 . . . 29 D2
Marley Ave DA7 . . . 146 D6
Marley Cl
Harringay N15 . . . 50 D5
Southall UB6 . . . 85 C4
Marley Ho 14 W11 . . . 112 D6
Marley Wlk NW2 . . . 68 C3
Marl Field Cl KT4 . . . 200 A1
Marlfield Ct KT3 . . . 199 D2
Marlin Cl TW16 . . . 171 C4
Marlin Ct 5 DA14 . . . 190 A6
Marling Ct TW12 . . . 173 B4
Marlingdene Cl TW12 . . . 173 C4
Marlings Cl BR7 . . . 211 C5
Marlings Park Ave BR7 . . . 211 C6
Marlin Ho SW15 . . . 157 A6
Marlins Cl 3 SM1 . . . 218 A3
Marloes Cl HA0 . . . 65 D4
Marloes Rd W8 . . . 113 D3 255 C5
Marlow Cl SE20 . . . 206 B6
Marlow Cres TW1 . . . 152 D5
Marlow Ct
Colindale NW9 . . . 45 D6
1 Ealing W7 . . . 108 C5
6 Finchley N3 . . . 29 C2
Harrow HA1 . . . 42 A3
Osidge N14 . . . 15 C4
Willesden NW6 . . . 68 D1
Marlow Dr SM3 . . . 216 D5
Marlowe Bsns Ctr 2 SE14 . . . 141 A5
Marlowe Cl BR7 . . . 189 B4
Marlowe Ct
Chelsea SW3 . . . 257 B3
2 Dulwich SE19 . . . 183 D5
6 Kingston u T KT2 . 175 D6
Marlowe Gdns SE9 . . . 166 C5
Marlowe Ho
Kingston u T KT1 . . . 197 D5
15 Stoke Newington N16 . . . 73 C4
Marlowe Lo CR0 . . . 223 A6
Marlowe Rd E17 . . . 54 A5
Marlowe Sq CR4 . . . 203 C5
Marlowes The NW8 . . . 92 B6 229 C6
Marlowe Way CR0 . . . 220 A6
Marlow Gdns UB3 . . . 105 B3
Marlow Ho
Bermondsey SE1 . . . 263 C6
15 Kensington W2 . . . 91 D1
44 Spitalfields E2 . . . 95 D4
Teddington TW11 . . . 175 A6
Wallington CR0 . . . 220 A5
Marlow Rd
Newham E6 . . . 100 B4
Penge SE20 . . . 184 B1
Southall UB2 . . . 107 B3
Marlow Studio Workshops 43 E2 . . . 95 D4
Marlow Way SE16 . . . 118 D4
Marl Rd SW18 . . . 136 A1
Marlston NW1 . . . 231 D1
Marlton St SE10 . . . 120 D1
Marlwood Cl DA15 . . . 167 C2
Marmadon Rd SE18, SE2 . . . 123 D2
Marmara Apts 4 E16 . . . 121 A6
Marmion App E4 . . . 35 C6
Marmion Ave E4 . . . 35 B6
Marmion Cl E4 . . . 35 B6
Marmion Ho 13 SW12 . . . 159 B4
Marmion Mews 4 SW11 . . . 137 A2
Marmion Rd SW11 . . . 137 A1
Marmont Rd SE15 . . . 140 A5
Marmora Ho E1 . . . 97 A2
Marmora Rd SE22 . . . 162 C5
Marmot Rd TW4 . . . 128 D2
Marncrest Ct KT5 . . . 198 B4
Marne Ave
Friern Barnet N11 . . . 31 B6
Welling DA16 . . . 146 A2
Marnell Way TW4 . . . 128 D2
Marner Prim Sch E3 . . 97 D3
Marne St W10 . . . 91 A4
Marney Rd SW11 . . . 137 A1
Marnfield Cres SW2 . . . 160 B3
Marnham Ave NW2 . . . 69 A4
Marnham Cres UB6 . . . 85 D5
Marnham Ct HA0 . . . 65 C3
Marnie Ct 11 E11 . . . 76 C6
Marnock Ho SE17 . . . 262 C2
Marnock Rd SE4 . . . 163 B6
Maroon St E14 . . . 97 A2
Maroons Way SE6 . . . 185 C5
Marqueen Twrs 1 SW16 . . . 182 B3
Marquess Rd N1 . . . 73 B2
Marquess Rd N N1 . . . 73 B2
Marquess Rd S 22 N1 . . . 73 A2
Marquis Cl HA0 . . . 66 B1
Marquis Ct
Barking IG11 . . . 79 C3
Finsbury Pk N4 . . . 50 B1
1 Kingston u T KT1 . . 198 A5
Stanwell TW19 . . . 148 A3
Marquis Rd
Bowes Pk N22 . . . 32 B4
Finsbury Pk N4 . . . 50 C1
Kentish Town NW1 . . . 71 D2
Marrabon Cl DA15 . . . 168 A3
Marrick Cl SW15 . . . 134 A1
Marrick Ho 19 NW6 . . . 91 D6
Marrilyne Ave EN3 . . . 7 B5
Marriner Ct UB3 . . . 105 C6
Marriott Cl TW14 . . . 149 B5
Marriott Ho 8 SE6 . . . 186 A6
Marriott Rd
Finsbury Pk N4 . . . 50 B1
Muswell Hill N10 . . . 30 D2
Newham E15 . . . 98 C6
Marriotts Cl NW9 . . . 45 D3
Marryat Cl TW3 . . . 129 B1
Marryat Ct 12 W6 . . . 112 B2
Marryat Ho SW1 . . . 259 A1
Marryat Pl SW19 . . . 179 A6
Marryat Rd SW19 . . . 179 A6
Marryat Sq SW6 . . . 264 A2
Marryatt Ct W5 . . . 88 B1
Marsala Rd SE13 . . . 141 D1
Marsalis Ho 3 E3 . . . 97 C4
Marsden Rd
Camberwell SE15 . . . 139 D2
Edmonton N9 . . . 18 B2
Marsden St NW5 . . . 71 A2
Marsden Way 2 BR6 . . . 227 D4
Marshall Cl
Brunswick Pk N11 . . . 15 B1
Harrow HA1 . . . 42 B2
Hounslow TW4 . . . 151 B6
Wandsworth SW18 . . . 158 A5
Marshall Ct SW4 . . . 270 B1
Marshall Dr UB4 . . . 83 D2
Marshall Ho
5 New Malden KT3 . . . 199 C5
Paddington NW6 . . . 91 B5
Shoreditch N1 . . . 235 D4
Walworth SE17 . . . 262 C2
Marshall Path 10 SE28 . . . 124 B6
Marshall Rd
Leyton E10 . . . 75 D4
Tottenham N17 . . . 33 B2
Marshalls Gr SE18 . . . 122 A2
Marshall's Pl SE16 . . 263 D5
Marshall's Rd SM1 . . . 217 D4
Marshall St W1 . . . 93 C1 239 B1
Marshalsea Rd SE1 . . . 117 A4 252 B2
Marsham Cl BR7 . . . 188 D5
Marsham Ct
19 Putney SW19 . . . 156 D3
Westminster SW1 . . . 259 D4
Marsham St SW1 . . . 115 D2 259 D4
Marsh Ave CR4 . . . 181 A1
Marshbrook Cl SE3 . . 143 D2
Marsh Cl NW7 . . . 11 D1
Marsh Ct Dalston E8 . . 74 A2
3 Merton SW19 . . . 180 A2
Marsh Dr NW9 . . . 45 D3
Marsh Farm Rd TW2 . . . 152 D3
Marshfield St E14 . . . 120 A3
Marsh Gate Bsns Ctr E15 . . . 98 A5
Marshgate Ctr The E15 . . . 97 D6
Marshgate La E15 . . . 75 D1
Marshgate Prim Sch TW10 . . . 154 B6
Marsh Green Prim Sch RM10 . . . 103 C5
Marsh Green Rd RM10 . . . 103 C6
Marsh Hall HA9 . . . 66 B5
Marsh Hill E9 . . . 75 A3
Marsh Ho
Nine Elms SW8 . . . 269 B2
Pimlico SW1 . . . 259 D1
Marsh La
Edgware NW7 . . . 11 C1
Leyton E10 . . . 75 C6
Stanmore HA7 . . . 25 C4
Tottenham N17 . . . 34 B2
Marsh Point HA5 . . . 41 B5
Marsh Rd Pinner HA5 . . 41 A5
Wembley HA0 . . . 87 D5
Marshside Cl N9 . . . 18 C3
Marsh St E14 . . . 119 D2
Marsh Wall E14 . . . 119 D4
Marshwood Ho 10 NW6 . . . 91 C6
Marsland Cl SE17 . . . 261 D1
Marsom Ho N1 . . . 235 C3
Marston Ave
Chessington KT9 . . . 214 A2
Dagenham RM10 . . . 81 C5
Marston Cl
Dagenham RM10 . . . 81 C5
South Hampstead NW6 . . . 70 A1
Marston Ct
Barnet EN5 . . . 13 C6
Sidcup DA14 . . . 189 D6
Walton-on-T KT12 . . . 194 C1
Marston Ho 23 SW9 . . 138 C3
Marston Rd TW11 . . . 175 B5
Marston SE17 . . . 262 B4
Marston Way SE19 . . . 183 A3
Marsworth Ave HA5 . . . 22 D2
Marsworth Cl UB4 . . . 85 A2
Marsworth Ho 8 E2 . . . 96 A6
Martaban Rd N16 . . . 73 D6
Martello St E8 . . . 74 B1
Martello Terr E8 . . . 74 B1
Martell Rd SE21 . . . 161 B1
Martel Pl E8 . . . 73 D2
Marten Rd E17 . . . 35 C1
Martens Ave DA7 . . . 147 D1
Martham Cl SE28 . . . 124 D6
Martha Rd E15 . . . 76 C2
Martha's Bldgs EC1 . 242 C6
Martha St E1 . . . 96 C1
Marthorne Cres HA3 . . 24 B1
Martin Bowes Rd SE9 . . . 144 B2
Martinbridge Trad Est EN1 . . . 18 A6
Martin Cl
Lower Edmonton N9 . . . 18 D3
Uxbridge UB10 . . . 82 A5
Martin Cres CR0 . . . 204 C1
Martin Ct
15 Cubitt Town E14 . . . 120 A4
Lewisham SE12 . . . 164 D4
Merton SW19 . . . 179 C3
Southall UB2 . . . 107 B4
Martindale Ave 2 E16 . . . 121 A6
Martindale Ho 23 E14 . . . 119 D6
Martindale SW14 . . . 155 A6
Martindale Rd
Balham SW12 . . . 159 B4
Hounslow TW4 . . . 129 A2
Martin Dene DA6 . . . 169 B6
Martin Dr UB5 . . . 63 B3
Martineau Cl KT10 . . . 212 B4
Martineau Dr TW1 . . . 131 B1
Martineau Ho SW1 . . 259 A1
Martineau Mews N5 . . 72 D4
Martineau Rd N5 . . . 72 D4
Martingale Cl TW16 . . 194 A5
Martingales Cl TW10 . . . 153 D1
Martin Gdns RM8 . . . 80 D4
Martin Gr SM4 . . . 201 C6
Martin Ho
Newington SE1 . . . 262 B5
7 New Malden KT3 . 199 C5
South Lambeth SW8 . 270 A4
Martini Dr EN3 . . . 7 C6
Martin Jun & Inf Schs N2 . . . 30 C1
Martin La EC4 . . . 252 D6
Martin Rd RM8 . . . 80 D4
Martin Rise DA6 . . . 169 B6
Martins Cl BR4 . . . 224 B6
Martins Mount EN5 . . . 1 D1
Martins Pl SE28 . . . 123 C5
Martin's Rd BR2 . . . 186 D1
Martins The Penge SE26 . . . 184 B5

Martins The *continued*
Wembley HA9 66 B5
Martin St SE28 123 C5
Martins Wlk
Muswell Hill N10 31 A2
Woolwich SE28 123 C5
Martin Way SW20,
SM4 201 B6
Martlesham N17 33 C1
Martlesham Wlk
NW9 27 C2
Martlet Gr 5 UB5 84 D4
Martlett Ct WC2 240 B1
Martlett Lo NW3 69 D4
Martley Dr IG2 56 D4
Martley Ho SW8 269 B2
Martock Cl HA3 43 A5
Martock Ct 10 SE15 140 B4
Martock Gdns N11 31 A5
Marton Cl SE6 163 C1
Marton Rd 2 N16 73 C5
Martyn Ct HA8 26 B6
Martyn Ho SE2 146 D6
Martynside 22 NW9 27 D2
Marvel Ho 5 SE5 139 B5
Marvell Ave UB4 84 A2
Marvels Cl SE12 165 B2
Marvels Lane Prim Sch
SE12 187 C6
Marvels La SE12 165 C1
Marville Rd
SW6 135 B5 264 C3
Marvin Ho 9 SE18 144 D6
Marvin St 3 E8 74 B2
Marwell Cl BR4 224 D6
Marwell Ct SE3 142 B3
Marwick Rd UB7 104 B4
Marwood Cl DA16 146 B2
Marwood Ct N3 29 D3
Marwood Dr NW7 28 D3
Mary Adelaide Cl
Kingston u T
SW15 155 C1
Kingston u T SW15 177 C6
Mary Adelaide Ho
W2 236 D4
Mary Ann Bldgs
SE8 141 C6
Maryatt Ave HA2 63 D6
Marybank SE18 122 B2
Mary Cl HA7 44 B5
Mary Datchelor Cl
SE5 139 B4
Mary Dine Ct SW8 270 D3
Mary Gn NW8 91 D6
Marygold Ho TW3 130 A4
Mary Ho
8 Hammersmith
W6 112 C1
6 Stockwell SW9 138 B3
Mary James Ho 32
E2 96 A5
Mary Jones Ho 20
E14 119 C6
Maryland Ct KT1 176 D1
Maryland Pk E15 76 C3
Maryland Point E15 76 C2
Maryland Prim Sch
E15 76 C3
Maryland Rd
Paddington W9 91 C3
South Norwood CR7 182 D2
Stratford New Town
E15 76 B3
Tottenham N22 32 C4
Marylands Ind Est
E15 76 C3
Maryland Sq E15 76 C3
Marylands Rd W9 91 D3
Maryland Sta E15 76 C2
Maryland St E15 76 C3
Maryland Way
TW16 172 A1
Maryland Wlk N1 235 A6
Mary Lawrenson Pl 1
SE3 143 A5
MARYLEBONE 93 B1
Marylebone Ct 3
HA0 66 A2
Marylebone Flyover
NW1 92 C2 237 A3
Marylebone High St
W1 93 A2 238 B4
Marylebone La
W1 93 A1 238 B2
Marylebone Mews
W1 238 C3
Marylebone Pas W1 239 B2
Marylebone Rd
NW1 92 D2 237 D4
Marylebone Sta
NW1 92 D3 237 C5
Marylebone St
W1 93 A2 238 B3
Marylee Way
SE11 116 B2 260 D3
Mary Macarthur Ho
8 Belvedere
DA17 125 C3
11 Dagenham RM10 81 C5
15 Globe Town E2 96 D4
Mary McArthur Ho 12
N19 49 D2
Mary Macarthur Ho
W14 264 A6
Marymount
International Sch
KT2 177 A3
Maryon Gr SE7 122 A2
Maryon Mews NW3 70 C4
Maryon Rd SE7 122 A2
Mary Peters Dr UB6 64 B3
Mary Pl W11 113 A6 244 A5
Mary Rose Cl TW12 173 C2
Mary Rose Mall E6 100 B2
Maryrose Way N20 14 B3
Mary's Ct NW8 237 B6
Mary Seacole Villas 19
NW10 67 B1
Mary Secole Cl 21
E8 95 D6
Mary Smith Ct SW5 255 B3
Mary St 5 E16 98 D2
Mary's Terr TW1 153 A4
Mary St N1 95 A6 235 B5
Mary Tates Cotts
CR4 202 D5
Mary Terr NW1 232 A5
Maryville DA16 145 D3
Mary Way WD19 22 C6
Mary Wharrie Ho 4
NW3 70 D1
Marzena Ct TW2 152 A6
Masbro' Rd W14 112 D3
Mascalls Ct 13 SE7 143 C6
Mascalls Rd SE7 143 C6
Mascotte Rd 2
SW15 134 D1
Mascotts Cl NW2 68 B5
Masefield Ave
Borehamwood
WD6 10 D6
Southall UB1 107 C6
Stanmore HA7 24 D5
Masefield Cres N14 15 C5
Masefield Ct
New Barnet EN5 2 A1
Stoke Newington N5 73 B3
19 Surbiton KT6 197 D2
Masefield Gdns E6 100 C3
Masefield Ho 4
NW6 91 C4
Masefield La UB4 84 C3
Masefield Rd TW13 173 B6
Masefield View
BR6 227 A5
Masefield Way
TW19 148 B3
Masham Ho 13
DA18 124 D4
Mashie Rd W3 89 C1
Maskall Cl SW2 160 C3
Maskani Wlk SW16 181 C3
Maskell Rd SW17 158 A1
Maskelyne Cl
SW11 136 C4 267 B2
Mason Cl
Bermondsey
SE16 118 A1
Bexleyheath DA7 147 D2
Hampton TW12 173 B2
Newham E16 121 A6
Wimbledon SW20 178 D2
Mason Ct
4 Penge SE19 183 D3
Wembley HA9 66 C6
Mason Ho
15 Bermondsey
SE1 118 A2
8 Friern Barnet N11 31 C5
16 Hackney E9 74 C1
Mason Rd
Sutton SM1 217 D3
Woodford IG8 36 C6
Mason's Arms Mews
W1 248 D6
Mason's Ave
City of London EC2 242 C2
Croydon CR0 221 A5
Masons Ave HA3 42 D5
Masons Hill
Bromley BR2 209 B5
13 Woolwich SE18 122 D2
Masons Ho NW9 44 D4
Mason's Pl
Finsbury EC1 235 A2
Mitcham CR4 180 D2
Mason St
SE17 117 B2 262 D4
Mason's Yd
Finsbury EC1 234 D2
St James SW1 249 B4
Wimbledon SW19 178 D5
Massey Cl N11 31 B5
Massey Ct 6 E6 99 C6
Massie Rd E8 74 A2
Massingberd Way
SW17 181 B6
Massinger St SE1,
SE17 263 A3
Massingham St E1 96 D3
Masson Ave HA4 62 C2
Mast Ct 17 SE16 119 A2
Master Gunner's Pl 1
SE18 144 A4
Masterman Ho 1
SE5 139 B5
Masterman Rd E6 100 A4
Masters Cl SW16 181 C4
Masters Ct HA4 61 C6
Masters Dr SE16 118 B1
Masters Lo 24 E1 96 C1
Master's St 16 E1 96 D2
Mast House Terr
E14 119 C2
Mastin Ho SW18 157 C3
Mastmaker Rd E14 119 C4
Maswell Park Cres
TW3 152 A6
Maswell Park Rd
TW3 130 A1
Matara Mews SE17 262 A1
Matcham Rd E11 76 D5
Matching Ct 14 E3 97 C4
Matchless Dr SE18 144 C5
Matfield Cl BR2 209 A4
Matfield Rd DA17 147 C6
Matham Gr SE22 139 D1
Matham Rd KT8 196 B4
Mathart Ct E4 36 B4
Matheson Lang Ho
SE1 251 A1
Matheson Rd
W14 113 B2 254 C3
Mathews Ave E6 100 C5
Mathews Park Ave
E15 76 D2
Mathews Yd WC2 240 A1
Mathieson Ct SE1 251 D1
Mathieson Ho 10 E4 20 C4
Mathilda Marks-
Kennedy Jewish Prim
Sch NW7 27 B5
Mathison Ho SW10 266 A4
Matilda Cl SE19 183 B3
Matilda Ho E1 118 A5
Matilda St N1 94 B6 233 D6
Matlock Cl
Barnet EN5 12 D6
Herne Hill SE24 139 A1
Matlock Cres SM3 217 A4
Matlock Ct
7 Herne Hill SE5 139 B1
St John's Wood NW8 229 A4
Woodford IG8 36 D2
Matlock Gdns SM1,
SM3 217 A4
Matlock Pl SM1,
SM3 217 A4
Matlock Rd E10 54 A3
Matlock St E14 97 A1
Matlock Way KT3 177 B2
Maton Ho SW6 264 C4
Matson Ct IG8 36 C3
Matson Ho
9 Bermondsey
SE16 118 B3
16 Homerton E9 74 D2
Matthew Cl W10 90 D3
Matthew Ct
Mitcham CR4 203 D4
4 Walthamstow E17 54 A6
Matthew Parker St
SW1 249 D1
Matthews Ct N5 73 A4
Matthews Ho 3 E14 97 C2
Matthews Rd UB6 64 B3
Matthews St SW11 136 D3
Matthias Ct 12
TW10 154 A5
Matthias Ho 2 N16 73 C3
Matthias Rd N16 73 C3
Mattingly Way 3
SE15 139 D5
Mattison Rd N4 50 D3
Mattock La W5,
W13 109 C5
Maud Cashmore Way
SE18 122 B3
Maude Ho 3 E2 96 A5
Maude Rd
Camberwell SE5 139 C4
Walthamstow E17 53 A4
Maudesville Cotts
W7 108 C5
Maude Terr E17 53 A5
Maud Gdns
Barking IG11 101 D5
Newham E13 98 D5
Maudlins Gn E1 118 A5
Maud Rd Leyton E10 76 A5
Newham E13 98 D5
Maudslay Rd SE9 144 B2
Maudsley Ho TW8 110 A1
Maudsley Hospl The
SE5 139 B3
Maud St E16 98 D2
Maud Wilkes Cl 10
NW5 71 C3
Maugham Ct 5 W3 111 A3
Mauleverer Rd SW2 160 A6
Maultway Ct KT19 215 B3
Maundeby Wlk
NW10 67 C2
Maunder Rd 4 W7 108 D5
Maunsel St
SW1 115 D2 259 C4
Maureen Campbell Ct
TW17 192 D4
Maurer Ct 2 SE10 120 D3
Mauretania Bldg 11
E1 118 D6
Maurice Ave N22 32 D1
Maurice Browne Cl
NW7 28 D4
Maurice Ct
3 Brentford
TW8 131 D5
4 Mile End E1 97 A4
Wood Green N22 32 C2
Maurice Ho
Hither Green
SE12 164 D5
1 Stockwell SW9 138 B3
Maurice St W12 90 B1
Maurice Wlk NW11 48 A5
Maurier Cl UB5 84 C6
Mauritius Rd SE10 120 C2
Maury Rd N16 74 A5
Mauveine Gdns
TW3 129 C1
Mavelstone Cl BR1 188 A2
Mavelstone Rd BR1 188 A2
Maverton Rd E3 97 C6
Mavery Ct 5 BR1 186 D3
Mavis Ave KT19 215 C3
Mavis Cl KT19 215 C3
Mavis Ct 33 NW9 27 D1
Mavis Wlk 9 E6 100 A2
Mavor Ho N1 233 D5
Mawbey Ho SE1 263 D1
Mawbey Pl
SE1 117 D1 263 D1
Mawbey Rd SE1 263 D1
Mawbey St SW8 270 A3
Mawdley Ho SE1 251 B1
Mawney Cl RM7 59 D6
Mawney Rd RM7 59 D6
Mawson Cl SW20 179 A1
Mawson Ct N1 235 D5
Mawson Ho EC1 241 A4
Mawson La W4 133 D6
Maxden Ct SE15 140 A2
Maxey Gdns RM9 81 A4
Maxey Rd
Dagenham RM9 81 A4
Plumstead SE18 123 A2
Maxfield Cl N20 14 A4
Maxim Apartments 3
BR2 209 B5
Maxim Rd N21 16 C5
Maxted Pk HA1 42 C2
Maxted Rd SE15 139 D2
Maxwell Cl
Croydon CR0 204 A1
Hayes UB3 106 A6
Maxwell Ct SE21 162 A3
Maxwell Gdns BR6 227 D5
Maxwell Ho
Bowes Pk N22 32 B4
Chislehurst BR7 188 D3
12 Shooters Hill
SE18 144 D6
Maxwell Rd
Ashford TW15 171 A4
Fulham
SW6 135 D5 265 D3
Welling DA16 146 A2
West Drayton UB7 104 B2
Maxwelton Ave NW7 27 B5
Maxwelton Cl NW7 27 B5
Maya Angelou Ct E4 36 A6
Maya Cl SE15 140 B3
Mayall Cl EN3 7 C5
Mayall Rd SE24 160 D6
Maya Pl N11 31 D3
Maya Rd N2 48 A5
Maybank Ave
Wembley HA0 65 A3
Woodford E18 37 B1
Maybank Gdns HA5 40 A4
Maybank Rd E18 37 C2
May Bate Ave KT2 175 D2
Maybells Commercial
Est IG11 102 D5
Mayberry Pl KT5 198 B2
Maybourne Cl SE26 184 B5
Maybourne Grange
CR0 221 C6
Maybrook Ct E11 77 B6
Maybury Cl Enfield EN1 6 B5
Petts Wood BR5 210 D4
Maybury Ct
Beckenham BR3 185 B3
Croydon CR2 220 D3
Harrow HA1 42 B3
Marylebone W1 238 B3
Maybury Gdns NW10 68 B2
Maybury Mews N6 49 C2
Maybury Rd
Barking IG11 102 A5
Newham E13 99 C3
Maybury St SW17 180 C5
Maychurch Cl HA7 25 D3
May Cl KT9 214 B2
Maycroft
2 Hayes BR2 208 D1
Pinner HA5 22 B1
Maycross Ave SM4 201 C5
May Ct 2 SW19 180 A2
Mayday Gdns SE3 144 A3
Mayday Rd CR0, CR7 204 D3
Mayday University
Hospl CR7 204 D3
Maydeb Ct RM6 59 B3
Maydew Ho SE16 118 C2
Maydwell Ho 6 E14 97 C2
Mayerne Rd SE9 165 D6
Mayesbrook Rd
Barking IG11 101 D6
Dagenham RM8, IG3 80 B5
Mayesford Rd RM6 58 C2
Mayespark Prim Sch
IG3 80 A5
Mayes Rd N22 32 B1
Mayeswood Rd
SE12 187 C6
MAYFAIR 115 B6
Mayfair Ave
Bexley DA7 146 D4
Dagenham RM6 58 D3
Ilford IG1 56 C1
New Malden KT4 200 A1
Twickenham TW2 152 A4
Mayfair Cl
Beckenham BR3 185 D2
Surbiton KT6 198 A1
Mayfair Ct
2 Beckenham
BR3 185 D2
7 Croydon CR0 221 D6
Edgware HA8 26 B5
13 Wimbledon
SW19 179 A3
Mayfair Gdns
Tottenham N17 33 B4
Woodford IG8 37 A3
Mayfair Ho 11 SE1 118 A2
Mayfair Pl W1 248 D4
Mayfair Terr N14 15 D4
Mayfield Ave
Broom Hill BR6 211 D2
Chiswick W4 111 C2
Harrow HA3 43 B4
North Finchley N12 30 B6
Osidge N14 15 D2
West Ealing W13 109 B4
Woodford IG8 37 A4
Mayfield Cl
Ashford TW15 170 D4
Clapham Pk SW4 159 D6
Dalston E8 73 D2
Hillingdon UB10 82 D4
Long Ditton KT7 197 B1
Penge SE20 184 B2
Mayfield Cres
Enfield N9 18 B5
Thornton Heath CR7 204 B4
Mayfield Ct SM2 218 A1
Mayfield DA7 147 B2
Mayfield Dr HA5 41 B5
Mayfield Gdns
Ealing W7 86 C2
Hendon NW4 46 D3
Mayfield Ho
31 Bethnal Green
E2 96 B5
Stamford Hill N16 51 C2
Mayfield Mans
SW15 157 B6
Mayfield Prim Sch
W7 86 B1
Mayfield Rd
Acton W3 110 D6
Bedford Pk W12 111 C4
Bromley BR1 210 A4
Chingford E4 20 B2
Dagenham RM8 58 C1
Dalston E8 73 D1
Enfield EN3 6 D3
Higham Hill E17 35 A1
Hornsey Vale N8 50 B3
Merton SW19 179 B2
Newham E13 98 D3
Mayfield Rd *continued*
South Croydon CR2 221 B1
Sutton SM2 218 B2
Thornton Heath CR7 204 B4
Mayfield Sch & Coll
RM8 58 C1
Mayfields Cl HA9 66 C6
Mayfields HA9 66 C6
Mayfield Villas
DA14 190 C4
Mayflower Cl
Bermondsey
SE16 118 D2
Ruislip HA4 39 A3
Mayflower Ho 2
IG11 101 B6
Mayflower Lo
Hendon N3 47 B6
Muswell Hill N10 31 A2
Mayflower Prim Sch
E14 97 D1
Mayflower Rd SW9 138 A2
Mayflower St 1
SE16 118 C4
Mayfly Cl HA5 40 C2
Mayfly Gdns 12 UB5 84 D4
Mayford Cl
Balham SW12 158 D4
Penge BR3 206 D6
Mayford NW1 232 B4
Mayford Rd SW12 159 A4
May Gdns Elstree WD6 9 D5
Wembley HA0 87 C4
Maygood Ho N1 234 A4
Maygood St
N1 94 C5 234 A4
Maygrove Rd NW6 69 B2
Mayhew Cl E4 19 C1
Mayhew Ct 2 SE5 139 B1
Mayhill Rd
Barnet EN5 13 A5
Greenwich SE7 143 B6
Mayland Mans 4
IG11 78 D1
Maylands Dr DA14 168 D1
Maylands Ho SW3 257 B3
Maylands Rd WD19 22 C6
Maylie Ho 4 SE16 118 B4
Maynard Cl
Fulham
SW6 135 D5 265 D3
Tottenham N15 51 C4
Maynard Ct EN3 7 C5
Maynard Ho
Mile End E1 97 A4
Plumstead SE18 123 A2
Maynard Rd E17 54 A4
Maynards Quay E1 118 C6
Mayne Ct E8 74 A4
Maynooth Gdns
CR4 202 D2
Mayo Ct W13 109 B3
Mayo Ho 10 E1 96 C2
Mayola Rd E5 74 C4
Mayo Rd
Thornton Heath
CR0 205 B4
Walton-on-T KT12 194 A2
Willesden NW10 67 C2
Mayow Rd SE23,
SE26 184 D6
Mayplace Cl DA7 147 D2
Mayplace La SE18 144 D6
Mayplace Rd W
DA7 147 C1
Maypole Ct UB2 107 B4
May Rd Chingford E4 35 C4
Newham E13 99 A5
Twickenham TW2 152 C3
Mayroyd Ave KT6 214 C6
May's Buildings Mews
SE10 142 B5
May's Ct SE10 142 B5
Mays Ct WC2 250 A5
May's Hill Rd BR2 208 C6
Mays La EN5 12 C5
Maysoule Rd SW11 136 B1
Mays Rd TW11,
TW12 174 B5
Maystocks E18 55 C6
Mayston Mews 3
SE10 121 A1
May St W14 254 D1
May Terr IG1 78 D4
Maythorne Cotts
SE13 164 B5
Maytime Prep Sch
IG1 78 C5
Mayton St N7 72 B5
Maytree Cl HA8 11 A1
Maytree Ct
Mitcham CR4 203 A6
Northolt UB5 85 A4
May Tree Ho SE4 141 B2

Maytree La HA7 ... 24 D3
Maytree Wlk SW2 ... 160 C2
Mayville Prim Sch E11 ... 76 C6
Mayville Rd
Ilford IG1 ... 78 D3
Leyton E11 ... 76 C6
Mayward Ho 7 SE5 ... 139 C4
May Wlk E13 ... 99 B5
Maywood Cl BR3 ... 185 D3
May Wynne Ho E16 ... 99 B1
Maze Hill Lodge 7 SE10 ... 142 B6
Maze Hill SE10, SE3 ... 142 C6
Maze Hill Sta SE10 ... 142 C6
Mazenod Ave NW6 ... 69 C1
Maze Rd TW9 ... 132 C5
Mead Cl
3 Camden Town NW1 ... 71 A1
Harrow HA3 ... 24 B2
Mead Cres
Carshalton SM1 ... 218 C4
Chingford E4 ... 36 A6
Meadcroft Ho 4 KT3 ... 199 C2
Meadcroft Rd SE17 ... 138 D6
Mead Ct NW9 ... 45 B4
Meade Cl W4 ... 132 C6
Meader Ct SE14 ... 140 D5
Meadfield HA8 ... 10 D2
Meadfield Gn HA8 ... 10 D2
Mead Field HA2 ... 63 B5
Meadfoot Rd SW16 ... 181 C2
Mead Gr RM6 ... 58 D6
Mead House La UB4 ... 83 B3
Mead Ho W11 ... 244 C4
Meadhurst Pk TW16 ... 171 C4
Mead Inf Sch The KT19 ... 215 D4
Meadlands Dr TW10 ... 153 D2
Meadlands Prim Sch TW10 ... 175 C6
Mead Lo W4 ... 111 B4
Meadow Ave CR0 ... 206 D3
Meadowbank Cl SW6 ... 134 C5
Meadowbank Gdns TW5 ... 128 B4
Meadowbank
Lewisham SE3 ... 142 D2
Primrose Hill NW3 ... 70 D1
Meadow Bank 8 SW15 ... 157 B6
Meadowbank Rd NW9 ... 45 B2
Meadowbanks EN5 ... 12 A6
Meadowbank
Southgate N21 ... 16 B5
Surbiton KT5 ... 198 B3
Meadowbrook Ct TW7 ... 130 D2
Meadow Cl
Barnet EN5 ... 13 B5
Bexley DA6 ... 169 B6
Catford SE6 ... 185 C5
Chingford E4 ... 19 D3
Chislehurst BR7 ... 188 D5
Enfield EN3 ... 7 A5
Hackney E9 ... 75 B3
Hinchley Wood KT10 ... 212 D5
Hounslow TW4 ... 151 C5
Northolt UB5 ... 85 C5
Richmond TW10 ... 154 A3
Ruislip HA4 ... 39 D3
Sutton SM1 ... 218 A6
West Barnes SW20 ... 200 C5
Meadowcourt Rd SE3 ... 142 D1
Meadow Croft BR1 ... 210 B6
Meadowcroft 9 W4 ... 110 C1
Meadowcroft Rd N13 ... 16 C2
Meadow Dr
Hendon NW4 ... 28 C1
Muswell Hill N10 ... 49 B6
Meadowford Cl SE28 ... 124 A6
Meadow Garth NW10 ... 67 B2
Meadowgate Cl NW7 ... 27 D5
Meadow Gate HA2 ... 63 D5
Meadowgate Sch SE4 ... 141 A2
Meadow Gdns HA8 ... 27 A4
Meadow High Sch UB8 ... 82 A2
Meadow Hill KT3 ... 199 C3
Meadow La SE12 ... 165 B1
Meadow Mews SW8 ... 270 C5
Meadow Pl
Chiswick W4 ... 133 C5
South Lambeth SW8 ... 138 A5 270 B4
Meadow Rd
Ashford TW15 ... 171 B5
Barking IG11 ... 80 A1
Beckenham BR2 ... 186 C1
Carshalton SM1 ... 218 C3
Claygate KT10 ... 212 C2
Dagenham RM9 ... 81 B2
Feltham TW13 ... 151 A2
Merton SW19 ... 180 A3
Pinner HA5 ... 41 A5
Southall UB1 ... 107 B6
South Lambeth SW8 ... 138 B5 270 C4
Meadow Row SE1 ... 262 A5
Meadows Cl E10 ... 75 C6
Meadows Ct DA14 ... 190 B4
Meadows End TW16 ... 172 A2
Meadowside
Eltham SE9 ... 143 C1
Twickenham TW1 ... 153 D4
Meadow Stile CR0 ... 221 A5
Meadowsweet Cl
3 Newham E16 ... 99 D2
West Barnes KT3 ... 200 C5
Meadow The BR7 ... 189 A4
Meadow View
Blackfen DA15 ... 168 B4
Harrow HA1 ... 42 C1
Meadowview Rd SE6 ... 185 C5
Meadow View Rd UB4 ... 83 B3
Meadowview Rd DA5 ... 169 B5
Meadow View Rd CR7 ... 204 D4
Meadowview Rd KT19 ... 215 C1
Meadowview TW17 ... 193 A2
Meadow Waye TW5 ... 129 A5
Meadow Way
Kingsbury NW9 ... 45 B4
Locksbottom BR6 ... 226 C5
Ruislip HA4 ... 40 B3
Meadow Way The HA3 ... 24 C2
Meadow Way HA9 ... 65 D4
Meadow Wlk
Dagenham RM9 ... 81 B2
Hackbridge SM6 ... 219 B5
Wanstead E18 ... 55 A5
West Ewell KT17, KT19 ... 215 D1
Meadow Wood Sch WD23 ... 8 A6
Mead Plat NW10 ... 67 A2
Mead Pl
Croydon CR0 ... 205 A1
Hackney E9 ... 74 C2
Mead Rd
Chislehurst BR7 ... 189 A4
Edgware HA8 ... 26 C4
Richmond TW10 ... 153 C1
Mead Road Inf Sch BR7 ... 189 A4
Mead Row SE1 ... 116 C3 261 A6
Meads Ct E15 ... 76 D2
Meadside Cl BR3 ... 185 A2
Meads La IG3 ... 57 D2
Meads Rd Enfield EN3 ... 7 A4
Tottenham N22 ... 32 D1
Meads The
Cheam SM3 ... 217 A5
Edgware HA8 ... 27 B4
Hillingdon UB8 ... 82 A3
Mead The
Beckenham BR3 ... 186 A2
Ealing W13 ... 87 B2
Finchley N2 ... 30 A1
Ickenham UB10 ... 60 C6
Wallington SM6 ... 219 D2
West Wickham BR4 ... 208 B1
Meadvale Rd
Croydon CR0 ... 206 A3
Ealing W5 ... 87 C3
Meadway
Ashford TW15 ... 170 C6
Barnet EN5 ... 1 C1
Beckenham BR3 ... 186 A2
Meadway Cl
Barnet EN5 ... 1 C1
Hampstead Garden Suburb NW11 ... 47 D3
Pinner HA5 ... 23 D4
Mead Way CR0 ... 223 A6
Meadway Ct
Dagenham RM8 ... 81 B6
Ealing W5 ... 88 B2
Hampstead Garden Suburb NW11 ... 47 D3
Meadway Enfield EN3 ... 6 D6
Meadway *continued*
Esher KT10 ... 212 A1
Meadway Gate NW11 ... 47 C3
Meadway Gdns HA4 ... 39 B3
Meadway NW11 ... 47 D3
Mead Way BR2 ... 209 A3
Meadway Ilford IG3 ... 79 C4
Palmers Green N14 ... 16 A2
Mead Way HA4 ... 39 B3
Meadway The
Buckhurst Hill IG9 ... 21 D3
Lewisham SE3 ... 142 B3
Meadway
Tolworth KT5 ... 199 A1
Twickenham TW2 ... 152 B3
West Barnes SW20 ... 200 C5
Woodford IG8 ... 37 C5
Meaford Way SE20 ... 184 B3
Meakin Est SE1 ... 263 A6
Meakin Ho N7 ... 72 B3
Meanley Rd E12 ... 78 A3
Meard St W1 ... 239 C1
Meath Ho SE24 ... 160 D5
Meath Rd Ilford IG1 ... 79 A5
Newham E15 ... 98 D5
Meath St SW11 ... 137 B4 268 C2
Mecklenburgh Pl WC1 ... 240 C6
Mecklenburgh Sq WC1 ... 94 B3 240 C6
Mecklenburgh St WC1 ... 240 C6
Medburn St NW1 ... 232 C4
Medcalf Rd EN3 ... 7 B6
Medcroft Gdns SW14 ... 133 A1
Medebourne Cl SE3 ... 143 A2
Mede Ho BR1 ... 187 B5
Medesenge Way N13 ... 32 D4
Medfield St SW15 ... 156 B4
Medhurst Cl 19 E3 ... 97 A5
Median Rd E5 ... 74 C3
Medina Ave KT10 ... 212 C5
Medina Ct N7 ... 72 C5
Medina Gr N7 ... 72 C5
Medina Ho SE15 ... 140 C1
Medina Rd N7 ... 72 C5
Medland Cl CR4 ... 203 A1
Medlar Cl 1 UB5 ... 84 D5
Medlar Ho 3 DA15 ... 168 A1
Medlar St SE5 ... 139 A4
Medley Rd NW6 ... 69 C2
Medora Rd SW2 ... 160 B4
Medresco Ho NW3 ... 70 B3
Medusa Rd SE6, SE13 ... 163 D5
Medway Bldgs E3 ... 97 A5
Medway Cl
Croydon CR0 ... 206 C3
Ilford IG1 ... 79 A3
Medway Ct
South Norwood SE25 ... 205 C4
St Pancras WC1 ... 233 A1
Medway Dr UB6 ... 86 D5
Medway Gdns HA0 ... 65 A4
Medway Ho
Bermondsey SE1 ... 252 D1
6 Kingston u T KT2 ... 175 D2
Paddington NW8 ... 237 A4
Stoke Newington N16 ... 73 B4
Medway Mews 35 E3 ... 97 A5
Medway Par 1 UB6 ... 86 D5
Medway Rd E3 ... 97 A5
Medway St SW1 ... 115 D3 259 D5
Medwin St SW4 ... 138 B1
Meecham Ct 1 SW11 ... 136 C3
Meerbrook Rd SE3 ... 143 C2
Meers Ct SW20 ... 178 C2
Meeson Rd E15 ... 76 D1
Meeson St E5 ... 75 A4
Meeting House Alley 7 E1 ... 118 B5
Meeting House La SE15 ... 140 B5
Mehetabel Rd E9 ... 74 C3
Meister Cl IG1 ... 57 B1
Melanda Cl BR7 ... 188 B5
Melanie Cl DA7 ... 147 A4
Melba Way SE13 ... 141 D4
Melbourne Ave
Bowes Pk N13 ... 32 B4
Ealing W13 ... 109 A5
Pinner HA2, HA5 ... 41 D6
Melbourne Cl
Broom Hill BR6 ... 211 C2
Ickenham UB10 ... 60 C4
Wallington SM6 ... 219 C3
Melbourne Ct
Hackney E5 ... 75 A4
Muswell Hill N10 ... 31 B3
Paddington W9 ... 236 B6
Penge SE20 ... 184 A3
Twickenham TW2 ... 152 B3
Melbourne Gdns RM6 ... 59 A4
Melbourne Gr SE22 ... 139 D1
Melbourne Ho
Hayes UB4 ... 84 C3
Kensington W8 ... 245 A3
South Norwood SE25 ... 205 D5
Melbourne Mews
Brixton SW9 ... 138 C4
Catford SE6 ... 164 A4
Melbourne Pl WC2 ... 240 D1
Melbourne Rd
Ilford IG1 ... 56 D1
Leyton E10 ... 53 D2
Merton SW19 ... 179 C2
Newham E6 ... 100 B5
Teddington TW11 ... 175 C4
Wallington SM6 ... 219 C3
Walthamstow E17 ... 53 A5
Melbourne Sq 21 SW9 ... 138 C4
Melbourne Way EN1 ... 17 D5
Melbray Mews 11 SW6 ... 135 B3
Melbreak Ho 11 SE22 ... 139 C2
Melbury Ave UB2 ... 107 D3
Melbury Cl
Claygate KT10 ... 213 B2
Elmstead BR7 ... 188 B4
Melbury Ct W8 ... 113 B3 254 D6
Melbury Dr SE5 ... 139 C5
Melbury Gdns SW20 ... 178 B2
Melbury Grange BR1 ... 188 A2
Melbury Ho
South Lambeth SW8 ... 270 C4
Twickenham TW2 ... 152 B2
Melbury Rd
Harrow HA3 ... 44 B4
Kensington W14 ... 113 B3 254 D6
Melchester Ho 1 N19 ... 71 D5
Melchester 5 W11 ... 91 B1
Melcombe Ct NW1 ... 237 C4
Melcombe Gdns HA3 ... 44 B3
Melcombe Ho SW8 ... 270 C3
Melcombe Pl NW1 ... 237 C4
Melcombe Prim Sch W6 ... 134 D6
Melcombe St NW1 ... 92 D3 237 D5
Meldex Cl NW7 ... 28 C4
Meldon Cl SW6 ... 265 D2
Meldone Cl KT5 ... 198 D3
Meldone KT3 ... 199 B1
Meldrum Rd IG3 ... 80 A6
Melfield Gdns SE6 ... 186 A5
Melford Ave IG11 ... 79 D2
Melford Cl KT9 ... 214 B3
Melford Ct
Bermondsey SE1 ... 263 B6
Dulwich SE22 ... 162 A4
Hackney E5 ... 74 B5
2 Sutton SM2 ... 218 A1
Melford Rd
Dulwich SE21, SE22 ... 162 A3
Ilford IG1 ... 79 B6
Leyton E11 ... 76 C6
Newham E6 ... 100 B4
Walthamstow E17 ... 53 B5
Melfort Ave CR7 ... 204 D6
Melfort Rd CR7 ... 204 D6
Melgund Rd N5 ... 72 C3
Melina Cl UB3 ... 83 B2
Melina Ct
Putney SW15 ... 134 A2
St John's Wood NW8 ... 229 C1
Melina Pl NW8 ... 92 B4 229 C1
Melina Rd W12 ... 112 B4
Melior Ct N6 ... 49 C3
Melior Pl SE1 ... 253 A2
Melior St SE1 ... 117 C4 253 A2
Meliot Rd SE6 ... 164 B2
Melisa Ct N6 ... 49 D2
Meller Cl SM6 ... 220 A5
Melling Dr EN1 ... 6 A4
Melling St SE18 ... 145 C6
Mellington Ct 2 N16 ... 74 A5
Mellis Ave TW9 ... 132 D4
Mellish Cl IG11 ... 101 D6
Mellish Ct KT6 ... 198 A3
Mellish Flats E10 ... 53 C2
Mellish Gdns IG8 ... 37 A5
Mellish Ho 2 E1 ... 96 B1
Mellish Ind Est SE18 ... 121 D3
Mellish St E14 ... 119 C3
Mellison Rd SW17 ... 180 C5
Mellitus St W12 ... 89 D1
Mellor Cl KT12 ... 195 B2
Mellor Ct 2 SW19 ... 180 A3
Mellor Ho 2 SE21 ... 183 C6
Mellow La E UB4 ... 83 A3
Mellow Lane Sch UB4 ... 83 A3
Mellow La W UB10 ... 83 A4
Mellows Rd
Redbridge IG5 ... 56 B6
Wallington SM6 ... 219 D3
Mells Cres SE9 ... 188 B6
Mell St 6 SE10 ... 120 C1
Melody La N5 ... 73 A3
Melody Rd SW18 ... 158 A6
Melon Pl W8 ... 245 B2
Melon Rd Leyton E11 ... 76 C5
Peckham SE15 ... 140 A4
Melrose Ave
Borehamwood WD6 ... 10 D6
Cricklewood NW2 ... 68 C3
Greenford UB6 ... 85 D5
Mitcham CR4 ... 181 B3
Thornton Heath SW16 ... 204 C6
Tottenham N22 ... 32 D2
Twickenham TW2 ... 151 D4
Wimbledon SW19 ... 157 C1
Melrose Cl
Greenford UB6 ... 85 D5
Grove Pk SE12 ... 165 B3
Hayes UB4 ... 84 A2
Melrose Cres BR6 ... 227 B3
Melrose Ct
5 Ealing W13 ... 109 A5
Wandsworth SW18 ... 157 B5
Melrose Dr UB1 ... 107 C5
Melrose Gdns
Edgware HA8 ... 26 D1
Hammersmith W6 ... 112 C3
Kingston u T KT3 ... 199 B6
Melrose Ho
Maida Vale NW6 ... 91 C4
Pimlico SW1 ... 258 D2
Melrose Rd
1 Barnes SW13 ... 133 D3
Merton SW19 ... 179 C2
Pinner HA5 ... 41 B5
Wandsworth SW18 ... 157 B5
Melrose Sch CR4 ... 202 C6
Melrose Terr W6 ... 112 C3
Melrose Tudor SM6 ... 220 A3
Melsa Rd SM4 ... 202 A3
Melthorne Dr HA4 ... 62 C5
Melthorpe Gdns SE3 ... 144 A4
Melton Cl HA4 ... 40 C1
Melton Ct
11 Croydon CR0 ... 221 D6
South Kensington SW7 ... 256 D3
Sutton SM2 ... 218 A1
1 Twickenham TW1 ... 153 B4
Melton Ho E5 ... 74 A6
Melton St NW1 ... 93 D4 232 C1
Melville Ave
Greenford UB6 ... 64 D3
South Croydon CR2 ... 221 D3
Wimbledon SW20 ... 178 A3
Melville Cl UB10 ... 61 B5
Melville Court Flats 8 W12 ... 112 B4
Melville Ct
4 Brentford W4 ... 110 C1
Rotherhithe SE8 ... 119 A2
Melville Gdns N13 ... 32 D5
Melville Ho
Lewisham SE10 ... 142 A4
New Barnet EN5 ... 14 B5
Melville Pl 4 N1 ... 73 A1
Melville Rd
Barnes SW13 ... 134 A4
Sidcup DA14 ... 168 C2
Stonebridge NW10 ... 67 B1
Walthamstow E17 ... 53 B6
Melville Villas Rd W3 ... 111 B5
Melvin Ct 11 TW9 ... 132 C4
Melvin Rd SE20 ... 184 C2
Melwood Ho 23 E1 ... 96 B1
Melyn Cl N7 ... 71 C4
Memel Ct EC1 ... 242 A5
Memel St EC1 ... 242 A5
Memess Path 4 SE18 ... 144 C6
Memorial Ave E15 ... 98 C4
Memorial Cl TW5 ... 129 B6
Memorial Hospl SE18 ... 144 C3
Memorial Hts IG2 ... 57 B3
Menai Pl 2 E3 ... 97 C5
Menard Ct EC1 ... 235 B1
Mendham Ho SE1 ... 263 A6
Mendip Cl
Forest Hill SE26 ... 184 C6
Harlington UB3 ... 127 B5
North Cheam KT4 ... 216 C6
Mendip Ct
12 Battersea SW11 ... 136 A2
Deptford SE14 ... 140 C6
1 East Barnet N20 ... 14 C2
Mendip Dr NW2, NW11 ... 69 A6
Mendip Ho HA3 ... 43 A3
Mendip Hos 12 E2 ... 96 C4
Mendip Ho 2 N4 ... 51 B2
Mendip Rd
Battersea SW11 ... 136 A2
Bushey WD23 ... 8 A5
Ilford IG2 ... 57 C4
Mendora Rd SW6 ... 135 B5 264 C4
Menelik Rd NW2 ... 69 B4
Menin Wks CR4 ... 180 D1
Menlo Gdns SE19 ... 183 B3
Mennie Ho SE18 ... 144 B4
Mennis Ho SM5 ... 218 C6
Menon Dr N9 ... 18 B1
Menorah Foundation Sch HA8 ... 27 A3
Menorah Prim Sch NW11 ... 47 A2
Menotti St 6 E2 ... 96 A3
Menteath Ho 9 E14 ... 97 C1
Mentmore Cl HA3 ... 43 C3
Mentmore Terr E8 ... 74 B1
Mentone Ct SW8 ... 270 B2
Meon Ct TW7 ... 130 C3
Meon Rd W3 ... 111 A4
Meopham Rd CR4, SW16 ... 181 C2
Mepham Cres HA3 ... 24 A3
Mepham Gdns HA3 ... 24 A3
Mepham St SE1 ... 116 C5 251 A3
Mera Dr DA7 ... 147 D1
Merantun Way SW19 ... 180 A2
Merbury Cl
Lewisham SE13 ... 164 B6
Woolwich SE28 ... 123 B5
Merbury Rd SE28 ... 123 C4
Mercator Pl 4 E14 ... 119 C1
Mercator Rd SE13 ... 142 B1
Mercer Cl KT7 ... 196 D2
Merceron Ho 3 E2 ... 96 C4
Merceron St E1 ... 96 B3
Mercer Pl HA5 ... 22 C1
Mercers Cl SE10 ... 120 D2
Mercer's Cotts 8 E3 ... 97 A1
Mercers Mews N7 ... 71 D4
Mercers Pl W6 ... 112 D2
Mercers Rd N19 ... 71 D5
Mercer St WC2 ... 94 A1 240 A1
Merchant Ct E1 ... 118 C5
Merchants Cl SE25 ... 206 A5
Merchants Ho SE10 ... 120 B1
Merchants Lo 5 E17 ... 53 C5
Merchant St E3 ... 97 B4
Merchant Taylors' Almshouses SE13 ... 142 C1
Merchant Taylors Hall* EC3 ... 242 D1
Merchiston Rd SE6 ... 164 B2
Merchland Rd SE9 ... 167 A3
Merchon Ho N7 ... 71 C4
Mercia Gr SE13 ... 142 A1
Mercia Ho
9 Camberwell SE5 ... 139 A3
Charlton TW15 ... 171 A2
Mercie Ct SE22 ... 162 A3
Mercier Rd SW15 ... 157 A6
Mercury Ct
8 Brixton SW9 ... 138 C4
10 Millwall E14 ... 119 C2
Mercury Ctr TW14 ... 150 A6
Mercury Ho
Brentford TW8 ... 109 D1
6 Old Ford E3 ... 97 C6
Mercury 23 NW9 ... 27 D2
Mercury Rd TW8 ... 109 C1
Mercury Way SE14 ... 140 D6
Mercy Terr SE13 ... 163 D6
Merebank La CR0, SM6 ... 220 B3
Mere Cl
Orpington BR6 ... 226 D6
Putney SW15, SW19 ... 156 D4
Meredith Ave NW2 ... 68 C3
Meredith Cl HA5 ... 22 D3
Meredith Ho 17 N16 ... 73 C3
Meredith Mews SE4 ... 141 B1
Meredith St
Finsbury EC1 ... 234 C1
Newham E13 ... 99 A4
Meredith Twr W3 ... 110 D3
Meredyth Rd SW13 ... 134 A3

Mere End CR0 ....206 D2
Mere Rd TW17 ....192 D3
Mereside BR6 ....226 C6
Mereside Pk TW15 .. 171 A6
Meretone Cl SE4 ....141 A1
Mereton Mans 6 SE8 ....141 C4
Meretune Ct SM4 ....201 B6
Merevale Cres SM4 ..202 A3
Mereway Industry TW2 ....152 C4
Mereway Rd TW2 ....152 C3
Merewood Cl BR1 ....188 C1
Merewood Gdns CR0 ....206 D2
Mereworth Cl BR2 ..208 D4
Mereworth Dr SE18 ..145 A5
Mereworth Ho 3 SE15 ....140 C6
Merganser Ct 17 SE8 ....141 B6
Merganser Gdns SE28 ....123 B3
Meridan Ct SE13 ....142 B1
Meriden Cl BR1 ....187 D3
Meriden Ct SW3 .... 257 A1
Meriden Ho
  4 Barnet EN5 ....1 A1
  25 Hoxton N1 ....95 C6
Meridian Building* SE10 ....142 B5
Meridian Ct
  4 Bermondsey SE16 .... 118 A4
  4 Catford SE6 .... 164 D3
  Croydon CR0 .... 220 C4
Meridian Ho SE10 ....120 C2
Meridian Pl E14 ....120 A4
Meridian Prim Sch SE10 ....142 B6
Meridian Rd SE7 ....143 D5
Meridian Sq E15 ....76 B1
Meridian Trad Est SE7 ....121 B2
Meridian Way
  Enfield EN3 ....19 A5
  Lower Edmonton N9, N18 ....18 D1
Meridian Wlk N17 ....33 C4
Merifield Rd SE9 ....143 C1
Merino Cl E11 ....55 C5
Merino Pl DA15 ....168 A6
Merioneth Ct 7 W7 ...86 D2
Merivale Rd
  Harrow HA1 ....42 A2
  Putney SW15 .... 135 A1
Merlewood Dr BR7 ...188 B2
Merley Ct NW9 ....45 A1
Merlin Cl
  Mitcham CR4 .... 202 C6
  4 Northolt UB5 ....84 C4
  South Croydon CR0 .. 221 C4
  Wallington SM6 ....220 B2
Merlin Cres HA8 ....26 B2
Merlin Ct
  Beckenham BR2 .... 208 D5
  6 Ealing W7 ....86 D3
  Mitcham CR4 .... 180 C2
  Ruislip HA4 ....61 B6
  Stanmore HA7 ....25 B5
  Wood Green N22 ....32 C2
Merling Cl KT9 ....213 D3
Merlin Gdns BR1 ....165 A1
Merlin Gr BR3 ....207 C4
Merlin Ho
  7 Chiswick W4 ....111 B1
  Enfield EN3 ....18 D6
  West Hampstead NW3 ....69 D4
Merlin 26 NW9 ....27 D2
Merlin Prim Sch BR1 .... 165 A1
Merlin Rd DA16 ....146 A1
Merlin Rd N DA16 ....146 A1
Merlin Rd E12 ....77 D6
Merlins Ave HA2 ....63 B5
Merlin Sch SW15 .... 157 A6
Merlins Ct WC1 .... 234 A1
Merlin St EC1 .. 94 C4 234 A1
Mermaid Ct
  Bermondsey SE1 .... 117 B4 252 C2
  Rotherhithe SE16 ....119 B5
  Stroud Green N4 ....50 C3
Mermaid Ho 8 E14 ..120 A6
Mermaid Twr 22 SE8 ....141 B6
Meroe Ct N16 ....73 C6
Merredene St SW2 ...160 B5
Merriam Ave 2 E9 ....75 B2
Merriam Cl E4 ....36 A5
Merrick Rd UB2 ....107 B3
Merricks Ct 5 SW14 ....132 D1
Merrick Sq SE1 ....117 B3 262 C6
Merridale SE12 ....164 D6
Merridene N21 ....16 D5
Merrielands Cres RM9 ....103 B5
Merrielands Ret Pk RM9 ....103 B5
Merrilands Rd KT4 ...200 C1
Merrilees Rd DA15 ...167 C4
Merrilyn Cl KT10 ....213 A2
Merriman Rd SE3 ....143 C4
Merrington Rd SW6. 265 B6
Merrion Ave HA7 ....25 D5
Merritt Gdns KT9 ....213 C2
Merritt Rd SE4 ....163 B6
Merrivale Ave IG4 .... 55 D5
Merrivale
  Camden Town NW1 .... 232 B5
  Southgate N14 ....15 D6
Merrow Ct CR4 ....180 B1
Merrow St SE17 ....117 B1 262 C1
Merrow Way CR0 .... 224 A2
Merrow Wlk SE17 ... 262 D2
Merrydown Way BR7 ....188 B2
Merry Fiddlers RM8 ... 81 B6
Merryfield Gdns HA7 .. 25 C5
Merryfield Ho SE12 ..165 C1
Merryfield SE3 ....142 D3
Merryhill Cl E4 ....19 D4
Merry Hill Rd WD23 ... 8 A3
Merryhills Ct N14 ....15 C6
Merryhills Dr EN2 .... 4 A1
Merryhills Prim Sch EN2 .... 4 B1
Merryweather Ct
  13 Dartmouth Pk N19 ....71 C5
  1 New Malden KT3 . 199 C4
Mersea Ho IG11 ....78 D2
Mersey Ct 10 KT2 ....175 D2
Mersey Ho 10 N7 ....72 C3
Mersey Rd E17 ....53 B6
Mersey Wlk UB5 ....85 C5
Mersham Dr NW9 ....44 D4
Mersham Pl
  Penge SE20 ....184 B2
  South Norwood CR7 ..183 B1
Mersham Rd CR7 ....183 B1
Merstone Ho SW18 ...157 D5
Merten Rd RM6 ....59 A2
Merthyr Terr SW13 ...134 B6
MERTON 179 C2
Merton Abbey Mills SW19 .... 180 A2
Merton Abbey Prim Sch SW19 .... 179 D2
Merton Ave
  Chiswick W4 .... 111 D2
  Hillingdon UB10 ....60 D1
  Northolt UB5 ....64 A3
Merton Coll SM4 ....201 B4
Merton Court Sch DA14 .... 190 C6
Merton Ct Barnet EN5 ... 1 D1
  Welling DA16 ....146 B3
Merton Gdns BR5 ....210 D4
Merton Hall Gdns SW20 ....179 A2
Merton Hall Rd SW19 ....179 A2
Merton High St SW19 ....180 A3
Merton Ho SW18 ....157 C3
Merton Ind Pk SW19 .... 180 A2
Merton La N6 ....70 D6
Merton Lo
  New Barnet EN5 ....14 A6
  3 Streatham SW16 . 182 A5
Merton Mans SW20 ..178 D1
MERTON PARK 179 C1
Merton Park Par SW19 ....179 B2
Merton Park Prim Sch SW19 .... 179 C1
Merton Park Sta SW19 .... 179 C2
Merton Pl 9 SW19 ...180 A3
Merton Rd
  Barking IG11 ....79 D1
  Croydon SE25 .... 206 A4
  Enfield EN2 .... 5 B5
  Harrow HA2 ....42 A1
  Ilford IG3 ....57 D2
  Leytonstone E17 ....54 A3
  Merton SW19 .... 179 D3
  Wandsworth SW18 ... 157 C4
Merton Rise NW3 ....70 C1
Merton Road Ind Est SW18 .... 157 C4
Merton Way
  East Molesey KT8 ... 196 A6
  Hillingdon UB10 ....60 D1
Merttins Rd SE15 ....162 D6
Meru Cl NW5 ....71 A3
Mervan Rd SW2 ....138 C1
Mervyn Ave SE9 ....167 A2
Mervyn Ct SE18 ....145 C6
Mervyn Rd
  Brentford W13 .... 109 A3
  Shepperton TW17 .... 193 A2
Mervyn Stockwood Ho 1 SE9 ....167 A2
Messaline Ave W3 ....89 A1
Messent Rd SE9 ....165 D6
Messer Ct CR0 ....220 D4
Messeter Pl SE9 ....166 C5
Messina Ave NW6 ....69 C1
Messiter Ho N1 .... 233 D5
Met Appts The SE12 ....164 D6
Metcalfe Ho 28 SW8 ....137 D3
Metcalfe Wlk 2 TW13 ....173 A6
Metcalf Rd TW15 ....170 D5
Meteor St SW11 ....137 A1
Meteor Way SM6 ....220 A1
Metford Cres EN3 .... 7 C5
Metherell Ho N21 ....17 B5
Metheringham Way NW9 ....27 C2
Methley Ho 8 N7 ....72 B6
Methley St SE11 ....116 C1 261 B1
Methodist Central Hall* SW1 .... 115 D4 249 D1
Methuen Cl HA8 ....26 C3
Methuen Pk N10 ....49 B6
Methuen Rd
  Belvedere DA17 .... 125 D2
  Bexleyheath DA6 ....147 B1
  Edgware HA8 ....26 C3
Methwold Rd W10 ....90 D2
Metro Bsns Ctr The SE26 ....185 B5
Metro Ctr UB4 .... 106 C6
Metro Ho E7 ....77 B2
Metro Ind Ctr TW7 ... 130 C3
Metropolis Apartments 5 SW12 ....159 B3
Metropolitan Benefit Societies Almshouses 3 N1 ....73 C2
Metropolitan Bsns Ctr 9 N1 ....73 C1
Metropolitan Cl 23 E14 ....97 C2
Metropolitan Ctr The UB6 ....85 D6
Metro Trad Ctr HA9 ...66 D4
Meudon Ct KT6 ....197 D4
Mews Pl IG8 ....37 A6
Mews St E1 ....118 A5
Mews The
  Beckenham BR3 .... 185 C2
  Hampton TW12 .... 174 A4
  Hornsey N8 ....50 C5
  Redbridge IG4 ....55 D4
  Shoreditch N1 .... 235 B6
  Thornton Heath SW16 ....182 B2
  Tottenham N15 ....51 C5
  5 Upper Holloway N19 ....50 A1
  Woolwich SE18 .... 122 D1
Mexborough NW1 .. 232 A5
Mexfield Rd SW15 ...157 B6
Meyer Gn EN1 .... 6 A5
Meyer Ho 1 SW12 ...159 B4
Meymott St SE1 ....116 D5 251 C3
Meynell Cres E9 ....74 D1
Meynell Gdns E9 ....74 D1
Meynell Rd E9 ....74 D1
Meyrick Ct CR7 ....204 C3
Meyrick Ho 8 E14 ....97 C2
Meyrick Rd
  Battersea SW11 .... 136 C2
  Willesden NW10 ....68 A2
Miah Terr 10 E1 ....118 A5
Miall Wlk SE26 ....185 A6
Micawber Ave UB8 ....82 C3
Micawber Ct N1 .... 235 B2
Micawber Ho 27 SE16 ....118 A4
Micawber St N1 ....95 A4 235 B2
Michael Cliffe Ho EC1 .... 234 B1
Michael Faraday Ho SE17 .... 262 D1
Michael Faraday Sch SE17 .... 117 B1 262 D1
Michael Gaynor Cl W7 ....108 D5
Michael Marshall Ho 2 SE9 ....167 A2
Michaelmas Cl SW20 ....200 C6
Michael Rd
  Leytonstone E11 ....54 D1
Michael Rd *continued*
  Parsons Green SW6 .... 135 D4 265 D2
  South Norwood SE25 .... 205 C6
Michaels Cl SE13 ....142 C1
Michael Sobell Sinai Sch HA3 ....44 C3
Michaelson Ho 4 SE21 ....183 C6
Michael Tippet Sch SE27 .... 161 A2
Michael Tippett Sch The SE11 .. 116 C2 261 B3
Michelangelo Ct 14 SE16 ....118 B1
Micheldever Rd SE12 ....164 D5
Michelham Gdns TW1 ....152 D1
Michelle Ct
  Acton W3 ....111 B6
  North Finchley N12 ....30 A5
Michell Ho TW1 ....152 D3
Michels Almshouses 11 TW10 ....154 A6
Michelsdale Dr 3 TW9 ....132 A1
Michelson Ho SE11 .. 260 D3
Michel's Row 2 TW9 ....132 A1
Michel Wlk SE18 ....122 D1
Michigan Ave E12 ....78 B4
Michigan Ho E14 ....119 C3
Michleham Down N12 ....29 B6
Mickledore NW1 .... 232 B3
Micklefield Ct CR0 ...204 D3
Mickleham Cl BR5 ....190 A1
Mickleham Gdns SM3 ....217 A2
Mickleham Rd BR5 ....190 A1
Mickleham Way CR0 ....224 B1
Micklethwaite Rd SW6 ....135 C6 265 B5
Mickleton Ho 30 W2 .. 91 C2
Midas Bsns Ctr RM10 .81 D4
Midas Metro Ctr SM4 .... 200 D2
Midcroft HA4 ....39 C1
Middle Dene NW7 ....11 B1
Middlefielde W13 ....87 B2
Middlefield Gdns IG2 ....56 D3
Middlefield NW8 ....92 B6 229 C6
Middle Green Cl 3 KT5 ....198 B3
Middleham Gdns N18 ....34 A4
Middleham Rd N18 ...34 A4
Middle La N8 ....50 A4
Middle Lane Mews N8 ....50 A4
Middle La TW11 ....174 D4
Middle Mill KT5 ....198 B6
Middle Park Ave SE9 ....165 D4
Middle Park Prim Sch SE9 .... 165 D4
Middle Rd
  East Barnet EN4 ....14 C5
  Finchley N10 ....30 C2
  Harrow HA2 ....42 B1
  Mitcham SW16 .... 181 D1
  12 Newham E13 ....99 A5
Middle Row Prim Sch W10 ....91 A3
Middle Row W10 ....91 A3
Middlesborough Rd N18 ....34 A4
Middlesex Bsns Ctr UB2 ....107 B4
Middlesex Cl UB6 ....85 D3
Middlesex Coll of Computing & Tech HA0 ....66 A3
Middlesex Ct
  5 Chiswick W4 .... 111 D2
  6 Harrow HA1 ....42 D4
Middlesex Cty Cricket Sch N3 ....29 D1
Middlesex Ho
  Marylebone W1 .... 239 B4
  4 Penge SE20 .... 184 C3
  Wembley HA0 ....87 D6
Middlesex Pas EC1 .. 241 D3
Middlesex Pl 18 E9 ....74 C2
Middlesex Rd CR4 ...204 A4
Middlesex St E1 ....95 D1 243 C2
Middlesex Univ (Cat Hill) EN4 ....15 A6
Middlesex Univ (Enfield Campus) EN3 ....18 C6
Middlesex Univ (Hendon Campus) NW4 ....46 B5
Middlesex Univ N17 ..33 D4
Middlesex Univ Trent Park EN4 .... 3 C3
Middle St
  Croydon CR0 .... 221 A5
  Holborn EC1 .... 242 A4
Middle Temple* EC4 .... 116 C6 251 A6
Middle Temple La EC4 ....116 C6 251 A6
Middleton Ave
  Chingford Green E4 .... 19 B1
  Greenford UB5 ....86 B5
  Sidcup DA14 .... 190 C5
Middleton Cl E4 ....19 B1
Middleton Ct
  Bromley BR1 ....187 B3
  New Barnet EN5 .... 2 A1
Middleton Dr
  Bermondsey SE16 .... 118 D4
  Pinner HA5 ....40 A6
Middleton Gdns IG2 .. 56 D3
Middleton Gr N7 ....72 A3
Middleton Ho
  Dalston E8 ....73 D1
  Newington SE1 .... 262 C5
Middleton Mews N7 .72 A3
Middleton Pl W1 ... 239 A3
Middleton Rd
  Carshalton CR4, SM5 ....202 B2
  Dalston E8 ....73 D1
  Golders Green NW11 ..47 C2
  Hayes UB3 ....83 B2
Middleton St E2 ....96 B4
Middleton Way SE13 ....142 B1
Middle Way UB4 ....84 C3
Middleway NW11 ....47 D4
Middle Way SW16 ....181 D1
Middle Way The HA3 ..24 D1
Middlewich Ho 7 UB5 ....85 B3
Midfield Prim Sch BR5 .... 190 A3
Midfield Way BR5 ....190 B2
Midford Ho 1 NW4 ...46 D5
Midford Pl W1 .... 239 B5
Midholm Cl NW11 ....47 D5
Midholm NW11 ....47 D5
Midholm Rd CR0 ....223 A6
Midholm HA9 ....44 C1
Midhope Ho WC1 .... 233 B1
Midhope St WC1 .... 233 B1
Midhurst Ave
  Muswell Hill N10 ....49 A6
  Thornton Heath CR0 . 204 C2
Midhurst Ct N8 ....50 A2
Midhurst Gdns UB10 ..61 A1
Midhurst Hill DA6 ....169 C6
Midhurst Ho 6 E14 ....97 B1
Midhurst Par N10 ....49 A6
Midhurst 1 SE26 ....184 C4
Midhurst Rd W13 ....109 A3
Midhurst Way E5 ....74 A4
Midland Mainline Terminal NW1 .... 93 D5 232 D3
Midland Pl E14 ....120 A1
Midland Rd
  Leytonstone E10 ....54 A2
  St Pancras NW1 .... 94 A4 233 A2
Midland Terr
  Cricklewood NW2 ....68 D5
  Dagenham NW10 ....89 C3
Midlea Ho EN3 .... 6 C4
Midleton Rd KT3 ....177 A1
Midlothian Ho NW2 ...68 B4
Midlothian Rd E3 ....97 B3
Midmoor Rd
  Merton SW19 .... 179 A2
  Streatham SW12 .... 159 C3
Midship Cl SE16 ....118 D5
Midship Point E14 ...119 C4
Midstrath Rd NW10 ...67 C4
Midsummer Apartments 7 SM2 ....217 C1
Midsummer Ave TW4 ....129 B1
Midsummer Ct
  Blackheath Pk SE12 .... 143 A1
  Edgware HA8 ....10 D1
  Harrow HA1 ....42 B4
Midway SM3 ....201 B2
Midway Ho EC1 .... 234 D2
Midwinter Cl 3 DA16 ....146 A2
Midwood Cl NW2 ....68 B5
Mighell Ave IG4 ....55 D4
Milan Ct N11 ....31 D2
Milan Rd UB1 ....107 B4
Milborne Gr SW10 .. 256 B1
Milborne Ho 11 E9 ....74 C2
Milborne St E9 ....74 C2
Milborough Cres SE12 ....164 C5
Milbourne La KT10 ..212 A3
Milbourne Lodge Jun Sch KT10 .... 212 A2
Milbourne Lodge Sen Sch KT10 ....212 B2
Milbrook Ct NW3 ....48 A1
Milbrook KT10 ....212 A2
Milburn Dr 1 UB7 ...104 A6
Milburn Ho SW20 ....178 B1
Milcote St SE1 .... 251 D1
Mildenhall Rd E5 ....74 C5
Mildmay Ave N1 ....73 B2
Mildmay Ct N1 ....73 B3
Mildmay Gr N N1 ....73 B3
Mildmay Gr S N1 ....73 B3
Mildmay Ho 6 SW15 ....156 C6
Mildmay Mission Hospl E2 ....95 D4
Mildmay Pk N1 ....73 B3
Mildmay Rd
  Ilford IG1 ....78 D5
  Stoke Newington N1 ...73 C3
Mildmay St N1 ....73 B2
Mildon Ho EN3 .... 6 C3
Mildred Ave
  Hayes UB3 ....105 B3
  Northolt UB5 ....63 D3
Mildura Ct N8 ....50 B5
MILE END 97 A3
Mile End Pl E1 ....96 D3
Mile End Rd E1, E3 ....96 D3
Mile End Sta E3 ....97 B4
Mile End The E17 ....34 D2
Mile Rd
  Hackbridge SM6 .... 203 A1
  Wallington CR0, CR4, CR9 .... 203 D1
Miles Bldgs NW1 .... 237 A4
Miles Cl SE28 ....123 B5
Miles Coverdale Prim Sch W12 .... 112 C4
Miles Ct
  Croydon CR0 .... 220 D6
  Stepney E1 ....96 B1
Miles Dr SE28 ....123 C5
Miles Ho 5 SE10 ....120 C1
Miles Lo Harrow HA1 ... 42 B4
  Stratford New Town E15 ....76 B3
Milespit Hill NW7 ....28 C5
Miles Pl NW8 .... 236 D4
Miles Rd Hornsey N8 ... 50 A6
  Mitcham CR4 .... 202 C6
Miles St SW8 ....138 A6 270 B5
Milestone Cl
  Edmonton N9 ....18 A2
  Sutton SM2 ....218 B1
Milestone Ct TW7 ....131 A4
Milestone Green SW14 ....133 B1
Milestone Ho KT1 ....197 D5
Milestone Rd SE19 ...183 D4
Miles Way N20 ....14 C2
Milfoil St W12 ....112 A6
Milford Cl SE2 ....147 A6
Milford Ct
  Southall UB1 .... 107 C5
  3 Stamford Hill N16 ..51 C1
Milford Gdns
  Croydon CR0 .... 206 D4
  Edgware HA8 ....26 C3
  Wembley HA0 ....65 D3
Milford Gr SM1 ....218 A4
Milford La WC2 ....116 C6 251 A6
Milford Mews SW16 ..160 B1
Milford Rd
  Ealing W13 ....109 B5
  Southall UB1 .... 107 C6
Milk St Bromley BR1 ...187 B4
  City of London EC2 ....95 A1 242 B2
  Newham E16 .... 122 D5
Milkwell Gdns IG8 .... 37 B3
Milkwell Yd 7 SE5 ...139 A4
Milkwood Rd SE24 ...138 D1
Milk Yd E1 ....118 C6
Millais Ave E12 ....78 C3
Millais Cres KT19 ....215 C3
Millais Ct 9 UB5 ....84 D5
Millais Gdns HA8 ....26 C1
Millais Rd Enfield EN1 ..17 D6
  Leyton E11 ....76 B4
  New Malden KT3 .... 199 C2
Millais Way KT19 ....215 A4
Milland Ho 11 SW15 ....156 A3

Millard Cl 21 N16 73 C3
Millard Terr RM10 81 C2
Millars Meadow Cl SE12 165 A6
Millbank Ho KT6 198 B2
Millbank Prim Sch SW1 115 D2 259 D3
Millbank SM6 219 D3
Millbank Way SE12 165 A6
Millbank SW1 116 A2 260 A3
Millbourne Rd TW13 173 A6
Mill Bridge EN5 13 B5
Millbrook Ave DA16 145 B1
Millbrooke Ct 7 SW15 157 A6
Millbrook Gdns RM6 59 A3
Millbrook Ho 4 SE15 140 A6
Millbrook Pl NW1 232 A4
Millbrook Rd
Brixton SW9 138 D2
Edmonton N9 18 B3
Millbrook 1 E18 55 A6
Mill Cl SM5 219 A6
Mill Cnr EN5 1 B4
Millcroft Ho SE6 185 D6
Mill Ct Hendon NW7 29 A2
Leyton E10 76 A5
14 Thamesmead SE28 124 B6
Millender Wlk SE16 118 C2
Millennium Bridge* SE1, EC4 252 A5
Millennium Bsns Ctr NW2 68 B6
Millennium City Acad W1 238 D3
Millennium Cl E16 99 B1
Millennium Dr E14 120 B2
Millennium Harbour E14 119 C4
Millennium Ho E17 52 D4
Millennium Pl 27 E2 96 B5
Millennium Prim Sch SE10 120 D3
Millennium Sq SE1 253 D2
Millennium Way SE10 120 C3
Miller Ave EN3 7 C5
Miller Cl
Bromley BR1 187 B5
Carshalton CR4 202 D2
Pinner HA5 22 C1
Miller Ct
Bexleyheath DA7 147 D2
8 Hendon NW9 46 A5
Miller Ho
Harringay N15 50 D5
9 Streatham SW2 160 A4
Miller Rd
Mitcham SW19 180 B4
Thornton Heath CR0 204 C1
Miller's Ave E8, N16 73 D3
Millers Cl NW7 28 A6
Miller's Ct 1 W4 111 D1
Millers Ct 3 HA0 88 A5
Millers Green Cl EN2 4 D2
Miller's House Visitor Ctr* 1 E3 98 A4
Millers Mead Ct SW19 180 B3
Miller's Terr 1 E8 73 D3
Miller St NW1 232 A4
Miller's Way W6 112 C4
Millers Wharf Ho E1 118 A5
Millers Yd N3 29 D3
Miller Wlk SE1 251 B3
Millet Rd UB6 85 D5
Mill Farm Ave TW16 171 C3
Millfarm Bsns Pk TW4 151 A4
Mill Farm Cl HA5 22 C1
Mill Farm Cres TW4 151 A3
Millfield Ave E17 35 B2
Millfield
Charlton TW16 171 B2
Finsbury Pk N4 72 C6
Kingston u T KT1 198 B6
Millfield La N6 70 D6
Millfield Pl N6 71 A6
Millfield Rd
Hendon HA8 27 A1
Twickenham TW4 151 B3
Millfields Com Sch E5 74 C4
Millfields Rd E5 74 C5
Mill Gdns SE26 162 B1
Mill Gn CR4 203 A2
Mill Green Bsns Pk CR4 203 A2
Mill Green Rd CR4 203 A2
Millgrove St 6 SW11 137 A3
Millharbour E14 119 D4
Millhaven Cl RM6 58 B3
MILL HILL 28 B5
Mill Hill SW13 134 A2
Mill Hill Broadway Sta NW7 27 C4
Mill Hill Circus NW7 27 D5
Mill Hill Cty High Sch NW7 11 C2
Mill Hill East Sta NW7 29 A3
Mill Hill Gr 11 W3 110 D5
Mill Hill Ind Est NW7 27 D4
Mill Hill Rd
Barnes SW13 134 A3
South Acton W3 110 D4
Mill Hill Sch NW7 28 B6
Mill Hill Terr 9 W3 110 D5
Mill Ho
4 Lewisham SE13 142 A2
Morden SM4 202 A5
Millhouse Pl SE27 182 D6
Mill Ho IG8 36 D5
Millicent Fawcett Ct N17 33 D2
Millicent Preston Ho 4 IG11 101 B6
Millicent Rd E10 53 B1
Milligan Ho SE23 163 B3
Milligan St E14 119 B6
Milliners Ho SW18 135 C1
Milling Rd HA8 27 B3
Millington Ho N16 73 B5
Millington Rd UB3 105 C3
Mill La
Brondesbury NW6 69 B3
Carshalton SM5 219 A5
Croydon CR0 220 C5
Dagenham RM6 59 A3
Mill Lane Trad Est CR0 220 B5
Mill La Sewardstone E4 7 D2
Woodford IG8 36 D5
Woolwich SE18 122 C1
Millman Ct
Bloomsbury WC1 240 C5
Greenwich SE3 143 B5
Millman Mews WC1 240 C5
Millman Pl WC1 240 D5
Millman St WC1 94 B3 240 C5
Millmark Gr SE14 141 A3
Millmarsh La EN3 7 B3
Millmead Bsns Ctr N17 52 B6
Millmead Ind Ctr N17 52 B6
Mill Mead Rd N17 52 B6
MILL MEADS 98 B5
Millner Ct SE4 141 B3
Mill Plat Ave TW7 131 A3
Mill Plat TW7 131 A3
Mill Pl
Chislehurst BR7 188 D2
Kingston u T KT1 198 B6
Limehouse E14 97 A1
Mill Pond Cl SW8 137 D5 269 D3
Millpond Est SE16 118 B4
Millpond Pl 2 SM6 219 A5
Mill Rd Ilford IG1 78 C5
Merton SW19 180 A3
Newham E16 121 B5
Twickenham TW2 152 A2
Mill Ridge HA8 26 C5
Mill River Trad Est EN3 7 A1
Mill Row N1 95 C6
Mills Cl UB10 82 C5
Mills Ct 9 Leyton E11 76 C5
Shoreditch EC2 95 C4
Mills Gr Hendon NW4 46 D6
1 South Bromley E14 98 A2
Mills Ho SW8 269 B2
Millshott Cl SW6 134 C4
Mills Ho E17 54 B6
Millside SM5 218 D6
Millside Pl TW7 131 B3
Millson Cl N20 14 B2
Mills Row W4 111 B2
Mill St
Bermondsey SE1 117 D4 253 D2
Kingston u T KT1 198 A6
Mayfair W1 249 A6
Millstream Cl N13 32 C5
Millstream Ho 14 SE16 118 B4
Millstream Rd SE1 117 D4 253 C1
Mill Trad Est The NW10 89 A4
Mill Vale BR2 186 D1
Mill View Cl KT17 215 D1
Mill View Gdns CR0 222 D5
MILLWALL 119 C3
Millwall Dock Rd E14 119 C3
Mill Way
Edgware NW7 27 C5
Feltham TW14 150 B6
Millway Gdns UB5 63 B2
Millwood Rd TW3, TW7 152 A6
Millwood St 10 W10 91 A2
Mill Yd E1 118 A6
Milman Cl HA5 40 D6
Milman Rd NW6 91 A5
Milman's Ho SW10 266 C5
Milman's St SW10 136 B6 266 C5
Milne Ct Enfield EN2 4 C3
4 Woodford E18 37 A2
Milne Field HA5 23 C3
Milne Gdns SE9 166 A6
Milne Ho 18 SE18 122 B2
Milner Bldg N16 73 B5
Milner Dr TW2 152 B4
Milner Ho
2 Battersea SW11 136 B2
Hayes UB4 84 B4
Milner Pl N1 94 C6 234 B6
Milner Rd
Dagenham RM8 80 C6
Kingston u T KT1 197 D6
Merton SW19 179 D2
Morden SM4 202 B4
Newham E15 98 C4
South Norwood CR7 205 B6
Milner Sq N1 72 D1
Milner St SW3 114 D2 257 C4
Milner Wlk SE9 167 B3
Milnthorpe Rd W4 133 B6
Milo Rd SE22 161 D5
Milrood Ho 5 E1 96 D2
Milroy Wlk SE1 251 C4
Milson Rd W14 113 A3 254 A6
Milsted Ho 23 E5 74 B3
Milton Ave
Barnet EN5 13 B6
Becontree NW10 89 B6
Carshalton SM1 218 C4
Crouch End N6 49 C2
Kingsbury NW9 45 A6
Plashet E6 78 A1
Thornton Heath CR0 205 B2
Milton Cl
Bermondsey SE1 117 D2 263 C3
Carshalton SM1 218 B5
Hampstead Garden Suburb N2 48 A3
Hayes UB4 84 A1
Milton Court Rd SE14 141 A6
Milton Cres IG2 57 A3
Milton Ct
Fulham SW6 135 A2
Ilford RM6 58 C2
Kingston u T KT2 176 A6
St Luke's EC2 242 C4
Twickenham TW2 152 C1
Uxbridge UB10 60 D5
9 Wandsworth SW18 157 C6
Milton Dr
Borehamwood WD6 10 D6
Littleton TW17 192 A5
Milton Gdns TW19 148 B3
Milton Gr
Friern Barnet N11 31 D5
Stoke Newington N16 73 C4
Milton Ho
12 Beckenham BR3 185 C3
19 Bethnal Green E2 96 C4
2 Camberwell SE5 139 B5
5 Kingston u T KT2 176 D4
Sutton SM1 217 C5
Milton House Mans E8 73 D4
Milton Lo
4 Sidcup DA14 190 A6
Southgate N21 16 D3
Twickenham TW1 152 D4
Milton Pk N6 49 C2
Milton Pl 3 N7 72 C3
Milton Rd Acton W3 111 B5
Belvedere DA17 125 C2
Bexley DA16 145 D4
Crouch End N6 49 C2
Ealing W7 108 D6
Hampton TW12 173 C3
Milton Rd *continued*
Harrow HA1 42 C5
1 Hendon NW9 46 A2
Mill Hill NW7 28 A5
Mitcham CR4 181 A3
Mortlake SW14 133 B2
Sutton SM1 217 C4
Thornton Heath CR0 205 B2
Tottenham N15 50 D6
Tulse Hill SE24 160 D6
Uxbridge UB10 60 D4
Wallington SM6 219 D2
Walthamstow E17 53 C5
Wimbledon SW19 180 A4
Milton St EC1, EC2 95 B2 242 C4
Milton Way UB7 104 B2
Milverton Dr UB10 61 A4
Milverton Gdns IG3 79 D6
Milverton Ho SE23 163 A1
Milverton NW5 71 A3
Milverton Rd NW6 68 C1
Milverton St SE11 116 C1 261 B1
Milverton Way SE9 188 C6
Milward St E1 96 B2
Milward Wlk 14 SE18 144 C6
Mimosa Ct
Colney Hatch N12 30 C4
South Lambeth SW4 270 B1
Mimosa Ho UB4 84 C2
Mimosa N15 51 B4
Mimosa Rd UB4 84 C2
Mimosa St SW6 135 B4 264 D1
Mina Rd SW19 179 C2
Minard Rd SE6 164 C3
Mina Rd SE17 117 C1 263 B2
Minchenden Cres N14 15 D1
Minchenden Ct N14 15 D2
Minchin Ho 10 E14 97 C1
Mincing La EC3 117 C6 253 A6
Minden Rd
Cheam SM3 217 B6
Penge SE20 184 B2
Minehead Ct HA2 63 C6
Minehead Rd
Harrow HA2 63 C5
Streatham SW16 182 B5
Mineral Cl EN5 12 C6
Mineral St SE18 123 C2
Minera Mews SW1 258 B4
Minerva Cl
Kennington SW9 138 C5
Sidcup DA14 189 C6
Minerva Rd
Becontree NW10 89 B4
Chingford E4 35 D3
Kingston u T KT1 176 B1
Minerva St E2 96 B5
Minerva Wlk EC1 241 D2
Minet Ave NW10 89 C5
Minet Ctry Pk UB2, UB3, UB4 106 C4
Minet Dr UB3 106 A5
Minet Gdns
Dagenham NW10 89 C5
Hayes UB3 106 B5
Minet Ho 20 E1 96 A1
Minet Jun & Inf Schs UB3 106 B5
Minet Rd SE5, SW9 138 D3
Minetta Ct 19 EN5 13 D6
Minford Gdns W14 112 D4
Mingard Wlk N7 72 B5
Ming St E14 119 C6
Minimax Cl TW14 150 A5
Ministry Way SE9 166 B2
Mink Ct TW4 128 C3
Minnie Bennett Ho SE3 143 C5
Minniedale KT5 198 B4
Minnow Wlk SE17 263 B3
Minories EC3 117 D6 253 C6
Minshaw Ct DA14 189 D6
Minshull Pl 23 BR3 185 C3
Minshull St SW8 269 C1
Minson Rd E9 96 D6
Minstead Gdns SW15 155 D4
Minstead Way KT3 199 C3
Minster Ave SM1 217 C6
Minster Ct EC3 253 B6
Minster Dr CR0 221 C4
Minster Gdns KT8 195 B5
Minsterley Ave TW16, TW17 193 C5
Minster Rd
Bromley BR1 187 B3
Brondesbury NW2 69 A3
Minster Wlk N8 50 A5
Minstrel Ct HA3 24 C1
Minstrel Gdns KT5 198 B5
Mint Bsns Pk 12 E16 99 A2
Mint Cl UB10 82 D4
Mintern Cl N13 16 D1
Minterne Ave UB2 107 C2
Minterne Rd HA3 44 B4
Minterne Waye UB4 84 C1
Mintern St N1 95 B5 235 D4
Minton Ho SE11 261 A4
Minton Mews 3 NW6 69 D2
Mint Rd SM5, SM6 219 B4
Mint St SE1 252 B2
Mint Wlk CR0 221 A5
Mirabel Rd SW6 135 B5 264 D4
Mirage Ctr The HA9 66 D4
Miranda Cl 19 E1 96 C2
Miranda Ct W3 88 B1
Miranda Ho
6 Belvedere DA17 125 C1
17 Hoxton N1 95 C5
Miranda Rd N19 49 C1
Mirfield Ct SE20 184 A1
Mirfield St SE7 121 D3
Miriam Ct DA14 190 B6
Miriam Rd SE18 123 C1
Mirravale Ct 11 IG9 21 C2
Mirravale Trad Est RM8 59 A2
Mirren Cl HA2 63 B5
Mirror Path SE12 165 C1
Misbourne Rd UB10 82 C6
Missenden Cl TW14 149 D3
Missenden Gdns SM4 202 A3
Missenden Ho NW8 237 A6
Missenden SE17 262 D1
Mission Gr E17 53 A4
Mission Grove Prim Sch E17 53 B5
Mission Pl SE15 140 A4
Mission Sq 13 TW8 132 A6
Mission The
13 Bermondsey SE16 118 B4
14 Poplar E14 97 B1
Missouri Ct HA5 40 C3
Misterton Ct SW11 266 D2
Mistletoe Cl CR0 206 D1
Mistley Thorn IG1 56 C2
Mistral Ct E4 19 D1
Mistral SE5 139 C4
Mistys Field KT12 194 C1
Mitali Pas 21 E1 96 A1
MITCHAM 202 D5
Mitcham Garden Village CR4 203 A4
Mitcham Ho 9 SE5 139 A4
Mitcham Ind Est CR4 181 A2
Mitcham Junction Sta CR4 203 A4
Mitcham La SW16 181 C5
Mitcham Pk CR4 202 C5
Mitcham Rd
Ilford IG3 57 D2
Newham E6 100 A4
Upper Tooting SW17 180 D5
Mitcham Sta CR4 202 C5
Mitchell Brook Prim Sch NW10 67 C2
Mitchellbrook Way NW10 67 B2
Mitchell Cl
Abbey Wood SE2 124 C2
Belvedere DA17 125 D3
Mitchell Ct SW14 133 C1
Mitchell Ho
Gunnersbury W4 110 D1
6 Islington N1 72 C1
31 Shepherd's Bush W12 112 B6
Mitchell 18 NW9 27 D2
Mitchell Rd
Edmonton N13 33 A5
Orpington BR6 227 D4
Mitchell's Pl SE21 161 C4
Mitchell St EC1 95 A3 242 B6
Mitchell Way
1 Bromley BR1 187 A2
Tokyngton NW10 67 A2
Mitchell Wlk E6 100 B2
Mitchison Rd N1 73 B2
Mitchley Rd N17 52 A6
Mitford Cl KT9 213 C2
Mitford Rd N19 72 A6
Mitre Bridge Ind Pk W10 90 B3
Mitre Cl
Shepperton TW17 193 B3
Sutton SM2 218 B1
Mitre Ct
Belvedere DA17 125 C1
1 Ilford RM6 58 B2
9 Woodford E18 37 A2
Mitre Ho RM7 59 D5
Mitre Rd
Lambeth SE1 116 C4 251 B2
Newham E15 98 C5
Mitre Sq EC3 243 B1
Mitre St EC3 95 C1 243 B1
Mitre The 9 E14 119 B6
Mitre Way W10 90 B2
Mizzen Ct E14 119 C4
Moatbridge Sch SE9 165 D5
Moat Cl BR6 227 D2
Moat Cres N3 47 D6
Moat Croft DA16 146 C2
Moat Ct Eltham SE9 166 B5
Sidcup DA15 167 D1
Moat Dr Harrow HA1 42 B5
5 Newham E13 99 C5
Ruislip HA4 39 C2
Moat Farm Rd UB5 63 B1
Moatfield NW6 69 A1
Moat Lodge The HA1 64 C6
Moat Pl Acton W3 88 D1
Stockwell SW9 138 B2
Moat Sch The SW6 135 A3
Moat Side Enfield EN3 6 D1
Feltham TW13 172 C6
Moat The KT3 177 C2
Moberly Rd SW4 159 D4
Mobey Ct SW4 270 A1
Moby Dick RM6 59 B5
Mocatta Ho 9 E1 96 B3
Modbury Gdns NW5 71 A2
Modder Pl SW15 134 D1
Model Cotts SW14 133 A2
Model Farm Cl SE9 166 A1
Modling Ho 8 E2 96 D5
Modoc Ho EN3 18 D6
Moelwyn Hughes Ct N7 71 D3
Moelyn Mews HA1 43 A4
Moffat Ct
Upper Tooting SW17 180 C6
Wimbledon SW19 179 C5
Moffat Ho 24 SE5 139 A5
Moffat Rd
Bowes Pk N13 32 A4
South Norwood CR7 183 B1
Upper Tooting SW17 180 D6
Mogden La TW7 152 D6
Mohammedi Pk Complex UB5 85 C6
Mohawk Ho 33 E3 97 A5
Mohmmad Khan Rd E11 54 D1
Mohr Ct N22 32 B3
Moidart Ct HA8 10 D2
Moineau 18 NW9 27 D2
Moira Cl N17 33 C1
Moira Ct SW17 159 A2
Moira Ho 18 SW9 138 C4
Moira Rd SE9 144 B1
Molasses Ho 1 SW11 136 A2
Molasses Row 2 SW11 136 A2
Mole Abbey Gdns KT8 195 D6
Mole Ct
2 Bedford Pk W12 111 C4
West Ewell KT19 215 A4
Mole Ho NW8 236 D5
Molember Ct KT7 196 C5
Molember Rd KT8 196 C4
Molescroft SE9 167 A1
Molesey Ave KT12, KT8 195 B4
Molesey Bsns Ctr KT8 195 B4
Molesey Dr SM3 217 A5
Molesey Ho E2 243 C6
Molesey Hospl KT8 195 C4
Molesey Park Ave KT8 195 D4
Molesey Park Cl KT8 196 A4
Molesey Park Rd KT8 196 A4
Molesey Rd KT12 195 A2
Molesford Rd SW6 265 A1
Molesham Cl KT8 195 D6
Molesham Way KT8 195 D6
Molesworth Ho 9 SE17 138 D6
Molesworth St SE13 142 A2
Moliner Ct 4 BR3 185 C3
Mollie Davis Ct SE19 183 D4

Mollison Ave EN3 7 B5
Mollison Dr SM6 220 A1
Mollison Sq SM6 219 D1
Mollison Way HA8 26 C1
Molly Huggins Cl SW12 159 C4
Molton Ho N1 233 D5
Molvic Ct BR3 185 B1
Molyneux Dr SW17 181 B6
Molyneux Ho W1 237 B2
Molyneux St W1 92 C2 237 B3
Monarch Cl
- Coney Hall BR4 224 D4
- East Bedfont TW14 149 C4

Monarch Ct
- Ealing W5 87 C2
- Hampstead Garden Suburb N2 48 A4

Monarch Dr E16 99 D2
Monarch Mews
- Walthamstow E17 53 D3
- West Norwood SW16 182 C5

Monarch Par CR4 180 D1
Monarch Pl
- Buckhurst Hill IG9 21 C2
- Sutton SM1 218 B3

Monarch Rd DA17 125 C3
Monarchs Ct
- 1 Edgware NW7 27 B5
- Harrow HA2 41 C2

Monarch's Way HA4 39 C1
Monarch Way IG2 57 B3
Mona Rd SE15 140 C3
Mona St E16 98 D2
Monastery Gdns EN2 5 B3
Monaveen Gdns KT8 195 D6
Monck's Row SW18 157 B5
Monck St SW1 115 D3 259 D5
Monckton Ct W14 254 C6
Monclar Rd SE5 139 B1
Moncorvo Cl SW7 114 C4 247 A1
Moncrieff Cl 4 E6 100 A1
Moncrieff St SE15 140 A3
Mondial Way UB7 127 A5
Mondragon Ho SW8 270 B2
Monega Prim Sch E12 77 D2
Monega Rd E7, E12 77 D2
Monet Ct 15 SE16 118 B1
Moneyer Ho N1 235 C2
Monica Ct SW16 181 D4
Monica James Ho 12 DA14 168 A1
Monica Shaw Ct NW1 232 D3
Monier Rd E3 75 C1
Monivea Rd BR3 185 B3
Monkbretton Ho E2 96 A4
Monk Ct W12 112 A5
Monk Dr E16 121 A6
MONKEN HADLEY 1 A3
Monken Hadley CE Prim Sch EN4 1 C4
Monkfrith Ave N14 15 B5
Monkfrith Cl N14 15 B4
Monkfrith Prim Sch N14 15 A4
Monkfrith Way N14 15 B4
Monkham's Ave IG8 37 B5
Monkham's Dr IG8 37 B5
Monkham's La IG8 37 B6
Monkleigh Rd SM4, SW20 201 A5
Monkridge 3 N8 49 D2
Monks Ave
- East Molesey KT8 195 B4
- New Barnet EN5 14 A5

Monks Cl
- Abbey Wood SE2 124 D2
- Enfield EN2 5 A3
- Harrow HA2 63 D6
- Ruislip HA4 62 D4

Monks Cres KT12 194 B1
Monksdene Gdns SM1 217 D5
Monks Dr W3 88 C1
Monksfield N4 72 C6
MONKS ORCHARD 207 A3
Monks Orchard Rd BR3, CR0 207 C2
Monks Orchard Sch CR0 206 D4
Monks Park Gdns HA9 66 D1
Monks Pk HA9 67 A2
Monks Rd EN2 5 A3
Monk St SE18 122 C2
Monks Way
- Beckenham BR3 207 C3
- Crofton BR5 211 B1
- Harmondsworth UB7 126 A6

Monks Way *continued*
- Temple Fortune NW11 47 B5

Monkswell Ct N10 31 A2
Monkswell Ho E2 96 A4
Monkswood Gdns
- Borehamwood WD6 11 B6
- Ilford IG5 56 C6

Monk Terr SE23 163 B2
Monkton Ho
- 32 Bermondsey SE16 118 D4
- 22 Hackney E5 74 B3

Monkton Rd DA16 145 D3
Monkton St SE11 116 C2 261 B4
Monkville Ave NW11 47 B5
Monkville Par 1 NW11 47 B5
Monkwell Sq EC2 242 B3
Monmouth Ave
- Teddington KT1 175 C3
- Wanstead E18 55 B6

Monmouth Cl
- Bedford Pk W4 111 B3
- Bexley DA16 146 A1
- Mitcham CR4, SW16 204 A5

Monmouth Ct 9 W7 86 D2
Monmouth Gr TW8 110 A2
Monmouth Ho
- 5 Camden Town NW5 71 B2
- Wandsworth SW18 157 C5

Monmouth Pl W2 91 D1
Monmouth Rd
- Dagenham RM9 81 B3
- Hayes UB3 105 D2
- Lower Edmonton N9 18 C2
- Newham E6 100 B4
- Notting Hill W2 91 C1

Monmouth St WC2 94 A1 240 A1
Monnery Rd N19 71 C5
Monnow Rd SE1 118 A2
Mono La TW13 150 B2
Monoux Almshouses E17 53 D5
Monoux Gr E17 35 C2
Monroe Cres EN1 6 B4
Monroe Dr SW14 154 D6
Monroe Ho
- 16 Crouch End N19 49 D2
- Lisson Gr NW8 230 B1

Monro Gdns HA3 24 C3
Monro Ho
- 16 Hampstead NW3 70 A4
- Putney SW15 156 B6

Monro Way E5 74 A4
Monsal Ct E5 75 A4
Monsell Ct 4 N4 72 D5
Monsell Rd N4, N5 72 D5
Monson Prim Sch SE14 140 D5
Monson Rd
- Deptford SE14 140 D5
- Willesden Green NW10 90 B5

Mons Way BR2 210 A3
Montacute Rd
- Bushey WD23 8 C4
- Carshalton SM4 202 B3
- Forest Hill SE6 163 B4

Montagu Cres N18 34 B6
Montagu Ct W1 237 D3
Montague Ave
- Brockley SE4 141 C1
- Ealing W7 108 D5

Montague Cl
- Borough The SE1 252 C4
- Walton-on-T KT12 194 A2

Montague Ct 18 DA14 168 A1
Montague Fell HA0 64 D4
Montague Gdns W3 110 C6
Montague Pl WC1 93 D2 239 D4
Montague Rd
- Ealing W13 87 B1
- Hanwell W7 108 D4
- Hornsey Vale N8 50 B4
- Hounslow TW3 129 D2
- Leytonstone E11 76 D6
- Merton SW19 179 D3
- Richmond TW10 154 A5
- Shacklewell E8 74 A3
- Southall UB2 107 A2
- Thornton Heath CR0 204 D1
- Tottenham Hale N15 52 A5
- Uxbridge UB8 60 A1

Montague Sq SE15 140 C5
Montague St
- Bloomsbury WC1 94 A2 240 A4
- City of London EC1 242 A3

Montague Terr 1 BR2 209 A5
Montague Waye UB2 107 A3
Montague Works HA0 88 B5
Montagu Gdns
- Edmonton N18 34 B6
- Wallington SM6 219 C4

Montagu Ind Est N18 34 C6
Montagu Mans W1 92 D2 237 D3
Montagu Mews N W1 237 D3
Montagu Mews S W1 237 D2
Montagu Mews W W1 237 D2
Montagu Pl W1 92 D2 237 D3
Montagu Rd
- Hendon NW4 46 A3
- Lower Edmonton N9, N18 18 C1

Montagu Row W1 237 D3
Montagu Sq W1 92 D1 237 D2
Montagu St W1 92 D1 237 D2
Montaigne Cl SW1 259 D3
Montalt Ho IG8 36 D6
Montalt Rd IG8 36 D5
Montana Bldg 4 SE13 141 D4
Montana Gdns
- Penge SE26 185 B5
- 5 Sutton SM1 218 A3

Montana Rd
- Upper Tooting SW17 159 A1
- Wimbledon SW20 178 C2

Montbelle Prim Sch SE9 188 C6
Montbelle Rd SE9 166 D1
Montcalm Cl
- Hayes BR2 209 A3
- Yeading UB4 84 B4

Montcalm Ho E14 119 C3
Montcalm Rd SE7 143 D5
Montclair Ct 21 N12 29 D6
Montclare St E2 95 D3 243 C6
Monteagle Ave IG11 79 A2
Monteagle Ct
- Barking IG11 79 A1
- 27 Hoxton N1 95 C5

Monteagle Prim Sch RM9 102 B6
Monteagle Way
- Nunhead SE15 140 B2
- Shacklewell E5 74 A5

Montefiore Ct 2 N16 51 D1
Montefiore St 2 SW8 137 B3
Montego Cl 10 SW2 138 C1
Montem Prim Sch N7 72 B5
Montem Rd
- Forest Hill SE23 163 B4
- New Malden KT3 199 C5

Montem St N4 50 B1
Montenotte Rd N8 49 C4
Monteray Studios W10 91 A5
Monterey Cl NW7 27 C5
Montesole Ct 7 HA5 22 C1
Montesquieu Terr 3 E16 98 D1
Montford Pl
- Kennington SE11 138 C6
- Kennington SE11 261 A1

Montford Rd TW16 194 A5
Montfort Ho
- 4 Bethnal Green E2 96 C4
- Cubitt Town E14 120 A3

Montfort Pl SW19 156 D3
Montgolfier Wlk UB5 85 A4
Montgomerie Ct 2 BR3 185 C2
Montgomery Ave KT10 212 C6
Montgomery Cl
- Blackfen DA15 167 D5
- Mitcham CR4 204 A5

Montgomery Ct W4 133 A6
Montgomery Gdns SM2 218 B1
Montgomery Ho 5 SW14 133 B2
Montgomery Lo 38 E1 96 C3
Montgomery Rd
- Acton W4 111 A2
- Edgware HA8 26 B4

Montholme Rd SW11 158 D5
Monthope Rd 17 E1 96 A2
Montolieu Gdns SW15 156 B6
Montpelier Ave
- Ealing W5 87 C2
- Sidcup DA5 168 D4

Montpelier Cl UB10 82 C6
Montpelier Ct
- 5 Beckenham BR2 208 D5
- Ealing W5 87 D2

Montpelier Gdns
- Ilford RM6 58 C2
- Newham E6 99 D4

Montpelier Gr NW5 71 C3
Montpelier Mews SW7 257 B6
Montpelier Pl
- Knightsbridge SW7 257 B6
- 21 Stepney E1 96 C1

Montpelier Prim Sch W5 87 D2
Montpelier Rd
- Ealing W5 87 D2
- Finchley N3 30 A2
- Peckham SE15 140 B4
- Sutton SM1 218 A4

Montpelier Rise
- Golders Green NW11 47 A2
- Wembley HA9 43 D1

Montpelier Row
- Blackheath Vale SE3 142 D3
- Twickenham TW1 153 C4

Montpelier Sq SW7 114 C4 247 B1
Montpelier St SW7 114 C3 257 B6
Montpelier Terr SW7 247 B1
Montpelier Vale SE3 142 D3
Montpelier Way NW11 47 A2
Montpelier Wlk SW7 114 C3 257 B6
Montpellier Ct KT12 194 B3
Montrave Rd SE20 184 C3
Montreal Ho
- Catford SE6 163 D3
- Hayes UB4 84 B4

Montreal Pl WC2 250 C6
Montreal Rd IG1 57 A2
Montrell Rd SW2 160 A3
Montrose Ave
- Falconwood DA16 145 C2
- Hendon HA8 27 B2
- Kensal Rise NW6 91 A5
- Sidcup DA15 168 A4
- Twickenham TW2 151 D4

Montrose Cl
- Ashford TW15 171 A5
- Falconwood DA16 145 D2
- Woodford IG8 37 A6

Montrose Cres
- Finchley N12 30 A4
- 1 Wembley HA0 66 A2

Montrose Ct
- 2 Catford SE6 164 D2
- Hendon NW9 27 A1
- Knightsbridge SW7 114 B4 246 D1
- Temple Fortune NW11 47 B5

Montrose Gdns
- Mitcham CR4 180 D1
- Sutton SM1 217 D6

Montrose Ho
- Belgravia SW1 248 B1
- Millwall E14 119 C3
- Twickenham TW2 151 D4

Montrose Pl SW1 115 A4 248 B1
Montrose Rd
- East Bedfont TW14 149 B5
- Harrow HA3 24 D1

Montrose Villas 5 W6 112 A1
Montrose Way SE23 162 D3
Montserrat Ave IG8 36 B3
Montserrat Cl SE19 183 B5
Montserrat Rd SW15 135 A1
Montway Hts SW19 179 D3
Monument Gdns SE13 164 A6
Monument Sta EC3 117 B6 252 D6
Monument St EC3 117 B6 252 D6
Monument The* EC3 252 D6
Monument Way N17 51 D6
Monza Bldg The E1 118 C6
Monza St E1 118 C6
Moodkee St SE16 118 C3
Moody Rd SE15 139 D4
Moody St E1 96 D4
Moon Ct SE12 143 A1
Moon Ho HA1 42 D5
Moon La EN5 1 B2
Moon St N1 94 D6 234 C6
Moorcroft Ct 4 N3 29 B1
Moorcroft HA8 26 D2
Moorcroft Gdns BR1 210 A4
Moorcroft La UB8 82 C2
Moorcroft Rd SW16 160 A1
Moorcroft Sch UB8 82 B1
Moorcroft Way HA5 41 A4
Moordown SE18 144 D4
Moore Cl
- Mitcham CR4 181 B1
- Mortlake SW14 133 A2
- Wallington SM6 220 A1

Moore Cres RM9 102 B6
Moore Ct N1 234 C5
Moorefield Rd N17 33 D1
Moore Ho
- 16 Bethnal Green E2 96 C4
- 5 Greenwich SE10 120 D1
- Hornsey N8 50 A5
- 7 Shadwell E1 118 C6
- Wandsworth SW17 158 B1
- 1 West Norwood SE27 183 A6

Mooreland Rd BR1 187 A2
Moore Park Ct SW6 265 D4
Moore Park Rd SW6 135 D5 265 C3
Moore Rd SE19 183 A4
Moore St SW3 114 D2 257 C4
Moore Wlk E7 77 A4
Moorey Cl 2 E15 98 D6
Moorfield Ave W5 87 D3
Moorfield Rd
- Chessington KT9 214 A3
- Enfield EN3 6 C4

Moorfields Ct 6 SW16 181 C6
Moorfields EC2 95 B2 242 C3
Moorfields Eye Hospl EC1 95 B4 235 C1
Moorfields Highwalk EC2 242 C3
Moorgate EC2 95 B2 242 C3
Moorgate Pl EC2 242 C2
Moorgate Sta EC2 95 B2 242 C3
Moorgreen Ho EC1 234 C2
Moorhead Way SE3 143 B2
Moorhouse 17 NW9 27 D2
Moorhouse Rd
- Harrow HA3 43 D6
- Notting Hill W2 91 C1

Moorings Ho 3 TW8 131 C5
Moorings The 5 E16 99 C2
Moor La
- Broadgate EC2 95 B2 242 C3
- Chessington KT9 214 A3

Moorland Cl TW4 151 C4
Moorland Ct N21 16 B5
Moorland Rd SW9 138 D1
Moorlands Ave NW7 28 B4
Moorlands
- Chislehurst BR7 188 D3
- Northolt UB5 85 A6
- 17 Wallington SM6 219 B2

Moor Lane Jun Sch KT9 214 B3
Moormead Dr KT19 215 C3
Moor Mead Rd TW1 153 A5
Moor Park Gdns KT2 177 C3
Moor Park Ho N21 16 D4
Moor Pl EC2 242 C3
Moorside Ct W13 109 C5
Moorside Rd BR1 186 D6
Moor St W1 239 D1
Moortown Rd WD19 22 C6
Moot Ct NW9 44 C4
Morant Ho SW9 138 B3
Morant Pl N22 32 B2
Morant St E14 119 C6
Mora Prim Sch NW2 68 C4
Mora Rd NW2 68 C4
Mora St EC1 95 A4 235 B1
Morat St SW9 138 B4 270 D2
Moravian Cl SW3 266 D5
Moravian Pl SW10 136 B6 266 D5
Moravian St 10 E2 96 C4
Moray Ave UB3 105 D5
Moray Cl HA8 10 D2
Moray Ho
- 11 Kingston u T KT6 198 A4
- 9 Mile End E1 97 A3

Moray Mews N4, N7 72 B6
Moray Rd N4, N7 72 B6
Mordaunt Gdns RM9 81 A1
Mordaunt Ho
- 4 Becontree NW10 89 B6
- 34 Clapham SW8 137 D3

Mordaunt Rd NW10 89 B6
Mordaunt St SW9 138 B2
MORDEN 201 D3
Morden Court Par SM4 201 D5
Morden Ct SM4 201 D5
Morden Gdns
- Greenford UB6 64 D3
- Mitcham CR4 202 B5

Morden Hall SW19 201 D6
Morden Hall Rd SM4 202 A5
Morden Hill SE13 142 A3
Morden Ho
- Morden SM4 201 C5
- 19 Tulse Hill SW2 160 C5

Morden La SE13 142 A4
Morden Lo BR2 186 B1
Morden Mount Prim Sch SE13 141 D3
MORDEN PARK 201 A3
Morden Park Sch Sports Ctr SM4 201 B4
Morden Prim Sch SM4 201 C4
Morden Rd
- Dagenham RM6 59 A2
- Kidbrooke SE3 143 A3
- Merton SW19 179 D1
- Mitcham CR4, SM4 202 B5

Morden Road Mews SE3 143 A3
Morden Road Sta SW19 179 D1
Morden South Sta SM4 201 C4
Morden Sta SW19 201 D6
Morden St SE13 141 D4
Morden Way SM3 201 C2
Morden Wharf Rd SE10 120 C3
Mordern Ho NW1 237 B5
Mordon Rd IG3 57 D2
Mordred Rd SE6 164 C2
Morecambe Cl 3 E1 96 D2
Morecambe Gdns HA7 25 D6
Morecambe St SE17 117 A1 262 B2
Morecambe Terr N18 33 B6
More Cl
- Canning Town E16 98 D1
- West Kensington W14 113 A2 254 A3

Morecoombe Cl KT2 176 D3
Morecroft TW2 152 A2
Moredown Ho 3 E8 74 A3
Moree Way N18 34 A6
More House Sch SW1 114 D3 257 D5
Moreland Ct 3 NW2 69 C5
Moreland Prim Sch EC1 94 D4 234 D1
Moreland St EC1 94 D4 234 D2
Moreland Way E4 20 A1
Morella Rd SW11, SW12 158 D4
Morell Ho 5 SW9 138 B3
Morello Ave UB8 82 D2
Morello Ct HA9 66 B5
Moremead Rd SE6 185 C6
Morena St SE6 163 D4
Moresby Ave KT5 198 D2
Moresby Rd E5 52 B1
Moresby Wlk 6 SW8 137 B3
More's Gdn SW3 266 D5
Moreton Ave TW7 130 C4
Moreton Cl
- Mill Hill NW7 28 C4
- Tottenham N15 51 B3
- Upper Clapton E5 52 C1

Moreton Ho
- Bermondsey SE16 118 B3
- Upper Tooting SW17 180 B6

Moreton Pl
SW1........115 C1 259 B2
Moreton Rd
Croydon CR2........221 B3
North Cheam KT4....216 B6
Tottenham N15.......51 B3
Moreton St
SW1........115 D1 259 C2
Moreton Terr Mews N
SW1..............259 B2
Moreton Terr Mews S
SW1..............259 B2
Moreton Terr
SW1........115 C1 259 B2
Moreton Twr 3
W3...............110 D5
Morford Cl HA4.......40 B2
Morford Way HA4.....40 B2
Morgan Ave E17......54 B5
Morgan Cl RM10......81 C1
Morgan Ct
Ashford TW15......170 D5
5 Battersea SW11...136 B3
Carshalton SM5.....218 D4
Morgan Ho
Nine Elms SW8.....269 B2
Pimlico SW1.......259 B3
Morgan Rd
Islington N7.........72 C3
Notting Hill W10.....91 B2
Plaistow BR1.......187 A3
Morgan's La UB3.....83 B2
Morgan St
Canning Town E16.....98 D2
Globe Town E3........96 D4
Morgan's Wlk SW11. 267 A3
Morgan Terr RM6......58 C4
Moriah Jewish Day Sch
The HA5..........41 A1
Moriatry Cl N7........72 A4
Morie St SW18.......157 D6
Morieux Rd E10.......53 B1
Moring Rd SW17.....181 A6
Morkyns Wlk SE21...161 C1
Morland Ave CR0....205 C1
Morland Cl
Golders Green
NW11.............47 D1
Hampton TW12......173 B5
Mitcham CR4.......202 C6
Morland Ct W12.....112 B4
Morland Est E8.......74 A1
Morland Gdns
Southall UB1.......107 D5
Stonebridge NW10....67 B1
Morland Ho
Kilburn NW6.........91 C6
Notting Hill W11......91 A1
Somers Town NW1...232 B3
Westminster SW1...260 A4
Morland Mews N1....72 C1
Morland Rd
Croydon CR0.......205 D2
Dagenham RM10......81 C1
Harrow HA3..........44 A5
Ilford IG1...........78 D6
Penge SE20........184 D4
Sutton SM1........218 A3
Walthamstow E17.....52 D4
Morley Ave
Chingford E4.........36 B3
Edmonton N18........34 A6
Tottenham N22.......32 D1
Morley Cl BR6.......226 D6
Morley Coll
SE1........116 C3 261 B6
Morley Cres HA8......11 A2
Morley Cres E HA7.....43 D6
Morley Cres HA4......62 C6
Morley Cres W HA7...43 C6
Morley Ct
Bromley BR3........186 B2
Chingford Hatch E4....35 B5
Lewisham SE13......142 A1
Shortlands BR2.....208 D5
Morley Hill EN2........5 B5
Morley Ho
Stoke Newington
N16.............74 A6
Streatham SW2.....160 A4
W1..............238 D2
Morley Rd
Barking IG11........101 B6
Cheam SM3.........201 B1
Chislehurst BR7.....189 A2
Dagenham RM6......59 A4
Lewisham SE13.....142 A1
Leytonstone E10......54 A1
Newham E15.........98 D5
Twickenham TW1....153 D5
Morley St
SE1.........116 C4 251 B1
Morna Rd SE5.......139 A3
Morning La E9........74 C2
Morningside Prim Sch
E9..................74 C2
Morningside Rd
KT4...............216 C6
Mornington Ave
Bromley BR1.......209 D6
Ilford IG1...........56 C2
Mornington Avenue
Mans W14........254 C3
Mornington Ave
W14........113 B2 254 C3
Mornington Cl IG8....37 A6
Mornington Cres
NW1........93 C5 232 A4
Mornington Crescent
Sta NW1.....93 C5 232 A4
Mornington Cres
TW5..............128 B4
Mornington Ct NW1. 232 A4
Mornington Gr E3....97 C4
Mornington Lo EN1....17 C6
Mornington Mews 2
SE5...............139 A4
Mornington Pl
4 New Cross
SE8..............141 B5
Regent's Pk NW1....232 A4
Mornington Rd
Ashford TW15......171 A5
Chingford E4.........20 B4
Greenford UB6.......85 D3
Leytonstone E11......54 D1
New Cross SE14,
SE8..............141 B5
Woodford IG8........36 D6
Mornington St
NW1........93 B5 231 D4
Mornington Terr
NW1........93 B5 231 D4
Mornington Wlk
TW10.............175 C6
Morocco St
SE1........117 C4 253 A1
Morpeth Gr E9.......96 D6
Morpeth Rd E9.......96 D6
Morpeth Sec Sch E2..96 C4
Morpeth St E2........96 D4
Morpeth Terr
SW1........115 C2 259 A4
Morpeth Wlk N17.....34 B3
Morrab Gdns IG3.....79 D5
Morrel Cl EN5..........2 A2
Morrel Ct 11 E2.......96 A5
Morris Ave E12.......78 B3
Morris Blitz Ct 2
N16................73 D4
Morris Cl
Croydon CR0.......207 A4
Orpington BR6......227 C5
Morris Ct
Chingford E4.........19 D1
Croydon CR0.......220 D4
3 Herne Hill SE5....139 B1
Morris Gdns SW18...157 C4
Morris Ho
17 Bethnal Green
E2................96 C4
Lisson Gr NW8.....237 A5
1 Stockwell SW4....138 A1
10 Tufnell Pk N19....71 C4
Morrish Rd SW2.....160 A4
Morrison Ave
Chingford E4.........35 C4
Tottenham N17.......51 C6
Morrison Bldgs 5
E1.................96 A1
Morrison Ct
7 Barnet EN5.........1 A1
Finchley N12.........30 C3
Morrison Ho SW2....160 C3
Morrison Rd
Barking IG11.......103 A5
24 Brixton SW9.....138 C3
Hayes UB4...........84 B4
Morrison St SW11...137 A2
Morrison Yd N17......33 D1
Morris Pl N4.........72 C6
Morris Rd
Bow Comm E14.......97 D2
Dagenham RM8.......81 B6
Isleworth TW7.......130 D2
Leyton E15...........76 C4
Morriss Ho
9 Bermondsey
SE16..............118 B4
5 Upper Clapton E5...74 B6
Morris St E1..........96 B1
Morris Stephany Ho 4
SE27..............182 D6
Morriston Cl WD19....22 C5
Morritt Ho 2 HA0....65 D3
Morse Cl E13.........99 A4
Morshead Mans W9...91 C4
Morshead Rd W9.....91 C4
Morson Rd EN3.......19 A5
Morston Gdns SE9...188 B6
Mortain Ho 9 SE16..118 B2
Morten Cl SW4......159 D5
Morteyne Rd N17.....33 B2
Mortgramit Sq
SE18..............122 C3
Mortham St E15......98 C6
Mortimer Cl
1 Child's Hill NW2....69 B5
Streatham SW16....159 D2
Mortimer Cres
Paddington NW6......91 D6
Worcester Pk KT4....215 B5
Mortimer Ct
St John's Wood
NW8.............229 B3
4 Whetstone N20.....14 A2
Mortimer Dr EN1......17 C6
Mortimer Est NW6....91 D6
Mortimer Ho
6 Shepherd's Bush
W11.............112 D5
West Kensington
W14.............254 B3
Mortimer Lo 11
SW19.............157 A3
Mortimer Market
WC1..............239 B5
Mortimer Pl NW6.....91 D6
Mortimer Rd
De Beauvoir Town
N1................73 C1
Ealing W13...........87 C1
Kensal Green NW10...90 C4
Mitcham CR4.......180 D2
Newham E6.........100 B4
Mortimer Sq W11....112 D6
Mortimer St
W1..........93 C2 239 B3
Mortimer Terr NW5...71 B4
MORTLAKE.........133 A2
Mortlake Cl CR0.....220 A5
Mortlake Dr CR4....180 C2
Mortlake High St
SW14..............133 B2
Mortlake Ho 7 W4..111 A2
Mortlake Rd
Ilford IG1...........79 B4
Newham E16.........99 B1
Richmond SW14,
TW9.............132 C4
Mortlake Sta SW14. 133 A2
Mortlake Terr TW9...132 C5
Mortlock Cl SE15....140 B4
Mortlock Ct E12......77 D4
Morton Cl
Hillingdon UB8........82 B3
Stepney E1...........96 C1
Wallington SM6......220 B1
Morton Cres N14......31 D6
Morton Ct UB5........64 A3
Morton Gdns SM6....219 C3
Morton Ho
Kennington SE17....138 D6
West Norwood SE27..183 B5
Morton Mews SW5...255 C3
Morton Pl SE1......261 A5
Morton Rd
Islington N1..........73 A1
Morden SM4........202 B4
Stratford E15.........76 D1
Morton Way N14......31 D6
Morvale Cl DA17.....125 B2
Morval Rd SW2......160 C6
Morven Rd SW17.....158 D1
Morville Ho SW18....158 B5
Morville St E3........97 C5
Morwell St WC1.....239 D3
Moscow Pl W2......245 C6
Moscow Rd
W2.........113 D6 245 C6
Mosedale NW1.....231 D1
Moseley Row SE10...120 D2
Moselle Ave N22......32 C1
Moselle Cl N8........50 B6
Moselle Ct N9........18 C1
Moselle Ho 2 N17.....33 D3
Moselle Pl N17.......33 D3
Moselle Sch (main site)
N17................33 C1
Moselle Sch (Upper)
N17................51 A6
Moselle St N17.......33 D3
Mosque Tower 26 E1..96 A2
Mossborough Cl N12..29 D4
Mossbourne Com Acad
E8..................74 A3
Mossbury Rd SW11..136 C2
Moss Cl Pinner HA5....23 A1
Spitalfields E1.......96 A2
Mossdown Cl DA17..125 C2
Mossford Ct IG6......56 D6
Mossford Gn IG6......57 A6
Mossford St E3.......97 B3
Moss Gdns
Feltham TW13......150 A2
South Croydon CR2..222 D1
Moss Hall Cres N12...30 A4
Moss Hall Ct N12.....29 D4
Moss Hall Gr N12.....29 D4
Moss Hall Inf Sch
N12................29 D4
Moss Hall Jun Sch
N3..................29 D4
Mossington Gdns
SE16..............118 C2
Moss La HA5.........23 A1
Mosslea Rd
Bromley Comm
BR2.............209 D4
Orpington BR6......227 A5
Penge SE20........184 C4
Mossop St
SW3.........114 C2 257 B4
Moss Rd RM10........81 C1
Mossville Gdns SM4..201 B5
Moswell Ho 4 N10....31 A3
Moston Cl UB3.......105 D1
Mostyn Ave HA9......66 B3
Mostyn Gdns NW10...90 D5
Mostyn Gr E3.........97 C5
Mostyn Lo N5........73 A4
Mostyn Rd
Brixton SW9.......138 C4
Bushey WD23.........8 A6
Grahame Pk HA8......27 C3
Merton SW19.......179 B1
Mosul Way BR2......210 A3
Motcomb St
SW1.........115 A3 258 A6
Moth Cl SM6........220 A1
Mothers Sq The 13
E5..................74 B4
Motley Ave EC2.....243 A6
Motley St SW8......137 C3
MOTSPUR PARK....200 A3
Motspur Park Sta
KT3...............200 B4
Motspur Pk KT3.....200 A3
MOTTINGHAM......165 D2
Mottingham Ct SE9...166 B3
Mottingham Gdns
SE9...............165 D3
Mottingham La SE9..165 C3
Mottingham Prim Sch
SE9...............166 B1
Mottingham Rd
Chislehurst SE9......166 B1
Ponders End N9.......18 D4
Mottingham Sta
SE9...............166 B3
Mottisfont Rd SE2...124 B2
Moules Ct SE5.......139 A5
Moulins Rd E9........74 C1
Moulsford Ho
5 Lower Holloway
N7...............72 A3
32 Paddington W2.....91 C2
Moulton Ave TW3,
TW5..............129 B3
Moundfield Rd N16....52 A3
Mound The SE9......166 C1
Mounsey Ho 13 W10..91 A4
Mountacre Cl SE26...183 D6
Mount Adon Pk SE21,
SE22..............162 A4
Mountague Pl 2
E14...............120 A6
Mountain Ho SE11..260 C2
Mountaire Ct NW9....45 B4
Mount Angelus Rd
SW15..............155 D4
Mount Ararat Rd
TW10..............154 A6
Mount Arlington 3
BR2...............186 C1
Mount Ash Rd SE26..162 B1
Mount Ave
Chingford E4.........19 D1
Ealing W5...........87 D2
Southall UB1.........85 C1
Mountbatten Cl
Plumstead Comm
SE18.............145 C6
6 West Norwood
SE19.............183 C5
Mountbatten Ct 8
IG9................21 D2
Mountbatten Gdns
BR3...............207 A5
Mountbatten Ho N6...49 A2
Mountbatten Mews
SW18..............158 A3
Mountbel Rd HA7.....25 A1
Mount Carmel 3 N7..72 B3
Mount Carmel RC Tech
Coll for Girls N19...49 D1
Mount Cl
Bromley BR1.......188 A2
Cockfosters EN4.......3 A1
Ealing W5...........87 C2
Mountcombe Cl
KT6...............198 A2
Mountcombe Ho
SW17..............180 B5
Mount Ct
6 Kingston u T
KT2.............176 D3
West Wickham BR4..224 C6
Mount Culver Ave
DA14..............190 D4
Mount Dr
Bexley DA6........169 A6
Harrow HA2, HA5.....41 B4
Welsh Harp HA9......67 A6
Mountearl Gdns SW16,
SW2...............160 B1
Mount Eaton Ct W5....87 C2
Mount Echo Ave E4...19 D3
Mount Echo Dr E4....19 D3
Mount Ephraim La
SW16..............159 D1
Mount Ephraim Rd
SW16..............159 D1
Mount Felix KT12....193 D1
Mountfield Cl SE6...164 B4
Mountfield Ct SE13..164 B5
Mountfield NW2......69 B6
Mountfield Rd
Ealing W5...........88 A1
East Finchley N3.....47 C6
Wallend E6.........100 C4
Mountford Ho EN2.....4 D1
Mount Ford St E1.....96 A1
Mountfort Cres N1....72 C1
Mountfort Terr 1
N1.................72 C1
Mount Gdns SE26....162 B1
Mount Gr HA8.........27 B6
Mountgrove Rd N5....73 A5
Mounthurst Rd BR2..208 D2
Mountier Ct 12 E11...55 A4
Mountington Park Cl
HA3................43 D3
Mountjoy Cl SE2.....124 B4
Mountjoy Ho EC2....242 A3
Mount Lodge SW4...137 D1
Mount Lo N6.........49 C3
Mount Mews TW12...173 D2
Mount Mills EC1....234 D1
Mount Nod Rd SW16,
SW2...............160 B1
Mount Olive Ct W7...108 C4
Mount Par EN4.........2 C1
Mount Park Ave HA1..64 C6
Mount Park Cres W5..87 D1
Mount Park Rd
Ealing W5...........87 D1
Harrow HA1..........64 B5
Pinner HA5..........40 A4
Mount Pk SM5.......219 A1
Mount Pl 7 W3.....110 D5
Mount Pleasant EN4....2 D1
Mount Pleasant Cotts
Osidge N14..........15 D4
Southall UB1.........85 C1
Mount Pleasant Cres
N4................50 B2
Mount Pleasant
WC1.........94 C3 241 A5
Mount Pleasant Hill
E5.................74 C6
Mount Pleasant IG1...79 A3
Mount Pleasant La
E5.................52 B1
Mount Pleasant Pl
SE18..............123 B2
Mount Pleasant Rd
Ealing W5...........87 C3
Higham Hill E17......35 A1
Kingston u T KT3....199 A6
Lewisham SE13.....164 A5
Tottenham N17.......33 C1
Willesden NW10.....90 C6
Mount Pleasant HA4..62 D6
Mount Pleasant Villas
N4................50 B2
Mount Pleasant
Wembley HA0........88 B6
West Norwood SE27.183 A6
Mount Prim Sch The
KT3...............199 A6
Mount Rd
Bexley DA6........169 A6
Chessington KT9.....214 B3
Dagenham RM8.......59 B1
Dollis Hill NW2.......68 C5
East Barnet EN4......14 C6
Feltham TW13......151 A1
Hayes UB3.........106 A4
Hendon NW4..........46 A3
Kingston u T KT3....199 B6
Mitcham CR4.......180 C1
South Norwood
SE19.............183 B4
Wimbledon SW18,
SW19............157 D2
Mount Row
W1.........115 B6 248 C5
Mount Sch NW7.......28 C5
Mountside HA7.......25 A2
Mounts Pond Rd SE3,
SE13..............142 B3
Mount Sq The 3
NW3...............70 A5
Mount Stewart Ave
HA3................43 D2
Mount Stewart Jun &
Inf Schs HA3........43 D2
Mount St
W1.........115 A6 248 B5
Mount Terr E1........96 B2
Mount The
Bexley DA6........169 D6
Cheam SM1.........217 C2
Chislehurst BR7.....188 C2
Finchley N2..........30 C1
Hampstead NW3.......70 A5
Harrow HA1..........64 C6
Kensington W8.....245 A3
Kingston u T KT3....199 D6
North Cheam KT4....216 B4
Northolt UB5.........63 D3
6 South Croydon
CR2.............221 A3
Upper Clapton E5.....74 B6
Welsh Harp HA9......67 A6
Whetstone N20.......14 A2
Mount Tyndal NW3....48 B1
Mount Vernon NW3...70 A4
Mountview Cl NW11..48 A1
Mountview Cotts
EN5................11 D5
Mountview Ct
Harringay N8.........50 D5
3 Whetstone N20.....14 A2
Mount View W5.......87 D3
Mountview NW7.......11 B1
Mount View EN2........4 B5
Mountview HA6.......22 A4
Mount View Rd
Chingford E4.........20 B4
Claygate KT10.......213 B1
Hornsey Vale N4......50 B3
Kingsbury NW9.......45 B4
Mount View UB2.....106 D2
Mountview 5
SW16..............160 B1
Mount Villas SE27....160 D1
Mountwood KT8.....195 D6
Mountwood Ho W5...87 D3
Mourne Ho NW3......70 A2
Movers La IG11......101 C6
Movers Lane (Flyover)
IG11...............101 C5
Mowat Ct KT4.......215 D6
Mowatt Cl N19.......49 D1
Mowbray Ct
South Norwood
SE19.............183 D2
Wood Green N22......32 C2
Mowbray Gdns UB5...85 C6
Mowbray Ho 5 N2....30 B1
Mowbray Rd
Brondesbury NW6.....69 A1
Edgware HA8.........26 C6
New Barnet EN5......14 A6
Richmond TW10......153 C1
South Norwood
SE19.............183 D2
Mowlem Prim Sch
E2..................96 C5
Mowlem St E2.......96 B5
Mowlem Trad Est
N17................34 C3
Mowll St SW9.......138 C5
Moxon Cl E13.........98 D5
Moxon St Barnet EN5....1 B2
Marylebone
W1.........93 A2 238 A3
Moye Cl 10 E2........96 A5
Moyers Rd E10.......54 A2
Moylan Rd
W6.........135 A6 264 B5
Moyle Ho SW1.......269 B6
Moyne Ho 10 SW9...138 D1
Moyne Pl NW10.......88 C5
Moynihan Dr N21.....16 A6
Moys Cl CR0........204 A3
Moyser Rd SW16.....181 B5
Mozart St W10.......91 B4
Mt Carmel RC Prim Sch
W5...............109 C3
Muchelney Rd SM4..202 A3
Mudchute Sta E14..119 D2
Mudie Ho 8 SW2...160 A4
Mudlarks Blvd 3
SE10..............120 D3
Muggeridge Cl CR2..221 B3
Muggeridge Rd
RM10...............81 D4
Muirdown Ave
SW14..............133 B1
Muir Dr SW18.......158 C5
Muirfield Cl
23 Bermondsey
SE16..............118 B1

Muirfield Cl *continued*
South Oxhey WD19 22 C6
Muirfield Cres E14 119 D3
Muirfield Gn WD19 22 C6
Muirfield W3 89 C1
Muirfield Rd WD19 22 C6
Muirhead Quay IG11 101 A5
Muirkirk Rd SE6 164 A3
Muir Rd E5 74 A5
Muir St E16 122 A5
Mulbarton Ct BR7 189 B4
Mulberry Ave TW19 148 A3
Mulberry Bsns Ctr SE16 118 D4
Mulberry Cl Barnet EN4 2 B1
Charlton SE7 143 D6
Chelsea SW3 266 D5
Chingford E4 19 C2
East Dulwich SE22 162 A5
Hampstead NW3 70 B4
Hendon NW4 46 C6
Hornsey N8 50 A4
Northolt UB5 85 A5
Streatham SW16 181 C6
Mulberry Cres
Brentford TW8 131 C5
West Drayton UB7 104 C4
Mulberry Ct
Barking IG11 79 D1
Bexley DA16 145 D3
Finchley N2 48 C6
Finsbury EC1 234 D1
Islington N5 72 D3
1 Leyton E11 76 B4
10 Paddington W9 91 B4
4 Surbiton KT6 197 D2
Twickenham TW1 152 D1
Willesden NW10 67 B2
Mulberry Ho
1 Bethnal Green E2 96 C4
8 Deptford SE8 141 B6
Mulberry House Sch The NW2 69 A3
Mulberry La CR0 205 D1
Mulberry Mews
New Cross SE14 141 B4
2 Wallington SM6 219 C2
Mulberry Par UB7 104 C4
Mulberry Pl
Chiswick W6 112 A1
Greenwich SE9 143 D1
Mulberry Prim Sch N17 34 A1
Mulberry Rd E8 73 D1
Mulberry Sch for Girls
Stepney E1 96 B1
St George in t East E1 118 B6
Mulberry St 7 E1 96 A1
Mulberry Trees TW17 193 B2
Mulberry Way
Ilford IG6 57 A5
Woodford E18 37 B1
Mulberry Wlk SW3 136 B6 266 D6
Mulgrave Chambers SM2 217 D2
Mulgrave Hall SM2 217 D2
Mulgrave Ho 19 SE18 122 B2
Mulgrave Manor SM2 217 D2
Mulgrave Prim Sch SE18 122 C2
Mulgrave Rd
Belmont SM2 217 C2
Ealing W5 87 D3
Harrow HA1 65 A6
South Croydon CR0 221 B5
West Kensington W14 264 C6
Willesden NW10 67 D4
Woolwich SE18 122 C2
Mulholland Cl CR4 181 B1
Mulkern Rd N19 49 D1
Mullard Ho WC1 239 C4
Mullards Cl CR4 202 D1
Mullens Ho 7 SW15 156 C6
Mullen Twr EC1 241 A5
Muller Ho SE18 122 C1
Muller Rd SW4 159 D5
Mullet Gdns 7 E2 96 A4
Mulletsfield WC1 233 B1
Mull Ho 17 E3 97 B5
Mullins Path SW14 133 B2
Mullion Cl HA3 23 D2
Mullion Wlk WD19 22 D6
Mulready St NW8 237 A5
Multi Way W3 111 C4
Multon Ho E9 74 C1
Multon Rd SW18 158 B4
Mulvaney Way SE1 252 D1
Mumford Rd SE24 160 D6
Muncaster Cl TW15 170 C6
Muncaster Rd
Ashford TW15 170 D5
Balham SW11 159 A6
Muncies Mews SE6 164 A2
Mundania Ct SE22 162 B5
Mundania Rd SE22 162 C5
Munday Ho SE1 262 C5
Munday Rd E16 121 A6
Munden Ho 5 E3 97 D4
Munden St W14 113 A2 254 A4
Mundesley Cl WD19 22 C6
Mundford Rd E5 74 C6
Mundon Gdns IG1 57 B1
Mund St W14 113 B1 254 D1
Mundy Ho 6 W10 91 A4
Mundy St N1 95 C4
Mungo-Park Cl WD23 8 A2
Munnery Way BR6 226 D6
Munning Ho 12 E16 121 B5
Munnings Gdns TW7 152 B6
Munro Ho
Bermondsey SE1 252 D1
Lambeth SE1 251 A1
Munro Mews W10 91 A2
Munro Rd WD23 8 A6
Munslow Gdns SM1 218 B4
Munstead Ct 12 SM2 218 A1
Munster Ave TW4 151 A6
Munster Ct
Fulham SW6 135 B3
Teddington TW11 175 C4
Munster Gdns N13 33 A6
Munster Ho N17 33 D2
Munster Rd
Fulham SW6 135 A5 264 B4
Teddington TW11 175 C4
Munster Residences SW6 264 B2
Munster Sq NW1 93 B3 238 D6
Munton Rd SE1, SE17 117 A2 262 B4
Murchison Ave DA5 169 A3
Murchison Ho 1 W10 91 A2
Murchison Rd E10 76 A6
Murdoch Ho 4 SE16 118 C3
Murdock Cl E16 98 D1
Murdock St SE15 140 B6
Murfett Cl SW19 157 A2
Muriel Ct 18 E10 53 D2
Muriel St N1 94 B6 233 D6
Murillo Rd SE13 142 C1
Murley Ct N21 17 A4
Murphy Ho SE1 261 D6
Murphy St SE1 116 C4 251 A1
Murray Ave
Bromley BR1 187 B1
Hounslow TW3 151 D6
Murray Cl SE28 123 C5
Murray Cres HA5 22 D2
Murray Ct
5 Harrow HA1 42 D3
Southall TW7 108 C3
Twickenham TW2 152 A2
Murray Grey Ho UB4 83 B2
Murray Gr N1 95 B5 235 C3
Murray Ho
1 North Finchley N12 30 B5
20 Woolwich SE18 122 B2
Murray Mews NW1 71 D1
Murray Rd
Brentford W5 109 C2
Richmond TW10 153 C2
Wimbledon SW19 178 D4
Murray Sq E16 121 B6
Murray St NW1 71 D1
Murray Terr NW3 70 B4
Musard Rd W6 135 A6 264 B6
Musbury St E1 96 C1
Muscal W6 264 A6
Muscatel Pl SE5 139 C4
Muschamp Prim Sch SM5 218 C6
Muschamp Rd
Camberwell SE15 139 D2
Carshalton SM5 218 C6
Muscott Ho 15 E2 96 A6
Muscovy Ho DA18 125 A4
Muscovy St EC3 253 B6
Museum Ho 7 E2 96 C4
Museum in Docklands* E14 119 C6
Museum Mans WC1 240 A3
Museum of Brands* W11 91 B1
Museum of Domestic Design & Architecture* EN4 15 A6
Museum St WC1 94 A1 240 A2
Musgrave Cl EN4 2 A4
Musgrave Cres SW6 135 C4 265 B2
Musgrave Ct SW11 267 A2
Musgrave Rd TW7 130 D4
Musgrove Ho 1 E9 74 D2
Musgrove Rd SE14 141 A4
Musical Mus The* TW8 132 A6
Musjid Rd 7 SW11 136 B3
Muslim Coll The W5 110 C6
Mus of Childhood (V&A)* E2 96 C4
Mus of Culinary History & Alimentation* NW1 232 B4
Mus of Garden History* SE1 260 C5
Mus of London* EC2 95 A2 242 A3
Mus of Richmond* TW10 153 D6
Mus of the Great Eastern Rly* E16 122 C4
Mus of the Order of St John* EC1 94 D3 241 C5
Musquash Way TW4 128 C3
Muston Rd E5 74 B6
Mustow Pl 2 SW6 135 B3
Muswell Ave N10 31 B1
MUSWELL HILL 49 A6
Muswell Hill Broadway N10 49 B6
Muswell Hill N10 49 C6
Muswell Hill Pl N10 49 B5
Muswell Hill Prim Sch N10 49 B6
Muswell Hill Rd N10 49 A4
Muswell Mews N10 49 B6
Muswell Rd N10 31 B1
Mutrix Rd NW6 91 C6
Mutton Pl NW1 71 A2
Muybridge Rd KT3 177 A1
Myatt Garden Prim Sch SE4 141 B3
Myatt Ho SE5 138 D3
Myatt Rd SW9 138 D4
Myatts Field Ct SE5 139 A4
Mycenae Rd SE3 143 A6
Mychell Ho 8 SW19 180 A3
Myddelton Ave EN1 5 C5
Myddelton Cl EN1 5 D4
Myddelton Gdns N21 17 A4
Myddelton Ho N8 50 A6
Myddelton Pas EC1 94 C4 234 B2
Myddelton Pk N20 14 B2
Myddelton Rd N8 50 A5
Myddelton Sq EC1 94 C4 234 B2
Myddelton St EC1 94 C4 234 B1
Myddleton Ave N4 73 A6
Myddleton Ho 14 N2 30 B1
Myddleton Mews N22 32 A3
Myddleton Rd N22 32 B3
Myers Ho 5 SE5 139 A5
Myers La SE14 140 D6
Myherin Ct SE23 163 B2
Mylis Cl SE26 184 B6
Mylius Cl SE14 140 C4
Mylne Cl W6 112 A1
Mylne Ho N21 17 B5
Mylne St EC1 234 A3
Mynterne Ct 16 SW19 156 D3
Myra St SE2 124 A2
Myrdle Ct 14 E1 96 A1
Myrdle St E1 96 A1
Myrna Cl SW19 180 C3
Myron Pl SE13 142 A2
Myrtle Alley SE18 122 C3
Myrtle Ave
Hatton TW14 149 C6
Ruislip HA4 40 B2
Myrtle Cl Barnet EN4 14 D3
Hillingdon UB8 82 B2
West Drayton UB7 104 B3
Myrtledene Rd SE2 124 A1
Myrtle Gdns W7 108 C5
Myrtle Gr Enfield EN2 5 B5
Kingston u T KT3 177 A1
Myrtle Ho SE14 140 D4
Myrtle Rd Acton W3 111 A5
Croydon CR0 223 C5
Edmonton N13 17 B1
Hampton TW12 174 A4
Myrtle Rd *continued*
Hounslow TW3 130 A3
Ilford IG1 78 D6
Newham E6 100 A6
Sutton SM1 218 A3
Walthamstow E17 53 A3
Myrtle Wlk 20 N1 95 C5
Mysore Rd SW11 136 D1
Myton Rd SE21 161 B1
Mytton Ho SW8 270 C3

N

N1 Shopping Ctr N1 94 C5 234 B4
Nacton Ct 2 RM6 58 C4
Nadine St SE7 121 C1
Nadir Ct E11 55 A2
Naffenton Rise IG10 21 D6
Nagle Cl E17 36 B1
Nags Head Ct EC1 242 B5
Nag's Head La DA16 146 B2
Nags Head N7 72 B4
Nags Head Rd EN3 6 D1
Nags Head Sh Ctr The N7 72 B4
Naima Jewish Prep Sch NW6 91 D5
Nainby Ho SE11 261 A3
Nairn Ct
3 Wallington SM6 219 C2
Wimbledon SW19 179 D4
Nairne Gr SE5, SE24 139 B1
Nairn Rd HA4 62 C2
Nairn St E14 98 A2
Naish Ct N1 233 B6
Naish Ho SW19 201 D6
Naldera Gdns SE3 143 A6
Nallhead Rd TW13 172 C5
Nalton Ho 4 NW6 70 A1
Namba Roy Cl SW16 182 B6
Namton Dr CR7, SW16 204 B5
Nan Clark's La NW7 11 D2
Nankin St E14 97 C1
Nansen Ct 1 E11 76 C6
Nansen Ho 8 NW10 67 B1
Nansen Rd SW11 137 A2
Nansen Village 5 N12 29 D6
Nant Ct NW2 69 B6
Nantes Cl SW18 136 A1
Nant Rd NW2 69 B6
Nant St E2 96 B4
Naomi Watts Ho 11 SW19 179 A3
Naoroji St WC1 234 A1
Napier Ave
Deptford E14 119 C1
Fulham SW6 135 B2
Napier Cl
New Cross SE14, SE8 141 B5
West Drayton UB7 104 B3
West Kensington W14 254 C6
Napier Ct
13 Croydon CR0 221 D6
Fulham SW6 135 B2
Grove Pk SE12 165 B1
Hayes UB4 84 C3
Shoreditch N1 235 C4
1 Surbiton KT6 197 D2
12 Wallington SM6 219 B2
Wembley HA0 65 D2
Napier Gr N1 95 A5 235 B4
Napier Ho
Eltham SE12 165 B1
Kennington SE17 138 D6
Napier Lo TW15 171 B4
Napier 15 NW9 27 D2
Napier Pl W14 113 B3 254 C5
Napier Rd
Ashford TW15 171 B3
Belvedere DA17 125 B2
Bromley BR2 209 B5
College Pk NW10 90 B4
Croydon SE25 206 B5
Enfield EN3 18 D6
Isleworth TW7 131 A1
Kensington W14 113 B3 254 C5
Leyton E11 76 C5
Newham E15 98 C5
South Croydon CR2 221 B1
Tottenham N17 51 C6
Wallend E6 100 C5
Wembley HA0 65 D2
Napier Terr N1 72 D1
Napier Wlk TW15 171 B3
Napoleon Rd
Hackney E5 74 B5
Twickenham TW1 153 B4
Napton Cl UB4 85 A3
Narbonne Ave SW4 159 C6
Narborough Cl UB10 61 A6
Narborough St SW6 135 D3
Narcissus Rd NW6 69 C3
Nardini 12 NW9 27 D2
Naresby Fold HA7 25 C4
Narford Rd E5 74 A6
Narrow Boat Cl SE28 123 B4
Narrow St
6 Acton W3 110 D5
Limehouse E14 119 A6
Narrow Way BR2 210 A3
Nascot St W12 90 C1
Naseby Cl
Hounslow TW7 130 C4
South Hampstead NW6 70 A1
Naseby Ct DA14 189 D6
Naseby Rd
Dagenham RM10 81 C5
South Norwood SE19 183 B4
NASH 225 A2
Nash Cl SM1 218 B5
Nash Ct HA3 43 B3
Nashe Ho SE1 262 C5
Nash Gn BR1 187 A4
Nash Ho
5 Millwall E14 119 C3
Pimlico SW1 258 D1
1 Walthamstow E17 53 D5
Nash La BR2 225 A2
Nash Rd
Brockley SE4 163 A6
Dagenham RM6 58 D5
Lower Edmonton N9 18 C2
Nash St NW1 231 D2
Nash Way HA3 43 B3
Nasmyth St W6 112 B3
Nassau Path 6 SE28 124 C5
Nassau Rd SW13 133 D4
Nassau St W1 239 A3
Nassington Rd NW3 70 D4
Natalie Cl TW14 149 B4
Natalie Mews TW2 152 B1
Natal Rd
Bowes Pk N11 32 A4
Ilford IG1 78 D4
South Norwood CR7 205 B6
Streatham SW16 181 D4
Nathan Ct N9 18 C4
Nathan Ho SE11 261 B3
Nathaniel Cl E1 243 D3
Nathaniel Ct E17 53 A3
Nathans Rd HA0 65 C6
Nathan Way SE28, SE18 123 D3
National Army Mus* SW3 136 D6 267 D6
National Fan Mus* SE10 142 A5
National Film Theatre* SE1 250 D4
National Gallery* W1 115 D6 249 D5
National Hospl The WC1 94 A3 240 B5
National Maritime Mus* SE10 142 B6
National Physical Laboratory TW11 174 C4
National Portrait Gallery (Annexe)* SW1 115 D5 249 D4
National Portrait Gallery* W1 115 D6 249 D5
National Theatre* SE1 116 B5 250 D4
National Wks TW4 129 B2
Nation Way E4 20 A3
Natural History Mus* SW7 114 B3 256 C5
Nat West Twr* EC2 243 A2
Nautilus Bldg The EC1 234 B2
Naval Row E14 120 A6
Navarino Gr E8 74 A2
Navarino Mans E8 74 A2
Navarino Rd E8 74 A2
Navarre Rd E6 100 A5
Navarre St E2 243 C6
Navenby Wlk 13 E3 97 C3
Navestock Cl E4 20 A1
Navestock Cres IG8 37 C3
Navestock Ho IG11 102 B5
Navigation Ct E16 123 A6
Navigator Dr UB2 108 A4
Navy St SW4 137 D2
Naxos Bldg 9 E14 119 C4
Nayland Ho SE6 186 A6
Naylor Bldg W 4 E1 96 A1
Naylor Gr EN3 18 D6
Naylor Ho
33 Clapham SW8 137 D3
Walworth SE17 262 D2
5 West Kilburn W10 91 B4
Naylor Rd
Peckham SE15 140 B5
Whetstone N20 14 A2
Nayor Bldg E 6 E1 96 A1
Nazareth Cl SE15 140 B3
Nazrul St E2 95 D4
Neal Ave UB1 85 B3
Neal Cl HA6 22 A2
Nealden St SW9 138 B2
Neale Cl N2 48 A6
Neale Ct
Dagenham RM9 80 B2
Muswell Hill N10 31 B3
Neal St WC2 94 A1 240 A1
Neal's Yd WC2 240 A1
Near Acre NW9 27 D2
NEASDEN 67 B4
Neasden Cl NW10 67 C3
Neasden Junc NW10 67 C4
Neasden La
Church End NW10 67 C3
Neasden NW10 67 B5
Neasden La N NW10 67 C5
Neasden Sta NW10 67 C3
Neasham Rd RM8 80 B3
Neate St SE5 139 D6
Neath Gdns SM4 202 A3
Neathouse Pl SW1 259 A4
Neats Acre HA4 39 B2
Neatscourt Rd E16 99 D2
Nebraska Bldg 11 SE13 141 D4
Nebraska St SE1 117 B4 252 C1
Neckinger Est SE16 263 D6
Neckinger SE16 117 D3 263 D6
Neckinger St SE1 263 D6
Nectarine Way SE13 141 D3
Nedahall Ct 4 NW11 47 B2
Needham Ct 20 EN3 7 C6
Needham Ho SE11 261 A3
Needham Rd W11 91 C1
Needham Terr NW2 68 D5
Needleman St SE16 118 D4
Needwood Ho N4 51 A1
Neela Cl UB10 60 D4
Neeld Cres
Hendon NW4 46 B4
Wembley HA9 66 C3
Neeld Ct HA9 66 C3
Neeld Par HA9 66 B3
Neil Cl TW15 171 A5
Neilson-Terry Ct 9 SW9 138 B1
Neil Wates Cres 17 SW2 160 C3
Nelgarde Rd SE6 163 C4
Nella Rd W6 134 D6
Nelldale Rd SE16 118 C2
Nellgrove Rd UB10 82 D3
Nell Gwynn Ave TW17 193 B3
Nell Gwynn Ho SW3 257 B3
Nello James Gdns SE27 183 B6
Nelson Cl
East Bedfont TW14 149 D3
Hillingdon UB10 82 D4
2 Paddington NW6 91 C4
Thornton Heath CR0 204 D1
Walton-on-T KT12 194 B1
Nelson Ct
5 Carshalton SM5 218 D5
Rotherhithe SE16 119 B5
Nelson Dock Pier SE16 119 B5
Nelson Gdns
Bethnal Green E2 96 A4
Twickenham TW3, TW4 151 C5
Nelson Grove Rd SW19 180 A2
Nelson Ho 1 W5 88 A4
Nelson Hospl SW20 179 B1
Nelson La UB10 82 D4
Nelson Mandela Cl N10 31 A1
Nelson Mandela Rd SE3 143 C2
Nelson Pas EC1 235 B2
Nelson Pl N1 234 D3
Nelson Prim Sch
Twickenham TW2 151 D5
Wallend E6 100 C5
Nelson Rd
Ashford TW15 170 A5

Nelson Rd *continued*
Bromley BR2 209 C5
Chingford E4 35 D4
Edmonton N9 18 B2
Enfield EN3 18 D5
Erith DA17 125 B1
Greenwich SE10 142 A6
Harmondsworth TW6 126 B4
Harrow HA1 42 C1
Hillingdon UB10 82 D4
Hornsey Vale N8 50 B3
Merton SW19 180 A3
New Malden KT3 199 B4
Sidcup DA14 190 A6
Stanmore HA7 25 C4
Tottenham N15 51 C5
Twickenham TW2, TW4 151 C5
Wanstead E11 55 B5
Nelson's Monument* WC2 250 A4
Nelson Sq SE1 116 D4 251 C2
Nelsons Row SW4 137 D1
Nelson St Barking E6 100 C6
Canning Town E16 120 D6
Newham E6 100 B5
Stepney E1 96 B1
Nelsons Yd NW1 232 A4
Nelson Terr N1 234 D3
Nelson Trad Est SW19 179 D2
Nemoure Rd W3 111 A6
Nene Gdns TW13 151 B2
Nene Rd TW6, UB7 126 D4
Nene Road Rdbt TW6 126 D4
Nepaul Rd 17 SW11 136 C2
Nepean St SW15 156 A4
Neptune Ct
Dagenham IG11 102 B4
13 Millwall E14 119 C2
Neptune Ho
2 Rotherhithe SE16 118 C3
14 Stoke Newington N16 73 C3
Neptune Rd
Harlington TW6 127 A4
Harrow HA1 42 B3
Neptune St SE16 118 C3
Nero Ct 6 TW8 131 D5
Nesbit Cl SE3 142 C2
Nesbit Rd SE9 143 D1
Nesbitt Ho DA6 169 D6
Nesbitt Sq SE19 183 C3
Nesham Ho 14 N1 95 C6
Nesham St E1 118 A5
Ness St 9 SE16 118 A3
Nesta Rd IG8 36 D4
Nestle's Ave UB3 105 D3
Nestor Ave N21 16 D5
Nestor Ho 18 E2 96 B5
Netheravon Rd
Chiswick W4 111 D1
Ealing W7 108 D5
Netheravon Rd S W4 111 D1
Netherbury Rd W5 109 D3
Netherby Gdns EN2 4 A1
Netherby Ho 23 SW8 137 D3
Netherby Rd SE23 162 C4
Nether Cl N3 29 C3
Nethercombe Ho 1 SE3 143 A6
Nethercott Ho 27 E3 97 D4
Nethercourt Ave N3 29 C4
Netherfield Gdns IG11 79 B1
Netherfield Rd
Finchley N12 29 D5
Upper Tooting SW17 159 A1
Netherford Rd SW4 137 C3
Netherhall Gdns NW3 70 A3
Netherhall Way NW3 70 A3
Netherlands Rd EN5 14 B5
Netherleigh Cl N6 49 B1
Nether St Finchley N3 29 D4
North Finchley N12 30 A5
Netherton Gr SW10 136 A6 266 B5
Netherton Ho 1 UB5 85 B4
Netherton Rd
Isleworth TW1 153 B6
Tottenham N15 51 B3
Netherwood 24 N2 30 B1
Netherwood Rd W14 112 D4
Netherwood St NW6 69 C2
Nethewode Ct DA17 125 D3
Netley Cl
Cheam SM3 216 D3
New Addington CR0 224 A1
Netley Ct IG2 57 B4
Netley Dr KT12 195 B2
Netley Gdns SM4 202 A2
Netley 18 SE5 139 C4
Netley Prim Sch NW1 93 C4 232 A1
Netley Rd
Brentford TW8 132 A6
Cheam SM4 202 A2
Ilford IG2 57 B4
Walthamstow E17 53 B4
Netley St NW1 93 C4 232 A1
Nettlecombe NW1 71 D1
Nettleden Ave HA9 66 C2
Nettleden Ho SW3 257 B3
Nettlefold Pl SE27 160 D1
Nettlestead Cl 16 BR3 185 C3
Nettleton Rd
Harlington TW6 126 D4
Ickenham UB10 60 B4
New Cross Gate SE14 140 D4
Nettlewood Rd SW16 181 D3
Neuchatel Rd SE6 163 B2
Nevada Cl KT3 199 A5
Nevada St SE10 142 A6
Nevena Ct 3 SW2 160 C6
Nevern Mans SW5 255 A2
Nevern Pl SW5 113 C2 255 B3
Nevern Rd SW5 255 A3
Nevern Sq SW5 113 C2 255 B3
Nevil Ho 7 SW9 138 D3
Nevill Ct SW10 266 A4
Neville Ave KT3 177 B2
Neville Cl Acton W3 111 A4
Hounslow TW3 129 D3
Leyton E11 76 D5
Paddington NW6 91 B5
Peckham SE15 140 A4
Sidcup DA15 189 D6
Somers Town NW1 232 D3
Neville Ct 10 SW12 159 C4
Neville Dr N2 48 A3
Neville Gdns RM8 80 D5
Neville Gill Cl SW18 157 D5
Neville Ho
Friern Barnet N11 31 A6
5 Twickenham TW1 153 A4
Neville Pl N22 32 B2
Neville Rd
Dagenham RM8 80 D5
Ealing W5 87 D3
Forest Gate E7 77 B1
Kingston u T KT1 176 C1
Paddington NW6 91 B5
Richmond TW10 153 C2
Thornton Heath CR0 205 B2
Neville's Ct NW2 68 A5
Neville St SW7 114 B1 256 C2
Neville Terr SW7 256 C2
Neville Wlk SM5 202 C2
Nevill Rd N16 73 C5
Nevin Dr E4 19 D3
Nevin Ho UB3 105 A3
Nevinson Cl SW18 158 B5
Nevis Rd SW17 159 A2
Nevitt Ho N1 235 D3
New Acres Rd SE28 123 C5
NEW ADDINGTON 224 B1
Newall Ho SE1 262 B6
Newall Rd TW6 127 A4
Newark Cres NW10 89 B4
Newark Ct KT12 194 C1
Newark Ho 3 SW9 138 D3
Newark Knok E6 100 C2
Newark Rd CR2 221 B2
Newark St E1 96 B2
Newark Way NW4 46 A6
New Ash Cl N2 48 B6
New Atlas Wharf E14 119 C3
New Barn Cl SM6 220 B2
NEW BARNET 14 A6
New Barnet Sta EN5 14 B6
New Barns Ave CR4 203 D5
New Barn St E13 99 B3
NEW BECKENHAM 185 A4
New Beckenham Sta BR3 185 B3
New Belmont Ho 4 SE23 162 C3
New Bentham Ct 10 N1 73 A1
Newbery Ho N1 73 A1
Newbiggin Path WD19 22 C6
Newbold Cotts 4 E1 96 C1
Newbolt Ave SM3 216 D3
Newbolt Ho SE17 262 C2
Newbolt Rd HA7 24 D5
New Bond St W1 115 B6 248 D6
Newborough Gn KT3 199 B5
Newborough Ho SW19 180 B3
New Brent St NW4 46 C4
Newbridge Ct SW17 180 A6
Newbridge Point 3 SE23 162 D1
Newbridge Sch RM6 58 B4
New Bridge St EC4 94 D1 241 C1
New Broad St EC2 95 C2 243 A3
New Broadway
Ealing W5 109 D6
7 Hillingdon UB10 82 D3
Teddington TW12 174 B5
New Bsns Ctr The NW10 89 D4
Newburgh Rd W3 111 A5
Newburgh St W1 239 B1
New Burlington Mews W1 249 A6
New Burlington Pl W1 249 A6
New Burlington St W1 249 A6
Newburn Ct N12 30 A3
Newburn Ho SE11 260 D2
Newburn St SE11 116 B1 260 D2
Newbury Ave EN3 7 B6
Newbury Cl UB5 63 B2
Newbury Cotts 4 IG2 57 A3
Newbury Ct
Hackney E5 75 A3
Sidcup DA14 189 D6
7 Wanstead E11 55 A5
Newbury Gdns KT19 215 D4
Newbury Ho
Barnet EN4 2 B1
Brixton SW9 138 D3
14 Kensington W2 91 D1
Wood Green N22 32 A2
Newbury Mews NW5 71 A2
NEWBURY PARK 57 B3
Newbury Park Prim Sch IG2 57 B3
Newbury Park Sta IG2 57 B3
Newbury Rd
Bromley BR2 209 A6
Chingford E4 36 A4
Harmondsworth TW6 126 B4
Ilford IG2 57 C3
Newbury St EC1 242 A4
Newbury Way UB5 63 B2
New Butt La SE8 141 C5
Newby Cl EN1 5 C3
Newby NW1 232 A2
Newby Pl E14 120 A6
Newby St SW8 137 B2
New Caledonian Wharf SE16 119 B3
New Campden Ct 9 NW3 70 A4
Newcastle Cl EC4 241 C2
Newcastle Ct EC4 252 B6
Newcastle Ho W1 238 A4
Newcastle Pl W2 92 B2 236 D4
Newcastle Row EC1 241 B5
New Cavendish St W1 93 B2 238 C3
New Change EC4 95 A1 242 A1
New Chapel Sq TW13 150 B3
New Charles St EC1 234 D2
NEW CHARLTON 121 C2
New Church Ct 3 SE19 184 A3
New Church Rd
32 Camberwell SE5 139 A5
Camberwell SE5 139 B6
New City Prim Sch E13 99 C4
New City Rd E13 99 C4
New Cl
Feltham TW13 173 A5
Morden SW19 202 A6
New Colebrooke Ct SM5 219 A1
New College Ct 6 NW3 70 A2
New College Mews 7 N1 72 C1
New College Par 1 NW3 70 B1
Newcombe Gdns TW3 129 B1
Newcombe Ho N5 73 A3
Newcombe Pk
Edgware NW7 27 C5
Wembley HA0 88 B6
Newcombe Rise UB7 82 A1
Newcombe St W8 245 B4
Newcome Gdns SW16 182 A6
Newcome Ho E5 74 B5
Newcomen Ho 5 NW5 71 B4
Newcomen Rd
Battersea SW11 136 B2
Leyton E11 76 D5
Newcomen St SE1 117 B4 252 C2
New Compton St WC2 94 A1 240 A1
New Concordia Wharf SE1 253 D2
Newcourt Ho 26 E2 96 B4
Newcourt St NW8 92 C5 230 A3
New Covent Garden Flower Market SW8 138 A6 270 A5
New Covent Garden Fruit & Vegetable Mkt SW8 137 D5 269 C3
New Crane Pl E1 118 C5
New Crescent Yd 1 NW10 89 D5
Newcroft Cl UB8 82 B2
Newcroft Ho 10 NW10 67 B1
NEW CROSS 141 B4
NEW CROSS GATE 140 D4
New Cross Gate SE14 140 D4
New Cross Gate Sta SE14 141 A5
New Cross Hospl SE14 140 C5
New Cross Rd SE14 141 A4
New Cross SE14 141 B5
New Cross Sta SE14 141 B5
New Ct
City of London EC4 241 A1
26 Hampstead NW3 70 A4
Northolt UB5 63 D3
Stoke Newington N16 51 B1
Newdales Cl N9 18 A2
Newdene Ave UB5 84 D5
New Den (Millwall FC) The SE16 118 C1
Newdigate Ho
6 Kingston u T KT2 176 D4
5 Poplar E14 97 B1
Newell St E14 97 B1
NEW ELTHAM 167 A2
New Eltham Sta SE9 166 D3
New End NW3 70 A5
New End Prim Sch NW3 70 A4
New End Sq NW3 70 B4
New England Est IG11 101 A5
Newent Cl
Camberwell SE15 139 C5
Carshalton SM5 202 D1
New Farm Ave BR2 209 A5
New Ferry App SE18 122 C3
New Fetter La EC4 94 C1 241 B2
Newfield Cl TW12 173 C2
Newfield Prim Sch NW10 67 D1
Newfield Rise NW2 68 B5
Newgale Gdns HA8 26 B2
New Garden Dr UB7 104 A4
Newgate Cl TW13 151 A1
Newgate CR0 205 A1
Newgate St
Chingford E4 20 C1
Holborn EC1 94 D1 241 D2
New Globe Wlk SE1 252 A4
New Goulston St E1 243 C2
New Green Pl SE19 183 C4
NEWHAM 98 D4
Newham Acad of Music E6 100 A6
Newham Coll of FE E6 100 B5
Newham Coll (Stratford Campus) E15 76 C1
Newham Ctr for Mental Health E16 99 D3
Newham General Hospl E13 99 C3
Newham Gn N22 32 C2
Newham Sch of Nursing E3 97 D3
Newham Sixth Form Coll E13 99 B3
Newham Sixth Form Coll (Stratford Ctr) E15 76 B1
Newham's Row SE1 253 B1
Newham Way
Beckton E6 100 B3
Canning Town E13 99 B2
Newhaven Cl UB3 105 D2
Newhaven Cres TW15 171 B5
Newhaven Gdns SE9 143 D1
Newhaven La 3 E16 99 A2
Newhaven Rd SE25 205 B4
New Heston Rd TW5 129 B5
New Horizons Ct TW8 131 A6
Newhouse Ave RM6 58 D6
Newhouse Cl KT3 199 C2
Newhouse 5 KT3 199 C2
Newhouse Wlk SM4 202 A2
Newick Cl DA5 169 D5
Newick Rd E5 74 C5
Newing Gn BR1 187 D3
NEWINGTON 116 D2
Newington Barrow Way N7 72 B5
Newington Butts SE1, SE11 116 D2 261 D3
Newington Cswy SE1 117 A3 262 A6
Newington Gn N16 73 B3
Newington Green Mans N16 73 B3
Newington Green Prim Sch N16 73 B3
Newington Green Rd N1 73 B3
Newington Ind Est SE17 262 A3
New Inn Broadway EC2 243 B6
New Inn Ct The KT8 196 B4
New Inn Sq EC2 243 B6
New Inn St EC2 243 B6
New Inn Yd EC2 95 C3 243 B6
New James Ct SE15 140 B2
New Jubilee Ct 1 IG8 37 A3
New Kelvin Ave TW11 174 C4
New Kent Rd SE1 117 A2 262 B4
New King's Prim Sch SW6 135 B3
New King's Rd SW6 135 C4 265 B1
New King St SE8 141 C6
Newland Cl HA5 23 B4
Newland Ct
St Luke's EC1 242 C6
Wembley HA9 66 C6
Newland Dr EN1 6 B4
Newland Gdns W13 109 A4
Newland Ho
17 Deptford SE14 140 D6
Hornsey N8 50 A6
Newland House Sch Annex TW1 174 D6
Newland House Sch TW1 174 D6
Newland Rd N8 50 A6
Newlands Ave KT7 196 C1
Newlands Cl
Edgware HA8 10 A1
Southall UB2 107 A1
Wembley HA0 65 C2
Newlands Croft SE20 184 D4
Newlands Ct
8 Eltham SE9 166 C5
6 Penge SE26 184 C4
Streatham SW16 182 A5
Newlands NW1 232 A2
Newlands Pk SE26 184 D5
Newlands Pl EN5 12 D6
Newlands Quay E1 118 C6
Newlands Rd
Thornton Heath SW16 182 A1
Woodford IG8 20 D2
Newlands The
Thames Ditton KT7 196 C1
Wallington SM6 219 D1
Newland St E16 122 B5
Newlands Way KT9 213 C3
Newling Cl E6 100 B1
New London St EC3 253 B6
New Lydenburg Commercial Est SE7 121 C3
New Lydenburg St SE7 121 C3
Newlyn Cl
Hillingdon UB8 82 C2
Orpington BR6 227 D4
Newlyn Gdns HA2 41 B2
Newlyn Ho
7 Pinner HA5 23 B3
7 Sutton SM1 218 A4
Newlyn NW1 232 B5
Newlyn Rd Barnet EN5 1 B1
Bexley DA16 145 D3
Tottenham N17 33 D2
NEW MALDEN 199 D5
New Malden Sta KT3 199 C6
Newman Ct
3 Bromley BR1 187 A2
8 Finchley N3 29 C2
Newman Ho 11 TW10 153 C1
Newman Pas W1 239 B3
Newman Rd
Bromley BR1 187 A2
Hayes UB3 106 B6
Newham E13 99 B4
Thornton Heath CR0 204 B1
Walthamstow E17 52 D4
Newman's Ct EC3 242 D1
Newman's Row WC2 240 D3
Newman St W1 93 C2 239 B3
Newman's Way EN4 2 A4
Newman Terr 9 CR4 202 D6
Newmarket Ave UB5 63 D3
Newmarket Gn SE9 165 D4
Newmarsh Rd SE28 123 D5
Newmill Ho E3 98 A3
New Mill Rd BR5 190 C2
Newminster Rd SM4 202 A3
Newmount NW3 70 B3
New Mount St E15 76 B1
Newnes Path SW15 134 B1
Newnham Ave HA4 40 C1
Newnham Cl
Loughton IG10 21 D5
Northolt UB5 64 A2
South Norwood CR7 183 A1
Newnham Gdns UB5 64 A2
Newnham Ho
Catford SE6 164 A1
Loughton IG10 21 D5
9 Putney SW15 156 D5
Newnham Jun & Inf Schs HA4 40 C1
Newnham Lo 10 DA17 125 C1
Newnham Mews N22 32 C2
Newnham Rd N22 32 C2
Newnhams Cl BR1 210 B6
Newnham Terr SE1 261 A6
Newnham Way HA3 44 A4
New North Com Sch The N1 73 B1
New North Pl EC2 243 A6
New North Rd N1 95 B6 235 C5
New North Road Bridge N1 235 C5
New North St WC1 94 B2 240 C4
Newnton Cl N4 51 B2
New Oak Rd N2 30 A1
New Oxford St WC1 94 A1 240 A2
New Palace Yd SW1 116 A4 250 A1
New Par TW15 170 B6
New Park Ave N13 17 B1
New Park Cl UB5 63 A2
New Park Ct 28 SW2 160 A4
New Park Est N18 34 C5
New Park Ho N13 32 B6
New Park Par 14 SW2 160 A4
New Park Rd
Ashford TW15 171 A5
Streatham SW2 160 A4
New Par UB7 104 A5
New Place Sq SE16 118 B3
New Pl CR0 223 C2
New Plaistow Rd E15 98 C6
New Pond Par HA4 62 A5
Newport Ave
Blackwall E14 120 B6
Newham E13 99 B3
Newport Cl EN3 7 A6
Newport Ct WC2 249 D6
Newport Ho 2 E3 97 A4

Newport Lo 2 EN1 .... 17 C6
Newport Mead
WD19 .... 22 D6
Newport Pl WC2 .... 249 D6
Newport Rd
Barnes SW13 .... 134 A4
Harmondsworth
TW6 .... 126 C4
Hayes UB4 .... 83 B2
Leyton E10 .... 76 B6
Walthamstow E17 .... 53 A5
Newport Sch E10,
E11 .... 76 A6
Newport St
SE11 .... 116 B2 260 D4
New Priory Ct 9
NW6 .... 69 C1
New Providence Wharf
E14 .... 120 B5
Newquay Cres HA2 .... 63 A6
Newquay Ho SE11 .... 261 A2
Newquay Rd SE6 .... 164 A2
New Quebec St W1 .... 237 D1
New Rd
Brentford TW8 .... 109 D1
Carshalton CR4 .... 203 A1
Chingford E4 .... 36 A6
Dagenham RM10 .... 103 D5
East Bedfont TW14 .... 149 B5
East Molesey KT8 .... 195 C6
Edmonton N9 .... 18 B2
Elstree WD6 .... 9 D5
Esher KT10 .... 212 A4
feltham TW14 .... 150 B3
Finchley N10 .... 30 C2
Hanworth TW13 .... 173 A5
Harlington TW6,
UB7 .... 127 A5
Harrow HA1 .... 64 D4
Hendon NW7 .... 29 A3
Hillingdon UB8 .... 83 A2
Hornsey N8 .... 50 A4
Hounslow TW3 .... 129 D1
Ilford IG3 .... 79 C6
Kingston u T KT2 .... 176 C3
Littleton TW17 .... 192 D6
Richmond TW10 .... 175 C6
Stepney E1 .... 96 B2
Tottenham N22 .... 33 A2
Welling DA16 .... 146 B3
West Heath SE2 .... 124 D1
New River Cres N13 .... 32 D6
New River Ct N5 .... 73 B4
New River Sports &
Recreation Ctr
N22 .... 32 D3
New River Way N4 .... 51 B2
New Row
WC2 .... 116 A6 250 A6
New Rush Hall Sch
IG1 .... 79 A6
Newry Rd TW1 .... 153 A6
New St Sq
EC4 .... 94 C1 241 B2
Newsam Ave N15 .... 51 B4
New Scotland Yard*
SW1 .... 115 D3 259 C6
New Shepherd's Bush
Mkt* 6 W12 .... 112 C4
Newsholme Dr N21 .... 16 B6
NEW SOUTHGATE 31 C6
New Southgate Ind Est
10 N11 .... 31 C5
New Southgate Sta
N11 .... 31 B5
New Spitalfields Mkt
E10 .... 75 C5
New Spring Gdns Wlk
SE11 .... 260 B1
New Sq
East Bedfont
TW14 .... 149 A3
St Giles WC2 .... 94 B1 240 D2
New Square Pas
WC2 .... 241 A2
Newstead Ave BR6 .... 227 C6
Newstead Cl N12 .... 30 C4
Newstead Ct UB5 .... 85 A4
Newstead Ho
Edmonton N9 .... 17 D1
Islington N1 .... 234 B4
Newstead Rd SE12 .... 164 D4
Newstead Way
SW19 .... 178 D6
Newstead Wlk SM5 .... 202 A2
Newstead Wood Sch for
Girls BR6 .... 227 B5
New St EC2 .... 95 C2 243 B3
New Street Hill BR1 .... 187 C5
Newton Ave
Acton W3 .... 111 A4
Muswell Hill N10 .... 31 B2
Newton Cl
Harrow HA2 .... 63 C6
Walthamstow E17 .... 53 A3
Newton Farm Fst & Mid
Sch HA2 .... 63 B6
Newton Gr W4 .... 111 C2
Newton Ho
22 Clapham SW8 .... 137 D3
Paddington NW8 .... 91 D6
1 Stepney E1 .... 118 B6
10 Walthamstow E17 .... 54 A6
Newton Ind Est RM6 .... 58 D5
Newton Pl E14 .... 119 C2
Newton Point 1 E16 .... 98 D1
Newton Prep Sch
SW8 .... 137 B4 268 D2
Newton Rd
Acton W3 .... 111 A4
Cricklewood NW2 .... 68 C5
Harrow HA3 .... 24 C1
Isleworth TW7 .... 130 D3
Kensington W2 .... 91 D1
South Tottenham N15 .... 52 A4
Stratford New Town
E15 .... 76 B3
Welling DA16 .... 146 A2
Wembley HA0 .... 66 B1
Wimbledon SW19 .... 179 A3
Newton St
WC2 .... 94 A1 240 B2
Newton's Yd 14
SW18 .... 157 C6
Newton Terr BR2 .... 209 D3
Newton Way N18 .... 33 A5
Newton Wlk HA8 .... 26 D2
New Tower Bldgs 21
E1 .... 118 B5
Newtown Ct
Battersea SW11 .... 268 C1
Clapham SW4 .... 159 B6
New Trinity Rd 1
N2 .... 30 B1
New Union Cl E14 .... 120 A3
New Union St EC2 .... 242 C3
New Victoria Hospl
KT3 .... 177 C2
New Wanstead E11 .... 55 A3
New Way Rd NW9 .... 45 C5
New Wharf Rd
N1 .... 94 A5 233 B4
New Woodlands Sch
BR1 .... 186 C6
NEWYEARS GREEN 38 B3
Newyears Green La
UB9 .... 38 B3
New Zealand Ave
KT12 .... 193 D1
Nexus Ct E11 .... 54 C2
Niagara Ave W5 .... 109 C2
Niagara Cl N1 .... 235 B4
Niagara Ct 6 SE16 .... 118 C3
Niagara Ho W5 .... 109 C2
Nibthwaite Rd HA1 .... 42 C4
Nicholas Cl UB6 .... 85 D5
Nicholas Ct
Chiswick W4 .... 133 C5
Golders Green NW11 .... 47 C2
Lewisham SE12 .... 165 A3
Newham E13 .... 99 B4
Nicholas Gdns W5 .... 109 D4
Nicholas Ho
Ealing W13 .... 87 C1
Penge SE26 .... 184 B4
2 Putney SW15 .... 156 A6
Nicholas La EC2, EC4 .... 252 D6
Nicholas Pas EC3 .... 252 D6
Nicholas Rd
Bethnal Green E1 .... 96 C3
Borehamwood WD6 .... 10 B6
Dagenham RM8 .... 81 B5
Wallington CR0 .... 220 A4
Nicholas Stacey Ho 3
SE7 .... 121 B1
Nicholay Rd N19 .... 49 D1
Nichol Cl N14 .... 15 D3
Nicholes Rd TW3 .... 129 C1
Nichol La BR1 .... 187 A3
Nicholl Ho N4 .... 51 A1
Nicholls Almshouses
NW7 .... 28 B5
Nicholls Ave UB8 .... 82 C3
Nicholls Point E15 .... 99 A6
Nicholl St E2 .... 96 A6
Nichols Cl
Chessington KT9 .... 213 C2
Finsbury Pk N4 .... 50 C1
Nichols Ct E2 .... 95 D5
Nichols Gn W5 .... 88 A2
Nicholson Ct 9 N17 .... 51 D6
Nicholson Ho SE17 .... 262 C2
Nicholson Mews
KT1 .... 198 A5
Nicholson Rd CR0 .... 205 D1
Nicholson St SE1 .... 251 C3
Nickelby Cl SE28 .... 102 C1
Nickleby Cl UB8 .... 82 D1
Nickleby Ho
18 Bermondsey
SE1 .... 118 A4
7 Shepherd's Bush
W11 .... 112 D5
Nickols Wlk SW18 .... 135 D1
Nicola Cl Harrow HA3 .... 24 B1
South Croydon CR2 .... 221 A2
Nicola Terr DA7 .... 147 A4
Nicol Cl 6 TW1 .... 153 B5
Nicole Ho SE25 .... 206 A6
Nicoll Ct
Dagenham NW10 .... 89 C6
Muswell Hill N10 .... 31 B3
Nicoll Pl NW4 .... 46 B2
Nicoll Rd NW10 .... 89 C6
Nicoll Way WD6 .... 11 B6
Nicolson Dr WD23 .... 8 A2
Nicolson 14 NW9 .... 27 D2
Nicosia Rd SW18 .... 158 C4
Niederwald Rd
SE26 .... 185 A6
Nield Rd UB3 .... 105 D4
Nigel Bldg EC1 .... 241 A4
Nigel Cl UB5 .... 85 A6
Nigel Ct N3 .... 29 D3
Nigel Fisher Way
KT9 .... 213 D1
Nigel Mews IG1 .... 78 D4
Nigel Playfair Ave
W6 .... 112 B1
Nigel Rd
Forest Gate E7 .... 77 C3
Peckham SE15 .... 140 A2
Nigeria Rd SE7 .... 143 D5
Nighthawk 16 NW9 .... 27 D2
Nightingale Ave
Chingford E4 .... 36 C5
Harrow HA1 .... 43 B1
Nightingale Cl
Carshalton SM5 .... 219 A6
Chingford E4 .... 36 C6
Chiswick W4 .... 133 A6
Pinner HA5 .... 40 C4
Nightingale Ct
14 Cubitt Town
E14 .... 120 A3
Finsbury Pk N4 .... 72 B6
1 Harrow HA1 .... 42 D3
Penge SE19 .... 183 D4
Sutton SM1 .... 218 A3
1 Wanstead E11 .... 55 B4
Nightingale Dr
KT19 .... 214 D2
Nightingale Gr
SE13 .... 164 B6
Nightingale Ho
Hayes UB3 .... 105 D2
21 Hoxton E1 .... 95 C6
4 North Kensington
W12 .... 90 C1
7 St George in t East
E1 .... 118 A5
Woolwich SE18 .... 122 C1
Nightingale La
Balham SW11,
SW12 .... 159 A5
Bromley BR1 .... 187 D1
Hornsey N8 .... 50 A6
Richmond TW10 .... 154 A4
Wanstead E11 .... 55 B4
Nightingale Lo
Edgware HA8 .... 27 A4
5 Paddington W9 .... 91 C2
Nightingale Mans 4
SW12 .... 159 A5
Nightingale Mews
1 Bow E3 .... 97 A5
Newington SE11 .... 261 C4
8 Wanstead E11 .... 55 B4
Nightingale Pl
Shooters Hill
SE18 .... 144 D6
West Brompton
SW10 .... 136 A6 266 B6
Nightingale Prim Sch
Shacklewell E5 .... 74 A4
Wanstead E18 .... 55 C5
Wood Green N22 .... 32 B2
Woolwich SE18 .... 122 D1
Nightingale Rd
Carshalton SM5 .... 219 A6
Dagenham NW10 .... 89 D5
Ealing W7 .... 108 D5
East Molesey KT8 .... 195 D4
Hackney E5 .... 74 B5
Hampton TW12 .... 173 C4
Orpington BR5 .... 211 A3
Ponders End N9 .... 18 C4
Walton-on-T KT12 .... 194 B2
Wood Green N22 .... 32 B3
Nightingale Sch
SW17 .... 158 C2
Nightingale Sq
SW12 .... 159 A4
Nightingales The
TW19 .... 148 B3
Nightingale Vale
SE18 .... 144 C6
Nightingale Way E6 .... 100 A2
Nightingale Wlk SW18,
SW4 .... 159 B5
Nile Cl N16 .... 73 D5
Nile Ct N12 .... 30 C4
Nile Dr N9 .... 18 C2
Nile Ho N1 .... 235 C2
Nile Path 6 SE18 .... 144 C6
Nile Rd E13 .... 99 C5
Nile St N1 .... 95 B4 235 C2
Nile Terr SE1,
SE15 .... 117 D1 263 D1
Nimegen Way 9
SE22 .... 161 C6
Nimmo Dr WD23 .... 8 B4
Nimrod Cl UB5 .... 84 D4
Nimrod 12 NW9 .... 27 C2
Nimrod Pas 4 N1 .... 73 C2
Nimrod Rd SW16 .... 181 B5
Nina Mackay Cl 10
E15 .... 98 C6
Nine Acres Cl E12 .... 78 A3
NINE ELMS 137 C5
Nine Elms Cl TW14 .... 149 D3
Nine Elms La
SW8 .... 137 D6 269 C5
Nineteenth Rd CR4 .... 204 A5
Ninhams Wood BR6 .... 226 C4
Ninth Ave UB3 .... 106 A6
Nisbet Ho E9 .... 74 D3
Nisbet 13 NW9 .... 27 C2
Nisbett Wlk DA14 .... 190 A6
Nita Ct SE12 .... 165 A3
Nithdale Rd SE18 .... 145 A5
Nithsdale Gr UB10 .... 61 A5
Niton Cl EN5 .... 12 D5
Niton Rd TW9 .... 132 C2
Niton St SW6 .... 134 D5
No 1 St SE18 .... 122 D3
No 2 Willow Rd*
NW3 .... 70 C4
Noam Prim Sch N12 .... 29 D6
Nobel Dr TW6 .... 127 C5
Nobel Ho 8 SE5 .... 139 A3
Nobel Rd N18 .... 34 C6
Noble Cnr TW5 .... 129 C4
Noble Ct
Mitcham CR4 .... 180 B1
Stepney E1 .... 118 B6
Noblefield Hts N2 .... 48 D4
Noble Ho 18 E1 .... 118 A6
Noble St EC2 .... 95 A1 242 A2
Noel Baker Ct 5 E11 .... 76 C6
Noel Coward Ho
SW1 .... 259 B3
Noel Ct TW4 .... 129 B2
Noel Dene W5 .... 109 C1
Noel Ho 8 NW3 .... 70 B1
Noel 13 NW9 .... 27 D2
NOEL PARK 32 D1
Noel Park Prim Sch
N22 .... 32 C1
Noel Park Rd N22 .... 32 C1
Noel Rd Acton W3 .... 88 C1
Islington N1 .... 94 D5 234 D4
Newham E6 .... 100 A3
Noel Sq RM8 .... 80 C4
Noel St W1 .... 93 C1 239 B1
Noel Terr
Forest Hill SE23 .... 162 C2
Sidcup DA14 .... 190 B6
Noko NW10 .... 90 D4
Nolan Way E5 .... 74 A4
Noll Ho N7 .... 72 B6
Nolton Pl HA8 .... 26 B2
Nonsuch Ct SM3 .... 217 A2
Nonsuch High Sch for
Girls SM3 .... 216 D1
Nonsuch Ho 5
SW19 .... 180 B2
Nonsuch Prim Sch
KT17 .... 216 B3
Nook The SW19 .... 180 A1
Noor Ul Islam Prim Sch
E10 .... 76 A6
Nora Gdns NW4 .... 46 D5
NORBITON 176 C1
Norbiton Ave KT1,
KT2 .... 176 C1
Norbiton Common Rd
KT1, KT3 .... 198 D6
Norbiton Hall KT2 .... 176 B1
Norbiton Rd E14 .... 97 B1
Norbiton Sta KT1 .... 176 C2
Norbreck Gdns
NW10 .... 88 B4
Norbreck Par NW10 .... 88 B4
Norbroke St W12 .... 111 D6
Norburn St W10 .... 91 A2
NORBURY 182 C2
Norbury Ave
Isleworth TW3 .... 130 B1
Thornton Heath CR7,
SW16 .... 182 C1
Norbury Cl SW16 .... 182 D2
Norbury Court Rd
SW16 .... 182 A1
Norbury Cres SW16 .... 182 C1
Norbury Cross
SW16 .... 204 A6
Norbury Ct N12 .... 30 A6
Norbury Gdns RM6 .... 58 D4
Norbury Gr NW7 .... 11 C1
Norbury Hill SW16 .... 182 D3
Norbury Manor Bsns &
Enterprise Coll For
Girls CR7 .... 182 C2
Norbury Manor Prim
Sch SW16 .... 182 A2
Norbury Rd
Chingford E4 .... 35 C5
Feltham TW13 .... 149 D1
South Norwood CR7 .... 205 A6
Norbury Rise SW16 .... 204 A6
Norbury Sch HA1 .... 42 C4
Norbury Sta SW16 .... 182 B2
Norbury Trad Est
SW16 .... 182 B1
Norcombe Gdns HA3 .... 43 C4
Norcombe Ho 2
N19 .... 71 D5
Norcott Cl UB4 .... 84 C3
Norcott Rd N16 .... 74 A5
Norcroft Gdns SE22 .... 162 A4
Norcutt Rd TW2 .... 152 C3
Norden Ho 25 E2 .... 96 B4
Norden Point NW2 .... 46 C1
Nore Ct NW10 .... 68 A1
Norfolk Ave
Edmonton N13 .... 32 D4
South Tottenham N15 .... 51 D3
Norfolk Cl
Cockfosters EN4 .... 3 A1
East Finchley N2 .... 48 C6
Edmonton N13 .... 32 D4
5 Twickenham
TW1 .... 153 B5
Norfolk Cres
Paddington
W2 .... 92 C1 237 B2
Sidcup DA15 .... 167 C4
Norfolk Ct
5 Barnet EN5 .... 1 A1
4 Ilford RM6 .... 58 B4
Surbiton KT5 .... 198 B3
Wembley HA0 .... 65 C2
Norfolk Gdns DA7 .... 147 B4
Norfolk Ho
13 Acton W3 .... 88 C1
Beckenham BR2 .... 208 D5
City of London EC4 .... 252 A6
Edgware HA8 .... 26 B3
Greenwich SE3 .... 142 C6
11 Merton SW19 .... 180 A3
Penge SE20 .... 184 C2
4 Putney SW15 .... 156 C4
Richmond TW10 .... 154 C6
Shacklewell E8 .... 73 D4
2 South Croydon
CR0 .... 221 B6
3 Stanmore HA7 .... 25 C5
St Johns SE8 .... 141 C4
Norfolk House Rd
SW16 .... 160 A1
Norfolk House Sch
N10 .... 31 B1
Norfolk Ho SW1 .... 259 D4
Norfolk Mans
Battersea SW11 .... 267 D1
10 Wandsworth
SW18 .... 157 C6
Norfolk Mews 12
W10 .... 91 A2
Norfolk Pl
Paddington
W2 .... 92 B1 236 D2
Welling DA16 .... 146 A3
Norfolk Rd
Barking IG11 .... 79 C1
Barnet EN5 .... 1 C2
Claygate KT10 .... 212 C3
Dagenham RM10 .... 81 D3
Enfield EN3 .... 18 B6
Feltham TW13 .... 150 C3
Harrow HA1 .... 41 D4
Higham Hill E17 .... 34 D1
Ilford IG3 .... 57 C2
Mitcham SW19 .... 180 C4
Newham E6 .... 100 B6
South Norwood CR7 .... 205 A6
St John's Wood
NW8 .... 92 B6 229 D5
Willesden NW10 .... 67 C1
Norfolk Row SE1,
SE11 .... 116 B2 260 C4
Norfolk Sq Mews
W2 .... 236 D1
Norfolk Sq
W2 .... 92 B1 236 D2
Norfolk St E7 .... 77 A3
Norgrove St SW12 .... 159 A4
Norhyrst Ave SE25 .... 205 D6
Norland Ho 13 W11 .... 112 D5
Norland Place Sch
W11 .... 113 A5 244 A3
Norland Pl
W11 .... 113 A5 244 B3
Norland Rd 16 W11 .... 112 D5
Norlands Cres BR7 .... 188 D2
Norland Sq
W11 .... 113 A5 244 B3
Norley Vale SW15 .... 156 A3
Norlington Rd E10,
E11 .... 54 B1
Norlington Sch for Boys
E10 .... 54 B1
Norman Ave
Feltham TW13 .... 151 B2
Southall UB1 .... 107 A6
Tottenham N22 .... 33 A2
Twickenham TW1 .... 153 C4
Norman Butler Ho 10
W10 .... 91 A3
Normanby Cl SW15 .... 157 B6
Normanby Rd NW10 .... 67 D4
Norman Cl
Orpington BR6 .... 227 A5
Tottenham N22 .... 33 A2
Norman Cres
Heston TW5 .... 128 D5
Pinner HA5 .... 22 C2
Norman Ct
Dulwich SE22 .... 162 A4
5 Finchley N3 .... 29 C2
Finsbury Pk N4 .... 50 C2
8 Hampton TW12 .... 173 C2
Ilford IG2 .... 57 B2
West Norwood
SW16 .... 182 C5
Willesden NW10 .... 68 A1
Woodford IG8 .... 37 B5
Normand Croft Com
Sch W14 .... 135 B6 264 D6
Normand Mews
W14 .... 264 B6
Normand Rd
W14 .... 135 B6 264 C6
Normandy Ave EN5 .... 1 B1
Normandy Cl SE26 .... 163 A1
Normandy Dr UB3 .... 83 A1
Normandy Ho
8 Cubitt Town
E14 .... 120 A4
4 Hendon NW4 .... 28 D1
Normandy Rd SW9 .... 138 C4
Normandy Terr E16 .... 99 B1
Norman Gr E3 .... 97 A5
Norman Ho
1 Cheam SM1 .... 217 C2
Feltham TW13 .... 151 B2
7 Leyton E11 .... 76 C6
Lower Halliford
TW17 .... 192 C2
South Lambeth SW8 .... 270 A4
Normanhurst TW15 .... 170 C5
Normanhurst Ave
DA7 .... 146 D4
Normanhurst Dr
TW1 .... 153 B6
Normanhurst Rd
St Paul's Cray
BR5 .... 190 B1
Streatham SW2 .... 160 B2
Walton-on-T KT12 .... 194 D1
Normanhurst Sch E4 .... 20 B4
Norman Par DA14 .... 168 D2
Norman Rd
Ashford TW15 .... 171 B4
Belvedere DA17 .... 125 D3
Greenwich SE10 .... 141 D5
Ilford IG1 .... 78 D3
Leyton E11 .... 76 C6
Merton SW19 .... 180 A3
Newham E6 .... 100 B3
South Tottenham N15 .... 51 D4
Sutton SM1 .... 217 C3
Thornton Heath CR7 .... 204 D4
Normans Cl
Hillingdon UB8 .... 82 A2
Willesden NW10 .... 67 B2
Normansfield Ave KT1,
KT8 .... 175 C3
Normanshire Dr E4 .... 35 D6
Normans Mead
NW10 .... 67 B2
Norman St
EC1 .... 95 A4 235 B1
Normanton Ave SW18,
SW19 .... 157 C2
Normanton Ct CR2 .... 221 C3
Normanton Ho 6
SW4 .... 159 C5
Normanton Pk E4 .... 20 C2
Normanton Rd CR2 .... 221 C2
Normanton St SE23 .... 162 D2
Norman Way
Acton W3 .... 88 D1
Palmers Green N14 .... 16 A2
Normington Cl
SW16 .... 182 C5
Norrice Lea N2 .... 48 B4

Norris Ho
 12 Hoxton N1 ....95 C6
 15 South Hackney E9 ..96 C6
Norris 11 NW9........27 D2
Norris St SW1 ...... 249 C5
Norroy Rd SW15 .....134 D1
Norrys Cl EN4 ....2 D1
Norrys Rd EN4..........2 D1
Norse Ho 13 SE5 .....139 A3
Norseman Cl 3 IG3...58 B1
Norseman Way UB6...85 D6
Norstead Pl SW15....156 A2
North Access Rd E17..52 D3
North Acre NW9 ......27 C2
NORTH ACTON 89 B4
North Acton Rd NW10.........89 B4
North Acton Sta W3..89 B2
Northampton Gr N1...73 B3
Northampton Pk N1 ..73 B2
Northampton Rd
 Croydon CR0 .... 222 A6
 Enfield EN3 ....7 A1
 Finsbury EC1..94 C3 241 B6
Northampton Sq EC1 ....94 D4 234 C1
Northampton St N1...73 A1
Northanger Rd SW16..............182 A4
North Audley St W1.........115 A6 248 A6
North Ave Ealing W13 ..87 B2
 Edmonton N18.........34 A6
 Harrow HA2 ....41 D3
 Hayes UB3......... 106 A6
 8 Richmond TW9... 132 C4
 Southall UB1 ....107 B6
 Wallington SM5...... 219 A1
Northaw Ho 4 W10...90 C3
North Bank NW8.........92 C4 230 A1
Northbank Rd E17 ....36 A1
North Beckton Prim Sch E6..................100 B2
North Birkbeck Rd E11..................76 B5
North Block 19 E1 ...118 C6
Northborough Rd SW16..............182 A1
Northbourne BR2....209 A2
Northbourne Ho
 21 Hackney E5 ....74 B3
 Osidge N14 ....15 D4
Northbourne Rd SW4...............159 D6
North Bridge House Sch NW3..............70 A2
North Bridge House Senior Sch NW1.........93 B6 231 C5
Northbrook CE Sch SE12............. 164 D6
Northbrook Rd
 Barnet EN5 ....13 A5
 Ilford IG1 ....78 C6
 Lewisham SE13...... 164 C6
 Thornton Heath CR0 ..205 B4
 Wood Green N22.......32 A3
Northburgh St EC1 ....94 D3 241 D6
Northbury Jun & Inf Schs IG11 ....79 A2
North Carriage Dr W2.........114 C6 247 B6
NORTH CHEAM 216 C6
Northchurch Ho 19 E2..................96 A6
Northchurch Rd
 De Beauvoir Town N1 ....73 B1
 Wembley HA9 ....66 C2
Northchurch SE17 .. 262 D2
Northchurch Terr N1 ....73 C1
North Circular Rd
 Edmonton N13........32 C5
 Finchley N2 ....30 B2
 Highams Pk E17 ......35 D2
 Ilford IG1, E12 ....78 C4
 Neasden NW2, NW10 ..67 C3
 Temple Fortune N3, NW2, NW4.............47 A4
 Woodford E18 ....37 C1
North Cl Barnet EN5 ....12 C6
 Bexley DA6 .... 146 D1
 Dagenham RM10.... 103 C6
 East Bedfont TW14 ...149 B5
Northcliffe Cl KT4 ...215 C5
Northcliffe Dr N20 ....13 B3
North Cl SM4 ....201 A5
North Colonnade The E14...............119 D5
North Common Rd
 Ealing W5 .... 110 A6
North Common Rd continued
 Uxbridge UB8 ....60 A3
Northcote Ave
 Ealing W5 .... 110 A6
 Isleworth TW7...... 153 A6
 Southall UB1 .... 107 A6
 Tolworth KT5....... 198 D2
Northcote Ho UB4 ....84 D2
Northcote Lodge Sch SW11............. 158 D5
Northcote 3 HA5.....22 C1
Northcote Rd
 Isleworth TW7...... 153 A6
 Kingston u T KT3 .....199 B6
 Sidcup DA14 .... 189 C6
 Thornton Heath CR0 ..205 B3
 Walthamstow E17.....53 A5
 Wandsworth SW11 .. 158 D6
 Willesden NW10 ......67 C1
Northcott Ave N22 ....32 A2
North Countess Rd E17.................35 B2
Northcourt W1 ..... 239 B4
NORTH CRAY 169 B1
North Cray Rd DA14..191 A5
North Cres
 Finchley N3 ....29 B1
 Marylebone WC1.... 239 C4
 Newham E16..........98 B3
Northcroft Ct 8 W12...............112 A4
Northcroft Rd
 Brentford W13.......109 B3
 West Ewell KT19...... 215 C1
North Crofts SE21....162 B3
North Cross Rd
 East Dulwich SE22............ 162 A6
 Ilford IG6 ....57 A5
North Ct SW1....... 260 A5
North Dene NW7......11 B1
Northdene Gdns N15..51 D3
North Dene TW5.....129 D4
Northdown Cl HA4 ....61 D5
Northdown Gdns IG2...................57 C4
Northdown Rd DA16 ....146 C3
Northdown St N1 ....94 B5 233 C3
North Dr
 Beckenham BR3 .... 207 D5
 Hounslow TW3, TW7 .... 130 A3
 Orpington BR6....... 227 C4
 Ruislip HA4 ....39 C2
 Streatham SW16.... 181 C6
North Dulwich Sta SE21...............161 B6
North Ealing Prim Sch W5.................87 B3
North Ealing Sta W3..88 B1
NORTH END 70 A6
North End Ave NW3 ....70 A6
North End IG9........21 C4
North End Cres W14.......113 B2 254 C3
North End CR0.......221 A6
North End Ho W14........113 A2 254 B3
North End La BR6....226 D1
Northend Lodge 2 HA5 ....40 D6
North End NW3.......70 A6
North End Par W14 . 254 B3
North End Rd
 Golders Green NW11............47 D1
 Wembley HA9 ....66 D5
 West Kensington W14..... 113 B1 254 D1
North End Way NW3 ..70 A6
Northern Ave N9......17 D2
Northernhay Wlk SM4...............201 A5
Northern Hts N8......49 D2
Northern Perimeter Rd TW6..............127 C4
Northern Perimeter Rd (W) TW6...........126 B4
Northern Rd E13...... 99 B5
Northern Relief Rd IG11...............79 A2
Northern Star Ho N11 ....31 B5
Northesk Ho 6 E1.... 96 B3
North Eyot Gdns 5 W6...............111 D1
Northey St E14 ....119 A6
NORTH FELTHAM 150 B6
North Feltham Trad Est TW14.............128 B1
Northfield Ave
 Pinner HA5 ....40 D5
 West Ealing W13, W5 ....109 B4
Northfield Cl
 Bromley BR1 .... 188 A2
 Hayes UB3......... 105 D3
Northfield Cres SM3................217 A4
Northfield Gdns RM9..81 B4
Northfield Hall N6 ....49 A2
Northfield Ho
 2 Newham E13 ......99 C5
 3 Peckham SE15 ... 140 A6
Northfield Ind Est HA0 ....88 C6
Northfield IG10........21 D6
Northfield Par UB3...105 D3
Northfield Path RM9 ..81 B4
Northfield Pk UB3 ...105 D3
Northfield Rd
 Cockfosters EN4 ....2 C2
 Dagenham RM9.......81 B4
 Enfield EN3 ....18 B6
 Heston TW5........ 128 D5
 Plashet E6...........78 B1
 Stamford Hill N16 .....51 C2
 West Ealing W13......109 B4
Northfields SW18 ....135 C1
Northfields Prospect SW18..............135 C1
Northfields Rd W3....89 A2
Northfields Sta W5 . 109 C3
NORTH FINCHLEY ...30 A6
Northfleet Ho SE1 .. 252 C2
North Flower Wlk W2.........114 B6 246 C5
Northgate Bsns Ctr EN1 ....6 B1
Northgate Ct 14 SW9..............138 C2
Northgate Dr NW9....45 C3
North Gate NW8.........92 C5 230 A3
North Gates N12......30 A2
North Gdns SW19....180 B3
North Glade The DA5 ....169 B3
North Gn NW9........27 C3
North Gower St NW1.........93 C4 232 B1
North Greenwich Sta SE10.............. 120 C4
North Gr Highgate N6 ..49 A2
 Tottenham N15 ....51 B4
North Harringay Prim Sch N8.............50 C5
NORTH HARROW 41 D2
North Harrow Sta HA2 ....41 D4
North Hill Ave N6.....48 D3
North Hill Ct N6 ......49 A2
NORTH HILLINGDON 61 A2
North Hill N6.........49 A3
North Ho 3 SE8 .....119 B1
NORTH HYDE 107 A1
North Hyde Gdns UB2, UB3 ....106 A3
North Hyde La UB2...107 A1
North Hyde Rd UB3 ..105 D3
Northiam N12 ....29 C6
Northiam St E9....... 96 B6
Northiam WC1...... 233 B1
Northington St WC1.........94 B3 240 D5
NORTH KENSINGTON 90 D2
Northlands Ave BR6 ....227 C4
Northlands 4 BR1 ...187 C1
Northlands St SE5 ...139 A3
North La TW11.......174 D4
Northleigh Ho 36 E3 ..97 D4
North Lo SW4 ....137 B1
North Lodge Cl SW15..............156 D6
North Lo N22.........31 D1
North London Bsns Pk N11 ....15 A1
North London Collegiate Sch The HA7, HA8............26 A5
North London Nuffield Hospl EN2...........4 C3
North Lo EN5 ....14 A6
North Mall The N9 ....18 B2
North Mews WC1.........94 B3 240 D5
North Middlesex University Hospl N18 ....33 C5
Northmoor 4 SE23 ..162 D1
North Mount N20 .....14 A2
Northolme Gdns HA8 ..26 C2
Northolme Rd N5.....73 A4
Northolme Rise BR6 ....227 C6
Northolm HA8 ....27 B6
NORTHOLT 63 C1
Northolt Ave HA4 .....62 B3
Northolt Gdns UB6....64 D3
Northolt High Sch UB5 ....63 B2
Northolt Park Inf Sch UB5 ....63 D3
Northolt Park Sta HA2 ....63 D4
Northolt Rd HA2 .....64 A5
Northolt Sta UB5 .....63 C2
Northolt N17 ....33 C1
Northolt Trad Est UB5 ....63 D1
Northover BR1.......164 D1
North Par
 Chessington KT9 .....214 B3
 Edgware HA8.........26 C1
 Southall UB1 ....85 C1
North Pas SW18 .....157 C6
North Pk SE9 ....166 C5
North Pl
 Mitcham SW19 ..... 180 D3
 Teddington TW11.... 174 D4
Northpoint BR1.....187 A2
Northpoint Cl SM1...218 A5
Northpoint Sq 8 NW1..................71 D2
North Point UB7..... 104 A5
North Pole La BR2 ...225 A2
North Pole Rd W10 ...90 C2
Northport St N1 .... 235 D5
North Prim Sch UB1 ....107 B6
North Rd
 Barnsbury N7 ....72 A2
 Brentford TW8...... 132 A6
 Bromley BR1 ....187 B2
 Dagenham RM6.......59 A4
 Ealing W5 .... 109 D3
 East Bedfont TW14 ...149 B5
 Edgware HA8.........26 D2
 Edmonton N9..........18 B3
 Erith DA17......... 125 D4
 Finchley N2 ....30 C2
 Hayes UB3...........83 B2
 Heston TW5........ 128 C6
 Highgate N6 ....49 A2
 Ilford IG3 ....79 C6
 Plumstead SE18 .... 123 C2
 Richmond TW9...... 132 C3
 Southall UB1 .... 107 C6
 Surbiton KT6 .... 197 D3
 West Drayton UB7....104 B3
 1 West Wickham BR4............ 207 D1
 Wimbledon SW19 ... 180 A4
North Residence IG3.. 58 B4
North Ride W2.........114 C6 247 A5
North Rise W2...... 237 B1
Northrop Rd TW6 ....127 C4
North Row W1.........115 A6 248 A6
NORTH SHEEN 132 C3
North Sheen Sta TW10.............. 132 C1
Northside Prim Sch N12 ....30 A5
Northside Rd BR1....187 A2
North Side Wandsworth Comm SW18 ....158 B6
Northspur Rd SM1 ...217 C5
North Sq Edmonton N9 . 18 B2
 Hampstead Garden Suburb NW11.......47 C4
North St Barking IG11 ..79 A1
 Bexleyheath DA7.... 147 C1
 Bromley BR1 .... 187 A2
 Carshalton SM5..... 218 D4
 Clapham SW4 ...... 137 C2
Northstead Rd SW2 ..160 C2
North St Hendon NW4 . 46 C4
 Isleworth TW7...... 131 A2
 Newham E13 ....99 B5
North Tenter St E1 .. 243 D1
North Terr SW3 ..... 257 A5
Northumberland Alley EC3 .... 243 B1
Northumberland Ave
 Enfield EN1 ....6 B4
 Falconwood DA16 .... 145 C2
 Hounslow TW7 ..... 130 D4
 Wanstead E12.........55 C1
 Westminster WC2..... 116 A5 250 A4
Northumberland Cl TW19...............148 A5
Northumberland Cres TW14..............149 C5
Northumberland Ct
 3 Hounslow TW3............ 129 D1
 South Croydon CR2 .. 221 C3
Northumberland Gdns
 Brentford TW7...... 131 A5
 Bromley BR1 .... 210 C5
 Edmonton N9.........17 D1
Northumberland Gdns continued
 Mitcham CR4....... 203 D4
Northumberland Gr N17 ....34 B3
Northumberland Heath Prim Sch DA8...... 147 D5
Northumberland Ho
 Finchley N12 ....29 D4
 Kentish Town NW5 ....71 C2
Northumberland Mans E5...................74 C4
Northumberland Park Com Sch N17.......34 A3
Northumberland Park Ind Est N17.........34 B3
Northumberland Park Sports Ctr N17......34 A3
Northumberland Park Sta N17...........34 B3
Northumberland Pk
 Erith DA8.......... 147 D5
 Tottenham N17 ....34 A3
Northumberland Pl
 Notting Hill W2 ....91 C1
 26 Richmond TW10.. 153 D6
Northumberland Rd
 Harrow HA2 ....41 C4
 New Barnet EN5 ......14 A4
 Newham E6........ 100 A1
 Walthamstow E17 .....53 C2
Northumberland St WC2............... 250 A4
Northumbria Ct 10 TW9...............132 A1
Northumbria St E14...97 C1
North Verbena Gdns 2 W6................112 A1
Northview Cres NW10................67 D4
Northview Dr IG8.....37 D1
North View W5 ....87 C3
Northview 1 N7.......72 A5
North View HA5.......40 C2
Northview Prim Sch NW10.................67 D4
North View Rd N8.....49 D6
North View SW19 ....178 C5
North Villas NW1.....71 D2
Northway Cir NW7 ....27 B6
Northway Cres NW7...27 C6
Northway Ct NW7.....27 B6
North Way N11 ....31 C4
Northway NW11 ......47 D4
North Way N9 ....18 D2
Northway SM4.......201 A5
North Way
 Pinner HA5 ....40 D5
 Queensbury NW9 .....44 D6
Northway Rd
 Camberwell SE5 .... 139 A2
 Croydon CR0 .... 205 D2
Northway Sch NW7 ...11 B1
Northways Par 2 NW3.................70 B1
North Way UB10 ......60 A1
Northway SM6.......219 C4
Northweald La KT2 ..175 D5
NORTH WEMBLEY ...65 C6
North Wembley Sta HA0, HA9 ....65 D5
North Western Ave (Tylers Way) WD23 ... 8 C6
North Western Ave (Watford By-Pass) WD6.................9 B4
Northwest Pl N1.... 234 B4
North Wharf Rd W2..........92 B2 236 C3
Northwick Ave HA3 ...43 B3
Northwick Circ HA3...43 C3
Northwick Cl
 Harrow HA1 ....43 B1
 Lisson Gr NW8.......92 B3 236 C6
Northwick Ho NW8 . 236 B6
Northwick Park Hospl HA1 ....43 A2
Northwick Park Rd HA1 ....42 D3
Northwick Park Sta HA3 ....43 B2
Northwick Rd
 South Oxhey WD19 ....22 C6
 Wembley HA0 ....87 D6
Northwick Terr NW8.........92 B3 236 C6
North Wlk
 Bayswater W2...... 114 A6 246 A5
 New Addington CR0 .. 224 A3
Northwold Dr HA5 ....40 C6
Northwold Prim Sch E5.................74 A6
Northwold Rd E5, N16 ....74 A6
NORTHWOOD 22 A3
Northwood Gdns
 Greenford UB6 ....64 D3
 Ilford IG5 ....56 C5
 North Finchley N12....30 B5
NORTHWOOD HILLS 22 A1
Northwood Hills Cir HA6 ....22 A2
Northwood Hills Sta HA6 ....22 A1
North Wood Lo NW3 ..69 D4
Northwood & Pinner Com Hospl HA6.....22 A2
Northwood Pl DA18 ..125 B3
Northwood Prim Sch DA18 ....125 B3
Northwood Rd
 Forest Hill SE23......163 B3
 Highgate N6 ....49 B2
 South Norwood CR7 . 183 A1
 Wallington SM5..... 219 A2
Northwood Sch HA6 ..22 A2
Northwood Twr 1 E17...................54 A5
Northwood Way
 Northwood HA6.......22 A3
 1 West Norwood SE19............. 183 C4
NORTH WOOLWICH 122 D4
North Woolwich Rdbt E16..................121 D5
North Woolwich Rd E16..................121 B5
North Worple Way SW14..............133 B2
Norton Ave KT5......198 D2
Norton Cl
 Chingford E4 ....35 C5
 Enfield EN1 ....6 B3
Norton Ct
 Beckenham BR3 .....185 B2
 Ilford IG2 ....57 B3
Norton Folgate E1 .. 243 B4
Norton Gdns SW16...182 A1
Norton Ho
 14 Globe Town E2.....96 D5
 6 New Malden KT3 . 199 C5
 30 Stepney E1........96 B1
 16 Stockwell SW9.....138 B3
Norton Rd
 Walthamstow E10 .....53 B1
 Wembley HA0 ....65 D2
Norval Gn 1 SW9....138 C3
Norval Rd HA0........43 B1
Norvic Ho 5 SE5 .....139 A3
Norway Gate SE16 ...119 A3
Norway Pl E14........97 B1
Norway St SE10......141 D6
Norwegian Sch The SW20.............. 178 C3
Norwich Cres RM6 ....58 B4
Norwich Ho 6 E14....97 D1
Norwich Mews IG3 ...58 A1
Norwich Pl 7 DA6 ...147 C1
Norwich Rd
 Forest Gate E7 ....77 A3
 Greenford UB6 ....85 D6
 Northwood HA6.......39 D6
 South Norwood CR7 . 205 A6
Norwich St EC4 ....94 C1 241 A2
Norwich Wlk HA8.....27 A3
Norwood Ave HA0 ....88 B5
Norwood Cl
 Cricklewood NW2 .....69 A5
 Southall UB2 .... 107 C2
 Twickenham TW2.....152 B2
Norwood Dr HA2......41 C3
Norwood Gdns
 Hayes UB4...........84 C3
 Southall UB2 ....107 B2
NORWOOD GREEN 107 C2
Norwood Green Inf Sch UB2 ....107 B1
Norwood Green Jun Sch UB2.......... 107 A1
Norwood Green Rd UB2 ....107 C2
Norwood Heights Sh Ctr 13 SE19........... 183 C4
Norwood High St SE27...............183 A6
Norwood Ho 25 E14..119 D6
Norwood Hospl SE19...............183 B4
Norwood Junction Sta SE25................ 206 A5
NORWOOD NEW TOWN 183 A4
Norwood Park Rd SE27...............183 A5
Norwood Rd
 Southall UB2 .... 107 C2
 West Norwood SE24, SE27............ 160 D3

Norwood Sch SE19 183 A5
Norwood Terr UB2 107 D2
Notley St SE5 139 B5
Notre Dame RC Girls Sch SE1 116 D3 261 D5
Notre Dame RC Prim Sch SE18 144 D6
Notson Rd SE25 206 B5
Notting Barn Rd W10 90 D3
Nottingdale Sq W11 244 A4
Nottingham Ave E16 99 C1
Nottingham Ct WC2 240 A1
Nottingham Ho
■33 Camberwell SE5 139 A3
Stoke Newington N4 51 A1
Nottingham Pl W1 93 A2 238 A4
Nottingham Rd
Croydon CR2 221 A3
Isleworth TW7 130 D3
Leytonstone E10 54 A3
Upper Tooting SW17 158 D3
Nottingham St W1 238 A4
Nottingham Terr NW1 238 A5
NOTTING HILL 113 B6
Notting Hill & Ealing High Sch W13 87 B2
Notting Hill Gate Sta W11 113 C5 245 A4
Notting Hill Gate W11 113 C5 245 A4
Nottingwood Ho W11 244 A6
Nova Bldg ■1 E14 119 C2
Nova Ct E ■3 E14 120 A5
Nova Ct W ■2 E14 120 A5
Nova Mews SM4 201 A2
Novar Cl BR6 211 D2
Nova Rd CR0 205 A2
Novar Rd SE9 167 A3
Novello St SW6 135 C4 265 A2
Nowell Rd SW13 134 A6
Nower Ct HA5 41 B5
NOWER HILL 41 B6
Nower Hill High Sch HA5 41 C5
Nower Hill HA5 41 B5
Noyna Rd SW17 158 D1
Nubia Way SE6 164 C1
Nucleus NW10 89 A4
Nuding Cl SE13 141 C2
Nuffield Ct TW5 129 B5
Nuffield Lo ■14 W9 91 C2
Nugent Ct
Streatham SW16 181 C6
■3 Upper Holloway N19 50 A1
Nugent Rd
Finsbury Pk N19 50 A1
South Norwood SE25 205 D6
Nugents Ct HA5 23 A2
Nugent's Pk HA5 23 B2
Nugent Terr NW8 92 A5 229 B3
Numa Ct TW8 131 D5
Nun Ct EC2 242 C2
Nuneaton Rd RM9 81 A1
Nuneham SW16 181 D6
NUNHEAD 140 C1
Nunhead Cres SE15 140 B2
Nunhead Gn SE15 140 B2
Nunhead Gr SE15 140 C2
Nunhead La SE15 140 B2
Nunhead Sta SE15 140 C3
Nunnington Cl SE9 166 A1
Nunn's Rd EN2 5 A3
Nupton Dr EN5 12 C5
Nurse Cl HA8 27 A2
Nursery Ave
Bexleyheath DA7 147 B2
Croydon CR0 222 D6
Finchley N3 30 A1
Nursery Cl
Broom Hill BR6 211 D2
Croydon CR0 222 D6
Dagenham RM6 58 D3
Enfield EN3 6 D4
Feltham TW14 150 B4
New Cross SE4 141 B3
Putney SW15 134 D1
Woodford IG8 37 B5
Nursery Ct
Ealing W13 87 A2
■8 Tottenham N17 33 D3
Nursery Gdns
Chislehurst BR7 188 D4
Enfield EN3 6 D4
Hampton TW13 173 B6
Hounslow TW4 151 B6
Sunbury TW16 171 D1
Nursery La
Forest Gate E7 77 A2
Hillingdon UB8 82 A3
North Kensington W10 90 C2
Shoreditch E2 95 D6
Nurserymans Rd N11 15 A2
Nursery Rd
Finchley N2 30 B2
Hackney E9 74 C2
Loughton IG10 21 C6
Merton SW19 179 D1
Mitcham CR4 202 C6
Osidge N14 15 C4
Pinner HA5 40 C6
South Norwood CR7 205 B5
Stockwell SW9 138 B1
Sunbury TW16 171 D1
Sutton SM1 218 A4
Wimbledon SW19 179 A3
Nursery Row SE17 262 C3
Nursery St N17 33 D3
Nursery Walk Ct NW4 46 B6
Nursery Wlk NW4 46 C6
Nurstead Rd DA8 147 C5
Nutborn Ho SW19 178 D4
Nutbourne St W10 91 A4
Nutbrook St SE15 140 A2
Nutbrowne Rd RM9 103 B6
Nutchford EN1 17 C5
Nutcroft Rd SE15 140 B5
Nutfield Cl
Carshalton SM5 218 C5
Edmonton N18 34 A4
Nutfield Gdns
Ilford IG3 80 A6
Northolt UB5 84 C5
Nutfield Pl ■1 CR7 204 D5
Nutfield Rd
Dollis Hill NW2 68 A5
East Dulwich SE22 139 D1
Leyton E15 76 A4
Thornton Heath CR7 204 D5
Nutfield Way BR6 226 D6
Nutford Pl W1 92 D1 237 C2
Nuthatch Cl TW19 148 B3
Nuthatch Gdns SE28 123 B4
Nuthurst Ave SW2 160 B2
Nutkin Wlk UB8 60 A1
Nutley Terr NW3 70 B2
Nutmeg Cl E16 98 C3
Nutmeg La E14 98 B1
Nuttall St N1 95 C5
Nutter La E11 55 C4
Nutt Gr HA8 9 D2
Nutt St SE15 139 D5
Nutty La TW17 193 A6
Nutwell St SW17 180 C5
Nuxley Rd DA17 125 C1
NW London Jewish Day Sch NW6 69 A1
Nyanza St SE18 145 B6
Nye Bevan Est E5 74 D5
Nye Bevan Ho SW6 264 C4
Nye's Wharf SE1, SE15 140 A6
Nylands Ave TW9 132 C3
Nymans Gdns SW20 200 B6
Nynehead St SE14 141 A5
Nyon Gr SE6 163 B2
Nyton Cl N19 50 A1

O

O2 Millennium Dome The* SE10 120 C5
Oak Apple Ct SE12 165 A3
Oak Ave
Croydon CR0 223 D6
Enfield EN2 4 B5
Hampton TW12, TW13 173 A4
Heston TW5 129 A5
Hornsey N8 50 A5
Muswell Hill N10 31 B3
Tottenham N17 33 C3
Uxbridge UB10 60 D6
West Drayton UB7 104 C3
Oakbank Ave KT12 195 B2
Oakbank Gr SE24 139 A1
Oak Bank CR0 224 A2
Oakbark Ho ■10 TW8 131 C5
Oakbrook ■8 BR3 185 D1
Oakbrook Cl BR1 187 B6
Oakbury Rd SW6 135 D3
Oak Cl
East Barnet N14 15 B4
Sutton SM1 218 A6
Oakcombe Cl KT3 177 C2
Oak Cottage Cl ■11 SE6 164 D3
Oak Cotts W7 108 C4
Oakcourt ■17 SE15 139 D5
Oak Cres E16 98 C2
Oakcroft Bsns Ctr KT9 214 B4
Oakcroft Cl HA5 22 B1
Oakcroft Ct SE3 143 A4
Oakcroft Ho ■8 KT3 199 C2
Oakcroft Rd
Chessington KT9 214 B4
Lewisham SE13 142 B3
Oakcroft SE12 165 B1
Oakcroft Villas KT9 214 B4
Oak Ct Bickley BR1 188 B1
Chingford E4 35 D4
Oakdale Ave
Harrow HA3 44 A4
Pinner HA6 22 A1
Oakdale BR3 186 A1
Oakdale Cl WD19 22 C6
Oakdale Ct
Chingford E4 36 A5
Upper Holloway N19 72 A6
Oakdale N14 15 B3
Oakdale Gdns E4 36 A5
Oakdale Inf Sch E18 37 B1
Oakdale Jun Sch E18 37 B1
Oakdale Lo NW4 29 A2
Oakdale Rd
Leyton E11 76 B6
Nunhead SE15 140 C2
South Oxhey WD19 22 C6
Streatham SW16 182 A5
Tottenham N4 51 B3
Upton E7 77 B1
Woodford E18 37 B1
Oakdale Way CR4 203 A2
Oakdene Ave
Chislehurst West BR7 188 C5
Thames Ditton KT7 197 A1
Oakdene Cl HA5 23 B3
Oakdene Ct
Feltham TW12 173 B6
■1 Streatham SW16 182 A5
Oakdene Dr KT5 199 A1
Oak Dene W13 87 B2
Oakdene Ho
Enfield EN2 4 D2
■11 Stamford Hill N16 51 C1
Oakdene Lo ■3 SE20 184 B3
Oakdene Mews SM3 201 B1
Oakdene ■3 SE15 140 B4
Oakdene Pk N3 29 B3
Oakdene Rd
Hillingdon UB10 82 D5
Orpington BR5 211 D4
Oakdene ■1 SE19 183 C5
Oakden St SE11 116 C2 261 B4
Oake Ct SW15 157 A6
Oakeford Ho W14 254 B5
Oakend Ho ■10 N4 51 B2
Oaken Dr KT10 212 D2
Oakenholt Ho ■1 SE2 124 D4
Oaken La KT10 212 C3
Oakenshaw Cl KT6 198 A2
Oakes Cl E6 100 B1
Oakeshott Ave N6 71 A6
Oakey La SE1 261 A6
Oak Farm WD6 11 A6
Oak Farm Jun & Inf Schs UB10 82 D6
Oakfield Ave HA3 43 B6
Oakfield E4 35 D5
Oakfield Cl
New Malden KT3 199 D4
Ruislip HA4 39 D3
Oakfield Ct
Clapham Pk SW4 160 A5
■2 Ealing W5 110 C5
Finchley N3 29 D2
Finsbury Pk N8 50 A2
Hendon NW2 46 D2
South Croydon CR2 221 A2
Oakfield Gdns
Beckenham BR3 207 C4
Carshalton SM5 202 D1
Edmonton N18 33 C6
Greenford UB6 86 B4
■3 West Norwood SE19 183 C5
Oakfield Ho ■2 IG1 78 D5
Oakfield La BR2 225 C4
Oakfield Lo ■8 IG1 78 D5
Oakfield Prep Sch SE21 161 B3
Oakfield Rd
Ashford TW15 170 D5
Croydon CR0 205 A1
Finchley N3 29 D2
Finsbury Pk N4 50 C2
Higham Hill E17 35 A1
Ilford IG1 78 D5
Newham E6 100 A6
Palmers Green N14 16 A2
Oakfield Rd *continued*
Penge SE20 184 B3
Wimbledon SW19 156 D1
Oakfield Road Ind Est ■11 SE20 184 B3
Oakfields Rd NW11 47 A3
Oakfield St SW10 136 A6 266 A6
Oakfields KT12 194 A1
Oakford Rd NW5 71 C4
Oak Gdns
Croydon CR0 223 C6
Hendon HA8 27 A1
Oak Grove Rd SE20 184 C1
Oak Gr Ruislip HA4 40 B1
Sunbury TW16 172 B3
West Hampstead NW2 69 A4
West Wickham BR4 208 A1
Oakhall Ct
Ashford TW16 171 D5
Wanstead E11 55 B3
Oakhall Dr TW16 171 D5
Oak Hall Rd E11 55 B3
Oakham Cl
Cockfosters EN4 2 D2
Forest Hill SE6 163 B2
Oakham Dr BR2 208 D5
Oakham Ho ■5 W10 90 C3
Oakhampton Rd NW7 28 D3
Oakhill Ave
Pinner HA5 23 A1
West Hampstead NW3 69 D4
Oak Hill IG8 36 C3
Oakhill KT10 213 A2
Oak Hill Cl IG8 36 B3
Oakhill Coll N14 15 A5
Oak Hill Cres
Chingford IG8 36 C3
Surbiton KT6 198 A2
Oak Hill Ct IG8 36 C3
Oakhill Ct
Honor Oak SE23 162 C5
Putney SW15 157 B6
■8 Surbiton KT6 198 A3
Wimbledon SW19 178 D3
Oak Hill Gdns E4 36 C2
Oak Hill Gr KT6 198 A3
Oakhill Ho BR5 190 A2
Oak Hill Lo NW3 69 D4
Oakhill Mans E4 14 C5
Oak Hill Park Mews NW3 70 A4
Oak Hill Pk NW3 69 D4
Oakhill Pl SW15 157 C6
Oakhill Prim Sch IG8 36 C4
Oakhill Rd
Beckenham BR3 186 A1
Orpington BR6 227 D6
Putney SW15 157 B6
Oak Hill Rd KT6 198 A3
Oakhill Rd
Sutton SM1 218 A5
Thornton Heath SW16 182 B2
Oak Hill KT6 198 A2
Oak Hill Way NW3 70 A4
Oak Ho
■13 Cubitt Town E14 120 A4
■11 Finchley N2 30 B1
■8 Maitland Pk NW3 70 D2
Penge SE20 184 B1
■2 Richmond TW9 132 D4
■13 Sidcup DA15 168 A1
■9 Stoke Newington N16 73 B6
Teddington TW11 175 C4
Oakhouse Rd DA6 169 C6
Oak Ho N22 32 A3
Oakhurst Ave
East Barnet EN4 14 C4
Erith DA7 147 A5
Oakhurst Cl
Chislehurst BR7 188 B2
Snaresbrook E17 54 C5
■4 Teddington TW11 174 C5
Oakhurst Ct E17 54 C5
Oakhurst Gdns
Chingford E4 20 D3
Erith DA7 147 A5
Snaresbrook E11, E17 54 C5
Oakhurst Gr SE22 140 A1
Oakhurst Rd KT19 215 B2
Oakington Ave
Harrow HA2 41 C2
Hayes UB3 105 B2
Wembley HA9 66 B5
Oakington Cl TW16 172 C1
Oakington Ct ■1 EN2 4 D3
Oakington Dr TW16 172 C1
Oakington ■14 KT1 176 C1
Oakington Manor Dr HA9 66 C3
Oakington Manor Prim Sch HA9 66 D3
Oakington Rd W9 91 C3
Oakington Way N8 50 A2
Oak La Finchley N2 30 B1
Friern Barnet N11 31 D4
Isleworth TW7 130 C1
Limehouse E14 119 B6
Oakland Pl IG9 21 A2
Oakland Rd E15 76 C4
Oaklands Ave
Enfield N9 18 B5
Hounslow TW7 130 D6
Sidcup DA15 167 D4
Thames Ditton KT10 196 B1
Thornton Heath CR7 204 C5
West Wickham BR4 223 D5
Oaklands BR7 189 B4
Oaklands Cl
Bexley DA6 169 B6
Chessington KT9 213 C4
Orpington BR5 211 C3
Oaklands CR0 220 D3
Oaklands Ct
Beckenham BR3 186 A1
Dagenham NW10 89 C6
Orpington BR6 227 A6
■5 Shepherd's Bush W12 112 B5
Wembley HA0 65 D3
Oaklands Dr TW2 152 A4
Oaklands W13 87 A2
Oaklands Gr W12 112 A5
Oaklands Ho SE4 141 B2
Oaklands Mews ■1 NW2 68 D4
Oaklands Park Ave IG1 79 A6
Oaklands Pas NW2 68 D4
Oaklands Pl ■8 SW4 137 D1
Oaklands Prim Sch W7 108 D4
Oaklands Rd
Barnet N20 13 B4
Bexley DA6 169 B6
Bromley BR1 186 C3
Cricklewood NW2 68 D4
Ealing W7 108 D4
Mortlake SW14 133 B2
West Ealing W7, W13 109 A4
Oaklands Sch
Hounslow TW3 130 B2
Loughton IG10 21 D6
Oaklands Sec Sch E2 96 B4
Oaklands
Southgate N21 16 B2
Twickenham TW2 152 A4
Oaklands Way SM6 219 D1
Oakland Way KT19 215 C2
Oak La TW1 153 A4
Oaklawn Ct HA7 25 B4
Oak La IG8 36 D6
Oakleafe Gdns IG6 56 D6
Oaklea Pas KT1 197 D6
Oakleigh Ave
East Barnet N20 14 C3
Edgware HA8 26 D2
Tolworth KT6 214 D6
Oakleigh Cl N20 14 D1
Oakleigh Cres N20 14 C1
Oakleigh Ct
East Barnet EN4 14 C5
Hendon HA8 27 A1
■7 Penge SE20 184 B3
Southall UB1 107 B5
Surbiton KT6 214 B6
Oakleigh Gdns
Edgware HA8 26 B5
Oakleigh Pk N20 14 B3
Orpington BR6 227 C4
Oakleigh Lodge IG3 80 A5
Oakleigh Mews ■2 N20 14 A2
OAKLEIGH PARK 14 B3
Oakleigh Park Ave BR7 188 C2
Oakleigh Park Sta EN4 14 C4
Oakleigh Pk N N20 14 B3
Oakleigh Pk S N20 14 C3
Oakleigh Rd UB10 61 A1
Oakleigh Rd N N20 14 C2
Oakleigh Rd HA5 23 B4
Oakleigh Rd S N11 31 A6
Oakleigh Sch N20 14 D1
Oakleigh Way
Mitcham CR4 181 B2
■1 Tolworth KT6 198 D1
Oakley Ave
Barking IG11 79 D1
Ealing W5 110 C6
Wallington CR0 220 A4
Oakley Cl
Chingford E4 20 A1
Ealing W7 108 C6
Hounslow TW7 130 B4
■7 Newham E6 100 A1
Oakley Cres EC1 234 D3
Oakley Ct
Carshalton CR4 203 A2
Harlington UB7 127 A5
Wembley HA0 65 A4
Oakley Dr
Keston Mark BR2 226 A5
Lewisham SE13 164 B5
New Eltham SE9 167 B3
Oakley Gdns
Chelsea SW3 136 C6 267 B6
Hornsey Vale N8 50 B4
Oakley Ho
Chelsea SW1 257 D4
Ealing W5 110 C6
Oakley Pk DA5 168 C4
Oakley Pl SE1 117 D1 263 C1
Oakley Rd
Croydon SE25 206 B4
De Beauvoir Town N1 73 B1
Harrow HA1 42 C3
Keston Mark BR2 226 A6
Oakley Sq NW1 93 C5 232 B4
Oakley St SW3 136 C6 267 A6
Oakley Wlk W6 134 D6
Oak Lo ■4 TW16 171 D3
Oak Lodge Cl HA7 25 C5
Oak Lodge Dr BR4 207 D2
Oak Lodge Sch
Balham SW12 159 A4
East Finchley N2 48 A5
Oaklodge Way NW7 27 D4
Oak Lodge ■14 SE21 161 B2
Oak Lo Southgate N21 16 B5
■10 Sutton SM1 218 A4
Wanstead E11 55 A2
■6 Wembley HA0 65 D3
Oakman Ho ■29 SW19 156 D3
Oakmead Ave BR2 209 A3
Oakmead Ct HA7 25 C6
Oakmeade HA5 23 C4
Oakmead Gdns HA8 27 B6
Oakmead HA1 64 B5
Oakmead Pl CR4 180 C2
Oakmead Rd
Balham SW12 159 B3
Wallington CR0 203 D3
Oakmere Rd SE2 146 A6
Oakmont Pl ■6 BR6 211 B1
Oak Park Gdns SW19 156 D3
Oak Park Mews N16 73 D5
Oak Rd Ealing W5 109 D6
Kingston u T KT3 177 B1
Oakridge Dr N2 48 B6
Oakridge La BR1 186 B5
Oakridge Rd BR1 186 C6
Oak Rise IG9 21 D1
Oak Row CR4 181 C1
Oaks Ave
Feltham TW13 151 A2
North Cheam KT4 216 B4
West Norwood SE19 183 C5
Oaksford Ave SE26 162 B1
Oaks Gr E4 20 C2
Oakshade Rd BR1 186 B6
Oakshaw Rd SW18 157 D4
Oakshott Ct NW1 232 C3
Oaks La Ilford IG2 57 C5
South Croydon CR0 222 C5
Oaks Park High Sch IG2 57 C4
Oaks Rd CR0 222 C4
Oaks Sh Ctr The W3 111 A5
Oaks The
Brondesbury Pk NW6 68 D1
Chingford IG8 36 C3
Enfield EN2 4 D2
Finchley N12 29 D6
Hayes UB4 83 A5
Long Ditton KT6 213 C5
Ruislip HA4 39 C2
Southborough BR2 210 C3
Wallington SM6 219 C4
Willesden NW10 68 B1
Wimbledon SW19 179 A4
Woolwich SE18 123 A1
Oaks Way
Surbiton KT6 197 D1
Wallington SM5 218 D1
Oakthorpe Ct N13 33 A5

Oakthorpe Prim Sch N13 33 A5
Oakthorpe Rd N13 32 C5
Oaktree Ave N13 16 D1
Oak Tree Ave N2 47 D6
Oak Tree Cl
Ealing W5 87 C1
Stanmore HA7 25 C3
Oak Tree Ct
Acton W3 110 D6
8 Clapham Pk SW4 160 A6
Elstree WD6 9 D5
Oak Tree Dell NW9 45 B4
Oak Tree Dr N20 13 D3
Oak Tree Gdns BR1 187 B5
Oaktree Gr IG1 79 B3
Oak Tree Ho W9 91 D3
Oak Tree Rd NW8 92 C4 230 A1
Oaktree Sch EN4 15 A5
Oaktrees Hostel HA8 11 A2
Oakview Gdns N2 48 B5
Oakview Gr CR0 207 A1
Oakview Lo NW11 47 B2
Oakview Rd SE6 185 D5
Oak Village NW5 71 A4
Oakway BR2 186 B1
Oakway Cl DA5 169 A5
Oak Way
Croydon CR0 206 D3
East Acton W3 111 C5
East Barnet N14 15 B4
East Bedfont TW14 149 C3
Oakways SE9 166 D5
Oakway SW20 200 C5
Oakwell Ho 24 SW8 137 D3
Oak Wlk CR4 203 A1
OAKWOOD 15 D6
Oakwood Ave
Beckenham BR2, BR3 186 A1
Bromley BR2 209 B6
Mitcham CR4 180 B1
Osidge N14 15 D4
Southall UB1 107 C6
Oakwood Cl
Chislehurst West BR7 188 C4
Lewisham SE13 164 B5
Southgate N14 15 C5
Oakwood Cres
Southgate N21 16 B5
Wembley UB6 65 B2
Oakwood Ct
Beckenham BR3 186 A1
6 Chingford E4 20 C4
Kensington W14 113 B3 254 C6
1 Newham E6 100 A6
17 Sutton SM1 218 A4
Oakwood Dr
Burnt Oak HA8 27 A4
West Norwood SE19 183 C4
Oakwood Gdns
Ilford IG3 79 D6
Orpington BR6 227 A6
Sutton SM1 217 C6
Oakwood La W14 113 B3 254 C6
Oakwood Park Rd N14 16 A5
Oakwood Pl CR0 204 C3
Oakwood Rd
Hampstead Garden Suburb NW11 47 D4
Orpington BR6 227 A6
Pinner HA5 22 B1
Thornton Heath CR0 204 C3
Wimbledon SW20 178 A2
Oakwood Sta N14 15 C6
Oakwood View N14 15 D4
Oakworth Rd W10 90 D2
Oarsman Pl KT8 196 C5
Oasis The 6 BR1 187 C1
Oast Ct 8 E14 119 B6
Oast Lo W4 133 C5
Oates Cl BR2 208 B6
Oatfield Ho 1 N15 51 C3
Oatfield Rd BR6 211 D1
Oat La EC2 95 A1 242 B2
Oatland Rise E17 35 A1
Oatlands Ct 3 SW19 156 D3
Oatlands Dr KT13 193 C1
Oatlands Rd EN3 6 C4
Oatwell Ho SW3 257 B3
Oban Cl E13 99 C3
Oban Ct HA8 10 D2
Oban Ho
5 Barking IG11 101 B5
South Bromley E14 98 B1
Oban Rd Newham E13 99 C4
South Norwood SE25 205 B5
Oban St E14 98 B1
Oberon Ho 5 N1 95 C5
Oberon Way TW17 192 A6
Oberstein Rd 15 SW11 136 B1
Oborne Cl SE24 160 D6
O'Brian Ho 10 E1 96 D4
Observatory Gdns W8 245 B2
Observatory Mews E14 120 B2
Observatory Rd SW14 133 A1
Occupation La
Brentford W5 109 D2
Shooters Hill SE18 144 D4
Occupation Rd
Newington SE17 117 A1 262 A2
West Ealing W13 109 B4
Ocean St E1 96 D2
Ocean Wharf E14 119 C4
Ochre Ct TW13 149 D1
Ockbrook 3 E1 96 C2
Ockendon Rd N1 73 B2
Ockham Dr BR5 190 A3
Ockley Ct
Sidcup DA14 167 C1
Sutton SM1 218 A4
Ockley Ho 8 KT2 176 D4
Ockley Rd
Streatham SW16 160 A1
Thornton Heath CR0 204 B2
Octagon Arc EC2 243 A3
Octagon The NW3 69 C4
Octavia Cl CR4 202 C4
Octavia Ho
Catford SE6 163 D4
Kensal Town W10 91 A3
Octavia Mews 1 W9 91 B3
Octavia Rd TW7 130 D2
Octavia St SW11 136 C4 267 B1
Octavia Way 12 SE28 124 B6
Octavius St SE8 141 C5
October Ct BR2 208 D6
October Pl NW4 46 D6
Odard Rd KT8 195 C5
Odell Cl IG11 79 D1
Odell Wlk SE13 142 A2
Odeon Ct
Dagenham NW10 89 C6
1 Newham E16 99 A2
Odeon Par
Eltham SE9 144 A1
Wembley UB6 65 B2
Odeon The IG11 79 B1
Odessa Inf Sch E7 77 A3
Odessa Rd Leyton E7 76 D4
Willesden Green NW10 90 A5
Odessa St SE16 119 B3
Odette Ct N20 14 A1
Odette Duval Ho 29 E1 96 C2
Odette Ho 6 SE27 183 B6
Odger St SW11 136 D3
Odhams Wlk WC2 240 B1
Odin Ho 6 SE5 139 A3
O'Donnell Ct WC1 240 B6
O'Driscoll Ho 4 W12 90 B1
Odyssey Bsns Pk HA4 62 B3
Offa's Mead E9 75 A4
Offenbach Ho 12 E2 96 D5
Offenham Rd BR7, SE9 188 B6
Offers Ct KT1 198 B6
Offerton Rd SW4 137 C2
Offham Ho SE17 263 A3
Offham Slope N12 29 B5
Offley Ho 10 E9 74 D2
Offley Pl TW7 130 B3
Offley Rd SW9 138 C5
Offord Cl N17 34 A4
Offord Rd N1 72 B1
Offord St N1 72 B1
Ogden Ho TW13 173 A6
Ogilby St SE18 122 B2
Ogilvie Ho 12 E1 96 D1
Oglander Rd SE15 139 D2
Ogle St W1 93 C2 239 A4
Oglethorpe Rd RM10 81 C5
O'Gorman Ho SW10 266 B4
O'Grady Ct 17 W13 109 A5
O'Grady Ho 17 E17 53 D6
Ohio Bldg 13 SE13 141 D4
Ohio Rd E13 98 D3
Oil Mill La W6 112 A1
Okeburn Rd SW17 181 A5
Okehampton Cl N12 30 B5
Okehampton Cres DA16 146 C4
Okehampton Rd NW10 90 D6
Okeover Manor SW4 137 B1
Olaf Palme Ho TW13 150 B1
Olaf St W11 112 D6
Old Bailey EC4 94 D1 241 D1
Old Barn Cl SM2 217 A1
Old Barrack Yd SW1 248 A1
Old Barrowfield 7 E15 98 C6
Old Bellgate Wharf E14 119 C3
Oldberry Rd HA8 27 B4
Old Bethnal Green Rd E2 96 B4
OLD BEXLEY 169 D4
Old Bexley Bsns Pk DA5 169 D4
Old Bexley CE Prim Sch DA5 169 B3
Old Billingsgate Wlk EC3 253 A5
Old Bldgs WC2 241 A2
Old Bond St W1 115 C6 249 A5
Oldborough Rd HA0 65 C5
Old Brewery Mews NW3 70 B4
Old Bridge Cl UB5 85 C5
Old Bridge St KT1 175 D1
Old Broad St EC2 95 B1 242 D2
Old Bromley Rd BR1 186 B5
Old Brompton Rd SW5, SW7 114 A2 256 B3
Old Burlington St W1 115 C6 249 A5
Oldbury Ct E9 75 A3
Oldbury Pl W1 93 A2 238 B4
Oldbury Rd EN1 6 A3
Old Castle St E1 95 D1 243 D2
Old Cavendish St W1 238 C1
Old Change Ct EC4 242 A1
Old Chapel Pl 2 N10 49 B6
Old Charlton Rd TW17 193 A4
Old Chiswick Yd W4 133 C6
Old Church Ct N11 31 B5
Old Church La
Ealing UB6 87 A4
Stanmore HA7 25 C4
Welsh Harp NW9 67 B6
Old Church Path KT10 212 A4
Old Church Rd
Chingford E4 19 C1
Stepney E1 96 D1
Old Church St SW3 256 D1
Old Claygate La KT10 213 A3
Old Clem Sq 12 SE18 144 C6
Old College Ct DA17 125 D1
Old Compton St W1 93 D1 239 C1
Old Cote Dr TW5 129 C6
Old Court Ho W8 245 C1
Old Court (Mus & Liby)* HA0 65 C3
Old Court Pl W8 113 D4 245 C1
Old Covent Gdn* WC2 250 B6
Old Ctyd The BR1 187 B2
Old Cty H* SE1 250 C2
Old Dairy Mews
5 Balham SW12 159 A3
4 Camden Town NW5 71 B2
Old Dairy Sq The N21 16 C4
Old Deer Park Gdns TW9 132 A2
Old Devonshire Rd SW12 159 B4
Old Dock Cl TW9 132 C6
Old Dover Rd SE3 143 B5
Oldegate Ho 1 E6 99 D6
Old Farm Ave
Osidge N14 15 C4
Sidcup DA15 167 C2
Old Farm Cl TW4 129 B1
Old Farm Ct UB2 107 D2
Old Farm Rd E DA15 168 A2
Old Farm Rd
Hampton TW12 173 C4
London N2 30 B2
Old Farm Rd W DA15 167 D2
Oldfield Cl
Bromley BR1 210 B5
Greenford UB6 64 C2
Stanmore HA7 25 A5
Oldfield Farm Gdns UB6 86 B6
Oldfield Gr SE16 118 D2
Oldfield Ho
14 Chiswick W4 111 C1
Streatham SW16 181 B6
Oldfield House Unit TW12 173 B2
Oldfield La N UB6 64 B1
Oldfield La S UB6 86 A4
Oldfield Mews N6 49 C2
Oldfield Prim Sch UB6 86 B5
Oldfield Rd
Bedford Pk W3, W12 111 D4
Bexleyheath DA7 147 A3
Bromley BR1 210 B5
Hampton TW12 173 B2
Stoke Newington N16 73 C5
Willesden NW10 67 D1
Wimbledon SW19 179 A4
Oldfields Cir UB5 64 A2
Oldfields Rd SM1, SM3 217 C6
Oldfields Trad Est SM1 217 C5
Old Fire Station The SE18 144 D5
Old Fish St Hill EC4 252 A6
Old Fleet La EC4 241 C2
Old Fold Cl EN5 1 B4
Old Fold La EN5 1 B4
OLD FORD 97 B6
Old Ford Ho CR0 220 A5
Old Ford Prim Sch E3 97 B5
Old Ford Rd E2, E3 96 D5
Old Ford Trad Ctr 13 E3 97 C6
Old Forge Cl HA7 25 A6
Old Forge Cres TW17 192 D3
Old Forge Mews W12 112 B4
Old Forge Rd
Enfield EN1 5 D5
Upper Holloway N19 71 D6
Old Forge Way DA14 190 B6
Old Gloucester St WC1 94 A2 240 B4
Old Hall Cl HA5 23 A2
Old Hall Dr HA5 23 A2
Oldham Ho 10 SE21 183 C6
Oldham Terr W3 111 A5
Old Hatch Manor HA4 40 A2
Old Hill
Chislehurst BR7 188 C2
Orpington BR6 227 C2
Oldhill St N16 52 A1
Old Homesdale Rd BR2 209 C5
Old Hospital Cl SW12, SW17 158 D3
Old Ho The BR7 189 B2
Old House Cl SW19 179 A5
Old House Gdns 9 TW1 153 C5
Old Howlett's La HA4 39 B3
Olding Ho 6 SW12 159 C4
Old Jamaica Bsns Est 23 SE16 118 A3
Old Jamaica Rd SE16 118 A3
Old James St SE15 140 B2
Old Jewry EC2 95 B1 242 C1
Old Kenton La NW9 44 D4
Old Kent Rd
Deptford SE1, SE15 140 B6
Walworth SE1 117 C1 263 B2
Old Kingston Rd KT4 215 A5
Old Laundry The 14 SW18 136 B1
Old Lodge Pl 7 TW1 153 B5
Old Lodge Way HA7 25 A5
Old London Rd KT2 176 A1
Old Maidstone Rd BR8, DA14 191 B3
OLD MALDEN 199 C1
Old Malden La KT4 215 C6
Oldman Ct SE12 165 B2
Old Manor Ct NW8 229 B4
Old Manor Dr TW7 152 A5
Old Manor House Mews TW17 192 C6
Old Manor Rd UB2 106 D2
Old Manor Way BR7, SE9 188 B5
Old Manor Yd SW5 255 C3
Old Market Ct SM1 217 D4
Old Market Sq 11 E2 95 D4
Old Marylebone Rd NW1 92 C2 237 B3
Oldmead Ho 8 RM10 81 D2
Old Mill Ct E18 55 C6
Old Mill Rd SE18 145 B6
Old Mitre Ct EC4 241 B1
Old Montague St E1 96 A2
Old Nichol St E2 95 D3 243 C6
Old North St WC1 240 C4
Old Nursery Pl TW15 170 D5
OLD OAK COMMON 89 D3
Old Oak Common La NW10 89 C3
Old Oak La NW10 89 D4
Old Oak Prim Sch W12 89 D1
Old Oak Rd W3 111 D6
Old Orchard Cl
Hadley Wood EN4 2 B5
Hillingdon UB8 82 C1
Old Orch TW16 172 C1
Old Orch The NW3 70 D4
Old Palace La TW9 153 C6
Old Palace Prim Sch E3 97 D4
Old Palace Rd CR0 221 A5
Old Palace Sch of John Whitgift CR9 220 D5
Old Palace Terr 8 TW9 153 D6
Old Palace Yd 2 TW9 153 D6
Old Paradise St SE11 116 B2 260 C4
Old Park Ave
Balham SW12 159 A5
Enfield EN2 5 A1
Old Park Gr EN2 5 A1
Old Park Ho N13 32 B6
Old Park La W1 115 B5 248 C3
Old Park Mews TW5 129 B5
Old Park Rd
Enfield EN2 4 D2
Palmers Green N13 32 B6
Plumstead Comm SE2 124 A1
Old Park Rd S EN2 4 D1
Old Park Ridings N21 17 A6
Old Park View EN2 4 D2
Old Perry St BR7 189 C3
Old Post Office La SE3 143 B2
Old Pound Cl TW7 131 A4
Old Priory UB9 38 D2
Old Pye Street Est SW1 259 C5
Old Pye St SW1 259 C6
Old Quebec St W1 237 D1
Old Queen St SW1 115 D4 249 D1
Old Rd Enfield EN3 6 C4
Lewisham SE13 142 C1
Old Rectory Gdns HA8 26 C4
Old Redding HA3 24 A6
Oldridge Rd SW12 159 B4
Old Royal Free Pl N1 234 B5
Old Royal Free Sq N1 94 C6 234 B5
Old Ruislip Rd UB5 84 C5
Old St Andrews Mans NW9 67 B6
Old School Cl
3 Beckenham BR3 185 A1
Merton SW19 179 C1
Old School Cres E7 77 A2
Old School Ct 8 N17 51 D6
Old School Ho CR4 202 C6
Old School Ho The EN2 4 D2
Old School Pl CR0 220 C4
Old School Rd UB8 82 B3
Old School Sq
12 Poplar E14 97 C1
Thames Ditton KT7 196 D3
Old School The
Bloomsbury WC1 240 D4
Merton SW19 179 C1
Old Seacoal La EC4 241 C1
Old South Cl HA5 22 D2
Old South Lambeth Rd SW8 138 A5 270 B4
Old Spitalfields Mkt E1 95 D2 243 D4
Old Sq WC2 241 A2
Old Stable Mews N5 73 A5
Old Station Rd UB3 105 D3
Old Station Yard The 11 E17 54 A5
Old St EC1 95 B3 242 D6
Oldstead Rd BR1 186 B6
Old St E13 99 B5
Old Street Sta EC1 95 B3 242 D6
Old Studio Cl CR0 205 B2
Old Sun Wharf E14 119 A6
Old Swan Wharf SW11 266 D2
Old Swan Yd SM5 218 D4
Old Theatre Ct SE1 252 B4
Old Town
Clapham SW4 137 C2
Croydon CR0 220 D5
Old Tramyard SE18 123 C2
Old Twelve Cl W7 86 C3
Old Vicarage Sch TW10 154 A5
Old Vicarage The CR4 202 C6
Old Woolwich Rd SE10 120 B1
Old York Rd SW18 157 D6
Oleander Cl BR6 227 B3
O'Leary Sq E1 96 C2
Oleastor Ct IG5 56 A6
Olga Prim Sch E3 97 A5
Olga St 20 E3 97 A5
Olinda Rd N16 51 D3
Oliphant St W10 91 A4
Olive Blythe Ho 14 W10 91 A3
Oliver Ave SE25 205 D6
Oliver Bsns Pk NW10 89 A5
Oliver Cl W4 132 D6
Oliver Ct
Isleworth TW7 130 D2
2 Penge SE26 184 C4
Plumstead SE18 123 A2
Olive Rd
Cricklewood NW2 68 C4
Ealing W5 109 D3
3 Merton SW19 180 A3
Newham E13 99 C4
Oliver Gdns E6 100 A2
Oliver Goldsmith Prim Sch
Camberwell SE5 139 D4
Kingsbury NW9 45 B4
Oliver Gr SE25 205 D5
Oliver Ho
22 Bermondsey SE16 118 A4
Notting Hill W11 244 A5
South Lambeth SW8 270 A4
Oliver House Prep Sch SW4 159 B5
Oliver Mews SE15 140 A3
Oliver Rd
Kingston u T KT3 177 A1
Leyton E10 75 D5
Sutton SM1 218 B4
Walthamstow E17 54 A4
Oliver's Yd EC1 242 D6
Olive Tree Ho
7 Deptford SE15 140 C6
Stroud Green N4 50 C3
Olive Tree Sch The SE13 163 D5
Olivette St 1 SW15 134 D1
Olive Waite Ho NW6 69 D1
Olivia Ct 1 EN5 1 B1
Ollard's Gr IG10 21 D6
Ollerton Gn E3 97 B6
Ollerton Rd N11 31 D5
Olley Cl SM6 220 A2
Ollgar Cl W12 111 D5
Olliffe St E14 120 A3
Olmar St SE1 140 A6
Olney Ho NW8 237 B6
Olney Rd SE17 139 A6
Olron Cres DA6 169 A6
Olven Rd SE18 145 A6
Olveston Wlk SM5 202 B3
Olwen Mews HA5 22 D1
Olyffe Ave DA16 146 A3
Olyffe Dr BR3 186 A2
Olympia Ex Ctr* W14 113 A3 254 B5
Olympia Ind Est N22 50 B6
Olympian Ct 8 E14 119 C2
Olympia Way W14 113 A3 254 B5
Olympia Yd W2 245 D5
Olympic Ho 10 W10 90 C1
Olympic Ret Pk HA9 66 D4
Olympic Way
Greenford UB6 85 D6
Wembley HA9 66 C4

Olympus Gr N22 ... 32 C2
Olympus Sq E5 ... 74 A5
Oman Ave NW2 ... 68 C4
Oman Ct NW4 ... 68 B4
Ombersley Ho N4 ... 51 A2
Omeara St SE1 ... 252 B3
Omega Cl E14 ... 119 D3
Omega Ho SW10 ... 266 B4
Omega Pl N1 ... 233 B3
Omega St SE14 ... 141 C4
Omega Works E3 ... 75 C1
Ommaney Rd SE14 ... 141 A4
Omnibus Bsns Ctr N7 ... 72 A3
Omnibus Way E17 ... 35 C1
Ondine Rd SE15 ... 139 D1
Onedin Point 10 E1 ... 118 A6
Onega Gate SE16 ... 119 A3
O'Neill Ho NW8 ... 229 D3
O'Neill Path 11 SE18 ... 144 C6
One Tree Cl SE23 ... 162 C5
Ongar Cl RM6 ... 58 C4
Ongar Ho 15 N1 ... 73 B2
Ongar Rd SW6 ... 135 C6 265 B6
Onra Rd E17 ... 53 C2
Onslow Avenue Mans 10 TW10 ... 154 A6
Onslow Ave TW10 ... 154 A6
Onslow Cl
Chingford E4 ... 20 B2
Notting Hill W9 ... 91 B4
Thames Ditton KT7 ... 196 C1
Onslow Cres BR7 ... 188 D2
Onslow Ct SW10 ... 256 B1
Onslow Dr DA14 ... 168 D2
Onslow Gdns
Chelsea SW7 ... 114 B1 256 C2
Cranley Gdns N10 ... 49 B4
Southgate N21 ... 16 C6
Thames Ditton KT7 ... 196 C1
Wallington SM6 ... 219 C1
Wanstead E18 ... 55 C6
Onslow Ho 1 KT2 ... 176 B2
Onslow Lo 23 SW2 ... 160 C4
Onslow Mews E SW7 ... 256 C3
Onslow Mews W SW7 ... 256 C3
Onslow Par N14 ... 15 B3
Onslow Rd
Richmond TW10 ... 154 A5
Thornton Heath CR0 ... 204 C1
West Barnes KT3 ... 200 A5
Onslow Sq SW7 ... 114 B2 256 D3
Onslow St EC1 ... 241 B5
Onslow Way KT7 ... 196 C1
Ontario St SE1 ... 116 D3 261 D6
Ontario Way E14 ... 119 C6
Onyx Ct N11 ... 31 D3
Onyx Ho KT4 ... 199 B1
Onyx Mews 4 E15 ... 76 D2
Opal Cl E16 ... 99 D1
Opal Ct N11 ... 31 D3
Opal Ho KT4 ... 199 B1
Opal Mews 2 IG1 ... 78 D6
Opal St SE11 ... 116 D1 261 C2
Open Air Theatre, Regent's Pk* NW1 ... 231 A1
Openshaw Rd SE2 ... 124 B2
Openview SW17, SW18 ... 158 B2
Opera Ct 7 N19 ... 71 D5
Operating Theatre Mus & Herb Garret* SE1 ... 117 B5 252 D3
Ophelia Gdns NW2 ... 69 A5
Ophir Terr SE15 ... 140 A4
Opie Ho NW8 ... 230 B4
Opossum Way TW4 ... 128 C2
Oppenheim Rd SE13 ... 142 A3
Oppidan Apartments NW6 ... 69 C2
Oppidans Rd NW3 ... 70 D1
Opus Studios E13 ... 99 A5
Orange Gr E11 ... 76 C5
Orange Hill Rd HA8 ... 27 A3
Orange Pl SE16 ... 118 C3
Orangery Gallery The* W8 ... 113 B4 244 C1
Orangery La SE9 ... 166 B6
Orangery The TW10 ... 153 C2
Orange St WC2 ... 115 D6 249 D5
Orange Yd WC2 ... 239 D1
Oransay Rd 23 N1 ... 73 A2
Oratory La SW3 ... 256 D2
Oratory RC Prim Sch SW3 ... 114 C1 257 A2
Oratory The* SW7 ... 114 C3 257 A5
Orbain Rd SW6 ... 135 A5 264 B3
Orbel St SW11 ... 136 C4 267 A1
Orb St SE17 ... 117 B2 262 C3
Orchard Ave
Ashford TW15 ... 171 A4
Carshalton CR4 ... 203 A1
Croydon CR0 ... 207 A1
East Finchley N3 ... 47 C6
Erith DA17 ... 147 B6
Hatton TW14 ... 149 B6
Heston TW5 ... 129 A5
Hinchley Wood KT7 ... 213 A6
Kingston u T KT3 ... 199 C6
Osidge N14 ... 15 C4
Southall UB1 ... 107 B5
Whetstone N20 ... 14 B2
Orchard Bsns Ctr SE26 ... 185 B5
Orchard Cl
Ashford TW15 ... 171 A4
Bexleyheath DA7 ... 147 A4
Bushey WD23 ... 8 B3
Chingford E4 ... 35 C6
Dollis Hill NW2 ... 68 A5
Edgware HA8 ... 26 A4
Honor Oak SE23 ... 162 C5
Islington N1 ... 73 A1
Kensal Town W10 ... 91 A2
Northolt UB5 ... 64 A2
Ruislip HA4 ... 39 A2
Thames Ditton KT7 ... 197 B2
Walton-on-T KT12 ... 194 B2
Wanstead E11 ... 55 B5
Wembley HA0 ... 88 A6
West Barnes SW20 ... 200 C5
West Ewell KT19 ... 214 D2
Orchard Cotts
Chislehurst BR7 ... 189 C4
Hayes UB3 ... 105 C4
Orchard Cres
Edgware HA8 ... 27 A5
Enfield EN1 ... 5 D4
Orchard Ct
Barnes SW13 ... 133 D2
Barnet EN5 ... 1 D2
Croydon BR3 ... 207 C1
Edgware HA8 ... 26 B5
Hounslow TW7 ... 130 B5
Marylebone W1 ... 238 A2
New Malden KT4 ... 200 A1
Penge SE26 ... 184 D5
Southgate N14 ... 15 C5
Wallington SM6 ... 219 B3
Walthamstow E10 ... 53 D1
1 Walton-on-T KT12 ... 193 D1
Wood Green N22 ... 32 A3
Orchard Dr
Blackheath Vale SE3 ... 142 C3
Edgware HA8 ... 26 B5
Upper Halliford TW17 ... 193 C6
Orchard Gate
Colindale NW9 ... 45 C5
Thames Ditton KT10 ... 196 B1
Wembley UB6 ... 65 B2
Orchard Gdns
Chessington KT9 ... 214 A4
Sutton SM1 ... 217 C3
Orchard Gn
Bromley BR1 ... 187 C2
Orpington BR6 ... 227 C6
Orchard Gr BR6 ... 227 D6
Croydon CR0 ... 207 A2
Edgware HA8 ... 26 D2
Harrow HA3 ... 44 B4
Orpington BR6 ... 211 D1
Penge SE20 ... 184 A3
Orchard Hill Coll SM6 ... 219 B2
Orchard Hill SE13 ... 141 D4
Orchard Ho
Camberwell SE5 ... 139 A4
11 Rotherhithe SE16 ... 118 C3
Shepherd's Bush W12 ... 112 A5
Orchard Inf Sch The KT8 ... 196 B5
Orchard Jun & Inf Sch The TW3 ... 151 C6
Orchard La
Thames Ditton KT8 ... 196 B3
Wimbledon SW20 ... 178 B2
Woodford IG8 ... 37 C6
Orchardleigh Ave EN3 ... 6 C3
Orchard Lo N12 ... 14 A1
Orchard Mead Ho NW11 ... 69 C6
Orchardmede N21 ... 17 B5
Orchard Mews N1 ... 73 B1
Orchard Pl
Canning Town E14 ... 120 C6
Tottenham N17 ... 33 D3
Orchard Prim Sch E9 ... 74 C1
Orchard Rd Barnet EN5 ... 1 B1
Belvedere DA17 ... 125 C2
Brentford TW8 ... 131 C6
Bromley BR1 ... 187 C2
Carshalton CR4 ... 203 A1
Chessington KT9 ... 214 A4
Dagenham RM10 ... 103 C6
Enfield EN3 ... 18 C6
Farnborough BR6 ... 226 D3
Feltham TW14 ... 150 A3
Hampton TW12 ... 173 B3
Hayes UB3 ... 106 A6
Highgate N6 ... 49 B2
Hounslow TW4 ... 151 C6
Isleworth TW1 ... 153 B6
Kingston u T KT1 ... 176 A1
Richmond TW9 ... 132 C2
Sidcup DA14 ... 189 C6
Sunbury TW16 ... 172 B3
Sutton SM1 ... 217 C4
Welling DA16 ... 146 B2
Orchard Rise CR0 ... 207 B1
Orchard Rise E DA15 ... 167 D6
Orchard Rise
Kingston u T KT2 ... 177 A2
Mortlake TW10 ... 132 D1
Pinner HA5 ... 39 D6
Orchard Rise W DA15 ... 167 C6
Orchard Sch DA14 ... 190 B5
Orchard School Sports Ctr SE20 ... 184 A2
Orchardson Ho NW8 ... 236 D5
Orchardson St NW8 ... 92 B3 236 D5
Orchard Sq W14 ... 254 C1
Orchard St
Marylebone W1 ... 238 B2
Walthamstow E17 ... 53 A5
Orchard Terr EN1 ... 18 A5
Orchard The
Acton Green W4 ... 111 B2
Ealing W5 ... 87 D2
East Barnet N14 ... 15 B6
Edgware HA8 ... 26 C5
Enfield N21 ... 17 B5
Ewell KT17 ... 215 D1
Hampstead Garden Suburb NW11 ... 47 C4
Hounslow TW3 ... 130 A3
Lewisham SE3 ... 142 B3
Totteridge N20 ... 13 D3
Orchard Villas BR7 ... 189 C4
Orchard Way
Ashford TW15 ... 148 B2
Croydon BR3, CR0 ... 207 A3
Enfield EN1 ... 5 C2
Esher KT10 ... 212 A2
Orchard Way Prim Sch CR0 ... 207 A2
Orchard Way SM1 ... 218 B4
Orchestra Ct HA8 ... 26 D3
Orchid Cl
Chessington KT9 ... 213 C1
1 Newham E6 ... 100 A2
Southall UB1 ... 85 A1
Orchid Ct
Catford BR1 ... 164 B1
Harrow HA3 ... 24 C2
Wembley HA9 ... 66 A6
Orchid Gdns TW3 ... 129 B1
Orchid Grange N14 ... 15 C4
Orchid Lo N14 ... 15 C4
Orchid Rd N14 ... 15 C4
Orchid St W12 ... 112 A6
Orde Hall St WC1 ... 94 B2 240 C4
Orde Ho 10 N16 ... 73 B4
Ordell Ct 36 E3 ... 97 B5
Ordell Rd E3 ... 97 B5
Orde 6 NW9 ... 27 D2
Ordnance Cl TW13 ... 150 A2
Ordnance Cres SE10 ... 120 C4
Ordnance Hill NW8 ... 92 B6 229 D5
Ordnance Mews NW8 ... 229 D4
Ordnance Rd
Canning Town E16 ... 98 D2
Enfield EN3 ... 7 B6
Shooters Hill SE18 ... 144 C6
Oregano Cl UB7 ... 104 B6
Oregano Dr E14 ... 98 B1
Oregon Ave E12 ... 78 B4
Oregon Bldg 5 SE13 ... 141 D4
Oregon Cl KT3 ... 199 A5
Oregon Sq BR6 ... 211 B1
Orestes Ct 9 E18 ... 55 A6
Orestes Mews 1 NW6 ... 69 C3
Orford Ct
Stanmore HA7 ... 25 C4
Wallington SM6 ... 219 C3
West Norwood SE27 ... 160 D2
Orford Gdns TW1 ... 152 D2
Orford Rd
Catford SE6 ... 163 D1
Walthamstow E17 ... 53 D4
Wanstead E18 ... 55 B6
Organ Crossroads KT17 ... 216 A1
Oriana Ct CR0 ... 221 B1
Oriana Ho 3 E14 ... 119 B6
Oriel Cl CR4 ... 203 D6
Oriel Ct
6 Croydon CR0 ... 205 B1
Hampstead NW3 ... 70 A4
Oriel Dr SW13 ... 134 C6
Oriel Gdns IG5 ... 56 B6
Oriel Jun & Inf Sch TW13 ... 151 A1
Oriel Rd Hackney E9 ... 75 A2
Homerton E9 ... 74 D2
Oriel Way UB5 ... 63 D1
Oriental City NW9 ... 45 B6
Oriental Rd E16 ... 121 D5
Orient Ind Pk E10 ... 75 C6
Orient St SE11 ... 116 D2 261 C4
Orient Way
Lea Bridge E5 ... 74 D5
Leyton E10 ... 75 B6
Oriole Way SE28 ... 124 B6
Orion Bsns Ctr SE14 ... 118 D1
Orion Ct 10 HA8 ... 26 D5
Orion Ctr The CR0 ... 220 A6
Orion Ho 20 E1 ... 96 B3
Orion Mews SM4 ... 201 C5
Orion Point 5 E14 ... 119 C2
Orion Prim Sch The NW9 ... 27 D2
Orion Rd N11 ... 31 A4
Orion Way HA6 ... 22 A6
Orissa Rd SE18 ... 123 C1
Orkney Ho N1 ... 233 C6
Orkney St SW11 ... 137 A3
Orlando Rd SW4 ... 137 C2
Orleans Cl KT10 ... 212 B6
Orleans Ct 9 TW1 ... 153 B4
Orleans House Gallery* TW1 ... 153 B3
Orleans Inf Sch TW1 ... 153 B4
Orleans Park Sch TW1 ... 153 B4
Orleans Rd
South Norwood SE19 ... 183 B4
Twickenham TW1 ... 153 C4
Orleston Mews N7 ... 72 C2
Orleston Rd N7 ... 72 C2
Orley Farm Rd HA1 ... 64 C5
Orley Farm Sch HA1 ... 64 B5
Orlop St SE10 ... 120 C1
Ormanton Rd SE26 ... 184 A6
Orme Ct Mews W2 ... 245 D5
Orme Ct W2 ... 113 D6 245 C5
Orme Ho 8 E8 ... 95 D6
Orme La W2 ... 113 D6 245 C5
Ormeley Rd SW12 ... 159 B3
Orme Rd
Kingston u T KT1, KT3 ... 176 D1
Sutton SM1 ... 217 D2
Ormerod Gdns CR4 ... 181 A2
Ormerod Ho 3 SW9 ... 138 A2
Ormesby Cl SE28 ... 124 D6
Ormesby Way HA3 ... 44 B4
Orme Sq W2 ... 245 C5
Ormiston Gr W12 ... 112 B5
Ormiston Rd SE10 ... 121 A1
Ormond Ave
Hampton TW12 ... 173 D2
23 Richmond TW10 ... 153 D6
Ormond Cl WC1 ... 240 B4
Ormond Cres TW12 ... 173 D2
Ormond Dr TW12 ... 173 D3
Ormonde Ave BR6 ... 227 A6
Ormonde Ct
Hendon NW4 ... 46 D6
Putney SW15 ... 134 C1
Ormonde Gate SW3 ... 114 D1 257 D1
Ormonde Mans WC1 ... 240 B4
Ormonde Pl SW1 ... 258 B3
Ormonde Rd SW14 ... 133 A2
Ormonde Rise IG9 ... 21 C3
Ormonde Terr NW8 ... 92 D6 230 C5
Ormond Ho 7 N16 ... 73 B6
Ormond Mans WC1 ... 240 C5
Ormond Mews WC1 ... 240 B5
Ormond Rd
Finsbury Pk N4, N19 ... 50 A1
Richmond TW10 ... 153 D6
Ormond Yd SW1 ... 249 B4
Ormrod Ct W11 ... 91 B1
Ormsby SM2 ... 217 D1
Ormsby Gdns UB6 ... 86 A5
Ormsby Lo 7 W4 ... 111 C3
Ormsby Pl N16 ... 73 D5
Ormsby Point 6 SE18 ... 122 D2
Ormsby St E2 ... 95 D5
Ormside St SE15 ... 140 C6
Ormskirk Rd WD19 ... 22 D5
Ornan Rd NW3 ... 70 C3
Orpen Ho SW5 ... 255 B3
Orpen Wlk N16 ... 73 C5
Orpheus Ho 25 N19 ... 49 D2
Orpheus St SE5 ... 139 B4
ORPINGTON ... 227 D6
Orpington Gdns N18 ... 17 C1
Orpington Hospl BR6 ... 227 D4
Orpington Mans N21 ... 16 C3
Orpington Rd
Southgate N21 ... 16 D3
St Paul's Cray BR7 ... 211 C6
Orpington Sta BR6 ... 227 C6
Orpwood Cl TW12 ... 173 B4
Orsett Mews W2 ... 92 A1 236 A2
Orsett St SE11 ... 116 B1 260 D2
Orsett Terr
Bayswater W2 ... 92 A1 236 A2
Woodford IG8 ... 37 C3
Orsman Rd N1 ... 95 C6
Orton Gr EN1 ... 6 A4
Orton St E1 ... 118 A5
Orville Rd SW11 ... 136 B3
Orwell Cl UB3 ... 105 C6
Orwell Ct Hackney E8 ... 96 A6
Highbury N5 ... 73 A4
Northolt UB5 ... 85 A6
Orwell Ho W12 ... 112 A6
Orwell Lo 2 E18 ... 55 A5
Orwell Rd E13 ... 99 C6
Osbaldeston Rd N16 ... 52 A1
Osberton Rd SE12 ... 165 A6
Osbert St SW1 ... 259 C3
Osborn Cl E8 ... 96 A6
Osborne Ave TW19 ... 148 B3
Osborne Cl
Beckenham BR3 ... 207 A5
Cockfosters EN4 ... 2 D2
Feltham TW13 ... 172 D5
Osborne Ct Ealing W5 ... 88 A2
10 Surbiton KT6 ... 198 A3
17 Walthamstow E10 ... 53 D2
Osborne Gdns CR7 ... 183 A1
Osborne Gr E17 ... 53 B5
Osborne Mews E17 ... 53 B5
Osborne Pl SM1 ... 218 B3
Osborne Rd
Buckhurst Hill IG9 ... 21 B3
Dagenham RM9 ... 81 B3
Enfield EN3 ... 7 A3
Erith DA17 ... 147 B6
Finsbury Pk N4 ... 50 C1
Forest Gate E7 ... 77 B3
Hackney E9 ... 75 B2
Hounslow TW3, TW4 ... 129 B2
Kingston u T KT2 ... 176 A3
Leyton E10 ... 75 D6
Palmers Green N13 ... 16 C1
South Acton W3 ... 110 D4
Southall UB1 ... 86 A1
South Norwood CR7 ... 183 A1
Walton-on-T KT12 ... 194 A1
Willesden NW2 ... 68 B2
Osborne Sq RM9 ... 81 B4
Osborne Terr 1 SW17 ... 181 A5
Osborne Way KT9 ... 214 B3
Osborn Gdns NW7 ... 28 D3
Osborn La SE23 ... 163 A4
Osborn St E1 ... 95 D2 243 D4
Osborn Terr SE3 ... 142 D1
Osbourne Ct HA2 ... 41 D5
Osbourne Ho
Richmond TW10 ... 154 C6
Twickenham TW2 ... 152 A2
Oscar Faber Pl 8 N1 ... 73 C1
Oscar St SE8 ... 141 C3
Oseney Cres NW5 ... 71 D2
Osgood Ave BR6 ... 227 D3
Osgood Gdns 1 BR6 ... 227 D3
OSIDGE ... 15 B2
Osidge Ct N14 ... 15 B3
Osidge La N14 ... 15 B3
Osidge Prim Sch N14 ... 15 C3
Osier Cres N10 ... 30 D2
Osier Ct E1 ... 96 D3
Osier La SE10 ... 120 D3
Osier Mews W4 ... 133 D6
Osiers Ct 3 KT1 ... 175 D2
Osiers Rd SW18 ... 135 C1
Osier St E1 ... 96 C3
Osier Way Leyton E10 ... 75 D5
Mitcham CR4 ... 202 D4
Oslac Rd SE6 ... 185 D5
Oslo Ct
Mitcham SW19 ... 180 B3
St John's Wood NW8 ... 230 A3
Oslo Ho 2 SE5 ... 139 A3
Oslo Sq SE16 ... 119 A3
Osman Cl N15 ... 51 B3
Osmani Prim Sch E1 ... 96 A2
Osman Rd
Edmonton N9 ... 18 A1
Hammersmith W6 ... 112 C3
Osmington Ho SW8 ... 270 D3
Osmond Cl HA2 ... 64 A6
Osmond Gdns SM6 ... 219 C3
Osmund St W12 ... 89 D2
Osnaburgh St NW1 ... 93 B3 238 D6
Osnaburgh Terr NW1 ... 238 D6
Osney Ho 4 SE2 ... 124 D4
Osney Wlk SM5 ... 202 B3
Osprey Cl
Cheam SM1 ... 217 B3
Higham Hill E17 ... 35 A3
Keston Mark BR2 ... 210 A1
Newham E6 ... 100 A2
Wanstead E11 ... 55 A5
West Drayton UB7 ... 104 A4
Osprey Ct
7 Ealing W7 ... 86 D3
Hampstead NW3 ... 69 D3
Thornton Heath SW16 ... 182 B1
Osprey Ho
Camberwell SE15 ... 139 D4
Isleworth TW7 ... 131 B2
3 Limehouse E14 ... 119 A6
Walthamstow E4 ... 35 B4
Osprey Mews EN3 ... 18 B6
Osprey 7 NW9 ... 27 D2
Ospringe Cl 6 SE20 ... 184 C3
Ospringe Ct SE9 ... 167 B5
Ospringe Ho SE1 ... 251 B3
Ospringe Rd NW5 ... 71 C4
Osram Ct W6 ... 112 C3
Osram Rd HA9 ... 65 D5
Osric Path 8 N1 ... 95 C5
Ossian Mews N4 ... 50 B2
Ossian Rd N4 ... 50 B2
Ossie Garvin Rdbt UB4 ... 106 C6
Ossington Bldgs W1 ... 238 A3
Ossington Cl W2 ... 245 B5
Ossington St W2 ... 113 D6 245 C5
Ossory Rd SE1 ... 140 A6
Ossulston St NW1 ... 93 D5 232 D4
Ossultan Pl N2 ... 48 A6
Ossulton Way N2 ... 48 A5
Ostade Rd SW2 ... 160 B4
Ostell Cres EN3 ... 7 C5
Osten Mews SW7 ... 113 D3 255 D5
OSTERLEY ... 130 B5
Osterley Ave TW7 ... 130 B5
Osterley Cl BR5 ... 190 A2
Osterley Cres TW7 ... 130 D4
Osterley Ct
Hounslow TW7 ... 130 B4
7 Northolt UB5 ... 84 C4
Osterley Gdns
Southall UB2 ... 108 A4
South Norwood CR7 ... 183 A1
Osterley Ho 5 E14 ... 97 D1
Osterley La
Isleworth TW7 ... 108 C1
Southall UB2, TW7 ... 107 D1
Osterley Lo 1 TW7 ... 130 C4
Osterley Park* TW7 ... 108 B1
Osterley Park Rd UB2 ... 107 B3
Osterley Park View Rd W7 ... 108 C4
Osterley Rd
Hounslow TW7 ... 130 C4
Stoke Newington N16 ... 73 C4
Osterley Sta TW7 ... 130 B5
Osterley Views UB2 ... 108 B4
Osterly Lodge UB2 ... 107 B3
Oster Terr E17 ... 52 D4

Ostlers Dr TW15 ... 171 A5
Ostliffe Rd N13 ... 33 A5
Oswald Bldg SW8 ... 268 C5
Oswald Rd UB1 ... 107 A5
Oswald's Mead E9 ... 75 A4
Oswald St E5 ... 74 D5
Oswald Terr NW2 ... 68 C5
Osward Pl N9 ... 18 B2
Osward Rd SW12, SW17 ... 158 D2
Oswell Ho 9 E1 ... 118 B5
Oswin St SE11 ... 116 D2 261 D4
Oswyth Rd SE5 ... 139 C3
Otford Cl Bexley DA5 ... 169 D5
Bromley BR1 ... 210 C6
Penge SE20 ... 184 C2
Otford Cres SE4 ... 163 B5
Otford Ho
Bermondsey SE1 ... 252 D1
6 Deptford SE15 ... 140 C6
Otha Ho 13 SW9 ... 138 A3
Othello Cl SE11 ... 261 C2
Otho Ct 5 TW8 ... 131 D5
Otis St E3 ... 98 A4
Otley App IG2 ... 56 D3
Otley Ct N11 ... 31 A4
Otley Dr IG2 ... 56 D3
Otley Ho N5 ... 72 D5
Otley Rd E16 ... 99 C1
Otley Terr E5 ... 74 D5
Ottawa Ho 4 HA4 ... 40 C1
Ottaway Ct E5 ... 74 A5
Ottaway St E5 ... 74 A5
Otterbourne Rd
Chingford E4 ... 20 B1
1 Croydon CR0 ... 221 A6
Otterburn Gdns TW7 ... 131 A5
Otterburn Ho 12 SE5 ... 139 A5
Otterburn St SW17 ... 180 D4
Otter Cl E15 ... 98 A6
Otterden Cl BR6 ... 227 C4
Otterden St SE6 ... 185 C6
Otterfield Rd UB7 ... 104 A6
Otter Rd UB6 ... 86 A3
Ottershaw Ho BR5 ... 190 B2
Otto Cl SE26 ... 162 B1
Ottoman Ct W5 ... 109 D2
Otto St SE17 ... 138 D6
Otway Ct N4 ... 50 B3
Otway Gdns WD23 ... 8 C4
Oulton Cl Erith SE28 ... 102 C1
Upper Clapton E5 ... 74 C6
Oulton Cres IG11 ... 79 D3
Oulton Rd N15 ... 51 B4
Oulton Way WD19 ... 23 B6
Oundle Ave WD23 ... 8 A5
Our Lady Immaculate RC Prim Sch KT6 ... 198 D1
Our Lady of Dolours RC Prim Sch W2 ... 91 D2
Our Lady of Grace RC Inf Sch NW2 ... 68 C6
Our Lady of Grace RC Jun Sch NW2 ... 68 B5
Our Lady of Grace RC Prim Sch SE7 ... 143 B6
Our Lady of Lourdes RC Prim Sch
Finchley N12 ... 30 A2
Friern Barnet N11 ... 31 C5
Lewisham SE13 ... 142 B2
Our Lady of Lourdes RC Sch NW10 ... 89 A6
Our Lady of Lourds RC Prim Sch E11 ... 55 A3
Our Lady of Muswell Prim Sch N10 ... 49 A6
Our Lady of Muswell RC Prim Sch N10 ... 31 A1
Our Lady of the Rosary RC Prim Sch DA15 ... 167 C5
Our Lady of the Visitation RC Prim Sch UB6 ... 86 A3
Our Lady of Victories RC Prim Sch
Putney SW15 ... 134 D1
South Kensington SW7 ... 114 A2 256 B3
Our Lady Queen of Heaven RC Sch SW19 ... 156 D4
Our Lady RC Prim Sch
Camden Town NW1 ... 93 C6 232 B6
Poplar E14 ... 97 B1
Our Lady & St John's RC Jun & Inf Sch TW8 ... 109 C1
Our Lady & St Joseph RC Prim Sch N1 ... 73 C2
Our Lady & St Philip Neri RC Prim Sch SE26 ... 185 A6
Our Lady's Convent RC High Sch N15 ... 51 C2
Ouseley Rd SW12 ... 158 D3
Outer Circ NW8 ... 92 D5 230 D3
Outgate Rd NW10 ... 67 D1
Outram Pl N1 ... 94 A6 233 B6
Outram Rd
Croydon CR0 ... 221 D6
Muswell Hill N22 ... 31 D2
Newham E6 ... 100 A6
Outwich St EC3 ... 243 B2
Outwood Ct CR2 ... 221 A1
Outwood Ho 3 SW2 ... 160 B4
Oval Ct Burnt Oak HA8 ... 27 A3
8 Teddington TW11 ... 174 D5
Oval Mans SE11 ... 270 D6
Oval Pl SW8 ... 138 B5 270 D4
Oval Prim Sch CR0 ... 205 C1
Oval Rd
Camden Town NW1 ... 93 B6 231 C6
Croydon CR0 ... 205 C1
Oval Rd N RM10 ... 103 D6
Oval Rd S RM10 ... 103 D5
Oval Sta SE11 ... 138 C6
Oval The Hackney E2 ... 96 B5
Sidcup DA15 ... 168 A4
Oval The (Surrey Cnty Crkt Gd) SE11 ... 138 C6
Oval Way SE11 ... 116 B1 260 D1
Overbrae BR3 ... 185 C5
Overbrook Wlk HA8 ... 26 C3
Overbury Ave BR3 ... 208 A6
Overbury 1 BR3 ... 208 A6
Overbury Ho 3 E5 ... 74 D4
Overbury Rd N4, N15 ... 51 B3
Overbury St E5 ... 74 D4
Overcliff Rd SE13 ... 141 C2
Overcourt Cl DA15 ... 168 B5
Overdale Ave KT3 ... 177 B1
Overdale Rd W5 ... 109 C3
Overdown Rd SE6 ... 185 D6
Overhill Rd SE21, SE22 ... 162 A4
Overhill Way BR3 ... 208 B4
Overlea Rd E5 ... 52 A2
Overmead DA15 ... 167 B4
Oversley Ho 17 W2 ... 91 C2
Overstand Cl BR3 ... 207 C4
Overstone Gdns CR0 ... 207 B2
Overstone Ho 10 E14 ... 97 C1
Overstone Rd W6 ... 112 C2
Overstrand Mans SW11 ... 268 A1
Overton Cl
Hounslow TW7 ... 130 D4
Tokyngton NW10 ... 67 A2
Overton Ct E11 ... 55 A2
Overton Dr
Ilford RM6 ... 58 C2
Wanstead E11 ... 55 B2
Overton Grange Sch SM2 ... 217 D1
Overton Ho SW15 ... 155 D4
Overton Rd
Abbey Wood SE2 ... 124 D3
Belmont SM2 ... 217 C1
Brixton SW9 ... 138 C3
Southgate N14 ... 16 A6
Walthamstow E10 ... 53 A1
Overton's Yd CR0 ... 221 A5
Overy Ho SE1 ... 251 C1
Ovesdon Ave HA2 ... 41 B1
Ovett Cl SE19 ... 183 C4
Ovex Cl E14 ... 120 A4
Ovington Ct SW3 ... 257 B5
Ovington Gdns SW3 ... 257 B5
Ovington Mews SW3 ... 257 B5
Ovington Sq SW3 ... 114 C3 257 B5
Ovington St SW3 ... 114 C2 257 B4
Owen Cl Hayes UB4 ... 84 B4
Northolt UB5 ... 63 A2
Thamesmead SE28 ... 124 C5
Thornton Heath CR0 ... 205 B3
Owen Ct UB4 ... 84 B4
Owen Ho
Feltham TW14 ... 150 A4
11 Tufnell Pk N19 ... 71 C4
5 Twickenham TW1 ... 153 B4
Owenite St SE2 ... 124 B2
Owen Rd
Edmonton N13 ... 33 A5
Hayes UB4 ... 84 B4
Owen's Ct EC1 ... 234 C2
Owens Mews 10 E11 ... 76 C6
Owen's Row EC1 ... 234 C2
Owen St EC1 ... 234 C3
Owens Way SE23 ... 163 A4
Owen Way NW10 ... 67 A3
Owen Wlk 7 SE20 ... 184 A3
Owgan Cl SE5 ... 139 B5
Oxberry Ave SW6 ... 135 A3
Oxbridge Ct 4 W4 ... 110 D1
Oxendon St SW1, W1 ... 115 D6 249 C5
Oxenford St SE15 ... 139 D2
Oxenham Ho 13 SE8 ... 141 C6
Oxenholme NW1 ... 232 B3
Oxenpark Ave HA9 ... 44 A2
Oxestalls Rd SE8 ... 119 A1
Oxford Ave
Harlington TW6 ... 127 D5
Hounslow TW5 ... 107 C1
Merton SW20 ... 179 A1
Southgate N14 ... 15 C3
Oxford & Cambridge Mans NW1 ... 237 B3
Oxford Circus Ave W1 ... 239 A1
Oxford Circus Sta W1 ... 93 C1 239 A1
Oxford Cir W1 ... 93 C1 239 A1
Oxford Cl
Edmonton N9 ... 18 B2
Littleton TW15, TW17 ... 171 A3
Mitcham CR4 ... 203 C6
Oxford Cres KT3 ... 199 B3
Oxford Ct
16 Acton W3 ... 88 C1
City of London EC4 ... 252 C6
8 Ealing W7 ... 86 D2
Gunnersbury W4 ... 110 D1
17 Kingston u T KT6 ... 198 A4
48 Paddington W2 ... 91 C2
Sidcup DA14 ... 189 D6
Oxford Dr
Bermondsey SE1 ... 253 A3
Ruislip HA4 ... 62 C6
Oxford Gardens Prim Sch W10 ... 90 D1
Oxford Gate W6 ... 112 D2
Oxford Gdns
Brentford W4 ... 132 C6
Edmonton N21 ... 17 A4
North Kensington W10 ... 90 D1
Oakleigh Pk N20 ... 14 B3
Oxford Ho N4 ... 50 C1
Oxford Mews DA5 ... 169 C4
Oxford Rd
Carshalton SM5 ... 218 C3
Ealing W5 ... 109 D6
Edmonton N9 ... 18 B2
Enfield EN3 ... 18 B6
Finsbury Pk N4 ... 50 C1
Harrow HA1 ... 42 A3
Ilford IG1 ... 79 A3
Oxford Rd N W4 ... 110 D1
Oxford Rd
Paddington NW6 ... 91 C5
Putney SW15 ... 135 A1
Sidcup DA14 ... 190 B5
Oxford Rd S W4 ... 110 D1
Oxford Rd
South Norwood SE19 ... 183 B4
Stratford E15 ... 76 B2
Teddington TW11, TW12 ... 174 B5
Wallington SM6 ... 219 C3
Wealdstone HA3 ... 42 D6
Woodford IG8 ... 37 D5
Oxford Sq W2 ... 92 C1 237 B1
Oxford St W1 ... 93 B1 238 D1
Oxford Way TW13 ... 172 D6
Oxford Wlk UB1 ... 107 B5
Oxgate Ct Par NW2 ... 68 A6
Oxgate Ctr NW2 ... 68 B6
Oxgate Ct NW2 ... 68 A6
Oxgate Gdns NW2 ... 68 B6
Oxgate La NW2 ... 68 B6
Oxhawth Cres BR2 ... 210 D3
Oxhey Dr S HA6 ... 22 B5
Oxhey Dr WD19 ... 22 B6
Oxhey La HA5 ... 23 C5
Oxhey Ridge Cl HA6 ... 22 B5
Oxhey Wood Prim Sch WD19 ... 22 C6
Oxleas Cl DA16 ... 145 B3
Oxleas E6 ... 100 D1
Oxleay Rd HA2 ... 41 C1
Oxleigh Cl KT3 ... 199 C4
Oxley Cl SE1 ... 118 A1
Oxleys Rd NW2 ... 68 B5
Oxlip Cl 2 CR0 ... 206 D1
Oxlow La RM10 ... 81 C4
Oxonian St SE22 ... 139 D1
Oxo Tower Wharf SE1 ... 251 B5
Oxo Twr* SE1 ... 251 B5
Oxted Cl CR4 ... 202 B6
Oxted Ct N16 ... 51 C1
Oxtoby Way SW16 ... 181 D2
OYH Prim Sch NW4 ... 46 D5
Oyster Catchers Cl E16 ... 99 B1
Oyster Catcher Terr IG5 ... 56 C6
Oyster Row E1 ... 96 C1
Ozolins Way E16 ... 99 A1

P

Pablo Neruda Cl 4 SE24 ... 138 D1
Pace Pl E1 ... 96 B1
Pacific Cl TW14 ... 149 D3
Pacific Ho 15 E1 ... 96 D3
Pacific Hts BR3 ... 185 C3
Pacific Rd E16 ... 99 A1
Pacific Wharf IG11 ... 78 D1
Pacific Wharf SE16 ... 118 D5
Packenham Ho
24 Crouch End N19 ... 49 D2
21 Spitalfields E2 ... 95 D4
Packham Ct KT4 ... 216 C5
Packington Sq N1 ... 95 A6 235 A6
Packington St N1 ... 94 D6 234 D5
Packmores Rd SE9 ... 167 B6
Padbury Cl TW14 ... 149 B3
Padbury Ct E2 ... 95 D4
Padbury Ho NW8 ... 237 B6
Padbury SE17 ... 263 B1
Padden Ct NW7 ... 28 D3
Paddenswick Ct 2 W6 ... 112 B3
Paddenswick Rd W6 ... 112 A3
PADDINGTON ... 92 A2
Paddington Acad
Paddington W2 ... 92 B2 236 C3
Paddington W9 ... 91 C3
Paddington Cl UB4 ... 84 D3
Paddington Com Hospl W9 ... 91 C2
Paddington Ct
10 Ealing W7 ... 86 D2
7 Wembley HA0 ... 66 A2
Paddington Gn W2 ... 92 B2 236 C4
Paddington Green Prim Sch NW8 ... 92 B3 236 C5
Paddington Sta W2 ... 92 B1 236 C2
Paddington St W1 ... 238 A4
Paddock Cl
Forest Hill SE26 ... 184 D6
Kidbrooke SE3 ... 143 A3
New Malden KT4 ... 199 C1
Northolt UB5 ... 85 C5
Orpington BR6 ... 226 D4
Paddock Ct SW20 ... 200 C5
Paddock Gdns SE19 ... 183 C4
Paddock Lo 13 EN1 ... 17 C6
Paddock Rd
Bexley DA6 ... 147 A1
Dollis Hill NW2 ... 68 A6
Ruislip HA4 ... 62 D5
Paddock Sch SW15 ... 133 D1
Paddocks Cl HA2 ... 63 D4
Paddocks Gn NW9 ... 44 D1
Paddocks The
Addington CR0 ... 223 C2
Cockfosters EN4 ... 2 D2
Preston HA9 ... 66 D6
Paddock The
Muswell Hill N10 ... 49 B6
Uxbridge UB10 ... 60 D4
Paddock Way
Chislehurst BR7 ... 189 B3
11 Putney SW15 ... 156 C4
Padfield Ct HA9 ... 66 B5
Padfield Rd SE5 ... 139 A2
Padley Cl KT9 ... 214 B3
Padnall Ct RM6 ... 58 D6
Padnall Rd RM6 ... 58 D5
Padstone Ho 50 E3 ... 97 D4
Padstow Cl BR6 ... 227 D4
Padstow Ho 12 E14 ... 119 B6
Padstow Rd EN2 ... 4 D4
Padstow Wlk TW14 ... 149 D3
Padua Rd SE20 ... 184 C2
Pagden St SW8 ... 268 D2
Pageant Ave NW9 ... 27 C2
Pageant Cres SE16 ... 119 B5
Pageantmaster Ct EC4 ... 241 C1
Pageant Wlk CR0 ... 221 C5
Page Cl
Dagenham RM9 ... 81 A3
Hampton TW12 ... 173 A4
Harrow HA3 ... 44 B3
Page Cres CR0 ... 220 D3
Page Ct NW7 ... 28 A3
Page Green Rd N15 ... 52 A4
Page Green Terr N15 ... 51 D4
Page Heath La BR1 ... 209 D6
Page Heath Villas BR1 ... 209 D6
Page High N22 ... 50 C6
Page Ho SE10 ... 142 A6
Pagehurst Rd CR0 ... 206 B2
Page Mdw NW7 ... 28 A3
Page Rd TW14 ... 149 B5
Page's Ct N10 ... 31 A1
Page's Hill N10 ... 31 A1
Page's La N10 ... 31 A1
Page St Hendon NW7 ... 28 A3
Westminster SW1 ... 115 D2 259 D4
Page's Wlk SE1 ... 117 C3 263 B5
Page's Yd W4 ... 133 C6
Paget Ave SM1 ... 218 B5
Paget Cl TW12 ... 174 B6
Paget Ct UB7 ... 104 A4
Paget Gdns BR7 ... 188 D2
Paget Ho 15 E2 ... 96 C5
Paget La TW7 ... 130 C2
Paget Pl
Kingston u T KT2 ... 177 A4
Thames Ditton KT7 ... 196 D1
Paget Rd
Hillingdon UB10 ... 83 A3
Ilford IG1 ... 78 D4
Stoke Newington N16 ... 51 B1
Paget Rise SE18 ... 144 C5
Paget St EC1 ... 234 C2
Paget Terr SE18 ... 144 D6
Pagham Ho 8 W10 ... 90 C3
Pagin Ho N15 ... 51 C4
Pagitts Gr EN4 ... 1 D4
Pagnell St SE14 ... 141 B5
Pagoda Ave TW9 ... 132 B2
Pagoda Gdns SE3 ... 142 B3
Pagoda Gr SE27 ... 161 A2
Paignton Rd
Ruislip HA4 ... 62 A5
Tottenham N15 ... 51 C3
Paine Ct SE3 ... 142 D6
Paines Cl HA5 ... 41 A6
Paine's La HA5 ... 23 A1
Pain's Cl CR4 ... 181 B1
Painsthorpe Rd 3 N16 ... 73 C5
Painswick Ct 1 SE15 ... 139 D5
Painters Mews SE16 ... 118 A2
Painters Rd IG2, RM6 ... 58 A6
Paisley Rd
Carshalton SM5 ... 202 B1
Tottenham N22 ... 32 D2
Paisley Terr SM5 ... 202 B2
Pakeman Ho SE1 ... 251 D2
Pakeman Prim Sch N7 ... 72 B5
Pakeman St N7 ... 72 B5
Pakenham Cl SW12 ... 159 A3
Pakenham St WC1 ... 94 B3 240 D6
Pakington Ho 22 SW9 ... 138 A3
Palace Ave W8 ... 113 D4 245 D2
Palace Court Gdns N10 ... 49 C6
Palace Ct
Bromley BR1 ... 187 B2
Eltham SE9 ... 166 B5
Hampstead NW3 ... 69 D3
Harrow HA3 ... 44 A3
Kensington W2 ... 113 D6 245 C5
South Norwood CR7 ... 205 B5
Streatham SW2 ... 160 C2
Palace Garden Mews W8 ... 245 B4
Palace Gate
Hampton KT8 ... 196 C6
Knightsbridge W8 ... 114 A4 246 A1
Palace Gate Mews 4 N8 ... 50 A5
Palace Gates Rd N22 ... 31 D2
Palace Gdns IG9 ... 21 D3
Palace Gdns Mews W8 ... 113 D5 245 D3
Palace Gdns Sh Ctr EN2 ... 5 B1
Palace Gn
Kensington W8 ... 113 D5 245 C3
New Addington CR0 ... 223 B1
Palace Gr
Bromley BR1 ... 187 B2
Penge SE19 ... 183 D3
Palace Mans W14 ... 254 B4
Palace Mews
Belgravia SW1 ... 258 B3
Fulham SW6 ... 264 D4
Walthamstow E17 ... 53 B5
Palace of Ind HA9 ... 66 C4
Palace Par E17 ... 53 C5
Palace Pl SW1 ... 259 A6
Palace Rd
Bromley BR1 ... 187 B2
East Molesey KT8 ... 196 B6
Hornsey N8 ... 49 D4
Kingston u T KT1 ... 197 D5
Penge SE19 ... 183 D3
Ruislip HA4 ... 63 A4
Streatham SE27, SW16, SW2 ... 160 C2
Wood Green N11 ... 32 A3
Palace Sq SE19 ... 183 D3
Palace St SW1 ... 115 C3 259 A6
Palace View
Bromley BR1 ... 209 B6
Croydon CR0 ... 223 B4
Grove Pk SE12 ... 165 A2
Palace View Rd E4 ... 35 D5
Palamos Rd E10 ... 53 C1
Palatine Ave N16 ... 73 C4
Palatine Rd N16 ... 73 C4
Palazzo Apartments 11 N1 ... 73 C1
Palemead Cl SW6 ... 134 D4
Palermo Rd NW10 ... 90 A5
Palestine Gr SW19 ... 180 B2
Palewell Cl BR5 ... 190 B1
Palewell Common Dr SW14 ... 155 B6
Palewell Pk SW14 ... 133 B1
Palfrey Pl SW8 ... 138 B5 270 D4
Palgrave Ave UB1 ... 107 C6
Palgrave Gdns NW1 ... 92 C3 237 B6
Palgrave Ho
7 Camberwell SE5 ... 139 A5
4 Maitland Pk NW3 ... 70 D3
Twickenham TW2 ... 152 A4
Palgrave Rd W12 ... 111 D3
Palissy St 33 E2 ... 95 D4
Palladino Ho 6 SW17 ... 180 C5
Pallant Ho SE1 ... 262 D5
Pallant Way BR6 ... 226 C5
Pallester Ct NW11 ... 47 A1
Pallet Way SE18 ... 144 A4
Palliser Ct W14 ... 254 A1
Palliser Ho
3 Greenwich SE10 ... 142 B6
21 Stepney E1 ... 96 D3
Palliser Rd W14 ... 113 A1 254 A1
Pallister Terr SW15 ... 155 D2
Pall Mall E SW1 ... 115 D5 249 D4
Pall Mall Pl SW1 ... 249 B3
Pall Mall SW1 ... 115 D5 249 C3
Palmar Cres DA7 ... 147 C3
Palmar Rd DA7 ... 147 C3
Palm Ave DA14 ... 190 D4
Palm Cl E10 ... 75 D5
Palm Ct
Beckenham BR3 ... 207 B6
18 Camberwell SE15 ... 139 D5
Stoke Newington N16 ... 73 B6
Wood Green N22 ... 32 B3
Palmeira Rd DA7 ... 146 D2
Palmer Ave KT4, SM3 ... 216 C4
Palmer Cl
Heston TW5 ... 129 C4
Northolt UB5 ... 63 A2
West Wickham BR4 ... 224 B6
Palmer Cres KT1 ... 198 A6
Palmer Gdns EN5 ... 12 D6
Palmer Ho
6 Deptford SE14 ... 140 D5
8 Kentish Town NW5 ... 71 C4
5 Tufnell Pk N19 ... 71 C5
Palmer Pl N7 ... 72 C3
Palmer Rd
Dagenham RM8 ... 58 D1
Newham E13 ... 99 B3
Palmer's Ct 11 N11 ... 31 C5
Palmers Gr KT8 ... 195 C5
PALMERS GREEN ... 16 A1

almers Green High Sch N21 ....16 C2
almers Green Sta N13 ....32 B6
almers La EN3 ....6 C4
almers Rd E2 ....96 D5
almer's Rd N11 ....31 C5
almers Rd
Mortlake SW14 ....133 A2
Thornton Heath SW16 ....182 B1
almerston Cres
Bowes Pk N13 ....32 B5
Woolwich SE18 ....145 A6
almerston Ct
2 Buckhurst Hill IG9 ....21 C2
22 Globe Town E3 ....96 D5
almerston Ctr HA3 ....42 D6
almerston Ct
9 Surbiton KT6 ....197 D2
7 Sutton SM1 ....218 A3
Walthamstow E17 ....53 B5
almerston Gr 11 SW19 ....179 C3
almerston Ho
Battersea SW11 ....268 B1
Kensington W8 ....245 A3
almerston Rd
Acton Green W3 ....111 A3
Bowes Pk N22 ....32 B4
Brondesbury NW6 ....69 B1
Buckhurst Hill IG9 ....21 C3
Farnborough BR6 ....227 A3
Hampstead NW6 ....69 C1
Harrow HA3 ....42 D6
Hounslow TW3 ....130 A4
Merton SW19 ....179 C3
Mortlake SW14 ....133 A1
Sutton SM1 ....218 A3
Thornton Heath CR0 ....205 B4
Twickenham TW2 ....152 C5
Upton E7 ....77 B2
Wallington SM5 ....219 A4
Walthamstow E17 ....53 B5
almerston Way SW8 ....268 D3
almer St SW1 ....259 C6
alm Gr W5 ....110 A3
alm Tree Ct 5 N17 ....33 D1
alm Tree Ho 2 SE14 ....140 D5
amela Ct
Finchley N12 ....29 D4
Willesden NW10 ....68 A1
amela Gdns HA5 ....40 B4
amela Ho 14 E8 ....95 D6
amir Ct 10 SM2 ....217 D2
amlion Ct N4 ....50 A2
ams Way KT19 ....215 B3
anama Ho 6 E1 ....96 D2
anbro Ho SE18 ....144 B4
ancras La EC2 ....242 C1
ancras Rd NW1 ....93 D5 232 D4
andian Way 4 NW5 ....71 D2
andora Ct 4 KT6 ....198 A3
andora Rd NW6 ....69 C2
anfield Mews IG2 ....56 C3
anfield Rd SE2 ....124 A3
angbourne Ave W10 ....90 C2
angbourne Ct
Oakleigh Pk N20 ....14 A4
Upper Tooting SW17 ....180 A6
angbourne Dr HA7 ....26 A5
angbourne Ho 4 N7 ....72 A3
angbourne NW1 ....232 A1
anhard Pl UB1 ....107 D6
ank Ave EN5 ....14 A6
ankhurst Ave 8 E16 ....121 B5
ankhurst Cl
7 Deptford SE14 ....140 D5
Isleworth TW7 ....130 D2
ankhurst Ho
2 Kensington NW10 ....90 C1
Streatham SW16 ....181 D5
ankhurst Rd KT12 ....194 C2
anmuir Rd SW20 ....178 B2
anmure Cl N5 ....72 D4
anmure Ct 11 UB1 ....86 A1
anmure Rd SE26 ....162 B1
anorama Ct N6 ....49 C3
ansy Gdns W12 ....112 A6
anther Dr NW10 ....67 B3
antiles Cl N13 ....32 D5
antiles The
Bickley BR1 ....210 A6
Bushey WD23 ....8 B3
Erith DA7 ....147 B5
Temple Fortune NW11 ....47 B4
Panton Cl CR0 ....204 D1
Panton St SW1 ....249 C5
Panyer Alley EC2 ....242 A2
Papermill Cl SM5 ....219 A4
Paper Mill Wharf E14 ....119 A6
Papillons Wlk SE3 ....143 A2
Papworth Gdns N7 ....72 B3
Papworth Way SW2 ....160 C4
Parade Mans
19 Camberwell SE5 ....139 A3
2 Hendon NW4 ....46 B4
Parade Mews SE27, SW2 ....160 D2
Parade The
Ashford TW16 ....171 D3
Battersea SW11 ....136 D5 267 D4
Claygate KT10 ....212 C2
Ilford IG2 ....57 B3
Thornton Heath CR0 ....204 A3
Thornton Heath CR7 ....204 C6
Waddon CR0 ....220 B3
Wembley UB6 ....65 B3
Paradise Pas N7 ....72 C3
Paradise Pl 13 SE7 ....122 A2
Paradise Rd
Richmond TW10 ....154 A6
South Lambeth SW4 ....138 A3
Paradise Row E2 ....96 B4
Paradise St SE16 ....118 B4
Paradise Wlk SW3 ....136 D6 267 D6
Paragon Cl E16 ....99 A1
Paragon Ct NW4 ....29 A2
Paragon Gr KT5 ....198 B3
Paragon Ho SE3 ....142 D3
Paragon N8 ....50 C5
Paragon Mews SE1 ....262 D4
Paragon Pl
Blackheath Vale SE3 ....142 D3
Surbiton KT5 ....198 B3
Paragon Rd E9 ....74 C2
Paragon The
Kidbrooke SE3 ....143 A3
Walworth SE17 ....262 D4
Paramount Bldg EC1 ....241 C6
Paramount Ct WC1 ....239 B5
Paramount Ho 10 E11 ....76 C5
Parbury Rd SE23 ....163 A5
Parbury Rise KT9 ....214 A2
Parchmore Rd CR7 ....205 A6
Parchmore Way CR7 ....182 D1
Pardes House Gram N3 ....29 B1
Pardes House Prim N3 ....29 B1
Pardoner St SE1 ....117 B3 262 D6
Pardon St EC1 ....241 D6
Parfett St E1 ....96 A1
Parfew Ct 2 SE22 ....162 B2
Parfitt Cl NW11 ....48 A1
Parfrey St W6 ....134 C6
Pargraves Ct HA9 ....66 C6
Parham Dr IG2 ....56 D4
Paris Gdn SE1 ....116 D5 251 C4
Parish CE Prim Sch BR1 ....187 A3
Parish Church CE Inf Sch CR0 ....220 D5
Parish Church CE Jun Sch CR0 ....220 D5
Parish Ct KT6 ....198 A3
Parish Gate Dr DA15 ....167 C5
Parish La SE20 ....184 D3
Paris Ho 12 E2 ....96 B5
Parish Wharf 6 SE7 ....122 A2
Park App DA16 ....146 B1
Park Ave Barking IG11 ....79 A2
Bromley BR6 ....226 C6
Edmonton N18 ....34 A6
Enfield EN1 ....17 C5
Park Ave E KT17 ....216 A2
Park Ave Finchley N3 ....29 D2
Golders Green NW11 ....47 D1
Ilford IG1 ....56 C1
Mitcham CR4 ....181 B3
Mortlake SW14 ....133 B1
Park Ave N
Dudden Hill NW10 ....68 B3
Hornsey N8 ....49 D5
Park Avenue Mews CR4 ....181 B3
Park Avenue Rd N17 ....34 B3
Park Ave
Palmers Green N13 ....16 C1
Plaistow BR1 ....187 A4
Park Ave *continued*
Ruislip HA4 ....39 C3
Park Ave S N8 ....49 D5
Park Ave
Southall UB1 ....107 C5
Stratford E15 ....76 C2
Twickenham TW3 ....151 D5
Upper Halliford TW17 ....193 C6
Wallend E6 ....100 C5
Wallington SM5 ....219 A2
West Wickham BR4 ....224 A6
Willesden NW2 ....68 C2
Woodford IG8 ....37 B5
Wood Green N22 ....32 B2
Park Ave W KT17 ....216 A2
Park Chase HA9 ....66 B4
Park Cl Dollis Hill NW2 ....68 B5
Ealing NW10 ....88 B4
Hampton TW12 ....174 A2
Harrow HA3 ....24 C2
Isleworth TW3, TW7 ....152 A6
Kensington W14 ....113 B3 254 D6
Kingston u T KT2 ....176 C2
Knightsbridge SW1 ....247 C1
North Finchley N12 ....30 B6
13 South Hackney E9 ....96 C6
Wallington SM5 ....218 D2
Park Cotts 10 TW1 ....153 B5
Park Crescent Mews E W1 ....238 D5
Park Crescent Mews W W1 ....238 C5
Park Cres Enfield EN2 ....5 B1
Finchley N3 ....30 A3
Harrow HA3 ....24 C2
Regent's Pk W1 ....93 B3 238 C5
Twickenham TW2 ....152 B3
Park Croft HA8 ....27 A2
Parkcroft Rd SE12 ....164 D4
Park Ct
Battersea SW11 ....268 C2
2 Beckenham BR3 ....207 D6
2 Chingford E4 ....20 A2
Clapham Pk SW4 ....159 D6
Dulwich SE21 ....161 B1
12 Hammersmith W6 ....112 A2
New Barnet EN5 ....14 B4
New Malden KT3 ....199 B5
North Finchley N12 ....30 B5
Teddington KT1 ....175 C2
Twickenham TW4 ....151 D6
Upper Tooting SW12 ....159 A3
Wallington SM6 ....220 A3
Walthamstow E17 ....53 D4
Wembley HA9 ....66 A3
Wood Green N11 ....31 D3
Parkdale Cres KT4 ....215 B5
Parkdale N11 ....31 D4
Parkdale Rd SE18 ....123 C1
Park Dr Acton W3 ....110 C3
Enfield N21 ....17 A5
Golders Green NW11 ....47 D1
Harrow HA2 ....41 C2
Mortlake SW14 ....133 B1
Stanmore HA3 ....24 C4
Woolwich SE7 ....144 A6
Park Dwellings 7 NW3 ....70 D3
Park End
Bromley BR1 ....186 D2
Hampstead NW3 ....70 C4
Parker Cl
Newham E16 ....122 A5
Wallington SM5 ....218 D2
Parker Ct
Shoreditch N1 ....235 B6
South Lambeth SW4 ....270 A1
Wimbledon SW19 ....179 A3
Parke Rd
Barnes SW13 ....134 A4
Sunbury TW16 ....194 A5
Parker Ho 4 SE18 ....122 D1
Parker Mews WC2 ....240 B2
Parker Rd CR0 ....221 A4
Parkers Rd N10 ....30 C2
Parker's Row SE1 ....253 D1
Parkers Row 15 SE16 ....118 A4
Parker St
Newham E16 ....122 A5
St Giles WC2 ....94 A1 240 B2
Park Farm Cl
East Finchley N2 ....48 A6
Pinner HA5 ....40 B4
Park Farm Ct UB3 ....105 C6
Park Farm Rd
Bromley BR1 ....187 D2
Kingston u T KT2 ....176 A3
Parkfield Ave
Feltham TW13 ....150 A1
Harrow HA2 ....24 A1
Parkfield Ave *continued*
Hillingdon UB10 ....82 D4
Mortlake SW14 ....133 C1
Northolt UB5 ....84 D5
Parkfield Cl
Edgware HA8 ....26 D4
Northolt UB5 ....85 A5
Parkfield Cres
Feltham TW13 ....150 A1
Harrow HA2 ....24 A1
Ruislip HA4 ....63 A5
Parkfield Ct SE14 ....141 B4
Parkfield Dr UB5 ....84 D5
Parkfield Gdns HA2 ....41 D6
Parkfield Ho HA2 ....23 D2
Parkfield 3 TW7 ....130 C4
Parkfield Ind Est SW11 ....137 A3
Parkfield Par TW13 ....150 A1
Parkfield Prim Sch NW4 ....46 B2
Parkfield Rd
Feltham TW13 ....150 A1
Harrow HA2 ....64 A5
New Cross SE14 ....141 B4
Northolt UB5 ....85 A5
Uxbridge UB10 ....60 D6
Willesden NW10 ....68 B1
Parkfields Ave
Welsh Harp NW9 ....45 B1
Wimbledon SW20 ....178 B1
Parkfields Cl SM5 ....219 A4
Parkfields
Croydon CR0 ....207 B1
Putney SW15 ....134 C1
Parkfields Rd KT2 ....176 B5
Parkfield St N1 ....94 C5 234 B4
Parkfield Way BR2 ....210 B4
Park Flats N6 ....48 C2
Parkgate Ave EN4 ....2 A4
Parkgate Cl KT2 ....176 D4
Parkgate Cres EN4 ....2 A4
Park Gate Ct TW12 ....174 A5
Park Gate Ealing W5 ....87 D2
East Finchley N2 ....48 B6
Parkgate Gdns SW14 ....155 B6
Parkgate House Sch SW11 ....137 A1
Parkgate SE3 ....142 D2
Parkgate Mews N6 ....49 C2
Parkgate Rd
Battersea SW11 ....136 C5 267 B3
Wallington SM5, SM6 ....219 B3
Park Gates HA2 ....63 C4
Park Gate N21 ....16 B4
Park Gdns
Kingston u T KT2 ....176 B5
Queensbury NW9 ....44 D6
Park Gr Bromley BR1 ....187 B2
Edgware HA8 ....26 B5
Newham E15 ....99 A6
Park Grove Rd E11 ....76 C6
Park Gr N11 ....31 D3
Park Hall Rd
Dulwich SE21 ....161 B1
East Finchley N2 ....48 C5
Park Hall Road Trad Est SE21 ....161 B1
Park Hall SE10 ....142 B5
Parkham Ct BR2 ....186 C1
Parkham St SW11 ....136 C4 267 A1
Parkham Way N10 ....31 C1
Park Heights Ct 21 E14 ....97 B1
Park High Sch HA7 ....25 D1
Park Hill
Bromley BR1 ....210 B5
Clapham Pk SW4 ....159 D6
Park Hill Cl SM5 ....218 C3
Park Hill Ct
Croydon CR0 ....221 C6
Ealing W5 ....87 D2
Upper Tooting SW17 ....158 D1
Park Hill Ealing W5 ....87 D2
Forest Hill SE23 ....162 C3
Parkhill Ho 1 SW16 ....182 C5
Parkhill Inf Sch IG5 ....56 C6
Park Hill Inf Sch CR0 ....221 C5
Parkhill Jun Sch IG5 ....56 C6
Park Hill Jun Sch CR0 ....221 C5
Park Hill IG10 ....21 D6
Park Hill Rd BR2 ....186 C1
Parkhill Rd
Chingford E4 ....20 A4
Maitland Pk NW3 ....70 D3
Old Bexley DA5 ....169 B4
Sidcup DA15 ....167 C1
Park Hill Rd
South Croydon CR0 ....221 C5
Wallington SM6 ....219 B1
Park Hill TW10 ....154 B5
Park Hill Rise CR0 ....221 D5
Park Hill Sch KT2 ....176 C3
Park Hill SM5 ....218 D2
Park Hill Wlk 10 NW3 ....70 D3
Park Ho
8 Camberwell SE5 ....139 B4
Finsbury Pk N4 ....72 D6
Forest Hill SE26 ....184 A5
35 Hackney E9 ....74 C1
Parkholme Rd E8 ....74 A2
Park Ho
Richmond TW10 ....154 A5
Sidcup DA14 ....190 A5
Southgate N21 ....16 B4
Park House Gdns TW1 ....153 C6
Parkhouse St SE5 ....139 B5
Park Hts NW4 ....46 B6
Parkhurst Ct N7 ....72 A4
Parkhurst Gdns 2 DA5 ....169 C4
Parkhurst Rd
Bowes Pk N22 ....32 B4
Friern Barnet N11 ....31 A5
Little Ilford E12 ....78 C4
Lower Holloway N7 ....72 A4
Sidcup DA5 ....169 C4
Sutton SM1 ....218 B4
Tottenham N17 ....34 A1
Walthamstow E17 ....53 A5
Parkin Ho SE20 ....184 D3
Parkinson Ct
Finsbury N1 ....235 C1
Shoreditch EC1 ....235 D2
Parkinson Ho 6 E9 ....74 C1
Park La Cheam SM3 ....217 A2
Cranford TW5 ....128 A5
Dagenham RM6 ....58 D3
Edmonton N9 ....17 D1
Harrow HA2 ....63 D5
Hayes UB4 ....83 C3
Mayfair W1 ....115 A6 248 A5
Mill Meads E15 ....98 B6
Parkland Ct
Kensington W14 ....244 A2
Stratford E15 ....76 C3
Parkland Gdns 12 SW19 ....156 D3
Parkland Gr
Ashford TW15 ....170 C6
Hounslow TW7 ....130 D4
Parkland Mead BR1 ....210 D6
Parkland Rd
Ashford TW15 ....170 C6
Woodford IG8 ....37 B3
Wood Green N22 ....32 B1
Parklands WD23 ....8 A5
Parklands Cl
Hadley Wood EN4 ....2 B5
Ilford IG2 ....57 A2
Mortlake SW14 ....155 A6
Parklands Ct TW5 ....128 D3
Parklands Dr N3 ....47 A6
Parklands
East Dulwich SE22 ....162 B6
Highgate N6 ....49 B2
Kingston u T KT5 ....198 B4
Parklands Par TW5 ....128 D3
Parklands Pl HA8 ....26 B6
Parklands Rd SW16 ....181 B5
Parklands Way KT4 ....215 C6
Parklands 5 N20 ....14 A2
Park Lane Cl N17 ....34 A3
Park Lane Mans CR0 ....221 B5
Park Lane Prim Sch HA9 ....66 A4
PARK LANGLEY 208 B4
Park La
Richmond TW9 ....131 D1
South Croydon CR0 ....221 B5
Stanmore HA7 ....9 A1
Teddington TW11 ....174 D4
Tottenham N17 ....34 A3
Wallington SM5, SM6 ....219 A3
Wembley HA9 ....66 A4
Park Lawn CR7 ....183 A1
Parklea Cl NW9 ....27 C2
Park Lea Ct N16 ....51 C2
Parkleigh Ct SW19 ....179 D1
Parkleigh Rd SW19 ....179 D1
Parkleys KT2, TW10 ....175 D6
Park Lo 3 W5 ....87 B3
Park Lofts 9 SW4 ....160 A6
Park Lo N12 ....30 A5
Park Lorne NW8 ....230 B1
Park Lo
11 South Hampstead NW8 ....70 B1
10 Wapping E1 ....118 B5
Willesden NW2 ....68 C4
Park Mans
Battersea SW11 ....267 C1
Bedford Pk W6 ....111 D3
Forest Hill SE26 ....162 C1
Fulham SW6 ....264 B1
5 Hendon NW4 ....46 B4
Knightsbridge SW1 ....247 C1
St John's Wood NW8 ....230 A3
Vauxhall SW8 ....270 B6
Park Mead DA15 ....168 B5
Parkmead Gdns NW7 ....27 D4
Park Mead HA2 ....63 D5
Parkmead SW15 ....156 B5
Park Mews
Chislehurst BR7 ....188 D4
Greenwich SE10 ....120 D1
Kensal Rise W10 ....91 A5
Stanwell TW19 ....148 B4
Parkmore BR7 ....188 D3
Parkmore Cl IG8 ....37 A6
Park Nook Gdns EN2 ....5 B6
Park Par Acton W3 ....110 C3
Dagenham NW10 ....89 D5
Hayes UB3 ....83 C1
Kingsbury NW9 ....45 B6
Park Place Dr W3 ....110 C3
Park Place Ho 8 SE10 ....142 B6
Park Place Villas W2 ....236 B4
Park Pl
Canary Wharf E14 ....119 C5
Ealing W5 ....109 D5
Gunnersbury W3 ....110 C2
Hampton TW12 ....174 A4
Shoreditch N1 ....235 D6
St James SW1 ....115 C5 249 A4
Wembley HA9 ....66 B4
Park Prim Sch E15 ....76 D1
Park Rd
Ashford TW15 ....170 D5
Beckenham BR3 ....185 C3
Bromley BR1 ....187 B2
Cheam SM3 ....217 A2
Chipping Barnet EN5 ....1 B1
Chislehurst BR7 ....188 D4
Chiswick W4 ....133 B6
Cockfosters EN4 ....2 C1
Dagenham NW10 ....89 C6
Park Rd E W3 ....111 A4
Park Rd Ealing W7 ....108 D6
East Finchley N2 ....48 B6
East Molesey KT8 ....196 A5
Edmonton N18 ....34 A6
Park Rd E UB10 ....82 A5
Park Rd
Feltham TW13 ....172 D6
Hackbridge SM6 ....219 B6
Hampton TW12 ....174 A5
Hampton Wick KT1 ....175 C2
Harringay N8, N15 ....50 D5
Hayes UB4 ....83 C2
Hendon NW4 ....46 B3
Hornsey N8 ....49 D4
Hounslow TW3, TW7 ....152 A6
Ilford IG1 ....79 B5
Isleworth TW7 ....131 B3
Kingsbury NW9 ....45 B2
Kingston u T KT2, TW10 ....176 C3
Leyton E10 ....53 C1
Lisson Gr NW1, NW8 ....92 C3 237 B6
Lower Halliford TW17 ....192 C1
Mitcham SW19 ....180 C4
Park Rd N W4 ....111 B1
Park Rd Newham E15 ....99 A6
New Malden KT3 ....199 B5
Park Rd N W3 ....110 D4
Park Rd Osidge N14 ....15 D4
Richmond TW10 ....154 B5
South Norwood SE25 ....205 C5
Sunbury TW16 ....172 B3
Teddington TW11 ....174 D4
Twickenham TW1 ....153 C5
Upton Pk E6 ....99 C6
Uxbridge UB8 ....60 A2
Wallington SM6 ....219 B3
Walthamstow E17 ....53 B4
Wanstead E12 ....77 B6
Wembley HA0 ....66 A2
Wood Green N11 ....31 D3
Park Ridings N8 ....50 C6

Park Rise
Forest Hill SE23 163 A3
Harrow HA3 24 C2
Park Rise Rd SE23 163 A3
Park Road E 11 W3 110 D4
Park Road Ho 3 KT2 176 C3
Park Row SE10 142 B6
PARK ROYAL 88 D4
Park Royal Bsns Ctr NW10 89 A3
Park Royal Metro Ctr NW10 88 D3
Park Royal Rd NW10, W3 89 A3
Park Royal Sta W5 88 D3
Park Royal NW10 88 D6
Park St James NW8 230 C5
Park Sch IG1 56 D1
Park Sheen 3 SW14 132 D1
Parkshot TW9 132 A1
Parkside Ave
Bromley BR1 210 A5
Wimbledon SW19 178 D5
Parkside 1 BR3 185 D1
Parkside Bsns Est SE8 141 A6
Parkside SM3 217 A2
Park Side IG9 21 B2
Parkside Cl SE20 184 C3
Parkside Cres
Highbury N7 72 C5
Tolworth KT5 199 A3
Parkside Ct
Bowes Pk N22 32 B4
2 Wanstead E11 55 A3
Park Side NW2 68 B4
Parkside Dr HA8 10 C1
Parkside Ealing W5 110 A6
East Acton W3 111 C5
Parkside Est E9 96 D6
Parkside N3 29 D3
Parkside Gdns
East Barnet EN4 15 A4
Wimbledon SW19 178 D6
Parkside
Greenwich SE3 142 D5
Hampton TW12 174 A5
Hayes UB3 105 C6
Hendon NW7 28 A4
Parkside Lo DA17 125 D1
Parkside Prep Sch N17 33 C2
Parkside (private) Hospl SW19 156 D1
Parkside Rd
Belvedere DA17 125 D2
Hounslow TW3 151 D6
Parkside DA14 168 B2
Parkside St SW11 268 A1
Parkside Terr N18 33 B6
Parkside Way HA2 42 A5
Parkside SW19 178 D6
Park Sq E NW1 93 B3 238 D6
Park Square Mews NW1 238 C5
Park Sq W NW1 93 B3 238 C5
Park S SW11 268 A1
Park St
Borough The SE1 117 A5 252 B4
Croydon CR0 221 A6
Parkstead Rd SW15 156 B6
Park St W1 115 A6 248 A5
Parkstone Ave N18 33 D5
Parkstone Rd
5 Peckham SE15 140 A3
Walthamstow E17 54 A6
Park Stps W2 247 B6
Park St TW11 174 C4
Park Terr
Carshalton SM5 218 C5
Enfield EN3 7 A5
New Malden KT4 200 A1
Park The Ealing W5 109 D5
Forest Hill SE23 162 C3
Golders Green NW11 47 D1
Highgate N6 49 A3
Sidcup DA14 190 A5
Wallington SM5 218 D3
Parkthorne Cl HA2 41 D3
Parkthorne Dr HA2 41 D3
Parkthorne Rd SW12 159 D4
Park Twrs W1 248 C3
Park View Acad N15 51 A5
Park View Cres N11 31 B6
Park View Ct N12 30 C6
Parkview Ct
Fulham SW6 135 A3

Parkview Ct *continued*
Harrow HA3 24 C3
Ilford IG2 57 C3
Park View Ct NW9 45 A5
Parkview Ct
Penge SE20 184 B2
Twickenham TW1 153 C4
Park View Ct SW18 157 C5
Park View W3 89 A2
Park View Dr CR4 180 B1
Parkview UB6 87 A4
Park View Gdns
Hendon NW4 46 D4
Redbridge IG4 56 B5
Wood Green N22 32 C2
Park View N5 73 A4
Park View Ho
Chingford E4 35 C5
Hampton TW12 174 A5
Streatham SE24 160 D5
Park View KT3 199 D6
Parkview Lo BR3 207 D6
Park View Mans N4 50 D2
Park View Mews 24 SW9 138 B3
Park View
Morden SM4 202 B4
Pinner HA5 23 B2
Park View Rd DA16 146 C2
Parkview Rd
Chislehurst SE9 166 D2
Croydon CR0 206 A1
Park View Rd
Ealing W5 88 A2
Finchley N3 29 D2
Hillingdon UB8 82 C1
Pinner HA5 22 B3
Southall UB1 107 C5
Tottenham N17 34 A1
Willesden NW10 67 D4
Park View
Southgate N21 16 B4
Wembley HA9 66 D3
Willesden NW2 68 C4
Yiewsley UB7 104 A6
Park Village E NW1 93 B5 231 D3
Park Village W NW1 93 B5 231 C4
Park Villas RM6 58 D3
Parkville Rd SW6 135 B5 264 C3
Park Vista Apartments E13 98 D4
Park Vista SE10 142 B6
Park Walk Prim Sch SW10 136 B6 266 C5
Parkway
Abbey Wood DA18 125 A3
Camden Town NW1 93 B6 231 C5
Park Way Ct HA4 39 D1
Park Way
East Molesey KT8 195 D6
Edgware HA8 26 D2
Enfield EN2 4 C3
Feltham TW14 150 B4
Friern Barnet N20 30 D6
Gunnersbury W3 110 C2
Parkway UB10 60 D1
Parkway Ho SW14 133 B1
Parkway Ilford IG3 79 D5
Palmers Green N14 16 A2
Parkway Prim Sch DA18 125 A3
Park Way Ruislip HA4 40 A1
Temple Fortune NW11 47 A4
Parkway The
Cranford TW5 128 B5
Hayes UB2, UB3, UB4, TW5 106 B3
Yeading UB4 84 D2
Parkway Trad Est TW5 128 C6
Parkway
West Barnes SW20 200 D5
Woodford IG8 37 C5
Park West Pl W1, W2 92 C1 237 B2
Park West W2 92 C1 237 B1
Park Wlk
Chelsea SW10 136 B6 266 C6
Highgate N6 49 A2
Parkwood Ave KT10 196 A1
Parkwood BR3 185 C3
Parkwood Gr TW16 194 A6
Parkwood Mews N6 49 B3
Parkwood NW8 230 C5
Parkwood Prim Sch N4 72 D6
Parkwood Rd
Hounslow TW7 130 D4

Parkwood Rd *continued*
Old Bexley DA5 169 B4
Wimbledon SW19 179 B5
Parliament Ct NW3 70 C4
Parliament Hill NW3 70 C4
Parliament Hill Mans NW5 71 A4
Parliament Hill Sch NW5 71 A4
Parliament Mews SW14 133 A3
Parliament Sq* SW1 116 A4 250 A1
Parliament St SW1 116 A4 250 A2
Parliament View Apartments SE11 260 C4
Parma Cres SW11 136 D1
Parminter Ind Est 24 E2 96 B5
Parmiter St E2 96 B5
Parmoor Ct EC1 242 A6
Parnall Ho 11 SE19 183 C6
Parnell Cl
Edgware HA8 27 A6
Hammersmith W12 112 B3
Parnell Ho WC1 239 D2
Parnell Rd E3 97 B6
Parnham Cl BR1 210 D6
Parnham St E14 97 A1
Parolles Rd N19 49 C1
Paroma Rd DA17 125 C3
Parr Cl N9 34 B6
Parr Ct
Feltham TW13 172 C6
Shoreditch N1 235 C4
Parrington Ho 1 SW4 159 D5
Parr Pl W4 111 D2
Parr Rd Newham E6 99 D6
Stanmore HA7 26 A2
Parr's Pl TW12 173 C3
Parr St N1 95 B5 235 C4
Parry Ave E6 100 B1
Parry Cl KT17 216 A1
Parry Ho 32 E1 118 B5
Parry Pl SE18 122 D2
Parry Rd
South Norwood SE25 205 C6
West Kilburn W10 91 A4
Parry St SW8 138 A6 270 B6
Parsifal Coll NW3 69 C4
Parsifal Ho NW3 69 C4
Parsifal Rd NW6 69 C3
Parsley Gdns CR0 206 D1
Parsloes Ave RM9 81 A3
Parsloes Prim Sch RM9 81 B2
Parsonage Cl UB3 83 D1
Parsonage Ct WD6 11 A6
Parsonage Gdns EN2 5 A3
Parsonage La
Enfield EN2 5 B3
Sidcup DA14 191 B6
Parsonage Manorway DA17 147 C6
Parsonage St E14 120 A2
Parsons Cl SM1 217 D5
Parsons Cres HA8 10 C1
Parsons Gn SW6 135 C4 265 A1
PARSONS GREEN 135 C4
Parsons Green La SW6 135 C4 265 A2
Parsons Green Sta SW6 135 C4 265 A1
Parsons Hill SE18 122 C3
Parsons Ho
Paddington W2 236 C5
21 Streatham SW12 160 A4
Parsons Lo NW6 69 D1
Parsons Mead KT8 196 A6
Parson's Mead CR0 204 D1
Parsons Rd
Edgware HA8 10 C1
Newham E13 99 C5
Parson St NW4 46 C6
Parthenia Rd SW6 135 C4 265 B1
Partingdale La NW7 28 D5
Partington Cl N19 49 D1
Parton Lo 14 E8 73 D2
Partridge Cl
Barnet EN5 12 C5
Bushey WD23 8 A3
1 Newham E16 99 D2
Stanmore HA7 26 A6
Partridge Ct EC1 241 C6
Partridge Dr BR6 227 A5
Partridge Gn SE9 166 C1
Partridge Ho 22 E3 97 B5
Partridge Rd
8 Hampton TW12 173 C4
Sidcup DA14 189 C6

Partridge Sq 3 E6 100 A2
Partridge Way N22 32 A2
Pasadena Cl UB3 106 B4
Pascall Ho SE17 139 A6
Pascal St SW8 137 D5 269 D4
Pascoe Rd SE13 164 B6
Pasley Cl SE17 262 A1
Pasquier Rd E17 53 A6
Passey Pl SE9 166 B5
Passfield Dr E14 97 D2
Passfield Ho SE18 123 B2
Passfield Path 13 SE28 124 B6
Passfields
Catford SE6 164 A1
West Kensington W14 254 C1
Passing Alley EC1 241 D5
Passingham Ho TW5 129 C6
Passmore Edwards Ho N11 31 D3
Passmore Gdns N11 31 D4
Passmore Ho 12 N9 18 A1
Passmore St SW1 115 A1 258 A2
Pasters Ct EN1 17 D5
Pasteur Cl NW9 27 C1
Pasteur Gdns N18 33 A5
Paston Cl SM6 219 C5
Paston Cres SE12 165 B4
Pastor Ct N6 49 C3
Pastor St SE1, SE11 116 D2 261 D4
Pasture Cl
Bushey WD23 8 A4
Wembley HA0 65 B5
Pasture Rd
Catford SE6 164 D3
Dagenham RM9 81 B3
Wembley HA0 65 B5
Pastures Mead UB10 60 C2
Pastures The N20 13 B3
Patcham Terr SW8 268 D2
Patch Cl UB10 82 B6
Patching Way UB4 85 A2
Pat Drew Ho BR1 187 C2
Patent Ho E14 97 D2
Paternoster La EC4 94 D1 241 D2
Paternoster Row EC2, EC4 95 A1 242 A1
Paternoster Sq EC4 94 D1 241 D2
Pater St W8 113 C3 255 A5
Pates Manor Dr TW14 149 B4
Pathfield Rd SW16 181 D4
Path The SW19 179 D2
Pathway Ho SW17 180 D4
Pathway Lo CR4 180 D2
Patience Rd SW11 136 C3
Patience Villas SE13 142 B2
Patio Cl SW4 159 D5
Patmore Ho 9 N16 73 C3
Patmore St SW8 137 C4 269 B2
Patmos Rd SW9 138 D4
Paton Cl E3 97 C4
Paton Ho 3 SW9 138 B3
Paton St EC1 235 A1
Patricia Ct
Chislehurst BR7 189 B2
Woolwich DA16 146 B5
Patrick Coman Ho EC1 234 C1
Patrick Connolly Gdns 41 E3 97 D4
Patrick Rd E13 99 C4
Patriot Sq E2 96 B5
Patrol Pl SE6 163 D5
Pat Shaw Ho 2 E1 96 D3
Patshull Pl NW5 71 C2
Patshull Rd NW5 71 C2
Patson Cl E5 74 D5
Pattenden Rd SE6 163 B3
Patten Ho N4 51 A1
Patten Rd SW18 158 C4
Patterdale Cl BR1 186 C4
Patterdale NW1 231 D1
Patterdale Rd SE15 140 C5
Patterson Ct SE19 183 D4
Patterson Rd SE19 183 D4
Pattina Wlk SE16 119 A5
Pattinson Point 10 E16 99 A2
Pattison Ho
Borough The SE1 252 B2
1 Stepney E1 96 D1
Pattison Rd NW2 69 C5
Pattison Wlk SE18 123 A1
Pat Williams Ho SE27 161 A1
Paul Byrne Ho 3 N2 48 A6
Paul Cl E15 76 C1

Paul Ct
7 Edmonton N18 34 A6
Hendon N3 29 A1
Paul Daisley Ct 2 NW6 69 A1
Paulet Rd SE5 138 D4
Paul Gdns CR0 221 D6
Paulhan Rd HA3 43 D5
Paul Ho 18 W10 91 A3
Paulin Dr N21 16 C4
Pauline Cres TW2 152 A3
Pauline Ho 21 E1 96 A2
Paulinus Cl BR5 190 C1
Paul Julius Cl E14 120 B6
Paul Robeson Cl E6 100 C4
Paulson Ho 7 IG11 78 D1
Paul St
Broadgate EC2 95 C3 243 A6
Newham E15 98 C6
Paultons Ho SW3 266 D6
Paultons Sq SW3 136 B6 266 D6
Paultons St SW3 136 B6 266 D5
Pauntley Ho 6 N19 49 C1
Pauntley St 4 N19 49 C1
Pavan Ct 28 E2 96 C4
Paved Ct 9 TW9 153 D6
Paveley Ct NW7 28 D3
Paveley Dr SW11 136 C5 267 A3
Paveley Ho N1 233 C3
Paveley St NW8 92 C3 237 B6
Pavement Mews 1 RM6 58 D2
Pavement Sq CR0 206 A1
Pavement The
Brentford W5 110 A3
Clapham SW4 137 C1
Leytonstone E11 54 A1
11 West Norwood SE27 183 A6
Pavet Cl RM10 81 D2
Pavilion Ct
Dagenham RM9 103 A6
7 Hampstead NW3 70 A4
Hampstead NW3 70 B3
3 Paddington NW6 91 C4
5 South Norwood SW16 182 B3
3 Wimbledon SW19 179 A3
Pavilion L Ctr The BR1 187 A1
Pavilion Lo HA2 42 B1
Pavilion Mans 10 SW9 138 B1
Pavilion Mews N3 29 C1
Pavilion Rd
Knightsbridge SW1 114 D3 257 D5
Redbridge IG1 56 B2
Pavilion Sq SW17 158 D1
Pavilions The BR3 185 C4
Pavilion St SW1 257 D5
Pavilion Terr
Ilford IG2 57 C4
8 North Kensington W12 90 C1
Pavilion Way
Burnt Oak HA8 27 A3
Ruislip HA4 62 C6
Pavillion Ct SW1 268 C6
Pavitt Ct NW10 68 A1
Pawleyne Cl SE20 184 C3
Pawsey Cl E13 99 A6
Pawson's Rd CR0 205 A4
Paxford Rd HA0 65 B6
Paxton Cl
Richmond TW9 132 B3
Walton-on-T KT12 194 C2
Paxton Ct
1 Forest Hill SE26 185 A6
Grove Pk SE9 165 C1
Mitcham CR4 180 D1
Paxton Ho SE17 262 B2
Paxton Pl SE27 183 C6
Paxton Prim Sch SE19 183 C4
Paxton Rd
Chiswick W4 133 C6
Forest Hill SE23 163 A1
Plaistow BR1 187 A3
Tottenham N17 34 A3
Paxton Terr SW1 268 D6
Paymal Ho 33 E1 96 C2
Payne Cl IG11 79 D1
Payne Ho N1 233 D5
Paynell Ct SE3 142 C2
Payne Rd E3 97 D5
Paynesfield Ave SW14 133 B2
Paynesfield Rd WD23 8 D4
Payne St SE8 141 B6

Paynes Wlk W6 135 A6 264 A
Payzes Gdns IG8 36 D
Peabody Ave SW1 115 B1 258 D
Peabody Bldgs
6 Camberwell SE5 139 B
Walworth SE17 262 C
Peabody Cl
Croydon CR0 206 C
SW1 268 D
Peabody Cotts N17 33 C
Peabody Ct
9 Camberwell SE5 139 B
25 Enfield EN3 7 C
St Luke's EC1 242 B
Peabody Est
18 Bethnal Green E2 96 B
Borough The SE1 252 A
Fulham SW6 135 B6 264 D
17 Hammersmith W6 112 C
Holborn EC1 241 B
Lambeth SE1 251 B
North Kensington W10 90 C
4 Ratcliff E1 118 D
7 St George in t East E1 118 A
St Luke's EC1 242 B
Strand WC2 240 C
Streatham SE24 161 A
Westminster SW1 259 B
Peabody Hill SE21 161 A
Peabody Sq SE1 251 C
Peabody Twr EC1 242 B
Peabody Yd N1 235 A
Peace Cl
East Barnet N14 15 B
Greenford UB6 86 B
South Norwood SE25 205 C
Peace Ct 10 NW9 46 A
Peace Gr HA9 66 D
Peacehaven Ct 8 N10 31 A
Peace St SE18 144 C
Peach Ct E4 35 C
Peaches Cl SM2 217 A
Peaches Ct SM2 217 A
Peach Gr E11 76 B
Peach Rd
Feltham TW14 150 A
London W10 91 A
Peach Tree Ave UB7 82 B
Peachum Rd SE3 142 D
Peach Walk Mews 24 E3 96 D
Peacock Ave TW14 149 B
Peacock Cl
Dagenham RM8 80 C
Walthamstow E4 35 B
Peacock Ct EN1 17 C
Peacock Ind Est N17 33 D
Peacock St SE17 116 D2 261 D
Peacock Wlk E16 99 B
Peacock Yd SE17 261 D
Peaketon Ave IG4 55 D
Peak Hill Ave SE26 184 C
Peak Hill SE26 184 C
Peak Hill Gdns SE26 184 C
Peak Ho N4 51 A
Peak The SE26 162 C
Peal Gdns W13 87 A
Peall Rd Ind Est CR0 204 B
Peall Rd CR0 204 B
Pear Ave TW17 193 C
Pearce Cl 2 CR4 181 A
Pearcefield Ave 5 SE23 162 C
Pearce Ho
Camden Town N19 71 C
7 Streatham SW2 160 A
Westminster SW1 259 D
Pear Cl
Kingsbury NW9 45 B
New Cross Gate SE14 141 A
Pearcroft Rd E11 76 B
Pear Ct 21 SE15 139 D
Peardon St SW8 137 B
Peareswood Gdns HA7 25 D
Pearfield Ho 1 N5 73 A
Pearfield Rd SE23 163 A
Pearl Cl Hendon NW2 46 D
Newham E6 100 C
Pearl Ct 18 NW9 46 A
Pearl Rd E17 53 C
Pearl St E1 118 B

Pearlstones Ct RM10 103 C6
Pearmain Cl TW17 192 D4
Pearmain Ho 9 SE13 142 A3
Pearman St SE1 116 C4 251 B1
Pear Pl SE1 251 A2
Pear Rd E11 76 C5
Pearscroft Ct SW6 135 D4 265 D1
Pearscroft Rd SW6 135 D4 265 D1
Pearse St 3 SE15 139 C6
Pearson Cl Barnet EN5 1 D2
 4 Camberwell SE5 139 A4
Pearson Ct SM4 201 D4
Pearson Ho SW15 134 C3
Pearson's Ave SE8, SE14 141 C4
Pearson St E2 95 D5
Pearson Way CR4 181 A2
Pears Rd TW3 130 A2
Pear Tree Ave UB7 82 B1
Peartree Ave SW17 158 A1
Pear Tree Cl
 Bromley BR2 209 D4
 Chessington KT9 214 C3
 Mitcham CR4 180 C1
 23 Shoreditch E2 95 D6
Pear Tree Ct
 Holborn EC1 241 B5
 Putney SW15 134 B1
 Woodford IG8 37 B2
Peartree Gdns RM8 80 B4
Pear Tree Ho
 Brockley SE4 141 B1
 Hayes UB8 83 A1
Peartree La E1 118 C6
Pear Tree Rd TW15 171 A5
Peartree Rd EN1 5 C2
Peartree St EC1 95 A3 242 A6
Peartree Way SE10 121 A2
Peary Ho 4 NW10 67 B1
Peary Pl E2 96 C4
Peaslake Ct SM2 218 A1
Peas Mead Terr E4 36 A6
Peatfield Cl DA15 167 C1
Pebworth Lo
 2 Belmont SM2 217 D1
 South Norwood SE25 205 D5
Pebworth Rd HA1 65 A6
Peckarmans Wood SE21, SE26 162 A1
Peckett Sq 3 N5 72 D4
Peckford Pl SW9 138 C3
PECKHAM 140 A4
Peckham Gr SE15 139 C5
Peckham High St SE15 140 A4
Peckham Hill St SE15 140 A5
Peckham Park Prim Sch SE15 140 A5
Peckham Park Rd SE15 140 A5
Peckham Rd SE5 139 C4
Peckham Rye
 East Dulwich SE22 140 A1
 Peckham SE15, SE22 140 B1
Peckham Rye Sta SE15 140 A3
Peckwater Ho 2 NW5 71 D2
Peckwater St NW5 71 C3
Pedlars Wlk N7 72 A3
Pedley Rd RM8 58 C1
Pedley St E1 95 D3 243 D5
Pedro St E5 74 D4
Pedworth Gdns 4 SE16 118 C2
Peebles Ct UB1 86 A1
Peek Cres SW19 178 D5
Peel Centre (Metropolitan Police Training Establishment) NW9 45 D6
Peel Cl Chingford E4 19 D2
 Edmonton N9 18 A1
Peel Ct UB6 86 A4
Peel Dr Colindale NW9 45 D6
 Redbridge IG5 56 A6
Peel Gr E2 96 C5
Peel Pass W8 245 A3
Peel Pl IG5 37 D1
Peel Prec NW6 91 C5
Peel Rd
 Farnborough BR6 227 A3
 Harrow HA3 42 D6
 Wembley HA0, HA9 65 D5
 Woodford E18 36 D2
Peel St W8 113 C5 245 A3

Peel Way UB8 82 A2
Peel Yates Ho 13 SE7 122 A2
Peerglow Est EN3 18 C6
Peerless St EC1 95 B4 235 C1
Pegamoid Rd N18 18 C1
Pegasus Cl N16 73 B4
Pegasus Ct
 11 Acton W3 89 A1
 Brentford TW8 110 B1
 2 Buckhurst Hill IG9 21 D2
 College Pk NW10 90 B4
 Edmonton N21 17 A4
 Harrow HA3 43 D4
 Kingston u T KT1 197 D6
 Sutton SM1 217 D6
Pegasus Ho 9 E1 96 D3
Pegasus Lo N21 17 A4
Pegasus Pl 2 SE11 138 C6
Pegasus Rd CR0, CR9 220 C2
Pegasus Way N11 31 B4
Peggotty Way UB8 82 D1
Pegg Rd TW5 128 D5
Peggy Quirke Ct 2 HA0 66 A2
Pegley Gdns SE12 165 A2
Pegwell Ho 19 E5 74 B3
Pegwell St SE18 145 C5
Pekin St E14 97 C1
Pekoe SE1 253 D3
Peldon Ct TW10 154 B6
Pele Ct N17 33 B3
Pelham Ave IG11 101 D6
Pelham Cl SE5 139 C2
Pelham Cotts DA5 169 D3
Pelham Cres SW7 257 A3
Pelham Ct SW3 257 A3
Pelham Ho W14 254 C3
Pelham Pl
 Chelsea SW7 257 A3
 8 Ealing W7 86 D3
Pelham Prim Sch
 Bexleyheath DA7 147 C2
 Merton SW19 179 C3
Pelham Rd
 Bexleyheath DA7 147 C2
 Ilford IG1 79 B6
 Merton SW19 179 C3
 Penge BR3, SE20 184 C1
 Tottenham N15 51 D5
 Wanstead E18 55 B6
 Wood Green N22 32 C1
Pelham St SW7 114 B2 256 D4
Pelican Ho 8 SE8 119 B2
Pelican Pas 3 E1 96 C3
Pelier St SE17 139 A6
Pelinore Rd SE6 164 C2
Pella Ho SE11 260 D2
Pellant Rd SW6 135 A5 264 B4
Pellatt Gr N22 32 C2
Pellatt Rd
 East Dulwich SE22 161 D6
 Wembley HA9 66 A6
Pellerin Rd N16 73 C3
Pellew Ho 15 E1 96 B3
Pellings Cl BR2 208 C6
Pelling St E14 97 C1
Pellipar Cl N13 16 C1
Pellipar Gdns SE18 122 B1
Pellipar Rd SE18 122 B1
Pelly Ct 4 E17 54 A5
Pelly Rd E13 99 A5
Pelter St E2 95 D4
Pelton Ct CR2 221 A2
Pelton Rd SE10 120 C1
Pembar Ave E17 53 A6
Pemberley Chase KT19 214 D3
Pemberley Cl KT19 214 D3
Pemberley Ho KT19 214 D3
Pember Rd NW10 90 D4
Pemberton Ct 18 E1 96 D4
Pemberton Gdns
 Camden Town N19 71 C5
 Dagenham RM6 59 A4
Pemberton Ho SE26 184 A6
Pemberton Pl
 Esher KT10 212 A5
 2 Hackney E8 74 B1
Pemberton Rd
 East Molesey KT8 196 A5
 Harringay N4 50 D4
Pemberton Row EC4 241 B2
Pemberton Terr N19 71 C5
Pembridge Ave TW4 151 B3
Pembridge Cres W11 113 C6 245 A6
Pembridge Gdns W2 113 C6 245 A5

Pembridge Hall Sch W2 113 C6 245 B5
Pembridge Mews W11 113 C6 245 A6
Pembridge Pl
 Notting Hill W2 113 C6 245 B6
 1 Wandsworth SW15 157 C6
Pembridge Rd W11 113 C6 245 A5
Pembridge Sq W2 113 C6 245 B5
Pembridge Villas W11 113 C6 245 A6
Pembroke Ave
 Enfield EN1 6 B4
 Harrow HA3 43 B6
 Islington N1 94 A6 233 B6
 Surbiton KT5 198 D4
Pembroke Bldgs NW10 90 A4
Pembroke Cl SW1 248 B1
Pembroke Ct 11 W7 86 D2
Pembroke Gdns Cl W8 255 A5
Pembroke Gdns
 Dagenham RM10 81 D5
 West Kensington W8 113 B2 254 D4
Pembroke Hall NW4 46 C6
Pembroke Ho
 Acton W3 111 A4
 Chelsea SW1 258 A5
 5 Clapham Pk SW2 160 A6
 17 Kensington W2 91 D1
 Putney SW15 156 A6
 Upper Tooting SW17 180 B5
Pembroke Lo 2 SW16 160 B1
Pembroke Mews
 8 Bow E3 97 A4
 Bromley BR1 187 D1
 Kensington W8 255 A5
 Muswell Hill N10 31 A2
Pembroke Pl
 Edgware HA8 26 C3
 Isleworth TW7 130 C3
 Kensington W8 255 A5
Pembroke Rd
 Bromley BR1 187 D1
 Edmonton N13 17 A1
 Greenford UB6 85 D3
 Hornsey N8 50 A5
 Ilford IG3 57 D2
 Kensington W8 113 C2 255 A4
 Mitcham CR4 181 A1
 Muswell Hill N10 31 A3
 Newham E6 100 B2
 Ruislip HA4 39 D1
 South Norwood SE25 205 C5
 South Tottenham N15 51 D4
 Walthamstow E17 53 D4
 Wembley HA9 65 D5
Pembroke Sq W8 113 C3 255 A5
Pembroke St N1 94 A6 233 B6
Pembroke Studios W8 254 D5
Pembroke Terr NW8 229 C5
Pembroke Villas
 Kensington W8 255 A4
 Richmond TW9 131 D1
Pembroke W14 254 D3
Pembroke Way UB3 105 A3
Pembroke Wlk W8 255 A4
Pembry Cl SW9 138 C4
Pembury Ave KT4 200 A2
Pembury Cl
 Hackney E5 74 B3
 Hayes BR2 208 D2
Pembury Cres DA14 169 A2
Pembury Ct UB3 127 B6
Pembury Ho
 Camberwell SE5 139 C3
 Keston Mark BR2 210 A1
Pembury Pl 15 E5, E8 74 B3
Pembury Rd
 Croydon SE25 206 A5
 Erith DA7 147 A6
 Hackney E5 74 B3
 Tottenham N17 33 D1
Pemdevon Rd CR0 204 C2
Pemell Cl 30 E1 96 C3
Pemell Ho 31 E1 96 C3
Pemerich Cl UB3 105 D1
Pempath Pl HA9 65 D6
Penair Lodge HA1 64 C5
Penally Pl N1 235 D6
Penang St E1 118 B5
Penard Rd UB2 107 D3
Penarth Ctr The SE15 140 C6

Penarth Ct SM2 218 A1
Penarth St SE15 140 C6
Penates KT10 212 B4
Penberth Rd SE6 164 A3
Penbury Rd UB2 107 B1
Penceat Ct SE20 184 C1
Pencombe Mews W11 244 D6
Pencraig Way SE15 140 B6
Pendall Cl EN4 2 C1
Penda Rd DA8 147 D5
Pendarves Rd SW20 178 C2
Penda's Mead E9 75 A4
Pendell Ave UB3 127 D5
Pendennis Ho 15 SE8 119 A2
Pendennis Rd
 Streatham SW16 182 A6
 Tottenham N17 51 B6
Penderel Rd TW3 151 C6
Penderry Rise SE6 164 B2
Penderyn Way N7 71 D4
Pendlebury Ho 5 SE18 144 A4
Pendle Ho 13 SE26 162 A1
Pendle Rd SW16 181 B5
Pendlestone Rd E17 53 D4
Pendley Ho 18 E2 96 A6
Pendolino Way NW10 66 D1
Pendragon Rd BR1 165 A1
Pendragon Sch BR1 165 A1
Pendragon Wlk NW9 45 C3
Pendrell Ho WC2 239 D1
Pendrell Rd SE4 141 A3
Pendrell St SE18 145 B6
Pendula Dr UB4 84 D3
Penelope Ho 20 SW9 138 C4
Penerley Rd SE6 163 D3
Penfield Lo 7 W9 91 C2
Penfields Ho N7 72 A2
Penfold Cl CR0 220 C5
Penfold Ct 7 CR4 181 A1
Penfold Ho 14 SE18 144 D6
Penfold La DA5 168 D3
Penfold Pl NW1 92 C2 237 A4
Penfold Rd N9 18 D3
Penfold St NW8 92 B3 236 D5
Penford Gdns SE9 143 D2
Penford St SE5 138 D3
Pengarth Rd DA5 168 D5
PENGE 184 D4
Penge East Sta SE20 184 C4
Penge La SE20 184 D3
Penge Rd
 Newham E13 99 C6
 South Norwood SE25 206 A6
Penge West Sta SE20 184 B4
Penhall Rd SE7 121 D2
Penhill Rd DA5 168 C4
Penhurst Mans SW6 264 C2
Penifather La UB6 86 B4
Peninsula Ct E14 119 D3
Peninsular Cl TW14 149 C5
Peninsular Park Rd SE7 121 A2
Penistone Rd SW16 182 A3
Penketh Dr HA1 64 B5
Penmayne Ho SE11 261 B2
Penmon Rd SE2 124 A3
Pennack Rd SE15 139 D6
Penn Almshouses 1 SE10 142 A4
Pennant Mews W8 113 D2 255 C4
Pennant Terr E17 35 B1
Pennard Mans 5 W12 112 C4
Pennard Rd W12 112 C4
Pennards The TW16 194 C6
Penn Cl
 Greenford UB6 85 D5
 Harrow HA3 43 C5
Penn Ct NW9 45 B6
Pennefather Ho N1 73 B2
Pennells Ct TW5 129 C6
Penner Cl SW19 157 A2
Penners Gdns KT6 198 A2
Pennethorne Cl E9 96 C6
Pennethorne Ho SW11 136 B2
Pennethorne Rd SE15 140 B5
Penn Gdns BR7 188 D1
Penn Ho
 7 Edmonton N9 18 A1
 Lisson Gr NW8 237 A5
Pennine Dr NW2 68 D6

Pennine La NW2 69 A6
Pennine Mans NW2 69 A6
Pennine Par NW2 69 A6
Pennine Way UB7 127 B5
Pennington Cl 10 SE27 183 B6
Pennington Ct
 4 Rotherhithe SE16 119 A5
 23 St George in t East E1 118 A6
Pennington Dr N21 16 A6
Pennington Lo 18 KT5 198 A4
Pennington St E1 118 B6
Pennington Way SE12 165 B2
Penniston Cl N17 33 A1
Penn La Bexley DA5 168 D5
 Sidcup DA5 169 A5
Penn Rd N7 72 A4
Penn St N1 95 B6 235 D5
Penny Ct SW10 266 B6
Pennyfields E14 119 C6
Pennyford Ct NW8 236 C6
Penny La TW17 193 C2
Penny Mews SW12 159 B4
Pennymore Wlk W9 91 B3
Penny Rd NW10 88 D4
Pennyroyal Ave E6 100 C1
Penny Royal SM6 219 D2
Penpoll Rd E8 74 B2
Penpool La DA16 146 B2
Penray EN5 1 A2
Penrhyn Ave E17 35 C2
Penrhyn Cres
 Mortlake SW14 133 A1
 Walthamstow E17 35 C2
Penrhyn Gdns KT1 197 D5
Penrhyn Gr E17 35 C2
Penrhyn Rd KT1 198 A6
Penrith Cl
 Beckenham BR3 185 D2
 Putney SW15 157 A6
Penrith Pl SE27 160 D2
Penrith Rd
 New Malden KT3 199 B5
 South Norwood CR7 183 A1
 Tottenham N15 51 B4
Penrith St SW16 181 C4
Penrose Gr SE17 117 A1 262 A1
Penrose Ho
 Camberwell SE17 262 A1
 Southgate N21 16 B6
Penrose St SE17 117 A1 262 A1
Penryn Ho SE11 261 C2
Penryn St NW1 93 D5 232 C4
Penry St SE1 263 B3
Pensbury Pl SW8 137 C3
Pensbury St SW8 137 C3
Pensford Ave TW9 132 C3
Penshurst Ave DA15 168 A5
Penshurst Ct
 Croydon CR2 220 D1
 1 Edgware HA8 26 D5
Penshurst Gdns HA8 26 D5
Penshurst Gn BR2 208 D4
Penshurst Ho 1 SE15 140 C6
Penshurst 2 NW5 71 A2
Penshurst Rd
 Erith DA7 147 B4
 Homerton E9 74 D1
 Thornton Heath CR7 204 D4
 Tottenham N17 33 D3
Penshurst Way SM2 217 C1
Penshurst Wlk 4 BR2 208 D4
Pensilver Cl EN4 2 C1
Penstemon Cl N3 29 C4
Pentavia Retail Pk NW7 27 D3
Pentelow Gdns TW14 150 A5
Pentire Rd E17 36 B2
Pentland Ave
 Edgware HA8 10 D2
 Littleton TW17 192 C4
Pentland Cl
 Cricklewood NW11 69 A6
 Lower Edmonton N9 18 C2
Pentland Gdns SW18 158 A5
Pentland Ho
 17 Camden Town NW5 71 A2
 7 Stamford Hill N16 51 D1
Pentland Pl UB5 85 A6
Pentland Rd
 Bushey WD23 8 A5
 1 Maida Vale NW6 91 C4
Pentlands BR3 186 A2
Pentlands Cl CR4 203 B6

Pentland St SW18 158 A5
Pentland Way UB10 61 A5
Pentlow St SW15 134 C2
Pentney Rd
 5 Chingford E4 20 B3
 Merton SW19, SW20 179 A2
 Streatham SW12 159 C3
Penton Gr N1 234 A3
Penton Ho
 3 Abbey Wood SE2 124 D4
 Islington N1 234 A3
 Sutton SM2 218 A1
Penton Pl SE17 116 D1 261 D2
Penton Rise WC1 94 B4 233 D2
Penton St N1 94 C5 234 A3
PENTONVILLE 94 B5
Pentonville Rd N1 94 B5 233 C3
Pentrich Ave EN1 6 A5
Pentridge St SE15 139 D5
Pentyre Ave N18 33 B5
Penwerris Ave TW5, TW7 130 A5
Penwerris Ct TW7 130 A5
Penwith Rd SW18 157 D2
Penwood Ct HA5 41 B5
Penwood Ho SW15 155 D5
Penwortham Ct 1 N22 32 C1
Penwortham Prim Sch SW17 181 B4
Penwortham Rd SW16 181 C4
Penylan Pl HA8 26 C3
Penywern Rd SW5 113 C1 255 B2
Penzance Ho SE11 261 B2
Penzance Pl W11 113 A5 244 B4
Penzance St W11 113 A5 244 A4
Peony Ct IG8 36 C3
Peony Gdns W12 112 A6
Peperfield WC1 233 C1
Pepler Ho 17 W10 91 A3
Pepler Mews SE1 263 C1
Peploe Rd NW6 90 D5
Pepper Cl E6 100 B2
Peppercorn Cl CR7 183 B1
Peppermead Sq SE13 163 C6
Peppermint Cl CR0 204 A2
Peppermint Pl 7 E11 76 C5
Pepper St
 Borough The SE1 252 A2
 Millwall E14 119 D3
Peppie Cl N16 73 C6
Pepsi Trocadero* W1 249 C5
Pepys Cl UB10 60 D4
Pepys Cres
 Barnet EN5 12 C6
 2 Newham E16 121 A5
Pepys Ct SW20 178 C1
Pepys Ent Ctr 13 SE8 119 B2
Pepys Ho
 14 Bethnal Green E2 96 C4
 Clapham Pk SW4 159 D6
Pepys Rd
 New Cross Gate SE14 140 D3
 Wimbledon SW20 178 C2
Pepys Rise BR6 211 D1
Pepys St EC3 117 C6 253 B6
Perak Ct KT5 199 A2
Peralte Terr CR4 204 A5
Perceval Ave NW3 70 C3
Perceval Ct UB5 63 C3
Percheron Cl TW7 130 D2
Percheron Ct 3 SW9 138 B2
Percheron Rd WD6 11 B5
Perch St E8 73 D4
Percival Ct N17 33 D3
Percival Gdns RM6 58 C3
Percival Ho 8 IG8 37 A6
Percival Rd Enfield EN1 5 D1
 Feltham TW13 149 D2
 Mortlake SW14 133 A1
 Orpington BR6 226 D6
Percival St EC1 94 D4 234 D1
Percival Way KT19 215 B4
Percy Ave TW15 170 C5
Percy Bilton Ct TW5 129 D4

Percy Bryant Rd TW16 171 C3
Percy Bush Rd UB7 104 B3
Percy Cir WC1 94 B4 233 D2
Percy Ct 1 KT5 198 B3
Percy Gdns
Enfield EN3 18 D6
Hayes UB4 83 C4
5 Isleworth TW7 131 A2
New Malden KT4 199 C1
Percy Ho 4 SW16 181 C6
Percy Laurie Ho 6 SW15 134 D1
Percy Mews W1 239 C3
Percy Pas W1 239 C3
Percy Rd
Bexleyheath DA7 147 A3
Carshalton CR4 203 A2
Croydon SE25 206 A4
Edmonton N21 17 A4
Hampton TW12 173 C3
Ilford IG3 58 A2
Isleworth TW7 131 A1
Leytonstone E11 54 C2
Newham E16 98 C2
North Finchley N12 30 A5
Penge SE20 184 D2
Romford RM7 59 D6
Shepherd's Bush W12 112 A4
Twickenham TW2 152 A3
Percy St W1 93 D2 239 C3
Percy Terr BR1 210 D6
Percy Way TW2 152 A3
Peregrine Cl NW10 67 B3
Peregrine Ct
Bexley DA16 145 D4
Streatham SW16 182 B6
Peregrine Gdns CR0 223 A6
Peregrine Ho
6 Battersea SW11 136 C2
Finsbury EC1 234 D2
Peregrine Rd
Sunbury TW16 171 D1
Tottenham N17 33 B3
Peregrine Way SW19, SW20 178 C3
Performing Arts & Tech Sch SE25 205 B3
Perham Rd W14 113 A1 254 B1
Peridot St E6 100 A2
Perifield SE21 161 A3
Perimeade Rd UB6 87 C5
Period Wks E10 53 A1
Periton Rd SE9 143 D1
PERIVALE 87 B5
Perivale Gdns W13 87 B3
Perivale Grange UB6 87 B5
Perivale Ind Pk UB6 87 B5
Perivale La UB6 87 A4
Perivale Lo UB6 87 A4
Perivale New Bsns Ctr UB6 87 C5
Perivale Prim Sch UB6 87 C5
Perivale Sta UB6 87 A5
Perivale UB6 86 D5
Perkin Cl
Hounslow TW3 129 D1
Wembley HA0 65 B3
Perkins Ct TW15 170 B5
Perkins Ho 15 E14 97 B2
Perkins Rd IG2 57 B4
Perkins Rents SW1 259 C5
Perkins Sq SE1 252 B4
Perks Cl SE3 142 C2
Perley Ho 9 E3 97 B2
Perotti Ho SW6 135 D2
Perpins Rd SE9 167 C5
Perran Rd SE24, SW2 160 D2
Perren St NW5 71 B2
Perrers Rd W6 112 B2
Perrin Cl TW15 170 B5
Perrin Ct TW15 170 C6
Perring Est E3 97 C2
Perrin Grange HA9 66 B6
Perrin Rd HA0 65 B4
Perrins Ct HA3 44 B2
Perrin's Ct 20 NW3 70 A4
Perrin's La NW3 70 A4
Perrin's Wlk NW3 70 A4
Perronet Ho SE1 261 D5
Perry Ave W3 89 B1
Perry Cl UB8 82 D1
Perry Ct
6 Isle of Dogs E14 119 C1
2 Kingston u T KT2 176 A1
Sutton SM1 217 C3
Perry Ct *continued*
2 Tottenham N15 51 C3
Perryfield Way
Richmond TW10 153 B2
West Hendon NW9 45 D3
Perry Garth UB5 84 C6
Perry Gdns N9 17 C1
Perry Hall Prim Sch BR6 211 D3
Perry Hill SE6 163 B1
Perry Ho 24 SW2 160 A4
Perry How KT4 199 D1
Perryman Ho
Barking IG11 101 A6
Tottenham N17 34 B3
Perrymans Farm Rd IG2 57 B4
Perry Mead
Bushey WD23 8 A5
Enfield EN2 4 D3
Perrymead St SW6 135 D4 265 C1
Perrymount Prim Sch SE23 162 D2
Perryn Ct 1 TW1 153 A4
Perryn Ho W3 111 C6
Perryn Rd Acton W3 111 B6
1 Bermondsey SE16 118 B3
Perry Rise SE23 163 A1
Perry's Pl W1 239 C2
Perry St BR7 189 C4
Perry Street Gdns BR7 189 C4
Perry Vale SE23 162 D2
Perrywood Ho 17 E5 74 B3
Persant Rd SE6 164 C2
Perseverance Pl SW9 138 C5
Perseverance Works 17 E2 95 C4
Pershore Cl IG2 56 D4
Pershore Gr SM5 202 B3
Pershore Ho 11 W13 109 A5
Pert Cl N10 31 B4
Perth Ave Hayes UB4 84 C3
Kingsbury NW9 45 B2
Perth Cl Northolt UB5 63 C3
Wimbledon SW20 178 A1
Perth Ct 5 SE5 139 B1
Perth Ho 12 Acton W3 88 C1
Barnsbury N1 72 B1
Perth Rd
Barking IG11 101 B6
Beckenham BR3 186 A1
Finsbury Pk N4 50 C1
Ilford IG2 56 D3
Newham E13 99 B5
Tottenham N22 32 D2
Walthamstow E10 53 B1
Perth Terr IG2 57 A2
Perwell Ave HA2 41 B1
Perystreete SE23 162 C2
Petavel Rd TW11 174 C4
Petchey Acad The E8 73 D3
Peter Ave NW10 68 B1
Peter Best Ho 1 E1 96 B1
Peterboat Cl SE10 120 C2
Peterborough Ct EC4 241 B1
Peterborough Gdns IG1 56 A2
Peterborough Mews SW6 135 C3
Peterborough Prim Sch SW6 135 C3
Peterborough Rd
Carshalton SM5 202 C3
Fulham SW6 135 C2
Harrow HA1 42 D2
Leytonstone E10 54 B3
Peterborough Villas SW6 265 C2
Peter Bradley Ct RM9 81 B1
Peter Butler Ho 9 SE1 118 A4
Peterchurch Ho SE15 140 B6
Peter Fagan Ho UB3 105 C3
Petergate SW11 136 A1
Peterhead Ct 12 UB1 86 A1
Peter Heathfield Ho 4 E15 98 B6
Peter Hills Ho 6 SE16 118 A2
Peter Hills with St Mary's & St Paul's CE Prim Sch SE16 118 D5
Peter Ho SW8 270 A4
Peter James Bsns Ctr UB3 106 A4
Peter James Ent Ctr NW10 89 A4
Peter Kennedy Ct CR0 207 B3
Peterley Bsns Ctr 21 E2 96 B5
Peter Lyell Ct HA4 62 B6
Peters Cl
Bexley DA16 145 C3
Dagenham RM8 58 D1
Stanmore HA7 25 D4
Peter's Ct SW4 160 A5
Peters Ct 9 W2 91 D1
Petersfield Cl N18 33 A5
Petersfield Rd W3 111 A4
Petersfield Rise SW15 156 B3
PETERSHAM 154 A3
Petersham Cl
Richmond TW10 153 D2
Sutton SM1 217 C3
Petersham Dr BR5 190 A1
Petersham Gdns BR5 189 D1
Petersham Ho SW7 256 C4
Petersham La SW7 256 A6
Petersham Mews SW7 114 A3 256 B5
Petersham Pl SW7 114 A3 256 B6
Petersham Rd TW10 154 A3
Petersham Terr CR0 220 A5
Peter's La EC1 241 D4
Peter's Lo HA8 26 B4
Peter's Path SE26 184 B6
Peterstone Rd SE2 124 B4
Peterstow Cl SW19 157 A2
Peter St W1 115 D6 249 C6
Peterwood Pk CR9 220 B6
Peterwood Way CR0 220 B6
Petherton Ct
Brondesbury Pk NW10 90 D6
10 Harrow HA1 42 D3
Petherton Ho N4 51 A1
Petherton Rd N5 73 A3
Petiver Cl 26 E9 74 C1
Petley Rd W6 134 D5
Peto Pl NW1 238 D6
Peto St N E16 98 D1
Petrel Ct 8 SE21 161 B2
Petrie Cl NW2 69 A2
Petrie Ho 3 SE18 144 C6
Petrie Mus of Egyptian Archaeology* WC1 93 D3 239 C5
Petros Gdns 1 NW3 70 A2
Pettacre Cl SE28 123 A3
Petticoat Lane Mkt* EC2 95 D2 243 C3
Petticoat Sq E1 243 C2
Petticoat Twr E1 243 C2
Pettit's Pl RM10 81 C3
Pettit's Rd RM10 81 C3
Pettiward Cl SW15 134 C1
Pettman Cres SE18, SE28 123 B3
Pettsgrove Ave HA0 65 C3
Pett's Hill UB5 63 D3
Petts La TW17 192 C5
Pett St SE7 122 A2
PETTS WOOD 211 B5
Petts Wood Rd BR5 211 B4
Petts Wood Sta BR5 211 A4
Petty France SW1 115 D3 259 C6
Petty Wales EC3 253 B5
Petworth Cl UB5 63 B1
Petworth Gdns
Hillingdon UB10 83 A6
West Barnes SW20 200 B6
Petworth Ho 16 SE22 139 C2
Petworth Rd
Bexley DA6 169 C6
Colney Hatch N12 30 C5
Petworth St SW11 136 C4 267 B2
Petyt Pl SW3 136 C6 267 A5
Petyward SW3 114 C2 257 B3
Pevensey Ave
Enfield EN1 5 C3
Friern Barnet N11 31 D5
Pevensey Cl TW7 130 A5
Pevensey Ct
4 South Acton W3 110 D4
West Norwood SW16 160 C1
10 Woodford E18 37 A2
Pevensey Ho 5 E1 97 A2
Pevensey Rd
Feltham TW13 151 A3
Pevensey Rd *continued*
Forest Gate E7 77 A4
Upper Tooting SW17 180 B6
Peverel Ho RM10 81 C6
Peverel E6 100 C1
Peverett Cl N11 31 B5
Peveril Dr TW11 174 B5
Peveril Ho SE1 262 D5
Pewsey Cl E4 35 C5
Pewsham Ho N4 51 A1
Pewterers Ct N3 29 B2
Peyton Ho N11 31 A6
Peyton Pl SE10 142 A5
Pharamond NW2 68 D2
Pharaoh Cl CR4 202 D2
Pheasant Cl E16 99 B1
Phelps Ho SW15 134 D2
Phelp St SE17 139 B6
Phelps Way UB3 105 D2
Phene St SW3 136 C6 267 B6
Philadelphia Ct SW10 266 B3
Philbeach Gdns SW5 113 C1 255 A2
Phil Brown Pl 3 SW8 137 B2
Philchurch Pl 36 E1 96 A1
Philia Ho 4 NW1 71 C1
Philimore Cl SE18 123 C1
Philip Blairman Ho E1 243 C5
Philip Ct Enfield EN2 5 B4
Paddington W2 236 C4
Philip Gdns CR0 223 B6
Philip Ho
East Barnet N20 14 D2
12 Paddington NW6 91 D6
Philip La N15 51 C6
Philipot Almshouse SE9 166 B5
Philipot Path SE9 166 B5
Philippa Gdns SE9 165 D6
Philips Cl CR4 203 A1
Philip St E13 99 A3
Philip Turner Est 28 E9 74 C1
Philip Wlk SE15 140 A2
Phillimore Ct W8 245 B1
Phillimore Gardens Cl W8 113 C3 255 A6
Phillimore Gdns
Kensington W8 113 C4 245 A1
Willesden NW10 90 C6
Phillimore Pl W8 113 C4 245 A1
Phillimore Terr W8 255 B6
Phillimore Wlk W8 113 C3 255 B6
Phillip Ho E1 243 D3
Phillipp St N1 95 C6
Phillips Ct
Edgware HA8 26 C4
Hayes UB4 84 B4
Phillipson Ho 6 N12 29 D5
Philpot La EC3 253 A6
Philpot Sq SW6 135 D2
Philpot St E1 96 B1
Philson Mans 13 E1 96 B1
Phineas Pett Rd SE9 144 A2
Phipp's Bridge Rd CR4, SW19 202 B6
Phipps Bridge Sta CR4 202 B6
Phipps Hatch La EN2 5 A5
Phipps Ho
1 Greenwich SE7 121 B1
15 Shepherd's Bush W12 112 B6
Phipp St EC2 95 C3 243 A6
Phoebeth Rd SE4 163 C6
Phoenix Bsns Ctr 22 E3 97 C2
Phoenix Cl
18 Shoreditch E8 95 D6
Walthamstow E17 35 B1
West Wickham BR4 224 C6
Phoenix Ct
4 Brentford TW8 110 A1
Chingford E4 19 D1
Croydon SE25 206 A4
2 Deptford SE14 141 A6
Enfield EN3 6 C5
Feltham TW13 171 C6
Millwall E14 119 C2
8 New Barnet EN5 2 A1
Phoenix Ctr The 1 SM6 220 A1
Phoenix Dr BR2 225 D5
Phoenix High Sch W12 112 A6
Phoenix Ho
Chelsea SW1 258 A4
Kingston u T KT3 199 D6
Phoenix Ind Est HA1 42 D5
Phoenix Lodge Mans 1 W6 112 C2
Phoenix Pk NW2 68 A6
Phoenix Pl WC1 94 B3 240 D6
Phoenix Rd
Penge SE20 184 C4
Somers Town NW1 93 D4 232 C2
Phoenix Sch E3 97 B4
Phoenix Sch The NW3 70 A2
Phoenix St WC2 239 D1
Phoenix Trad Est UB6 87 D6
Phoenix Trad Pk TW8 109 D1
Phoenix Way TW5 128 D6
Phoenix Wharf Rd SE1 253 D1
Phyllis Ave KT3 200 B4
Phyllis Ho CR0 220 D4
Phyllis Hodges Ho NW1 93 D5 232 C3
Physic Pl SW3 136 D6 267 C6
Picador Ho 1 RM10 81 D2
Picardy Manorway DA17 125 D4
Picardy Rd DA17 125 C2
Picardy St DA17 125 C3
Piccadilly Arc SW1 249 A4
Piccadilly Circus Sta SW1 115 D6 249 C5
Piccadilly Cir* W1 115 D6 249 C5
Piccadilly Ct 5 N7 72 B2
Piccadilly Pl W1 249 B5
Piccadilly W1 115 C5 249 A4
Pickard Cl N14 15 D3
Pickard St EC1 234 D2
Pickering Ave E6 100 C4
Pickering Cl E9 74 D1
Pickering Ct N22 32 D2
Pickering Gdns
Croydon SE25 205 D3
Friern Barnet N11 31 A4
Pickering Ho
Brentford W5 109 C2
18 Kensington W2 91 D1
Stoke Newington N4 51 B2
4 Woolwich SE18 122 C2
Pickering Mews 9 W2 91 D1
Pickering Pl SW1 249 B3
Pickering St N1 234 D6
Pickets Cl WD23 8 C3
Pickets St SW12 159 B4
Pickett Croft HA7 25 D2
Pickett's Lock La N9 18 D2
Pickford Cl DA7 147 A3
Pickford La DA7 147 A3
Pickford Rd DA7 147 A2
Pickfords Wharf N1 235 A3
Pickhurst Gn BR2 208 D2
Pickhurst Inf Sch BR2 208 D3
Pickhurst Jun Sch BR2 208 D3
Pickhurst La BR2, BR3, BR4 208 C2
Pickhurst Mead BR2 208 D2
Pickhurst Pk BR2 208 D4
Pickhurst Rise BR4 208 B1
Pickwick Cl TW4 151 A6
Pickwick Ct SE9 166 B3
Pickwick Ho
21 Bermondsey SE16 118 A4
3 Shepherd's Bush W11 112 D5
Pickwick Mews N18 33 C5
Pickwick Pl HA1 42 C2
Pickwick Rd SE21 161 C4
Pickwick St SE1 252 A1
Pickwick Way BR7 189 A4
Pickworth Cl SW8 270 B3
Picton Ho 1 SW4 160 A4
Picton Pl
Marylebone W1 238 B1
Tolworth KT6 198 C1
Picton St SE5 139 B5
Picture Ho 6 SW16 160 A2
Pied Bull Ct WC1 240 B3
Pied Bull Yd WC1 240 B3
Piedmont Rd SE18 123 B1
Pield Heath Ave UB8 82 C3
Pield Heath House Sch UB8 82 A3
Pield Heath Rd UB8 82 B3
Pier Head E1 118 B5
Pierhead Wharf 37 E1 118 B5
Pier Ho SW3 267 B5
Piermont Pl BR1 188 A1
Piermont Rd SE22 162 B6
Pier Par 3 E16 122 C5
Pierpoint Bldg 4 E14 119 C4
Pier Rd
Feltham TW14 150 B6
Newham E16 122 C4
Pierrepoint Rd W3 110 D6
Pierrepoint Row N1 234 C4
Pierrepoint SE25 205 C6
Pierson Ho 12 SE19 183 C4
Pier St E14 120 A2
Pier Terr SW18 136 A1
Pier Way SE18 123 B3
Pigeon Ct E4 36 A4
Pigeon La TW12 173 C6
Piggott Ho 2 E2 96 D5
Pigott St E14 97 C1
Pike Cl Bromley BR1 187 B5
Hillingdon UB10 82 B6
Pike Rd NW7 27 B6
Pike's End HA5 40 B5
Pikestone Cl UB4 85 A3
Pikethorne 1 SE23 162 D2
Pilgrimage St SE1 117 B4 252 C1
Pilgrim Cl SM4 201 D2
Pilgrim Hill SE27 183 A6
Pilgrim Ho SE1 262 D5
Pilgrims Cl UB5 64 A3
Pilgrims Cloisters 10 SE5 139 C5
Pilgrims Cl N13 32 B6
Pilgrims Ct Enfield EN1 5 B3
Greenwich SE3 143 A4
Pilgrim's La NW3 70 B4
Pilgrims Mews 12 E14 120 B6
Pilgrim's Pl 6 NW3 70 B4
Pilgrim's Rise EN4 14 C6
Pilgrim St EC4 241 C1
Pilgrims Way 5 E6 100 A6
Pilgrims Way Prim Sch SE15 140 C6
Pilgrim's Way CR2 221 D3
Pilgrims Way
Upper Holloway N19 49 D1
Wembley HA9 44 D1
Pilkington Ct 1 NW9 46 A5
Pilkington Rd
Orpington BR6 227 A6
4 Peckham SE15 140 B3
Pillions La UB4 83 B3
Pilot Ind Ctr NW10 89 C3
Pilsden Cl SW19 156 D3
Piltdown Rd WD19 22 D6
Pilton Est The CR0 220 D6
Pilton Pl SE17 262 B2
Pimento Ct W5 109 D3
Pimlico Sta SW1 115 D1 259 C2
PIMLICO 115 C1
Pimlico Rd SW1 115 A1 258 B2
Pimlico Sch SW1 115 C1 259 B1
Pimlico Wlk 1 N1 95 C4
Pinchbeck Rd BR6 227 D2
Pinchin St E1 118 A6
Pincombe Ho SE17 262 C2
Pincott Pl SE4 140 D2
Pincott Rd
8 Bexley DA6 147 C1
Merton SW19 180 A2
Pindar St EC2 95 C2 243 A4
Pindock Mews W9 91 D3
Pine Apple Ct SW1 259 A6
Pine Ave
Stratford New Town E15 76 B3
West Wickham BR4 207 D1
Pine Cl
11 Dartmouth Pk N19 71 C6
London E10 75 D6
Osidge N14 15 C4
3 Penge SE20 184 C2
Stanmore HA7 25 B6
Pine Coombe CR0 222 D4
Pinecrest Gdns BR6 226 D4
Pinecroft Cres EN5 1 A1
Pinecroft
East Wickham DA16 146 A5
Harrow HA3 44 B4
Pine Ct UB5 85 A4
Pinedene 2 SE15 140 B4
Pinefield Cl E14 119 C6
Pine Gdns Ruislip HA4 62 B6
Surbiton KT5 198 C

Pine Glade BR6 ... 226 B4
Pine Gr
Finsbury Pk N4,
N19 ... 72 B6
Totteridge N20 ... 13 C3
Wimbledon SW19 ... 179 B5
Pine Ho Bow E3 ... 97 A6
21 Rotherhithe
SE16 ... 118 C4
Pinehurst BR7 ... 188 D4
Pinehurst Ct 6 W11 ... 91 B1
Pinehurst HA7 ... 25 A5
Pinehurst Wlk 4
BR6 ... 211 B1
Pinelands Cl 7 SE3 ... 142 D5
Pine Lo SW15 ... 157 A5
Pinemartin Cl NW2 ... 68 C5
Pine Pl UB4 ... 83 D3
Pine Rd
Brunswick Pk N11 ... 15 A2
Cricklewood NW2 ... 68 D4
Pine Ridge SM5 ... 219 A1
Pines Ct 14 SW19 ... 156 D3
Pines Rd BR1 ... 188 A1
Pine St EC1 ... 94 C3 241 A6
Pines The
Southgate N14 ... 15 C6
South Norwood
SE19 ... 182 D4
Sunbury TW16 ... 194 A6
Surbiton KT6 ... 214 A5
Woodford IG8 ... 21 A1
Pine Tree Cl TW5 ... 128 B4
Pine Tree Ho SE14 ... 140 D5
Pine Tree Lo BR2 ... 208 D5
Pine Trees Dr UB10 ... 60 A4
Pineview Ct 5 E4 ... 20 A3
Pine Wlk KT5 ... 198 C3
Pinewood Ave
Hillingdon UB8 ... 82 B1
Pinner HA5 ... 23 D4
Sidcup DA15 ... 167 C3
Pinewood BR7 ... 188 C4
Pinewood Cl
Crofton BR6 ... 211 B1
Croydon CR0 ... 223 A5
Pinner HA5 ... 23 D4
South Oxhey HA6 ... 22 B5
Pinewood Ct
Clapham Pk SW4 ... 159 D5
Enfield EN2 ... 4 D2
Merton SW19 ... 179 D3
Pinewood Dr BR6 ... 227 C3
Pinewood Gr W5 ... 87 C1
Pinewood Lo WD23 ... 8 B3
Pinewood Pl KT19 ... 215 B4
Pinewood Rd
Bromley BR2 ... 209 A5
Feltham TW13 ... 150 B1
West Heath SE2 ... 146 D6
Pine Wood TW16 ... 172 A2
Pinfold Rd SW16 ... 182 A6
Pinglestone Cl UB7 ... 126 A5
Pinkcoat Cl TW13 ... 150 B1
Pinkerton Ct KT2 ... 176 D1
Pinkerton Pl SW16 ... 181 D6
Pinkham Mans W4 ... 110 C1
Pinkham Way (North
Circular Rd) N12 ... 31 A4
Pinkwell Ave UB3 ... 105 B2
Pinkwell La UB3 ... 105 B2
Pinkwell Prim Sch
UB3 ... 105 A2
Pinley Gdns RM9 ... 102 B6
Pinnace Ho E14 ... 120 A3
Pinnacle Hill DA7 ... 147 D1
Pinnacle Hill N DA7 ... 147 D1
Pinnacle Ho EC3 ... 253 A5
Pinnacle The
Dagenham RM6 ... 59 A3
7 Kingsland N1 ... 73 B2
Pinnell Rd SE9 ... 143 D1
PINNER ... 41 A6
Pinner Ct
Paddington NW8 ... 236 C6
Pinner HA5 ... 41 C5
Pinner Gn HA5 ... 22 C1
PINNER GREEN ... 22 C1
Pinner Gr HA5 ... 41 A4
Pinner Hill HA5 ... 22 B3
Pinner Hill Rd HA5 ... 22 C1
Pinner Ho
30 Camberwell
SE5 ... 139 A3
Pinner HA5 ... 41 A6
Pinner Park Ave HA2 ... 24 A1
Pinner Park Fst & Mid
Schs HA5 ... 41 D6
Pinner Park Gdns
HA2 ... 24 A1
Pinner Rd
Harrow HA1, HA2 ... 42 A3
Northwood HA6 ... 22 A1
Pinner HA2, HA5 ... 41 C5
Pinner Sta HA5 ... 41 A5
Pinner View HA1,
HA2 ... 42 A4
PINNERWOOD PARK
... 22 C3
Pinner Wood Sch
HA5 ... 22 C2
Pinn Way HA4 ... 39 C2
Pintail Cl E6 ... 100 A2
Pintail Ct 39 SE8 ... 141 B6
Pintail Rd IG8 ... 37 B3
Pintail Way UB4 ... 84 D2
Pinter Ho 30 SW9 ... 138 A3
Pinto Cl WD6 ... 11 B5
Pinto Way SE3 ... 143 B1
Pioneer Cl W12 ... 90 B1
Pioneers Ind Pk
CR0 ... 204 A1
Pioneer St SE15 ... 140 A4
Pioneer Way W12 ... 90 C1
Piper Cl N7 ... 72 B3
Piper Rd KT1 ... 198 C6
Pipers Gdns CR0 ... 207 A2
Pipers Gn NW9 ... 45 A4
Pipers Green La HA8 ... 10 A1
Pipers Ho SE10 ... 120 B1
Piper Way IG1 ... 57 B1
Pipewell Rd SM5 ... 202 C3
Pippenhall SE9 ... 166 D5
Pippin Cl
Croydon CR0 ... 207 B1
Dollis Hill NW2 ... 68 B5
Pippin Ct 5 EN4 ... 2 C1
Pippin Ho 17 W10 ... 112 D6
Pippins Ct TW15 ... 170 D4
Piquet Rd SE20 ... 184 C1
Pirbright Cres CR0 ... 224 A2
Pirbright Ho 11 KT2 ... 176 D4
Pirbright Rd SW18 ... 157 C3
Pirie St 6 E16 ... 121 B5
Pitcairn Cl RM7 ... 59 C5
Pitcairn Ct CR4 ... 180 D3
Pitcairne Ct N21 ... 16 B6
Pitcairn Ho 1 E9 ... 74 C1
Pitcairn Rd CR4 ... 180 D3
Pitchford St E15 ... 76 C1
Pitfield Cres SE28 ... 124 A5
Pitfield Ho N5 ... 73 A3
Pitfield St N1 ... 95 C5
Pitfield Way
Enfield EN3 ... 6 C4
Tokyngton NW10 ... 67 A2
Pitfold Cl SE12 ... 165 B5
Pitfold Rd SE12 ... 165 A4
Pit Ho NW10 ... 67 B5
Pitlake CR0 ... 220 D6
Pitman Ho
Southgate N21 ... 16 B6
4 St Johns SE8 ... 141 C4
Pitman St SE5 ... 139 A5
Pitmaston Ho 2
SE13 ... 142 A3
Pitsea Pl E1 ... 96 D1
Pitsea St E1 ... 96 D1
Pitshanger Ct 2 W5 ... 87 C3
Pitshanger La W5 ... 87 C3
Pitshanger Manor Mus
& Art Gallery*
W5 ... 109 D5
Pitt Cres SW19 ... 179 D6
Pitt Ho 4 SW11 ... 136 B1
Pittman Gdns IG1 ... 79 A3
Pitt Rd Harrow HA2 ... 64 A6
Orpington BR6 ... 227 A4
Thornton Heath CR0,
CR7 ... 205 A4
Pitt's Head Mews
W1 ... 248 B3
Pittsmead Ave BR2 ... 209 A2
Pitt St W8 ... 113 C4 245 B2
Pittville Gdns SE25 ... 206 A6
Pixfield Ct BR2 ... 186 D1
Pixham Ct 5 SW19 ... 179 B5
Pixley St E14 ... 97 B1
Pixton 14 NW9 ... 27 C2
Pixton Way CR2 ... 223 B1
Place Farm Ave BR5,
BR6 ... 211 B1
Plains The 7 E4 ... 20 C4
PLAISTOW E13 ... 99 B4
BR1 ... 187 A4
Plaistow Gr
Bromley BR1 ... 187 B3
West Ham E15 ... 98 D6
Plaistow Hospl E13 ... 99 C5
Plaistow La BR1 ... 187 C2
Plaistow Park Rd
E13 ... 99 B5
Plaistow Prim Sch
E13 ... 99 B5
Plaistow Rd E13, E15 ... 98 D5
Plaistow Sta E13 ... 98 D5
Plane St SE26 ... 162 B1
Plane Tree Cres
TW13 ... 150 B1
Planetree Ct W6 ... 112 D2
Plane Tree Ho
Deptford SE8 ... 141 A6
Greenwich SE7 ... 121 D1
Plane Tree Wlk 4
SE19 ... 183 C4
Plantagenet Cl
KT19 ... 215 B4
Plantagenet Gdns
RM6 ... 58 D2
Plantagenet Ho
SE18 ... 122 B3
Plantagenet Pl RM6 ... 58 D2
Plantagenet Rd EN5 ... 2 A1
Plantain Gdns E11 ... 76 B5
Plantain Pl SE1 ... 252 C2
Plantation La EC3 ... 253 A6
Plantation The SE3 ... 143 A3
Plasel Ct E13 ... 99 B6
PLASHET ... 78 A2
Plashet Gr E6 ... 77 D1
Plashet Rd E13 ... 77 B1
Plashet Sch E6 ... 78 A1
Plassy Rd SE6 ... 163 D4
Platehouse The 3
E14 ... 119 D1
Platina St EC2 ... 242 D6
Platinum Ct RM7 ... 59 D6
Plato Pl 1 SW6 ... 135 B3
Plato Rd SW2 ... 138 A1
Platt Halls (a) 35
NW9 ... 27 D1
Platt Halls (b) 37
NW9 ... 27 D1
Platt Halls (c) 38
NW9 ... 27 D1
Platt's Eyot TW12 ... 173 C1
Platt's La NW3 ... 69 C5
Platts Rd EN3 ... 6 C4
Platt St NW1 ... 232 C4
Plaxdale Ho SE17 ... 263 A3
Plaxtol Cl BR1 ... 187 C2
Plaxtol Rd DA8 ... 147 C5
Plaxton Ct E11 ... 76 D5
Playfair St W6 ... 112 C1
Playfield Cres SE22 ... 161 D6
Playfield Rd HA8 ... 27 A1
Playford Rd
Finsbury Pk N4 ... 72 B6
Finsbury Pk N4 ... 72 C6
Playgreen Way SE6 ... 185 C6
Playground Cl BR3 ... 184 D1
Playhouse Yd EC4 ... 241 C1
Plaza Bsns Ctr EN3 ... 7 B3
Plaza Hts E10 ... 76 A5
Plaza Sh Ctr
W1 ... 93 C1 239 B2
Plaza Wlk NW9 ... 45 A6
Pleasance Rd
Putney SW15 ... 156 B6
St Paul's Cray BR5 ... 190 B1
Pleasance The
SW15 ... 134 B1
Pleasant Gr CR0 ... 223 B5
Pleasant Pl N1 ... 72 D1
Pleasant Row NW1 ... 231 D5
Pleasant View BR6 ... 227 A3
Pleasant View Pl
BR6 ... 227 A3
Pleasant Way HA0 ... 87 C5
Pleasaunce Ct SE9 ... 144 B1
Plender Ct NW1 ... 232 B5
Plender St
NW1 ... 93 C6 232 B5
Pleshey Rd N7 ... 71 D4
Plevna Cres N15 ... 51 C3
Plevna Ho 1 N9 ... 18 A1
Plevna Rd
Edmonton N9 ... 18 B1
Hampton TW12 ... 173 D2
Plevna St E14 ... 120 A3
Pleydell Ave
Chiswick W6 ... 111 D2
Penge SE19 ... 183 D3
Pleydell Ct EC4 ... 241 B1
Pleydell Gdns SE19 ... 183 D4
Pleydell St EC4 ... 241 B1
Plimsoll Cl E14 ... 97 D1
Plimsoll Rd N4 ... 72 D5
Plough Ct EC3 ... 252 D6
Plough Farm Cl HA4 ... 39 B3
Plough La SE22 ... 161 D5
Plough Lane Cl CR0,
SM6 ... 220 A3
Plough La
7 Teddington
TW11 ... 175 A5
Wallington CR0,
SM6 ... 220 A3
Wimbledon SW17,
SW19 ... 180 A6
Ploughmans Cl NW1 232 C6
Ploughmans End
TW7 ... 152 B6
Plough Mews 19
SW11 ... 136 B1
Plough Pl EC4 ... 241 B2
Plough Rd
Battersea SW11 ... 136 B1
West Ewell KT19 ... 215 B1
Plough St 18 E1 ... 96 A1
Plough Terr SW11 ... 136 B1
Plough Way SE16 ... 119 A2
Plough Yd EC2 ... 243 B5
Plover Ho 4 SW9 ... 138 C5
Plover Way
Hayes UB4 ... 84 D2
Rotherhithe SE16 ... 119 A3
Plowman Cl N18 ... 33 B5
Plowman Ho SW19 ... 156 D2
Plowman Way RM8 ... 58 C1
Plumbers Row E1 ... 96 A1
Plumbridge St 7
SE10 ... 142 A4
Plum Cl TW14 ... 150 A3
Plumcroft Prim Sch
SE18 ... 145 A6
Plume Ho SE10 ... 141 D6
Plum Garth TW8 ... 109 D2
Plum La SE18 ... 145 A5
Plummer Ct SE13 ... 163 D5
Plummer La CR4 ... 180 D1
Plummer Rd SW4 ... 159 D4
Plumpton Cl UB5 ... 63 C2
Plumpton Ct SE23 ... 163 A4
Plumpton Lo E5 ... 74 D5
Plumpton Way SM5 ... 218 C5
PLUMSTEAD ... 123 C2
PLUMSTEAD COMMON
... 145 D6
Plumstead Common Rd
SE18 ... 145 A6
Plumstead High St SE18,
SE2 ... 123 C2
Plumstead Manor/
Negus Sch SE18 ... 145 B6
Plumstead Rd SE18,
SE28 ... 123 A2
Plumstead Road
Covered Mkt
SE18 ... 122 D2
Plumstead Sta SE18 ... 123 B2
Plumtree Cl
Dagenham RM10 ... 81 D2
Wallington SM6 ... 219 D1
Plumtree Ct EC4 ... 241 C2
Plymen Ho KT8 ... 195 C4
Plymouth Ho
10 Barking IG11 ... 80 A1
20 Lewisham SE10 ... 141 D4
Plymouth Rd
Bromley BR1 ... 187 B2
Newham E16 ... 99 A2
Plymouth Wharf
E14 ... 120 B2
Plympton Ave NW6 ... 69 B1
Plympton Cl 8
DA17 ... 125 A3
Plympton Pl NW1 ... 237 A5
Plympton Rd NW6 ... 69 B1
Plympton St NW8 ... 237 A5
Plymstock Rd DA16 ... 146 C5
Pocklington Cl NW9 ... 27 C1
Pocklington Ct
SW15 ... 156 A3
Pocklington Lo 6
W12 ... 112 A3
Pocock Ave UB7 ... 104 B3
Pocock St
SE1 ... 116 D4 251 D2
Podmore Rd SW18 ... 136 A1
Poets Cnr* SW1 ... 260 A6
Poet's Rd N5 ... 73 B3
Poets Way HA1 ... 42 C5
Pointalls Cl N3 ... 30 A1
Point Cl SE10 ... 142 A4
Pointer Cl SE28 ... 102 D1
Pointer Sch The
SE3 ... 143 A5
Pointers Cl E14 ... 119 D1
Point Hill SE10 ... 142 A4
Point Ho SE10 ... 142 A4
Point Pleasant
SW18 ... 135 C1
Point Pl HA9 ... 66 D1
Point Terr E7 ... 77 B3
Point The HA4 ... 62 A4
Point Wharf La
TW8 ... 132 A5
Poland Ho 3 E15 ... 98 B6
Poland St W1 ... 93 C1 239 B1
Polaris Ct EN4 ... 14 B6
Polebrook Rd SE3 ... 143 C2
Polecroft La SE6 ... 163 B2
Polehamptons The
TW12 ... 174 A2
Pole Hill Rd
Chingford E4 ... 20 A4
Hillingdon UB4 ... 83 A4
Polesden Gdns
SW20 ... 178 B1
Polesworth Ho 16
W2 ... 91 C2
Polesworth Rd RM9 ... 80 D1
Polish Inst & Sikorski
Mus* SW7 ... 246 D1
Polish Univ Abroad
W6 ... 112 A2
Polish War Meml
HA4 ... 62 C2
Pollard Cl
Islington N7 ... 72 B4
Newham E16 ... 121 A6
Pollard Ct SM4 ... 202 C4
Pollard Ho
Cheam KT4 ... 216 C4
Islington N1 ... 233 C3
Pollard Rd
East Barnet N20 ... 14 C2
Morden SM4 ... 202 B4
Pollard Row E2 ... 96 A4
Pollards Cl IG10 ... 21 C6
Pollards Cres SW16 ... 204 A6
Pollards Hill E
SW16 ... 204 B6
Pollards Hill N
SW16 ... 204 B6
Pollards Hill S
SW16 ... 204 B6
Pollards Hill W
SW16 ... 204 B6
Pollard St E2 ... 96 A4
Pollards Wood Rd
SW16 ... 204 A6
Pollard Wlk DA14 ... 190 C4
Pollen St W1 ... 238 D1
Pollitt Dr
NW8 ... 92 B3 236 D6
Pollock Ho W10 ... 91 A3
Polperro Cl BR6 ... 211 D3
Polperro Mans 3
NW6 ... 69 C3
Polperro Mews
SE11 ... 261 C4
Polsted Rd SE6 ... 163 B4
Polsten Mews 2 EN3 ... 7 C6
Polthorne Gr SE18 ... 123 B2
Polworth Rd SW16 ... 182 A5
Polygon Rd
NW1 ... 93 D5 232 C3
Polygon The
1 Clapham SW4 ... 137 C1
St John's Wood NW8 229 D6
Polytechnic St SE18 ... 122 C2
Pomell Way E1 ... 243 D2
Pomeroy Cl TW1 ... 131 B1
Pomeroy Ct W11 ... 91 A1
Pomeroy Ho 5 E2 ... 96 D5
Pomeroy St SE14 ... 140 C4
Pomfret Rd SE5 ... 138 D2
Pomoja La N19 ... 72 A6
Pomona Ho 10 SE8 ... 119 A2
Pond Cl
Colney Hatch N12 ... 30 C4
Kidbrooke SE3 ... 143 A3
Pond Cottage La BR3,
BR4 ... 207 C1
Pond Cotts SE21 ... 161 C3
PONDERS END ... 18 D6
Ponders End Ind Est
EN3 ... 19 A6
Ponders End Sta
EN3 ... 19 A6
Ponder St 5 N7 ... 72 B1
Pond Farm Est E5 ... 74 C5
Pondfield End IG10 ... 21 C4
Pondfield Ho
4 Islington N5 ... 73 A3
West Norwood SE27 ... 183 A5
Pondfield Rd
Dagenham RM10 ... 81 D3
Locksbottom BR6 ... 226 D5
West Wickham BR2 ... 208 C1
Pond Gn HA4 ... 61 C6
Pond Hill Gdns SM3 ... 217 A2
Pond Ho
Chelsea SW3 ... 257 A3
Stanmore HA7 ... 25 B4
Pond Mead SE21 ... 161 B5
Pond Path BR7 ... 188 D4
Pond Pl
SW3 ... 114 C2 257 A3
Pond Rd
Blackheath Vale
SE3 ... 142 D3
Newham E15 ... 98 C5
Pondside Cl UB3 ... 127 B6
Pond Sq N6 ... 49 A1
Pond St NW3 ... 70 C3
Pond Way TW11 ... 175 C4
Pondwood Rise
BR6 ... 211 C2
Ponler St E1 ... 96 B1
Ponsard Rd NW10 ... 90 B4
Ponsford St E9 ... 74 C2
Ponsonby Ho 13 E2 ... 96 C5
Ponsonby Pl
SW1 ... 115 D1 259 D2
Ponsonby Rd SW15 ... 156 B4
Ponsonby Terr SW1 ... 259 D2
Pontefract Ct UB5 ... 63 D3
Pontefract Rd BR1 ... 186 D5
Ponton Ho SW2 ... 160 C3
Ponton Rd
SW8 ... 137 D6 269 D5
Pontoon Dock Sta
E16 ... 121 C5
Pont St Mews SW1 ... 257 C5
Pont St SW1. 114 D3 257 D5
Pontypool Pl SE1 ... 251 C2
Pool Cl
Beckenham BR3 ... 185 C5
East Molesey KT8 ... 195 B4
Pool Ct SE6 ... 163 C2
Poole Cl HA4 ... 61 C6
Poole Court Rd
TW5 ... 129 A3
Poole Ct
De Beauvoir Town
N1 ... 73 C1
Hounslow TW5 ... 129 A3
Poole Ho SE11 ... 260 D5
Pool End Cl TW17 ... 192 C4
Poole Rd
Homerton E9 ... 74 D2
West Ewell KT19 ... 215 B2
Pooles Bldgs EC1 ... 241 A5
Pooles Ct IG3 ... 80 A5
Pooles La SW10 ... 266 A3
Pooles Park Prim Sch
N4 ... 72 B6
Pooles Pk N4 ... 72 C6
Poole St N1 ... 95 B6 235 C5
Poole Way UB4 ... 83 C4
Pooley Ho E1 ... 96 D4
Pool Ho NW8 ... 236 D4
Poolmans St SE16 ... 118 D4
Pool Rd
East Molesey KT12,
KT8 ... 195 B4
Harrow HA1 ... 42 B2
Poolsford Rd NW9 ... 45 C5
Poonah St E1 ... 96 C1
Pope Cl
East Bedfont
TW14 ... 149 D3
Mitcham SW17,
SW19 ... 180 B4
Pope Ct 10 KT2 ... 175 D6
Pope Ho
7 Bermondsey
SE16 ... 118 B2
8 Camberwell SE5 ... 139 B5
Pope John RC Prim Sch
W12 ... 112 B6
Pope Rd BR2 ... 209 D4
Pope's Ave TW2 ... 152 C2
Popes Ct TW2 ... 152 C2
Popes Dr N3 ... 29 C2
Popes Gr CR0 ... 223 B5
Pope's Gr TW1, TW2 ... 152 D2
Pope's Head Alley
EC3 ... 242 D1
Pope's La W5 ... 110 A3
Pope's Rd SW9 ... 138 C2
Pope Street Ct SE9 ... 166 B3
Pope St SE1 ... 253 B1
Popham Cl TW13 ... 151 B1
Popham Ct N16 ... 73 C5
Popham Gdns TW9 ... 132 D2
Popham Rd
N1 ... 95 A6 235 A6
Popham St
Islington N1 ... 234 D6
Shoreditch
N1 ... 95 A6 235 A6
Pop In Bsns Ctr HA9 ... 66 D3
POPLAR ... 97 C1
Poplar Ave
Mitcham CR4 ... 180 D2
Orpington BR6 ... 226 D6
Southall UB2 ... 107 D3
Yiewsley UB7 ... 104 B6
Poplar Bath St 11
E14 ... 119 D6
Poplar Bsns Pk E14. 120 A6
Poplar Cl Hackney E9 ... 75 B3
Pinner HA5 ... 22 D2
Poplar Cres KT19 ... 215 A2
Poplar Ct
Chingford E4 ... 35 D4
Northolt UB5 ... 84 C5
4 Streatham SW16 ... 160 B1
13 Twickenham
TW1 ... 153 C5
Wimbledon SW19 ... 179 C5
Poplar Farm Cl
KT19 ... 215 A2
Poplar Gdns KT3 ... 177 B1
Poplar Gr
Friern Barnet N11 ... 31 A4
Hammersmith W6 ... 112 C4
Kingston u T KT3 ... 199 B6
Wembley HA9 ... 67 A5
Poplar High St E14 ... 119 D6
Poplar Ho
Brockley SE4 ... 141 B1
19 Rotherhithe
SE16 ... 118 D4

Poplar Mews 4 W12 ... 112 C5
Poplar Mount DA17 .. 125 D2
Poplar Pl Hayes UB3 .. 106 A6
Kensington W2 ... 113 D6 245 D6
Woolwich SE28 ... 124 C6
Poplar Prim Sch SW19 ... 201 C6
Poplar Rd
Ashford TW15 ... 171 A5
Cheam SM3 ... 201 B1
Herne Hill SE24 ... 139 A1
Merton SW19 ... 179 C1
Poplar Rd S SW19 ... 201 C6
Poplars Cl HA4 ... 39 C1
Poplars Ho 14 E17 ... 53 D6
Poplars Rd E17 ... 53 D3
Poplar Sta E14 ... 119 D6
Poplars The
East Barnet N14 ... 15 B6
Kentish Town NW5 ... 71 C3
Poplar View HA9 ... 65 D6
Poplar Way
Feltham TW13 ... 150 B1
Ilford IG6 ... 57 A5
Poplar Wlk
Croydon CR0 ... 205 A1
Herne Hill SE24 ... 139 A1
Poppins Ct EC4 ... 241 C1
Poppleton Rd E11 ... 54 C3
Poppy Cl
Belvedere DA17 ... 125 D4
Hackbridge SM6 ... 203 A1
Northolt UB5 ... 63 B2
Poppy Ct HA3 ... 42 C6
Poppy La CR0 ... 206 C1
Porchester Ct W2 ... 91 D1
Porchester Gate W2 246 A5
Porchester Gdn Mews W2 ... 91 D1
Porchester Gdns W2 ... 113 D6 245 D6
Porchester Ho 3 E1 .. 96 B1
Porchester Mead BR3 ... 185 D4
Porchester Mews W2 ... 91 D1
Porchester Pl W2 ... 237 B1
Porchester Rd
Kensington W2 ... 91 D1
Kingston u T KT1 ... 176 D1
Porchester Sq W2 ... 91 D1
Porchester Terr N W2 ... 91 D1
Porchester Terr W2 ... 114 A6 246 A6
Porch Way N20 ... 14 D1
Porcupine Cl SE9 ... 166 A2
Porden Rd SW2 ... 138 B1
Porland Ct SE1 ... 262 C6
Porlock Ave HA1, HA2 ... 42 A1
Porlock Ho 5 SE26 .. 162 A1
Porlock Rd EN1 ... 17 D4
Porlock St SE1 ... 117 B4 252 D2
Porrington Cl BR7 ... 188 C2
Porson Ct SE13 ... 141 D2
Portal Cl
Hillingdon UB10 ... 60 B1
Ruislip HA4 ... 62 B4
West Norwood SE27 . 160 C1
Portal Way W3 ... 89 B2
Portbury Cl 17 SE15 .. 140 A4
Portchester Cl SE24 .. 139 B1
Port Cres E13 ... 99 B3
Portcullis Lodge Rd EN1 ... 5 B2
Portelet Ct 1 N1 ... 95 C6
Portelet Rd E1 ... 96 D4
Porten Hos W14 ... 254 A5
Porten Rd W14 ... 254 A5
Porte 10 NW9 ... 27 D2
Porter Rd E6 ... 100 B1
Porters Ave RM8, RM9 ... 80 C3
Porter Sq N19 ... 50 A1
Porter St
Borough The SE1 ... 117 A5 252 B4
Marylebone W1 ... 237 D4
Porters & Walters Almshouses N22 ... 32 B3
Porters Way UB7 ... 104 B4
Porteus Rd W2 ... 236 B4
Portfleet Pl 34 N1 ... 95 C6
Portgate Cl W9 ... 91 B3
Porthallow Cl BR6 ... 227 D4
Porthcawe Rd SE26 .. 185 B6
Porthkerry Ave DA16 ... 146 A1
Port Ho 6 SW11 ... 136 A2
Port House The 6 E14 ... 119 D1
Portia Ct 12 IG11 ... 80 A1
Portia Way E3 ... 97 B3
Porticos The SW3 ... 266 C5
Portinscale Rd SW15 ... 157 B6
Portishead Ho 29 W2 ... 91 C2
Portland Ave
Blackfen DA15 ... 168 A5
New Malden KT3 ... 199 D2
Stamford Hill N16 ... 51 D2
Portland Cl
Dagenham RM6 ... 59 A4
New Malden KT4 ... 200 B2
Portland Commercial Est IG11 ... 102 C5
Portland Cotts
Feltham TW13 ... 173 A5
Wallington CR0 ... 203 D2
Portland Cres
1 Chislehurst SE9 ... 166 A2
Feltham TW13 ... 171 B6
Southall UB6 ... 86 A2
Stanmore HA7 ... 25 D1
Portland Cres W HA7 ... 43 D6
Portland Ct
7 De Beauvoir Town N1 ... 73 C1
1 Deptford SE14 ... 141 A6
1 Sutton SM2 ... 217 D2
Portland Dr EN2 ... 5 C5
Portland Gdns
Harringay N4 ... 50 D3
Ilford RM6 ... 58 D4
Portland Gr SW8 ... 138 B4 270 C2
Portland Hospl for Women & Children The W1 ... 238 D5
Portland Ho 19 SW2 ... 160 C3
Portland Mans SE25 ... 206 B4
Portland Mews W1 . 239 B1
Portland Place Schs W1 ... 93 B2 238 D4
Portland Place Sch W1 ... 93 B2 238 D3
Portland Pl
Croydon SE25 ... 206 A5
Marylebone W1 ... 93 B2 238 D3
Portland Rd
Ashford TW15 ... 148 A1
Bromley BR1 ... 187 C5
Chislehurst SE9 ... 166 A2
Croydon SE25 ... 206 B4
Hayes UB4 ... 83 C4
Kingston u T KT1 ... 198 B6
Mitcham CR4 ... 180 C1
Notting Hill W11 ... 113 A5 244 B4
Notting Hill W11 ... 113 A6 244 A5
Southall UB2 ... 107 B3
Tottenham N15 ... 51 D5
Portland Rise N4 ... 51 A1
Portland Sq 4 E1 ... 118 B5
Portland St SE17 ... 117 B1 262 C1
Portland Terr
Edgware HA8 ... 26 C3
Richmond TW9 ... 131 D1
Portland Village W6 ... 112 C3
Portman Ave SW14 ... 133 B2
Portman Cl
Bexley DA7 ... 147 A2
Marylebone W1 ... 93 A1 238 A2
Portman Dr IG8 ... 37 D1
Portman Gate NW1 . 237 B5
Portman Gdns
Hendon NW9 ... 27 B1
Hillingdon UB10 ... 60 C1
Portman Hall HA3 ... 24 B5
Portman Hts 1 NW3 .. 69 C5
Portman Lo N21 ... 16 D6
Portman Mews S W1 ... 238 A1
Portman Pl E2 ... 96 C4
Portman Rd KT1 ... 176 B1
Portman Sq W1 ... 93 A1 238 A2
Portman St W1 ... 93 A1 238 A1
Portman The NW11 ... 47 C2
Portman Twrs W1 ... 237 D2
Portmeadow Wlk SE2 ... 124 D4
Portmeers Cl E17 ... 53 C3
Portnall Rd W9 ... 91 B4
Portobello Ct Est W11 ... 91 B1
Portobello Ho 6 SW27 ... 182 D5
Portobello Mews W11 ... 245 A5
Portobello Rd W11 ... 113 B6 244 D6
Portobello Road Mkt* W10 ... 91 A2
Porton Ct KT6 ... 197 C3
Portpool La EC1 ... 94 C2 241 A4
Portree Cl N22 ... 32 B3
Portree St E14 ... 98 B1
Port Royal Pl 3 N16 .. 73 C3
Portrush Ct 9 UB1 ... 86 A1
Portsdown Ave NW11 ... 47 B3
Portsdown HA8 ... 26 C5
Portsdown Mews NW11 ... 47 B3
Portsea Hall W2 ... 237 B1
Portsea Ho 3 SW15 ... 156 B3
Portsea Mews W2 .. 237 B1
Portsea Pl W2 ... 237 B1
Portslade Rd SW8 ... 137 C3
Portsmouth Ave KT7 ... 197 A2
Portsmouth Rd
Esher KT10 ... 212 A5
Putney SW15 ... 156 C4
Thames Ditton KT6, KT7 ... 197 C3
Portsmouth St WC2 . 240 D1
Portsoken St E1, EC3 253 C6
Portswood Pl SW15 .. 155 D5
Portugal Gdns TW2 .. 152 A2
Portugal St WC2 ... 94 B1 240 D1
Portway E15 ... 98 D6
Portway Gdns SE18 .. 143 D5
Portway Prim Sch E13 ... 98 D6
Poseidon Ct
Dagenham IG11 ... 102 B4
9 Millwall E14 ... 119 C2
Postern Gn EN2 ... 4 C2
Postern The EC2 ... 242 B3
Post La TW2 ... 152 B3
Postmasters Lodge HA5 ... 41 A2
Postmill Cl CR0 ... 222 D5
Post Office App E7 ... 77 B3
Post Office Way SW8 ... 137 D5 269 C4
Post Rd UB2 ... 107 D3
Postway Mews 1 IG1 ... 78 D5
Potier St SE1 ... 262 D5
Potter Cl CR4 ... 181 B1
Potteries The EN5 ... 13 C6
Potterill Ct TW11 ... 175 B3
Potterne Cl 5 SW19 ... 156 D4
Potters Cl
5 Camberwell SE15 ... 139 C5
Croydon CR0 ... 207 A1
Pottersfield EN1 ... 5 C1
Potters Fields SE1 ... 117 C5 253 B3
Potters Gr KT3 ... 199 A5
Potters Heights Cl HA5 ... 22 B3
Potter's La Barnet EN5 .. 1 C1
Streatham SW16 ... 181 D4
Potters Lo E14 ... 120 A1
Potters Mews 4 WD6 .. 9 D5
Potter's Rd EN5 ... 1 D1
Potters Rd SW6 ... 136 A3
Potter St HA5 ... 22 B2
Potter Street Hill HA5 ... 22 B3
Pottery La W11 ... 113 A5 244 B4
Pottery Rd TW8 ... 132 A6
Pottery St SE16 ... 118 B4
Pott St E2 ... 96 B4
Poulett Gdns TW1 ... 153 A3
Poulett Rd E6 ... 100 B5
Poullett Ho SW2 ... 160 D3
Poulters Wood BR2 .. 225 D3
Poulton Ave SM1 ... 218 B5
Poulton Cl E8 ... 74 B2
Poultry EC2 ... 95 B1 242 C1
Pound Cl
Long Ditton KT6 ... 197 C1
Orpington BR6 ... 227 B6
Pound Court Dr BR6 ... 227 B6
Pound Farm Cl KT10 ... 196 B1
Pound Green Ct 4 DA5 ... 169 C4
Pound La NW10 ... 68 A2
Pound Park Rd SE7 .. 121 D2
Pound Pl SE9 ... 166 C5
Pound St SM5 ... 218 D3
Pountney Rd SW11 ... 137 A2
Poverest Rd BR5 ... 211 D4
Povey Ho
Tulse Hill SW2 ... 160 C5
Walworth SE17 ... 263 A3
Powder Mill La TW2, TW4 ... 151 C3
Powell Cl
Chessington KT9 ... 213 D3
Edgware HA8 ... 26 B4
Wallington SM6 ... 220 A1
Powell Ct
Croydon CR2 ... 221 A4
19 Walthamstow E17 .. 53 D6
Powell Gdns RM10 ... 81 C4
Powell Ho 10 SW19 .. 179 A4
Powell Rd
Buckhurst Hill IG9 ... 21 C4
Hackney E5 ... 74 B5
Powell's Wlk W4 ... 133 D6
Powell Terr CR4 ... 204 A5
Powergate Bsns Pk NW10 ... 89 B4
Power Ho 13 TW9 ... 132 C4
Power Ho The W4 ... 111 D2
Power Rd W4 ... 110 C2
Powerscroft Rd
Lower Clapton E5 ... 74 C4
Sidcup DA14 ... 190 C4
Powers Ct TW1 ... 153 D4
Powis Ct Bushey WD23 .. 8 B3
Edgware HA8 ... 26 B6
Powis Gdns
Golders Green NW11 ... 47 B2
Notting Hill W11 ... 91 B1
Powis Ho WC2 ... 240 B2
Powis Mews W11 ... 91 B1
Powis Pl WC1 . 94 A3 240 B5
Powis Rd E3 ... 97 D4
Powis Sq W11 ... 91 B1
Powis St SE18 ... 122 D2
Powis Terr W11 ... 91 B1
Powlesland Ct 21 E14 ... 97 A1
Powle Terr IG1 ... 79 B3
Powlett Ho NW1 ... 71 B2
Powlett Pl NW1 ... 71 B1
Pownall Gdns TW3 ... 129 D1
Pownall Rd
Hackney E8 ... 96 A6
Hounslow TW3 ... 129 D1
Pownsett Terr IG1 ... 79 A3
Powrie Ho 4 SW11 .. 136 B3
Powster Rd BR1 ... 187 B5
Powys Cl DA7 ... 146 D6
Powys Ct N11 ... 32 A5
Powys La
Bowes Pk N13 ... 32 A5
Palmers Green N14 ... 32 A6
Poynder Ct 3 N7 ... 72 A3
Poynder Lo TW7 ... 131 A4
Poynders Ct 9 SW4 ... 159 C5
Poynders Gdns SW12 ... 159 C4
Poynders Rd SW12, SW4 ... 159 D4
Poynings Rd N19 ... 71 C5
Poynings Way N12 ... 29 C5
Poyntell Cres BR7 ... 189 B2
Poynter Ct 11 UB5 ... 84 D5
Poynter Ho
Paddington NW8 ... 236 C6
10 Shepherd's Bush W11 ... 112 D5
Poynter Rd EN1 ... 18 A6
Poynton Rd N17 ... 34 A1
Poyntz Rd SW11 ... 136 D3
Poyser St E2 ... 96 B5
Praed Mews W2 ... 236 D2
Praed St W2 ... 92 B1 236 D2
Pragel St E13 ... 99 C5
Pragnell Rd SE12 ... 165 B2
Prague Pl SW2 ... 160 A6
Prah Rd N4 ... 72 C6
Prairie St SW8 ... 137 B3
Pratt Mews NW1 ... 232 A5
Pratt St NW1 .. 93 C6 232 A6
Pratt Wlk SE1, SE11 ... 116 B2 260 D4
Prayle Gr NW2 ... 46 D1
Preachers Ct EC1 ... 241 D5
Prebend Gdns W4, W6 ... 111 D2
Prebend Mans 4 W4 ... 111 D2
Prebend St N1 ... 95 A6 235 A6
Precinct Rd UB3 ... 106 A6
Precincts The SM4 ... 201 C3
Precinct The
Islington N1 ... 235 A5
Islington N5 ... 72 D3
Premier Corner NW6 .. 91 B5
Premier Ct EN3 ... 6 D5
Premier Ho 25 N1 ... 72 D1
Premier League Hall of Fame* SE1 ... 250 C2
Premier Lo N3 ... 29 C2
Premier Park Rd NW10 ... 88 D5
Premier Pk NW10 ... 88 D5
Premier Pl 17 E14 ... 119 C6
Prendergast Ho 7 SW4 ... 159 D4
Prendergast Rd SE3 ... 142 C2
Prendergast Sch SE4 ... 141 C1
Prentice Ct 2 SW19 ... 179 B5
Prentis Rd SW16 ... 181 D6
Prentiss Ct SE7 ... 121 D2
Presburg Rd KT3 ... 199 C4
Prescelly Pl HA8 ... 26 B2
Prescot St E1 ... 117 D6 253 D6
Prescott Ave BR5 ... 210 D3
Prescott Ho
Croydon CR0 ... 220 C5
13 Kennington SE17 . 138 D6
Prescott Pl
Clapham SW4 ... 137 D1
Streatham SW16 ... 182 A3
Presentation Mews SW2 ... 160 B3
Preshaw Cres CR4 ... 202 C6
President Dr E1 ... 118 B5
President Ho EC1 ... 234 D1
President St EC1 ... 235 A2
Prespa Cl N9 ... 18 C2
Press Ho NW10 ... 67 B5
Press Rd NW10 ... 67 B5
Prestage Way 13 E14 ... 120 A6
Prestbury Rd E7 ... 77 C1
Prestbury Sq SE9 ... 188 B6
Prested Rd SW11 ... 136 C1
PRESTON ... 44 A1
Preston Ave E4 ... 36 B4
Preston Cl
Twickenham TW2 ... 152 C1
Walworth SE1 ... 263 A4
Preston Ct
5 New Barnet EN5 ... 2 A1
Northwood Hills HA6 .. 22 A1
Sidcup DA14 ... 189 D6
Walton-on-T KT12 ... 194 C1
Preston Dr
Bexley DA7 ... 146 D4
Wanstead E11 ... 55 C4
West Ewell KT19 ... 215 D2
Preston Gdns
Enfield EN3 ... 7 A6
Redbridge IG1 ... 56 A3
Willesden NW10 ... 67 C2
Preston Hill HA3 ... 44 B3
Preston Ho
Bermondsey SE1 ... 263 C6
3 Dagenham RM10 ... 81 C5
Walworth SE1 ... 263 A4
1 Woolwich SE18 ... 122 C2
Preston Manor High Sch HA9 ... 66 B6
Preston Park Prim Sch HA9 ... 43 D1
Preston Pl
Richmond TW10 ... 154 A6
Willesden NW2 ... 68 A2
Preston Rd
Leytonstone E11 ... 54 C3
Littleton TW17 ... 192 C4
South Norwood SE19 ... 182 D4
Wembley HA3, HA9 ... 66 A6
Wimbledon SW20 ... 177 D3
Preston Road Sta HA3 ... 44 A1
Prestons Rd BR2 ... 225 A6
Preston's Rd E14 ... 120 A5
Preston Waye HA3 ... 44 A1
Prestwich Terr SW4 ... 159 D6
Prestwick Cl UB2 ... 107 A1
Prestwick Ct
Southall UB1 ... 108 A6
Tottenham N17 ... 34 A3
Prestwick Rd WD19 ... 22 D6
Prestwood Ave HA3 ... 43 B5
Prestwood Cl
East Wickham SE18 ... 146 A6
Harrow HA3 ... 43 B5
Prestwood Gdns CR0 ... 205 A2
Prestwood Ho 3 SE16 ... 118 B3
Prestwood St N1 ... 235 B3
Pretoria Ave E17 ... 53 A5
Pretoria Cres E4 ... 20 A3
Pretoria Ho 3 HA4 ... 40 C
Pretoria Rd
Chingford E4 ... 20 B
Ilford IG1 ... 78 D
Leytonstone E11 ... 54 B
Pretoria Rd N N18 ... 33 D
Pretoria Rd
Newham E16 ... 98 D
Streatham SW16 ... 181 C
Tottenham N17 ... 33 D
Pretty Cnr HA6 ... 22 A
Prevost Rd N11 ... 15 A
Priam Ho 17 E2 ... 96 B
Price Cl Finchley NW7 .. 29 A
Upper Tooting SW17 ... 158 D
Price Ct HA1 ... 43 A
Price Ho N1 ... 235 A
Price Rd CR0 ... 220 D
Prices Ct SW11 ... 136 B
Price's St SE1 ... 251 D
Price's Yd N1 ... 233 D
Price Way TW12 ... 173 A
Prichard Ct
Battersea SW11 ... 266 D
Islington N7 ... 72 B
Pricklers Hill EN5 ... 13 D
Prickley Wood BR2 .. 208 D
Priddy's Yd 4 CR0 .. 221 A
Prideaux Ho WC1 ... 233 D
Prideaux Pl
Acton W3 ... 111 B
St Pancras WC1 ... 94 B4 233 D
Prideaux Rd SW9 ... 138 A
Pride Ct N1 ... 234 B
Pridham Rd CR7 ... 205 B
Priestfield Rd SE23 .. 163 A
Priestlands Park Rd DA15 ... 167 D
Priestley Cl N16 ... 51 D
Priestley Gdns RM6 ... 58 B
Priestley Ho
2 Camden Town NW5 ... 71 B
St Luke's EC1 ... 242 B
3 Wembley HA9 ... 67 A
Priestley Rd CR4 ... 181 A
Priestley Way
Hendon NW2 ... 46 A
Walthamstow E17 ... 52 D
Priestman Point 25 E3 ... 97 D
Priestmead Fst & Mid Schs HA3 ... 43 B
Priest Park Ave HA2 .. 63 C
Priests Bridge SW14 ... 133 C
Priest's Ct EC2 ... 242 A
Prima Rd SW9 ... 138 C
Primrose Ave
Enfield EN2 ... 5 C
Ilford RM6 ... 58 B
Primrose Cl
6 Bow E3 ... 97 C
Catford SE6 ... 186 A
Finchley N3 ... 29 D
Hackbridge SM6 ... 203 B
Harrow HA2 ... 63 B
Primrose Ct
2 Child's Hill NW2 ... 69 B
New Malden KT4 ... 200 A
Primrose Hill NW8 .. 230 C
11 Streatham SW12 . 159 D
Primrose Gdns
Hampstead NW3 ... 70 C
Ruislip HA4 ... 62 C
PRIMROSE HILL ... 70 D
Primrose Hill Ct NW3 ... 70 D
Primrose Hill EC4 ... 241 B
Primrose Hill Rd
Primrose Hill NW1, NW3 ... 70 D
Primrose Hill NW1, NW3 ... 230 C
Primrose Hill Sch NW1 ... 93 A6 231 B
Primrose Hill Studios NW1 ... 231 A
Primrose Ho
7 Peckham SE15 ... 140 A
1 Richmond TW9 ... 132 B
Primrose La CR0 ... 206 D
Primrose Mans SW11 ... 268 A
Primrose Mews 9 NW1 ... 70 D
Primrose Pl TW7 ... 130 D
Primrose Rd
Walthamstow E10 ... 53 D
Woodford E18 ... 37 B
Primrose Sq E9 ... 96 C
Primrose St EC2 ... 95 C2 243 B

imrose Way HA0 87 D5
imrose Wlk
Ewell KT17 215 D1
6 New Cross Gate
SE14 141 A5
imula St W12 90 A1
ince Albert Ct
Primrose Hill NW8 230 C5
Sunbury TW16 171 C3
ince Albert Rd
NW8 92 D6 230 C5
ince Arthur Ct 18
NW3 70 A4
ince Arthur Mews 17
NW3 70 A4
ince Arthur Rd
NW3 70 A3
ince Charles Dr
NW2 46 C2
ince Charles Rd
SE3 142 D4
ince Charles Way
SM6 219 B5
ince Consort Dr
BR7 189 B2
ince Consort Ho
SE1 260 B2
ince Consort Rd
SW7 114 B3 256 C6
incedale Rd
W11 113 A5 244 B4
ince Edward Mans
W2 245 B6
ince Edward Rd
E9 75 B2
ince George Ave
N14 15 D6
ince George Rd
N16 73 C4
ince George's Ave
SW20 178 C1
ince Georges Rd
SW19 180 B2
ince Henry Rd
SE7 143 D5
ince Imperial Rd
Chislehurst BR7 188 D3
Kidbrooke SE18 144 B4
ince John Rd SE9 166 A6
incelet St
E1 95 D2 243 D4
ince of Orange La 3
SE10 142 A5
ince Of Wales Cl
W4 46 B5
ince of Wales Dr
SW11 137 A4 268 A2
ince of Wales Mans
Battersea SW11 268 B2
Clapham SW4 159 B6
ince of Wales Pas
NW1 232 A1
ince of Wales Prim
Sch EN3 7 B6
ince of Wales Rd
Blackheath Vale
SE3 142 D4
Camden Town NW5 71 A2
ince Of Wales' Rd
SM1 218 B6
ince Of Wales Rd
E16 99 C1
ince Of Wales Terr
Chiswick W4 111 C1
Kensington W8 245 D1
ince Rd SE25 205 C4
ince Regent Ct 2
SE16 119 A5
ince Regent La
E13 99 C3
ince Regent Mews
NW1 232 A1
ince Regent E16 99 C2
ince Regent Rd
TW3 130 A2
ince Regent Sta
E16 121 C6
ince Rupert Rd
SE9 144 B1
inces Arc SW1 249 B4
inces Ave
Acton W3 110 C3
Edmonton N13 32 C5
Finchley N3 29 D2
Muswell Hill N10 49 B6
Orpington BR5 211 C4
Queensbury NW9 44 D5
ince's Ave UB1 85 D1
inces Ave
Tolworth KT6 214 C6
Wallington SM5 218 D1
Woodford IG8 37 C6
Wood Green N22 31 D2
inces Cir
WC2 94 A1 240 A2

Princes Cl
Edgware HA8 26 C5
Finsbury Pk N4 50 D1
Queensbury NW9 44 C5
Sidcup DA14 168 D1
Prince's Cl TW11,
TW12 174 B6
Princes Coll WC1 240 A2
Princes Court Bsns Ctr
14 E1 118 B6
Princes Ct
Brondesbury NW2 69 A3
Hampstead NW3 70 B4
Kingston u T KT3 199 D6
Prince's Ct SE16 119 B3
Princes Ct
Stepney E1 118 B6
Wembley HA9 66 A3
Princes Dr HA1 42 C6
Princes Gate Ct
SW7 246 D1
Princes Gate Mews
SW7 114 B3 256 D6
Princes Gate
SW7 114 B4 246 D1
Prince's Gate
SW7 114 C4 247 A1
Princes Gdns
Acton W3 88 C2
Brompton
SW7 114 B3 256 D6
Ealing W5 87 C3
Princes Ho W11 245 A5
Princes La N10 49 B6
Prince's Mews 1
W6 112 B1
Princes Mews TW3 129 C1
Prince's Mews
W2 113 D6 245 C6
Princes Park Ave
Hayes UB3 105 B6
Temple Fortune
NW11 47 A4
Princes Park Circ
UB3 105 B6
Princes Park Cl
UB3 105 B6
Princes Park La
UB3 105 B6
Princes Park Par
UB3 105 B6
Princes Par NW11 47 A3
Prince's Plain BR2 210 A1
Princes Plain Prim Sch
BR2 210 A2
Princes Pl
Notting Hill
W11 113 A5 244 A4
St James SW1 249 B4
Princes Rd
Ashford TW15 170 B5
Buckhurst Hill IG9 21 C2
Ealing W13 109 B5
Edmonton N18 34 C6
Feltham TW13 149 D1
Ilford IG6 57 B5
Kew TW9 132 B4
Kingston u T KT2 176 C3
Prince's Rd SW14 133 B2
Princes Rd
Penge SE20 184 D4
Richmond TW10 154 B6
Prince's Rd
Teddington TW11,
TW12 174 B6
Wimbledon SW19 179 C4
Princes Rise SE13 142 A3
Princes Riverside Rd 7
SE16 118 D5
Princessa Ct EN2 17 B6
Princess Alexandra
School of Nursing
The E1 96 B2
Princess Alice Ho 1
W10 90 C3
Princess Alice Way
SE28 123 B4
Princess Ave HA9 66 A6
Princess Beatrice Ho
SW10 255 C1
Princess Cl SE28 102 D1
Princess Cres N4 72 D6
Princess Ct
Catford BR1 186 C4
3 Croydon CR0 221 D6
Hampstead NW6 69 D1
Hounslow TW4 128 C2
Kensington W2 245 D6
Marylebone W1 237 C3
11 Wimbledon
SW19 178 D3
Princess Frederica CE
Prim Sch NW10 90 C5
Princess Grace Hospl
The W1 93 A3 238 A5
Princess La HA4 39 C1

Princess Louise Cl
W2 236 D4
Princess Louise Hospl
W10 90 C2
Princess Mary Ho
SW1 259 D3
Princess May Prim Sch
N16 73 D4
Princess May Rd
N16 73 C4
Princess Mews
Hampstead NW3 70 B2
Kingston u T KT1 198 B6
Princess Par RM10 103 C5
Princess Park Manor
N11 31 A5
Princess Par BR6 226 C5
Prince's Sq
W2 113 D6 245 C6
Princess Rd
Camden Town
NW1 93 A6 231 B6
Paddington NW6 91 C5
Thornton Heath CR0 205 A3
Princess Royal
University Hospl
BR6 226 C5
Princess St
Bexley DA7 147 B2
Newington SE1 261 D5
Princes St DA7 147 B1
Prince's St
EC2 95 B1 242 C1
Princes St W1 238 D1
Prince's St TW10,
TW9 154 A6
Princes St
Sutton SM1 218 B4
Tottenham N17 33 C4
Prince's Terr E13 99 B6
Prince St SE8 141 B6
Princes Way
Acton W3 110 C3
Buckhurst Hill IG9 21 C2
Coney Hall BR4 224 D5
Croydon CR0 220 B3
Putney SW15, SW19 157 A3
Ruislip HA4 63 A4
Princes Yd W11 244 B3
Princethorpe Ho W2 91 D2
Princethorpe Rd
SE26 184 D6
Princeton Ct SW15 134 D2
Princeton Mans
WC1 240 C3
Princeton Mews 3
KT2 176 C2
Princeton St
WC1 94 B2 240 C4
Prince William Ct
TW15 170 B5
Principal Cl N14 15 C3
Principal Sq E9 74 D3
Pringle Gdns SW16 181 C6
Pringle Ho N21 16 B6
Printers Mews E3 97 A6
Printer St EC4 241 B2
Printinghouse La
UB3 105 C4
Printing House Yd 16
E2 95 C4
Printon Ho 10 E3 97 B2
Print Village Ind Est
SE15 139 D3
Priolo Rd SE7 121 C1
Prior Ave SM2, SM5 218 C1
Prior Bolton St N1 72 D2
Prioress Ho 2 E3 97 D4
Prioress Rd SE27 160 D1
Prioress St SE1 262 D5
Prior Rd IG1 78 C5
Priors Croft E17 35 B1
Priors Field UB5 63 A2
Priors Gdns HA4 62 C3
Priors Lo 4 TW10 154 A5
Priors Mead EN1 5 C4
Prior St SE10 142 A5
Priors Wood KT10 212 D6
Prior Weston Prim
Sch
Broadgate
EC1 95 B3 242 C6
St Luke's EC1 95 A3 242 B5
Priory Ave
Bedford Pk W4 111 C3
Cheam SM3 216 D4
Chingford E4 19 C1
Hornsey N8 49 D5
Petts Wood BR5 211 B3
Walthamstow E17 53 C4
Wembley HA0 64 D4
Priory CE Prim Sch
SW19 179 D5
Priory Cl
Ashford TW16 172 A3
Barnet N20 13 B4

Priory Cl *continued*
Beckenham BR3 207 A6
Chingford Green E4 19 B1
Chislehurst BR7 188 B2
East Barnet N14 15 B6
Finchley N3 29 B2
Hampton TW12 173 B2
Hayes UB3 106 B6
3 Merton SW19 179 D2
Ruislip HA4 39 D1
Stanmore HA7 8 D1
Wembley HA0 64 D4
Woodford E18 37 A2
Priory Cres
Cheam SM3 216 D4
South Norwood
SE19 183 A3
Wembley HA0 65 A5
Priory Ct Bushey WD23 8 A3
Cheam SM3 217 A4
City of London EC4 241 D1
Hampton TW12 173 C3
Highgate N6 49 B3
Homerton E9 74 D3
Hounslow TW3 129 D2
Ilford RM6 58 B3
Newham E6 99 D6
Nunhead SE15 140 C1
Roehampton SW15 133 D1
South Lambeth
SW8 137 D4 269 D2
Walthamstow E17 35 B1
4 Wembley HA0 88 A5
Priory Dr
Stanmore HA7 8 D1
West Heath SE2 124 D1
Priory Field Dr HA8 26 D6
Priory Gdns
Ashford TW15 171 B5
Barnes SW13 133 D2
6 Chiswick W4 111 C2
Ealing W5 88 A4
Hampton TW12 173 B2
Highgate N6 49 B3
South Norwood
SE25 205 D5
Wembley HA0 65 A4
Priory Gn N1 233 C4
Priory Grange N2 48 D6
Priory Gr Barnet EN5 13 C6
South Lambeth
SW8 138 A4 270 A1
Priory Hill HA0 65 A4
Priory Ho
3 Charlton SE7 143 C6
Clerkenwell EC1 241 C6
Pimlico SW1 259 C2
Spitalfields E1 243 C4
Priory Hospl Hayes
Grove The BR2 225 A6
Priory Hospl The
SW15 133 D1
Priory House Ct
SE6 163 D3
Priory Htss N1 233 D4
Priory La
East Molesey KT8 195 D5
Roehampton SW15 155 D6
Priory Leas SE9 166 A3
Priory Lo
7 Brentford W4 110 C1
Coney Hall BR4 224 C5
Ealing W5 87 C1
Priory Mans
17 Maitland Pk
NW3 70 D2
South Kensington
SW10 256 B1
Priory Park Rd
Kilburn NW6 91 B6
Wembley HA0 65 A4
Priory Pk SE3 142 D2
Priory Rd
Barking IG11 79 B1
Bedford Pk W4 111 B3
Cheam SM3 216 D4
Chessington KT9 214 A5
Hampstead NW6 69 D1
Hampton TW12 173 C3
Hornsey N8 49 D5
Hounslow TW3 152 A6
Mitcham SW19 180 B3
Newham E6 99 D5
Richmond TW9 132 C5
Thornton Heath CR0 204 C2
Priory Ret Pk SW19 180 B3
Priory Sch SE25 205 D5
Priory St 16 E3 97 D4
Priory Terr NW6 91 D6
Priory The
Croydon CR0 220 C5
Hornsey N8 49 D5
21 Kingston u T KT6 198 A4
Lambeth SE1 251 C1
Lewisham SE3 142 D1
Priory View WD23 8 C4
Priory Villas N11 30 D5

Priory Way
Harmondsworth
UB7 126 A6
Harrow HA2 41 D5
Southall UB2 106 D3
Priory Wlk
South Kensington
SW10 114 A1 256 B1
Sunbury TW16 172 A3
Priscilla Cl N15 51 A4
Priscilla Ho 8
TW16 171 D3
Pritchard Ho 23 E2 96 A5
Pritchard's Rd E2 96 A5
Pritchett Cl 13 EN3 7 C6
Priter Rd SE16 118 A3
Priter Road Hostel 14
SE16 118 A3
Private Rd EN1 17 C6
Probert Rd SW2 160 C6
Probyn Ho SW1 259 D4
Probyn Rd SW2 160 D2
Procter Ho 12 SE5 139 B5
Procter St
WC1 94 B2 240 C3
Proctor Cl CR4 181 A2
Proctor Ho 5 SE1 118 A1
Proctors Cl TW14 150 A3
Prodger 8 NW9 27 D2
Progress Bsns Pk
CR9 220 B6
Progress Way
Croydon CR0 220 B6
Enfield EN1 18 A6
Wood Green N22 32 C2
Prologis Pk
Hounslow TW4 128 C1
Wallington CR0 203 D2
Prome Ho 3 N16 73 B4
Promenade Approach
Rd W4 133 C5
Promenade Mans
HA8 26 C5
Promenade The
W4 133 C4
Pronto Trad Est UB4 83 C2
Prospect Cl
Belvedere DA17 125 C2
Forest Hill SE26 184 B6
Hounslow TW5 129 B4
Ruislip HA4 40 D2
Prospect Cotts
SW18 135 C1
Prospect Cres TW2 152 A5
Prospect Hill E17 53 D5
Prospect Ho
1 Dalston E8 73 D2
Islington N1 234 A3
3 Mitcham SW19 180 B2
Newington SE1 261 D5
14 North Kensington
W10 90 D1
Prospect House Sch
SW15 156 D4
Prospect Ho 9 E17 54 A6
Prospect Pl
Bromley BR2 209 B6
5 Child's Hill NW2 69 B5
2 Chiswick W4 111 B1
6 Deptford SE8 141 B6
East Finchley N2 48 B5
12 Hampstead NW3 70 A4
7 Lower Holloway
N7 72 A4
Tottenham N17 33 C3
Wapping E1 118 C5
Wimbledon SW20 178 B3
Prospect Quay
SW18 135 C1
Prospect Rd
Barnet EN5 1 D1
Child's Hill NW2 69 C5
Kingston u T KT6 197 C3
Woodford IG8 37 C5
Prospect Ring N2 48 B6
Prospect St SE16 118 B4
Prospect Vale SE7,
SE18 122 A2
Prospect Wharf E1 118 C6
Prospero Ho 7
DA17 125 C1
Prospero Rd N19 49 D1
Protea Cl E16 98 D3
Protheroe Ho 11 N17 51 D6
Prothero Gdns NW4 46 B4
Prothero Ho 15
NW10 67 B1
Prothero Rd
SW6 135 B5 264 C4
Proud Ho 16 E1 96 B1
Prout Gr NW10 67 D4
Prout Rd E5 74 B5
Provence St N1 235 A4
Providence Ave HA2 41 C1
Providence Cl E9 96 D6

Providence Ct
Harlington UB3 127 B5
Islington N1 234 C5
Mayfair W1 248 B6
Providence La UB3 127 B5
Providence Pl N1 234 C5
Providence Rd UB7 104 B5
Providence Row Cl 30
E1 96 B4
Providence Row N1 233 C3
Providence 1 SE16 118 A4
Providence Sq 36
SE1 118 A4
Providence Yd 1 E2 96 A4
Provident Ind Est
UB3 106 A4
Provincial Terr 2
SE20 184 D3
Provost Ct NW3 70 D2
Provost Rd NW3 70 D1
Provost St N1 95 B4 235 C2
Prowse Ave WD23 8 A2
Prowse Pl NW1 71 C1
Prudence La BR6 226 C4
Pruden Cl N14 15 C2
Prudent Pas EC2 242 B1
Prusom's Island 8
E1 118 C5
Prusom St E1 118 B5
Pryors The NW3 70 B5
Public Record Office
TW9 132 D5
Puccinia Ct TW19 148 A3
Pudding La EC3 252 D6
Pudding Mill La E15 97 D6
Pudding Mill Lane Sta
E15 97 D6
Puddle Dock
EC4 116 D6 251 D6
Puffin Cl
Barking IG11 102 B4
Beckenham BR3 206 D4
Puffin Ct 9 W13 86 D3
Puffin Terr IG5 56 C6
Puget Ct N12 30 A5
Pugin Ct N1 72 C1
Pulborough Rd
SW18 157 B4
Pulborough Way
TW4 128 C1
Pulford Rd N15 51 B3
Pulham Ave N2 48 B5
Pulham Ho SW8 270 C3
Puller Rd EN5 1 A3
Pulleyns Ave E6 100 A4
Pullman Ct SW2 160 B3
Pullman Gdns
SW15 156 C5
Pullman Mews
SE12 165 B1
Pullman Pl SE9 166 A6
Pulross Rd SW9 138 B2
Pulteney Cl
3 Isleworth
TW7 131 A2
20 Old Ford E3 97 B6
Pulteney Gdns 9
E18 55 B6
Pulteney Rd E18 55 B6
Pulteney Terr
N1 94 B6 233 D6
Pulton Ho SE4 141 A1
Pulton Pl
SW6 135 C5 265 A3
Puma Ct E1 243 C4
Puma Trade Pk CR4 202 B5
Pump Alley 3 TW8 131 D5
Pump Cl UB5 85 C5
Pump Ct EC4 241 A1
Pump House Cl
Bromley BR2 186 D1
Rotherhithe SE16 118 C4
Pumphouse Educational
Mus The* SE16 119 A5
Pumping Ho 3 E14 120 B6
Pumping Station Rd
W4 133 C6
Pump La
Deptford SE14 140 C5
Hayes UB3 106 A4
Pump Pail N CR0 221 A5
Pump Pail S CR0 221 A5
Punchard Cres EN3 7 D5
Punderson's Gdns E2 96 B4
Puran Ho E13 99 C5
Purbeck Ave KT3 199 D3
Purbeck Ct 2 N20 14 C2
Purbeck Dr NW2 68 D6
Purbeck Ho SW8 270 C3
Purbrook Est SE1 253 B1
Purbrook Ho 2
SW15 156 B3
Purbrook St SE1 263 B6

Purcell Cres SW6 135 A5 264 A4
Purcell Ho
  Chelsea SW10 266 C5
  Isleworth TW2 152 B5
  Southall UB1 85 C1
Purcell Mews 2 NW10 67 C1
Purcell Rd UB6 85 D2
Purcells Ave HA8 26 C5
Purcell St N1 95 C5
Purchese St NW1 93 D5 232 D3
Purday Ho 4 W10 91 B4
Purdey Ct 3 KT4 200 A1
Purdon Ho 11 SE15 140 A4
Purdy St E3 97 D3
Purkis Cl UB3 105 A6
Purland Cl RM8 59 B1
Purland Rd SE28, SE18 123 D4
Purley Ave NW2 69 A6
Purley Oaks Prim Sch CR2 221 B1
Purley Pl N1 72 D1
Purley Rd
  Edmonton N9 17 C1
  South Croydon CR2 221 B1
Purley View Terr CR2 221 B1
Purley Way Cres CR0 204 B2
Purley Way
  Croydon CR0, CR9 220 C3
  Thornton Heath CR0 204 B1
Purneys Rd SE9 143 D1
Purrett Rd SE18 123 D1
Purser Ho 3 SW2 160 C5
Pursers Cross Rd SW6 135 B4 264 D2
Pursewardens Cl W13 109 C5
Pursley Rd NW7 28 B3
Purves Rd NW10 90 C5
Purvis Ho CR0 205 B2
Pusey Ho 20 E14 97 C1
Puteaux Ho 6 E2 96 D5
PUTNEY 156 C6
Putney Bridge App SW6 135 A2
Putney Bridge Rd SW15 135 B1
Putney Bridge Sta SW6 135 B2
Putney Comm SW15 134 C2
Putney Exchange Shopping Ctr SW15 134 D1
Putney Gdns RM6 58 B4
PUTNEY HEATH 156 C4
Putney Heath La SW15 156 D5
Putney Heath SW15 156 C5
Putney High Sch SW15 156 D6
Putney High St SW15 135 A1
Putney Hill SW15 156 D6
Putney Park Ave SW15 134 A1
Putney Park La SW15 156 B6
Putney Park Sch SW15 134 B1
Putney Pier SW15 135 A2
Putney School of Art & Design SW15 135 A1
Putney Sta SW15 135 A1
PUTNEY VALE 156 A1
Putney Wharf Twr SW15 135 A2
Pycombe Cnr N12 29 B6
Pycroft Way N9 34 A6
Pykewell Lo 13 E8 74 A3
Pylbrook Rd SM1 217 D5
Pylon Trad Est E16 98 B2
Pylon Way CR0 204 A1
Pym Cl EN4 14 B6
Pymers Mead SE21 161 A3
Pymmes Brook Dr EN4 2 C1
Pymmes Brook Ho 3 N10 31 A3
Pymmes Cl
  Bowes Pk N13 32 B5
  Tottenham N17 34 B2
Pymmes Gdns N N9 17 D1
Pymmes Gdns S N9 17 D1
Pymmes Green Rd N11 15 C1
Pymmes Mews N13 32 A5
Pymmes Rd N13 32 A5
Pynchester Cl UB10 60 C6
Pyne Rd KT6 198 C1
Pynfolds SE16 118 B4
Pynham Cl SE2 124 B3
Pynnacles Cl HA7 25 B5
Pynnersmead SE24 161 A6
Pyramid Ho N12 30 A6
Pyrford Ho 12 SW9 138 D1
Pyrland Rd
  Richmond TW10 154 B5
  Stoke Newington N5 73 B3
Pyrmont Gr SE27 160 D1
Pyrmont Rd W4 132 C6
Pytchley Cres SE19 183 A4
Pytchley Rd SE22 139 C2

Q

Quadrangle Cl SE1 263 A4
Quadrangle Ho The E15 76 C2
Quadrangle Lo SW19 179 C4
Quadrangle The
  Chelsea SW10 266 B2
  Fulham SW6 264 A3
  Herne Hill SE24 161 A6
  3 North Kensington W12 90 C1
  Paddington W2 237 A2
  Stanmore HA7 25 C3
  Walthamstow E17 35 B1
Quadrant Arc W1 249 B5
Quadrant Bsns Ctr NW6 91 A6
Quadrant Cl NW4 46 B4
Quadrant Gr NW5 70 D3
Quadrant Ho E15 98 C4
Quadrant Rd
  Richmond TW9 131 D1
  Thornton Heath CR7 204 D5
Quadrant The
  4 Kensal Green W10 90 D4
  Richmond TW9 132 A1
  Sutton SM2 218 A2
  West Heath DA7 146 D5
  Wimbledon SW20 179 A2
Quad Rd HA9 65 D5
Quaggy Wlk SE3 143 A1
Quainton Hall Sch HA1 42 C4
Quainton St NW10 67 B5
Quaker Ct EC1 242 B6
Quaker La UB2 107 C3
Quakers Course NW9 27 D2
Quaker's Pl E7 77 D3
Quaker St E1 95 D3 243 C5
Quakers Wlk N21 17 B5
Quality Ct WC2 241 A2
Quantock Cl UB3 127 B5
Quantock Ct
  4 East Barnet N20 14 C2
  Greenford UB6 64 C3
Quantock Dr KT4 216 C6
Quantock Gdns NW2 68 D6
Quantock Ho N16 51 D1
Quantock Mews 3 SE15 140 A3
Quarles Park Rd RM6 58 C3
Quarrendon St SW6 135 C3
Quarr Rd SM5 202 C3
Quarry Park Rd SM1 217 B2
Quarry Rd SW18 158 A5
Quarry Rise SM1 217 B2
Quarterdeck The E14 119 C4
Quartermain Ho SM4 202 A4
Quartermile La E10, E15 75 D4
Quayside Ct 6 SE16 118 D5
Quay West Ct TW11 175 B5
Quebec & Crown Wharves E14 97 B1
Quebec Ind Est SE16 119 A3
Quebec Mews W1 237 D1
Quebec Rd
  Hayes UB4 84 C1
  Ilford IG1 57 A2
Quebec Way SE16 119 A4
Quebec Wharf 32 E8 95 C6
Quedgeley Ct 3 SE15 139 D6
Queen Adelaide Ct SE20 184 C4
Queen Adelaide Rd SE20 184 C3
Queen Alexandra Mans WC1 233 A1
Queen Alexandra's Ct SW19 179 B5
Queen Anne Ave BR2 208 D6
Queen Anne Dr KT10 212 C1
Queen Anne Gate DA7 146 D2
Queen Anne Mews W1 238 D3
Queen Anne Rd E9 74 D2
Queen Annes Cl TW2 152 B1
Queen Anne's Gate SW1 115 D4 249 C1
Queen Anne's Gdns
  Bedford Pk W4 111 C3
  Ealing W5 110 A4
  Enfield EN1 17 C5
  Mitcham CR4 202 D6
Queen Anne's Gr
  Bedford Pk W4 111 C3
  Ealing W5 110 A4
  Enfield EN1 17 C5
Queen Anne's Pl EN1 17 C5
Queen Anne St W1 93 B2 238 C3
Queen Anne Terr 9 E1 118 B6
Queenborough Gdns
  Chislehurst BR7 189 B4
  Ilford IG2 56 C5
Queen Caroline St W6 112 C1
Queen Charlottes & Chelsea Hospl W12 90 A1
Queen Ct WC1 240 B5
Queen Elizabeth Ct
  Barnet EN5 1 B1
  5 Kingsland N1 73 B2
Queen Elizabeth Gdns SM4 201 C5
Queen Elizabeth Hall & Purcell Room* SE1 250 D4
Queen Elizabeth Ho SW12 159 A4
Queen Elizabeth Hospl SE18 144 A5
Queen Elizabeth II Con Ctr SW1 249 D1
Queen Elizabeth II Jubilee Sch W9 91 B3
Queen Elizabeth II Pier SE10 120 D5
Queen Elizabeth Rd
  Kingston u T KT2 176 B1
  Walthamstow E17 53 A6
Queen Elizabeth's Cl N16 73 B6
Queen Elizabeth's Coll 15 SE10 142 A5
Queen Elizabeth's Dr N14 16 A3
Queen Elizabeth's Girls Sch EN5 1 B1
Queen Elizabeth's Hunting Lodge Mus* E4 20 D4
Queen Elizabeth St SE1 117 D4 253 C2
Queen Elizabeth's Wlk
  Stoke Newington N16 73 B6
  Wallington SM6 219 D4
Queen Elizabeth Wlk SW13 134 B4
Queenhithe EC4 252 B6
Queen Margaret Flats 22 E2 96 B4
Queen Margarets Ct N1 73 C3
Queen Margaret's Gr N1 73 C3
Queen Mary Ave SM4 200 D4
Queen Mary Cl KT9 214 C5
Queen Mary Ct TW19 148 A3
Queen Mary Rd
  Charlton TW17 171 A1
  South Norwood SE19 182 D4
Queen Mary's Ave SM5 218 D1
Queen Mary's Gdns* NW1 231 A1
Queen Mary's Hospl
  Hampstead NW3 70 A5
  Sidcup DA14 190 A4
Queen Mary's Univ Hospl SW15 156 A5
Queen Mary, Univ of London E1 97 A3
Queen of Denmark Ct SE16 119 B3
Queens Acre SM3 217 A1
Queen St Pl EC4 252 B6
Queens Ave TW13 172 C6
Queen's Ave N3 30 A2
Queens Ave N10 49 B6
Queen's Ave
  Southall UB1 86 A1
  Southgate N21 16 D3
Queens Ave
  Stanmore HA7 25 C1
  Whetstone N20 14 B2
Queen's Ave IG8 37 B5
Queensberry Ho 6 TW9 153 D6
Queensberry Mews W SW7 256 C4
Queensberry Pl
  Chelsea SW7 114 B2 256 C4
  Plashet E12 78 A3
Queensberry Way SW7 256 C4
Queensborough Ct N3 47 B5
Queensborough Mews W2 246 A6
Queensborough Pas W2 246 A6
Queensborough Terr W2 113 D6 245 D6
Queensbridge Ct 1 E2 95 D5
Queensbridge Inf Sch E8 73 D1
Queensbridge Pk TW7 152 C6
Queensbridge Rd
  Dalston E8 73 D1
  Shoreditch E2, E8 95 D6
QUEENSBURY 44 B6
Queensbury IG9 21 B3
Queensbury Circ Par HA3 44 A6
Queensbury Ct CR7 183 A1
Queensbury Rd
  Kingsbury NW9 45 B2
  Wembley HA0 88 B5
Queensbury Sta HA7, HA8 44 B6
Queensbury Station Par HA8 44 B6
Queensbury St N1 73 A1
Queen's CE Prim Sch The TW9 132 C5
Queen's Cir SW11 137 B5 268 C3
Queen's Cl HA8 26 C5
Queen's Club Gdns W14 135 A6 264 B6
Queen's Club The W14 113 A1 254 B1
Queen's Cl SM6 219 B3
Queen's Coll W1 93 B2 238 C3
Queenscourt HA9 66 A4
Queen's Cres NW5 71 A2
Queens Cres TW10 154 B6
Queenscroft Rd SE9 165 D5
Queen's Ct SW13 134 A2
Queens Ct SW11 268 C2
Queen's Ct BR3 185 C2
Queens Ct
  Beckenham BR3 185 D3
  Camberwell SE5 139 C3
Queen's Ct
  Croydon CR2 221 A3
  8 Ealing W5 87 C2
  Hampstead Garden Suburb NW11 47 C4
  Kensington W2 245 D5
  1 Kingston u T KT2 176 C3
Queens Ct E10 53 C2
Queen's Ct E11 54 C2
Queens Ct 4 E14 119 B6
Queen's Ct 3 TW10 154 B5
Queens Ct
  Sidcup DA14 190 A6
  Stanmore HA7 25 B1
Queen's Ct NW8 229 C4
Queens Ct 8 NW11 47 B4
Queen's Ct CR7 204 C4
Queens Ct E17 53 C4
Queensdale Cres W11 112 D5
Queensdale W11 112 D5
Queensdale Pl W11 244 A3
Queensdale Rd
  Notting Hill W11 112 D5
  Notting Hill W11 113 A5 244 A3
Queensdale Wlk W11 244 A3
Queensdown Rd E5 74 B4
Queen's Dr Acton W3 88 C1
Queen's Dr *continued*
  Finsbury Pk N4 72 D6
Queens Dr KT5 198 C3
Queen's Dr KT7 197 A3
Queens Dr E10 53 C2
Queen's Elm Par SW3 256 D2
Queen's Elm Sq SW3 256 D1
Queensferry Wlk N17 52 B5
Queensfield Ct SM3 216 C4
Queen's Gallery* SW1 115 B4 248 D1
Queensgate Ct N12 29 D5
Queens Gate Gdns BR7 189 B2
Queensgate Gdns SW15 134 B1
Queen's Gate Gdns SW7 114 A3 256 B5
Queensgate Ho 34 E3 97 B5
Queen's Gate Mews SW7 114 A3 256 B6
Queensgate Pl 10 NW6 69 C1
Queen's Gate Pl Mews SW7 114 A3 256 B5
Queen's Gate Pl SW7 114 A3 256 B5
Queens Gate IG4 56 B5
Queen's Gate Sch SW7 256 C4
Queen's Gate SW7 114 A3 256 B5
Queen's Gate Terr SW7 114 A3 256 B6
Queens Gate Villas E9 75 A1
Queen's Gdns
  Bayswater W2 114 A6 246 A6
  Ealing W5 87 C3
  Heston TW5 129 A4
Queens Gdns NW4 46 C4
Queen's Gr NW8 92 B6 229 D5
Queen's Grove Rd E4 20 B3
Queen's Head Pas EC2 242 A2
Queen's Head St N1 94 D6 234 D5
Queen's Head Yd SE1 252 C3
Queens Ho 1 SE17 139 B6
Queen's Ho TW11 174 D4
Queen's House The* SE10 142 B6
Queens Keep 10 TW1 153 C5
Queens La
  2 Ashford TW15 170 B6
  Muswell Hill N10 49 B6
Queensland Ave
  Edmonton N18 33 A4
  Merton SW19 179 D2
Queensland Cl E17 35 B1
Queensland Ct N10 31 B3
Queensland Ho 2 E16 122 C5
Queensland Rd N7 72 C4
Queens Lo HA7 25 A5
Queens Manor Sch SW6 134 D5
Queen's Mans W6 112 D2
Queens Mans
  Hampstead NW6 69 D3
  Hendon NW4 46 B4
Queen's Mans N10 49 A6
Queensmead TW15 170 B5
Queens Mead HA8 26 B4
Queen's Mead Rd BR2 186 D1
Queensmead Sch HA4 62 D4
Queensmead NW8 92 B6 229 D6
Queensmere Cl SW19 156 D2
Queensmere Ct SW13 134 A6
Queensmere Rd SW19 156 D2
Queensmere 4 SM1 217 D3
Queens Mews 5 IG9 21 C2
Queen's Mews W2 113 D6 245 C6
Queensmill Rd SW6 134 D5
Queensmill Sch SW6 135 C3
Queen's Mkt E13 99 C6
Queens Parade Cl N11 30 D5
Queens Par W5 88 B1
Queen's Par 3 N11 30 D5
Queens Par 7 NW4 46
Queens Park Com Sch NW6 90
Queens Park Ct 5 W10 90
Queens Park Gdns TW13 149
Queen's Park Prim Sch W10 91
Queen's Park Sta NW6 91
Queens Par 3 NW2 68
Queen's Par N11 32
Queen's Pas BR7 188
Queen's Pl SM4 201
Queen's Quay EC4 252
Queen Sq WC1 94 A2 240
Queen's Rd
  Barking IG11 79
  Beckenham BR3 185
  Bowes Pk N11 32
  Bromley BR1 187
  Buckhurst Hill IG9 21
  Chislehurst BR7 188
  Ealing W5 88
  Edmonton N9 18
  Enfield EN1 5
  Feltham TW13 150
  Finchley N3 30
  Hampton TW12 173
Queens Rd UB3 83
Queen's Rd
  Hendon NW4 46
  Hounslow TW3 129
  Kingston u T KT2 176
  Leytonstone E11 54
  Mitcham CR4 202
Queens Rd SM4 201
Queen's Rd
  Mortlake SW14 133
  New Cross Gate SE14, SE15 140
  Newham E13 99
  New Malden KT3 199
  Richmond KT2, TW10 176
  Richmond TW10 154
  Southall UB2 107
  Teddington TW11 174
  Thames Ditton KT7 196
  Thornton Heath CR0 205
Queens Rd TW1 153
Queen's Rd
  Wallington SM6 219
  Walthamstow E17 53
  Welling DA16 146
Queens Rd UB7 104
Queen's Rd SW19 179
Queen's Rd W E13 99
Queens Reach KT8 196
Queen's Ride SW13 134
Queen's Rise TW10 154
Queen's Road Sta SE15 140
Queen's Row SE17 139
Queen St
  Bexleyheath DA7 147
  City of London EC4 117 A6 252
  Croydon CR0 221
Queens Terr Cotts W7 108
Queens Terr HA3 24
Queen's Terr TW7 131
Queens Terr
  Newham E13 99
  St John's Wood NW8 92 B5 229
Queensthorpe Rd SE26 184
Queen St W1 115 B5 248
Queenstown Mews SW8 268
Queenstown Rd SW8 137 B5 268
Queenstown Road Sta SW8 137 B4 268
Queen St N17 33
Queensville Rd SW12, SW4 159
Queens Walk Ho W5 87
Queensway Bsns Ctr EN3 6
Queensway
  Coney Hall BR4 224
  Croydon CR0 220
  Enfield EN3 6
Queens Way
  Feltham TW13 172
  Hendon NW4 46
Queensway
  Kensington W2 113 D6 245
  Orpington BR5 211

Queensway Sta
W2 113 D6 245 D5
Queensway TW16 172 B1
Queens Well Ave
N20 30 C6
Queenswell Jun & Inf Schs N20 14 B2
Queens Wlk
Ashford TW15 170 A6
Chingford E4 20 B3
Queen's Wlk W5 87 C2
Queens Wlk
Harrow HA1 42 C5
Ruislip HA4 62 C5
Queen's Wlk
SW1 115 C5 249 A3
Queens Wlk NW9 67 A6
Queenswood Ave
Chingford E17 36 A2
Hampton TW12 173 D4
Hounslow TW3, TW5 129 B3
Thornton Heath CR7 204 C4
Wallington CR0, SM6 219 D4
Queenswood Ct
7 Clapham Pk SW4 160 A6
11 West Norwood SE27 183 B6
Queenswood Gdns
E11 55 B1
Queenswood Pk N3 29 A2
Queenswood Rd
Blackfen DA15 167 D5
Forest Hill SE23 163 A1
Queen's Wood Rd N6 49 B3
Queens Yd E9 75 C2
Queen's Yd W1 239 B5
Queen Victoria Ave
HA0 65 D1
Queen Victoria Meml*
SW1 249 A2
Queen Victoria St
EC4 117 A6 252 A6
Queen Victoria Terr 12
E1 118 B6
Quelch Ho 2 N19 71 D3
Quemerford Rd N7 72 B3
Quendon Ho 9 W10 90 C3
Quenington Ct 5
SE15 139 D6
Quenington Mans
SW6 264 C2
Quennel Ho 7
SW12 159 C4
Quentin Pl SE13 142 C2
Quentin Rd SE13 142 C2
Quernmore Cl BR1 187 A4
Quernmore Rd
Plaistow BR1 187 A4
Stroud Green N4 50 C3
Querrin St SW6 136 A3
Quested Ct 27 E8 74 B3
Quex Mews NW6 91 C6
Quex Rd NW6 91 C6
Quick Rd W4 111 C1
Quicks Rd SW19 179 D3
Quick St N1 94 D5 234 D3
Quick Street Mews
N1 234 C3
Quickswood NW3 70 C1
Quiet Nook BR2 225 D5
Quill La SW15 134 D1
Quill St Ealing W5 88 A5
Highbury N4 72 C5
Quilp St SE1 252 A2
Quilter St
Bethnal Green E2 96 A4
Plumstead Comm SE18 123 D1
Quilting Ct 23 SE16 118 D4
Quince Ho TW13 150 A3
Quince Rd SE13 141 D3
Quinta Dr EN5 12 C6
Quintin Ave SW20 179 B2
Quintin Cl HA5 40 B4
Quintin Ct W4 133 A5
Quintin Kynaston Sch
NW8 92 B6 229 C5
Quintock Ho 2
TW9 132 C4
Quinton Cl
Beckenham BR3 208 A6
Cranford TW5 128 B5
Wallington SM6 219 B4
Quinton Ho SW8 270 A4
Quinton Rd KT7 197 A1
Quinton St SW18 158 A2
Quixley St 1 E14 120 B6
Quorn Rd SE22 139 C2
Quwwat-Ul-Islam Girls Sch E7 77 B2

R

Rabbit Row W8 245 B4
Rabbits Rd E12 78 A4
Rabbs Farm Prim Sch
UB7 104 A6
Rabinal Ho EN3 18 D6
Rabournmead Dr
UB5 63 A3
Raby Rd KT3 199 B5
Raby St E14 97 A1
Raccoon Way TW4 128 C3
Rachel Cl IG6 57 B6
Rachel Ct SM2 218 B1
Racine 15 SE5 139 C4
Rackham Cl DA16 146 B3
Rackham Mews
SW16 181 C4
Racs Flats 9 SE1 118 A2
Racton Rd
SW6 135 C6 265 A5
Radbourne Ave W5 109 C2
Radbourne Cl E5 74 D4
Radbourne Cres E17 36 B1
Radbourne Ct HA3 43 B3
Radbourne Rd
SW12 159 D3
Radcliff Bldg EC1 241 A4
Radcliffe Ave
Enfield EN2 5 A4
Willesden Green NW10 90 A5
Radcliffe Coll
Marylebone W1 93 C1 239 A1
Soho W1 93 D1 239 C2
Radcliffe Gdns SM5 218 C1
Radcliffe Ho 10
SE16 118 B2
Radcliffe Path 5
SW8 137 B3
Radcliffe Rd
Bermondsey SE1 263 B6
Harrow HA3 25 A1
South Croydon CR0 221 D5
Southgate N21 16 D3
Radcliffe Sq SW15 156 D5
Radcliffe Way UB5 84 D4
Radcliff Mews
TW12 174 A5
Radcot Point 2
SE23 162 D1
Radcot St SE11 261 B1
Raddington Rd W10 91 A2
Radfield Way DA15 167 B4
Radford Ho
7 Bow Comm E14 97 D2
Islington N7 72 B3
Radford Rd SE13 164 A5
Radford Way IG11 101 D4
Radipole Rd
SW6 135 B4 264 C2
Radius Pk TW6 127 D1
Radland Rd E16 99 A1
Radlet Ave SE23 162 B2
Radlett Cl E7 76 D2
Radlett Pl
NW8 92 C6 230 A6
Radley Ave IG3 80 A4
Radley Cl TW14 149 D3
Radley Ct
4 Catford BR1 186 A6
25 Rotherhithe SE16 118 D4
Radley Gdns HA3 44 A5
Radley Ho
11 Abbey Wood SE2 124 D4
Marylebone NW1 237 C6
Radley Lo 30 SW19 156 D3
Radley Mews W8 255 B5
Radley Rd N17 33 C1
Radley's La E18 37 A1
Radleys Mead RM10 81 D2
Radley Sq E5 74 C6
Radley Terr 1 E16 98 D2
Radlix Rd E10 53 C1
Radnor Ave
Bexley DA16 168 B6
Harrow HA1 42 C4
Radnor Cl
Chislehurst BR7 189 C4
Mitcham CR4 204 A5
Radnor Cres
Redbridge IG4 56 B4
Woolwich SE18 146 A5
Radnor Ct Ealing W7 86 D1
6 Forest Hill SE23 162 D1
Harrow HA3 24 D2
Radnor Gdns
Enfield EN1 5 C4
Twickenham TW1 152 D2
Radnor Gr UB10 82 C5
Radnor Ho
East Molesey KT8 196 B5
Radnor Ho *continued*
Thornton Heath SW16 182 B1
Radnor Lo W2 236 D1
Radnor Mews
W2 92 B1 236 D1
Radnor Pl W2 92 C1 237 A1
Radnor Rd
Harrow HA1 42 C4
Kensal Rise NW6 91 A6
Peckham SE15 140 A5
Twickenham TW1 152 D2
Radnor St
EC1 95 A4 235 B1
Radnor Terr
W14 113 B2 254 C4
Radnor Way NW10 88 D3
Radnor Wlk
Chelsea SW3 114 D1 257 C1
Croydon CR0 207 A3
21 Millwall E14 119 C2
Radstock Ave HA3 43 B6
Radstock Cl N11 31 A4
Radstock St SW11 267 A3
Radway Ho 38 W2 91 C2
Radwell Ho SW2 160 C6
Raebarn Ct 6
SW16 160 A1
Raebarn Gdns EN5 12 B6
Raeburn Ave KT5 198 D3
Raeburn Cl
Hampstead Garden Suburb NW11 48 A3
Teddington KT1 175 D3
Raeburn Ho
5 Belmont SM2 217 D1
6 Northolt UB5 84 D5
Raeburn Rd
Edgware HA8 26 C2
Hayes UB4 83 B5
Sidcup DA15 167 C5
Raeburn St SW2 138 A1
Raffles Ct HA8 26 B6
Raffles Ho NW4 46 B5
Rafford Way BR1 209 B6
RAF Mus* NW9 28 A1
Ragged School Mus The* E3 97 A2
Raggleswood BR7 188 C2
Raglan Cl TW4 151 B6
Raglan Ct
Brixton SW9 138 C2
Croydon CR0, CR2 220 D3
Lee SE12 165 A6
Wembley HA9 66 C5
Raglan Jun & Inf Schs
EN1 17 C4
Raglan Prim Sch
BR2 209 D5
Raglan Rd
Belvedere DA17 125 B2
Bromley BR2 209 C5
Enfield EN1 17 D4
Walthamstow E17 54 B4
Woolwich SE18 123 A1
Raglan St NW5 71 B2
Raglan Terr HA2 63 D4
Raglan Way UB5 64 A2
Ragley Cl W3 111 A4
Ragwort Ct 1 SE26 184 B5
Rahere Ho EC1 235 A2
Railey Mews NW5 71 C3
Railshead Rd TW1, TW7 131 B1
Railton Rd SE24 160 D6
Railway App
Bermondsey SE1 252 D4
Harrow HA1, HA3 42 D5
Stroud Green N4 50 C3
11 Twickenham TW1 153 A4
Wallington SM6 219 B3
Railway Ave SE16 118 C4
Railway Cotts
Hammersmith W6 112 C4
Ilford IG6 57 B6
Railway Gr SE14 141 B5
Railway Pl DA17 125 C3
Railway Rd TW11 174 D6
Railway Rise SE22 139 C1
Railway Side SW13 133 C2
Railway St Ilford RM6 58 C2
King's Cross N1 233 B3
Railway Terr
Chingford E17 36 A2
Feltham TW13, TW14 150 A3
Ladywell SE13 163 D6
Rainborough Cl
NW10 67 A2
Rainbow Ave E14 119 D1
Rainbow Ct 3 SE14 141 A6
Rainbow Ind Est
SW20 178 B1
Rainbow Quay SE16 119 A3
Rainbow Sch The
SW17 158 A2
Rainbow St SE5 139 C5
Rainbow Works N15 52 A4
Raine Gdns 4 IG8 37 A6
Raines Ct N16 73 D6
Raine's Foundation Lower Sch E2 96 B5
Raine's Foundation Sch
E2 96 C5
Raine St E1 118 B5
Rainford Ho 9 N7 72 B6
Rainham Cl
Sidcup SE9 167 C5
Wandsworth SW11 158 C5
Rainham Ho NW1 232 B5
Rainham Rd NW10 90 C4
Rainham Rd N RM10 81 D6
Rainham Rd S RM10 81 D4
Rainhill Way E3 97 C4
Rainsborough Ave
SE8 119 A2
Rainsford Cl HA7 25 C5
Rainsford Ct NW10 88 D5
Rainsford Ho 14
SW2 160 B6
Rainsford Rd NW10 88 D5
Rainsford St W2 237 A2
Rainstar Est N18 34 C6
Rainton Rd SE7 121 A1
Rainville Rd W6 134 C6
Raisins Hill HA5 40 C6
Raith Ave N14 15 D1
Raleigh Ave
Hayes UB4 84 B2
Wallington SM6 219 D4
Raleigh Cl
Hendon NW4 46 C4
Pinner HA5 40 D2
Ruislip HA4 61 D6
Raleigh Ct
Beckenham BR3 185 D2
4 Dulwich SE19 183 D5
Ealing W13 87 B2
7 Hammersmith W12 112 B4
2 Rotherhithe SE16 118 D5
Wallington SM6 219 B2
Raleigh Dr
East Barnet N20 14 C1
Esher KT10 212 B3
Tolworth KT5 199 A1
Raleigh Gdns
Mitcham CR4 202 D6
Tulse Hill SW2 160 B5
Raleigh Ho
30 Clapham SW8 137 D3
Isle of Dogs E14 119 D4
1 Thames Ditton KT7 197 A2
Raleigh Mews
Islington N1 234 D5
6 Orpington BR6 227 D3
Raleigh Rd Enfield EN2 5 B1
Feltham TW13 149 D2
Finchley N10 30 C2
Hornsey N8 50 C5
Penge SE20 184 D3
Richmond TW9 132 B2
Southall UB2 107 A1
Raleigh St N1 94 D6 234 D5
Raleigh Way
Feltham TW13 172 C5
Southgate N14 16 A3
Ralph Ct 8 W2 91 D1
Ralph Perring Ct
BR3 207 C5
Ralston St SW3 257 C1
Ramac Ind Est SE7 121 B1
Rama Cl SW16 182 A3
Rama Ct HA1 64 C6
Ramac Way SE7 121 B1
Rama La SE19 183 D3
Ramar Ho 12 E1 96 A2
Rambler Cl SW16 181 C6
Rambler Ct 11 NW9 46 A5
Rame Cl SW17 181 A5
Ramilles Cl SW2 160 A5
Ramilles Ho W1 239 B1
Ramillies Pl
W1 93 C1 239 A1
Ramillies Rd
Bedford Pk W4 111 B3
Blackfen DA15 168 B5
Edgware NW7 11 C2
Ramillies St W1 239 A1
Ramney Dr EN3 7 A6
Rampart St E1 96 B1
Ram Pas KT1 175 D1
Rampayne St SW1 259 C2
Rampton Cl E4 19 C1
Ramsay Ho NW8 230 A4
Ramsay Rd
Acton W3 111 A4
Leyton E7 76 D4
Ramscroft Cl N9 17 C4
Ramsdale Rd SW17 181 A5
Ramsdean Ho 1
SW15 156 B3
Ramsden Rd
Balham SW12 159 A4
Friern Barnet N11 30 D5
Ramsey Cl
Greenford UB6 64 B3
West Hendon NW9 45 D3
Ramsey Ct
Croydon CR0 220 D6
Hornsey N8 49 D4
Putney SW15 156 C5
6 Upper Holloway N19 71 D6
Ramsey Ho
5 Battersea SW11 136 B1
14 Kennington SW9 138 C5
7 Merton SW19 179 D2
Ramsey Rd CR7 204 B3
Ramsey St E2 96 A3
Ramsey Way N14 15 C4
Ramsfort Ho 4
SE16 118 B2
Ramsgate Cl 10 E16 121 B5
Ramsgate St E8 73 D2
Ramsgill App IG2 57 D5
Ramsgill Dr IG2 57 D5
Rams Gr RM6 59 A5
Ram St SW18 157 D6
Ramulis Dr UB4 84 D3
Ramus Wood Ave
BR6 227 C3
Rance Ho 12 SE7 122 A2
Rancliffe Gdns SE9 144 A1
Rancliffe Rd E6 100 A5
Randal Cremer JMI Sch
E2 95 D5
Randall Ave NW2 67 D5
Randall Cl
SW11 136 C4 267 A2
Randall Ct NW7 28 A3
Randall 9 NW9 27 D2
Randall Pl SE10 142 A5
Randall Rd
SE11 116 B2 260 C3
Randall Row SE11 260 C3
Randell's Rd
N1 94 A6 233 B6
Randisbourne Gdns
SE6 163 D1
Randle Rd TW10 175 C6
Randlesdown Rd
SE6 163 D1
Randmore Ct 6
BR3 185 C3
Randolf Ct
Paddington NW6 91 D5
St John's Wood NW8 229 A5
Randolph App E16 99 C1
Randolph Ave
W9 92 A4 229 A1
Randolph Cl KT2 177 A5
Randolph Cres
W9 92 A3 236 A6
Randolph Ct HA5 23 C3
Randolph Gdns NW6 91 D5
Randolph Gr RM6 58 C4
Randolph Mews
W9 92 A3 236 B5
Randolph Rd
Bromley BR2 210 B1
Paddington W9 92 A3 236 B5
Southall UB1 107 B4
Walthamstow E17 53 D4
Randolph St NW1 71 C1
Randon Cl HA2 23 D1
Ranelagh Ave
Barnes SW13 134 A3
Fulham SW6 135 B2
Ranelagh Cl HA8 26 C6
Ranelagh Ct HA8 26 C6
Ranelagh Dr
Edgware HA8 26 C6
Twickenham TW1 153 C6
Ranelagh Gardens Mans
SW6 135 A2
Ranelagh Gardens (site of Chelsea Flower Show)*
SW1 115 A1 258 B1
Ranelagh Gdns
3 Bedford Pk W6 111 D3
Chiswick W4 133 A5
Fulham SW6 135 B2
Ilford IG1 56 C1
Wanstead E11 55 C4
Ranelagh Gr
SW1 115 A1 258 B2
Ranelagh Ho SW3 257 C2
Ranelagh Mans 4
SW6 135 B3
Ranelagh Pl KT3 199 C4
Ranelagh Prim Sch
E15 98 C5
Ranelagh Rd
Dagenham NW10 89 D5
Ealing W5 109 D4
Leyton E11 76 C4
Newham E15 98 C5
Pimlico SW1 115 C1 259 B1
Southall UB1 106 D5
Tottenham N17 51 C6
Wallend E6 100 C5
Wembley HA0 65 D2
Wood Green N22 32 B2
Ranfurly Rd SM1 217 C6
Rangdon St EC3 243 C1
Rangefield Prim Sch
BR1 186 C5
Rangefield Rd BR1 186 D5
Rangemoor Rd N15 51 D4
Ranger's House (The Wernher Collection)*
SE10 142 B4
Ranger's Rd
Buckhurst Hill IG9, IG10 21 A4
Chingford E4 20 D4
Rangers Sq SE10 142 B4
Range Villas TW17 192 A2
Range Way TW17 192 C2
Rangeworth Pl
DA15 167 D1
Rangoon Ho 5 N16 73 B4
Rankin Cl NW9 45 C6
Rankine Ho SE1 262 A5
Ranleigh Gdns DA7 147 B5
Ranmere St SW12 159 B3
Ranmoor Cl HA1 42 B5
Ranmoor Gdns HA1 42 C5
Ranmore Ave CR0 221 D5
Ranmore Ct
Kingston u T KT6 197 D4
3 Wimbledon SW20 178 D2
Rann Ho 1 SW14 133 B2
Rannoch Cl HA8 10 D2
Rannoch Ct 9 KT6 198 A4
Rannoch Rd W6 134 D6
Rannock Ave NW9 45 C2
Ransford Ho 16
SE21 183 C6
Ransomes Dock Bsns Ctr SW11 267 B3
Ransomes Mews
SW11 267 B4
Ransom Rd 1 SE7 121 C1
Ranston St NW1 237 A4
Ranulf Rd NW2 69 B4
Ranwell Cl 18 E3 97 B6
Ranwell Ho 17 E3 97 B6
Ranworth Rd N9 18 C2
Ranyard Cl KT9 214 B5
Raphael Ct 9 SE16 118 B1
Raphael Dr KT7 196 D2
Raphael St SW7 247 C1
Rapide 15 NW9 27 C2
Rapley Ho 14 E2 96 A4
Rashleigh Ct 8
SW8 137 B2
Rashleigh Ho WC1 233 A1
Rasper Rd N20 14 A2
Rastell Ave SW12 159 D3
RATCLIFF 118 D6
Ratcliffe Cl SE12 165 A4
Ratcliffe Cross St E1 96 D1
Ratcliffe Ho 10 E14 97 A1
Ratcliffe La 16 E14 97 A1
Ratcliffe Orch 9
E1 118 D6
Ratcliff Rd E7 77 C3
Rathbone Ho
5 Canning Town E16 98 D1
Kilburn NW6 91 C6
10 Wimbledon SW19 178 D3
Rathbone Mkt 3
E16 98 D2
Rathbone Pl
W1 93 D1 239 C2
Rathbone St
Canning Town E16 98 D1
Fitzrovia W1 93 C2 239 B3
Rathcoole Ave N8 50 B4
Rathcoole Gdns N8 50 B4
Rathfern Prim Sch
SE6 163 B3
Rathfern Rd SE6 163 B3
Rathgar Ave W13 109 C5
Rathgar Cl N3 29 B1
Rathgar Rd SW9 138 D2
Rathmell Dr SW4 159 D5
Rathmore Rd SE7 121 B1

Ratier 16 NW9 27 C2
Rattray Ct 3 SE6 164 D2
Rattray Rd SW2 160 C6
Raul Rd SE15 140 A4
Raveley St NW5 71 C4
Raven Cl NW9 27 C1
Ravendale Rd TW16 171 D1
Ravenet Ct
 Battersea SW11 268 C1
 Clapham SW4 159 B6
Ravenet St
 SW11 137 B4 268 C1
Ravenfield Rd
 SW17 158 D1
Ravenhill Rd E13 99 C5
Raven Ho 10 SE16 118 D2
Ravenings Par IG3 58 A1
Ravenna Rd SW15 156 D6
Ravenor Ct UB6 85 D3
Ravenor Park Rd
 UB6 86 A4
Ravenor Prim Sch
 UB6 85 C4
Raven Rd E18 37 C1
Raven Row E1 96 B2
Ravensbourne Ave
 Bromley BR2,
 BR3 186 C2
 Catford BR2 186 B3
 Stanwell TW19 148 A3
Ravensbourne Bsns Ctr
 BR2 225 D4
Ravensbourne Coll of Design & Communication
 BR7 188 B5
Ravensbourne Ct
 SE6 163 C4
Ravensbourne Gdns
 W13 87 B2
Ravensbourne Ho
 10 Catford BR1 186 B5
 Paddington NW8 237 A4
 3 Twickenham TW1 153 C5
Ravensbourne Mans 9
 SE8 141 C6
Ravensbourne Park Cres SE6 163 B4
Ravensbourne Pk
 SE6 163 C4
Ravensbourne Pl
 SE13 141 D3
Ravensbourne Rd
 Bromley BR1,
 BR2 209 A6
 Forest Hill SE23 163 B3
 Twickenham TW1 153 C5
Ravensbourne Sch The
 BR2 209 B5
Ravensbourne Sta
 BR3 186 B3
Ravensbury Ave
 SM4 202 A4
Ravensbury Ct CR4 202 B5
Ravensbury Gr CR4 202 B5
Ravensbury La CR4 202 B5
Ravensbury Rd
 Orpington BR5 211 D5
 Wandsworth SW18 157 D2
Ravensbury Terr
 SW18 157 D2
Ravenscar Lo 14
 SW19 178 D3
Ravenscar NW1 232 A5
Ravenscar Rd
 Catford BR1 186 C6
 Surbiton KT6 214 B6
Ravens Cl
 Bromley BR2 186 D1
 Enfield EN1 5 C3
 Kingston u T KT6 197 D3
Ravenscourt Ave
 W6 112 A2
Ravenscourt Cl HA4 39 A2
Ravenscourt Gdns
 W6 112 A2
Ravenscourt Ho 13
 W6 112 B2
Ravenscourt Park Mans
 1 W6 112 B3
Ravenscourt Park Prep Sch W6 112 A2
Ravenscourt Park Sta
 W6 112 B2
Ravenscourt Pk W6 112 A2
Ravenscourt Pl W6 112 B2
Ravenscourt Rd
 Hammersmith W6 112 B2
 St Paul's Cray BR5 190 B1
Ravenscourt 1 N16 74 A5
Ravenscourt Sq W6 112 A3
Ravenscourt TW16 171 D2
Ravenscourt Theatre Sch W6 112 B2
Ravenscraig Rd N11 31 C6
Ravenscroft Ave
 Golders Green NW11 47 B2
 Wembley HA9 44 B2
Ravenscroft Cl 4
 E16 99 A2
Ravenscroft Cres
 SE9 166 B1
Ravenscroft Ct NW11 47 B2
Ravenscroft Pk EN5 1 A1
Ravenscroft Point 26
 E9 74 D2
Ravenscroft Prim Sch
 E16 99 A3
Ravenscroft Rd
 Acton W4 111 A2
 Newham E16 99 A2
 Penge BR3 184 D1
Ravenscroft Sch a Tech Coll The N20 13 B4
Ravenscroft St E2 95 D4
Ravensdale Ave N12 30 B6
Ravensdale Commercial Est N16 52 A3
Ravensdale Gdns
 Hounslow TW4 129 A2
 South Norwood SE19 183 B3
Ravensdale Mans N8 50 A3
Ravensdale Rd
 Hounslow TW4 129 A2
 South Tottenham N16 51 D3
Ravensdon St
 SE11 116 C1 261 B1
Ravensfield Cl RM9 80 D4
Ravensfield Gdns
 KT19 215 C4
Ravenshaw St NW6 69 B3
Ravenshill BR7 188 D2
Ravens Ho KT1 175 D1
Ravenshurst Ave
 NW4 46 C5
Ravenside Cl N18 34 D5
Ravenside KT6 197 D4
Ravenside Ret Pk
 N18 34 D5
Ravenslea Rd SW11,
 SW12 158 D4
Ravensleigh Gdns
 BR1 187 B5
Ravensmead Rd
 BR2 186 B3
Ravensmede Way
 W4 111 D2
Ravensroost SE19 183 B2
Ravenstone Prim Sch
 SW12 159 A2
Ravenstone Rd
 Hornsey N8 50 C6
 West Hendon NW9 45 D3
Ravenstone
 SE17 117 C1 263 B1
Ravenstone St
 SW12 159 A3
Ravensview Ct KT6 197 D4
Ravens Way SE3,
 SE12 165 A6
Ravenswood Ave
 Tolworth KT6 214 C6
 West Wickham BR4 208 A1
Ravenswood N22 32 B4
Ravenswood Cres
 Harrow HA2 63 B6
 West Wickham BR4 208 A1
Ravenswood Gdns
 TW7 130 C4
Ravenswood Ind Est 5
 E17 54 A5
Ravenswood Pk HA6 22 A4
Ravenswood Rd
 Balham SW12 159 B4
 Croydon CR0 220 D5
 Walthamstow E17 54 A5
Ravens Wood Sch
 BR2 225 D5
Ravenswood DA5 169 A3
Ravensworth Ct
 SW6 265 A3
Ravensworth Rd
 Chislehurst SE9 188 B6
 College Pk NW10 90 B4
Raven Wharf SE1 253 C2
Ravey St EC2 95 C3 243 A6
Ravine Gr SE18 145 C6
Rav Pinter Cl N16 51 C2
Rawlings Cl
 Beckenham BR3 208 A4
 3 Orpington BR6 227 D3
Rawlings Cres HA9 66 D5
Rawlings St
 SW3 114 D2 257 C4
Rawlins Cl Hendon N3 47 A6
 South Croydon CR2 223 B1
Rawlinson Ct NW2 46 C2
Rawlinson Ho SE13 142 B1
Rawlinson Point 8
 E16 98 D2
Rawnsley Ave CR4 202 C4
Rawreth Wlk N1 235 B6
Rawson Ct SW11 268 B1
Rawson St
 SW11 137 B4 268 C1
Rawsthorne Cl E16 122 B5
Rawstone Wlk 5
 E13 99 A5
Rawstorne Pl EC1 234 C2
Rawstorne St
 EC1 94 D4 234 C2
Raybell Ct TW7 130 D3
Rayburne Ct
 1 Buckhurst Hill
 IG9 21 C3
 West Kensington
 W14 254 A6
Ray Cl KT9 213 C2
Ray Ct Ealing W13 109 B5
 Stanmore HA7 25 B5
 Woodford IG8 37 D4
Raydean Rd EN5 13 D6
Raydons Gdns RM9 81 A3
Raydons Rd RM9 81 A3
Raydon St N19 71 B6
Rayfield Cl BR2 210 A3
Rayford Ave SE12 164 D4
Ray Gdns
 Barking IG11 102 A5
 Stanmore HA7 25 B5
Ray Ho
 7 North Kensington
 W10 90 D1
 Shoreditch N1 235 D5
Rayleas Cl SE18 144 D4
Rayleigh Ave TW11 174 C4
Rayleigh Cl N13 17 B1
Rayleigh Ct
 2 Kingston u T
 KT1 176 B1
 Tottenham N22 33 A2
Rayleigh Rd
 Edmonton N13 17 B1
 Merton SW19 179 B2
 5 Newham E16 121 B5
 Woodford IG8 37 C3
Rayleigh Rise CR2 221 C2
Ray Lodge Prim Sch
 IG8 37 D4
Ray Lodge Rd IG8 37 D4
Ray Massey Way 3
 E6 100 A6
Raymead Ave CR7 204 C4
Raymede Twr W10 90 D2
Raymere Gdns SE18 145 C5
Raymond Ave
 Brentford W13 109 A3
 Woodford E18 36 D1
Raymond Bldgs
 WC1 240 D4
Raymond Cl SE26 184 C5
Raymond Ct N10 31 A3
Raymond Postgate Ct
 5 SE28 124 B6
Raymond Rd
 Beckenham BR3 207 A5
 Ilford IG2 57 B2
 Newham E13 99 C6
 Wimbledon SW19 179 A4
Raymond Way KT10 213 A2
Raymouth Rd SE16 118 B2
Raynald Ho 15
 SW16 160 A1
Rayne Ct
 Bermondsey SE1 253 C2
 Snaresbrook E18 54 D5
Rayne Ho
 1 Balham SW12 159 A5
 Paddington W9 91 D3
Rayner Ct 10 W12 112 C4
Rayners Cl HA0 65 D3
Rayners Cres UB5 84 B4
Rayners Gdns UB5 84 B4
Rayners La HA2 63 D6
RAYNERS LANE 41 B1
Rayners Lane Sta
 HA5 41 B2
Rayners La HA5 41 B3
Rayner's Rd SW15 157 A6
Rayner Twrs E10 53 C2
Raynes Ave E11 55 C2
Raynes Ct NW2 69 A4
Raynesfield SW20 200 C6
RAYNES PARK 200 C6
Raynes Park High Sch
 SW20 200 B6
Raynes Park Sta
 SW20 178 C1
Raynham Ave N18 34 A5
Raynham Ho 1 E1 96 D3
Raynham Prim Sch
 N18 34 A5
Raynham Rd
 Edmonton N18 34 A5
Raynham Rd *continued*
 Hammersmith W6 112 B2
Raynham Terr N18 34 A5
Raynham W2 237 A2
Raynor Cl UB1 107 B5
Raynor Pl N1 235 B6
Raynton Cl
 Harrow HA2 41 A2
 Hayes UB4 83 D3
Raynton Dr
 Hayes UB4 83 C5
 Hayes UB4 83 D3
Raynton Rd EN3 6 D6
Ray Rd KT8 195 D4
Rays Ave N18 34 C6
Rays Rd
 Edmonton N18 34 C6
 West Wickham BR4 208 A2
Ray St EC1 241 B5
Ray Wlk N7 72 B6
Raywood Cl UB7 127 A5
Reachview Cl 17
 NW1 71 C1
Read Cl KT7 197 A2
Read Ct E17 53 D3
Reade Ct 6 W3 111 A3
Reade Wlk 5 NW10 67 C1
Read Ho
 Friern Barnet N11 30 D6
 4 Kennington SE11 138 C6
Reading Ho
 Paddington W2 236 A1
 Peckham SE15 140 A6
Reading La E8 74 B2
Reading Rd
 Northolt UB5 64 A3
 Sutton SM1 218 A3
Reading Way NW7 29 A5
Readman Ct 8
 SE20 184 B2
Reads Cl IG1 78 D5
Reapers Cl NW1 232 C6
Reapers Way TW7 152 B6
Reardon Ho 5 E1 118 B5
Reardon Path 31 E1 118 B5
Reardon St E1 118 B5
Reaston St SE14 140 D5
Reay Prim Sch
 SW9 138 B5 270 D3
Rebecca Ct
 3 Beckenham
 BR3 185 C2
 Sidcup DA14 190 B6
Rebecca Ho 12 N12 29 D6
Reckitt Rd W4 111 C1
Record St SE16 140 C6
Recovery St SW17 180 C5
Recreation Rd
 Bromley BR2 186 D1
 Forest Hill SE26 184 D6
 Southall UB2 107 A2
Recreation Way CR4,
 SW16 204 A6
Rector St N1 95 A6 235 A5
Rectory Bsns Ctr 5
 DA14 190 B6
Rectory Cl
 Chingford E4 19 C1
 Finchley N3 29 B2
 Littleton TW17 192 C6
 Long Ditton KT6 197 C1
 Sidcup DA14 190 B6
 Stanmore HA7 25 B5
 West Barnes SW20 200 C6
Rectory Cres E11 55 C3
Rectory Ct
 Cranford TW5 128 C3
 Feltham TW13 172 C6
 Leyton E11 76 D5
 Wallington SM6 219 C4
 West Drayton UB7 104 A4
 Woodford E18 36 D2
Rectory Field Cres
 SE7 143 C5
Rectory Gdns
 Beckenham BR3 185 C2
 6 Clapham SW4 137 C2
 Hornsey N8 50 A5
 Northolt UB5 85 B6
Rectory Gn BR3 185 B2
Rectory Gr
 Clapham SW4 137 C2
 Croydon CR0 220 D6
 Hampton TW12,
 TW13 173 B6
Rectory La
 Edgware HA8 26 C4
 Long Ditton KT6 197 C1
 Sidcup DA14 190 C6
 Stanmore HA7 25 B5
 Upper Tooting
 SW17 181 A5
 Wallington SM6 219 C4
Rectory Orch SW19 179 A6
Rectory Paddock Sch
 BR5 190 C1
Rectory Park Ave
 UB5 85 B4
Rectory Pl SE18 122 C2
Rectory Rd
 Barnes SW13 134 A3
 Beckenham BR3 185 C2
 Cranford TW5 128 C3
 Dagenham RM10 81 D1
 Hayes UB3 84 A1
 Keston BR2 225 D1
 Little Ilford E12 78 B3
 1 London W3 111 A5
 Shacklewell N16 73 D5
 Southall UB2 107 B3
 Sutton SM1 217 D5
 Walthamstow E17 53 D5
Rectory Road Sta
 N16 73 D5
Rectory Sq E1 96 D2
Rectory Way UB10 60 D5
Reculver Ho 2
 SE15 140 C6
Reculver Mews N18 34 A6
Reculver Rd SE16 118 D1
Red Anchor Cl SW3 267 A5
Redan Pl W2 91 D1
Redan St W14 112 D3
Redan Terr SE5 138 D3
Red Barracks Rd 4
 SE18 122 B2
Redberry Gr SE23,
 SE26 162 C1
Redbourne Ave N3 29 C2
Redbourne Dr SE28 102 D1
Redbourne Ho
 Finchley N3 29 C2
 7 Poplar E14 97 B1
Redbourn Ho 10
 W10 90 C3
REDBRIDGE 55 C3
Redbridge Coll RM6 58 B4
Redbridge Ct IG1 55 D3
Redbridge Ent Ctr
 IG1 79 A6
Redbridge Foyer IG1 79 A6
Redbridge Gdns
 SE5 139 C5
Redbridge La E IG4 56 A4
Redbridge La W E11 55 C3
Redbridge Prim Sch
 IG4 56 A4
Redbridge Rdbt IG4 55 D3
Redbridge Sta IG4 55 D3
Redburn St
 SW3 136 D6 267 C6
Redburn Trad Est
 EN3 18 D5
Redcar Cl UB5 63 D2
Redcar Ho SE26 184 B4
Redcar St SE5 139 A5
Redcastle Cl E1 118 C6
Red Cedars Rd BR6 211 C2
Redchurch St
 E2 95 D3 243 C6
Redcliffe Cl SW5 255 C1
Redcliffe Ct 2 E5 74 B5
Redcliffe Gdns
 Chiswick W4 132 D5
 Fulham
 SW10 135 D6 265 D6
 Ilford IG1 56 C1
Redcliffe Mews
 SW10 255 D1
Redcliffe Pl SW10 266 A5
Redcliffe Rd
 SW10 136 A6 266 B6
Redcliffe Sch
 SW10 136 A6 266 A6
Redcliffe Sq
 SW10 113 D1 255 D1
Redcliffe St SW10 265 D6
Redclose Ave SM4 201 C4
Redclyffe Rd E6 99 C6
Redclyffe Terr 2
 SM2 217 C1
Redclyf Ho 13 E1 96 C3
Redcroft 5 NW6 69 C2
Redcroft Rd UB1 86 A1
Red Cross Cotts SE1 252 B2
Redcross Way
 SE1 117 A5 252 B3
Redding Ho SE18 122 A3
Reddings Ave WD23 8 A6
Reddings Cl NW7 27 D6
Reddings The NW7 11 D1
Reddins Rd SE15 140 A6
Reddons Rd BR3 185 A3
Rede Pl W2 113 C6 245 B6
Redesdale Gdns
 TW7 131 A5
Redesdale St SW3 267 C6
Redfern Ave TW2,
 TW4 151 C4
Redfern Ho 6 E13 98 D6
Redfern Rd
 Catford SE6 164 A4
 Willesden NW10 67 C1
Redfield La
 SW5 113 D2 255 C4
Redfield Mews SW5 255 B4
Redfiff Est SE16 119 B3
Redford Ave
 Thornton Heath
 CR7 204 B5
 Wallington SM6 220 A2
Redford Cl TW13 149 D2
Redford Wlk N1 235 A6
Redgate Dr BR2 225 B6
Red Gates Sch CR9 220 C3
Redgate Terr SW15 156 D5
Redgrave Cl SE25 205 D3
Redgrave Rd SW15 134 D2
Red Hill BR7 188 D5
Redhill Ct SW2 160 C2
Redhill Dr HA8 27 A1
Red Hill Prim Sch
 BR7 188 D5
Redhill St
 NW1 93 B4 231 D2
Red House* DA6 147 A1
Red House La DA6 147 A1
Red House Rd CR0 203 D3
Red House Sq 20 N1 73 A1
Redif Ho RM10 81 D4
Redington Gdns
 NW3 69 D4
Redington Ho N1 233 D4
Redington Rd NW3 69 D4
Redknap Ho TW10 153 C1
Red La KT10 213 A2
Redland Gdns KT8 195 B5
Redlands Ct BR1 186 D3
Redlands Prim Sch
 E1 96 C2
Redlands Rd EN3 7 A4
Redlands TW11 175 A4
Redlands The 5
 BR3 185 D1
Redlands N15 51 B3
Redlands Way SW2 160 B4
Redleaf Cl DA17 147 C6
Redleaves Ave
 TW15 170 D4
Redlees Cl TW7 131 A1
Red Leys UB8 60 A1
Red Lion Bsns Ctr
 KT6 214 B5
Red Lion Cl 9 SE17 139 B6
Red Lion Ct
 Holborn EC4 241 B1
 Hounslow TW3 129 D2
Red Lion Hill N2 30 B1
Red Lion La SE18 144 C4
Red Lion Pl SE18 144 C4
Red Lion Rd KT6 214 C
Red Lion Row SE17 139 A6
Red Lion Sq
 WC1 94 B2 240 C
Red Lion St
 Gray's Inn
 WC1 94 B2 240 C
 Richmond TW10 153 D
Red Lion Yd W1 248 B
Red Lodge Rd BR3,
 BR4 208 B
Red Lo Ealing W5 88 A
 West Wickham BR4 208 A
Redlynch Ct
 W14 113 A4 244 B
Redlynch Ho 27
 SW9 138 C
Redman Bldg EC1 241 A
Redman Cl UB5 84 C
Redman Ho SE1 252 B
Redman's Rd E1 96 C
Redmayne Ho 15
 SW9 138 B
Redmead La E1 118 A
Redmead Rd UB3 105 C
Redmill Ho 24 E1 96 B
Redmond Ho N1 233 D
Redmore Rd W6 112 B
Red Oak Cl BR6 226 D
Redo Ho 3 E12 78 C
Red Pl W1 248 A
Redpoll Way DA18 124 D
Red Post Hill SE21,
 SE24 161 B
Red Post Ho E6 77 D
Redriffe Rd E13 98 D
Redriff Prim Sch
 SE16 119 A
Redriff Rd SE16 119 A
Redroofs Cl BR3 185 D
Redrose Trad Ctr 1
 EN4 14 B
Red Rover SW13 134 A
Redrup Ho 21 SE14 140 C
Redruth Cl N22 32 B
Redruth Gdns KT10 212 D
Redruth Ho SM2 217 D
Redruth Rd E9 96 C
Red Sq The N16 73 B

Redstart Cl
New Cross Gate SE14 141 A5
Newham E6 100 A2
Redston Rd N8 49 D5
Redvers Rd N22 32 C1
Redvers St E2 95 C4
Redwald Rd E5 74 D4
Redway Dr TW2 152 A4
Redwing Path SE28 123 B4
Redwing Rd SM6 220 B1
Redwood Cl
4 Bow E3 97 C5
Chigwell IG9 21 B2
Hillingdon UB10 82 D5
Osidge N14 15 D4
Rotherhithe SE16 119 A5
Sidcup DA15 168 A3
South Oxhey WD19 22 D6
Redwood Ct
Brondesbury NW6 69 A1
Crouch End N19 49 D2
Northolt UB5 85 A4
10 Surbiton KT6 197 D2
edwood Est TW5 128 B6
edwood Gdns E4 19 D5
edwood Gr W5 109 B2
edwood Mews
Ashford TW15 171 B3
2 Clapham SW4 137 B2
edwoods SW15 156 A3
edwood Way EN5 12 D6
edwood Wlk KT6 197 D1
eece Mews SW7 256 C4
eed Ave BR6 227 C5
eed Cl Lee SE12 165 A6
Newham E16 99 A2
eede Gdns RM10 81 D3
eede Rd RM10 81 D2
eede Way RM10 81 D2
eedham Cl N17 52 B5
eedham St SE15 140 A2
eedholm Villas N16 73 B4
eed Ho SW15 156 A5
eed Mans 6 E11 55 A3
eed Pl
Clapham SW4 137 D1
Lower Halliford TW17 192 B1
eed Rd N17 33 D1
eedsfield Cl TW15 148 D1
eedsfield Rd TW15 170 D6
eed's Pl NW1 71 C1
eedworth St SE11 116 C2 261 B3
eef Ho E14 120 A3
eenglass Rd HA7 25 D6
ees Dr HA7 26 A6
ees Gdns CR0 205 D3
ees Ho 6 N17 33 D3
eesland Cl E12 78 C2
ees St N1 95 A6 235 B5
eets Farm Cl NW9 45 C3
eeves Ave NW9 45 B2
eeves Cnr CR0 220 D6
eeves Cnr Sta CR0 220 D6
eeves Ho
Lambeth SE1 251 A1
Mayfair W1 248 A5
eeves Mews W1 115 A6 248 B5
eeves Rd Bromley E3 97 D3
Shooters Hill SE18 144 D6
eflection Ho 9 E2 96 A3
eflection The E16 122 D4
eflex Apartments 1 BR2 209 B5
eform Row N17 33 D1
eform St SW11 136 D3
egal Cl Ealing W5 87 D2
Spitalfields E1 96 A2
egal Cres SM6 219 B5
egal Ct
Edmonton N18 33 D5
2 Mitcham CR4 202 D6
Wembley HA0 65 D4
egal Dr N11 31 B5
egal Ho IG2 57 B3
egal La NW1 231 B5
egal Pl
3 Tower Hamlets E3 97 B4
Walham Green SW6 265 D3
egal Way HA3 44 A3
egan Ho 1 N18 33 D4
egan Way N1 95 C5
egatta Ho TW11 175 A6
egatta Point TW8 132 B6
egel Ct NW7 29 A2
egency Cl Ealing W5 88 A1
Hampton TW12 173 B5
egency Cres 3 NW4 28 D1
egency Ct
9 Bow E3 97 B5
Enfield EN1 17 B6

Regency Ct *continued*
4 Kingston u T KT5 198 B4
4 Penge SE19 184 A3
14 South Hackney E9 96 C6
Sutton SM1 217 D5
Wimbledon SW19 179 B3
2 Woodford E18 37 A1
Regency Dr HA4 39 C1
Regency Gdns KT12 194 C1
Regency Ho
Finchley N3 29 B1
Marylebone NW1 238 D6
Regency Lo
1 Buckhurst Hill IG9 21 D2
Harrow HA3 42 C6
South Hampstead NW3 70 B1
Regency Mews
Beckenham BR3 186 A2
Camberwell SW9 138 D5
Isleworth TW7 152 C6
1 Willesden NW10 68 A2
Regency Pl SW1 259 D4
Regency St SW1 115 D2 259 D3
Regency Terr SW7 256 C2
Regency Way DA6 147 A2
Regency Wlk
Croydon CR0 207 B3
8 Richmond TW10 154 A6
Regeneration Rd SE16 118 D1
Regent Ave UB10 60 D1
Regent Bsns Ctr UB3 106 A4
Regent Cl
Cranford TW4 128 B4
Harrow HA3 44 A3
North Finchley N12 30 A5
Regent Ct
4 Finchley N3 29 D3
Lisson Gr NW8 230 A1
South Norwood SE19 182 D4
1 Stamford Hill N16 51 D2
Regent Gdns IG3 58 A2
Regent Ho W14 254 A4
Regent Pl
Croydon CR0 205 D1
St James W1 249 B6
Wimbledon SW19 180 A5
Regent Rd
Surbiton KT5 198 C4
Tulse Hill SE24 160 D6
Regents Ave N13 32 C5
Regents Bridge Gdns SW8 270 B4
Regents Canal Ho 19 E14 97 A1
Regents Cl Hayes UB4 83 C2
South Croydon CR2 221 C2
Regent's Coll NW1 93 A3 238 A6
Regents Ct
22 Beckenham BR3 185 C3
Bromley BR1 186 D3
Edgware HA8 26 A6
Hackney E8 96 A6
1 Kingston u T KT2 176 A2
Regent's Ct HA5 22 D1
Regents Dr BR2 225 D3
Regents Gate Ho 20 E14 119 A6
Regents Lo 9 SW2 160 B3
Regents Mews NW8 92 A5 229 B4
REGENT'S PARK 93 B4
Regent's Park Barracks NW1 231 D3
Regent's Park* NW1 93 A5 231 A3
Regent's Park Rd
Camden Town NW1 93 A6 231 A6
Hendon N3 47 B6
Primrose Hill NW3 71 A1
Regent's Park Sta NW1 93 B3 238 C5
Regent's Park Terr NW1 231 C6
Regents Plaza 2 NW6 91 D5
Regents Pl IG10 21 D4
Regent's Pl SE3 143 A3
Regent Sq
Belvedere DA17 125 D2
23 Bromley E3 97 D4
St Pancras WC1 94 A4 233 B1
Regent's Row E8 96 A6
Regent St
Brentford W4 110 C1
7 Kensal Green NW10 90 D4
Mayfair W1 115 C6 249 A6

Regents Wharf
3 Hackney E2 96 B6
Islington N1 233 C4
Regina Coeli RC Prim Sch CR2 220 D1
Regina Ct TW11 174 C5
Reginald Ct BR3 186 A2
Reginald Pl 6 SE8 141 C5
Reginald Rd
Deptford SE8 141 C5
Forest Gate E7 77 A2
Reginald Sorenson Ho E11 54 B2
Reginald Sq SE8 141 C5
Regina Point SE16 118 C3
Regina Rd
Ealing W13 109 A5
Finsbury Pk N4 50 B1
Southall UB2 107 A2
South Norwood SE25 206 A6
Regina Terr W13 109 B5
Regis Ct
East Bedfont TW14 149 B5
Hornsey N8 50 B5
Marylebone NW1 237 C4
Mitcham SW19 180 C2
Regis Pl 17 SW2 138 B1
Regis Rd NW5 71 B3
Regnart Bldgs NW1 232 B1
Regnolruf Ct KT12 194 A2
Reid Cl Hayes UB3 83 C1
Pinner HA5 40 A5
Reid Ct SW14 133 A3
Reidhaven Rd SE18 123 C2
Reigate Ave SM1 201 C1
Reigate Rd
Catford BR1 164 D1
Grove Pk BR1, SE12 165 A2
Ilford IG3 79 D6
Reigate Way SM6 220 A3
Reighton Rd E5 74 A6
Reizel Cl N16 51 D1
Relay Rd W12 112 C5
Relf Rd SE15 140 A2
Reliance Sq E2 243 B6
Relko Gdns SM1 218 B3
Relton Ct W3 110 C4
Relton Mews SW7 257 B6
Rembrandt Cl E14 120 B3
Rembrandt Ct
10 Bermondsey SE16 118 B1
Harrow HA3 43 A3
West Ewell KT19 215 D2
Rembrandt Rd
Edgware HA8 26 C1
Lewisham SE13 142 C1
Rembrant Cl SW1 258 A3
Remembrance Ave N2 47 D6
Remington Rd
Newham E6 100 A1
Tottenham N15 51 B3
Remington St N1 94 D5 234 D3
Remnant St WC2 240 C2
Remsted Ho 7 NW6 91 D6
Remus Rd E3 75 C1
Renaissance Ct SM1 202 A1
Renaissance Wlk 4 SE10 120 D3
Renbold Ho 5 SE10 142 A4
Rendlebury Ho 17 SE18 122 B2
Rendle Cl CR0 206 A4
Rendlesham Ho 3 E5, N16 74 A5
Rendlesham Rd
Enfield EN2 4 D4
Shacklewell E5 74 A5
Renforth St SE16 118 C4
Renfree Way TW17 192 C2
Renfrew Cl E6 122 C6
Renfrew Ct TW5 129 A3
Renfrew Ho
Paddington NW6 91 D5
Walthamstow E17 35 B1
Renfrew Rd
Hounslow TW5 129 A3
Kingston u T KT2 177 A3
Newington SE11 116 D2 261 C3
Renmuir St SW17 180 D4
Rennell Ho 18 E9 74 D2
Rennell St SE13 142 A2
Renness Rd E17 53 A6
Rennets Cl SE9 167 C6
Rennets Wood Ho SE9 167 B6
Rennets Wood Rd SE9 167 B6
Rennie Cotts 29 E1 96 C3

Rennie Ct
Holdbrook EN3 7 C5
Lambeth SE1 251 C4
Rennie Ho SE1 262 A5
Rennie St SE1 116 D5 251 C4
Renoir Ct 7 SE16 118 B1
Renovation The E16 122 D4
Renown Cl CR0 204 D1
Rensburg Rd E17 52 D3
Rensburg Villas E17 52 D4
Renshaw Cl 7 DA17 147 B6
Renshaw Cnr CR4 181 A2
Renshaw Ct SW19 179 A6
Renshaw Ho 11 SW27 182 D5
Renters Ave NW4 46 C3
Renton Cl SW2 160 B5
Renwick Rd IG11 102 B4
Repens Way UB4 84 D3
Rephidim St SE1 263 A5
Replingham Rd SW18 157 C3
Reporton Rd SW6 135 A5 264 B3
Repository Rd SE7, SE18 122 B1
Repton Ave
Hayes UB3 105 B2
Wembley HA0 65 C4
Repton Cl SM5 218 C3
Repton Ct
Beckenham BR3 185 D2
Southgate N21 16 C3
Repton Ho SW1 259 B3
Repton Rd
Harrow HA3 44 B5
Orpington BR6 227 D5
Repton St E14 97 A1
Reservoir Cl CR7 205 B5
Reservoir Rd
New Cross Gate SE4 141 A3
Ruislip HA4 39 B5
Southgate N14 15 C6
Reservoir Studios 14 E1 96 D1
Resham Cl UB2 106 C3
Resolution Way 14 SE8 141 C5
Resolution Wlk SE18 122 B3
Restell Cl SE3 142 C6
Restmor Way SM5, SM6 219 A6
Reston Pl SW7 246 A1
Restons Cres DA15, SE9 167 C5
Restoration Sq SW11 266 D1
Restormel Cl TW3 151 C6
Retcar Pl N19 71 B6
Retford St E2 95 C5
Retingham Way E4 19 D2
Retlas Ct HA1 42 B2
Retreat Cl HA3 43 C4
Retreat Cvn Site The IG9 21 A3
Retreat Ho 5 E9 74 C2
Retreat Pl E9 74 C2
Retreat Rd TW9 153 D6
Retreat The
Harrow HA2 41 C2
Kingsbury NW9 45 B4
Mortlake SW14 133 C2
North Cheam KT4 216 B6
South Norwood CR7 205 B5
Surbiton KT5 198 B3
Reunion Row E1 118 B6
Reveley Sq SE16 119 A4
Revell Rd
Cheam SM1 217 B2
Kingston u T KT1 176 D2
Revell Rise SE18 145 D6
Revelon Rd SE4 141 A2
Revelstoke Rd SW18, SW19 157 C2
Reventlow Rd SE9 167 A3
Reverdy Rd SE1 118 A2
Reverend Cl HA2 63 D5
Revesby Rd SM5 202 C3
Review Lo RM10 103 D5
Review Rd
Dagenham RM10 103 D6
Willesden NW2 67 D6
Rewell St SW6 136 A5 266 A3
Rewley Rd SM4 202 B3
Rew Lo 25 N2 30 B1
Rex Ave TW15 170 C5
Rex Ho TW13 151 A1
Rex Par 2 IG8 37 C4
Rex Pl W1 115 A5 248 B4
Reydon Ave E11 55 C3
Reygate Ct N4 51 A3

Reynard Cl
Brockley SE4 141 A2
Bromley BR1 210 C6
Reynard Dr SE19 183 D3
Reynard Mills Trad Est TW8 109 C1
Reynard Pl SE14 141 A6
Reynardson Rd N17 33 A3
Reynardson's Ct 10 N17 51 D6
Reynolah Gdns SE7 121 B1
Reynolds Ave
Chessington KT9 214 A1
Ilford RM6 58 C2
Little Ilford E12 78 C3
Reynolds Cl
Carshalton SM5 202 D1
Golders Green NW11 47 D2
Mitcham SW19 180 B2
Reynolds Ct
Ilford RM6 58 D6
Leyton E11 76 D5
Reynolds Dr HA8 44 B6
Reynolds Ho
Enfield EN1 18 A6
Finsbury Pk N4 50 A1
18 South Hackney E2 96 C5
St John's Wood NW8 229 D3
Westminster SW1 259 D3
Reynolds Pl
Greenwich SE3 143 B5
12 Richmond TW10 154 B5
Reynolds Rd
Acton Green W4 111 A3
Hayes UB4 84 C3
New Malden KT3 199 B2
Nunhead SE15 140 C1
Reynolds Way CR0 221 C4
Rheidol Mews N1 235 A4
Rheidol Terr N1 95 A6 235 A5
Rhein Ho N8 50 A6
Rheola Cl N17 33 D2
Rhoda St E2 95 D3 243 D6
Rhodes Avenue Prim Sch N22 31 C2
Rhodes Ave N22 31 C2
Rhodes Ho
Shepherd's Bush W12 112 B5
Shoreditch N1 235 C2
Rhodesia Rd
Leyton E11 76 B6
Stockwell SW9 138 A3
Rhodes-Moorhouse Ct SM4 201 C3
Rhodes St N7 72 B3
Rhodeswell Rd E14 97 B1
Rhodrons Ave KT9 214 A3
Rhondda Gr E3 97 B4
Rhyl Prim Sch NW5 71 A2
Rhyl Rd UB6 86 D5
Rhyl St NW5 71 A2
Rhys Ave N11 31 D3
Rialto Rd CR4 181 A1
Ribble Cl IG8 37 C4
Ribblesdale Ave
Friern Barnet N11 31 A4
Northolt UB5 63 D2
Ribblesdale Ho 11 NW6 91 C6
Ribblesdale Rd
Hornsey N8 50 B5
Streatham SW16 181 B5
Ribbon Dance Mews SE5 139 B4
Ribchester Ave UB6 86 D4
Ribston Cl BR2 210 B1
Ribstone Ho 12 E9 74 D2
Ricardo Path 5 SE28 124 C5
Ricardo St E14 97 D1
Ricards Lodge High Sch SW19 179 B5
Ricards Rd SW19 179 B5
Riccall Ct 2 NW9 27 C2
Riceyman Ho WC1 234 A1
Richard Alibon Prim Sch RM10 81 C3
Richard Anderson Ct 1 SE14 140 D5
Richard Atkins Prim Sch SW2 160 A4
Richard Burbidge Mans SW13 134 C6
Richard Burton Ct 4 IG9 21 C2
Richard Challoner Sch KT3 199 B2
Richard Cloudesley Sch EC1 95 A3 242 A5
Richard Cl SE18 122 A2
Richard Cobden Prim Sch NW1 93 C6 232 B5
Richard Ct
Ashford TW15 170 B5
1 Barnet EN5 1 A2

Richard Fell Ho 3 E12 78 C4
Richard Fox Ho N4 73 A5
Richard Ho 10 SE16 118 C2
Richard House Dr E16 100 A1
Richard Knight Ho SW6 265 B2
Richard Neale Ho 2 E1 118 B6
Richard Neve Ho 2 SE18 123 C2
Richards Cl
Bushey WD23 8 B4
Harlington UB3 127 B6
Harrow HA1 43 A4
Hillingdon UB10 82 C6
Richards Ct BR3 184 D2
Richard Sharples Ct 16 SM2 218 A1
Richardson Cl 19 E8 95 D6
Richardson Ct 20 SW4 138 A3
Richardson Gdns 12 RM10 81 D2
Richardson Ho
Isleworth TW7 130 D2
10 Poplar E14 97 C2
Richardson Rd E15 98 C5
Richardson's Mews W1 239 A5
Richards Pl E17 53 C6
Richard's Pl SW3 257 B4
Richard St 20 E1 96 B1
Richbell Pl WC1 240 C4
Richbell WC1 240 B4
Richborne Terr SW8 138 B5 270 D4
Richborough Ho
10 Deptford SE15 140 C6
14 Hackney E5 74 B4
Richborough Rd NW2 69 A4
Richbourne Ct W1 237 B2
Richens Cl TW3 130 B3
Riches Rd IG1 79 A6
Richfield Ct
4 Beckenham BR3 185 B2
Wembley HA0 66 A2
Richfield Rd WD23 8 A4
Richford Gate W6 112 C3
Richford Rd E15 98 D6
Richford St W6 112 C3
Richings Ho BR5 190 A2
Richland Ho 4 SE15 140 A4
Richlands Ave KT17 216 A4
Rich La SW5 255 C2
Richman Ho 10 SE8 119 B1
RICHMOND 131 C1
Richmond Adult Com Coll TW9 131 D1
Richmond Ave
Chingford E4 36 B5
Feltham TW14 149 C5
Hillingdon UB10 60 D2
Islington N1 94 B6 233 D6
Willesden NW10 68 C2
Wimbledon SW20 179 A2
Richmond Bldgs W1 239 C1
Richmond Bridge Mans 1 TW1 153 D5
Richmond Bridge TW1 153 D5
Richmond Circus TW9 132 A1
Richmond Cl
Borehamwood WD6 11 B6
Walthamstow E17 53 B3
Richmond Coll
Kensington W8 113 D3 255 D6
Richmond TW10 154 A4
Richmond Cres
Chingford E4 36 B5
Edmonton N9 18 A3
Islington N1 94 C6 234 A6
Richmond Ct
Bromley BR1 187 B3
12 Kingston u T KT2 176 C3
Knightsbridge SW1 247 D1
1 Loughton IG10 21 D6
Mitcham CR4 202 B6
4 New Southgate N11 31 A4
Wembley HA9 66 B6
Wimbledon SW20 178 B1
Richmond Dr TW17 193 B3
Richmond Gate TW10 154 B4

Richmond Gdns
Harrow HA3 24 D3
Hendon NW4 46 A4
Richmond Gn CR0 220 A5
Richmond Gr
Islington N1 72 D1
Surbiton KT5 198 B3
Richmond Healthcare Hamlet Hospl TW9 132 A2
RICHMOND HILL 154 A5
Richmond Hill Ct 5 TW10 154 B3
Richmond Hill TW10 154 A5
Richmond Ho 12 SE26 162 A1
Richmond Ho (Hampton Com Coll) TW12 173 B5
Richmond Ho
Regent's Pk NW1 231 D3
Walworth SE17 262 C2
Richmond International Bsns Ctr 9 TW9 132 B1
Richmond Mans
Earl's Ct SW5 255 C2
Putney SW15 135 A2
13 Twickenham TW1 153 D5
Richmond Mews W1 239 C1
Richmond Park* TW10 155 A3
Richmond Park Rd
Kingston u T KT2 176 A3
Mortlake SW14 133 B1
Richmond Pk IG10 21 D4
Richmond Pl SE18 123 A2
Richmond Rd
Bowes Pk N11 32 A4
Chingford E4 20 B3
Dalston E8 74 A1
Ealing W5 110 A4
Finchley N2 30 A1
Forest Gate E7 77 B3
Ilford IG1 79 A5
Isleworth TW7 131 A2
Kingston u T KT2 176 A4
Leyton E11 76 B6
New Barnet EN5 14 A6
Thornton Heath CR7 204 D5
Tottenham N15 51 C3
Twickenham TW1 153 C4
Wallington CR0 220 A5
Wimbledon SW20 178 B2
Richmond Sta TW9 132 A1
Richmond St E13 99 A5
Richmond Terr SW1 116 A4 250 A2
Richmond upon Thames Coll TW2 152 C4
Richmond Way
Hammersmith W12, W14 112 D4
Wanstead E11 77 A6
Richmount Gdns SE3 143 A2
Rich St E14 119 B6
Rickard Cl
Hendon NW4 46 A5
Streatham SW2 160 C3
Rickards Cl KT6 214 A6
Rickett St SW6 265 B6
Rickman Ho 23 E2 96 C3
Rickman St 24 E1 96 C3
Rickmansworth Rd HA5 22 C1
Rick Roberts Way E15 98 B5
Rickthorne Rd 7 N19 72 A6
Rickyard Path SE9 144 A1
Riddell Ct SE1 263 C2
Riddell Lo EN2 4 D3
Ridding La UB6 64 D3
Riddons Rd SE12 187 C6
Rideout St SE18 122 B2
Rider Cl DA15 167 C5
Ride The
Brentford TW8 109 C1
Enfield EN3 6 D2
Ridgdale St E3 97 D5
Ridge Ave N21 17 B4
Ridgebrook Rd SE3, SE9 143 D2
Ridge Cl Hendon NW4 28 D1
Kingsbury NW9 45 B5
Plumstead SE28 123 B4
Ridge Crest EN2 4 B4
Ridge Hill NW11 47 A1
Ridge Ho 4 KT2 176 D3
Ridgeleigh Ct 3 EN5 1 A2
Ridgemead Cl N13, N14 16 A2
Ridgemont Gdns HA8 27 A6
Ridgemount Ave CR0 222 D6
Ridgemount Cl 4 SE20 184 B3
Ridgemount Gdns EN2 4 D3
Ridgeon Ct N22 32 B4
Ridge Rd
Cheam SM3 201 B1
Child's Hill NW2 69 B5
Edmonton N21 17 B3
Hornsey Vale N8 50 B3
Mitcham CR4 181 B3
Ridges The E4 35 C6
Ridge Terr N21 17 A4
Ridge The Barnet EN5 13 B6
Old Bexley DA5 169 B4
Orpington BR6 227 B6
Surbiton KT5 198 C4
Twickenham TW2 152 B4
Ridgeview Cl EN5 12 D5
Ridgeview Ct EN4 15 C6
Ridgeview Rd N20 14 A1
Ridgeway Ave EN4 14 D5
Ridgeway Cres BR6 227 C5
Ridgeway Crescent Gdns BR6 227 C5
Ridgeway Ct HA5 23 C3
Ridgeway Dr
Acton W3 110 C3
Grove Pk BR1 187 B6
Ridgeway E DA15 167 D6
Ridge Way TW13 151 A1
Ridgeway Gdns
Crouch End N6 49 C2
Redbridge IG4 56 A4
Ridgeway BR2 225 A6
Ridgeway Rd TW7 130 C4
Ridgeway Rd N TW7 130 C5
Ridgeway 11 TW10 154 A5
Ridgeway The
Acton W3 110 C3
Chingford E4 20 A3
Enfield EN2 4 B5
Finchley N3 29 D3
Friern Barnet N11 30 D6
Golders Green NW11 47 B1
Kenton HA3 43 C3
Kingsbury NW9 45 B5
Mill Hill NW7 28 B6
North Harrow HA2 41 D3
Palmers Green N14 16 A2
Pinner HA2 41 B4
Ruislip HA4 40 A2
Stanmore HA7 25 C4
Wallington CR0 220 B5
Ridgeway KT12 193 D1
Ridgeway W DA15 167 C6
Ridge Way 7 SE19 183 C4
Ridgeway Wlk UB5 63 A2
Ridgeway IG8 37 C6
Ridgewell Cl
Dagenham RM10 103 D6
Forest Hill SE26 185 B6
Shoreditch N1 235 B6
Ridgmount Gdns WC1 93 D2 239 C4
Ridgmount Pl WC1 239 C4
Ridgmount Rd SW18 157 D6
Ridgmount St WC1 93 D2 239 C4
Ridgway Ct SW19 178 D4
Ridgway Gdns SW19 178 D3
Ridgway Pl SW19 179 A4
Ridgway Rd SW9 138 D2
Ridgway The SM2 218 B1
Ridgway SW19, SW20 178 D4
Ridgwell Rd E16 99 C2
Riding House St W1 93 C2 239 A3
Ridings Ave N21 17 A6
Ridings Cl N6 49 C2
Ridings The
Ealing W5 88 B3
Oakleigh Pk EN4 14 B4
Sunbury TW16 172 A2
Surbiton KT5 198 C4
Riding The NW11 47 B2
Ridler Rd EN1 5 C5
Ridley Ave W13 109 B3
Ridley Cl IG11 79 D1
Ridley Ct
Orpington BR6 227 A4
Streatham SW16 182 A4
Ridley Ho 14 SW11 136 C2
Ridley Rd
Beckenham BR2 208 D6
Dalston E8 73 D3
Forest Gate E7 77 C4
Ridley Rd *continued*
Merton SW19 179 D3
Welling DA16 146 B4
Willesden Green NW10 90 A5
Ridley Road Mkt E8 73 D3
Ridsdale Rd SE20 184 B2
Riefield Rd SE9 167 A6
Riesco Dr CR0 222 C2
Riffel Rd NW2 68 C3
Rifle Ct SE11 138 C6
Rifle Pl W11 112 D5
Rifle St E14 97 D2
Riga Ho 12 E1 96 D2
Rigault Rd SW6 135 A3
Rigby Cl CR0 220 C5
Rigby Ho 2 N17 51 D6
Rigby La UB3 105 A4
Rigby Mews IG1 78 C6
Rigby Pl 8 EN3 7 C6
Rigden St E14 97 D1
Rigeley Rd NW10 90 A4
Rigg App E10 53 A1
Rigge Pl SW4 137 D1
Rigg Ho 2 SW4 160 A4
Riggindale Rd SW16 181 D6
Rignold Ho 6 SE5 139 C3
Riley Ho 9 Bow E3 97 C3
Chelsea SW10 266 C5
1 Streatham SW4 159 D4
Riley Rd
Bermondsey SE1 117 D3 263 C6
Enfield EN3 6 C5
Riley St SW10 136 B5 266 C4
Rill Ho 16 SE5 139 C5
Rimini Ct SW12 158 D3
Rinaldo Rd SW12 159 B4
Ring Cl BR1 187 B3
Ringcroft St N7 72 C3
Ringer's Rd BR1 209 A6
Ringford Ho SW18 157 B6
Ringford Rd SW18 157 C5
Ring Ho 15 E1 118 C6
Ringlet Cl E16 99 B2
Ringlewell Cl EN1 6 B3
Ringmer Ave SW6 135 A4 264 B1
Ringmer Gdns 3 N19 72 A6
Ringmer Ho 15 SE22 139 C2
Ringmer Pl N21 17 B6
Ringmer Way BR1 210 B4
Ringmore Rise SE23 162 B4
Ring Rd W12 112 C5
Ringsfield Ho SE17 262 B1
Ringslade Rd N22 32 B1
Ringstead Bldgs SE6 163 D4
Ringstead Ct SM1 218 B3
Ringstead Rd
Catford SE6 163 D4
Sutton SM1 218 B3
Ring Way N11 31 C4
Ringway UB2 107 A1
Ringwold Cl BR3 185 A3
Ringwood Ave
Muswell Hill N2 48 D6
Thornton Heath CR0 204 A2
Ringwood Cl HA5 40 C6
Ringwood Gdns
17 Millwall E14 119 C2
Roehampton SW15 156 A3
Ringwood Rd E17 53 B3
Ringwood Way
Hampton TW12 173 C6
Southgate N21 16 D4
Ripley Cl
Bromley BR1 210 B4
New Addington CR0 224 A2
Ripley Ct 1 CR4 180 B1
Ripley Gdns
Mortlake SW14 133 B2
Sutton SM1 218 A4
Ripley Ho
13 Kingston u T KT2 176 D4
Mortlake SW14 133 C2
Nine Elms SW1 269 A6
5 Penge SE26 184 B5
Ripley Mews E11 54 C3
Ripley Rd
Belvedere DA17 125 C2
Enfield EN2 5 A4
Hampton TW12 173 C3
Ilford IG3 79 D6
Newham E16 99 C1
Riplington Ct SW15 156 B4
Ripon Cl UB5 63 C2
Ripon Ct 10 N11 31 A4
Ripon Gdns
Chessington KT9 213 D3
Redbridge IG1 56 A2
Ripon Rd
Edmonton N9 18 B4
Shooters Hill SE18 144 D6
Tottenham N17 51 B6
Ripon Way WD6 11 B6
Rippersley Rd DA16 146 A4
Ripple Ct 10 IG11 101 B6
Ripple Jun & Inf Schs IG11 79 C1
Ripple Rd
Barking IG11 79 A1
Barking IG11 101 C6
Castle Green RM9 102 A6
Rippleside Commercial Est IG11 102 C5
Ripplevale Gr N1 72 B1
Rippolson Rd SE18 123 D1
Ripston Rd TW15 171 B5
Risborough Cl 4 N10 49 B6
Risborough Ct 5 N10 49 B6
Risborough Dr KT4 200 A2
Risborough Ho NW8 237 B6
Risborough SE17 262 A4
Risborough St SE1 251 D2
Risdon Ho 26 SE16 118 C4
Risdon St 27 SE16 118 C4
Risedale Rd DA7 147 D2
Riseholme Ct E9 75 B2
Riseholme Ho 14 SE22 139 C2
Riseldine Rd SE23 163 A5
Rise The
Borehamwood WD6 10 B6
Buckhurst Hill IG9 21 D4
Chingford E4 20 C3
Edgware HA8 26 D5
Edmonton N13 32 C6
Harrow HA2 24 A1
Hendon NW7 27 D4
Hillingdon UB10 82 B5
Neasden NW10 67 B5
Sidcup DA5 168 C4
Wanstead E11 55 A4
Wembley HA0, UB6 65 A3
Risinghill St N1 234 A4
Risingholme Cl HA3 24 C2
Risingholme Rd HA3 24 C1
Risings The E17 54 B5
Rising Sun Ct EC1 241 D3
Risley Avenue Prim Sch N17 33 C2
Risley Ave N17 33 B2
Risley Ho 7 E9 74 D2
Rita Rd SW8 138 B5 270 C4
Ritches Rd N15 51 A4
Ritchie Ho
Crouch End N19 49 D2
8 Rotherhithe SE16 118 C3
12 South Bromley E14 98 B1
Ritchie Rd CR0 206 B3
Ritchie St N1 94 C5 234 B4
Ritchings Ave E17 53 A5
Ritherdon Rd SW17 159 B2
Ritson Ho N1 233 C5
Ritson Rd E8 74 A2
Ritter St SE18 144 C6
Ritz Par W5 88 B3
Rivaz Pl E9 74 C2
Riven Ct 10 W2 91 D1
Rivenhall Gdns E11, E18 54 D5
Riverains The SW11 266 C1
River Ave
Southgate N13 16 D1
Thames Ditton KT7 197 A2
Riverbank KT8 196 C5
River Bank N21 17 A4
Riverbank Rd BR1 165 A1
River Bank KT7 196 D4
Riverbank Way TW8 131 C6
River Barge Cl E14 120 A4
River Brent Bsns Pk W7 108 C3
River Cl Ruislip HA4 39 D3
Southall UB2 108 A4
Wanstead E11 55 C3
River Cotts BR5 190 C1
Rivercourt Rd W6 112 B1
River Crane Way TW13 151 B2
River Ct
Kingston u T KT6 197 D4
Lambeth SE1 251 C5
Shepperton TW17 193 A2
Wanstead E11 55 C3
Riverdale Cl IG11 102 B3
Riverdale Ct N21 17 B6
Riverdale Dr SW18 157 D3
Riverdale Gdns TW1 153 C6
Riverdale Rd
Erith DA8 125 D1
Feltham TW13 173 B6
Plumstead Comm SE18 123 D1
Sidcup DA5 169 B5
Twickenham TW1 153 C5
Riverdene HA8 11 A1
Riverdene Rd IG1 78 D5
Riverfleet WC1 233 B2
Riverford Ho 28 W2 91 C2
River Front EN1 5 C2
River Gdns Bsns Ctr TW14 128 B1
River Gdns
Carshalton SM5 219 A5
Feltham TW14 150 B6
River Grove Pk BR3 185 B2
Riverhead Cl E17 34 D1
River Ho
Barnes SW13 133 C3
1 Forest Hill SE26 162 B1
Riverholme KT8 196 C6
Riverhope Mans SE18 122 A3
Riverine Lo HA7 25 A5
River La TW10 153 D3
Riverleigh Ct E4 35 A5
Rivermead Cl TW11 175 B5
Rivermead Ct
Ealing UB6 87 A4
Fulham SW6 135 B2
Rivermead KT8 196 A6
Rivermead Ho
Hackney E9 75 A3
Sunbury TW16 194 C6
Rivermead KT6 197 D4
River Meads Ave TW13, TW2 151 D1
River Mount KT12 193 D2
Rivernook Cl KT12 194 C4
River Park Gdns BR2 186 B3
River Park Rd N22 32 B1
River Plate Ho EC2 242 D3
River Pl N1 73 A1
River Rd
Barking IG11 101 D3
Buckhurst Hill IG9 21 D3
River Reach TW11 175 C5
River Road Bsns Pk IG11 101 D4
Riversdale Gdns N22 32 C2
Riversdale Prim Sch SW18 157 C3
Riversdale Rd
Highbury N5 73 A5
Thames Ditton KT7 197 A3
Riversdene N5 73 A5
Riversfield Rd EN1 5 C2
Rivers Ho 11 TW8 110 C1
Riverside Apartments N13 32 B5
Riverside Ave KT8 196 B4
Riverside SW11 267 B4
Riverside Bsns Ctr SW18 157 D3
Riverside Bsns Pk SW19 180 A2
Riverside Cl
Chislehurst BR5 190 C1
Ealing W7 86 C3
Hackbridge SM6 219 B5
Kingston u T KT1 197 D5
Upper Clapton E5 74 C6
Riverside Ct
Chingford E4 19 D5
Lewisham SE12 142 D1
Nine Elms SW8 269 D6
Richmond TW11 175 C5
Riverside Dr
Chiswick W4 133 C4
Mitcham CR4 202 C4
Richmond TW10 153 B1
Temple Fortune NW11 47 A3
Riverside Est EN3 19 A5
Riverside SE6 185 B6
Riverside Gdns
Enfield EN2 5 A3
Hammersmith W6 112 B1
Hendon N3 47 A6
Wembley HA0 88 A5
Riverside
Greenwich SE7 121 B3
Hendon NW4 46 B2
Riverside Ho
Finchley N12 29 D6
14 Islington N1 73 A1
Morden SW19 202 A5
30 Richmond TW10 153 D6
Riverside Ind Est IG11 102 A4
Riverside Mans 4 E1 118 C5
Riverside TW17 193 C2
Riverside Pl
New Southgate N11 15 C
Stanwell TW19 148 A
Riverside Prim Sch SE16 118
Riverside Rd
Mill Meads E15 98
Sidcup DA14 169
South Tottenham N15 52
Stanwell TW19 148
Wandsworth SW17, SW19 158
Riverside
11 Rotherhithe SE16 118
St Pancras WC1 233
Sunbury TW16 172 D
Riverside The KT8 196
Riverside TW1 153
Riverside Wlk
Isleworth TW7 130
3 West Wickham BR4 207 D
Riverside Works IG11 78
Riverside Workshops SE1 252
River St EC1 94 C4 234
Riverstone Cl HA2 64
Riverstone Ct KT2 176
Riverston Sch SE12 165
River Terr W6 112
Riverton Cl W9 91
Riverview CE Prim Sch KT19 215
Riverview Ct 14 DA17 125
River View EN2 5
Riverview Gdns SW13 134
River View Gdns TW1 152
Riverview Gr W4 132
Riverview Hts SE18 144
Riverview Lo NW9 67
Riverview Pk SE6 163
Riverview Rd
Chiswick W4 132
West Ewell KT19 215
Riverview TW17 193
River Way SE10 120
Riverway N13 32
River Way
Twickenham TW13, TW2 151
West Ewell KT19 215
River Wlk KT12 194
Riverwood La BR7 189
Rivet Ho SE1 263
Rivington Ave IG8 37
Rivington Cres NW7 27
Rivington Ct
17 Dagenham RM10 81
Willesden Green NW10 90
Rivington Pl EC2 95
Rivington St EC2 95
Rivington Wlk 4 E8 96
Rivulet Rd N17 33
Rixon Ho SE18 144
Rixon St N7 72
Rixsen Rd E12 78
Roach Rd E3 75
Roads Pl N19 72
Roan Ind Est CR4 180
Roan St SE10 142
Robart Ho 2 N12 30
Robarts Cl HA5 40
Robbins Hall EN3 18
Robb Rd HA7 25
Robert Adam St W1 238
Roberta St E2 96
Robert Bell Ho 2 SE16 118
Robert Blair Prim Sch N7 72
Robert Browning Prim Sch SE17 117 B1 262
Robert Burns Ho N17 34
Robert Clack Lower Sch RM8 81
Robert Clack Upper Sch RM8 59
Robert Cl
Barking IG11 79
Paddington W9 236
Robert Dashwood Way SE17 262
Robert Gentry Ho W14 254
Robert Gerard Ho 7 SE27 183
Robert Ho 12 HA1 42

Robert Jones Ho [3] SE16 . . . 118 A2
Robert Keen Cl [18] SE15 . . . 140 A4
Robert Lowe Cl SE14 . . . 140 D5
Roberton Dr BR1 . . . 187 C2
Robert Owen Ho
Fulham SW6 . . . 134 D4
[8] Spitalfields E2 . . . 95 D4
Robert Owen Lo [4] E5 . . . 74 B4
Robertsbridge Rd SM5 . . . 202 B2
Roberts Cl
Cheam SM3 . . . 216 D1
New Eltham SE9 . . . 167 B3
South Norwood CR7 . . . 205 B6
Yiewsley UB7 . . . 104 A5
Roberts Ct
Chessington KT9 . . . 213 D3
Ealing W5 . . . 88 A1
Islington N1 . . . 234 D5
Penge SE20 . . . 184 C2
Willesden NW10 . . . 67 C2
Roberts Ho
Dagenham RM10 . . . 81 D1
Friern Barnet N11 . . . 31 B5
[6] Kidbrooke SE18 . . . 144 A4
[5] West Norwood SE27 . . . 160 D1
Roberts Mews SW1 . . . 258 A5
Robertson Ho
Kidbrooke SE18 . . . 144 B4
[11] Lewisham SE10 . . . 142 A4
[1] Upper Tooting SW17 . . . 180 C5
Robertson Rd E15 . . . 98 A6
Robertson St SW8 . . . 137 B3
Roberts Pl RM10 . . . 81 C2
Robert's Pl EC1 . . . 241 B6
Roberts Rd
Belvedere DA17 . . . 125 C1
Finchley NW7 . . . 29 A4
Highams Pk E17 . . . 35 D2
Robert St
Croydon CR0 . . . 221 A5
Newham E16 . . . 122 D5
Plumstead SE18 . . . 123 B2
Regent's Pk NW1 . . . 93 B4 231 D1
Strand WC2 . . . 250 B5
Robert Sutton Ho [20] E1 . . . 96 C1
Robeson St [7] E3 . . . 97 B2
Robina Cl DA6 . . . 146 D1
Northwood HA6 . . . 22 A2
Robin Cl
Edgware NW7 . . . 11 C1
Hampton TW12 . . . 173 A5
Robin Cres E16 . . . 99 D2
Robin Ct
[15] Cubitt Town E14 . . . 120 A3
Wallington SM6 . . . 219 C2
Wood Green N22 . . . 32 B3
Robin Gr
Brentford TW8 . . . 131 C6
Dartmouth Pk N6 . . . 71 A6
Harrow HA3 . . . 44 B3
Robin Hill Dr BR7 . . . 188 A4
Robin Ho NW8 . . . 230 A3
Robinhood Cl CR4 . . . 203 C6
Robin Hood Ct [2] SM1 . . . 217 D3
Robin Hood Dr HA3 . . . 24 D3
Robin Hood Gdns [12] E14 . . . 120 A6
Robin Hood Inf Sch SM1 . . . 217 C3
Robin Hood Jun Sch SM1 . . . 217 D3
Robin Hood SW15 . . . 155 C1
Robin Hood La
Bexley DA6 . . . 169 A6
Blackwall E14 . . . 120 A6
Kingston u T SW15 . . . 177 C6
Robinhood La CR4 . . . 203 C6
Robin Hood La SM1 . . . 217 D3
Robin Hood Prim Sch SW15 . . . 177 C5
Robin Hood Way (Kingston By Pass) KT2, SW15, SW20 . . . 177 C5
Robin Hood Way UB6 . . . 64 D2
Robinia Cl SE20 . . . 184 A2
Robinia Cres E10 . . . 75 D6
Robin La NW4 . . . 46 D6
Robinscroft Mews [18] SE10 . . . 141 D4
Robin's Ct
Beckenham BR3 . . . 186 B1
Clapham Pk SW4 . . . 160 A5
Robins Ct
Grove Pk SE12 . . . 165 C1
Richmond TW10 . . . 154 A5
Robins Ct *continued*
South Croydon CR2 . . . 221 C4
Robinsfield Inf Sch NW8 . . . 92 C5 230 A4
Robins Gr BR4 . . . 225 A5
Robinson Cl
Enfield EN2 . . . 5 A2
[11] Leyton E11 . . . 76 C5
Robinson Cres WD23 . . . 8 A3
Robinson Ct
[5] Barnet EN4 . . . 14 D3
Islington N1 . . . 234 D6
[4] Richmond TW9 . . . 132 B1
Thornton Heath CR0 . . . 204 D3
Robinson Ho
[4] North Kensington W10 . . . 90 D1
[12] Tower Hamlets E14 . . . 97 C2
Robinson Rd
Dagenham RM10 . . . 81 C4
Mitcham SW19 . . . 180 C4
South Hackney E2 . . . 96 C5
Robinson's Cl W13 . . . 87 A2
Robinson St SW3 . . . 267 C6
Robinwood Gr UB8 . . . 82 B3
Robinwood Pl SW15 . . . 177 B6
Robsart St SW9 . . . 138 C3
Robson Ave NW10 . . . 68 A1
Robson Cl Enfield EN2 . . . 4 D3
Newham E6 . . . 100 A1
Robson Ct N12 . . . 30 A5
Robson Rd SE21, SE27 . . . 161 A1
Roby Ho EC1 . . . 242 A6
Roch Ave HA8 . . . 26 B1
Rochdale Rd
Abbey Wood SE2 . . . 124 B2
Walthamstow E17 . . . 53 C2
Rochdale Way [4] SE8 . . . 141 C5
Rochdale [8] SE19 . . . 183 C4
Roche Ho [15] E14 . . . 119 B6
Rochelle Cl SW11 . . . 136 B1
Rochelle Ct
Beckenham BR3 . . . 185 D3
[14] Stepney E1 . . . 96 C1
Rochelle St [31] E2 . . . 95 D4
Rochemont Wlk [2] E8 . . . 96 A6
Roche Rd SW16 . . . 182 B2
Roche Sch The SW18 . . . 157 C6
Rochester Ave
Bromley BR1 . . . 187 B1
Feltham TW13 . . . 149 D2
Newham E13 . . . 99 C6
Rochester Cl
[1] Blackfen DA15 . . . 168 B5
Enfield EN1 . . . 5 C4
Streatham SW16 . . . 182 A3
Rochester Ct
[1] Bethnal Green E2 . . . 96 B3
[9] Camden Town NW1 . . . 71 C1
Finchley N3 . . . 29 A1
Kingsbury NW9 . . . 45 B4
South Norwood SE25 . . . 184 A1
Rochester Dr
Old Bexley DA5 . . . 169 C5
Pinner HA5 . . . 40 D4
Rochester Gdns
Redbridge IG1 . . . 56 B2
South Croydon CR0 . . . 221 C5
Rochester Ho
Bermondsey SE1 . . . 252 D1
[18] Deptford SE15 . . . 140 C6
Rochester Mews NW1 . . . 71 C1
Rochester Par TW13 . . . 150 A1
Rochester Pl NW1 . . . 71 C1
Rochester Rd
Carshalton SM5 . . . 218 D4
Kentish Town NW1 . . . 71 C2
Northwood HA6 . . . 39 D6
Rochester Row SW1 . . . 115 C2 259 B4
Rochester Sq NW1 . . . 71 C1
Rochester St SW1 . . . 259 C5
Rochester Terr NW1 . . . 71 C2
Rochester Way
Eltham SE9 . . . 144 C2
Kidbrooke SE3, SE9 . . . 143 D2
Rochester Wlk SE1 . . . 252 C4
Roche Wlk SM5 . . . 202 B3
Rochford Ave RM6 . . . 58 C4
Rochford Cl [2] E6 . . . 99 D5
Rochford N17 . . . 33 C1
Rochford Way CR0 . . . 204 A3
Rochford Wlk [8] E8 . . . 74 A1
Rochfort Ho [4] SE8 . . . 119 B1
Rock Ave [13] SW14 . . . 133 B2
Rockbourne Rd SE23 . . . 162 D3
Rock Cl CR4 . . . 180 B1
Rockell's Pl SE22 . . . 162 B5
Rockfield Ho
Greenwich SE10 . . . 142 A6
[2] Hendon NW4 . . . 46 D5
Rockford Ave UB6 . . . 87 B5
Rock Gdns RM10 . . . 81 D3
Rock Grove Way SE16 . . . 118 A2
Rockhall Rd NW2 . . . 68 D4
Rockhampton Cl [4] SE27 . . . 182 C6
Rockhampton Rd
South Croydon CR2 . . . 221 C2
West Norwood SE27, SW16 . . . 182 C6
Rock Hill SE19 . . . 183 D6
Rockingham Cl SW15 . . . 133 D1
Rockingham Ct [19] BR3 . . . 185 C3
Rockingham Gate WD23 . . . 8 A5
Rockingham St SE1 . . . 117 A3 262 A5
Rockland Rd SW15 . . . 135 A1
Rocklands Dr HA7 . . . 25 C1
Rocklands N3 . . . 29 B3
Rockley Ct [9] W14 . . . 112 D4
Rockley Rd W14 . . . 112 D4
Rockliffe Manor Prim Sch SE18 . . . 145 D6
Rockmount Prim Sch SE19 . . . 183 B4
Rockmount Rd
Plumstead Comm SE18, SE2 . . . 123 D1
South Norwood SE19 . . . 183 B4
Rocks La SW13 . . . 134 A2
Rock St N4 . . . 72 C6
Rockstraw Ho [5] NW3 . . . 70 D1
Rockware Ave UB6 . . . 86 C6
Rockware Bsns Ctr UB6 . . . 86 B6
Rockways EN5 . . . 11 D5
Rockwell Gdns SE19 . . . 183 C6
Rockwell Rd RM10 . . . 81 D3
Rockwood Ct N16 . . . 52 A2
Rocliffe St N1 . . . 94 D5 234 D3
Rocombe Cres SE23 . . . 162 C4
Rocque Ho SW6 . . . 264 C4
Rocque La SE3 . . . 142 D2
Rodborough Rd NW11 . . . 47 C1
Rodd Est TW17 . . . 193 B4
Roden Gdns CR0 . . . 205 C3
Rodenhurst Ct SW4 . . . 159 D6
Rodenhurst Rd SW4 . . . 159 D5
Roden St Ilford IG1 . . . 78 C5
Upper Holloway N7 . . . 72 B5
Roderick Ho [3] SE16 . . . 118 C2
Roderick Rd NW3 . . . 70 D4
Rodgers Cl WD6 . . . 9 D5
Rodgers Ho [4] SW4 . . . 159 D4
Rodin Ct N1 . . . 234 C5
Roding Ct [6] W12 . . . 111 C4
Roding Ho N1 . . . 234 A5
Roding Hospl IG4 . . . 55 D6
Roding La IG9 . . . 21 D3
Roding La N IG8 . . . 37 D1
Roding La S IG4 . . . 55 D5
Roding Lo IG1 . . . 55 D3
Roding Mews E1 . . . 118 A5
Roding Prim Sch RM8 . . . 80 C3
Roding Rd
Hackney E5 . . . 75 A3
Newham E6 . . . 100 D2
Rodings Ct E4 . . . 36 B5
Rodings Row EN5 . . . 1 A1
Rodings The [4] IG8 . . . 37 C4
Roding Valley Sta IG9 . . . 37 D6
Roding View IG9 . . . 21 D3
Rodmarton St W1 . . . 92 D2 237 D3
Rodmell Cl UB4 . . . 85 A3
Rodmell Slope N12 . . . 29 B5
Rodmell WC1 . . . 233 B1
Rodmere St SE10 . . . 120 C1
Rodmill La SW2 . . . 160 A4
Rodney Cl
New Malden KT3 . . . 199 C4
Pinner HA5 . . . 41 A2
Thornton Heath CR0 . . . 204 D1
Walton-on-T KT12 . . . 194 C1
Rodney Ct NW8 . . . 236 B6
Rodney Gdns
Hayes BR4 . . . 225 A4
Pinner HA5 . . . 40 C4
Rodney Ho
[4] Cubitt Town E14 . . . 119 D2
Islington N1 . . . 233 D3
Notting Hill W11 . . . 245 A6
Rodney Pl
Merton SW19 . . . 180 A2
Newington SE17 . . . 117 A2 262 B4
Walthamstow E17 . . . 35 B1
Rodney Rd
Mitcham CR4 . . . 202 C6
New Malden KT3 . . . 199 C4
Twickenham TW4 . . . 151 C4
Walton-on-T KT12 . . . 194 C1
Walworth SE17 . . . 117 B2 262 C3
Wanstead E11 . . . 55 B5
Rodney St N1 . . . 94 B5 233 D3
Rodwall Pl HA8 . . . 26 C3
Rodway Rd
Bromley BR1 . . . 187 B2
Putney SW15 . . . 156 A4
Rodwell Cl [2] HA4 . . . 40 C1
Rodwell Rd SE22 . . . 161 D5
Roebourne Way E16 . . . 122 C4
Roebuck Cl
Feltham TW13 . . . 172 B6
Tottenham N17 . . . 33 D4
Roebuck Ct
Chingford E4 . . . 36 A3
[2] New Malden KT3 . . . 199 C4
Roebuck Hts IG10 . . . 21 C4
Roebuck La IG9 . . . 21 C3
Roebuck Rd KT9 . . . 214 C3
Roedean Ave EN3 . . . 6 C5
Roedean Cl EN3 . . . 6 C4
Roedean Cres SW15 . . . 155 C6
Roe End NW9 . . . 45 A5
Roe Gn NW9 . . . 45 A4
Roe Green Jun & Inf Schs NW9 . . . 44 D5
ROEHAMPTON . . . 155 C4
Roehampton CE Prim Sch SW15 . . . 156 B4
Roehampton Cl SW15 . . . 134 A1
Roehampton Ct SW13 . . . 134 A2
Roehampton Dr BR7 . . . 189 A4
Roehampton Gate SW15 . . . 155 C5
Roehampton High St SW15 . . . 156 A4
Roehampton La
Putney SW15 . . . 156 A5
Roehampton SW15 . . . 156 B3
Roehampton Univ (Digby Stuart Coll) SW15 . . . 156 A6
Roehampton Univ (Froebel Coll) SW15 . . . 155 D5
Roehampton Univ (Southlands Coll) SW15 . . . 156 A6
Roehampton Univ (Whitelands Coll) SW15 . . . 156 A4
Roehampton Vale SW15 . . . 155 D2
Roe La NW9 . . . 45 A5
Roe [5] NW9 . . . 27 D2
Roe Way SM6 . . . 220 A2
Roffey Ct [9] NW9 . . . 46 A5
Roffey St E14 . . . 120 A4
Rogate Ho E5 . . . 74 A5
Roger Ascham Prim Sch E17 . . . 35 B2
Roger Dowley Ct [8] E2 . . . 96 C5
Roger's Almshouses [2] SW9 . . . 138 B1
Rogers Ct [16] E14 . . . 119 C6
Rogers Est [28] E2 . . . 96 C4
Rogers Gdns RM10 . . . 81 C3
Rogers Ho
[9] Dagenham RM10 . . . 81 C5
Westminster SW1 . . . 259 D4
Rogers Rd
Canning Town E16 . . . 98 D1
Dagenham RM10 . . . 81 C3
Upper Tooting SW17 . . . 180 C6
Roger Stone Ct NW10 . . . 67 B6
Roger St WC1 . . . 94 B3 240 D5
Rogers Wlk N12 . . . 13 D1
Rohan Pl [4] IG4 . . . 56 B4
Rojack Rd SE23 . . . 162 D3
Rokeby Gdns IG8 . . . 37 A2
Rokeby Ho
[9] Balham SW12 . . . 159 B4
Bloomsbury WC1 . . . 240 C5
Rokeby Pl SW20 . . . 178 B3
Rokeby Rd SE4 . . . 141 B3
Rokeby Sch
Kingston u T KT2 . . . 177 A3
Stratford E15 . . . 76 B1
Rokeby St E15 . . . 98 C6
Rokeland Ho SE4 . . . 141 A1
Rokell Ho BR3 . . . 185 D5
Roker Park Ave UB10 . . . 60 A4
Rokesby Cl DA16 . . . 145 B3
Rokesby Pl HA0 . . . 65 D3
Rokesly Ave N8 . . . 50 A4
Rokesly Jun & Inf Schs N8 . . . 50 A4
Roland Ct SE19 . . . 183 D2
Roland Gdns SW7 . . . 114 A1 256 B2
Roland Ho SW7 . . . 256 B2
Roland Mews [1] E1 . . . 96 D2
Roland Rd E17 . . . 54 B5
Roland Way
South Kensington SW7 . . . 114 A1 256 B2
Walworth SE17 . . . 262 D1
Worcester Pk KT4 . . . 215 D6
Roles Gr RM6 . . . 59 A5
Rolfe Cl EN4 . . . 2 C1
Rolfe Ho N11 . . . 30 D6
Rolinsden Way BR2 . . . 225 D4
Rolland Ho W7 . . . 86 C2
Rollesby Rd KT19, KT9 . . . 214 C2
Rollesby Way SE28 . . . 102 C1
Rolleston Ave BR5 . . . 210 D3
Rolleston Cl BR5 . . . 210 D2
Rolleston Rd CR2 . . . 221 B1
Roll Gdns IG2 . . . 56 C4
Rollins St SE15 . . . 140 C6
Rollit Cres TW3 . . . 151 C6
Rollit Ho N7 . . . 72 C3
Rollit St N7 . . . 72 C3
Rollo Ct SW11 . . . 268 C1
Rolls Bldgs EC4 . . . 241 B2
Rollscourt Ave SE24 . . . 161 A6
Rolls Ct The E4 . . . 36 A5
Rolls Park Ave E4 . . . 35 D5
Rolls Park Rd E4 . . . 35 D5
Rolls Pas EC4 . . . 241 A2
Rolls Rd SE1 . . . 117 D1 263 D2
Rolt St SE8 . . . 141 A6
Rolvenden Gdns BR1 . . . 187 D3
Rolvenden Pl N17 . . . 34 A2
Roman Cl
Feltham TW14 . . . 150 C6
South Acton W3 . . . 110 D4
Roman Ct [4] N7 . . . 72 B2
Romanfield Rd SW2 . . . 160 B4
Romanhurst Ave BR2 . . . 208 C5
Romanhurst Gdns BR2, BR3 . . . 208 C5
Roman Ind Est CR0 . . . 205 C2
Roman Lo [6] IG9 . . . 21 C3
Roman Rd
Chiswick W4 . . . 111 D2
Finchley N12 . . . 30 C2
Globe Town E2, E3 . . . 96 D5
Ilford IG1 . . . 78 D2
Muswell Hill N10 . . . 31 B3
Newham E6 . . . 100 A3
[25] Old Ford E3 . . . 97 B6
Willesden NW2 . . . 68 C5
Roman Rise SE19 . . . 183 B4
Roman Road Prim Sch E6 . . . 99 D3
Roman Sq SE28 . . . 124 A5
Roman Square Mkt [1] E3 . . . 97 B5
Roman Way
Barnsbury N7 . . . 72 B2
Croydon CR0 . . . 220 D6
[4] Deptford SE15 . . . 140 C5
Enfield EN1 . . . 17 D6
Romany Gdns
Cheam SM3 . . . 201 C2
[1] Higham Hill E17 . . . 35 A2
Romany Ho [8] N9 . . . 18 A1
Romany Prospect SE19 . . . 183 B4
Romany Rise BR5 . . . 211 A1
Roma Rd E17 . . . 53 A6
Roma Read Cl SW15 . . . 156 B4
Romayne Ho SW4 . . . 137 D2
Romberg Rd SW17 . . . 159 A1
Romborough Gdns SE13 . . . 164 A6
Romborough Way SE13 . . . 164 A6
Romeland Ct WD6 . . . 9 D5
Romeland WD6 . . . 9 D5
Romer Ho [9] SW2 . . . 160 B6
Romero Cl SW9 . . . 138 B2
Romero Sq SE9 . . . 143 C1
Romeyn Rd SW16 . . . 160 B1
ROMFORD . . . 59 D4
Romford Ho [17] N1 . . . 73 B2
Romford Rd
Forest Gate E7, E12 . . . 77 C3
Stratford E15 . . . 76 D2
Romford St E1 . . . 96 B2
Romilly Dr WD19 . . . 23 A6
Romilly Rd N4 . . . 72 D6
Romilly St W1 . . . 249 D6
Romily Ct SW6 . . . 135 A3
Rommany Ct SE27 . . . 183 B6
Rommany Rd SE27 . . . 183 B6
Romney Cl
Ashford TW15 . . . 171 A5
Chessington KT9 . . . 214 A4
[7] Deptford SE14 . . . 140 C5
Harrow HA2 . . . 41 C2
North End NW11 . . . 48 A1
Tottenham N17 . . . 34 B2
Romney Ct
[9] Hammersmith W12 . . . 112 C4
[9] Hampstead NW3 . . . 70 C2
[15] Northolt UB5 . . . 84 D5
Romney Dr
Bromley BR1 . . . 187 D3
Harrow HA2 . . . 41 C2
Romney Gdns DA7 . . . 147 B4
Romney Ho
[2] Blackwall E14 . . . 120 B6
Enfield EN1 . . . 18 A6
Sutton SM2 . . . 217 D2
Romney Mews W1 . . . 238 A4
Romney Par UB4 . . . 83 B5
Romney Rd
Greenwich SE10 . . . 142 B6
Hayes UB4 . . . 83 B5
New Malden KT3 . . . 199 B3
Romney Row NW2 . . . 68 D6
Romney St SW1 . . . 116 A3 260 A5
Romola Rd SE24, SW2 . . . 160 D3
Romsey Cl BR6 . . . 226 D4
Romsey Gdns RM9 . . . 102 D6
Romsey Rd
Dagenham RM9 . . . 102 D6
Ealing W13 . . . 109 A6
Romulus Ct [7] TW8 . . . 131 D5
Ronald Ave E15 . . . 98 C4
Ronald Cl BR3 . . . 207 B4
Ronald Ct EN5 . . . 1 D2
Ronald Ho
Eltham SE9 . . . 143 C1
[4] Sutton SM1 . . . 218 B3
Ronald Ross Prim Sch SW19 . . . 157 A4
Ronaldshay N4 . . . 50 C1
Ronalds Rd
Bromley BR1 . . . 187 A2
Islington N5 . . . 72 C3
Ronald St E1 . . . 96 C1
Ronaldstone Rd DA15 . . . 167 C5
Rona Rd NW3 . . . 71 A4
Ronart St HA3 . . . 42 D6
Rona Wlk [20] N1 . . . 73 B2
Rondu Rd NW2 . . . 69 A3
Ronelean Rd KT6 . . . 214 B5
Ron Leighton Way E6 . . . 100 A6
Ronnie La E12 . . . 78 C4
Ron Todd Cl RM10 . . . 103 C6
Ronver Lo E4 . . . 20 C1
Ronver Rd SE12 . . . 164 D3
Rood La EC3 . . . 117 C6 253 A6
Rookby Ct N21 . . . 16 D2
Rook Cl HA9 . . . 66 D5
Rookeries Cl TW13 . . . 150 C1
Rookery Cl NW9 . . . 45 D4
Rookery Cotts EN4 . . . 3 B2
Rookery Cres RM10 . . . 81 D1
Rookery Dr BR7 . . . 188 C2
Rookery La BR2 . . . 209 D3
Rookery Rd SW4 . . . 137 C1
Rookery Way NW9 . . . 45 D4
Rooke Way SE10 . . . 120 D1
Rookfield Ave N10 . . . 49 C5
Rookfield Cl N10 . . . 49 C5
Rook Lo IG1 . . . 55 D3
Rooks Heath High Sch HA2 . . . 63 C5
Rooksmead Rd TW16 . . . 172 A1
Rooks Terr UB7 . . . 104 A4
Rookstone Rd SW17 . . . 180 D5

Rook Wlk E6 ... 100 A1
Rookwood Ave
Wallington SM6 ... 219 D4
West Barnes KT3 ... 200 A5
Rookwood Gdns E4 ... 20 D2
Rookwood Ho 2
IG11 ... 101 B5
Rookwood Rd N16 ... 52 A2
Roosevelt Ct 15
SW19 ... 157 A3
Rootes Dr W10 ... 90 D2
Ropemaker Rd
SE16 ... 119 A3
Ropemaker's Fields 7
E14 ... 119 B6
Ropemaker St
EC2 ... 95 B2 242 C4
Roper Ho 13 SE21 ... 183 C6
Roper La
SE1 ... 117 C4 253 B1
Ropers Ave E4 ... 36 A5
Roper's Orch SW3 ... 267 A5
Roper St 1 SE9 ... 166 C5
Ropers Wlk 13 SE24 ... 160 C4
Roper Way CR4 ... 181 A1
Ropery Bsns Pk
SE7 ... 121 C2
Ropery St E3 ... 97 B3
Rope St SE16 ... 119 A3
Ropewalk Gdns 18
E1 ... 96 A1
Rope Yard Rails
SE18 ... 122 D3
Ropley St 6 E2 ... 96 A5
Rosa Alba Mews N5 ... 73 A4
Rosa Ave TW15 ... 170 C6
Rosa Freedman Ctr
NW2 ... 46 C1
Rosalind Ct 6 IG11 ... 80 A1
Rosalind Ho 25 N1 ... 95 C5
Rosaline Rd
SW6 ... 135 A5 264 B3
Rosaline Terr SW6 ... 264 B3
Rosamond St SE26 ... 162 B1
Rosamund Cl CR2 ... 221 B4
Rosamun St UB2 ... 107 A2
Rosa Parks Ho 8
SW9 ... 138 B3
Rosary Cl TW3,TW5 ... 129 A3
Rosary Ct 17 E1 ... 96 D2
Rosary Gdns
Ashford TW15 ... 170 D6
Bushey WD23 ... 8 C4
South Kensington
SW7 ... 114 A2 256 B3
Rosary RC Inf Sch
TW5 ... 129 C6
Rosary RC Jun Sch
TW5 ... 129 C6
Rosary RC Prim Sch
NW3 ... 70 C3
Rosaville Rd
SW6 ... 135 B5 264 C3
Rosbury SW15 ... 157 A5
Roscastle Rd SE4 ... 163 A6
Roscoe St
EC1 ... 95 A3 242 B5
Roscoff Cl HA8 ... 27 A2
Roscommon Ho 2
NW3 ... 70 B3
Roseacre Cl
Ealing W13 ... 87 B2
Littleton TW17 ... 192 C4
Roseacre Lo EN3 ... 6 C1
Roseacre Rd DA16 ... 146 B2
Rose Alley
Borough The SE1 ... 252 B4
Broadgate EC2 ... 243 B3
Rose Ave
Mitcham CR4 ... 180 D2
Morden SM4 ... 202 A4
Woodford E18 ... 37 B1
Rosebank Ave HA0 ... 64 D4
Rosebank Cl
Colney Hatch N12 ... 30 C5
Teddington TW11 ... 175 A4
Rosebank
2 Dagenham W3 ... 89 B1
Fulham SW6 ... 134 C5
Rosebank Gdns
Bow E3 ... 97 B5
1 Dagenham W3 ... 89 B1
Rosebank Gr E17 ... 53 B6
Rosebank SE20 ... 184 B3
Rosebank Rd
Hanwell W7 ... 108 C4
Walthamstow E17 ... 53 D3
Rosebank Villas E17 ... 53 C5
Rosebank Way W3 ... 89 B1
Rosebank Wlk
Camden Town
NW1 ... 71 D1
14 Woolwich SE7 ... 122 A2
Rose Bates Dr NW9 ... 44 C5
Rosebay Ho 20 E3 ... 97 C2
Roseberry Gdns
Harringay N4 ... 50 D3
Orpington BR6 ... 227 C5
Roseberry Pl E8 ... 73 D2
Roseberry St SE16 ... 118 B2
Rosebery Ave
Finsbury
EC1 ... 94 C4 234 B1
Harrow HA2 ... 63 B4
Kingston u T KT3 ... 199 D6
Plashet E12 ... 78 B2
Sidcup DA15 ... 167 C4
South Norwood CR7 ... 183 A1
Tottenham N17 ... 34 A1
Rosebery Cl SM4 ... 200 D3
Rosebery Ct
Chessington KT9 ... 214 B3
Holborn EC1 ... 241 A6
Mayfair W1 ... 248 C4
Rosebery Gdns
Ealing W13 ... 87 A1
Hornsey N8 ... 50 A4
Sutton SM1 ... 217 D4
Rosebery Ho 21 E2 ... 96 C5
Rosebery Ind Pk N17 ... 34 B1
Rosebery Mews N10 ... 31 C1
Rosebery Rd
Cheam SM1, SM2 ... 217 B2
Clapham Pk SW2 ... 160 A5
Isleworth TW3,
TW7 ... 152 A6
Kingston u T KT1 ... 176 D1
Muswell Hill N10 ... 31 C1
Rosebery Sq
Holborn EC1 ... 241 A5
Kingston u T KT1 ... 176 D1
Rosebine Ave TW2 ... 152 B4
Rosebriars KT10 ... 212 A3
Rose Bruford Coll
DA15 ... 168 B3
Rosebury Ct SW16 ... 182 B2
Rosebury Rd SW6 ... 135 D3
Rosebury Vale HA4 ... 62 A6
Rose Bush Ct NW3 ... 70 D3
Rose Cotts KT10 ... 212 B3
Rosecourt Rd CR0 ... 204 B3
Rosecroft Ave NW3 ... 69 C5
Rosecroft Gdns
Dollis Hill NW2 ... 68 A5
Twickenham TW2 ... 152 B3
Rosecroft Rd UB1 ... 85 C3
Rosecroft Wlk
Pinner HA5 ... 40 D4
Wembley HA0 ... 65 D3
Rosecroft N22 ... 32 B2
Rose & Crown Ct
EC2 ... 242 A2
Rose & Crown Yd
SW1 ... 249 B3
Rose Ct 7 Dalston E8 ... 73 D1
Harrow HA2 ... 64 A6
Ilford IG1 ... 78 D2
Islington N1 ... 234 C5
Muswell Hill N10 ... 31 B3
3 Pinner HA5 ... 40 C6
Spitalfields E1 ... 243 D3
7 Wembley HA0 ... 88 A5
10 Wimbledon
SW19 ... 179 B5
Rosedale Ave UB3 ... 83 B2
Rosedale Cl
Abbey Wood SE2 ... 124 B3
Hanwell W7 ... 108 D4
Stanmore HA7 ... 25 B4
Rosedale Cnr BR7 ... 188 B2
Rosedale Coll UB3 ... 83 C1
Rosedale Ct N5 ... 72 D4
Rosedale Dr RM9 ... 80 B1
Rosedale Gdns RM9 ... 80 B1
Rosedale Ho N16 ... 51 B1
Rosedale Lo N14 ... 15 B4
Rose Dale BR6 ... 226 D6
Rosedale Pl CR0 ... 206 D2
Rosedale Rd
Dagenham RM9 ... 80 B1
Forest Gate E7 ... 77 C3
Richmond TW9 ... 132 A1
Stoneleigh KT17 ... 216 A3
Rosedale Terr W6 ... 112 B3
Rosedene Ave
Morden SM4 ... 201 C4
Southall UB6 ... 85 C4
Streatham SW16 ... 160 B1
Thornton Heath CR0 ... 204 A2
Rosedene Ct HA4 ... 39 C1
Rosedene Gdns IG2 ... 56 C5
Rosedene NW6 ... 90 D6
Rosedene Terr E10 ... 75 D6
Rosedew Rd W6 ... 134 D6
Rose End KT4 ... 200 D1
Rosefield Cl SM5 ... 218 C3
Rosefield Ct EN4 ... 2 D1
Rosefield Gdns E14 ... 119 C6
Roseford Ct 16
W12 ... 112 D4
Rose Garden Cl HA8 ... 26 A4
Rosegate Ho 32 E3 ... 97 B5
Rose Gdns
Ealing W5 ... 109 D3
Feltham TW13 ... 150 A2
Southall UB1 ... 85 C3
Rose Glen NW9 ... 45 B5
Rosehart Mews 8
W11 ... 91 C1
Rosehatch Ave RM6 ... 58 D6
Roseheath Rd TW4 ... 151 B6
ROSEHILL ... 202 A1
Rosehill Ave SM1,
SM5 ... 202 A1
Rose Hill
Carshalton SM4,
SM5 ... 202 A2
Cheam SM1 ... 201 D1
Rosehill KT10 ... 213 A2
Rosehill Ct SM4 ... 202 A2
Rosehill Gdns
Greenford UB6 ... 64 D3
Sutton SM1 ... 218 A6
Rosehill TW12 ... 173 C2
Rose Hill Park W
SM1 ... 218 A6
Rosehill Rd SW18 ... 158 A6
Rose La RM6 ... 59 A5
Roseland Cl N17 ... 33 B3
Roseland Ho SW6 ... 135 A2
Rose Lawn WD23 ... 8 A3
Roseleigh Ave N5 ... 72 D4
Roseleigh Cl 15
TW1 ... 153 D5
Roselle Ct W5 ... 88 A1
Rosemary Ave
East Finchley NW2 ... 47 D5
East Molesey KT8 ... 195 C5
Edmonton N9 ... 18 B3
Enfield EN2 ... 5 C4
Finchley N3 ... 29 D1
Hounslow TW4 ... 128 D3
Rosemary Branch
Bridge N1 ... 235 D6
Rosemary Cl
Hillingdon UB8 ... 82 C2
Thornton Heath CR0 ... 204 A3
Rosemary Cotts 4
SW19 ... 178 C3
Rosemary Ct 35 SE8 ... 141 B6
Rosemary Dr
Redbridge IG4 ... 55 D4
16 South Bromley
E14 ... 98 B1
Rosemary Gdns
Chessington KT9 ... 214 A4
Dagenham RM8 ... 59 B1
Mortlake SW14 ... 133 A2
Rosemary Ho
Shoreditch N1 ... 235 D5
Willesden NW10 ... 90 B6
Rosemary La SW14 ... 133 A2
Rosemary Rd
Bexley DA16 ... 145 D4
Camberwell SE15 ... 139 D5
Wandsworth SW17 ... 158 A1
Rosemary St N1 ... 235 D6
Rosemary Works Sch
N1 ... 95 B6 235 D5
Rosemead Ave
Feltham TW13 ... 149 D2
Mitcham CR4 ... 181 C1
Wembley HA9 ... 66 A3
Rosemead NW9 ... 46 A2
Rosemead Prep Sch
SE27 ... 161 A2
Rose Mews N18 ... 34 B6
Rosemont Ave N12 ... 30 A4
Rosemont Mans 11
NW3 ... 69 D2
Rosemont Rd
Acton W3 ... 110 D6
Kingston u T KT3 ... 199 A6
Richmond TW10 ... 154 A5
South Hampstead
NW3 ... 70 A2
Wembley HA0 ... 88 A6
Rosemoor Ho 14
W13 ... 109 A5
Rosemoor St
SW3 ... 114 D2 257 C3
Rosemount Ct
2 Acton W3 ... 110 D5
South Norwood
SE25 ... 205 C6
Rosemount Dr BR1 ... 210 B5
Rosemount Lo W3 ... 110 D6
Rosemount Point 10
SE23 ... 162 D1
Rosemount Rd W13 ... 87 A1
Rosemount Twrs 5
SM6 ... 219 C2
Rosenau Cres SW11 ... 267 C1
Rosenau Rd
SW11 ... 136 D4 267 C2
Rosendale Prim Sch
SE21 ... 161 A4
Rosendale Rd SE21,
SE24 ... 161 A3
Roseneath Ave N21 ... 16 D3
Roseneath Pl 2
SW16 ... 182 B6
Roseneath Rd
SW11 ... 159 A5
Roseneath Wlk EN1 ... 5 C1
Rosens Wlk HA8 ... 10 D1
Rosenthal Ho SE6 ... 163 D5
Rosenthal Rd SE6 ... 164 A5
Rosenthorpe Rd
SE15 ... 162 D6
Roserton St E14 ... 120 A4
Rosery The CR0 ... 206 D3
Rose Sq SW7 ... 256 D2
Roses The IG8 ... 36 D3
Rose St Holborn EC4 ... 241 D2
Strand WC2 ... 116 A6 250 A6
Rosethorn Cl SW12 ... 159 D4
Rosetta Cl SW8 ... 270 B3
Rosetta Ct SE19 ... 183 C3
Rosetta Prim Sch
E16 ... 99 B2
Rosetti Terr RM8 ... 80 B4
Roseveare Rd SE12 ... 187 C6
Roseville Ave TW3,
TW4 ... 151 C6
Roseville Rd UB3 ... 106 A2
Roseville N21 ... 16 C3
Rosevine Rd SW20 ... 178 C2
Rosewall Ct SW19 ... 179 D5
Rose Way
Edgware HA8 ... 27 A6
Lee SE12 ... 165 A6
Roseway SE21 ... 161 B5
Rosewell Cl SE20 ... 184 B3
Rose Wlk
Surbiton KT5 ... 198 D4
West Wickham BR4 ... 224 B6
Rosewood Ave UB6 ... 65 A2
Rosewood Cl DA14 ... 168 C1
Rosewood Ct
Bromley BR1 ... 187 D2
Dagenham RM6 ... 58 C4
Kingston u T KT2 ... 176 C3
2 Leyton E11 ... 76 B4
Rosewood Dr TW17 ... 192 B4
Rosewood Gdns
SE13 ... 142 A3
Rosewood Gr SM1 ... 218 A6
Rosewood Ho 9
NW3 ... 69 D2
Rosewood Sq W12 ... 90 A1
Rosher Cl E15 ... 76 B1
Roshni Ho SW17 ... 180 C4
Rosh Pinah Prim Sch
Edgware HA8 ... 10 D1
Edgware HA8 ... 26 C6
Rosina Ct SW17 ... 180 C5
Rosina St E9 ... 74 D2
Roskeen Ct 1
SW19 ... 178 C3
Roskell Rd SW15 ... 134 D2
Roskild Ct HA9 ... 66 B4
Roslin Ho 2 E1 ... 118 D6
Roslin Rd W3 ... 110 D3
Roslin Way BR1 ... 187 A5
Roslyn Cl CR4 ... 180 B1
Roslyn Rd N15 ... 51 C4
Rosmead Rd
W11 ... 113 A6 244 B6
Rosoman Pl EC1 ... 241 B6
Rosoman St EC1 ... 234 B1
Rossal Ct 2 SE20 ... 184 B3
Rossall Cres NW10 ... 88 B4
Rossanne Ho N3 ... 29 D3
Ross Ave
Dagenham RM8 ... 59 B1
Finchley NW7 ... 29 A5
Ross Cl Harrow HA3 ... 24 A3
Hayes UB3 ... 105 B2
Northolt UB5 ... 64 B4
Ross Ct
Chislehurst BR7 ... 188 B3
Colindale NW9 ... 45 C6
Ealing W13 ... 87 B2
Edgware HA8 ... 10 D2
1 Hackney E5 ... 74 B4
4 Putney SW15 ... 156 D4
South Croydon CR2 ... 221 A2
Rossdale SM1 ... 218 C3
Rossdale Dr
Ponders End N9 ... 18 C5
Welsh Harp NW9 ... 45 A1
Rossdale Rd SW15 ... 134 C1
Rosse Gdns SE13 ... 164 B5
Rosse Mews SE3 ... 143 B4
Rossendale Cl EN2 ... 4 D6
Rossendale Ho 7 E5 ... 74 B6
Rossendale St E5 ... 74 B6
Rossendale Way
NW1 ... 93 C6 232 B6
Rossendon Ct 1
SM6 ... 219 C2
Rossetti Ct WC1 ... 239 C4
Rossetti Gdns Mans
SW3 ... 267 C6
Rossetti Ho SW1 ... 259 D3
Rossetti Mews NW8 ... 229 D5
Rossetti Rd SE16 ... 118 B1
Rossetti Studios
SW3 ... 267 B6
Ross Ho
2 Kidbrooke
SE18 ... 144 A4
Twickenham TW2 ... 151 D2
18 Wapping E1 ... 118 B5
Rossignol Gdns
SM5 ... 219 A6
Rossindel Rd TW3 ... 151 C6
Rossington Cl EN1 ... 6 B5
Rossington St E5 ... 74 A6
Rossiter Fields EN5 ... 13 B5
Rossiter Rd SW12 ... 159 B3
Rossland Cl DA6 ... 169 D6
Rosslyn Ave
Barnes SW13 ... 133 D2
Chingford E4 ... 20 D2
Dagenham RM8 ... 59 C2
East Barnet EN4 ... 14 C5
Feltham TW14 ... 150 A5
Rosslyn Cl
Ashford TW16 ... 171 C4
Coney Hall BR4 ... 224 D5
Hayes UB3 ... 83 B2
Rosslyn Cres
Harrow HA1 ... 42 D5
Wembley HA9 ... 66 A4
Rosslyn Ct NW3 ... 70 C3
Rosslyn Hill NW3 ... 70 B3
Rosslyn Ho 8 TW9 ... 132 B4
Rosslyn Mans
8 Hampstead
NW3 ... 70 A2
South Hampstead
NW6 ... 70 A2
Rosslyn Mews 7
NW3 ... 70 B4
Rosslyn Park Mews
NW3 ... 70 B3
Rosslyn Rd
Barking IG11 ... 79 B1
Twickenham TW1 ... 153 C5
Walthamstow E17 ... 54 A5
Rossmore Cl EN3 ... 6 D1
Rossmore Ct NW1 ... 237 C6
Rossmore Rd
NW1 ... 92 C3 237 B6
Ross Par SM6 ... 219 B2
Ross Rd
South Norwood
SE25 ... 205 C6
Twickenham TW2 ... 152 A3
Wallington SM6 ... 219 C3
Rossway Dr WD23 ... 8 B6
Ross Way SE9 ... 144 A2
Rosswood Gdns
SM6 ... 219 C2
Rosswood Ho 13
SM6 ... 219 B2
Rosswood Lo CR0 ... 222 D6
Rostella Rd SW17 ... 180 B6
Rostrever Gdns
UB3 ... 105 C5
Rostrevor Ave N15 ... 51 D3
Rostrevor Gdns
UB2 ... 107 A1
Rostrevor Mans
SW6 ... 264 C2
Rostrevor Mews
SW6 ... 264 C1
Rostrevor Rd
Fulham
SW6 ... 135 B4 264 C2
Wimbledon SW19 ... 179 C5
Rotary Ct KT8 ... 196 C6
Rotary Lo 12 SE27 ... 160 D1
Rotary St SE1 ... 261 D6
Rothay NW1 ... 231 D2
Rothbury Gdns
TW7 ... 131 A5
Rothbury Rd E9 ... 75 C1
Rothbury Wlk N17 ... 34 A3
Rotheley Ho 39 E9 ... 74 C1
Rotherfield Ct
De Beauvoir Town
N1 ... 73 B1
Shoreditch
N1 ... 95 B6 235 C6
Rotherfield Prim Sch
N1 ... 95 A6 235 B6
Rotherfield Rd
Enfield EN3 ... 6 D6
Wallington SM5 ... 219 A3
Rotherfield St
Islington N1 ... 73 A1
Shoreditch
N1 ... 95 A6 235 B6
Rotherham Wlk SE1 ... 251 C3
Rotherhill Ave
SW16 ... 181 D4
ROTHERHITHE ... 118 D3
Rotherhithe Bsns Est 6
SE16 ... 118 C2
Rotherhithe New Rd
SE16 ... 118 B1
Rotherhithe Old Rd
SE16 ... 118 D2
Rotherhithe Prim Sch
SE16 ... 118 D2
Rotherhithe Sta
SE16 ... 118 C4
Rotherhithe St
SE16 ... 118 C4
Rotherhithe Tunnel
SE16 ... 118 D5
Rother Ho SE15 ... 140 B1
Rotherwick Hill W5 ... 88 B3
Rotherwick Rd NW11 ... 47 C2
Rotherwood Cl
SW20 ... 179 A2
Rotherwood Rd
SW15 ... 134 D2
Rothery St N1 ... 234 D6
Rothesay Ave
Merton SW20 ... 179 A1
Mortlake SW14,
TW10 ... 132 D1
Northolt UB6 ... 64 B2
Rothesay Ct
4 Catford SE6 ... 164 D2
Grove Pk SE12 ... 165 B1
13 Kennington SE11 ... 138 C6
Rothesay Rd SE25 ... 205 C5
Rothley Ct NW8 ... 236 C6
Rothsay Rd E7 ... 77 C2
Rothsay St
SE1 ... 117 C3 263 A5
Rothsay Wlk 19 E14 ... 119 C2
Rothschild Rd W4 ... 111 A3
Rothschild St SE27 ... 182 D6
Rothwell Ct
2 Bromley BR1 ... 187 B2
4 Harrow HA1 ... 42 D4
Rothwell Gdns RM9 ... 102 C6
Rothwell Ho TW5 ... 129 C6
Rothwell Rd RM9 ... 102 C6
Rothwell St
10 Hampstead
NW1 ... 70 D1
Primrose Hill NW1 ... 230 D6
Roth Wlk N7 ... 72 B6
Rotten Row
SW1 ... 114 D4 247 C2
Rotterdam Dr E14 ... 120 A3
Rouel Rd
Bermondsey
SE16 ... 118 A2
Bermondsey SE16 ... 118 A3
Rougemont Ave
SM4 ... 201 C3
Roundabout Ho HA6 ... 22 A2
Roundacre SW19 ... 156 D2
Roundel Cl SE4 ... 141 B1
Roundell Ho 14
SE21 ... 183 C6
Rounders Ct 7
RM10 ... 81 D2
Round Gr CR0 ... 206 D2
Roundhay Cl SE23 ... 162 D2
Roundhedge Way EN2 ... 4 B5
Roundhill Dr EN2 ... 4 B1
Round Hill SE23 ... 162 C1
ROUNDSHAW ... 220 B1
Roundshaw Ctr
SM6 ... 220 A1
Roundtable Rd BR1 ... 164 D1
Roundtree Rd HA0 ... 65 B3
Roundways HA4 ... 61 D5
Roundway The
Claygate KT10 ... 212 D2
Tottenham N17 ... 33 B2
Roundwood Ave
UB11 ... 105 A5
Roundwood BR7 ... 188 D1
Roundwood Cl HA4 ... 39 B2
Roundwood Rd
NW10 ... 67 D1
Rounton Rd E3 ... 97 C3
Rountree Ct 9 UB1 ... 85 D1
Roupell Ho 7 KT2 ... 176 B3
Roupell Rd SW2 ... 160 B3
Roupell St
SE1 ... 116 C5 251 B3
Rousden St NW1 ... 71 C1
Rouse Gdns SE21 ... 183 C6
Routemaster Cl E13 ... 99 B4
Routh Ct TW14 ... 149 B3
Routh Rd SW18 ... 158 C4
Routh St E6 ... 100 B2
Rover Ho 26 N1 ... 95 C6
Rowallan Ct 3 SE6 ... 164 D3
Rowallan Rd
SW6 ... 135 A5 264 A3
Rowallen Par RM8 ... 58 C1
Rowan Ave E4 ... 35 B4
Rowan Cl Ealing W5 ... 110 A4
Harrow HA7 ... 24 D4
Ilford IG1 ... 79 B

Rowan Cl *continued*
Kingston u T KT3 177 C1
Streatham SW16 181 C2
Wembley HA0 65 A5
Rowan Cres SW16 181 C2
Rowan Ct
10 Camberwell
SE15 139 D5
Forest Hill SE26 184 C6
11 Kingston u T KT2 176 C3
Newham E13 99 B5
Twickenham TW4 151 D6
Wandsworth SW11 158 D5
Wimbledon SW20 178 B1
Rowan Dr NW9 46 A6
Rowan Gdns CR0 221 D5
Rowan Ho 9 Bow E3 97 B6
Dagenham NW10 89 C3
East Bedfont TW14 149 B5
Ilford IG1 79 B3
5 Maitland Pk NW3 70 D2
Sidcup DA14 167 D1
Rowan N10 31 B1
Rowan Pl UB3 105 D6
Rowan Rd
Brentford TW8 131 B5
Brook Green W6 112 D2
DA7 147 A2
Mitcham SW16 181 C1
West Drayton UB7 104 A2
Rowans The
Ashford TW16 171 D5
Edmonton N13 17 A1
7 Sutton SM2 217 D2
Rowan Terr W6 112 D2
Rowantree Cl N21 17 B3
Rowantree Rd
Edmonton N21 17 B3
Enfield EN2 4 D3
Rowan Way RM6 58 C6
Rowan Wlk BR2 226 B5
7 Dartmouth Pk N19 71 C6
Hampstead Garden
Suburb N2 48 A4
Kensal Town W10 91 A3
1 New Barnet EN5 13 D6
Rowanwood Ave
DA15 168 A3
Rowanwood Mews
EN2 4 D3
Rowben Cl N20 13 D3
Rowberry Cl SW6 134 C5
Rowcross St
SE1 117 D1 263 D2
Rowdell Rd UB5 85 C6
Rowden Par E4 35 C4
Rowden Park Gdns
E4 35 C4
Rowden Rd
Beckenham BR3 185 B2
Chingford E4 35 D4
West Ewell KT19 215 A4
Rowditch La SW11 137 A3
Rowdon Ave NW10 68 B1
Rowdowns Rd RM9 81 B1
Rowe Gdns IG11 102 A5
Rowe Ho E9 74 C2
Rowe La E9 74 C3
Rowena Cres SW11 136 C3
Rowe Wlk HA2 63 C5
Rowfant Rd SW12,
SW17 159 A2
Rowhill Mans 11 E5 74 B4
Rowhill Rd E5 74 B4
Rowington Cl W2 91 D2
Rowland Ave HA3 43 C6
Rowland Ct E16 98 D3
South Croydon CR0 221 C6
Rowland Gr SE26 162 B1
Rowland Hill
Almshouses 7
TW15 170 C5
Rowland Hill Ave
N17 33 B4
Rowland Hill Ho
SE1 251 C2
Rowland Hill St NW3 70 C3
Rowlands Ave HA5 23 D4
Rowlands Cl
Hendon NW7 28 A3
Highgate N6 49 A3
Rowlands Rd RM8 81 B6
Rowland Way
Ashford TW15 171 B3
Merton SW19 179 D2
Rowley Ave DA15 168 B4
Rowley Cl HA0 66 B1
Rowley Ct EN1 17 C6
Rowley Gdns N4 51 A2
Rowley Green Rd
EN5 12 A6
Rowley Ho SE8 141 C6
Rowley Ind Pk W3 110 D3
Rowley La EN5 11 D6
Rowley Rd N15 51 A4
Rowley Way NW8 229 A6
Rowlheys Pl UB7 104 A3

Rowlls Rd KT1 198 B6
Rowney Gdns RM9 80 C2
Rowney Rd RM9 80 B2
Rowntree Clifford Cl 7
E13 99 B4
Rowntree Cl NW6 69 C2
Rowntree Path 1
SE28 124 B5
Rowntree Rd TW2 152 C3
Rowse Cl E15 98 A6
Rowsham Ct HA1 64 C5
Rowsley Ave NW4 46 C6
Rowstock Gdns N7 71 D3
Rowstock 1 NW5 71 D2
Rowton Rd SE18 145 A5
Roxborough Ave
Harrow HA1 42 C2
Hounslow TW7 130 D5
Roxborough Pk HA1 42 C2
Roxborough Rd HA1 42 B3
Roxbourne Cl UB5 62 D2
Roxbourne Fst & Mid
Schs HA2 63 A6
Roxburgh Rd SE27 182 D5
Roxburn Way HA4 61 D5
Roxby Pl
SW6 135 C6 265 B6
ROXETH 64 A6
Roxeth Ct 6 TW15 170 C5
Roxeth Fst & Mid Sch
HA2 64 B6
Roxeth Green Ave
HA2 63 D6
Roxeth Gr HA2 63 D4
Roxeth Hill HA2 64 C6
Roxeth Manor Fst & Mid
Schs HA2 63 C5
Roxeth Mead Sch
HA2 64 B6
Roxford Cl TW17 193 C4
Roxford Ho 2 E3 97 D3
Roxley Rd SE13 163 D5
Roxton Gdns CR0 223 C3
Roxwell 10 NW1 71 B2
Roxwell Rd
Barking IG11 102 A5
Shepherd's Bush
W12 112 A4
Roxwell Trad Pk E10 53 A2
Roxwell Way IG8 37 C3
Roxy Ave RM6 58 C2
Royal Academy of
Dramatic Art*
WC1 93 D2 239 C4
Royal Acad of Arts*
W1 115 C6 249 A5
Royal Acad of Dance
SW11 266 D1
Royal Acad of Music
NW1 238 B5
Royal Albert Hall*
SW7 114 B4 246 C1
Royal Albert Sta
E16 122 A6
Royal Albert Way
E6 122 B6
Royal Arc W1 249 A5
Royal Armouries The*
E1 253 C5
Royal Avenue Ho
SW3 257 C2
Royal Ave
SW3 114 D1 257 C2
Worcester Pk KT4 215 C6
Royal Ballet Sch The
Hammersmith
W14 112 D1
St Giles WC2 94 A1 240 B1
Royal Ballet Sch (White
Lodge) The TW10 155 B3
Royal Brompton
Hospl
Chelsea
SW3 114 B1 256 C2
Chelsea
SW3 114 C1 257 A2
Royal Cir SE27 160 D1
Royal Cl
Deptford SE8 141 B6
Hillingdon UB7 82 B1
Ilford IG3 58 A2
Locksbottom BR6 226 D4
Putney SW19 156 D2
Stamford Hill N16 51 C1
Worcester Pk KT4 215 C6
Royal College of
Physicians Liby
NW1 93 B3 238 D6
Royal College St
NW1 93 C6 232 B6
Royal Coll of
Anaesthetists
WC1 240 C3
Royal Coll of Art
Sculpture Sch
SW11 136 C5 267 A3

Royal Coll of Art
SW7 114 B4 246 C1
Royal Coll of Midwives
W1 93 B2 238 C3
Royal Coll of Music
SW7 114 B3 256 C6
Royal Coll of
Obstetricians &
Gynaecologists
NW1 92 D3 237 C6
Royal Coll of
Ophthalmologists
NW1 238 A5
Royal Coll of
Paediatrics & Child
Health W1 238 D4
Royal Coll of
Pathologists
SW1 115 D5 249 C3
Royal Coll of Physicians
NW1 93 B3 238 D6
Royal Coll of
Radiologists W1 238 D4
Royal Coll of Science
SW7 114 B3 256 C6
Royal Coll of Speech
Language Therapists
SE1 252 C3
Royal Coll of Surgeons
WC2 94 B1 240 D2
Royal Connaught Apts
E16 121 D5
Royal Courts of Justice
WC2 94 C1 241 A1
Royal Crescent Mews
W11 112 D5
Royal Cres Ilford IG2 57 B3
Ruislip HA4 63 A5
Royal Crest Ho SM2 217 A1
Royal Cres
W11 113 A5 244 A3
Royal Ct
City of London EC3 242 D1
Enfield EN1 17 C5
9 Kingston u T KT2 176 D3
Mottingham SE9 166 B3
Rotherhithe SE16 119 B3
Ruislip HA4 40 A2
Royal Docks Com Sch
The E16 99 C1
Royal Docks Rd E6 100 D2
Royal Dr N11 31 A5
Royal Duchess Mews
SW12 159 B4
Royal Exchange Bldgs
EC3 242 D1
Royal Exchange*
EC3 242 D1
Royal Festival Hall*
SE1 116 B5 250 D3
Royal Free Hospl
NW3 70 C3
Royal Fusiliers Mus*
E1 253 C5
Royal Gdns W7 109 A3
Royal Geographical
Society SW7 246 D1
Royal Hill Ct 2
SE10 142 A5
Royal Hill SE10 142 A5
Royal Horticultural
Society (Lawrence
Hall & Conf Ctr)
SW1 259 C5
Royal Horticultural
Society (Lindley Hall)
SW1 259 C4
Royal Hospital (Army
Pensioners)*
SW1 115 A1 258 A1
Royal Hospital Rd
SW3 114 D1 257 D1
Royal Hospl and Home
SW15 157 A5
Royal La
Hillingdon UB7 82 B1
Hillingdon UB8 82 B3
Royal Langford
Apartments 3
NW6 91 D5
Royal London Est The
NW10 89 B5
Royal London Est
N17 34 B4
Royal London
Homeopathic Hospl
The WC1 94 A2 240 B4
Royal London Hospl
Archives & Mus*
E1 96 B2
Royal London Hospl
(Mile End) The E2 96 D4
Royal London Hospl (St
Clements) The E3 97 B4
Royal London Hospl
(Whitechapel) The
E1 96 B2

Royal Marsden Hospl
SW3 114 B1 256 D2
Royal Mews KT8 196 C6
Royal Mews The*
SW1 115 B3 258 D6
Royal Military Sch of
Music (Kneller Hall)
TW2 152 B5
Royal Mint Pl 6 E1 118 A6
Royal Mint St
E1 117 D6 253 D6
Royal National
Orthopaedic Hospl
Regent's Pk
W1 93 B3 238 D5
Stanmore HA7 9 C2
Royal National TNE
Hospl The
WC1 94 B4 233 C2
Royal Nat TN&E Hospl
The W5 87 C2
Royal Naval Pl SE14 141 B5
Royal Oak Ct
Dagenham RM8 80 C6
9 Shoreditch N1 95 C4
Royal Oak Mews 9
TW11 175 A5
Royal Oak Pl SE22 162 B5
Royal Oak Rd
Bexley DA6 147 C1
DA6 169 B6
5 Hackney E8 74 B2
Royal Oak Sta W2 91 D2
Royal Oak Yd SE1 253 A1
Royal Obsy The*
SE10 142 B5
Royal Opera Arc
SW1 249 C4
Royal Orchard Cl
SW18 157 A4
Royal Par
Blackheath Vale
SE3 142 D3
Chislehurst BR7 189 A3
11 Dagenham RM10 81 D2
Ealing W5 88 A4
Fulham SW6 264 A4
Royal Park Prim Sch
DA14 169 A1
Royal Par 12 TW9 132 C4
Royal Pl 11 SE10 142 A5
Royal Rd
Kennington SE17 138 D6
Newham E16 99 D1
Sidcup DA14 168 D1
Teddington TW11 174 B5
Royal Route HA9 66 B4
Royal Russell Sch
CR0 222 B3
Royal Sch Hampstead
The NW3 70 B4
Royal St SE1 116 B3 260 D6
Royal Tower Lo 3
SE1 118 A6
Royalty Ho W1 239 C1
Royalty Mews W1 239 C1
Royalty Studios W11 91 A1
Royal United Services
Mus* SW1 250 A3
Royal Veterinary Coll
NW1 93 D6 232 C5
Royal Victoria Pl 7
E16 121 B5
Royal Victoria Sq
E16 121 B6
Royal Victoria Sta
E16 121 A6
Royal Victor Pl E3 96 D5
Royal Wlk SM6 219 B5
Roycraft Ave IG11 101 D5
Roycroft Cl
Streatham SW2 160 C3
Woodford E18 37 B2
Roydene Rd SE18 123 C1
Roydon Cl 7 SW11 136 D3
Roy Gdns IG2 57 D4
Roy Gr TW12 173 D4
Royle Cres W13 87 A3
Roymount Ct TW2 152 C1
Roy Ridley Ho 6
SW4 137 D2
Roy Sq E14 119 A6
Royston Ave
Carshalton SM1 218 B5
Chingford E4 35 D5
Wallington SM6 219 D4
Royston Cl
Cranford TW5 128 B4
Walton-on-T KT12 194 A1
Royston Ct
Hinchley Wood
KT10 212 D6
New Cross SE4 141 B3
1 Newham E13 99 A6
Redbridge IG1 55 D3

Royston Ct *continued*
3 Richmond TW9 132 B4
Ruislip HA5 40 C2
Tolworth KT6 214 C6
Royston Gdns IG1 55 D3
Royston Gr HA5 23 C4
Royston Ho
Friern Barnet N11 31 A6
14 SE15 140 A6
Royston Lo SW19 180 A4
Royston Park Rd
HA5 23 C5
Royston Par IG1 55 D3
Royston Prim Sch
SE20 184 D2
Royston Rd
Penge SE20 184 D2
Richmond TW10 154 A6
Royston St 24 E2 96 C5
Roystons The KT5 198 D4
Rozel Ct 3 N1 95 C6
Rozelle Ct 1 CR7 204 C3
Rozel Rd SW4 137 C2
Rubastic Rd UB2 106 C3
Rubens Rd UB5 84 D5
Rubens St SE6 163 B2
Rubin Pl 14 EN3 7 C6
Ruby Ct TW13 149 D1
Ruby Rd E17 53 C6
Ruby St SE15 140 B6
Stonebridge NW10 67 A1
Ruby Triangle SE15 140 B6
Ruckholt Cl E10 75 D5
Ruckholt Rd E10 75 D5
Rucklidge Ave NW10 90 A5
Rudall Cres NW3 70 B4
Rudbeck Ho 11
SE15 140 A5
Ruddington Cl E5 75 A4
Ruddock Cl HA8 27 A3
Ruddstreet Cl SE18 123 A2
Rudge Ho 1 SE16 118 A3
Rudgwick Terr
NW8 92 C6 230 B5
Rudhall Ho 4 SW2 160 C5
Rudland Rd DA7 147 D2
Rudloe Rd SW12 159 C4
Rudolf Pl SW8 270 B5
Rudolph Ct SE22 162 B4
Rudolph Rd E13 98 D5
Paddington NW6 91 C5
Rudstone Ho 10 E3 97 D4
Rudyard Ct SE1 252 D1
Rudyard Gr NW7 27 A4
Ruegg Ho 5 SE18 144 C6
Ruffetts Cl CR2 222 B1
Ruffetts The CR2 222 B1
Ruffle Cl UB7 104 B4
Rufford Cl HA3 43 A3
Rufford St N1 94 A6 233 B6
Rufford Street Mews
N1 72 A1
Rufford Twr 5 W3 110 D5
Rufforth Ct 1 NW9 27 C2
Rufus Bsns Ctr
SW18 157 D2
Rufus Cl HA4 63 A5
Rufus Ho SE1 263 D6
Rufus St N1 95 C4
Rugby Ave
Edmonton N9 17 D3
Northolt UB6 64 B2
Wembley HA0 65 C4
Rugby Cl HA1 42 C5
Rugby Gdns RM9 80 C2
Rugby Mans W14 254 B4
Rugby Rd
Bedford Pk W4 111 C4
Dagenham RM9 80 C2
Queensbury NW9 44 D5
Twickenham TW1, TW2,
TW7 152 C5
Rugby St WC1 94 B3 240 C5
Rugg St E14 119 C6
Rugless Ho 2 E14 120 A4
Rugmere 4 NW1 71 A1
RUISLIP 39 B2
Ruislip Cl UB6 85 D3
RUISLIP COMMON 39 B4
Ruislip Ct HA4 61 D6
RUISLIP GARDENS 61 D5
Ruislip Gardens Prim
Sch HA4 61 D4
Ruislip Gardens Sta
HA4 62 A4
Ruislip Lido Rly*
HA4 39 B5
Ruislip Lido* HA4,
HA5 39 B5
RUISLIP MANOR 40 A1
Ruislip Manor Sta
HA4 40 A1
Ruislip Rd E
Ealing UB6, W7 86 D3
Greenford UB6 86 B3
Ruislip Rd UB6, UB5 85 C4
Ruislip Sta HA4 39 D1

Ruislip St SW17 180 D6
Rumball Ho 14 SE5 139 C5
Rumbold Rd
SW6 135 D5 265 D3
Rum Cl E1 118 C6
Rumford Ho SE1 262 A5
Rumsey Cl TW12 173 B4
Rumsey Rd SW9 138 B2
Runacres Ct SE17 262 A1
Runbury Circ NW9 67 B6
Runcorn Cl N17 52 B5
Runcorn Pl W11 244 A6
Rundell Cres NW4 46 B4
Rundell Twr SW8 270 C2
Runes Cl CR4 202 C5
Runnelfield HA1 64 C5
Running Horse Yd 12
TW8 132 A6
Runnymede Cl TW2 151 D4
Runnymede Cres
SW16 182 A2
Runnymede Ct
Roehampton
SW15 156 A3
1 Wallington SM6 219 B2
Runnymede Gdns
Greenford UB6 86 C5
Twickenham TW2 151 D4
Runnymede Ho
Hackney E9 75 A4
Richmond TW10 154 C6
Runnymede SW19 180 B2
Runnymede Rd
TW2 151 D5
Runway The HA4 62 C3
Rupack St 3 SE16 118 C4
Rupert Ave 6 HA9 66 A3
Rupert Ct W1 249 C6
Rupert Gdns SW9 138 D3
Rupert Ho SE11 261 B3
8 Upper Holloway
N19 71 D5
Rupert Rd
Bedford Pk W4 111 C3
Paddington NW6 91 B5
Upper Holloway N19 71 D6
Rupert St
W1 115 D6 249 C6
Rural Way SW16 181 B3
Rusbridge Cl E8 74 A3
Ruscoe Ho 12 SW27 182 D5
Ruscoe Rd E16 98 D1
Ruscombe Way
TW14 149 D4
Rusham Rd SW12 158 D4
Rushbrook Cres E17 35 B2
Rushbrook Ho 20
SW8 137 D3
Rushbrook Rd SE9 167 A2
Rushbury Ct 4
TW12 173 C2
Rushby Ct SW4 270 A1
Rush Common Mews 18
SW2 160 B4
Rushcroft Rd
Brixton SW2,
SW9 138 C1
Chingford E4 35 D3
Rush Croft Sch E4 35 D3
Rushcutters Ct 18
SE16 119 A2
Rushden Cl SE19 183 B3
Rushdene Ave EN4 14 C4
Rushdene Cl UB5 84 C5
Rushdene Cres UB5 84 C4
Rushdene Rd HA5 40 D3
Rushdene SE2 124 D3
Rushden Gdns
Ilford IG5 56 C6
Mill Hill NW7 28 C4
Rushen Wlk SM5 202 B1
Rushet Rd BR5 190 A1
Rushett Cl KT7 197 B1
Rushett Rd KT7 197 B2
Rushey Cl KT3 199 B5
Rushey Gn SE6 163 D4
Rushey Green Prim Sch
SE6 163 D3
Rushey Hill EN2 4 B1
Rushey Mead SE4 163 C6
Rushford Rd SE4 163 B5
Rush Green Rd RM7, RM8,
RM10 59 D1
Rushgrove Ave NW9 45 D5
Rushgrove Ct NW9 45 C4
Rushgrove St SE18 122 B2
Rush Hill Mews 3
SW11 137 A2
Rush Hill Rd SW11 137 A2
Rushlake Ho 3
SW11 137 A3
Rushley Cl BR2 226 A4
Rushman Villas
KT3 199 D5

Rushmead 5 E2 96 B4
Rushmead Cl CR0 221 D4
Rushmead TW10 153 B1
Rushmere Ct KT4 216 A6
Rushmere Ho 2
SW15 156 A3
Rushmere Pl SW19 178 D5
Rushmon Pl SM3 217 A2
Rushmoor Cl HA5 40 B5
Rushmore Cl BR1 210 A6
Rushmore Cres 9
E5 74 D4
Rushmore Ho
9 Kentish Town
N7 71 D3
W14 254 B5
Rushmore Prim Sch
E5 74 D4
Rushmore Rd
Clapton Pk E5 74 D4
Hackney E5 75 A4
Rusholme Ave RM10 81 C5
Rusholme Gr SE19 183 C5
Rusholme Rd SW15 157 A5
Rushout Ave HA3 43 B3
Rush The SW20 179 B2
Rushton Ho 26 SW8 137 D3
Rushton St
N1 95 B5 235 D4
Rushworth St
SE1 116 D4 251 D1
Rushy Meadow La
SM5 218 C5
Rushy Meadow Prim
Sch SM5 218 C5
Ruskin Ave DA16 146 A3
Feltham TW14 149 D5
Plashet E12 78 A2
Richmond TW9 132 C5
Ruskin Cl NW11 47 D3
Ruskin Ct
Herne Hill SE5 139 B2
SE9 166 B5
Southgate N21 16 B4
Ruskin Dr
North Cheam KT4 216 C6
Orpington BR6 227 C5
Welling DA16 146 A2
Ruskin Gdns
Ealing W5 87 D3
Harrow HA3 44 B5
Ruskin Gr DA16 146 A3
Ruskin Ho SW1 259 D3
Ruskin Par CR0 221 B3
Ruskin Park Ho SE5 139 B2
Ruskin Rd
Belvedere DA17 125 C2
Croydon CR0 220 D6
Isleworth TW7 130 D2
Southall UB1 107 A6
Tottenham N17 33 D2
Wallington SM5 219 A3
Ruskin Way SW19 180 B2
Ruskin Wlk BR2 210 B3
Edmonton N9 18 A2
Herne Hill SE24 161 A6
Rusland Ave BR6 227 B5
Rusland Hts HA1 42 C5
Rusland Park Rd
HA1 42 C5
Rusper Cl
Cricklewood NW2 68 C5
Stanmore HA7 25 C6
Rusper Ct SW9 138 A3
Rusper Rd
Dagenham RM9 80 C2
Tottenham N17, N22 51 A6
Russel Cl BR3 208 A6
Russel Ct N14 15 D6
Russell Ave N22 32 D1
Russell Cl
Bexleyheath DA7 147 C1
Chiswick W4 133 D6
Greenwich SE7 143 C5
Ruislip HA4 62 C6
Stonebridge NW10 67 A1
Russell Ct
Battersea SW11 268 B1
Bloomsbury WC1 240 A5
Bromley BR1 186 D3
12 New Barnet EN5 2 A1
5 Peckham SE15 140 B3
St James SW1 249 B3
Streatham SW16 182 B5
Surbiton KT6 198 A2
Wallington SM6 219 C3
4 Walthamstow E10 53 D2
Wembley HA0 66 A1
Russell Gdns
East Barnet N20 14 C2
Ilford IG2 57 B2
Russell Gdns Mews
W14 113 A3 254 A6
Russell Gdns
Richmond TW10 153 C2
Temple Fortune
NW11 47 A3
W14 113 A3 254 A6
West Drayton UB7 104 C1
Russell Gr
33 Brixton SW9 138 C4
Edgware NW7 27 C6
Russell Ho
21 Poplar E14 97 C1
SW1 259 A2
Russell Kerr Cl W4 133 A5
Russell La N20 14 D2
Russell Lo
5 Chingford E4 20 A2
SE1 262 C6
Russell Mans WC1 240 B4
Russell Mead HA3 24 D2
Russell Par NW11 47 A3
Russell Pickering Ho 2
SW4 138 A2
Russell Pl
Hampstead NW3 70 C3
Rotherhithe SE16 119 A3
Russell Rd
Bowes Pk N13 32 B4
Buckhurst Hill IG9 21 C3
Chingford Hatch E4 35 B6
Crouch End N8 49 D3
East Barnet N20 14 C2
Enfield EN1 5 D5
Leyton E10 53 D3
Merton SW19 179 C3
Mitcham CR4 202 C6
Newham E16 99 B1
Northolt UB5 64 A3
Shepperton TW17 193 A2
Tottenham N15 51 C4
Twickenham TW1,
TW2 152 D5
W14 113 A3 254 B5
Walthamstow E17 53 B6
Walton-on-T KT12 194 A3
West Hendon NW9 45 D3
Russell Sch The
TW10 153 D3
Russell Square Ho
WC1 240 A5
Russell Square Mans
WC1 240 B4
Russell Square Sta
WC1 94 A3 240 A5
Russell Sq
WC1 94 A3 240 A5
Russell St
WC2 116 A6 250 B6
Russell's Wharf 2
W9 91 B3
Russell Way SM1 217 D3
Russell Wlk 4
TW10 154 B5
Russet Ave TW16,
TW17 193 C6
Russet Cl UB10 83 A3
Russet Cres N7 72 B3
Russet Ct
6 Barnet EN4 2 C1
Dollis Hill NW2 68 B5
Feltham TW13 149 C1
Russet Dr CR0 207 A1
Russet Ho TW3 129 B1
Russet House Sch EN1 6 B4
Russets Cl E4 36 B6
Russettings 1 HA5 23 B3
Russett Way SE13 141 D3
Russia Dock Rd
SE16 119 A5
Russia La E2 96 C5
Russia Row EC2 242 B1
Russington Rd
TW17 193 B3
Rusthall Ave W4 111 B3
Rusthall Cl CR0 206 C3
Rusthall Mans 3
W4 111 B2
Rustic Ave SW16 181 B3
Rustic Pl HA0 65 D4
Rustic Wlk E16 99 B1
Rustington Wlk
SM4 201 B2
Ruston Ave KT5 198 D2
Ruston Gdns N14 15 A5
Ruston Mews W11 91 A1
Ruston Rd SE18 122 A3
Ruston St E3 97 B6
Rust Sq SE5 139 B5
Rutford Rd SW16 182 A5
Ruth Cl HA7 44 B5
Ruth Ct 16 E3 97 A5
Rutherford Cl
Hillingdon UB8 82 B3
Sutton SM2 218 B2
Rutherford Ct
Mitcham SW19 180 B3
Southgate N21 16 B6
Rutherford Ho
12 Bethnal Green
E1 96 B3
Teddington TW11 174 D5
4 Wembley HA9 67 A5
Rutherford St
SW1 115 D2 259 C4
Rutherford Twr 8
UB1 85 D1
Rutherford Way
Bushey WD23 8 C3
Wembley HA9 66 C4
Rutherglen Rd SE2 146 A6
Rutherwyke Cl
KT17 216 A2
Ruth Ho W10 91 A3
Ruthin Cl NW9 45 C3
Ruthin Rd SE3 143 A6
Ruthven St E9 96 D6
Rutland Ave DA15 168 A4
Rutland Cl
Chessington KT9 214 B2
DA5 168 D3
Mitcham SW19 180 C3
Mortlake SW14 133 A2
Rutland Ct
15 Acton W3 88 C1
Chislehurst BR7 188 C2
Enfield EN3 18 B6
Herne Hill SE5 139 B1
Sidcup SE9 167 A2
SW7 247 B1
Twickenham TW2 152 C1
Rutland Dr
Morden SM4 201 C2
Richmond TW10 154 A3
Rutland Gate
Beckenham BR2 208 D5
Belvedere DA17 125 D1
Rutland Gate Mews
SW7 247 A1
Rutland Gate
SW7 114 C4 247 B1
Rutland Gdns
Dagenham RM8 80 C3
Ealing W13 87 A2
Rutland Gdns Mews
SW7 247 B1
Rutland Gdns
South Croydon
CR0 221 C4
Stoke Newington N4 51 A3
SW7 114 C4 247 B1
Rutland Gr W6 112 B1
Rutland Ho
Edgware HA8 26 B4
6 Northolt UB5 63 C2
2 Penge SE20 184 C2
10 Putney SW15 156 C4
Tolworth KT6 198 C1
W8 255 C5
15 Woolwich SE18 122 B2
Rutland Lo
Forest Hill SE6 163 B2
Teddington TW11 174 C5
Rutland Mews E
SW7 257 B6
Rutland Mews S
SW7 257 A6
Rutland Mews W
SW7 257 A6
Rutland Park Gdns 1
NW2 68 C2
Rutland Park Mans 2
NW2 68 C2
Rutland Pk
Forest Hill SE6 163 B2
Willesden NW2 68 C2
Rutland Pl
Bushey WD23 8 B3
EC1 241 D4
Rutland Rd
Forest Gate E7 77 D1
Harrow HA1 42 A3
Hayes UB3 105 B2
Ilford IG1 78 D5
Mitcham SW19 180 C3
Southall UB1 85 C2
South Hackney E9 96 D6
Twickenham TW2 152 B2
Walthamstow E17 53 C3
Wanstead E11 55 B4
Rutland St SW7 257 B6
Rutland Studios
NW10 90 A4
Rutland Wlk SE6 163 B2
Rutley Cl SE11 138 D6
Rutlish Rd SW19 179 C2
Rutlish Sch SW20 179 B1
Rutter Gdns CR4 202 B5
Rutters Cl UB7 104 C4
Rutt's Terr SE14 140 D4
Rutts The WD23 8 B3
Ruvigny Gdns SW15 134 D2
Ruvigny Mans
SW15 134 D2
Ruxbury Ct TW15 148 A1
RUXLEY 191 A3
Ruxley Cl
Chessington
KT19 214 D3
Sidcup DA14 191 A4
Ruxley Cnr DA14 191 A4
Ruxley Corner Ind Est
DA14 190 D4
Ruxley Cres KT10 213 B1
Ruxley Ct KT19 215 A3
Ruxley Gdns TW17 193 A4
Ruxley La KT19 215 B3
Ruxley Mews KT19 214 D3
Ruxley Ridge KT10 213 A1
Ryall's Ct N20 14 D1
Ryan Cl Ruislip HA4 40 B1
SE9 143 C1
Ryan Ct SW16 182 A3
Ryan Dr TW8 131 A6
Ryan Ho 3 HA1 42 D4
Ryarsh Cres BR6 227 C4
Rycott Path SE22 162 A4
Rycroft Way N17 51 D6
Ryculff Sq SE3 142 D3
Rydal Cl NW4 29 A2
Rydal Cres UB6 87 C5
Rydal Ct Edgware HA8 26 B5
Wembley HA9 44 A2
Rydal Dr DA7 147 C4
West Wickham BR4 224 C6
Rydal Gdns
Kingsbury NW9 45 C4
Kingston u T SW15 177 C5
Twickenham TW2,
TW3 151 D5
Wembley HA9 43 C1
Rydal Ho 25 SW8 137 D3
Rydal Lo N17 34 A3
Rydal Rd SW16 181 D6
Rydal Water NW1 232 A1
Rydal Way Enfield EN3 18 C5
Ruislip HA4 62 C4
Ryde Ho 1 NW6 91 C6
Rydens Ho SE9 165 C1
Rydens Rd KT12 194 D1
Ryde Pl TW1 153 D5
Ryder Cl BR1 187 B5
Ryder Ct Leyton E10 75 D6
SW1 249 B4
Ryder Dr SE16 118 B1
Ryder Ho
18 Bethnal Green
E1 96 C3
5 Merton SW19 179 D2
Ryder's Terr
NW8 92 A5 229 A4
Ryder St SW1 249 B4
Ryder Yd SW1 249 B4
Ryde Vale Rd SW12 159 C2
Rydon Mews SW19 178 C3
Rydons Cl SE9 144 A2
Rydon St N1 235 B6
Rydston Cl 2 N7 72 B1
Rye Cl DA5 169 D5
Ryecotes Mead
SE21 161 C3
Ryecroft Ave TW2 151 D3
Ryecroft Cres EN5 12 B6
Ryecroft Rd BR5 211 B3
Lewisham SE13 164 A6
South Norwood
SW16 182 C4
Ryecroft St
SW6 135 D4 265 C1
Rye Ct BR3 185 B2
Ryedale Ct 7 TW12 173 C2
Ryedale SE22 162 B5
Ryefield Ave UB10 60 D1
Ryefield Cres HA5,
HA6 22 A1
Ryefield Ct HA6 22 A1
Ryefield Path 7
SW15 156 A3
Ryefield Prim Sch
UB10 83 B6
Ryefield Rd SE19 183 A4
Ryegates 2 SE15 140 B3
Ryehill Ct KT3 199 D2
Rye Hill Pk SE15 140 C1
Rye Ho 17 SE16 118 C4
Rye La SE15 140 A3
Ryeland Cl UB7 82 A1
Ryelands Cres SE12 165 C5
Ryelands Prim Sch
SE25 206 B4
Rye Lane Mkt SE15 140 A3
Rye Oak Sch SE15 140 B2
Rye Rd SE15 140 D1
Rye The N14 15 C4
Rye Way HA8 26 B4
Rye Wlk SW15 156 D6
Ryfold Rd SW19 157 C1
Ryhope Rd N11 31 B6
Ryland Cl TW13 171 D6
Rylandes Rd NW2 68 A5
Ryland Ho 11 SW16 181 C5
Ryland Rd NW5 71 B2
Rylett Cres W12 111 D3
Rylett Rd W12 111 D3
Rylston Rd
Edmonton N13 17 B1
SW6 135 B6 264 C5
Rylton Ho KT12 194 A1
Rymer Rd CR0 205 C2
Rymer St SE24 160 D5
Rymill St E16 122 C5
Rysbrack St SW1 257 C6
Rythe Cl KT9 213 C1
Rythe Ct KT7 197 A2
Rythe Ho 7 BR1 186 B5
Rythe Rd KT10 212 C3

S

Saatchi Gallery Duke of
York's HQ*
SW3 114 D1 257 D2
Sabah Ct TW15 170 C6
Sabbarton St 9 E16 98 D1
Sabella Ct E3 97 B5
Sabine Rd SW11 137 A2
Sable Cl TW4 128 C2
Sable Ct 3 KT3 199 C4
Sable St N1 72 D1
Sach Rd E5 74 B6
Sacketts Ho 24
SW9 138 C4
Sackville Ave BR2 209 A1
Sackville Cl HA2 64 B5
Sackville Gdns IG1 56 B1
Sackville Ho
Hornsey N8 50 A5
16 Streatham SW16 160 A1
Sackville Rd SM2 217 C1
Sackville St
W1 115 C6 249 B5
Sacred Heart High Sch
W6 112 C2
Sacred Heart Jun Sch
W6 112 D2
Sacred Heart Language
Coll The HA3 24 C1
Sacred Heart Prim Sch,
Battersea SW11 136 C3
Sacred Heart RC Prim
Sch
East Barnet N20 14 C2
Islington N7 72 B3
Putney SW15 156 A6
Ruislip HA4 61 C6
Teddington TW11 175 B3
West Barnes KT3 200 A5
Sacred Heart RC Sec
Sch SE5 139 A4
Saddlebrook Pk
TW16 171 C3
Saddlers Cl
Barnet EN5 12 B6
Borehamwood WD6 11 B5
Pinner HA5 23 C5
Saddlers Mews SW8 270 B2
Teddington KT1 175 C2
Wembley HA0 64 D4
Saddlers Path WD6 11 B6
Saddlescombe Way
N12 29 C5
Sadler Cl CR4 180 D1
Sadler Ho
17 Bromley E3 97 D4
EC1 234 C2
Sadlers Ho EN1 17 C6
Sadlers Ride KT8 174 A1
Saffron Ave E14 120 B6
Saffron Cl
Temple Fortune
NW11 47 B3
Thornton Heath CR0 204 A3
Saffron Ct
East Bedfont
TW14 149 A4
10 Kingsland N1 73 B2
Stratford E15 76 C3
Saffron Hill
EC1 94 C2 241 B4
Saffron Ho 6 TW9 132 D4
Saffron St EC1 241 B4
Saffron Way KT6 197 D1
Saffron Wharf SE1 253 D2
Sage Cl 7 E6 100 B2
Sage Mews SE22 161 D6
Sage St E1 118 C6
Sage Way WC1 233 C1
Sage Yd KT6 198 B1
Sahara Ct UB1 107 A6
Saigasso Cl E16 99 D1
Sailacre Ho 10
SE10 120 D1
Sail Ct 10 E14 120 B6
Sailmakers Ct SW6 136 A2
Sail St SE11 116 B2 260 D4
Saimet 3 NW9 27 D2
Sainfoin Rd SW17 159 A2
Sainsbury Rd SE19 183 C5
St Agatha's Dr KT2 176 B4
St Agatha's Gr SM5 202 D1
St Agatha's RC Prim Sch
KT2 176 B4
St Agnes Cl E9 96 C6
St Agnes Pl SE11 138 D6
St Agnes RC Prim Sch
E3 97 D4
St Agnes RC Sch
NW2 69 A5
St Aidans Ct IG11 102 B5
St Aidan's Prim Sch
N4 50 C2
St Aidan's RC Prim Sch
IG1 57 B1
St Aidan's Rd
East Dulwich
SE22 162 B6
West Ealing W13 109 B4
St Aiden's Ct W13 109 C4
St Albans Ave
Bedford Pk W4 111 B3
Feltham TW13 172 D5
St Alban's Ave E6 100 C4
St Alban's CE Prim Sch
EC1 94 C2 241 A4
St Alban's Cl NW11 47 C1
St Alban's Cres IG8 37 A2
St Albans Cres N22 32 C2
St Alban's Gdns
TW11 175 A5
St Alban's Gr
Carshalton SM5 202 C2
W8 113 D3 255 D6
St Albans Ho 2
SW16 182 C6
St Albans La NW11 47 C1
St Albans Mans W8 255 D6
St Alban's Pl
N1 94 D6 234 C5
St Alban's RC Prim Sch
KT8 196 A4
St Albans Rd
Barnet EN5 1 A3
Cheam SM1 217 B4
St Alban's Rd
Dagenham NW10 89 C6
Dartmouth Pk NW5 71 B5
St Albans Rd
Ilford IG3 57 D2
Kingston u T KT2 176 A4
St Alban's Rd IG8 37 A3
St Alban's St SW1 249 C5
St Albans Studios
W8 255 D6
St Albans Terr W6 264 A6
St Alban's Villas
NW5 71 A5
St Alfege Pas SE10 142 A6
St Alfege Rd SE7 143 D6
St Alfege with St Peter's
CE Prim Sch
SE10 142 A
St Aloysius RC Coll
N19 49 C
St Aloysius RC Inf Sch
NW1 93 D4 232 C
St Aloysius RC Jun Sch
NW1 93 D5 232 C
St Alphage Ct NW9 45 B
St Alphage Gdn EC2 242 B
St Alphage Highwalk
EC2 242 B
St Alphage Wlk HA8 27 A
St Alphege Rd N9 18 C
St Alphonsus Rd
SW4 137 D
St Amunds Cl SE6 185 C
St Andrew & St Francis
CE Prim Sch NW2 68 A
St Andrews Ave HA0 65 A
St Andrew's (Barnsbury)
CE Prim Sch
N1 94 B6 233 D
St Andrew's CE Prim
Sch
Enfield EN1 5 C
Osidge N14 15 D
Stockwell SW9 138 A
St Andrew's CE Sch
N20 13 B
St Andrews Chambers
W1 239 B
St Andrews Cl 25
SE16 118 B
St Andrew's Cl NW2 68 B
St Andrews Cl SE28 102 D
St Andrew's Cl 2
TW7 130 C
St Andrews Cl KT7 197 B
St Andrew's Cl N12 30 A
St Andrews Cl
Ruislip HA4 62 D
Stanmore HA7 25 C
St Andrew's Cl
TW17 193 B

St Andrews Cl SW19 179 D4
St Andrew's Ct SM5 218 C5
St Andrews Ct W4 133 A4
St Andrew's Ct
  2 Higham Hill E17 35 A1
  Kingston u T KT3 199 D6
  2 Wandsworth SW18 158 A2
St Andrews Dr HA7 25 C2
St Andrew's Greek Sch NW1 71 C2
St Andrew's Gr N16 51 B1
St Andrew's High Sch CR0 220 D4
St Andrew's Hill EC4 94 D1 241 D1
St Andrews Ho
  11 Bermondsey SE16 118 B3
  Bromley BR1 187 B4
St Andrew's Hospl E3 97 D3
St Andrews Mans 9 E5 74 B4
St Andrew's Mans W1 238 A3
St Andrews Mews SE3 143 A5
St Andrew's Mews N16 51 C1
St Andrews Mews 4 SW12 159 D3
St Andrew's Pl NW1 238 D6
St Andrews RC Prim Sch SW16 182 A5
St Andrews Rd SM5 218 C5
St Andrew's Rd 3 CR0 221 A4
St Andrews Rd DA14 168 D1
St Andrew's Rd
  Dagenham W3 89 C1
  Enfield EN1 5 B2
  Hanwell W7 108 C4
St Andrews Rd E17 35 A1
St Andrew's Rd
  Hillingdon UB10 82 B6
  Leytonstone E11 54 C3
  Newham E13 99 B4
St Andrews Rd N9 18 C4
St Andrew's Rd
  Redbridge IG1 56 B2
  Surbiton KT6 197 D3
  Temple Fortune NW11 47 B3
St Andrews Rd UB10 60 B1
St Andrew's Rd W14 264 B6
St Andrews Rd NW9 45 B1
St Andrew's Rd NW2 68 B2
St Andrew's & St Mark's CE Jun Sch KT6 197 D4
St Andrew's Sq
  Notting Hill W11 91 A1
  Surbiton KT6 197 D3
St Andrew St EC4 241 B3
St Andrews Terr WD19 22 C5
St Andrew's Twr UB1 108 A6
St Andrews Way E3 97 D3
St Andrew's Wharf SE1 253 D2
St Angela's Ursuline Convent Sch E7 77 B2
St Anna Rd EN5 12 D6
St Anne RC Prim Sch E1 96 A3
St Annes Catholic High Sch for Girls (Upper) N13 32 C6
St Anne's CE Prim Sch SW18 157 D6
St Anne's Cl N6 71 A5
St Annes Cl WD19 22 C6
St Anne's Ct NW6 91 A6
St Annes Ct 8 SM2 217 D2
St Anne's Ct W1 239 C1
St Anne's Flats NW1 232 C2
St Annes Gdns NW10 88 B4
St Anne's Pas E14 97 B1
St Anne's RC High Sch for Girls EN2 5 B1
St Anne's RC Prim Sch SE11 138 B6 270 C6
St Anne's Rd
  Leyton E11 76 B6
  Wembley HA0 65 D3
St Anne's Row E14 97 B1
St Anne St E14 97 B1
St Anne's Trad Est 25 E14 97 B1
St Ann's IG11 101 A6
St Ann's CE Prim Sch N15 51 B4
St Ann's Cres SW18 158 A5
St Ann's Ct NW4 46 B6
St Ann's Ctr HA1 42 C3
St Ann's Gdns NW5 71 A2
St Ann's General Hospl N4, N15 51 A4
St Ann's Hill SW18 158 A5
St Ann's Ho WC1 234 A1
St Ann's La SW1 259 D5
St Ann's Park Rd SW18 158 A5
St Ann's Rd 2 IG11 101 A6
St Anns Rd SW13 133 D4
St Ann's Rd
  Edmonton N9 17 D3
  Harrow HA1 42 C3
  Shepherd's Bush W11 112 D6
  Tottenham N15 51 B4
St Ann's Sch
  Ealing W7 108 C5
  Morden SM4 201 D4
St Ann's St SW1 115 D3 259 D6
St Ann's Terr NW8 92 B5 229 D4
St Ann's Villas W11 113 A5 244 A3
St Ann's Way CR2 220 D2
St Anselm RC Prim Sch UB2 107 B3
St Anselm's Ct SW16 182 A5
St Anselm's Pl W1 248 C6
St Anselm's RC Prim Sch
  Harrow HA1 42 C2
  Upper Tooting SW17 159 A1
St Anselms Rd UB3 105 D4
St Anthony's Ave IG8 37 C3
St Anthony's Cl 8 E1 118 A5
St Anthonys Cl SW17 158 C2
St Anthony's Ct
  2 Balham SW12 159 A5
  Orpington BR6 226 D6
  Upper Tooting SW17 159 A2
St Anthony's Flats NW1 232 C3
St Anthony's Hospl KT4 200 D1
St Anthony's RC Prim Sch
  East Dulwich SE22 162 A5
  Penge SE20 184 B2
  Upton E7 77 B1
St Anthony's Way TW14 127 D1
St Antony's RC Prim Sch IG8 37 A6
St Antony's Rd E7 77 B1
St Arvans Cl CR0 221 C5
St Asaph Ct SE4 140 D2
St Asaph Rd SE4 140 D2
St Aubins Ct N1 235 D6
St Aubyn's Ave
  Hounslow TW3, TW4 151 C6
  Wimbledon SW19 179 B5
St Aubyns Cl BR6 227 D5
St Aubyn's Ct SW19 179 A4
St Aubyns Gdns BR6 227 D6
St Aubyns E18 54 D5
St Aubyn's Rd SE19 183 D4
St Aubyn's Sch IG8 36 D3
St Audrey Ave DA7 147 C3
St Augustine of Canterbury CE Prim Sch DA17 125 B2
St Augustine's Ave
  BR1, BR2 210 A4
  Ealing W5 88 A4
  South Croydon CR2 221 A1
  Wembley HA9 66 A5
St Augustine's CE High Sch NW6 91 C5
St Augustine's CE Prim Sch NW6 91 D5
St Augustines Ct BR3 185 A1
St Augustine's Ct E11 54 D1
St Augustines Ct 4 EN5 14 A6
St Augustine's Ho NW1 232 C2
  Upper Tooting SW17 180 D6
St Augustine's RC Prim Sch
  Ilford IG2 56 D4
  W6 135 A6 264 B5
St Augustine's Rd
  Camden Town NW1 71 D1
  DA17 125 B2
St Augustines's RC Prim Sch SE6 186 A5
St Austell Cl HA8 26 B1
St Austell Rd SE13 142 B3
St Awdry's Rd IG11 79 B1
St Barnabas CE Prim Sch SW1 115 A1 258 B2
St Barnabas Cl
  Beckenham BR3 186 A1
  11 Dulwich Village SE22 161 C6
St Barnabas Ct HA3 24 A2
St Barnabas' Gdns KT8 195 C4
St Barnabas Ho CR4 181 A3
St Barnabas Rd
  Mitcham CR4 181 A3
  Sutton SM1 218 B3
  Walthamstow E17 53 C3
  Woodford IG8 37 C3
St Barnabas & St Philip's CE Prim Sch W8 113 C3 255 A5
St Barnabas St SW1 258 B2
St Barnabas Terr E9 74 D3
St Barnabas Villas SW8 138 A4 270 B2
St Bartholomew's CE Prim Sch SE26 184 C6
St Bartholomews CE Prim Sch SE26 162 C1
St Bartholomew's Cl SE26 184 C6
St Bartholomews Ct 6 E6 100 A6
St Bartholomew's Hospl EC1 94 D2 241 D3
St Bartholomew's Rd E6 100 B5
St Bede's RC Inf Sch SW12 159 D3
St Bede's RC Prim Sch RM6 58 C4
St Benedict's Cl SW17 181 A5
St Benedict's Jun Sch W5 87 C2
St Benedict's Sch W5 87 D2
St Benets Cl SW17 158 C2
St Benet's Gr SM5 202 A2
St Benet's Pl EC3 252 D6
St Bernadette RC Jun Sch SW12 159 C4
St Bernadette's Prim Sch HA3 44 B5
St Bernadette's RC Prim Sch UB10 82 D6
St Bernard Ho 6 E14 120 A3
St Bernards Cl 8 SE27 183 B6
St Bernards Ho 1 KT6 214 A6
St Bernard's Rd E6 99 D6
St Bernards CR0 221 C5
St Blaise Ave BR1 187 B1
St Bonaventure's RC Sch E7 77 A1
St Boniface RC Prim Sch SW17 180 D5
St Botolph St E1, EC3 95 D1 243 C2
St Brelades Ct N1 235 D6
St Bride's Ave EC4 241 C1
  Edgware HA8 26 B2
St Brides Cl DA18 124 D4
St Bride's Pas EC4 241 C1
St Bride St EC4 94 D1 241 C2
St Catherines Cl
  Chessington KT9 213 D2
  Upper Tooting SW17 158 C2
St Catherines Ct TW13 150 A3
St Catherine's Ct 8 W4 111 C3
St Catherine's Dr SE14 140 D3
St Catherines Farm Ct HA4 39 A3
St Catherines Mews SW3 257 C4
St Catherine's RC Sch EN5 1 C1
St Catherine's RC Sch for Girls DA6 169 D6
St Catherines Rd
  Chingford E4 19 C2
  Ruislip HA4 39 B3
St Catherine's Sch TW1 153 A2
St Catherines Twr 5 E10 53 D2
St Cecilia's CE Sch SW18 157 B3
St Cecilia's Cl SM3 201 A1
St Cecilia's RC Prim Sch SM3 216 D6
St Chads Cl KT6 197 C2
St Chad's Gdns RM6 59 A2
St Chad's Pl WC1 233 C2
St Chad's RC Prim Sch SE25 205 C4
St Chad's Rd RM6 59 A2
St Chad's St WC1 233 B2
St Charles' Hospl W10 90 D2
St Charles Pl W10 91 A2
St Charles RC Prim Sch W10 90 D2
St Charles RC Sixth Form Coll W10 90 D2
St Charles Sq W10 90 D2
St Christina's Sch NW8 92 C5 230 B4
St Christopher's Cl TW7 130 C4
St Christophers Ct 15 N19 71 C5
St Christophers Dr UB3 106 B6
St Christophers Gdns CR7 204 C6
St Christopher's Ho NW1 232 C3
St Christopher's Mews SM6 219 C3
St Christopher's Pl W1 238 B2
St Christopher's Sch
  Beckenham BR3 186 A1
  Hampstead NW3 70 B3
  Wembley HA9 66 B5
St Clair Dr KT4 216 B4
St Clair Ho 17 E3 97 B4
St Clair Rd E13 99 B5
St Clair's Rd CR0 221 C6
St Clare Bsns Pk TW12 174 A4
St Clare St EC3 243 C1
St Clement Danes CE Prim Sch WC2 94 B1 240 C1
St Clement & St James CE Prim Sch W11 113 A5 244 A4
St Clements Ct N7 72 B2
St Clement's Ct EC3 252 D6
St Clements Ct
  7 SE14 140 D6
  8 Shepherd's Bush W11 112 D6
St Clements Ho E1 243 C3
  Walton-on-T KT12 194 A2
St Clement's Hts SE26 184 A6
St Clement's La WC2 240 D1
St Clements Mans 3 SW6 134 D6
St Clements St N7 72 C1
St Cloud Rd SE27 183 B6
St Columba's Ct E15 76 C4
St Columbas Ho 2 E17 53 D5
St Columba's RC Boys Sch DA6 169 D6
St Columb's Ho 11 W10 91 A2
St Crispins Cl NW3 70 C4
St Crispin's Cl UB1 85 B1
St Crispins Ct 1 UB1 85 B1
St Cross St EC1 94 C2 241 B4
St Cuthberts Gdns 2 HA5 23 B3
St Cuthberts Rd N13 32 C4
St Cuthbert's Rd NW2 69 B2
St Cuthbert with St Matthias Prim Sch SW5 113 D1 255 C2
St Cyprian's Greek Orthodox Prim Sch CR7 183 A2
St Cyprian's St SW17 180 D6
St Davids Cl
  27 Bermondsey SE16 118 B1
  Wembley HA9 67 A5
St David's Cl BR4 207 D2
St David's Coll BR4 207 D2
St David's Ct
  Bromley BR1 210 D6
  8 Southall UB1 86 A1
St David's Ct *continued*
  1 Walthamstow E17 54 A6
St Davids Ct 5 E11 55 B4
St David's Dr HA8 26 B2
St David's Pl NW4 46 B2
St David's Sch TW15 148 B1
St David's Sq E14 119 D1
St Denis Rd SE27 183 B6
St Dionis Rd SW6 135 B3
St Domingo Ho SE18 122 B3
St Dominic RC Prim Sch NW5 70 D3
St Dominics RC Prim Sch E9 75 A2
St Dominic's Sixth Form Coll (RC) HA1 64 C6
St Donatt's Rd SE14 141 B4
St Dunstan's Alley EC3 253 A5
St Dunstan's Ave W3 111 B6
St Dunstan's CE Prim Sch SM3 217 A1
St Dunstans SM1 217 B2
St Dunstans Cl UB3 105 D2
St Dunstan's Coll SE6 163 C3
St Dunstan's Ct EC4 241 B1
St Dunstan's Gdns W3 111 B6
St Dunstan's Hill
  Cheam SM1, SM3 217 A3
  EC3 253 A5
St Dunstan's La
  Beckenham BR3 208 A4
  EC3 253 A5
St Dunstan's Rd
  Cranford TW5 128 B3
  Feltham TW13 149 D1
  Hammersmith W6 112 D1
  Hanwell W7 108 C4
St Dunstans Rd E7 77 C2
St Dunstan's Rd SE25 205 D5
St Edmund RC Sch E14 119 C2
St Edmunds Ave HA4 39 B3
St Edmunds Cl DA18 124 D4
St Edmund's Cl NW8 230 C5
St Edmunds Cl SW17 158 C2
St Edmund's Ct NW8 230 C5
St Edmunds Dr HA7 25 A2
St Edmund's La TW2 151 D4
St Edmund's RC Prim Sch
  Edmonton N9 18 B3
  Twickenham TW2 151 D4
St Edmunds Rd N9 18 A4
St Edmund's Rd IG1 56 B3
St Edmund's Sq SW13 134 C6
St Edmund's Terr NW8 92 D6 230 C5
St Edward's CE Comp Sch RM7 59 C3
St Edward's Cl NW11 47 C3
St Edwards Ct 3 E10 54 A2
St Edward's Ct NW11 47 C3
St Edwards RC Prim Sch E6 99 C6
St Edward's RC Prim Sch NW1 92 C3 237 B5
St Egberts Way E4 20 A3
St Elizabeth Ct
  North Finchley N12 30 A6
  9 Walthamstow E10 53 D2
St Elizabeth RC Prim Sch E2 96 C5
St Elizabeth's RC Prim Sch TW10 154 B5
St Elmo Rd W12 111 D4
St Elmos Rd SE16 119 A4
St Elphege's RC Inf Sch SM6 220 A2
St Elphege's RC Jun Sch SM6 220 A2
SS Peter & Paul's RC Prim Sch
  Ilford IG1 79 B5
  Mitcham CR4 202 D5
St Erkenwald Mews IG11 101 B6
St Erkenwald Rd IG11 101 B6
St Ermin's Hill SW1 259 C6
St Ervan's Rd W10 91 B2
St Eugene de Mazenod Rc Prim Sch NW6 69 C1
St Faith's CE Prim Sch SW18 158 A6
St Faith's Cl EN2 5 A4
St Faith's Rd SE24 160 D3
St Fillans Rd SE6 164 A4
St Francesca Cabrini Prim Sch SE23 162 C5
St Francis Cl BR5 211 C3
St Francis de Sales RC Jun & Inf Sch N17 33 D3
St Francis' Ho NW1 232 C3
St Francis Lodge HA0 64 D5
St Francis of Assisi RC Prim Sch W11 112 D6
St Francis Pl SW12 159 B5
St Francis RC Prim Sch
  SE15 140 A5
  Stratford E15 76 C3
St Francis Rd SE22 139 C1
St Francis Way IG1 79 B4
St Francis Xavier Sixth Form Coll SW12 159 B5
St Frideswides Mews 5 E14 98 A1
St Gabriel's CE Prim Sch SW1 115 C1 259 A1
St Gabriels Cl 3 E14 97 D2
St Gabriel's Cl E11 55 B1
St Gabriels Ct N11 31 D3
St Gabriel's Rd NW2 68 D3
St George Ho SW11 268 B1
ST GEORGE IN THE EAST 118 A6
St George's Ave
  Ealing W5 109 D4
  Kingsbury NW9 45 B5
  Southall UB1 107 B6
  Tufnell Pk N7 71 D4
  Upton E7 77 B1
St George's Battersea CE Prim Sch SW8 137 C5 269 B3
St George's Bickley CE Prim Sch BR1 187 D1
St George's Bldgs SE11 261 D5
St George's Cath NW1 231 D2
St George's Cath RC Jun & Inf Sch SE1 116 D3 261 C6
St George's CE Prim Sch SE5 139 C5
St George's Circ SE1 116 D3 261 C6
St Georges Cl SE28 102 D1
St George's Cl NW11 47 B3
St Georges Cl
  Nine Elms SW8 269 B2
  Wembley HA0 65 A5
St Georges Coll N7 72 C5
St George's Ct SW3 257 A4
St Georges Ct HA3 43 A3
St George's Ct SW7 256 A5
St Georges Ct E6 100 B3
St George's Ct SE1 261 C5
St Georges Ct
  Penge SE20 184 B2
  Putney SW15 135 B1
  Walthamstow E17 54 B4
St George's Dr
  Ickenham UB10 60 B6
  South Oxhey WD19 23 A6
  SW1 115 C1 259 A2
St George's Field W2 92 C1 237 B1
St George's Gdns KT6 214 D6
St George's Gr SW17 158 B1
St Georges Hanover Sq Sch W1 115 A6 248 B5
St George's Ho NW1 232 B3
St George's Hospl SW17 180 B5
St George's Ind Est KT2 175 D5
St Georges Ind Est N22 32 D3
St George's La EC3 253 A6
St George's Lo N10 49 C5
St Georges Mews 11 NW1 70 D1
St George's Mews
  2 Rotherhithe SE8 119 B2
  SE1 261 B6
St Georges Pl N7 71 D4
St George's RC Cath SE1 116 C3 261 B6
St George's RC Prim Sch
  Enfield EN2 5 B3
  Harrow HA1 64 D5

St George's RC Sec Sch W9 .... 91 D5
St George's Rd W4 ... 111 B4
St George's Rd BR3 .. 185 D2
St Georges Rd BR1 ... 210 B6
St Georges Rd Ctr RM9 .... 81 B4
St Georges Rd RM9 ... 81 A4
St George's Rd
Ealing W7 .... 108 D5
Enfield EN1 .... 5 D5
Feltham TW13 .... 172 D6
Isleworth TW1 .... 153 B6
2 Kingston u T KT2 . 176 C3
Leyton E10 .... 76 A5
Mitcham CR4 .... 203 B6
Newington SE1 .... 116 D3 261 C5
Palmers Green N13 .... 16 B2
St Georges Rd BR5 .... 211 B3
St George's Rd
Redbridge IG1 .... 56 B2
Richmond TW9 .... 132 B2
Sidcup DA14 .... 190 D4
Temple Fortune NW11 .... 47 B3
Upton E7 .... 77 B2
Wallington SM6 .... 219 B3
St Georges Rd W BR1 .... 188 A1
St George's Rd SW19 .... 179 B4
St George's Residences 4 SW2 .... 160 C6
St Georges's Ct EC4. 241 C2
St Georges Sh & L Ctr HA1 .... 42 C3
St Georges Sq 1 E14 .... 119 A6
St George's Sq
Kingston u T KT3 .... 199 C6
Rotherhithe SE8 .... 119 B2
SW1 .... 115 D1 259 C1
St George's Square Mews SW1 .... 259 C1
St George's Sq E7 .... 77 B1
St Georges Terr
Hampstead NW1 .... 70 D1
NW1 .... 230 D6
St George St W1 .... 115 B6 248 D6
St George's Way SE15 .... 139 C6
St George's Wlk CR0 .... 221 A5
St George the Martyr CE Prim Sch WC1 .... 94 B3 240 D5
St George Wharf SW8 .... 270 A6
St Gerards Cl SW4 .... 159 C6
St German's Pl SE3 .. 143 A4
St German's Rd SE23 .... 163 A3
St Gildas' RC Jun Sch N8 .... 50 A2
ST GILES 94 A1
St Giles Ave
Dagenham RM10 .... 81 D1
Uxbridge UB10 .... 61 A4
St Giles Cir WC1 .... 93 D1 239 D2
St Giles Cl BR6 .... 227 B3
Dagenham RM10 .... 81 D1
Heston TW3 .... 129 A5
St Giles Coll WC1 .... 94 A2 240 B4
St Giles Ct
Ealing W13 .... 109 C5
WC2 .... 240 A2
St Giles High St WC2 .... 93 D1 239 D2
St Giles Ho 2 EN5 .... 2 A1
St Giles Hospl SE5 .. 139 C4
St Giles Ho SW16 .... 160 A1
St Giles Pas WC2 .... 239 D1
St Giles Rd SE5 .... 139 C4
St Giles' Sch CR2 ... 220 D2
St Giles Twr 3 SE5 ... 139 C4
St Gilles Ho 15 E2 .... 96 D5
St Gothard Rd SE21, SE27 .... 183 B6
St Gregory Cl HA4 .... 62 C4
St Gregory RC High Sch HA3 .... 43 D4
St Gregory's RC Prim Sch W5 .... 87 D2
St Helena Ho WC1 ... 234 A1
St Helena Pier TW9. 153 D6
St Helena Rd SE16 ... 118 D2
St Helena St WC1 ... 234 A1
St Helena Terr 31 TW9 .... 153 D6
St Helens Coll UB10 .. 60 C1
St Helen's Cres SW16 .... 182 B2
St Helen's Gdns W10 .. 90 D1
St Helen's Pl EC3 ... 243 A2
St Helen's RC Inf Sch E17 .... 54 A4
St Helen's RC Prim Sch E13 .... 99 A3
St Helen's RC Sch SW9 .... 138 C2
St Helens Rd 5 DA18 .... 124 D4
St Helen's Rd
Ealing W13 .... 109 C5
Redbridge IG1 .... 56 B3
Thornton Heath SW16 .... 182 B2
St Helens KT7 .... 196 D2
ST HELIER 202 B2
St Helier Ave SM4 .... 202 A3
St Helier Ct 4 N1 .... 95 C6
St Helier Hospl SM5 .... 202 A1
St Heliers Ave TW3, TW4 .... 151 C6
St Helier's Rd E10 .... 54 A3
St Helier Sta SM4 .. 201 C3
St Hilary's Ct BR1 .... 210 D6
St Hilda's Ave TW15 .. 170 A5
St Hilda's Cl NW6 .... 68 D1
St Hildas Cl SW17 .... 158 C2
St Hilda's Rd SW13 .. 134 B6
St Hildas Wharf E1 ... 118 C5
St Hubert's Ho 2 E14 .... 119 C3
St Hughes Cl SW17 ... 158 C2
St Hugh's Rd SE20 ... 184 B3
St Ignatius Coll EN1 ... 6 B6
St Ignatius' RC Prim Sch N15 .... 51 D3
St Ignatius RC Prim Sch TW16 .... 172 A2
St Ives Ct NW2 .... 69 A2
St Ivian Ct 3 N10 .... 31 B1
ST JAMES 115 C5
St James Apartments 2 E17 .... 53 A4
St James' Ave W13 ... 109 A5
St James Ave
East Barnet N20 .... 14 C1
Sutton SM1 .... 217 C3
St James CE Jun Sch E7 .... 77 A3
St James CE Prim Sch EN3 .... 6 C3
St James' CE Prim Sch SE16 .... 118 A3
St James Cl Barnet EN4 . 2 B1
East Barnet N20 .... 14 C1
St James' Cl
New Malden KT3 .... 199 D4
Ruislip HA4 .... 62 C6
St James' Ct W4 .... 111 B3
St James Ct
26 Bethnal Green E2 .... 96 A4
10 Brentford W4 .... 110 C1
1 Bromley BR2 .... 187 A1
Forest Hill SE23 .... 163 A3
St James' Ct 7 KT1 .. 198 A6
St James Ct SE3 .... 143 B4
St James' Ct SW1 ... 259 B6
St James Ct
Thornton Heath CR0 .... 204 D2
Wanstead E12 .... 77 C6
St James Gate IG9 .... 21 B3
St James Gdns IG6 .... 58 B5
St James' Gdns HA0 ... 66 A1
St James Ho N5 .... 72 C3
St James Hts 3 SE18 .... 123 A1
St James Independent Schs W14 .. 113 A2 254 B4
St James Ind Mews 16 SE1 .... 118 A1
St James Ind Sch for Boys TW1 .... 153 A2
St James' Mans NW6 .. 69 C1
St James Mews E14 .... 120 A3
St James' RC High Sch NW9 .... 27 D2
St James RC Prim Sch BR5 .... 210 D4
St James Rd SM5 .... 218 C5
St James' Rd
Edmonton N9 .... 18 B2
Forest Gate E15 .... 76 D3
St James Rd KT1 .... 175 D1
St James' Rd
Mitcham CR4 .... 181 A3
Surbiton KT6 .... 197 D3
St James Rd SM1, SM2 .... 217 C3
St James's App EC2. 243 A5
St James's Ave
Beckenham BR3 .... 207 A6
Hampton TW12 .... 174 A5
South Hackney E2 .... 96 C5
St James's CE Prim Sch N10 .... 49 A5
St James School Flats 5 N7 .... 72 C3
St James's Cl NW8 .. 230 C5
St James's Cloisters 2 SE22 .... 139 D1
St James's Cl
Upper Tooting SW17 .... 158 D2
Woolwich SE18 .... 123 A1
St James's Cotts 14 TW10 .... 153 D6
St James's Cres SW9 .... 138 C2
St James's Ct
8 Edmonton N18 .... 34 A5
Harrow HA1 .... 43 A3
St James's Dr
Balham SW12, SW17 .... 158 D4
Upper Tooting SW17 .... 158 D3
St James's Gdns W11 .... 113 A5 244 A4
St James's Gr SW11 .. 136 D3
St James's Hatcham CE Prim Sch SE14 .... 141 A4
St James's La N10 .... 49 B5
St James's SE14 .... 141 A4
St James's Market SW1 .... 249 C5
St James's Mews E17 .... 53 A4
St James's Pal* SW1 .... 115 C5 249 B3
St James's Park Sta SW1 .... 115 D3 259 C6
St James's Pas EC3. 243 B1
St James's Pk* SW1 .... 249 C2
St James's Pk CR0 ... 205 A2
St James's Pl SW1 .... 115 C5 249 A3
St James's RC Prim Sch TW2 .... 152 C1
St James's Rd
Bermondsey SE1, SE16 .... 118 A2
Hampton TW12 .... 173 D5
Peckham SE1 .... 140 A6
Thornton Heath CR0 .. 205 B2
St James's & St Michael's CE Prim Sch W2 .... 114 A6 246 B6
St James's Sq SW1 .... 115 C5 249 B4
St James's St SW1 .... 115 C5 249 A4
Walthamstow E17 .... 53 A4
St James's Terrace Mews NW8 .... 230 C5
St James's Terr NW8 .... 230 C6
2 Upper Tooting SW12 .... 159 A3
St James St W6 .... 112 C1
St James Street Sta E17 .... 53 A4
St James The Great RC Prim Sch
Camberwell SE15 .... 139 D4
South Norwood CR7 . 182 D1
St James Way DA14 .. 191 A5
St James Wlk EC1 .. 241 C6
St Jerome's Gr UB3 ... 83 A1
St Joachim's RC Prim Sch E16 .... 99 C1
St Joan of Arc RC Prim Sch N5 .... 73 A4
St Joan's Rd N9 .... 17 D2
St John Baptist CE Prim Sch BR1 .... 186 A6
St John Evangelist RC Prim Sch N1 .... 94 D5 234 C4
St John Fisher RC Fst & Mid Sch HA5 .... 41 C5
St John Fisher RC Prim Sch
DA18 .... 125 A3
Wembley UB6 .... 87 C4
West Barnes SW20 .. 200 D4
St John of Jerusalem CE Prim Sch E9 .... 74 C1
ST JOHNS 141 C3
St John & St James CE Prim Sch
Edmonton N18 .... 33 D5
Hackney E9 .... 74 C3
St John's Angell Town CE Prim Sch SW9. 138 C3
St John's Ave
Dagenham NW10 .... 89 D6
Friern Barnet N11 .... 30 D5
Putney SW15 .... 156 D6
St John's CE First Sch HA7 .... 25 A6
St John's CE JMI Sch N11 .... 30 D6
St John's CE Prim Sch
Buckhurst Hill IG9 .... 21 B3
Croydon CR0 .... 222 D5
Enfield EN2 .... 4 D6
Fulham SW6 .... 135 A4 264 B2
Kingston u T KT1 .... 198 A6
Penge SE20 .... 184 C3
SE17 .... 117 A2 262 B3
South Hackney E2 .... 96 C5
Whetstone N20 .... 14 A2
St John's CE Sch Stanmore HA7 .... 25 A6
St John's Church Rd E9 .... 74 C3
St Johns Cl N14 .... 15 C5
St John's Cl SW6 ... 265 A4
Wembley HA9 .... 66 A3
St Johns Concert Hall* SW1 .... 260 A5
St John's Cotts 2 SE20 .... 184 C3
St John's Cres SW9 .. 138 C2
St John's Ct IG9 .... 21 B3
St Johns Ct 39 E1 .... 118 B5
St John's Ct
Finsbury Pk N4 .... 72 D6
Hammersmith W6 .... 112 B2
2 Harrow HA1 .... 42 D3
Saint John's Ct N5 .... 72 D4
St John's Ct
Isleworth TW7 .... 130 D3
Kingston u T KT1 .... 198 A5
Lewisham SE13 .... 142 A3
Leytonstone E11 .... 54 D1
5 South Hampstead NW3 .... 70 A2
St Johns Dr KT12 .... 194 C1
St John's Dr SW18 .... 157 D3
St John's Est SE1 .... 253 C1
St John's Gdns W11 .... 113 B6 244 C5
St John's Gr
3 Barnes SW13 .... 133 D3
1 Richmond TW9 .... 132 A1
Upper Holloway N19 ... 71 C6
St John's Highbury Vale CE Prim Sch N5 .... 72 D5
St John's Hill Gr SW11 .... 136 B1
St John's Hill SW11 .. 136 B1
St John's Ho 1 E14 .... 120 A2
St Johns Ho 5 SE17 .... 139 B6
Streatham SW16 .... 182 A4
St John's La EC1 .... 94 D2 241 D4
St John's Lodge 8 SE8 .... 141 C4
St John's Mans E5 .... 74 C3
St John's Par W13 ... 109 B5
St John's Park Mans N19 .... 71 C5
St John's Par 3 DA14 .... 190 B6
St John's Path EC1 .. 241 C5
St John's Pk SE3 .... 143 A5
St John's Pl EC1 .... 241 C5
St John's Prim Sch W13 .... 109 A6
St John's RC Prim Sch SE16 .... 119 A4
St John's Rd
Barking IG11 .... 101 C6
Battersea SW11 .... 136 C1
Canning Town E16 .... 99 A1
Carshalton SM5 .... 218 C5
Chingford E4 .... 35 D6
Croydon CR0 .... 220 D5
DA16 .... 146 B2
East Ham E6 .... 100 A6
East Molesey KT8 .... 196 B5
Feltham TW13 .... 173 B6
Harrow HA1 .... 42 D3
St Johns Rd IG2 .... 57 C2
St John's Rd TW7 .... 130 D3
St Johns Rd KT3 .... 199 A6
St John's Rd
Orpington BR5 .... 211 C3
Penge SE20 .... 184 C4
Richmond TW9 .... 132 A1
Sidcup DA14 .... 190 B6
Southall UB2 .... 107 A3
Sutton SM1 .... 217 D6
Teddington KT1 .... 175 C1
St John's Rd *continued*
Temple Fortune NW11 .... 47 B3
Tottenham N15 .... 51 C3
Walthamstow E17 .... 36 A1
Wembley HA9 .... 66 A3
Wimbledon SW19 ... 179 A4
St John's & St Clements CE Prim Sch SE15 .... 140 A2
St John's Sch HA6 .... 22 B4
St John's Sq EC1 .... 94 D3 241 C5
St Johns Sta SE8 ... 141 C3
St John St EC1 .... 94 D3 241 C6
St John's Terr
Enfield EN2 .... 5 B6
North Kensington W10 .... 90 D3
SE18 .... 145 B6
Upton E7 .... 77 B2
St Johnstone Ho 17 N12 .... 29 D6
St John's Upper Holloway CE Prim Sch N19 .... 71 D6
St John's Vale SE8 ... 141 C3
St John's Villas
4 Friern Barnet N11 .... 30 D5
Upper Holloway N19 ... 71 D6
W8 .... 255 D5
St John's Way N19 .... 49 D1
ST JOHN'S WOOD 92 B5
St John's Wood Ct NW8 .... 229 D1
St John's Wood High St NW8 .... 92 C5 230 A3
St John's Wood Park NW8 .... 92 B6 229 C6
St John's Wood Pre-Prep Sch NW8 .... 92 C4 230 A2
St John's Wood Rd NW8 .... 92 B4 229 D1
St John's Wood Sta NW8 .... 92 B5 229 C4
St John's Wood Terr NW8 .... 92 C5 230 A4
St John the Baptist CE Jun Sch KT1 .... 175 D3
St John the Baptist CE Prim Sch N1 .... 95 B5 235 D3
St John the Divine CE Jun & Inf Sch SE5 .... 138 D5
St John Vianney RC Prim Sch N8 .... 50 D5
St Joseph RC Prim Sch W7 .... 108 C5
St Joseph's Acad SE3 .... 142 C2
St Josephs Cl BR6 ... 227 D4
St Joseph's Cl W10 ... 91 A2
St Joseph's Coll Mill Hill Missionaries NW7 .. 27 D6
St Joseph's Convent Sch E11 .... 55 A3
St Joseph's Ct E4 .... 20 B4
St Josephs Ct
3 Dagenham NW10 .... 89 D5
20 Walthamstow E10 .. 53 D2
St Joseph's Dr UB1 .. 107 B5
St Joseph's Flats NW1 .... 232 C2
St Josephs Gr NW4 .... 46 B5
St Joseph's Ho W6 ... 112 D2
St Joseph's Hospice E9, E8 .... 96 B6
St Joseph's RC Coll SW16 .... 182 D4
St Joseph's RC Fst & Mid Sch HA3 .... 25 A1
St Joseph's RC Inf & Jun Schs
Hendon NW4 .... 46 B5
SE5 .... 139 A5
St Joseph's RC Inf Sch
Leyton E10 .... 75 C6
South Norwood SE19 .... 183 A4
St Joseph's RC Jun & Inf Schs HA9 .... 66 B3
St Joseph's RC Jun Sch
South Norwood SE19 .... 183 A4
Walthamstow E10 .... 53 D1
St Joseph's RC Prim Sch
Barking IG11 .... 101 A6
St Joseph's RC Prim Sch *continued*
Bermondsey SE16 .... 118 A4
Bromley BR1 .... 187 B3
Chelsea SW3 .... 114 D2 257 C3
Dagenham RM9 .... 81 B4
Deptford SE8 .... 141 C5
Greenwich SE10 .... 120 C1
Kingston u T KT1 .... 176 B1
Paddington W9 .... 92 A4 229 A1
Rotherhithe SE16 .... 118 C3
St Giles WC2 .. 94 A1 240 B2
Upper Holloway N19 ... 49 B1
Wandsworth SW18 ... 157 C6
Willesden NW10 .... 67 C1
St Joseph's Rd N9 .... 18 C3
St Joseph's St SW8 . 268 D2
St Joseph's Vale SE3 .... 142 B2
St Jude & St Paul's CE Prim Sch N1 .... 73 C2
St Jude's CE Prim Sch SE24 .... 160 D6
St Judes Ho 6 W10 ... 91 B4
St Jude's Prim Sch SE1 .... 116 D3 261 C5
St Jude's Rd E2 .... 96 B5
St Jude St N16 .... 73 C3
St Julian's Cl SW16 .. 182 C6
St Julian's Farm Rd SE27, SW16 .... 182 D6
St Julian's Rd NW6 ... 91 C6
St Katharine's Ho N1 .... 234 A4
St Katharine's Prec NW1 .... 231 C4
St Katharine's Way E1 .... 117 D5 253 D4
St Katherines Rd DA18 .... 124 D4
St Katherine's Row EC3 .... 243 B1
St Katherine's Wlk 1 W11 .... 112 D5
St Keverne Rd SE9 ... 188 A6
St Kilda Rd BR6 .... 211 D1
Ealing W13 .... 109 A4
St Kilda's Rd
Harrow HA1 .... 42 C3
Stamford Hill N16 .... 51 C1
St Kitts Terr SE19 .... 183 C5
St Laurence's Cl NW6 .... 90 D6
St Lawrence CE Jun Sch KT8 .... 196 B5
St Lawrence Cl HA8 ... 26 B3
St Lawrence Ct N1 .. 235 D6
St Lawrence Dr HA5 .. 40 B4
St Lawrence Ho SE1 263 B6
St Lawrence RC Prim Sch TW13 .... 150 B2
St Lawrence St E14 .. 120 A5
St Lawrence Terr W10 .... 91 A2
St Lawrence Way SW9 .... 138 C3
St Leonard's Ave E4 ... 36 B4
St Leonards Ave HA3 .. 43 C4
St Leonard's CE Prim Sch SW16 .... 181 D5
St Leonards Cl 4 DA16 .... 146 A2
St Leonards Ct SW14 .... 133 A2
St Leonard's Ct N1 .. 235 D2
St Leonard's Gdns TW5 .... 129 A4
St Leonards Gdns IG1 .... 79 A3
St Leonard's Hospl N1 .... 95 C5
St Leonard's Rd
Becontree NW10 .... 89 B3
Claygate KT10 .... 212 D2
Croydon CR0 .... 220 D5
Ealing W13 .... 109 C6
Kingston u T KT6 .... 197 D4
St Leonards Rd SW14 .... 133 A2
St Leonard's Rd
South Bromley E14 .... 98 A2
Thames Ditton KT7 .. 197 A2
St Leonards Rise BR6 .... 227 C4
St Leonard's Sq
Camden Town NW5 .... 71 A2
Kingston u T KT6 .... 197 D4
St Leonard's St E3 .... 97 D4
St Leonard's Terr SW3 .... 114 D1 257 D1
St Leonard's Wlk SW16 .... 182 B3
St Loo Ave SW3 .... 136 C6 267 B6

St Loo Ct SW3 267 C6
St Louis Rd SE27 183 B6
St Loy's Rd N17 51 D6
St Lucia Dr E15 98 D6
St Luke Prim Sch E16 98 D1
ST LUKE'S 95 A3
St Luke's Ave
Clapham SW4 137 D1
Enfield EN2 5 B5
Ilford IG1 78 D3
St Luke's CE Prim Sch
Cubitt Town E14 120 B2
Kingston u T KT2 176 B2
Paddington W9 91 B4
Shoreditch EC1 95 A4 235 B1
West Norwood SE27 183 A5
St Luke's Cl
Croydon SE25 206 B3
St Luke's EC1 95 A3 242 B6
St Luke's Ct W11 91 B1
St Lukes Ct 6 E10 53 D2
St Luke's Hospl W1 93 C3 239 A5
St Luke's Mews W11 91 B1
St Luke's Path 1 IG1 78 D3
St Luke's RC Sixth Form Coll DA14 189 D5
St Luke's Rd
Notting Hill W11 91 B2
Uxbridge UB10 60 A1
St Luke's Sq E16 98 D1
St Luke's St SW3 257 B2
St Luke's Woodside Hospl N10 49 A5
St Malo Ave N9 18 C1
St Margaret Clitherow RC Prim Sch
Neasden NW10 67 B4
Woolwich SE28 124 B5
ST MARGARETS 153 A5
St Margarets Ave TW15 170 D5
St Margaret's Ave SM3 217 A5
St Margarets Ave DA15 167 B1
St Margaret's Ave
Harringay N8, N15 50 D5
Harrow HA2 64 A5
St Margarets Ave
Hillingdon UB8 82 C3
Whetstone N20 14 A3
St Margarets IG11 101 B6
St Margarets Bsns Ctr 11 TW1 153 B5
St Margaret's CE Prim Sch
Barking IG11 79 A1
Woolwich SE18 123 A1
St Margaret's Cres SW15 156 B6
St Margaret's Ct
Leyton E15 76 C4
Putney SW15 134 B1
SE1 252 C3
9 Twickenham TW1 153 B5
St Margaret's Dr TW1 153 B6
St Margaret's Gr
Leyton E11 76 D5
SE18 145 A6
Twickenham TW1 153 A5
St Margaret's La W8 113 D3 255 C5
St Margaret's Lee CE Prim Sch SE13 142 C1
St Margarets Lo W3 110 D4
St Margaret's Pass SE13 142 C2
St Margaret's Path 4 SE18 123 A1
St Margaret's Rd SE4 141 B1
St Margarets Rdbt TW1 153 B6
St Margarets Rd HA8 26 D5
St Margaret's Rd
Hanwell W7 108 C4
Isleworth TW1 153 B6
Kensal Green NW10 90 C4
St Margarets Rd HA4 39 B3
St Margaret's Rd
Tottenham N17 51 C6
Wanstead E12 77 C6
St Margaret's Sch NW3 69 D4
St Margaret's Sta TW1 153 B5
St Margaret's Terr SE18 123 A1
St Margaret St SW1 250 A1
St Margret's Ct N11 31 A6
St Mark's CE Acad CR4 181 B1
St Mark's CE Prim Sch
Bromley BR2 209 A6
Croydon SE25 206 A5
Kennington SE11 138 B6 270 D6
St Mark's Cl
Barnet EN5 1 D2
Harrow HA1 43 B1
St Marks Cl 5 SE10 142 A5
St Mark's Cres NW1 93 A6 231 B6
St Mark's Ct
Hanwell W7 108 C4
8 Walthamstow E10 53 D2
St Marks Gate E9 75 B1
St Mark's Gr SW10 135 D5 265 D4
St Mark's Hill KT6 198 A3
St Mark's Ho 8 E17 54 A5
St Marks Ho 6 SE17 139 B6
St Mark's Hospl EC1 94 D4 234 D2
St Mark's Hts 25 KT6 198 A4
St Marks Ind Est E16 121 D5
St Mark's Mans 14 N4 72 B6
St Mark's Pl
Notting Hill W11 91 A1
Wimbledon SW19 179 B4
St Mark's Prim Sch
Hanwell W7 108 C4
Mitcham CR4 180 D1
Upper Holloway N19 72 A6
St Mark's RC Sch TW3 129 C2
St Mark's Rd
Bromley BR2 209 B6
Croydon SE25 206 A5
Ealing W5 110 A5
Enfield EN1 17 D6
Hanwell W7 108 C4
Mitcham CR4 181 A1
St Marks Rd 15 NW10 90 D1
St Mark's Rd
North Kensington W10 90 D2
Notting Hill W11 91 A1
Teddington TW11 175 B3
St Mark's Rise E8 73 D3
St Mark's Sq NW1 231 A5
St Mark St E1 95 D1 243 D1
St Martha's Convent Jun Sch EN5 1 A1
St Martha's Senior Sch EN4 1 C4
St Martin-in-the-Fields High Sch for Girls SW2 160 C3
St Martin of Porres RC Prim Sch N11 31 C4
St Martin's Almshouses NW1 232 A6
St Martin's App HA4 39 C2
St Martin's Ave E6 99 D5
St Martins Cl DA18 124 D4
St Martin's Cl
Enfield EN1 6 B4
NW1 232 A6
St Martins Cl WD19 22 C6
St Martins Ct N1 95 C6
St Martin's Ct WC2 250 A6
West Norwood SE27 160 D2
St Martins La BR3 207 D4
St Martin's La WC2 116 A6 250 A5
St Martin's Le Grand EC1 242 A2
St Martin's Pl WC2 250 A5
St Martin's Rd
Edmonton N9 18 B2
Finchley N2 30 B2
Stockwell SW9 138 B3
St Martin's Sch NW7 27 B5
St Martin's St WC2 249 D5
St Martin's Way SW17 158 A1
St Mary Abbots CE Prim Sch W8 113 D4 245 C1
St Mary Abbot's Ct W14 254 C5
St Mary Abbot's Pl W8 254 D5
St Mary Abbots Terr W14 254 D5
St Mary at Hill EC3 117 C6 253 A5
St Mary Ave SM6 219 B5
St Mary Axe EC3 95 C1 243 B2
St Marychurch St SE16 118 C4
St Mary Graces Ct E1 253 D5
St Marylebone CE Sch The W1 93 A2 238 B4
St Mary le Bow Church* EC2 242 B1
St Mary- le-Park Ct SW11 267 B3
St Mary Magdalene CE Prim Sch
Islington N7 72 C2
Paddington W2 91 D2
Peckham SE15 140 B3
Woolwich SE18 122 C2
St Mary Magdalen's RC Prim Sch
Brockley SE4 141 A1
Mortlake SW14 133 B2
St Mary Magdelen's RC Jun Sch NW2 68 B2
St Mary Newington Cl SE17 263 B2
St Mary of the Angels RC Prim Sch W2 91 C1
St Mary RC Prim Sch W10 91 A3
St Mary Rd E17 53 D5
St Mary & St Joseph's RC Sch DA14 189 D5
St Mary & St Michael Prim Sch E1 96 C1
St Mary & St Pancras CE Prim Sch NW1 93 D5 232 C3
St Mary's App E12 78 B3
St Mary's Ave
Beckenham BR2 208 C6
Finchley N3 29 B1
St Marys Ave UB2 107 D2
St Mary's Ave
Teddington TW11 174 D4
Wanstead E11 55 B2
St Marys IG11 101 B6
St Mary's Bryanston Square CE Sch W1 92 D2 237 C4
St Mary's CE High Sch (Lower & Upper) NW4 46 C6
St Mary's CE High Sch (Middle) NW4 46 C6
St Mary's CE Inf Sch N8 50 B5
St Mary's CE Jun Sch N8 50 A5
St Mary's CE Prim Sch
Chessington KT9 214 B2
East Barnet EN4 14 C5
Finchley N3 29 B3
St Mary's CE Prim Sch (Inf) TW1 153 A4
St Mary's CE Prim Sch N1 94 D6 234 D6
St Mary's CE Prim Sch (Jun) TW1 153 B4
St Mary's CE Prim Sch
Long Ditton KT7 197 B1
Putney SW15 134 D2
Walthamstow E17 53 D5
Willesden NW10 67 C2
St Mary's Church Ho 11 E17 53 D5
St Mary's Cl BR5 190 B1
Chessington KT9 214 B1
Ewell KT17 215 D1
Sunbury TW16 194 A5
Tottenham N17 34 A2
St Mary's Coll TW1 152 D1
St Mary's Cottage Hospl TW12 173 B2
St Mary's Cres
Hayes UB3 105 D6
Hendon NW4 46 B6
Hounslow TW7 130 C5
St Marys Ct SE2 124 D2
St Mary's Ct
Bedford Pk W6 111 D3
Ealing W5 109 D4
Finchley N12 30 A3
Kingston u T KT3 199 C6
Leytonstone E11 54 D1
St Marys Ct
Newham E6 100 B3
SE7 143 D5
St Mary's Ct SM6 219 C4
St Mary's Dr TW14 149 A4
St Mary's Est 2 SE16 118 C4
St Mary's Flats NW1 232 C2
St Mary's Gate W8 255 C5
St Mary's Gdns SE11 261 B4
St Mary's Gn 1 N2 48 A6
St Mary's Gr
Barnes SW13 134 B2
Chiswick W4 132 D6
Islington N1 72 D2
Richmond TW10, TW9 132 B1
St Mary's Ho
Ealing W5 109 D3
N1 234 D6
St Mary's Hospl Medical Sch W2 92 B1 236 D2
St Mary's Hospl W2 92 B1 236 D2
St Mary's Kilburn CE Prim Sch NW6 91 C6
St Mary's Lewisham CE Prim Sch SE13 163 D6
St Mary's Lo E11 55 B3
St Mary's Mans
Dagenham NW10 89 C6
Paddington W2 92 B2 236 C4
St Mary's Mews NW6 69 D1
St Mary's Path N1 234 D6
St Mary's Pl
Ealing W5 109 D4
Eltham SE9 166 C5
Kensington W8 113 D3 255 C5
St Mary's RC High Sch CR0 205 A1
St Mary's RC Inf Sch
Carshalton SM5 218 D4
Croydon CR0 205 B1
St Mary's RC Jun & Inf Schs N15 51 B4
St Mary's RC Jun Sch
Croydon CR0 205 B1
Wallington SM5 218 D3
Walthamstow E17 54 A6
St Mary's RC Prim Sch
Beckenham BR3 186 A3
Chingford E4 20 B3
Chiswick W4 133 C6
Clapham Pk SW4 159 C6
Clapham SW8 137 B4 268 D2
Enfield EN3 6 D1
Hammersmith W14 112 D3
Isleworth TW7 131 A2
Merton SW19 179 C3
Paddington NW6 91 C5
SE9 166 C6
St Mary's Rd
Dagenham NW10 89 C6
Ealing W5 109 D5
East Barnet EN4 14 D4
East Molesey KT8 196 B4
Finchley N2 30 B2
Golders Green NW11 47 A2
Hayes UB3 105 D6
Hornsey N8 50 A5
St Marys Rd IG1 79 B6
St Mary's Rd
Leyton E10 76 A6
Long Ditton KT6 197 C1
Lower Edmonton N9 18 C3
Newham E13 99 B5
Nunhead SE15 140 C3
South Norwood SE25 205 C6
Surbiton KT6 197 D3
Wimbledon SW19 179 B5
Worcester Pk KT4 215 C6
St Mary's & St John's CE Prim Sch NW4 46 B4
St Mary's & St Peter's CE Prim Sch TW11 174 D5
St Mary's Sch Hampstead NW3 70 B3
St Mary's Sq
Ealing W5 109 D4
W2 236 C4
St Mary's Stoke Newington CE Prim Sch N16 73 C6
St Mary's Terr W2 236 C4
St Mary St SE18 122 C2
St Mary's Twr EC1 242 B5
St Marys View HA3 43 C4
St Mary's Wlk
Hayes UB3 105 D6
SE11 261 B4
St Matthew's Ave KT6 198 B1
St Matthew's CE Prim Sch
Enfield EN3 18 C6
Surbiton KT6 198 A2
St Matthew's CE Prim Sch *continued*
Wimbledon SW20 178 A2
Yiewsley UB7 104 A5
St Matthew's Ct 1 TW15 170 C5
St Matthews Ct
Muswell Hill N10 31 A1
SE1 262 A5
2 Stratford E15 76 D1
7 Walthamstow E10 53 D2
St Matthews Dr BR1 210 B6
St Matthew's Ho 8 SE17 139 B6
St Matthew's Lo NW1 232 B4
St Matthew's Rd
Clapham Pk SW2 160 B6
Ealing W5 110 A5
St Matthew's Row E2 96 A3
St Matthews Sch Westminster SW1 115 D3 259 D6
St Matthew St SW1 259 C5
St Matthias CE Prim Sch E2 95 D3 243 D6
St Matthias Cl NW9 45 D4
St Matthias's CE Prim Sch N16 73 C4
St Mauritius Ho SE13 164 A6
St Maur Rd SW6 135 B4 264 D1
St Mellion Cl SE28 102 D1
St Merryn Cl SE18 145 B5
St Merryn Ct BR3 185 C3
St Michael-at-Bowes CE Jun Sch N13 32 C4
St Michael RC Prim Sch TW15 170 C5
St Michael & St Martin RC Prim Sch TW4 129 B2
St Michael's Alley EC3 242 D1
St Michaels Ave N9 18 C4
St Michael's Ave HA9 66 C2
St Michael's CE Prim Sch
Camden Town NW1 93 C6 232 A6
Enfield EN2 5 A4
Forest Hill SE26 185 A6
Highgate N6 49 A2
Wandsworth SW18 157 B4
Wood Green N22 32 B2
St Michaels Cl BR1 210 A6
St Michael's Cl
Colney Hatch N12 30 C5
DA18 124 D4
Finchley N3 29 B1
St Michaels Cl
4 Newham E16 99 D2
Worcester Pk KT4 215 D6
St Michael's Cres HA5 41 A3
St Michael's Ct N11 15 A1
St Michaels Ct 2 E14 98 A2
St Michael's Ct NW11 47 B2
St Michael's East Wickham CE Prim Sch DA16 146 C4
St Michael's Flats NW1 232 C3
St Michael's Gdns W10 91 A2
St Michaels Ho SE26 185 B6
St Michael's Hospl EN2 5 B4
St Michael's RC Gram Sch N12 30 A5
St Michael's RC Prim Sch E6 100 B5
St Michael's RC Sch SE16 118 A4
St Michaels Rd TW15 170 C5
St Michael's Rd
Cricklewood NW2 68 C4
Croydon CR0 205 A1
DA16 146 B2
Stockwell SW9 138 B3
Wallington SM6 219 C2
St Michael's Rise DA16 146 B4
St Michael's St W2 92 C1 237 A2
St Michael Steiner Sch The SW18 157 C6
St Michael's Terr N22 32 A2
St Mildred's Ct EC2 242 C1
St Mildreds Rd SE12, SE6 164 D4
St Mirren Ct 8 EN5 14 A6
St Monica's RC Prim Sch
Palmers Green N14 16 A1
Shoreditch N1 95 C4
St Nicholas CE Prim Sch TW17 192 D3
St Nicholas Cl WD6 9 D5
St Nicholas Ct E4 36 A4
St Nicholas Ctr 7 SM1 217 D3
St Nicholas Dr TW17 192 C2
St Nicholas Elstree CE Prim Sch WD6 9 D5
St Nicholas' Flats NW1 232 C3
St Nicholas Glebe SW17 181 A4
St Nicholas Ho SE8 141 C6
St Nicholas Mans SW17 158 D2
St Nicholas Rd
Plumstead SE18 123 D2
Sutton SM1 217 D3
Thames Ditton KT7 196 D3
St Nicholas Sch NW9 67 A6
St Nicholas St SE8 141 C4
St Nicholas Way SM1 217 D3
St Nicolas La BR7 188 A2
St Ninian's Ct N20 14 D1
St Norbert Gn SE4 141 A1
St Norbert Rd SE4 141 A1
St Olaf's Rd SW6 135 A5 264 B3
St Olave's Ct EC2 242 C1
St Olaves Ct W2 245 C5
St Olave's Est SE1 253 B2
St Olave's Gdns SE11 261 A4
St Olave's Mans SE11 261 A4
St Olaves Prep Sch SE9 166 D2
St Olave's Rd E6 100 C6
St Olave's Wlk SW16 181 D1
St Olav's Sq 32 SE16 118 C4
St Osmund's RC Prim Sch SW13 133 D4
St Oswald's Pl SE11 116 B1 260 C1
St Oswald's Rd SW16 182 D2
St Oswulf St SW1 259 D3
St Owen Ho SE1 263 B6
ST PANCRAS 94 A4
St Pancras Almshouses 13 NW5 70 D3
St Pancras Commercial Ctr NW1 232 B6
St Pancras Ct
Finchley N2 30 B1
6 Wembley HA0 66 A2
St Pancras Hospl NW1 93 D6 232 C5
St Pancras International Sta WC1 94 A4 233 A2
St Pancras Way NW1 93 D6 232 C6
St Patrick's Coll W1 93 D1 239 C2
St Patricks Ct IG8 36 C3
St Patrick's RC Prim Sch
Camden Town NW5 71 B3
Plumstead SE18 123 B2
Walthamstow E17 53 A5
St Paul's Acad SE2 146 A6
St Paul's & All Hallows CE Jun & Inf Schs N17 34 A3
St Paul's Ave
Harrow HA3 44 B5
Rotherhithe SE16 118 D5
Willesden NW2 68 C2
St Paul's Cath* EC4 95 A1 242 A1
St Paul's Cath Sch EC4 95 A1 242 A1
St Paul's CE Jun Sch KT2 176 C3
St Pauls CE Prim Sch TW8 131 D6
St Paul's CE Prim Sch
Chessington KT9 214 A4
Friern Barnet N11 31 B5
Hammersmith W6 112 C1

St Paul's CE Prim Sch *continued*
Hampstead NW3 ......70 D1
Mill Hill NW7 ......28 B6
SE17 ...... 117 A1 262 A2
Southgate N21 ......16 D4
St Paul's Church Yd EC4 ......95 A1 242 A1
St Paul's Cl
Ashford TW15 ......171 A5
Borehamwood WD6 ......11 A6
Carshalton SM5 ......202 C1
Chessington KT9 ......213 D4
St Pauls Cl W5 ......110 B4
St Paul's Cl SE7 ......121 D1
St Pauls Cl UB3 ......105 B1
St Paul's Cl TW3, TW4 ......129 A3
ST PAUL'S CRAY 190 A1
St Paul's Cray Rd BR7 ......189 B2
St Pauls Cres NW1 ......71 D1
St Paul's Ct
Clapham SW4 ......137 D1
Hounslow TW4 ......129 A2
6 Upper Holloway N19 ......72 A6
St Paul's Dr E15 ......76 B3
St Paul's Girls' Sch W6 ......112 D2
St Pauls Ho N17 ......34 A3
St Pauls Mews NW1 ......71 D1
St Paul's Pl N1 ......73 B2
St Paul's RC Coll TW16 ......172 A2
St Paul's RC Prim Sch
Thames Ditton KT7 ......196 C2
Wood Green N22 ......32 B1
St Pauls Rd IG11 ......101 A6
St Paul's Rd
Brentford TW8 ......131 D6
Canonbury N1 ......73 A2
St Pauls Rd TW9 ......132 B2
St Paul's Rd
South Norwood CR7 ......205 A6
Tottenham N17 ......34 A2
St Pauls Rise N13 ......32 D4
St Paul's Sch SW13 . 112 A1
St Paul's Sq BR2 ......187 A1
St Paul's Sta EC2 ......95 A1 242 A2
St Paul's Terr SE17 ...138 D6
St Paul St N1 ......235 B5
St Paul's Twr 14 E10 ...53 D2
St Pauls View WC1 ...234 A1
St Paul's Way Com Sch E3 ......97 C2
St Paul's Way
Finchley N3 ......29 D3
Tower Hamlets E3 ......97 C2
St Paul's Whitechapel CE Prim Sch E1 ... 118 A6
St Paul's with St Michael's Prim Sch E8 ......96 A6
St Paul's Wood Hill BR5 ......189 D1
St Paul with St Luke CE Prim Sch E3 ......97 B2
St Peter Chanel RC Prim Sch DA14 .... 190 C5
St Peter in Chains RC Inf Sch N8 ......50 A3
St Peter & Paul RC Prim Sch BR5 ......189 C1
St Peter & St Paul RC Prim Sch EC1 ......94 D3 241 D6
St Peter's Alley EC3 . 242 D1
St Peter's Ave
Edmonton N18 ......34 A6
37 Hackney E2 ......96 A5
St Peters Ave N12 ......30 C3
St Peter's Ave E17 ......54 C5
St Petersburgh Mews W2 ......245 C6
St Petersburgh Pl W2 ......113 D6 245 C5
St Peter's CE Prim Sch
Chiswick W6 ......112 A1
Paddington W9 ......91 C3
SE17 ......117 B1 262 C1
St Peter's Church Ct N1 ......234 D5
St Peter's Cl EN5 ......12 B6
St Peters Cl BR7 ......189 B3
St Peter's Cl
Bushey WD23 ......8 B3
Hackney E2 ......96 A5
St Peters Cl IG2 ......57 D5
St Peter's Cl HA4 ......62 D6
St Peters Cl SW17 ......158 C2
St Peters Ct KT8 ......195 C5
St Peter's Ct
Hendon NW4 ......46 C4
Lewisham SE12 ......164 D6
St Peters Ct
New Cross SE4 ......141 B3
28 Stepney E1 ......96 C3
St Peter's Eaton Square Prim Sch SW1 ......115 B3 258 D5
St Peter's Gdns SE27 ......160 C1
St Peter's Gr W6 ......112 A2
St Peter's Ho
4 SE17 ......139 B6
Stamford Hill N16 ......51 C2
St Peters Ho
Tottenham Hale N15 ......52 A5
WC1 ......233 B1
St Peters La BR5 ......190 A1
St Peter's London Docks CE Prim Sch E1 ... 118 C5
St Peters Mews N4 ......50 D4
St Peter's Pl W9 ......91 D3
St Peter's Prim Sch CR2 ......221 C2
St Peter's RC Prim Sch
Dagenham RM9 ......103 B6
Woolwich SE18 ......122 D2
St Peter's Rd
Chiswick W6 ......112 A1
Croydon CR0 ......221 B4
East Molesey KT8 ...195 C5
Edmonton N9 ......18 B3
Isleworth TW1 ......153 B6
St Peters Rd KT1 ......176 C1
St Peter's Rd UB1 ......85 C2
St Peter's Sq
Chiswick W6 ......111 D1
Hackney E2 ......96 A5
St Peter's St
Croydon CR2 ......221 B3
Islington N1 .. 94 D6 234 D5
St Peter's Street Mews N1 ......234 D4
St Peter's Terr SW6 . 264 B3
St Peter's Villas 5 W6 ......112 A2
St Peter's Way
De Beauvoir Town N1 ......73 C1
Ealing W5 ......87 D2
St Peters Way UB3 ...105 B1
St Peter's Wharf 8 W6 ......112 A1
St Philip Ho WC1 ...234 A1
St Philip's Ave KT4 ...216 B6
St Philips Gate KT4 ..216 B6
St Philip Sq 1 SW8 ..137 B3
St Philip's Rd
Dalston E8 ......74 A2
Surbiton KT6 ......197 D3
St Philip's Sch
Chessington KT9 ......213 D2
SW7 ......114 A2 256 B3
St Philip St SW8 ......137 B3
St Philip's Way N1 ... 235 B5
St Philomena's Sch SM5 ......218 C3
St Quentin Ho SW18 ......158 B5
St Quentin Rd DA16 ..145 D2
St Quintin Ave W10 ...90 D2
St Quintin Gdns 21 W10 ......90 C2
St Quintin Rd E13 ......99 B5
St Raphaels Ho W13 ......109 C5
St Raphael's RC Prim Sch UB5 ......84 B5
St Raphael's Way NW10 ......67 A3
St Regis Cl N10 ......31 B1
St Regis Hts NW3 ......69 D5
St Richards Ct TW10 ......153 B1
St Richard's Ho NW1 ......232 C2
St Richard's with St Andrew's CE Prim Sch TW10 ......153 B1
St Robert Southwell RC Prim Sch NW9 ......45 A3
St Ronans Cl EN4 ......2 B5
St Ronans Cres IG8 ...37 A3
St Ronan's 2 N3 ......29 C2
St Rule St SW8 ......137 C3
St Savior's CE Inf Sch W5 ......109 D6
St Saviour's CE Prim Sch
Bow Comm E14 ......97 D2
Camberwell SE24 ... 139 A2
St Saviour's CE Prim Sch *continued*
Paddington W9 ......91 D3
Walthamstow E17 ......53 B2
St Saviour's Coll SE27 ......183 B6
St Saviours Ct
Harrow HA1 ......42 C4
Muswell Hill N22 ......31 D1
St Saviours Ho 35 SE1 ......118 A4
St Saviours SW4 ......137 B1
St Saviour's RC Prim Sch SE13 ......142 A1
St Saviour's Rd
Clapham Pk SW2 ......160 B6
Thornton Heath CR0 . 205 A3
St Saviours & St Olaves CE Sch SE1 ......117 B3 262 D5
St Saviour's Wharf SE1 ......253 D2
St Scholastica's RC Prim Sch E5 ......74 A5
Saints Cl SE27 ......182 D6
Saints Dr E7 ......77 D3
St Silas Pl NW5 ......71 A2
St Simon's Ave SW15 ......156 C6
St Stephen's Ave
Ealing W13 ......87 B1
Shepherd's Bush W12 ......112 B4
Walthamstow E17 ......54 A4
St Stephen's CE Jun Sch TW1 ......153 B5
St Stephen's CE Prim Sch
Paddington W2 ......91 C2
Shepherd's Bush W12 ......112 C4
St Johns SE8 ......141 C3
SW8 ......138 B5 270 C4
St Stephen's Cl
Maitland Pk NW5 ......70 D3
NW8 ......230 B5
Southall UB1 ......85 C2
Walthamstow E17 ......53 D4
St Stephen's Cres
Notting Hill W2 ......91 C1
Thornton Heath CR7 . 204 C6
St Stephens Ct
Ealing W13 ......87 B1
Enfield EN1 ......17 C5
Hornsey Vale N8 ......50 B3
St Stephen's Gdns
Notting Hill W2 ......91 C1
4 Putney SW15 ......157 B6
Twickenham TW1 ......153 C5
St Stephen's Gr SE13 ......142 A2
St Stephens Ho 7 SE17 ......139 B6
St Stephen's Mews 34 W2 ......91 C2
St Stephens Par E6 ...77 C1
St Stephens Prim Sch E6 ......77 C1
St Stephen's RC Prim Sch DA16 ......146 A3
St Stephens Rd EN5 ...12 D6
St Stephen's Rd
Bow E3 ......97 B5
Ealing W13 ......87 C1
Enfield EN3 ......6 D6
Hounslow TW3, TW4 ......151 C6
St Stephens Rd E6 ......77 C1
St Stephen's Rd
Walthamstow E17 ......53 D4
Yiewsley UB7 ......104 A5
St Stephen's Row EC4 ......242 C1
St Stephen's Terr SW8 ......270 C3
St Stephen's Wlk SW7 ......256 A4
St Swithin's La EC4 ......117 B6 252 C6
St Swithun's Rd SE13 ......164 B6
St Swithun Wells RC Prim Sch HA4 ......62 D5
St Teresa's RC Fst & Mid Sch HA3 ......24 A2
St Teresa's RC Prim Sch SM4 ......202 B3
St Teresa's RC Prim Sch The RM8 ......80 C4
St Theresa Ct E4 ......20 B4
St Theresa's RC Sch N3 ......47 D6
St Theresa's Rd TW14 ......127 D1
St Thomas a Beckett RC Prim Sch SE2 ......124 A3
St Thomas Becket RC Prim Sch SE25 ......206 A3
St Thomas' CE Prim Sch W10 ......91 A3
St Thomas' Cl KT6 ....198 B1
St Thomas Ct 14 NW1 ......71 C1
St Thomas' Ct HA5 ....23 A2
St Thomas Ct
Sidcup DA5 ......169 C4
11 Walthamstow E10 ..53 D2
St Thomas' Dr BR5 ...211 A1
Pinner HA5 ......23 A2
St Thomas Gdns IG1 ..79 A2
St Thomas Ho 2 E1 ...96 D1
St Thomas More Language Coll SW3 ......114 D2 257 C3
St Thomas More RC Comp Sch SE9 ......166 C5
St Thomas More RC Prim Sch
Bexley DA7 ......147 B3
SE9 ......144 A2
St Thomas More Sch N22 ......32 C3
St Thomas of Canterbury RC Prim Sch
Mitcham CR4 ......203 A6
SW6 ......135 B5 264 C4
St Thomas' Rd W4 ...133 A6
St Thomas Rd
Newham E16 ......99 A1
Osidge N14 ......15 D4
St Thomas's Gdns NW5 ......71 A2
St Thomas's Hospl Medical Sch SE1 ......116 B3 260 C5
St Thomas's Hospl SE1 ......116 B3 260 C6
St Thomas's Pl 20 E9 ..74 C1
St Thomas's Rd
Dagenham NW10 ......89 C6
Highbury N4, N5 ......72 C5
St Thomas's Sq E9 ....74 C1
St Thomas St SE1 ......117 B5 252 D3
St Thomas's Way SW6 ......135 B5 264 D4
St Thomas the Apostle Coll The SE15 ......140 C4
St Timothy's Mews 3 BR1 ......187 B2
St Ursula Gr HA5 ......41 A4
St Ursula Rd UB1 ......85 C1
St Ursula's Convent Sch SE10 ......142 B5
St Vincent Cl SE27 ...182 D5
St Vincent De Paul Ho 24 E1 ......96 C2
St Vincent De Paul RC Prim Sch SW1 ......115 C3 259 B6
St Vincent Ho SE1 ... 263 C6
St Vincent Rd TW2 ...152 A5
St Vincent's Hospl HA5 ......39 D6
St Vincents La NW7 ...28 C6
St Vincent's RC Prim Sch
Acton W3 ......110 D6
Dagenham RM8 ......80 C6
Marylebone W1 ......93 A2 238 B3
St Vincents RC Prim Sch SE9 ......188 A6
St Vincent's RC Sch NW7 ......28 C5
St Vincent St W1 ....238 B3
St Wilfrid's Cl EN4 ....14 C6
St Wilfrid's Rd EN4 ....14 C6
St William of York RC Prim Sch SE23 ....163 A3
St Winefride's Ave E12 ......78 B3
St Winefride's RC Prim Sch E12 ......78 B3
St Winifred's RC Inf Sch SE12 ......164 C6
St Winifred's RC Jun Sch SE12 ......164 D4
St Winifred's Rd TW11 ......175 B4
Sakura Dr N22 ......31 D2
Sala Ho SE3 ......143 B1
Salamanca Pl SE1 .. 260 C3
Salamanca St SE1, SE11 ......116 B2 260 C3
Salamander Cl KT2 ..175 C5
Salamander Quay KT1 ......175 D2
Salcombe Dr
Dagenham RM6 ......59 B3
Salcombe Dr *continued*
North Cheam SM4 ... 200 D1
Salcombe Gdns
Clapham SW4 ......137 B1
Mill Hill NW7 ......28 C4
Salcombe Ho 6 SE23 ......162 C2
Salcombe Lo NW5 ......71 A4
Salcombe Pk IG10 ......21 D6
Salcombe Rd
Ashford TW15 ......148 A1
23 Stoke Newington N16 ......73 C3
Walthamstow E17 ......53 B2
Salcombe Sch N14 ...15 B4
Salcombe Villas 13 TW10 ......154 A6
Salcombe Way
Hayes UB4 ......83 C4
Ruislip HA4 ......62 A6
Salcot N4 ......72 B6
Salcott Rd
Wallington CR0 ......220 B4
Wandsworth SW11 .. 158 D6
Salehurst Cl HA3 ......44 A4
Salehurst Rd SE4 ......163 B5
Salem Ho 13 E9 ......74 D2
Salem Pl CR0 ......221 A5
Salem Rd W2 ......113 D6 245 D6
Sale Pl W2 ......92 C1 237 A2
Salesian Coll SW11 ......136 C4 267 A1
Sale St E2 ......96 A3
Salford Ho 5 E14 ......120 A2
Salford Rd SW12, SW2 ......159 D3
Salhouse Cl SE28 ......102 C1
Salisbury Ave
Barking IG11 ......79 C1
Cheam SM1, SM2 ......217 B2
Hendon N3 ......47 B6
Salisbury Cl SE17 ... 262 C4
Worcester Pk KT4 ... 215 D5
Salisbury Ct
15 Bermondsey SE16 ......118 A3
Chiswick W4 ......111 C2
EC4 ......241 C1
Edgware HA8 ......26 B6
Enfield EN2 ......5 B1
Finchley N3 ......29 B1
Hackney E9 ......75 A3
Northolt UB5 ......63 D3
Salisbury Gdns
5 Buckhurst Hill IG9 ......21 D2
Wimbledon SW19 ... 179 A3
Salisbury Hall Gdns E4 ......35 C4
Salisbury Ho
2 Islington N1 ......72 D2
Islington N1 ......234 C6
3 Poplar E14 ......97 D1
1 Ruislip HA4 ......40 C1
Stanmore HA7 ......25 A4
5 Wallington SM6 ...219 B3
Westminster SW1 ... 259 D2
Wimbledon SW19 ... 156 D1
Salisbury Lower Sch N9 ......18 C4
Salisbury Mans
Edmonton N9 ......18 A1
Harringay N4, N15 ....50 D4
Salisbury Mews
Bromley Comm BR2 ......210 A4
Fulham SW6 ......264 C3
Salisbury Pl
Camberwell SW9 ....138 D5
Marylebone W1 ......237 C4
Salisbury Prim Sch E12 ......78 A3
Salisbury Rd
Barnet EN5 ......1 A2
Bromley Comm BR2 .. 210 A4
Chingford E4 ......19 C1
Croydon SE25 ......206 A3
Dagenham RM10 ......81 D2
East Bedfont TW6 ... 149 A5
Enfield EN3 ......7 B6
Feltham TW13 ......150 C3
Forest Gate E7 ......77 A2
Harringay N4 ......50 D4
Harrow HA1 ......42 B4
Hounslow TW4 ......128 C2
Ilford IG3 ......79 C6
Kingston u T KT3 ......199 B6
Leyton E10 ......76 A6
Old Bexley DA5 ......169 C3
Pinner HA5 ......40 A5
Plashet E12 ......77 D3
Richmond TW9 ......132 A1
Southall UB2 ......107 A2
Tottenham N22 ......32 D1
Wallington SM5 ......218 D2
Walthamstow E17 ......54 A4
Salisbury Rd *continued*
West Ealing W13 ......109 B4
Wimbledon SW19 ... 179 A3
Worcester Pk KT4 ... 215 C5
Salisbury Sq EC4 .... 241 B1
Salisbury St
10 Acton W3 ......111 A4
NW8 ......237 A5
Salisbury Terr SE15 ..140 C2
Salisbury Upper Sch N9 ......18 C4
Salisbury Wlk N19 ....71 C6
Salix Cl TW16 ......172 B3
Salix Ct N3 ......29 C4
Salliesfield TW2 ......152 B5
Sally Murray Cl E12 ...78 C4
Salmen Rd E13 ......98 D5
Salmond Cl HA7 ......25 A4
Salmon La E14 ......97 A1
Salmon Rd DA17 ......125 C1
Salmons Brook Ho EN2 ......4 D2
Salmons Rd
Chessington KT9 .... 214 A2
Edmonton N9 ......18 A3
Salmon St
Kingsbury NW9 ......45 A2
13 Poplar E14 ......97 B1
Salomons Rd 2 E13 ..99 C2
Salop Rd E17 ......52 D3
Saltash Cl SM1 ......217 B4
Saltash Rd DA16 ......146 C4
Saltcoats Rd W4 ......111 C4
Saltcroft Cl HA9 ......44 D1
Saltdene N4 ......50 B1
Salter Cl HA2 ......63 B4
Salterford Rd SW17 ..181 A4
Salter Ho 8 SW16 ...181 C6
Saltern Ct IG11 ......102 B4
Salter Rd SE16 ......119 A5
Salters' Hall Ct EC4 . 252 C6
Salter's Hill SE19 ....183 B5
Salters Rd
North Kensington W10 ......90 D3
Walthamstow E17 ......54 B5
Salter St
College Pk NW10 .....90 A4
11 Poplar E14 ......119 C6
Salterton Rd N7 ......72 B5
Salt Hill Cl UB8 ......60 A3
Saltley Cl E6 ......100 A1
Saltoun Rd SW2, SW9 ......138 C1
Saltram Cl N15 ......51 D5
Saltram Cres W9 .....91 C4
Saltwell St E14 ......119 C6
Saltwood Gr SE17 ... 262 C1
Saltwood Ho 19 SE15 ......140 C6
Salusbury Prim Sch NW6 ......91 B6
Salusbury Rd NW6 ....91 A6
Salutation Rd SE10 ...120 C2
Salvador SW17 ......180 D5
Salvatorian RC Coll HA3 ......24 C1
Salvia Gdns UB6 ......87 A5
Salvin Rd SW15 ......134 D2
Salway Cl IG8 ......37 A3
Salway Ho E10 ......75 D6
Salway Pl E15 ......76 C2
Salway Rd E15 ......76 B2
Salween Ho 2 N16 ...73 B4
Samantha Cl E17 .....53 B2
Samantha Ct E11 .....54 C2
Samaritan Hospl for Women NW1 ...... 237 C4
Sam Bartram Cl SE7 ......121 C1
Sambrooke Ct EN1 ....17 D6
Sambrook Ho 25 E1 ...96 C2
Sambruck Mews SE6 ......163 D3
Samels Ct W6 ......112 A1
Samford Ho N1 ..... 234 A5
Samford St NW8 .... 237 A5
Samira Cl E17 ......53 C3
Sam Manners Ho 7 SE10 ......120 C1
Sam March Ho 5 E14 ......98 B1
Samos Rd SE20 ......184 B1
Sampson Ave EN5 .....12 D6
Sampson Cl DA17 ....125 A3
Sampson Ct TW17 ...193 A4
Sampson St E1 ......118 A5
Samson Ct 5 DA17 ..125 C2
Samson Ho SE18 ......123 A2
Samson St E13 ......99 C5
Samuel Cl SE14 ......140 D6
Shoreditch E8 ......95 D6
Woolwich SE18 ......122 A2
Samuel Ct
Beckenham BR3 .... 207 D6
Shoreditch N1 ......95 C4

Samuel Gray Gdns KT2 175 D2
Samuel Ho
15 Shoreditch E8 95 D6
3 West Norwood SE27 182 D6
Samuel Johnson Cl SW16 182 B6
Samuel Jones Ind Est 7 SE15 139 C5
Samuel Lewis Bldgs N1 72 C2
Samuel Lewis Trust Dwellings
6 Camberwell SE5 139 A4
Chelsea SW3 257 A3
Walham Green SW6 135 C5 265 B4
West Kensington W14 254 B4
Samuel Lewis Trust Est N15 51 C3
Samuel Lo N3 29 B1
Samuel Rhodes Sch N1 94 C6 234 A6
Samuel Richardson Ho W14 254 C3
Samuel's Cl 2 W6 112 C2
Samuel St SE15 139 D5
Woolwich SE18 122 B2
Sancroft Cl NW2 68 B5
Sancroft Ct SW11 267 B2
Sancroft Ho SE11 260 D2
Sancroft Rd HA3 25 A1
Sancroft St SE11 116 B1 260 D2
Sanctuary Mews 15 E8 73 D2
Sanctuary Rd TW19, TW6 148 C5
Sanctuary St SE1 252 B2
Sanctuary The
Morden SM4 201 C3
Sidcup DA5 168 D5
35 Wapping E1 118 B5
Westminster SW1 115 D3 259 D6
Sandale Cl N16 73 B5
Sandall Cl W5 88 A3
Sandall Ho 7 E3 97 A5
Sandall Rd Ealing W5 88 A3
Kentish Town NW5 71 C2
Sandal Rd
Edmonton N18 34 A5
New Malden KT3 199 C5
Sandal St E15 98 C6
Sandalwood Cl 11 E1 97 A3
Sandalwood Dr HA4 39 A2
Sandalwood Ho
DA15 167 D1
6 Hampstead NW3 69 D2
Sandalwood Rd TW13 150 B1
Sandbach Pl SE18 123 A1
Sandbourne Ave SW19 179 D1
Sandbourne
4 Kensington W11 91 C1
14 Paddington NW8 91 D6
Sandbourne Rd SE4 141 A3
Sandbrook Cl NW7 27 B4
Sandbrook Rd N16 73 C5
Sandby Ct BR3 185 B2
Sandby Gn SE9 144 A2
Sandby Ho
11 Camberwell SE5 139 C4
6 Kilburn NW6 91 C6
Sandcroft Cl N13 32 D4
Sandells Ave
Ashford TW15 171 A6
Ashford TW15 171 A6
Sandell St SE1 251 A2
Sanderling Ct
20 SE8 141 B6
Woolwich SE28 124 C6
Sanders Cl TW12 174 A5
Sanders Ho
Streatham SW16 182 A4
WC1 234 A2
Sanders La NW7 28 C3
Sanderson Cl NW5 71 B4
Sanderson Ho 7 SE8 119 B1
Sanderson Sq BR1 210 C6
Sanderstead Ave NW2 69 A6
Sanderstead Cl SW12 159 C4
Sanderstead Rd
South Croydon CR2 221 B1
Walthamstow E10 53 A1
Sanders Way 3 N19 49 D1
Sandfield Gdns CR7 204 D6
Sandfield Pl CR7 205 A6
Sandfield Rd CR7 204 D6
Sandfield WC1 233 B1
Sandford Ave N22 33 A2
Sandford Cl E6 100 B3
Sandford Ct
Barnet EN5 1 D2
Stamford Hill N16 51 C1
Sandford Rd
Bexley DA7 147 A2
BR2 209 A5
Newham E6 100 B4
Sandford Row SE17 262 D2
Sandford St SW6 265 D3
Sandgate Ho
14 Beckenham BR3 185 C3
Ealing W5 87 C2
15 Hackney E5 74 B4
Sandgate La SW17, SW18 158 C3
Sandgate Rd DA16 146 C5
Sandgate St SE15 140 B6
Sandgate Trad Est SE15 140 B6
Sandham Ct SW4 270 B1
Sandham Point 10 SE18 122 D2
Sandhills Mdw TW17 193 A2
Sandhills The SW10 266 B6
Sandhills CR0, SM6 219 D4
Sandhurst Ave
Harrow HA2 41 D3
Tolworth KT5 198 D2
Sandhurst Cl
Queensbury NW9 44 C6
South Croydon CR2 221 C1
Sandhurst Ct SW2 138 A1
Sandhurst Dr IG3 79 D4
Sandhurst Ho 12 E1 96 C2
Sandhurst Jun & Inf Schs SE6 164 C3
Sandhurst Mkt SE6 164 A3
Sandhurst Rd
Bexley DA5 168 D6
Catford SE6 164 B3
DA15 168 A1
Ponders End N9 18 D5
Queensbury HA8, NW9 44 C6
Sandhurst Way CR2 221 C1
Sandifer Dr NW2 68 D5
Sandiford Rd SM3 217 B6
Sandiland Cres BR2 224 D6
Sandilands Rd SW6 135 D4 265 C1
Sandilands CR0 222 A5
Sandilands Sta CR0 221 D6
Sandison St SE15 140 A2
Sandland St WC1 240 D3
Sandling Rise SE9 166 C1
Sandlings Cl SE15 140 B3
Sandlings The
Tottenham N22 50 D6
5 Wood Green N22 32 C1
Sandmartin Way CR4 203 A1
Sandmere Rd SW4 138 A1
Sandon Cl KT10 196 B1
Sandon Ct IG3 80 A5
Sandon Ho 5 SW2 160 A4
Sandow Commercial Est UB3 105 D3
Sandow Cres UB3 105 D3
Sandown Ave KT10 212 A3
Sandown Cl TW5 128 A4
Sandown Ct 12 SM2 217 D1
Sandown Gate KT10 212 B5
Sandown Ho
2 Acton Green W4 111 A1
Esher KT10 212 A4
Penge SE26 184 B4
Sandown Park KT10 212 A6
Sandown Rd
Croydon SE25 206 B4
Esher KT10 212 A4
Sandown Way UB5 63 B3
Sandpiper Cl
Higham Hill E17 34 D3
Rotherhithe SE16 119 B4
Sandpiper Ct
13 Cubitt Town E14 120 A3
1 SE8 141 C5
Sandpiper Rd SM1 217 B3
Sandpiper Terr IG5 56 D6
Sandpit Pl SE7 122 A1
Sandpit Rd BR1 186 C5
Sandpits Rd
Richmond TW10 153 D2
South Croydon CR0 222 D4
Sandra Cl
Hounslow TW3 151 D6
Tottenham N17 33 A2
Sandra Ho KT8 196 B4
Sandridge Cl
Hadley Wood EN4 2 C6
Harrow HA1 42 C5
Sandridge St 3 N19 71 C6
Sandringham Ave SW20 179 A1
Sandringham Cl
Enfield EN1 5 C3
Ilford IG6 57 A6
1 Putney SW19 156 D3
Sandringham Cres HA2 63 D6
Sandringham Ct
3 Beckenham BR3 186 A2
Edgware HA8 26 D6
Hillingdon UB10 83 A3
Kingston u T KT2 176 A2
Marylebone W1 239 B1
Putney SW15 156 D5
18 Rotherhithe SE16 118 D5
St John's Wood W9 229 B1
2 Twickenham TW1 153 A3
Sandringham Dr
Ashford TW15 170 A6
DA16 145 C3
Sandringham Flats WC2 249 D6
Sandringham Gdns
Cranford TW5 128 A4
East Molesey KT8 195 C5
Finchley N12 30 B4
Hornsey Vale N8 50 A3
Ilford IG6 57 A6
Sandringham Ho
Richmond TW10 154 C6
W14 254 A4
Sandringham Lo BR6 226 C4
Sandringham Mews TW12 173 B2
Sandringham Prim Sch E7 77 C3
Sandringham Rd
Barking IG11 79 D2
BR1 187 A5
Dalston E8 73 D3
Forest Gate E7 77 C3
Golders Green NW11 47 A2
Leytonstone E10 54 B3
Northolt UB5 63 C1
Stanwell TW19, TW6 148 A6
Thornton Heath CR0 205 A4
Tottenham N22 33 A1
Willesden NW2 68 B2
Worcester Pk KT4 216 A5
Sandrock Pl CR0 222 D4
Sandrock Rd SE13 141 C2
SANDS END 136 A2
Sands End La SW6 135 D4 265 D2
Sandstone La E16 121 B6
Sandstone Pl N19 71 B6
Sandstone Rd SE12 165 B2
Sandstone TW9 132 C5
Sandtoft Rd SE7 143 B6
Sandways 6 TW9 132 C4
Sandwell Cres 2 NW6 69 C2
Sandwell Mans 3 NW6 69 C2
Sandwich Ho
15 Rotherhithe SE16 118 C4
WC1 233 A1
Sandwich St WC1 94 A4 233 A1
Sandwick Cl NW7 28 A3
Sandy Bury BR6 227 B5
Sandycombe Ctr TW9 132 C2
Sandycombe Rd
East Bedfont TW14 150 A3
Richmond TW9 132 C3
Sandycoombe Rd TW1 153 C5
Sandycroft SE2 146 A6
Sandy Dr TW14 149 C3
Sandy Hill Ave SE18 122 D1
Sandy Hill La SE18 122 D2
Sandyhill Rd IG1 78 D4
Sandy Hill Rd SE18 122 D1
Sandy La
Belmont SM2 217 A1
BR5 190 D2
Eastbury HA6 22 A6
Harrow HA3 44 C3
Mitcham CR4 181 A2
Sandy Lane N SM6 219 D3
Sandy Lane S SM6 219 C1
Sandy La
Richmond TW10 153 D2
Teddington KT8, TW11 175 B3
Walton-on-T KT12 194 C3
Sandy Lo N6 49 C2
Sandymount Ave HA7 25 D5
Sandy Rd NW3 69 D6
Sandy Ridge BR7 188 C4
Sandy's Row E1 243 B3
Sandy Way
Croydon CR0 223 B5
Walton-on-T KT12 193 D1
Sanford La 3 N16 73 D6
Sanford St SE14, SE8 141 A6
Sanford Terr N16 73 D5
Sanford Wlk SE14 141 A6
4 Stoke Newington N16 73 D6
Sangam Cl UB2 107 A3
Sanger Ave KT9 214 B4
Sangley Rd
Catford SE6 164 A3
South Norwood SE25 205 C5
Sangora Rd 17 SW11 136 B1
San Ho 29 E9 74 D2
Sankey Ho 22 E2 96 C5
Sansom Rd E11 76 D6
Sansom St
Camberwell SE5 139 B4
SE5 139 B5
Sans Wlk EC1 94 D3 241 C6
Santana SE18 144 D5
Santley Ho SE1 251 B1
Santley St SW4 138 B1
Santos Rd SW18 157 C6
Sapcote Trad Ctr NW10 67 D2
Saperton Wlk SE11 260 D4
Saphora Cl BR6 227 B3
Sapperton Ct EC1 242 A6
Sapphire Cl
Dagenham RM8 58 C1
Newham E6 100 C1
Sapphire Ct 13 E1 118 A6
Sapphire Rd
Rotherhithe SE8 119 A2
Willesden NW10 67 A1
Saracen Cl CR0 205 B3
Saracen St E14 97 C1
Sarah Bonnell Sch E15 76 C2
Sarah Ct UB5 85 B6
Sarah Ho
Roehampton SW15 133 D1
8 Stepney E1 96 B1
Sarah Swift Ho SE1 252 D2
Sarah Turnbull Ho 2 SE18 122 B2
Sara Lane Ct 31 N1 95 C5
Saratoga Rd E5 74 C4
Sardeson Ho 13 SW27 182 D5
Sardinia Ho WC2 240 C1
Sardinia St WC2 240 C2
Sargents Hill N2 30 C2
Sarita Cl HA3 24 B1
Sarjant Path SW19 156 D2
Sark Cl TW5 129 C5
Sark Ho
9 Canonbury N1 73 A2
Enfield EN3 6 D5
Sark Twr SE28 123 A4
Sark Wlk E16 99 B1
Sarnersfield Ho SE15 140 B6
Sarnes Ct 4 N11 31 B6
Sarnesfield Rd EN2 5 B2
Sarratt Ho 6 W10 90 C2
Sarre Rd NW2 69 B3
Sarsden Bldgs W1 238 B1
Sarsen Ave TW3 129 C3
Sarsfeld Rd SW12, SW17 158 D3
Sarsfield Rd UB6 87 C5
Sartor Rd SE15 140 D1
Sarum Hall Sch NW3 70 C1
Sarum Ho W11 244 D5
Sarwan Ho 1 E7 77 C1
Sassoon Ho SE15 140 C3
Sassoon 4 NW9 27 D2
Satanita Cl E16 99 D1
Satchell Mead NW9 27 D2
Satchwell Rd 17 E2 96 A4
Satin Ct NW9 45 D5
Saturn Ho 4 E3 97 C6
Saul Ct 4 SE15 139 D6
Sauls Gn E11 76 C5
Saunders Cl
Ilford IG1 57 B1
Saunders Cl *continued*
14 Limehouse E14 119 B6
Saunders Ho 11 SW2 160 C3
Saunders Ness Rd E14 120 B2
Saunders Rd
Hillingdon UB10 82 B6
Plumstead Comm SE18 123 D1
Saunders St SE11 261 A4
Saunders Way SE28 124 B6
Saunderton Rd HA0 65 B3
Saunton Ave UB3 127 D5
Saunton Ct UB1 108 A6
Savage Gdns EC3 253 B6
Newham E6 100 B1
Savana N16 73 C6
Savannah Cl 9 SE15 139 D5
Savernake Ct HA7 25 B4
Savernake Ho N4 51 B2
Savernake Rd
Enfield N9 18 A5
Maitland Pk NW3 70 D4
Savery Dr KT6 197 C2
Savile Cl
New Malden KT3 199 C4
Thames Ditton KT7 197 A1
Savile Gdns CR0 221 D6
Savill Ct IG8 36 D4
Saville Cres TW15 171 B4
Saville Ho E16 122 D5
Saville Rd
Bedford Pk W4 111 B3
Dagenham RM6 59 B2
Newham E16 122 A5
Twickenham TW1 152 D3
Saville Row
Enfield EN3 6 D3
Hayes BR2 208 D1
W1 115 C6 249 A6
Savill Gdns SW20 200 A6
Savill Ho 2 SW4 159 D5
Savill Row IG8 36 D4
Savin Lo 7 SM2 218 A1
Savona Cl 16 SW19 178 D3
Savona Ct SW20 178 D2
Savona St SW8 137 C5 269 A3
Savoy Ave UB3 105 C1
Savoy Circus W3 111 D6
Savoy Cl Edgware HA8 26 C5
Newham E15 98 C6
Savoy Ct
Earl's Ct SW5 255 B4
Strand WC2 250 B5
Savoy Hill WC2 250 C5
Savoy Mews SW9 138 A2
Savoy Par EN1 5 C2
Savoy Pier WC2 250 C5
Savoy Pl WC2 116 B6 250 C5
Savoy Row WC2 250 C6
Savoy Stps WC2 250 C5
Savoy St WC2 116 B6 250 C5
Savoy Way WC2 250 C5
Sawbill Cl UB4 84 D2
Sawkins Cl SW19 157 A2
Sawley Rd W12 112 A5
Sawmill Yd E3 97 A6
Sawtry Cl SM5 202 C2
Sawyer Cl N9 18 A2
Sawyer Ho 15 SE21 183 C6
Sawyer's Hill TW10 154 B4
Sawyers Lawn W13 87 A1
Sawyer St SE1 117 A4 252 A2
Saxby Rd SW2 160 A4
Saxham Rd IG11 101 D5
Saxlingham Rd E4 20 B1
Saxon Ave TW13 151 B2
Saxon Bsns Ctr SW19 180 A2
Saxonbury Ave TW16 172 B1
Saxonbury Cl CR4 202 B6
Saxonbury Ct
16 Kentish Town N7 71 D3
2 Lower Holloway N7 72 A3
Saxonbury Gdns KT6 197 C1
Saxon Cl
Hillingdon UB8 82 A2
Surbiton KT6 197 D3
Walthamstow E17 53 C2
Saxoncroft Ho SW16 159 D1
Saxon Ct
Colney Hatch N12 30 C5
4 Edgware HA8 26 D5
Saxon Dr W3 88 D2
Saxonfield Cl SW2 160 B4
Saxon Gdns UB1 107 A6
Saxon Hall W2 245 C5
Saxon Ho
4 Clapham SW4 137 D1
Feltham TW13 151 B2
Saxon Prim Sch TW17 192 C4
Saxon Rd
Ashford TW15 171 B4
Bow E3 97 B5
Bromley BR1 186 D3
Ilford IG1 78 D3
Kingston u T KT2 176 A2
Newham E6 100 B3
Southall UB1 107 A6
South Norwood SE25 205 B4
Tottenham N22 32 D2
Wembley HA9 67 A5
Saxon Terr SE6 163 B2
Saxon Way N14 15 D5
Saxon Wlk DA14 190 C4
Saxony Par UB3 83 A2
Saxton Cl SE13 142 B2
Saxville Rd BR5 190 B1
Sayer Ho SE4 141 A1
Sayers Ho 4 N2 30 B1
Sayer's Wlk TW10 154 B4
Sayesbury La N18 34 A5
Sayes Court St SE8 141 B6
Sayes Ct SE8 141 B6
Sayline Ct CR0 221 B5
Scadbury Gdns BR5 190 A1
Scadbury Park Nature Reserve* BR7 189 D4
Scads Hill Cl BR6 211 D3
Scafell NW1 232 A2
Scala St W1 239 B4
Scales Rd N17 52 A6
Scampston Mews 5 W10 90 D1
Scandrett St 38 E1 118 B5
Scarba Wlk N1 73 B2
Scarborough Rd
East Bedfont TW6 149 A5
Finsbury Pk N4 50 C1
Leytonstone E11 54 B1
Ponders End N9 18 C4
Scarborough St E1 243 D1
Scarbrook Rd CR0 221 A5
Scardale Ho 12 E5 74 B6
Scarle Rd HA0 65 D2
Scarlet Rd SE6 164 C1
Scarlette Manor Wlk 10 SE24 160 C4
Scarsbrook Ho 2 SW2 160 C5
Scarsbrook Rd SE3 143 D2
Scarsdale Pl W8 255 C6
Scarsdale Rd HA2 64 A5
Scarsdale Villas W8 113 C3 255 B5
Scarth Rd SW13 133 D2
Scawen Cl SM5 219 A4
Scawen Rd SE8 119 A1
Scawfell St E2 95 D5
Scaynes Link N12 29 C6
Sceptre Ho 10 E1 96 C3
Sceptre Rd E2 96 C4
Schiller International Univ SE1 116 C5 251 A3
Schofield Wlk SE3 143 A5
Sch of Pharmacy WC1 94 A3 240 B6
Scholars Cl EN5 1 A1
Scholars Ct 5 N19 49 D1
Scholars Ho 6 E4 20 B3
Scholars Rd
Chingford E4 20 B3
Streatham SW12 159 C3
Scholefield Rd N19 71 D6
Scholey Ho SW11 136 C2
Schomberg Ho SW1 259 D4
Schonfeld Sq N16 51 B1
School App 21 E2 95 C4
Schoolbank Rd SE10 120 D2
School Bell Cloisters 17 E3 97 A5
Schoolbell Mews 18 E3 97 A5
School Cotts
Bromley BR1 187 A3
Sidcup DA14 190 C5
School Flats SW8 270 A1
School Ho SE1 263 A4
Schoolhouse La E1 118 D6
School House La TW11 175 C3
Schoolhouse Yd 9 SE18 122 D1
School La DA16 146 B2
Lower Halliford TW17 192 D2
Pinner HA5 41 A5

School La *continued*
Surbiton KT6 ... 198 B1
Teddington KT1 ... 175 C2
School Pas
3 Kingston u T KT1 ... 176 B1
Southall UB1 ... 107 B6
School Rd
Ashford TW15 ... 170 D4
Becontree NW10 ... 89 B3
BR7 ... 189 A3
Dagenham RM10 ... 103 D6
East Molesey KT8 ... 196 B5
Hampton TW12 ... 174 A4
Hounslow TW3 ... 130 A2
Ilford E12 ... 78 B4
Littleton TW15 ... 170 D3
Teddington KT1 ... 175 C2
School Road Ave TW12 ... 174 A4
School Sq SE10 ... 120 D3
School Way RM8 ... 80 C5
Schoolway N12 ... 30 B4
School Wlk TW16 ... 193 D6
Schooner Cl
Barking IG11 ... 102 B4
Cubitt Town E14 ... 120 B3
1 Rotherhithe SE16 ... 118 D4
Schubert Rd
Elstree WD6 ... 9 D5
Putney SW15 ... 157 B6
Science Mus* SW7 ... 114 B3 256 C5
Scilly Isles KT10 ... 212 C6
Sclater St E1 ... 243 D6
Scoles Cres SW2 ... 160 C3
Scope Way KT1 ... 198 A5
Scoresby St SE1 ... 251 C3
Scoresdale SE19 ... 183 C2
Scorton Ave UB6 ... 87 A5
Scorton Ho 2 N1 ... 95 C5
Scotch Comm W13 ... 87 B2
Scotch Ho SW1 ... 114 D4 247 C1
Scoter Cl IG8 ... 37 B3
Scoter Ct 23 SE8 ... 141 B6
Scot Gr HA5 ... 22 D3
Scotia Bldg 10 E1 ... 118 D6
Scotia Ct 3 SE16 ... 118 C3
Scotia Rd 24 SW2 ... 160 C4
Scotland Gn N17 ... 33 D1
Scotland Green Rd EN3 ... 18 D6
Scotland Green Rd N EN3 ... 7 A1
Scotland Pl SW1 ... 250 A3
Scotland Rd IG9 ... 21 C3
Scotney Cl BR6 ... 226 C4
Scotney Ho E9 ... 74 C2
Scots Cl TW19 ... 148 A3
Scotsdale Cl
Belmont SM3 ... 217 A1
BR5 ... 211 C5
Scotsdale Rd SE12 ... 165 B6
Scotson Ho SE11 ... 261 A3
Scotswood St EC1 ... 94 C3 241 B6
Scotswood Wlk N17 ... 34 A3
Scott Cl
Thornton Heath SW16 ... 182 B2
West Drayton UB7 ... 104 B2
West Ewell KT19 ... 215 A3
Scott Ct Acton W4 ... 111 B4
4 Clapham SW11 ... 137 B3
17 Stoke Newington N16 ... 73 C5
Scott Ellis Gdns NW8 ... 92 B4 229 C1
Scottes La RM8 ... 58 D1
Scott Farm Cl KT7 ... 197 B1
Scott Gdns TW5 ... 128 D5
Scott Ho
2 Barnsbury N7 ... 72 B2
3 Edmonton N18 ... 34 A5
4 Erith DA17 ... 125 B1
Islington N1 ... 235 C6
Lisson Gr NW8 ... 237 A5
17 Millwall E14 ... 119 C4
6 Newham E13 ... 99 A5
Richmond TW10 ... 153 C2
3 Stonebridge NW10 ... 67 B1
Scott Lidgett Cres SE16 ... 118 A4
Scott Rd HA8 ... 26 D1
Scott's Ave
Ashford TW16 ... 171 C3
Beckenham BR2 ... 186 B1
Scotts Ct 6 W12 ... 112 B4
Scotts Dr TW12 ... 173 D3
Scotts Farm Rd KT19 ... 215 A2
Scotts Ho DA16 ... 146 C4
Scott's La BR2, BR3 ... 186 B1
Scotts Park Prim Sch BR1 ... 187 C2
Scotts Rd BR1 ... 187 A3
Scott's Rd
Leytonstone E10 ... 54 A1
Shepherd's Bush W12 ... 112 B4
Scotts Rd UB2 ... 106 D3
Scott's Sufferance Wharf SE1 ... 253 D1
Scott St E1 ... 96 B3
Scott's Way TW16 ... 171 C3
Scott's Yd EC4 ... 252 C6
Scott Trimmer Way TW3 ... 129 A3
Scottwell Dr NW9 ... 45 D4
Scott Wilkie Prim Sch E16 ... 99 C1
Scoulding Ho 12 E14 ... 119 C3
Scoulding Rd E16 ... 99 A1
Scouler St E14 ... 120 B6
Scout App NW10 ... 67 C4
Scout La SW4 ... 137 C2
Scout Way NW7 ... 27 B6
Scovell Cres SE1 ... 252 A1
Scovell Rd SE1 ... 252 A1
Scratchwood Nature Trail* NW7 ... 11 B4
Scrattons Terr IG11 ... 103 A5
Scriven Ct 2 E8 ... 95 D6
Scriven St E8 ... 95 D6
Scrooby St SE6 ... 163 D5
Scrope Bldg EC1 ... 241 A4
Scrubs La NW10, W10, W12 ... 90 B3
Scrutton Cl SW12 ... 159 D4
Scrutton St EC2 ... 95 C3 243 A5
Scudamore La NW9 ... 45 A5
Scutari Rd SE22 ... 162 C6
Scylla Cres TW6&TW14 ... 148 D4
Scylla Rd
East Bedfont TW14, TW6 ... 148 D5
Nunhead SE15 ... 140 B2
Seabright St 27 E2 ... 96 B4
Seabrook Dr BR4 ... 224 C6
Seabrook Gdns RM7 ... 59 C2
Seabrook Rd RM8 ... 80 D5
Seacole Cl W3 ... 89 B2
Seacole Ct N15 ... 51 D4
Seacole Lo N21 ... 16 B6
Seacon Twr 8 E14 ... 119 C4
Seacourt Rd SE2 ... 124 D4
Seacroft Gdns WD19 ... 22 D6
Seafield Rd N11 ... 31 D6
Seaford Cl HA4 ... 61 B6
Seaford Ho 13 SE16 ... 118 C4
Seaford Rd
Ealing W13 ... 109 B5
Enfield EN1 ... 5 C1
Tottenham N15 ... 51 C4
Walthamstow E17 ... 53 D6
Seaford St WC1 ... 233 B1
Seaforth Ave KT3 ... 200 B5
Seaforth Cres N5 ... 73 A3
Seaforth Gdns
Southgate N21 ... 16 C3
Woodford IG8 ... 37 C5
Worcester Pk KT19 ... 215 D3
Seaforth Lo 2 SW13 ... 133 D3
Seaforth Pl SW1 ... 259 B6
Seagrave Lo SW6 ... 265 B6
Seagrave Rd SW6 ... 135 C6 265 B6
Seagrove Cl E1 ... 96 D2
Seagry Rd E11 ... 55 B2
Seagull Cl IG11 ... 102 A4
Seagull La E16 ... 121 A6
Sealand Rd TW6 ... 148 C5
Sealand Wlk UB5 ... 85 A4
Seal Ho SE1 ... 262 D6
Seal St E8 ... 73 D4
Searle Ct 2 CR4 ... 180 C2
Searle Pl N4 ... 50 B1
Searles Cl SW11 ... 136 C5 267 B3
Searles Dr E6 ... 100 D2
Searles Rd SE1 ... 262 D4
Searson Ho SE17 ... 261 D3
Sears Ret Pk UB6 ... 86 C6
Sears St SE5 ... 139 B5
Seasalter Ho 10 SW9 ... 138 C4
Seasprite Cl 10 UB5 ... 84 D4
Seath Ho 4 SE26 ... 184 B5
Seaton Ave IG3 ... 79 D3
Seaton Cl
Isleworth TW2 ... 152 B5
6 Newham E13 ... 99 A3
Roehampton SW15 ... 156 B4
Seaton Dr TW15 ... 148 A2
Seaton Gdns HA4 ... 62 A6
Seaton Point E5 ... 74 A4
Seaton Rd
Bexley DA16 ... 146 C5
Hayes UB3 ... 105 B3
Mitcham CR4 ... 180 C1
Twickenham TW2 ... 152 A5
Wembley HA0 ... 88 A5
Seaton Sq NW7 ... 28 D3
Seaton St N18 ... 34 A5
Seavington Ho 3 SE5 ... 139 C2
Sebastian Ct 11 IG11 ... 79 D1
Sebastian Ho 22 N1 ... 95 C5
Sebastian St EC1 ... 94 D4 234 D1
Sebastopol Rd N9 ... 34 A6
Sebbon St N1 ... 72 D1
Sebergham Gr NW7 ... 28 A3
Sebert Rd E7 ... 77 B4
Sebright Ho 22 E2 ... 96 A5
Sebright Pas 29 E2 ... 96 A5
Sebright Rd EN5 ... 1 A2
Sebright Sch E2 ... 96 A5
Secker Cres HA3 ... 24 A2
Secker Ho SW9 ... 138 D3
Secker St SE1 ... 251 A3
Second Ave
Chadwell Heath RM6 ... 58 C4
Dagenham RM10 ... 103 D5
East Acton W3 ... 111 D5
Edmonton N18 ... 34 C6
Enfield EN1 ... 17 D6
Hayes UB3 ... 105 D5
Hendon NW4 ... 46 D5
Kensal Town W10 ... 91 A3
Manor Pk E12 ... 78 A3
Mortlake SW14 ... 133 C2
Newham E13 ... 99 A4
Walthamstow E17 ... 53 C4
Walton-on-T KT12 ... 194 B3
Wembley HA9 ... 65 D6
Second Cl KT8 ... 196 A5
Second Cross Rd TW2 ... 152 C2
Second Way HA9 ... 66 D4
Secrett Ho 6 TW10 ... 153 C1
Sedan Way SE17 ... 117 C1 263 A2
Sedcombe Cl DA14 ... 190 C6
Sedcote Rd EN3 ... 18 D6
Sedding St SW1 ... 258 A4
Seddon Ho EC2 ... 242 A4
Seddon Rd SM4 ... 202 B4
Seddon St WC1 ... 94 B4 233 D1
Sedgebrook Rd SE3 ... 143 D2
Sedgecombe Ave HA3 ... 43 C4
Sedgefield Ct UB5 ... 63 D3
Sedgeford Rd W12 ... 111 D5
Sedgehill Rd SE6 ... 185 D5
Sedgehill Sch SE6 ... 185 D5
Sedgemere Ave N2 ... 48 A6
Sedgemere Rd SE2 ... 124 C3
Sedgemoor Dr RM10 ... 81 C4
Sedge Rd N17 ... 34 C3
Sedgeway SE6 ... 164 D3
Sedgewick Ho SW19 ... 156 D2
Sedgewood Cl BR2 ... 208 D2
Sedgley Ho N4 ... 72 B6
Sedgmoor Pl SE5 ... 139 C5
Sedgwick Ave UB10 ... 60 D1
Sedgwick Rd E10 ... 76 A6
Sedgwick St E9 ... 74 D3
Sedleigh Rd SW18 ... 157 B5
Sedlescombe Rd SW6 ... 135 C6 265 A6
Sedley Cl EN1 ... 6 B5
Sedley Ct SE26 ... 162 B2
Sedley Ho SE11 ... 260 D2
Sedley Pl W1 ... 238 C1
Sedum Cl NW9 ... 44 D4
Seeley Dr SE21 ... 183 C6
Seelig Ave NW9 ... 46 A2
Seely Rd SW17 ... 181 A4
Seething La EC3 ... 117 C6 253 B6
SEETHING WELLS ... 197 D3
Seething Wells Halls of Residence KT6 ... 197 C3
Seething Wells La KT6 ... 197 C3
Sefton Ave
Edgware NW7 ... 27 B5
Harrow HA3 ... 24 B2
Sefton Cl BR5 ... 211 D5
Sefton Ct TW5 ... 129 D4
Sefton Lo 2 TW1 ... 153 C5
Sefton Rd
Croydon CR0 ... 206 A1
Orpington BR5 ... 211 D5
Sefton St SW15 ... 134 C2
Segal Cl SE23 ... 163 A4
Sekforde St EC1 ... 94 D3 241 C6
Sekhon Terr TW13 ... 151 C1
Selan Gdns UB4 ... 84 B2
Selbie Ave NW10 ... 67 D3
Selborne Ave DA5 ... 169 A3
Little Ilford E12 ... 78 C4
Walthamstow E17 ... 53 B5
Selborne Gdns
Hendon NW4 ... 46 A5
Wembley UB6 ... 87 A5
Selborne Ho SE1 ... 252 C1
Selborne 2 SW11 ... 137 A2
Selborne Prim Sch UB6 ... 86 D5
Selborne Rd
1 Camberwell SE5 ... 139 B3
Ilford IG1 ... 78 C6
Kingston u T KT3 ... 177 C1
Palmers Green N14 ... 16 A1
Sidcup DA14 ... 190 B6
South Croydon CR0 ... 221 D5
Walthamstow E17 ... 53 C4
Wood Green N22 ... 32 B2
Selborne Wlk E17 ... 53 B5
Selborne Wlk Sh Ctr E17 ... 53 B5
Selbourne Ave KT6 ... 214 C5
Selbridge Ct SW19 ... 179 C4
Selby Chase HA4 ... 62 B6
Selby Cl BR7 ... 188 C4
Chessington KT9 ... 214 A1
14 Newham E6 ... 100 A2
Selby Ct TW2 ... 152 B2
Selby Gdns UB1 ... 85 C3
Selby Gn SM5 ... 202 C2
Selby Ho 10 SW4 ... 159 C5
Selby Rd
Ashford TW15 ... 171 A4
Carshalton SM5 ... 202 C2
Ealing W5 ... 87 C3
Leyton E11 ... 76 C5
Newham E13 ... 99 B2
Penge SE20 ... 184 A1
Tottenham N17 ... 33 C4
Selby Sq 1 W10 ... 91 A4
Selby St E1 ... 96 A3
Selden Ho 2 SE15 ... 140 C3
Selden Rd SE15 ... 140 C3
Selden Wlk N7 ... 72 B6
Seldon Ho
Nine Elms SW8 ... 269 A3
Pimlico SW1 ... 259 A1
Selena Ct N20 ... 14 D1
SELHURST ... 205 B4
Selhurst Cl SW19 ... 156 D3
Selhurst New Ct SE25 ... 205 C3
Selhurst New Rd SE25 ... 205 C3
Selhurst Park (Crystal Palace FC) SE25 ... 205 C5
Selhurst Pl SE25 ... 205 C3
Selhurst Rd
Edmonton N9 ... 17 C1
South Norwood SE25 ... 205 C4
Selhurst Sta SE25 ... 205 C4
Selina Ho NW8 ... 236 D6
Selinas La RM8 ... 59 B2
Selkirk Ct N17 ... 33 C1
Selkirk Ho N1 ... 233 C6
4 Stoke Newington N16 ... 73 C5
Selkirk Rd
Twickenham TW2 ... 152 A3
Upper Tooting SW17 ... 180 C6
Sellers Hall Cl N3 ... 29 C3
Sellincourt Prim Sch SW17 ... 180 C4
Sellincourt Rd SW17 ... 180 C4
Sellindge Cl BR3 ... 185 B3
Sellons Ave NW10 ... 89 D6
Sellsby Ct N11 ... 31 B5
Sellwood Dr EN5 ... 12 D6
Selma Ho 7 W12 ... 90 B1
Selman Ho 3 E9 ... 75 A2
SELSDON ... 223 A1
Selsdon Ave CR2 ... 221 B2
Selsdon Cl KT6 ... 198 A4
Selsdon High Sch CR2 ... 222 D1
Selsdon Park Rd CR0, CR2 ... 223 B1
Selsdon Rd
Newham E13 ... 99 C5
South Croydon CR2 ... 221 B2
Wanstead E11 ... 55 A2
West Norwood SE27 ... 182 D6
Willesden NW2 ... 67 D6
Selsdon Road Ind Est CR2 ... 221 B2
Selsdon Way E14 ... 119 D3
Selsea Pl N16 ... 73 C3
Selsey Cres DA16 ... 146 D4
Selsey St E14 ... 97 C2
Selvage La NW7 ... 27 B6
Selway Cl HA5 ... 40 B6
Selway Ho SW8 ... 270 B2
Selwood Ho
Chislehurst BR7 ... 189 A4
1 Stoke Newington N4 ... 51 B2
Selwood Pl SW7 ... 114 B1 256 C2
Selwood Rd
Cheam SM3 ... 201 B1
Chessington KT9 ... 213 D4
Croydon CR0 ... 206 B1
Selwood Terr SW7 ... 256 C2
Selworthy Cl E11 ... 55 A4
Selworthy Ho SW11 ... 266 D2
Selworthy Rd SE6 ... 163 B1
Selwyn Ave
Chingford E4 ... 36 A4
Ilford IG3 ... 57 D3
Richmond TW9 ... 132 B2
Selwyn Cl TW4 ... 129 A1
Selwyn Cres DA16 ... 146 B1
Selwyn Ct
Edgware HA8 ... 26 D3
Lewisham SE3 ... 142 D2
8 Richmond TW10 ... 154 B6
Walthamstow E17 ... 53 C4
Wembley HA9 ... 67 A5
Selwyn Ho 3 SW15 ... 156 D5
Selwyn Inf Sch E4 ... 36 A4
Selwyn Jun Sch E4 ... 36 A4
Selwyn Prim Sch E13 ... 99 A6
Selwyn Rd Bow E3 ... 97 B5
Newham E13 ... 99 B6
New Malden KT3 ... 199 B4
Willesden NW10 ... 67 C1
Semley Gate E9 ... 75 B2
Semley Ho SW1 ... 258 C3
Semley Pl SW1 ... 115 B2 258 C3
Thornton Heath SW16 ... 182 B1
Semley Rd SW16 ... 182 A1
Senate St SE15 ... 140 C3
Senators Lo 31 E3 ... 97 A5
Senator Wlk 2 SE28 ... 123 B3
Sencler Ho SE2 ... 146 D6
Sendall Ct 13 SW11 ... 136 B2
Seneca Rd CR7 ... 205 A5
Senga Rd SM6 ... 203 A1
Senhouse Rd SM3 ... 216 D5
Senior St W2 ... 91 D2
Senlac Rd SE12 ... 165 B3
Sennen Rd EN1 ... 17 D4
Sennen Wlk SE9 ... 166 A1
Senrab St E1 ... 96 D1
Sentinel Cl UB5 ... 85 A3
Sentinel Ho NW4 ... 46 C5
Sentinel Sq NW4 ... 46 C5
September Ct UB1 ... 107 D5
September Way HA7 ... 25 B4
Sequoia Cl WD23 ... 8 B3
Sequoia Gdns BR6 ... 211 D2
Sequoia Pk HA5 ... 23 D4
Seraph Ct EC1 ... 95 A4 235 A2
Serbin Cl E10 ... 54 A2
Serenaders Rd 20 SW9 ... 138 C3
Sergeant Ind Est The SW18 ... 157 D5
Serica Ct 14 SE10 ... 142 A5
Serjeants' Inn EC4 ... 241 B1
Serlby Ct W14 ... 254 C6
Serle St WC2 ... 94 B1 240 D2
Sermon La EC4 ... 242 A1
Serpentine Ct 10 SE16 ... 118 D4
Serpentine Gallery* W2 ... 114 B4 246 D2
Serpentine Rd W2 ... 114 D5 247 C3
Serpentine The* W2 ... 114 C5 247 B3
Service Route No 1 E15 ... 76 B1
Service Route No 2 1 E15 ... 76 B1
Service Route No 3 2 E15 ... 76 B1
Serviden Dr BR1 ... 187 D2
Servite Ho
Beckenham BR3 ... 185 B2
Bromley BR1 ... 188 B1
East Barnet N14 ... 15 B6
Lewisham SE13 ... 141 D4
Penge SE26 ... 184 C4
Worcester Pk KT4 ... 215 D6
Servite RC Prim Sch SW10 ... 136 A6 266 A6
Servius Ct 2 TW8 ... 131 D5
Sessions Terr CR4 ... 180 D2
Setchell Rd SE1 ... 117 D2 263 C4
Setchell Way SE1 ... 263 C4
Seth St 25 SE16 ... 118 C4
Seton Ct 3 NW9 ... 46 A5
Seton Gdns RM9 ... 80 C1
Settle Point 11 E13 ... 99 A5
Settlers Ct 11 E14 ... 120 B6
Settles St E1 ... 96 A1
Settrington Rd SW6 ... 135 D3
Seven Acres
Carshalton SM5 ... 218 C6
Northwood HA6 ... 22 A4
Seven Dials WC2 ... 94 A1 240 A1
SEVEN KINGS ... 57 D2
Seven Kings High Sch IG2 ... 57 B2
Seven Kings Rd IG3 ... 79 D6
Seven Kings Sta IG3 ... 57 C1
Seven Kings Way KT2 ... 176 A2
Seven Mills Prim Sch E14 ... 119 C4
Sevenoaks Rd BR6 ... 227 D4
Catford SE4 ... 163 B5
Sevenoaks Way BR5 ... 190 C1
Seven Sisters N15 ... 51 D4
Seven Sisters Prim Sch N15 ... 51 B4
Seven Sisters Rd
Finsbury Pk N4 ... 72 D6
Stoke Newington N4, N7, N15 ... 51 A2
Seven Sisters Sta N15 ... 51 C4
Seven Stars Cnr W12 ... 112 A3
Seven Stars Yd E1 ... 243 D4
Seventh Ave
Hayes UB3 ... 106 A5
Ilford E12 ... 78 B4
Seven Ways Par IG2 ... 56 C4
Severnake Cl E14 ... 119 C2
Severn Ave 2 W10 ... 91 A4
Severn Ct 11 KT2 ... 175 D2
Severn Dr Enfield EN1 ... 6 A5
Hinchley Wood KT10 ... 213 A6
Severn Way NW10 ... 67 D3
Severus Rd SW11 ... 136 C1
Seville Ho 11 E1 ... 118 A5
Seville Mews N1 ... 73 C1
Seville St SW1 ... 247 D1
Sevington Rd NW4 ... 46 B3
Sevington St W9 ... 91 D3
Seward Rd
Penge BR3 ... 184 D1
West Ealing W7 ... 109 A4
Seward St EC1 ... 95 A4 235 A1
SEWARDSTONEBURY ... 20 C6
Sewardstone Gdns E4 ... 19 D6
Sewardstone Rd
Chingford E4 ... 19 D6
South Hackney E2 ... 96 C5
Sewdley St E5 ... 74 D5
Sewell Ho 2 N16 ... 73 C3
Sewell Rd SE2 ... 124 B4
Sewell St E13 ... 99 A4
Sextant Ave E14 ... 120 B2
Sexton Ct 7 E14 ... 120 B6
Sexton's Ho 5 SE13 ... 142 A6
Seychelle Ct BR3 ... 185 D3
Seymour Ave
Tottenham N17 ... 34 A1
West Barnes SM4 ... 200 D2
Seymour Cl
East Molesey KT8 ... 196 A4
Pinner HA5 ... 23 B2
Seymour Ct
Chingford E4 ... 20 D2
Dollis Hill NW2 ... 68 B6
Muswell Hill N10 ... 31 A1
Putney SW15 ... 134 B1
Southgate N21 ... 16 B5
Upper Clapton N16 ... 52 A1
Seymour Dr BR2 ... 210 B1
Seymour Gdns
Brockley SE4 ... 141 A2
Feltham TW13 ... 172 C6
Kingston u T KT5 ... 198 B4
Redbridge IG1 ... 56 B1
Ruislip HA4 ... 40 D1
Twickenham TW1 ... 153 B4
Seymour Ho
Bloomsbury WC1 ... 240 A6
1 Clapham SW8 ... 137 C3
Ruislip HA4 ... 40 A5
Somers Town NW1 ... 232 D1
Seymour Lo 14 KT1 ... 175 D2
Seymour Mews W1 ... 238 A2

Seymour Pl
Croydon SE25 .... 206 B5
Paddington
W1....... 92 D1 237 C2
Seymour Rd
Acton W4......... 111 A2
Carshalton CR4..... 203 A2
Chingford E4........ 19 D3
East Molesey KT8... 196 A4
Edmonton N9......... 18 B2
Finchley N3.......... 29 D3
Hampton TW12..... 174 A5
Harringay N8........ 50 D4
Newham E6.......... 99 D6
Teddington KT1..... 175 D2
Wallington SM5..... 219 A3
Walthamstow E10..... 53 B1
Wandsworth SW18... 157 B5
Wimbledon SW19... 156 D1
Seymour St
Paddington
W1....... 92 D1 237 D1
Woolwich SE18...... 123 A3
Seymour Terr SE20... 184 B2
Seymour Villas
SE20........... 184 A2
Seymour Way TW16.. 171 C3
Seymour Wlk
SW10....... 136 A6 266 A6
Seyssel St E14........ 120 A2
Shaa Rd W3.......... 111 B6
Shabana Ct 3 W12.. 112 B5
Shacklegate La
TW11.......... 174 C6
Shackleton Cl SE23.. 162 B2
Shackleton Ct
3 Dulwich SE21..... 161 B2
2 Isle of Dogs E14 . 119 C1
4 Shepherd's Bush
W12.......... 112 B4
7 Stanwell TW19... 148 A5
Shackleton Ho
5 Stonebridge
NW10........... 67 B1
5 Wapping E1 ..... 118 C5
Shackleton Lo
SW16.......... 181 D5
Shackleton Rd UB1.. 107 B6
SHACKLEWELL 73 D4
Shacklewell Ho 3
E8........... 73 D4
Shacklewell La E8.... 73 D3
Shacklewell Prim Sch
E8........... 73 D4
Shacklewell Rd N16... 73 D4
Shacklewell Row E8.. 73 D4
Shacklewell St 30 E2.. 95 D4
Shadbolt Ave E4...... 35 A5
Shadbolt Cl KT4..... 215 D6
Shad Thames
SE1........ 117 D4 253 D2
SHADWELL 118 C6
Shadwell Ct UB5...... 85 B5
Shadwell Dr UB5...... 85 B4
Shadwell Gdns E1 ... 118 C6
Shadwell Pierhead
E1........... 118 C6
Shadwell Pl 1 E1.... 118 C6
Shadwell Sta E1...... 118 B6
Shady Bush Cl WD23... 8 A4
Shaef Way TW11..... 175 A3
Shaftesbury Ave
Enfield EN3.......... 6 D3
Feltham TW14...... 150 A5
Kenton HA3.......... 44 A3
New Barnet EN5....... 2 A1
Southall UB2........ 107 C3
W1........ 115 D6 249 D6
West Harrow HA1,
HA2............ 42 A1
Shaftesbury Circ
HA2............ 42 A1
Shaftesbury Ct
Borough The SE1.... 262 C6
1 Herne Hill SE5..... 139 B1
Ilford RM6........... 58 C2
Newham E6......... 100 C1
Shaftesbury Ctr
NW10........... 90 D3
Shaftesbury Ct
Shoreditch N1...... 235 C3
Streatham SW16.... 159 D1
3 Thamesmead
SE28........... 124 C5
Shaftesbury Gdns
NW10........... 89 C3
Shaftesbury High Sch
HA3........... 23 D2
Shaftesbury Ho
11 Canning Town
E16........... 98 D1
Croydon SE25 ...... 206 A3
13 Stoke Newington
N16............ 73 C5
Upper Tooting SW17.. 180 B6
W2........... 245 D6
Shaftesbury Lo 9
E14........... 97 D1
Shaftesbury Mews
2 Clapham Pk
SW4........... 159 C6
W8.............. 255 B5
Shaftesbury Park
Chambers 1
SW11........... 137 A2
Shaftesbury Point
E13........... 99 B5
Shaftesbury Prim Sch
E7........... 77 C1
Shaftesbury Rd
Beckenham BR3..... 185 B1
Carshalton SM5...... 202 C2
Chingford E4......... 20 B3
Edmonton N18........ 33 D4
Finsbury Pk N4, N19... 50 A1
Leyton E10........... 53 C1
Richmond TW9...... 132 A2
Upton E7............ 77 C1
Walthamstow E17..... 53 D3
Shaftesburys The
IG11........... 101 A5
Shaftesbury St N1 .. 235 C3
Shaftesbury Waye
UB4............. 84 C1
Shaftesbury Way
TW2........... 152 B1
Shafteswood Ct
SW17.......... 158 D1
Shafto Mews SW1 .. 257 D5
Shafton Rd E9........ 96 D6
Shaftsbury Park Prim
Sch SW11......... 137 A3
Shafts Ct EC3....... 243 A1
Shahjalal Ho 18 E2.... 96 A5
Shakespeare Ave
7 Becontree
NW10........... 89 B6
Feltham TW14...... 150 A5
Friern Barnet N11..... 31 C5
Hayes UB4........... 84 B2
Shakespeare Cl HA3 .. 44 C2
Shakespeare Cres
E12............ 78 B2
Shakespeare Ct EN5 ... 1 D2
Shakespeare Dr HA3 .. 44 B3
Shakespeare Gdns
N2............. 48 D5
Shakespeare Ho
1 Erith DA17....... 125 B1
3 Hackney E9 .... 74 C1
Osidge N14.......... 15 D2
Shakespeare Rd
Acton W3.......... 111 A5
Brixton SE24....... 138 D1
DA7............. 147 A4
Ealing W7.......... 108 D6
Finchley N3.......... 29 C2
Higham Hill E17....... 34 D1
Mill Hill NW7......... 28 A6
Shakespeare's Globe
Theatre (site of)*
SE1 .... 252 B4
Shakespeare Twr
EC2 .... 242 B4
Shakespeare Way
TW13........... 172 C6
Shakspeare Mews 7
N16............. 73 C4
Shakspeare Wlk N16.. 73 C4
Shalbourne Sq E9..... 75 B2
Shalcomb St
SW10....... 136 A6 266 B5
Shalden Ho SW15.... 155 D5
Shaldon Dr
Ruislip HA4.......... 62 C5
West Barnes SM4... 201 A4
Shaldon Rd HA8...... 26 B1
Shalfleet Dr W10 .... 112 D6
Shalford Cl BR6...... 227 A4
Shalford Ct N1 ..... 234 C4
Shalford Ho SE1.... 262 D6
Shalford
Willesden Green
NW10........... 90 A6
3 Woodford IG8....... 37 C4
Shalimar Gdns W3... 111 A6
Shalimar Lo W3 ..... 111 A6
Shalimar Rd W3 ..... 111 A6
Shallons Rd SE9..... 188 D6
Shalstone Rd SW14,
TW9........... 132 D2
Shalston Villas KT5,
KT6........... 198 B3
Shamrock Ct E7 ...... 77 D3
Shamrock Ho
East Barnet N14...... 15 B4
Forest Hill SE26..... 184 A6
Shamrock Rd CR0.... 204 B3
Shamrock St SW4.... 137 D2
Shamrock Way N14 ... 15 B3
Shandon Ct SE4 ..... 141 A3
Shandon Rd SW4 .... 159 C5
Shand St
SE1........ 117 C4 253 B2
Shandy St E1......... 96 D3
Shane Ct EN2.......... 5 A3
Shan Ho WC1....... 240 C5
Shanklin Gdns WD19.. 22 C6
Shanklin Ho E17...... 35 B1
Shanklin Rd
Hornsey N8.......... 49 D4
Tottenham Hale N15... 52 A5
Shannon Cl
Cricklewood NW2..... 68 D5
Southall UB2....... 106 D1
Shannon Cnr Ret Pk
KT3............ 200 A5
Shannon Cnr KT3.... 200 A5
Shannon Commercial
Ctr KT3........... 200 A5
Shannon Ct
Croydon CR0....... 205 A1
11 Peckham SE15... 139 D5
Stoke Newington N16.. 73 C5
Willesden NW10...... 68 A2
Shannon Gr SW9 .... 138 B1
Shannon Pl
NW8......... 92 C5 230 B4
Shannon Way BR3 ... 185 D4
Shanti Ct SW18...... 157 C3
Shap Cres SM5 ...... 202 D1
Shapland Way N13.... 32 B5
Shapla Prim Sch
E1............ 118 A6
Shapwick Cl N11...... 30 D5
Shardcroft Ave
SE24........... 160 D6
Shardeloes Rd SE14.. 141 B3
Shard's Sq SE15 ..... 140 A6
Sharebourne Ho
SW2............ 160 C6
Sharland Cl CR7..... 204 C3
Sharman Ct DA14..... 190 A6
Sharman Ho 18 E14... 98 A1
Sharnbrooke Cl
DA16........... 146 C2
Sharnbrook Ho W6 . 265 A6
Sharon Cl KT6....... 197 C1
Sharon Ct 1 N12..... 30 A4
Sharon Gdns E9...... 96 C6
Sharon Rd
Chiswick W4......... 111 B1
Enfield EN3........... 7 A3
Sharpe Cl W7........ 86 D2
Sharp Ho SW8....... 137 B2
Sharples Hall St 8
NW1............ 70 D1
Sharpness Cl UB4..... 85 A2
Sharpness Ct 2
SE15........... 139 D5
Sharps La HA4........ 39 B2
Sharratt St SE15..... 140 C6
Sharsted St
SE17........ 116 D1 261 C1
Sharvel La UB5 ...... 84 B6
Sharwood WC1...... 233 D3
Shaver's Pl SW1 .... 249 C5
Shaw Ave IG11 ...... 103 A5
Shawbrooke Rd
SE9............ 143 D1
Shawbury Cl 9 NW9.. 27 C2
Shawbury Ct SE22 .. 161 D6
Shawbury Rd SE22... 161 D6
Shaw Cl Bushey WD23... 8 C2
Woolwich SE28...... 124 B5
Shaw Cotts SE23..... 163 A1
Shaw Cres 6 E14..... 97 A1
Shaw Ct
8 Acton Green
W3........... 111 A3
12 Battersea SW11... 136 B2
Cheam SM4......... 202 A2
Upper Holloway N19... 72 A6
Shaw Dr KT12 .... 194 C2
Shawfield Ct UB7 ... 104 A3
Shawfield Pk BR1.... 187 D1
Shawfield St
SW3........ 114 C1 257 B1
Shawford Ct 8
SW15........... 156 A4
Shawford Rd KT19 .. 215 B2
Shaw Gdns IG11 ..... 103 A5
Shaw Ho
6 Erith DA17........ 125 B1
5 Newham E16 ..... 122 C5
Shaw Path BR1 ...... 164 D1
Shaw Rd
Camberwell SE22 ... 139 C1
Catford BR1........ 164 D1
Enfield EN3........... 6 D4
Shaw Sq E17 .... 35 A2
Shaws Wood Cotts
EN4............... 3 C3
Shaw Way SM6 ...... 220 A1
Shearing Dr SM4 .... 202 A2
Shearling Way N7 .... 72 A2
Shearman Rd SE3.... 142 D2
Shears Ct TW16...... 171 C3
Shearsmith Ho 19
E1........... 118 A6
Shears The TW16.... 171 C3
Shears Way TW16.... 171 C2
Shearwater Cl IG11.. 102 A4
Shearwater Ct 24
SE8........... 141 B6
Shearwater Rd SM1.. 217 B3
Shearwater Way
UB4........... 84 D1
Sheaveshill Ave NW9.. 45 C5
Sheaveshill Ct NW9.. 45 C5
Sheaveshill Par NW9.. 45 C5
Sheba Ct N17......... 34 A4
Sheba Pl E1......... 243 D5
Sheen Common Dr SW14,
TW10.......... 154 C6
Sheen Court Rd
TW10.......... 132 C1
Sheen Ct TW10 ...... 132 C1
Sheendale Rd TW9... 132 B1
Sheenewood SE26 ... 184 B6
Sheen Gate Gdns
SW14........... 133 A1
Sheengate Mans
SW14........... 133 B1
Sheen Gr N1 .. 94 C6 234 A6
Sheen La SW14...... 133 A1
Sheen Mount Prim Sch
SW14........... 154 D6
Sheen Pk TW10,
TW9........... 132 A1
Sheen Rd
Orpington BR5...... 211 D5
Richmond TW10,
TW9........... 132 B1
Sheen Way SM6 ..... 220 B3
Sheen Wood SW14... 155 A6
Sheepcote Cl TW5... 128 A5
Sheepcote La SW11.. 136 D3
Sheepcote Rd HA1.... 42 D3
Sheepcotes Rd RM6... 59 A5
Sheephouse Way
KT3........... 199 C2
Sheep La E8......... 96 B6
Sheep Walk Mews 7
SW19.......... 179 A4
Sheepwalk TW17 .... 192 B3
Sheerness Mews
E16............ 122 D4
Sheerwater Rd E16 ... 99 D2
Sheffield Ho 15
SE15........... 139 D4
Sheffield Rd TW14,
TW6........... 149 A6
Sheffield Sq 2 E3.... 97 B4
Sheffield St WC2.... 240 C1
Sheffield Terr
W8........ 113 C5 245 B3
Sheffield Way TW14,
TW6........... 149 B6
Shefton Rise HA6..... 22 A3
Shelbey Ct BR1...... 186 D2
Shelbourne Cl HA5.... 41 B6
Shelbourne Ho 20
N19............ 49 D2
Shelbourne Rd N17... 34 B2
Shelburne Ct SW15 .. 156 D6
Shelburne Dr TW4... 151 C5
Shelburne Ho 9
SW16.......... 181 C5
Shelburne Rd N7 ..... 72 B4
Shelbury Cl DA14.... 168 A1
Shelbury Rd SE22.... 162 B6
Sheldon Ave N6 ...... 48 D3
Sheldon Cl
Penge SE20......... 184 B2
SE12............ 165 B6
Sheldon Ct Barnet EN5.. 1 D1
SW8............ 270 A3
Sheldon Ho
Chingford E4......... 36 C4
9 Homerton E9...... 74 D2
Teddington TW11.... 175 A4
Sheldon Pl E2........ 96 B5
Sheldon Rd
Cricklewood NW2..... 68 D4
DA7............ 147 B4
Dagenham RM9........ 81 A1
Edmonton N18........ 33 C6
Sheldon Sq W2 ..... 236 B3
Sheldon St CR0...... 221 A5
Sheldrake Cl E16 .... 122 B5
Sheldrake Ho 15
SE16........... 118 D2
Sheldrake Pl
W8........ 113 C4 245 A2
Sheldrick Cl CR4..... 180 B1
Shelduck Cl E15 ...... 76 D3
Shelduck Ct 37 SE8 .. 141 B6
Sheldwich Terr
BR2............ 210 A3
Shelford Ct 7 E5 ..... 52 B1
Shelford 20 KT1...... 176 C1
Shelford Pl N16....... 73 B5
Shelford Rd EN5 ..... 12 C5
Shelford Rise SE19... 183 D3
Shelgate Rd SW11 ... 158 D6
Shell Cl BR2......... 210 A3
Shell Ctr SE1....... 250 D3
Shellduck Cl NW9..... 27 C1
Shelley Ave
Greenford UB6 .... 86 B4
Plashet E12.......... 78 A2
Shelley Cl BR6....... 227 C5
Edgware HA8......... 26 C6
Greenford UB6 .... 86 B4
Hayes UB4........... 84 A2
Peckham SE15....... 140 B3
Shelley Cres
Heston TW5........ 128 D4
Southall UB1 .... 85 B1
Shelley Ct
Finsbury Pk N4 .... 50 B1
9 Kingston u T KT2 . 175 D6
SW3............ 267 D6
13 Walthamstow E10 .. 53 D2
8 Wanstead E11 ..... 55 A5
Wembley HA0 .... 65 C4
West Barnes KT3 .... 200 A4
Shelley Dr DA16 .... 145 C4
Shelley Gdns HA0..... 65 C6
Shelley Ho
21 Bethnal Green
E2............. 96 C4
Chelsea SW1....... 269 A6
9 Stoke Newington
N16............. 73 C4
Walworth SE17 ..... 262 B2
Shelley N8 .... 50 A6
Shelley Rd NW10...... 89 B6
Shelley Way SW17 ... 180 B4
Shellgrove Rd N16.... 73 C3
Shellness Rd E5 ...... 74 B3
Shell Rd SE13........ 141 D2
Shellwood Rd
SW11........... 136 D3
Shelly Lo EN2.......... 5 B4
Shelmerdine Cl E3.... 97 C2
Shelson Ave TW13 ... 171 D6
Shelton Ct N21 .... 16 C4
Shelton Rd SW19 .... 179 C2
Shelton St
WC2......... 94 A1 240 A1
Shene Bldg EC1..... 241 A4
Shene Sch SW14 .... 133 C1
Shenfield Ho 3
SE18........... 143 D5
Shenfield Rd IG8 ..... 37 B3
Shenfield St N1....... 95 C5
Shenley Ave HA4...... 39 D1
Shenley Ho 3
SW16........... 182 B6
Shenley Rd
Camberwell SE5 .... 139 C4
Heston TW5........ 129 A4
Shenstone W13....... 109 C5
Shenstone Gdns IG2 .. 57 D4
Shenstone Ho
SW16........... 181 C5
Shepard Ho 18
SW11........... 136 B2
Sheperdess Pl N1... 235 B2
Shepherd Cl
Feltham TW13...... 173 A6
W1............ 248 A6
Shepherdess Wlk
N1.......... 95 A5 235 B3
Shepherd Ho
Barnsbury N7 .... 72 A2
10 Poplar E14 .... 97 D1
Shepherd Mkt W1 ... 248 C3
SHEPHERD'S BUSH
.... 112 B5
Shepherd's Bush
(Central Line) Sta
W12........... 112 D4
Shepherd's Bush Gn
W12............ 112 C4
Shepherd's Bush
(Hamm & City) Sta
W12........... 112 C5
Shepherd's Bush Market
W12............ 112 C4
Shepherd's Bush Pl
W12............ 112 D4
Shepherd's Bush Rd
W6............. 112 C3
Shepherds Cl RM6 .... 58 D5
Shepherd's Cl N6...... 49 B3
Shepherds Cl
Orpington BR6...... 227 D5
Shepperton TW17 ... 192 D3
Stanmore HA7........ 25 A5
Shepherds Ct
8 Hammersmith
W12........... 112 D4
13 Harrow HA1....... 42 D3
Shepherds Gn BR7 ... 189 B3
Shepherd's Hill N6.... 49 C3
Shepherd's La E9..... 74 D2
Shepherds La SE28... 123 C5
Shepherds Leas
SE9............ 145 B1
Shepherds Path UB5.. 63 A2
Shepherds Pl W1... 248 A6
Shepherd St
W1......... 115 B5 248 C3
Shepherds Way
CR2............ 222 D1
Shepherds Wlk
Bushey WD23.......... 8 B2
Dollis Hill NW2........ 68 A6
Shepherd's Wlk NW3 . 70 B4
Shepiston La UB3.... 105 A1
Shepley Cl SM5...... 219 A5
Shepley Ct SW16..... 181 C6
Shepley Mews EN3..... 7 C6
Sheppard Cl
Enfield EN1........... 6 B5
Kingston u T KT6.... 198 A5
Sheppard Dr SE16 ... 118 B1
Sheppard Ho
31 Hackney E2 .... 96 A5
8 Streatham SW2.. 160 C3
Sheppard's Ct
Harrow HA1 .... 42 C2
Wembley UB6 .... 64 D2
Sheppard St E16...... 98 D3
SHEPPERTON 193 A3
Shepperton Bsns Park
TW17........... 193 A4
Shepperton Court Dr
TW17........... 192 D4
Shepperton Ct
TW17........... 192 D3
SHEPPERTON GREEN
.... 192 D5
Shepperton Rd
Littleton TW17,
TW18.......... 192 A5
Orpington BR5...... 211 A3
Shoreditch
N1 .... 95 B6 235 C6
Shepperton Sta
TW17........... 193 A4
Shepperton Studios
TW17........... 192 B6
Sheppey Gdns RM9... 80 C1
Sheppey Ho 16 E5 .... 74 B4
Sheppey Rd RM9...... 80 C1
Shepton Ct SW11 ... 266 D2
Shepton Hos 11 E2.... 96 C4
Sherard Ct N19 .... 72 A5
Sherard Ho 24 E9 ..... 74 C1
Sherard Rd SE9...... 166 A6
Sheraton Bsns Ctr
UB6............. 87 C5
Sheraton Cl WD6 ..... 10 B6
Sheraton Ho SW1... 268 D6
Sheraton Lo HA3...... 42 C6
Sheraton St W1 .... 239 C1
Sheraton The 22
KT6............ 198 A4
Sherborne Ave
Enfield EN3........... 6 C3
Southall UB2....... 107 C2
Sherborne Cl UB4..... 84 C1
Sherborne Cres
SM5............ 202 C2
Sherborne Ct SE20... 184 C1
Sherborne Gdns
Ealing W13 .... 87 B2
Queensbury NW9 ..... 44 C6
Sherborne Ho
Pimlico SW1 .... 258 D2
South Lambeth SW8 . 270 C3
Sherborne La EC4... 252 D6
Sherborne Rd BR5 ... 211 D4
Cheam SM3........ 201 C1
Chessington KT9.... 214 A3
East Bedfont TW14... 149 B3
Sherborne St
N1.......... 95 B6 235 C6
Sherboro Rd 1 N15... 51 D3
Sherbourne Ct
1 Hampton
TW12........... 173 C2
9 Sutton SM2 ..... 218 A2
SW5............ 255 C4
Sherbourne Gdns
TW17........... 193 C2
Sherbourne Pl HA7 ... 25 A4
Sherbrooke Cl DA7... 147 C1
Sherbrooke Ho 9
E2.............. 96 C5
Sherbrooke Rd
SW6........ 135 A5 264 B3
Sherbrooke Terr
SW6............ 264 B3
Sherbrooke Way
KT4............ 200 B2
Sherbrook Gdns N21.. 16 D4
Sherbrook Ho 2 N3 .. 29 D3
Shere Cl KT9 .... 213 D3
Sheredan Rd E4 ...... 36 C5
Shere Ho SE1....... 262 C6
Shere Lo 1 SW19.... 180 C3

Shere Rd IG2 56 C4
Sherfield Cl KT3 198 D5
Sherfield Gdns SW15 155 D5
Sheridan Bldgs WC2 240 B1
Sheridan Cl UB10 83 A3
Sheridan Cres BR7 188 D1
Sheridan Ct
Ealing W7 108 D6
Earl's Ct SW5 255 C3
Harrow HA1 42 B3
Hounslow TW4 151 A6
South Hampstead NW6 70 A1
South Lambeth SW9 270 D1
Sheridan Gdns HA3 43 D3
Sheridan Ho SE11 261 B3
7 Stoke Newington N16 73 C5
Sheridan Lo
Barnet EN5 1 D1
Bromley BR2 209 C5
East Barnet N14 15 B4
Sheridan N8 50 C5
Sheridan Mews E11 55 B3
Sheridan Pl
Barnes SW13 133 D2
Hampton TW12 174 A2
Harrow HA1 42 C2
Sheridan Rd
Belvedere DA17 125 C2
DA7 147 A2
Leyton E7 76 D5
Little Ilford E12 78 B3
Merton SW19 179 B2
Richmond TW10 153 C1
Sheridan St 34 E1 96 B1
Sheridan Terr UB5 63 D3
Sheridan Way 5 BR3 185 B2
Sheridan Wlk
Golders Green NW11 47 C3
Wallington SM5 218 D3
Sheringdale Prim Sch SW18 157 B3
Sheringham Ave
Feltham TW13 150 A1
Little Ilford E12 78 B3
Southgate N14 15 D5
Twickenham TW2 151 C3
Sheringham Ct 1 N3 29 C2
Sheringham Dr IG11 80 A3
Sheringham Ho NW1 237 B4
Sheringham Jun Sch E12 78 B4
Sheringham Mews 4 SW18 158 A2
Sheringham NW8 229 D6
Sheringham Rd
Islington N7 72 C2
Penge SE20 206 C6
Sheringham Twr UB1 107 D6
Sherington Ave HA5 23 C3
Sherington Prim Sch SE7 143 B6
Sherington Rd SE7 143 B6
Sheriton Ct SM1 217 C5
Sherland Rd TW1 152 D3
Sherleys Ct HA4 61 C6
Sherlies Ave BR6 227 C6
Sherlock Ct NW8 229 C6
Sherlock Holmes Mus* NW1 92 D3 237 D5
Sherlock Mews W1 238 A4
Sherman Gdns RM6 58 C3
Sherman Rd BR1 187 A2
Shernhall St E17 54 A5
Sherwood Ho 1 E18 55 A5
Sherrard Rd E7, E12 77 D2
Sherrards Way EN5 13 D5
Sherren Ho 35 E1 96 C3
Sherrick Green Rd NW10 68 B3
Sherriff Ct NW6 69 C2
Sherriff Rd NW6 69 C2
Sherringham Ave N17 34 A1
Sherrin Rd E10 75 D4
Sherrock Gdns NW4 46 A5
Sherry Mews IG11 79 B1
Sherston Ct
Finsbury WC1 234 A1
Newington SE1 261 D4
Sherwin Ho 1 SE11 138 C6
Sherwin Rd SE14 140 D4
Sherwood Ave
Greenford UB6 64 C3
Hayes UB4 84 B3
Sherwood Ave *continued*
Mitcham SW16 181 D2
Ruislip HA4 39 C3
Wanstead E18 55 B6
Sherwood
3 Barnet EN5 1 D1
Brondesbury NW6 69 A1
Sherwood Cl
Barnes SW13 134 B2
DA5 168 C5
Ealing W13 109 B5
Walthamstow E17 35 B1
Sherwood Ct
11 Battersea SW11 136 A2
Colney Hatch N12 30 C5
2 South Croydon CR2 221 A3
St Johns SE13 141 D3
Sutton SM1 217 C3
W1 237 C3
6 West Wickham BR4 207 D1
Sherwood Gdns
Barking IG11 79 B1
Bermondsey SE16 118 B1
Millwall E14 119 C2
Sherwood Hall 7 N2 48 A6
Sherwood Ho N4 51 A2
Sherwood KT6 213 D6
Sherwood Park Ave DA15 168 B5
Sherwood Park Prim Sch DA15 168 B5
Sherwood Park Rd
Mitcham CR4 203 D5
Sutton SM1 217 C3
Sherwood Park Sch SM6 219 D5
Sherwood Rd
Croydon CR0 206 B1
DA16 145 C2
Hampton TW12 174 A5
Harrow HA2 64 A6
Hendon NW4 46 C6
Ilford IG6 57 B5
Merton SW19 179 B3
Sherwood Sch The CR4 203 C5
Sherwood St W1 249 B6
Whetstone N20 14 B1
Sherwood Terr N20 14 B1
Sherwood Way BR4 224 A6
Shetland Cl WD6 11 B5
Shetland Rd Bow E3 97 B5
East Bedfont TW6 149 A5
Shield Dr TW8 131 A6
Shieldhall St SE2 124 C2
Shield Rd TW15 171 B6
Shifford Path SE23 162 D1
Shillaker Ct W3 111 D5
Shillibeer Ct N18 34 B5
Shillibeer Pl W1 237 B3
Shillingford Cl NW7 28 D3
Shillingford Ho 40 E3 97 D4
Shillingford St 23 N1 72 D1
Shilling Pl TW8 109 A5
Shillingstone Ho W14 254 B5
Shine Ho 3 N3 29 D3
Shinfield St W12 90 C1
Shinglewell Rd DA8 147 C5
Shinners Cl SE25 206 A4
Shipka Rd SW12 159 B3
Shiplake Ct SW17 180 B6
Shiplake Ho 45 E2 95 D4
Ship La SW14 133 A3
Shipley Ct SE20 184 A1
Shipley Ho 32 SW8 137 D3
Shipman Rd
Forest Hill SE23 162 D2
Newham E16 99 C1
Ship & Mermaid Row SE1 253 A2
Ship St SE8 141 C4
Ship Tavern Pas EC3 253 A6
Shipton Cl RM8 80 D5
Shipton Ho
7 Camden Town NW5 71 A2
14 Haggerston E2 95 D5
Shipton Rd UB8 60 B4
Shipton St E2 95 D4
Shipwright Rd SE16 119 A4
Shipwright Yd SE1 253 A3
Shirburn Cl SE23 162 C4
Shirbutt St E14 119 D6
Shirebrook Rd SE3 143 D2
Shire Ct DA18 124 D3
Ewell KT17 215 D1
Shirehall Cl NW4 46 D3
Shirehall Gdns NW4 46 D3
Shirehall La NW4 46 D3
Shirehall Pk NW4 46 D3
Shire Ho E11 76 D5
Shire Horse Way TW7 130 D2
Shire La BR6 227 B2
Shiremeade WD6 10 B6
Shire Mews TW2 152 A5
Shire Pl
12 Brentford TW8 131 C5
Wandsworth SW18 158 A4
Shires The TW10 176 A6
Shirland Mews W9 91 B4
Shirland Rd W9 91 C3
SHIRLEY 206 C1
Shirley Ave
Carshalton SM1 218 C4
Croydon CR0 206 D1
DA5 168 D3
Shirley Church Rd CR0 223 A5
Shirley Cl
Hounslow TW3 152 A6
Walthamstow E17 53 D4
Shirley Cres BR3 207 A5
Shirley Ct
8 Ealing W13 109 A5
Ilford IG2 57 B4
Kingsbury NW9 45 B4
2 South Norwood SW16 182 B3
Thornton Heath SW16 204 B6
Shirley Dr TW3 152 A6
Shirley Gdns
Barking IG11 79 C2
Ealing W7 108 D5
Shirley Gr
Clapham SW11 137 A2
Ponders End N9 18 D4
Shirley High Sch Performing Arts Coll CR0 222 D5
Shirley Hills Rd CR0 222 D3
Shirley Ho 13 SE5 139 B5
Shirley House Dr SE7 143 C5
Shirley Hts 6 DA6 147 A1
Shirley Lo 4 SE26 185 A6
SHIRLEY OAKS 207 A1
Shirley Oaks Hospl CR0 206 C2
Shirley Oaks Rd CR0 222 D6
Shirley Park Rd CR0 206 C1
Shirley Rd Acton W4 111 B4
Croydon CR0 206 B1
Enfield EN2 5 A2
Sidcup DA15 167 C1
Stratford E15 76 C1
Shirley St E16 98 D1
Shirley Way CR0 223 B5
Shirlock Rd NW3 70 D4
Shirwell Cl NW7 28 D3
Shobden Rd N17 33 B2
Shobroke Cl NW2 68 C5
Shoebury Rd E6 78 B1
Shoe La EC4 94 C1 241 B2
Shoelands Ct NW9 45 B6
Shona Ho E16 99 C2
Shooters Ave HA3 43 C5
SHOOTERS HILL 145 A4
Shooters Hill Rd
Blackheath Vale SE3, SE10 142 C4
SE18, SE3, SE7 143 D5
Shooters Hill SE18 144 C4
Shooters Rd EN2 4 D4
Shoot-Up Hill NW2 69 A2
Shopstop SW11 136 C1
Shore Bsns Ctr 31 E9 74 C1
Shore Cl
Feltham TW14 150 A4
Hampton TW12 173 A5
Shorediche Cl UB10 60 B5
SHOREDITCH 95 B5
Shoreditch Ct 2 E8 73 D1
Shoreditch High St E2 95 C3 243 B6
Shoreditch Ho N1 235 D1
Shore Gr TW13 151 C2
Shoreham Cl
Croydon CR0 206 C3
DA5 168 D3
Wandsworth SW18 157 D6
Shoreham Rd BR5 190 B1
Shoreham Rd (E) TW6 148 A6
Shoreham Rd (W) TW6 148 A6
Shoreham Way BR2 209 A3
Shore Ho SW8 137 B2
Shore Mews 30 E9 74 C1
Shore Pl E9 74 C1
Shore Point 2 IG9 21 B2
Shore Rd E9 74 C1
Shore Way 26 SW9 138 C3
Shorncliffe Rd SE1 117 D1 263 C2
Shorndean St SE6 164 A3
Shorne Cl 3 DA15 168 B5
Shornefield Cl BR1 210 C6
Shornells Way SE2 124 C1
Shorrolds Rd SW6 135 B5 264 D4
Shortcroft Mead Ct NW10 68 A3
Shortcroft Rd KT17 215 D1
Shortcrofts Rd RM9 81 B2
Shorter St EC3 117 D6 253 D6
Shortgate N12 29 B6
SHORTLANDS 208 C6
Shortlands W6 112 D2
Shortlands Cl DA17 125 B3
Edmonton N18 17 B1
Shortlands Gdns BR2 186 C1
Shortlands Gr BR2 208 B6
Shortlands UB3 127 B6
Shortlands Rd
Beckenham BR2, BR3 208 C6
Kingston u T KT2 176 B3
Walthamstow E10 53 D2
Shortlands Sta BR2 186 C1
Short La TW15, TW19 148 B3
Short Path SE18 144 D6
Short Rd
Chiswick W4 133 C6
Leyton E11 76 C6
Stanwell TW19 148 A5
Shorts Croft NW9 44 D5
Shorts Gdns WC2 94 A1 240 A1
Shorts Rd SM5 218 C3
Short St
7 Hendon NW4 46 C5
SE1 251 B2
Short Way N12 30 C4
Shortway SE9 144 A2
Short Way TW2 152 A4
Shotfield SM6 219 B2
Shott Cl SM1 218 A3
Shottendane Rd SW6 135 C4 265 A2
Shottery Cl SE9 166 A1
Shottfield Ave SW14 133 C1
Shottsford 1 W11 91 C1
Shoulder of Mutton Alley 10 E14 119 A6
Shouldham St W1 92 C2 237 B3
Showers Way UB3 106 A5
Shrapnel Cl SE18 144 A5
Shrapnel Rd SE9 144 B2
Shreveport Ho 23 N19 49 D2
Shrewsbury Ave
Harrow HA3 44 A5
Mortlake SW14 133 B1
Shrewsbury Cl KT6 214 A6
Shrewsbury Ho
Chelsea SW3 267 A5
Kennington SE11 270 D5
Shrewsbury House Sch KT6 214 A6
Shrewsbury La SE18 144 D4
Shrewsbury Mews 33 W2 91 C2
Shrewsbury Rd
Beckenham BR3 207 A6
Carshalton SM5 202 C2
Friern Barnet N11 31 D4
Harlington TW14, TW6 149 B5
Notting Hill W2 91 C1
Plashet E7 77 D2
Shrewsbury St W10 90 C3
Shrewsbury Wlk 9 TW7 131 A2
Shrewton Rd SW17 180 D3
Shri Swaminarayan Mandir* NW10 67 B2
Shroffold Rd BR1 164 D1
Shropshire Cl CR4 204 A5
Shropshire Ct W7 86 D1
Shropshire Ho WC1 239 B5
Shropshire Rd N22 32 B3
Shroton St NW1 92 C2 237 B4
Shrubberies The
Ilford IG2 57 D4
Woodford E18 37 A1
Shrubbery Cl N1 235 B5
Shrubbery Gdns N21 16 D4
Shrubbery Rd
Edmonton N9 18 A1
Southall UB1 107 C5
Shrubbery Rd *continued*
Streatham SW16 182 A6
Shrubbery The
2 Surbiton KT6 198 A1
7 Wanstead E11 55 B4
Shrub Ct 5 SM2 218 A2
Shrubland Gr KT4 216 C5
Shrubland Rd
Hackney E8 96 A6
Leyton E10 53 C2
Walthamstow E17 53 C4
Shrublands Ave CR0 223 C4
Shrublands Cl
Forest Hill SE26 162 C1
Whetstone N20 14 B2
Shrubsall Cl SE9 166 A3
Shrubs Ho SW1 259 D3
Shurland Ave EN4 14 B5
Shurland Gdns SE15 139 D5
Shurlock Dr BR6 227 A4
Shuters Sq W14 254 C1
Shuttle Cl DA15 167 D4
Shuttlemead DA5 169 B4
Shuttle St E1 96 A3
Shuttleworth Rd SW11 136 C3
Sibella Rd SW4 137 D3
Sibford Ct 5 CR4 202 D6
Sibley Cl Bexley DA6 169 A6
Bromley BR1 210 A4
Sibley Ct
Beckenham BR3 186 C1
Hillingdon UB8 83 A2
Sibley Gr E12 78 A1
Sibthorpe Rd SE12 165 C4
Sibthorp Rd 2 CR4 180 D1
Sibton Rd SM5 202 C2
Sicilian Ave WC1 240 B3
Sidbury St SW6 135 A4 264 A2
SIDCUP 190 A5
Sidcup By Pass Rd
Sidcup DA14 189 C6
St Paul's Cray BR5, BR7 190 B3
Sidcup Hill DA14 190 B5
Sidcup Hill Gdns DA14 190 C5
Sidcup Pl DA14 190 A5
Sidcup Rd SE9 166 A3
Sidcup Sta DA15 168 A2
Sidcup Tech Ctr DA14 190 D4
Siddeley Dr TW4 129 A3
Siddons Ct WC2 240 C1
Siddons Ho 8 NW3 70 D3
Siddons La NW1 92 D3 237 D5
Siddons Rd
Croydon CR0 220 D5
Forest Hill SE23 163 A2
Tottenham N17 34 A2
Side Rd E17 53 B4
Sidewood Rd SE9 167 B3
Sidford Ho SE1 260 D5
Sidford Pl SE1 116 B3 260 D5
Sidgwick Ho 26 SW9 138 A3
Sidi Ct 2 N15 50 D6
Sidings Mews N7 72 C4
Sidings The E11 54 A1
Sidlaw Ho N16 51 D1
Sidmouth Ave TW7 130 C3
Sidmouth Dr HA4 62 A5
Sidmouth Ho
18 Camberwell SE15 140 A5
Marylebone W1 237 B2
26 Streatham SW2 160 C4
Sidmouth Mews WC1 233 C1
Sidmouth Par NW2 68 C1
Sidmouth Rd
Bexley DA16 146 C5
Leyton E10 76 A5
Willesden NW2 68 C1
Sidmouth St WC1 94 B4 233 C1
Sidney Ave N13 32 B5
Sidney Boyd Ct NW6 69 C1
Sidney Elson Way E6 100 C5
Sidney Gdns TW8 131 D6
Sidney Godley (VC) Ho 31 E2 96 C4
Sidney Gr EC1 234 C3
Sidney Ho
4 Globe Town E2 96 D5
SE18 144 B4
Sidney Miller Ct 8 W3 110 D5
Sidney Rd
Beckenham BR3 185 A1
Croydon SE25 206 A4
Sidney Rd *continued*
Harrow HA2 42 A6
Stockwell SW9 138 B3
Twickenham TW1 153 B5
Walton-on-T KT12 194 B1
Wanstead E7 77 A5
Wood Green N22 32 B3
Sidney Sq E1 96 C2
Sidney St E1 96 C2
Sidworth St 6 E8 74 B1
Siebert Rd SE3 143 A6
Siedle Ho 9 SE18 144 C6
Siege Ho 14 E1 96 B1
Siemens Rd SE18 121 D3
Sienna Ct TW13 149 D1
Sienna SE28 123 D3
Sierra Dr RM9 103 D5
Sigdon Rd E8 74 A3
Sigers The HA5 40 B3
Signal Ho
9 London E8 74 B1
SE1 252 A1
Signmakers Yd NW1 231 D5
Sigrist Sq 4 KT2 176 A2
Silbury Ave CR4 180 C2
Silbury Ho 9 SE26 162 A1
Silbury St N1 235 C2
Silchester Ct
Stanwell TW15 148 A2
Thornton Heath CR7 204 C5
Silchester Rd W10 90 D1
Silecroft Rd DA7 147 C4
Silesia Bldgs E8 74 B1
Silex St SE1 116 D4 251 D1
Silicone Bsns Ctr UB6 87 C5
Silk Cl SE12 165 A5
Silkfield Rd NW9 45 C4
Silk Ho NW9 45 B6
Silk Mills Path SE13 142 A2
Silk Mills Sq E9 75 B2
Silks Ct E11 54 C1
Silk St EC2 95 A2 242 B4
Silkstream Par HA8 27 A2
Silkstream Rd HA8 27 A2
Sillitoe Ho N1 235 D5
Silsoe Ho NW1 231 D3
Silsoe Rd N22 50 B6
Silverbell Ct 1 N12 29 D5
Silver Birch Ave E4 35 B4
Silver Birch Cl
Forest Hill SE6 163 B1
Friern Barnet N11 31 A4
Ickenham UB10 60 A4
SE28 124 A5
Silver Birch Ct EN3 18 D6
Silver Birch Gdns E6 100 B3
Silverbirch Wlk 1 NW3 71 A2
Silverburn Ho 4 SW9 138 D4
Silver Cl HA3 24 B3
Silvercliffe Gdns EN4 2 C1
Silver Cl SE14 141 A5
Silver Cres W4 110 D2
Silver Ct N19 71 C5
Silverdale Ave IG3 57 D4
Silverdale Cl
Cheam SM1 217 B4
1 Ealing W7 108 D5
Northolt UB5 63 B3
Silverdale Ct EC1 241 D6
Silverdale Dr
Chislehurst SE9 166 A2
Sunbury TW16 172 B1
Silverdale EN2 4 A1
Silverdale Factory Ctr UB3 106 A3
Silverdale SE26 184 C6
Silverdale Gdns UB3 106 A4
Silverdale Ind Est UB3 106 A4
Silverdale NW1 232 A2
Silverdale Par IG3 57 D4
Silverdale Rd
Bexleyheath DA7 147 D3
Chingford E4 36 B4
Hayes UB3 106 A4
Petts Wood BR5 211 A5
Silverhall St TW7 131 A2
Silverholme Cl HA3 44 A2
Silver Ind Est N17 33 D1
Silver Jubilee Way TW4 128 B3
Silverland St E16 122 B5
Silver La BR4 224 B6
Silverleigh Rd CR7 204 B4
Silvermead 7 E18 37 A2
Silvermere Rd SE6 163 D5
Silver Pl W1 249 B6
Silver Rd
Shepherd's Bush W12 112 D6
St Johns SE13 141 D2

Silvers 4 IG9 ....21 C3
Silver Spring Cl DA8 ....147 D6
Silver St
Edmonton N18........33 C6
Enfield EN1 ....5 B2
Silverstone Ct 8 BR1 ....187 C1
Silverston Way HA7...25 C4
Silver Street Sta N18 .33 D5
Silverthorne Lo EN1...17 C6
Silverthorne Rd SW8......137 B3
Silverthorne Gdns E4 ..19 C2
Silverthorn 17 NW6 ...91 D6
Silverton Lo SE19....183 C3
Silverton Rd W6 .....134 D6
SILVERTOWN 121 B4
Silvertown Way E16.......121 A5
Silvertree La UB6 .....86 B4
Silver Way
Hillingdon UB10.......82 D5
Romford RM7 ....59 D6
Silver Wing Ind Est CR0 ....220 B2
Silver Wlk SE16.......119 B5
Silverwood Cl BR3 ...185 C3
Silvester Ho
27 Bethnal Green E2.........96 C4
1 Notting Hill W11 ...91 B1
Pinner HA5 ....40 A5
6 Stepney E1........96 B1
Silvester Rd SE22 ....161 D6
Silvester St SE1.....252 C1
Silwex Ho E1 ......243 C5
Silwood St SE16 .....118 C1
Simba Ct TW1 ......152 D3
Simla Ho SE1.......252 D1
Simmil Rd KT10......212 C3
Simmonds Ct SW5 ..255 C3
Simmons Cl
Chessington KT9 .....213 C2
East Barnet N20 ......14 C3
Simmons Dr RM8 .....81 A5
Simmons Gate KT10 ....212 A3
Simmons Ho
20 Bethnal Green E2.........96 A4
Finsbury Pk N7 ....72 B6
Simmons La E4........20 B2
Simmons Rd SE18....122 D1
Simmons' Way N20 ...14 C2
Simms Cl SM5 ....218 C6
Simms Ct SW6.......135 A2
Simms Gdns N2 ......30 A1
Simms Rd SE1.......118 A2
Simnel Rd SE12......165 B4
Simon Cl W11........113 B6 244 D6
Simon Ct
Paddington W9 ....91 C4
5 Woolwich SE28 ...124 B5
Simonds Rd E10 ......75 C6
Simone Cl BR1.......187 D2
Simon Lo 31 SW19 ...156 D3
Simon Marks Jewish Prim Sch N16.......73 D6
Simons Wlk E15 ......76 B3
Simpson Cl N21 ....16 B6
Simpson Dr W3.......89 B1
Simpson Ho
Lisson Gr NW8 .....230 A1
Vauxhall SE11 ......260 C1
Wembley HA9 ....65 D6
Simpson Rd
Hounslow TW4 ......151 B5
Richmond TW10.....175 C6
Simpson's Rd BR2 ...209 A6
Poplar E14........119 D6
Simpson St SW11....136 C3
Simpson Way KT6....197 C3
Sim's Cotts KT10.....212 D2
Sims Wlk SE3........142 D1
Sinclair Ct
21 Beckenham BR3............185 C3
Canonbury N5 ....73 A2
5 Croydon CR0 .... 221 D6
Sinclair Gdns W14 ...112 D4
Sinclair Gr NW11 .....46 D3
Sinclair Ho
Harrow HA7 ....24 D4
3 South Norwood SW16...........182 B3
1 Streatham SW12 . 159 D3
Sinclair Mans 13 W12..........112 D4
Sinclair Pl SE4.......163 C5
Sinclair Rd
Chingford Hatch E4....35 B5
W14....... 113 A3 254 A6
Sinclairs Ho 18 E3 ....97 B5
Sinclare Cl EN1........5 D4
Singapore Rd W13...109 A5
Singer St EC2....... 235 D1
Singlegate Prim Sch SW19............180 B3
Singleton Cl
Mitcham SW17 ..... 180 D3
Thornton Heath CR0 . 205 A2
Singleton Rd RM9......81 B3
Singleton Scarp N12..29 C5
Sinnott Rd E17 ....34 D2
Sion Ct TW1 ....153 B3
Sion Ho SE13 ....142 A1
Sion-Manning RC Sch for Girls
Kensal Town W10 .....91 A2
North Kensington W10 ....90 D2
Sion Rd TW1 ....153 B3
Sippetts Ct IG1.......57 B1
SIPSON 126 C6
Sipson Cl UB7 ....126 C6
Sipson La UB3, UB7 ...126 D6
Sipson Rd
Harmondsworth UB7 .... 126 C6
West Drayton UB7....104 B2
West Drayton UB7... 104 C1
Sipson Way UB7 .....126 C5
Sir Abraham Dawes Cotts SW15 ....135 A1
Sir Alexander Cl W3...............111 D5
Sir Alexander Rd W3...............111 D5
Sir Arthur Bliss Ct 4 SW19..............180 D1
Sir Cyril Black Way 2 SW19..............179 C3
Sirdar Rd
Mitcham CR4....... 181 A4
Tottenham N22 ....33 A1
W11....... 113 A6 244 A5
Sir Francis Drake Prim Sch SE8 .... 119 A1
Sir George Monoux Sixth Form Coll E17.................35 D1
Sir Henry Floyd Ct HA7 ....9 B2
Sirinham Point SW8 270 D5
Sirius Bldg 13 E1 ....118 D6
Sir James Barrie Prim Sch SW8... 137 C4 269 B1
Sir John Cass Foundation & Redcoat CE Sec Sch E1..................96 D2
Sir John Cass's Foundation Prim Sch EC3 ....95 C1 243 B1
Sir John Heron Prim Sch E12 ....78 B4
Sir John Kirk Cl 33 SE5...............139 A5
Sir John Lillie Prim Sch SW6......... 135 A6 264 B5
Sir Martin Bowes Ho 9 SE18...............122 C2
Sir Oswald Stoll Foundation The SW6................. 265 C4
Sir Thomas Abney Sch N16...................51 B1
Sir Thomas More Est SW3...........136 B6 266 D5
Sirus Rd HA6 ....22 A5
Sir William Burrough Prim Sch E14 .... 97 A1
Sir William Powell's Almshos SW6 ......135 A2
Sise La EC4.......... 242 C1
Siskin Ho
Edmonton N9.........18 D3
14 Rotherhithe SE16............ 118 D2
Sisley Rd IG11 ....101 D6
Sispara Gdns SW18 ..157 B5
Sissinghurst Cl BR1..186 C5
Sissinghurst Ho 17 SE15..............140 C6
Sissinghurst Rd CR0 ....206 A2
Sissulu Ct 8 E6 ......99 C6
Sister Mabel's Way 15 SE15................140 A5
Sisters Ave SW11 ....136 D1
Sistova Rd SW12.....159 B3
Sisulu Pl SW9 ....138 C2
Sitarey Ct 4 W12....112 B5
Site of Changing of the Guard* SW1 ...... 249 A1
Sittingbourne Ave EN1 ....17 B5
Sitwell Gr HA7........24 D5
Siverst Cl UB5 ....63 D2
Sivill Ho 9 E2.........95 D4
Siviter Way RM10 .....81 D1
Siward Rd
Bromley BR2....... 209 C6
Tottenham N17 ....33 B2
Wandsworth SW17 .. 158 A1
Six Bridges Ind Est 15 SE1.................118 A1
Sixpenny Ct IG11 ....79 A2
Sixth Ave Hayes UB3 ..105 D5
Ilford E12 ....78 B4
West Kilburn W10......91 A4
Sixth Cross Rd TW2 ..152 A1
Skardu Rd NW2.......69 A3
Skeena Hill SW18, SW19.................157 A4
Skeffington Rd E6 ...100 B6
Skeffington St SE18..123 A3
Skeggs Ho 5 E14....120 A3
Skegness Ho 3 N7 ....72 B1
Skelbrook St SW18...158 A2
Skelgill Rd SW15.....135 B1
Skelley Rd E15........76 D1
Skelton Cl 7 E8 ......73 D2
Skelton Ho N16.......73 C3
Skelton Rd E7 ....77 A2
Skelton's La E10......53 D2
Skelwith Rd W6 .....134 C6
Skenfrith Ho SE15 ....140 B6
Skerne Rd KT2.......175 D2
Skerne Wlk KT2......175 D2
Sketchley Gdns SE16...............118 D1
Sketty Rd EN1 ....5 D2
Skiers St E15.........98 C6
Skiffington Cl SW2...160 C3
Skillen Lodge HA5 ....22 D2
Skinner Ct E17 ....53 C4
Skinner Pl SW1..... 258 A3
Skinners Almshouses N13 ....16 C1
Skinners Company Sch (Upper) N16.......51 D2
Skinner's Company's Lower Sch E5........52 B1
Skinners La EC4 .... 252 B6
Hounslow TW5 ..... 129 D4
Skinner St EC1 ....94 C3 241 B6
Skipper Ct 6 IG11....101 A6
Skipsea Ho SW18 ....158 B5
Skipsey Ave E6 ......100 B4
Skipton Cl N11 ....31 A4
Skipton Dr UB3.......105 A3
Skipton Ho SE4.......141 A1
Skipwith Bldg EC1 .. 241 A4
Skipworth Rd E9.......96 C6
Skua Ct 33 SE8.......141 B6
Skyline Ct SE1....... 263 C5
Skyline Plaza Bldg 19 E1.................96 A1
Skylines E14..........120 A4
Sky Peals Rd IG8 ......36 B3
Sky Studios E16 .....122 C4
Sladebrook Rd SE3 ..143 D2
Slade Ct Barnet EN5 .....1 D2
Brondesbury NW2.......69 A3
Muswell Hill N10.......31 B3
Sladedale Rd SE18 ...123 C1
Slade Ho TW4 ....151 B5
Sladen Pl 12 E5.......74 B4
Slades Cl EN2 ....4 C2
Slades Dr BR7 ....189 A6
Slades Gdns EN2.......4 C2
Slades Hill EN2 ....4 C2
Slades Rise EN2 ....4 C2
Slade The SE18 ......145 C6
Slade Twr E10 ....75 C6
Slade Way CR4 ....181 A2
Slagrove Pl SE13......163 D6
Slaidburn St SW10........136 A6 266 B5
Slaithwaite Rd SE13..................142 A1
Slaney Ct NW10.......68 C1
Slaney Pl 1 N7.......72 C3
Slater Cl 18 SE18.....122 C2
Slatter 1 NW9 ....27 D2
Slattery Rd TW13 ....150 C3
Sleaford Ho 16 E3.....97 C3
Sleaford Ind Est SW8......... 137 C5 269 B3
Sleaford St SW8..........137 C5 269 B3
Sleat Ho 11 E3........97 B5
Sledmere Ct TW14....149 C3
Slievemore Cl 8 SW4..................137 D2
Sligo Ho 8 E1.........96 D3
Slingsby Pl WC2 ..... 250 A6
Slippers Pl SE16 .....118 B3
Slipway Ho 1 E14 ...119 D1
Sloane Avenue Mans SW3................ 257 C3
Sloane Ave SW3........114 C2 257 B3
Sloane Ct E SW3.... 258 A2
Sloane Ct W SW3 ... 258 A2
Sloane Gate Mans SW1............. 258 A4
Sloane Gdns
Belgravia SW1..... 115 A2 258 A3
Orpington BR6....... 227 A5
Sloane Ho 7 E9 ....74 C1
Sloane Hospl BR3 ...186 B2
Sloane Sq SW1 ..... 257 D3
Sloane Square Sta SW1....... 115 A2 258 A3
Sloane St SW1....... 114 D3 257 D5
Sloane Terr Mans SW1................ 258 A4
Sloane Terr SW1 .... 258 A4
Sloane Wlk CR0.......207 B3
Sloan Ho RM10 ....81 D1
Slocum Cl SE28......124 C6
Slough La NW9 ....45 A3
Sly St 17 E1..........96 B1
Smaldon Cl UB7 .....104 C3
Smallberry Ave TW7...................130 D3
Smallberry Green Prim Sch The TW7...... 131 A4
Smallbrook Mews W2................ 236 C1
Smallbugh Mans HA0 ....65 B4
Smalley Cl N16 ....73 D5
Smallwood Prim Sch SW17.................180 B6
Smallwood Rd SW17.................180 B6
Smarden Cl DA17 ....125 C1
Smarden Gr SE9 .....188 B6
Smart's Pl
Edmonton N18........34 A5
WC1, WC2........... 240 B2
Smart St E2 ....96 D4
Smeaton Cl KT9 .....213 D2
Smeaton Ct SE1 ..... 262 A5
Smeaton Rd
Holdbrook EN3 ....7 C6
Wandsworth SW18 .. 157 C4
Smeaton St E1 ....118 B5
Smedley St SW4 .....137 D3
Smeed Rd E3.........75 C1
Smiles Pl SE13.......142 A3
Smith Cl SE16 ....118 D5
Smithers Ho 3 SE20.................184 D3
Smithfield Mkt EC1 241 D3
Smithfield St EC1 ....94 D2 241 C3
Smithies Ct E15.......76 A3
Smithies Rd SE2 .....124 B2
Smith's Ct W1...... 249 C6
Smithson Rd N17 .....33 B2
Smiths Point E13 .....99 A6
Smith Sq SW1........116 A3 260 A5
Smith St
Surbiton KT5 ....198 B3
SW3....... 114 D1 257 C1
Smith's Yd SW18.....158 A2
Smith Terr SW3.........114 D1 257 C1
Smithwood Cl SW19...............157 A2
Smithy St E1 ....96 C2
Smithy Street Sch E1....................96 C2
Smock Wlk CR0......205 A3
Smoothfield TW3 ....129 C1
Smugglers Way SW18..................135 D1
Smyrk's Rd SE17....... 117 C1 263 B1
Smyrna Mans 8 NW6...................69 C1
Smyrna Rd NW6 ......69 C1
Smythe St E14.......119 D6
Snakes La E IG8 ......37 C4
Snakes La EN4, N14.....3 C1
Snakes La W IG8......37 B4
Snakey La TW13 .....172 B6
SNARESBROOK 54 D6
Snaresbrook Coll E18...................37 A1
Snaresbrook Dr HA7 ..26 A6
Snaresbrook Hall 12 E18.................55 A6
Snaresbrook Ho E18 ..54 D5
Snaresbrook Prim Sch E18..................55 A5
Snaresbrook Rd E11 ..54 D5
Snaresbrook Sta E11 .55 A4
Snarsgate St W10.....90 C2
Sneath Ave NW11 .....47 B2
Snell's Pk N18........33 D4
Sneyd Rd NW2........68 C4
Snowberry Cl E11.....76 B4
Snowbury Rd 6 SW6.................135 D3
Snow Ct 4 HA0.......65 D3
Snowden Ave UB10 ....82 D5
Snowden St EC2 ....95 C3 243 A5
Snowdon Cres UB3 ..105 A3
Snowdon Dr NW9.....45 C3
Snowdon Rd TW6.....149 A5
Snowdown Cl SE20...184 D2
Snowdrop Cl 2 TW12...............173 C4
Snowe Ho SE27 ......160 D1
Snow Hill EC1 .94 D2 241 C3
Snowman Ho NW6 ....91 D6
Snowsfields Prim Sch SE1......... 117 C4 253 A2
Snowsfields SE1.........117 B4 252 D2
Snowshill Rd E12 .....78 A3
Snowy Fielder Waye TW7...................131 B3
Soames St SE15 .....139 D2
Soames Wlk KT3.....177 C2
Soane Cl W5 ....109 D4
Soane Ct 10 NW1 .....71 C1
Soane Ho SE17 ..... 262 D1
Soane Mus The* WC2.........94 B1 240 C2
Soaphouse La TW8 ..132 A5
Soham Rd EN3......... 7 B6
SOHO 93 D1
Soho Mills SM6......203 B1
Soho Parish CE Prim Sch W1.... 115 D6 249 C6
Soho Sq W1 ...93 D1 239 C2
Soho St W1 .... 239 C2
Soho* W1..... 93 D1 239 C2
Sojourner-Truth Cl 11 E8..................74 B2
Sola Ct 8 CR0 ....205 B1
Solander Gdns
13 Shadwell E1..... 118 C6
Stepney E1 ....118 B6
Solar Ct N3...........29 D3
Soldene Ct N7.........72 B2
Solebay St E1 ....97 A3
Solent Ct SW16 ....182 B1
Solent Ho 6 E1 ......97 A2
Solent Rd NW6 ....69 C3
Solent Rise E13.......99 A4
Soley Mews WC1 ..... 234 A2
Solidarity Ho 5 NW10...................68 C2
Solna Ave SW15 .....156 C6
Solna Rd N21 ....17 B4
Solomon Ave N9......34 A6
Solomons Ct N12 .....30 A3
Solomon's Pas SE15 .140 B1
Solon New Rd SW4 ..138 A1
Solon Rd SW2 ....138 A1
Solway Cl TW4 ......129 A2
Solway Ho 12 E1......96 D3
Solway Rd
East Dulwich SE22............. 140 A1
Tottenham N22 ....32 D2
Somaford Gr EN4 .....14 B5
Somali Rd NW2.......69 B3
Somborne Ho 11 SW15.................156 A4
Sombrook Ho SE11 . 261 A3
Somerby Rd IG11.....79 B1
Somercoates Cl EN4 ...2 C2
Somer Ct SW6....... 265 A5
Somerfield Rd N4......72 D6
Somerfield St SE16 ..118 D1
Somerford Cl HA5 ....40 A5
Somerford Grove Est N16 ....73 D4
Somerford Gr
Shacklewell N16 ......73 D4
Tottenham N17 ....34 A3
Somerford St E1......96 B3
Somerford Way SE16.................119 A4
Somerhill Ave DA15 ..168 B4
Somerhill Rd DA16...146 B3
Somerleyton Rd SW9..................138 C1
Somersby Est SE20...184 C3
Somersby Gdns IG4...56 B4
Somers Cl NW1..... 232 C4
Somers Cres W2.... 237 A1
Somerset Ave
Chessington KT9 .... 213 D4
DA16 .... 145 D1
Wimbledon SW20 ....178 B1
Somerset Cl
New Malden KT3.... 199 C3
Tottenham N17 ....33 B1
Woodford IG8 ....37 A2
Somerset Ct
10 Buckhurst Hill IG9..................21 C2
Ealing W7 ....86 D1
2 Hampton TW12 ... 173 C2
Somerset Gdns
Highgate N6 ....49 A2
St Johns SE13 ...... 141 D3
Somerset Gdns *continued*
Teddington TW11.... 174 C5
Thornton Heath SW16..............204 B6
Tottenham N17 ....33 C3
Somerset Hall N17....33 C3
Somerset Ho WC2......... 116 B6 250 D6
Somerset Ho SW19 ..157 A1
Somerset Lo
9 Brentford TW8 .... 131 D6
5 New Barnet EN5 ...14 A6
Putney SW15........134 B1
Somerset Rd
Bedford Pk W4 ......111 B3
Brentford TW8...... 131 C6
Ealing W13 .... 109 C5
Edmonton N18........33 D5
Harrow HA1 ....42 A4
Hendon NW4.........46 C5
Holdbrook EN3 ....7 C5
Kingston u T KT1.....176 B1
New Barnet EN5 ......14 A6
Southall UB1 ....85 C2
Teddington TW11.... 174 C5
Tottenham N17 ....51 D6
Walthamstow E17 .....53 C3
Wimbledon SW19 ... 157 A1
Somerset Sq W14........113 B4 244 C1
Somerset Waye TW5...................129 A5
Somersham Rd DA7...................147 A3
Somers Pl SW2......160 B4
Somers Rd
Tulse Hill SW2.......160 B5
Walthamstow E17.....53 B5
SOMERS TOWN 93 D4
Somers Town Est NW1.........93 C5 232 B3
Somers Way WD23.....8 A4
Somerton Ave TW9 ..132 D2
Somerton Rd
Cricklewood NW2 .....69 A5
Nunhead SE15.......140 B1
Somertrees Ave SE12..................165 B2
Somervell Rd HA2 ....63 C3
Somerville Ave SW13.................134 C6
Somerville Ct SW16 .181 D4
Somerville Ho 10 SW15................156 D5
Somerville Point SE16..................119 B4
Somerville Rd
Dagenham RM6.......58 C4
Penge SE20.........184 D3
Sonderburg Rd 13 N7 ....72 B6
Sondes St SE17......139 B6
Songhurst Cl CR0 ....204 B3
Sonia Ct Edgware HA8..26 B3
North Finchley N12 ....30 A6
Sonia Gdns
Heston TW5......... 129 C5
North Finchley N12 ....30 A6
Willesden NW10 ....67 D4
Sonning Ct CR0......222 A6
Sonning Gdns TW12...................173 A4
Sonning Ho 32 E2.....95 D4
Sonning Rd CR0 .....206 A3
Soper Cl
Chingford Hatch E4....35 B5
4 Forest Hill SE23.. 162 D2
Soper Mews EN3 ......7 C5
Sophia Cl N7 ....72 B2
Sophia Ho
10 Hammersmith W6 .... 112 C1
Tottenham N15 ....51 D5
Sophia Rd
Newham E13..........99 B2
Walthamstow E10 .....53 D1
Sophia Sq 14 SE16 ...119 A6
Sopwith Ave KT9......214 A3
Sopwith Cl KT2 ......176 B5
Sopwith 2 NW9 ......27 D2
Sopwith Rd TW5.....128 C5
Sopwith Way
Battersea SW8..... 137 B5 268 C4
Kingston u T KT2.... 176 A2
Sorbus Ct EN2..........4 D3
Sorensen Ct 2 E10 ....75 D6
Sorrel Cl SE28........124 A5
Sorrel Gdns E6 ......100 A2
Sorrel Ho TW3.......130 A4
Sorrel La 17 E14 ......98 B1
Sorrell Cl
6 Brixton SW9..... 138 C3

Sorrell Cl *continued* SE14 141 A5
Sorrento Rd SM1 217 D5
Soseki Mus* SW4 137 B2
Sotheby Rd N5 73 A4
Sotheran Cl E8 96 A6
Sotheron Pl SW6 265 D3
Soudan Rd SW11 136 D4 267 C1
Souldern Rd 10 W14 112 D3
South Access Rd E17 53 A3
South Acre NW9 27 D1
Southacre Way HA5 22 C2
SOUTH ACTON 110 D3
South Acton Sta W3, W4 111 A3
South Africa Rd W12 112 B6
SOUTHALL 107 A5
Southall Ct UB1 107 B6
Southall Ent Ctr UB2 107 C4
Southall La TW5 106 B1
Southall Norwood Hospl UB2 107 B3
Southall Pl SE1 252 C1
Southall Sta UB1 107 B4
Southall & West London Coll UB1 107 A5
Southam Ho 9 W10 91 A3
Southampton Bldgs WC2 241 A3
Southampton Gdns CR4 204 A4
Southampton Mews E16 121 B5
Southampton Pl WC1 240 B3
Southampton Rd
Maitland Pk NW5 70 D3
Stanwell TW19, TW6 148 B5
Southampton Row WC1 94 A2 240 B4
Southampton St WC2 250 B6
Southampton Way SE5 139 C5
Southam St W10 91 A3
South Audley St W1 115 A5 248 B4
South Ave
Chingford E4 20 A4
East Finchley NW11 47 D5
South Avenue Gdns UB1 107 B6
South Ave
Richmond TW9 132 C3
Southall UB1 107 B6
Wallington SM5 219 A1
SOUTH BANK 116 B4
South Bank Bsns Ctr SW8 137 D6 269 D5
Southbank International Sch NW3 70 A2
Southbank International Sch (Westminster Campus) W1 93 B2 238 C4
Southbank Int Sch W11 113 C6 245 A5
South Bank Lo 2 KT6 198 A3
South Bank KT6 198 A3
South Bank Terr KT6 198 A3
Southbank KT7 197 B2
South Bank Univ
London SW8 137 D4 269 D2
SE1 116 D3 261 D6
SOUTH BEDDINGTON 219 C2
South Bermondsey Sta SE16 118 C1
South Birkbeck Rd E11 76 B5
South Black Lion La 7 W6 112 A1
South Bldg SW1 259 B6
South Block 20 E1 118 C6
South Bolton Gdns SW10 255 D2
SOUTHBOROUGH 197 D1 210 B3
Southborough Cl KT6 197 D1
Southborough High Sch KT6 214 A5
Southborough Ho SE17 263 B2
Southborough La BR1, BR2 210 B4
Southborough Prim Sch BR2 210 C4
Southborough Rd
Bromley BR1, BR2 210 A5
South Hackney E9 96 D6
Surbiton KT6 198 A1
Southborough Rd (The Lane) KT6 198 A1
Southbourne Ave NW9 27 B1
Southbourne Cl HA5 41 A2
Southbourne Cres NW4 47 A5
Southbourne Ct NW9 27 A1
Southbourne Gdns
Ilford IG1 79 A3
Ruislip HA4 40 B1
SE12 165 B6
Southbourne BR2 209 A2
Southbridge Pl CR0 221 A4
Southbridge Rd CR0 221 A4
Southbridge Way UB2 107 A4
SOUTH BROMLEY 98 B2
Southbrook Mews SE12 164 D5
Southbrook Rd
Hither Green SE12 164 D5
Thornton Heath SW16 182 A2
South Building* SE10 142 B5
Southbury Ave EN1 6 A1
Southbury NW8 229 B6
Southbury Prim Sch EN3 6 C1
Southbury Rd
Enfield EN1 5 D2
Enfield EN1, EN3 6 B1
Southbury Sta EN3 6 B1
South Camden Com Sch NW1 93 D5 232 C4
South Carriage Dr SW1, SW7 114 D4 247 C2
South Chelsea Coll SW9 138 B1
Southchurch Ct
Bowes Pk N13 32 B5
Newham E6 100 B5
Southchurch Rd E6 100 B5
South Cl Barnet EN5 1 B2
DA6 146 D1
Dagenham RM10 103 C6
Highgate N6 49 B3
Morden SM4 201 C3
Pinner HA5 41 B2
Twickenham TW2 151 C1
West Drayton UB7 104 C3
South Colonnade The E14 119 D5
Southcombe St W14 254 A4
South Common Rd UB8 60 A2
Southcote Ave
Feltham TW13 150 A2
Tolworth KT5 198 D2
Southcote Rd
Croydon SE25 206 B3
Tufnell Pk N19 71 C4
Walthamstow E17 53 A4
Southcote Rise HA4 39 B2
Southcott Ho
31 Bromley E3 97 D4
W9 236 B5
South Countess Rd E17 53 B6
South Cres
Newham E16 98 B3
WC1 239 C3
Southcroft Ave
DA16 145 C2
West Wickham BR4 224 A6
Southcroft SM1 218 C3
Southcroft Rd BR6 227 C5
Streatham SW17 181 A4
South Cross Rd IG6 57 A4
South Croxted Rd SE21 183 B6
SOUTH CROYDON 221 B1
South Croydon Sta CR2 221 B3
South Ct 17 SW15 156 D5
Southdean Gdns SW19 157 B2
Southdene Ct N11 15 C1
South Dene NW7 11 B1
Southdown Ave W7 109 A3
Southdown Cres
Harrow HA2 42 A1
Ilford IG2 57 C4
Southdown Dr SW20 178 D3
Southdown N7 72 A2
Southdown Rd SW20 178 D2
South Dr
Orpington BR6 227 C3
Ruislip HA4 39 C1
South Ealing Cemy W5 109 D2
South Ealing Rd W5 109 D3
South Ealing Sta W5 109 D3
South Eastern Ave N9 17 D1
South Eastern Univ N7 72 B5
South Eaton Pl SW1 115 A2 258 B4
South Eden Park Rd BR3 207 D4
South Edwardes Sq W8 255 A5
SOUTHEND 186 B6
South End Cl NW3 70 C4
Southend Cl SE9 166 D5
Southend Cres SE9 166 D5
South End CR0 221 A4
South End Gn NW3 70 C4
Southend Ho SE9 166 C4
Southend La SE6 185 C6
Southend Rd BR3 185 C2
South End Rd NW3 70 C4
Southend Rd
Plashet E6 78 B1
Woodford IG8 37 D1
Southend Road (North Circular Rd) E17, E18 36 C2
South End Row W8 113 D3 255 D6
South End W8 113 D3 255 D6
Southern Ave
East Bedfont TW14 150 A3
South Norwood SE25 205 D6
Southerngate Way SE14 141 A5
Southern Gr E3 97 B3
Southernhay IG10 21 D6
Southern Perimeter Rd
Hatton TW14, TW6 149 B6
West Bedfont TW19, TW6 148 C5
Southern Rd
Fortis Green N2 48 D5
Newham E13 99 B5
Southern Road Prim Sch E13 99 B5
Southern Row W10 91 A3
Southern St N1 233 C4
Southern Way
Greenwich SE10 120 D3
Romford RM7 59 C3
Southerton Rd W6 112 C2
South Esk Rd E7 77 C2
Southey Ho SE17 262 B2
Southey Mews E16 121 A5
Southey Rd
Brixton SW9 138 C4
Merton SW19 179 C3
Tottenham N15 51 C4
Southey St SE20 184 D3
Southfield EN5 12 D5
Southfield Cl UB8 82 C4
Southfield Cotts W7 108 D4
Southfield Ct E11 76 D5
Southfield Gdns TW1, TW2 174 D6
Southfield Lo W4 111 B4
Southfield Pk HA2 41 D5
Southfield Prim Sch W4 111 C4
Southfield Rd
Acton W4 111 B4
Enfield EN3 18 C5
St Paul's Cray BR7 211 D6
SOUTHFIELDS 157 D3
Southfields Ave TW15 170 D4
Southfields Com Coll SW18 157 C3
Southfields Ct SM3 217 C6
Southfields NW4 46 B6
Southfields Rd SW18 157 C5
Southfields Sta SW18 157 B3
Southfields KT8 196 C3
Southfleet Rd BR6 227 C4
SOUTHGATE 16 B4
South Gate Ave TW13 171 B6
Southgate Cir 3 N14 15 D3
Southgate Coll N14 15 D2
Southgate Ct N1 73 B1
Southgate Gr N1 73 B1
Southgate Ho 7 E17 54 A6
Southgate Rd N1 95 B6 235 D6
Southgate Sch EN4 15 B6
Southgate Sta N14 15 D3
Southgate Way N2 30 C2
South Gdns
Mitcham SW19 180 B3
Wembley HA9 66 C6
South Gipsy Rd DA16 146 D2
South Glade The DA5 169 B3
South Gn NW9 27 C2
South Greenford Sta UB6 86 C4
South Gr N6 49 A1
South Grove Ho N6 49 A1
South Grove Prim Sch E17 53 B3
South Gr
Tottenham N15 51 B4
Walthamstow E17 53 B4
SOUTH HACKNEY 96 C6
SOUTH HAMPSTEAD 70 A1
South Hampstead High Sch Jun Dept NW3 70 A2
South Hampstead High Sch NW3 70 B2
South Hampstead Sta NW8 70 A1
South Harringay Jun & Inf Schs N4 50 D4
SOUTH HARROW 63 D5
South Harrow Sta HA2 64 A5
South Hill Ave HA1, HA2 64 B5
South Hill BR7 188 B4
South Hill Gr HA1 64 C4
South Hill Pk Gdns NW3 70 C4
South Hill Pk NW3 70 C4
South Hill Rd BR2 208 C5
Southholme Cl SE19 183 C2
Southill La HA5 40 B5
Southill Rd BR7 188 B3
Southill St E14 97 D1
South Island Pl SW9 138 C5
SOUTH KENSINGTON 114 A1
South Kensington Sta SW7 114 B2 256 D4
South Kensington Station Arc SW7 256 D4
South Kenton Sta HA9 43 C1
South La KT1 197 D6
SOUTH LAMBETH 138 A4
South Lambeth Pl SW8 270 B6
South Lambeth Rd SW8 138 A5 270 B4
Southland Rd SE18 145 D5
Southlands Ave BR6 227 C3
Southlands Ct BR2 209 D5
Southlands Dr SW19 156 D2
Southlands Gr BR1 210 A6
Southlands Rd BR1, BR2 209 D5
Southland Way TW7 152 B6
South La KT3 199 B3
South La W KT3 199 B5
South Lodge Ave CR4, CR7, SW16 204 A5
South Lodge Cres EN2 3 D1
South Lodge Dr N14 15 D6
South London Montessori Sch SW11 267 A1
South Lo
6 New Barnet EN5 13 D6
NW8 229 C2
Twickenham TW2 152 A5
South Mall The N9 18 A1
South Mead NW9 27 D2
Southmead Prim Sch SW19 157 A3
Southmead Rd SW19 157 A3
South Mead KT19 215 D1
South Merton Sta SW20 201 B6
South Molton La W1 93 B1 238 C1
South Molton Rd E16 99 A1
South Molton St W1 93 B1 238 C1
Southmont Rd KT10 212 C5
Southmoor Way E9 75 B3
South Mount N20 14 A2
SOUTH NORWOOD 205 C6
South Norwood Ctry Pk* SE25 206 C5
South Norwood Hill SE19, SE25 183 D1
South Norwood Prim Sch SE25 206 A5
South Oak Rd SW16 182 B6
Southold Rise SE9 166 B1
Southolm St SW11 137 B4 268 D1
South Ordnance Rd EN3 7 C5
Southover BR1 187 A5
Finchley N12 29 C6
SOUTH OXHEY 22 B6
South Par W4 111 B2
South Parade SW3 114 B1 256 D2
South Par HA8 26 C1
South Park Bsns Ctr IG3 79 C6
South Park Cres
Catford SE6 164 D3
Ilford IG1 79 C5
South Park Ct 24 BR3 185 C3
Southpark Ct SW19 179 C4
South Park Dr IG3 79 C4
South Park Gr KT3 199 A5
South Park Hill Rd CR2 221 B4
South Park Mews SW6 135 D2
South Park Prim Sch IG3 79 C5
South Park Rd
Ilford IG1 79 B5
Wimbledon SW19 179 D4
South Park Terr IG1 79 C5
South Park Villas IG3 79 C4
South Park Way HA4 62 C3
South Par SM6 219 C2
South Pl
Broadgate EC2 95 B2 242 D3
Enfield EN3 18 C6
South Pl Mews EC2 242 D3
South Pl KT5 198 B2
Southport Rd SE18 123 B2
South Quay Plaza E14 119 D4
South Quay Sta E14 119 D4
South Rd
Brentford W5 109 D2
Edgware HA8 26 D2
Edmonton N9 18 A3
Feltham TW13 172 D5
Forest Hill SE23 162 D2
Hampton TW12 173 B4
Heston TW5 128 D6
Mitcham SW19 180 B4
Southall UB1 107 B5
Twickenham TW2 152 B1
West Drayton UB7 104 C3
South Residence IG3 58 B4
South Ridge BR2 209 C5
Southridge Pl SW20 178 D3
South Rise Prim Sch SE18 123 B1
South Rise W2 247 B6
South Rise Way SE18 123 B2
South Row SE3 142 D3
SOUTH RUISLIP 62 D4
South Ruislip Sta HA4 62 C3
Southsea Rd KT1 198 A5
South Sea St SE16 119 B3
Southside Comm SW19 178 D4
Southside Ind Est SW8 269 A2
Southside N7 71 D4
South Side W6 111 D3
Southside Quarter 4 SW11 136 D3
Southside Sh Ctr SW18 157 D5
Southspring DA15 167 B4
South Sq
Hampstead Garden Suburb NW11 47 D3
WC1 241 A3
South St
Bromley BR1 187 A1
Enfield EN3 18 D6
Isleworth TW7 131 A2
Mayfair W1 115 A5 248 B4
South Tenter St E1 95 D1 243 D1
South Terr
Muswell Hill N22 31 D1
Surbiton KT6 198 A3
SW7 114 C2 257 A4
South Thames Coll (Battersea Ctr) SW11 136 D4 267 D1
South Thames Coll (Putney Ctr) SW15 156 D6
South Thames Coll (Roehampton Ctr) SW15 156 A5
South Thames Coll (Tooting Ctr) SW17 180 C5
South Thames Coll (Wandsworth Ctr) SW18 157 D6
SOUTH TOTTENHAM 51 D3
South Tottenham Sta N15 51 D4
South Vale HA1 64 C4
Southvale Rd SE3 142 C3
South Vale SE19 183 C4
Southview Ave NW10 67 D3
South View BR1 187 C1
South View Cl DA5 169 B5
Southview Cl SW17 181 A5
South View Cres IG2 56 D3
South View Ct
8 Forest Hill SE23 162 C3
South Norwood SE19 183 A3
Southview Dr E18 55 B6
Southview Gdns SM6 219 C1
Southview Rd BR1 186 B6
South View Rd
Hornsey N8 50 A6
Pinner HA5 22 B4
South View SW19 178 D4
South Villas NW1 71 D2
Southville Cl
East Bedfont TW14 149 C3
West Ewell KT19 215 B1
Southville Cres TW14 149 C3
Southville Jun & Inf Schs TW14 149 D3
Southville SW8 137 D4 269 D1
Southville Rd
East Bedfont TW14 149 C4
Thames Ditton KT7 197 B2
SOUTHWARK 117 B5
Southwark Bridge Rd SE1 117 A5 252 B3
Southwark Bridge SE1, EC4 117 A6 252 B5
Southwark Cath* SE1 117 B5 252 C4
Southwark Coll (Blackfriars Ctr) SE1 251 C3
Southwark Coll (Camberwell Ctr) SE5 139 C5
Southwark Coll (Grange Ctr) SE1 263 B5
Southwark Coll SE1 116 D4 251 C2
Southwark Coll (Surrey Docks Ctr) SE16 118 B3
Southwark Park Est 11 SE16 118 B2
Southwark Park Prim Sch SE16 118 B3
Southwark Park Rd SE16 118 A2
Southwark Pl BR1 210 B6
Southwark St SE1 117 A5 252 A3
Southwater Cl
Beckenham BR3 185 D3
8 Poplar E14 97 B1
Southway Cl 9 W12 112 B4
South Way
Croydon CR0 223 A5
Friern Barnet N11 31 C4
Southway NW11 47 D4
South Way HA2 41 C5
Southway BR2 209 A2
South Way N9 18 C2

Southway
Totteridge N20 ....13 C2
Wallington SM6.....219 C4
South Way HA9.......66 C3
Southway SW20 .....200 D5
Southwell Ave UB5....63 C2
Southwell Gdns
SW7..........256 A3
Southwell Grove Rd
E11.............76 C6
Southwell Ho
8 Bermondsey
SE16.........118 B2
13 Stoke Newington
N16.........73 C3
Southwell Rd
Camberwell SE5 ....139 A2
Harrow HA3 ....43 D3
Thornton Heath CR0 . 204 C3
South Western Rd
TW1..........153 B5
Southwest Rd E11 ....54 B1
South Wharf Rd
W2.........92 B1 236 D2
Southwick Mews
W2..........236 D2
Southwick Pl W2 ... 237 A1
Southwick St
W2.........92 C1 237 A2
Southwick Yd W2... 237 A1
SOUTH WIMBLEDON
.........179 D4
South Wimbledon Sta
SW19..........179 D3
South Wlk
Coney Hall BR4 ....224 C5
Hayes UB3.........83 B2
Southwold Dr IG11 ...80 A3
Southwold Mans W9..91 C4
Southwold Prim Sch
E5...........74 B6
Southwold Rd DA5...169 D5
Upper Clapton E5 .....74 C6
Southwood Ave
Highgate N6 ....49 B2
Kingston u T KT2,
KT3.........177 A2
Southwood Cl BR1...210 B5
North Cheam KT4 ...200 D1
Southwood Ct EC1..234 C1
Hampstead Garden
Suburb NW11.......47 D4
Southwood Dr KT5...199 A1
South Woodford Sta
E18..........37 B1
Southwood Gdns
Hinchley Wood
KT10.........213 A5
Ilford IG2 ....56 D5
Southwood Hall N6...49 B3
Southwood Ho
New Eltham SE9 ....166 D2
Notting Hill W11....244 A6
Southwood Hospl
(Geriatric) N6 ......49 A2
Southwood Hts N6....49 B2
Southwood La N6.....49 A2
Southwood Lawn Rd
N6 ....49 B2
Southwood Mans N6..49 B3
Southwood Park N6 ..49 A2
Southwood Prim Sch
RM9.........81 A4
Southwood Rd SE9...166 D2
Woolwich SE28 ......124 B5
Southwood Smith Ho 4
E2..........96 B4
Southwood Smith St
N1 ....234 C5
South Worple Ave
SW14.........133 C2
Southwyck Ho SW9..138 C1
South Yd EC1.......242 C4
Sovereign Bsns Ctr
EN3 ....7 B2
Sovereign Cl
Ealing W5 ....87 C2
Ruislip HA4 ....39 C1
Stepney E1 ....118 B6
Sovereign Cres
SE16.........119 A6
Sovereign Ct BR2....210 B3
East Molesey KT8 ...195 B5
Harlington UB7 .....126 D5
3 Richmond TW9....132 B1
13 Stepney E1.......118 B6
Sovereign Gr HA0.....65 D5
Sovereign Ho
Ashford TW15 ......170 A6
23 Bethnal Green E1...96 B3
Chislehurst BR7......189 B3
Edgware NW7.......27 B6
3 Wimbledon
SW19..........179 A4
Woolwich SE18 ......122 B3
Sovereign Mews
Barnet EN4 ....2 D2

Sovereign Mews
continued
6 Haggerston E2....95 D5
Sovereign Pk NW10...88 D3
Sovereign Pl HA1.....42 D4
Sovereign Rd IG11...102 C4
Sovreign Ct HA6 .....22 A2
Sowerby Cl SE9......166 B6
Space Apartments
N22 ....32 B3
Space Bsns Pk NW10 .88 D4
Spa Central 1
SW16.........182 A3
Space Waye TW14 ...150 B6
Spa Cl SE19 ....183 C2
Spa Ct
12 Bermondsey
SE16.........118 A3
Streatham SW16.....182 B6
Spafield St EC1.....241 A6
Spa Hill CR7, SE19....183 B2
Spalding Cl HA8 .....27 C3
Spalding Ct HA8 .....26 B6
Spalding Ho SE4.....163 A6
Spalding Rd
Hendon NW4.........46 C3
Streatham SW17.....181 B5
Spanby Rd E3 ....97 C3
Spangate SE3 ....142 D2
Spaniards Cl NW11...48 B1
Spaniards End NW3...48 B1
Spaniards Rd NW3....70 A6
Spanish Pl W1......238 B2
Spanish Rd SW18....158 A6
Spanswick Lo 2
N15 ....50 D5
Spa Rd SE16. 117 D3 263 D5
Sparkbridge Rd HA1 ..42 C5
Sparkes Cl BR2 .....209 B5
Sparke Terr 2 E16 ....98 D1
Sparkford Gdns N11 ..31 A5
Sparkford Ho SW11 ..266 D2
Sparks Cl Acton W3....89 B1
Dagenham RM8.......80 D6
Hampton TW12 .....173 A4
Sparrow Cl TW12 ....173 A4
Sparrow Ct E4.......36 A4
Sparrow Dr BR5 .....211 B1
Sparrow Farm Com Jun
Sch KT17 ....216 B4
Sparrow Farm Dr
TW14.........150 D4
Sparrow Farm Inf Sch
TW14.........150 C4
Sparrow Farm Jun Sch
TW14.........150 C4
Sparrow Farm Rd KT17,
KT4 ....216 B4
Sparrow Gn RM10.....81 D5
Sparrow's Farm L Ctr
SE9.........167 A4
Sparrows Herne
WD23..........8 A4
Sparrows La SE9.....167 A3
Sparrows Way WD23 ...8 A4
Sparsholt Rd
Barking IG11.......101 C6
Finsbury Pk N19 ......50 B1
Sparta St SE10.......142 A4
Spa Sch SE1.........118 A2
Spa View 6 SW16....160 B1
Speakers' Corner*
W1........114 D6 247 D6
Speaker's Ct 3 CR0..205 B1
Speakman Ho SE4 ...141 A2
Spearman St 8
SE18.........144 C6
Spear Mews
SW5........113 C2 255 B3
Spearpoint Gdns IG2..57 D5
Spears Rd N19.......50 A1
Speart La TW5.......129 A5
Spectacle Works
E13.........99 C4
Spectrum Ho NW5 ....71 A4
Spectrum Twr 1
IG1.........79 A6
Spedan Cl NW3.......70 A5
Speechly Mews E8.....73 D3
Speed Ho EC2 ......242 C4
Speedwell Ct 9 N12 ..29 D6
Speedwell Ho 11
N12 ....29 D6
Speedwell St 5
SE8.........141 C5
Speedy Pl WC1 .....233 A1
Speer Rd KT7.......196 D3
Speirs Cl KT3........199 D3
Spekehill SE9........166 B1
Speke Rd CR7 ....183 B1
Speldhurst Cl 2
BR2 ....208 D4
Speldhurst Rd
Bedford Pk W4 ......111 B3
Homerton E9.........74 D1
Spellbrook Wlk N1.. 235 B6
Spelman Ho 15 E1 ....96 A2

Spelman St E1.......96 A2
Spelthorne Coll
TW15.........170 B6
Spelthorne Gr
TW16.........171 D3
Spelthorne Inf Sch
TW15.........171 B4
Spelthorne Jun Sch
TW15.........171 B4
Spelthorne La TW15,
TW17.........171 A2
Spence Cl SE16......119 B4
Spencer Ave
Bowes Pk N13.......32 B4
Hayes UB4..........84 A2
Spencer Cl BR6 ......227 D6
Church End N3........29 C1
Ealing NW10 ....88 B4
Woodford IG8 ....37 C5
Spencer Ct 5 BR6 ....227 A3
6 Finchley N3 ....29 D3
Wimbledon SW20 ....178 B2
Spencer Dr N2 ....48 A3
Spencer Gdns
SW14.........155 A6
Spencer Hill Rd
SW19.........179 A3
Spencer Hill SW19...179 A3
Spencer Ho
31 Clapham SW8 ...137 D3
Hendon NW4.........46 B4
24 Putney SW19....156 D3
Spencer House Mus*
SW1.......115 C5 249 A3
Spencer Ho
Vale of Health NW3....70 B5
Wimbledon SW19 ...156 D1
Spencer Mews
Fulham W6 ....264 A6
South Lambeth SW9 .270 C1
Spencer Park Ct
SW18.........158 B6
Spencer Pk
East Molesey KT8 ...196 A4
Wandsworth SW18 ...158 B6
Spencer Pl
16 Islington N1.......72 D1
SW1.........259 B5
Thornton Heath CR0 ..205 B2
Spencer Rd
Acton W3.........111 A5
Bromley BR1 ....186 D3
Carshalton CR4 .....203 A2
Chingford E17 ....36 A1
Chiswick W4 ....133 A5
East Molesey KT8 ...196 A4
Friern Barnet N11.....31 B6
Harrow HA3 ....24 C1
Hornsey Vale N8 ......50 B4
Hounslow TW3, TW5,
TW7 ....130 A4
Ilford IG3 ....57 D1
Mitcham CR4.......203 A6
Newham E6 ....99 D6
South Croydon CR2 ..221 C3
Tottenham N17 ....34 A2
Twickenham TW2.....152 C2
Wandsworth SW18 ...158 B6
Wembley HA0 ....65 C6
Wimbledon SW20 ....178 B2
Spencer Rise NW5 ....71 B5
Spencer St
Finsbury
EC1.......94 D4 234 C1
Southall UB2 ....106 D4
Spencer Wlk
23 Hampstead
NW3.........70 A4
Putney SW15.......134 D1
Spencer Yd SE3......142 D3
Spenlow Ho 2
SE16.........118 A3
Spenser Ct 5
TW10.........175 D6
Spenser Gr N16.......73 C4
Spenser Mews SE21..161 B3
Spenser Rd SE24......160 D6
Spenser St SW1 ....259 B6
Spens Ho WC1 ......240 C5
Spensley Wlk N16.....73 B5
Speranza St SE18 ....123 D1
Sperling Rd N17 ......33 C1
Spert St E14........119 A6
Speyside N14.........15 C5
Spey St E14 ....98 A2
Spezia Rd NW10 ......90 A5
Spice Ct
10 Battersea
SW11 ....136 A2
2 St George in t East
E1...........118 A5
Spice Quay Htss
SE1.........253 D3
Spicer Cl
Brixton SE5, SW9 ...138 D3
Walton-on-T KT12 ...194 C3
Spicer Ct EN1 ....5 C2

Spicer Ho E2 ....96 A4
Spices Yd CR0 ....221 A4
Spigurnell Rd N17 ....33 B2
Spikes Bridge Rd
UB1 ....107 A6
Spilsby Cl NW9 ....27 C1
Spindle Cl SE18......122 A3
Spindle Ho 8 DA15...168 A1
Spindlewood Gdns
CR0 ....221 C4
Spindrift Ave E14 ....119 D2
Spinel Cl SE18.......123 D1
Spinnaker Cl IG11 ...102 B4
Spinnaker Ct 2
KT1 ....175 D2
Spinnaker Ho 21
E14.........119 C4
Spinnells Rd HA2 .....41 B1
Spinney Cl
Beckenham BR3 ....207 D5
New Malden KT3.....199 C4
Worcester Pk KT4...215 D6
Yiewsley UB7.......104 A6
Spinney Dr TW14 ....149 A4
Spinney Gdns
Dagenham RM9.......81 A3
Dulwich SE19.......183 D5
Spinney Oak BR1 ....188 A1
Spinneys The BR1....188 B1
Spinney The
Barnes SW13 ....134 B6
Barnet EN5 ....1 D3
Cheam SM3........216 C4
DA14 ....191 A5
Edgware HA7.........26 A6
Southgate N21........16 C4
Streatham SW16.....159 D1
Sunbury TW16.......172 A2
Wembley HA0 ....65 A5
Spire Ct 10 TW10....154 A5
Spire Ho W2........246 B6
Spires The EN5 ....1 A2
Spirit Quay E1.......118 B5
SPITALFIELDS 95 D2
Spital Sq E1...95 C2 243 B4
Spital St E1 ....96 A2
Spital Yd E1 ....243 B4
Spitfire Bsns Pk
CR0 ....220 C2
Spitfire Est The
TW5.........106 C1
Spitfire Rd SM6......220 A1
Spitfire Way TW5 ....106 C1
Splendour Wlk
SE16.........118 C1
Spode Ho SE11 .....261 A5
Spode Wlk NW3 ......69 D3
Spondon Rd N15......52 A5
Spoonbill Way UB4 ...84 D2
Spooner Ho TW5 ....129 C6
Spooner 8 NW9......27 D3
Spooner Wlk SM6....219 D3
Sporle Ct 6 SW11 ...136 B2
Sportsbank St SE6 ...164 A4
Spottons Gr N17 ......33 A2
Spout Hill CR0.......223 C3
Spratt Hall Rd E11 ....55 A3
Spray St SE18........122 D2
Spreighton Rd KT8...195 D5
Sprewell SW15 ....157 A5
Spriggs Ho 14 N1 .....72 D1
Sprimont Pl
SW3........114 D1 257 C2
Springall St 9
SE15.........140 B5
Springalls Wharf 2
SE16.........118 A4
Springbank Rd
SE13.........164 C5
Springbank N21 ......16 B5
Springbank Wlk
NW1.........71 D1
Springbourne Ct
BR3 ....186 A2
Spring Bridge Rd
W5.........109 D6
Spring Cl Barnet EN5...12 D6
Dagenham RM8.......58 D1
Springclose La SM3..217 A2
Spring Cnr TW13 ....149 D1
Spring Cott 10 W12 ..112 A4
Spring Cotts KT6.....197 D4
Spring Court Rd EN2...4 C5
Springcroft Ave N2 ...48 D5
Spring Ct
Brondesbury NW2.....69 B2
Ealing W7 ....108 B6
Edgware HA8.........26 B5
10 Wanstead E18 .....55 B6
Springdale Rd N16....73 B4
Spring Dr HA5........40 A3
Springett Ho 15
SW2.........160 B6
Springfield Ave
Hampton TW12 .....173 D4
Hornsey N10 ....49 C6
Merton SW20 ....201 B6

Springfield WD23 ......8 B3
Springfield Cl
Finchley N12 ....29 D5
Stanmore HA7.........9 A1
Springfield Com Prim
Sch N16 ....52 A3
Springfield Ct
7 Dagenham W3 .....89 A1
1 Friern Barnet N20 ..14 D1
Hampstead NW3......70 C1
2 Ilford IG1.........78 D3
9 Kingston u T KT1 . 198 A6
Upper Clapton E5 .....52 B1
Wallington SM6......219 B3
Springfield Dr IG2 ....57 A3
Springfield Gdns
BR1 ....210 B5
Kingsbury NW9.......45 B4
Ruislip HA4 ....40 B1
Upper Clapton E5 .....52 B1
West Wickham BR4 ..223 D6
Woodford IG8 ....37 C3
Springfield Gr SE7 ...143 C6
Sunbury TW16.......172 A2
Springfield Ho
Acton W3..........111 A5
1 Camberwell SE5..139 C3
13 Dalston E8 ....73 D2
Springfield Hospl
SW17.........158 C1
Springfield La NW6 ...91 D6
Springfield Mount
NW9.........45 C4
Springfield Pl KT3 ...199 A5
Springfield Prim Sch
TW16.........171 D1
Springfield Rd
Ashford TW15 ....170 B5
Bexleyheath DA7.....147 D1
Bromley BR1 ....210 B5
Chingford E4 ....20 C4
Ealing W7 ....108 C5
Friern Barnet N11.....31 C5
Harrow HA1 ....42 C3
Hayes UB4..........106 C5
Kingston u T KT1 ...198 A6
Newham E15 ....98 C4
Penge SE26 ....184 B5
Plashet E6...........78 B1
South Norwood CR7 . 183 A2
St John's Wood
NW8.......92 A6 229 B5
8 Teddington
TW11 ....175 A5
Tottenham Hale N15...52 A5
Twickenham TW2....151 C3
Wallington SM6......219 B3
Walthamstow E17 .....53 B3
Welling DA16........146 B2
Wimbledon SW19 ....179 B5
Springfield Rise
SE26.........162 B1
Springfields 16 EN5 ...13 D6
Springfield
South Norwood
SE25.........206 A6
Upper Clapton E5 .....52 B1
Springfield Wlk
3 BR6 ....211 B1
Paddington NW6 ......91 D6
Spring Gdns
East Molesey KT8 ...196 A5
Islington N5 ....73 A3
SW1.......116 A5 250 A4
Wallington SM6.....219 C3
Woodford IG8 ....37 C3
Spring Gr
Brentford W4.......132 C6
Hampton TW12 .....173 D2
Loughton IG10.......21 D5
Mitcham CR4.......181 A2
SPRING GROVE 130 C3
Spring Grove Cres TW3,
TW5.........130 A4
Spring Grove Prim Sch
TW7.........130 B3
Spring Grove Rd
Hounslow TW3, TW5,
TW7 ....130 A4
Richmond TW10......154 B6
Springhallow Sch
W13.........87 A1
Springhill Cl SE5.....139 B2
Spring Hill
Forest Hill SE26.....184 C6
Upper Clapton E5 .....52 A2
Spring Ho
Merton SW19 ....179 B2
WC1.........234 A1
Springhurst Cl CR0 ..223 B4
Spring La SE25 ......206 B3
Spring Lake HA7......25 B6
Spring La
Muswell Hill N10.....49 A6
Upper Clapton E5 .....52 B1
Spring Mews W1 ....237 D4

SPRING PARK 223 B5
Spring Park Ave
CR0 ....222 D6
Springpark Dr
Beckenham BR3 ....208 A6
Stoke Newington N4...51 A1
Spring Park Prim Sch
CR0 ....223 C5
Spring Park Rd CR0..222 D6
Spring Pl
Camden Town NW5....71 B3
Church End N3........29 C1
Springpond Rd RM9...81 A3
Spring Rd TW13 .....149 D1
Springrice Rd SE13 ..164 B5
Spring Shaw Rd
BR5 ....190 A2
Spring St W2..92 B1 236 C1
Spring Terr TW10 ....154 A6
Springtide Cl 10
SE15.........140 A4
Springvale Ave
TW8.........110 A1
Springvale Ct SE12...143 A1
Spring Vale DA7 .....147 D1
Springvale Terr 5
W14.........112 D3
Spring Villa Rd HA8 ..26 C3
Springwater Cl
SE18.........144 C4
Springwater WC1...240 C4
Springway HA1 ....42 B2
Springwell Ave
NW10.........89 D6
Springwell Cl SW16..182 B6
Springwell Ct TW5...128 D3
Springwell Jun & Inf
Schs TW5.........129 A5
Springwell Rd
Heston TW5........128 D4
West Norwood
SW16 ....182 C5
Spring Wlk E1........96 A2
Springwood Cl 8 E3..97 C5
Springwood Cres
HA8 ....11 A2
Springwood Ct CR2..221 C4
Sprowston Mews E7 ..77 A3
Sprowston Rd E7 .....77 A3
Spruce Ct W5 ....110 A3
Sprucedale Gdns
CR0 ....222 D4
Spruce Hills Rd E17...36 A1
Spruce Ho
2 Brentford
TW8 ....131 C5
15 Rotherhithe
SE16.........118 D4
Spruce Pk BR2 ......208 D5
Sprules Rd SE4 .....141 A3
Spurfield KT8........195 D6
Spurgeon Ave SE19 ..183 B2
Spurgeon Rd SE19 ..183 B3
Spurgeon's Coll
SE25.........183 C1
Spurgeon St
SE1.......117 B3 262 C6
Spur Ho 10 SW19 ....179 D2
Spurling Rd
Dagenham RM9.......81 B2
East Dulwich SE22...139 D1
Spur Rd
Brentford TW7.......131 B5
Edgware HA8.........26 A6
Feltham TW14 ....128 B1
SE1 ......116 C4 251 A2
Tottenham N15 ....51 B5
Wallend IG11 ......101 A4
Spurstowe Rd E8 .....74 B2
Spurstowe Terr E8 ....74 B3
Spurway Par 2 IG2...56 B4
Square Rigger Row 7
SW11.........136 A2
Square The
Hammersmith
W6 ....112 C1
Hayes UB11.........105 B5
Ilford IG1 ....56 C2
Leyton E10...........76 A5
12 Richmond TW10...153 D6
SW6.........265 A1
Wallington SM5......219 A3
Woodford IG8 ....37 A5
Squarey St SW17.....158 A1
Squire Ct 2 CR0.....205 C1
Squire Gdns NW8....229 C1
Squire's Almshouses 7
E17.........53 D5
Squires Bridge Rd
KT17 ....192 B5
Squires Ct
Finchley N3 ....30 A2
SW4.........270 B1
Wimbledon SW19 ...179 C6

Squires Ho 3 SE18 ..144 D6
Squires La N3 ....30 A2
Squire's Mount NW3..70 B5
Squire's Rd TW17....192 C5
Squires The RM7......59 D3
Squires Wlk TW15 ...171 B3
Squires Wood Dr
BR7 ....188 B3
Squirrel Cl TW4......128 C2
Squirrel Mews W13..109 A6
Squirrels Cl
Hillingdon UB10.......60 C1
North Finchley N12....30 A6
Orpington BR6........211 C1
Squirrels Ct KT4 ......215 D6
Squirrels Gn KT4......216 A6
Squirrel's La IG9 .....21 D1
Squirrels The
Bushey WD23 ....8 B5
Lewisham SE13......142 B2
Pinner HA5 ....41 B6
Squirrels Trad Est
UB3 ....105 D3
Squirries St E2 ....96 A4
Stable Cl
Kingston u T KT2.....176 B4
Northolt UB5..........85 C5
Stable Ct 4 SM6.....219 A5
Stable Ho 9 SE16....118 C4
Stable Mews
Twickenham TW1.... 152 D3
West Norwood SE27 . 183 A5
Stables End BR6.....227 A5
Stables The IG9.......21 C4
Stables Way
SE11........116 C1 261 A2
Stable Way W10 ......90 C1
Stable Wlk N2........30 B2
Stable Yd Rd
SW1........115 C4 249 B2
Staburn Ct HA8.......27 A1
Stacey Ave N18.......34 C6
Stacey Cl E10.........54 B4
Stacey St Highbury N7..72 C5
Soho WC2 ... 93 D1 239 D1
Stack Ho SW1 ...... 258 B3
Stackhouse St SW1 . 257 C6
Stacy Path 13 SE5....139 C5
Staddon Cl BR3.......207 A5
Stadium Bsns Ctr
HA9 ....66 D5
Stadium Rd E NW2....46 C2
Stadium Rd
Hendon NW2.........46 C2
SE7, SE18 ....144 B6
Stadium Ret Pk HA9..66 C5
Stadium St
SW10.......136 A5 266 B3
Stadium Way HA9.....66 C4
Staffa Rd E10.........53 A1
Stafford Cl
Cheam SM3........ 217 A2
Maida Vale NW6......91 C4
Southgate N14........15 C6
Walthamstow E17......53 B3
Stafford Cripps Ho
30 Bethnal Green
E2................96 C4
SW6............. 264 D5
Stafford Cross Bsns Pk
CR0 ....220 B3
Stafford Cross CR0...220 B3
Stafford Ct
Croydon CR0....... 220 C4
Ealing W7 ....86 D1
Kensington W8 ..... 255 B6
South Lambeth SW8 . 270 A2
Stafford Gdns CR0 ...220 B3
Stafford Ho SE1 .... 263 D2
Stafford Mans
13 Hammersmith
W14.......... 112 D3
14 Stockwell SW4... 138 A1
SW11............ 267 C3
Stafford Morris Ho 9
E15..............98 C6
Stafford Pl
Richmond TW10......154 B4
SW1....... 115 C3 259 A6
Stafford Rd Bow E3....97 B5
Harrow HA3 ....24 A3
Kingston u T KT3.... 199 A6
Maida Vale NW6......91 C4
Plashet E7...........77 D2
Ruislip HA4 ....61 D4
Sidcup DA14 .... 189 C6
Wallington CR0,
SM6 .... 220 A3
Staffordshire Ho N3 ..47 A6
Staffordshire St
Peckham SE15...... 140 A4
Peckham SE15.......140 B4
Stafford St W1 ..... 249 A4
Stafford Terr
W8.........113 C3 255 A6
Stag Cl HA8 ....27 A1
Stag Ct 16 SM6 ......219 B2
Stagg Hill EN4.........2 C6
Stag Hts 1 IG9.........21 B2
Stag La Chigwell IG9 ...21 B2
Edgware HA8, NW9....45 A6
Stag Lane Fst & Mid
Schs HA8 ....26 C1
Stag La SW15.........155 D2
Stags Ct KT7.........197 A2
Stagshaw Ho 17
SE22...............139 C2
Stags Way TW7 ......130 D6
Stainbank Rd CR4....203 B6
Stainby Cl UB7.......104 A3
Stainby Rd N15.......51 D5
Staincliffe Ho 5
SM1...............218 A4
Stainer Ho SE9 ......143 C1
Stainer St SE1 ...... 252 D3
Staines Ave SM3 .....216 D6
Staines By-Pass
TW15..............170 A4
Staines Rd TW14.....149 B4
Staines Rd E TW12,
TW16..............172 C2
Staines Rd
Feltham TW14,
TW3 .... 150 C6
Hounslow TW3 ..... 129 C1
Ilford IG1 ....79 B4
Twickenham TW2.... 152 A1
Twickenham TW13,
TW2 .... 151 D1
Staines Rd W TW15 ..171 B3
Staines Wlk DA14....190 C4
Stainford Cl TW15 ...171 B5
Stainforth Rd
Ilford IG2 ....57 B2
Walthamstow E17......53 C5
Staining La EC2..... 242 B2
Stainmore Cl BR7....189 B2
Stainsbury St 25 E2 ...96 C5
Stainsby Rd E14 .....97 C1
Stainton Rd
Enfield EN3 ....6 C4
Lewisham SE13......164 B4
Stalbridge Flats W1. 238 B1
Stalbridge Ho NW1 . 232 A3
Stalbridge St NW1.. 237 B4
Stalham St SE16 .....118 B3
Stambourne Ho
SW8.............. 270 B2
Stambourne Way
Penge SE19........ 183 D3
West Wickham BR4.. 224 A5
Stamford Bridge
Stadium (Chelsea FC)
SW6....... 135 D5 265 C4
Stamford Brook Ave
W6................111 D3
Stamford Brook Gdns
1 W6 ....111 D3
Stamford Brook Mans
2 W6 ....111 D2
Stamford Brook Rd
W6................111 D3
Stamford Brook Sta
W6............... 111 D2
Stamford Cl
Harrow HA3 ....24 C3
2 London NW3 ......70 A5
Southall UB1 .... 107 C6
Tottenham Hale N15...52 A5
Stamford Cotts
SW10............. 265 D4
Stamford Ct
Chiswick W6 .... 112 A2
Edgware HA8........26 B6
Stamford Dr BR2.....208 D5
Stamford Gdns RM9...80 C1
Stamford Gr E 1
N16 ....52 A1
Stamford Gr W 4
N16 ....52 A1
STAMFORD HILL 51 C1
Stamford Hill N16....51 D1
Stamford Hill Mans 1
N16 ....51 D1
Stamford Hill Prim Sch
N15 ....51 B3
Stamford Hill Sta
N16 ....51 C2
Stamford Ho N15 .....52 A4
Stamford Hospl W6. 112 A2
Stamford Lo 2 N16...51 D2
Stamford Mans 2
N16 ....52 A1
Stamford Rd
Dagenham RM9.......80 C1
Kingsland N1.........73 C2
Newham E6.........100 A6
South Tottenham N15 ..52 A4
Stamford St
SE1........116 C5 251 B4
Stamp Pl E2..........95 D4
Stanard Cl N16 ....51 C2
Stanborough Cl
TW12..............173 B4
Stanborough Ho 4
E3.................97 D3
Stanborough Pas E8 ..73 D2
Stanborough Rd TW3,
TW7...............130 B2
Stanbridge Mans
SW15..............134 C2
Stanbridge Pl N21 ....16 D2
Stanbridge Rd
SW15..............134 C2
Stanbrook Ct W1 ... 249 A4
Stanbrook Rd SE2 ...124 B4
Stanburn Fst & Mid
Schs HA7...........25 C3
Stanbury Ct 16 NW3...70 D2
Stanbury Rd
Nunhead SE15...... 140 C3
Peckham SE15.......140 B3
Stancroft NW9........45 C4
Standale Gr HA4......39 A4
Standard Ind Est
E16...............122 B4
Standard Pl 13 EC2....95 C4
Standard Rd
Becontree NW10......89 B3
Belvedere DA17 .... 125 C1
DA6 .... 147 A1
Enfield EN3 ....7 A6
Hounslow TW4 ..... 129 A2
Standen Rd SW18....157 C4
Standfield Gdns
RM10...............81 C2
Standfield Rd RM10...81 C3
Standish Ho
6 Chiswick W6..... 112 A2
SE9 ....143 B1
Standish Rd W6 .....112 A2
Standlake Point 1
SE23...............162 D1
Standor Ho 7 CR4...202 D6
Stane Cl SW19.......179 D3
Stanedge Ct SW16 ...182 A5
Stane Gr SW4 ....138 A3
Stanesgate Ho 20
SE15...............140 A5
Stanetta Ct 3 RM6....58 B2
Stane Way SE18......144 A5
Stanfield Ho
8 Northolt UB5......84 D5
NW8 .... 236 D6
Stanfield Rd 14 E3 ....97 A5
Stanford Cl
Hampton TW12......173 B4
Romford RM7 ....59 D3
Ruislip HA4 ....39 A3
Stanford Ct
Friern Barnet N11.....31 A5
Kensington W8 ..... 255 D5
Walham Green SW6 . 265 D1
Stanford Ho IG11 ....102 B5
Stanford Pl
SE1.........117 C2 263 A3
Stanford Prim Sch
SW16............. 181 D2
Stanford Rd
Friern Barnet N11.....30 D5
Thornton Heath
SW16............ 182 A1
W8.......... 113 D3 255 D6
Stanford St SW1.... 259 C3
Stanford Way SW16 ..181 D1
Stangate Cres WD6 ...11 C6
Stangate Gdns HA7 ...25 B6
Stangate Lo N21......16 B4
Stangate Mansi
TW1...............152 D1
Stangate SE1....... 260 D6
Stanger Rd SE25......206 A5
Stanhope Ave
Harrow HA3 ....24 B2
Hayes BR2.......... 209 A1
Hendon N3 ....47 B6
Stanhope Cl 28
SE16...............118 D4
Stanhope Ct N3........29 B1
Stanhope Gate W1... 248 B4
Stanhope Gdns
Crouch End N6........49 C3
Dagenham RM8........81 B5
Edgware NW7.........27 D5
Redbridge IG1........56 B1
Stoke Newington N4 ...51 A3
SW7....... 114 A2 256 B4
Stanhope Gr BR3 ....207 B5
Stanhope Ho
Crouch End N6........49 C3
5 Friern Barnet N11 ..31 B6
4 Putney SW15.... 156 C6
SE8 ....141 B5
Stanhope Mews E
SW7........114 A2 256 B4
Stanhope Mews S
SW7.............. 256 B3
Stanhope Mews W
SW7........114 A2 256 B4
Stanhope Park Rd
UB6 ....86 A3
Stanhope Par NW1.. 232 A2
Stanhope Pl W2 .... 237 C1
Stanhope Prim Sch
UB6 ....86 A3
Stanhope Rd
Barnet EN5 ....12 D5
Crouch End N6.......49 C2
DA7 .... 147 A3
Dagenham RM8.......81 B5
North Finchley N12....30 A5
Sidcup DA15 .... 190 A6
Southall UB6 ....86 A2
South Croydon CR0 .. 221 C5
Wallington SM5...... 219 A1
Walthamstow E17 .....53 D4
Stanhope Row W1 .. 248 C3
Stanhope St
NW1........93 C4 232 A1
Stanhope Terr
W2.........114 B6 246 D6
Stanier Cl SW5 ..... 254 D1
Stanlake Mews 7
W12...............112 C5
Stanlake Rd W12 ....112 C5
Stanlake Villas 8
W12...............112 C5
Stanley Ave
Barking IG11....... 101 D5
Beckenham BR2,
BR3............ 208 A6
Dagenham RM8.......59 B2
Greenford UB6 ....86 A6
Wembley HA0 ....66 A1
West Barnes KT3 ... 200 A4
Stanley Bldgs NW1.. 233 A3
Stanley Cl
Eltham SE9 .... 167 A3
SW8.............. 270 C5
Wembley HA0 ....66 A1
Stanley Cohen Ho
EC1 .... 242 A5
Stanley Cres
W11........113 B6 244 C6
Stanleycroft Cl
TW7...............130 C4
Stanley Ct
Belmont SM2....... 217 D1
11 Ealing W5........87 C2
Wallington SM5..... 219 A1
Wimbledon SW19 ... 179 C4
Stanley Gardens Rd
TW11..............174 C5
Stanley Gdns
Bedford Pk W3 ..... 111 C4
Cricklewood NW2 .....68 C3
Mitcham CR4...... 181 A4
W11.............. 244 C6
Wallington SM6..... 219 C2
Stanley Glynn Ct
BR7 ....188 C5
Stanley Gr
Clapham SW11 ..... 137 A3
Thornton Heath CR0 . 204 C3
Stanley Ho
35 Clapham SW8 ... 137 D3
Leytonstone E11 ......54 C3
Stanley Holloway Ct
E16.................99 A1
Stanley Ho
22 Poplar E14........97 C1
Wembley HA0 ....66 A1
Stanley Inf Sch
KT11 .... 174 C6
Stanley Jun Sch
KT11 .... 174 C6
Stanley Mans SW10 . 266 B6
Upper Tooting
SW17........... 158 D2
Stanley Park Dr HA0 .. 88 B6
Stanley Park High Sch
SM5 .... 219 A2
Stanley Park Inf Sch
SM5 .... 218 D1
Stanley Park Jun Sch
SM5 .... 218 D1
Stanley Park Rd SM5,
SM6 ....219 A1
Stanley Rd
Acton Green W3 .... 111 A3
Ashford TW15 ...... 170 A5
Belmont SM2....... 217 D1
BR6 .... 211 D1
Bromley BR2 .... 209 C5
Chingford E4 ....20 B3
East Finchley N2 ......48 B6
Edmonton N9..........17 D2
Enfield EN1 ....5 C2
Friern Barnet N11.....31 D5
Harringay N15........50 D5
Harrow HA2 ....64 A6
2 Hendon NW9 ....46 A2
Ilford IG1 ....79 B6
Isleworth TW3...... 130 A1
Stanley Rd *continued*
Mill Meads E15 ....98 B6
Mitcham CR4....... 181 A3
Morden SM4 .... 201 C5
Mortlake SW14...... 132 D1
Muswell Hill N10.......31 B3
Northwood HA6.......22 A2
Plashet E12..........78 A3
Sidcup DA14 .... 168 A1
Southall UB1 .... 107 A6
Teddington TW11,
TW2 .... 174 C5
Thornton Heath CR0 . 204 C3
Twickenham TW2.....152 B1
Wallington SM5..... 219 A1
Walthamstow E10 .....53 D3
Wembley HA9 ....66 B2
Wimbledon SW19 ... 179 C4
Woodford E18 ....36 D2
Stanley St SE14, SE8 ..141 B5
Stanley Studios
SW10............. 266 B6
Stanley Tech High Sch
for Boys SE25..... 205 D6
Stanley Terr 8 N19 ...72 A6
Stanliff Ho 8 E14.....119 C3
Stanmer St SW11 ....136 C3
STANMORE 25 A5
Stanmore Coll HA7 ...25 C4
Stanmore Gdns
Richmond TW9.......132 B2
Sutton SM1 .... 218 A5
Stanmore Hill HA7 ....25 A6
Stanmore Ho 21
SW8...............137 D3
Stanmore Lo HA7 ..... 25 B6
Stanmore Pl NW1... 231 D6
Stanmore Rd
Harringay N15........50 D5
Leytonstone E11 ......54 D1
Richmond TW9.......132 B2
Stanmore Sta HA7....25 D6
Stanmore St
N1 .... 94 B6 233 C6
Stanmore Terr 3
BR3 ....185 C1
Stanmuir Lo NW9......45 A4
Stannard Cotts 27 E1..96 C3
Stannard Ct SE6 .....163 D3
Stannard Mews E8....74 A2
Stannard Rd E8.......74 A2
Stannary Pl SE11 ... 261 B1
Stannary St
SE11........116 C1 261 B1
Stannet Way SM6 ....219 C4
Stansbury Sq 3 W10..91 A4
Stansfeld Ho SE1 ... 263 D3
Stansfeld Rd E6 ......99 D1
Stansfield Rd
Cranford TW4,
TW5 ....128 B3
Stockwell SW9 ......138 B2
Stansgate Rd RM10 ...81 C5
Stanstead Cl BR2 ....208 D3
Stanstead Gr SE23 ...163 B3
Stanstead Ho E3......98 A3
Stanstead Manor
SM1...............217 C2
Stanstead Rd
Forest Hill SE23,
SE6............. 163 A3
Wanstead E11.........55 B4
Stansted Cres DA5...168 D3
Stansted Express
Terminal EC2 ..... 243 A4
Stansted Rd TW6 ....148 B5
Stanswood Gdns
SE5...............139 C5
Stanthorpe Cl
SW16..............182 A5
Stanthorpe Rd
SW16..............182 A5
Stanton Ave TW11 ...174 C4
Stanton Cl
Chessington
KT19........... 214 D3
North Cheam KT4 ... 200 D1
Stanton Ct 5 DA15 ...168 A1
Finchley N3 ....29 C2
Stoke Newington N16 ..51 B2
Stanton Ho 9 SE10 ..142 A6
Stanton Rd
Barnes SW13 ...... 133 D3
Thornton Heath CR0 . 205 A2
Wimbledon SW20 ... 178 D2
Stanton Sq SE26.....185 B6
Stanton Way SE26 ...185 B6
Stanway Ct 23 N1 .....95 C5
Stanway Gdns
Acton W3 .... 110 C5
Edgware HA8.........27 A5
Stanway St N1........95 C5
STANWELL 148 A3
Stanwell Fields CE Prim
Sch TW19......... 148 A4
Stanwell Rd
Ashford TW15 ...... 170 A6
Stanwell Rd *continued*
East Bedfont TW14, TW19,
TW6 .... 148 D4
Stanwell TW15 ..... 148 A1
Stanwick Rd
W14........113 B2 254 C3
Stanworth Ct TW5 ...129 C5
Stanworth St SE1 ... 253 D1
Stanyhurst SE23 .....163 A3
Stapenhill Rd HA0 ....65 B5
Staplefield Cl
Pinner HA5 ....23 A3
3 Streatham SW2 .. 160 A3
Stapleford Ave IG2....57 C4
Stapleford Cl
Chingford E4 ....20 A1
Kingston u T KT1 ... 198 C6
Putney SW19....... 157 A4
Stapleford Rd HA0 ....65 D1
Stapleford N17 ....33 C1
Stapleford Way
IG11...............102 B4
Staplehurst Ct
SW11..............158 D5
Staplehurst Ho 18 E5..74 B3
Staplehurst Rd
Lewisham SE13..... 164 C6
Sutton SM5 .... 218 C1
Staple Inn Bldgs
WC2.............. 241 A3
Staple Inn WC2 ..... 241 A3
Staples Cl SE16......119 A5
Staples Corner Bsns Pk
NW2...............46 B1
Staples Corner (East)
NW2...............46 B1
Staples Corner Ret Pk
NW2...............46 B1
Staples Corner (West)
NW2...............46 B1
Staple St
SE1........117 B4 252 D1
Stapleton Gdns
CR0 ....220 C3
Stapleton Hall N4.....50 B2
Stapleton Hall Rd N4..50 B2
Stapleton Ho 19 E2 ...96 B4
Stapleton Rd DA7....147 B6
Orpington BR6...... 227 D5
Upper Tooting
SW17........... 159 A1
Stapley Rd DA17.....125 C1
Stapylton Rd EN5 ......1 A2
Star Alley EC3 ...... 253 B6
Star and Garter Hill
TW10..............154 A4
Starboard Way E14 ..119 C3
Starbuck Cl SE9 .....166 C4
Star Cl EN3...........18 C5
Starcross St
NW1........93 C4 232 B1
Star Ct UB10..........83 A3
Stardome* NW1 .... 238 A5
Starfield Rd W12 .....112 A4
Star & Garter Mans
SW15..............134 D2
Star La E16...........98 C3
Starliner Ct N7 ....72 C2
Starling Cl
Beckenham BR3 .... 207 A3
Buckhurst Hill IG9.....21 A3
Pinner HA5 ....40 C6
Starling Ct E13 ......99 B6
Starling Ho NW8.... 230 A4
Starling Wlk TW12 ...173 A5
Starmans Cl RM9 ....103 A6
Star Path UB5 ....85 C5
Star Pl E1 ....118 A6
Star Prim Sch E16....98 C3
Star Rd
Hillingdon UB10.......83 A3
Hounslow TW7 ......130 B3
W14....... 113 B1 254 C1
Star St W2 ....92 C1 237 A2
Starts Cl BR6 ....226 C5
Starts Hill Ave BR6...226 D4
Starts Hill Rd BR6....226 D4
Starveall Cl UB7 .....104 B3
Star Works NW10.....90 A4
Star Yd WC2...94 C1 241 A2
State Farm Ave
BR6...............227 A4
Stateland Ct 10 N11...31 B6
Staten Gdns TW1 ....152 D3
Statham Ct N7........72 A5
Statham Gr
Edmonton N18........33 C5
Stoke Newington N16 ..73 B5
Statham Ho SW8.... 269 A2
Station App
Ashford TW15 ....170 B6
Belmont SM2....... 217 A1
Bexleyheath DA7..... 147 A3
Chislehurst BR7..... 188 C1
Dagenham NW10 .....89 D4
Elmstead BR7 ...... 188 A4
20 Finchley N12 ......29 D6

Station App *continued*
Forest Gate E7 77 B4
Friern Barnet N11 31 B5
Fulham SW6 135 A2
Greenford UB6 64 B1
Hampton TW12 173 C2
Hayes BR2 209 A1
Hayes Town UB3 105 D3
Hinchley Wood KT10 212 D5
4 Kingston u T KT1, KT2 176 C2
Lewisham SE3 143 B2
Mottingham SE9 166 B3
New Barnet EN5 2 A1
6 New Malden KT4 200 A1
Orpington BR6 227 D6
Penge SE26 185 B5
Pinner HA5 41 A6
Richmond TW9 132 C4
Station Approach Rd W4 133 A5
Station App
Ruislip HA4 39 D1
Shepperton TW17 193 A4
3 South Croydon CR0 221 B6
South Ruislip HA4 62 B3
Streatham SW16 181 D5
Sunbury TW16 172 A2
1 Surbiton KT6 198 A3
Walthamstow E17 53 C4
Wanstead E11 55 A4
Welling DA16 146 A3
Wembley HA0 65 B2
2 Woodford E18 37 B1
Woodford IG8 37 B4
Woodford IG9 37 D6
Worcester Pk KT19 216 A3
Yiewsley UB7 104 A5
Station Ave
5 Brixton SW9 138 D2
Kingston u T KT3 199 C6
14 Richmond TW9 132 C4
West Ewell KT19 215 D1
Station Bldgs
Catford SE6 163 C4
Merton SW20 178 C1
Station Blgs W5 110 B5
Station Cl Finchley N3 29 C2
Hampton TW12 173 D2
Station Cres
Ashford TW15 170 A6
Greenwich SE3 121 A1
Tottenham N15 51 B5
Wembley HA0 65 B2
Station Ct
Mitcham CR4 202 C5
5 Nunhead SE15 140 C3
South Tottenham N15 51 D4
Wembley HA9 43 C1
Stationers Hall Ct EC4 241 D1
Station Estate Rd TW14 150 B3
Station Est BR3 206 D5
Station Est 1 E18 37 B1
Station Gdns W4 133 A5
Station Gr HA0 66 A2
Station Hill BR2 225 A6
Station House Mews N9 34 A6
Station Mans 9 N3 29 C2
Station Mews Terr 4 SE3 121 A1
Station Par Acton W3 88 C1
1 Ashford TW15 170 B6
Barking IG11 79 A1
Belmont HA3 25 A1
Cockfosters EN4 3 A1
Cricklewood NW2 68 C2
Dagenham RM10 81 C2
Ealing W5 110 B5
Edgware HA8 26 A3
Feltham TW14 150 B4
Northolt UB5 63 D4
4 Osidge N14 15 D3
Richmond TW9 132 C4
Ruislip HA4 61 B6
South Harrow HA2 63 D4
4 Upper Tooting SW12 159 A3
2 Wanstead E11 55 A4
Woodford IG9 37 D6
Station Pas
New Cross Gate SE15 140 C4
Woodford E18 37 B1
Station Pl N4 72 C6
Station Rd
Ashford TW15 170 B6
Barkingside IG6 57 B6
Barnes SW13 133 D3
Beckenham BR2 186 C1
Belvedere DA17 125 C3
Bexleyheath DA7 147 A2
Bromley BR1 187 A2

Station Rd *continued*
Camden Town N19 71 C5
Carshalton SM5 218 D4
Chadwell Heath RM6 58 D2
Chessington KT9 214 A3
Chingford E4 20 B3
Church End N3 29 C1
Claygate KT10 212 C3
Croydon CR0 205 A1
Edgware HA8 26 C4
Edgware NW7 27 C4
Esher KT10 212 B6
Forest Gate E7 77 A4
Friern Barnet N11 31 B5
Greenhill HA1 42 D4
Hampton TW12 173 D2
Hampton Wick KT1 175 D2
Hanwell W7 108 C5
Harlesden NW10 89 D5
Hayes UB3 105 C2
Hendon NW4 46 A4
Hounslow TW3 129 D1
Ilford IG1 78 D5
Kingston u T KT2 176 C2
Lewisham SE13 142 A2
Leyton E10 76 A5
Manor Pk E12 78 A4
Merton SW19 180 A2
Station Rd N DA17 125 D3
Station Rd
New Barnet EN5 13 D6
North Harrow HA1, HA2 41 D4
Orpington BR6 227 D6
Penge SE20 184 C4
Shepperton TW17 193 A4
Sidcup DA14, DA15 168 A1
Southgate N21 16 D3
South Norwood SE25 205 D5
Sunbury TW16 172 A3
Teddington TW11 175 A4
Thames Ditton KT7 196 D2
Tottenham Hale N17 52 A6
Twickenham TW1 152 D4
Walthamstow E17 53 A4
West Acton W5 88 B1
West Barnes KT3 200 B4
West Drayton UB7 104 A4
West Wickham BR4 208 A1
Wood Green N22 32 B1
Station Rise SE27 160 D2
Station Sq BR5 211 A4
Station St
Newham E16 122 D5
Stratford E15 76 B1
Station Terr
Camberwell SE5 139 A4
Kensal Rise NW10 90 D5
Station View UB6 86 B6
Station Way
Cheam SM2, SM3 217 A1
Claygate KT10 212 C2
Woodford IG9 37 D6
Station Yd TW1 153 A4
Staton Ct 1 E10 53 D2
Staunton Ho SE17 263 A3
Staunton Rd KT2 176 B3
Staunton St SE8 141 B6
Staveley Cl
Hackney E9 74 C3
Lower Holloway N7 72 A4
New Cross Gate SE15 140 C4
8 Peckham SE15 140 B4
Staveley Ct 4 E11 55 A4
Staveley Gdns W4 133 B4
Staveley Ho SE4 163 A6
Staveley NW1 232 A2
Staveley Rd
Ashford TW15 171 B4
Chiswick W4 133 B5
Stavers Ho 31 E3 97 B5
Staverton Rd NW2 68 C1
Stave Yard Rd SE16 119 A5
Stavordale Lo W14 254 D6
Stavordale Rd
Carshalton SM5 202 A2
Highbury N5 72 D4
Stayner's Rd E1 96 D3
Stayton Rd SM1 217 C5
Steadfast Rd KT1 175 D2
Steadman Ct EC1 242 B6
Steadman Ho 4 RM10 81 C5
Stead St SE17 117 B2 262 C3
Steam Farm La TW14 127 D1
Stean St E8 95 D6
Stebbing Ho 8 W11 112 D5
Stebbing Way IG11 102 A5
Stebondale St E14 120 A2
Stebon Prim Sch E14 97 C2
Stedham Pl WC1 240 A2

Stedman Cl UB10 60 C5
Steedman St SE17 117 A2 262 A3
Steeds Rd N10 30 D2
Steel App IG11 102 B5
Steele Rd
Acton Green W4 111 A3
Becontree NW10 89 A5
Isleworth TW7 131 A1
Leyton E11 76 C4
Tottenham N17 51 C6
Steele's Mews N NW3 70 D2
Steele's Mews S NW3 70 D2
Steele's Rd NW3 70 D2
Steele Wlk DA8 147 D5
Steel's La 23 E1 96 C1
Steen Way 7 SE22 161 C6
Steep Cl BR6 227 D2
Steep Hill
South Croydon CR0 221 C4
Streatham SW16 159 D1
Steeple Cl
Fulham SW6 135 A3
Wimbledon SW19 179 A5
Steeple Ct
19 Bethnal Green E1 96 B3
Wimbledon SW19 179 A5
Steeplestone Cl N18 33 A5
Steepleton Ct E11 54 A1
Steeple Wlk N1 235 B6
Steerforth St SW18 158 A2
Steering Cl N9 18 C3
Steers Mead CR4 180 D2
Steers Way SE16 119 A4
Steetley Ct 14 SM2 218 A1
Steinman Ct TW7 130 D2
Stelfax Ho WC1 233 D2
Stella Cl UB8 82 D2
Stella Rd SW17 180 D4
Stellar Ho 4 N17 33 D4
Stellman Cl E5 74 A5
Stembridge Rd SE20 184 B1
Sten Cl 12 EN3 7 C6
Stephan Cl E8 96 A6
Stephen Cl BR6 227 D5
Stephen Ct 18 SW19 156 D3
Stephendale Rd SW6 136 A3
Stephen Fox Ho 7 W4 111 C1
Stephen Hawking Sch E14 97 A1
Stephen Mews W1 239 C3
Stephen Pl SW4 137 C2
Stephen Saunders Ct SW11 158 C6
Stephens Ct
Brockley SE4 141 A2
E16 98 D3
Stephens Lo N12 14 A1
Stephenson Ct SM2 217 B1
Stephenson Ho
2 Gospel Oak NW5 71 B4
6 Maitland Pk NW3 70 D3
Newington SE1 262 A6
West Heath SE2 124 D1
Stephenson Rd
Ealing W7 86 D1
Twickenham TW4 151 C4
Walthamstow E17 53 A4
Stephenson St
Dagenham NW10 89 D4
Newham E16 98 C2
Stephenson Way NW1 93 C3 239 B6
Stephen's Rd E15 98 C6
Stephen St W1 239 C3
STEPNEY 96 D2
Stepney City E1 96 C2
Stepney Cswy E1 96 D1
Stepney Gn E1 96 D2
Stepney Greencoat CE Prim Sch The E14 97 B1
Stepney Green Ct 4 E1 96 D2
Stepney Green Sch E1 96 D2
Stepney Green Sta E1 96 D3
Stepney High St E1 96 D2
Stepney Way
Mitcham CR4 181 A2
Stepney E1 96 C2
Sterling Ave HA8 26 B6
Sterling Cl NW10 68 A1
Sterling Gdns SE14 141 A6
Sterling Ho SE9 143 B1
Sterling Ind Est RM10 81 D4
Sterling Pl W5 110 A2

Sterling Rd EN2 5 B5
Sterling St SW7 257 B6
Sterling Way (North Circular Rd) N18 33 C5
Stern Cl IG11 102 C5
Sterndale Rd W14 112 D3
Sterne St W12 112 D4
Sternhall La SE15 140 A2
Sternhold Ave SW12, SW2 159 D2
Sterry Cres RM10 81 C3
Sterry Dr
Thames Ditton KT7 196 C3
Worcester Pk KT19 215 C4
Sterry Gdns RM10 81 C2
Sterry Rd
Barking IG11 101 D6
Dagenham RM10 81 C3
Sterry St SE1 252 C1
Steucers La SE23 163 A3
Stevanne Ct 1 DA17 125 C1
Steve Biko Ct W10 90 D3
Steve Biko La SE6 185 C6
Steve Biko Lodge 13 E13 99 A5
Steve Biko Rd N7 72 C5
Steve Biko Way TW3 129 C2
Stevedale Rd DA16 146 C3
Stevedore St 3 E1 118 B5
Stevenage Rd
Fulham SW6 134 D4
Wallend E6 78 C2
Stevens Ave E9 74 C2
Stevens Cl
Beckenham BR3 185 C4
Hampton TW12 173 B4
Pinner HA5 40 C4
Stevens Ct BR3 185 C4
Stevens Gn WD23 8 A3
Stevens Ho KT1 175 D1
Stevens' La KT10 213 A2
Stevenson Cl EN5 14 B4
Stevenson Cres SE16 118 B1
Stevenson Ho
1 Battersea SW11 136 D3
6 Clapham Pk SW2 160 A6
NW8 229 A6
Wembley HA9 65 D6
Stevens Rd RM8 80 C5
Stevens St SE1 263 B6
Steventon Rd W12 111 D6
Stewards Holte Wlk 3 N11 31 B6
Stewart Ave TW17 192 C5
Stewart Cl BR7 188 D6
Hampton TW12 173 A4
Kingsbury NW9 45 A3
Stewart Fleming Prim Sch SE20 206 C6
Stewart Headlam Prim Sch E1 96 B3
Stewart Ho SE1 263 A5
Stanmore HA7 25 B5
Stewart Quay UB3 105 C4
Stewart Rainbird Ho 1 E12 78 C3
Stewart Rd E15 76 B4
Stewartsby Cl N18 33 A5
Stewart's Gr SW3 114 C1 257 A2
Stewart's Rd SW8 137 C4 269 A2
Stewart St E14 120 A4
Stew La EC4 252 A6
Steyne Ho
15 Acton W3 110 D5
11 Acton W3 111 A5
Steyne Rd W3 110 D5
Steyning Gr SE9 188 B6
Steynings Way N12 29 C5
Steyning Way TW4 128 C1
Steynton Ave DA5 168 D2
Stickland Rd DA17 125 C2
Stickleton Cl UB6 85 D4
Stifford Ho E1 96 C2
Stilecroft Gdns HA0 65 B5
Stile Hall Gdns W4 110 C1
Stile Hall Par 6 W4 110 C1
Stileman Ho 4 E3 97 B2
Stile Path TW16 194 A5
Stiles Cl BR2 210 B3
Erith DA8 125 D1
Stillingfleet Rd SW13 134 A6
Stillington St SW1 115 C2 259 B4
Stillness Jun & Inf Schs SE23 163 A5
Stillness Rd SE23 163 B5
Stilwell Dr UB8 82 B3
Stilwell Rdbt UB8 104 D6

Stipularis Dr UB4 84 D3
Stirling Ave
Pinner HA5 41 A2
Upper Halliford TW17 193 C6
Wallington SM6 220 A1
Stirling Cl
Sidcup DA14 189 D6
Streatham SW16 181 C2
Stirling Cnr EN5, WD6 11 B5
Stirling Ct
Clerkenwell EC1 241 C6
Ealing W13 109 B6
Strand WC2 240 C1
Stirling Gr TW3 130 A3
Stirling Ho 5 SE18 122 D1
Stirling Ind Ctr WD6 11 B6
Stirling Lo 7 EN5 14 A6
Stirling Mans NW6 70 A2
Stirling Rd
Harrow HA3 42 D6
Hayes UB3 106 B6
Newham E13 99 B5
South Acton W3 110 D3
Stanwell TW19, TW6 148 B5
Stockwell SW9 138 A3
Tottenham N17 34 A2
Twickenham TW2 151 D4
Walthamstow E17 53 A6
Wood Green N22 32 D2
Stirling Ret Pk WD6 11 B5
Stirling Way
Borehamwood WD6 11 B6
Thornton Heath CR0 204 A2
Stiven Cres HA2 63 B5
Stoatley Ho 10 SW15 156 A3
Stockbeck NW1 232 B3
Stockbridge Ho EN2 4 D3
Stockbury Rd CR0 206 C3
Stockdale Rd RM8 81 B6
Stockdove Way UB6 86 D4
Stocker Gdns RM9 80 C1
Stockfield Rd
Claygate KT10 212 C3
Streatham SW16 160 B1
Stockford Ave NW7 28 D3
Stockholm Ho E1 118 A6
Stockholm Rd SE16 118 C1
Stockholm Way 9 E1 118 A5
Stockhurst Cl SW15 134 D3
Stockingswater La EN3 7 B2
Stockleigh Hall NW8 230 B4
Stockley Acad UB8 82 B1
Stockley Cl UB7 104 D4
Stockley Ctry Pk UB7 104 C6
Stockley Farm Rd UB7 104 D3
Stockley Park Bsns Pk UB11 105 A5
Stockley Rd UB7, UB8, UB11 104 D4
Stock Orchard Cres N7 72 B3
Stock Orchard St N7 72 B3
Stockport Rd SW16 181 D2
Stocks Ct 5 E1 96 D3
Stocksfield Rd E17 54 A6
Stocks Pl
Hillingdon UB10 82 C6
16 Limehouse E14 119 B6
Stock St E13 99 A5
Stockton Cl EN5 2 A1
Stockton Gdns
Edgware NW7 11 C1
Tottenham N17 33 A3
Stockton Ho 16 E2 96 B4
Harrow HA2 41 C1
Stockton Rd
Edmonton N18 34 B4
Tottenham N17 33 A3
STOCKWELL 138 A2
Stockwell Ave SW9 138 B2
Stockwell Cl BR1 187 B1
Stockwell Gdns SW9 138 B4 270 C1
Stockwell Gn SW9 138 B3
Stockwell La SW9 138 B3
Stockwell Park Cres SW9 138 B3
Stockwell Park Rd SW9 138 B4 270 D1
Stockwell Park Sch SW9 138 B4 270 C1
Stockwell Park Wlk SW9 138 C2
Stockwell Prim Sch SW9 138 B2
Stockwell Rd SW9 138 B3
Stockwell Sta SW4 138 A3
Stockwell St SE10 142 A6

Stockwell Terr SW9 270 C1
Stodart Rd SE20 184 C2
Stoddart Ho SW8 270 D5
Stodmarsh Ho 28 SW9 138 C4
Stofield Gdns SE9 165 D1
Stoford Cl SW19 157 A4
Stokenchurch St SW6 135 D4 265 C1
STOKE NEWINGTON 73 C6
Stoke Newington Church St N16 73 C6
Stoke Newington Comm N16 73 D6
Stoke Newington High St N16 73 D5
Stoke Newington Rd N16 73 D4
Stoke Newington Sch N16 73 B5
Stoke Newington Sta N16 73 D6
Stoke Pl NW10 89 D4
Stoke Rd KT2 177 A3
Stokesby Rd KT9 214 B2
Stokes Ct N2 48 C5
Stokesley St W12 89 D1
Stokes Rd
Croydon CR0 206 D3
Newham E6 100 A3
Stokley Ct N8 50 A5
Stoll Cl NW2 68 C5
Stoms Path SE6 185 C5
Stonard Rd
Dagenham RM8 80 B4
Palmers Green N13 16 C1
Stondon Pk SE23 163 A5
Stondon Wlk 4 E6 99 D5
Stonebanks KT12 194 A2
Stone Bldgs WC2 94 B2 240 D3
STONEBRIDGE 89 A6
Stonebridge Ct 9 NW10 67 B1
Stonebridge Ctr 6 NW10 89 B6
Stonebridge Ctr The N15 52 A4
Stonebridge Park Sta NW10 66 D1
Stonebridge Park HA9 66 D1
Stonebridge Pk NW10 67 B1
Stonebridge Rd N15 51 D4
Stonebridge Sch The NW10 89 B6
Stonebridge Way HA9 66 D2
Stonechat Sq 6 E6 100 A2
Stone Cl
Clapham SW4 137 C3
Dagenham RM8 81 B6
Yiewsley UB7 104 B5
Stonecot Cl SM3 201 A1
Stonecot Hill SM3 201 A1
Stone Cres TW14 149 D4
Stonecroft Way CR0 204 A2
Stonecrop Cl NW9 45 B6
Stone Ct
Southgate N21 16 B6
4 Stratford E15 76 D1
Stonecutter St EC4 241 C2
Stonefield Cl DA7 147 C2
Ruislip HA4 63 A3
Stonefield N4 72 B6
Stonefield Mans N1 234 A5
Stonefield St N1 94 C6 234 B6
Stonefield Way
Ruislip HA4 63 A3
SE7 143 D5
Stonegate 8 NW5 71 A2
Stone Gr HA8 26 B5
Stone Grove Ct HA8 26 B5
Stonegrove Gdns HA8 26 A5
Stonegrove Ho HA8 26 B5
Stonehall Ave IG1 56 A3
Stone Hall Rd N21 16 C4
Stoneham Rd N11 31 C5
Stonehaven BR3 185 D1
Stonehill Bsns Pk N18 34 D5
Stonehill Cl SW14 155 B6
Stonehill Ct E4 19 D4
Stonehill Rd
Brentford W4 110 C1
Mortlake SW14 155 B6
Stonehills Ct SE21 161 C1
Stonehill's Mans 3 SW16 160 A2

Stonehill Woods Pk DA14 .... 191 D4
Stonehorse Rd EN3 ... 18 C6
Stonehouse Ct EC2 . 243 B2
Stonehouse Ho 27 W2 ... 91 C2
Stonehouse NW1 ... 232 B5
Stone Lake Ind Pk SE7 ... 121 C2
Stone Lake Ret Pk SE7 ... 121 C2
STONELEIGH ... 216 A3
Stoneleigh Ave
Enfield EN1 ... 6 B4
North Cheam KT17, KT4 ... 216 A5
Stoneleigh Broadway KT17 ... 216 A3
Stoneleigh Cres KT19 ... 215 D3
Stoneleigh Ct
Redbridge IG5 ... 56 A6
6 Tottenham N17 ... 33 D1
Stoneleigh Fst Sch KT17 ... 216 B4
Stoneleigh Lo 13 TW9 ... 132 B4
Stoneleigh Mews 15 E3 ... 97 A5
Stoneleigh Park Ave CR0 ... 206 D3
Stoneleigh Park Rd KT19, KT4 ... 216 A3
Stoneleigh Pl W11 ... 112 D6
Stoneleigh Rd
Bromley BR1 ... 210 D6
Carshalton SM5 ... 202 C2
Redbridge IG5 ... 56 B6
Tottenham N17 ... 33 D1
Stoneleigh Sta KT19 ... 216 A3
Stoneleigh St W11 ... 112 D6
Stoneleigh Terr N19 ... 71 B6
Stonell's Rd SW11 ... 158 D6
Stonemasons Cl N15 ... 51 B5
Stonenest St N4 ... 50 B1
Stone Park Ave BR3 ... 207 D5
Stone Pl KT4 ... 216 A6
Stone Rd BR2 ... 208 D4
Stones End St SE1 .. 252 A1
Stonewall E6 ... 100 C2
Stoneworth Ct SE25 .. 206 A3
Stoney Alley SE18 ... 144 C3
Stoneyard La E14 ... 119 D6
Stoneycroft Cl SE12 .. 164 D4
Stoney Deep TW11 ... 175 A6
Stoneydown Ave E17 .. 53 A5
Stoneydown Ho 2 E17 ... 53 A5
Stoneydown E17 ... 53 A5
Stoneydown Park Sch E17 ... 53 A5
Stoneyfields Gdns HA8 ... 27 A6
Stoneyfields La HA8 ... 27 A6
Stoney La E1 ... 243 B2
Penge SE19 ... 183 D4
Stoney St SE1 ... 117 B5 252 C4
Stonhouse St SW4 ... 137 D1
Stonor Rd W14 ... 113 B2 254 C3
Stonycroft Cl EN3 ... 7 A3
Stopes St SE15 ... 139 D5
Stopford Rd
Newham E13 ... 99 A6
SE17 ... 261 D1
Stopher Ho SE1 ... 251 D1
Storace Ho 6 SW4 ... 138 A1
Store Rd E16 ... 122 C4
Storers Quay E14 ... 120 B2
Store St
Bloomsbury WC1 ... 93 D2 239 C4
Stratford New Town E15 ... 76 B3
Storey Ct NW8 ... 229 C1
Storey Ho 13 E14 ... 119 D6
Storey Prim Sch E16 ... 122 D5
Storey Rd
Highgate N6 ... 48 D3
Walthamstow E17 ... 53 B5
Storey's Gate SW1 ... 115 D4 249 D1
Storey St E16 ... 122 C4
Stories Rd SE5 ... 139 C2
Stork Rd E7 ... 77 A2
Storksmead Rd HA8 ... 27 C3
Storks Rd SE16 ... 118 A3
Stormont House Sch E5 ... 74 B4
Stormont Rd
Clapham SW11 ... 137 A1
Highgate N6 ... 48 D2
Stormont Way KT9 ... 213 C3
Stormount Dr UB3 ... 105 A4
Storrington Rd CR0 .. 205 D1
Storrington WC1 ... 233 B1
Story St N1 ... 72 B1
Stotfold BR1 ... 188 A2
Stothard Ho 25 E1 ... 96 C3
Stothard Pl E1 ... 243 B4
Stothard St 12 E1 ... 96 C3
Stott Cl SW18 ... 158 B5
Stoughton Ave SM3 .. 217 A3
Stoughton Cl
Roehampton SW15 ... 156 A3
SE11 ... 260 D3
Stour Ave UB2 ... 107 C3
Stourbridge Ho 8 UB5 ... 85 B3
Stour Cl BR2 ... 225 C4
Stourcliffe Cl W1 ... 237 C2
Stourcliffe St W1 ... 237 C1
Stour Ct UB1 ... 86 B1
Stourhead Cl 6 SW19 ... 156 D4
Stourhead Gdns SW20 ... 200 A6
Stour Rd
Dagenham RM10 ... 81 C6
Hackney Wick E3 ... 75 C1
Stourton Ave TW13 .. 173 B6
Stowage SE8 ... 141 D6
Stow Cres E17 ... 35 A3
Stowe Cres HA4 ... 39 A3
Stowe Gdns N9 ... 17 D3
Stowe Ho
Hampstead Garden Suburb NW11 ... 48 A3
11 Stoke Newington N16 ... 73 C5
Stowell Ho 2 N8 ... 50 A5
Stowe Pl N15 ... 51 C6
Stowe Rd W12 ... 112 B4
Stowford Coll SM2 .. 218 A1
Stowting Rd BR6 ... 227 C4
Stox Mead HA3 ... 24 B2
Stracey Rd
Becontree NW10 ... 89 B6
Forest Gate E7 ... 77 A4
Strachan Pl SW19, SW20 ... 178 C4
Stradbroke Gr
Buckhurst Hill IG9 ... 21 D3
Redbridge IG5 ... 56 C6
Stradbroke Rd N5 ... 73 A4
Stradbrook Cl HA2 ... 63 B5
Stradella Rd SE24 ... 161 A5
Straffan Lo 8 NW3 ... 70 C2
Strafford Ho 9 SE8 .. 119 B1
Strafford Rd
Acton W3 ... 111 A4
Barnet EN5 ... 1 A2
Hounslow TW3 ... 129 B2
Twickenham TW1 ... 153 A4
Strafford St E14 ... 119 C4
Strahan Rd E3 ... 97 A4
Straightsmouth SE10 ... 142 A5
Straight The UB2 ... 107 A4
Strait Rd E6 ... 122 B6
Straker's Rd SE15 ... 140 B1
Strale Ho 17 N1 ... 95 C6
STRAND ... 116 B6
Strand Ct SE18 ... 123 D1
Strand Dr TW9 ... 132 D5
Strandfield Cl SE18 .. 123 C1
Strand Ho SE28 ... 123 B5
Strand La WC2 ... 250 D6
STRAND ON THE GREEN ... 132 C6
Strand-on-the-Green W4 ... 132 C6
Strand-on-the-Green Schs W4 ... 132 C6
Strand Pl N18 ... 33 C6
Strand
Strand WC2 ... 116 B6 250 C6
Strand WC2 ... 240 D1
Strang Ho N1 ... 235 A5
Strangways Terr W14 ... 254 C5
Stranraer Way
Barnsbury N1 ... 72 A1
1 Stanwell TW6 ... 148 A5
Strasburg Rd SW11 ... 137 B4 268 C1
Stratfield Ho SE12 ... 165 A2
Stratfield Park Cl N21 ... 16 D4
STRATFORD ... 76 A2
Stratford Ave UB10 ... 82 B5
Stratford Bus Sta E15 ... 76 B1
Stratford Cir (Newham 6th Form Coll) E15 .. 76 B2
Stratford Cl IG11 ... 80 A1
Stratford Ct KT3 ... 199 B5
Stratford Gr SW15 ... 134 D1
Stratford House Ave BR1 ... 210 A6
Stratford International Sta E15 ... 76 A2
STRATFORD MARSH ... 97 D6
STRATFORD NEW TOWN ... 76 A3
Stratford Office Village The 1 E15 ... 76 C1
Stratford Pl W1 ... 238 C1
Stratford Rd
Harlington TW6 ... 149 A6
Hayes UB4 ... 84 B3
Hendon NW4 ... 46 D5
Newham E13 ... 99 A6
Southall UB2 ... 107 A2
Thornton Heath CR7 . 204 D6
W8 ... 113 C3 255 B5
Stratford Sch (Annexe) E7 ... 77 B2
Stratford Sch E7 ... 77 A1
Stratford Sh Ctr E15 .. 76 B1
Stratford Sta E15 ... 76 B1
Stratford Studios W8 ... 255 C5
Stratford Villas NW1 .. 71 D1
Stratford Workshops E15 ... 98 B6
Strathan Cl SW18 ... 157 A5
Strathaven Rd SE12 .. 165 B5
Strathblaine Rd SW11 ... 136 B1
Strathbrook Rd SW16 ... 182 B3
Strathcona Rd HA9 ... 65 D6
Strathdale SW16 ... 182 B5
Strathdon Dr SW17 .. 158 B1
Strathearn Ave
Harlington UB3 ... 127 D5
Twickenham TW2 ... 152 A3
Strathearn Ho W2 .. 247 A6
Strathearn Pl W2 ... 114 C6 247 A6
Strathearn Rd
Sutton SM1 ... 217 C3
Wimbledon SW19 ... 179 C6
Stratheden Par SE3 .. 143 A5
Stratheden Rd SE3 ... 143 A5
Strathfield Gdns IG11 ... 79 B2
Strathleven Rd SW2 ... 160 A6
Strathmore Ct NW8 .. 230 A2
Strathmore Gdns
Edgware HA8 ... 26 D1
Finchley N3 ... 29 D2
W8 ... 245 B4
Strathmore Rd
Teddington TW11, TW2 ... 174 C6
Thornton Heath CR0 .. 205 B2
Wimbledon SW19 ... 157 C1
Strathmore Sch TW10 ... 153 D2
Strathnairn St SE1 ... 118 A2
Strathray Gdns NW3 .. 70 C2
Strath Terr SW11 ... 136 C1
Strathville Rd SW18 .. 157 D2
Strathyre Ave SW16 .. 204 C6
Stratton Ave EN2 ... 5 B6
Stratton Cl
DA7 ... 147 A2
Edgware HA8 ... 26 B4
Heston TW5 ... 129 C4
Merton SW19 ... 179 C1
Walton-on-T KT12 ... 194 C1
Stratton Ct
4 De Beauvoir Town N1 ... 73 C1
10 Kingston u T KT6 . 198 A4
10 Pinner HA5 ... 23 B3
Strattondale St E14 .. 120 A3
Stratton Dr IG11 ... 79 D2
Stratton Gdns UB1 ... 85 C1
Stratton Ho HA8 ... 26 B6
Stratton Lo 10 EN5 ... 1 D1
Stratton Rd
DA7 ... 147 A2
Merton SW19 ... 179 C1
Sunbury TW16 ... 171 D1
Stratton St W1 ... 115 B5 248 D4
Strauss Rd W4 ... 111 B4
Strawberry Fields BR6 ... 226 D3
STRAWBERRY HILL ... 152 D1
Strawberry Hill Cl TW1 ... 152 D1
Strawberry Hill Rd TW1 ... 152 D1
Strawberry Hill Sta TW2 ... 152 D1
Strawberry La SM5 .. 219 A5
Strawberry Terr N10 .. 30 D2
Strawberry Vale
Finchley N2 ... 30 B2
Twickenham TW1 ... 153 A1
Strayfield Rd EN2 ... 4 D6
Streakes Field Rd NW2 ... 68 A6
Streamdale SE2 ... 146 B6
Stream La HA8 ... 26 D5
Streamline Mews SE22 ... 162 A3
Streamside Cl BR2 .. 209 A5
Edmonton N9 ... 17 D3
Stream Way DA17 ... 147 C6
Streatfeild Ave E6 ... 100 B6
Streatfield Rd HA3, HA7 ... 43 D6
STREATHAM ... 182 A4
Streatham & Clapham High Sch SW16 ... 159 D1
Streatham Cl SW16 .. 160 A2
Streatham Common N SW16 ... 182 B5
Streatham Common S SW16 ... 182 B4
Streatham Common Sta SW16 ... 181 D3
Streatham Ct SW16 .. 160 A1
Streatham High Rd SW16, SW2 ... 182 A5
STREATHAM HILL ... 160 A3
Streatham Hill & Clapham High Sch SW2 ... 160 B3
Streatham Hill Sta SW2 ... 160 A2
Streatham Hill SW2 .. 160 A3
STREATHAM PARK ... 181 C6
Streatham Pl SW2 ... 160 A4
Streatham Rd CR4 ... 181 A2
Streatham Sta SW16 ... 181 D5
Streatham St WC1 .. 240 A2
STREATHAM VALE ... 181 D3
Streatham Vale SW16 ... 181 D3
Streathbourne Rd SW17 ... 159 A1
Streathem Wells Prim Sch SW2 ... 160 C2
Streatleigh Par 4 SW16 ... 160 A2
Streatley Pl
27 Hampstead NW3 ... 70 A4
Hampstead NW3 ... 70 B4
Streatley Rd NW6 ... 69 B1
Streeters La SM6 ... 219 D5
Streetfield Mews SE3 ... 143 A2
Streimer Rd E15 ... 98 A5
Strelley Way W3 ... 111 C6
Stretford Ct 1 SW19 ... 179 A3
Stretton Lo W13 ... 109 B6
Stretton Mans 16 SE8 ... 141 C6
Stretton Rd
Croydon CR0 ... 205 C2
Richmond TW10 ... 153 C2
Strickland Ct SE15 ... 140 A2
Strickland Ho 26 E2 ... 95 D4
Strickland Row SW18 ... 158 B4
Strickland St SE8 ... 141 C4
Strickland Way 4 BR6 ... 227 D4
Stride Rd E13 ... 98 D5
Strimon Cl N9 ... 18 C2
Stringer Hos 19 N1 ... 95 C6
Strode Cl N10 ... 31 A3
Strode Ho 3 SW2 ... 160 C3
Strode Rd
Forest Gate E7 ... 77 A4
SW6 ... 135 A5 264 A4
Tottenham N17 ... 33 C1
Willesden NW10 ... 68 A2
Strome Ho NW6 ... 91 D5
Strone Rd E7, E12 ... 77 D2
Strone Way UB4 ... 85 A3
Strongbow Cres SE9 ... 166 B6
Strongbow Rd SE9 ... 166 B6
Strongbridge Cl HA2 .. 41 C1
Stronsa Rd W12 ... 111 D4
Strood Ho
9 Penge SE20 ... 184 C3
SE1 ... 252 D1
Stroud Cres SW15 ... 156 A1
Stroudes Cl KT4 ... 199 D2
Stroud Field UB5 ... 63 A2
Stroud Gate HA2 ... 63 D4
STROUD GREEN ... 50 C3
Stroud Green Gdns CR0 ... 206 C2
Stroud Green Prim Sch N4 ... 50 C1
Stroud Green Rd N4 .. 50 C1
Stroud Green Way CR0 ... 206 C3
Stroudley Ho SW8 .. 269 B2
Stroudley Wlk E3 ... 97 D4
Stroud Rd
Croydon SE25 ... 206 A3
Wimbledon SW19 ... 157 C1
Strouds Cl RM6 ... 58 B4
Stroud Way TW15 ... 171 A4
Strout's Pl 2 E2 ... 95 D4
Struan Ho 15 E11 ... 55 A4
Strudwick Ct SW4 .. 270 B1
Strutton Ground SW1 ... 115 D3 259 C5
Strype St E1 ... 243 C3
Stuart Ave
Ealing W5 ... 110 B4
Harrow HA2 ... 63 B5
Hayes BR2 ... 209 A1
Hendon NW9 ... 46 A2
Walton-on-T KT12 ... 194 B1
Stuart Cl UB10 ... 60 C2
Stuart Cres
Croydon CR0 ... 223 B5
Hayes UB3 ... 83 A1
Wood Green N22 ... 32 B2
Stuart Ct Chingford E4 .. 20 D2
6 Croydon CR0 ... 220 D5
2 Elstree WD6 ... 9 D5
Stuart Evans Cl DA16 ... 146 C2
Stuart Gr TW11 ... 174 C5
Stuart Ho
Hammersmith W6 ... 112 C3
1 Homerton E9 ... 74 D1
Queensbury NW9 ... 44 C5
5 Stockwell SW4 ... 138 A1
W14 ... 254 A4
Stuart Lo SE25 ... 183 C1
Stuart Mill Ho N1 ... 233 C3
Stuart Pl CR4 ... 180 D2
Stuart Rd Acton W3 ... 111 A5
Barking IG11 ... 79 D1
DA16 ... 146 B4
East Barnet EN4 ... 14 D4
Harrow HA3 ... 42 D6
Maida Vale NW6 ... 91 C4
Nunhead SE15 ... 140 C1
Richmond TW10 ... 153 B1
South Norwood CR7 . 205 A5
Wimbledon SW19 ... 157 C1
Stubbs Cl NW9 ... 45 A4
Stubbs Dr SE16 ... 118 B1
Stubbs Ho
Finsbury Pk N4 ... 50 B1
1 Globe Town E2 ... 96 D4
Stubbs Mews RM8 ... 80 B4
Stubbs Point E13 ... 99 B3
Stubbs Way SW19 ... 180 B2
Stucley Pl 19 NW1 ... 71 B1
Stucley Rd TW5, TW7 ... 130 A5
Studdridge St SW6 ... 135 C3
Studd St N1 ... 94 D6 234 C6
Studholme Ct NW3 ... 69 C4
Studholme St SE15 ... 140 B5
Studio Mews 5 NW4 .. 46 C5
Studio Pl SW1 ... 247 D1
Studios NW8 ... 229 A4
Studios Rd TW17 ... 192 B6
Studios The
4 Clapham SW4 ... 137 C1
SW8 ... 269 D1
Studland Cl DA15 ... 167 D1
Studland Ho E14 ... 97 A1
Studland Rd
Ealing W7 ... 86 C1
Forest Hill SE26 ... 184 D5
Kingston u T KT2 ... 176 A4
Studland SE17 ... 262 C2
Studland St W6 ... 112 B2
Studley Ave E4 ... 36 B3
Studley Cl E5 ... 75 A3
Studley Ct
13 Blackwall E14 ... 120 B6
DA14 ... 190 B5
Redbridge IG4 ... 55 D3
Studley Dr IG4 ... 55 D3
Studley Grange Rd W7 ... 108 D4
Studley Rd
Dagenham RM9 ... 80 D1
South Lambeth SW4 . 138 A3
Upton E7 ... 77 B2
Study Prep Sch The SW19 ... 178 C5
Study Sch The KT3 .. 199 C4
Stukeley Rd E7 ... 77 B1
Stukeley St WC2 ... 94 A1 240 B2
Stumps Hill La BR3 .. 185 C
Stunell Ho 23 SE14 ... 140 D
Sturdee Ho 2 E2 ... 96 A
Sturdy Ho 28 E3 ... 97 A
Sturdy Rd SE15 ... 140 B
Sturge Ave E17 ... 35 D
Sturgeon Rd SE17 ... 117 A1 262 A
Sturges Field BR7 ... 189 B
Sturgess Ave NW4 ... 46 B
Sturge St SE1 ... 117 A4 252 A
Sturmer Way N7 ... 72 B
Sturminster Cl UB4 ... 84 C
Sturminster Ho SW8 ... 270 D
Sturrock Cl N15 ... 51 B
Sturry St E14 ... 97 D
Sturt St N1 ... 235 B
Stutfield St E1 ... 96 A
Stuttle Ho 14 E1 ... 96 A
Styles Gdns SW9 ... 138 D
Styles Ho SE1 ... 251 C
Styles Way BR3 ... 208 A
Stylus Apartments 25 E1 ... 96 C
Sudbourne Prim Sch SW2 ... 160 B
Sudbourne Rd SW2 .. 160 B
Sudbrooke Rd SW12 ... 159 A
Sudbrook Gdns TW10 ... 154 A
Sudbrook La TW10 ... 154 A
SUDBURY ... 65 A
Sudbury Ave HA0 ... 65 D
Sudbury Court Dr HA1 ... 65 A
Sudbury Court Rd HA1 ... 65 A
Sudbury Cres BR1 ... 187 A
Wembley HA0 ... 65 B
Sudbury Croft HA0 ... 64 D
Sudbury Ct
1 Ilford RM6 ... 58 B
SW8 ... 269 D
Sudbury Gdns CR0 ... 221 C
Sudbury & Harrow Road Sta HA0 ... 65 B
Sudbury Heights Ave UB6 ... 65 A
Sudbury Hill Cl HA0 ... 64 D
Sudbury Hill HA1 ... 64 C
Sudbury Hill Harrow Sta HA1 ... 64 C
Sudbury Hill Sta HA1 . 64 C
Sudbury Ho SW18 ... 157 D
Sudbury E6 ... 100 C
Sudbury Prim Sch HA0 ... 65 B
Sudbury Rd IG11 ... 79 D
Sudbury Town Sta UB6 ... 65 B
Sudeley St N1 ... 94 D5 234 D
Sudlow Rd SW18 ... 157 C
Sudrey St SE1 ... 252 A
Suez Ave UB6 ... 86 D
Suez Rd EN3 ... 7 A
Suffield Ho SE17 ... 261 D
Suffield Rd
Chingford E4 ... 35 D
Penge SE20 ... 184 C
2 South Tottenham N15 ... 51 D
Suffolk Cl WD6 ... 11 B
Suffolk Ct
3 Dagenham RM6 ... 58 C
Ilford IG3 ... 57 C
Walthamstow E17 ... 53 C
3 West Norwood SW16 ... 182 C
Suffolk Ho
11 Acton W3 ... 88 C
Beckenham BR2 ... 208 D
8 Dartmouth Pk NW5 ... 71 C
Edgware HA8 ... 26 B
Penge SE20 ... 184 C
4 South Croydon CR0 ... 221 B
Suffolk La EC4 ... 252 C
Suffolk Park Rd E17 ... 53 A
Suffolk Pl SW1 ... 249 D
Suffolk Rd
Barking IG11 ... 79 B
Barnes SW13 ... 134 A
Dagenham RM10 ... 81 D
Enfield EN3 ... 18 B
Harrow HA2 ... 41 C
Ilford IG3 ... 57 C
4 Newham E13 ... 99 A
Sidcup DA14 ... 190 C
South Norwood SE25 ... 205 D
Tottenham N15 ... 51 B
Willesden NW10 ... 67 C

Suffolk Rd *continued*
Worcester Pk KT4 215 D6
Suffolks Prim Sch EN1 6 B3
Suffolk St
Forest Gate E7 77 A4
SW1 115 D5 249 D4
Sugar House La E15 98 A5
Sugar Loaf Wlk 6 E2 96 C4
Sugden Rd
Clapham SW11 137 A1
Long Ditton KT7 197 B1
Sugden Way IG11 101 D5
Sulby Ho SE4 141 A1
Sulgrave Gdns 11 W6 112 C4
Sulgrave Rd W6 112 C3
Sulina Rd SW2 160 A4
Sulivan Ct SW6 135 C3
Sulivan Ent Ctr SW6 135 C2
Sulivan Prim Sch SW6 135 C3
Sulivan Rd SW6 135 C2
Sulkin Ho 11 E2 96 D4
Sullivan Ave E16 99 D2
Sullivan Cl
Battersea SW11 136 C2
Hayes UB4 84 C2
Sullivan Ct
1 Croydon CR0 206 A1
Stamford Hill N16 51 D1
SW5 255 B4
Sullivan Ho
Chelsea SW1 268 D6
Isleworth TW2 152 B5
Vauxhall SE11 260 D3
Sullivan Rd SE11 116 C2 261 B4
Sullivans Reach KT12 193 D2
Sullivan Way WD6 9 C5
Sultan Ho SE1 118 A1
Sultan Rd E11 55 B5
Sultan St Penge BR3 184 D1
SE5 139 A5
Sumal Ct E9 76 B6
Sumatra Rd NW6 69 C2
Sumburgh Rd SW12 159 A5
Summer Ave KT8 196 C4
Summercourt Rd E1 96 C1
Summer Crossing KT7 196 C4
Summerene Cl SW16 181 C3
Summerfield Ave
Colney Hatch N12 30 C4
Kensal Rise NW6 91 A5
Summerfield 6 BR1 187 B2
Summerfield Ho RM9 80 D4
Summerfield La KT6 213 D6
Summerfield Rd
Ealing W5 87 B3
Loughton IG10 21 D5
Summerfield St SE12 164 D4
Summer Gdns KT8 196 C4
Summer Gr WD6 9 D5
Summer Hill
Borehamwood WD6 10 C6
BR7 188 C1
Summerhill Cl BR6 227 C5
Summerhill Gr EN1 17 C5
Summerhill Rd N15 51 B5
Summerhill Villas BR7 188 D2
Summerhill Way CR4 181 A2
Summer Ho SE13 142 B1
Summerhouse Ave TW5 129 A4
Summerhouse Rd N16 73 C6
Summerland Gdns N10 49 B6
Summerland Grange N10 49 B6
Summerlands Ave W3 111 A6
Summerlands Lo BR6 226 C4
Summerlee Ave N2 48 D5
Summerlee Gdns N2 48 D5
Summerley St SW18 157 D2
Summer Rd
East Molesey KT8 196 B4
Thames Ditton KT7, KT8 196 D4
Summersby Rd N6 49 B3
Summers Cl
Belmont SM2 217 C1

Summers Cl *continued*
Wembley HA9 44 D1
Summersell Ho SE27 183 B5
Summerside Prim Sch N12 30 B4
Summerskille Cl N9 18 B2
Summers La N12 30 B3
Summers Row N12 30 C4
Summers St EC1 241 A5
SUMMERSTOWN 158 A1
Summerstown SW17 180 A6
Summerton Way SE28 102 D1
Summer Trees TW16 172 B2
Summerville Gdns SM1 217 B2
Summerwood Rd TW1, TW7 152 D5
Summit Ave NW9 45 B4
Summit Bsns Pk The TW16 172 A3
Summit Cl
Edgware HA8 26 C3
Kingsbury NW9 45 B5
Osidge N14 15 C2
Summit Ct
5 Barnet EN5 1 B2
Brondesbury NW2 69 A3
Summit Dr IG8 37 D1
Summit Est N16 52 A2
Summit Rd
Northolt UB5 63 C1
Walthamstow E17 53 D5
Summit Way
Brunswick Pk N14 15 B2
South Norwood SE19 183 C3
Sumner Ave SE15 139 D4
Sumner Bldgs SE1 252 A4
Sumner Cl BR6 227 A4
Sumner Ct SW8 270 A2
Sumner Gdns CR0 204 C1
Sumner Ho 1 E3 97 D2
Sumner Place Mews SW7 256 D3
Sumner Pl SW7 114 B2 256 D3
Sumner Rd
Harrow HA1 42 A2
SE15 139 D5
Sumner Rd S CR0 204 C1
Sumner Rd CR0 204 D1
Sumner St SE1 117 A5 252 A4
Sumpter Cl NW3 70 A2
Sun Alley 6 TW9 132 A1
Sun Alliance Ho WC2 241 A2
Sunbeam Cres W10 90 C3
Sunbeam Rd NW10 89 B3
SUNBURY 194 B6
Sunbury Ave
Edgware NW7 27 B6
Mortlake SW14 133 B1
Sunbury Cl KT12 194 A3
SUNBURY COMMON 171 D3
Sunbury Court Island TW16 194 D6
Sunbury Court Mews TW16 172 D1
Sunbury Court Rd TW16 172 C1
Sunbury Cres TW13 171 D6
Sunbury Cross TW16 172 A3
Sunbury Cross Ctr 9 TW16 171 D3
Sunbury Ct 3 EN5 1 A1
Sunbury Ct (Con Ctr) TW16 172 D1
Sunbury Ct 3 SE14 140 D6
Sunbury TW16 172 D1
Sunbury Gdns NW7 27 B5
Sunbury Ho 38 E2 95 D4
Sunbury Int Bsns Ctr TW16 171 C2
Sunbury La
Battersea SW11 136 B4 266 D2
Walton-on-T KT12 194 A3
Sunbury Manor Sch TW16 171 D2
Sunbury Rd
Cheam SM3 217 A5
Feltham TW13 171 D6
Sunbury Sta TW16 172 A2
Sunbury St SE18 122 B3
Sunbury Way TW13 172 C5
Sunbury Workshops 39 E2 95 D4
Suncroft Pl SE26 162 C1
Sun Ct EC3 242 D1

Sunderland Ct
Dulwich SE22 162 A4
12 Stanwell TW19 148 A5
Sunderland Ho 26 W2 91 C2
Sunderland Mount SE23 162 D2
Sunderland Point E16 123 A5
Sunderland Rd
Ealing W5 109 D3
Forest Hill SE23 162 D2
Sunderland Terr W2 91 D1
Sunderland Way E12 77 D6
Sundew Ave W12 112 A6
Sundew Ct 9 HA0 88 A5
Sundial Ave SE25 205 D6
Sundial Ct KT5 214 D6
Sundorne Rd SE7 121 C1
Sundown Rd TW15 171 A5
Sundra Wlk 26 E1 96 D3
SUNDRIDGE 187 C4
Sundridge Ave
Bromley BR1, BR7 188 A3
DA16 145 B2
Sundridge Ho
Bromley BR1 187 B5
4 Homerton E9 74 D1
Sundridge Par BR1 187 B3
Sundridge Park Sta BR1 187 B3
Sundridge Rd CR0 206 A1
Sunfields Pl SE3 143 B5
Sun in the Sands SE3 143 B5
Sunken Rd CR0 222 C3
Sunland Ave DA6 147 A1
Sun La SE3 143 B5
Sunleigh Ct HA0 88 A6
Sunleigh Rd HA0 88 A6
Sunley Gdns UB6 87 A6
Sunley Ho E1 243 D3
Sun Life Trad Est TW14 128 A2
Sunlight Cl SW19 180 A4
Sunlight Sq 29 E2 96 B4
Sunmead Rd TW16 194 A6
Sunna Gdns TW16 172 B1
Sunna Lo TW16 171 D3
Sunniholme Ct CR2 221 A3
Sunningdale Ave
Barking IG11 79 B1
East Acton W3 111 C6
Feltham TW13 151 A2
Ruislip HA4 40 C1
Sunningdale Cl
22 Bermondsey SE16 118 B1
Erith SE28 103 A1
Newham E6 100 B4
Stanmore HA7 25 A3
3 Surbiton KT6 214 A6
Sunningdale Ct
18 Kingston u T KT2 176 C3
13 Southall UB1 86 A1
Sunningdale
Ealing W13 87 B2
Friern Barnet N14 31 D5
Sunningdale Gdns
Kingsbury NW9 45 A4
W8 255 B5
Sunningdale Lo HA8 26 B5
Sunningdale Rd
BR1, BR2 210 A4
Cheam SM1 217 B4
Sunningfields Cres NW4 28 B1
Sunningfields Rd NW4 46 B6
Sunninghill Ct 9 W3 111 A4
Sunninghill Gdns IG2 57 D4
Sunninghill Rd SE13 141 D3
Sunny Bank SE25 206 A6
Sunny Cres NW10 67 A1
Sunnycroft Rd
Hounslow TW3 129 D3
Southall UB1 85 C2
South Norwood SE25 206 A6
Sunnydale BR6 226 C6
Sunnydale Gdns NW7 27 C4
Sunnydale Rd SE12 165 B6
Sunnydene Ave
Chingford E4 36 B5
Ruislip HA4 62 A6
Sunnydene Gdns HA0 65 C2
Sunnydene St SE26 185 A6
Sunnyfield NW7 27 D6
Sunnyfields Prim Sch NW4 46 B6

Sunny Gardens Par NW4 28 B1
Sunny Gardens Rd NW4 46 C6
Sunnyhill Cl E5 75 A4
Sunny Hill Ct NW4 28 B1
Sunny Hill NW4 46 B6
Sunnyhill Prim Sch SW16 182 B6
Sunnyhill Rd SW16 182 A6
Sunnyhurst Cl SM1 217 C5
Sunnymead Ave CR4 203 D6
Sunnymead Ct W5 109 D6
Sunnymead Rd
Kingsbury NW9 45 B2
Putney SW15 156 B6
Sunnymede Ave KT19 215 C1
Sunnymede Dr IG6 56 D5
Sunny Nook Gdns CR2 221 B2
Sunny Pl NW4 46 C5
Sunny Rd The EN3 6 D4
Sunnyside 4 NW2 69 B5
Sunnyside Dr E4 20 A4
Sunnyside Ho 3 NW2 69 B5
Sunnyside Pl SW19 179 A4
Sunnyside Rd
Crouch End N19 49 D2
Ealing W5 109 D5
Sunnyside Rd E N9 18 A1
Sunnyside Rd IG1 79 B5
Sunnyside Rd N N9 18 A1
Sunnyside Rd S N9 18 A1
Sunnyside Rd
Teddington TW11 174 B6
Walthamstow E10 53 C1
Sunnyside
Walton-on-T KT12 194 C4
Wimbledon SW19 179 A4
Sunny View NW9 45 B4
Sunny Way N12 30 C3
Sun Pas 8 SE16 118 A3
Sunray Ave BR2 210 B3
Herne Hill SE5, SE24 139 B1
Tolworth KT5 214 D6
Sun Rd W14 113 B1 254 C1
Sunrise Cl TW13 151 B1
Sunrise View NW7 27 D4
Sun St Pas EC2 95 C2 243 A3
Sunset Ave
Chingford E4 19 D3
Woodford IG8 36 D6
Sunset Ct 4 IG8 37 C3
Sunset Gdns SE25 183 D1
Sunset Ho HA3 42 C6
Sunset Rd
Herne Hill SE5 139 B1
SE28 124 A5
Wimbledon SW19 178 B5
Sunset View EN5 1 A3
Sunshine Way CR4 180 D1
Sun St EC2 95 B2 242 D4
Sunwell Cl SE15 140 B4
Superior Dr 4 BR6 227 D2
Suraj Ho 6 N22 32 C1
SURBITON 198 A2
Surbiton Boys Prep Sch KT6 198 A4
Surbiton Cres KT1, KT6 198 A5
Surbiton Ct KT6 197 D3
Surbiton Hall Cl KT1 198 A5
Surbiton High Sch Jun Girls Sch KT1 198 A5
Surbiton High Sch KT1 198 A5
Surbiton Hill Pk KT5 198 C4
Surbiton Hill Rd KT6 198 A4
Surbiton Hospl KT6 198 A3
Surbiton Par 11 KT6 198 A3
Surbiton Rd KT1 198 A5
Surbiton Sta KT6 198 A3
Surcot Ho 2 SW4 137 D3
Surlingham Cl SE28 124 D6
Surma Cl E1 96 A3
Surmans Cl RM9 102 C6
Surrendale Pl W9 91 C3
Surrey Canal Rd SE14, SE16, SE8 140 D6
Surrey Cl N3 47 A6
Surrey Cres 1 W4 110 C1
Surrey Ct 15 SM6 219 B2
Surrey Gdns N4 51 A3
Surrey Gr
Carshalton SM1 218 B5
SE17 263 A1
Surrey Ho
Edgware HA8 26 B4

Surrey Ho *continued*
8 Rotherhithe SE16 118 D5
Surrey La SW11 136 C4 267 B1
Surrey Lo SW20 178 C1
Surrey Mews SE27 183 C6
Surrey Mount SE23 162 B3
Surrey Quays Rd SE16 118 D4
Surrey Quays Sh Ctr SE16 118 D3
Surrey Quays Sta SE16 118 D2
Surrey Rd
Barking IG11 79 C1
Dagenham RM10 81 D3
Harrow HA1 42 A4
Honor Oak SE15 162 D6
West Wickham BR4 207 D1
Surrey Row SE1 116 D4 251 D2
Surrey Sq SE17 117 C1 263 B2
Surrey Square Inf Sch SE17 117 C1 263 A2
Surrey Square Jun Sch SE17 117 C1 263 A2
Surrey St
Croydon CR0 221 A5
4 Newham E13 99 B4
WC2 116 B6 250 D6
Surrey Terr SE17 263 B2
Surrey Water Rd SE16 118 D5
Surrey Wharf SE1 140 A6
Surridge Ct 15 SW9 138 A3
Surridge Gdns SE19 183 B4
Surr St N7 72 A3
Sury Basin KT2 176 A2
Susan Constant Ct 18 E14 120 B6
Susan Lawrence Ho 4 E12 78 C4
Susannah St E14 98 A1
Susan Rd SE3 143 B3
Susan Wood BR7 188 C2
Sussex Ave TW7 130 C2
Sussex Cl
New Malden KT3 199 C5
Redbridge IG4 56 B4
4 Twickenham TW1 153 B5
Upper Holloway N19 72 A6
Sussex Cres UB5 63 C2
Sussex Ct
4 Barnes SW13 133 D3
Greenwich SE10 142 A6
Mitcham CR4 204 A4
Paddington W2 236 C1
Sussex Gate N6 48 D4
Sussex Gdns
Chessington KT9 213 D2
Fortis Green N6 48 D4
Harringay N4 51 A4
Paddington W2 92 B1 236 D1
Sussex Ho
Edgware HA8 26 B4
Hampstead NW3 70 C2
Richmond TW9 132 B3
Sussex House Sch SW3 114 D2 257 C4
Sussex Lo W2 236 D1
Sussex Mans
South Kensington SW7 256 C3
Strand WC2 250 B6
Sussex Mews E W2 236 D1
Sussex Mews SE6 163 C3
Sussex Mews W W2 246 D6
Sussex Pl
22 Hammersmith W6 112 C1
Lisson Gr NW1 92 D3 237 C6
New Malden KT3 199 C5
Paddington W2 92 B1 236 D1
Sussex Rd
Barking E6 100 C6
Erith DA8 147 D5
Harrow HA1 42 A4
Mitcham CR4 204 A3
New Malden KT3 199 C5
Sidcup DA14 190 B5
Southall UB2 106 D3
South Croydon CR2 221 B2
Uxbridge UB10 61 A3
Wallington SM5 218 D2
2 West Wickham BR4 207 D1
Sussex Ring N12 29 C5
Sussex Sq W2 114 B6 246 D6
Sussex St
Newham E13 99 B4

Sussex St *continued*
SW1 258 D2
Sussex Way
Cockfosters EN4 15 B6
Upper Holloway N7 72 B5
Upper Holloway N7, N19 72 A6
Upper Holloway N19 49 D1
Sutcliffe Cl NW11 47 D4
Sutcliffe Ho UB3 84 A1
Sutcliffe Rd
Bexley DA16 146 C3
SE18 145 C6
Sutherland Ave
Ealing W13 87 B1
Falconwood DA16 145 C1
Hayes UB3 106 A2
Orpington BR5 211 D4
Paddington W9 92 A3 236 A6
Sunbury TW16 171 D1
Sutherland Cl EN5 1 A1
Sutherland Ct
Kingsbury NW9 44 D4
3 Paddington W9 91 C3
Stoke Newington N16 73 B5
Sutherland Dr SW19 180 B2
Sutherland Gdns
Mortlake SW14 133 C2
North Cheam KT4 200 B1
Sunbury TW16 171 D1
Sutherland Gr
Putney SW18, SW19 157 B4
Teddington TW11 174 C5
Sutherland Ho
Ealing W13 109 A6
Kensington W8 255 C5
Kidbrooke SE18 144 B4
7 Putney SW15 156 C4
Richmond TW10 153 C2
9 South Hampstead NW6 70 A2
Sutherland Pl W2 91 C1
Sutherland Rd
Belvedere DA17 125 C3
Chiswick W4 133 C6
Ealing W13 87 A1
Edmonton N9 18 B3
Enfield EN3 18 D6
Southall UB1 85 B1
Thornton Heath CR0 204 C2
Tottenham N17 34 A2
Walthamstow E17 53 A6
Sutherland Row SW1 258 D2
Sutherland Sq SE17 117 A1 262 A1
Sutherland St SW1 115 B1 258 D2
Sutherland Wlk SE17 262 B1
Sutlej Rd SE7 143 C5
Sutterton St N7 72 B2
SUTTON 218 A2
Sutton Cl
Beckenham BR3 185 D2
Pinner HA5 40 A4
Sutton Coll of Liberal Arts SM1 217 D3
Sutton Common Rd
Cheam SM3 201 C1
Sutton SM1, SM3 217 D6
Sutton Common Sta SM1 217 D6
Sutton Courtenay Ho SW17 180 B6
Sutton Court Mans W4 133 A6
Sutton Court Rd
Chiswick W4 133 A6
Hillingdon UB10 82 D6
Newham E13 99 C4
Sutton SM1 218 A2
Sutton Cres EN5 12 D6
Sutton Ct
Chiswick W4 133 A6
Ealing W5 110 A5
East Molesey KT8 195 B4
8 Hackney E5 74 B4
Penge SE19 183 D3
Sutton SM2 218 A2
Sutton Dene TW3 129 D4
Sutton Est SW3 114 C1 257 B2
Sutton Est The 8 W10 90 C2
Sutton Gdns
Barking IG11 101 C5
Croydon CR0 205 D4
Sutton Gn IG11 101 C6
Sutton Gram Sch For Boys SM1 218 A3

Sutton Gr SM1 .... 218 B3
Sutton Hall Rd TW5 .. 129 C5
Sutton High Sch
SM1 .... 217 D2
Sutton Ho N21 .... 16 B6
Sutton House* E9 .... 74 C3
Sutton Hts SM2 .... 218 B1
Sutton La EC1 .... 241 D5
Hounslow TW3, TW4,
TW5 .... 129 B3
Sutton La N W4 .... 111 A1
Sutton La S W4 .... 133 A6
Sutton Park Rd SM1,
SM2 .... 217 D2
Sutton Par NW4 .... 46 C5
Sutton Pl E9 .... 74 C3
Sutton Rd
Barking IG11 .... 101 C6
E13 .... 98 D3
Heston TW5 .... 129 C4
Higham Hill E17 .... 34 D2
Muswell Hill N10 .... 31 A2
Sutton Row W1 .... 239 D2
Sutton Sq Hackney E9 .. 74 C3
Hounslow TW5 .... 129 B4
Sutton Sta SM2 .... 218 A2
Sutton St E1 .... 96 C1
Suttons Way EC1 .... 242 B5
Sutton Way
Hounslow TW5 .... 129 B4
North Kensington
W10 .... 90 C2
Sutton Wlk
SE1 .... 116 B5 250 D3
Swaby Rd SW17,
SW18 .... 158 A2
Swaffham Ct 1 RM6 .. 58 C4
Swaffield Prim Sch
SW18 .... 158 A4
Swaffield Rd SW18 ... 158 A4
Swain Cl SW16 .... 181 B4
Swain Ho CR4 .... 180 D3
Swain Rd CR7 .... 205 A4
Swains Cl UB7 .... 104 A4
Swain's La N6 .... 71 B6
Swainson Ho N7 .... 72 C4
Swainson Rd W3 .... 111 D4
Swains Rd CR4,
SW17 .... 180 D3
Swain St NW8 . 92 C3 237 A6
Swakeleys Dr UB10 ... 60 C3
Swakeleys Rdbt UB8,
UB10 .... 60 A4
Swakeleys Rd UB10 ... 60 C5
Swakeleys Sch UB10 .. 82 D5
Swaledale Cl N11 .... 31 A4
Swallands Rd SE6 .... 163 C1
Swallowbrook Bsns Ctr
UB4 .... 106 D5
Swallow Cl
Bushey WD23 .... 8 A3
New Cross Gate
SE14 .... 140 D4
Swallow Ct
Chingford IG8 .... 36 B3
Ilford IG2 .... 56 D4
4 Paddington W9 .... 91 C2
5 Ruislip HA4 .... 40 C1
1 SE12 .... 165 A4
Swallow Dr
Northolt UB5 .... 85 C5
Willesden NW10 .... 67 B2
Swallowfield NW1 .. 231 D1
Swallowfield Rd
SE7 .... 121 B1
Swallowfield Way
UB3 .... 105 B4
Swallow Gdns
SW16 .... 181 D5
Swallow Ho
Hornsey N8 .... 50 B6
NW8 .... 230 A4
Swallow Pk KT6 .... 214 B5
Swallow Pl
24 Poplar E14 .... 97 B1
W1 .... 238 D1
Swallows Ct 5
SE20 .... 184 D3
Swallow St
Newham E6 .... 100 A2
W1 .... 115 C6 249 B5
Swaminarayan Sch The
NW10 .... 67 B2
Swanage Ct 5 N1 .... 73 C1
Swanage Ho SW8 ... 270 C3
Swanage Rd
Chingford E4 .... 36 A3
Wandsworth SW18 .. 158 A5
Swanage Waye UB4 ... 84 C1
Swan And Pike Rd
EN3 .... 7 C5
Swan App E6 .... 100 A2
Swanbourne Ho
NW8 .... 237 A6
Swanbourne SE17 .. 262 A3
Swanbridge Rd
DA7 .... 147 C4
Swan Bsns Ctr 8
W4 .... 111 B2
Swan Cl
Croydon CR0 .... 205 C2
Feltham TW13 .... 173 A6
Higham Hill E17 .... 35 A3
Swan Ct Chelsea SW3 257 B1
Parsons Green SW6 . 265 A3
Poplar E14 .... 97 B1
Swan Ctr SW17 .... 158 A1
Swan Ct N20 .... 14 A2
Swandon Way
SW18 .... 135 D1
Swan Dr NW9 .... 27 C1
Swanfield St E2 .... 95 D4
Swan Ho
De Beauvoir Town
N1 .... 73 B1
Enfield EN3 .... 18 C6
Swan La EC4 . 117 B6 252 D5
Loughton IG10 .... 21 C4
Swan Lane Pier
EC4 .... 117 B6 252 C5
Swan La N20 .... 14 A1
Swanlea Sec Sch E1 .. 96 B3
Swanley Ho SE17 ... 263 B2
Swanley Rd DA16 .... 146 C4
Swan Mead
SE1 .... 117 C3 263 A5
Swan Mews
Stockwell SW9 .... 138 B3
SW6 .... 265 A2
Swanmore Ct SW18 .. 158 A5
Swann Ct 3 TW7 .... 131 A2
Swanne Ho 12 SE10 .. 142 A5
Swan Pas 5 E1 .... 118 A6
Swan Pl SW13 .... 133 D3
Swan Rd
Feltham TW13 .... 173 A6
Greenwich SE18 .... 121 D3
Rotherhithe SE16 ... 118 C4
Southall UB1 .... 85 D1
West Drayton UB7 ... 104 A4
Swanscombe Ho
1 BR5 .... 190 B1
11 Shepherd's Bush
W11 .... 112 D5
Swanscombe Point 7
E16 .... 98 D2
Swanscombe Rd
5 Chiswick W4 .... 111 C1
Shepherd's Bush
W11 .... 112 D5
Swansea Ct E16 .... 122 D5
Swansea Rd
Enfield EN3 .... 6 C1
Harlington TW14,
TW6 .... 149 B5
Swansland Gdns 2
E17 .... 35 A2
Swan St TW7 .... 131 B2
Swanston Ct TW1 .... 152 D4
Swan St SE1 .. 117 A4 252 B1
Swan The BR4 .... 224 A6
Swanton Gdns
SW19 .... 156 D3
Swanton Rd DA8 .... 147 D5
Swan Way EN3 .... 6 D3
Swanwick Cl SW15 ... 155 D4
Swan Wlk
Oatlands Pk
TW17 .... 193 C2
SW3 .... 136 D6 267 C6
Swan Yd N1 .... 72 D2
Swaton Rd E3 .... 97 C3
Swaylands Rd DA17 .. 147 C6
Swaythling Cl N18 .... 34 B6
Swaythling Ho
SW15 .... 155 D5
Swedenborg Gdns
E1 .... 118 B6
Sweden Gate SE16 ... 119 A2
Swedish Quays
SE16 .... 119 A3
Swedish Sch The
SW13 .... 134 A6
Sweeney Cres SE1 .. 253 D1
Sweet Briar Gn N9 ... 17 D1
Sweet Briar Gr N9 .... 17 D1
Sweet Briar Wlk N18 .. 33 D6
Sweetcroft La UB10 ... 60 C1
Sweetmans Ave HA5 .. 40 D6
Sweets Way N20 .... 14 B2
Swell Ct E17 .... 53 D3
Swetenham Wlk
SE18 .... 123 A1
Swete St E13 .... 99 A5
Sweyn Pl SE3 .... 143 A3
Swift Cl Harrow HA2 ... 63 D6
Hayes UB3 .... 83 D1
Higham Hill E17 .... 35 A3
Thamesmead SE28 ... 124 B6
Swift Ct SM2 .... 217 D1
Swift Ctr CR0 .... 220 B1
Swift Ho
16 Stepney E1 .... 96 C1
15 Stoke Newington
N16 .... 73 C5
1 SW9 .... 138 C5
8 Wanstead E18 .... 55 B6
Swift Rd
Feltham TW13 .... 173 A6
Southall UB2 .... 107 B3
Swiftsden Way BR1 .. 186 C4
Swift St SW6 . 135 B4 264 C2
Swinbrook Rd W10 ... 91 A2
Swinburne Cres
CR0 .... 206 C3
Swinburne Ct 4
SE5 .... 139 B1
Swinburne Ho 15 E2 .. 96 C4
Swinburne Rd
SW15 .... 134 A1
Swinderby Rd HA0 .... 66 A2
Swindon Cl IG3 .... 57 C1
Swindon Rd TW6 .... 149 A6
Swindon St W12 .... 112 C5
Swinfield Cl TW13 ... 173 A6
Swinford Gdns
SW9 .... 138 D2
Swingate La SE18 .... 145 C5
Swingfield Ct BR2 ... 209 D4
Swingfield Ho 4 E9 .. 96 C6
Swinley Ho NW1 .... 231 D2
Swinnerton St E9 .... 75 A3
Swinson Ho 12 N11 ... 31 C5
Swinton Cl HA9 .... 44 D1
Swinton Ho 21 E2 .... 96 A4
Swinton Pl WC1 .... 233 C2
Swinton St
WC1 .... 94 B4 233 C2
Swires Shaw BR2 .... 225 D4
Swiss Cottage NW3 ... 70 B1
Swiss Cottage Sch
South Hampstead
NW3 .... 70 B1
St John's Wood
NW8 .... 92 B6 229 D6
Swiss Cottage Sta
NW3 .... 70 B1
Swiss Re Building*
EC2 .... 95 C1 243 B2
Swiss Terr 7 NW3 .... 70 B1
Switch Ho 4 E14 .... 120 B6
Swithland Gdns
SE9 .... 188 C6
Swyncombe Ave
W5 .... 109 B2
Swynford Gdns 7
NW4 .... 46 A5
Sybil Elgar Sch UB2 . 107 B3
Sybil Mews N4 .... 50 D3
Sybil Phoenix Cl
SE8 .... 118 D1
Sybil Thorndike Casson
Ho SW5 .... 255 B1
Sybil Thorndike Ho 12
N1 .... 73 A2
Sybourn Inf Sch Annexe
E10 .... 53 A1
Sybourn Jun & Inf Schs
E17 .... 53 B2
Sybourn St E17 .... 53 B2
Sycamore Ave
DA15 .... 167 D5
Ealing W5 .... 109 D3
East Finchley N3 .... 47 D6
Hayes UB3 .... 105 C6
Old Ford E3 .... 97 B6
Sycamore Cl
Carshalton SM5 .... 218 D4
Chislehurst SE9 .... 166 A2
East Acton W3 .... 111 C5
2 Edgware HA8 .... 27 A6
Edmonton N9 .... 34 A6
Feltham TW13 .... 150 A1
New Barnet EN4 .... 14 B5
Newham E16 .... 98 C3
Northolt UB5 .... 85 A6
South Croydon CR2 .. 221 C3
Yiewsley UB7 .... 104 B6
Sycamore Ct
4 Beckenham
BR3 .... 185 C2
Forest Gate E7 .... 77 A2
3 Forest Hill SE26 .. 184 C6
Golders Green NW11 .. 47 A3
Hendon NW4 .... 28 C1
Hillingdon UB8 .... 82 C3
Hither Green SE12 ... 164 D5
Hounslow TW4 .... 129 A1
Kilburn NW6 .... 91 C6
Surbiton KT6 .... 198 A2
Tufnell Pk N19 .... 71 D5
10 West Norwood
SW16 .... 182 C5
Sycamore Gdns
Hammersmith W6,
W12 .... 112 B3
Mitcham CR4 .... 180 B1
Sycamore Gdns *continued*
Tottenham N15 .... 51 D5
Sycamore Gr
Kingsbury NW9 .... 45 A2
Kingston u T KT3 .... 199 C6
Lewisham SE6 .... 164 A5
Penge SE20 .... 184 A2
Sycamore Hill N11 .... 31 A4
Sycamore Ho
4 Buckhurst Hill
IG9 .... 21 D2
23 Finchley N2 .... 30 B1
10 Maitland Pk NW3 ... 70 D2
Penge SE20 .... 184 D4
17 Rotherhithe
SE16 .... 118 D4
3 Shepherd's Bush
W6 .... 112 B4
2 Stoke Newington
N16 .... 73 B6
Teddington TW11 .... 175 C3
Twickenham TW1 .... 152 D2
Sycamore Lo 7
TW16 .... 171 D3
Sycamore Lodge
HA2 .... 64 B6
Sycamore Lo SW15 .. 134 B2
Sycamore Mews 4
SW4 .... 137 C2
Sycamore Rd SW19,
SW20 .... 178 C4
Sycamore St EC1 .... 242 A5
Sycamore Way
TW11 .... 175 C4
Sycamore Wlk
Ilford IG6 .... 57 A5
1 Kensal Town W10 ... 91 A3
Sydcote SE21 .... 161 A3
Sydenham Ave
Penge SE26 .... 184 B5
Southgate N21 .... 16 B6
Sydenham High Sch
SE26 .... 162 B1
Sydenham High Sch
GDST SE26 .... 184 B5
Sydenham Hill SE21, SE22,
SE23, SE26, SE19 .... 162 A1
Sydenham Hill Sta
SE21 .... 161 D1
Sydenham Ho 16
KT6 .... 197 D2
Sydenham Ind Est
SE26 .... 185 B5
Sydenham Park Mans
2 SE26 .... 162 C1
Sydenham Park Rd SE23,
SE26 .... 162 C1
Sydenham Pk SE26 .. 162 C1
Sydenham Rd
Forest Hill SE26 .... 185 A6
Thornton Heath CR0 .. 205 B2
Sydenham Rise
SE23 .... 162 B2
Sydenham Sta SE26 . 184 C6
Sydenham Station App
4 SE26 .... 184 C6
Sydmons Ct SE23 .... 162 C4
Sydner Mews N16 .... 73 D4
Sydner Rd N16 .... 73 D4
Sydney Chapman Way
EN5 .... 1 B3
Sydney Cl SW3 .... 256 D3
Sydney Cotts KT10 .. 212 D2
Sydney Cres TW15 .. 170 D4
Sydney Ct Hayes UB4 .. 84 C3
Surbiton KT6 .... 214 A6
Sydney Gr NW4 .... 46 C4
Sydney Ho
4 Chiswick W4 .... 111 C2
Muswell Hill N10 .... 31 B3
Sydney Mews SW3 .. 256 D3
Sydney Pl SW7 .... 257 A3
Sydney Rd
Abbey Wood SE2 .... 124 D3
Bexley DA6 .... 146 D1
Ealing W13 .... 109 A4
East Bedfont TW14 .. 150 A3
Enfield EN2 .... 5 B1
Hornsey N8 .... 50 C5
Muswell Hill N10 .... 31 B3
Richmond TW10,
TW9 .... 132 A1
Sidcup DA14 .... 189 C6
Sutton SM1 .... 217 C4
Teddington TW11 .... 174 D5
Wanstead E11 .... 55 B3
West Barnes SW20 .. 178 D1
Woodford IG8 .... 37 A6
Sydney Russell Sch The
RM9 .... 80 D3
Sydney St
SW3 .... 114 C1 257 A2
Sydney Terr KT10 ... 212 D2
Sylva Cotts 3 SE8 ... 141 C4
Sylva Ct 3 SW15 .... 156 D4
Sylvana Cl UB10 .... 82 B6
Sylvan Ave
Church End N3 .... 29 C1
Dagenham RM6 .... 59 B3
Edgware NW7 .... 27 D4
Wood Green N22 .... 32 C3
Sylvan Ct
Finchley N12 .... 29 D6
1 Kilburn NW6 .... 91 D6
South Croydon CR2 .. 221 A2
Sylvan Gdns KT6 .... 197 D2
Sylvan Gr
Hampstead NW2 .... 68 D4
SE15 .... 140 B6
Sylvan Hill SE19 .... 183 C2
Sylvan Ho N21 .... 16 B6
Sylvan Rd Ilford IG1 ... 79 A6
South Norwood
SE19 .... 183 D2
Upton E7 .... 77 B2
Walthamstow E17 .... 53 C4
Wanstead E11 .... 55 A4
Sylvan Way
Coney Hall BR4 .... 224 C4
Dagenham RM8 .... 80 B5
Sylvan Wlk BR1 .... 210 B6
Sylverdale Rd CR0 ... 220 D5
Sylvester Ave BR7 .... 188 B4
Sylvester Ct HA0 .... 65 D3
Sylvester Ho 7 E8 ... 74 B2
Sylvester Path 8 E8 .. 74 B2
Sylvester Rd
Finchley N2 .... 30 B1
Hackney E8 .... 74 B2
Walthamstow E17 .... 53 B2
Wembley HA0 .... 65 C3
Sylvestrus Cl KT1 .... 176 C1
Sylvia Ave HA5 .... 23 B4
Sylvia Ct N1 .... 235 C3
Wembley HA9 .... 66 D1
Sylvia Gdns HA9 .... 66 D1
Sylvia Lawla Ct N22 .. 32 B1
Sylvia Pankhurst Ho
10 Dagenham
RM10 .... 81 C5
14 Globe Town E2 .... 96 D4
Sylvia Young Theatre
Sch NW1 .... 237 B5
Symes Mews NW1 .... 232 A4
Symington Ho SE1 ... 262 C5
Symington Mews E9 .. 74 D3
Symister Mews N1 .... 95 C4
Symons St
SW3 .... 114 D2 257 D3
Symphony Cl HA8 .... 26 D3
Symphony Mews 15
W10 .... 91 A4
Syon Gate Way TW7,
TW8 .... 131 B5
Syon Ho & Pk*
TW8 .... 131 C4
Syon La
Brentford TW7,
TW8 .... 131 B5
Hounslow TW7 .... 130 D6
Syon Lane Sta TW7 . 131 A5
Syon Lo 6 SE12 .... 165 A4
Syon Park Cotts
TW8 .... 131 C4
Syon Park Gdns
TW7 .... 130 D5
Syon Park Sch TW7 .. 131 B4
Syringa Ho SE4 .... 141 B2

T

Tabard Ct 6 E14 .... 98 A1
Tabard Ho SE1 .... 262 D6
Teddington KT1 .... 175 C2
Tabard St
SE1 .... 117 B3 262 C6
Tabernacle Ave 7
E13 .... 99 A3
Tabernacle St
EC2 .... 95 B3 242 D6
Tableer Ave SW4 .... 159 D6
Tabley Rd N7 .... 72 A4
Tabor Ct 3 SM3 .... 217 A2
Tabor Gdns SM2,
SM3 .... 217 B1
Tabor Gr SW19 .... 179 B3
Tabor Rd W6 .... 112 B3
Tachbrook Est
SW1 .... 115 D1 259 D1
Tachbrook Mews
SW1 .... 259 A4
Tachbrook Rd
East Bedfont
TW14 .... 149 D4
Southall UB2 .... 106 D2
Tachbrook St
SW1 .... 115 C2 259 B3
Tack Mews SE4 .... 141 C2
Tadbourne Ct 1
HA8 .... 27 A3
Tadema Ho NW8 .... 236 D5
Tadema Rd
SW10 .... 136 A5 266 B
Tadlow KT1 .... 198 C
Tadmor Cl TW16 .... 193 D
Tadmor St W12 .... 112 D
Tadworth Ave KT3 ... 199 D
Tadworth Ct 5 N11 ... 31 A
Tadworth Ho SE1 .... 251 C
Tadworth Rd NW2 .... 68 A
Taeping St E14 .... 119 D
Taffrail Ho 2 E14 .... 119 D
Taffy's How CR4 .... 202 C
Taft Way 4 E3 .... 97 D
Taggs Ho KT1 .... 175 D
Tailors Ct 9 SW16 .... 181 C
Tailworth St 16 E1 .... 96 A
Tait Ct 16 Old Ford E3 ... 97 B
SW8 .... 269 D
Tait Ho SE1 .... 251 B
2 Tufnell Pk N19 .... 71 C
Tait 7 NW9 .... 27 D
Tait Rd CR0 .... 205 C
Tait Rd Ind Est CR0 . 205 C
Takhar Mews SW11 .. 136 C
Talacre Rd NW5 .... 71 A
Talbot Ave N2 .... 48 B
Talbot Cl N15 .... 51 D
Talbot Cres NW4 .... 46 A
Talbot Ct EC3 .... 252 D
Neasden NW9 .... 67 B
Talbot Gdns IG3 .... 80 A
Talbot Grove Ho 10
W11 .... 91 A
Talbot Ho
Highbury N7 .... 72 C
Poplar E14 .... 97 D
Talbot Pl SE3 .... 142 C
Talbot Rd
Ashford TW15 .... 170 A
Camberwell SE22 .... 139 C
Dagenham RM9 .... 81 B
Ealing W13 .... 109 A
Forest Gate E7 .... 77 A
Harrow HA3 .... 24 D
Highgate N6 .... 49 A
Isleworth TW1,
TW7 .... 131 A
Notting Hill W2 .... 91 C
Notting Hill W11 .... 91 B
Southall UB2 .... 107 A
South Norwood CR7 .. 205 B
Tottenham N15 .... 51 D
Twickenham TW2 .... 152 C
Wallend E6 .... 100 C
Wallington SM5 .... 219 A
Wembley HA0 .... 65 D
Wood Green N22 .... 32 C
Talbot Sq W2 . 92 B1 236 C
Talbot Wlk
Notting Hill W11 .... 91 A
Willesden NW10 .... 67 C
Talbot Yd SE1 .... 252 C
Talcott Path 12
SW2 .... 160 C
Talfourd Pl SE15 .... 139 D
Talfourd Rd SE15 .... 139 D
Talgarth Rd
Hammersmith
W6 .... 112 C
W14 .... 113 A1 254 B
Talgarth Wlk NW9 .... 45 C
Talia Ho E14 .... 120 A
Talina Ctr SW6 .... 266 A
Talisman Cl 2 IG3 .... 58 B
Talisman Sq SE26 .... 184 A
Talisman Way HA9 .... 66 B
Tallack Cl HA3 .... 24 C
Tallack Rd E10 .... 53 B
Tall Elms Cl BR2 .... 208 D
Talleyrand Ho SE5 ... 139 A
Tallis Cl E16 .... 99 B
Tallis Gr SE7 .... 143 B
Tallis St EC4 .... 251 B
Tallis View NW10 .... 67 B
Tallow Rd TW8 .... 131 C
Tall Trees SW16 .... 204 B
Talma Gdns TW2 .... 152 C
Talmage Cl SE23 .... 162 C
Talman Gr HA7 .... 25 D
Talma Rd SW2 .... 138 C
Talmud Torah Chaim
Meirim Sch N16 .... 51 D
Talmud Torah
Machzikei Hadass
Sch E5 .... 52 A
Talmud-Torah Yetev-
Lev N16 .... 52 A
Talwin St E3 .... 97 D
Tamar Cl 24 E3 .... 97 B
Tamar Ho
10 Cubitt Town
E14 .... 120 A
SE11 .... 261 B
Tamarind Ct 8 W3 .... 89 A
Tamarind Ho 4
SE15 .... 140 A
Tamarind Yd 5 E1 .... 118 A

amarisk Sq W12 .... 111 D6
amar Sq IG8 .... 37 B4
amar St SE7 .... 122 A2
amar Way N17 .... 52 A6
ame Ho 3 UB5 .... 85 B4
amesa Ho TW17 .... 192 C2
amesis Gdns KT4 .... 215 C6
amian Ind Est TW4 .... 128 C1
amian Way TW4 .... 128 C1
amil Ho SE6 .... 163 C2
amworth Ave IG8 .... 36 C4
amworth La CR4 .... 203 B6
amworth N7 .... 72 A2
amworth Pk CR4 .... 203 B6
amworth Pl 3 CR0 .... 221 A6
amworth Rd CR0 .... 221 A6
amworth St SW6 .... 135 C6 265 A5
ancred Rd N4 .... 50 D3
andem Ctr SW19 .... 180 B2
andridge Ct SM2 .... 217 D2
andridge Dr BR6 .... 211 B1
andridge Pl 2 BR6 .... 211 B1
anfield Ave NW2 .... 67 D5
anfield Rd CR0 .... 221 A4
angier Rd TW10 .... 132 D2
angleberry Cl BR1 .... 210 B5
angle Tree Cl N3 .... 29 D1
anglewood Cl
Hillingdon UB10 .... 82 C3
South Croydon CR0 .... 222 C5
Stanmore HA7 .... 8 C2
anglewood Lo HA8 .... 27 A4
anglewood Way TW13 .... 150 B1
angley Gr SW15 .... 155 D4
angley Park Rd TW12 .... 173 B4
anglyn Ave TW17 .... 192 D4
angmere Gdns UB5 .... 84 C5
angmere Gr KT2 .... 175 D5
angmere N17 .... 33 B1
angmere Way NW9 .... 27 C1
angmere WC1 .... 233 C1
anhurst Ho 27 SW2 .... 160 A4
anhurst Wlk SE2 .... 124 D3
ankerton Rd KT6 .... 214 B6
ankerton St WC1 .... 233 B1
ankerton Terr CR0 .... 204 B3
ankerville Rd SW16 .... 182 A3
ankridge Rd NW2 .... 68 B6
anner Ho
1 Merton SW19 .... 180 A2
SE1 .... 253 B1
anner Point E13 .... 99 A6
anners Cl KT12 .... 194 B3
anners End La N18 .... 33 C5
anner's Hill SE8 .... 141 C4
anners La IG6 .... 57 A6
anners Mews SE8 .... 141 B4
anner St
Barking IG11 .... 79 A2
SE1 .... 117 C4 253 B1
anners Yd 3 E2 .... 96 B5
annery Cl
Beckenham BR3, CR0 .... 206 D4
Dagenham RM10 .... 81 D5
annery Ho 22 E1 .... 96 A2
annington Terr N5 .... 72 C5
annsfeld Rd SE26 .... 184 D5
ansley Cl N7 .... 71 D3
answell St SE1 .... 251 A1
ansy Cl E6 .... 100 C1
antallon Rd SW12 .... 159 A3
ant Ave E16 .... 98 D1
antony Gr RM6 .... 58 D6
anworth Gdns HA5 .... 22 C1
anyard Ho 8 TW8 .... 131 C5
an Yard La DA5 .... 169 C4
anza Rd NW3 .... 70 D4
apestry Cl SM2 .... 217 D1
apley Ho 11 SE1 .... 118 A4
aplow Ct CR4 .... 202 C5
aplow Ho 36 E2 .... 95 D4
aplow NW3 .... 70 B1
aplow Rd N13 .... 33 A6
aplow St N1 .... 95 A5 235 B3
appesfield Rd SE15 .... 140 C2
apping Cl 5 KT2 .... 176 C3
app St E1 .... 96 B3
apster St EN5 .... 1 B2
ara Ct 4 BR3 .... 185 D1
aranto Ho 14 E1 .... 96 D2
arati Ct HA0 .... 65 D1
arbert Rd SE22 .... 161 C6
arbert Wlk E1 .... 118 C6
Target Cl TW14 .... 149 C5
Target Ho W13 .... 109 B5
Target Rdbt UB5 .... 85 B6
ariff Rd N17 .... 34 A4
Tarleton Ct 2 N22 .... 32 C1
Tarleton Gdns SE23 .... 162 B3
Tarling Cl DA14 .... 168 B1
Tarling Rd
Canning Town E16 .... 98 D1
Finchley N2 .... 30 A1
Tarling St E1 .... 96 C1
Tarnbank EN2 .... 16 A6
Tarnbrook Ct SW1 .... 258 A3
Tarns The NW1 .... 232 A2
Tarn St SE1 .... 117 A3 262 A5
Tarnwood Pk SE9 .... 166 B3
Tarplett Ho 22 SE14 .... 140 D6
Tarquin Ho SE26 .... 184 A6
Tarragon Cl SE14 .... 141 A5
Tarragon Gr SE26 .... 184 D4
Tarranbrae NW6 .... 69 A1
Tarrant Ho E2 .... 96 C4
Tarrant Pl W1 .... 237 C3
Tarrantt Ho W14 .... 254 A6
Tarriff Cres SE8 .... 119 B2
Tarrington Cl SW16 .... 159 D1
Tartan Ho 12 E14 .... 98 A1
Tarver Rd
SE17 .... 116 D1 261 D2
Tarves Way SE10 .... 141 D5
Tash Pl N11 .... 31 B5
Tasker Cl UB7 .... 127 A5
Tasker Ho
3 Barking IG11 .... 101 B5
17 Poplar E14 .... 97 B2
Tasker Lo W8 .... 245 A2
Tasker Rd NW3 .... 70 D3
Tasman Ct
Ashford TW16 .... 171 C3
9 Cubitt Town E14 .... 119 D2
Tasman Ho 17 E1 .... 118 B5
Tasmania Terr N18 .... 33 A4
Tasman Rd SW9 .... 138 A2
Tasman Wlk E16 .... 99 D1
Tasso Rd
W6 .... 135 A6 264 A6
Tasso Yd W6 .... 264 A5
Tatam Rd NW10 .... 67 B1
Tatchbury Ho SW15 .... 155 D5
Tate Britain*
SW1 .... 116 A2 260 A3
Tate Gdns WD23 .... 8 C4
Tate Ho 13 E2 .... 96 D5
Tate Modern*
EC4 .... 116 D5 251 D4
Tate Rd Newham E16 .... 122 B5
Sutton SM1 .... 217 C3
Tatham Pl
NW8 .... 92 B5 229 D4
Tatnell Rd SE23 .... 163 A5
Tattersall Cl SE9 .... 166 A6
Tatton Cres E5, N16 .... 51 D2
Tatum St
SE17 .... 117 B2 262 D3
Tauheed Cl N4 .... 73 A6
Taunton Ave
Hounslow TW3 .... 130 A3
Wimbledon SW20 .... 178 B1
Taunton Cl SM3 .... 201 C1
Taunton Dr Enfield EN2 .... 4 C2
Finchley N2 .... 30 A1
Taunton Ho W2 .... 236 A1
Taunton Mews NW1 .... 237 C5
Taunton Pl
NW1 .... 92 D3 237 C6
Taunton Rd
Greenford UB6 .... 85 D6
Lewisham SE12 .... 164 D6
Taunton Way HA7 .... 26 A1
Tavern Cl SM5 .... 202 C2
Tavern Ct SE1 .... 262 B5
Taverner Ho N16 .... 73 B5
Taverners Cl W11 .... 244 A3
Taverners Ct HA9 .... 66 B6
Taverners Lo EN4 .... 15 A6
Taverner Sq 4 N5 .... 73 A4
Taverners Way E4 .... 20 C3
Tavern La SW9 .... 138 C3
Tavistock Ave
Mill Hill NW7 .... 28 D3
Walthamstow E17 .... 53 A6
Wembley UB6 .... 87 A5
Tavistock Cl N16 .... 73 C3
Tavistock Cres
Mitcham CR4 .... 204 A5
Notting Hill W11 .... 91 B2
Tavistock Ct
1 Croydon CR0 .... 205 B1
WC1 .... 239 D6
Tavistock Gdns IG3 .... 79 C4
Tavistock Gr CR0 .... 205 B2
Tavistock Ho 3 W11 .... 91 B2
Tavistock Mews 3
W11 .... 91 B1
Tavistock Pl
Bloomsbury
WC1 .... 94 A3 240 A6
East Barnet N14 .... 15 B5
Tavistock Rd
4 Beckenham
BR2 .... 208 D5
Tavistock Rd *continued*
Carshalton SM5 .... 202 B1
Croydon CR0 .... 205 B1
DA16 .... 146 C4
Dagenham NW10 .... 89 D5
Edgware HA8 .... 26 C2
Leyton E7 .... 76 D4
Notting Hill W11 .... 91 B2
Stratford E15 .... 76 D2
Tottenham N4, N15 .... 51 B3
Uxbridge UB10 .... 61 A3
Wanstead E18 .... 55 A6
Tavistock Sq
WC1 .... 93 D3 239 D6
Tavistock St
WC2 .... 116 A6 250 B6
Tavistock Terr N19 .... 71 D5
Tavistock Twr SE16 .... 119 A3
Tavistock Wlk SM5 .... 202 B1
Taviton St
WC1 .... 93 D3 239 C6
Tavy Bridge SE2 .... 124 C4
Tavy Cl SE11 .... 261 B2
Tawney Rd SE28 .... 124 B6
Tawny Cl Ealing W13 .... 109 B5
Feltham TW13 .... 150 A1
Tawny Way SE16 .... 118 D2
Tayben Ave TW2 .... 152 C5
Taybridge Rd SW11 .... 137 A1
Tayburn Cl E14 .... 98 A1
Tayfield Cl UB10 .... 61 A5
Tay Ho 10 E3 .... 97 B5
Tayler Ct NW8 .... 229 C6
Taylor Ave TW9 .... 132 D3
Taylor Cl
Deptford SE8 .... 141 B6
Hampton TW12 .... 174 A5
Hounslow TW3 .... 130 A4
3 Orpington BR6 .... 227 D4
Tottenham N17 .... 34 A3
Taylor Ct Ealing W13 .... 109 C5
Penge SE20 .... 184 C1
Stratford New Town
E15 .... 76 A3
Taylor Ho
Carshalton SM5 .... 218 C6
10 Streatham SW2 .... 160 C3
Taylor Rd
Mitcham CR4 .... 180 C3
Wallington SM6 .... 219 B3
Taylor's Bldgs SE18 .... 122 D2
Taylors Cl DA14 .... 167 D1
Taylors Ct TW13 .... 150 A2
Taylor's Gn W3 .... 89 C1
Taylor's La Barnet EN5 .... 1 B4
Forest Hill SE26 .... 184 B6
Willesden NW10 .... 67 C1
Taylorsmead NW7 .... 28 A5
Taymount Grange 2
SE23 .... 162 C2
Taymount Rise
SE23 .... 162 C2
Tayport Cl N1 .... 72 A1
Tayside Ct 6 SE5 .... 139 B1
Tayside Dr HA8 .... 10 D2
Taywood Rd UB5 .... 85 B3
Teak Cl SE16 .... 119 A5
Tealby Ct N7 .... 72 B2
Teal Cl Enfield EN3 .... 6 C6
Newham E16 .... 99 D2
Teal Ct 30 SE8 .... 141 B6
Wallington SM6 .... 219 C3
Willesden NW10 .... 67 B2
Teale St E2 .... 96 A5
Tealing Dr KT19 .... 215 B4
Teal Pl SM1 .... 217 B3
Teal St 1 SE10 .... 120 D3
Teasel Cl CR0 .... 206 D1
Teasel Cres SE28 .... 123 C5
Teasel Way E15 .... 98 C4
Teather St 12 SE5 .... 139 C5
Tebbs Ho 14 SW2 .... 160 C4
Tebworth Rd N17 .... 33 D3
Technology Pk NW9 .... 45 C6
Teck Cl TW7 .... 131 A3
Tedder Cl
Chessington KT9 .... 213 C3
Hillingdon UB10 .... 60 B1
Tedder 5 NW9 .... 27 D3
Tedder Rd CR2 .... 222 D1
TEDDINGTON 175 C5
Teddington Meml Hospl
TW11 .... 174 C4
Teddington Park Rd
TW11 .... 174 D6
Teddington Pk
TW11 .... 174 D5
Teddington Sch
TW11 .... 175 C4
Teddington Sta
TW11 .... 175 A4
Ted Hennem Ho
RM10 .... 81 D5
Tedman Ct SE13 .... 142 A1
Ted Roberts Ho 25
E2 .... 96 B5
Tedworth Gdns SW3 .... 257 C1
Tedworth Sq
SW3 .... 114 D1 257 C1
Tees Ave UB6 .... 86 D5
Tees Ct W7 .... 86 B1
Teesdale Ave TW7 .... 131 A4
Teesdale Cl E2 .... 96 B5
Teesdale Gdns
Isleworth TW7 .... 131 A4
South Norwood
SE25 .... 183 C1
Teesdale Rd E11 .... 54 D2
Teesdale St E2 .... 96 B5
Teesdale Yd 31 E2 .... 96 B5
Teeswater Ct DA18 .... 124 D3
Tee The W3 .... 89 C1
Teevan Cl CR0 .... 206 A2
Teevan Rd CR0 .... 206 A2
Teign Mews SE9 .... 166 A2
Teignmouth Cl
6 Clapham SW4 .... 137 D1
Edgware HA8 .... 26 B1
Teignmouth Gdns
UB6 .... 87 A4
Teignmouth Par UB6 .... 87 B5
Teignmouth Rd
Bexley DA16 .... 146 C3
Brondesbury NW2 .... 68 D2
Tejas Ct N3 .... 47 A5
Tej Ct E7 .... 77 D3
Telcote Way HA4 .... 40 C2
Telegraph Hill NW3 .... 69 D5
Telegraph La KT10 .... 212 D3
Telegraph Mews
Ilford IG3 .... 58 A1
Seven Kings IG3 .... 57 D1
Telegraph Pl E14 .... 119 D2
Telegraph Rd SW15 .... 156 C4
Telegraph St EC2 .... 242 C2
Telemann Sq SE3 .... 143 B2
Telephone Pl SW6 .... 264 D6
Telfer Cl 4 W3 .... 111 A4
Telfer Ho
8 Dulwich SE21 .... 183 C6
EC1 .... 234 D1
Telferscot Prim Sch
SW12 .... 159 D3
Telferscot Rd SW12 .... 159 D3
Telford Avenue Mans 7
SW2 .... 160 A3
Telford Ave SW12,
SW2 .... 160 A3
Telford Cl
Penge SE19 .... 183 D4
Walthamstow E17 .... 53 A2
Telford Ct EN5 .... 13 C6
Telford Dr KT12 .... 194 C2
Telford Ho
2 Belvedere
DA17 .... 125 C3
8 Kensal Town W10 .... 91 A2
SE1 .... 262 A6
Telford Parade Mans 8
SW2 .... 160 A3
Telford Rd
3 Hendon NW9 .... 46 A3
Kensal Town W10 .... 91 A2
Telford Rd (North
Circular Rd) N11 .... 31 C5
Telford Rd
Sidcup SE9 .... 167 B2
Southall UB1 .... 85 D1
Twickenham TW4 .... 151 C4
Telford's Yd 21 SE1 .... 118 A6
Telford Terr SW1 .... 269 A6
Telford Way
Dagenham W3 .... 89 C2
Hayes UB4 .... 85 A2
Telham Rd E6 .... 100 C5
Tell Gr SE22 .... 139 D1
Tellson Ave SE18 .... 144 A4
Telscombe Cl BR6 .... 227 C6
Telscombe Ho SW11 .... 268 A1
Temair Ho 1 SE10 .... 142 A5
Temeraire Pl TW8 .... 110 B1
Temeraire St SE16 .... 118 C4
Tempelhof Ave NW2 .... 46 C2
Temperley Rd
SW12 .... 159 A4
Templar Ct RM7 .... 59 D5
Templar Dr SE28 .... 102 D1
Templar Ho
Hampstead NW2 .... 69 B2
6 Upper Clapton E5 .... 74 C6
Templar Pl TW12 .... 173 C3
Templars Ave NW11 .... 47 B3
Templars Cres N3 .... 29 C1
Templars Dr HA3 .... 24 B4
Templars Ho E15 .... 75 D3
Templar St SE5 .... 138 D3
Temple Ave
Croydon CR0 .... 223 B5
Dagenham RM8 .... 59 C1
EC4 .... 116 C6 251 B6
Oakleigh Pk N20 .... 14 B4
Temple Cl Finchley N3 .... 29 B1
Leytonstone E11 .... 54 C2
Woolwich SE18 .... 123 A3
Templecombe Rd E9 .... 96 C6
Templecombe Way
SM4 .... 201 A4
Templecroft TW15 .... 171 B4
Temple Ct Stepney E1 .... 96 D2
SW8 .... 270 A3
Templedene BR2 .... 186 B1
Temple Dwellings 7
E2 .... 96 B5
TEMPLE FORTUNE 47 A4
Temple Fortune Ct 9
NW11 .... 47 B4
Temple Fortune Hill
NW11 .... 47 C4
Temple Fortune Ho 3
NW11 .... 47 B4
Temple Fortune La
NW11 .... 47 C3
Temple Fortune Par 5
NW11 .... 47 B4
Temple Gdns
Dagenham RM8 .... 80 D5
Edmonton N21 .... 16 D2
Temple Fortune
NW11 .... 47 B3
Temple Gr Enfield EN2 .... 4 D2
Golders Green NW11 .... 47 C3
Temple Hall Ct E4 .... 20 B2
Temple Ho
13 Battersea
SW11 .... 136 C2
4 Tufnell Pk N7 .... 71 C5
11 Walthamstow E17 .... 53 D6
Temple La
EC4 .... 94 C1 241 B1
Temple Lo EN5 .... 14 B4
Templeman Rd W7 .... 86 D2
Templemead Cl W3 .... 89 C1
Temple Mead Cl HA7 .... 25 B4
Templemead Ho E9 .... 75 A4
Temple Mill La E10,
E15 .... 76 A4
TEMPLE MILLS 75 D3
Temple Mills Rd E9 .... 75 C4
Templemore DA14 .... 190 B5
Temple Par EN5 .... 14 B4
Temple Pk UB8 .... 82 C4
Temple Pl
WC2 .... 116 B6 250 D6
Temple Rd
Acton Green W4 .... 111 A3
Cricklewood NW2 .... 68 C5
Croydon CR0 .... 221 B4
Ealing W5 .... 109 D3
Hornsey N8 .... 50 B5
Isleworth TW3 .... 130 A1
Newham E6 .... 100 A6
Richmond TW9 .... 132 B2
Temple Sheen
SW14 .... 155 A6
Temple Sheen Rd
SW14 .... 133 A1
Temple Sta
WC2 .... 116 C6 251 A6
Temple St E2 .... 96 B5
Temple Terr N22 .... 32 C1
Templeton Ave E4 .... 35 D6
Templeton Cl
South Norwood
SE19 .... 183 B2
25 Stoke Newington
N16 .... 73 C3
Templeton Ct
Enfield EN3 .... 6 C5
Walthamstow E10 .... 53 D1
Templeton Pl
SW5 .... 113 C2 255 B3
Templeton Rd N4,
N15 .... 51 B3
Temple Way SM1 .... 218 B5
Temple West Mews
SE11 .... 261 C5
Templewood Ave
NW3 .... 69 D5
Templewood W13 .... 87 B2
Templewood Gdns
NW3 .... 69 D5
Templewood Point
NW2 .... 69 B6
Tempsford Cl EN2 .... 5 A2
Tempsford Ct HA1 .... 42 D3
Temsford Cl HA2 .... 24 A1
Tenbury Cl E7 .... 77 D3
Tenbury Ct SW12 .... 159 D3
Tenby Ave HA3 .... 25 B1
Tenby Cl
Dagenham RM6 .... 59 A3
Tottenham N15 .... 51 D5
Tenby Ct E17 .... 53 A4
Tenby Gdns UB5 .... 63 C2
Tenby Ho Hayes UB3 .... 105 A3
Islington N7 .... 72 C4
W2 .... 236 A1
Tenby Rd DA16 .... 146 D4
Dagenham RM6 .... 59 A3
Edgware HA8 .... 26 B1
Enfield EN3 .... 6 C1
Tenby Rd *continued*
Walthamstow E17 .... 53 A4
Tench St E1 .... 118 B5
Tenda Rd SE16 .... 118 B2
Tendring Ho SW2 .... 160 C5
Tendring Way RM6 .... 58 C4
Tenham Ave SW2 .... 159 D2
Tenison Ct W1 .... 249 A6
Tenison Way SE1 .... 251 A3
Tenniel Cl W2 .... 245 D6
Tennison Ave WD6 .... 10 D6
Tennison Rd SE25 .... 205 D4
Tennis St
SE1 .... 117 B4 252 C2
Tenniswood Rd EN1 .... 5 C4
Tennyson Ave
Kingsbury NW9 .... 45 A6
Plashet E12 .... 78 A1
Twickenham TW1 .... 152 D3
Wanstead E11 .... 55 A2
West Barnes KT3 .... 200 B4
Tennyson Cl DA16 .... 145 D4
Enfield EN3 .... 18 D6
Feltham TW14 .... 150 A5
Tennyson Ct 3
TW10 .... 175 D6
Tennyson Ho
2 Erith DA17 .... 125 B1
SE17 .... 262 B2
Southall UB1 .... 85 C1
Tennyson Rd
Ashford TW15 .... 170 A5
Ealing W7 .... 108 D6
Hounslow TW3 .... 130 A3
Kilburn NW6 .... 91 B6
Leyton E10 .... 75 D6
Mill Hill NW7 .... 28 A5
Penge SE20 .... 184 D3
Stratford E15 .... 76 C1
Walthamstow E17 .... 53 B3
Wimbledon SW19 .... 180 A4
Tennyson St SW8 .... 137 B3
Tensing Ct TW19 .... 148 A3
Tensing Ho N1 .... 72 D2
Tensing Rd UB2 .... 107 C3
Tentelow La UB2 .... 107 D3
Tenterden Cl
Hendon NW4 .... 46 D6
SE9 .... 188 B6
Tenterden Dr NW4 .... 46 D6
Tenterden Gdns
Croydon CR0 .... 206 A2
Hendon NW4 .... 46 D6
Tenterden Gr NW4 .... 46 D6
Tenterden Ho SE17 .... 263 B2
Tenterden Rd
Croydon CR0 .... 206 A2
Dagenham RM8 .... 81 B6
Tottenham N17 .... 33 D3
Tenterden St W1 .... 238 D1
Tenter Ground E1 .... 243 C3
Tent Peg La BR5 .... 211 A4
Tent St E1 .... 96 B3
Tenzing Ct 4 SE9 .... 166 A2
Tequila Wharf E14 .... 97 A1
Terborch Way 6
SE22 .... 161 C6
Tercelet Terr NW3 .... 70 A4
Teredo St SE16 .... 118 D3
Terence Ct 6 DA17 .... 147 B6
Teresa Mews E17 .... 53 C5
Teresa Wlk N10 .... 49 B4
Terling Cl E11 .... 76 D5
Terling Ho 9 W10 .... 90 C2
Terling Rd RM8 .... 81 C6
Terling Wlk N1 .... 235 A6
Terminal Four Rdbt
TW6 .... 149 A5
Terminus Pl SW1 .... 258 D5
Tern Ho 9 SE15 .... 139 D4
Terrace Gdns SW13 .... 133 D3
Terrace Ho 2 N20 .... 14 A1
Terrace La TW10 .... 154 A5
Terrace Rd
Hackney E9 .... 74 C1
Newham E13 .... 99 B6
Walton-on-T KT12 .... 194 B3
Terraces The 6
SW20 .... 178 D3
Terrace The
Barnes SW13,
SW14 .... 133 C3
Chingford E4 .... 20 C1
Cranley Gdns N2 .... 49 A5
EC4 .... 241 B1
Kilburn NW6 .... 91 C6
10 Rotherhithe SE8 .... 119 B2
1 Woodford IG8 .... 37 A4
Terrace Wlk RM9 .... 81 A3
Terrall Apartments 7
N17 .... 51 D6
Terrano Ho 1 TW9 .... 132 D4
Terrapin Ct SW17 .... 159 B1
Terrapin Rd SW17 .... 159 B1

Terrapins KT6 197 D2
Terrick Rd N22 32 A2
Terrick St W12 90 B1
Terrilands HA5 41 B6
Territorial Ho SE11 261 B3
Terront Rd N15 51 A5
Terry Ct 8 SM6 219 C2
Terry Ho SW2 160 C3
Terry Lodge 2 CR7 204 C4
Tersha St TW9 132 B1
Tessa Sanderson Pl 6 SW8 137 B2
Tessa Sanderson Way UB6 64 B3
Testerton Wlk 3 W11 112 D6
Testwood Ct W7 108 C6
Tetcott Rd SW10 136 A5 266 A3
Tetherdown N10 49 A6
Tetherdown Prim Sch N10 49 A5
Tetty Way BR1, BR2 187 A1
Teversham La SW8 138 A4 270 B2
Teviot Cl DA16 146 B4
Teviot St E14 98 A2
Tewkesbury Ave
Forest Hill SE23 162 B4
Pinner HA5 41 A4
Tewkesbury Cl
Barnet EN4 2 B1
Tottenham N15 51 B3
Tewkesbury Ct N11 31 D4
Tewkesbury Gdns NW9 44 D6
Tewkesbury Rd
Carshalton SM5 202 B1
Ealing W13 109 A6
Tottenham N15 51 B3
Tewkesbury Terr N11 31 D4
Tewson Rd SE18 123 C1
Teyham Ct SW11 158 D5
Teynham Ave EN1 17 B5
Teynham Ct N12 30 A6
Teynham Gn BR2 209 A4
Teynham Ho SE9 167 B5
Teynton Terr N17 33 A2
Thackeray Ave N17 34 A1
Thackeray Cl
Hayes UB8 82 D1
Isleworth TW7 131 A3
Wimbledon SW19 178 D3
Thackeray Ct
Chelsea SW3 257 C2
Ealing W5 88 B1
West Kensington W14 254 A5
Thackeray Dr RM6 58 B2
Thackeray Ho
College Pk NW10 90 A4
WC1 240 A6
Thackeray Manor SM1 218 A3
Thackeray Mews E8 74 A2
Thackeray Rd
Clapham SW8 137 B3
Newham E6 99 D5
Thackeray's Almshouses SE6 163 D5
Thackeray St W8 255 D6
Thackery Lo TW14 149 B5
Thackrah Cl N2 30 A1
Thakeham Cl SE26 184 B5
Thalia Cl SE10 142 B6
Thame Rd SE16 118 D4
Thames Ave
Dagenham RM9 103 D3
Sands End SW10 136 A4 266 B2
Wembley UB6 86 D5
Thames Bank SW14 133 A3
Thamesbank Pl SE28 102 C1
Thames Barrier Visitor Ctr* SE18 121 D3
Thames Christian Coll SW11 136 B2
Thames Circ E14 119 C2
Thames Cl TW12 173 D1
Thames Cnr TW16 194 C6
Thames Cres W4 133 C5
Thames Ct Ealing W7 86 C1
Edmonton N9 18 C1
10 SE15 139 D5
West Molesey KT8 173 D1
THAMES DITTON 197 B2
Thames Ditton Fst Sch KT7 196 D3
Thames Ditton Island KT7 197 A3
Thames Ditton Jun Sch KT7 196 D2
Thames Ditton Sta KT7 196 D2
Thames Dr HA4 39 A3
Thames Eyot 8 TW1 153 A3
Thamesfield Ct TW17 193 A2
Thamesfield Ho TW17 193 A2
Thamesfield Mews TW17 193 A2
Thamesgate Cl TW10 175 B6
Thames Gateway Pk RM9 103 B4
Thames Haven KT6 197 D4
Thames Hts SE1 253 C2
Thameside Ctr TW8 132 B6
Thameside Ind Est E16 121 D4
Thameside Pl KT1 175 D2
Thameside TW11 175 D3
Thames Link Ho 7 TW9 132 A1
Thames Mdw KT12, TW17 193 C1
THAMESMEAD 124 A5
Thames Meadow KT8 195 C6
Thamesmead Sec Sch TW17 193 B3
Thamesmead Sh Ctr SE28 124 A6
Thames Mead KT12 194 A3
Thamesmere Dr SE28 124 A6
Thames Pl SW15 134 D2
Thamespoint TW11 175 D3
Thames Quay
Millwall E14 119 D4
SW10 266 B1
Thames Rd
Barking IG11 102 A4
Chiswick W4 132 D6
Newham E16 121 D5
Thames Reach
Fulham W6 134 C6
Woolwich SE28 123 C4
Thames Road Ind Est E16 121 D4
Thames Row TW9 132 B6
Thames Side
Teddington KT1 175 D2
Thames Ditton KT7 197 B3
Thames St
Hampton TW12 173 D1
Kingston u T KT1, KT2 175 D1
SE10 141 D6
Sunbury TW16 194 B6
Walton-on-T KT12 193 D2
Thamesvale Cl TW3 129 C3
Thames Valley Univ W5 109 D5
Thames View Ho TW12 194 A3
Thames View 2 IG1 79 A6
Thames View Inf Sch IG11 102 A5
Thames View Jun Sch IG11 101 D5
Thames View Lo IG11 101 C4
Thames Village W4 133 A4
Thames Wlk SW11 136 C5 267 A4
Thane Mans N7 72 B5
Thanescroft Gdns CR0 221 C5
Thanet Ct 14 W3 88 C1
Thanet Dr BR2 225 D5
Thanet Ho WC1 233 A1
1 West Norwood SE27 160 D1
Thanet Lo NW2 69 A2
Thanet Pl CR0 221 A4
Thanet Rd DA5 169 C4
Thanet St WC1 94 A4 233 A1
Thane Villas N7 72 B5
Thane Works N7 72 B5
Thanington Ct DA15 167 C5
Thant Cl E10 75 D5
Tharp Rd SM6 219 D3
Thatcham Ct N20 14 A4
Thatcham Gdns N20 14 A4
Thatcher Cl UB7 104 A4
Thatchers Way TW7 152 B6
Thatches Gr RM6 59 A5
Thavies Inn EC4 241 B2
Thaxted Ct N1 235 D3
Thaxted Ho
Bermondsey SE16 118 C2
Dagenham RM10 81 D1
Thaxted Lo 3 E18 55 B6
Thaxted Pl 9 SW20 178 D3
Thaxted Rd
Buckhurst Hill IG9 21 D4
SE9 167 A2
Thaxton Rd W14 135 B6 264 D6
Thayers Farm Rd BR3 185 A2
Thayer St W1 93 A1 238 B2
Theatre Sq E15 76 B2
Theatre St SW11 136 D2
Theberton St N1 94 D6 234 C6
Theed St SE1 116 C5 251 B3
Thelbridge Ho 28 E3 97 D4
Thelma Gdns SE3 144 A4
Thelma Gr TW11 175 A4
Theobald Cres HA3 24 A2
Theobald Rd
Croydon CR0 220 D6
Walthamstow E17 53 C2
Theobalds Ave N12 30 A6
Theobalds Ct N4 73 A6
Theobalds Park Rd EN2 4 D6
Theobald's Rd WC1 94 B2 240 C4
Theobald St SE1 262 C5
Theodora Way HA5 39 D6
Theodore Ct SE13 164 B5
Theodore Ho 1 SW15 156 A6
Theodore Rd SE13 164 B5
Therapia Lane Sta CR0 204 A2
Therapia La
Thornton Heath CR0 204 A2
Thornton Heath CR0 204 A3
Wallington CR0 203 D2
Therapia Rd SE22 162 C5
Theresa Rd W6 112 A2
Therfield Ct N4 73 A6
Thermopylae Gate E14 119 D2
Theseus Ho
2 South Bromley E14 98 B1
Theseus Wlk N1 234 D3
Thesiger Rd SE20 184 D3
Thessaly Ho SW8 269 A3
Thessaly Rd SW8 137 C4 269 B2
Thetford Cl N13 32 D4
Thetford Ct
3 Dulwich SE21 162 B2
New Malden KT3 199 C4
Thetford Gdns RM9 103 A6
Thetford Ho SE1 263 C6
Thetford Rd
Ashford TW15 148 A1
Dagenham RM9 80 D1
New Malden KT3 199 C4
Thetis Terr TW9 132 C6
Theydon Gr IG8 37 C4
Theydon Rd E5 74 C6
Theydon St E17 53 B2
Thicket Cres SM1 218 A4
Thicket Ct 14 SM1 218 A4
Thicket Gr
Dagenham RM9 80 C2
Penge SE20 184 A3
Thicket Rd
Penge SE20 184 B3
Sutton SM1 218 A4
Thicket The UB7 82 A1
Third Ave
Chadwell Heath RM6 58 C3
Dagenham RM10 103 D5
East Acton W3 111 D5
Enfield EN1 17 D6
Hayes UB3 105 D5
Little Ilford E12 78 B3
3 Newham E13 99 A4
Walthamstow E17 53 C4
Wembley HA9 65 D6
West Kilburn W10 91 A4
Third Cl KT8 196 A5
Third Cross Rd TW2 152 B2
Third Way HA9 66 D4
Thirleby Rd
Hendon HA8 27 B2
SW1 115 C3 259 B5
Thirlestane Ct N10 31 A1
Thirlestane Ho TW12 173 D6
Thirlmere Ave UB6 87 C4
Thirlmere Gdns HA9 43 D1
Thirlmere Ho
Isleworth TW1 152 D6
19 Stoke Newington N16 73 B4
Thirlmere NW1 231 D2
Thirlmere Rd
Muswell Hill N10 31 B2
Streatham SW16 181 D6
Thirlmere Rise BR1 186 D4
Thirsk Cl UB5 63 C2
Thirsk Rd
Clapham SW11 137 A1
Mitcham CR4 181 A3
South Norwood SE25 205 B5
Thistlebrook Ind Est SE2 124 C4
Thistlebrook SE2 124 C3
Thistlecroft Gdns HA7 25 D1
Thistle Ct N17 52 B5
Thistledene Ave HA2 63 A5
Thistledene KT7 196 C3
Thistledown Ct SE25 205 C6
Thistlefield Cl DA5 168 D3
Thistle Gr SW7 256 B1
Thistle Ho 10 E14 98 A1
Thistlemead BR7 188 D1
Thistlewaite Rd E5 74 B5
Thistlewood Cl 3 N7 72 B6
Thistleworth Cl TW7 130 B5
Thistley Cl N12 30 C4
Thistly Ct SE8 141 D6
Thomas a' Beckett Cl HA0 64 D4
Thomas Arnold Prim Sch RM9 81 B1
Thomas Baines Rd SW11 136 B2
Thomas Burt Ho 9 E2 96 B4
Thomas Buxton Jun & Inf Sch E1 96 A3
Thomas Cribb Mews E6 100 B1
Thomas Crowell Ct 29 N1 73 C3
Thomas Ct RM8 80 C6
Thomas Dean Rd SE26 185 B6
Thomas Dinwiddy Rd SE12 165 B2
Thomas Doyle St SE1 261 D6
Thomas Fairchild Com Sch N1 95 A5 235 B4
Thomas Gamuel Prim Sch E17 53 C3
Thomas Hardy Ho N22 32 B2
Thomas Hewlett Ho HA1 64 C4
Thomas Ho
9 Belmont SM2 217 D1
3 Hackney E9 74 C2
Thomas Hollywood Ho 3 E2 96 C5
Thomas Ho 4 SW4 138 A1
Thomas Jones Prim Sch W11 91 A1
Thomas' La SE6 163 C4
Thomas Lo E17 53 D4
Thomas Milner Ho 8 SE15 140 A5
Thomas More Bldg The HA4 39 C1
Thomas More Ho EC2 242 A3
Thomas More Sq E1 118 A6
Thomas More St E1 118 A5
Thomas More Way N2 48 A6
Thomas North Terr 4 E16 98 D2
Thomas Pl W8 255 C5
Thomas Pooley Ct KT6 198 A2
Thomas Rd E14 97 C2
Thomas Road Ind Est 2 E14 97 C1
Thomas Shearley Ct DA5 169 D4
Thomas's London Day Schs SW11 136 B4 266 D1
Thomas's Prep Sch Clapham SW11 158 D6
Thomas St SE18 122 D2
Thomas Tallis Sch SE3 143 B2
Thomas Wall Cl SM1 217 D3
Thomas Watson Cottage Homes The EN5 13 A6
Thompson Ave
Richmond TW9 132 C2
6 SE5 139 A5
Thompson Cl
Ilford IG1 79 A6
Morden SM3 201 C1
Thompson Ho
11 Kensal Town W10 91 A3
SE14 140 D6
Southall UB1 107 A6
Thompson Rd
Dagenham RM9 81 B5
Dulwich Village SE22 161 D5
Hounslow TW3 129 D1
Uxbridge UB10 60 A1
Thomson Cres CR0 204 C1
Thomson Ct 4 E8 74 A2
Thomson Ho
Pimlico SW1 259 D1
Walworth SE17 263 A3
Thomson Rd HA3 42 C6
Thorburn Ho SW1 248 A1
Thorburn Sq SE1 118 A2
Thorburn Way SW19 180 B2
Thoresby Ho N16 73 B5
Thoresby St N1 95 A4 235 B2
Thorkhill Gdns KT7 197 B1
Thorkhill Rd KT7 197 B2
Thornaby Gdns N18 34 B5
Thornaby Ho 15 E2 96 B4
Thorn Ave WD23 8 A3
Thornbill Ho 1 SE15 140 A5
Thornbridge Ct 10 EN5 13 D6
Thornbury Ave TW7 130 B5
Thornbury Cl
Edgware NW7 28 D3
Stoke Newington N16 73 C3
Thornbury Ct
Croydon CR2 221 B3
Hounslow TW7 130 C5
W11 245 A6
Thornbury Ho N6 49 C1
Thornbury Lo EN2 4 D2
Thornbury 3 NW4 46 C5
Thornbury Rd
Clapham Pk SW2 160 A5
Hounslow TW7 130 B4
Thornbury Sq N6 49 C1
Thornby Rd E5 74 C5
Thorn Cl BR2 210 C3
Thorncliffe Ct SW2 160 A5
Thorncliffe Rd
Clapham Pk SW2 160 A5
Southall UB2 107 B1
Thorn Cl UB5 85 B4
Thorncombe Rd SE22 161 C6
Thorncroft HA2 64 A5
Thorncroft Rd SM1 217 D4
Thorncroft St SW8 138 A5 270 A3
Thorndale BR7 188 B3
Thorndale Ho 10 N16 51 C1
Thorndean St SW18 158 A2
Thorndene Ave N11 15 A3
Thorndike Ave UB5 84 D6
Thorndike Cl SW10 136 A5 266 A4
Thorndike Ho SW1 259 C2
Thorndike Rd 21 N1 73 B2
Thorndike St SW1 115 D2 259 C3
Thorndon Cl BR5 189 D1
Thorndon Gdns KT19 215 C4
Thorndon Rd BR5 189 D1
Thorndyke Ct HA5 23 B3
Thorne Cl
Claygate KT10 213 A1
DA8 147 D6
Leyton E11 76 C4
Littleton TW15 171 A3
Newham E16 99 A1
Thorne Ho
34 Bethnal Green E2 96 C4
4 Cubitt Town E14 120 A3
Thorneloe Gdns CR0, CR9 220 D3
Thorne Pas 7 SW13 133 D3
Thorne Rd SW8 138 A5 270 B3
Thorne's Cl BR3 208 A6
Thorness Ct SW18 158 A5
Thorne St SW13, SW14 133 C2
Thornet Wood Rd BR1 210 C6
Thornewill Ho 8 E1 118 C6
Thorney Cres SW11 136 B5 266 D3
Thorneycroft Cl KT12 194
Thorneycroft Dr EN3 7
Thorneycroft Ho 11 W4 111
Thorney Ct W8 246
Thorney Hedge Rd W4 110
Thorney St SW1 116 A2 260
Thornfield Ave NW7 29
Thornfield Ct NW7 29
Thornfield Ho 5 E14 119
Thornfield Par NW7 29
Thornfield Rd W12 112
Thornford Rd SE13 164
Thorngate Rd W9 91
Thorngrove Rd E13 99
Thornham Gr E15 76
Thorn Ham Ho SE1 262
Thornham St SE10 141
Thornhaugh St WC1 239
Thornhill Ave SE18 145
Surbiton KT6 214
Thornhill Bridge Wharf N1 233
Thornhill Cres N1 72
Thornhill Ct N8 49
Thornhill Gdns
Barking IG11 79
Leyton E10 75
Thornhill Gr N1 72
Thornhill Ho
12 Chiswick W4 111
Islington N1 72
Thornhill Mews SW15 135
Thornhill Prim Sch N1 72
Thornhill Rd
Ickenham UB10 60
Islington N1 94 C6 234
Leyton E10 75
Surbiton KT6 214
Thornton Heath CR0 205
Thornhill Sq N1 72
Thornhill Way TW17 192
Thornicroft Ho 12 SW9 138
Thornlaw Rd SE27 182
Thornley Cl N17 34
Thornley Dr HA2 63
Thornley Pl 2 SE10 120
Thornsbeach Rd SE6 164
Thornsett Pl SE20 184
Thornsett Rd
Penge SE20 184
Wandsworth SW18 157
Thornsett Terr SE20 184
Thornton Ave
Chiswick W4 111
Streatham SW2 159
Thornton Heath CR0 204
West Drayton UB7 104
Thornton Cl UB7 104
Thornton Ct
Lower Holloway N7 72 A
West Barnes SW20 200 D
Thornton Dene BR3 185 C
Thornton Gdns SW12 159 D
Thornton Gr HA5 23 C
THORNTON HEATH 204 D
Thornton Heath Pond CR7 204 C
Thornton Heath Sta CR7 205 A
Thornton Hill SW19 179 A
Thornton Ho SE17 263 A
7 Wanstead E11 55 A
Thornton Lo
South Norwood CR7 205 A
8 Wimbledon SW19 179 A
Thornton Pl W1 237 D
Thornton Rd
Barnet EN5 1 A
Belvedere DA17 125 D
BR1 187 A
Carshalton SM5 202 B
Thornton Rd E SW19 178 D
Thornton Rd IG1 78 D
Thornton Rd Ind Est CR0 204 B
Thornton Rd
Leyton E11 76 B
Lower Edmonton N18 18 C
Mortlake SW14 133 B
Streatham SW12, SW2 159 D

Thornton Rd *continued*
Thornton Heath CR0, CR7 204 B3
Wimbledon SW19 178 D3
Thornton Row CR7 204 C4
Thornton St SW9 138 C3
Thornton Way NW11 47 D4
Thorntree Ct W5 88 A2
Thorntree Prim Sch SE7 121 D1
Thorntree Rd SE7 121 D1
Thornville Gr CR4 180 B1
Thornville St SE8 141 C4
Thornwell Ct W7 108 C4
Thornwood Cl E18 37 B1
Thornwood Gdns W8 245 A2
Thornwood Lo W8 245 A2
Thornwood Rd SE13 164 C6
Thornycroft Ct TW9 132 B3
Thorogood Gdns E15 76 C3
Thorold Ho SE1 252 A2
6 Streatham SW2 160 A4
Thorold Rd Ilford IG1 57 A1
Wood Green N22 32 A3
Thorparch Rd SW8 137 D5 269 D3
Thorpebank Rd W12 112 A5
Thorpe Cl BR6 227 C6
Forest Hill SE26 184 D6
Notting Hill W10 91 A1
Thorpe Coombe Hospl E17 54 A6
Thorpe Cres E17 35 B1
Thorpe Ct Enfield EN2 4 D2
Upper Tooting SW17 180 C6
Thorpedale Gdns IG6 56 D5
Thorpedale Rd N4 50 B1
Thorpe Hall W5 87 D2
Thorpe Hall Prim Sch E17 36 B2
Thorpe Hall Rd E17 36 A2
Thorpe Ho N1 233 D5
Thorpe Rd
Barking IG11 79 B1
Chingford E17 36 A1
Kingston u T KT2 176 A3
Leyton E7 76 D4
Newham E6 100 B6
Tottenham N15 51 C3
Thorpewood Ave SE23, SE26 162 B2
Thorpland Ave UB10 61 A5
Thorsden Way 2 SE19 183 C5
Thorverton Rd NW2 69 A5
Thoydon Rd E3 97 A5
Thrale Almshouses SW16 182 A5
Thrale Rd SW16 181 C5
Thrale St SE1 252 B3
Thrasher Cl 20 E8 95 D6
Thrawl St E1 95 D2 243 D3
Thrayle Ho 2 SW9 138 B2
Threadgold Ho 8 N1 73 B2
Threadneedle St EC2, EC3 95 B1 242 D1
Three Bridges Bsns Ctr UB2 108 A4
Three Bridges Prim Sch UB2 107 D3
Three Colts La E2 96 B3
Three Colt St E14 119 B6
Three Corners DA7 147 D3
Three Cups Yd WC1 240 D3
Three Kings Yd W1 248 C6
Three Meadows Mews HA7 24 D2
Three Mill La E3 98 A4
Three Mills Studios E14 98 A4
Three Nun Ct EC2 242 B2
Three Oak La SE1 253 C2
Three Oaks Cl UB10 60 B5
Threshers Pl W11 244 A6
Thriffwood SE23, SE26 162 D1
Thrigby Rd KT9 214 B2
Thring Ho 2 SW9 138 B3
Throckmorten Rd E16 99 B1
Throgmorton Ave EC2 95 B1 242 D2
Throgmorton St EC2 95 B1 242 D2
Throwley Cl SE2 124 C3
Throwley Rd SM1 217 D3
Throwley Way SM1 217 D3
Thrupp Cl CR4 181 B1
Thrush Gn HA2 41 C5
Thrush St SE17 262 A2
Thunderer Rd RM9 103 B3
Thurbarn Rd SE6 185 D5
Thurbin Ho UB4 83 B2
Thurland Ho 3 SE16 118 B2
Thurland Rd SE16 118 A3
Thurlby Cl HA1 43 A3
Thurlby Croft NW4 46 C6
Thurlby Rd
Wembley HA0 65 D2
West Norwood SE27 182 C6
Thurleigh Ave SW12 159 A5
Thurleigh Ct SW12 159 A5
Thurleigh Rd SW12 159 A5
Thurleston Ave SM4 201 A4
Thurlestone Ave
Colney Hatch N12 30 D4
Ilford IG3 79 D4
Thurlestone Cl TW17 193 A3
Thurlestone Ct 1 UB1 85 D1
Thurlestone Par TW17 193 A3
Thurlestone Rd SE27 182 C6
Thurloe Cl SW7 257 A4
Thurloe Ct SW3 257 A3
Thurloe Place Mews SW7 256 D4
Thurloe Pl SW7 114 B2 256 D4
Thurloe Sq SW7 114 C2 257 A4
Thurloe St SW7 114 B2 256 D4
Thurlow Cl E4 35 D4
Thurlow Ct 5 E11 55 A4
Thurlow Gdns HA0 65 D3
Thurlow Hill SE21 161 A2
Thurlow Ho 17 SW16 160 A1
Thurlow Park Rd SE21, SE24 161 A2
Thurlow Rd
Hampstead NW3 70 B3
West Ealing W7 109 A4
Thurlow St SE17 117 C1 263 A1
Thurlow Terr NW5 71 A3
Thurlow Twrs SE27 160 C1
Thurlow Wlk SE17 263 A1
Thurlston Rd HA4 62 A5
Thurnby Ct TW2 152 C1
Thurnscoe NW1 232 A5
Thursland Rd DA14 191 A5
Thursley Cres CR0 224 B1
Thursley Gdns SW19 156 D2
Thursley Ho
3 Kingston u T KT2 176 D3
10 Streatham SW2 160 B4
Thursley Rd SE9 166 B1
Thurso Ho NW6 91 D5
Thurso St SW17 180 B6
Thurstan Rd SW20 178 B3
Thurston Ho 4 BR3 185 D4
Thurston Ind Est SE13 141 D2
Thurston Rd
Southall UB1 85 B1
St Johns SE8, SE13 141 D3
Thurtle Rd E2 95 D5
Thurza Ct TW7 130 D3
Thyer Cl BR6 227 A4
Thyme Cl SE3 143 C2
Thyme Ct NW7 29 A3
Thyra Gr N12 29 D4
Tibbatt's Rd E3 97 D3
Tibbenham Pl SE6 163 C2
Tibbenham Wlk E13 98 D5
Tibberton Sq N1 235 A6
Tibbets Cl SW19 156 D3
Tibbet's Corner SW19 156 D4
Tibbet's Ride SW19 156 D4
Tiber Cl 10 E3 97 C6
Tiber Gdns N1 233 B5
Ticehurst Cl BR5 190 A3
Ticehurst Rd SE23 163 A2
Tickford Cl SE2 124 C4
Tickford Ho NW8 230 A1
Tidal Basin Rd E16 120 D6
Tidbury Ct SW8 269 A3
Tideham Ho SE28 123 B5
Tidelock Ho SE28 123 B4
Tidemill Prim Sch SE8 141 C5
Tidenham Gdns CR0 221 C5
Tideside Ct SE18 122 A3
Tideslea Path SE28 123 B5
Tideslea Twr SE28 123 A4
Tideswell 10 NW5 71 B4
Tideswell Rd
Croydon CR0 223 C5
Putney SW15 134 C1
Tideway Cl TW10 175 C6
Tideway Ct 9 SE16 118 D5
Tideway Ho E14 119 C4
Tideway Ind Est SW8 137 C6 269 B5
Tideway Wharf SW13 133 C3
Tideway Yd SW13 133 C3
Tidey St E3 97 C2
Tidford Rd DA16 145 D3
Tidworth Ho 18 SE22 139 C2
Tidworth Rd E3 97 C3
Tiepigs La BR2, BR4 208 D1
Tierney Ct 4 CR0 221 D6
Tierney Rd SW2 160 A3
Tierney Terr SW2 160 A3
Tiffin Girls' Sch The KT2 176 A4
Tiffin Sch KT2 176 B1
Tiger Ho WC1 232 D1
Tiger La BR2 209 B5
Tiger Way E5 74 B4
Tignel Ct W3 110 C4
Tigris Cl N9 18 C2
Tilbrook Rd SE3 143 C2
Tilbury Cl
14 Camberwell SE15 139 D5
St Paul's Cray BR5 190 B1
Tilbury Ho 4 SE14 140 D6
Tilbury Rd
Leytonstone E10 54 A2
Newham E6 100 B5
Tildesley Rd SW15 156 C5
Tile Farm Rd BR6 227 B5
Tilehurst NW1 231 D1
Tilehurst Point 2 SE2 124 C4
Tilehurst Rd
Cheam SM3 217 A3
Wandsworth SW17, SW18 158 B3
Tile Kiln La
Edmonton N13 33 A5
Harefield UB9 38 D2
Upper Holloway N6 49 C1
Tileyard Rd N7 72 A1
Tilford Ave CR0 224 A1
Tilford Gdns SW19 156 D3
Tilford Ho 8 SW2 160 B4
Tilia Cl SM1 217 B3
Tilia Rd E5 74 B4
Tilia Wlk 21 SW9 138 D1
Tiller Ho 28 N1 95 C6
Tiller Rd E14 119 C3
Tillet Sq SE16 119 A4
Tillett Cl NW10 67 A2
Tillet Way 6 E2 96 A4
Tilley Rd TW14 150 A3
Tillingbourne Gdns N3 47 B6
Tillingbourne Way N3 47 B5
Tillingham Way N12 29 D6
Tilling Ho 1 SE15 140 B2
Tilling Rd NW2 46 C2
Tilling Way HA9 65 D6
Tillman Ho 8 SW2 160 B3
Tillman St E1 96 B1
Tilloch St 9 N1 72 B1
Tillotson Ct SW8 269 D3
Tillotson Rd
Edmonton N9 17 D2
Harrow HA3 23 D3
Ilford IG1 56 C2
Tilney Ct EC1 242 B6
Kingston u T KT6 197 D4
Woodford IG9 21 A2
Tilney Dr IG9 21 A2
Tilney Gdns 12 N1 73 B2
Tilney Rd
Dagenham RM9 81 B2
Southall UB2 106 C2
Woodford IG9 21 A2
Tilney St W1 248 B4
Tilson Cl 2 SE15 139 C5
Tilson Gdns SW2, SW4 160 A4
Tilson Ho SW2 160 A4
Tilson Rd N17 34 A2
Tilston Cl E11 76 D5
Tilton St SW6 264 B5
Tiltwood The W3 111 A6
Tilt Yard App SE9 166 B5
Timber Cl BR7 188 C1
Timbercroft La SE18 145 C5
Timbercroft Prim Sch SE18 145 C5
Timbercroft KT19 215 C4
Timberdene NW4 28 D1
Timberland Cl 16 SE15 140 A5
Timberland Rd E1 96 B1
Timber Mill Way SW4 137 D2
Timber Pond Rd SE16 118 D4
Timber St EC1 242 A6
Timberwharf Rd N16 52 A3
Time Sq E8 73 D3
Times Sq SM1 217 D3
Timor Ct UB1 107 D5
Timothy Cl
Bexley DA6 169 A6
1 Clapham Pk SW4 159 C6
Timothy Ho DA18 125 A4
Timsbury Wlk 5 SW15 156 A3
Tina Ct
Forest Hill SE6 163 B4
West Norwood SW16 160 C1
Tindal St SW9 138 D4
Tinniswood Cl N5 72 C3
Tinsley Cl SE25 206 B6
Tinsley Rd E1 96 C2
Tintagel Cres SE22 139 D1
Tintagel Ct EC1 241 C6
Tintagel Dr HA7 25 D6
Tintagel Ho SE20 184 A3
Tintern Ave NW9 44 D6
Tintern Cl
Putney SW15 157 A6
Wimbledon SW19 180 A4
Tintern Ct W13 109 A6
Tintern Gdns N14 16 A4
Tintern Ho
Belgravia SW1 258 C3
Regent's Pk NW1 231 D3
Tintern Path NW9 45 C3
Tintern Rd
Carshalton SM5 202 B1
Tottenham N22 33 A2
Tintern St SW4 138 A1
Tintern Way HA2 41 D1
Tinto Rd E16 99 A3
Tinwell Mews WD6 11 B6
Tinworth St SE11 116 A1 260 B2
Tippett Ct E6 100 B5
Tippetts Cl EN2 5 A4
Tipthorpe Rd SW11 137 A2
Tipton Dr CR0 221 C4
Tiptree Cl E4 20 A1
Tiptree Cres IG5 56 C6
Tiptree Ct EN2 5 B1
Tiptree Dr EN2 5 B1
Tiptree 7 NW1 71 B1
Tiptree Rd HA4 62 B4
Tirlemont Rd CR2 221 A1
Tirrell Rd CR0 205 A3
Tisbury Ct W1 249 C6
Tisbury Rd SW16 182 A1
Tisdall Pl SE17 117 B2 262 D3
Tissington Ct 4 SE16 118 D2
Titan Bsns Est 3 SE8 141 C5
Titan Ct TW8 110 B1
Titchborne Row W2 237 B1
Titchfield Rd
Carshalton SM5 202 B1
Enfield EN3 7 A6
Paddington NW8 92 D6 230 C6
Titchfield Wlk SM5 202 B2
Titchwell Rd SW18 158 B3
Tite St SW3 136 D6 267 C6
Tithe Barn Cl KT2 176 B2
Tithe Barn Way UB5 84 B5
Tithe Cl Hayes UB4 83 D2
Hendon NW7 28 A2
Walton-on-T KT12 194 B3
Tithe Ct NW4 28 A2
Tithe Farm Ave HA2 63 C5
Tithe Farm Cl HA2 63 C5
Tithe Wlk NW7 28 A2
Titian Ave WD23 8 C4
Titley Cl E4 35 C5
Titmus Cl UB8 83 A1
Titmuss Ave SE28 124 B6
Titmuss St W12 112 C4
Tivendale N8 50 A6
Tiverton Ave IG5 56 C6
Tiverton Cl CR0 205 D2
Tiverton Dr SE9 167 A3
Tiverton Prim Sch N15 51 B3
Tiverton Rd
Brondesbury Pk NW6, NW10 90 D6
Edgware HA8 26 B1
Edmonton N18 33 C5
Hounslow TW3 130 A3
Ruislip HA4 62 A5
Tottenham N4, N15 51 B3
Wembley HA0 88 A5
Tiverton St SE1 117 A3 262 A6
Tiverton Way
Chessington KT9 213 D3
Edgware NW7 28 D3
Tivoli Ct SE16 119 B5
Tivoli Gdns 11 SE7 122 A2
Tivoli Rd Hornsey N8 49 D4
Hounslow TW4 129 A1
West Norwood SE27 183 A5
Toad La TW4 129 B1
Tobago St 12 E14 119 C4
Tobin Cl NW3 70 C1
Toby Ct N9 18 C4
Toby La E1 97 A3
Toby Way KT5, KT6 214 D6
Todber Ho W14 254 A6
Todd Ho 3 N2 30 B1
Todds Wlk N7 72 B6
Tokenhouse Yd EC2 242 C2
TOKYNGTON 66 D2
Tokyngton Ave HA9 66 C2
Toland Sq SW15 156 A6
Tolcairn Ct 2 DA17 125 C1
Tolcarne Dr HA5 40 B6
Tolchurch 2 W11 91 C1
Toldos Yakov Yosef sch N16 51 C1
Toley Ave HA3, HA9 44 A2
Tolhurst Dr 4 W10 91 A4
Tollbridge Cl W10 91 A3
Tollesbury Gdns IG6 57 B6
Tollet St E1 96 D3
Tollgate Dr
Dulwich SE21 161 C2
Hayes UB4 106 D6
Tollgate Ho 1 NW6 91 D5
Tollgate Prim Sch
Croydon CR0 206 C3
Newham E13 99 C3
Tollgate Rd E6 100 A2
Tollhouse Way N19 71 C6
Tollington Ct N4 72 B6
Tollington Ho 4 N19 72 A5
Tollington Pk N4 72 B6
Tollington Pl N4 72 B6
Tollington Rd N7 72 B4
Tollington Way N7 72 A5
Tolmers Sq NW1 93 C3 239 B6
Tolpaide Ho SE11 261 A3
Tolpuddle Ave 1 E13 99 C6
Tolpuddle St N1 94 C5 234 A4
Tolsford Rd E5 74 B3
Tolson Ho 4 TW7 131 A2
Tolson Rd TW7 131 A2
Tolverne Rd SW20 178 C2
TOLWORTH 214 C6
Tolworth Broadway KT6 198 D1
Tolworth Cl KT6 198 D1
Tolworth Gdns RM6 58 D4
Tolworth Girls' Sch KT6 214 B5
Tolworth Hospl KT6 214 C6
Tolworth Inf Sch KT6 198 B1
Tolworth Junc KT6 214 D6
Tolworth Jun Sch KT6 198 B1
Tolworth Par RM6 59 A4
Tolworth Park Rd KT6 214 B6
Tolworth Rd KT6 214 A6
Tolworth Rise N KT5 198 D1
Tolworth Rise S KT5 198 D1
Tolworth Sta KT5 214 D6
Tolworth Underpass KT5, KT6 214 D6
Tomahawk Gdns 4 UB5 84 D4
Tom Coombs Cl SE9 144 A1
Tom Cribb Rd SE18, SE28 123 B3
Tom Groves Cl E15 76 B3
Tom Hood Cl E15 76 B3
Tom Hood Sch E11 76 D5
Tom Jenkinson Rd 5 E16 121 A5
Tomkyns Ho SE11 261 A3
Tomline Ho SE1 252 A3
Tomlin's Gr E3 97 C4
Tomlinson Cl
5 Gunnersbury W4 110 D1
Spitalfields E2 95 D4
Tomlins Orch IG11 101 A6
Tomlin's Terr E14 97 A1
Tomlins Wlk 4 N7 72 B6
Tom Mann Cl IG11 101 C6
Tom Nolan Cl E15 98 C5
Tompion Ho EC1 241 D6
Tompion St EC1 234 D1
Tom Smith Cl SE10 142 C6
Tom Smith Ho 3 E17 54 A4
Tomson Ho SE1 263 C6
Tom Williams Ho SW6 264 C5
Tonbridge Cres HA3 44 A5
Tonbridge Hos WC1 233 A1
Tonbridge Rd KT12, KT8 195 B5
Tonbridge St WC1 94 A4 233 A1
Toneborough 16 NW8 91 D6
Tonfield Rd SM3 201 B1
Tonge Cl BR3 207 C4
Tonsley Hill SW18 157 D6
Tonsley Pl SW18 157 D6
Tonsley Rd SW18 157 D6
Tonsley St SW18 157 D6
Tonstall Rd CR4 181 A1
Tony Law Ho SE12 165 A6
Tooke Cl HA5 23 A2
Tookey Cl HA3 44 B2
Took's Ct EC4 241 A2
Tooley St SE1 117 C5 253 A3
Toorack Rd HA3 24 B1
Tooting Bec Gdns SW16 181 D6
Tooting Bec Lido SW16 181 C6
Tooting Bec Rd
Furzedown SW17 181 B6
Streatham SW16 181 C5
Tooting Bec Sta SW17 159 A1
Tooting Broadway Sta SW17 180 C5
Tooting Broadway SW17 180 D5
TOOTING GRAVENEY 180 B5
Tooting Gr SW17 180 C5
Tooting High St SW17, SW19 180 C5
Tooting Mkts SW17 180 D6
Tooting Sta SW17 180 D4
Tootswood Rd BR2, BR3 208 C5
Topaz Ct TW13 149 D1
Topaz Ho KT4 199 B1
Topaz Wlk NW2 46 D2
Topcliffe Dr BR6 227 B4
Topham Ho 8 SE10 142 A5
Topham Sq N17 33 A2
Topham St EC1 241 A6
Top House Rise E4 20 A4
Topiary Sq TW9 132 B2
Topley St SE9 143 D1
Topmast Point 23 E14 119 C4
Top Pk BR3 208 C4
Topsfield Cl N8 49 D4
Topsfield Par N8 50 A3
Topsfield Rd N8 50 A4
Topsham Rd SW17 181 A6
Tora Ct 9 IG9 21 C2
Torbay Ct 13 NW1 71 B1
Torbay Mans NW6 91 B6
Torbay Rd
Brondesbury NW6 69 B1
Harrow HA2 63 A6
Torbay St 15 NW1 71 B1
Torbitt Way IG2 57 D4
Torbridge Cl HA8 26 A3
Torbrook Cl DA5 169 A5
Torcross Dr SE23 162 C2
Torcross Rd HA4 62 C5
Tor Ct W8 245 B2
Torfell 5 E18 36 D1
Tor Gdns W8 113 C4 245 A2
Tor Gr SE28 123 C5
Tor Ho N6 49 B3
Tormead Cl SM1 217 C2
Tormount Rd SE18 145 C6
Tornay Ho
Hackney E9 74 C1
N1 233 C4
Toronto Ave E12 78 B4
Toronto Rd IG1 57 A1
Torquay Gdns IG4 55 D5
Torquay Ho 1 SM6 219 D3
Torquay St W2 91 D2
Tor Rd DA16 146 C4
Torrence Ho 6 N19 71 C6
Torrens Ct SE5 139 B2
Torrens Rd
Clapham Pk SW2 160 B6
Stratford E15 76 D2
Torrens Sq E15 76 D2

Torrens St EC1 . . . 94 D5 234 C3
Torres Sq E14 . . . 119 C1
Torre Wlk SM5 . . . 202 C1
Torrey Dr SW9 . . . 138 C3
Torriano Ave NW5 . . . 71 D3
Torriano Cotts NW5 . . . 71 C3
Torriano Jun & Inf Schs NW5 . . . 71 D3
Torriano Mews NW5 . . 71 C3
Torridge Gdns SE15 . . 140 C1
Torridge Rd CR7 . . . 204 D4
Torridon Ct HA8 . . . 10 D2
Torridon Ho NW6 . . . 91 D5
Torridon Jun & Inf Schs SE6 . . . 164 B2
Torridon Rd SE13, SE6 . . . 164 B3
Torrington Ave N12 . . . 30 B5
Torrington Cl
Claygate KT10 . . . 212 C2
North Finchley N12 . . . 30 B6
Torrington Ct
Forest Hill SE26 . . . 184 A5
Harrow HA2 . . . 63 D5
North Finchley N12 . . . 30 B6
Torrington Dr HA2 . . . 63 D5
Torrington Gdns
Friern Barnet N11 . . . 31 C4
Wembley UB6 . . . 65 C1
Torrington Gr N12 . . . 30 C5
Torrington Pk N12 . . . 30 B6
Torrington Pl
Bloomsbury WC1 . . . 93 D2 239 C4
St George in t East E1 . . . 118 A5
Torrington Rd
Claygate KT10 . . . 212 C2
Dagenham RM8 . . . 59 B1
Ruislip HA4 . . . 62 A5
Wanstead E18 . . . 55 A6
Wembley UB6 . . . 87 C6
Torrington Sq
Bloomsbury WC1 . . . 93 D3 239 D5
Thornton Heath CR0 . . 205 B2
Torrington Way SM4 . . . 201 C3
Torr Rd SE20 . . . 184 D3
Tortington Ho 1 SE15 . . . 140 B5
Torver Rd HA1 . . . 42 C5
Torver Way BR6 . . . 227 B5
Torwood Rd SW15 . . . 156 A6
Totham Lo SW20 . . . 178 B2
Tothill Ho SW1 . . . 259 D4
Tothill St SW1 . . . 115 D4 249 D1
Totland Ho SW18 . . . 157 D5
Totnes Rd DA16 . . . 146 C5
Totnes Villas N11 . . . 31 C5
Totnes Wlk N2 . . . 48 B5
Tottan Terr E1 . . . 96 D1
Tottenhall Inf Sch N13 . . . 32 C4
Tottenhall 5 NW1 . . . 71 A1
Tottenhall Rd N13 . . . 32 D4
TOTTENHAM . . . 33 D1
Tottenham Court Rd W1 . . . 93 C2 239 B4
Tottenham Court Road Sta W1 . . . 93 D1 239 D2
Tottenham Gn E 3 N15 . . . 51 D5
Tottenham Gn E South Side 4 N15 . . . 51 D5
TOTTENHAM HALE . . . 52 A6
Tottenham Hale N15 . . 52 A5
Tottenham Hale Ret Pk N15 . . . 52 A5
Tottenham Hale Sta N17 . . . 52 B6
Tottenham La N8 . . . 50 B4
Tottenham Mews W1 . . . 239 B4
Tottenham Rd N1 . . . 73 C2
Tottenham St W1 . . . 93 C2 239 B4
Totterdown St SW17 . . . 180 D5
TOTTERIDGE . . . 13 C3
Totteridge Comm N20 . . . 12 C3
Totteridge Gn N20 . . . 13 C2
Totteridge Ho
Barnet N20 . . . 13 B3
Battersea SW11 . . . 136 B3
Totteridge La N20 . . . 13 D3
Totteridge Pk N20 . . . 12 D3
Totteridge Rd EN3 . . . 6 D6
Totteridge Village N20 . . . 13 B3
Totteridge & Whetstone Sta N20 . . . 14 A2
Totternhoe Cl HA3 . . . 43 C4
Totton Rd CR7 . . . 204 C6
Toucan Cl NW10 . . . 88 C4
Touchard Ho N1 . . . 235 D1
Toulmin St SE1 . . . 117 A4 252 A1
Toulon St SE5 . . . 139 A5
Toulouse Ct 2 SE16 . . . 118 B1
Tounson Ct SW1 . . . 259 D3
Tournay Rd SW6 . . . 135 B5 264 D4
Toussaint Wlk 18 SE16 . . . 118 A3
Tovil Cl SE20 . . . 184 B1
Tovy Ho 6 SE1 . . . 118 A1
Towcester Rd E3 . . . 98 A3
Tower 42* EC2 . . . 95 C1 243 A2
Tower Bldgs 22 E1 . . . 118 B5
Tower Br App E1, EC3 . . . 253 C5
Tower Bridge Bsns Complex SE16 . . . 118 B3
Tower Bridge Bsns Sq SE16 . . . 118 B2
Tower Bridge* E1, EC3, SE1 . . . 117 D5 253 C4
Tower Bridge Mews HA0 . . . 64 D4
Tower Bridge Piazza SE1 . . . 253 C3
Tower Bridge Prim Sch SE1 . . . 117 D4 253 C2
Tower Bridge Rd SE1 . . . 117 C4 253 A1
Tower Bridge Sq SE1 . . . 253 C2
Tower Bridge Wharf E1 . . . 118 A5
Tower Cl
Hampstead NW3 . . . 70 B3
Orpington BR6 . . . 227 D5
Penge SE20 . . . 184 B3
Tower Ct
Brockley SE4 . . . 141 A1
Stamford Hill E5 . . . 51 D2
St Giles WC2 . . . 240 A1
St John's Wood NW8 . 230 B4
Tower Gardens Rd N17 . . . 33 B2
Towergate Cl UB8 . . . 60 A3
Towergate Ho 35 E3 . . . 97 B5
Towergate SE1 . . . 263 A4
Tower Gateway Sta EC3 . . . 117 D6 253 C6
Tower Gdns KT10 . . . 213 A1
Tower Gr KT13 . . . 193 C1
TOWER HAMLETS . . . 97 B2
Tower Hamlets Coll
Poplar E14 . . . 97 D1
Poplar E14 . . . 119 D6
Stepney E1 . . . 96 D1
Tower Hamlets Rd
Forest Gate E7 . . . 76 D3
Walthamstow E17 . . . 53 C6
Tower Hill EC3 . . . 117 D6 253 D5
Tower Hill Sta EC3 . . . 117 D6 253 C6
Tower La HA9 . . . 65 D5
Tower Mans SE1 . . . 263 C5
Tower Mews
Hackney E5 . . . 75 A3
Walthamstow E17 . . . 53 C5
Tower Millennium Pier EC3 . . . 117 C5 253 B4
Tower Mill Rd 1 SE15 . . . 139 C5
Tower Pl E EC3 . . . 253 B5
Tower Pl W EC3 . . . 253 B5
Tower Rd DA7 . . . 147 D1
Orpington BR6 . . . 227 D5
Twickenham TW1, TW2 . . . 152 D1
Willesden NW10 . . . 68 A1
Tower Rise TW9 . . . 132 A2
Tower Royal EC4 . . . 252 C6
Towers Ave UB10 . . . 83 A4
Towers Bsns Pk HA9 . . 66 D4
Towers Ct UB10 . . . 83 A4
Towers Pl TW10 . . . 154 A6
Towers Rd
Pinner HA5 . . . 23 A2
Southall UB1 . . . 85 C3
Towers The
Dartmouth Pk NW5 . . . 71 B5
1 Richmond TW9 . . . 132 B1
Tower St WC2 . . . 240 A1
Tower Terr
Brockley SE4 . . . 141 A1
Wood Green N22 . . . 32 B1
Tower The* EC3 . . . 117 D6 253 C5
Tower View
Bushey WD23 . . . 8 C4
Croydon CR0 . . . 207 A2
Towerview SE13 . . . 163 C6
Tower Wharf SE1 . . . 253 C2
Tower Wlk SE1 . . . 263 A4
Towfield Ct TW13 . . . 151 B2
Towfield Rd TW13 . . . 151 B2
Towncourt Cres BR5 . . . 211 B5
Towncourt La BR5 . . . 211 B2
Towncourt Path N4 . . . 51 A1
Townend Ct 6 BR1 . . 186 D2
Towney Mead Ct UB5 . . . 85 B5
Towney Mead UB5 . . . 85 B5
Townfield Rd UB3 . . . 105 D5
Townfield Sq UB3 . . . 105 D6
Town Field Way TW7 . . . 131 A3
Town Hall Approach Rd N15 . . . 51 D5
Townhall Ave 3 W4 . . . 111 B1
Town Hall Rd SW11 . . 136 D2
Townholm Cres W7 . . 108 D3
Town Hos EC1 . . . 241 D5
Town La TW19 . . . 148 A2
Townley Ct E15 . . . 76 D2
Townley Gram Sch for Girls DA6 . . . 169 B6
Townley Rd DA6 . . . 169 B6
Dulwich Village SE22 . . . 161 C6
Townley St SE17 . . . 117 B1 262 C2
Townmead Bsns Ctr SW6 . . . 136 A2
Town Meadow TW8 . . 131 D5
Townmead Rd
Richmond TW9 . . . 132 D3
Sands End SW6 . . . 136 A3
Town Quay IG11 . . . 100 D6
Town Quay Wharf IG11 . . . 100 D6
Town Rd N9 . . . 18 B2
Townsend Ave N14 . . . 31 D6
Townsend Ct NW9 . . . 45 B2
Townsend Ho 14 SE1 . . . 118 A2
Townsend Ind Est NW10 . . . 89 A5
Townsend La NW9 . . . 45 B3
Townsend Mews 3 SW18 . . . 158 A2
Townsend Prim Sch SE17 . . . 117 C2 263 A4
Townsend Rd
Ashford TW15 . . . 170 A5
Southall UB1 . . . 107 A5
South Tottenham N15 . . 51 D4
Townsend St SE1, SE17 . . . 117 C2 263 A4
Townsend Way HA6 . . . 22 A3
Townsend Yd N6 . . . 49 B1
Townshend Cl DA14 . . . 190 C4
Townshend Ct NW8 . . 230 B4
Townshend Est NW8 . . . 92 C5 230 A4
Townshend Ho 16 SE18 . . . 122 B2
Townshend Rd
Chislehurst BR7 . . . 188 D5
Primrose Hill NW8 . . . 92 C6 230 A5
Richmond TW9 . . . 132 B1
Townshend Terr TW9 . . . 132 B1
Towns Ho 4 SW4 . . . 137 D2
Townson Ave UB5 . . . 84 B5
Townson Way UB5 . . . 84 A5
Town The EN2 . . . 5 B2
Town Tree Rd TW15 . . . 170 C5
Towpath TW17 . . . 192 B1
Towpath Way CR0 . . . 205 D4
Towpath Wlk E9 . . . 75 B3
Towton Rd SE27 . . . 161 A2
Toxteth Ho N4 . . . 51 A2
Toynbec Cl BR7 . . . 188 D6
Toynbee Rd SW19, SW20 . . . 179 A2
Toynbee St E1 . . . 95 D2 243 C3
Toyne Way N6 . . . 48 D3
Tracey Ave NW2 . . . 68 C3
Tracy Ct HA7 . . . 25 C3
Tracy Ho 15 E3 . . . 97 B4
Trade Cl N13 . . . 32 C6
Trader Rd E6 . . . 100 D1
Tradescant Ho 15 E9 . . 74 C1
Tradescant Rd SW8 . . . 138 A5 270 B3
Trade Twr 8 SW11 . . . 136 A2
Trade Winds Ct 1 E1 . . . 118 A5
Trading Estate Rd NW10 . . . 89 A3
Traemore Ct SW16 . . . 160 C1
Trafalgar Ave
North Cheam KT4, SM3, SM4 . . . 200 D1
SE15 . . . 139 D6
Tottenham N17 . . . 33 C4
Trafalgar Bsns Ctr IG11 . . . 101 D3
Trafalgar Cl 1 SE16 . . . 119 A2
Trafalgar Ct
Barking E6 . . . 100 C6
Hounslow TW3 . . . 129 B2
West Barnes KT3 . . . 200 B6
Trafalgar Gdns
Stepney E1 . . . 96 D2
W8 . . . 255 D6
Trafalgar Gr SE10 . . . 142 B6
Trafalgar Ho
Barking IG11 . . . 102 B4
SE17 . . . 262 B2
Trafalgar Inf Sch TW2 . . . 152 B2
Trafalgar Jun Sch TW2 . . . 152 B2
Trafalgar Mews E9 . . . 75 B2
Trafalgar Pl
Edmonton N18 . . . 34 A5
Wanstead E11 . . . 55 A5
Trafalgar Point 2 N1 . . . 73 B1
Trafalgar Rd
Greenwich SE10 . . . 120 C1
Merton SW19 . . . 180 A3
Twickenham TW2 . . . 152 B2
Trafalgar Sq* SW1 . . . 115 D5 249 D4
Trafalgar St SE17 . . . 117 B1 262 D2
Trafalgar Terr HA1 . . . 42 C1
Trafalgar Trad Est EN3 . . . 7 A1
Trafalgar Way
Canary Wharf E14 . . . 120 A5
Croydon CR0 . . . 220 C6
Trafford Cl E15 . . . 75 D3
Trafford Ho N1 . . . 235 D4
Trafford Rd CR7 . . . 204 B4
Trafford Villas CR0 . . . 204 B4
Tragail SW15 . . . 157 A6
Traherne Lo 5 TW11 . . . 174 D5
Trahorn Cl E1 . . . 96 B3
Traitors Gate* EC3 . . . 117 D5 253 C4
Tralee Ct 31 SE16 . . . 118 B1
Tramsheds Ind Est The CR0, CR4 . . . 203 D2
Tramway Ave
Ponders End N9 . . . 18 C4
Stratford E15 . . . 76 B1
Tramway Cl SE20 . . . 184 C2
Tramway Path CR4 . . . 202 C5
Trance Way W3 . . . 110 C3
Tranmere Ct 5 SM2 . . . 218 A1
Tranmere Ho 7 N7 . . . 72 C3
Tranmere Rd
Edmonton N9 . . . 17 D4
Twickenham TW2 . . . 151 D4
Wandsworth SW17, SW18 . . . 158 A2
Tranquil Pas SE3 . . . 142 D3
Tranquil Vale SE3 . . . 142 C3
Transept St NW1 . . . 237 B3
Transmere Cl BR5 . . . 211 A3
Transmere Rd BR5 . . . 211 A3
Transom Cl SE16 . . . 119 A2
Transom Sq E14 . . . 119 D1
Transport Ave TW8 . . 131 B6
Tranton Rd SE16 . . . 118 B3
Trappes Ho 2 SE16 . . 118 B2
Traps La KT2, KT3 . . . 177 C2
Travellers Way TW5 . . . 128 C3
Travers Cl E17 . . . 34 D2
Travers Ho 6 SE10 . . . 142 B6
Travers Rd N7 . . . 72 C5
Travis Ho SE10 . . . 142 A4
Treacy Cl WD23 . . . 8 A2
Treadgold Ho 7 W11 . . . 112 D6
Treadgold St W11 . . . 112 D6
Treadway St E2 . . . 96 B5
Treasury Bldgs SW1 250 A2
Treasury Cl SM6 . . . 219 D3
Treaty Ctr TW3 . . . 129 D2
Treaty St N1 . . . 94 B6 233 C5
Trebeck St W1 . . . 248 C3
Treborough Ho W1 . 238 A4
Trebovir Rd SW5 . . . 113 C2 255 B3
Treby St E3 . . . 97 B3
Trecastle Way 2 N7 . . 71 D4
Tredegar Mews 10 E3 . . . 97 B4
Tredegar Rd Bow E3 . . . 97 B5
Wood Green N11 . . . 31 D3
Tredegar Sq E3 . . . 97 B4
Tredegar Terr E3 . . . 97 B4
Trederwen Rd E8 . . . 96 A6
Tredown Rd SE26 . . . 184 C5
Tredwell Cl BR2 . . . 210 A5
Tredwell Rd SE27 . . . 182 D6
Tree Cl TW10 . . . 153 D3
Treehouse Sch N10 . . . 49 A5
Treen Ave SW13 . . . 133 D2
Tree Rd E16 . . . 99 C1
Trees The N16 . . . 51 B2
Treetops Cl SE2 . . . 125 A1
Treetops Ct CR7 . . . 205 A4
Treetops View IG10 . . . 21 D4
Tree Tops 1 IG8 . . . 37 A6
Treeview Cl SE19 . . . 183 C2
Treewall Gdns BR1 . . . 187 B6
Trefgarne Rd RM10 . . . 81 C6
Trefil Wlk N7 . . . 72 A4
Trefoil Ho DA18 . . . 125 A4
Trefoil Rd SW18 . . . 158 A6
Trefusis Ct TW5 . . . 128 B4
Tregaron Ave N8 . . . 50 A3
Tregaron Gdns KT3 . . 199 C5
Tregarvon Rd SW11 . . 137 A1
Tregenna Ave HA2 . . . 63 C4
Tregenna Cl 1 N14 . . . 15 C6
Tregenna Ct HA2 . . . 63 C4
Tregony Rd BR6 . . . 227 D4
Trego Rd E9 . . . 75 C1
Tregothnan Rd SW9 . . . 138 A2
Tregunter Rd SW10 . . . 114 A1 256 A1
Treherne Ct
Brixton SW9 . . . 138 D4
Upper Tooting SW17 . . . 181 A6
Trehern Rd 12 SW14 . . . 133 B2
Trehurst St E5 . . . 75 A3
Trelawney Cl E17 . . . 53 D5
Trelawney Est E9 . . . 74 C2
Trelawney Ho SE1 . . . 252 A2
Trelawn Rd
Leyton E10 . . . 76 A5
Tulse Hill SW2 . . . 160 C6
Trellis Ho SW19 . . . 180 A3
Trellis Sq 1 E3 . . . 97 B4
Treloar Gdns SE19 . . . 183 B4
Tremadoc Rd SW4 . . . 137 D1
Tremaine Cl SE4 . . . 141 C3
Tremaine Rd SE20 . . . 184 B1
Trematon Ho SE11 . . . 261 B2
Trematon Pl TW11 . . . 175 C3
Tremlett Gr N19 . . . 71 C5
Tremlett Mews N19 . . . 71 C5
Trenance Gdns IG3 . . . 80 A5
Trenchard Ave HA4 . . . 62 B4
Trenchard Cl
Grahame Pk NW9 . . . 27 C2
Stanmore HA7 . . . 25 B4
Trenchard Ct SM4 . . . 201 C3
Trenchard St SE10 . . . 120 B1
Trenchold St SW8 . . . 138 A6 270 A5
Trend Ct W13 . . . 109 B5
Trendell Ho 8 E14 . . . 97 C1
Trenholme Cl 6 SE20 . . . 184 B3
Trenholme Rd SE20 . . 184 B3
Trenholme Terr SE20 . . . 184 B3
Trenmar Gdns NW10 . . 90 B4
Trent Ave W5 . . . 109 C3
Trent CE Prim Sch EN4 . . . 2 D1
Trent Ctry Pk* EN4 . . . 3 A3
Trent Ct
1 South Croydon CR2 . . . 221 A3
Wanstead E11 . . . 55 A4
Trent Gdns N14 . . . 15 B5
Trentham Ct W3 . . . 89 B2
Trentham Lo 8 EN1 . . . 17 C6
Trentham St SW18 . . . 157 C3
Trent Ho
4 Kingston u T KT2 . . . 175 D2
Nunhead SE15 . . . 140 C1
Trent Rd
Buckhurst Hill IG9 . . . 21 B3
Clapham Pk SW2 . . . 160 B6
Trent Way Hayes UB4 . . 83 C4
North Cheam KT4 . . . 216 C5
Trentwood Side EN2 . . . 4 B2
Treport St SW18 . . . 157 D4
Tresco Cl BR1 . . . 186 C4
Trescoe Gdns HA2 . . . 41 A2
Tresco Gdns IG3 . . . 80 A6
Tresco Ho SE11 . . . 261 A2
Tresco Rd SE15 . . . 140 B1
Tresham Cres NW8 . . . 92 C3 237 A6
Tresham Rd IG11 . . . 79 D1
Tresham Wlk E9 . . . 74 C3
Tresidder Ho 10 SW4 . . . 159 D4
Tresilian Ave N21 . . . 16 B6
Tressel Cl 20 N1 . . . 72 D1
Tressillian Cres SE4 . . . 141 C2
Tressillian Rd SE4 . . . 141 C2
Trestis Cl UB4 . . . 84 D2
Treswell Rd RM9 . . . 103 A6
Tretawn Gdns NW7 . . . 11 C1
Tretawn Pk NW7 . . . 27 C6
Trevallyn Lo 1 KT2 . . 176 D2
Trevanion Rd W14 . . 254 B2
Treve Ave HA1 . . . 42 B2
Trevelyan Ave E12 . . . 78 B4
Trevelyan Cres HA3 . . . 43 D2
Trevelyan Ct KT3 . . . 199 D2
Trevelyan Gdns NW10 . . . 90 C6
Trevelyan Ho
16 Globe Town E2 . . . 96 D4
SE5 . . . 138 D5
6 Twickenham TW1 . . . 153 C5
Trevelyan Rd
Leyton E15 . . . 76 D4
Upper Tooting SW17 . . . 180 D4
Trevenna Ho 13 SE23 . . . 162 D1
Trevera Ct EN3 . . . 19 A6
Treveris St SE1 . . . 251 D3
Treversh Ct 7 BR1 . . 186 D2
Treverton St W10 . . . 90 D3
Treverton Twr W10 . . . 90 D2
Treves Cl N21 . . . 16 B6
Treves Ho E1 . . . 96 A3
Treville St SW15 . . . 156 B4
Treviso Rd SE23 . . . 163 A2
Trevithick Cl TW14 . . 149 D3
Trevithick Ho
13 Bermondsey SE16 . . . 118 B2
3 Gospel Oak NW5 . . . 71 B4
SW8 . . . 269 C2
Trevithick St SE8 . . . 141 C6
Trevone Gdns HA5 . . . 41 A3
Trevor Cl Harrow HA3 . . 24 D3
Hayes BR2 . . . 209 A2
Isleworth TW7 . . . 152 D6
New Barnet EN4 . . . 14 B5
Northolt UB5 . . . 84 C5
Trevor Cres HA4 . . . 61 D4
Trevor Gdns
Hendon HA8 . . . 27 B2
Northolt UB5 . . . 84 C5
Ruislip HA4 . . . 62 A4
Trevor Pl SW7 . . . 114 C4 247 B1
Trevor Rd
Hayes UB3 . . . 105 C4
Hendon HA8 . . . 27 B2
Wimbledon SW19 . . . 179 A3
Woodford IG8 . . . 37 A3
Trevor Roberts Tutorial Coll NW8 . . . 70 B1
Trevor Sq SW7 . . . 114 C4 247 B1
Trevor St SW7 . . . 114 C4 247 B1
Trevose Ho SE11 . . . 260 D2
Trevose Rd E17 . . . 36 B2
Trewenna Dr KT9 . . . 213 D3
Trewince Rd SW20 . . . 178 C2
Trewint St SW18 . . . 158 A2
Trewsbury Ho 2 SE2 . . . 124 D4
Trewsbury Rd SE26 . . 184 D5
Triandra Way UB4 . . . 84 D2
Triangle Ct 4 E16 . . . 99 C2
Triangle Ctr UB1 . . . 108 B5
Triangle Ct SE1 . . . 252 B3
Triangle Est The SE11 . . . 261 A1
Triangle Ho SE1 . . . 253 C2
Triangle Pl SW4 . . . 137 D1
Triangle Rd 7 E8 . . . 96 B6
Triangle The
Barking IG11 . . . 79 A2
Crouch End N19 . . . 49 D2
EC1 . . . 241 D6
Hackney E8 . . . 96 B6
Kingston u T KT3 . . . 177 A1
Tribune Ct 16 NW9 . . . 46 A5
Tricorn Ho SE28 . . . 123 B5
Trident Bsns Ctr SW17 . . . 180 D5
Trident Gdns 6 UB5 . . 84 D4
Trident Ho
14 South Bromley E14 . . . 98 A1
Woolwich SE28 . . . 123 B5
Trident St SE16 . . . 118 D2

Trident Way UB2 . . . 106 B3
Trieste Ct SW12 . . . 158 D3
Trig La EC4 . . . 252 A6
Trigon Rd
SW8 . . . 138 B5 270 D4
Trilby Rd SE23 . . . 162 D2
Trillington Ho W12 . . . 112 A5
Trillo Ct IG1 . . . 57 C2
Trimdon NW1 . . . 232 B5
Trimmer Ct TW7 . . . 130 D2
Trimmer Wlk 11
TW8 . . . 132 A6
Trim St SE8 . . . 141 B6
Trinder Gdns N19 . . . 50 A1
Trinder Mews 10
TW11 . . . 175 A5
Trinder Rd
Barnet EN5 . . . 12 C6
Finsbury Pk N4, N19 . . . 50 A1
Tring Ave Ealing W5 . . . 110 B5
Southall UB1 . . . 85 B1
Wembley HA9 . . . 66 C2
Tring Cl IG2 . . . 57 B4
Tring Ct TW1 . . . 175 A6
Trinidad Ho 17 E14 . . . 119 B6
Trinidad St E14 . . . 119 B6
Trinity Ave
East Finchley N2 . . . 48 B6
Enfield EN1 . . . 17 D5
Trinity Church Rd
SW13 . . . 134 B6
Trinity Church Sq
SE1 . . . 117 A3 262 B6
Trinity Cl
3 Clapham SW4 . . . 137 C1
Hounslow TW4 . . . 129 A1
Keston Mark BR2 . . . 210 A1
Lewisham SE13 . . . 142 B1
Leyton E11 . . . 76 C6
Trinity Cotts TW9 . . . 132 B2
Trinity Cres SW17 . . . 159 A2
Trinity Ct
8 Chingford E4 . . . 20 A2
Edmonton N18 . . . 33 D4
Eltham SE9 . . . 166 D5
Finsbury WC1 . . . 240 C6
Forest Hill SE23 . . . 162 C1
Greenwich SE7 . . . 121 D2
2 Hoxton N1 . . . 95 C6
Rotherhithe SE16 . . . 119 A4
Southgate N21 . . . 16 D3
Thornton Heath
SE25 . . . 205 C3
Twickenham TW2 . . . 152 C2
Wallington SM6 . . . 219 C1
Willesden NW2 . . . 68 C3
Wimbledon SW19 . . . 179 C4
Trinity Dr UB8 . . . 83 A1
Trinity Gdns E16 . . . 98 D2
Stockwell SW2, SW9 . . 138 B1
11 Wanstead E18 . . . 55 B6
Trinity Gn E1 . . . 96 C2
Trinity Gr 8 SE10 . . . 142 A4
Trinity Homes 14
SW2 . . . 138 B1
Trinity Ho SE1 . . . 262 B6
5 Walthamstow E17 . . 53 D6
Trinity Mews
Penge SE20 . . . 184 B2
SE9 . . . 167 B5
Wandsworth SW18 . . . 157 C3
Trinity Par TW3 . . . 129 D2
Trinity Pl
Bexleyheath DA6 . . . 147 B1
City of London EC3 . . 253 C5
Trinity RC High Sch
(Lower) IG8 . . . 37 A6
Trinity RC High Sch
(Upper Sch) IG8 . . . 36 D6
Trinity RC High Sch
(Upper) IG8 . . . 37 A6
Trinity Rd
East Finchley N2 . . . 48 B6
Ilford IG6 . . . 57 A6
Richmond TW9 . . . 132 B2
Southall UB1 . . . 107 A5
Wandsworth SW17,
SW18 . . . 158 C4
Wimbledon SW19 . . . 179 C4
Wood Green N22 . . . 32 A3
Wood Green N22 . . . 32 B2
Trinity Rise SE24,
SW2 . . . 160 D4
Trinity St Mary's CE
Prim Sch SW12 . . . 159 A3
Trinity Sch
Croydon CR0 . . . 222 C6
Dagenham RM10 . . . 81 C4
Trinity Sq
EC3 . . . 117 C6 253 B6
Trinity St Enfield EN2 . . . 5 A3
9 Newham E16 . . . 99 A2
SE1 . . . 117 B3 262 C6
Trinity Terr IG9 . . . 21 B4
Trinity Way
East Acton W3 . . . 111 D6
Walthamstow E4 . . . 35 B4
Trio Pl SE1 . . . 117 A4 252 B1
Triscott Ho UB3 . . . 106 A5
Tristan Ct 34 SE8 . . . 141 B6
Tristan Sq SE3 . . . 142 C2
Tristram Cl E17 . . . 54 B6
Tristram Dr N9 . . . 18 A1
Tristram Rd BR1 . . . 186 D6
Triton Ct EC2 . . . 242 D5
Woodford IG9 . . . 21 A2
Triton Ho 2 E14 . . . 119 D2
Triton Sq NW1 . . . 239 A6
Tritton Ave CR0 . . . 220 A4
Tritton Ho N21 . . . 17 B5
Tritton Rd SE21,
SE27 . . . 161 B1
Triumph Cl UB7 . . . 127 A4
Triumph Ho IG11 . . . 102 A4
Triumph Rd E6 . . . 100 B1
Triumph Trad Est
N17 . . . 34 A4
Trocette Mans SE1 . . 263 B6
Trojan Ct
Brondesbury NW6 . . . 69 A1
9 Ealing W7 . . . 109 A5
Trojan Ind Est NW10 . . 67 D2
Trojan Way CR0 . . . 220 B5
Troon Cl
31 Bermondsey
SE16 . . . 118 B1
Erith SE28 . . . 102 D1
Troon Ct UB1 . . . 108 A6
Troon Ho 9 E14 . . . 97 A1
Troon St E1 . . . 97 A1
Tropical Ct 2 W10 . . . 90 D4
Trosley Rd DA17 . . . 147 C6
Trossachs Rd SE22 . . . 161 C6
Trothy Rd SE1 . . . 118 A2
Trotman Ho 1
SE14 . . . 140 C4
Trott Rd N10 . . . 31 A3
Trott St
SW11 . . . 136 C4 267 A1
Trotwood Ho 3
SE16 . . . 118 B4
Troubridge Ct 12
W4 . . . 111 A1
Troughton Rd SE7 . . . 121 B1
Troutbeck NW1 . . . 231 D1
Troutbeck Rd SE14 . . . 141 A4
Trouville Rd SW4 . . . 159 C5
Trowbridge Rd E9 . . . 75 B2
Trower Ho 5 E9 . . . 75 A2
Trowlock Ave TW11 . . 175 C4
Trowlock Island
TW11 . . . 175 D4
Trowlock Way
TW11 . . . 175 D4
Troy Ct W8 . . . 255 A6
5 Woolwich SE18 . . . 122 D2
Troyes Ho NW3 . . . 70 D3
Troy Rd SE19 . . . 183 B4
Troy Town Flats
SE15 . . . 140 A2
Troy Town SE15 . . . 140 A2
Trubshaw Rd UB2 . . . 107 D3
Trulock Ct N17 . . . 34 A3
Trulock Rd N17 . . . 34 A3
Truman Cl 2 HA8 . . . 27 A3
Truman's Rd 24 N16 . . . 73 C3
Trumpers Way W7 . . . 108 D3
Trumpeters Inn
TW9 . . . 153 C6
Trumpington Rd E7 . . . 76 D4
Trump St EC2 . . . 242 B1
Trundlers Way WD23 . . . 8 C3
Trundle St SE1 . . . 252 A2
Trundley's Rd SE8 . . . 118 D1
Trundleys Rd SE8 . . . 141 A6
Trundley's Terr SE8 . . 118 D2
Truro Ct 2 N8 . . . 49 D4
Truro Gdns IG1 . . . 56 A2
Truro Ho
25 Paddington W2 . . . 91 C2
Pinner HA5 . . . 23 B2
Truro Rd
Walthamstow E17 . . . 53 B5
Wood Green N22 . . . 32 B3
Truro St NW5 . . . 71 A2
Truro Way UB4 . . . 83 C4
Truscott Ho 3 CR7 . . . 204 C3
Trusedale Rd E6 . . . 100 B1
Truslove Rd SE27 . . . 182 D5
Trussley Rd W6 . . . 112 C3
Trust Wlk SE21 . . . 160 D3
Tryfan Cl IG4 . . . 55 D4
Tryon Cres E9 . . . 96 C6
Tryon St
SW3 . . . 114 D1 257 C2
Trystings Cl KT10 . . . 213 A2
Tuam Rd SE18 . . . 145 B6
Tubbenden Cl BR6 . . . 227 C5
Tubbenden Dr BR6 . . . 227 B4
Tubbenden Jun & Inf
Schs BR6 . . . 227 B4
Tubbenden La BR6 . . . 227 C5
Tubbenden La S
BR6 . . . 227 B3
Tubbs Rd NW10 . . . 89 D5
Tudor Ave
Hampton TW12 . . . 173 C3
North Cheam KT4 . . . 216 B4
Tudor Cl
Ashford TW15 . . . 170 A6
BR7 . . . 188 B2
Cheam SM3 . . . 217 A2
Chessington KT9 . . . 214 A3
Crouch End N6 . . . 49 C2
Hampstead NW3 . . . 70 C2
Hampton TW12 . . . 174 A5
Hendon NW7 . . . 28 A4
Pinner HA5 . . . 40 A4
Tulse Hill SW2 . . . 160 B5
Wallington SM6 . . . 219 C1
Welsh Harp NW9 . . . 67 A6
Woodford IG8 . . . 37 B5
Tudor Coll WC1 . . . 233 A1
Tudor Court N HA9 . . . 66 C3
Tudor Court S HA9 . . . 66 C3
Tudor Cres EN2 . . . 5 A4
Tudor Ct 2 Barnet EN5 . . 1 B1
3 Ealing W13 . . . 87 C1
Feltham TW13 . . . 172 C6
Kingsland N1 . . . 73 C2
5 Rotherhithe
SE16 . . . 118 D5
Sidcup DA14 . . . 168 A1
South Acton W5 . . . 110 C4
4 Stanwell TW19 . . . 148 A5
Teddington TW11 . . . 174 D4
Walthamstow E17 . . . 53 B2
Tudor Dr
Kingston u T KT2 . . . 176 A5
Walton-on-T KT12 . . . 194 D1
West Barnes SM4 . . . 201 A3
Tudor Ent Pk HA3 . . . 42 B6
Tudor Est NW10 . . . 88 D5
Tudor Gables NW7 . . . 27 D6
Tudor Gdns Acton W3 . . 88 C1
Harrow HA3 . . . 24 B1
Mortlake SW14 . . . 133 C2
Twickenham TW1 . . . 152 D3
Welsh Harp NW9 . . . 67 A6
West Wickham BR4 . . . 224 A5
Tudor Gr E9 . . . 74 C1
Tudor Ho
Brook Green W14 . . . 112 D2
Feltham TW13 . . . 172 C6
34 Hackney E9 . . . 74 C1
Mitcham CR4 . . . 181 A2
6 Muswell Hill N10 . . . 31 A3
Queensbury NW9 . . . 44 C5
Tolworth KT6 . . . 198 C1
Tudor Lo 4 N12 . . . 29 D5
Tudor Mews
Walthamstow E17 . . . 53 B5
2 Willesden NW10 . . . 68 A2
Tudor Par
Dagenham RM6 . . . 58 D2
SE9 . . . 144 A1
Tudor Pl SW19 . . . 180 C3
Tudor Prim Sch
Finchley N3 . . . 30 A2
Southall UB1 . . . 107 A6
Tudor Rd
Ashford TW15 . . . 171 B4
Barking IG11 . . . 101 D6
Barnet EN5 . . . 1 D2
Beckenham BR3 . . . 208 A6
Chingford E4 . . . 35 D4
Croydon SE25 . . . 206 B4
Hackney E9 . . . 96 B6
Hampton TW12 . . . 173 C3
Harrow HA3 . . . 24 B1
Hayes UB3 . . . 83 B1
Isleworth TW3 . . . 130 B1
Kingston u T KT2 . . . 176 C3
Newham E6 . . . 99 C6
Penge SE19 . . . 183 D3
Pinner HA5 . . . 22 C1
Ponders End N9 . . . 18 C4
Southall UB1 . . . 107 A6
Tudor Sq UB3 . . . 83 B2
Tudor St
EC4 . . . 116 C6 251 B6
Tudors The 2 BR3 . . . 185 D1
Tudor Way BR5 . . . 211 B3
Hillingdon UB10 . . . 60 C2
Osidge N14 . . . 15 D3
South Acton W3 . . . 110 C4
Tudor Well Cl HA7 . . . 25 B5
Tudor Wlk DA5 . . . 169 A5
Tudway Rd SE3, SE9 . . 143 C1
Tufnell Ct 19 E3 . . . 97 B6
Tufnell Mans 7 N7 . . . 71 D4
TUFNELL PARK . . . 71 D4
Tufnell Park Mans 2
N7 . . . 72 A5
Tufnell Park Prim Sch
N7 . . . 71 D4
Tufnell Park Rd N19,
N7 . . . 71 D4
Tufnell Park Sta N19 . . 71 C4
Tufton Ct SW1 . . . 260 A5
Tufton Gdns KT8 . . . 173 D1
Tufton Rd E4 . . . 35 C6
Tufton St
SW1 . . . 116 A3 260 A5
Tugboat St SE28 . . . 123 C4
Tugela Rd CR0 . . . 205 B3
Tugela St SE6 . . . 163 B2
Tugmutton Cl BR6 . . . 226 D4
Tuke Sch SE15 . . . 140 B4
Tulip Cl Croydon CR0 . . 206 D1
Hampton TW12 . . . 173 B4
5 Newham E6 . . . 100 B2
Southall UB2 . . . 108 A4
Tulip Ct 1 HA5 . . . 40 C6
Tulip Gdns
Chingford E4 . . . 20 B1
Ilford IG1 . . . 78 D2
Tullis Ho 12 E9 . . . 74 C1
Tull St CR4 . . . 202 D2
Tulse Cl BR3 . . . 208 A6
TULSE HILL . . . 160 D4
Tulse Hill Sta SE27 . . 160 D2
Tulse Hill
Tulse Hill SW2 . . . 160 C4
Tulse Hill SW27 . . . 160 D2
Tulse Ho SW2 . . . 160 C5
Tulsemere Rd SE21,
SE27 . . . 161 A2
Tumbling Bay KT12 . . 194 A3
Tummons Gdns
SE25 . . . 183 C1
Tump Ho SE28 . . . 123 C5
Tunbridge Ct 1
SE26 . . . 162 A1
Tunbridge Ho EC1 . . . 234 C2
Tuncombe Rd N18 . . . 33 C6
Tunis Rd W12 . . . 112 B5
Tunley Gn 12 E14 . . . 97 B2
Tunley Rd
Dagenham NW10 . . . 89 C6
Upper Tooting SW12,
SW17 . . . 159 A2
Tunmarsh La E13 . . . 99 C4
Tunnan Leys E6 . . . 100 C1
Tunnel Avenue Trad Est
SE10 . . . 120 B4
Tunnel Gdns N11 . . . 31 C3
Tunnel Link Rd
TW6 . . . 148 C5
Tunnel Rd E TW6 . . . 126 D3
Tunnel Rd SE16 . . . 118 C4
Tunnel Rd W TW6 . . . 126 D4
Tunstall Cl BR6 . . . 227 C4
Tunstall Ct 14 TW9 . . . 132 B4
Tunstall Rd
Croydon CR0 . . . 205 C1
Stockwell SW9 . . . 138 B1
Tunstall Wlk 10
TW8 . . . 132 A6
Tunstock Way DA17 . . 125 A3
Tunworth Cl NW9 . . . 45 A3
Tunworth Cres
SW15 . . . 155 D5
Tun Yd SW8 . . . 137 B2
Tupelo Rd E10 . . . 75 D6
Tupman Ho 26 SE16 . . 118 A4
Tuppy St SE28 . . . 123 A3
Turberville Ho 1
SW9 . . . 138 B2
Turenne Cl SW18 . . . 136 A1
Turin Rd N9 . . . 18 C4
Turin St E2 . . . 96 A4
Turkey Oak Cl SE19 . . 183 C2
Turkey St EN1, EN3 . . . 6 C6
Turkey Street Sta EN3 . 6 C6
Turks Cl UB8 . . . 82 C4
Turk's Head Yd EC1 . . 241 C4
Turks Row
SW3 . . . 114 D1 257 D2
Turle Rd
Finsbury Pk N4 . . . 72 B6
Thornton Heath
SW16 . . . 182 A1
Turlewray Cl N4 . . . 50 B1
Turley Cl E15 . . . 98 C6
Turnagain La EC4 . . . 241 C2
Turnage Rd RM8 . . . 59 A1
Turnant Rd N17 . . . 33 A2
Turnberry Cl
24 Bermondsey
SE16 . . . 118 B1
Hendon NW4 . . . 28 D1
Turnberry Quay 1
E14 . . . 119 D3
Turnberry Way BR6 . . 211 B1
Turnbull Ho N1 . . . 234 D6
Turnbury Cl SE28 . . . 102 D1
Turnchapel Mews 1
SW4 . . . 137 B2
Turner Ave
Mitcham CR4 . . . 180 D2
Tottenham N15 . . . 51 C5
Twickenham TW2 . . . 152 A1
Turner Cl
7 Brixton SW9 . . . 138 D4
Hampstead Garden
Suburb NW11 . . . 47 D3
Hillingdon UB4 . . . 83 A4
Turner Cl *continued*
Wembley HA0 . . . 65 D2
Turner Ct
9 Herne Hill SE5 . . . 139 B1
24 Rotherhithe
SE16 . . . 118 C4
Turner Dr NW11 . . . 47 D3
Turner Ho
Finsbury Pk N4 . . . 50 B1
24 Millwall E14 . . . 119 C4
St John's Wood NW8 . . 230 A4
Strand WC2 . . . 250 B5
6 Twickenham
TW1 . . . 153 D5
Westminster SW1 . . . 259 D3
Turner Lo 10 SW19 . . . 156 D3
Turner Mews SM2 . . . 217 D1
Turner Pl SW11 . . . 158 C6
Turner Rd
Edgware HA8 . . . 26 B1
New Malden KT3 . . . 199 B2
Walthamstow E17 . . . 54 A6
Turners Cl N20 . . . 14 D1
Turners Ct Leyton E15 . . 76 A4
New Barnet EN5 . . . 13 D5
Tottenham N15 . . . 51 B4
Turners Meadow Way
BR3 . . . 185 B2
Turner's Rd E3 . . . 97 B2
Turner St
Canning Town E16 . . . 98 D1
Stepney E1 . . . 96 B2
Turners Way CR0 . . . 220 C6
Turneville Rd
W14 . . . 135 B6 264 C6
Turney Prim & Sec
Specl Sch SE21 . . . 161 A4
Turney Rd SE21 . . . 161 B4
Turnham Green Sta
W4 . . . 111 C2
Turnham Green Terr
W4 . . . 111 C2
Turnham Ho SE4 . . . 141 A1
Turnham Prim Sch
SE4 . . . 141 A1
Turnham Rd SE4 . . . 141 A1
Turnmill Ho 8
SW2 . . . 160 C6
Turnmill St
EC1 . . . 94 D2 241 C4
Turnour Ho 31 E1 . . . 96 B1
Turnpike Cl SE8 . . . 141 B5
Turnpike Ct DA6 . . . 146 D1
Turnpike Ho EC1 . . . 234 D1
Turnpike La N8 . . . 50 C6
Turnpike Lane Sta
N15 . . . 50 D6
Turnpike La
Sutton SM1 . . . 218 A3
Uxbridge UB10 . . . 82 A5
Turnpike Link CR0 . . . 221 C6
Turnpike Mews N8 . . . 50 C6
Turnpike Way TW7 . . . 131 A4
Turnpin La 3 SE10 . . . 142 A6
Turnstone Cl
Edgware NW9 . . . 27 C1
Newham E13 . . . 99 A4
Uxbridge UB10 . . . 60 D3
Turnstone Terr 11
W13 . . . 86 D3
Turpentine La
SW1 . . . 115 B1 258 D1
Turpin Cl 15 EN3 . . . 7 C6
Turpington Cl BR2 . . . 210 A2
Turpington La BR2 . . . 210 A3
Turpin Ho SW11 . . . 268 C2
Turpin Rd TW14 . . . 149 D5
Turpin Way
Upper Holloway
N19 . . . 49 D1
Wallington SM6 . . . 219 B1
Turquand St SE17 . . . 262 B3
Turret Gr SW4 . . . 137 C2
Turret Ho KT2 . . . 176 A4
Turton Ho 5 SE18 . . . 144 D6
Turton Rd HA0 . . . 66 A3
Turville Ho NW8 . . . 237 A6
Turville St E2 . . . 243 C6
Tuscan Ho 36 E2 . . . 96 C4
Tuscan Rd SE18 . . . 123 B1
Tuscany Ho E17 . . . 35 B1
Tuskar St SE10 . . . 120 C1
Tutorial Coll of West
London UB1 . . . 107 B5
Tuttlebee La IG9 . . . 21 A2
Tuttle Ho SW1 . . . 259 D1
Tweedale Ct E15 . . . 76 A3
Tweed Ct W7 . . . 86 C1
Tweeddale Gr UB10 . . . 61 A5
Tweeddale Prim Sch
SM5 . . . 202 B2
Tweeddale Rd SM5 . . . 202 B1
Tweed Ho E14 . . . 98 A3
Tweedmouth Rd E13 . . . 99 B5
Tweedy Cl EN1 . . . 17 D6
Tweedy Rd BR1 . . . 187 A2
Tweezer's Alley
WC2 . . . 251 A6
Twelve Acre Ho 5
E12 . . . 78 C5
Twelvetrees Bsns Pk
E16 . . . 98 B3
Twelvetrees Cres E3 . . 98 A3
Twentyman Cl IG8 . . . 37 A5
Twice Times
Montessori Sch
SW6 . . . 135 C3
TWICKENHAM . . . 152 D4
Twickenham Bridge
TW9 . . . 153 C6
Twickenham Cl CR0 . . 220 B5
Twickenham Gdns
Harrow HA3 . . . 24 C3
Wembley UB6 . . . 65 A3
Twickenham Pl
KT7 . . . 212 D6
Twickenham Prep Sch
TW12 . . . 174 A2
Twickenham Rd
Isleworth TW1,
TW7 . . . 131 A2
Leyton E11 . . . 76 B6
Richmond TW1,
TW9 . . . 131 C1
Teddington TW11 . . . 175 A6
Twickenham TW13 . . . 151 B1
Twickenham Rugby
Football Union
Ground TW2 . . . 152 C5
Twickenham Sta
TW1 . . . 153 A4
Twickenham Trad Ctr
TW1 . . . 152 D5
Twig Folly Cl 21 E2 . . . 96 D5
Twilley St SW18 . . . 157 D4
Twine Cl IG11 . . . 102 B4
Twine Ct E1 . . . 118 C6
Twineham Gn N12 . . . 29 C6
Twining Ave TW2 . . . 152 B1
Twinn Rd NW7 . . . 29 A4
Twin Tumps Way
SE28 . . . 124 A6
Twisden Rd NW5 . . . 71 B4
Twiss Ho 6 SE18 . . . 122 D1
Twist Ho E10 . . . 75 D6
Two Bridges Ind Est
CR0 . . . 221 B2
Twybridge Way
NW10 . . . 67 A1
Twyford Abbey Rd
NW10 . . . 88 B4
Twyford Ave
Acton W3 . . . 110 C6
Muswell Hill N2 . . . 48 D6
Twyford CE High Sch
W3 . . . 110 D5
Twyford Cres W3 . . . 110 C5
Twyford Ct
Acton W3 . . . 110 C6
Muswell Hill N10 . . . 49 A6
6 Wembley HA0 . . . 88 A5
Twyford Ho
Highbury N5 . . . 72 D5
6 Tottenham N15 . . . 51 C3
Twyford Par KT6 . . . 198 C1
Twyford Rd
Carshalton SM5 . . . 202 B1
Harrow HA2 . . . 41 D2
Ilford IG1 . . . 79 A3
Twyford St
N1 . . . 94 B6 233 C6
Twynholm Mans
SW6 . . . 264 A4
Tyas Rd E16 . . . 98 D3
Tybenham Rd SW19 . . 201 C6
Tyberry Rd EN3 . . . 6 C2
Tyburn La HA1 . . . 42 D2
Tyburn Tree (site of)*
W2 . . . 247 C6
Tyburn Way W1 . . . 247 D6
Tye La BR6 . . . 227 A3
Tyer's Est SE1 . . . 253 A2
Tyers Gate
SE1 . . . 117 C4 253 A1
Tyers Ho 1 SW16 . . . 181 C5
Tyers St
SE11 . . . 116 B1 260 C2
Tyers Terr
SE11 . . . 116 B1 260 D1
Tyeshurst Cl SE2 . . . 125 A1
Tylecroft Rd SW16 . . . 182 A1
Tylehurst Gdns IG1 . . . 79 A3
Tyler Cl Erith DA8 . . . 147 D5
Haggerston E2 . . . 95 D5
Tyler Ho SE3 . . . 142 B3
Tyler Rd UB2 . . . 107 D3
Tylers Ct
4 Walthamstow
E17 . . . 53 C5

Tylers Ct *continued*
5 Wembley HA0 88 A5
Tylers Gate HA3 44 A3
Tylers Path SM5 218 D4
Tyler St
Greenwich SE10 120 C1
SE10 142 C6
Tylney Ave SE19 183 D5
Tylney Ho 10 E1 96 B1
Tylney Rd BR1 187 D1
Forest Gate E7 77 C4
Tymperley Ct SW19 157 A3
Tynamara KT1 197 D5
Tynan Cl TW14 150 A3
Tyndale La N1 72 D1
Tyndale Mans N1 72 D1
Tyndale Terr 13 N1 72 D1
Tyndall Gdns E10 76 A6
Tyndall Rd DA16 145 D2
Leyton E10 76 A6
Tyne Ct W7 86 C1
Tyneham Cl 10
SW11 137 A2
Tyneham Rd SW11 137 A2
Tyne Ho 8 KT2 175 D2
Tynemouth Cl E6 100 D1
Tynemouth Dr EN1 6 A5
Tynemouth Rd
Mitcham CR4 181 A3
Plumstead Comm
SE18 123 C1
Tottenham N15 51 D5
Tynemouth St SW6 136 A3
Tynemouth Terr 9
N15 51 D5
Tyne St E1 243 D2
Tynsdale Rd NW10 67 C2
Tynte Ct E9 75 A3
Tynwald Ho 14
SE26 162 A1
Type St E2 96 D5
Tyrawley Rd SW6 265 C2
Tyrell Cl HA1 64 C4
Tyrell Ct SM5 218 D4
Tyrells Ct 3 SE15 140 B2
Tyrols Rd SE23 162 D3
Tyrone Ct SW16 181 D5
Tyrone Rd E6 100 B4
Tyron Way DA14 189 D5
Tyrrell Ave DA16 168 B6
Tyrrell Ho
Catford BR3 185 D5
SW1 269 B6
Tyrrell Rd SE22 140 A1
Tyrrell Sq CR4 180 C2
Tyrrel Way NW9 46 A2
Tyrwhitt Rd SE4 141 C2
Tysoe Ave EN3 7 B6
Tysoe St EC1 234 B1
Tyson Rd SE23 162 C4
Tyssen Com Prim Sch
N16 52 A1
Tyssen Rd N16 73 D5
Tyssen St Dalston E8 73 D2
Hoxton N1 95 C5
Tysson Ho E9 75 A1
Tytherton 20 E2 96 C5
Tytherton Rd N19 71 D5

U

Uamvar St E14 97 D2
Uckfield Gr CR4 181 A2
Uckfield Rd EN3 6 D6
Udall St SW1 259 B3
Udimore Ho 11 W10 90 C2
Udney Park Rd
TW11 175 A4
Uffington Rd
West Norwood
SE27 182 C6
Willesden Green
NW10 90 B6
Ufford Cl HA3 23 D3
Ufford Rd HA3 23 D3
Ufford St
SE1 116 C4 251 B2
Ufton Ct UB5 84 D4
Ufton Gr N1 73 B1
Ufton Rd N1 73 C1
Uhura Sq 19 N16 73 C5
Ujima Ct
Finsbury Pk N19 50 A1
Streatham SW16 182 A6
Ujima Ho SW16 182 A6
UK Coll of Bsns &
Computing IG2 56 C3
Uk Cotts UB3 105 B4
Ullathorne Rd
SW16 181 C6
Ulleswater Rd N14 16 B1
Ullin St E14 98 A2
Ullswater Cl
Bromley BR1 186 C3
Hayes UB4 83 C5
Kingston u T KT2,
SW15 177 B6
Ullswater Cres
SW15 177 B6
Ullswater Ct
Harrow HA2 41 C2
2 Woodford E18 37 A1
Ullswater Ho SE15 140 C6
Ullswater SW15 156 D5
Ullswater Rd
Barnes SW13 134 A5
West Norwood SE27,
SW16 160 D2
Ulster Ct KT2 175 D4
Ulster Gdns N13 33 A6
Ulster Pl NW1 238 C5
Ulster Terr NW1 238 C6
Ulundi Rd SE3 142 C6
Ulva Rd SW15 134 D1
Ulverscroft Rd SE22 162 A6
Ulverstone Rd SE27 160 D2
Ulverston Rd E17 36 B1
Ulysses Rd NW6 69 B3
Umberston St E1 96 B1
Umbria St SW15 156 A5
Umfreville Rd N4 50 D3
Umoja Ho N22 32 B1
Una Ho 7 NW5 71 B2
Undercliff SE10 142 A4
Undercliff Rd SE13 141 D2
UNDERHILL 13 C6
Underhill EN5 13 C6
Underhill Ct EN5 13 C6
Underhill Ho 7 E14 97 C2
Underhill Jun & Inf
Schs EN5 13 A6
Underhill Pas NW1 231 D6
Underhill Rd SE21,
SE22 162 B4
Underhill St NW1 231 D5
Underne Ave N14 15 B2
Undershaft
EC3 95 C1 243 A1
Undershaw Rd BR1 164 D1
Underwood Ct 3
E10 53 D1
Underwood Ho
East Molesey KT8 195 C4
Hammersmith W6 112 B3
Underwood CR0 224 A3
Underwood Rd
Bethnal Green E1 96 A3
Chingford E4 35 D5
Woodford IG8 37 D3
Underwood Row N1 235 B2
Underwood St
N1 95 A4 235 B2
Underwood The
SE9 166 B2
Undine Rd E14 119 D2
Undine St SW17 180 D5
Uneeda Dr UB6 86 B6
Unicorn Bldg 14 E1 118 D6
Unicorn Prim Sch
BR3 207 D4
Unicorn Sch TW9 132 B4
Unicorn Works N17 34 C3
Union Cl E11 76 B4
Union Ct
45 Paddington W2 91 C2
2 Richmond TW10 154 A6
South Lambeth SW4 138 A3
Union Dr E1 97 A3
Union Gr SW8 137 D3
Union Mews 32
SW9 138 A3
Union Pk 11 SE10 120 D1
Union Rd BR2 209 D4
Clapham SW8 137 D3
Friern Barnet N11 31 D4
Northolt UB5 85 C5
Thornton Heath CR0 205 A2
Wembley HA0 66 A2
Union Sq N1 95 A6 235 B5
Union St Barnet EN5 1 A2
Kingston u T KT1 175 D1
Mill Meads E15 98 B6
SE1 117 A5 252 A3
Union Terr HA2 41 C1
Union Wharf N1 235 B4
Union Wlk E2 95 C4
Union Yd W1 238 D1
Unity Cl
West Norwood
SE19 183 A5
Willesden NW10 68 A2
Unity Mews NW1 232 C4
Unity Rd EN3 6 C6
Unity Terr HA2 63 D6
Unity Way SE18 121 D3
Univ Coll Jun Sch
NW3 70 A4
Univ Coll London
Bloomsbury
WC1 93 D3 239 C6
Bloomsbury
WC1 94 A3 240 B6
Univ Coll London
(Windeyer Inst)
W1 93 C2 239 B4
Univ Coll London
(Wolfson Ho)
NW1 93 C4 232 B1
University Cl NW7 27 D3
University Coll Hospl
WC1 93 C3 239 B6
University Coll Sch
NW3 70 A3
University Gdns
DA5 169 B4
University Mans
SW15 134 D2
University Pl DA8 147 D5
University Rd SW19 180 B4
University St
WC1 93 C3 239 B5
University Way E16 122 D6
Univ of California
WC1 93 D2 239 D3
Univ of East London
RM8 80 A4
Univ of East London
(Duncan Ho) E15 98 B6
Univ of East London
(Holbrook Ctr)
E15 98 D5
Univ of East London
Newham E16 122 C6
Stratford E15 76 C2
Univ of Greenwich
Avery Hill Campus
Mansion Site SE9 167 A5
Univ of Greenwich
Avery Hill Campus
Southwood Site
SE9 167 B4
Univ of Greenwich
Rachel Mcmillan
Campus SE8 141 C6
Univ of Greenwich
Riverside Ho Annexe
SE18 122 C3
Univ of Greenwich
SE10 142 B6
Univ of London (King's
Coll Hall) SE5 139 B2
Univ of London Obsy
NW7 27 D4
Univ of London (Queen
Mary & Westfield
Coll) E1 97 A3
Univ of London
WC1 93 D3 239 D5
Univ of Westminster
(Cavendish Campus)
W1 93 C2 239 A4
Univ of Westminster
(Harrow Campus)
HA1 43 A2
Univ of Westminster
(Marylebone Campus)
W1 93 A2 238 A4
Univ of Westminster
NW1 93 C3 239 A6
Univ of Westminster
(Regent Campus,
Univ HQ)
W1 93 B1 238 D2
Univ of Westminster
(Regent Campus)
W1 93 C2 239 A3
Uno Apartments 4
BR1 187 A2
Unwin Ave TW14 149 B6
Unwin Cl SE15 140 A6
Unwin Rd
Isleworth TW7 130 C2
SW7 114 B3 256 D6
Upbrook Mews
W2 92 A1 236 B1
Upcerne Rd
SW10 136 A5 266 B3
Upchurch Cl 8
SE20 184 B3
Upcott Ho
33 Bromley E3 97 D4
4 Hackney E9 74 C1
Upcroft Ave HA8 27 A6
Updale Rd DA14 189 D6
Upfield Rd W7 86 D2
Upfield CR0 222 B5
Upgrove Manor Way 12
SE24 160 C4
Uphall Prim Sch IG1 78 D3
Uphall Rd IG1 78 D3
Upham Park Rd W4 111 C2
Uphill Dr
Edgware NW7 27 C5
Uphill Dr *continued*
Kingsbury NW9 45 A4
Uphill Gr NW7 27 C6
Uphill Rd NW7 27 C6
Upland Ct SE23 162 C2
Upland Prim Sch
DA7 147 B2
Upland Rd
Croydon CR2 221 B3
DA7 147 B2
East Dulwich SE22 162 A5
8 Newham E13 99 A3
Sutton SM2 218 B1
Uplands Ave E17 34 D1
Uplands BR3 185 C1
Uplands Bsns Pk E17 52 D6
Uplands Cl SW14 154 D6
Uplands Ct N21 16 C4
Uplands Park Rd EN2 4 C3
Uplands Rd
East Barnet EN4 15 A3
Hornsey Vale N8 50 B4
Ilford RM6 58 D6
Woodford IG8 37 D3
Uplands The HA4 40 A1
Uplands Way N21 16 C6
Uplands SE18 122 D1
Upnall Ho 16 SE15 140 C6
Upney Ct 2 IG11 79 D1
Upney La IG11 79 D1
Upney Sta IG11 79 D1
Upnor Way SE17 263 B2
Uppark Dr IG2 57 A3
Upper Abbey Rd
DA17 125 C2
Upper Addison Gdns
W14 113 A4 244 A2
Upper Bank St E14 119 D5
Upper Bardsey Wlk 7
N1 73 A2
Upper Belgrave St
SW1 115 A3 258 B6
Upper Berkeley St
W1 92 D1 237 D1
Upper Beulah Hill
SE19 183 C2
Upper Brighton Rd
KT6 198 A2
Upper Brockley Rd
SE4 141 B3
Upper Brook St
W1 115 A6 248 A6
Upper Butts TW8 131 C6
Upper Caldy Wlk 18
N1 73 A2
Upper Camelford Wlk
14 W10 91 A1
Upper Cavendish Ave
N3 47 C6
Upper Cheyne Row
SW3 136 C6 267 A6
UPPER CLAPTON 52 B1
Upper Clapton Rd E5 74 B6
Upper Clarendon Wlk
12 W11 91 A1
Upper Dengie Wlk
N1 235 A6
UPPER EDMONTON 34 B5
UPPER ELMERS END
207 B3
Upper Elmers End Rd
BR3 207 A4
Upper Farm Rd KT8 195 B5
Upper Fosters NW4 46 C5
Upper Gn W CR4 180 D1
Upper Grosvenor St
W1 115 A6 248 A5
Upper Grotto Rd
TW1 152 D2
Upper Ground
SE1 116 C5 251 A4
Upper Grove Rd
DA17 147 B6
Upper Gr SE25 205 D5
Upper Gulland Wlk 23
N1 73 A2
UPPER HALLIFORD
193 B5
Upper Halliford Rd
TW17 193 C6
Upper Halliford Sta
TW16 171 C1
Upper Hampstead Wlk
29 NW3 70 A4
Upper Ham Rd KT2,
TW10 175 D6
Upper Handa Wlk 2
N1 73 A2
Upper Harley St
NW1 238 B5
Upper Hawkwell Wlk
N1 235 B6
UPPER HOLLOWAY 71 D6
Upper Holloway Sta
N19 71 D6
Upper Holly Hill Rd
DA17 125 D1
Upper James St W1 249 B6
Upper John St W1 249 B6
Upper Lismore Wlk 8
N1 73 A2
Upper Lodge Mews
TW12 174 A4
Upper Mall W6 112 B1
Upper Marsh
SE1 116 B3 260 D6
Upper Montague St
W1 92 D2 237 C3
Upper Mulgrave Rd
SM2 217 A1
Upper North St E3,
E14 97 C2
UPPER NORWOOD 183 C3
Upper Park Rd
Belvedere DA17 125 D2
BR1 187 C2
Friern Barnet N11 31 C5
Kingston u T KT2 176 C4
Maitland Pk NW3 70 D3
Upper Phillimore Gdns
W8 113 C4 245 A1
Upper Pk IG10 21 D6
Upper Ramsey Wlk 19
N1 73 B2
Upper Rawreth Wlk
N1 235 B6
Upper Rd Finchley N2 30 C2
Newham E13 99 A4
Wallington SM6 219 D3
Upper Richmond Rd
SW15 134 C1
Upper Richmond Rd W
TW10, SW14, SW15 133 A1
UPPER RUXLEY 191 C3
Upper St Martin's La
WC2 250 A6
Upper Selsdon Rd
CR2 221 D1
Upper Sheridan Rd 3
DA17 125 C2
UPPER SHIRLEY 222 D4
Upper Shirley Rd
CR0 222 D5
Upper Sq TW7 131 A2
Upper St N1 94 D6 234 C5
Upper Sunbury Rd
TW12 173 C2
Upper Sutton La
TW5 129 C4
UPPER SYDENHAM
184 A6
Upper Tachbrook St
SW1 259 B4
Upper Talbot Wlk 7
W10 91 A1
Upper Teddington Rd
KT1, KT8 175 C2
Upper Terr NW3 70 A5
Upper Thames St
EC4 117 A6 252 B6
Upper Tollington Pk
N4 50 C1
Upperton Rd DA14 189 D5
Upperton Rd E E13 99 C4
Upperton Rd W E13 99 C4
UPPER TOOTING 158 D1
Upper Tooting Park
Mans 1 SW17 159 A2
Upper Tooting Pk
SW17 158 D2
Upper Tooting Rd
SW17 158 D1
Upper Town Rd UB6 85 D3
Upper Tulse Hill
SW2 160 B3
Upper Vernon Rd
SM1 218 B3
UPPER WALTHAMSTOW
54 C6
Upper Walthamstow Rd
E17 54 B6
Upper Wickham La
DA16 146 B4
Upper Wimpole St
W1 93 A2 238 B4
Upper Woburn Pl NW1,
WC1 93 D4 232 D1
Uppingham Ave HA7 25 C1
Upsdell Ave N13 32 C4
Upshire Ho E17 35 B1
Upstall St SE5 138 D4
UPTON 77 B1
Upton Ave E7 77 A1
Upton Cl
Cricklewood NW2 69 A5
Sidcup DA5 169 B5
Upton Cross E13 99 A6
Upton Cross Prim Sch
E13 99 B6
Upton Ct
Penge SE20 184 C3
Southall UB1 107 D5
4 Wimbledon
SW19 178 D3
Upton Day Hospl
DA6 147 A1
Upton Dene SM2 217 D1
Upton Gdns HA3 43 C3
Upton Hts E7 77 A1
Upton La E7 77 A1
Upton Lodge Cl WD23 8 A4
Upton Lo E7 77 A2
UPTON PARK 99 D6
Upton Park Rd E7 77 B1
Upton Park Sta E13 99 C6
Upton Prim Sch
DA5 169 B6
Upton Rd
Bexley DA6 169 A6
Edmonton N18 34 A5
Hounslow TW3 129 C2
SE18 145 A6
South Norwood CR7 183 B1
Upton Rd S DA5 169 B5
Upton Villas 4 DA6 147 A1
Upway N12 30 C4
Upwood Rd SE12 165 A5
Thornton Heath
SW16 182 A2
Urban Mews N4 50 D2
Urlwin St SE5 139 A6
Urlwin Wlk SW9 138 D4
Urmston Dr SW19 157 A3
Urmston Ho 4 E14 120 A2
Urquhart Ct BR3 185 B3
Ursula Lo DA14 190 B5
Ursula Mews N4 51 A1
Ursula St
SW11 136 C4 267 A1
Ursuline High Sch
SW20 178 D2
Ursuline Prep Sch
SW19 178 D3
Urswick Gdns RM9 81 A1
Urswick Rd
Dagenham RM9 81 A1
Hackney E5, E9 74 C3
Usborne Mews SW8 270 D4
Usher Hall NW4 46 B5
Usher Rd E3 97 B5
Usk Rd SW11 136 A1
Usk St E2 96 D4
Utah Bldg 3 SE13 141 D4
Utopia Ho 3 NW2 68 A2
Utopia Village
NW1 93 A6 231 A6
Uvedale Rd
Dagenham RM10 81 C5
Enfield EN2 17 B6
Uverdale Rd
SW10 136 A5 266 B3
UXBRIDGE 82 A6
Uxbridge Coll
Hayes UB3 106 A6
Uxbridge UB8 60 A2
Uxbridge High Sch
UB8 82 A5
Uxbridge Rd
Acton W3, W5 110 C5
Ealing W13 109 C6
Feltham TW13 150 D2
Hampton TW12,
TW13 173 D5
Hayes UB4 106 C6
Hillingdon UB10, UB4 83 C2
Kingston u T KT1,
KT6 197 D4
Shepherd's Bush
W12 112 B5
Southall UB1, UB2, W5,
W7 108 B5
Stanmore HA7 25 A5
Uxbridge Road (Harrow
Weald) HA3 24 B3
Uxbridge Road (Hatch
End) HA5 23 B3
Uxbridge Road (Pinner)
HA5 22 D1
Uxbridge St
W8 113 C5 245 A4
Uxendon Cres HA3,
HA9 44 A1
Uxendon Hill HA9 44 B2
Uxendon Manor Prim
Sch HA3 44 A4

V

Vadnie Bish Ho NW5 71 C2
Vaine Ho 4 E9 75 A2
Valance Ave E4 20 D3
Valan Leas BR2 208 C6
Vale Ave WD6 10 D6
Vale Cl
Muswell Hill N2 48 D6
Orpington BR6 226 C4
St John's Wood
W9 92 A4 229 A1
Twickenham TW1 153 A1
Vale Cres SW15 177 C6

le Croft
Claygate KT10 212 D1
Pinner HA5 41 A4
le Ct Barnet EN5 1 D1
East Acton W3 111 D5
St John's Wood
W9 92 A4 229 A1
Wembley HA0 65 C5
le Dr EN5 13 C6
le End SE22 139 D1
le Est The W3 111 C5
le Farm Sports Ctr
HA0 65 B4
le Gr Acton W3 111 B5
Stoke Newington N4 51 A2
le La W3 88 C2
le Lo SE23 162 C2
lence Ave RM8 80 D6
lence Cir RM8 81 A5
lence House Mus*
RM8 81 A6
lence Jun & Inf Schs
RM8 80 D6
lence Wood Rd
RM8 81 A5
lencia Rd HA7 25 C6
lens Ho 1 SW2 160 C3
lentia Pl SW9 138 C1
lentine Ave DA5 169 A3
lentine Ct
Elstree WD6 9 D5
3 Forest Hill SE23 162 D2
lentine Ho
11 Clapham Pk
SW4 159 C5
26 Old Ford E3 97 B6
lentine Pl
SE1 116 D4 251 C2
lentine Rd
Harrow HA2 64 A5
Homerton E9 74 D2
lentine Row SE1 251 C1
lentines High Sch
IG2 56 C3
lentines Rd IG1 56 D1
ALE OF HEALTH 70 B5
ale of Health NW3 70 B5
ale Rd BR1 188 C1
Claygate KT10 212 D1
Mitcham CR4 203 D5
ale Rd N KT6 214 A6
ale Rd S KT6 214 A6
ale Rd
Stoke Newington
N4 51 A2
Sutton SM1 217 D4
Upton E7 77 B2
Worcester Pk KT19,
KT4 215 D5
alerian Way E15 98 C4
alerie Ct
Belmont SM2 217 D1
Bushey WD23 8 A4
ale Rise NW11 47 B1
ale Row N5 72 D5
ale Royal N7 72 A1
alery Pl TW12 173 C3
ale Sch The SW7 256 A5
aleside Ct 2 EN5 1 D1
aleswood Rd BR1 186 D5
ale Terr N4 51 A3
ale The
Ashford TW16 172 A4
Cricklewood NW11 69 A6
Croydon CR0 222 D6
East Acton W3 111 C5
Feltham TW14 150 B5
Heston TW5 129 A6
Muswell Hill N10 31 A2
Ruislip HA4 62 C4
Southgate N14 16 A4
SW3 136 B6 266 D6
Woodford IG8 37 A3
aletta Gr E13 99 A5
aletta Rd W3 111 D4
alette Ct N10 49 B5
alette Ho E9 74 C2
alette St E8 74 B2
aliant Cl 18 UB5 84 D4
aliant Ho
9 Cubitt Town
E14 120 A4
5 Greenwich SE7 121 C1
SW11 266 D1
aliant Way E6 100 B2
allance Rd
Bethnal Green E1 96 A3
Muswell Hill N22 31 C1
allentin Rd E17 54 A5
alley Ave N12 30 B6
alley (Charlton
Athletic FC) The
SE7 121 C1
alley Cl HA5 22 B1
alley Ct IG8 37 B3
alley Dr NW9 44 D3

Valleyfield Rd
SW16 182 B5
Valley Fields Cres
EN2 4 C3
Valley Gdns
Mitcham SW19 180 B3
Wembley HA0 66 B1
Valley Gr SE7 121 C1
Valley Ho
4 Edmonton N9 18 A1
Upper Clapton E5 52 C1
Valleylink Est EN3 19 A5
Valley Mews TW1 153 A2
Valley Pl KT6 198 A3
Valley Point Ind Est
CR0 204 A2
Valley Prim Sch
BR2 186 D1
Valley Prospect 3
SE19 183 C4
Valley Rd
Beckenham BR2 186 C1
BR5 190 B2
Streatham SW16 182 B6
Uxbridge UB10 82 A5
Valley Side E4 19 C3
Valleyside SE7 121 D1
Valley Side Par E4 19 C2
Valley View EN5 13 A5
Valley Wlk CR0 222 C6
Valliere Rd NW10 90 A4
Valliers Wood Rd
DA15 167 C3
Vallis Way
Chessington KT9 213 D4
Ealing W13 87 A2
Val McKenzie Ave
N7 72 C5
Valmar Rd SE5 139 A4
Valmar Trad Est
SE5 139 A4
Valnay St SW17 180 D5
Valognes Ave E17 35 A2
Valois Ho SE1 263 C6
Valonia Gdns SW18 157 B5
Vambery Rd SE18 145 A6
Vanbern Ho NW5 71 A2
Vanborough Ct 4
SM2 218 A2
Vanbrough Cres UB5 84 C6
Vanbrugh Cl 2 E16 99 D2
Vanbrugh Ct SE11 261 B3
Vanbrugh Dr KT12 194 C3
Vanbrugh Fields
SE3 142 D5
Vanbrugh Hill SE10,
SE3 142 D6
Vanbrugh Ho 8 E9 74 C1
Vanbrugh Mews
KT12 194 C2
Vanbrugh Park Rd
SE3 142 D5
Vanbrugh Park Rd W
SE3 142 D5
Vanbrugh Pk SE3 142 D5
Vanbrugh Rd W4 111 B3
Vanbrugh Terr SE3 142 D4
Vanburgh Cl BR6 211 C1
Vanburgh Ct 6 EN5 1 A1
Vanburgh Ho E1 243 C4
Vancouver Rd
Edgware HA8 26 D2
Forest Hill SE23 163 B2
Hayes UB4 84 B3
Richmond TW10 175 C6
Vancover Ho 33 E1 118 B5
Vanderbilt Rd
SW18 158 A3
Vanderbilt Villas 1
W12 112 D4
Vanderville Gdns N2 30 B1
Vandome Cl E16 99 B1
Vandon Ct SW1 259 B6
Vandon Pas SW1 259 B6
Vandon St SW1 259 B6
Van Dyck Ave KT3 199 B2
Vandyke Cl SW15 156 D5
Vandyke Cross SE9 166 A6
Vandy St EC2 243 A5
Vane Cl
Hampstead NW3 70 B4
Harrow HA3 44 B3
Vane Ho 18 N2 30 B1
Vanessa Cl DA17 125 C1
Vane St SW1 259 B4
Vanfame Ct KT3 199 D6
Vange Ho 12 W10 90 C2
Van Gogh Cl 11
TW7 131 A2
Van Gogh Ct E14 120 B3
Vanguard Bldg 6
E14 119 C4
Vanguard Cl
Newham E16 99 B2
Thornton Heath CR0 204 D1
Vanguard Ho
11 Hackney E8 74 B1

Vanguard Ho *continued*
7 Merton SW19 180 A3
6 Stanwell TW19 148 A5
Vanguard St SE8 141 C4
Vanguard Trad Ctr
E15 98 A6
Vanguard Way
Hatton TW6 127 C3
Wallington SM6 220 A1
Van Lang Ho EN3 18 D6
Vanneck Sq SW15 156 A6
Vanner Point 27 E9 74 D2
Vanoc Gdns BR1 187 A6
Vansittart Rd E7 77 A4
Vansittart St 7
SE14 141 A5
Vanston Pl
SW6 135 C5 265 B4
Vantage Ct
Harlington UB3 127 C5
4 South Norwood
SW16 182 B3
Vantage Mews 7
E14 120 A5
Vantage Pl W8 255 B5
Vant Rd SW17 180 D5
Vantrey Ho SE11 261 A3
Varcoe Rd SE16 118 C1
Vardens Rd SW11 136 B1
Varden St E1 96 B1
Vardon Cl W3 89 B1
Vardon Ho SE10 142 A4
Vardy Ho HA7 25 B5
Varey Ho E1 97 A4
Varley Ho 5 NW6 91 C6
Varley Par NW9 45 C5
Varley Rd E16 99 B1
Varley Way CR4 180 B1
Varma Ct SE3 143 A4
Varna Rd
Hampton TW12 173 D2
SW6 135 B5 264 C3
Varndell St
NW1 93 C4 232 A2
Varsity Dr TW1,
TW7 152 D5
Varsity Row SW14 133 A3
Vartry Rd N15 51 C3
Vascroft Est NW10 88 D3
Vassall Ho 3 E3 97 A4
Vassall Rd SW9 138 C5
Vat Ho SW8 270 B4
Vauban Est SE16 263 D5
Vauban St
SE16 117 D3 263 D5
Vaudeville Ct N4 72 C6
Vaughan Almshouses
TW15 170 D5
Vaughan Ave
Chiswick W6 111 D2
Hendon NW4 46 A4
Vaughan Cl TW12 173 A4
Vaughan Est 3 E2 95 D4
Vaughan Fst & Mid Sch
HA1 42 A3
Vaughan Gdns IG1 56 B2
Vaughan Ho SE1 251 C2
Vaughan Rd
Camberwell SE5 139 A2
DA16 145 D3
Harrow HA1 42 B3
Stratford E15 76 D2
Thames Ditton KT7 197 B2
Vaughan St SE16 119 B4
Vaughan Way E1 118 A5
Vaughan Williams Cl
SE8 141 C5
VAUXHALL 116 A1
Vauxhall Bridge Rd
SW1 115 C2 259 B3
Vauxhall Cross SE1,
SW8 116 A1 260 B1
Vauxhall Gdns CR2 221 A2
Vauxhall Gr
SW8 138 B6 270 C6
Vauxhall Prim Sch
SE11 116 B1 260 D2
Vauxhall Sta
SE11 116 A1 260 B1
Vauxhall St
SE11 116 B1 260 D2
Vauxhall Wlk SE11 260 C2
Vawdrey Cl E1 96 C3
Vaynor Ho N7 72 A4
Veals Mead CR4 180 C2
Vectis Ct SW18 157 D5
Vectis Gdns SW17 181 B4
Vectis Rd SW17 181 B4
Veda Rd SE13 141 C1
Vega Cres HA6 22 A5
Vega Rd WD23 8 A4
Veitch Cl TW14 149 D4
Veldene Way HA2 63 B5
Velde Way 1 SE22 161 C6
Vellacott Ho 3 W12 90 B1
Velletri Ho 11 E2 96 D5
Vellum Dr SM5 219 A5

Venables Cl RM10 81 D4
Venables St
NW8 92 B2 236 D4
Vencourt Pl W6 112 A2
Venetian Rd SE5 139 A3
Venetia Rd
Ealing W5 109 D4
Harringay N4 50 D3
Venice Ct 14 SE5 139 A5
Venita Manor SE27 182 C5
Venmead Ct 7
DA17 125 C2
Venner Rd SE26 184 C5
Venn Ho N1 233 D5
Venn St SW4 137 C1
Ventnor Ave HA7 25 B1
Ventnor Dr N20 13 D2
Ventnor Gdns IG11 79 C2
Ventnor Mans IG11 79 C2
Ventnor Rd
Belmont SM2 217 D1
SE14 140 D5
Ventnor Terr N15 52 A5
Ventura Ho 12 SW2 138 A1
Venture Cl DA5 169 A4
Venture Ct 3 SE12 165 A4
Venue St E14 98 A2
Venus Ho
7 Millwall E14 119 C2
8 Old Ford E3 97 C6
Venus Mews CR4 202 C6
Venus Rd SE18 122 B3
Vera Ave N21 16 C6
Vera Ct
1 Kensington W2 91 D1
Tottenham N22 32 D2
Vera Lynn Cl 5 E7 77 A4
Vera Rd
SW6 135 A4 264 B2
Verbena Cl E16 98 D3
Verbena Gdns 4
W6 112 A1
Verdant Ct 3 SE6 164 C4
Verdant La SE6 164 C3
Verdayne Ave CR0 222 D6
Verdi Cres W10 91 A5
Verdun Rd
Barnes SW13 134 A5
SE18 146 A6
Vere Bank SW19 157 B3
Vereker Dr TW16 194 A6
Vereker Rd W14 254 B1
Vere St W1 93 B1 238 C1
Verity Cl W11 91 A1
Verity Ct N9 18 D3
Verity Ho 20 E3 97 B4
Vermeer Ct E14 120 B3
Vermillion Ct TW13 149 D1
Vermont Cl EN2 4 D1
Vermont Ho E17 35 B1
Vermont Rd
Sutton SM1 217 D5
Wandsworth SW18 157 D5
West Norwood SE19 183 C4
Verne Ct 9 W3 111 A3
Verneer Gdns SE15 140 C1
Verney Gdns RM9 81 A4
Verney Ho
Isleworth TW3 130 A1
Lisson Gr NW8 237 A6
South Kensington
SW10 266 A6
Verney Rd
Bermondsey SE16 118 B1
Dagenham RM9 81 A4
Verney St NW10 67 B5
Verney Way SE16 118 B1
Vernham Rd SE18 145 A6
Vernon Ave Ilford E12 78 B4
West Barnes SW20 178 D1
Woodford IG8 37 B3
Vernon Cl
Stanwell TW19 148 A3
West Ewell KT19 215 A2
Vernon Cres EN4 15 A5
Vernon Ct
Child's Hill NW2 69 B5
Ealing W5 109 C6
Stanmore HA7 25 B2
Vernon Dr HA7 25 A2
Vernon Ho
Hyde The NW9 45 D4
SE11 260 D1
Vernon House Sch
NW10 67 B3
Vernon Mews W14 254 B3
Vernon Pl WC1 240 B3
Vernon Rd Bow E3 97 B5
Feltham TW13 149 D2
Hornsey N8 50 C6
Ilford IG3 57 D1
Leytonstone E11 54 C1
Mortlake SW14 133 B2
Stratford E15 76 C1
Sutton SM1 218 B3
Walthamstow E17 53 B4

Vernon Rise
Greenford UB6 64 B3
WC1 233 D2
Vernon Sq WC1 233 D2
Vernon St
W14 113 A2 254 B3
Vernon Yd
W11 113 B6 244 C6
Veroan Rd DA7 147 A3
Verona Ct
Chiswick W4 111 C1
10 SE14 140 D6
Verona Dr KT6 214 A6
Verona Rd E7 77 A1
Veronica Gdns CR4,
SW16 181 C2
Veronica Ho
Brockley SE4 141 B2
46 Bromley E3 97 D4
Veronica Rd SW17 159 B2
Veronique Gdns IG6 57 A4
Verran Rd SW12 159 B4
Versailles Rd SE20 184 A3
Verulam Ave E17 53 B2
Verulam Bldgs WC1 240 D4
Verulam Ct
Hendon NW9 46 A2
4 Southall UB1 86 A1
Verulam Ho 1 W6 112 C4
Verulam Rd UB6 85 C3
Verulam St
EC1 94 C2 241 A4
Vervain Ho 2 SE15 140 A5
Verwood Dr EN4 2 D2
Verwood Ho SW8 270 D3
Verwood Lo 1 E14 120 B2
Verwood Rd HA2 24 A1
Veryan Ct 3 N8 49 D4
Vesage Ct EC1 241 B3
Vesey Path 15 E14 97 D1
Vespan Rd W12 112 A4
Vesta Ct SE1 253 A1
Vesta Ho 9 E3 97 C6
Vesta Rd SE4, SE14 141 A3
Vestris Rd SE23 162 D2
Vestry House (Mus)*
E17 53 D5
Vestry Mews 12
SE5 139 C4
Vestry Rd
Camberwell SE5 139 C4
Walthamstow E17 53 D5
Vestry St N1 95 B4 235 C2
Vevey St SE23, SE6 163 B2
Veysey Gdns RM10 81 C5
Viaduct Pl 28 E2 96 B4
Viaduct Rd N2 30 C1
Viaduct St E2 96 B4
Viaduct The
Harrow HA2 64 A5
Woodford E18 37 B1
Vian St SE13 141 D2
Vibart Gdns SW2 160 B4
Vibart Wlk N1 233 B6
Vicarage Ave SE3 143 A5
Vicarage Cl
New Malden KT4 199 C1
Northolt UB5 63 B1
Ruislip HA4 39 B2
Vicarage Cres
SW11 136 B4 266 C1
Vicarage Ct
Beckenham BR3 207 A6
East Bedfont TW14 149 A4
Finchley N12 29 D5
7 Putney SW15 156 A4
W8 245 C2
Vicarage Dr
Barking IG11 79 A1
Beckenham BR3 185 C2
Mortlake SW14 155 B6
Vicarage Farm Ct
TW5 129 B5
Vicarage Farm Rd TW3,
TW4, TW5 129 A4
Vicarage Field Sh Ctr
The IG11 79 A1
Vicarage Fields
KT12 194 C3
Vicarage Gate
W8 113 D5 245 C3
Vicarage Gdns
Mitcham CR4 202 C6
Mortlake SW14 155 B6
W8 245 B3
Vicarage Gr SE5 139 B4
Vicarage Ho 1 KT1 176 B1
Vicarage La
Ilford IG1 57 B1
Stratford E15 76 D1
Wallend E6 100 C4
Vicarage Mans N15 51 A5
Vicarage Pk SE18 123 A1
Vicarage Prim Sch
E6 100 B4
Vicarage Rd
Ashford TW16 171 D4

Vicarage Rd *continued*
Croydon CR0 220 C5
DA5 169 D3
Dagenham RM10 81 D1
Hampton Wick KT1 175 C2
Hendon NW4 46 A3
Kingston u T KT1 175 D1
Mortlake SW14 155 B6
Stratford E15 76 D1
Sutton SM1 217 D5
Teddington TW11 175 A5
Tottenham N17 34 A2
Walthamstow E10 53 D1
Woolwich SE18 123 A1
Vicarage The N8 50 B3
Vicarage Way
Harrow HA2 41 C2
Neasden NW10 67 B5
Vicarage Wlk
SW11 136 B4 266 D2
Vicars Bridge Cl HA0 88 A5
Vicar's Cl Enfield EN1 5 C3
Newham E15 99 A6
South Hackney E9 96 C6
Vicar's Green Prim Sch
HA0 87 C5
Vicars Hill SE13 141 D1
Vicar's Moor La N21 16 D4
Vicars Oak Rd SE19 183 C4
Vicar's Rd NW5 71 A3
Vicar's Wlk RM8 80 B5
Viceroy Cl N2 48 C6
Viceroy Ct
5 Croydon CR0 205 B1
NW8 230 B4
Viceroy Lo 6 KT6 198 A4
Viceroy Par N2 48 C6
Viceroy Rd
SW8 138 A4 270 A2
Vic Johnson Ho 21
E3 97 B6
Vickers Cl SM6 220 B1
Vickers Ct 10 TW19 148 A5
Vickery Ct EC1 242 B6
Vickery Ho 13 SW4 138 A1
Vickery's Wharf 3
E14 97 C1
Victor Cazalet Ho
N1 234 C6
Victor Gr HA0 66 A1
Victor Ho 2 N20 14 D1
Victoria & Albert Mus*
SW7 114 B3 256 D5
Victoria Arc SW1 258 D5
Victoria Ave
Barnet EN4 2 B1
East Molesey KT8 195 D6
EC2 243 B3
Finchley N3 29 B2
Hackbridge SM5,
SM6 219 A5
Hillingdon UB10 60 D1
Hounslow TW3,
TW4 151 C6
Newham E6 99 D6
Surbiton KT6 197 D3
Wembley HA9 66 D2
Victoria Bglws
DA14 191 B3
Victoria Bldgs 13 E8 96 B6
Victoria Bsns Ctr
DA16 146 B3
Victoria Chambers
EC2 243 A6
Victoria Cl Barnet EN4 2 B1
East Molesey KT8 195 C6
Harrow HA1 42 D3
Hayes UB3 83 B1
Victoria Coach Sta
SW1 115 B2 258 C3
Victoria Coll WC2 241 A2
Victoria Cotts
Ilford IG6 57 A4
Muswell Hill N10 31 A1
7 Richmond TW9 132 C4
3 Spitalfields E1 96 A2
Victoria Cres
Tottenham N15 51 C4
West Norwood SE19 183 C4
Victoria Ct
5 Clapham Pk
SW4 159 D5
3 Penge SE26 184 C4
South Acton W3 110 C4
4 St George in t East
E1 118 A6
1 Wanstead E18 55 B6
Wembley HA9 66 C2
Victoria Dock Rd
E16 121 B6
Victoria Dr SW19 156 D3
Victoria Emb
WC2 116 C6 251 A5

Victoria Gdns
Heston TW5 129 A4
W11 113 C5 245 A4
Victoria Gr Mews
W2 245 C5
Victoria Gr
North Finchley N12 30 B5
W8 114 A3 256 A6
Victoria Hall 15 E16 121 A5
Victoria Ho
6 Clapham Pk SW4 159 D5
Edgware HA8 26 D4
2 Shepherd's Bush W12 112 A4
SW1 258 C2
Victoria Ind Est W3 89 C2
Victoria Jun Sch TW13 150 B3
Victoria La Barnet EN5 1 B1
Hayes UB3 105 B1
Victoria Lo 5 SW19 178 C3
Victoria Mans
8 Islington N7 72 C3
Willesden NW10 68 B1
Victoria Mews
Kilburn NW6 91 C6
Wandsworth SW18 158 A3
Victoria Mills 1 E15 98 B6
Victorian Gr N16 73 C5
Victorian Hts 7 SW8 137 B3
Victorian Rd N16 73 D5
Victoria Park Ct 11 E9 74 C1
Victoria Park Ind Ctr E9 75 B1
Victoria Park Lofts E9 96 D6
Victoria Park Rd E9 74 D1
Victoria Park Sq E2 96 C4
Victoria Pas NW8 236 C6
Victoria Place Sh Ctr SW1 115 B2 258 D4
Victoria Pl 17 TW10 153 D6
Victoria Point 10 E13 99 A5
Victoria Rd
Barking IG11 78 D2
Barnet EN4 2 B1
Bexley DA6 147 C1
Bromley Comm BR2 209 D4
Buckhurst Hill IG9 21 D2
Chingford E4 20 C3
Chislehurst West BR7 188 C5
Dagenham RM10 81 D3
Ealing W5 87 B2
Edgware NW7 27 D5
Edmonton N9 17 D1
Feltham TW13 150 B3
Finsbury Pk N4 50 B1
Hendon NW4 46 D5
Kensington W8 114 A3 256 A6
Kilburn NW6 91 B6
Kingston u T KT1 176 B1
Leyton E11 76 C4
Mitcham CR4 180 D3
Mortlake SW14 133 B2
Muswell Hill N22 31 D2
Newham E13 99 A5
North Acton NW10 89 C3
Ruislip HA4 62 B4
Sidcup DA15 168 A1
Southall UB2 107 B3
Surbiton KT6 197 D3
Sutton SM1 218 B3
Teddington TW11 175 A4
Tottenham Hale N15 52 A5
Twickenham TW1 153 B4
Walthamstow E17 36 A1
Wanstead E18 55 B6
Victoria Ret Pk HA4 62 D3
Victoria Rise SW4 137 B2
Victoria Sq SW1 258 D6
Victoria Sta SW1 115 B2 258 D4
Victoria St
Erith DA17 125 B1
Stratford E15 76 C1
SW1 115 C3 259 B5
Victoria Terr
Dagenham NW10 89 C3
Finsbury Pk N4 50 C1
Harrow HA1 42 C1
Victoria (Underground) SW1 115 B3 258 D5
Victoria Villas TW9 132 B1
Victoria Way SE7 143 C6
Victoria Wharf E14 119 A6
Victoria Yd 28 E1 96 A1
Victor Mills Cotts BR8 191 C3
Victor Rd
College Pk NW10 90 B4
Harrow HA2 42 A6
Penge SE20 184 D3
Teddington TW11 174 C6
Victors Dr TW12 173 A4
Victor Seymour Inf Sch SM5 218 D4
Victors Way EN5 1 B2
Victor Villas N9 17 B1
Victory Ave SM4 202 A4
Victory Bsns Ctr The TW7 130 D1
Victory Cl TW19 148 A3
Victory Ct IG11 102 B4
Victory Pl
6 Limehouse E14 119 A6
SE17 117 B2 262 C4
West Norwood SE19 183 C4
Victory Rd
Merton SW19 180 A3
Wanstead E11 55 B5
Victory Road Mews 5 SW19 180 A3
Victory Sch SE17 117 A2 262 B4
Victory Way
Hounslow TW5 106 C1
Rotherhithe SE16 119 A4
Victory Wlk SE8 141 C4
Video Ct N4 50 A2
Vidler Cl KT9 213 C2
Vienna Cl IG5 37 D1
View Cl Harrow HA1 42 B5
Highgate N6 48 D2
View Cres N8 49 D4
Viewfield Cl HA3 44 A2
Viewfield Rd DA5 168 C3
Wandsworth SW18 157 B5
Viewland Rd SE18 123 D1
Viewpoint Ct 8 HA5 22 C1
Viewpoint Ealing W5 110 B6
3 Islington N5 72 D3
Lewisham SE3 142 D2
View Point N20 14 A4
View Rd N6 48 D3
Viewside Lo N6 49 C3
View The SE2 125 A1
Viga Rd N21 16 C5
Vigilant Cl SE26 184 A6
Vignoles Rd RM7 59 C2
Vigo St W1 115 C6 249 A5
Vi & John Rubens Ho IG2 56 C3
Viking Cl 18 E3 97 A5
Viking Ct
Hampton TW12 173 D2
New Barnet EN4 14 B6
Viking Gdns E6 100 A3
Viking Ho
3 Camberwell SE5 139 A3
3 Woolwich SE7 122 A2
Viking Pl E10 53 B1
Viking Prim Sch UB5 84 D4
Viking Rd UB1 107 A6
Villacourt Rd SE18 146 A6
Village Arc The 2 E4 20 B3
Village Cl
Chingford E4 36 A5
Hampstead NW3 70 B3
Village Ct
Blackheath SE3 142 C2
Walthamstow E17 53 D4
Village Gate TW17 192 D4
Village Home The IG6 57 A6
Village Hts IG8 36 D5
Village Inf Sch RM10 81 C1
Village Mount 19 NW3 70 A4
Village Park Cl EN1 17 C5
Village Rd Enfield EN1 17 C6
Hendon N3 29 A1
Village Row SM2 217 C1
Village Sch The NW3 70 D2
Village The
Battersea SW11 136 D2
SE7 143 D6
Village Way
Ashford TW15 170 C6
Beckenham BR3 207 C6
Dulwich Village SE21 161 B5
Village Way E HA2 41 C2
Village Way
Ilford IG6 57 A6
Pinner HA5 41 B2
Willesden NW10 67 B4
Villa Rd SW9 138 C2
Villas On The Heath NW3 70 A5
Villas Rd SE18 123 A2
Villa St SE17 117 B1 262 D1
Villiers Ave
Kingston u T KT5 198 B5
Twickenham TW2 151 B3
Villiers Cl
Kingston u T KT5 198 B5
Leyton E10 75 C6
Villiers Ct
Oakleigh Pk N20 14 A4
SW11 267 B2
Villiers High Sch UB1 107 B5
Villiers Ho W5 109 D6
Villiers Rd
Isleworth TW7 130 C3
Kingston u T KT1 198 B6
Penge BR3 184 D1
Southall UB1 107 B5
Willesden NW2 68 A2
Villiers St WC2 250 B4
Vincam Cl TW2 151 C4
Vince Ct N1 235 D1
Vincent Ave KT5 215 A6
Vincent Cl
Avery Hill DA15 167 C3
Barnet EN5 1 D2
Bromley BR2 209 B5
Harmondsworth UB7 126 C6
Vincent Ct
Finsbury Pk N4 50 A1
Hendon NW4 46 D5
Marylebone W1 237 C2
Ruislip HA4 62 B3
South Lambeth SW9 270 D1
Vincent Dr
Hillingdon UB10 82 B6
Upper Halliford TW17 193 C6
Vincent Gdns NW2 67 D5
Vincent Ho KT3 199 D5
Vincent Mews 1 E3 97 C5
Vincent Rd
Acton Green W3 111 A3
Chingford E4 36 B4
Croydon CR0 205 C2
Dagenham RM9 81 A1
Hounslow West TW4 128 D2
Kingston u T KT1 198 C6
Osterley TW7 130 B4
Tottenham N15 51 A5
Wembley HA0 66 B1
Wood Green N22 32 C1
Woolwich SE18 122 D2
Vincent Row TW12 174 A5
Vincents Cl SE16 119 A4
Vincents Path UB5 63 A2
Vincent Sq
SW1 115 D2 259 C4
Wood Green N22 32 C1
Vincent St
Canning Town E16 98 D2
Westminster SW1 115 D2 259 D4
Vincent Terr N1 94 D5 234 D4
Vince St EC1 95 B4 235 D1
Vine Cl Surbiton KT5 198 B3
Sutton SM1 218 A5
West Drayton UB7 104 C2
Vine Cotts
3 Ealing W7 108 C5
Southall UB2 107 D2
Vine Ct Harrow HA3 44 A3
Spitalfields E1 96 A2
Vinegar St E1 118 B5
Vinegar Yd SE1 253 A2
Vine Gdns IG1 79 A3
Vine Gr UB10 60 C1
Vine Hill EC1 241 A5
Vine La
Hillingdon UB10 82 B6
SE1 117 C5 253 B3
Uxbridge UB10 60 B1
Vine Lo N12 30 A4
Vine Pl Ealing W5 110 A5
Hounslow TW3 129 D1
Vine Rd
Barnes SW13 133 D2
BR6 227 D2
East Molesey KT8 196 A5
Stratford E15 76 D1
Vineries Bank NW7 28 B5
Vineries Cl
Dagenham RM9 81 B2
Harmondsworth UB7 126 C6
Vineries The
Enfield EN1 5 C2
Southgate N14 15 C5
Viners Cl KT12 194 C3
Vine St Bridge EC1 241 B5
Vines Ave N3 29 D2
Vine Sq W14 254 D1
Vines Sch The SW11 137 A1
Vine St W1 249 B5
Vine St *continued*
Whitechapel EC3 95 D1 243 C1
Vinewood Ct E17 54 B4
Vineyard Ave NW7 29 A3
Vineyard Cl
Forest Hill SE6 163 C3
Kingston u T KT1 198 B6
Vineyard Gr N3 29 D2
Vineyard Hill Rd SW19 179 C6
Vineyard Path SW14 133 B2
Vineyard Rd TW13 150 A1
Vineyard Row KT1, KT8 175 C2
Vineyard Sch The TW10 154 A5
Vineyards The TW13 150 A1
Vineyard Studios 3 E7 77 C1
Vineyard The TW10 154 A6
Vineyard Wlk EC1 241 A6
Viney Ct 9 SW4 159 D5
Vine Yd SE1 252 B2
Viney Rd SE13 141 D2
Vining St SW2, SW9 138 C1
Vinlake Ave UB10 60 C5
Vinson Ho N1 235 D3
Vinter Ct TW17 192 C4
Vintners Ct EC4 252 B6
Vintry Mews 3 E17 53 C5
Viola Ave
Feltham TW14 150 C5
SE2 124 B1
Stanwell TW19 148 A3
Viola Ct HA8 26 D3
Viola Sq W12 111 D6
Violet Ave Enfield EN2 5 B5
Hillingdon UB8 82 B2
Violet Cl Cheam SM3 201 A1
Hackbridge SM6 203 A1
Newham E16 98 C3
32 SE8 141 B6
Violet Ct 2 E15 76 C1
Violet Gdns CR0 220 D3
Violet Hill Ho NW8 229 A3
Violet Hill
NW8 92 A5 229 A3
Violet La CR0 220 D3
Violet Rd Bromley E3 97 D3
Walthamstow E17 53 C3
Woodford E18 37 B1
Violet St E2 96 B3
Violet Terr UB8 82 C2
Violette Szabo Ho 4 SE27 183 B6
VIP Trad Est SE7 121 C2
Virgil Pl W1 237 C3
Virgil St SE1 116 B3 260 D6
Virginia Cl KT3 199 A5
Virginia Ct
Ashford TW15 170 A6
7 Rotherhithe SE16 118 D4
Virginia Ho
3 Blackwall E14 120 A6
Teddington TW11 175 A5
Virginia Prim Sch E2 95 D4
Virginia Rd
South Norwood CR7 182 D2
19 Spitalfields E2 95 D4
Virginia St E1 118 A6
Virginia Wlk SW2 160 B5
Viridian Ct TW13 149 D1
Viscount Cl N11 31 B5
Viscount Ct
9 Kensington W11 91 C1
1 Littleton TW15 171 A3
Viscount Dr E6 100 B2
Viscount Gr 3 UB5 84 D4
Viscount Point 6 SW19 179 C3
Viscount Rd TW19 148 A3
Viscount St EC1 242 A4
Viscount Way TW6 127 C1
Vista Ave EN3 6 D3
Vista Bldgs 19 E3 97 B4
Vista Bldg The 14 SE18 122 C2
Vista Dr IG4 55 D4
Vista Ho 2 SW19 180 B2
Vista Hts SE23 163 A4
Vista The Chingford E4 20 B4
SE9 165 D4
Sidcup DA14 189 D5
Vista Way HA3 44 A3
Vitae Apartments 7 W6 112 A3
Vita Et Pax Sch N14 15 B6
Vittoria Ho N1 233 D5
Vittoria Prim Sch N1 94 C5 234 A4
Viveash Cl UB3 105 D3
Vivian Ave
Hendon NW4 46 B4
Wembley HA9 66 C2
Vivian Comma Cl 3 N4 72 D5
Vivian Ct Finchley N12 29 D5
Paddington NW6 91 D5
Vivian Gdns HA9 66 C3
Vivian Ho N4 51 B2
Vivian Mans 1 NW4 46 B4
Vivian Rd E3 97 A5
Vivian Sq SE15 140 B2
Vivian Way N2 48 B4
Vivien Cl KT9 214 A1
Vivienne Cl TW1 153 D5
Voce Rd SE18 145 B5
Voewood Cl KT3 199 D3
Vogans Mill SE1 253 D2
Vogler Ho 3 E1 118 C6
Vogue Ct 8 BR1 187 B2
Vollasky Ho 5 E1 96 A2
Volta Cl N9 18 C1
Voltaire 2 SE5 139 D4
Voltaire Ct 13 SW11 137 A3
Voltaire Rd SW4 137 D2
Voltaire 15 TW9 132 B4
Voltaire Way UB3 105 C6
Volt Ave NW10 89 C4
Volta Way CR0 204 B1
Voluntary Pl E11 55 A3
Vora Ho HA0 65 D2
Vorley Rd N19 71 C6
Voss Ct SW16 182 A4
Voss St E2 96 A4
Voyager Bsns Est 10 SE16 118 A3
Voyagers Cl IG11 102 C1
Voysey Cl N3 47 A6
Vulcan Cl E6 100 C1
Vulcan Gate EN2 4 C3
Vulcan Rd SE4 141 B3
Vulcan Sq E14 119 C2
Vulcan Terr SE4 141 B3
Vulcan Way N7 72 B2
Vyne Ho SM5 218 D2
Vyner Ct E5 74 A6
Vyner Rd W3 111 B6
Vyners Sch UB10 60 B4
Vyner St E2 96 B6
Vyners Way UB10 60 C3
Vyne The DA7 147 D2
Vyvyan Ho SE18 144 C4

W

Wadbrook St KT1 175 D1
Wadcroft Ct SE4 141 B2
Waddesdon Lo HA3 43 A3
Wadding St
SE17 117 B2 262 C3
Waddington Cl EN1 5 C1
Waddington Rd E15 76 B2
Waddington St E15 76 B2
Waddington Way SE19 183 B2
WADDON 220 C4
Waddon Cl CR0 220 C5
Waddon Court Rd CR0 220 C5
Waddon Inf Sch CR9 220 C3
Waddon Marsh Sta CR0 220 C6
Waddon Marsh Way CR0 204 B1
Waddon New Rd CR0 220 D6
Waddon Park Ave CR0 220 C5
Waddon Rd CR0 220 D5
Waddon Sta CR0 220 C4
Waddon Way CR0, CR2, CR9 220 D2
Wade Ct
Muswell Hill N10 31 B3
Wembley HA0 65 D5
Wade Ho
16 Bermondsey SE1 118 A4
1 Enfield EN1 17 C6
Wade's Gr N21 16 C4
Wade's Hill N21 16 C4
Wade's La TW11 175 A5
Wadeson St E2 96 B5
Wade's Pl E14 119 D6
Wadeville Ave RM6 59 B2
Wadeville Cl DA17 125 C1
Wadham Ave E17 35 D3
Wadham Cl TW17 193 A2
Wadham Gdns
Greenford UB6 64 B2
Primrose Hill NW3 92 C6 230 A6
Wadham Ho N18 33 D5
Wadham Rd
Highams Pk E17 35 D2
Wadham Rd *continued*
Putney SW15 135
Wadhurst Cl SE20 184
Wadhurst Ct E6 100
Wadhurst Rd W4 111
Wadley Rd E11 54
Wadsworth Bsns Ctr UB6 87
Wadsworth Cl
Enfield EN3 18
Wembley UB6 87
Wadsworth Ct E10 54
Wadsworth Rd UB6 87
Wager St E3 97
Waggoners Rdbt TW5 128
Waggon Mews N14 15
Waggon Rd EN4 2
Waghorn Rd
Harrow HA3 43
Newham E13 99
Waghorn St SE15 140
Wagner St SE15 140
Wagon Rd EN4, EN5 1
Wagstaff Gdns RM9 80
Wagtail Cl NW9 27
Wagtail Wlk BR3 208
Waights Ct KT2 176
Waikato Lo IG9 21
Wainford Cl SW19 156
Wainwright Gr TW7 130
Wainwright Ho 3 E1 118
Waite Davies Rd SE12 164
Waitelands Ho KT3 199
Waite St SE15 139
Waithman St EC4 241
Wakefield Ct 4 SE26 184
Wakefield Gdns
Redbridge IG1 56
South Norwood SE19 183
Wakefield Ho
Dulwich SE22 162
6 Peckham SE15 140
Wakefield Mews WC1 233
Wakefield Rd
Friern Barnet N11 31
20 Richmond TW10 153
South Tottenham N15 51
Wakefield St
Edmonton N18 34
Newham E6 100
St Pancras WC1 94 A4 233
Wakeford Cl SW4 159
Wakehams Hill HA5 41
Wakeham St 9 N1 73
Wakehurst Rd SW11 158
Wakeling Ct E7 77
Wakeling Ho 8 SE27 160
Wakeling La HA0 65
Wakeling Rd W7 86
Wakeling St 11 E14 97
Wakelin Ho
Forest Hill SE23 163
19 Islington N1 72
Wakelin Rd E15 98
Wakeman Ho HA8 26
Wakeman Rd NW10 90
Wakemans Hill Ave NW9 45
Wakering Rd IG11 79
Wakerley Cl 6 E6 100
Wakley St EC1 94 D4 234
Walberswick St SW8 270
Walbrook Ct 22 N1 95
Walbrook EC4 252
Walbrook Ho N9 18
Walbrook 10 E18 55
Walbrook Wharf EC4 252
Walburgh St E1 96
Walcorde Ave SE17 262
Walcot Ct CR0 222
Walcot Gdns SE11 261
Walcot Ho 9 SE22 139
Walcot Rd EN3 7
Walcot Sq SE11 116 C2 261
Walcott St SW1 259
Waldair Ct E16 122
Waldeck Gr SE27 160
Waldeck Rd
Brentford W4 132
Ealing W13 87
Mortlake SW14 133
Tottenham N15 50
Waldeck Terr SW14 133

Waldegrave Ct
11 Barking IG11 . . . . . 101 B6
1 Teddington
TW11 . . . . 174 D5
Waldegrave Gdns
TW1 . . . . 152 D1
Waldegrave Ho 5
SW15 . . . . 156 C6
Waldegrave Pk
TW1 . . . . 174 D6
Waldegrave Rd BR1 . . 210 B5
Dagenham RM8 . . . . . . 80 C6
Ealing W5 . . . . 110 B6
Hornsey N8 . . . . 50 C6
Penge SE19 . . . . 183 D3
Teddington TW11 . . . . 174 D6
Waldegrave Sch
TW2 . . . . 152 B1
Waldegrove CR0 . . . . . 221 D5
Waldemar Ave
Ealing W13 . . . . 109 C5
Fulham SW6 . . . . 135 A3
Waldemar Avenue Mans
SW6 . . . . 264 A1
Waldemar Rd SW19 . . 179 C5
Walden Ave BR7 . . . . . 188 B6
Edmonton N13 . . . . 33 A6
Walden Cl DA17 . . . . . 125 B1
Walden Ct SW8 . . . . . . 269 D2
Walden Gdns CR7,
SW16 . . . . 204 B5
Walden Ho Barnet EN4 . . 2 C1
8 Clapham SW11 . . . 137 A3
SW1 . . . . 258 B3
Walden Rd BR7 . . . . . . 188 B4
Tottenham N17 . . . . 33 B2
Waldenshaw Rd
SE23 . . . . 162 C3
Walden St E1 . . . . 96 B1
Walden Way NW7 . . . . . 28 D4
Waldo Cl SW4 . . . . 159 C6
Waldo Ind Est BR1 . . 209 D6
Waldo Pl SW19 . . . . . 180 C3
Waldo Rd BR1 . . . . . . 209 D6
College Pk NW10 . . . . . 90 B4
Waldorf Cl CR2 . . . . . . 220 D1
Waldram Cres SE23 . . 162 C3
Waldram Park Rd
SE23 . . . . 162 D3
Waldram Pl 6
SE23 . . . . 162 C3
Waldrist Way DA18 . . . 125 B4
Waldron Gdns BR2 . . . 208 B6
Waldron Ho 17 SW2 . . 160 B6
Waldronhyrst CR0,
CR2 . . . . 220 D4
Waldron Mews SW3 . 266 D6
Waldron Rd
Harrow HA1, HA2 . . . . . 42 C1
Wandsworth SW18 . . 158 A1
Waldrons The CR0 . . . 221 A4
Waldron's Yd HA2 . . . . 64 B6
Waldstock Rd SE28 . . 124 A6
Waleran Cl HA7 . . . . . . 24 D4
Walerand Rd SE13 . . . 142 A3
Waleran Flats SE1 . . 263 A4
Wales Ave SM5 . . . . . . 218 C3
Wales Cl SE15 . . . . . . 140 B6
Wales Farm Rd W3 . . . 89 B2
Waleton Acres SM6 . . 219 C2
Waley St 1 E1 . . . . 97 A2
Walfield Ave N20 . . . . . 13 D4
Walfield Ho N20 . . . . . . 14 A4
Walford Ho 28 E1 . . . . . 96 B1
Walford Rd N16 . . . . . . 73 C4
Walfrey Gdns RM9 . . . . 81 A1
Walham Ct 15 NW3 . . . . 70 D2
WALHAM GREEN . . . 135 D5
Walham Green Arc
SW6 . . . . 265 B4
Walham Gr
SW6 . . . . 135 C5 265 A4
Walham Rise 1
SW19 . . . . 179 A4
Walham Yd SW6 . . . . 265 A4
Walkden Rd BR7 . . . . 188 C5
Walker Cl Ealing W7 . . 108 C5
East Bedfont TW14 . . 149 D4
Friern Barnet N11 . . . . 31 C6
Hampton TW12 . . . . . 173 B4
Plumstead SE18 . . . . 123 A2
Walker Ho NW1 . . . . . 232 C3
Walker Mews 9
SW2 . . . . 160 C6
Walker Prim Sch
N14 . . . . 15 D2
Walkerscroft Mead
SE21 . . . . 161 A3
Walker's Ct W1 . . . . . 249 C6
Walkers Lo 18 E14 . . 120 A4
Walker's Pl SW15 . . . 135 A1
Walkinshaw Ct 9
N1 . . . . 73 A1
Walks The N2 . . . . 48 B6
Walk The
Ashford TW16 . . . . . . 171 D3
Palmers Green N13 . . . . 16 C1
Walkynscroft 1
SE15 . . . . 140 B3
Wallace Cl SE28 . . . . . 124 D6
Upper Halliford
TW17 . . . . 193 B5
Uxbridge UB10 . . . . 82 A5
Wallace Collection*
W1 . . . . 238 A2
Wallace Cres SM5 . . . 218 D3
Wallace Ct
19 Enfield EN3 . . . . 7 C6
NW1 . . . . 237 B3
Wallace Ho N7 . . . . 72 B2
Wallace Lo N4 . . . . 50 C1
Wallace Rd N1, N5 . . . . 73 A2
Wallasey Cres UB10 . . . 60 C5
Wallbrook Bsns Ctr
TW4 . . . . 128 B2
Wallbutton Rd SE4 . . . 141 A3
Wallcote Ave NW2 . . . . 46 D1
Wall Ct N4 . . . . 50 B1
Walled Garden Cl
BR3 . . . . 207 D5
Walled Gdn The*
TW16 . . . . 194 B6
WALLEND 100 C6
Wall End Ct E6 . . . . . . 100 C6
Wall End Rd E6 . . . . . . 78 C1
Waller Dr HA6 . . . . 22 A2
Waller Rd SE14 . . . . . 140 D3
Wallers Cl RM9 . . . . . 103 B6
Wallett Ct 11 NW1 . . . . 71 C1
Wallflower St W12 . . . 111 D6
Wallgrave Rd SW5 . . 255 C3
Wallingford Ave
W10 . . . . 90 D1
WALLINGTON 219 A2
Wallington Cl HA4 . . . . 39 A3
Wallington Ct 10
SM6 . . . . 219 B2
Wallington Cty Gram
Sch SM6 . . . . 219 B5
Wallington Green
SM6 . . . . 219 B4
Wallington Rd IG3 . . . . 57 D2
Wallington Sq 4
SM6 . . . . 219 C2
Wallington Sta SM6 . 219 B2
Wallis Alley SE1 . . . . 252 B2
Wallis Cl SW11 . . . . . 136 B2
Wallis Ho
5 New Cross Gate
SE14 . . . . 141 A4
Ruislip HA4 . . . . 39 A1
Ruislip HA4 . . . . 39 B1
Wallis Rd
Hackney Wick E9 . . . . . 75 C2
Southall UB1 . . . . 85 D1
Wallorton Gdns
SW14 . . . . 133 B1
Wallside EC2 . . . . 242 B3
Wall St N1 . . . . 73 B2
Wallwood Rd E11 . . . . . 54 B2
Wallwood St E14 . . . . . 97 B2
Walmar Cl EN4 . . . . 2 B4
Walmer Cl BR6 . . . . . . 227 B4
Chingford E4 . . . . 19 D2
Walmer Gdns W13 . . . 109 A4
Walmer Ho
8 North Kensington
W10 . . . . 90 D1
8 Penge SE20 . . . . . 184 C3
Walmer Pl W1 . . . . . . 237 C4
Walmer Rd
North Kensington
W10 . . . . 90 C1
W11 . . . . 113 A6 244 A5
Walmer Terr SE18 . . . 123 B2
Walmgate Rd UB6 . . . . 87 B6
Walmington Fold
N12 . . . . 29 C4
Walm La NW2 . . . . 68 C2
Walmsley Ho 1
SW16 . . . . 181 C6
Walney Wlk 6 N1 . . . . 73 A2
Walnut Ave UB7 . . . . . 104 C3
Walnut Cl
Hayes UB3 . . . . 105 C6
Ilford IG6 . . . . 57 A5
SE8 . . . . 141 B6
Wallington SM5 . . . . . 218 D3
Walnut Ct 2 E17 . . . . . 54 A5
Walnut Gdns E15 . . . . . 76 C3
Walnut Gr EN1 . . . . 17 B6
Walnut Ho 11 E3 . . . . . 97 B6
Walnut Mews SM2 . . . 218 A1
Walnut Rd E10 . . . . 75 D6
Walnut Tree Ave
CR4 . . . . 202 C6
Walnut Tree Cl
Barnes SW13 . . . . . . 133 D4
Chislehurst BR7 . . . . . 189 A2
Walnut Tree Cotts
SW19 . . . . 179 A5
Walnut Tree Ho
SW10 . . . . 265 D6
Walnut Tree Rd
Brentford TW8 . . . . . . 132 A6
Charlton TW17 . . . . . . 171 A1
Dagenham RM8 . . . . . . 81 A6
Greenwich SE10 . . . . . 120 C1
Heston TW5 . . . . 129 B6
Walnut Tree Walk Prim
Sch SE11 . . 116 C2 261 A4
Walnut Tree Wlk
SE11 . . . . 116 C2 261 A4
Walnut Way
Buckhurst Hill IG9 . . . . 21 D1
Ruislip HA4 . . . . 62 C2
Walpole Ave TW9 . . . . 132 B3
Walpole Cl
Pinner HA5 . . . . 23 C4
West Ealing W13 . . . . 109 C4
Walpole Cres 10
TW11 . . . . 174 D5
Walpole Ct
Ealing W5 . . . . 109 D5
7 Hammersmith
W14 . . . . 112 D3
South Hampstead
NW6 . . . . 70 A1
Twickenham TW2 . . . . 152 C2
2 Wallington SM6 . . . 219 B3
Walpole Gdns
Acton Green W4 . . . . 111 A1
Twickenham TW2 . . . . 152 C1
Walpole Ho
Chislehurst BR7 . . . . . 189 B2
East Molesey KT8 . . . 195 C4
Walpole Lo W13 . . . . . 109 C5
Walpole Mews NW8 . 229 C5
Walpole Pl
9 Teddington
TW11 . . . . 174 D5
3 Woolwich SE18 . . . 122 D2
Walpole Rd BR2 . . . . . 209 D4
Mitcham SW19 . . . . . . 180 B4
South Croydon CR0 . . 221 B6
Surbiton KT6 . . . . 198 A3
Teddington TW11 . . . . 174 D5
Tottenham N17 . . . . 33 A1
Tottenham N17 . . . . 51 A6
Twickenham TW2 . . . . 152 C2
Upton E6 . . . . 77 C1
Walthamstow E17 . . . . . 53 A5
Woodford E18 . . . . 36 D2
Walpole St
SW3 . . . . 114 D1 257 D2
Walrond Ave HA9 . . . . . 66 A3
Walsham Cl SE28 . . . . 124 D6
Upper Clapton N16 . . . . 52 A1
Walsham Ho
New Cross Gate
SE14 . . . . 140 D3
SE17 . . . . 262 C2
Walsham Rd
Feltham TW14 . . . . . . 150 B4
New Cross Gate
SE14 . . . . 140 D3
Walsh Lodge HA4 . . . . . 40 B3
Walsingham Gdns
KT19 . . . . 215 D3
Walsingham Ho
Chingford E4 . . . . 20 B4
Twickenham TW2 . . . . 152 B2
Walsingham Lo
SW13 . . . . 134 A4
Walsingham Mans
SW6 . . . . 265 D4
Walsingham NW8 . . . 229 D6
Walsingham Pk
BR7 . . . . 189 B1
Walsingham Pl SW4,
SW11 . . . . 159 A5
Walsingham Rd
BR5 . . . . 190 B2
Ealing W13 . . . . 109 A5
Enfield EN2 . . . . 17 B6
Mitcham CR4 . . . . 202 D4
Shacklewell E5 . . . . . . 74 A5
Walsingham Wlk
DA17 . . . . 147 C6
Walter Besant Ho 20
E1 . . . . 96 D4
Walter Ct 3 W3 . . . . . . 89 A1
Walter Green Ho
SE15 . . . . 140 C4
Walter Ho SW10 . . . . 266 C4
Walter Hurford Par 5
E12 . . . . 78 C4
Walter Northcott Ho 2
NW6 . . . . 69 C3
Walter Rodney Cl
E12 . . . . 78 B2
Walter Savill Twr
E17 . . . . 53 C3
Walters Cl
Hayes UB3 . . . . 105 D4
SE17 . . . . 262 B3
Walters Ho
3 Camberwell
SE5 . . . . 139 C3
Islington N1 . . . . 234 D6
Walters Ho continued
10 Kennington SE17 . 138 D6
Walter Sickert Hall
N1 . . . . 235 A3
Walters Rd EN3 . . . . 6 C1
Walter's Rd SE25 . . . . 205 C5
Walter St
Globe Town E2 . . . . . . 96 D4
2 Kingston u T KT2 . 176 A2
Walters Way SE23 . . . 162 D5
Walters Yd BR1 . . . . . 187 A1
Walter Taylor Ct
SE4 . . . . 141 B1
Walter Terr E1 . . . . 96 D1
Walterton Rd W9 . . . . . 91 C3
Walter Wlk HA8 . . . . . . 27 A4
Waltham Ave
Hayes UB3 . . . . 105 B3
Preston NW9 . . . . 44 C3
Waltham Ct
Chingford E17 . . . . 36 A2
Whetstone N20 . . . . . . 14 B1
Waltham Dr HA8 . . . . . 44 C6
Waltham Forest Coll
E17 . . . . 35 D1
Waltham Gdns EN3 . . . . 6 C6
Waltham Green Ct
SW6 . . . . 265 C3
Waltham Ho NW8 . . . 229 A6
10 Stockwell SW9 . . . 138 B3
Waltham Park Way
E17 . . . . 35 C3
Waltham Pk E17 . . . . . . 35 C2
Waltham Rd
Carshalton SM5 . . . . . 202 C1
Southall UB2 . . . . 107 A3
WALTHAMSTOW 53 D6
Walthamstow Acad
E17 . . . . 35 B2
Walthamstow Ave
E4 . . . . 35 C3
Walthamstow Ave
(North Circular Rd)
E4 . . . . 35 B4
Walthamstow Bsns Ctr
E17 . . . . 36 A1
Walthamstow Central
Sta E17 . . . . 53 C4
Walthamstow Mkt
E17 . . . . 53 C5
Walthamstow Queens
Road Sta E17 . . . . . . 53 C4
Walthamstow Sch for
Girls E17 . . . . 53 D5
Waltham Way E4 . . . . . 19 C2
Waltheof Ave N17 . . . . 33 B2
Waltheof Gdns N17 . . . 33 B2
Walton Ave
Cheam SM3 . . . . 217 B5
Harrow HA2 . . . . 63 B4
New Malden KT3 . . . . 199 D5
Wembley HA9 . . . . 66 D5
Walton Bridge Rd KT12,
TW17 . . . . 193 C2
Walton Cl
Dollis Hill NW2 . . . . . . 68 B6
Harrow HA1 . . . . 42 B5
Lea Bridge E5 . . . . 74 D5
SW8 . . . . 138 A5 270 B4
Walton Croft HA1 . . . . . 64 C4
Walton Ct EN5 . . . . 14 A6
Walton Dr
Harrow HA1 . . . . 42 B5
Willesden NW10 . . . . . 67 B2
Walton Gdns
Acton W3 . . . . 88 D2
Feltham TW13 . . . . . . 171 D6
Wembley HA9 . . . . 66 A6
Walton Gn CR0 . . . . . 224 A1
Walton Ho E2 . . . . 243 D6
Ealing W5 . . . . 109 D2
1 Edmonton N9 . . . . . . 34 A6
1 Kingston u T KT2 . 176 A3
Upper Holloway N7 . . . . 72 B5
10 Walthamstow E17 . . 53 D6
Wandsworth SW18 . . 157 C5
Walton La
Oatlands Pk KT13,
TW17 . . . . 193 B1
Shepperton TW17 . . . 193 B2
Walton Oak Prim Sch
KT12 . . . . 194 C1
WALTON-ON-THAMES
. . . . 194 C2
Walton Pl SW3 . . . . . . 257 C6
Walton Rd
East Molesey KT8,
KT12 . . . . 195 C5
Harrow HA1 . . . . 42 B5
Little Ilford E12 . . . . . . 78 C4
Newham E13 . . . . 99 C5
Sidcup DA14 . . . . 168 C1
Tottenham N15 . . . . 51 D5
Walton-on-T
KT12&KT8 . . . . 194 D4
Walton St Enfield EN2 . . . 5 B4
SW3 . . . . 114 C3 257 B5
Walton Way
Acton W3 . . . . 88 D2
Mitcham CR4 . . . . 203 C5
Walt Whitman Cl 6
SE24 . . . . 138 D1
WALWORTH 117 B1
Walworth Pl
SE17 . . . . 117 A1 262 B1
Walworth Rd
SE17 . . . . 117 A1 262 B2
Walworth Sch
SE17 . . . . 117 C1 263 B1
Walwyn Ave BR1 . . . . 209 D6
Wanborough Dr
SW15 . . . . 156 B3
Wanderer Dr IG11 . . . 102 C4
Wandle Bank
Mitcham SW19 . . . . . 180 B3
Wallington CR0 . . . . . 220 A5
Wandle Court Gdns
CR0 . . . . 220 A5
Wandle Ct
4 Bedford Pk
W12 . . . . 111 C4
Wallington CR0 . . . . . 220 A5
West Ewell KT19 . . . . 215 A4
Wandle Ho
6 Catford BR1 . . . . . 186 B5
NW8 . . . . 237 A4
Wandsworth SW18 . . 157 D4
Wandle Lodge SM6 . . 219 B6
Wandle Lo CR0 . . . . . 220 A5
Wandle Pk Sta CR0 . 220 C6
Wandle Rd
Croydon CR0 . . . . 221 A5
Hackbridge SM6 . . . . . 219 B6
Morden SM4 . . . . 202 B4
Upper Tooting
SW17 . . . . 158 C2
Wallington CR0 . . . . . 220 A5
Wandle Side
Hackbridge SM6 . . . . . 219 B5
Wallington CR0 . . . . . 220 B5
Wandle Tech Pk
CR4 . . . . 202 D2
Wandle Trad Est
CR4 . . . . 202 D2
Wandle Valley Sch
SM5 . . . . 202 C2
Wandle Way
Mitcham CR4 . . . . 202 D4
Wandsworth SW18 . . 157 D3
Wandon Rd
SW6 . . . . 135 D5 265 D3
WANDSWORTH 157 C5
Wandsworth Bridge Rd
SW6 . . . . 135 D4 265 C1
Wandsworth Common
Sta SW12 . . . . 158 D4
Wandsworth Common
West Side SW18 . . . . 158 A6
Wandsworth Gyratory
SW18 . . . . 157 D6
Wandsworth High St
SW18 . . . . 157 D6
Wandsworth Mus*
SW18 . . . . 157 D6
Wandsworth Plain
SW18 . . . . 157 D6
Wandsworth Rd
SW8 . . . . 138 A5 270 A3
Wandsworth Road Sta
SW4 . . . . 137 C3
Wandsworth Town Sta
SW18 . . . . 135 D1
Wangey Rd RM6 . . . . . . 58 D2
Wangford Ho 13
SW9 . . . . 138 D1
Wanless Rd SE24 . . . . 139 A2
Wanley Rd SE5 . . . . . . 139 B1
Wanlip Rd E13 . . . . 99 B3
Wansbeck Ct EN2 . . . . . . 4 D2
Wansbeck Rd E3, E9 . . . 75 B1
Wansdown Pl
SW6 . . . . 135 D5 265 C4
Wansey St
SE17 . . . . 117 A2 262 B3
Wansford Rd IG8 . . . . . 37 C2
WANSTEAD 55 C3
Wanstead Church Sch
E11 . . . . 55 A4
Wanstead Cl BR1 . . . . 187 C1
Wanstead High Sch
E11 . . . . 55 C3
Wanstead Hospl E11 . . 55 B5
Wanstead Hts 8 E11 . . 55 A4
Wanstead La IG1 . . . . . 56 A3
Wanstead Park Ave
E12 . . . . 77 D6
Wanstead Park Rd
IG1 . . . . 56 A1
Wanstead Park Sta
E7 . . . . 77 B4
Wanstead Pl E11 . . . . . 55 A4
Wanstead Rd BR1 . . . . 187 C1
Wanstead Sta E11 . . . . 55 B3
Wantage Rd SE12 . . . . 164 D6
Wantz Rd RM10 . . . . . . 81 D3
WAPPING 118 B5
Wapping Dock St 19
E1 . . . . 118 B5
Wapping High St
E1 . . . . 118 B5
Wapping La E1 . . . . . . 118 B5
Wapping Sta E1 . . . . . 118 C5
Wapping Wall E1 . . . . 118 C5
Warbank La KT2 . . . . . 177 D3
Warbeck Rd W12 . . . . 112 B4
Warberry Rd N22 . . . . . 32 B1
Warboys App KT2 . . . . 176 D4
Warboys Cres E4 . . . . . 36 A5
Warboys Rd KT2 . . . . . 176 D4
Warburg Ho E2 . . . . 96 A4
Warburton Cl
6 Kingsland N1 . . . . . . 73 C2
Stanmore HA3 . . . . 24 B4
Warburton Ct
Peckham SE15 . . . . . . 140 A2
Ruislip HA4 . . . . 62 A6
Warburton Ho 5 E8 . . . 96 B6
Warburton Rd
8 Hackney E8 . . . . 96 B6
Twickenham TW2 . . . . 151 D3
Warburton St 6 E8 . . . 96 B6
Warburton Terr E17 . . . 35 D1
Wardalls Ho 12 SE8 . . 141 B6
Ward Cl CR2 . . . . 221 C3
Wardell Cl NW7 . . . . . . 27 C3
Wardell Ct N2 . . . . 48 B6
Wardell Ho 7 SE10 . . . 142 A6
Warden Ave HA2 . . . . . . 41 B1
Warden Rd NW5 . . . . . . 71 A2
Wardens Field Cl 2
BR6 . . . . 227 D2
Wardens Gr SE1 . . . . . 252 A3
Wardle St E9 . . . . 74 D3
Wardley Lo E11 . . . . . . 54 D3
Wardley St SW18 . . . . 157 D4
Wardlow 8 NW5 . . . . . . 71 B4
Wardo Ave
SW6 . . . . 135 A4 264 A2
Wardour Mews W1 . . 239 B1
Wardour St
W1 . . . . 93 D1 239 C1
Ward Point SE11 . . . . 261 A3
Ward Rd
Camden Town N19 . . . . 71 C5
Mill Meads E15 . . . . . . 98 B6
Wardrew Ct 9 EN5 . . . 14 A6
Wardrobe Pl EC4 . . . . 241 D1
Wardrobe Terr EC4 . . 251 D6
Wardrobe The 3
TW9 . . . . 153 D6
Wards Cotts TW19 . . . 148 B4
Wards Rd IG2 . . . . 57 B2
Wards Wharf App
E16 . . . . 121 D4
Ware Ct Cheam SM1 . . 217 B4
Edgware HA8 . . . . 26 A6
Wareham Cl TW3 . . . . 129 D1
Wareham Ct 2 N1 . . . . 73 C1
Wareham Ho SW8 . . . 270 C4
Warehouse W E16 . . . 121 B6
Waremead Rd IG2 . . . . 56 D4
Ware Point Dr SE28 . . 123 B4
Warfield Rd
East Bedfont
TW14 . . . . 149 C4
Hampton TW12 . . . . . 173 D2
Kensal Green NW10 . . . 90 D4
Warfield Yd 6
NW10 . . . . 90 D4
Wargrave Ave N15 . . . . 51 D3
Wargrave Ho 16 E2 . . . 95 D4
Wargrave Rd HA2 . . . . . 64 A5
Warham Rd
Croydon CR2 . . . . 221 A3
Harringay N4 . . . . 50 D4
Harrow HA3 . . . . 24 D1
Warham St SE5 . . . . . 138 D5
Waring Cl BR6 . . . . . . 227 D2
Waring Dr BR6 . . . . . . 227 D2
Waring Ho 25 E2 . . . . . 96 A4
Waring Rd DA14 . . . . . 190 C4
Waring St SE27 . . . . . 183 A6
Warkworth Gdns
TW7 . . . . 131 A5
Warkworth Rd N17 . . . . 33 B3
Warland Rd SE18 . . . . 145 C5
Warley Ave
Dagenham RM8 . . . . . . 59 B2
Hayes UB4 . . . . 84 A1
Warley Cl E10 . . . . 53 B1
Warley Ho N1 . . . . 73 B2
Warley Rd Hayes UB4 . . 84 A2
Lower Edmonton N9 . . . 18 C2
Woodford IG8 . . . . 37 B3
Warley St E2 . . . . 96 D4
Warlingham Rd
CR7 . . . . 204 D5
Warlock Rd W9 . . . . 91 C3

Warlow Cl 6 EN3 7 C6
Warlters Cl N7 72 A4
Warlters Rd N7 72 A4
Warltersville Mans N19 50 A2
Warltersville Rd N4, N8, N19 50 A2
War Meml Homes W4 133 B5
Warming Cl E5 74 D5
Warmington Rd SE24 161 A5
Warmington St 3 E13 99 A3
Warminster Gdns SE25 184 A1
Warminster Rd SE25 184 A1
Warminster Sq SE25 184 A1
Warminster Way CR4 181 B1
Warmsworth NW1 232 A6
Warmwell Ave NW9 27 C2
Warndon St SE16 118 C2
Warneford Rd HA3 44 A6
Warneford St E9 96 B6
Warne Pl 4 DA15 168 B5
Warner Ave SM3 217 A6
Warner Cl
Hampton TW12 173 B5
Harlington UB3 127 B5
Hendon NW9 46 A2
Stratford E15 76 C3
Warner Ct SM3 217 A6
Warner Ho
1 Beckenham BR3 185 D4
Harrow HA1 42 B2
4 Homerton E9 74 D2
Lewisham SE13 141 D3
NW8 229 A2
Warner Pl E2 96 A4
Warner Rd
Bromley BR1 186 D3
Camberwell SE5 139 A4
Hornsey N8 49 D5
Walthamstow E17 53 A5
Warners Cl IG8 37 A5
Warner St EC1 94 C3 241 A5
Warner Yd EC1 241 A5
Warnford Ho SW15 155 C5
Warnford Ind Est UB3 105 C4
Warnford Rd BR6 227 D3
Warnham Court Rd SM5 218 D1
Warnham Ho 6 SW2 160 B4
Warnham Rd N12 30 C5
Warnham WC1 233 C1
Warple Mews W3 111 C4
Warple Way W3, W12 111 C4
Warren Ave
Bromley BR1 186 C3
Leyton E11 76 B5
Mortlake SW14, TW10 132 D1
Orpington BR6 227 D3
South Croydon CR2 222 D1
Warren Cl DA6 169 C6
Esher KT10 212 A4
Hayes UB4 84 C2
Ponders End N9 18 D4
Wembley HA9 65 D6
West Norwood SE21 161 A4
Warren Comp Sch The RM6 59 B4
Warren Cres N9 17 D4
Warren Ct
17 Beckenham BR3 185 C3
5 Croydon CR0 205 C1
6 Ealing W5 87 C2
Greenwich SE7 143 C6
N1 234 A4
Tottenham Hale N17 52 A6
Warren Cutting KT2 177 B3
Warrender Prim Sch HA4 39 D2
Warrender Rd N19 71 C4
Warrender Way HA4 40 A2
Warren Dr UB6 86 A3
Warren Dr N KT5, KT6 198 D1
Warren Dr HA4 40 D2
Warren Dr S KT5 199 A1
Warren Dr The E11 55 C2
Warren Farm Cotts RM6 59 B5
Warren Fields HA7 25 C6
Warren Gdns E15 76 B3
Warren Hill IG10 21 C6
Warren Ho 21 E3 97 D4
Warren Jun Sch RM6 59 B4
Warren La
Stanmore HA7 9 A2
Woolwich SE18 122 D3
Warren Mews W1 239 A5
Warren Park Rd SM1 218 C2
Warren Pk KT2 177 A4
Warren Pond Rd E4 20 D4
Warren Rd
Ashford TW15 171 C3
Bexleyheath DA6 169 C6
Bushey WD23 8 B3
Chingford E4 20 A2
Croydon CR0 205 D1
Hayes BR2 225 A6
Ickenham UB10 60 B4
Ilford IG6 57 B4
Isleworth TW2 152 B5
Kingston u T KT2 177 A4
Leyton E10 76 A5
Mitcham SW19 180 C4
Sidcup DA14 168 C1
Wanstead E11 55 C2
Willesden NW2 67 D6
Warren Rise KT3 177 B2
Warren Road Prim Sch BR6 227 D4
Warrens Shawe La HA8 10 D2
Warren Street Sta NW1 93 C3 239 B6
Warren St W1 93 C3 239 A5
Warren Terr RM6 58 D5
Warren The
Hayes UB4 84 A1
Heston TW5 129 B5
Manor Pk E12 78 A4
Worcester Pk KT19 215 B5
Warren Way
Edgware HA8 26 D1
Finchley NW7 29 A4
Warren Wlk 1 SE7 143 C6
Warren Wood Cl BR2 225 A6
Warriner Dr N9 18 A1
Warriner Gdns SW11 137 A4 268 A1
Warrington Cres W9 92 A3 236 A6
Warrington Ct
4 Croydon CR0 220 D5
13 Merton SW19 179 C3
Warrington Gdns W9 236 A5
Warrington Rd
Croydon CR0 220 D5
Dagenham RM8 81 A6
Harrow HA1 42 C4
22 Richmond TW10 153 D6
Warrington Sq RM8 80 D6
Warrior Cl SE28 123 C5
Warrior Sq E12 78 C4
Warsaw Cl HA4 62 B2
Warspite Ho 3 E14 119 D2
Warspite Rd SE18 122 A3
Warton Rd E15 98 A6
Warwall E6 100 D1
Warwick Ave
Edgware HA8 11 A1
Harrow HA2 63 B4
Warwick Avenue Sta W9 92 A3 236 A5
Warwick Ave W9 92 A3 236 A5
Warwick Bldg SW8 268 C5
Warwick Chambers W8 255 A6
Warwick Cl
Bushey WD23 8 C4
DA5 169 B4
Hampton TW12 174 A3
New Barnet EN4 14 B6
Warwick Cres
Hayes UB4 83 D3
Little Venice W2 92 A2 236 A4
Warwick Ct
1 Beckenham BR2 186 C1
Ealing W7 86 D1
5 East Finchley N2 48 A6
Friern Barnet N11 31 D4
Harrow HA1 42 C6
Merton SW19 179 B2
13 New Barnet EN5 13 D6
Northolt UB5 63 C3
Surbiton KT6 214 A6
3 Upper Clapton E5 74 B6
WC1 240 D3
Warwick Dene W5 110 A5
Warwick Dr SW15 134 B2
Warwick Gdns
Harringay N4 51 A4
Warwick Gdns *continued*
Ilford IG1 56 D1
Thames Ditton KT7 196 D4
Thornton Heath CR7 204 C5
W14 113 B2 254 D4
Warwick Gr
Surbiton KT5 198 B2
Upper Clapton E5 52 B1
Warwick Ho
9 Acton W3 88 C1
10 Brixton SW9 138 C3
6 Kingston u T KT2 176 A2
6 Putney SW15 156 C4
Stoke Newington N4 51 A1
Warwick House St SW1 249 D4
Warwick Ho 5 SW19 179 A3
Warwick La EC4 94 D1 241 D1
Warwick Lo
Brondesbury NW2 69 A3
Cheam SM1 217 B4
Twickenham TW2 151 D1
Warwick Mans SW5 255 A4
Warwick Par HA7 25 B1
Warwick Pas EC4 241 D2
Warwick Pl
Ealing W5 109 D4
Little Venice W9 92 A2 236 A4
Warwick Pl N SW1 259 A3
Warwick Rd
Ashford TW15 170 A5
Barnet EN5 1 D1
Bexley DA16 146 C2
Chingford E4 35 C5
Ealing W5 110 A5
Edmonton N18 33 D6
Enfield EN3 7 B6
Friern Barnet N11 31 D4
Hounslow TW4 128 B2
Kingston u T KT3 199 A6
Penge SE20 206 B6
Plashet E12 78 A3
Sidcup DA14 190 B5
Southall UB2 107 B3
Stratford E15 76 D2
Sutton SM1 218 A3
Teddington KT1 175 C2
Thames Ditton KT7 196 D4
Thornton Heath CR7 204 C6
Twickenham TW2 152 C3
Walthamstow E17 35 B1
Wanstead E11 55 B4
West Kensington W14, SW5 113 B2 254 D4
Yiewsley UB7 104 A5
Warwick Row SW1 115 B3 258 D6
Warwick Sch for Boys E17 54 A5
Warwickshire Path SE8 141 B5
Warwick Sq EC4 241 D2
Warwick Sq Mews SW1 259 A3
Warwick Sq SW1 115 C1 259 A2
Warwick St W1 115 C6 249 B6
Warwick Terr
Leytonstone E17 54 B4
SE18 145 B6
Warwick W14 113 B2 254 D3
Warwick Way SW1 115 B2 258 D4
Warwick Yd EC1 242 B5
Wasdale NW1 231 D1
Washbourne Ct N9 18 A2
Washbrook Ho SW2 160 C5
Washington Ave E12 78 B4
Washington Bldg 1 SE13 141 D4
Washington Cl 45 E3 97 D4
Washington Ct SW17 180 D4
Washington Ho SW1 247 C1
Walthamstow E17 35 B1
Washington Rd
Barnes SW13 134 A5
Kingston u T KT1 176 C1
North Cheam KT4 200 B1
Upton E6 77 C1
2 Woodford E18 36 D1
Wastdale Rd SE23 162 D3
Watchfield Ct 7 W4 111 A1
Watcombe Cotts TW9 132 C6
Watcombe Rd SE25 206 B4
Waterbank Rd SE6 186 A6
Waterbeach Rd RM9 80 C2
Water Brook La NW4 46 C4
Watercress Pl N1 73 C1
Waterdale Rd SE2 146 A6
Waterden Cres E9 75 C3
Waterden Rd E15 75 C2
Waterer Ho 7 SE6 186 A6
Waterer Rise SM6 219 D2
Waterfall Cl N14 15 C1
Waterfall Cotts SW19 180 B4
Waterfall Rd
Mitcham SW19 180 B4
New Southgate N11, N14 15 C1
Waterfall Terr SW17 180 C4
Waterfield Cl
Belvedere DA17 125 C3
Woolwich SE28 124 B5
Waterfield Gdns SE25 205 C4
Waterford Ct 16 W13 109 A5
Waterford Rd SW6 135 D5 265 C3
Waterford Way NW10 68 A3
Watergardens The KT2 177 A4
Water Gardens The W2 92 C1 237 B2
Watergardens The IG8 37 A5
Watergate EC4 251 C6
Watergate Ho 5 SE18 122 C2
Watergate Sch SE6 185 D5
Watergate St SE8 141 C6
Watergate Wlk WC2 250 B4
Water Gdns HA7 25 B4
Waterglade Ctr The W5 109 D6
Waterhall Ave E4 36 C6
Waterhall Cl E17 34 D2
Waterhead NW1 232 A2
Waterhedge Mews EN1 17 D6
Waterhouse Cl
Hammersmith W6 112 D1
Hampstead NW3 70 B3
Newham E16 99 D2
Waterhouse Ct 7 TW11 174 D5
Wateridge Cl E14 119 C3
Wateringbury Cl BR5 190 B1
Water La
16 Camden Town NW1 71 B1
Edmonton N9 18 B4
Ilford IG3 79 D5
Water Lane Ho 29 TW10 153 D6
Water La
Richmond TW10, TW9 153 D6
SE14 140 C5
Sidcup DA14 169 B2
Stratford E15 76 C2
Teddington KT1 175 D2
Twickenham TW1 153 A3
Water Lily Cl UB2 108 A4
Waterloo Bridge SE1, WC2 116 B6 250 D5
Waterloo Cl
East Bedfont TW14 149 D3
Hackney E9 74 C3
Waterloo Ct 4 HA0 66 A2
Waterloo East Sta SE1 116 C5 251 B3
Waterloo Gdns
26 Islington N1 72 D1
South Hackney E2 96 C5
Waterloo Int Sta SE1 116 B4 250 D2
Waterloo Pier SE1 250 C2
Waterloo Pl
Kew TW9 132 C6
9 Richmond TW9 132 A1
SW1 115 D5 249 C4
Waterloo Rd
Dollis Hill NW2 68 A6
Forest Gate E7 76 D3
SE1 116 C4 251 B2
Sutton SM1 218 B3
Upton E6 77 C1
Walthamstow E10 53 C2
Waterloo Sta SE1 116 C4 251 A2
Waterloo Terr N1 72 D1
Waterlow Ct NW11 47 D2
Waterlow Rd N19 49 C1
Waterman Bldg 2 E14 119 C4
Watermans Ct
12 Brentford TW8 131 D6
Watermans Ct *continued*
2 Brentford TW8 132 A6
Watermans Mews 1 W5 110 A6
Waterman St SW15 134 D2
Waterman Way E1 118 B5
Watermark Ct RM6 58 B3
Watermead TW14 149 C3
Watermead Ho E9 75 B3
Watermead La CR4 202 D2
Watermeadow La SW6 136 A3
Watermead Rd SE6 186 A6
Watermead Way N17 34 B1
Watermen's Sq 1 SE20 184 C3
Water Mews SE15 140 C1
Watermill Bsns Ctr EN3 7 B3
Watermill Cl TW10 153 C1
Watermill Ct SE13 141 D2
Watermill La N18 33 C5
Water Mill Way TW13 151 C2
Watermill Way SW19 180 A2
Watermint Quay N16 52 A2
Water Rd HA0 88 B6
Water's Edge SW6 134 C4
Watersedge KT19 215 A4
Watersfield Way HA8 26 A3
Waters Gdns RM10 81 C3
Watershipdown Ho 4 E11 54 D2
Waterside Ave BR3 207 D4
Waterside 11 BR3 185 C2
Waterside Cl
Barking IG11 80 A4
30 Bermondsey SE16 118 A4
Northolt UB5 85 B4
Old Ford E3 97 B6
Surbiton KT6 214 A6
Woolwich SE28 123 D5
Waterside Ct
3 Hackbridge SM6 219 A5
Lewisham SE13 142 B1
Waterside Dr KT12 194 B4
Waterside N1 235 A3
Waterside Pl NW1 231 B6
Waterside Point SW11 267 B4
Waterside Rd UB2 107 C3
Waterside Sch SE18 123 B1
Waterside Trad Ctr W7 108 C3
Waterside E17 52 C3
Waterside Way SW17 180 A5
Watersmeet Way SE28 102 D1
Waterson St E2 95 D4
Watersplash Cl KT1 198 A6
Watersplash La
Hayes UB3 106 A2
Southall TW5 106 B1
Watersplash Rd TW17 192 C5
Waters Pl SW15 134 C3
Waters Rd
Catford SE6 164 C1
Kingston u T KT1 176 D1
Waters Sq KT1 198 D6
Water St WC2 251 A6
Water View Cl DA6 168 D6
Waterview Ho 13 E14 97 A2
Waterville Lo 6 N12 30 A5
Waterways Bsns Ctr EN3 7 C5
Waterworks Cnr E17 36 C1
Waterworks La E5 74 D6
Waterworks Rd SW2 160 B5
Waterworks Yd 4 CR0 221 A5
Watery La DA14 190 B4
Hayes UB3 105 B1
Merton SW19, SW20 179 B1
Northolt UB5 84 C5
Wates Way CR4 202 D3
Wateville Rd N17 33 A2
Watford Cl SW11 267 B2
Watford Rd
Elstree WD6 9 C5
Harrow HA1 43 A1
Newham E16 99 A2
Northwood HA6 22 A4
Sudbury HA0, HA1 65 B4
Watford Way (Barnet By-Pass) NW9 27 D3
Watford Way NW4 46 A5
Watkin Mews 18 EN3 7 C6
Watkin Rd HA9 66 D5
Watkins Ho
11 Cubitt Town E14 120 A4
Harrow HA1 42 D4
Watkinson Rd N7 72 B2
Watling Ave HA8 27 B2
Watling Ct EC4 242 B1
1 Elstree WD6 9 D5
Watling Gate NW9 45 C5
Watling Gdns NW2 69 A2
Watling Ho 10 SE18 144 C6
Watlings Cl CR0 207 A3
Watling St
Bexleyheath DA7 147 D1
4 Camberwell SE15 139 C6
City of London EC4 95 A1 242 B1
Watlington Gr SE26 185 A5
Watney Cotts SW14 133 A2
Watney Mkt* E1 96 B1
Watney Rd SW14 133 A2
Watneys Rd CR4 203 D4
Watney St E1 96 B1
Watson Ave
Cheam SM3 217 A6
Wallend E6 78 C1
Watson Cl
Mitcham SW19 180 C3
Stoke Newington N16 73 B3
Watson Ho 3 SW2 160 A4
Watsons Lo 4 RM10 81 D2
Watsons Mews W1 237 B3
Watsons Rd N22 32 B2
Watson's St SE8 141 C5
Watson St E13 99 B5
Wattisfield Rd E5 74 C5
Watts Cl N15 51 C4
Wattsdown Cl E13 99 A6
Watts Gr E3 97 D2
Watts Ho 6 W10 91 A2
Watt's La
Chislehurst BR7 189 A2
Teddington TW11 175 A5
Watts Rd KT7 197 A2
Watts St SE15 139 D4
Wapping E1 118 B5
Wat Tyler Ho N8 50 A6
Wat Tyler Rd SE10 142 B4
Wauthier Cl N13 32 D5
Wavel Ct
7 Streatham SW16 160 A1
7 Wapping E1 118 C5
Wavell Dr DA15 167 C5
Wavell Ho N6 49 A3
Wavel Mews
Hampstead NW6 69 D1
Hornsey N8 49 D5
Wavel Pl SE26 183 D6
Wavendon Ave W4 111 B1
Waveney Ave SE15 140 B1
Waveney Cl E1 118 A5
Waveney Ho SE15 140 B1
Waverley Ave
Chingford Hatch E4 35 B6
Sutton SM1 217 D6
Tolworth KT5 199 A3
Twickenham TW2, TW4 151 C3
Walthamstow E17 54 B6
Wembley HA9 66 B3
Waverley Cl BR2 209 D4
East Molesey KT8 195 C4
Hayes UB3 105 B2
Woodford E18 37 C1
Waverley Cres SE18 123 B1
Waverley Ct
5 Brondesbury NW6 69 A1
Enfield EN2 5 A2
North Finchley N12 30 B6
W1 238 B4
Waverley Gdns
Barking IG11 101 C5
Ealing NW10 88 B5
Ilford IG6 57 B6
Newham E6 100 A2
Northwood HA6 22 A2
Waverley Gr N3 47 A6
Waverley Ind Pk HA1 42 B6
Waverley Pl
Finsbury Pk N4 50 D1
St John's Wood NW8 92 B5 229 C4
Waverley Rd
Croydon SE25 206 B6
Enfield EN2 4 D2
Finsbury Pk N8 50 A2
Harrow HA2 41 A1
Plumstead SE18 123 B1
Southall UB1 107 C6
Stoneleigh KT17, KT4 216 B3
Tottenham N17 34 B3
Walthamstow E17 54 A6
Woodford E18 37 C2

Waverley Sch EN3 6 C1
Waverley Way SM5 218 C2
Waverly Ct NW3 70 D2
Waverton Ho 2 E3 97 B6
Waverton Rd SW18 158 A4
Waverton St
W1 115 B5 248 C4
Wavertree Ct 9
SW2 160 A3
Wavertree Rd
Streatham SW2 160 B3
Woodford E18 37 A1
Waxham NW5 70 D3
Waxlow Cres UB1 85 C1
Waxlow Ho UB4 84 C2
Waxlow Rd NW10 89 B5
Waxlow Way UB5 85 B3
Waxwell Cl HA5 22 D1
Waxwell La HA5 22 D1
Wayatt Point 1
SE28 123 A3
Wayborne Gr HA4 39 A3
Waye Ave TW5 128 A4
Wayfarer Rd UB5 85 A4
Wayfield Link SE9 167 B5
Wayford St SW11 136 C3
Wayland Ave E8 74 A3
Wayland Ho 12
SW9 138 C3
Waylands Ct IG1 79 B4
Waylands UB3 83 B2
Waylands Mead
BR3 185 D2
Waylett Ho SE11 261 A1
Waylett Pl
Wembley HA0 65 D4
West Norwood
SE27 160 D1
Wayman Ct E8 74 B2
Wayne Cl BR6 227 D5
Waynflete Ave CR0 220 D5
Waynflete Sq
18 North Kensington
W10 90 D1
16 Shepherd's Bush
W10 112 D6
Waynflete St SW18 158 A2
Wayside Ave WD23 8 B5
Wayside BR7 189 B2
Wayside Cl N14 15 C5
Wayside Commercial
Est IG11 102 A5
Wayside Ct
Isleworth TW7 130 C3
Twickenham TW1 153 C5
Wembley HA9 66 C5
Wayside Gdns RM10 81 C3
Wayside NW11 47 A1
Wayside Gr BR7,
SE9 188 B6
Wayside Mews IG2 56 C4
Wayside
Mortlake SW14 155 A6
New Addington CR0 223 D2
Weald Cl
16 Bermondsey
SE16 118 B1
BR2 226 A6
Weald Fst & Mid Schs
HA3 24 D3
Weald La HA3 24 B2
Weald Rd UB10 82 C5
Weald Rise HA3 24 D2
Weald Sq E5 74 B6
WEALDSTONE 42 D6
Wealdstone Rd
SM3 217 B6
Weald The BR7 188 B4
Weald Way
Hayes UB4 83 C4
Romford RM7 59 D3
Wealdwood Gdns
HA5 23 D4
Weale Rd E4 20 B1
Weall Ct HA5 41 A5
Weardale Ct EN5 12 C6
Weardale Gdns EN2 5 B4
Weardale Ho N4 51 A2
Weardale Rd SE13 142 B1
Wearmouth Ho 1
E3 97 B2
Wear Pl 15 E2 96 B4
Wearside Rd SE13 141 D1
Weatherbury Ho 3
N19 71 D5
Weatherbury 6 W2 91 C1
Weatherill Ct SE25 206 B3
Weatherley Cl E3 97 B2
Weathersfield Ct
SE9 166 B5
Weaver Cl
Newham E16 122 D6
South Croydon CR0 221 D4
Weaver Ct 2 E2 96 B3
Weaver Ho
12 Bethnal Green
E1 96 A3

Weaver Ho *continued*
1 Northolt UB5 85 B3
Weavers Cl TW7 130 C1
Weavers Ho 4 E11 55 A3
Weaver's La
SE1 117 C5 253 B3
Weaver St E1 96 A3
Weavers Way
6 Camden Town
NW1 71 D1
NW1 232 C6
Weaver Wlk SE27 182 D6
Webb Cl NW10 90 C3
Webb Ct 6 SE28 124 B6
South Acton W3 110 D4
Webber Cl WD6 9 D5
Webber Ho 6 IG11 78 D1
Webber Row
SE1 116 D4 251 C1
Webber St
SE1 116 D4 251 C1
Webb Est E5 52 A2
Webb Gdns 1 E13 99 A3
Webb Ho
2 Dagenham
RM10 81 C5
Feltham TW13 151 A1
SW8 269 D3
Webb Pl NW10 89 D4
Webb Rd SE3 142 D6
Webbscroft Rd RM10 81 D4
Webbs Rd UB4 84 B4
Webb's Rd SW11 158 D6
Webb St SE1 117 C3 263 A5
Webheath 6 NW6 69 B1
Webley Ct 22 EN3 7 C6
Webster Gdns W5 109 D5
Webster Ho 16 N16 73 C3
Webster Rd
Bermondsey
SE16 118 A3
Leyton E11 76 A5
Weddell Ho 23 E1 96 D3
Wedderburn Rd
Barking IG11 101 C6
Hampstead NW3 70 B3
Wedgewood Ct
1 Beckenham
BR2 208 D5
DA5 169 B4
Wedgewood Ho
SW1 259 A1
Thames Ditton KT7 196 D1
Wedgewood Mews
W1 239 D1
Wedgewood Wlk
NW3 69 D3
Wedgwood Ho
17 Globe Town E2 96 D4
SE11 261 A5
Wedgwood Way
SE19 183 A3
Wedlake St W10 91 A3
Wedmore Gdns N19 71 D6
Wedmore Rd UB6 86 B4
Wedmore St N19 71 D5
Weech Rd NW6 69 C4
Weedington Rd NW5 71 A3
Weedon Ho W12 90 A1
Weekley Sq SW11 136 B2
Weeks Ho TW10 175 C6
Weigall Rd SE12,
SE3 143 A1
Weighhouse St W1 238 B1
Weighton Rd
Harrow HA3 24 B2
Penge SE20 184 B1
Weihurst Ct SM1 218 C3
Weihurst Gdns SM1 218 B3
Weimar St SW15 135 A2
Weirdale Ave N20 14 D2
Weir Hall Ave N18 33 B4
Weir Hall Gdns N18 33 B5
Weir Hall Rd N18 33 B4
Weir Ho 8 SW12 159 C4
Weir Rd Sidcup DA5 169 D4
Streatham SW12 159 C4
Walton-on-T KT12 194 A3
Wimbledon SW18,
SW19 157 D1
Weir's Pas NW1 232 D2
Weiss Rd SW15 134 D2
Welbeck Ave
Grove Pk BR1 187 B6
Hayes UB4 84 B3
Sidcup DA15 168 A3
Welbeck Cl
New Malden KT3 199 D4
North Finchley N12 30 B5
Stoneleigh KT17 216 A1
Welbeck Ct
Hayes UB4 84 B3
W14 254 C4
Welbeck Mans 10
NW6 69 C3
Welbeck Rd
Carshalton SM1 218 B6

Welbeck Rd *continued*
Carshalton SM5 202 C1
East Barnet EN4 14 C5
Harrow HA2 41 D1
Newham E6 99 D4
Welbeck St
W1 93 B1 238 C2
Welbeck Villas N21 17 A3
Welbeck Way W1 238 C2
Welbeck Wlk SM5 202 B1
Welbourne Prim Sch
N17 52 A6
Welbury Ct E8 73 C1
Welby Ho N19 49 D2
Welby St SE5 138 D4
Welch Pl HA5 22 C2
Welcome Ct E17 53 C2
Weldon Cl HA4 62 B2
Weldon Ct
Southgate N21 16 B6
St Johns SE8 141 C3
7 Sutton SM1 218 B3
Thornton Heath CR7 204 D4
Weldon Dr KT8 195 B5
Weld Pl N11 31 B5
Welfare Rd E15 76 C1
Welford Cl E5 74 D5
Welford Ct
12 Camden Town
NW1 71 B1
7 Clapham SW8 137 C3
Welford Ho 4 UB5 85 B3
Welford Pl SW19 179 A6
Welham Rd SW16,
SW17 181 B4
Welhouse Rd SM5 202 C1
Wellacre Rd HA3 43 B3
Wellan Cl DA15,
DA16 168 B6
Welland Ct SE6 163 B2
Welland Gdns UB6 86 D5
Welland Ho SE15 140 C1
Welland Mews E1 118 A5
Wellands Cl BR1 188 B1
Welland St SE10 142 A6
Well App EN5 12 C6
Wellbrook Rd BR6 226 C4
Wellby Cl N9 18 A3
Wellby Ct 1 E13 99 C5
Wellclose Sq E1 118 A6
Wellclose St 20 E1 118 A6
Well Cl Ruislip HA4 63 A5
Streatham SW16 182 B6
Well Cottage Cl E11 55 C2
Well Ct EC4 242 B1
Wellday Ho 2 E9 75 A2
Welldon Cres HA1 42 C3
Welldon Ct
Harrow HA1 42 C4
1 West Dulwich
SE21 161 B2
Welldon Park Fst Sch
HA2 64 A4
Welldon Park Mid Sch
HA2 64 A4
Weller Ho 23 SE16 118 A4
Weller Mews 6
BR2 209 B5
Weller St SE1 252 A2
Welles Ct 15 E14 119 C6
Wellesley Ave W6 112 B3
Wellesley Cl 8 SE7 121 C1
Wellesley Court Rd 1
CR0 221 B6
Wellesley Cres TW2 152 C1
Wellesley Ct
Cheam SM3 201 A1
St John's Wood
W9 92 A4 229 A2
Twickenham TW2 152 C1
Wellesley Gr CR0 221 B6
Wellesley Ho NW1 232 C1
12 Wimbledon
SW19 179 A3
Wellesley Park Mews
EN2 4 D3
Wellesley Pl
Camden Town
NW5 71 A3
NW1 232 C1
Wellesley Rd
Croydon CR0 205 A1
Gospel Oak NW5 71 A3
Gunnersbury W4 110 D1
Harrow HA1 42 C4
Ilford IG1 57 A1
Sutton SM2 218 A2
Twickenham TW2 152 C1
Walthamstow E17 53 C3
Wanstead E11 55 A4
Wood Green N22 32 C1
Wellesley Road Sta
CR0 221 B6
Wellesley St E1 96 D2
Wellesley Terr
N1 95 A4 235 B2
Wellfield Ave N10 49 B6

Wellfield Rd SW16 182 B6
Wellfit St 6 SE24 138 D2
Wellgarth Rd NW11 47 D1
Wellgarth UB6 65 B2
Well Gr N20 14 B3
Wellgrove Sch N20 14 B3
Well Hall Par SE9 144 B1
Well Hall Pleasaunce*
SE9 144 A1
Well Hall Rd SE9 144 B1
Well Ho 11 N9 18 A1
Wellhouse Rd BR3 207 C5
Wellhurst Cl BR6 227 D1
WELLING 146 B2
Wellingfield Ct 1
DA16 146 A2
Welling High St
DA16 146 B2
Welling Sch DA16 146 B4
Wellings Ho UB3 106 B5
Welling Sta DA16 146 A3
Wellington Arch*
SW1 248 B2
Wellington Ave
Chingford E4 19 D2
DA15 168 A5
Edmonton N9 18 B1
Hounslow TW3,
TW4 151 C6
North Cheam KT4 216 C5
Pinner HA5 23 B2
South Tottenham N15 52 A3
Wellington Bldgs
15 Bow E3 97 C4
SW1 258 B1
Wellington Cl
Kensington W11 91 C1
New Cross Gate
SE14 140 D4
Walton-on-T KT12 193 D1
Wellington Cres
KT3 199 A6
Wellington Ct
Ashford TW15 170 A6
Knightsbridge SW1 247 C1
Stanwell TW19 148 A4
St John's Wood NW8 229 D3
Strand WC2 250 A6
5 Surbiton KT6 198 A3
Teddington TW12 174 B5
4 Upper Tooting
SW17 180 C4
Wandsworth SW18 158 C6
Wellington Gdns
Greenwich SE7 121 C1
Teddington TW12,
TW2 174 B6
Wellington 1 NW9 27 D3
Wellington Gr SE10 142 B5
Wellington Ho
4 Ealing W5 88 A4
18 Maitland Pk NW3 70 D2
Northolt UB5 63 C1
Wellington N8 50 A5
Wellington Ho 6
HA4 40 C1
Wellington Hospl The
NW8 92 B5 229 D3
Wellington Ho HA7 9 A1
Wellington Mans
Shacklewell N16 73 D4
1 Walthamstow E10 53 C1
Wellington Mews
East Dulwich
SE22 140 A1
3 Islington N7 72 B2
SE7 143 C6
Streatham SW16 159 D1
Wellington Mus (Apsley
Ho)* SW1 115 A4 248 B2
Wellington Par
DA15 168 A6
Wellington Park Est
NW2 68 A6
Wellington Pas 7
E11 55 A4
Wellington Pl
East Finchley N2 48 C4
St John's Wood
NW8 92 B4 229 D2
Wellington Prim Sch
Bow E3 97 C4
Chingford E4 19 D2
Hounslow TW3 129 B3
Wellington Rd
Ashford TW15 170 A5
Bexley DA5 168 D6
Brentford W5 109 C3
Bromley BR2 209 C5
Enfield EN1 17 C6
Erith DA17 125 B1
Harrow HA3 42 C6
Hatton TW14 149 C6
Kensal Green NW10 90 D4
Leyton E7 76 D4
Newham E6 100 B5

Wellington Rd N
TW4 129 B2
Wellington Rd HA5 23 B2
Wellington Rd S
TW4 151 B6
Wellington Rd
St John's Wood
NW8 92 B5 229 D3
Teddington TW12,
TW2 174 B6
Thornton Heath CR0 204 D2
Walthamstow E10 53 A1
Walthamstow E17 53 A5
Wanstead E11 55 A4
Wimbledon SW19 157 C2
Wellington Row E2 96 A4
Wellington Sq
SW3 114 D1 257 C2
Wellington St
1 Barking IG11 101 A6
WC2 116 B6 250 C6
Woolwich SE18 122 C2
Wellington Terr
Harrow HA1 42 B1
2 Wapping E1 118 B5
Wellington Way E3 97 C4
Welling Way DA16 145 B2
Well La SW14 155 A6
Wellmead IG3 58 A2
Wellmeadow Rd
Brentford W7 109 A2
Catford SE13, SE6 164 C3
Wellow Wlk SM5 202 B1
Well Rd Barnet EN5 12 C6
Vale of Health NW3 70 B5
Wells Cl
2 Northolt UB5 84 C4
South Croydon CR2 221 C3
Wells Ct
21 Hampstead
NW3 70 A4
4 Mitcham CR4 180 C2
1 Paddington NW6 91 C5
Stoke Newington N1 73 C3
Wells Dr NW9 45 B1
Wells Gdns
Dagenham RM10 81 D3
Redbridge IG1 56 A2
Wells Ho
4 Barking IG11 80 A1
Ealing W5 109 D6
Finsbury EC1 234 C2
12 Kensal Town W10 91 A3
New Cross Gate SE4 141 A3
Plaistow BR1 187 B5
9 Rotherhithe
SE16 118 C3
Wells Ho The 2
NW3 70 B4
Wells House Rd
NW10 89 C2
Wellside Gdns
SW14 155 A6
Wells Mews W1 239 B2
Wellsmoor Gdns
BR1 210 C6
Wells Park Ct SE26 184 B6
Wells Park Rd SE26 184 B6
Wells Pl SW18 158 A4
Wells Prim Sch IG8 37 A6
Wellspring Cres HA9 66 D5
Wells Rd BR1 188 B1
Hammersmith W12 112 C4
Wells Rise
NW8 92 D6 230 C5
Wells Sq WC1 233 D1
Wells St W1 93 C1 239 B2
Wellstead Ave N9 18 D4
Wellstead Rd E6 100 C5
Wells Terr N4 72 C6
Well St E9 74 C1
Wells The N14 15 D4
Well St E15 76 C2
Wells Way
Brompton
SW7 114 B3 256 C6
Camberwell SE5 139 C6
Well Wlk NW3 70 B5
Wellwood Ct SW15 134 C1
Wellwood Rd IG3 58 A2
Welmar Works
SW4 137 D1
Welsby Ct W5 87 C2
Welsford St SE1 118 A2
Welsh Cl E13 99 A4
WELSH HARP 45 C1
Welsh Harp Field
Centre NW9 45 B1
Welsh Ho 14 E1 118 B5
Welshpool Ho 22 E8 96 A6
Welshpool St 1 E8 96 B6
Welshside NW9 45 C3
Welshside Wlk NW9 45 C3
Welstead Ho 29 E1 96 B1
Welstead Way W4 111 D2
Weltje Rd W6 112 A1
Welton Ct SE5 139 C4

Welton Ho E1 96 D2
Welton Rd SE18 145 C5
Welwyn Ave TW14 149 D5
Welwyn St E2 96 C4
Welwyn Way UB4 83 C3
WEMBLEY 65 D2
Wembley Arena HA9 66 C4
Wembley Central Sta
HA9 66 A3
Wembley Commercial
Ctr HA9 65 D6
Wembley Conference
Ctr HA9 66 C4
Wembley Exhibition
Halls HA9 66 C4
Wembley High Tech
Coll HA0 65 C5
Wembley Hill Rd
HA9 66 B4
Wembley Hospl HA0 65 D2
Wembley Mkt
1 Wembley HA0 66 A3
1 Wembley Pk HA9 66 C4
WEMBLEY PARK 66 C5
Wembley Park Bsns Ctr
HA9 66 D5
Wembley Park Dr
HA9 66 B5
Wembley Park Sta
HA9 66 C5
Wembley Prim Sch
HA9 66 A5
Wembley Rd TW12 173 C2
Wembley Stadium Ind
Est
Wembley HA9 66 C5
Wembley HA9 66 D4
Wembley Stadium Sta
HA9 66 B3
Wembley Stadium
HA9 66 C3
Wembley Way HA9 66 D2
Wembley HA0 65 D2
Wemborough Rd
HA7 25 C3
Wembury Mews N6 49 C2
Wembury Rd N6 49 B2
Wemyss Rd SE3 142 D3
Wendela Ct HA1 64 C6
Wendell Park Prim Sch
W12 111 D4
Wendell Rd W12 111 D4
Wenderholme CR2 221 B3
Wendle Ct SW8 270 A5
Wendling NW5 70 D3
Wendling Rd SM1 218 B6
Wendon Ct 13 SM6 219 C2
Wendon St E3 97 B6
Wendover Cl UB4 85 A3
Wendover Ct
Acton W3 88 D3
Becontree W3 89 A3
Bromley BR2 209 B6
4 Child's Hill NW2 69 C5
W1 238 A3
Wendover Dr KT3 199 D3
Wendover Ho
Bowes Pk N22 32 B5
W1 238 A3
Wendover Lo NW9 45 D3
Wendover Rd
Blackheath SE9 143 D2
Bromley BR1, BR2 209 B6
Dagenham NW10 89 D5
Wendover
SE17 117 C1 263 A1
Wendover Way
Bexley DA16 146 A1
Bushey WD23 8 A5
Wendy Cl EN1 17 D5
Wendy Ho 8 N12 30 B5
Wendy Way HA0 88 A6
Wengham Ho W12 112 A6
Wenham Ho SW8 269 A3
Wenlake Ho EC1 242 A6
Wenlock Ct N1 235 D3
Wenlock Gdns 13
NW4 46 A5
Wenlock Rd
Burnt Oak HA8 27 A4
Shoreditch
N1 95 A5 235 B3
Wenlock St
N1 95 B5 235 C3
Wennington Rd E3 96 D5
Wensdale Ho E5 74 A6
Wensley Ave IG8 37 A3
Wensley Cl
6 Barnet N11 31 A4
SE9 166 B5
Wensleydale Gdns
TW12 173 D3
Wensleydale Ho 8
N4 51 A2

Wensleydale Rd TW12 .... 173 D3
Wensley Rd N18 .... 34 B4
Wentland Cl SE6 .... 164 B2
Wentland Rd SE6 .... 164 B2
Wentway Ct W13 .... 87 A3
Wentwood Ho 1 E5 .... 74 B6
Wentworth Ave
Borehamwood WD6 .... 10 B6
Finchley N3 .... 29 C3
Wentworth Cl
Ashford TW15 .... 170 D6
Finchley N3 .... 29 D3
Hayes BR2 .... 225 A6
Long Ditton KT6 .... 213 D6
Morden SM4 .... 201 C2
Orpington BR6 .... 227 C3
Thamesmead SE28 .... 102 D1
Wentworth Cres
Hayes UB3 .... 105 B3
SE15 .... 140 A5
Wentworth Ct
Barnet EN5 .... 1 A2
7 Chingford E4 .... 36 B5
20 Kingston u T KT6 .... 198 A4
Southall UB2 .... 106 C2
2 Surbiton KT6 .... 214 A6
Twickenham TW2 .... 152 C1
W6 .... 264 A5
Wandsworth SW18 .... 157 D5
Wentworth Dr HA5 .... 40 A4
Wentworth Dwellings E1 .... 243 C2
Wentworth Gdns N13 .... 16 D1
Wentworth Hall NW7 .... 28 C5
Wentworth Hill HA9 .... 44 B1
Wentworth Ho
Enfield EN1 .... 17 C5
4 Greenwich SE3 .... 143 A5
Wentworth Lo N3 .... 29 D3
Wentworth Mews E3 .... 97 B4
Wentworth Pk N3 .... 29 D3
Wentworth Pl HA7 .... 25 B4
Wentworth Rd
Manor Pk E12 .... 77 D4
Southall UB2 .... 106 D2
Temple Fortune NW11 .... 47 B3
Thornton Heath CR0 .... 204 C2
Wentworth St E1 .... 95 D2 243 D3
Wentworth Tutorial Coll NW11 .... 46 D3
Wentworth Way HA5 .... 41 A5
Wenvoe Ave DA7 .... 147 D3
Wepham Cl UB4 .... 84 D2
Wernbrook St SE18 .... 145 A6
Werndee Rd SE25 .... 206 A5
Werneth Hall Rd IG5 .... 56 C6
Werrington St NW1 .... 93 C5 232 B3
Werter Rd SW15 .... 135 A1
Wesleyan Pl NW5 .... 71 B4
Wesley Ave
Becontree NW10 .... 89 B4
Hounslow TW3 .... 129 B3
Newham E16 .... 121 B5
Wesley Cl
Finsbury Pk N7 .... 72 B6
Harrow HA2 .... 64 A6
SE17 .... 261 D3
Wesley Ct W1 .... 238 B3
Wesley Ho SE24 .... 161 B5
Wesley Rd
Becontree NW10 .... 89 A6
Finchley N10 .... 30 C2
Hayes UB3 .... 84 A1
Leytonstone E10 .... 54 A2
Wesley Sq W11 .... 91 A1
Wesley St W1 .... 238 B3
Wessex Ave SW19 .... 201 C6
Wessex Cl
Hinchley Wood KT10, KT7 .... 212 D6
Ilford IG3 .... 57 C3
Kingston u T KT1, KT2 .... 176 D2
Wessex Ct
Putney SW15 .... 156 D6
5 Stanwell TW19 .... 148 A5
Wembley HA9 .... 66 B6
Wessex Dr HA5 .... 23 A3
Wessex Gardens Prim Sch NW11 .... 47 A1
Wessex Gdns NW11 .... 47 A1
Wessex Ho SE1 .... 263 D1
4 Tufnell Pk N19 .... 71 D5
Wessex La UB6 .... 86 B5
Wessex St E2 .... 96 C4
Wessex Way NW11 .... 47 A1
Wesson Ho 3 CR0 .... 206 A1
West 12 Sh Ctr W12 .... 112 D4
Westacott Cl N19 .... 49 D1
Westacott UB4 .... 83 C2
WEST ACTON 88 C1
West Acton Prim Sch W3 .... 88 D1
West Acton Sta W3 .... 88 C1
West App BR5 .... 211 A4
West Arbour St E1 .... 96 D1
West Ave
East Finchley N2 .... 47 D6
Finchley N3 .... 29 C4
Hayes UB3 .... 105 D6
Hendon NW4 .... 46 D4
West Avenue Rd E17 .... 53 D5
West Ave Pinner HA5 .... 41 B2
Southall UB1 .... 107 B6
Wallington SM6 .... 220 A3
Walthamstow E17 .... 53 D4
West Bank
Barking IG11 .... 100 D6
Enfield EN2 .... 5 A3
Westbank Rd TW12 .... 174 A4
West Bank N16 .... 51 C2
WEST BARNES 200 C4
West Barnes La KT3, SW20 .... 200 B5
WEST BEDFONT 148 B4
Westbeech Rd N22 .... 50 C6
Westbere Ct HA7 .... 25 D5
Westbere Dr HA7 .... 25 D5
Westbere Rd NW2 .... 69 A3
West Block 18 E1 .... 118 C6
Westbourne Ave
Cheam SM3 .... 217 A6
Dagenham W3 .... 89 B1
Westbourne Cl UB4 .... 84 C3
Westbourne Cres W2 .... 246 C6
Westbourne Ct
Cheam SM3 .... 217 A6
W2 .... 236 A2
Westbourne Dr SE23 .... 162 D2
Westbourne Gdns W2 .... 91 D1
WESTBOURNE GREEN 91 D3
Westbourne Gr Mews 7 W11 .... 91 C1
Westbourne Gr W2, W11 .... 91 C1
Westbourne Gr Terr W2 .... 91 D1
Westbourne Gr W11 .... 113 B6 244 D6
Westbourne Ho
Heston TW5 .... 129 C6
SW1 .... 258 C2
8 Twickenham TW1 .... 153 B4
Westbourne Par 4 UB10 .... 82 D3
Westbourne Park Rd
Notting Hill W2 .... 91 C1
Notting Hill W11 .... 91 B1
Westbourne Park Sta W11 .... 91 B2
Westbourne Park Villas W2 .... 91 D2
Westbourne Pl N9 .... 18 B1
Westbourne Prim Sch SM1 .... 217 C5
Westbourne Rd
Barnsbury N7 .... 72 B2
Croydon CR0 .... 205 D3
DA7 .... 147 A5
Feltham TW13 .... 149 D1
Hillingdon UB8 .... 82 D3
Penge SE26 .... 184 D4
Westbourne St W2 .... 114 B6 246 C6
Westbourne Terrace Mews W2 .... 236 A2
Westbourne Terrace Rd W2 .... 92 A2 236 A3
Westbourne Terr W2 .... 92 A1 236 B2
Westbridge Cl W12 .... 112 A5
Westbridge Prim Sch SW11 .... 267 A2
Westbridge Rd SW11 .... 136 C4 267 A2
WEST BROMPTON 135 D6
West Brompton Sta SW5 .... 113 C1 255 B1
Westbrook Ave TW12 .... 173 B3
Westbrook Cl EN4 .... 2 B2
Westbrook Cres EN4 .... 2 B2
Westbrook Ct SE3 .... 143 B4
Westbrooke Cres DA16 .... 146 C2
Westbrooke Rd
Bexley DA16 .... 146 C2
DA15 .... 167 B2
Westbrooke Sch DA16 .... 146 D2
Westbrook Ho
5 Bethnal Green E2 .... 96 C4
5 Clapham Pk SW4 .... 159 C6
Westbrook Rd
Heston TW5 .... 129 B5
SE3 .... 143 B4
South Norwood CR7 .... 183 B1
Westbrook Sq EN4 .... 2 B2
West Brow BR7 .... 188 D5
Westbury Ave
Claygate KT10 .... 212 D2
Southall UB1 .... 85 C3
Tottenham N22 .... 32 D1
Wembley HA0 .... 66 A1
Westbury Cl
Ruislip HA4 .... 40 A2
Shepperton TW17 .... 192 D3
Westbury Ct
3 Barking IG11 .... 101 B6
Beckenham BR3 .... 185 D2
1 Buckhurst Hill IG9 .... 21 C2
Clapham SW4 .... 159 B5
11 New Barnet EN5 .... 14 A6
Tottenham N22 .... 33 A1
Westbury Gr N12 .... 29 C4
Westbury House Sch KT3 .... 199 B4
Westbury Ho
1 Walthamstow E17 .... 53 C5
6 Willesden NW10 .... 67 C1
Westbury La IG9 .... 21 C2
Westbury Lodge Cl HA5 .... 40 D6
Westbury Pl 2 TW8 .... 131 D6
Westbury Rd
Barking IG11 .... 101 B6
Beckenham BR3 .... 207 A6
Bowes Pk N11 .... 32 A4
Bromley BR1 .... 187 D2
Buckhurst Hill IG9 .... 21 C3
Ealing W5 .... 88 A1
Feltham TW13 .... 150 D3
Finchley N12 .... 29 D5
Ilford IG1 .... 78 C6
New Malden KT3 .... 199 B4
Penge SE20 .... 184 D2
Thornton Heath CR0 .... 205 B3
Upton E7 .... 77 B2
Walthamstow E17 .... 53 C5
Wembley HA0 .... 66 A1
Westbury Terr E7 .... 77 B2
Westbush Ct 1 W12 .... 112 B4
West Carriage Dr W2 .... 114 C5 247 A4
West Central St WC1 .... 240 A2
West Chantry HA3 .... 23 D2
Westchester Ct NW4 .... 46 D6
Westchester Dr NW4 .... 46 D6
Westchester Ho W2 .... 237 C1
West Cl
Ashford TW15 .... 170 A6
Barnet EN5 .... 12 B6
Cockfosters EN4 .... 3 A1
Edmonton N9 .... 17 D1
Greenford UB6 .... 86 A5
Hampton TW12 .... 173 A4
Westcliff Ho 13 N1 .... 73 B2
West Cl HA9 .... 44 B1
Westcombe Ave CR0 .... 204 B2
Westcombe Ct 1 SE3 .... 142 D5
Westcombe Dr EN5 .... 13 C6
Westcombe Hill SE3, SE10 .... 143 A6
Westcombe Lodge Dr UB4 .... 83 B2
Westcombe Park Rd SE3 .... 142 D5
Westcombe Park Sta SE3 .... 121 A1
West Common Rd BR2 .... 225 B5
Westcoombe Ave SW20 .... 177 D2
Westcote Rd SW16 .... 181 C5
Westcote Rise HA4 .... 39 A2
Westcott Cl BR1 .... 210 A4
2 South Tottenham N15 .... 51 D3
Westcott Cres W7 .... 86 C2
Westcott Ho 1 E14 .... 119 D6
Westcott Rd SE17 .... 138 D6
West Cotts NW6 .... 69 C3
Westcroft Cl
Enfield EN3 .... 6 C5
West Hampstead NW2 .... 69 A4
Westcroft Ct
3 Chiswick W6 .... 112 A2
Westcroft Ct *continued*
Kingsbury NW9 .... 44 D4
Westcroft Gdns SM4 .... 201 B5
Westcroft Ho 2 SM5 .... 219 A4
Westcroft Rd SM5, SM6 .... 219 A4
Westcroft Sq W6 .... 112 A2
Westcroft 1 SM5 .... 219 A4
Westcroft Way NW2 .... 69 A4
West Cromwell Rd W14 .... 113 B1 254 D2
West Cross Ctr TW8 .... 131 B6
West Cross Route W10, W11 .... 112 D6
West Cross Way TW8 .... 131 B6
West Croydon Sta CR9 .... 205 A1
West Ct
Hounslow TW7 .... 130 A5
Sunbury TW16 .... 172 B1
Walthamstow E17 .... 53 D5
Wembley HA0 .... 65 C6
Westdale Rd SE18 .... 144 D6
Westdean Ave SE12 .... 165 C3
Westdean Cl SW18 .... 157 D5
Westdown Rd
Catford SE6 .... 163 C4
Leyton E15 .... 76 A4
WEST DRAYTON 104 B4
West Drayton Park Ave UB7 .... 104 A3
West Drayton Prim Sch UB7 .... 104 A4
West Drayton Rd UB8 .... 82 D1
West Drayton Sta UB7 .... 104 A5
West Drive Gdns HA3 .... 24 B4
West Dr
Stanmore HA3 .... 24 B4
Streatham SW16 .... 181 C6
WEST DULWICH 161 A2
West Dulwich Sta SE21 .... 161 B3
WEST EALING 109 B5
West Ealing Bsns Ctr W13 .... 109 A6
West Ealing Sta W13 .... 109 B6
West Eaton Pl Mews SW1 .... 258 A4
West Eaton Pl SW1 .... 258 A4
West Ella Rd NW10 .... 67 C1
West End Ave
Leytonstone E10 .... 54 B4
Pinner HA5 .... 40 D5
West End Cl
Stonebridge NW10 .... 67 A1
Willesden NW10 .... 67 A1
West End Ct
Hampstead NW6 .... 69 D1
Pinner HA5 .... 40 D5
West End Gdns UB5 .... 84 C5
West End La
Hampstead NW6 .... 69 D2
Harlington UB7 .... 127 A5
Pinner HA5 .... 40 D5
West End Rd
Ruislip HA4, UB5 .... 62 A4
Ruislip UB5 .... 62 C1
Southall UB1 .... 107 A5
Westerdale Ct N5 .... 72 D4
Westerdale Rd 2 SE10 .... 121 A1
Westerfield Rd 1 N15 .... 51 D4
Westergate W5 .... 88 A2
Westergate Rd SE2 .... 147 A6
Westerham Ave N9 .... 17 C1
Westerham Dr DA15 .... 168 C5
Westerham Ho SE1 .... 262 D6
Westerham 18 KT6 .... 198 A4
Westerham Lo 10 BR3 .... 185 C3
Westerham NW1 .... 232 A5
Westerham Rd
Keston BR2 .... 225 D2
Walthamstow E10 .... 53 D2
Westerley Cres SE26 .... 185 B5
Westerley Ct HA4 .... 62 B3
Western Ave
Dagenham W3 .... 89 B1
Hendon NW11 .... 46 D3
Hillingdon HA4, UB4, UB5, UB10 .... 61 C1
Northolt UB5, UB6 .... 85 B6
Western Avenue Bsns Pk W3 .... 88 D3
Western Ave
Ruislip UB8, UB9, UB10 .... 60 B3
Wembley UB6 .... 87 C4
Western Beach Apts E16 .... 121 A5
Western Ct
4 Dagenham W3 .... 89 B1
Finchley N3 .... 29 C4
3 Kilburn W9 .... 91 B5
Southall UB2 .... 107 A3
Western Dr TW17 .... 193 B3
Western Eye Hospl The NW1 .... 92 D2 237 C4
Western Gateway E16 .... 121 A6
Western Gdns W5 .... 110 C6
Western Ho 3 W9 .... 91 B3
Western Hts SM1 .... 217 C3
Western International Market UB2 .... 106 B2
Western La SW12 .... 159 A4
Western Mews W9 .... 91 B3
Western Par EN5 .... 13 D6
Western Pl 19 SE16 .... 118 C4
Western Rd
Becontree NW10 .... 89 A3
Brixton SW9 .... 138 C2
Ealing W5 .... 109 D6
Fortis Green N2 .... 48 D5
Mitcham CR4, SW19 .... 180 C1
Newham E13 .... 99 C5
Southall UB2 .... 106 D2
Sutton SM1 .... 217 C3
Walthamstow E17 .... 54 A4
Wood Green N22 .... 32 B1
Western Terr 3 W6 .... 112 A1
Western View UB3 .... 105 D4
Westernville Gdns IG2 .... 57 A2
Western Way
New Barnet EN5 .... 13 D5
Plumstead SE28 .... 123 C4
Western Wharf 2 SE15 .... 140 A6
WEST EWELL 215 C1
West Ewell Inf Sch KT19 .... 215 B3
West Farm Ct EN4 .... 2 D2
Westferry Cir E14 .... 119 C5
Westferry Rd E14 .... 119 C3
Westferry Sta E14 .... 119 C6
Westfield 1 BR6 .... 227 A3
Westfield Cl
Cheam SM1 .... 217 B4
Enfield EN3 .... 7 A2
Kingsbury NW9 .... 45 A6
SW10 .... 266 A3
Westfield Ct
1 Kensal Green W10 .... 90 D4
Kingston u T KT6 .... 197 D4
Westfield Dr HA3 .... 43 D5
Westfield Gdns
Harrow HA3 .... 43 D5
Ilford RM6 .... 58 C3
Westfield Ho 6 SE16 .... 118 D2
Westfield La HA3 .... 43 D5
Westfield IG10 .... 21 C6
Westfield Pk HA5 .... 23 B3
Westfield Rd
Beckenham BR3 .... 185 B1
Cheam SM1 .... 217 B4
Croydon CR0 .... 220 D6
Dagenham RM9 .... 81 B4
Ealing W13 .... 109 A5
Edgware NW7 .... 11 C1
Kingston u T KT6 .... 197 D4
Mitcham CR4 .... 180 D1
Walton-on-T KT12 .... 195 A2
Westfields Ave SW13 .... 133 C2
Westfields SW13 .... 133 D2
Westfields Rd W3 .... 88 D2
Westfield St SE18 .... 121 D3
Westfield Way
Mile End E1 .... 97 A3
Ruislip HA4 .... 61 D5
Westfield NW3 .... 69 C4
West Finchley Sta N3 .... 29 D4
West Garden Pl W2 .... 237 B1
Westgate Bsns Ctr
2 Kensal Town W10 .... 91 A3
North Kensington W10 .... 90 D3
Westgate Ct
6 Beckenham BR3 .... 186 A2
15 Brixton SW9 .... 138 C2
Lewisham SE12 .... 165 A3
West Gate W5 .... 88 A4
Westgate Est TW14 .... 148 D3
Westgate Rd
Beckenham BR3 186
Croydon SE25 206
Westgate St E8 96
Westgate Terr SW10 .... 135 D6 265
West Gdns
Mitcham SW19 180
Stepney E1 118
Westglade Ct HA3 43
WEST GREEN 51
West Green Pl UB6 86
West Green Prim Sch N15 51
West Green Rd N15 51
West Gr SE10 142
Westgrove La SE10 142
West Grove Prim Sch N14 15
West Gr IG8 37
West Halkin St SW1 .... 115 A3 258
West Hallowes SE9 166
West Hall Rd TW9 132
WEST HAM 99
West Ham Church Prim Sch E15 98
West Ham La E15 76
WEST HAMPSTEAD 69
West Hampstead Mews NW6 69
West Hampstead Sta NW6 69
West Hampstead Thameslink Sta NW6 69
West Ham Sta E15 98
West Harding St EC4 241
WEST HARROW 42
West Harrow Sta HA1 42
West Hatch Manor HA4 39
Westhaven SM1 217
Westhay Gdns SW14 154
WEST HEATH 146
West Heath Ave NW11 47
West Heath Cl NW3 69
West Heath Ct NW11 47
West Heath Dr NW11 47
West Heath Gdns NW3 69
West Heath Rd
SE2, DA7 146
West Hampstead NW3 69
WEST HENDON 45
WEST HILL 157
West Hill Ct N6 71
Westhill Ct W11 244
West Hill Hall HA2 64
West Hill Harrow HA2 64
Highgate N6 49
Westhill Pk
Dartmouth Pk N6 71
Highgate N6 70
West Hill Prim Sch SW18 157
West Hill SW15 157
West Hill Rd SW18 157
West Hill CR2 221
West Hill Way N20 13
West Hill HA9 44
West Ho IG11 78
Westholme BR6 211
Westholme Gdns HA4 40
Westholm NW11 47
Westhope Ho 29 E2 96
West Ho 4 SE20 184
Westhorne Ave SE9, SE12 165
Westhorpe Gdns NW4 46
Westhorpe Rd SW15 134
West Ho 9 SW12 159
West House Cl SW19 157
Westhurst Dr BR7 188
West India Ave E14 119
West India Dock Rd E14 119
West India Ho 1 E14 119
West India Quay Sta E14 119
WEST KENSINGTON 113
West Kensington Ct W14 254
West Kensington Mans W14 254

West Kensington Sta W14 113 B1 254 C2
WEST KILBURN 91 A4
Westlake Cl
Hayes UB4 85 A3
Palmers Green N13 16 C1
Westlake Rd HA9 65 D6
Westlake 12 SE16 118 C2
Westland Cl TW19 148 A5
Westland Ct 9 UB5 84 D4
Westland Dr BR2, BR4 224 D6
Westland Ho 1 E16 122 C5
Westland Lo 1 BR1 187 C1
Westland Pl N1 235 C2
Westlands Cl UB3 106 A2
Westlands Ct KT8 196 C5
Westlands Terr 3 SW12 159 C5
West La SE16 118 B4
Westlea Rd W7 109 A3
West Lea Sch N9 17 C1
Westleigh Ave SW15 156 C6
Westleigh Ct
Finchley N12 29 D4
16 Wanstead E11 55 A4
Westleigh Dr BR1 188 A2
Westleigh Gdns HA8 26 C1
West Links HA0 87 D4
Westlinton Cl NW7 29 A4
West Lodge Ave W3 110 C5
West Lodge Ct W3 110 C5
West Lodge Fst & Mid Schs HA5 40 D5
West Lodge Sch DA15 168 A1
West London Acad
Northolt UB5 63 A1
Northolt UB5 85 A6
West London Shooting Grounds UB5 84 B5
Westly Ct NW2 68 D2
Westly Ho N9 18 B3
Westmacott Dr TW14 149 D3
Westmacott Ho NW8 236 D5
West Mall W11 245 B4
Westmark Point 13 SW15 156 B3
Westmead Cnr SM5 218 C4
Westmead SW15 156 B5
Westmead Rd SM1 218 B4
West Mead
Ruislip HA4 62 C4
West Ewell KT19 215 C2
Westmeath Ho NW2 68 A5
Westmere Dr NW7 11 B1
West Mersea Cl 9 E16 121 B5
West Mews SW1 259 A3
West Middlesex Univ Hosp TW7 131 A3
Westmill Ct N4 73 A6
WESTMINSTER 115 C4
Westminster Abbey Choir Sch SW1 115 D3 259 D6
Westminster Abbey* SW1 116 A3 260 A6
Westminster Acad NW1 92 C2 237 A4
Westminster Acad (Sch of English) W1 93 C1 239 B2
Westminster Ave CR7 182 D1
Westminster Boating Base SW1 269 C6
Westminster Bridge Rd SE1 116 B4 250 C1
Westminster Bridge SE1, SW1 116 A4 250 B1
Westminster Cath Choir Sch SW1 115 C2 259 B4
Westminster Cath RC Prim Sch SW1 115 D1 259 D2
Westminster Cath* SW1 115 C3 259 A5
Westminster City Hall SW1 259 B6
Westminster City Sch SW1 259 B6
Westminster Cl
East Bedfont TW14 150 A3
Teddington TW11 175 A5
Westminster Coll of Computing HA9 66 A3
Westminster Ct
22 Rotherhithe SE16 118 D5
South Norwood CR7 183 A1
5 Wandsworth SW18 157 C6
Wanstead E11 55 B3
Westminster Dr N13 32 A5
Westminster Gdns
Barking IG11 101 C5
Chingford E4 20 C3
SW1 260 A4
Westminster Ind Est SE18 121 D3
Westminster Kingsway Coll SW11 137 A4 268 B2
Westminster Kingsway Coll (Regent's Park Ctr) NW1 93 C3 239 A6
Westminster Kingsway Coll WC1 94 B4 233 C1
Westminster Pier SW1 250 B1
Westminster Rd
Carshalton SM1 218 B6
Ealing W7 108 C5
Edmonton N9 18 B3
Westminster Sch SW1 116 A3 260 A6
Westminster Sta SW1 116 A4 250 B1
Westminster Under Sch SW1 115 D2 259 C3
Westmoat Cl BR3 186 A3
WEST MOLESEY 195 C5
Westmont Rd KT10 212 C6
Westmoor Gdns EN3 6 D3
Westmoor Rd EN3 6 D3
Westmoor St SE7 121 D3
Westmore Ct SW15 157 A6
Westmoreland Ave DA16 145 C1
Westmoreland Dr SM2 217 D1
Westmoreland Ho NW10 90 A4
Westmoreland Pl
5 Bromley BR1 209 A6
Ealing W5 87 D2
Pimlico SW1 258 D1
Westmoreland Rd
Barnes SW13 134 A4
Beckenham BR2, BR3 208 D5
Bromley BR2 209 A5
Camberwell SE17 139 B6
Queensbury NW9 44 B5
Westmoreland St W1 238 B3
Westmoreland Terr
10 Penge SE20 184 B3
SW1 115 B1 258 D1
Westmorland Cl
3 Twickenham TW1 153 B5
Wanstead E12 77 D6
Westmorland Ct
12 Surbiton KT6 197 D2
Sutton SM1 218 A5
Westmorland Rd
BR2 209 A5
Harrow HA1 41 D4
Walthamstow E17 53 C3
Westmorland Way CR4 203 D4
Westmount Ct W5 88 B2
Westmount Rd SE9 144 C1
WEST NORWOOD 161 A1
West Norwood Sta SE27 160 D1
West Oak BR3 186 B2
Westoe Rd N9 18 B2
Weston Ave
East Molesey KT8 195 B5
Thames Ditton KT10, KT7 196 C2
Westonbirt Ct 6 SE15 139 D6
Weston Ct
Highbury N4 73 A5
3 Kingston u T KT1 198 A6
Oakleigh Pk N20 14 A4
Weston Dr HA7 25 B2
Weston Ed Ctr The SE5 139 A3
West One Ho W1 239 A3
Westone Mans 6 IG11 79 D1
West One Sh Ctr W1 93 B1 238 C1
Weston Gdns TW7 130 C4
Weston Gn
Dagenham RM9 81 B4
Thames Ditton KT7 196 C1
Weston Gr 1 BR1 186 D2
WESTON GREEN 196 D1
Weston Green Prep Sch KT7 196 C1
Weston Green Rd KT7 196 C2
Weston Ho
6 Brondesbury NW6 69 A1
8 South Hackney E9 96 C6
Weston Lo KT7 196 D1
Weston Park Cl KT7 196 C1
Weston Park Prim Sch N8 50 B4
Weston Pk
Hornsey Vale N8 50 B3
Kingston u T KT1 176 A1
Thames Ditton KT10, KT7 196 C1
Weston Rd
Acton Green W4 111 A3
Bromley BR1 186 D3
Dagenham RM9 81 A4
Enfield EN2 5 B3
Thames Ditton KT7 196 C1
Weston Rise N1, WC1 94 B4 233 D2
Weston St SE1 117 B4 252 D2
Weston Wlk 3 E8, E9 74 B1
Westover Hill NW3 69 C6
Westover Rd SW18 158 A5
Westow Hill SE19 183 D4
Westow St SE19 183 C4
West Park Ave TW9 132 D4
West Park Cl
Heston TW5 129 B6
Ilford RM6 58 D4
Westpark W5 87 D1
West Park Rd
Richmond TW9 132 C4
Southall UB2 108 B5
West Parkside
Greenwich SE10 120 D3
Greenwich SE10 121 A2
West Pk SE9 166 A3
West Plaza E14 119 D5
West Pl SW19 178 C5
Westpoint Apartments N8 50 B5
Westpoint
Beckenham BR2 208 B6
Putney SW15 156 D5
West Point 2 SE1 118 A1
Westpoint Trad Est W3 88 D2
Westpole Ave EN4 3 B1
Westport Ct UB4 84 C3
Westport Rd E13 99 B3
Westport St E1 96 D1
West Poultry Ave EC1 241 C3
West Quarters W12 90 A1
West Quay Dr UB4 85 A2
West Ramp TW6 126 C4
West Rd
Chelsea SW3 136 D6 267 D6
Clapham Pk SW4 159 D6
Dagenham RM6 59 A3
Ealing W5 88 A2
East Barnet EN4 15 A3
East Bedfont TW14 149 B4
Finchley N2 30 B2
Kingston u T KT2, KT3 177 A2
Tottenham N17 34 B4
West Drayton UB7 104 B3
West Ham E15 98 D6
West Ridge Gdns UB6 86 A5
Westrow Dr IG11 80 A2
Westrow Gdns IG3 79 D5
Westrow SW15 156 C5
West Row W10 91 A3
WEST RUISLIP 61 B6
West Ruislip Ct HA4 61 B6
West Ruislip Elementary Sch UB10 61 A5
West Ruislip Sta HA4 61 A6
West Sheen Vale TW9 132 B1
West Side Comm SW19 178 C5
Westside Ct 1 W9 91 C3
Westside
11 Hammersmith W6 112 A2
Hendon NW4 28 B1
Muswell Hill N2 48 D6
West Silvertown Sta E16 121 A5
West Smithfield EC1 94 D2 241 D3
West Sq SE11 116 D3 261 C5
West St
30 Bethnal Green E2 96 B5
Bexleyheath DA7 147 B2
Bromley BR1 187 A1
Carshalton SM5 218 D4
Croydon CR0 221 A4
Harrow HA1 42 C1
Leyton E11 76 C5
West Street La SM5 218 D4
West Street Pl 1 CR0 221 A4
West St
Soho WC2 93 D1 239 D1
Sutton SM1 217 D3
Walthamstow E17 53 D4
West Surrey Est TW15 171 A2
West Sutton Sta SM1 217 C4
West Temple Sheen SW14 154 D6
West Tenter St E1 95 D1 243 D1
West Terr DA15 167 C3
West Thames Coll TW7 130 C4
West Thamesmead Bsns Pk SE28 123 D3
West Thornton Prim Sch CR0 204 B3
West Towers HA5 40 D3
West Twyford Prim Sch NW10 88 C5
Westvale Mews W3 111 C4
Westview Cl
North Kensington W10 90 C1
Willesden NW10 67 D3
Westview Cres N9 17 C4
Westview Ct
3 Elstree WD6 9 D5
1 Whetstone N20 14 A2
West View RM6 58 C4
Westview Dr IG8 37 D1
Westview W7 86 C1
West View TW14 149 A4
West View Gdns WD6 9 D5
Westville Rd
Shepherd's Bush W12 112 A4
Thames Ditton KT7 197 A2
Westward Rd E4 35 B5
Westward Way HA3 44 A3
West Warwick Pl SW1 259 A3
West Way BR5 211 B4
Burnt Oak HA8 27 A4
Westway Cl SW20 200 B6
West Way CR0 223 A5
Westway Ct UB5 85 C6
West Way N18 33 B6
Westway (Elevated Rd) W10 91 B2
West Way Gdns CR0 222 D6
West Way TW5 129 B4
Westway Lo 35 W2 91 C2
West Way
Neasden NW10 67 B5
Pinner HA5 40 D5
Ruislip HA4 39 D1
Westway W10, W12 112 A6
West Way TW17 193 B3
West Ways HA6 22 A1
Westways KT19 215 D4
Westway SW20 200 C5
West Way BR4 208 C3
Westwell 4 NW5 71 A2
Westwell Rd SW16 182 A4
Westwell Road App SW16 182 A4
Westwick Gdns
Cranford TW4, TW5 128 B3
Hammersmith W14 112 D4
WEST WICKHAM 224 C6
West Wickham Sta BR3 208 A2
Westwick 7 KT1 176 C1
West Wimbledon Prim Sch SW20 200 B6
West Wlk
East Barnet EN4 15 A3
Hayes UB3 106 A5
Westwood Ave
Harrow HA2 63 D4
South Norwood SE19 183 A2
Westwood Bsns Ctr NW10 89 C3
Westwood Cl BR1 209 D6
Esher KT10 212 A5
Ruislip HA4 38 D3
Westwood Coll DA16 145 C1
Westwood Ct
Enfield EN1 17 C5
3 Forest Hill SE23 162 C3
7 Wimbledon SW19 179 B5
Westwood Gdns SW13 133 D2
Westwood Hill SE26 184 B6
Westwood Ho
6 Shepherd's Bush W12 112 C5
5 Stoke Newington N4 51 B2
Westwood La DA16 145 D1
Westwood Language College for Girls SE19 183 B3
Westwood Lo N12 30 C5
Westwood Park Trad Est W3 88 D3
Westwood Pk SE23 162 B4
Westwood Pl SE26 184 A6
Westwood Rd
Barnes SW13 133 D2
Ilford IG3 58 A2
Westwood Sch WD23 8 B2
West Woodside DA5 169 A3
Wetheral Ct SW17 180 B6
Wetheral Dr HA7 25 C1
Wetherby Cl UB5 63 D2
Wetherby Ct SE25 183 C1
Wetherby Gdns SW5 114 A2 256 A3
Wetherby Mans SW5 255 C2
Wetherby Mews SW5 255 D2
Wetherby Pl SW7 114 A2 256 B3
Wetherby Rd EN2 5 A4
Wetherby Way KT9 214 A1
Wetherden St E17 53 B2
Wetherell Rd E9 96 D6
Wetherill Rd N10 31 A2
Wevco Wharf SE15 140 B6
Wexford Ho 11 E1 96 C2
Wexford Rd SW12 158 D4
Weybourne St SW18 158 A2
Weybridge Ct 19 SE16 118 B1
Weybridge Ho N4 51 A2
Weybridge Point 11 SW11 136 D3
Weybridge Rd CR7 204 C5
Wey Ct KT19 215 A4
Weydown Cl SW19 157 A3
Weyhill Ho 26 SE5 139 A3
Weyhill Rd 11 E1 96 A1
Wey Ho
6 Northolt UB5 85 B3
NW8 236 D5
Weylands Cl KT12 195 B1
Weylond Rd RM8 81 B5
Weyman Rd SE3 143 C4
Weymarks The N17 33 B4
Weymouth Ave
Brentford W5 109 C3
Edgware NW7 27 C5
Weymouth Cl 1 E6 100 D1
Weymouth Ct
Belmont SM2 217 C1
5 Haggerston E2 95 D5
15 Streatham SW2 160 B4
Weymouth Ho
Bromley BR2 186 D1
Edgware HA8 26 B4
Fitzrovia W1 238 D4
South Lambeth SW8 270 C3
Weymouth Mews W1 93 B2 238 C4
Weymouth Rd UB4 83 C4
Weymouth St W1 93 B2 238 C4
Weymouth Terr E2 95 D5
Weymouth Wlk HA7 25 A4
Whadcoat St N4 72 C6
Whaddon Ho
10 Camberwell SE5 139 C2
SW1 247 D1
Whalebone Ave RM6 59 B3
Whalebone Gr RM6 59 B3
Whalebone La E15 76 C1
Whalebone Lane N RM6 59 A6
Whalebone Lane S RM6, RM8 59 B2
Whales Yd E15 76 C1
Wharfdale Cl N11 31 A4
Wharfdale Rd N1 94 A5 233 B4
Wharfedale Ct 5 E5 74 D4
Wharfedale Gdns CR7, SW16 204 B6
Wharfedale St SW10 255 C1
Wharf La
19 Poplar E14 97 B1
Twickenham TW1 153 A3
Wharf Pl E2 96 B6
Wharf Rd Enfield EN3 19 A5
King's Cross NW1 93 D6 232 D5
Shoreditch N1 95 A5 235 A3
Wharf Road NW1 94 A5 233 A4
Wharfside Rd E16 98 C2
Wharfside HA0 88 A6
Wharf St E16 98 C2
Wharf View Ct 15 E14 98 A1
Wharncliffe Dr UB1 108 B5
Wharncliffe Gdns SE25 183 C1
Wharncliffe Ho 3 SW15 156 C6
Wharncliffe Rd SE25 183 C1
Wharton Cl NW10 67 C2
Wharton Ho SE1 263 C6
Wharton Rd BR1 187 B2
Wharton St WC1 94 B4 233 D1
Whateley Rd
East Dulwich SE22 161 D6
Penge SE20 184 D3
Whatley Ave SW20 201 A6
Whatman Ho 10 E14 97 B1
Whatman Rd SE23 162 D4
Wheatcroft Ct SM1 201 D1
Wheatfields
Enfield EN3 7 A3
Newham E6 100 D1
Wheatfield Way KT1 176 A1
Wheathill Ho SE20 184 B1
Wheathill Rd SE20 206 B6
Wheat Ho TW19 148 A3
Wheatland Ho 7 SE22 139 C2
Wheatlands TW5 129 C6
Wheatlands Rd SW17 159 A1
Wheatley Cl NW4 28 A1
Wheatley Cres UB3 106 A6
Wheatley Gdns N9 17 C2
Wheatley Ho
Gospel Oak NW5 71 B4
3 Putney SW15 156 A4
Wheatley Mans 8 IG11 80 A1
Wheatley Rd TW7 130 D2
Wheatley St W1 238 B3
Wheat Sheaf Cl E14 119 D2
Wheatsheaf Cl UB5 63 A3
Wheatsheaf La
Fulham SW6 134 C5
SW8 270 B4
Wheatsheaf Par 7 BR4 207 D1
Wheatsheaf Terr SW6 264 D3
Wheatstone Cl SW19 180 C2
Wheatstone Ho 7 W10 91 A2
Wheatstone Rd W10 91 A2
Wheeler Ct 5 SW11 136 B2
Wheeler Gdns N1 233 B6
Wheeler La E1 243 C4
Wheeler 2 NW9 27 D3
Wheeler Pl 2 BR2 209 B5
Wheelers Cross IG11 101 B5
Wheelers Dr HA4 39 A3
Wheeler's St SM1 217 C5
Wheelhouse The 4 E14 119 D1
Wheelock Cl DA8 147 D5
Wheelwright St N7 72 B1
Whelan Way SM6 219 D5
Wheldon Ct SE1 253 C2
Wheler Ho E1 243 C5
Wheler St E1 95 D3 243 C5
Whellock Rd W4 111 C3
Whernside Cl SE28 124 C6
WHETSTONE 14 A2
Whetstone Cl N20 14 B2
Whetstone Park WC2 94 B1 240 C2
Whetstone Rd SE3 143 D4
Whewell Rd N19 72 A6
Whichcote St SE1 251 A3
Whidborne Bldgs WC1 233 A1

Whidborne Cl SE8 ... 141 C3
Whidborne St WC1 ... 233 B1
Whimbrel Cl SE28 ... 124 C6
Whimbrel Way UB4 ... 84 D2
Whinchat Rd SE18, SE28 ... 123 B3
Whinfell Cl SW16 ... 181 D5
Whinyates Rd SE9 ... 144 A2
Whippendell Cl BR5 ... 190 B2
Whippendell Way BR5 ... 190 B1
Whippingham Ho 22 E3 ... 97 B4
Whipps Cross Ho E17 ... 54 B4
Whipps Cross Hospl E10, E11 ... 54 B3
Whipps Cross E17 ... 54 B4
Whipps Cross Rd E11 ... 54 C3
Whiskin St EC1 ... 94 D4 234 C1
Whisperwood Cl HA3 ... 24 C3
Whistler Gdns HA8 ... 26 B1
Whistler Mews
Dagenham RM8 ... 80 B3
23 SE15 ... 139 D5
Whistlers Ave SW11 ... 136 B5 266 D3
Whistler St N5 ... 72 D3
Whistler Twr SW10 ... 266 A3
Whistler Wlk SW10 ... 266 B4
Whiston Ho 18 N1 ... 72 D1
Whiston Rd E2 ... 96 A6
Whitakers Lo EN2 ... 5 B4
Whitbread Cl N17 ... 34 A2
Whitbread Ctr EC1 ... 242 C5
Whitbread Rd SE4 ... 141 B1
Whitburn Rd SE13 ... 142 A1
Whitby Ave NW10 ... 88 D4
Whitby Ct
6 Lower Holloway N7 ... 72 A4
3 New Southgate N11 ... 31 A4
Whitby Gdns
Carshalton SM1 ... 218 B6
Queensbury NW9 ... 44 C6
Whitby Ho NW8 ... 229 A5
Whitby Par HA4 ... 62 C6
Whitby Rd
Carshalton SM1 ... 218 B6
Harrow HA2 ... 64 A5
Ruislip HA4 ... 62 C6
Woolwich SE18 ... 122 B2
Whitby St E1 ... 243 C6
Whitcher Cl SE14 ... 141 A6
Whitcher Pl NW1 ... 71 C2
Whitchurch Ave HA8 ... 26 B3
Whitchurch Cl HA8 ... 26 B4
Whitchurch Ct SW17 ... 180 B6
Whitchurch Fst & Mid Schs HA7 ... 25 D3
Whitchurch Gdns HA8 ... 26 B4
Whitchurch Ho
Catford SE6 ... 164 A1
16 North Kensington W10 ... 90 D1
Whitchurch La HA8 ... 26 B3
Whitchurch Par HA8 ... 26 C3
Whitchurch Rd W11 ... 112 D6
Whitcomb Ct W1 ... 249 D5
Whitcomb St WC2 ... 115 D6 249 D5
Whitcome Mews TW9 ... 132 D4
Whiteacre Mews SE11 ... 261 B1
Whiteadder Way E14 ... 119 D2
Whitear Wlk E15 ... 76 B2
Whitebarn La RM10 ... 103 C6
Whitebeam Ave BR2 ... 210 C3
Whitebeam Cl SW9 ... 270 D3
Whitebeam Ho 3 NW3 ... 70 D2
White Bear Pl 1 NW3 ... 70 B4
White Bear Yd EC1 ... 241 A5
White Bridge Ave CR4 ... 202 B6
White Bridge Cl TW14 ... 149 D5
White Butts Rd HA4 ... 62 D5
WHITECHAPEL ... 95 D1
Whitechapel High St E1 ... 95 D1 243 D2
Whitechapel Mkt E1 ... 96 A2
Whitechapel Rd E1 ... 96 B2
Whitechapel Sta E1 ... 96 B2
Whitechurch La 3 E1 ... 96 A1
Whitechurch Pas 1 E1 ... 96 A1
White City Cl W12 ... 112 C6
White City Est W12 ... 112 B6
White City W10 ... 90 C1
White City Rd W12 ... 112 C6
White City Sta W12 ... 112 C6
Whitecliff Ho SW18 ... 157 D5
White Conduit St N1 ... 234 B4
Whitecote Rd UB1 ... 86 A1
White Craig Cl HA5 ... 23 C5
Whitecroft Cl BR3 ... 208 B5
Whitecroft Way BR3 ... 208 B5
Whitecross Pl EC2 ... 242 D4
Whitecross St EC1 ... 95 A3 242 B5
White Cube The, Art Gallery* N1 ... 95 C4
Whitefield Ave NW2 ... 46 C1
Whitefield Cl SW15 ... 157 A5
Whitefield Sch
Chingford E17 ... 36 A1
Hendon NW2 ... 46 D2
Whitefoot La BR1 ... 164 B1
Whitefoot Terr BR1 ... 164 D1
Whitefriars Ave HA3 ... 24 C1
Whitefriars Ct 9 N12 ... 30 B5
Whitefriars Dr HA3 ... 24 C1
Whitefriars Fst & Mid Sch HA3 ... 24 C1
Whitefriars St EC4 ... 94 C1 241 B1
Whitefriars Trad Est HA3 ... 24 B1
White Gate Gdns HA3 ... 24 D3
Whitegates 4 EN5 ... 13 D6
White Gdns RM10 ... 81 C2
Whitehall Cres KT9 ... 213 D3
Whitehall Ct SW1 ... 116 A5 250 B3
Whitehall Gdns
Acton W3 ... 110 C5
Chingford E4 ... 20 C3
Chiswick W4 ... 132 D6
SW1 ... 250 A3
Whitehall La IG9 ... 21 A2
Whitehall Lo
Muswell Hill N10 ... 49 A6
Woodford IG8 ... 21 A1
Whitehall Mans 3 N19 ... 49 C1
Whitehall Park Rd W4 ... 132 D6
Whitehall Pk N19 ... 49 C1
Whitehall Pl
Wallington SM5 ... 219 B4
WC2, SW1 ... 116 A5 250 A3
Whitehall Prim Sch E4 ... 20 C2
Whitehall Rd
Bromley BR2 ... 209 D5
Chingford E4 ... 20 C2
Harrow HA1 ... 42 C2
Thornton Heath CR7 ... 204 C4
West Ealing W7 ... 109 A4
Woodford IG8 ... 21 A1
Whitehall St N17 ... 33 D3
Whitehall SW1 ... 250 A2
White Hart Ave SE28, SE18 ... 123 D3
White Hart La SW13 ... 133 C2
White Hart Lane Sec Sch N22 ... 32 D3
White Hart Lane Sta N17 ... 33 D3
White Hart Lane (Tottenham Hotspur FC) N17 ... 34 A3
White Hart La NW10 ... 67 D2
Whitehart Lo SW19 ... 180 A4
White Hart Rdbt UB5 ... 84 D5
White Hart Rd SE18 ... 123 C2
White Hart St
Holborn EC4 ... 241 D2
Kennington SE11 ... 116 C1 261 B2
White Hart Terr N17 ... 33 D3
White Hart Yd SE1 ... 252 C3
Whitehaven Cl BR2 ... 209 A5
Whitehaven Ct 5 DA6 ... 147 A1
Whitehaven St NW8 ... 237 A5
Whitehead Cl
Edmonton N18 ... 33 B5
Wandsworth SW18 ... 158 A4
Whitehead Ct
Muswell Hill N10 ... 31 A2
Twickenham TW1 ... 152 D4
Whitehead Ho 8 SW15 ... 156 D6
Whitehead's Gr SW3 ... 114 C2 257 B3
White Heart Ave UB8 ... 83 A2
Whiteheath Ave HA4 ... 39 A2
Whiteheath Inf Sch HA4 ... 39 A3
Whiteheath Jun Sch HA4 ... 39 A2
White Heron Mews TW11 ... 174 D4
White Ho
2 Battersea SW11 ... 136 B3
Lower Edmonton N9 ... 18 C2
Whitehorn Ho 6 E1 ... 118 C5
White Horse Hill BR7, SE9 ... 188 C6
White Horse La E1 ... 96 D2
Whitehorse La SE25 ... 205 C5
Whitehorse Manor Inf Sch CR7 ... 205 B5
Whitehorse Manor Jun Sch CR7 ... 205 B5
Whitehorse Mews SE1 ... 261 C6
White Horse Rd
Limehouse E1 ... 97 A1
Newham E6 ... 100 B4
Whitehorse Rd
South Norwood CR0, CR7 ... 205 B3
Tower Hamlets E1 ... 97 A2
White Horse St W1 ... 115 B5 248 D3
White Horse Yd EC2 ... 242 C2
White Ho 3 SW4 ... 159 D4
White Ho The NW1 ... 238 D6
Tottenham N17 ... 51 C6
Upper Tooting SW17 ... 180 D5
White House Ct
1 Beckenham BR3 ... 186 A2
Osidge N14 ... 15 D2
White House Dr HA7 ... 25 C6
Whitehouse Est E10 ... 54 A3
Whitehouse La EN2 ... 5 A4
Whitehouse Way N14 ... 15 B1
White Kennett St E1 ... 243 B2
Whitelands Cres SW18 ... 157 A4
Whitelands Ho SW3 ... 257 D2
Whiteledges W13 ... 87 C1
Whitelegg Rd E13 ... 98 D5
Whiteley Ho 9 SW4 ... 159 D4
Whiteley Rd SE19 ... 183 B5
Whiteleys Ctr 19 W2 ... 91 D1
Whiteleys Ho TW13 ... 151 C1
Whiteleys Par 5 UB10 ... 82 D3
Whiteleys Way TW13 ... 151 C1
White Lion Ct EC3 ... 243 A1
White Lion Hill EC4 ... 116 D6 251 D6
White Lion St N1 ... 94 C5 234 B3
Whitelock Ho 21 E9 ... 74 D2
White Lodge Cl
Hampstead Garden Suburb N2 ... 48 B3
Isleworth TW7 ... 131 A3
Sutton SM2 ... 218 A1
White Lodge Ct TW16 ... 172 C2
White Lo
7 Ealing W5 ... 87 C2
Golders Green NW11 ... 47 B1
South Norwood SE19 ... 182 D3
Whitely Ct TW13 ... 151 B1
White Lyon Ct EC2 ... 242 A4
Whiteness Ho 18 SW9 ... 138 C4
White Oak Dr BR3 ... 186 A1
White Oak Gdns DA15 ... 167 D4
Whiteoak Ho SE19 ... 183 A3
Whiteoaks La UB6 ... 86 B5
White Orchards
Barnet N20 ... 13 B3
Stanmore HA7 ... 25 A5
White Post La E9 ... 75 C2
White Post St SE14, SE15 ... 140 C5
White Rd E15 ... 76 C1
Whites Ave IG2 ... 57 C3
Whites Dr BR2 ... 208 D2
White's Grounds Est SE1 ... 253 B2
White's Grounds SE1 ... 117 C4 253 B2
White's Mdw BR1 ... 210 C5
Whitespar DA14 ... 189 D6
White's Row E1 ... 95 D2 243 C3
White's Sq SW4 ... 137 D1
Whitestile Rd TW8 ... 109 D1
Whitestone La NW3 ... 70 A5
Whitestone Wlk NW3 ... 70 A5
White St UB1 ... 106 D4
Whitethorn Ave UB7 ... 104 B6
Whitethorn Gdns
Croydon CR0 ... 222 B6
Enfield EN2 ... 17 B6
Whitethorn Pl UB7 ... 104 B5
Whitethorn St E3 ... 97 C2
Whiteways NW4 ... 46 D5
Whitewebbs Way BR5 ... 189 D2
Whitfield Ct
3 Dulwich SE21 ... 183 C6
Redbridge IG1 ... 56 B2
SW4 ... 270 A1
West Barnes SW20 ... 178 D1
Whitfield Gdns W1 ... 239 B4
Whitfield Ho NW8 ... 237 A5
Whitfield Pl W1 ... 239 B5
Whitfield Rd DA7 ... 147 B5
Upton E6 ... 77 C1
Whitfield St W1 ... 93 C2 239 B4
Whitford Gdns CR4 ... 202 D6
Whitgift Ave CR2 ... 221 A3
Whitgift Ct CR2 ... 221 A3
Whitgift Ctr CR0 ... 221 A6
Whitgift Ho
Battersea SW11 ... 267 A2
Croydon CR2 ... 221 A3
Lambeth SE11 ... 260 C4
Whitgift Sch CR2 ... 221 A3
Whitgift St
Croydon CR0 ... 221 A5
SE11 ... 116 B2 260 C4
Whiting Ave IG11 ... 78 D1
Whitings Hill Prim Sch EN5 ... 12 C6
Whitings Rd EN5 ... 12 C6
Whitings The IG2 ... 57 C4
Whitings Way E6 ... 100 C2
Whitington Ave EC3 ... 243 A1
Whitland Rd SM5 ... 202 B1
Whitley Cl TW19 ... 148 A5
Whitley Ho SW1 ... 269 B6
Whitley Rd N17 ... 33 C1
Whitlock Dr SW19 ... 157 A3
Whitman Ho 20 E2 ... 96 C4
Whitman Rd E3 ... 97 A3
Whitmead Cl CR2 ... 221 C2
Whitmore Cl N11 ... 31 B5
Whitmore Gdns NW10 ... 90 C5
Whitmore High Sch HA1, HA2 ... 42 A1
Whitmore Ho
Friern Barnet N11 ... 30 D6
20 Hoxton E1 ... 95 C6
Whitmore Prim Sch N1 ... 95 B6 235 D5
Whitmore Rd
Beckenham BR3 ... 207 B6
Harrow HA1 ... 42 A2
Hoxton N1 ... 95 C6
Whitnell Ct 7 SW15 ... 156 D6
Whitnell Way SW15 ... 156 D6
Whitney Ave IG4 ... 55 D5
Whitney Ho 6 SE22 ... 139 C2
Whitney Rd E10 ... 53 D2
Whitney Wlk DA14 ... 191 A4
Whitstable Cl
Beckenham BR3 ... 185 B2
Ruislip HA4 ... 61 C6
Whitstable Ho 11 W10 ... 90 D1
Whitstable Pl 9 CR0 ... 221 A4
Whitsters Ho SE1 ... 253 C2
Whitstone La BR3 ... 207 D4
Whittaker Ave TW10, TW9 ... 153 D6
Whittaker Ct SW4 ... 270 B1
Whittaker 3 NW9 ... 27 D3
Whittaker Pl 28 TW10 ... 153 D6
Whittaker Rd
Cheam SM3 ... 217 B5
Forest Gate E6 ... 77 D1
Whittaker St SW1 ... 258 A3
Whittaker Way 19 SE1 ... 118 A2
Whittam Ho SE27 ... 183 A5
Whitta Rd E12 ... 77 D4
Whittell Gdns SE26 ... 162 C1
Whitten Lo N12 ... 30 C6
Whittingham Com Prim Sch E17 ... 35 A2
Whittingham Ct W4 ... 133 C5
Whittingham 6 N17 ... 34 B3
Whittingstall Mans SW6 ... 264 D1
Whittingstall Rd SW6 ... 135 B4 264 D1
Whittington Ave UB4 ... 83 D2
Whittington Ct
Fortis Green N2 ... 48 D4
Penge SE20 ... 184 B1
Whittington Hospl The N19 ... 71 C6
Whittington Mews N12 ... 30 A6
Whittington Rd N22 ... 32 A3
Whittington Way HA5 ... 41 A4
Whittlebury Cl SM5 ... 218 D1
Whittlebury Ho N4 ... 51 A2
Whittle Cl
Southall UB1 ... 85 D1
Walthamstow E17 ... 53 A2
Whittle 4 NW9 ... 27 D3
Whittle Rd
Heston TW5 ... 128 C5
Southall UB2 ... 107 D4
Whittlesea Cl HA3 ... 24 A3
Whittlesea Path HA3 ... 24 A2
Whittlesea Rd HA3 ... 24 A2
Whittlesey St SE1 ... 116 C5 251 B3
WHITTON ... 152 A4
Whitton Ave W UB5, UB6 ... 64 B3
Whitton Cl UB6 ... 65 B2
Whitton Dene TW3, TW7 ... 152 B6
Whitton Dr UB6 ... 65 A2
Whitton NW3 ... 70 D1
Whitton Manor Rd TW7 ... 152 A5
Whitton Rd
Hounslow TW3 ... 151 D6
Twickenham TW1 ... 153 A4
Whitton Road Rdbt TW1 ... 152 D5
Whitton Sch TW2 ... 151 D2
Whitton Sta TW2 ... 152 A4
Whitton Waye TW2, TW3 ... 151 C5
Whitton Wlk E3 ... 97 C4
Whitwell Ho 11 E5 ... 74 B6
Whitwell Rd E13 ... 99 A4
Whitworth Cres 1 EN3 ... 7 C6
Whitworth Ho SE1 ... 262 B5
Whitworth Rd SE18 ... 144 C5
South Norwood SE25 ... 205 D5
Whitworth St SE10 ... 120 C1
Whorlton Rd SE15 ... 140 B2
Whychcote Point NW2 ... 46 C2
Whymark Ave N22 ... 50 D6
Whytecroft TW5 ... 128 D5
Whyteville Ho E7 ... 77 B2
Whyteville Rd E7 ... 77 B2
Whytlaw Ho 10 E3 ... 97 B2
Wickersley Rd SW11 ... 137 A3
Wickers Oake SE19 ... 183 D6
Wicker St 24 E1 ... 96 B1
Wicket Rd UB6 ... 87 A4
Wickets The TW15 ... 170 A6
Wicket The CR0 ... 223 C3
Wickfield Ho 32 SE16 ... 118 A4
Wickford Ho 6 E1 ... 96 C3
Wickford St E1 ... 96 C3
Wickford Way E17 ... 52 D5
Wickham Ave
Cheam KT4, SM3 ... 216 C3
Croydon CR0 ... 207 A1
Wickham Chase BR4 ... 208 C2
Wickham Cl
Enfield EN3 ... 6 C2
New Malden KT3 ... 199 D4
Stepney E1 ... 96 C2
Wickham Common Prim Sch BR4 ... 225 A4
Wickham Court Rd BR4 ... 224 A6
Wickham Court Sch BR4 ... 224 B4
Wickham Cres BR4 ... 224 A6
Wickham Ct DA16 ... 145 C3
Wickham Gdns SE4 ... 141 B2
Wickham Ho SW15 ... 156 D5
Wickham La SE2 ... 146 A6
Wickham Mews SE4 ... 141 B3
Wickham Rd
Beckenham BR3 ... 207 D6
Brockley SE4 ... 141 B2
Wickham Rd *continued*
Chingford E4 ... 36 A3
Croydon CR0 ... 207 B1
Harrow HA3 ... 24 B1
Wickham St
Bexley DA16 ... 145 C3
Vauxhall SE11 ... 116 B1 260 C2
Welling DA16 ... 146 A4
Wickham Way BR3 ... 208 A4
Wick Ho 1 KT1 ... 175 D2
Wick La Hackney E3 ... 75 B1
Stratford Marsh E3 ... 97 C6
Wickliffe Ave N3 ... 29 A1
Wickliffe Gdns HA9 ... 66 D6
Wicklow Ct SE26 ... 184 C5
Wicklow Ho N16 ... 51 D1
Wicklow St WC1 ... 94 B4 233 C2
Wick Rd Hackney E9 ... 74 D2
Hackney E9 ... 75 A2
Teddington TW11 ... 175 C3
Wicks Cl SE12 ... 187 D6
Wickstead Ho TW8 ... 110 B1
Wicksteed Ho SE1 ... 262 B5
Wickway Ct 7 SE15 ... 139 D6
Wickwood St SE5 ... 138 D3
Widdenham Rd N7 ... 72 B4
Widdicombe Ave HA2 ... 63 A6
Widdin St E15 ... 76 C1
Widecombe Ct N2 ... 48 B4
Widecombe Gdns IG4 ... 56 A5
Widecombe Ho 32 SE5 ... 139 A3
Widecombe Rd SE9 ... 166 A1
Widecombe Way N2 ... 48 B5
Widegate St E1 ... 243 B3
Widenham Cl HA5 ... 40 C4
Wide Way CR4 ... 203 D6
Widewing Cl TW11 ... 175 B3
Widford Ho N1 ... 234 C3
Widford 8 NW1 ... 71 B2
Widgeon Cl E16 ... 99 B1
Widgeon Path SE28 ... 123 B3
Widley Rd W9 ... 91 C3
Widmer Ct TW5 ... 129 A3
WIDMORE ... 188 A1
Widmore Lodge Rd BR1 ... 187 D1
Widmore Rd BR1 ... 187 C1
Hillingdon UB8 ... 82 D3
Widnes Ho 6 N7 ... 72 C3
Wieland Rd HA6 ... 22 A3
Wigan Ho E5 ... 52 B1
Wigeon Way UB4 ... 84 D1
Wiggins La TW10 ... 153 C2
Wiggins Mead NW9 ... 27 D3
Wigginton Ave HA9 ... 66 D2
Wigham Ho IG11 ... 79 A1
Wightman Rd N4, N8 ... 50 C4
Wighton Mews TW7 ... 130 C3
Wigley Rd TW13 ... 150 D3
Wigmore Ct 4 W13 ... 109 A5
Wigmore Hall* W1 ... 238 C2
Wigmore Pl W1 ... 93 B1 238 C2
Wigmore Rd SM5 ... 202 C1
Wigmore St W1 ... 93 A1 238 B2
Wigmore Wlk SM5 ... 218 B6
Wigram Ct SW11 ... 267 A2
Wigram Ho 7 E14 ... 119 D6
Wigram Rd E11 ... 55 C3
Wigram Sq E17 ... 54 A6
Wigston Cl N18 ... 33 C5
Wigston Rd E13 ... 99 B3
Wigton Gdns HA7 ... 26 A2
Wigton Pl SE11 ... 261 B1
Wigton Rd E17 ... 35 B2
Wilberforce Ct
Edgware HA8 ... 26 B6
2 SE28 ... 124 C5
Wilberforce Ho 4 SW11 ... 136 B2
Wilberforce Mews 9 SW4 ... 137 D1
Wilberforce Prim Sch W10 ... 91 A4
Wilberforce Rd
Finsbury Pk N4 ... 72 D6
Hendon NW9 ... 46 A3
Highbury N4, N5 ... 73 A5
Wilberforce Way SW19 ... 178 D4
Wilbraham Ho SW8 ... 270 A3
Wilbraham Pl SW1 ... 258 A4
Wilbury Prim Sch N18 ... 33 B5
Wilbury Way N18 ... 33 B5
Wilby Mews W11 ... 113 B5 244 D4
Wilcox Cl SW8 ... 270 B4

Wilcox Gdns TW17...192 B6
Wilcox Ho 5 E3......97 B2
Wilcox Pl SW1......259 B5
Wilcox Rd
Sutton SM1........217 D4
SW8.......138 A5 270 A4
Teddington TW11.....174 B6
Wildcroft Gdns HA8...25 D4
Wildcroft Manor
SW15.............156 C4
Wildcroft Rd SW15...156 C4
Wild Ct WC2...94 B1 240 C2
Wilde Cl E8..........96 A6
Wilde Pl
Edmonton N13........32 D4
Wandsworth SW18...158 B4
Wilder Cl HA4........40 B1
Wilde Rd DA8.......147 D5
Wilderness Mews
SW4..............137 B1
Wilderness Rd BR7..188 D3
Wilderness The
East Molesey KT8...196 A4
Hampton TW12.....173 D6
Wilderton Rd N16.....51 C2
Wildes Cotts SM3....217 A2
Wildfell Rd SE6......163 D4
Wild Goose Dr
SE14.............140 C4
Wild Hatch NW11.....47 C3
Wilding Ho 17 E9.....74 D2
Wild Marsh Ct EN3.....7 A6
Wild's Rents
SE1.......117 C3 263 A6
Wild St WC2...94 B1 240 C1
Wildwood Cl SE12...164 D4
Wildwood Gr NW3....48 A1
Wildwood Rd NW11...48 A2
Wildwood Rise
NW11..............48 A1
Wildwood Terr NW3...48 A1
Wilford Cl EN2........5 B2
Wilford Ho 3 SE18...122 D1
Wilford Rd CR0......205 A2
Wilfred Fienburgh Ho
N7.................71 D4
Wilfred Owen Cl
SW19.............180 A4
Wilfred St
SW1.......115 C3 259 A6
Wilfrid Gdns W3......89 A2
Wilkes Rd 3 TW8....132 A6
Wilkes St E1...95 D2 243 D4
Wilkie Ho SW1......259 D2
Wilkins Cl
Hayes UB3........105 D1
Mitcham CR4.......180 C2
Wilkins Ho SW1.....269 A6
Wilkinson Cl UB10....83 A6
Wilkinson Ct SW17...180 B6
Wilkinson Gdns
CR7..............183 C2
Wilkinson Ho
Isleworth TW7......130 D2
N1................235 D3
Twickenham TW2.....152 B2
Wilkinson Rd E16.....99 C1
Wilkinson St
SW8........138 B5 270 C3
Wilkinson Way W4...111 B4
Wilkin St NW5........71 B2
Wilks Gdns CR0......207 A1
Wilks Pl N1..........95 C5
Willan Rd N17........33 C1
Willan Wall E16......120 D6
Willard St SW8......137 B2
Willbury Ho 4 N7....71 D3
Willcocks Cl KT9.....214 A5
Willcott Rd W3......110 D5
Will Crooks Gdns
SE9..............143 D1
Willenfield Rd NW10..89 A5
Willenhall Ave EN5....14 A5
Willenhall Ct EN5.....14 A5
Willenhall Dr UB3....105 C6
Willenhall Rd SE18...122 D1
Willersley Ave
Blackfen DA15......167 D4
Orpington BR6.......227 B5
Willersley Cl DA15...167 D3
WILLESDEN.........67 D1
Willesden Community
Hospl The NW10....68 A1
WILLESDEN GREEN..90 B6
Willesden Green Sta
NW2...............68 C2
Willesden Junction Sta
NW10..............89 D4
Willesden La NW2,
NW6...............68 D2
Willes Rd NW5........71 B2
Willett Cl BR5.......211 C3
3 Northolt UB5......84 C4
Willett Ho
7 Newham E13......99 A5
Stockwell SW9.....138 A2
Willett Pl CR7.......204 C4
Willett Rd CR7.......204 C4
Willett Way BR5.....211 C3
William Allen Ho
HA8................26 B3
William Ash Cl RM9...80 B2
William Atkinson Ho
N17................33 C3
William Banfield Ho 10
SW6..............135 B3
William Barefoot Dr
SE9..............166 C1
William Bellamy Jun &
Inf Schs RM10......81 C6
William Blake Ho 2
SE15.............140 A3
William Bonney Est 10
SW4..............137 D1
William Booth Meml
Training Coll SE5..139 B3
William Booth Rd
SE20.............184 A2
William Brown Ct
SE27.............160 D2
William Byrd Sch
UB3..............127 A6
William Carey Way
HA1................42 C3
William Caslon Ho 28
E2.................96 B5
William Channing Ho 6
E2.................96 B4
William C Harvey Sch
N17................33 B1
William Cl
26 Finchley N2.......30 B1
Lewisham SE13.....142 A2
Southall UB2.......108 A4
William Covell Cl EN2..4 B5
William Ct
4 Belvedere
DA17.............125 C2
4 Ealing W5.........87 C2
Ilford IG6...........57 B5
William Davies Prim
Sch E7.............77 D2
William Davis Prim Sch
E2.................96 A3
William Dromey Ct
NW6...............69 B1
William Dr HA7.......25 B5
William Dunbar Ho
NW6...............91 B5
William Dyce Mews 1
SW16.............181 D6
William Ellis Sch
NW5...............71 A5
William Ellis Way 16
SE16..............118 A3
William Evans Ho 9
SE8...............118 D2
William Ford CE Jun
Sch RM10...........81 C1
William Gdns SW15..156 B6
William Guy Gdns 47
E3.................97 D4
William Harvey Ho 1
SW19.............157 A3
William Ho N13.......32 D4
William Hogarth Prim
Sch The W4........111 C1
William Hunt Mans
SW13.............134 C6
William IV St
WC2.......116 A6 250 A5
William Margrie Cl 1
SE15..............140 A3
William Marsden Ho 2
SE27..............182 D6
William Mews
SW1........114 D4 247 D1
William Morley Cl
E6.................99 D6
William Morris Acad
W6................112 D1
William Morris Cl
E17................53 B6
William Morris
Gallery* E17........53 C6
William Morris Ho
W6................134 D6
William Morris Prim
Sch CR4..........203 D6
William Morris Sch
E17................35 A2
William Morris Way
SW6..............136 A3
William Patten Prim
Sch N16............73 D6
William Perkin Ct
UB6................64 C2
William Pl 37 E3......97 B5
William Rainbird Ho 9
N17................33 D3
William Rathbone Ho 3
E2.................96 B4
William Rd
Regent's Pk
NW1......93 C4 232 A1
Sutton SM1........218 A3
Wimbledon SW19...179 A3
William Rushbrooke Ho
4 SE16............118 A2
Williams Ave E17.....35 B2
William Saville Ho 2
NW6...............91 B5
William's Bldgs 1
E2.................96 C3
Williams Cl
SW6.......135 A5 264 B4
Williams Coll EC1...241 B3
Williams Dr TW3.....129 C1
Williams Gr
Kingston u T KT6....197 C3
Wood Green N22......32 C2
Williams Ho
10 Bow E3...........97 C4
9 Hackney E9........96 B6
14 Streatham SW2..160 C3
7 Tottenham N17....33 D3
Willesden NW2.......68 C5
Williams La
Morden SM4.......202 A4
Mortlake SW14.....133 A3
William Smith Ho 10
DA17..............125 C3
Williamson Cl SE10..120 D1
Williamson Ct SE17..262 A1
Williamson Rd N4....50 D3
Williamson St N7.....72 A4
Williamson Way
NW7................29 A4
William Sq 15 SE16...119 A6
William's Rd W13....109 A5
Williams Rd UB2.....107 A2
William St
Barking IG11.........79 A1
Carshalton SM5.....218 D5
Williams Terr CR0....220 C2
William St
SW1.......114 D4 247 D1
Tottenham N17.......33 D3
Walthamstow E10.....53 D3
William Torbitt Prim
Sch IG2.............57 D4
William Tyndale Prim
Sch N1.............72 D1
William Wilberforce Ho
1 SE27.............182 D6
William Winter Ct 29
SW2...............160 C4
William Wood Ho 3
SE26..............162 C1
Willifield Way NW11..47 C4
Willingale Cl IG8.....37 C4
Willingdon Rd N22....32 D1
Willingham Cl 4
NW5................71 C3
Willingham Terr
NW5................71 C3
Willingham Way
KT1...............176 C1
Willington Ct E5......75 A5
Willington Prep Sch
SW19..............179 B5
Willington Rd SW9...138 A2
Willis Ave SM2, SM5..218 C2
Willis Ct CR7........204 C3
Willis Ho
2 Ilford E12..........78 C5
8 Poplar E14.......119 D6
Willis Rd E15.........98 D5
Thornton Heath CR0.205 A2
Willis St E14..........97 D1
Willis Yd N14.........15 D4
Willows The CR0.....223 A6
Will Miles Ct 6
SW19..............180 A3
Willmore End SW19..179 D1
Willoughby Ave
CR0...............220 B4
Willoughby Gr N17....34 B3
Willoughby Ho EC2..242 C3
34 Wapping E1......118 B5
Willoughby La N17....34 B3
Willoughby Mews
N17................34 B3
Willoughby Park Rd
N17................34 B3
Willoughby Rd
Hampstead NW3......70 B4
Hornsey N8..........50 C5
Kingston u T KT2....176 B2
Twickenham TW1....153 D6
Willoughbys The
SW14..............133 C1
Willoughby St WC1..240 A3
Willoughby Way
SE7...............121 B2
Willow Ave
Barnes SW13......133 D3
DA15..............168 A5
Yiewsley UB7.......104 B6
Willowbank SW6.....135 A2
Willowbank Rd
SE15..............139 D6
Willow Bank TW10...153 B1
Willowbay Cl EN5.....12 D5
Willow Bridge Rd N1..73 A2
Willow Brook Prim Sch
E10................53 C1
Willowbrook Rd
Southall UB2.......107 C3
Stanwell TW19.....148 A2
Willow Bsns Pk
SE26..............162 C1
Willow Cl BR2.......210 B4
Brentford TW8......131 C6
Buckhurst Hill IG9....21 D1
12 Catford SE6.....164 D3
Sidcup DA5........169 B5
Willow Cotts
Carshalton CR4.....202 D2
Feltham TW13......151 A1
Richmond TW9.....132 C6
Willowcourt Ave HA3..43 B4
Willowcroft SE3.....142 D1
Willow Ct
Ashford TW16......171 C3
5 Beckenham BR3..185 C2
Brixton SW9........138 C4
Chiswick W4........133 C5
8 Dagenham RM8....58 D2
EC2...............243 A6
Edgware HA8.........26 A6
6 Finchley N12.......29 D6
Harrow HA3..........24 D2
Headstone HA2.......24 A1
Ilford IG1...........79 A3
Islington N7.........72 B3
Kingston u T KT3....198 D6
8 London E11........76 C6
Mitcham CR4.......202 C5
40 Paddington W2.....91 C2
Willow Ctr The CR4..202 D3
Willow Ct
3 Streatham
SW16..............160 B1
Thornton Heath CR7..205 B4
Willow Dean HA5.....22 D1
Willow Dene WD23.....8 C4
Willowdene Cl TW2..152 A4
Willowdene Ct N20....14 A4
Willowdene
Highgate N6.........48 D2
1 Peckham SE15.....140 B4
Willow Dene Sch
SE18..............145 C4
Willowdene 5
SE15..............140 B5
Willow Dr EN5..........1 A1
Willow End
Northwood HA6.......22 A4
Surbiton KT6.......198 A1
Totteridge N20.......13 C2
Willow Farm La
SW15..............134 B2
Willowfields Cl
SE18..............123 C1
Willowfield Sec Sch
E17................52 D6
Willow Gdns
Heston TW5........129 C4
Ruislip HA4..........61 D6
Willow Gn
Borehamwood
WD6................11 B6
Grahame Pk NW9.....27 C2
Willow Gr BR7.......188 D4
Newham E13.........99 A5
Ruislip HA4..........39 D1
Willow Hall NW3......70 B4
Willowhayne Dr
KT12..............194 B2
Willowhayne Gdns
KT4...............216 C4
Willow Ho TW14.....150 B6
Willow Ho
17 Finchley N2.......30 B1
9 Maitland Pk NW3...70 D2
North Kensington
W10................90 D3
Teddington TW11....175 C3
Willow La
Mitcham CR4.......202 D3
Woolwich SE18.....122 C2
Willow Lo 6 TW16...171 D3
Willow Lodge 10
SW8...............137 B2
Willow Lo
Fulham SW6.......134 D4
New Barnet EN5......14 A6
Putney SW15........134 B2
Willow Manor SM1...217 B4
Willowmead Cl W5...87 D2
Willowmere
Esher KT10........212 A4
Ladywell SE13......163 D6
Willow Mount CR0...221 C5
Willow Pl
SW1........115 C2 259 B4
Willow Rd
Dagenham RM6.......59 A3
Ealing W5.........110 A4
Enfield EN1...........5 C3
Hampstead NW3......70 B4
New Malden KT3....199 A5
Wallington SM6.....219 B1
Willows Ave SM4....201 D4
Willows Cl HA5.......22 C1
Willows Ct 3 SW19..179 C3
Willows Sch The
UB4................84 D3
Willow St
Broadgate
EC2.......95 C3 243 A6
Chingford E4.........20 B4
Willows Terr NW10....89 D5
Willows The
Beckenham BR3.....185 C2
Claygate KT10......212 C2
Loughton IG10........21 D6
Wallend E12..........78 C1
Whetstone N20........14 A1
Willow Tree Cl
Hayes UB4............84 C3
Northolt UB5.........63 A2
14 Old Ford E3......97 B6
Willowtree Cl UB10...61 A5
Willow Tree Cl
SW18..............157 D3
Willow Tree Ct
DA14..............189 D5
5 Wembley HA0.....65 D3
Willow Tree La UB4...84 C3
Willow Tree Prim Sch
UB5................63 A2
Willowtree Way
SW16..............182 C2
Willow Tree Wlk
BR1...............187 B2
Willow Vale BR7.....188 D4
Shepherd's Bush
W12...............112 A5
Willow View SW19...180 B2
Willow Way
Finchley N3..........29 D3
Forest Hill SE26.....162 C1
9 Shepherd's Bush
W11...............112 D6
Sunbury TW16......194 A5
Twickenham TW2....151 D2
Wembley HA0.........65 A5
West Ewell KT19.....215 B2
Willow Wlk
Bermondsey
SE1........117 D2 263 C4
Cheam SM1, SM3....217 B5
15 Finchley N2.......30 B1
Harringay N15........50 D5
Locksbottom BR6....226 D5
Southgate N21........16 B5
Walthamstow E17.....53 B4
Willow Wood Cres
SE25..............205 C3
Willridge Ct E11.....54 B2
Willrose Cres SE2...124 B1
Willsbridge Ct 1
SE15..............139 D6
Wills Cres TW3......151 D5
Wills Gr NW7.........28 B5
Will Thorne Pav The
E16...............100 A1
Wilman Gr E8.........74 A1
Wilmar Cl UB4........83 B3
Wilmar Gdns BR4....207 D1
Wilmcote Ho W2......91 D2
Wilment Ct NW2......68 C5
Wilmer Cl KT2.......176 B5
Wilmer Cres KT2.....176 B5
Wilmer Gdns 22 N1....95 C6
Wilmer Ho 6 E3......97 A5
Wilmer Lea Cl E15....76 B1
Wilmer Pl N16........73 D6
Wilmers Ct 5 NW10...89 B6
Wilmer Way N14......31 D5
Wilmington Ave
W4................133 B5
Wilmington Ct
SW16..............182 A3
Wilmington Gdns
IG11...............79 C1
Wilmington Sq
WC1.........94 C4 234 A1
Wilmington St WC1..234 A1
Wilmot Cl Finchley N2..30 A1
SE15..............140 A5
Wilmot Ho 14 SM2....218 A2
Wilmot Pl
Camden Town
NW1................71 C1
Ealing W7..........108 C5
Wilmot Rd Leyton E10..75 D6
Tottenham N17........51 B6
Wallington SM5......218 D3
Wilmot St E2.........96 B3
Wilmount St SE18....122 D2
Wilna Rd SW18......158 A4
Wilnett Ct 4 RM6.....58 B2
Wilnett Villas 5 RM6..58 B2
Wilsham St
W11........113 A5 244 A4
Wilshaw Cl NW4......46 A6
Wilshaw Ho 10 SE8...141 C5
Wilshaw St SE14.....141 C4
Wilsmere Dr
Harrow HA3..........24 C3
Northolt UB5.........63 A3
Wilson Ave CR4......180 C2
Wilson Cl
Croydon CR2........221 B3
Wembley HA9.........44 B2
Wilson Ct 9 SE28....123 A3
Wilson Dr HA9........44 B2
Wilson Gdns HA1.....42 A2
Wilson Gr SE16......118 B4
Wilson Ho
39 Clapham SW8....137 D3
2 SE7..............143 C6
South Hampstead
NW6................70 A1
Wilson Rd
Camberwell SE5.....139 C4
Chessington KT9.....214 B2
Newham E6...........99 D4
Redbridge IG1........56 B2
Wilson's Ave 4 N17...33 D1
Wilson's Pl E14.......97 B1
Wilson's Rd W6......112 D1
Wilson's Sch SM6...220 A2
Wilson St
Broadgate
EC2.......95 B2 242 D4
Southgate N21........16 C4
Walthamstow E17.....54 A4
Wilstone Cl UB4......85 A3
Wiltern Ct NW2.......69 A2
Wilthorne Gdns
RM10...............81 D1
Wilton Ave W4.......111 C1
Wilton Cres
Merton SW19.......179 B2
SW1........115 A4 248 A1
Wilton Ct
3 Edgware HA8......26 D5
Muswell Hill N10......31 A1
4 Richmond TW10..154 A6
7 Stepney E1........96 B1
7 Woodford IG8......37 A4
Wilton Est E8........74 A2
Wilton Gdns
East Molesey KT8...195 C6
Walton-on-T KT12...194 D1
Wilton Gr
Merton SW19.......179 B2
New Malden KT3....199 D3
Wilton Ho
8 Camberwell
SE22..............139 C2
Chislehurst BR7.....189 B2
Ealing W13.........109 B6
Wilton Mews
SW1........115 A3 258 B6
Wilton Par TW13.....150 B2
Wilton Pl
2 Beckenham
BR3...............208 A6
4 Harrow HA1........42 D3
SW1........115 A4 248 A1
Wilton Rd
Abbey Wood SE2....124 C2
Cockfosters EN4.......2 D1
Hounslow TW4......128 D2
Mitcham SW19......180 C3
Muswell Hill N10......31 A1
Westminster
SW1........115 C2 259 A4
Wilton Row SW1.....248 A1
Wilton Sq N1..95 B6 235 C6
Wilton St
SW1........115 B3 258 C6
Wilton Terr SW1.....258 A6
Wilton Villas N1.....235 C5
Wilton Way E8........74 A2
Wiltshire Cl
Edgware NW7........27 D5
SW3...............257 C3
Wiltshire Ct
Barking IG11.........79 A2
2 Finsbury Pk N4....50 B1
Wiltshire Gdns
Stoke Newington
N4.................51 A3
Twickenham TW2....152 A3
Wiltshire La
Pinner HA5...........40 A5
Ruislip HA4..........39 D6
Wiltshire Rd
Brixton SW9........138 C2
Thornton Heath CR7..204 C6

Wiltshire Row
N1 ... 95 B6 235 D5
Wilverley Cres KT3 ... 199 C3
Wimbart Rd SW2 ... 160 B4
WIMBLEDON ... 179 B4
Wimbledon Bridge
SW19 ... 179 B4
Wimbledon Central
SW19 ... 179 B4
Wimbledon Chase Prim
Sch SW20 ... 179 A2
Wimbledon Chase Sta
SW20 ... 179 A1
Wimbledon Cl 2
SW20 ... 178 D3
Wimbledon Coll
SW19 ... 178 D3
Wimbledon Common
Prep Sch SW19 ... 178 D3
Wimbledon Common*
SW19 ... 178 B6
Wimbledon High Sch
SW19 ... 179 A4
Wimbledon Hill Rd
SW19 ... 179 B4
Wimbledon Lawn
Tennis Mus*
SW19 ... 157 A1
Wimbledon Park Ct
SW19 ... 157 B3
Wimbledon Park
Montessori Sch
SW18 ... 157 C2
Wimbledon Park Prim
Sch SW19 ... 157 D2
Wimbledon Park Rd
SW18, SW19 ... 157 B3
Wimbledon Park Side
SW19 ... 156 D3
Wimbledon Park Sta
SW19 ... 157 C1
Wimbledon Rd
SW17 ... 180 A6
Wimbledon Sch of Art
Annexe SW19 ... 179 C3
Wimbledon Sch of Art
SW19 ... 179 A2
Wimbledon Stadium
Bsns Ctr SW17 ... 157 D1
Wimbledon Stad
SW17 ... 180 A6
Wimbledon Sta
SW19 ... 179 B4
Wimbledon Windmill
Mus* SW19 ... 156 C1
Wimbolt St E2 ... 96 A4
Wimborne Ave
Hayes UB4 ... 84 B1
Southall UB2 ... 107 C2
St Paul's Cray BR5,
BR7 ... 211 D5
Wimborne Cl
Buckhurst Hill IG9 ... 21 C2
Lewisham SE12 ... 164 D6
North Cheam KT4 ... 200 C1
Wimborne Ct 1 UB5 ... 63 C2
Wimborne Dr
Pinner HA5 ... 41 A2
Queensbury NW9 ... 44 C6
Wimborne Gdns W13 ... 87 B2
Wimborne Ho
Canning Town
E16 ... 120 D6
Croydon CR0 ... 206 C4
Marylebone NW1 ... 237 B5
South Lambeth SW8 ... 270 D3
Upper Tooting
SW12 ... 159 C1
Wimborne Rd
Edmonton N9 ... 18 A2
Tottenham N17 ... 33 C1
Wimborne 2 DA14 ... 190 B6
Wimborne Way
BR3 ... 207 A5
Wimbourne Ct
Mitcham SW19 ... 180 B3
N1 ... 235 C4
South Croydon CR2 ... 221 C2
Wimbourne St
N1 ... 95 B5 235 C4
Wimbush Ho 3 N12 ... 29 D5
Wimpole Cl
Bromley BR2 ... 209 C5
1 Kingston u T KT1 ... 176 C1
Wimpole Mews
W1 ... 93 B2 238 C3
Wimpole St
W1 ... 93 B1 238 C2
Wimshurst Cl CR0 ... 204 A1
Winans Wlk SW9 ... 138 C3
Winant Ho 19 E14 ... 119 D6
Wincanton Cres UB5 ... 63 C3
Wincanton Ct 2 N11 ... 31 A4
Wincanton Gdns IG6 ... 56 D6
Wincanton Rd
SW18 ... 157 B4
Winchcombe Rd
SM5 ... 202 C1
Winchcomb Gdns
SE9 ... 143 D2
Winchelsea Ave
DA7 ... 147 B5
Winchelsea Cl
SW15 ... 156 D6
Winchelsea Ho 16
SE16 ... 118 C4
Winchelsea Rd
Becontree NW10 ... 89 B6
Forest Gate E7 ... 77 A4
Tottenham N17 ... 51 C6
Winchelsey Rise
CR2 ... 221 D2
Winchendon Rd
Fulham
SW6 ... 135 B4 264 D2
Teddington TW11,
TW12 ... 174 B6
Winchester Ave
Brondesbury NW6 ... 69 A1
Heston TW5 ... 129 B6
Queensbury NW9 ... 44 C6
Winchester Cl
Beckenham BR2 ... 208 D6
Enfield EN1 ... 17 C6
Kingston u T KT2 ... 176 D3
11 Newham E6 ... 100 B1
SE17 ... 261 D3
Winchester Ct
15 Belvedere
DA17 ... 125 C1
5 Higham Hill E17 ... 35 A2
Richmond TW9 ... 132 B2
W8 ... 245 C2
Winchester Dr HA5 ... 40 D4
Winchester Ho
5 Barking IG11 ... 80 A1
Bayswater W2 ... 236 A1
Chelsea SW3 ... 266 D5
1 Greenwich SE18 ... 143 D5
24 Tower Hamlets E3 ... 97 B4
Twickenham TW1 ... 153 C4
Winchester Mews
KT4 ... 216 D6
Winchester Pal*
SE1 ... 252 C4
Winchester Pk BR2 ... 208 D6
Winchester Pl
6 Dalston E8 ... 73 D3
Highgate N6 ... 49 B1
Winchester Rd
Beckenham BR2 ... 208 D6
Bexley DA7 ... 146 D3
Chingford E4 ... 36 A3
Edmonton N9 ... 18 A3
Harlington UB3 ... 127 C5
Harrow HA3 ... 44 A5
Highgate N6 ... 49 B1
Ilford IG1 ... 79 B5
Northwood HA6 ... 40 A6
South Hampstead
NW3 ... 70 B1
St Margarets TW1 ... 153 B5
Twickenham TW13 ... 151 B1
Walton-on-T KT12 ... 194 A1
Winchester Sq SE1 ... 252 C4
Winchester St
Acton W3 ... 111 A4
SW1 ... 115 B1 258 D2
Winchester Wlk SE1 ... 252 C4
Winchet Wlk CR0 ... 206 C3
Winchfield Cl HA3 ... 43 C3
Winchfield Ho
SW15 ... 155 D5
Winchfield Rd SE26 ... 185 A5
Winch Ho
Isle of Dogs E14 ... 119 D3
SW10 ... 266 B4
Winchilsea Cres
KT8 ... 174 A1
Winchilsea Ho NW8 ... 229 D1
WINCHMORE HILL ... 16 D4
Winchmore Hill Rd N14,
N21 ... 16 A4
Winchmore Hill Sta
N21 ... 16 D4
Winchmore Sch N21 ... 17 A2
Winchmore Villas
N21 ... 16 B4
Winchstone Cl
TW17 ... 192 B5
Winckley Cl HA3 ... 44 B4
Wincott St
SE11 ... 116 C2 261 B3
Wincrofts Dr SE9 ... 145 B1
Windall Cl SE20 ... 184 A2
Windborough Rd
SM5 ... 219 A1
Windcott Ct HA3 ... 43 C2
Windermere Ave
Golders Green N3 ... 47 C6
Kensal Rise NW6 ... 91 A6
Windermere Ave
continued
Merton SW19 ... 201 D6
Ruislip HA4 ... 40 D2
Wembley HA9 ... 43 C1
Windermere Cl BR6 ... 226 D5
East Bedfont TW14 ... 149 D3
Stanwell TW19 ... 148 A2
Windermere Ct
Barnes SW13 ... 133 D6
Barnet EN5 ... 1 D1
Carshalton SM5 ... 219 A5
Wembley HA9 ... 43 C2
Windermere Gdns
IG4 ... 56 A4
Windermere Gr HA9 ... 43 C1
Windermere Hall
HA8 ... 26 B5
Windermere Ho
Isleworth TW1 ... 152 D6
Tower Hamlets E3 ... 97 B3
Windermere NW1 ... 231 D2
Windermere Point 3
SE15 ... 140 C5
Windermere 12
SW15 ... 156 D5
Windermere Rd
Brentford W5 ... 109 C3
Croydon CR0 ... 205 D1
Kingston u T SW15 ... 177 C5
Mitcham SW16 ... 181 D1
Muswell Hill N10 ... 31 B2
Southall UB1 ... 85 B2
Upper Holloway N19 ... 71 C6
West Wickham BR4 ... 224 C6
Windermere Way
UB7 ... 104 B5
Winders Rd SW11 ... 136 C3
Windfield Cl SE26 ... 184 D6
Windham Rd TW9 ... 132 B2
Winding Way RM8 ... 80 C5
Windlass Pl SE8 ... 119 A2
Windlesham Gr
SW19 ... 156 D3
Windley Cl SE23 ... 162 C2
Windmill Alley 7
W4 ... 111 C2
Windmill Ave UB2 ... 108 A4
Windmill Bridge Ho 1
CR0 ... 205 C1
Windmill Bsns Ctr
UB2 ... 108 A5
Windmill Bsns Village
TW16 ... 171 C2
Windmill Cl
Ashford TW16 ... 171 C3
12 Bermondsey SE1 ... 118 A2
Kingston u T KT6 ... 197 C2
4 Lewisham SE13 ... 142 A3
Windmill Ct
Brentford W5 ... 109 C2
Brondesbury NW2 ... 69 A2
Bushey WD23 ... 8 B3
Windmill Dr BR2 ... 225 C4
Clapham SW4 ... 159 B6
Cricklewood NW2 ... 69 A5
Windmill Gdns
Brixton SW2 ... 160 B5
Enfield EN2 ... 4 C2
Windmill Gr CR0 ... 205 A3
Windmill Hill
Enfield EN2 ... 5 A2
1 Hampstead NW3 ... 70 A4
Hampstead NW3 ... 70 A5
Ruislip HA4 ... 39 D1
Windmill Ho
4 Millwall E14 ... 119 C2
SE1 ... 251 B3
Windmill La
Barnet Gate EN5 ... 11 D5
Bushey WD23 ... 8 C3
Greenford UB6 ... 86 A2
Isleworth TW7, UB2,
W7 ... 108 C2
Southall UB2 ... 108 A4
Stratford E15 ... 76 B2
Thames Ditton KT7 ... 197 B2
Windmill Lo TW16 ... 171 C2
Windmill Pas 10
W4 ... 111 C2
Windmill Pl UB1 ... 108 A5
Windmill Rd
Brentford TW8,
W5 ... 109 C1
Charlton TW16 ... 171 C2
Chiswick W4 ... 111 C2
Edmonton N18 ... 33 B6
Hampton TW12 ... 174 A5
Mitcham CR4 ... 203 C5
Roehampton SW19 ... 156 B3
Thornton Heath CR0 ... 205 A2
Wandsworth SW18 ... 158 B5
Windmill Rd W
TW16 ... 171 C1
Windmill Rise KT2 ... 176 D3
Windmill Row SE11 ... 261 A1
Windmill St
Bloomsbury
W1 ... 93 D2 239 C3
Bushey WD23 ... 8 C3
Windmill Terr
TW17 ... 193 C2
Windmill Trad Est
CR4 ... 203 C5
Windmill Way HA4 ... 39 D1
Windmill WC1 ... 240 C4
Windmill Wlk SE1 ... 251 B2
Windmore Cl HA0 ... 65 A3
Windrose Cl SE16 ... 118 D4
Windrush Cl
Battersea SW11 ... 136 B1
Chiswick W4 ... 133 A5
Ickenham UB10 ... 60 B4
Windrush Ho NW8 ... 236 D4
Windrush KT3 ... 199 A5
Windrush La SE23 ... 162 D1
Windrush Prim Sch
SE28 ... 124 B5
Windrush Rd NW10 ... 89 B6
Windsock Cl 1
SE16 ... 119 B2
Windsor Ave
Cheam SM3 ... 217 A5
East Molesey KT8 ... 195 C6
Edgware HA8 ... 10 D1
Higham Hill E17 ... 35 A1
Hillingdon UB10 ... 60 D1
Merton SW19 ... 180 A2
New Malden KT3 ... 199 A4
Windsor Cl
Brentford TW8 ... 131 B6
Chislehurst BR7 ... 188 D5
Harrow HA2 ... 63 C5
Hendon N3 ... 29 A1
Pinner HA6 ... 22 A1
West Norwood SE27 ... 183 A6
Windsor Cres
Harrow HA2 ... 63 C5
Wembley HA9 ... 66 D5
Windsor Ct
Battersea SW11 ... 136 B3
Bayswater W2 ... 245 C6
Bickley BR1 ... 210 A6
Bushey WD23 ... 8 A4
Chelsea SW3 ... 257 B2
2 Clapham SW4 ... 137 C1
Edgware HA8 ... 26 B3
Friern Barnet N11 ... 30 D5
Fulham SW6 ... 135 A2
Osidge N14 ... 15 C4
20 Rotherhithe
SE16 ... 118 D5
Windsor Ctr The
SE27 ... 183 A6
Windsor Ct
17 Sidcup DA14 ... 168 A1
South Norwood
SE19 ... 183 C2
Sunbury TW16 ... 172 A3
Temple Fortune
NW11 ... 47 A3
Walthamstow E17 ... 53 B6
4 Wandsworth
SW18 ... 157 C6
West Hampstead
NW3 ... 69 C4
5 West Wickham
BR4 ... 207 D1
Windsor Dr EN4 ... 14 D5
Windsor Gdns
Hayes UB3 ... 105 B3
Paddington W9 ... 91 C3
Wallington CR0 ... 220 A5
Windsor Gr SE27 ... 183 A6
Windsor Hall 11
E16 ... 121 B5
Windsor Ho
4 Acton Green
W4 ... 111 A1
Brondesbury NW2 ... 69 A2
4 Globe Town E2 ... 96 D4
2 Hendon NW4 ... 28 D1
7 Northolt UB5 ... 63 C2
Queensbury NW9 ... 44 C5
Regent's Pk NW1 ... 231 D2
Shoreditch N1 ... 235 B4
Stanmore HA7 ... 25 B5
Stoke Newington N4 ... 51 A1
Windsor Lo KT3 ... 199 A4
Windsor Mews
Catford SE6 ... 164 A3
Forest Hill SE23 ... 163 A3
Windsor Park Rd
UB3 ... 127 D5
Windsor Pk SW19 ... 180 A2
Windsor Pl SW1 ... 259 B4
Windsor Rd
Ashford TW16 ... 172 A4
Barnet EN5 ... 12 D5
Chingford E4 ... 35 D6
Cranford TW4, TW5 ... 128 C3
DA6 ... 147 A1
Dagenham RM8 ... 81 A5
Windsor Rd *continued*
Ealing W5 ... 110 A6
Forest Gate E7 ... 77 C3
Harrow HA3 ... 24 B2
Hendon N3 ... 29 A1
Ilford IG1 ... 79 A4
Kingston u T KT2 ... 176 A3
Leyton E10 ... 75 D6
Palmers Green N13 ... 16 C1
Richmond TW9 ... 132 B3
Southall UB2 ... 107 B3
South Norwood CR7 ... 182 D1
Teddington TW11 ... 174 B5
Tottenham N17 ... 34 A1
Upper Holloway N7 ... 72 A5
Wanstead E11 ... 77 A6
Willesden NW2 ... 68 B2
Worcester Pk KT4 ... 216 A6
Windsor St
N1 ... 94 D6 234 D6
Windsor Terr
N1 ... 95 A4 235 B2
Windsor Way
W14 ... 113 A2 254 A4
Windsor Wharf E9 ... 75 B3
Windsor Wlk
Camberwell SE5 ... 139 B3
Walton-on-T KT12 ... 194 D1
Windspoint Dr SE15 ... 140 B6
Windus Rd N16 ... 51 D1
Windus Wlk N16 ... 51 D1
Windy Ridge BR1 ... 188 A2
Windy Ridge Cl
SW19 ... 178 D5
Wine Cl E1 ... 118 C6
Wine Office Ct EC4 ... 241 B2
Winery La KT1 ... 198 B6
Winey Cl KT9 ... 213 C1
Winfield Ho 3
SW11 ... 136 B3
Winford Ct 16 SE15 ... 140 A4
Winford Ho E3 ... 75 B1
Winford Par 6 UB1 ... 85 D1
Winforton St SE10 ... 142 A4
Winfrith Rd SW18 ... 158 A3
Wingate Cres CR0 ... 204 A3
Wingate Ho
26 Bromley E3 ... 97 D4
8 Stoke Newington
N16 ... 73 B4
Wingate Rd
Hammersmith W6 ... 112 B3
Ilford IG1 ... 78 D3
Sidcup DA14 ... 190 C4
Wingate Trad Est 11
N17 ... 33 D3
Wingfield Ct
5 Blackwall E14 ... 120 B6
Sidcup DA15 ... 167 D3
Wingfield Ho
Paddington NW6 ... 91 D5
16 Spitalfields E2 ... 95 D4
Wingfield Mews
SE15 ... 140 A2
Wingfield Prim Sch
SE3 ... 143 B2
Wingfield Rd
Kingston u T KT2 ... 176 C4
Leyton E15 ... 76 C4
Walthamstow E17 ... 53 D4
Wingfield St SE15 ... 140 A2
Wingfield Way HA4 ... 62 B2
Wingford Rd SW2 ... 160 A5
Wingham Ho 3
SE26 ... 184 B5
Wingham 3 NW5 ... 71 A2
Wingmore Rd SE24 ... 139 A2
Wingrad Ho 18 E1 ... 96 C2
Wingrave Rd W6 ... 134 C6
Wingrave SE17 ... 262 C3
Wingreen 15 NW8 ... 91 D6
Wingrove Ho E4 ... 19 D4
Wingrove Rd SE6 ... 164 C2
Wings Cl SM1 ... 217 C4
Winicotte Ho W2 ... 236 D4
Winifred Cl EN5 ... 11 D5
Winifrede Paul Ho 7
NW5 ... 71 B4
Winifred Pl N12 ... 30 A5
Winifred Rd
Dagenham RM8 ... 59 A1
Hampton TW12 ... 173 C6
Merton SW19 ... 179 C2
Winifred St E16 ... 122 B5
Winifred Terr EN1 ... 17 D4
Winkfield Rd
Newham E13 ... 99 B5
Wood Green N22 ... 32 C2
Winkley Ct
Cranley Gdns N10 ... 49 B5
Harrow HA2 ... 63 C5
Winkley St 6 E2 ... 96 B5
Winkworth Cotts 14
E1 ... 96 C3
Winlaton Rd BR1 ... 186 B6
Winmill Rd RM8 ... 81 B5
Winn Bridge Cl IG8 ... 37 D2
Winn Common Rd
SE18 ... 145 C6
Winnett St W1 ... 249 C6
Winningales Ct IG5 ... 56 A6
Winnings Wlk UB5 ... 63 A2
Winnington Cl N2 ... 48 B3
Winnington Ho
19 Kensal Town
W10 ... 91 A3
8 SE5 ... 139 A5
Winnington Rd
Enfield EN3 ... 6 C6
Hampstead Garden
Suburb N2 ... 48 B3
Winnipeg Dr 3
BR6 ... 227 D2
Winnipeg Ho UB4 ... 84 B3
Winn Rd SE12 ... 165 B3
Winns Ave E17 ... 53 B6
Winns Mews N15 ... 51 C5
Winns Prim Sch The
E17 ... 35 B1
Winns Terr E17 ... 53 C6
Winsbeach E17 ... 36 B1
Winscombe Cres W5 ... 87 D3
Winscombe Ct W5 ... 87 D3
Winscombe St N19 ... 71 B6
Winscombe Way
HA7 ... 25 A5
Winsford Rd SE6 ... 163 B1
Winsford Terr N18 ... 33 B5
Winsham Gr SW11 ... 159 A6
Winsham Ho NW1 ... 232 D2
Winslade Ho 4 E5 ... 74 B6
Winslade Rd SW2 ... 160 A6
Winslade Way SE6 ... 163 D4
Winsland Mews W2 ... 236 C2
Winsland St
W2 ... 92 B1 236 C2
Winsley St W1 ... 239 B2
Winslow Cl
2 Neasden NW10 ... 67 C5
Pinner HA5 ... 40 B3
Winslow Gr E4 ... 20 C2
Winslow Rd W6 ... 134 C6
Winslow SE17 ... 263 A1
Winslow Way TW13 ... 151 A1
Winsmoor Ct EN2 ... 4 D2
Winsor Prim Sch
E6 ... 100 C1
Winsor Terr E6 ... 100 C2
Winstanley Rd
SW11 ... 136 B2
Winston Ave NW9 ... 45 C2
Winston Cl
Harrow HA3 ... 24 D4
Romford RM7 ... 59 D5
Winston Ct 7 BR1 ... 187 B2
Harrow HA3 ... 23 D3
Winston Ho WC1 ... 239 D6
Winston Rd N16 ... 73 B4
Winston Way IG1 ... 79 A5
Winston Wlk 2 W4 ... 111 B2
Winter Ave E6 ... 100 A6
Winterberry Ct 22
N12 ... 29 D6
Winterborne Ave
BR6 ... 227 B5
Winterbourne Ho
W11 ... 244 A5
Winterbourne Inf Sch
CR7 ... 204 C5
Winterbourne Jun Boys'
Sch CR7 ... 204 C5
Winterbourne Jun Girls'
Sch CR7 ... 204 C5
Winterbourne Rd
Dagenham RM8 ... 80 C6
Forest Hill SE6 ... 163 B3
Thornton Heath CR7 ... 204 C5
Winter Box Wlk
TW10 ... 154 B6
Winterbrook Rd
SE24 ... 161 A5
Winterburn Cl N11 ... 31 A4
Winterfold Cl SW19 ... 157 A2
Wintergreen Cl 7
E6 ... 100 A2
Winterleys 7 NW6 ... 91 B5
Winter Lo 17 SE16 ... 118 A1
Winter's Ct E4 ... 19 D1
Winterslow Ho 20
SE5 ... 139 A3
Winters Rd KT7 ... 197 B2
Winterstoke Gdns
NW7 ... 28 A5
Winterstoke Rd SE6 ... 163 B3
Winterton Ct KT1 ... 175 D2
Winterton Ho 15 E1 ... 96 C1
Winterton Pl SW10 ... 266 B6
Winterwell Rd SW2 ... 160 A6
Winthorpe Rd
SW15 ... 135 A1
Winthrop Ho 10
W12 ... 112 B6
Winthrop St E1 ... 96 B2
Winthrop Wlk HA9 ... 66 A5

Winton Ave N11 31 C3
Winton Cl N9 18 D4
Winton Ct 15 KT6 197 D2
Winton Gdns HA8 26 B3
Winton Prim Sch N1 94 B5 233 C3
Winton Rd BR6 226 D4
Winton Way SW16 182 C5
Wintour Ho HA9 65 D6
Wirrall Ho 15 SE26 162 A1
Wirral Wood Cl BR7 188 C4
Wisbeach Rd CR0 205 B4
Wisbech 5 N4 50 B1
Wisden Ho SW8 270 D5
Wisdom Ct 7 TW7 131 A2
Wisdons Cl RM7, RM9 59 D1
Wise La NW7 28 A4
Wiseman Ct 12 SE19 183 C5
Wiseman Rd E10 75 C6
Wise Rd E15 98 B6
Wiseton Rd SW17 158 D3
Wishart Rd SE3 143 D3
Wishaw Wlk N13 32 A4
Wisley Ho SW1 259 C2
Wisley Rd
Balham SW11 159 A6
St Paul's Cray BR5 190 B3
Wistaria Cl BR6 226 D6
Wisteria Cl
Edgware NW7 27 D4
Ilford IG1 78 D3
Wisteria Ho SE4 141 A2
Wisteria Rd SE13 142 B1
Wistow Ho 14 E2 96 A6
Witanhurst La N6 49 A1
Witan St E2 96 B4
Witchwood Ho 10 SW9 138 C2
Witcombe Point 14 SE15 140 A4
Witham Ct Leyton E10 75 D5
Upper Tooting SW17 158 D1
Witham Ho 34 SE5 139 A3
Witham Rd
Dagenham RM10 81 C3
Ealing W13 109 B5
Hounslow TW7 130 B4
Penge SE20 206 C6
Witherby Cl CR0 221 C4
Witherington Rd N5 72 C3
Withers Cl KT9 213 C2
Withers Mead NW9 27 D2
Withers Pl EC1 242 B6
Witherston Way SE9 166 C1
Withington Rd N2 30 C2
Withycombe Rd SW19 156 D4
Withy Ho 4 E1 96 D3
Withy La HA4 39 A4
Withy Mead E4 20 B1
Witley Cres CR0 224 A2
Witley Ct
Southall UB2 107 B2
WC1 240 A5
Witley Gdns UB2 107 B2
Witley Ho 2 SW2 160 B4
Witley Ind Est UB2 107 B2
Witley Point 8 SW15 156 B3
Witley Rd N19 71 C6
Witney Cl
Ickenham UB10 60 B4
Pinner HA5 23 B4
Witney Path SE23 162 D1
Wittenham Way E4 20 B1
Witten Ho KT3 199 B1
Wittering Cl KT2 175 D5
Wittering Ho 9 SW11 136 D3
Wittersham Rd BR1 186 D5
Witts Ho KT2 198 B6
Wivenhoe Cl SE15 140 B2
Wivenhoe Ct TW4 129 B1
Wivenhoe Rd IG11 102 B5
Wiverton Rd SE26 184 C5
Wixom Ho SE9 143 C1
Wix Prim Sch SW4 137 B1
Wix Rd RM9 102 D6
Wix's La SW4 137 B1
Woburn Cl
Bushey WD23 8 A5
SE28 102 D1
Wimbledon SW19 180 A4
Woburn Ct
32 Bermondsey SE16 118 B1
Croydon CR0 205 A1
1 DA6 147 A1
Richmond TW9 132 B2
4 Woodford E18 37 A1
Woburn W13 87 B2
Woburn Pl WC1 94 A3 240 A5
Woburn Rd
Carshalton SM5 202 C1
Croydon CR0 205 A1
Woburn Sq WC1 93 D3 239 D5
Woburn Twr 14 UB5 84 D4
Woburn Wlk WC1 232 D1
Wodeham Gdns 1 E1 96 B2
Wodehouse Ave SE15 139 D4
Wodehouse Ct 10 W3 111 A3
Woffington Cl KT1, KT8 175 C2
Woking Cl SW15 133 D1
Wolcot Ho NW1 232 B3
Woldham Pl BR2 209 C5
Woldham Rd BR2 209 C5
Wolds Dr BR6 226 C4
Wolfe Cl Hayes BR2 209 A3
Yeading UB4 84 B4
Wolfe Cres
Greenwich SE7 121 D1
34 Rotherhithe SE16 118 D4
Wolfe Ho 19 W12 112 B6
Wolferton Rd E12 78 B4
Wolffe Gdns 2 E15 76 D2
Wolf Fields Prim Sch UB2 107 B2
Wolfington Rd SE27 182 D6
Wolfram Cl SE13 164 C6
Wolfson Ct
4 Barnet EN4 14 D3
Golders Green NW11 47 A2
SE1 253 D2
Wolfson Hillel Prim Sch N14 15 D5
Wolftencroft Cl SW11 136 B2
Wollaston Cl SE1 262 A4
Wollotan Ho N1 234 B4
Wolmer Cl HA8 26 D6
Wolmer Gdns HA8 10 C1
Wolmer Rd HA8 26 D6
Wolseley Ave SW18, SW19 157 C2
Wolseley Gdns W4 132 D6
Wolseley Rd
Acton W4 111 A2
Carshalton CR4 203 A2
Harrow HA3 42 C6
Hornsey N8 49 D4
Upton E7 77 B1
Wood Green N22 32 B2
Wolseley St SE1 117 D4 253 D1
Wolsey Ave
Thames Ditton KT7 196 D4
Wallend E6 100 C4
Walthamstow E17 53 B6
Wolsey Cl
Isleworth TW3 130 A1
Kingston u T KT2 176 D2
Southall UB2 108 A3
Wimbledon SW20 178 B3
Worcester Pk KT19, KT4 216 A4
Wolsey Cres SM4 201 B2
Wolsey Ct
Bromley BR1 186 D3
SE9 166 B5
South Hampstead NW6 70 A1
Wolsey Dr
Kingston u T KT2 176 A4
Walton-on-T KT12 194 D1
Wolsey Gr HA8 27 B3
Wolsey Ho
2 Hampton TW12 173 D4
3 Kentish Town NW5 71 D2
Wolsey Inf Sch CR0 224 A1
Wolsey Jun Sch CR0 224 A1
Wolsey Mews
Kentish Town NW5 71 C2
Orpington BR6 227 D3
Wolsey Rd
Ashford TW15 170 B6
East Molesey KT8 196 B5
Enfield EN1 6 B3
Hampton TW12 174 A4
Stoke Newington N1 73 B3
Sunbury Comm TW16 171 D4
Wolsey St E1 96 C2
Wolsey Way KT9 214 C3
Wolstenholme HA7 25 B5
Wolstonbury N12 29 C5
Wolvercote Rd SE2 124 D4
Wolverley St E2 96 B4
Wolverton Ave KT2 176 C2
Wolverton Gdns
Brook Green W6 112 D2
Ealing W5 110 B6
Wolverton Mans W5 110 B5
Wolverton Rd HA7 25 B3
Wolverton SE17 263 A2
Wolverton Way N14 15 C6
Wolves La N22 32 C4
Womersley Rd N4, N8 50 B3
Wonford Cl KT2, KT3 177 C2
Wontner Cl 5 N1 73 A1
Wontner Rd SW12, SW17 158 D2
Wooburn Cl UB8 82 D3
Wooburn Ct N14 15 D3
Woodall Cl
Chessington KT9 213 D2
15 Poplar E14 119 D6
Woodall Ho TW7 130 D2
Woodall Rd EN3 18 D5
Woodbank Rd BR1 164 D1
Woodbastwick Rd SE26 185 A5
Woodberry Ave
Edmonton N21 16 D2
Harrow HA2 42 A5
Woodberry Cl
Ashford TW16 172 A4
Mill Hill NW7 28 D3
Woodberry Cres N10 49 B6
Woodberry Down Com Prim Sch N4 51 A2
Woodberry Down N4 51 A2
Woodberry Gdns N12 30 A4
Woodberry Gr
Finchley N12 30 A4
Stoke Newington N4 51 A2
Woodberry View N6 49 A3
Woodberry Way
Chingford E4 20 A4
Finchley N12 30 A4
Woodbine Cl TW2 152 B2
Woodbine Gr
Enfield EN2 5 B5
Penge SE20 184 B3
Woodbine La KT4 216 C5
Woodbine Pl E11 55 A3
Woodbine Rd DA15 167 C3
Woodbines Ave KT1 197 D6
Woodbine Terr E9 74 C2
Woodborough Rd SW15 134 B1
Woodbourne Ave SW16 159 D1
Woodbourne Cl SW16 160 A1
Woodbourne Dr KT10 212 D2
Woodbourne Gdns SM6 219 B1
Woodbridge Cl
4 Dollis Hill NW2 68 A5
10 Finsbury Pk N7 72 B6
Woodbridge Ct
Forest Gate E7 77 D3
Stoke Newington N16 73 B5
Woodbridge High Sch IG8 37 B3
Woodbridge Ho E11 54 D1
Woodbridge Rd IG11 79 D3
Woodbridge St EC1 94 D3 241 C6
Woodbrook Rd SE2 146 B6
Woodbrook Sch BR3 185 B2
Woodburn Cl NW4 46 D4
Woodbury Cl
Croydon CR0 221 D6
Wanstead E11 55 B5
Woodbury Ct 1 W13 87 B3
Woodbury Gdns
Bromley SE12 187 B6
Eltham SE12 165 B1
Woodbury Ho 4 SE26 162 B1
Woodbury Park Rd W13 87 B3
Woodbury Rd E17 53 D5
Woodbury St SW17 180 C5
Woodchester Sq W2 91 D2
Woodchurch Cl DA14 167 B1
Woodchurch Dr BR1 187 D3
Woodchurch Ho 15 SW9 138 C4
Woodchurch Rd NW6 69 D1
Wood Cl
Bethnal Green E2 96 A3
Harrow HA1 42 B2
Kingsbury NW9 45 B2
Woodclyffe Dr BR7 188 C1
Woodcock Ct HA3 44 A2
Woodcock Dell Ave HA3 43 D2
Woodcock Hill HA3 43 C3
Woodcock Ho 4 E14 97 C2
Woodcocks E16 99 D2
Woodcombe Cres SE23 162 C3
Woodcote Ave
Mill Hill NW7 28 C4
Thornton Heath CR7 204 D5
Wallington SM6 219 B1
Woodcote Cl
Enfield N9 18 C5
Kingston u T KT2 176 B5
Woodcote Ct 14 SM6 219 B2
Woodcote Dr BR6 211 B2
Woodcote Ho 4 SE8 141 B6
Woodcote Mews
Loughton IG10 21 D4
Wallington SM6 219 B2
Woodcote Pl 1 SE27 182 D5
Woodcote Rd
Wallington SM6 219 C1
Wanstead E11 55 A2
Woodcott Ho 1 SW15 156 A4
Woodcroft Ave
Edgware NW7 27 C4
Stanmore HA7 25 A2
Woodcroft Cres UB10 82 D6
Woodcroft Mews SE8 119 A2
Woodcroft Prim Sch HA8 27 C3
Woodcroft Rd CR7 204 D3
Woodcroft SE9 166 B1
South Croydon CR0 221 C5
Southgate N21 16 C3
17 Stanmore HA7 25 C5
Wembley UB6 65 A2
Wood Dene 6 SE15 140 B4
Wood Dr BR7 188 A4
Woodedge Cl E4 20 D3
WOOD END 83 D1
Wood End Ave HA2 64 A4
Wood End Cl UB5 64 B3
Woodend Gdns EN2 4 A1
Wood End Gdns UB5 64 A3
WOOD END GREEN 83 C2
Wood End Green Rd UB3 83 C1
Wood End UB3 83 C1
Wood End Inf Sch UB5 64 B3
Wood End Jun Sch UB6 64 B3
Wood End La UB5 63 D3
Wood End Park Com Sch UB3 105 A6
Woodend Rd E17 36 A1
Wood End Rd HA1, UB5 64 B4
Woodend
South Norwood SE19 183 A4
Sutton SM1 218 A6
Thames Ditton KT10 212 A6
Wood End Way UB5 64 A3
Wooder Gdns E7 77 A4
Wooderson Cl SE25 205 C5
Wooderson Ct 9 BR3 185 C2
Woodfall Ave EN5 13 B6
Woodfall Rd N4 72 C6
Woodfall St SW3 257 C1
Woodfarrs SE5 139 B1
Woodfield Ave
Colindale NW9 45 C5
Ealing W5 87 C3
Streatham SW16 159 D1
Wallington SM5 219 A1
Wembley HA0 65 C5
Woodfield Cl
1 Enfield EN1 5 C1
South Norwood SE19 183 A3
Woodfield Cres W5 87 D3
Woodfield Ct SW16 159 D1
Woodfield Dr EN4 15 A3
Woodfield Gdns KT3 199 D4
Woodfield Gr SW16 159 D1
Woodfield Ho
11 Forest Hill SE23 162 D1
Hinchley Wood KT7 212 D6
New Malden KT3 199 D4
6 Upper Clapton E5 74 B6
Wood Green N11 31 D4
Wood Field NW3 70 D3
Woodfield Pl W9 91 B3
Woodfield Rd
Cranford TW4, TW5 128 B3
Ealing W5 87 C3
Hinchley Wood KT10, KT7 212 D6
Kensal Town W9 91 B2
Woodfield Rise WD23 8 B4
Woodfield Sch NW9 45 C1
Woodfields Ct SM1 218 A5
Woodfield SW16 182 B2
Woodfield Way N11 31 D3
WOODFORD 37 D5
Woodford Ave IG2, IG4, IG5, IG8 56 B5
Woodford Bridge Rd IG4 56 A5
Woodford Cres HA5 22 B1
Woodford Ct 15 W12 112 D4
Woodford Cty High Sch IG8 36 D4
Woodforde Ct UB3 105 B1
WOODFORD GREEN 37 B3
Woodford Green Prep Sch IG8 37 A4
Woodford Green Sch IG8 36 D5
Woodford Ho
13 SE18 144 D6
5 Wanstead E18 55 A5
Woodford New Rd
Upper Walthamstow E17 54 C6
Woodford E18 36 D3
Woodford Pl HA9 44 A1
Woodford Rd
Forest Gate E7 77 B4
Wanstead E18 55 A6
Woodford Sta IG8 37 B4
Woodford Trad Est IG8 37 D1
WOODFORD WELLS 21 B1
Woodgate Ave KT9 213 D3
Woodgate Cres HA6 22 A4
Woodgate Dr SW16 181 D3
Woodgate Ho 12 KT6 198 A3
Woodger Rd W12 112 C4
Woodget Cl E6 100 A1
Woodglen SM4 202 C4
Woodgrange Ave
Ealing W5 110 C5
Enfield EN1 18 A5
Finchley N12 30 B4
Harrow HA3 43 D4
Woodgrange Cl HA3 43 D4
Woodgrange Ct 1 BR2 208 D1
Woodgrange Gdns EN1 18 A5
Woodgrange Ho W5 110 B5
Woodgrange Inf Sch E7 77 B4
Woodgrange Mans HA3 43 C4
Woodgrange Park Sta E12 77 D3
Woodgrange Rd E7 77 A3
Woodgrange Terr EN1 18 A5
WOOD GREEN 32 B2
Wood Green Sh City N22 32 C1
Wood Green Sta N22 32 C1
Woodhall Ave
Dulwich SE21 161 D1
Pinner HA5 23 A2
Woodhall Dr
Dulwich SE21 161 D1
Pinner HA5 23 A2
Woodhall Gate HA5 22 D3
Woodhall Ho SW18 158 B5
Woodhall La WD19 23 A6
Woodhall NW1 232 A1
Woodhall Prim Sch WD19 23 A6
Woodhall Rd HA5 22 D4
Woodham Ct E11 54 D5
Woodham Rd SE6 164 A1
Woodhatch Cl 16 E6 100 A2
Woodhaven Gdns IG6 57 A5
Woodhayes BR7 188 D4
Woodhayes Rd SW19, SW20 178 C4
Woodhead Dr BR6 227 C6
Woodheyes Rd NW10 67 C3
Woodhill Cres HA3 43 D3
Woodhill Prim Sch SE18 122 A2
Woodhill SE7, SE18 122 A2
Wood Ho
4 Clapham SW4 137 D3
6 Paddington NW6 91 B5
Woodhouse Ave UB6 86 D5
Woodhouse Cl
Hayes UB3 105 C3
Wembley UB6 86 D5
Woodhouse Eaves HA6 22 A5
Woodhouse Gr E12 78 A2
Woodhouse Rd
Colney Hatch N12 30 C4
Leyton E11 76 D5
Woodhouse Sixth Form Coll N12 30 B4
Woodhurst Ave BR5 211 A3
Woodhurst Rd
Acton W3 111 A6
SE2 124 A2
Woodington Cl SE9 166 C5
Woodison St E3 97 A3
Woodknoll Dr BR7 188 B2
Wood La
Dagenham RM10 81 A5
Highgate N6 49 B3
Hounslow TW7 130 D5
Kingsbury NW9 45 B2
Woodland App UB6 65 A2
Woodland Cl
Kingsbury NW9 45 A3
Uxbridge UB10 60 D6
West Ewell KT19 215 C2
West Norwood SE19 183 C4
Woodford IG8 21 B1
Woodland Cres
18 Rotherhithe SE16 118 D4
SE10 142 C6
Woodland Ct
Cheam SM1 217 C2
Temple Fortune NW4 47 A4
13 Wanstead E11 55 A4
Woodland Gdns
Cranley Gdns N10 49 B4
Isleworth TW7 130 C2
Woodland Gr SE10 120 C1
Woodland Hill SE19 183 C4
Woodland Hts SE3 142 C6
Woodland Mews SW16 160 A1
Woodland Rd
Chingford E4 20 A3
Friern Barnet N11 31 B5
Penge SE19 183 D4
Thornton Heath CR7 204 C5
Woodland Rise
Cranley Gdns N10 49 B5
Wembley UB6 65 A2
WOODLANDS 130 C2
Woodlands Ave
Acton W3 110 D5
DA15 167 C3
Dagenham RM6 59 A2
Finchley N3 30 A2
Kingston u T KT3 177 B2
Ruislip HA4 40 D2
Wanstead E11 55 B1
Worcester Pk KT4 216 A6
Woodlands
Beckenham BR3 185 D3
Clapham SW4 137 B1
Woodlands Cl BR1 188 B1
Claygate KT10 212 D1
Temple Fortune NW11 47 A4
Woodlands Ct
9 Bromley BR1 186 D2
Brondesbury Pk NW10 90 D6
Dulwich SE22 162 B4
Southall UB1 107 C6
Woodlands Dr
Harrow HA7 24 D4
Sunbury TW16 172 C1
Woodlands N12 30 A4
Woodlands Fst & Mid Sch HA8 26 B2
Woodlands Gdns E17 54 C5
Woodlands Gr TW7 130 C3
Woodlands Gt SW15 157 B6
Woodlands HA2 41 C5
Woodlands Jun & Inf Schs IG1 79 B3
Woodlands Par TW15 171 A4
Woodlands Park Rd
SE10 142 C6
Tottenham N15 51 A4
Woodlands Rd
Barnes SW13 133 D2
Bexleyheath DA7 147 A2

Woodlands Rd *continued*
Bickley BR1 188 B1
Enfield EN2 5 B4
Harrow HA1 42 D4
Ilford IG1 79 A5
Isleworth TW7 130 C3
Leyton E11 76 C6
Lower Edmonton N9 18 C3
Southall UB1 106 D5
Surbiton KT6 197 D2
Walthamstow E17 54 A6
Woodlands St SE13 164 B4
Woodlands NW11 47 A4
Woodlands The
East Barnet N14 15 B3
Harrow HA1 64 C6
Highbury N5 73 A4
12 Hornsey N8 50 A2
Isleworth TW7 130 D3
Lewisham SE13 164 B4
Mitcham CR4 203 A6
South Norwood SE19 183 A3
Stanmore HA7 25 B5
Thames Ditton KT10 212 A6
Woodland St 2 E8 73 D2
Woodlands E11 54 B2
Woodlands Way SW15 157 B6
Woodlands SW20 200 D5
Woodland Terr SE7 122 A2
Woodland Way
Abbey Wood SE2 124 D2
Croydon CR0 207 A1
Edgware NW7 27 D4
Merton SM4 201 B5
Mitcham CR4 181 A3
Petts Wood BR5 211 A4
Southgate N21 16 C2
Tolworth KT5 214 D6
West Wickham BR4 224 A5
Woodford IG8 21 B1
Woodland Wlk
Chessington KT19 214 C2
9 Greenwich SE10 120 C1
Hampstead NW3 70 C3
Wood Lane High Sch W12 90 B1
Wood La Ruislip HA4 61 C6
Shepherd's Bush W12 112 C6
Stanmore HA7 9 B2
Woodlawn Cl SW15 157 B6
Woodlawn Cres TW2 151 D2
Woodlawn Dr TW13 150 D2
Woodlawn Rd SW6 134 D4
Wood La IG8 36 D5
Woodlea Dr BR2 208 C4
Woodlea Lo EN1 17 C5
Woodlea Rd N16 73 C5
Woodleigh Ave N12 30 C4
Woodleigh Ct N22 32 B2
Woodleigh Gdns SW16 160 A1
Woodleigh
1 Kingston u T KT5 198 B4
3 Woodford E18 37 A2
Woodley Cl SW17 180 D3
Woodley La SM1, SM5 218 C5
Wood Lodge Gdns BR1 188 A3
Wood Lodge La BR4 224 A5
Woodlodge 4 SW19 179 B5
Woodman La E4 20 C6
Woodman Mews TW9 132 D4
Woodman Par 4 E16 122 C5
Woodmans Ct HA7 44 A6
Woodmans Gr NW10 67 D3
Woodmans Mews W12 90 B2
Woodmansterne Prim Sch SW16 181 D2
Woodmansterne Rd
Mitcham SW16 181 D2
Sutton SM5 218 C1
Woodman St E16 122 C5
Wood Mead N17 34 A4
Woodmere Ave CR0 206 D2
Woodmere Cl
11 Clapham SW11 137 A2
Croydon CR0 206 D2
Woodmere Ct N14 15 B4
Woodmere Gdns CR0 206 D2
Woodmere SE9 166 B3
Woodmere Way BR3 208 B4
Woodnook Rd SW16 181 B5
Woodpecker Cl
Bushey WD23 8 A3
Enfield N9 18 B5
Harrow HA3 24 D2
Woodpecker Ct TW2 151 D4
Woodpecker Ho E17 53 C6
Woodpecker Mews SE13 142 B1
Woodpecker Rd
6 SE14 141 A6
Woolwich SE28 124 C6
Wood Point 8 E16 99 A2
Woodquest Ave SE24 161 A6
Wood Rd
Littleton TW17 192 C5
Willesden NW10 67 A1
Wood Retreat SE18 145 B5
Wood Ride Barnet EN4 2 B4
Orpington BR5 211 C5
Woodridge Cl EN2 4 C4
Woodridge Prim Sch N12 13 C1
Woodridings Ave HA5 23 B2
Woodridings Cl HA5 23 B3
Woodridings Ct N22 31 D2
Woodriffe Rd E11 54 B2
Wood Rise HA5 40 A4
Woodrow Ave UB4 83 D3
Woodrow Cl UB6 65 B1
Woodrow Ct 3 N17 34 B3
Woodrow SE18 122 B2
Woodruff Ho 12 SW2 160 C5
Woodrush Cl 4 SE14 141 A5
Woodrush Way RM6 58 D5
Woodseer St E1 96 A2
Woodsford SE17 262 C1
Woodsford Sq W14 113 A4 244 B2
Woodshire Rd RM10 81 D5
Woods Ho SW8 269 A2
WOODSIDE 206 A4
Woodside Ave
Chislehurst BR7 189 A5
Croydon SE25 206 B4
Fortis Green N6 48 D5
North Finchley N12 30 A6
Thames Ditton KT10 196 C2
Wembley HA0 88 A6
Woodside IG9 21 C2
Woodside Cl
Ruislip HA4 39 B3
Stanmore HA7 25 B5
Tolworth KT5 199 A2
Wembley HA0 88 A6
Woodside Court Rd CR0 206 A2
Woodside Cres DA15 167 C1
Woodside Ct
Ealing W5 110 A5
Enfield EN2 4 D4
10 Finchley N12 29 D6
Palmers Green N13 16 C1
Wanstead E12 55 C1
Woodside End HA0 88 A6
Woodside Gdns
Chingford E4 35 D4
Tottenham N17 33 D1
Woodside Gn SE25 206 A3
Woodside Grange Rd N12 29 D6
Woodside Gr N12 14 A1
Woodside NW11 47 C4
Woodside Ho SW19 179 B4
Woodside Jun & Inf Sch CR0 206 A2
Woodside La DA5 168 D5
Whetstone N12 14 A1
Woodside N10 49 A6
WOODSIDE PARK 29 C6
Woodside Park Ave E17 54 B5
Woodside Park Int Sch N11 30 D5
Woodside Park Rd N12 30 A6
Woodside Pk SE25 206 B3
Woodside Pl HA0 88 A6
Woodside Rd BR1 210 A4
Coombe KT3 177 C1
Croydon SE25 206 B3
Kingston u T KT2 176 A3
Newham E13 99 C3
Northwood HA6 22 A3
Sidcup DA15 167 C1
Sutton SM1 218 A5
Woodford IG8 37 A6
Wood Green N22 32 C3
Woodside Sch
Belvedere DA17 125 D2
Walthamstow E17 54 A6
Woodside Sta SE25 206 B3
Woodside KT12 194 A1
Woodside Way
Croydon CR0 206 C3
Streatham CR4 181 C2
Woodside SW19 179 B5
Wood's Mews W1 115 A6 248 A6
Woodsome Rd NW5 71 B5
Wood's Pl SE1 263 B5
Woodspring Rd SW19 157 A2
Wood's Rd SE15 140 B4
Woodstar Ho 3 SE15 140 A5
Wood St Barnet EN5 1 A1
Carshalton CR4 203 A2
Chiswick W4 111 C1
City of London EC2 95 A1 242 B2
Custom Ho E16 121 B6
Woodstead Gr HA8 26 A4
Woods The
Eastbury HA6 22 A5
Uxbridge UB10 60 D4
Wood St
Kingston u T KT1 175 D1
Kingston u T KT2 176 A2
Woodstock Ave
Brentford W13 109 A3
Cheam SM3 201 B2
Golders Green NW11 47 A2
Isleworth TW7 153 A6
Southall UB1 85 B4
Woodstock Cl DA5 169 B3
Stanmore HA7 26 A1
Woodstock Cres N9 18 B5
Woodstock Ct
Kingston u T KT2 176 D1
Lee SE12 165 A5
Vauxhall SE11 260 D2
Woodstock Dr UB10 60 B4
Woodstock Gdns
Beckenham BR3 185 D3
Hayes UB4 83 D2
Ilford IG3 80 A6
Woodstock Grange W5 110 A5
Woodstock Gr W12 112 D4
Woodstock Ho
Hayes UB3 83 B2
2 Highbury N5 73 A4
Woodstock Lane N KT6 213 C6
Woodstock Lane S KT6, KT9, KT10 213 C4
Woodstock Mews W1 238 B3
Woodstock Rd
Bedford Pk W4 111 C3
Bushey WD23 8 D4
Chingford E17 36 B1
Finsbury Pk N4 50 C1
Golders Green NW11 47 B1
South Croydon CR0 221 B5
Upton E7 77 C1
Wallington SM5, SM6 219 A3
Wembley HA0 66 B1
Woodstock Rise SM3 201 B2
Woodstock Studios 17 W12 112 D4
Woodstock St W1 238 C1
Woodstock Terr E14 119 D6
Woodstock The SM3 201 B2
Woodstock Way CR4 181 C1
Woodstone Ave KT17, KT4 216 A3
Wood Street Sta E17 54 B5
Wood St E17 54 B5
Woodsyre SE26 183 D6
Woodthorpe Rd
Ashford TW15 170 A6
Putney SW15 134 B1
Woodtree Cl NW4 28 C1
Woodvale Ave SE25 183 D1
Wood Vale N10 49 C4
Woodvale Ct BR1 187 B1
South Norwood SE25 205 D6
Wood Vale SE22 162 B4
Woodvale Way NW11 68 D5
Woodvale Wlk SE27 183 A5
Woodview Ave E4 36 A6
Woodview Cl
Finsbury Pk N4 50 D2
Kingston u T SW15 177 B6
Orpington BR6 227 A6
Woodville Cl SE12 165 A6
Woodville Cl *continued*
Teddington TW11 175 A6
Woodville Ct
3 Lewisham SE10 142 A4
Southgate N14 15 C6
Woodville Gdns
Ealing W5 88 A1
Hendon NW11 46 D2
Ilford IG6 56 D5
Ruislip HA4 39 A2
Surbiton KT6 197 D2
Woodville Gr 2 DA16 146 A2
Woodville Ho SE1 263 C6
Sutton SM1 217 D4
Woodville Rd
Barnet EN5 1 D2
Ealing W5 87 D1
Golders Green NW11 47 A2
Leytonstone E11 54 D1
Morden SM4 201 C5
Paddington NW6 91 B5
Richmond TW10 153 C1
South Norwood CR7 205 B6
Stoke Newington N16 73 C3
Walthamstow E17 53 B5
Woodford E18 37 B1
Woodville SE3 143 B4
Woodville St 16 SE7 122 A2
Woodville The W5 87 D1
Woodward Ave NW4 46 A4
Woodward Cl KT10 212 D2
Woodwarde Rd SE22 161 C5
Woodward Gdns
Dagenham RM9 80 C1
Harrow HA7 24 D3
Woodward Rd RM9 80 C1
Wood Way BR6 226 C6
Woodway Cres HA1 43 A3
Woodwell St SW18 158 A6
Wood Wharf SE10 142 A6
Woodyard Cl NW5 71 A3
Woodyard La SE21 161 C4
Woodyates Rd SE12 165 B4
Woolacombe Rd SE3 143 C3
Woolacombe Way UB3 105 C2
Woolcombes Ct 4 SE16 118 D5
Woolden Ho 2 E4 20 C4
Wooler St SE17 117 B1 262 D2
Woolf Cl SE28 124 B5
Woolf Ct 7 W3 111 A3
Woolf Mews WC1 240 A6
Woollaston Rd N4 50 D3
Woolley Ho SW9 138 D2
Woollon Ho 1 E1 96 C1
Woolmead Ave NW9 46 A2
Woolmer Gdns N18 34 A5
Woolmer Ho 2 E5 74 B6
Woolmer Rd N18 34 A5
Woolmore Prim Sch E14 120 A6
Woolmore St E14 120 A6
Woolneigh St SW6 135 D3
Woolpack Ho 1 E9 74 C2
Wool Rd SW20 178 B4
Woolridge Way E9 74 C1
Woolstaplers Way SE16 118 A2
Woolston Cl E17 34 D1
Woolstone Ho 7 E2 96 A6
Woolstone Rd SE23 163 A2
Woolven Ho SE3 142 D6
WOOLWICH 122 D3
Woolwich Arsenal Sta SE18 122 D2
Woolwich Church St SE7, SE18 122 A3
Woolwich Comm SE18 144 C6
Woolwich Ct EN3 7 C5
Woolwich Dockyard Ind Est SE18 122 A3
Woolwich Dockyard Sta SE18 122 B2
Woolwich High St SE18 122 C3
Woolwich Manor Way E6 100 C1
Woolwich Manorway E16 122 D4
Woolwich Manor Way E16 122 D5
Woolwich New Rd SE18 122 D2
Woolwich Poly Sch for Boys SE28 124 A5
Woolwich Rd
Belvedere DA17 125 C1
DA7 147 C2
Erith SE2 125 B1
Woolwich Rd *continued*
Greenwich SE7, SE10 121 C2
Wooster Gdns E14 98 B1
Wooster Mews HA2 42 A6
Wooster Pl SE1 262 D4
Wootton KT10 212 A4
Wootton Gr N3 29 C2
Wootton Ho SE9 167 B5
Wootton St SE1 116 C5 251 B3
Worbeck Rd SE20 184 C1
Worcester Ave N17 34 A3
Worcester Cl
Croydon CR0 223 C6
Dollis Hill NW2 68 B5
Mitcham CR4 181 A1
Worcester Cres
Edgware NW7 11 C1
Woodford IG8 37 C6
Worcester Ct
Ashford TW15 170 D5
Ealing W7 86 D1
Finchley N12 29 D5
Harrow HA1 42 C6
44 Paddington W2 91 C2
12 Sutton SM2 217 D2
Walton-on-T KT12 194 C1
Worcester Pk KT4 215 C5
Worcester Dr
Ashford TW15 170 D5
Bedford Pk W4 111 C4
Worcester Gdns
Northolt UB6 64 B2
Redbridge IG1 56 A2
Wandsworth SW11 158 D6
Worcester Pk KT4 215 C5
Worcester Ho
Bayswater W2 236 A1
3 Islington N1 73 A1
Lambeth SE11 261 A5
9 Putney SW15 156 C4
Worcester Mews 2 NW6 69 D2
WORCESTER PARK 215 C4
Worcester Park Rd KT4 215 B5
Worcester Park Sta KT4 200 A1
Worcester Rd
Belmont SM2 217 D1
Higham Hill E17 34 D1
Ilford E12 78 B4
11 Wimbledon SW19 179 B5
Worcesters Ave EN1 6 A5
Worcesters Prim Sch EN1 5 D5
Wordsworth Ave
Greenford UB6 86 B5
Plashet E12 78 A1
Snaresbrook E18 54 D6
Wordsworth Ct
Harrow HA1 42 B2
New Barnet EN5 14 A6
Wordsworth Dr KT4, SM3 216 C4
Wordsworth Gdns WD6 10 C6
Wordsworth Ho
Maida Vale NW6 91 C4
15 SE18 144 C6
Wordsworth N8 50 C5
Wordsworth Par 1 N15 50 D5
Wordsworth Pl 11 NW5 70 D3
Wordsworth Rd
Bermondsey SE1 263 D3
Bexley DA16 145 C4
Hampton TW12, TW13 173 B6
Penge SE20 184 D3
Stoke Newington N16 73 C4
Wallington SM6 219 D2
Wordsworth Way UB7 104 B2
Wordsworth Wlk NW11 47 C5
Worfield St SW11 136 C5 267 B3
Worgan St
Rotherhithe SE16 118 D2
SE11 116 B1 260 C2
Working Men's Coll The NW1 93 C5 232 B4
Worland Rd E15 76 C1
World Bsns Ctr TW6 127 A4
WORLD'S END 4 C1
World's End La EN2 4 B1
Worlds End La BR6 227 D1
World's End Pas SW10 266 C4
World's End Pl SW10 266 B4
World Trade Ctr London E14 119 D4
Worley Ct NW2 68 D5
Worleys Dr BR6 227 B4
Worlidge St W6 112 C1
Worlingham Rd SE22 139 D1
Wormholt Park Prim Sch W12 112 A6
Wormholt Rd W12 112 A5
Wormwood St EC2 243 A2
Wornington Rd W10 91 A2
Woronzow Rd NW8 92 C6 230 A5
Worple Ave
Isleworth TW7 153 A6
Wimbledon SW19 178 D3
Worple Cl HA2 41 B1
Worple Ct SW19 179 A4
Worple Prim Sch TW7 131 A1
Worple Rd
Isleworth TW7 131 A1
Wimbledon SW19, SW20 178 D2
Worple Road Mews SW19 179 B4
Worple St SW14 133 B2
Worple Way
Harrow HA2 41 B1
Richmond TW10 132 A1
Worship St EC2 95 C3 243 A5
Worslade Rd SW17 180 B6
Worsley Bridge Jun Sch BR3 185 C3
Worsley Bridge Rd BR3, SE6 185 C5
Worsley Ct N3 29 D4
Worsley Grange BR7 189 A4
Worsley Gr E5 74 A4
Worsley Ho 9 SE23 162 B2
Worsley Rd E11 76 C4
Worsopp Dr SW4 159 C6
Worth Cl BR6 227 C4
Worthfield Cl KT19 215 B1
Worth Gr SE17 262 C1
Worthing Cl 5 E15 98 C6
Worthing Rd TW5 129 B6
Worthington Cl CR4 203 B6
Worthington Ho
EC1 234 B2
16 Streatham SW2 160 C4
Worthington Rd KT6 198 B1
Wortley Rd
Forest Gate E6 77 D1
Thornton Heath CR0 204 C2
Worton Ct TW7 130 C1
Worton Gdns TW7 130 B3
Worton Hall Ind Est TW7 130 C1
Worton Rd TW7 130 C2
Worton Way TW3, TW7 130 B3
Wotton Ct 10 E14 120 B6
Wotton Rd
Cricklewood NW2 68 C5
18 SE8 141 B6
Wouldham Rd E16 98 D1
Wragby Rd E11 76 C5
Wrampling Pl N9 18 A3
Wrangthorne Wlk CR0 220 C4
Wray Ave IG5 56 C6
Wrayburn Ho 28 SE16 118 A4
Wray Cres N4 72 B6
Wray Ct N4 72 B6
Wrayfield Rd SM3 216 D5
Wray Ho 11 SW2 160 A3
Wraysbury Cl TW4 151 A6
Wrays Way UB4 83 C3
Wrekin Rd SE18 145 A5
Wren Ave
Cricklewood NW2 68 C4
Southall UB2 107 B2
Wren Cl E16 98 D1
Lower Edmonton N9 18 D3
Wren Cres WD23 8 A3
Wren Ct
1 Barnet EN4 14 D3
Croydon CR0 221 B4
Wren Gdns RM9 80 D3
Wren Ho 29 Bow E3 97 A5
4 Hampton TW12 173 D4
SW1 259 C1
Wren Landing E14 119 C5
Wrenn Ho SW13 134 C6
Wren Path SE28 123 B4
Wren Rd
Camberwell SE5 139 B4
Dagenham RM9 80 D3
Sidcup DA14 168 C1
Wrens Ave TW15 171 A6
Wren's Park Ho E5 74 B6

Wren St WC1 . . 94 B3 240 D6
Wrentham Ave NW10 . . . 90 D5
Wrenthorpe Rd BR1 . . . 186 C6
Wren View N6 . . . 49 C1
Wrenwood Way HA5 . . 40 B5
Wrestlers Ct EC3 . . . 243 A2
Wrexham Rd E3 . . . 97 C5
Wricklemarsh Rd SE3 . . . 143 D4
Wrigglesworth St SE14 . . . 140 D5
Wright Cl SE13 . . . 142 B1
Wright Gdns TW17 . . 192 C4
Wright Ho SW15 . . . 156 B6
Wrighton Ct SM1 . . . 217 B2
Wright Rd TW5 . . . 128 C5
Wrights Cl RM10 . . . 81 D4
Wright's Gn SW4 . . . 137 D1
Wright's La W8 . . . 113 D3 255 C6
Wrights Pl NW10 . . . 67 A2
Wright's Rd E3 . . . 97 B5
Wrights Rd SE25 . . . 205 C6
Wrights Row SM5 . . . 219 B4
Wrights Wlk SW14 . . . 133 B2
Writtle Ho 36 NW9 . . . 27 D1
Wrotham Ho
Beckenham BR3 . . . 185 B3
SE1 . . . 262 D6
Wrotham Rd
Barnet EN5 . . . 1 A3
13 Camden Town NW1 . . . 71 C1
DA16 . . . 146 C4
Ealing W13 . . . 109 C5
Wrottesley Rd SE18 . . 145 A6
Willesden Green NW10 . . . 90 A5
Wroughton Rd SW11 . . . 158 D5
Wroughton Terr NW4 . . . 46 B5
Wroxall Rd RM9 . . . 80 C2
Wroxham Gdns N11 . . . 31 D3
Wroxham Rd SE28 . . . 124 D6
Wroxton Rd SE15 . . . 140 C3
Wr Twr Cl UB8 . . . 60 A3
Wr Twr Hill CR0 . . . 221 B4
Wr Twr Pl N1 . . . 234 C5
Wrythe Gn 2 SM5 . . . 218 D5
Wrythe Green Rd SM5 . . . 218 D5
Wrythe La SM1, SM5, SM4 . . . 218 C5
WRYTHE THE . . . 218 D6
Wulfstan St W12 . . . 89 D1
Wyatt Cl Bushey WD23 . . . 8 C4
Feltham TW13 . . . 150 D3
Hayes UB4 . . . 84 A2
Rotherhithe SE16 . . . 119 B4
Wyatt Ct HA0 . . . 66 A1
Wyatt Dr SW13 . . . 134 B5
Wyatt Ho
Blackheath Vale SE3 . . . 142 D3
NW8 . . . 236 D5
Wyatt Park Mans 1 SW2 . . . 160 A2
Wyatt Park Rd SW2 . . 160 B2
Wyatt Rd
Forest Gate E7 . . . 77 A2
Highbury N5 . . . 73 A5
Wyatt's La E17 . . . 54 A6
Wybert St NW1 . . . 239 A6
Wyborne Ho NW10 . . . 67 A1
Wyborne Prim Sch SE9 . . . 166 D3
Wyborne Way NW10 . . 67 A1
Wyburn Ave EN5 . . . 1 B2
Wyche Gr CR2 . . . 221 A1
Wycherley Cl SE3 . . . 142 D5
Wycherley Cres EN5 . . 13 D5
Wychwood Ave
Edgware HA8 . . . 25 D4
South Norwood CR7 . 205 A6
Wychwood Cl
Ashford TW16 . . . 172 A4
Edgware HA8 . . . 25 D4
Wychwood End N6 . . . 49 C2
Wychwood Gdns IG5 . . 56 C5
Wychwood Ho N4 . . . 51 A2
Wychwood Way SE19 . . . 183 B4
Wyclif Ct EC1 . . . 234 C1
Wycliffe Cl DA16 . . . 145 D4
Wycliffe Ho 13 N16 . . . 73 C4
Wycliffe Rd
Battersea SW11 . . . 137 A3
Wimbledon SW19 . . . 179 D4
Wyclif St EC1 . . . 234 C1
Wycombe Ct SE3 . . . 143 A5
Wycombe Gdns NW11 . . . 69 C6
Wycombe Ho NW8 . . . 237 A6
Wycombe Pl SW18 . . . 158 A5
Wycombe Rd
Redbridge IG2 . . . 56 B4
Tottenham N17 . . . 34 A2
Wembley HA0 . . . 88 C6
Wycombe Sq W8 . . . 245 A3
Wydehurst Rd CR0 . . . 206 B2
Wydell Cl SM4 . . . 200 D3
Wydeville Manor Rd SE12 . . . 187 B6
Wye Cl
Ashford TW15 . . . 170 D6
BR6 . . . 211 D2
Ruislip HA4 . . . 39 A3
Wye Ct W13 . . . 87 B2
Wyemead Cres E4 . . . 20 C2
Wyersdale Ho N4 . . . 51 A2
Wye St SW11 . . . 136 B3
Wyevale Cl HA5 . . . 40 A6
Wyfold Ho 8 SE2 . . . 124 D4
Wyfold Rd SW6 . . . 135 A5 264 A3
Wyke Cl TW7 . . . 130 D6
Wyke Gdns W7 . . . 109 A3
Wykeham Ave RM9 . . . 80 C2
Wykeham Cl UB7 . . . 126 C6
Wykeham Ct
Chislehurst BR7 . . . 189 C4
Hendon NW4 . . . 46 C4
Wykeham Gn RM9 . . . 80 C2
Wykeham Hill HA9 . . . 44 B1
Wykeham Ho SW19 . . . 179 C2
Wykeham Prim Sch NW10 . . . 67 C5
Wykeham Rd
Harrow HA3 . . . 43 B5
Hendon NW4 . . . 46 C4
Wykeham Rise N20 . . . 13 A3
Wykehurst Ho SW17 . . . 180 B5
Wyke Rd
Hackney Wick E3 . . . 75 C1
Merton SW20 . . . 178 C1
Wylchin Cl HA5 . . . 39 D6
Wyldes Cl NW11 . . . 48 A1
Wyldfield Gdns N9 . . . 17 D2
Wyld Way HA9 . . . 66 D2
Wyleu St SE23 . . . 163 A4
Wylie Rd UB2 . . . 107 C3
Wyllen Cl E1 . . . 96 C3
Wylo Dr EN5 . . . 12 A5
Wymering Mans 9 W9 . . . 91 C4
Wymering Rd W9 . . . 91 C4
Wymondham Ct NW8 . . . 229 D6
Wymond St SW15 . . . 134 C2
Wynan Rd E14 . . . 119 D1
Wynash Gdns SM5 . . . 218 C3
Wynaud Ct N22 . . . 32 B4
Wynbourne Ct SE20 . . . 184 B1
Wyncham Ave DA15 . . . 167 C3
Wynchgate
Harrow HA3 . . . 24 C3
Southgate N14 . . . 16 A4
Wyncroft Cl BR1 . . . 210 B6
Wyndale Ave NW9 . . . 44 C3
Wyndcliff Rd SE7 . . . 143 B6
Wyndcroft Cl EN2 . . . 4 D2
Wyndham Cl
Belmont SM2 . . . 217 C1
Orpington BR6 . . . 211 A1
Wyndham Cres
Camden Town N19 . . . 71 C5
Hounslow TW4 . . . 151 C5
Wyndham Ct
Brentford W7 . . . 109 A2
1 Thornton Heath CR0 . . . 204 D3
Wyndham Deedes Ho 30 E2 . . . 96 A5
Wyndham Ho SW1 . . . 258 A3
Wyndham Lo TW7 . . . 130 C4
Wyndham Mews W1 . . . 237 C3
Wyndham Pl W1 . . . 237 C3
Wyndham Rd
Barnet EN4 . . . 14 D3
Brentford W13 . . . 109 B3
Wyndham Rd *continued*
Forest Gate E6 . . . 77 D1
Kingston u T KT2 . . . 176 B3
SE5 . . . 139 A5
Wyndhams Ct 4 E8 . . . 73 D1
Wyndham St W1 . . . 92 D2 237 C4
Wyndham Yd W1 . . . 237 C3
Wyndhurst Cl CR2 . . . 220 D1
Wyneham Rd SE24 . . . 161 B6
Wynell Rd SE23 . . . 162 D1
Wynford Pl DA17 . . . 147 C6
Wynford Rd N1 . . . 94 B5 233 D4
Wynford Way SE9 . . . 166 B1
Wynlie Gdns HA5 . . . 22 B1
Wynndale Rd E18 . . . 37 B2
Wynne Ct 6 TW7 . . . 131 A2
Wynne Ho SE14 . . . 140 D4
Wynne Rd SW9 . . . 138 C3
Wynn's Ave DA15 . . . 168 A6
Wynnstay Gdns W8 . . . 113 C3 255 B6
Wynter Ho 20 SW9 . . . 138 B3
Wynter St SW11 . . . 136 A1
Wynton Gdns SE25 . . . 205 D4
Wynton Pl W3 . . . 88 D1
Wynyard Ho SE11 . . . 260 D2
Wynyard Terr SE11 . . . 260 D2
Wynyatt Ho EC1 . . . 234 C2
Wynyatt St EC1 . . . 94 D4 234 C2
Wyre Gr Edgware HA8 . . . 10 D1
Hayes UB3 . . . 106 A2
Wyresdale Cres UB6 . . . 86 D4
Wyteleaf Cl HA4 . . . 39 A3
Wytham Ho NW8 . . . 236 D5
Wythburn Ct W1 . . . 237 C2
Wythburn Pl W1 . . . 237 C2
Wythenshawe Rd RM10 . . . 81 C5
Wythens Wlk SE9 . . . 166 D5
Wythes Cl BR1 . . . 188 B1
Wythes Rd E16 . . . 122 A5
Wythfield Rd SE9 . . . 166 B5
Wyvenhoe Rd HA2 . . . 64 A5
Wyvern Est The KT3 . . . 200 A5
Wyvil Prim Sch SW8 . . . 138 A5 270 B4
Wyvil Rd SW8 . . . 138 A5 270 A4
Wyvis St E14 . . . 97 D2

X

Xavier Ho E17 . . . 35 B1

Y

Yabsley St E14 . . . 120 A5
Yaldam Ho SE1 . . . 263 A3
Yalding Ho 20 E5 . . . 74 B3
Yalding Rd SE16 . . . 118 A2
Yale Cl TW4 . . . 151 B6
Yale Ct NW6 . . . 69 D3
Yarborough Rd 1 SW19 . . . 180 B2
Yardley Cl E4 . . . 19 D6
Yardley Ct SM3 . . . 216 D4
Yardley La E4 . . . 19 D6
Yardley Prim Sch E4 . . . 20 A5
Yardley St WC1 . . . 234 A1
Yard The N1 . . . 233 B3
Yarlington Ct N11 . . . 31 A5
Yarmouth Cres N17 . . . 52 B4
Yarmouth Pl W1 . . . 248 C3
Yarnfield Sq 15 SE15 . . . 140 A4
Yarnton Way DA17, DA18 . . . 125 B3
Yarrow Cres E6 . . . 100 A2
Yarrow Ho
12 Cubitt Town E14 . . . 120 A3
16 North Kensington W10 . . . 90 C2
Yateley St SE18 . . . 121 D3
Yatesbury Ct E5 . . . 75 A3
Yates Ct NW2 . . . 68 D2
Yates Ho 22 E2 . . . 96 A4
Yatton Ho 15 W10 . . . 90 C2
YEADING . . . 84 D3
Yeading Ave HA2 . . . 41 A1
Yeading Ct UB4 . . . 84 C3
Yeading Fork UB4 . . . 84 C3
Yeading Gdns UB4 . . . 84 B2
Yeading Ho UB4 . . . 84 D2
Yeading Jun & Inf Schs UB4 . . . 84 C2
Yeading La
Hayes UB4 . . . 84 B2
Northolt UB4, UB5 . . . 84 C4
Yeadon Ho 14 W10 . . . 90 C2
Yeames Cl W13 . . . 87 A1
Yearby Ho W10 . . . 90 C3
Yeate St N1 . . . 73 B1
Yeatman Rd N6 . . . 48 D3
Yeats Cl NW10 . . . 67 C2
Yeend Cl KT8 . . . 195 C5
Yeldham Ho W6 . . . 112 D1
Yeldham Rd W6 . . . 112 D1
Yellowhammer Ct NW9 . . . 27 C1
Yelverton Lo TW1 . . . 153 C4
Yelverton Rd SW11 . . . 136 B3
Ye Market CR0 . . . 221 B3
Yenston Cl SM4 . . . 201 C3
Yeoman Cl
Newham E16 . . . 122 D6
West Norwood SE27 . . . 160 D1
Yeoman Ct
Heston TW5 . . . 129 B5
8 Sutton SM1 . . . 218 B3
Yeoman Dr TW19 . . . 148 A3
Yeoman Rd UB5 . . . 63 A1
Yeomans Acre HA4 . . . 40 A3
Yeomans Mews TW7 . . . 152 B6
Yeoman's Row SW3 . . . 114 C3 257 B5
Yeoman St SE8 . . . 119 A2
Yeomans Way EN3 . . . 6 C3
Yeoman's Yd E1 . . . 253 D6
Yeo St E3 . . . 97 D2
Yeovil Cl BR6 . . . 227 C6
Yeovil Ho
Finsbury Pk N7 . . . 72 B6
North Kensington W10 . . . 90 C3
Yeovilton Pl KT2 . . . 175 C5
Yerbury Prim Sch N19 . . . 71 D5
Yerbury Rd N19 . . . 71 D5
Yeshivo Horomo Tadmudical Coll N16 . . . 51 B1
Yesodey Hatorah Sch N16 . . . 51 D2
Yester Dr BR7 . . . 188 A3
Yester Pk BR7 . . . 188 B4
Yester Rd BR7 . . . 188 B3
Yet Lev Ct E5 . . . 52 A1
Yew Ave UB7 . . . 104 A6
Yew Cl IG9 . . . 21 D2
Yewdale Cl BR1 . . . 186 C4
Yewfield Rd NW10 . . . 67 D2
Yew Gr NW2 . . . 68 D4
Yew Ho SE14 . . . 141 B3
Yews The TW15 . . . 170 D6
Yew Tree Ave N2 . . . 47 D6
Yew Tree Cl DA16 . . . 146 A4
Yewtree Cl HA2 . . . 41 D5
Yew Tree Cl
3 Lewisham SE13 . . . 142 A2
New Malden KT4 . . . 199 C1
Southgate N21 . . . 16 C4
Yewtree Cl N22 . . . 31 C2
Yew Tree Cotts KT10 . . . 212 B6
Yew Tree Ct
Elstree WD6 . . . 9 D5
8 Stoke Newington N16 . . . 73 B6
8 Sutton SM2 . . . 218 A1
4 Temple Fortune NW11 . . . 47 B4
Yew Tree Gdns RM6 . . . 59 A4
Yew Tree Grange 2 W5 . . . 109 C6
Yew Tree Ho
New Malden KT4 . . . 199 C1
5 Surbiton KT6 . . . 198 A1
Yew Tree Lo 10 SW16 . . . 181 C6
Yewtree Rd BR3 . . . 207 B6
Yew Tree Rd
East Acton W12 . . . 111 D6
Hillingdon UB10 . . . 82 B6
Yew Trees TW17 . . . 192 B5
Yew Tree Wlk TW4 . . . 151 B6
Yew Wlk HA1 . . . 42 C1
YIEWSLEY . . . 104 A6
Yiewsley Ct UB7 . . . 104 A5
Yoakley Rd N16 . . . 73 C6
Yoke Cl N7 . . . 72 A2
Yolande Gdns SE9 . . . 166 A6
Yonge Pk N4, N7 . . . 72 C5
York Ave Ealing W7 . . . 108 C5
Hayes UB3 . . . 83 A1
Mortlake SW14 . . . 155 A6
Sidcup DA15 . . . 167 D2
Stanmore HA7 . . . 25 B1
Walworth SE17 . . . 262 B2
York Bldgs WC2 . . . 116 A6 250 B5
York Bridge NW1 . . . 93 A3 238 A6
York Cl
17 Camberwell SE5 . . . 139 A3
Ealing W7 . . . 108 C5
Morden SM4 . . . 201 D5
Newham E6 . . . 100 B1
York Ct
Beckenham BR3 . . . 186 B2
Kingston u T KT2 . . . 175 D4
Palmers Green N13 . . . 16 A1
Wallington SM6 . . . 219 C3
York Gate NW1 . . . 238 B5
Southgate N14 . . . 16 A4
York Gr SE15 . . . 140 C4
York Hill SE27, SW16 . . . 160 D1
York Ho Acton W3 . . . 111 A6
Chelsea SW3 . . . 257 D2
Chingford E4 . . . 35 C6
Edgware HA8 . . . 26 B4
Enfield EN2 . . . 5 B4
Forest Hill SE26 . . . 184 C5
1 Hendon NW4 . . . 28 D1
1 Ilford IG1 . . . 78 D6
Islington N5 . . . 72 C3
Kensington W8 . . . 245 C2
11 Kentish Town N7 . . . 71 D2
Kew TW9 . . . 132 C4
4 Kingston u T KT2 . . . 176 B3
Lambeth SE1 . . . 116 B3 260 D5
Marylebone W1 . . . 237 C4
Pentonville N1 . . . 233 C3
Richmond TW10 . . . 154 C6
South Norwood SE25 . . . 205 C5
York House Pl W8 . . . 113 D4 245 C2
York Ho 10 W3 . . . 88 C1
Yorkland Ave DA16 . . . 145 D1
Yorkley Ho 3 W10 . . . 90 C3
York Mans
Battersea SW11 . . . 268 B2
2 Hendon NW9 . . . 46 A3
Marylebone W1 . . . 238 A4
Walworth SE17 . . . 262 B2
York Mews
Camden Town NW5 . . . 71 B3
Ilford IG1 . . . 78 C5
York Par
Brentford TW8 . . . 109 D1
Hendon NW9 . . . 46 A3
York Place Mans NW1 . . . 237 D4
York Pl
Battersea SW11 . . . 136 B2
Ilford IG1 . . . 78 C6
WC2 . . . 250 B5
York Rd
Battersea SW11, SW18 . . . 136 B2
Belmont SM1, SM2 . . . 217 C1
Brentford TW8 . . . 109 D1
Chingford E4 . . . 35 C5
Dagenham W3 . . . 89 B1
Ealing W5 . . . 109 C3
Edmonton N18 . . . 34 B5
Forest Gate E7 . . . 77 A2
Friern Barnet N11 . . . 31 D4
Hounslow TW3 . . . 129 D2
Ilford IG1 . . . 78 C6
Kingston u T KT2 . . . 176 B3
Leyton E10 . . . 76 A5
New Barnet EN5 . . . 14 B6
Pinner HA6 . . . 22 A1
4 Richmond TW10 . . . 154 B6
SE1 . . . 116 B4 250 D2
Southgate N21 . . . 17 B4
Teddington TW11 . . . 174 C6
York Rd *coninued*
Thornton Heath CR0 . 204 C2
Walthamstow E17 . . . 52 D4
Wimbledon SW19 . . . 180 A4
York Rise BR6 . . . 227 C6
Dartmouth Pk NW5 . . . 71 B5
York Road Bsns Ctr SW11 . . . 136 B3
York St Chambers W1 . . . 237 C4
Yorkshire Cl N16 . . . 73 C5
Yorkshire Gdns N18 . . . 34 B5
Yorkshire Grey SE9 . . . 165 D6
Yorkshire Grey Pl 13 NW3 . . . 70 A4
Yorkshire Grey Yd WC1 . . . 240 C3
Yorkshire Rd
Limehouse E14 . . . 97 A1
Mitcham CR4 . . . 204 A5
York Sq 12 E14 . . . 97 A1
York St
Carshalton CR4 . . . 203 A2
Paddington W1 . . . 92 D2 237 D4
Twickenham TW1 . . . 153 A3
York Terr EN2 . . . 5 A5
York Terr E NW1 . . . 93 A3 238 B5
York Terr W NW1 . . . 93 A3 238 A5
Yorkton St E2 . . . 96 A5
York Way
Barnsbury N1, N7, NW1 . . . 72 A1
Chessington KT9 . . . 214 A1
York Way Ct
Islington N1 . . . 233 C5
Islington N1 . . . 233 B5
York Way
Friern Barnet N20 . . . 14 D1
N1 . . . 233 B5
Twickenham TW13 . . . 151 B1
Youngmans Cl EN2 . . . 5 A4
Young Rd E16 . . . 99 C1
Young's Bldgs EC1 . . . 242 B6
Youngs Brewery Visitor Ctr* SW18 . . . 157 D6
Youngs Ct SW11 . . . 268 B1
Youngs Rd IG2 . . . 57 B4
Young St W8 . . . 113 D4 245 C1
Yoxall Ho 2 W10 . . . 90 C3
Yoxford Ct 6 RM6 . . . 58 B4
Yoxley App IG2 . . . 57 A3
Yoxley Dr IG2 . . . 57 A3
Yukon Rd SW12 . . . 159 B4
Yunus Khan Cl E17 . . . 53 C4

Z

Zambezie Dr N9 . . . 18 C1
Zampa Rd SE16 . . . 118 C1
Zander Ct E2 . . . 96 A4
Zangwill Ho NW6 . . . 91 B5
Zangwill Rd SE18, SE3 . . . 143 D4
Zealand Ave UB7 . . . 126 A5
Zealand Ho
11 Camberwell SE5 . . . 139 A3
4 Woolwich SE7 . . . 122 A2
Zealand Rd E3 . . . 97 A5
Zenith Lo 7 N3 . . . 29 D3
Zennor Rd SW12 . . . 159 C3
Zenoria St SE22 . . . 139 D1
Zermatt Rd CR7 . . . 205 A5
Zetland Ho W8 . . . 255 C6
Zetland St E14 . . . 98 A2
Zeus Ho N1 . . . 235 C1
Zion Ho 6 E1 . . . 96 C1
Zion Pl CR7 . . . 205 B5
Zion Rd CR7 . . . 205 B5
Zircon Ct N11 . . . 31 D3
ZK Pk CR0 . . . 220 B5
Zoar St SE1 . . . 117 A5 252 A4
Zodiac Ct CR0 . . . 204 D1
Zodiac Ho 3 E3 . . . 97 C3
Zoffany St N19 . . . 71 D6

List of numbered locations

This atlas shows thousands more place names than any other London street atlas. In some busy areas it is impossible to fit the name of every place.

Where not all names will fit, some smaller places are shown by a number. If you wish to find out the name associated with a number, use this listing.

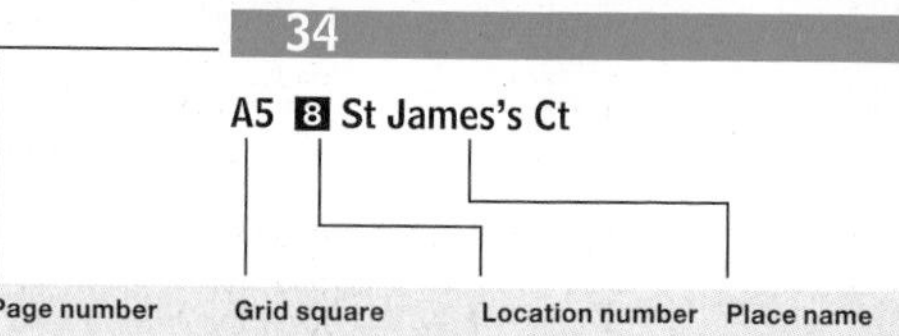

The places in this list are also listed normally in the Index.

1

A1 1 Hertswood Ct
2 Abingdon Lo
3 Sunbury Ct
4 Meriden Ho
5 Norfolk Ct
6 Vanburgh Ct
7 Morrison Ct
8 Kingshill Ct
9 Baronsmere Ct
10 Chartwell Ct
A2 1 Richard Ct
2 Alston Ct
3 Ridgeleigh Ct
4 Bartletts Cotts
5 Leathersellers Cl
6 Holkham Ho
7 Leinster Mews
B1 1 Olivia Ct
2 Tudor Ct
3 Gordon Mans
B2 1 Brake Shear Ho
2 Durham Ct
3 Huntingdon Ct
4 Cambridge Ct
5 Summit Ct
D1 1 Cranleigh Ct
2 Valeside Ct
3 Sherwood
4 Bradbury Ct
5 Chester Ho
6 Graham Ho
7 Highfield Ct
8 Amberley Ho
9 Hadley View
10 Stratton Lo
11 Gainsborough Ct
12 Christopher Ct
13 Bowmar Lo

2

A1 1 Hanover Ho
2 St Giles Ho
3 Henrietta Ho
4 Byron Ct
5 Preston Ct
6 Clivedon Ct
7 Battle House Mews
8 Phoenix Ct
9 Landsdown Cl
10 Comer Ho
11 Basil Ct
12 Russell Ct
13 Alice Cl
C1 1 Braeburn Ct
2 Bramley Ct
3 Cox Ct
4 Golden Ct
5 Pippin Ct
6 Russet Ct
7 High Birch Ct
8 Joystone Ct
9 Mark Lo
10 Edgeworth Ct

4

D3 1 Oakington Ct
2 Elderberry Ct
3 Blueberry Ct
4 Butterfield Ho

5

C1 1 Woodfield Cl
2 Fielders Cl

7

A2 1 Amethyest Ct
2 Bradmore Ct
3 Acer Ct
4 Cornell Ct
5 Durnsford Ct
6 Feldspar Ct
C6 1 Whitworth Cres
2 Polsten Mews
3 Aldis Mews
4 Dundas Mews
5 Colt Mews
6 Warlow Cl
7 Barrass Cl
8 Rigby Pl
9 Gunner Dr
10 Colgate Pl
11 Baddeley Cl
12 Sten Cl
13 Pritchett Cl
14 Rubin Pl
15 Turpin Cl
16 Island Centre Way
17 Hispano Mews
18 Watkin Mews
19 Wallace Ct
20 Needham Ct
21 Dryer Ct
22 Webley Ct
23 Frosbery Ct
24 Jacob Ct
25 Peabody Ct
26 Greener Ct
27 Bren Ct

9

D5 1 Watling Ct
2 Stuart Ct
3 Westview Ct
4 Potters Mews

13

D6 1 Rowan Wlk
2 Ford Ho
3 Glenwood Ho
4 Whitegates
5 Lisa Lo
6 South Lo
7 Hockington Ct
8 Lysander Ct
9 Ashwood Lo
10 Thornbridge Ct
11 Invergarry Ct
12 Eysham Ct
13 Warwick Ct
14 Chaucer Ct
15 Coleridge Ct
16 Springfields
17 Bure Ct
18 Florence Ct
19 Minetta Ct

14

A1 1 Belmont Ct
2 Terrace Ho
3 Croft Mews
4 Bluebell Ct
A2 1 Westview Ct
2 Oakleigh Mews
3 Mountview Ct
4 Mortimer Ct
5 Parklands
A6 1 Chiltern Ct
2 Gills Ct
3 Beaufort Ct
4 St Augustines Ct
5 Somerset Lo
6 Carlyle Lo
7 Stirling Lo
8 St Mirren Ct
9 Wardrew Ct
10 Apex Lo
11 Westbury Ct
B2 1 Davis Ct
2 Deerings Ct
3 Ashcroft Ct
B6 1 Redrose Trad Ctr
2 Lancaster Road Ind Est
C2 1 Mendip Ct
2 Purbeck Ct
3 Brendon Ct
4 Quantock Ct
5 Malvern Ct
6 Chiltern Ct
C5 1 Feline Ct
2 Brookhill Ct
3 Littlegrove Ct
4 Desmond Ho
D1 1 Springfield Ct
2 Victor Ho
3 Malborough Ho
4 Coopers Ct
5 Joiners Ct
D2 1 Bantock Ct
2 Burgess Ct
3 Heaton Ct
4 Bordley Ct
5 Garside Ct
6 Cranston Ct
7 Gleave Ct
D3 1 Wren Ct
2 Homerton Ct
3 Emmanuel Ct
4 Wolfson Ct
5 Robinson Ct
6 Gonville Ct

15

C6 1 Tregenna Cl
2 Catherine Ct
3 Conisbee Ct
4 Ashmead
D3 1 Dennis Par
2 Broadway The
3 Southgate Cir
4 Station Par
5 Bourneside
6 Bourneside Cres

17

C6 1 Wade Ho
2 Newport Lo
3 Halcyon Ho
4 Lerwick Ct
5 Anchor Ct
6 Grassmere Ct
7 Datchworth Ct
8 Trentham Lo
9 Austin Ct
10 Cedar Grange
11 Brookview Ct
12 Chestbrook Ct
13 Paddock Lo
14 Hamlet Ct
15 Haven Lo

18

A1 1 Plevna Ho
2 Lea Ho
3 Brook Ho
4 Valley Ho
5 Chiltern Ho
6 Blenheim Ho
7 Penn Ho
8 Romany Ho
9 Gilpin Ho
10 Anvil Ho
11 Well Ho
12 Passmore Ho
13 Durbin Ho
A2 1 Market Par
2 Beechwood Mews
3 Keats Par
4 Cedars Rd
5 Cross Keys Cl
6 Dorman Pl
7 Concourse The

20

1 Lea Ct
2 Park Ct
3 Conference Cl
4 Berrybank Cl
5 Russell Lo
6 Brunswick Lo
7 Kenilworth Ct
8 Trinity Ct
9 Kingsmead Lo
10 Fairlawns
A3 1 Knight Ct
2 Grant Ct
3 Chantry The
4 Bowyer Ct
5 Pineview Ct
6 Ellen Ct
7 Leeview Ct
8 Chelsea Ct
9 Bramley Ct
10 Garenne Ct
11 Kendal Ct
12 Fairways
13 Avon Ct
B3 1 Maddox Ct
2 Village Arc The
3 Cambridge Rd
4 Crown Bldgs
5 Pentney Rd
6 Scholars Ho
7 Cranworth Cres
C4 1 Connaught Ct
2 Woolden Ho
3 Fairmead Ct
4 Lockhart Lo
5 Cavendish Ct
6 Oakwood Ct
7 Plains The
8 Hadleigh Ct
9 Forest Ho
10 Mathieson Ho

21

B2 1 Stag Hts
2 Shore Point
3 Buckhurst Hill Ho
4 Beech Ave
5 High Road Buckhurst Hill
6 Highclears
C2 1 Westbury Ct
2 Palmerston Ct
3 Ibrox Ct
4 Richard Burton Ct
5 Queens Mews
6 Gunnels Ct & Hastingwood Ct
7 Marlborough Ct
8 Avenue The
9 Tora Ct
10 Somerset Ct
11 Mirravale Ct
C3 1 Rayburne Ct
2 Laurels The
3 Mablin Lo
4 Silvers
5 Makinen Ho
6 Roman Lo
D1 1 Highview Ho
1 Hornbeam Ho
2 Highview Ho
3 Bourne Ho
D2 1 Regency Lo
2 Kings Ct
3 Beech Ct
4 Sycamore Ho
5 Salisbury Gdns
6 Pegasus Ct
7 Buckhurst Ct
8 Mountbatten Ct
9 Atrium
D6 1 Richmond Ct
2 Highview Ct
3 Collins Ct
4 Lower Park Rd
5 Homecherry Ho

22

C1 1 Daniel Ho
2 Hawthorn Ct
3 Northcote
4 Edwin Ware Ct
5 Chalfont Wlk
6 Maple Ct
7 Montesole Ct
8 Viewpoint Ct

23

B3 1 Russettings
2 St Cuthberts Gdns
3 Cherry Croft Gdns
4 Claire Ct
5 Cornwall Ct
6 Falmouth Ho
7 Newlyn Ho
8 Chestnuts The
9 Dunford Ct
10 Stratton Ct
11 Hanover Ct

25

C5 1 Belgrave Gdns
2 Heywood Ct
3 Norfolk Ho
4 Garden Ct
5 Chatsworth Ct
6 Chartridge Ct
7 Hardwick Cl
8 Cheltenham Ct
9 Cargrey Ho
10 Holbein Ho
11 Goodwood Cl
12 Ascot Pl
13 Longchamp Ct
14 Halfacre
15 Burnham Ct
16 Dingle Ct
17 Woodcroft
18 Daneglen Ct
19 Buckingham Par
C6 1 Bickley Ct
2 Kelmscott Ct
3 Elstree Ho
4 Brompton Ct
5 Kenmare Ct
6 Burlington Park Ho
7 Gressenham Ct
8 Amora

26

D5 1 Penshurst Ct
2 Cranbourne Ct
3 Wilton Ct
4 Saxon Ct
5 Abbey Ct
6 Kenlor Ct
7 Daniel Ct
8 Hillcrest Ct
9 Hunters Lo
10 Orion Ct

27

A1 1 Colesworth Ho
2 Crokesley Ho
3 Curtlington Ho
4 Clare Ho
5 Kedyngton Ho
A3 1 Tadbourne Ct
2 Truman Cl
3 Lords Ct
4 Hutton Row
5 Compton Cl
6 Botham Cl
7 Bradman Row
A6 1 Iris Wlk
2 Sycamore Cl
3 Aster Ct
4 Firethorn Cl
5 Berberry Cl
6 Hibiscus Cl
B5 1 Monarchs Ct
2 Kensington Ct
3 Grosvenor Ct
4 Chasewood Ct
C2 1 Rufforth Ct
2 Riccall Ct
3 Lindholme Ct
4 Driffield Ct
5 Jack Ashley Ct
6 Folkingham La
7 Debden Cl
8 Holbeach Cl
9 Shawbury Cl
10 Daniel Ct
11 Leander Ct
12 Nimrod
13 Nisbet
14 Pixton
15 Rapide
16 Ratier
D1 1 Gauntlet
2 Guilfoyle
3 Grebe
4 Gates
5 Galy
6 Folland
7 Firefly
8 Halifax
9 Debussy
10 Crosbie
11 Grant Ct
12 Ham Ct
13 Deal Ct
14 Ember Ct
15 Canterbury Ct
16 Beaumont Ct
17 Cirrus
18 Defiant
19 Dessouter
20 Douglas
21 Cobham
22 Clayton
23 Camm
24 Bradon
25 Boarhound
26 Bodmin
27 Bleriot
28 Blackburn
29 Audax
30 Anson
31 Albatross
32 Arran Ct
33 Mavis Ct
34 Goosander Ct
35 Platt Halls (a)
36 Writtle Ho
37 Platt Halls (b)
38 Platt Halls (c)
D2 1 Slatter
2 Sopwith
3 Saimet
4 Sassoon
5 Roe
6 Orde
7 Osprey
8 Prodger
9 Randall
10 Porte
11 Norris
12 Nardini
13 Noel
14 Nicolson
15 Napier
16 Nighthawk
17 Moorhouse

18 Moineau
19 Mitchell
20 Lysander
21 Lillywhite
22 Martynside
23 March
24 Kemp
25 Mercury
26 Merlin
27 Hudson
28 Hawker
29 Hawfinch
30 Heracles
31 Hector
32 Concourse The
D3 1 Wellington
2 Wheeler
3 Whittaker
4 Whittle
5 Tedder
6 Cranwell Ct
7 Tait
8 Spooner

28

D1 1 York Ho
2 Windsor Ho
3 Regency Cres
4 Normandy Ho
5 Allerton Ct
6 Beaulieu Ho
7 Dewlands Ct
8 Knightshayes Ho

29

A3 2 Frances & Dick James Ct
3 Farthing Ct
4 Coniston Ct
B1 1 Carlisle Lo
2 Laburnum Lo
3 Eden Ct
4 Moorcroft Ct
5 Clifford Lo
6 Acacia Lo
7 Cumberland Ct
8 Little Dell Lo
9 Cyprus Ct
10 Cyprus Ho
C2 1 Sheringham Ct
2 St Ronan's
3 Crescent Rise
4 Elm Ct
5 Norman Ct
6 Marlow Ct
7 Dancastle Ct
8 Newman Ct
9 Station Mans
10 Alice Ct
D3 1 Hadley Ct
2 Sherbrook Ho
3 Shine Ho
4 Regent Ct
5 Lodge Mead Ct
6 Spencer Ct
7 Zenith Lo
8 Burberry Ct
D5 1 Silverbell Ct
2 Inverey Ho
3 Wimbush Ho
4 Tudor Lo
5 Duncan Ct
6 Phillipson Ho
D6 1 Brookfield Ct
2 Magnolia Ct
3 Dunbar Ct
4 Haughmond
5 Nansen Village
6 Willow Ct
7 Birch Ct
8 Beechcroft Ct
9 Speedwell Ct
10 Woodside Ct
11 Speedwell Ho
12 Rebecca Ho
13 Ashbourne Ct
14 Forest Ct
15 Beecholme
16 Greville Lo
17 St Johnstone Ho
18 Ashbourne Cl
19 Clements Cl
20 Station App
21 Montclair Ct
22 Winterberry Ct
23 Caroline Ct

30

A4 1 Sharon Ct
2 Lydia Ct
3 Beatrice Lo
4 Grange Ct
5 Blissland Ct
A5 1 Archgate Bsns Ctr
2 Robart Ho
3 Danescroft
4 Cornelius Ct
5 Gable Lo
6 Waterville Lo
7 Chand Ho
B1 1 New Trinity Rd
2 Garden Ho
3 Todd Ho
4 Sayers Ho
5 Mowbray Ho
6 Bouchier Ho
7 Cleveland Ho
8 Goodyear Ho
9 Lochleven Ho
10 Berwick Ho
11 Oak Ho
12 Hilton Ho
13 East View Ho
14 Myddleton Ho
15 Willow Wlk
16 Craven Ho
17 Willow Ho
18 Vane Ho
19 Adelphi Ct
20 Annette White Lo
21 Foskett Ho
22 Elmfield Ho
23 Sycamore Ho
24 Netherwood
25 Rew Lo
26 William Cl
B5 1 Murray Ho
2 Damon Ho
3 Wendy Ho
4 Lychgate Ct
5 Clarence Ct
6 Carley Ct
7 Hermiston Ct
8 Cardrew Ct
9 Whitefriars Ct
D5 1 Halliwick Ct
2 Halliwick Court Par
3 Queen's Par
4 St John's Villas
5 Hartland Ct
6 Kennard Mans
7 Bensley Cl
8 Leadbeaters Cl
9 Gibson Ct
10 Burton Ct
11 Knights Ct
12 Constable Cl
13 Alderman Ct

31

A3 1 Campe Ho
2 Betstyle Ho
3 Pymmes Brook Ho
4 Mosswell Ho
5 Cavendish Ho
6 Tudor Ho
7 Kingsfield Ho
8 Peacehaven Ct
9 Hatch Ho
10 Hampden Ct
11 Crown Ct
A4 1 Cheddar Cl
2 Wincanton Ct
3 Whitby Ct
4 Richmond Ct
5 Tadworth Ct
6 Wensley Cl
7 Howeth Ct
8 Kilnsey Ct
9 Harrogate Ct
10 Ripon Ct
B1 1 Cedar Ct
2 Carisbrook
3 St Ivian Ct
4 Barrington Ct
5 Essex Lo
B6 1 Grovefield
2 Lapworth
3 Stewards Holte Wlk
4 Sarnes Ct
5 Stanhope Ho
6 Holmsdale Ho
7 Crosby Ct
8 Leyland Ct
9 Boundary Ct
10 Stateland Ct
C5 1 Barbara Martin Ho
2 Jerome Ct
3 Limes Cl
4 Arnos Grove Ct
5 Cedar Ct
6 Betspath Ho
7 Curtis Ho
8 Mason Ho
9 Danford Ho
10 New Southgate Ind Est
11 Palmer's Ct
12 Swinson Ho
13 Jackson Ho

32

A4 1 Brownlow Lo
2 Brownlow Ct
3 Latham Ct
4 Fairlawns
5 Beaumaris
C1 1 Penwortham Ct
2 Tarleton Ct
3 Holmeswood Ct
4 Kwesi Johnson Ct
5 Sandlings The
6 Suraj Ho
C6 1 Hazelwood Ct
2 Ashbourne Lo
3 Mapledurham Ct

33

D1 1 Kenmare Dr
2 Ashling Ho
3 Honeysett Rd
4 Wilson's Ave
5 Palm Tree Ct
6 Stoneleigh Ct
7 Brook St
D3 1 Charles Ho
2 Moselle Ho
3 Ermine Ho
4 Kathleen Ferrier Ct
5 Concord Ho
6 Rees Ho
7 Williams Ho
8 Nursery Ct
9 William Rainbird Ho
10 Gibson Bsns Ctr
11 Wingate Trad Est
D4 1 Regan Ho
2 Isis Ho
3 Boundary Ct
4 Stellar Ho
5 Cooperage Cl

34

A5 1 Angel Pl
2 Cross St
3 Scott Ho
4 Beck Ho
5 Booker Rd
6 Bridport Ho
7 Cordwain Ho
8 St James's Ct
9 Highmead
A6 1 Walton Ho
2 Alma Ho
3 Brompton Ho
4 Field Ho
5 Bradwell Mews
6 Angel Corner Par
7 Paul Ct
8 Cuthbert Rd
9 Brockenhurst Mews
B3 1 Kenneth Robbins Ho
2 Charles Bradlaugh Ho
3 Woodrow Ct
4 Cheviot
5 Corbridge
6 Whittingham
7 Eastwood Cl
8 Alnwick
9 Bamburgh
10 Bellingham
11 Briaris Cl

35

A1 1 Clayton Ct
2 St Andrew's Ct
3 Aranya Ct
4 Fitzwilliam Ho
A2 1 Romany Gdns
2 Swansland Gdns
3 Garnett Way
4 Claymore Ct
5 Winchester Ct
C5 1 Ainslie Ho
2 Lewis Ho

36

B5 1 Hedgemoor Ct
2 Hewitt Ho
3 Castle Ho
4 Bailey Ct
5 Harcourt Ho
6 Gerboa Ct
7 Wentworth Ct
D1 1 Chatham Rd
2 Washington Rd
3 Cherry Tree Ct
4 Grosvenor Lo
5 Torfell
D2 1 Hillboro Ct
2 Dorchester Ct

37

A1 1 Chiltons The
2 Ullswater Ct
3 Leigh Ct
4 Woburn Ct
5 Alveston Sq
6 Eaton Ct
7 Regency Ct
8 Cowley Ct
9 High Oaks Lo
A2 1 Lindal Ct
2 Hockley Ct
3 Woodleigh
4 Milne Ct
5 Cedar Ct
6 Elizabeth Ct
7 Silvermead
8 Laurel Mead Ct
9 Mitre Ct
10 Pevensey Ct
11 Lyndhurst Ct
12 Manor Court Lo
A3 1 New Jubilee Ct
2 Chartwell Ct
3 Greenwood
4 Clementine Wlk
A4 1 Terrace The
2 Broomhill Ct
3 Clifton Ct
4 Fairstead Lo
5 Hadleigh Lo
6 Broadmead Ct
7 Wilton Ct
8 Fairfield Ct
9 Higham Ct
10 Aston Ct
A6 1 Tree Tops
2 Cranfield Ct
3 Percival Ho
4 Raine Gdns
B1 1 Station Est
2 Station App
3 James Ct
C3 1 Liston Way
2 Elizabeth Ct
3 Coopersale Cl
4 Sunset Ct
5 Lambourne Ct
C4 1 Hope Cl
2 Rex Par
3 Shalford
4 Rodings The
5 Lawrence Ct
6 Cowan Lo

40

C1 1 Salisbury Ho
2 Rodwell Cl
3 Pretoria Ho
4 Ottawa Ho
5 Swallow Ct
6 Wellington Ho
7 Canberra Ho
C6 1 Tulip Ct
2 Hyacinth Ct
3 Rose Ct
4 Iris Ct
D6 1 Ashburton Ct
2 Northend Lodge

42

D3 1 Nightingale Ct
2 St John's Ct
3 Gayton Ct
4 Wilton Pl
5 Murray Ct
6 Cymbeline Ct
7 Knowles Ct
8 Charville Ct
9 Lime Ct
10 Petherton Ct
11 Garth Ct
12 Chalfont Ct
13 Shepherds Ct
D4 1 Crystal Ctr The
2 Blue Point Ct
3 Ryan Ho
4 Rothwell Ct
5 Bruce Ho
6 Middlesex Ct
7 Ingram Ho
8 Arless Ho
9 Leaf Ho
10 Becket Fold
11 Brandan Ho
12 Robert Ho

46

A2 1 Milton Rd
2 Stanley Rd
A3 1 Mapesbury Mews
2 York Mans
3 Telford Rd
A5 1 Pilkington Ct
2 Cousins Ct
3 Seton Ct
4 Frensham Ct
5 Chatton Ct
6 Geraldine Ct
7 Swynford Gdns
8 Miller Ct
9 Roffey Ct
10 Peace Ct
11 Rambler Ct
12 Lion Ct
13 Wenlock Gdns
14 Dogrose Ct
15 Harry Ct
16 Tribune Ct
17 Bonville Gdns
18 Pearl Ct
B4 1 Vivian Mans
2 Parade Mans
3 Georgian Ct
4 Florence Mans
5 Park Mans
6 Cheyne Cl
7 Queens Par
8 Central Mans
C5 1 Courtney Ho
2 Golderton
3 Thornbury
4 Ferrydale Lo
5 Studio Mews
6 Brampton La
7 Short St
8 Belle Vue Rd
9 Longford Ct
10 Ashwood Ho
D5 1 Midford Ho
2 Rockfield Ho
3 Lisselton Ho
4 Acrefield Ho

47

B2 1 Berkeley Ct
2 Exchange Mans
3 Beechcroft Ct
4 Nedahall Ct
B3 1 Charlton Lo
2 Clifton Gdns
B4 1 Hallswelle Par
2 Belmont Par
3 Temple Fortune Ho
4 Yew Tree Ct
5 Temple Fortune Par
6 Courtleigh
7 Arcade Ho
8 Queens Ct
9 Temple Fortune Ct
B5 1 Monkville Par
2 Ashbourne Par

48

A6 1 St Mary's Gn
2 Dunstan Cl
3 Paul Byrne Ho
4 Longfield Ct
5 Warwick Ct
6 Branksome Ct
7 Sherwood Hall

49

B6 1 Dorchester Ct
2 Old Chapel Pl
3 Athenaeum Pl
4 Risborough Cl
5 Risborough Ct
C1 1 Calvert Ct
2 Academy The
3 Whitehall Mans
4 Pauntley St
5 Archway Hts
6 Pauntley Ho
D1 1 Louise White Ho
2 Levison Way
3 Sanders Way
4 Birbeck Ho
5 Scholars Ct
D2 1 Eleanor Rathbone Ho
2 Christopher Lo
3 Monkridge
4 Marbleford Ct
5 High London
6 Garton Ho
7 Hilltop Ho
8 Caroline Martyn Ho
9 Arthur Henderson Ho
10 Margaret Mcmillan Ho
11 Enid Stacy Ho
12 Mary McArthur Ho
13 Bruce Glasier Ho
14 John Wheatley Ho
15 Keir Hardie Ho
16 Monroe Ho
17 Iberia Ho
18 Lygoe Ho
19 Lambert Ho
20 Shelbourne Ho
21 Arkansas Ho
22 Lafitte Ho
23 Shreveport Ho
24 Packenham Ho
25 Orpheus Ho
26 Fayetville Ho
27 Bayon Ho
D4 1 Kelland Cl
2 Truro Ct
3 Veryan Ct
4 Coulsdon Ct

50

A1 1 Beeches The
2 Lambton Ct
3 Nugent Ct
4 Lambton Mews
5 Mews The
A2 1 Marie Lloyd Gdns
2 Edith Cavell Cl
3 Marie Stopes Ct
4 Jessie Blythe La
5 Barbara Rudolph Ct
6 Hetty Rees Ct
7 Leyden Mans
8 Brambledown
9 Lochbie
10 Lyngham Ct
11 High Mount
12 Woodlands The
A4 1 Margaret Hill Ho
2 Manray Ct
3 Hermiston Ct
4 Carleton Ho
A5 1 Mackenzie Ho
2 Stowell Ho
3 Campsbourne Ho
4 Palace Gate Mews
B1 1 Lawson Ct
2 Wiltshire Ct
3 Fenstanton
4 Hutton Ct
5 Wisbech
D5 1 Wordsworth Par
2 Spanswick Lo
3 Barker Ho
D6 1 Langham Cl
2 Sidi Ct
3 Ince Terr

51

A2 1 Finmere Ho
2 Keynsham Ho
3 Kilpeck Ho
4 Knaresborough Ho
5 Leighfield Ho
6 Lonsdale Ho
7 Groveley Ho
8 Wensleydale Ho
9 Badminton Ct
B2 1 Selwood Ho
2 Mendip Ho
3 Ennerdale Ho
4 Delamere Ho
5 Westwood Ho
6 Bernwood Ho
7 Allerdale Ho
8 Chattenden Ho
9 Farningham Ho
10 Oakend Ho
C1 1 Godstone Ct
2 Farnham Ct
3 Milford Ct
4 Cranleigh Ct
5 Haslemere Ct
6 Belmont Ct
7 Hockworth Ho
8 Garratt Ho
9 Fairburn Ho
10 Thorndale Ho
11 Oakdene Ho
12 Briardale Ho
C3 1 Oatfield Ho
2 Perry Ct
3 Henrietta Ho
4 Bournes Ho
5 Chisley Rd
6 Twyford Ho
7 Langford Cl
8 Hatchfield Ho
D1 1 Stamford Hill Mans
2 Montefiore Ct
3 Berwyn Ho
4 Clent Ho
5 Chiltern Ho
6 Laindon Ho
7 Pentland Ho
D2 1 Regent Ct
2 Stamford Lo
3 Holmwood Ct
D3 1 Sherboro Rd
2 Westcott Cl
3 Cadoxton Ave
D4 1 Westerfield Rd
2 Suffield Rd
D5 1 Laseron Ho
2 Greenway Cl
3 Tottenham Gn E
4 Tottenham Gn E South Side
5 Deaconess Ct
6 Elliot Ct
7 Bushmead Cl
8 Beaufort Ho
9 Tynemouth Terr

D6 1 Holcombe Rd
2 Rigby Ho
3 Chaplin Rd
4 Keswick Apartments
5 Ambleside Cl
6 Lauriston Apartments
7 Terrall Apartments
8 Old School Ct
9 Nicholson Ct
10 Reynardson's Ct
11 Protheroe Ho

52

A1 1 Stamford Gr E
2 Stamford Mans
3 Grove Mans
4 Stamford Gr W
B1 1 Hawkwood Mount
2 Holmbury View
3 High Hill Ferry
4 Leaside Ho
5 Courtlands
6 Ivy Ho
7 Shelford Ct

53

A4 1 Hammond Ct
2 St James Apartments
3 Grange The
A5 1 Bristol Park Rd
2 Stoneydown Ho
3 Callonfield
4 Hardyng Ho
C1 1 Wellington Mans
2 Clewer Ct
3 Cochrane Ct
C5 1 Westbury Ho
2 Hatherley Ho
3 Vintry Mews
4 Tylers Ct
5 Merchants Lo
6 Gillards Mews
7 Blacksmiths Ho
8 Central Par
D1 1 Fitzgerald Ct
2 Bechervaise Ct
3 Underwood Ct
D2 1 Staton Ct
2 Howell Ct
3 Atkinson Ct
4 Russell Ct
5 St Catherines Twr
6 St Lukes Ct
7 St Matthews Ct
8 St Mark's Ct
9 St Elizabeth Ct
10 Emanuel Ct
11 St Thomas Ct
12 Beaumont Ho
13 Shelley Ct
14 St Paul's Twr
15 Flack Ct
16 King Ct
17 Osborne Ct
18 Muriel Ct
19 All Saints Twr
20 St Josephs Ct
D5 1 Nash Ho
2 St Columbas Ho
3 Attlee Terr
4 Astins Ho
5 Lindens The
6 Kevan Ct
7 Squire's Almshouses
8 Berry Field Cl
9 Connaught Ct
10 Holmcroft Ho
11 St Mary's Church Ho
D6 1 Hallingbury Ct
2 Mace Ho
3 Gaitskell Ho
4 Hancocke Ho
5 Trinity Ho
6 Fanshaw Ho
7 Hilltop
8 Batten Ho
9 Bradwell Ho
10 Walton Ho
11 Temple Ho
12 Gower Ho
13 Maple Ho
14 Poplars Ho
15 Cedars Ho
16 Kimm Ho
17 O'Grady Ho
18 Latham Ho
19 Powell Ct
20 Crosbie Ho

54

A2 1 Ayerst Ct
2 Dare Ct
3 St Edwards Ct
A4 1 Collard's Almshouses
2 Ellen Miller Ho
3 Tom Smith Ho
A5 1 Northwood Twr
2 Walnut Ct
3 Albert Whitcher Ho
4 Pelly Ct
5 Ravenswood Ind Est
6 Holland Ct
7 Emberson Ho
8 St Mark's Ho
9 Alfred Villas
10 Leonard Ho
11 Old Station Yard The
A6 1 St David's Ct
2 Golden Par
3 Chestnuts Ct
4 Matthew Ct
5 Gilbert Ho
6 Manning Ho
7 Southgate Ho
8 Boyden Ho
9 Prospect Ho
10 Newton Ho
D2 1 Buxton Ct
2 Hanbury Dr
3 Forest Lea
4 Watershipdown Ho

55

A3 1 Aldham Hall
2 Parkside Ct
3 Mapperley Cl
4 Weavers Ho
5 Cyna Ct
6 Reed Mans
7 Thornton Ho
8 Hardwick Ct
A4 1 Kingsley Grange
2 Station Par
3 Gwynne Ho
4 Staveley Ct
5 Thurlow Ct
6 Devon Ho
7 Wellington Pas
8 Wanstead Hts
9 Hollies The
10 Little Holt
11 Hunter Ct
12 Mountier Ct
13 Woodland Ct
14 Dudley Ct
15 Struan Ho
16 Westleigh Ct
A5 1 Shernwood Ho
2 Orwell Lo
3 Hermitage Ct
4 Gowan Lea
5 Woodford Ho
6 Eagle Ct
7 Newbury Ct
8 Shelley Ct
9 Hardy Ct
10 Dickens Ct
11 Byron Ct
A6 1 Millbrook
2 Half Acre
3 Elmbrook
4 Grange The
5 Glenavon Lo
6 Glenwood Ct
7 Ferndown
8 Embassy Ct
9 Orestes Ct
10 Walbrook
11 Helmsley
12 Snaresbrook Hall
B4 1 Nightingale Ct
2 Chelston Ct
3 Grosvenor Ct
4 Louise Ct
5 St Davids Ct
6 Cedar Ct
7 Shrubbery The
8 Nightingale Mews
B5 1 Great Hall The
2 Clock Ct
3 Langham Ho
B6 1 Victoria Ct
2 Kenwood Gdns
3 Thaxted Lo
4 Albert Rd
5 Albert Ho
6 Falcon Ct
7 Deborah Ct
8 Swift Ho
9 Pulteney Gdns
10 Spring Ct
11 Trinity Gdns

56

B4 1 High View Par
2 Spurway Par
3 Florence Root Ho
4 Rohan Pl
5 Homeheather Ho

57

A3 1 Catherine Ct
2 Lincoln Ct
3 Ivy Terr
4 Newbury Cotts

58

B1 1 Caledonian Cl
2 Talisman Cl
3 Norseman Cl
4 Frank Slater Ho
5 Brook's Mans
6 Brook's Par
B2 1 Mitre Ct
2 Coppins The
3 Stanetta Ct
4 Wilnett Ct
5 Wilnett Villas
B4 1 Sudbury Ct
2 Dunwich Ct
3 Cromer Terr
4 Norfolk Ct
5 Framlingham Ct
6 Yoxford Ct
C4 1 Swaffham Ct
2 Nacton Ct
3 Suffolk Ct
D2 1 Pavement Mews
2 Chadview Ct
3 Granary Ct
4 Bedwell Ct
5 Chapel La
6 Faulkner Cl
7 Maple Ct
8 Willow Ct
9 Cedar Terr

63

C2 1 Wimborne Ct
2 Haydock Green Flats
3 Brighton Dr
4 Blaydon Ct
5 Fakenham Cl
6 Rutland Ho
7 Windsor Ho

65

D3 1 Lowry Lo
2 Morritt Ho
3 Charles Goddard Ho
4 Snow Ct
5 Willow Tree Ct
6 Oak Lo

66

A2 1 Montrose Cres
2 Peggy Quirke Ct
3 Marylebone Ct
4 Waterloo Ct
5 Euston Ct
6 St Pancras Ct
7 Paddington Ct
8 Copland Mews
9 Coronet Par
10 Aylestone Ct
11 Charlotte Ct
A3 1 Wembley Mkt
2 Market Way
3 Lodge Ct
4 Central Sq
5 Manor Ct
6 Rupert Ave
7 Lily Ho
C4 1 Wembley Mkt

67

A5 1 Curie Ho
2 Darwin Ho
3 Priestley Ho
4 Rutherford Ho
5 Fleming Ho
6 Lister Ho
7 Edison Ho
B1 1 Biko Ho
2 Kingthorpe Terr
3 Scott Ho
4 Peary Ho
5 Shackleton Ho
6 Amundsen Ho
7 Brentfield Ho
8 Nansen Ho
9 Stonebridge Ct
10 Newcroft Ho
11 Magellan Ct
12 Leadbetter Ct
13 Jefferies Ho
14 Cowan Ct
15 Prothero Ho
16 Crawford St
17 Clark Ct
18 Diamond St
19 Mary Seacole Villas
C1 1 Beveridge Rd
2 Purcell Mews
3 George Lansbury Ho
4 Charles Hobson Ho
5 Reade Wlk
6 Westbury Ho
7 Bridge Ct
C4 1 Grange Ct
2 Green Ct
C5 1 Hazelwood Ct
2 Winslow Cl

68

A2 1 Regency Mews
2 Tudor Mews
3 Utopia Ho
4 Bell Flats
5 Angel Ct
A5 1 Bourne Ho
2 Carton Ho
3 Bidwell Ho
4 Woodbridge Cl
5 Mackenzie Ho
6 Banting Ho
C2 1 Rutland Park Gdns
2 Rutland Park Mans
3 Queens Par
4 Harcourt Ho
5 Solidarity Ho
6 Electra Ct
7 Cassandra Ct
8 Carlton Ct
D4 1 Oaklands Mews
2 Acer Ct
3 Maple Ct
4 Argyle Mans

69

A1 1 Christ Church Ct
2 Paul Daisley Ct
3 Fountain Ho
4 Kingston Ho
5 Waverley Ct
6 Weston Ho
7 Mapes Ho
8 Athelstan Gdns
9 Leff Ho
B1 1 Alma Birk Ho
2 Brooklands Ct
3 Brooklands Court Apartments
4 Cleveland Mans
5 Buckley Ct
6 Webheath
B5 1 Mortimer Cl
2 Primrose Ct
3 Sunnyside Ho
4 Sunnyside
5 Prospect Pl
C1 1 Linstead St
2 Embassy Ho
3 Acol Ct
4 Kings Wood Ct
5 Douglas Ct
6 King's Gdns
7 Carlton Mans
8 Smyrna Mans
9 New Priory Ct
10 Queensgate Pl
11 Brondesbury Mews
C2 1 Dene Mans
2 Sandwell Cres
3 Sandwell Mans
4 Hampstead West
5 Redcroft
C3 1 Orestes Mews
2 Walter Northcott Ho
3 Polperro Mans
4 Lyncroft Mans
5 Marlborough Mans
6 Alexandra Mans
7 Cumberland Mans
8 Cavendish Mans
9 Ambassador Ct
10 Welbeck Mans
11 Inglewood Mans
12 Dennington Park Mansions
C5 1 Portman Hts
2 Hermitage Ct
3 Moreland Ct
4 Wendover Ct
D2 1 Beswick Mews
2 Worcester Mews
3 Minton Mews
4 Doulton Mews
5 Laurel Ho
6 Sandalwood Ho
7 Iroko Ho
8 Banyan Ho
9 Rosewood Ho
10 Ebony Ho
11 Rosemont Mans
12 Exeter Mews

70

A1 1 Harrold Ho
2 Glover Ho
3 Byron Ct
4 Nalton Ho
A2 1 Petros Gdns
2 Heath Ct
3 Imperial Twrs
4 Fairhurst
5 St John's Ct
6 New College Ct
7 Chalford
8 Rosslyn Mans
9 Sutherland Ho
A4 1 Windmill Hill
2 Highgrove Point
3 Gainsborough Ho
4 Holly Bush Hill
5 Heath Mans
6 Holly Bush Steps
7 Pavilion Ct
8 Holly Berry La
9 New Campden Ct
10 Holly Bush Vale
11 Benham's Pl
12 Prospect Pl
13 Yorkshire Grey Pl
14 Gardnor Mans
15 Ellerdale Cl
16 Monro Ho
17 Prince Arthur Mews
18 Prince Arthur Ct
19 Village Mount
20 Perrin's Ct
21 Wells Ct
22 Bakers Pas
23 Spencer Wlk
24 Bird In Hand Yd
25 Kings Well
26 New Ct
27 Streatley Pl
28 Mansfield Pl
29 Upper Hampstead Wlk
A5 1 Hampstead Sq
2 Stamford Cl
3 Mount Sq The
B1 1 New College Par
2 Northways Par
3 Noel Ho
4 Campden Ho
5 Centre Hts
6 Hickes Ho
7 Swiss Terr
8 Leitch Ho
9 Jevons Ho
10 Langhorne Ct
11 Park Lo
12 Avenue Lo
B2 1 Belsize Park Mews
2 Baynes Mews
3 McCrone Mews
B3 1 Belsize Court Garages
2 Roscommon Ho
3 Akenside Ct
B4 1 White Bear Pl
2 Wells Ho The
3 Boades Mews
4 Flask Cotts
5 Coach House Yd
6 Pilgrim's Pl
7 Rosslyn Mews
C2 1 Banff Ho
2 Glenloch Ct
3 Havercourt
4 Holmefield Ct
5 Gilling Ct
6 Howitt Cl
7 Manor Mans
8 Straffan Lo
9 Romney Ct
10 Lancaster Stables
11 Eton Garages
D1 1 Hancock Nunn Ho
2 Higginson Ho
3 Duncan Ho
4 Mary Wharrie Ho
5 Rockstraw Ho
6 Cleaver Ho
7 Chamberlain St
8 Sharples Hall St
9 Primrose Mews
10 Rothwell St
11 St Georges Mews
D2 1 Alder Ho
2 Hornbeam Ho
3 Whitebeam Ho
4 Aspen Ho
5 Rowan Ho
6 Beech Ho
7 Chestnut Ho
8 Oak Ho
9 Willow Ho
10 Sycamore Ho
11 Maple Ho
12 Hazel Ho
13 Elaine Ct
14 Faircourt
15 Walham Ct
16 Stanbury Ct
17 Priory Mans
18 Wellington Ho
19 Grange The
D3 1 Cayford Ho
2 Du Maurier Ho
3 Isokon Flats
4 Palgrave Ho
5 Garnett Ho
6 Stephenson Ho
7 Park Dwellings
8 Siddons Ho
9 Mall Studios
10 Park Hill Wlk
11 Wordsworth Pl
12 Fraser Regnart Ct
13 St Pancras Almshouses

71

A1 1 Bridge Ho
2 Hardington
3 Mead Cl
4 Rugmere
5 Tottenhall
6 Beauvale
7 Broomfield
A2 1 Silverbirch Wlk
2 Penshurst
3 Wingham
4 Westwell
5 Chislet
6 Burmarsh
7 Shipton Ho
8 Stonegate
9 Leysdown
10 Headcorn
11 Lenham
12 Halstow
13 Fordcombe
14 Cannington
15 Langridge
16 Athlone Ho
17 Pentland Ho
18 Beckington
19 Hawkridge
20 Edington
B1 1 Ferdinand Ho
2 Harmood Ho
3 Hawley Rd
4 Hawley Mews
5 Leybourne St
6 Barling
7 Tiptree
8 Havering
9 Candida Ct
10 Lorraine Ct
11 Donnington Ct
12 Welford Ct
13 Torbay Ct
14 Bradfield Ct
15 Torbay St
16 Water La
17 Leybourne Rd
18 Haven St
19 Stucley Pl
20 Lawrence Ho
B2 1 Ashington
2 Priestley Ho
3 Leonard Day Ho
4 Old Dairy Mews
5 Monmouth Ho
6 Alpha Ct
7 Una Ho
8 Widford
9 Heybridge
10 Roxwell
11 Hamstead Gates
B4 1 Denyer Ho
2 Stephenson Ho
3 Trevithick Ho
4 Brunel Ho
5 Newcomen Ho
6 Faraday Ho
7 Winifrede Paul Ho
8 Wardlow
9 Fletcher Ct
10 Tideswell
11 Grangemill
12 Hambrook Ct
13 Calver
C1 1 Cherry Tree Ct
2 Chichester Ct
3 Durdans Ho
4 Philia Ho
5 Bernard Shaw Ct
6 Foster Ct
7 Bessemer Ct
8 Hogarth Ct
9 Rochester Ct
10 Soane Ct
11 Wallett Ct
12 Inwood Ct
13 Wrotham Rd
14 St Thomas Ct
15 Caulfield Ct
16 Bruges Pl
17 Reachview Cl
18 Lawfords Wharf
C3 1 Eleanor Ho

2 Falkland Pl
3 Kensington Ho
4 Willingham Cl
5 Kenbrook Ho
6 Aborfield
7 Great Field
8 Appleford
9 Forties The
10 Maud Wilkes Cl
11 Dunne Mews
12 Dowdeny Cl
C4 1 Benson Ct
2 Tait Ho
3 Manorfield Cl
4 Greatfield Cl
5 Longley Ho
6 Lampson Ho
7 Davidson Ho
8 Palmer Ho
9 Lambourn Cl
10 Morris Ho
11 Owen Ho
C5 1 Hunter Ho
2 Fisher Ho
3 Lang Ho
4 Temple Ho
5 Palmer Ho
6 Carlisle Ho
7 Durham Ho
8 Suffolk Ho
9 Lincoln Ho
10 Llewellyn Ho
11 Fell Ho
12 Aveling Ho
13 Merryweather Ct
14 Brennands Ct
15 St Christophers Ct
16 Francis Terrace Mews
C6 1 Flowers Mews
2 Archway Cl
3 Sandridge St
4 Bovingdon Cl
5 Cavell Ct
6 Torrence Ho
7 Rowan Wlk
8 Laurel Cl
9 Forest Way
10 Larch Cl
11 Pine Cl
12 Alder Mews
13 Aspen Cl
D1 1 Hillier Ho
2 Gairloch Ho
3 Cobham Mews
4 Bergholt Mews
5 Blakeney Cl
6 Weavers Way
7 Allensbury Pl
D2 1 Rowstock
2 Peckwater Ho
3 Wolsey Ho
4 Pandian Way
5 Busby Mews
6 Caledonian Sq
7 Canal Bvd
8 Northpoint Sq
9 Lock Mews
10 Carters Cl
11 York Ho
12 Hungerford Rd
13 Cliff Road Studios
14 Cliff Ct
15 Camelot Ho
16 Church Studios
17 Camden Terr
D3 1 Blake Ho
2 Quelch Ho
3 Lee Ho
4 Willbury Ho
5 Howell Ho
6 Holmsbury Ho
7 Leith Ho
8 Betchworth Ho
9 Rushmore Ho
10 Dugdale Ho
11 Horsendon Ho
12 Colley Ho
13 Coombe Ho
14 Ivinghoe Ho
15 Buckhurst Ho
16 Saxonbury Ct
17 Charlton Ct
18 Apollo Studios
19 Barn Cl
20 Long Meadow
21 Landleys Field
22 Margaret Bondfield Ho
23 Haywood Lo
D4 1 Fairlie Ct
2 Trecastle Way
3 Dalmeny Avenue Est
4 Hyndman Ho
5 Carpenter Ho
6 Graham Ho
7 Tufnell Mans
D5 1 Melchester Ho
2 Norcombe Ho
3 Weatherbury Ho
4 Wessex Ho
5 Archway Bsns Ctr
6 Harford Mews
7 Opera Ct
8 Rupert Ho
9 All Saints Church
D6 1 Bowerman Ct
2 Gresham Pl
3 Hargrave Mans
4 Church Garth
5 John King Ct
6 Ramsey Ct

72

A3 1 Kimble Ho
2 Saxonbury Ct
3 Poynder Ct
4 Pangbourne Ho
5 Moulsford Ho
A4 1 Arcade The
2 Macready Pl
3 Cardwell Rd
4 Mcmorran Ho
5 Crayford Ho
6 Whitby Ct
7 Prospect Pl
A5 1 Northview
2 Tufnell Park Mans
3 Fulford Mans
4 Tollington Ho
A6 1 Bracey Mews
2 Christie Ct
3 Ringmer Gdns
4 Kingsdown Rd
5 Cottenham Ho
6 St Paul's Ct
7 Rickthorne Rd
8 Stanley Terr
9 Arundel Lo
10 Landseer Ct
B1 1 Kerwick Cl
2 Rydston Cl
3 Skegness Ho
4 Frederica St
5 Ponder St
6 Kings Ct
7 Freeling St
8 Coatbridge Ho
9 Tilloch St
B2 1 Burns Ho
2 Scott Ho
3 Wellington Mews
4 Roman Ct
5 Piccadilly Ct
B3 1 Culverin Ct
2 Garand Ct
3 Mount Carmel
B4 1 Buckmaster Ho
2 Loreburn Ho
3 Cairns Ho
4 Halsbury Ho
5 Chelmsford Ho
6 Cranworth Ho
B6 1 Berkeley Wlk
2 Lazar Wlk
3 Thistlewood Cl
4 Tomlins Wlk
5 Andover Ho
6 Barmouth Ho
7 Chard Ho
8 Methley Ho
9 Rainford Ho
10 Woodbridge Cl
11 Allerton Wlk
12 Falconer Wlk
13 Sonderburg Rd
14 St Mark's Mans
15 Athol Ct
C1 1 Mountfort Terr
2 Avon Ho
3 Buckland Ho
4 Dovey Lo
5 Carfree Cl
6 Mitchell Ho
7 New College Mews
8 Lofting Ho
9 Brooksby Ho
10 Cara Ho
C3 1 Slaney Pl
2 Eastwood Cl
3 Milton Pl
4 Hartnoll Ho
5 St James School Flats
6 Widnes Ho
7 Tranmere Ho
8 Victoria Mans
9 Formby Ct
10 Mersey Ho
11 Birkenhead Ho
12 Drayton Park Mews
C6 1 Brookfield
2 Churnfield
D1 1 Islington Park Mews
2 Evelyn Denington Ct
3 Bassingbourn Ho
4 Cadmore Ho
5 Adstock Ho
6 Garston Ho
7 Flitton Ho
8 Datchworth Ho
9 Battishill St
10 Almeida St
11 Edward's Cotts
12 Hyde's Pl
13 Tyndale Terr
14 Spriggs Ho
15 Barratt Ho
16 Spencer Pl
17 Chadston Ho
18 Whiston Ho
19 Wakelin Ho
20 Tressel Cl
21 Canonbury Ct
22 Halton Ho
23 Shillingford St
24 Highburty Mans
25 Premier Ho
26 Waterloo Gdns
D2 1 Hampton Ct
2 Salisbury Ho
D3 1 De Barowe Mews
2 Fieldview Ct
3 Viewpoint
4 Ashurst Lo
D4 1 Chestnuts The
2 Bowen Ct
3 Peckett Sq
D5 1 Hurlock Ho
2 Blackstock Ho
3 Vivian Comma Cl
4 Monsell Ct

73

A1 1 Astey's Row
2 Lincoln Ho
3 Worcester Ho
4 Melville Pl
5 Wontner Cl
6 Hedingham Cl
7 Laundry La
8 Base Apartments
9 Walkinshaw Ct
10 New Bentham Ct
11 Bentham Ct
12 Haslam Ho
13 Horsfield Ho
14 Riverside Ho
15 Eric Fletcher Ct
16 Annette Cres
17 Ashby Ho
18 Lindsey Mews
19 Cardigan Wlk
20 Red House Sq
A2 1 Crowline Wlk
2 Upper Handa Wlk
3 Handa Wlk
4 Lismore Wlk
5 Bardsey Wlk
6 Walney Wlk
7 Upper Bardsey Wlk
8 Upper Lismore Wlk
9 Sark Ho
10 Guernsey Ho
11 Guernsey Rd
12 Sybil Thorndike Ho
13 Clephane Rd
14 Florence Nightingale Ho
15 Jersey Ho
16 Jethou Ho
17 Islay Wlk
18 Upper Caldy Wlk
19 Caldy Wlk
20 Alderney Ho
21 Gulland Wlk
22 Marquess Rd S
23 Upper Gulland Wlk
24 Church Rd
25 Oransay Rd
A3 1 Pearfield Ho
2 Larchfield Ho
3 Beresford Terr
4 Pondfield Ho
5 Ashfield Ho
6 Elmfield Ho
A4 1 Fountain Mews
2 Woodstock Ho
3 Henson Ct
4 Taverner Sq
B1 1 Downham Ct
2 Trafalgar Point
B2 1 John Kennedy Ct
2 John Kennedy Lo
3 Ball's Pond Pl
4 Haliday Wlk
5 Queen Elizabeth Ct
6 Canonbury Hts
7 Pinnacle The
8 Threadgold Ho
9 Wakeham St
10 Saffron Ct
11 Callaby Terr
12 Tilney Gdns
13 Westcliff Ho
14 Ilford Ho
15 Ongar Ho
16 Greenhills Terr
17 Romford Ho
18 Bute Wlk
19 Upper Ramsey Wlk
20 Rona Wlk
21 Thorndike Rd
B4 1 Ledo Ho
2 Salween Ho
3 Prome Ho
4 Arakan Ho
5 Rangoon Ho
6 Mandalay Ho
7 Karen Ho
8 Wingate Ho
9 Jubet Ho
10 Orde Ho
11 Chindit Ho
12 Mabel Thornton Ho
13 Crawshay Ho
14 Avon Ho
15 Connaught Mans
16 Jonson Ho
17 Herrick Ho
18 Donne Ho
19 Thirlmere Ho
20 Grasmere Ho
B6 1 Chestnut Cl
2 Sycamore Ho
3 Lordship Ho
4 Clissold Ho
5 Beech Ho
6 Laburnum Ho
7 Ormond Ho
8 Yew Tree Ct
9 Oak Ho
C1 1 Dorchester Ct
2 Wareham Ct
3 Dorset Ct
4 Stratton Ct
5 Swanage Ct
6 Blandford Ct
7 Portland Ct
8 Oscar Faber Pl
9 Metropolitan Bsns Ctr
10 Lancaster Cl
11 Palazzo Apartments
C2 1 Kingsland Gn
2 Kingsland Pas
3 Metropolitan Benefit Societies Almshouses
4 Nimrod Pas
5 De Beauvoir Pl
6 Warburton Cl
7 Buckingham Mews
8 Aztec Ct
C3 1 Hewling Ho
2 Matthias Ho
3 Port Royal Pl
4 Cressington Cl
5 King Henry's Yd
6 Bronte Ho
7 Sewell Ho
8 Lydgate Ho
9 Patmore Ho
10 Congreve Ho
11 Elton St
12 Conrad Ho
13 Southwell Ho
14 Neptune Ho
15 Campion Ho
16 Webster Ho
17 Meredith Ho
18 Beckford Ho
19 Ashley Ct
20 Hayling Cl
21 Millard Cl
22 Lydford Cl
23 Salcombe Rd
24 Truman's Rd
25 Templeton Cl
26 John Campbell Rd
27 Gillett Pl
28 Bradbury St
29 Thomas Crowell Ct
C4 1 Londesborough Ho
2 Knebworth Ho
3 Knebworth Rd
4 Bransby Ct
5 Imperial Ave
6 Leonard Pl
7 Shakspeare Mews
8 Binyon Ho
9 Shelley Ho
10 Browning Ho
11 Burns Ho
12 Andrew Marvell Ho
13 Wycliffe Ho
14 Blake Ho
15 Marlowe Ho
16 Fletcher Ho
17 Chaucer Ct
C5 1 Gujarat Ho
2 Marton Rd
3 Painsthorpe Rd
4 Selkirk Ho
5 Defoe Ho
6 Edward Friend Ho
7 Sheridan Ho
8 Barrie Ho
9 Arnold Ho
10 MacAulay Ho
11 Stowe Ho
12 Carlyle Ho
13 Shaftesbury Ho
14 Lillian Cl
15 Swift Ho
16 Dryden Ho
17 Scott Ct
18 Kingsfield Ho
19 Uhura Sq
20 Hartopp Ct
D1 1 Hilborough Rd
2 Shoreditch Ct
3 Evergreen Sq
4 Wyndhams Ct
5 Festival Ct
6 Fortune Ct
7 Rose Ct
8 Ability Plaza
D2 1 Prospect Ho
2 Woodland St
3 Crosby Wlk
4 Kirkland Wlk
5 Bowness Cl
6 Carlisle Wlk
7 Skelton Cl
8 Camerton Cl
9 Buttermere Wlk
10 Houghton Cl
11 Hayton Cl
12 Kingsland Sh Ctr
13 Springfield Ho
14 Parton Lo
15 Sanctuary Mews
D3 1 Miller's Terr
2 Chow Sq
3 Drysdale Flats
4 Gateway Mews
5 Birkbeck Mews
6 Winchester Pl
D4 1 Coronation Ave
2 Morris Blitz Ct
3 Shacklewell Ho
4 Alexandra Ct
D5 1 Lawrence Bldgs
2 Cottage Wlk
3 Batley Pl
D6 1 Garnham St
2 Garnham Cl
3 Sanford La
4 Sanford Wlk
5 Abney Gdns
6 Fleet Wood

74

A1 1 Aldington Ct
2 Bayton Ct
3 Rochford Wlk
A2 3 Burdon Ct
4 Thomson Ct
5 Bruno Ct
A3 1 Kingsdown Ho
2 Glendown Ho
3 Moredown Ho
4 Blakeney Cl
5 Beeston Cl
6 Benabo Ct
7 David Devine Ho
8 Kreedman Wlk
9 Hermitage Row
10 Grafton Ct
11 Lushington Terr
12 Aspen Ct
13 Pykewell Lo
14 Albion Works Studios
A5 1 Ravenscourt
2 Mellington Ct
3 Rendlesham Ho
4 Carroll Ct
A6 1 Cazenove Mans
2 Chedworth Ho
3 Aldergrove Ho
4 Abbotstone Ho
5 Briggeford Cl
6 Inglethorpe Ho
7 Ashdown Ho
8 Epping Ho
9 Cypress Cl
B1 1 Fortescue Ave
2 Pemberton Pl
3 Weston Wlk
4 Bayford St Ind Ctr
5 Bayford St
6 Sidworth St
7 Helmsley St
8 Cyntra Pl
9 Signal Ho
10 All Nations Ho
11 Vanguard Ho
12 Hacon Sq
B2 1 Bohemia Pl
2 Graham Mans
3 Marvin St
4 Boscobel Ho
5 Royal Oak Rd
6 Colonnades The
7 Sylvester Ho
8 Sylvester Path
9 Doctor Spurstowe Almshouses
10 Great Eastern Bldgs
11 Sojourner-Truth Cl
B3 1 Birchington Ho
2 Bicknor Ho
3 Boxley Ho
4 Adisham Ho
5 Cranbrook Ho
6 Marden Ho
7 Broome Ho
8 Crandale Ho
9 Cheriton Ho
10 Ditton Ho
11 Langley Ho
12 Dymchurch Ho
13 Elham Ho
14 Davina Ho
15 Pembury Pl
16 Downs Ct
17 Perrywood Ho
18 Staplehurst Ho
19 Pegwell Ho
20 Yalding Ho
21 Northbourne Ho
22 Monkton Ho
23 Milsted Ho
24 Athlone Cl
25 Clarence Pl
26 Gould Terr
27 Quested Ct
28 Brett Pas
29 Marcon Ct
30 Appleton Ct
B4 1 Ross Ct
2 Downs La
3 Gaviller Pl
4 Robert Owen Lo
5 Apprentice Way
6 Arrowe Ct
7 Gilwell Ct
8 Sutton Ct
9 St Andrews Mans
10 Kinnoull Mans
11 Rowhill Mans
12 Sladen Pl
13 Mothers Sq The
14 Richborough Ho
15 Sandgate Ho
16 Sheppey Ho
B5 1 De Vere Ct
2 Redcliffe Ct
3 Greville Ct
4 Anthony Kendal Ho
B6 1 Wentwood Ho
2 Woolmer Ho
3 Warwick Ct
4 Winslade Ho
5 Morriss Ho
6 Woodfield Ho
7 Rossendale Ho
8 Ettrick Ho
9 Charnwood Ho
10 Boyne Ho
11 Whitwell Ho
12 Scardale Ho
13 Hendale Ho
14 Brampton Cl
15 Aveley Ct
16 Aldeburgh Cl
17 Dennington Cl
C1 1 Pitcairn Ho
2 Lyme Grove Ho
3 Shakespeare Ho
4 Upcott Ho
5 Loddiges Ho
6 Parkinson Ho
7 Sloane Ho
8 Vanbrugh Ho
9 Cambridge Pas
10 Lyttleton Ho
11 Victoria Park Ct
12 Tullis Ho
13 Fairchild Ho
14 Forsyth Ho
15 Tradescant Ho
16 Mason Ho
17 Capel Ho
18 Cordwainers Ct
19 Bridgeman Ho
20 St Thomas's Pl
21 Barclay Ho

22 Clayton Ho
23 Danby Ho
24 Sherard Ho
25 Catesby Ho
26 Petiver Cl
27 Leander Ct
28 Philip Turner Est
29 Grendon Ho
30 Shore Mews
31 Shore Bsns Ctr
32 Kendal Ho
33 Classic Mans
34 Tudor Ho
35 Park Ho
36 Enterprise Ho
37 Alpine Gr
38 Clarendon Cl
39 Rotheley Ho
40 Bernie Grant Ho
C2 1 Woolpack Ho
2 Elvin Ho
3 Thomas Ho
4 Hockley Ho
5 Retreat Ho
6 Butfield Ho
7 Brooksbank Ho
8 Cresset Ho
9 Brooksbank St
10 Lennox Ho
11 Milborne Ho
12 Collent Ho
13 Middlesex Pl
14 Elsdale Ho
15 Devonshire Hall
16 Brent Ho
C6 1 Haybridge Ho
2 Framlingham Cl
3 Halesworth Cl
4 Harleston Cl
5 Lowestoft Cl
6 Howard Ho
7 Templar Ho
D1 1 Stuart Ho
2 Gascoyne Ho
3 Chelsfield Point
4 Sundridge Ho
5 Banbury Ho
6 Lauriston Ho
D2 1 Musgrove Ho
2 Cheyney Ho
3 Haynes Ho
4 Warner Ho
5 Gilby Ho
6 Gadsden Ho
7 Risley Ho
8 Baycliffe Ho
9 Sheldon Ho
10 Offley Ho
11 Latimer Ho
12 Ribstone Ho
13 Salem Ho
14 Fieldwick Ho
15 Lever Ct
16 Matson Ho
17 Wilding Ho
18 Rennell Ho
19 Dycer Ho
20 Granard Ho
21 Whitelock Ho
22 Harrowgate Ho
23 Cass Ho
24 Lofts on the Park
25 Heathcote Point
26 Ravenscroft Point
27 Vanner Point
28 Hensley Point
29 San Ho
D4 1 Cromford Path
2 Longford Ct
3 Overbury Ho
4 Heanor Ct
5 Wharfedale Ct
6 Ladybower Ct
7 Ilkeston Ct
8 Derby Ct
9 Rushmore Cres
10 Blackwell Cl
11 Belper Ct

75

A2 1 Chigwell Ct
2 Wellday Ho
3 Selman Ho
4 Vaine Ho
5 Trower Ho
B2 1 Mallard Cl
2 Merriam Ave
3 Gainsborough St
D6 1 Hammond Ct
2 Sorensen Ct
3 Hinton Ct

76

B1 1 Service Route No 2
2 Service Route No 3
B4 1 Mulberry Ct
2 Rosewood Ct
3 Gean Ct
4 Blackthorn Ct
5 Cypress Ct
C1 1 Stratford Office Village The
2 Violet Ct
3 Mandrake Way
4 Brimstone Ho
5 Hibiscus Lo
6 Glasier Ct
C3 1 Bordeaux Ho
2 Luxembourg Mews
3 Basle Ho
C5 1 Acacia Bsns Ctr
2 Brook Ct
3 Gainsfield Ct
4 Artesian Wlk
5 Doreen Capstan Ho
6 Apollo Pl
7 Peppermint Pl
8 Denmark St
9 Mills Ct
10 Paramount Ho
11 Robinson Cl
C6 1 Nansen Ct
2 Mallinson Ct
3 Barbara Ward Ct
4 Caradon Cl
5 Noel Baker Ct
6 Corigan Ct
7 Norman Ho
8 Willow Ct
9 Lime Ct
10 Owens Mews
11 Marnie Ct
12 Cotton Cl
D1 1 Flint Cl
2 St Matthews Ct
3 Ammonite Ho
4 Stone Ct
D2 1 Common The
2 Wolffe Gdns
3 College Pt
4 Onyx Mews
5 Candlelight Ct
6 Boltons The

77

A4 1 Bronte Cl
2 Anna Neagle Cl
3 Brownlow Rd
4 Carrington Gdns
5 Vera Lynn Cl
C1 1 Sarwan Ho
2 Bridgepoint Lofts
3 Vineyard Studios

78

C3 1 Stewart Rainbird Ho
2 Abraham Fisher Ho
3 Redo Ho
4 George Comberton Wlk
C4 1 Cardamom Ct
2 Annie Taylor Ho
3 Richard Fell Ho
4 Susan Lawrence Ho
5 Walter Hurford Par
6 John Cornwell VC Ho
7 Alfred Prior Ho
C5 1 Charlbury Ho
2 Willis Ho
3 Arthur Walls Ho
4 Blakesley Ho
5 Twelve Acre Ho
6 Beech Ct
7 Golding Ct
D1 1 Aveley Mans
2 Harlow Mans
3 Danbury Mans
4 Mayland Mans
5 Bowers Ho
6 Webber Ho
7 Paulson Ho
8 Collins Ho
9 Jack Cook Ho
D3 1 St Luke's Path
2 Springfield Ct
D5 1 Postway Mews
2 Oakfield Ho
3 Janice Mews
4 Kenneth More Rd
5 Clements Ct
6 Handforth Rd
7 Churchill Ct
8 Oakfield Lo
9 Langdale Ct
10 Ilford Chambers
D6 1 York Ho
2 Opal Mews
3 Florentine Ho
4 Kingsley Mews
5 Hainault Bridge Par

79

A6 1 Spectrum Twr
2 Thames View
3 City View
4 Centreway
D1 1 Gibbards Cott
2 Upney Ct
3 Edgefield Ct
4 Manor Ct
5 Lambourne Gdns
6 Westone Mans
7 Loveland Mans
8 Edward Mans
9 Clarke Mans
10 Dawson Gdns
11 Sebastian Ct

80

A1 1 Bristol Ho
2 Canterbury Ho
3 Durham Ho
4 Wells Ho
5 Winchester Ho
6 Rosalind Ct
7 Exeter Ho
8 Wheatley Mans
9 Greenwood Mans
10 Plymouth Ho
11 Graham Mans
12 Portia Ct

81

C5 1 Markham Ho
2 Webb Ho
3 Preston Ho
4 Steadman Ho
5 Hyndman Ho
6 Clynes Ho
7 Henderson Ho
8 Blatchford Ho
9 Rogers Ho
10 Sylvia Pankhurst Ho
11 Mary Macarthur Ho
12 Ellen Wilkinson Ho
D2 1 Picador Ho
2 Centurion Lodge
3 Louis Ct
4 Watsons Lo
5 Carpenters Ct
6 Bell Ho
7 Rounders Ct
8 Oldmead Ho
9 Jervis Ct
10 Bartletts Ho
11 Royal Par
12 Richardson Gdns
13 Forsyth Ct
14 Eldridge Ct
15 Madison Ct
16 Bowery Ct
17 Rivington Ct

82

D3 1 Marlborough Par
2 Blenheim Par
3 Lea Ct
4 Westbourne Par
5 Whiteleys Par
6 Hillingdon Par
7 New Broadway

84

C4 1 Dilston Cl
2 Wells Cl
3 Willett Cl
4 Merlin Cl
5 Glyndebourne Ct
6 Albury Ct
7 Osterley Ct
8 Hatfield Ct
9 Gayhurst Ct
D4 1 Caravelle Gdns
2 Farman Gr
3 Viscount Gr
4 Tomahawk Gdns
5 Martlet Gr
6 Trident Gdns
7 Latham Ct
8 Jupiter Ct
9 Westland Ct
10 Seasprite Cl
11 Convair Wlk
12 Mayfly Gdns
13 Valiant Cl
14 Woburn Twr
15 Brett Cl
16 Friars Cl
D5 1 Medlar Cl
2 Cranberry Cl
3 Lely Ho
4 Girtin Ho
5 Cotman Ho
6 Raeburn Ho
7 Gainsborough Twr
8 Stanfield Ho
9 Millais Ct
10 Hunt Ct
11 Poynter Ct
12 Hogarth Ho
13 Constable Ho
14 Bonnington Ct
15 Romney Ct
16 Landseer Ho

85

B1 1 St Crispins Ct
B3 1 Weaver Ho
2 Caldon Ho
3 Ashby Ho
4 Welford Ho
5 Hertford Ho
6 Wey Ho
7 Middlewich Ho
8 Stourbridge Ho
B4 1 Netherton Ho
2 Keadby Ho
3 Tame Ho
4 Dorset Ct
D1 1 Thurlestone Ct
2 Disley Ct
3 Burgess Ct
4 Bayliss Cl
5 Lytham Ct
6 Winford Par
7 Brunel Pl
8 Rutherford Twr
9 Rountree Ct

86

A1 1 Farnham Ct
2 Gleneagles Twr
3 Birkdale Ct
4 Verulam Ct
5 Hartsbourne Ct
6 Ferndown Ct
7 Deal Ct
8 St David's Ct
9 Portrush Ct
10 Alnmouth Ct
11 Panmure Ct
12 Peterhead Ct
13 Sunningdale Ct
D2 1 Denbigh Ct
2 Devon Ct
3 Dorset Ct
4 Glamorgan Ct
5 Gloucester Ct
6 Hereford Ct
7 Merioneth Ct
8 Oxford Ct
9 Monmouth Ct
10 Paddington Ct
11 Pembroke Ct
12 Chadwick Cl
13 Cotts Cl
D3 1 Berkshire Ct
2 Buckingham Ct
3 Cardigan Ct
4 Carmarthen Ct
5 Cornwall Ct
6 Merlin Ct
7 Osprey Ct
8 Pelham Pl
9 Puffin Ct
10 Fulmar Ct
11 Turnstone Terr
D5 1 Medway Par
2 Brabstone Ho
3 Cotswold Ct

87

B3 1 Woodbury Ct
2 Edward Ct
3 Park Lo
C1 1 Hurley Ct
2 Amherst Gdns
3 Tudor Ct
4 Hilton Ho
C2 1 Hutton Ct
2 Cain Ct
3 Langdale Ct
4 William Ct
5 Castlebar Ct
6 Warren Ct
7 White Lo
8 Queen's Ct
9 King's Ct
10 Cheriton Cl
11 Stanley Ct
12 Juniper Ho
C3 1 Holtoake Ct
2 Pitshanger Ct
3 Holtoake Ho

88

A4 1 Nelson Ho
2 Gordon Ho
3 Frobisher Ho
4 Wellington Ho
5 Fairfax Ho
A5 1 Carlyon Mans
2 Ainslie Ct
3 Millers Ct
4 Priory Ct
5 Tylers Ct
6 Twyford Ct
7 Rose Ct
8 Laurel Ct
9 Sundew Ct
10 Campion Ct
11 Foxglove Ct
C1 1 Buckingham Ho
2 Chester Ct
3 Devon Ct
4 Essex Ho
5 Fife Ct
6 Gloucester Ct
7 Hereford Ho
8 Inverness Ct
9 Warwick Ho
10 York Ho
11 Suffolk Ho
12 Perth Ho
13 Norfolk Ho
14 Thanet Ct
15 Rutland Ct
16 Oxford Ct

89

A1 1 Avon Ct
2 Bromley Lo
3 Walter Ct
4 Lynton Terr
5 Acton Ho
6 Fells Haugh
7 Springfield Ct
8 Tamarind Ct
9 Lynton Ct
10 Aspen Ct
11 Pegasus Ct
12 Friary Park Ct
B1 1 Rosebank Gdns
2 Rosebank
3 Edinburgh Ho
4 Western Ct
5 Kilronan
B6 1 Carlyle Rd
2 Bernard Shaw Ho
3 Longlents Ho
4 Mordaunt Ho
5 Wilmers Ct
6 Stonebridge Ctr
7 Shakespeare Ave
C5 1 Futters Ct
2 Barrett Ct
3 Elms The
4 Fairlight Ct
D5 1 New Crescent Yd
2 Harlesden Plaza
3 St Josephs Ct
4 Jubilee Cl
5 Ellery Cl

90

B1 1 Holborn Ho
2 Clement Danes Ho
3 Vellacott Ho
4 O'Driscoll Ho
5 King Ho
6 Daley Ho
7 Selma Ho
8 Garrett Ho
C1 1 Latimer Ind Est
2 Pankhurst Ho
3 Quadrangle The
4 Nightingale Ho
5 Gordon Ct
6 Ducane Cl
7 Browning Ho
8 Pavilion Terr
9 Ivebury Ct
10 Olympic Ho
C2 1 Galleywood Ho
2 Edgcott Ho
3 Cuffley Ho
4 Addlestone Ho
5 Hockliffe Ho
6 Sarratt Ho
7 Firle Ho
8 Sutton Est The
9 Terling Ho
10 Danes Ho
11 Udimore Ho
12 Vange Ho
13 Binbrook Ho
14 Yeadon Ho
15 Yatton Ho
16 Yarrow Ho
17 Clement Ho
18 Danebury
19 Coronation Ct
20 Calderon Pl
21 St Quintin Gdns
C3 1 Princess Alice Ho
2 Yoxall Ho
3 Yorkley Ho
4 Northaw Ho
5 Oakham Ho
6 Markyate Ho
7 Letchmore Ho
8 Pagham Ho
9 Quendon Ho
10 Redbourn Ho
11 Ketton Ho
12 Hillman Dr
D1 1 Kelfield Ct
2 Downing Ho
3 Crosfield Ct
4 Robinson Ho
5 Scampston Mews
6 Girton Villas
7 Ray Ho
8 Walmer Ho
9 Goodrich Ct
10 Arthur Ct
11 Whitstable Ho
12 Kingsnorth Ho
13 Bridge Cl
14 Prospect Ho
15 St Marks Rd
16 Whitchurch Ho
17 Blechynden Ho
18 Waynflete Sq
19 Bramley Ho
20 Dixon Ho
D4 1 Westfield Ct
2 Tropical Ct
3 Chamberlayne Mans
4 Quadrant The
5 Queens Park Ct
6 Warfield Yd
7 Regent St
8 Cherrytree Ho
9 Artisan Mews
10 Artisan Quarter

91

A1 1 Malton Mews
2 Lancaster Lo
3 Manning Ho
4 Galsworthy Ho
5 Hudson Ho
6 Cambourne Mews
7 Upper Talbot Wlk
8 Kingsdown Cl
9 Lower Clarendon Wlk
10 Talbot Grove Ho
11 Clarendon Wlk
12 Upper Clarendon Wlk
13 Camelford Wlk
14 Upper Camelford Wlk
15 Camelford Ct
A2 1 Murchison Ho
2 MacAulay Ho
3 Chesterton Ho
4 Chiltern Ho
5 Lionel Ho
6 Watts Ho
7 Wheatstone Ho
8 Telford Ho
9 Golborne Mews
10 Millwood St
11 St Columb's Ho
12 Norfolk Mews
13 Lionel Mews
A3 1 Sycamore Wlk
2 Westgate Bsns Ctr
3 Buspace Studios
4 Bosworth Ho
5 Golborne Gdns
6 Appleford Ho
7 Adair Twr
8 Gadsden Ho
9 Southam Ho
10 Norman Butler Ho
11 Thompson Ho
12 Wells Ho
13 Paul Ho
14 Olive Blythe Ho
15 Katherine Ho
16 Breakwell Ct
17 Pepler Ho
18 Edward Kennedy Ho
19 Winnington Ho
A4 1 Selby Sq
2 Severn Ave
3 Stansbury Sq
4 Tolhurst Dr
5 John Fearon Wlk
6 Mundy Ho
7 Macfarren Ho
8 Bantock Ho
9 Banister Ho
10 Batten Ho
11 Croft Ho
12 Courtville Ho
13 Mounsey Ho
14 Bliss Mews
15 Symphony Mews
B1 1 Silvester Ho
2 Golden Cross Mews
3 Tavistock Mews
4 Clydesdale Ho
5 Melchester
6 Pinehurst Ct
7 Denbigh Ho

B2 1 Blagrove Rd
2 All Saints Ho
3 Tavistock Ho
4 Leamington Ho
B3 1 Octavia Mews
2 Russell's Wharf
3 Western Ho
4 Kelly Mews
B4 1 Boyce Ho
2 Farnaby Ho
3 Danby Ho
4 Purday Ho
5 Naylor Ho
6 St Judes Ho
7 Leeve Ho
8 Longhurst Ho
9 Harrington Ct
10 Mulberry Ct
11 Kilburn Ho
B5 1 Claremont Ct
2 William Saville Ho
3 Western Ct
4 Bond Ho
5 Crone Ct
6 Wood Ho
7 Winterleys
8 Carlton Ho
9 Fiona Ct
C1 1 Shottsford
2 Tolchurch
3 Casterbridge
4 Sandbourne
5 Anglebury
6 Weatherbury
7 Westbourne Gr Mews
8 Rosehart Mews
9 Viscount Ct
10 Hereford Mans
11 Hereford Mews
C2 1 Ascot Ho
2 Ashgrove Ct
3 Lockbridge Ct
4 Swallow Ct
5 Nightingale Lo
6 Hammond Lo
7 Penfield Lo
8 Harvey Lo
9 Hunter Lo
10 Barnard Lo
11 Falcon Lo
12 Johnson Lo
13 Livingstone Lo
14 Nuffield Lo
15 Finch Lo
16 Polesworth Ho
17 Oversley Ho
18 Derrycombe Ho
19 Buckshead Ho
20 Combe Ho
21 Culham Ho
22 Dainton Ho
23 Devonport Ho
24 Honwell Ho
25 Truro Ho
26 Sunderland Ho
27 Stonehouse Ho
28 Riverford Ho
29 Portishead Ho
30 Mickleton Ho
31 Keyham Ho
32 Moulsford Ho
33 Shrewsbury Mews
34 St Stephen's Mews
35 Westway Lo
36 Langley Ho
37 Brindley Ho
38 Radway Ho
39 Astley Ho
40 Willow Ct
41 Larch Ct
42 Elm Ct
43 Beech Ct
44 Worcester Ct
45 Union Ct
46 Leicester Ct
47 Kennet Ct
48 Oxford Ct
49 Fazerley Ct
C3 1 Westside Ct
2 Byron Mews
3 Sutherland Ct
4 Fleming Cl
5 Hermes Cl
C4 1 Pentland Rd
2 Nelson Cl
3 Pavilion Ct
4 Masefield Ho
5 Austen Ho
6 Fielding Ho
7 Argo Bsns Ctr
8 John Ratcliffe Ho
9 Wymering Mans
C5 1 Wells Ct
2 Cambridge Ct
3 Ely Ct
4 Durham Ct
C6 1 Ryde Ho
2 Glengall Pass
3 Leith Yd
4 Daynor Ho
5 Varley Ho
6 Sandby Ho
7 Colas Mews
8 Bishopsdale Ho
9 Lorton Ho
10 Marshwood Ho
11 Ribblesdale Ho
12 Holmesdale Ho
13 Kilburn Vale Est
14 Kilburn Bridge
D1 1 Vera Ct
2 Alexander Mews
3 Gurney Ho
4 Burdett Mews
5 Greville Lo
6 Hatherley Ct
7 Bridge Field Ho
8 Ralph Ct
9 Peters Ct
9 Pickering Mews
10 Riven Ct
11 Inver Ct
12 Cervantes Ct
13 Bishops Ct
14 Newbury Ho
15 Marlow Ho
16 Lynton Ho
17 Pembroke Ho
18 Pickering Ho
19 Whiteleys Ctr
D3 1 Ellwood Ct
D5 1 Tollgate Ho
2 Regents Plaza
3 Royal Langford Apartments
D6 1 Sylvan Ct
2 Birchington Ct
3 Farndale Ho
4 Abbey Rd Motorist Ctr
5 Greville Mews
6 Goldsmith's Pl
7 Remsted Ho
8 Bradwell Ho
9 Cheshunt Ho
10 Haliwell Ho
11 Broadoak Ho
12 Philip Ho
13 Hillsborough Ct
14 Sandbourne
15 Wingreen
16 Toneborough
17 Silverthorn
18 Kington Ho
19 Marrick Ho

95

C4 1 Pimlico Wlk
2 Aske Ho
3 Hathaway Ho
4 Haberdasher Pl
5 Fairchild Ho
6 Burtt Ho
7 Enfield Cloisters
8 McGregor Ct
9 Royal Oak Ct
10 Hoxton Mkt
11 Bath Pl
12 Chapel Pl
13 Standard Pl
14 Cleeve Workshops
15 Cleeve Ho
16 Printing House Yd
17 Perseverance Works
18 Crooked Billet Yd
19 Drysdale Ho
20 Castlefrank Ho
21 School App
22 Basing House Yd
23 Mail Coach Yd
C5 1 Bracer Ho
2 Scorton Ho
3 Fern Cl
4 Macbeth Ho
5 Oberon Ho
6 Buckland Ct
7 Crondall Ct
8 Osric Path
9 Caliban Twr
10 Celia Ho
11 Juliet Ho
12 Bacchus Wlk
13 Malcolm Ho
14 Homefield St
15 Crondall Pl
16 Blanca Ho
17 Miranda Ho
18 Falstaff Ho
19 Charmian Ho
20 Myrtle Wlk
21 Arden Ho
22 Sebastian Ho
23 Stanway Ct
24 Jerrold St
25 Rosalind Ho
26 Cordelia Ho
27 Monteagle Ct
28 John Parry Ct
29 James Anderson Ct
30 Ben Jonson Ct
31 Sara Lane Ct
32 Walbrook Ct
C6 1 Portelet Ct
2 Trinity Ct
3 Rozel Ct
4 St Helier Ct
5 Corbiere Ho
6 Kenning Ho
7 Higgins Ho
8 Cavell Ho
9 Girling Ho
10 Fulcher Ho
11 Francis Ho
12 Norris Ho
13 Kempton Ho
14 Nesham Ho
15 Crossbow Ho
16 Catherine Ho
17 Strale Ho
18 Horner Hos
19 Stringer Hos
20 Whitmore Ho
21 Nightingale Ho
22 Wilmer Gdns
23 Arrow Ho
24 Archer Ho
25 Meriden Ho
26 Rover Ho
27 Bowyer Ho
28 Tiller Ho
29 Canalside Studios
30 Kleine Wharf
31 Benyon Wharf
32 Quebec Wharf
33 Belvedere Ct
34 Portfleet Pl
D4 1 Gorsuch Pl
2 Strout's Pl
3 Vaughan Est
4 George Loveless Ho
5 Baroness Rd
6 James Brine Ho
7 Arthur Wade Ho
8 Robert Owen Ho
9 Sivill Ho
10 Georgina Gdns
11 Old Market Sq
12 Cuff Point
13 Bakers Rents
14 Leopold Bldgs
15 Dunmore Point
16 Wingfield Ho
17 Gascoigne Pl
18 Mandela Ho
19 Virginia Rd
20 Briggs Ho
21 Packenham Ho
22 Gowan Ho
23 Kirton Gdns
24 Chambord Ho
25 Ducal St
26 Strickland Ho
27 Alliston Ho
28 Gibraltar Wlk
29 Equity Sq
30 Shacklewell St
31 Rochelle St
32 Sonning Ho
33 Culham Ho
34 Hurley Ho
35 Palissy St
36 Taplow Ho
37 Chertsey Ho
38 Sunbury Ho
39 Sunbury Workshops
40 Datchett Ho
41 Hocker St
42 Coll Sharp Ct
43 Marlow Studio Workshops
44 Marlow Ho
45 Shiplake Ho
46 Wargrave Ho
47 Iffley Ho
D5 1 Queensbridge Ct
2 Godwin Ho
3 Kent Ct
4 Brunswick Ho
5 Weymouth Ct
6 Sovereign Mews
7 Dunloe Ct
8 Cremer Bsns Ctr
9 James Hammett Ho
10 Allgood St
11 Horatio St
12 Cadell Ho
13 Horatio Ho
14 Shipton Ho
D6 1 Hilborough Ct
2 Scriven Ct
3 Livermere Ct
4 Angrave Ct
5 Angrave Pas
6 Benfleet Ct
7 Belford Ho
8 Orme Ho
9 Clemson Ho
10 Longman Ho
11 Lowther Ho
12 Lovelace Ho
13 Harlowe Ho
14 Pamela Ho
15 Samuel Ho
16 Acton Ho
17 Loanda Cl
18 Phoenix Cl
19 Richardson Cl
20 Thrasher Cl
21 Mary Secole Cl
22 Canal Path
23 Pear Tree Cl
24 Hebden Ct
25 Charlton Ct
26 Laburnum Ct
27 Mansfield Ct
28 Garden Pl
29 Amber Wharf
30 Haggerston Studios

96

A1 1 Whitechurch Pas
2 Manningtree St
3 Whitechurch La
4 Naylor Bldg W
5 Morrison Bldgs
6 Nayor Bldg E
7 Mulberry St
8 Albany Ct
9 Cornell Bldg
10 Dryden Bldg
11 Weyhill Rd
12 Colefax Bldg
13 Fordham St
14 Myrdle Ct
15 Buckle St
16 Plough St
17 Goodman's Stile
18 Ropewalk Gdns
19 Skyline Plaza Bldg
20 Minet Ho
21 Mitali Pas
22 Basil Ho
23 Bernhard Baron Ho
24 Hogarth Ct
25 Delafield Ho
26 Chandlery Ho
27 Berner Terr
28 Victoria Yd
29 Batson Ho
30 Harkness Ho
31 Drewett Ho
32 Dowler Ho
33 Everard Ho
34 Bicknell Ho
35 Danvers Ho
36 Philchurch Pl
37 Hadfield Ho
38 Kindersley Ho
39 Langmore Ho
40 Halliday Ho
A2 1 Arthur Deakin Ho
2 Albert Cotts
3 Victoria Cotts
4 Boden Ho
5 Vollasky Ho
6 Daplyn St
7 Hobsons Pl
8 Hanbury Ho
9 Huguenot Ct
10 Links Yd
11 Casson Ho
12 Ramar Ho
13 Greatorex Ho
14 Chicksand Ho
15 Spelman Ho
16 Tailworth St
17 Monthope Rd
18 Evelyn Ho
19 Bloomfield Ho
20 Davenant Ho
21 Pauline Ho
22 Tannery Ho
23 Don Gratton Ho
24 Green Dragon Yd
25 Fieldgate Mans
26 Mosque Tower
A3 1 Bentworth Ct
2 Hawksmoor Pl
3 Kerbela St
4 Fuller Cl
5 Kinsham Ho
6 Menotti St
7 Barwell Ho
8 Grimsby St
9 Reflection Ho
10 Fleet Street Hill
11 Bratley St
12 Weaver Ho
13 Cornerstone Ct
14 Stuttle Ho
15 McGlashon Ho
16 John Pritchard Ho
A4 1 Providence Yd
2 Lygon Ho
3 Brabner Ho
4 Delta St
5 Delta Point
6 Tillet Way
7 Mullet Gdns
8 Lampern Sq
9 Kite Pl
10 Elver Gdns
11 Cobden Ho
12 Eversley Ho
13 Lorden Wlk
14 Rapley Ho
15 Dence Ho
16 McKinnon Wood Ho
17 Satchwell Rd
18 Dickinson Ho
19 Hutton Ho
20 Simmons Ho
21 Swinton Ho
22 Yates Ho
23 Johnson Ho
24 Jeremy Bentham Ho
25 Waring Ho
26 St James Ct
27 Ebony Ho
28 Azure Ho
29 Westhope Ho
30 Hague St
A5 1 London Terr
2 Sturdee Ho
3 Maude Ho
4 Haig Ho
5 Jellicoe Ho
6 Ropley St
7 Guinness Trust Bldgs
8 Ion Ct
9 Columbia Rd
10 Moye Cl
11 Morrel Ct
12 Courtauld Ho
13 Drummond Ho
14 Gurney Ho
15 Atkinson Ho
16 Halley Ho
17 Goldsmith's Sq
18 Shahjalal Ho
19 Ken Wilson Ho
20 April Ct
21 Crofts Ho
22 Sebright Ho
23 Beechwood Ho
24 Gillman Ho
25 Cheverell Ho
26 Besford Ho
27 Dinmont Ho
28 Elizabeth Mews
29 Sebright Pas
30 Wyndham Deedes Ho
31 Sheppard Ho
32 Mary James Ho
33 Hadrian Est
34 Blythendale Ho
35 George Vale Ho
36 Lion Mills
37 St Peter's Ave
38 Pritchard Ho
A6 1 Broke Wlk
2 Rochemont Wlk
3 Marlborough Ave
4 Rivington Wlk
5 Magnin Cl
6 Gloucester Sq
7 Woolstone Ho
8 Marsworth Ho
9 Cheddington Ho
10 Linslade Ho
11 Cosgrove Ho
12 Blisworth Ho
13 Eleanor Ct
14 Wistow Ho
15 Muscott Ho
16 Boxmoor Ho
17 Linford Ho
18 Pendley Ho
19 Northchurch Ho
20 Debdale Ho
21 Broadway Market Mews
22 Welshpool Ho
23 Ada Ho
B1 1 Peter Best Ho
2 Mellish Ho
3 Porchester Ho
4 Dickson Ho
5 Joscoyne Ho
6 Silvester Ho
7 Wilton Ct
8 Sarah Ho
9 Bridgen Ho
10 Tylney Ho
11 Greenwich Ct
12 Damien Ct
13 Philson Mans
14 Siege Ho
15 Jacob Mans
16 Proud Ho
17 Sly St
18 Barnett St
19 Kinder St
20 Richard St
21 Hungerford St
22 Colstead Ho
23 Melwood Ho
24 Wicker St
25 Langdale St
26 Chapman Ho
27 Burwell Cl
28 Walford Ho
29 Welstead Ho
30 Norton Ho
31 Turnour Ho
32 Luke Ho
33 Dunch St
34 Sheridan St
35 Brinsley St
B2 1 Wodeham Gdns
2 Castlemaine St
3 Court St
B3 1 Rochester Ct
2 Weaver Ct
3 Greenheath Bsns Ctr
4 Glass St
5 Herald St
6 Northesk Ho
7 Codrington Ho
8 Heathpool Ct
9 Mocatta Ho
10 Harvey Ho
11 Blackwood Ho
12 Rutherford Ho
13 Bullen Ho
14 Fremantle Ho
15 Pellew Ho
16 Ashington Ho
17 Dinnington Ho
18 Bartholomew Sq
19 Steeple Ct
20 Orion Ho
21 Fellbrigg St
22 Eagle Ho
23 Sovereign Ho
24 Redmill Ho
25 Berry Ho
26 Grindall Ho
27 Collingwood Ho
B4 1 Charles Dickens Ho
2 Adrian Bolt Ho
3 William Rathbone Ho
4 Southwood Smith Ho
5 Rushmead
6 William Channing Ho
7 John Cartwright Ho
8 Charles Darwin Ho
9 Thomas Burt Ho
10 John Fielden Ho
11 Gwilym Maries Ho
12 Joseph Priestley Ho
13 Wear Pl
14 John Nettleford Ho
15 Thornaby Ho
16 Stockton Ho
17 Barnard Ho
18 Gainford Ho
19 Stapleton Ho
20 James Middleton Ho
21 Kedleston Wlk
22 Queen Margaret Flats
23 Hollybush Ho
24 Horwood Ho
25 Norden Ho
26 Newcourt Ho
27 Seabright St
28 Viaduct Pl
29 Sunlight Sq
30 Providence Row Cl
B5 1 Dinmont St
2 Marian St
3 Claredale Ho
4 Keeling Ho
5 Maple St
6 Winkley St
7 Temple Dwellings
8 Argos Ho
9 Helen Ho
10 Lysander Ho
11 Antenor Ho
12 Paris Ho
13 Nestor Ho
14 Hector Ho
15 Ajax Ho
16 Achilles Ho
17 Priam Ho
18 Peabody Est
19 Felix St

96 B5

20 Cambridge Cres
21 Peterley Bsns Ctr
22 Beckwith Ho
23 Brookfield Ho
24 Parminter Ind Est
25 Ted Roberts Ho
26 Cambridge Ct
27 Millennium Pl
28 William Caslon Ho
29 Hugh Platt Ho
30 West St
31 Mayfield Ho
32 Apollo Ho
33 Tanners Yd
34 Teesdale Yd
B6 1 Welshpool St
2 Broadway Ho
3 Regents Wharf
4 London Wharf
5 Warburton Ho
6 Warburton St
7 Triangle Rd
8 Warburton Rd
9 Williams Ho
10 Booth Cl
11 Albert Cl
12 King Edward Mans
13 Victoria Bldgs
14 Andrews Wharf
C1 1 Woollon Ho
2 Dundalk Ho
3 Anne Goodman Ho
4 Newbold Cotts
5 Kerry Ho
6 Zion Ho
7 Longford Ho
8 Bromehead St
9 Athlone Ho
10 Jubilee Mans
11 Harriott Ho
12 Brayford Sq
13 Clearbrook Way
14 Rochelle Ct
15 Winterton Ho
16 Swift Ho
17 Brinsley Ho
18 Dean Ho
19 Foley Ho
20 Robert Sutton Ho
21 Montpelier Pl
22 Glastonbury Pl
23 Steel's La
24 Masters Lo
25 Stylus Apartments
26 Arta Ho
C2 1 Fulneck
2 Gracehill
3 Ockbrook
4 Fairfield
5 Dunstan Hos
6 Cressy Ct
7 Cressy Hos
8 Callahan Cotts
9 Lindley Ho
10 Mayo Ho
11 Wexford Ho
12 Sandhurst Ho
13 Addis Ho
14 Colverson Ho
15 Beckett Ho
16 Jarman Ho
17 Armsby Ho
18 Wingrad Ho
19 Miranda Cl
20 Drake Ho
21 Ashfield Yd
22 Magri Wlk
23 Jean Pardies Ho
24 St Vincent De Paul Ho
25 Sambrook Ho
26 Louise De Marillac Ho
27 Dagobert Ho
28 Le Moal Ho
29 Odette Duval Ho
30 Charles Auffray Ho
31 Boisseau Ho
32 Clichy Ho
33 Paymal Ho
C3 1 William's Bldgs
2 Donegal Ho
3 Pelican Pas
4 Frederick Charrington Ho
5 Wickford Ho
6 Braintree Ho
7 Doveton Ho
8 Doveton St
9 Cephas Ho
10 Sceptre Ho
11 Bancroft Ho
12 Stothard St
13 Redclyf Ho
14 Winkworth Cotts
15 Amiel St
16 Hadleigh Ho
17 Hadleigh Cl
18 Ryder Ho
19 Mantus Cl
20 Kenton Ho
21 Colebert Ho
22 Ibbott St
23 Rickman Ho
24 Rickman St
25 Stothard Ho
26 Barbanel Ho
27 Stannard Cotts
28 St Peters Ct
29 Rennie Cotts
30 Pemell Cl
31 Pemell Ho
32 Leatherdale St
33 Gouldman Ho
34 Lamplighter Cl
35 Sherren Ho
36 Marlborough Lo
37 Hamilton Lo
38 Montgomery Lo
39 Cleveland Gr
40 Cromwell Lo
41 Bardsey Pl
42 Charrington Ho
43 Hayfield Yd
44 Allport Mews
45 Colin Winter Ho
C4 1 Mulberry Ho
2 Gretton Ho
3 Merceron Ho
4 Montfort Ho
5 Westbrook Ho
6 Sugar Loaf Wlk
7 Museum Ho
8 Burnham Est
9 Globe Terr
10 Moravian St
11 Shepton Hos
12 Mendip Hos
13 Academy Ct
14 Pepys Ho
15 Swinburne Ho
16 Moore Ho
17 Morris Ho
18 Burns Ho
19 Milton Ho
20 Whitman Ho
21 Shelley Ho
22 Keats Ho
23 Dawson Ho
24 Bradbeer Ho
25 Forber Ho
26 Hughes Ho
27 Silvester Ho
28 Rogers Est
29 Pavan Ct
30 Stafford Cripps Ho
31 Sidney Godley (VC) Ho
32 Butler Ho
33 Butler St
34 Thorne Ho
35 Bevin Ho
36 Tuscan Ho
C5 1 Evesham Ho
2 James Campbell Ho
3 Thomas Hollywood Ho
4 James Docherty Ho
5 Ebenezer Mussel Ho
6 Jameson Ct
7 Edinburgh Cl
8 Roger Dowley Ct
9 Sherbrooke Ho
10 Calcraft Ho
11 Burrard Ho
12 Dundas Ho
13 Ponsonby Ho
14 Barnes Ho
15 Paget Ho
16 Maitland Ho
17 Chesil Ct
18 Reynolds Ho
19 Cleland Ho
20 Goodrich Ho
21 Rosebery Ho
22 Sankey Ho
23 Cyprus Pl
24 Royston St
25 Stainsbury St
26 Hunslett St
27 Baildon
28 Brockweir
29 Tytherton
30 Malmesbury
31 Kingswood
32 Colville Ho
C6 1 Halkett Ho
2 Christchurch Sq
3 Helena Pl
4 Swingfield Ho
5 Greenham Ho
6 Dinmore Ho
7 Anstey Ho
8 Weston Ho
9 Carbroke Ho
10 Bluebell Cl
11 Cherry Tree Cl
12 Georgian Ct
13 Park Cl
14 Regency Ct
15 Norris Ho
D1 1 Pattison Ho
2 St Thomas Ho
3 Arbour Ho
4 Bladen Ho
5 Antill Terr
6 Majorie Mews
7 Billing Ho
8 Dowson Ho
9 Lipton Rd
10 Chalkwell Ho
11 Corringham Ho
12 Ogilvie Ho
13 Edward Mann Cl
14 Reservoir Studios
15 Lighterman Mews
D2 1 Roland Mews
2 Beatrice Ho
3 Morecambe Cl
4 Stepney Green Ct
5 Milrood Ho
6 Panama Ho
7 Galway Ho
8 Jacqueline Ho
9 Crown Mews
10 Caspian Ho
11 Darien Ho
12 Riga Ho
13 Flores Ho
14 Taranto Ho
15 Aden Ho
16 Master's St
17 Rosary Ct
D3 1 Raynham Ho
2 Pat Shaw Ho
3 Colmar Cl
4 Withy Ho
5 Stocks Ct
6 Downey Ho
7 Bay Ct
8 Sligo Ho
9 Pegasus Ho
10 Barents Ho
11 Biscay Ho
12 Solway Ho
13 Bantry Ho
14 Aral Ho
15 Pacific Ho
16 Magellan Ho
17 Levant Ho
18 Adriatic Ho
19 Genoa Ho
20 Hawke Ho
21 Palliser Ho
22 Ionian Ho
23 Weddell Ho
24 Carlyle Mews
25 Greencourt Ho
26 Sundra Wlk
D4 1 Stubbs Ho
2 Holman Ho
3 Clynes Ho
4 Windsor Ho
5 Gilbert Ho
6 Chater Ho
7 Ellen Wilkinson Ho
8 George Belt Ho
9 Ayrton Gould Ho
10 O'Brian Ho
11 Sulkin Ho
12 Jenkinson Ho
13 Bullards Pl
14 Sylvia Pankhurst Ho
15 Mary Macarthur Ho
16 Trevelyan Ho
17 Wedgwood Ho
18 Pemberton Ct
19 Leatherdale St
20 Walter Besant Ho
21 Barber Beaumont Ho
22 Brancaster Ho
23 Litcham Ho
D5 1 Kemp Ho
2 Piggott Ho
3 Mark Ho
4 Sidney Ho
5 Pomeroy Ho
6 Puteaux Ho
7 Doric Ho
8 Modling Ho
9 Longman Ho
10 Ames Ho
11 Alzette Ho
12 Offenbach Ho
13 Tate Ho
14 Norton Ho
15 St Gilles Ho
16 Harold Ho
17 Velletri Ho
18 Bridge Wharf
19 Gathorne St
20 Bow Brook The
21 Twig Folly Cl
22 Palmerston Ct
23 Lakeview
24 Peach Walk Mews
25 Caesar Ct

97

A1 1 Hearnshaw St
2 Berry Cotts
3 Causton Cotts
4 Elizabeth Blount Ct
5 Carr St
6 Shaw Cres
7 Darnley Ho
8 Mercer's Cotts
9 Troon Ho
10 Ratcliffe Ho
11 Wakeling St
12 York Sq
13 Anglia Ho
14 Cambria Ho
15 Caledonia Ho
16 Ratcliffe La
17 Bekesbourne St
18 John Scurr Ho
19 Regents Canal Ho
20 Basin App
21 Powlesland Ct
A2 1 Waley St
2 Edith Ramsay Ho
3 Andaman Ho
4 Atlantic Ho
5 Pevensey Ho
6 Solent Ho
7 Lorne Ho
8 Cromarty Ho
9 Dakin Pl
10 Greaves Cotts
11 Donaghue Cotts
12 Ames Cotts
13 Waterview Ho
14 Limehouse Fields Est
A3 1 Formosa Ho
2 Galveston Ho
3 Arabian Ho
4 Greenland Ho
5 Coral Ho
6 Anson Ho
7 Cambay Ho
8 Lindop Ho
9 Moray Ho
10 Azov Ho
11 Sandalwood Cl
12 Broadford Ho
A4 1 Imperial Ho
2 Newport Ho
3 Vassall Ho
4 Maurice Ct
5 Creed Ct
6 Christopher France Ho
7 Beaumont Ct
8 Pembroke Mews
A5 1 Nightingale Mews
2 Bunsen Ho
3 Bunsen St
4 Beatrice Webb Ho
5 Margaret Bondfield Ho
6 Wilmer Ho
7 Sandall Ho
8 Butley Ct
9 Josseline Ct
10 Dalton Ho
11 Brine Ho
12 Ford Cl
13 Viking Cl
14 Stanfield Rd
15 Stoneleigh Mews
16 Ruth Ct
17 School Bell Cloisters
18 Schoolbell Mews
19 Medhurst Cl
20 Olga St
21 Conyer St
22 Diamond Ho
23 Daring Ho
24 Crane Ho
25 Exmoor Ho
26 Grenville Ho
27 Hyperion Ho
28 Sturdy Ho
29 Wren Ho
30 Ardent Ho
31 Senators Lo
32 Hooke Ho
33 Mohawk Ho
34 Ivanhoe Ho
35 Medway Mews
B1 1 Dora Ho
2 Flansham Ho
3 Gatwick Ho
4 Ashpark Ho
5 Newdigate Ho
6 Midhurst Ho
7 Redbourne Ho
8 Southwater Cl
9 Andersens Wharf
10 Whatman Ho
11 Butler Ho
12 Fitzroy Ho
13 Salmon St
14 Mission The
15 Aithan Ho
16 Britley Ho
17 Cheadle Ho
18 Elland Ho
19 Wharf La
20 Docklands Ct
21 Park Heights Ct
22 Grosvenor Ct
23 Lime House Ct
24 Swallow Pl
25 St Anne's Trad Est
B2 1 Wearmouth Ho
2 Elmslie Point
3 Grindley Ho
4 Stileman Ho
5 Wilcox Ho
6 Huddart St
7 Robeson St
8 Couzens Ho
9 Perley Ho
10 Whytlaw Ho
11 Booker Cl
12 Tunley Gn
13 Callingham Cl
14 Bowry Ho
15 Perkins Ho
16 Printon Ho
17 Tasker Ho
B4 1 Trellis Sq
2 Sheffield Sq
3 Howcroft Ho
4 Astra Ho
5 Frye Ct
6 Byas Ho
7 George Lansbury Ho
8 Regal Pl
9 Coborn Mews
10 Tredegar Mews
11 Cavendish Terr
12 Lyn Mews
13 Buttermere Ho
14 Coniston Ho
15 Tracy Ho
16 Hanover Pl
17 St Clair Ho
18 Longthorne Ho
19 Vista Bldgs
20 Verity Ho
21 Icarus Ho
22 Whippingham Ho
23 Hamilton Ho
24 Winchester Ho
B5 1 Roman Square Mkt
2 John Bond Ho
3 McKenna Ho
4 Dennis Ho
5 McAusland Ho
6 McBride Ho
7 Libra Rd
8 Dave Adams Ho
9 Regency Ct
10 Tay Ho
11 Sleat Ho
12 Brodick Ho
13 Ewart Pl
14 Lunan Ho
15 Cruden Ho
16 Anglo Rd
17 Mull Ho
18 Sinclairs Ho
19 Driftway Ho
20 Clayhall Ct
21 Berebinder Ho
22 Partridge Ho
23 Barford Ho
24 Gullane Ho
25 Gosford Ho
26 Dornoch Ho
27 Dunnet Ho
28 Enard Ho
29 Fraserburgh Ho
30 Forth Ho
31 Stavers Ho
32 Rosegate Ho
33 Crowngate Ho
34 Queensgate Ho
35 Towergate Ho
36 Ordell Ct
37 William Pl
B6 1 Hampstead Wlk
2 Waverton Ho
3 Elton Ho
4 Locton Gn
5 Birtwhistle Ho
6 Clare Ho
7 Magpie Ho
8 Hornbeam Sq
9 Rowan Ho
10 Barge La
11 Walnut Ho
12 Birdsfield La
13 Atkins Ct
14 Willow Tree Cl
15 Jasmine Sq
16 Tait Ct
17 Ranwell Ho
18 Ranwell Cl
19 Tufnell Ct
20 Pulteney Cl
21 Vic Johnson Ho
22 Lea Sq
23 Iceni Ct
24 Tamar Cl
25 Roman Rd
26 Valentine Ho
C1 1 Landin Ho
2 Thomas Road Ind Est
3 Vickery's Wharf
4 Abbotts Wharf
5 Limehouse Ct
6 Charlesworth Ho
7 Gurdon Ho
8 Trendell Ho
9 Menteath Ho
10 Minchin Ho
11 Donne Ho
12 Old School Sq
13 Anglesey Ho
14 Gough Wlk
15 Baring Ho
16 Gladstone Ho
17 Hopkins Ho
18 Granville Ho
19 Overstone Ho
20 Pusey Ho
21 Russell Ho
22 Stanley Ho
C2 1 Bredel Ho
2 Linton Ho
3 Matthews Ho
4 Woodcock Ho
5 Limborough Ho
6 Maydwell Ho
7 Underhill Ho
8 Meyrick Ho
9 Ambrose Ho
10 Richardson Ho
11 Carpenter Ho
12 Robinson Ho
13 Bellmaker Ct
14 Lime Tree Ct
15 Bracken Ho
16 Bramble Ho
17 Berberis Ho
18 Bilberry Ho
19 Ladyfern Ho
20 Rosebay Ho
21 Invicta Cl
22 Phoenix Bsns Ctr
23 Metropolitan Cl
24 Busbridge Ho
C3 1 Fairmont Ho
2 Healy Ho
3 Zodiac Ho
4 Buick Ho
5 Consul Ho
6 Bentley Ho
7 Cresta Ho
8 Daimler Ho
9 Riley Ho
10 Jensen Ho
11 Lagonda Ho
12 Ireton St
13 Navenby Wlk
14 Burwell Wlk
15 Leadenham Ct
16 Sleaford Ho
17 Bow Triangle Bsns Ctr
C4 1 Bow Ho
2 Denmark Pl
3 Marsalis Ho
4 Lovette Ho
5 Drapers Almhouses
6 Mallard Point
7 Creswick Wlk
8 Bevin Ho
9 Huggins Ho
10 Williams Ho
11 Harris Ho
12 Marina Ct
13 Electric Ho
14 Matching Ct
15 Wellington Bldgs
16 Grafton Ho
17 Berkeley Ho
18 Columbia Ho
C5 1 Vincent Mews
2 Menai Pl
3 Heathfield Ct
4 Redwood Cl
5 Acorn Ct
6 Primrose Cl
7 Briar Ct

8 Springwood Cl
C6 1 Ironworks
2 Juno Ho
3 Chariot Cl
4 Saturn Ho
5 Hadrian Cl
6 Mercury Ho
7 Forum Cl
8 Venus Ho
9 Vesta Ho
10 Tiber Cl
11 Gemini Ho
12 Crown Close Bsns Ctr
13 Old Ford Trad Ctr
D1 1 Colebrook Ho
2 Essex Ho
3 Salisbury Ho
4 Maidstone Ho
5 Osterley Ho
6 Norwich Ho
7 Clarissa Ho
8 Elgin Ho
9 Shaftesbury Lo
10 Shepherd Ho
11 Jeremiah St
12 Elizabeth Cl
13 Chilcot Cl
14 Fitzgerald Ho
15 Vesey Path
16 Ennis Ho
17 Kilmore Ho
18 Cygnet House N
19 Cygnet House S
D2 1 Sumner Ho
2 David Hewitt Ho
3 St Gabriels Cl
4 Limehouse Cut
5 Colmans Wharf
6 Foundary Ho
7 Radford Ho
D3 1 Broxbourne Ho
2 Roxford Ho
3 Biscott Ho
4 Stanborough Ho
5 Hillstone Ct
D4 1 Bradley Ho
2 Prioress Ho
3 Alton Ho
4 Foxley Ho
5 Munden Ho
6 Canterbury Ho
7 Corbin Ho
8 Barton Ho
9 Jolles Ho
10 Rudstone Ho
11 Baxter Ho
12 Baker Ho
13 Insley Ho
14 Hardwicke Ho
15 Glebe Ct
16 Priory St
17 Sadler Ho
18 Ballinger Point
19 Henshall Point
20 Dorrington Point
21 Warren Ho
22 Fairlie Ct
23 Regent Sq
24 Hackworth Point
25 Priestman Point
26 Wingate Ho
27 Nethercott Ho
28 Thelbridge Ho
29 Bowden Ho
30 Kerscott Ho
31 Southcott Ho
32 Birchdown Ho
33 Upcott Ho
34 Langmead Ho
35 Limscott Ho
36 Northleigh Ho
37 Huntshaw Ho
38 Chagford Ho
39 Ashcombe Ho
40 Shillingford Ho
41 Patrick Connolly Gdns
42 Lester Ct
43 Franklin St
44 Taft Way
45 Washington Cl
46 Veronica Ho
47 William Guy Gdns
48 Denbury Ho
49 Holsworthy Ho
50 Padstone Ho

98

A1 1 Glenkerry Ho
2 Carradale Ho
3 Langdon Ho
4 Balfron Twr
5 St Frideswides Mews
6 Tabard Ct
7 Delta Bldg
8 Findhorn St
9 Kilbrennan Ho
10 Thistle Ho
11 Heather Ho
12 Tartan Ho
13 Sharman Ho
14 Trident Ho
15 Wharf View Ct
A2 1 Mills Gr
2 St Michaels Ct
3 Duncan Ct
A4 1 Miller's House Visitor Ctr
B1 1 Lansbury Gdns
2 Theseus Ho
3 Adams Ho
4 Jones Ho
5 Sam March Ho
6 Arapiles Ho
7 Athenia Ho
8 Julius Ho
9 Jervis Bay Ho
10 Helen Mackay Ho
11 Gaze Ho
12 Ritchie Ho
13 Blairgowrie Ct
14 Circle Ho
15 Dunkeld Ho
16 Rosemary Dr
17 Sorrel La
18 East India Dock Road Tunnel
B3 1 Crescent Court Bsns Ctr
2 Ashmead Bsns Ctr
3 Forward Bsns Ctr The
B6 1 Victoria Mills
2 Hallings Wharf Studios
3 Poland Ho
4 Peter Heathfield Ho
5 Burford Rd
C5 1 Abbey Lane Commercial Est
2 Greenway Ct
C6 1 Barnby Sq
2 Barnby St
3 Brassett Point
4 David Lee Point
5 Worthing Cl
6 Bexhill Wlk
7 Old Barrowfield
8 Elmgreen Cl
9 Stafford Morris Ho
10 Nina Mackay Cl
11 Lime Wlk
D1 1 Newton Point
2 Sparke Terr
3 Montesquieu Terr
4 Crawford Point
5 Rathbone Ho
6 George St
7 Emily St
8 Fendt Cl
9 Sabbarton St
10 Briary Ct
11 Shaftesbury Ho
D2 1 Radley Terr
2 Bernard Cassidy St
3 Rathbone Mkt
4 Thomas North Terr
5 Mary St
6 Hughes Terr
7 Swanscombe Point
8 Rawlinson Point
9 Kennedy Cox Ho
10 Cooper St
D6 1 Harris Cotts
2 Moorey Cl
3 Euro Bsns Ctr
4 Ladywell St
5 Caistor Ho
6 Redfern Ho

99

A2 1 Odeon Ct
2 Edward Ct
3 Newhaven La
4 Ravenscroft Cl
5 Douglas Rd
6 Ferrier Point
7 Harvey Point
8 Wood Point
9 Trinity St
10 Pattinson Point
11 Clinch Ct
12 Mint Bsns Pk
A3 1 Webb Gdns
2 Eric Shipman Terr
3 Warmington St
4 Jellicoe Rd
5 Frank St
6 Seaton Cl
7 Tabernacle Ave
8 Upland Rd
9 Clove St
10 Edward St
A4 1 Bob Anker Cl
2 Lea Ct
3 Third Ave
4 Suffolk Rd
A5 1 Lettsom Wlk
2 Ashburton Terr
3 Grasmere Rd
4 Dimsdale Wlk
5 Rawstone Wlk
6 Scott Ho
7 Willett Ho
8 James Cl
9 Cordwainers Wlk
10 Victoria Point
11 Settle Point
12 Middle Rd
13 Steve Biko Lodge
14 Lady Helen Seymour Ho
A6 1 Royston Ct
B4 1 Barbers Alley
2 Grengate Lodge
3 Augurs La
4 Surrey St
5 Dongola Rd W
6 Bemersyde Point
7 Rowntree Clifford Cl
C2 1 Alliance Rd
2 Salomons Rd
3 Barnes Ct
4 Triangle Ct
5 Moorings The
C5 1 Wellby Ct
2 Northfield Ho
3 Bishop Wilfred Wood Ct
4 Castle Point
5 Moat Dr
C6 1 Tolpuddle Ave
2 Crown Mews
3 Lilac Ct
4 Hamara Ghar
5 Greenleaf Rd
6 Massey Ct
7 Florence Rd
8 Sissulu Ct
9 Austin Ct
D2 1 Partridge Cl
2 Vanbrugh Cl
3 Meadowsweet Cl
4 St Michaels Cl
5 Long Mark Rd
6 Congreve Wlk
D5 1 Foxcombe Cl
2 Rochford Cl
3 Kylemore Cl
4 Stondon Wlk
5 Imperial Mews
6 Dominica Cl
D6 1 Oldegate Ho
2 Gaitskell Ho
3 Cabot Way

100

A1 1 Hadleigh Wlk
2 Hawksmoor Cl
3 Fraser Cl
4 Moncrieff Cl
5 Burlington Cl
6 Dundonald Cl
7 Oakley Cl
8 Ashwell Cl
A2 1 Orchid Cl
2 Bellflower Cl
3 Partridge Sq
4 Larkspur Cl
5 Lobelia Cl
6 Stonechat Sq
7 Wintergreen Cl
8 Garnet Wlk
9 Mavis Wlk
10 Beacons Cl
11 Abbess Cl
12 Elmley Cl
13 Chetwood Wlk
14 Selby Cl
15 Denny Cl
16 Woodhatch Cl
A6 1 Oakwood Ct
2 Harrow Rd
3 Ray Massey Way
4 Madge Gill Way
5 Pilgrims Way
6 St Bartholomews Ct
B1 1 Bowers Wlk
2 Barton Cl
3 Clayton Cl
4 Dixon Cl
5 Gautrey Sq
6 Wakerley Cl
7 Canterbury Cl
8 Goose Sq
9 Coventry Cl
10 Butterfield Sq
11 Winchester Cl
B2 1 Fleetwood Ct
2 Lymington Cl
3 Holyhead Cl
4 Bondfield Rd
5 Tulip Cl
6 Ambrose Cl
7 Sage Cl
8 Lindwood Cl
D1 1 Weymouth Ct
2 Founder Cl
3 Admirals Ct

101

A6 1 Wellington St
2 St Ann's Rd
3 Cooke St
4 Gateway Ho
5 Ardleigh Ho
6 Skipper Ct
7 Hewetts Quay
B5 1 Anderson Ho
2 Rookwood Ho
3 Tasker Ho
4 Crispe Ho
5 Oban Ho
6 Earlsdown Ho
B6 1 Jarvis Cl
2 Mayflower Ho
3 Westbury Ct
4 Millicent Preston Ho
5 Louise Graham Ho
6 Grange Ho
7 Basing Ho
8 Barnes Ho
9 Lexham Ho
10 Ripple Ct
11 Waldegrave Ct
12 Howard Ct

104

A6 1 Milburn Dr
2 Cousins Cl
3 Leacroft Cl

108

C5 1 Marlow Ct
2 Andrewes Ct
3 Vine Cotts
4 Benjamin Ct
5 Broadway Bldgs
6 Clocktower Mews
7 Amberley Ho
8 Diamond Ct
D5 1 Silverdale Cl
2 Burdett Cl
3 Hopefield
4 Maunder Rd
5 Clare Ho

109

A5 1 Glastonbury Ct
2 Evesham Ct
3 Lacock Ct
4 Wigmore Ct
5 Melrose Ct
6 Brownlow Rd
7 Chignell Pl
8 Shirley Ct
9 Trojan Ct
10 Hatfield Rd
11 Pershore Ho
12 Hyde Ho
13 Hugh Clark Ho
14 Rosemoor Ho
15 Leeland Mans
16 Waterford Ct
17 O'Grady Ct
C6 1 Abbey Lo
2 Yew Tree Grange
3 Abinger Ct

110

A1 1 Burford Ho
2 Hope Cl
3 Centaur Ct
4 Phoenix Ct
A6 1 Watermans Mews
2 Hills Mews
3 Grosvenor Ct
4 Elton Lo
5 Hambledon Ct
C1 1 Surrey Cres
2 Forbes Ho
3 Haining Cl
4 Melville Ct
5 London Stile
6 Stile Hall Par
7 Priory Lo
8 Kew Bridge Ct
9 Meadowcroft
10 St James Ct
11 Rivers Ho
C5 1 Grosvenor Par
2 Oakfield Ct
3 Hart Grove Ct
4 Grosvenor Ct
D1 1 Churchdale Ct
2 Cromwell Cl
3 Cambridge Rd S
4 Oxbridge Ct
5 Tomlinson Cl
6 Gunnersbury Mews
7 Grange The
8 Gunnersbury Cl
9 Bellgrave Lo
D4 1 Cheltenham Pl
2 Beaumaris Twr
3 Arundel Ho
4 Pevensey Ct
5 Jerome Twr
6 Anstey Ct
7 Bennett Ct
8 Gunnersbury Ct
9 Barrington Ct
10 Hope Gdns
11 Park Road E
D5 1 Lantry Ct
2 Rosemount Ct
3 Moreton Twr
4 Acton Central Ind Est
5 Rufford Twr
6 Narrow St
7 Mount Pl
8 Sidney Miller Ct
9 Mill Hill Terr
10 Cheltenham Pl
11 Mill Hill Gr
12 Benjamin Ho
13 Arlington Ct
14 Lombard Ct
15 Steyne Ho

111

A1 1 Arlington Park Mans
2 Sandown Ho
3 Goodwood Ho
4 Windsor Ho
5 Lingfield Ho
6 Ascot Ho
7 Watchfield Ct
8 Belgrave Ct
9 Beverley Ct
10 Beaumont Ct
11 Harvard Rd
12 Troubridge Ct
13 Branden Lo
14 Fromow's Cnr
A2 1 Chiswick Green Studios
2 Bell Ind Est
3 Fairlawn Ct
4 Dukes Gate
5 Dewsbury Ct
6 Chiswick Terr
7 Mortlake Ho
A3 1 Blackmore Twr
2 Bollo Ct
3 Kipling Twr
4 Lawrence Ct
5 Maugham Ct
6 Reade Ct
7 Woolf Ct
8 Shaw Ct
9 Verne Ct
10 Wodehouse Ct
11 Greenock Rd
12 Garden Ct
13 Barons Gate
14 Cleveland Rd
15 Carver Cl
16 Chapter Cl
17 Beauchamp Cl
18 Holmes Ct
19 Copper Mews
A4 1 Belgrave Cl
2 Buckland Wlk
3 Frampton Ct
4 Telfer Cl
5 Harlech Twr
6 Corfe Twr
7 Barwick Ho
8 Charles Hocking Ho
9 Sunninghill Ct
10 Salisbury St
11 Jameson Pl
12 Castle Cl
A5 1 Rectory Rd
2 Derwentwater Mans
3 Market Pl
4 Hooper's Mews
5 Cromwell Pl
6 Locarno Rd
7 Edgecote Cl
8 Harleyford Manor
9 Coopers Ct
10 Avingdor Ct
11 Steyne Ho
B1 1 Chatsworth Lo
2 Prospect Pl
3 Townhall Ave
4 Devonhurst Pl
5 Heathfield Ct
6 Horticultural Pl
7 Merlin Ho
8 Garth Rd
9 Autumn Rise
B2 1 Disraeli Cl
2 Winston Wlk
3 Rusthall Mans
4 Bedford Park Mans
5 Essex Place Sq
6 Holly Rd
7 Homecross Ho
8 Swan Bsns Ctr
9 Jessop Ho
C1 1 Glebe Cl
2 Devonshire Mews
3 Binns Terr
4 Ingress St
5 Swanscombe Rd
6 Brackley Terr
7 Stephen Fox Ho
8 Manor Gdns
9 Coram Ho
10 Flaxman Ho
11 Thorneycroft Ho
12 Thornhill Ho
13 Kent Ho
14 Oldfield Ho
C2 1 Chestnut Ho
2 Bedford Ho
3 Bedford Cnr
4 Sydney Ho
5 Bedford Park Cnr
6 Priory Gdns
7 Windmill Alley
8 Castle Pl
9 Jonathan Ct
10 Windmill Pas
11 Chardin Rd
12 Gable Ho
C3 1 Fleet Ct
2 Ember Ct
3 Emlyn Gdns
4 Clone Ct
5 Brent Ct
6 Abbey Ct
7 Ormsby Lo
8 St Catherine's Ct
9 Lodge The
C4 1 Longford Ct
2 Mole Ct
3 Lea Ct
4 Wandle Ct
5 Beverley Ct
6 Roding Ct
7 Crane Ct
D1 1 Miller's Ct
2 British Grove Pas
3 British Grove S
4 Berestede Rd
5 North Eyot Gdns
D2 1 Flanders Mans
2 Stamford Brook Mans
3 Linkenholt Mans
4 Prebend Mans
5 Middlesex Ct
D3 1 Stamford Brook Gdns
2 Hauteville Court Gdns
3 Ranelagh Gdns

112

A1 1 Chisholm Ct
2 North Verbena Gdns
3 Western Terr
4 Verbena Gdns
5 Montrose Villas
6 Hammersmith Terr
7 South Black Lion La
8 St Peter's Wharf
A2 1 Hamlet Ct
2 Derwent Ct
3 Westcroft Ct
4 Black Lion Mews
5 St Peter's Villas
6 Standish Ho
7 Chambon Pl
8 Court Mans
9 Longthorpe Ct
10 Charlotte Ct
11 Westside
12 Park Ct
13 London Ho
A3 1 Elizabeth Finn Ho
2 Ashchurch Ct
3 King's Par
4 Inver Ct
5 Ariel Ct
6 Pocklington Lo
7 Vitae Apartments
A4 1 Becklow Gdns
2 Victoria Ho
3 Lycett Pl
4 Kylemore Ct
5 Alexandra Ct
6 Lytten Ct
7 Becklow Mews
8 Northcroft Ct
9 Bailey Ct
10 Spring Cott

112 A4

11 Landor Wlk
12 Laurence Mews
13 Hadyn Park Ct
14 Askew Mans
15 Malvern Ct
B1 1 Prince's Mews
2 Aspen Gdns
3 Hampshire Hog La
4 Blades Ct
B2 1 Albion Gdns
2 Flora Gdns
3 Lamington St
4 Felgate Mews
5 Galena Ho
6 Albion Mews
7 Albion Ct
8 King Street Cloisters
9 Dimes Pl
10 Clarence Ct
11 Hampshire Hog La
12 Marryat Ct
13 Ravenscourt Ho
B3 1 Ravenscourt Park Mans
2 Paddenswick Ct
3 Ashbridge Ct
B4 1 Westbush Ct
2 Goldhawk Mews
3 Sycamore Ho
4 Shackleton Ct
5 Drake Ct
6 Scotts Ct
7 Raleigh Ct
8 Melville Court Flats
9 Southway Cl
B5 1 Arlington Ho
2 Lugard Ho
3 Shabana Ct
4 Sitarey Ct
5 Oaklands Ct
6 Davenport Mews
B6 1 Abercrombie Ho
2 Bathurst Ho
3 Brisbane Ho
4 Bentinck Ho
5 Ellenborough Ho
6 Lawrence Cl
7 Mackenzie Cl
8 Carteret Ho
9 Calvert Ho
10 Winthrop Ho
11 Auckland Ho
12 Blaxland Ho
13 Havelock Cl
14 Hargraves Ho
15 Hudson Cl
16 Phipps Ho
17 Lawson Ho
18 Hastings Ho
19 Wolfe Ho
20 Malabar Ct
21 Commonwealth Ave
22 Charnock Ho
23 Canning Ho
24 Cornwallis Ho
25 Commonwealth Ave
26 Champlain Ho
27 Grey Ho
28 Durban Ho
29 Baird Ho
30 Campbell Ho
31 Mitchell Ho
32 Denham Ho
33 Mackay Ho
34 Evans Ho
35 Davis Ho
36 Mandela Cl
C1 1 Bridge Avenue Mans
2 Bridgeview
3 College Ct
4 Beatrice Ho
5 Amelia Ho
6 Edith Ho
7 Joanna Ho
8 Mary Ho
9 Adela Ho
10 Sophia Ho
11 Henrietta Ho
12 Charlotte Ho
13 Alexandra Ho
14 Bath Pl
15 Elizabeth Ho
16 Margaret Ho
17 Peabody Est
18 Eleanor Ho
19 Isabella Ho
20 Caroline Ho
21 Chancellors Wharf
22 Sussex Pl
C2 1 Phoenix Lodge Mans
2 Samuel's Cl
3 Broadway Arc
4 Brook Ho
5 Hammersmith Broadway
6 Broadway Ctr The
7 Cambridge Ct
8 Ashcroft Sq
C4 1 Verulam Ho
2 Grove Mans
3 Frobisher Ct
4 Library Mans
5 Pennard Mans
6 New Shepherd's Bush Mkt
7 Kerrington Ct
8 Granville Mans
9 Romney Ct
10 Rayner Ct
11 Sulgrave Gdns
12 Bamborough Gdns
13 Hillary Ct
14 Market Studios
15 Lanark Mans
C5 1 Linden Ct
2 Frithville Ct
3 Blomfield Mans
4 Poplar Mews
5 Hopgood St
6 Westwood Ho
7 Stanlake Mews
8 Stanlake Villas
9 Alexandra Mans
D3 1 Grosvenor Residences
2 Blythe Mews
3 Burnand Ho
4 Bradford Ho
5 Springvale Terr
6 Ceylon Rd
7 Walpole Ct
8 Bronte Ct
9 Boswell Ct
10 Souldern Rd
11 Brook Green Flats
12 Haarlem Rd
13 Stafford Mans
14 Lionel Mans
15 Barradell Ho
D4 1 Vanderbilt Villas
2 Bodington Ct
3 Kingham Cl
4 Clearwater Terr
5 Lorne Gdns
6 Cameret Ct
7 Bush Ct
8 Shepherds Ct
9 Rockley Ct
10 Grampians The
11 Charcroft Ct
12 Addison Park Mans
13 Sinclair Mans
14 Fountain Ct
15 Woodford Ct
16 Roseford Ct
17 Woodstock Studios
D5 1 St Katherine's Wlk
2 Dorrit Ho
3 Pickwick Ho
4 Dombey Ho
5 Caranday Villas
6 Mortimer Ho
7 Nickleby Ho
8 Stebbing Ho
9 Boxmoor Ho
10 Poynter Ho
11 Swanscombe Ho
12 Darnley Terr
13 Norland Ho
14 Hume Ho
15 Boundary Ho
16 Norland Rd
17 Helix Ct
D6 1 Frinstead Ho
2 Hurstway Wlk
3 Testerton Wlk
4 Grenfell Wlk
5 Grenfell Twr
6 Barandon Wlk
7 Treadgold Ho
8 St Clements Ct
9 Willow Way
10 Florence Ho
11 Dora Ho
12 Carton Ho
13 Agnes Ho
14 Marley Ho
15 Estella Ho
16 Waynflete Sq
17 Pippin Ho
18 Baseline Business Studios

118

A1 1 Hope Ct
2 West Point
3 Centre Point
4 East Point
5 Proctor Ho
6 Tovy Ho
7 Avondale Pavement
8 Brettinghurst
9 Colechurch Ho
10 Harman Cl
11 Avondale Ho
12 Lanark Ho
13 George Elliston Ho
14 Eric Wilkins Ho
15 Six Bridges Ind Est
16 St James Ind Mews
17 Winter Lo
18 Fern Wlk
19 Ivy Ct
20 Fallow Ct
21 Culloden Cl
22 Archers Lo
A2 1 Cadbury Way
2 Robert Bell Ho
3 Robert Jones Ho
4 William Rushbrooke Ho
5 Helen Taylor Ho
6 Peter Hills Ho
7 Charles Mackenzie Ho
8 Drappers Way
9 Racs Flats
10 Abbey Gdns
11 Mayfair Ho
12 Windmill Cl
13 Maria Cl
14 Townsend Ho
15 Mason Ho
16 Kotree Way
17 Hannah Mary Way
18 Langdon Way
19 Whittaker Way
A3 1 Rudge Ho
2 Spenlow Ho
3 Darnay Ho
4 Carton Ho
5 Giles Ho
6 Bowley Ho
7 Casby Ho
8 Sun Pas
9 Ness St
10 Voyager Bsns Est
11 Dockley Road Ind Est
12 Spa Ct
13 Discovery Bsns Pk
14 Priter Road Hostel
15 Salisbury Ct
16 William Ellis Way
17 John McKenna Wlk
18 Toussaint Wlk
19 Gillison Wlk
20 Bromfield Ct
21 Ben Smith Way
22 Major Rd
23 Old Jamaica Bsns Est
A4 1 Providence
2 Springalls Wharf
3 Flockton St
4 Meridian Ct
5 East La
6 Luna Ho
7 Axis Ct
8 Farthing Alley
9 Peter Butler Ho
10 Brownlow Ho
11 Tapley Ho
12 Copperfield Ho
13 Dombey Ho
14 Fleming Ho
15 Parkers Row
16 Wade Ho
17 Bardell Ho
18 Nickleby Ho
19 John Felton Rd
20 Flockton St
21 Pickwick Ho
22 Oliver Ho
23 Weller Ho
24 Haredale Ho
25 Havisham Ho
26 Tupman Ho
27 Micawber Ho
28 Wrayburn Ho
29 Dartle Ct
30 Waterside Cl
31 Burnaby Ct
32 Wickfield Ho
33 Fountain Ho
34 Fountain Green Sq
35 St Saviours Ho
36 Providence Sq
A5 1 Trade Winds Ct
2 Spice Ct
3 Leeward Ct
4 Bridgeport Pl
5 Tamarind Yd
6 Cape Yd
7 Nightingale Ho
8 St Anthony's Cl
9 Stockholm Way
10 Miah Terr
11 Seville Ho
12 Douthwaite Sq
13 Codling Cl
14 Hermitage Ct
15 Capital Wharf
16 Cinnabar Wharf East
17 Cinnabar Wharf Central
18 Cinnabar Wharf West
19 Halcyon Wharf
A6 1 Conant Mews
2 Hanson Ho
3 Royal Tower Lo
4 Victoria Ct
5 Swan Pas
6 Royal Mint Pl
7 Peabody Est
8 Florin Ct
9 Flank St
10 Onedin Point
11 Liberty Ho
12 Ensign Ct
13 Sapphire Ct
14 Graces Alley
15 George Leybourne Ho
16 Fletcher St
17 Hatton Ho
18 Noble Ho
19 Shearsmith Ho
20 Wellclose St
21 Telford's Yd
22 Breezer's Ct
23 Pennington Ct
B1 1 Hockney Ct
2 Toulouse Ct
3 Lowry Ct
4 Barry Ho
5 Lewis Ct
6 Gainsborough Ct
7 Renoir Ct
8 Blake Ct
9 Raphael Ct
10 Rembrandt Ct
11 Constable Ct
12 Da Vinci Ct
13 Gaugin Ct
14 Michelangelo Ct
15 Monet Ct
16 Weald Cl
17 Jasmin Lo
18 Birchmere Lo
19 Weybridge Ct
20 Florence Ho
21 Gleneagles Cl
22 Sunningdale Cl
23 Muirfield Cl
24 Turnberry Cl
25 St Andrews Cl
26 Kingsdown Cl
27 St Davids Cl
28 Galway Cl
29 Edenbridge Cl
30 Birkdale Cl
31 Tralee Ct
32 Woburn Ct
33 Belfry Cl
34 Troon Cl
35 Holywell Cl
B2 1 Market Pl
2 Trappes Ho
3 Thurland Ho
4 Ramsfort Ho
5 Hambley Ho
6 Holford Ho
7 Pope Ho
8 Southwell Ho
9 Mortain Ho
10 Radcliffe Ho
11 Southwark Park Est
12 Galleywall Road Trad Est
13 Trevithick Ho
14 Barlow Ho
15 Donkin Ho
16 Landmann Ho
17 Fitzmaurice Ho
18 Dodd Ho
B3 1 Perryn Rd
2 Chalfont Ho
3 Prestwood Ho
4 Farmer Ho
5 Gataker Ho
6 Gataker St
7 Cornick Ho
8 Glebe Ho
9 Matson Ho
10 Hickling Ho
11 St Andrews Ho
B4 1 Butterfield Cl
2 Janeway Pl
3 Trotwood Ho
4 Maylie Ho
5 Cranbourn Pas
6 Cranbourn Ho
7 Cherry Garden Ho
8 Burton Ho
9 Morriss Ho
10 Dixon's Alley
11 King Edward The Third Mews
12 Cathay St
13 Mission The
14 Millstream Ho
B5 1 China Ct
2 Wellington Terr
3 Stevedore St
4 Portland Sq
5 Reardon Ho
6 Lowder Ho
7 Meeting House Alley
8 Farthing Fields
9 Oswell Ho
10 Park Lo
11 Doughty Ct
12 Inglefield Sq
13 Chopin's Ct
14 Welsh Ho
15 Hilliard Ho
16 Clegg St
17 Tasman Ho
18 Ross Ho
19 Wapping Dock St
20 Bridewell Pl
21 New Tower Bldgs
22 Tower Bldgs
23 Chimney Ct
24 Jackman Ho
25 Fenner Ho
26 Franklin Ho
27 Frobisher Ho
28 Flinders Ho
29 Chancellor Ho
30 Beechey Ho
31 Reardon Path
32 Parry Ho
33 Vancover Ho
34 Willoughby Ho
35 Sanctuary The
36 Dundee Ct
37 Pierhead Wharf
38 Scandrett St
39 St Johns Ct
B6 1 Newton Ho
2 Richard Neale Ho
3 Maddocks Ho
4 Cornwall St
5 Brockmer Ho
6 Dellow Ho
7 Bewley Ho
8 Artichoke Hill
9 Queen Anne Terr
10 King Henry Terr
11 King Charles Terr
12 Queen Victoria Terr
13 Sovereign Ct
14 Princes Court Bsns Ctr
15 Kingsley Mews
C2 1 Damory Ho
2 Antony Ho
3 Roderick Ho
4 Pedworth Gdns
5 Banner Ct
6 Rotherhithe Bsns Est
7 Beamish Ho
8 Corbetts Pas
9 Gillam Ho
10 Richard Ho
11 George Walter Ho
12 Westlake
13 Adron Ho
14 McIntosh Ho
C3 1 Blick Ho
2 Neptune Ho
3 Scotia Ct
4 Murdoch Ho
5 Edmonton Ct
6 Niagara Ct
7 Columbia Point
8 Ritchie Ho
9 Wells Ho
10 Helen Peele Cotts
11 Orchard Ho
12 Dock Offices
13 Landale Ho
14 Courthope Ho
15 Hithe Gr
16 China Hall Mews
C4 1 Mayflower St
2 St Mary's Est
3 Rupack St
4 Frank Whymark Ho
5 Adams Gardens Est
6 Hatteraick St
7 East India Ct
8 Bombay Ct
9 Stable Ho
10 Grannary The
11 Riverside
12 Cumberland Wharf
13 Seaford Ho
14 Hythe Ho
15 Sandwich Ho
16 Winchelsea Ho
17 Rye Ho
18 Kenning St
19 Western Pl
20 Ainsty St
21 Pine Ho
22 Beech Ho
23 Larch Ho
24 Turner Ct
25 Seth St
26 Risdon Ho
27 Risdon St
28 Aylton Est
29 Manitoba Ct
30 Calgary Ct
31 Irwell Est
32 St Olav's Sq
33 City Bsns Ctr
C5 1 John Rennie Wlk
2 Malay Ho
3 Wainwright Ho
4 Riverside Mans
5 Shackleton Ho
6 Whitehorn Ho
7 Wavel Ct
8 Prusom's Island
C6 1 Shadwell Pl
2 Gosling Ho
3 Vogler Ho
4 Donovan Ho
5 Knowlden Ho
6 Chamberlain Ho
7 Moore Ho
8 Thornewill Ho
9 Fisher Ho
10 All Saints Ct
11 Coburg Dwellings
12 Lowood Ho
13 Solander Gdns
14 Chancery Bldgs
15 Ring Ho
16 Juniper St
17 Gordon Ho
18 West Block
19 North Block
20 South Block
21 Ikon Ho
D2 1 John Kennedy Ho
2 Brydale Ho
3 Balman Ho
4 Tissington Ct
5 Harbord Ho
6 Westfield Ho
7 Albert Starr Ho
8 John Brent Ho
9 William Evans Ho
10 Raven Ho
11 Egret Ho
12 Fulmar Ho
13 Dunlin Ho
14 Siskin Ho
15 Sheldrake Ho
16 Buchanan Ct
17 Burrage Ct
18 Biddenham Ho
19 Ayston Ho
20 Empingham Ho
21 Deanshanger Ho
22 Codicote Ho
23 Buryfield Ct
D4 1 Schooner Cl
2 Dolphin Cl
3 Clipper Cl
4 Deauville Ct
5 Colette Ct
6 Coniston Ct
7 Virginia Ct
8 Derwent Ct
9 Grantham Ct
10 Serpentine Ct
11 Career Ct
12 Lacine Ct
13 Fairway Ct
14 Harold Ct
15 Spruce Ho
16 Cedar Ho
17 Sycamore Ho
18 Woodland Cres
19 Poplar Ho
20 Adelphi Ct
21 Basque Ct
22 Aberdale Ct
23 Quilting Ct
24 Chargrove Cl
25 Radley Ct
26 Greenacre Sq
27 Maple Leaf Sq
28 Stanhope Cl
29 Hawke Pl
30 Drake Cl
31 Brass Talley Alley
32 Monkton Ho
33 James Ho
34 Wolfe Cres
D5 1 Clarence Mews
2 Raleigh Ct
3 Katherine Cl
4 Woolcombes Ct

5 Tudor Ct
6 Quayside Ct
7 Princes Riverside Rd
8 Surrey Ho
9 Tideway Ct
10 Edinburgh Ct
11 Falkirk Ct
12 Byelands Cl
13 Gwent Ct
14 Lavender Ho
15 Abbotshade Rd
16 Bellamy's Ct
17 Blenheim Ct
18 Sandringham Ct
19 Hampton Ct
20 Windsor Ct
21 Balmoral Ct
22 Westminster Ct
23 Beatson Wlk
6 1 Barnardo Gdns
2 Roslin Ho
3 Glamis Est
4 Peabody Est
5 East Block
6 Highway Trad Ctr The
7 Highway Bsns Pk The
8 Cranford Cotts
9 Ratcliffe Orch
10 Scotia Bldg
11 Mauretania Bldg
12 Compania Bldg
13 Sirius Bldg
14 Unicorn Bldg
15 Keepier Wharf

119

2 1 Trafalgar Cl
2 Hornblower Cl
3 Cunard Wlk
4 Caronia Ct
5 Carinthia Ct
6 Freswick Ho
7 Graveley Ho
8 Husbourne Ho
9 Crofters Ct
10 Pomona Ho
11 Hazelwood Ho
12 Cannon Wharf Bsns Ctr
13 Bence Ho
14 Clement Ho
15 Pendennis Ho
16 Lighter Cl
17 Mast Ct
18 Rushcutters Ct
19 Boat Lifter Way
5 1 Edward Sq
2 Prince Regent Ct
3 Codrington Ct
4 Pennington Ct
5 Cherry Ct
6 Ash Ct
7 Beech Ct
8 Hazel Ct
9 Laurel Ct
6 1 St Georges Sq
2 Drake Ho
3 Osprey Ho
4 Fleet Ho
5 Gainsborough Ho
6 Victory Pl
7 Challenger Ho
8 Conrad Ho
9 Lock View Ct
10 Shoulder of Mutton Alley
11 Frederick Sq
12 Helena Sq
13 Elizabeth Sq
14 Sophia Sq
15 William Sq
16 Lamb Ct
17 Lockside
18 Adriatic Bldg
19 Ionian Bldg
20 Regents Gate Ho
1 1 Gransden Ho
2 Daubeney Twr
3 North Ho
4 Rochfort Ho
5 Keppel Ho
6 Camden Ho
7 Sanderson Ho
8 Berkeley Ho
9 Strafford Ho
10 Richman Ho
11 Hurleston Ho
12 Grafton Ho
13 Fulcher Ho
14 Citrus Ho
2 1 Windsock Cl
2 St George's Mews
3 Linberry Wlk
4 Lanyard Ho
5 Golden Hind Pl
6 James Lind Ho
7 Harmon Ho
8 Pelican Ho
9 Bembridge Ho
10 Terrace The
11 George Beard Rd
12 Colonnade The
13 Pepys Ent Ctr
B6 1 Hamilton Ho
2 Imperial Ho
3 Oriana Ho
4 Queens Ct
5 Brightlingsea Pl
6 Faraday Ho
7 Ropemaker's Fields
8 Oast Ct
9 Mitre The
10 Bate St
11 Joseph Irwin Ho
12 Padstow Ho
13 Bethlehem Ho
14 Saunders Cl
15 Roche Ho
16 Stocks Pl
17 Trinidad Ho
18 Grenada Ho
19 Kings Ho
20 Dunbar Wharf
21 Limekiln Wharf
22 Belgrave Ct
23 Eaton Ho
C1 1 Hudson Ct
2 Shackleton Ct
3 De Gama Pl
4 Mercator Pl
5 Maritime Quay
6 Perry Ct
7 Amundsen Ct
C2 1 Nova Bldg
2 Apollo Bldg
3 Gaverick Mews
4 Windmill Ho
5 Orion Point
6 Galaxy Bldg
7 Venus Ho
8 Olympian Ct
9 Poseidon Ct
10 Mercury Ct
11 Aphrodite Ct
12 Cyclops Mews
13 Neptune Ct
14 Artemis Ct
15 Hera Ct
16 Ares Ct
17 Ringwood Gdns
18 Dartmoor Wlk
19 Rothsay Wlk
20 Ashdown Wlk
21 Radnor Wlk
22 Ironmonger's Pl
23 Britannia Rd
24 Deptford Ferry Rd
25 Magellan Pl
26 Dockers Tanner Rd
C3 1 Bowsprit Point
2 St Hubert's Ho
3 John Tucker Ho
4 Broadway Wlk
5 Nash Ho
6 Fairlead Ho
7 Crosstrees Ho
8 Stanliff Ho
9 Keelson Ho
10 Clara Grant Ho
11 Gilbertson Ho
12 Scoulding Ho
13 Hibbert Ho
14 Cressall Ho
15 Alexander Ho
16 Kedge Ho
C4 1 Anchorage Point
2 Waterman Bldg
3 Jefferson Bldg
4 Pierpoint Bldg
5 Franklin Bldg
6 Vanguard Bldg
7 Edison Bldg
8 Seacon Twr
9 Naxos Bldg
10 Express Wharf
11 Hutching's Wharf
12 Tobago St
13 Bellamy Cl
14 Dowlen Ct
15 Cochrane Ho
16 Beatty Ho
17 Scott Ho
18 Laybourne Ho
19 Ensign Ho
20 Beaufort Ho
21 Spinnaker Ho
22 Bosun Cl
23 Topmast Point
24 Turner Ho
25 Constable Ho
26 Knighthead Point
C6 1 West India Ho
2 Berber Pl
3 Birchfield Ho
4 Elderfield Ho
5 Thornfield Ho
6 Gorsefield Ho
7 Arborfield Ho
8 Colborne Ho
9 East India Bldgs
10 Compass Point
11 Salter St
12 Garland Ct
13 Bogart Ct
14 Fonda Ct
15 Welles Ct
16 Rogers Ct
17 Premier Pl
18 Kelly Ct
19 Flynn Ct
20 Mary Jones Ho
21 Cannon Dr
22 Horizon Bldg
D1 1 Slipway Ho
2 Taffrail Ho
3 Platehouse The
4 Wheelhouse The
5 Chart House The
6 Port House The
7 Beacon Ho
8 Blasker Wlk
9 Maconochies Rd
D2 1 Brassey Ho
2 Triton Ho
3 Warspite Ho
4 Rodney Ho
5 Conway Ho
6 Exmouth Ho
7 Akbar Ho
8 Arethusa Ho
9 Tasman Ct
10 Cutty Sark Ho
D3 1 Turnberry Quay
2 Balmoral Ho
3 Aegon Ho
4 Marina Point
D6 1 Westcott Ho
2 Corry Ho
3 Malam Gdns
4 Blomfield Ho
5 Devitt Ho
6 Leyland Ho
7 Wigram Ho
8 Willis Ho
9 Balsam Ho
10 Finch's Ct
11 Poplar Bath St
12 Lawless St
13 Storey Ho
14 Abbot Ho
15 Woodall Cl
16 Landon Wlk
17 Goodhope Ho
18 Goodfaith Ho
19 Winant Ho
20 Goodspeed Ho
21 Lubbock Ho
22 Goodwill Ho
23 Martindale Ho
24 Holmsdale Ho
25 Norwood Ho
26 Constant Ho

120

A2 1 St John's Ho
2 Betty May Gray Ho
3 Castleton Ho
4 Urmston Ho
5 Salford Ho
6 Capstan Ho
7 Frigate Ho
8 Galleon Ho
9 Barons Lo
A3 1 Cardale St
2 Hickin St
3 John McDonald Ho
4 Thorne Ho
5 Skeggs Ho
6 St Bernard Ho
7 Kimberley Ho
8 Kingdon Ho
9 Killoran Ho
10 Alastor Ho
11 Lingard Ho
12 Yarrow Ho
13 Sandpiper Ct
14 Nightingale Ct
15 Robin Ct
16 Heron Ct
17 Ferndown Lo
18 Crosby Ho
A4 1 Llandovery Ho
2 Rugless Ho
3 Ash Ho
4 Elm Ho
5 Cedar Ho
6 Castalia Sq
7 Aspect Ho
8 Normandy Ho
9 Valiant Ho
10 Tamar Ho
11 Watkins Ho
12 Alice Shepherd Ho
13 Oak Ho
14 Ballin Ct
15 Martin Ct
16 Grebe Ct
17 Kingfisher Ct
18 Walkers Lo
19 Antilles Bay
A5 1 Lumina Bldg
2 Nova Ct W
3 Nova Ct E
4 Aurora Bldg
5 Arran Ho
6 Kintyre Ho
7 Vantage Mews
8 Managers St
9 Horatio Pl
10 Concordia Wharf
A6 1 Discovery Ho
2 Mountague Pl
3 Virginia Ho
4 Collins Ho
5 Lawless Ho
6 Carmichael Ho
7 Commodore Ho
8 Mermaid Ho
9 Bullivant St
10 Anderson Ho
11 Mackrow Wlk
12 Robin Hood Gdns
13 Prestage Way
B2 1 Verwood Lo
2 Fawley Lo
3 Lyndhurst Lo
4 Blyth Cl
5 Farnworth Ho
6 Francis Cl
B6 1 Quixley St
2 Romney Ho
3 Pumping Ho
4 Switch Ho
5 Wingfield Ct
6 Explorers Ct
7 Sexton Ct
8 Keel Ct
9 Bridge Ct
10 Sail Ct
11 Settlers Ct
12 Pilgrims Mews
13 Studley Ct
14 Wotton Ct
15 Cape Henry Ct
16 Bartholomew Ct
17 Adventurers Ct
18 Susan Constant Ct
19 Atlantic Ct
C1 1 Bellot Gdns
2 Thornley Pl
3 King William La
4 Bolton Ho
5 Miles Ho
6 Mell St
7 Sam Manners Ho
8 Hatcliffe Almshouses
9 Woodland Wlk
10 Earlswood Cl
D1 1 Baldrey Ho
2 Christie Ho
3 Dyson Ho
4 Cliffe Ho
5 Moore Ho
6 Collins Ho
7 Lockyer Ho
8 Halley Ho
9 Kepler Ho
10 Sailacre Ho
11 Union Pk
D3 1 Teal St
2 Maurer Ct
3 Mudlarks Blvd
4 Renaissance Wlk
5 Alamaro Lo

121

A1 1 Layfield Ho
2 Westerdale Rd
3 Mayston Mews
4 Station Mews Terr
A5 1 Capulet Mews
2 Pepys Cres
3 De Quincey Mews
4 Hardy Ave
5 Tom Jenkinson Rd
6 Kennacraig Cl
7 Charles Flemwell Mews
8 Gatcombe Rd
9 Badminton Mews
10 Holyrood Mews
11 Britannia Gate
12 Dalemain Mews
13 Bowes-Lyon Hall
14 Lancaster hall
15 Victoria Hall
A6 1 Clements Ave
2 Martindale Ave
3 Balearic Apts
4 Marmara Apts
5 Baltic Apts
6 Coral Apts
7 Aegean Apts
8 Capital East Apts
B1 1 Phipps Ho
2 Hartwell Ho
3 Nicholas Stacey Ho
4 Frank Burton Cl
B5 1 Beaulieu Ave
2 Charles Whincup Rd
3 Audley Dr
4 Julia Garfield Mews
5 Rayleigh Rd
6 Pirie St
7 Royal Victoria Pl
8 Pankhurst Ave
9 West Mersea Cl
10 Ramsgate Cl
11 Windsor Hall
12 Munning Ho
13 Drake Hall
14 Jane Austen Hall
15 Eastern Quay
C1 1 Ransom Rd
2 Linton Cl
3 Cedar Pl
4 Gooding Ho
5 Valiant Ho
6 Chaffey Ho
7 Benn Ho
8 Wellesley Cl
9 Gollogly Terr

122

A2 1 Harden Ct
2 Albion Ct
3 Viking Ho
4 Zealand Ho
5 Glenalvon Way
6 Parish Wharf
7 Elsinore Ho
8 Lolland Ho
9 Denmark Ho
10 Jutland Ho
11 Tivoli Gdns
12 Rance Ho
13 Peel Yates Ho
14 Rosebank Wlk
15 Paradise Pl
16 Woodville St
B2 1 Bowling Green Row
2 Sarah Turnbull Ho
3 Brewhouse Rd
4 Red Barracks Rd
5 Marine Dr
6 Hastings Ho
7 Centurion Ct
8 Cambridge Ho
9 Churchill Ct
10 Elizabeth Ct
11 Cambridge Barracks Rd
12 Len Clifton Ho
13 Granby Ho
14 Harding Ho
15 Rutland Ho
16 Townshend Ho
17 Rendlebury Ho
18 Milne Ho
19 Mulgrave Ho
20 Murray Ho
21 Chatham Ho
22 Biddulph Ho
23 Carew Ho
24 Eleanor Wlk
C2 1 Preston Ho
2 Lindsay Ho
3 Fraser Ho
4 Pickering Ho
5 Watergate Ho
6 Grinling Ho
7 Glebe Ho
8 Elliston Ho
9 Sir Martin Bowes Ho
10 Jim Bradley Cl
11 Bathway
12 Limavady Ho
13 Slater Cl
14 Vista Bldg The
C5 1 Westland Ho
2 Queensland Ho
3 Pier Par
4 Woodman Par
5 Shaw Ho
6 Glen Ho
7 Brocklebank Ho
D1 1 Branham Ho
2 Ford Ho
3 Wilford Ho
4 Parker Ho
5 Stirling Ho
6 Twiss Ho
7 Hewett Ho
8 De Haviland Dr
9 Schoolhouse Yd
D2 1 Beresford Sq
2 Central Ct
3 Walpole Pl
4 Anglesea Ave
5 Troy Ct
6 Ormsby Point
7 Haven Lo
8 Green Lawns
9 Eardley Point
10 Sandham Point
11 Bingham Point
12 Anglesea Mews
13 Masons Hill
14 Maritime Ho

123

A1 1 Glenmount Path
2 Claymill Ho
3 St James Hts
4 St Margaret's Path
5 George Akass Ho
A3 1 Wayatt Point
2 Albert Ho
3 Building 50
4 Building 49
5 Building 48
6 Building 47
7 Building 36
8 Blenheim Ho
9 Wilson Ct
B1 1 Bert Reilly Ho
B3 1 Apollo Way
2 Senator Wlk
3 Mallard Path
4 Fortune Wlk
C1 1 Fox Hollow Cl
2 Goldsmid St
C2 1 Gavin Ho
2 Richard Neve Ho
3 Bateson St
4 Lewin Ct

124

B5 1 Rowntree Path
2 MacAulay Way
3 Manning Ct
4 Chadwick Ct
5 Simon Ct
B6 1 Beveridge Ct
2 Hammond Way
3 Leonard Robbins Path
4 Lansbury Ct
5 Raymond Postgate Ct
6 Webb Ct
7 Curtis Way
8 Lytton Strachey Path
9 Keynes Ct
10 Marshall Path
11 Cross Ct
12 Octavia Way
13 Passfield Path
14 Mill Ct
15 Besant Ct
C3 1 Hermitage Cl
2 Chantry Cl
C4 1 Binsey Wlk
2 Tilehurst Point
3 Blewbury Ho
4 Coralline Wlk
5 Evenlode Ho
C5 1 Kingsley Ct
2 Wilberforce Ct
3 Shaftesbury Ct
4 Hazlitt Ct
5 Ricardo Path
6 Nassau Path
7 Malthus Path
8 Bright Ct
9 Cobden Ct
D4 1 Oakenholt Ho
2 Trewsbury Ho
3 Penton Ho
4 Osney Ho
5 St Helens Rd
6 Clewer Ho
7 Maplin Ho
8 Wyfold Ho
9 Hibernia Point
10 Duxford Ho
11 Radley Ho
12 Limestone Wlk
13 Masham Ho
14 Jacob Ho

125

A3 1 Harlequin Ho
2 Dexter Ho
3 Argali Ho
4 Mangold Way
5 Lucerne Ct
6 Holstein Way
7 Abbotswood Cl
8 Plympton Cl

125 A3
9 Benedict Cl
B1 1 Shakespeare Ho
2 Tennyson Ho
3 Dickens Ho
4 Scott Ho
5 Lansbury Ho
6 Shaw Ho
7 Chestnuts The
C1 1 Stevanne Ct
2 Tolcairn Ct
3 Chalfont Ct
4 Alonso Ho
5 Ariel Ct
6 Miranda Ho
7 Prospero Ho
8 Laurels The
9 Camden Ct
10 Newnham Lo
11 Court Lo
12 Flaxman Ct
13 Hertford Wlk
14 Riverview Ct
15 Winchester Ct
C2 1 Brushwood Lo
2 Bletchington Ct
3 Upper Sheridan Rd
4 William Ct
5 Samson Ct
6 Cowper Rd
7 Venmead Ct
C3 1 Cressingham Ct
2 Telford Ho
3 Kelvin Ho
4 Faraday Ho
5 Jenner Ho
6 Keir Hardie Ho
7 Lennox Ho
8 Mary Macarthur Ho
9 Elizabeth Garrett Anderson Ho
10 William Smith Ho
11 Baden Powell Ho
12 Baird Ho
13 Boyle Ho

129
D1 1 Heathwood Ct
2 Aldermead
3 Northumberland Ct

130
C4 1 Osterley Lo
2 St Andrew's Cl
3 Parkfield
4 Fairways
5 Granwood Ct
6 Grovewood Ct

131
A2 1 Brewery Mews Bsns Ctr
2 Forge Lo
3 Pulteney Cl
4 Tolson Ho
5 Percy Gdns
6 Wynne Ct
7 Wisdom Ct
8 Swann Ct
9 Shrewsbury Wlk
10 King's Terr
11 Van Gogh Cl
12 Holme Ct
C5 1 Canute Ho
2 Spruce Ho
3 Moorings Ho
4 Jessops Wharf
5 Corsell Ho
6 Barnes Qtr
7 Dorey Ho
8 Tanyard Ho
9 Booth Ho
10 Oakbark Ho
11 Bordeston Ct
12 Shire Pl
D5 1 Galba Ct
2 Servius Ct
3 Maurice Ct
4 Leo Ct
5 Otho Ct
6 Nero Ct
7 Romulus Ct
8 Pump Alley
D6 1 Brockshot Cl
2 Westbury Pl
3 Brook La N
4 Braemar Ct
5 Brook Ct
6 Clifden Ho
7 Cedar Ct
8 Cranbrook Ct
9 Somerset Lo
10 Alexandra Rd
11 Berkeley Ho
12 Watermans Ct
13 Ferry Quays Ctyd

132
A1 1 St John's Gr
2 Michel's Row
3 Michelsdale Dr
4 Blue Anchor Alley
5 Clarence St
6 Sun Alley
7 Thames Link Ho
8 Benns Wlk
9 Waterloo Pl
10 Northumbria Ct
A6 1 Ferry Sq
2 Watermans Ct
3 Wilkes Rd
4 Albany Par
5 Charlton Ho
6 Albany Ho
7 Alma Ho
8 Griffin Ct
9 Cressage Ho
10 Tunstall Wlk
11 Trimmer Wlk
12 Running Horse Yd
13 Mission Sq
14 Distillery Wlk
B1 1 Towers The
2 Longs Ct
3 Sovereign Ct
4 Robinson Ct
5 Calvert Ct
6 Bedford Ct
7 Hickey's Almshouses
8 Church Estate Almshouses
9 Richmond International Bsns Ctr
10 Abercorn Mews
B4 1 Primrose Ho
2 Lawman Ct
3 Royston Ct
4 Garden Ct
5 Capel Lo
6 Devonshire Ct
7 Celia Ct
8 Rosslyn Ho
9 Branstone Ct
10 Lamerton Lo
11 Kew Lo
12 Dunraven Ho
13 Stoneleigh Lo
14 Tunstall Ct
15 Voltaire
C4 1 Clarendon Ct
2 Quintock Ho
3 Broome Ct
4 Lonsdale Mews
5 Elizabeth Cotts
6 Sandways
7 Victoria Cotts
8 North Ave
9 Grovewood
10 Hamilton Ho
11 Melvin Ct
12 Royal Par
13 Power Ho
14 Station Ave
15 Blake Mews
D1 1 Hershell Ct
2 Deanhill Ct
3 Park Sheen
4 Furness Lo
5 Merricks Ct
D4 1 Terrano Ho
2 Oak Ho
3 Aura Ho
4 Maple Ho
5 Cedar Ho
6 Saffron Ho
7 Lime Ho
8 Lavender Ho
9 Juniper Ho

133
B2 1 Rann Ho
2 Craven Ho
3 John Dee Ho
4 Kindell Ho
5 Montgomery Ho
6 Avondale Ho
7 Addington Ct
8 Dovecote Gdns
9 Firmston Ho
10 Glendower Gdns
11 Chestnut Ave
12 Trehern Rd
13 Rock Ave
D3 1 Melrose Rd
2 Seaforth Lo
3 St John's Gr
4 Sussex Ct
5 Carmichael Ct
6 Hampshire Ct
7 Thorne Pas
8 Brunel Ct
9 Beverley Path

134
D1 1 Olivette St
2 Mascotte Rd
3 Glegg Pl
4 Crown Ct
5 Charlwood Terr
6 Percy Laurie Ho
D6 1 Cobb's Hall
2 Dorset Mans
3 St Clements Mans
4 Bothwell St
5 Hawksmoor St

135
B3 1 Plato Pl
2 Mustow Pl
3 Laurel Bank Gdns
4 Ranelagh Mans
5 Churchfield Mans
6 Bear Croft Ho
7 Elysium Gate
8 Ethel Rankin Ct
9 Arthur Henderson Ho
10 William Banfield Ho
11 Melbray Mews
D3 1 Brightwells
2 Broughton Road App
3 Bulow Ct
4 Langford Rd
5 Elizabeth Barnes Ct
6 Snowbury Rd

136
A2 1 Molasses Ho
2 Molasses Row
3 Cinnamon Row
4 Calico Ho
5 Calico Row
6 Port Ho
7 Square Rigger Row
8 Trade Twr
9 Ivory Ho
10 Spice Ct
11 Sherwood Ct
12 Mendip Ct
13 Chalmers Ho
14 Coral Row
15 Ivory Sq
16 Kingfisher Ho
B1 1 Burke Ho
2 Fox Ho
3 Buxton Ho
4 Pitt Ho
5 Ramsey Ho
6 Beverley Cl
7 Florence Ho
8 Linden Ct
9 Dorcas Ct
10 Johnson Ct
11 Agnes Ct
12 Hilltop Ct
13 Courtyard The
14 Old Laundry The
15 Oberstein Rd
16 Fineran Ct
17 Sangora Rd
18 Harvard Mans
19 Plough Mews
B2 1 Benham Cl
2 Milner Ho
3 McManus Ho
4 Wilberforce Ho
5 Wheeler Ct
6 Sporle Ct
7 Holliday Sq
8 John Parker Sq
9 Carmichael Cl
10 Fenner Sq
11 Clark Lawrence Ct
12 Shaw Ct
13 Sendall Ct
14 Livingstone Rd
15 Farrant Ho
16 Jackson Ho
17 Darien Ho
18 Shepard Ho
19 Ganley Ct
20 Arthur Newton Ho
21 Chesterton Ho
22 John Kirk Ho
23 Mantua St
24 Heaver Rd
25 Candlemakers
B3 1 Archer Ho
2 White Ho
3 Winfield Ho
4 Powrie Ho
5 Morgan Ct
6 Fairchild Cl
7 Musjid Rd
C2 1 Kiloh Ct
2 Lanner Ho
3 Griffon Ho
4 Kestrel Ho
5 Kite Ho
6 Peregrine Ho
7 Hawk Ho
8 Inkster Ho
9 Harrier Ho
10 Eagle Hts
11 Kingfisher Ct
12 Lavender Terr
13 Temple Ho
14 Ridley Ho
15 Eden Ho
16 Hertford Ct
17 Nepaul Rd
C3 1 Meecham Ct
2 McKiernan Ct
3 Banbury St
4 Colestown St
5 Crombie Mews
6 Frere St
D3 1 Stevenson Ho
2 Ambrose Mews
3 Harling Ct
4 Southside Quarter
5 Latchmere St
6 Dovedale Cotts
7 Roydon Cl
8 Castlemaine
9 Wittering Ho
10 Berry Ho
11 Weybridge Point

137
A2 1 Shaftesbury Park Chambers
2 Selborne
3 Rush Hill Mews
4 Marmion Mews
5 Crosland Pl
6 Craven Mews
7 Garfield Mews
8 Audley Cl
9 Basnett Rd
10 Tyneham Cl
11 Woodmere Cl
A3 1 Hopkinson Ho
2 MacDonald Ho
3 Rushlake Ho
4 Bishopstone Ho
5 Dresden Ho
6 Millgrove St
7 Farnhurst Ho
8 Walden Ho
9 Kennard St
10 Langhurst Ho
11 Atkinson Ho
12 Kennard Ho
13 Voltaire Ct
14 Barloch Ho
15 London Stone Bsns Est
B2 1 Turnchapel Mews
2 Redwood Mews
3 Phil Brown Pl
4 Bev Callender Cl
5 Keith Connor Cl
6 Tessa Sanderson Pl
7 Daley Thompson Way
8 Rashleigh Ct
9 Abberley Mews
10 Willow Lodge
11 Beaufoy Rd
B3 1 St Philip Sq
2 Montefiore St
3 Gambetta St
4 Scott Ct
5 Radcliffe Path
6 Moresby Wlk
7 Victorian Hts
C1 1 Polygon The
2 Windsor Ct
3 Trinity Cl
4 Studios The
5 Bourne Ho
C2 1 Clapham Manor Ct
2 Clarke Ho
3 Gables The
4 Sycamore Mews
5 Maritime Ho
6 Rectory Gdns
7 Floris Pl
C3 1 Seymour Ho
2 Lucas Ho
3 Durrington Twr
4 Amesbury Twr
5 Fovant Ct
6 Allington Ct
7 Welford Ct
8 Ilsley Ct
9 Blake Ct
10 Brooklands Ct
D1 1 Kendoa Rd
2 Felmersham Cl
3 Abbeville Mews
4 Saxon Ho
5 Gifford Ho
6 Teignmouth Cl
7 Holwood Pl
8 Oaklands Pl
9 Wilberforce Mews
10 William Bonney Est
D2 1 Chelsham Ho
2 Lynde Ho
3 Greener Ho
4 Towns Ho
5 Hugh Morgan Ho
6 Roy Ridley Ho
7 Lendal Terr
8 Slievemore Cl
9 Cadmus Cl
10 Clapham North Bsns Ctr
D3 1 Haltone Ho
2 Surcot Ho
3 Kingsley Ho
4 Wood Ho
5 Dalemain Ho
6 Fallodon Ho
7 Dartington Ho
8 Esher Ho
9 Kneller Ho
10 Lostock Ho
11 Croxteth Ho
12 Donnington Ho
13 Farnley Ho
14 Hardwick Ho
15 Bradfield Ho
16 Brocket Ho
17 Colchester Ho
18 Clive Ho
19 Chessington Ho
20 Rushbrook Ho
21 Stanmore Ho
22 Newton Ho
23 Netherby Ho
24 Oakwell Ho
25 Rydal Ho
26 Rushton Ho
27 Harcourt Ho
28 Metcalfe Ho
29 Lydwell Ho
30 Raleigh Ho
31 Spencer Ho
32 Shipley Ho
33 Naylor Ho
34 Mordaunt Ho
35 Stanley Ho
36 Alderley Ho
37 Effingham Ho
38 Grant Ho
39 Wilson Ho
40 Fraser Ho

138
A1 1 Morris Ho
2 Gye Ho
3 Clowes Ho
4 Thomas Ho
5 Stuart Ho
6 Storace Ho
7 Bedford Ho
8 Ascot Ct
9 Ascot Par
10 Ashmere Ho
11 Ashmere Gr
12 Ventura Ho
13 Vickery Ho
14 Stafford Mans
15 Beresford Ho
A2 1 Callingham Ho
2 Russell Pickering Ho
3 Ormerod Ho
4 Lopez Ho
5 Coachmaker Mews
A3 1 Barling Ct
2 Jeffrey's Ct
3 Brooks Ct
4 Dalmeny Ct
5 Fender Ct
6 Fishlock Ct
7 Bedser Ct
8 Gover Ct
9 Clarence Wlk
10 Barton Ct
11 Allom Ct
12 Garden Ho
13 Otha Ho
14 Hayward Ct
15 Surridge Ct
16 Knox Ct
17 Jephson Ct
18 Holmes Ct
19 McIntyre Ct
20 Richardson Ct
21 Cassell Ho
22 Pakington Ho
23 Bain Ho
24 Enfield Ho
25 Fawcett Ho
26 Sidgwick Ho
27 Jowett Ho
28 Beckett Ho
29 Arden Ho
30 Pinter Ho
31 Barrington Ct
32 Union Mews
B1 1 Freemens Hos
2 Roger's Almshouses
3 Gresham Almshouse
4 Exbury Ho
5 Glasbury Ho
6 Dalbury Ho
7 Fosbury Ho
8 Chalbury Ho
9 Neilson-Terry Ct
10 Pavilion Mans
11 Daisy Dormer Ct
12 George Lashwood C
13 Marie Lloyd Ct
14 Trinity Homes
15 Lethaby Ho
16 Edmundsbury Ct Est
17 Regis Pl
18 Marlborough Mews
19 Alpha Ho
20 Beta Pl
21 Cedars Ho
B2 1 Turberville Ho
2 Thrayle Ho
3 Percheron Ct
4 Draymans Ct
B3 1 Maurice Ho
2 Thring Ho
3 Paton Ho
4 Huxley Ho
5 Morell Ho
6 Mary Ho
7 Beale Ho
8 Rosa Parks Ho
9 Birrell Ho
10 Waltham Ho
11 Burford Ho
12 Thornicroft Ho
13 Addington Ho
14 Goffton Ho
15 Redmayne Ho
16 Norton Ho
17 Aytoun Ct
18 Colwall Ho
19 Burrow Ho
20 Wynter Ho
21 Crowhurst Ho
22 Lidcote Gdns
23 Cumnor Cl
24 Park View Mews
C1 1 Electric Mans
2 Electric La
3 Connaught Mans
4 Clifton Mans
5 Hereford Ho
6 Chaplin Ho
7 Brixton Oval
8 Lord David Pitt Ho
9 Marcus Garvey Way
10 Montego Cl
11 Bob Marley Way
12 Leeson Rd
C2 1 Buckmaster Cl
2 Albemarle Ho
3 Goodwood Mans
4 Angell Park Gdns
5 Fyfield Rd
6 Howard Ho
7 Harris Ho
8 Broadoak Ct
9 Burgate Ct
10 Witchwood Ho
11 Blacktree Mews
12 Chartham Ct
13 Chilham Ct
14 Northgate Ct
15 Westgate Ct
16 Dover Mans
C3 1 Norval Gn
2 Hilda Terr
3 Burton La
4 Church Gn
5 Lord Holland La
6 Sorrell Cl
7 Burton Rd
8 Holles Ho
9 Leys Ct
10 Warwick Ho
11 Fairfax Ho
12 Wayland Ho
13 Dudley Ho
14 Denchworth Ho
15 Fitzgerald Ho
16 Lambert Ho
17 Chute Ho
18 Bedwell Ho
19 Ferrey Mews
20 Serenaders Rd
21 Boatemah Wlk
22 Ireton Ho
23 Marston Ho
24 Morrison Rd
25 Fir Grove Rd
26 Shore Way
C4 1 Hector Ct
2 Jason Ct
3 Creon Ct
4 Hermes Ct
5 Argos Ct

6 Cadmus Ct
7 Appollo Ct
8 Mercury Ct
9 County Ho
10 Seasalter Ho
11 Downbarton Ho
12 Garlinge Ho
13 Moira Ho
14 Alvanley Ho
15 Woodchurch Ho
16 Durlock Ho
17 Hallam Ho
18 Whiteness Ho
19 Bromstone Ho
20 Penelope Ho
21 Melbourne Sq
22 Cloisters The
23 Cliffsend Ho
24 Sacketts Ho
25 Hanway Ho
26 Brickworth Ho
27 Redlynch Ho
28 Stodmarsh Ho
29 Kingsgate Ho
30 Chardin Ho
31 Annesley Ho
32 Knowlton Ho
33 Russell Gr
34 Eamann Casey Ho
C5 1 Swift Ho
2 Listowel Cl
3 Deal Wlk
4 Plover Ho
5 Aigburth Mans
6 Glencoe Mans
7 Glenshaw Mans
8 Cleveland Mans
9 Leda Ct
10 Jupiter Ct
11 Juno Ct
12 Healy Ho
13 Ashton Ho
14 Ramsey Ho
15 Annesley Ho
16 Cowley Rd
C6 1 Sherwin Ho
2 Pegasus Pl
3 Kilner Ho
4 Read Ho
5 Lohmann Ho
6 Hornby Ho
7 Abel Ho
8 Blythe Ho
9 Key Ho
10 Lockwood Ho
11 Alverstone Ho
12 Blades Ho
13 Rothesay Ct
D1 1 Mahatma Gandhi Ind Est
2 Dylan Rd
3 Bessemer Park Ind Est
4 Pablo Neruda Cl
5 Langston Hughes Cl
6 Walt Whitman Cl
7 James Joyce Wlk
8 Alice Walker Cl
9 Louise Bennett Cl
10 Chadacre Ho
11 Burwood Ho
12 Pyrford Ho
13 Wangford Ho
14 Ashford Ho
15 Kenwood Ho
16 Moyne Ho
17 Elveden Ho
18 Carrara Cl
19 Broughton Dr
20 Angela Davis Ind Est
21 Tilia Wlk
22 County Ho
D2 1 Mallams Mews
2 Amberley Ct
3 Harper Ho
4 Leicester Ho
5 Station Ave
6 Wellfit St
7 Loughborough Ct
8 Belinda Rd
9 Higgs Ind Est
D3 1 Langport Ho
2 Iveagh Ho
3 Newark Ho
4 Edgehill Ho
5 Hopton Ho
6 Ashby Ho
7 Nevil Ho
D4 1 Fairbairn Gn
2 Hammelton Gn
3 Foxley Sq
4 Silverburn Ho
5 Butler Ho
6 Dalkeith Ho
7 Turner Cl
8 Bathgate Ho
9 Black Roof Ho
D6 1 Faunce Ho
2 Garbett Ho
3 Harvard Ho
4 Doddington Pl
5 Kean Ho
6 Jephson Ho
7 Cornish Ho
8 Bateman Ho
9 Molesworth Ho
10 Walters Ho
11 Cruden Ho
12 Brawne Ho
13 Prescott Ho
14 Chalmer's Wlk
15 Copley Cl
16 King Charles Ct

139

A3 1 Bergen Ho
2 Oslo Ho
3 Viking Ho
4 Jutland Ho
5 Norvic Ho
6 Odin Ho
7 Baltic Ho
8 Nobel Ho
9 Mercia Ho
10 Kenbury Gdns
11 Zealand Ho
12 Elsinore Ho
13 Norse Ho
14 Denmark Mans
15 Dane Ho
16 Canterbury Cl
17 York Cl
18 Kenbury Mans
19 Parade Mans
20 Winterslow Ho
21 Lilford Ho
22 Bartholomew Ho
23 Guildford Ho
24 Boston Ho
25 Hereford Ho
26 Weyhill Ho
27 Lichfield Ho
28 Lansdown Ho
29 Honiton Ho
30 Pinner Ho
31 Baldock Ho
32 Widecombe Ho
33 Nottingham Ho
34 Witham Ho
35 Barnet Ho
36 Empress Mews
A4 1 Bertha Neubergh Ho
2 Mornington Mews
3 Badsworth Rd
4 Pearson Cl
5 Elm Tree Ct
6 Samuel Lewis Trust Dwellings
7 Milkwell Yd
8 Keswick Ho
9 Mitcham Ho
A5 1 Boundary Ho
2 Day Ho
3 Burgess Ho
4 Carlyle Ho
5 Myers Ho
6 Thompson Ave
7 Palgrave Ho
8 Winnington Ho
9 Brantwood Ho
10 Lowell Ho
11 Jessie Duffett Ho
12 Otterburn Ho
13 Crossmount Ho
14 Venice Ct
15 Bowyer St
16 Livingstone Ho
17 Gothic Ct
18 Coniston Ho
19 Harlynwood
20 Carey Ct
21 Finley Ct
22 Grainger Ct
23 Hayes Ct
24 Moffat Ho
25 Marinel Ho
26 Hodister Cl
27 Arnot Ho
28 Lamb Ho
29 Kipling Ho
30 Keats Ho
31 Kenyon Ho
32 New Church Rd
33 Sir John Kirk Cl
B1 1 Shaftesbury Ct
2 Mayhew Ct
3 Morris Ct
4 Swinburne Ct
5 Perth Ct
6 Tayside Ct
7 Matlock Ct
8 Hunter Ct
9 Turner Ct
B3 1 Selborne Rd
2 Hascombe Terr
B4 1 Joiners Arms Yd
2 Butterfly Wlk
3 Cuthill Wlk
4 Colonades The
5 Artichoke Mews
6 Peabody Bldgs
7 Brighton Ho
8 Park Ho
9 Peabody Ct
10 Lomond Ho
11 Lamb Ho
12 Kimpton Ct
13 Belham Wlk
14 Datchelor Pl
15 Harvey Rd
B5 1 Masterman Ho
2 Milton Ho
3 Pope Ho
4 Chester Ct
5 Marvel Ho
6 Flecker Ho
7 Landor Ho
8 Leslie Prince Ct
9 Evelina Mans
10 Langland Ho
11 Drinkwater Ho
12 Procter Ho
13 Shirley Ho
14 Drayton Ho
15 Bridges Ho
16 Cunningham Ho
17 Hood Ho
18 Herrick Ho
19 Dekker Ho
20 Houseman Way
21 Coleby Path
B6 1 Queens Ho
2 Arnside Ho
3 Horsley St
4 St Peter's Ho
5 St Johns Ho
6 St Marks Ho
7 St Stephens Ho
8 St Matthew's Ho
9 Red Lion Cl
10 Boyson Rd
11 Bradenham
C2 1 Harfield Gdns
2 Karen Ct
3 Seavington Ho
4 Appleshaw Ho
5 Birdsall Ho
6 Whitney Ho
7 Wheatland Ho
8 Wilton Ho
9 Walcot Ho
10 Whaddon Ho
11 Melbreak Ho
12 Ledbury Ho
13 Tidworth Ho
14 Riseholme Ho
15 Ringmer Ho
16 Petworth Ho
17 Stagshaw Ho
18 Ivybridge Ho
19 Inwood Ho
20 Gatcombe Ho
21 Felbridge Ho
22 Cowdray Ho
C3 1 Springfield Ho
2 Craston Ho
3 Walters Ho
4 Edgecombe Ho
5 Fowler Ho
6 Rignold Ho
7 Chatham Ho
C4 1 Barnwell Ho
2 Brunswick Villas
3 St Giles Twr
4 Bentley Ho
5 Dawson Ho
6 Dryden Ho
7 Mayward Ho
8 Longleigh Ho
9 Fairwall Ho
10 Bodeney Ho
11 Sandby Ho
12 Vestry Mews
13 Netley
14 Lakanal
15 Racine
C5 1 Tower Mill Rd
2 Tilson Cl
3 Granville Sq
4 Edgar Wallace Cl
5 Potters Cl
6 Dorton Cl
7 Samuel Jones Ind Est
8 Dibden Ho
9 Marchwood Cl
10 Pilgrims Cloisters
11 Beacon Ho
12 Teather St
13 Stacy Path
14 Rumball Ho
15 Ballow Cl
16 Rill Ho
C6 1 Downend Ct
2 Andoversford Ct
3 Pearse St
4 Watling St
5 Gandolfi St
D1 1 Dulwich Mews
2 St James's Cloisters
D4 1 Colbert
2 Voltaire
3 Finch Mews
4 Charles Coveney Rd
5 Bamber Rd
6 Crane St
7 Curlew Ho
8 Mallard Ho
9 Tern Ho
10 Crane Ho
11 Falcon Ho
12 Bryanston Ho
13 Basing Ct
14 Marcus Ho
15 Sheffield Ho
D5 1 Painswick Ct
2 Sharpness Ct
3 Mattingly Way
4 Hordle Prom N
5 Burcher Gale Gr
6 Calypso Cres
7 Hordle Prom S
8 Cinnamon Cl
9 Savannah Cl
10 Thames Ct
11 Shannon Ct
12 Amstel Ct
13 Danube Ct
14 Tilbury Cl
15 Hordle Prom E
16 Indus Ct
17 Oakcourt
18 Palm Ct
19 Rowan Ct
20 Blackthorn Ct
21 Pear Ct
22 Lidgate Rd
23 Whistler Mews
24 Boathouse Wlk
D6 1 Willsbridge Ct
2 Cam Ct
3 Quedgeley Ct
4 Saul Ct
5 Quenington Ct
6 Westonbirt Ct
7 Wickway Ct

140

A3 1 William Margrie Cl
2 William Blake Ho
3 Quantock Mews
4 Choumert Sq
5 Parkstone Rd
6 Atwell Rd
A4 1 Canal Head Public Sq
2 Angelina Ho
3 Jarvis Ho
4 Richland Ho
5 Honeywood Ho
6 Wakefield Ho
7 Primrose Ho
8 Hardcastle Ho
9 Dunstall Ho
10 Springtide Cl
11 Purdon Ho
12 Flamborough Ho
13 Lambrook Ho
14 Witcombe Point
15 Yarnfield Sq
16 Winford Ct
17 Portbury Cl
18 Robert Keen Cl
A5 1 Thornbill Ho
2 Vervain Ho
3 Woodstar Ho
4 Tamarind Ho
5 Hereford Retreat
6 Haymerle Ho
7 Furley Ho
8 Thomas Milner Ho
9 Applegarth Ho
10 Freda Corbett Cl
11 Rudbeck Ho
12 Henslow Ho
13 Lindley Ho
14 Collinson Ho
15 Sister Mabel's Way
16 Timberland Cl
17 Hastings Cl
18 Sidmouth Ho
19 Budleigh Ho
20 Stanesgate Ho
21 Breamore Ho
22 Ely Ho
23 Gisburn Ho
A6 1 Bowles Rd
2 Western Wharf
3 Northfield Ho
4 Millbrook Ho
5 Denstone Ho
6 Deerhurst Ho
7 Caversham Ho
8 Battle Ho
9 Cardiff Ho
10 Bridgnorth Ho
11 Exeter Ho
12 Grantham Ho
13 Aylesbury Ho
14 Royston Ho
B2 1 Tilling Ho
2 Goodwin Ho
3 Tyrells Ct
4 Citron Terr
5 Basswood Cl
6 Cheam St
B3 1 Walkynscroft
2 Ryegates
3 Hathorne Cl
4 Pilkington Rd
5 Russell Ct
6 Heaton Ho
7 Magdalene Cl
8 Iris Ct
B4 1 Willowdene
2 Pinedene
3 Oakdene
4 Beechdene
5 Hollydene
6 Wood Dene
8 Staveley Cl
9 Carnicot Ho
10 Martock Ct
11 Cherry Tree Ct
12 Kendrick Ct
B5 1 Tortington Ho
2 Credenhill Ho
3 Bromyard Ho
4 Hoyland Cl
5 Willowdene
6 Ashdene
7 Acorn Par
8 Havelock Ct
9 Springall St
10 Harry Lambourn Ho
11 Grenier Apartments
C3 1 Honiton Gdns
2 Selden Ho
3 Hathway Ho
4 Hathway St
5 Station Ct
C4 1 Trotman Ho
2 Boddington Ho
3 Heydon Ho
4 Boulter Ho
5 Astbury Bsns Pk
C5 1 Ambleside Point
2 Grasmere Point
3 Windermere Point
4 Roman Way
5 Laburnum Cl
6 Juniper Ho
7 Romney Cl
8 Hammersley Ho
9 Hutchinson Ho
10 Hammond Ho
11 Fir Tree Ho
12 Glastonbury Ct
13 Highbridge Ct
14 Filton Ct
15 Chiltern Ct
16 Cheviot Ct
C6 1 Penshurst Ho
2 Reculver Ho
3 Mereworth Ho
4 Camber Ho
5 Chiham Ho
6 Otford Ho
7 Olive Tree Ho
8 Aspen Ho
9 Lewis Silkin Ho
10 Richborough Ho
11 Dover Ho
12 Eynsford Ho
13 Horton Ho
14 Lamberhurst Ho
15 Canterbury Ind Pk
16 Upnall Ho
17 Sissinghurst Ho
18 Rochester Ho
19 Saltwood Ho
20 Leybourne Ho
21 Lullingstone Ho
D1 1 Laxton Path
2 Barlings Ho
3 Bayfield Ho
4 Coston Wlk
5 Coverham Ho
6 Gateley Ho
7 Dereham Ho
8 Greenwood Ho
9 Hilton Ho
10 Goodall Ho
11 Horsley Ho
12 Jordan Ho
D5 1 Richard Anderson Ct
2 Palm Tree Ho
3 Edward Robinson Ho
4 Antony Ho
5 Gerrard Ho
6 Palmer Ho
7 Pankhurst Cl
D6 1 Harrisons Ct
2 Grantley Ho
3 Sunbury Ct
4 Tilbury Ho
5 Graham Ct
6 Connell Ct
7 St Clements Ct
8 Henderson Ct
9 Jemotts Ct
10 Verona Ct
11 Heywood Ho
12 Francis Ct
13 Hind Ho
14 Donne Ho
15 Carew Ct
16 Burbage Ho
17 Newland Ho
18 Dobson Ho
19 Dalton Ho
20 Greene Ct
21 Redrup Ho
22 Tarplett Ho
23 Stunell Ho
24 Gasson Ho
25 Bryce Ho
26 Barnes Ho
27 Barkwith Ho
28 Bannister Ho
29 Apollo Ind Bsns Ctr

141

A4 1 Archer Ho
2 Browning Ho
3 Hardcastle Ho
4 Brooke Ho
5 Wallis Ho
A5 1 Batavia Ho
2 Marlowe Bsns Ctr
3 Batavia Mews
4 Woodrush Cl
5 Alexandra St
6 Primrose Wlk
7 Vansittart St
8 Granville Ct
9 Cottesbrook St
10 Ewen Henderson Ct
11 Fordham Ho
A6 1 Portland Ct
2 Phoenix Ct
3 Rainbow Ct
4 Hawke Twr
5 Chubworthy St
6 Woodpecker Rd
7 Hercules Ct
B5 1 Austin Ho
2 Exeter Way
3 Crossleigh Ct
4 Mornington Pl
5 Maple Ho
B6 1 Chester Ho
2 Lynch Wlk
3 Arlington Ho
4 Woodcote Ho
5 Cornbury Ho
6 Prospect Pl
7 Akintaro Ho
8 Mulberry Ho
9 Laurel Ho
10 Linden Ho
11 Ashford Ho
12 Wardalls Ho
13 Magnolia Ho
14 Howard Ho
15 Larch Cl
16 Ibis Ct
17 Merganser Ct
18 Wotton Rd
19 Kingfisher Sq
20 Sanderling Ct
21 Dolphin Twr
22 Mermaid Twr
23 Scoter Ct
24 Shearwater Ct
25 Brambling Ct
26 Kittiwake Ct
27 Diana Cl
28 Guillemot Ct
29 Marine Twr
30 Teal Ct
31 Lapwing Twr
32 Violet Cl
33 Skua Ct
34 Tristan Ct
35 Rosemary Ct
36 Cormorant Ct
37 Shelduck Ct
38 Eider Ct
39 Pintail Ct
C4 1 Admiralty Cl

141 C4
2 Harton Lodge
3 Sylva Cotts
4 Pitman Ho
5 Heston Ho
6 Mereton Mans
7 Indiana Bldg
8 St John's Lodge
C5 1 Sandpiper Ct
2 Flamingo Ct
3 Titan Bsns Est
4 Rochdale Way
5 Speedwell St
6 Reginald Pl
7 Fletcher Path
8 Frankham Ho
9 Cremer Ho
10 Wilshaw Ho
11 Castell Ho
12 Holden Ho
13 Browne Ho
14 Resolution Way
15 Lady Florence Ctyd
16 Covell Ct
17 Albion Ho
C6 1 Dryfield Wlk
2 Blake Ho
3 Hawkins Ho
4 Grenville Ho
5 Langford Ho
6 Mandarin Ct
7 Bittern Ct
8 Lamerton St
9 Ravensbourne Mans
10 Armada St
11 Armada Ct
12 Benbow Ho
13 Oxenham Ho
14 Caravel Mews
15 Hughes Ho
16 Stretton Mans
D4 1 Washington Bldg
2 California Bldg
3 Utah Bldg
4 Montana Bldg
5 Oregon Bldg
6 Dakota bldg
7 Idaho Bldg
8 Atlanta Bldg
9 Colorado Bldg
10 Arizona Bldg
11 Nebraska Bldg
12 Alaska Bldg
13 Ohio Bldg
14 Charter Bldgs
15 Flamsteed Ct
16 Friendly Pl
17 Dover Ct
18 Robinscroft Mews
19 Doleman Ho
20 Plymouth Ho
D5 1 Finch Ho
2 Jubilee The
3 Maitland Cl
4 Ashburnham Retreat

142

A2 1 Bankside Ave
2 Elder Wlk
3 Yew Tree Cl
4 Mill Ho
A3 1 Ellison Ho
2 Pitmaston Ho
3 Aster Ho
4 Windmill Cl
5 Hertmitage The
6 Burnett Ho
7 Lacey Ho
8 Darwin Ho
9 Pearmain Ho
A4 1 Penn Almshouses
2 Jervis Ct
3 Woodville Ct
4 Darnall Ho
5 Renbold Ho
6 Lindsell St
7 Plumbridge St
8 Trinity Gr
9 Hollymount Cl
10 Cade Tyler Ho
11 Robertson Ho
A5 1 Temair Ho
2 Royal Hill Ct
3 Prince of Orange La
4 Lambard Ho
5 St Marks Cl
6 Ada Kennedy Ct
7 Arlington Pl
8 Topham Ho
9 Darnell Ho
10 Hawks Mews
11 Royal Pl
12 Swanne Ho
13 Maribor
14 Serica Ct
15 Queen Elizabeth's Coll
A6 1 Crescent Arc
2 Greenwich Mkt
3 Turnpin La
4 Durnford St
5 Sexton's Ho
6 Bardsley Ho
7 Wardell Ho
8 Clavell St
9 Stanton Ho
10 Macey Ho
11 Boreman Ho
12 Clipper Appts
B6 1 Frobisher Ct
2 Hardy Cotts
3 Palliser Ho
4 Bernard Angell Ho
5 Corvette Sq
6 Travers Ho
7 Maze Hill Lodge
8 Park Place Ho
D5 1 Westcombe Ct
2 Kleffens Ct
3 Ferndale Ct
4 Combe Mews
5 Mandeville Cl
7 Pinelands Cl

143

A5 1 Mary Lawrenson Pl
2 Bradbury Ct
3 Dunstable Ct
4 Wentworth Ho
A6 1 Nethercombe Ho
2 Holywell Cl
B6 1 Capella Ho
2 Collington Ho
C6 1 Warren Wlk
2 Wilson Ho
3 Priory Ho
4 Mar Ho
5 Langhorne Ho
6 Games Ho
7 Erskine Ho
8 Ducie Ho
9 Downe Ho
10 Bayeux Ho
11 Elliscombe Mount
12 Harold Gibbons Ct
13 Mascalls Ct
14 Leila Parnell Pl
15 East Mascalls
16 Birch Tree Ho
17 Cherry Tree Ct
18 Elm Tree Ct
19 Cedar Ct
D5 1 Winchester Ho
2 Brentwood Ho
3 Shenfield Ho
4 Chesterford Ho

144

A4 1 Master Gunner's Pl
2 Ross Ho
3 Dickson Ho
4 Horne Ho
5 Pendlebury Ho
6 Roberts Ho
7 Maple Tree Pl
C6 1 Lawson Ho
2 Mabbett Ho
3 Petrie Ho
4 Memess Path
5 Ruegg Ho
6 Nile Path
7 Leslie Smith Sq
8 Spearman St
9 Siedle Ho
10 Watling Ho
11 O'Neill Path
12 Old Clem Sq
13 Jefferson Wlk
14 Milward Wlk
15 Wordsworth Ho
16 Fenwick Cl
D6 1 Acworth Ho
2 Griffiths Ho
3 Squires Ho
4 Cowen Ho
5 Turton Ho
6 Alford Ho
7 Boxshall Ho
8 MacAllister Ho
9 Marvin Ho
10 Kelham Ho
11 Kimber Ho
12 Maxwell Ho
13 Woodford Ho
14 Penfold Ho

146

A2 1 Wellingfield Ct
2 Woodville Gr
3 Midwinter Cl
4 St Leonards Cl

147

A1 1 Woburn Ct
2 Arundel Ct
3 Longleat Ct
4 Upton Villas
5 Whitehaven Ct
6 Shirley Hts
7 Louise Ct
8 Bethany Ct
B6 1 Bevercote Wlk
2 Lullingstone Rd
3 Benjamin Ct
4 Charton Cl
5 Terence Ct
6 Renshaw Cl
7 Grove Rd
C1 1 Friswell Pl
2 Market Pl
3 Geddes Pl
4 Janet Ct
5 Broadway Sh Ctr
6 Mall The
7 Norwich Pl
8 Pincott Rd

148

A5 1 Stranraer Way
2 Deri Dene Cl
3 Lord Knyvetts Ct
4 Tudor Ct
5 Wessex Ct
6 Vanguard Ho
7 Shackleton Ct
8 Fleetwood Ct
9 Clifton Ct
10 Vickers Ct
11 Bristol Ct
12 Sunderland Ct

153

A3 1 Katharine Rd
2 Sandringham Ct
3 Garfield Rd
4 Arragon Rd
5 Flood La
6 John Wesley Ct
7 King Street Par
8 Thames Eyot
A4 1 Perryn Ct
2 Ivybridge Cl
3 Heritage Ho
4 Brook Ho
5 Neville Ho
6 Latham Cl
7 March Rd
8 Berkley Ct
9 Cole Court Lo
10 Cheltenham Ave
11 Railway App
A5 1 Greenways The
2 Cole Park View
B4 1 Melton Ct
2 Amyand Park Gdns
3 Crown Ct
4 Burrell Ho
5 Owen Ho
6 Brentford Ho
7 Leeson Ho
8 Westbourne Ho
9 Orleans Ct
10 Lebanon Ct
B5 1 Grove The
2 Cumberland Cl
3 Westmorland Cl
4 Sussex Cl
5 Norfolk Cl
6 Nicol Cl
7 Old Lodge Pl
8 Kelvin Ct
9 St Margaret's Ct
10 Park Cotts
11 St Margarets Bsns Ctr
12 Amyand Cotts
C1 1 Benson Ho
2 Bowes Lyon Ho
3 Cavendish Ho
4 Bentinck Ho
5 Clarke Ho
6 Secrett Ho
7 Edwards Ho
8 Field Ho
9 Greig Ho
10 Hawkins Ho
11 Newman Ho
12 Leyland Ho
13 Hornby Ho
14 Hatch Ho
C5 1 Howmic Ct
2 Sefton Lo
3 Ravensbourne Ho
4 Arlington Ct
5 Georgina Ct
6 Trevelyan Ho
7 Caradon Ct
8 Green Hedges
9 Old House Gdns
10 Queens Keep
11 Beresford Ct
12 Langham Ct
13 Poplar Ct
D5 1 Richmond Bridge Mans
2 Heatherdene Mans
3 Kenton Ct
4 Lennox Ho
5 Leicester Ct
6 Turner Ho
7 Blanchard Ho
8 Arosa Rd
9 Ashe Ho
10 Bevan Ct
11 Lawley Ho
12 Darling Ho
13 Richmond Mans
14 Beaulieu Cl
15 Roseleigh Cl
16 Mallard Ct
D6 1 Garrick Cl
2 Old Palace Yd
3 Wardrobe The
4 Maids of Honour Row
5 Hunters Ct
6 Queensberry Ho
7 Green The
8 Old Palace Terr
9 Paved Ct
10 Golden Ct
11 Brewers La
12 Square The
13 Lower George St
14 St James's Cotts
15 Church Wlk
16 Church Ct
17 Victoria Pl
18 Castle Yd
19 Lewis Rd
20 Wakefield Rd
21 Church Terr
22 Warrington Rd
23 Ormond Ave
24 Glovers Lo
25 Holbrooke Pl
26 Northumberland Pl
27 Heron Sq
28 Whittaker Pl
29 Water Lane Ho
30 Riverside Ho
31 St Helena Terr

154

A5 1 Lancaster Cotts
2 Lancaster Mews
3 Bromwich Ho
4 Priors Lo
5 Richmond Hill Ct
6 Glenmore Ho
7 Hillbrow
8 Heathshott
9 Friars Stile Pl
10 Spire Ct
11 Ridgeway
12 Matthias Ct
A6 1 Lichfield Terr
2 Union Ct
3 Carrington Lo
4 Wilton Ct
5 Egerton Ct
6 Beverley Lo
7 Bishop Duppa's Almshouses
8 Regency Wlk
9 Clear Water Ho
10 Onslow Avenue Mans
11 Michels Almshouses
12 Albany Pas
13 Salcombe Villas
B5 1 Chester Cl
2 Evesham Ct
3 Queen's Ct
4 Russell Wlk
5 Charlotte Sq
6 Jones Wlk
7 Hilditch Ho
8 Isabella Ct
9 Damer Ho
10 Eliot Ho
11 Fitzherbert Ho
12 Reynolds Pl
13 Chisholm Rd
B6 1 Alberta Ct
2 Beatrice Rd
3 Lorne Rd
4 York Rd
5 Connaught Rd
6 Albany Terr
7 Kingswood Ct
8 Selwyn Ct
9 Broadhurst Cl

156

A3 1 Farnborough Ho
2 Rushmere Ho
3 Horndean Cl
4 Highcross Way
5 Timsbury Wlk
6 Foxcombe Rd
7 Ryefield Path
8 Greatham Wlk
9 Gosport Ho
10 Stoatley Ho
11 Milland Ho
12 Clanfield Ho
13 Fareham Ho
14 Grayswood Point
A4 1 Woodcott Ho
2 Lyndhurst Ho
3 Wheatley Ho
4 Allbrook Ho
5 Bordon Wlk
6 Chilcombe Ho
7 Vicarage Ct
8 Shawford Ct
9 Eastleigh Wlk
10 Kings Ct
11 Somborne Ho
A6 1 Theodore Ho
2 Nicholas Ho
3 Bonner Ho
4 Downing Ho
5 Jansen Ho
6 Fairfax Ho
7 Devereux Ho
8 David Ho
9 Leigh Ho
10 Clipstone Ho
11 Mallet Ho
12 Arton Wilson Ho
B3 1 Ramsdean Ho
2 Purbrook Ho
3 Portsea Ho
4 Blendworth Point
5 Eashing Point
6 Hindhead Point
7 Hilsea Point
8 Witley Point
9 Buriton Ho
10 Grateley Ho
11 Hascombe Ho
12 Dunhill Point
13 Westmark Point
14 Longmoor Point
15 Cadnam Point
C4 1 Cumberland Ho
2 Devonshire Ho
3 Cornwall Ho
4 Norfolk Ho
5 Leicester Ho
6 Warwick Ho
7 Sutherland Ho
8 Carmarthen Ho
9 Worcester Ho
10 Rutland Ho
11 Paddock Way
C6 1 Inglis Ho
2 Ducie Ho
3 Wharncliffe Ho
4 Stanhope Ho
5 Waldegrave Ho
6 Mildmay Ho
7 Mullens Ho
D3 1 Sandringham Cl
2 Eastwick Ct
3 Oatlands Ct
4 Banning Ho
5 Grantley Ho
6 Caryl Ho
7 Duncombe Ho
8 Chilworth Ct
9 Kent Lo
10 Turner Lo
11 Marlborough
12 Parkland Gdns
13 Lewesdon Cl
14 Pines Ct
15 Ashtead Ct
16 Mynterne Ct
17 Arden
18 Stephen Ct
19 Marsham Ct
20 Doradus Ct
21 Acorns The
22 Heritage Ho
23 Conifer Ct
24 Spencer Ho
25 Chartwell
26 Blenheim
27 Chivelston
28 Greenfield Ho
29 Oakman Ho
30 Radley Lo
31 Simon Lo
32 Admirals Ct
D4 1 Brett Ho
2 Brett House Cl
3 Sylva Ct
4 Ross Ct
5 Potterne Cl
6 Stourhead Cl
7 Fleur Gates
8 Greenwood
D5 1 Balmoral Cl
2 Glenalmond Ho
3 Selwyn Ho
4 Keble Ho
5 Bede Ho
6 Gonville Ho
7 Magdalene Ho
8 Armstrong Ho
9 Newnham Ho
10 Somerville Ho
11 Balliol Ho
12 Windermere
13 Little Combe Cl
14 Classinghall Ho
15 Chalford Ct
16 Garden Royal
17 South Ct
18 Anne Kerr Ct
19 Ewhurst
D6 1 Geneva Ct
2 Laurel Ct
3 Cambalt Ho
4 Langham Ct
5 Lower Pk
6 King's Keep
7 Whitnell Ct
8 Whitehead Ho
9 Halford Ho
10 Humphry Ho
11 Jellicoe Ho

157

A3 1 William Harvey Ho
2 Highview Ct
3 Cameron Ct
4 Galgate Cl
5 Green Ho The
6 King Charles Wlk
7 Florys Ct
8 Augustus Ct
9 Albert Ct
10 Hertford Lo
11 Mortimer Lo
12 Allenswood
13 Ambleside
14 Hansler Ct
15 Roosevelt Ct
A6 1 Claremont
2 Downside
3 Cavendish Cl
4 Ashcombe Ct
5 Carltons The
6 Espirit Ho
7 Millbrooke Ct
8 Coysh Ct
9 Keswick Hts
10 Lincoln Ho
11 Avon Ct
B6 1 Keswick Broadway
2 Burlington Mews
3 Cambria Lo
4 St Stephen's Gdns
5 Atlantic Ho
6 Burton Lo
7 Manfred Ct
8 Meadow Bank
9 Hooper Ho
10 Aspire Bld
C6 1 Pembridge Pl
2 Adelaide Rd
3 London Ct
4 Windsor Ct
5 Westminster Ct
6 Fullers Ho
7 Bridge Pk
8 Lambeth Ct
9 Milton Ct
10 Norfolk Mans
11 Francis Snary Lo
12 Bush Cotts
13 Downbury Mews
14 Newton's Yd
D6 1 Fairfield Ct
2 Blackmore Ho
3 Lancaster Mews
4 Cricketers Mews
5 College Mews
6 Arndale Wlk

158

A2 1 Beemans Row
2 St Andrew's Ct
3 Townsend Mews
4 Sheringham Mews

159

1 Upper Tooting Park Mans
2 Cecil Mans
3 Marius Mans
4 Boulevard The
5 Elmfield Mans
6 Holdernesse Rd
7 Lumiere Ct
A3 1 Heslop Ct

2 St James's Terr
3 Boundaries Mans
4 Station Par
5 Old Dairy Mews
4 1 Hollies Way
2 Endlesham Ct
5 1 Rayne Ho
2 St Anthony's Ct
3 Earlsthorpe Mews
4 Nightingale Mans
3 1 Holbeach Mews
2 Hildreth Street Mews
3 Coalbrook Mans
4 Hub Buildings The
5 Metropolis Apartments
4 1 Meyer Ho
2 Faraday Ho
3 Hales Ho
4 Frankland Ho
5 Graham Ho
6 Gibbs Ho
7 Dalton Ho
8 Ainslie Wlk
9 Rokeby Ho
10 Caistor Ho
11 Ivanhoe Ho
12 Catherine Baird Ct
13 Marmion Ho
14 Devonshire Ct
15 Blueprint Apartments
4 1 Limerick Ct
2 Homewoods
3 Jewell Ho
4 Glanville Ho
5 Dan Bryant Ho
6 Olding Ho
7 Quennel Ho
8 Weir Ho
9 West Ho
10 Neville Ct
11 Friday Grove Mews
5 1 Joseph Powell Cl
2 Cavendish Mans
3 Westlands Terr
4 Cubitt Ho
5 Hawkesworth Ho
6 Normanton Ho
7 Eastman Ho
8 Couchman Ho
9 Poynders Ct
10 Selby Ho
11 Valentine Ho
12 Gorham Ho
13 Deauville Mans
14 Deauville Ct
6 1 Timothy Cl
2 Shaftesbury Mews
3 Brook Ho
4 Grover Ho
5 Westbrook Ho
6 Hewer Ho
7 Batten Ho
8 Mandeville Ho
9 George Beare Lo
3 1 Sinclair Ho
2 MacGregor Ho
3 Ingle Ho
4 St Andrews Mews
4 1 Riley Ho
2 Bennett Ho
3 White Ho
4 Rodgers Ho
5 Dumphreys Ho
6 Homan Ho
7 Prendergast Ho
8 Hutchins Ho
9 Whiteley Ho
10 Tresidder Ho
11 Primrose Ct
12 Angus Ho
13 Currie Ho
5 1 Parrington Ho
2 Savill Ho
3 Blackwell Ho
4 Bruce Ho
5 Victoria Ct
6 Victoria Ho
7 Belvedere Ct
8 Ingram Lo
9 Viney Ct
10 Bloomsbury Ho
11 Belgravia Ho
12 Barnsbury Ho

160

A1 1 De Montfort Ct
2 Leigham Hall Par
3 Leigham Hall
4 Endsleigh Mans
5 John Kirk Ho
6 Raebarn Ct
7 Wavel Ct
8 Homeleigh Ct
9 Howland Ho
10 Beauclerk Ho
11 Bertrand Ho
12 Drew Ho
13 Dowes Ho
14 Dunton Ho
15 Raynald Ho
16 Sackville Ho
17 Thurlow Ho
18 Astoria Mans
A2 1 Wyatt Park Mans
2 Broadlands Mans
3 Stonehill's Mans
4 Streatleigh Par
5 Dorchester Ct
6 Picture Ho
A3 1 Beaumont Ho
2 Christchurch Ho
3 Staplefield Cl
4 Chipstead Ho
5 Coulsdon Ho
6 Conway Ho
7 Telford Avenue Mans
8 Telford Parade Mans
9 Wavertree Ct
10 Hartswood Ho
11 Wray Ho
A4 1 Picton Ho
2 Rigg Ho
3 Watson Ho
4 MacArthur Ho
5 Sandon Ho
6 Thorold Ho
7 Pearce Ho
8 Mudie Ho
9 Miller Ho
10 Lycett Ho
11 Lafone Ho
12 Lucraft Ho
13 Freeman Ho
14 New Park Par
15 Argyll Ct
16 Dumbarton Ct
17 Kintyre Ct
18 Cotton Ho
19 Crossman Hos
20 Cameford Ct
21 Parsons Ho
22 Brindley Ho
23 Arkwright Ho
24 Perry Ho
25 Brunel Ho
26 New Park Ct
27 Tanhurst Ho
28 Hawkshaw Cl
A6 1 King's Mews
2 Clapham Court Terr
3 Clapham Ct
4 Clapham Park Terr
5 Pembroke Ho
6 Stevenson Ho
7 Queenswood Ct
8 Oak Tree Ct
9 Park Lofts
10 Ashby Mews
B1 1 Carisbrooke Ct
2 Pembroke Lo
3 Willow Ct
4 Poplar Ct
5 Mountview
6 Spa View
B3 1 Charlwood Ho
2 Earlswood Ho
3 Balcombe Ho
4 Claremont Cl
5 Holbrook Ho
6 Gwynne Ho
7 Kynaston Ho
8 Tillman Ho
9 Regents Lo
10 Hazelmere Ct
11 Dykes Ct
B4 1 Archbishop's Pl
2 Witley Ho
3 Outwood Ho
4 Dunsfold Ho
5 Deepdene Lo
6 Warnham Ho
7 Albury Lo
8 Tilford Ho
9 Elstead Ho
10 Thursley Ho
11 Brockham Ho
12 Capel Lo
13 Leith Ho
14 Fairview Ho
15 Weymouth Ct
16 Ascalon Ct
17 China Mews
18 Rush Common Mews
B6 1 Beatrice Ho
2 Florence Ho
3 Evelyn Ho
4 Diana Ho
5 Brixton Hill Ct
6 Austin Ho
7 Manor Ct
8 Camsey Ho
9 Romer Ho
10 Gale Ho
11 Byrne Ho
12 Farnfield Ho
13 Marchant Ho
14 Rainsford Ho
15 Springett Ho
16 Mannering Ho
17 Waldron Ho
C3 1 Valens Ho
2 Loveday Ho
3 Strode Ho
4 Ethelworth Ct
5 Harbin Ho
6 Brooks Ho
7 Godolphin Ho
8 Sheppard Ho
9 McCormick Ho
10 Taylor Ho
11 Saunders Ho
12 Talcott Path
13 Derrick Ho
14 Williams Ho
15 Baldwin Ho
16 Churston Cl
17 Neil Wates Cres
18 Burnell Ho
19 Portland Ho
C4 1 Ellacombe Ho
2 Booth Ho
3 Hathersley Ho
4 Brereton Ho
5 Holdsworth Ho
6 Dearmer Ho
7 Cherry Cl
8 Greenleaf Cl
9 Longford Wlk
10 Scarlette Manor Wlk
11 Chandlers Way
12 Upgrove Manor Way
13 Ropers Wlk
14 Tebbs Ho
15 Bell Ho
16 Worthington Ho
17 Courier Ho
18 Mackie Ho
19 Hamers Ho
20 Kelyway Ho
21 Harriet Tubman Cl
22 Estoria Cl
23 Leckhampton Pl
24 Scotia Rd
25 Charles Haller St
26 Sidmouth Ho
27 Hunter Ct
28 Onslow Lo
29 William Winter Ct
30 Langthorne Lo
C5 1 Eccleston Ho
2 Scarsbrook Ho
3 Purser Ho
4 Rudhall Ho
5 Hardham Ho
6 Heywood Ho
7 Haworth Ho
8 Birch Ho
9 Lansdell Ho
10 Lomley Ho
11 Laughton Ho
12 Woodruff Ho
13 Bascome St
14 Dudley Mews
15 Herbert Mews
16 Blades Lo
17 Dick Shepherd Ct
18 Charman Ho
19 Morden Ho
20 Bishop Ct
21 Blackburn Ct
22 Leigh Ct
23 John Conwey Ho
24 Bristowe Cl
C6 1 Crownstone Ct
2 Brockwell Ct
3 Nevena Ct
4 St George's Residences
5 Hanover Mans
6 Fleet Ho
7 Langbourne Ho
8 Turnmill Ho
9 Walker Mews
10 Cossar Mews
11 Carter Ho
D1 1 Thanet Ho
2 Chapman Ho
3 Beaufoy Ho
4 Easton Ho
5 Roberts Ho
6 Lloyd Ct
7 Kershaw Ho
8 Wakeling Ho
9 Edridge Ho
10 Jeston Ho
11 Lansdowne Wood Cl
12 Rotary Lo

161

B2 1 Welldon Ct
2 Coppedhall
3 Shackleton Ct
4 Bullfinch Ct
5 Gannet Ct
6 Fulmar Ct
7 Heron Ct
8 Petrel Ct
9 Falcon Ct
10 Eagle Ct
11 Dunnock Ct
12 Dunlin Ct
13 Cormorant Ct
14 Oak Lodge
15 Corfe Lodge
C6 1 Velde Way
2 Delft Way
3 Arnhem Way
4 Isel Way
5 Kempis Way
6 Terborch Way
7 Steen Way
8 Deventer Cres
9 Nimegen Way
10 Hilversum Cres
11 St Barnabas Cl

162

A1 1 Tunbridge Ct
2 Harrogate Ct
3 Bath Ct
4 Leamington Ct
5 Porlock Ho
6 Cissbury Ho
7 Eddisbury Ho
8 Dundry Ho
9 Silbury Ho
10 Homildon Ho
11 Highgate Ho
12 Richmond Ho
13 Pendle Ho
14 Tynwald Ho
15 Wirrall Ho
16 Greyfriars
A6 1 Dorothy Charrington Ho
2 Keswick Ct
3 Kendall Ct
4 Halliwell Ct
B1 1 River Ho
2 Fordington Ho
3 Arbury Terr
4 Woodbury Ho
5 Gainsborough Mews
6 Forest Hill Ct
B2 1 Bromleigh Ct
2 Parfew Ct
3 Thetford Ct
4 Attleborough Ct
5 Dunton Ct
6 Frobisher Ct
7 Julian Taylor Path
8 Grizedale Terr
9 Worsley Ho
C1 1 Forest Lo
2 Sydenham Park Mans
3 William Wood Ho
C2 1 Fitzwilliam Hts
2 Taymount Grange
3 McLeod Ho
4 Featherstone Ave
5 Kingswear Ho
6 Salcombe Ho
7 Glynwood Ct
C3 1 Harlech Ct
2 Angela Ct
3 Westwood Ct
4 New Belmont Ho
5 Pearcefield Ave
6 Waldram Pl
7 Horniman Grange
8 South View Ct
9 Heron Ct
10 Katherine Ct
D1 1 Standlake Point
2 Radcot Point
3 Newbridge Point
4 Northmoor
5 Kelmscott
6 Radnor Ct
7 Heathwood Point
8 Ashleigh Point
9 Deepdene Point
10 Rosemount Point
11 Woodfield Ho
12 Clairville Point
13 Trevenna Ho
14 Hyndewood
D2 1 Pikethorne
2 Andrew Ct
3 Valentine Ct
4 Soper Cl

164

C4 1 Beaumont Terr
2 Littlebourne
3 Verdant Ct
D2 1 Kinross Ct
2 Montrose Ct
3 Rattray Ct
4 Rothesay Ct
D3 1 Edinburgh Ct
2 McMillan Ct
3 Rowallan Ct
4 Meridian Ct
5 Braemar Ct
6 Barrow Ct
7 Blair Ct
8 Darlington Ct
9 Hamilton Ct
10 Inverness Ct
11 Oak Cottage Cl
12 Willow Cl
13 Keswick Ct

165

A4 1 Swallow Ct
2 Honeysuckle Ct
3 Venture Ct
4 Cheriton Ct
5 Askham Lo
6 Syon Lo

166

A2 1 Portland Cres
2 Bourdillon Ct
3 Hillary Ct
4 Tenzing Ct
5 John Hunt Ct
6 Everest Ct
A6 1 Horsfeld Gdns
2 Foxhole Rd
C5 1 Roper St
2 Arcade The
3 Elm Terr
4 Imber Ct
5 Ashcroft Ct
6 Fairlands Ct
7 Brecon Ct
8 Newlands Ct
9 Harvard Ct
10 Garden Ct
11 Chiltern Ct
12 Fairway Ct

167

A2 1 Mervyn Stockwood Ho
2 Michael Marshall Ho
3 Keith Sutton Ho

168

A1 1 Ham Shades Cl
2 Aspen Ho
3 Medlar Ho
4 Cornel Ho
5 Stanton Ct
6 Hornbeam Ho
7 Beech Ho
8 Spindle Ho
9 Hunters Lo
10 Edam Ct
11 Monica James Ho
12 Oak Ho
13 Crescent Ct
14 Freeland Ct
15 Montague Ct
16 Windsor Ct
B5 1 Rochester Cl
2 Cobham Cl
3 Shorne Cl
4 Warne Pl

169

C4 1 Close The
2 Parkhurst Gdns
3 Chichester Ct
4 Pound Green Ct

170

B6 1 Station Par
2 Queens La
3 Copthorne Chase
4 Canterbury Ct
5 Church Par
C5 1 St Matthew's Ct
2 Dencliffe
3 Crest Ho
4 Bourne Ho
5 Elms The
6 Roxeth Ct
7 Rowland Hill Almshouses

171

A3 1 Viscount Ct
2 Blackthorne Ct
D3 1 Bishops Ct
2 Ash Lo
3 Lime Lo
4 Oak Lo
5 Elm Ct
6 Willow Lo
7 Sycamore Lo
8 Priscilla Ho
9 Sunbury Cross Ctr
10 Isobel Ho

173

A6 1 Gabriel Cl
2 Metcalfe Wlk
3 Dunmow Cl
4 Burgess Cl
5 Chamberlain Wlk
C2 1 Sherbourne Ct
2 Somerset Ct
3 Jubilee Ho
4 Rushbury Ct
5 Blenheim Ct
6 Hemming Cl
7 Ryedale Ct
8 Norman Ct
C4 1 Begonia Pl
2 Snowdrop Cl
3 Hyacinth Cl
4 Cyclamen Cl
5 Jonquil Gdns
6 Gladioli Cl
7 Daffodil Pl
8 Partridge Rd
D4 1 Acorn Cl
2 Wolsey Ho
3 Lytton Ho
4 Wren Ho
5 Faraday Ho

174

C5 1 Knaggs Ho
2 Keeling
3 Elizabeth Ct
4 Oakhurst Cl
5 Charles Ct
6 Harold Ct
D5 1 Waldegrave Ct
2 Luther Mews
3 Alice Mews
4 Gresham Ho
5 Traherne Lo
6 Fishers Ct
7 Waterhouse Ct
8 Oval Ct
9 Walpole Pl
10 Walpole Cres
11 Bychurch End

175

A5 1 Cherrywood Ct
2 Cambridge Ho
3 Cairngorm Cl
4 Gleneagles Ct
5 Christchurch Ave
6 Hales Ct
7 Plough La
8 Springfield Rd
9 Royal Oak Mews
10 Trinder Mews
C3 1 Belgravia Ho
2 Ash Ho
3 Crieff Ct
4 Maples The
D2 1 Wick Ho
2 Spinnaker Ct
3 Osiers Ct
4 Trent Ho
5 Arun Ho
6 Medway Ho
7 Avon Ho
8 Tyne Ho
9 Clyde Ho
10 Mersey Ct
11 Severn Ct
12 John William Cl
13 Henry Macaulay Ave
14 Seymour Lo
15 Falmouth Ho
16 Earlsfield Ho
D6 1 Byron Ct
2 Coleridge Ct
3 Tennyson Ct
4 Herrick Ct
5 Spenser Ct
6 Marlowe Ct
7 Brooke Ct
8 Gray Ct
9 Shelley Ct
10 Pope Ct
11 Dryden Ct

176

A1 1 Cleave's Almshos
2 Perry Ct
3 Drovers Ct
4 Gough Ho
5 Eden Wlk
6 Alderman Judge Mall
7 Lady Booth Rd
8 Caversham Ho
9 Littlefield Cl
10 Bentall Sh Ctr The

11 Adams Wlk
12 Ceres Ct
A2 1 Regents Ct
2 Walter St
3 Canbury Bsns Pk
4 Sigrist Sq
5 Ashway Ctr
6 Warwick Ho
7 Hedingham Ho
8 Alexander Ho
9 Bramber Ho
10 Carisbrooke Ho
11 Dartmouth Ho
12 Garland Ho
A3 1 Walton Ho
2 Berkeley Cl
3 Canbury Ct
4 King's Penny Ho
B1 1 Vicarage Ho
2 Rayleigh Ct
3 School Pas
4 Chippenham
5 Camm Gdns
B2 1 Onslow Ho
2 Dowler Ct
B3 1 McDonald Ho
2 Elm Ho
3 Dale Ct
4 York Ho
5 Florence Ho
6 Florence Rd
7 Roupell Ho
8 Delft Ho
C1 1 Wimpole Cl
2 Burwell
3 Caldecote
4 Fordham
5 Connington
6 Chesterton Terr
7 Westwick
8 Eureka Rd
9 Fulbourn
10 Comberton
11 Madingley
12 Grantchester
13 Cambridge Grove Rd
14 Oakington
15 Harston
16 Graveley
17 Croxton
18 Brinkley
19 Impington
20 Shelford
21 Duxford
22 Cascadia Ho
C2 1 Farthings The
2 Brae Ct
3 Princeton Mews
4 Station App
C3 1 Queen's Ct
2 St George's Rd
3 Park Road Ho
4 Dagmar Rd
5 Tapping Cl
6 Arthur Rd
7 Borough Rd
8 Belvedere Ct
9 Braywick Ct
10 Dean Ct
11 Rowan Ct
12 Richmond Ct
13 Sunningdale Ct
14 Hawker Ct
15 Cromwell Ct
16 Kings Ct
D2 1 Trevallyn Lo
2 Chichester Ho
3 Beechcroft
4 Cedars The
5 Liddlesdale Ho W
6 Liddlesdale Ho E
7 Deerhurst
8 Brockworth
9 Alderton
D3 1 Bramley Ho
2 Abinger Ho
3 Thursley Ho
4 Ridge Ho
5 Clone The
6 Mount Ct
7 Hillside Ct
8 Hill Ct
9 Royal Ct
10 Lakeside
11 High Ashton
D4 1 Godstone Ho
2 Hambledon Ho
3 Kingswood Ho
4 Leigh Ho
5 Milton Ho
6 Newdigate Ho
7 Farleigh Ho
8 Ockley Ho
9 Effingham Ho
10 Dunsfold Ho
11 Pirbright Ho
12 Clandon Ho
13 Ripley Ho

178

C3 1 Roskeen Ct
2 Chimneys Ct
3 Aston Ct
4 Rosemary Cotts
5 Victoria Lo
D2 1 Beaufort Ho
2 Kinnear Ct
3 Ranmore Ct
4 Lantern Ct
5 Crescent Ho
D3 1 Kings View Ct
2 Wimbledon Cl
3 Beryl Harding Ho
4 Upton Ct
5 Marian Lo
6 Terraces The
7 Lanherne Ho
8 Cumberland Cl
9 Thaxted Pl
10 Rathbone Ho
11 Princess Ct
12 Claremont Lo
13 Downs Ct
14 Ravenscar Lo
15 Haverley
16 Savona Cl
17 Beaumont Ct
18 Gordon Ct
D5 1 Lancaster Pl
2 Haygarth Pl
3 Allington Cl
4 Homefield Pl

179

A3 1 Stretford Ct
2 Brunswick Ct
3 Pavilion Ct
4 Louie Black Ho
5 Warwick Ho
6 Erica Ho
7 Adyar Ct
8 Thornton Lo
9 Ash Ct
10 Broughton Ho
11 Naomi Watts Ho
12 Wellesley Ho
13 Mayfair Ct
A4 1 Walham Rise
2 Grosvenor Ct
3 Sovereign Ho
4 Holly Lo
5 Florence Ct
6 Linden Cotts
7 Sheep Walk Mews
8 Emerson Ct
9 Hill Ct
10 Powell Ho
B4 1 Aspen Lo
2 Gladebury Ct
3 Centre Court Sh Ctr
B5 1 Lawns The
2 Prentice Ct
3 Catherine Ct
4 Woodlodge
5 Pixham Ct
6 Lake Cl
7 Westwood Ct
8 Brambles The
9 Lismore
10 Rose Ct
11 Worcester Rd
12 Leopold Ct
C3 1 Ashbourne Terr
2 Sir Cyril Black Way
3 Willows Ct
4 Harefield Ct
5 Broadway Ho
6 Viscount Point
7 Carrington Ho
8 Cloisters Ho
9 Downing Ho
10 Bickley Ct
11 Palmerston Gr
12 Gladstone Ct
13 Warrington Ct
D2 1 Gilbert Cl
2 Becket Cl
3 Priory Cl
4 Hudson Ct
5 Ryder Ho
6 Eleanor Ho
7 Ramsey Ho
8 Colborne Ct
9 Falcon Ho
10 Spur Ho
D3 1 Hamilton Road Mews
2 Dowman Cl
3 Burleigh Lo
4 Horatio Ho

180

A2 1 Tanner Ho
2 May Ct
3 Marsh Ct
4 Lovell Ho
A3 1 Fiske Ct
2 Mellor Ct
3 Olive Rd
4 Allerton Ho
5 Victory Road Mews
6 Will Miles Ct
7 Vanguard Ho
8 Mychell Ho
9 Merton Pl
10 De Burgh Ho
11 Norfolk Ho
12 Hotham Road Mews
B1 1 Ripley Ct
2 Brooklands Ct
3 Horner La
B2 1 Yarborough Rd
2 Vista Ho
3 Prospect Ho
4 Independence Ho
5 Nonsuch Ho
6 Baron Ho
C2 1 Linford Ct
2 Searle Ct
3 Gunnell Ct
4 Wells Ct
5 Hartley Ct
C3 1 Shere Lo
2 Goodwin Ct
3 Cairn Ho
C4 1 Douglas Ct
2 Lannock Ct
3 Gateway Ho
4 Wellington Ct
C5 1 Robertson Ho
2 Dewar Ho
3 Jean Ho
4 Marion Ct
5 Gravenel Gdns
6 Palladino Ho
D1 1 Elms Cotts
2 Sibthorp Rd
3 Armfield Cotts
4 Sir Arthur Bliss Ct
5 Fountain Ho
6 Gladstone Ho
7 Chart Ho

181

A1 1 Kennedy Cl
2 Pearce Cl
3 Mainwaring Ct
4 Coningsby Ct
5 Laburnum Ct
6 Beaumont Ct
7 Penfold Ct
8 Fitch Ct
10 Lea Cotts
A5 1 Osborne Terr
2 Limetree Wlk
C5 1 Tyers Ho
2 Boothby Ho
3 Adams Ho
4 Burney Ho
5 Boswell Ho
6 Chesterfield Ho
7 Garrick Ho
8 Levett Ho
9 Shelburne Ho
10 Marchmont Ho
11 Ryland Ho
12 Flather Cl
13 Bank Bldgs
14 Carriage Pl
15 Locarno Cl
C6 1 Walmsley Ho
2 Chambers Ho
3 Fordyce Ho
4 Percy Ho
5 Langton Ho
6 Moorfields Ct
7 Hidaburn Ct
8 Salter Ho
9 Tailors Ct
10 Yew Tree Lo
D6 1 William Dyce Mews
2 Doctor Johnson Ho

182

A3 1 Spa Central
A5 1 Oakdene Ct
2 Hopton Par
3 Merton Lo
4 Bouverie Ct
5 Deerhurst
6 Farnan Hall
A6 1 Central Mans
2 Central Par
B3 1 Marqueen Twrs
2 Shirley Ct
3 Sinclair Ho
4 Vantage Ct
5 Pavilion Ct
B6 1 Ashleigh Ho
2 Roseneath Pl
3 Shenley Ho
4 Blytheswood Pl
C5 1 Parkhill Ho
2 Ash Ct
3 Alder Ct
4 Beech Ct
5 Acacia Ct
6 Blackthorn Ct
7 Cypress Ct
8 Hawthorn Ct
9 Hazel Ct
10 Sycamore Ct
11 Maple Ct
12 Laburnam Ct
13 Fern Lo
14 Colyton La
C6 1 James Boswell Cl
2 St Albans Ho
3 Suffolk Ct
4 Rockhampton Cl
5 Delphian Ct
6 Heather Ct
D5 1 Woodcote Pl
2 Joe Hunte Ct
3 Cork Tree Ho
4 Lake Ho
5 Cedars Ho
6 Portobello Ho
7 Cooper Ho
8 Farnsworth Ho
9 Hook Ho
10 Crest The
11 Renshaw Ho
12 Ruscoe Ho
13 Sardeson Ho
D6 1 William Wilberforce Ho
2 William Marsden Ho
3 Samuel Ho
4 Morris Stephany Ho
5 Church Ct

183

A6 1 Moore Ho
2 Chaucer Ho
3 Bushell Ho
4 Bligh Ho
5 Hobbs Rd
6 Hogarth Ho
7 Goodbehere Ho
8 Astley Ho
9 Elder Gdns
10 Elderberry Gr
11 Pavement The
12 Dunkirk St
B6 1 Josef Perrin Ho
2 Jean Humbert Ho
3 Charles Staunton Ho
4 Violette Szabo Ho
5 Lilian Rolfe Ho
6 Odette Ho
7 Robert Gerard Ho
8 St Bernards Cl
9 Champness Cl
10 Pennington Cl
11 Queenswood Ct
C4 1 Northwood Way
2 High Limes
3 Valley Prospect
4 Plane Tree Wlk
5 City Prospect
6 Bankside Way
7 Ridge Way
8 Rochdale
9 Barrington Wlk
10 Gatestone Ct
11 Childs La
12 Carberry Rd
13 Norwood Heights Sh Ctr
C5 1 Oakdene
2 Thorsden Way
3 Oakfield Gdns
4 Georgetown Cl
5 Bridgetown Cl
6 Mountbatten Cl
7 Brabourne Cl
8 Alexandra Wlk
9 Compton Ct
10 Battenburg Wlk
11 Burma Terr
12 Wiseman Ct
C6 1 Linley Ct
2 Mellor Ho
3 Whitfield Ct
4 Michaelson Ho
5 Holberry Ho
6 Hovenden Ho
7 Huntley Ho
8 Telfer Ho
9 Markham Ho
10 Oldham Ho
11 Parnall Ho
12 Pierson Ho
13 Roper Ho
14 Roundell Ho
15 Sawyer Ho
16 Ransford Ho
17 Carmichael Ho
18 Bonne Marche Terr Mews
D3 1 Hetley Gdns
2 Claybourne Mews
3 Highland Lo
4 Mason Ct
5 Kendall Ct
6 High View
D5 1 Glenhurst Ct
2 Marlowe Ct
3 Grenville Ct
4 Raleigh Ct
5 Beechwoods Ct
6 Burntwood View

184

A3 1 Hanover Ct
2 Brunswick Ct
3 New Church Ct
4 Regency Ct
7 Owen Wlk
8 Bargrove Cl
9 Beaver Cl
B2 1 Dorset Ho
2 Collingwood Cl
3 Chartwell Way
4 Essex Twr
5 Appletree Cl
6 Ditton Pl
7 Kelvin Ct
8 Readman Ct
9 Glen Ct
10 Kingsbridge Ho
11 Carlton Ct
12 Benhurst Ct
13 Carole Ho
14 Dover Ho
15 Bettswood Ct
B3 1 Avery Ct
2 Rossal Ct
3 Oakdene Lo
4 Ridgemount Cl
5 Blakewood Ct
6 Trenholme Cl
7 Oakleigh Ct
8 Upchurch Cl
9 Devon Ho
10 Westmoreland Terr
11 Oakfield Road Ind Est
B5 1 Ragwort Ct
2 Firs The
3 Wingham Ho
4 Seath Ho
5 Ripley Ho
6 Lathwood Ho
7 Hurst Ho
8 George Ho
9 Browne Ho
10 Beacon Ho
11 Bailey Ho
12 Agate Ho
C2 1 Challin St
2 Rutland Ho
3 Pine Cl
C3 1 Watermen's Sq
2 St John's Cotts
3 Gladstone Mews
4 Middlesex Ho
5 Bethesda Ct
6 Ospringe Cl
7 Goudhurst Ho
8 Walmer Ho
9 Strood Ho
10 Greatstone Ho
11 John Baird Ho
C4 1 Midhurst
2 Oliver Ct
3 Victoria Ct
4 Wakefield Ct
5 Fountain Ct
6 Newlands Ct
C6 1 Homewalk Ho
2 Grace Path
3 Sycamore Ct
4 Sydenham Station App
5 Greenways
6 Faircroft
D3 1 Groombridge Ho
2 Provincial Terr
3 Smithers Ho
4 West Ho
5 Swallows Ct
6 Hornbeam Ho
7 Blenheim Centre

185

A1 1 Clock House Ct
2 Blandford Ave
3 Old School Cl
4 Lynsted Ct
5 Florence Rd
A6 1 Paxton Ct
2 Kenton Ct
3 Grove Ct
4 Shirley Lo
B2 1 Ashton Ct
2 Coombe Ct
3 Fontaine Ct
4 Richfield Ct
5 Sheridan Way
C1 1 Christ Church Rd
2 Lea Rd
3 Stanmore Terr
C2 1 Erindale Ct
2 Montgomerie Ct
3 Rebecca Ct
4 Sycamore Ct
5 Willow Ct
6 Marlborough Ct
7 Bearsted Terr
8 Berwick Ct
9 Wooderson Ct
10 Beck River Pk
11 Waterside
C3 1 Gardenia Ct
2 Brackendale Ct
3 Daniel Ct
4 Moliner Ct
5 Chartwell Lo
6 Randmore Ct
7 Dover Ho
8 Lucerne Ct
9 Malling Ho
10 Westerham Lo
11 Brasted Lo
12 Milton Ho
13 Bradsole Ho
14 Sandgate Ho
15 Adelaide Ct
16 Nettlestead Cl
17 Warren Ct
18 Alton Ct
19 Rockingham Ct
20 Camellia Ct
21 Sinclair Ct
22 Regents Ct
23 Minshull Pl
24 South Park Ct
D1 1 Parkside
2 Tudors The
3 Oakbrook
4 Tara Ct
5 Redlands The
6 Cambria
7 Hillworth
8 Kelsey Gate
9 Burrells
10 Lincoln Lo
11 Courtlands
12 Fairleas
13 Ashdown Cl
14 Barons
D2 1 Clifton Ct
2 Mayfair Ct
3 Lait Ho
4 Fire Station Mews
D4 1 Warner Ho
2 Clifford Ho
3 Lloyd Ho
4 Thurston Ho
5 Byron Ho
6 Blake Ho
7 Keats Ho

186

A2 1 White House Ct
2 Hunters The
3 Sandringham Ct
4 Glenhurst
5 Copperfields
6 Westgate Ct
A6 1 Dedham Ho
2 Flatford Ho
3 Langthorne Ct
4 Radley Ct
5 Hoover Ho
6 Brunner Ho
7 Waterer Ho
8 Marriott Ho
9 Bourbon Ho
B5 1 Longford Ho
2 Ingrebourne Ho
3 Brent Ho
4 Darent Ho
5 Beverley Ho
6 Wandle Ho
7 Rythe Ho
8 Ember Ho
9 Crane Ho
10 Ravensbourne Ho
C1 1 Warwick Ct
2 Maplehurst
3 Mount Arlington
4 Arundel Ct
D2 1 Weston Gr
2 Gibbs Ho
3 Longfield
4 Hammelton Ct

5 Bracken Hill Cl
6 Townend Ct
7 Treversh Ct
8 Cameron Ho
9 Woodlands Ct
10 Blythwood Pk
11 Bromley Pk
D3 1 Homecoppice Ho
2 Linden Ct
3 Kimberley Gate
4 Inglewood Ct
5 Mavery Ct
6 Glen Ct
7 Marlborough Ct
8 Cawston Ct
9 Blendon Path

187

A1 1 St James Ct
A2 1 Mitchell Way
2 Harrington Ho
3 Newman Ct
4 Uno Apartments
5 Bromley Ho
B2 1 Dainton Cl
2 Rothwell Ct
3 St Timothy's Mews
4 Andringham Lo
5 Kendall Lo
6 Summerfield
7 Winston Ct
8 Vogue Ct
9 Laurels The
C1 1 Westland Lo
2 Eastland Ct
3 Dairsie Ct
4 Northlands
5 Beechfield Cotts
6 Oasis The
7 Cromarty Ct
8 Silverstone Ct

188

A6 1 Beaconsfield Par
2 Cranley Par
3 Kimmeridge Gdns
4 King & Queen Cl
C2 1 Ivybridge Ct
2 Greenbank Lo

190

A6 2 Cyril Lo
3 Hazlemere
4 Milton Lo
5 Marlin Ct
6 Conroy Ct
7 Glenwood Ct
8 Culverton Ct
9 Holmbury Manor
B1 1 Swanscombe Ho
2 Haverstock Ct
3 Arrandene Ho
4 Broomfield Ho
5 Headley Ho
6 Kenley Ho
7 Ladywell Ho
B6 1 Chudleigh
2 Wimborne
3 St John's Par
4 Holly Ct
5 Rectory Bsns Ctr

193

D1 1 Orchard Ct
2 Bridge Ct

197

A2 1 Raleigh Ho
2 Leicester Ho
3 Gresham Ho
D2 1 Napier Ct
2 Darlington Ho
3 Charminster Ct
4 Mulberry Ct
5 Leander Ct
6 Clinton Ho
7 Hollingsworth Ct
8 Gloucester Ct
9 Palmerston Ct
10 Redwood Ct
11 Hursley Ct
12 Westmorland Ct
13 Lawson Ct
14 Alexander Ct
15 Winton Ct
16 Sydenham Ho
17 Caroline Ct
18 Ellswood Ct
19 Masefield Ct

198

A1 1 Ash Tree Cl
2 Shrubbery The
3 Malvern Ct
4 Gate Ho
5 Yew Tree Ho
A3 1 Station App
2 South Bank Lo
3 Bramshott Ct
4 Pandora Ct
5 Wellington Ct
6 Glenbuck Ct
7 Leighton Ho
8 Oakhill Ct
9 Downs View Lo
10 Osborne Ct
11 Surbiton Par
12 Woodgate Ho
13 Godwyn Ho
14 Ashby Ho
A4 1 Effingham Lo
2 Maple Ho
3 Channon Ct
4 Falconhurst
5 Ferndown
6 Viceroy Lo
7 Frensham Ho
8 Kingsley Ho
9 Rannoch Ct
10 Stratton Ct
11 Moray Ho
12 Dulverton Ct
13 Westerham
14 Hill Ct
15 Assheton-Bennett Ho
16 Hatfield Ho
17 Oxford Ct
18 Pennington Lo
19 Austin Ho
20 Wentworth Ct
21 Priory The
22 Sheraton The
23 Christopher Ct
24 Hobart Ho
25 St Mark's Hts
A5 1 Marquis Ct
2 Garrick Ho
A6 1 College Rdbt
2 Edinburgh Ct
3 Weston Ct
4 Grebe Terr
5 Heron Ct
6 Agar Ho
7 St James' Ct
8 Grove Ct
9 Springfield Ct
10 College Wlk
B3 1 Percy Ct
2 Holmwood
3 Middle Green Cl
4 Herbert Ct
B4 1 Woodleigh
2 Highcroft
3 Caernarvon Ct
4 Regency Ct
D1 1 Oakleigh Way
2 Chandler Ct

199

C2 1 Goodland Ho
2 Furzeland Ho
3 Oakcroft Ho
4 Meadcroft Ho
5 Newhouse
C4 1 Merryweather Ct
2 Roebuck Ct
3 Sable Ct
C5 1 Acacia Ho
2 Kingston Lo
3 Carrington Ct
4 Fairholme Ho
5 Marshall Ho
6 Norton Ho
7 Martin Ho

200

A1 1 Brookside Cres
2 Beverley Gdns
3 Purdey Ct
4 Avenue The
5 Briarwood Ct
6 Station App

202

D6 1 Fair Green Ct
2 Regal Ct
3 Lewes Ct
4 Esher Mews
5 Sibford Ct
6 Deseret Ho
7 Standor Ho
8 Langdale Par
9 Newman Terr

204

A2 1 Barcom Trad Est
2 Croydon Valley Trade Pk
C3 1 Rozelle Ct
2 Dunheved Ct
3 Truscott Ho
C4 1 Brigstock Par
2 Terry Lodge
3 Justin Ct
D3 1 Wyndham Ct
D5 1 Nutfield Pl
2 Braidwood Ho
3 Elliott Ho

205

B1 1 Tavistock Ct
2 Chartwell Cl
3 Speaker's Ct
4 Cumberland Ct
5 Viceroy Ct
6 Oriel Ct
7 Cherry Orchard Gdns
8 Sola Ct
9 Gamma Ct
C1 1 Windmill Bridge Ho
2 Squire Ct
3 Houston Ct
4 Warren Ct
D1 1 Hastings Pl
2 Grant Pl
3 Clive Ho
4 Havelock Ho
5 Bellmore Ct
6 Hereford Ct
7 Chequers Ct
8 Havelock Hall

206

A1 1 Farleycroft
2 Edgecumbe Ct
3 Wesson Ho
4 Sullivan Ct
5 Kenley Ho
6 Christopher Ct
7 Jayson Ct
A6 1 Leybourne Ct
2 Lestock Cl
3 Croftside The
D1 1 Cottongrass Cl
2 Oxlip Cl
3 Eyebright Cl

207

1 North Rd
2 Sussex Rd
3 Riverside Wlk
4 Christie Ho
5 Windsor Ct
6 Sherwood Ct
7 Wheatsheaf Par
D6 1 Linden Ct
2 Park Ct
3 Chilchester Ct
4 Iveagh Ct

208

A6 1 Overbury
2 Wilton Pl
D1 1 Woodgrange Ct
2 Maycroft
3 Farnborough Cres
D4 1 Knowlton Gn
2 Speldhurst Cl
3 Bidborough Cl
4 Penshurst Wlk
D5 1 Wedgewood Ct
2 Birches The
3 Eccleshill
4 Tavistock Rd
5 Montpelier Ct

209

A5 1 Montague Terr
2 Chatsworth Ho
A6 1 Marina Cl
2 Cheveney Wlk
3 Bromley Manor Mans
4 Mall The
5 Westmoreland Pl
B5 1 Reflex Apartments
2 Wheeler Pl
3 Maxim Apartments
4 Exchange Apartments
5 Axiom Apartments
6 Weller Mews

211

B1 1 Gleneagles Gn
2 Tandridge Pl
3 Springfield Wlk
4 Pinehurst Wlk
5 Cromer Pl
6 Oakmont Pl

214

A6 1 St Bernards Ho
2 Wentworth Ct
3 Sunningdale Cl
4 Arklow Mews
5 Edward Pinner Ct

216

1 Lansdowne Copse
2 Lansdowne Ct

217

A2 1 Cheam Court Flats
2 Farnham Ct
3 Tabor Ct
C1 1 Lancaster Ct
2 Redclyffe Terr
3 Kenilworth Terr
4 Lincoln Terr
5 Garden Ct
6 Ashwood Pk
7 Midsummer Apartments
8 Lyndhurst Ct
9 Lorraine Ct
10 Gloucester Ct
11 Banbury Ct
12 Camilla Ct
13 Lorac Ct
14 Kingswood Mans
15 Claremont Ho
16 Holly Ct
17 Castle Ho
18 Balmoral Ct
19 Davington Ct
20 Hereford Ct
C2 1 Norman Ho
2 Hawthorns The
3 Limes The
4 Alexa Ct
5 Kristina Ct
6 Beverley Ct
7 Chestnut Ct
D1 1 Holmeswood
2 Pebworth Lo
3 Addison Ct
4 Kingslee Ct
5 Raeburn Ho
6 Girtin Ho
7 Leith Towers
8 Courtlands
9 Thomas Ho
10 Grayshott Ct
11 Hadrian Ct
12 Sandown Ct
13 Magnolia Ct
14 Dunsfold Ct
15 Camberley Ct
16 Berrylands Ct
17 Brockham Ct
18 Alford Ct
19 Lansdowne Ho
20 Larchvale Ct
D2 1 Portland Ct
2 Durnston Ct
3 Barton Ct
4 Aplin Ct
5 Hannah Ct
6 Honeysuckle Ct
7 Rowans The
8 St Annes Ct
9 Bonnington Ho
10 Pamir Ct
11 Bradbourne Ct
12 Worcester Ct
D3 1 Marian Ct
2 Robin Hood Ct
3 Distin Ct
4 Queensmere
5 Grosvenor Ho
6 Cromer Mans
7 St Nicholas Ctr
D5 1 Dorothy Pettingel Ho
2 Margaret Ho

218

A1 1 Beauclere Ho
2 Melford Ct
3 Elmhurst Lo
4 Mansard Manor
5 Tranmere Ct
6 Beechcroft Lo
7 Savin Lo
8 Yew Tree Ct
9 Avondale Ct
10 Devonshire Ho
11 Hidcote Ho
12 Munstead Ct
13 Lodden Lo
14 Steetley Ct
15 Grampian Cl
16 Richard Sharples Ct
A2 1 Grosvenor Ct
2 Forest Dene Ct
3 Cedar Ct
4 Vanborough Ct
5 Shrub Ct
6 Evergreen Ct
7 Grasmere Ct
8 Heathfield Ct
9 Sherbourne Ct
10 Kinsale Grange
11 Linden Ct
12 Jubilee Ct
13 Langley Ct
14 Wilmot Ho
15 Farendon Ho
16 Alexander Ho
A3 1 Goossens Cl
2 Cliffe Wlk
3 Marlins Cl
4 Clowser Cl
5 Montana Gdns
6 Bournemouth Ct
7 Palmerston Ct
A4 1 Lodge The
2 Hazelwood Ho
3 Chesterton Ho
4 Clevedon Ho
5 Staincliffe Ho
6 Denewood Ho
7 Newlyn Ho
8 Manor Ct
9 Glenrose Ho
10 Oak Lo
11 Briar The
12 Fernhead
13 Branch Ho
14 Thicket Ct
15 Adam Ct
16 Arndell Ho
17 Oakwood Ct
B3 1 Hogarth Ho
2 Gillray Ho
3 Cramhurst Ho
4 Ronald Ho
5 Blythewood
6 Hillsde
7 Weldon Ct
8 Yeoman Ct
D5 1 Kynersley Cl
2 Wrythe Gn
3 Bedford Villas
4 Chateau The
5 Nelson Ct
6 Errington Manor
7 Leeds Ct
8 Blair Ct

219

A4 1 Westcroft
2 Westcroft Ho
A5 1 Burnside Ct
2 Millpond Pl
3 Waterside Ct
4 Stable Ct
5 Manor Ct
B2 1 Runnymede Ct
2 Dolphin Ct
3 Kings Ct
4 Cheyne Ct
5 Hendfield Ct
6 Ellerslie Ct
7 Embassy Ct
8 Chandler Ct
9 Hambledon Ct
10 Wallington Ct
11 Jasmine Ct
12 Napier Ct
13 Rosswood Ho
14 Woodcote Ct
15 Surrey Ct
16 Stag Ct
17 Moorlands
B3 1 Cornelion Cotts
2 Walpole Ct
3 Farmstead Ct
4 Derby Ho
5 Salisbury Ho
6 Chatham Ho
B4 1 Loraine Ho
2 Harcourt Lo
3 Coniston Ct
4 Alcester Ct
5 Friars Ct
6 Campbell Ho
7 Brodie Ho
8 Lesley Ct
9 Birch Ct
10 Airborne Ho
C2 1 Rossendon Ct
2 Mulberry Mews
3 Nairn Ct
4 Wallington Sq
5 Rosemount Twrs
6 Connell Ho
7 Ashby Grange
8 Terry Ct
9 Leigham Cl
10 Clyde Works
11 Chandos Bsns Ctr
12 Beech Ho
13 Wendon Ct
D3 1 Torquay Ho
2 Ashburton Ho
D5 1 Goodwood Lo
2 Haydock Lo
3 Kempton Lo

220

A1 1 Phoenix Ctr The
2 Ensign Way
3 Hunter Cl
4 Cirrus Cl
D5 1 Latimer Rd
2 Cromwell Ho
3 Arundel Ct
4 Warrington Ct
5 Grace Ct
6 Stuart Ct
7 Bridge Par

221

A3 1 Trent Ct
2 Sherwood Ct
3 Archers Ct
4 Keepers Ct
5 Lincoln Ct
6 Mount The
7 Fairhaven Ct
8 Brockham Ct
9 Chelwood Ct
10 Marey Ct
11 Landau Ct
A4 1 West Street Pl
2 Maple Ct
3 St Andrew's Rd
4 Albury Ct
5 Chestnut Ct
6 Elgin Ct
7 Beechfield Ct
8 Barham Ct
9 Whitstable Pl
10 Ledbury Pl
A5 1 Fellmongers Yd
2 Halstead Cl
3 Mann Cl
4 Waterworks Yd
5 Chanderia Ct
6 Katherine Ho
A6 1 Otterbourne Rd
2 Charrington Rd
3 Tamworth Pl
4 Priddy's Yd
5 Hospital of the Holy Trinity (Almshouses)
B6 1 Wellesley Court Rd
2 Norfolk Ho
3 Station App
4 Suffolk Ho
5 Cherry Orchard Gdns
6 Harrington Ct
D6 1 Cheyne Ct
2 Fourways
3 Princess Ct
4 Tierney Ct
5 Sinclair Ct
6 Guinness Ct
7 Mayfair Ct
8 Bishopscourt
9 Gloucester Lo
10 Beverley Hyrst
11 Melton Ct
12 Cecil Ct
13 Napier Ct

227

A3 1 Westfield
2 Farnborough Ct
3 Fern Hill Pl
4 Churchill Ct
5 Spencer Ct
6 Ladycroft Gdns
7 Crabbs Croft Cl
8 Clifton Cl
D2 1 Brittenden Cl
2 Wardens Field Cl
3 Winnipeg Dr
4 Superior Dr
5 Huron Cl
6 Manitoba Gdns
7 Lynne Cl
8 Flint Cl
9 Bakers Mews
D3 1 Osgood Gdns
2 Amberley Cl
3 Rawlings Cl
4 Beblets Cl
5 Fir Tree Cl
6 Raleigh Mews
7 King Henry Mews
D4 1 Healy Dr
2 Marsden Way
3 Taylor Cl
4 Strickland Way
5 Dryland Ave
6 Adcot Wlk
7 Lichlade Cl

Hospitals

Hospitals with Accident and Emergency departments

Central Middlesex Hospital 89 A4
Acton Lane, Park Royal, London NW10 7NS
020 8965 5733

Charing Cross Hospital 112 D1
Fulham Palace Road, London W6 8RF
(A&E entrance off St Dunstan's Road)
020 8846 1234

Chase Farm Hospital 4 C5
The Ridgeway, Enfield, Middlesex EN2 8JL
020 8375 1010

Chelsea and Westminster Hospital 136 A6 266 B5
369 Fulham Road, London SW10 9NH
020 8746 8080

Ealing Hospital 108 B4
Uxbridge Road, Southall, Middlesex UB1 3HW
020 8967 5613

Hammersmith Hospital 90 B1
Du Cane Road, London W12 0HS
020 8383 1111

Hillingdon Hospital 82 B2
Pield Heath Road, Uxbridge, Middlesex UB8 3NN
01895 238282

Homerton University Hospital 74 D3
Homerton Row, E9 6SR
020 8510 5555

King George Hospital 58 A4
Barley Lane, Goodmayes, Ilford, Essex IG3 8YB
020 8983 8000

King's College Hospital 139 B3
Denmark Hill, (A&E in Ruskin Wing) SE5 9RS
020 3299 9000

Kingston Hospital 176 D2
Galsworthy Road, Kingston-upon-Thames, Surrey KT2 7QB
020 8546 7711

Lewisham Hospital 163 D6
High Street, Lewisham, London SE13 6JH
020 8333 3000

Mayday University Hospital 204 D3
Mayday Road, Thornton Heath CR7 7YE
020 8401 3000

Moorfields Eye Hospital (eyes only) 95 B4 235 C1
162 City Rd, London EC1V 2PO
020 7253 3411

Newham General Hospital 99 C3
Glen Road, Plaistow, London E13 8SL
020 7476 4000

North Middlesex University Hospital 33 C5
Sterling Way, Edmonton, London, N18 1QX
020 8887 2000

Northwick Park Hospital 43 A2
Watford Road, Harrow, Middlesex HA1 3UJ
020 8864 3232

Princess Royal University Hospital 226 C5
Farnborough Common, Orpington BR6 8ND
01689 863000

Queen Elizabeth Hospital 144 A5
Stadium Rd, Woolwich SE18 4QH
020 8836 6000

Queen Mary's Hospital 190 A4
Frognal Avenue, Sidcup,Kent DA14 6LT
020 8302 2678

Royal Free Hospital 70 C3
Pond Street, London NW3 2QG
020 7794 0500

Royal London Hospital (Whitechapel) 96 B2
Whitechapel Road, London E1 1BB
020 7377 7000

St George's Hospital 180 B5
Blackshaw Road, London SW17 0QT
020 8672 1255

St Helier Hospital 202 A1
Wrythe Lane, Carshalton, Surrey SM5 1AA
020 8296 2000

St Mary's Hospital 92 B1 236 D2
Praed Street, Paddington W2 1NY
(A&E entrance on South Wharf Rd)
020 7886 6666

St Thomas' Hospital 116 B3 260 C6
Lambeth Palace Road, London SE1 7EH
020 7188 7188

University College Hospital 93 C3 239 B6
235 Euston Rd, London NW1 2BU
0845 155 5000

West Middlesex University Hospital 131 A3
Twickenham Road, Isleworth, Middlesex TW7 6AF
020 8560 2121

Whipps Cross Hospital 54 B3
Whipps Cross Road, Leytonstone London E11 1NR
020 8539 5522

Whittington Hospital 71 C6
Highgate Hill, London, N19 5NF
020 7272 3070

Acton Hospital W3 110 C4
Ashford Hospital TW15 3AA 148 A2
Athlone House (The Middlesex Hospital) N6 48 D1
Atkinson Morley Hospital SW20 178 B3
Barking Hospital IG11 79 D1
Barnes Hospital SW14 133 C2
Beckenham Hospital BR3 185 B1
Bethlem Royal Hospital The BR3 207 C2
Blackheath Hospital SE3 142 C2
Bolingbroke Hospital The SW11 158 C6
Bowden House Hospital (Private) HA1 64 C6
British Home and Hospital for Incurables SW16 182 D5
Bromley Hospital BR2 9AJ 209 B5
Brompton Hospital SW3 114 B1 256 D2
BUPA Bushey Hospital WD2 8 D3
Carshalton, War Memorial Hospital SM5 218 D2
Cassel Hospital TW10 175 D6
Castlewood Day Hospital SE18 144 C4
Central Middlesex Hospital NW10 7NS 89 A4
Central Public Health Laboratory NW9 45 C6
Chadwell Heath Hospital RM6 58 B4
Charing Cross Hospital W6 8RF 112 D1
Charter Nightingale Hospital The NW1 92 C2 237 B4
Chase Farm Hospital EN2 8JL 4 C5
Chelsea Hospital for Women SW3 114 C1 257 A2
Chelsea and Westminster Hospital SW10 9NH 136 A6 266 B5
Chingford Hospital E4 20 A1
Chiswick Maternity Hospital W4 111 D1
Clayponds Hospital and Day Treatment Ctr TW8 110 A2
Clementine Churchill Hospital The HA1 64 D5
Colindale Hospital NW9 45 C6
Connaught Day Hospital E11 54 C3
Coppetts Wood Hospital N10 30 D2
Cromwell Hospital SW5 113 D2 255 C4
Devonshire Hospital W1 93 A2 238 B4
Dulwich Hospital SE22 139 C1
Ealing Hospital UB1 3HW 108 B4
East Ham Memorial Hospital E7 77 D1
Eastman Dental Hospital WC1 94 B4 240 C6
Edgware General Hospital HA8 26 D3
Elizabeth Garrett Anderson and Obstetric Hospital WC1 93 C3 235 B5
Farnborough Hospital BR6 226 C4
Finchley Memorial Hospital N12 30 A3
Fitzroy Nuffield Hospital W1 92 D1 237 C2
Garden Hospital The NW4 46 C6
Goldie Leigh Hospital SE2 146 C6
Goodmayes Hospital IG3 58 A4
Gordon Hospital The SW1 115 D2 259 C3
Great Ormond St Hospital for Children WC1 94 B3 240 C5
Grovelands Priory N14 16 A3
Guy's Hospital SE1 117 B5 252 D2
Hackney Hospital E9 75 A3
Hamlet (Day) Hospital The TW9 132 A2
Hammersmith Hospital W12 90 B1
Harrow Hospital HA2 64 C6
The Heart Hospital W1 93 B2 238 C3
Hillingdon Hospital UB8 82 B2
Homerton University Hospital E9 74 D3

Hornsey Central Hospital N8 49 D4
Hospital for Tropical Diseases WC1 232 C5
Hospital of St John and St Elizabeth NW8 92 B5 229 C3
Inverforth House Hospital NW3 70 A6
Jewish Home and Hospital at Tottenham The N15 51 D5
King George Hospital IG3 58 A4
King's College Hospital SE5 139 B3
Kings Oak Hospital (Private) The EN2 4 C5
Kingsbury Hospital NW9 44 C5
Kingston Hospital KT2 176 D2
Langthorne Hospital E11 76 B5
Lewisham Hospital SE13 163 D6
Lister Hospital SW1 115 B1 258 C1
London Bridge Hospital SE1 117 B5 252 D4
London Chest Hospital E2 96 C5
London Clinic NW1 93 A3 238 B5
London Foot Hospital W1 93 C3 239 A5
London Hospital (Mile End) The E2 96 D4
London Hospital (St Clements) The E3 97 B4
London Independent Hospital The E1 96 D2
Maida Vale Psychiatric Hospital W9 92 A3 236 B6
Manor House Hospital NW11 47 D1
Marlborough Day Hospital NW8 92 A5 229 A4
Maudsley Hospital The SE5 139 B3
Mayday University Hospital CR7 204 D3
Memorial Hospital SE18 144 C3
Mildmay Mission Hospital E2 95 D4
Molesey Hospital KT8 195 C4
Moorfields Eye Hospital EC1 95 B4 235 C1
Morland Road Day Hospital RM10 103 C6
National Hospital for Neurology and Neurosurgery N2 48 C5
National Hospital The WC1 94 A3 240 B5
National Physical Laboratory TW11 174 C4
Nelson Hospital SW20 179 B1
New Cross Hospital SE14 140 C5
New Victoria Hospital KT3 177 C2
Newham General Hospital E13 99 C3
Normansfield Hospital KT8 175 C3
North London Nuffield Hospital EN2 4 C3
North Middlesex University Hospital N18 33 C5
Northwick Park Hospital HA1 43 A2
Northwood Pinner and District Cottage Hospital HA6 22 A2
Norwood Hospital SE19 183 B4
Orpington Hospital BR6 227 D4
Paddington Com Hospital W9 91 C2
Penny Sangam Day Hospital UB2 107 B3
Plaistow Hospital E13 99 C5
Portland Hospital for Women and Children The W1 93 B3 238 D5
Princess Grace Hospital The W1 93 A3 238 A5
Princess Louise Hospital W10 90 C2
Princess Royal University Hospital BR6 226 C5
Priory Hospital The SW15 133 D1
Putney Hospital SW15 134 C2
Queen Charlotte's Hospital W12 90 B1
Queen Elizabeth Hospital for Children The E2 96 A5
Queen Elizabeth Hospital SE18 144 A5
Queen Mary's Hospital DA14 6LT 190 A4
Queen Mary's Hospital NW3 70 A5
Queen Mary's University Hospital SW15 156 A5
Queen's Hospital CR0 205 A3

Roding Hospital IG4 55 D6
Royal Brompton and Nat Heart Hospital The SW3 114 C1 257 A2
Royal Ear Hospital WC1 93 C3 239 B5
Royal Free Hospital NW3 70 C3
Royal Hospital SW15 157 A5
Royal London Homeopathic Hospital The WC1 94 A2 240 B4
Royal London Hospital(Whitechapel) E1 96 B2
Royal Marsden Hospital SW3 114 B1 256 D2
Royal Masonic Hospital W6 112 A2
Royal National Orthopaedic Hospital HA7 9 C2
Royal National Orthopaedic Hospital W1 93 B3 238 D5
Royal Nat TN&E Hospital The W5 87 C2
Royal Nat TN&E Hospital The WC1 94 B4 233 C2
St Andrew's Hospital E3 97 D3
St Ann's General Hospital N4, N15 51 A4
St Anthony's Hospital KT4 200 D1
St Bartholomew's Hospital EC1 94 D2 241 D3
St Charles' Hospital W10 90 D2
St Christopher's Hospice SE26 184 C5
St George's Hospital SW17 180 B5
St Giles Hospital SE5 139 C4
St Helier Hospital SM5 202 A1
St Joseph's Hospice E9, E8 96 B6
St Leonard's Hospital N1 95 C5
St Luke's Hospital W1 93 C3 239 A5
St Luke's Woodside Hospital N10 49 A5
St Mark's Hospital EC1 94 D4 234 D2
St Mark's Hospital HA1 43 A2
St Mary's Cottage Hospital TW12 173 B2
St Mary's Hospital W2 92 B1 236 D2
St Michael's Hospital EN2 5 B4
St Pancras Hospital NW1 93 D6 232 C5
St Thomas's Hospital SE1 116 B3 260 C6
St Vincent's Hospital HA5 39 D6
Samaritan Hospital for Women NW1 237 C4
Shirley Oaks Hospital CR0 206 C2
Sloane Hospital BR3 186 B2
South Western Hospital SW9 138 B2
Southwood Hospital (Geriatric) N6 49 A2
Springfield Hospital SW17 158 C1
Stepney Day Hospital E1 96 C1
Surbiton Hospital KT6 198 A3
Teddington Memorial Hospital TW11 174 C4
Thorpe Coombe Hospital E17 54 A6
Tolworth Hospital KT6 214 C6
Travel Clinic, Hospital for Tropical Diseases WC1 93 C3 239 B5
University College Hospital WC1 93 C3 239 B6
Upton Day Hospital DA6 147 A1
Wanstead Hospital E11 55 B5
Wellington Hospital (North) NW8 92 B5 229 D3
Wellington Hospital (South) NW8 92 B5 229 D3
Wembley Hospital HA0 65 D2
West Middlesex University Hospital TW7 6AF 131 A3
Western Hospital The NW1 92 D2 237 C4
Whipps Cross Hospital E11 1NR 54 B3
Whittington Hospital N19 5NF 71 C6
Willesden Community Hospital The NW10 68 A1
Winifred House Hospital EN5 11 D5

Places of interest

Central

West End

Admiralty Arch SW1 ... 249 D4
Apple Market WC2 ... 250 B6
Banqueting House SW1 ... 250 A3
Big Ben SW1 ... 250 B1
British Library NW1 ... 93 D4 232 D2
British Mus WC1 ... 94 A2 240 A3
BT Tower W1 ... 93 C2 239 A4
Buckingham Palace SW1 . 115 C4 249 A1
Cabinet War Rooms SW1 . 115 D4 249 D2
Carnaby Street W1 ... 93 C1 239 A1
Cenotaph SW1 ... 250 A2
Changing of the Guard (site of) SW1 ... 249 A1
Chinatown W1 ... 115 D6 249 D6
Clarence House SW1 ... 115 C5 249 B3
Cleopatra's Needle WC2 .. 116 B5 250 C5
Courtauld Galleries WC2 ... 250 C6
Covent Garden WC2 ... 116 A6 250 B6
Dickens House Mus WC1 ... 94 B3 240 D5
Downing Street SW1 ... 116 A4 250 A2
Eros W1 ... 115 D6 249 C5
Green Park SW1,W1 ... 115 B4 248 D2
Guards Mus SW1 ... 115 C4 249 B1
Holocaust Memorial Garden W2 ... 114 D4 247 D2
Horse Guards Parade SW1 ... 115 D5 249 D3
Houses of Parliament SW1 ... 116 A3 260 B6
Hyde Park W2 ... 114 D5 247 C3
Leicester Square WC2 ... 115 D6 249 D5
London's Transport Mus WC2 ... 250 B6
Marble Arch W1 ... 114 D6 247 D6
Methodist Central Hall SW1 ... 115 D4 249 D1
National Gallery W1 ... 115 D6 249 D5
National Portrait Gallery W1 ... 115 D6 249 D5
Nelson's Monument WC2 ... 250 A4
New Scotland Yard SW1 .. 115 D3 259 C6
Parliament Square SW1 .. 116 A4 250 A1
Pepsi Trocadero W1 ... 249 C5
Piccadilly Circus W1 ... 115 D6 249 C5
Queen Victoria Memorial SW1 ... 249 A2
Queen's Gallery SW1 ... 115 B4 248 D1
Rotten Row SW1 ... 114 D4 247 C2
Royal Academy of Arts W1 115 C6 249 A5
Royal Mews SW1 ... 115 B3 258 D6
Royal United Services Mus SW1 ... 250 A3
St James's Palace SW1 ... 115 C5 249 B3
St James's Park SW1 ... 249 C2
Serpentine Gallery W2 ... 114 B4 246 D2
Soho W1 ... 93 D1 239 C2
Somerset House WC2 ... 116 B6 250 D6
Speakers' Corner W1 ... 114 D6 247 D6
Tate Britain SW1 ... 116 A2 260 A3
Theatre Mus WC2 ... 250 B6
Trafalgar Square SW1 ... 115 D5 249 D4
Tyburn Tree (site of) W2 ... 247 C6
Wallace Collection W1 ... 238 A2
Wellington Arch SW1 ... 248 B2
Wellington Mus (Apsley House) SW1 ... 115 A4 248 B2
Westminster Abbey SW1 .. 116 A3 260 A6
Westminster Cathedral SW1 ... 115 C3 259 A5

City

Bank of England EC2 ... 242 C1
Barbican Arts and Conference Centre EC2 ... 95 A2 242 B4
Central Criminal Court (Old Bailey) EC4 ... 94 D1 241 D2
Custom House EC3 ... 117 C6 253 A5
Dr Johnson's House EC4 ... 241 B1
Gray's Inn WC1 ... 94 B2 240 D4
Guildhall EC2 ... 95 A1 242 B2
Inner Temple EC4 ... 251 A6
John Wesley's House & Mus EC1 ... 242 D6
Lincoln's Inn WC2 ... 94 B1 240 D2
Lloyd's Building EC3 ... 95 C1 243 A1
Mansion House EC4 ... 242 C1
Merchant Taylors Hall EC2R ... 242 D1
Middle Temple EC4 ... 116 C6 251 A6
Monument, The EC3 ... 252 D6
Mus of London EC2 ... 95 A2 242 A3
Nat West Tower EC2 ... 243 A2
National Postal Mus EC1 ... 95 A1 242 A2
Petticoat Lane Market EC2 95 D2 243 C3
Public Record Office Mus EC4,WC2 ... 241 A2
Royal Exchange EC3 ... 242 D1
St Katharine Dock E1 ... 117 D5 253 D4
St Mary le Bow Church EC2 ... 242 B1
St Paul's Cathedral EC4 ... 95 A1 242 A1
Sir John Soane's Mus WC2 ... 94 B1 240 C2
Spitalfields Market E1 ... 95 D2 243 C4
Stock Exchange EC2 ... 241 D1
Tower Bridge E1,EC3,SE1 .. 117 D5 253 C4
Tower of London EC3 ... 117 D6 253 C5
Traitors Gate EC3 ... 117 D5 253 C4
Ye Olde Cheshire Cheese EC4 ... 241 B2

Northern

Business Design Centre N1 94 C6 234 B5
Camden Market NW1 ... 93 B6 231 D6
London Canal Mus N1 ... 94 A5 233 B4
London Central Mosque NW8 ... 92 C4 230 B1
London Zoo NW1 ... 93 A5 231 A4
Lord's Cricket Ground NW8 92 B4 229 D2
Madame Tussaud's NW1 ... 93 A3 238 A5
Open Air Theatre, Regent's Park NW1 ... 231 A1
Planetarium NW1 ... 93 A3 238 A5
Primrose Hill NW1 ... 92 D6 230 C6
Queen Mary's Gardens NW1 ... 231 A1
Regent's Park NW1 ... 93 A4 231 A3
St George's Cathedral NW1 ... 231 D2
Sherlock Holmes Mus NW1 ... 92 D3 237 D5

Southern

Battersea Park SW11 ... 137 A5 268 A3
Battersea Power Station SW8 ... 137 B6 268 D6
Brompton Oratory SW7 ... 114 C3 257 A5
Bear Gardens Mus SE1 ... 117 A5 252 A4
Bermondsey Market SE1 .. 117 C3 263 B8
Borough Market SE1 ... 252 C3
Design Mus SE1 ... 117 D4 253 D2
Florence Nightingale Mus SE1 ... 250 D1
Gabriel's Wharf SE1 ... 251 A4
George Inn SE1 ... 252 C3
Globe Theatre SE1 ... 252 A5
Hayward Gallery SE1 ... 116 B5 250 D4
HMS Belfast SE1 ... 253 B4
Imperial War Mus SE1 ... 116 C3 261 B5
Lambeth Palace SE1 ... 116 B3 260 C5
London Aquarium SE1 ... 250 C1
London Dungeon SE1 ... 117 B5 252 D4
London Eye SE1 ... 116 B4 250 C2
London Peace Pagoda SW11 ... 267 D4
Millennium Bridge SE1,EC4 ... 252 A5
Mus of Garden History SE1 ... 260 C5
National Film Theatre SE1 ... 250 D4
National Theatre SE1 ... 116 B5 250 D4
Old County Hall SE1 ... 250 C2
Operating Theatre Mus and Herb Garret SE1 ... 117 B5 252 D3
Oxo Tower SE1 ... 251 B5
Royal Festival Hall SE1 ... 116 B5 250 D3
Saatchi Gallery SE1 ... 250 C2
St George's RC Cathedral SE1 ... 116 C3 261 B6
Shakespeare's Globe Theatre (site of) SE1 ... 252 B4
Southwark Cathedral SE1 117 B5 252 C4
Tate Modern SE1 ... 116 D6 251 D4
Vinopolis SE1 ... 117 B5 252 C4

Western

Albert Memorial SW7 ... 114 B4 246 C1
Carlyle's House SW3 ... 267 A5
Chelsea Barracks SW1 ... 115 A1 258 B1
Chelsea Physic Garden SW3 ... 115 A1 267 C6
Commonwealth Institute W8 ... 113 C3 255 A6
Geological Mus SW7 ... 114 B3 256 D5
Kensington Gardens W2 .. 114 A5 246 B3
Kensington Palace W8 ... 113 D5 245 D3
Leighton House W14 ... 254 D6
Lindsey House SW10 ... 266 D4
Little Venice W9 ... 92 A2 236 A4
National Army Mus SW3 ... 136 D6 267 D6
Natural History Mus SW7 ... 114 B3 256 C5
Ranelagh Gardens SW1 .. 115 A1 258 B1
Royal Albert Hall SW7 ... 114 B4 246 C1
Royal Hospital (Army Pensioners) SW1 ... 115 A1 258 A1
Science Mus SW7 ... 114 B3 256 C5
Victoria and Albert Mus SW7 ... 114 B3 256 D5

East

Canary Wharf E14 ... 119 D5
Docklands Mus E14 ... 119 D6
Epping Forest IG10 ... 21 B6
Geffrye Mus E2 ... 95 D5
London Docklands Visitor Centre E14 ... 120 A4
London Gas Mus E16 ... 98 B3
Mus of Childhood (V&A) E2 ... 96 C4
Museum of the Great Eastern Railway E16 ... 122 C4
Queen Elizabeth's Hunting Lodge Mus E4 ... 20 D4
Ragged School Mus E3 ... 97 A2
Vestry House (Mus) E17 ... 53 D5
Whitechapel Art Gallery E1 ... 95 D1

North

Alexandra Palace N22 ... 31 D1
Barnet Mus EN5 ... 1 A1
Battle of Britain Mus NW9 ... 27 D1
Bruce Castle Mus N17 ... 33 C2
Church Farm House Mus NW4 ... 46 B6
Coppetts Centre N12 ... 30 D3
Forty Hall EN2 ... 5 D6
Freud Mus NW3 ... 70 A2
Grange Mus of Community History NW10 ... 67 D4
Hampstead Heath NW3 ... 70 B6
Harrow Mus and Heritage Centre HA2 ... 42 A6
Highgate Cemetery N19 ... 71 B6
Kensal Green Cemetery (All Souls) NW10 ... 90 C4
Kenwood House NW3 ... 48 C1
Old Court (Mus and Library) HA0 .. 65 C3
RAF Mus NW9 ... 28 A1
Ruislip Lido HA4,HA5 ... 39 B5
Ruislip Lido Railway HA4 ... 39 B5
White Cube N1 ... 95 C4

South east

Blackheath SE3 ... 142 C4
Brockwell Park SE24 ... 160 D5
Cutty Sark SE10 ... 142 A6
Docklands Heritage Mus SE16 ... 119 B5
Dulwich Picture Gallery SE21 ... 161 C4
Eltham Palace SE9 ... 166 A4
Flamsteed House SE10 ... 142 B5
Gipsy Moth IV SE10 ... 142 A6
Greenwich Park SE10 ... 142 C5
Horniman Mus and Gardens SE23 162 B3
Livesey Mus SE15 ... 140 B6
Meridian Building SE10 ... 142 B5
Millennium Dome SE10 ... 120 C5
National Maritime Mus SE10 ... 142 B6
Old Royal Observatory Greenwich SE10 ... 142 B5
Queen's House SE10 ... 142 B6
Rotunda Mus SE18 ... 122 B1
Scadbury Park Nature Reserve BR7 ... 189 D4
South Norwood Country Park SE25 ... 206 C5
Thames Barrier Visitor Centre SE18 ... 121 D3
Well Hall Pleasaunce SE9 ... 144 A1

South west

Barnes Common SW13 ... 134 A2
Clapham Common SW4 ... 137 C1
Fulham Palace SW6 ... 135 A3
Hampton Court Palace KT8 ... 196 D6
Kingston Mus KT1 ... 176 A1
Wandsworth Mus SW15 ... 135 A1
Wetland Centre SW13 ... 134 B5
Wimbledon Common SW19 ... 178 B6
Wimbledon Lawn Tennis Mus SW19 ... 157 A1
Wimbledon Windmill Mus SW19 .. 156 C1

West

Chiswick House W4 ... 133 B6
Eel Pie Island TW1 ... 153 A3
Gunnersbury Park Mus W3 ... 110 C3
Ham House TW10 ... 153 C2
Kew Bridge Steam Mus TW8 ... 110 B1
Kew Gardens (Royal Botanic Gardens) TW9 ... 132 A4
Kew Observatory TW9 ... 131 C2
Kew Palace TW9 ... 132 A5
London Butterfly House TW8 ... 131 B4
Marble Hill TW1 ... 153 C4
Mus of Richmond TW10 ... 153 D6
Musical Mus TW8 ... 132 A6
Osterley Park TW7 ... 108 B1
Pitshanger Manor Mus and Art Gallery W5 ... 109 D5
Portobello Road Market W10 ... 91 A2
Richmond Park TW10 ... 155 A3
Syon House TW8 ... 131 C4
Walled Garden TW16 ... 194 B6

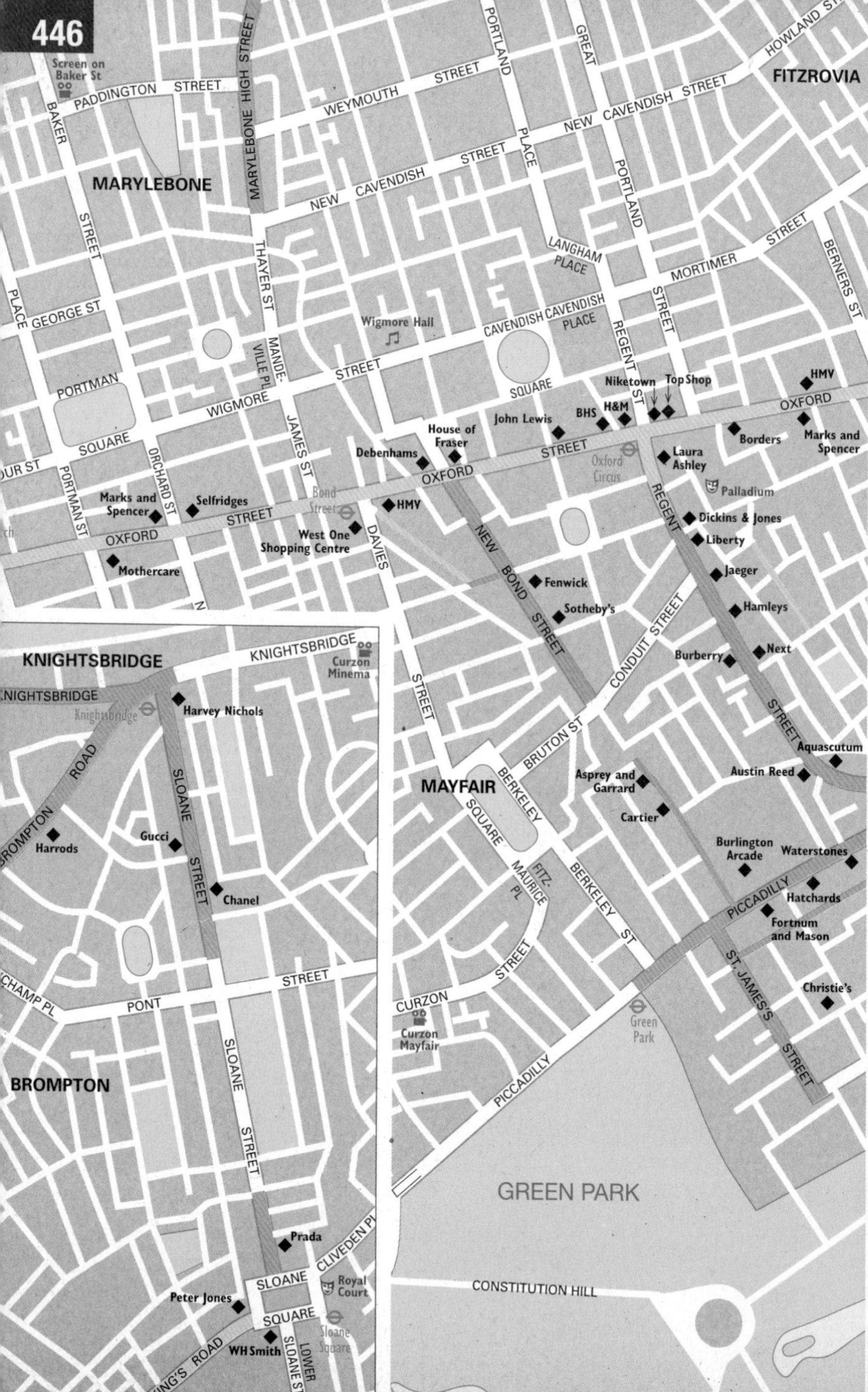
Screen on Baker St
PADDINGTON STREET
BAKER STREET
MARYLEBONE HIGH STREET
WEYMOUTH STREET
PORTLAND PLACE
GREAT PORTLAND STREET
HOWLAND ST
FITZROVIA
NEW CAVENDISH STREET
MARYLEBONE
THAYER ST
LANGHAM PLACE
MORTIMER STREET
BERNERS ST
PLACE
GEORGE ST
Wigmore Hall
CAVENDISH SQUARE
CAVENDISH PLACE
REGENT ST
MANDEVILLE PL
PORTMAN SQUARE
WIGMORE STREET
Niketown
TopShop
HMV
JAMES ST
John Lewis
BHS
H&M
OXFORD STREET
House of Fraser
Debenhams
Borders
Marks and Spencer
ORCHARD ST
PORTMAN ST
Laura Ashley
Oxford Circus
Bond Street
Palladium
Marks and Spencer
Selfridges
HMV
West One Shopping Centre
DAVIES STREET
Dickins & Jones
Liberty
Mothercare
NEW BOND STREET
Fenwick
Jaeger
Sotheby's
CONDUIT STREET
Hamleys
REGENT STREET
KNIGHTSBRIDGE
Curzon Minema
Next
Burberry
Harvey Nichols
Knightsbridge
BROMPTON ROAD
SLOANE STREET
BRUTON ST
Aquascutum
Austin Reed
Asprey and Garrard
MAYFAIR
BERKELEY SQUARE
Cartier
Harrods
Gucci
Burlington Arcade
Waterstones
Chanel
FITZMAURICE PL
BERKELEY ST
PICCADILLY
Hatchards
Fortnum and Mason
ST. JAMES'S STREET
CURZON STREET
Christie's
PONT STREET
CHAMP PL
Curzon Mayfair
Green Park
BROMPTON
GREEN PARK
Prada
CLIVEDEN PL
Royal Court
CONSTITUTION HILL
SLOANE SQUARE
Peter Jones
Sloane Square
KING'S ROAD
WH Smith
SLOANE ST
LOWER

Cinemas, theatres shopping streets

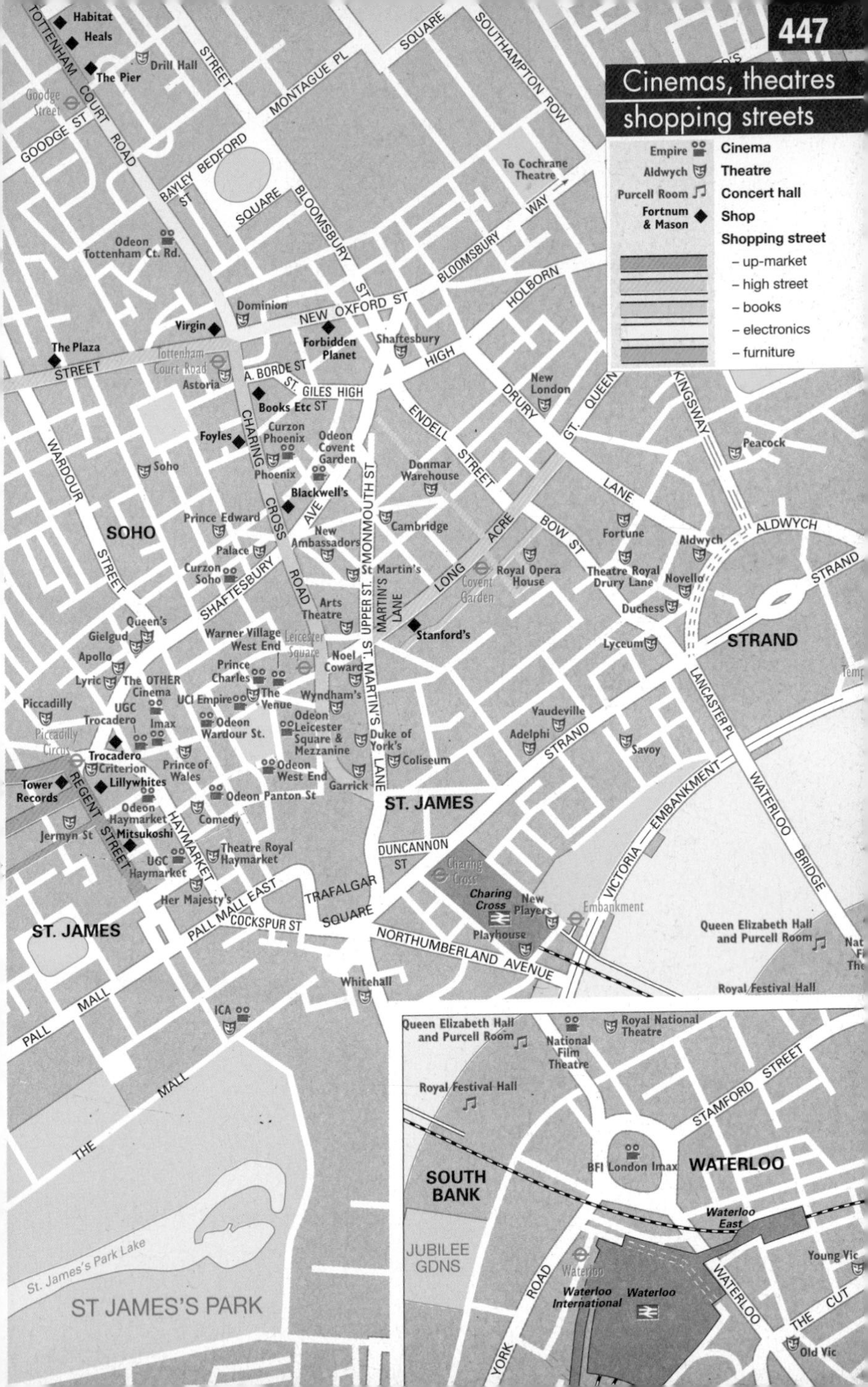

Empire	Cinema
Aldwych	Theatre
Purcell Room	Concert hall
Fortnum & Mason	Shop
	Shopping street
	– up-market
	– high street
	– books
	– electronics
	– furniture

Habitat
Heals
The Pier
Drill Hall
Goodge Street
Tottenham Court Road
Goodge St
Street
Montague Pl
Square
Southampton Row
Bayley St
Bedford Square
Bloomsbury St
To Cochrane Theatre
Bloomsbury Way
Odeon Tottenham Ct. Rd.
Holborn
Dominion
New Oxford St
Virgin
Forbidden Planet
Shaftesbury
The Plaza
Street
Tottenham Court Road
Astoria
A. Borde St
St. Giles High St
High
New London
Drury
Gt. Queen
Kingsway
Books Etc
Curzon Phoenix
Odeon Covent Garden
Foyles
Charing Cross Road
Phoenix
Soho
Wardour Street
Blackwell's
Upper St. Martin's Lane
St. Martin's Lane
Monmouth St
Endell Street
Donmar Warehouse
Peacock
Lane
Cambridge
Ave
Shaftesbury
New Ambassadors
Prince Edward
SOHO
Palace
Curzon Soho
St Martin's
Long Acre
Covent Garden
Royal Opera House
Bow St
Fortune
Aldwych
Theatre Royal Drury Lane
Novello
Aldwych
Strand
Arts Theatre
Stanford's
Duchess
Queen's
Gielgud
Warner Village West End
Leicester Square
Noel Coward
Lyceum
STRAND
Apollo
Prince Charles
Lyric
The OTHER Cinema
The Venue
Wyndham's
Piccadilly
UCI Empire
UGC Trocadero
Imax
Odeon Wardour St.
Odeon Leicester Square & Mezzanine
Duke of York's
Vaudeville
Adelphi
Strand
Savoy
Lancaster Pl
Piccadilly Circus
Trocadero
Coliseum
Criterion
Prince of Wales
Odeon West End
Garrick
Victoria — Embankment
Waterloo Bridge
Tower Records
Regent Street
Lillywhites
Odeon Panton St
ST. JAMES
Odeon Haymarket
Comedy
Jermyn St
Haymarket
Mitsukoshi
Theatre Royal Haymarket
Duncannon St
UGC Haymarket
Charing Cross
Her Majesty's
Trafalgar Square
Charing Cross
New Players
Embankment
Pall Mall East
Cockspur St
Queen Elizabeth Hall and Purcell Room
ST. JAMES
Playhouse
Northumberland Avenue
Whitehall
Royal Festival Hall
Pall Mall
ICA
The Mall
St. James's Park Lake
ST JAMES'S PARK

Queen Elizabeth Hall and Purcell Room
National Film Theatre
Royal National Theatre
Stamford Street
Royal Festival Hall
BFI London Imax
WATERLOO
SOUTH BANK
Waterloo East
JUBILEE GDNS
Waterloo
Young Vic
Road
Waterloo International
Waterloo
Waterloo
The Cut
York
Old Vic

ST JOHN'S WOOD
REGENT'S PARK
London Zoo
Lord's Cricket Ground
London Mosque
Regent's Park Lake
Queen Mary's Gardens
Open Air Theatre
MAIDA VALE
Madame Tussaud's
Marylebone
Little Venice
National Heart Hospital
PADDINGTON
St Mary's Hospital
Paddington
Wallace Collection
BAYSWATER
MARBLE ARCH
KENSINGTON GARDENS
HYDE PARK
The Serpentine
Kensington Palace
Serpentine Gallery
Princess Diana Memorial Fountain
Apsley House and Wellington Museum
Albert Memorial
KNIGHTSBRIDGE
Royal Albert Hall
Science Museum
Natural History Museum
Brompton Oratory
Victoria and Albert Museum
BROMPTON
BELGRAVIA
MAY
Hospital of St John and Elizabeth

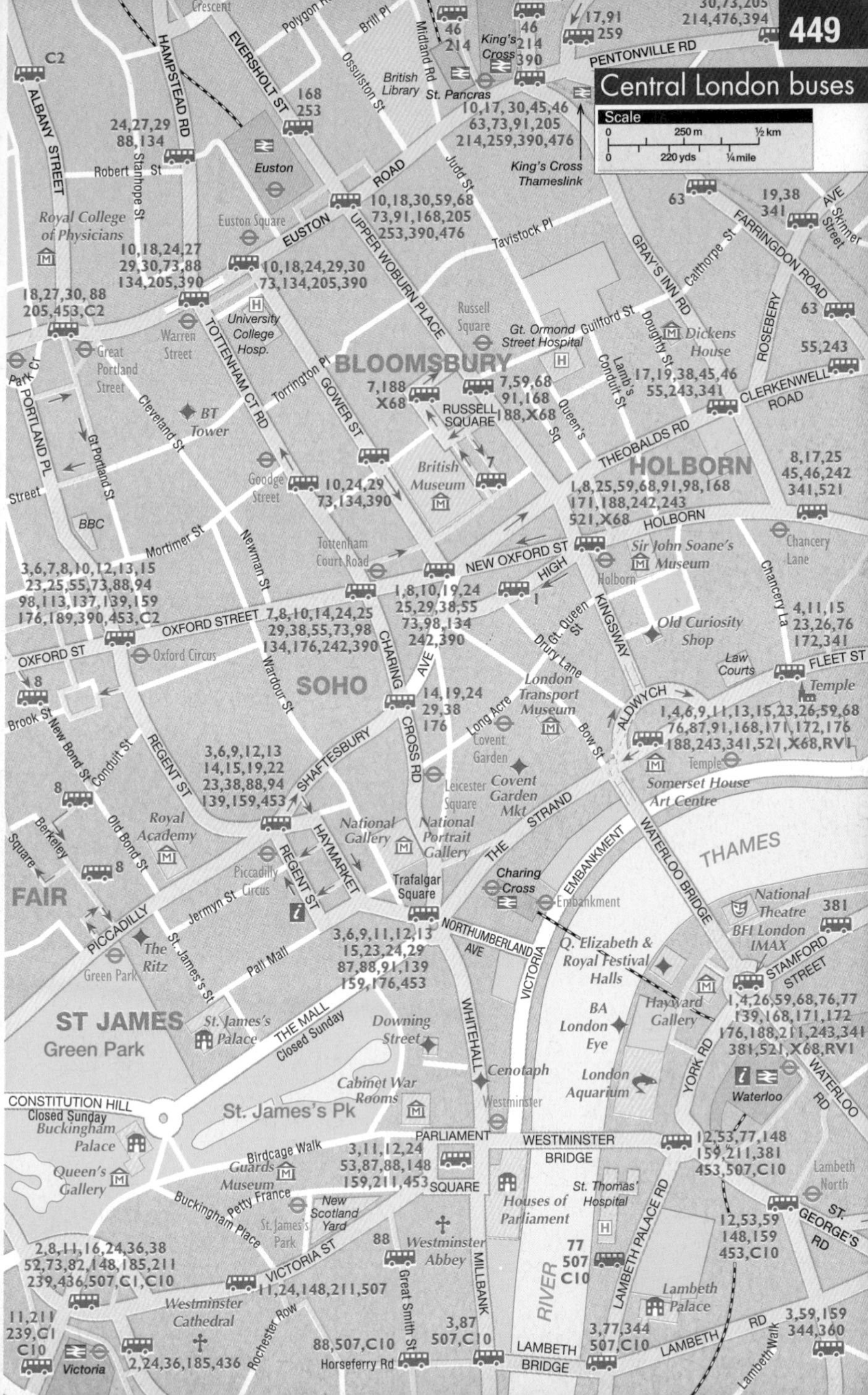

449
Central London buses
Scale
250 m
½ km
220 yds
¼ mile
Crescent
Polygon Rd
Brill Pl
Midland Rd
PENTONVILLE RD
HAMPSTEAD RD
EVERSHOLT ST
Ossulston St
British Library
St. Pancras
King's Cross
King's Cross Thameslink
ALBANY STREET
Stanhope St
Robert St
Euston
EUSTON ROAD
Judd St
Euston Square
UPPER WOBURN PLACE
Tavistock Pl
Royal College of Physicians
Russell Square
Gt. Ormond Street Hospital
Guilford St
GRAY'S INN RD
Calthorpe St
FARRINGDON ROAD
Skinner Street
AVE
Doughty St
Dickens House
ROSEBERY
Lamb's Conduit St
Queen's Sq
CLERKENWELL ROAD
THEOBALDS RD
University College Hosp.
Warren Street
Great Portland Street
TOTTENHAM CT RD
Torrington Pl
GOWER ST
BLOOMSBURY
RUSSELL SQUARE
Park Cr
PORTLAND PL
Gt Portland St
Cleveland St
BT Tower
British Museum
HOLBORN
Goodge Street
Street
BBC
Mortimer St
Newman St
Tottenham Court Road
NEW OXFORD ST
HIGH
Sir John Soane's Museum
Holborn
Chancery Lane
Chancery La
KINGSWAY
Gt. Queen St
Drury Lane
Old Curiosity Shop
Law Courts
FLEET ST
Temple
OXFORD STREET
OXFORD ST
Oxford Circus
Wardour St
CHARING CROSS RD
AVE
SOHO
London Transport Museum
ALDWYCH
Brook St
New Bond St
Conduit St
REGENT ST
SHAFTESBURY
Long Acre
Covent Garden
Bow St
Temple
Somerset House Art Centre
Leicester Square
Covent Garden Mkt
THE STRAND
Berkeley Square
Old Bond St
Royal Academy
HAYMARKET
National Gallery
National Portrait Gallery
EMBANKMENT
WATERLOO BRIDGE
THAMES
Piccadilly Circus
REGENT ST
FAIR
Jermyn St
Trafalgar Square
Charing Cross
Embankment
National Theatre
BFI London IMAX
PICCADILLY
The Ritz
St. James's St
NORTHUMBERLAND AVE
Pall Mall
VICTORIA
Q. Elizabeth & Royal Festival Halls
STAMFORD STREET
Green Park
ST JAMES
Green Park
St. James's Palace
THE MALL Closed Sunday
Downing Street
WHITEHALL
BA London Eye
Hayward Gallery
YORK RD
Cenotaph
London Aquarium
Waterloo
WATERLOO RD
CONSTITUTION HILL Closed Sunday
Buckingham Palace
Cabinet War Rooms
St. James's Pk
Westminster
PARLIAMENT SQUARE
WESTMINSTER BRIDGE
Birdcage Walk
Guards Museum
Queen's Gallery
Petty France
New Scotland Yard
St. James's Park
Houses of Parliament
St. Thomas' Hospital
LAMBETH PALACE RD
Lambeth North
ST. GEORGE'S RD
Buckingham Place
Westminster Abbey
RIVER
VICTORIA ST
Great Smith St
MILLBANK
Lambeth Palace
Westminster Cathedral
Rochester Row
LAMBETH RD
Lambeth Walk
Victoria
Horseferry Rd
LAMBETH BRIDGE
C2
24,27,29 88,134
10,18,24,27 29,30,73,88 134,205,390
18,27,30, 88 205,453,C2
168 253
46 214
46 214 390
17,91 259
30,73,205 214,476,394
10,17,30,45,46 63,73,91,205 214,259,390,476
10,18,30,59,68 73,91,168,205 253,390,476
10,18,24,29,30 73,134,205,390
63
19,38 341
63
55,243
7,188 X68
7,59,68 91,168 188,X68
17,19,38,45,46 55,243,341
7
10,24,29 73,134,390
8,17,25 45,46,242 341,521
1,8,25,59,68,91,98,168 171,188,242,243 521,X68
3,6,7,8,10,12,13,15 23,25,55,73,88,94 98,113,137,139,159 176,189,390,453,C2
7,8,10,14,24,25 29,38,55,73,98 134,176,242,390
1,8,10,19,24 25,29,38,55 73,98,134 242,390
1
4,11,15 23,26,76 172,341
8
14,19,24 29,38 176
1,4,6,9,11,13,15,23,26,59,68 76,87,91,168,171,172,176 188,243,341,521,X68,RV1
3,6,9,12,13 14,15,19,22 23,38,88,94 139,159,453
8
8
3,6,9,11,12,13 15,23,24,29 87,88,91,139 159,176,453
381
1,4,26,59,68,76,77 139,168,171,172 176,188,211,243,341 381,521,X68,RV1
3,11,12,24 53,87,88,148 159,211,453
12,53,77,148 159,211,381 453,507,C10
12,53,59 148,159 453,C10
88
77 507 C10
2,8,11,16,24,36,38 52,73,82,148,185,211 239,436,507,C1,C10
11,24,148,211,507
3,59,159 344,360
11,211 239,C1 C10
3,87 507,C10
3,77,344 507,C10
88,507,C10
2,24,36,185,436

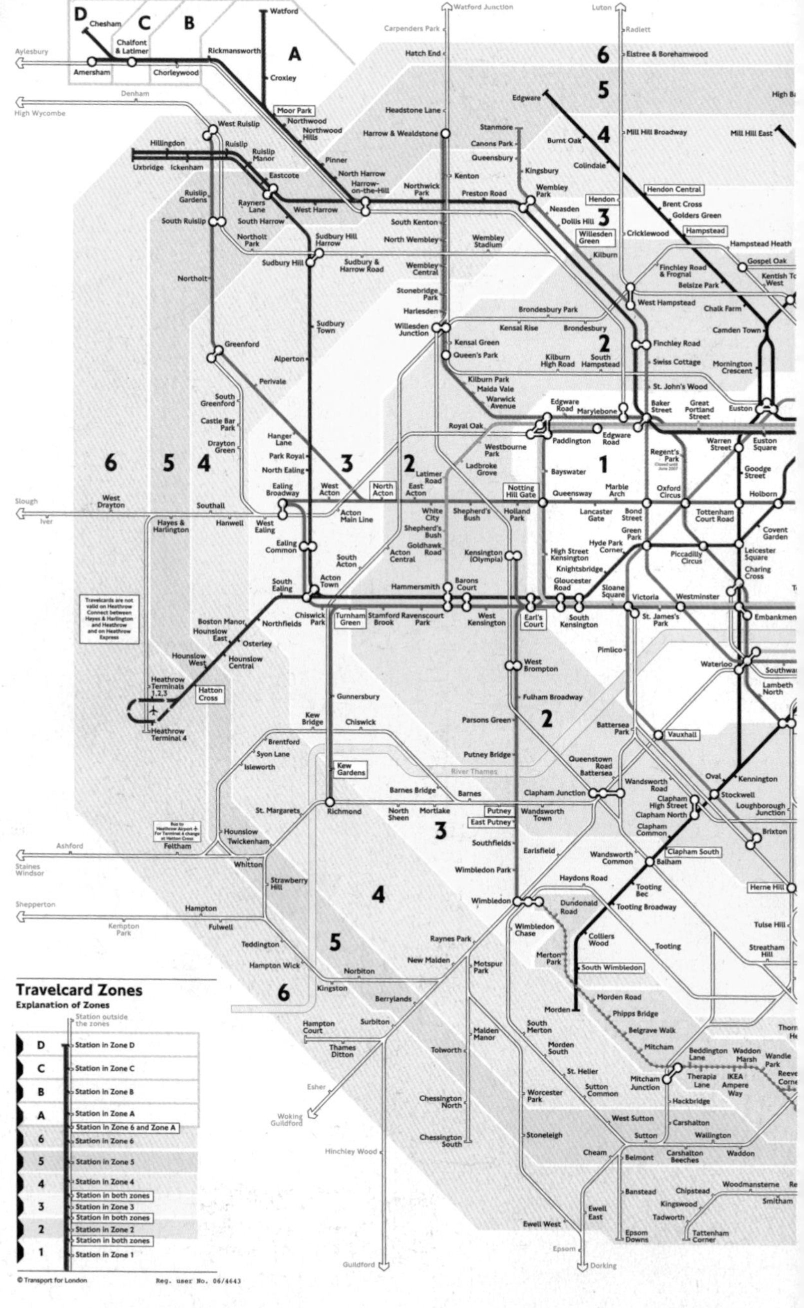

MAYOR OF LONDON

24 hour travel information 020 7222 1234

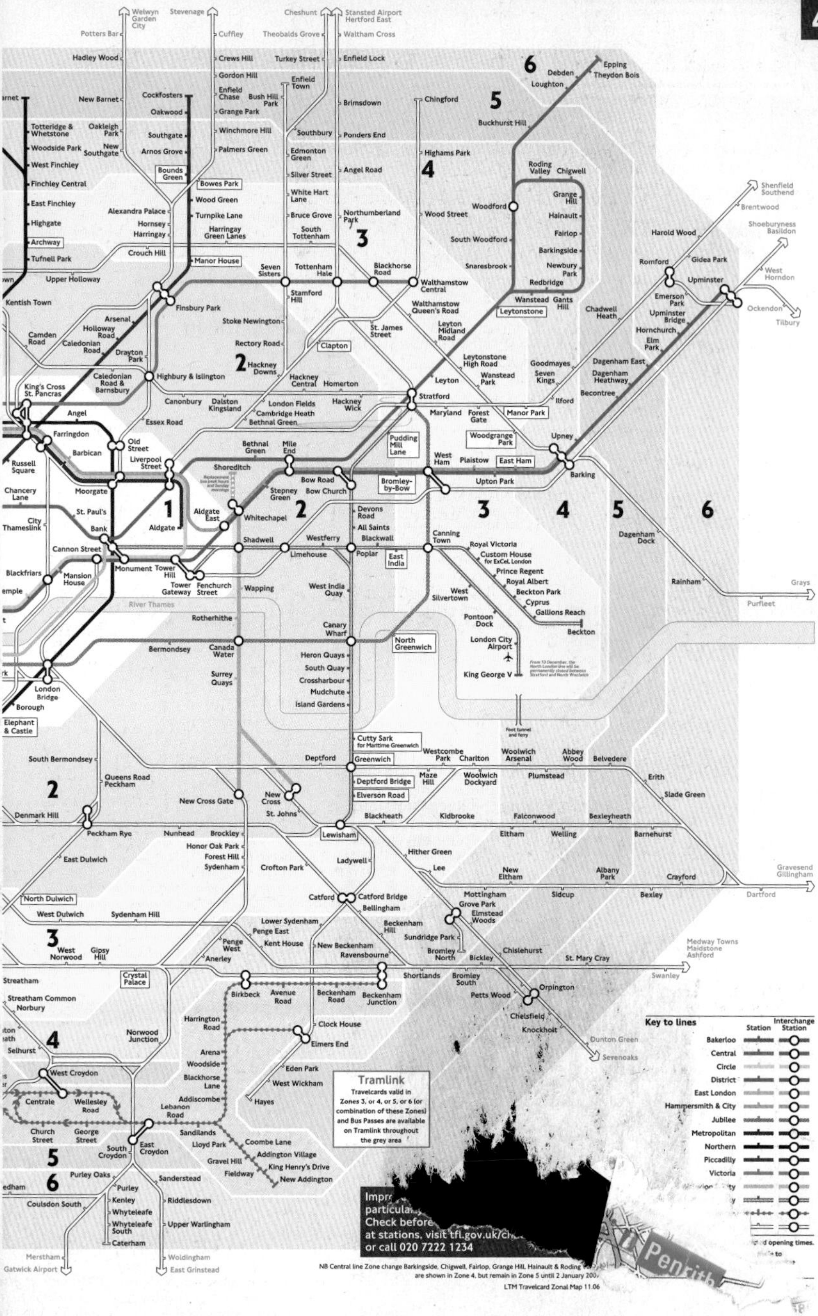

Tramlink

Travelcards valid in Zones 3, or 4, or 5, or 6 (or combination of these Zones) and Bus Passes are available on Tramlink throughout the grey area

Key to lines

	Station	Interchange Station
Bakerloo		
Central		
Circle		
District		
East London		
Hammersmith & City		
Jubilee		
Metropolitan		
Northern		
Piccadilly		
Victoria		

Impr… particula… Check before… at stations, visit tfl.gov.uk/ch… or call 020 7222 1234

NB Central line Zone change Barkingside, Chigwell, Fairlop, Grange Hill, Hainault & Roding … are shown in Zone 4, but remain in Zone 5 until 2 January 200…

LTM Travelcard Zonal Map 11.06